Tolley's Employment Handbook

by

Elizabeth A Slade QC MA (*Oxon*)

Deputy High Court Judge,
A Recorder of the Crown Court,
A Master of the Bench of the Inner Temple,
Honorary Vice-President of the
Employment Law Bar Association

Twenty-First Edition

by

members of
11 KBW, 11 King's Bench Walk

and

Dominic Regan
Solicitor, employment law consultant to Brabners

LexisNexis®
Tolley

Members of the LexisNexis Group worldwide

United Kingdom	LexisNexis Butterworths, a Division of Reed Elsevier (UK) Ltd, Halsbury House, 35 Chancery Lane, London, WC2A 1EL, and London House, 20–22 East London Street, Edinburgh EH7 4BQ
Argentina	LexisNexis Argentina, Buenos Aires
Australia	LexisNexis Butterworths, Chatswood, New South Wales
Austria	LexisNexis Verlag ARD Orac GmbH & Co KG, Vienna
Benelux	LexisNexis Benelux, Amsterdam
Canada	LexisNexis Canada, Markham, Ontario
Chile	LexisNexis Chile Ltda, Santiago
China	LexisNexis China, Beijing and Shanghai
France	LexisNexis SA, Paris
Germany	LexisNexis Deutschland GmbH, Munster
Hong Kong	LexisNexis Hong Kong, Hong Kong
India	LexisNexis India, New Delhi
Italy	Giuffrè Editore, Milan
Japan	LexisNexis Japan, Tokyo
Malaysia	Malayan Law Journal Sdn Bhd, Kuala Lumpur
Mexico	LexisNexis Mexico, Mexico
New Zealand	LexisNexis NZ Ltd, Wellington
Poland	Wydawnictwo Prawnicze LexisNexis Sp, Warsaw
Singapore	LexisNexis Singapore, Singapore
South Africa	LexisNexis Butterworths, Durban
USA	LexisNexis, Dayton, Ohio

© Reed Elsevier (UK) Ltd and Elizabeth Slade QC 2007

Published by LexisNexis Butterworths

A CIP Catalogue record for this book is available from the British Library.

ISBN 13: 978 0 7545 3265 1

Typeset by Letterpart Ltd, Reigate, Surrey

Printed and bound in Great Britain by William Clowes Limited, Beccles, Suffolk

Visit LexisNexis Butterworths at www.lexisnexis.co.uk

List of contributors

Members of 11 King's Bench Walk Chambers

Andrew Blake BA, LLM, barrister - Holidays (29)

James Boddy BA (Hons) Dunelm - Insolvency of Employer (31)

Akhlaq Choudhury BSc, LLB, barrister - Disability Discrimination (10)

Joanne Clement BA (Hons) Oxon, BCL - Less-Favourable Treatment of Part-Time Workers (32)

James Cornwell MA (Oxon), MPhil (London), DPhil (Oxon), Dip Law, barrister - Discrimination and Equal Opportunities III (14)

Harini Iyengar MA (Oxon), BCL (Oxon), barrister - Time Off Work (49), Unfair Dismissal I to III (53, 54, 55)

Seán Jones BA, BCL (Oxon), barrister - Discrimination and Equal Opportunities I (12)

Richard Leiper LLB, MJuris, barrister - Public Sector Employees (37), Transfer of Undertakings (52)

Jane McCafferty MA (Cantab) - Equal Pay (24), European Community Law (25)

Alistair McGregor QC, LLB (London) - Restraint of Trade (41)

Julian Milford MA, barrister - Continuous Employment (7), Redundancy I and II (38, 39)

Paul Nicholls LLB, BCL (Oxon), barrister - Collective Agreements (6), Contract of Employment (8), Employee or Self-Employed? (17), Engagement of Employees (23), Probationary Employees (36), References (40)

Nigel Porter MA, LLM, barrister - Introduction (1), Advisory, Conciliation and Arbitration Service (2), Codes of Practice (5), Disclosure of Information (11), Employees' Past Criminal Convictions (19), Human Rights (30), Pay I and II (34, 35), Temporary and Seasonal Employees (47)

Anya Proops MA (Cantab), PhD, barrister - Employee Participation (18), Foreign Employees (26), Vicarious Liability (56)

Tom Restrick BA (Oxon) - Dispute Resolution (15)

Clive Sheldon BA, LLM, barrister - Maternity Rights (33), Sickness and Sick Pay (44), Termination of Employment (48), Wrongful Dismissal (58)

Daniel Stilitz BA, MA, barrister - Strikes and Industrial Action (45), Trade Unions I and II (50, 51)

Judy Stone BA (Hons) Oxon - Age Discrimination (3), Directors (9), Retirement (42)

Holly Stout MA (Cantab), DipLaw - Discrimination and Equal Opportunities II (13), Equal Pay (24), Restraint of Trade (41), Wrongful Dismissal (58)

Peter Wallington MA, LLM, barrister - Employment Tribunals I to III (20, 21, 22), Working Time (57)

List of contributors

Other contributors

Stephen Barc LLB, solicitor, senior legal editor, LexisNexis Butterworths - Children and Young Persons (4), Education and Training (16), Service Lettings (43)

Sarah Bradford BA (Hons), ACA, CTA (Fellow), Director of Writetax Ltd - Taxation (46)

Dominic Regan BA (Hons), Law, sweet and Maxwell Prizeman, solicitor, employment law consultant to Brabners - Health and Safety at Work I and II (27, 28)

Preface

With this edition we say goodbye to a long-standing contributor: Stephen Hardy. I am exceptionally grateful to him for the hard work he put in since joining the Tolley's team. The book will not be the same without him. It was hard to find a replacement author with matching dedication and verve but we are confident we have done so in Dominic Regan, someone whose reputation, if you have a professional interest in Employment Law, will already be known to you. His enthusiasm and insight will be immediately apparent from his re-working of the chapters on Health and Safety.

Readers should once again expect to see all of the last year's major developments (legislative and judicial) reflected in this latest revision. As has come to be expected, there was plenty happening in the world of equal opportunities.

The difficult question of the burden of proof was addressed in a number of significant EAT cases including *Laing v Manchester City Council* [2006] ICR 1519 and by the Court of Appeal in *Madarassy v Nomura International Plc* [2007] EWCA Civ 33, [2007] IRLR 246.

In *Equal Opportunities Commission v Secretary of State for Trade and Industry* [2007] EWHC 483 (Admin); [2007] IRLR 327, the Divisional Court politely informed the Government that a number of key aspects of its recent amendments to the *Sex Discrimination Act 1975* did not comply with the European legislation that it was intended to implement. The decision has a broad impact as the arguments that prevailed apply equally to the other anti-discrimination measures.

There has been a surprising focus on extreme right wing politics in this year's crop of cases. The Court of Appeal in *Redfearn v Serco Ltd* [2006] EWCA Civ 659, [2006] ICR 1367 overturned the EAT and determined that it was not open to an employee dismissed, in essence, for being a member of the British National Party, to complain that he had been dismissed on grounds of race. That was not the only reverse to which the BNP were subject. In *Associated Society of Locomotive Engineers & Firemen v United Kingdom* [2007] IRLR 361, the European Court of Human Rights held that the UK law breached Article 11 by preventing a union from expelling a member on grounds that he was a member of the BNP.

Legislation prohibiting discrimination on grounds of religion or belief has been amended to make it clear that atheists are protected alongside theists. The prohibition has been the subject of a further extension (of uncertain scope) so that where an employee complains of less favourable treatment on grounds of belief they no longer need to establish that the relevant belief is 'similar' to a religious belief. The new Gender Equality Duty imposed on public authorities is also considered in this edition.

In the area of equal pay, the decisions in *Secretary of State for Trade and Industry v Rutherford (No 2)* [2006] IRLR 551; *Cadman v Health and Safety Executive* [2006] IRLR 969; and *Redcar & Cleveland Borough Council v Bainbridge* [2007] IRLR 91, EAT have all been subject to detailed consideration in this edition's revisions.

In a blow to a number of barristers' High Court practices, the Court of Appeal decided in *Commerzbank v Keen* [2007] IRLR 132, that the Unfair Contract Terms Act does not apply to employment contracts and proceeded to take a narrow view of the circumstances in which a court should interfere with an employer's exercise of a discretion as to bonus.

Preface

I would like to thank the editorial team at LexisNexis for their continued support. They have become adept at prodding tardy chapter authors with just the right mix of velvet and steel and have endured the annual wearing through of their patience with good grace and understanding. I express my gratitude on behalf of all the contributors.

I would also like to thank those who have used our feedback email address (tolleysfeedback@11kbw.com) to provide us with their own insights, comments and, occasionally, corrections. I would like, in particular, to thank Robert Foulke, Andrew Sladen, Susan Kerr and Nicola Bocking.

Seán Jones

Contents

Table of Statutes   ix
Table of EU Legislative Material   xxxvii
Table of Statutory Instruments   xliii
Table of Cases   lxix
Abbreviations and References   clxxix

1 Introduction   1
2 Advisory, Conciliation and Arbitration Service (ACAS)   8
3 Age Discrimination   16
4 Children and Young Persons   52
5 Codes of Practice   63
6 Collective Agreements   69
7 Continuous Employment   73
8 Contract of Employment   86
9 Directors   119
10 Disability Discrimination   142
11 Disclosure of Information   178
12 Discrimination and Equal Opportunities – I   193
13 Discrimination and Equal Opportunities – II   249
14 Discrimination and Equal Opportunities – III   295
15 Dispute Resolution   337
16 Education and Training   353
17 Employee, Self-Employed or Worker?   360
18 Employee Participation   374
19 Employee's Past Criminal Convictions   395
20 Employment Tribunals – I   401
21 Employment Tribunals – II   450
22 Employment Tribunals – III   517
23 Engagement of Employees   537
24 Equal Pay   539
25 European Community Law   588
26 Foreign Employees   605
27 Health and Safety at Work – I   619
28 Health and Safety at Work – II   646
29 Holidays   668
30 Human Rights   677
31 Insolvency of Employer   689
32 Less-Favourable Treatment of Part-Time Workers   698
33 Maternity and Parental Rights   711
34 Pay – I   728
35 Pay – II   756

Contents

36 Probationary Employees   762
37 Public Sector Employees   764
38 Redundancy – I   773
39 Redundancy – II   784
40 References   795
41 Restraint of Trade, Confidentiality and Employee Inventions   800
42 Retirement   834
43 Service Lettings   857
44 Sickness and Sick Pay   866
45 Strikes and Industrial Action   875
46 Taxation   896
47 Temporary and Seasonal Employees   915
48 Termination of Employment   928
49 Time Off Work   941
50 Trade Unions – I   957
51 Trade Unions – II   981
52 Transfer of Undertakings   997
53 Unfair Dismissal – I   1019
54 Unfair Dismissal – II   1039
55 Unfair Dismissal – III   1074
56 Vicarious Liability   1097
57 Working Time   1102
58 Wrongful Dismissal   1129

Index   1155

Table of Statutes

Access to Health Records
Act 1990 .... 11.1, 54.8
  s 2–6 .... 11.15
    8 .... 11.15

Access to Justice Act 1999
  s 55 .... 22.26
    90 .... 35.3
  Sch 13
    para 64 .... 35.3
       66 .... 35.3

Access to Medical Reports
Act 1988 .... 11.1, 54.8
  s 1 .... 11.15
    3(1) 11.15
    4 .... 11.15
    5(1), (2) 11.15
    8 .... 11.15

Administration of Justice Act 1982
  s 10(i) 44.16

Agricultural Wages Act 1948
  s 3, 4 .... 29.7
    11 .... 29.7

Agriculture (Safety, Health and
Welfare Provisions) Act 1956
  s 3 .... 28.29
    5 .... 28.29
    25(3) 28.29
    (6) 28.29

Air Force Act 1955 .... 37.2

Apportionment Act 1870 .... 29.49
  s 2 .... 8.24, 34.22
    5 .... 8.24, 34.22
    7 .... 8.24, 34.22

Arbitration Act 1950
  Pt I (ss 1–34) 2.6
  s 4 .... 58.38

Arbitration Act 1975
  s 1 .... 58.38

Arbitration Act 1996 .... 21.37

Armed Forces Act 1966 .... 37.2

Armed Forces Act 1991 .... 37.2

Armed Forces Act 1996 .... 24.2, 37.2
  s 24 .... 24.4

Army Act 1955 .... 37.2

Asylum and Immigration
Act 1996 .... 12.12
  s 8 .... 26.10
    (4)–(6B) 26.9
    8A 26.9, 26.10

Attachment of Earnings Act 1971 ... 35.11
  s 1(1)–(3) 35.1
    5(1) 35.1
    6 .... 35.3
    (2) 35.1
    7(1) 35.6
    (2) 35.7
    (4)(a), (b) 35.9
    9(2) 35.6
    12(3) 35.6
    14(1)(b) 35.7
    15(c) 35.7
    16(1)–(3) 35.2
    23(5) 35.8
    24(1), (2) 35.2
  Sch 3
    Pt 1 .... 35.4
    Pt 2
    para 7, 8 .... 35.5

Betting, Gaming and Lotteries
Act 1963 .... 8.5
  Sch 5A 8.25

Capital Allowances Act 2001
  s 262 .... 46.2

Child Support Act 1991 .... 35.1, 35.11

Child Support, Pensions and Social
Security Act 2000
  s 74, 75 .... 46.17

Table of Statutes

Children Act 1989
s 3 .... 49.19
Sch 13
  para 32 .... 4.3

**Children and Young Persons
  Act 1933**
s 18(1) 4.2, 57.3
  (2) 4.3
  (2A) 4.2
21 .... 4.3
23–26 .... 4.4

**Children and Young Persons
  Act 1963** 4.2, 4.3
s 37–42 .... 4.4

**Children and Young Persons
  Act 1969** 4.3

**Children and Young Persons
  (Scotland) Act 1937** 57.3

Chiropractors Act 1994
s 40(2) 19.4
  (4) 19.4

**Civil Jurisdiction and Judgments
  Act 1982** 26.12

**Civil Jurisdiction and Judgments
  Act 1991** 26.12

**Civil Liability (Contribution)
  Act 1978** 27.10
s 1(1), (2) 56.3

Civil Partnership Act 2004
s 1 .... 12.6
  212–218 .... 13.13
  246, 247 .... 38.10
  251(1), (2) 12.2, 12.7
Sch 20 .... 13.13
Sch 21 .... 38.10

Civil Procedure Act 1997
s 1–4 .... 35.1

Companies Act 1985 .... 9.1, 9.17, 11.1,
                                        12.12
s 144(3), (4) 9.18
  170–177 .... 9.17
  234 .... 10.15, 11.9
  (4) 18.3

Companies Act 1985 – *contd*
s 246(3) 9.23
  247(3) 9.23, 9.25
  247A 9.23
  287(1) 9.7
  303, 304 .... 9.26
  309(1), (2) 18.2
  310(1) 9.18
    (3)(a), (b) 9.18
  312 .... 9.27
  313 .... 9.30
  314, 315 .... 9.31
  316(3) 9.27, 9.30, 9.31
  317(3) 9.7
  318(4) 9.8
    (8), (9) 9.8
  319 .... 8.3, 9.11, 58.14
    (1)–(3) 9.12
    (5) 9.12
  379 .... 9.26
  727 .... 9.18, 9.19
    (2) 9.19
Sch 6 .... 9.27
  Pt 1 .... 9.22
  para 1(1)(a) 9.22, 9.23
          (b) 9.22
          (c), (d) 9.22, 9.23
       (2)(b) 9.22, 9.23
       (3) 9.22
  2 .... 9.23
    (1), (2) 9.22
  5 .... 9.22
  7 .... 9.25
  8(1) 9.28
  Pt 2, 3 .... 9.22
Sch 7
  para 9 .... 10.15, 11.9
  11 .... 11.9, 18.3
Sch 7A 9.22
  para 6(1)(d) 9.27
  13 .... 9.25
  14 .... 9.27

Companies Act 1989 .... 9.1
s 137(1) 9.18

Companies Act 2006 .... 9.1, 9.7
s 170–177 .... 9.17

**Company Directors Disqualification
  Act 1986**
s 2(1) 27.38

Compensation Act 2006 .... 20.2
  s 3 .... 27.8
  Pt 2 (ss 4–15) 21.40

Competition Act 1998
  Pt I (ss 1–60) 41.1

Constitutional Reform Act 2005 .... 20.7

Consumer Protection Act 1987
  s 36 .... 27.21
  Sch 3 .... 27.21

Contempt of Court Act 1981 .... 30.5

Continental Shelf Act1964
  s 1(7) 12.12

Contracts (Applicable Law)
  Act 1990
  s 2(2) 26.11

County Courts Act 1984
  s 55(1), (2) 14.27
  69 .... 58.31

Courts and Legal Services
  Act 1990 .... 3.45, 14.33
  Sch 17
    para 5 .... 35.3

Crime and Disorder Act 1998
  s 31, 32 .... 28.28

Criminal Justice Act 1982
  s 37(2) 1.10
  77, 78 .... 19.1
  Sch 14
    para 36 .... 19.1
  Sch 16 .... 19.1

Criminal Justice Act 1991
  s 17 .... 1.10
  18 .... 1.10

Criminal Justice Act 1993
  s 65 .... 1.10

Criminal Justice Act 2003
  s 321 .... 49.5
  Sch 33 .... 49.5

Criminal Law Act 1977
  s 32(1) 1.10

Criminal Justice and Public Order
  Act 1994 .... 12.12, 28.28
  s 126 .... 37.2
  Sch 9
    para 11(2) 19.6

Crown Proceedings Act 1947 .... 13.32

Data Protection Act 1984 ..... 11.1, 11.13,
                       11.15, 44.7
  s 5(1), (2) 11.12
  21–23 .... 11.12
  Sch 1
  Pt 1
    para 7 .... 11.12

Data Protection Act 1998 ..... 11.1, 11.12,
                28.1, 40.6, 44.7
  s 1(1) 11.14
  Pt II(ss 7–15) 11.14
  s 7 .... 11.14
  10 .... 11.14
  12–14 .... 11.14
  51(3)(b) 5.14
  Sch 1 .... 11.14
  Sch 3 .... 11.14, 19.8
  Sch 8 .... 11.13

Deregulation and Contracting Out
  Act 1994 ...... 4.5, 20.11, 49.21, 54.3,
                           57.1
  s 20 .... 8.25
  Sch 10
    para 1 .... 47.3

Disability Discrimination
  Act 1995 .... 1.6, 10.1, 10.9, 10.10,
              10.11, 10.22, 13.9,
              13.21, 14.26, 15.4,
              17.1, 20.29, 21.9,
            21.18, 21.29, 23.1,
            23.2, 24.12, 25.7,
            36.1, 40.4, 42.4,
          42.7, 54.8, 57.13
  s 1(1) 10.2, 10.6
  (2) 10.3
  2(1) 10.5, 10.7
  (4), (5) 10.6
  3(3) 10.4
  Pt II (ss 3A–18D) 14.26, 20.22
  s 3A(1) 42.10
    (a), (b) 10.15
  (2) 10.12
  (3) 10.11, 10.15

Table of Statutes

Disability Discrimination Act 1995 –
contd

s 3a (4) 10.10
  (5) 10.10, 10.15
  (6) 10.11
 3B 10.21
 4(1) 10.19, 42.10
  (2) 10.20, 42.10
   (d) 10.21
  (3), (4) 10.24
  (5) 10.21
  (6) 10.24, 26.11
 4A 10.13, 10.15
  (1) 10.12, 42.10
  (2) 10.12, 10.14
  (3)(b) 10.15
 4B(1)–(3) 10.25
 4G 10.20, 42.10
 4H 10.20, 42.10
  (1) 10.14
 4I 42.10
 4J 42.10
  (4) 10.20
 5(6) 10.11
 6 .... 10.14, 10.23, 25.6
  (1) 10.15
 6A–7D 10.24
 8(2)–(4) 10.34
  (5) 10.34, 21.66
  (6) 10.34
 9 .... 8.17, 26.13
  (1) 10.36
  (2), (3) 10.37
 13(1)–(3) 10.26
 14 .... 10.26
 14A(3) 10.26
 14B 10.26
 15A–15C 10.24
 16 .... 10.13
 16A 10.17
 16B 10.18, 14.30
 16C 10.27, 14.30
 17A 20.11
  (1) 10.18, 10.34
  (1C) 10.15, 10.34
  (4) 10.18
  (5) 10.20, 42.10
 17B(1) 10.18
 18 .... 10.20
 18A 10.26, 10.34
  (2) 10.13
 18B(2) 10.14
  (6) 10.14
 18C 10.24

Disability Discrimination Act 1995 –
contd

s 18D(2) 10.12
Pt III (ss 19–28) 14.26, 14.30, 20.13
s 21B–21E 10.24
Pt IV (ss 28A–31C) 14.26
s 49A 10.24
 53 .... 5.12
  (4)–(6) 5.13
 53A 5.12
  (8), (8A) 10.32
 56 .... 21.8
  (2) 10.35
  (3)(a) 10.35
   (b) 10.35, 21.9
 57 .... 10.29
  (4) 10.27, 10.28, 10.30
  (5) 10.30
 58(1) 10.27, 56.1
  (2), (3) 10.28
  (5) 10.27
 59(1) 10.24
  (2A) 10.24
  (3) 10.24
 55(1)–(4) 10.16
 61(7) 10.3
  (b) 10.8
  (8) 10.3
 64 .... 37.2
  (7) 10.24
 68 .... 26.13
  (1) 10.17, 16.2
  (2), (2A) 10.24
  (4) 10.24
Sch 1
 para 1(1), (2) 10.2
  2(1)–(4) 10.2
  3(3) 10.7
  4(1), (2) 10.2
  5 .... 10.2
  6(1), (2) 10.7
   (3)(a) 10.7
  7(1), (2) 10.8
   (5) 10.8
  8(1) 10.7
Sch 3 .... 20.11
 para 2(1), (2) 10.33
  3(1) 10.34
   (2) 10.34, 20.29, 20.30
  (3), (4) 10.34
Sch 3A
 para 2 .... 21.33
Sch 4
 para 2 .... 10.34

Disability Discrimination Act 1995 –
contd
Sch 6
  para 4 .... 10.15

Disability Discrimination
  Act 2005 .... 10.1
s 1–3 .... 10.24
  10(2) 10.18
  11 .... 10.20
  17 .... 10.35
  18 .... 10.8
    (2) 10.2
    (3) 10.7

Disability Rights Commission
  Act 1999 .... 10.31
s 1–3 .... 10.31
  4 .... 10.31, 20.11
  5–7 .... 10.31
  9 .... 10.31
Sch 3
  para 23, 24 .... 10.31

Disabled Persons (Employment)
  Act 1944 .... 10.3, 10.8

Education Act 1996
  s 8 .... 4.1
  Pt II Ch V (ss 101–126) 37.2
  s 558 .... 4.1
  559(1)–(4) 4.3
  560(4), (5) 4.2
  579(1) 4.1

Education Act 2002 .... 15.4
s 31 .... 15.5, 15.10
  32 .... 15.5
    (2), (3) 15.11, 15.13
    (4) 15.11
    (6) 15.11
  40 .... 15.1
  119–130 .... 37.2
Sch 3 .... 15.5, 15.10, 15.11
Sch 4 .... 15.5

Education and Inspections
  Act 2006 .... 16.5

Education (Work Experience)
  Act 1973
  s 1 .... 4.2

Employers' Liability (Compulsory
  Insurance) Act 1969 .... 28.16

Employers' Liability (Defective
  Equipment) Act 1969
  s 1(3) 27.6

Employment Act 1980 .... 33.1, 51.3
  s 20 .... 7.1
  Sch 2 .... 7.1

Employment Act 1982 .... 51.3

Employment Act 1988 .... 51.3

Employment Act 1989 .... 4.5, 16.4
  s 3(2) 13.3
    (3) 13.18
  8 .... 13.9
  10(3)(b), (c) 4.5
    (4) 4.5
  11(1), (2) 12.5, 13.12
    (5) 28.4
  12(1), (2) 28.4
Sch 3
  Pt III 4.4

Employment Act 1990 .... 51.3

Employment Act 2002 .... 2.9, 2.10, 5.2,
                8.4, 15.11, 20.2,
           20.6, 20.16, 21.34,
                21.37, 29.6,
            33.2749.19, 54.4,
         54.10, 55.10, 57.23
  s 17(1) 33.20
  21(1), (2) 33.16
  22 .... 20.3
  24 .... 20.3, 21.29
  26 .... 20.3, 20.10
  27, 28 .... 20.3
  Pt III (ss 29–40) 15.1
  s 29 .... 20.19, 20.25, 51.15
  30 .... 8.5, 8.13, 8.25. 54.3
    (2) 8.17
    (3) 54.3
  31 .... 20.3, 57.22
    (2) 15.12, 55.13
    (c)(ii) 54.15
    (3), (4) 15.12, 55.13
    (6) 55.13

Table of Statutes

Employment Act 2002 – *contd*
s 32 .... 10.34, 14.9, 15.14, 20.3, 20.5,
　　　　20.16, 20.18, 20.19,
　　　　20.20, 20.23, 20.24,
　　　　20.25, 20.30, 20.31,
　　　　21.10, 32.20, 51.15,
　　　　53.2, 57.22
(2), (3) 15.13, 51.15
(4) 15.13, 20.19, 51.15
(5) 20.19
(6) 20.19, 51.16
(8) 20.19
33 .... 20.3, 20.16, 20.18, 20.19, 20.20,
　　　　20.23, 20.30, 21.10
34 .... 54.3, 54.4, 54.11, 55.13
(3), (4) 55.5
(6) 55.8
35, 36 .... 8.5
38 .... 55.16
(2), (3) 55.13
(5) 55.13
Sch 2 ... 8.23, 14.9, 20.23, 20.19, 24.22,
　　　　39.8, 53.15, 57.22
para 1 .... 15.2
2(1)–(4) 15.2
3 .... 15.8
(2)–(5) 15.2
4 .... 15.2
5 .... 15.8
(1)–(4) 15.2
6 .... 15.4, 15.9, 53.7
7 .... 15.9, 53.7
(1)–(4) 15.4
8 .... 15.9, 53.7
(1)–(4) 15.4
9 .... 15.4, 53.7
10 .... 15.4
11–13 .... 15.2
Pt 3 .... 54.3
para 14 .... 15.2, 54.3
15(1) 15.5
(2) 15.4
Sch 3 .... 20.32, 32.21, 57.22
Sch 4 .... 15.13, 20.19, 20.32, 32.20,
　　　　32.21, 57.22
Sch 5 .... 8.9

Employment Agencies Act 1973
s 3–3D 47.3
5(2) 47.5
6 .... 47.3
13 .... 17.3
(2), (3) 47.5

Employment and Training Act 1963
s 2 .... 3.40

Employment and Training Act 1973
s 2 .... 13.30
8, 9 .... 16.5
10 .... 13.30, 16.5
10A, 10B 16.5

Employment of Children Act 1973
s 2(2), (2A) 4.3
(3) 4.3

**Employment of Women, Young
　Persons and Children Act 1920**
s 1(1), (2) 4.4
3(2) 4.4
Schedule 4.4

Employment Protection Act 1975 ...... 2.1,
　　　　5.2, 18.1, 33.1,
　　　　34.23, 38.1, 50.4,
　　　　50.19
s 97 (5) 29.7
Sch 9
Pt I 29.7

**Employment Protection
　(Consolidation) Act 1978** ... 1.6, 25.2,
　　　　25.7, 33.1, 38.1,
　　　　53.1, 54.3
s 8 .... 34.16
140(1) 53.19
151 .... 7.1
(3) 7.3
Sch 3 .... 48.12
Sch 9
para 1(5A) 14.11
Sch 13 .... 7.1, 38.4, 38.13
para 9(1)(b), (c) 7.7
17(2) 7.9
Sch 14 .... 34.34, 38.13, 48.15

Employment Relations Act 1999 .... 2.4,
　　　　12.12, 33.1, 47.3,
　　　　50.11, 50.19, 51.10,
　　　　55.7
s 1 .... 18.29
(2) 53.11, 54.3, 54.11
3, 4 .... 51.10
5 .... 18.29, 50.38
10 .... 7.13, 15.3, 22.1, 51.21, 53.11,
　　　　54.3, 54.10
(2B), (2c) 51.21

Employment Relations Act 1999 – *contd*
s 10 (4) 15.7, 51.21
 (5) 51.21
 (6) 49.2, 51.21
11 .... 20.11, 54.3, 54.10
 (1), (2) 51.21
12 .... 51.21, 54.2
 (4) 7.13, 53.11
13(4) 51.21
16 .... 7.13, 53.11, 53.17, 54.3
18(1) 53.15
19–21 .... 32.1
22 .... 34.10
23 .... 53.3
24 .... 50.25
28 .... 51.17
30 .... 18.1, 18.30
32(3) 53.15
34(1) 55.16
 (4) 55.10
37 .... 54.3
 (1) 55.10, 55.16
 (4) 51.4
38 .... 52.1
128 .... 15.8
Sch 1 .... 18.29, 50.19, 50.25, 51.17,
 53.11, 54.3, 54.11
 para 30, 31 .... 6.2
Sch 2 .... 51.17
Sch 3 .... 45.14
Sch 5 .... 7.13, 53.11, 53.17, 53.18, 54.3

Employment Relations Act 2004 .... 5.4,
 50.19, 50.25, 53.17,
 53.18
s 22 .... 45.14, 45.15
29 .... 30.4, 51.17
38 .... 22.1

Employment Rights Act 1996 ..... 1.6, 7.1,
 10.22, 12.12, 13.33,
 14.19, 17.1, 20.11,
 20.22, 21.34, 25.6,
 25.7, 26.3, 26.11,
 26.13, 27.1, 28.7,
 31.1, 33.1, 34.14,
 34.23, 38.1, 53.1,
 53.6, 54.3, 54.8,
 57.31
s 1 .... 8.7, 8.9, 9.6, 9.8, 52.22
 (1), (2) 8.4
 (3) 8.5
 (4) 8.5
 (d)(i) 29.9

Employment Rights Act 1996 – *contd*
s 1(4)(d) (ii), (iii) 8.6
 (e) 8.6
 (5) 8.5
2 .... 9.6
 (1) 8.5
 (2), (3) 8.6
 (4)–(6) 8.4
3 .... 8.4, 9.6
 (1) 8.5
 (2) 8.5, 8.23
 (5) 8.5
4 .... 8.9, 9.6
 (1) 8.7, 38.12
 (3) 8.7
 (6) 8.7
 (8) 8.7
5 .... 9.6
 (1) 8.8
6 .... 9.6
7 .... 8.5
7A(1)(c) 8.4
7B 8.4
8 .... 34.16, 35.9
9 .... 35.9
 (1)–(4) 34.17
11 .... 20.9, 34.8, 34.20
 (1), (2) 8.9, 34.19
 (4) 8.9, 34.19
12(1), (2) 8.9
 (3)–(5) 34.20
Pt II (ss 13–27) 8.17, 8.23, 20.9,
 20.11, 20.31, 21.29,
 29.6, 34.2, 34.6,
 34.12, 51.20
s 13 .... 8.9, 24.9, 48.11
 (1) 34.6, 34.8, 34.12
 (2)–(4) 34.6
14 .... 8.9, 34.6, 48.11
15 .... 8.9, 48.11
 (1) 34.6, 34.8
 (2) 34.6
 (5) 34.6
16 .... 8.9, 48.11
17 .... 8.9, 48.11
 (1)–(3) 34.7
18 .... 8.9, 48.11
 (1)–(3) 34.7, 34.8
19 .... 8.9, 48.11
 (1) 34.7
20 .... 8.9, 48.11
 (1) 34.7, 34.8
 (2), (3) 34.7
 (5) 34.7

Table of Statutes

Employment Rights Act 1996 – *contd*

s 21 .... 8.9, 48.11
 (1) 34.7, 34.8
 (3) 34.7
22 .... 8.9, 48.11
 (1)–(4) 34.7
23 .... 8.9, 20.9, 34.8, 34.20, 41.1,
 48.11
 (1) 34.8
 (3) 20.31, 29.6, 34.8
 (4) 20.31
24 .... 8.9, 34.8, 34.20, 48.11
25 .... 8.9, 34.8, 34.20
 (1), (2) 34.8
 (3) 34.6, 34.8
 (4), (5) 34.8
26 .... 8.9, 34.8, 48.11
27 .... 8.9, 34.12, 48.11
 (1)–(3) 34.6
 (5) 34.6
Pt III (ss 28–35) 31.2, 31.5, 34.2
s 28 .... 21.29
 (1)–(5) 34.24
29(1) 7.13, 34.25
 (2) 34.25
 (3)–(5) 34.26
30(1) 21.63, 34.27
 (2)–(5) 34.27
31, 32 .... 34.27
34 .... 20.9, 51.4
 (1)–(3) 34.28
35 .... 34.27
36–39 .... 8.25, 57.1
40 .... 57.1
41 .... 57.1
 (2), (3) 8.25
42 .... 57.1
 (2) 8.25
43 .... 8.25, 57.1
Pt IVA (ss 43A–43L) 15.4, 40.4
s 43A 7.13, 18.10, 18.12, 18.26,
 53.11, 54.3, 54.11
 43B 7.13, 28.9, 53.11, 54.3, 54.11
 (1)(b) 11.18
 (2)–(4) 11.18
 43C–43F 7.13, 11.18, 28.9, 53.11,
 54.3, 54.11
 43G 7.13, 11.18, 28.9, 53.11, 54.3,
 54.11
 (2)(a)–(c) 11.18
 (3)–(4) 11.18
 43H 7.13, 11.18, 28.9, 53.11, 54.3,
 54.11
 43I 7.13, 53.11, 54.3, 54.11

Employment Rights Act 1996 – *contd*

s 43J 7.13, 11.18, 53.11, 54.3, 54.11
 43K 7.13, 17.1, 28.9, 53.11, 54.3,
 54.11
 43L 7.13, 53.11, 54.3, 54.11
44 .... 11.18
 (2), (3) 28.8
 45(1)–(8) 8.25
45A 57.23
46 .... 42.12
47 .... 52.23
47A 4.9
47B 11.17, 11.18, 21.29, 28.9, 40.4,
 57.23
47C 49.19
47E 49.19
48 .... 4.9, 8.25, 33.9, 34.12
 (1), (1A) 28.10
 (2)–(4) 28.10
49 .... 18.11, 18.27, 28.10, 33.9, 34.12,
 57.23, 57.24
50 .... 21.29
 (4) 49.5
51(1)–(3) 49.6
52 .... 21.29
 (1), (2) 49.7
53 .... 21.29, 31.2
 (1)–(6) 49.7
 (7) 49.8
54(1), (2) 49.8
 (4) 49.8
55 .... 21.29, 49.11
 (1) 33.2, 33.3, 33.5
 (2)(a), (b) 33.3
56 .... 21.29, 31.2
 (1) 33.2, 33.3, 33.5
 (2)–(4) 33.4
 (5), (6) 33.5
57 .... 7.13
 (1)–(5) 33.5
57A 49.18, 54.3
 (1)–(6) 49.17
57B(1)–(4) 49.18
58 .... 42.12, 47.12
 (1), (2) 49.12
59 .... 42.12, 47.12
 (1)–(4) 49.12
 (6) 49.13
60 .... 42.12, 47.12
 (1)–(5) 49.13
61 .... 49.14, 52.23
62 .... 52.23
 (1) 49.14
63 .... 52.23

Employment Rights Act 1996 – *contd*
s 63A(1) 4.7, 4.9
   (2)(c) 4.7
   (3) 4.7, 4.9
   (4), (5) 4.7
   (7) 4.7
  63B(1)–(4) 4.7, 4.9
  63C 4.7
   (1)–(5) 4.8
  Pt VII (ss 64–70) 31.2
s 64 .... 21.29
   (3) 34.29
   (5) 34.30
  65(1) 7.13, 34.30
   (2) 34.30
   (3) 34.31
   (4)(a), (b) 34.31
  66 .... 24.4, 33.23
   (1) 33.6
   (2) 33.6, 33.8
  67 .... 24.4, 57.13
   (1), (2) 33.24
  68 .... 21.29, 24.4, 33.25
  69 .... 24.4
   (1)–(3) 33.25, 34.32
  70 .... 20.9, 24.4
   (1)–(3) 33.25, 34.33
   (4)–(7) 33.24
  71 .... 7.6, 33.8, 33.17, 33.18, 48.19,
                        53.4
   (1) 12.5, 12.6
   (4) 42.9
   (c) 33.20
   (5) 42.9
  72 .... 33.17, 33.20, 49.19
   (1) 12.5, 12.6, 24.14
   (5) 33.20
  73 .... 7.6, 33.17, 49.19
   (1) 12.5, 12.6
  74, 75 .... 33.17
  75A, 75B 7.6, 49.19
  75C, 75D 49.19
  76 .... 49.19
  80 .... 2.4
  80A, 80B 49.19
  80C 49.19
   (1) 7.6
  80D, 80E 49.19
  80F–80H 2.10, 49.19, 54.3
  80I 2.10, 47.19
  86 .... 3.47, 31.5, 53.13, 54.3, 58.16,
                       58.27
   (1) 48.7
   (a) 44.5

Employment Rights Act 1996 – *contd*
s 86 (2) 48.17
   (3) 48.7, 58.16, 58.21
   (4) 7.13, 44.5
   (5) 48.8
   (6) 38.4
  87(1) 7.13, 48.12, 58.27
   (2) 48.12
   (4) 48.12, 58.27
  88–90 .... 48.12, 58.27
  91(1)–(4) 48.12
   (5) 48.12, 58.27
  92 .... 32.17
   (1) 46.14, 46.15, 48.14, 48.15
   (3) 7.13, 48.15
   (4) 48.14
   (7) 7.6, 55.7
  93 .... 40.8
   (1)–(3) 48.15
  94(1) 53.3
  95 .... 39.4, 52.25
   (1) 48.18, 53.4
   (a), (b) 15.3, 15.5
   (c) 28.11
   (2) 53.5
  97(1) 20.23, 38.4, 53.13
   (2) 7.6, 53.13
   (4) 53.13, 55.7
  98(1) 54.1, 54.2
   (b) 47.7, 54.13, 54.14
   (2) 54.2, 54.14
   (ba) 3.48, 42.3
   (d) 54.13
   (3) 54.5
   (3A) 54.4
   (4) 21.59, 22.17, 30.7, 32.19,
                 36.2, 41.1, 54.4,
                  54.9, 54.11
   (b) 47.7
   (6) 36.2
  98A 15.11, 55.5, 55.8
   (1) 54.3, 55.13
   (2) 54.4, 54.11, 55.13
  98B 7.13, 53.18, 54.3, 54.11
  98ZA–98ZF 42.3
  98ZG 54.4
  98ZH 3.13, 42.3
  99 .... 53.18, 54.3, 54.11
  100 .... 53.15, 53.18, 54.11, 55.10,
                      55.16
   (1)(a), (b) 55.8, 55.9, 55.16
   (d), (e) 54.3
   (2)–(3) 54.3
  101 .... 54.3, 54.11

Table of Statutes

Employment Rights Act 1996 – *contd*

s 101 (1)–(3) 8.25
101A 54.3, 54.11, 57.24
(1)(d) 53.18, 55.8, 55.9, 55.16
102 .... 42.12, 54.3, 54.11
(1) 55.8, 55.9, 55.16
103 .... 52.23, 53.18, 54.3, 54.11, 55.8,
55.9, 55.16
103A 11.18, 21.29, 53.15, 53.18,
54.3, 54.11, 55.10,
55.16
104 .... 34.6, 53.18, 54.11, 57.24
(1)–(3) 54.3
(4) 8.25
104A 34.12, 54.3, 54.11
104B 54.3, 54.11
104C 49.19, 53.19, 54.3
105 .... 54.3, 54.11
(1) 8.25
(c) 54.3
(3) 55.10, 55.16
(4) 8.25
(6A) 21.29, 54.3, 55.10, 55.16
(7D) 54.3
106 .... 33.22, 47.7
107 .... 54.16
108(2) 7.13, 53.11
(3) 8.25, 33.7
(aa) 53.11
(b)–(l) 7.13, 53.11
(m), (n) 7.13, 53.11
(o) 7.13, 53.11
109 .... 13.8, 24.10
(1) 42.2, 42.4, 53.14
(2) 8.25, 33.7, 42.5
110 .... 15.3, 54.3
111 .... 20.23
(2) 20.25, 53.2
(3) 20.24, 20.32
112 .... 21.37
(1) 55.1
(5) 55.5
113 .... 21.37
114 .... 21.37
(1) 55.2
(3) 55.2
(4) 55.4
115 .... 21.37
(1), (2) 55.3
(3) 55.4
116 .... 21.37
(1) 55.2
(2) 55.3
(4) 55.3

Employment Rights Act 1996 – *contd*

s 116 (5), (6) 55.4
117 .... 21.37, 55.14
(1) 55.4
(2) 55.4, 55.5
(2A) 55.5
(3), (4) 21.66, 55.4, 55.5
(5) 21.66
(7) 55.5
118 .... 21.37
(1) 55.6
119 .... 21.37
(2), (3) 55.7
120 .... 21.37, 55.9
(1)–(1B) 55.8
121 .... 21.37, 55.8
122 .... 21.37
(1)–(3) 55.9
(3A) 55.8, 55.9
(4) 55.8, 55.9
123 .... 21.37
(1) 55.11, 55.13
(2), (3) 55.11
(6), (7) 55.13
(8) 55.5
124 .... 21.37, 51.16
(1A) 11.18, 54.3, 55.16
(3) 55.4
(4), (5) 55.10
124A 15.10, 55.13
127A 58.30
127B 11.18
128 .... 20.9, 20.18, 54.3, 55.18
(2)–(5) 55.18
129–132 .... 20.9, 20.18, 55.18
Pt XI (ss 135–181) 31.3, 52.11
s 135 .... 3.26, 38.2
136(1) 38.6, 48.18
(2), (3) 38.6
(5) 38.6
138(1) 7.6, 38.6, 55.8
(2) 38.6, 38.12
(3) 38.6
(4) 38.6, 38.12
(5) 38.6
(6) 38.6, 38.12
139(1) 38.7
140(1)–(3) 38.10
141 .... 55.8
(1) 38.10, 38.12
(2) 38.10
(3), (4) 38.10, 38.12
(4) 38.10, 38.12
142(1), (2) 38.6

Employment Rights Act 1996 – *contd*
s 145 .... 20.27, 38.4
 (5) 7.6, 38.4
145A, 145B 54.3
146(1) 38.6
 (2) 38.12
147(2) 38.8
148 .... 38.8, 38.9
149 .... 38.9
150(1) 38.8
 (3) 38.8
152(1)(b) 38.9
155 .... 7.13, 38.2, 38.4
156 .... 13.8, 24.10
157 .... 31.4, 38.10
38.13 159–161 .... 38.10
162(1)–(3) 3.26, 38.13
163 .... 20.9, 21.29
 (1) 38.14
 (2) 38.7
164 .... 20.22, 21.29, 31.4
 (1), (2) 20.27, 38.11
 (3) 20.27
166 .... 31.5
 (5)–(8) 31.4
167 .... 7.12
 (3), (4) 31.4
169 .... 31.4
170 .... 20.9, 31.4
Pt XII (ss 182–190) 31.3, 31.4, 31.7,
 52.11
s 182 .... 17.3, 31.5
183 .... 31.5
184(1)(a) 31.5
 (2) 31.5
185–187 .... 31.5
188 .... 20.9, 31.7
189, 190 .... 31.5
191 .... 37.2, 37.3, 58.43
192 .... 37.2
193 .... 37.6
196 .... 53.15
 (2), (3) 34.8, 34.18
 (5) 53.15
197(1) 53.15
198 .... 8.4, 8.8
199 .... 8.8, 48.8, 53.15
 (2) 34.18, 38.10, 53.15
 (4) 34.18
200 .... 53.15
 (1) 34.18, 37.2
 (2) 37.2
201 .... 53.15
202 .... 37.6

Employment Rights Act 1996 – *contd*
s 203 .... 8.25, 21.33, 21.34, 21.35,
 32.23, 48.7, 55.19
 (1) ... 2.4, 8.17, 21.32, 34.8, 38.14,
 46.2, 53.19
 (2) ... 2.4, 8.17, 34.8, 38.14, 53.15,
 53.20
 (f) 21.33
 (3), (4) 21.33
205(2) 34.8
206(4) 20.9
Pt XIV (ss 210–235) 47.14
s 210 .... 7.1, 38.13, 53.12
 (1)–(3) 7.2
 (4) 7.5, 7.12
 (5) 7.5
211 .... 7.1, 38.13, 53.12
 (1) 7.3
 (2) 7.3, 38.4
 (3) 7.3, 7.11
212 .... 7.1, 38.13, 53.12
 (1) 7.6
 (3) 7.6, 7.7
 (a) 7.7
 (b) 7.7, 47.8
 (c) 7.7
 (4) 7.6
213 .... 7.1, 38.13, 53.12
214 .... 7.1, 7.12, 38.13, 53.12
 (2) 38.13
215 .... 7.1, 7.5, 7.12, 53.12
 (1)(a) 7.10
 (2)(a), (b) 7.10
216 .... 7.1, 7.5, 7.12, 38.1, 38.13,
 53.12
 (1)–(3) 7.10
217 .... 7.1, 7.5, 7.12, 38.13, 53.12
218 .... 3.25, 7.1, 38.13, 53.12
 (2)–(6) 7.9
 (8)–(10) 37.2
219 .... 7.1, 7.6, 38.13, 53.12, 55.4
220 .... 34.32
221 .... 29.4, 34.12, 34.32, 34.34,
 38.13, 48.15, 55.7
 (2), (3) 34.35, 34.36
222 ... 34.34, 34.35, 38.13, 48.15, 55.7
223 .... 34.34, 38.13, 48.15, 55.7
 (1), (2) 34.35
 (3) 34.36
224 .... 29.4, 34.34, 34.37, 38.13,
 48.15, 55.7
225 .... 34.12, 34.34, 34.38, 38.13,
 48.15, 55.7
226 .... 34.12, 34.34, 38.13, 55.7

Table of Statutes

Employment Rights Act 1996 – *contd*
s 226 (2) 48.15
227 .... 34.12, 34.34, 38.13, 48.15,
51.16, 55.7
(1) 50.38, 51.21, 55.7
(b) 42.3
228, 229 ... 34.12, 34.34, 38.13, 48.15,
55.7
230 .... 17.1, 17.9, 32.2
(1) 38.3, 53.3
(2) 16.2, 17.2
(3) 34.6, 34.12, 54.3
231 .... 7.9, 34.38
232(1) 8.25
(3) 8.25
(6) 8.25
233(1), (2) 8.25
234 .... 29.4
(1)–(3) 34.36
235 .... 7.5
(1) 33.18, 33.19, 55.3
240 .... 35.5
Sch 1
para 3 .... 35.4
56 .... 53.17
Sch 2
para 16 .... 37.2
Sch 7

**Employment Rights (Dispute
Resolution) Act 1998** 20.1, 20.2,
21.33, 24.2
s 2 .... 20.10
4 .... 20.8
7 .... 2.10, 21.37
9 .... 14.33
11 .... 2.4
15 .... 55.9
Sch 1
para 2, 3 .... 21.34
9 .... 21.34
11 .... 21.34
22 .... 55.9
24 .... 21.34

Employment Tribunals Act 1996 .... 1.6,
20.6, 20.7
s 3 .... 58.38
4 .... 20.5, 20.9, 34.12, 37.6
(2) 20.9
(5) 20.9
(6A) 20.10
6 .... 21.55
7(3A) 20.10

Employment Tribunals Act 1996 – *contd*
s 7 (4) 21.4
10 .... 37.6
11 .... 14.11
(1)(a) 21.19
(2) 21.18
(6) 14.11, 21.18
12 .... 21.18
(1)–(2) 10.34
(3) 10.34, 21.18
(7) 10.34
15 .... 21.66
18 .... 2.4, 7.6
(1) 2.4, 14.10
(2) 2.4, 14.10, 21.29
(2A) 21.29
(3) 2.4, 14.10, 21.29
(4)–(5) 2.4
(7) .... 2.4, 14.10 , 21.29
21 .... 22.1
22(1)(c) 22.2
28 .... 37.6
(3), (4) 22.2
29(1) 22.14
(2) 22.21
30(3) 22.1
32 .... 10.34, 21.18
33 .... 21.77, 30.7
35 .... 22.21
(1) 22.11
37(1), (2) 22.26
218(7)–(10) 7.9

Enterprise Act 2002 .... 41.1

**Enterprise and New Towns
(Scotland) Act 1990**
s 2(3) 13.30

Equal Pay Act 1970 .... 1.6, 5.8, 5.9, 8.13,
8.17, 12.10, 12.12,
13.8, 13.10, 13.33,
14.24, 14.33, 20.19,
20.22, 21.29, 21.34,
24.1, 24.2, 24.5,
24.10, 24.11, 24.14,
24.17, 24.19, 24.22,
24.23, 25.2, 25.7,
32.1, 32.11, 42.12,
52.19
s 1 .... 24.9, 24.25, 26.11, 26.13
(1) 24.4, 24.5
(2)(a), (b) 24.5
(c) 24.5, 24.8

Equal Pay Act 1970 – *contd*
s 1(2) (d)–(f) 24.14
  (3) 24.5, 24.10, 24.12, 24.22
    (a), (b) 24.11
  (4) 24.6, 32.10
  (5) 24.7
  (6) 24.9
    (a) 24.4
    (c) 24.9
  (6A)–(6C) 24.4
  (11) 24.4
  (13) 24.4
2 .... 14.29, 14.33, 20.11, 24.17
  (1), (1A) 24.20
  (2), (3) 24.20
  (4) 20.28, 24.13, 24.19, 24.20
  (5) 24.9, 24.19, 24.20
2A 20.11, 24.17
  (1) 24.22
  (2) 24.8, 24.22
  (2A) 24.23
2ZA 24.20
  (2)–(7) 20.28
2ZB 24.20
3 .... 24.25
5 .... 24.21
5A, 5B 24.14
7A 37.2
7B 21.8, 24.23
  (4) 21.9
11(2A) 20.28

Equal Pay Act (Northern Ireland) 1970 .... 24.4

Equality Act 2006 .... 13.1, 13.33, 14.1,
                   14.23, 20.11
Pt I (ss 1–43) 14.26
s 1–5 .... 14.26
  6(1)–(3) 14.27
  (6) 14.27
8 .... 14.27, 14.31
  (1) 14.26
9 .... 14.27, 14.31
  (4) 14.26
10 .... 14.27, 14.31
11, 12 .... 14.26
14(1) 14.26
  (6), (7) 14.26
15(4) 14.26
16(1), (2) 14.27
17 .... 14.31
20(1)–(5) 14.27
21 .... 14.27, 14.28

Equality Act 2006 – *contd*
s 21 (1), (2) 14.28
  (4)–(7) 14.28
21 .... 14.27, 14.28
22(2), (3) 14.28
  (5) 14.28
  (6)(b), (c) 14.28
  (7) 14.28
  (9) 14.28
23 .... 14.29
  (1) 14.28
24(1)–(3) 14.29
25(1)–(6) 14.30
26(1)–(3) 14.30
28(1) 14.31
  (4) 14.31
  (6), (7) 14.31
  (12), (13) 14.31
29 .... 14.31
30 .... 14.26
31, 32 .... 14.27
33(1) 14.26
34 .... 14.26
36 .... 10.31, 14.26
37, 38 .... 14.26
40 .... 14.26
Pt II (ss 44–80) 14.26, 14.30
s 54, 55 .... 14.30
  77(2) 12.6
Pt III (ss 81–82) 14.26
Sch 1
  para 32 .... 14.26
Sch 2
  para 2, 3 .... 14.27
    6–11 .... 14.27
    12(2) 14.27
    13 .... 14.27
    15, 16 .... 14.27
    18, 19 .... 14.27
Sch 3 .... 14.26

European Communities Act 1972 ..... 25.1
s 2(1) 25.2
  (2) 52.1

European Communities (Amendment) Act 1986 .... 25.1

European Communities (Amendment) Act 1993 .... 25.1

Factories Act 1961 .... 4.5
s 1–7 .... 28.29
  18 .... 28.29

Table of Statutes

Factories Act 1961 – *contd*
s 28, 29 .... 28.29
57–60 .... 28.29
69 .... 28.29
175(5) 28.29

**Fair Employment (Northern Ireland)
Act 1976** 12.8

Family Law Reform Act 1969
s 1 .... 4.1

Finance Act 1988
s 74 .... 48.10

Finance Act 2000
s 47 .... 46.31
58 .... 46.33
62 .... 46.32
Sch 8 .... 46.31
Sch 12 .... 46.35
Sch 14 .... 46.32

Finance Act 2001
s 62 .... 46.32
Sch 14 .... 46.32

Finance Act 2003
s 136 .... 46.35
Sch 21 .... 46.29, 46.31
para 16 .... 46.30
Sch 22 .... 46.29, 46.31

Finance Act 2004
s 78, 79 .... 46.23
Pt IV (ss 149–284) 42.7, 42.11
Sch 13 .... 46.23

Financial Services Act 1986
s 189 .... 19.4
Sch 14 .... 19.4

**Financial Services and Markets
Act 2000**
Pt IV (ss 40–55) 9.23
Pt VI (ss 72–103) 9.22

Fire Precautions Act 1971 .... 27.38, 28.13
s 23 .... 28.13

Gender Recognition Act 2004 .... 24.13
s 9 .... 13.5
14 .... 13.5

Health Act 2006 .... 28.23

**Health and Safety at Work etc
Act 1974** 5.10, 18.1, 20.4, 27.1,
27.3, 27.16, 27.25,
28.13, 33.23, 56.1,
57.20, 57.21
Pt I (ss 1–54) 27.17, 27.29
s 1(1) 27.17
2 ...... 27.28, 27.37, 27.43, 28.2, 28.28
(1) 27.18
(2) 27.18
(c) 11.7
(e) 28.23
(3) 11.7, 27.18
(4) 28.21
(6) 28.21
3 .... 27.28, 27.37, 27.43
(1) 27.19, 27.37
(2), (3) 27.19
4 .... 27.20, 27.28, 27.37, 27.43
5 .... 27.28, 27.37, 27.43
6 .... 27.28, 27.37, 27.43
(8), (8A) 27.21
7 .... 27.22, 27.28, 27.37, 27.43
8 .... 27.23, 27.37, 27.43
9 .... 27.24, 27.37, 28.12
10 .... 27.26
14(1) 27.26
(2) 27.26
(a), (b) 27.40
16 .... 5.10, 27.28
17 .... 5.11
(2) 27.37
20 .... 27.37
(2)(a)–(i) 27.30
(4) 27.30
(7), (8) 27.30
21 .... 27.31, 27.32
22 .... 27.32
23(2)(a) 27.32
(5) 27.33
24(2) 27.34
(3)(a), (b) 27.35
(4) 27.34
25 .... 27.37
(1) 27.30
27 .... 27.27
(1) 27.37
(4) 27.37
28 .... 27.37
33 .... 27.37
(1) 11.7
(a) 27.37

Health and Safety at Work etc Act 1974 – *contd*
s 33(1) (b) 27.23, 27.37, 27.39
    (c)–(f) 27.37
    (g) 27.37, 27.41
    (h)–(o) 27.37
    (1A) 11.7, 27.37
    (2) 27.37
    (2A) 27.37, 27.39
    (3) 11.7, 27.37
    (b) 27.23
    (4)(a)–(c) 27.37
    (7) 27.37
  34(1)–(3) 27.40
  37 .... 27.38
  40 .... 27.41
  42(1), (2) 27.39
    (4) 27.37
  47(1)(a) 27.43
    (2) 27.43
    (5) 27.43
  53(1) 27.29
  Sch 1 .... 27.17, 27.29, 27.37, 27.38

Highways Act 1980
s 137(1) 45.12

Housing Act 1980 .... 43.5
  s 52 .... 43.5
  55 .... 43.6

Housing Act 1985
  Sch 1
    para 2(1)–(3) 43.7
    5(1) 43.7

Housing Act 1988 .... 43.1, 43.5
  s 1 .... 43.5
  7 .... 43.6
  9 .... 43.6
  13, 14 .... 43.8
  19A 43.5
  20, 20A 43.5
  21 .... 43.6
  22 .... 43.8
  24, 25 .... 43.9
  27 .... 43.3
  29 .... 43.3
  32 .... 43.4
  Sch 2
    Ground 16 .... 43.6
  Sch 2A 43.5

Housing Act 1996
  s 96, 97 .... 43.5
  98, 99 .... 43.6
  100 .... 43.8
  103 .... 43.9

Human Rights Act 1998 .... 1.7, 2.10,
              11.14, 12.10, 13.33,
              20.7, 21.16, 21.37,
              27.37, 28.3, 30.1,
              30.5, 45.1
  s 1, 2 .... 30.6
  3 .... 30.6, 30.7
  4 .... 22.1, 30.6
    (5) 30.7
  6 .... 20.13, 21.51
    (3) 30.6
  7 .... 20.13, 30.6
  8 .... 30.6
  10 .... 30.6
  19 .... 30.6

Immigration and Asylum Act 1999
  s 22 .... 26.9, 26.11
  15–26 .... 26.10

Income and Corporation Taxes Act 1988 .... 17.1, 46.1
  s 148 .... 48.10, 58.32
  150 .... 44.6
  188 .... 58.32
    (4) 48.10
  198 .... 46.28
  588 .... 16.1

Income Tax (Earnings and Pensions) Act 2003 .... 46.1
  s 7 .... 46.2
  44–47 .... 46.2
  48–61 .... 46.2, 46.35
  62 .... 46.2, 46.23
  63 .... 46.2, 46.3
  64–66 .... 46.2
  67, 68 .... 46.2, 46.3
  69 .... 46.2
  70–83 .... 46.2, 46.21
  84 .... 46.2, 46.21
    (2A) 46.23
  85–98 .... 46.2, 46.21
  99, 100 .... 46.2, 46.21, 46.23
  101–113 .... 46.2, 46.21
  114–148 .... 46.2, 46.21, 46.25
  149–153 .... 46.2, 46.21, 46.26
  154 .... 46.2, 46.21

Table of Statutes

Income Tax (Earnings and Pensions) Act 2003 – *contd*
s 155–170 .... 46.2, 46.21, 46.27
171–200 .... 46.2, 46.21
201, 202 .... 46.2
203, 204 .... 46.2, 46.2, 46.21
205 .... 46.2, 46.21
206–215 .... 46.2
216–220 .... 46.2, 46.3
221–223 .... 46.2
225, 226 .... 46.2
229–232 .... 46.21
235, 236 .... 46.21
237 .... 46.23
242–248 .... 46.23
248A 46.27
250–264 .... 46.23
270A 46.23
271–289 .... 46.21, 46.23
313 .... 46.23
316, 317 .... 46.23
318–318D 46.23
319, 320 .... 46.23
325 .... 46.21, 46.23
333–336 .... 46.28
386–400 .... 46.2
401–403 .... 46.2, 46.8
404–417 .... 46.2
418 .... 46.2, 46.31
419–487 .... 46.2
488–515 .... 46.2, 46.31
516–520 .... 46.2, 46.29
521–526 .... 46.2, 46.30
527–541 .... 46.2, 46.32
542–554 .... 46.2
684 .... 46.4
686 .... 46.4
708 .... 46.4
713–715 .... 46.33
Sch 2 .... 46.31
Sch 3 .... 46.29
Sch 4 .... 46.30
Sch 5 .... 46.32

Industrial Courts Act 1919 .... 50.6

Industrial Relations Act 1971 ..... 5.1, 5.2, 51.3, 53.1
s 134 .... 45.10

Industrial Training Act 1982
s 5(1), (2) 16.4
(4)(d) 16.4
6(1) 16.4

Industrial Training Act 1982 – *contd*
s 11 .... 16.4

Infants Relief Act 1874 .... 4.10

Insolvency Act 1986 .... 30.1
s 19 .... 9.27, 31.11
29(2) 31.11
44 .... 9.27
(2) 31.11
s 386 .... 31.2
Sch 1B
para 10 .... 31.11
14 .... 31.11
22 .... 31.11
9(5)(a) 31.11
Sch 6 .... 31.2
para 9–15 .... 31.2

Insolvency Act 1994 .... 9.28

Judgments Act 1838 .... 21.67

Law of Property Act 1925
s 146 .... 43.5

Law Reform (Contributory Negligence) Act 1945
s 1(1) 27.44

Law Reform (Frustrated Contracts) Act 1943
s 1(3) 48.3

Law Reform (Personal Injuries) Act 1948
s 1(3) 27.7

Learning and Skills Act 2000 ... 16.5, 16.9

Limitation Act 1980 .... 31.11
s 5 .... 58.40
33 .... 20.30
(3) 14.7

Limited Partnerships Act 1907
s 3 .... 3.35

Local Government Act 1972
s 112 .... 37.2
116 .... 37.2

Local Government Act 1988
s 17 .... 14.32

Local Government Act 1988 – *contd*
Pt II(ss 24–26) 51.19

Local Government and Housing Act 1989
s 1–3 .... 37.2
7 .... 10.24, 37.2
10 .... 49.5
12 .... 37.2

Magistrates' Courts Act 1980
s 32(2) 11.7

Merchant Shipping Act 1979
s 39 .... 35.2

Merchant Shipping Act 1995
s 55(1A) 4.4
85 .... 57.32, 57.33
314(2) 35.2
Sch 13
para 46 .... 35.2

Minors' Contracts Act 1987
s 1 .... 4.10

Misuse of Drugs Act 1971
s 8 .... 28.2

National Health Service and Community Care Act 1990
s 6(1) 8.13

National Minimum Wage Act 1998 .... 7.13, 16.2, 17.1, 17.9, 20.11, 26.3, 29.2, 53.11, 54.11, 57.5, 57.22
s 2, 3 .... 34.10
5–8 .... 34.10
9, 10 .... 34.11
11(2) 34.11
12 .... 34.11
13(1)(b) 34.13
14, 15 .... 34.13
18 .... 20.31, 34.12
19 .... 20.31
(4)–(9) 34.13
20 .... 34.13
21(3) 34.13
(5)–(7) 34.13
22 .... 34.13
23, 24 .... 34.12
25 .... 34.12, 54.3

National Minimum Wage Act 1998 – *contd*
s 27 .... 34.12
28 .... 34.10, 34.12
31 .... 54.3
(1)–(5) 34.13
(9) 34.13
32 .... 34.13
33(1) 34.13
34 .... 34.10, 47.6
35–44A 34.10
45 .... 34.10
49(3), (4) 21.33
54 .... 34.9
(3) 34.10, 34.12, 47.6
Sch 1 .... 34.10

National Minimum Wage (Enforcement Notices) Act 2003 .... 34.13

Nationality, Immigration and Asylum Act 2002
s 147 .... 26.9

Naval Discipline Act 1957 .... 37.2

Occupiers' Liability Act 1957 .... 27.1, 27.12
s 2(2), (3) 27.14
(4)(b) 27.15

Occupiers' Liability Act 1984 .... 27.1, 27.12

Offices, Shops and Railway Premises Act 1963 .... 4.5
s 4–16 .... 28.29

Offshore Safety Act 1992
s 4 .... 27.37, 27.39

Offshore Safety (Protection against Victimisation) Act 1992 .... 54.3

Osteopaths Act 1993
s 39(2) 19.4
(4) 19.4

Partnership Act 1890
s 4 .... 3.35

Payment of Wages Act 1960
s 1 .... 34.4

Payment of Wages Act 1960 – *contd*
s 11 .... 34.3

Pension Schemes Act 1993 ..... 20.11, 42.7
s 124(1)–(3A) 31.7
  (4), (5) 31.7
126 .... 31.7
127(1) 31.7
145–151 .... 42.14
190 .... 35.2
Sch 8
  para 4 .... 35.2

Pensions Act 1995 ...... 13.31, 24.2, 24.16,
                    24.18, 24.19, 31.7,
                    42.1, 42.7, 49.12
s 1 .... 42.12
10 .... 42.8
16–21 .... 42.12
46(5) 54.3
50 .... 42.14
62 .... 13.10, 20.11, 42.14
  (1)–(4) 24.17
  (6) 24.17
63 .... 20.11
  (1), (2) 24.17
  (4) 24.17
  (6) 24.17
64 .... 13.10, 20.11
  (2), (3) 24.17
65 .... 20.11
124(1) 14.22
126 .... 24.17
157 .... 42.12

Pensions Act 2004 .... 31.1, 42.7, 42.9
Pt II Ch III (ss 126–181) 31.9
s 241, 242 .... 42.12
257, 258 .... 52.19
273 .... 42.14

Petroleum Act 1998
s 10(8) 12.12
11(2) 12.12
50 .... 12.12
Sch 4
  para 8 .... 12.12
  11 .... 12.12

Police Act 1996 .... 43.7
s 15 .... 37.2
64(4A), (4B) 37.2
88 .... 56.1, 56.2
91 .... 37.2

Police Act 1997
Pt V (ss 112–127) 19.7
s 112 .... 19.7
113(2)–(5) 19.7
114 .... 19.7
115(2)–(4) 19.7
  (5)(a)–(g) 19.7
  (7)–(9) 19.7
116–121 .... 19.7
122(1), (2) 19.7
123–127 .... 19.7

**Police and Criminal Evidence
    Act 1984**
s 54(9) 13.5

**Powers of Criminal Courts
    Act 1973**
s 30 .... 1.10

**Private International Law
    (Miscellaneous Provisions)
    Act 1995**
s 11(1) 26.11
12(1) 26.11

Protection from Eviction Act 1977
s 1(2)–(3B) 43.3
2 .... 43.3
3(1) 43.3
5 .... 43.5
  (1A) 43.4
8(2) 43.3

**Protection from Harassment
    Act 1997** 3.8, 12.12, 28.28
s 3 .... 28.25, 56.1

**Public Interest Disclosure
    Act 1998** ... 11.1, 11.18, 18.26, 20.11,
                                    21.7
s 1 .... 11.18, 28.9, 54.3
2 .... 11.17, 11.18, 28.9
3 .... 28.10
5 .... 11.17, 11.18, 54.3
7 .... 11.17
8(4) 11.18
11 .... 11.17
13 .... 11.17

Public Order Act 1986
s 4A 28.28
Pt II (ss 11–16) 45.12

Race Relations Act 1965 .... 12.2

Race Relations Act 1968 .... 12.2

Race Relations Act 1976 .... 1.6, 3.5, 10.9,
10.10, 10.12, 10.16,
10.17, 12.2, 12.5,
12.6, 12.8, 13.1,
13.4, 13.6, 13.8,
13.19, 14.1, 14.3,
14.26, 21.9, 21.29,
23.1, 23.2, 25.7,
26.9, 30.7, 32.11,
36.1, 40.4,
s 1(1)(a) 12.4, 12.6
 (b) 12.7
  (ii) 13.8
 (1A) 12.7
 (c) 13.8
 (2) 12.5
2(1), (2) 12.10
3(1) 12.6
 (4) 12.5, 12.10
3A(1) 12.11
 (2) 12.11
4 .... 13.15, 25.4, 26.13
 (1) 13.34
 (2) 20.29
 (b) 12.12, 13.17
 (c) 12.11, 12.12, 12.13
 (3) 10.24, 13.11
 (4) 12.1213.17
 (4A) 12.12
4A(2)(a) 13.4
5 .... 13.4
 (2)(d) 13.5
 (3)–(4) 13.5
6 .... 13.11
 (2) 12.12
7(1) 13.21
 (2)(a) 13.22
 (3), (3A) 13.21
 (5) 13.21
8 .... 26.13
 (1) 12.12, 13.15, 25.4
 (1A) 12.12, 13.15
 (3) 12.12, 13.15
 (4) 12.12
 (5) 12.12, 13.15
9 .... 12.12
 (1) 13.11
 (3) 13.11
 (5) 13.11
10(1)–(1B) 13.25

Race Relations Act 1976 – *contd*
 s 10 (2)–(6) 13.25
Pt II (ss 11–16) 12.13, 14.26, 14.30,
17.1, 20.22
 s 11 .... 13.27
 (1)–(4) 13.26
 12(1), (1A) 13.27
 (2) 13.27
 13(1)–(3) 13.28
 14(1), (1A) 13.29
 (2) 13.30
 (3)–(6) 13.29
 15(1), (1A) 13.30
 (2) 13.30
 16 .... 12.13, 37.2
 (1) 12.12
Pt III (ss 17–27) 14.26
 s 20 .... 13.17
 25 .... 13.27
 26A(1)–(3A) 13.24
 (4) 13.24
 26B 13.24
Pt IV (ss 27A–33) 14.26
 s 27A(1) 13.33
 (2) 12.12, 13.33
 (3) 13.33
 28 .... 12.13, 14.27, 14.29
 (3) 13.40
 29 .... 14.27, 14.30
 (1) 12.12, 13.34
 (2) 13.34
 (3)–(5) 12.12, 13.34
 30 .... 12.13, 13.40, 14.27, 14.30
 31 .... 14.27, 14.30
 (1), (2) 12.13, 13.40
 32 .... 12.13, 14.2
 (1) 12.13, 13.23, 13.35, 56.1
 (2) 12.13, 13.38
 (3) 12.13, 13.35, 13.38
 33 .... 14.2
 (1) 12.13, 13.36
 (2) 13.37
 (3) 12.13, 13.36
 (4) 13.36
 35 .... 13.9
 37 .... 12.5, 13.9
 38(1)–(4) 12.5, 13.9
 (5) 13.9
 39 .... 13.11
 40(1) 12.12
 41(1), (1A) 13.18
 (2) 13.18
 (d), (e) 13.18
 43(1) 14.25

Table of Statutes

Race Relations Act 1976 – *contd*
s 47 .... 5.6
  (1) 14.25
  (10) 5.7, 14.25
48 .... 14.27
49(2)–(4) 14.27
50(2)(a), (b) 14.27
  (3)(a), (b) 14.27
  (5), (6) 14.27
51(1) 14.27
52(1)–(3) 14.27
53(1), (2) 14.1
54 .... 14.28, 20.11
  (1) 14.2
  (2) 13.27, 14.2
56(1) 14.30
   (a), (b) 14.12
   (c) 14.12, 14.30
  (2) 14.13
  (4) 21.66
   (a), (b) 14.21
57(3) 14.14
  (4) 14.16
58(2) 14.28
  (4), (5) 14.28
59 .... 20.11
  (1)–(4) 14.28
60 .... 14.27, 14.28
61(4) 14.28
62(1) 14.29, 14.30
63 .... 12.12, 13.34, 13.40, 20.11
  (1), (2) 14.30
  (4), (5) 14.30
64(1) 14.30
65 .... 21.8
  (2)(a) 14.9
   (b) 14.9, 21.9
66 .... 14.31
68(1) 14.4, 20.29
  (4), (5) 14.30
  (6) 14.7, 14.30, 20.30
  (7) 14.4, 20.29
   (b) 14.6
71 .... 14.26
  (1) 13.33
71A 13.33
71C 13.33
71D, 71E 13.34
72 .... 8.17, 8.18
  (1) 14.32
  (3) 14.32
  (4) 14.33
   (a) 2.4
   (aa) 21.33

Race Relations Act 1976 – *contd*
s 72 (4A) 21.33
  (5) 14.32
72A 8.18, 14.17
75 .... 37.2
  (2)–(9B) 13.32
75A, 75B 13.32
76(2)–(9) 13.22
76ZA(1)–(6) 13.22
   (7)(b) 13.22
   (8)(c) 13.22
   (9)(a), (b) 13.22
76A(2) 13.23
   (3)(b) 13.23
   (4)–(6) 13.23
76B(3) 13.23
78 .... 12.11, 12.12
  (1) 12.12, 13.26, 13.34, 16.2
  (4) 13.33

Race Relations (Amendment)
  Act 2000 .... 5.6, 12.13, 13.33

Race Relations (Remedies)
  Act 1994 .... 14.13

Railways and Transport Safety
  Act 2003 .... 28.26

Railways Act 2005 .... 57.20
Sch 3 .... 28.26

Redundancy Payments Act 1965 ...... 38.1

Rehabilitation of Offenders
  Act 1974 .... 19.5, 19.7
s 1(1) 19.1
  4(1) 19.2
  (2) 19.2, 19.4
   (a), (b) 19.7
  (3) 19.4
   (a) 19.2
   (b) 19.3
  (6) 19.2
  5 .... 19.6
  (1) 19.1
  8(3) 19.2
  (5) 19.2

Rent Act 1977 .... 17.8, 43.1, 43.5
s 1 .... 43.3
  44 .... 43.8
Pt IV (ss 62–75) 43.8
s 98(2) 43.6

Rent Act 1977 – *contd*
s 100 .... 43.6
Sch 15
  Pt I
    Case 8 .... 43.6
      19 .... 43.6
    Pt II 43.6

Rent (Agriculture) Act 1976 .... 43.9

Reserve Forces Act 1996
s 27 .... 32.2

Reserve Forces (Safeguard of Employment) Act 1985
s 1(2) 49.20
  3–5 .... 49.20
  7–10 .... 49.20

Road Safety Act 2005 .... 28.1

Schools Standards and Framework Act 1998 .... 37.2

Sex Discrimination Act 1975 ...... 1.6, 3.5,
                          10.9, 10.10, 10.12,
                          10.16, 10.17, 10.27,
                          12.5, 12.7, 12.8,
                          12.11, 13.1, 13.3,
                          13.4, 13.7, 13.8,
                          13.33, 14.1, 14.3,
                          14.26, 17.1, 21.29,
                          23.1, 23.2, 24.2,
                          24.5, 24.9, 24.10,
                          24.11, 24.17, 25.7,
                          32.11, 33.21, 36.1,
                          40.4,
s 1 .... 12.11, 25.6
  (1) 12.6
    (a) 12.4, 12.5, 12.6
    (b) 32.1
  (2) 13.8, 25.6
    (a) 12.4, 12.5, 12.6
    (b) 12.7
      (ii) 13.8
  (2) 12.5, 13.9
  (3) 12.12
2A 12.2, 12.4, 13.25, 24.2, 24.13
  (1) 12.6
  (3) 12.5
3 .... 12.2, 12.6, 13.9
  (1)(a) 12.4, 12.6
    (b) 12.7
  (2) 12.6

Sex Discrimination Act 1975 – *contd*
s 3A 12.2
  (1) 12.6
    (a), (b) 12.4, 12.5
  (2) 12.4, 12.5, 12.6
  (3)(a)–(c) 12.5, 12.6
4(1) 12.10
  (a) 12.6
  (2) 12.10
  (4)–(6) 24.2
  (8) 24.2
4A(1) 12.11, 56.1
  (2)–(4) 12.11
5(3) 12.5, 12.6
Pt II (ss 6–20A) 14.26, 14.30, 20.22
s 6 .... 12.13, 13.33, 26.11
  (1) 13.15, 24.13
  (2) 12.12
    (a) 12.5, 13.17
    (b) 12.6, 12.11, 12.12, 12.13,
                                    13.5
  (4) 13.10, 24.17
  (4A) 24.17, 24.25
  (5) 13.10
  (6) 13.10, 24.5
  (7) 12.12, 13.17
  (8) 13.10
6A 12.12
  (1)(b) 12.12
  (2)–(7) 12.12
7(2), (3) 13.3
  (4) 13.3, 13.5
7A(1)(b) 13.5
  (3), (4) 13.5
7B(1)(a) 13.5
  (3) 13.5
9(2), (2A) 13.21
  (3)–(3B) 13.21
  (4) 13.21
10 .... 24.4, 26.13
  (1) 12.12, 13.15, 24.13
  (1A) 12.12
  (2) 12.12
    (a), (b) 13.15
  (4), (5) 12.12
10A(2)–(5) 13.22
10B(1)–(9) 13.22
  (11) 13.22
11(1), (2) 13.25
  (2A) 13.25
  (3)–(3B) 13.25
  (4)–(6) 13.25
12(1)–(4) 13.26
13(1), (1A) 13.27

Table of Statutes

Sex Discrimination Act 1975 – *contd*

s 13 (2), (3) 13.27
14(1)(a) 13.28
(1A), (1B) 13.28
(2) 13.28
15(1), (1A) 13.29
(2) 13.30
(3)–(6) 13.29
16(1), (1A) 13.30
(2) 13.30
17 .... 37.2
(1) 13.23
(1A)(b) 13.23
(2), (3) 13.10
(4)–(5A) 13.23
(6), (7) 13.23
(9) 13.23
18(1), (2) 13.10
(1) 13.10
(3), (4) 13.10
20A 12.12
Pt III (ss 21A–36) 14.26
s 29 .... 13.17
35A(1)–(4) 13.24
35B 13.24
Pt IV (ss 37–42) 14.26
s 37 .... 14.27, 14.29
(3) 13.40
38 .... 12.12, 14.27, 14.28, 14.30
(1) 12.12, 13.34
(2) 13.34
(3)–(5) 12.12, 13.34
39 .... 12.13, 13.40, 14.27, 14.30
40 .... 12.13, 13.40, 14.27, 14.30
(1) 13.40
(2) 12.13, 13.40
41 .... 14.2, 14.3
(1) 12.13, 13.35, 56.1
(2) 12.13, 13.38
(3) 12.13, 13.35, 13.38
42 .... 14.2, 14.3
(1) 12.13
(2) 13.36, 13.37
(3) 12.13, 13.36
(4) 13.36
44 .... 13.10
46(3)–(6) 13.10
47(4) 13.9
48(1)–(3) 13.9
49(1), (2) 13.9
50(1) 12.12
51(1)(c)(ii) 13.18
52(1), (2) 13.19
53 .... 14.24

Sex Discrimination Act 1975 – *contd*

s 55, 56 .... 14.24
56A 5.8, 5.9
(10) 14.3, 14.24
57(1) 14.27
58(2)–(3A) 14.27
59(2)(a), (b) 14.27
(3)(a), (b) 14.27
(4) 14.27
(6) 14.27
60(1) 14.27
61(1)–(3) 14.27
62(1), (2) 14.1
63 .... 14.28, 14.29, 20.11
(1) 14.2
(2) 13.27, 14.2
63A 12.5, 14.2, 25.6
(2) 14.3
65 .... 12.6
(1)(a) 14.12, 14.30
(b) 14.12
(c) 14.12, 14.30
(1B) 14.14
(3) 21.66
(a), (b) 14.22
66(4) 14.16
67(2) 14.28
(4), (5) 14.28
68 .... 20.11
(1)–(4) 14.28
69 .... 14.27, 14.28
70(4) 14.28
71(1) 14.29, 14.30
72 .... 12.12, 13.34, 13.40, 20.11
(1), (2) 14.30
(4), (5) 14.30
73(1) 14.30
74 .... 14.9, 21.8
(2)(a) 14.9
(b) 14.3, 14.9, 21.9
75 .... 14.31
(2) 14.2, 14.9
(2A) 14.9
76 .... 14.6
(1) 14.4, 20.29, 24.13
(3), (4) 14.30
(5) 14.7, 14.30, 20.30, 24.13
(6) 14.4, 20.29
(c) 14.5
76A 14.26
(1) 13.33
(5), (6) 13.33
76B 13.33, 14.26
76C 14.26

Sex Discrimination Act 1975 – *contd*
s 76D 13.34
76E 13.33
77 .... 8.17, 8.18, 24.25
(1) 14.32
(3) 14.32, 24.23
(4) 24.23
(a) 2.4
(aa) 14.33, 21.33, 24.23
(4A) 21.33, 24.23
(5) 14.32
82(1) 12.6, 12.11, 12.12, 13.26,
13.34, 16.2, 24.13
(4) 14.28
85 .... 13.32, 37.2
(2) 13.32
(4) 13.10, 13.32
(5) 13.10
(7)–(9E) 13.32
85A, 85B 13.32
86(1), (2) 13.22
Sch 3 .... 14.24

Sex Discrimination Act 1986 .... 24.2,
24.25
s 1(2) 13.3
2 .... 42.1
(1) 24.17
6 .... 6.6, 8.18, 14.32, 24.25
9 .... 24.25

Shops Act 1950 .... 4.5, 57.1

Social Security Act 1975 .... 35.10

Social Security Act 1985
s 18(2)(d) 44.4
21 .... 35.2
Sch 4
para 1 .... 35.2

Social Security Act 1986 .... 42.7
Sch 10
para 102 .... 35.2

Social Security Act 1989 .... 24.2, 33.10
s 5A, 5B 42.9
Sch 5 .... 24.18, 42.9
para 2 .... 33.1
5, 6 .... 24.17, 33.1

**Social Security Administration
Act 1992**
s 14(3) 44.8

Social Security Administration Act 1992 –
contd
s 15 .... 33.13
(2) 33.15
113 .... 44.13

**Social Security Contributions and
Benefits Act 1992** ... 7.10, 33.1, 33.10
s 4(1) 44.6
5(1) 42.11
10 .... 46.17
10ZA 46.17
151(2) 44.3
152 .... 44.3, 44.5
153(2) 44.5
(12) 44.5
155(1), (2) 44.5
156 .... 44.3
157(1) 44.6
164(1), (2) 33.11
(4) 33.13
(6) 33.11
166 .... 33.14
167 .... 33.16
171(1) 33.11
Sch 11 .... 44.3
para 2(c) 44.6
Sch 12 .... 44.5
para 2 .... 44.9
Sch 13
para 3 .... 33.14

**Social Security (Incapacity for
Work) Act 1994** 44.5
s 8(1) 44.6

Social Security Pensions Act 1975
s 65 .... 35.2

State Immunity Act 1978 .... 13.1, 30.4
s 16(1)(a) 13.20

Statutory Sick Pay Act 1994 .... 44.6
s 1 .... 44.4

Sunday Trading Act 1994 .... 8.5, 54.3
s 4 .... 8.25
Sch 4 .... 8.25

Superannuation Act 1972 .... 37.2, 42.7

Supreme Court Act 1981
s 35A 58.31
42(1A) 21.77

Table of Statutes

Tax Credits Act 1999 .... 7.13, 53.11, 54.3

Tax Credits Act 2002 .... 53.11, 54.11
  s 47 .... 35.2
  Sch 1
    para 1 .... 35.2

Teaching and Higher Education
  Act 1998
  s 32 .... 4.7

Trade Descriptions Act 1968 .... 27.38

Trade Disputes Act 1906
  s 3 .... 45.1

Trade Union and Labour Relations
  Act 1974 .... 5.2, 51.3

Trade Union and Labour Relations
  (Consolidation) Act 1992 .... 1.6, 2.1,
                 5.2, 11.1, 14.33,
           18.12, 20.11, 20.22,
           30.4, 38.7, 45.1,
           45.13, 51.3
  s 1 .... 50.1, 49.22
  2 .... 50.21
  5 .... 50.22, 54.3
  6 .... 50.26
    (1) 50.21
    (3) 50.21
    (4) 50.23
    7(1) 50.24
  9 .... 50.24
  10(1) 50.2
  12(1) 50.2
    (2) 50.17
  14 .... 49.11
  15 .... 45.16
    (2), (3) 50.18
    (5) 50.18
  16 .... 50.2
  20 .... 45.17
    (1) 50.16
    (2) 45.14, 50.16, 53.18
    (3) 50.16
    (6) 45.16
  21 .... 53.18
    (1)–(6) 50.16
  22(2), (3) 50.17
  23(1), (2) 50.17
  24 .... 50.12
    (3) 50.13
  25(5A) 50.13

Trade Union and Labour Relations
  (Consolidation) Act 1992 – *contd*
  s 26(4) 50.13
  27, 28 .... 50.12
  30 .... 51.2
  32, 32A 50.12
  33 .... 50.12
  37A–37E 50.3
  40 .... 50.12
  45 .... 50.3, 48.14
  45A 50.3
  45B 50.14
  45C(5A) 50.14
  45D 50.13, 50.14
  46 .... 50.12
    (1) 50.14
    (3), (4) 50.14
    (4A) 50.14
  47–50 .... 50.14
  51(6) 50.14
  52 .... 48.14
  54 .... 50.14
  55(2), (3) 50.14
    (5A) 50.14
  56(3), (4) 50.14
  56A 50.14
  62 .... 45.18, 51.2
    (2), (3) 45.17
    (5), (6) 45.17
    (8) 45.17
  63(1)–(4) 51.15
  64(1), (2) 51.16
    (4), (5) 51.16
  65 .... 51.13
    (2) 51.9, 51.16
    (3)–(6) 51.16
  66 .... 51.14
    (1)–(3) 51.16
  67(1) 51.16
    (3) 51.16
    (5)–(9) 51.16
  68 .... 21.29, 54.3
    (1)–(4) 51.20
  68A 20.9
    (1)–(3) 51.20
  69 .... 51.2
  70A 50.11
  70B 2.4, 18.29, 50.38, 51.1
  71 .... 50.12, 50.15
  72, 72A 50.15
  73–81 .... 50.15
  82(2), (3) 50.15
  84(1), (2) 50.15
  86 .... 50.15, 54.3

Trade Union and Labour Relations (Consolidation) Act 1992 – *contd*

s 87 .... 50.15
97–105 .... 50.39
108A–108C 50.3
109 .... 51.17
117 .... 50.2
119 .... 50.14, 50.16, 49.22
137(1)(b) 51.4
(3)–(6) 51.4
(7)(a), (b) 51.4
138 .... 51.4
138A 53.11
139(1) 51.4
140(1)(b) 51.4
(2), (3) 51.4
141, 142 .... 51.4
143(2)–(4) 51.4
144 .... 45.7, 51.19
145 .... 45.7
(1)–(5) 51.19
145A, 145B 51.17, 54.3, 55.15
145C–145F 51.17
146 .... 54.3
(1) 51.17
(a) 30.4
(c) 51.8
(3) 51.8, 51.17
(5) 51.8, 51.18
147 .... 51.18
148 .... 51.17
(1), (2) 51.18
(3) 49.18
149, 150 .... 51.18
152 .... 54.3, 54.11, 55.8, 55.15, 55.16,
(1)(c) 51.5
(2) 54.3
(3) 51.6, 55.15
(4) 51.5
153 ...... 51.5, 55.8, 55.9, 55.15, 55.16
154 .... 7.13, 51.5, 53.11, 54.3
155 .... 51.7, 55.15
156 .... 51.7
(1) 51.16, 55.8, 55.9
(2) 55.9
160 .... 51.7, 54.16
(1) 21.23
(2) 21.23, 55.17
(3) 55.17
161 .... 20.9, 20.18
(1)–(3) 55.18
162 .... 20.18
(1)–(4) 55.18
163 .... 20.18, 55.18

Trade Union and Labour Relations (Consolidation) Act 1992 – *contd*

s 164 .... 55.18
165, 166 .... 20.9, 55.18
168 .... 21.29, 54.3
(1)–(3) 49.2
(4) 49.2, 49.6
168A 49.2, 54.3
169 .... 21.29, 24.3, 31.2, 54.3
(4) 49.2
(5) 49.2, 49.6
170 .... 21.29, 52.21, 54.3
(1) 49.3
(2) 49.3
(2A)–(2C) 49.3
(3) 49.3
(4) 49.3, 49.6
171 .... 49.6
172(1) 49.6
(2) 47.6, 49.6, 51.13
(3) 49.6
174 .... 51.11
(1)–(3) 51.13
(4) 51.13, 51.14
175 .... 51.13, 51.14
176 .... 51.13
(1)–(3) 51.14
(5) 51.14
177(2) 51.13
(5) 51.13
Pt IV (ss 178–218) 50.19
Pt IV Ch I (ss 178–187) 11.2
s 178 .... 6.1, 50.27
(1) 39.4, 50.20
(2) 3.45, 39.4, 49.2, 50.20, 57.4
(3) 39.4, 50.20
179 .... 52.20
(1), (2) 6.2
180 .... 6.5
181 .... 11.3, 50.6, 50.8, 50.19
182(1), (2) 11.3
183 .... 48.6, 48.8
(1) 11.5
(2) 2.5, 11.5, 50.8
(3)–(5) 11.5, 50.8
184 .... 11.5, 48.8
(2) 50.8
(4) 50.8
185 .... 50.9
(1) 11.5
(2) 11.5, 50.8
(3) 11.5, 50.8
(4), (5) 11.5, 50.8
186 .... 45.7, 51.19

Table of Statutes

Trade Union and Labour Relations (Consolidation) Act 1992 – *contd*

s 187 .... 45.7
   (3) 51.19
Pt IV Ch II (ss 188–198) ... 39.3, 47.14,
                                54.3, 55.18
s 188 .... 15.3, 18.7, 20.33, 25.8, 39.3,
                  39.6, 39.7, 39.8,
               49.2, 52.19, 52.23,
                      54.3, 54.11
   (1)–(1B) 39.4
   (2) 39.4
   (4) 39.4, 39.6
   (7), (7A) 39.6
   (7B) 39.4
188A 18.7, 39.4, 39.5, 39.6
   (1), (2) 39.5
189 .... 18.7, 25.8, 31.2, 39.6
   (1A) 39.6
   (2) 39.6
   (4) 39.6
   (5) 20.33, 39.6
190 .... 18.7, 25.8
   (1)–(3) 39.6
   (5) 39.6
191 .... 18.7, 25.8
   (1)–(7) 39.6
192 .... 18.7, 20.9, 21.29, 25.8
   (1)–(3) 39.6
193 .... 25.8, 39.2
   (1), (2) 39.7
   (4) 39.7
   (7) 39.7
194 .... 25.8
   (1) 39.7
195 .... 25.8
   (1), (2) 39.3
196 .... 25.8
   (2) 39.4
197, 198 .... 25.8
199 .... 2.9, 5.15
   (4) 39.4
200 .... 5.2
201 .... 5.2, 5.15
202 .... 5.15
203 .... 5.4, 5.15, 50.14, 50.32
204 .... 45.14, 50.14, 50.32
   (2) 5.4
205, 206 .... 5.15
207(1) 5.3, 5.5
   (2) 5.3
   (3) 5.5
208(2) 5.4
209 .... 2.1

Trade Union and Labour Relations (Consolidation) Act 1992 – *contd*

s 210 .... 2.3
212(1) 2.6
   (b) 50.7
   (2), (3) 2.6
   (4)(b) 2.6
   (5) 2.6
212A 2.10, 2.45, 21.37
213 .... 2.7
214(1), (2) 2.8
219 ..... 45.3, 45.4, 45.8, 45.16, 45.20,
                     50.16, 53.17
   (3) 45.9
220 .... 45.9, 45.10, 45.12, 45.16
   (1)(b) 45.6, 45.9
221(1), (2) 45.16
222(1), (3) 45.7
223 .... 45.8
224(1) 45.6, 45.9
   (2) 45.6
   (3) 45.9
   (4)–(6) 45.6
225 .... 45.7
226(1) 45.14
   (2)(b) 45.14
   (3) 45.14
226A 45.14
226B, 226C 45.14, 45.17
227 .... 45.17
   (1) 45.14
228 .... 45.17
   (4) 45.14
228A 45.14, 45.17
229 .... 45.17
   (1A) 45.14
   (2) 45.14
   (4) 45.14
230 .... 45.17
   (1), (2) 45.14
   (4)(a) 45.14
231–231B 45.14, 45.17
232 .... 45.14, 45.17
232A(C) 45.14
232B 45.14
233 .... 45.14, 45.17
   (3)(a) 45.15
234(1) 45.15, 45.17
   (2)–(6) 45.15
234A 45.15
235A(1)–(5) 45.18
236 .... 6.5, 8.24, 45.16
237 .... 45.8, 45.16
   (2)–(6) 53.18

Trade Union and Labour Relations (Consolidation) Act 1992 – *contd*

s 238 .... 45.16, 53.17, 53.18
  (2) 15.3, 54.3
238A 7.13, 45.16, 53.17, 54.3
  (2) 15.3
  (7) 53.17
239(1) 53.17
240(1) 45.20
  (3) 45.20
241(1)(d) 45.12
  (2) 45.12
244(1) 45.4
  (2) 37.2
  (3) 45.4
  (5) 45.4
245 .... 37.3, 45.2
247 .... 2.1
248 .... 2.2
251A 2.1
254 .... 50.3
258 .... 50.3
259 .... 50.4
260 .... 50.5, 50.25
282 .... 7.13
285(1) 51.4
288 .... 8.17, 50.9, 51.4
  (2A), (2B) 21.33
291(2) 51.4
296(1) 50.26
Sch A1 .... 50.11, 50.19, 50.20, 50.23,
            50.25, 50.38, 51.1
para 1–4 .... 50.27
  5, 6 .... 50.29
  7 .... 50.29
  (1) 50.26
  8 .... 50.28, 50.29
  9 .... 50.29
  10 .... 50.28
  11, 12 .... 50.29
  15 .... 50.29
  18 .... 50.29
  19 .... 50.29, 50.30
  20 .... 50.30, 50.31
  21–24 .... 50.31
  25–29 .... 50.32
  30–32 .... 50.33
  33–42 .... 50.29
  43–50 .... 50.30
  52 .... 50.34
  55, 56 .... 50.34
  58–63 .... 50.34
  64–89 .... 50.35
  99–153 .... 50.36

Trade Union and Labour Relations (Consolidation) Act 1992 – *contd*

Sch A1 – *contd*
  para 156 .... 2.4, 50.37
  157–159 .... 50.37
  161 .... 7.13, 50.37, 54.3
  162 .... 7.13, 50.37, 53.11, 54.11
  163–165 .... 50.37
  171 .... 50.25
Sch 3
  para 5 .... 6.2
  7 .... 50.6

Trade Union Reform and Employment Rights Act 1993 .... 2.1,
           16.5, 20.1, 21.18,
           21.33, 25.2, 25.9,
           33.1, 39.2
s 14 .... 51.11
28 .... 54.3
29 .... 54.3
32 .... 6.6, 24.25
33 .... 11.6
34 .... 54.11
  (2)(a) 39.4
    (c) 39.6
  (3) 39.6
  (4) 39.7
  (5) 39.3
43(1) 2.1
  (2) 2.7
44 .... 2.1
Sch 5 .... 54.3
Sch 7
  para 15 .... 5.9
Sch 8
  para 77 .... 53.17

Transport and Works Act 1992 .... 28.2

Truck Act 1831
s 1 .... 34.3
3 .... 34.4
9 .... 34.4
20 .... 34.5
23 .... 34.5

Truck Amendment Act 1887
s 4 .... 34.5

Unfair Contract Terms Act 1977 ... 58.17,
           58.37
s 11 .... 8.21
  (3) 40.5

Table of Statutes

Wages Act 1986 .... 8.23, 20.11, 34.2,
                                        48.11
  s 11 .... 34.3
Water Act 1989 .... 37.7
Water Industry Act 1991 .... 37.7
Welfare Reform and Pensions
    Act 1999
  Pt I (ss 1–8) 42.7, 42.8

Welfare Reform and Pensions Act 1999 –
    contd
  s 3(8) 42.8
    75 .... 46.35

Work and Families Act 2006 .... 33.1

Young Persons (Employment)
    Act 1938 .... 4.5

Table of EU Legislation

Primary Legislation

Treaties Agreements and Conventions

Convention on Jurisdiction and the
    Enforcement of Judgments in
    Civil and Commercial Matters
    (Brussels, 27 September 1968)
    art 5(1) 26.12
       (3) 26.12
      17 .... 26.12
      18(2) 26.12
      21 .... 26.12

Convention on Jurisdiction and the
    Enforcement of Judgments in
    Civil and Commercial Matters
    (Lugano, 16 September
    1988) 26.12

Council of Europe Social Charter
    (Turin, 18 October 1961) 30.8

European Convention for the
    Protection of Human Rights
    and Fundamental Freedoms
    (Rome, 4 November 1950) 1.7,
                12.6, 21.2, 28.3,
             30.1, 30.2, 30.5, 37.2
    art 3 .... 30.4
      6 .... 20.7, 20.13, 21.16, 21.42, 21.77
       (1) 13.20, 30.4, 30.7
       (2) 30.7
      8 .... 12.6, 19.7, 21.51, 30.4, 30.6,
                         30.7
       (2) 30.4
      9 .... 30.7
       (1) 12.6
      10 .... 30.4, 30.6, 30.7
      11 .... 30.6, 30.7, 45.1, 45.12, 50.19,
                     51.13, 51.17
       (1), (2) 30.4, 45.4
      12, 13 .... 30.4
      14 .... 30.4, 30.6
      17 .... 30.7
    First Protocol
      art 1 .... 30.7, 34.9, 34.21

European Economic Area
    Agreement (Oporto, 1970) 57.35

Rome Convention on the Law
    Applicable to Contractual
    Obligations (Rome,
    19 June1980)
    art 3(1) 26.11
       (3) 26.11
      6(1), (2) 26.11
      7(1) 26.11
      17 .... 26.11

Single European Act 1986 .... 25.1

Treaty Establishing the European
    Economic Community (EEC
    Treaty) (Rome, 25 March
    1957) 25.3
    art 2 .... 25.6
      3(2) 25.6
      10(5) 25.5
      11(1), (2) 45.4
      13 .... 25.1, 25.6
       (1) 12.2
      39 .... 25.4
       (4) 26.2, 37.7
      40–42 .... 25.4
      48 ..... 12.12, 13.15, 24.4, 26.2, 37.7
      81 .... 41.1
      87 .... 46.35
      94 .... 25.1
      95 .... 25.1
      118A 57.1
      136 .... 25.1
      137 .... 25.1, 27.25, 57.1
      138–140 .... 25.1
      141 ...... 7.1, 12.2, 20.12, 24.1, 24.3,
                     24.4, 24.5, 24.6,
                 24.9, 24.10, 24.11,
               24.13, 24.14, 24.16,
               24.17, 24.18, 24.19,
               25.1, 25.2, 25.6,
               30.5, 42.1, 42.2,
               42.7, 42.9, 49.4,
               53.11, 53.14
       (1) 13.9
       (4) 13.9
      226, 227 .... 25.2

Table of EU Legislation

Treaty Establishing the European
    Economic Community (EEC Treaty)
    (Rome, 25 March 1957) – *contd*
  art 234 .... 22.27, 25.2
  251 .... 25.1, 25.6
  302 .... 25.1

Treaty of Amsterdam (Amsterdam,
    2 October 1997) 12.2, 25.1, 25.3,
                              27.25

Treaty of Nice (Nice, 26 February
    2001) 27.25

Treaty on European Union
    (Maastricht Treaty,
    1 November 1993) 25.1, 25.3,
                              27.25
  Social Chapter 30.8

Secondary Legislation

Decisions

Council Decision 88/591/EEC
    (Establishing a Court of First
    Instance of the European
    Communities) 37.8

Directives

Council Directive 68/360/EEC
    (Abolition of Restrictions on
    Movement and Residence
    Directive) 26.2

Council Directive 75/117/EEC
    (Equal Pay Directive) 24.1, 24.3,
                              42.7
  art 1 .... 25.6

Council Directive 75/129/EEC
    (Collective Redundancy
    Directive) 25.8, 39.2

Council Directive 76/207/EEC
    (Equal Treatment Directive) 7.1,
                     12.2, 12.5, 12.6,
                  12.12, 13.16, 13.33,
                  14.1, 14.11, 20.12,
                  24.3, 25.2, 25.3,
             25.5, 25.6, 42.6, 42.8
  art 1((2) 12.11
  2(2) 13.8, 13.10
  (4) 12.5, 13.9
  (8) 13.9
  5(1) 12.5, 24.3
  6 .... 13.19, 21.18

Council Directive 77/187/EEC
    (Acquired Rights Directive) 18.28,
                  25.9, 42.4, 52.3,
                  52.6, 52.7, 52.14
  art 1–7 .... 52.1

Council Directive 79/7/EEC (Social
    Security Directive) 12.5, 25.5

Council Directive 80/987/EEC
    (Insolvency Protection
    Directive) 25.7, 31.1, 31.3

Council Directive 83/189/EEC
    (Provision of Information in
    the Field of Technical
    Standards and Regulations
    Directive) 25.2

Council Directive 86/378/EEC
    (Principle of Equal Treatment
    for Men and Women in
    Occupational Social Security
    Schemes) 24.3, 24.18, 25.5, 25.6,
                                  33.1

Council Directive 87/164/EEC
    (Amending 80/987 on Account
    of the Accession of Spain) 31.5

Council Directive 89/48/EEC (First
    Diploma Directive) 25.4

Council Directive 89/391/EEC
    (Health and Safety Framework
    Directive) 28.17
  art 5(4) 27.25

Council Directive 89/654/EEC
(Minimum Safety and Health
Requirements for the
Workplace) 27.25, 28.29
Annex II 28.14

Council Directive 89/655/EEC
(Directive Relating to the use
of Machines and Equipment) ....
27.25, 28.12

Council Directive 89/656/EEC
(Minimum health and safety
requirements for the use by
workers of personal protective
equipment at the workplace) ... 27.25,
28.12

Council Directive 90/269/EEC
(Minimum Health and Safety
Requirements for the Manual
Handling of Loads) 27.25
Annex II 28.18

Council Directive 90/270/EEC
(Directive Relating to the Use
of Display Screen
Equipment) 27.25
art 2(a) 28.5

Council Directive 90/364/EEC
(Right of Residence
Directive) 26.2

Council Directive 90/365/EEC
(Right of Residence for
Employees and Self-Employed
Persons who Have Ceased their
Occupational Activity) 26.2

Council Directive 90/394/EEC
(Protection of Workers from
the Risks Related to Exposure
to Carcinogens at Work) 27.25

Council Directive 90/679/EEC
(Protection of Workers from
Risks Related to Exposure to
Biological Agents at Work) 27.25

Council Directive 91/353/EEC
(Proof of Employment
Directive) 25.7

Council Directive 91/383/EEC
(Temporary Workers'
Directive) 28.17

Council Directive 92/51/EEC
(Second Diploma Directive) 25.4

Council Directive 92/56/EEC
(Amending 75/129) 25.8, 39.2

Council Directive 92/57/EEC
(Minimum Safety and Health
Requirements at Temporary or
Mobile Work Sites) 27.25, 28.4

Council Directive 92/58/EEC
(Minimum Requirements for
the Provision of Safety and/or
Health Signs at Work) 27.25,
28.30, 39.4

Council Directive 92/85/EEC
(Pregnant Workers Directive) ... 25.6,
27.25, 28.17, 33.10,
42.9
art 10 .... 12.5
11(2)(b) 24.14

Council Directive 93/104/EC
(Working Time Directive) 4.6,
25.11, 28.15, 7.1,
57.2, 57.5, 57.6,
57.7, 57.15, 57.31
art 1(3) 57.3
7 .... 29.2, 57.1
13 .... 57.18

Council Directive 94/33/EC (Young
Workers Directive on the
Protection of Young People at
Work) 4., 4.6, 28.15, 28.17, 57.2,
57.3
Annex 4.5

Council Directive 94/45/EC
(European Works Council
Directive) 18.1, 18.4, 18.6, 18.21,
25.3, 25.12

Council Directive 95/46/EC (Data
Protection Directive) 11.12, 11.13

Council Directive 95/63/EC
(amending 89/655) 25.10, 28.12

Council Directive 96/34/EC
(Directive on Parental Leave) ... 18.4,
25.3, 25.6, 33.26,
49.19

Council Directive 96/71/EC
(Directive on the Posting of
Workers) 13.15, 25.7
art 1 .... 26.3
3 .... 26.3
6 .... 26.3

Council Directive 96/82/EC 28.26

Council Directive 96/96/EC
(Amending 77/388) 24.3, 24.18,
25.6

Council Directive 97/42/EC
(Amending 90/394) 27.25

Council Directive 97/74/EC
(Extending to the UK and
Northern Ireland, 94/45) 18.21
art 4(2) 18.22

**Council Directive 97/80/EC(Burden
of Proof Directive)** 14.3, 24.10,
25.3, 25.6

Council Directive 97/81/EC
(Part-time Work Directive) 25.6,
32.1, 32.20

Council Directive 98/23/EC
(Part Time Work Directive) 32.1,
32.2, 32.11

Council Directive 98/59/EC
(Approximation of the Laws of
the Member States Relating to
Collective Redundancies) 25.8,
39.2, 39.4

Council Directive 99/63/EC
(Hearings provided for in
17/62) 25.11, 57.1, 57.3, 57.31

Council Directive 99/70/EC
(Directive on Fixed-term
Contracts) 25.3, 25.7, 47.9

Council Directive 99/95/EC
(Seafarers' Hours of Work) 57.31

Council Directive 2000/34/EC
(Amending 93/104) 25.11, 57.1,
57.2

**Council Directive 2000/43/EC (Race
Discrimination Framework
Directive)** 12.7, 13.16, 25.3, 25.6
art 2(2)(b) 13.8
3(2) 12.2
5 .... 13.9, 25.6
6 .... 25.6
7(1) 12.2

**Council Directive 2000/78/EC
(Equal Treatment in
Employment and Occupation
Directive)** 3.22, 10.1, 12.2, 12.12,
13.4, 13.7, 13.13,
14.1, 25.3, 25.6
recital 2 .... 13.13
14 .... 3.23
art 2(2)(b) 13.8
6 .... 3.2
(1) 3.4
7 .... 13.9

**Council Directive
2000/79/EC(Mobile Workers in
Civil Aviation and its Domestic
Implementation)** 57.1, 57.3, 57.32,
57.33, 57.34

Council Directive 2001/23/EC
(Transfers Directive) 18.28, 25.9
art 1(1)(b) 52.1
(c) 37.2, 52.9

Council Directive 2001/44/EC
(European Physical Agents
(Vibration) Directive) 28.27

Council Directive 2001/45/EC
(Amending 89/655) 25.10

Council Directive 2001/86/EC
(Directive on Worker
Involvement) 18.1, 18.4, 18.13

Council Directive 2002/14/EC
(Information and Consultation
Directive) 11.11, 18.4, 25.12

Council Directive 2002/15/EC
(Organisation of the Working
Time of Persons Performing
Mobile Road Transport
Activities).... 57.1, 57.3, 57.34, 57.35

Council Directive 2002/73/EC
(Amending 76/207)........ 12.5, 12.11,
13.8, 13.9, 25.3, 25.6

Council Directive 2002/74/EC
(Amending 80/987)... 25.7, 31.1, 31.3

Council Directive 2003/88/EC
(Organisation of Working
Time Directive)...... 25.11, 29.2, 57.1

Council Directive 2006/54/EC (on
the implementation of the
principle of equal opportunities
and equal treatment of men
and women in matters of
employment and occupation)..... 12.2

Regulations

Council Regulation (EEC)
No 1612/68 (Freedom of
movement for Workers within
the Community).................... 26.2
art 8..................................... 51.2

Council Regulation (EEC)
No 1251/70 (Right of Workers
to Remain in the Territory of a
Member State after having
been Employed in that State).... 26.2

Council Regulation (EEC)
No 574/72 (Fixing the
Procedure for Implementing
1408/71)............................. 25.5

Council Regulation (EEC)
No 3820/85 (Drivers' Hours
Regulations)................. 57.1, 57.35

Council Regulation (EC)
No 44/2001 (Brussels I
Regulation)
art 2................................... 26.12
5(1)................................ 26.12
(3)................................ 26.12
17................................... 26.12
18(2)............................. 26.12
21................................... 26.12
28................................... 26.12

Council Regulation (EC)
No 2157/2001 (Regulation
establishing a European
Company Statute)......... 18.1, 18.13

Table of Statutory Instruments

ACAS Arbitration Scheme (Great
Britain) Order 2004,
SI 2004/753 .... 2.10, 21.37
Schedule
para 17–28 .... 21.37
34–40 .... 21.37
42–59s 21.37
63 .... 21.37
65 .... 21.37
67 .... 21.37
73 .... 21.37
76–77 .... 21.37
81 .... 21.37
85 .... 21.37
97 .... 21.37
100 .... 21.37
106–112s 21.37
170 .... 21.37
201s–204s 21.37
206s–208s 21.37
210s 21.37

ACAS (Flexible Working)
Arbitration Scheme (England
and Wales) Order 2003,
SI 2003/694 .... 2.10, 21.37

ACAS (Flexible Working)
Arbitration Scheme (Great
Britain) Order 2004,
SI 2004/2333 .... 21.37

Accession (Immigration and Worker
Registration) Regulations 2004,
SI 20041219 .... 26.1

Act of Sederunt (Interest on Sheriff
Court Decrees or Extracts)
1975, SI 1975/948 .... 14.20, 24.20

Armed Forces Act 1996
(Commencement No 3 and
Transitional Provisions)
Order 1997, SI 1997/2164 .... 24.4

Attachment of Earnings
(Employer's Deduction)
Order 1991, SI 1999/356
art 2 .... 35.9

Charitable Deductions (Approved
Schemes) Regulations 1986,
SI 1986/2211 .... 46.33

Chemicals (Hazard Information and
Packaging for Supply)
(Amendment)
Regulations 1996,
SI 1996/1092 .... 28.26

Chemicals (Hazard Information and
Packaging for Supply)
(Amendment)
Regulations 1997,
SI 1997/1460 .... 28.26

Chemicals (Hazard Information and
Packaging for Supply)
(Amendment)
Regulations 1998,
SI 1998/3106 .... 28.26

Chemicals (Hazard Information and
Packaging for Supply)
(Amendment)
Regulations 2000,
SI 2000/2381 .... 28.26

Chemicals (Hazard Information and
Packaging for Supply)
(Amendment)
Regulations 1999,
SI 1999/197 .... 28.26

Chemicals (Hazard Information and
Packaging for Supply)
Regulations 1994,
SI 1994/3247 .... 28.26

Child Support (Collection and
Enforcement)
Regulations 1992,
SI 1992/1989 .... 35.11

Children (Protection at Work)
(No 2) Regulations 2000,
SI 2000/2548 .... 4.2

Table of Statutory Instruments

Children (Protection at Work)
Regulations 1998,
SI 1998/276 .... 4.2, 4.4

Children (Protection at Work)
Regulations 2000,
SI 2000/1333 .... 4.2, 4.4,

Civil Aviation (Working Time)
Regulations 2004,
SI 2004/756 .... 57.33
reg 2 .... 29.8

Civil Jurisdiction and Judgments
Order 2001, SI 2001/3929 ...... 26.12

Civil Partnership Act 2004
(Commencement No 2)
Order 2005, SI 2005/3175
art 2(1) 12.2
Sch 1 .... 12.2

Civil Procedure Rules 1998,
SI 1998/3132 .... 21.1, 21.71
Pt 3
r 3.9 .... 21.16
(1) 14.7
Pt 6
r 6.19, 6.20 .... 26.12
6.21(2A) 26.12
Pt 23 .... 41.17
Pt 24 .... 8.23, 21.15, 21.17, 58.41
Pt 25 .... 41.17
r 26.6 .... 58.41
Pt 31 .... 21.11
Pt 36 .... 58.41
Pt 52
r 52.3 .... 22.26
Pt 53 .... 37.4
Pt 54 .... 14.28
Sch 1
Rules of the Supreme Court
Ord 14, 14A 8.23
Sch 2
County Court Rules
Ord 27
r 7(9) 35.1

Code of Practice on Equal Pay
Order 2003, SI 2003/2865 .... 5.8

Collective Redundancies and
Transfer of Undertakings
(Protection of Employment)
(Amendment)
Regulations 1995,
SI 1995/2587 .... 7.13, 11.6, 18.28,
25.8, 25.9, 39.4,
39.6, 39.7, 52.1,
54.3, 54.11
reg 8 .... 7.1

Collective Redundancies and
Transfer of Undertakings
(Protection of Employment)
(Amendment)
Regulations 1999,
SI 1999/1925 .... 18.28, 31.9, 39.4,
39.5, 39.6, 52.1

Community Charge and Council
Tax (Administration and
Enforcement) (Amendment)
(Jobseeker's Allowance)
Regulations 1996,
SI 1996/2405 .... 35.10

Companies (Inspection and Copying
of Registers, Indices and
Documents) Regulations 1991,
SI 1991/1998 .... 9.8

Companies Act 1985 (Accounts of
Small and Medium-sized
Companies and Minor
Accounting Amendments)
Regulations 1997,
SI 1997/220 .... 9.23

Companies Act 1985 (Accounts of
Small and Medium-Sized
Enterprises and Publication of
Accounts in ECUs)
Regulations 1992,
SI 1992/2452 .... 9.23

Companies (Tables A to F)
Regulations 1985, SI 1985/805
Schedule
Table A 9.1
art 82 .... 9.20
83 .... 9.18
84 .... 9.2, 9.3, 9.20
87 .... **9.25**

Company Accounts (Disclosure of
  Directors' Emoluments)
  Regulations 1997,
  SI 1997/570 .... 9.22, 9.23, 9.26, 9.28

Compromise Agreements
  (Description of Person)
  Order 2004, SI 2004/754 .... 14.33

Conduct of Employment Agencies
  and Employment Businesses
  Regulations 1976,
  SI 1976/715 .... 47.3, 47.4

Conduct of Employment Agencies
  and Employment Businesses
  Regulations 2003,
  SI 2003/3319 .... 47.3, 47.4
  reg 2 .... 47.5
    5 .... 47.5
    6 .... 45.5
    12 .... 47.5
    14 .... 17.3
      (2) 47.5
      (4)–(6) 47.5
    15 .... 17.3, 47.5
    17 .... 47.5
    19 .... 47.5
    20(2)–(6) 47.5
    21(1)(a)(i) 47.5
    22 .... 47.5
    26(3) 47.5
      (5), (6) 47.5
    28 .... 47.5
    30(1) 47.5
    31(1), (2) 47.5
    32(1) 47.5
      (9) 47.5
      (12) 47.5
  Sch 3 .... 47.5

Construction (Design and
  Management)
  Regulations 1994,
  SI 1994/3140 .... 28.4

Construction (Design and
  Management) (Amendment)
  Regulations 2002,
  SI 2002/2380 .... 28.4

Construction (Head Protection)
  Regulations 1989,
  SI 1989/2209 .... 28.4

Construction (Health, Safety and
  Welfare) Regulations 1996,
  SI 1996/1592 .... 25.10, 28.4

Control of Asbestos at Work
  Regulations 1987,
  SI 1987/2115 .... 28.26

Control of Asbestos at Work
  Regulations 2002,
  SI 2002/2675 .... 27.17

Control of Industrial Major
  Accident Hazards
  Regulations 1984,
  SI 1984/1902 .... 27.20

Control of Lead at Work
  Regulations 1980,
  SI 1980/1248
  reg 16 .... 34.29

Control of Lead at Work
  Regulations 1998,
  SI 1998/543 .... 28.26

Control of Major Accident Hazards
  Regulations 1999,
  SI 1999/743 .... 27.20, 28.1, 28.26

Control of Noise at Work
  Regulations 2005,
  SI 2005/1643 .... 28.19

Control of Substances Hazardous to
  Health Regulations 1988,
  SI 1988/1657 .... 27.17
  reg 11 .... 34.29

Control of Substances Hazardous to
  Health Regulations 2002,
  SI 2002/2677
  reg 2(1) 28.26
    3 .... 28.26
    4 .... 28.26
    6 .... 28.26
    7(1)–(4) 28.26
    8(1), (2) 28.26
    9–12 .... 28.26
    14 .... 28.26
    20 .... 28.26

Control of Vibration at Work
  Regulations 2005,
  SI 2005/1093 .... 28.27

Table of Statutory Instruments

Council Tax (Administration and
  Enforcement)
  Regulations 1992, SI 1992/613
  reg 32(1) 35.10
    34 .... 35.10
    37(1)–(3) 35.10
    38 .... 35.10
    39(1), (2) 35.10
    (4) 35.10
    (6) 35.10
    40, 42 .... 35.10
    56(2) 35.10
  Sch 4 .... 35.10

Court Funds Rules 1987,
  SI 1987/821
  r 27(1) 14.20, 21.67, 24.20

Criminal Justice and Public Order
  Act 1994 (Commencement
  No 5 and Transitional
  Provisions) Order 1995,
  SI 1995/127 .... 19.6

Dangerous Substances and
  Preparations (Safety)
  (Consolidation) and Chemicals
  (Hazard Information and
  Packaging for Supply)
  (Amendment)
  Regulations 2000,
  SI 2000/2897 .... 28.26

Dangerous Substances (Notification
  and Markings of Sites)
  Regulations 1990,
  SI 1990/304 .... 28.26

Deregulation (Deduction from Pay
  of Union Subscriptions)
  Order 1998, SI 1998/1529
  reg 3(1)–(3) 51.20

Directors' Remuneration Report
  Regulations 2002,
  SI 2002/1986 .... 9.22

Disability Discrimination Act 1995
  (Amendment)
  Regulations 2003,
  SI 2003/1673 .... 10.1
  reg 6 .... 10.24
    16 .... 10.31
    27 .... 10.24

Disability Discrimination Act 1995
  (Pensions) Regulations 2003,
  SI 2003/2770 .... 10.14

Disability Discrimination (Blind and
  Partially Sighted Persons)
  Regulations 2003,
  SI 2003/712 .... 10.8

Disability Discrimination
  (Description of Insurance
  Services) Regulations 1999,
  SI 1999/2114 .... 10.20

Disability Discrimination
  (Employment Field) (Leasehold
  Premises) Regulations 2004,
  SI 2004/153
  reg 3 .... 10.11, 10.20
    7 .... 10.13
    9 .... 10.13

Disability Discrimination
  (Employment)
  Regulations 1996,
  SI 1996/1456 .... 10.11, 42.10

Disability Discrimination (Meaning
  of Disability)
  Regulations 1996,
  SI 1996/1455
  reg 3(1), (2) 10.2
    4 .... 10.20
    (1) 10.2
    5 .... 10.7

Disability Discrimination
  (Questions and Replies)
  Order 2004, SI 2004/1168 ...... 10.35

Education (Modification of
  Enactments Relating to
  Employment) Order 2003,
  SI 2003/1964 .... 10.24, 37.2

Electricity at Work
  Regulations 1989,
  SI 1989/635 .... 27.17, 28.6
  reg 4 .... 28.6
    6–9 .... 28.6
    12–16 .... 28.6

Employers' Health and Safety
Policy Statements (Exception)
Regulations 1975,
SI 1975/1584 .... 27.18

Employers' Liability (Compulsory
Insurance) Regulations 1998,
SI 1998/2573 .... 28.16

Employment Act 1989
(Amendments and Revocations)
Order 1989, SI 1989/2311 .... 4.5

Employment Act 2002 (Amendment
of Schedules 3, 4 and 5)
Order 2007, SI 2007/30 .... 15.5,
20.19

Employment Act 2002 (Dispute
Resolution) Regulations 2004,
SI 2004/752 .... 2.9, 15.1, 20.3, 20.15,
20.19, 20.25, 20.30,
21.10, 32.21, 52.22,
55.13, 57.22, 57.23
reg 1(2) 15.3
2(1) 15.3, 15.4, 15.5, 15.11, 54.3
(2) 15.4
3(1) 15.3, 54.3
(2) 54.3
(a)–(d) 15.3
4 .... 39.8
(1)(a)–(g) 15.3, 54.3
5(1) 15.8, 54.3
(b) 55.18
(2), (3) 15.8, 54.3
6 .... 53.7
(1) 15.5
(3)–(6) 15.5
7 .... 53.7
(1), (2) 15.5
8 .... 53.7
(1), (2) 15.7
9 .... 20.19, 53.7
(1), (2) 15.9
10 .... 20.19, 53.7
(a) 15.9
11(1), (2) 15.7
(3)(a)–(c) 15.7, 20.19
(4) 54.3
12(1) 15.7, 54.3
(3) 15.7, 54.3
(4) 54.3
13(1) 15.7, 54.3
(2) 15.7

Employment Act 2002 (Dispute
Resolution) Regulations 2004,
SI 2004/752 – *contd*
reg 13 (3), (4) 15.7, 54.3
14 .... 14.9, 15.4, 20.19, 24.22
15 ..... 4.6, 14.3, 14.9, 20.20, 20.25,
20.31, 20.32, 53.2,
54.3
(1) 15.14
(a), (b) 15.13
(2) 15.14, 54.15
(3)(a), (b) 15.13
(4)(a), (b) 15.14
(5) 15.14
16 .... 15.7
18 .... 15.14, 20.20
(b) 20.19

Employment Appeal Tribunal
Rules 1993, SI 1993/2854 ...... 21.18,
22.4
r 3(1) 22.5
(3) 22.5
(7) 22.8, 22.9
(8)–(10) 22.8
6(12) 22.6
(14)–(16) 22.6
19–20 .... 22.8
21 .... 22.6, 22.8
23 .... 21.18, 22.13
(2), (3) 14.11, 22.13
(5), (5A) 14.11, 22.13
(5B), (5C) 22.13
23A 21.18
24 .... 22.9
25 .... 22.9
30 .... 37.6
33 .... 22.25
34(3)–(6) 22.22
34A 22.23
(1)–(3) 22.22
34B 22.23
(1), (2) 22.22
34C 22.4, 22.22, 22.24
34D 22.22
(2)–(5) 22.23
(7) 22.23
37(1A) 22.5
39 .... 22.9
Schedule
Form 1 .... 22.5

Table of Statutory Instruments

Employment Appeal Tribunal
(Amendment) Rules 1996,
SI 1996/3216 .... 10.34

Employment Appeal Tribunal
(Amendment) Rules 2001,
SI 2001/1128 .... 22.4

Employment Appeal Tribunal
(Amendment) Rules 2004,
SI 2004/2526 .... 21.74, 22.3, 22.4,
22.22
r 15 .... 14.7
24 .... 22.5

Employment (Appointed Day)
Order 2006, SI 2006/630 .... 14.25

Employment Code of Practice
(Access and Unfair Practices
during Recognition and
Derecognition Ballots)
Order 2005, SI 2005/2421 ...... 50.32

Employment Code of Practice
(Access to Workers during
Recognition and Derecognition
Ballots) Order 2000,
SI 2000/1443 .... 45.14

Employment Code of Practice
(Industrial Action Ballots and
Notice to Employers)
Order 1995, SI 1995/2729 .... 5.4,
45.14

Employment Code of Practice
(Picketing) Order 1992,
SI 1992/476 .... 5.4, 45.11

Employment Codes of Practice
(Revocation) Order 1991,
SI 1991/1264 .... 5.2, 5.4

Employment Equality (Age)
Regulations 2006,
SI 2006/1031 .... 3.1, 3.2, 3.3, 3.4,
3.16, 3.17, 20.22,
21.29, 25.6, 38.13,
42.1, 42.2, 42.3,
42.14, 53.14, 53.20
reg 2(2) 3.10, 3.11
3(1) 42.3, 42.11
(a) 3.4

Employment Equality (Age)
Regulations 2006, SI 2006/1031 –
contd
reg 3(1) (b) 3.5
(3)(a), (b) 3.5
4(1), (2) 3.7
6(1), (2) 3.8
Pt II (regs 7–24) 3.23, 3.41, 3.45
reg 7(1) 3.9, 3.12
(2) 3.9, 3.13
(3) 3.13
(6), (7) 3.13
(8) 3.12
8(2) 3.17
9(1)–(5) 3.29
10(1), (2) 3.11
(3)(a), (b) 3.11
(4)–(6) 3.11
(8)(a), (b) 3.30
11 .... 42.11
(1), (2) 3.34
12(1)–(7) 3.30
(10)(a)–(e) 3.30
13 .... 37.2
(1)(a), (b) 3.31
(2) 3.31
(3)(b) 3.31
(4)–(7) 3.31
14(1), (2) 3.32
15(1)–(5) 3.33
16 .... 3.33
17(1), (2) 3.35
(4)–(8) 3.35
18 .... 3.37, 3.40
(1)–(4) 3.36
19 .... 3.37, 3.45
(1)–(3) 3.37
20(1)–(4) 3.38
21(1)–(5) 3.39
(6)(a), (b) 3.39
22(1) 3.40
(3) 3.40
Pt III (regs 24–26) 3.23
reg 24 .... 3.9, 3.15
(1)–(3) 3.21
25 .... 56.1
(1)–(3) 3.42
26(1)–(4) 3.43
28 .... 3.21
29(1)–(3) 3.22
30(2) 3.23, 3.48, 42.3
31 .... 3.24
32(1)–(3) 3.25
(4)(a)–(c) 3.25

**Employment Equality (Age)
Regulations 2006, SI 2006/1031 –**
contd
reg 32 (7) 3.25
   33(1)(a) 3.26
    (4)(a)–(c) 3.26
   34(1), (2) 3.27
   35 .... 3.44
   36(1) 20.11
   37(2) 3.44
   38(1)(b) 3.44
    (2) 3.44
    (3) 3.44, 21.66
   39(3) 3.44
   41 .... 21.9
    (2) 3.44
    (b) 21.9
    (4)(a) 3.44
    (b)(i) 3.44
    (5), (6) 3.44
   42(1) 3.44, 20.29
    (3) 3.44, 20.30
    (4) 3.44, 20.29
   44 .... 3.46, 37.2
   45, 46 .... 3.46
Sch 2 .... 3.34, 3.49
  para 2(1), (2) 42.11
   4(1)(b) 3.45
   5 .... 42.11
   6 .... 3.45
   (4) 42.11
  Pt 2 .... 42.11
  para 3A(2) 42.11
   7(a), (b) 42.11
   8, 9 .... 42.11
   10(a)–(c) 42.11
   11–229 .... 42.11
  Pt 3 .... 42.11
Sch 3 .... 3.44
Sch 4 .... 3.44
  para 4(1)(c) 3.45
Sch 5
  para 1(1)–(3) 3.45
   2 .... 21.33
   (3)–(5) 3.45
   (8), (9) 3.45
   3 .... 3.45
   4(1) 3.45
   (2)(c) 3.45
   5 .... 3.45
   7–10 .... 3.45
Sch 6 .... 7.13
  para 1(1) 3.47
   2 .... 3.48

**Employment Equality (Age)
Regulations 2006, SI 2006/1031 –**
contd
Sch 6 – *contd*
  para 2 (1) 3.47, 42.3
   4 .... 3.47, 3.48, 42.3
   5 .... 42.3
   (2), (3) 3.47
   6–8 .... 3.47, 3.48, 42.3
   9 .... 3.47, 42.3, 54.11
   10 .... 3.47
   11 .... 3.47, 20.11, 42.3
Sch 7
  para 2–5 .... 3.47
Sch 8 .... 38.13

**Employment Equality (Religion or
Belief) Regulations 2003,
SI 2003/1660** 12.12, 12.13, 13.1,
      13.8, 13.34, 14.1,
      14.3, 14.26, 17.1,
      21.29, 23.1, 23.2,
      25.6, 37.2, 40.4
reg 1(2) 12.2
  2(1)(a)–(c) 12.6
   (3) 12.12
  3(1)(a) 12.4, 12.6
   (b) 12.7
   (iii) 13.8
   (2) 12.6
   (3) 12.5, 12.7
  4(1), (2) 12.10
  5(1), (2) 12.11
Pt II (regs 6–21) 14.26
reg 6(1) 12.12
  (2)(b) 13.17
  (d) 12.12
  (4) 12.12, 13.17
  (5) 12.12
  7(2)(b), (c) 13.6
  (3)(b), (c) 13.6
  8(1)–(4) 13.21
  9 .... 26.12, 26.13
  (1) 13.15
  (2) 12.12, 13.15
  (3)(a) 12.12, 13.15
  (b) 13.15
  (4), (5) 13.15
  9A(1), (2) 13.31
  (4) 14.22
  10(1)–(4) 13.22
  (6)–(9) 13.22
  (10)(a)–(d) 13.22
  11 .... 13.32, 37.2

Table of Statutory Instruments

Employment Equality (Religion or Belief) Regulations 2003, SI 2003/1660 – *contd*

reg 11 (1)–(8)	13.23
12(1)–(5)	13.24
13	13.24
14(1)–(6)	13.25
(8)	13.25
15(1)–(4)	13.26
16(1)–(3)	13.27
17(1)–(4)	13.28
18(1)–(6)	13.29
19(1)–(3)	13.30
21	14.22
(1)	13.33
(2)	12.12, 13.33
(3)	13.33
Pt III (regs 22–23)	14.26
reg 22	14.2, 56.1
(1)	12.13, 13.35
(2)	12.13, 13.38
(3)	12.13, 13.35, 13.38
23	14.2
(1)	12.13, 13.36
(2)	1.27
(3), (4)	12.13, 13.36
24	13.19
25(1), (2)	12.5, 13.9
26(1)–(4)	12.5, 13.12
27(2)	14.1, 14.22
28	20.11
(1)	14.2
(2)	13.27
(a)	14.2
30	14.14
(1)(a)–(c)	14.12
(3)	14.21, 21.66
33(2)(b)	21.9
(3), (4)	14.9
34(1)	14.4, 20.29
(1A)	14.4
(3)	14.7, 20.30
(4)	14.4, 20.29
35	14.32, 14.33
36	13.10, 13.32, 14.2
(2)	13.32
(4)	13.32
(7)–(10)	13.32
37, 38	13.32
Sch 1A	
para 1–5	13.31
6	14.22
7(1)(b)	14.22
Sch 2	14.9

Employment Equality (Religion or Belief) Regulations 2003, SI 2003/1660 – *contd*

Sch 3	14.9
Sch 4	
Pt 1	8.18
para 1(1)	14.32
(3)	8.17, 14.32
2	14.33, 21.33
3(1)	14.32
Pt 2	8.18, 14.32
para 5	20.11

Employment Equality (Religion or Belief) (Amendment) Regulations 2003, SI 2003/2828 .... 13.31, 14.22

Employment Equality (Religion or Belief) Regulations 2003 (Amendment) (No 2) Regulations 2004, SI 2004/2520 .... 14.33

Employment Equality (Sex Discrimination) Regulations 2005, SI 2005/2467 .... 12.5, 13.5, 13.25, 13.28, 24.2, 25.6, 26.13, 33.6, 56.1

reg 3	12.7, 13.8
4	12.2, 12.5
5	12.6, 12.11
8	12.12
11	12.12, 13.15
(2)	24.4
13	13.22
18	13.29
21	12.12
33	12.11
34	13.10
35	24.4
36	24.14

Employment Equality (Sexual Orientation) (Amendment) Regulations 2003, SI 2003/2827 .... 12.2, 13.31, 14.22

reg 6(2)	12.12
(4)	12.12
9	26.13
(4), (5)	12.12

Employment Equality (Sexual Orientation) Regulations 2003, SI 2003/1661 .... 12.2, 12.13, 13.1, 13.8, 13.22, 13.34, 14.1, 14.3, 14.26, 17.1, 21.29, 23.1, 23.2, 25.6, 37.2, 40.4
reg 2 .... 12.6
  (3) 12.12
  3(1) 12.6
    (a) 12.4
    (b) 12.7
      (iii) 13.8
  (2) 12.5
  4(1), (2) 12.10
  5(1) 12.11
Pt II (regs 6–21) 14.26
reg 6(1) 12.12
  (2)(b) 13.17
  (d) 12.12
  (4) 12.12, 13.17
  (5) 12.12
  7(2) 13.7
  (3)(a)–(c) 13.7
  8(1)–(4) 13.21
  9 .... 26.12
  (1) 13.15
  (2) 12.12, 13.15
  (3) 12.12
    (a), (b) 13.15
  (4), (5) 13.15
  9A 42.7
  (1), (2) 13.31
  (4) 14.22
  10(1)–(4) 13.22
  (6), (7) 13.22
  (8)(a), (b) 13.22
  (9) 13.22
  (10)(a)–(d) 13.22
  11 .... 13.32, 37.2
  (1)–(8) 13.23
  12(1)–(5) 13.24
  13 .... 13.24
  14(1)–(6) 13.25
  (8) 13.25
  15(1)–(4) 13.26
  16(1)–(4) 13.27
  17(1)–(4) 13.28
  18(1)–(6) 13.29
  19(1)–(3) 13.30
  21 .... 14.22
  (1) 13.33
  (2) 12.12, 13.33
  (3) 13.33

Employment Equality (Sexual Orientation) Regulations 2003, SI 2003/1661 – *contd*
Pt III (regs 22–23) 14.26
reg 22 .... 14.2, 56.1
  (1) 12.13, 13.35
  (2) 12.13, 13.38
  (3) 12.13, 13.35, 13.38
  23 .... 14.2
  (1) 12.13, 13.36
  (2) 13.37
  (3), (4) 12.13, 13.36
  24 .... 13.19
  25 .... 12.9, 13.13, 42.7
  26(1) 12.5, 13.9
  (2), (3) 13.9
  27(2) 14.1, 14.22
  28 .... 20.11
  (1) 14.2
  (2) 13.27
    (a) 14.2
  30 .... 14.14
  (1)(a)–(c) 14.12
  (3) 14.21, 21.66
  33 .... 21.9
  (2) 14.5
    (b) 21.9
  (4) 14.9
  34(1) 14.4, 20.29
  (1A) 14.4
  (3) 14.7, 20.30
  (4) 14.4, 20.29
  35 .... 8.17, 8.18, 14.32, 14.33
  36 .... 13.10, 14.2
  (4) 13.32
  (7)–(10) 13.32
  37, 38 .... 13.32
Sch 1A 42.7
  para 1–5 .... 13.31
    6 .... 14.22
    7(1)(b) 14.22
Sch 2 .... 14.9
Sch 3 .... 14.9
Sch 4 .... 8.18
  para 1 .... 14.33
    (1) 8.17, 14.32
    (3) 14.32
    2 .... 14.33, 21.33
    3(1) 14.32
  Pt 2 .... 8.18, 14.32
  para 5 .... 20.11

Employment Equality (Sexual
Orientation) Regulations 2003
(Amendment)
Regulations 2004,
SI 2004/2519 .... 14.33

Employment Protection Code of
Practice (Disclosure of
Information) Order 1998,
SI 1998/45 .... 11.4

Employment Protection Code of
Practice (Time Off)
Order 1998, SI 1998/46 .... 5.2

Employment Protection Code of
Practice (Time Off)
Order 2003, SI 2003/1191 ... 2.9, 5.2,
49.2

Employment Protection (Continuity
of Employment)
Regulations 1996,
SI 1996/3147 .... 7.6, 7.12

Employment Protection (National
Health Service) Order 1996,
SI 1996/638 .... 7.9

Employment Protection (Offshore
Employment) Order 1976,
SI 1976/766 .... 53.15

Employment Protection (Part-time
Employees) Regulations 1995,
SI 1995/31 .... 7.1, 38.4

Employment Protection
(Recoupment of Jobseeker's
Allowance and Income
Support) Regulations 1996,
SI 1996/2349 .... 21.68, 55.6

Employment Relations Act 1999
(Commencement No 2 and
Transitional and Saving
Provisions) Order 1999,
SI 1999/2830
Sch 3
para 2 .... 53.15

Employment Relations Act 1999
(Commencement No 5 and
Transitional Provision)
Order 2000, SI 2000/875
art 3 .... 53.17

Employment Relations Act 1999
(Commencement No 6 and
Transitional Provision)
Order 2000, SI 2000/1338 ...... 53.11

Employment Rights (Increase of
Limits) Order 2003,
SI 2003/3038 .... 31.5

Employment Rights (Increase of
Limits) Order 2006,
SI 2006/3045 ...... 31.5, 34.27, 34.39,
38.13, 51.4, 55.7,
55.10

Employment Tribunals Act 1996
(Application of Conciliation
Provisions) Order 2000,
SI 2000/1337 .... 2.4

Employment Tribunals (Constitution
and Rules of Procedure)
Regulations 1993,
SI 1993/2687 .... 21.18
Sch 1
r 14(1A), (1B) 10.34
Sch 6 .... 14.28

Employment Tribunals (Constitution
and Rules of Procedure)
Regulations 2001,
SI 2001/1171 .... 20.2, 20.3, 21.1,
21.17, 21.69, 21.70,
24.22
Sch 1
r 15(1) 21.18
19(3) 21.24
Sch 3 .... 24.8, 24.22
Sch 5 .... 27.31
r 2(1), (2) 27.34

Employment Tribunals (Constitution
and Rules of Procedure)
Regulations 2004,
SI 2004/1861 .... 20.3, 20.5, 20.14,
20.18, 21.7, 21.10,
21.17, 22.3, 24.22
reg 2(2) 21.71
3 .... 20.14, 21.1, 24.22
4 .... 20.6
6, 7 .... 20.6
8(5) 20.7
9(3) 20.8
10, 11 .... 20.7

Employment Tribunals (Constitution and Rules of Procedure) Regulations 2004, SI 2004/1861 – *contd*

reg 14 .... 20.15
    (1)(c) 20.16
    15(5) 21.38
    (6) 21.15, 22.5
    17 .... 21.65
    19 .... 26.12
    20 .... 21.62, 24.22
    (2)–(5) 21.69
    37(1) 21.64
    61(4)(h) 26.13
Sch 1 .... 20.2, 21.27, 21.72, 22.3
  r 1 .... 24.22
    (1), (2) 20.21
    (3) 20.16
    (4) 20.15
    (7) 20.15
    2(1) 20.16
    (2) 20.16, 20.34
    3(1) 20.16
    (5) 20.34
    (9) 20.16
    (10) 22.2
    4 .... 24.22
    (1), (2) 20.35
    (4) 20.36, 20.37, 21.21
    (5), (6) 20.35
    6(1) 20.35
    (2), (3) 20.37
    7 .... 20.32
    8 .... 20.10
    (1)–(6) 20.38
    9 .... 20.38
    10 .... 21.30
    (1) 21.20
    (2) 21.2
    (c) 21.4
    (d) 21.4, 21.11
    (e) 21.21
    (h) 21.22
    (j) 21.24
    (k), (l) 21.23
    (n) 21.7, 21.15
    (r) 21.23
    (5) 21.2
    (7) 21.2, 21.24
    (8) 21.3
    11 .... 20.36, 21.30
    (1) 21.3
    (3) 21.8
    (4) 21.2

Employment Tribunals (Constitution and Rules of Procedure) Regulations 2004, SI 2004/1861 – *contd*

Sch 1 – *contd*
  r 12(2) 21.3, 21.10
    (3) 21.3, 21.41
    13(1) 21.4, 21.71
    (b) 21.16
    (2) 21.4, 21.16
    (5) 21.74
    14 .... 20.34
    (2), (3) 21.6, 21.52
    (4) 21.6, 21.38
    (5) 21.6, 21.46, 21.47
    (6) 21.47
    15 .... 21.6, 21.49
    16 .... 21.6
    (1), (2) 21.51
    17(1) 21.2, 21.51
    (2) 21.2, 21.5, 21.18, 21.70
    18 .... 21.5, 21.17, 21.75
    (1) 21.6, 21.51
    (2) 20.18
    (3) 20.9, 21.6
    (6) 21.6
    (7) 21.2, 21.6, 21.55
    (a) 21.23
    (b)–(d) 21.17
    (f) 21.17
    (g) 21.18
    (9) 21.15
    19 .... 20.11, 21.2
    (1) 21.6, 21.16
    20 .... 22.2
    (1)–(5) 21.15
    21 .... 21.25
    22(1) 21.29
    (2), (3) 21.29, 21.30
    (4)–(6) 21.29
    (7), (8) 21.30
    23(1) 21.30
    24 .... 21.30
    25 .... 21.75
    (3) 21.28
    (4) 20.10, 21.28
    (5) 21.28
    26(3) 21.51
    27(2) 21.52
    (3) 21.49
    (4) 21.57
    (5) 20.10, 21.54
    (6) 21.54
    28 .... 21.2

Table of Statutory Instruments

Employment Tribunals (Constitution and Rules of Procedure) Regulations 2004, SI 2004/1861 – *contd*

Sch 1 – *contd*

r 28 (1)(a) 21.75
   (2) 20.10
   (4) 21.62
 30(1) 21.3
    (b) 21.62
   (2) 21.3
   (3) 21.3
    (b) 21.63, 22.11
   (5) 21.62
   (6) 21.63
 31(1), (2) 21.65
 33(2), (3) 20.38
   (5)–(7) 20.38
 34 .... 20.34, 20.37, 21.15
   (1)(b) 21.75
   (3) 20.14, 20.34, 21.75
    (d) 22.16
   (4) 20.34
   (5) 21.75
 35(1), (2) 20.34, 21.75
   (3) 21.75
 36(2) 21.75
   (3) 20.34, 21.75
 37 .... 21.76
 38(1)(a) 21.70
    (b) 21.71
   (2) 21.70
   (5) 21.70
   (7)–(10) 21.71
 39 .... 55.4
 40(1)–(3) 21.71
 41(1) 21.71
   (3) 21.71
 42–44 .... 21.73
 45(2)–(4) 21.73
 46(1) 21.70
   (2) 21.70, 21.71
 47 .... 21.71
 48 .... 22.24
   (1)–(6) 21.74
   (9) 21.74
 49 .... 14.11, 21.19, 21.65, 22.13
 50 .... 21.18, 22.13
   (1) 14.11
    (b) 21.18
   (2)–(6) 14.11, 21.18
   (7) 21.18
   (8)(a)–(c) 21.18
   (9) 14.11

Employment Tribunals (Constitution and Rules of Procedure) Regulations 2004, SI 2004/1861 – *contd*

Sch 1 – *contd*

r 50 (11) 14.11
 51 .... 21.18
 54 .... 37.6
   (1)(a) 21.51
 55 .... 21.22
 57 .... 20.11
 60(1) 21.18, 21.20, 21.52
 61(4)(h) 26.12
Sch 2 .... 20.4, 21.78
Sch 3 .... 20.4
Sch 4 .... 20.4
Sch 5 .... 14.28, 20.4
Sch 6 .... 20.2, 20.4, 21.14, 21.78
r 3 .... 24.22
 4(4) 24.22
 5 .... 24.22
 6(2) 24.22
 7(3)–(6) 24.22
 9(1)–(3) 24.22
 10(1) 24.22
   (3)–(6) 24.22
 11(1)–(6) 24.22
 12(4), (5) 24.22
 13(2) 24.22
 14 .... 24.22

Employment Tribunals (Constitution and Rules of Procedure) (Amendment) Regulations 1996, SI 1996/1757 .... 10.34, 22.29

Employment Tribunals (Constitution and Rules of Procedure) (Amendment) Regulations 2004, SI 2004/2351 .... 20.2, 20.4, 24.22

Employment Tribunals (Constitution and Rules of Procedure) (Amendment) Regulations 2005, SI 2005/435 .... 20.2

Employment Tribunals (Constitution and Rules of Procedure) (Amendment) (No 2) Regulations 2005, SI 2005/1865 .... 20.2, 21.2, 21.29

Employment Tribunals (Constitution
and Rules of Procedure)
(Scotland) Regulations 2001,
SI 2001/1170 .... 20.2

Employment Tribunals Extension of
Jurisdiction (England and
Wales) Order 1994,
SI 1994/1623 .... 20.9, 20.11, 41.1,
42.14
art 3 .... 26.12
(c) 8.23
4 .... 8.23, 58.38
5 .... 8.23
7 .... 8.23, 20.32, 58.40
8 .... 8.23, 20.32

Employment Tribunals Extension of
Jurisdiction (Scotland)
Order 1994, SI 1994/1624 ...... 58.38
art 7 .... 58.40

Employment Tribunals (Interest on
Awards in Discrimination
Cases) Regulations 1996,
SI 1996/2803 ...... 3.44, 14.13, 21.67,
24.13, 24.20
reg 2(1)(b) 21.67
3(1) 14.20, 24.20
(2) 14.20, 21.67, 24.20
(3) 14.20, 21.67
4 .... 14.20, 24.20
6 .... 21.67
(1)(a) 14.20, 24.20
(b) 14.20, 24.20
(2) 14.20, 24.20
(3) 24.20
7 .... 21.63
8 .... 21.67

Employment Tribunals (Interest)
Order 1990, SI 1990/479 .... 21.67

Equal Opportunities (Employment
Legislation) (Territorial Limits)
Regulations 1999,
SI 1999/3163 .... 24.4, 25.7

Equal Pay Act 1970 (Amendment)
Regulations 2003,
SI 2003/1656 .... 20.28, 24.2, 24.20

Equal Pay Act 1970 (Amendment)
Regulations 2004,
SI 2004/2352 .... 24.22

Equal Pay (Amendment)
Regulations 1983,
SI 1983/1794 .... 24.2

Equal Pay (Complaints to
Employment Tribunals) (Armed
Forces) Regulations 1997,
SI 1997/2162 .... 24.4, 37.2

Equal Pay (Questions and Replies)
Order 2003, SI 2003/722 .... 24.2,
24.10, 24.22

European Communities
(Employment in the Civil
Service) Order 1991,
SI 1991/1221 .... 37.7

European Cooperative Society
(Involvement of Employees)
Regulations 2006,
SI 2006/2059 .... 53.11
reg 31 .... 54.3, 54.11

European Public Limited Liability
Company Regulations 2004,
SI 2004/2326 .... 7.13, 18.1, 15.5,
53.11
Pt 3 .... 18.13
reg 17(1)–(3) 18.13
18(1)–(3) 18.14
19(1), (2) 18.14
20 .... 18.16
21(1)–(6) 18.15
22(1)–(4) 18.15
23(4), (5) 18.15
24 .... 18.15
25(1)–(8) 18.15
27(2) 18.16
(3) 18.16, 18.17
28(4) 18.16
29(1)–(6) 18.16
30(1)–(4) 18.18
31(1), (2) 18.16
32 .... 18.17
33(1)–(6) 18.19
39, 40 .... 18.20, 49.14
42 .... 18.20, 54.3, 54.11
Sch 3 .... 18.17

Fire Precautions (Workplace)
Regulations 1997,
SI 1997/1840 .... 28.13

Table of Statutory Instruments

Fire Precautions (Workplace)
(Amendment)
Regulations 1999,
SI 1999/1877 .... 28.13

Fishing Vessels (Working Time:
Sea-fishermen)
Regulations 2004,
SI 2004/1713 ...... 54.3, 54.11, 57.23,
57.31

Fixed-term Employees (Prevention
of Less Favourable Treatment)
Regulations 2002,
SI 2002/2034 .... 7.13, 20.32, 25.7,
32.7, 47.1, 47.7,
47.8, 47.9, 53.11,
54.14
reg 1 .... 47.9, 53.6
2 .... 47.9
3(2), (3) 47.9
(6), (7) 47.9
4 .... 47.9
5 .... 21.9
(1), (2) 47.9
6 .... 54.3
(2) 47.9
(3) 47.9, 54.11
7 .... 20.11, 20.22
(2), (3) 47.9
(6) 47.9
(7)(c) 47.9
(10) 47.9
(13) 47.9
8 .... 21.33
(2) 47.9
(4), (5) 47.9
9 .... 20.32
(1)–(4) 47.9
(5) 20.11
(6) 20.32
(a), (b) 47.9
11 .... 53.15
12(1)–(3) 47.9
14 .... 47.9
18 .... 47.9
19(3) 47.9
20 .... 47.9
Sch 2
Pt 1
para 3(1) 53.15
(15) 53.15
Sch 2
Pt 2

Fixed-term Employees (Prevention of Less
Favourable Treatment)
Regulations 2002, SI 2002/2034 –
contd
Sch 2 – contd
para 5 .... 53.15

Flexible Working (Eligibility,
Complaints and Remedies)
Regulations 2002, SI 2002/
3236 49.19
reg 15 .... 22.1

Flexible Working (Procedural
Requirements)
Regulations 2002,
SI 2002/3207 .... 49.19

Health and Safety at Work etc
Act 1974 (Application outside
Great Britain) Order 2001,
SI 2001/2127 .... 13.12, 27.41
art 8(1)(a) 12.5

Health and Safety (Consultation
with Employees)
Regulations 1996,
SI 1996/1513 .... 11.8, 18.28, 28.8,
28.20, 28.21, 49.9,
54.3
reg 4–8 .... 28.22
Sch 2
para 2–5 .... 49.10

Health and Safety (Display Screen
Equipment) Regulations 1992,
SI 1992/2792 .... 28.17, 28.31
reg 1(2) 28.5
3 .... 28.5

Health and Safety (Enforcing
Authority) Regulations 1989,
SI 1989/1903 .... 27.29

Health and Safety (Enforcing
Authority) Regulations 1998,
SI 1998/494
Sch 1 .... 27.29

Health and Safety (First-Aid)
Regulations 1981,
SI 1981/917 .... 27.17, 28.17
reg 3, 4 .... 28.14

Health and Safety Information for
Employees (Modifications and
Repeals) Regulations 1995,
SI 1995/2923 .... 27.18

Health and Safety Information for
Employees Regulations 1989,
SI 1989/682 .... 27.18

Health and Safety Inquiries
(Procedure) (Amendment)
Regulations 1976,
SI 1976/246 .... 27.26

Health and Safety Inquiries
(Procedure) Regulations 1975,
SI 1975/335 .... 27.26

Health and Safety (Miscellaneous
Amendments)
Regulations 2002,
SI 2002/2174 .... 28.17
reg 2 .... 28.14
3 .... 28.5
4 .... 28.18
6 .... 28.29

Health and Safety (Safety Signs
and Signals) Regulations 1996,
SI 1996/341 .... 28.30

Health and Safety (Training for
Employment)
Regulations 1990,
SI 1990/1380 .... 16.7, 27.17

Health and Safety (Young Persons)
Regulations 1997,
SI 1997/135 .... 4.5

Immigration (European Economic
Area) Regulations 2006,
SI 2006/1003 .... 26.1, 26.2

Immigration (Restrictions on
Employment) Order 1996,
SI 1996/3225 .... 12.12, 26.8

Immigration (Restrictions on
Employment) Order 2004,
SI 2004/755
Schedule
para 4 .... 26.9

Income Tax (Benefits in Kind)
(Exemption for Welfare
Counselling) Regulations 2000,
SI 2000/2080 .... 46.23

Income Tax (Employments)
Regulations 1993,
SI 1993/744 .... 46.4

Income Tax (Exemption of Minor
Benefits) Regulations 2002,
SI 2002/205 .... 46.23

Income Tax (Pay As You Earn)
Regulations 2003,
SI 2003/2682 .... 46.4
reg 41, 42 .... 46.14
47–53 .... 46.14
70 .... 46.14
80 .... 46.14
82, 83 .... 46.14

Industrial Training Levy
(Construction Industry
Training Board) Order 2007,
SI 2007/607 .... 16.4

Industrial Training Levy
(Engineering Construction
Industry Training Board)
Order 2007, SI 2007/609 .... 16.4

Information and Consultation of
Employees Regulations 2004,
SI 2004/3426 .... 7.13, 11.11, 15.5,
18.1, 25.12, 39.4,
50.6, 53.11
reg 2 .... 18.4
4(1)–(3) 18.4
5 .... 18.5, 18.12
6 .... 18.5
7(1)–(5) 18.5
8(1) 18.8
(b), (c) 11.11
(2)–(4) 11.11, 18.8
(5)(b), (c) 18.8
(6)–(9) 18.8
9(1)–(3) 18.8
10(1), (2) 18.8
(3)(a), (b) 18.8
(c)(i) 18.8
11(1), (2) 18.5
12(1), (2) 18.5
13(1)–(3) 18.5

Table of Statutory Instruments

Information and Consultation of
Employees Regulations 2004,
SI 2004/3426 – contd
reg 14(1)–(5) 18.6
(6) 18.5
15(1), (2) 18.6
16(1) 11.11, 18.6
(2) 11.11, 18.6
(3)–(6) 18.6
17(1), (2) 18.6
18(1) 18.7
(2) 18.5
19(1) 18.7
(3)–(6) 18.7
20(1) 18.7
(3)–(5) 18.7
21 .... 18.6
22(1)–(7) 18.11
23(3) 18.11
25 .... 11.11
(1)–(4) 18.10
(6), (7) 18.10
26 .... 11.11
(1)–(4) 18.10
27, 28 .... 18.12, 49.14
29(1) 18.12
(2)(a) 18.12
(3)–(5) 18.12
30 .... 18.12, 54.3, 54.11
32(4) 18.12
33 .... 18.12
Sch 1 .... 18.4
Sch 2 .... 18.7

Insolvency Proceedings (Monetary
Limits) Order 1986,
SI 1986/1996
art 4 .... 31.2

Insolvency Rules 1986,
SI 1986/1925 .... 31.2

Insurance Companies (Third
Insurance Directives)
Regulations 1994,
SI 1994/1696 .... 19.4

Ionising Radiations
Regulations 1985,
SI 1985/1333
reg 16 .... 34.29

Jobseeker's Allowance
Regulations 1996,
SI 1996/207 .... 12.5

Lifting Operations and Lifting
Equipment Regulations 1998,
SI 1998/2307 .... 28.12, 28.17

Local Authorities (Contracting
Outof Tax Billing, Collection
and Enforcement Functions)
Order 1996, SI 1996/1880 ...... 35.10

Local Authorities (Goods and
Services) (Public Bodies)
Order 1992, SI 1992/2830 ...... 55.10

Local Government Changes for
England (Community Charge
and Council Tax,
Administration and
Enforcement)
Regulations 1995,
SI 1995/247 .... 35.9

Local Government (Discretionary
Payments) Regulations 1996,
SI 1996/1680 .... 37.2

Local Government Officers
(Political Restrictions)
Regulations 1990,
SI 1990/851 .... 37.2

Local Government Pension Scheme
Regulations 1997,
SI 1997/578 .... 42.6

Management of Health and Safety
at Work Regulations 1992,
SI 1992/2051 .... 4.5, 5.10, 28.2,
28.17, 28.21, 28.25,
28.28, 33.23
reg 13A(3) 33.23
13B 33.23

Management of Health and Safety
at Work Regulations 1999,
SI 1999/3242 .... 4.1, 4.5, 12.5, 27.18,
28.4, 57.11
reg 3 .... 28.17
(5) 4.5
4–8 .... 28.17
9 .... 28.17, 57.13

Management of Health and Safety at Work Regulations 1999, SI 1999/3242 – *contd*

reg 10 .... 28.17
(2) 4.4
11–15 .... 28.17
16 .... 28.17, 33.23
17 .... 28.17, 57.13
19 .... 28.17
(1)–(3) 4.5
21, 22 .... 28.17
Sch 1 .... 28.17

Management of Health and Safety at Work (Amendment) Regulations 1994, SI 1994/2865 .... 33.23

Manual Handling Operations Regulations 1992, SI 1992/2793 .... 28.17
reg 4(3) 28.18
Sch 1 .... 28.18

Maternity and Parental Leave etc. and the Paternity and Adoption Leave (Amendment) Regulations 2006, SI 2006/2014 .... 33.22A

Maternity and Parental Leave Regulations 1999, SI 1999/3312 .... 25.3, 25.6, 33.1,
33.26
reg 4 .... 49.19
5 .... 49.19
8 .... 49.19
9 .... 13.33
(3) 42.9
10 .... 33.6
13 .... 33.26
14(1) 33.26, 49.19
15(1)(a) 33.26
(2) 33.46
16 .... 49.19
17 .... 7.6, 12.12, 13.33, 33.26,
49.19, 53.4
18(3) 49.19
(5) 49.19
19 .... 33.8
(2)(e) 49.19
(ii) 33.26
20 .... 54.3
(1)(b) 33.6

Maternity and Parental Leave Regulations 1999, SI 1999/3312 – *contd*

reg 20 (2) 49.19
(e)(ii) 33.26
(3) 49.19
(7), (8) 33.6
21 .... 49.19
Sch 1 .... 49.19
Sch 2 .... 33.26
para 6 .... 49.19
8 .... 49.19

Maternity and Parental Leave (Amendment) Regulations 2001, SI 2001/4010 .... 13.33, 33.26

Maternity and Parental Leave (Amendment) Regulations 2002, SI 2002/2789 .... 33.26

Merchant Shipping and Fishing Vessels (Health and Safety at Work) (Employment of Young Persons) Regulations 1998, SI 1998/2411 .... 4.5
reg 6 .... 4.6

Merchant Shipping and Fishing Vessels (Manual Handling Operations) Regulations 1998, SI 1998/2857 .... 28.18

Merchant Shipping and Fishing Vessels (Personal Protective Equipment) Regulations 1999, SI 1999/2205 .... 28.12

Merchant Shipping (Hours of Work: Inland Waterways) Regulations 2003, SI 2003/3049 .... 57.32

Merchant Shipping (Hours of Work) Regulations 2002, SI 2002/2125 .... 4.4
reg 3(1) 57.31
18(1) 57.31

Table of Statutory Instruments

Merchant Shipping (Working Time
: Inland Waterways)
Regulations 2003,
SI 2003/3049 .... 54.3, 54.11, 57.3,
57.23, 57.33

National Health Service Pension
Scheme Regulations 1995,
SI 1995/300 .... 24.18

National Minimum Wage (Offshore
Employment) Order 1999,
SI 1999/1128 .... 34.10

National Minimum Wage
Regulations 1999, SI 1999/584
reg 3–6 .... 34.9
9 .... 34.9
10, 11 .... 34.9
12 .... 34.10
(2) 16.2, 34.9
13(1) 34.9
28 .... 34.12
30–37 .... 34.9
38(2) 34.11

National Minimum Wage
Regulations 1999 (Amendment)
Regulations 2000,
SI 2000/1989
reg 31 .... 34.12

National Minimum Wage
Regulations 1999 (Amendment)
Regulations 2001,
SI 2001/1108 .... 34.9

National Minimum Wage
Regulations 1999 (Amendment)
Regulations 2004,
SI 2004/1161 .... 34.9

National Minimum Wage
Regulations 1999 (Amendment)
Regulations 2006,
SI 2006/2001
reg 5 .... 34.9

Noise at Work Regulations 1989,
SI 1989/1790 .... 28.19

Notices to Quit, etc (Prescribed
Information) Regulations 1988,
SI 1988/2201 .... 43.4, 43.5

Notification of New Substances
Regulations 1993,
SI 1993/3050 .... 28.26

Occupational and Personal Pension
Schemes (Consultation by
Employers and Miscellaneous
Amendment) Regulations 2006,
SI 2006/349 .... 7.13, 15.5
reg 12(2)(a) 49.14
(3) 49.14
13(2) 49.14
Schedule
para 2, 3 .... 49.14
5 .... 54.3
(6) 54.11

Occupational Pension Schemes
(Disclosure of Information)
Regulations 1986,
SI 1986/1046 .... 11.1

Occupational Pension Schemes
(Disclosure of Information)
Regulations 1996,
SI 1996/1655
reg 3–6 .... 11.10
Sch 1–3 .... 11.10

Occupational Pension Schemes
(Equal Access to Membership)
Amendment Regulations 1995,
SI 1995/1215 .... 24.16, 24.17

Occupational Pension Schemes
(Equal Treatment)
Regulations 1995,
SI 1995/3183 .... 42.14
reg 3–7 .... 24.17
9–12 .... 24.17

Occupational Pension Schemes
(Internal Dispute Resolution
Procedures) Regulations 1996,
SI 1996/1270 .... 42.14

Occupational Pension Schemes
(Member-nominated Trustees
and Directors)
Regulations 1996,
SI 1996/1216 .... 42.12

**Occupational Pension Schemes
(Member-nominated Trustees
and Directors)
Regulations 2006,
SI 2006/714** 42.12

**Offshore Electricity and Noise
Regulations 1997,
SI 1997/1993** 28.6

**Part-time Workers (Prevention of
Less Favourable Treatment)
Regulations 2000,
SI 2000/1551** 7.13, 20.32, 24.2,
24.15, 25.6, 32.1,
32.11, 32.19, 32.23,
47.1, 53.11
reg 1(2) 32.2
2(1), (2) 24.15, 32.7
(3) 32.7
(a)–(c) 32.9
(d) 24.15, 32.9
(4)(a)(ii) 24.15
(b) 24.15, 32.8
3 .... 24.15, 32.13, 32.21
4 .... 24.15, 32.13, 32.21
5 .... 32.13, 32.20, 32.21
(1) 24.15
(a), (b) 32.4
(2) 24.15
(a) 32.14
(b) 24.15
(3) 24.15
(4) 24.15, 32.6
6 .... 21.9, 32.17
7 .... 54.3
(1) 32.2
(2) 32.18, 32.20, 32.21
(3) 54.11
8 .... 20.11, 20.22
(1) 32.20
(2)–(4) 32.21
(6) 32.21
(7)(a)–(c) 32.22
(9)–(14) 32.22
9 .... 21.33, 32.24
12 .... 32.2
13(1)–(3) 32.2
14–17 .... 32.2

**Part-time Workers (Prevention of
Less Favourable Treatment)
Regulations 2000 (Amendment)
Regulations 2002,
SI 2002/2035** 24.15, 47.1

**Paternity and Adoption Leave
Regulations 2002,
SI 2002/2788** 33.27
reg 4–11 .... 49.19
12 .... 7.6, 49.19
13 .... 33.27, 49.19
14–17 .... 49.19
18 .... 33.27, 49.19
19 .... 7.6, 49.19
20 .... 49.19
21 .... 7.6, 49.19
22–27 .... 49.19
28 .... 33.27, 49.19
29 .... 33.27, 49.19, 54.3

**Pension Protection Fund
(Compensation)
Regulations 2005,
SI 2005/670** 31.9

**Pension Protection Fund (Pension
Compensation Cap)
Order 2007, SI 2007/989** 31.9

**Pensions Act 1995 (Commencement
No 2) Order 1995,
SI 1995/3104** 24.17

**Personal and Occupational Pensions
Schemes (Pensions
Ombudsman)
Regulations 1996,
SI 1996/2475** 42.14

**Personal Protective Equipment at
Work Regulations 1992,
SI 1992/2966** 28.17
reg 4 .... 28.12
7(1) 28.12

**Police Act 1997 (Commencement
No 9) Order 2002,
SI 2002/413** 19.7

**Police Act 1997 (Criminal Records)
(Registration)
Regulations 2001,
SI 2001/1194** 19.7

**Police Act 1997 (Criminal Records)
(Registration) (Amendment)
Regulations 2001,
SI 2001/2498** 19.7

Table of Statutory Instruments

Police Act 1997 (Criminal Records)
Regulations 2002,
SI 2002/233 .... 19.7

Police Act 1997 (Enhanced Criminal
Record Certificates)
(Protection of Vulnerable
Adults) Regulations 2002,
SI 2002/446 .... 19.7

Police (Conduct) Regulations 1999,
SI 1999/730 .... 12.12

Police (Discipline)
Regulations 1985,
SI 1985/518 .... 12.12

Police (Health and Safety)
Regulations 1999,
SI 1999/860 .... 28.21

Protection from Harassment
Act 1997 (Commencement
No 1) Order 1997,
SI 1997/1418 .... 12.12

Provision and Use of Work
Equipment Regulations 1992,
SI 1992/2932 .... 27.38, 28.12

Provision and Use of Work
Equipment Regulations 1998,
SI 1998/2306
reg 4 .... 28.12
5(1) 28.12
6–24 .... 28.12

Public Interest Disclosure
(Compensation)
Regulations 1999,
SI 1999/1548 .... 11.18

Public Interest Disclosure
(Prescribed Persons)
Order 1999, SI 1999/1549 ...... 11.18

Quarries Regulations 1999,
SI 1999/2024 .... 28.17

Race Relations Act 1976
(Amendment)
Regulations 2003,
SI 2003/1626 .... 12.2, 12.7, 12.13,
13.4, 13.11, 13.18,
13.33, 14.5, 25.6

Race Relations (Complaints to
Employment Tribunals) (Armed
Forces) Regulations 1997,
SI 1997/2161 .... 13.10, 14.2, 37.2

Race Relations (Formal
Investigations)
Regulations 1977,
SI 1977/841 .... 14.27

Race Relations (Offshore
Employment) Order 1987,
SI 1987/929 .... 12.12

Race Relations (Questions and
Replies) Order 1977,
SI 1977/842
art 5 .... 14.9
Sch 1, 2 .... 14.9

Recognition and Derecognition
Ballots (Qualified Persons)
Order 2000, SI 2000/1306 ...... 50.32

Redundancy Payments Pensions
Regulations 1965,
SI 1965/1932 .... 38.13

Rehabilitation of Offenders
Act 1974 (Exceptions)
Order 1975, SI 1975/1023 .... 19.4

Rehabilitation of Offenders
Act 1974 (Exceptions)
(Amendment) Order 1986,
SI 1986/1249 .... 19.4

Rehabilitation of Offenders
Act 1974 (Exceptions)
(Amendment) Order 2002,
SI 2002/441 .... 19.4

Rehabilitation of Offenders
Act 1974 (Exceptions)
(Amendment No 2)
Order 1986, SI 1986/2268 .... 19.4

Reinstatement in Civil Employment
(Procedure) Regulations 1944,
SR & O 1944/880 .... 49.20

Reporting of Injuries, Diseases and
Dangerous Occurrences
Regulations 1985,
SI 1985/2023 .... 28.1

Reporting of Injuries, Diseases and Dangerous Occurrences Regulations 1995, SI 1995/3163 .... 27.17
  reg 3–7 .... 28.1
    10 .... 28.1
  Sch 1–4 .... 28.1

Right to Time Off for Study or Training Regulations 1999, SI 1999/986 .... 4.7

Right to Time Off for Study or Training Regulations 2001, SI 2001/2801
  Schedule 4.7

Road Transport (Working Time) Regulations 2005, SI 2005/639 .... 57.1, 57.3, 57.35

Safety Representatives and Safety Committees Regulations 1977, SI 1977/500 .... 5.10, 18.28 28.20, 49.9
  reg 3(1), (4) 28.21
    4(1), (2) 28.21
    4A 28.21
    7(1)–(3) 11.8
    8(2) 28.21
    9 .... 28.21
    11(1)–(4) 49.10

Sex Discrimination Act 1975 (Application to Armed Forces, etc) Regulations 1994, SI 1994/3276 .... 13.10, 25.6

Sex Discrimination (Amendment) Order 1988, SI 1988/249 .... 13.19

Sex Discrimination and Equal Pay (Miscellaneous Amendments) Regulations 1996, SI 1996/438 .... 14.14

Sex Discrimination and Equal Pay (Offshore Employment) Order 1987, SI 1987/930 .... 12.12

Sex Discrimination and Equal Pay (Remedies) Regulations 1993, SI 1993/2798 .... 14.13, 24.2, 24.20

Sex Discrimination (Complaints to Employment Tribunals) (Armed Forces) Regulations 1997, SI 1997/2163 .... 13.10, 14.2, 37.2

Sex Discrimination (Formal Investigations) Regulations 1975, SI 1975/1993 .... 14.27

Sex Discrimination (Gender Reassignment) Regulations 1999, SI 1999/1102 .... 12.2, 13.5, 24.2

Sex Discrimination (Indirect Discrimination and Burden of Proof) Regulations 2001, SI 2001/2660 .... 25.3, 25.6

Sex Discrimination (Questions and Replies) Order 1975, SI 1975/2048
  art 5 .... 14.9
  Sch 1, 2 .... 14.9

Social Security Act 1989 (Commencement No 5) Order 1994, SI 1994/1661 .... 33.1

Social Security (Claims and Payments) Regulations 1979, SI 1979/628
  reg 25 .... 28.1

Social Security Contributions (Intermediaries) Regulations 2000, SI 2000/727 .... 46.35

Social Security Contributions, Statutory Maternity Pay and Statutory Sick Pay (Miscellaneous Amendments) Regulations 1996, SI 1996/777
  reg 2 .... 44.7
    3 .... 44.3
    4 .... 33.11

Social Security Maternity Benefits and Statutory Sick Pay (Amendment) Regulations 1994, SI 1994/1367
  reg 3 .... 33.11, 33.14

Table of Statutory Instruments

Social Security (Refunds)
(Repayment of Contractual
Maternity Pay)
Regulations 1990,
SI 1990/536 .... 33.10

Stakeholder Pensions Scheme
Regulations 2000,
SI 2000/1403 .... 42.8

Statutory Maternity Pay
(Compensation of Employers)
Amendment Regulations 2003,
SI 2003/672 .... 33.16

Statutory Maternity Pay
(Compensation of Employers)
and Miscellaneous Amendment
Regulations 1994,
SI 1994/1882
reg 5 .... 33.16

Statutory Maternity Pay (General)
Regulations 1986,
SI 1986/1960
reg 3 .... 33.11
    4 .... 33.11, 33.18
    (3) 33.14
    6 .... 33.18
    (3) 33.21
    7 .... 31.8, 33.15, 33.18
    (4) 33.21
    (6), (7) 33.21
    8 .... 33.20
    9 .... 33.11, 33.18
    10 .... 33.19
    12 .... 33.21
    18A 33.18, 33.21
    21 .... 33.18, 33.21
    25A 33.15
    27 .... 33.14
    29 .... 33.14
    30 .... 31.8, 33.15

Statutory Maternity Pay (General)
Amendment Regulations 1990,
SI 1990/622 .... 33.15

Statutory Maternity Pay (General)
Amendment Regulations 1996,
SI 1996/1335
reg 2 .... 33.14

Statutory Maternity Pay (General)
Amendment Regulations 2005,
SI 2005/729 .... 33.14

Statutory Maternity Pay (Medical
Evidence) Regulations 1987,
SI 1987/235 .... 33.13

Statutory Maternity Pay (Persons
Abroad and Mariners)
Regulations 1987,
SI 1987/418 .... 33.11

Statutory Paternity Pay and
Statutory Adoption Pay
(Administration)
Regulations 2002,
SI 2002/2820 .... 49.19

Statutory Paternity Pay and
Statutory Adoption Pay
(Weekly Rates)
Regulations 2002,
SI 2002/2818 .... 33.28, 49.19

Statutory Paternity Pay and
Statutory Adoption Pay
(General) Regulations 2002,
SI 2002/2822 .... 33.28, 49.19
reg 43 .... 31.8

Statutory Sick Pay and Statutory
Maternity Pay (Decisions)
Regulations 1999,
SI 1999/776 .... 33.15, 44.8

Statutory Sick Pay (General)
Regulations 1982,
SI 1982/894 .... 44.3, 44.5, 44.13
reg 3(3) 44.5
    7 .... 44.3
    9B 31.8
    13 .... 44.7
    15 .... 44.4, 44.5
    15A 44.12

Statutory Sick Pay (General)
Amendment Regulations 1986,
SI 1986/477 ... 44.3, 44.4, 44.5, 44.13
reg 5 .... 44.7

Statutory Sick Pay (General)
Amendment Regulations 1996,
SI 1996/3042
reg 2 .... 44.7

Statutory Sick Pay (General)
Amendment (No 2)
Regulations 1987,
SI 1987/868 .... 44.3

Statutory Sick Pay (Medical
Evidence) Regulations 1985,
SI 1985/1604 .... 44.8

Suspension from Work (on
Maternity Grounds)
Order 1994, SI 1994/2930 ...... 28.17,
33.23

Teachers (Compensation for
Redundancy and Premature
Retirement) Regulations 1997,
SI 1997/311 .... 37.2

Teaching and Higher Education
Act 1998 (Commencement
No 5) Order 1999,
SI 1999/987 .... 4.7

Trade Union Ballots and Elections
(Independent Scrutineer
Qualifications) Order 1993,
SI 1993/1909 .... 45.14, 50.14

Trade Union Recognition (Method
of Collective Bargaining)
Order 2000, SI 2000/1300 ...... 50.33,
50.34

Trade Unions and Employers'
Association (Amalgamations,
etc) Regulations 1975,
SI 1975/536 .... 50.39

Transfer of Employment (Pension
Protection) Regulations 2005,
SI 2005/649 .... 52.19

Transfer of Undertakings
(Protection of Employment)
Regulations 1981,
SI 1981/1794 .... 6.4, 7.12, 11.1, 9.33,
18.4, 18.28, 20.28,
21.33, 24.19, 25.9,
39.6, 42.7, 48.1,
49.2, 52.1, 52.7,
52.25, 53.20, 55.7
reg 2(1) 52.13
4 .... 31.10

Transfer of Undertakings (Protection of
Employment) Regulations 1981,
SI 1981/1794 – *contd*
reg 5 .... 8.22
(1) 41.3
6(a) 6.6
8(1) 7.1, 7.13
(2)(b) 54.14
10 .... 11.6, 18.7, 55.18
11 .... 11.6, 18.7, 21.33, 55.18
(5) 20.9, 21.29
(8) 20.32
12 .... 18.7, 21.33

Transfer of Undertakings
(Protection of Employment)
Regulations 2006,
SI 2006/246 .... 9.32, 20.28, 21.6,
25.2, 25.9, 41.3,
42.4, 49.2, 50.19,
52.1, 54.3
reg 2(1) 52.3
3(1)(a) 52.5
(b) 52.3
(3)(a), (b) 52.3
(4)(a), (b) 52.6
(5) 52.9
(6)(a) 52.7
(b) 52.8
4 .... 52.11, 52.15
(1) 41.3, 52.14
(2) 52.18
(a) 38.5
(3) 52.12, 52.14
(4), (5) 52.29
(6) 52.19
(7)–(8) 52.16
(9) 52.16, 52.25
(10) 52.16
(11) 52.16, 52.25
5 .... 52.22
(b) 52.20
6 .... 52.21
7 .... 52.11, 52.14
(1)(a), (b) 52.26, 54.3
(4) 52.26
8 .... 31.10
(1)–(7) 52.11
9 .... 31.10
10 .... 52.19
11 .... 11.6, 52.22
(4) 52.22
(6) 52.22
12 .... 11.6, 20.11, 52.22

Table of Statutory Instruments

Transfer of Undertakings (Protection of Employment) Regulations 2006, SI 2006/246 – *contd*

reg 13 .... 11.6, 49.14, 52.22, 52.23
(2) 52.23
(3)(b) 52.23
(4) 21.23, 52.23
(5), (6) 52.23
(9) 52.23
(11) 52.23
14 .... 11.6, 49.14, 52.22, 52.23
15 .... 11.6, 20.11, 49.14, 52.22
(1) 52.23
(3), (4) 52.23
(5) 21.23, 52.23
(9)–(12) 52.23
16 .... 11.6, 49.14, 52.22
(3) 52.23
18 .... 21.33, 52.28
Sch 5
para 1 .... 42.5

Transfer of Undertakings (Protection of Employment) (Amendment) Regulations 1987, SI 1987/442 .... 31.9, 52.1, 52.8

Transnational Information and Consultation of Employees Regulations 1999, SI 1999/3323 .... 7.13, 18.1, 25.3, 25.12

reg 5(1) 18.23
6(1)(b) 18.22
(2), (3) 18.22
7 .... 18.6, 18.27
8 .... 18.22
9(1)–(3) 18.23
(5) 18.23
10 .... 18.23
12–16 .... 18.24
17(4), (5) 18.25
18–21 .... 18.25
22(2) 18.25
23, 24 .... 18.26
25–27 .... 18.27, 49.16
28 .... 18.27, 53.11, 54.3
(6) 54.3
31(1)–(6) 18.27
32 .... 18.27
38(8) 18.25
39(1) 18.25
41 .... 18.27

Transnational Information and Consultation of Employees Regulations 1999, SI 1999/3323 – *contd*

reg 44, 45 .... 18.21
Schedule
para 7(3) 18.25

Unfair Dismissal and Statement of Reasons for Dismissal (Variation of Qualifying Period) Order 1999, SI 1999/1436 .... 7.1, 48.14, 53.11

Wages Act 1986 (Commencement) Order 1986, SI 1986/1998 .... 34.3

Welfare Reform and Pensions Act 1999 (Commencement No 2) Order 1999, SI 1999/3420 .... 46.35

Working Time Regulations 1998, SI 1998/1833 .... 4.6, 8.17, 8.24, 17.1, 17.6, 17.9, 20.22, 25.11, 26.3, 28.15, 29.1, 29.8, 29.9, 34.6, 54.3, 54.11, 55.8, 57.2, 57.3, 57.28, 57.32, 57.33, 57.35

reg 2(1) 29.2, 57.3, 57.4, 57.9, 57.33
(a) 57.5
4(1) 57.6, 57.7, 57.21
(2) 57.6, 57.7, 57.8, 57.21
(3), (4) 57.6
(5) 57.6, 57.29
(6), (7) 57.6
5(2), (3) 57.7
5A 4.6, 57.6
(2) 57.6
(4) 57.21
6(1) 57.10
(2) 57.10, 57.21
(3)–(5) 57.10
(7) 57.11, 57.21
(8) 57.11
6A 4.6, 57.10
7(1) 57.12, 57.21
(2) 4.6, 57.12, 57.21
(4), (5) 57.12
(6) 57.13, 57.21
8 .... 57.18, 57.21
9 .... 57.7, 57.8, 57.13, 57.21

Working Time Regulations 1998,
  SI 1998/1833 – *contd*
reg 10(1) 57.15, 57.22
  (2) 4.6, 57.15, 57.22
  (3) 57.15
  11(1), (2) 57.16, 57.22
  (3) 4.6, 57.16, 57.22
  (4) 57.16
  (6)–(8) 57.16
  12 .... 57.29
  (1)–(3) 57.17
  (4) 4.6, 57.17
  (5) 57.6, 57.17
  13 .... 4.2, 21.29, 57.19
  (1) 29.2, 29.3, 57.22
  (3) 29.3
  (5) 29.3
  (7), (8) 29.2
  (9) 29.3
  14 .... 29.3
  (2) 21.29, 57.22
  (3) 29.4
  15(1)–(5) 29.5
  15A 29.3
  16 .... 21.29
  (1) 57.22
  (4), (5) 29.4
  18 .... 57.3
  (1)(b) 57.31
  (c) 57.32
  (2)(b) 57.32, 57.33
  19 .... 4.6, 57.30
  20 .... 57.15
  (1) 57.28
  (2) 28.15, 57.2, 57.6, 57.28
  21 .... 57.15, 57.29, 57.33
  22(1) 57.16
  (a) 57.15
  (c) 57.15
  23 .... 57.10, 57.11, 57.15, 57.16,
                                      57.17
  (b) 57.6
  24 .... 57.4, 57.15, 57.16, 57.17,
                          57.21, 57.22, 57.34
  24A 57.15, 57.16, 57.21, 57.22,
                          57.29, 57.34, 57.36
  (3) 57.15
  25 .... 57.22
  (2), (3) 4.6
  25A(1) 57.6
  27 .... 57.15, 57.17, 57.22
  (2) 4.6
  27A 57.10

Working Time Regulations 1998,
  SI 1998/1833 – *contd*
reg 27a (1)–(3) 4.6
  (4)(a) 57.21
  (b) 4.6
  28 .... 57.20, 57.21
  29 .... 57.21
  29A–29E 57.20, 57.21
  30 .... 4.6, 20.9, 20.11, 20.31
  (1) 29.6, 57.22
  (a), (b) 57.22
  (2) 29.6
  (4) 29.4
  (5) 29.4, 29.6
  31 .... 20.11, 57.23
  32 .... 20.11, 54.3
  (1), (2) 57.24
  35 .... 57.25
  (1)(a) 29.4
  (2)(b) 21.33
  (3) 21.33
  35A 57.1, 57.26
  36–42 .... 57.3
  43 .... 57.19
Sch 1 .... 54.3, 55.18
  para 3 .... 57.4
Sch 2 .... 29.7, 57.19
Sch 3 .... 57.20, 57.21

Working Time (Amendment)
  Regulations 2001,
  SI 2001/3256 .... 29.2

Working Time (Amendment)
  Regulations 2002,
  SI 2002/3128 .... 4.6, 25.11, 57.3

Working Time (Amendment)
  Regulations 2003,
  SI 2003/1684 .... 57.2, 57.3, 57.26

Working Time (Amendment)
  Regulations 2006, SI 2006/99 ... 57.2,
                                      57.28

Working Time (Amendment No 2)
  Regulations 2006,
  SI 2006/2389 .... 57.3

Workplace (Health, Safety and
  Welfare) Regulations 1992,
  SI 1992/3004 .... 28.17
reg 4–25 .... 28.29

Table of Cases

A

A v B [2003] IRLR 405, [2003] All ER (D) 184 (May), EAT 54.9
A v B, ex p News Group Newspapers Ltd [1998] ICR 55, sub nom
    Chessington World of Adventures Ltd v Reed [1997] IRLR 556, EAT 22.1
A v Chief Constable of West Yorkshire Police [2002] EWCA Civ 1584,
    [2003] 1 All ER 255, [2003] 1 CMLR 782, [2003] ICR 161, [2003] IRLR
    32, [2002] 3 FCR 751, [2003] 1 FLR 223, [2003] Fam Law 98,
    [2003] 01 LS Gaz R 24, (2002) Times, 14 November, 146 Sol Jo LB 254,
    [2002] All ER (D) 50 (Nov); affd [2004] UKHL 21, [2004] 3 All ER 145,
    [2004] 2 WLR 1209, [2004] 2 CMLR 884, [2004] ICR 806, [2004] IRLR
    573, [2004] 2 FCR 160, [2004] 20 LS Gaz R 34, [2004] NLJR 734, 148
    Sol Jo LB 572, (2004) Times, 7 May, [2004] All ER (D) 47 (May) 12.6, 13.5,
                                                                            21.18, 30.4
A v Company B Ltd [1997] IRLR 405, 577 IRLB 8 .... 8.23
A to B Travel Ltd v Kennedy (11 Ocotber 2006, unreported) 15.9
AB v CD [2001] IRLR 808, [2001] All ER (D) 354 (May) 50.14
ADI (UK) Ltd v Willer [2001] EWCA Civ 971, [2001] 3 CMLR 139,
    [2001] IRLR 542, [2001] All ER (D) 237 (Jun) 52.5
AGCO Ltd v Massey Ferguson Works Pension Trust Ltd [2003] EWCA Civ
    1044, [2004] ICR 15, [2003] IRLR 783, [2003] 35 LS Gaz R 37, (2003)
    Times, 24 July, 147 Sol Jo LB 1085, [2003] OPLR 199, [2003] All ER (D)
    292 (Jul) 42.1
AGR Regeling v Bestuur van der Bedrijfsvereniging voor de
    Metaallnijverheid: C-125/97 [1998] ECR I-4493, [1999] 1 CMLR 1410,
    [1999] ICR 605, [1999] IRLR 379, [1998] All ER (D) 336, ECJ 31.5
ALM Medical Services Ltd v Bladon [2002] EWCA Civ 1085, [2002] ICR
    1444, [2002] IRLR 807, (2002) Times, 29 August, [2002] All ER (D) 400
    (Jul) 21.7
AM v WC [1999] ICR 1218, [1999] IRLR 410, EAT 13.36
AMICUS v GBS Tooling Ltd (in administration) EAT/100/05 .... 39.6
Abbey Life Assurance Co Ltd v Tansell. See MHC Consulting Services Ltd v
    Tansell
Abbey National plc v Fairbrother [2007] IRLR 320, sub nom Fairbrother v
    Abbey National plc [2007] All ER (D) 24 (Jan), EAT 10.11
Abbey National plc v Formoso [1999] IRLR 222, EAT 12.5, 14.15
Abbott v Cheshire and Wirral Partnership NHS Trust [2006] EWCA Civ 523,
    [2006] ICR 1267, [2006] IRLR 546, (2006) Times, 10 May, 150 Sol Jo LB
    471, [2006] All ER (D) 32 (Apr) 12.8, 24.10
Abdoulaye v Régie nationale des usines Renault SA: C-218/98 [1999] ECR
    I-5723, [2001] 2 CMLR 372, [2001] ICR 527, [1999] IRLR 811, [1999]
    All ER (D) 1014, ECJ 24.14
Abels v Administrative Board of the Bedrijfsvereniging voor de
    Metaalindustrie en de Electrotechnische Industrie: 135/83 [1985] ECR
    469, [1987] 2 CMLR 406, ECJ 52.11
Aberdeen Steak Houses Group plc v Ibrahim [1988] ICR 550, [1988] IRLR
    420, [1988] NLJR 151, EAT 21.52
Abernethy v Mott, Hay and Anderson [1974] ICR 323, [1974] IRLR 213, 118
    Sol Jo 294, CA 54.1
Abler v Sodexho MM Catering Betriebsgesellschaft mbH: C-340/01
    [2004] IRLR 168, [2003] All ER (D) 277 (Nov), ECJ 52.5

Table of Cases

Abrahams v Performing Right Society [1995] ICR 1028, [1995] IRLR
   486, CA 48.9, 58.21
Abrahamsson v Fogelqvist: C-407/98 [2000] ECR I-5539, [2002] ICR 932,
   [2000] IRLR 732, ECJ 12.12, 13.9
Ackinclose v Gateshead Metropolitan Borough Council [2005] IRLR 79,
   [2004] All ER (D) 397 (Oct), EAT 52.20
Adams v British Airways plc [1996] IRLR 574, CA 6.3
Adams v Hackney London Borough Council [2003] IRLR 402, [2003] All
   ER (D) 54 (Feb), EAT 50.37, 51.14, 51.18
Adams v Lancashire County Council [1997] ICR 834, sub nom Adams v
   Lancashire County Council and Bet Catering Services Ltd [1997] IRLR
   436, CA 52.19
Adams v West Sussex County Council [1990] ICR 546, [1990] IRLR 215,
   [1990] 17 LS Gaz R 32, EAT 22.19
Adamson v B & L Cleaning Services Ltd [1995] IRLR 193, EAT 8.13
Adcock v Coors Brewers Ltd [2007] EWCA Civ 19, [2007] All ER (D) 190
   (Jan), sub nom Coors Brewers Ltd v Adcock [2007] IRLR 440 .... 34.6
Addey and Stanhope School Governing Body v Vakante [2003] ICR 290,
   [2002] All ER (D) 79 (Oct), EAT 13.16
Addis v Gramophone Co Ltd [1909] AC 488, 78 LJKB 1122,
   [1908–10] All ER Rep 1, 101 LT 466, HL 55.12, 58.29
Addison v Babcock FATA Ltd [1988] QB 280, [1987] 2 All ER 784,
   [1987] 3 WLR 122, [1987] ICR 805, 131 Sol Jo 538,
   [1987] LS Gaz R 1409, sub nom Babcock FATA Ltd v Addison
   [1987] IRLR 173, [1987] 1 FTLR 505, CA 55.13
Addison v Denholm Ship Management (UK) Ltd [1997] ICR 770,
   [1997] IRLR 389, EAT 53.15
Adebayo v Dresdner Kleinwort Wasserstein Ltd [2005] IRLR 514, [2005] All
   ER (D) 371 (Mar), EAT 14.3
Adekeye v Post Office [1993] ICR 464, [1993] IRLR 324, EAT 14.6
Adekeye v Post Office (No 2). See Post Office v Adekeye
Adeneler v Ellinikos Organismos Galaktos: C-212/04 [2007] All ER (EC) 82,
   [2006] 3 CMLR 867, [2006] IRLR 716, [2006] All ER (D) 25 (Jul),
   ECJ 25.2, 47.9
Adin v Sedco Forex International Resources Ltd [1997] IRLR 280, Ct of
   Sess 8.13
Adlington v British Bakeries (Northern) Ltd. See British Bakeries
   (Northern) Ltd v Adlington
Affleck v Newcastle Mind [1999] ICR 852, [1999] IRLR 405, EAT 21.24
Afolabi v Southwark London Borough Council [2003] EWCA Civ 15,
   [2003] ICR 800, [2003] IRLR 220, [2003] 11 LS Gaz R 32, (2003) Times,
   30 January, 147 Sol Jo LB 115, [2003] All ER (D) 217 (Jan) 14.7, 20.30
Agrico UK Ltd v Ireland EAT/0042/05 .... 20.25
Ahmed v United Kingdom (Application 22954/93) (1998) 29 EHRR 1,
   [1999] IRLR 188, 5 BHRC 111, ECtHR 37.2
Ainsworth v Glass Tubes and Components Ltd [1977] ICR 347, [1977] IRLR
   74, EAT 24.9
Air Canada v Secretary of State for Trade [1983] 2 AC 394, [1983] 2 WLR
   494, 126 Sol Jo 709, sub nom Air Canada v Secretary of State for Trade
   (No 2) [1983] 1 All ER 161, CA; affd [1983] 2 AC 394, [1983] 1 All ER
   910, sub nom Air Canada v Secretary of State for Trade [1983] 2 WLR
   494, 127 Sol Jo 205, HL 37.6
Airlie v Edinburgh District Council [1996] IRLR 516, EAT 8.22

Akinmolasire v Camden and Islington Mental Health & Social Care Trust
[2004] EWCA Civ 1351, [2004] All ER (D) 59 (Oct) 14.8
Ako v Rothschild Asset Management Ltd [2002] EWCA Civ 236,
[2002] 2 All ER 693, [2002] ICR 899, [2002] IRLR 348,
[2002] 17 LS Gaz R 36, [2002] All ER (D) 07 (Mar) 8.23, 21.26
Alabaster v Barclays Bank plc [2005] EWCA Civ 508, [2005] IRLR 576,
(2005) Times, 27 May, 149 Sol Jo LB 579, [2005] All ER (D) 02 (May),
sub nom Alabaster v Barclays Bank plc (formerly Woolwich plc)
[2005] ICR 1246 .... 24.9, 25.2, 33.14
Alabaster v Woolwich plc and Secretary of State for Social Security
[2000] ICR 1037, [2000] IRLR 754, EAT; on appeal [2002] EWCA Civ
211, [2002] IRLR 420; refd C-147/02 [2004] 2 CMLR 186, [2005] ICR
695, [2004] IRLR 486, [2004] All ER (D) 558 (Mar), ECJ 24.14, 33.14
Alamo Group (Europe) Ltd v Tucker [2003] ICR 829, [2003] IRLR 266,
[2003] All ER (D) 367 (Apr), EAT 39.6
Albion Hotel (Freshwater) Ltd v Maia E Silva [2002] IRLR 200, [2001] All
ER (D) 265 (Nov), EAT 21.52
Alboni v Ind Coope Retail Ltd [1998] IRLR 131, CA 54.4, 54.14
Alcan Extrusions v Yates [1996] IRLR 327, EAT 8.22, 48.1, 53.5
Alcock v Chief Constable of South Yorkshire Police [1992] 1 AC 310,
[1991] 4 All ER 907, [1991] 3 WLR 1057, 8 BMLR 37,
[1992] 3 LS Gaz R 34, 136 Sol Jo LB 9, HL 27.8
Alderson v Secretary of State for Trade and Industry [2003] EWCA Civ
1767, [2004] 1 All ER 1148, [2004] 1 CMLR 1180, [2004] LGR 389,
[2004] ICR 512, [2004] 03 LS Gaz R 33, (2003) Times, 12 December, 147
Sol Jo LB 784, [2003] All ER (D) 137 (Dec) 52.4
Aldred v Nacanco [1987] IRLR 292, CA 56.2
Alexander v Bridgen Enterprises Ltd [2006] ICR 1277, [2006] IRLR 422,
[2006] All ER (D) 224 (Apr), EAT 15.2, 15.10, 54.3, 54.4
Alexander v Home Office [1988] 2 All ER 118, [1988] 1 WLR 968,
[1988] ICR 685, [1988] IRLR 190, 132 Sol Jo 1147, CA 14.13
Alexander v Jarvis Hotels plc (unreported) 57.5
Alexander v Midland Bank plc [1999] IRLR 723 .... 28.31
Alexander v Standard Telephones and Cables plc [1990] ICR 291,
[1990] IRLR 55 .... 6.3, 8.23
Alexander v Standard Telephones and Cables Ltd (No 2) [1991] IRLR 286 .... 6.3,
8.22, 58.19, 58.25
Alexanders Holdings Ltd v Methven EAT/782/93 .... 20.25
Ali v Christian Salvesen Food Services Ltd [1997] 1 All ER 721, [1997] ICR
25, [1997] IRLR 17, 140 Sol Jo LB 231, sub nom Christian Salvesen
Food Services Ltd v Ali [1996] 41 LS Gaz R 29, CA 6.3
Ali v Office of National Statistics [2004] EWCA Civ 1363, [2005] IRLR 201,
148 Sol Jo LB 1250, [2004] All ER (D) 274 (Oct) 14.8, 20.17, 21.10
Ali v Southwark London Borough Council [1988] ICR 567, [1988] IRLR
100 .... 8.23
Allan v Newcastle-upon-Tyne City Council [2005] ICR 1170, [2005] IRLR
504, [2005] NLJR 619, [2005] All ER (D) 197 (Apr), EAT 14.18, 20.28
Allan Janes LLP v Johal [2006] EWHC 286 (Ch), [2006] ICR 742,
[2006] IRLR 599, [2006] NLJR 373, [2006] All ER (D) 345 (Feb) 41.3, 41.5
Allders Department Stores Ltd, Re [2005] EWHC 172 (Ch), [2005] 2 All ER
122, [2005] ICR 867, (2005) Times, 2 March, [2005] All ER (D) 231
(Feb) 31.11

Table of Cases

Allen v Amalgamated Construction Co Ltd: C-234/98 [2000] All ER (EC) 97,
[1999] ECR I-8643, [2000] 1 CMLR 1, [2000] IRLR 119, 632 IRLB 2,
ECJ 52.6
Allen v National Australia Group Europe Ltd [2004] IRLR 847, [2004] All
ER (D) 13 (Sep) 47.9
Allied Dunbar (Frank Weisinger) Ltd v Weisinger [1988] IRLR 60 .... 41.8, 41.10
Allonby v Accrington and Rossendale College [2001] EWCA Civ 529,
[2001] 2 CMLR 559, [2001] ICR 1189, [2001] IRLR 364, [2001] All ER
(D) 285 (Mar); sub nom refd Allonby v Accrington and Rossendale
College C-256/01: [2005] All ER (EC) 289, [2004] ECR I-873,
[2004] 1 CMLR 1141, [2004] ICR 1328, [2004] IRLR 224, ECJ 12.8, 13.8,
                                               13.21, 24.9, 24.17, 24.19, 25.2
Allsop v North Tyneside Metropolitan Borough Council (1992) 90 LGR 462,
[1992] ICR 639, [1992] RVR 104, CA 37.2
Allué and Coonan v Università degli Studi di Venezia: 33/88 [1989] ECR
1591, [1991] 1 CMLR 283, ECJ 37.7
Amber Size and Chemical Co Ltd v Menzel [1913] 2 Ch 239, 82 LJ Ch 573,
30 RPC 433, 57 Sol Jo 627, 109 LT 520, 29 TLR 590 .... 41.13
American Cyanamid Co v Ethicon Ltd [1975] AC 396, [1975] 1 All ER 504,
[1975] 2 WLR 316, [1975] FSR 101, [1975] RPC 513, 119 Sol Jo
136, HL 8.23, 41.17
Anandarajah v Lord Chancellor's Department [1984] IRLR 131, EAT 36.2
Anderson v Dalkeith Engineering Ltd [1985] ICR 66, [1984] IRLR
429, EAT 52.26
Anderson v Newham College of Further Education [2002] EWCA Civ 505,
[2003] ICR 212, [2002] All ER (D) 381 (Mar) 27.44
Anderson v Pringle of Scotland Ltd [1998] IRLR 64, 1998 SLT 754, OH 8.23
Andreou v Lord Chancellor's Department [2002] EWCA Civ 1192,
[2002] IRLR 728, [2002] All ER (D) 309 (Jul) 21.54, 30.7
Andrews v King (Inspector of Taxes) [1991] STC 481, [1991] ICR 846, 135
Sol Jo LB 84 .... 8.1, 17.3
Angel (Morris) & Son Ltd v Hollande [1993] 3 All ER 569, [1993] ICR 71,
[1993] IRLR 169, CA 41.3, 52.13, 52.17
Angestelltenbetriebsrat der Wiener Gebietskrankenkasse v Wiener
Gebietskrankenkasse: C-309/97 [1999] ECR I-2865, [1999] 2 CMLR
1173, [1999] IRLR 804, [1999] All ER (D) 483, ECJ 24.6
Anglian Home Improvements Ltd v Kelly [2004] IRLR 763, CA 21.62
Angus Council v Edgley EAT/289/99 .... 28.2
Aniagwu v Hackney London Borough [1999] IRLR 303, EAT 14.7, 20.30
Anker v Germany: C-47/02 [2003] ECR I-10447, [2004] 2 CMLR 845, [2003]
All ER (D) 62 (Oct), ECJ 37.7
Annandale Engineering v Samson [1994] IRLR 59, EAT 8.15
Ansar v Lloyds TSB Bank plc [2006] EWCA Civ 1462, [2007] IRLR 211,
[2006] All ER (D) 88 (Oct) 21.50, 22.12
Antal International Ltd, Re [2003] EWHC 1339 (Ch), [2003] 2 BCLC 406,
[2003] BPIR 1067, [2003] All ER (D) 56 (May) 31.11
Anya v University of Oxford [2001] EWCA Civ 405 , [2001] ICR 847,
[2001] IRLR 377, [2001] All ER (D) 266 (Mar) 14.3, 21.63

Anyanwu and Ebuzoeme v South Bank Students' Union and South Bank
University (Commission for Racial Equality interveners) [2000] 1 All ER
1, [2000] ICR 221, [2000] IRLR 36, [1999] 43 LS Gaz R 34, 143 Sol Jo
LB 271, CA; revsd sub nom Anyanwu v South Bank Student Union
(Commission for Racial Equality, interveners) [2001] UKHL 14,
[2001] 2 All ER 353, [2001] 1 WLR 638, [2001] ICR 391, [2001] IRLR
305, [2001] 21 LS Gaz R 39, 151 NLJ 501, [2001] All ER (D) 272
(Mar) 12.13, 13.36, 21.17
Aon Training Ltd (formerly Totalamber plc) v Dore [2005] EWCA Civ 411,
[2005] IRLR 891, [2005] All ER (D) 328 (Mar) 55.13
Aparau v Iceland Frozen Foods plc [1996] IRLR 119, EAT; revsd
[2000] 1 All ER 228, [2000] IRLR 196, [1999] 45 LS Gaz R 31, CA 8.13, 8.22,
22.19, 42.5
Apelogun-Gabriels v Lambeth London Borough Council [2001] EWCA Civ
1853, [2002] ICR 713, [2002] IRLR 116, [2001] All ER (D) 350 (Nov) 14.7,
20.30
Appiah v Bishop Douglass Roman Catholic High School [2007] EWCA Civ
10, [2007] IRLR 264, [2007] All ER (D) 240 (Jan) 14.3
Apple Corpn Ltd v Apple Computer Inc [1992] FSR 431 .... 41.9
Appleyard v F M Smith (Hull) Ltd [1972] IRLR 19, IT 54.7
Arafa v Potter. See Potter v Arafa
Arbeiterwohlfahrt der Stadt Berlin e V v Bötel: C-360/90 [1992] ECR I-3589,
[1992] 3 CMLR 446, [1992] IRLR 423, [1993] 21 LS Gaz R 45, ECJ ... 24.3, 24.10
Arbuthnot Fund Managers Ltd v Rawlings [2003] EWCA Civ 518, [2003] All
ER (D) 181 (Mar) 41.17
Archer v Marsh (1837) 6 Ad & El 959, 6 LJKB 244, 2 Nev & PKB 562, Will
Woll & Dav 641 .... 41.10
Archibald v Fife Council [2004] UKHL 32, [2004] 4 All ER 303, [2004] ICR
954, [2004] IRLR 651, [2004] 31 LS Gaz R 25, 148 Sol Jo LB 826, [2004]
All ER (D) 32 (Jul) 10.12, 10.14, 10.24, 10.32
Argyll Training Ltd v Sinclair [2000] IRLR 630, EAT 52.5
Armitage v Weir Valves and Controls (UK) Ltd [2004] ICR 371, [2003] All
ER (D) 80 (Dec), EAT 21.16
Armour v Skeen [1977] IRLR 310, 1977 JC 15, 1977 SLT 71, JC 27.38
Armstrong v Newcastle Upon Tyne NHS Hospital Trust [2005] EWCA Civ
1608, [2006] IRLR 124, [2005] All ER (D) 341 (Dec) 24.5, 24.9, 24.11
Armstrong (W A) & Sons v Borril [2000] ICR 367, EAT 34.39
Arnold v Barnfield College [2004] All ER (D) 63 (Jul), EAT 13.9
Arnold v Beecham Group Ltd [1982] ICR 744, [1982] IRLR 307, EAT 24.7
Arnold Clark Automobiles v Stewart (unreported), EAT 15.4
Arnold Clark Automobiles Ltd v Glass (7 June 2007, unreported) 15.13
Arora v Rockwell Automation Ltd (21 April 2006, unreported) EAT 34.8
Arthur v A-G [1999] ICR 631, EAT 13.27
Arthur v London Eastern Rly Ltd (t/a One Stansted Express) [2006] EWCA
Civ 1358, [2007] ICR 193, [2007] IRLR 58, [2006] All ER (D) 300
(Oct) 14.6
Artisan Press Ltd v Srawley [1986] ICR 328, [1986] IRLR 126, EAT 55.4
Asda Stores Ltd v Thompson [2002] IRLR 245, [2002] All ER (D) 32
(Feb), EAT 21.12
Asda Stores Ltd v Thompson [2004] IRLR 598, [2003] All ER (D) 434
(Nov), EAT 21.12, 54.10
Ashburn Anstalt v Arnold [1989] Ch 1, [1988] 2 All ER 147, [1988] 2 WLR
706, 55 P & CR 137, [1987] 2 EGLR 71, 284 Estates Gazette 1375,
[1988] 16 LS Gaz R 43, 132 Sol Jo 416, CA 43.2

Table of Cases

Ashby v Addison (t/a Brayton News) [2003] ICR 667, [2003] IRLR 211,
    [2003] NLJR 145, (2003) Times, 24 January, [2003] All ER (D) 98
    (Jan), EAT 4.2, 29.2, 57.3
Ashley v Ministry of Defence [1984] ICR 298, [1984] IRLR 57, EAT 49.2
Ashmore v British Coal Corpn [1990] 2 QB 338, [1990] 2 All ER 981,
    [1990] 2 WLR 1437, [1990] ICR 485, [1990] IRLR 283, CA 21.24
Ashton v Chief Constable of West Mercia Constabulary [2001] ICR 67 .... 12.6
Askew v Governing Body of Clifton Middle School. See Clifton Middle
    School Governing Body v Askew
Aslan v Murphy [1989] 3 All ER 130, [1990] 1 WLR 766, 59 P & CR 407, 21
    HLR 532, [1989] 2 EGLR 57, [1989] 38 EG 109, [1989] NLJR
    936, CA 43.2
Aspden v Webbs Poultry and Meat Group (Holdings) Ltd [1996] IRLR
    521 .... 8.13, 42.13, 44.15, 58.19
Aspland v Mark Warner Ltd [2006] IRLR 87, [2006] All ER (D) 02
    (Mar), EAT 15.4
Associated British Ports v Palmer [1995] 2 AC 454, [1995] 2 All ER 100,
    [1995] 2 WLR 354, [1995] ICR 406, [1995] IRLR 258,
    [1995] 17 LS Gaz R 48, [1995] NLJR 417, HL 51.17
Associated British Ports v Transport and General Workers' Union
    [1989] 3 All ER 796, [1989] 1 WLR 939, [1989] ICR 557, [1989] IRLR
    305, CA; revsd [1989] 3 All ER 822, [1989] 1 WLR 939, [1989] ICR 557,
    [1989] IRLR 399, HL 45.2, 45.3, 45.4, 45.5, 45.14, 45.16, 45.20
Associated Newspapers Ltd v Wilson [1995] 2 AC 454, [1995] 2 All ER 100,
    [1995] 2 WLR 354, [1995] ICR 406, [1995] IRLR 258,
    [1995] 17 LS Gaz R 48, [1995] NLJR 417, HL 51.18
Associated Society of Locomotive Engineers and Firemen v United
    Kingdom (Application No 11002/05) [2007] IRLR 361, (2007) Times,
    9 March, [2007] All ER (D) 348 (Feb), ECtHR 30.4, 51.13
Assoukou v Select Services Partners Ltd [2006] EWCA Civ 1442 (unreported,
    11 October 2006) 14.16
Astle v Cheshire County Council [2005] IRLR 12, [2004] All ER (D) 134
    (Jun), EAT 52.5
Astles v AG Stanley Ltd IDS Brief No 588 .... 21.54
Astley v Celtec Ltd [2002] EWCA Civ 1035, [2002] 3 CMLR 366, [2002] ICR
    1289, [2002] IRLR 629, [2002] 37 LS Gaz R 38, (2002) Times, 9 August,
    [2002] All ER (D) 287 (Jul) 7.9
Athinaiki Chartopoiia AE v Panagiotidis: C-270/05 [2007] IRLR 284, [2007]
    All ER (D) 186 (Feb), ECJ 39.4
Atkinson (Octavius) & Sons Ltd v Morris [1989] ICR 431, [1989] IRLR
    158, CA 48.13, 53.13
Atos Origin IT Services UK Ltd v Haddock [2005] ICR 277, [2005] IRLR
    20, [2004] All ER (D) 369 (Oct), EAT 22.4
A-G v Blake (Jonathan Cape Ltd third party) [2001] 1 AC 268,
    [2000] 4 All ER 385, [2000] 2 All ER (Comm) 487, [2000] 3 WLR 625,
    [2001] IRLR 36, [2000] NLJR 1230, [2000] 32 LS Gaz R 37, 144 Sol Jo
    LB 242, [2001] 1 LRC 260, [2000] EMLR 949, [2000] IP & T 1261,
    [2000] All ER (D) 1074, HL 8.24, 41.19
A-G v Wheen [2000] IRLR 461, [2000] All ER (D) 767, EAT; affd
    [2001] IRLR 91, [2000] All ER (D) 2186, CA 21.77, 30.7
A-G of Commonwealth of Australia v Adelaide Steamship Co Ltd
    [1913] AC 781, 83 LJPC 84, 12 Asp MLC 361, [1911–13] All ER Rep
    1120, 109 LT 258, 29 TLR 743, PC 41.5

A-G's Reference (No 2 of 1999) [2000] QB 796, [2000] 3 All ER 182,
    [2000] 3 WLR 195, [2000] IRLR 417, [2000] 2 BCLC 257, [2000] 2 Cr
    App Rep 207, [2000] Crim LR 475, [2000] 09 LS Gaz R 39, CA 27.42
Attridge Law (a firm) v Coleman. See Coleman v Attridge Law (a firm)
Attwood v Lamont [1920] 3 KB 571, 90 LJKB 121, [1920] All ER Rep 55, 65
    Sol Jo 25, 124 LT 108, 36 TLR 895, CA 41.7
Austin Knight (UK) Ltd v Hinds [1994] FSR 52 .... 41.8
Austin Rover Group Ltd v HM Inspector of Factories [1990] 1 AC 619,
    [1989] 3 WLR 520, [1990] ICR 133, [1989] IRLR 404, sub nom Mailer v
    Austin Rover Group plc [1989] 2 All ER 1087, HL 27.20
Australian Commercial Research and Development Ltd v ANZ McCaughan
    Merchant Bank Ltd [1989] 3 All ER 65 .... 8.23
Automatic Switching Ltd v Brunet [1986] ICR 542, EAT 21.22
Automotive Products Ltd v Peake. See Peake v Automotive Products Ltd
Avon County Council v Foxall [1989] ICR 407, [1989] IRLR 435, EAT 24.8, 24.22
Avon County Council v Howlett [1983] 1 All ER 1073, [1983] 1 WLR 605,
    81 LGR 555, [1983] IRLR 171, 127 Sol Jo 173, 133 NLJ 377, CA 34.15
Avonmouth Construction Co Ltd v Shipway [1979] IRLR 14, EAT 54.11
Aziz v Bethnal Green City Challenge Co Ltd [2000] IRLR 111, CA 22.6
Aziz v Trinity Street Taxis Ltd [1989] QB 463, [1988] 2 All ER 860,
    [1988] 3 WLR 79, [1988] ICR 534, [1988] IRLR 204, 132 Sol Jo 898,
    [1988] 26 LS Gaz R 42, CA 12.10
Azmi v Kirklees Metropolitan Borough Council (30 March 2007, unreported)
    EAT 13.8

B
B v BA [2006] EWCA Civ 132, [2006] All ER (D) 300 (Feb) 14.3
BCCI SA (in liquidation) v Ali (No 3) [2002] EWCA Civ 82, [2002] 3 All ER
    750, [2002] ICR 1258, [2002] IRLR 460 .... 8.23
BG plc v O'Brien [2001] IRLR 496, [2001] All ER (D) 169 (May), EAT; affd
    sub nom O'Brien v Transco plc (formerly BG plc) [2002] EWCA Civ
    379, [2002] ICR 721, [2002] IRLR 444, [2002] All ER (D) 80 (Mar) 53.7
BHS Ltd v Walker (2005) IDS Brief No 787 .... 14.6
BL Cars Ltd v Brown [1983] ICR 143, [1983] IRLR 193, 80 LS Gaz
    R 94, EAT 12.12
BMK Ltd v Logue [1993] ICR 601, [1993] IRLR 477, EAT 58.7
BNP Paribas v Mezzotero [2004] IRLR 508, 148 Sol Jo LB 666, [2004] All
    ER (D) 226 (Apr), EAT 14.9, 21.13, 55.22
BP Chemicals Ltd v Gillick [1995] IRLR 128, EAT 13.21
BSC Sports and Social Club v Morgan [1987] IRLR 391, EAT 48.5, 58.1
BSG Property Services v Tuck [1996] IRLR 134, EAT 52.5, 52.26
BT Fleet Ltd v McKenna [2005] EWHC 387 (Admin), (2005) Times, 5 April,
    [2005] All ER (D) 284 (Mar) 27.32
BUPA Care Homes (BNH) Ltd v Cann [2006] IRLR 248, [2006] All ER (D)
    299 (Feb), EAT 15.11, 20.19
Babcock FATA Ltd v Addison. See Addison v Babcock FATA Ltd
Babula v Waltham Forest College [2007] EWCA Civ 174 .... 11.18
Bache v Essex County Council [2000] 2 All ER 847, [2000] IRLR 251,
    [2000] 05 LS Gaz R 33, [2000] NLJR 99, CA 21.40, 21.55, 22.12, 30.7
Bachnak v Emerging Markets Partnership (Europe) Ltd (27 January 2006,
    unreported), EAT 11.18
Bacica v Muir [2006] IRLR 35, EAT 29.2
Baggs v Fudge (No 1400114/05) 12.6

Table of Cases

Bahl v Law Society [2003] IRLR 640, 147 Sol Jo LB 994, [2003] All ER (D) 570 (Jul), EAT; affd [2004] EWCA Civ 1070, [2004] IRLR 799, [2004] NLJR 1292, 148 Sol Jo LB 976, [2003] All ER (D) 570 (Jul) 12.5, 14.3, 21.63

Bailey v BP Oil (Kent Refinery) Ltd [1980] ICR 642, [1980] IRLR 287, CA 54.10

Bailey v Home Office [2005] EWCA Civ 327, [2005] ICR 1057, [2005] IRLR 369, (2005) Times, 8 April, [2005] All ER (D) 356 (Mar) 24.10

Bainbridge v Circuit Foil UK Ltd [1997] ICR 541, [1997] IRLR 305, CA 44.14

Bainbridge v Redcar and Cleveland Borough Council (UKEAT/0424/06/LA) (23 March 2007, unreported) 15.7, 15.10, 24.19

Bakers' Union v Clarks of Hove Ltd. See Clarks of Hove Ltd v Bakers' Union

Balamoody v UK Central Council for Nursing, Midwifery and Health Visiting [2001] EWCA Civ 2097, [2002] ICR 646, [2002] IRLR 288, [2001] All ER (D) 80 (Dec) 12.5, 21.17

Baldwin v Brighton and Hove City Council [2007] ICR 680, [2007] IRLR 232, [2006] All ER (D) 220 (Dec), EAT 8.13

Balfour v Foreign and Commonwealth Office [1994] 2 All ER 588, [1994] 1 WLR 681, [1994] ICR 277, [1994] 2 LRC 48, CA 21.13, 37.6

Balfour Beatty Power Networks v Wilcox [2006] EWCA Civ 1240, [2007] IRLR 63, [2006] All ER (D) 275 (Jul) 52.5

Balfron Trustees Ltd v Peterson [2001] IRLR 758, [2002] Lloyd's Rep PN 1, [2001] NLJR 1180, [2001] All ER (D) 103 (Jul) 56.2

Balgobin v Tower Hamlets London Borough Council [1987] ICR 829, [1987] IRLR 401, [1987] LS Gaz R 2530, EAT 12.13, 13.35

Ball v Street [2005] EWCA Civ 76, [2005] All ER (D) 73 (Feb) 28.12

Balston Ltd v Headline Filters Ltd [1987] FSR 330 .... 8.13, 41.13

Bamsey v Albion Engineering and Manufacturing plc [2004] EWCA Civ 359, [2004] 2 CMLR 1353, [2004] ICR 1083, [2004] IRLR 457, [2004] 17 LS Gaz R 31, (2004) Times, 15 April, 148 Sol Jo LB 389, [2004] All ER (D) 482 (Mar) 29.4

Bangs v Connex South Eastern Ltd [2005] EWCA Civ 14, [2005] 2 All ER 316, [2005] IRLR 389, (2005) Times, 15 February, 149 Sol Jo LB 148, [2005] All ER (D) 263 (Jan), sub nom Connex South Eastern Ltd v Bangs [2005] ICR 763 .... 20.13, 21.62, 22.18

Bank of Credit and Commerce International SA, Re [1994] IRLR 282 ..... 8.24, 34.14, 34.22

Bank of Credit and Commerce International SA (in liquidation) v Ali [1999] 4 All ER 83, [1999] IRLR 508, [1999] 30 LS Gaz R 28; affd [2002] EWCA Civ 82, [2002] 3 All ER 750, [2002] ICR 1258, [2002] IRLR 460, (2002) Times, 15 February, [2002] All ER (D) 308 (Jan) 58.29

Banking Insurance and Finance Union v Barclays Bank plc [1987] ICR 495, [1987] LS Gaz R 901, EAT 52.23

Banks v Lavin IDS Brief No 410, EAT 48.15

Banks v Tesco Stores Ltd [2000] 1 CMLR 400, [1999] ICR 1141, EAT 24.14

Barber v Guardian Royal Exchange Assurance Group: C-262/88 [1991] 1 QB 344, [1990] 2 All ER 660, [1991] 2 WLR 72, [1990] ECR I-1889, [1990] 2 CMLR 513, [1990] ICR 616, [1990] IRLR 240, [1990] NLJR 925, ECJ 24.3, 24.5, 24.16, 25.2, 42.1, 42.5

Barber v RJB Mining (UK) Ltd [1999] 2 CMLR 833, [1999] ICR 679, [1999] IRLR 308, 143 Sol Jo LB 141, [1999] All ER (D) 244 .... 57.21, 57.22

Barber v Staffordshire County Council [1996] 2 All ER 748, [1996] IRLR 209, [1996] 06 LS Gaz R 26, sub nom Staffordshire County Council v Barber [1996] ICR 379, CA 8.23, 20.12, 21.17, 21.26, 25.2

Barber v Thames Television plc [1992] ICR 661, [1992] IRLR 410, CA 22.15, 53.14

Barclay v City of Glasgow District Council [1983] IRLR 313, EAT 48.5, 53.10

Barclays Bank plc v Kapur [1991] 2 AC 355, [1991] 1 All ER 646, [1991] 2 WLR 401, [1991] ICR 208, [1991] IRLR 136, HL 12.12, 14.6, 20.29

Barclays Bank plc v O'Brien. See O'Brien v Barclays Bank plc

Barke v SEETEC Business Technology Centre Ltd [2005] EWCA Civ 578, [2005] ICR 1373, [2005] IRLR 633, (2005) Times, 26 May, [2005] All ER (D) 216 (May) 21.63, 22.11

Barker v Service Children's Schools: C-374/95 unreported, ECJ 12.12

Barking and Dagenham London Borough v Oguoko [2000] IRLR 179, EAT 21.58, 24.14

Barnsley Metropolitan Borough Council v Prest [1996] ICR 85, EAT 55.9

Barracks v Coles (Secretary of State for the Home Department intervening) [2006] EWCA Civ 1041, [2007] ICR 60, [2007] IRLR 73, (2006) Times, 7 August, [2006] All ER (D) 310 (Jul) 21.12, 30.7

Barralet v A-G [1980] 3 All ER 918, sub nom Re South Place Ethical Society, Barralet v A-G [1980] 1 WLR 1565, 54 TC 446, [1980] TR 217, 124 Sol Jo 744 .... 12.6

Barretts & Baird (Wholesale) Ltd v Institution of Professional Civil Servants [1987] IRLR 3, [1988] NLJR 357 .... 45.2

Barros D'Sa v University Hospital and Warwickshire NHS Trust [2001] EWCA Civ 983, [2001] IRLR 691, 62 BMLR 39, [2001] All ER (D) 173 (Jun) 8.23

Barry v Midland Bank plc [1998] 1 All ER 805, [1999] ICR 319, [1998] IRLR 138, CA; affd [1999] 3 All ER 974, [1999] 1 WLR 1465, [1999] ICR 859, [1999] IRLR 581, [1999] 31 LS Gaz R 36, [1999] NLJR 1253, 143 Sol Jo LB 221, HL 12.9, 24.10, 24.11

Bartholomew v London Borough of Hackney [1999] IRLR 246, CA 40.4

Bartholomew v Southwark London Borough Council [2004] ICR 358, [2003] All ER (D) 190 (Dec), EAT 21.76

Barton v Investec Henderson Crosthwaite Securities Ltd [2003] ICR 1205, [2003] IRLR 332, [2003] 22 LS Gaz R 29, (2003) Times, 16 April, [2003] All ER (D) 61 (Apr), EAT 12.6, 14.3, 24.11

Base Metal Trading Ltd v Shamurin [2003] EWHC 2419 (Comm), [2004] 1 All ER (Comm) 159, [2003] All ER (D) 364 (Oct); affd [2004] EWCA Civ 1316, [2005] 1 All ER (Comm) 17, [2005] 1 WLR 1157, [2005] 2 BCLC 171, (2004) Times, 1 November, 148 Sol Jo LB 1281, [2004] All ER (D) 178 (Oct) 26.11

Basingstoke Press Ltd (in administration) v Clarke (9 January 2007, unreported) 15.11

Bass Leisure Ltd v Thomas [1994] IRLR 104, EAT 8.13, 22.25, 38.7

Bass Taverns Ltd v Burgess [1995] IRLR 596, CA 54.3

Batchelor v British Railways Board [1987] IRLR 136, CA 53.13

Battersby v Campbell [2001] STC (SCD) 189 .... 46.35

Baxter v Harland & Wolff plc [1990] IRLR 516, NICA 27.2

Baynham v Philips Electronics (UK) Ltd (1995) IDS Brief No 551 .... 42.6

Baynton v Saurus General Engineers Ltd [2000] ICR 375, [1999] IRLR 604, EAT 10.11

Baynton v South West Trains Ltd [2005] ICR 1730, [2005] All ER (D) 253 (Jun), EAT 14.6

Table of Cases

Beacard Property Management and Construction Co Ltd v Day [1984] ICR
  837, EAT 21.16
Beckett Investment Management Group Ltd v Hall [2007] EWHC 241 (QB),
  [2007] All ER (D) 178 (Mar) 41.8
Beckmann v Dynamco Whicheloe MacFarlane Ltd: C-164/00 [2002] All ER
  (EC) 865, [2002] ECR I-4893, [2002] 2 CMLR 1152, [2003] ICR 50,
  [2002] IRLR 578, (2002) Times, 17 June, [2002] All ER (D) 05 (Jun),
  ECJ 42.4, 52.19
Beaumont v Amicus MSF (2004) 148 Sol Jo LB 1063, [2004] All ER (D) 34
  (Aug), EAT 51.14, 51.16
Beedell v West Ferry Printers Ltd [2000] IRLR 650, EAT 54.4
Bell v Department of Health and Social Security (1989) Times, 13 June 27.3
Bell v Lever Bros Ltd [1932] AC 161, 101 LJKB 129, 37 Com Cas 98,
  [1931] All ER Rep 1, 76 Sol Jo 50, 146 LT 258, 48 TLR 133, HL 58.42
Bennett v Southwark London Borough Council [2002] EWCA Civ 223,
  [2002] ICR 881, [2002] IRLR 407, (2002) Times, 28 February, 146 Sol Jo
  LB 59 .... 21.16, 21.17, 21.40, 21.50, 21.55, 22.12
Benson v Secretary of State for Trade and Industry [2003] ICR 1082,
  [2003] IRLR 748, [2003] All ER (D) 113 (May), EAT 31.5
Benteler Automotive UK and ISTC, Re (2000) IDS Brief No 677 .... 50.30
Bentley Engineering Co Ltd v Mistry [1979] ICR 47, [1978] IRLR
  437, EAT 54.10
Benton v Sanderson Kayser Ltd [1989] ICR 136, [1989] IRLR 19, CA 38.12
Bentwood Bros (Manchester) Ltd v Shepherd [2003] EWCA Civ 380,
  [2003] ICR 1000, [2003] IRLR 364, [2003] All ER (D) 398 (Feb) 14.15, 14.20,
                                                                                                       55.12
Benveniste v University of Southampton [1989] ICR 617, [1989] IRLR
  122, CA 24.11
Berg and Busschers v Besselsen: 144/87 and 145/87 [1988] ECR 2559,
  [1989] 3 CMLR 817, [1990] ICR 396, [1989] IRLR 447, ECJ 52.6, 52.14
Bernadone v Pall Mall Services Group Ltd [2001] ICR 197 .... 52.18
Bernard v A-G of Jamaica [2004] UKPC 47, [2005] IRLR 398, 148 Sol Jo
  LB 1281, [2005] 2 LRC 561, [2004] All ER (D) 96 (Oct) 56.2
Bernstein v Immigration Appeal Tribunal and Department of Employment
  [1988] Imm AR 449, CA 25.2
Berriman v Delabole Slate Ltd [1985] ICR 546, sub nom Delabole Slate Ltd
  v Berriman [1985] IRLR 305, CA 52.26
Berwick Salmon Fisheries Co Ltd v Rutherford [1991] IRLR 203, EAT 7.7
Best v Tyne and Wear Passenger and Transport Executive (t/a Nexus)
  [2007] ICR 523, [2006] All ER (D) 362 (Dec), EAT 24.10
Bestuur van het Algemeen Burgerlijk Pensioenfonds v Beune: C-7/93 [1995]
  All ER (EC) 97, [1994] ECR I-4471, [1995] 3 CMLR 30, [1995] IRLR
  103, ECJ 24.18
Betriebsrat der Bofrost Josef H Boquoi Deutschland West GmbH & Co KG
  v Bofrost Josef H Boquoi Deutschland West GmbH & Co KG: C-62/99
  [2001] ECR I-2579, [2004] 2 CMLR 1223, [2001] IRLR 403, [2001] All
  ER (D) 350 (Mar), ECJ 18.22
Betriebsrat der Firma ADS Anker GmbH v ADS Anke GmbH (2004) IDS
  Brief No 763 .... 18.22
Betts v Brintel Helicopters Ltd (t/a British International Helicopters)
  [1997] 2 All ER 840, [1997] ICR 792, [1997] IRLR 361, [1997] NLJR
  561, sub nom Betts v Brintel Helicopters Ltd and KLM ERA
  Helicopters (UK) Ltd [1998] 2 CMLR 22, CA 52.5
Beveridge v KLM UK Ltd [2000] IRLR 765, EAT 34.6

Bewley v HM Prison Service [2004] ICR 422, (2004) Times, 4 February,
[2004] All ER (D) 22 (Mar), EAT 57.4
Bhatt v Chelsea and Westminster Health Care NHS Trust [1998] ICR 576,
[1997] IRLR 660, EAT 53.15
Biggs v Somerset County Council [1995] ICR 811, [1995] IRLR 452, EAT;
affd [1996] 2 All ER 734, [1996] 2 CMLR 292, [1996] ICR 364,
[1996] IRLR 203, [1996] 06 LS Gaz R 27, [1996] NLJR 174, 140 Sol Jo
LB 59, CA 20.12, 20.18, 20.25, 20.30, 25.2
Bilka-Kaufhaus GmbH v Weber von Hartz: 170/84 [1986] ECR 1607,
[1986] 2 CMLR 701, [1987] ICR 110, [1986] IRLR 317, ECJ 12.9, 13.8, 24.3,
24.10, 24.11
Bingham v Hobourn Engineering Ltd [1992] IRLR 298, EAT 22.16, 55.12
Birch v University of Liverpool [1985] ICR 470, [1985] IRLR 165, 129 Sol Jo
245, CA 48.2, 53.8
Birds Eye Walls Ltd v Harrison [1985] ICR 278, [1985] IRLR 47, EAT 21.11
Birds Eye Walls Ltd v Roberts: C-132/92 [1993] ECR I-5579, [1993] 3 CMLR
822, [1994] IRLR 29, sub nom Roberts v Birds Eye Walls Ltd
[1994] ICR 338, ECJ 24.12, 24.17, 24.18
Birmingham City Council v Equal Opportunities Commission [1989] AC
1155, [1989] 2 WLR 520, 87 LGR 557, [1989] IRLR 173, 133 Sol Jo 322,
[1989] 15 LS Gaz R 36, [1989] NLJR 292, sub nom Equal Opportunities
Commission v Birmingham City Council [1989] 1 All ER 769, HL 12.5
Birmingham Optical Group plc v Johnson [1995] ICR 459, EAT 20.25
Bisset v Martins and Castlehill Housing Association Ltd (18 August 2006,
unreported) (UKEAT/0022/06) 15.11, 20.20
Blackpool and Fylde College v National Association of Teachers in Further
and Higher Education [1994] ICR 648, [1994] IRLR 227, CA 45.14, 45.15
Blaik v Post Office [1994] IRLR 280, EAT 21.17
Bliss v South East Thames Regional Health Authority [1987] ICR 700,
[1985] IRLR 308, CA 53.7, 55.12
Blockleys plc v Miller [1992] ICR 749, [1992] 34 LS Gaz R 39, EAT 22.25
Blue Circle Staff Association v Certification Officer [1977] 2 All ER 145,
[1977] 1 WLR 239, [1977] ICR 224, [1977] IRLR 20, 121 Sol Jo
52, EAT 50.23
Bodhu v Hampshire Area Health Authority [1982] ICR 200, EAT 20.25
Bolch v Chipman [2004] IRLR 140, [2003] All ER (D) 122 (Nov), EAT 21.17
Bolton School v Evans. See Evans v Bolton School
Bond v CAV Ltd [1983] IRLR 360 .... 8.13
Bone v Fabcon Projects Ltd [2007] 1 All ER 1071, [2006] ICR 1421,
[2006] IRLR 908, [2006] All ER (D) 167 (Oct), EAT 20.35
Bonner v H Gilbert Ltd [1989] IRLR 475, EAT 38.10
Boorman v Allmakes Ltd [1995] ICR 842, [1995] IRLR 553, CA 55.9
Boote v Ministry of Defence (3 March 2004, unreported) 13.8
Booth v United States of America [1999] IRLR 16, 611 IRLB 9, EAT 7.7
Borders Regional Council v Maule [1993] IRLR 199, EAT 49.2, 49.5
Bork (P) International A/S v Foreningen af Arbejdsledere i Danmark: 101/87
[1988] ECR 3057, [1990] 3 CMLR 701, [1989] IRLR 41, ECJ 52.6, 52.10
Bossa v Nordstress Ltd [1998] ICR 694, [1998] IRLR 284, EAT 12.12, 13.15, 25.4
Bostock v Bryant (1990) 61 P & CR 23, 22 HLR 449, [1990] 2 EGLR 101,
[1990] 39 EG 64, CA 43.2
Boston Deep Sea Fishing and Ice Co v Ansell (1888) 39 Ch D 339,
[1886–90] All ER Rep 65, 59 LT 345, CA 58.6, 58.20

Table of Cases

Botham v Ministry of Defence [2006] UKHL 3, [2006] 1 All ER 823,
  [2006] IRLR 289, [2006] 06 LS Gaz R 36, [2006] NLJR 184, 150 Sol Jo
  LB 131, [2006] All ER (D) 184 (Jan) 26.13
Botzen v Rotterdamsche Droogdok Maatschappij BV: 186/83 [1985] ECR
  519, [1986] 2 CMLR 50, ECJ 52.15
Bouchaala v Trusthouse Forte Hotels Ltd [1980] ICR 721, [1980] IRLR
  382, EAT 54.13
Boulding v Land Securities Trillium Ltd EAT/0023/06 .... 21.17
Bowater plc v Charlwood [1991] ICR 798, [1991] IRLR 340, EAT 21.22
Bowden v Tuffnells Parcels Express Ltd [2000] IRLR 560, EAT; refd
  C-133/00: [2001] All ER (EC) 865, [2001] ECR I-7031, [2001] 3 CMLR
  1342, [2001] IRLR 838, [2001] All ER (D) 32 (Oct), ECJ 57.3
Bower v Stevens (6 April 2004, unreported) 7.9
Bowman v Harland & Wolff plc [1992] IRLR 349 .... 27.2
Boxfoldia Ltd v National Graphical Association [1988] ICR 752,
  [1988] IRLR 383 .... 45.16, 50.17
Boyle v Equal Opportunities Commission: C-411/96 [1998] All ER (EC) 879,
  [1998] ECR I-6401, [1998] 3 CMLR 1133, [1999] ICR 360, [1998] IRLR
  717, [1999] 1 FCR 581, [1999] 1 FLR 119, 608 IRLB 5, [1998] All ER
  (D) 500, ECJ 24.14, 42.9
Boyo v Lambeth London Borough Council [1994] ICR 727, [1995] IRLR
  50, CA 8.23, 48.19, 53.9, 58.7, 58.18, 58.25
Boys and Girls Welfare Society v Macdonald [1997] ICR 693, EAT 54.9
Brace v Calder [1895] 2 QB 253, 59 JP 693, 64 LJQB 582, 14 R 473,
  [1895–9] All ER Rep 1196, 72 LT 829, 11 TLR 450, CA 58.8
Bracebridge Engineering Ltd v Darby [1990] IRLR 3, EAT 12.12, 13.35
Bradford City Metropolitan Council v Arora [1991] 2 QB 507,
  [1991] 3 All ER 545, [1991] 2 WLR 1377, [1991] ICR 226, [1991] IRLR
  165, CA 14.18
Bradford Hospitals NHS Trust v Al-Shabib [2003] IRLR 4, [2002] All ER
  (D) 68 (Oct), EAT 12.6
Bradley v National and Local Government Officers Association [1991] ICR
  359, [1991] IRLR 159, EAT 51.14
Bradley v Secretary of State for Employment [1989] ICR 69,
  [1989] 3 LS Gaz R 43, EAT 31.4
Brady v Associated Society of Locomotive Engineers and Firemen
  [2006] IRLR 576, [2006] All ER (D) 14 (Apr), EAT 54.9
Brasserie du Pecheur SA v Germany: C-46/93 [1996] QB 404, [1996] All ER
  (EC) 301, [1996] 2 WLR 506, [1996] ECR I-1029, [1996] 1 CMLR 889,
  [1996] IRLR 267, ECJ 25.2
Bratko v Beloit Walmsley Ltd [1996] ICR 76, [1995] IRLR 629, EAT 42.5, 53.14
Braund (Walter) (London) Ltd v Murray [1991] ICR 327, [1991] IRLR
  100, EAT 55.10
Breach v Epsylon Industries Ltd [1976] ICR 316, [1976] IRLR 180, EAT ... 8.13, 58.21
Brennan v J H Dewhurst Ltd [1984] ICR 52, [1983] IRLR 357, EAT 12.12
Brent London Borough Council v Charles (1997) 29 HLR 876, CA 43.7
Bridge v Deacons (a firm) [1984] AC 705, [1984] 2 WLR 837, 128 Sol Jo 263,
  [1984] LS Gaz R 1291, 134 NLJ 723, sub nom Deacons (a firm) v
  Bridge [1984] 2 All ER 19, PC 41.8
Brigden v American Express Bank Ltd [2000] IRLR 94, 631 IRLB 13, [1999]
  All ER (D) 1130 .... 58.37
Bridgen v Lancashire County Council [1987] IRLR 58, CA 53.7
Briggs v North Eastern Education and Library Board [1990] IRLR 181,
  NICA 12.8

Briggs v Oates [1991] 1 All ER 407, [1990] ICR 473, [1990] IRLR 472,
    [1990] NLJR 208 .... 48.1, 58.8
Brind v Secretary of State for the Home Department. See R v Secretary of
    State for the Home Department, ex p Brind
Briscoe v Lubrizol Ltd [2002] EWCA Civ 508, [2002] IRLR 607, [2002] All
    ER (D) 190 (Apr) 44.14, 44.15, 58.17
British Aerospace plc v Green [1995] ICR 1006, [1995] IRLR 433, CA 21.12, 54.11
British Aircraft Corpn v Austin [1978] IRLR 332, EAT 27.1, 27.18, 28.11
British Airways Engine Overhaul Ltd v Francis [1981] ICR 278, [1981] IRLR
    9, EAT 54.3
British Airways (European Operations at Gatwick) Ltd v Moore [2000] ICR
    678, [2000] IRLR 296, EAT 24.4, 33.24
British Airways plc v Grundy (4 August 2005, unreported) 13.8
British Airways plc v Grundy (11 October 2005, unreported), EAT 13.8
British Airways plc v Noble [2006] EWCA Civ 537, [2006] ICR 1227,
    [2006] IRLR 533, [2006] All ER (D) 110 (May) 29.4
British Airways plc v Starmer (23 August 2005, unreported), EAT 13.8
British Association of Advisers and Lecturers in Physical Education v
    National Union of Teachers [1986] IRLR 497, CA 50.1
British Bakeries Ltd v Nascimento EAT/0888/04 .... 20.9
British Bakeries (Northern) Ltd v Adlington [1989] ICR 438, sub nom
    Adlington v British Bakeries (Northern) Ltd [1989] IRLR 218, CA 49.2
British Reinforced Concrete Engineering Co Ltd v Schelff [1921] 2 Ch 563,
    91 LJ Ch 114, [1921] All ER Rep 202, 126 LT 230 .... 41.7
BBC v Hearn [1978] 1 All ER 111, [1977] 1 WLR 1004, [1977] ICR 685,
    [1977] IRLR 273, 121 Sol Jo 374, CA 45.4
BBC v Kelly-Phillips [1998] 2 All ER 845, [1998] ICR 587, [1998] IRLR 294,
    [1998] NLJR 658, 592 IRLB 6, CA 53.15
BBC Scotland v Souster [2001] IRLR 150, Ct of Sess 12.6
British Coal Corpn v British Coal Staff Superannuation Scheme Trustees Ltd
    [1995] 1 All ER 912, [1994] ICR 537 .... 42.13
British Coal Corpn v Cheesbrough [1990] 2 AC 256, [1990] 1 All ER 641,
    [1990] 2 WLR 407, [1990] ICR 317, [1990] IRLR 148, 134 Sol Jo 661,
    [1990] 11 LS Gaz R 39, HL 34.36, 34.39
British Coal Corpn v Keeble [1997] IRLR 336, EAT 14.7, 20.30
British Coal Corpn v Smith [1996] 3 All ER 97, [1996] ICR 515,
    [1996] IRLR 404, [1996] NLJR 843, HL 24.9
British Gas plc v McCarrick [1991] IRLR 305, CA 22.17
British Gas plc v Sharma [1991] ICR 19, [1991] IRLR 101, EAT 14.21, 21.59
British Gas Services Ltd v McCaull [2001] IRLR 60 .... 10.15, 10.34, 20.29, 54.8
British Home Stores Ltd v Burchell [1980] ICR 303n, [1978] IRLR 379, 13
    ITR 560, EAT 40.4, 54.9, 54.10
British Judo Association v Petty [1981] ICR 660, [1981] IRLR 484, EAT 13.27
British Leyland (UK) Ltd v Swift [1981] IRLR 91, CA 54.4
British Nursing Association v Inland Revenue (National Minimum Wage
    Compliance Team) [2002] EWCA Civ 494, [2002] IRLR 480, [2003] ICR
    19 .... 34.12, 34.13
British Publishing Co Ltd v Fraser [1987] ICR 517, EAT 22.20
British Railways Board v National Union of Railwaymen [1989] ICR 678,
    [1989] IRLR 349, CA 45.14
British Road Services Ltd v Loughran [1997] IRLR 92, CA 24.11
British School of Motoring v Fowler EAT/0059/06 .... 22.22
British Sugar plc v Kirker [1998] IRLR 624, EAT 10.22, 10.34

Table of Cases

British Telecommunications plc v Communication Workers Union
[2003] EWHC 937 (QB), [2004] IRLR 58 .... 45.4
British Telecommunications plc v Grant (1994) IDS Brief No 518, EAT 12.10
British Telecommunications plc v Reid [2003] EWCA Civ 1675, [2004] IRLR
327, [2003] 41 LS Gaz R 33, (2003) Times, 9 October, [2003] All ER (D)
91 (Oct) 14.16
British Telecommunications plc v Roberts [1996] ICR 625, [1996] IRLR
601, EAT 12.9, 32.21
British Telecommunications plc v Sheridan [1990] IRLR 27, CA 22.17
British Telecommunications plc v Ticehurst [1992] ICR 383,
[1992] 15 LS Gaz R 32, 136 Sol Jo LB 96, sub nom Ticehurst and
Thompson v British Telecommunications plc [1992] IRLR 219, CA 8.13, 8.24,
34.14, 45.16
British Telecommunications plc v Williams [1997] IRLR 668, EAT 12.5
Brock v Minerva Dental Ltd [2007] ICR 917 .... 15.3, 15.5, 15.11
Bromley v H & J Quick Ltd [1988] 2 CMLR 468, [1988] ICR 623,
[1988] IRLR 249, CA 24.7
Bromley v Smith [1909] 2 KB 235, 78 LJKB 745, [1908–10] All ER Rep 384,
100 LT 731 .... 4.10
Brompton v AOC Internaional Ltd [1997] IRLR 639, CA 8.13, 42.13, 58.7
Brook v Haringey London Borough Council [1992] IRLR 478, EAT 12.5
Brook Lane Finance Co Ltd v Bradley [1988] ICR 423, [1988] IRLR 283,
[1988] 15 LS Gaz R 35, EAT 52.12
Brooker v Charrington Fuel Oils Ltd [1981] IRLR 147, Cty Ct 34.4
Brookes v Borough Care Services and CLS Care Services Ltd [1998] ICR
1198, [1998] IRLR 636, EAT 52.10
Brooks v British Telecommunications plc [1992] ICR 414, [1992] IRLR
66, CA 53.14
Broome v DPP [1974] AC 587, [1974] 1 All ER 314, [1974] 2 WLR 58,
[1974] ICR 84, [1974] IRLR 26, [1974] Crim LR 311, 118 Sol Jo
50, HL 45.10
Brown v Chief Adjudication Officer [1997] ICR 266, [1997] IRLR 110,
[1996] 42 LS Gaz R 28, 140 Sol Jo LB 221, CA 44.5
Brown v Croydon London Borough Council (20 February 2006,
unreported), EAT 12.5
Brown v JBD Engineering Ltd [1993] IRLR 568, EAT 53.7, 58.22
Brown v Knowsley Borough Council [1986] IRLR 102, EAT 53.10
Brown v London Borough of Croydon [2007] EWCA Civ 32, [2007] IRLR
259, [2007] All ER (D) 239 (Jan) 12.5, 14.3
Brown v Merchant Ferries Ltd [1998] IRLR 682, NICA 53.7
Brown v Rentokil Ltd: C-394/96 [1998] All ER (EC) 791, [1998] ECR I-4185,
[1998] 2 CMLR 1049, [1998] ICR 790, [1998] IRLR 445, [1999] 1 FCR
49, [1998] 2 FLR 649, [1998] Fam Law 597, 48 BMLR 126,
[1998] 34 LS Gaz R 34, [1998] All ER (D) 313, ECJ 12.5
Brown v Southall and Knight [1980] ICR 617, [1980] IRLR 130, EAT 53.13, 58.5
Brown v Tower Hamlets London Borough Council (17 November 2006,
unreported) 15.5
Brown (John) Engineering Ltd v Brown [1997] IRLR 90, EAT 54.11
Bruce v Wiggins Teape (Stationery) Ltd [1994] IRLR 536, EAT 34.6, 58.24
Brumfitt v Ministry of Defence [2005] IRLR 4, 148 Sol Jo LB 1028, [2004]
All ER (D) 479 (Jul), EAT 12.5
Brunnhofer v Bank der österreichischen Postsparkasse AG: C-381/99
[2001] ECR I-4961, [2001] All ER (EC) 693, [2001] 3 CMLR 173,
[2001] IRLR 571, ECJ 24.6, 24.11

Bruton v London and Quadrant Housing Trust [2000] 1 AC 406, [1999] 3 All ER 481, [1999] 3 WLR 150, 31 HLR 902, [1999] 2 EGLR 59, [1999] 30 EG 91, [1999] EGCS 90, [1999] NLJR 1001, 78 P & CR D21, HL 43.2

Bryant v Housing Corpn. See Housing Corpn v Bryant

Buchan v Secretary of State for Employment [1997] IRLR 80, 565 IRLB 2, EAT 31.4

Buchanan-Smith v Schleicher & Co International Ltd [1996] ICR 613, [1996] IRLR 547, EAT 52.15

Budd v Scotts Co (UK) Ltd [2004] ICR 299, [2003] IRLR 145, EAT 48.12, 58.27

Budgen & Co v Thomas [1976] ICR 344, [1976] IRLR 174, EAT 54.10

Bullivant (Roger) Ltd v Ellis [1987] FSR 172, [1987] ICR 464, [1987] IRLR 491, CA 41.15

Bullock v Alice Ottley School (1993) 91 LGR 32, [1993] ICR 138, [1992] IRLR 564, CA 12.5, 24.17

Bulwick v Mills & Allen Ltd (8 June 2000, unreported), EAT 39.4

Bunce v Postworth Ltd (t/a Skyblue) [2005] EWCA Civ 490, [2005] IRLR 557, 149 Sol Jo LB 578, [2005] All ER (D) 38 (May) 17.3, 47.2

Burgoine v Waltham Forest London Borough Council (1996) 95 LGR 520, [1997] 2 BCLC 612, [1997] BCC 347 .... 37.2

Burlo v Langley [2006] EWCA Civ 1778, [2007] 2 All ER 462, [2007] ICR 390, [2007] IRLR 145, [2006] All ER (D) 366 (Dec) 55.12, 55.13

Burns v Royal Mail Group plc (formerly Consignia plc) [2004] ICR 1103, sub nom Burns v Consignia plc (No 2) [2004] IRLR 425, (2004) Times, 24 June, [2004] All ER (D) 453 (Mar), EAT 21.63, 22.11

Burrett v West Birmingham Health Authority [1994] IRLR 7, EAT 12.5

Burton v De Vere Hotels Ltd [1997] ICR 1, [1996] IRLR 596, EAT 12.12, 12.13

Burton Group Ltd v Smith [1977] IRLR 351, EAT 48.5, 58.5

Busch v Klinikum Neustadt GmbH & Co Betriebs-KG: C-320/01 [2003] All ER (EC) 985, [2003] ECR I-2041, [2003] 2 CMLR 481, [2003] IRLR 625, [2004] 1 FCR 54, [2003] All ER (D) 394 (Feb), ECJ 12.5

Business Seating (Renovations) Ltd v Broad [1989] ICR 729 .... 41.8

Bux v Slough Metals Ltd [1974] 1 All ER 262, [1973] 1 WLR 1358, [1974] 1 Lloyd's Rep 155, 117 Sol Jo 615, CA 27.5, 27.44

Buxton v Equinox Design Ltd [1999] ICR 269, [1999] IRLR 158, EAT 10.34

Byrne v Birmingham City District Council (1987) 85 LGR 729, [1987] ICR 519, [1987] IRLR 191, CA 7.7

Byrne v BOC Ltd [1992] IRLR 505, EAT 54.10

Byrne v Financial Times Ltd [1991] IRLR 417, EAT 21.8

Byrne Bros (Formwork) Ltd v Baird [2002] ICR 667, [2002] IRLR 96, [2001] All ER (D) 321 (Nov), EAT 17.9, 29.2, 57.3

C

CIA Security International SA v Signalson: C-194/94 [1996] All ER (EC) 557, [1996] ECR I-2201, [1996] 2 CMLR 781, ECJ 25.2

CPL Distribution Ltd v Evans [2002] EWCA Civ 1481, [2003] IRLR 28, [2002] All ER (D) 100 (Oct) 52.15

CPS Recruitment Ltd v Bowen [1982] IRLR 54, EAT 38.6

Cable & Wireless plc v Muscat [2006] EWCA Civ 220, [2006] IRLR 354, 150 Sol Jo LB 362, [2006] All ER (D) 127 (Mar) 8.3, 17.3, 47.2

Cadman v Health and Safety Executive [2004] EWCA Civ 1317, [2004] All ER (D) 191 (Oct) 13.8, 24.11

Table of Cases

Cadman v Health and Safety Executive: C-17/05 [2007] All ER (EC) 1,
[2007] 1 CMLR 530, [2006] ICR 1623, [2006] IRLR 969, (2006) Times,
6 October, [2006] All ER (D) 17 (Oct), ECJ 3.4, 24.11

Cadoux v Central Regional Council [1986] IRLR 131, 1986 SLT 117, Ct of
Sess 6.4

Cain v Leeds Western Health Authority [1990] ICR 585, [1990] IRLR
168, EAT 54.9

Cairns v Visteon UK Ltd [2007] ICR 616, [2007] IRLR 175, [2007] All ER
(D) 39 (Jan), EAT 17.3, 47.2

Caisse Nationale d'Assurance Vieillesse des Travailleurs Salaries v Thibault:
C-136/95 [1998] All ER (EC) 385, [1998] ECR I-2011, [1998] 2 CMLR
516, [1998] IRLR 399, [1998] All ER (D) 167, sub nom Thibault v
Caisse Nationale d'Assurance Vieillesse des Travailleurs Salaries
(CNAVTS) [1999] ICR 160, ECJ 12.5

Calder v James Finlay Corpn Ltd [1989] ICR 157n, [1989] IRLR 55, EAT 14.4,
14.12

Calder v Rowntree Mackintosh Confectionery Ltd [1993] ICR 811,
[1993] IRLR 212, CA 24.11

Caledonia Bureau Investment and Property v Caffrey [1998] ICR 603,
[1998] IRLR 110, 591 IRLB 6, EAT 12.5, 33.6

Caledonian Mining Co Ltd v Bassett [1987] ICR 425, [1987] IRLR
165, EAT 48.2

Callagan v Glasgow City Council [2001] IRLR 724, [2001] All ER (D) 101
(Aug), EAT 10.24

Cambridge and District Co-operative Society Ltd v Ruse [1993] IRLR
156, EAT 38.12

Camelot Group plc v Centaur Communications Ltd [1999] QB 124,
[1998] 1 All ER 251, [1998] 2 WLR 379, [1998] IRLR 80,
[1997] 43 LS Gaz R 30, [1997] NLJR 1618, 142 Sol Jo LB 19,
[1998] EMLR 1, CA 30.5

Campbell v Dunoon and Cowal Housing Association Ltd [1992] IRLR 528,
1992 SLT 1136n, Ct of Sess 22.26

Campbell v Dunoon and Cowal Housing Association Ltd [1993] IRLR 496,
Ct of Sess 54.11

Campbell & Smith Construction Group Ltd v Greenwood [2001] IRLR 588,
[2001] All ER (D) 240 (May), EAT 34.6

Campion v Hamworthy Engineering Ltd [1987] ICR 966, CA 22.26

Canada Life Ltd v Gray [2004] ICR 673, sub nom Gray v Canada Life Ltd
[2004] All ER (D) 36 (Jan), EAT 29.6

Canary Wharf Management v Edebi EAT/0708/05 .... 15.4, 15.11, 20.19, 21.10

Canniffe v East Riding of Yorkshire Council [2000] IRLR 555, EAT 12.13, 13.35

Capek v Lincolnshire County Council [2000] ICR 878, [2000] IRLR 590,
[2000] 24 LS Gaz R 39, CA 8.23, 20.32

Capper Pass Ltd v Lawton [1977] QB 852, [1977] 2 All ER 11, [1977] 2 WLR
26, [1977] ICR 83, [1976] IRLR 366, 11 ITR 316, 120 Sol Jo 768, EAT 24.6

Carden v Pickerings Europe Ltd [2005] IRLR 720, [2005] All ER (D) 145
(May), EAT 10.7

Cardiff Women's Aid v Hartup [1994] IRLR 390, EAT 12.12, 13.34

Care First Partnership Ltd v Roffey [2001] ICR 87, [2001] IRLR 85, CA 20.2

Carlisle-Morgan v Cumbria County Council [2007] IRLR 314, [2007] All ER
(D) 248 (Jan), EAT 11.18

Carmichael v National Power plc [1999] 4 All ER 897, [1999] 1 WLR 2042,
[1999] ICR 1226, [2000] IRLR 43, [1999] 46 LS Gaz R 38, 143 Sol Jo
LB 281, 632 IRLB 18, HL 17.3

Carrington v Harwich Dock Co Ltd [1998] ICR 1112, [1998] IRLR
567, EAT 7.6
Carrington v Helix Lighting Ltd [1990] ICR 125, [1990] IRLR 6,
[1990] 1 LS Gaz R 30, EAT 14.9, 21.12
Carroll v Manek (12 July 1999, unreported) 43.4
Carter v Credit Change Ltd [1980] 1 All ER 252, [1979] ICR 908,
[1979] IRLR 361, 123 Sol Jo 604, CA 21.22
Carter v Reiner Moritz Associates Ltd [1997] ICR 881, EAT 21.32, 21.66
Cartlidge v Chief Adjudication Officer [1986] QB 360, [1986] 2 All ER 1,
[1986] 2 WLR 558, [1986] ICR 256, [1986] IRLR 182, 130 Sol Jo
185, CA 45.19
Cartwright v G Clancey Ltd [1983] ICR 552, [1983] IRLR 355, EAT 34.27
Caruana v Manchester Airport plc [1996] IRLR 378, EAT 12.5
Carver (née Mascarenhas) v Saudi Arabian Airlines [1999] 3 All ER 61,
[1999] ICR 991, [1999] IRLR 370, 615 IRLB 4, CA 13.15
Casella London Ltd v Banai [1990] ICR 215, [1990] 4 LS Gaz R 39, EAT 21.64
Casey v Morane Ltd [2001] ICR 316, [2001] IRLR 166, [2000] All ER (D)
615, CA 27.44
Cassell & Co Ltd v Broome [1972] AC 1027, [1972] 1 All ER 801,
[1972] 2 WLR 645, 116 Sol Jo 199, HL 37.5
Cast v Croydon College [1998] ICR 500, [1998] IRLR 318,
[1998] 16 LS Gaz R 26, 142 Sol Jo LB 119, CA 14.6, 20.29
Catamaran Cruisers Ltd v Williams [1994] IRLR 386, EAT 17.3, 54.14
Catherall v Michelin Tyres plc [2003] ICR 28, [2003] IRLR 61, EAT 10.21, 20.29
Caulfield v Marshalls Clay Products Ltd. See Marshalls Clay Products Ltd v
Caulfield
Celtec Ltd v Astley: C-478/03 [2005] ICR 1409, [2005] IRLR 647, (2005)
Times, 9 June, [2005] All ER (D) 400 (May), ECJ 7.9, 52.12
Cerberus Software Ltd v Rowley [2000] ICR 35, [1999] IRLR 690, EAT;
revsd sub nom Rowley v Cerberus Software Ltd [2001] EWCA Civ 78,
[2001] ICR 376, [2001] IRLR 160, (2001) Times, 20 February, [2001] All
ER (D) 80 (Jan) 48.7, 55.13, 58.16, 58.21
Chadwick v Bayer plc [2002] All ER (D) 88 (Jun), EAT 21.10
Chairman and Governors of Amwell View School v Dogherty. See Dogherty
v Chairman and Governors of Amwell View School
Chamberlin Solicitors v Emokpae [2004] IRLR 592, [2004] All ER (D) 110
(Jun), EAT 12.6
Chan v Hackney London Borough Council [1997] ICR 1014, EAT 14.15
Chaplin v H J Rawlinson Ltd [1991] ICR 553, EAT 55.13
Chaplin v Leslie Frewin (Publishers) Ltd [1966] Ch 71, [1965] 3 All ER 764,
[1966] 2 WLR 40, 109 Sol Jo 871, CA 4.10
Chapman v Simon [1994] IRLR 124, CA 14.8, 20.14
Chapman and Elkin v CPS Computer Group plc [1987] IRLR 462, CA 52.17
Charlton v Forrest Printing Ink Co Ltd [1980] IRLR 331, CA 27.8
Chaudhary v Specialist Training Authority Appeal Panel [2005] EWCA Civ
282, [2005] ICR 1086, [2005] All ER (D) 256 (Mar) 14.2
Cheesman v R Brewer Contracts Ltd [2001] IRLR 144, [2000] All ER (D)
2047, EAT 52.5
Chelminski v Gdynia America Shipping Lines (London) Ltd [2004] EWCA
Civ 871, [2004] 3 All ER 666, [2004] IRLR 725, [2004] All ER (D) 83
(Jul), sub nom Gdynia America Shipping Lines (London) Ltd v
Chelminski [2004] ICR 1523, 148 Sol Jo LB 877 .... 22.5
Chelsea Football Club and Athletic Co Ltd v Heath [1981] ICR 323,
[1981] IRLR 73, EAT 55.9

Table of Cases

Chessington World of Adventures Ltd v Reed. See A v B, ex p News Group
    Newspapers Ltd
Chief Constable of Avon and Somerset Constabulary v Chew (2002) IDS
    Brief No 701 .... 12.8
Chief Constable of Bedfordshire Constabulary v Graham [2002] IRLR 239,
    [2001] All ER (D) 89 (Sep), EAT 12.6
Chief Constable of Bedfordshire Police v Liversidge [2002] EWCA Civ 894,
    [2002] ICR 1135, [2002] IRLR 651, [2002] All ER (D) 395 (May) 12.13, 13.23
Chief Constable of Cumbria v McGlennon [2002] ICR 1156, [2002] All ER
    (D) 231 (Jul), EAT 13.23
Chief Constable of Greater Manchester Police v Hope [1999] ICR
    338, EAT 14.15
Chief Constable of Kent Constabulary v Baskerville [2003] EWCA Civ 1354,
    [2003] ICR 1463, [2003] 39 LS Gaz R 38, (2003) Times, 10 September,
    147 Sol Jo LB 1028, [2003] All ER (D) 27 (Sep) 13.38
Chief Constable of Lincolnshire Police v Stubbs [1999] ICR 547,
    [1999] IRLR 81, EAT 12.13, 13.35
Chief Constable of Thames Valley Police v Kellaway [2000] IRLR
    170, EAT 22.7
Chief Constable of West Yorkshire Police v A [2001] ICR 128, [2000] IRLR
    465, EAT 14.11
Chief Constable of West Yorkshire Police v Khan [2001] UKHL 48,
    [2001] 1 WLR 1947, [2001] ICR 1065, [2001] IRLR 830,
    [2001] 42 LS Gaz R 37, 145 Sol Jo LB 230, [2001] All ER (D) 158 (Oct),
    sub nom Khan v Chief Constable of West Yorkshire Police
    [2001] 4 All ER 834 .... 12.10, 32.14
Chief Constable of West Yorkshire Police v Vento [2002] IRLR 177, [2001]
    All ER (D) 20 (Dec), EAT; revsd sub nom Vento v Chief Constable of
    West Yorkshire Police [2002] EWCA Civ 1871, [2003] ICR 318,
    [2003] IRLR 102, [2003] 10 LS Gaz R 28, (2002) Times, 27 December,
    147 Sol Jo LB 181, [2002] All ER (D) 363 (Dec) 11.18, 14.15, 14.16
Chohan v Derby Law Centre [2004] IRLR 685, [2004] All ER (D) 132
    (Apr), EAT 14.7, 20.30
Chorion plc v Lane IDS Brief No 642 .... 21.22
Christie v John E Haith Ltd [2003] IRLR 670, [2003] All ER (D) 267
    (Jul), EAT 24.11
Church v West Lancashire NHS Trust [1998] ICR 423, [1998] IRLR 4, 588
    IRLB 7, EAT 38.7
City and Hackney Health Authority v Crisp [1990] ICR 95, [1990] IRLR
    47, EAT 55.3
City Equitable Fire Insurance Co Ltd, Re [1925] Ch 407, 94 LJ Ch 445,
    [1925] B & CR 109, [1924] All ER Rep 485, 133 LT 520, 40 TLR
    853, CA 9.15
City of Bradford Metropolitan District Council v Pratt [2007] IRLR 192,
    [2007] All ER (D) 19 (Jan), EAT 15.4, 20.19
Civil Service Union v Central Arbitration Committee [1980] IRLR 274 .... 11.3
Civilian War Claimants Association Ltd v R [1932] AC 14, 101 LJKB 105,
    [1931] All ER Rep 432, 75 Sol Jo 813, 146 LT 169, 48 TLR 83, HL 25.2
Clancy v Cannock Chase Technical College [2001] IRLR 331, [2001] All ER
    (D) 36 (Mar), EAT 14.19, 55.2, 55.12
Clapson v British Airways plc [2001] IRLR 184, EAT 21.14, 21.57
Clark v BET plc [1997] IRLR 348 .... 58.25
Clark v Civil Aviation Authority [1991] IRLR 412, EAT 54.4

Clark v Fahrenheit 451 (Communications) Ltd (1999) IDS Brief
No 666, EAT 48.6
Clark v Midland Packaging Ltd [2005] 2 All ER 266, [2005] All ER (D) 10
(Mar), EAT 22.1
Clark v Nomura International plc [2000] IRLR 766, EAT 34.6, 58.28
Clark v Novacold Ltd [1999] 2 All ER 977, [1999] ICR 951, [1999] IRLR
318, 48 BMLR 1, CA 10.11, 10.12, 10.15, 10.32, 24.12
Clark v Oxfordshire Health Authority [1998] IRLR 125, 41 BMLR 18, CA 17.3
Clark v Secretary of State for Employment. See Secretary of State for
Employment v Clark
Clark & Tokeley Ltd (t/a Spellbrook) v Oakes [1998] 4 All ER 353,
[1999] ICR 276, [1998] IRLR 577, 142 Sol Jo LB 253, [1998] All ER (D)
376, CA 7.9
Clarke v Hampshire Electro-Plating Co Ltd [1992] ICR 312, [1991] IRLR
490, EAT 14.6
Clarke v Newland [1991] 1 All ER 397, CA 41.6
Clarke v Redcar and Cleveland Borough Council [2006] IRLR 324,
[2006] ICR 897, [2006] All ER (D) 309 (Feb), EAT 2.4, 14.10, 21.29, 21.32
Clarke v Watford Borough Council (4 May 2000, unreported), EAT 21.59
Clarke v Yorke (1882) 52 LJ Ch 32, 31 WR 62, 47 LT 381 .... 8.23
Clarke and Powell v Eley (IMI) Kynoch Ltd [1982] IRLR 131, IT; revsd sub
nom Clarke v Eley (IMI) Kynoch Ltd [1983] ICR 165, [1982] IRLR
482, EAT 12.9
Clarks of Hove Ltd v Bakers' Union [1979] 1 All ER 152, [1978] 1 WLR
1207, [1978] ICR 1076, 13 ITR 356, sub nom Bakers' Union v Clarks of
Hove Ltd [1978] IRLR 366, 122 Sol Jo 643, CA 39.6
Clay Cross (Quarry Services) Ltd v Fletcher [1979] 1 All ER 474,
[1978] 1 WLR 1429, [1979] ICR 1, 122 Sol Jo 776, sub nom Fletcher v
Clay Cross (Quarry Services) Ltd [1978] 3 CMLR 1, [1978] IRLR
361, CA 24.11
Clayton v Vigers [1989] ICR 713, [1990] IRLR 177, EAT 33.6
Clayton (Herbert) & Jack Waller Ltd v Oliver [1930] AC 209, 99 LJKB 165,
[1930] All ER Rep 414, 74 Sol Jo 187, 142 LT 585, 46 TLR 230, HL 58.29
Clements v London and North Western Rly Co [1894] 2 QB 482, 58 JP 818,
63 LJQB 837, 9 R 641, 42 WR 663, 38 Sol Jo 562, 70 LT 896, 10 TLR
539, [1891–4] All ER Rep Ext 1461, CA 4.10
Cleveland Ambulance NHS Trust v Blane [1997] ICR 851, [1997] IRLR
332, EAT 51.18
Cleveland County Council v Springett [1985] IRLR 131, EAT 50.20
Clifford v Union of Democratic Mineworkers [1991] IRLR 518, CA 8.1
Clifton Middle School Governing Body v Askew [2000] LGR 96, [2000] ICR
286, [1999] ELR 425, [1999] 33 LS Gaz R 30, sub nom Askew v
Governing Body of Clifton Middle School [1999] IRLR 708, [1999] All
ER (D) 825, CA 52.13
Clymo v Wandsworth London Borough Council [1989] 2 CMLR 577,
[1989] ICR 250, [1989] IRLR 241, [1989] 19 LS Gaz R 41, EAT 12.9
Cobb v Secretary of State for Employment [1989] ICR 506, [1989] IRLR
464, [1989] NLJR 868, EAT 13.8
Cobley v Forward Technology Industries plc [2003] EWCA Civ 646,
[2003] ICR 1050, [2003] IRLR 706, [2003] 29 LS Gaz R 36, (2003)
Times, 15 May, 147 Sol Jo LB 696, [2003] All ER (D) 175 (May) 54.14
Cocking v Sandhurst (Stationers) Ltd [1974] ICR 650, [1975] ITR 6, NIRC 21.10
Codemasters Software Co Ltd v Wong (EAT/0639/06) 20.20
Cofone v Spaghetti House Ltd [1980] ICR 155, EAT 34.16

Table of Cases

Coker v Lord Chancellor. See Lord Chancellor v Coker and Osamor
Cold Drawn Tubes Ltd v Middleton [1992] ICR 318, [1992] IRLR
    160, EAT 55.2
Coldridge v HM Prison Service IDS Brief No 788 .... 20.25
Coleman v Attridge Law (a firm) [2007] ICR 654, (2007) Times, 12 January,
    [2006] All ER (D) 326 (Dec), sub nom Attridge Law (a firm) v Coleman
    [2007] IRLR 88, EAT 10.9, 10.27, 22.27
Coleman v Skyrail Oceanic Ltd (t/a Goodmos Tours). See Skyrail
    Oceanic Ltd v Coleman
Coleman and Stephenson v Magnet Joinery Ltd [1974] ICR 25, [1973] IRLR
    361, 17 KIR 11, 9 ITR 74, NIRC; affd [1975] ICR 46, [1974] IRLR 343,
    [1975] KILR 139, CA 55.2
Colen v Cebrian (UK) Ltd [2003] EWCA Civ 1676, [2004] ICR 568,
    [2004] IRLR 210, [2004] 02 LS Gaz R 27, (2003) Times, 27 November,
    [2003] All ER (D) 294 (Nov) 8.15, 13.16
College of Ripon and York St John v Hobbs [2002] IRLR 185, [2001] All ER
    (D) 259 (Nov), EAT 10.2
Collier v Sunday Referee Publishing Co Ltd [1940] 2 KB 647,
    [1940] 4 All ER 234, 109 LJKB 974, 84 Sol Jo 538, 164 LT 10, 57 TLR
    2 .... 58.21
Collino v Telecom Italia SpA: C-343/98 [2001] All ER (EC) 405, [2000] ECR
    I-6659, [2002] 3 CMLR 997, [2002] ICR 38, [2000] IRLR 788, [2000] All
    ER (D) 1196, ECJ 18.4, 37.2, 52.9
Collins v John Ansell & Partners Ltd IDS Brief No 659 .... 52.20
Collins v National Trust (17 January 2006, unreported), EAT 11.18
Collison v BBC [1998] ICR 669, [1998] IRLR 238, EAT 7.5
Coloroll Pension Trustees Ltd v Russell: C-200/91 [1995] All ER (EC) 23,
    [1994] ECR I-4389, [1995] 2 CMLR 357, [1995] ICR 179, [1994] IRLR
    586, [1995] 42 LS Gaz R 23, (1994) Times, 30 November, ECJ 24.18, 42.7
Coltman v Bibby Tankers Ltd, The Derbyshire [1988] AC 276,
    [1987] 3 All ER 1068, [1987] 3 WLR 1181, [1988] 1 Lloyd's Rep 109,
    [1988] ICR 67, 131 Sol Jo 1658, [1988] 3 LS Gaz R 36, [1987] NLJ Rep
    1157, 1 S & B AvR I/165, HL 27.6
Commercial Plastics Ltd v Vincent [1965] 1 QB 623, [1964] 3 All ER 546,
    [1964] 3 WLR 820, 108 Sol Jo 599, CA 41.3, 41.13
Commerzbank AG v Keen. See Keen v Commerzbank AG
Commission for Racial Equality v Amari Plastics Ltd [1982] QB 265,
    [1981] 3 WLR 511, [1981] ICR 767, [1981] IRLR 340, 125 Sol Jo
    694, EAT; affd [1982] QB 1194, [1982] 2 All ER 499, [1982] 2 WLR 972,
    [1982] ICR 304, [1982] IRLR 252, 126 Sol Jo 227, CA 14.28
Commission for Racial Equality v Dutton [1989] QB 783, [1989] 1 All ER
    306, [1989] 2 WLR 17, [1989] IRLR 8, 133 Sol Jo 19,
    [1989] 1 LS Gaz R 38, CA 12.6, 12.9
Commission for Racial Equality v Imperial Society of Teachers of Dancing
    [1983] ICR 473, [1983] IRLR 315, EAT 12.13, 13.40
Commotion Ltd v Rutty [2006] ICR 290, sub nom Rutty v Commotion Ltd
    [2006] IRLR 171, [2006] All ER (D) 122 (Jan), EAT 15.4, 20.19, 49.19
Compton v St Regis Paper Co Ltd (23 February 2000, unreported) 57.22
Conlin v United Distillers [1994] IRLR 169, Ct of Sess 21.63
Connex South Eastern Ltd v Bangs. See Bangs v Connex South Eastern Ltd
Connolly v Sellars Arenascene Ltd [2001] EWCA Civ 184, [2001] ICR 760,
    [2001] IRLR 222, 145 Sol Jo LB 37, [2001] All ER (D) 25 (Feb) 9.4, 17.3, 31.4
Constantine v McGregor Cory Ltd [2000] ICR 938, EAT 55.1

Construction Industry Training Board v Labour Force Ltd [1970] 3 All ER
220, 114 Sol Jo 704, DC 17.3
Construction Industry Training Board v Leighton [1978] 2 All ER 723,
[1978] IRLR 60, sub nom Leighton v Construction Industry Training
Board [1978] ICR 577, EAT 8.9
Conway v Rimmer [1968] AC 910, [1968] 1 All ER 874, [1968] 2 WLR 998,
112 Sol Jo 191, HL 37.6
Cook v Square D Ltd [1992] ICR 262, [1992] PIQR P33, 135 Sol Jo LB 180,
sub nom Square D Ltd v Cook [1992] IRLR 34, CA 27.3
Cook (James W) & Co (Wivenhoe) Ltd (in liquidation) v Tipper [1990] ICR
716, [1990] IRLR 386, CA 20.25, 20.26, 54.11, 55.13
Cooke v Glenrose Fish Co [2004] ICR 1188, [2004] IRLR 866, [2004] All ER
(D) 19 (Jun), EAT 21.54
Cooper v Metropolitan Police Comr (1985) 82 Cr App Rep 238, DC 45.12
Coors Brewers Ltd v Adcock. See Adcock v Coors Brewers Ltd
Coote v Granada Hospitality Ltd: C-185/97 [1998] All ER (EC) 865,
[1998] ECR I-5199, [1998] 3 CMLR 958, [1999] ICR 100, [1998] IRLR
656, ECJ; apld Coote v Granada Hospitality Ltd (No 2) [1999] 3 CMLR
334, [1999] ICR 942, [1999] IRLR 452, EAT 12.12, 13.33, 40.4
Copsey v WWB Devon Clays Ltd [2005] EWCA Civ 932, [2005] ICR 1789,
[2005] IRLR 811, [2005] NLJR 1484, (2005) Times, 25 August, [2005]
All ER (D) 350 (Jul) 30.7
Coral Leisure Group Ltd v Barnett [1981] ICR 503, [1981] IRLR 204, 125
Sol Jo 374, EAT 8.15
Corner v Buckinghamshire County Council (1978) 77 LGR 268, [1978] ICR
836, [1978] IRLR 320, 13 ITR 421, EAT 49.6
Cornwall County Care Ltd v Brightman [1998] ICR 529, [1998] IRLR
228, EAT 52.29
Cornwall County Council v Prater [2006] EWCA Civ 102, [2006] IRLR 362,
[2006] NLJR 372, [2006] All ER (D) 358 (Feb) 47.8
Corporate Express Ltd v Day [2004] EWHC 2943 (QB), [2004] All ER (D)
290 (Dec) 41.17, 41.18
Cort (Robert) & Son Ltd v Charman [1981] ICR 816, [1981] IRLR
437, EAT 48.9, 53.13
Costain Building and Civil Engineering Ltd v Smith [2000] ICR 215, EAT 17.3,
47.2
Cotswold Developments Construction Ltd v Williams [2006] IRLR 181,
[2005] All ER (D) 355 (Dec), EAT 17.3, 29.2
Council of Civil Service Unions v Minister for the Civil Service [1985] AC
374, [1984] 3 All ER 935, [1984] 3 WLR 1174, [1985] ICR 14, 128 Sol Jo
837, [1985] LS Gaz R 437, sub nom R v Secretary of State for Foreign
and Commonwealth Affairs, ex p Council of Civil Service Unions
[1985] IRLR 28, HL 37.3, 37.4, 37.6
Countrywide Assured Financial Services Ltd v Smart [2004] EWHC 1214
(Ch) 41.8
Courage Take Home Trade Ltd v Keys [1986] ICR 874, [1986] IRLR
427, EAT 55.22
Courtaulds Northern Spinning Ltd v Sibson [1988] ICR 451, [1988] IRLR
305, 132 Sol Jo 1033, CA 8.13
Coutts & Co plc v Cure [2005] ICR 1098, (2004) Times, 25 October, [2004]
All ER (D) 393 (Oct), EAT 20.18
Cowan v Scargill [1985] Ch 270, [1984] 2 All ER 750, [1984] 3 WLR 501,
[1984] ICR 646, [1984] IRLR 260, 128 Sol Jo 550 .... 42.10

Table of Cases

Cowen v Haden Ltd [1983] ICR 1, [1982] IRLR 225, 126 Sol Jo 411, EAT;
    revsd [1983] ICR 1, 126 Sol Jo 725, sub nom Haden Ltd v Cowen
    [1982] IRLR 314, CA 38.7
Cowley v Manson Timber Ltd [1995] ICR 367, [1995] IRLR 153, CA 55.1
Cox v Post Office, IDS Brief No 609 .... 10.14
Cox v Sun Alliance Life Ltd [2001] EWCA Civ 649, [2001] IRLR 448, [2001]
    All ER (D) 108 (May) 40.4
Cox Toner (W E) (International) Ltd v Crook [1981] ICR 823, [1981] IRLR
    443, EAT 53.7
Coxall v Goodyear Great Britain Ltd [2002] EWCA Civ 1010, [2003] 1 WLR
    536, [2003] ICR 152, [2002] IRLR 742, (2002) Times, 5 August, [2002]
    All ER (D) 303 (Jul) 27.8
Coy v Department of Health and Social Security [1985] AC 776,
    [1985] 2 WLR 866, [1985] ICR 419, [1985] IRLR 263, 129 Sol Jo
    315, HL 53.14
Crawford v Secretary of State for Employment [1995] IRLR 523, EAT 20.27, 31.4
Crawford v Swinton Insurance Brokers Ltd [1990] ICR 85, [1990] IRLR
    42, EAT 52.26
Credit Suisse Asset Management Ltd v Armstrong [1996] ICR 882,
    [1996] IRLR 450, [1996] 23 LS Gaz R 36, 140 Sol Jo LB 140, CA 41.14, 58.21
Credit Suisse First Boston (Europe) Ltd v Lister [1999] ICR 794,
    [1998] IRLR 700, [1998] 44 LS Gaz R 35, 142 Sol Jo LB 269, CA 8.22
Crees v Royal London Mutual Insurance Society Ltd [1998] ICR 848,
    [1998] IRLR 245, [1998] 15 LS Gaz R 33, 142 Sol Jo LB 94, 590 IRLB
    11, CA 33.21
Cresswell v Inland Revenue Board [1984] 2 All ER 713, [1984] ICR 508,
    [1984] IRLR 190, 128 Sol Jo 431 .... 8.13
Criddle v Epcot Leisure Ltd EAT/0275/05 .... 21.16, 21.69, 21.71
Croft v Royal Mail Group plc [2003] EWCA Civ 1045, [2003] ICR 1425,
    [2003] IRLR 592, (2003) Times, 24 July, 147 Sol Jo LB 904, [2002] All
    ER (D) 179 (Sep) 12.5
Crofton v Yeboah [2002] EWCA Civ 794, [2002] IRLR 634, (2002) Times,
    20 June, [2002] All ER (D) 512 (May) 12.13, 13.37
Crofts v Cathay Pacific Airways Ltd [2005] EWCA Civ 599, [2005] ICR 1436,
    [2005] IRLR 624, (2005) Times, 31 May, [2005] All ER (D) 305 (May) 26.12,
                                                                                              26.13, 53.15
Crofts v Veta Ltd [2006] UKHL 3, [2006] 1 All ER 823, [2006] IRLR 289,
    [2006] 06 LS Gaz R 36, [2006] NLJR 184, 150 Sol Jo LB 131, [2006] All
    ER (D) 184 (Jan) 26.13
Cromie v Moroak (t/a Blake Envelopes). See Moroak (t/a Blake Envelopes) v
    Cromie
Cross v British Airways plc [2005] IRLR 423, [2005] All ER (D) 10
    (Apr), EAT 13.8, 42.2
Cross v British Airways plc [2006] EWCA Civ 549, [2006] ICR 1239,
    [2006] IRLR 804, [2006] 21 LS Gaz R 24, (2006) Times, 5 June, [2006]
    All ER (D) 148 (May) 24.11, 52.17
Cross v Highlands and Islands Enterprise [2001] IRLR 336, Ct of Sess 27.8
Cross v Redpath Dorman Long (Contracting) Ltd [1978] ICR 730, EAT 47.2
Crossley v Faithful & Gould Holdings Ltd [2004] EWCA Civ 293,
    [2004] 4 All ER 447, [2004] IRLR 377, [2004] NLJR 653, (2004) Times,
    29 March, 148 Sol Jo LB 356, [2004] All ER (D) 295 (Mar) 8.13
Crosville Motor Services Ltd v Ashfield [1986] IRLR 475, EAT 51.5
Crosville Wales Ltd v Tracey (No 2). See Tracey v Crosville Wales Ltd
Crouch v British Rail Engineering Ltd [1988] IRLR 404, CA 27.5

Crown Estate Comrs v Dorset County Council [1990] Ch 297,
[1990] 1 All ER 19, [1990] 2 WLR 89, 88 LGR 132, 60 P & CR 1 .... 21.22
Crown Suppliers (Property Services Agency) v Dawkins [1993] ICR 517, sub
nom Dawkins v Department of the Environment [1993] IRLR
284, CA 12.6
Crowther & Nicholson Ltd, Re (1981) Times, 10 June 58.28
Croydon Health Authority v Jaufurally [1986] ICR 4, EAT 20.25
Cruickshank v VAW Motorcast Ltd [2002] ICR 729, [2002] IRLR 24, [2001]
All ER (D) 372 (Oct), EAT 10.2, 10.6
Curling v Securicor Ltd [1992] IRLR 549, EAT 8.13
Curr v Marks & Spencer plc [2002] EWCA Civ 1852, [2003] ICR 443,
[2003] IRLR 74, [2002] All ER (D) 205 (Dec) 7.7

D
DJM International Ltd v Nicholas [1996] ICR 214, [1996] IRLR 76, EAT 52.18
DMC Business Machines plc Plummer (EAT 0381/06) 15.11, 20.16, 20.19
Dabell v Vale Industrial Services (Nottingham) Ltd [1988] IRLR 439, CA 7.9
Dacas v Brook Street Bureau (UK) Ltd [2003] IRLR 190, [2003] All ER (D)
241 (Jan), EAT; revsd [2004] EWCA Civ 217, [2004] IRLR 358, (2004)
Times, 19 March, [2004] All ER (D) 125 (Mar) 8.3, 17.3, 47.2
Dairy Crest Ltd v Pigott [1989] ICR 92, CA 41.8
Dakri (A) & Co Ltd v Tiffen [1981] ICR 256, [1981] IRLR 57, EAT 38.8
Daley v A E Dorsett (Almar Dolls) Ltd [1982] ICR 1, [1981] IRLR
385, EAT 55.12, 55.13
Daley v Allied Suppliers Ltd [1983] ICR 90, [1983] IRLR 14, EAT 12.12
Dalgleish v Lothian and Borders Police Board [1991] IRLR 422, 1992 SLT
721, Ct of Sess 11.16
Darr v LRC Products Ltd [1993] IRLR 257, EAT 55.14, 55.15
Dattani v Chief Constable of West Mercia Police [2005] IRLR 327, [2005]
All ER (D) 95 (Feb), EAT 14.3, 14.9, 21.9
Dave v Robinska [2003] ICR 1248, [2003] NLJR 921, [2003] All ER (D) 35
(Jun), EAT 13.25
David (Lawrence) Ltd v Ashton [1991] 1 All ER 385, [1989] ICR 123,
[1989] IRLR 22, CA 41.8, 41.17
David-John v North Essex Health Authority [2004] ICR 112, [2003] All ER
(D) 84 (Aug), EAT 13.21, 17.3
Davies v Asda Stores Ltd (IDS Brief 801) 51.17
Davies v Davies (1887) 36 Ch D 359, 56 LJ Ch 962, 36 WR 86, 58 LT 209, 3
TLR 839, CA 41.7
Davies v M J Wyatt (Decorators) [2000] IRLR 759, EAT 34.6
Davies v McCartneys [1989] ICR 705, [1989] IRLR 439, EAT 24.11
Davies v Neath Port Talbot County Borough Council [1999] ICR 1132,
[1999] IRLR 769, EAT 24.3
Davies v Presbyterian Church of Wales [1986] 1 All ER 705, [1986] 1 WLR
323, [1986] ICR 280, [1986] IRLR 194, 130 Sol Jo 203, HL 17.3
Davy v Spelthorne Borough Council [1984] AC 262, [1983] 3 All ER 278,
[1983] 3 WLR 742, 82 LGR 193, 47 P & CR 310, 127 Sol Jo 733, [1984]
JPL 269, HL 37.4
Dawkins v Department of the Environment. See Crown Suppliers (Property
Services Agency) v Dawkins
Dawnay, Day & Co Ltd v de Braconier d'Alphen [1997] IRLR 285; affd
[1998] ICR 1068, [1997] IRLR 442, [1997] 26 LS Gaz R 30, 141 Sol Jo
LB 129, CA 41.4, 41.8

Table of Cases

Day v T Pickles Farms Ltd [1999] IRLR 217, EAT 28.17
Daynecourt Insurance Brokers Ltd v Iles [1978] IRLR 335, EAT 48.15
Days Medical Aids Ltd v Pihsiang Machinery Manufacturing Co Ltd
    [2004] EWHC 44 (Comm), [2004] 1 All ER (Comm) 991, [2004] All ER
    (D) 282 (Jan) 41.1
Deacons (a firm) v Bridge. See Bridge v Deacons (a firm)
Deane v Ealing London Borough Council [1993] ICR 329, [1993] IRLR
    209, EAT 12.13, 14.18, 13.37, 37.5
Deary v Mansion Hide Upholstery Ltd [1983] ICR 610, [1983] IRLR 195,
    147 JP 311 .... 27.41
Deaway Trading Ltd v Calverley [1973] 3 All ER 776, [1973] ICR 546,
    NIRC 31.10
Dedman v British Building and Engineering Appliances Ltd [1974] 1 All ER
    520, [1974] 1 WLR 171, [1974] ICR 53, [1973] IRLR 379, 16 KIR 1, 9
    ITR 100, 117 Sol Jo 938, CA 20.23, 20.25, 53.13
De Francesco v Barnum (1890) 45 Ch D 430, 60 LJ Ch 63, 39 WR 5,
    [1886–90] All ER Rep 414, 63 LT 438, 6 TLR 463 .... 4.10
Defrenne v Sabena: 43/75 [1981] 1 All ER 122, [1976] ECR 455,
    [1976] 2 CMLR 98, [1976] ICR 547, ECJ 24.19, 24.20, 25.2
Degnan v Redcar and Cleveland Borough Council [2005] ICR 1170,
    [2005] IRLR 504, [2005] NLJR 619, [2005] All ER (D) 197
    (Apr), EAT 24.20
Degnan v Redcar and Cleveland Borough Council [2005] EWCA Civ 726,
    [2005] IRLR 615, [2005] All ER (D) 167 (Jun) 24.5
De Grasse v Stockwell Tools Ltd [1992] IRLR 269, EAT 54.11
De Haney v Brent Mind [2003] EWCA Civ 1637, [2004] ICR 348,
    [2003] 45 LS Gaz R 29, (2003) Times, 11 November, 147 Sol Jo LB
    1275, [2003] All ER (D) 444 (Oct) 20.8, 22.2
De Keyser Ltd v Wilson [2001] IRLR 324, [2001] All ER (D) 237
    (Mar), EAT 10.2, 21.14, 30.7
Dekker v Stichting Vormingscentrum voor Jong Volwassenen (VJV-Centrum)
    Plus: 177/88 [1990] ECR I-3941, [1992] ICR 325, [1991] IRLR 27, ECJ 12.5
Delabole Slate Ltd v Berriman. See Berriman v Delabole Slate Ltd
Delaney v Staples (t/a De Montfort Recruitment) [1991] 2 QB 47,
    [1991] 1 All ER 609, [1991] 2 WLR 627, [1991] ICR 331, [1991] IRLR
    112, CA; affd [1992] 1 AC 687, [1992] 1 All ER 944, [1992] 2 WLR 451,
    [1992] ICR 483, [1992] IRLR 191, [1992] 15 LS Gaz R 32, 136 Sol Jo
    LB 91, HL 31.11, 34.6, 46.8, 48.9, 48.10
Delauche v EC Commission: 111/86 [1987] ECR 5345, [1989] 2 CMLR 565,
    ECJ 37.8
Dellas v Premier Ministre: C-14/04 [2006] IRLR 225, [2005] All ER (D) 19
    (Dec), ECJ 57.5
Dench v Flynn & Partners [1998] IRLR 653, CA 55.12
Denham v Midland Employers' Mutual Assurance Ltd [1955] 2 QB 437,
    [1955] 2 All ER 561, [1955] 3 WLR 84, [1955] 1 Lloyd's Rep 467, 99 Sol
    Jo 417, CA 47.2
Denise v M J Wyatt (Decorators) Ltd [2000] IRLR 759, EAT 29.4
Dentmaster (UK) Ltd v Kent [1997] IRLR 636, CA 41.8
Department for Constitutional Affairs v Jones (24 November 2006,
    unreported) 15.4, 15.5
Department for Work and Pensions v Thompson [2004] IRLR 348, EAT 12.5, 20.8
Department for Work and Pensions v Webley [2004] EWCA Civ 1745,
    [2005] ICR 577, [2005] IRLR 288, (2005) Times, 17 January, [2004] All
    ER (D) 368 (Dec) 47.9

Department of Education and Science v Taylor [1992] IRLR 308 .... 21.17, 21.24
Department of Health v Bruce (1992) Times, 31 December, EAT 37.3
Department of Health and Social Security v Hughes. See Hughes v
    Department of Health and Social Security
Department of Transport v Gallacher [1994] ICR 967, [1994] IRLR
    231, CA 51.17
Depledge v Pye Telecommunications Ltd [1981] ICR 82, [1980] IRLR
    390, EAT 49.2
Derby Daily Telegraph Ltd v Foss, IDS Brief No 471 .... 55.21
Derby Daily Telegraph Ltd v Pensions Ombudsman [1999] ICR 1057,
    [1999] IRLR 476, [1999] All ER (D) 300 .... 42.4
Derby Specialist Fabrication Ltd v Burton [2001] 2 All ER 840, [2001] ICR
    833, [2001] IRLR 69, [2000] All ER (D) 1348, EAT 20.29
Derbyshire, The. See Coltman v Bibby Tankers Ltd, The Derbyshire
Derbyshire County Council v Times Newspapers Ltd [1993] AC 534,
    [1993] 1 All ER 1011, [1993] 2 WLR 449, 91 LGR 179,
    [1993] 14 LS Gaz R 46, [1993] NLJR 283, 137 Sol Jo LB 52, 81, HL 30.5
Deria v General Council of British Shipping [1986] 1 WLR 1207, [1986] ICR
    172, [1986] IRLR 108, 130 Sol Jo 649, [1986] LS Gaz R 2996, CA 13.15
De Souza v Automobile Association [1986] ICR 514, [1986] IRLR 103, 130
    Sol Jo 110, [1986] LS Gaz R 288, CA 12.12
D'Souza v Lambeth London Borough [1997] IRLR 677, EAT; revsd sub
    nom Lambeth London Borough v D'Souza [1999] IRLR 240, CA 14.13, 14.19
D'Souza v Lambeth London Borough (2001) IDS Brief No 688 .... 12.10
D'Souza v Lambeth London Borough Council [2003] UKHL 33,
    [2003] 4 All ER 1113, [2003] 2 CMLR 1329, [2003] ICR 867,
    [2003] IRLR 484, 74 BMLR 109, [2003] 30 LS Gaz R 30, (2003) Times,
    23 June, 147 Sol Jo LB 782, [2003] All ER (D) 258 (Jun) 10.17, 12.12, 13.33
Dethier (Jules) Equipement SA v Dassy and Sovam SPRL (in liquidation):
    C-319/94 [1998] All ER (EC) 346, [1998] ECR I-1061, [1998] 2 CMLR
    611, [1998] ICR 541, [1998] IRLR 266, ECJ 52.11, 52.20
d'Urso v Ercole Marelli Elettromeccanica Generale SpA: C-362/89
    [1991] ECR I-4105, [1993] 3 CMLR 513, [1992] IRLR 136, ECJ 52.26, 52.28
Deutsche Telekom AG v Schröder: C-50/96 [2000] ECR I-743,
    [2002] 2 CMLR 583, [2000] IRLR 353, ECJ 24.18
Devenney v United Kingdom (Application 24265/94) (2002) Times, 11 April,
    ECtHR 30.4
Devine v Designer Flowers Wholesale Florist Sundries Ltd [1993] IRLR
    517, EAT 55.12
Devis (W) & Sons Ltd v Atkins [1977] AC 931, [1977] 2 All ER 321,
    [1977] 2 WLR 70, [1977] ICR 377, [1976] IRLR 428, 12 ITR 12, 121 Sol
    Jo 52, CA; affd [1977] AC 931, [1977] 3 All ER 40, [1977] 3 WLR 214,
    [1977] ICR 662, [1977] IRLR 314, 13 ITR 71, 121 Sol Jo 512, 8 BLR
    57, HL 5.3, 54.1, 54.10, 55.13
Devlin v United Kingdom (Application 29545/95) [2002] IRLR 155, (2001)
    Times, 9 November, [2001] ECHR 29545/95 , ECtHR 30.4
Devon County Council v Cook [1977] IRLR 188, EAT 58.5
Devonald v Rosser & Sons [1906] 2 KB 728, 75 LJKB 688, [1904–7] All ER
    Rep 988, 50 Sol Jo 616, 95 LT 232, 22 TLR 682, CA 58.21
Devonshire v Trico-Folberth Ltd [1989] ICR 747, sub nom
    Trico-Folberth Ltd v Devonshire [1989] IRLR 396, CA 55.13
Dewhirst Group v GMB Trade Union EAT/486/03 .... 39.4
Dhaliwal v British Airways Board [1985] ICR 513, EAT 54.9

Table of Cases

Dhatt v McDonalds Hamburgers Ltd [1991] 3 All ER 692, [1991] 1 WLR
    527, [1991] ICR 238, [1991] IRLR 130, CA 12.5, 13.18
Dibro Ltd v Hore [1990] ICR 370, [1990] IRLR 129,
    [1990] 13 LS Gaz R 43, EAT 24.8
Dick v Boots the Chemist Ltd IDS Brief No 451 .... 54.11
Dick v University of Glasgow [1993] IRLR 581, Ct of Sess 54.4
Diem v Crystal Services plc EAT/0398/95 .... 21.52, 22.12
Dietman v Brent London Borough Council [1987] ICR 737, [1987] IRLR
    259; affd [1988] ICR 842, [1988] IRLR 299, CA 8.23, 58.7, 58.17, 58.18
Dietrich v Westdeutscher Rundfunk: C-11/99 [2000] ECR I-5589, ECJ 28.5
Dietz v Stichting Thuiszorg Rotterdam: C-435/93 [1996] ECR I-5223,
    [1997] 1 CMLR 199, [1996] IRLR 692, 563 IRLB 13, ECJ 24.17, 24.18
Digital Equipment Co Ltd v Clements (No 2) [1998] ICR 258, [1998] IRLR
    134, [1998] 03 LS Gaz R 24, CA 14.15, 22.25, 55.13
Dignity Funerals v Bruce [2005] IRLR 189, 2004 SLT 1223, 148 Sol Jo LB
    1313, [2005] All ER (D) 427 (Apr), Ct of Sess 55.12
Dillenkofer v Germany: C-178/94, C-179/94, C-188/94, C-189/94 and
    C-190/94 [1997] QB 259, [1996] All ER (EC) 917, [1997] 2 WLR 253,
    [1996] ECR I-4845, [1996] 3 CMLR 469, [1997] IRLR 60, ECJ 25.2
Dimbleby & Sons Ltd v National Union of Journalists [1984] 1 All ER 117,
    [1984] 1 WLR 67, [1984] ICR 386, [1984] IRLR 67, 128 Sol Jo 64,
    [1984] LS Gaz R 515, CA; affd [1984] 1 All ER 751, [1984] 1 WLR 427,
    [1984] ICR 386, [1984] IRLR 161, 128 Sol Jo 189, HL 45.16
Dimskal Shipping Co SA v International Transport Workers' Federation,
    The Evia Luck (No 2) [1992] 2 AC 152, [1991] 4 All ER 871,
    [1991] 3 WLR 875, [1992] 1 Lloyd's Rep 115, [1992] ICR 37,
    [1992] IRLR 78, HL 45.16
Dimtsu v Westminster City Council [1991] IRLR 450, EAT 14.6
Dines v Initial Health Care Services [1995] ICR 11, [1994] IRLR 336, CA 52.5
Diosynth Ltd v Thomson [2006] CSIH 5, [2006] IRLR 284, 2006 SLT 323,
    [2006] All ER (D) 165 (Feb) 54.9
DPP v Fidler [1992] 1 WLR 91, 94 Cr App Rep 286, 156 JP 257,
    [1992] Crim LR 62, DC 45.12
DPP v Jones [1999] 2 AC 240, [1999] 2 All ER 257, [1999] 2 WLR 625,
    [1999] 2 Cr App Rep 348, 163 JP 285, [1999] Crim LR 672,
    [1999] 11 LS Gaz R 71, [1999] 13 LS Gaz R 31, 6 BHRC 513,
    [1999] EGCS 36, 143 Sol Jo LB 98, [1999] 3 LRC 699, HL 45.12
DPP v Marshall [1998] ICR 518, EAT 20.30
Discount Tobacco and Confectionery Ltd v Armitage [1990] IRLR 15,
    [1995] ICR 431n, EAT 54.3
Discount Tobacco and Confectionery Ltd v Williamson [1993] ICR 371,
    [1993] IRLR 327, EAT 34.6
Dispatch Management Services (UK) Ltd v Douglas [2002] IRLR 389, [2001]
    All ER (D) 26 (Dec), EAT 21.55, 30.7
Divine-Bortey v Brent London Borough Council [1998] ICR 886,
    [1998] IRLR 525, [1998] 22 LS Gaz R 29, 142 Sol Jo LB 152, CA 14.8, 21.26
Dixon v BBC [1979] QB 546, [1979] 2 All ER 112, [1979] 2 WLR 647,
    [1979] ICR 281, [1979] IRLR 114, 122 Sol Jo 713, CA 53.6
Dixon and Shaw v West Ella Developments Ltd [1978] ICR 856,
    [1978] IRLR 151, 13 ITR 235, EAT 54.3
Dixon Stores Group v Arnold EAT/772/93 .... 20.26
Dobie v Burns International Security Services (UK) Ltd [1984] 3 All ER 333,
    [1985] 1 WLR 43, [1984] ICR 812, [1984] IRLR 329, 128 Sol Jo
    872, CA 22.19

Dodds v Bank Of Toyko-Mitsubishi Ltd EAT/0480/05 .... 22.6
Dogherty v Chairman and Governors of Amwell View School [2007] ICR
    135, (2006) Times, 5 October, [2006] All ER (D) 112 (Sep), sub nom
    Chairman and Governors of Amwell View School v Dogherty
    [2007] IRLR 198, EAT 30.7, 54.10
Doherty v British Midland Airways Ltd [2006] IRLR 90, [2005] All ER (D)
    12 (Apr), EAT 8.13
Dolphin v Hartlepool Borough Council (9 August 2006, unreported) 37.2
Donaldson v Perth and Kinross Council [2004] ICR 667, [2004] IRLR 121,
    [2003] All ER (D) 416 (Dec) 52.11
Donnelly v Kelvin International Services [1992] IRLR 496, EAT 7.7
Doolan v United Kingdom [2002] IRLR 580, ECtHR 30.4
Dore v Aon Training Ltd [2005] EWCA Civ 411, [2005] IRLR 891, [2005] All
    ER (D) 328 (Mar) 14.15
Doshoki v Draeger Ltd [2002] IRLR 340, [2002] All ER (D) 139
    (Mar), EAT 14.16
Doughty v Rolls-Royce plc [1992] 1 CMLR 1045, [1992] IRLR 126, sub nom
    Rolls-Royce plc v Doughty [1992] ICR 538, CA 37.7
Doyle v White City Stadium Ltd [1935] 1 KB 110, 104 LJKB 140,
    [1934] All ER Rep 252, 78 Sol Jo 601, 152 LT 32, CA 4.10
Drage v Governors of Greenford High School [2000] ICR 899, [2000] IRLR
    314, 144 Sol Jo LB 165, [2000] All ER (D) 343, CA 20.23
Draper v Mears Ltd [2006] IRLR 869, [2006] All ER (D) 273 (Oct), EAT 15.2
Drew v St Edmundsbury Borough Council [1980] ICR 513, [1980] IRLR
    459, EAT 54.3
Drinkwater Sabey Ltd v Burnett [1995] ICR 328, [1995] IRLR 238, EAT 21.10
Driskel v Peninsula Business Services Ltd [2000] IRLR 151, EAT 12.12
Dryden v Greater Glasgow Health Board [1992] IRLR 469, EAT 28.23
Dudley Bower Building Services Ltd v Lowe [2003] ICR 843, [2003] IRLR
    260, [2003] All ER (D) 243 (Feb), EAT 52.5
Duffy v Yeomans & Partners Ltd [1993] ICR 862, [1993] IRLR 368, EAT;
    affd [1995] ICR 1, [1994] IRLR 642, CA 21.60, 54.4, 54.11
Dugdale v Kraft Foods Ltd [1977] 1 All ER 454, [1976] 1 WLR 1288,
    [1977] ICR 48, [1976] IRLR 368, 11 ITR 309, 120 Sol Jo 780, EAT 24.6
Dugmore v Swansea NHS Trust [2002] EWCA Civ 1689, [2003] 1 All ER
    333, [2003] ICR 574, [2003] IRLR 164, 72 BMLR 22,
    [2003] 05 LS Gaz R 30, (2002) Times, 9 December, 146 Sol Jo LB 271,
    [2002] All ER (D) 307 (Nov) 28.26
Duke v GEC Reliance Ltd (formerly Reliance Systems Ltd) [1988] AC 618,
    [1988] 1 All ER 626, [1988] 2 WLR 359, [1988] 1 CMLR 719,
    [1988] ICR 339, [1988] IRLR 118, 132 Sol Jo 226,
    [1988] 11 LS Gaz R 42, HL 25.2
Duncan Web Offset (Maidstone) Ltd v Cooper [1995] IRLR 633, EAT 52.15
Dundon v GPT Ltd [1995] IRLR 403, EAT 54.3, 54.11
Dunham v Ashford Windows [2005] IRLR 608, [2005] All ER (D) 104
    (Jun), EAT 10.2
Dunk v George Waller & Son Ltd [1970] 2 QB 163, [1970] 2 All ER 630,
    [1970] 2 WLR 1241, 114 Sol Jo 356, CA 16.2, 58.29
Dunlop Pneumatic Tyre Co Ltd v New Garage and Motor Co Ltd [1915] AC
    79, 83 LJKB 1574, [1914–15] All ER Rep 739, 111 LT 862, 30 TLR
    625, HL 58.26
Dunlop Tyres Ltd v Blows [2001] EWCA Civ 1032, [2001] IRLR 629, [2001]
    All ER (D) 179 (Jun) 6.3, 8.10, 34.6

Table of Cases

Dunn v R [1896] 1 QB 116, 60 JP 117, 65 LJQB 279, 44 WR 243,
[1895–9] All ER Rep 907, 40 Sol Jo 129, 73 LT 695, 12 TLR 101, CA 37.3
Dunnachie v Kingston-Upon-Hull City Council [2004] EWCA Civ 84,
[2004] 2 All ER 501, [2004] ICR 481, [2004] IRLR 287, [2004] NLJR
248, (2004) Times, 26 February, 148 Sol Jo LB 233, [2004] All ER (D)
185 (Feb); revsd [2004] UKHL 36, [2004] 3 All ER 1011, [2004] 3 WLR
310, [2004] ICR 1052, [2004] IRLR 727, [2004] 33 LS Gaz R 34,
[2004] NLJR 1156, 148 Sol Jo LB 909, [2004] All ER (D) 251 (Jul) 8.23, 55.12,
58.29
Duport Steels Ltd v Sirs [1980] 1 All ER 529, [1980] 1 WLR 142, [1980] ICR
161, [1980] IRLR 116, 124 Sol Jo 133, HL 45.5
Durant v Clariston Clothing Co Ltd [1974] IRLR 360, IT 54.14
Duru v Granada Retail Catering Ltd EAT/281/00, IDS Brief No 697 .... 21.32
Dutton v Hawker Siddeley Aviation Ltd [1978] ICR 1057, [1978] IRLR
390, EAT 49.7
Dutton & Clark Ltd v Daly [1985] ICR 780, [1985] IRLR 363, EAT 8.13, 28.28
Dyke v Hereford and Worcester County Council [1989] ICR 800, EAT 37.1, 54.11
Dyson Technology Ltd v Strutt [2005] EWHC 2814 (Ch), [2005] All ER (D)
355 (Nov) 41.6

E

EC Commission v Belgium: C-229/89 [1991] ECR I-2205, [1993] 2 CMLR
403, [1991] IRLR 393, ECJ 13.8
EC Commission v Belgium: C-173/91 [1993] IRLR 404, ECJ 24.3
EC Commission v United Kingdom: 165/82 [1984] 1 All ER 353, [1983] ECR
3431, [1984] 1 CMLR 44, [1984] ICR 192, [1984] IRLR 29, ECJ 25.6
EC Commission v United Kingdom: C-382/92 [1994] ECR I-2435,
[1995] 1 CMLR 345, [1994] ICR 664, [1994] IRLR 392, ECJ 18.28, 25.2
EC Commission v United Kingdom: C-383/92 [1994] ECR I-2479,
[1995] 1 CMLR 345, [1994] ICR 664, [1994] IRLR 412, ECJ 25.8, 25.9
EC Commission v United Kingdom: C-484/04 unreported, ECJ 57.2, 57.15
EC Commission v United Kingdom of Great Britain and Northern Ireland:
61/81 [1982] ECR 2601, [1982] 3 CMLR 284, [1982] ICR 578,
[1982] IRLR 333, ECJ 25.6
ECM (Vehicle Delivery Service) v Cox [1999] 4 All ER 669, [2000] 1 CMLR
224, [1999] ICR 1162, [1999] IRLR 559, [1999] All ER (D) 838, CA 52.5
EFTA Surveillance Authority v Norway: E-1/02 [2003] 1 CMLR 725,
[2003] IRLR 318, EFTA Ct 12.12, 13.9
EMI Group Electronics Ltd v Coldicott (Inspector of Taxes) [2000] 1 WLR
540, [1999] STC 803, 71 TC 455, [1999] IRLR 630,
[1999] 32 LS Gaz R 34, 143 Sol Jo LB 220, [1999] All ER (D)
803, CA 46.8, 48.10, 58.21
Eagland v British Telecommunications plc [1993] ICR 644, [1992] IRLR
323, CA 8.9
Ealing London Borough v Race Relations Board [1972] AC 342,
[1972] 1 All ER 105, [1972] 2 WLR 71, 116 Sol Jo 60, HL 12.6
Earl v Slater & Wheeler (Airlyne) Ltd [1973] 1 All ER 145, [1973] 1 WLR 51,
[1972] ICR 508, [1972] IRLR 115, 13 KIR 319, 8 ITR 33, 117 Sol Jo 14,
NIRC 54.2
East Berkshire Health Authority v Matadeen [1992] ICR 723, [1992] IRLR
336, [1992] 29 LS Gaz R 24, EAT 22.7, 22.17
East Lindsey District Council v Daubney [1977] ICR 566, [1977] IRLR 181,
12 ITR 359, EAT 54.8

Eastham v Newcastle United Football Club Ltd [1964] Ch 413,
  [1963] 3 All ER 139, [1963] 3 WLR 574, 107 Sol Jo 574, Aus HC 41.5
Eastwood v Magnox Electric plc [2004] UKHL 35, [2004] 3 All ER 991,
  [2004] 3 WLR 322, [2004] ICR 1064, [2004] IRLR 733, [2004] NLJR
  1155, 148 Sol Jo LB 909, [2004] All ER (D) 268 (Jul) 8.13, 8.23, 53.7
Eaton v Robert Eaton Ltd [1988] ICR 302, [1988] IRLR 83, EAT 31.2
Eaton Ltd v Nuttall [1977] 3 All ER 1131, [1977] 1 WLR 549, [1977] ICR
  272, [1977] IRLR 71, 12 ITR 197, 121 Sol Jo 353, EAT 24.6
Ebac Ltd v Wymer [1995] ICR 466, EAT 38.12
Ecclestone v National Union of Journalists [1999] IRLR 166 .... 50.14
Edebi v Canary Wharf Management Ltd [2006] ICR 719, [2006] IRLR 416,
  [2006] All ER (D) 03 (Apr), EAT 15.12, 20.19
Edge v Pensions Ombudsman [2000] Ch 602, [1999] 4 All ER 546,
  [2000] 3 WLR 79, [2000] ICR 748, [1999] PLR 215,
  [1999] 35 LS Gaz R 39, [1999] NLJR 1442, CA 42.14
Edmonds v Lawson [2000] IRLR 18, [1999] 39 LS Gaz R 38, 143 Sol Lo LB
  234, [1999] All ER (D) 1035; revsd [2000] QB 501, [2000] 2 WLR 1091,
  [2000] ICR 567, [2000] IRLR 391, 144 Sol Jo LB 151, [2000] All ER (D)
  312, CA 16.2, 34.9
Edwards v Derby City Council [1999] ICR 114, EAT 24.14
Edwards v National Coal Board [1949] 1 KB 704, [1949] 1 All ER 743, 93
  Sol Jo 337, 65 TLR 430, CA 27.5
Edwards v Society of Graphical and Allied Trades [1971] Ch 354,
  [1970] 3 All ER 689, [1970] 3 WLR 713, 114 Sol Jo 618, CA 51.12
Egg Stores (Stamford Hill) Ltd v Leibovici [1977] ICR 260, [1976] IRLR 376,
  11 ITR 289, EAT 48.3
Eidesund v Stavanger Catering A/S: E-2/95 [1997] 2 CMLR 672,
  [1996] IRLR 684, EFTA Ct 52.19
Ekpe v Metropolitan Police Comr [2001] ICR 1084, [2001] All ER (D) 353
  (May), [2001] IRLR 605, EAT 10.2, 10.4
Elkouil v Coney Island Ltd [2002] IRLR 174, [2001] All ER (D) 181
  (Nov), EAT 55.13
Elliott Turbomachinery Ltd v Bates [1981] ICR 218, EAT 38.7
Elsner-Lakeberg v Land Nordrhein-Westfalen: C-285/02 [2004] 2 CMLR 874,
  [2005] IRLR 209, [2004] All ER (D) 423 (May), ECJ 24.5
Eltek (UK) Ltd v Thomson [2000] ICR 689, EAT 21.10
Elvidge v Coventry City Council [1994] QB 241, [1993] 4 All ER 903,
  [1993] 3 WLR 976, [1994] ICR 68, 26 HLR 281, CA 43.7
Ely v YKK Fasteners (UK) Ltd [1993] IRLR 500, CA 54.1
Emmott v Minister for Social Welfare and A-G: C-208/90 [1991] ECR
  I-4269, [1991] 3 CMLR 894, [1993] ICR 8, [1991] IRLR 387, ECJ 20.18, 25.2
Employees of the Consiglio Nazionale delle Ricerche, Re, EC Commisison v
  Italy: 225/85 [1988] ECR 2271, [1988] 3 CMLR 635, ECJ 37.7
Employment Service v Nathan EAT/1316/95, IDS Brief No 568 .... 21.38
Enderby v Frenchay Health Authority [1991] 1 CMLR 626, [1991] ICR 382,
  [1991] IRLR 44, EAT; on appeal [1994] ICR 112, [1992] IRLR 15, CA;
  refd C-127/92: [1994] 1 All ER 495, [1993] ECR I-5535, [1994] 1 CMLR
  8, [1994] ICR 112, [1993] IRLR 591, ECJ 22.27, 24.10, 24.11
Enderby v Frenchay Health Authority (No 2) [1999] IRLR 155, EAT; affd
  [2000] ICR 612, [2000] IRLR 257, CA 24.5, 24.9
English v Emery Reimbold & Strick Ltd [2002] EWCA Civ 605,
  [2002] 3 All ER 385, [2003] IRLR 710 .... 21.63, 22.11
English v UNISON (2000) IDS Brief No 668 .... 51.21

Table of Cases

English, Welsh and Scottish Railway Ltd v National Union of Rail,
  Maritime and Transport Workers [2004] EWCA Civ 1539, 148 Sol Jo LB
  1246, [2004] All ER (D) 203 (Oct) 45.14
Equal Opportunities Commission v Birmingham City Council. See
  Birmingham City Council v Equal Opportunities Commission
Equal Opportunities Commission v Secretary of State for Employment. See
  R v Secretary of State for Employment, ex p Equal Opportunities
  Commission
Equal Opportunities Commission v Secretary of State for Trade and
  Industry [2007] EWHC 483 (Admin), [2007] IRLR 327, [2007] All ER
  (D) 183 (Mar) 12.5, 12.11, 12.12, 25.2, 25.5, 56.1
Equal Opportunities Commission for Northern Ireland's Application, Re
  [1989] IRLR 64 .... 24.11
Essa v Laing Ltd [2003] ICR 1110, [2003] IRLR 346, [2003] 18 LS Gaz R 34,
  (2003) Times, 7 April, [2003] All ER (D) 215 (Feb), EAT; affd
  [2004] EWCA Civ 02, [2004] ICR 746, [2004] IRLR 313, (2004) Times,
  29 January, 148 Sol Jo LB 146, [2004] All ER (D) 155 (Jan) 14.17
Esso Petroleum Co Ltd v Harper's Garage (Stourport) Ltd [1968] AC 269,
  [1967] 1 All ER 699, [1967] 2 WLR 871, 111 Sol Jo 174, 201 Estates
  Gazette 1043, HL 41.3
Esso Petroleum Co Ltd v Jarvis EAT 0831/0 .... 47.2
Etam plc v Rowan [1989] IRLR 150, EAT 13.3
Euro-Diam Ltd v Bathurst [1990] 1 QB 1, [1988] 2 All ER 23, [1988] 2 WLR
  517, [1988] 1 Lloyd's Rep 228, 132 Sol Jo 372,
  [1988] 9 LS Gaz R 45, CA 8.15
Euroguard Ltd v Rycroft IDS Brief No 498 .... 54.11
European Commission v Germany: C-341/02 [2005] All ER (D) 172 (Apr),
  ECJ 26.3
European Commission v United Kingdom: C-484/04 [2006] 3 CMLR 1322,
  [2007] ICR 592, [2006] IRLR 888, (2006) Times, 21 September, [2006]
  All ER (D) 32 (Sep), ECJ 25.11, 57.2, 57.15, 57.26
Europieces SA v Saunders IDS Brief No 627, ECJ 52.11
Evans v Bolton School [2006] EWCA Civ 1653, [2007] ICR 641, 150 Sol Jo
  LB 1532, [2006] All ER (D) 198 (Nov), sub nom Bolton School v Evans
  [2007] IRLR 140 .... 11.18
Evans v Malley Organisation Ltd (t/a First Business Support) [2002] EWCA
  Civ 1834, [2003] ICR 432, [2003] IRLR 156, (2003) Times, 23 January,
  [2002] All ER (D) 397 (Nov) 29.4
Evening Standard Co Ltd v Henderson [1987] ICR 588, [1987] IRLR
  64, CA 8.24
Everson v Secretary of State for Trade and Industry: C-198/98 [1999] ECR
  I-8903, [2000] All ER (EC) 29, [2000] 1 CMLR 489, [2000] IRLR 202,
  ECJ 31.3
Evia Luck (No 2), The. See Dimskal Shipping Co SA v International
  Transport Workers' Federation, The Evia Luck (No 2)
Export Credits Guarantee Department v Universal Oil Products Co
  [1983] 2 All ER 205, [1983] 1 WLR 399, [1983] 2 Lloyd's Rep 152, 127
  Sol Jo 408, 23 BLR 106, 133 NLJ 662, HL 58.26
Express and Echo Publications Ltd v Tanton [1999] ICR 693, [1999] IRLR
  367, [1999] 14 LS Gaz R 31, [1999] All ER (D) 256, CA 17.3
Express and Star Ltd v National Graphical Association [1986] ICR 589,
  [1986] IRLR 222, [1986] LS Gaz R 2083, CA 45.16, 50.16
Express Newspapers v Keys [1980] IRLR 247 .... 45.4

Express Newspapers Ltd v McShane [1980] AC 672, [1980] 1 All ER 65,
[1980] 2 WLR 89, [1980] ICR 42, 124 Sol Jo 30, sub nom McShane and
Ashton v Express Newspapers Ltd [1980] IRLR 35, HL 45.5

F

FS Consulting v McCaul [2002] STC (SCD) 138 .... 46.35
Faccenda Chicken Ltd v Fowler [1987] Ch 117, [1986] 1 All ER 617,
[1986] 3 WLR 288, [1986] FSR 291, [1986] ICR 297, [1986] IRLR 69,
130 Sol Jo 573, CA 41.13
Faccini Dori v Recreb Srl: C-91/92 [1995] All ER (EC) 1, [1994] ECR I-3325,
[1995] 1 CMLR 665, ECJ 25.2
Facey v Midas Retail Security [2001] ICR 287, [2000] IRLR 812, EAT 22.12
Fadipe v Reed Nursing Personnel [2001] EWCA Civ 1885, [2005] ICR 1760,
[2001] All ER (D) 23 (Dec) 11.18
Fairbrother v Abbey National plc. See Abbey National plc v Fairbrother
Fairchild v Glenhaven Funeral Services Ltd [2001] EWCA Civ 1881,
[2002] 1 WLR 1052, [2002] ICR 412, [2002] IRLR 129, [2001] All ER
(D) 125 (Dec); revsd [2002] UKHL 22, [2003] 1 AC 32, [2002] 3 All ER
305, [2002] ICR 798, [2002] IRLR 533, 67 BMLR 90, [2002] NLJR 998,
[2003] 1 LRC 674, [2002] All ER (D) 139 (Jun) 27.8, 27.14
Fairfield Ltd v Skinner [1992] ICR 836, [1993] IRLR 4,
[1992] 34 LS Gaz R 39, EAT 34.6
Fairhurst Ward Abbotts Ltd v Botes Building Ltd [2004] EWCA Civ 83,
[2004] ICR 919, [2004] IRLR 304, 148 Sol Jo LB 235, [2004] All ER (D)
225 (Feb)... 52.4
Falconer v ASLEF and NUR [1986] IRLR 331, [1986] BTLC 258, Cty Ct 45.18
Falkirk Council v Whyte [1997] IRLR 560, EAT 12.8
Family Benefits for Community Civil Servants, Re, EC Commission v
Belgium: 186/85 [1987] ECR 2029, [1988] 2 CMLR 759, ECJ 37.8
Fantask A/S v Industriministeriet (Erhvervsministeriet): C-188/95 [1998] All
ER (EC) 1, [1997] ECR I-6783, [1998] 1 CMLR 473, ECJ 25.2
Farnsworth (F W) Ltd v McCoid [1998] IRLR 362, EAT; affd [1999] ICR
1047, [1999] IRLR 626, [1999] 16 LS Gaz R 35, CA 51.17
Farrant v Woodroffe School [1998] ICR 184, [1998] IRLR 176, EAT 54.9
Farrell Matthews & Weir (a firm) v Hansen [2005] ICR 509, [2005] IRLR
160, [2004] All ER (D) 365 (Oct), EAT 34.6
Farrow v Wilson (1869) LR 4 CP 744, 38 LJCP 326, 18 WR 43,
[1861–73] All ER Rep 846, 20 LT 810 .... 58.8
Faust v Power Packing Casemakers. See Power Packing Casemakers v Faust
Fay v North Yorkshire County Council (1986) 85 LGR 87, [1986] ICR 133,
sub nom North Yorkshire County Council v Fay [1985] IRLR
247, CA 47.7, 54.14
Federatie Nederlandse Vakbeweging v Netherlands: C-124/05 [2006] All ER
(D) 69 (Apr), ECJ 29.3
Fellowes & Son v Fisher [1976] QB 122, [1975] 2 All ER 829, [1975] 3 WLR
184, 119 Sol Jo 390, CA 41.8
Fennelly v Connex South Eastern Ltd [2001] IRLR 390, [2000] All ER (D)
2233, CA 56.2
Fentiman v Fluid Engineering Products Ltd [1991] ICR 570, [1991] IRLR
150, EAT 55.12
Fenton v Stablegold Ltd (t/a Chiswick Court Hotel) [1986] ICR 236,
[1986] IRLR 64, EAT 55.7

Table of Cases

Ferenc-Batchelor v London Underground Ltd [2003] ICR 656, [2003] IRLR
252, [2003] All ER (D) 252 (Mar), EAT 51.21
Ferguson v Gateway Training Centre Ltd [1991] ICR 658, EAT 21.60
Ferguson v Prestwick Circuits Ltd [1992] IRLR 266, EAT 54.11
Ferguson v Welsh [1987] 3 All ER 777, [1987] 1 WLR 1553, 86 LGR 153,
[1988] IRLR 112, 131 Sol Jo 1552, [1987] LS Gaz R 3581, [1987] NLJ
Rep 1037, HL 27.15
Fernandez v McDonald [2003] EWCA Civ 1219, [2003] 4 All ER 1033,
[2004] 1 WLR 1027, [2004] HLR 189, [2003] 42 EG 128,
[2003] 34 LS Gaz R 33, (2003) Times, 9 October, 147 Sol Jo LB 995,
[2003] All ER (D) 94 (Aug) 43.6
Fernandez v Office of the Parliamentary Commissioner for Administration
and the Health Service Comr [2006] All ER (D) 460 (Jul), EAT 14.3
Ferranti International plc, Re. See Talbot v Cadge
Finalarte Sociedade de Construção Civil Lda v Urlaubs- und
Lohnausgleichskasse der Bauwirtschaft: C-49/98, C-50/98, C-52/98 to
C-54/98 and C-68/98 to C-71/98 [2001] ECR I-7831, [2003] 2 CMLR
333, [2001] All ER (D) 361 (Oct), ECJ 26.3
Financial Techniques (Planning Services) Ltd v Hughes [1981] IRLR
32, CA 53.7
Financial Times Ltd v Byrne (No 2) [1992] IRLR 163, EAT 24.11
Fire Brigades Union v Fraser [1998] IRLR 697, Ct of Sess 13.26
First Castle Electronics Ltd v West [1989] ICR 72, EAT 21.22
First Hampshire and Dorset Ltd v Feist (5 October 2006, Unreported) 57.3, 57.15,
                                                                       57.29, 57.34
First Point International Ltd v Department of Trade and Industry
(1999) 164 JP 89, [1999] All ER (D) 898, DC 47.3
Fisher-Karpark Industries Ltd v Nichols [1982] FSR 351 .... 41.15
Fisscher v Voorhuis Hengelo BV: C-128/93 [1995] All ER (EC) 193,
[1994] ECR I-4583, [1995] 1 CMLR 881, [1995] ICR 635, [1994] IRLR
662, ECJ 20.12, 24.18, 25.2
Fitch v Dewes [1921] 2 AC 158, 90 LJ Ch 436, [1921] All ER Rep 13, 65 Sol
Jo 626, 125 LT 744, 37 TLR 784, HL 41.8
Fitzgerald v Hall, Russell & Co Ltd [1970] AC 984, [1969] 3 All ER 1140,
[1969] 3 WLR 868, [1969] 2 Lloyd's Rep 514, 7 KIR 263, 5 ITR 1, 113
Sol Jo 899, 1970 SC 1, 1970 SLT 37, HL 47.8
Fitzgerald v University of Kent at Canterbury [2004] EWCA Civ 143,
[2004] ICR 737, [2004] IRLR 300, [2004] 11 LS Gaz R 34, (2004) Times,
4 March, 148 Sol Jo LB 237, [2004] All ER (D) 262 (Feb) 20.23, 53.13
Fitzpatrick v British Railways Board [1992] ICR 221, [1991] IRLR
376, CA 54.3
Flack v Kodak Ltd [1986] 2 All ER 1003, [1987] 1 WLR 31, [1986] ICR 775,
[1986] IRLR 255, 130 Sol Jo 713, [1986] LS Gaz R 2238, CA 7.7
Fletcher v Clay Cross (Quarry Services) Ltd. See Clay Cross (Quarry
Services) Ltd v Fletcher
Fletcher v NHS Pensions Agency [2005] ICR 1458, sub nom Fletcher v
Blackpool Fylde & Wyre Hospitals NHS Trust [2005] IRLR 689, [2005]
All ER (D) 57 (Jun), EAT 12.5, 13.27
Flett v Matheson [2005] ICR 1134, [2005] IRLR 412, [2005] All ER (D) 188
(Apr), EAT; revsd [2006] EWCA Civ 53, [2006] IRLR 277, [2006] All
ER (D) 88 (Feb) 16.2, 17.3, 58.15
Fogarty v United Kingdom (Application 37112/97) [2002] IRLR 148, 12
BHRC 132, ECtHR 13.20, 30.4
Folami v Nigerline (UK) Ltd [1978] ICR 277, EAT 9.4

c

Forbuoys Ltd v Rich EAT/144/01 .... 57.22

Ford v Milthorn Toleman Ltd [1980] IRLR 30, CA 53.7

Ford v Stakis Hotels and Inns Ltd [1987] ICR 943, [1988] IRLR 46,
[1987] LS Gaz R 2192, EAT 20.21

Ford v Warwickshire County Council [1983] 2 AC 71, [1983] 1 All ER 753,
[1983] 2 WLR 399, 81 LGR 326, [1983] ICR 273, [1983] IRLR 126, 127
Sol Jo 154, HL 7.7, 47.8

Foreningen af Arbejdsledere i Danmark v Daddy's Dance Hall A/S: 324/86
[1988] ECR 739, [1989] 2 CMLR 517, [1988] IRLR 315, ECJ 52.6, 52.29

Forshaw v Archcraft Ltd [2006] ICR 60, [2005] IRLR 600, [2005] All ER (D)
105 (May), EAT 41.1

Forster v Cartwright Black [2004] ICR 1728, [2004] IRLR 781, [2004] All ER
(D) 93 (Aug), EAT 49.17

Fosca Services (UK) Ltd v Birkett [1996] IRLR 325, EAT 8.23, 58.25

Foster v British Gas plc: C-188/89 [1991] 1 QB 405, [1990] 3 All ER 897,
[1991] 2 WLR 258, [1990] ECR I-3313, [1990] 2 CMLR 833, [1991] ICR
84, [1990] IRLR 353, ECJ; apld [1991] 2 AC 306, [1991] 2 All ER 705,
[1991] 2 WLR 1075, [1991] 2 CMLR 217, [1991] ICR 463, [1991] IRLR
268, [1991] 18 LS Gaz R 34, HL 25.2, 37.7

Foster v D & H Travel Ltd [2006] ICR 1537, [2006] All ER (D) 15
(Aug), EAT 20.38, 21.16

Foster v South Glamorgan Health Authority [1988] ICR 526, [1988] IRLR
277, [1988] 15 LS Gaz R 37, EAT 20.30

Foster Bryant Surveying Ltd v Bryant [2007] EWCA Civ 200, [2007] IRLR
425, [2007] All ER (D) 213 (Mar) 8.13, 9.16

Foster Clark Ltd's Indenture Trusts, Re, Loveland v Horscroft
[1966] 1 All ER 43, [1966] 1 WLR 125, 110 Sol Jo 108 .... 31.10, 58.9

Four Seasons Healthcare Ltd (formerly Cotswold Spa Retirement
Hotels Ltd) v Maughan [2005] IRLR 324, [2005] All ER (D) 24
(Jan), EAT 48.3

Fox v Rangecroft [2006] EWCA Civ 1112, (unreported, 13 July 2006) 14.3

Fozard v Greater Manchester Police Authority IDS Brief No 601 .... 10.11

Francis v Kennedy Scott Ltd [2007] All ER (D) 162 (Jun) 15.4

Francovich and Bonifaci v Italy: C-6/90 and C-9/90 [1991] ECR I-5357,
[1993] 2 CMLR 66, [1995] ICR 722, [1992] IRLR 84, ECJ 25.2

Franks v Reuters Ltd [2003] EWCA Civ 417, [2003] ICR 1166, [2003] IRLR
423, [2003] 25 LS Gaz R 45, (2003) Times, 23 April, 147 Sol Jo LB 474,
[2003] All ER (D) 160 (Apr) 8.3, 17.3, 47.2

Fraser v HLMAD Ltd [2006] EWCA Civ 738, [2007] 1 All ER 383,
[2006] ICR 1395, [2006] IRLR 687, 150 Sol Jo LB 809, [2006] All ER
(D) 152 (Jun) 21.26, 58.39

Freeman v Sovereign Chicken Ltd [1991] ICR 853, [1991] IRLR 408, EAT 21.32

Freer v Glover [2005] EWHC 3341 (QB), [2006] IRLR 521, [2005] All ER
(D) 271 (Dec) 2.4

French v Barclays Bank plc [1998] IRLR 646, CA 55.12

Freud v Bentalls Ltd [1983] ICR 77, [1982] IRLR 443, EAT 54.11

Friend v Institution of Professional Managers and Specialists [1999] IRLR
173 .... 51.22

Table of Cases

Frost v Chief Constable of South Yorkshire Police [1998] QB 254,
  [1997] 1 All ER 540, [1997] 3 WLR 1194, [1997] IRLR 173, 33 BMLR
  108, [1996] NLJR 1651, CA; revsd sub nom White v Chief Constable of
  South Yorkshire Police [1999] 2 AC 455, [1999] 1 All ER 1,
  [1998] 3 WLR 1509, [1999] ICR 216, [1999] IRLR 110, 45 BMLR 1,
  [1999] 02 LS Gaz R 28, [1998] NLJR 1844, [1999] 3 LRC 644, sub nom
  Frost v Chief Constable of South Yorkshire Police 143 Sol Jo LB
  51, HL 27.8
Fry v Foreign and Commonwealth Office [1997] ICR 512, EAT 21.51
Fullarton Computer Industries Ltd v Central Arbitration Committee
  [2001] IRLR 752, Ct of Sess 50.10, 50.31
Fuller v Lloyds Bank plc [1991] IRLR 336, EAT 54.4
Fyfe v Scientific Furnishings Ltd [1989] ICR 648, [1989] IRLR 331, EAT 55.13,
                                                                                                                    58.30
Fytche v Wincanton Logistics plc [2004] UKHL 31, [2004] 4 All ER 221,
  [2004] ICR 975, [2004] IRLR 817, [2004] 31 LS Gaz R 25, (2004) Times,
  2 July, 148 Sol Jo LB 825 .... 28.12

                                                    G
GEC Ferranti Defence Systems Ltd v MSF [1993] IRLR 101, EAT 39.4
GFI Group Inc v Eaglestone [1994] IRLR 119 .... 41.14
GKN Sankey v National Society of Motor Mechanics [1980] ICR 148,
  [1980] IRLR 8, EAT 39.4
GMB v Lambeth Service Team Ltd [2005] All ER (D) 153 (Jul), EAT 39.6
GMB v MAN Truck and Bus UK Ltd [2000] ICR 1101, [2000] IRLR
  636, EAT 39.3
GMB v Susie Radin Ltd [2004] EWCA Civ 180, [2004] 2 All ER 279,
  [2004] ICR 893, [2004] 11 LS Gaz R 34, 148 Sol Jo LB 266, [2004] All
  ER (D) 353 (Feb), sub nom Susie Radin Ltd v GMB [2004] IRLR 400,
  (2004) Times, 16 March 39.6, 52.23
GMB and Amicus v Beloit Walsmsley Ltd [2004] IRLR 18, EAT 39.6
GMM v Hamm IDS Brief No 682 .... 20.25
Galaxy Showers Ltd v Wilson [2006] IRLR 83, [2005] All ER (D) 260
  (Dec), EAT 15.4, 20.19
Gale v Northern General Hospital NHS Trust. See Northern General
  Hospital NHS Trust v Gale
Gallagher v Alpha Catering Services Ltd (t/a Alpha Flight Services)
  [2004] ICR 1489, [2004] All ER (D) 262 (May), EAT; affd [2004] EWCA
  Civ 1559, [2005] ICR 673, [2005] IRLR 102, [2004] All ER (D) 121
  (Nov) 57.2, 57.5, 57.17, 57.29
Galt v Philp [1984] IRLR 156, 1984 SLT 28, JC 45.12
Ganase v Kent Community Housing Trust [2001] All ER (D) 07
  (Jul), EAT 21.17
Gardiner v London Borough of Merton. See Merton London Borough
  Council v Gardiner
Gardiner-Hill v Roland Beiger Technics Ltd [1982] IRLR 498, EAT 55.13, 58.30
Garland v British Rail Engineering Ltd [1983] 2 AC 751, [1982] 2 WLR 918,
  [1981] 2 CMLR 542, [1982] ICR 420, HL; refd 12/81: [1983] 2 AC 751,
  [1982] 2 All ER 402, [1982] 2 WLR 918, [1982] ECR 359,
  [1982] 1 CMLR 696, [1982] ICR 420, [1982] IRLR 111, ECJ; apld
  [1983] 2 AC 751, [1982] 2 All ER 402, [1982] 2 WLR 918,
  [1982] 2 CMLR 174, [1982] ICR 420, [1982] IRLR 257, 126 Sol Jo
  309, HL 42.6

Garrett v Camden London Borough Council [2001] EWCA Civ 395, [2001]
All ER (D) 202 (Mar) 28.25
Gascol Conversions Ltd v Mercer [1974] ICR 420, [1974] IRLR 155, [1975]
KILR 149, 9 ITR 282, 118 Sol Jo 219, CA 34.36
Gate Gourmet London Ltd v Transport and General Workers Union
[2005] EWHC 1889 (QB), [2005] IRLR 881, [2005] 35 LS Gaz R 41,
[2005] All ER (D) 117 (Aug) 30.7
Gateway Hotels Ltd v Stewart [1988] IRLR 287, EAT 52.20
Gbaja-Biamila v DHL International (UK) Ltd [2000] ICR 730, EAT 14.13, 14.18
Gdynia America Shipping Lines (London) Ltd v Chelminski. See Chelminski
v Gdynia America Shipping Lines (London) Ltd
Gee v Shell UK Ltd [2002] EWCA Civ 1479, [2003] IRLR 82,
[2002] 49 LS Gaz R 19, (2002) Times, 4 November, 146 Sol Jo LB 245,
[2002] All ER (D) 350 (Oct) 21.61
General Billposting Co Ltd v Atkinson [1909] AC 118, 78 LJ Ch 77,
[1908–10] All ER Rep 619, 99 LT 943, 25 TLR 178, HL 41.11, 58.34
General Cleaning Contractors Ltd v Christmas [1953] AC 180,
[1952] 2 All ER 1110, [1953] 2 WLR 6, 51 LGR 109, 97 Sol Jo 7, HL ... 27.3, 27.5
General Engineering Services Ltd v Kingston and St Andrew Corpn
[1988] 3 All ER 867, [1989] 1 WLR 69, [1989] ICR 88, [1989] IRLR 35,
133 Sol Jo 20, [1989] 4 LS Gaz R 44, PC 56.2
General of the Salvation Army v Dewsbury [1984] ICR 498, [1984] IRLR
222, EAT 7.3, 23.3, 53.11
General Rolling Stock Co, Re, Chapman's Case (1866) LR 1 Eq 346, 35 Beav
207, 12 Jur NS 44 .... 31.10, 58.9
Genower v Ealing, Hammersmith and Hounslow Area Health Authority
[1980] IRLR 297, EAT 54.14
Georgiou v Colman Coyle (2002) IDS Brief No 705 .... 12.9
Gerster v Freistaat Bayern: C-1/95 [1997] ECR I-5253, [1998] 1 CMLR 303,
[1998] ICR 327, [1997] IRLR 699, ECJ 24.3, 24.11
Gesamtbetriebsrat Der Kühne & Nagel AG & Co KG v Kühne & Nagel AG
& Co KG: C-440/00 [2004] 2 CMLR 1242, [2004] IRLR 332 , [2004] All
ER (D) 31 (Jan), ECJ 18.22
Gibbons v Associated British Ports [1985] IRLR 376 .... 6.4
Gibbs (t/a Jarlands Financial Services) v Harris (EAT0023/07) (unreported) 15.4,
20.19
Gibson v East Riding of Yorkshire Council [2000] ICR 890, [2000] IRLR
598, [2000] All ER (D) 846, CA 29.2, 57.1
Gibson v Motortune Ltd [1990] ICR 740, EAT 7.9
Gibson v Scottish Ambulance Service EATS/0052/04 .... 32.4, 32.14
Gilbank v Miles [2006] EWCA Civ 543, [2006] ICR 1297, [2006] IRLR 538,
[2006] All ER (D) 160 (May) 12.12, 21.23
Gilbert v Kembridge Fibres Ltd [1984] ICR 188, [1984] IRLR 52, EAT 2.4
Gilford Motor Co Ltd v Horne [1933] Ch 935, 102 LJ Ch 212, [1933] All ER
Rep 109, 149 LT 241, CA 41.8
Gilham v Kent County Council [1985] IRLR 16. See Kent County Council v
Gilham
Gilham v Kent County Council (No 2) [1985] ICR 233, [1985] IRLR
18, CA 54.4
Gilham v Kent County Council (No 3) [1986] ICR 52, [1986] IRLR
56, EAT 55.12
Gill v Cremadez [2000] CLY 3876 .... 43.5
Gill v Ford Motor Co Ltd [2004] IRLR 840, [2004] 33 LS Gaz R 34, [2004]
All ER (D) 131 (Jul), EAT 34.6

Table of Cases

Gillespie v Northern Health and Social Services Board: C-342/93 [1996] All
ER (EC) 284, [1996] ECR I-475, [1996] 2 CMLR 969, [1996] ICR 498,
[1996] IRLR 214, ECJ 24.14, 33.14, 42.9
Gillespie v Northern Health and Social Services Board (No 2) [1997] IRLR
410, NICA 24.14
Gimber (W) & Sons Ltd v Spurrett (1967) 2 ITR 308, DC 38.7
Ging v Ellward Lancs Ltd [1991] ICR 222n, 13 ITR 265, EAT 55.12
Giraud UK Ltd v Smith [2000] IRLR 763, EAT 8.24, 48.16, 58.26
Gladwell v Secretary of State for Trade and Industry [2007] ICR 264, [2006]
All ER (D) 154 (Nov), EAT 17.3, 20.9, 31.4
Glasgow City Council v Marshall [2000] 1 All ER 641, [2000] 1 WLR 333,
[2000] LGR 229, [2000] ICR 196, [2000] IRLR 272,
[2000] 07 LS Gaz R 39, 2000 SC (HL) 67, 2000 SLT 429, HL 24.11
Glasgow City Council v Zafar [1998] 2 All ER 953, [1997] 1 WLR 1659,
[1998] ICR 120, [1997] 48 LS Gaz R 29, 1998 SC (HL) 27, 1998 SLT
135, 142 Sol Jo LB 30, sub nom Zafar v Glasgow City Council
[1998] IRLR 36, HL 12.5, 14.3
Gledhow Autoparts Ltd v Delaney [1965] 3 All ER 288, [1965] 1 WLR 1366,
109 Sol Jo 571, CA 41.3
Glenboig Union Fireclay Co Ltd v Stewart (1971) 6 ITR 14, Ct of Sess 58.8
Glendale Managed Services v Graham [2003] EWCA Civ 773, [2003] IRLR
465, (2003) Times, 4 June, [2003] All ER (D) 225 (May) 52.18
Glennie v Independent Magazines (UK) Ltd [1999] IRLR 719, [1999] All ER
(D) 637, CA 22.15
Glenrose (Fish Merchants) Ltd v Chapman IDS Brief No 438 .... 53.17
Gloystane & Co Ltd v Martin [2001] IRLR 15, EAT 21.32
Gogay v Hertfordshire County Council [2000] IRLR 703, [2001] 1 FCR 455,
[2000] Fam Law 883, [2000] All ER (D) 1057, CA 8.13, 8.23
Goldman Sachs Services Ltd v Montali [2002] ICR 1251, CA 21.3, 21.7
Gómez v Continental Industrias del Caucho SA: C-342/01 [2004] ECR
I-2605, [2004] 2 CMLR 38, [2005] ICR 1040, [2004] IRLR 407, [2004]
All ER (D) 350 (Mar), ECJ 29.5, 33.18
Goodeve v Gilsons [1985] ICR 401, 129 Sol Jo 283, CA 38.10
Goodwin v Cabletel UK Ltd [1998] ICR 112, [1997] IRLR 665, EAT 28.8, 54.3
Goodwin v Patent Office [1999] ICR 302, [1999] IRLR 4, EAT 10.2, 10.32
Goodwin v United Kingdom (Application 17488/90) (1996) 22 EHRR 123, 1
BHRC 81, ECtHR 30.5
Goodwin v United Kingdom (Application 28957/95) [2002] IRLR 664,
[2002] 2 FCR 577, [2002] 2 FLR 487, [2002] Fam Law 738, 35 EHRR
447, 13 BHRC 120, 67 BMLR 199, [2002] NLJR 1171, (2002) Times,
12 July, [2002] All ER (D) 158 (Jul), ECtHR 12.6, 24.13, 30.4
Goold (W A) (Pearmak) Ltd v McConnell [1995] IRLR 516, EAT 8.13
Gorictree Ltd v Jenkinson [1985] ICR 51, [1984] IRLR 391, EAT 52.27
Goring v British Actors Equity Association [1987] IRLR 122 .... 51.12, 51.15
Gothard v Mirror Group Newspapers Ltd [1988] ICR 729, [1988] IRLR
396, CA 48.11, 58.21
Gover v Propertycare Ltd [2006] EWCA Civ 286, [2006] All ER (D) 408
(Mar) 22.26
Government Communications Staff Federation v Certification Officer
[1993] ICR 163, [1993] IRLR 260, [1993] 5 LS Gaz R 41, EAT 50.22
Graf v Filzmoser Maschinenbau GmbH: C-190/98 [2000] All ER (EC) 170,
[2000] ECR I-493, [2000] 1 CMLR 741, ECJ 26.2
Grant v In 2 Focus Sales Development Services Ltd (EAT0310/06) 20.16, 20.34,
22.4

Grant v South-West Trains Ltd: C-249/96 [1998] All ER (EC) 193,
    [1998] ECR I-621, [1998] 1 CMLR 993, [1998] ICR 449, [1998] IRLR
    206, [1998] 1 FCR 377, [1998] 1 FLR 839, [1998] Fam Law 392, 3
    BHRC 578, ECJ 30.5
Graphical, Paper and Media Union v Derry Print Ltd [2002] IRLR 380 .... 50.30
Gray v Canada Life Ltd. See Canada Life Ltd v Gray
Greater Manchester Police Authority v Lea [1990] IRLR 372, EAT 12.8
Green v Deustche Bank [2006] EWHC 1898 .... 28.25
Green v Hackney London Borough Council EAT/182/98 .... 21.16
Green (E) & Son (Castings) Ltd v Association of Scientific, Technical and
    Managerial Staffs [1984] ICR 352, [1984] IRLR 135, EAT 39.4, 39.6
Greenaway Harrison Ltd v Wiles [1994] IRLR 380, 501 IRLIB 2, EAT 53.7
Greenhof v Barnsley Metropolitan Borough Council [2006] IRLR 98,
    [2006] ICR 1514, [2005] All ER (D) 347 (Oct), EAT 8.13, 10.15, 14.19
Greenwood v British Airways plc [1999] ICR 969, [1999] IRLR 600 .... 10.4
Gregory v Tudsbury Ltd [1982] IRLR 267, IT 33.3
Gregory v Wallace [1998] IRLR 387, CA 58.21
Greig v Insole [1978] 3 All ER 449, [1978] 1 WLR 302, 122 Sol Jo 163 .... 41.5
Griffin v London Pensions Fund Authority [1993] 2 CMLR 571, [1993] ICR
    564, [1993] IRLR 248, [1993] 11 LS Gaz R 44, EAT 24.18
Griffin v South West Water Services Ltd [1995] IRLR 15 .... 37.7, 39.4
Griffiths v Secretary of State for Social Services [1974] QB 468,
    [1973] 3 All ER 1184, [1973] 3 WLR 831, 117 Sol Jo 873 .... 31.10, 58.9
Griffiths-Henry v Network Rail Infrastructure Ltd [2006] IRLR 865, [2006]
    All ER (D) 15 (Jul), EAT 14.3
Grimaldi v Fonds des Maladies Professionnelles: 322/88 [1989] ECR 4407,
    [1991] 2 CMLR 265, [1990] IRLR 400, ECJ 25.1
Grimmer v KLM Cityhopper UK [2005] IRLR 596, [2005] All ER (D) 218
    (May), EAT 20.16
Group 4 Nightspeed Ltd v Gilbert [1997] IRLR 398, 574 IRLB 13, EAT ... 20.31, 34.8
Gruber v Silhouette International Schmeid GmbH & Co: C-249/97 (1999)
    IDS Brief No 647 .... 24.14
Grundy v British Airways plc EAT/0676/04RN (19 August 2005,
    unreported) 24.10
Grundy (Teddington) Ltd v Plummer [1983] ICR 367, [1983] IRLR
    98, EAT 54.11
Gryf-Lowczowski v Hinchingbrooke Healthcare NHS Trust [2005] EWHC
    2407 (QB), [2006] IRLR 100, 87 BMLR 46, [2005] All ER (D) 21
    (Nov) 48.3, 58.23
Guinness plc v Saunders [1990] 2 AC 663, [1990] 1 All ER 652,
    [1990] 2 WLR 324, [1990] BCLC 402, 134 Sol Jo 457,
    [1990] 9 LS Gaz R 42, HL 9.3, 58.36
Guinness (Arthur) Son & Co (Great Britain) Ltd v Green [1989] ICR 241,
    [1989] IRLR 288, EAT 21.64, 55.12
Guney-Gorres v Securicor Aviation (Germany) Ltd: C-232/04 and C-233/04
    [2006] IRLR 305, [2005] All ER (D) 230 (Dec), ECJ 52.5
Gunning v Mirror Group Newspapers Ltd [1986] 1 All ER 385, sub nom
    Mirror Group Newspapers Ltd v Gunning [1986] 1 WLR 546,
    [1986] ICR 145, [1986] IRLR 27, 130 Sol Jo 242, CA 12.12
Gunton v Richmond-upon-Thames London Borough Council [1981] Ch 448,
    [1980] 3 All ER 577, [1980] 3 WLR 714, 79 LGR 241, [1980] ICR 755,
    [1980] IRLR 321, CA 48.19, 53.9, 58.7, 58.18, 58.25
Gutzmore v J Wardley (Holdings) Ltd [1993] ICR 581, CA 21.64

H

HM Prison Service v Barua [2007] ICR 671, [2007] IRLR 4, [2006] All ER
  (D) 199 (Nov), EAT 15.13, 20.19
HM Prison Service v Beart [2005] IRLR 171, [2004] All ER (D) 370
  (Oct), EAT; affd [2003] EWCA Civ 119, [2003] ICR 1068, [2003] IRLR
  238, (2003) Times, 7 March, [2003] All ER (D) 191 (Jan) 10.12, 14.19
HM Prison Service v Davis (2000) IDS Brief No 666, EAT 12.13, 13.35
HM Prison Service v Dolby [2003] IRLR 694, [2003] All ER (D) 156
  (Jul), EAT 21.17
HM Prison Service v Johnson [1997] ICR 275, [1997] IRLR 162, 567 IRLB
  13, EAT 14.16
HM Prison Service v Salmon [2001] IRLR 425, [2001] All ER (D) 154
  (Apr), EAT 14.17
HMRC v Stringer (13 December 2006, unreported) 29.3
HSBC Bank plc (formerly Midland Bank plc) v Madden [2001] 1 All ER
  550, [2000] ICR 1283, [2000] IRLR 827, [2000] All ER (D) 1137, CA ... 54.4, 54.9
Haddon v Van den Bergh Foods Ltd [1999] ICR 1150, [1999] IRLR 672, 628
  IRLB 3, EAT 54.4
Haden Ltd v Cowen. See Cowen v Haden Ltd
Hadjioannous v Coral Casinos Ltd [1981] IRLR 352, EAT 54.9
Haigh (Catherine) Harlequin Hair Design v Seed [1990] IRLR 175, EAT 48.15
Hair Colour Consultants Ltd v Mena [1984] ICR 671, [1984] IRLR 386,
  [1984] LS Gaz R 2147, EAT 7.9
Hairsine v Kingston upon Hull City Council [1992] ICR 212, [1992] IRLR
  211, EAT 49.2
Halford v Sharples [1992] ICR 146, EAT; affd [1992] 3 All ER 624,
  [1992] 1 WLR 736, [1992] ICR 583, CA 21.13, 21.50, 37.6
Halford v United Kingdom (Application 20605/92) (1997) 24 EHRR 523,
  [1997] IRLR 471, [1998] Crim LR 753, 94 LS Gaz R 24, 3 BHRC 31,
  ECtHR 30.4
Halfpenny v IGE Medical Systems Ltd [1999] ICR 834, [1999] IRLR 177,
  [1999] 1 FLR 944, 143 Sol Jo LB 38, [1998] All ER (D) 769, CA; revsd
  [2001] ICR 73, [2001] IRLR 96, [2000] All ER (D) 2284, HL 12.12, 13.33,
                                                                                  33.21
Hall (Inspector of Taxes) v Lorimer [1994] 1 All ER 250, [1994] 1 WLR 209,
  [1994] STC 23, 66 TC 349, [1994] ICR 218, [1994] IRLR 171,
  [1993] 45 LS Gaz R 45, 137 Sol Jo LB 256, CA 17.3
Hall v Woolston Hall Leisure Ltd [2000] 4 All ER 787, [2001] 1 WLR 225,
  [2001] ICR 99, [2000] IRLR 578, [2000] 24 LS Gaz R 39, [2000] NLJR
  833, CA 8.15, 13.16
Hallam v Avery [2000] 1 WLR 966, [2000] LGR 452, [2000] ICR 583,
  [2000] 01 LS Gaz R 23, 144 Sol Jo LB 32; affd [2001] UKHL 15,
  [2001] 1 WLR 655, [2001] LGR 278, [2001] ICR 408,
  [2001] 21 LS Gaz R 39, 145 Sol Jo LB 116, [2001] IRLR 312 .... 12.13, 13.36
Hamill v EC Commission: 180/87 [1990] 1 All ER 982, [1988] ECR 6141,
  [1990] 1 CMLR 982, ECJ 37.8
Hamilton v Futura Floors Ltd [1990] IRLR 478, OH 6.3
Hamlet v General Municipal Boilermakers and Allied Trades Union
  [1987] 1 All ER 631, [1987] 1 WLR 449, [1987] ICR 150, [1986] IRLR
  293, 131 Sol Jo 470, [1987] LS Gaz R 1327 .... 51.12, 51.15
Hamling v Coxlease School Ltd [2007] ICR 108, [2007] IRLR 8, EAT 20.16, 20.34
Hammersmith and Fulham London Borough Council v Farnsworth
  [2000] IRLR 691, [2000] All ER (D) 812, EAT 10.15

Hampson v Department of Education and Science [1990] 2 All ER 25,
[1989] ICR 179, [1989] IRLR 69, 133 Sol Jo 151,
[1989] 13 LS Gaz R 43, CA; revsd [1991] 1 AC 171, [1990] 2 All ER 513,
[1990] 3 WLR 42, [1990] ICR 511, [1990] IRLR 302, 134 Sol Jo 1123,
[1990] 26 LS Gaz R 39, [1990] NLJR 853, HL 13.8, 13.18
Hancill v Marcon Engineering Ltd [1990] ICR 103, [1990] IRLR 51, EAT 7.9
Handels-og Kontorfunktionaerernes Forbund i Danmark v Dansk
Arbejdsgiverforening, acting on behalf of Danfoss: 109/88 [1989] ECR
3199, [1991] 1 CMLR 8, [1991] ICR 74, [1989] IRLR 532, ECJ 24.11
Handels-og Kontorfunktionaerernes Forbund i Danmark (acting on behalf
of Hoj Pedersen) v Faellesforeningen for Danmarks Brugsforeninger
(acting on behalf of Kvickly Skive): C-66/96 [1998] ECR I-7327,
[1999] 2 CMLR 326, [1999] IRLR 55, sub nom Pedersen v Kvickly Skive
[1999] All ER (EC) 138, [1998] All ER (D) 614, ECJ 24.14
Haniff v Robinson [1993] QB 419, [1993] 1 All ER 185, [1992] 3 WLR 875,
26 HLR 386, [1992] 2 EGLR 111, [1992] 45 EG 145, CA 43.3
Hannah Blumenthal, The. See Wilson (Paal) & Co A/S v Partenreederei
Hannah Blumenthal, The Hannah Blumenthal
Hannan v TNT-IPEC (UK) Ltd [1986] IRLR 165, EAT 54.1
Harada Ltd (t/a Chequepoint UK) v Turner EAT/516/99 .... 26.12
Harding v Wealands [2006] UKHL 32, [2006] 4 All ER 1, [2006] 3 WLR 83,
[2006] RTR 422, [2006] NLJR 1136, (2006) Times, 6 July, [2006] All ER
(D) 40 (Jul) 26.11
Hardman v Mallon (t/a Orchard Lodge Nursing Home) [2002] IRLR 516 .... 12.5
Hardy v Polk (Leeds) Ltd [2004] IRLR 420, [2004] All ER (D) 282
(Mar), EAT 55.13
Hardy v Tourism South East [2005] IRLR 242, [2005] All ER (D) 201
(Jan), EAT 39.4
Hardys & Hansons plc v Lax [2005] EWCA Civ 846, [2005] ICR 1565,
[2005] IRLR 726, (2005) Times, 26 July, [2005] All ER (D) 83 (Jul) 13.8, 33.21
Harford v Swiftrim Ltd [1987] ICR 439, [1987] IRLR 360,
[1987] LS Gaz R 820, EAT 7.9
Haringey Council (Haringey Design Partnership Directorate of Technical
and Environmental Services) v Al-Azzawi (2002) IDS Brief No 703 .... 12.13,
13.35
Harland and Wolff Pension Trustees Ltd v Aon Consulting Financial
Services Ltd [2006] EWHC 1778 (Ch), [2007] ICR 429, [2006] All ER
(D) 216 (Jul) 24.17
Harmer v Cornelius (1858) 22 JP 724, 5 CBNS 236, 28 LJCP 85, 4 Jur NS
1110, 6 WR 749, 141 ER 94, [1843–60] All ER Rep 624, 32 LTOS 62 .... 58.17
Harmony Healthcare plc v Drewery EAT/886/00 .... 21.17
Harper v Virgin Net Ltd [2004] EWCA Civ 271, [2005] ICR 921,
[2004] IRLR 390, (2004) Times, 16 March, 148 Sol Jo LB 353, [2004] All
ER (D) 184 (Mar) 8.23, 53.11, 58.33
Harris v Courage (Eastern) Ltd [1982] ICR 530, [1982] IRLR 509, CA 54.9
Harris v Shuttleworth [1994] ICR 991, [1994] IRLR 547, CA 42.4, 42.14
Harris v Towergate London Market Ltd [2007] All ER (D) 222 (Jun) 15.13
Harris & Russell Ltd v Slingsby [1973] 3 All ER 31, [1973] ICR 454,
[1973] IRLR 221, 15 KIR 157, 8 ITR 433, NIRC 53.5
Harrison v Boots the Chemist Ltd EAT/1098/97 .... 22.15
Harrison v Kent County Council [1995] ICR 434, EAT 51.4
Harrison v Norwest Holst Group Administration Ltd. See Norwest Holst
Group Administration Ltd v Harrison
Harrison Bowden Ltd v Bowden [1994] ICR 186, EAT 52.14

Table of Cases

Harrison (T C) (Newcastle-under-Lyme) Ltd v Ramsey [1976] IRLR 135,
IT 27.36
Harrods Ltd v Remick [1998] 1 All ER 52, [1998] ICR 156, [1997] IRLR
583, CA 13.21
Harrow London Borough v Cunningham [1996] IRLR 256, EAT 54.9
Hart v A R Marshall & Sons (Bulwell) Ltd [1978] 2 All ER 413,
[1977] 1 WLR 1067, [1977] ICR 539, [1977] IRLR 51, 12 ITR 190, 121
Sol Jo 677, EAT 48.3
Hart v English Heritage (Historic Buildings and Monuments Commission for
England) [2006] ICR 655, [2006] IRLR 915, [2006] All ER (D) 343
(Feb), EAT 21.3, 21.7, 21.10, 21.75
Hartlebury Printers Ltd (in liquidation), Re [1993] 1 All ER 470, [1992] ICR
559, [1992] IRLR 516, [1993] BCLC 902, [1992] BCC 428 .... 25.2, 39.2, 39.4, 39.6
Hartwell v A-G of the British Virgin Islands [2004] UKPC 12, [2004] 1 WLR
1273, (2004) Times, 27 February, 148 Sol Jo LB 267, [2004] All ER (D)
372 (Feb) 56.2
Harvest Press Ltd v McCaffrey [1999] IRLR 778, EAT 28.8, 54.3
Harvest Town Circle Ltd v Rutherford [2001] 3 CMLR 691, [2002] ICR 123,
[2001] IRLR 599, [2001] All ER (D) 112 (Jul), EAT 12.8, 53.14
Harvey v Institute of the Motor Industry (No 2) [1996] ICR 981,
[1995] IRLR 416, EAT 14.13
Harvey v Port of Tilbury (London) Ltd [1999] ICR 1030, [1999] IRLR
693, EAT 21.10
Harvey's Household Linens Ltd v Benson [1974] ICR 306, 16 KIR 228, 9
ITR 234, NIRC 20.25
Haseltine Lake & Co v Dowler [1981] ICR 222, [1981] IRLR 25, EAT 53.5, 53.8,
                                                                                                         58.5
Hasley v Fair Employment Agency [1989] IRLR 106, NICA 7.9, 24.9
Hatton v Sutherland [2002] EWCA Civ 76, [2002] 2 All ER 1, [2002] ICR
613, 68 BMLR 115, (2002) Times, 11 February, [2002] All ER (D) 53
(Feb), sub nom Sutherland v Hatton [2002] IRLR 263 .... 28.25
Hawkes v Southwark London Borough (20 February 1998,
unreported), CA 28.18
Hawkins v Ball and Barclays Bank plc [1996] IRLR 258, EAT 14.7, 20.30, 22.10,
                                                                                                         22.14
Hawley v Luminar Leisure Ltd [2006] EWCA Civ 18, [2006] Lloyd's Rep IR
307, [2006] IRLR 817, 150 Sol Jo LB 163, [2006] All ER (D) 158 (Jan) 56.1,
                                                                                                         56.3
Hay v George Hanson (Building Contractors) Ltd [1996] IRLR 427, EAT 52.16
Hay v Surrey County Council [2007] EWCA Civ 93, [2007] All ER (D) 199
(Feb) 10.15
Hayes v Malleable Working Men's Club and Institute [1985] ICR 703,
[1985] IRLR 367, EAT 12.5
Haynes v Doman [1899] 2 Ch 13, 68 LJ Ch 419, 43 Sol Jo 553, 80 LT 569, 15
TLR 354, [1895–9] All ER Rep Ext 1468, CA 41.6, 41.8
Hayward v Cammell Laird Shipbuilders Ltd [1988] AC 894, [1988] 2 All ER
257, [1988] 2 WLR 1134, [1988] ICR 464, [1988] IRLR 257, 132 Sol Jo
750, [1988] NLJR 133, HL 24.5, 24.8, 32.12
Healey v Française Rubastic SA [1917] 1 KB 946, 86 LJKB 1254, 117 LT 92,
33 TLR 300 .... 9.16, 58.28
Health Development Agency v Parish [2004] IRLR 550, [2004] All ER (D)
106 (Jan), EAT 21.70
Heasmans v Clarity Cleaning Co Ltd [1987] ICR 949, [1987] IRLR 286,
[1987] BTLC 174, [1987] NLJ Rep 101, CA 56.2

Heath v Metropolitan Police Comr [2004] EWCA Civ 943, [2005] ICR 329,
  [2005] IRLR 270, 148 Sol Jo LB 913, [2004] All ER (D) 359 (Jul) 14.2
Heathmill Multimedia ASP Ltd v Jones [2003] IRLR 856, [2003] All ER (D)
  440 (Oct), EAT 51.21
Hedley Byrne & Co Ltd v Heller & Partners Ltd [1964] AC 465,
  [1963] 2 All ER 575, [1963] 3 WLR 101, [1963] 1 Lloyd's Rep 485, 107
  Sol Jo 454, HL 40.5
Heggie v Uniroyal Englebert Tyres Ltd [1998] IRLR 425, EAT; revsd
  [1999] IRLR 802, Ct of Sess 55.13
Heinz (H J) Co Ltd v Kenrick [2000] ICR 491, [2000] IRLR 144, 635 IRLB
  10, EAT 10.11, 10.15, 54.8
Hellyer Bros Ltd v Atkinson and Dickinson [1992] IRLR 540, EAT; revsd
  [1994] IRLR 88, CA 48.2
Hellyer Bros Ltd v McLeod [1987] 1 WLR 728, [1987] ICR 526, 131 Sol Jo
  805, [1987] LS Gaz R 1056, sub nom McLeod v Hellyer Bros Ltd
  [1987] IRLR 232, CA 17.3, 47.8
Helmet Integrated Systems Ltd v Tunnard [2006] EWCA Civ 1735,
  [2007] IRLR 126, [2006] All ER (D) 228 (Dec) 8.13, 9.16, 41.13
Hely-Hutchinson v Brayhead Ltd [1968] 1 QB 549, [1967] 2 All ER 14,
  [1967] 2 WLR 1312, 111 Sol Jo 329; affd [1968] 1 QB 549,
  [1967] 3 All ER 98, [1967] 3 WLR 1408, 111 Sol Jo 830, CA 9.7
Hempell v W H Smith & Sons Ltd [1986] ICR 365, [1986] IRLR 95, EAT 38.12
Henderson v Henderson (1843) 3 Hare 100, [1843–60] All ER Rep 378, 1
  LTOS 410 .... 14.8, 21.26
Hendricks v Metropolitan Police Comr [2002] EWCA Civ 1686,
  [2003] 1 All ER 654, [2003] ICR 530, [2003] IRLR 96,
  [2003] 05 LS Gaz R 30, (2002) Times, 6 December, 146 Sol Jo LB 274,
  [2002] All ER (D) 407 (Nov) 14.6, 20.29
Hendry v Scottish Liberal Club [1977] IRLR 5, IT 19.3
Henfdrickson Europe Ltd v Pipe UKEAT/0272/02 .... 32.4, 32.19
Henke v Gemeinde Schierke and Verwaltungsgemeinschaft Brocken:
  C-298/94 [1997] All ER (EC) 173, [1996] ECR I-4989, [1997] 1 CMLR
  373, [1997] ICR 746, [1996] IRLR 701, ECJ 18.4, 37.2, 52.9
Hennessy v Craigmyle & Co Ltd [1986] ICR 461, [1986] IRLR 300, 130 Sol
  Jo 633, [1986] LS Gaz R 2160, CA 2.4, 22.26
Henry v London General Transport Services Ltd [2002] EWCA Civ 488,
  [2002] IRLR 472, [2002] All ER (D) 322 (Mar) 6.3, 34.6
Hereford and Worcester County Council v Neale. See Neale v Hereford and
  Worcester County Council
Heron v Citilink-Nottingham [1993] IRLR 372, EAT 54.11
Heron Corpn Ltd v Commis [1980] ICR 713, EAT 13.11
Herrero (Sarkatzis) v Instituto Madrileno de la Salud (Imsalud): C-294/04
  [2006] IRLR 296, [2006] All ER (D) 220 (Feb), ECJ 12.5
Hertaing v Benoidt: C-305/94 [1997] All ER (EC) 40, [1996] ECR I-5927,
  [1997] 1 CMLR 329, [1997] IRLR 127, ECJ 52.13
Hewcastle Catering Ltd v Ahmed and Elkamah [1992] ICR 626,
  [1991] IRLR 473, CA 8.15
Hewlett Packard Ltd v O'Murphy [2002] IRLR 4, [2001] All ER (D) 91
  (Sep), EAT 17.3, 47.2
Hidalgo v Asociacion de Servicios Aser and Sociedad Cooperativa Minerva:
  C-173/96 [1998] ECR I-8237, [2002] ICR 73, [1999] IRLR 136, ECJ 52.5
High Table Ltd v Horst [1998] ICR 409, [1997] IRLR 513, sub nom Horst v
  High Table Ltd [1997] 28 LS Gaz R 25, 141 Sol Jo LB 161, CA 8.13, 21.63,
                                                                                                    38.7

Table of Cases

Higham v Horton. See Horton v Higham

Hilde Schönheit v Stadt Frankfurt am Main: C-4/02 and C-5/02 [2003] ECR I-12575, [2004] IRLR 983, [2003] All ER (D) 401 (Oct), ECJ 13.8, 24.11, 42.9

Hill v Chapell [2003] IRLR 19, [2002] All ER (D) 461 (May), EAT 29.4

Hill v General Accident Fire and Life Assurance Corpn plc [1998] IRLR 641, 1999 SLT 1157, 1998 SCLR 1030, 609 IRLB 8, OH 8.13, 42.13, 44.15, 58.19

Hill v Revenue Comrs: C-243/95 [1998] All ER (EC) 722, [1998] ECR I-3739, [1998] 3 CMLR 81, [1999] ICR 48, [1998] IRLR 466, [1998] 34 LS Gaz R 33, [1998] All ER (D) 277, ECJ 24.3

Hill (William) Organisation Ltd v Tucker [1999] ICR 291, [1998] IRLR 313, [1998] 20 LS Gaz R 33, 142 Sol Jo LB 140, CA 8.13, 8.24, 58.21

Hillingdon London Borough Council v Commission for Racial Equality [1982] AC 779, [1982] 3 WLR 159, 80 LGR 737, [1982] IRLR 424, 126 Sol Jo 449, HL 14.27, 14.28

Hillman v London General Transport Services Ltd (14 April 1999, unreported), EAT 37.7

Hills v Co-operative Wholesale Society Ltd [1940] 2 KB 435, [1940] 3 All ER 233, 109 LJKB 972, 84 Sol Jo 658, 163 LT 167, 56 TLR 875, CA 8.23, 58.39

Hillsdown Holdings plc v Pensions Ombudsman [1997] 1 All ER 862, [1996] PLR 427 .... 42.13

Hilton v Shiner Ltd Builders Merchants [2001] IRLR 727, [2001] All ER (D) 316 (May), EAT 8.13

Hilton International Hotels (UK) Ltd v Faraji [1994] ICR 259, [1994] IRLR 267, EAT 55.12, 55.13

Hilton International Hotels (UK) Ltd v Protopapa [1990] IRLR 316, EAT 53.7

Hilton UK Hotels Ltd v McNaughton [2006] All ER (D) 327 (May) 14.33, 21.34

Hindle Gears Ltd v McGinty [1985] ICR 111, [1984] IRLR 477, EAT 53.5, 58.5

Hinton v University of East London [2005] EWCA Civ 532, [2005] ICR 1260, [2005] IRLR 552, [2005] NLJ 827, 149 Sol Jo LB 637, [2005] All ER (D) 83 (May) 21.34, 53.20, 55.22

Hitchcock v Post Office [1980] ICR 100, EAT 17.3

Hivac Ltd v Park Royal Scientific Instruments Ltd [1946] Ch 169, [1946] 1 All ER 350, 115 LJ Ch 241, 90 Sol Jo 175, 174 LT 422, 62 TLR 231, CA 9.16

Hockenjos v Secretary of State for Social Security [2004] EWCA Civ 1749, [2005] IRLR 471, [2005] 1 FCR 286, (2005) Times, 4 January, [2004] All ER (D) 331 (Dec) 13.8

Hodgson v Scarlett (1818) 1 B & Ald 232 .... 40.4

Hoeffler v Kwik Save Stores Ltd EAT/803/97 .... 21.35

Hogg v Dover College [1990] ICR 39, EAT 8.22, 48.1

Holc-Gale v Makers UK Ltd [2006] ICR 462, [2006] IRLR 178, [2005] All ER (D) 361 (Dec), EAT 15.11

Holdsworth (Harold) & Co (Wakefield) Ltd v Caddies [1955] 1 All ER 725, [1955] 1 WLR 352, 99 Sol Jo 234, HL 9.5

Holland v Glendale Industries Ltd [1998] ICR 493, EAT 48.19, 53.7

Hollister v National Farmers' Union [1979] ICR 542, [1979] IRLR 238, CA 54.14

Homan v Al Bacon Co Ltd [1996] ICR 721, EAT 55.6

Home Counties Dairies Ltd v Skilton [1970] 1 All ER 1227, [1970] 1 WLR 526, 114 Sol Jo 107, CA 41.3, 41.6

Home Office v Ayres [1992] ICR 175, [1992] IRLR 59, EAT 34.6

Home Office v Bailey [2005] IRLR 757, [2005] All ER (D) 499 (Jul), EAT 24.7, 24.11

Home Office v Coyne [2000] ICR 1443, [2000] IRLR 838, [2000] All ER (D) 1081, CA 12.12
Home Office v Robinson [1982] ICR 31, [1981] IRLR 524, EAT 37.2
Home Office v Saunders [2006] ICR 318, EAT 12.5
Hone v Six Continents Retail Ltd [2005] EWCA Civ 922, [2006] IRLR 49 .... 57.21
Hooper v British Railways Board [1988] IRLR 517, CA 8.10, 54.4
Hoover Ltd v Forde [1980] ICR 239, EAT 55.13
Hopkins v Norcros plc [1994] ICR 11, [1994] IRLR 18, CA 55.13, 58.30
Hopley Dodd v Highfield Motors (Derby) Ltd (1969) 4 ITR 289 .... 58.9
Holc-Gale v Makers UK Ltd [2006] ICR 462, [2006] IRLR 178, [2005] All
 ER (D) 361 (Dec), EAT 14.9, 15.4, 20.19, 24.22
Horcal Ltd v Gatland [1984] IRLR 288, [1984] BCLC 549, CA 9.16
Horkulak v Cantor Fitzgerald International [2003] EWHC 1918 (QB),
 [2004] ICR 697, [2003] IRLR 756, [2003] All ER (D) 542 (Jul); revsd in
 part [2004] EWCA Civ 1287, [2005] ICR 402, [2004] IRLR 942, 148 Sol
 Jo LB 1218, [2004] All ER (D) 170 (Oct) 8.13, 53.7, 58.25, 58.28
Horst v High Table Ltd. See High Table Ltd v Horst
Horton v Higham [2004] EWCA Civ 941, [2004] 3 All ER 852, [2004] All ER
 (D) 261 (Jul), sub nom 1 Pump Court Chambers v Horton
 [2004] 33 LS Gaz R 34, sub nom Higham v Meurig Lestyn Horton 148
 Sol Jo LB 911 .... 13.9
Horton v Taplin Contracts Ltd [2002] EWCA Civ 1604, [2003] ICR 179,
 [2003] 01 LS Gaz R 24, [2003] PIQR P180, [2003] BLR 74, (2002)
 Times, 25 November, 146 Sol Jo LB 256, [2002] All ER (D) 122 (Nov) 28.12
Hotson v Wisbech Conservative Club [1984] ICR 859, [1984] IRLR
 422, EAT 20.35
Hough v Leyland DAF Ltd [1991] ICR 696, [1991] IRLR 194, EAT 22.17, 39.2,
 39.4, 54.11
Hounslow London Borough Council v Miller (EAT0645/06) (unreported) 20.16
Hounslow London Borough Council v Bhatt [2001] IDS Brief
 No 692, EAT 12.10
Housing Corpn v Bryant [1999] ICR 123, sub nom Bryant v Housing Corpn
 [1998] 26 LS Gaz R 31, 142 Sol Jo LB 181, CA 14.8, 21.10
Housing Services Agency v Cragg [1997] ICR 1050, [1997] IRLR 380, 569
 IRLB 8, EAT 53.15
Howard v Millrise Ltd (t/a Colourflow) (in liquidation) [2005] ICR 435,
 [2005] IRLR 84, [2004] All ER (D) 436 (Nov), EAT 52.23
Howlett Marine Services Ltd v Bowlam [2001] ICR 595, [2001] IRLR 201,
 [2000] All ER (D) 2494, EAT 20.25, 20.26, 20.33, 39.6
Howman & Son v Blyth [1983] ICR 416, [1983] IRLR 139, EAT 44.2
Hoyland v Asda Stores Ltd [2005] ICR 1235, [2005] IRLR 438, [2005] All
 ER (D) 219 (Apr) 12.5, 24.5, 33.8
Huddersfield Fine Worsteds Ltd, Re, Krasner v McMath [2005] EWCA Civ
 1072, [2005] 4 All ER 886, [2006], ICR 205, [2005] NLJR 1355, [2005]
 All ER (D) 65 (Aug) 31.11
Hudson v GMB [1990] IRLR 67 .... 51.12
Hudson v Ridge Manufacturing Co Ltd [1957] 2 QB 348, [1957] 2 All ER
 229, [1957] 2 WLR 948, 101 Sol Jo 409 .... 27.7
Hugh-Jones v St John's College Cambridge [1979] ICR 848, 123 Sol Jo
 603, EAT 13.18
Hughes v Department of Health and Social Security [1985] AC 776,
 [1985] 2 WLR 866, [1985] ICR 419, 129 Sol Jo 315, sub nom
 Department of Health and Social Security v Hughes [1985] IRLR
 263, HL 53.14

Table of Cases

Hughes v Greenwich London Borough Council [1994] 1 AC 170,
[1993] 4 All ER 577, [1993] 3 WLR 821, 92 LGR 61, 69 P & CR 487,
[1994] ICR 48, 26 HLR 99, [1993] 46 LS Gaz R 38, [1993] NLJR 1571n,
137 Sol Jo LB 244, HL 43.7
Hughes v Southwark London Borough Council [1988] IRLR 55 .... 8.23
Hunter v British Coal Corpn [1999] QB 140, [1998] 2 All ER 97,
[1998] 3 WLR 685, [1999] ICR 72, [1998] 12 LS Gaz R 27, 142 Sol Jo
LB 85, CA 27.8
Hurley v Mustoe (No 2) [1983] ICR 422, EAT 14.12
Hurt v Sheffield Corpn (1916) 85 LJKB 1684 .... 29.9
Hussain v Elonex plc [1999] IRLR 420, CA 54.10
Hussain v HM Prison Service (2002) IDS Brief No 713, EAT 12.13, 13.39
Hussain v New Taplow Paper Mills Ltd [1987] 1 All ER 417, [1987] 1 WLR
336, [1987] ICR 28, 131 Sol Jo 358, [1987] LS Gaz R 1242, CA; affd
[1988] AC 514, [1988] 1 All ER 541, [1988] 2 WLR 266, [1988] ICR 259,
[1988] IRLR 167, 132 Sol Jo 226, [1988] 10 LS Gaz R 45, [1988] NLJR
45, HL 44.9
Hussman Manufacturing Ltd v Weir [1998] IRLR 288, 599 IRLB 5, EAT 34.6
Hutchinson v Westward Television Ltd [1977] ICR 279, [1977] IRLR 69, 12
ITR 125, EAT 20.30
Hutton v Parker (1839) 7 Dowl 739 .... 41.10
Hyde v Lehman Bros Ltd [2004] All ER (D) 40 (Aug), EAT 20.31
Hydra plc v Anastasi [2005] EWHC 1559 (QB), [2005] All ER (D) 276
(Jul) 41.8
Hynd v Armstrong [2007] CSIH 16, [2007] IRLR 338 .... 52.26

I

ICTS (UK) Ltd v Tchoula [2000] IRLR 643, [2000] All ER (D) 614, EAT 14.16,
14.18
Ibe v McNally [2005] EWHC 1551 (Ch), [2005] STC 1426, sub nom
Redundant Employee v McNally (Inspector of Taxes) [2005] All ER (D)
389 (Mar) 46.8
Ibex Trading Co Ltd v Walton [1994] ICR 907, [1994] IRLR 564, [1994]
BCC 982, EAT 52.26
Iceland Frozen Foods Ltd v Jones [1983] ICR 17, [1982] IRLR 439, EAT 54.4
Igbo v Johnson Matthey Chemicals Ltd [1986] ICR 505, [1986] IRLR 215,
130 Sol Jo 524, [1986] LS Gaz R 2089, CA 53.19
Iggesund Converters Ltd v Lewis [1984] ICR 544, [1984] IRLR 431, EAT 21.60
Imperial Group Pension Trust Ltd v Imperial Tobacco Ltd [1991] 2 All ER
597, [1991] 1 WLR 589, [1991] ICR 524, [1991] IRLR 66 .... 42.13
Income Tax Special Purposes Comrs v Pemsel [1891] AC 531, 3 TC 53, 55 JP
805, 61 LJQB 265, [1891–4] All ER Rep 28, 65 LT 621, 7 TLR
657, HL 12.6
Industrial Rubber Products v Gillon [1977] IRLR 389, 13 ITR 100, EAT 53.7
Ingram v Bristol Street Parts [2007] All ER (D) 345 (May) 15.2, 15.10
Ingram v Foxon [1984] ICR 685, [1985] IRLR 5, EAT 7.7
Initial Electronic Security Systems Ltd v Avdic [2005] IRLR 671, [2005] All
ER (D) 335 (Jul), EAT 20.25
Initial Supplies Ltd v McCall 1992 SLT 67 .... 52.10
IRC v Ainsworth [2005] EWCA Civ 441, [2005] ICR 1149, [2005] IRLR 465,
[2005] NLJR 744 .... 20.9, 20.31, 29.3, 29.6, 57.22

IRC v Bebb Travel plc [2002] 4 All ER 534, [2003] ICR 201, [2002] IRLR
    783, [2002] NLJR 1350, (2002) Times, 30 October, [2002] All ER (D)
    105 (Aug), EAT; affd [2003] EWCA Civ 563, [2003] 3 All ER 546,
    [2003] ICR 1271, [2003] NLJR 633, (2003) Times, 25 April, 147 Sol Jo
    LB 505, [2003] All ER (D) 291 (Apr) 34.13
IRC v Post Office Ltd [2003] ICR 546, [2003] IRLR 199, [2002] All ER (D)
    282 (Dec), EAT 34.9
IRC v St Hermans Estate Co Ltd [2002] IRLR 788, [2002] All ER (D) 58
    (Jul), EAT 34.13
Inner London Education Authority v Gravett [1988] IRLR 497, EAT 54.9
Insitu Cleaning Co Ltd v Heads [1995] IRLR 4, EAT 12.12
Institution of Professional Civil Servants v Secretary of State for Defence
    [1987] 3 CMLR 35, [1987] IRLR 373 .... 52.23
Inter-Environnement Wallonie ASBL v Region Wallonie: C-129/96
    [1997] ECR I-7411, [1998] All ER (EC) 155, [1998] 1 CMLR 1057,
    ECJ 25.2
Intercity West Coast Ltd v National Union of Rail, Maritime and Transport
    Workers [1996] IRLR 583, CA 45.14
International Computers v Kennedy [1981] IRLR 28, EAT 58.5
International Consulting Services (UK) Ltd v Hart [2000] IRLR 227 .... 41.8
International Packaging Corpn (UK) Ltd v Balfour [2003] IRLR 11, [2002]
    All ER (D) 146 (Nov) 34.6
International Sports Co Ltd v Thomson [1980] IRLR 340, EAT 54.8
Investors' Compensation Scheme Ltd v West Bromwich Building Society
    [1998] 1 All ER 98, [1998] 1 WLR 896, [1998] 1 BCLC 493,
    [1997] NLJR 989, [1997] CLC 1243, [1997] PNLR 541, HL 8.9
Irani v Southampton and South West Hampshire Health Authority
    [1985] ICR 590, [1985] IRLR 203 .... 8.23
Iron and Steel Trades Confederation v ASW Ltd (in liquidation)
    [2004] IRLR 926, [2004] All ER (D) 101 (Sep), EAT 22.22
Ironmonger v Movefield Ltd (t/a Deering Appointments) [1988] IRLR
    461, EAT 17.3, 47.2
Ironsides Ray & Vials v Lindsay [1994] ICR 384, [1994] IRLR 318, EAT 20.18,
                                                                                        21.76
Irving and Irving v Post Office [1987] IRLR 289, CA 13.35
Iske v P & O European Ferries (Dover) Ltd [1997] IRLR 401, EAT 12.5, 24.14
Isles of Scilly Council v Brintel Helicopters Ltd [1995] ICR 249, [1995] IRLR
    6, EAT 52.5
Item Software (UK) Ltd v Fassihi [2002] EWHC 3116 (Ch), [2003] IRLR
    769, [2003] 2 BCLC 1, [2002] All ER (D) 62 (Dec); revsd in part
    [2004] EWCA Civ 1244, [2005] ICR 450, [2004] IRLR 928,
    [2005] 2 BCLC 91, [2004] 39 LS Gaz R 34, (2004) Times, 21 October,
    148 Sol Jo LB 1153, [2004] All ER (D) 187 (Sep) ... 8.13, 9.16, 34.22, 58.20, 58.28
Ivory v Palmer [1975] ICR 340, 119 Sol Jo 405, CA 43.4
Iwanuszezak v General Municipal Boilermakers and Allied Trades Union
    [1988] IRLR 219, CA 51.2
Ixora Trading Inc v Jones [1990] FSR 251 .... 8.13

                                            J
JMCC Holdings Ltd v Conroy [1990] ICR 179, EAT 21.22
Jackson v Ghost Ltd [2003] IRLR 824, [2003] All ER (D) 17 (Sep), EAT 53.15
Jackson v Invicta Plastics Ltd [1987] BCLC 329 .... 58.17

Table of Cases

Jaffrey v Department of the Environment Transport, and the Regions
[2002] IRLR 688, [2002] All ER (D) 111 (Jul), EAT 12.7
Jakeman v South West Thames Regional Health Authority and London
Ambulance Service [1990] IRLR 62 .... 8.23, 34.14
James v Blockbuster Entertainment Ltd [2006] EWCA Civ 684, [2006] IRLR
630, [2006] All ER (D) 360 (May)... 21.16, 21.17
James v Eastleigh Borough Council [1990] 2 AC 751, [1990] 2 All ER 607,
[1990] 3 WLR 55, 88 LGR 756, [1990] ICR 554, [1990] IRLR 288,
[1990] 27 LS Gaz R 41, [1990] NLJR 926, HL 12.6
James v Great Eastern Railway UKEAT/0496/04/SM 32.5, 32.6
James v Greenwich London Borough Council [2007] ICR 577, [2007] IRLR
168, [2007] All ER (D) 12 (Jan), EAT 17.3, 47.2
James v Redcats (Brands) Ltd [2007] IRLR 296, [2007] All ER (D) 270
(Feb), EAT 17.3, 17.9, 29.2, 34.10
Jämställdhetsombudsmannen v Örebro läns landsting: C-236/98 [2000] ECR
I-2189, [2000] 2 CMLR 708, [2001] ICR 249, [2000] IRLR 421, ECJ 24.5
Janata Bank v Ahmed [1981] ICR 791, [1981] IRLR 457, CA 8.24
Janciuk v Winerite Ltd [1998] IRLR 63, EAT 8.23, 58.25
Janes Solicitors v Lamb-Simpson (1996) 541 IRLB 15, EAT 29.9
Jarnell v Department of the Environment [1985] AC 776, [1985] 2 WLR 866,
[1985] ICR 419, [1985] IRLR 263, 129 Sol Jo 315, HL 53.14
Jeetle v Elster [1985] ICR 389, [1985] IRLR 227, EAT 7.9, 52.3
Jenkins v Kingsgate (Clothing Production) [1981] 1 WLR 1485,
[1980] 1 CMLR 81, [1981] ICR 715, [1980] IRLR 6, 125 Sol Jo
587, EAT 24.10, 24.11
Jenkins v P & O European Ferries (Dover) Ltd [1991] ICR 652, EAT 22.25
Jenvey v Australian Broadcasting Corpn [2002] EWHC 927 (QB), [2003] ICR
79, [2002] IRLR 520, [2002] All ER (D) 179 (Apr)................................ 8.13
Jeremiah v Ministry of Defence. See Ministry of Defence v Jeremiah
Jiad v Byford [2003] EWCA Civ 135, [2003] IRLR 232, [2003] All ER (D)
299 (Jan) 12.12
Jiménez Melgar v Ayuntamiento de Los Barrios: C-438/99 [2001] ECR
I-6915, [2003] 3 CMLR 67, [2004] ICR 610, [2001] IRLR 848, [2001] All
ER (D) 42 (Oct), ECJ... 12.5
Jiminez v Southwark London Borough Council [2003] EWCA Civ 502,
[2003] ICR 1176, [2003] IRLR 477, [2003] 23 LS Gaz R 37, (2003)
Times, 1 May, 147 Sol Jo LB 476, [2003] All ER (D) 123 (Apr) 21.61
John v Rees [1970] Ch 345, [1969] 2 All ER 274, [1969] 2 WLR 1294, 113 Sol
Jo 487 .... 55.13
Johnson v Chief Adjudication Officer (No 2): C-410/92 [1995] All ER (EC)
258, [1994] ECR I-5483, [1995] 1 CMLR 725, [1995] ICR 375,
[1995] IRLR 157, ECJ.. 25.2
Johnson v Coventry Churchill International Ltd [1992] 3 All ER 14 .... 26.11
Johnson v Ryan [2000] ICR 236, EAT 17.8
Johnson v Unisys Ltd [2001] UKHL 13, [2003] 1 AC 518, [2001] 2 All ER
801, [2001] 2 WLR 1076, [2001] ICR 480, [2001] IRLR 279 ...... 8.13, 8.23, 55.12,
58.18, 58.29
Johnson Underwood Ltd v Montgomery [2001] EWCA Civ 318, [2001] ICR
819, [2001] 20 LS Gaz R 40, [2001] All ER (D) 101 (Mar), sub nom
Montgomery v Johnson Underwood Ltd [2001] IRLR 269, ... 17.1, 17.3, 47.2
Johnston v Chief Constable of the Royal Ulster Constabulary: 222/84
[1987] QB 129, [1986] 3 All ER 135, [1986] 3 WLR 1038, [1986] ECR
1651, [1986] 3 CMLR 240, [1987] ICR 83, [1986] IRLR 263, 130 Sol Jo
953, [1987] LS Gaz R 188, ECJ 13.19, 25.6

Johnstone v Bloomsbury Health Authority [1992] QB 333, [1991] 2 All ER
    293, [1991] 2 WLR 1362, [1991] ICR 269, [1991] IRLR 118, [1991] 2
    Med LR 38, CA 8.13
Jones v Associated Tunnelling Co Ltd [1981] IRLR 477, EAT 8.13, 8.22
Jones v DAS Legal Expenses Insurance Co Ltd [2003] EWCA Civ 1071,
    [2004] IRLR 218, 147 Sol Jo LB 932, [2003] All ER (D) 425 (Jul).... 21.50, 22.12,
                                                                                                30.7
Jones v Friends Provident Life Office [2004] IRLR 783, NICA 13.21
Jones v Governing Body of Burdett Coutts School [1997] ICR 390, 571
    IRLB 9, EAT; revsd [1999] ICR 38, [1998] IRLR 521,
    [1998] 18 LS Gaz R 32, 142 Sol Jo LB 142, CA 22.15, 38.12
Jones v Gwent County Council [1992] IRLR 521 .... 8.23
Jones v Mid-Glamorgan County Council [1997] ICR 815, [1997] IRLR
    685, CA 53.8
Jones v Post Office [2001] EWCA Civ 558, [2001] ICR 805, [2001] IRLR 384,
    [2001] All ER (D) 133 (Apr) 10.11
Jones v Secretary of State for Employment [1982] ICR 389, EAT 31.4
Jones v 3M Healthcare Ltd [2003] UKHL 33, [2003] 4 All ER 1113,
    [2003] 2 CMLR 1329, [2003] ICR 867, [2003] IRLR 484, 74 BMLR 109,
    [2003] 30 LS Gaz R 30, (2003) Times, 23 June, 147 Sol Jo LB 782, [2003]
    All ER (D) 258 (Jun) 10.17, 12.12
Jones v Tower Boot Co Ltd [1995] IRLR 529, EAT; revsd [1997] 2 All ER
    406, [1997] ICR 254, [1997] IRLR 168, [1997] NLJR 60, CA 12.13, 13.35, 56.1
Jones v University of Manchester [1993] ICR 474, [1993] IRLR 218,
    [1993] 10 LS Gaz R 33, 137 Sol Jo LB 14, CA 12.8, 13.8
Jørgensen v Foreningen af Speciallæger: C-226/98 [2000] ECR I-2447,
    [2002] 1 CMLR 1151, [2000] IRLR 726, ECJ 13.8
Jowett (Angus) & Co Ltd v National Union of Tailors and Garment
    Workers [1985] ICR 646, [1985] IRLR 326, EAT 39.6, 52.19
Jowitt v Pioneer Technology (UK) Ltd [2003] EWCA Civ 411, [2003] ICR
    1120, [2003] IRLR 356, [2003] All ER (D) 263 (Mar) 44.14, 44.17
Judge v Crown Leisure Ltd [2005] EWCA Civ 571, [2005] IRLR 823, [2005]
    All ER (D) 283 (Apr) 8.3
Junk v Kuhnel: C-188/03 [2005] IRLR 310, [2005] All ER (D) 264 (Jan),
    ECJ 39.4
Jupiter General Insurance Co Ltd v Shroff [1937] 3 All ER 67, PC 58.17
Justfern Ltd v D'Ingerthorpe [1994] ICR 286, [1994] IRLR 164, EAT 7.9, 55.13

K

KB v National Health Service Pensions Agency: C-117/01 [2004] All ER
    (EC) 1089, [2004] 1 CMLR 931, [2004] ICR 781, [2004] IRLR 240,
    [2004] 1 FLR 683, (2004) Times, 15 January, [2004] All ER (D) 03 (Jan),
    ECJ 24.13, 42.7
Kachelmann v Bankhaus Hermann Lampe KG: C-322/98 [2000] ECR
    I-7505, [2002] 1 CMLR 155, [2001] IRLR 49, ECJ 12.9
Kalanke v Freie Hansestadt Bremen: C-450/93 [1996] All ER (EC) 66,
    [1995] ECR I-3051, [1996] 1 CMLR 175, [1996] ICR 314, [1995] IRLR
    660, ECJ 12.5, 12.12, 13.9, 37.2
Kalliope Schöning-Kougebetopoulou v Freie und Hansestadt Hamburg. See
    Schöning-Kougebetopoulou v Freie und Hansestadt Hamburg
Kapadia v Lambeth London Borough Council [2000] IRLR 14, EAT; affd
    [2000] IRLR 699, 57 BMLR 170, [2000] All ER (D) 785, CA 10.7

Table of Cases

Kapfunde v Abbey National plc [1999] ICR 1, [1998] IRLR 583, 46 BMLR
176, CA 40.7
Kapur v Shields [1976] 1 All ER 873, [1976] 1 WLR 131, [1976] ICR 26, 120
Sol Jo 96 .... 53.15
Katsikas v Konstantinidis: C-132/91, C-138/91 and C-139/91 [1992] ECR
I-6577, [1993] 1 CMLR 845, [1993] IRLR 179, ECJ 52.16
Kaur v MG Rover Group Ltd [2004] IRLR 279 .... 6.3
Kavanagh v Hiscock [1974] QB 600, [1974] 2 All ER 177, [1974] 2 WLR 421,
[1974] ICR 282, [1974] IRLR 121, 16 KIR 31, [1974] Crim LR 255, 118
Sol Jo 98 .... 45.10
Keeley v Fosroc International Ltd [2006] EWCA Civ 1277, [2006] IRLR 961,
[2006] 40 LS Gaz R 33, 150 Sol Jo LB 1328, [2006] All ER (D) 65
(Oct) 8.11
Keen v Commerzbank AG [2006] EWCA Civ 1536, [2007] ICR 623, [2006]
All ER (D) 239 (Nov), sub nom Commerzbank AG v Keen
[2007] IRLR 132 .... 8.13, 8.21
Kells v Pilkington plc [2002] IRLR 693, [2002] All ER (D) 33 (May), EAT 24.9
Kelly-Madden v Manor Surgery [2007] ICR 203, [2007] IRLR 17, [2006] All
ER (D) 232 (Oct), EAT 54.4, 55.13
Kelly v Northern Ireland Housing Executive [1999] 1 AC 428, [1998] 3 WLR
735, [1998] ICR 828, [1998] IRLR 593, [1998] 36 LS Gaz R 31, 142 Sol
Jo LB 254, HL 12.12
Kelly v Upholstery and Cabinet Works (Amesbury) Ltd [1977] IRLR
91, EAT 39.4, 54.11
Kelman v Care Contract Services Ltd [1995] ICR 260, EAT 52.5
Kenny v Hampshire Constabulary [1998] ICR 27, [1999] IRLR 76, EAT 10.11,
10.14
Kenny v South Manchester College [1993] ICR 934, [1993] IRLR 265 .... 52.5
Kent County Council v Gilham [1985] ICR 227, sub nom Gilham v Kent
County Council [1985] IRLR 16, CA 48.14
Kent Free Press v NGA [1987] IRLR 267 .... 45.16
Kent Management Services Ltd v Butterfield [1992] ICR 272, [1992] IRLR
394, EAT 34.6
Kerr v Sweater Shop (Scotland) Ltd [1996] IRLR 424, EAT 34.6
Kerry Foods Ltd v Creber [2000] ICR 556, [2000] IRLR 10, EAT 39.6, 52.26
Kerry Foods Ltd v Lynch [2005] IRLR 680, [2005] All ER (D) 351
(Jun), EAT 53.7
Keywest Club Ltd (t/a Veeraswamys Restaurant) v Choudhury [1988] IRLR
51, EAT 34.35
Khan v Chief Constable of West Yorkshire Police. See Chief Constable of
West Yorkshire Police v Khan
Khan v General Medical Council [1996] ICR 1032, [1994] IRLR 646, CA 13.27,
14.2
Khan v Heywood and Middleton Primary Care Trust [2006] IRLR 345 .... 21.28
Khan v Trident Safeguards Ltd [2004] EWCA Civ 624, [2004] ICR 1591,
[2004] IRLR 961, (2004) Times, 28 May, 148 Sol Jo LB 634 .... 14.2
Khanum v Mid-Glamorgan Area Health Authority [1979] ICR 40,
[1978] IRLR 215, 13 ITR 303, EAT 54.10
Khudados v Leggate [2005] ICR 1013, [2005] IRLR 540, [2005] All ER (D)
241 (Feb), EAT 22.5
Kidd v Axa Equity and Law Life Assurance Society plc [2000] IRLR 301 .... 40.4
Kidd v DRG (UK) Ltd [1985] ICR 405, [1985] IRLR 190, EAT 12.9

Kien Tran v Greenwich Vietnam Community Project [2002] EWCA Civ 553, [2002] ICR 1101, [2002] IRLR 735, [2002] 21 LS Gaz R 31, [2002] All ER (D) 238 (Apr) 21.63, 22.11

Kigass Aero Components Ltd v Brown [2002] ICR 697, [2002] IRLR 312, [2002] All ER (D) 341 (Feb), EAT 29.3

King v Eaton Ltd [1996] IRLR 199, 1997 SLT 654, Ct of Sess 21.12, 54.11

King v Eaton Ltd (No 2) [1998] IRLR 686, 1999 SLT 656, Ct of Sess 55.13

King v Great Britain-China Centre [1992] ICR 516, [1991] IRLR 513, CA 14.3

King v Smith [1995] ICR 339, CA 27.5

King v University Court of the University of St Andrews [2002] IRLR 252, Ct of Sess 8.23

King's College London v Clark (2003) IDS Brief No 747 .... 24.11

Kingston v British Railways Board [1982] ICR 392, [1982] IRLR 274, EAT; affd [1984] ICR 781, [1984] IRLR 146, CA 12.13, 13.35, 54.14

Kingston-upon-Hull City Council v Dunnachie (No 3) [2004] ICR 227, [2003] IRLR 843, 147 Sol Jo LB 992, EAT 21.69

Kirby v National Probation Service [2006] IRLR 508, [2006] All ER (D) 111 (Mar), EAT 12.10

Kirton v Tetrosyl Ltd [2003] EWCA Civ 619, [2003] ICR 1237, [2003] IRLR 353, (2003) Times, 28 April, 147 Sol Jo LB 474, [2003] All ER (D) 190 (Apr) 10.7

Knapton v ECC Card Clothing Ltd [2006] ICR 1084, [2006] IRLR 756, EAT 55.12

Knight v Central London Bus Co Ltd EAT/443/00 .... 22.12

Knight v Department of Social Security [2002] IRLR 249, [2001] All ER (D) 473 (Nov), EAT 21.12

Knowles v Liverpool City Council [1993] 4 All ER 321, [1993] 1 WLR 1428, 91 LGR 629, [1994] 1 Lloyd's Rep 11, [1994] ICR 243, [1993] IRLR 588, [1993] NLJR 1479n, [1994] PIQR P8, HL 27.6

Konski v Peet [1915] 1 Ch 530, 84 LJ Ch 513, 59 Sol Jo 383, 112 LT 1107 .... 41.8

Kopel v Safeway Stores plc [2003] IRLR 753, [2003] All ER (D) 05 (Sep), EAT 21.36, 21.72, 55.22

Kording v Senator für Finanzen: C-100/95 [1997] ECR I-5289, [1998] 1 CMLR 395, [1997] IRLR 710, ECJ 24.3

Kores Manufacturing Co Ltd v Kolok Manufacturing Co Ltd [1957] 3 All ER 158, [1957] 1 WLR 1012, [1957] RPC 431, 101 Sol Jo 799, [1957] CLY 1285; affd [1959] Ch 108, [1958] 2 All ER 65, [1958] 2 WLR 858, [1958] RPC 200, 102 Sol Jo 362, 1958 SLT 221, [1958] JBL 306, CA 41.5

Kovacs v Queen Mary and Westfield College [2002] EWCA Civ 352, [2002] ICR 919, [2002] IRLR 414, [2002] 19 LS Gaz R 29, (2002) Times, 12 April, 146 Sol Jo LB 91, [2002] All ER (D) 368 (Mar) 20.3, 21.36, 21.69

Kowalska v Freie und Hansestadt Hamburg: C-33/89 [1990] ECR I-2591, [1992] ICR 29, [1990] IRLR 447, ECJ 24.23, 24.24

Krasner v McMath. See Huddersfield Fine Worsteds Ltd, Re; Krasner v McMath

Kraus v Penna plc [2004] IRLR 260, [2003] All ER (D) 275 (Nov), EAT 11.18

Kuddus v Chief Constable of Leicestershire Constabulary [2001] UKHL 29, [2002] 2 AC 122, [2001] 3 All ER 193, [2001] 2 WLR 1789, [2001] 28 LS Gaz R 43, [2001] NLJR 936, 145 Sol Jo LB 166, [2001] All ER (D) 30 (Jun) 14.13, 14.18, 37.5

Kuratorium für Dialyse und Nierentransplantation eV v Lewark: C-457/93 [1996] ECR I-243, [1996] IRLR 637, ECJ 24.3, 49.4

Table of Cases

Kutz-Bauer v Freie und Hansestadt Hamburg: C-187/00 [2003] ECR I-2741,
  [2003] IRLR 368, [2003] All ER (D) 327 (Mar), ECJ 13.8
Kuzel v Roche Products Ltd [2007] IRLR 309, [2007] All ER (D) 32
  (Mar), EAT 11.18
Kwamin v Abbey National plc [2004] ICR 841, [2004] IRLR 516,
  [2004] NLJR 418, [2004] All ER (D) 189 (Mar), EAT 20.13, 21.62, 30.7
Kwik-Fit (GB) Ltd v Lineham [1992] ICR 183, [1992] IRLR 156,
  [1992] 4 LS Gaz R 31, EAT 48.5
Kwik Save Stores Ltd v Swain [1997] ICR 49, EAT 20.37

L

LMC Drains Ltd v Waugh [1991] 3 CMLR 172, EAT 52.6
Labour Party v Oakley [1988] ICR 403, sub nom Oakley v Labour Party
  [1988] IRLR 34, CA 54.14
Ladd v Marshall [1954] 3 All ER 745, [1954] 1 WLR 1489, 98 Sol Jo
  870, CA 22.16
Laher v Hammersmith and Fulham London Borough EAT/215/91, IDS Brief
  No 531 .... 21.52
Laing v Manchester City Council [2006] ICR 1519, [2006] IRLR 748, [2006]
  All ER (D) 452 (Jul), EAT 12.5, 14.3
Laird v A K Stoddart Ltd [2001] IRLR 591, [2001] All ER (D) 261
  (Jan), EAT 34.12
Lake v British Transport Police [2007] ICR 47, [2006] All ER (D) 04
  (Oct), EAT; revsd [2007] EWCA Civ 424, [2007] All ER (D) 77 (May) 14.2
Lambeth London Borough v D'Souza. See D'Souza v Lambeth London
  Borough
Lambeth London Borough Council v Commission for Racial Equality
  (1989) 87 LGR 862, [1989] ICR 641, [1989] IRLR 379,
  [1989] 29 LS Gaz R 44, EAT; affd [1990] ICR 768, [1990] IRLR
  231, CA 12.5, 12.8, 13.4, 13.9, 13.14
Lambeth London Borough Council v Corlett (EAT0396/06) [2007] ICR 88 .... 15.5,
                                                                           15.11, 20.20
Lambeth London Borough Council v Miller (20 March 2007, unreported)
  (UKEAT/0016/06) 15.11
Lamont v Fry's Metals Ltd [1985] ICR 566, [1985] IRLR 470, CA 21.64
Lana v Positive Action Training In Housing (London) Ltd [2001] IRLR 501,
  [2001] All ER (D) 23 (Jun), EAT 12.13, 13.38
Lancashire Fire Ltd v SA Lyons & Co Ltd [1997] IRLR 113, CA 41.13
Lancaster v DEK Printing Machines Ltd EAT/623/99 .... 20.25
Land Brandenburg v Sass: C-284/02 [2005] IRLR 147, [2004] All ER (D) 310
  (Nov), ECJ 12.5, 12.12
Land Securities Trillium Ltd v Thornley [2005] IRLR 765, [2005] All ER (D)
  194 (Jun), EAT 53.7
Landeshauptstadt Kiel v Jaeger: C-151/02 [2004] All ER (EC) 604,
  [2003] ECR I-8389, [2003] 3 CMLR 493, [2004] ICR 1528, [2003] IRLR
  804, 75 BMLR 201, [2003] All ER (D) 72 (Sep), ECJ 57.4, 57.14
Lane v Shire Roofing Co (Oxford) Ltd [1995] IRLR 493, [1995] PIQR
  P417, CA 27.2
Lange v Georg Schünemann GmbH: C-350/99 [2001] ECR I-1061, [2001] All
  ER (EC) 481, [2001] IRLR 244, [2001] All ER (D) 90 (Feb), ECJ 8.9
Langston v Amalgamated Union of Engineering Workers [1974] 1 All ER
  980, [1974] 1 WLR 185, [1974] ICR 180, [1974] IRLR 15, 16 KIR 139,
  118 Sol Jo 97, CA 8.13, 58.21

Lansing Linde Ltd v Kerr [1991] 1 All ER 418, [1991] 1 WLR 251,
[1991] ICR 428, [1991] IRLR 80, [1990] NLJR 1458, CA 8.23, 41.13, 41.17
Landon v Lill EAT/1486/00 .... 20.18
Lanton Leisure Ltd v White and Gibson [1987] IRLR 119, EAT 53.13
Larsen v Henderson [1990] IRLR 512, sub nom Larsen's Executrix v
Henderson 1990 SLT 498, Ct of Sess 31.11
Lasertop Ltd v Webster [1997] ICR 828, [1997] IRLR 498, 572 IRLB
14, EAT 13.3
Latchman v Reed Business Information Ltd [2002] ICR 1453 .... 10.6
Laurie v Holloway [1994] ICR 32, EAT 21.52
Lavarack v Woods of Colchester Ltd [1967] 1 QB 278, [1966] 3 All ER 683,
[1966] 3 WLR 706, 1 KIR 312, 110 Sol Jo 770, CA 58.25
Law Hospital NHS Trust v Rush [2001] IRLR 611, Ct of Sess 10.2
Lawal v Northern Spirit Ltd [2003] UKHL 35, [2004] 1 All ER 187,
[2003] ICR 856, [2003] IRLR 538, [2003] 28 LS Gaz R 30, [2003] NLJR
1005, (2003) Times, 27 June, 147 Sol Jo LB 783, [2003] All ER (D) 255
(Jun) 22.2, 30.7
Lawrence v HM Prison Service (26 March 2007, unreported) 15.5
Lawrence v Regent Office Care Ltd: C-320/00 [2002] ECR I-7325,
[2002] 3 CMLR 761, [2003] ICR 1092, [2002] IRLR 822, (2002) Times,
10 October, [2002] All ER (D) 84 (Sep), ECJ 24.9
Lawrence David Ltd v Ashton [1989] ICR 123 .... 41.8
Lawrie-Blum v Land Baden-Württemberg: 66/85 [1986] ECR 2121,
[1987] 3 CMLR 389, [1987] ICR 483, ECJ 24.4
Laws v London Chronicle (Indicator Newspapers) Ltd [1959] 2 All ER 285,
[1959] 1 WLR 698, 103 Sol Jo 470, CA 58.17
Lawson v Serco Ltd [2004] EWCA Civ 12, [2004] 2 All ER 200, [2004] ICR
204, [2004] IRLR 206, (2004) Times, 30 January, 148 Sol Jo LB 148,
[2004] All ER (D) 217 (Jan); revsd [2006] UKHL 3, [2006] 1 All ER 823,
[2006] IRLR 289, [2006] 06 LS Gaz R 36, [2006] NLJR 184, 150 Sol Jo
LB 131, [2006] All ER (D) 184 (Jan) 26.3, 26.13, 53.15
Learoyd v Brook [1891] 1 QB 431, 55 JP 265, 60 LJQB 373, 39 WR 480, 64
LT 458, 7 TLR 236 .... 58.44
Ledernes Hovedorganisation (acting for Rygard) v Dansk
Arbejdsgiverforening (acting for Sto Molle Akustik A/S): C-48/94
[1995] ECR I-2745, [1996] 3 CMLR 45, [1996] ICR 333, [1996] IRLR
51, ECJ 52.5
Lee v GEC Plessey Telecommunications [1993] IRLR 383 .... 6.4, 8.22
Lee v Showmen's Guild of Great Britain [1952] 2 QB 329, [1952] 1 All ER
1175, 96 Sol Jo 296, [1952] 1 TLR 1115, CA 51.12
Lee Ting Sang v Chung Chi-Keung [1990] 2 AC 374, [1990] 2 WLR 1173,
[1990] ICR 409, [1990] IRLR 236, 134 Sol Jo 909,
[1990] 13 LS Gaz R 43, PC 17.3
Leech v Preston Borough Council [1985] ICR 192, [1985] IRLR 337, EAT 53.13
Leeds Private Hospital Ltd v Parkin [1992] ICR 571, EAT 12.5
Leefe v NSM Music Ltd (2005) 150 Sol Jo LB 400, [2006] All ER (D) 57
(Feb), EAT 20.37
Legal and General Assurance Ltd v Kirk [2001] EWCA Civ 1803,
[2002] IRLR 124, [2001] All ER (D) 212 (Nov) 30.7
Legal and General Assurance Society Ltd v Pensions Ombudsman
[2000] 2 All ER 577, [2000] 1 WLR 1524, [1999] 46 LS Gaz R 40,
[1999] NLJR 1733, 144 Sol Jo LB 8 .... 42.14
Lehman Brothers Ltd v Smith EAT/0486/05 .... 20.18, 21.10
Leicester University v A [1999] ICR 701, [1999] IRLR 352, EAT 14.11, 21.18

Leighton v Charalambous [1995] ICR 1091, [1996] IRLR 67, EAT 8.15
Leighton v Construction Industry Training Board. See Construction Industry
  Training Board v Leighton
Leighton v Michael [1995] ICR 1091, [1996] IRLR 67, EAT 8.15, 13.16
Leisure Employment Services Ltd v Revenue and Customs Comrs
  [2007] EWCA Civ 92, [2007] IRLR 450, (2007) Times, 7 March, [2007]
  All ER (D) 202 (Feb) 34.9
Leisure Leagues UK Ltd v Maconnachie [2002] IRLR 600, (2002) Times,
  3 May, [2002] All ER (D) 223 (Mar), EAT 29.9, 34.14, 34.22
Leng (Sir W C) & Co Ltd v Andrews [1909] 1 Ch 763, 78 LJ Ch 80, 100 LT
  7, 25 TLR 93, CA 41.5
Lennon v Birmingham City Council [2001] EWCA Civ 435, [2001] IRLR
  826, [2001] All ER (D) 321 (Mar) 8.23, 21.26
Leonard v Southern Derbyshire Chamber of Commerce [2001] IRLR 19,
  [2000] All ER (D) 1327, EAT 10.2
Leonard v Strathclyde Buses Ltd [1998] IRLR 693, 1999 SC 57, 1999 SLT
  734, 606 IRLB 8, Ct of Sess 55.13
Leonard (Cyril) & Co v Simo Securities Trust Ltd [1971] 3 All ER 1313,
  [1972] 1 WLR 80, 115 Sol Jo 911, CA 58.20
Letheby & Christopher Ltd v Bond [1988] ICR 480, EAT 7.7
Leverton v Clwyd County Council [1989] AC 706, [1989] 2 WLR 47,
  [1988] 2 CMLR 811, 87 LGR 269, [1989] ICR 33, [1988] IRLR 239, CA;
  affd [1989] AC 706, [1989] 1 All ER 78, [1989] 2 WLR 47, 87 LGR 269,
  [1989] ICR 33, [1989] IRLR 28, 133 Sol Jo 45,
  [1989] 19 LS Gaz R 41, HL 24.7, 24.9, 24.11
Levez v T H Jennings (Harlow Pools) Ltd: C-326/96 [1999] All ER (EC) 1,
  [1998] ECR I-7835, [1999] 2 CMLR 363, [1999] ICR 521, [1999] IRLR
  36, 608 IRLB 3, [1998] All ER (D) 662, ECJ 20.12
Levez v T H Jennings (Harlow Pools) Ltd (No 2) [1999] 3 CMLR 715,
  [2000] ICR 58, [1999] IRLR 764, 629 IRLB 7, EAT 24.9
Lewen v Denda: C-333/97 [1999] ECR I-7243, [2000] All ER (EC) 261,
  [2000] 2 CMLR 38, [2000] IRLR 67, ECJ 12.12, 24.14
Lewicki v Brown & Root Wimpey Highland Fabricators Ltd 1996 STC 145,
  [1996] IRLR 565, OH 44.16
Lewis v Motorworld Garages Ltd [1986] ICR 157, [1985] IRLR 465, CA 53.7
Lewis and Britton v E Mason & Sons [1994] IRLR 4, EAT 53.17
Lewis (John) plc v Coyne [2001] IRLR 139, EAT 54.9
Lewisham and Guys Mental NHS Trust v Andrews [2000] ICR 707, CA 14.2
Lewisham London Borough Council v Colbourne (UKEAT/339/06) 15.13
Leyland DAF Ltd, Re. See Talbot v Cadge
Leyland Vehicles Ltd v Jones [1981] ICR 428, [1981] IRLR 269, EAT 51.5
Libyan Arab Foreign Bank v Bankers Trust Co [1989] QB 728,
  [1989] 3 All ER 252, [1989] 3 WLR 314, [1988] 1 Lloyd's Rep 259, 133
  Sol Jo 568 .... 58.15
Lightfoot v D & J Sporting Ltd [1996] IRLR 64, EAT 8.15
Lightways (Contractors) Ltd v Associated Holdings Ltd [2000] IRLR 247, Ct
  of Sess 52.5
Linbourne v Constable [1993] ICR 698, EAT 21.10
Lincoln v Daniels [1962] 1 QB 237, [1961] 3 All ER 740, [1961] 3 WLR 866,
  105 Sol Jo 647, CA 2.4
Lincoln Mills (Australia) Ltd v Gough [1964] VR 193 .... 9.28
Lindsay v Alliance and Leicester plc [2000] ICR 1234, [2000] All ER (D)
  282, EAT 12.10

Linfood Cash and Carry Ltd v Thomson [1989] ICR 518, [1989] IRLR
235, EAT 54.10
Lipkin Gorman (a firm) v Karpnale Ltd [1991] 2 AC 548, [1992] 4 All ER
512, [1991] 3 WLR 10, [1991] NLJR 815, 135 Sol Jo LB 36, HL 34.15
Lipscombe v Forestry Commission [2007] EWCA Civ 428, [2007] All ER (D)
132 (May) 22.15
Lisk-Carew v Birmingham City Council [2004] EWCA Civ 565,
[2004] 20 LS Gaz R 35, (2004) Times, 7 June, [2004] All ER (D) 215
(Apr) 14.19
List Design Group Ltd v Douglas [2002] ICR 686, [2003] IRLR 14, [2002]
All ER (D) 215 (Mar), EAT 29.6, 34.6
Lister v Hesley Hall Ltd [2001] UKHL 22, [2002] 1 AC 215, [2001] 2 All ER
769, [2001] 1 WLR 1311, [2001] ICR 665, [2001] IRLR 472,
[2001] 2 FCR 97, [2001] 2 FLR 307, [2001] Fam Law 595, [2001] NPC
89, [2001] NLJR 728, (2001) Times, 10 May, 145 Sol Jo LB 126, [2001]
All ER (D) 37 (May) 12.13, 13.35, 56.1, 56.2
Litster v Forth Dry Dock and Engineering Co Ltd [1990] 1 AC 546,
[1989] 1 All ER 1134, [1989] 2 WLR 634, [1989] ICR 341, [1989] IRLR
161, 133 Sol Jo 455, [1989] NLJR 400, 1989 SC (HL) 96, HL 7.9, 25.2, 52.6,
52.12, 52.14
Little v Charterhouse Magna Assurance Co Ltd [1980] IRLR 19, EAT 8.13
Littlewoods Organisation Ltd v Harris [1978] 1 All ER 1026, [1977] 1 WLR
1472, 121 Sol Jo 727, CA 41.6, 41.8
Littlewoods Organisation plc v Traynor [1993] IRLR 154, EAT 14.6
Liverpool City Council v Irwin [1977] AC 239, [1976] 2 All ER 39,
[1976] 2 WLR 562, 74 LGR 392, 32 P & CR 43, 13 HLR 38, 120 Sol Jo
267, 238 Estates Gazette 879, 963, HL 8.13
Living Design (Home Improvements) Ltd v Davidson [1994] IRLR 69, Ct of
Sess 41.7
Livingstone v Hepworth Refractories Ltd [1992] 3 CMLR 601, [1992] ICR
287, [1992] IRLR 63, [1992] 5 LS Gaz R 31, EAT 2.4, 20.12
Lloyd v Grace, Smith & Co [1912] AC 716, 81 LJKB 1140, [1911–13] All ER
Rep 51, 56 Sol Jo 723, 107 LT 531, 28 TLR 547, HL 56.2
Lloyd v Taylor Woodrow Construction [1999] IRLR 782, EAT 54.11
Locabail (UK) Ltd v Bayfield Properties Ltd [2000] QB 451, [2000] 1 All ER
65, [2000] 2 WLR 870, [2000] IRLR 96, [2000] 3 LRC 482, 7 BHRC 583,
[1999] All ER (D) 1279, CA 21.50
Lock v Cardiff Rly Co [1998] IRLR 358, 599 IRLB 6, EAT 54.4, 54.10
Lock v Connell Estate Agents [1994] ICR 983, [1994] IRLR 444, EAT 55.9, 55.13,
58.30
Lockwood v Crawley Warren Group (2001) IDS Brief No 680 .... 12.9
Lodwick v Southwark London Borough Council [2004] EWCA Civ 306,
[2004] ICR 884, [2004] IRLR 554, (2004) Times, 9 April, 148 Sol Jo LB
385, [2004] All ER (D) 349 (Mar) 21.71, 22.12
Logan v Customs and Excise Comrs [2003] EWCA Civ 1068, [2004] ICR 1,
[2004] IRLR 63, [2003] 37 LS Gaz R 31, (2003) Times, 4 September,
[2003] All ER (D) 388 (Jul) 21.59
Lommers v Minister van Landbouw, Natuurbeheer en Visserij: C-476/99
[2002] ECR I-2891, [2004] 2 CMLR 1141, [2002] IRLR 430, [2002] All
ER (D) 280 (Mar), ECJ 24.3
London Ambulance Service v Charlton [1992] ICR 773, [1992] IRLR
510, EAT 49.2
London and Mashonaland Exploration Co Ltd v New Mashonaland
Exploration Co Ltd [1891] WN 165 .... 9.16

Table of Cases

London Fire and Civil Defence Authority v Betty [1994] IRLR 384, EAT 54.8

London Fire and Civil Defence Authority v Samuels EAT/450/00, IDS Brief No 669 .... 21.38, 21.42

London International College v Sen [1993] IRLR 333, CA 20.25

London Probation Board v Kirkpatrick [2005] ICR 965, [2005] IRLR 443, [2005] All ER (D) 148 (Feb), EAT 20.23

London Transport Executive v Clarke [1981] ICR 355, [1981] IRLR 166, CA 48.19, 53.9, 58.7

London Underground Ltd v Edwards [1995] ICR 574, [1995] IRLR 355, EAT 12.8, 14.14

London Underground Ltd v Edwards (No 2) [1999] ICR 494, [1998] IRLR 364, [1998] 25 LS Gaz R 32, [1998] NLJR 905, 142 Sol Jo LB 182, [1998] All ER (D) 231, CA 12.8

London Underground Ltd v National Union of Rail, Maritime and Transport Workers [2001] EWCA Civ 211, [2001] ICR 647, [2001] IRLR 228, [2001] All ER (D) 191 (Feb) 45.14

London Underground Ltd v National Union of Railwaymen [1989] IRLR 341 .... 45.14

London Underground Ltd v National Union of Railwaymen, Maritime and Transport Workers [1996] ICR 170, CA 45.14

London Underground Ltd v Noel [2000] ICR 109, [1999] IRLR 621, sub nom Noel v London Underground Ltd [1999] 31 LS Gaz R 38, CA 20.25

Longden v Ferrari Ltd [1994] ICR 443, [1994] BCC 250, sub nom Longden and Paisley v Ferrari Ltd and Kennedy International Ltd [1994] IRLR 157, EAT 52.14

Lonrho Ltd v Shell Petroleum Co Ltd (No 2) [1982] AC 173, [1981] 2 All ER 456, [1981] 3 WLR 33, 125 Sol Jo 429, HL 45.2

Lonrho plc v Fayed [1992] 1 AC 448, [1991] 3 All ER 303, [1991] 3 WLR 188, [1991] BCLC 779, [1991] BCC 641, 135 Sol Jo LB 68, HL 45.2

Lord Chancellor v Coker and Osamor [2001] ICR 507, [2001] IRLR 116, [2001] All ER (D) 68 (Jan), EAT; affd sub nom Coker v Lord Chancellor [2001] EWCA Civ 1756, [2002] ICR 321, [2002] IRLR 80, (2001) Times, 3 December, 145 Sol Jo LB 268, [2001] All ER (D) 334 (Nov) 12.8, 12.9

Loughran v Northern Ireland Housing Executive [1999] 1 AC 428, [1998] 3 WLR 735, [1998] ICR 828, [1998] IRLR 593, [1998] 36 LS Gaz R 31, 142 Sol Jo LB 254, HL 12.12

Louies v Coventry Hood and Seating Co Ltd [1990] ICR 54, [1990] IRLR 324, EAT 54.10

Lubbe v Cape plc [2000] 4 All ER 268, [2000] 1 WLR 1545, [2000] 2 Lloyd's Rep 383, 144 Sol Jo LB 250, [2000] 5 LRC 605, HL 26.12

Lucas (T) & Co Ltd v Mitchell [1974] Ch 129, [1972] 3 All ER 689, [1972] 3 WLR 934, 116 Sol Jo 711, CA 41.7

Lucas and Gandiya v Ministry of Defence (2004) IDS Brief No 763 .... 13.15

Luce v Bexley London Borough Council (1990) 88 LGR 909, [1990] ICR 591, [1990] IRLR 422, [1990] 27 LS Gaz R 41, EAT 49.3

Lunt v Merseyside Tec Ltd [1999] ICR 17, [1999] IRLR 458, EAT 14.33, 21.34

Lyfar v Brighton and Sussex University Hospitals Trust [2006] EWCA Civ 1548, [2006] All ER (D) 182 (Nov) 14.6, 20.29

Lynock v Cereal Packaging Ltd [1988] ICR 670, [1988] IRLR 510, EAT 54.8

Lytlarch Ltd v Reid [1991] ICR 216, EAT 55.12

M

M v Vincent [1998] ICR 73, EAT 21.18

M and S Drapers (a firm) v Reynolds [1956] 3 All ER 814, [1957] 1 WLR 9,
  101 Sol Jo 44, CA 41.10

MHC Consulting Services Ltd v Tansell [1999] ICR 1211, [1999] IRLR
  677, EAT; affd [2000] ICR 789, 144 Sol Jo LB 205, sub nom Abbey Life
  Assurance Co Ltd v Tansell [2000] IRLR 387, [2000] All ER (D)
  483, CA 10.25, 13.21

MPB Structure Ltd v Munro [2002] IRLR 601, [2002] All ER (D) 264 (Apr);
  affd sub nom Munro v MPB Structures Ltd [2004] 2 CMLR 1032,
  [2004] ICR 430, [2003] IRLR 350, (2003) Times, 24 April, 2003 SLT 551,
  2003 SCLR 542 .... 22.1, 29.4, 57.25

MRS Environmental Services Ltd v Marsh [1997] 1 All ER 92,
  [1997] 2 CMLR 842, [1997] ICR 995, [1996] 29 LS Gaz R 29, 140 Sol Jo
  LB 186, CA 7.1

MSF v Refuge Assurance plc [2002] ICR 1365, [2002] IRLR 324, [2002] All
  ER (D) 209 (Feb), EAT 39.4

Mabey Plant Hire Ltd v Richens IDS Brief No 495 .... 55.12

Mabirizi v National Hospital for Nervous Diseases [1990] ICR 281,
  [1990] IRLR 133, EAT 55.5

Macari v Celtic Football Athletic Co Ltd [1999] IRLR 787, 2000 SLT 80,
  2000 SCLR 209 .... 58.17

McAuley v Eastern Health and Social Services Board [1991] IRLR 467,
  NICA 24.8

McBrearty v Thomson IDS Brief No 450 .... 48.15

McCabe v Cornwall County Council [2004] UKHL 35, [2004] 3 All ER 991,
  [2004] 3 WLR 322, [2004] ICR 1064, [2004] IRLR 733, [2004] NLJR
  1155, 148 Sol Jo LB 909, [2004] All ER (D) 268 (Jul) 8.13, 8.23, 58.29

McCarthy v British Insulated Callenders Cables plc [1985] IRLR 94, EAT 55.10

MacCartney v Oversley House Management [2006] ICR 510, [2006] All ER
  (D) 246 (Jan), EAT 34.12, 57.5, 57.17

McCausland v Dungannon District Council [1993] IRLR 583, NICA 12.8

McClaren v Home Office [1990] ICR 824, [1990] IRLR 338, CA 37.3, 37.4

McClelland v Northern Ireland General Health Services Board
  [1957] 2 All ER 129, [1957] 1 WLR 594, 55 LGR 281, [1957] NI 100,
  101 Sol Jo 355, HL 58.15

McClory v Post Office [1993] 1 All ER 457, [1992] ICR 758, [1993] IRLR
  159 .... 8.13

McConnell v Police Authority for Northern Ireland [1997] IRLR 625,
  NICA 14.18

McCook v Lobo [2002] EWCA Civ 1760, [2003] ICR 89, [2002] All ER (D)
  272 (Nov) 27.2

McDermid v Nash Dredging and Reclamation Co Ltd [1987] AC 906,
  [1987] 2 All ER 878, [1987] 3 WLR 212, [1987] 2 Lloyd's Rep 201,
  [1987] ICR 917, [1987] IRLR 334, 131 Sol Jo 973,
  [1987] LS Gaz R 2458, HL 27.3, 56.1

MacDonald v Ministry of Defence [2001] 1 All ER 620, [2001] ICR 1,
  [2000] IRLR 748, [2000] All ER (D) 1494, EAT; on appeal [2002] ICR
  174, [2001] IRLR 431, 2002 SC 1, 2001 SLT 819, Ct of Sess; on appeal
  sub nom Macdonald v Advocate General for Scotland [2003] UKHL 34,
  [2004] 1 All ER 339, [2003] ICR 937, [2003] IRLR 512,
  [2003] 29 LS Gaz R 36, (2003) Times, 20 June, 2003 SLT 1158, 2003
  SCLR 814, 147 Sol Jo LB 782, [2004] 2 LRC 111, [2003] All ER (D) 259
  (Jun) 12.5, 12.6, 12.12, 12.13, 13.39, 30.5

Table of Cases

Macer v Abafast Ltd [1990] ICR 234, [1990] IRLR 137, EAT 7.9, 52.12, 52.14
McFadden v Greater Glasgow Passenger Transport Executive [1977] IRLR
    327, IT 33.6
McFarlane v Glasgow City Council [2001] IRLR 7, EAT 17.3
McGhee v Midlands British Road Services Ltd [1985] ICR 503, [1985] IRLR
    198, EAT 51.13
McGowan v Scottish Water [2005] IRLR 167, [2004] All ER (D) 130 (Nov) 30.7
McGuigan v T G Boynes & Sons (1999) IDS Brief No 633, EAT 12.5
Machine Tool Industry Research Association v Simpson [1988] ICR 558,
    [1988] IRLR 212, CA 20.25
McHugh v Hempsall Bulk Transport Ltd IDS Brief No 480 .... 38.12
McIntosh v John Brown Engineering Ltd IDS Brief No 441 .... 11.15
Mack Trucks (Britain) Ltd, Re [1967] 1 All ER 977, [1967] 1 WLR 780, 111
    Sol Jo 435 .... 31.10, 58.9
McKechnie v UBM Building Supplies (Southern) Ltd [1991] 2 CMLR 668,
    [1991] ICR 710, [1991] IRLR 283, EAT 24.3
McLeod v Hellyer Bros Ltd. See Hellyer Bros Ltd v McLeod
McManus v Daylay Foods Ltd EAT/82/95 .... 25.2
McMaster v Manchester Airport plc [1998] IRLR 112, 593 IRLB 17, EAT 20.18,
    20.23, 53.13
McMeechan v Secretary of State for Employment [1997] ICR 549,
    [1997] IRLR 353, CA 17.3, 47.2
McMenemy v Capita Business Services Ltd [2006] IRLR 761, EAT; affd
    [2007] IRLR 400 .... 32.5, 32.11, 32.14
Macmillan v Ministry of Defence (11 November 2003, unreported), EAT 13.8
Macmillan Inc v Bishopsgate Investment Trust plc [1993] 4 All ER 998,
    [1993] 1 WLR 837, [1993] IRLR 393, [1993] 11 LS Gaz R 44, sub nom
    Macmillan Inc v Bishopsgate Investment Trust plc (No 2) [1993] ICR
    385; affd sub nom Macmillan Inc v Bishopsgate Investment Trust plc
    [1993] 4 All ER 998, [1993] 1 WLR 1372, [1993] 31 LS Gaz R 39, CA 8.13
Madarassy v Nomura International plc [2007] EWCA Civ 33, [2007] IRLR
    246, [2007] All ER (D) 226 (Jan) 12.5, 14.3
McNicol v Balfour Beatty Rail Maintenance Ltd [2002] ICR 381,
    [2001] IRLR 644, [2001] All ER (D) 404 (Jul), EAT; affd [2002] EWCA
    Civ 1074, [2002] ICR 1498, [2002] IRLR 711, 71 BMLR 1, (2002)
    Times, 26 August, [2002] All ER (D) 407 (Jul) 10.2, 21.52
McPherson v BNP Paribas (London Branch) [2004] EWCA Civ 569,
    [2004] 3 All ER 266, [2004] IRLR 558, (2004) Times, 31 May, [2004] All
    ER (D) 175 (May) 21.17, 21.70, 21.72
MacPherson v London Borough of Lambeth [1988] IRLR 470 .... 8.23, 34.14
MacRae (Kenneth) & Co Ltd v Dawson [1984] IRLR 5, EAT 38.8
McShane and Ashton v Express Newspapers Ltd. See Express
    Newspapers Ltd v McShane
McVitae v UNISON [1996] IRLR 33 .... 51.15
Madden v Preferred Technical Group CHA Ltd [2004] EWCA Civ 1178,
    [2005] IRLR 46, 148 Sol Jo LB 1064, [2004] All ER (D) 153 (Aug) 12.5
Madhewoo v NHS Trust Direct (1 March 2006, unreported)
    (UKEAT/0030/06/LA) 15.14
Magorrian v Eastern Health and Social Services Board: C-246/96 [1998] All
    ER (EC) 38, [1997] ECR I-7153, [1998] ICR 979, [1998] IRLR 86,
    ECJ 20.12
Mahlburg v Land Mecklenburg-Vorpommern: C-207/98 [2000] ECR I-549,
    [2001] 3 CMLR 887, [2001] ICR 1032, [2000] IRLR 276, [2000] All ER
    (D) 116, ECJ 12.5

Mailer v Austin Rover Group plc. See Austin Rover Group Ltd v HM
    Inspector of Factories
Mailway (Southern) Ltd v Willsher [1978] ICR 511, [1978] IRLR 322, 122
    Sol Jo 79, EAT 34.24
Majrowski v Guy's and St Thomas's NHS Trust [2006] UKHL 34,
    [2006] 3 WLR 125 .... 56.1
Malik v BCCI SA (in liquidation) [1998] AC 20, [1997] 3 All ER 1,
    [1997] 3 WLR 95, [1997] ICR 606, [1997] IRLR 462,
    [1997] 94 LS Gaz R 33, [1997] NLJR 917, HL 8.13, 8.23, 55.12, 58.29
Malik v Post Office Counters Ltd [1993] ICR 93, EAT 13.27
Mandla v Dowell Lee [1983] 2 AC 548, [1983] 1 All ER 1062, [1983] 2 WLR
    620, [1983] ICR 385, [1983] IRLR 209, 127 Sol Jo 242, HL 12.6
Manel v Memon (2000) 33 HLR 235, [2000] 2 EGLR 40, [2000] 33 EG 74,
    80 P & CR D22, [2000] All ER (D) 481, CA 43.5
Mangold v Helm: C-144/04 [2006] All ER (EC) 383, [2006] IRLR 143, [2005]
    All ER (D) 287 (Nov), ECJ 3.2, 3.4, 25.1, 25.2
Mann v Secretary of State for Employment. See Secretary of State for
    Employment v Mann
Manor Bakeries Ltd v Nazir [1996] IRLR 604, EAT 24.3, 49.4
Manpower Ltd v Hearne [1983] ICR 567, [1983] IRLR 281, EAT 55.12
Maresca v Motor Insurance Repair Research Centre [2004] 4 All ER 254,
    [2005] ICR 197, [2004] All ER (D) 20 (Mar), EAT 21.16, 21.76
Market Force (UK) Ltd v Hunt [2002] IRLR 863, [2002] All ER (D) 06
    (Jul), EAT 21.60
Market Investigations Ltd v Minister of Social Security [1969] 2 QB 173,
    [1968] 3 All ER 732, [1969] 2 WLR 1, 112 Sol Jo 905 .... 17.3
Marks & Spencer plc v Williams-Ryan [2005] EWCA Civ 470, [2005] ICR
    1293, [2005] IRLR 562, 149 Sol Jo LB 511, [2005] All ER (D) 248
    (Apr) 20.25
Marleasing SA v La Comercial Internacional de Alimentacion SA: C-106/89
    [1990] ECR I-4135, [1992] 1 CMLR 305, [1993] BCC 421, 135 Sol Jo 15,
    ECJ 25.2
Marler (E T) Ltd v Robertson [1974] ICR 72, NIRC 21.72
Marley v Forward Trust Group Ltd [1986] ICR 891, [1986] IRLR 369, CA 6.3
Marley Tile Co Ltd v Johnson [1982] IRLR 75, CA 41.8
Marley Tile Co Ltd v Shaw [1980] ICR 72, [1980] IRLR 25, 123 Sol Jo
    803, CA 54.3
Marley (UK) Ltd v Anderson [1996] ICR 728, [1996] IRLR 163,
    [1996] 02 LS Gaz R 28, 140 Sol Jo LB 26, CA 20.25, 20.26
Marlow v East Thames Housing Group Ltd [2002] IRLR 798, [2002] All ER
    (D) 393 (May) 8.13, 44.14
Marriott v Oxford and District Co-operative Society Ltd (No 2) [1970] 1 QB
    186, [1969] 3 All ER 1126, [1969] 3 WLR 984, 113 Sol Jo 655, CA 48.19
Marschall v Land Nordrhein-Westfalen: C-409/95 [1997] All ER (EC) 865,
    [1997] ECR I-6363, [1998] 1 CMLR 547, [2001] ICR 45, [1998] IRLR
    39, ECJ 12.12, 13.9
Marsh v National Autistic Society [1993] ICR 453 .... 48.19, 58.7
Marsh & McLennan Companies UK Ltd v Pensions Ombudsman
    [2001] IRLR 505, [2001] All ER (D) 299 (Feb) 42.14
Marshall v Harland & Wolff Ltd [1972] 2 All ER 715, [1972] 1 WLR 899,
    [1972] ICR 101, [1972] IRLR 90, 7 ITR 150, 116 Sol Jo 484, NIRC 48.3
Marshall v Harland & Wolff Ltd (No 2) (Practice Note) [1972] ICR 97, 7
    ITR 132, NIRC 22.6

Marshall v NM Financial Management Ltd [1997] 1 WLR 1527, [1997] ICR
1065, [1997] IRLR 449, CA 41.3, 41.7
Marshall v Southampton and South West Hampshire Area Health Authority
(Teaching): 152/84 [1986] QB 401, [1986] 2 All ER 584, [1986] 2 WLR
780, [1986] ECR 723, [1986] 1 CMLR 688, [1986] ICR 335, [1986] IRLR
140, 130 Sol Jo 340, ECJ 20.12, 25.6, 37.7
Marshall v Southampton and South West Hampshire Area Health Authority
(No 2): C-271/91 [1994] QB 126, [1993] 4 All ER 586, [1993] 3 WLR
1054, [1993] ECR I-4367, [1993] 3 CMLR 293, [1993] ICR 893,
[1993] IRLR 445, ECJ; apld sub nom Marshall v Southampton and
South-West Hampshire Area Health Authority (Teaching) (No 2)
[1994] 1 AC 530n, [1994] 1 All ER 736n, [1994] 2 WLR 392, [1994] ICR
242n, HL 14.13, 20.12, 21.67, 25.5
Marshall (Cambridge) Ltd v Hamblin [1994] ICR 362, [1994] IRLR
260, EAT 8.13, 48.9, 53.5, 58.21
Marshall (Thomas) (Exports) Ltd v Guinle [1979] Ch 227, [1978] 3 All ER
193, [1978] 3 WLR 116, [1979] FSR 208, [1978] ICR 905, [1978] IRLR
174, 122 Sol Jo 295 .... 9.16, 48.19, 53.9, 58.7
Marshalls Clay Products Ltd v Caulfield [2004] ICR 436, sub nom Caulfield
v Marshalls Clay Products Ltd [2003] IRLR 552, EAT; on appeal sub
nom Caulfield v Marshalls Clay Products Ltd [2004] EWCA Civ 422,
[2004] 2 CMLR 1040, [2004] ICR 1502, [2004] IRLR 564, 148 Sol Jo LB
539, [2004] All ER (D) 292 (Apr) 22.1, 29.4, 57.25
Martin v British Railways Board [1989] ICR 24, [1989] IRLR 198, EAT 22.5
Martin v Class Security Installations Ltd (16 March 2006, unreported) 15.4
Martin v Glynwed Distribution Ltd [1983] ICR 511, sub nom Martin v MBS
Fastings (Glynwed) Distribution Ltd [1983] IRLR 198, CA 53.8
Martin v South Bank University: C-4/01 [2004] 1 CMLR 472, [2004] ICR
1234, [2004] IRLR 74, [2003] All ER (D) 85 (Nov), ECJ 42.4, 52.19, 52.29
Martin v Yeoman Aggregates Ltd [1983] ICR 314, [1983] IRLR 49, EAT 48.20,
53.10
Martin v Yorkshire Imperial Metals Ltd [1978] IRLR 440, EAT 27.23, 28.11
Martins v Marks & Spencer plc [1998] ICR 1005, [1998] IRLR 326, CA 12.5, 21.7
Masiak v City Restaurants (UK) Ltd [1999] IRLR 780, EAT 28.8, 54.3, 58.16
Mason v Governing Body of Ward End Primary School [2006] ICR 1128,
[2006] IRLR 432, [2006] All ER (D) 199 (Apr), EAT 54.4
Mason v Provident Clothing and Supply Co Ltd [1913] AC 724, 82 LJKB
1153, [1911–13] All ER Rep 400, 57 Sol Jo 739, 109 LT 449, 29 TLR
727, HL 41.4, 41.6
Massey v Crown Life Insurance Co [1978] 2 All ER 576, [1978] 1 WLR 676,
[1978] ICR 590, [1978] IRLR 31, 13 ITR 5, 121 Sol Jo 791, CA 17.3
Matthews v Kent and Medway Towns Fire Authority [2004] ICR 257,
[2003] IRLR 732, [2003] All ER (D) 90 (Aug), EAT; affd [2004] EWCA
Civ 844, [2004] 3 All ER 620, [2005] ICR 84, [2004] IRLR 697, (2004)
Times, 8 July, 148 Sol Jo LB 876, [2004] All ER (D) 47 (Jul); revsd in
part [2006] UKHL 8, [2006] 2 All ER 171, [2006] IRLR 367,
[2006] NLJR 420, (2006) Times, 2 March, [2006] All ER (D) 15 (Mar) 24.15,
32.5, 32.9, 32.10, 32.12, 32.14
Mattis v Pollock (t/a Flamingos Nightclub) [2003] EWCA Civ 887,
[2004] 4 All ER 85, [2003] 1 WLR 2158, [2003] ICR 1335, [2003] IRLR
603, (2003) Times, 16 July, 147 Sol Jo LB 816, [2003] All ER (D) 10
(Jul) 56.2
Matty v Tesco Stores IDS Brief No 609 .... 10.11
Mau v Bundessanstaltfur Arbeit: C-160/01 [2004] 1 CMLR 34 .... 31.5

Maund v Penwith District Council [1984] ICR 143, [1984] IRLR 24, 134
    NLJ 147, CA 54.1, 54.3
Maurissen and European Public Service Union v Court of Auditors of the
    European Communities: 193/87 [1989] ECR 1045, ECJ 37.8
Maxwell Fleet and Facilities Management Ltd (in administration) (No 2), Re
    [2000] 2 All ER 860, [2000] 2 BCLC 155, [2000] ICR 717,
    [2000] 06 LS Gaz R 35 .... 52.7
May (Greg) (Carpet Fitters and Contractors) Ltd v Dring [1990] ICR 188,
    [1990] IRLR 19, EAT 34.6
Mayo-Deman v University of Greenwich [2005] IRLR 845 .... 14.33, 21.32
Mayeur v Association Promotion de l'Information Messine (APIM):
    C-175/99 [2002] ICR 1316, [2000] IRLR 783, ECJ 18.4, 52.9
Mayhew v Suttle (1854) 19 JP 38, 4 E & B 347, 24 LJQB 54, 1 Jur NS 303, 3
    WR 108, 3 CLR 59, 24 LTOS 159, Ex Ch 43.2
Mazzoleni (criminal proceedings against): C-165/98 [2001] ECR I-2189,
    ECJ 26.3
Meacham v Amalgamated Engineering and Electrical Union [1994] IRLR
    218 .... 51.15
Meade-Hill and National Union of Civil and Public Servants v British
    Council [1996] 1 All ER 79, [1995] ICR 847, [1995] IRLR 478, CA 12.9
Mears v Safecar Security Ltd [1983] QB 54, [1982] 2 All ER 865,
    [1982] 3 WLR 366, [1982] ICR 626, [1982] IRLR 183, 126 Sol Jo 496,
    [1982] LS Gaz R 921, CA 8.9, 44.2
Measures Bros Ltd v Measures [1910] 2 Ch 248, 79 LJ Ch 707, 18 Mans 40,
    54 Sol Jo 521, 102 LT 794, 26 TLR 488, [1908–10] All ER Rep Ext
    1188, CA 31.10
Medical Protection Society v Sadek. See Sadek v Medical Protection Society
Meek v City of Birmingham District Council [1987] IRLR 250, CA 21.63, 22.18
Meer v Tower Hamlets London Borough Council [1988] IRLR 399, CA 12.8
Meikle v Nottinghamshire County Council [2004] EWCA Civ 859,
    [2004] 4 All ER 97, [2005] ICR 1, (2004) Times, 15 July, [2004] All ER
    (D) 123 (Jul), sub nom Nottinghamshire County Council v Meikle
    [2004] IRLR 703, 80 BMLR 129, 148 Sol Jo LB 908 .... 8.13, 10.21, 14.6, 20.29
Melhuish v Redbridge Citizens Advice Bureau [2005] IRLR 419, [2004] All
    ER (D) 116 (Aug), EAT 17.3
Melia v Magna Kansei Ltd [2005] ICR 874, [2005] IRLR 449, [2005] All ER
    (D) 92 (Mar), EAT; revsd in part [2005] EWCA Civ 1547, [2006] IRLR
    117, (2005) Times, 14 November, [2005] All ER (D) 75 (Nov) 21.67, 55.13
Mennell v Newell & Wright (Transport Contractors) Ltd [1997] ICR 1039,
    [1997] IRLR 519, [1997] 33 LS Gaz R 26, CA 34.6, 54.3
Mensah v East Hertfordshire NHS Trust [1998] IRLR 531, [1998] All ER
    (D) 260, CA 14.8, 21.52
Merckx v Ford Motors Co Belgium SA: C-171/94 and C-172/94 [1996] All
    ER (EC) 667, [1996] ECR I-1253, [1997] ICR 352, [1996] IRLR 467,
    ECJ 52.5, 52.16
Mercury Communications Ltd v Scott-Garner [1984] Ch 37, [1984] 1 All ER
    179, [1983] 3 WLR 914, [1984] ICR 74, [1983] IRLR 485; revsd
    [1984] Ch 37, [1984] 1 All ER 179, [1983] 3 WLR 914, [1984] ICR 74,
    [1983] IRLR 494, 127 Sol Jo 764, CA 45.4
Merkur Island Shipping Corpn v Laughton [1983] 2 AC 570, [1983] 2 All ER
    189, [1983] 2 WLR 778, [1983] 2 Lloyd's Rep 1, [1983] ICR 490,
    [1983] IRLR 218, 127 Sol Jo 306, HL 45.2
Mersey Dock and Harbour Co v Verrinder [1982] IRLR 152 .... 45.2

Table of Cases

Mersey Docks and Harbour Board v Coggins & Griffiths (Liverpool) Ltd
[1947] AC 1, [1946] 2 All ER 345, 115 LJKB 465, 90 Sol Jo 466, 175 LT
270, 62 TLR 533, HL 47.2, 56.3
Merseyside and North Wales Electricity Board v Taylor [1975] ICR 185,
[1975] IRLR 60, 10 ITR 52, 119 Sol Jo 272 .... 54.8
Merton London Borough Council v Gardiner [1981] QB 269, [1981] 2 WLR
232, 79 LGR 374, [1981] ICR 186, sub nom Gardiner v London
Borough of Merton [1980] IRLR 472, 125 Sol Jo 97, CA 7.9
Meteorological Office v Edgar [2002] ICR 149, [2001] All ER (D) 06
(Aug), EAT 11.18
Methven v Cow Industrial Polymers Ltd [1980] ICR 463, [1980] IRLR 289,
124 Sol Jo 374, CA 24.11
Metrobus Ltd v Cook (unreported) 15.10
Metropolitan Police Comr v Harley [2001] ICR 927, [2001] IRLR 263, [2001]
All ER (D) 216 (Feb), EAT 20.29
Metropolitan Police Comr v Locker [1993] 3 All ER 584, [1993] ICR 440,
[1993] IRLR 319, [1993] NLJR 543, EAT 37.6
Metropolitan Police Comr v Lowrey-Nesbitt [1999] ICR 401, EAT 37.2
Metropolitan Police Service v Hendricks (2002) IDS Brief No 707 .... 14.6
Metropolitan Police Service v Hendricks [2003] ICR 999 .... 14.6
Metropolitan Police Service v Shoebridge EAT/0234/03, [2004] ICR 1680 .... 13.33
Mettoy Pension Trustees Ltd v Evans [1991] 2 All ER 513, [1990] 1 WLR
1587 .... 42.13
Meyers v Adjudication Officer: C-116/94 [1995] All ER (EC) 705,
[1995] ECR I-2131, [1996] 1 CMLR 461, [1995] IRLR 498, ECJ 25.5
Mezey v South West London and St George's Mental Health NHS Trust
[2007] EWHC 62 (QB), [2007] IRLR 237 .... 8.23
Michael (John) Design plc v Cooke [1987] 2 All ER 332, [1987] ICR 445, 131
Sol Jo 595, [1987] LS Gaz R 1492, CA 41.8
Midas IT Services Ltd v Opus Portfolios Ltd (21 December 1999,
unreported) 41.15
Middlebrook Mushrooms Ltd v Transport and General Workers' Union
[1993] ICR 612, [1993] IRLR 232, CA 30.4, 45.2
Middlesbrough Borough Council v Transport and General Workers Union
[2002] IRLR 332, [2001] All ER (D) 79 (May), EAT 39.4
Midland Bank plc v Madden [2000] IRLR 288 .... 54.4
Midland Counties District Bank Ltd v Attwood [1905] 1 Ch 357, 74 LJ
Ch 286, 12 Mans 20, [1904–7] All ER Rep 648, 92 LT 360, 21 TLR
175 .... 31.10, 58.9
Midland Mainline Ltd v National Union of Rail, Maritime and Transport
Workers [2001] EWCA Civ 1206, [2001] IRLR 813,
[2001] 38 LS Gaz R 37, [2001] All ER (D) 352 (Jul) 45.14
Mid-Staffordshire General Hospitals NHS Trust v Cambridge [2003] IRLR
566, [2003] All ER (D) 06 (Sep), EAT 10.15
Mihlenstedt v Barclays Bank International Ltd and Barclays Bank plc
[1989] IRLR 522, [1989] PLR 124, CA 42.4, 42.13
Mikeover Ltd v Brady [1989] 3 All ER 618, 59 P & CR 218, 21 HLR 513,
[1989] 2 EGLR 61, [1989] 40 EG 92, CA 43.2
Miles v Gilbank [2006] ICR 12, EAT 14.13, 14.16
Miles v Wakefield Metropolitan District Council [1987] AC 539,
[1987] 1 All ER 1089, [1987] 2 WLR 795, 85 LGR 649, [1987] ICR 368,
[1987] IRLR 193, 131 Sol Jo 408, [1987] LS Gaz R 1239, [1987] NLJ
Rep 266, HL 8.24, 34.14, 45.16

Millam v Print Factory (London) 1991 Ltd [2007] EWCA Civ 322, [2007] All ER (D) 132 (Apr) 52.10

Miller v Harry Thornton (Lollies) Ltd [1978] IRLR 430, IT 34.24

Miller v Karlinski (1945) 62 TLR 85, CA 8.15

Miller Bros and F P Butler Ltd v Johnston [2002] ICR 744, [2002] IRLR 386, (2002) Times, 18 April, [2002] All ER (D) 220 (Mar), EAT 8.23, 20.32, 21.34

Mills v Dunham [1891] 1 Ch 576, 60 LJ Ch 362, 39 WR 289, 64 LT 712, 7 TLR 238, CA 41.6

Milsom v Leicestershire County Council [1978] IRLR 433, IT 34.20

Mingeley v Pennock and Ivory (t/a Amber Cars) [2004] EWCA Civ 328, [2004] ICR 727, [2004] IRLR 373, [2004] 11 LS Gaz R 33, (2004) Times, 4 March, [2004] All ER (D) 132 (Feb) 12.12

Mining Supplies (Longwall) Ltd v Baker [1988] ICR 676, [1988] IRLR 417, EAT 55.13

Ministry of Defence v Anderson [1996] IRLR 39, EAT 14.16

Ministry of Defence v Armstrong [2004] IRLR 672, [2004] All ER (D) 146 (Apr), EAT 24.10

Ministry of Defence v Cannock [1995] 2 All ER 449, [1994] ICR 918, [1994] IRLR 509, EAT 14.15

Ministry of Defence v Hunt [1996] ICR 544, EAT 14.15

Ministry of Defence v Jeremiah [1980] QB 87, [1979] 3 All ER 833, [1979] 3 WLR 857, [1980] ICR 13, 123 Sol Jo 735, sub nom Jeremiah v Ministry of Defence [1979] IRLR 436, CA 12.12

Ministry of Defence v Meredith [1995] IRLR 539, EAT 14.18, 21.12

Ministry of Defence v O'Hare (No 2) [1997] ICR 306, EAT 14.16

Ministry of Defence v Pope [1997] ICR 296, EAT 12.5

Ministry of Defence v Wheeler [1998] 1 All ER 790, [1998] 1 WLR 637, [1998] ICR 242, [1998] IRLR 23, [1997] 45 LS Gaz R 27, 142 Sol Jo LB 13, CA 14.15

Miriki v General Council of the Bar [2001] EWCA Civ 1973, [2002] ICR 505, (2002) Times, 22 January, [2001] All ER (D) 364 (Dec) 22.9

Mirror Group Newspapers Ltd v Gunning. See Gunning v Mirror Group Newspapers Ltd

Mitchell v Arkwood Plastics (Engineering) Ltd [1993] ICR 471, EAT 54.8

Mitie Managed Services Ltd v French [2002] ICR 1395 .... 52.18

Mock v IRC [1999] IRLR 785, EAT 22.6

Moenich v Fenestre (1892) 61 LJ Ch 737, 2 R 102, 67 LT 602, 8 TLR 804, CA 41.6

Monie v Coral Racing Ltd [1981] ICR 109, [1980] IRLR 464, CA 54.9

Mono Pumps Ltd v Froggatt and Radford [1987] IRLR 368, EAT 55.12

Monsanto plc v Transport and General Workers' Union [1987] 1 All ER 358, [1987] 1 WLR 617, [1987] ICR 269, [1986] IRLR 406, 131 Sol Jo 690, [1987] LS Gaz R 1572, [1986] NLJ Rep 917, CA 45.14

Mont (J A) (UK) Ltd v Mills [1993] FSR 577, [1993] IRLR 172, CA 41.1, 41.6, 41.8

Montgomery v Johnson Underwood Ltd. See Johnson Underwood Ltd v Montgomery

Montgomery v Lowfield Distribution Ltd (1996) IDS Brief No 576 .... 24.11

Moonsar v Fiveways Express Transport Ltd [2005] IRLR 9, [2004] All ER (D) 110 (Nov), EAT 12.5, 14.16

Moore v Duport Furniture Products Ltd [1982] ICR 84, [1982] IRLR 31, 126 Sol Jo 98, HL 2.4, 21.32

Table of Cases

Moore's (Wallisdown) Ltd v Pensions Ombudsman [2002] 1 All ER 737,
[2002] 1 WLR 1649, [2002] ICR 773, (2002) Times, 1 March, [2001] All
ER (D) 372 (Dec) 42.14
Moores v Bude Stratton Town Council [2001] LGR 129, [2001] ICR 271,
[2000] IRLR 676, [2000] All ER (D) 404, EAT 8.13, 56.1
Moroak (t/a Blake Envelopes) v Cromie [2005] ICR 1226, sub nom Cromie v
Moroak (t/a Blake Envelopes) [2005] IRLR 535, [2005] All ER (D) 233
(May), EAT 20.37, 21.21
Morgan v Electrolux Ltd [1991] ICR 369, [1991] IRLR 89, CA 22.19
Morgan v Staffordshire University [2002] ICR 475, [2002] IRLR 190, [2001]
All ER (D) 119 (Dec), EAT 10.2
Morgan v West Glamorgan County Council [1995] IRLR 68, EAT 34.6
Morganite Electrical Carbon Ltd v Donne [1988] ICR 18, [1987] IRLR
363, EAT 55.15
Morley v Heritage plc [1993] IRLR 400, CA 8.5, 29.9
Moroni v Collo GmbH: C-110/91 [1993] ECR I-6591, [1995] 2 CMLR 357,
[1995] ICR 137, [1994] IRLR 130, [1995] 42 LS Gaz R 23, ECJ 24.18
Morris v Acco Ltd [1985] ICR 306, EAT 55.13
Morris v Breaveglen Ltd (t/a Anzac Construction Co) [1993] ICR 766,
[1993] IRLR 350, [1993] PIQR P294, 137 Sol Jo LB 13, CA 56.3
Morris v C W Martin & Sons Ltd [1966] 1 QB 716, [1965] 2 All ER 725,
[1965] 3 WLR 276, [1965] 2 Lloyd's Rep 63, 109 Sol Jo 451, CA 56.2
Morris v John Grose Group Ltd [1998] ICR 655, [1998] IRLR 499, EAT 52.26
Morris v Secretary of State for Employment [1985] ICR 522, [1985] IRLR
297, EAT 31.5
Morris v Walsh Western UK Ltd [1997] IRLR 562, EAT 7.5, 7.7
Morris (Herbert) Ltd v Saxelby [1916] 1 AC 688, 85 LJ Ch 210,
[1916–17] All ER Rep 305, 60 Sol Jo 305, 114 LT 618, 32 TLR
297, HL 41.4, 41.8
Morrison v Amalgamated Transport and General Workers Union
[1989] IRLR 361, NICA 54.10, 55.13
Morrison (William B) & Son Ltd (1999) IDS Brief No 648 .... 12.5
Morrow v Safeway Stores plc [2002] IRLR 9, [2001] All ER (D) 63
(Sep), EAT 8.13, 53.7, 58.6
Morse v Wiltshire County Council [1998] ICR 1023, [1998] IRLR 352, 44
BMLR 58, EAT 10.12
Morton Sundour Fabrics Ltd v Shaw (1966) 2 KIR 1, 2 ITR 84, DC 48.5, 58.5
Mossman v Bray Management Ltd EAT/0477/04 .... 20.21
Motorola Ltd v Davidson [2001] IRLR 4, EAT 17.3, 47.2
Mowat-Brown v University of Surrey [2002] IRLR 235, [2001] All ER (D)
115 (Dec), EAT 10.7
Mowlem Northern Ltd v Watson [1990] ICR 751, [1990] IRLR 500, EAT 48.5
Moyhing v Barts and London NHS Trust [2006] IRLR 860, [2006] All ER
(D) 64 (Jun), EAT 14.16
Moyling v Homerton University Hospitals NHS Trust, City University
(25 August 2005, unreported), EAT 13.28
Muffett (S H) Ltd v Head [1987] ICR 1, [1986] IRLR 488,
[1986] LS Gaz R 2653, EAT 55.12
Mugford v Midland Bank plc [1997] ICR 399, [1997] IRLR 208, EAT 54.11
Mulox IBC Ltd v Geels: C-125/92 [1993] ECR I-4075, [1994] IRLR 422,
ECJ 26.12
Munir v Jang Publications [1989] ICR 1, [1989] IRLR 224, CA 21.22
Munro v MPB Structures Ltd. See MPB Structure Ltd v Munro

Murphy v Bord Telecom Eireann: 157/86 [1988] ECR 673, [1988] 1 CMLR
    879, [1988] ICR 445, [1988] IRLR 267, ECJ 24.6, 24.8
Murphy v Slough Borough Council [2004] ICR 1163, [2004] All ER (D) 393
    (May), EAT 10.24
Murphy v Slough Borough Council [2005] EWCA Civ 122, [2005] ICR 721,
    [2005] IRLR 382, (2005) Times, 6 April, [2005] All ER (D) 244 (Feb) 37.2
Murray v Foyle Meats Ltd [2000] 1 AC 51, [1999] 3 All ER 769,
    [1999] 3 WLR 356, [1999] ICR 827, [1999] IRLR 562,
    [1999] 31 LS Gaz R 36, 143 Sol Jo LB 214, HL 38.7
Murray v Leisureplay plc [2005] EWCA Civ 963, [2005] IRLR 946, [2005] All
    ER (D) 428 (Jul) 8.23, 8.24, 9.28, 58.26
Murray v Powertech (Scotland) Ltd [1992] IRLR 257, EAT 14.16

N

N v Chief Constable of Merseyside Police [2006] EWHC 3041 (QB), [2006]
    All ER (D) 421 (Nov) 56.2
NACODS v Gluchowski [1996] IRLR 252, EAT 51.13
NALGO v Secretary of State for the Environment (1992) 5 Admin LR 785 .... 30.4
NRG Victory Reinsurance Ltd v Alexander [1992] ICR 675, EAT 55.1
NUMAST v P & O Scottish Ferries [2005] ICR 1270, sub nom National
    Union of Maritime Aviation and Shipping Transport v P & O Scottish
    Ferries [2005] All ER (D) 27 (Apr), EAT 52.5
NUPE and COHSE's Application, Re [1989] IRLR 202 .... 37.4
NWL Ltd v Woods, The Nawala [1979] 3 All ER 614, [1979] 1 WLR 1294,
    [1980] 1 Lloyd's Rep 1, [1979] ICR 867, [1979] IRLR 478, 123 Sol Jo
    751, HL 45.4, 45.16
Nagarajan v London Regional Transport [1998] IRLR 73, CA; revsd
    [2000] 1 AC 501, [1999] 4 All ER 65, [1999] 3 WLR 425, [1999] ICR 877,
    [1999] IRLR 572, [1999] 31 LS Gaz R 36, 143 Sol Jo LB 219, HL 12.6, 12.10,
                                                                        20.17, 24.11
Nagle v Feilden [1966] 2 QB 633, [1966] 1 All ER 689, [1966] 2 WLR 1027,
    110 Sol Jo 286, CA 51.12
Nairne v Highland and Islands Fire Brigade [1989] IRLR 366, 1989 SLT 754,
    Ct of Sess 55.13
Naomi Campbell v Vanessa Frisbee [2002] EWHC 328 .... 41.11
Napier v National Business Agency Ltd [1951] 2 All ER 264, 30 ATC 180, 44
    R & IT 413, 95 Sol Jo 528, CA 8.15
National and Local Government Officers' Association v Courtney-Dunn
    [1991] ICR 784, [1992] IRLR 114, EAT 51.16
National and Local Government Officers' Association v Killorn [1991] ICR
    1, [1990] IRLR 464, EAT 51.16
National Coal Board v Galley [1958] 1 All ER 91, [1958] 1 WLR 16, 102 Sol
    Jo 31, CA 45.16
National Coal Board v National Union of Mineworkers [1986] ICR 736,
    [1986] IRLR 439 .... 6.3
National Coal Board v Sherwin [1978] ICR 700, [1978] IRLR 122, EAT 24.6
National Dock Labour Board v Pinn & Wheeler Ltd [1989] BCLC 647, 5
    BCC 75 .... 7.9
National Federation of Self-Employed and Small Businesses Ltd v Philpott
    [1997] ICR 518, [1997] IRLR 340, EAT 13.26
National Grid Co plc v Mayes [2001] UKHL 20, [2001] 2 All ER 417,
    [2001] 1 WLR 864, [2001] ICR 544, [2001] IRLR 394, [2001] NLJR 572,
    (2001) Times, 10 April, 145 Sol Jo LB 98, [2001] All ER (D) 28 (Apr) 42.13

Table of Cases

National Grid Co plc v Virdee [1992] IRLR 555, EAT 21.16

National Union of Gold, Silver and Allied Trades v Albury Bros Ltd
[1979] ICR 84, [1978] IRLR 504, 122 Sol Jo 662, CA 39.4, 50.20

National Union of Maritime Aviation and Shipping Transport v P & O
Scottish Ferries. See NUMAST v P & O Scottish Ferries

National Union of Mineworkers (Yorkshire Area) v Millward [1995] ICR
482, [1995] IRLR 411, EAT 50.39

National Union of Teachers v Avon County Council (1978) 76 LGR 403,
[1978] ICR 626, [1978] IRLR 55, EAT 39.4, 54.11

National Union of Teachers v St Mary's Church of England (Aided) Junior
School (Governing Body) [1997] ICR 334, [1997] IRLR 242, [1997] ELR
169, CA 25.2, 37.7

National Vulcan Engineering Insurance Group Ltd v Wade [1979] QB 132,
[1978] 3 All ER 121, [1978] 3 WLR 214, [1978] ICR 800, [1978] IRLR
225, 13 ITR 212, 122 Sol Jo 470, CA 24.11

Navas v Eurest Colectividades SA: C-13/05 [2007] All ER (EC) 59,
[2006] 3 CMLR 1123, [2007] ICR 1, [2006] IRLR 706, (2006) Times,
9 August, [2006] All ER (D) 132 (Jul), ECJ 25.6

Nawala, The. See NWL Ltd v Woods, The Nawala

Neale v Hereford and Worcester County Council [1986] ICR 471, sub nom
Hereford and Worcester County Council v Neale [1986] IRLR
168, CA 22.17, 54.4

Neary v Dean of Westminster [1999] IRLR 288 .... 58.17

Neath v Hugh Steeper Ltd: C-152/91 [1994] 1 All ER 929, [1993] ECR
I-6935, [1995] 2 CMLR 357, [1995] ICR 158, [1994] IRLR 91,
[1995] 42 LS Gaz R 23, ECJ 22.27, 24.18

Neil v Strathclyde Borough Council. See Strathclyde Regional Council v Neil

Nelhams v Sandells Maintenance Ltd (1995) Times, 15 June, CA 27.10

Nelson v BBC (No 2) [1980] ICR 110, [1979] IRLR 346, 123 Sol Jo
552, CA 55.13

Nelson v Carillion Services Ltd [2003] EWCA Civ 544, [2003] ICR 1256,
[2003] IRLR 428, [2003] 26 LS Gaz R 36, (2003) Times, 2 May, 147 Sol
Jo LB 504, [2003] All ER (D) 253 (Apr) 24.10, 24.22

Nelson v James Nelson & Sons Ltd [1914] 2 KB 770, 83 LJKB 823, 110 LT
888, 30 TLR 368, CA 9.3

Nerva v RL & G Ltd [1997] ICR 11, [1996] IRLR 461,
[1996] 23 LS Gaz R 35, 140 Sol Jo LB 140, CA 34.21

Nerva v United Kingdom (Application 42295/98) [2002] IRLR 815, 13
BHRC 246, (2002) Times, 10 October, [2002] All ER (D) 137 (Sep),
ECtHR 30.7, 34.9, 34.21

Nethermere (St Neots) Ltd v Gardiner [1984] ICR 612, sub nom Nethermere
(St Neots) Ltd v Taverna and Gardiner [1984] IRLR 240, CA 17.3

New Century Cleaning Co Ltd v Church [2000] IRLR 27, [1999] All ER (D)
345, CA 34.6

New Southern Railway Ltd v Quinn [2006] IRLR 266, [2005] All ER (D) 367
(Nov), EAT 12.5, 33.23

New Southern Railways Ltd (formerly South Central Trains) v Rodway
[2005] EWCA Civ 443, [2005] ICR 1162, sub nom Rodway v New
Southern Railways Ltd [2005] IRLR 583, (2005) Times, 21 April, [2005]
All ER (D) 216 (Apr) 33.26, 49.19

New Testament Church of God v Stewart [2007] IRLR 178, sub nom
Stewart v New Testament Church of God [2006] All ER (D) 362
(Oct), EAT 17.8

New Victoria Hospital v Ryan [1993] ICR 201, [1993] IRLR 202,
[1993] 5 LS Gaz R 41, EAT 21.13
Newell v Gillingham Corpn [1941] 1 All ER 552, 39 LGR 191, 165 LT 184 .... 58.44
Newham London Borough Council v National and Local Government
Officers' Association [1993] ICR 189, [1993] IRLR 83, CA 45.4
Newham London Borough Council v Skingle [2003] EWCA Civ 280,
[2003] 2 All ER 761, [2003] ICR 1008, [2003] IRLR 359, 147 Sol Jo LB
300, [2003] All ER (D) 287 (Feb) 42.7
Newland v Simons & Willer (Hairdressers) Ltd [1981] ICR 521, [1981] IRLR
359, EAT 8.15
Newman v Polytechnic of Wales Students Union [1995] IRLR 72, EAT 20.23
Newns v British Airways plc [1992] IRLR 575, CA 52.25
News Group Newspapers Ltd v Society of Graphical and Allied Trades 1982
[1986] ICR 716, [1986] IRLR 227, 130 Sol Jo 407,
[1986] LS Gaz R 1726, CA 45.16
News Group Newspapers Ltd v Society of Graphical and Allied Trades '82
(No 2) [1987] ICR 181, [1986] IRLR 337 .... 45.2, 50.1
Nicoll v Cutts [1985] BCLC 322, 1 BCC 99,427, [1985] PCC 311, CA 31.10
Nimz v Freie und Hansestadt Hamburg: C-184/89 [1991] ECR I-297,
[1992] 3 CMLR 699, [1991] IRLR 222, ECJ 6.6, 24.3, 24.11, 24.23, 24.24
Noel v London Underground Ltd. See London Underground Ltd v Noel
Noel (Auguste) Ltd v Curtis [1990] ICR 604, [1990] IRLR 326, EAT 54.9
Noone v North West Thames Regional Health Authority (No 2). See North
West Thames Regional Health Authority v Noone
Noorani v Merseyside Tec Ltd [1999] IRLR 184, CA 21.14
Nordenfelt v Maxim Nordenfelt Guns and Ammunition Co Ltd [1894] AC
535, 63 LJ Ch 908, 11 R 1, [1891–4] All ER Rep 1, 71 LT 489, 10 TLR
636, HL 41.2
Norris v Checksfield [1991] 4 All ER 327, [1991] 1 WLR 1241, 63 P & CR
38, [1991] ICR 632, 23 HLR 425, [1992] 1 EGLR 159, [1991] NLJR 707,
[1992] 01 EG 97, CA 43.2, 43.4
North East Midlands Co-operative Society Ltd v Allen [1977] IRLR
212, EAT 39.4, 54.11
North Essex Health Authority v David-John. See David-John v North Essex
Health Authority
North West Thames Regional Health Authority v Noone [1988] ICR 813,
sub nom Noone v North West Thames Regional Health Authority
(No 2) [1988] IRLR 530, CA 14.13, 14.21
North Yorkshire County Council v Fay. See Fay v North Yorkshire County
Council
North Yorkshire County Council v Ratcliffe [1994] ICR 810, [1994] IRLR
342, CA; revsd sub nom Ratcliffe v North Yorkshire County Council
[1995] 3 All ER 597, 93 LGR 571, 159 LG Rev 1009, [1995] IRLR 439,
[1995] 30 LS Gaz R 34, [1995] NLJR 1092, 139 Sol Jo LB 196, sub nom
North Yorkshire County Council v Ratcliffe [1995] ICR 833, HL 24.9, 24.11,
37.2
Northern General Hospital NHS Trust v Gale [1994] ICR 426, sub nom
Gale v Northern General Hospital NHS Trust [1994] IRLR 292, CA 7.9, 8.13,
52.15
Northern Joint Police Board v Power [1997] IRLR 610, EAT 12.6
Norton Tool Co Ltd v Tewson [1973] 1 All ER 183, [1973] 1 WLR 45,
[1972] ICR 501, [1972] IRLR 86, 117 Sol Jo 33, NIRC 55.12

Table of Cases

Norwest Holst Group Administration Ltd v Harrison [1985] ICR 668, sub
  nom Harrison v Norwest Holst Group Administration Ltd [1985] IRLR
  240, CA 53.7, 53.8
Norwich Pharmacal Co v Customs and Excise Comrs [1974] AC 133,
  [1972] 3 All ER 813, [1972] 3 WLR 870, [1972] RPC 743, 116 Sol Jo
  823, CA; revsd [1974] AC 133, [1973] 2 All ER 943, [1973] 3 WLR 164,
  [1973] FSR 365, [1974] RPC 101, 117 Sol Jo 567, HL 8.23
Notcutt v Universal Equipment Co (London) Ltd [1986] 3 All ER 582,
  [1986] 1 WLR 641, [1986] ICR 414, [1986] IRLR 218, 130 Sol Jo 392,
  [1986] LS Gaz R 1314, [1986] NLJ Rep 393, CA 48.3
Notting Hill Housing Trust v Roomus [2006] EWCA Civ 407, [2006] 1 WLR
  1375, [2006] All ER (D) 432 (Mar) 43.6
Nottingham University v Fishel [2000] ICR 1462, [2000] IRLR 471,
  [2000] ELR 385, [2001] RPC 367, [2000] All ER (D) 269 .... 8.13
Nottinghamshire County Council v Bowly [1978] IRLR 252, EAT 54.9
Nottinghamshire County Council v Meikle. See Meikle v Nottinghamshire
  County Council
Nu-Swift International Ltd v Mallinson [1979] ICR 157, [1978] IRLR 537,
  122 Sol Jo 744, EAT 33.5
Nuttall (Edmund) Ltd v Butterfield [2005] IRLR 751, [2005] All ER (D) 488
  (Jul), EAT 10.2, 10.11

O

OBG Ltd v Allan [2007] UKHL 21, [2007] All ER (D) 44 (May) 45.2
Oakley v Labour Party. See Labour Party v Oakley
O'Brien v Associated Fire Alarms Ltd [1969] 1 All ER 93, [1968] 1 WLR
  1916, 3 KIR 223, 3 ITR 182, 112 Sol Jo 232, CA 8.13
O'Brien v Barclays Bank plc [1995] 1 All ER 438, sub nom Barclays
  Bank plc v O'Brien [1994] ICR 865, [1994] IRLR 580, CA 42.2, 42.3, 53.14
O'Brien v Sim-Chem Ltd [1980] 3 All ER 132, [1980] 1 WLR 1011,
  [1980] ICR 573, [1980] IRLR 373, 124 Sol Jo 560, HL 24.7
O'Brien v Transco plc (formerly BG plc). See BG plc v O'Brien
Odoemelam v The Whittington Hospital NHS Trust (6 February 2007,
  unreported) (UKEAT/0016/06) 15.4, 15.11, 15.14, 20.20
O'Donoghue v Redcar and Cleveland Borough Council [2001] EWCA Civ
  701, [2001] IRLR 615, [2001] All ER (D) 192 (May) 14.15, 14.16, 55.13
Office Angels Ltd v Rainer-Thomas and O'Connor [1991] IRLR 214, CA ... 41.4, 41.8
O'Hanlon v Revenue and Customs Comrs [2007] EWCA Civ 283,
  [2007] IRLR 404, [2007] All ER (D) 516 (Mar) 10.11, 10.14, 10.23
Ojutiku v Manpower Services Commission [1982] ICR 661, [1982] IRLR
  418, CA 13.8
O'Kelly v Trusthouse Forte plc [1984] QB 90, [1983] 3 All ER 456,
  [1983] 3 WLR 605, [1983] ICR 728, [1983] IRLR 369, 127 Sol Jo 632,
  [1983] LS Gaz R 2367, CA 17.3
O'Laoire v Jackel International Ltd (No 2) [1991] ICR 718, [1991] IRLR
  170, CA, CA 58.33
Oliver v J P Malnick & Co [1983] 3 All ER 795, [1983] ICR 708,
  [1983] IRLR 456, 127 Sol Jo 646, EAT 16.2
Omilaju v Waltham Forest London Borough Council [2004] EWCA Civ
  1493, [2005] 1 All ER 75, [2005] ICR 481, 148 Sol Jo LB 1370, [2004]
  All ER (D) 174 (Nov), sub nom Waltham Forest London Borough
  Council v Omilaju [2005] IRLR 35

O'Neill v DSG Retail Ltd [2002] EWCA Civ 1139, [2003] ICR 222,
[2002] 40 LS Gaz R 32, (2002) Times, 9 September, [2002] All ER (D)
500 (Jul) 28.18
O'Neill v Governors of St Thomas More RCVA Upper School [1997] ICR
33, [1996] IRLR 372, EAT 12.5
O'Neill v Symm & Co Ltd [1998] ICR 481, [1998] IRLR 232, EAT 10.15
Onwuka v Spherion Technology UK Ltd [2005] ICR 567, [2004] All ER (D)
153 (Dec), EAT 21.3, 21.7, 21.75
Optikinectics Ltd v Whooley [1999] ICR 984 .... 55.13
O'Reilly v Mackman [1983] 2 AC 237, [1982] 3 All ER 680, [1982] 3 WLR
604, 126 Sol Jo 311; on appeal AC 237, [1982] 3 All ER 680,
[1982] 3 WLR 604, 126 Sol Jo 578, CA; affd [1983] 2 AC 237,
[1982] 3 All ER 1124, [1982] 3 WLR 1096, 126 Sol Jo 820, HL 37.4
Orlando v Didcot Power Station Sports and Social Club [1996] IRLR
262, EAT 14.16
Orphanos v Queen Mary College [1985] AC 761, [1985] 2 All ER 233,
[1985] 2 WLR 703, [1986] 2 CMLR 73, [1985] IRLR 349, 129 Sol Jo
284, [1985] LS Gaz R 1787, HL 13.8
Orthet Ltd v Vince-Cain [2005] ICR 374, [2004] IRLR 857, [2004] All ER
(D) 143 (May), EAT 14.16, 14.19
Osborn & Co Ltd v Dior [2003] EWCA Civ 281, [2003] HLR 649,
[2003] 05 EG 144 (CS), [2003] All ER (D) 185 (Jan), CA 43.5
Osborne v Valve (Engineering) Services Ltd (24 November 2000,
unreported) 8.23
Osterreichischer Gewerkschaftsbund v Wirtschaftskammer Osterreich (2004)
IDS Brief No 760 .... 24.14
Outram v Academy Plastics [2001] ICR 367, [2000] IRLR 499, CA 42.13
Owusu v London Fire and Civil Defence Authority [1995] IRLR 574, EAT 14.6,
20.29
Oxford v Department of Health and Social Security [1977] ICR 884,
[1977] IRLR 225, 12 ITR 436, EAT 14.9
Oy Liikenne Ab v Liskojärvi: C-172/99 [2001] All ER (EC) 544, [2001] ECR
I-745, [2001] 3 CMLR 807, [2002] ICR 155, [2001] IRLR 171, [2001] All
ER (D) 168 (Jan), ECJ 52.5

P

P (a minor) v National Association of Schoolmasters/Union of Women
Teachers [2003] UKHL 8, [2003] 2 AC 663, [2003] 1 All ER 993,
[2003] 2 WLR 545, [2003] ICR 386, [2003] IRLR 307, [2003] ELR 357,
(2003) Times, 6 March, [2003] NLJR 350, [2003] All ER (D) 384 (Feb) 45.4,
45.14
P v Nottinghamshire County Council [1992] ICR 706, [1992] IRLR
362, CA 54.9
P v S: C-13/94 [1996] All ER (EC) 397, [1996] ECR I-2143, [1996] 2 CMLR
247, [1996] ICR 795, [1996] IRLR 347, [1997] 2 FCR 180, [1996] 2 FLR
347, ECJ 1.2, 12.6, 22.27, 24.2
P & O European Ferries (Dover) Ltd v Iverson (1999) IDS Brief No 640 .... 24.14
P & O Property Ltd v Allen [1997] ICR 436, EAT 52.16
P & O Trans European Ltd v Initial Transport Service Ltd [2003] IRLR 128,
sub nom P&O Trans European Ltd v Initial Transport Service Ltd
[2002] All ER (D) 116 (Nov), EAT 52.5
PSM International plc v Whitehouse [1992] FSR 489, [1992] IRLR
279, CA 41.15

Table of Cases

Pacitti Jones v O'Brien (a firm) [2005] CSIH 56, [2005] IRLR 888, [2005] All
    ER (D) 141 (Jul) 53.11
Page v Freight Hire (Tank Haulage) Ltd [1981] 1 All ER 394, [1981] ICR
    299, [1981] IRLR 13, EAT 13.18
Page v Hull University Visitor. See R v Hull University Visitor, ex p Page
Page v Smith [1996] AC 155, [1995] 2 All ER 736, [1995] 2 WLR 644,
    [1995] RTR 210, [1995] 2 Lloyd's Rep 95, 28 BMLR 133, [1995] PIQR
    P329, [1995] 23 LS Gaz R 33, [1995] NLJR 723, ... 27.8
Paggetti v Cobb [2002] IRLR 861, (2002) Times, 12 April, [2002] All ER (D)
    394 (Mar), EAT 34.12
Paine v Colne Valley Electricity Supply Co Ltd and British Insulated
    Cables Ltd [1938] 4 All ER 803, 37 LGR 200, 83 Sol Jo 115, 160 LT
    124, 55 TLR 181 .... 27.3
Pakenham-Walsh v Connell Residential [2006] EWCA Civ 90,
    [2006] 11 LS Gaz R 25, [2006] All ER (D) 275 (Feb) 57.21
Palfrey v Greater London Council [1985] ICR 437 .... 44.9
Palfrey v Transco plc [2004] IRLR 916, [2004] All ER (D) 150 (Jul), EAT ... 48.5, 53.5
Palihakkara v British Telecommunications plc (EAT/0185/06) (2007) 823 IDS
    Brief 18 .... 14.33, 21.34
Palmer v Southend-on-Sea Borough Council [1984] 1 All ER 945,
    [1984] 1 WLR 1129, [1984] ICR 372, [1984] IRLR 119, 128 Sol Jo
    262, CA 20.25
Palmer, Wyeth and National Union of Rail, Maritime and Transport
    Workers v United Kingdom [2002] IRLR 568, ECtHR 30.4
Pambakian v Brentford Nylons Ltd [1978] ICR 665, 122 Sol Jo 177, EAT 31.10
Panama v London Borough of Hackney [2003] EWCA Civ 273, [2003] IRLR
    278, [2003] All ER (D) 224 (Feb) 54.9
Paramount Airways Ltd (No 3), Re. See Powdrill v Watson
Parkins v Sodexho Ltd [2002] IRLR 109, [2001] All ER (D) 377
    (Jun), EAT 11.18
Parkinson v March Consulting Ltd [1998] ICR 276, [1997] IRLR 308, CA 54.1
Parliamentary Comr for Administration v Fernandez [2004] 2 CMLR 59,
    [2004] ICR 123, [2004] IRLR 22, [2003] All ER (D) 115 (Oct), EAT 24.11,
                                                                              24.12
Parr v Whitbread & Co plc [1990] ICR 427, [1990] IRLR 39, EAT 54.9
Parry v National Westminster Bank plc [2004] EWCA Civ 1563, [2005] ICR
    396, [2005] IRLR 193, (2004) Times, 4 November, 148 Sol Jo LB 1314,
    [2004] All ER (D) 22 (Nov) 55.5
Parsons v Albert J Parsons & Sons Ltd [1979] FSR 254, [1979] ICR 271,
    [1979] IRLR 117, 122 Sol Jo 812, CA 9.4, 17.3
Parsons v BNM Laboratories Ltd [1964] 1 QB 95, [1963] 2 All ER 658,
    [1963] 2 WLR 1273, 42 ATC 200, [1963] TR 183, 107 Sol Jo 294, CA 58.30
Patefield v Belfast City Council [2000] IRLR 664, NICA 13.21
Patel v Clemence Hoare Cummings (EAT 0214/06) 15.14
Patel v Nagesan [1995] ICR 989, [1995] IRLR 370, CA 20.23
Patel v RCMS Ltd [1999] IRLR 161, EAT 20.32
Paterson v Islington London Borough (23 April 2004, unreported), EAT ... 24.7, 24.11
Patterson v Legal Services Commission [2003] EWCA Civ 1558, [2004] ICR
    312, [2004] IRLR 153, [2004] 02 LS Gaz R 28, (2003) Times,
    20 November, 147 Sol Jo LB 1364, [2003] All ER (D) 140 (Nov) 13.27
Paul v East Surrey District Health Authority [1995] IRLR 305, 30 BMLR
    41, CA 54.9
Paul v National and Local Government Officers' Association [1987] IRLR
    43 .... 50.12

Pay v Lancashire Probation Service [2004] ICR 187, [2004] IRLR 129, (2003)
  Times, 27 November, [2003] All ER (D) 468 (Oct), EAT 30.7
Payne v Secretary of State for Employment [1989] IRLR 352, CA 7.9
Peace v City of Edinburgh Council [1999] IRLR 417, 1999 SLT 712, OH 8.23
Peach Grey & Co (a firm) v Sommers [1995] 2 All ER 513, [1995] ICR 549,
  [1995] IRLR 363, [1995] 13 LS Gaz R 31 .... 21.14
Peake v Automotive Products Ltd [1977] QB 780, [1977] 2 WLR 751,
  [1977] ICR 480, [1977] IRLR 105, 12 ITR 259, 121 Sol Jo 222, EAT;
  revsd [1978] QB 233, [1978] 1 All ER 106, [1977] 3 WLR 853,
  [1977] ICR 968, 121 Sol Jo 644, sub nom Automotive Products Ltd v
  Peake [1977] IRLR 365, 12 ITR 428, CA 24.5
Pearson v Kent County Council [1993] IRLR 165, CA 7.7
Pedersen v Camden London Borough Council [1981] ICR 674, [1981] IRLR
  173, CA 53.7
Pedersen v Kvickly Skive See Handels-og Kontorfunktionaerernes Forbund i
  Danmark (acting on behalf of Hoj Pedersen) v Faellesforeningen for
  Danmarks Brugsforeninger (acting on behalf of Kvickly Skive)
Pendragon plc v Copus EAT/0317/05 .... 20.38
Peninsula Business Services Ltd v Sweeney [2004] IRLR 49, EAT 8.23, 41.1, 41.3
Pepper (Inspector of Taxes) v Hart [1993] AC 593, [1993] 1 All ER 42,
  [1992] 3 WLR 1032, [1992] STC 898, 65 TC 421, [1993] ICR 291,
  [1993] IRLR 33, [1993] NLJR 17, [1993] RVR 127, HL 46.21
Percival-Price v Department of Economic Development [2000] NI 141,
  [2000] IRLR 380, NICA 24.4, 25.2
Percy v Board of National Mission of the Church of Scotland [2005] UKHL
  73, [2006] 2 WLR 353, [2006] ICR 134, [2006] IRLR 195, (2005) Times,
  16 December, 2006 SLT 11, 150 Sol Jo LB 30, [2005] All ER (D) 229
  (Dec) 12.12, 13.10, 17.3, 17.8
Perera v Civil Service Commission [1983] ICR 428, [1983] IRLR 166, CA 12.7
Perkin v St George's Healthcare NHS Trust [2005] EWCA Civ 1174,
  [2006] ICR 617, [2005] IRLR 934, [2005] All ER (D) 112 (Oct) 54.14
Pertemps Groups plc v Nixon IDS Brief No 506 .... 47.2
Pestle and Mortar, The v Turner EAT/0652/05 .... 20.38
Petia Chickerova v Holovachuk (21 February 2007, unreported)
  (UKEAT/0016/07/ZT) 15.11
Petch v Customs and Excise Comrs [1993] ICR 789, 137 Sol Jo LB
  120, CA 42.13
Peterborough Regional College v Gidney IDS Brief No 644 .... 20.23
Peters v Sat Katar Co Ltd [2003] ICR 1574, [2003] IRLR 574,
  [2003] 33 LS Gaz R 28, (2003) Times, 1 July, [2003] All ER (D) 271
  (Jun), CA 22.6
Peters (Michael) Ltd v Farnfield [1995] IRLR 190, EAT 52.15
Petrofina (Great Britain) Ltd v Martin [1966] Ch 146, [1966] 1 All ER 126,
  [1966] 2 WLR 318, 109 Sol Jo 126, [1966] Brewing Tr Rev 145, CA 41.16
Pfaffinger v City of Liverpool Community College [1997] ICR 142,
  [1996] IRLR 508, EAT 38.7, 53.7
Pfeiffer v Deutsches Rotes Kreuz, Kreisverband Waldshut eV: C-397/01 to
  C-403/01 [2005] ICR 1307, [2005] IRLR 137, [2004] All ER (D) 52
  (Oct), ECJ 57.3
Photo Production Ltd v Securicor Transport Ltd [1980] AC 827,
  [1980] 1 All ER 556, [1980] 2 WLR 283, [1980] 1 Lloyd's Rep 545, 124
  Sol Jo 147, 130 NLJ 188, HL 41.11
Photostatic Copiers (Southern) Ltd v Okuda and Japan Office
  Equipment Ltd (in liquidation) [1995] IRLR 11, EAT 52.13

Table of Cases

Pickford v Imperial Chemical Industries plc [1998] 3 All ER 462,
[1998] 1 WLR 1189, [1998] ICR 673, [1998] IRLR 435,
[1998] 31 LS Gaz R 36, [1998] NLJR 978, 142 Sol Jo LB 198, [1998] All
ER (D) 302, HL 28.31
Pickstone v Freemans plc [1989] AC 66, [1987] 3 All ER 756, [1987] 3 WLR
811, [1987] 2 CMLR 572, [1987] ICR 867, [1987] IRLR 218, 131 Sol Jo
538, [1987] LS Gaz R 1409, [1987] NLJ Rep 315, CA; affd [1989] AC 66,
[1988] 2 All ER 803, [1988] 3 WLR 265, [1988] 3 CMLR 221,
[1988] ICR 697, [1988] IRLR 357, 132 Sol Jo 994, [1988] NLJR
193, HL 20.12
Pickwell v Lincolnshire County Council (1993) 91 LGR 509, [1993] ICR 87,
[1992] 41 LS Gaz R 36, EAT 38.6, 52.18
Piggott Bros & Co Ltd v Jackson [1992] ICR 85, [1991] IRLR 309, CA 22.7, 22.14,
22.17, 28.11
Pinkney v Sandpiper Drilling Ltd [1989] ICR 389, [1989] IRLR 425, EAT 7.9
Pinkus v Crime Reduction Initiative (unreported) 15.5
Pinnington v Swansea City Council [2005] EWCA Civ 135, [2005] ICR 685,
(2005) Times, 9 March, [2005] All ER (D) 58 (Feb) 11.18, 28.9
Piscitellia v Zilli Fish Ltd (21 December 2005, unreported)
(UKEAT/0638/05:21) 15.13, 20.20
Plowman (GW) & Son Ltd v Ash [1964] 2 All ER 10, [1964] 1 WLR 568,
108 Sol Jo 216, CA 41.6, 41.8
Polentarutti v Autokraft Ltd [1991] ICR 757, [1991] IRLR 457, EAT 55.13
Polkey v A E Dauton (or Dayton) Services Ltd [1988] AC 344,
[1987] 3 All ER 974, [1987] 3 WLR 1153, [1988] ICR 142, [1987] IRLR
503, 131 Sol Jo 1624, [1988] 1 LS Gaz R 36, [1987] NLJ Rep
1109, HL 39.4, 54.4, 54.11, 55.13
Porcelli v Strathclyde Regional Council [1986] ICR 564, sub nom Strathclyde
Regional Council v Porcelli [1986] IRLR 134, Ct of Sess 12.12
Port of London Authority v Payne [1994] ICR 555, [1994] IRLR 9, CA 55.2, 55.5,
55.17
Porter v Bandridge Ltd [1978] 1 WLR 1145, [1978] ICR 943, [1978] IRLR
271, 13 ITR 340, 122 Sol Jo 592, CA 20.25
Porter v Cannon Hygiene Ltd [1993] IRLR 329, NICA 25.2
Porter v Magill [2001] UKHL 67, [2002] 2 AC 357, [2002] 1 All ER 465,
[2002] 2 WLR 37, [2002] LGR 51, [2001] All ER (D) 181 (Dec) 22.12, 30.7
Porter and Nanyakkara v Queen's Medical Centre (Nottingham University
Hospital) [1993] IRLR 486 .... 52.26
Portsea Island Mutual Co-operative Society Ltd v Leyland (1978) 77 LGR
164, [1978] ICR 1195, [1978] IRLR 556, [1978] Crim LR 554, 122 Sol Jo
486, DC 4.3
Portugaia Construções Lda, Re: C-164/99 [2002] ECR I-787, [2003] 2 CMLR
1093, ECJ 26.3
Post Office v Adekeye [1997] ICR 110, 140 Sol Jo LB 262, sub nom Adekeye
v Post Office (No 2) [1997] IRLR 105, CA 12.12, 40.4
Post Office v Fennell [1981] IRLR 221, CA 54.9
Post Office v Foley 2001] 1 All ER 550, [2000] ICR 1283, [2000] IRLR 827,
[2000] All ER (D) 1137, CA 54.4, 54.9
Post Office v Marney [1990] IRLR 170, EAT 54.4, 54.9, 54.15
Post Office v Moore [1981] ICR 623, EAT 20.21
Post Office v Mughal [1977] ICR 763, [1977] IRLR 178, 12 ITR 130, EAT 36.2
Post Office v Roberts [1980] IRLR 347, EAT 8.13
Post Office v Strange [1981] IRLR 515, EAT 53.7

Post Office v Union of Communication Workers [1990] 3 All ER 199, [1990] 1 WLR 981, [1990] ICR 258, [1990] IRLR 143, CA 45.14

Postcastle Properties Ltd v Perridge (1985) 18 HLR 100, [1985] 2 EGLR 107, 276 Estates Gazette 1063, CA 43.2

Potter v Arafa [1995] IRLR 316, sub nom Arafa v Potter [1994] PIQR Q73, CA 58.30

Potter v Hunt Contracts Ltd [1992] ICR 337, [1992] IRLR 108, EAT 34.6, 34.8

Potter v R J Temple plc (in liquidation) (2004) Times, 11 February, [2003] All ER (D) 327 (Dec), EAT 20.23

Powdrill v Watson [1994] 2 BCLC 118, sub nom Re Paramount Airways Ltd (No 3) [1993] BCC 662; affd sub nom Powdrill v Watson [1994] 2 All ER 513, [1994] ICR 395, [1994] IRLR 295, [1994] 2 BCLC 118, 138 Sol Jo LB 76, [1994] 15 LS Gaz R 35, sub nom Powdrill v Watson, Re Paramount Airways Ltd (No 3) [1994] BCC 172, CA; on appeal sub nom Powdrill v Watson [1995] 2 AC 394, [1995] 2 All ER 65, [1995] 2 WLR 312, [1995] ICR 1100, [1995] 1 BCLC 386, [1995] NLJR 449, [1995] 17 LS Gaz R 47, sub nom Powdrill and Atkinson (as joint administrators of Paramount Airways Ltd) v Watson [1995] IRLR 269, sub nom Powdrill v Watson (Paramount Airways Ltd) [1995] BCC 319, HL 9.28, 31.11

Powell v Brent London Borough Council [1988] ICR 176, [1987] IRLR 466, CA 8.23

Power v Panasonic UK Ltd [2003] IRLR 151, 72 BMLR 1, [2002] All ER (D) 297 (Nov), EAT 10.2

Power v Panasonic UK Ltd EAT/439/04 .... 21.72

Power v Regent Security Services Ltd [2007] IRLR 226, [2007] All ER (D) 262 (Jan), EAT 52.29

Power Packing Casemakers v Faust [1983] QB 471, [1983] 2 All ER 166, [1983] 2 WLR 439, [1983] ICR 292, 127 Sol Jo 187, sub nom Faust v Power Packing Casemakers [1983] IRLR 117, CA 53.17

Powerhouse Retail Ltd v Burroughs [2006] UKHL 13, [2006] IRLR 381, 150 Sol Jo LB 364 .... 20.28

Practice Direction [2003] IRLR 65 .... 22.3

Prakash v Wolverhampton City Council EAT/0140/06 .... 21.10

Prater v Cornwall County Council [2006] EWCA Civ 102, [2006] 2 All ER 1013, [2006] ICR 731, [2006] IRLR 362, [2006] NLJR 372, [2006] All ER (D) 358 (Feb) 17.3

Premier Motors (Medway) Ltd v Total Oil Great Britain Ltd [1984] 1 WLR 377, [1984] ICR 58, [1983] IRLR 471, 128 Sol Jo 151, EAT 52.25

Premium Care Homes Ltd v Osborne EAT/0077/06 .... 21.16

Prescription Pricing Authority v Ferguson [2005] IRLR 464, 2005 SLT 63, [2005] All ER (D) 355 (Feb) 20.11

Presley v Llanelli Borough Council [1979] ICR 419, [1979] IRLR 381, EAT 20.23

Prestige Group plc, Re, Commission for Racial Equality v Prestige Group plc [1984] 1 WLR 335, [1984] ICR 473, [1984] IRLR 166, 128 Sol Jo 131, HL 14.27

Table of Cases

Preston v Wolverhampton Healthcare NHS Trust and Secretary of State for
    Health [1996] IRLR 484, EAT; affd [1997] 2 CMLR 754, [1997] ICR
    899, [1997] IRLR 233, CA; on appeal [1998] 1 All ER 528,
    [1998] 1 WLR 280, [1998] ICR 227, [1998] IRLR 197,
    [1998] 08 LS Gaz R 33, 142 Sol Jo LB 82, 566 IRLB 12, HL; refd sub
    nom Preston v Wolverhampton Healthcare NHS Trust: C-78/98
    [2001] 2 AC 415, [2000] All ER (EC) 714, [2001] 2 WLR 408,
    [2000] ECR I-3201, [2000] 2 CMLR 837, [2000] ICR 961, [2000] IRLR
    506, ECJ; apld sub nom Preston v Wolverhamptom Healthcare NHS
    Trust (No 2) [2001] UKHL 5, [2001] 2 AC 455, [2001] 3 All ER 947,
    [2001] 2 WLR 448, [2001] ICR 217, [2001] IRLR 237, (2001) Times,
    8 February, 145 Sol Jo LB 55 .... 20.28, 24.19, 24.20, 25.2
Preston v Wolverhampton Healthcare Trust (No 2) [2004] EWCA Civ 1281,
    [2005] ICR 222, (2004) Times, 27 October, 148 Sol Jo LB 1212, [2004]
    All ER (D) 73 (Oct), sub nom Powerhouse Retail Ltd v Burroughs
    [2004] IRLR 979 .... 24.19, 52.19
Prestwick Circuits Ltd v McAndrew [1990] IRLR 191, 1990 SLT 654, Ct of
    Sess 8.13
Price v Civil Service Commission (No 2) [1978] IRLR 3, IT 12.9
Printers and Finishers Ltd v Holloway [1964] 3 All ER 54n, [1965] 1 WLR 1,
    [1965] RPC 239, 108 Sol Jo 521 .... 41.8, 41.13
Prison Officers' Association and Securicor Custodial Services Ltd, Re (2000)
    IDS Brief 670 .... 50.29
Procter v British Gypsum Ltd [1992] IRLR 7, EAT 54.9
Property Guards Ltd v Taylor and Kershaw [1982] IRLR 175, EAT 19.3
Provident Financial Group plc v Hayward [1989] 3 All ER 298, [1989] ICR
    160, [1989] IRLR 84, CA 8.24, 41.3, 41.14
Pruden v Cunard Ellerman Ltd [1993] IRLR 317, EAT 20.18
Prudential Assurance Co Ltd v London Residuary Body [1992] 2 AC 386,
    [1992] 3 All ER 504, [1992] 3 WLR 279, 64 P & CR 193, [1992] 2 EGLR
    56, [1992] 33 LS Gaz R 36, [1992] NLJR 1087, [1992] 36 EG 129, 136
    Sol Jo LB 229, HL 43.2
Prudential Assurance Co Ltd v Lorenz (1971) 11 KIR 78 .... 45.3
Pugh v National Assembly for Wales (EAT0251/06) 20.29
Puglia v James & Sons [1996] ICR 301, [1996] IRLR 70, EAT 55.12, 55.13
Puttick v Eastbourne Borough Council (COIT 3106/2) (1995) unreported 12.9

Q

Qualcast (Wolverhampton) Ltd v Haynes [1959] AC 743, [1959] 2 All ER 38,
    [1959] 2 WLR 510, 103 Sol Jo 310, HL 27.5
Quarcoopome v Sock Shop Holdings Ltd [1995] IRLR 353, EAT 14.8, 21.10
Quinn v Ministry of Defence [1998] PIQR P387, HL 37.2
Quinn v Schwarzkopf Ltd [2001] IRLR 67, [2000] All ER (D) 1607, EAT;
    revsd [2002] IRLR 602, Ct of Sess 10.15
Quirk v Burton Hospital NHS Trust [2002] EWCA Civ 149, [2002] IRLR
    353, (2002) Times, 19 February, [2002] All ER (D) 149 (Feb) 24.18

R

R v Associated Octel Co Ltd [1996] 4 All ER 846, [1996] 1 WLR 1543,
    [1996] ICR 972, [1997] IRLR 123, [1997] Crim LR 355, [1996] NLJR
    1685, HL 27.19
R v A-G for Northern Ireland, ex p Burns [1999] IRLR 315 .... 20.12, 57.9

R v Boal [1992] QB 591, [1992] 3 All ER 177, [1992] 2 WLR 890, 95 Cr App
Rep 272, [1992] ICR 495, [1992] IRLR 420, 156 JP 617, [1992] BCLC
872, [1992] 21 LS Gaz R 26, 136 Sol Jo LB 100, CA 27.38, 28.13
R v Bow Street Metropolitan Stipendiary Magistrate, ex p Pinochet Ugarte
(No 2) [2000] 1 AC 119, [1999] 1 All ER 577, [1999] 2 WLR 272, 6
BHRC 1, [1999] 1 LRC 1, sub nom Re Pinochet Ugarte [1999] NLJR
88, [1999] All ER (D) 18, HL 22.12
R v BBC, ex p Lavelle [1983] 1 All ER 241, [1983] 1 WLR 23, [1983] ICR 99,
[1982] IRLR 404, 126 Sol Jo 836 .... 8.23, 37.4, 58.18
R v British Coal Corpn, ex p Vardy [1993] 1 CMLR 721, [1993] ICR 720,
sub nom R v British Coal Corpn and Secretary of State for Trade and
Industry, ex p Vardy [1993] IRLR 104 .... 37.4, 39.4
R v British Coal Corpn and Secretary of State for Trade and Industry,
ex p Price [1994] IRLR 72, DC 37.4, 39.4
R v British Steel plc [1995] 1 WLR 1356, [1995] ICR 586, [1995] IRLR 310,
[1995] Crim LR 654, CA 27.19, 27.38
R v Burke [1991] 1 AC 135, [1990] 2 All ER 385, [1990] 2 WLR 1313, 90 Cr
App Rep 384, 154 JP 798, [1990] Crim LR 877, 22 HLR 433, 134 Sol Jo
1106, [1990] 24 LS Gaz R 43, [1990] NLJR 742, HL 43.3
R v Central Arbitration Committee, ex p BTP Tioxide Ltd [1981] ICR 843,
[1982] IRLR 60 .... 11.3, 50.8
R v Certification Officer for Trade Unions and Employers' Associations,
ex p Electrical Power Engineers' Association [1990] ICR 682,
[1990] IRLR 398, HL 50.14
R v Chief Constable of West Midlands Police, ex p Wiley [1995] 1 AC 274,
[1994] 3 All ER 420, [1994] 3 WLR 433, 159 LG Rev 181, [1995] 1 Cr
App Rep 342, [1994] 40 LS Gaz R 35, [1994] NLJR 1008, 138 Sol Jo LB
156, HL 21.13, 37.6
R v Civil Service Appeal Board, ex p Bruce [1988] 3 All ER 686, [1988] ICR
649, DC; affd sub nom R v Civil Service Appeal Board, ex p Bruce
(A-G intervening) [1989] 2 All ER 907, [1989] ICR 171, CA 37.3
R v Civil Service Appeal Board, ex p Chance [1993] COD 116 .... 37.4
R v Civil Service Appeal Board, ex p Cunningham [1991] 4 All ER 310,
[1992] ICR 816, [1991] IRLR 297, [1991] NLJR 455, CA 37.4
R v Commission for Racial Equality, ex p Cottrell and Rothon
[1980] 3 All ER 265, [1980] 1 WLR 1580, 124 Sol Jo 882, 255 Estates
Gazette 783 .... 14.28
R v Commission for Racial Equality, ex p Westminster City Council
[1984] ICR 770, [1984] IRLR 230; affd [1985] ICR 827, [1985] IRLR
426, CA 12.6, 14.28
R v Crown Prosecution Service, ex p Hogg (1994) Times, 14 April, [1994] 6
Admin LR 778, CA 37.4
R v Davies (David Janway) [2002] EWCA Crim 2949, [2003] ICR 586,
[2003] IRLR 170, 147 Sol Jo LB 29, [2003] 09 LS Gaz R 27 .... 27.37
R v Department of Health, ex p Gandhi [1991] 4 All ER 547, [1991] 1 WLR
1053, [1991] ICR 805, [1991] IRLR 431, DC 13.27, 14.2
R v Derbyshire County Council, ex p Noble (1990) 154 LG Rev 575,
[1990] ICR 808, [1990] IRLR 332, 4 BMLR 103, CA 37.4
R v Director of Government Communications Headquarters, ex p Hodges
[1988] COD 123, (1988) Times, 26 July, DC 37.4
R v DPP, ex p Jones [2000] IRLR 373, [2000] Crim LR 858 .... 27.42
R v East Berkshire Health Authority, ex p Walsh [1985] QB 152,
[1984] 3 All ER 425, [1984] 3 WLR 818, [1984] ICR 743, [1984] IRLR
278, CA 37.4

Table of Cases

R v F Howe & Son (Engineers) Ltd [1999] 2 All ER 249, [1999] 2 Cr App
Rep (S) 37, [1999] IRLR 434, 163 JP 359, [1999] Crim LR 238,
[1998] 46 LS Gaz R 34, [1998] All ER (D) 552, CA 27.37
R v Gateway Foodmarkets Ltd [1997] 3 All ER 78, [1997] 2 Cr App Rep 40,
[1997] ICR 382, [1997] IRLR 189, [1997] Crim LR 512,
[1997] 03 LS Gaz R 28, 141 Sol Jo LB 28, CA 27.18
R v Ghosh [1982] QB 1053, [1982] 2 All ER 689, [1982] 3 WLR 110, 75 Cr
App Rep 154, 146 JP 376, [1982] Crim LR 608, 126 Sol Jo 429, CA 54.9
R v Gough [1993] AC 646, [1993] 2 All ER 724, [1993] 2 WLR 883, 97 Cr
App Rep 188, 157 JP 612, [1993] Crim LR 886, [1993] NLJR 775, 137
Sol Jo LB 168, HL 22.12
R v Greater London Council, ex p Westminster City Counil (1984) Times,
27 December 37.2
R v Hammersmith and Fulham London Borough Council, ex p NALGO
[1991] IRLR 249, [1991] COD 397, 37.4
R v Hull University Visitor, ex p Page [1991] 4 All ER 747, [1991] 1 WLR
1277, [1992] ICR 67, CA; on appeal sub nom R v Lord President of the
Privy Council, ex p Page [1993] AC 682, [1992] 3 WLR 1112, [1993] ICR
114, [1993] 10 LS Gaz R 33, 137 Sol Jo LB 45, sub nom Page v Hull
University Visitor [1993] 1 All ER 97, [1993] NLJR 15, HL 8.12
R v Islington London Borough, ex p Building Employers' Confederation
[1989] IRLR 382, 45 BLR 45, DC 14.32
R v Kirk: 63/83 [1985] 1 All ER 453, [1984] ECR 2689, [1984] 3 CMLR 522,
ECJ 30.5
R v Liverpool City Corpn, ex p Ferguson and Ferguson [1985] IRLR 501 .... 37.4
R v Local Authority and Police Authority in the Midlands, ex p LM
[2000] 1 FCR 736, [2000] 1 FLR 612, [2000] Fam Law 83 .... 19.7
R v London (North) Industrial Tribunal, ex p Associated Newspapers Ltd
[1998] ICR 1212, [1998] IRLR 569, [1998] All ER (D) 181 ..... 14.11, 21.18, 21.51
R v Lord Chancellor's Department, ex p Nangle [1992] 1 All ER 897,
[1991] ICR 743, [1991] IRLR 343 .... 37.2, 37.3
R v Lord President of the Privy Council, ex p Page. See R v Hull University
Visitor, ex p Page
R v Mara [1987] 1 All ER 478, [1987] 1 WLR 87, [1987] ICR 165,
[1987] IRLR 154, 131 Sol Jo 132, [1986] LS Gaz R 3751, CA 27.19, 27.38
R v Nelson Group Services (Maintenance) Ltd [1998] 4 All ER 331,
[1999] 1 WLR 1526, [1999] ICR 1004, [1999] IRLR 646, CA 27.19
R v North Thames Regional Health Authority, ex p L (an infant) [1996] 7
Med LR 385 .... 37.2
R v Registrar General, ex p Segerdal [1970] 2 QB 697, [1970] 3 All ER 886,
[1970] 3 WLR 479, [1970] RA 439, 114 Sol Jo 703, CA 12.6
R v Rhone-Poulenc Rorer Ltd [1996] ICR 1054, [1996] Crim LR 656,
[1996] 02 LS Gaz R 27, 140 Sol Jo LB 39, CA 27.19
R v Rollco Screw and Rivet Co Ltd [1999] 2 Cr App Rep (S) 436,
[1999] IRLR 439, CA 27.37, 27.38
R v Science Museum (Board of Trustees) [1994] IRLR 25, 158 JP 39, CA 27.19
R v Secretary of State for Education and Science, ex p Prior [1994] ICR 877,
[1994] ELR 231, [1994] COD 197 .... 37.4
R v Secretary of State for Employment, ex p Equal Opportunities
Commission [1995] 1 AC 1, [1994] 2 WLR 409, [1995] 1 CMLR 391, 92
LGR 360, [1994] IRLR 176, [1994] NLJR 358, sub nom Equal
Opportunities Commission v Secretary of State for Employment
[1994] 1 All ER 910, [1994] ICR 317, HL 7.1, 12.9, 14.24, 24.11, 25.2, 25.6,
37.4, 38.4

R v Secretary of State for Employment, ex p Seymour-Smith: C-167/97
[1999] 2 AC 554, [1999] All ER (EC) 97, [1999] 3 WLR 460, [1999] ECR
I-623, [1999] 2 CMLR 273, [1999] ICR 447, [1999] IRLR 253, ECJ; apld
sub nom R v Secretary of State for Employment, ex p Seymour-Smith
(No 2) [2000] 1 All ER 857, [2000] 1 WLR 435, [2000] 1 CMLR 770,
[2000] ICR 244, [2000] IRLR 263, [2000] 09 LS Gaz R 40, HL 7.1, 12.8, 13.8,
24.3, 24.10, 25.2, 53.11
R v Secretary of State for Foreign and Commonwealth Affairs, ex p Council
of Civil Service Unions. See Council of Civil Service Unions v Minister
for the Civil Service
R v Secretary of State for the Home Department, ex p Attard [1990] COD
261, CA 37.4
R v Secretary of State for the Home Department, ex p Brind [1991] 1 AC
696, [1990] 1 All ER 469, [1990] 2 WLR 787, [1989] NLJR 1751, CA;
affd [1991] 1 AC 696, [1991] 2 WLR 588, 135 Sol Jo 250, sub nom Brind
v Secretary of State for the Home Department [1991] 1 All ER
720, HL 30.5
R v Secretary of State for the Home Department, ex p Moore [1994] COD
67 .... 37.4
R v Secretary of State for the Home Department, ex p Narin
[1990] 2 CMLR 233, [1990] Imm AR 403, [1990] COD 417, CA 26.2
R v Secretary of State for Trade and Industry, ex p Trades Union Congress
[2001] 1 CMLR 5, [2000] Eu LR 698, [2000] IRLR 565; affd
[2001] 1 CMLR 8, CA 25.6
R v Secretary of State for Trade and Industry, ex p UNISON
[1997] 1 CMLR 459, [1996] ICR 1003, [1996] IRLR 438 .... 7.1, 39.6
R v Secretary of State for Transport, ex p Factortame Ltd: C-48/93
[1996] QB 404, [1996] All ER (EC) 301, [1996] 2 WLR 506, [1996] ECR
I-1029, [1996] 1 CMLR 889, [1996] IRLR 267, ECJ; apld
[1998] 1 All ER 736n, [1998] 1 CMLR 1353, [1997] Eu LR 475, DC; on
appeal [1999] 2 All ER 640n, [1998] 3 CMLR 192, [1998] NPC 68,
[1998] Eu LR 456, CA; affd [2000] 1 AC 524, [1999] 4 All ER 906,
[1999] 3 WLR 1062, [1999] 3 CMLR 597, [1999] 43 LS Gaz R 32, HL 25.2
R v Securities and Futures Authority Ltd, ex p Fleurose [2001] EWCA Civ
2015, [2002] IRLR 297 .... 30.7
R v Southampton Industrial Tribunal, ex p INS News Group Ltd
[1995] IRLR 247 .... 21.18, 21.51
R v Transco [2006] All ER (D) 416 (Mar), CA 27.38
R v Walsall Metropolitan Borough Council, ex p Yapp [1994] ICR 528, 92
LGR 110, CA 37.2
R (on the application of the BBC) v Central Arbitration Committee
[2003] EWHC 1375 (Admin), [2003] ICR 1542, [2003] IRLR 460, (2003)
Times, 12 June, [2003] All ER (D) 71 (Jun) 50.26
R (on the application of Kwik-Fit (GB) Ltd) v Central Arbitration
Committee [2002] EWCA Civ 512, [2002] ICR 1212, [2002] IRLR 395,
(2002) Times, 29 March, [2002] All ER (D) 272 (Mar) 50.30
R (on the application of National Union of Journalists) v Central
Arbitration Committee [2005] EWCA Civ 1309, [2006] ICR 1,
[2006] IRLR 53, [2005] All ER (D) 299 (Jul) 50.29
R (on the application of Ultraframe (UK) Ltd) v Central Arbitration
Committee [2005] EWCA Civ 560, [2005] ICR 1194, [2005] IRLR 641,
(2005) Times, 11 May, [2005] All ER (D) 326 (Apr) 50.32

Table of Cases

R (on the application of X) v Chief Constable of the West Midlands Police
  [2004] EWCA Civ 1068, [2005] 1 All ER 610, [2005] 1 WLR 65,
  [2004] 35 LS Gaz R 34, (2004) Times, 18 August, 148 Sol Jo LB 1119,
  [2004] All ER (D) 576 (Jul) 19.7
R (on the application of Unison) v First Secretary of State [2006] EWHC
  2373 (Admin), [2006] IRLR 926, [2006] All ER (D) 127 (Sep) 3.4
R (on the application of Professional Contractors Group) v IRC
  [2001] EWCA Civ 1945, [2002] STC 165, 74 TC 393,
  [2002] 09 LS Gaz R 31, 146 Sol Jo LB 21, [2001] All ER (D) 356
  (Dec) 46.35
R (on the application of L) v Metropolitan Police Comr [2006] EWHC 482
  (Admin), [2006] All ER (D) 262 (Mar); affd sub nom R (on the
  application of L) v Metropolitan Police Comr [2007] EWCA Civ 168,
  (2007) Times, 28 March, [2007] All ER (D) 19 (Mar) 19.7
R (on the application of Manson) v Ministry of Defence [2005] EWHC 427
  (Admin), [2005] All ER (D) 270 (Feb); affd [2005] EWCA Civ 1678,
  [2005] All ER (D) 69 (Nov) 25.2, 32.2, 32.16, 32.20
R (on the application of Elias) v Secretary of State for Defence
  [2005] EWHC 1435 (Admin), [2005] IRLR 788, (2005) Times,
  25 August, [2005] All ER (D) 94 (Jul) 13.8
R (on the application of Elias) v Secretary of State for Defence
  [2006] EWCA Civ 1293, [2006] 1 WLR 3213, [2006] IRLR 934, (2006)
  Times, 17 October, [2006] All ER (D) 104 (Oct) 12.7, 14.16
R (on the application of Mohammed) v Secretary of State for Defence
  [2007] EWCA Civ 983, 151 Sol Jo LB 610, [2007] All ER (D) 09
  (May) 13.18
R (on the application of Williamson) v Secretary of State for Education and
  Employment [2001] EWHC Admin 960, [2002] 1 FLR 493,
  [2002] Fam Law 257, [2002] ELR 214, [2001] All ER (D) 405 (Nov); affd
  [2002] EWCA Civ 1926, [2003] QB 1300, [2003] 1 All ER 385,
  [2003] 3 WLR 482, [2003] 1 FCR 1, [2003] 1 FLR 726,
  [2003] 09 LS Gaz R 27, (2002) Times, 18 December, [2002] All ER (D)
  192 (Dec) 12.6
R (on the application of B) v Secretary of State for the Home Department
  [2006] EWHC 579 (Admin), [2006] All ER (D) 370 (Mar) 19.7
R (on the application of the Broadcasting, Entertainment, Cinematographic
  and Theatre Union) v Secretary of State for Trade and Industry:
  C-173/99 [2001] All ER (EC) 647, [2001] 1 WLR 2313, [2001] ECR
  I-4881, [2001] 3 CMLR 109, [2001] ICR 1152, [2001] IRLR 559, [2001]
  All ER (D) 272 (Jun), ECJ 25.11, 29.2
R (on the application of Amicus – MSF section) v Secretary of State for
  Trade and Industry [2004] EWHC 860 (Admin), [2004] IRLR 430,
  [2004] All ER (D) 238 (Apr) 13.7, 13.13, 30.7
R (on the application of Malik) v Waltham Forest Primary Care Trust
  [2006] EWHC 487 (Admin), [2006] 3 All ER 71, [2006] ICR 1111,
  [2006] IRLR 526, 90 BMLR 49, (2006) Times, 26 May, [2006] All ER
  (D) 260 (Mar); revsd [2007] EWCA Civ 265, [2007] All ER (D) 462
  (Mar) 30.7
RCO Support Services Ltd v UNISON [2000] ICR 1502, [2000] IRLR
  624, EAT; affd [2002] EWCA Civ 464, [2002] ICR 751, [2002] IRLR
  401, [2002] All ER (D) 50 (Apr) 52.5
RS Components Ltd v Irwin [1974] 1 All ER 41, [1973] ICR 535,
  [1973] IRLR 239, NIRC 54.14

Rabahallah v British Telecommunications plc [2005] ICR 440, [2005] IRLR
184, [2004] All ER (D) 411 (Nov), EAT 20.8
Radin (Susie) Ltd v GMB. See GMB v Susie Radin Ltd
Rai v Somerfield Stores Ltd [2004] ICR 656, [2004] IRLR 124, EAT 20.23, 48.5
Rainey v Greater Glasgow Health Board [1987] AC 224, [1987] 1 All ER 65,
[1986] 3 WLR 1017, [1987] 2 CMLR 11, [1987] ICR 129, [1987] IRLR
26, 130 Sol Jo 954, [1987] LS Gaz R 188, [1986] NLJ Rep 1161, 1987 SC
(HL) 1, 1987 SLT 146, HL 13.8, 24.11
Ralton v Havering College of Further and Higher Education [2001] 3 CMLR
1452, [2001] IRLR 738, [2001] All ER (D) 297 (Jun), EAT 52.29
Ramdoolar v Bycity Ltd [2005] ICR 368, [2004] All ER (D) 21 (Nov), EAT 33.6
Rank Xerox Ltd v Churchill [1988] IRLR 280, EAT 8.13
Rank Xerox (UK) Ltd v Stryczek [1995] IRLR 568, EAT 55.3
Rankin v British Coal Corpn [1995] ICR 774, [1993] IRLR 69, EAT 25.2
Rao v Civil Aviation Authority [1994] ICR 495, [1994] IRLR 240, CA 55.13
Rask and Christensen v ISS Kantineservice A/S: C-209/91 [1992] ECR
I-5755, [1993] IRLR 133, ECJ 52.5
Raspin v United News Shops Ltd [1999] IRLR 9, 611 IRLB 4, EAT 58.33
Ratcliffe v North Yorkshire County Council. See North Yorkshire County
Council v Ratcliffe
Ravenseft Properties Ltd v Hall [2001] EWCA Civ 2034, [2002] HLR 624,
[2002] 11 EG 156, (2002) Times, 15 January, [2001] All ER (D) 318
(Dec) 43.5
Rayware Ltd v Transport and General Workers' Union [1989] 3 All ER 583,
[1989] 1 WLR 675, [1989] ICR 457, [1989] IRLR 134,
[1989] 29 LS Gaz R 44, CA 45.9
Read v Astoria Garage (Streatham) Ltd [1952] Ch 637, [1952] 2 All ER 292,
[1952] 2 TLR 130, CA 9.3, 58.10
Read v Phoenix Preservation Ltd [1985] ICR 164, [1985] IRLR 93,
[1985] LS Gaz R 43, EAT 54.9
Read (Richard) (Transport) Ltd v National Union of Mineworkers (South
Wales Area) [1985] IRLR 67 .... 45.16
Ready Mixed Concrete (South East) Ltd v Minister of Pensions and
National Insurance [1968] 2 QB 497, [1968] 1 All ER 433, [1968] 2 WLR
775, 112 Sol Jo 14 .... 17.3
Red Bank Manufacturing Co Ltd v Meadows [1992] ICR 204, [1992] IRLR
209, EAT 22.12
Reda v Flag Ltd [2002] UKPC 38, [2002] IRLR 747, [2002] All ER (D) 201
(Jul) 8.13, 48.6, 58.15
Redcar and Cleveland Borough Council v Bainbridge [2007] IRLR 91, [2006]
All ER (D) 197 (Nov), EAT 15.7, 24.8, 24.11
Reddington v Straker & Sons Ltd [1994] ICR 172, EAT 21.3, 21.10, 21.41
Redfearn v Serco Ltd (t/a West Yorkshire Transport Service) [2005] IRLR
744, [2005] All ER (D) 98 (Sep), EAT 13.8
Redfearn v Serco Ltd (t/a West Yorkshire Transport Service) [2006] EWCA
Civ 659, [2006] ICR 1367, [2006] IRLR 623, (2006) Times, 27 June, 150
Sol Jo LB 703, [2006] All ER (D) 366 (May) 30.7
Redmond (Dr Sophie) Stichting v Bartol: C-29/91 [1992] ECR I-3189,
[1994] 3 CMLR 265, [1992] IRLR 366, ECJ 52.4, 52.5
Reed and Bull Information Systems v Stedman [1999] IRLR 299 .... 12.12
Rees v Apollo Watch Repairs plc [1996] ICR 466, EAT 12.5
Refreshment Systems Ltd v Wolstenholme EAT/608/03 .... 22.1
Reid v Camphill Engravers [1990] ICR 435, [1990] IRLR 268, EAT 20.31, 34.8

Table of Cases

Reid v Explosives Co Ltd (1887) 19 QBD 264, 56 LJQB 388, 35 WR 509,
[1886–90] All ER Rep 712, 57 LT 439, 3 TLR 588, CA 31.10, 58.9
Reid v Rush & Tompkins Group plc [1989] 3 All ER 228, [1990] 1 WLR 212,
[1990] RTR 144, [1989] 2 Lloyd's Rep 167, [1990] ICR 61, [1989] IRLR
265, CA 28.16
Relaxion Group plc v Rhys-Harper [2003] UKHL 33, [2003] 4 All ER 1113,
[2003] 2 CMLR 1329, [2003] ICR 867, [2003] IRLR 484, 74 BMLR 109,
[2003] 30 LS Gaz R 30, (2003) Times, 23 June, 147 Sol Jo LB 782, [2003]
All ER (D) 258 (Jun) 10.17, 11.18, 12.12, 14.6
Rentokil Ltd v Mackin [1989] IRLR 286, EAT 54.9
Retarded Children's Aid Society Ltd v Day [1978] 1 WLR 763, [1978] ICR
437, [1978] IRLR 128, 122 Sol Jo 385, CA 22.17
Rewe-Zentralfinanz GmbH v Landwirtschaftskammer für Saarland: 33/76
[1976] ECR 1989, [1977] 1 CMLR 533, CMR 8382, ECJ 25.2
Rhys Harper v Relaxion Group plc [2003] UKHL 33, [2003] 4 All ER 1113,
[2003] 2 CMLR 1329, [2003] ICR 867, [2003] IRLR 484, 74 BMLR 109,
[2003] 30 LS Gaz R 30, 147 Sol Jo LB 782 .... 11.18, 13.33, 40.5
Richardson (Inspector of Taxes) v Delaney [2001] STC 1328, 74 TC 167,
[2001] IRLR 663, [2001] All ER (D) 74 (Jun) 48.10, 58.32
Richardson v Koefod [1969] 3 All ER 1264, [1969] 1 WLR 1812, 113 Sol Jo
898, CA 58.15
Richardson v U Mole Ltd [2005] IRLR 668, [2005] All ER (D) 80
(Jul), EAT 20.16, 20.34, 22.4
Richmond Precision Engineering Ltd v Pearce [1985] IRLR 179, EAT 54.14
Rickard v PB Glass Supplies Ltd [1990] ICR 150, CA 34.8
Ridout v T C Group [1998] IRLR 628, EAT 10.12, 10.15, 10.32
Rigby v Ferodo Ltd [1988] ICR 29, [1987] IRLR 516, HL 8.22, 48.19, 58.7, 58.24
Riley v Tesco Stores Ltd [1980] ICR 323, [1980] IRLR 103, CA 20.25
Rinner-Kühn v FWW Spezial-Gebäudereinigung GmbH & Co KG: 171/88
[1989] ECR 2743, [1993] 2 CMLR 932, [1989] IRLR 493, ECJ 24.3
Riordan v War Office [1959] 3 All ER 552, [1959] 1 WLR 1046, 103 Sol Jo
921; affd [1960] 3 All ER 774n, [1961] 1 WLR 210, CA ... 48.20, 53.5, 53.10, 58.5,
58.43
Roach v CSB (Moulds) Ltd [1991] ICR 349, [1991] IRLR 200, EAT 7.6
Robb v Green [1895] 2 QB 1, 59 JP 695, 64 LJQB 593, 44 WR 26, 39 Sol Jo
382, 72 LT 686, 11 TLR 330; affd [1895] 2 QB 315, 59 JP 695, 64 LJQB
593, 14 R 580, 44 WR 25, [1895–9] All ER Rep 1053, 39 Sol Jo 653, 73
LT 15, 11 TLR 517, CA 41.13
Robb v Hammersmith and Fulham London Borough Council [1991] ICR
514, [1991] IRLR 72 .... 8.23
Roberts v Birds Eye Walls Ltd. See Birds Eye Walls Ltd v Roberts
Roberts v Skelmersdale College [2003] EWCA Civ 954, [2003] ICR 1127,
[2004] IRLR 69, [2003] All ER (D) 272 (Jun) 21.54
Roberts v West Coast Trains Ltd [2004] EWCA Civ 900, [2005] ICR 254,
[2004] IRLR 788, [2004] 28 LS Gaz R 33, (2004) Times, 25 June, [2004]
All ER (D) 147 (Jun) 55.2
Robertson v Bexley Community Centre (t/a Leisure Link) [2003] EWCA Civ
576, [2003] IRLR 434, [2003] All ER (D) 151 (Mar) 14.7, 20.29, 20.30
Robertson v Blackstone Franks Investment Management Ltd [1998] IRLR
376, CA 34.6, 34.8
Robertson v British Gas Corpn [1983] ICR 351, [1983] IRLR 302, CA 6.4, 8.5
Robertson v Department for Environment Food and Rural Affairs
[2005] EWCA Civ 138, [2005] ICR 750, [2005] IRLR 363, (2005) Times,
2 March, [2005] All ER (D) 335 (Feb) 24.9

Robertson v Magnet Ltd (Retail Division) [1993] IRLR 512, EAT 54.4, 55.13

Robertson and Rough v Forth Road Bridge Joint Board [1995] IRLR 251, Ct of Sess 27.8

Robins v Secretary of State for Work and Pensions: C-278/05 [2007] 2 CMLR 269, [2007] IRLR 270, (2007) Times, 30 January, [2007] All ER (D) 195 (Jan), ECJ 25.2

Robinson v Oddbins Ltd [1996] 27 DCLD 1 .... 12.9

Robinson v Post Office [2000] IRLR 804 , [2000] All ER (D) 1304, EAT ... 14.7, 20.30

Robinson v Ulster Carpet Mills Ltd [1991] IRLR 348, NICA 54.4, 54.11

Robinson-Steele v RD Retail Services Ltd: C-131/04 [2006] IRLR 386, [2006] All ER (D) 238 (Mar), ECJ 22.1, 22.27, 29.4, 57.25

Rock Refrigeration Ltd v Jones [1997] 1 All ER 1, [1997] ICR 938, [1996] IRLR 675, [1996] 41 LS Gaz R 29, 140 Sol Jo LB 226, CA 41.11, 58.34

Rockfon A/S v Specialarbejderforbundet i Danmark: C-449/93 [1995] ECR I-4291, [1996] ICR 673, [1996] IRLR 168, ECJ 39.4

Rock-it Cargo Ltd v Green [1997] IRLR 581, EAT 8.23, 21.34

Rodway v New Southern Railways Ltd. See New Southern Railways Ltd (formerly South Central Trains) v Rodway

Roebuck v National Union of Mineworkers (Yorkshire Area) [1977] ICR 573, 121 Sol Jo 709 .... 51.15

Roith (W & M) Ltd, Re [1967] 1 All ER 427, [1967] 1 WLR 432, 110 Sol Jo 963 .... 58.36

Rolls Royce Ltd v Walpole [1980] IRLR 343, EAT 54.8

Rolls-Royce Motor Cars Ltd v Price [1993] IRLR 203, EAT 54.11

Rolls-Royce Motors Ltd v Dewhurst [1985] ICR 869, [1985] IRLR 184, EAT 54.11

Rolls-Royce plc v Doughty. See Doughty v Rolls-Royce plc

Rookes v Barnard [1964] AC 1129, [1964] 1 All ER 367, [1964] 2 WLR 269, [1964] 1 Lloyd's Rep 28, 108 Sol Jo 93, HL 14.18, 37.5

Rose v Plenty [1976] 1 All ER 97, [1976] 1 WLR 141, [1976] 1 Lloyd's Rep 263, [1975] ICR 430, [1976] IRLR 60, 119 Sol Jo 592, CA 56.2

Ross v Delrosa Caterers Ltd [1981] ICR 393, EAT 7.12

Rousillon v Rousillon (1880) 14 Ch D 351, 44 JP 663, 49 LJ Ch 338, 28 WR 623, 42 LT 679 .... 41.12

Rovenska v General Medical Council [1998] ICR 85, [1997] IRLR 367, CA 14.6, 20.29

Rowan v Machinery Installations (South Wales) Ltd [1981] ICR 386, [1981] IRLR 122, EAT 7.12

Rowell v Hubbard Group Services Ltd [1995] IRLR 195, EAT 54.11

Rowley v Cerberus Software Ltd. See Cerberus Software Ltd v Rowley

Roy v Kensington and Chelsea and Westminster Family Practitioner Committee [1992] 1 AC 624, [1992] 1 All ER 705, [1992] 2 WLR 239, [1992] IRLR 233, 8 BMLR 9, [1992] 17 LS Gaz R 48, 136 Sol Jo LB 62, HL 37.4

Royal and Sun Alliance Insurance Group v Payne [2005] IRLR 848, (2005) Times, 12 October, [2005] All ER (D) 07 (Aug), EAT 42.2, 42.5

Royal Bank of Sctoland plc v Theobald (EAT/0444/06) 20.25, 20.26

Royal Liverpool Children's NHS Trust v Dunsby [2006] IRLR 351, [2006] All ER (D) 244 (Jan), EAT 10.23

Royal Mail Group plc v Lynch UKEAT/0426/03 .... 32.11

Royal National Lifeboat Institution v Bushaway [2005] IRLR 674, [2005] All ER (D) 307 (Apr), EAT 17.3, 47.2

Royal National Orthopaedic Hospital Trust v Howard [2002] IRLR 849, [2002] All ER (D) 54 (Aug), EAT 21.32

Table of Cases

Royal Philanthropic Society v County (1985) 18 HLR 83, 129 Sol Jo 854,
  [1985] 2 EGLR 109, 276 Estates Gazette 1068, CA 43.2
Royal Society for the Prevention of Cruelty to Animals v Cruden [1986] ICR
  205, [1986] IRLR 83, EAT 54.10
Royal Society for the Protection of Birds v Croucher [1984] ICR 604,
  [1984] IRLR 425, EAT 54.10
Rubenstein and Roskin (t/a McGuffies Dispensing Chemists) v McGloughlin
  [1996] ICR 318, [1996] IRLR 557, EAT 22.25, 55.13
Rummler v Dato-Druck GmbH: 237/85 [1987] ICR 774, [1987] IRLR 32,
  ECJ 24.7
Runciman v Walter Runciman plc [1992] BCLC 1084, [1993] BCC 223 .... 9.7, 58.28,
                                                                                 58.36
Rushton v Harcros Timber and Building Supplies Ltd [1993] ICR 230,
  [1993] IRLR 254, [1993] 8 LS Gaz R 40, EAT 55.13
Russell v Elmdon Freight Terminal Ltd [1989] ICR 629, EAT 7.9
Rutherford v Radio Rentals Ltd 1993 SLT 221 .... 44.14
Rutherford v Secretary of State for Trade and Industry [2003] 3 CMLR 933,
  [2003] 42 LS Gaz R 31, [2003] NLJR 1633, sub nom Secretary of State
  for Trade and Industry v Rutherford [2003] IRLR 858, EAT; on appeal
  Rutherford v Secretary of State for Trade and Industry [2004] EWCA
  Civ 1186, [2004] 3 CMLR 1158, [2004] IRLR 892, [2004] All ER (D) 23
  (Sep), sub nom Secretary of State for Trade and Industry v Rutherford
  (No 2) [2005] ICR 119, sub nom Rutherford v Towncircle Ltd 148 Sol Jo
  LB 1065; affd sub nom Rutherford v Secretary of State for Trade and
  Industry [2006] UKHL 19, [2006] All ER (D) 30 (May) 12.8, 13.8, 24.10, 42.2,
                                                                           53.14, 53.15
Rutherford v Towncircle Ltd (t/a Harvest) (in liquidation) and Secretary of
  State for Trade and Industry (No 2) [2003] 2 CMLR 877, [2002] IRLR
  768, EAT 38.13
Rutten v Cross Medical Ltd: C-383/95 [1997] All ER (EC) 121, [1997] ECR
  I-57, [1997] ICR 715, [1997] IRLR 249, ECJ 26.12
Rutty v Commotion Ltd. See Commotion Ltd v Rutty
Ryan v Shipboard Maintenance Ltd [1980] ICR 88, [1980] IRLR 16, EAT 53.10
Rybak v Jean Sorelle Ltd [1991] ICR 127, sub nom Jean Sorelle Ltd v Rybak
  [1991] IRLR 153, EAT 20.25
Ryford Ltd v Drinkwater [1996] IRLR 16, EAT 49.2, 49.6
Rygard v Sto Molle Akustik. See Ledernes Hovedorganisation (acting for
  Rygard) v Dansk Arbejdsgiverforening (acting for Sto Molle Akustik
  A/S)

                                          S
S and U Stores Ltd v Wilkes [1974] 3 All ER 401, [1974] ICR 645,
  [1974] IRLR 283, [1975] KILR 117, 9 ITR 415, NIRC 34.39
SIP Industrial Products Ltd v Swinn [1994] ICR 473, [1994] IRLR
  323, EAT 34.6
ST v North Yorkshire County Council. See Trotman v North Yorkshire
  County Council
Sadek v Medical Protection Society [2004] EWCA Civ 865, [2004] 4 All ER
  118, [2005] IRLR 57, (2004) Times, 2 September, [2004] All ER (D) 163
  (Jul), sub nom Medical Protection Society v Sadek [2004] ICR 1263, 148
  Sol Jo LB 878 .... 13.26
Sadler v Imperial Life Assurance Co of Canada Ltd [1988] IRLR 388 .... 41.3

Safeway Stores plc v Burrell [1997] ICR 523, [1997] IRLR 200, 567 IRLB
   8, EAT 38.7
Saggar v Ministry of Defence [2005] EWCA Civ 413, [2005] ICR 1073,
   [2005] IRLR 618, (2005) Times, 9 May, [2005] All ER (D) 382 (Apr) 12.12,
                                                                                   13.15, 26.13
Sahatciu v DPP Restaurants Ltd [2007] All ER (D) 224 (Jun) 15.1, 15.2
Sainsbury (J) Ltd v Savage [1981] ICR 1, [1980] IRLR 109, CA 20.23, 53.13, 54.15
Sainsbury (J) plc v Moger [1994] ICR 800, EAT 22.20
St Anne's Board Mill Co Ltd v Brien [1973] ICR 444, [1973] IRLR 309,
   NIRC 54.10
St Helens Metropolitan Borough Council v Derbyshire [2005] EWCA Civ
   977, [2006] ICR 90, [2005] IRLR 801, (2005) Times, 26 August, [2005]
   All ER (D) 468 (Jul) 12.10
St John of God (Care Services) Ltd v Brooks [1992] ICR 715, [1992] IRLR
   546, [1992] 29 LS Gaz R 24, EAT 54.14
St Matthias Church of England School (Board of Governors) v Crizzle
   [1993] ICR 401, [1993] IRLR 472, [1993] 15 LS Gaz R 39, EAT 13.8
Sajid v Sussex Muslim Society [2001] EWCA Civ 1684, [2002] IRLR 113,
   [2001] All ER (D) 19 (Oct) 8.23, 21.26, 58.39
Salinas v Bear Stearns International Holdings Inc [2005] ICR 1117, [2004]
   All ER (D) 296 (Oct), EAT 21.72
Salgueiro da Silva Mouta v Portugal [2001] 1 FCR 653, ECtHR 30.4
Salton v Durham County Council [1989] IRLR 99, EAT 53.19
Salvesen v Simons [1994] ICR 409, [1994] IRLR 52, EAT 8.15
Salvesen (Christian) Food Services Ltd v Ali. See Ali v Christian Salvesen
   Food Services Ltd
Sampson v Wilson [1996] Ch 39, [1995] 3 WLR 455, 70 P & CR 359, 29
   HLR 18, CA 43.3
Sanni v SmithKline Beecham Ltd EAT/656/98 .... 21.16
Santamera v Express Cargo Forwarding (t/a IEC Ltd) [2003] IRLR 273,
   (2003) Times, 13 January, [2002] All ER (D) 379 (Nov), EAT 54.10
Sarker v South Tees Acute Hospitals NHS Trust [1997] ICR 673,
   [1997] IRLR 328, EAT 8.23, 23.5
Saunders v Richmond-upon-Thames London Borough Council [1978] ICR
   75, [1977] IRLR 362, 12 ITR 488, EAT 12.12
Savage v British India Steam Navigation Co Ltd (1930) 46 TLR 294 .... 58.17
Savoia v Chiltern Herb Farms Ltd [1982] IRLR 166, CA 53.7
Sawyer v Ahsan [2000] ICR 1, [1999] IRLR 609, EAT 13.27
Sayers v Cambridgeshire County Council [2006] EWHC 2029 (QB),
   [2007] IRLR 29 .... 57.21
Sayers v International Drilling Co NV [1971] 3 All ER 163, [1971] 1 WLR
   1176, [1971] 2 Lloyd's Rep 105, 115 Sol Jo 466, CA 26.11
Scally v Southern Health and Social Services Board [1992] 1 AC 294,
   [1991] 4 All ER 563, [1991] 3 WLR 778, [1991] ICR 771, [1991] IRLR
   522, 135 Sol Jo LB 172, HL 8.9, 8.13, 24.19, 42.13
Scanfuture UK Ltd v Secretary of State for the Department of Trade and
   Industry [2001] ICR 1096, [2001] IRLR 416, [2001] All ER (D) 296
   (Mar), EAT 30.7
Schmidt v Austicks Bookshops Ltd [1978] ICR 85, [1977] IRLR 360, EAT 12.5
Schmidt v Spar und Leihkasse der früheren Amter Bordesholm, Kiel und
   Cronshagen: C-392/92 [1994] ECR I-1311, [1995] 2 CMLR 331,
   [1995] ICR 237, [1994] IRLR 302, ECJ 52.5

Table of Cases

Schöning-Kougebetopoulou v Freie und Hansestadt Hamburg: C-15/96
  [1998] All ER (EC) 97, [1998] 1 CMLR 931, sub nom Kalliope
  Schöning-Kougebetopoulou v Freie und Hansestadt Hamburg
  [1998] ECR I-47, ECJ 26.2
Schroeder (A) Music Publishing Co Ltd v Macaulay [1974] 3 All ER 616,
  [1974] 1 WLR 1308, 118 Sol Jo 734, HL 41.9
Schuler-Zgraggen v Switzerland (Application 14518/89) (1993) 16 EHRR
  405, [1994] 1 FCR 453, ECtHR 30.4
Schultz v Esso Petroleum Ltd [1999] 3 All ER 338, [1999] ICR 1202,
  [1999] IRLR 488, CA 20.25
Science Research Council v Nassé [1980] AC 1028, [1979] 3 All ER 673,
  [1979] 3 WLR 762, [1979] IRLR 465, [1979] ICR 921, 123 Sol Jo
  768, HL 14.9, 21.12
Scope v Thornett. See Thornett v Scope
Scorer v Seymour-Johns [1966] 3 All ER 347, [1966] 1 WLR 1419, 1 KIR
  303, 110 Sol Jo 526, CA 41.8
Scotch Premier Meat Ltd v Burns [2000] IRLR 639, EAT 39.4
Scott v Coalite Fuels and Chemicals Ltd [1988] ICR 355, [1988] IRLR
  131, EAT 48.2, 53.19
Scott v Creager [1979] ICR 403, [1979] IRLR 162, EAT 34.20
Scott v IRC [2004] EWCA Civ 400, [2004] IRLR 713, (2004) Times, 19 April,
  148 Sol Jo LB 474, [2004] All ER (D) 46 (Apr) 14.18, 21.11
Scottbridge Construction Ltd v Wright [2003] IRLR 21, Ct of Sess 34.12
Scott-Davies v Redgate Medical Services [2007] ICR 348, [2006] All ER (D)
  29 (Dec), EAT 15.1, 15.8
Scottish Daily Record and Sunday Mail (1986) Ltd v Laird [1996] IRLR 665,
  1997 SLT 345, Ct of Sess 54.9
Scullard v Knowles [1996] ICR 399, [1996] IRLR 344, EAT 24.3, 24.9, 25.2, 25.6
Scully UK Ltd v Lee [1998] IRLR 259, CA 41.7, 41.8
Sealy v Consignia plc [2002] EWCA Civ 878, [2002] 3 All ER 801,
  [2002] ICR 1193, [2002] IRLR 624, (2002) Times, 3 July, [2002] All ER
  (D) 129 (Jun) 20.21, 20.25
Secretary of State for Employment v Associated Society of Locomotive
  Engineers and Firemen (No 2) [1972] 2 QB 455, [1972] 2 All ER 949,
  [1972] 2 WLR 1370, [1972] ICR 19, 13 KIR 1, 116 Sol Jo 467, CA 8.13, 45.16
Secretary of State for Employment v Banks [1983] ICR 48, EAT 38.11
Secretary of State for Employment v Chapman [1989] ICR 771, CA 7.9
Secretary of State for Employment v Clark [1997] 1 CMLR 613, sub nom
  Clark v Secretary of State for Employment [1997] ICR 64, [1996] IRLR
  578, CA 24.3, 24.14
Secretary of State for Employment v Cooper [1987] ICR 766, EAT 31.5
Secretary of State for Employment v Doulton Sanitaryware Ltd [1981] ICR
  477, [1981] IRLR 365, EAT 33.11
Secretary of State for Employment v Globe Elastic Thread Co Ltd
  [1980] AC 506, [1979] 2 All ER 1077, [1979] 3 WLR 143, [1979] ICR
  706, [1979] IRLR 327, 123 Sol Jo 504, HL 7.5, 7.7, 38.13
Secretary of State for Employment v Helitron Ltd [1980] ICR 523, EAT 39.7
Secretary of State for Employment v John Woodrow & Sons (Builders) Ltd
  [1983] ICR 582, [1983] IRLR 11, EAT 34.39
Secretary of State for Employment v Mann [1996] ICR 197, [1996] IRLR
  4, EAT; on appeal [1997] ICR 209, [1997] IRLR 21, CA; affd sub nom
  Mann v Secretary of State for Employment [1999] ICR 898,
  [1999] IRLR 566, HL 20.12, 25.2, 31.5
Secretary of State for Employment v Reeves [1993] ICR 508, EAT 31.6

Secretary of State for Employment v Spence [1987] QB 179, [1986] 3 All ER
  616, [1986] 3 WLR 380, [1986] 3 CMLR 647, [1986] ICR 651,
  [1986] IRLR 248, 130 Sol Jo 407, [1986] LS Gaz R 2084, CA 52.12
Secretary of State for Employment v Staffordshire County Council. See
  Staffordshire County Council v Secretary of State for Employment
Secretary of State for Employment v Stewart [1996] IRLR 334, EAT 31.5
Secretary of State for Employment v Wilson [1997] ICR 408, [1996] IRLR
  330, EAT 31.5
Secretary of State for Scotland v Taylor [2000] 3 All ER 90, [2000] ICR 595,
  2000 SC (HL) 139, 2000 SLT 708, sub nom Taylor v Secretary of State
  for Scotland [2000] IRLR 502, HL 8.11, 42.1
Secretary of State for Scotland and Greater Glasgow Health Board v Wright
  and Hannah [1993] 2 CMLR 257, [1991] IRLR 187, EAT 25.2, 37.4
Secretary of State for Trade and Industry v Bottrill [2000] 1 All ER 915,
  [1999] ICR 592, [1999] IRLR 326, [2000] 2 BCLC 448, [1999] BCC 177,
  143 Sol Jo LB 73, CA 9.4, 17.3, 31.4
Secretary of State for Trade and Industry v Cook [1997] 3 CMLR 1465,
  [1997] ICR 288, [1997] IRLR 150, 562 IRLB 12, EAT 52.13
Secretary of State for Trade and Industry v Forde [1997] ICR 231,
  [1997] IRLR 387, EAT 31.4
Secretary of State for Trade and Industry v Lassman (Pan Graphics
  Industries Ltd, in receivership) [2000] ICR 1109, [2000] IRLR 411, CA 7.12
Secretary of State for Trade and Industry v Rutherford. See Rutherford v
  Secretary of State for Trade and Industry
Secretary of State for Trade and Industry v Walden [2000] IRLR 168, EAT 31.4
Securicor Guarding Ltd v R [1994] IRLR 633, EAT 21.18
Securicor Omega Express Ltd v GMB [2004] IRLR 9, [2003] All ER (D) 181
  (Sep), EAT 39.4
Seide v Gillette Industries [1980] IRLR 427, EAT 12.6
Selfridges Ltd v Malik [1998] ICR 268, [1997] IRLR 577, EAT 55.5
Selkent Bus Co Ltd v Moore [1996] ICR 836, [1996] IRLR 661, EAT 21.10, 21.41
Senior Heat Treatment Ltd v Bell [1997] IRLR 614, EAT 7.12, 52.16
Serco Group plc v Wild (19 December 2006, unreported) 15.4
Setiya v East Yorkshire Health Authority [1995] ICR 799, [1995] IRLR
  348, EAT 22.6
Sevince v Staatssecretaris van Justitie: C-192/89 [1990] ECR I-3461,
  [1992] 2 CMLR 57, ECJ 26.2
Shakespeare v British Coal Corpn (1988) Times, 5 April, CA 5.3
Shamoon v Chief Constable of the Royal Ulster Constabulary [2003] UKHL
  11, [2003] 2 All ER 26, [2003] ICR 337, [2003] IRLR 285, (2003) Times,
  4 March, 147 Sol Jo LB 268, [2003] All ER (D) 410 (Feb) 12.4, 12.5, 12.12
Sharifi v Strathclyde Regional Council [1992] IRLR 259, EAT 14.13
Sharma v Hindu Temple IDS Brief No 464 .... 8.15
Sharp v Caledonia Group Services Ltd [2006] IRLR 4, [2005] All ER (D) 09
  (Nov), EAT 24.11
Sharp (G F) & Co Ltd v McMillan [1998] IRLR 632, EAT 48.3
Shawkat v Nottingham City Hospital Trust [2001] EWCA Civ 954,
  [2002] ICR 7, [2001] IRLR 555, [2001] All ER (D) 214 (Jun) 38.7
Sheffield v Oxford Controls Co Ltd [1979] ICR 396, [1979] IRLR
  133, EAT 48.2, 53.8
Sheikh v Chief Constable of Greater Manchester Police [1990] 1 QB 637,
  [1989] 2 All ER 684, [1989] 2 WLR 1102, [1989] ICR 373, 133 Sol Jo
  784, CA 12.12, 37.2
Sheiky v Argos Distributions Ltd (1997) IDS Brief No 597 .... 12.12

Table of Cases

Shepherd v North Yorkshire County Council [2006] IRLR 190, [2005] All
  ER (D) 354 (Dec), EAT 12.13
Shepherd (F C) & Co Ltd v Jerrom [1987] QB 301, [1986] 3 All ER 589,
  [1986] 3 WLR 801, [1986] ICR 802, [1986] IRLR 358, 130 Sol Jo
  665, CA 48.3
Shepherds Investments Ltd v Walters [2006] EWHC 836 (Ch), [2006] IRLR
  110, [2006] All ER (D) 213 (Apr)... 8.13, 9.16
Shergold v Fieldway Medical Centre [2006] IRLR 76, EAT 15.1, 15.4, 15.11, 20.19
Sheridan v Stanley Cole (Wainfleet) Ltd [2003] ICR 297, [2003] IRLR 52,
  [2002] All ER (D) 11 (Nov), EAT; affd [2003] EWCA Civ 1046,
  [2003] 4 All ER 1181, [2003] ICR 1449, [2003] IRLR 885,
  [2003] 38 LS Gaz R 33, (2003) Times, 5 September 21.52, 53.7
Sheriff v Klyne Tugs (Lowestoft) Ltd [1999] ICR 1170, [1999] IRLR 481, 625
  IRLB 6, [1999] All ER (D) 666, CA 14.17, 21.26
Shillcock v Uppingham School [1997] Pens LR 207 .... 24.17
Shillito v Van Leer (UK) Ltd [1997] IRLR 495, EAT 28.8
Shindler v Northern Raincoat Co Ltd [1960] 2 All ER 239, [1960] 1 WLR
  1038 .... 9.4, 58.10, 58.30
Shipping Co Uniform Inc v International Transport Workers' Federation,
  The Uniform Star [1985] 1 Lloyd's Rep 173, [1985] ICR 245,
  [1985] IRLR 71 .... 45.14
Shomer v B & R Residential Lettings Ltd [1992] IRLR 317, CA 12.5
Shove v Downs Surgical plc [1984] 1 All ER 7, [1984] ICR 532, [1984] IRLR
  17 .... 55.12, 58.28, 58.32
Showboat Entertainment Centre Ltd v Owens [1984] 1 All ER 836,
  [1984] 1 WLR 384, [1984] ICR 65, [1984] IRLR 7, 128 Sol Jo 152,
  [1983] LS Gaz R 3002, 134 NLJ 37, EAT 12.6
Sibson v United Kingdom (Application 14327/88) (1993) 17 EHRR 193,
  ECtHR 30.4
Sidhu v Aerospace Composite Technology Ltd [2001] ICR 167, [2000] IRLR
  602, [2000] 25 LS Gaz R 38, [2000] All ER (D) 744, CA 12.6, 12.13, 13.35
Sigurjonsson v Iceland (Application 16130/90) (1993) 16 EHRR 462,
  ECtHR 30.4
Sillars v Charringtons Fuels Ltd [1989] ICR 475, [1989] IRLR 152, CA 7.7, 47.8
Silman v ICTS (UK) Ltd EAT/0630/05 .... 15.2
Silvey v Pendragon plc [2001] EWCA Civ 784, [2001] IRLR 685 .... 8.23, 58.21
Sim v Rotherham Metropolitan Borough Council [1987] Ch 216,
  [1986] 3 All ER 387, [1986] 3 WLR 851, 85 LGR 128, [1986] ICR 897,
  [1986] IRLR 391, 130 Sol Jo 839, [1986] LS Gaz R 3746 .... 8.24, 34.14, 45.16
Sime v Sutcliffe Catering Scotland Ltd [1990] IRLR 228, 1990 SLT 687n, Ct
  of Sess 56.3
Simmons v Hoover Ltd [1977] QB 284, [1977] 1 All ER 775, [1976] 3 WLR
  901, [1977] ICR 61, [1976] IRLR 266, 10 ITR 234, 120 Sol Jo
  540, EAT 58.17
Simms v Transco plc [2001] All ER (D) 245 (Jan), EAT 14.7
Simon v Brimham Associates [1987] ICR 596, [1987] IRLR 307, CA 12.6
Simper (Peter) & Co Ltd v Cooke [1986] IRLR 19, EAT 22.12
Simrad Ltd v Scott [1997] IRLR 147, EAT 55.13
Sinclair Roche & Temperley v Heard [2004] IRLR 763 .... 13.36, 14.3, 21.58, 22.19
Sindicato de Médicos de Asistencia Pública (Simap) v Conselleria de Sanidad
  y Consumo de la Generalidad Valenciana: C-303/98 [2001] All ER (EC)
  609, [2000] ECR I-7963, [2001] 3 CMLR 932, [2001] ICR 1116,
  [2000] IRLR 845, [2000] All ER (D) 1236, ECJ 57.5, 57.7
Singh v British Rail Engineering Ltd [1986] ICR 22, EAT 13.8

Singh v Guru Nanak Gurdwara [1990] ICR 309, CA 17.3
Singh (t/a Rainbow International) v Taylor (27 June 2006, unreported)
    (UKEAT/0183/06/MAA) 15.13, 20.20
Sirdar v Army Board and Secretary of State for Defence: C-273/97 [1999] All
    ER (EC) 928, [1999] ECR I-7403, [1999] 3 CMLR 559, [2000] ICR 130,
    [2000] IRLR 47, 7 BHRC 459, [1999] All ER (D) 1156, ECJ 13.10, 13.19
Sisley v Britannia Security Systems Ltd [1983] ICR 628, [1983] IRLR
    404, EAT 13.3
Sita (GB) Ltd v Burton [1998] ICR 17, [1997] IRLR 501, EAT 52.25
Skiggs v South West Trains Ltd [2005] IRLR 459, [2005] All ER (D) 96
    (Mar), EAT 49.6, 51.21
Skyrail Oceanic Ltd v Coleman [1981] ICR 864, sub nom Coleman v Skyrail
    Oceanic Ltd (t/a Goodmos Tours) [1981] IRLR 398, 125 Sol Jo
    638, CA 12.9, 14.16
Slack v Greenham (Plant Hire) Ltd [1983] ICR 617, [1983] IRLR
    271, EAT 2.4
Slater v Leicestershire Health Authority [1989] IRLR 16, CA 54.10
Slaughter v C Brewer & Sons Ltd [1990] ICR 730, [1990] IRLR 426, EAT 55.13
Slaven v Thermo Engineers Ltd [1992] ICR 295, HC 49.20
Smith v A J Morrisroes & Sons Ltd [2005] ICR 596, [2005] IRLR 72, [2004]
    All ER (D) 291 (Dec), EAT 29.4
Smith v Avdel Systems Ltd: C-408/92 [1995] All ER (EC) 132, [1994] ECR
    I-4435, [1995] 3 CMLR 543, [1995] ICR 596, [1994] IRLR 602, ECJ 22.27,
                                                                          24.18, 42.5
Smith v Bexley London Borough Council IDS Brief No 448 .... 34.14
Smith v Cherry Lewis Ltd [2005] IRLR 86, EAT 39.6
Smith v Churchills Stairlifts plc [2005] EWCA Civ 1220, [2006] ICR 524,
    [2006] IRLR 41, [2005] All ER (D) 318 (Oct) 10.12
Smith v City of Glasgow District Council [1987] ICR 796, [1987] IRLR 326,
    1987 SC (HL) 175, 1987 SLT 605, HL 54.4
Smith v Gardner Merchant Ltd [1998] 3 All ER 852, [1999] ICR 134,
    [1998] IRLR 510, [1998] 32 LS Gaz R 29, 142 Sol Jo LB 244, [1998] All
    ER (D) 338, CA 12.5
Smith v Gwent District Health Authority [1996] ICR 1044, EAT 21.41
Smith v Hayle Town Council [1978] ICR 996, [1978] IRLR 413, 77 LGR 52,
    122 Sol Jo 642, CA 54.3
Smith v Network Rail Infrastructure Ltd [2007] All ER (D) 253 (May) 15.5
Smith v Safeway plc [1996] ICR 868, [1996] IRLR 456, CA 12.5
Smith v Secretary of State for Trade and Industry [2000] ICR 69,
    [2000] IRLR 6, EAT 30.7, 31.4
Smith v Seghill Overseers (1875) LR 10 QB 422, 40 JP 228, 44 LJMC 114, 23
    WR 745, [1874–80] All ER Rep 373, 32 LT 859 .... 43.2
Smith v Stages [1989] AC 928, [1989] 1 All ER 833, [1989] 2 WLR 529,
    [1989] ICR 272, [1989] IRLR 177, 133 Sol Jo 324,
    [1989] 15 LS Gaz R 42, [1989] NLJR 291, HL 56.2
Smith v United Kingdom [1999] IRLR 734 .... 12.6
Smith v Zeneca (Agrochemicals) Ltd [2000] ICR 800, [2000] All ER (D)
    163, EAT 14.8, 21.10
Smith and Grady v United Kingdom (Applications 33985/96 and 33986/96)
    (1999) 29 EHRR 493, [1999] IRLR 734, 11 Admin LR 879, ECtHR 30.4
Smiths Industries Aerospace and Defence Systems v Rawlings [1996] IRLR
    656, EAT 54.11

Table of Cases

Snoxell v Vauxhall Motors Ltd [1978] QB 11, [1977] 3 All ER 770,
[1977] 3 WLR 189, [1977] 1 CMLR 487, [1977] ICR 700, [1977] IRLR
123, 12 ITR 235, 121 Sol Jo 354, EAT 24.11
Sodexho plc v Gibbons [2005] IRLR 836 ... 20.10, 20.14, 20.34, 20.37, 21.3, 21.6, 21.7,
21.15, 21.75, 21.76
Sogbetun v Hackney London Borough [1998] ICR 1264, [1998] IRLR
676, EAT 20.9
Solectron Scotland Ltd v Roper [2004] IRLR 4, EAT 8.13, 8.22, 52.28
Solihull Metropolitan Borough v National Union of Teachers [1985] IRLR
211 .... 45.16
Somjee v United Kingdom (Application 42116/98) [2002] IRLR 886, [2002]
All ER (D) 214 (Oct), ECtHR 20.13, 30.4
Sorelle (Jean) Ltd v Rybak. See Rybak v Jean Sorelle Ltd
Soros v Davison [1994] ICR 590, [1994] IRLR 264, EAT 55.13
Soteriou v Ultrachem Ltd [2004] EWHC 983 (QB), [2004] IRLR 870, [2004]
All ER (D) 278 (Apr) 21.16, 21.22, 30.7
Sothern v Franks Charlesly & Co [1981] IRLR 278, CA 48.5, 53.10
Sougrin v Haringey Health Authority [1992] ICR 650, [1992] IRLR
416, CA 14.6
South Ayrshire Council v Morton [2001] IRLR 28, [2000] All ER (D)
1899, EAT; affd [2002] IRLR 256, (2002) Times, 1 March, Ct of Sess 24.9
South Durham Health Authority v UNISON [1995] ICR 495, [1995] IRLR
407, EAT 20.33, 52.23
South East Essex College v Abegaze [2006] ICR 468, EAT 12.12
South Holland District Council v Stamp EAT/1097/02 .... 57.5
South Place Ethical Society, Re, Barralet v A-G. See Barralet v A-G
South Tyneside Metropolitan Borough Council v Anderson
(UKEAT/0684/05/ZT and o525/06/ZT) (26 March 2007, unreported) 24.19
South Tyneside Metropolitan Borough Council v Toulson [2003] 1 CMLR
867, [2002] All ER (D) 437 (Nov), EAT 29.2
South West Launderettes Ltd v Laidler [1986] ICR 455, [1986] IRLR
305, CA 7.9
Southampton City College v Randall [2006] IRLR 18, [2005] All ER (D) 87
(Nov), EAT 10.12, 10.14, 10.15, 10.23
Southern Foundries (1926) Ltd v Shirlaw [1940] AC 701, [1940] 2 All ER
445, 109 LJKB 461, 84 Sol Jo 464, 164 LT 251, 56 TLR 637, HL 9.3, 58.10
Southwark London Borough v O'Brien [1996] IRLR 420, EAT 34.6
Southwark London Borough Council v Bartholomew [2004] ICR
358, EAT 21.54
Sovereign Distribution Services Ltd v Transport and General Workers'
Union [1990] ICR 31, [1989] IRLR 334, EAT 39.4, 39.6
Sovereign House Security Services Ltd v Savage [1989] IRLR 115, CA 48.5, 58.5
Spafax Ltd v Harrison [1980] IRLR 442, CA 41.8
Spano v Fiat Geotech SpA and Fiat Hitachi Excavators SpA: C-472/93
[1995] ECR I-4321, ECJ 52.28
Specialarbejderforbundet i Danmark v Dansk Industri acting for Royal
Copenhagen A/S: C-400/93 [1995] ECR I-1275, [1995] All ER (EC) 577,
[1996] 1 CMLR 515, [1996] ICR 51, [1995] IRLR 648, ECJ 24.10
Speciality Care plc v Pachela [1996] ICR 633, [1996] IRLR 248, EAT 54.3
Spencer v HM Prison Service EAT/0812/02 .... 20.29
Spencer v Marchington [1988] IRLR 392 .... 8.13, 41.8, 58.21
Spencer v Paragon Wallpapers Ltd [1977] ICR 301, [1976] IRLR 373, EAT 54.8
Spencer and Griffin v Gloucestershire County Council [1985] IRLR
393, CA 38.12

Spicer v Government of Spain [2004] EWCA Civ 1046, [2005] ICR 213,
(2004) Times, 10 September, [2004] All ER (D) 526 (Jul) 12.5
Spijkers v Gebroeders Benedik Abbatoir CV and Alfred Benedik en
Zonen BV: 24/85 [1986] ECR 1119, [1986] 2 CMLR 296, ECJ 52.5
Spiliada Maritime Corpn v Cansulex Ltd, The Spiliada [1987] AC 460,
[1986] 3 All ER 843, [1986] 3 WLR 972, [1987] 1 Lloyd's Rep 1, 130 Sol
Jo 925, [1987] LS Gaz R 113, [1986] NLJ Rep 1137, [1987] LRC
(Comm) 356, HL 26.12
Spillers-French (Holdings) Ltd v Union of Shop, Distributive and Allied
Workers [1980] 1 All ER 231, [1980] ICR 31, [1979] IRLR 339, 123 Sol
Jo 654, EAT 39.6
Sports Club v HM Inspector of Taxes [2000] STC (SCD) 443 .... 46.35
Spring v Guardian Assurance plc [1995] 2 AC 296, [1994] 3 All ER 129,
[1994] 3 WLR 354, [1994] ICR 596, [1994] IRLR 460,
[1994] 40 LS Gaz R 36, [1994] NLJR 971, 138 Sol Jo LB 183, HL 40.4, 42.13
Spring Grove Service Group plc v Hickinbottom [1990] ICR 111, EAT 21.64
Springboard Sunderland Trust v Robson [1992] ICR 554, [1992] IRLR
261, EAT 24.7
Square D Ltd v Cook. See Cook v Square D Ltd
Squibb UK Staff Association v Certification Officer [1979] 2 All ER 452,
[1979] 1 WLR 523, [1979] ICR 235, [1979] IRLR 75, 123 Sol Jo
352, CA 50.22
Stacey v Babcock Power Ltd [1986] QB 308, [1986] 2 WLR 207, [1986] ICR
221, [1986] IRLR 3, 130 Sol Jo 71, EAT 54.4, 54.11
Stadt Lengerich v Helmig: C-399/92, C-409/92, C-425/92, C-34/93, C-50/93,
and C-78/93 [1994] ECR I-5727, [1995] 2 CMLR 261, [1996] ICR 35,
[1995] IRLR 216, ECJ 24.11, 32.6
Staffordshire County Council v Barber. See Barber v Staffordshire County
Council
Staffordshire County Council v Black [1995] IRLR 234, EAT 24.10
Staffordshire County Council v Secretary of State for Employment
[1989] ICR 664, sub nom Secretary of State for Employment v
Staffordshire County Council [1989] IRLR 117, CA 53.13
Staffordshire Sentinel Newspapers Ltd v Potter [2004] IRLR 752, [2004] All
ER (D) 131 (May), EAT 17.3
Stankovic v Westminster City Council (17 October 2001, unreported) 38.7
Stannard v Fisons Pension Trust Ltd [1992] IRLR 27, [1991] PLR 225, CA 42.13
Stannard & Co (1969) Ltd v Wilson [1983] ICR 86, EAT 22.25
Stansbury v Datapulse plc [2003] EWCA Civ 1951, [2004] ICR 523,
[2004] IRLR 466, [2004] 06 LS Gaz R 32, (2004) Times, 28 January, 148
Sol Jo LB 145 .... 21.52, 21.56, 22.12
Stapp v Shaftesbury Society [1982] IRLR 326, CA 53.13
Stark v Post Office [2000] ICR 1013, [2000] PIQR P105,
[2000] 14 LS Gaz R 41, 144 Sol Jo LB 150, CA 28.12
Starmer v British Airways plc [2005] IRLR 862, [2005] All ER (D) 323
(Jul), EAT 12.8, 13.8
Steel Stockholders (Birmingham) Ltd v Kirkwood [1993] IRLR 515, EAT 55.13
Steenhorst-Neerings v Bestuur van de Bedrijfsvereniging voor Detailhandel,
Ambachten en Huisvrouwen: C-338/91 [1993] ECR I-5475,
[1995] 3 CMLR 323, [1994] IRLR 244, ECJ 25.2
Steinicke v Bundesanstalt fur Arbeit: C-77/02 [2003] IRLR 892, [2003] All
ER (D) 87 (Sep), ECJ 24.3
Stenhouse Australia Ltd v Phillips [1974] AC 391, [1974] 1 All ER 117,
[1974] 2 WLR 134, [1974] 1 Lloyd's Rep 1, 117 Sol Jo 875, PC 41.3, 41.8

Table of Cases

Stephenson v Delphi Diesel Systems Ltd [2003] ICR 471, [2003] All ER (D) 84 (Mar), EAT 17.3

Stephenson (SBJ) Ltd v Mandy [2000] FSR 286, [2000] IRLR 233 .... 41.19, 58.21

Sterling Developments (London) Ltd v Pagano (EAT/0511/06) 20.9

Stevedoring and Haulage Services Ltd v Fuller [2001] EWCA Civ 651, [2001] IRLR 627, [2001] All ER (D) 106 (May) 17.3

Stevens v Bexley Health Authority [1989] ICR 224, [1989] IRLR 240, EAT 14.7, 25.2

Stevenson v United Road Transport Union [1977] 2 All ER 941, [1977] ICR 893, CA 51.15

Stevenson (or Stephenson) Jordan and Harrison Ltd v MacDonald and Evans (1952) 69 RPC 10, [1952] 1 TLR 101, CA 9.4

Stewart v Cleveland Guest (Engineering) Ltd [1994] ICR 535, [1994] IRLR 440, EAT 22.17

Stewart v Glentaggart (1963) 42 ATC 318, [1963] TR 345, 1963 SC 300, 1963 SLT 119, Ct of Sess 58.32

Stewart v Moray Council [2006] IRLR 592, EAT 11.11

Stewart v New Testament Church of God. See New Testament Church of God v Stewart

Stewart v YMCA Training Ltd (2006) 2007] IRLR 185, sub nom YMCA Training Ltd v Stewart [2007] IRLR 185, sub nom Stewart v YMCA Training Ltd [2006] All ER (D) 69 (Dec), EAT 15.2

Stewart (Rex) Jeffries Parker Ginsberg Ltd v Parker [1988] IRLR 483, CA 58.21

Stocker v Lancashire County Council [1992] IRLR 75, CA 54.4, 54.10

Stokes v Guest, Keen and Nettlefold (Bolts and Nuts) Ltd [1968] 1 WLR 1776, 5 KIR 401, 112 Sol Jo 821 .... 27.8

Stolt Offshore Ltd v Miklaszewicz [2002] IRLR 344, 2002 SC 232, 2002 SLT 103 .... 11.18, 54.3

Stonehill Furniture Ltd v Phillippo [1983] ICR 556, EAT 21.75

Storer v British Gas plc [2000] 2 All ER 440, [2000] 1 WLR 1237, [2000] ICR 603, [2000] IRLR 495, CA 20.8, 21.51

Stowe v Voith Turbo Ltd [2005] ICR 543, [2005] All ER (D) 152 (Jan), sub nom Voith Turbo Ltd v Stowe [2005] IRLR 228, EAT 14.16, 55.13

Strange (SW) Ltd v Mann [1965] 1 All ER 1069, [1965] 1 WLR 629, 109 Sol Jo 352 .... 41.5

Stratford (J T) & Son Ltd v Lindley [1965] AC 269, [1964] 2 All ER 209, [1964] 2 WLR 1002, [1964] 1 Lloyd's Rep 237, 108 Sol Jo 298, CA; revsd [1965] AC 269, [1964] 3 All ER 102, [1964] 3 WLR 541, [1964] 2 Lloyd's Rep 133, 108 Sol Jo 636, HL 45.2

Strathclyde Regional Council v Neil [1984] IRLR 11; affd sub nom Neil v Strathclyde Borough Council [1984] IRLR 14, 1983 SLT (Sh Ct) 89 .... 16.3

Strathclyde Regional Council v Porcelli. See Porcelli v Strathclyde Regional Council

Strathclyde Regional Council v Wallace [1998] 1 All ER 394, [1998] 1 WLR 259, [1998] ICR 205, [1998] IRLR 146, [1998] 07 LS Gaz R 32, 1998 SC (HL) 72, 142 Sol Jo LB 83, sub nom West Dunbartonshire Council v Wallace 1998 SLT 421, HL 24.11, 24.12

Street v Derbyshire Unemployed Workers' Centre [2004] EWCA Civ 964, [2004] 4 All ER 839, [2005] ICR 97, [2004] IRLR 687, (2004) Times, 6 September, [2004] All ER (D) 377 (Jul) 11.18, 28.9

Street v Mountford [1985] AC 809, [1985] 2 All ER 289, [1985] 2 WLR 877, 50 P & CR 258, 17 HLR 402, 129 Sol Jo 348, [1985] 1 EGLR 128, [1985] LS Gaz R 2087, [1985] NLJ Rep 460, 274 Estates Gazette 821, HL 43.2

Stribling v Wickham (1989) 21 HLR 381, [1989] 2 EGLR 35, [1989] 27 EG
   81, CA 43.2
Strouthos v London Underground Ltd [2004] EWCA Civ 402, [2004] IRLR
   636, [2004] All ER (D) 366 (Mar) 54.9
Strudwick v Iszatt Bros Ltd (or IBL) [1988] ICR 796, [1988] IRLR
   457, EAT 7.9
Suffritti v Istituto Nazionale della Previdenza Sociale (INPS): C-140/91,
   C-141/91, C-278/91 and C-279/91 [1992] ECR I-6337, [1993] IRLR 289,
   ECJ 25.2
Sun Alliance and London Insurance Ltd v Dudman [1978] ICR 551,
   [1978] IRLR 169, EAT 24.5
Sunderland Polytechnic v Evans [1993] ICR 392, [1993] IRLR 196, EAT 34.6
Sunley Turriff Holdings Ltd v Thomson [1995] IRLR 184, EAT 52.15
Surrey County Council v Lamond (1998) 31 HLR 1051, [1999] 1 EGLR 32,
   [1999] 12 EG 170, [1998] EGCS 185, 78 P & CR D3, CA 43.7
Sutcliffe v Big C's Marine Ltd [1998] ICR 913, [1998] IRLR 428, EAT 20.9, 20.18,
   22.13
Sutherland v British Telecommunications plc (1989) Times, 30 January 40.4
Sutherland v Hatton. See Hatton v Sutherland
Sutherland v Network Appliance Ltd [2001] IRLR 12, [2000] All ER (D)
   1000, EAT 21.35, 58.42
Sutton v The Ranch Ltd [2006] ICR 1170, [2006] All ER (D) 195
   (Jun), EAT 21.69, 22.22
Suzen v Zehnacker Gebaudereinigung GmbH Krankenhausservice: C-13/95
   [1997] All ER (EC) 289, [1997] ECR I-1259, [1997] 1 CMLR 768,
   [1997] ICR 662, [1997] IRLR 255, ECJ 52.5
Swain v Denso Marston Ltd [2000] ICR 1079, [2000] PIQR P129, CA 28.18
Swain v Hillman [2001] 1 All ER 91, [2000] PIQR P51, (1999) Times,
   4 November, CA 21.15, 21.17
Swainston v Hetton Victory Club Ltd [1983] 1 All ER 1179, [1983] ICR 341,
   [1983] IRLR 164, 127 Sol Jo 171, CA 20.21
Sweater Shop (Scotland) Ltd v Park [1996] IRLR 424, EAT 34.6
Sweeney v J & S Henderson (Concessions) Ltd [1999] IRLR 306, EAT 7.6
Sweetin v Coral Racing [2006] IRLR 252, [2006] All ER (D) 74 (Mar) 52.23
Sweetlove v Redbridge and Waltham Forest Area Health Authority
   [1979] ICR 477, [1979] IRLR 195, EAT 55.13
Swift v Chief Constable of Wiltshire Constabulary [2004] ICR 909,
   [2004] IRLR 540, [2004] All ER (D) 299 (Feb), EAT 10.4, 10.6
Swithland Motors plc v Clarke [1994] ICR 231, [1994] IRLR 275, EAT 14.5, 20.29
Sybron Corpn v Rochem Ltd [1984] Ch 112, [1983] 2 All ER 707,
   [1983] 3 WLR 713, [1983] ICR 801, [1983] IRLR 253, [1983] BCLC 43,
   127 Sol Jo 391, CA 8.13, 9.16
Systems Reliability Holdings plc v Smith [1990] IRLR 377 .... 41.8, 41.13

T

T v North Yorkshire County Council. See Trotman v North Yorkshire
   County Council
TFS Derivatives Ltd v Morgan [2004] EWHC 3181 (QB), [2005] IRLR 246,
   [2004] All ER (D) 236 (Nov) 41.6, 41.8, 41.14
TGWU v Lambeth Service Team Ltd [2005] All ER (D) 153 (Jul), EAT 39.6
TSB Bank plc v Harris [2000] IRLR 157, EAT 40.4, 48.19
TSC Europe (UK) Ltd v Massey [1999] IRLR 22 .... 41.8

Table of Cases

Tagro v Cafane [1991] 2 All ER 235, [1991] 1 WLR 378, 23 HLR 250,
[1991] 1 EGLR 279, CA 43.3

Talbot v Cadge [1995] 2 AC 394, [1995] 2 WLR 312, [1995] ICR 1100, sub
nom Re Leyland DAF Ltd, [1994] 4 All ER 300, [1994] NLJR 1311; sub
nom Re Leyland DAF Ltd (No 2) [1994] 2 BCLC 760, sub nom Re
Leyland Daf Ltd, Talbot v Cadge [1994] BCC 658; on appeal sub nom
Talbot v Grundy [1995] 2 AC 394, [1995] 2 WLR 312, [1995] ICR 1100,
[1995] IRLR 269, [1995] 17 LS Gaz R 47, sub nom Re Leyland
DAF Ltd [1995] 2 All ER 65, [1995] NLJR 449, sub nom Re Leyland
DAF Ltd (No 2) [1995] 1 BCLC 386, sub nom Talbot v Cadge (Leyland
DAF Ltd) [1995] BCC 319, HL 9.28, 31.11

Tan v Sitkowski [2007] EWCA Civ 30, (2007) Times, 15 February, [2007] All
ER (D) 16 (Feb) 43.3

Tanks and Drums Ltd v Transport and General Workers' Union [1992] ICR
1; affd [1992] ICR 1, [1991] IRLR 372, 135 Sol Jo LB 68, CA 45.15

Tanna v Post Office [1981] ICR 374, EAT 12.12

Tanner v D T Kean Ltd [1978] IRLR 110, EAT 58.5

Taplin v C Shippam Ltd [1978] ICR 1068, [1978] IRLR 450, 13 ITR
532, EAT 55.21

Tarbuck v Sainsbury Supermarkets Ltd [2006] IRLR 664, [2006] All ER (D)
50 (Jun), EAT 10.12, 10.14, 10.15, 10.34

Tarling v Wisdom Toothbrushes Ltd (COIT 1500148/97) (24 June 1997,
unreported) 10.14

Tarmac Roadstone Holdings Ltd v Peacock [1973] 2 All ER 485,
[1973] 1 WLR 594, [1973] ICR 273, [1973] IRLR 157, 14 KIR 277, 8
ITR 300, 117 Sol Jo 186, CA 34.36

Tattari v Private Patients Plan Ltd [1998] ICR 106, [1997] IRLR 586, 38
BMLR 24, CA 13.27

Taupo Totara Timber Co Ltd v Rowe [1978] AC 537, [1977] 3 All ER 123,
[1977] 3 WLR 466, 121 Sol Jo 692, [1977] 2 NZLR 453, PC 9.28

Taylor v Connex South Eastern Ltd IDS Brief No 670 .... 52.26

Taylor v East Midlands Offender Employment [2000] IRLR 760, EAT 8.24, 29.9

Taylor v National Union of Mineworkers (Derbyshire Area) [1984] IRLR
440 .... 51.15

Taylor v OCS Group Ltd [2006] EWCA Civ 702, [2006] ICR 1602,
[2006] IRLR 613, (2006) Times, 12 July, 150 Sol Jo LB 810, [2006] All
ER (D) 51 (Aug) 10.15, 54.10

Taylor v Secretary of State for Scotland. See Secretary of State for Scotland
v Taylor

Taylor v Serviceteam Ltd [1998] PIQR P201 .... 52.18

Taylor Gordon & Co Ltd (t/a Plan Personnel) v Timmons [2004] IRLR 180,
[2003] 44 LS Gaz R 32, (2003) Times, 7 November, [2003] All ER (D) 05
(Oct), EAT 20.11, 34.6, 44.8

Taylorplan Services Ltd v Jackson [1996] IRLR 184, EAT 20.31, 34.8

Tehrani v United Kingdom Central Council for Nursing, Midwifery and
Health Visiting [2001] IRLR 208, 2001 SLT 879, Ct of Sess 30.7

Teinaz v Wandsworth London Borough Council [2002] EWCA Civ 1040,
[2002] ICR 1471, [2002] IRLR 721, (2002) Times, 21 August, [2002] All
ER (D) 238 (Jul) 21.54, 30.7

Tejani v Superintendent Registrar for the District of Peterborough
[1986] IRLR 502, CA 12.6

Tele Danmark A/S v Handels- og Kontorfunktionærernes Forbund i
    Danmark (HK): C-109/00 [2001] All ER (EC) 941, [2001] ECR I-6993,
    [2002] 1 CMLR 105, [2004] ICR 610, [2001] IRLR 853, [2001] All ER
    (D) 37 (Oct), ECJ 12.5
Tele-Trading Ltd v Jenkins [1990] IRLR 430, CA 55.13
Telephone Information Services Ltd v Wilkinson [1991] IRLR 148, EAT 21.17,
    21.72, 55.1
Temco Service Industries SA v Imzilyen: C-51/00 [2002] ECR I-969,
    [2004] 1 CMLR 877, [2002] IRLR 214, [2002] All ER (D) 199 (Jan),
    ECJ 52.7
Ten Oever v Stichting Bedrijfspensioenfonds voor het Glazenwassers- en
    Schoonmaakbedrijf: C-109/91 [1993] ECR I-4879, [1995] 2 CMLR 357,
    [1995] ICR 74, [1993] IRLR 601, [1995] 42 LS Gaz R 23, ECJ 24.18
Tennants Textile Colours Ltd v Todd [1989] IRLR 3, NI CA 24.22
Terry v East Sussex County Council [1977] 1 All ER 567, 75 LGR 111,
    [1976] ICR 536, [1976] IRLR 332, 12 ITR 265, EAT 47.7, 54.14
Tesco Stores Ltd v Pook [2003] EWHC 823 (Ch), [2004] IRLR 618, [2003]
    All ER (D) 233 (Apr) 8.13
Tesco Supermarkets Ltd v Nattrass [1972] AC 153, [1971] 2 All ER 127,
    [1971] 2 WLR 1166, 69 LGR 403, 135 JP 289, 115 Sol Jo 285, HL 27.38
Thames Water Utilities v Reynolds [1996] IRLR 186, EAT 8.24, 29.9, 34.14, 34.22
Thibault v Caisse Nationale d'Assurance Viellesse des Travailleurs Salaries
    (CNAVTS). See Caisse Nationale d'Assurance Vieillesse des Travailleurs
    Salaries v Thibault
Thomas v Bristol Aeroplane Co Ltd [1954] 2 All ER 1, [1954] 1 WLR 694,
    52 LGR 292, 98 Sol Jo 302, CA 27.3
Thomas v Farr plc [2007] EWCA Civ 118, [2007] IRLR 419, (2007) Times,
    27 February, [2007] All ER (D) 240 (Feb) 41.8
Thomas v National Coal Board [1987] ICR 757, [1987] IRLR 451,
    [1987] LS Gaz R 2045, EAT 24.6
Thomas v National Union of Mineworkers (South Wales Area) [1986] Ch 20,
    [1985] 2 All ER 1, [1985] 2 WLR 1081, [1985] ICR 886, [1985] IRLR
    136, 129 Sol Jo 416, [1985] LS Gaz R 1938 .... 5.5, 45.2, 45.12
Thomas & Betts Manufacturing Ltd v Harding [1980] IRLR 255, CA 54.11
Thompson v SCS Consulting Ltd [2001] IRLR 801, [2001] All ER (D) 03
    (Sep), EAT 52.26
Thompson v Walon Car Delivery [1997] IRLR 343, EAT 53.20
Thomson (D C) & Co Ltd v Deakin [1952] Ch 646, [1952] 2 All ER 361,
    [1952] 2 TLR 105, CA 45.2
Thornett v Scope [2006] EWCA Civ 1600, [2007] ICR 236, [2006] All ER (D)
    357 (Nov), sub nom Scope v Thornett [2007] IRLR 155 .... 55.12, 55.13
Thorpe v Dul [2003] ICR 1556, [2003] All ER (D) 14 (Jul), EAT 16.2
Tice v Cartwright [1999] ICR 769, EAT 7.9
Ticehurst and Thompson v British Telecommunications plc. See British
    Telecommunications plc v Ticehurst
Timeplan Education Group Ltd v National Union of Teachers [1997] IRLR
    457, CA 45.2
Tipper v Roofdec Ltd [1989] IRLR 419, EAT 7.5
Titchener v Secretary of State for Trade and Industry [2002] ICR 225,
    [2002] IRLR 195, [2001] All ER (D) 93 (Sep), EAT 31.5
Tocher v General Motors Scotland Ltd [1981] IRLR 55, EAT 6.3
Todd v British Midland Airways Ltd [1978] ICR 959, [1978] IRLR 370, 13
    ITR 553, 122 Sol Jo 661, CA 53.15
Toffel v London Underground Ltd IDS Brief No 609 .... 10.11

Table of Cases

Tomlinson v Dick Evans U Drive Ltd [1978] ICR 639, [1978] IRLR
77, EAT 8.15
Torquay Hotel Co Ltd v Cousins [1969] 2 Ch 106, [1968] 3 All ER 43,
[1968] 3 WLR 540, 4 KIR 635, 112 Sol Jo 688; affd [1969] 2 Ch 106,
[1969] 1 All ER 522, [1969] 2 WLR 289, 6 KIR 15, 113 Sol Jo 52, CA 45.2
Tottenham Green Under Fives' Centre v Marshall [1989] ICR 214,
[1989] IRLR 147, [1989] 15 LS Gaz R 39, EAT 13.4
Tottenham Green Under Fives' Centre v Marshall (No 2) [1991] ICR 320,
[1991] IRLR 162, EAT 13.4
Tower Hamlets Health Authority v Anthony [1989] ICR 656, [1989] IRLR
394, CA 54.9
Tower Hamlets London Borough Council v Qayyum [1987] ICR 729, EAT 12.8
Tracey v Crosville Wales Ltd [1998] AC 167, [1997] 4 All ER 449,
[1997] 3 WLR 800, [1997] ICR 862, [1997] 41 LS Gaz R 28,
[1997] NLJR 1582, sub nom Crosville Wales Ltd v Tracey (No 2)
[1997] IRLR 691, HL 55.13
Tradewinds Airways Ltd v Fletcher [1981] IRLR 272, EAT 55.12
Trafford v Sharpe & Fisher (Building Supplies) Ltd [1994] IRLR 325, EAT 52.26
Trafford Carpets Ltd v Barker IDS Brief No 440 .... 2.4
Trafigura Beheer BV v Kookmin Bank Co [2006] EWHC 1450 (Comm),
[2006] 2 All ER (Comm) 1008, [2006] 2 Lloyd's Rep 455, [2006] All ER
(D) 183 (Jun) 26.11
Transco plc (formerly BG plc) v O'Brien [2002] EWCA Civ 379, [2002] ICR
721, [2002] IRLR 444 .... 8.13
Transocean International v Russell (unreported), EATS 57.3
Transport and General Workers' Union v Asda [2004] IRLR 836 .... 50.29
Transport and General Workers' Union v Brauer Coley Ltd [2007] ICR 226,
[2007] IRLR 207, [2006] All ER (D) 254 (Nov), EAT 39.6
Transport and General Workers' Union v Howard [1992] ICR 106,
[1992] IRLR 170, EAT 51.7, 55.15, 55.19
Transport and General Workers' Union v Ledbury Preserves (1928) Ltd
[1985] IRLR 412, EAT 39.4
Transport and General Workers' Union v Ledbury Preserves (1928) Ltd
[1986] ICR 855, [1986] IRLR 492, EAT 39.6
Transport and General Workers' Union v McKinnon [2001] ICR 1281,
[2001] IRLR 597, [2001] All ER (D) 275 (Jun) 39.6, 52.18
Travers v Planning Inspectorate (9 December 2002, unreported) 24.10
Treganowan v Robert Knee & Co Ltd [1975] ICR 405, [1975] IRLR 247, 10
ITR 121, 119 Sol Jo 490 .... 48.5, 58.1
Trego v Hunt [1896] AC 7, 65 LJ Ch 1, 44 WR 225, [1895–9] All ER Rep
804, 73 LT 514, 12 TLR 80, HL 41.8
Trevelyans (Birmingham) Ltd v Norton [1991] ICR 488, EAT 20.25
Trico-Folberth Ltd v Devonshire. See Devonshire v Trico-Folberth Ltd
Triesman v Ali [2002] EWCA Civ 93, [2002] ICR 1026, [2002] IRLR 489,
(2002) Times, 11 March, [2002] All ER (D) 87 (Feb) 13.27
Trimble v Supertravel Ltd [1982] ICR 440, [1982] IRLR 451, EAT 20.14, 21.76,
                                                                                           55.13
Trotman v North Yorkshire County Council [1999] LGR 584,
[1998] 32 LS Gaz R 29, 142 Sol Jo LB 218, sub nom ST v North
Yorkshire County Council [1999] IRLR 98, sub nom T v North
Yorkshire County Council 49 BMLR 150, CA 56.2
Trotter v Forth Ports Authority [1991] IRLR 419, Ct of Sess 48.7
Trussed Steel Concrete Co Ltd v Green [1946] Ch 115, 44 LGR 263, 110 JP
144, 115 LJ Ch 123, 90 Sol Jo 80, 174 LT 122, 62 TLR 128 .... 9.4

Trustees of Uppingham School Retirement Benefit Scheme for Non-Teaching
    Staff v Shillcock [2002] EWHC 641 (Ch), [2002] IRLR 702, [2002] All
    ER (D) 147 (Apr) 24.17, 24.18
Tuck (A & G) Ltd v Bartlett [1994] ICR 379, [1994] IRLR 162, EAT 52.14
Tucker v British Leyland Motor Corpn Ltd [1978] IRLR 493, Cty Ct 29.9
Tunstall v Condon [1980] ICR 786, EAT 58.8
Turner v Commonwealth & British Minerals Ltd [2000] IRLR 114, [1999]
    All ER (D) 1097, CA 41.6, 41.8
Turner v Grovit: C-159/02 [2004] All ER (EC) 485, [2004] 2 All ER (Comm)
    381, [2004] 2 Lloyd's Rep 169, [2004] IRLR 899, (2004) Times, 29 April,
    [2004] All ER (D) 259 (Apr), ECJ 26.12
Turner v Labour Party and Labour Party Superannuation Society
    [1987] IRLR 101, CA 12.9
Turvey v C W Cheyney & Son Ltd [1979] ICR 341, [1979] IRLR 105, EAT 38.12
Tyagi v BBC World Service [2001] EWCA Civ 549, [2001] IRLR 465 .... 14.6, 20.29
Tyldesley v TML Plastics Ltd [1996] ICR 356, [1996] IRLR 395, EAT 24.11
Tyne and Wear Autistic Society v Smith [2005] ICR 663, [2005] IRLR
    336, EAT 20.21
Tyson v Concurrent Systems Incorporated Ltd EAT/0028/03 .... 32.11, 32.22

U

UNECTEF v Heylens. See Union Nationale des Entraîneurs et Cadres
    Techniques Professionnels du Football (UNECTEF) v Heylens
UNIFI v Union Bank of Nigeria [2001] IRLR 713 .... 50.47
Unison v Gallagher (2005) IDS Brief No 791 .... 50.3
Unison v Leicestershire County Council [2005] IRLR 920,
    [2005] 42 LS Gaz R 24, [2005] All ER (D) 175 (Sep), EAT 39.4
Unison v Leicestershire County Council [2006] EWCA Civ 825, [2006] IRLR
    810, [2006] All ER (D) 339 (Jun) 22.15, 39.4
Unison v United Kingdom [2002] IRLR 497, ECtHR 30.4, 30.7, 45.4
Ulsterbus Ltd v Henderson [1989] IRLR 251, NICA 54.4, 54.9
Uniform Star, The. See Shipping Co Uniform Inc v International Transport
    Workers' Federation, The Uniform Star
Union Nationale des Entraîneurs et Cadres Techniques Professionnels du
    Football (UNECTEF) v Heylens: 222/86 [1987] ECR 4097,
    [1989] 1 CMLR 901, ECJ 25.4
Union Traffic Ltd v Transport and General Workers' Union [1989] ICR 98,
    [1989] IRLR 127, CA 45.2, 45.9, 45.16
United Arab Emirates v Abdelghafar [1995] ICR 65, [1995] IRLR
    243, EAT 22.6
United Bank Ltd v Akhtar [1989] IRLR 507, EAT 8.13, 58.22
United Kingdom v EU Council: C-84/94 [1996] All ER (EC) 877,
    [1996] ECR I-5755, [1996] 3 CMLR 671, [1997] ICR 443, [1997] IRLR
    30, ECJ 25.11, 57.1
University College London Hospital NHS Trust v UNISON [1999] ICR 204,
    [1999] IRLR 31, [1998] 41 LS Gaz R 45, 142 Sol Jo LB 270, [1998] All
    ER (D) 450, CA 45.4
University College of Swansea v Cornelius [1988] ICR 735, EAT 21.50
University of Cambridge v Murray [1993] ICR 460, EAT 20.18
University of Central England v National and Local Government Officers'
    Association [1993] IRLR 81 .... 45.14
University of Huddersfield v Wolff [2004] ICR 828, [2004] IRLR 534, [2003]
    All ER (D) 245 (Oct), EAT 14.3

Table of Cases

University of Nottingham v Eyett [1999] 2 All ER 437, [1999] 1 WLR 594,
[1999] ICR 721, [1999] IRLR 87, [1999] ELR 141,
[1999] 01 LS Gaz R 24, [1998] All ER (D) 584 .... 8.13, 42.13
University of Oxford (Chancellor, Master and Scholars) v Humphreys
[2000] 1 All ER 996, [2000] 1 CMLR 647, [2000] ICR 405, [2000] IRLR
183, CA 52.16, 52.25

V

Vakante v Addey and Stanhope School [2004] ICR 279, [2003] All ER (D)
352 (Dec), EAT; affd [2004] EWCA Civ 1065, [2004] 4 All ER 1056,
[2005] 1 CMLR 62, [2005] ICR 231, [2004] 36 LS Gaz R 33, (2004)
Times, 28 September, [2004] All ER (D) 561 (Jul) 8.15, 13.16, 26.9
Vaseghi v Brunel University [2007] EWCA Civ 482, [2007] All ER (D) 377
(May) 14.9, 21.13
Vauxhall Motors Ltd v Ghafoor [1993] ICR 376, EAT 54.10
Vauxhall Motors Ltd v Transport and General Workers Union [2006] IRLR
674, [2006] All ER (D) 214 (Apr), EAT 39.7
Venables v Hornby (Inspector of Taxes) [2003] UKHL 65, [2004] 1 All ER
627, [2003] 1 WLR 3022, [2004] STC 84, [2004] ICR 42, (2003) Times,
5 December, 147 Sol Jo LB 1431, [2003] All ER (D) 86 (Dec) 42.1
Vento v Chief Constable of West Yorkshire Police. See Chief Constable of
West Yorkshire Police v Vento
Verdin v Harrods Ltd [2006] IRLR 339, [2005] All ER (D) 349 (Dec), EAT 21.28
Verholen v Sociale Versekeringsbank Amsterdam: C-87/90, C-99/90, and
C-89/90 [1991] ECR I-3757, [1994] 1 CMLR 157, [1992] IRLR 38,
ECJ 25.2
Viasystems (Tyneside) Ltd v Thermal Transfer (Northern) Ltd [2005] EWCA
Civ 1151, [2005] 4 All ER 1181, [2006] 2 WLR 428, [2005] IRLR 983,
[2005] 44 LS Gaz R 31, [2005] All ER (D) 93 (Oct) 56.1, 56.3
Vicary v British Telecommunications plc [1999] IRLR 680, EAT 10.4, 10.7
Vidal (Francisco Hernandez) SA v Perez: C-127/96, C-229/96 and C-74/97
[1998] ECR I-8179, [1999] IRLR 132, ECJ 52.5
Vidler v UNISON [1999] ICR 746 .... 21.77
Viggosdottir v Islandspostur HF [2002] IRLR 425 .... 37.2, 52.9
Villalba v Merrill Lynch & Co Inc [2007] ICR 469, [2006] IRLR 437, 150 Sol
Jo LB 742, [2006] All ER (D) 486 (Mar), EAT 12.5, 12.10, 24.11
Villella v MFI Furniture Centres Ltd [1999] IRLR 468 .... 8.13, 42.13, 44.14, 48.19,
58.19
Virdi v Metropolitan Police Comr [2007] IRLR 24, [2006] All ER (D) 214
(Oct), EAT 14.6
Virgo Fidelis Senior School v Boyle [2004] ICR 1210, [2004] IRLR 268,
(2004) Times, 26 February, [2004] All ER (D) 214 (Jan), EAT 11.18, 14.18
Visa International Service Association v Paul [2004] IRLR 42, [2003] All ER
(D) 265 (May), EAT 14.15, 53.7
Vogt v Germany (Application 17851/91) (1995) 21 EHRR 205, [1996] ELR
232, ECtHR 30.4
Voith Turbo Ltd v Stowe. See Stowe v Voith Turbo Ltd
Vokes Ltd v Bear [1974] ICR 1, [1973] IRLR 363, 15 KIR 302, 9 ITR 85,
NIRC 54.11
Von Horn v Cinnamond: C-163/95 [1998] QB 214, [1997] All ER (EC) 913,
[1998] 2 WLR 104, [1997] ECR I-5451, ECJ 26.12
Voteforce Associates Ltd v Quinn [2002] ICR 1, [2001] All ER (D) 483
(Jul), EAT 29.2

Vroege v NCIV Institut voor Volkshuisvesting BV: C-57/93 [1995] All ER
   (EC) 193, [1994] ECR I-4541, [1995] 1 CMLR 881, [1995] ICR 635,
   [1994] IRLR 651, ECJ 24.10

W

Wadcock v London Borough of Brent [1990] IRLR 223 .... 8.23
Waddington v Leicester Council for Voluntary Services [1977] 2 All ER 633,
   [1977] 1 WLR 544, [1977] ICR 266, [1977] IRLR 32, 12 ITR 65, 121 Sol
   Jo 84, EAT 24.6
Wadman v Carpenter Farrer Partnership [1993] 3 CMLR 93, [1993] IRLR
   374, EAT 12.12, 25.1
Wain v Guernsey Ship Management Ltd [2007] EWCA Civ 294, [2007] All
   ER (D) 35 (Apr) 52.4
Waite v Government Communications Headquarters [1983] 2 AC 714,
   [1983] 2 All ER 1013, [1983] 3 WLR 389, 81 LGR 769, [1983] ICR 653,
   [1983] IRLR 341, 127 Sol Jo 536, [1983] LS Gaz R 2516, 133 NLJ
   745, HL 53.14
Wakeman v Quick Corpn [1999] IRLR 424, [1999] All ER (D) 158, CA 12.5
Walden Engineering Co Ltd v Warrener [1993] 3 CMLR 179, [1993] ICR
   967, [1993] IRLR 420, [1992] OPLR 1, EAT 52.19
Walker v Josiah Wedgwood & Sons Ltd [1978] ICR 744, [1978] IRLR 105, 13
   ITR 271, EAT 53.7
Walker v Northumberland County Council [1995] 1 All ER 737, [1995] ICR
   702, [1995] IRLR 35, [1995] ELR 231, [1994] NLJR 1659 .... 8.13,
                                                                           27.8Walk-
                           er (J H) Ltd v Hussain [1996] ICR 291,
                                   [1996] IRLR 11, EAT 14.14
Wall v British Compressed Air Society [2003] EWCA Civ 1762, [2004] ICR
   408, [2004] IRLR 147, [2004] 05 LS Gaz R 28, [2003] NLJR 1903,
   (2004) Times, 9 January, [2003] All ER (D) 169 (Dec) 42.2, 53.14
Wallace v C A Roofing Services Ltd [1996] IRLR 435 .... 16.2, 58.44
Walls Meat Co Ltd v Khan [1979] ICR 52, [1978] IRLR 499, 122 Sol Jo
   759, CA 20.25
Walls Meat Co Ltd v Selby [1989] ICR 601, CA 54.11
Walmsley v C & R Ferguson Ltd [1989] IRLR 112, 1989 SLT 258, Ct of
   Sess 48.16
Walter v Secretary of State for Social Security [2001] EWCA Civ 1913,
   [2002] ICR 540, (2001) Times, 13 December, [2001] All ER (D) 71
   (Dec) 12.5
Waltham Forest London Borough Council v Omilaju. See Omilaju v
   Waltham Forest London Borough Council
Walton v Airtours plc [2002] EWCA Civ 1659, [2004] Lloyd's Rep IR 69,
   [2003] IRLR 161, [2002] All ER (D) 34 (Nov) 44.17
Walton v Independent Living Organisation [2003] EWCA Civ 199,
   [2003] ICR 688, [2003] IRLR 469, (2003) Times, 27 February, 147 Sol Jo
   LB 266, [2003] All ER (D) 373 (Feb) 34.12
Waltons and Morse v Dorrington [1997] IRLR 488, EAT 8.13, 28.23, 53.7
Wandsworth London Borough Council v D'Silva [1998] IRLR 193, CA 8.11, 8.22
Wandsworth London Borough Council v National Association of
   Schoolmasters/Union of Women Teachers (1994) 92 LGR 91,
   [1994] ICR 81, [1993] IRLR 344, [1994] ELR 170, [1993] NLJR
   655n, CA 37.2, 45.20
Warner v Adnet Ltd [1998] ICR 1056, [1998] IRLR 394, CA 52.26, 54.11

Table of Cases

Warnes v Trustees of Cheriton Oddfellows Social Club [1993] IRLR
58, EAT 53.5, 53.7
Warnock v Scarborough Football Club [1989] ICR 489, EAT 20.26, 21.22
Warren v Mendy [1989] 3 All ER 103, [1989] 1 WLR 853, [1989] ICR 525,
[1989] IRLR 210, CA 8.13, 8.24
Waters v Metropolitan Police Comr [1997] ICR 1073, [1997] IRLR 589, CA;
revsd [2000] 4 All ER 934, [2000] 1 WLR 1607, [2000] ICR 1064, [000]
IRLR 720, HL 8.13, 12.10, 12.13, 13.35, 37.2
Watts v High Quality Lifestyles Ltd [2006] IRLR 850, [2006] All ER (D) 216
(Apr), EAT 10.10
Way v Crouch [2005] ICR 1362, [2005] IRLR 603, [2005] NLJR 937, [2005]
All ER (D) 40 (Jun), EAT 14.13, 21.23
Weathersfield Ltd (t/a Van and Truck Rentals) v Sargent [1999] ICR 425,
[1999] IRLR 94, 143 Sol Jo LB 39, CA 12.6, 12.13, 13.40, 48.19
Webb v EMO Air Cargo (UK) Ltd [1992] 4 All ER 929, [1993] 1 WLR 49,
[1993] 1 CMLR 259, [1993] ICR 175, [1993] IRLR 27,
[1993] 9 LS Gaz R 44, 137 Sol Jo LB 48, HL; refd C-32/93: [1994] QB
718, [1994] 4 All ER 115, [1994] 3 WLR 941, [1994] ECR I-3567,
[1994] 2 CMLR 729, [1994] ICR 770, [1994] IRLR 482, [1994] NLJR
1278, ECJ; apld sub nom Webb v EMO Air Cargo (UK) Ltd (No 2)
[1995] 4 All ER 577, [1995] 1 WLR 1454, [1996] 2 CMLR 990,
[1995] ICR 1021, [1995] IRLR 645, [1995] 42 LS Gaz R 24, 140 Sol Jo
LB 9, HL 12.5, 25.2
Weber v Universal Ogden Services Ltd: C-37/00 [2002] QB 1189, [2002] All
ER (EC) 397, [2002] 3 WLR 931, [2002] ECR I-2013, [2002] ICR 979,
[2002] IRLR 365, [2002] All ER (D) 377 (Feb), ECJ 26.12
Weddel (W) & Co Ltd v Tepper [1980] ICR 286, [1980] IRLR 96, 124 Sol Jo
80, CA 54.9
Weir v Bettison (sued as Chief Constable of Merseyside Police)
[2003] EWCA Civ 111, [2003] ICR 708, [2003] 12 LS Gaz R 32, (2003)
Times, 4 February, 147 Sol Jo LB 145, [2003] All ER (D) 273 (Jan) 56.2
Wellcome Foundation v Darby [1996] IRLR 538, EAT 20.18
Wessex Dairies Ltd v Smith [1935] 2 KB 80, 104 LJKB 484, [1935] All ER
Rep 75, 153 LT 185, 51 TLR 439, CA 41.8
West v Kneels Ltd [1987] ICR 146, [1986] IRLR 430,
[1986] LS Gaz R 2488, EAT 53.13, 58.5
West Dunbartonshire Council v Wallace. See Strathclyde Regional Council v
Wallace
West Midland Co-operative Society Ltd v Tipton [1986] AC 536,
[1986] 1 All ER 513, [1986] 2 WLR 306, [1986] ICR 192, [1986] IRLR
112, 130 Sol Jo 143, [1986] LS Gaz R 780, [1986] NLJ Rep 163, HL 53.13,
54.4, 54.10, 54.15
West Midlands Passenger Executive v Singh [1988] 2 All ER 873, sub nom
West Midlands Passenger Transport Executive v Singh [1988] 1 WLR
730, [1988] ICR 614, [1988] IRLR 186, 132 Sol Jo 933, CA 14.9, 21.12
West Midlands Travel Ltd v Transport and General Workers' Union
[1994] ICR 978, [1994] IRLR 578, CA 45.14
Western Excavating (ECC) Ltd v Sharp [1978] QB 761, [1978] 1 All ER 713,
[1978] 2 WLR 344, [1978] ICR 221, [1978] IRLR 27, 121 Sol Jo
814, CA 53.7
Westminster City Council v Cabaj [1996] ICR 960, [1996] IRLR 399, CA 54.10,
58.1
Westminster City Council v Haywood [1998] Ch 377, [1997] 2 All ER 84,
[1997] 3 WLR 641, [1998] ICR 920, CA 42.14

Westminster City Council v UNISON [2001] EWCA Civ 443, [2001] LGR
378, [2001] ICR 1046, [2001] IRLR 524, [2001] 20 LS Gaz R 41, [2001]
All ER (D) 250 (Mar) 45.4
Weston v Vega Space Systems Engineering Ltd [1989] IRLR 429, EAT 53.15
Westwood v Secretary of State for Employment [1985] AC 20,
[1984] 1 All ER 874, [1984] 2 WLR 418, [1985] ICR 209, [1984] IRLR
209, 128 Sol Jo 221, HL 31.5, 58.27, 58.30
Wheeler v Patel [1987] ICR 631, [1987] IRLR 211,
[1987] LS Gaz R 1240, EAT 52.12, 52.26
Whelan (t/a Cheers Off Licence) v Richardson [1998] ICR 318, [1998] IRLR
114, EAT 55.12
Whent v T Cartledge Ltd [1997] IRLR 153, EAT 6.4, 52.20
Werhof v Freeway Traffic Systems GmbH & Co KG: C-499/04 [2006] IRLR
400, [2006] All ER (D) 145 (Mar), ECJ 52.20
Whiffen v Milham Ford Girls' School [2001] EWCA Civ 385, [2001] LGR
309, [2001] ICR 1023, [2001] IRLR 468, [2001] All ER (D) 256 (Mar) 13.8
Whitbread & Co plc v Mills [1988] ICR 776, [1988] IRLR 501, EAT 54.9, 54.10
Whitbread & Co plc v Thomas [1988] ICR 135, [1988] IRLR 43,
[1987] LS Gaz R 3500, EAT 54.9
Whitbread plc (t/a Whitbread Medway Inns) v Hall [2001] EWCA Civ 268,
[2001] ICR 699, [2001] IRLR 275, [2001] 16 LS Gaz R 32, 145 Sol Jo
LB 77, [2001] All ER (D) 338 (Feb) 54.4
Whitbread West Pennines Ltd v Reedy [1988] ICR 807, 20 HLR 642, CA 43.4
White v Bristol Rugby Ltd [2002] IRLR 204 .... 48.19
White v Chief Constable of South Yorkshire Police. See Frost v Chief
Constable of South Yorkshire Police
White v Holbrook Precision Castings [1985] IRLR 215, CA 27.2
White v Reflecting Roadstuds Ltd [1991] ICR 733, [1991] IRLR 331, EAT 8.13
White v South London Transport Ltd [1998] ICR 293, EAT 54.4, 54.11
White (Marion) Ltd v Francis [1972] 3 All ER 857, [1972] 1 WLR 1423, 116
Sol Jo 822, CA 41.16
Whitefield v General Medical Council [2002] UKPC 62, [2003] IRLR 39, 72
BMLR 7, (2002) Times, 29 November, [2002] All ER (D) 220 (Nov) 30.7
Whitehouse v Blatchford & Sons Ltd [2000] ICR 542 .... 52.26
Whitely v Marton Electrical Ltd [2003] ICR 495, [2003] IRLR 197, (2003)
Times, 2 January, [2002] All ER (D) 370 (Nov), EAT 16.2, 17.3
Whitewater Leisure Management Ltd v Barnes [2000] ICR 1049,
[2000] IRLR 456, [2000] All ER (D) 568, EAT 52.5
Whittaker v Watson and Watson (t/a P & M Watson Haulage) [2002] ICR
1244, 67 BMLR 28, [2002] All ER (D) 424 (Feb), EAT 20.13, 22.1, 30.7
Whittle v Manpower Services Commission [1987] IRLR 441, EAT 53.14
Wickens v Champion Employment [1984] ICR 365, 134 NLJ 544, EAT 47.2
Wigan Borough Council v Davies [1979] ICR 411, [1979] IRLR 127, EAT 53.7
Wignall v British Gas Corpn [1984] ICR 716, [1984] IRLR 493, EAT 49.2
Wilding v British Telecommunications plc [2002] EWCA Civ 349, [2002] ICR
1079, [2002] IRLR 524, [2002] All ER (D) 278 (Mar) 55.5, 55.13
Wileman v Minilec Engineering Ltd [1988] ICR 318, [1988] IRLR
144, EAT 14.16, 21.76, 22.16
Williams v Channel 5 Engineering Services Ltd IDS Brief No 609 .... 10.14
Williams v Compair Maxam Ltd [1982] ICR 156, [1982] IRLR 83, EAT 54.11
Williams v Ferrosan Ltd [2004] IRLR 607, [2004] All ER (D) 272
(May), EAT 20.14, 21.76, 22.25

Table of Cases

Williams v J Walter Thompson Group Ltd [2005] EWCA Civ 133,
[2005] IRLR 376, (2005) Times, 5 April, 149 Sol Jo LB 237, [2005] All
ER (D) 261 (Feb) 10.11, 10.15
Williams v Watsons Luxury Coaches Ltd [1990] ICR 536, [1990] IRLR
164, EAT 48.3
Williams-Drabble v Pathway Care Solutions Ltd IDS Brief No 776 .... 13.8
Willment Bros Ltd v Oliver [1979] ICR 378 .... 55.13
Willow Oak Developments Ltd (t/a Windsor Recruitment) v Silverwood
[2006] IRLR 28, [2005] All ER (D) 252 (Oct), EAT; affd [2006] EWCA
Civ 660, [2006] IRLR 607, [2006] All ER (D) 351 (May) 54.14
Wilson (Inspector of Taxes) v Clayton [2004] EWHC 898 (Ch), [2004] STC
1022, [2004] IRLR 611, [2004] 19 LS Gaz R 29, (2004) Times, 7 June,
[2004] All ER (D) 313 (Apr); affd [2004] EWCA Civ 1657, [2005] STC
157, 77 TC 1, [2005] IRLR 108, (2005) Times, 12 January, 149 Sol Jo LB
24, [2004] All ER (D) 94 (Dec) 55.22
Wilson v Ethicon Ltd [2000] IRLR 4, EAT 54.4
Wilson v Mars UK Ltd (t/a Masterfoods) [2007] ICR 370, [2006] All ER (D)
35 (Dec), EAT 15.2, 15.3
Wilson v Maynard Shipbuilding Consultants AB [1978] QB 665,
[1978] 2 All ER 78, [1978] 2 WLR 466, [1978] ICR 376, [1977] IRLR
491, 13 ITR 23, 121 Sol Jo 792, CA 53.15
Wilson v Post Office [2000] IRLR 834 .... 54.2
Wilson v Racher [1974] ICR 428, [1974] IRLR 114, 16 KIR 212, CA 58.17
Wilson v St Helens Borough Council [1999] 2 AC 52, [1998] 4 All ER 609,
[1998] 3 WLR 1070, [1999] 1 CMLR 918, [1999] LGR 255, [1998] ICR
1141, [1998] IRLR 706, [1998] All ER (D) 516, HL 52.26
Wilson (Joshua) & Bros Ltd v Union of Shop, Distributive and Allied
Workers [1978] 3 All ER 4, [1978] ICR 614, [1978] IRLR 120, 13 ITR
229, EAT 50.20
Wilson (Paal) & Co A/S v Partenreederei Hannah Blumenthal, The Hannah
Blumenthal [1983] 1 AC 854, [1982] 3 All ER 394, [1982] 3 WLR 49,
[1982] 1 Lloyd's Rep 582, 126 Sol Jo 292, CA; varied [1983] 1 AC 854,
[1983] 1 All ER 34, [1982] 3 WLR 1149, [1983] 1 Lloyd's Rep 103, 126
Sol Jo 835, HL 48.3
Wilson and National Union of Journalists v United Kingdom (Applications
30668/96, 30679/61 and 30678/96) [2002] IRLR 568, 13 BHRC 39,
(2002) Times, 5 July, [2002] All ER (D) 35 (Jul), ECtHR 30.4, 50.19, 51.18
Wilton (Arthur H) Ltd v Peebles EAT/835/93 .... 20.31
Wiltshire County Council v National Association of Teachers in Further and
Higher Education (1980) 78 LGR 445, [1980] ICR 455, [1980] IRLR
198, CA 53.6
Wiluszynski v Tower Hamlets London Borough Council (1989) 88 LGR 14,
[1989] ICR 493, [1989] IRLR 259, 133 Sol Jo 628, CA 8.24, 34.14, 45.16
Winfield v London Philharmonic Orchestra Ltd [1979] ICR 726, EAT 17.3
Wippel v Peek & Cloppenburg Gmbh & Co Kg: C-313/02 [2005] ICR 1604,
[2005] IRLR 211, ECJ 12.12, 32.2, 32.9, 32.11
Wise v Union of Shop, Distributive and Allied Workers [1996] ICR 691,
[1996] IRLR 609 .... 50.14
Wise Group v Mitchell [2005] ICR 896, [2005] All ER (D) 168 (Feb), EAT 58.25,
                                                                                        58.33
Wishart v National Association of Citizens Advice Bureaux Ltd [1990] ICR
794, [1990] IRLR 393, CA 8.23, 40.9
Witley and District Men's Club v Mackay [2001] IRLR 595, [2001] All ER
(D) 31 (Jun), EAT 29.4

Wolstenholme v Post Office Ltd [2003] ICR 546, EAT 17.3, 29.2
Wong v BAE Systems Operations Ltd [2004] IRLR 840,
    [2004] 33 LS Gaz R 34, [2004] All ER (D) 131 (Jul), EAT 34.6
Wong v Codemasters Software Co Ltd [2007] All ER (D) 102 (Jan) 15.13
Wong v Igen Ltd (Equal Opportunities Commission intervening)
    [2005] EWCA Civ 142, [2005] 3 All ER 812, [2005] ICR 931,
    [2005] IRLR 258, (2005) Times, 3 March, 149 Sol Jo LB 264, [2005] All
    ER (D) 300 (Feb) 3.44, 12.5, 12.10, 14.3
Wood v Coverage Care Ltd [1996] IRLR 264, EAT 19.4, 54.11
Wood v Cunard Line Ltd [1991] ICR 13, [1990] IRLR 281, CA 53.11, 53.15
Wood Group Heavy Industrial Turbines Ltd v Crossan [1998] IRLR
    680, EAT 55.2
Woodrup v Southwark London Borough Council [2002] EWCA Civ 1716,
    [2003] IRLR 111, 146 Sol Jo LB 263, [2002] All ER (D) 181 (Nov) 10.7, 20.13
Woods v Suffolk Mental Health Partnership NHS Trust (26 September 2006,
    unreported) 22.5
Woods v WM Car Services (Peterborough) Ltd [1982] ICR 693, [1982] IRLR
    413, [1982] Com LR 208, CA 53.7
Woodward v Abbey National plc [2005] IRLR 782, [2005] All ER (D) 64
    (Aug), EAT 22.1, 22.5, 22.6
Woodward v Abbey National plc [2006] EWCA Civ 822, [2006] 4 All ER
    1209, [2006] ICR 1436, [2006] IRLR 677, (2006) Times, 11 July, 150 Sol
    Jo LB 857, [2006] All ER (D) 253 (Jun) 11.18, 40.4, 57.23
Woolf (Lewis) Griptight Ltd v Corfield [1997] IRLR 432, EAT 12.5
Worlsey (E) & Co Ltd v Cooper [1939] 1 All ER 290 .... 41.13
Wright v London General Omnibus Co (1877) 2 QBD 271, 41 JP 486, 46
    LJQB 429, 25 WR 647, 36 LT 590, [1874–80] All ER Rep Ext 1721 .... 8.23
Wright v Redrow Homes (Yorkshire) Ltd [2004] EWCA Civ 469,
    [2004] 3 All ER 98, [2004] ICR 1126, [2004] IRLR 720, 148 Sol Jo LB
    666, [2004] All ER (D) 221 (Apr) 17.9, 29.2, 57.3
Wright (Frank) & Co (Holdings) Ltd v Punch [1980] IRLR 217, EAT 58.22
Wyatt v Kreglinger and Fernau [1933] 1 KB 793, 102 LJKB 325,
    [1933] All ER Rep 349, 148 LT 521, 49 TLR 264, CA 41.4
Wynnwith Engineering Co Ltd v Bennett [2002] IRLR 170, [2001] All ER
    (D) 134 (Dec), EAT 52.4

X

X v Metropolitan Police Comr [2003] ICR 1031, [2003] NLJR 719, [2003] All
    ER (D) 374 (Apr), sub nom X v Stevens [2003] IRLR 411, EAT 14.11, 21.18,
                                                                           22.1
X v United Kingdom 11 DR 55 (1977) 12.6
X v Y [2004] EWCA Civ 662, [2004] ICR 1634, [2004] IRLR 625, [2004]
    UKHHR 1172, 148 Sol Jo LB 697, [2004] All ER (D) 449 (May) 20.13, 30.7,
                                                                            54.9
X v Z Ltd [1998] ICR 43, CA 21.18
X and Church of Scientology v Sweden (Application 7805/77) 16 DR 68
    (1979), EComHR 12.6
XXX v YYY [2004] IRLR 137, [2003] All ER (D) 07 (Sep), EAT; revsd
    [2004] EWCA Civ 231, [2004] IRLR 471, [2004] All ER (D) 144 (Feb) 21.51

Y

YMCA Training Ltd v Stewart. See Stewart v YMCA Training Ltd

Table of Cases

Yearwood v Metropolitan Police Comr [2004] ICR 1660, [2004] All ER (D)
   457 (May), EAT 12.13
Yeboah v Crofton [2002] EWCA Civ 794, [2002] IRLR 634 ... 12.13, 13.37, 22.7, 22.17
Yell Ltd v Garton [2004] EWCA Civ 87, (2004) Times, 26 February, 148 Sol
   Jo LB 180, [2004] All ER (D) 80 (Feb) 22.14
Yemm v British Steel plc [1994] IRLR 117, EAT 34.6
Yenula Properties Ltd v Naidu [2002] EWCA Civ 719, [2003] HLR 229,
   [2002] 42 EG 162, [2002] 27 LS Gaz R 34, [2002] 23 EGCS 121, (2002)
   Times, 5 June, [2002] All ER (D) 366 (May) 43.5
York Trailer Co Ltd v Sparkes [1973] ICR 518, NIRC 55.12
York Truck Equipment Ltd, Re IDS Brief No 439 .... 12.10
Yorkshire Blood Transfusion Service v Plaskitt [1994] ICR 74, EAT 24.11
Young v Charles Church (Southern) Ltd (1997) 33 BMLR 101, CA 27.8
Young v National Power plc [2001] 2 All ER 339, [2001] ICR 328,
   [2001] IRLR 32, (2000) Times, 23 November, [2000] All ER (D)
   1727, CA 20.28
Young v Timmins (1831) 1 Cr & J 331, 9 LJOS Ex 68, 1 Tyr 226 .... 41.3
Young & Woods Ltd v West [1980] IRLR 201, CA 17.3
Young, James and Webster v United Kingdom (Applications 7601/76,
   7806/77) (1981) 4 EHRR 38, [1981] IRLR 408, ECtHR 30.4
Young, James and Webster v United Kingdom [1983] IRLR 35 .... 30.4

                                         Z
Zafar v Glasgow City Council. See Glasgow City Council v Zafar
Zaiwalla & Co v Walia [2002] IRLR 697, (2002) Times, 1 August, [2002] All
   ER (D) 103 (Aug), EAT 14.16
Zarb and Samuels v British and Brazilian Produce Co (Sales) Ltd
   [1978] IRLR 78, EAT 7.9
Zarczynska v Levy [1979] 1 All ER 814, [1979] 1 WLR 125, [1979] ICR 184,
   [1978] IRLR 532, 143 JP 297, 122 Sol Jo 776, EAT 12.6, 12.13, 13.40
Zahedi v McGee EAT/465/94, IDS Brief No 551 .... 22.12
Zurich Insurance Co v Gulson [1998] IRLR 118, EAT 21.56

Decisions of the European Court of Justice are listed below numerically.
These decisions are also listed alphabetically in the preceding Table of Cases.

43/75: Defrenne v Sabena [1981] 1 All ER 122, [1976] ECR 455,
   [1976] 2 CMLR 98, [1976] ICR 547, ECJ 24.19, 24.20, 25.2
33/76: Rewe-Zentralfinanz GmbH v Landwirtschaftskammer für Saarland
   [1976] ECR 1989, [1977] 1 CMLR 533, CMR 8382, ECJ 25.2
12/81: Garland v British Rail Engineering Ltd [1983] 2 AC 751,
   [1982] 2 All ER 402, [1982] 2 WLR 918, [1982] ECR 359,
   [1982] 1 CMLR 696, [1982] ICR 420, [1982] IRLR 111, ECJ; apld
   [1983] 2 AC 751, [1982] 2 All ER 402, [1982] 2 WLR 918,
   [1982] 2 CMLR 174, [1982] ICR 420, [1982] IRLR 257, 126 Sol Jo
   309, HL 42.5
61/81: EC Commission v United Kingdom of Great Britain and Northern
   Ireland [1982] ECR 2601, [1982] 3 CMLR 284, [1982] ICR 578,
   [1982] IRLR 333, ECJ 25.6
165/82: EC Commission v United Kingdom [1984] 1 All ER 353, [1983] ECR
   3431, [1984] 1 CMLR 44, [1984] ICR 192, [1984] IRLR 29, ECJ 25.6

63/83: R v Kirk [1985] 1 All ER 453, [1984] ECR 2689, [1984] 3 CMLR 522, ECJ.. 30.5

135/83: Abels v Administrative Board of the Bedrijfsvereniging voor de Metaalindustrie en de Electrotechnische Industrie [1985] ECR 469, [1987] 2 CMLR 406, ECJ... 52.11

186/83: Botzen v Rotterdamsche Droogdok Maatschappij BV [1985] ECR 519, [1986] 2 CMLR 50, ECJ... 52.15

152/84: Marshall v Southampton and South West Hampshire Area Health Authority (Teaching) [1986] QB 401, [1986] 2 All ER 584, [1986] 2 WLR 780, [1986] ECR 723, [1986] 1 CMLR 688, [1986] ICR 335, [1986] IRLR 140, 130 Sol Jo 340, ECJ.. 20.12, 25.6, 37.7

170/84: Bilka-Kaufhaus GmbH v Weber von Hartz [1986] ECR 1607, [1986] 2 CMLR 701, [1987] ICR 110, [1986] IRLR 317, ECJ...... 12.9, 13.8, 24.3, 24.10, 24.11

222/84: Johnston v Chief Constable of the Royal Ulster Constabulary [1987] QB 129, [1986] 3 All ER 135, [1986] 3 WLR 1038, [1986] ECR 1651, [1986] 3 CMLR 240, [1987] ICR 83, [1986] IRLR 263, 130 Sol Jo 953, [1987] LS Gaz R 188, ECJ.. 13.19, 25.6

24/85: Spijkers v Gebroeders Benedik Abbatoir CV and Alfred Benedik en Zonen BV [1986] ECR 1119, [1986] 2 CMLR 296, ECJ........................... 52.5

66/85: Lawrie-Blum v Land Baden-Württemberg [1986] ECR 2121, [1987] 3 CMLR 389, [1987] ICR 483, ECJ...................................... 24.4

186/85: Family Benefits for Community Civil Servants, Re, EC Commission v Belgium [1987] ECR 2029, [1988] 2 CMLR 759, ECJ.......................... 37.8

225/85: Employees of the Consiglio Nazionale delle Ricerche, Re, EC Commisison v Italy [1988] ECR 2271, [1988] 3 CMLR 635, ECJ............. 37.7

237/85: Rummler v Dato-Druck GmbH [1987] ICR 774, [1987] IRLR 32, ECJ.. 24.7

111/86: Delauche v EC Commission [1987] ECR 5345, [1989] 2 CMLR 565, ECJ.. 37.8

157/86: Murphy v Bord Telecom Eireann [1988] ECR 673, [1988] 1 CMLR 879, [1988] ICR 445, [1988] IRLR 267, ECJ.................................. 24.6, 24.8

222/86: Union Nationale des Entraîneurs et Cadres Techniques Professionnels du Football (UNECTEF) v Heylens [1987] ECR 4097, [1989] 1 CMLR 901, ECJ.. 25.4

324/86: Foreningen af Arbejdsledere i Danmark v Daddy's Dance Hall A/S [1988] ECR 739, [1989] 2 CMLR 517, [1988] IRLR 315, ECJ............ 52.6, 52.29

101/87: P Bork International A/S v Foreningen af Arbejdsledere i Danmark [1988] ECR 3057, [1990] 3 CMLR 701, [1989] IRLR 41, ECJ............ 52.6, 52.14

144/87 and 145/87: Berg and Busschers v Besselsen [1988] ECR 2559, [1989] 3 CMLR 817, [1990] ICR 396, [1989] IRLR 447, ECJ............ 52.6, 52.18

180/87: Hamill v EC Commission [1990] 1 All ER 982, [1988] ECR 6141, [1990] 1 CMLR 982, ECJ... 37.8

193/87: Maurissen and European Public Service Union v Court of Auditors of the European Communities [1989] ECR 1045, ECJ.......................... 37.8

33/88: Allué and Coonan v Università degli Studi di Venezia [1989] ECR 1591, [1991] 1 CMLR 283, ECJ.. 37.7

109/88: Handels-og Kontorfunktionaerernes Forbund i Danmark v Dansk Arbejdsgiverforening, acting on behalf of Danfoss [1989] ECR 3199, [1991] 1 CMLR 8, [1991] ICR 74, [1989] IRLR 532, ECJ....................... 24.11

171/88: Rinner-Kühn v FWW Spezial-Gebäudereinigung GmbH & Co KG [1989] ECR 2743, [1993] 2 CMLR 932, [1989] IRLR 493, ECJ.................. 24.3

Table of Cases

177/88: Dekker v Stichting Vormingscentrum voor Jong Volwassenen
(VJV-Centrum) Plus [1990] ECR I-3941, [1992] ICR 325, [1991] IRLR
27, ECJ 12.5
C-262/88: Barber v Guardian Royal Exchange Assurance Group [1991] 1 QB
344, [1990] 2 All ER 660, [1991] 2 WLR 72, [1990] ECR I-1889,
[1990] 2 CMLR 513, [1990] ICR 616, [1990] IRLR 240, [1990] NLJR
925, ECJ 24.3, 24.5, 24.16, 25.2, 42.1, 42.5
322/88: Grimaldi v Fonds des Maladies Professionnelles [1989] ECR 4407,
[1991] 2 CMLR 265, [1990] IRLR 400, ECJ 25.1
C-33/89: Kowalska v Freie und Hansestadt Hamburg [1990] ECR I-2591,
[1992] ICR 29, [1990] IRLR 447, ECJ 24.23, 24.24
C-106/89: Marleasing SA v La Comercial Internacional de Alimentacion SA
[1990] ECR I-4135, [1992] 1 CMLR 305, [1993] BCC 421, 135 Sol Jo 15,
ECJ 25.2
C-184/89: Nimz v Freie und Hansestadt Hamburg [1991] ECR I-297,
[1992] 3 CMLR 699, [1991] IRLR 222, ECJ 6.6, 24.3, 24.11, 24.23, 24.24
C-188/89: Foster v British Gas plc [1991] 1 QB 405, [1990] 3 All ER 897,
[1991] 2 WLR 258, [1990] ECR I-3313, [1990] 2 CMLR 833, [1991] ICR
84, [1990] IRLR 353, ECJ; apld [1991] 2 AC 306, [1991] 2 All ER 705,
[1991] 2 WLR 1075, [1991] 2 CMLR 217, [1991] ICR 463, [1991] IRLR
268, [1991] 18 LS Gaz R 34, HL 25.2, 37.7
C-192/89: Sevince v Staatssecretaris van Justitie [1990] ECR I-3461,
[1992] 2 CMLR 57, ECJ 26.2
C-229/89: EC Commission v Belgium [1991] ECR I-2205, [1993] 2 CMLR
403, [1991] IRLR 393, ECJ 13.8
C-362/89: d'Urso v Ercole Marelli Elettromeccanica Generale SpA
[1991] ECR I-4105, [1993] 3 CMLR 513, [1992] IRLR 136, ECJ 52.26, 52.28
C-6/90 and C-9/90: Francovich and Bonifaci v Italy [1991] ECR I-5357,
[1993] 2 CMLR 66, [1995] ICR 722, [1992] IRLR 84, ECJ 25.2
C-87/90, C-99/90, and C-89/90: Verholen v Sociale Versekeringsbank
Amsterdam [1991] ECR I-3757, [1994] 1 CMLR 157, [1992] IRLR 38,
ECJ 25.2
C-208/90: Emmott v Minister for Social Welfare and A-G [1991] ECR
I-4269, [1991] 3 CMLR 894, [1993] ICR 8, [1991] IRLR 387, ECJ 20.18, 25.2
C-360/90: Arbeiterwohlfahrt der Stadt Berlin e V v Bötel [1992] ECR I-3589,
[1992] 3 CMLR 446, [1992] IRLR 423, [1993] 21 LS Gaz R 45, ECJ ... 24.3, 24.10
C-29/91: Redmond (Dr Sophie) Stichting v Bartol [1992] ECR I-3189,
[1994] 3 CMLR 265, [1992] IRLR 366, ECJ 52.4, 52.5
C-109/91: Ten Oever v Stichting Bedrijfspensioenfonds voor het
Glazenwassers- en Schoonmaakbedrijf [1993] ECR I-4879,
[1995] 2 CMLR 357, [1995] ICR 74, [1993] IRLR 601,
[1995] 42 LS Gaz R 23, ECJ 24.18
C-110/91: Moroni v Collo GmbH [1993] ECR I-6591, [1995] 2 CMLR 357,
[1995] ICR 137, [1994] IRLR 130, [1995] 42 LS Gaz R 23, ECJ 24.18
C-132/91, C-138/91 and C-139/91: Katsikas v Konstantinidis [1992] ECR
I-6577, [1993] 1 CMLR 845, [1993] IRLR 179, ECJ 52.16
C-140/91, C-141/91, C-278/91 and C-279/91: Suffritti v Istituto Nazionale
della Previdenza Sociale (INPS) [1992] ECR I-6337, [1993] IRLR 289,
ECJ 25.2
C-152/91: Neath v Hugh Steeper Ltd [1994] 1 All ER 929, [1993] ECR
I-6935, [1995] 2 CMLR 357, [1995] ICR 158, [1994] IRLR 91,
[1995] 42 LS Gaz R 23, ECJ 22.27, 24.18
C-173/91: EC Commission v Belgium [1993] IRLR 404, ECJ 24.3

C-200/91: Coloroll Pension Trustees Ltd v Russell [1995] All ER (EC) 23,
[1994] ECR I-4389, [1995] 2 CMLR 357, [1995] ICR 179, [1994] IRLR
586, [1995] 42 LS Gaz R 23, (1994) Times, 30 November, ECJ 24.18, 42.7
C-209/91: Rask and Christensen v ISS Kantineservice A/S [1992] ECR
I-5755, [1993] IRLR 133, ECJ 52.5
C-271/91: Marshall v Southampton and South West Hampshire Area Health
Authority (No 2) [1994] QB 126, [1993] 4 All ER 586, [1993] 3 WLR
1054, [1993] ECR I-4367, [1993] 3 CMLR 293, [1993] ICR 893,
[1993] IRLR 445, ECJ; apld sub nom Marshall v Southampton and
South-West Hampshire Area Health Authority (Teaching) (No 2)
[1994] 1 AC 530n, [1994] 1 All ER 736n, [1994] 2 WLR 392, [1994] ICR
242n, HL 14.13, 20.12, 21.67, 25.5
C-338/91: Steenhorst-Neerings v Bestuur van de Bedrijfsvereniging voor
Detailhandel, Ambachten en Huisvrouwen [1993] ECR I-5475,
[1995] 3 CMLR 323, [1994] IRLR 244, ECJ 25.2
C-91/92: Faccini Dori v Recreb Srl [1995] All ER (EC) 1, [1994] ECR I-3325,
[1995] 1 CMLR 665, ECJ 25.2
C-125/92: Mulox IBC Ltd v Geels [1993] ECR I-4075, [1994] IRLR 422,
ECJ 26.12
C-127/92: Enderby v Frenchay Health Authority [1994] 1 All ER 495,
[1993] ECR I-5535, [1994] 1 CMLR 8, [1994] ICR 112, [1993] IRLR
591, ECJ 22.27, 24.10, 24.11
C-132/92: Birds Eye Walls Ltd v Roberts [1993] ECR I-5579, [1993] 3 CMLR
822, [1994] IRLR 29, sub nom Roberts v Birds Eye Walls Ltd
[1994] ICR 338, ECJ 24.12, 24.17, 24.18
C-382/92: EC Commission v United Kingdom [1994] ECR I-2435,
[1995] 1 CMLR 345, [1994] ICR 664, [1994] IRLR 392, ECJ 18.28, 25.2
C-383/92: EC Commission v United Kingdom [1994] ECR I-2479,
[1995] 1 CMLR 345, [1994] ICR 664, [1994] IRLR 412, ECJ 25.8, 25.9
C-392/92: Schmidt v Spar und Leihkasse der früheren Amter Bordesholm,
Kiel und Cronshagen [1994] ECR I-1311, [1995] 2 CMLR 331,
[1995] ICR 237, [1994] IRLR 302, ECJ 52.5
C-399/92, C-409/92, C-425/92, C-34/93, C-50/93, and C-78/93: Stadt
Lengerich v Helmig [1994] ECR I-5727, [1995] 2 CMLR 261, [1996] ICR
35, [1995] IRLR 216, ECJ 24.11, 32.6
C-408/92: Smith v Avdel Systems Ltd [1995] All ER (EC) 132, [1994] ECR
I-4435, [1995] 3 CMLR 543, [1995] ICR 596, [1994] IRLR 602, ECJ 22.27,
24.18, 42.5
C-410/92: Johnson v Chief Adjudication Officer (No 2) [1995] All ER (EC)
258, [1994] ECR I-5483, [1995] 1 CMLR 725, [1995] ICR 375,
[1995] IRLR 157, ECJ 25.2
C-7/93: Bestuur van het Algemeen Burgerlijk Pensioenfonds v Beune [1995]
All ER (EC) 97, [1994] ECR I-4471, [1995] 3 CMLR 30, [1995] IRLR
103, ECJ 24.18
C-32/93: Webb v EMO Air Cargo (UK) Ltd [1994] QB 718, [1994] 4 All ER
115, [1994] 3 WLR 941, [1994] ECR I-3567, [1994] 2 CMLR 729,
[1994] ICR 770, [1994] IRLR 482, [1994] NLJR 1278, ECJ; apld sub
nom Webb v EMO Air Cargo (UK) Ltd (No 2) [1995] 4 All ER 577,
[1995] 1 WLR 1454, [1996] 2 CMLR 990, [1995] ICR 1021, [1995] IRLR
645, [1995] 42 LS Gaz R 24, 140 Sol Jo LB 9, HL 12.5, 25.2
C-46/93: Brasserie du Pecheur SA v Germany [1996] QB 404, [1996] All ER
(EC) 301, [1996] 2 WLR 506, [1996] ECR I-1029, [1996] 1 CMLR 889,
[1996] IRLR 267, ECJ 25.2

Table of Cases

C-48/93: R v Secretary of State for Transport, ex p Factortame Ltd
[1996] QB 404, [1996] All ER (EC) 301, [1996] 2 WLR 506, [1996] ECR
I-1029, [1996] 1 CMLR 889, [1996] IRLR 267, ECJ; apld
[1998] 1 All ER 736n, [1998] 1 CMLR 1353, [1997] Eu LR 475, DC; on
appeal [1999] 2 All ER 640n, [1998] 3 CMLR 192, [1998] NPC 68,
[1998] Eu LR 456, CA; affd [2000] 1 AC 524, [1999] 4 All ER 906,
[1999] 3 WLR 1062, [1999] 3 CMLR 597, [1999] 43 LS Gaz R 32, HL 25.2
C-57/93: Vroege v NCIV Institut voor Volkshuisvesting BV [1995] All ER
(EC) 193, [1994] ECR I-4541, [1995] 1 CMLR 881, [1995] ICR 635,
[1994] IRLR 651, ECJ 24.10
C-128/93: Fisscher v Voorhuis Hengelo BV [1995] All ER (EC) 193,
[1994] ECR I-4583, [1995] 1 CMLR 881, [1995] ICR 635, [1994] IRLR
662, ECJ 20.12, 24.18, 25.2
C-342/93: Gillespie v Northern Health and Social Services Board [1996] All
ER (EC) 284, [1996] ECR I-475, [1996] 2 CMLR 969, [1996] ICR 498,
[1996] IRLR 214, ECJ 24.14, 33.14, 42.8
C-400/93: Specialarbejderforbundet i Danmark v Dansk Industri acting for
Royal Copenhagen A/S [1995] ECR I-1275, [1995] All ER (EC) 577,
[1996] 1 CMLR 515, [1996] ICR 51, [1995] IRLR 648, ECJ 24.10
C-435/93: Dietz v Stichting Thuiszorg Rotterdam [1996] ECR I-5223,
[1997] 1 CMLR 199, [1996] IRLR 692, 563 IRLB 13, ECJ 24.17, 24.18
C-444/93: Megner and Scheffel v Innungskrankenkasse Vorderpfalz [1996]
All ER (EC) 212, [1995] ECR I-4741, [1996] IRLR 236, ECJ 25.2
C-449/93: Rockfon A/S v Specialarbejderforbundet i Danmark [1995] ECR
I-4291, [1996] ICR 673, [1996] IRLR 168, ECJ 39.4
C-450/93: Kalanke v Freie Hansestadt Bremen [1996] All ER (EC) 66,
[1995] ECR I-3051, [1996] 1 CMLR 175, [1996] ICR 314, [1995] IRLR
660, ECJ 12.5, 12.12, 13.9, 37.2
C-457/93: Kuratorium für Dialyse und Nierentransplantation eV v Lewark
[1996] ECR I-243, [1996] IRLR 637, ECJ 24.3, 49.4
C-472/93: Spano v Fiat Geotech SpA and Fiat Hitachi Excavators SpA
[1995] ECR I-4321, ECJ 52.28
C-13/94: P v S [1996] All ER (EC) 397, [1996] ECR I-2143, [1996] 2 CMLR
247, [1996] ICR 795, [1996] IRLR 347, [1997] 2 FCR 180, [1996] 2 FLR
347, ECJ 12.2, 12.6, 22.27, 24.2
C-48/94: Ledernes Hovedorganisation (acting for Rygard) v Dansk
Arbejdsgiverforening (acting for Sto Molle Akustik A/S) [1995] ECR
I-2745, [1996] 3 CMLR 45, [1996] ICR 333, [1996] IRLR 51, ECJ 52.5
C-84/94: United Kingdom v EU Council [1996] All ER (EC) 877,
[1996] ECR I-5755, [1996] 3 CMLR 671, [1997] ICR 443, [1997] IRLR
30, ECJ 25.11, 57.1
C-116/94: Meyers v Adjudication Officer [1995] All ER (EC) 705,
[1995] ECR I-2131, [1996] 1 CMLR 461, [1995] IRLR 498, ECJ 25.5
C-171/94 and C-172/94: Merckx v Ford Motors Co Belgium SA [1996] All
ER (EC) 667, [1996] ECR I-1253, [1997] ICR 352, [1996] IRLR 467,
ECJ 52.5, 52.16
C-178/94, C-179/94, C-188/94, C-189/94 and C-190/94: Dillenkofer v
Germany [1997] QB 259, [1996] All ER (EC) 917, [1997] 2 WLR 253,
[1996] ECR I-4845, [1996] 3 CMLR 469, [1997] IRLR 60, ECJ 25.2
C-194/94: CIA Security International SA v Signalson [1996] All ER (EC)
557, [1996] ECR I-2201, [1996] 2 CMLR 781, ECJ 25.2
C-298/94: Henke v Gemeinde Schierke and Verwaltungsgemeinschaft
Brocken [1997] All ER (EC) 173, [1996] ECR I-4989, [1997] 1 CMLR
373, [1997] ICR 746, [1996] IRLR 701, ECJ 18.4, 37.2, 52.9

C-305/94: Hertaing v Benoidt [1997] All ER (EC) 40, [1996] ECR I-5927,
[1997] 1 CMLR 329, [1997] IRLR 127, ECJ 52.13
C-319/94: Dethier (Jules) Equipement SA v Dassy and Sovam SPRL (in
liquidation) [1998] All ER (EC) 346, [1998] ECR I-1061,
[1998] 2 CMLR 611, [1998] ICR 541, [1998] IRLR 266, ECJ 52.11, 52.26
C-1/95: Gerster v Freistaat Bayern [1997] ECR I-5253, [1998] 1 CMLR 303,
[1998] ICR 327, [1997] IRLR 699, ECJ 24.3, 24.11
E-2/95:Eidesund v Stavanger Catering A/S: [1997] 2 CMLR 672,
[1996] IRLR 684, EFTA Ct 52.19
C-13/95: Suzen v Zehnacker Gebaudereinigung GmbH Krankenhausservice
[1997] All ER (EC) 289, [1997] ECR I-1259, [1997] 1 CMLR 768,
[1997] ICR 662, [1997] IRLR 255, ECJ 52.5
C-100/95: Kording v Senator für Finanzen [1997] ECR I-5289,
[1998] 1 CMLR 395, [1997] IRLR 710, ECJ 24.3
C-136/95: Caisse Nationale d'Assurance Vieillesse des Travailleurs Salaries v
Thibault [1998] All ER (EC) 385, [1998] ECR I-2011, [1998] 2 CMLR
516, [1998] IRLR 399, [1998] All ER (D) 167, sub nom Thibault v
Caisse Nationale d'Assurance Viellesse des Travailleurs Salaries
(CNAVTS) [1999] ICR 160, ECJ 12.5
C-163/95: Von Horn v Cinnamond [1998] QB 214, [1997] All ER (EC) 913,
[1998] 2 WLR 104, [1997] ECR I-5451, ECJ 26.12
C-188/95: Fantask A/S v Industriministeriet (Erhvervsministeriet) [1998] All
ER (EC) 1, [1997] ECR I-6783, [1998] 1 CMLR 473, ECJ 25.2
C-243/95: Hill v Revenue Comrs [1998] All ER (EC) 722, [1998] ECR I-3739,
[1998] 3 CMLR 81, [1999] ICR 48, [1998] IRLR 466,
[1998] 34 LS Gaz R 33, [1998] All ER (D) 277, ECJ 24.3
C-374/95: Barker v Service Children's Schools unreported, ECJ 12.12
C-383/95: Rutten v Cross Medical Ltd [1997] All ER (EC) 121, [1997] ECR
I-57, [1997] ICR 715, [1997] IRLR 249, ECJ 26.12
C-409/95: Marschall v Land Nordrhein-Westfalen [1997] All ER (EC) 865,
[1997] ECR I-6363, [1998] 1 CMLR 547, [2001] ICR 45, [1998] IRLR
39, ECJ 12.12, 13.9
C-15/96: Schöning-Kougebetopoulou v Freie und Hansestadt Hamburg:
[1998] All ER (EC) 97, [1998] 1 CMLR 931, sub nom Kalliope
Schöning-Kougebetopoulou v Freie und Hansestadt Hamburg
[1998] ECR I-47, ECJ 26.2
C-50/96: Deutsche Telekom AG v Schröder [2000] ECR I-743,
[2002] 2 CMLR 583, [2000] IRLR 353, ECJ 24.18
C-66/96: Handels-og Kontorfunktionaerernes Forbund i Danmark (acting on
behalf of Hoj Pedersen) v Faellesforeningen for Danmarks
Brugsforeninger (acting on behalf of Kvickly Skive) [1998] ECR I-7327,
[1999] 2 CMLR 326, [1999] IRLR 55, sub nom Pedersen v Kvickly Skive
[1999] All ER (EC) 138, [1998] All ER (D) 614, ECJ 24.14
C-127/96, C-229/96 and C-74/97: Vidal (Francisco Hernandez) SA v Perez
[1998] ECR I-8179, [1999] IRLR 132, ECJ 52.5
C-129/96:Inter-Environnement Wallonie ASBL v Region Wallonie
[1997] ECR I-7411, [1998] All ER (EC) 155, [1998] 1 CMLR 1057,
ECJ 25.2
C-173/96: Hidalgo v Asociacion de Servicios Aser and Sociedad Cooperativa
Minerva [1998] ECR I-8237, [2002] ICR 73, [1999] IRLR 136, ECJ 52.5
C-246/96: Magorrian v Eastern Health and Social Services Board [1998] All
ER (EC) 38, [1997] ECR I-7153, [1998] ICR 979, [1998] IRLR 86,
ECJ 20.12

Table of Cases

C-249/96: Grant v South-West Trains Ltd [1998] All ER (EC) 193,
[1998] ECR I-621, [1998] 1 CMLR 993, [1998] ICR 449, [1998] IRLR
206, [1998] 1 FCR 377, [1998] 1 FLR 839, [1998] Fam Law 392, 3
BHRC 578, ECJ 30.5
C-326/96: Levez v TH Jennings (Harlow Pools) Ltd [1999] All ER (EC) 1,
[1998] ECR I-7835, [1999] 2 CMLR 363, [1999] ICR 521, [1999] IRLR
36, 608 IRLB 3, [1998] All ER (D) 662, ECJ 20.12
C-394/96: Brown v Rentokil Ltd [1998] All ER (EC) 791, [1998] ECR I-4185,
[1998] 2 CMLR 1049, [1998] ICR 790, [1998] IRLR 445, [1999] 1 FCR
49, [1998] 2 FLR 649, [1998] Fam Law 597, 48 BMLR 126,
[1998] 34 LS Gaz R 34, [1998] All ER (D) 313, ECJ 12.5
C-411/96: Boyle v Equal Opportunities Commission [1998] All ER (EC) 879,
[1998] ECR I-6401, [1998] 3 CMLR 1133, [1999] ICR 360, [1998] IRLR
717, [1999] 1 FCR 581, [1999] 1 FLR 119, 608 IRLB 5, [1998] All ER
(D) 500, ECJ 24.14, 42.9
C-125/97: AGR Regeling v Bestuur van der Bedrijfsvereniging voor de
Metaallnijverheid [1998] ECR I-4493, [1999] 1 CMLR 1410, [1999] ICR
605, [1999] IRLR 379, [1998] All ER (D) 336, ECJ 31.5
C-167/97: R v Secretary of State for Employment, ex p Seymour-Smith
[1999] 2 AC 554, [1999] All ER (EC) 97, [1999] 3 WLR 460, [1999] ECR
I-623, [1999] 2 CMLR 273, [1999] ICR 447, [1999] IRLR 253, ECJ; apld
sub nom R v Secretary of State for Employment, ex p Seymour-Smith
(No 2) [2000] 1 All ER 857, [2000] 1 WLR 435, [2000] 1 CMLR 770,
[2000] ICR 244, [2000] IRLR 263, [2000] 09 LS Gaz R 40, HL 7.1, 12.8, 13.8,
24.3, 24.10, 25.2, 53.11
C-185/97: Coote v Granada Hospitality Ltd [1998] All ER (EC) 865,
[1998] ECR I-5199, [1998] 3 CMLR 958, [1999] ICR 100, [1998] IRLR
656, ECJ; apld Coote v Granada Hospitality Ltd (No 2) [1999] 3 CMLR
334, [1999] ICR 942, [1999] IRLR 452, EAT 12.12, 13.33, 40.4
C-249/97: Gruber v Silhouette International Schmeid GmbH & Co (1999)
IDS Brief 647 .... 24.14
C-273/97: Sirdar v Army Board and Secretary of State for Defence [1999] All
ER (EC) 928, [1999] ECR I-7403, [1999] 3 CMLR 559, [2000] ICR 130,
[2000] IRLR 47, 7 BHRC 459, [1999] All ER (D) 1156, ECJ 13.10, 13.19
C-309/97: Angestelltenbetriebsrat der Wiener Gebietskrankenkasse v Wiener
Gebietskrankenkasse [1999] ECR I-2865, [1999] 2 CMLR 1173,
[1999] IRLR 804, [1999] All ER (D) 483, ECJ 24.6
C-333/97: Lewen v Denda [2000] All ER (EC) 261, [1999] ECR I-7243,
[2000] 2 CMLR 38, [2000] IRLR 67, ECJ 12.12, 24.14
C-49/98, C-50/98, C-52/98 to C-54/98 and C-68/98 to C-71/98: Finalarte
Sociedade de Construção Civil Lda v Urlaubs- und Lohnausgleichskasse
der Bauwirtschaft [2001] ECR I-7831, [2003] 2 CMLR 333, [2001] All
ER (D) 361 (Oct), ECJ 26.3
C-78/98: Preston v Wolverhampton Healthcare NHS Trust: [2001] 2 AC 415,
[2000] All ER (EC) 714, [2001] 2 WLR 408, [2000] ECR I-3201,
[2000] 2 CMLR 837, [2000] ICR 961, [2000] IRLR 506, ECJ; apld sub
nom Preston v Wolverhamptom Healthcare NHS Trust (No 2)
[2001] UKHL 5, [2001] 2 AC 455, [2001] 3 All ER 947, [2001] 2 WLR
448, [2001] ICR 217, [2001] IRLR 237, (2001) Times, 8 February, 145
Sol Jo LB 55 .... 20.28, 24.19, 24.20, 25.2
C-165/98: Mazzoleni (criminal proceedings against) [2001] ECR I-2189,
ECJ 26.3
C-190/98: Graf v Filzmoser Maschinenbau GmbH [2000] All ER (EC) 170,
[2000] ECR I-493, [2000] 1 CMLR 741, ECJ 26.2

C-198/98: Everson v Secretary of State for Trade and Industry [1999] ECR
I-8903, [2000] All ER (EC) 29, [2000] 1 CMLR 489, [2000] IRLR 202,
ECJ 31.3
C-207/98: Mahlburg v Land Mecklenburg-Vorpommern [2000] ECR I-549,
[2001] 3 CMLR 887, [2001] ICR 1032, [2000] IRLR 276, [2000] All ER
(D) 116, ECJ 12.5
C-218/98: Abdoulaye v Régie nationale des usines Renault SA [1999] ECR
I-5723, [2001] 2 CMLR 372, [2001] ICR 527, [1999] IRLR 811, [1999]
All ER (D) 1014, ECJ 24.14
C-226/98: Jørgensen v Foreningen af Speciallæger [2000] ECR I-2447,
[2002] 1 CMLR 1151, [2000] IRLR 726, ECJ 13.8
C-234/98: Allen v Amalgamated Construction Co Ltd [2000] All ER (EC) 97,
[1999] ECR I-8643, [2000] 1 CMLR 1, [2000] IRLR 119, 632 IRLB 2,
ECJ 52.6
C-236/98: Jämställdhetsombudsmannen v Örebro läns landsting [2000] ECR
I-2189, [2000] 2 CMLR 708, [2001] ICR 249, [2000] IRLR 421, ECJ 24.5
C-303/98: Sindicato de Médicos de Asistencia Pública (Simap) v Conselleria
de Sanidad y Consumo de la Generalidad Valenciana [2001] All ER
(EC) 609, [2000] ECR I-7963, [2001] 3 CMLR 932, [2001] ICR 1116,
[2000] IRLR 845, [2000] All ER (D) 1236, ECJ 57.5, 57.7
C-322/98: Kachelmann v Bankhaus Hermann Lampe KG [2000] ECR
I-7505, [2002] 1 CMLR 155, [2001] IRLR 49, ECJ 12.9
C-343/98: Collino v Telecom Italia SpA [2001] All ER (EC) 405, [2000] ECR
I-6659, [2002] 3 CMLR 997, [2002] ICR 38, [2000] IRLR 788, [2000] All
ER (D) 1196, ECJ 18.4, 37.2, 52.9
C-407/98: Abrahamsson v Fogelqvist [2000] ECR I-5539, [2002] ICR 932,
[2000] IRLR 732, ECJ 12.12, 13.9
C-11/99: Dietrich v Westdeutscher Rundfunk [2000] ECR I-5589, ECJ 28.5
C-62/99: Betriebsrat der Bofrost Josef H Boquoi Deutschland West GmbH
& Co KG v Bofrost Josef H Boquoi Deutschland West GmbH & Co
KG [2001] ECR I-2579, [2004] 2 CMLR 1223, [2001] IRLR 403, [2001]
All ER (D) 350 (Mar), ECJ 18.22
C-164/99: Portugaia Construções Lda, Re [2002] ECR I-787, [2003] 2 CMLR
1093, ECJ 26.3
C-172/99: Oy Liikenne Ab v Liskojärvi [2001] All ER (EC) 544, [2001] ECR
I-745, [2001] 3 CMLR 807, [2002] ICR 155, [2001] IRLR 171, [2001] All
ER (D) 168 (Jan), ECJ 52.5
C-173/99: R (on the application of the Broadcasting, Entertainment,
Cinematographic and Theatre Union) v Secretary of State for Trade and
Industry [2001] All ER (EC) 647, [2001] 1 WLR 2313, [2001] ECR
I-4881, [2001] 3 CMLR 109, [2001] ICR 1152, [2001] IRLR 559, [2001]
All ER (D) 272 (Jun), ECJ 25.11, 29.2
C-175/99: Mayeur v Association Promotion de l'Information Messine
(APIM): [2002] ICR 1316, [2000] IRLR 783, ECJ 18.4, 52.9
C-350/99: Lange v Georg Schünemann GmbH [2001] All ER (EC) 481,
[2001] ECR I-1061, [2001] IRLR 244, [2001] All ER (D) 90 (Feb),
ECJ 8.9
C-381/99: Brunnhofer v Bank der österreichischen Postsparkasse AG [2001]
All ER (EC) 693, [2001] ECR I-4961, [2001] 3 CMLR 173, [2001] IRLR
571, ECJ 24.6, 24.11
C-438/99: Jiménez Melgar v Ayuntamiento de Los Barrios [2001] ECR
I-6915, [2003] 3 CMLR 67, [2004] ICR 610, [2001] IRLR 848, [2001] All
ER (D) 42 (Oct), ECJ 12.5

Table of Cases

C-476/99: Lommers v Minister van Landbouw, Natuurbeheer en Visserij
[2002] ECR I-2891, [2004] 2 CMLR 1141, [2002] IRLR 430, [2002] All
ER (D) 280 (Mar), ECJ 24.3
C-37/00: Weber v Universal Ogden Services Ltd [2002] QB 1189, [2002] All
ER (EC) 397, [2002] 3 WLR 931, [2002] ECR I-2013, [2002] ICR 979,
[2002] IRLR 365, [2002] All ER (D) 377 (Feb), ECJ 26.12
C-51/00: Temco Service Industries SA v Imzilyen [2002] ECR I-969,
[2004] 1 CMLR 877, [2002] IRLR 214, [2002] All ER (D) 199 (Jan),
ECJ 52.7
C-109/00: Tele Danmark A/S v Handels- og Kontorfunktionærernes Forbund
i Danmark (HK) [2001] All ER (EC) 941, [2001] ECR I-6993,
[2002] 1 CMLR 105, [2004] ICR 610, [2001] IRLR 853, [2001] All ER
(D) 37 (Oct), ECJ 12.5
C-133/00: Bowden v Tuffnells Parcels Express Ltd [2001] All ER (EC) 865,
[2001] ECR I-7031, [2001] 3 CMLR 1342, [2001] IRLR 838, [2001] All
ER (D) 32 (Oct), ECJ 57.3
C-164/00: Beckmann v Dynamco Whicheloe MacFarlane Ltd [2002] All ER
(EC) 865, [2002] ECR I-4893, [2002] 2 CMLR 1152, [2003] ICR 50,
[2002] IRLR 578, (2002) Times, 17 June, [2002] All ER (D) 05 (Jun),
ECJ 42.4, 52.19
C-187/00: Kutz-Bauer v Freie und Hansestadt Hamburg [2003] ECR I-2741,
[2003] IRLR 368, [2003] All ER (D) 327 (Mar), ECJ 13.8
C-320/00: Lawrence v Regent Office Care Ltd [2002] ECR I-7325,
[2002] 3 CMLR 761, [2003] ICR 1092, [2002] IRLR 822, (2002) Times,
10 October, [2002] All ER (D) 84 (Sep), ECJ 24.9
C-440/00: Gesamtbetriebsrat Der Kühne & Nagel AG & Co KG v Kühne &
Nagel AG & Co KG [2004] 2 CMLR 1242, [2004] IRLR 332 , [2004] All
ER (D) 31 (Jan), ECJ 18.22
C-4/01: Martin v South Bank University [2004] 1 CMLR 472, [2004] ICR
1234, [2004] IRLR 74, [2003] All ER (D) 85 (Nov), ECJ 42.4, 52.19, 52.29
C-117/01: KB v National Health Service Pensions Agency [2004] All ER
(EC) 1089, [2004] 1 CMLR 931, [2004] ICR 781, [2004] IRLR 240,
[2004] 1 FLR 683, (2004) Times, 15 January, [2004] All ER (D) 03 (Jan),
ECJ 24.13, 42.7
C-160/01: Mau v Bundessanstaltfur Arbeit [2004] 1 CMLR 34 .... 31.5
C-256/01: Allonby v Accrington and Rossendale College [2004] ECR I-873,
[2005] All ER (EC) 289, [2004] 1 CMLR 1141, [2004] ICR 1328,
[2004] IRLR 224, [2004] All ER (D) 47 (Jan), ECJ 12.8, 13.8, 13.21, 24.9,
                                                                          24.17, 24.19, 25.2
C-320/01: Busch v Klinikum Neustadt GmbH & Co Betriebs-KG [2003] All
ER (EC) 985, [2003] ECR I-2041, [2003] 2 CMLR 481, [2003] IRLR
625, [2004] 1 FCR 54, [2003] All ER (D) 394 (Feb), ECJ 12.5
C-340/01: Abler v Sodexho MM Catering Betriebsgesellschaft mbH
[2004] IRLR 168, [2003] All ER (D) 277 (Nov), ECJ 52.5
C-342/01: Gómez v Continental Industrias del Caucho SA [2004] ECR
I-2605, [2004] 2 CMLR 38, [2005] ICR 1040, [2004] IRLR 407, [2004]
All ER (D) 350 (Mar), ECJ 29.5, 33.18
C-397/01 to C-403/01: Pfeiffer v Deutsches Rotes Kreuz, Kreisverband
Waldshut eV [2005] ICR 1307, [2005] IRLR 137, [2004] All ER (D) 52
(Oct), ECJ 57.3
E-1/02: EFTA Surveillance Authority v Norway [2003] 1 CMLR 725,
[2003] IRLR 318, EFTA Ct 13.9
C-4/02 and C-5/02 : Hilde Schönheit v Stadt Frankfurt am Main [2003] ECR
I-12575, [2004] IRLR 983, [2003] All ER (D) 401 (Oct), ECJ 13.8, 24.11, 42.9

C-47/02: Anker v Germany [2003] ECR I-10447, [2004] 2 CMLR 845, [2003]
All ER (D) 62 (Oct), ECJ 37.7
C-77/02: Steinicke v Bundesanstalt fur Arbeit [2003] IRLR 892, [2003] All
ER (D) 87 (Sep), ECJ 24.3
C-147/02: Alabaster v Woolwich plc [2004] 2 CMLR 186, [2005] ICR 695,
[2004] IRLR 486, [2004] All ER (D) 558 (Mar), ECJ 24.14, 33.14
C-151/02: Landeshauptstadt Kiel v Jaeger [2004] All ER (EC) 604,
[2003] ECR I-8389, [2003] 3 CMLR 493, [2004] ICR 1528, [2003] IRLR
804, 75 BMLR 201, [2003] All ER (D) 72 (Sep), ECJ 57.4, 57.14
C-159/02: Turner v Grovit [2004] All ER (EC) 485, [2004] 2 All ER (Comm)
381, [2004] 2 Lloyd's Rep 169, [2004] IRLR 899, (2004) Times, 29 April,
[2004] All ER (D) 259 (Apr), ECJ 26.12
C-284/02: Land Brandenburg v Sass [2005] IRLR 147, [2004] All ER (D) 310
(Nov), ECJ 12.12
C-285/02: Elsner-Lakeberg v Land Nordrhein-Westfalen [2004] 2 CMLR 874,
[2005] IRLR 209, [2004] All ER (D) 423 (May), ECJ 24.5
C-313/02: Wippel v Peek & Cloppenburg Gmbh & Co Kg [2005] ICR 1604,
[2005] IRLR 211, ECJ 12.12, 32.2, 32.9, 32.11
C-341/02: European Commission v Germany [2005] All ER (D) 172 (Apr),
ECJ 26.3
C-188/03: Junk v Kuhnel [2005] IRLR 310, [2005] All ER (D) 264 (Jan),
ECJ 39.4
C-478/03: Celtec Ltd v Astley [2005] ICR 1409, [2005] IRLR 647, (2005)
Times, 9 June, [2005] All ER (D) 400 (May), ECJ 52.12
C-14/04: Dellas v Premier Ministre [2006] IRLR 225, [2005] All ER (D) 19
(Dec), ECJ 57.5
C 131/04: Robinson-Steele v RD Retail Services Ltd [2006] IRLR 386, [2006]
All ER (D) 238 (Mar), ECJ 22.1, 22.27, 29.4, 57.25
C-144/04: Mangold v Helm [2006] All ER (EC) 383, [2006] IRLR 143, [2005]
All ER (D) 287 (Nov), ECJ 3.2, 3.4, 25.1, 25.2
C-212/04: Adeneler v Ellinikos Organismos Galaktos [2007] All ER (EC) 82,
[2006] 3 CMLR 867, [2006] IRLR 716, [2006] All ER (D) 25 (Jul),
ECJ 25.2, 47.9
C-232/04 and C-233/04: Guney-Gorres v Securicor Aviation (Germany) Ltd:
[2006] IRLR 305, [2005] All ER (D) 230 (Dec), ECJ 52.5
C-294/04: Herrero (Sarkatzis) v Instituto Madrileno de la Salud (Imsalud)
[2006] IRLR 296, [2006] All ER (D) 220 (Feb), ECJ 12.5
C-484/04: European Commission v United Kingdom [2006] 3 CMLR 1322,
[2007] ICR 592, [2006] IRLR 888, (2006) Times, 21 September, [2006]
All ER (D) 32 (Sep), ECJ 25.11, 57.2, 57.15, 57.26
C-499/04: Werhof v Freeway Traffic Systems GmbH & Co KG [2006] IRLR
400, [2006] All ER (D) 145 (Mar), ECJ 52.20
C-13/05: Navas v Eurest Colectividades SA [2007] All ER (EC) 59,
[2006] 3 CMLR 1123, [2007] ICR 1, [2006] IRLR 706, (2006) Times,
9 August, [2006] All ER (D) 132 (Jul), ECJ 25.6
C-17/05: Cadman v Health and Safety Executive [2007] All ER (EC) 1,
[2007] 1 CMLR 530, [2006] ICR 1623, [2006] IRLR 969, (2006) Times,
6 October, [2006] All ER (D) 17 (Oct), ECJ 3.4, 24.11
C-124/05: Federatie Nederlandse Vakbeweging v Netherlands [2006] All ER
(D) 69 (Apr), ECJ 29.3
C-270/05: Athinaiki Chartopoiia AE v Panagiotidis [2007] IRLR 284, [2007]
All ER (D) 186 (Feb), ECJ 39.4

Table of Cases

C-278/05: Robins v Secretary of State for Work and Pensions
   [2007] 2 CMLR 269, [2007] IRLR 270, (2007) Times, 30 January, [2007]
   All ER (D) 195 (Jan), ECJ.. 25.2

Abbreviations and References

ABBREVIATIONS – GENERAL

ACAS	=	Advisory, Conciliation and Arbitration Service
CA	=	Court of Appeal
CAC	=	Central Arbitration Committee
COET	=	Central Office of the Employment Tribunals
CRE	=	Commission for Racial Equality
DfEE	=	Department for Education and Employment
DRC	=	Disability Rights Commission
DSS	=	Department of Social Security
DTI	=	Department of Trade and Industry
EAT	=	Employment Appeal Tribunal
EEC	=	European Economic Community
EC	=	European Community
ECJ	=	European Court of Justice
EOC	=	Equal Opportunities Commission
HL	=	House of Lords
Pt	=	Part
Sch	=	Schedule
SI	=	Statutory Instrument
SR & O	=	Statutory Rules and Orders

ABBREVIATIONS – STATUTES

DDA	=	Disability Discrimination Act 1995
DRCA	=	Disability Rights Commission Act 1999
EA	=	Employment Act (with date)
EPA	=	Employment Protection Act 1975
EPCA	=	Employment Protection (Consolidation) Act 1978
ETA	=	Employment Tribunals Act 1996
EqPA	=	Equal Pay Act 1970
ERA 1996	=	Employment Rights Act 1996
ERA 1999	=	Employment Relations Act 1999
FA	=	Finance Act (with date)
HSWA	=	Health and Safety at Work etc. Act 1974
HRA	=	Human Rights Act 1998
ICTA	=	Income and Corporation Taxes Act 1988
OLA	=	Occupiers' Liability Act 1957
OSRPA	=	Offices, Shops and Railway Premises Act 1963
PIDA	=	Public Interest Disclosure Act 1998
RRA	=	Race Relations Act 1976
SBA	=	Supplementary Benefits Act 1976
SDA	=	Sex Discrimination Act 1975
SDA 1986	=	Sex Discrimination Act 1996
SSA	=	Social Security Act 1975
SSA 1986	=	Social Security Act 1986
SSAA	=	Social Security Administration Act 1992

Abbreviations and References

SSCBA	=	Social Security Contributions and Benefits Act 1992
SSHBA	=	Social Security and Housing Benefits Act 1982
SSPA	=	Social Security Pensions Act 1975
TUA	=	Trade Union Act 1984
TULRA	=	Trade Union and Labour Relations Act 1974
TULR(A)A	=	Trade Union and Labour Relations (Amendment) Act 1976
TULRCA	=	Trade Union and Labour Relations (Consolidation) Act 1992
TURERA	=	Trade Union Reform and Employment Rights Act 1993
UCTA	=	Unfair Contract Terms Act 1977
WA	=	Wages Act 1986

LAW REPORTS – SERIES REFERRED TO

AC	=	Law Reports, Appeal Cases
All ER	=	All England Law Reports
ATC	=	Annotated Tax Cases
BCLC	=	Butterworths Company Law Cases
Ch	=	Law Reports, Chancery Division
CMLR	=	Common Market Law Reports
Cr App Rep	=	Criminal Appeal Reports
FSR	=	Fleet Street Reports
ICR	=	Law Reports, Industrial Cases Reports
IDS	=	Incomes Data Services
IRLB	=	Industrial Relations Law Bulletin
IRLR	=	Industrial Relations Law Reports
ITR	=	Industrial Tribunal Reports
LJKB	=	Law Journal Reports, New Series, King's Bench (ended 1949)
Lloyd's Rep	=	Lloyd's List Law Reports
LS Gaz	=	Law Society's Gazette
PCC	=	Palmer's Company Cases
QB/KB	=	Law Reports, Queen's (King's) Bench Division
TLR	=	Times Law Reports (last year of publication 1952)
WLR	=	Weekly Law Reports

1   Introduction

1.1   SCOPE AND AIMS OF THIS BOOK

Employment law is fully recognised today as a subject of the greatest importance. Legislation passed in recent years has transformed the law and created entirely new statutory rights and obligations. Employment law continues to develop at a rapid pace, with new domestic legislation creating or modifying statutory rights being enacted each year. Further, EC legislation and decisions of the European Court have had, and will continue to have, an important impact on certain areas of domestic employment law. Inevitably, a wealth of reported tribunal and court decisions on the meaning and effect of these new provisions has also built up.

This handbook seeks to explain the legislation in its context, along with the common law and the EC law on employment matters. It is intended as a reference guide for the employer, company secretary, manager or personnel officer involved daily in decisions concerning the rights of employees. It is also intended to serve as a comprehensive handbook on employment law for solicitors, employees, trade union officials, and all kinds of advisers and professional people.

The remainder of this chapter serves as an introduction to the subject by examining a number of fundamental aspects of current employment law. It concludes with a checklist of the areas of law relevant to the various stages of employment and a brief explanation of the standard scale of maximum fines which may be imposed upon conviction of an adult of a summary offence.

Employment law and trade union law. The main emphasis of this book is on the law affecting the individual employment relationship, ie directly applying to employers and their employees. It therefore provides detailed coverage of the law governing the contract of employment, termination of employment, redundancy, unfair dismissal, equal pay, sex and race discrimination and other individual employment rights. The importance of trade unions is nonetheless fully recognised, and the status, functions and liabilities of trade unions and the law relating to trade union membership are considered in appropriate chapters.

1.2   WHAT CONSTITUTES EMPLOYMENT?

One of the most fundamental questions asked is whether a particular worker is an employee or not. An employee is a person who agrees to work for another person pursuant to a *contract of employment* (or 'contract of service' to use the more traditional term). It is important to be able to distinguish a contract of employment from other types of agreement under which services are rendered. There are a number of characteristics which enable a contract of employment to be identified. One problem which can often arise is deciding whether a particular person doing work for another is working as an employee, ie under a contract of employment, or as an independent contractor (or 'self-employed' person) under a contract *for services*. These matters are discussed further in EMPLOYEE, SELF-EMPLOYED OR WORKER? (17).

1.3   The contract of employment

The most important matters to be borne in mind are the following.

1.4   Introduction

(a)   In general, the parties are free to agree whatever contractual terms they wish – this means, among other things, that they may agree that work is to be done either by an employee or by an independent contractor.

(b)   However, *all the terms* of the contract, and the way in which it is performed, will be looked at in deciding whether it is in substance a contract of employment or not, so it will not be sufficient merely to state that the contract is a contract for services and not a contract of employment.

(c)   Whether or not the contract is a contract of employment, certain further terms may be implied, if not expressly agreed.

(d)   If the contract *is* a contract of employment, all the statutory employment rights are capable of applying, if the relevant pre-conditions are satisfied, and (subject to limited exceptions) any term of the contract excluding these rights is usually *ineffective*.

(e)   If the contract *is not* a contract of employment, the main statutory employment rights cannot apply, because they apply only for the benefit of people working under a contract of employment. However, there are some important statutory provisions which also apply to self-employed persons and/or 'workers' as defined in the relevant legislation.

For further details, see CONTRACT OF EMPLOYMENT (8) and EMPLOYEE, SELF-EMPLOYED OR WORKER? (17).

1.4   SOURCES OF EMPLOYMENT LAW

The legal rules governing employment law are derived from three principal sources:

(a)   the common law, including the law of contract pursuant to which the contract of employment is enforced, and the law of torts (wrongful acts which cause damage or loss) which governs (for example) an employer's liability for acts of his employees, civil liability for industrial accidents and for strikes and other forms of industrial action;

(b)   statute law, ie Acts of Parliament and Regulations, which operate outside the contract (eg the law on unfair dismissal); and

(c)   European legislation and judgments of the European Court of Justice ('ECJ').

Some elements of these three sources are considered briefly below.

1.5   Terms of the contract of employment

Generally, the employer and employee are free to agree whatever terms they wish. Therefore, the most basic legal rules governing the employment relationship are those agreed by the parties themselves, for example, the type of work to be done, place of work, rate of pay, etc. In practice, the more detailed terms and conditions of the contract are often not discussed and agreed individually with each employee. Many employers have written standard terms and conditions of employment for all employees, sometimes drawn up and agreed in consultation with officials of recognised trade unions.

In cases where a disagreement arises, the main problem is often evidential. If an employer does not provide written particulars of the terms and conditions of employment, or if a particular matter was agreed orally but never put in writing, years later memories will have faded and there may be no reliable evidence of precisely what was agreed. This is one reason why employers are under a statutory obligation to provide a written summary of the main contractual terms to each employee within a short time after he begins his job. They must notify changes in the same way. (See 8.7 CONTRACT OF EMPLOYMENT.)

1.6 **Domestic employment legislation**

The main statutory employment rights are found in the *Employment Rights Act 1996* as amended.

In addition, there is a considerable amount of anti-discrimination primary legislation affecting employment. The main domestic statutory provisions are:

Equal Pay Act 1970, as amended

Sex Discrimination Act 1975, as amended

Race Relations Act 1976, as amended

Disability Discrimination Act 1995, as amended.

In addition a substantial number of statutory instruments provide important and specific rights in relation to employment and are considered, where relevant, in the chapters of the book.

The main Act governing trade unions and trade disputes is the:

Trade Union and Labour Relations (Consolidation) Act 1992 as amended.

The Act governing the presentation of complaints to an employment tribunal is the:

Employment Tribunals Act 1996.

This book provides an account of the effect of all of these main legislative provisions, with references to the specific provisions and to decided cases. However, a reader who is called upon to consider the law in detail would probably be well advised to obtain copies of the Acts themselves in addition. The Acts are obtainable from the Stationery Office or through bookshops. Legislation, including Statutory Instruments, enacted after 1988 is available online from the Office of Public Sector Information website (www.opsi.gov.uk). For people requiring a complete reprint of all the relevant legislation, compendia of employment legislation are published commercially by a number of law publishers. As mentioned in the Preface, in a particular case of doubt or difficulty the reader should consult a professional adviser.

Leaflets. The Department of Trade and Industry ('DTI') produces a large number of free explanatory leaflets dealing with particular aspects of employment legislation (eg unfair dismissal, redundancy payments). This book gives the name and reference number of each leaflet at the beginning of the relevant chapter. They may also be useful, for example, to provide to employees to explain their rights. Leaflets become out of date when the law changes and they are then reprinted or discontinued. There is a very real danger in using a leaflet that is out of date: it is important to ensure that any leaflet being used is the latest reprint available. Guidance on various areas of employment law (including copies of the explanatory documents) is also available online from the DTI website (www.dti.gov.uk) which also provides information on forthcoming employment legislation and consultation.

1.7 Introduction

1.7 European law

European legislative instruments. Where English domestic legislation has failed fully to implement EC Treaty obligations, individuals may rely in the English courts upon the EC Treaty, and, where the employer is the State, upon certain EC directives. (See EUROPEAN COMMUNITY LAW (25).)

In the employment context, this has been done in particular to establish claims for equal pay and equal treatment (see EQUAL PAY (19)).

EC legislation is also important where a business is transferred from one employer to another (see TRANSFER OF UNDERTAKINGS (52)). Other areas influenced by EC legislation include HEALTH AND SAFETY AT WORK – II (28), HOLIDAYS (29), the rules on written particulars of employment (see 8.4 CONTRACT OF EMPLOYMENT) and requirements for consultation in redundancy situations (see 39.2 REDUNDANCY – II).

Judgments of the European Court. The ECJ is the final arbiter in matters of interpretation of European legislation. Thus, its judgments are of importance in interpreting directly applicable European legislative instruments and also domestic legislation which implements European law obligations.

The *European Convention on Human Rights* is also relevant; the *Human Rights Act 1998* requires the court to interpret United Kingdom law in accordance with the Convention. This has clear implications in the employment context (see HUMAN RIGHTS (30)).

1.8 GEOGRAPHICAL SCOPE OF THIS BOOK

This book seeks to explain the law applying in England and Wales. Much of the relevant legislation applies, without significant differences, to *Scotland*. However, Scotland has a quite different legal system from that of England and Wales, and different legal traditions. It also has a separate system of courts and tribunals. This book should not be regarded as authoritative on the law applying in Scotland because specific matters of Scottish law have not been taken into consideration. For example, the explanation of attachment of earnings for payment of debts (PAY – II (35)) relates to England and Wales only: different procedures apply in Scotland.

The legal system and legal traditions of *Northern Ireland* are much more similar to those of England and Wales than are those of Scotland, but the legislation discussed in this book generally does not apply to Northern Ireland. It has a separate legislative code, although on employment law its provisions are co-ordinated with those of Great Britain. Northern Ireland also has a separate system of courts and tribunals. Therefore, while the law will often be similar, this book is not authoritative on Northern Ireland employment law and any reader in Northern Ireland is advised to consult the specific Northern Ireland legal sources on any particular issue.

This book does not contain an account of the laws relating to employment applying in the Channel Islands or the Isle of Man, nor of those foreign systems of law which may apply where an English employee is sent to work abroad. For the rules determining which system of law governs an employment relationship with international elements, see 26.9 FOREIGN EMPLOYEES.

1.9 STAGES OF EMPLOYMENT – CHECKLIST

The chapters of this book are arranged in alphabetical order to assist the reader in tracing all the areas of law that may relate to a particular problem. The following checklist sets out the chronological stages of employment, from selection for appointment to termination, and beyond, together with a list of chapters relevant to each stage.

All stages	
General	Contract of Employment (8) Employee, Self-Employed or Worker? (17)
Discrimination	Disability Discrimination (10) Equal Pay (24) Discrimination andEqual Opportunities– I, II and III (12, 13, 14) European Community Law (25)
Statutory rights	Continuous Employment (7) Pay – I (34)
Chronological stages	
Selection for appointment	Children and Young Persons (4) Disability Discrimination (10) Employee's Past Criminal Convictions (19) Foreign Employees (26)
Terms of engagement	Contract of Employment (8) Employee, Self-Employed or Worker? (17) Engagement of Employees (23) Probationary Employees (36)
Duration of employment	Continuous Employment (7) Temporary and Seasonal Employees (47) Transfer of Undertakings (52)
Pay, etc	Equal Pay (24) Pay – I and II (34, 35) Sickness and Sick Pay (44) Taxation (46)
Terms and conditions (other than pay)	Collective Agreements (6) Contract of Employment (8) Directors (9) Equal Pay (24) Holidays (29) Public Sector Employees (37) Restraint of Trade, Confidentiality and Employee Inventions (41) Service Lettings (43) Transfer of Undertakings (52)

1.9 Introduction

All stages	
Safety and welfare	Children and Young Persons (4) Education and Training (11) Health and Safety at Work – I and II (27, 28) Maternity and Parental Rights (33) Pay – I (34) Sickness and Sick Pay (44) Time Off Work (49) Vicarious Liability (56) Working Time (57)
General management	Advisory, Conciliation and Arbitration Service (2) Codes of Practice (5) Employee Participation (18)
Trade unions	Disclosure of Information (11) Health and Safety at Work – II (28) Trade Unions – I and II (50, 51)
Trade disputes	Advisory, Conciliation and Arbitration Service (2) Codes of Practice (5) Strikes and Industrial Action (45)
Lay-offs	Pay – I (34) Redundancy – I (38)
Discipline and breach of contract	Termination of Employment (48) Unfair Dismissal – II (54)
Termination of employment (generally)	Trade Unions – I (50) Maternity and Parental Rights (33) References (40) Restraint of Trade, Confidentiality and Employee Inventions (41) Termination of Employment (48) Transfer of Undertakings (52) Unfair Dismissal – I, II and III (53, 54, 55) Wrongful Dismissal (58)
Redundancy	Redundancy – I and II (38, 39) Unfair Dismissal – II (54)
Retirement	Retirement (42)
Claims against employer –Dismissals	Employment Tribunals: Practice and Procedure (20)
	Redundancy – I and II (38, 39) Unfair Dismissal – I, II and III (53, 54, 55) Wrongful Dismissal (58)
Insolvency of employer	Insolvency of Employer (31)

1.10 **STANDARD SCALE OF FINES**

At various points in the book, reference is made to the standard scale of maximum fines which may be imposed upon conviction of an adult of a summary offence (that is, one which falls to be tried by magistrates rather than by the Crown Court).

The standard scale of maximum fines is as follows.

Level on the scale	Amount of maximum fine (£)
1	200
2	500
3	1,000
4	2,500
5	5,000

(*Criminal Justice Act 1982, s 37(2)*), as substituted by *Criminal Justice Act 1991, s 17*.)

Where the Crown Court tries an offence and imposes a fine following a conviction there is no maximum amount in the absence of some specific provision to the contrary (*Powers of Criminal Courts Act 1973, s 30*; *Criminal Law Act 1977, s 32(1)*).

Before a court (magistrates' court or Crown Court) fixes the amount of any fine, it must inquire into the financial circumstances of the offender. The amount must reflect the court's opinion of the seriousness of the offence, and the court must also take account of the circumstances of the case, including the financial circumstances of the offender. (*Criminal Justice Act 1991, s 18*, as substituted by *Criminal Justice Act 1993, s 65*.)

2 Advisory, Conciliation and Arbitration Service (ACAS)

2.1 The Advisory, Conciliation and Arbitration Service was established pursuant to powers conferred by the *Employment Protection Act 1975*. Its activities are now regulated by the *Trade Union and Labour Relations (Consolidation) Act 1992* (*'TULRCA 1992'*), as amended by the *Trade Union Reform and Employment Rights Act 1993* (*'TURERA 1993'*). ACAS continues in existence under *TULRCA 1992, s 247*. Its duties are to promote the improvement of industrial relations, in particular by exercising its functions in relation to the settlement of trade disputes (*TULRCA 1992, s 209* as amended by *TURERA 1993, s 43(1)*).

ACAS may charge fees for the exercise of its functions to persons who benefit from that exercise, and may be directed to do so by the Secretary of State (*TULRCA 1992, s 251A* as inserted by *TURERA 1993, s 44*). Fees are charged at present only for certain publications and seminars, and thus not for the key function of conciliation.

2.2 CONSTITUTION

The Secretary of State for Trade and Industry appoints the members of the Council of ACAS in accordance with the requirements laid down in *TULRCA 1992, s 248*. Those requirements ensure that both employers' organisations and workers' organisations are consulted before appointments are made and that a balance is maintained between employers' and workers' interests.

2.3 CONCILIATION

One function of ACAS is to conciliate in trade disputes. ACAS may appoint either an independent person or an officer of the Service to offer assistance to the parties to the dispute. During the course of conciliation the parties will be encouraged to use any existing agreed procedures to resolve the conflict (*TULRCA 1992, s 210*).

2.4 CONCILIATION IN EMPLOYMENT TRIBUNAL COMPLAINTS

ACAS appoints conciliation officers to conciliate on matters which are or could be the subject of proceedings before an employment tribunal. The *ACAS Annual Report 2005-06* reveals that, during the course of that year, ACAS was involved in the individual conciliation of 76,134 claims presented to the employment tribunals. Of that total number some 36% were settled via ACAS conciliation, a fall of 8% compared to the data in the previous Annual Report. Some 24% of cases referred for conciliation went to a full hearing. Requests for conciliation in collective disputes continued to fall (down to 952). The *Annual Report* is available on the ACAS website (www.acas.org.uk).

Conciliation officers may (and must if required to do so by a party to the complaint) take action to conciliate on most claims which can be brought before an employment tribunal, including claims of sex or race discrimination and complaints against trade unions (*Employment Tribunals Act 1996* (*'ETA 1996'*), *s 18*). Either the person making the complaint or the person against whom the complaint or application is made may request the assistance of a conciliation officer. *Section 11* of the *Employment Rights (Dispute Resolution) Act 1998* extended the duties of ACAS conciliation officers to include redundancy payment cases with effect from October 1998 (see 38.4 REDUNDANCY – I).

The *Employment Tribunals Act 1996 (Application of Conciliation Provisions) Order 2000 (SI 2000/1337)* extends conciliation under *s 18* of *ETA 1996* to issues relating to training (as introduced by the *Employment Relations Act 1999*; see *TULRCA 1992, s 70B*), detriment arising out of participation or involvement in a trade union recognition procedure pursuant to *TULRCA 1992, Sch A1 para 156* and complaints relating to failure to permit parental leave (see *ERA 1999, s 80*).

Before a complaint is presented to an employment tribunal, the conciliation officer will only take action if requested to do so by a party to the potential complaint (*ETA 1996, s 18(3), (5)*). He must conciliate if requested to do so by both parties to the potential complaint or if he considers that he could conciliate with a reasonable prospect of success. He may conciliate (at the request of either party) as soon as action has been taken in respect of which a person could present a complaint to an employment tribunal (*ETA 1996, s 18(3), (5)*). The requirement for action to have been taken in respect of which a complaint could be made will generally mean that ACAS will decline to become involved where a dismissal is contemplated but has not yet taken place. Once a complaint has been presented to an employment tribunal, a conciliation officer must conciliate whether or not he is requested to do so if he considers that he could conciliate with a reasonable prospect of success or when he is requested to do so by both parties (*ETA 1996, s 18(1), (2)*).

Where the complaint is one of unfair dismissal, and the complainant has ceased to be employed by the employer against whom the complaint is made, the conciliation officer is required to seek the complainant's reinstatement or re-engagement. Where the complainant does not wish for either of these remedies, or where reinstatement or re-engagement is not practicable, the conciliation officer will attempt to obtain for him a sum by way of compensation (*ETA 1996, s 18(4)*).

Thus, if a complaint is presented to an employment tribunal, the respondent employer will often be contacted by a conciliation officer. The conciliation officer will usually outline the complainant's grievance and may convey the respondent's comments back to the complainant. If the respondent does not want his comments conveyed to the complainant he should make this clear to the conciliation officer. Nothing communicated to a conciliation officer in connection with the performance of his functions is admissible in evidence in any proceedings before an employment tribunal, except with the consent of the person who communicated it to the officer (*ETA 1996, s 18(7)*). It may also be of some comfort to those involved in the settlement of claims through ACAS to know that such communications attract absolute privilege for the purposes of any defamation proceedings as held in *Freer v Glover* [2005] EWHC 3341 (QB), [2006] IRLR 521 in which a solicitor acting for the employer involved in negotiations through ACAS was sued in defamation by the employee. Incidental publication of the alleged defamatory statement to ACAS staff was also protected by the privilege (*Lincoln v Daniels* [1962] 1 QB 237 (CA) applied).

The important role of conciliation officers is emphasised by the fact that, subject to one important exception, an agreement to settle an employment tribunal complaint will only normally be binding on the parties if the agreement relates to a complaint or potential complaint where a conciliation officer has taken action in accordance with his statutory powers. The important exception concerns settlements reached after the employee has received advice from a relevant independent adviser (see EMPLOYMENT TRIBUNALS – I (20)). In other cases, an agreement to settle a claim or a potential claim is unenforceable, leaving the complainant free to pursue his claim before an employment tribunal (*ERA 1996, s 203(1), (2)*; *SDA 1975, s 77(4)(a)*; *RRA 1976, s 72(4)(a)*). In *Moore v Duport Furniture Products Ltd* [1982] ICR 84, a conciliation officer was considered to have taken such action in circumstances where the parties had already reached a settlement. In that case, the officer ascertained that they had truly reached agreement, which he then recorded in writing on a form designed for the purpose (Form COT 3). Where a conciliation officer assisted the parties in reaching an oral agreement, that agreement was held to be binding, notwithstanding that it had not been recorded in writing (*Gilbert v Kembridge Fibres Ltd* [1984] ICR 188; see also *Hennessy v Craigmyle & Co Ltd* [1986] ICR 461). A conciliation officer is not under a duty to advise an employee on the relevant legislation, but an agreement reached with his assistance may be set aside if he acts partially or adopts unfair methods (*Slack v Greenham (Plant Hire) Ltd* [1983] ICR 617). Nor will a tribunal be bound by a sham COT 3 designed to mislead a government department (*Trafford Carpets Ltd v Barker* IDS 440, p 16).

An attack upon the binding nature of a COT3 agreement on the basis that the conciliation officer had not advised the employees properly as to their rights was rejected by the EAT in *Clark v Redcar and Cleveland Borough Council* [2006] IRLR 324 (EAT). As part of an overall settlement negotiated in equal pay claims the employees signed COT3 agreements limiting the amount of back pay to be paid. Subsequently they sought to set them aside on the basis of ACAS failing to provide advice that they could achieve considerably more in compensation by proceeding with the claims. The EAT reaffirmed that the function of ACAS was to promote settlement and not to advise upon the merits of a party's case and to do so might compromise the role of the conciliation officer. While best practice might sometimes suggest that the conciliation officer should caution the employee to take further advice, failure to do so would not provide grounds to set aside the COT3 which would only be set aside in cases of bad faith or impropriety by the conciliation officer.

Thus, in order to ensure that an agreement to settle a complaint or potential complaint is enforceable, parties should normally seek the assistance of a conciliation officer to promote a settlement and have him record the agreement on the appropriate form.

In *Livingstone v Hepworth Refractories plc* [1992] ICR 287, it was held that a COT 3 made where the conciliation officer was acting under *EPCA* was only effective to settle discrimination or equal pay claims if it was expressly stated to include such claims, whether brought under domestic or European law.

2.5   Conciliation in complaints to Central Arbitration Committee

ACAS will seek to promote a settlement of complaints by recognised trade unions of failure to disclose information (*TULRCA 1992, s 183(2)*; see TRADE UNIONS – I (50)).

2.6   **ARBITRATION**

Where a trade dispute exists or is apprehended, ACAS may, with the consent of all parties to the dispute, refer the matters in dispute for the arbitration of:

(*a*)   an independent arbitrator or arbitrators, not being an employee of ACAS; or (*b*)   the Central Arbitration Committee.

(*TULRCA 1992, s 212(1).*)

However, ACAS will first consider the likelihood of the dispute being settled by conciliation and, in the absence of special reasons, a matter will not be referred to arbitration until any agreed disputes procedure has been exhausted (*TULRCA 1992, s 212(2), (3)*).

An award by an arbitrator may be published if ACAS so decides and all the parties concerned consent (*TULRCA 1992, s 212(4)(b)*).

The *Arbitration Act 1950, Part I* does not apply to such an arbitration (*TULRCA 1992, s 212(5)*).

2.7   ADVICE

ACAS is empowered, on request or on its own initiative, to give such advice as it thinks appropriate to employers, workers and their organisations on matters concerned with or affecting or likely to affect industrial relations. It may also publish general advice on matters connected with or affecting or likely to affect industrial relations (*TULRCA 1992, s 213* as substituted by *TURERA 1993, s 43(2)*). ACAS's helpline is extremely popular, with close to one million calls answered in the previous year (908,553 calls: Annual Report 2005–06).

ACAS publishes a number of guides in relation to various employment law issues with a series of advisory booklets, leaflets and handbooks, the latter directed particularly to small firms. In addition, ACAS has recently published a DVD guide to the Employment Tribunals giving advice on presentation and preparation for a claim and the hearing and has a series of e-learning packages available on its website. These publications are available from ACAS Public Enquiry Points and also from the ACAS website (www.acas.org.uk).

In addition, since July 2001, the Race Relations Employment Advisory Service ('RREAS') and Equality Direct (the telephone helpline for equality issues at work) form part of ACAS.

2.8   INQUIRY

ACAS may, if it thinks fit, inquire into any question relating to industrial relations generally or to industrial relations in any particular industry or in any particular undertaking or part of any undertaking (*TULRCA 1992, s 214(1)*).

The findings of such an inquiry, together with any advice given in connection with those findings, may be published by ACAS if it appears to it that publication is desirable for the improvement of industrial relations. Before deciding whether to publish, ACAS must send a draft of the findings to all the parties appearing to ACAS to be concerned, and take account of their views (*TULRCA 1992, s 214(2)*).

2.9   CODES OF PRACTICE

ACAS has a general power to issue new or revised Codes of Practice to give practical guidance for promoting the improvement of industrial relations (*TULRCA 1992, s 199*). It has issued three Codes of Practice so far:

No 1: Disciplinary and Grievance Procedures

No 2: Disclosure of Information

2.10   Advisory, Conciliation and Arbitration Service (ACAS)

No 3: Time Off for Trade Union Duties (revised version)

The Codes have not remained static since their first issue in 1985 and have been the subject of a number of revisions. Revised versions of the three ACAS Codes of Practice were issued with effect from 5 February 1998. Code of Practice No 3 was further revised with effect from 27 April 2003 (*SI 2003/1191*) in the light of changes to time off rights introduced by the *Employment Act 2002*. Code of Practice No 1 has been substantially revised to take into account the changes to disciplinary and grievance procedures introduced by the implementation of the relevant provisions of Part 3 of the *Employment Act 2002* (with effect from 1 October 2004) by the *Employment Act 2002* (*Dispute Resolution*) *Regulations 2004* (*SI 2004/752*). This is discussed more fully in the chapter on CODES OF PRACTICE (5).

For the legal effect of these Codes of Practice and the procedure to be followed in issuing them, see 5.3 CODES OF PRACTICE.

2.10   THE EMPLOYMENT RIGHTS (DISPUTE RESOLUTION) ACT 1998

By *s 7* of the *Employment Rights* (*Dispute Resolution*) *Act 1998* (which came into force on 1 August 1998), ACAS was given the power to draw up a scheme for the voluntary (but binding) arbitration of unfair dismissal disputes subject to the approval of the Secretary of State. Following ACAS consultation on the scheme, which was expressed to be intended to be 'voluntary, speedy, informal, confidential and free from legal argument', the arbitration scheme came into effect in England and Wales on 21 May 2001. Copies of the scheme (running to some 70 pages) are available from the DTI website (www.dti.gov.uk/er). The application of the scheme was, from 6 April 2004, extended to Scotland by the *ACAS Arbitration Scheme* (*Great Britain*) *Order 2004* (*SI 2004/753*). The scheme may be summarised (in brief outline) as follows (for further detail see EMPLOYMENT TRIBUNALS – I (20)).

First, it is important to note that the scheme is voluntary and is limited to unfair dismissal claims. If a claim for unfair dismissal is to be determined under the scheme then any other claim (even if raised at the same time or on related facts) must go to the Employment Tribunal or be settled. If other related claims are to be heard in the Employment Tribunal, then the arbitration proceedings may be postponed pending the Tribunal's determination. On submission of a claim to arbitration, both parties must waive in writing the right they would otherwise have in relation to an unfair dismissal claim. This includes waiver of the right to raise jurisdictional issues such as time limits, continuity of service and whether, in fact, the employee was dismissed.

The scheme provides for hearings to take place in private (unlike the normal tribunal procedure) and are intended to be speedy, non-legalistic and cost effective. The scheme is not intended for claims involving legal complexity or EC law; such claims, according to the Schedule, should remain the province of the Employment Tribunal. The arbitrators will be appointed by ACAS from the ACAS Arbitration panel. In contrast to tribunal proceedings, the arbitration may take place anywhere, including the employee's place of work. There is no mechanism for compulsory attendance of witnesses or production of documents (although failure to produce/attend may be taken into account by the arbitrator in reaching his decision). Evidence will not be subject to the formality of tribunal procedure and will be given unsworn and without cross-examination. The arbitrator will, however, have the power to question witnesses or parties to determine the facts.

The arbitrator's decision will not take the form of detailed reasons. The arbitrator must, in reaching his decision, apply the recognised principles of fairness in the employment context (including ACAS Codes of Practice) and, additionally, must apply the *Human Rights Act 1998* and relevant EC law. The remedies available to a successful employee are the same as in the Employment Tribunal (reinstatement, re-engagement and compensation). The arbitrator's decision is final; there is no mechanism for appeal from the decision. The parties remain free to settle the matter at any time during the arbitration, however. To date the scheme has not proved to be very popular: the *ACAS Annual Report 2005-06* reveals that in that year only six unfair dismissal cases have been the subject of arbitration (up from 4 in 2004–05 and down from 7 in 2003–2004 and 23 in 2002–2003).

The potential role of ACAS to arbitrate has, however, been increased. From 6 April 2003 and the introduction of the right to request flexible working (see *ERA 1996, ss 80F-80I* as inserted by the *Employment Act 2002*) a new right has been created to have these matters determined by ACAS arbitration. The new scheme, introduced pursuant to *s 212A* of *TULRCA* (see the *ACAS (Flexible Working) Arbitration Scheme (England and Wales) Order 2003 (SI 2003/694)*) is similar in form and operation to the scheme relating to unfair dismissal. An arbitrator hears the claim and give a final decision with limited rights of appeal or challenge available to the parties. If the parties have elected to go to arbitration, there is no right to go to the Employment Tribunal. The remedies and compensation which may be awarded by the arbitrator mirror those in the Employment Tribunal. The *ACAS Annual Report 2005-06* reveals that in that year no flexible working claims went to arbitration (down from one complaint the previous year according to the *2004–05 Annual Report*).

2.11 CONTACTING ACAS

ACAS headquarters are at Brandon House, 180 Borough High Street, London SE1 1LW. Tel: 020 7210 3613. However, for enquiries, leaflets, etc, a person should contact one of the public enquiry points or main offices, as listed below.

ACAS Public Enquiry Points

Birmingham	Tel: (0121) 456 5856
Bristol	Tel: (0117) 946 9500
Cardiff	Tel: (029) 2076 1126
Fleet	Tel: (01252) 811868
Glasgow	Tel: (0141) 204 2677
Leeds	Tel: (0113) 243 1371
Liverpool	Tel: (0151) 427 8881
London	Tel: (020) 7396 5100
Manchester	Tel: (0161) 833 8585
Newcastle upon Tyne	Tel: (0191) 261 2191
Nottingham	Tel: (0115) 969 3355

ACAS main offices

Midlands Region

Warwick House,
6 Highfield Road,
Edgbaston,
Birmingham
B15 3ED

2.11 Advisory, Conciliation and Arbitration Service (ACAS)

Anderson House,
Clinton Avenue,
Nottingham
NG5 1AW

Northern Region

Commerce House,
St Albans Place,
Leeds
LS2 8HH

Cross House,
Westgate Road,
Newcastle upon Tyne
NE1 4XX

North West Region

Commercial Union House,
2–10 Albert Square,
Manchester
M60 8AD

Cressington House,
249 St Mary's Road,
Garston,
Liverpool
L19 0NF

South and West Region

Regent House,
27a Regent Street,
Clifton,
Bristol
BS8 4HR

Westminster House,
Fleet Road,
Fleet,
Hants
GU13 8PD

London, Eastern and Southern Areas

Clifton House,
83–117 Euston Road,
London
NW1 2RB

39 King Street,
Thetford,
Norfolk
IP24 2AU

Suites 3–5,
Business Centre,
1–7 Commercial Road,
Paddock Wood,
Kent
TN12 6EN

Scotland

Franborough House,
123–157
Bothwell Street,
Glasgow
G2 7JR

Wales

3 Purbeck House,
Lambourne Crescent,
Llanishen,
Cardiff
CF4 5GJ

3 Age Discrimination

3.1 INTRODUCTION

The *Employment Equality (Age) Regulations 2006* ('*Regulations*') represent an important step in the expansion of the scope of discrimination law. Until recently, there had been a near complete absence of legal protection against discrimination on the basis of age.

The *Regulations* came into force on 1 October 2006.

It is still too early to judge the full effect of the *Regulations*. Nevertheless, they are likely to have a widespread and significant effect on employment practices. This is particularly so with regard to indirect discrimination. A number of practices which have, until now, been considered standard could now become subject to scrutiny. These might include:

(*a*)   a requirement that an employee have 5 years' experience of a particular kind of work;

(*b*)   only considering graduate applicants for a post;

(*c*)   confining appointments to those with a certain number of years of experience, for example, requiring a barrister of at least 10 years' call;

(*d*)   recruiting primarily through university visits;

(*e*)   requiring health checks;

(*f*)   requiring IT skills where these are not strictly relevant to the post;

(*g*)   the recruitment of staff to project a particular youthful image; and

(*h*)   a last in, first out redundancy policy.

If an employee is able to show that such a practice amounts to less favourable treatment on the basis of age, or that the practice puts those of a certain age group at a particular disadvantage, these practices are now unlawful unless the employer is able to justify the policy. An employer can only do this by showing that the measure pursues a legitimate aim and is proportionate to that aim. A measure is proportionate if it is appropriate and necessary for achieving the aim.

3.2 BACKGROUND

On 27 November 2000 the EU Framework Directive on equal treatment in employment and occupation (*Council Directive No 2000/78/EC: 'the Equality Directive'*) came into force. This required member states to enact legislation prohibiting, among other things, age discrimination in employment. Implementation was required by December 2003, but with an option (which the United Kingdom exercised) to defer implementation until 2006.

The *2006 Regulations* were made as the United Kingdom's response to the Equality Directive. They have been in force since 1 October 2006.

Among other things, the Directive prohibits direct discrimination, indirect discrimination and harassment on the grounds of age in the sphere of employment and vocational training. The Directive recognises that discrimination on the grounds of age can be justified in certain circumstances. A list of possible justifications is set out in *art 6* of the *Directive*. It also allows for positive action to be taken to prevent or compensate for disadvantages suffered as the result of previous discrimination.

Following the case of *Mangold v Helm* [2006] IRLR 143 in the European Court of Justice, there is some question as to whether the *Equality Directive* made it unlawful to discriminate on the grounds of age even prior to 1 October 2006. This is a matter of some controversy and is not addressed in detail here. For a recent discussion by the Attorney General of the European Court of Justice, see *Case C-411/05 Félix Palacios de la Villa v Cortefiel Servicios SA* at paras 79 to 100.

3.3   MEANING OF DISCRIMINATION AND HARASSMENT

The most important distinction between age discrimination and most other forms of discrimination in UK law is that both direct and indirect age discrimination may be justified.

Discrimination under the *2006 Regulations* is divided into three different types: direct discrimination, indirect discrimination and victimisation. The *2006 Regulations* also define harassment.

3.4   **Direct discrimination**

A person ('A') directly discriminates against another person ('B') if, on the grounds of B's age, A treats B less favourably than he treats or would treat other persons and A cannot show the treatment is a proportionate means of achieving a legitimate aim *(reg 3(1)(a))*.

Less favourable treatment

For guidance on the meaning of 'less favourable treatment' see 12.5 DISCRIMINATION AND EQUAL OPPORTUNITIES – I.

On grounds of age

The primary question is always whether or not the less favourable treatment afforded to B was caused by considerations of age. The burden of proof in determining that question rests on the complainant only to a limited extent: once he has proved facts from which the tribunal could conclude, in the absence of an adequate explanation by the respondent, that the less favourable treatment was on the grounds of age, the court or tribunal must uphold the complaint, unless the respondent establishes that he did not act unlawfully (see further 'Burden of Proof' below).

However, in the absence of any direct evidence of discrimination on the grounds of age, a complainant will often need to ask a court or tribunal to draw an inference. Guidance on the extent to which it is legitimate to draw such an inference may be gleaned from the case law on other forms of discrimination: see DISCRIMINATION AND EQUAL OPPORTUNITIES – I (12).

The respondent will then only be able to show that there was no discrimination if it can show that the treatment was in no way whatsoever on the grounds of age.

Proportionate means of achieving a legitimate aim

In the context of age discrimination, a discriminatory act or provision, criterion or practice is not unlawful where the respondent is able to show that it was a 'proportionate means of achieving a legitimate aim'. What the provisions require is that the tribunal carry out a balancing exercise between the discriminatory effects of a measure and the importance of the aim pursued.

There is no restriction on the possible motivations that can constitute a legitimate aim. It will therefore be open to employers to demonstrate that any aim they seek to pursue is legitimate. This is consistent with the fact that justification must be applied on a case by case basis and that it is very difficult to anticipate all possible justifications.

Article 6(1) of the *Directive* sets out a list of examples of possible legitimate aims. These were repeated in the original drafts of the *Regulations* but did not find their way into the final provisions. The examples themselves are somewhat difficult to understand and would in any event be difficult to apply in practice.

The DTI, in its July 2005 Consultation Paper Equality and Diversity: Coming of Age ('the Consultation Paper') suggested various potential legitimate aims. These include:

(a)   health, welfare and safety;

(b)   facilitation of employment planning;

(c)   particular training requirements;

(d)   encouraging and rewarding loyalty;

(e)   the need for a reasonable period of employment before retirement; and

(f)   recruiting or retaining older people.

The Consultation Paper emphasises that less favourable treatment on the grounds of age cannot be justified by an aim which is itself related to age discrimination.

In *Mangold v Helm* [2006] IRLR 143, the European Court of Justice agreed that encouraging the recruitment of older persons would potentially constitute a legitimate aim.

It will not be sufficient for an employer to show that the complainant was less favourably treated on grounds of age for a legitimate aim. The employer must also show that the treatment was appropriate and reasonably necessary in order to achieve that aim.

In particular:

(a)   the treatment must actually contribute to the pursuit of the legitimate aim. For example, the employer must, if using an age-related condition to promote safety, be convinced that the condition actually promotes safety;

(b)   the importance of the aim being pursued should be balanced against the discriminatory effect of the treatment; and

(c)   if the aim could have been achieved by other means, without treating those in a particular age group less favourably (or with a lesser effect), the treatment will not be justified.

In *Mangold*, a measure aimed to encourage the recruitment of older persons was held to be disproportionate as it applied to all old people, regardless of whether they had been out of employment.

In *R (on the application of Unison v the First Secretary of State* [2006] EWHC 2373 (Admin), [2006] IRLR 926, the Secretary of State had changed the Local Government Pension Scheme, considering this to be necessary in order to comply with the Equality Directive and the *Regulations*. The Secretary of State considered that the scheme would not be justified by the aim of rewarding loyalty as it treated those who remained in service in the same way as those who had left. The Court held that this position was not irrational.

See also *Cadman v Health and Safety Executive* [2007] All ER (EC) 1 on whether evidence is needed to justify the use of length of service criteria (in the different context of equal pay).

Questions of legitimate aim and proportionality are likely to generate considerable case law as the concepts are somewhat vague. Further, the degree of latitude that courts and tribunals will allow employers in the justification of less favourable treatment is unclear. This is particularly in view of the fact that considerations of age and age-related considerations (such as experience) form a central part of working life. In *Mangold*, the European Court of Justice emphasised that Member States enjoy a broad discretion in this area.

For further guidance on justification, see 13.8 DISCRIMINATION AND EQUAL OPPORTUNITIES – II.

3.5   **Indirect discrimination**

Indirect discrimination occurs where B applies to A a provision, criterion or practice which he applies or would apply equally to a person not of the same age group as B, but which:

(a)   puts or would put persons of the same age group as B at a particular disadvantage when compared with other persons, and

(b)   puts B at that disadvantage,

and A cannot show the treatment or, as the case may be, provision, criterion or practice to be a proportionate means of achieving a legitimate aim (*reg 3(1)(b)*).

'Age group' is defined at *reg 3(3)(a)* as 'a group of persons by reference to age, whether by reference to a particular age or a range of ages'. The reference to B's age includes B's apparent age: *reg 3(3)(b)*.

Provision, criterion of practice

The formula is identical to that in the *SDA 1975* (as amended by the *Sex Discrimination (Indirect Discrimination and Burden of Proof) Regulations 2001 (SI 2001/2660)* and the *RRA 1976* (as amended by the *Race Relations Act 1976 (Amendment) Regulations 2003 (SI 2003/1626)*. Readers are referred to the discussion of those provisions in the chapters on discrimination (DISCRIMINATION AND EQUAL OPPORTUNITIES – I, II, III (12, 13, 14)).

Disparity of effect

The Regulations require only that persons of the same age group as the complainant are put 'at a particular disadvantage'. Unlike the equivalent provisions of the *SDA 1975* and the *RRA 1976*, there is no requirement that any particular proportion of people of that age group would be disadvantaged. It will therefore be sufficient for the complainant to adduce evidence of a likelihood of a particular disadvantage.

3.6   Age Discrimination

Personal disadvantage

Hypothetical cases cannot be brought; the complainant must herself have been put at a disadvantage.

Proportionate means of achieving a legitimate aim

Like direct discrimination, indirect discrimination can also be justified. The same considerations will apply. See above at 3.4.

3.6   Instructions to discriminate

A also discriminates against B if he treats that B less favourably than he treats or would treat other persons in the same circumstances, and does so by reason that:

(a)   B has not carried out (in whole or in part) an instruction to do an act which is unlawful by virtue of the Regulations, or

(b)   B, having been given an instruction to do such an act, complains to A or to any other person about that instruction.

(*Regulation 5*)

3.7   Victimisation

Victimisation occurs where a respondent treats a complainant less favourably than he treats or would treat other person in the same circumstances, and does so by reason that the complainant has:

(a)   brought proceedings against the respondent or any other person under or by virtue of the *Regulations*;

(b)   given evidence or information in connection with proceedings brought by any person against the respondent or any other person under or by virtue of the *Regulations*;

(c)   otherwise done anything under or by reference to these *Regulations* in relation to the respondent or any other person; or

(d)   alleged that the respondent or any other person has committed an act which (whether or not the allegation so states) would amount to a contravention of these Regulations.

or by reason that the respondent knows that the complainant intends to do any of these things, or suspects that he has done or intends to do any of these things (*reg 4(1)*).

No protection is afforded to anyone who gives false evidence or information or makes a false allegation which was not made (or given) in good faith (*reg 4(2)*).

The provisions are virtually identical to their equivalents in other discrimination legislation and the case law with regard to those provisions will be relevant (see DISCRIMINATION AND EQUAL OPPORTUNITIES – I, II, III (12, 13, 14)).

3.8   Harassment

Harassment is defined by *reg 6(1)* as occurring where, on the grounds of age, the respondent engages in unwanted conduct which has the purpose or effect of:

(a)   violating the complainant's dignity; or

(b)   creating an intimidating, hostile, degrading, humiliating or offensive environment for the complainant.

Conduct is regarded as having the effect specified in (a) or (b) only if, having regard to all the circumstances, including in particular the complainant's perception, it should reasonably be considered as having that effect (*reg 6(2)*).

There is no need for a complainant to show less favourable treatment or to identify a comparator.

Unwanted conduct

The conduct must be unwanted by the complainant, but there is no requirement that the complainant make that clear at the time, nor that the respondent be aware that the conduct is unwanted. Whether conduct was 'unwanted' would be a matter of fact for the tribunal or court.

Purpose or effect

The unwanted conduct may be unlawful either where it is intended to have the specified effects or where it has any of those effects, regardless of the respondent's intention. This protection is wider, in this respect, than the generally available civil law in the *Protection from Harassment Act 1997,* in that there is no requirement in the *Regulations* that the respondent is aware, or even that a reasonable person would be aware, that the conduct might amount to harassment.

However, an over-sensitive complainant may not succeed in proving a complaint of harassment. This is because of the effect of *reg 6(2)*. In deciding whether the conduct has one or more of the requisite effects, a tribunal or court must apply an objective standard of reasonableness, taking into account all the circumstances including, in particular, the complainant's perception.

Types of harassment

Two types of harassment are outlawed: harassment that violates dignity, and harassment that creates an offensive (or other unwelcome) environment for the complainant. The two types of harassment are unlikely to differ in practice. However, it may be that a single slight against someone on the grounds of age could undermine dignity, without necessarily creating an offensive working environment. Conversely, an ageist work environment might be generally offensive to an older (or younger) person, without necessarily violating an individual's dignity.

3.9   **DISCRIMINATION AND HARASSMENT IN EMPLOYMENT**

The *Regulations* are confined to age discrimination in the fields of employment, vocational training and certain types of education. The *Regulations* do not extend to discrimination in connection with the provision of goods and services. This means that, for example, they will not prevent cinemas from selling reduced price tickets to students.

The following classes of complainant are protected against discrimination in relation to employment:

(a)   applicants for employment at an establishment in Great Britain (*reg 7(1)*);

(b)   those employed at an establishment in Great Britain (*reg 7(2)*);

(c)   in certain circumstances, those formerly employed at an establishment in Great Britain (*reg 24*);

(d)   members or prospective members of an occupational pension scheme (see further below).

3.10 Meaning of 'employment'

'Employment' is defined to mean 'employment under a contract of service or of apprenticeship or a contract personally to do any work' (*reg 2(2)*). This is virtually identical to that in other discrimination legislation and the case law in those contexts will be likely to apply (see DISCRIMINATION AND EQUAL OPPORTUNI-TIES – I, II, III (12, 13, 14)).

3.11 Meaning of 'at an establishment in Great Britain'

'Establishment' is not defined in the *Regulations*. Employment is to be regarded as being at an establishment in Great Britain if the employee-

(a)   does his work wholly or partly in Great Britain; or

(b)   does his work wholly outside Great Britain; but:

    (i)   the employer has a place of business at an establishment in Great Britain;

    (ii)   the work is for the purposes of the business carried on at that establishment; and

    (iii)   the employee is ordinarily resident in Great Britain:

        (1)   at the time when he applies for or is offered the employment, or

        (2)   at any time during the course of his employment (*reg 10(1)* and (*2*).

'Great Britain' includes such territorial waters of the United Kingdom as are adjacent to Great Britain (*reg 2(2)*).

Where employment is on board a ship, it only counts as employment at an establishment in Great Britain if the ship is registered at a port of registry in Great Britain (*reg 10(3)(a)*). Where employment is on an aircraft or hovercraft it only qualifies if the aircraft or hovercraft is registered in the United Kingdom and operated by a person who has his principal place of business, or is ordinarily resident in Great Britain (*reg 10(3)(b)*).

There are specific provisions relating to the exploration of the sea-bed or sub-soil and the Frigg Gas Field (*reg 10(4)*, (*5*) and (*6*)).

3.12 Unlawful discrimination against applicants for employment

It is unlawful for an employer, in relation to employment by him at an establishment in Great Britain, to discriminate against a person:

(a)   in the arrangements he makes for the purpose of determining to whom he should offer employment;

(b)   in the terms on which he offers that person employment; or

(c)   by refusing to offer, or deliberately not offering, him employment.

(*Regulation 7(1)*).

(a) and (b) do not apply in relation to an employee whose age is greater than the employer's normal retirement age or, if the employer does not have a normal retirement age, the age of 65; or who would, within a period of six months from the date of his application to the employer, reach the employers' normal retirement age, or if the employer does not have a normal retirement age, the age of 65. 'Normal retirement age' is an age of 65 or more which is the age at which employees in the employer's undertaking who hold, or have held, the same kind of position as the employee are normally required to retire (see *reg 7(8)* and *s 98ZH ERA 1996* (as inserted)).

3.13   **Unlawful discrimination against employees**

It is unlawful for an employer, in relation to a person whom he employs at an establishment in Great Britain, to discriminate against that person:

(a)   in the terms of employment which he affords him;

(b)   in the opportunities which he affords him for promotion, a transfer, training, or receiving any other benefit;

(c)   by refusing to afford him, or deliberately not affording him, any such opportunity; or

(d)   by dismissing him, or subjecting him to any other detriment.

(*Regulation 7(2)*).

Benefits

The 'benefits' referred to at (b) do not include benefits of any description if the employer is concerned with the provision (for payment or not) of benefits of that description to the public, or to a section of the public which includes the employee in question, unless:

(a)   that provision differs in a material respect form the provision of the benefits by the employer to his employees; or

(b)   the provision of the benefits to the employee in question is regulated by his contract of employment; or

(c)   the benefits relate to training.

(*Regulation 7(6)*).

Dismissal

Reference to the dismissal of a person from employment includes reference-

(a)   to the termination of that person's employment by the expiration of any period (including a period expiring by reference to an event or circumstance), not being a termination immediately after which the employment is renewed on the same terms; and

(b)   to the termination of that person's employment by any act of his (including the giving of notice) in circumstances such that he is entitled to terminate it without notice by reason of the conduct of the employer.

(*Regulation 7(7)*).

3.14 Unlawful harassment of employees and applications for employment

It is unlawful for an employer, in relation to employment by him at an establishment in Great Britain, to subject to harassment a person whom he employs or who has applied to him for employment (*reg 7(3)*).

For the definition of harassment, see 3.8 above.

3.15 Unlawful discrimination against former employees

The protection extends to acts of discrimination against those who were until recently in an employment (or vocational training) relationship, but have since ceased to be in that relationship. Liability is confined to where the discrimination or harassment is 'closely connected to that relationship' (*reg 24*). There is no time limit for complaints of post-termination discrimination and harassment. However, the greater the time that has passed, the less likely that the complainant will be able to establish the necessary close connection.

3.16 EXCEPTIONS

The Exceptions are among the most complex aspects of the *Regulations*. This chapter has already discussed the huge potential significance of the *Regulations* in terms of their effects on standard employment practices. By way of these Exceptions, the *Regulations* seek to permit the continuance of some of those standard practices. It must be stressed that not all such 'standard' practices are exempted. For example, the practice of requiring a degree or relevant experience for an appointment is not among the exceptions. Accordingly, an employer will need to justify any such requirement.

3.17 Exception for genuine occupational requirement

The *Regulations* recognise that there may be circumstances in which being of a particular age group may be a genuine requirement of the job. Such cases are an exception to the general protection afforded by the *Regulations*. It is important to remember that it is not a licence to discriminate. The existence of a genuine occupational requirement is no defence to discrimination taking one of the following forms:

(a)   discrimination on the terms on which employment is offered;

(b)   discrimination in the terms of employment afford to an employee;

(c)   subjecting the employee to a detriment other than dismissal; and

(d)   harassing the employee.

The defence is *potentially* available where the discrimination takes one or more of the following forms:

(a)   discrimination in the arrangements made for determining to whom employment should be offered;

(b)   discrimination by refusing to offer, or deliberately not offering, employment;

(c)   discrimination in the opportunities offered an employee for promotion, transfer, or training;

(d)   discrimination by refusing to afford, or deliberately not offering, an opportunity; and

(e)   discrimination by dismissal.

The *Regulations* do not list the circumstances in which such a principle might apply. Instead, they describe a general principle. Where, having regard to the nature of the employment, or the context in which the employment is carried out, possessing a characteristic related to age is a *genuine and determining* occupational requirement, a genuine occupational requirement might exist. However, the existence of the requirement is not in itself sufficient. It must also be proportionate to apply that requirement in the particular case (*reg 8(2)*).

As an exception to the law against discrimination, it is expected that tribunals and courts will take a strict interpretation of this provision. It is only where an employer can show that the requirement really is genuine and determining that discrimination would be found to be lawful.

3.18   Benefits provided to the public

See 3.13 above at the sub-heading 'Benefits'.

3.19   Employment outside Great Britain

See 3.11 above.

3.20   Statutory authority

A discriminatory act is not unlawful if it is done in order to comply with a requirement of any statutory provision. A statutory provision means any provision of an Act or an Act of the Scottish Parliament, an instrument made by a Minister of the Crown under an Act; and an instrument made under an Act or an act of the Scottish Parliament by the Scottish Ministers of a member of the Scottish Executive. This would include, for example, the minimum age requirement to become a licensee of a public house.

3.21   National security

A discriminatory act is not unlawful if it is done for the purpose of safeguarding national security, if the act is justified by that purpose (*reg 28*). (It should be noted that the *Regulations* do not apply to the armed services.)

3.22   Positive action

The *Regulations*, like the Directive, allow positive action in a limited range of circumstances. It must reasonably appear to the person doing the act that it prevents or compensates for disadvantages linked to age suffered by persons of that age or age group doing that work or likely to take up the work. The positive action must cover providing facilities for training which would help fit employee for particular work; or encouraging person of a particular age or age group to take advantage of opportunities for doing particular work (*reg 29(1)*).

There is a specifically defined exception for acts done by trade organisations (see *reg 29(2)* and *(3)*).

3.23   Retirement

By virtue of *reg 30(2)*, nothing in *Parts 2* or *3* of the *Regulations* 'shall render unlawful the dismissal of a person to whom this regulation applies at or over the age of 65 where the reason for the dismissal is retirement'.

3.24   Age Discrimination

There are specific and detailed provisions determining whether or not the reason for a dismissal is retirement. These are discussed below at 3.38.

This is the somewhat notorious provision which creates a national default retirement age ('NDRA'). There has been considerable discussion as to whether such a provision is lawful in accordance with the *Equality Directive*. A challenge to the NDRA on this basis was brought by an organisation called 'Heyday'. At a hearing on 6 December 2006 before the Administrative Court, the question of the legality of the NDRA was referred to the European Court of Justice for a preliminary ruling. It is likely to take some time before the point is determined. However, the Attorney General has delivered a recent opinion in a somewhat similar Spanish case, *Case C-411/05 Félix Palacios de la Villa v Cortefiel Servicios SA*. The question was whether a national law which allowed compulsory retirement clauses to be included in collective agreements was in breach of the *Equality Directive*. Advocate General Mazák held that retirement ages fall outside the scope of the *Equality Directive* since they were excluded by the 14th recital, and that the Spanish law would have been justified in any event.

It should be stressed that no such exception applies to employers who are dismissed by reason of retirement at or below the age of 65. This means that any such policy will constitute unlawful discrimination unless the employer can show that it is objectively justified. (It should also be noted that this exception applies only to employees and not, for example, to office-holders.)

3.24   National minimum wage

The National Minimum Wage ('NMW') legislation allows for lower sums to be paid to younger workers. *Regulation 31* allows employers to retain different pay between the bands but only if the younger workers are being paid less than the adult NMW. Surprisingly, if the employer pays the younger workers more than the adult NMW, but less than older employees, this will require objective justification.

3.25   Certain benefits based on length of service

Regulation 32 makes some provision for employers to provide benefits to employees by reference to the length of their service.

The exception applies where a person ('A'), in relation to the award of any benefit by him, puts a worker ('B') at a disadvantage when compared to another worker ('C') if and to the extent that the disadvantage suffered by B is because B's length of service is less than that of C (*reg 32(1)*).

However, where B's length of service is longer than 5 years, it must reasonably appear to A that the way in which the criterion of length of service is used fulfils a business need. Examples are given of encouraging loyalty or motivation, or rewarding experience (*reg 32(2)*).

'Benefit' does not include any benefit awarded to a worker by virtue of his ceasing to work for A (*reg 32(7)*).

There is some complication about the identification of the relevant 5 year period. The employer can decide whether to determine this by reference to the total length of time the worker has been working for the employer, or the length of time the worker has been working for him doing work which he reasonably considers to be at or above a particular level (*reg 32(3)*).

In calculating the length of time a worker has been working for him, a person must calculate the length of time in terms of the number of weeks during the whole or part of which the worker was working for him (*reg 32(4)(a)*). The employer may discount any period during which the worker was absent from work (unless in all the circumstances, including the way in which other workers' similar absences have been treated, it is not reasonable to do so) (*reg 32(4)(b)*). The employer may also discount any period during which the worker was present at work where that preceded a period of absence and, in all the circumstances including the length of the absence, the reason for the absence, its effect on the worker's ability to discharge his duties, and the way in which other workers are treated, it is reasonable for the period to be discounted (*reg 32(4)(c)*).

Further, a worker must be treated as having worked for A during any period during which he worked for another, if required to do so by *s 218 ERA 1996* (see CONTINUOUS EMPLOYMENT (7)).

3.26   Enhanced redundancy benefits

Regulation 33 makes provision for employers to provide 'qualifying employees' with enhanced redundancy payments.

A 'qualifying employee' is an employee who is entitled to a redundancy payment by virtue of *s 135* of the *ERA 1996*, or who would be so entitled but does not have the two year qualifying period, or to an employee who agrees to the termination of his employment in circumstances where, had he been dismissed, he would have fallen into one of the former two categories.

Regulation 33 allows employers to give enhanced redundancy payments only to those who are entitled to a redundancy payment by virtue of *s 135 ERA 1996*, or those who agree to termination when, had they been dismissed, they would have been so entitled.

Employers may also give qualifying employees an enhanced redundancy payment which is less than that given to another such employee, so long as they are both 'calculated in the same way' (*reg 33(1)(a)*).

There are rules as to how the amounts must be calculated. The amount must be calculated as in the relevant provisions of the *ERA 1996* (*ss 162(1)–(3)*). However, in making the calculation, the employer may treat a week's pay as not being subject to a maximum amount, and/or multiply the appropriate amount allowed for each year of employment by a figure of more than one (reg *33(4)(a)* and (*b*)). Having made the calculation, the employer may also increase the amount calculated by multiplying it by a figure of more than one (*reg 33(4)(c)*).

3.27   Provision of life assurance cover to retired workers

Regulation 34 provides an exception for the provision of life assurance to retired workers. Where an employer arranges for workers to be provided with life assurance after their early retirement on grounds of ill health, it is not unlawful to arrange for such cover to cease when the workers reach a normal retirement age, if one exists, or age 65, where there is no retirement age (*reg 34(1)*).

'Normal retirement age' means the age at which workers in the undertaking who held the same kind of position as the worker held at the time of his retirement were normally required to retire (*reg 34(2)*).

3.28 NON-EMPLOYEES COVERED BY THE EMPLOYMENT RULES

The *Regulations* also cover a number of non-employees. The exceptions set out above do not apply to all of the non-employees covered. Where exceptions do apply, these are set out below.

3.29 Contract workers

In recent times, there has been a marked trend towards the use of contract workers. Contract workers are normally parties to a tri-partite arrangement. The first party is the person who has work which needs doing. He is known as the 'principal'. The principal enters into a contract with a second party who is obliged to supply his own employees to perform the work. The employees are known as 'contract workers' (see *reg 9(5)*).

It is unlawful for a principal, in relation to contract work at an establishment in Great Britain, to discriminate against a contract worker:

(a)   in the terms on which he allows him to do that work;

(b)   by not allowing him to do it or continue to do it;

(c)   in the way he affords him access to any benefits or by refusing or deliberately not affording him access to them; or

(d)   by subjecting him to any other detriment.

(*Regulation 9(1)*).

A genuine occupational requirement defence is available to the principal with regard to para (b) above, but not to the other acts (*reg 9(3)*). It can be relied upon if it would have been available had the contract worker been directly employed by the principal.

'Benefits' do not include benefits of any description if the principal is concerned with the provision (for payment or not) of benefits of that description to the public, or to a section of the public to which the contract worker belongs, unless that provision differs in a material respect from the provision of the benefits by the principal to his contract workers (*reg 9(4)*).

It is also unlawful for a principal to subject a contract worker to harassment (*reg 9(2)*).

3.30 Office-holders

The *Regulations* cover discrimination against office holders. Overwhelmingly, office holders are public sector appointees, often those with specific statutory powers or responsibilities. They are considered not to be employed in a post but, rather, as holding an office which exists independently of the terms of their appointment.

Meaning of 'office holder'

The *Regulations* encompass any office or post to which person are appointed to discharge functions personally under the direction of another person, and in respect of which they are entitled to remuneration, and also to any office or post to which appointments are made by (or on the recommendation of or subject to the approval of) a Minister of the Crown, a government department, the National Assembly for Wales or any part of the Scottish administration (*reg 10(8)(a)* and (*b*)).

Excluded from the definition are political offices and any office which (but for the operation of any other provision of the regulations) would fall within the scope of the protections conferred on applicants and employees, contract workers, barristers, advocates or partners (*reg 10(8)*).

The holder of an office or post:

(a)   is to be regarded as discharging his functions under the direction of another person if that other person is entitled to direct him as to when and where he discharges those functions;

(b)   is not to be regarded as entitled to remuneration merely because he is entitled to payments:

    (i)   in respect of expenses incurred by him in carrying out the function of the office or post; or

    (ii)   by way of compensation for the loss of income or benefits he would or might have received from any person had he not been carrying out the functions of the office or post.

Regulation 12(10)(b) contains an exhaustive list of those offices which are considered to be 'political offices'.

Meaning of relevant persons

In the provisions dealing with office holders, references to employers are replaced with references to the 'relevant person'. The relevant person in relation to an office or post means:

(a)   any person with power to make or terminate appointments to the office or post, or to determine the terms of appointment;

(b)   any person with power to determine the working conditions of a person appointed to the office or post in relation to opportunities for promotion, a transfer, training or for receiving any other benefit; and

(c)   any person or body on whose recommendation or subject to whose approval appointments are made to the office or post.

(*Regulation 12(10)(c)*).

Meaning of appointment

Similarly, references to 'employment' are replaced by references to 'appointment'. Appointment is defined to mean appointment to an office or post but excluding election to an office or post (*reg 12(10)(a)*).

Unlawful discrimination against applicants for an appointment

It is unlawful for a 'relevant person', in relation to an appointment to an office or post to discriminate against a person:

(a)   in the arrangements which he makes for the purpose of determining to whom the appointment should be offered;

(b)   in the terms on which he offers him the appointment; or

(c)   by refusing to offer him the appointment.

(*Regulation 12(1)*).

There is an exception where, if the office or post had constituted employment, the act would by lawful by virtue of the genuine occupational requirement defence (*reg 12(5)*).

Unlawful discrimination in relation to recommendations for appointment

It is unlawful, in relation to an appointment to an office or post to which appointments are made by (or on the recommendation of or subject to the approval of) a Minister of the Crown, a government department, the National Assembly of Wales or any part of the Scottish Administration, for a relevant person on whose recommendation (or subject to whose approval) appointments to the office or post are made, to discriminate against a person:

(a)   in the arrangements which he makes for the purpose of determining who should be recommended or approved in relation to the appointment; or

(b)   in making or refusing to make a recommendation, or giving or refusing to give an approval, in relation to the appointment.

(*Regulation 12(2)*).

References to making a recommendation include references to making a negative recommendation (*reg 12(10)(d)*) and references to refusal include references to deliberate omission (*reg 12(10)(e)*).

An act in relation to an office or post falling within any of the categories set out immediately above will nevertheless be lawful where, if the office or post constituted employment, it would be lawful by virtue of the existence of the genuine occupational requirement to refuse to offer the person such employment (*reg 12(5)*).

Unlawful discrimination against holders of an appointment

It is unlawful for a relevant person, in relation to a person who has been appointed to an office or post to which this regulation applies, to discriminate against him:

(a)   in the terms of the appointment;

(b)   in the opportunities which he affords him for promotion, a transfer, training or receiving any other benefit, or by refusing to afford him any such opportunity;

(c)   by terminating the appointment; or

(d)   by subjecting him to any other detriment in relation to the appointment.

(*Regulation 12(3)*).

An act in relation to an office or post falling within any of the categories set out immediately above will nevertheless not be unlawful where, if the office or post had constituted employment, that act would be lawful as a result of a genuine occupational requirement (*reg 12(5)*).

The reference to 'benefits' in sub-para (b) immediately above does not apply to benefits of any description if the relevant person is concerned with the provision (for payment or not) of benefits of that description to the public, or a section of the public to which the person appointed belongs unless:

(a)   that provision differs in a material respect from the provision of the benefits by the relevant person to persons appointed to offices or posts which are the same as, or not materially different from, that which the person appointed holds; or

(b)   the provisions of the benefits to the person appointed is regulated by the terms and conditions of his appointment; or

(c)   the benefits relate to training.

(*Regulation 12(6)*).

'Termination of the appointment' is deemed to refer also to:

(a)   the termination of the appointment by the expiration of any period (including a period expiring by reference to an event or circumstance), not being a termination immediately after which the appointment is renewed on the same terms and conditions; and

(b)   the termination of the appointment by any act of the person appointed (including the giving of notice) in circumstances such that he is entitled to terminate the appointment without notice by reason of the conduct of the relevant person.

(*Regulation 12(7)*).

Unlawful harassment of applicants for appointment or holders of an appointment

It is unlawful for a relevant person, in relation to an office or post to subject to harassment a person:

(a)   who has been appointed to the office or post;

(b)   who is seeking or being considered for appointment to the office or post; or

(c)   who is seeking or being considered for a recommendation or approval in relation to an appointment to an office or post to which appointments are made by (or on the recommendation of or subject to the approval of) a Minister of the Crown, a government department, the National Assembly of Wales or any part of the Scottish Administration.

(*Regulation 12(4)*).

3.31   **Police**

Those holding the office of police constables are office-holders and not employees. However, the *Regulations* deem them to be employees (*reg 13(1)*). Police cadets are also treated as employees for the purposes of the *Regulations* (*reg 13(6)*).

Where the discriminatory act is an act of the relevant chief officer of police, the chief officer is deemed to be the constable's employer (*reg 13(1)(a)*). 'Chief officer of police' is defined:

(*a*)   in relation to a person appointed, or an appointment falling to be made, under a specified Act, as in the *Police Act 1996*.

(*b*)   in relation to a person appointed, or an appointment falling to be made, under the *Police (Scotland) Act 1967*, as the chief constable of the relevant police force;

(c)   in relation to any other person or appointment, as the officer or other person who has the direction and control of the body of constables or cadets in question.

(*Regulation 13(7)*).

Where the discriminatory act is an act of the relevant police authority, the authority is deemed to be the constable's employer (*reg 13(1)(b)*). 'Police authority' is defined:

(a)   in relation to a person appointed, or an appointment falling to be made, under a specified act, as in the *Police Act 1996*;

(b)   in relation to a person appointed, or an appointment falling to be made, under the *Police (Scotland) Act 1967*, as in that Act;

(c)   in relation to any other person or appointment, as the authority by whom the person in question is or on appointment would be paid.

(*Regulation 13(7)*).

The relevant chief officer of police is vicariously liable for the actions of those police officers for whom he is responsible and he is treated as their employer for that purpose (*reg 13(2)* and see 3.43 below). Broadly, an employer is vicariously liable for any act of the employee performed in the course of their employment. For present purposes, anything done by a police officer in the performance, or purported performance, of his functions shall be treated as done in the course of that employment (*reg 13(3)(b)*).

Where proceedings are brought against a chief officer of police, any compensation, costs or expenses ordered against the chief officer are payable from the police fund. The chief officer can also recover the costs of successfully contesting proceedings from the fund in so far as they are not recovered from the complainant or other party. Finally, he can recover the cost of compromising any proceedings against him, subject to having obtained the approval of the relevant police authority (*reg 13(3)*).

Any proceedings under the *Regulations* which would lie against a chief officer of police should be brought against whoever holds the post of chief officer of police for the time being. If the post is vacant, proceedings should be brought against the person for the time being performing the functions of that office (*Reg 13(4)*).

A police authority may, in such cases and to such extent as appear to it to be appropriate, pay out of the police fund:

(a)   any compensation, costs or expenses awarded in proceedings under the *Regulations* against a person under the direction and control of the chief officer of police;

(b)   any costs or expenses incurred and not recovered by such a person in such proceedings; and

(c)   any sum required in connection with the settlement of a claim that has or might have given rise to such proceedings.

(*Regulation 13(5)*).

3.32 **Serious Organised Crime Agency**

Where a constable or other person has been seconded to the Serious Organised Crime Agency ('SOCA') to serve as a member of its staff, he is treated as an employee of SOCA (*reg 14(1)*).

For the purposes of vicarious liability, any constable or other person seconded to SOCA to serve as a member of its staff is treated as being employed by SOCA and by no one else. Anything done by such a person in the performance or purported performance of his functions is treated as done in the course of that employment (*reg 14(2)*).

3.33 **Barristers**

Regulation 15 contains provisions relating to barristers. It only extends to England and Wales. There are similar provisions for Scottish advocates in *reg 16*.

In the provisions concerning barristers, the following definitions are used. 'Barrister's clerk' includes any person carrying out any of the persons of a barrister's clerk. 'Pupil', 'pupillage' and 'set of chambers' have the meanings commonly associated with their use in the context of barristers practising in independent practice. 'Tenancy' and 'tenant' have the meanings commonly associated with their use in the context of barristers practising in independent practice, but also include reference to any barrister permitted to work in a set of chambers who is not a tenant (*reg 15(5)*).

Unlawful discrimination against applicants for pupillage or tenancy

It is unlawful for a barrister or barrister's clerk, in relation to any offer of a pupillage or tenancy, to discriminate against a person:

(a)　in the arrangements which are made for the purpose of determining to whom the pupillage or tenancy should offered;

(b)　in respect of any terms on which it is offered; or

(c)　by refusing, or deliberately not offering, it to him.

(*Regulation 15(1)*).

Unlawful discrimination against pupils or tenants

It is unlawful for a barrister or barrister's clerk, in relation to a pupil or tenant in the set of chambers in question, to discriminate against him:

(a)　in respect of any terms applicable to him as a pupil or tenant;

(b)　in the opportunities for training, or gaining experience, which are afforded or denied to him;

(c)　in the benefits which are afforded or denied to him; or

(d)　by terminating his pupillage, or by subjecting him to any pressure to leave the chambers or other detriment.

(*Regulation 15(2)*).

Unlawful harassment of pupils, tenants or applicants for pupillage or tenancy

It is unlawful for a barrister or barrister's clerk, in relation to a pupillage or tenancy in the set of chambers in question, to subject to harassment a person who is, or has applied to be, a pupil or tenant (*reg 15(3)*).

3.34 Age Discrimination

Unlawful discrimination by those instructing barristers

It is unlawful for any person, in relation to the giving, withholding or acceptance of instructions to a barrister, to discriminate against any person by subjecting him to a detriment, or to subject him to harassment (*reg 15(4)*).

3.34 NON-EMPLOYERS COVERED BY THE EMPLOYMENT RULES

Trustees and managers of occupational pension schemes

It is unlawful for the trustees or managers of an occupational pension scheme to discriminate against a member or prospective member of the scheme in carrying out any of their functions in relation to it including, in particular, their functions relating to the admission of members to the scheme and the treatment of members of it (*reg 11(1)*). There is an exception, however, for rights accrued or benefits payable in respect of period of service prior to the coming into force of the *Regulations*.

It is also unlawful for the trustees or managers of an occupational pension scheme, in relation to the scheme, to subject any member or prospective member to harassment (*reg 11(2)*).

Schedule 2 to the *Regulations* contains detailed provisions defining the terms, exempting certain practices, including a 'non-discrimination rule in each scheme, giving trustees and managers power to change the scheme to secure conformity with that rule, and making provision as to enforcement. These provisions are discussed more fully in RETIREMENT (42).

3.35 Partnerships

Definitions

In the provisions concerning partnerships, the following definitions are used. 'Firm' has the meaning given by *s 4* of the *Partnership Act 1890* (*reg 17(7)*). *Regulation 17* defines firm so as to include persons proposing to form themselves into a partnership. Also within the scope of the Regulations are limited liability partnerships (*reg 17(6)*).

In the case of a limited partnerships, references to a 'partner' are to be construed as references to a 'general partner' as defined in *s 3* of the *Limited Partnerships Act 1907* (*reg 17(5)*). In the case of limited liability partnerships, such references are to be construed as references to a member of the limited liability partnership (*reg 17(6)*).

Unlawful discrimination against partners and candidates for partnership

It is unlawful for a firm, in relation to a position as partner in the firm, to discriminate against a person-

(a)   in the arrangements they make for the purpose of determining to whom they should offer that position;

(b)   in the terms on which they offer him that position;

(c)   by refusing to offer, or deliberately not offering, him that position; or in a case where the person already holds that position-

   (i)   in the way they afford him access to any benefits or by refusing to afford, or deliberately not affording, him access to them; or

(ii)   by expelling him from that position, or subjecting him to any other detriment.

(*Regulation 17(1)*).

An act falling into one of the categories set out immediately above will not be unlawful if, had the complainant been an employee or applicant for employment, a genuine occupational requirement defence would have been available (*reg 17(4)*).

'Expulsion' is defined additionally to refer to:

(a)   the termination of that person's partnership by the expiration of any period (including a period expiring by reference to an event or circumstance), not being a termination immediately after which the partnership is renewed on the same terms; and

(b)   the termination of that person's partnership by any act of his (including the giving of notice) in circumstances such that he is entitled to terminate it without notice by reason of the conduct of the other partners.

(*Regulation 17(8)*).

Unlawful harassment of partners and candidates for partnership

It is unlawful for a firm, in relation to a position of partner in the firm, to subject to harassment anyone who holds or has applied for that position (*reg 17(2)*).

3.36   **Trade organisations**

Definition

A trade organisation is 'an organisation of workers, an organisation of employers or any other organisation whose members carry on a particular profession or trade for the purposes of which the organisation exists' (*reg 18(4)*). The *Regulations* define 'profession' to include 'any vocation or occupation', and 'trade' to include 'any business'.

Unlawful discrimination against applicants for membership of the organisation

It is unlawful for a trade organisation to discriminate against a person:

(a)   in the terms on which it is prepared to admit him to membership of the organisation; or

(b)   by refusing to accept, or deliberately not accepting, his application for membership.

(*Regulation 18(1)*).

Unlawful discrimination against members

It is unlawful for a trade organisation, in relation to a member of the organisation, to discriminate against him:

(a)   in the way it affords him access to any benefits or by refusing or deliberately omitting to afford him access to them;

(b)   by depriving him of membership, or varying the terms on which he is a member; or

(c)   by subjecting him to any other detriment.

(*Regulation 18(2)*).

3.37 Age Discrimination

Unlawful harassment of members and applicants for membership

It is unlawful for a trade organisation, in relation to a person's membership or application for membership of that organisation, to subject that person to harassment (*reg 18(3)*).

3.37 Qualifications bodies

A qualifications body is 'any authority or body which can confer a professional or trade qualification', excluding institutions of further and higher education and schools (*reg 19(3)*). 'Confer' is defined to include 'renew' and 'extend'. 'Professional or trade qualification' means any authorisation, qualification, recognition, registration, enrolment, approval or certification which is needed for, or facilitates engagement in, a particular profession or trade. Finally 'profession' and 'trade' have the same meaning as they do in *reg 18*.

It is unlawful for a qualifications body to discriminate against a person:

(*a*) in the terms on which it is prepared to confer a professional or trade qualification on him;

(*b*) by refusing or deliberately not granting any application by him for such a qualification; or

(*c*) by withdrawing such a qualification from him or varying the terms on which he hold it.

(*Regulation 19(1)*).

It is also unlawful for a qualifications body, in relation to a professional or trade qualification conferred by it, to subject to harassment a person who holds or applies for such a qualification (*reg 19(2)*).

3.38 Providers of vocational training

A 'training provider' is any person who provides or makes arrangements for the provision of training, but excluding the complainant's employer in relation to training for persons employed by him; any institution of further or higher education and any school (*reg 20(4)*). 'Training' means all types and all levels of training which would help fit a person for any employment, vocational guidance, facilities for training, practical work experience, and any assessment related to the award of any professional or trade qualification (*reg 20(4)*).

Unlawful discrimination against anyone undergoing or seeking to undergo vocational training

It is unlawful, in relation to a person seeking or undergoing training, for any training provider to discriminate against him:

(a) in the arrangements he makes for the purpose of determining to whom he should offer training;

(b) in the terms on which the training provider affords him access to any training;

(c) by refusing or deliberately not affording him such access;

(d) by terminating his training; or

(e) by subjecting him to any other detriment during his training.

(*Regulation 20(1)*).

The provider has a defence where the discrimination concerns training that would only fit a person for employment which, by virtue of the operation of the exception for a genuine occupational requirement, the employer could lawfully refuse to offer the person seeking training (*reg 20(3)*).

Unlawful harassment

It is also unlawful for a training provider, in relation to a person seeking or undergoing training, to subject him to harassment (*reg 20(2)*).

3.39   **Employment agencies, careers guidance, etc**

Employment agencies are addressed in *reg 21*. For the purposes of the *Regulations*, an employment agency is defined as 'a person who, for profit or not, provides services for the purpose of finding employment for workers or supplying employers with workers', excluding institutions of further and higher education and schools (*reg 21(6)(a)*). References to the services of an employment agency include guidance on careers and other services related to employment (*reg 21(6)(b)*).

Unlawful discrimination against users and potential users of an employment agency

It is unlawful for an employment agency to discriminate against a person:

(a)   in the terms on which the agency offers to provide any of its services;

(b)   by refusing or deliberately not providing any of its services; or

(c)   in the way it provides any of its services.

(*Regulation 21(1)*).

The agency will have a defence where the alleged discrimination only concerns employment which the employer could lawfully refuse to offer the person in question by virtue of a genuine occupational requirement (*reg 21(3)*). The agency is not subject to any liability if it proves that it acted in reliance on a statement made to it by the employer to the effect that the act would not be unlawful due to the existence of a genuine occupational requirement but only if it was reasonable for the agency to rely on that statement (*reg 21(4)*).

A person who knowingly or recklessly makes a statement such as this which is false or misleading in a material respect commits an offence punishable by a fine not exceeding level 5 on the standard scale (*reg 21(5)*).

Unlawful harassment of users and potential users of an employment agency

It is also unlawful for an employment agency, to subject a person to whom it provides its services, or who has requested it to provide its services, to harassment (*reg 21(2)*).

3.40   **Secretary of State: Assisting persons to gain employment**

It is unlawful for the Secretary of State to discriminate against any person by subjecting him to a detriment, or to subject a person to harassment, in the provision of facilities or services under *s 2* of the *Employment and Training Act 1973* (arrangements for assisting persons to obtain employment) (*reg 22(1)*).

3.41 Age Discrimination

Excluded from this potential head of liability are circumstances where either *reg 20* (the provision of vocational training) applies or where the Secretary of State is acting as an employment agency within the meaning of *reg 18* (*reg 22(3)*).

3.41 RELATIONSHIPS WHICH HAVE COME TO AN END

Regulation 24 provides that, even where a relationship has come to an end, the risk of liability may, in appropriate circumstances, remain. The regulation is concerned with 'relevant relationships'. A 'relevant relationship' is any relationship 'during the course of which an act of discrimination against or harassment of one party to the relationship ('B') by the other party to it ('A') is unlawful by virtue of any preceding provision of [Part 2 of the Regulations]' (*reg 24(1)*).

Where a relevant relationship has come to an end, it is unlawful for A:

(a)   to discriminate against B by subjecting him to a detriment; or

(b)   to subject B to harassment,

where the discrimination or harassment arises out of, and is closely connected to, that relationship (*reg 24(2)*).

The *Regulations* do not provide any guidance as to when a sufficiently close connection will be established.

Reference to an act of discrimination or harassment which is unlawful includes, in the case of a relationship which has come to an end before the coming into force of the *Regulations*, reference to an act of discrimination which would, after that date, be unlawful (*reg 24(3)*).

3.42 OTHER UNLAWFUL ACTS

Vicarious liability

Liability of employers

Employers are liable for the discriminatory acts of their employees provided those acts are done 'in the course of the [relevant] employment'. Employers are treated as having done what their employees have done. That is so, whether or not the act was done with the employer's knowledge or approval (*reg 25(1)*).

Liability of principals

Anything done by a person as agent for another person with the authority (whether express or implied, and whether precedent or subsequent) of that other person is treated for the purposes of the Regulations as done by that other person as well as by him (*reg 25(2)*).

However, the employer or principal will have a defence where he proves that he took such steps as were reasonably practicable to prevent the employee from doing that act, or from doing acts of that description in the course of his employment (*reg 25(3)*).

3.43 Knowingly aiding unlawful acts

A person who knowingly aids another person to do an act made unlawful by the *Regulations* is treated as if he had committed the unlawful act himself (*reg 26(1)*).

Regulation 26(2) produces a rather unusual set of liabilities. An employee who commits an act of unlawful discrimination is made liable for his own act. So long as the act is performed in the course of employment, the employer is vicariously liable for the employee's act. *Regulation 26(2)* then deems that the wrongdoing employee has 'aided' his employer to commit the act of unlawful discrimination for which the employer is liable. Further, the employee remains liable for aiding an unlawful act on the part of his employer even where the employer escapes liability by making out the 'reasonable steps' defence set out above.

A person is not treated as knowingly aiding another to do an unlawful act where:

(*a*)   he acts in reliance on a statement made to him by that other person that, by reason of any provision of the *Regulations*, the act which he aids would not be unlawful; and

(*b*)   it is reasonable for him to rely on that statement.

(*Regulation 26(3)*).

A person who knowingly or recklessly makes a statement such as this which is false or misleading in a material respect commits an offence, and is liable on summary conviction to a fine not exceeding level 5 on the standard scale (*reg 26(4)*).

3.44   ENFORCEMENT

The *Regulations* set out exhaustively the ways in which proceedings may be brought. Save for a general reservation of the possibility of bringing judicial review proceedings, a complainant can only bring proceedings in the manner and in the circumstances stipulated in the *Regulations* (*reg 35*). Thus, where the *Regulations* provide that the tribunal is to have exclusive jurisdiction in relation to particular types of claim, the complainant cannot commence proceedings dealing with those matters in the courts.

The jurisdiction of the employment tribunals

The tribunal has exclusive jurisdiction over claims of unlawful discrimination of the many types described in the paragraphs above. The exclusive jurisdiction encompasses claims based on vicarious liability and on the aiding of unlawful acts (*reg 36(1)*).

Time limit

An employment tribunal must not consider a complaint of discrimination unless the complaint is presented to the tribunal before the end of the period of three months beginning when the act complained of was done (*reg 42(1)*). However, the tribunal has a very broad discretion to extend time if, in all the circumstances of the case it considers that it is just and equitable to do so (*reg 42(3)*).

Regulation 42(4) makes provision for determining when an act may be said to be 'done' for the purposes of calculating the time limit:

(*a*)   when the making of a contract is, by reason of the inclusion of any term, an unlawful act, that act is treated as extending throughout the duration of the contract; and

(*b*)   any act extending over a period is treated as done at the end of that period; and

(*c*)   a deliberate omission is treated as done when the person in question decided upon it, and, in the absence of evidence establishing the contrary, a person is taken to decide upon an omission when he does an act inconsistent with doing the omitted act or, if he has not performed an inconsistent act, when the period expires within which he might reasonably have been expected to do the omitted act if it was to be done.

Proving discrimination: the questionnaire

The principal difficulty encountered by complainants is obtaining the information necessary to assess the strength of their case and to conduct it successfully once they are satisfied of its merit. The questionnaire procedure is a very powerful tool which aims to address that difficulty.

A person who considers that he may have been discriminated against, or subjected to harassment, can serve on the respondent (or prospective respondent) to a claim in the employment tribunal, questions either in the form set out in *Sch 3* to the *Regulations*, or in a similar form adapted to the circumstances of the case. There are time limits applicable to the service of such questions. Where proceedings have not yet been issued, the questions must be served within three months of the date on which the allegedly discriminatory act was done (*reg 41(4)(a)*). Where proceedings have been commenced, the questions must be served within 21 days of the claim having been presented (*reg 41(4)(b)(i)*). The latter time limit may be extended with the leave of the tribunal.

Schedule 4 to the *Regulations* sets out a form which the respondent can use to assist in structuring his answers to the questions.

The questions, together with any answers given by the respondent, are admissible as evidence in the proceedings. Furthermore, if it appears to the tribunal that the respondent deliberately, and without reasonable excuse, omitted to reply within eight weeks of the service of the questions, or that his reply is evasive or equivocal, the tribunal may draw any inference from that fact that it considers it just and equitable to draw, including an inference that the respondent committed an unlawful act (*reg 41(2)*).

Regulation 41(5) makes detailed provision as to how questions and answers may be served on the other party. Service may be effected:

(*a*)   by delivering the questions or answers to the other party;

(*b*)   by sending it by post at the party's usual or last known address;

(*c*)   where the person served is a body corporate or a trade union or employers' association, by delivering them to the secretary or clerk of that body, union or association at its registered or principal office or by sending it by post to the secretary or clerk at that office;

(*d*)   where the person to be served is acting by a solicitor, by delivering it at, or by sending it by post to, the solicitor's address for service; or

(*e*)   where the person to be served is the person aggrieved, by delivering the reply, or sending it by post, to him at his address for reply as stated by him in the document containing the questions.

The provisions set out above are without prejudice to 'any other enactment or rule of law regulating interlocutory or preliminary matters in proceedings before [an] employment tribunal, and have effect subject to any enactment or rule of law regulating the admissibility of evidence in such proceedings' (*reg 41(6)*).

Proving discrimination: the burden of proof

The burden of proof on an employee bringing a claim of age discrimination will be the same as that in most other forms of discrimination. Where, on the hearing of a complaint, the complainant proves facts from which the tribunal could conclude in the absence of an adequate explanation that the respondent:

(*a*)   has committed an unlawful act against the complainant falling within the jurisdiction of the employment tribunal; or

(*b*)   is either vicariously liable for such an act or has knowingly aided the commission of such an act;

the tribunal should uphold the complaint unless the respondent proves that he did not commit, or as the case may be, is not to be treated as having committed, the act (*reg 37(2)*).

General guidance on the application of this test was provided in *Wong v Igen* [2005] EWCA Civ 142, [2005] ICR 931. For a more detailed consideration of the burden of proof in discrimination cases, see 13.3 DISCRIMINATION AND EQUAL OPPORTUNITIES – II.

Remedies available from the employment tribunal

Where an employment tribunal finds that a complaint presented to it is well-founded, the tribunal must provide one or more of the remedies set out below. It should exercise its discretion as to remedy by focusing on what is just and equitable. The possible remedies are:

(*a*)   an order declaring the rights of the complainant and the respondent in relation to the act to which the complaint relates ('a declaration');

(*b*)   an order requiring the respondent to pay to the complaint compensation of an amount corresponding to any damages he could have been ordered by a county court to pay to the complainant if the complaint had fallen to be dealt with under the jurisdiction of the county court; and

(*c*)   a recommendation that the respondent take within a specified period action appearing to the tribunal to be practicable for the purpose of obviating or reducing the adverse effect on the complainant of any act of discrimination or harassment to which the complaint relates ('a recommendation').

(*Regulation 38(1)*).

In cases of indirect discrimination, the tribunal's power to award compensation is more limited where the respondent is able to establish that he had no intention of treating the complainant unfavourably on grounds of age. In essence, the tribunal is required first to consider whether, if it had no power to order compensation, it would make a declaration and/or recommendation. If it decides that it would not do so, it can move on to consider compensation. If it decides that it would do so, it should first make the declaration or recommendation and then ask itself whether it is just and equitable to make an award of compensation as well (*reg 38(2)*).

If, without reasonable justification, the respondent to a complaint fails to comply with a recommendation made by an employment tribunal, then, if it thinks it just and equitable to do so:

(a)   the tribunal may increase the amount of compensation required to be paid to the complainant; or

(b)   if a compensation order was not made, the tribunal may make one.

(*Regulation 38(3)*).

The tribunal may award interest on the award subject to, and in accordance with, the provisions of the *Employment Tribunals* (*Interest on Awards in Discrimination Cases*) *Regulations 1996* (*SI 1996/2803*).

The employment tribunal would appear to be able to make an award for injury to feelings (see *reg 38(1)(b)*) read with *reg 39(3)*).

3.45   **VALIDITY OF CONTRACTS, COLLECTIVE AGREEMENTS AND RULES OF UNDERTAKINGS**

Validity and revision of contracts

Schedule 5 to the *Regulations* makes detailed provision as to the fate of discriminatory contractual terms.

Where:

(*a*)   the making of the contract is, by reason of the inclusion of the term, unlawful by virtue of the *Regulations*;

(*b*)   a particular term is included in furtherance of an act which is unlawful by virtue of the *Regulations*; or

(*c*)   the term provides for the doing of an act which is unlawful by virtue of the *Regulations*;

the relevant term of the contract is void (*para 1(1)* of *Sch 5*).

This principle does not apply to a term the inclusion of which constitutes, or is in furtherance of, or provides for, unlawful discrimination against, or harassment of a party to the contract. However, that term is unenforceable against that party (*para 1(2)* of *Sch 5*).

Where a party to a contract considers that a term is void or unenforceable for one of the reasons set out above, it can apply to the county court to obtain an order removing or modifying the offending term (*para 3*).

A term in a contract which purports to exclude or limit any provision of the *Regulations* is unenforceable by any person in whose favour the term would operate (*para 1(3)*). However, there is an exception for compromise contracts which are made with the assistance of a conciliation officer (so called COT3 agreements) and for compromise agreements which satisfy the following conditions:

(*a*)   the contract is in writing;

(*b*)   the contract relates to the particular complaint;

(*c*)   the complainant has received advice from a relevant independent adviser as to the terms and effect of the proposed contract and in particular its effect on his ability to pursue a complaint before an employment tribunal;

(*d*)   there must be in force, when the adviser gives the advice, a contract of insurance, or an indemnity provided for members of a profession or professional body, covering the risk of a claim by the complainant in respect of loss arising in consequence of the advice;

(*e*)   the contract must identify the adviser; and

(*f*)   the contract must state that the conditions regulating compromise contracts under *Sch 5* are satisfied (*Sch 4, para 2*).

A person is a 'relevant independent adviser' if:

(*a*)   he is a qualified lawyer;

(*b*)   he is an officer, official, employee or member of an independent trade union who has been certified in writing by the trade union as competent to give advice and as authorised to do so on behalf of the trade union; or

(*c*)   he works at an advice centre (whether as an employee or a volunteer) and has been certified in writing by the centre as competent to give advice and as authorised to do so on behalf of the centre.

(*Sch 5 para 2(3)*).

A person is not a 'relevant independent adviser':

(*a*)   if he is employed by, or is acting in the matter for the other party, or is a person who is connected with the other party;

(*b*)   in the case of a person within (b) and (c) immediately above, if the trade union or advice centre is the other party or a person who is connected with the other party; or

(*c*)   in the case of a person within sub-para (c) immediately above, if the complainant makes a payment for the advice received from him.

(*Sch 5, para 2(4)*).

Any two persons are to be treated as connected if one is a company of which the other (directly or indirectly) has control, or else if both are companies of which a third person (directly or indirectly) has control (*Sch 5, para 2(8)*).

'Qualified lawyer' means a barrister (whether in practice as such or employed to give legal advice), a solicitor who holds a practising certificate, or a person other than a barrister or solicitor who is an authorised advocate or authorised litigator (within the meaning of the *Courts and Legal Services Act 1990*)(*Sch 5, para 2(5)*).

'Independent trade union' has the same meaning as in the *Trade Unions and Labour Relations (Consolidation) Act 1992* (see TRADE UNIONS – I, II (50, 51)).

An agreement under which the parties agree to submit a dispute to arbitration is regarded as being a contract settling a complaint if the dispute is covered by a scheme having effect by virtue of an order under *s 212A* of the *Trade Union and Labour Relations (Consolidation) Act 1992* and the agreement is to submit it to arbitration in accordance with the scheme. However, in other cases, it is not regarded as being nor including such a contract (*para 2(9)*).

Collective agreements and rules of undertakings

Provision in relation to collective agreements and the rules of undertakings are set out in *Sch 5 Part 2* to the *Regulations*. That part of the *Schedule* applies to:

(*a*)   any term of a collective agreement, including an agreement which was not intended, or is presumed not to have been intended, to be a legally enforceable contract;

(*b*)   any rule made by an employer for application to all or any of the persons who are employed by him or who apply to be, or are, considered by him for employment;

(c)   any rule made by a trade organisation (within the meaning of *reg 18*) or a qualifications body (within the meaning of *reg 19*) for application to:

   (i)   all or any of its members or prospects members; or

   (ii)   all or any of the persons on whom it has conferred professional or trade qualifications (within the meaning of *reg 19*) or who are seeking the professional or trade qualifications which it has power to confer.

(*Para 4(1)*).

Any term or rule to which Part 2 applies is void where:

(a)   the making of the collective agreement is, by reason of the inclusion of the term, unlawful by virtue of the *Regulations*;

(b)   the term or rule is included in furtherance of an act which is unlawful by virtue of the *Regulations*; or

(c)   the term or rule provides for the doing of an act which is unlawful by virtue of the *Regulations*;

This rule applies whether the agreement was entered into, or the rule made, before of after the date on which the *Regulations* come into force (ie 1 October 2006). However, in the case of an agreement entered into, or a rule made, before the date on which the *Regulations* came into force, that sub-paragraph does not apply in relation to any period before that date (*Sch 5, Pt 2, para 4*).

Para 5 of Sch 5 allows for presentation of a complaint to an employment tribunal where the complainant has reason to believe:

(a)   that the term or rule may at some future time have effect in relation to him; and

(b)   where he alleges that it is void by virtue of *para 4(2)(c)* that:

   (i)   an act for the doing of which it provides, may at some such time by done in relation to him; and

   (ii)   the act would be unlawful by virtue of the *Regulations* if done in relation to him in present circumstances.

In the case of a complaint about:

(a)   a term of a collective agreement made by or on behalf of:

   (i)   an employer,

   (ii)   an organisation of employers of which the employer is a member, or

   (iii)   an association of such organisations, one of which the employer is a member, or

(b)   a rule made by an employer within the meaning of *para 4(1)(b)* of *Pt 2* of *Sch 2*,

a complaint to the tribunal may be made by any person who is, or is genuinely and actively seeking to become, one of his employees (*para 6, Sch 2*).

In the case of a complaint about a rule made by an organisation or body to which *para 4(1)(c)* of *Part 2* of *Sch 4* applies, a complaint to the tribunal may be made by any person:

(a)   who is, or is genuinely and actively seeking to become, a member of the organisation or body;

(b)   on whom the organisation or body has conferred a professional or trade qualification (within the meaning of *reg 19*); or

(c)   who is genuinely and actively seeking such a professional or trade qualification which the organisation or body has to confer.

(*Para 7*).

When an employment tribunal finds that a complaint presented to it is well-founded the tribunal makes an order declaring that the term or rule is void. The order may include provision in relation to any period before the making of the order (but after the coming into force of the *Regulations*) (*para 8*).

The avoidance of any term or rule which provides for any person to be discriminated against is without prejudice to the following rights (except in so far as they enable any person to require another person to be treated less favourably than himself):

(a)   such of the rights of the person to be discriminated against; and

(b)   such of the rights of any person who will be treated more favourably in direct or indirect consequence of the discrimination,

as are conferred by, or in respect of, a contract made or modified wholly or partly in pursuance of, or by reference to, that term or rule (*para 9*).

'Collective agreement' means 'any agreement relating to one or more of the matters mentioned in *Trade Union and Labour Relations* (*Consolidation*) *Act 1992, s 178(2)* (meaning of trade dispute), being an agreement made by or on behalf of one or more employers or one or more organisations of employers or associations of such organisations with one or more organisations of workers or associations of such organisations' (*para 10*).

3.46   APPLICATION TO CROWN SERVANTS AND HOUSE OF COMMONS AND HOUSE OF LORDS STAFF

Regulations 44 to *46* make detailed provision in relation to Crown servants (but not members of the armed forces) and House of Commons and House of Lords staff which are beyond the scope of this work.

3.47   RETIREMENT DISMISSALS AND AGE DISCRIMINATION

The *Regulations* also contain extremely complicated provisions relating to the retirement of individuals. This matter is addressed in more detail in RETIREMENT (42), particularly at 41.3. The following paragraphs summarise the key provisions.

Employers' duty to notify

An employer will be under a duty to notify the employee of an upcoming retirement. An employer who intends to retire an employee has a duty to notify the employee in writing of the date on which he intends the employee to retire and of the employee's right to request to work beyond that date. This notification must be made not more than one year and not less than six months before that date: *para 2(1), Sch 6* to the *Regulations*.

Paragraph 4 of *Sch 6* to the *Regulations* provides that, where an employer has failed to give such notice, there is a continuing duty to notify the employee in writing until the fourteenth day before the date of termination. The phrase used is the 'operative date of termination'. This means either the date upon which the notice is to expire or, if there is no notice, the date on which the termination of the employment contract takes effect: see *para 1(1)* of *Sch 6*.

It should be noted that an employee may present a complaint to the Employment Tribunal that his employer has failed to comply with the duty to notify under *para 2*. The Tribunal may award compensation of an amount up to 8 weeks' pay: *para 11* of *Sch 6*.

Employees' right to request continued working

An employee has the right to make a request not to retire on the intended date of termination. The request must be in writing and must state that it is made under the relevant paragraph. It must state whether the employee wishes the employment to continue indefinitely, for a stated period or until a stated date. An employee may make only one such request in relation to any one intended date of retirement: see *para 5* of *Sch 6*. There are also provisions as to the necessary timing of such a request.

Employers' duty to consider the request

Where a request is made, an employer is under a duty to consider the request: *para 6*. The requirement that the employer consider the request 'in good faith' does not appear in the latest version of the *Regulations*. Unless the employer and employee agree the employment will continue indefinitely, the employer must, in most circumstances, hold a meeting with the employee to discuss the request within a reasonable period.

Following that meeting (or, where applicable, the employer's consideration) the employee must give the employee notice of his decision. If the request is accepted, the notice must state this. If the request is refused, the notice must confirm the employer's wish to retire the employee and the date on which the dismissal is to take effect. The notice must be dated. If the employer does not fully accede to the employee's request, the notice must inform the employee of the right to appeal (*para 7* of *Sch 6*).

Appeals

An employee is entitled to appeal against an employer's refusal of his or her request by giving notice as soon as reasonably practicable after notice has been given (*para 8* of *Sch 6*). An appeal notice must set out the grounds of appeal.

In most cases, the employer must hold a meeting with the employee to discuss the appeal. This duty applies in the same situations as the duty to hold a meeting to discuss the original request.

Where meetings are held to consider requests or appeals, the employee has a right to be accompanied (*para 9* of *Sch 6*). If an employer fails, or threatens to fail, to comply with the provisions concerning the right to be accompanied, a tribunal may make an award of up to two weeks' pay if the employee brings a complaint.

Transitional provisions

There are detailed transitional provisions set out in *Sch 7*. They are included here as ongoing cases may relate to matters that arose during the transitional period. These provisions use the term 'expiry date'. This means the date on which notice of dismissal given by an employer expires.

Where:

(*a*)   an employer has given notice of the dismissal before 1 October 2006 of:

   (i)   at least the period required by the contract of employment; or

   (ii)   where the period required by the contract exceeds four weeks, at least four weeks;

(*b*)   the expiry date falls before 1 April 2007; and

(*c*)   the employer has made the employee aware, before 1 October 2006, that the employer considers that the employee is being retired on the expiry date;

then, if the employer on or as soon as is practicable after 1 October 2006, notifies the employee in writing of the employee's right to make a request under *para 5* of *Sch 6*:

(*a*)   the employer will be treated as having complied with the duty to notify the employee;

(*b*)   a request will be treated as having been made under *para 5* of *Sch 6* provided it:

   (i)   is made after the employer notified the employee of his right to make a request;

   (ii)   satisfies the requirements of *sub-paras* (*2*) and (*3*) of *para 5* of *Sch 6*; and

   (iii) is made:

      (1)   where practicable, at least four weeks before the expiry date; or

      (2)   where that is not practicable, as soon as reasonably practicable (whether before or after the expiry date) after the employer notified the employee of his right to make a request, but not more than four weeks after the expiry date.

However, if in otherwise similar circumstances, the employer does not, on or as soon as is practicable after 1 October 2006, notify the employee in writing of the employee's right to make a request:

(*a*)   the duty to notify in accordance with *para 2* of *Sch 6* does not apply;

(*b*)   the duty to notify in accordance with *para 4* of *Sch 6* applies as if

   (i)   the employer had failed to notify in accordance with *para 2* of *Sch 6*; and

   (ii)   the duty was to notify at any time before the expiry date;

(*c*)   a request will be treated as being a request under *para 5* of *Sch 6* if it satisfies the requirements of *sub-paras* (*2*) and (*3*) of *Sch 6* and is made:

   (i)   before any notification given in accordance with *para 4* of *Sch 6*; or

   (ii)   after such notification and:

      (1)   where practicable, at least four weeks before the expiry date; or

      (2)   where that is not practicable, as soon as reasonably practicable (whether before or after the expiry date) after the employer

notified the employee of his right to make a request, but not more than four weeks after the expiry date.

(*Para 2, Sch 7*).

The next situation is where an employer has given notice of dismissal to the employee before 1 October 2006, the expiry date falls before 1 April 2007, but the period of notice given is shorter than the minimum period of notice required by the contract of employment or, where that notice exceeds four weeks, at least four weeks.

In this situation:

(*a*)   the duty to notify in accordance with *para 2* of *Sch 6* does not apply;

(*b*)   the duty to notify in accordance with *para 4* of *Sch 6* applies as if:

    (i)   the employer had failed to notify in accordance with *para 2* of *Sch 6*; and

    (ii)   the duty was to notify at any time before the expiry date

(*c*)   a request will be treated as being a request under *para 5* of *Sch 6* if it satisfies the requirements of *sub-paras* (2) and (3) of *Sch 6* and is made:

    (i)   before any notification given in accordance with *para 4* of *Sch 6*; or

    (ii)   after such notification and:

        (1)   where practicable, at least four weeks before the expiry date; or

        (2)   where that is not practicable, as soon as reasonably practicable (whether before or after the expiry date) after the employer notified the employee of his right to make a request, but not more than four weeks after the expiry date.

(*Para 3, Sch 7*).

The situation is different again where notice of dismissal is given on or after 1 October 2006 of at least the period required by the contract of employment or, if longer, the period required by *s 86, ERA 1996* and the expiry date falls before 1 April 2007.

In this case, if the employer notifies the employee in writing of the employee's right to make a request under *para 5* of *Sch 6* before, or on the same day as, the date on which notice of dismissal is given:

(*a*)   the employer will be treated as having complied with the duty to notify the employee;

(*b*)   a request will be treated as having been made under *para 5* of *Sch 6* provided it:

    (i)   is made after the employer notified the employee of his right to make a request;

    (ii)   satisfies the requirements of *sub-paras* (2) and (3) of *para 5* of *Sch 6*; and

    (iii)   is made-

        (1)   where practicable, at least four weeks before the expiry date; or

        (2)   where that is not practicable, as soon as reasonably practicable (whether before or after the expiry date) after the employer

notified the employee of his right to make a request, but not more than four weeks after the expiry date.

However, if in this same situation, the employer does not notify the employee in writing of the employee's right to make a request before, or on the same day as, the day on which notice of dismissal is given:

(*a*)   the duty to notify in accordance with *para 2* of *Sch 6* does not apply;

(*b*)   the duty to notify in accordance with *para 4* of *Sch 6* applies as if:

   (i)   the employer had failed to notify in accordance with *para 2* of *Sch 6*; and

   (ii)   the duty was to notify at any time before the expiry date;

(*c*)   a request will be treated as being a request under *para 5* of *Sch 6* if it satisfies the requirements of *sub-paras* (*2*) and (*3*) of *Sch 6* and is made:

   (i)   before any notification given in accordance with *para 4* of *Sch 6*; or

   (ii)   after such notification and-

      (1)   where practicable, at least four weeks before the expiry date; or

      (2)   where that is not practicable, as soon as reasonably practicable (whether before or after the expiry date) after the employer notified the employee of his right to make a request, but not more than four weeks after the expiry date.

(*Para 4, Sch 7*).

The final situation addressed in the transitional provisions is where notice of dismissal is given on or after 1 October 2006 and is for a period shorter than that required by the contract of employment or, if longer, that required by *ERA 1996, s 86* and the period of notice expires on a date falling before 1 April 2007. In this case:

(*a*)   the duty to notify in accordance with *para 2* of *Sch 6* does not apply;

(*b*)   the duty to notify in accordance with *para 4* of *Sch 6* applies as if:

   (i)   the employer had failed to notify in accordance with *para 2* of *Sch 6*; and

   (ii)   the duty was to notify at any time before the expiry date;

(*c*)   a request will be treated as being a request under *para 5* of *Sch 6* if it satisfies the requirements of *sub-paras* (*2*) and (*3*) of *Sch 6* and is made:

   (i)   before any notification given in accordance with *para 4* of *Sch 6*; or

   (ii)   after such notification and-

      (1)   where practicable, at least four weeks before the expiry date; or

      (2)   where that is not practicable, as soon as reasonably practicable (whether before or after the expiry date) after the employer notified the employee of his right to make a request, but not more than four weeks after the expiry date.

(*Para 5, Sch 7*).

In all of these situations, *para 10* of *Sch 6* does not apply and the employer is under a duty to consider any request made by the employee to continue working in accordance with *paras 7* to *9* of *Sch 6* (see further above at 3.37).

3.48 UNFAIR DISMISSAL AND AGE DISCRIMINATION

The *Regulations* will also make significant amendments to the *ERA 1996*. Most importantly, the age limit on bringing claims of unfair dismissal will be abolished. New provisions are then inserted to make retirement a potentially fair reason for the dismissal. There are detailed provisions as to when retirement is the reason for a dismissal and whether a dismissal by reason of retirement will be fair.

With regard to unfair dismissal, the first question to ask is whether retirement is the reason for the dismissal. It is only then that the question of fairness can be addressed.

Is retirement the reason for the dismissal?

Retirement will be a potentially fair reason for dismissal (*s 98(2)(ba)*, *ERA 1996*). There are complicated provisions to determine the circumstances in which retirement is the reason for the dismissal. The structure of the *Regulations* is that, in some circumstances, retirement is taken to be the only reason for the dismissal, in others, retirement cannot be a reason for the dismissal while in others, the Tribunal will be required to consider whether retirement is the principal reason for the dismissal.

Retirement is the only reason for the dismissal in the following circumstances:

(*a*) the employee has no 'normal retirement age', the date of termination falls after the employee's 65th birthday, the employer has properly notified the employee of the intended retirement in accordance with *para 2* of *Sch 6*, and the employment contract terminates on the intended date (above);

(*b*) there is a 'normal retirement age', that age is 65 or higher, the date of termination falls after the employee reaches the normal retirement age, the employer has properly notified the employee, and the employment contract terminates on the intended date; or

(*c*) there is a 'normal retirement age' of under 65, this retirement age is justified, the date of termination is on or after the employee reached this age, the employer has properly notified the employee and the employment contract terminates on the intended date.

('Normal retirement age' means the age at which employees in the employer's undertaking who hold, or have held, the same kind of position as the employee are normally required to retire (*ERA 1996, s 98ZH*).)

However, retirement is not the reason for the dismissal if:

(*a*) the employee has no 'normal retirement age' and the date of termination falls before the date when the employee reaches the age of 65;

(*b*) the contract of employment terminates before the intended date of retirement, whether or not there is a 'normal retirement age', whether or not that age is above or below 65 and regardless of whether the employer has properly notified the employee; or

(*c*) there is a 'normal retirement age', and the date of termination falls before the date on which the employee reaches that age;

(*d*)   there is a 'normal retirement age' of under 65 and it constitutes unlawful discrimination under the Regulations for the employee to have that normal retirement age (ie that it cannot be justified).

The apparent effect of (d) immediately above is that, where there is a normal retirement age of under 65 which is not justified, the employer will *never* be able to retire an employee, even when he is over the age of 65. (*Regulation 30(2)* will not assist the employer as it only applies where retirement is the reason for the retirement in accordance with the provisions summarised above.)

In other cases, the Tribunal (or court) must consider whether or not retirement was the reason for the dismissal. In so doing, particular regard must be had to:

(*a*)   whether the employer informed the employee of the intended retirement more than 14 days before the intended date of retirement;

(*b*)   how long before the notified retirement date the notification was given;

(*c*)   whether or not the employer followed the procedures relating to the duty to consider a request to work beyond retirement.

Fairness

If the reason or principal reason for a dismissal is retirement, the employee is regarded as unfairly dismissed if and only if there has been a failure on the part of the employer to comply with one or more of the following provisions of *Sch 6* to the *Regulations*:

(*a*)   the continuing duty to notify the employee of the retirement until 14 days before the intended date of retirement (*para 4*, if not already given under *para 2*);

(*b*)   the duty to consider the employee's request not to be retired (*para 6* and *7*);

(*c*)   the duty to consider an appeal against the decision to refuse a request not to be retired (*para 8*).

In all other circumstances, a retirement dismissal will be fair.

3.49   PENSIONS AND AGE DISCRIMINATION

Schedule 2 to the *Regulations* sets out the provisions as they apply to occupational pensions schemes. For guidance as to the application of these provisions, see RETIREMENT (42).

4   Children and Young Persons

The employment of children and young persons is restricted by legislation, the most important of which is summarised below. In addition, a new right for young persons in employment to take time off from work for study or training is outlined. Also summarised is the contractual capacity of children and young persons, insofar as it concerns contracts of employment.

Cross-reference. See EDUCATION AND TRAINING (16) for the 'New Deal' and other training schemes.

4.1   DEFINITIONS

Child. For the purposes of the statutory provisions relating to the employment of children, a child is a person not over compulsory school age (at present, 16 years – see *Education Act 1996, s 8*) (*Education Act 1996, s 558*).

Young person. A person who has ceased to be a child and who is under the age of 18 years (*Education Act 1996, s 579(1)*). (However, note that there is a different definition in the *Management of Health and Safety at Work Regulations 1999* – see 4.5 below.)

Minor. A person who is under the age of 18 years (ie a child or young person) (*Family Law Reform Act 1969, s 1*).

4.2   RESTRICTIONS ON EMPLOYMENT OF CHILDREN

The *Children (Protection at Work) Regulations 1998* (*SI 1998/276*), which came into force on 4 August 1998, amended the *Children and Young Persons Acts 1933 and 1963* in order to implement the provisions of the *EC Young Workers Directive on the Protection of Young People at Work* (*94/33*) relating to the employment of children. At the same time that these *Regulations* were introduced, the Government announced that it would be conducting a general review of child employment legislation, which was completed in the summer of 1999. The response of the Government to the review's findings is still awaited. In the meantime, the *Children (Protection at Work) Regulations 2000* (*SI 2000/1333*) and the *Children (Protection at Work) (No 2) Regulations 2000* (*SI 2000/2548*), which came into force on 7 June 2000 and 11 October 2000, respectively, made some additional minor amendments to the *Children and Young Persons Act 1933* so as to give further effect to the *EC Directive 94/33* referred to above.

The main provisions restricting the employment of children, as amended by the above-mentioned *Regulations*, are outlined below.

In general, no child may be employed whether paid or not:

(*a*)   if he is under the age of 14 years; or

(*b*)   to do any work other than light work; or

(*c*)   before the close of school hours on any day on which he is required to attend school; or

(*d*)   before seven o'clock in the morning or after seven o'clock in the evening on any day; or (*e*)   for more than two hours on any day on which he is required to attend school; or

(*f*)   for more than 12 hours in any week in which he is required to attend school; or

(*g*)   for more than two hours on any Sunday; or

(*h*)   for more than eight hours or, if he is under the age of 15 years, for more than five hours on any day (other than Sunday) on which he is not required to attend school; or

(*i*)   for more than 35 hours or, if he is under the age of 15 years, for more than 25 hours in any week in which he is not required to attend school; or

(*j*)   for more than four hours in any day without a rest break of at least one hour; or

(*k*)   at any time in a year unless at that time, he has had (or could still have), during a school holiday, at least two consecutive weeks without employment.

'Light work' is defined by reference to the *EC Directive 94/33* referred to above, and means work which (on account of the inherent nature of the tasks which are involved and the particular conditions under which they are performed) is not likely to be harmful to a child's safety, health, development, attendance at school or participation in work experience.

(*Children and Young Persons Act 1933, s 18(1)*, *(2A)* as amended; see also 4.3 below.)

In *Addison v Ashby* [2003] IRLR 211, the EAT held that a 15-year old paper boy was not a 'worker' within the meaning of the *Working Time Regulations 1998*, and was therefore not entitled to four weeks' paid annual leave in accordance with *reg 13* (see 29.2 HOLIDAYS). The definition of 'young person' in those regulations (ie a person who is over compulsory school age and under 18 — see 4.6 below) was not intended to include a child. Children are provided for by separate legislation, namely the *Children and Young Persons Act 1933, s 18(1)* which had been amended to give effect to the *EC Young Workers Directive* and which provided, in relation to holidays, that during a school holiday a child must have two consecutive weeks without employment (see (*k*) above).

The *Education Act 1996, s 560* (replacing the *Education (Work Experience) Act 1973, s 1*) provides that, with certain exceptions, the enactments relating to the prohibition or regulation of the employment of a child in his last two years of compulsory schooling shall not apply where the employment is in pursuance of arrangements made or approved by the local education authority, or by the governing body of a school on behalf of such an authority, with a view to providing him with work experience as a part of his education. However, the enactments regulating the employment of young persons apply to a child on a work experience programme (*Education Act 1996, s 560(4), (5)*).

4.3   Local authority powers

Local authorities are empowered under the *Children and Young Persons Acts 1933–1969* (as amended) to pass bye-laws restricting the employment of children. Among other matters, any such bye-laws may authorise:

4.3 Children and Young Persons

(*a*) the employment on an occasional basis of children aged 13 years (notwith-standing anything in 4.2(a) above) by their parents or guardians in light agricultural or horticultural work;

(*b*) the employment of children aged 13 years (notwithstanding anything in 4.2(a) above) in categories of light work specified in the bye-law; and

(*c*) the employment of children for not more than one hour before the commencement of school hours on any day on which they are required to attend school (notwithstanding anything in 4.2(c) above).

(*Children and Young Persons Act 1933, s 18(2), as amended.*)

The employer who breaches such a bye-law will be guilty of a criminal offence as will any person (other than the person employed) by whose act or default a contravention took place (*Children and Young Persons Act 1933, s 21*).

In *Portsea Island Mutual Co-operative Society Ltd v Leyland* [1978] IRLR 556, the Divisional Court quashed the convictions recorded against the company under *s 21, CYPA 1933*. A milk roundsman, exceeding his authority and contrary to the company's instructions, had engaged a boy of 10 years of age to deliver milk on a Sunday before 9 am, contrary to the local authority's bye-laws. Talbot J held ([1978] IRLR 556 at 558) that an employer can be liable for such a contravention only if either he employed the child or if an agent of his who is engaged to take persons into his employment (e g a personnel manager) did so.

If it appears to a local education authority that a child is being employed in such a manner as to be prejudicial to his health, or otherwise to render him unfit to obtain the full benefit of the education provided for him, the authority may serve a notice in writing on the employer: (*a*) prohibiting him from employing the child, or (*b*) imposing such restrictions upon his employment of the child as appear to be expedient in the child's interests (*Education Act 1996, s 559(1)*). A local education authority may serve a notice in writing on the parent or employer of a child requiring the parent or employer to provide the authority, within such period as may be specified in the notice, with such information as appears to be necessary for enabling them to ascertain whether the child is being employed in such a manner as to render him unfit to obtain the full benefit of the education provided for him (*Education Act 1996, s 559(2)*). A person who (i) employs a child in contravention of any prohibition or restriction imposed under *s 559(1)*, or (ii) fails to comply with the requirements of a notice served under *s 559(2)*, is guilty of an offence and liable on summary conviction to a fine or imprisonment or both (*Education Act 1996, s 559(3), (4)*). The provisions of *s 559* will cease to have effect when *s 2* of the *Employment of Children Act 1973* (see below) comes into force.

Employment of Children Act 1973. When the *Employment of Children Act 1973* comes into force, each local education authority will be given the following powers to supervise the employment of children in its area.

(*a*) *Requiring particulars.* It will be able to require particulars of how the child is employed, or is about to be employed, and at what times and for what periods from:

(i) the child's parent or any person responsible for the child (ie with parental responsibility for the child or care of him); or

54

(ii)   the person appearing to have the child in his employment or to be about to employ him.

(*Employment of Children Act 1973, s 2(2), (2A)*, as amended by *Children Act 1989, Sch 13 para 32.*)

(b)   *Prohibiting or restricting employment.* If it appears to the authority that a child is currently employed, or is about to become employed, in a way (or at times or for periods) which is not unlawful but is unsuitable for the child (by reference to his age or state of health), or otherwise prejudicial to his education, by a notice served on either the parent or the employer it will be able to:

(i)   prohibit the child's employment in any manner specified in the notice; or

(ii)   require his employment to be subject to such conditions (specified in the notice and to be complied with by the person served with it) as the authority thinks fit to impose in the interests of the child.

(*Employment of Children Act 1973, s 2(3).*)

4.4   Other provisions

(a)   No child may be employed in any industrial undertaking unless the undertaking is one in which only members of the same family are employed (*Employment of Women, Young Persons and Children Act 1920, ss 1(1), 3(2), Sch*).

(b)   No child may be employed in any sea-going United Kingdom ship (*Merchant Shipping Act 1995, s 55(1A)*, inserted by the *Merchant Shipping (Hours of Work) Regulations 2002 (SI 2002/2125)*).

(c)   Special provisions regulate the employment of children in entertainment (*Children and Young Persons Act 1933, ss 23–26* as amended by *EA 1989, Sch 3 Part III* and *SI 2000/1333; Children and Young Persons Act 1963, ss 37–42* as amended by *SI 1998/276* (see above)).

(d)   The *Management of Health and Safety at Work Regulations 1999* also apply to the employment of children (see 4.5 below). In addition to his other obligations, every employer must, before employing a child, provide comprehensible and relevant information to the parents of (or those with parental responsibility for) the child on the outcome of the risk assessment, and on the control measures that the employer has introduced (*reg 10(2)*).

4.5   EMPLOYMENT OF YOUNG PERSONS

Health and safety

Until recently, the employment of young persons in factories and shops was governed by the *Shops Act 1950*, the *Factories Act 1961* and the *Offices, Shops and Railway Premises Act 1963* ('*OSRPA 1963*'), as amended by *EA 1989*. The *Young Persons (Employment) Act 1938* ('*YPEA 1938*') governed a wide variety of employments, but was repealed by *EA 1989*, which also repealed many of the restrictions contained in the *Factories Act 1961*. The remaining restrictions in the *Factories Act 1961*, together with those in the *Offices, Shops and Railway Premises Act 1963*, were repealed by the *Health and Safety (Young Persons) Regulations 1997 (SI 1997/135)*, which are dealt with below. The provisions of the *Shops*

Act 1950 governing employment in shops, including the employment of young persons, were repealed by the *Deregulation and Contracting Out Act 1994.*

The Secretary of State has power to repeal statutory provisions relating to the employment of persons or classes of persons who have not attained the age of 18 (or a specified lower age not less than 16); he may also amend such provisions so that they refer to school-leaving age rather than a specific age (*EA 1989, s 10(3)(b), (c)*). But the exercise of those powers may not affect provisions relating to the employment of persons under school-leaving age (*EA 1989, s 10(4)*). The powers given have so far been used to amend and revoke a number of statutory instruments (*Employment Act 1989 (Amendments and Revocations) Order 1989 (SI 1989/2311)*).

The *Health and Safety (Young Persons) Regulations 1997 (SI 1997/135)*, which came into force on 3 March 1997, implemented the health and safety provisions of the *EC Directive on the Protection of Young People at Work (94/33)*. They were based on proposals set out in a consultative document published by the Health and Safety Commission in March 1996. They extended the risk assessment and information requirements of the *Management of Health and Safety at Work Regulations 1992* by amending those *Regulations*, and they also removed various provisions relating to the health and safety of young persons which were regarded as outdated and unnecessary.

The *1992 Regulations* were revoked and replaced by the *Management of Health and Safety at Work Regulations 1999 (SI 1999/3242)* with effect from 29 December 1999; the *1999 Regulations* also revoked the *Health and Safety (Young Persons) Regulations 1997*, having incorporated the changes originally made by those Regulations. References below are to the *1999 Regulations*; note that in the *1999 Regulations* 'young person' means any person under 18, so that they also apply to the employment of children. The *1999 Regulations* do not apply to the master or crew of a ship (*reg 2*); for separate provisions governing the health and safety of young persons engaged as workers on United Kingdom ships, see the *Merchant Shipping and Fishing Vessels (Health and Safety at Work) (Employment of Young Persons) Regulations 1998 (SI 1998/2411)*. The last-named Regulations also prescribe rest periods for young persons so engaged: see 4.6 below.

Before young persons start work, the employer is required to assess the risks to their health and safety, taking particular account of:

(*a*)   their inexperience, their absence of awareness of existing or potential risks, and their immaturity;

(*b*)   the fitting-out and layout of the workplace and the workstation;

(*c*)   the nature, degree and duration of exposure to physical, biological and chemical agents;

(*d*)   the form, range and use of work equipment and the way in which it is handled;

(*e*)   the organisation of processes and activities;

(*f*)   the extent of the health and safety training provided or to be provided to young persons; and

(*g*)   risks from agents, processes and work listed in the Annex to *Directive 94/33* (referred to above).

(*Regulation 3(5)*.)

In addition, every employer must ensure that young persons employed by him are protected at work from any risks to their health or safety which are a consequence of the factors referred to in (*a*) above (*reg 19(1)*). Furthermore, the employment of young persons is prohibited for work:

(i)　which is beyond their physical or psychological capacity;

(ii)　involving harmful exposure to agents which are toxic or carcinogenic, cause heritable genetic damage or harm to the unborn child, or which in any other way chronically affect human health;

(iii)　involving harmful exposure to radiation;

(iv)　involving the risk of accidents which it may reasonably be assumed cannot be recognised or avoided by young persons owing to their insufficient attention to safety or lack of experience or training; or

(v)　in which there is a risk to health from extreme cold or heat, noise or vibration.

In determining whether work will involve harm or risk for these purposes, the employer must have regard to the results of the assessment referred to above (*reg 19(2)*).

However, the prohibition in *reg 19(2)* does not apply in relation to young persons over school-leaving age where (i) the work is necessary for their training, (ii) the young person will be supervised by a competent person, and (iii) the risks are reduced to their lowest practicable level (*reg 19(3)*).

4.6　Rest periods, breaks and night work

Following the publication in February 1997 by the DTI of a consultation document to implement the provisions of *Directive 94/33* (see above) which cover night work, and entitlement to rest periods, for young persons, the DTI subsequently announced that it intended to implement those provisions by including them in the regulations for implementing the *EC Working Time Directive (93/104)*.

Both Directives were implemented by the *Working Time Regulations 1998 (SI 1998/1833)*, which came into force on 1 October 1998. With regard to young persons (referred to in those *Regulations* as 'young workers'), *Directive 94/33* sets a limit on working time of eight hours per day and 40 hours per week, and prohibits night work altogether. However, in the draft *Regulations* which were originally issued for consultation, the Government stated that it proposed to take advantage of the opt-outs available in the *Directive* which disapplied those limits, as it believed 'that the working time limits set out in the Working Time Directive provide sufficient protection for all workers'. Thus, the original wording of the *Working Time Regulations 1998* did not provide for separate limits on working time for young workers, and the adult limits were applicable to them. (For a summary of the adult limits, see 28.15 HEALTH AND SAFETY AT WORK – II.)

The opt-outs referred to above ceased to be available on 22 June 2000, and the Government issued a consultation document in December 2000 seeking views on how the remaining provisions of the *Directive* should be implemented. In June 2002, the Government issued a further consultation document (see www.dti.gov.uk/er/work_time_regs) to which draft amending *Regulations* were annexed. These amending *Regulations* were subsequently issued as the *Working Time (Amendment) Regulations 2002 (SI 2002/3128)* and came into force on 6 April 2003. From that date the *1998 Regulations* were amended so as to:

4.6 Children and Young Persons

(a) limit the working hours of young workers to no more than 40 hours per week, or eight hours in any one day – an employer must take all reasonable steps, in keeping with the need to protect the health and safety of workers, to ensure that these limits are complied with in respect of each young worker employed by him (*reg 5A*); and

(b) prohibit night working by young workers between 10pm to 6am (or 11pm to 7am) (*reg 6A*).

These new provisions protecting young workers were added to the existing special entitlements in the *1998 Regulations* which apply to young workers, which are set out below:

(c) a health and capacities assessment before being required to perform night work, and periodically thereafter (*reg 7(2)*);

(d) a minimum daily continuous rest period of 12 hours (*reg 10(2)*);

(e) two days off per week (*reg 11(3)*); and

(f) a minimum 30-minute rest break after 4½ hours of continuous work (*reg 12(4)*).

Note that the protections and entitlements set out in (a) to (f) above are subject to the following exceptions.

Domestic servants. Regulations 5A, 6A, and *7(2)* do not apply in relation to a young worker employed as a domestic servant in a private household (*reg 19,* as amended).

Armed forces. Regulations 5A, 6A, 10(2) and *11(3)* do not apply in relation to a young worker serving as a member of the armed forces, although where such a young worker is accordingly required to work during the restricted period, or is not permitted the minimum rest period provided for in *reg 10(2)* or *11(3)*, he must be allowed an appropriate period of compensatory rest (*reg 25(2),* as amended).

Force majeure. Regulations 5A, 6A, 10(2) and *12(4)* do not apply in relation to a young worker where his employer requires him to undertake work which no adult worker is available to perform and which:

(i) is occasioned by either an occurrence due to unusual and unforeseeable circumstances, beyond the employer's control, or exceptional events, the consequences of which could not have been avoided despite the exercise of all due care by the employer;

(ii) is of a temporary nature; and

(iii) must be performed immediately.

Where the application of *regs 5A, 6A, 10(2)* or *12(4)* is excluded by virtue of (i) to (iii) above, and a young worker is accordingly required to work during a period which would otherwise be a rest period or rest break, his employer must allow him to take an equivalent period of compensatory rest within the following three weeks (*reg 27,* as amended).

Other restrictions applicable to young workers. Regulation 5A does not apply in relation to a young worker:

(1) where the young worker's employer requires him to undertake work which is necessary either to maintain continuity of service or production or to respond to a surge in demand for a service or product;

(2)   where no adult worker is available to perform the work; and

(3)   where performing the work would not adversely affect the young worker's education or training.

(*Regulation 27A(1)*, inserted by *SI 2002/3128*).

In addition, in the circumstances referred to in (1) to (3) above:

(*a*)   *reg 6A* does not apply in relation to a young worker employed—

   (i)   in a hospital or similar establishment; or

   (ii)   in connection with cultural, artistic, sporting or advertising activities; and

(*b*)   *reg 6A* does not apply, except in so far as it prohibits work between midnight and 4am, in relation to a young worker employed in—

   (i)   agriculture;

   (ii)   retail trading;

   (iii)   postal or newspaper deliveries;

   (iv)   a catering business;

   (v)   a hotel, public house, restaurant, bar or similar establishment; or

   (vi)   a bakery.

(*Regulation 27A(2)(3)*, inserted by *SI 2002/3128*.)

Where the application of *reg 6A* is excluded by para (*a*) or (*b*) above, and a young worker is accordingly required to work during a period which would otherwise be a rest period or rest break—

   (i)   he must be supervised by an adult worker where such supervision is necessary for the young worker's protection; and

   (ii)   he must be allowed an equivalent period of compensatory rest.

(*Regulation 27A(4)*, inserted by *SI 2002/3128*.)

Remedies. *Regulation 30* (as amended) provides that a young worker may complain to an employment tribunal where his employer has refused to permit him to exercise any right he has:

(*a*)   under *reg 10(2), 11(3),* or *12(4)*; or

(*b*)   to compensatory rest under *reg 25(3), 27A(4)(b)* or *27(2)*.

The time limit for the presentation of such a complaint is three months beginning with the day on which it is alleged that the exercise of the right should have been permitted (or in the case of a rest period or leave extending over more than one day, the date on which it should have been permitted to begin). If the tribunal is satisfied that it was not reasonably practicable for the complaint to be presented within the period of three months (see 20.7 EMPLOYMENT TRIBUNALS – I), then this time may be extended. In certain circumstances, the time limit may be extended by virtue of *reg 15* of the *Employment Act 2002 (Dispute Resolution) Regulations 2004 (SI 2004/752)*.

Where the tribunal finds the complaint well-founded, it must make a declaration to that effect, and may make an award of compensation to be paid by the employer to the worker. The amount of the compensation will be such as the tribunal considers just and equitable in all the circumstances having regard to—

(i)   the employer's default in refusing to permit the worker to exercise his right; and

(ii)   any loss sustained by the worker which is attributable to the matters complained of.

(For separate provisions governing rest periods for young persons engaged as workers on United Kingdom ships, see the *Merchant Shipping and Fishing Vessels (Health and Safety at Work) (Employment of Young Persons) Regulations 1998 (SI 1998/2411), reg 6*.)

4.7   TIME OFF FOR YOUNG PERSONS FOR STUDY OR TRAINING

A new right for young persons in employment to take time off from work for study and training, by virtue of *ERA 1996, ss 63A–63C* (inserted by the *Teaching and Higher Education Act 1998, s 32*), came into effect on 1 September 1999 (see *SI 1999/987*).

An employee who:

(*a*)   is aged 16 or 17;

(*b*)   is not receiving full-time secondary or further education; and

(*c*)   has not attained the prescribed standard of achievement,

is entitled to be permitted by his employer to take time off during the employee's working hours in order to undertake study or training leading to a relevant qualification (*ERA 1996, s 63A(1)*). The study or training may be either on the premises of the employer (or principal – see below) or elsewhere (*ERA 1996, s 63A(7)*). For the 'prescribed standard of achievement', see the *Right to Time Off for Study or Training Regulations 2001 (SI 2001/2801)*, which revoked and replaced the *1999 Regulations (SI 1999/986)* with effect from 1 September 2001.

A 'relevant qualification' means an external qualification the attainment of which (i) would contribute to the attainment of the prescribed standard referred to in (*c*) above, or (ii) would be likely to enhance the employee's employment prospects, whether with his employer or otherwise (*ERA 1996, s 63A(2)(c)*). An 'external qualification' means an academic or vocational qualification awarded or authenticated by such person or body as may be specified in *Regulations* (as to which, see the *Schedule to SI 2001/2801* referred to above).

An employee who satisfies the requirements in (*a*) to (*c*) above, and is subcontracted by his employer to another person ('the principal'), is entitled to be permitted by the principal to take time off for the purposes specified in *s 63A(1), ERA 1996 (ERA 1996, s 63A(3)*). An 18-year-old employee who is undertaking study or training leading to a relevant qualification which he began before attaining that age has a similar right to time off (*ERA 1996, s 63A(4)*).

The amount of time off that an employee is to be permitted to take, and the occasions on which and the conditions under which time off is to be taken, are those that are reasonable in the circumstances having regard, in particular, to (*a*) the requirements of the employee's study or training, and (*b*) the circumstances of the business of the employer (or the principal) and the effect of the employee's time off on the running of that business (*ERA 1996, s 63A(5)*).

An employee who is allowed time off is entitled to be paid for the time taken off at the 'appropriate hourly rate', ie one week's pay divided by the number of normal working hours in a week for that employee when employed under the contract of employment in force on the day when the time off is taken (*ERA 1996, s 63B(1), (2)*). (For the calculation of the normal hourly rate where the number of normal working hours differs from week to week or over a longer period, see *ERA 1996, s 63B(3), (4)*.)

4.8 **Remedy for refusal of, or remuneration for, time off**

If the employer (or principal) has unreasonably refused the employee time off or has refused to pay him, the employee may present a complaint to an employment tribunal (*ERA 1996, s 63C(1)*). The time limit for the presentation of such a complaint is three months beginning with the day on which it is alleged the time off should have been allowed. If the tribunal is satisfied that it was not reasonably practicable for the complaint to be presented within the period of three months (see 20.7 EMPLOYMENT TRIBUNALS – I), then this time may be extended (*ERA 1996, s 63C(2)*).

If the employment tribunal finds the complaint well-founded, it will make a declaration to that effect (*ERA 1996, s 63C(3)*). If the complaint is of an unreasonable refusal to permit the employee to take time off, the tribunal will also order the employer or principal to pay the employee remuneration for the period during which the time off should have been allowed (*ERA 1996, s 63C(4)*). If the complaint is of a refusal to pay the employee for the time off, the tribunal will also order the employer or principal to pay the employee the amount due to him (*ERA 1996, s 63C(5)*).

4.9 **Right not to suffer detriment**

By virtue of *ERA 1996, s 47A* (inserted by the *Teaching and Higher Education Act 1998, s 44*), an employee who is entitled to (i) time off under *ERA 1996, s 63A(1)* or *63A(3)* and (ii) remuneration under *ERA 1996, s 63B(1)* for that time off (see 4.7 above), has the right not to be subjected to a detriment (ie an action short of dismissal) by his employer or principal on the ground that the employee exercised (or proposed to exercise) that right or received (or sought to receive) such remuneration.

If the employee suffers such a detriment, the remedy is to complain to an employment tribunal pursuant to *ERA 1996, s 48*. (For details, see 28.10 HEALTH AND SAFETY AT WORK – II.)

4.10 **CONTRACTS OF EMPLOYMENT, AND MINORS**

Contracts of employment form an important exception to the general principle that any contract made by a minor is unenforceable against him during his minority.

A contract of service or apprenticeship which enables a minor to earn a living is likely to be upheld, as being for his benefit (*Doyle v White City Stadium Ltd* [1935] 1 KB 110; this principle was followed by analogy in *Chaplin v Leslie Frewin (Publishers) Ltd* [1966] Ch 71, which concerned a contract for the publication of a book). The effect of the entire contract must be considered; the contract will be upheld if on the whole it is for the minor's benefit (*Clements v London and North Western Rly Co* [1894] 2 QB 482), but it will not be binding on the minor if it is not in his interests, or is clearly unreasonable or oppressive (*De Francesco v Barnum* (1890) 45 Ch D 430). Where a contract is, on the whole, for the minor's benefit, but it contains invalid covenants which are severable, such covenants may be struck out and the remainder of the contract upheld (see *Bromley v Smith* [1909] 2 KB 235).

The *Minors' Contracts Act 1987* made some limited amendments to the law relating to minors' contracts generally. In particular, it repealed the *Infants Relief Act 1874*, thereby enabling a minor, on or after reaching the age of majority, to ratify an otherwise unenforceable contract which he had entered into as a minor (*MCA 1987, s 1*).

5   Codes of Practice

Cross-references. See 11.4 DISCLOSURE OF INFORMATION for details of ACAS Code No 2 and 11.14 DISCLOSURE OF INFORMATION for the Codes of Practice in relation to Data Protection issued by the information Commissioner; 28.21 HEALTH AND SAFETY AT WORK – II for the HSC Code on Safety Representatives and Safety Committees; 49.2, 49.3 and 49.9 TIME OFF WORK for ACAS Code No 3 and the HSC Code on Time Off for Training of Safety Representatives. See also 10.32 DISABILITY DISCRIMINATION for the Code of Practice for the elimination of discrimination in the field of employment against disabled persons or persons who have had a disability.

5.1   The first Code of Practice (now revoked) was introduced under powers conferred by the *Industrial Relations Act 1971*. Since then a number of other Codes have been issued. Codes of Practice are written in clear terms for the layman in order to give practical guidance. Employers are advised to read the existing and any new Codes of Practice issued and to follow their provisions whenever applicable. Although following a Code of Practice does not guarantee success in any potential claim in an employment tribunal, the employer who can show that he has followed its provisions will be on firm ground.

In broad terms, these Codes of Practice cannot be enforced by law. Nor does breach of a Code *of itself* give rise to any liability. However, Codes may be taken into account in legal proceedings. This chapter considers the powers which exist enabling specified bodies or people to issue Codes and the particular legal effect of the different Codes.

5.2   **THE CODES OF PRACTICE ISSUED BY ACAS**

Power to issue the Codes

The original *Industrial Relations Code of Practice* was issued under the *Industrial Relations Act 1971* and continued in force on the repeal of that Act by the *Trade Union and Labour Relations Act* (the predecessor statute to *TULRCA*: see below) and then by the *Employment Protection Act 1975*. However, having become largely superseded, it was revoked by the *Employment Codes of Practice* (*Revocation*) *Order 1991* (*SI 1991/1264*).

The *Employment Protection Act 1975* gave ACAS the power to issue Codes of Practice, subject to approval by both Houses of Parliament. That power is now contained in the *Trade Union and Labour Relations* (*Consolidation*) *Act 1992* (*'TULRCA 1992'*), *s 199*. Three such Codes (as amended) have been issued:

ACAS Code of Practice No 1 on Discipline and Grievance Procedures (which was substantially revised in the light of the implementation, with effect from 1 October 2004, of the dispute resolution procedures in Part 3 of the *Employment Act 2002*) (see *The Employment Act 2002* (*Dispute Resolution*) *Regulations 2004* (*SI 2004/752*)). The new Code of Practice No 1 represents a substantial departure from the previous form of Code No 1 and provides helpful guidance on the complicated provisions relating to the conduct of disciplinary hearings after 1 October 2004, and has particular relevance for unfair dismissal claims.

ACAS Code of Practice No 2 on Disclosure of Information to Trade Unions for Collective Bargaining Purposes.

5.3   Codes of Practice

ACAS Code of Practice No 3 on Time Off for Trade Union Duties and Activities. This Code was amended in the light of changes made to rights to time off work introduced by the provisions of the *Employment Act 2002* (see FURTHER TIME-OFF WORK (49)). The new Code of Practice No 3 came into force on 27 April 2003 (*SI 2003/1191*).

As each of the three Codes has during their history been the subject of substantial revision, in all cases the most up-to-date versions of the Codes should always be consulted.

Each of the revised Codes is available for download in pdf format from the ACAS website (www.acas.org.uk).

Where ACAS proposes to issue a Code, or a revised Code, it must first publish a draft and consider any representations made to it. If ACAS decides to proceed, the draft (modified if need be) is transmitted to the Secretary of State, who may either approve it or publish his reasons for withholding approval. If the Secretary of State approves the draft, it is laid before Parliament (*TULRCA 1992, ss 200, 201*).

The legal status of the Codes remains unchanged – they do not have legal effect but may be taken into account by an employment tribunal in determining the fairness of any dismissal (see 5.3 below).

5.3   Legal effect

TULRCA 1992, s 207(1), (2) states that breach of the ACAS Codes does not render a person liable to proceedings but that the Codes shall be admissible and are to be taken into account if relevant in any proceedings before an employment tribunal or the Central Arbitration Committee ('CAC').

Non-compliance with a Code will not necessarily render a dismissal unfair, but 'a failure to follow a procedure prescribed in the Code may lead to the conclusion that a dismissal was unfair, which, if that procedure had been followed, would have been held to have been fair' (*W Devis & Sons Ltd v Atkins* [1977] AC 931 at 955).

However, a tribunal does not err in law if it fails to take account of the Codes in a case where their provisions are not relied upon by the parties (*Shakespeare v British Coal Corpn* (1998) Times, 5 April).

5.4   CODES ISSUED BY THE DTI

Power to issue the Codes

TULRCA 1992, ss 203 and *204* empower the Secretary of State to issue Codes of Practice, after consultation with ACAS, to be approved by both Houses of Parliament. Such Codes are to contain practical guidance for the purpose of promoting the improvement of industrial relations or promoting desirable practices in relation to the conduct by trade unions of ballots and elections. The Codes currently applicable are The *Code on Picketing* (*1992*), the *Code of Practice on Industrial Action Ballots and Notice to Employers* (*2005*) and the *Code of Practice on Access and Unfair Practices During Recognition Ballots* (*2005*). The *Code on Picketing* is a reissued and revised version of the previous Code (see *Employment Code of Practice (Picketing) Order 1992* (*SI 1992/476*)). The other two Codes were laid before Parliament on 18 July 2005 and came into force on 1 October 2005 replacing the previous Codes: *Industrial Action Ballots and Notice to Employers* (2000) and: *Access to Workers during Recognition and Derecognition*

Ballots (*2000*) which, pursuant to TULRCA s 208(2) ceased to have effect on that date. The 2005 Codes incorporate changes made by the Employment Relations Act 2004 (see TRADE UNIONS – I, II (50, 51)) as well as updating and revising the earlier Codes. Care should be taken to ensure that the 1 October 2005 versions of these Codes are consulted. The new Codes are currently available at www.dti.gov.uk/er/union.htm.

A previously issued Code – *Code on Closed Shop Agreements and Arrangements* was revoked by the *Employment Codes of Practice* (*Revocation*) *Order 1991* (*SI 1991/1264*) and accordingly should not be consulted.

Copies of the revised code on Picketing may be obtained from the DTI website at www.dti.gov.uk/er/union/picketing-pl928.htm.

The Department of Trade and Industry Codes may supersede any part of or all of a Code issued by ACAS or a previous DTI or Department of Employment Code (*TULRCA 1992, s 208(2)*) (see above).

5.5   Legal effect

Although a failure to comply with the Codes issued by the Secretary of State does not itself render a person liable to proceedings, the Codes are stated to be admissible in evidence and to be taken into account, if relevant, in any proceedings not only before an employment tribunal or the CAC but also, in the case of a DTI or Department for Education and Employment Code, in any court (*TUL-RCA 1992, s 207(1),* (*3*)). Thus, in *Thomas v National Union of Mineworkers (South Wales Area)* [1985] ICR 886 at 920–921 Scott J granted an injunction, following violent picketing, to restrain the union from organising pickets in greater numbers than were suggested by the relevant Code.

5.6   CODES ISSUED BY THE COMMISSION FOR RACIAL EQUALITY

Power to issue the Codes

The *Race Relations Act 1976, s 47* empowers the Commission for Racial Equality to issue Codes of Practice containing practical guidance for either or both of the following purposes:

(*a*)   the elimination of discrimination in the field of employment; and

(*b*)   the promotion of equality of opportunity in that field between persons of different racial groups.

The Commission for Racial Equality ('CRE') had issued a Code of Practice back in April 1984 which had remained in force for over twenty years. Following a period of consultation beginning in 2004, with effect from 6 April 2006 a new Code of Practice on Racial Equality in Employment (2005) has been issued replacing the 1984 Code for England Wales and Scotland. The text of the new Code of Practice may be found on the CRE's website (www.cre.gov.uk/gdpract/employmentcode2005.html)

The CRE has also published a Code of Practice on the Duty to Promote Racial Equality (in force from May 2002) as a consequence of the duty imposed by *the Race Relations (Amendment) Act 2000* on public bodies to promote racial equality. (See DISCRIMINATION AND EQUAL OPPORTUNITIES – I, II, III (12, 13, 14).)

5.7 Codes of Practice

5.7 Legal effect

The *Race Relations Act 1976, s 47(10)* provides that a failure to observe any provision in a Code of Practice shall not of itself render a person liable to proceedings. However, such Codes are admissible in evidence and, where relevant, are to be taken into account in any proceedings before an employment tribunal. In any proceedings commenced after 6 April 2006 the provisions of the new Code of Practice will be used.

5.8 CODES ISSUED BY THE EQUAL OPPORTUNITIES COMMISSION

Power to issue the Codes

The *Sex Discrimination Act 1975, s 56A* empowers the Equal Opportunities Commission to issue Codes of Practice containing practical guidance for either or both of the following purposes:

(*a*)the elimination of discrimination in the field of employment; and

(*b*)the promotion of equality of opportunity in that field between men and women.

The Equal Opportunities Commission has issued a Code of Practice which came into force on 30 April 1985. (See DISCRIMINATION AND EQUAL OPPORTUNITIES – I, II, III (12, 13, 14).)

More recently, the Equal Opportunities Commission has issued a new Code of Practice on Equal Pay, which was brought into force on 1 December 2003 by the *Code of Practice on Equal Pay Order 2003* (*SI 2003/2865*). The new Code is admissible in evidence in any proceedings under the *SDA 1975* or the *Equal Pay Act 1970* (see 4.9 below) and new additions include information on equal pay for pregnant women and those on maternity leave, the Equal Pay Questionnaire procedure and equal pay reviews and grievance procedures. (See EQUAL PAY (24).)

5.9 Legal effect

The *Sex Discrimination Act 1975, s 56A* (as amended by *TURERA 1993, Sch 7 para 15*) provides that a failure to observe any provision in a Code of Practice shall not of itself render a person liable to proceedings. However, such Codes are admissible in evidence and, where relevant, are to be taken into account in any proceedings before an employment tribunal under that *Act* or the *Equal Pay Act 1970*.

5.10 CODES ISSUED BY THE HEALTH AND SAFETY COMMISSION

Power to issue the Codes

Regulations made under the *Health and Safety at Work, etc Act 1974* ('*HSWA 1974*') are sometimes supplemented by Codes of Practice approved and/or issued by the Health and Safety Commission (for details of which see 27.28 HEALTH AND SAFETY AT WORK – I) (*HSWA 1974, s 16*). A full consideration of these Codes is beyond the scope of this book. Two such Codes are directly relevant to employment law: the HSC *Code of Practice on Safety Representatives and Safety Committees* and the HSC *Code of Practice on Time Off for Training Safety Representatives*. They both supplement the *Safety Representatives and Safety Committees Regulations 1977* (*SI 1977/500*) as amended by *SI 1992/2051*, made under *HSWA 1974*.

5.11   **Legal effect**

Non-compliance with a relevant HSC Code does not of itself render a person liable to any civil or criminal proceedings. However, where in any criminal proceedings a person is alleged to have committed an offence by contravening a provision for which a Code of Practice was in force, if breach of the Code is established, the offence is proved unless the court is satisfied that the requirement or prohibition was complied with otherwise than by observance of the Code (*HSWA 1974, s 17*).

CODES ISSUED BY THE DEPARTMENT FOR EDUCATION AND EMPLOYMENT AND THE DISABILITY RIGHTS COMMISSION

5.12   **Power to issue the Codes**

The *Disability Discrimination Act 1995, s 53* empowered the Secretary of State to issue Codes of Practice containing such practical guidance as he considers appropriate with a view to:

(*a*)   eliminating discrimination in the field of employment against disabled persons and persons who have had a disability; and

(*b*)   encouraging good practice in relation to the employment of disabled persons and persons who have had a disability.

The Secretary of State had issued a Code of Practice which came into effect on 2 December 1996. That Code was repealed from October 2004 (SI 2004/2300).

The current relevant Code of Practice is the Disability Rights Commission Code of Practice on Employment and Occupation promulgated under powers conferred by *s 53A* of the *Disability Discrimination Act 1995* (as added by the *Disability Rights Commission Act 1999*). By *s 53A* the Disability Rights Commission is empowered to issue codes of practice giving practical guidance on how to avoid unlawful discrimination and guidance on the operation of the Disability Discrimination Act and on promoting the equalisation of opportunities for disabled persons and for the purpose of encouraging good practice. (see DISABILITY DISCRIMINATION (10)).

5.13   **Legal effect**

A failure on the part of any person to observe any provision of a Code of Practice does not of itself make that person liable to any proceedings. However, such a Code is admissible in evidence in any proceedings under the *DDA 1995* before an employment tribunal, a county court or a sheriff court and, where relevant, it is to be taken into account in determining any question arising in any such proceedings (*DDA 1995, s 53A(8)* and (*8A*) and for the predecessor code see *DDA, s 53(4)–(6)*).

5.14   **CODES ISSUED BY THE INFORMATION COMMISSIONER**

The Information Commissioner issued the Employment Practices Data Protection Code in four parts. Part 1: Recruitment and Selection: March 2002. Part 2: Employment Records: August 2002. Part 3: Monitoring at Work: June 2003. Part 4: Information about Workers Health: December 2004. The Code is issued pursuant to statutory authority conferred on the Information Commissioner by *s 51(3)(b)* of the *Data Protection Act 1998*. The Codes promulgated by the Information Commissioner do not have formal legal status or effect unlike the other codes of practice considered above. The Information Commissioner is, however, the enforcing authority for the purposes of the Data Protection Act 1998 and the Code may reasonably be assumed to represents the views of the

Information Commissioner in relation to the standards of practice to be expected of employers in relation to the subject matters covered by the Code.

5.15 **REVISION AND REVOCATION OF CODES**

Provision has been made for the revision by the appropriate authority of those Codes which are issued under *TULRCA 1992, s 203* (ie the Department of Employment or DTI Codes; see 5.4 above) or which are issued under *TULRCA 1992, s 199* (ie the ACAS Codes; see 5.2 above). ACAS may revise its Codes under *TULRCA 1992, s 201* and the Secretary of State may revise the Department of Employment or DTI Codes under *TULRCA 1992, s 205*. Similar procedural provisions apply as in the case of making new Codes. The Secretary of State may, with Parliamentary approval, revoke either an ACAS or a Department of Employment Code (*TULRCA 1992, ss 202, 206*). In the case of an ACAS Code, he may do so only at the request of ACAS.

6   Collective Agreements

6.1   In large industries, the wage rates and terms and conditions of employment of workers in those industries are frequently determined by collective agreements. These are negotiated by the trade unions and employers or employers' associations in the industry concerned. The collective agreements may form the basis for the individual worker's contract of employment if it is agreed between the parties that they should do so.

For the purposes of the *Trade Union and Labour Relations (Consolidation) Act 1992* ('*TULRCA 1992*'), a collective agreement is defined in *s 178* as 'any arrangement or agreement made by or on behalf of one or more trade unions and one or more employers or employers' associations' which relates to one or more of the following matters:

'(a)   terms and conditions of employment, or the physical conditions in which any workers are required to work;

(b)   engagement or non-engagement, or termination or suspension of employment or the duties of employment, of one or more workers;

(c)   allocation of work or the duties of employment between workers or groups of workers;

(d)   matters of discipline;

(e)   a worker's membership or non-membership of a trade union;

(f)   facilities for officials of trade unions; and

(g)   facilities for negotiation or consultation, and other procedures, relating to any of the above matters, including the recognition by employers or employers' associations of the right of a trade union to represent workers in such negotiation or consultation or in the carrying out of such procedures.'

6.2   Legal effect

Any collective agreement made before 1 December 1971, or after 16 September 1974, will be conclusively presumed not to have been intended by the parties to the agreement to be a legally enforceable contract unless the agreement:

(a)   is in writing; and

(b)   contains a provision which (however expressed) states that the parties intend that the agreement shall be a legally enforceable contract,

in which event it is conclusively presumed to be legally enforceable (*TULRCA 1992, s 179(1)(2), Sch 3 para 5*). Condition (b) is not satisfied by a mere statement in the agreement that the parties are to be bound by it (*NCB v NUM* [1986] ICR 736).

However, where an employer is required to recognise a trade union in accordance with the provisions of *Sch 1* to the *Employment Relations Act 1999* (see TRADE UNIONS – I (50)), any agreement reached concerning collective bargaining will have effect as a legally enforceable contract made between the parties. The only remedy for breach will be specific performance (*Employment Relations Act 1999, Sch 1 paras 30–31*).

6.3   Effect on individual contracts of employment

Although collective agreements may not be legally enforceable by the union against the employer or vice versa, they may have legally binding consequences as between the employer and the individual employee. Their terms may be incorporated into individual contracts of employment either because the contract expressly provides for such incorporation, or because incorporation is an implied term of the contract deriving from custom and practice in the industry. In either case, the collective agreement will be incorporated, notwithstanding that the particular employee may not approve of what the union has negotiated, or may even have ceased to belong to the relevant union (see, e g *Tocher v General Motors (Scotland) Ltd* [1981] IRLR 55). A collective agreement will not be incorporated into individual contracts of employment merely because the employer belongs to the association which negotiated that agreement (*Hamilton v Futura Floors Ltd* [1990] IRLR 478). In *Marley v Forward Trust Group Ltd* [1986] ICR 891, the Court of Appeal held that an employee could enforce the terms of a collective agreement on redundancy which was incorporated into his contract, even though the agreement itself was expressed to be 'binding in honour only'.

However, some terms of collective agreements, such as the terms of conciliation schemes, may not be apt to become enforceable by or against individual employees, and will not be treated as incorporated (*NCB v NUM* [1986] ICR 736). Provisions dealing with, for example, relations between an employer and a union operate at a collective level and are inappropriate for incorporation as terms of individual contracts. In order to decide whether a particular provision in a collective agreement is incorporated into a contract, it is necessary to consider the context in which the provision arises. The greater the extent to which the surrounding terms are not apt for incorporation, the less likely it will be that any individual term is apt for incorporation into an individual contract. It is also necessary to consider the particular term in question and whether it is formulated in a way which permits enforcement as part of an individual contract. In *Alexander v Standard Telephones and Cables plc* the judge hearing an application for an interlocutory injunction considered it arguable that a 'last in first out' clause in a collective agreement was incorporated into individual contracts ([1990] ICR 291), but when the case came to trial it was held on the facts that there was no such incorporation ([1991] IRLR 286). Similarly in *Kaur v MG Rover Group Ltd* [2005] IRLR 40 a provision in a collective agreement which stated that 'there will be no compulsory redundancy' did not have effect as a term of the individual contracts of employment between the employer and each employee. See also *Keeley v Fosroc International Ltd* [2006] IRLR 961.

The principles applicable to the construction of collective agreements are the same as those which apply to other contracts. One construes the words used in their factual context (*Adams v British Airways plc* [1996] IRLR 574). Where the terms of a collective agreement are truly ambiguous, it is permissible to look at a clearly established practice, which continues both before and after an agreement is made, as evidence of what the parties meant by the agreement (*Dunlop Tyres Ltd v Blows* [2001] EWCA Civ 1032, [2001] IRLR 629; see also CONTRACT OF EMPLOYMENT (8)).

In the case of *Ali v Christian Salvesen* [1997] ICR 25, [1997] IRLR 17, the Court of Appeal addressed the question of implying terms into collective agreements and took a restrictive approach. The court acknowledged that such agreements are reached between the two sides of industry and will inevitably involve compromises between their interests. The case concerned an 'annualised hours' contract. Under that contract, the employees were employed to work a notional 40-hour week but in fact were expected to work far more flexible hours. There would be no entitlement to overtime pay until the number of hours calculated over a year exceeded a specified figure. The individual workers in the case had worked for more than 40 hours per week, but their contracts had been terminated before the number of hours worked in the year exceeded the specified figure. The question was whether they could claim overtime in respect of the number of hours which they had worked in excess of 40 per week. There was no express term which governed what should happen in this situation. The employees therefore based their case on an implied term. The Court of Appeal rejected the implication of a term to cover this situation. Waite LJ pointed out that this was one of several situations for which the collective agreement had not made provision. However, he refused to imply a term, stating that when a matter had not been covered in a collective agreement, the natural inference was that it had been intentionally omitted because it was either too controversial or too complicated to justify inclusion. This decision shows that courts will be reluctant to fill perceived gaps in collective agreements by the use of implied terms and that if the parties to an agreement wish to deal with a particular situation, it is incumbent on them to make express provision for it.

In *Henry v London General Transport Services* [2002] EWCA Civ 488, [2002] IRLR 472, the employers entered into negotiations with a union, the TGWU, in preparation for a management buy-out. There had been a history of negotiations with the TGWU but there was no express incorporation of terms collectively agreed. The TGWU and the employers agreed a framework agreement which contained new and less advantageous terms and conditions, including reduced pay. The tribunal held that the terms of the framework agreement were so fundamental that the past practice of negotiations leading to the incorporation of terms collectively agreed was not such as to enable these changes to be incorporated into individual contracts. The Court of Appeal disagreed. The matters which were the subject of the framework agreement were apt for incorporation into individual contracts. Further if the appropriate custom and practice was established, it could be expected to cover all contractual terms. The tribunal had been wrong to draw a distinction between fundamental and other terms without identifying a basis for that distinction.

6.4   Changes to collective agreements

Once the terms of a collective agreement are incorporated into individual contracts, the relevant contractual terms are, as a matter of general principle, unaffected by the termination of the collective agreement (*Robertson v British Gas Corpn* [1983] ICR 351; *Gibbons v Associated British Ports* [1985] IRLR 376; *Lee v GEC Plessey Telecommunications* [1993] IRLR 383). A further example of this principle is shown by *Whent v T Cartledge Ltd* [1997] IRLR 153. In that case individual terms were expressed to be determined in accordance with a collective agreement which had transferred from the original employer to another pursuant to the *Transfer of Undertakings (Protection of Employment) Regulations 1981 (SI 1981/1794)* (see TRANSFER OF UNDERTAKINGS (52)). The transferee employer withdrew recognition from the trade union and pulled out of the collective agreement. The EAT nonetheless held that individuals retained the right under their individual contracts of employment to the benefits provided for by the

6.5 Collective Agreements

collective agreement. However, the true construction of the contract of employment may be that it incorporates the collective agreement between employer and union which is for the time being in force. In such a case, agreed variations in the collective agreement will be effective to alter the terms of the individual contracts of employment.

Where the document which is incorporated is not a collective agreement but a set of rules promulgated by the employer, and the employer is entitled unilaterally to amend those rules, the employee cannot enforce any contractual rights where the employer changes the rules so as to withdraw benefits under them (*Cadoux v Central Regional Council* [1986] IRLR 131)(see CONTRACT OF EMPLOYMENT (8)).

6.5 'No strike' clauses

Any provision of a collective agreement which prohibits or restricts the right of workers to engage in a strike or other industrial action, or has the effect of prohibiting or restricting that right, will by law be excluded from forming any part of the contract of employment of an individual worker with an individual employer. This restriction will apply unless the collective agreement:

(*a*)   is in writing; and

(*b*)   contains a provision stating that those terms shall or may be incorporated in such a contract; and

(*c*)   is reasonably accessible at his place of work to the worker to whom it applies and is available for him to consult during working hours; and

(*d*)   is one where each trade union which is a party to the agreement is an independent trade union (see 46.22 TRADE UNIONS – I); and

(*e*)   the individual contract with the worker expressly or impliedly incorporates those terms of the collective agreement relating to strikes.

(*TULRCA 1992, s 180.*)

Despite the fact that a collective agreement and an individual's contract of employment may comply with all the requirements of *s 180*, no court will order specific performance of a contract of employment or grant an injunction restraining a breach, or threatened breach, of such a contract which would have the effect of compelling an employee to do any work or attend at any place for the doing of any work (*TULRCA 1992, s 236*).

6.6 Miscellaneous

Subject to certain preconditions, collective agreements are automatically transferred from vendor to purchaser on the transfer of an undertaking (*Transfer of Undertakings (Protection of Employment) Regulations 1981 (SI 1981/1794), reg 6(a)*) (see TRANSFER OF UNDERTAKINGS (52)).

Terms in collective agreements which are discriminatory between men and women are void, and a complaint to that effect may be made to the tribunal (*Sex Discrimination Act 1986, s 6* as amended by *TURERA 1992, s 32*). (See *Nimz v Freie und Hansestadt Hamburg* [1991] IRLR 222; and DISCRIMINATION AND EQUAL OPPORTUNITIES – I, II, III (12, 13, 14).)

7 Continuous Employment

(See DTI booklet 'Rules governing continuous employment and a week's pay' (URN 96/754).)

7.1 Many of the statutory employment protection rights such as the right to claim a redundancy payment and compensation for unfair dismissal are conferred only on those employees who have accrued sufficient continuous employment. Further, the calculation of a redundancy payment and of the basic award in unfair dismissal proceedings is based on the employee's length of continuous service. The length of an employee's period of continuous employment is calculated with a few exceptions according to provisions in *ERA 1996, ss 210–219*. The rules relating to continuous employment were previously contained in *EPCA 1978, s 151* and *Sch 13* as amended by *EA 1980, s 20* and *Sch 2*.

The provisions in *EPCA 1978, Sch 13*, as originally drafted, defined continuous employment in such a way as to exclude part-time workers from protection, or to make it more difficult for them to acquire the relevant rights. This result was achieved by incorporating, in the definition of continuous employment, a qualifying threshold of two years' continuous employment for at least 16 hours per week, or five years' continuous employment for between 8 and 16 hours per week. However, in *R v Secretary of State for Employment, ex p Equal Opportunities Commission* [1994] ICR 317, the House of Lords (reversing the Court of Appeal) held that those parts of *EPCA 1978, Sch 13* which differentiated between part-time and full-time workers contravened *art 141* (formerly *art 119*) of the EC Treaty.

As a result of the House of Lords' ruling, the Government introduced the *Employment Protection (Part-time Employees) Regulations 1995 (SI 1995/31)*. With effect from 6 February 1995, these *Regulations, inter alia,* deleted *paras 3* and *5–8* from *EPCA 1978, Sch 13* (together with a reference in *para 4* to the 16 hours threshold), thereby providing that periods of part-time employment, irrespective of the number of hours worked per week, will count in the computation of continuous employment under *EPCA 1978*. Accordingly, there are no special rules relating to continuity for part-time employees in *ERA 1996*.

Principles of European law formed the basis for another, and separate, challenge to the orthodox approach to continuity of employment. In *Milligan v Securicor Cleaning Ltd* [1995] IRLR 288, the Employment Appeal Tribunal held that if the transfer of an undertaking is the reason or principal reason for an employee's dismissal, a claim for unfair dismissal could be brought pursuant to *reg 8(1)* of the *Transfer of Undertakings (Protection of Employment) Regulations 1981* (see TRANSFER OF UNDERTAKINGS (52)), even if the employee did not otherwise have the requisite continuity of employment for an unfair dismissal claim (at that time, two years). However, with effect from 26 October 1995, the decision in *Milligan* was in effect overruled by the *Collective Redundancies and Transfer of Undertakings (Protection of Employment) (Amendment) Regulations 1995 (SI 1995/2587)*, which amended the *1981 Regulations* so as to provide that claims for unfair dismissal following the transfer of a business can be made only by employees who meet the general qualifying conditions for such claims. Subsequently in *MRS Environmental Services Ltd v Marsh* [1997] 1 All ER 92, the Court of Appeal overruled *Milligan* and held that the normal continuity threshold applied to dismissals which took place in the context of the transfer of an undertaking.

A further challenge to the legislative provisions dealing with continuity of employment occurred in *R v Secretary of State for Employment, ex p Seymour-Smith* [1995] ICR 889, where the Court of Appeal held that the qualifying condition for unfair dismissal claims of two years' continuous employment indirectly discriminated against the female applicants, so that the qualifying condition was declared to be incompatible with *EC Directive 76/207* (the *Equal Treatment Directive*) in May 1991 when the applicants were dismissed. On appeal, however, the House of Lords discharged the declaration on the grounds that it served no purpose since it neither enabled the employees to sue for unfair dismissal (the Directive not having direct effect against the applicants' private employers), nor told the Government (or any other interested party) that UK legislation needed to be changed (see *R v Secretary of State for Employment, ex p Seymour-Smith* [1997] ICR 371). The House of Lords, however, adjourned consideration of whether the qualifying period, as applied to the applicants, was contrary to *art 141* of the *Treaty of Rome*, until the European Court of Justice ruled, *inter alia*, on whether unfair dismissal compensation was 'pay' for the purposes of *art 141*.

The European Court of Justice held in *R v Secretary of State for Employment, ex p Seymour Smith* [1999] IRLR 253 that unfair dismissal compensation was, indeed, 'pay' for the purposes of *art 141* of the *EU Treaty of Rome* (formerly *art 119*). However, the ECJ referred the case back to the House of Lords to consider whether or not the two-year qualifying period for unfair dismissal as applied to these employees contravened *art 141*. If so, then the applicants would be able to rely on this finding to bring unfair dismissal claims against their private sector employers so as to disapply the two-year requirement, since (unlike a *Directive*) *art 141* has direct effect against all employers, public and private.

The House of Lords finally decided the case of *Seymour-Smith* (*R v Secretary of State for Employment, ex p Seymour-Smith and Perez* [2000] IRLR 263) in the light of the guidance given by the European Court of Justice. The House of Lords rejected the argument that the two-year qualifying period was incompatible with *art 141* (formerly *art 119*) of the EU Treaty. The majority of their Lordships held that, whilst the qualifying period did indirectly discriminate against Ms Seymour-Smith and Ms Perez, the Government could justify the discriminatory effect of the limit both at the time of its introduction in 1985 and when it applied to the applicants in 1991.

A similar challenge to the lawfulness of the two-year qualifying period (intro-duced by *reg 8* of the *Collective Redundancies and Transfer of Undertakings (Protection of Employment) (Amendment) Regulations 1995* (*SI 1995/2587*)) for bringing an unfair dismissal claim in respect of a dismissal occurring because of a transfer of an undertaking failed in the case of *R v Secretary of State for Trade and Industry, ex p Unison* [1996] ICR 1003. The challenge was dismissed on the grounds that the available evidence for 1995 failed to show that the qualifying period had a disparate adverse impact on women contrary to European law. (See DISCRIMINATION AND EQUAL OPPORTUNITIES – I, II, III (12, 13, 14), EUROPEAN COMMUNITY LAW (25), and PUBLIC SECTOR EMPLOYEES (37).)

Following the proposals in the *Fairness at Work* White Paper, the *Unfair Dismissal and Statement of Reasons for Dismissal (Variation of Qualifying Period) Order 1999* (*SI 1999/1436*) was made. This reduced the qualifying period for unfair dismissal complaints (and for a written statement of reasons for dismissal) from two years to one year from 1 June 1999.

The more important provisions relating to continuity of employment are set out in this chapter.

7.2   COMPUTATION OF PERIODS OF EMPLOYMENT

Questions arising as to whether an employee's employment is of a kind which counts towards a period of continuous employment, or whether periods are to be treated as forming a single period of continuous employment, are still to be determined week by week, but the length of an employee's period of employment is to be computed in *calendar months* and *years of twelve months* (*ERA 1996, s 210(1)*, *(2)*, *(3)*).

7.3   Beginning and end of a period of continuous employment

Subject to the provisions of *ERA 1996, s 211(2)*, *(3)* an employee's period of continuous employment for the purpose of calculating his entitlement to any right under *ERA 1996* begins with the day on which he actually starts work and ends with the day by reference to which the length of his period of continuous employment falls to be ascertained for the purposes of the employment right in question (*ERA 1996, s 211(1)*). It is important to note that the day on which an employee actually started work must be included in the reckoning under *ERA 1996, s 211*, so that if, for example, an employee starts work on 2 April, and is dismissed on 1 April the following year, he will have one year's continuous employment (see *Pacitti Jones v O'Brien* [2005] IRLR 888). In *General of the Salvation Army v Dewsbury* [1984] ICR 498, the EAT held that 'starts work' in *EPCA 1978, s 151(3)* (the predecessor to *ERA 1996, s 211(1)*) was not intended to refer to the undertaking of the full-time duties of employment but was intended to refer to the beginning of the employee's employment under her contract of employment, which in that case was earlier than the former date.

7.4   EVENTS AFFECTING A PERIOD OF EMPLOYMENT

The rest of this chapter sets out the events which may affect the period of employment. The following matters are considered:

— weeks which count (see 7.6 below);

— change of employer (see 7.9 below);

— weeks, or part weeks, which do not count but which do not break continuity (see 7.10 below);

— events which break continuity (see 7.12 below).

7.5   PRELIMINARY POINTS

Presumption of continuity. A person's employment (by a particular employer) is presumed to have been continuous unless the contrary is shown (*ERA 1996, s 210(5)*). Except as provided in *ERA 1996, ss 215–217*, any week which does not count in computing a period of employment breaks the continuity of the period of employment (*ERA 1996, s 210(4)*).

Meaning of 'week'. For these purposes, a week runs from Sunday to Saturday (*ERA 1996, s 235*). So long as the employee is employed by the employer in two successive weeks, it does not matter that one job may have ended and another begun, nor how the first job ended (*Tipper v Roofdec Ltd* [1989] IRLR 419).

7.6 Continuous Employment

Statutory concept. The concept of continuity of employment is a statutory concept (see *Secretary of State for Employment v Globe Elastic Thread Co Ltd* [1979] ICR 706). This means that parties cannot destroy it by means of a contractual agreement (see *Collison v BBC* [1998] IRLR 238), or seek to preserve it by means of a contractual agreement (see *Morris v Walsh Western UK Ltd* [1997] IRLR 562). (See 7.7 below.)

7.6   WEEKS WHICH COUNT

The following weeks count towards a period of continuous employment.

(a) Any week during the whole or part of which the employee's relations with his employer are governed by a contract of employment (*ERA 1996, s 212(1)*).

In *Roach v CSB (Moulds) Ltd* [1991] ICR 349, the EAT held that continuity had been broken where in two successive weeks the applicant had been employed first by the respondent, then by a third party, then by the respondent again in a different job. However, the EAT in Scotland held in *Sweeney v J & S Henderson (Concessions) Ltd* [1999] IRLR 306 that the long-criticised *Roach* decision was wrongly decided and that, so long as during the relevant weeks there is at least one day governed by a contract of employment with the relevant employer, it does not matter how the gap was created nor what the employee did during its currency (see also *Carrington v Harwich Dock Co Ltd* [1998] IRLR 567).

(b) Periods in which there is no contract of employment may count as periods of employment in certain circumstances. If in any week the employee is, for the whole or part of the week:

   (i) incapable of work in consequence of illness or injury; or

   (ii) absent from work on account of a temporary cessation of work; or

   (iii) absent from work in circumstances such that, by arrangement or custom, he is regarded as continuing in the employment of his employer for all or any purposes,

that week will count as a period of employment (*ERA 1996, s 212(3)*).

Not more than 26 weeks count under (b)(i) above between any periods of employment which themselves count for continuity purposes (*ERA 1996, s 212(4)*). The problems arising from these provisions are considered in more detail in 6.7 below.

(c) An employee's contract of employment is deemed to continue during maternity leave with appropriate amendments so that there is no need for special provisions preserving continuity during the maternity period (*ss 71 and 73, ERA 1996* and *reg 17* of the *Maternity and Parental Leave Regulations 1999*). The same position applies in respect of continuity during any statutory parental leave period (*ss 75A-B, ERA 1996* and *regs 19 and 21* of the *Paternity and Adoption Leave Regulations 2002* (*SI 2002/2788*)), and during paternity leave (*s 80C(1), ERA 1996* and *reg 12* of the *Paternity and Adoption Leave Regulations*).

(d) Intervals in employment where employment is deemed to continue by virtue of the provisions of *ERA 1996, ss 92(7), 97(2), 138(1)* and *145(5)* respectively also count. *Sections 92(7), 97(2)* and *145(5), ERA 1996* operate to treat an employee's employment as continuing until the expiry of the statutory minimum period of notice in circumstances where notice should have been given but was not, and the employee was thereby deprived of the minimum qualifying period of employment for claims for a written statement of reasons for dismissal, unfair dismissal and redundancy payments respectively. *Section 138(1), ERA 1996* operates to preserve continuity where an employee dismissed for redundancy has his contract renewed or is re-engaged after an interval of not more than four weeks. If a dismissed employee is reinstated or re-engaged in consequence of the presentation of a complaint of unfair dismissal, or as a result of action taken by a conciliation officer under *Employment Tribunals Act 1996, s 18*, or as a result of a relevant compromise contract (see 21.27 EMPLOYMENT TRIBUNALS – II), the employee's continuity of employment is preserved and the weeks in any intervening period count. Further, if the employee has been paid a redundancy payment and it is a term of his reinstatement or re-engagement that he repay that sum, the continuity of his employment for redundancy payments purposes is not broken (*Employment Protection (Continuity of Employment) Regulations 1996 (SI 1996/3147)*; *ERA 1996, s 219*).

7.7   Periods of 'no employment'

The true meaning of *ERA 1996, s 212(3)*, formerly *EPCA 1978, Sch 13 para 9* (see 7.6(B) above) has given rise to various difficulties of interpretation.

Generally. Section 212(3) applies only where there is no contract of employment in existence and not where there is a contract of employment in existence, but the employee is not required to perform any work under that contract (*Ford v Warwickshire County Council* [1983] ICR 273; *Pearson v Kent County Council* [1993] IRLR 165). In *Pearson*, the Court of Appeal held that the critical question is why there is no contract during the week in question, and not why the previous contract of employment came to an end.

Illness and injury (s 212(3)(a)). This provision can apply so long as the employee is unfit for the work for which he was previously employed. Thus, continuity may be preserved even where the employee takes a temporary job with another employer until he is capable of returning to his former work (*Donnelly v Kelvin International Services* [1992] IRLR 496; see also *Pearson*, above).

Temporary cessation of work (s 212(3)(b)). In *Ford* the House of Lords held that the continuity of employment of a teacher whose contract came to an end at the end of every summer term but who was re-engaged in the autumn term was preserved during the summer vacation by *EPCA 1978, Sch 13 para 9(1)(b)*, now *s 212(3)(b), ERA 1996*. Lord Diplock at 285 said that 'temporary' meant lasting only for a relatively short time, and that it was necessary to ask whether the interval between the two contracts was short in relation to their combined duration. This has become known as the 'mathematical' approach.

In *Flack v Kodak Ltd* [1986] ICR 775 the Court of Appeal had to consider whether six workers in the photo-finishing department of Kodak Ltd had sufficient continuous employment to pursue their employment protection rights. They had been employed intermittently over a number of years. Their period of employment depended on the extent of the department's work. The court decided that the correct approach in deciding whether a gap in an employee's employment, during which he is absent from work on account of a cessation of work, is a temporary cessation for the purposes of *EPCA 1978, Sch 13 para 9(1)(b)*, now *s 212(3)(b), ERA 1996*, is to take into account all the relevant circumstances and in particular to consider the length of the period of absence in the context of the period of employment as a whole. Thus, the court did not apply a strictly 'mathematical' approach and held that the periods of absence did not break the continuity of employment (see also *Berwick Salmon Fisheries Co Ltd v Rutherford* [1991] IRLR 203).

However, in *Sillars v Charringtons Fuels Ltd* [1989] ICR 475 the Court of Appeal held that it was still open to an employment tribunal, after considering the matter in the round, to conclude that the 'mathematical' approach should be applied in an appropriate case (for example, where there was a systematic pattern of events). That there was an intention to re-employ the applicant later did not necessarily mean that the cessation of work was temporary in the sense of being for a relatively short time.

The 'cessation of work' must involve a reduction in the employer's overall quantum of work, and not merely a decision to allocate work to some other employee (*Byrne v Birmingham City District Council* [1987] ICR 519). *Byrne* was followed in *Letheby & Christopher Ltd v Bond* [1988] ICR 480.

Regarded as continuing in employment (s 212(3)(c)). This provision might apply to, for example, a period of unpaid leave. However, it was held in *Letheby* (see above) that an employee employed under single separate contracts, who went on holiday at a time convenient to her employers, was not absent from work in circumstances such that by arrangement or custom she was regarded as continuing in employment, where there was no prior agreement between the parties that after each holiday period there was to be some continuation of her employment.

The Court of Appeal in *Curr v Marks & Spencer plc* [2002] EWCA Civ 1852, [2003] IRLR 74 has stressed that *s 212(3)(c)* requires a mutual arrangement between employer and employee prior to the absence from work in question; and a 'meeting of minds' by the arrangement that both parties regard the ex-employee as continuing in employment for some purpose. The Court did not regard it as helpful to refer to the test of *s 212(3)(c)* as involving consideration of whether an employment relationship continues (regarded as the 'key question' by the EAT in *Letheby* and *Booth v United States of America* [1999] IRLR 16): this was not the statutory test. In *Curr*, an employee absent on a four-year maternity break scheme did not fall within *s 212(3)(c)*, although she was required to work for at least two weeks in each year of the break; was prohibited from accepting other paid employment without consulting her manager; and was in regular contact with the employer. This was because the other terms on which she took her maternity break clearly showed that employment was not regarded as continuing. On commencement of her break, she was required to resign, and was given her P45. At the end of the break, she had an option to be re-employed by the employer, but the scheme's emphasis on 're-employment' in fact showed that she was not regarded as continuing in employment during the break.

Consistent with *Curr*, the EAT in *Morris v Walsh Western UK Ltd* [1997] IRLR 562 held that a retrospective agreement to treat the period of an employee's absence as continuous is insufficient to preserve continuity of employment under *s 212(3)(c)* (because continuity of employment is a statutory concept – see *Secretary of State for Employment v Globe Elastic Thread Co Ltd* [1979] ICR 706). The EAT in *Morris* criticised *Ingram v Foxon* [1984] ICR 685, in which it was held that the period between an employee's dismissal and his reinstatement on terms that his continuity of employment would be regarded as unbroken was a period falling within *para 9(1)(c) of Sch 13, EPCA 1978* (the predecessor to *s 212(3)(c)*). In the light of *Curr*, *Ingram* must be regarded as wrongly decided.

7.8   **Part-timers and EC law**

As mentioned in 7.1 above, there is no longer any difference in the provisions for calculating periods of continuous employment, in relation to their application to part-time employees as against full-time employees.

7.9   **CHANGE OF EMPLOYER**

Normally, to be continuous, employment must be with one employer. Separate companies must normally be treated as quite distinct entities. The 'corporate veil' may only be pierced if it is a mere facade concealing the true facts (*National Dock Labour Board v Pinn & Wheeler Ltd* [1989] BCLC 647). However, note the following points.

(*a*)   *Associated employers.* If an employee of an employer is taken into the employment of another employer who, at the time when the employee enters his employment is an 'associated' employer of the former employer, that change will not break the continuity of the employee's employment (*ERA 1996, s 218(6)*).

For the purposes of *ERA 1996*, any two employers are to be treated as associated if one is a company of which the other (directly or indirectly) has control, or if both are companies of which a third person (directly or indirectly) has control (*ERA 1996, s 231*). The definition of 'control' in *s 231* has been problematic over the years. The EAT held in *Hair Colour Consultants Ltd v Mena* [1984] ICR 671 that 'control' means voting control by a majority of shares (see also *South West Launderettes Ltd v Laidler* [1986] ICR 455). However, the Court of Appeal in *Payne v Secretary of State for Employment* [1989] IRLR 352 and in *Secretary of State for Employment v Chapman* [1989] ICR 771 held that whilst voting control is the usual and normal test for determining whether two employers are associated, that test is not conclusive. Further, the EAT held in *Tice v Cartwright* [1999] ICR 769 that the word 'control' in *s 231* dealt with practical rather than theoretical control so that two brothers in partnership controlled the company in which they each had a 50% shareholding. (See also, *Hartford v Swiftrim Ltd* [1987] ICR 439; and *Zarb v British Brazilian Produce Co (Sales) Ltd* [1978] IRLR 78 cf *Strudick v IBL* [1988] ICR 796; and *Russell v Elmdon Freight Terminal Ltd* [1989] ICR 629.)

The EAT has been willing to treat the term 'company' as including both a partnership of companies (*Pinkney v Sandpiper Drilling Ltd* [1989] IRLR 425) and a foreign entity equivalent to an English company (*Hancill v Marcon Engineering Ltd* [1990] ICR 103). However, not all bodies corporate (such as local authorities) are 'companies' within *ERA 1996, s 231* (*Gardiner v London Borough of Merton* [1980] IRLR 472). In *Hasley v Fair Employment Agency* [1989] IRLR 106, the Northern Ireland Court of Appeal pointed out that the section only requires the employer which is *controlled* to be a company; the *controlling* employer may be some other type of legal person.

(*b*)   *Transfers of a business.* If a trade or business or an undertaking is transferred from one person to another, the period of employment of an employee in the trade or business or undertaking at the time of the transfer counts as a period of employment with the transferee and is regarded as unbroken (*ERA 1996, s 218(2)*). In *Dabell v Vale Industrial Services (Nottingham) Ltd* [1988] IRLR 439, the Court of Appeal upheld a tribunal's decision that there was such a transfer when there was a substantive handing over of the business but no finally concluded agreement as to the transfer of ownership. Domestic case law has warned against artificial attempts to break continuity. In *Macer v Abafast Ltd* [1990] ICR 234 and *Gibson v Motortune Ltd* [1990] ICR 740, the EAT stated that the machinery of *EPCA, Sch 13 para 17(2)*, the predecessor to *ERA 1996, s 218(2)*, could operate even where the machinery of transfer led to a gap of more than one week between periods of employment, in conformity with the purposive approach in *Litster v Forth Dry Dock and Engineering Co Ltd* [1990] 1 AC 546. This approach was adopted by the Court of Appeal in *Clark & Tokeley Ltd v Oakes* [1998] IRLR 577 and *Astley v Celtec Ltd* [2002] IRLR 629, in which the court held that the 'time of transfer' was not confined to a particular moment, but could be spread over a longer period of a week (*Clark*), or indeed several years (*Astley*). However, all these cases must now be regarded with caution in the light of the ECJ's findings on the 'time of transfer' in the *Astley* case, on a reference from the House of Lords (*Celtec Ltd v Astley C-478/03* [2005] IRLR 647). In *Astley*, the ECJ has stated that the 'date of transfer' for the purposes of *Directive 77/187/EC* refers to a particular point in time, representing the date on which responsibility as employer for carrying on the business of the unit transferred moves from the transferor to the transferee (applied by the House of Lords on resumed hearing of the appeal: see *Celtec Ltd v Astley* [2006] ICR 993, HL). Accordingly, an employee cannot be considered employed in a transferring undertaking at the time of transfer, purely on the basis of a holding that the transfer has taken place over an extended period (though the purposive approach in *Litster* may of course still apply to preserve continuity): see also TRANSFER OF UNDERTAKINGS (52).

(c)   *Substitution of employer by statute.* If by or under an Act of Parliament, whether public or local, a contract of employment between any body corporate and an employee is modified and some other body corporate is substituted as the employer, the period of employment of the employee at the time when the modification takes effect counts as a period of employment with the second body corporate and is regarded as unbroken (*ERA 1996, s 218(3)*). For a case where, on the facts, the predecessor provision to s 218(3) was held not to apply, see *Gale v Northern General Hospital NHS Trust* [1994] IRLR 292.

(d)   *Employment in schools/the National Health Service.* If an employee of the governing body of a maintained school is taken into the employment of the local authority responsible for the school, or vice versa, continuity of employment is preserved (*ERA 1996, s 218(7)*). Similarly, in certain circumstances, continuity of employment is preserved when an employee's employment switches from one health service employer to another, if he is undergoing professional training which involves successive employment by a number of different health service employers (*ERA 1996, ss 218(8)- 218(10)* and *Employment Protection (National Health Service) Order 1996 (SI 1996/638)*).

(e)   *Death of employer, partnerships, etc.* If, on the death of the employer, the employee passes into the employment of the personal representatives or trustees of the deceased, continuity is not broken. A change in partners, personal representatives or trustees does not break the continuity of an employee's employment (*ERA 1996, s 218(4), (5)*). The provision in *ERA 1996, s 218(5)* for preservation of continuity on a change in partners covers the situation where, after the change, there are no partners, but only a sole proprietor: see *Bower v Stevens* (6 April 2004, CA) and *Jeetle v Elster* [1985] ICR 389.

7.10   WEEKS WHICH DO NOT BREAK CONTINUITY

The following weeks do not count in the computation but do not break continuity. (This applies also where the events occur in only part of the week.)

(*a*)   Any week during which the employee takes part in a strike (*ERA 1996, s 216(1), (2)*).

(*b*)   Any week during which the employee is absent from work because of a lock out (*ERA 1996, s 216(3)*).

(*c*)   For the purpose of calculating the qualifying period for pursuing a claim to a redundancy payment and for the purpose of calculating the amount of the payment, any week during which the employee (i) was employed outside Great Britain (*ERA 1996, s 215(2)(a)*), and (ii) was not an employed earner for the purposes of the *Social Security Contributions and Benefits Act 1992* in respect of whom a secondary Class 1 contribution was payable under that Act (whether or not the contribution was in fact paid) (*ERA 1996, s 215(2)(b)*). For all other purposes, continuity continues during periods in which the employee is engaged in work wholly or mainly outside Great Britain (*ERA 1996, s 215(1)(a)*).

7.11   'Postponement' of start of employment

If an employee's period of continuous employment includes one or more periods which do not count in computing the length of the period but do not break continuity, the beginning of the period is treated as *postponed* by the number of days falling within that intervening period, or, as the case may be, by the aggregate number of days falling within those periods (*ERA 1996, s 211(3)*).

7.12   EVENTS WHICH BREAK CONTINUITY

Except as is otherwise specifically provided in *ERA 1996, ss 215–217*, any week which does not count in the computation breaks the continuity of a period of employment (*ERA 1996, s 210(4)*).

The receipt of a redundancy payment breaks continuity for redundancy qualification and payment purposes (*ERA 1996, s 214*). However, *s 214* does not apply where an employee, having received a redundancy payment (or equivalent payment), is reinstated or re-engaged by his employer on terms which include a requirement to repay the amount of that payment, and that requirement is complied with (*Employment Protection (Continuity of Employment) Regulations 1996 (SI 1996/3147)* – see also 7.6(D) above). *Section 214* also does not apply where a 'redundancy payment' paid by the employer is not a payment which he is statutorily obliged to make (*Rowan v Machinery Installations (South Wales) Ltd* [1981] ICR 386; *Ross v Delrosa Caterers Ltd* [1981] ICR 393). Further, given that a 'redundancy payment' in this context means a statutory redundancy payment, and a right to such a payment depends on there having been a dismissal, it follows that where an employee's employment is transferred pursuant to *TUPE 1981*, there is no dismissal and therefore any payment received by the employee is not a statutory redundancy payment and will not break continuity under *s 214* (*Senior Heat Treatment v Bell* [1997] IRLR 614). However, this will not be the case where the Secretary of State has paid the equivalent of a statutory redundancy payment to an employee of an insolvent employer under *ERA 1996, s 167* (*Secretary of State for Trade and Industry v Lassman* [2000] IRLR 411).

7.13 **TABLE OF QUALIFYING PERIODS FOR STATUTORY EMPLOYMENT PROTECTION RIGHTS**

Employment right	Qualifying period
	NB Not all statutory employment protection rights require a qualifying period of continuous employment. For example, neither the general right to maternity leave nor the right to written particulars of employment depends upon 'continuous' employment as defined by *ERA 1996*.
Guarantee payments/Payments during medical suspension	One month ending with the day before the period for which guarantee payment, etc is claimed (*ERA 1996, s 29(1)* and *s 65(1)*).
Minimum period of notice	One month (*ERA 1996, ss 86(1), 87(1)*). Any contract of a person who has been employed for three months which is a contract for a fixed term of one month or less is deemed for the purposes of *s 86* to have effect as if it were for an indefinite period and thus subject to the notice provisions (*ERA 1996, s 86(4)*).
Unfair dismissal	One year.
Written reasons for dismissal	(*ERA 1996, s 108(1)* and *92(3)*).
	If an employee is dismissed by reason of a medical suspension requirement or recommendation under an enactment or a Code of Practice providing for health and safety at work, the qualifying period is one month (*ERA 1996, s 108(2)*). In certain other cases of unfair dismissal, no qualifying period is necessary. These are where the reason or principal reason for the dismissal:

(*a*) was a union-related reason (*TULRCA 1992, s 154*; and see 54.3(A) UNFAIR DISMISSAL – II);

(*b*) was the assertion of a statutory right (*ERA 1996, s 108(3)(g)*; and see 54.3(C) UNFAIR DISMISSAL – II);

(*c*) was a health and safety-related reason (*ERA 1996, s 108(3)(c)*; and see 54.3(B) UNFAIR DISMISSAL – II);

(*d*) was a reason related to pregnancy, childbirth or maternity; maternity leave; adoption leave; parental leave; paternity leave; or time off for dependants under *ERA 1996, s 57* (*ERA 1996, s 108(3)(b)*; and see 33.6 MATERNITY AND PARENTAL RIGHTS);

Employment right   Qualifying period

(*e*)   was a reason connected with the performance by an employee who is a pension scheme trustee of his functions as such a trustee (*ERA 1996, s 108(3)(e)*; see 54.3(E) UNFAIR DISMISSAL – II);

(*f*)   was a reason connected with the performance by an employee representative (see 39.4 REDUNDANCY – II and 52.18 TRANSFER OF UNDERTAKINGS), or a candidate in an election for such an employee representative, of his functions as such an employee representative or candidate (*ERA 1996, s 108(3)(f)*; see 54.3(F) UNFAIR DISMISSAL – II);

(*g*)   was a reason connected with the refusal of Sunday work by a shop worker or betting worker (*ERA 1996, s 108(3)(d)*; see 54.3(G) UNFAIR DISMISSAL – II);

(*h*)   was a reason related to working time (*ERA 1996, s 108(3)(dd)*; and see 54.3(H) UNFAIR DISMISSAL – II);

(*j*)   was a reason connected with the assertion of rights under the *National Minimum Wage Act 1998* (*ERA 1996, s 108(3)(gg)*; see 54.3(M) UNFAIR DISMISSAL – II);

(*k*)   was a reason connected with the making of a protected disclosure under *ERA 1996, ss 43A–43L* (*ERA 1996, s 108(3)(ff)*; see 54.3(N) UNFAIR DISMISSAL – II);

(*l*)   was a reason connected with the assertion of rights under the *Tax Credits Act 1999* (*ERA 1996, s 108(3) (gh)*; see 54.3(T) UNFAIR DISMISSAL – II);

(*m*)   was a reason connected with the assertion of rights under the *Transnational Information and Consultation of Employees Regulations 1999* (*ERA 1996, s 108(3)(hh)*; see 54.3(U) UNFAIR DISMISSAL – II);

(n)   was a reason connected with the assertion of rights under the *Part-time Workers (Prevention of Less Favourable Treatment) Regulations 2000* (*SI 2000/1551*) (*ERA 1996, s 108(3)(i)*; see 54.3(S) UNFAIR DISMISSAL – II);

(o)   was a reason connected with the assertion of rights under the *Fixed-term Employees (Prevention of Less Favourable Treatment) Regulations 2002* (*SI 2002/2034*) (*ERA 1996, s 108(3)(j)*; see 54.3(V) UNFAIR DISMISSAL – II);

7.13 Continuous Employment

Employment right	Qualifying period

(*p*) was a reason connected with the assertion of flexible working rights under *ERA 1996, ss 80F-80G* (*ERA 1996, s 108(3)(gi)*; see 54.3 UNFAIR DISMISSAL – II);

(*q*) was a reason connected with trade union recognition or bargaining arrangements (*TULRCA 1992, Sch A1, paras 161–162* (see 54.3(O) UNFAIR DISMISSAL – II);

(*r*) was that the employee exercised or sought to exercise the right, pursuant to *Employment Relations Act 1999, s 10*, to be accompanied to a disciplinary or grievance hearing or that the employee accompanied or sought to accompany another worker to such a hearing (*Employment Relations Act 1999, s 12(4)*. See 54.3(P) UNFAIR DISMISSAL – II);

(*s*) was that the employee was dismissed for taking part in protected industrial action in the circumstances set out in *TULRCA 1992, s 238A*, introduced by the *Employment Relations Act 1999, s 16* and *Sch 5*. (See 54.3(Q) UNFAIR DISMISSAL – II; or

(*t*) was a reason connected with the exercise of various negotiation or consultation rights within a "European Company" as defined in the *European Public Limited-Liability Company Regulations 2004* (*SI 2004/2326*). (See 54.3 UNFAIR DISMISSAL – II);

(*u*) was a reason connected with the exercise of various negotiation or consultation rights under the *Information and Consultation of Employees Regulations 2004* (*SI 2004/3426*). (See 54.3 UNFAIR DISMISSAL – II);

(*v*) was the fact that the employee has been summoned for jury service, or has been absent on jury service in the circumstances set out in *ERA 1996, s 98B*. (See 54.3 UNFAIR DISMISSAL – II (applying to dismissals from 6 April 2005));

(*w*) was a selection for redundancy for a reason which would have been automatically unfair if it had been the reason for dismissal (*ERA 1996, s 108(3)(h)*);

Employment right	Qualifying period

Qualifying period

(*x*) was a reason connected with an employee's performance of various functions or exercise of various entitlements as a consulted representative or a candidate in an election to elect representatives for the purposes of consultation about occupational or personal pension schemes under the *Occupational and Personal Pension Schemes* (*Consultation by Employers and Miscellaneous Amendment*) *Regulations 2006* (*SI 2006/349*): see *ERA 1996, s 108(3)(m)* (applying to dismissals from 6 April 2006);

(*y*) was the fact that the employee exercised or sought to exercise his right to be accompanied, or accompanied or sought to accompany another employee, at a meeting to discuss a statutory right to request not to retire: see the *Employment Equality* (*Age*) *Regulations 2006* (*SI 2006/1031*), *Sch 6* and *ERA 1996, s 108(3)(n)* (applying to dismissals from 1 October 2006).

If the reason or principal reason for dismissal is the transfer of an undertaking or a reason connected with it, so that dismissal is automatically unfair by operation of *reg 8(1)* of the *Transfer of Undertakings* (*Protection of Employment*) *Regulations 1981*, the normal qualifying period applies (*Collective Redundancies and Transfer of Undertakings* (*Protection of Employment*) (*Amendment*) *Regulations 1995* (*SI 1995/2587*), effectively overruling *Milligan v Securicor Cleaning Ltd* [1995] IRLR 288 – see 7.1 above).

Redundancy payment — Two years (*ERA 1996, s 155*).

Consultation of appropriate representatives and notification of Secretary of State on redundancy — Three months, but only where the employment is under a fixed-term contract of three months or less or one made in contemplation of a specific task not expected to last for more than three months (*TULRCA 1992, s 282*).

8   Contract of Employment

(See also DTI booklet No 1 'Written statement of employment particulars' (PL 700).)

Cross-references. See CHILDREN AND YOUNG PERSONS (4) for statutory restrictions on their employment; RESTRAINT OF TRADE, CONFIDENTIALITY AND EMPLOYEE INVENTIONS (41); and COLLECTIVE AGREEMENTS (6) for their respective effects on individual contracts; 23.4 EQUAL PAY for the statutory equality clause; 34.6 PAY – I for illegal deductions from wages; 45.16 STRIKES AND INDUSTRIAL ACTION for the effect of industrial action on contracts; and 55.2–55.5 UNFAIR DISMISSAL – III for reinstatement and re-engagement orders. See TERMINATION OF EMPLOYMENT (48) and WRONGFUL DISMISSAL (58) for termination of contract rules. For restrictions on contracting out of statutory provisions, see 24.15 EQUAL PAY, 38.14 REDUNDANCY – I and 53.19 UNFAIR DISMISSAL – I.

8.1   The contract between an employer and an employee is usually referred to as a contract of employment or a contract of service. Three main categories of question may arise regarding a contract of employment.

(*a*)   The question whether a particular agreement under which a person works is a 'contract of employment' or not, which is considered in EMPLOYEE, SELF-EMPLOYED OR WORKER? (17).

(*b*)   Questions relating to the terms or form of a particular contract of employment, which are considered in this chapter. This chapter also considers the requirement to provide certain written particulars of the contract terms if there is no written contract (see 8.4–8.8 below).

(*c*)   Questions relating to the remedies available for breach of the contract of employment (see 8.23 below).

The question of the identity of the employer may arise in relatively rare cases where it is unclear which of a number of companies or other legal persons is the employer under the contract. In such cases, the employer is likely to be the person who has power to control the employee's activities (see *Clifford v Union of Democratic Mineworkers* [1991] IRLR 518; *Andrews v King* [1991] ICR 846).

See 26.10 FOREIGN EMPLOYEES for the rules as to which country's system of law governs the contract of employment.

8.2   **FREEDOM TO EMPLOY**

An employer may engage or refuse to engage any person, subject only to the statutory provisions relating to CHILDREN AND YOUNG PERSONS (4), discrimination on grounds of race or sex or disability or religion or belief or sexual orientation or trade union membership or non-membership (see DISCRIMINATION AND EQUAL OPPORTUNITIES – I, II, III (12, 13, 14), DISABILITY DISCRIMINATION (10), 50.2 TRADE UNIONS – I) and the provisions relating to the employment of foreign nationals (see FOREIGN EMPLOYEES (26)).

8.3   **THE FORM OF THE CONTRACT**

A contract of employment may be either written or oral, or a mixture of the two. This means that its form may range from a document drawn up by solicitors and signed by both parties, to a chat over a cup of tea in the canteen. There must, however, be certainty as to the terms. In *Judge v Crown Leisure Ltd* [2005] EWCA Civ 571, [2005] IRLR 823, a case where there was an extant contract of employment, it was held that vague statements made at a Christmas party did not amount to a contractually binding agreement to increase the employee's pay. It is usual for senior executives to be employed pursuant to written agreements drafted by solicitors to meet the specific circumstances. These agreements are often for a fixed term. Note that a provision for the employment of a director for more than two years is void, unless the term has been approved by a resolution of the members of the company (see 9.3 DIRECTORS) (*Companies Act 2006, s 188*). Such agreements frequently contain provisions dealing with the tenure by the employee of a directorship of the employing company. They may also contain restrictive covenants (see RESTRAINT OF TRADE, CONFIDENTIALITY AND EMPLOYEE INVENTIONS (41)). Less senior employees may be asked to sign a standard form of contract of employment. In other cases, the contract will be contained in an exchange of letters, or terms may be agreed orally at an interview. Provided that the parties are in agreement over the essential terms of the contract, such as hours and wages, there will be a valid contract of employment enforceable by either party. However, an employer is under a duty to give his employees particulars *in writing* of certain important terms of their contracts (see 8.4 below). A contract of employment may also be implied from the parties' conduct: *Franks v Reuters Ltd* [2003] EWCA Civ 417, [2003] IRLR 423, *Dacas v Brook Street Bureau* [2004] EWCA Civ 217, [2004] IRLR 358 and *Cable & Wireless plc v Muscat* [2006] EWCA Civ 220, [2005] IRLR 354 (see EMPLOYEE, SELF-EMPLOYED OR WORKER? (17)).

8.4   WRITTEN PARTICULARS OF CONTRACT

Although the law does not require the contract itself to be in writing, every employer has for some time been required to give each employee a written statement of particulars of certain terms of his contract not later than two months after the beginning of the employee's employment (see *ERA 1996, s 1* and CONTINUOUS EMPLOYMENT (7)).

Under *ERA 1996, s 1(1), (2)*, the written statement of particulars must be given to the employee not later than two months after the beginning of the employment. If, during that period, the employee is to begin work outside the UK for more than a month, the statement must be given to him not later than the time he leaves the UK to begin work (*ERA 1996, s 2(5)*).

The statement may be given in instalments during the two-month period (*ERA 1996, s 1(1)*). However, certain of the particulars must be included in a single document. These are the names of the parties, the dates when employment and continuous employment began, the particulars of remuneration, hours and holidays, the job title or description, and the place of work (*ERA 1996, s 2(4)*).

If employment ends within the two-month period, a statement must still be given (*ERA 1996, s 2(6)*), unless the employment continued for less than one month (*ERA 1996, s 198*).

Amendments to the *ERA 1996* introduced by the *Employment Act 2002* permit the use of documents as an alternative to a statement of particulars. If the employer gives the employee a contract of employment or an engagement letter which contains the information required by *ERA 1996, s 1* at the time when employment commences (*ERA 1996, s 7B*) or afterwards (*ERA 1996, s 7A(1)(c)*) that is sufficient to meet the obligations under *s 1*. If the document contains the material required by *s 3* (disciplinary procedure, etc) that is sufficient to comply with that section.

8.5   Particulars which must be given

The written statement must:

(*a*)   name the employer and the employee;

(*b*)   specify the date when the employment began; and

(*c*)   specify the date on which the employee's period of *continuous* employment began (taking into account any employment with a previous employer which counts towards that period).

(*ERA 1996, s 1(3)*.)

(For the day on which employment 'begins', see 7.3 CONTINUOUS EMPLOYMENT.)

It must also give the following particulars of terms of employment which are applicable as at a specified date not more than seven days before the date on which the statement is given:

(*d*)   the scale or rate of remuneration, or the method of calculating remuneration;

(*e*)   the intervals at which remuneration is paid (that is whether weekly, or monthly or at other specified intervals);

(*f*)   any terms and conditions relating to hours of work (including any terms and conditions relating to normal working hours);

(*g*)   any terms and conditions relating to:

    (i)   entitlement to holidays, including public holidays and holiday pay (the particulars being sufficient to enable the employee's entitlement, including any entitlement to accrued holiday pay on the termination of employment, to be precisely calculated);

    (ii)   incapacity for work due to sickness or injury, including any provisions for sick pay; and

    (iii)   pensions and pension schemes (unless the employee's pension rights depend on the terms of a pension scheme established under statute, and he is employed by a body or authority required under statute to give information concerning pension rights to new employees);

(*h*)   the length of notice which the employee is obliged to give and entitled to receive to terminate his contract of employment;

(*j*)   the title of the job which the employee is employed to do or a brief description of the work for which the employee is employed;

(*k*)   where the employment is not intended to be permanent, the period for which it is expected to continue or, if it is for a fixed term, the date when it is to end;

(*l*)   either the place of work or, where the employee is required or permitted to work at various places, an indication of that and of the employer's address;

(*m*) any collective agreements which directly affect the terms and conditions of the employment, including the persons by whom they were made where the employer is not a party; and

(*n*) where the employee is required to work outside the UK for more than a month, certain further particulars concerning that period, the currency of remuneration, any additional remuneration and benefits, and any terms and conditions relating to return.

(*ERA 1996, s 1(4), (5)*.)

The Secretary of State may add to the list of particulars to be given (*ERA 1996, s 7*).

Contracting-out certificate. The written particulars must include a note stating whether a contracting-out certificate is in force for the particular employment concerned (*ERA 1996, s 3(5)*). Such a certificate is issued where there is in place an occupational pension scheme which satisfies certain conditions.

Disciplinary and complaints procedures. The *ERA 1996* (as amended by *s 35, Employment Act 2002*) further requires that every statement given to an employee shall contain a note:

(A) specifying any disciplinary rules applicable to the employee or referring to a document which is reasonably accessible to the employee and which specifies such rules. The employer must also specify any procedure applicable to the taking of disciplinary actions relating to the employee, or to a decision to dismiss the employee, or refer the employee to the provisions of another document which specifies such a procedure; and

(B) specifying, by description or otherwise:

  (i) a person to whom the employee can apply if he is dissatisfied with any disciplinary decision relating to him or any decision to dismiss him; and

  (ii) a person to whom the employee can apply for the purpose of seeking redress of any grievance relating to his employment and the manner in which any such application should be made,

and where there are further steps to be taken in any such application, explaining those steps or referring to a document which is reasonably accessible to the employee and which explains them (*ERA 1996, s 3(1)*).

Statutory disciplinary and grievance procedures. The *Employment Act 2002* introduces statutory rules for disciplinary and grievance procedures. By *s 30* of the *Employment Act 2002* 'every contract of employment shall have effect to require the employer and employee to comply ... with the requirements of the [statutory] procedure'. The government has indicated that it has no present intention to bring *s 30* into force.

The requirement to give a note of disciplinary and complaints procedures does not apply to rules, disciplinary decisions, decisions to dismiss, grievances or procedures relating to HEALTH AND SAFETY AT WORK – II (27) (*ERA 1996, s 3(2)*).

Previously, employers who (together with any associated employer) employed less than 20 persons were exempted from the obligations in respect of informing employees of disciplinary procedures. That exemption is abolished by *s 36, Employment Act 2002*.

8.6 Contract of Employment

ERA 1996 does not require there to be provisions in the contract on all these matters (see *Morley v Heritage plc* [1993] IRLR 400). It simply requires notice of such provisions that do exist to be given to the employee. Where there are no provisions relating to any of the matters listed above, that fact must be stated, e g where no contractual sick pay is provided (*ERA 1996, s 2(1)*).

In *Robertson v British Gas Corpn* [1983] ICR 351, the Court of Appeal held that the statutory written statement of particulars is neither the contract itself nor conclusive evidence of it. For obvious reasons, however, an employer may have difficulty in going behind the written statement.

Certain classes of employee are also entitled to a statement setting out their right to refuse to work on Sundays under the provisions formerly in the *Sunday Trading Act 1994* and the *Betting, Gaming and Lotteries Act 1963* which have now been consolidated in the *ERA 1996* (see 8.25 below).

8.6 Alternatives to inclusion of particulars in written statement

ERA 1996, s 2(2), (3) provides that the written statement of particulars:

(*a*)   may refer the employee to the provisions of some other document which he has reasonable opportunities of reading in the course of his employment, or which is made reasonably accessible to him in some other way, for particulars of any of the matters specified in *ERA 1996, s 1(4)(d)(ii)* and (*iii*) (sickness, sick pay and pensions); and

(*b*)   may refer the employee to the law or to a collective agreement which directly affects his terms and conditions for particulars of the matters specified in *s 1(4)(e), ERA 1996* (length of notice), provided that any such collective agreement is one which he has reasonable opportunities of reading in the course of his employment or which is made reasonably accessible to him in some other way.

8.7 Changes in contract terms

Any changes in the contractual terms or in other matters of which written particulars must be given must be the subject of a written statement given to the employee at the earliest opportunity and in any event not later than one month after the change (or the time of leaving the UK to work for more than one month, if that is the cause of the change) (*ERA 1996, s 4(1), (3)*). Similar provisions concerning the documents in which particulars may be set out again apply.

A mere change of the employer's name, or a mere change in employer which does not break CONTINUOUS EMPLOYMENT (7), does not require a complete new statement under *ERA 1996, s 1*, but does require a statement of change under *s 4* (*ERA 1996, s 4(6), (8)*).

No change in an employee's contractual terms may be made without his consent (see 8.22 below).

8.8 Exceptions

The requirement to give written particulars applies to all employees except:

(*a*)   seamen of various kinds (*ERA 1996, s 199, s 5(1)*); and

(*b*)   a person whose employment continues for less than one month (*ERA 1996, s 198*).

8.9   **Employees' remedies for failure to give particulars**

An employee who has not been provided with the particulars specified in the Act may make a complaint relating to the failure to an employment tribunal (*ERA 1996, s 11(1)*). An application may be made by either the employer or the employee if a statement of particulars has purportedly been given, but a question arises as to the particulars which ought to have been included or referred to in it (*ERA 1996, s 11(2)*). Where no *express* term has been agreed, it may be that the tribunal is able to *imply* a term after considering all the facts and circumstances of the relationship between the employer and the employee concerned (*Mears v Safecar Security Ltd* [1982] ICR 626). However, if there has been no express or implied agreement upon a particular term, the tribunal has no power to invent a term for the parties (*Eagland v British Telecommunications plc* [1993] ICR 644; and see 8.12 below). Nor is *s 11* to be used as a means of clarifying or interpreting an ambiguous term (*Construction Industry Training Board v Leighton* [1978] IRLR 60).

An employer's failure to include a term in the statement of particulars does not mean that the employer is unable to enforce that term: *Lange v Georg Schüneman GmbH* [2001] IRLR 244, ECJ.

The tribunal will, if it finds such a complaint under *s 11* well-founded, state the particulars which should have been given and the employer will be deemed to have given a statement including those particulars (*ERA 1996, s 12(1), (2)*). If the employer has been in breach of any of those terms, the employee may bring an action against him in the county court or the High Court or, if the breach involves a deduction from pay, in the tribunal under *ERA 1996, ss 13–27* (the former *Wages Act* provisions) (see 34.6 PAY – I). The right to present a complaint for failure to provide written particulars may be exercised by an employee who has been employed for more than two months. If the employment has ceased, the application to the tribunal must be made before the end of the period of three months beginning with the date on which the employment ceased or within such further period as the tribunal considers reasonable where it was not reasonably practicable for the application to be made within three months (*ERA 1996, s 11(4)*). (See 20.7 EMPLOYMENT TRIBUNALS.)

There is no right to claim damages for a breach of the statutory duty to give written particulars, although in certain special circumstances an employer may be under a contractual duty to take reasonable steps to publicise a term (*Scally v Southern Health and Social Services Board* [1991] ICR 771, HL).

In the event that an employee brings a claim of a type specified in *Sch 5* to the *Employment Act 2002* (a wide range of claims including, but not limited to, unfair dismissal, discrimination and breach of contract cases) against an employer which is resolved in favour of the employee and, at the time when the proceedings were commenced, the employer was in breach either of his duty to provide a statement of particulars under *ERA 1996, s 1* or to a statement of changes under *ERA 1996, s 4*, then the tribunal must award the employee two weeks' pay (and may award four weeks' pay) even if it makes no other award. If the tribunal does make an award in favour of the employee, it must increase that award by two weeks' pay (and may increase it by four weeks' pay). However, if there are exceptional circumstances that would make the award or the increase to the award unjust or inequitable, then the tribunal does not have to order the additional award.

Claims under *s 11* are a relatively speedy way of having contractual employment rights determined.

8.10   **TERMS OF THE CONTRACT**

Freedom to agree

The parties are free to agree any terms they wish, subject to certain limitations set out below. If an employment tribunal is called upon to interpret the terms of a contract, it must apply the same principles as an ordinary court. This means, for example, the words used must be interpreted in the context which existed and was known to both parties at the time when the contract was made (*Investors Compensation Scheme Ltd v West Bromwich Building Society* [1998] 1 All ER 98, HL) but that the parties' subsequent conduct is not admissible in construing their original written agreement (*Hooper v British Railways Board* [1988] IRLR 517). However, where the terms of a written contract are truly ambiguous, it is permissible to construe what the parties meant by using evidence of a clearly established practice, which continued both before and after the contract was made (*Dunlop Tyres Ltd v Blows* [2001] IRLR 629, CA; see also COLLECTIVE AGREEMENTS (6)).

8.11   **Employer handbooks and policies**

Employees will often be provided with a substantial volume of documentation upon commencing employment. These documents may be presented under a variety of titles, such as employer policies and company handbooks. In practice, they are often more voluminous than the statement of written particulars or any document which is according to its own terms a contractual document. In many cases, it may be a matter of considerable practical importance to know whether or not these documents have contractual effect. This question may arise, for example, when the employer seeks to vary the provisions of a policy or of the handbook. If the policy or handbook is contractual, it may not be unilaterally varied. The question may also arise when an employer is seeking to dismiss an employee. Where the handbook provides, for example, a disciplinary procedure, and the employer proposes to dismiss in breach of that procedure, the employee may seek an injunction to restrain dismissal (see 8.23 below). Such an injunction can only be granted where the procedure relied upon is contractual. If the procedure does not have contractual force, there is no legal foundation for such an injunction.

A code of policy is only to be regarded as having contractual effect when it may be regarded as conferring rights on employees. If it lays down standards of good practice which an employer would be expected to follow, it does not have contractual effect (*Wandsworth London Borough Council v D'Silva* [1998] IRLR 193, CA). In *D'Silva* the employer sought unilaterally to alter the terms of a sickness policy. The employee alleged that this would be in breach of contract. The Court of Appeal held that since the policy was not intended to confer rights but was only a statement of good practice, the employer could alter the terms without securing the agreement of the employees.

In *Keeley v Fosroc International Ltd* [2006] EWCA Civ 1277. [2006] IRLR 961, the Court of Appeal held that even where a handbook was expressly incorporated, that did not mean that the full content of the handbook had contractual effect. It was particularly relevant to consider the importance of the provision for the employee. If it was clearly worded as conferring an entitlement on the employee, it was likely to have contractual effect. It was not determinative that the passage in the handbook was described as a policy.

Even where the policy is contractual, its effect will depend on the construction of the contract as a whole. Thus, the House of Lords held in *Taylor v Secretary of State for Scotland* [2000] IRLR 502 that the inclusion in the contract of an equal opportunities policy which undertook that there should be no discrimination on the grounds of age did not prevent the employer from dismissing an employee on the grounds that he had reached the minimum retirement age.

8.12   Express or implied terms

The terms of the contract may be express or implied or incorporated.

Express terms are those that the parties specifically deal with and agree upon. The express terms of the contract may be found in a document described as the contract of employment or in an offer letter. The provisions set out in a statement of written particulars will be evidence of the express terms, albeit that the statement of written particulars is not the contract itself. The parties may agree upon certain points by reference to a document such as a collective agreement which thereby becomes incorporated into the agreement between the parties (see 6.2 COLLECTIVE AGREEMENTS).

In *R v Hull University Visitor, ex p Page* [1992] ICR 67 at 80D–80F, Staughton LJ was of the view that a job advertisement should be read together with a letter of appointment (the case later went to the House of Lords: [1993] ICR 114). Implied and incorporated terms are dealt with below.

8.13   Common implied terms

Frequently, many terms of the contract will not be specifically set out or stated. There may be many rights and obligations on either side which are left unexpressed and unspecified. The general rule is that a term will be implied into a contract if it is so obvious that both parties would have regarded it as a term even though they had not expressly stated it as a term or if it is *necessary* to imply the term in order to give the contract business efficacy (*Liverpool City Council v Irwin* [1977] AC 239; *Scally v Southern Health and Social Services Board* [1991] ICR 771 at 781). Terms also may be implied if they are customary in the trade or calling, or form the usual practice of the particular employer, if it is sufficiently well known. Such a custom or practice must be 'reasonable, certain and notorious' (*Bond v CAV Ltd* [1983] IRLR 360). In order to become an implied term, a custom must be followed with regularity such that it becomes legitimate to infer that the parties follow the practice because they regard it as a legal obligation rather than that the practice is followed as a matter of policy: *Solectron Scotland Ltd v Roper* [2004] IRLR 4.

Terms commonly implied are the *employee's* duties of:

(a)   fidelity;

(b)   obedience;

(c)   working with due diligence and care;

(d)   not using or disclosing the employer's trade secrets or confidential information;

and the *employer's* duty:

(e)   not to destroy the relationship of trust and confidence between the employer and the employee (see below under 'Employer's duties' for more detail);

(f)   to take care for the employee's health and safety;

and the duty of *both parties:*

(*g*)   to give a reasonable period of notice of termination, when no specific notice has been agreed.

The above list is not exhaustive: other duties can arise in various circumstances. Some of them are dealt with below.

Employee's duties. An employee has a duty to serve his employer faithfully and not to act against the interests of the employer's business. Thus, it would be in breach of an implied term of the contract of employment for the employee to set up a rival business to that of his employer during the period of his employment, unless he had been expressly permitted to do so, or to take more than preparatory steps towards doing so: *Balston Ltd v Headline Filters Ltd* [1990] FSR 385. However, mere preparations to set up a competing business after the termination of the employment are not necessarily a breach of contract (*Ixora Trading Inc v Jones* [1990] FSR 251).

The line between legitimate and illegitimate steps may be difficult to draw. It has been held that it is not decisive to consider whether the acts done by the employee are described as preparatory: *Helmet Integrated Systems v Tunnard* [2007] IRLR 126. It is a question for decision in each case whether the employee's conduct in seeking to set up a new business is legitimate or illegitimate. In the *Tunnard* case it was held that an employee did not act in breach of contract when he designed a product intended to compete with his employer's. The Court reached this view partly on the basis that the contract of employment did not sufficiently restrict his ability to prepare for future competition. That analysis does not sit happily with the existence of the implied duty of fidelity and the position that breach of that implied term is sufficient. The Court also noted that he was a salesman and not a technical designer. In principle, an employee crosses the line and acts unlawfully when his acts are inconsistent with his duty of fidelity (see *Shepherds Investments Ltd v Walters* [2006] IRLR 110, [2006] EWHC 836, Ch, a case concerned primarily with directors). Another example (albeit that this was a case about a director's fiduciary duty) is *Foster Bryant Surveying Ltd v Bryant* [2007] EWCA Civ 200, [2007] IRLR 425. It is also a breach of contract for an employee to tender for future business from a customer of the employer in competition with the employer (*Adamson v B & L Cleaning Services Ltd* [1995] IRLR 193. For the implied obligation not to use or disclose the employer's trade secrets or confidential information, see 41.12 RESTRAINT OF TRADE, CONFIDENTIALITY AND EMPLOYEE INVENTIONS.

The employee is also obliged by the implied terms of his contract of employment to obey the reasonable instructions of his employer and to carry out his work conscientiously and honestly. In *Sybron Corpn v Rochem Ltd* [1984] Ch 112, it was held that the terms and nature of a particular employment might be such that there was a contractual duty to disclose the misconduct of other employees (see also *Item Software (UK) Ltd v Fassihi* [2005] EWCA Civ 1244, [2005] ICR 450).

A work to rule or withdrawal of goodwill may amount to a breach of the implied obligation to serve the employer faithfully (*Secretary of State for Employment v ASLEF (No 2)* [1972] ICR 19; *British Telecommunications plc v Ticehurst* [1992] ICR 383).

The duties of obedience and fidelity are also owed to an employer to whom the employee is seconded (*Macmillan Inc v Bishopsgate Investment Trust plc* [1993] IRLR 393).

A distinction must be drawn between the duty to serve the employer in good faith, which is owed by all employees, and fiduciary duties, which are not an incident of every employment relationship. When a person is a fiduciary (such as a trustee or a company director), he is obliged to pursue another's interests at the expense of his own. In the case of an employee, his obligation is to comply with the express and implied terms of his contract (for a discussion of the distinction, see *Nottingham University v Fishel* [2000] IRLR 471). By way of further example of the difference, an employee is not under an implied obligation to reveal his own misconduct, but a fiduciary is under such an obligation (*Tesco Stores Ltd v Pook* [2004] IRLR 618); *Item Software (UK) Ltd v Fassihi* [2005] EWCA Civ 1244, [2005] ICR 450). Senior employees may owe fiduciary obligations by reason of their seniority even if they are not directors: *Shepherds Investments Ltd v Walters* [2006] IRLR 110.

In *Cresswell v Board of Inland Revenue* [1984] ICR 508, it was held that an employee was expected to adapt to new methods and techniques in performing his duties, provided the employer arranged for him to receive the necessary training in the new skills and the nature of the work did not alter so radically that it was outside the contractual obligation of the employee. If the employer has an express power to transfer the employee to other duties, he is not subject to an implied requirement to exercise that power reasonably, provided that he has some proper grounds for the exercise of the express power and he does not exercise it in such a way as to destroy trust and confidence between himself and the employee (*White v Reflecting Roadstuds Ltd* [1991] ICR 733). Similarly, an express right in the employer to require a particular number of hours per week to be worked must be construed as being subject to the employer's duty to safeguard the employee's health and safety (*Johnstone v Bloomsbury Health Authority* [1991] ICR 269).

There must be some contractual term, express or implied, dealing with the place where the employee may be required to work. If there is no express term, that term will be implied which the parties would have agreed if they had directed their minds to the problem. All the circumstances of the case will be considered, including the nature of the business, the nature of the employee's duties and his status, what the employee was told when employed and whether he has in fact been moved from time to time, and whether there is any provision for the payment of expenses for working away from home. The term implied may be that the employee can be required to work anywhere within reasonable daily travelling distance of his home (*O'Brien v Associated Fire Alarms Ltd* [1969] 1 All ER 93; *Jones v Associated Tunnelling Co Ltd* [1981] IRLR 477; *Courtaulds Northern Spinning Ltd v Sibson* [1988] ICR 451). See also *Little v Charterhouse Magna Assurance Co Ltd* [1980] IRLR 19 and *Rank Xerox Ltd v Churchill* [1988] IRLR 280. However, such a 'mobility clause' (whether express or implied) may be matched by implied obligations to give reasonable notice of the move (see *United Bank Ltd v Akhtar* [1989] IRLR 507; *Prestwick Circuits Ltd v McAndrew* [1990] IRLR 191; and cf *White*, above). Although there must be a term which identifies where the employee is to work, it is not necessary in every case to imply a mobility clause. Whether or not it is necessary to imply such a clause will depend on the nature of the work and the other facts of the case (*Aparau v Iceland Frozen Foods plc* [1996] IRLR 119). It appears that an employer may only effectively rely upon a mobility clause if he makes it clear that he is doing so (*Curling v Securicor Ltd* [1992] IRLR 549).

In *Bass Leisure Ltd v Thomas* [1994] IRLR 104, the EAT held that the place where an employee works is a question of fact to be determined by considering where the employee in fact works rather than where she can be required to work (see 38.7 REDUNDANCY – I). This approach was approved by the Court of Appeal in *High Tables Ltd v Horst* [1997] IRLR 513. (Compare *Gale v Northern General*

Hospital NHS Trust [1994] IRLR 292, which was concerned specifically with the construction of *National Health Service and Community Care Act 1990, s 6(1)*.)

Employer's duties: trust and confidence. It is now well established that there is a term implied into a contract of employment that the parties to that contract will not, without reasonable and proper cause, conduct themselves in a manner calculated or likely to destroy or seriously damage the relationship of confidence and trust which should exist between employer and employee. This implied term has been approved by the House of Lords in the landmark decision of *Malik v BCCI* [1997] IRLR 462. In *Eastwood v Magnox Electric plc* [2004] UKHL 35, [2004] IRLR 733, the term was referred to as one which obliged the employer to treat his employees fairly and to act responsibly and in good faith towards them. (The term is that the parties will not act in a way calculated **or** likely to destroy or seriously damage the relationship of trust and confidence. In *Malik* Lord Steyn said the term applied to conduct calculated **and** likely to have that effect. But by reference to other cases, the EAT has re-confirmed that it is 'calculated or likely' and not 'calculated and likely': *Baldwin v Brighton and Hove Council* [2007] IRLR 232. It has also been held that the test for determining whether the employer has acted in breach of this term is a severe one: the conduct of the employer must be such as to destroy or seriously damage the relationship, and there must have been no reasonable and proper cause for the conduct (*Gogay v Hertfordshire County Council* [2000] IRLR 703, CA, paras 53–55). This term is fundamental to the employment relationship and any breach of it is likely to be repudiatory of the contract: *Morrow v Safeway Stores plc* [2002] IRLR 9, EAT. However, it is important to bear in mind that both limbs of the term are important: conduct which destroys trust and confidence is not in breach of contract if there is a reasonable cause (*Hilton v Shiner Ltd Builders Merchants* [2001] IRLR 727). The Court of Appeal has deprecated the use of loose language in some cases which may appear to extend the scope of the implied term (into, for example, an obligation of 'fair dealing'). The proper approach is to apply the language of the House of Lords in *Malik*: see *Transco plc v O'Brien* [2002] EWCA Civ 379, [2002] ICR 721. However, in *Eastwood v Magnox* [2004] IRLR 733, Lord Steyn preferred the formulation 'the implied obligation of good faith'.

The implied term that the employer will not act in a manner calculated or likely to destroy or seriously to damage the relationship of trust and confidence between employer and employee is capable of being relevant in a very wide range of circumstances. Breaches of this implied term are often cited in constructive dismissal cases and a number of examples are given in that context (see 53.7 UNFAIR DISMISSAL – I).

It has been held that an employer's failure to adhere to statutory obligations may give rise to a breach of the implied term. Thus in *Nottinghamshire County Council v Meikle* [2004] IRLR 703 it was held that an employer's continuing failure to make the reasonable adjustments which were required to be made in order to accommodate the employee's disability was in breach of contract. (See also *Greenhof v Barnsley Metropolitan Borough Council* [2006] IRLR 98.) This case should not be pushed too far. It is wrong to suggest that every breach by an employer of his statutory obligations involves a breach of contract – *Doherty v British Midland Airways Ltd* [2006] IRLR 90.

In *Hill v General Accident Fire & Life Assurance Co plc* [1998] IRLR 641, the Court of Session specifically rejected a submission that, as a result of *Malik*, a new approach had to be taken to the interpretation of contracts of employment and that they had to be construed in a way which furthered mutual trust. The English courts have shown similar restraint. In *University of Nottingham v Eyett*

[1999] IRLR 87, it was held that there had been no breach of the implied term by an employer who failed to advise the employee that if he delayed his retirement by a short time, he would be paid a higher pension than that which he actually received. An employer can be held in breach of this term by reason of a failure to act.

In considering the extent of the implied term of trust and confidence, it is important to bear in mind that the obligation in question relates to the maintenance of the trust and confidence which should exist in an employment relationship. There is no implied obligation on the employer to act reasonably: see *Post Office v Roberts* [1980] IRLR 347. The Privy Council appears importantly to have limited the scope of the implied term. Where there is an untrammelled express power in a contract (for example, to dismiss without cause or to require an employee to move location) the implied term cannot operate to limit the scope of that power: *Reda v Flag Ltd* [2002] UKPC 38, [2002] IRLR 747. This is a timely re-affirmation of the rule that implied terms in contracts must give way to and may not contradict express terms.

There is a further crucial limitation on the efficacy of the implied term of trust and confidence. It is inoperative in connection with decisions to terminate employment: *Johnson v Unisys Ltd* [2001] UKHL 13, [2001] ICR 480. The reason for this is purely policy. Since Parliament has enacted the right not to be unfairly dismissed, it would be an abuse of the judicial function to develop or apply an implied term that co-existed with the statutory provisions in regulating the manner of dismissal. It would be wrong, for example, for the common law to develop a right which overlapped with the right not to be unfairly dismissed but which was not subject to the same limitations, in respect of, for example, continuity of employment and time limits for the presentation of claims, which Parliament has decided should apply to unfair dismissal claims.

Thus, an employee cannot complain that his dismissal was in breach of the implied term of trust and confidence. It is, however, possible to formulate a claim for breach of the implied term of trust and confidence in respect of things done by the employer prior to dismissal. A line is drawn between unfairness in respect of dismissal, which can only be the subject of a statutory claim of unfair dismissal and unfairness before the dismissal which gives rise to a separate cause of action. Usually, it is the employer's decision to dismiss, rather than any earlier act, which gives rise to loss. There may be exceptional cases where this is not so. Examples might include cases of unjustified suspension (as in *Gogay v Hertfordshire County Council* [2000] IRLR 703) or cases where an employee suffers psychiatric illness as a result of pre-dismissal unfairness. Examples of the latter are *Eastwood v Magnox Electric plc* and *McCabe v Cornwall County Council* [2004] UKHL 35, [2004] IRLR 733. In both cases employees alleged that they had suffered psychiatric illness as a result of the ways in which the employers had conducted investigations and disciplinary proceedings. The claims were originally struck out as having no basis in law in the light of *Johnson* but the House of Lords held that the claims, being based on allegations about pre-dismissal conduct, did disclose a cause of action and could proceed to trial.

In some cases, where a breach of this duty is alleged the question may arise whether the employer is liable for the act said to constitute the breach. Thus, in *Moores v Bude-Stratton Town Council* [2000] IRLR 676 an individual councillor verbally abused an employee. When the employee resigned and claimed constructive dismissal, the issue arose whether the council was liable for the acts of the individual back-bench councillor. A majority of the EAT (Lindsay J dissenting) held that the council was liable. For the parameters of an employer's liability, see

VICARIOUS LIABILITY (55). Even if the employer is not vicariously liable for the acts complained of, he may be directly liable for failing to supervise or prevent those acts: see *Waters v Metropolitan Police Comr* [2000] IRLR 720. In *Waters*, the House of Lords held that an employer might be liable to his employee in negligence if he knew of or foresaw acts being done by other employees which might cause physical or mental harm to the employee but did nothing to prevent or supervise such acts when it was in his power to do so. The argument in *Waters* was concerned with the tort of negligence. However, in that case there was no contract between the police officer and the commissioner. One can see how, in a case where there was a contract of employment, the implied term of trust and confidence would impose a similar duty in contract on the employer.

Other implied terms. The contract of employment will also be held to include an implied term that the employer will take reasonable steps to ensure the employee's safety (see comments in *Dutton & Clark Ltd v Daly* [1985] IRLR 363, *Johnstone v Bloomsbury Health Authority* [1991] ICR 269 and HEALTH AND SAFETY AT WORK – I (27)). This includes providing a safe system of work. The duty to provide a safe system of work should not be limited to preventing physical injury. Employers also owe a duty to take reasonable care not to cause psychiatric harm to an employee by reason of the volume or character of work imposed on the employee. The standard of care depends on what is reasonable conduct for a person in the employer's position. What is reasonable depends on the nature of the relationship, the magnitude of the risk of injury that was reasonably foreseeable, the serious-ness of the consequences for the employee if that injury should occur, and the cost and practicability of preventing the risk (*Walker v Northumberland County Council* [1995] IRLR 35).

In *Waltons & Morse v Dorrington* [1997] IRLR 488, it was held that a term was to be implied into every contract of employment that 'the employer will provide and monitor for employees, so far as is reasonably practicable, a working environment which is reasonably suitable for the performance by them of their contractual duties'. In that case, the employer acted in breach of the term by requiring a non-smoking secretary to work in a smoke-filled environment.

In *WA Goold (Pearmak) Ltd v McConnell* [1995] IRLR 516, the EAT held that it was an implied term that the employer would 'reasonably and promptly afford a reasonable opportunity to their employees to obtain redress of any grievance they may have'. The basis for the implication of this term was the statutory obligation to include in the written statement of terms, a note specifying to whom and in what manner an employee might apply for the purpose of seeking redress of any grievance relating to employment (see 8.5 above).

In some cases, it may be argued that there is no duty upon an employer to provide work. In other words, so long as the employee is fully remunerated, the employer can ask him to stay at home without being in breach of contract. However, a contract of employment may be subject to an implied obligation to provide work where earnings vary according to the work done, where an individual such as an actor is dependent upon publicity, or where the employee has skills that may atrophy through lack of use. See *Langston v AUEW (Nos 1 and 2)* [1974] ICR 180 and 510; *Breach v Epsylon Industries Ltd* [1976] ICR 316; *Spencer v Marchington* [1988] IRLR 392; and cf *Warren v Mendy* [1989] ICR 525. The range of cases in which the court will imply an obligation to provide work may expand following the decision of the Court of Appeal in *William Hill Organisation v Tucker* [1998] IRLR 313. There it was held that the question of whether there was an obligation to provide work depended on the facts of each case. The question was whether the consideration moving from the employer extended to an obligation to permit the employee to do the work or whether it was confined to a duty to pay the agreed remuneration.

In *McClory v Post Office* [1992] ICR 758, the court was prepared to imply a term that the employer's express right to suspend the employee must be exercised on reasonable grounds, although not to imply any term that the employer should when exercising that power observe the principles of natural justice. The case also contains a useful discussion of the circumstances in which an employee may have a contractual right to work overtime.

In *Marshall (Cambridge) Ltd v Hamblin* [1994] IRLR 260, the EAT held by a majority that an employee who has resigned has no right to work out his notice period (in the absence, of course, of any express term or custom and practice to the contrary). The employee's only right was to pay in lieu of notice, even though the majority of the employee's income was based on commission.

In *Scally v Southern Health and Social Services Board* [1991] ICR 771, the House of Lords held that the employer was under an implied duty to take reasonable steps to bring to the employee's attention a right which he had (in that case, to purchase extra years' service for superannuation purposes) but which he would lose unless he took certain action, given that the employee could not reasonably have been expected to be aware of the relevant contractual term without it being drawn to his attention.

However, there is no implied term that the employer will take reasonable care of his employees' economic well-being: *Crossley v Faithful & Gould Holdings* [2004] EWCA Civ 293, [2004] IRLR 377.

Where a contract of employment contains terms entitling the employee to benefits during a period of ill health and the continued receipt of such benefits is dependent on the individual remaining in the employer's employment, a term will be implied that the employer will not dismiss the employee while he remains incapacitated so as to deprive him of the continued receipt of those benefits (*Aspden v Webbs Poultry & Meat Group (Holdings) Ltd* [1996] IRLR 521). A similar approach was taken in Scotland in *Adin v Sedco Forex International Resources Ltd* [1997] IRLR 280 (and see *Brompton v AOC International* [1997] IRLR 639, para 38).

The extent to which an employer may dismiss an employee who is in receipt of sick pay and/or who anticipates that, if his contract of employment continues in force, he will in due course be entitled to early retirement or to some other benefit was the issue in the Court of Session case of *Hill v General Accident Fire and Life Assurance Corpn plc* [1998] IRLR 641. The employee in that case was in receipt of sick pay. If he had remained employed and in receipt of sick pay for a further four months, he would have been entitled to an ill-health retirement pension or to sickness and accident benefit. The employer terminated his contract by reason of redundancy. Mr Hill sued alleging that the termination of his employment was in breach of the implied duty of trust and confidence and that, whilst he was absent sick and in receipt of sick pay or with an anticipation of early retirement or other benefits, his employment could be terminated only by reason of his own repudiatory breach of contract. The court held that a person in Mr Hill's position could not be dismissed by reason of his absence, or for a specious reason, or for no reason at all. The power to dismiss included, but was not limited to, the case where the employee acted in repudiatory breach of contract. Accordingly, a dismissal by reason of redundancy was not in breach of the implied term of trust and confidence. In *Villella v MFI Furniture Centre Ltd* [1999] IRLR 468, a case concerning Permanent Health Insurance, the High Court formulated an implied term that the employer would not terminate the contract of employment, save for cause other than ill health, in circumstances which would deprive the employee of his continuing entitlement to benefit.

It has also been held that where an employer provides a benefit such as PHI and the insurer fails to pay, there is an implied obligation on the employer to pursue the insurer for payment, including, if need be, by litigation: *Marlow v East Thames Housing Group* [2002] IRLR 798. The extent of the obligation would of course depend on the merits of the employee's argument.

The *Aspden* line of cases has been applied by analogy to the case where an employer proposes to dismiss for redundancy and employees have the benefit of a contractual redundancy package. In *Jenvey v Australian Broadcasting Corpn* [2002] EWHC 927 (QB), [2003] ICR 79 it was held that where the employer had proposed to dismiss for redundancy with the consequence that the employee would enjoy a contractual payment, it was an implied term that the employer would not then dismiss for any other reason (apart from cause) if to do so would defeat those contractual rights.

In the absence of any express term governing the notice required to be given to terminate the contract, it is an implied term that reasonable notice of termination will be given. Reasonable notice will not be implied if to do so would contradict an express term, eg a term giving a party the right to terminate at any time without cause. The implication of the term is necessary in order to provide a means by which a contract of otherwise indefinite duration may be terminated. If the express terms make provision, there is no need to imply a term: *Reda v Flag Ltd* [2002] UKPC 38, [2002] IRLR 747. What is reasonable will depend on all the facts of the case (see 48.6 TERMINATION OF EMPLOYMENT).

Contracts providing an entitlement to bonus often confer a discretion on the employer in relation to the amount of the bonus. It is an implied term that such a discretion will be exercised rationally and lawfully: *Horkulak v Cantor Fitzgerald International* [2004] IRLR 942, CA. In that case, damages for breach of contract by not making a bonus payment were assessed on the basis of what the employer would have paid had it exercised the discretion genuinely and rationally. The court stood in the shoes of the employer and decided what sums would have been awarded once it was established that the sum awarded by the employer was in breach of contract.

However, the Court of Appeal has stressed the limited role of the Court in such claims. It is no part of the Court's function to decide what bonus should have been awarded. The Court is concerned only to ensure that the employer complies with its legal obligation to exercise its discretion in good faith and rationally. It was emphasised that the employer had a wide discretion and that the burden of establishing that a bonus paid was irrational was 'a very high one': *Keen v Commerzbank AG* [2006] EWCA Civ 1536, [2007] ICR 623, sub nom Commerzbank AG v Keen [2007] IRLR 132.

Incorporated terms. These are terms which are incorporated into the contract rather than being agreed individually between the parties. There are two principal sources of incorporated terms. One is collective agreements (see COLLECTIVE AGREEMENTS (6)), and the other is statute. Thus the *Equal Pay Act* incorporates into every contract of employment an 'equality clause'. The *Employment Act 2002, s 30* appears to incorporate into contracts of employment a contractual obligation to comply with the statutory disciplinary and grievance procedures laid down by that *Act*.

8.14   Terms automatically varied by statute

Terms which, although they are agreed between the parties, are in breach of certain statutory provisions take effect as if varied to comply with those provisions. For example:

(*a*)   terms which are less advantageous than those which apply to a member of the opposite sex doing the same or like work, or work of equal value (see 24.5 EQUAL PAY), or which infringe the law on sex discrimination; or

(*b*)   terms providing for the employment of directors for a fixed period of more than five years (see 9.3 DIRECTORS).

8.15   Terms which are unlawful or contrary to public policy

A contract the terms of which are unlawful (e g to do an unlawful act) or which are contrary to public policy (e g a contract for an immoral purpose) is unenforceable in a court of law. The same may be true where the contract, although capable of being performed lawfully, has in fact been performed illegally. Further, relief will not be granted to a party if to do so would 'affront the public conscience'. The general law as to illegality was summarised by the Court of Appeal in *Euro-Diam v Bathurst* [1990] 1 QB 1. In *Colen v Cebrian (UK) Ltd* [2003] EWCA Civ 1676, [2004] ICR 568, the Court of Appeal gave the following guidance. In order for a contract to become unenforceable by reason of illegality, it must be shown either that the contract was entered into with the object of committing an illegal act or that it was performed with that objective. If the contract was lawful when entered into and was intended to be performed lawfully, some illegal act done does not in every case make the entire contract unenforceable. It is necessary to consider the intentions of the parties to the contract. The court will not assist a party who has to rely on his own illegal act for the purposes of his claim. If he does not have to pray in aid the unlawful act, it is a question of fact in each case whether the method of performance of the contract or the degree of participation in the illegal act means that the contact is unenforceable by reason of illegality. The burden of establishing that the contract was illegal rests on the person making that allegation.

For example, contracts which are a fraud on the Inland Revenue cannot be relied upon to pursue claims for wrongful or unfair dismissal (*Napier v National Business Agency Ltd* [1951] 2 All ER 264; *Tomlinson v Dick Evans U Drive Ltd* [1978] ICR 639). A foreign employee knowingly working illegally without a work permit will not be able to complain of unfair dismissal (*Sharma v Hindu Temple*, IDS Brief 464, p 5; for work permits, see 26.4 FOREIGN EMPLOYEES). Similarly, the contract of employment of an employee taking employment in breach of the terms on which he has been permitted entry to the UK is unlawful (*Vakante v Governing Body of Addey and Stanhope School* [2005] ICR 231, CA). If the employee was not aware of the fact that the contract was being performed unlawfully by the employer (by, for example, not deducting tax from remuneration) the employee may rely on the contract for the purposes of claiming employment protection rights (*Newland v Simons and Willer (Hairdressers) Ltd* [1981] ICR 521). However, ignorance of the law as opposed to the facts is no excuse (*Miller v Karlinski* (1945) 62 TLR 85). Nor is the fact that the parties did not intend to break the law relevant (*Salvesen v Simon* [1994] ICR 409). The mere fact that in the course of performing an otherwise lawful contract, the employee has committed an unlawful or immoral act does not bar him from bringing a claim for unfair dismissal (*Coral Leisure Group Ltd v Barnett* [1981] ICR 503; *Hewcastle Catering Ltd v Ahmed* [1992] ICR 626). Thus, the fact that an employee did not pay tax on occasional payments received outside his contract of employment did not have the effect of rendering the contract of employment illegal in *Annandale Engineering v Samson* [1994] IRLR 59. Further, the claim may be brought if the employer's conduct in participating in an illegal contract is so reprehensible in comparison with that of the employee that it would be wrong to allow the employer to rely on the illegality (cf *Euro-Diam*, above).

The distinction between unlawful tax evasion and lawful tax avoidance must be borne in mind. The fact that an employee lawfully arranges matters so as to minimise liability to tax does not render the contract of employment illegal (*Lightfoot v D & J Sporting Ltd* [1996] IRLR 64).

The fact that a contract is unenforceable by reason of illegality does not preclude a person employed under such a contract from bringing claims of sex (or presumably race or disability or religion or belief or sexual orientation) discrimination. The reason for this is that such actions do not seek to enforce the unenforceable contract (*Leighton v (1) Michael and (2) Charalambous* [1996] IRLR 67) unless the claim arises out of or is inextricably bound up with the conduct which causes the contract to be illegal (see *Hall v Woolston Hall Leisure Ltd* [2000] IRLR 578, CA, in which *Leighton* was approved).

8.16 UNENFORCEABLE TERMS

Certain terms, while not being unlawful in the sense of rendering an employer liable to criminal prosecution or a civil action, may be unenforceable by him, as set out in 8.17–8.20 below.

8.17 Restrictions upon contracting out of certain statutory provisions

With some exceptions, for instance where a conciliation officer (see 2.3 ADVISORY, CONCILIATION AND ARBITRATION SERVICE) has exercised his statutory powers in the settlement of certain claims or where there has been a valid compromise agreement (see 20.27 EMPLOYMENT TRIBUNALS), an employer or employee may not contract out of the following Acts.

> *Sex Discrimination Act 1975* (see *s 77*)
>
> *Equal Pay Act 1970* (see *SDA 1975, s 77*)
>
> *Race Relations Act 1976* (see *s 72*)
>
> *ERA 1996, Part II* (see *s 203(1), (2)*)
>
> *Trade Union and Labour Relations (Consolidation) Act 1992* (see *s 288*)
>
> *Disability Discrimination Act 1995* (see *s 9*)
>
> *Working Time Regulations 1998* (save insofar as the *Regulations* permit the parties to agree that the operation of the *Regulations* is to be excluded or limited)
>
> *Employment Act 2002* (see *s 30(2)*)
>
> *Employment Equality (Religion or Belief) Regulations 2003* (see *sch 4 pt 1, para 1(3)*)
>
> *Employment Equality (Sexual Orientation) Regulations 2003* (see *reg 35 and sch 4, para 1(1)*)

Any attempt to do so will be ineffective.

8.18   Discriminatory terms

Terms in contracts which are contrary to the provisions of the discrimination legislation are void and unenforceable against the person discriminated against. See *Sex Discrimination Act 1975, s77; Race Relations Act 1976, s 72; Disability Discrimination Act 1995, Sch 3A; Religion or Belief Regulations, Sch 4, Pt 1; Sexual Orientation Regulations, reg 35 and Sch 4*. Similarly, any term in a collective agreement which discriminates on grounds of sex, sexual orientation or religion or belief is void and unenforceable against the party discriminated against (see *SDA 1986, s 6; RRA s 72A; DDA 1995, Sch 3A; Religion or Belief Regulations, Sch 4, Pt 2; Sexual Orientation Regulations, Sch 4, Pt 2*).

8.19   Terms in restraint of trade

Sometimes, a contract will contain a term restricting the employee's freedom to work after he leaves his employment. Such terms will be regarded as 'in restraint of trade' and therefore unenforceable if their main purpose is simply to restrain competition. However, if the main purpose is to protect something in which the employer has a legitimate interest, such as trade secrets or confidential information, or to protect the employer's goodwill or *'customer connection'* (as it is called in this context), then such a term may be enforceable. These questions are discussed in more detail in RESTRAINT OF TRADE, CONFIDENTIALITY AND EMPLOYEE INVENTIONS (41).

8.20   Restrictions on industrial action

Provisions in collective agreements which purport to restrict the right to take industrial action cannot form part of the individual contract of employment unless certain conditions are satisfied (see 6.5 COLLECTIVE AGREEMENTS).

8.21   Unfair Contract Terms Act 1977

The effect of the *Unfair Contract Terms Act 1977* ('*UCTA 1977*') is to render certain types of contractual term unenforceable, and others unenforceable unless they satisfy a test of reasonableness laid down in *UCTA 1977, s 11* (namely, that the term was a fair and reasonable one to be included having regard to the circumstances which were, or ought reasonably to have been, known to or in the contemplation of the parties when the contract was made; in applying this test the court is directed to have regard to certain specific considerations).

Despite earlier indications to the contrary, it has now been held that *UCTA* does not apply to contracts of employment. The reason for this is that *UCTA* applies only to those who either 'deal as a consumer' or deal 'on the other [party's] written standard terms of business'. In *Keen v Commerzbank AG* [2006] EWCA Civ 1536, [2007] ICR 623, sub nom Commerzbank AG v Keen [2007] IRLR 132, the Court of Appeal held that an employee neither dealt as a consumer nor on his employer's standard terms of business. Employers do not deal with their employees as consumers; the business of an employer is not employing its staff.

In the light of this judgment, no further consideration will be given to *UCTA* in this work

8.22   CHANGE IN TERMS OF CONTRACT

No change in the terms of an employee's contract may be made without his consent. Such consent may be *express*, by the employee agreeing to the change orally or, preferably, in writing. Alternatively, it may be *implied*, by the employee continuing to work for the employer without protest for a significant period of time whilst being aware of the change.

If the change in contractual terms is of great importance to the employer, the only course of action open to him in circumstances in which the employee does not consent, is to give notice to terminate the original contract and offer new terms. Great care must be taken to adhere to a fair procedure when doing this so as to avoid a successful claim for unfair dismissal (see UNFAIR DISMISSAL – II (54)).

Where a change is imposed by the employer and the employee continues to work without objection, it may be that the employee will be held impliedly to have consented to the change. Where the change is one which has an immediate effect on the employee, continuing to work without protest may very well indicate consent. However, where the change is one which does not have an immediate practical effect, the court should exercise caution before inferring consent (*Jones v Associated Tunnelling Co Ltd* [1981] IRLR 477, *Aparau v Iceland Frozen Foods plc* [1996] IRLR 119 and *Solectron Scotland Ltd v Roper* [2004] IRLR 4).

Any change in terms to which the employee does not consent is *prima facie* a breach of contract. If the change is a significant one, the employee may be entitled to resign and allege that he has been constructively dismissed (see 48.19 TERMINATION OF EMPLOYMENT). However, where an employer unilaterally imposes radically different terms of employment, it may be that the correct interpretation is that the employer has terminated the original contract and replaced it with another. Accordingly, there would be a dismissal by the employer (and immediate re-employment) which entitled the employee to bring unfair dismissal proceedings (*Hogg v Dover College* [1990] ICR 39; *Alcan Extrusions v Yates* [1996] IRLR 327; and see UNFAIR DISMISSAL – I (53)).

Although, in *Alexander v Standard Telephones and Cables Ltd (No 2)* [1991] IRLR 286, a High Court judge held that a clear statement by an employer that he is only willing to continue to employ an employee after a period amounting to the notice period on revised terms was equivalent to giving notice to terminate the existing contract, it is doubted that the same view of such a statement would be taken in other cases. *Rigby v Ferodo Ltd* [1988] ICR 29, a relevant decision in the House of Lords, is not referred to in the judgment.

In *Lee v GEC Plessey Telecommunications* [1993] IRLR 383, the High Court held that there was good consideration for any pay rise which followed pay negotiations, so that the employer was legally bound by the increased rate of pay. It was also held that an express power to vary the terms of the contract could only be enforced where it was clearly specified. In *Airlie v Edinburgh District Council* [1996] IRLR 517, the EAT in Scotland held that a contract could be varied without consent where it contained a term permitting unilateral variation. This case should be approached with caution for it seems to be a dilution of *Lee*.

In some contracts, the employer will expressly reserve the power to vary the terms. The Court of Appeal has indicated that a strict approach should be taken to the interpretation of such provisions. First, it will require clear words to create a power unilaterally to alter the terms of the contract. Second, the court is unlikely to favour an interpretation which does more than vary the contractual provisions with which the employer is required to comply. A court is unlikely to allow an interpretation which goes further and which may affect the rights of the employee under the contract (*Wandsworth London Borough Council v D'Silva* [1998] IRLR 193). Thus, the extent to which an employer will be permitted to rely on an express provision entitling him to vary the terms of a contract, and so to evade the general rule that changes to contracts must be mutually agreed, is likely to be limited.

A particular question which has caused difficulty is whether a change in terms and conditions mutually agreed between the parties can be enforced in the context of the transfer of an undertaking under the *Transfer of Undertakings* (*Protection of Employment*) *Regulations 1981* (*SI 1981/1794*) (*'TUPE 1981'*). This subject is considered fully in TRANSFER OF UNDERTAKINGS (52). The law appears to be that, where there is a transfer of an undertaking, the employer and employee have no power to agree to vary the terms of the contract of employment. This is so even if the variation is to the advantage of the employee. Thus, in *Crédit Suisse First Boston (Europe) Ltd v Lister* [1998] IRLR 700, an employer sought an injunction to enforce a restrictive covenant agreed with the defendant employee as part of the takeover by the employer of the business which previously employed the defendant. That covenant purported to prevent the employee from taking up employment with a competing business. The employee's contract with his previous employer had not contained such a provision. The Court of Appeal refused to grant an injunction on the basis that the provision introducing the restrictive covenant was unenforceable. Enforcement of a new restrictive covenant would be inconsistent with *reg 5* of *TUPE 1981*, which provides that, after a transfer, the employees of the transferor are to be employed by the transferee on the terms of their contract with the transferor. It made no difference that the employee had been paid a substantial sum of money or that other new terms were beneficial to him. The employee and transferee employer had no power to contract out of the mandatory effect of *reg 5*.

8.23   REMEDIES FOR BREACH OF CONTRACT OF EMPLOYMENT

Employee's remedies

If an employer is in breach of contract, his employee may bring proceedings in the High Court or the county court for sums due under the contract and for damages. The employee can bring such an action while remaining in employment. However, if the employer's breach of contract is sufficiently serious, the employee may treat himself as dismissed, leave, and bring proceedings for his prospective loss (see WRONGFUL DISMISSAL (56)) as well as for any sums outstanding at the date of dismissal. The courts are also able to grant declaratory relief. If the breach of contract involves a deduction from pay, the employee may present a complaint to the employment tribunal under *Part II* of the *ERA 1996* (which contains provisions formerly found in the *Wages Act 1986*) (see 27.6 PAY – I). Employment tribunals now also have jurisdiction in relation to certain claims for damages arising on the termination of an employee's employment, as to which see below.

Damages. Where an employee is dismissed summarily in breach of contract, the *prima facie* measure of damages is the sum which the employer would have had to pay in order to bring the contract to an end lawfully – that is to say, the sum payable in respect of the notice period. However, it will often be a term of the contract that the employer must follow a disciplinary or other procedure prior to dismissal. In such cases, if the employee can show that the conduct of the procedure would take time and, therefore, extend the period of employment, he may be able to claim as damages lost wages for the time which the disciplinary or other procedure would have taken, in addition to pay for the notice period (see *Boyo v London Borough of Lambeth* [1995] IRLR 50 and *Focsa Services (UK) Ltd v Birkett* [1996] IRLR 325). However, in assessing compensation, the tribunal must work on the basis that the outcome of the pursuit of the disciplinary or other procedure would have been the same (*Janciuk v Winerite* [1998] IRLR 63). This means that an employee cannot be compensated in a breach of contract claim on the basis that, had a contractual disciplinary procedure been pursued, he would not have been dismissed. The limit of compensation is the time which would have been taken to pursue the procedure.

Damages payable will include damages for loss of pension rights that would have accrued had the employee not been dismissed summarily in breach of contract: *Silvey v Pendragon plc* [2001] EWCA Civ 784, [2001] IRLR 685.

Of course, an employee need not actually have commenced duties in order to be able to bring a claim. So, for example, where an offer of employment is made and accepted, there is a valid contract of employment even if the start date is postponed. If the contract is terminated before the actual start date, the employee will have a claim for wrongful dismissal. He may also have other claims such as discrimination or unfair dismissal for an inadmissible reason (see *Sarker v South Tees Acute Hospitals NHS Trust* [1997] IRLR 328 and 23.5 ENGAGEMENT OF EMPLOYEES).

No damages for loss of the chance to claim unfair dismissal. Sometimes, employers dismiss employees summarily in order to prevent the employee from accruing a sufficient period of qualifying employment to bring a claim for unfair dismissal. Thus, for example, a person with a month's notice period might be summarily dismissed two weeks before accruing one year's continuous employment. However, it has been held that a claim for damages for breach of contract cannot include damages for the loss of a chance to bring an unfair dismissal claim: *Harper v Virgin Net Ltd* [2004] EWCA Civ 271, [2004] IRLR 390, CA.

Damages for loss of reputation. In *Malik v BCCI SA* [1997] IRLR 462, the House of Lords accepted that it might be possible to recover damages for loss of reputation caused by a breach of contract, provided that a relevant breach of contract could be established and that requirements of causation, remoteness and mitigation are satisfied. It was not necessary that the conduct relied upon be directed at the employees. In that case, the individual employees alleged that their employer had run a corrupt and dishonest business and that, as a result, the employees were tainted by their involvement with their former employer and were at a disadvantage in the job market. These facts were assumed to be true for the purposes of the argument, although no findings were made in respect of them. The Lords held that it would be a breach of the implied term of trust and confidence to operate a dishonest business and that the employees were entitled to argue that they could recover damages for any consequent loss as a result of damage inflicted on their employment prospects. The correct measure of damages where the breach affects employment prospects is to ask: but for the breach by the employer, what would prospective employers considering the claimant's application have done and what would have been the outcome for the employee? (*BCCI SA v Ali (No 3)* [2002] EWCA Civ 82, [2002] IRLR 460).

Damages for the manner of dismissal. The *Malik* case does not alter the principle that damages are not recoverable for the manner of a dismissal, according to the House of Lords in *Johnson v Unisys Ltd* [2001] UKHL 13, [2003] 1 AC 518. By a majority of four to one, their Lordships held that there was no right at common law to recover damages for injury to feeling (even in the case where that injury manifested itself as a psychological injury) caused by dismissal. The House of Lords declined to hold that the implied term of trust and confidence extended to dismissal. Therefore, the general rule precluding recovery of damages for non-pecuniary losses caused by dismissal or the manner of dismissal remained good law. The principal reason for this conclusion was policy. It would be wrong to develop by judicial invention a right to such compensation in circumstances where Parliament had already intervened by creating the right not to be unfairly dismissed. The courts ought not to allow persons to side-step the limits on that right which Parliament had put in place by the creation of a common law right which overlapped to a substantial degree. Lord Hoffmann expressed the view (*obiter*) that damages for unfair dismissal should include 'in an appropriate case … compensation for distress, humiliation, damage to reputation in the community or to family life'. Those who thought unfair dismissal compensation was for purely financial loss had taken too narrow an approach. However, the House of Lords declined to follow Lord Hoffmann's *obiter* comment and has re-affirmed that damages for unfair dismissal are limited to financial losses: *Dunnachie v Kingston upon Hull City Council* [2004] UKHL 36, [2004] IRLR 727.

Johnson v Unisys Ltd has led to some hard cases. Following cases such as *Gogay v Hertfordshire County Council* [2000] IRLR 703, CA an employee might seek to recover damages for psychological injury as a consequence of the manner in which an allegation of misconduct was investigated. The employee would be entitled to rely on the implied term of trust and confidence during the employment to give rise to such a remedy. However, an employee who suffered psychological injury as a result of being dismissed would not be able to recover damages for that injury at common law.

A number of cases in which employees alleged that they had suffered psychiatric injury as a consequence of the investigative or disciplinary process followed by their employer, rather than their dismissal, were struck out at first instance on the ground that they were barred by *Johnson*. However, the House of Lords has now ruled that the effect of *Johnson* is only to preclude common law claims where the employee seeks to recover damages consequent on dismissal. Where it is possible to claim that loss or injury has flowed not from dismissal but from pre-dismissal steps (such as suspension or the anterior conduct of disciplinary procedures), then *Johnson* does not prevent claims being brought: *Eastwood v Magnox Electric plc* and *McCabe v Cornwall County Council* [2004] UKHL 35, [2004] IRLR 733. (See also *King v University Court of University of St Andrews* [2002] IRLR 252.) Nonetheless the position remains that an employee dismissed unfairly may, because of statutory limitations, recover less compensation than a person treated unfairly prior to dismissal.

Express terms regarding damages. In some contracts, most usually those of senior executives, there is a term which provides for sums payable by the employer on breach. A question may arise whether such terms are liquidated damages clauses, which are valid, or penalties, which are unenforceable. A clause is a liquidated damages clause where it represents a genuine pre-estimate of a party's loss in the event of breach. Where the amount to be paid appears designed to deter or punish the wrong-doer rather than to compensate the innocent party, the clause is a penalty. In *Murray v Leisureplay plc* [2005] EWCA Civ 963, [2005] IRLR 946 a clause entitling an executive to three years' pay on termination without the obligation to mitigate was held not to be a penalty. The Court held that a useful test was whether the sum to be paid was extravagant and unconscionable.

Injunctions. In certain circumstances, the courts will grant an employee an injunction to restrain the employer from taking action in breach of contract. This may be done to restrain the implementation of a dismissal where a contractual disciplinary or disputes procedure has not been exhausted (see, eg *Irani v Southampton and South-West Hampshire Health Authority* [1985] ICR 590 and observations in *R v BBC, ex p Lavelle* [1983] ICR 99). In *Barros D'Sa v University*

Hospital Coventry and Warwickshire NHS Trust [2001] EWCA Civ 983, [2001] IRLR 691, there was a two-stage disciplinary procedure. The first stage involved an investigation by an inquiry panel. The second stage involved a disciplinary hearing at which decisions would be taken as to the appropriate course of action depending upon the circumstances and the inquiry panel's recommendations. At the second stage, the employer sought to introduce new material and new allegations against the employee which had not been considered at the inquiry panel stage. The Court of Appeal granted an injunction to prevent that new material and allegation being considered. An employer was not entitled to depart from a contractual disciplinary procedure on the ground that he considered that the relationship of trust and confidence had broken down.

In *Mezey v South West London and St George's Mental Health NHS Trust* [2007] EWHC 62 (QB), [2007] IRLR 237, 244 the Court of Appeal upheld the grant of an injunction to restrain a suspension on full pay on the basis that the decision to suspend, even if permitted by the express terms of the contract, could involve a breach of the implied term of trust and confidence.

An injunction has also been granted to restrain the enforcement of an instruction the employer was not contractually entitled to give (see *Hughes v London Borough of Southwark* [1988] IRLR 55) and to prevent a dismissal which would be in breach of a contractual redundancy selection procedure (*Anderson v Pringle of Scotland* [1998] IRLR 64). However, an injunction will only be granted in the exceptional case where the employer still has full confidence in the employee's continuing ability and other necessary attributes (*Powell v Brent London Borough Council* [1988] ICR 176; *Alexander v Standard Telephones & Cables plc* [1990] ICR 291). In *Robb v Hammersmith and Fulham London Borough Council* [1991] ICR 514, it was suggested that this might not be necessary where the employee will merely be remaining at home under suspension pending a disciplinary hearing. The better view is that no injunction should be granted unless trust and confidence remain between the employer and the employee. To grant an injunction in circumstances where trust and confidence did not remain would be inconsistent with the general rule that there cannot be specific performance of a contract of service. However, within modern contracts of employment, there are often a number of provisions which may be enforced by an injunction without compelling the parties to a contract of employment to perform their obligations to employ and/or to work. Where the parties are in agreement that the contract of employment subsists, albeit in a qualified form (such as where the employee is suspended), then the court may enforce by order parts of the contract which do not compel the parties to co-operate any more than they would be prepared to do in any event. Thus if, for example, the parties agree that the contract subsists albeit that the employee is suspended, then the court may enforce contractual provisions relating to, for example, discipline. Enforcement of such provisions in those circumstances does not require a reluctant employer to employ or a reluctant employee to work (see *Peace v City of Edinburgh Council* [1999] IRLR 417).

In previous cases, injunctions have been granted only to restrain the breach of a *contractual* disciplinary procedure. When *s 30* of the *Employment Act 2002* is brought into force (which the government has indicated it has no present intention to do), it will mean that there is a contractual obligation to comply with the statutory discipline and dismissal procedure. This is because *s 30* provides that contracts shall have effect to require the parties to follow the statutory procedures. If that is correct, then it would appear that an injunction could be granted to restrain *any* dismissal until the disciplinary procedure laid down by *Employment*

Act 2002, Sch 2 had been followed. The injunction may, if necessary, be made conditional upon the employee undertaking to work in accordance with instructions (*Wadcock v London Borough of Brent* [1990] IRLR 223). Similarly, if new working practices are introduced in breach of contract, an injunction will not be granted where, for practical purposes, the old system cannot be restored (*MacPherson v London Borough of Lambeth* [1988] IRLR 470). See also *Dietman v Brent London Borough Council* [1988] ICR 842, *Ali v London Borough of Southwark* [1988] ICR 567 and *Wishart v National Association of Citizens Advice Bureaux Ltd* [1990] ICR 794.

The court will usually first be asked to grant an *interlocutory* injunction, ie one which seeks to restrain the alleged breach of contract pending the trial (which may not happen for several months or even longer). At the interlocutory stage, the judge does not hear oral evidence and will not have time to determine complex questions that may arise. The correct approach is therefore to decide, first, whether there is a serious question to be tried and, second, whether any injustice caused by granting or refusing to grant the injunction could be properly compensated by an award of damages later. A 'serious question to be tried' means that there is an arguable case that the plaintiff is entitled to the relief sought. There must be evidence which supports each of the constituent parts of the plaintiff's claim. The judge will not determine whether the plaintiff's evidence is true. He will, however, have to see that there is at that stage a sufficient basis in fact and law to mean that the claim has some merit. If there is a serious question and damages would not be an adequate remedy, the court may grant an injunction, and the decision whether to do so will depend upon the 'balance of convenience'. This will often lead it to preserve the *status quo* (see *American Cyanamid Co v Ethicon Ltd* [1975] AC 396). Somewhat different considerations may apply where the decision at the interlocutory stage will effectively determine the dispute in favour of one party or the other. In those circumstances, the court will do its best to form a view as to which party has the stronger case (see *Lansing Linde Ltd v Kerr* [1991] ICR 428). Also, where the dispute turns upon a question of law or the construction of a document, the court has power to make a final determination of that question at an interlocutory stage (*Civil Procedure Rules, part 24*, formerly *RSC Ord 14, 14A*). For an example of this course being taken in an employment dispute, see *Jones v Gwent County Council* [1992] IRLR 521.

The courts will not generally make mandatory interlocutory orders for the continued payment of wages where these are sought as an indirect means of obtaining an injunction (see *Alexander*, above; *Jakeman v South West Thames Regional Health Authority and London Ambulance Service* [1990] IRLR 62).

Jurisdiction of employment tribunals. Employment tribunals have jurisdiction to hear claims for breach of contracts of employment or contracts 'connected with employment' other than personal injury claims (*Employment Tribunals Extension of Jurisdiction (England and Wales) Order 1994 (SI 1994/1623)*).

The claim must be one which 'arises or is outstanding on the termination of the employee's employment' (*art 3(c)*). This means that the employee must have an enforceable but unsatisfied claim at the date of termination. The formulation does not enable tribunals to determine claims which, at the termination of employment, are contingent: *Peninsula Business Services v Sweeney* [2004] IRLR 49. *Article 5* specifically excludes a claim relating to:

(*a*)   a term requiring the employer to provide living accommodation for the employee;

(b)   a term imposing an obligation on the employer or the employee in connection with living accommodation;

(c)   a term relating to intellectual property;

(d)   a term imposing an obligation of confidence; and

(e)   a term which is in restraint of trade.

Article 7 provides that an employee must present a contract claim:

(i)   within three months of the effective date of termination of the contract giving rise to the claim (see 51.13 UNFAIR DISMISSAL – I);

(ii)   where there is no effective date of termination, within three months of the date when the employee last worked in the employment which has been terminated; or

(iii)   within such further period as the tribunal considers reasonable, where it was not reasonably practicable for the employee to present a claim in time (see 20.7 EMPLOYMENT TRIBUNALS – I).

The tribunal has jurisdiction only in respect of contracts of employment or those connected with employment (*ERA 1996, s 3(2)*). Thus, an agreement compromising a wrongful dismissal claim effected during employment falls within the tribunal's jurisdiction: *Rock-it Cargo Ltd v Green* [1997] IRLR 581.

The provisions as to the time when a claim must be made mean that the employment tribunal does not have jurisdiction to consider a claim made during the currency of employment. Its jurisdiction is limited to claims submitted after the termination of the employment: see *Capek v Lincolnshire County Council* [2000] ICR 878, CA. Further, the claim must arise or be outstanding on the termination of employment. This means that the tribunal does not have jurisdiction to entertain claims that only arise for the first time after the employment has terminated, eg a settlement of a dismissal claim made after the employment has ended: *Miller Bros and F P Butler v Johnston* [2002] IRLR 386.

Employers are entitled to counterclaim (*arts 4, 8*). Counterclaims must be made at a time when a contract claim by an employee is already before the tribunal and has not been settled or withdrawn. The counterclaim must arise out of a contract with the employee who has made the contract claim.

The time limit for presenting counterclaims is six weeks from the date when the employer (or other respondent to the employee's contract claim) received a copy of the originating application in respect of that employee's contract claim. This period is subject to extension where it was not reasonably practicable for the employer's counterclaim to be presented in time (see 20.7 EMPLOYMENT TRIBUNALS – I).

The Order contains specific provisions relating to death and bankruptcy.

The maximum award which a tribunal may make in respect of a contract claim, or a number of contract claims relating to the same contract, is £25,000 (*art 10*). In many cases, the potential value of a contractual claim may exceed £25,000. The question may arise whether a successful employee in the tribunal who recovers the maximum award may then bring fresh proceedings in the High Court for the remainder of the value of the contractual claim. In *Fraser v HLMAD Ltd* [2006] IRLR 687, [2006] ICR 1395, the Court of Appeal held that no further claim may be brought in the civil courts once a tribunal has ruled on a wrongful dismissal claim. The key point is that, once the court has decided a matter, a claimant may not ask another court to deal with that same matter again. The reason for this is that the employee no longer has a cause of action which he is able to litigate. The cause of action – breach of contract – has been replaced by, or 'merged in' the judgment of the tribunal. The concept of a cause of action merging in a judgment, so precluding a further action being brought in respect of the same cause of action, is well established in law (see *Halsbury's Laws*, Vol 26, paras 550–551). Further, there are several cases in which a party who has succeeded in one forum which has a limited power to award damages has been precluded from seeking to institute fresh proceedings in respect of the same matter in another forum in order to recover the shortfall. In *Hills v Co-operative Wholesale Society Ltd* [1940] 2 KB 435, an employee brought an action in the High Court and in the county court against his employer in respect of the same complaint. A defence of common employment was available to the employer in the High Court but not in the county court. The employer paid into the county court the maximum sum which the employee could recover in that forum and the employee accepted that sum. The Court of Appeal held that the employee could not continue with the High Court proceedings. His cause of action had been completely satisfied when he accepted the payment made in respect of the county court proceedings, notwithstanding that there was a limit on the sum that the county court could award. See also *Wright v London General Omnibus Co* (1877) 2 QBD 271; *Clarke v Yorke* (1882) 52 LJ Ch 32.

It is suggested that a person should not be entitled to bring the same cause of action simultaneously in the tribunal and in the county court or the High Court. Rather, he should be put to his election. An analogy is to be found in *Australian Commercial Research and Development Ltd v ANZ McCaughan Merchant Bank Ltd* [1989] 3 All ER 65 where a plaintiff who had commenced proceedings based on the same cause of action in both England and Queensland was put to his election. It is important that a person chooses carefully in which forum to begin, since cause of action estoppel may be created where an application to the tribunal is dismissed upon withdrawal by the applicant (*Barber v Staffordshire County Council* [1996] ICR 379, followed in *Osborne v Valve (Engineering) Services Ltd* (24 November 2000, unreported), EAT). In *Osborne* the court held that: (1) the principles of *res judicata* bar an employee from bringing High Court wrongful dismissal proceedings after the same cause of action has been determined by the tribunal; and (2) a 'determination' by the tribunal includes a dismissal by the tribunal following withdrawal of the claim. Therefore, the safest course to adopt in a case where an applicant wishes to pursue High Court wrongful dismissal proceedings after having already commenced tribunal proceedings is to invite the tribunal to stay the case before it. A stay does not determine the proceedings. It simply prevents further steps being taken until the stay is lifted.

However, a number of cases have suggested a more flexible approach to those who commence proceedings in the tribunal and withdraw in order to sue in the civil courts; the cases are not wholly easy to reconcile. In *Sajid v Sussex Muslim Society* [2002] IRLR 113, an applicant presented a breach of contract claim to a tribunal and later withdrew it. His express reason for withdrawing was in order to present the claim in a court whose jurisdiction to award damages was not limited to £25,000. The Court of Appeal held that his claim was entitled to proceed. The second proceedings did not offend the principle of *res judicata*, which was finality in litigation. Since it was clear that the purpose of withdrawal of the tribunal claim was so as to bring county court proceedings, the principle behind *res judicata* was not engaged. Unlike the applicant in *Barber*, Mr Sajid had not intended by withdrawing his claim to abandon his cause of action.

A different analysis prevailed in *Lennon v Birmingham City Council* [2001] EWCA Civ 435, [2001] IRLR 826, decided by the Court of Appeal before *Sajid* but not referred to in the latter case. In *Lennon*, the applicant brought and subsequently withdrew a complaint in which she alleged that she had been harassed and bullied by her employer. This was regarded by the employer as a complaint of sex discrimination. A tribunal dismissed the claim on withdrawal. Later she brought a claim in the county court in which she relied on the same allegations which had provided the foundation for her tribunal claim. The Court of Appeal held that the claim was rightly struck out under the doctrine of issue estoppel. The court expressly rejected the argument that the reason for the withdrawal of the complaint could be relevant: all that mattered was the simple fact of the dismissal of the claim by the tribunal on withdrawal.

The Court of Appeal has sought to reconcile the apparent tension between *Sajid* and *Lennon* in *Ako v Rothschild Asset Management Ltd* [2002] EWCA Civ 236, [2002] ICR 899. In that case, the applicant lodged a complaint of discrimination, which was subsequently dismissed on withdrawal. A week after the dismissal of the first complaint, she lodged a second complaint containing the same allegations against the same respondent but also added a new respondent. It was found that her intention had not been to cease the litigation against Rothschild, but only to add in the additional respondent. The Court of Appeal held that, as a matter of general legal principle, a court could review the matrix of fact surrounding a legal act in order to understand its effect. Therefore, there could be cases where the circumstances surrounding the withdrawal of a claim meant that the cause of action was not exhausted. The court drew attention to procedural rules in the common law courts, which enabled proceedings that had been discontinued to be revived with permission. There was no such rule in the tribunal. Its omission meant that the strict application of the rules of estoppel could work an injustice.

Disclosure. This section is principally concerned with the remedies of the employee against the employer when the latter has acted in breach of contract. However, the situation may also arise when the employer has become mixed up in alleged wrongdoing by third parties. In *A v Company B Ltd* [1997] IRLR 405, an employee was dismissed by his employer after allegations of gross misconduct had been made to the employer by a third party. The employer did not identify the complainant or specify the nature of the complaints that had been made. The employee took the view that false allegations had been made about him and wished to institute an action against the third party alleging defamation. In order that the employee could prosecute that action, the High Court ordered that the employer disclose details of the allegations which had been made about him by the third party, following the principles laid down in *Norwich Pharmacal Co v Customs and Excise Comrs* [1974] AC 133.

8.24   Employer's remedies

Withholding or deduction of wages. If an employee does not perform any of his contractual duties, he is not entitled to his contractual wage. Thus, an employee is not entitled to be paid for days when he is on strike.

If the employee refuses to perform the full range of his contractual duties, particularly if this refusal is in pursuance of industrial action, the purpose of which is to disrupt the employer's business, the employee will not be entitled to his full contractual wage (see *Miles v Wakefield Metropolitan District Council* [1987] ICR 368). In *Wiluszynski v Tower Hamlets London Borough Council* [1989] IRLR 259, the Court of Appeal held that the Council was entitled to withhold the whole of the employee's wages when the employee refused to perform a substantial part of his duties and it was clear that the employer was not accepting the work which was performed as substantial performance of the contract. In *British Telecommunications plc v Ticehurst* [1992] ICR 383, it was held that a manager who intended to continue participating in a withdrawal of goodwill could be sent home without pay.

Alternatively, the employer may be able to deduct from the employee's wages a sum representing the financial loss suffered by him as a result of the employee's breach of contract (see *Sim v Rotherham Metropolitan Borough Council* [1986] ICR 897).

The question sometimes arises regarding what is the appropriate amount of the deduction from the employee's pay. In the case of a one-day strike, for example, should it be 1/365th on the basis that there are 365 days in the year, or a fraction based on the number of days actually worked by the employee in an ordinary year? In *Miles v Wakefield Metropolitan District Council* (above), Lord Templeman suggested (at 387) that it would be appropriate to divide the annual salary by 365. However, that was in the context of a person such as an ambassador or a judge who might be required to work on any day of the year. It is suggested that the better view is that the amount of the deduction should be a fraction based on the number of days actually worked. It is by working for that number of days that an employee earns his pay. Self-evidently, he does not earn an entitlement to be paid otherwise than by working. Therefore, in the case of a person who works, say, 240 days per year, each day earns the employee 1/240th of his annual salary. By refusing to work for one day, the employee disentitles himself to 1/240th of his salary. From the employer's perspective, the employee is paid a salary in return for 240 days' work. Therefore, if the employee fails to work for one day, the loss which the employer suffers is 1/240th of the benefit for which he has bargained.

The strongest argument against this analysis is the *Apportionment Act 1870, s 2* which provides that '... All rents, annuities [which include salaries (*s 5*)], dividends and other periodical payments in the nature of income ... shall ... be considered as accruing from day to day, and shall be apportionable in respect of time accordingly'. In *Thames Water Utilities v Reynolds* [1996] IRLR 186, the EAT held that a day for the purposes of the *Apportionment Act 1870* meant a calendar day and not a working day. Accordingly, for the purposes of calculating the amount of accrued holiday pay to which a person was entitled on termination of employment, the value of one day's pay was 1/365th of annual salary. That case followed a decision of the High Court in *Re BCCI SA* [1994] IRLR 282 (at 290–291) which concerned payment of arrears of salary. Evans-Lombe J held that the arrears were to be calculated on the basis of 1/365th for each day. His Lordship distinguished *Miles v Wakefield Metropolitan District Council* (above) and *Sim v Rotherham Metropolitan Borough Council* (above) on the basis that the principles on which a claim for arrears of salary should be calculated differed from those relevant to the deduction of wages where an employee is in breach of contract. For that reason, neither *Re BCCI SA* (above) nor *Thames Water Utilities v Reynolds* (above) is determinative of the question of what fraction of salary an employer should deduct in the case of a breach of contract by the employee such as a strike. In any event, the *Apportionment Act 1870, s 7* provides that the *Act* shall not apply where it is expressly stipulated that no apportionment shall take place. Where the terms of a contract are such that it would be inconsistent to hold that apportionment should take place, this section may be relied upon to displace the rule in *s 2*.

The decision of the EAT in *Thames Water Utilities v Reynolds* [1996] IRLR 186 – that pay accrues from one calendar day to another rather than from one working day to another – has been followed in *Taylor v East Midlands Offender Employment* [2000] IRLR 760. Like *Reynolds*, that was a case about holiday pay. But the decision may also be relevant to the question of what deduction an employer may make from the pay of an employee who fails to attend for work. In *Taylor*, the EAT held that where an employee was entitled to pay in respect of 10 days' accrued holiday, that is to say, pay for 10 working days, the correct approach was first to divide the year's pay by 365 in order to identify the value of a day's pay. Next, one had to multiply the resultant figure by 14. The reason for this is that the tribunal must 'gross up' to a 7-day working week. Where, as in this case, a person was due 10 days' holiday, that would of necessity involve weekends prior to the commencement of the first period of 5 days' holiday and between two periods of 5 days' holiday. The contract of employment is not suspended between those periods and the employee is therefore entitled to pay. The EAT also drew comfort from observing that this approach is consistent with that required by the *Working Time Regulations 1998*.

(See also 28.14 PAY – I.)

Acceptance of fundamental breach. If the employee is in fundamental breach of his contractual obligations, the employer can accept the breach and bring the contract to an end. Such a fundamental breach will generally consist of gross misconduct, extreme incompetence, or a major failure to carry out the work required of the employee. To go on strike will generally amount to a fundamental breach of contract. See also 45.12 STRIKES AND INDUSTRIAL ACTION and 58.6, 58.7 WRONGFUL DISMISSAL.

Damages. An employer may bring proceedings against an employee for damages for breach of contract (see, e g *Janata Bank v Ahmed* [1981] ICR 791). Situations which may give rise to such proceedings are a breach of the employee's duty of fidelity, breach of his duty of care and failure to give the notice of termination he is contractually obliged to give. In practice, such claims are rare. What is more common is an application for an injunction to restrain disclosure of confidential information or to enforce a restrictive covenant (see RESTRAINT OF TRADE, CONFIDENTIALITY AND EMPLOYEE INVENTIONS (41)).

Parties to contracts are entitled to make their own provision for compensation in the event of breach by one party. Such provisions will be enforced to the extent that they are genuine pre-estimates of loss and not penalties. The law distinguishes between clauses designed to deter or punish a wrongdoer and clauses designed to compensate the innocent party. The former are penalties and unenforceable. The latter are liquidated damages clauses and legitimate. A payment to an employee on dismissal is likely to be regarded as a penalty if it is extravagant and unconscionable: *Murray v Leisureplay plc* [2005] EWCA Civ 963, [2005] IRLR 946. These clauses are not too common in employment contracts. However, in *Giraud UK Ltd v Smith* [2000] IRLR 763, the contract provided that in the event that the employee failed to give and work the notice period stipulated by the contract, there would be a deduction from his final payment 'equivalent to the number of days short'. The employee left without notice. The employer refused to make any final payment to the employee. The employer argued that it was entitled to a payment from the employee of four weeks' pay. The EAT upheld the decision of the Employment Tribunal that this was a penalty clause rather than a genuine pre-estimate of loss and unenforceable. The EAT held that employment contracts may contain liquidated damages clauses. However, in order to be enforced, the clauses must comply with the general law relating to penalties. In this case, the clause was a penalty because there was no limit of liability to the employer's actual loss.

Injunction or specific performance. In no circumstances may the employee be compelled to work by injunction or specific performance being ordered. That was the common law and the principle is enacted in *TULRCA 1992, s 236.* That applies also if such compulsion will be the practical result of granting an injunction against a third party, eg the only alternative employer (*Warren v Mendy* [1989] ICR 525); the court will not make an order which would prevent the employee from earning his living. However, the Court of Appeal held in *Evening Standard Co Ltd v Henderson* [1987] ICR 588 that it may be possible to restrain an employee who does not give proper notice (see 48.17 TERMINATION OF EMPLOY-MENT) from working elsewhere during his notice period so long as the employer will provide him with all his contractual benefits without his actually having to work. The *Henderson* principle was approved in *Provident Financial Group plc and Whitegates Estate Agency Ltd v Hayward* [1989] ICR 160, where an express contractual prohibition was relied upon. However, the Court of Appeal indicated that no injunction would be granted if the plaintiff's business had nothing to do with that of the new employer. It also recognised that an employee might need to work and exercise his skills (the employer in *Hayward* had put the employee on 'garden leave' during his notice period, whereas in *Henderson* work was available if the employee wanted it), and refused to grant an injunction after considering the non-competitive nature of the job the employee wished to take up, and the length of the unexpired notice period (see also *Warren*, and see 8.12 above).

In *William Hill Organisation Ltd v Tucker* [1998] IRLR 313, the Court of Appeal appeared to impose further limitations on the availability of the 'garden leave injunction' remedy. The court held that it was necessary to consider in each case whether the consideration moving from the employer obliged the employer to permit the employee to do work, or whether the full extent of the obligation is to pay the employee. If the employer was obliged to permit the employee to carry out work, then the court would be unlikely to grant a garden leave injunction in the absence of an express provision which entitled the employer not to provide work and/or required the employee to agree not to attend work during the notice period. It was unlikely that such a provision would be implied. However, even where an express term was present, the court would not grant relief to any greater extent than would be granted in respect of a justifiable covenant in restraint of trade (see 41.6 RESTRAINT OF TRADE, CONFIDENTIALITY AND EMPLOYEE INVENTIONS).

The same general principles relating to the grant of interlocutory injunctions apply as are discussed under 'Employee's remedies', above (see also RESTRAINT OF TRADE, CONFIDENTIALITY AND EMPLOYEE INVENTIONS (41)).

Account of profits. In some cases, the appropriate remedy for a breach of contract may be the restitutionary remedy of an account of profits. An account was ordered by the House of Lords in *A-G v Blake* [2001] IRLR 36. Such a remedy will only be available in exceptional circumstances where the normal remedies of damages, specific performance and injunction do not provide an adequate remedy. The case of Blake, a spy who had published a book in breach of his contractual duties to the Crown, was such an exceptional case.

8.25   CONTRACTS OF EMPLOYMENT AND SUNDAY TRADING

The *Sunday Trading Act 1994* relaxed the previously restrictive rules relating to Sunday trading. *Section 4* and *Sch 4* of the *Sunday Trading Act* introduced provisions relating to contracts of employment. Similar provisions relating to those who work in the betting industry were introduced into the *Betting, Gaming and Lotteries Act 1963* (new *Sch 5A*) by *s 20* of the *Deregulation and Contracting Out Act 1994*. These provisions have now been consolidated in the *ERA 1996*.

The relevant provisions apply to two types of worker: shop workers and betting workers. These terms are defined in *ERA 1996, s 232(1)* and *ERA 1996, s 233(1)*, respectively. A shop worker is someone who, under his contract of employment, is or may be required to do 'shop work'. That term is defined to mean work in or about a 'shop', and a 'shop' is defined to include any premises where any retail trade or business is carried on (*ERA 1996, s 232(3)*). 'Retail trade or business' includes barbers and hairdressers, the hiring of goods otherwise than for use in the course of a trade or business and retail sales by auction but it excludes catering business or the sale at theatres and places of amusement of programmes, catalogues and similar items (*ERA 1996, s 232(6)*).

A betting worker is a person who, under his contract of employment, is or may be required to do betting work. 'Betting work' means work at a track in England or Wales for a bookmaker on a day when the bookmaker acts as such at the track and which consists of or includes dealing with betting transactions, and work in a licensed betting office (*ERA 1996, s 233(2)*). A bookmaker is a person who receives or negotiates bets or conducts pool-betting operations or holds himself out as doing so.

The *Act* provides protection to two types of shop workers and betting workers. The first is the 'protected shop workers and betting workers'. This is a shop worker or betting worker who either:

(*a*)   was employed as a shop worker on 25 August 1994 or as a betting worker on 2 January 1995 (ie the day before the relevant provisions came into force) but was not on that day employed solely to work Sundays. He must also remain employed as a shop worker or betting worker at the 'appropriate date' and have been continuously employed between those two dates. In relation to cases of dismissal or the subjection of the employee to another detriment, the appropriate date is the effective date of termination or the date when the detrimental act or omission occurs, respectively; or

(*b*)   is a shop worker or betting worker who does not work Sundays and could not be required so to work.

(*ERA 1996, s 36.*)

The second type of protected shop worker or betting worker is an 'opted-out shop worker or betting worker'. This is a shop worker or betting worker who:

(i)   is or may be required to work on Sunday, but is not employed solely to work on Sundays; and

(ii)   has given a written 'opting-out notice', signed and dated by the employee, registering his objection to working on Sundays.

(*ERA 1996, s 41.*)

An opting-out notice takes effect three months after it has been given (*ERA 1996, s 41(3)*). A worker who has given an opting-out notice is then an opted-out worker for as long as he remains continuously employed under a contract of employment as a shop worker or a betting worker between the date of giving the notice and the appropriate date (*ERA 1996, s 41*).

A shop worker or betting worker ceases to be protected if:

(i)   he gives his employer a written 'opting-in notice', signed and dated by the employee, in which he expressly states that he wishes to work on Sundays or that he has no objection to being required so to work; and

(ii)   subsequently expressly agrees with his employer to do shop work or betting work on Sundays or on a particular Sunday.

(*ERA 1996, s 41(2)*.)

A shop worker or betting worker is entitled not to be dismissed (*ERA 1996, s 101(1)–(3)*) or to be subjected to any other detriment (*ERA 1996, s 45(1)–(8)*) by reason of his refusal to work Sundays, whether as a protected shop worker or betting worker or as an opted-out shop worker or betting worker. The right not to be dismissed includes a right not to be selected for redundancy where the reason or the principal reason for selection is the employee's refusal to work Sundays (*ERA 1996, s 105(1), (4)*) (see UNFAIR DISMISSAL – II (54)). Dismissal of a shop worker or a betting worker for asserting the statutory rights created for the protection of such workers would be automatically unfair (*ERA 1996, s 104(4)*) (see UNFAIR DISMISSAL – II (54)).

It is not a detriment to refuse to pay the employee in respect of Sundays which he does not work, nor is it a detriment to pay those employees who do work Sundays a higher rate of pay or to offer them enhanced benefits (*ERA 1996, s 45(5), (6)*). Thus, employers are free to offer economic incentives to employees to work Sundays.

The qualifying periods and upper age limits which generally apply to unfair dismissal claims do not apply to the right not to be dismissed by reason of a refusal to work Sundays (*ERA 1996, ss 108(3), 109(2)*) (see UNFAIR DISMISSAL – I (53)).

Employers are required to give those shop workers and betting workers who are or may be required to work Sundays (but not those employed only to work on Sundays) a written statement setting out their right to opt out of working Sundays and not to be dismissed or subjected to any other detriment as a result of doing so. This requirement also applies to those employees who have given opting-in notices. The terms in which the statement must be given are prescribed by the *Act*. The statement must be given within two months of the date when the employee became a shop worker or a betting worker. If the employer fails to comply with this time limit and in the interim a shop worker or a betting worker serves an opting-out notice, that notice takes effect after only one month, rather than the three-month period laid down by *ERA 1996, s 41(3)* (*ERA 1996, s 42(2)*).

After the commencement date, any term in a contract of employment of a shop worker or betting worker who is not employed only to work on a Sunday which requires that worker to work Sundays is unenforceable. Similarly, any agreement by such a shop worker or betting worker that he will work Sundays is unenforceable. Where an employee has given an opting-in notice, the contract of employment is taken to be varied to the extent necessary to give effect to that notice (*ERA 1996, s 37*).

After a shop worker or a betting worker has given an opting-out notice, any term in his contract of employment requiring him to work Sundays after the elapse of the three-month notice period is unenforceable. Any other agreement between an employer and an opted-out shop worker or a betting worker to the effect that the worker is required to work Sundays is likewise unenforceable (*ERA 1996, s 43*).

Where a shop worker or a betting worker has worked a fixed number of hours each week (including Sundays) and the effect of ceasing to work on Sundays is to reduce the total hours which he works, there is no obligation on the employer to increase the hours the employee is required to work on weekdays to compensate for that reduction. Further, where an employee who has previously worked Sundays ceases to do so after the commencement of the *Schedule*, and it is not clear from the contract of employment what the employee's pay was in respect of working Sundays, an employer is entitled to reduce the employee's pay proportionately to take account of the fact that the employee no longer works on Sundays (*ERA 1996, ss 38, 39*).

A protected or opted-out shop worker may complain to an employment tribunal in respect of any detriment he suffers by reason of his refusal to work Sundays (*ERA 1996, s 48*). Complaints must be brought within three months of the act or failure to act complained of, subject to an extension of time where it was not reasonably practicable to present the claim in time.

Any agreement purporting to contract out of the rights created for shop workers and betting workers is void unless either a conciliation officer has intervened or the parties have entered an agreement which satisfies the requirements of *ERA 1996, s 203*. (See 53.20 UNFAIR DISMISSAL – I and 20.28 EMPLOYMENT TRIBU-NALS – I.)

9   Directors

9.1   INTRODUCTION

Directors of companies are office-holders. They are not necessarily employees. However, directors often enter into service agreements with their company, thereby becoming employees in addition to holding office. The appointment of a director is nevertheless independent of any contract of employment between a director and a company, although the contract of employment may contain provisions which have application to the office.

The provisions regulating the appointment to, and removal from, the office of a director are set out in the *Companies Acts 1985* (*'CA 1985'*) and *1989*. These will be supplemented by further provisions in the company's articles of association. *Table A* of the *Companies* (*Tables A to F*) *Regulations 1985* (*SI 1985/805*) sets out 'default' articles of association. A company may adopt for its articles the whole or any part of Table A. This chapter will refer to the provisions of Table A. However, it will be necessary to look at the precise terms of the articles of a company in order to determine the position in any particular case.

The *Companies Act 2006* (*'CA 2006'*) will (among a number of other changes) codify, and to some degree alter, the rules governing the duties directors owe to their companies. The relevant provisions are not yet in force and so are not addressed in detail in this chapter. However, it should be noted that many of the important provisions will come into force in October 2008. Accordingly, directors and those advising them may wish to acquaint themselves with the new law in this area.

This chapter concerns the position of directors as employees. It does not set out the numerous responsibilities of directors under company law, nor address the power of the courts to control delinquent directors.

9.2   APPOINTMENT

A director may be employed by the other directors of a company under the authority of one of the articles of association. Such a director is often referred to as an executive director. The relevant provision in *Table A* is *art 84*. It provides:

'Subject to the provisions of the Act, the directors may appoint one or more of their number to the office of managing director or to any other executive office under the company and may enter into an agreement or arrangement with any director for his employment by the company or for provision by him of any services outside the scope of the ordinary duties of a director. Any such appointment, agreement or arrangement may be made upon such terms as the directors determine and they may remunerate any such director for his services as they think fit. Any appointment of a director to an executive office shall terminate if he ceases to be a director but without prejudice to any claim to damages for breach of the contract of service between the director and the company. A managing director and a director holding any executive office shall not be subject to retirement by rotation.'

As explained above, *Table A* may or may not be incorporated into the articles of a particular company. Even where *Table A* is not incorporated into the articles, executive directors are not usually subject to retirement by rotation. However, where a company is listed, the Combined Code (see 9.21 below) recommends that all directors should be required to submit themselves for re-election at regular intervals, and at least every three years.

Usually, the terms of the director's appointment will be recorded in a letter written under the authority of the board of directors, or in a service agreement which the board has approved. Where a board resolution contains the terms of the appointment, this may be sufficient evidence of the terms of the contract between the director and the company.

9.3 Relationship between articles and contracts of employment

Where the articles do not confer the directors with a power to employ one of their number, or if that power is not properly exercised, the employment contract between the employed director and the company will be void for want of authority. An example of this situation is *Guinness plc v Saunders* [1990] 1 All ER 652. In *Guinness v Saunders*, a committee of the board purported to grant a director special remuneration pursuant to an alleged oral contract. The House of Lords held that this alleged contract was void. This was because the board had no power under the articles to delegate this power to the committee. Since there was no binding contract, their Lordships refused to permit the director to claim payment for actual services which he had performed (on a *quantum meruit* basis). He also could not claim an equitable allowance because it would be inequitable to permit the director to take advantage of his directorship in order to claim remuneration in such circumstances. This was in accordance with the general equitable principle that a director may not profit from the holding of his office. (This principle is often modified by the articles of association.)

The articles and board resolutions are deemed to be known by each director. Accordingly, a director cannot rely on ostensible authority, implied authority or assume that another director, the committee or the board have powers which they do not have: *Guinness v Saunders*, above, at 658, per Lord Templeman. When considering the position of an employed director, it is necessary to examine carefully the relationship between the articles and terms of any service agreement. In order to avoid any doubt, service agreements should expressly provide for the circumstances in which they can be terminated. They must be drafted having regard to the articles which are then in force. (It should also be noted that the employers of directors are obliged to provide a written statement of the particulars of employment, see further below at 9.6.)

An example is *Read v Astoria Garage (Streatham) Ltd* [1952] Ch 637, where a managing director was appointed by a board resolution. This resolution contained no terms as to how the post might be terminated. A resolution of the board, later approved by the company in general meeting, removed the managing director from post. The relevant article provided that the appointment

> 'shall be subject to determination *ipso facto* if he ceases for any cause to be a director or if the Company in general meeting resolves that the tenure of office as managing director ... be determined'.

In the absence of an express term in the original resolution, the director was taken to have contracted on the terms of the articles. He therefore had no claim for wrongful dismissal since the employment had been terminated in accordance with the articles. By contrast, the director in *Nelson v James Nelson & Sons Ltd* [1914] 2 KB 770, CA was appointed in accordance with an article which enabled the board to make an appointment 'for such period as they think fit, and may revoke such appointment'. The duration of the agreement by which the director was appointed was for an indefinite period. It was held that the board had an unfettered power to appoint for such period as it deemed fit. However, the right to revoke only existed if the contract so provided. Since the contract did not contain a power to revoke, the director was entitled to damages for wrongful dismissal when his appointment was terminated.

The position must be judged by considering the articles as they are at the date of entering into the contract of service with the director. In *Southern Foundries (1926) Ltd v Shirlaw* [1940] AC 701, the company, subsequent to the appointment of a director, had adopted new articles which were less favourable to an employed director. It was held that the adoption of these new articles could not worsen the contractual position of an employed director. Accordingly, a dismissal taking place under the new articles was wrongful.

Service agreements may also contain implied terms. For example, in *Shindler v Northern Raincoat Co Ltd* [1960] 1 WLR 1038, a director sold his shares in the company to a different company under a contract of sale which provided that he would be appointed managing director for a period of ten years. This second company was subsequently resold to a third company. The third company did not wish to retain the director's services. In the director's successful claim for wrongful dismissal, it was held that it had become an implied term of his contract of service that the company would not do anything of its own motion to cause him to be removed as managing director in breach of the contract of sale. Diplock J distinguished *Read v Astoria Garage* (above) on the basis that, in *Shindler* and unlike in *Read,* there was evidence of a contract between the company and the director which was inconsistent with the articles. On the basis of the reasoning in Southern *Foundries v Shirlaw*, the director had been wrongfully dismissed in breach of that contract.

9.4   Employed or not?

Articles, such as Article 84, usually give the directors a very broad discretion as to the terms of appointment of one of their number. In particular, such articles often provide a power to employ a director pursuant to a contract of employment or, instead, to enter into a agreement for the provision of services. A director may, in respect of additional services, be engaged as either an employee or as an independent contractor. The question of whether the director is an employee or an independent contractor may be of great importance. Many statutory employment rights, such as the right to claim unfair dismissal, are only conferred on employees.

It should also be noted that whether or not an individual is 'employed' may depend on the context in which the question is asked. This is because the definition of an 'employee' may vary.

This matter is addressed in detail in EMPLOYEE, SELF-EMPLOYED OR WORKER? (17)). However, the questions pertaining to directors are to some degree distinct and merit separate attention.

Where there is no formal agreement, evidence as to the employment status of a director may be gleaned from board resolutions or minutes, correspondence between the parties and the manner in which the individual is paid and taxed. The courts have tended to consider that directors who work full-time for a company and are paid a salary are employees: *Trussed Steel Concrete Co Ltd v Green* [1946] Ch 115. An example is *Folami v Nigerline (UK) Ltd* [1978] ICR 277, where an accountant from a holding company was appointed managing director of the company's subsidiary and it was held that, having been paid by the subsidiary, the managing director was an employee for the purposes of statutory employment rights. A director who was remunerated by way of director's fees and had not been treated as an employee for the purposes of national insurance was held not to be an employee for the purpose of exercising statutory employment rights in *Parsons v Albert J Parsons & Sons Ltd* [1979] IRLR 117. The Court of Appeal has held that a person who is a controlling shareholder can also be an employee of that company. The fact that he is a controlling shareholder may point against the relationship being one of employment, but it is only one of the relevant factors and is not determinative: *Secretary of State for Trade and Industry v Bottrill* [1999] IRLR 326. A similar conclusion was reached by the Court of Appeal in *Connolly v Sellars Arenascene Ltd* [2001] EWCA Civ 184, [2001] IRLR 222.

With regard to directors, the 'control test' (see further 17.3) is not particularly appropriate for determining whether a director is employed. This is because a director may be largely in control of the day-to-day running of the company or part of it. Indeed, a controlling share-holder, such as in *Secretary of State for Trade and Industry v Bottrill*, above, can even ultimately decide whether or not he is dismissed. The 'organisation test', also known as the 'integration test' may be more appropriate. This test was set out by Denning LJ in *Stevenson Jordan and Harrison v MacDonald and Evans* [1952] 1 TLR 101 as follows:

> 'Under a contract of service, a man is employed as part of the business and his work is done as an integral part of the business; whereas, under a contract for services, his work, although done for the business, is not integrated into it but is an accessory to it'.

Accordingly, a director who provides consultancy or advisory services to the company is likely to be an independent contractor, whereas an executive director who is engaged for the purposes of managing the business (or a part of it), and whose work forms an integral part of the business is likely to be an employee.

Clear written agreements may assist in clarifying the issues. However, courts are likely to look to the substance of the agreement rather than simply its form.

9.5   Scope of employment

The scope of a director's employment will be determined by the terms of any service agreement, and any board resolutions which are in force from time to time which grant him or her authority. The powers and duties of a director may be subject to variation by the board. Directors may be appointed to an executive function such as finance director of the company or group. Subject to the terms of the service agreement, the scope of the employment is capable of being completely changed, expanded or narrowed. Even the executive function may be subject to change in some circumstances.

It *Harold Holdsworth & Co (Wakefield) Ltd v Caddies* [1955] 1 WLR 352, it was held that the board could confine the responsibilities of a managing director to the affairs of a subsidiary where the contract provided that he was:

> 'appointed a managing director of the Company and as such managing director he shall perform the duties and exercise the powers in relation to the business of the company and the business.. of its existing subsidiary company … which may from time to time be assigned to or vested in him by the board of directors..'

(The court noted that Mr Caddies had been appointed 'a' rather than 'the' managing director.)

9.6   Written particulars

The employer of a director, like that of other employees, is obliged to provide a written statement of the particulars of the employment. The provisions of *ss 1 to 6* of the *Employment Rights Act 1996* apply to the employment of directors (see CONTRACT OF EMPLOYMENT (8)).

9.7   DIRECTORS' SERVICE CONTRACTS

Disclosure

A director must disclose any direct or indirect interest of his in a contract or proposed contract with the company: s *317* of the *CA 1985*. (This provision (as well a number of the others referred to in what follows) will be repealed and replaced with new provisions by *CA 2006*.) This disclosure must be made by declaring the nature of the interest at the meeting of the directors at which the question of entering into the contract is first taken into consideration or at the first meeting held after the director became interested. Disclosure must be made before the full board of directors and not merely to a sub-committee: see *Guinness plc v Saunders*, above.

A director may instead give a general notice to the directors of an interest; *s 317(3) CA 1985*. Such a notice may be addressed to the company's registered office: *s 287(1), CA 1985*. However, a general notice will only have effect if it is given at a meeting of the directors or the director takes reasonable steps to secure that it is brought up and read at the next meeting after it is given.

The disclosure obligation applies even where it is plain and obvious that the director has an interest such as in the case of service agreement: see *Runciman v Walter Runciman plc* [1992] BCLC 1084. *Section 317* also applies where there is a variation of a service agreement.

The failure of a director to declare his interest renders a contract voidable at the instance of the company: see *Hely-Hutchinson v Brayhead Ltd* [1968] 1 QB 549, CA at 589, 594.

9.8   Inspection

Under s *318* of the *CA 1985*, directors' contracts of service with the company (or with a subsidiary of the company) must be made available for inspection. This obligation does not apply where the unexpired portion of the term for which the contract is to be in force is less than 12 months, or at a time at which the contract can be terminated by the company without payment of compensation within the next ensuing 12 months. It is unclear whether 'compensation' here includes unfair dismissal compensation or only applies to damages under the contract. Where this section applies, the contract (or, if it is not in writing, a written memorandum setting out its terms) must be kept at the same 'appropriate place'. 'Appropriate places' are the company's registered office, the place where its register of members is kept, and its principal place of business: *CA 1985, s 318(3)*. Unless service agreements are kept at the company's registered office, the Register of Companies must be informed of the place where they are kept and of any change to that place (*CA 1985, s 318(4)*).

'Contract of service' is not defined in *s 318*. It should be taken to embrace all documents with contractual effect including the original contract, any 'side letters' containing enforceable terms and any subsequent variations. It would probably not include employee benefit plans such as pension scheme trust deeds and share option scheme rules.

Section 318 does not specify the terms which are to be included in any memorandum setting out the terms of a service agreement where this is not in writing (except in the case of directors who work wholly or mainly outside the United Kingdom). Nevertheless, a memorandum should specify the main terms of the employment pertaining to salary, benefits and duration. It could also contain all the written particulars required by *s 1* of the *Employment Rights Act 1996*.

If a service contract requires a director to work wholly or mainly outside the United Kingdom, the company is only required to keep a memorandum giving the director's name and the provisions of the contract relating to duration, where the service contract is with the company. Where the service contract is with a subsidiary, such a memorandum must also state the place of incorporation of the subsidiary (*CA 1985, s 318(5)*). This memorandum must be kept at the same place as copies and memoranda of the service contracts of other directors.

All copies and memoranda which are required to be kept must be open to inspection to any member of the company without charge (*CA 1985, s 318(7)*).

If a company fails to comply with any of the above provisions, the company and every officer who is in default is liable to a fine and, for continued contravention to a daily default fine (*CA 1985, s 318(8)*). If inspection of a copy or memorandum is refused, the court may order an immediate inspection (*CA 1985, s 318(9)*).

9.9 Listing Rule requirements

The Financial Services Authority ('FSA') is the United Kingdom's Listing Authority ('UKLA'). It makes rules governing the admission and continuing obligations of listed companies. These are known as the *Listing Rules*. They can be found on the FSA's website at www.fsa.gov.uk. These have sometimes included provisions as to directors' service contracts. Companies would be well advised to check the detailed provisions as they change from time to time.

In particular, according to the current version of the rules, a listed company must notify a Regulatory Information Service (RIS) of any change including:

(*a*) the appointment of a new director stating the appointee's name and whether the position is executive, non-executive or chairman and the nature of any specific function or responsibility of the position;

(*b*) the resignation, removal or retirement of a director;

(*c*) important changes to the role, functions or responsibilities of a director; and

(*d*) the effective date of the change if it is not with immediate effect (LR 9.6.11).

This notification must take place as soon as possible and in any event by the end of the business day following the decision or receipt of notice about the change by the company.

If the effective date of the change is not known, the notification should state the fact and the company should notify a RIS as soon as the date has been decided. (LR 9.6.12)

A listed company must also notify a RIS of the following information in respect of any new director appointed to the board:

(a)   details of all directorships held by the director in any other publicly quoted company at any time in the previous five years, indicating whether or not he is still a director;

(b)   any unspent convictions in relation to indictable offences;

(c)   details of any receiverships, compulsory liquidations, creditors voluntary liquidations, administrations, company voluntary arrangements or any composition or arrangement with its creditors generally or any class of its creditors of any company where the director was an executive director at the time of, or within the 12 months preceding, such events;

(d)   details of any compulsory liquidations, administrations or partnership voluntary arrangements of any partnerships where the director was a partner at the time of, or within the 12 months preceding, such events;

(e)   details of receiverships of any asset of such person or of a partnership of which the director was a partner at the time of, or within the 12 months preceding, such event; and

(f)   details of any public criticisms of the director by statutory or regulatory authorities (including designated professional bodies) and whether the director has ever been disqualified by a court from acting as a director of a company or from acting in the management or conduct of the affairs of any company (LR 9.6.13)

This notification must be given as soon as possible following the decision to appoint the director and in any event within five business days of the decision.

If there is no such information that requires to be disclosed about a director, then this should be notified to the RIS (LR 9.6.15)

Any changes in such information should also be disclosed with respect to a current director (LR 9.6.14)

9.10   Take-over Code

During the course of an offer, or even before the date of the offer if the board of an offeree company has reason to believe that a *bona fide* offer might be made imminently, *rule 21* of the *City Code on Take-overs and Mergers* will apply. Where *rule 21* applies, the board must not enter into contracts other than in the ordinary course of business without the approval of the shareholders of the company in general meeting (or in pursuant of a contract entered into earlier).

Note 6 of the notes to *Rule 21* indicates that the Panel on Take-Overs and Mergers will regard amending or entering into a service contract with, or creating or varying the terms of employment of, a director as entering into a contract 'otherwise than in the ordinary course of business' for the purpose of *Rule 21* if the new or amended contract or terms constitute an abnormal increase in the director's emoluments or a significant improvement in the terms of service. Accordingly, during an offer period, extending the duration of a service agreement or increasing a director's salary should not be effected without the prior agreement of the Panel.

The notes go on to state that this will not prevent any such increase or improvement which results from a genuine promotion or new appointment. However, the Panel must be consulted in advance in such cases.

9.11   Directors

9.11   Duration of director's service agreement

The duration of a service agreement will be largely a matter of contract between the company and the director concerned. This may be subject, however, to any restrictions in the articles as well as to *s 319* of *CA 1985*, discussed further below.

9.12   *Section 319*

Shareholder approval is required for any service agreement which can last for more than five years pursuant to *CA 1985, s 319*. This provision applies to contracts 'for services' (ie agreements with non-employees), as well as to contracts of employment (*CA 1985, s 319(7)*). This provision applies wherever the employ-ment is to continue, or may be continued, otherwise than at the instance of the company, for a period of more than five years during which the employment cannot be terminated by the company by notice, or can be terminated but only in specified circumstances. The section therefore applies to contracts terminable by notice, and to contracts with a minimum duration but which are intended to continue thereafter upon notice, as well as to fixed-term contracts. Specified circumstances would include, for example, the right to terminate for gross misconduct or incapacity. Therefore, any right to terminate on these grounds would not avoid the need for shareholder approval.

Section 319(2) sets out a situation in which serial contracts are, to some degree, aggregated in determining the duration of the agreement. Where someone is employed under an agreement which cannot be terminated by notice (or can be so terminated but only in specified circumstances) and, more than 6 months before the expiration of the period of employment, a further employment contract with the company (or group) is entered, then, *s 319* applies as if the period of employment under the further agreement is added to the period equal to the unexpired period of the original agreement (*CA 1985, s 319(2)*). The scope of this provision is somewhat uncertain. It would seem that it only applies to fixed-term contracts. The aim appears to be to catch the situation whereby a company attempts to circumvent s 319 by employing a director on a series of short term contracts. There may be problems of 'double-counting' the overlap where an existing agreement is terminated and a new agreement is simultaneously entered into. In such circumstances, it may be safer to wait for a short period to elapse in between the termination of an original contract and entering into the new agreement (with a duration of less than five years) in order to avoid the aggregation.

Where s 319 requires a term to be approved, it must be approved by a resolution of the company in general meeting, or, where the director is or is to be employed by the holding company, by a resolution of the holding company in general meeting (*CA 1985, s 319(3)*). Before a resolution is passed, a written memoran-dum setting out the proposed agreement incorporating the term must be available for inspection by members of the company both at the company's registered office for not less than 15 days ending before the date of the meeting, and at the meeting itself (*CA 1985, s 319(5)*).

If a term is incorporated into an agreement in contravention of *s 319*, it is void, and is, in certain circumstances, replaced by a term entitling the company to terminate the employment at any time by giving reasonable notice (*CA 1985, s 319(6)*). This provision incorporates the common law concept of reasonable notice which is discussed in WRONGFUL DISMISSAL (58).

9.13   *Recommendations*

Currently, there are no other statutory restrictions on the duration of a director's service agreement. However, the Combined Code on Corporate Governance 2006 ('Combined Code') recommends that companies should set notice periods at one year or less. The Combined Code was published in October 2006 and applies in respect of reporting years commencing on or after 1 November 2006. It replaces the previous Code which was based on a review by Sir Derek Higgs of the role and effectiveness of non-executive directors and a review of audit committees by a group led by Sir Robert Smith.

Listed companies must, in order to comply with the *Listing Rules*, make a disclosure statement setting out how the principles of the Combined Code are applied, and either confirming compliance with its provisions, or providing an explanation for non-compliance (LR 9.8.6(5) and (6) of the *Listing Rules*). This is often described as 'comply or explain'.

Paragraph B.1.6 of the Combined Code recommends that notice or contract periods should be set at one year or less. That paragraph also states that, if it is necessary to offer longer notice or contract periods to new directors recruited from outside a company, such period should reduce to one year or less after the initial period.

Since a company is only required to 'comply or explain', departures may be made from these provisions in certain circumstances. A departure from the provisions of para B.1.6 may be justified, for example, where a new recruit is only prepared to contract with the company on terms other than those recommended. If a company decides to set a longer notice or contract period than the recommendation, an explanation for this must of course be given in the company's disclosure statement.

9.14   **DIRECTORS' DUTIES**

Whether or not a director is employed by the company, he owes it duties. The nature and extent of the duties will depend on the circumstances of an individual case. He or she will owe the general duties owed by all directors to their companies as well as any additional or specific duties imposed by reason of the articles of association or any relevant board resolution. He or she may also have express or implied duties under the contract of employment or other service agreement.

The provisions of CA 2006 will codify, and to a certain extent alter, the existing law in this area. The relevant provisions are not yet in force. They will come into force in October 2008.

9.15   **General duties of care and skill**

The classic exposition of the general (implied) duties of a director was stated by Romer J in *Re City Equitable Fire Insurance Co Ltd* [1925] Ch 407:

'In order therefore to ascertain the duties that a person appointed to the board of an established company undertakes to perform, it is necessary to consider not only the nature of the company's business but also the manner in which the work of the company is in fact distributed between the directors and other officials of the company, provided also that this distribution is a reasonable one in the circumstances and not inconsistent with any express provisions in the articles of association. In discharging the duties of his position thus ascertained, a director must, of course, act honestly; he must also exercise some degree of both skill and diligence. To the question of what is the particular degree of skill and diligence required of him, the authorities do not I think give any clear answers. It has been laid down that so long as a director acts honestly he cannot be made responsible in damages unless guilty of gross or culpable negligence in a business sense'.

Romer J went on to set out the following specific principles:

'(1)   A director need not exhibit in the performance of his duties a greater degree of skill than may reasonably be expected from a person of his knowledge and experience. A director of a life insurance company, for instance, does not guarantee that he has the skill of an actuary or physician ...

(2)   A director is not bound to give continuous attention to the affairs of his company. His duties are of an intermittent nature to be performed at periodical board meetings, and at meetings of any committee of the board upon which he happens to be placed ...

(3)   In respect of all duties that, having regard to the exigencies of the business, and the articles of association, may properly be left to some other official, a director is, in the absence of grounds for suspicion, justified in trusting that official to perform such duties honestly.'

A director's general duties are therefore not set at a high level. They are also determined in the context of the particular knowledge and experience of the individual concerned. However, where a director is also an employee, the legal position is different. This is because an employee impliedly undertakes that he possesses, and will exercise, reasonable skill and competence in the work which he undertakes (*Harmer v Cornelius* (1858) 5 CBNS 236 and *Lister v Romford Ice and Cold Storage Co Ltd* [1957] AC 555). He owes an implied duty to his employer to take such reasonable care and skill in his work. (For other implied duties of employees SEE CONTRACT OF EMPLOYMENT (8)). These duties go beyond those set out in *Re City Equitable*. These higher duties would apply to a director who is also an employee. Any breach of these implied duties may constitute a repudiatory breach of the contract, and therefore justify a company in terminating the employment contract without notice. If the contract is terminated, the director will usually be under a contractual obligation to resign his office with the company.

9.16   Duty of good faith

Like other employees, an employed director owes a duty of good faith to the company. This duty arises both in his or her capacity as an employee, and as a director by which he or she owes various fiduciary duties to the company. An executive director must act in good faith in the interests of the company, and must not engage in competition with it or make secret profits. Such a duty may be more extensive than the parallel duty of a director who is not employed. (See, for example, *London and Mashonaland Exploration Co v new Mashonaland Exploration Co Ltd* [1891] WN 165, where it was held that a director (albeit a dummy director who did not attend board meetings) did not commit any breach of duty by being appointed a director of a competing company.) If a full time employee works for a competing company part-time without the consent of his full-time employer, this amounts to a serious breach of his contract *Hivac Ltd v Park Royal Scientific Instruments Ltd* [1946] Ch 169. This principle also applies to employed directors. For example, in *Thomas Marshall (Export) Ltd v Guinle* [1979] Ch 227, a managing director traded on his own account on behalf of two other companies which he had set up in competition with the company. His service agreement had expressly provided that, while employed as a managing director, he would not engage in any other business without the company's consent. He was held to be in breach of his obligation of fidelity and good faith as an employee and in breach of his fiduciary duty as a director.

The precise duties owed by an employed director will depend on the articles of association, memorandum, and relevant board minutes as well as the express and implied terms of the service agreement.

There is no separate and independent duty requiring an employed director to disclose his own wrongdoing. However, the fundamental duty to act in good faith in the interests of the company may require an employed director to disclose his own wrongdoing in certain circumstances, particularly where the wrongdoing constitutes a breach of fiduciary duties. For example, in *Item Software (UK) Ltd v Fassihi* [2004] EWCA Civ 1244, [2005] ICR 450, [2004] IRLR 928, the Court of Appeal held that an employed director was under a duty to disclose his own misconduct in seeking to divert a contract from the company to another company which he himself owned. In these circumstances, the company could recover damages for loss caused by the breach of duty. (Such a duty may also apply to senior employees, see *Tesco Stores plc v Pook* [2004] IRLR 618 and *Helmet Integrated Systems Ltd v Tunnard* [2007] IRLR 126.)

Directors (and senior employees) may be under a duty not to prepare to take preparatory steps to compete with their existing employers and, if they do so, to disclose their wrongdoing to their employer. Whether or not such a duty exists and whether or not a director will be found to be in breach of the duty depends very much upon the circumstances of an individual case. For contrasting recent examples, see *Tunnard* (where the employee was not in breach) and *Shepherds Investments Ltd v Walters* [2007] IRLR 110 (where the director was in breach).

Senior employees and directors may also be under a duty to disclose the wrongdoing of their colleagues, whether subordinate or superior (for an example, see *Walters*, above). This duty applies even where this would inevitably involve the disclosure of the director's own misconduct (*Sybron Corpn v Rochem Ltd* [1983] 2 All ER 707).

A breach of any duty to disclose may lead to a subsequent agreement for payment to a director being avoided on grounds of mistake. This could include, for example, a termination payment. The Court of Appeal accepted in *Horcal Ltd v Gatland* [1984] IRLR 288 that a director was not under a duty to disclose his own *intended* wrongdoing. Accordingly, the company was not entitled to recover a termination payment in a situation where the director had not committed any wrongful act at the date of the termination agreement. A company may even be liable to the director for any unpaid salary earned by the director from the time of a breach of duty until termination, even where the breach could have justified summary dismissal had the company been aware of it (*Healey v Francaise Rubastic SA* [1917] 1 KB 946).

In the recent case of *Foster Bryant Surveying Ltd v Bryant* [2007] IRLR 425, the Court of Appeal reviewed the law relating to a director's fiduciary duties during a period of notice after he had resigned but before he had left office. In general terms, the director must act towards his company with honesty, good faith and loyalty, and must avoid any conflict of interest. On the facts of *Bryant,* a director who had resigned in innocent circumstances was not in breach of fiduciary duty when he agreed to be retained by a company's main client after his resignation became effective.

9.17 The Companies Act 2006

On 8 November 2006, *CA 2006* received the Royal Assent. All parts of *CA 2006* will be in force by October 2008 (albeit that some provisions will come into force in October 2007). At the time of writing, the Department of Trade and Industry is consulting as to the detail of some of the secondary legislation.

The background to *CA 2006* was a number of major reports which indicated the need for a statutory codification of directors' duties. These were the Law Commission's report of September 1999 (Company Directors: Regulating Conflicts of Interest and Formulating a Statement of Duties, Report No 261) and the second report of the Company Law Review Steering Group of March 2000 (Modern Company Law for a Competitive Economy: Developing the Framework). On 16 July 2002, the Government stated its core proposals for reform in a White Paper 'Modernising Company Law' (Cm 5553).

The Government published a further White Paper, 'Company Law Reform' in March 2005, setting out proposals for a comprehensive reform of the framework of company law. The White Paper indicated the intention to introduce a Company Law Reform Bill which would, *inter alia,* include provisions setting out the duties of directors.

On 1 November 2005, the Company Law Reform Bill was placed before the House of Lords. The Bill ran to 855 clauses and 15 schedules. The Bill has now become the *Companies Act 2006*.

CA 2006 will repeal and replace most of *CA 1985*. Principally, *CA 2006* aims to simplify the administrative burden on smaller private companies, facilitate shareholder engagement and update and clarify the law in various areas, particularly in relation to directors' duties. For the first time, the duties owed by directors to their company will be set out in statute, hopefully making them clearer and more accessible.

Sections 170 to *177* of *CA 1985* are intended to 'codify' the duties that have been established in the cases to date, although there will be slight changes in relation to conflicts of interest.

Directors will be obliged to:

(*a*)   act within their powers under the company's constitution, and only exercise powers for the purposes for which they are conferred (*s 171*); and

(*b*)   act in the way in which they consider, in good faith, would be most likely to promote the success of the company for the benefit of the members as a whole, having regard (so far as is reasonably practicable) to:

    (i)   the likely consequences of any decision in the long term;

    (ii)   the interests of the company's employees;

    (iii)   the need to foster the company's relationships with customers, suppliers and others;

    (iv)   the impact of the company's operations on the community and the environment;

    (v)   the desirability of the company maintaining a reputation for high standards of business conduct; and

    (vi)   the need to act fairly as between the members of the company (*s 172*).

A director will also be required to:

(*a*)   exercise independent judgement and not fetter his discretion except pursuant to an agreement that was considered to be in the best interests of the company when it was entered into (*s 173*);

(*b*)   exercise reasonable care, skill and diligence (*s 174*);

(*c*)   avoid conflicts of interest (*s 175*);

(*d*)   not accept benefits from third parties (*s 176*); and

(*e*)   declare any interest in any proposed transaction or agreement (*s 177*).

Section 177 of *CA 2006* will require an interested director to disclose the nature of his interest to the rest of the board before a transaction is approved. However, disclosure will not need to be made if the interest cannot reasonably be regarded as likely to give rise to a conflict of interest, if the other directors are already aware of the director's interest, or if it concerns terms of his service agreement that have been or are to be considered by a meeting of the directors or a committee of directors appointed for this purpose.

Although the new duties will displace those formulated in the case law, some of the authorities will remain relevant to some degree. Where the duties have not been reformulated, the case law will assist in of determining how these duties should be applied in individual cases.

9.18   **Indemnity**

An employee is entitled to be indemnified by his employer in respect of expenses, costs and claims incurred by him on behalf of his employer during the proper performance of his duties as an employee. An employed director is similarly entitled to such an indemnity. This entitlement may be expressly set out under the articles. For example, under *art 83* of *Table A*, directors may be paid all travelling, hotel and other expenses properly incurred by them in connection with their attendance at meetings of the directors (or committees of the directors), or general meetings, or separate meetings of the holders of any class of shares or of debentures of the company, or otherwise in connection with their duties.

However, there is a statutory limit on the scope of indemnities that may be afforded to a director (whether or not he is employed). *Section 309A* of *CA 1985* (inserted by *s 19(1)* of the *Companies (Audit, Investigations and Community Enterprise) Act 2004* and in force from 6 April 2005) applies in relation to any liability attaching to a director of a company in connection with any negligence, default, breach of duty or breach of trust by him in relation to the company. By consequence *of s 309A(3)*, any provision (whether or not it is in the articles or in any contract) by which a company directly or indirectly provides to any extent an indemnity for a director of the company or an associated company (a subsidiary, holding company or a subsidiary of the same holding company) against any such liability is void unless one of two exceptions apply. The first exception is that this does not prevent a company from purchasing and maintaining insurance against any such liability for a director of the company (or an associated company). The second exception is a 'qualifying third party indemnity provision'. A 'qualifying third party indemnity provision' is one in relation to which the following three conditions are satisfied:

Condition A: The provision does not provide any indemnity against a liability incurred by the director to the company or to any associated company.

Condition B: The provision does not provide any indemnity against any liability incurred by the director to pay a fine imposed in criminal proceedings or a sum payable to a regulatory body by way of penalty in respect of non-compliance with any requirement of a regulatory nature.

Condition C: The provision does not provide any indemnity against any liability incurred by the director in defending any criminal proceedings in which he is convicted (and the conviction has become final) or in defending any civil proceedings brought by the company or an associated company in which judgment is given against him, or in connection with any application under any specified provisions in which the court refuses to grant him relief. These provisions are *s 144(3)* or *(4)* of *CA 1985* (acquisition of shares by innocent nominee) or *s 727 CA 1985* (general power to grant relief in case of honest and reasonable conduct). (With regard to *s 727*, see further 9.19, below.)

(*CA 1985, s 309B.*)

9.19 Relief from liability

Section 727 of *CA 1985* applies where a director is facing proceedings for negligence, default, breach of duty or breach of trust. In such circumstances, if it appears to the court hearing the case that the director has acted honestly and reasonably and, in all the circumstances (including those connected with his appointment) he ought fairly to be excused, that court may relieve him either wholly or partly from his liability on such terms as it thinks fit. Where such a director is tried by a judge with a jury, the judge may withdraw the case in whole or in part from the jury if satisfied that relief should be granted, and direct that judgment be entered for the defendant on such terms as are considered appropriate (*CA 1985, s 727(3)*).

If a director has reason to believe that any such proceedings will or might be made against him, he may apply to the court for relief and the court has the same power of relief as set out above (*CA 1985, s 727(2)*).

9.20 REMUNERATION

There is nothing in the Companies Act 1985 to restrict or determine the amount of remuneration which may be paid to a director. *Article 82* of *Table A* provides in relation to non-executive directors that:

'The director shall be entitled to such remuneration as the company may by ordinary resolution determine and, unless the resolution provides otherwise, the remuneration shall be deemed to accrue from day to day'.

With regard to executive directors appointed in accordance with *art 84* (see 9.2 above), the amount of remuneration is a matter for the board. So long as the board exercises its power in good faith in accordance with *art 84*, the company will be unable to avoid the terms agreed for remuneration. If remuneration is set at an excessive level, this might provide evidence of a failure to exercise the power in good faith.

9.21 *Recommendations*

A brief explanation of the operation of the Combined Code is set out at para 9.13 above. With regard to directors' remuneration, the Combined Code recommends that the board of directors should establish a remuneration committee with delegated responsibility for setting remuneration levels for all executive directors and the chairman. This should include pension rights and any compensation payments. In relation to the level and make-up of remuneration for executive directors, the Combined Code recommends that:

(*a*) levels of remuneration should be sufficient to attract, retain and motivate directors of the quality required to run the company successfully, but should not be more than necessary (*para B.1*);

(*b*) remuneration committees should judge where to position their company relative to other companies but such comparisons should be made with caution as they can result in an upwards ratchet of remuneration levels with no corresponding improvement in performance. They should also be sensitive to pay and employment conditions elsewhere in the group especially when determining salary increases (*para B.1*);

(*c*) performance-related elements of remuneration should form a significant proportion of the total remuneration package and should be designed to align their interests with those of shareholders and to give these directors keen incentives to perform at the highest levels. (*para B.1.1*);

(*d*) executive share options should not be offered at a discount save as permitted by the *Listing Rules* (*para B.1.2*);

(*e*) remuneration committees should consider whether directors should be eligible for annual bonuses. If so, performance conditions should be relevant, stretching and designed to enhance shareholder value. Upper limits should be set and disclosed (*para 1 of Sch A*);

(*f*) consideration should be given as to whether directors should be eligible for benefits under long term incentive schemes. Traditional share option schemes should be weighed against other kinds of long-term incentive scheme. In normal circumstances, shares granted or other forms of deferred remuneration should not vest, and options should not be exercisable, in less than three years. Directors should be encouraged to hold their shares for a further period after vesting or exercise, subject to the need to finance any costs of acquisition and associated tax liabilities (*para 2 of Sch A*);

(*g*) any new long-term incentive schemes proposed should be approved by shareholders and should preferably replace any existing schemes or at least form part of a well considered overall plan, incorporating existing schemes. The total awards potentially available should not be excessive (*para 3 of Sch A*);

(*h*) pay-outs or grants under all incentive schemes should be subject to challenging criteria and consideration should be given to criteria which reflect the company's objectives. Consideration should be given to criteria which reflect the company's performance relative to a group of comparator companies in some key variables such as shareholder return (*para 4 of Sch A*);

(i) grants under executive share option and other long-term incentive schemes should normally be phased rather than awarded in one large block (*para 5 of Sch A*);

(*j*) in general only basic salary should be pensionable (*para 6 of Sch A*); and

(*k*) consideration should be given to the pensions consequences and associated costs of basic salary increases and other changes in pensionable remuneration, especially for directors close to retirement (*para 7 of Sch A*).

9.22   **Disclosure of directors' remuneration**

Details of emoluments and other benefits to directors and others must be disclosed in companies' annual accounts pursuant to *Part I of Sch 6 of CA 1985* (as amended).

The *Directors' Remuneration Report Regulations 2002* (*SI 2002/1986*) exempt a quoted company from most of the requirements of *Part I of Sch 6*. Instead, a quoted company is required to set out a large part of the information concerning directors' remuneration in a directors' remuneration report. The requirements for such reports are set out in *Sch 7A*. Part I of *Sch 6* continues to apply to companies which are not quoted. *Parts II and III of Sch 6* apply to both quoted and unquoted companies.

For both quoted and unquoted companies, para 1(1) of Sch 6 requires the notes to the accounts to show:

(*a*)   the aggregate amount of emoluments paid to or receivable by directors in respect of qualifying services;

(*b*)   for quoted and AIM listed companies only, the aggregate amount of gains made by directors on the exercise of share options;

(*c*)   the aggregate of:

   (i)   the amount of money paid to or receivable by directors under long term incentive schemes in respect of qualifying services; and

   (ii)   the net value of assets (which for unlisted companies excludes shares) other than money and share options, received or receivable by directors under such schemes in respect of such services;

(*d*)   the aggregate of any company contributions paid, or treated as paid, to a pension scheme in respect of directors' qualifying services, being contributions by reference to which the rate or amount of any money purchase benefits that may become payable will be calculated; and

(*e*)   the number of directors to whom benefits are accruing in respect of qualifying services under money purchase and defined benefit schemes.

(*Sch 6, para 1(1) and 1(2)(a)*.)

With regard to an unquoted company, where the aggregates shown under *paras* (*a*), (*b*) and (*c*) amount to £200,000 or more, the following information must also be shown in the notes to the accounts:

(1)   the amount attributable to the highest paid director, and the amount attributable to him in relation to pension contribution (calculated as at para (*d*) above); and

(2)   where the highest paid director has performed qualifying services during the financial year by reference to which the rate or amount of any defined benefits which may become payable will be calculated, the amount of his accrued pension and any accrued lump sum at the end of the year.

(*Sch 6, para 2(1) and (2)*.)

In addition, unlisted companies whose aggregates under *para 1(1)(a) to (c)* amount to £200,000 or more must show:

   (i)   whether the highest paid director exercised any share options; and

(ii)   whether any shares were received or receivable by that director in respect of qualifying services under a long term incentive scheme.

(*Sch 6, para 2(3)*)

Unquoted companies and those not listed on AIM must also show:

(i)   the number of directors who exercised share options, and

(ii)   the number of directors in respect of whose qualifying services shares were received or receivable under long term incentive schemes.

(*Sch 6, para 1(2)(b)*.)

'Emoluments' for these purposes includes salary, fees and bonuses, sums payable by way of expenses allowance (to the extent that they are chargeable to UK income tax) and the estimated money value of any other benefits received by him otherwise than in cash, but does not include:

(i)   the value of any share options granted to him, or the amount of any gains made on the exercise of those options;

(ii)   any company contributions paid or treated as paid, in respect of him under any pension scheme or any benefits to which he is entitled under any such scheme; or

(iii)   any money or other assets paid to or receivable by him under any long term incentive scheme.

(*Sch 6, para 1(3)*.)

'Qualifying services' means services as a director of the company or, while a director of the company, as a director of any of its subsidiary undertakings, or otherwise in connection with the management of the affairs of the company or any of its subsidiary undertakings (*Sch 6, para 5*).

A 'quoted company' means a company whose equity share capital:

(I)   has been included in the official list in accordance with the provisions of Part VI of the Financial Services and Markets Act 2000;

(II)   is officially listed in an EEA State; or

(III)   is admitted to dealing on either the New York Stock Exchange or Nasdaq.

9.23   *Special Provisions for Small Companies*

Special provisions for small companies are contained in *s 246 of CA 1985* (as substituted and amended). By virtue of *s 246(3)*, a small company need only give the total of the aggregates required by *paras (a), (c)* and *(d)* of *para 1(1)* of *Sch 6*, instead of giving those aggregates individually. In addition, small companies are exempted from being required to set out the information in the notice of their accounts that would otherwise be required by the following paragraphs of *Sch 6*:

(*a*)   *para 1(2)(b)* (the numbers of directors exercising share options and receiving shares under long term incentive schemes); and

(*b*)   *para 2* (the details of highest paid director's emoluments).

A 'small company' is defined as a company which satisfies in the first financial year, or, in any subsequent year and the preceding year, two or more of the following requirements:

(i)   turnover of not more than £5.6 million;

(ii) balance sheet total of not more than £2.8 million; and

(iii) not more than 50 employees.

(*CA 1985, s 247(3)* as amended)

The special provisions for small companies do not, however, apply to ineligible companies. These are public companies, companies with permission under Part 4 of the Financial Services and Markets Act 2000 to carry on a regulated activity, and companies who carry on an insurance market activity (*s 247A* of *CA 1985* as inserted and amended). The special provisions do not apply to a group if any of its members fall within this definition of an ineligible company (or if any of the members is a body corporate other than a company with power under its constitution to offer its shares or debentures to the public and may lawfully exercise the power).

9.24 *Listing Rules requirements*

Listed companies must make a disclosure statement stating whether they have complied with the Combined Code and, if not, providing an explanation for non-compliance ((LR 9.8.6(5) and (6) of the *Listing Rules*, discussed further above at 9.13.

Further, *rule 9.8.6* of the *Listing Rules* requires a company to include with its annual reports and accounts a report to the shareholders of the board containing a statement setting out all the beneficial and non-beneficial interests of each director of the listed company, including all changes in the beneficial and non-beneficial interests that have occurred between the end of the period under review and one month prior to the date of the notice of the annual general meeting; or a statement that there have been no such changes.

Rule 9.8.8 requires the report to a shareholder of the Board to contain information in tabular form, unless inappropriate, on:

(*a*) the amount of each element in the remuneration package of each director by name, including but not restricted to, basic salary and fees, the estimated money value of benefits in kind, annual bonuses, deferred bonuses, compensation for loss of office and payments for breach of contract or other termination payments;

(*b*) the total remuneration for each director;

(*c*) any significant payments made to former directors;

(*d*) any share options, including 'Save as you earn' options for each director by name;

(*e*) details of any long-term incentive schemes, other than share options;

(*f*) details of any entitlements or awards granted and commitments made under any long-term incentive schemes;

(*g*) details of the monetary value and number of shares, cash payments or other benefits received by each director under any long-term incentive schemes;

(*h*) details of the interests of each director in the long-term incentive scheme at the end of the period;

(*i*) an explanation and justification of any element of a director's remuneration, other than basic salary, which is pensionable;

(*j*)   details of any director's service contract with a notice period in excess of one year or with provisions for pre-determined compensation on termination which exceeds one year's salary and benefits in kind, giving the reasons for such notice period;

(*k*)   details of the unexpired term of any service contract of a director proposed for election or re-election;

(*l*)   a statement of the company's policy on the granting of options or awards under its employees' share scheme or other long term investment scheme, explaining and justifying any departure and any change in policy from the previous year;

(*m*)   for money purchase schemes, details of the contribution or allowance payable or made by the listed company in respect of each director;

(*n*)   for defined benefits schemes, details of the amount of increase during the period under review and of the accumulated total amount at the end of the period in respect of the accrued benefit to which each director would be entitled on leaving service or is entitled having left service; and

(*o*)   either the transfer value of the relevant increase in accrued benefit or so much of the specified information as is necessary to make a reasonable assessment of the transfer value.

These requirements are additional to the information required by statute.

9.25 Pensions

The making of pension arrangements for directors is expressly authorised by *Article* 87 of *Table A*. Usually, the making of such arrangements will be regulated by the company's articles of association. *Article 87* of *Table A* provides:

'The directors may provide benefits, whether by the payment of gratuities or pensions or by insurance or otherwise, for any director who has held but no longer holds any executive office or employment with the company or with any body corporate which is or has been a subsidiary of the company or a predecessor in business of the company or of any such subsidiary, and for any member of his family (including a spouse and a former spouse) or any person who is or was dependent on him, and may (as well before as after he ceases to hold such office or employment) contribute to any fund and pay premiums for the purchase or provision of any such benefit'.

For unquoted companies, the notes of accounts must show the excess retirement benefits paid to or receivable by directors or past directors (*para 7 of Sch 6 to CA 1985*). The notes must disclose the aggregate of:

(*a*)   the amount of retirement benefits paid to or receivable by directors under pension schemes; and

(*b*)   the amount of retirement benefits paid to or receivable by past directors under such schemes,

as, in each case, is in excess of the retirement benefits to which they were each entitled on the date the benefits first became payable or 31 March 1997, whichever is the later.

The aggregate need not include excess amounts if:

(i)   the funding of the scheme was such that the amounts were or could have been paid without recourse to additional contributions; and

(ii) the amounts were paid to or receivable by all pensioner members of the scheme on the same basis.

Companies which fall within the definition of 'small companies' (see 9.23 above) within the meaning of *s 247(3)* of *CA 1985* are not obliged to disclose this information.

With regard to quoted companies, similar provisions apply to the disclosure of excess retirement benefits in respect of the directors' remuneration report (see *para 13* of *Sch 7A* of the *Companies Act 1985*).

9.26 TERMINATION OF DIRECTORS' OFFICE

A company may, by ordinary resolution, remove a director from office under s *303* of *CA 1985*. This power applies regardless of any contrary provisions in the articles of association or in any service agreement. However, the section does not deprive a person removed under it of compensation or damages payable to him in respect of the termination of his appointment, or as derogating from any power to remove a director which may exist apart from it (*CA 1985, s 303(5)*). Such a power may, for example, derive its authority under the articles.

The ordinary resolution may only be proposed if special notice of it has been given (pursuant to *CA 1985, s 379*). A director has specified rights to protest against a proposal to remove him from office (see *CA 1985, s 304*).

Any service agreement will usually be terminated by the removal of a director from office. However, this is not invariably so. The outcome will depend on the terms of the service agreement. A person cannot, for example, continue as managing director if he or she is not a director. By contrast, there may be situations in which the office of director is wholly separate from the employment relationship. This might be the case where a manager has no right under his employment contract to be appointed or remain as a director. Such a person may continue in his employment as a manager despite the termination of his directorship. If the companies intend that the employment should end if the employee ceases to be a director, the service agreement should include a clause stating this. The converse position may also occur where the employment of an executive director may terminate whilst he or she remains in office. Usually, the board is responsible for terminating the executive appointment of a director, by a majority of the board. Again, if it is intended that the executive appointment should be co-terminous with the appointment as a director, the service agreement should so provide. Service agreements often provide that the executive is required to resign from office as a director (and all other offices held by him in the company) in the event that the employment terminates.

9.27 Termination payments

It is not lawful for a company to make to a director any payment by way of compensation for loss of office, or as consideration for or in connection with his retirement from office, without particulars of the proposed payment (including the amount) being disclosed to members of the company and the proposal being approved by the company. This restriction is by virtue of s *312* of *CA 1985*. These payments do not, however, include any payment made in good faith by way of damages for breach of contract or by way of pension in respect of past services (*CA 1985, s 316(3)*).

In *Taupo Totara Timber Co Ltd v Rowe* [1978] AC 537, a director was given the right, under the terms of his service agreement, to resign his office following a takeover. Further, he would then be entitled to a payment equivalent to five times his annual salary to be paid tax free. Following a takeover, the director sought to enforce this provision by giving notice. The Privy Council held that the payment did not require shareholder approval since it had been contractually agreed by the company. In that case, there was no suggestion that this was a liquidated damages clause – such a clause might amount to a penalty and therefore be unenforceable.

The Privy Council approved the decision in *Taupo Totara Timber Co Ltd v Rowein* the Australian case of *Lincoln Mills (Aust) Ltd v Gough* [1964] VR 193 in which it was held that the similar (but non-identical) provision in Victorian companies legislation applied only to payment to a director for loss of office and not in respect of loss of the employment.

In *Murray v Leisureplay plc* [2005] EWCA Civ 963, [2005] IRLR 946, the Court of Appeal considered an argument that a clause in a chief executive director's contract providing for the payment of one year's gross salary in the event of termination was unenforceable as a penalty. The Court of Appeal there held that a clause will only be held to be a penalty if the party seeking to avoid it can demonstrate that the sum payable on breach is extravagant or unconscionable.

There is no English case which holds that *s 312* should be construed in this narrow way. It would be prudent to assume that *s 312* does apply to termination payments to executive directors unless they fall within the exception set out in *CA 1985, s 316(3)*.

If an employed director is dismissed following the appointment of an administrator, he or she may be entitled to enforce provisions of the service agreement against the administrator personally. Before 15 March 1994, administrators of an insolvent company were deemed to have 'adopted' employment contracts within the meaning of *ss 19* and *44* of the *Insolvency Act 1986* if they did not change the terms and conditions within 14 days of their appointment (*Powdrill v Watson, Re Leyland DAF Ltd, Re Ferranti International plc* [1995] 2 All ER 65). In relation to contracts of employment adopted on or after 15 March 1994, administrators are personally liable on any contract of employment if his liability is to pay a sum by way of wages or salary or contribution to an occupational pension scheme which was incurred while he is in office and is in respect of services rendered wholly or partly after the adoption of the contract. (See further INSOLVENCY OF EMPLOYER (31)).

In respect of unquoted companies, details of compensation paid to directors for loss of office must be shown in notes to the accounts (under *Sch 6* to the *CA 1985* as amended). There must be shown the aggregate amount of any compensation to director or past directors including compensation receivable for:

(*a*)   loss of office as a director of the company; or

(*b*)   loss, while a director of the company or on or in connection with his ceasing to be a director of it, of any other office in connection with the management of the company's affairs, or any office as director or otherwise in connection with the management of the affairs of any subsidiary undertaking of the company.

References to compensation include benefits otherwise than in cash and in relation to such compensation, references to its amount are to the estimated money value of the benefit. The nature of any such compensation must be disclosed. References to compensation for loss of office include:

(i) compensation in consideration for, or in connection with, a person's retirement from office;

(ii) where that retirement is as a result of a breach of the person's contract with the company or with a subsidiary undertaking, payments by way of damages or settlement in respect of the breach.

With regard to quoted companies, similar disclosures must be made in the directors' remuneration report (provisions apply to the disclosure of excess retirement benefits in respect of the directors' remuneration report (see *paras 6(1)(d)* and *14* of *Sch 7A* to *CA 1985*).

9.28 *Recommendations*

Paragraph B.1.5 of the Combined Code recommends that remuneration committees consider what compensation commitments, including pension contributions, their directors' terms of appointment would entail in the event of early termination. The aim should be to avoid rewarding poor performance. It is recommended that committees should take a robust line on reducing compensation to reflect the departing directors' obligations to mitigate loss.

9.29 *Listing Rules*

The *Listing Rules* require listed companies to disclose in their report to shareholders any significant payments made to former directors and any compensation paid to directors for loss of office (rule 9.8.8).

9.30 **Company approval for property transfer**

Payments to a director by way of compensation for loss of office, or as consideration for or in connection with retirement from office, where made in connection with the transfer of the whole or any part of the undertaking or property of a company, must have shareholder approval (*CA 1985, s 313*). Shareholder approval is not required, however, where payment is made of *bona fide* damages for breach of contract or by way of pension for past services (*s 316(3)*). If approval is required but not obtained, the amount received is deemed to be held by the director in trust for the company.

9.31 **Payments on takeover**

A director has a specific duty under *s 314* of *CA 1985* where a payment is made to him or her by way of compensation for loss of office, or as consideration for or in connection with retirement for office, in connection with the transfer of all or any of the company's shares resulting from

(*a*) an offer made to the general body of shareholders;

(*b*) an offer made by or on behalf of some other body corporate with a view to the company becoming its subsidiary or a subsidiary of its holding company;

(*c*) an offer made by or on behalf of an individual with a view to his obtaining the right to exercise or control the exercise of not less than one-third of the voting power at any general meeting of the company; or

(*d*) any other offer which is conditional to a given extent.

The duty is to take all reasonable steps to secure that particulars of the proposed payment (including the amount) are included or sent with any notice of the offer made for their shares which is given to any shareholders. Failing to comply with this duty is an offence, punishable by a fine.

This duty does not apply where a payment is made of *bona fide* damages for breach of contract or by way of pension for past services (*CA 1985, s 316(3)*).

If the director does not comply with this duty, or if the payment is not approved, the director is deemed to hold any payment in trust for those persons who have sold their shares as a result of the offer made. He or she is also required to bear the expenses incurred in distributing that sum (*CA 1985, s 315*).

9.32   TRANSFER OF UNDERTAKING

If an undertaking is sold or otherwise transferred, the employment of all those employed in the undertaking automatically transfers from the transferor company to the transferee under the *Transfer of Undertakings* (*Protection of Employment*) *Regulations 2006* (*SI 2006/246* (*'TUPE'*)). For the purposes of TUPE, a contract of employment is defined as any agreement between an employee and his or her employer which determines the conditions of employment. An 'employee' is any individual who works for another person whether under a contract of service or apprenticeship or otherwise but does not include anyone who provides services under a contract for services. Accordingly, an employed director will be an employee for the purposes of TUPE. Therefore, if the undertaking or part of undertaking in which the director is employed is transferred, the directors' employment contract will transfer to the transferee.

If the director is entitled under the contract of employment to be appointed director of the company which employs him or her, then failure to appoint him as a director of the transferee will amount to a repudiatory breach of contract, entitling the director to resign and claim constructive dismissal. The director will also be required to resign as a director of the transferor company or otherwise be removed from office.

Service agreements often contain provisions dealing with reconstructions. A typical agreement will exclude any claim brought by a director if he or she is offered employment with the successor company on no less favourable terms and conditions. In any event, TUPE would be likely to apply in these circumstances to the same effect.

(TUPE is addressed in detail in TRANSFER OF UNDERTAKINGS (52).)

10   Disability Discrimination

(See also the Disability Discrimination Act 1995 Code of Practice Employment and Occupation (*'Code of Practice'*) issued by the Disability Rights Commission. The *Code of Practice* provides comprehensive coverage of the application of the law as from 1 October 2004 and is essential reading for anyone advising in this area. A wide range of useful information is also available from the Disability Rights Commission website: www.drc-gb.org, and the Government website: www.disability.gov.uk.

10.1   The *Disability Discrimination Act 1995* (*'DDA 1995'*) renders it unlawful to discriminate against disabled persons in employment and other areas. *Council Directive 2000/78/EC*, which establishes a general framework for equal treatment in employment, includes discrimination on the grounds of disability within its scope. In compliance with its obligations under the *Directive*, the Government has made the *Disability Discrimination Act 1995 (Amendment) Regulations 2003* (*SI 2003/1673*) (*'Amendment Regulations'*). The *Amendment Regulations* came into force on 1 October 2004 and made significant modifications to some of the key parts of *DDA 1995*. Readers should also note that the *Disability Discrimination Act 2005* (*'DDA 2005'*) introduced significant modifications to *DDA 1995* (in relation, in particular, to the definition of 'disability' and to the duties of public authorities) and some of these are mentioned below. However, readers are advised to refer both to *DDA 1995* as amended by the *Amendment Regulations* and to *DDA 2005* for a full account of the changes.

10.2   **DEFINITION OF 'DISABILITY' AND 'DISABLED PERSON'**

Subject to the provisions of *DDA 1995, Sch 1*, a person has a disability for the purposes of *DDA 1995* if he has a physical or mental impairment which has a substantial and long-term adverse effect on his ability to carry out normal day-to-day activities (*DDA 1995, s 1(1)*). The requirement that a mental illness had to be a clinically well-recognised illness before it could be a mental impairment was repealed as from 5 December 2005 (*DDA 2005, s 18(2)*). The effect of an impairment is a long-term effect if it has lasted at least 12 months, or if it is likely to last at least that long, or if it is likely to last for the rest of the affected person's life, or if it is likely to recur if in remission (*DDA 1995 Sch 1 para 2(1), (2)*). An impairment is to be taken to affect the ability to carry out normal day-to-day activities only if it affects one of the following:

(*a*)   mobility;

(*b*)   manual dexterity;

(*c*)   physical co-ordination;

(*d*)   continence;

(*e*)   the ability to lift, carry or otherwise move everyday objects;

(*f*)   speech, hearing or eyesight;

(*g*)   memory or ability to concentrate, learn or understand; or

(*h*)   perception of the risk of physical danger.

(*DDA 1995, Sch 1 para 4(1)*.)

Where there is a substantial effect on one of the capacities listed in (*a*) to (*h*) above, it is not necessary to demonstrate that there is a substantial effect on another. (The ECJ gave its first decision on disability discrimination in *Chacon Navas v Eurest Collectividades SA* [2006] IRLR 706, and held that sickness as such is not a disability. It is unlikely that the long-established (and broader) definition of 'disability' under *DDA 1995* will be affected by this decision.)

In addition to the above definitions, Regulations may make provision, for the purposes of the *DDA 1995*:

(i) for conditions of a prescribed description to be treated as amounting to or not amounting to impairments (*DDA 1995, Sch 1 para 1(2)*);

(ii) for prescribing circumstances in which the effect of an impairment is or is not to be treated as a long-term effect (*DDA 1995, Sch 1 para 2(4)*);

(iii) for prescribing circumstances in which the likelihood of a substantial adverse effect recurring is to be disregarded (*DDA 1995, Sch 1 para 2(3)*);

(iv) for prescribing circumstances in which an impairment is to be taken to affect or not to affect the ability to carry out normal day-to-day activities (*DDA 1995, Sch 1 para 4(2)*); and

(v) for prescribing the kinds of effect on the ability to carry out normal day-to-day activities which are to be treated as a substantial adverse effect (*DDA 1995, Sch 1 para 5*).

The power to make regulations features prominently throughout the *DDA 1995*, and readers should refer to relevant regulations, to guidance issued by the Secretary of State (see 10.4 below), and to the *Code of Practice* to determine what amounts to a disability for the purposes of the *DDA 1995*.

The *Disability Discrimination* (*Meaning of Disability*) *Regulations* (*SI 1996/1455*) ('*Meaning Regulations*') were the first Regulations to be made under these powers. These specifically provide that addiction to alcohol, nicotine or any other substance (except where the addiction originally resulted from the administration of medically prescribed drugs) is to be treated as not amounting to an impairment for the purposes of *DDA 1995* (*Meaning Regulations, reg 3(1)*, (*2*)). Certain personality disorders such as pyromania, kleptomania, a tendency to physical or sexual abuse of other persons, exhibitionism and voyeurism are to be treated as not amounting to impairments (*Meaning Regulations, reg 4(1)*). Hayfever and similar conditions are also to be treated as not amounting to impairments. An employee may have a condition eg a depressive illness that does amount to a disability within the meaning of *DDA 1995* but which was in fact caused by or was the result of an excluded condition, eg addiction to alcohol. The EAT (Ms Recorder Slade QC presiding) has confirmed that an employee in these circumstances would be disabled notwithstanding the link with the excluded condition because it is not relevant to consider the cause of a particular disability (*Power v Panasonic (UK) Ltd* [2003] IRLR 151). Conversely, a person might have an excluded condition that is caused by or is a manifestation of an impairment that falls within the scope of *DDA 1995*. (See *Edmund Nuttall Ltd v Butterfield* [2005] IRLR 751, where the excluded condition – in that case, exhibitionism – was caused by depression; and see 10.7 below).

Chronic fatigue syndrome or 'ME', asthma, epilepsy, dyslexia, post-traumatic stress disorder and depression are all capable of amounting to a disability within the meaning of *DDA 1995*. This does not mean, however, that such conditions will always amount to a disability. It will be a question of fact for the tribunal in each case to determine whether the condition has a substantial and long-term adverse effect on the person's ability to carry out normal day-to-day activities.

Impairment. 'Impairment' is not defined in *DDA 1995*. Guidance issued by the Secretary of State provides that the term 'mental or physical impairment' should be give its ordinary meaning and that it may not always be possible, nor is it necessary, to categorise a condition as either a physical or mental impairment. (See also *McNicol v Balfour Beatty Rail Maintenance Ltd* [2002] EWCA Civ 1074, [2002] ICR 1498). In *College of Ripon and York St John v Hobbs* [2002] IRLR 185, the EAT held that the task of ascertaining whether there is a physical impairment within the meaning of *DDA 1995* did not involve drawing any rigid distinctions between an underlying fault or defect in the body on the one hand, and evidence of the manifestations or effects of that fault or defect on the other. Thus, an impairment can be something that consists simply of the effects of an illness as opposed to the illness itself. In that case, there was clear evidence that there was something physically wrong with the applicant's body. However, there was no conclusive medical evidence as to the precise cause. Notwithstanding this lacuna in the evidence, the EAT held that it was open to the tribunal to find that there was a physical impairment simply on the basis of the evidence that there was something wrong with the applicant physically (see also *Rugamer v Sony Music Entertainment UK Ltd* [2002] ICR 381, [2001] IRLR 644). This rather relaxed approach to ascertaining a physical impairment is to be contrasted with the more rigid approach recommended in cases of mental impairment. In *Morgan v Staffordshire University* [2002] IRLR 190, the EAT held (no doubt to the relief of employers faced with a barrage of medical certificates merely citing 'stress' or 'anxiety' as the reason for absence) that the occasional use of terms such as 'anxiety', 'stress' or 'depression' even by GPs will not amount to proof of a mental impairment within the meaning of *DDA 1995*. In particular, it was held that the occasional mention in medical notes or reference in the World Health Organisation's International Classification of Diseases of or to such terms would not be sufficient in the absence of informed medical evidence that said more. The EAT in that case also provided some detailed guidance for those seeking to establish a mental impairment. Readers are referred to the report of the *Morgan* case for the full details. In essence, however, the guidance reiterates the importance of expert medical evidence in this area. Both the *College of Ripon* and *Morgan* cases were noted with approval by the Court of Appeal in *McNicol* (see above). (See also *De Keyser Ltd v Wilson* [2001] IRLR 324.) However, readers should also refer to the more recent decision of *Dunham v Ashford Windows* [2005] ICR 1584, [2005] IRLR 608, in which the EAT held that a person might have a mental impairment (such as learning difficulties) which did not amount to a mental illness. In such cases, the EAT suggested that there is no requirement to establish a clinically well-recognised illness since the impairment is not based on mental illness at all. The Code of Practice appears to support this distinction between a mental impairment and mental illness (Code of Practice, Appendix B). The requirement that a mental illness must be clinically well-recognised was in any case repealed as from 5 December 2005 (*DDA 2005, s 18(2)*).

The 'Goodwin v Patent Office' Guidance. The EAT in *Goodwin v Patent Office* [1999] IRLR 4 laid down detailed guidance as to the approach to be taken by employment tribunals in determining whether or not an applicant is disabled within the meaning of *DDA 1995*. Readers should refer to this case for the full details of the EAT's guidance. In summary, the EAT held that in determining whether or not an applicant is disabled, the tribunal should look carefully at what the parties have said in the pleadings and clarify the issues, in most cases after standard directions to this effect or at a directions hearing; they should take a purposive approach to the construction of *DDA 1995*; they should refer expressly to any relevant provisions of the Guidance and Code of Practice which have been taken into account (see 10.4 and 10.32 below); in determining whether or not an impairment has an adverse effect on a person's ability to carry out activities, they should bear in mind that the fact that a person can, with difficulty or great effort, carry out these activities does not mean that his ability to carry them out has not been impaired; they should bear in mind that disabled persons are likely to play down the effect that a disability has on their activities; in determining what is a day-to-day activity, the tribunal's inquiry should not focus only on a particular or a special set of circumstances such as activities carried on in the home; in determining whether an adverse effect is substantial the tribunal may, where the applicant still claims to be suffering from the same degree of impairment as at the time of the events complained of, take into account how the applicant appears to the tribunal to 'manage' his condition; where an applicant is or had been on medication, the tribunal should, in determining whether there is an adverse effect, examine how the applicant's abilities were affected whilst on medication and how those activities would have been affected without the medication; and when addressing each of the conditions under *DDA 1995, s 1(1)*, namely the 'impairment' condition, the 'adverse effect' condition, the 'substantial' conditions and the 'long-term' condition, the tribunal should be careful not to lose sight of the overall picture.

The EAT in the case of *Leonard v Southern Derbyshire Chamber of Commerce* [2001] IRLR 19 emphasised that in considering whether an impairment had a substantial adverse effect on the ability to carry out normal day-to-day activities, the tribunal must concentrate on what the applicant cannot do or can only do with difficulty. An approach that looks mainly to what the applicant can do may lead to the erroneous conclusion that because the applicant can still do many things, the adverse effect cannot be substantial. Similarly, the mere fact that an employee can perform the duties of his job does not necessarily mean that he is not disabled. (See *Law Hospital NHS Trust v Rush* [2001] IRLR 611 and *Ekpe v Metropolitan Police Comr* [2001] IRLR 605.) In *Cruickshank v VAW Motorcast Ltd* [2002] IRLR 24, the EAT considered the position of an employee whose impairment (an asthmatic complaint) was such that he only appeared to suffer substantial adverse effects whilst present at the workplace. The employment tribunal had held that the employee was not a disabled person within the meaning of *DDA 1995* because it could not be said that there was an adverse effect on his normal day-to-day activities. The EAT disagreed and held that the tribunal had been wrong to confine its analysis of the applicant's ability to carry out normal day-to-day activities to his activities outside of the work environment. In general terms, the principle that normal day-to-day activities are not to be determined only on the basis of a particular environment must be correct. However, where there is evidence that an employee only suffers substantial adverse effects when in a particular work environment (in the form, say, of a severe allergic reaction to the carpets in a particular office) and nowhere else, it might still be possible to argue that there was no *substantial* adverse effect on normal day-to-day activities or that the effects were not long term. The better approach in these circumstances (as suggested by the EAT in *Cruickshank*) would be to consider whether any reasonable adjustments could be made rather than attempting to argue that there is no disability.

10.3   The definition of 'disabled person' under the *Disabled Persons (Employment) Act 1944 ('DPEA 1944')* was repealed, upon the coming into force of *DDA 1995, s 61(7)*. A 'disabled person' is a person who has a disability as defined above (*DDA*

1995, s 1(2)), and all references to 'disabled person' in subordinate legislation making reference to *DPEA 1944* are to be construed accordingly *(DDA 1995, s 61(8)).*

10.4 Guidance

The Secretary of State has issued guidance pursuant to *DDA 1995, s 3* about matters to be taken into account in determining questions relating to the definition of disability. Guidance originally issued in 1996 was revoked with effect from 30 April 2006 and replaced by revised Guidance which came into force on 1 May 2006 and which takes into account many of the points established by case law in recent years. Under *DDA 1995, s 3(3)* an employment tribunal is obliged to take into account any of the Guidance which appears to it to be relevant (see *Goodwin v Patent Office* above).

Guidance on the meaning of 'substantial' adverse effect. The Guidance provides that a 'substantial' effect is one that is greater than the effect which would be produced by the sort of physical or mental conditions experienced by many people which have only 'minor' or 'trivial' effects. In assessing whether the effect of an impairment is substantial, consideration is to be given to the time taken to carry out an activity, the way in which the activity is carried out, the cumulative effects of an impairment, the effects of the environment, the extent to which a person can reasonably be expected to modify behaviour to prevent or reduce the effects of an impairment on normal day-to-day activities, and the effect of treatment. Readers should refer to the Guidance for further examples.

Guidance on the meaning of 'long-term effects'. It is not necessary for the effect of an impairment to be the same throughout the relevant period. Thus the effect may change or disappear temporarily but there would still be a long-term effect if the impairment continues to have, or is likely to have, such an effect throughout the period. An event is 'likely' to happen if it is more probable than not that it will happen. When an effect has ceased, the likelihood of recurrence is to be taken into account. If it is likely that the substantial adverse effect will recur, it is to be treated as long term. It is important to recognise here that the relevant question is not whether the *illness* is likely to recur, but whether the *substantial adverse effect* is likely to do so. Theoretically, therefore, whilst a person may stage a full recovery from an illness there may be an ongoing likelihood of recurrence of the adverse effect. (See *Swift v Chief Constable of Wiltshire Constabulary* [2004] IRLR 540.) In determining whether the effect of an impairment is likely to last for at least 12 months, an employment tribunal should consider the adverse effects of the applicant's condition up to and including the tribunal hearing (see *Greenwood v British Airways plc* [1999] IRLR 600 and 10.6 below, 'Disabled at the Relevant Time').

Guidance on the meaning of 'normal day-to-day activities'. Such activities do not include those which are normal only for a particular person or group of people. In deciding whether an activity is a 'normal day-to-day activity', account shall be taken of how far the activity is normal for most people. In this context 'normal' is to be given its ordinary, everyday meaning. The Guidance provides numerous examples (which are purely illustrative) of effects on activities which it would or would not be reasonable to regard as having a substantial adverse effect. These include: total inability to walk or difficulty walking other than at a slow pace or with unsteady or jerky movements; difficulty in going up or down steps, stairs or gradients; difficulty in using one or more forms of public transport; difficulty pressing the buttons on keyboards or keypads at the same speed as someone who does not have an impairment; infrequent loss of control of the bowels; difficulty carrying a moderately loaded tray steadily; difficulty giving clear basic instructions orally to colleagues; difficulty hearing and understanding another person speaking clearly over the telephone (without the use of a hearing aid or similar device); inability to distinguish any colours at all (as opposed to red/green colour-blindness); and difficulty recognising by sight a known person across a moderately-sized room (unless this can be corrected by glasses). The above are all examples of adverse effects which it *would* be reasonable to regard as substantial. It would *not* be reasonable, however, to regard as having a substantial adverse effect: an inability to articulate fluently due to a lisp or other minor speech impediment; an inability to reach typing speeds standardised for secretarial work; simple clumsiness; infrequent and minor leakage from the bladder; an inability to carry heavy luggage without assistance; an inability to concentrate on a task requiring application over several hours; or a fear of significant heights. Readers should refer to the Guidance for further examples.

The decision of the EAT in the case of *Vicary v British Telecommunications plc* [1999] IRLR 680 cautions employment tribunals against taking too literal an approach to the Guidance issued by the Secretary of State. In *Vicary*, the employment tribunal (wrongly) found that DIY tasks, filing nails, tonging hair, ironing, shaking quilts, grooming animals, polishing furniture, knitting and sewing, and cutting with scissors were *not* normal day-to-day activities 'as set out in the Guidance'. The EAT held that the tribunal had misunderstood the nature of the Guidance (as it then was) in that it was meant to be illustrative of the kinds of things that would be regarded as day-to-day activities, and was not intended to be exhaustive. The kinds of activities which the applicant in *Vicary* had difficulty with plainly were normal day-to-day activities since they are all activities which most people would do on a frequent or regular basis. (See *Guidance*, paras D4 to 10 and also *Ekpe v Metropolitan Police Comr* [2001] IRLR 605, where the EAT held that it was an error of law to conclude that an activity only done by women was not a normal day-to-day activity.)

In *Leonard v Southern Derbyshire Chamber of Commerce*, the employment tribunal had considered the examples given in the Guidance (as it then was) in determining whether or not the applicant's condition had a substantial adverse effect on her day-to-day activities. In deciding that the applicant was not disabled, the employment tribunal had balanced those examples in the Guidance that the applicant could do (such as being able to eat and drink) against those which the applicant could not do (such as negotiate pavement edges properly). The EAT held that this balancing exercise was inappropriate, 'since her ability to catch a ball did not diminish her inability to negotiate pavement edges safely'. As stated above, the correct approach involves considering all matters, but paying particular attention to those activities that the applicant cannot do.

10.5   Past disabilities

The provisions of the *DDA 1995* in respect of discrimination in connection with employment also apply to persons who have had a disability but have recovered, and all references to disabled persons are to be read accordingly (*DDA 1995, s 2(1)*). This applies even if the person recovered before the *Act* came into force. For example, a woman who four years ago, experienced a mental illness which amounted to a disability, but who has experienced no recurrence of the condition, is still entitled to the protection afforded by *DDA 1995*. (See *Guidance*, para A15).

10.6 Disability Discrimination

10.6 Disabled at 'the relevant time'

In any proceedings under the employment-related provisions of the *DDA 1995*, the question whether a person had a disability at a particular time ('the relevant time') shall be determined as if the provisions of, or made under, the *Act* in force when the act complained of was done had been in force at the relevant time (*DDA 1995, s 2(4)*). The relevant time may be a time before the passing of the *Act* (*DDA 1995, s 2(5)*).

The EAT in *Cruickshank v VAW Motorcast Ltd* [2002] IRLR 24 confirmed that in determining whether a person is disabled for the purposes of *DDA 1995*, the court should apply the appropriate test to the applicant's condition as at the date of the alleged discriminatory act and not as at the date of the hearing. This approach can present difficulties particularly where the effects of a particular condition tend to fluctuate or last for uncertain periods. The fact that by the date of the hearing, an adverse effect had in fact lasted for 12 months is not necessarily conclusive of it having been likely to have lasted that long as at the date of the discriminatory act. If, on the basis of information as to the person's condition that would reasonably have been available at the time of the discriminatory act, it would *not* have been possible to conclude at that stage that the adverse effect was *likely* to last for 12 months, then the longevity requirement of *s 1(1)* of the *DDA 1995* would not be satisfied (see *Latchman v Reed Business Information Ltd* [2002] ICR 1453). In *Swift v Chief Constable of Wiltshire Constabulary* [2004] IRLR 540 (in which *Latchman* was cited), the EAT confirmed that in determining whether at a particular point in time a substantial adverse effect was likely to recur, the Tribunal was entitled to take account of evidence of what had happened since that time. However, the EAT went on to say that evidence showing that the effect *did* recur would not necessarily be conclusive.

10.7 Other disabilities

Severe disfigurement. Subject to Regulations made under the *DDA 1995*, an impairment which consists of a severe disfigurement is to be treated as a disability (*DDA 1995, Sch 1 para 3*). This might not apply to disfigurements which have been deliberately acquired (*DDA 1995, Sch 1 para 3(3)*). Disfigurement could include limb or postural deformation (*Guidance*, para B21). A disfigurement which consists of a tattoo (which has not been removed) or a piercing of the body for decorative or other non-medical purposes is not to be considered a severe disfigurement (*Meaning Regulations, reg 5*).

Controlled or corrected impairments. An impairment which is controlled or corrected by, for example, medical treatment or the use of a prosthesis or any other aid, is to be treated, unless prescribed otherwise, as a disability if the impairment would have a substantial adverse effect on the ability to carry out normal day-to-day activities were it not controlled or corrected ('the deduced effect') (*DDA 1995, Sch 1 para 6(1), (2)*). The EAT in *Vicary v British Telecommunications plc* [1999] IRLR 680, commented (*obiter*) that the words 'or any other aid' in this context (*DDA 1995, Sch 1 para 6(1), (2)*) are probably intended to refer to aids such as Zimmerframes or sticks or wheelchairs and not to labour-saving household devices such as electric can-openers. An 'aid' in this context can also include surgically inserted plates and pins. (*Carden v Pickerings Europe Ltd* [2005] IRLR 720). The EAT in *Kapadia v Lambeth London Borough Council* [2000] IRLR 14 found that counselling sessions conducted by a consultant psychologist amounted to 'medical treatment' within the meaning of the *DDA 1995*, notwithstanding the fact that the counselling only comprised 'talking' to the applicant and the fact that no drugs were administered. An asthmatic employee would probably be regarded as disabled within the meaning of the Act if his condition was such that if it were not controlled through the use of inhalers and medication, it would have a substantial adverse effect on his normal day-to-day activities. Impaired eyesight which is correctable by spectacles or contact lenses, however, will not be treated as a disability (*DDA 1995, Sch 1 para 6(3)(a)*). It should be noted that where a deduced effect is alleged, the employee is required to prove the disability with some particularity and clear medical evidence will usually be necessary. A mere assertion by the employee as to what would happen if the treatment ceased will probably not be sufficient (*Woodrup v Southwark London Borough Council* [2003] IRLR 111, CA). In *Abadeh v British Telecommunications plc* [2001] ICR 156, the EAT provided guidance on the approach to be taken in determining the deduced effect in circumstances where the medical treatment had ceased. Nelson J clarified in that case that the applicant could only rely on a deduced effect if the medical treatment is ongoing. Where treatment has ceased, the employment tribunal should take into account the effect of the treatment in order to assess whether there is a disability. Thus, if a person has had medical treatment that has had the effect of restoring his ability to carry out normal day-to-day activities and that treatment has ceased, then he cannot rely on the effects of his impairment as they were without the medical treatment. (See *Guidance*, para B15 and also *Carden v Pickerings Europe Ltd* [2005] IRLR 720). The EAT in *Abadeh* did not deal expressly with the fact that persons who have had a disability in the past are still protected for the purposes of *DDA 1995* (*DDA 1995, s 2(1)* and see 10.5 above). However, the existence of such protection means that the EAT's guidance in respect of applicants whose treatment has ceased can only apply where as at the particular date in respect of which the employment tribunal is considering whether or not the applicant was disabled, the applicant has not already had a disability within the meaning of *DDA 1995*.

Further guidance was provided by the EAT in *Abadeh* (see above) in respect of those applicants whose treatment is continuing. Where the tribunal is satisfied that the effect of the continuing medical treatment is to create a permanent improvement rather than a temporary improvement, such permanent improvement should be taken into account. Readers are referred to the full decision for examples given by the EAT to illustrate this principle.

Progressive conditions. A person having a progressive condition (such as cancer or muscular dystrophy), which is likely to result in a disability, may be taken as having a disability even if the condition has not yet had a substantial adverse effect on the person's ability to carry out normal day-to-day activities (*DDA 1995, Sch 1 para 8(1)*). It is important, however, that there is some effect before *DDA 1995* can apply. As from 5 December 2005, persons with multiple sclerosis, HIV infection or cancer (other than prescribed forms of cancer) will be deemed to have a disability (*DDA 2005, s 18(3)*). (See 10.8, Persons Deemed to be Disabled). Mere diagnosis of a progressive condition (other than one of the conditions giving rise to a deemed disability) would not be sufficient in itself. In *Mowat-Brown v University of Surrey* [2002] IRLR 235, the EAT in fact held that it is not enough simply for an applicant to establish that he has a progressive condition and that it has or has had an effect on his ability to carry out normal day-to-day activities. An applicant with a progressive condition must go on to show that it is more likely than not that at some stage in the future there will be a substantial adverse effect on his ability to carry out normal day-to-day activities. The Guidance (at para B17) provides that in such cases, medical prognosis of the likely impact of the condition will be the normal route to establishing protection under the progressive conditions provisions. A person may be taken as having a disability even where the substantial adverse effect is as a result of the treatment for a progressive condition (eg an operation for prostrate cancer that results in urinary incontinence) rather than the progressive condition itself (see *Kirton v Tetrosyl Ltd* [2003] EWCA Civ 619, [2003] ICR 1237, [2003] IRLR 353).

10.8 **Persons deemed to be disabled**

Any person on the old *DPEA 1944* register of disabled persons both on 12 January 1995 and on 2 December 1996, shall be deemed, for a period of three years, to have a disability for the purposes of the Act, and afterwards, to have had a disability and hence to have been a disabled person during that period (*DDA 1995, Sch 1 para 7(1)(2)*). Thus, although *DPEA 1944* registration provisions have been repealed (*DDA 1995, s 61(7)(b)*), registered persons will not necessarily be obliged to re-establish their disability to avail themselves of protection under the *Act*. Regulations may provide for other persons who are to be deemed to be disabled (*DDA 1995, Sch 1 para 7(5)*). Unsurprisingly, a person who is certified as blind or partially sighted by a consultant ophthalmologist in accordance with relevant guidance or who is registered as blind will be deemed to have a disability (*Disability Discrimination (Blind and Partially Sighted Persons) Regulations 2003 (SI 2003/712)*). As from 5 December 2005 persons with multiple sclerosis, HIV infection or cancer (other than prescribed forms of cancer) will also be deemed to have a disability (*DDA 2005, s 18(3)*).

10.9 **MEANING OF DISCRIMINATION IN EMPLOYMENT**

Disability discrimination by an employer may take place in any one of five ways: direct discrimination, disability-related discrimination, discrimination by way of the employer's failure to comply with the duty to make reasonable adjustments, harassment and discrimination by way of victimisation. It is now only open to the employer to show that disability-related discrimination is justified (see 10.11 below).

Code of Practice. The *Code of Practice* issued by the Disability Rights Commission on 1 October 2004 gives extensive practical guidance on the application of *DDA 1995* and provides numerous examples of how the *Act* is likely to work in practice, including guidance on the meaning of discrimination in employment. Readers are advised to refer to the *Code of Practice* for such examples, some of which are referred to below.

Although there is no provision in *DDA 1995* corresponding to the indirect discrimination provisions of the *Sex Discrimination Act 1975 ('SDA 1975')* and *Race Relations Act 1976 ('RRA 1976')*, the duty to make reasonable adjustments under *DDA 1995* arises wherever a provision, criterion or practice places a disabled person at a substantial disadvantage as compared to a non-disabled person. (See 10.12.)

The question whether a person who is not herself disabled can bring a claim under *DDA 1995* by reason of having been treated less favourably on the grounds that she was a carer for a disabled person has been referred to the European Court of Justice. The EAT held that *DDA 1995* is capable of interpretation so as to include 'associative discrimination' and that the employment tribunal had not erred in making such a reference to the ECJ (*Attridge Law v Coleman* [2007] IRLR 88).

10.10 **Direct discrimination**

Prior to 1 October 2004, 'direct discrimination' under DDA was the same as what is now referred to in the *Code of Practice* as 'disability-related discrimination' (see

10.11 below). Under the present legislation, an employer directly discriminates against a disabled person if, on the ground of the disabled person's disability, he treats the disabled person less favourably than he treats or would treat a person not having that particular disability whose relevant circumstances, including his abilities, are the same as, or not materially different from, those of the disabled person. The justification defence is *not* available for discrimination under *DDA 1995, s 3A(5)* (*DDA 1995, s 3A(4)*). This type of direct discrimination does bear some similarity to direct discrimination as it is understood under *SDA 1975* and *RRA 1976*. In particular, there is a requirement to compare like with like in that the relevant circumstances of the disabled employee and the comparator must be the same or not materially different. Relevant circumstances here expressly include the disabled employee's abilities. Thus, if a disabled typist and a non-disabled typist could both type at 30wpm, then their respective abilities would be the same. If an employer were to treat the non-disabled typist more favourably (eg by offering him a job) than the disabled typist, that would amount to direct discrimination. (See *Code of Practice, paras 4.20 and 4.21*). Such discrimination could not be justified and would be unlawful. As with other discrimination legislation, *DDA* enables a comparison to be made with a hypothetical comparator.

Watts v High Quality Lifestyles Ltd [2006] IRLR 850, [2006] All ER (D) 216 (Apr), EAT is the first appellate decision to consider direct discrimination under DDA 1995. In that case, the claimant was a support worker who had suffered a number of injuries including cuts and bites in the course of his work with persons with learning difficulties. Upon revealing to management that he was HIV+, he was suspended and later dismissed on the grounds that his position was untenable after a risk assessment concluded that injuries involving broken skin were commonplace. The employment tribunal found that such treatment was on the grounds of disability and upheld his claim. However, the EAT found that the employment tribunal had failed to consider whether there had in fact been less favourable treatment than a hypothetical comparator. The EAT also found that in identifying the appropriate comparator, the Employment Tribunal should have found that the comparator had 'some attribute, whether caused by medical condition or otherwise, which is not HIV+ ...[which] must carry the same risk of causing to others illness or injury of the same gravity, here serious and possibly fatal'. It is thought that this approach to identifying comparators might be to construe 'relevant circumstances' under *s 3A(5)* too narrowly. A comparator with an attribute carrying precisely the same risk of causing illness or injury to others would almost always be likely to be treated the same as the claimant, in which case the claim of direct discrimination would fail. The EAT's approach to comparator in this case, which requires that the comparator is effectively someone who is HIV+ by another name, could also let discrimination based on the stigma of being HIV+ slip through the net.

10.11 **Disability-related discrimination**

'Disability-related discrimination' is a term that will not be found in *DDA*. It is a convenient shorthand adopted by the *Code of Practice* to describe the type of discrimination that prior to 1 October 2004 was referred to as 'direct discrimination'. (*Code of Practice, para 4.28*). Care should be taken when referring to authorities decided prior to 1 October 2004 since references to 'direct discrimination' will in fact be references to 'disability-related discrimination' rather than the type of discrimination described in the previous paragraph.

An employer engages in disability-related discrimination if, for a reason which relates to the disabled person's disability, he treats him less favourably than he treats or would treat others to whom that reason does not or would not apply, and the employer cannot show that such treatment is justified (*DDA 1995, s 3A(1)*). A reason relating to disability may include, for example, the disabled person's poor time-keeping due to lack of mobility. In *Clark v Novacold Ltd* [1999] IRLR 318, the first decision of the Court of Appeal under *DDA 1995*, the court provided important guidance as to the meaning of discrimination under what is now *DDA 1995, s 3A(1)*. The Court of Appeal confirmed that for a disabled person to establish that there has been less favourable treatment for a reason relating to disability there is no need to identify an able-bodied comparator (or a person with a different disability) who has or would have been treated differently. All that a disabled person has to show is that, for a reason related to his disability, he was treated less favourably than another to whom that reason, ie the reason for the treatment, does not apply. The application of this approach can be demonstrated by using the example of the employee who has poor time-keeping because of his disability. If the employee is dismissed because of poor time-keeping, he would have been less favourably treated for a reason related to his disability. A person to whom 'that reason' did not apply would be a person who did not have poor time-keeping. Such a person clearly would not have been dismissed and the disabled person would have established disability-related discrimination. The onus would then fall on the employer to show that the treatment was justified. Indeed, the critical question in many disability-related discrimination cases brought under *DDA 1995, s 3A(1)* will be one of justification. In *Abbey National plc v Fairbrother* [2007] IRLR 320, the Court of Appeal found that a person who had been subject to taunts relating to her obsessive compulsive disorder had not been treated less favourably because another person who did not have the disorder was also subject to such taunts. It is arguable (given the decision in *Clark v Novacold* above) that the appropriate comparator in this case is in fact a person who was not disabled and was not therefore subjected to any taunts at all rather than (as the Court of Appeal found) a person who was subjected to taunts for a different reason. Where a person is suffering from a legitimate impairment and an excluded condition (eg addiction to alcohol), less favourable treatment by reason only of the excluded condition might not give rise to disability-related discrimination. That was the conclusion of the EAT in *Edmund Nuttall Ltd v Butterfield* [2005] IRLR 751 in a case where the Tribunal appeared to find that the excluded condition (exhibition-ism) stemmed from a disability within the meaning of *DDA 1995*, namely mental illness. Although the facts of that case were unusual, it could be argued that the EAT there took an unduly restrictive approach to causation in a case of disability-related discrimination, where all that needs to be shown is that the less favourable treatment was for a reason *related to* disability and not by reason of or on the grounds of disability. As such, if the excluded condition arose out of or was a manifestation of a legitimate disability, then it could be said that any less favourable treatment in connection with the excluded condition was indeed treatment that was for a reason *related* to the disability.

Justification. In order to establish the defence of justification, the employer must show that the reason for the treatment in question of the disabled person is both material in the circumstances and substantial (*DDA 1995, s 3A(3)*). A minor difference in productivity between the disabled person and his colleagues (even after making reasonable adjustments) is unlikely to be regarded as a substantial reason. Treatment for a reason based on a general assumption about people with a particular condition, eg an assumption that blind people cannot use computers or that the condition poses a health and safety risk, would not be a material reason because it is not related to the particular circumstances of the person receiving the treatment (*Code of Practice, paras 6.3 to 6.7*). In *H J Heinz Co Ltd v*

Kenrick [2000] IRLR 144, the EAT considered the issue of justification and, in particular, the threshold for establishing justification under what is now *DDA 1995, s 3A(3)*. It was held that, in view of the statutory language of *s 3A(3)*, which provides that treatment 'is' justified (rather than 'can be' or 'may be' justified) if the reason for it is both material and substantial to the circumstances, treatment *must* be taken to be justified in a case of disability-related discrimination if the requirements of materiality and substance are made out. The EAT also stated that, although a balancing exercise between the interests of the disabled employee and the employer (as advocated by the EAT in the earlier case of *Baynton v Saurus General Engineers Ltd* [1999] IRLR 604) may be carried out, the comparatively limited requirements of *s 3A(3)* must be borne in mind. The practical effect of this restrictive (although probably correct) approach to the meaning of *DDA 1995, s 3A(3)* is that tribunals have no discretion as to whether or not treatment is justified if the employer manages to satisfy the requirements of materiality and substance. Since 'substantial' in this context means only 'more than minor or trivial', it can be seen that in many cases justification under *DDA 1995, s 3A(3)* should not be difficult to establish. (It should be noted that as from 1 October 2004, this defence of justification is only available in cases of disability-related discrimination. Direct discrimination on the grounds of a person's disability where the relevant circumstances are the same or not materially different can never be justified. See 10.10.)

Regulations may prescribe circumstances in which treatment is to be taken as justified for these purposes (*DDA 1995, s 5(6)*). The first such Regulations were the *Disability Discrimination (Employment) Regulations 1996 (SI 1996/1456)* which provided, among other things, for circumstances where treatment of a disabled employee (or a failure to make adjustments to premises) was justified. However, these Regulations have now been revoked (*Disability Discrimination (Employment Field) (Leasehold Premises) Regulations 2004 (SI 2004/153), reg 3*).

In the case of an employer who has not complied with his duty to make adjustments (see 10.12 below), the defence of justification is only available if the treatment in question would have been justified even if the duty had been complied with (*DDA 1995, s 3A(6)*). Thus, where an employee using a wheelchair is not promoted solely because the workstation for the more senior post is inaccessible to wheelchairs, the refusal to promote would not be justified if the furniture could be rearranged to make the workstation accessible.

The following are cases where a defence of justification has been accepted:

(i)   failure to employ a diabetic as a fitter at a distribution centre was justified because the risk of injury to a diabetic employee in the low-temperature environment could not be reduced by supplying or modifying equipment (*Matty v Tesco Stores*, IDS Brief 609, p 14);

(ii)   rejection of an applicant with congenital myotonic dystrophy (a condition which reduced dexterity and caused learning difficulties) for a job as a word processor was justified because an essential requirement of the job was accuracy in written work (*Fozard v Greater Manchester Police Authority*, IDS Brief 601, p 10);

(iii)   withdrawal of a job offer from an applicant with cerebral palsy was justified because of the impossibility of providing the assistance of another person for the applicant's toilet needs (*Kenny v Hampshire Constabulary* [1999] IRLR 76); and

(iv)   refusal to offer a post as a train guard to an applicant being treated for depression was justified because of the risk of the side effects of the treatment and the employer's responsibility for the safety of passengers (*Toffel v London Underground Ltd*, IDS Brief 609, p 13).

Jones v Post Office [2001] EWCA Civ 558, [2001] ICR 805. In this case, an insulin-dependent diabetic postman was removed from driving duties as the employer believed, on the basis of medical evidence available at the time, that there was a risk to safety. It was accepted that the postman was less favourably treated for a reason related to his disability. The issue was whether such treatment was justified. In considering this issue, the employment tribunal had the benefit of the latest medical information as to the effect of requiring insulin. It concluded that the greater risk posed by the fact that insulin was required was negligible and that, therefore, the employer had not been justified in removing driving duties for that reason. The Court of Appeal held that the tribunal was wrong to engage in its own analysis of the risk to safety and that its task was simply to consider whether the employer's justification meets the statutory criteria of materiality and substance. 'Where a properly conducted risk assessment provides a reason [for the treatment of the applicant] which is on its face both material and substantial, and is not irrational, the tribunal cannot substitute its own appraisal.' A reason may be material and substantial within the meaning of *DDA 1995* even if the tribunal would have come to a different conclusion as to the extent of the risk. This decision, as the Court of Appeal acknowledged, places a constraint upon the power of tribunals to uphold challenges to justification. It emphasises that the tribunal's role is to consider whether the employer had acted within the range of reasonable responses open to an employer complying with the statutory criteria and its role is not to consider what it would regard as material and substantial. The 'range of reasonable responses' test (familiar to those dealing with unfair dismissals) now applies to the question of justification in disability-related discrimination. *Jones v Post Office* was followed recently in another decision of the Court of Appeal, *Williams v J Walter Thompson Group Ltd* [2005] EWCA Civ 133, [2005] IRLR 376. The EAT in *O'Hanlon v Revenue and Customs Comrs* [2006] IRLR 840 found that a challenge to justification was effectively doomed to fail once the employment tribunal found that the claimed reasonable adjustment was not in the circumstances an adjustment a reasonable employer would be required to make. It would appear therefore that it will only be in rare cases that the requirement of justification would not be satisfied if there were no reasonable adjustments that could be made (*O'Hanlon v Comr for HM Revenue & Customs* was upheld by the Court of Appeal ([2007] EWCA Civ 283, [2007] IRLR 404)).

In *Jones v Post Office*, Arden LJ further stated that for a reason to be 'material', there must be a 'reasonably strong connection between that reason and the circumstances of the individual case', and for it to be 'substantial', it 'must carry real weight and thus be of substance' although it need not necessarily be the best possible conclusion that could be reached in the light of all known medical science.

10.12 Duty of employer to make adjustments

An employer is under a duty to take such steps as are reasonable to prevent any provision, criterion or practice applied by him or on his behalf, or any physical feature of the employer's premises from placing the disabled person concerned at a substantial disadvantage in comparison to those persons who are not disabled (*DDA 1995, s 4A(1)*). Failure to comply with this duty in relation to a disabled person amounts to discrimination against that person (*DDA 1995, s 3A(2)*).

Unlike the position as it was prior to 1 October 2004, a failure to make reasonable adjustments cannot be justified. (Earlier authorities such as *Morse v Wiltshire County Council* [2003] EWCA Civ 119, [1998] IRLR 352 and *HM Prison Service v Beart* [2003] IRLR 238 which provided guidance as to the approach to be taken by Tribunals in determining whether there has been discrimination by way of a failure to make reasonable adjustments should not be followed in so far as they refer to the possibility of justifying such failure). The 'disabled person concerned' in this context means, in the case of a provision, criterion or practice for determining to whom employment should be offered, any disabled person who is an applicant for that employment or who has notified the employer that he may be an applicant. In all other cases, the 'disabled person concerned' is any applicant for the employment concerned or an employee of the employer concerned. (*DDA 1995, s 4A(2)*). The phrase 'provision, criterion or practice' replaces the previous terminology of 'arrangements' (although the latter is expressly included within the meaning of the former (*DDA 1995, s 18D(2)*)) and is consistent with the terminology used in the indirect discrimination provisions under *SDA 1975* and *RRA 1976*). It would appear that a 'provision, criterion or practice' could include an implied condition that a person is fit for the job they are employed to do. If it transpires that a person through disability can no longer fulfil that condition (ie the person is no longer capable of doing the job for which they were employed) then there may be a duty to consider any adjustments that could be made to remove the disadvantage caused by that implied condition. This could involve offering the employee an alternative job at a higher grade which she is capable of doing without requiring her to undergo a competitive interview. In certain circumstances (eg where there is an ongoing reorganisation) it could even involve the creation of an entirely new job (*Southampton City College v Randall* [2006] IRLR 18). Whilst this might amount to treating the disabled employee more favourably than other employees, there is nothing in *DDA 1995* which suggests that adjustments which have that effect should not be made if it would otherwise be reasonable in all the circumstances to make it. To that extent, there is little doubt that *DDA 1995* does introduce an element of positive discrimination as far as disabled employees are concerned (see *Archibald v Fife Council* [2004] UKHL 32, [2004] ICR 954, HL and see 10.14 below). However, there is no obligation on an employer to create a post specifically, which is not otherwise necessary, merely to create a job for a disabled person (*Tarbuck v Sainsbury's Supermarkets Ltd* [2006] IRLR 664). Employers should also be careful to identify what arrangement or what provision, criterion or practice is actually placing the disabled employee at a disadvantage in order that the appropriate adjustments can be considered. In *Paul v Probation Service* [2004] IRLR 190, a tribunal rejected the claim of an applicant who had been refused a job after failing an occupational health assessment. The tribunal concluded that the applicant had not been placed at a disadvantage as compared to others since all job applicants had to undergo an assessment. The EAT held that the tribunal had wrongly regarded the relevant arrangement as being the requirement to undergo an assessment. It was not the fact of the assessment that had placed the applicant at a disadvantage but the health adviser's assessment that the applicant's depressive illness rendered him unsuitable for the job. By focusing on the wrong 'arrangement' the tribunal omitted to consider whether there were any reasonable adjustments that the employer could have made (eg by obtaining specialist advice from the applicant's consultant on his fitness for the job). (See also *Smith v Churchills Stairlifts plc* [2005] EWCA Civ 1220, [2006] IRLR 41, where the Court of Appeal confirmed that the comparator for these purposes is readily identified by reference to the disadvantage caused by the relevant arrangements.)

The term 'physical features' includes anything on the premises (whether temporary or permanent) arising from a building's design or construction or from an approach to, exit from or access to such a building, fixtures, fittings, furnishings, furniture, equipment or materials, and any other physical element or quality of land comprised in the premises (*DDA 1995, s 18D(2)*). The EAT has held that whether or not any adjustments were reasonable in the circumstances will be determined by the employment tribunal objectively (see *Morse v Wiltshire County Council* [1998] IRLR 352). Thus, it may not be sufficient for an employer simply to assert that adjustments were considered and thought to be unreasonable if the tribunal finds that there were other reasonable adjustments which could have been made by the employer (see also *Ridout v TC Group* [1998] IRLR 628, discussed at 10.15 below, for further guidance as to the circumstances in which the employer's duty will arise). The employment tribunal will not be entitled, however, to rely upon a failure to make a reasonable adjustment where the particular adjustment in question was not raised as an issue and the parties have not had an opportunity to make submissions in relation to that adjustment (*Tarbuck v Sainsbury's Supermarkets Ltd* [2006] IRLR 664).

A complaint of discrimination by way of a failure to make reasonable adjustments under what is now *DDA 1995, s 3A(2)* is an entirely separate cause of action from disability-related discrimination under what is now *DDA 1995, s 3A(1)* and a *s 3A(2)* claim is not dependant on successfully establishing a claim under *DDA 1995, s 3A(1)* (see *Clark v Novacold Ltd* [1999] IRLR 318; However cf *Archibald v Fife Council* [2004] UKHL 32, [2004] ICR 954 at 961G where Lord Rodger of Earlsferry stated that in a case where the alleged failure of duty relates to the procedures leading up to dismissal, it is 'not possible' to divorce the alleged discrimination in terms of *DDA 1995, s 3A(1)* from the duty to take steps under *s 4A* and hence from the alleged discrimination in terms of *s 3A(2)*).

10.13 Employer occupying premises under a lease or sub-lease

A difficulty for employers occupying premises under a lease may be that the employer is not entitled under the terms of the lease to make the alterations to premises necessary for compliance with the *s 4A* duty. In these circumstances, *DDA 1995, s 18A* (previously *s 16*) provides that the lease shall have effect as if it provided for the occupier to be entitled to make alterations with the written consent of the lessor, and for such consent not to be withheld unreasonably. Such written consent must be obtained upon the employer having made a written application to the lessor (*DDA 1995, s 18A(2)*). The lessor may attach reasonable conditions to the giving of consent, such as obtaining any necessary planning permission, allowing the lessor a reasonable opportunity to inspect the work when completed or that the lessor be reimbursed for reasonable costs incurred in connection with the giving of his consent or (in a case where it would be reasonable for the lessor to withhold consent) a condition that the occupier must reinstate any altered part to its former state when the lease expires (*Leasehold Premises Regulations, reg 7*). Similar provisions apply where an employer occupies premises under a sub-lease or sub-tenancy (*DDA 1995, s 18A as modified by the Leasehold Premises Regulations, reg 9*).

10.14 Steps to be taken by an employer

In order to comply with his duty not to place a disabled applicant or employee at a substantial disadvantage, an employer may have to:

(*a*) make adjustments to premises (e g widening a doorway or relocating light switches);

(*b*)   allocate some of the disabled person's duties to another person;

(*c*)   transfer him to fill an existing vacancy (eg where no reasonable adjustment would enable the employee to continue doing the current job. A purposive meaning is to be given to 'transferring' in this context and it should not be construed as being limited to a transfer to a post at the same pay grade or at the same level of seniority (see *Archibald v Fife Council* [2004] UKHL 32, [2004] ICR 954). Indeed, there may even be rare circumstances in which it would be reasonable to go as far as to devise an entirely new job for the employee (see *Southampton City College v Randall* [2006] IRLR 18 but cf *Tarbuck v Sainsbury's Supermarkets Ltd* [2006] IRLR 664 where it was held that there was no obligation to create a post specifically, which is not otherwise necessary, merely to create a job for a disabled person);

(*d*)   alter his working hours (eg allowing the disabled person to work flexible hours to enable additional breaks to overcome fatigue arising from the disability);

(*e*)   assign him to a different place of work (eg moving a workstation to make it more accessible);

(*f*)   allow him to be absent during working hours for rehabilitation, assessment or treatment;

(*g*)   giving, or arranging for, training or mentoring (whether for the disabled person or any other person) (eg training in the use of particular pieces of equipment unique to the disabled person, or training appropriate for all employees, but which needs to be longer or slightly different for the disabled person because of the disability or paying for a disabled person to see a work mentor to help with loss of confidence following the onset of disability);

(*h*)   acquire or modify equipment (eg adapted keyboards or telephones. Note that there is no requirement to provide or modify equipment for personal purposes unconnected with work, such as providing a wheelchair if a person needs one in any event but does not have one);

(*i*)   modify instructions or reference manuals (eg producing instructions in Braille or on audio tape);

(*j*)   modify procedures for testing or assessment (eg allowing a person with restricted manual dexterity to give oral, rather than written, responses to a test);

(*k*)   provide a reader or interpreter; or

(*l*)   provide supervision (eg for someone whose disability leads to uncertainty or lack of confidence).

(*DDA 1995, s 18B(2); Code of Practice, para 5.18.*)

In determining whether it is reasonable for an employer to have to take steps such as those above, regard shall be had, in particular, to the extent to which taking the step would prevent the effect in relation to which the duty is imposed, the extent to which it would be practicable for the employer to take such steps, the costs incurred, the disruption to the employer's activities, the employer's financial and other resources, the availability to the employer of financial and other assistance and the nature of the employer's activities and the size of its undertaking (*DDA 1995, s 18B*). Where the step would be taken in relation to a private household, the extent to which taking the step would disrupt the household or disturb any person living there shall be taken into account. The *Code of Practice* suggests that it would be reasonable for an employer to spend at least as much on an adjustment to enable the retention of a disabled person, including any retraining, as might be spent on recruiting and training a replacement. It is also suggested that it would generally be reasonable for a large employer with many staff to make an adjustment with significant cost than for an employer with fewer resources, and to make significant efforts to re-allocate duties, identify a suitable alternative post or provide supervision from existing staff. A disabled person is not required to contribute to the cost of a reasonable adjustment (*Code of Practice, paras 5.24 to 5.41*). The *Code of Practice* also mentions other factors that could be taken into account which are not expressly referred to in *DDA 1995*. These include the effect on other employees, the fact that there are several employees with mobility problems – this may render it reasonable to make significant structural changes to the workplace – and the extent to which the disabled person is willing to co-operate. If a reasonable adjustment is made and the disabled person does not co-operate (e g the disabled person refuses to work at a more accessible workstation), and there is no other adjustment that can reasonably be made, the employer will not have to do any more (*Code of Practice, para 5.42*). It should be emphasised that the *Act* does not impose any general duty to make adjustments, the breach of which might be actionable. The duties are only imposed for the purposes of determining whether an employer has discriminated against a disabled person (*DDA 1995, s 18B(6)*).

The duty to make adjustments also applies in relation to any provision, criterion or practice applied by or on behalf of the trustees or managers of an occupational pension scheme which places a relevant disabled person at a substantial disadvantage in comparison with persons who are not disabled. (*Disability Discrimination Act 1995 (Pensions) Regulations 2003 (SI 2003/2770)* ('*Pensions Regulations*'); *DDA 1995, s 4H(1)* as amended by the *Pensions Regulations*). As for discrimination against disabled persons in respect of the membership of and treatment under an occupational pension scheme, see 10.20 below.

Archibald v Fife Council [2004] UKHL 32, [2004] ICR 954, HL(Sc) is the first decision under *DDA 1995* to reach the House of Lords. The applicant was employed by the council as a road sweeper. She became disabled following an operation and was no longer able to carry out her duties as a road sweeper. She was, however, assessed as capable of undertaking sedentary work. Such work was at a higher grade than the manual work that she had been doing and the council's procedures required appointments to higher grades to be made on competitive interview. The applicant could not secure such work despite making over 100 applications. Eventually, she was dismissed for incapacity. In her claim to the tribunal, the applicant alleged that she had been discriminated against contrary to what is now *s 4A(2)* in that the council failed to make an adjustment that would have enabled her to obtain a sedentary post without having to undergo a competitive interview. The tribunal and the EAT dismissed her claim on the basis that there was nothing in the arrangements for determining who should be offered the sedentary job which placed her at a substantial disadvantage since the arrangements applied equally to everyone. The Court of Session dismissed the appeal on the basis of a very narrow construction of the duty to consider transferring an employee to fill a vacancy: It held that the duty to make reasonable adjustments did not arise at all if there was nothing the employer could do to make it possible for the applicant to carry out the tasks of her job as a road sweeper. This was notwithstanding the express references in the *Code of Practice* to transferring employees to fill other posts. The reasoning of the tribunal was rejected by the House of Lords. The House of Lords acknowledged that *DDA 1995* entails 'a measure of positive discrimination'. It went on to find that it was an 'implied condition' or arrangement of the council that the applicant was capable of fulfilling the tasks of her job description. Upon becoming incapable of fulfilling that condition (and thereby becoming liable to be dismissed), the applicant was placed at a substantial disadvantage compared to other non-disabled employees (since they were not liable to be dismissed). Accordingly, it was held that the duty to make adjustments was triggered and it remained to be determined whether it would have been reasonable in all the circumstances to transfer the applicant to an existing vacancy at a slightly higher grade without competitive interview. The case was remitted to the tribunal to determine that issue. This is clearly an important decision in the annals of *DDA 1995* even though it deals with the pre-October 2004 provisions. It establishes that the duty to make adjustments can extend to the point of treating a person *more* favourably than others if that would be reasonable in all the circumstances. It also re-emphasises the importance of referring to the *Code of Practice* in determining the scope of *DDA 1995*.

The following have all been held by employment tribunals to be reasonable adjustments:

(i)   provision of subtitled training videos for Channel 5 Television re-tuners (*Williams v Channel 5 Engineering Services Ltd*, IDS Brief 609, p 13);

(ii) discounting of disability-related absences in assessing absence record (*Cox v Post Office*, IDS Brief 609, p 14 but see *O'Hanlon v Revenue and Customs Comrs* [2007] IRLR 404 and 10.23 below); and

(iii) provision of a special 'Grahl' chair costing £1,000 for an employee with a club foot (*Tarling v Wisdom Toothbrushes Ltd*, 24 June 1997, COIT 1500148/97).

The employer's duty to make reasonable adjustments is confined to those which are 'job related' (see *Kenny v Hampshire Constabulary* [1999] IRLR 76). A disabled person may be in a position to obtain employment if he was provided with transport to get to the place of employment. However, the employer's duty under *DDA 1995, s 6* in relation to that person, whilst extending to the making of adjustments to enable access to the employer's premises, would not extend to the provision of transport to get there from home. In *Kenny*, the job applicant had cerebral palsy and required assistance in carrying out his toilet functions. The EAT held that whilst there may be a duty to consider physical adjustments to enable access to the toilets, the employer was not under a duty to provide a personal carer to assist the applicant with his toilet needs. Such provision would address the applicant's personal needs but would not be job-related.

10.15 **Employer's knowledge of disability**

An important question for parties contemplating bringing or defending proceedings under the *DDA 1995* is the extent to which an employer must know of an employee's disability before liability can arise, ie can an employer be liable for discriminating against a disabled person if he has no knowledge of the disability? The question arises in the context of disability-related and direct discrimination under *DDA 1995, s 3A(1),(5)* and in the context of the duty to make reasonable adjustments under *DDA 1995, s 4A*.

Knowledge and disability-related discrimination under DDA 1995, s 3A(1). This has been considered in several cases. In the first of these, *O'Neill v Symm Co Ltd* [1998] IRLR 233, it was held by the EAT that knowledge was a relevant factor in determining whether there had been discrimination under (what is now) *DDA 1995, s 3A(1)*. However, that decision has now effectively been overruled and can no longer be regarded as correct. In *H J Heinz Co Ltd v Kenrick* [2000] IRLR 144, the applicant was suffering from chronic fatigue syndrome (CFS) and was dismissed by his employer after being absent for almost a year. By the time of his dismissal, CFS had not been diagnosed and the employer resisted the claim of disability discrimination on the grounds that at the time of dismissal they were not aware that the employee had a disability. The employment tribunal noted that the applicant had made the employer's medical adviser aware of his symptoms, and concluded that the employer had sufficient knowledge of the manifestation of the applicant's disability at the time of dismissal for it to be held that they had treated him less favourably for a reason related to his disability within the meaning of *DDA 1995, s 3A(1)(a)*. The EAT (having regard to the decision in *Clark v Novacold Ltd* [1999] IRLR 318) upheld the tribunal's decision on discrimination. It was held that (what is now) *s 3A(1)(a)* did not require the employer to have knowledge of the disability as such. The test for determining whether treatment was related to disability was an objective one and did not depend on the subjective viewpoint of the employer. If this were not the case, then there would be difficulties in establishing there had been discrimination in cases involving employers who failed to recognise or acknowledge the obvious. The view that knowledge of disability was irrelevant at the stage of determining whether there had been less favourable treatment (ie at the *DDA 1995, s 3A(1)(a)* stage) was confirmed in the recent decision of the EAT in *Hammersmith and Fulham London Borough Council v Farnsworth* [2000] IRLR 691. (See also *Code of Practice, para 4.31*). Although knowledge of disability is not a requirement in a claim of disability-related discrimination, it would appear from the Court of Appeal's decision in *Taylor v OCS Group Ltd* [2006] IRLR 613 that the employer's state of knowledge is not entirely irrelevant in determining whether there has been such discrimination. In *Taylor*, a profoundly deaf employee had been dismissed for misconduct after illicitly copying personal emails. The EAT (disagreeing with the employment tribunal on this point) found that the dismissal was also related to his disability because the employee had been unable, on account of his deafness, to give a proper explanation for his actions during the disciplinary hearing. The Court of Appeal rejected the EAT's reasoning and stated that, 'Discrimination requires that the employer should have a certain state of mind. In the context of the DDA, an employer cannot discriminate against an employee unless he treats the disabled employee differently for a reason (present in ... the employer's mind) which is related to the employee's disability ...'. The Court of Appeal went on to hold that as the reason for dismissal was misconduct (which was unrelated to the employee's disability) the employer did not have a disability-related reason in mind when it dismissed the employee and had therefore not discriminated against him.

As for the relevance of knowledge at the justification stage, Charles J in the *Farnsworth* case held that 'knowledge or lack of knowledge of the disability of the relevant person is not a necessary ingredient for the purposes of [*ss 3A(1)(b)* and (3) *DDA*]...'. The Court of Appeal in *Jones v Post Office* (see above) held that the task of the tribunal is simply to test the employer's reason for the less favourable treatment against the statutory criteria of materiality and substance. Knowledge of the disability itself does not come into the question and it may be possible for the treatment to be justified notwithstanding the fact that at the time of meting out the treatment, the employer was ignorant of the disability. The earlier decision of the Scottish EAT in *Quinn v Schwarzkopf Ltd* [2001] IRLR 67, which stated that knowledge of the disability was necessary before a defence of justification could be accepted, has now been overruled ([2002] IRLR 602). The position now is clear that a justification defence in respect of disability-related discrimination may be put forward irrespective of the employer's actual knowledge of the disability at the relevant time.

The effect of the decisions in *Heinz* and *Farnsworth* is that employers cannot rely on the lack of formal confirmation by an employee that he is disabled in order to avoid a finding that they have discriminated. Indeed, employers must be aware of the potential discriminatory impact of their decisions whenever less favourable treatment is meted out. As suggested by the EAT in *Heinz*, an employer is required to pause before dismissing an employee or treating an employee in a less favourable way in order to consider whether the reason for the dismissal or treatment might relate to disability and, if it might, to reflect on the *DDA 1995* and the *Code of Practice* before dismissing or treating the employee in that way.

Knowledge and direct discrimination under DDA 1995, s 3A(5). Direct discrimination occurs where an act of less favourable treatment is 'on the ground of disability'. This suggests that the discriminator has based his decision to discriminate (consciously or otherwise) on the fact of the disabled person's disability. However, that raises the question whether it is necessary for the employer to know of the disability before direct discrimination can be made out. The answer is probably 'no'. Direct discrimination under *s 3A(5)* can only occur where the relevant circumstances of the disabled person are the same as or not materially different from a person not having that particular disability. In these circumstances, if it is established that the disabled person was treated less favourably, then an application of the burden of proof provisions (*DDA 1995, s 17A(1C)*) will result in the presumption of discrimination, which the employer will then have to disprove. The employer who is unable to put forward a cogent reason for the treatment will be liable, irrespective of the state of his knowledge. If there is a cogent reason for the treatment which is not discriminatory, then arguably the relevant circumstances were not the same or were materially different in the first place. The *Code of Practice* expressly acknowledges that direct discrimination can occur even where the employer is not aware of the disability of the disabled person concerned. An internal recruitment advertisement which places a blanket ban on all people with a history of mental illness might preclude an employee with a history of schizophrenia (of which the employer was unaware) from applying even though his ability to do the advertised job is the same as or not materially different from other non-disabled employees. This would amount to unlawful direct discrimination that could not be justified (*Code of Practice, para 4.11*).

Knowledge and the duty to make reasonable adjustments. The *Act* does not impose any duty on an employer in relation to a disabled person if the employer does not know and could not reasonably be expected to know that that person has a disability placing him at a substantial disadvantage (*DDA 1995, s 4A(3)(b)*). Clearly, if an employer's agent or employee knows in that capacity of an employee's disability, then the employer cannot claim that he does not know of that person's disability. This is so even if the disabled employee specifically requests that information about his disability be kept confidential. The *Code of Practice* envisages that in such circumstances of confidentiality, it may be necessary for the agent with knowledge of the disability to arrange for reasonable adjustments to be made by, for example, the disabled person's line manager without informing the line manager why such adjustments are being made (*Code of Practice, para 5.15*).

The extent to which tribunals should take into account the actual or assumed knowledge of an employer in the context of the duty to make reasonable adjustments has been considered by the EAT in *Ridout v TC Group* [1998] IRLR 628. In that case, a job applicant had disclosed in her application that she was disabled and had photosensitive epilepsy controlled by a daily dose of Epilim. She was shortlisted for an interview. Upon entering the room in which the interview was to be held, the applicant, who was wearing sunglasses around her neck, commented that she might be disadvantaged by the fluorescent lighting in the room. However, the applicant did not use the sunglasses during her interview nor did she say that she felt in any way disadvantaged. The applicant complained to the tribunal that the employer had failed in its duty to make reasonable adjustments in respect of the physical arrangements for the interview. The tribunal dismissed the complaint. The EAT held that the tribunal was correct to find that the employer was not in breach of its duty to make reasonable adjustments notwithstanding that it knew of the applicant's condition. The EAT added that the provisions of *DDA 1995, s 6* require the tribunal to measure the extent of the duty, if any, against the actual or assumed knowledge of the employer both as to the disability and its likelihood of causing the individual a substantial disadvantage in comparison with persons who are not disabled. In this case, no reasonable employer could be expected to know, without being told in terms by the applicant, that the arrangements which were made for her interview might disadvantage her. Thus, it would appear that the extent of the duty to make reasonable adjustments will depend partly on the amount of information volunteered by the disabled person as to any disadvantages being suffered. However, this does not mean that the employer can simply wait to be told of such disadvantages before a duty will arise. On the facts in *Ridout*, it may have been reasonable for the employer itself not to make further inquiries as to any disadvantage. Whether or not this will be so in other cases will be a question of fact for the tribunal. In *Mid-Staffordshire General Hospitals NHS Trust v Cambridge* [2003] IRLR 566, the EAT went so far as to hold that 'A proper assessment of what is required to eliminate the disabled person's disadvantage is ... a necessary part of the duty imposed by *s 6(1)* since that duty cannot be complied with unless the employer makes a proper assessment of what needs to be done.' However, this decision (which was followed by the EAT in *Southampton City College v Randall* [2006] IRLR 18) was held by the EAT in *Tarbuck v Sainsbury's Supermarkets Ltd* [2006] IRLR 664 to have been incorrectly decided. Elias J concluded in *Tarbuck* that '... there is no separate and distinct duty' to consult employees and that the single question under section 3A(1) was whether the employer had complied with his obligations there set out (see *Hay v Surrey County Council* [2007] EWCA Civ 93, [2007] All ER (D) 199 (Feb) in which the EAT's reasoning in *Tarbuck* was approved and it was held that there is, similarly, no separate duty to undertake a risk assessment, although an employer who had failed to conduct such an assessment could not use ignorance by reason of that failure to excuse non compliance). The effect of these decisions is that consultation and/or risk assessments clearly remain prudent practice in any case where an employer was made aware of a disability, although the failure to take such steps would not of itself amount to a breach of the duty (see *Code of Practice, paras 5.12 and 7.29*). Indeed, the Court of Appeal has stated that a failure to conduct adequate investigations or assessments into the adjustments that can be made can amount to unjustified treatment of an employee. (See *Williams v J Walter Thompson Group Ltd* [2005] EWCA Civ 133, [2005] IRLR 376, which was not referred to in Hay *v Surrey County Council*). The EAT has stated that there was almost bound to be a breach of the implied term of trust and confidence where the employer had over a period of time seriously breached its obligation to make reasonable adjustments (*Greenhof v Barnsley Metropolitan Borough Council* [2006] IRLR 98).

It is to be noted that ignorance of the disability does not mean that the duty to make reasonable adjustments can never be complied with. In *British Gas Services Ltd v McCaull* [2001] IRLR 60, the EAT held that there is no automatic breach of the duty to make reasonable adjustments simply because the employer was unaware of that duty. If an employer does not know that there is a disability and is therefore unaware of its duty to make reasonable adjustments, it is not precluded from arguing that, notwithstanding its ignorance, the duty has been complied with or that there were no reasonable steps that could have been taken. The test under *DDA 1995, s 4A* is an objective one and requires the tribunal to consider whether the employer took such steps as it is reasonable for him to have taken. It is the steps taken or not taken that are to be tested and not the employer's state of mind in taking or not taking such steps.

Company reports. Companies which employ, on average, more than 250 employees in the financial year are obliged to include in their annual report a policy statement on the employment of disabled persons (*Companies Act 1985, s 234, Sch 7 para 9* as amended by *DDA 1995, Sch 6 para 4*).

10.16 Discrimination by victimisation

An employer ('A') discriminates against another person ('B') if he treats B less favourably than he treats or would treat other persons, whose circumstances are the same as B's (and for this purpose, if B is a disabled person, his disability shall be disregarded: *DDA 1995, s 55(3)*) and does so by reason that B has:

(*a*) brought proceedings against A or any other person under the *Act*;

(*b*) given evidence or information in connection with such proceedings brought by any person;

(*c*) otherwise done anything under or by reference to the *Act* in relation to A or any other person; or

(*d*) alleged that A or any other person has contravened the *Act*,

or by reason that A believes or suspects that B has done or intends to do any of these things (*DDA 1995, s 55(1)(2)* and (*6*) as amended by the *Amendment Regulations, reg 21*; cf DISCRIMINATION AND EQUAL OPPORTUNITIES – I (12)). This provision is very similar to the victimisation provisions in *SDA 1975* and *RRA 1976*, and readers should refer to relevant decisions under those Acts (see *Code of Practice, para 4.33*).

A person is not protected under (*d*) above where it is established that the allegation made by him was false and not made in good faith (*DDA 1995, s 55(4)*).

10.17 DISCRIMINATION IN EMPLOYMENT

The *Act* prohibits discrimination by an employer against a disabled person at every stage of employment 'Employment' is defined in *DDA 1995, s 68(1)* as employment under a contract of service or of apprenticeship or a contract personally to do any work, and thus carries a broader meaning than it does in some other employment protection legislation. However, the definition is subject to any prescribed provision. Hence, this broader definition, which appears in *RRA 1976* and *SDA 1975* without the proviso, may be restricted by regulations. Until the issue of such regulations, however, decisions under the corresponding provisions of *RRA 1976* and *SDA 1975* as to what constitutes employment for the purposes of the Act would appear to be relevant (cf DISCRIMINATION AND EQUAL OPPORTUNITIES – I (12)). Prior to 1 October 2004, case law had established that it is also unlawful to discriminate against former employees if there is a substantive connection between the discriminatory conduct and the employment relationship. (*Relaxion Group plc v Rhys-Harper, D'Souza v Lambeth London Borough Council, Jones v 3M Healthcare Ltd* [2003] UKHL 33, [2003] ICR 867, [2003] IRLR 484, HL). The Act now expressly reflects this development in the law with the insertion of *s 16A* which deals with relationships which have come to an end. *DDA 1995, s 16A* provides that where there has been a relevant relationship between a disabled person and the 'relevant person' and that relationship has come to an end, it is unlawful for the 'relevant person' to discriminate against the disabled person by subjecting him to a detriment or to harassment where the discrimination or harassment arises out of and is closely connected to the relevant relationship. The 'relevant person' will usually mean the former employer although the relevant person can be any person who was in a position to discriminate against the disabled person during the course of the relationship. The obvious instance of such post-relationship discrimination is where the former employer provides an unfair reference to a disabled employee that had brought proceedings against the former employer (*Code of Practice, para 8.29*). It is to be noted that the requirement that the discrimination or harassment has to arise out of and be closely connected to the relevant relationship means that not all post-relationship discrimination or harassment will be unlawful. For instance, disability-related abuse from an employer directed towards a former employee attending a public football match probably would not be unlawful under *DDA*. Although such abuse probably arises out of the former relationship, the circumstances are such that the abuse is not closely connected with the former employment. The post-relationship duty not to discriminate extends to the duty to make reasonable adjustments if any provision, criterion or practice or physical features of premises place the disabled former employee at a substantial disadvantage compared to others in the same position who are not disabled (*Code of Practice, para 8.30*).

10.18 **Advertisements suggesting discrimination**

As from 5 December 2005 it is unlawful for a person to publish or be caused to be published an advertisement which invites applications for a relevant appointment or benefit and which indicates, or might reasonably be understood to indicate, that an application will or may be determined to any extent by reference to:

(i)   the applicant not having any disability or any particular disability, or

(ii)   the applicant not having had any disability, or any particular disability, or

(iii) any reluctance of the person determining the application to comply with a duty to make adjustments (or in relation to employment services) with the duty imposed by *DDA 1995, s 21* as modified by *DDA 1995, s 21A(6)* (*DDA 1995, s 16B(1)* as amended by DDA 2005, s 10).

'Advertisement' in this context includes every form of advertisement or notice, whether to the public or not. A discriminatory internal vacancy notice would therefore be unlawful (*DDA 1995, s 16B(4)*). This marks a change from the previous (pre-October 2004) position where the placing of a discriminatory advertisement merely raised a presumption against the employer. Now, the placing of the advertisement itself is unlawful. Another change is that the power to enforce these provisions now lies exclusively with the DRC (*DDA 1995, ss 16B, 17B(1)*).

10.19 **Engagement**

It is unlawful for an employer to discriminate against a disabled person:

(*a*)   in the arrangements he makes for the purpose of determining who should be offered that employment; or

(*b*)   in the terms on which employment is offered; or

(*c*)   by refusing or deliberately omitting to offer employment.

(*DDA 1995, s 4(1)*; cf DISCRIMINATION AND EQUAL OPPORTUNITIES – I (12))

Note that the *Code of Practice* envisages that seemingly innocuous stipulations in job specifications such as a requirement that applicants be 'team players' or 'active and energetic' could amount to discrimination where the requirement is marginal or unrelated to the main duties of the job (*Code of Practice, para 7.7*). Whilst it probably would not be discriminatory in itself for an employer to include a question on an application form asking whether someone is disabled, the *Code of Practice* discourages the asking of such a broad question as 'Do you have a disability?' on the basis that the answer is unlikely to yield any useful information. The recommended approach is to ask such questions only if they are or may be relevant to a person's ability to do the job, after a reasonable adjustment if necessary. If there are medical requirements that must be met by the job holder, the *Code of Practice* suggests that applicants should not be required to complete a medical questionnaire until after a conditional offer of employment is made. However, it is considered good practice to ask those attending interviews if there are any reasonable adjustments that might enable the interviewee to participate fully in the process (*Code of Practice, paras 7.27 to 7.29*). It may be a reasonable adjustment to provide information about a job in a more accessible format to an applicant whom the employer knows to be disabled as it would to accept an application from a disabled person in a non-standard form (eg on tape or by telephone) (*Code of Practice, paras 7.16, 7.17*).

10.20 **Training and other benefits**

An employer may not discriminate against a disabled employee in the terms of employment offered to him, or in the opportunities for promotion, training or the receipt of any other benefit afforded to him, or by refusing to afford him or deliberately not affording him, any such opportunity (*DDA 1995, s 4(2)*) (cf DIS-CRIMINATION AND EQUAL OPPORTUNITIES – I (12)).

Membership of occupational pension schemes. DDA 1995, s 4G provides that every occupational pension scheme shall be taken to include a 'non-discrimination' rule containing the requirements that the trustees or managers of the scheme refrain from discriminating against a relevant disabled person in carrying out any of their functions in relation to the scheme (including their functions in relation to the admission to the scheme and the treatment of members of the scheme) and that they do not subject a relevant disabled person to harassment in relation to the scheme. It is unlawful for the trustees or managers of the scheme to discriminate against a disabled person contrary to the requirements of the non-discrimination rule. This new provision which came into force on 1 October 2004 strengthens the position of disabled persons vis-à-vis their rights in relation to such schemes since it applies to *any* of the functions of the trustees or managers. However, this non-discrimination rule does not apply in relation to rights accrued, or benefits payable, in respect of periods of service before 1 October 2004. Readers should refer to the earlier incarnation of the non-discrimination rule for rights accruing before that date (*DDA 1995, s 4G*). Previously, regulations prescribed that less favourable treatment of a disabled person being considered for admission to a scheme is taken to be justified where, by reason of the disabled person's disability, the cost of providing any benefit under a scheme is likely to be substantially greater than it would be for a comparable person without that disability (*Disability Regulations, reg 4*). However, this has now been revoked (*Leasehold Premises Regulations, reg 3*). In addition, there is now a duty on the trustees and managers of such schemes to make reasonable adjustments where any provision, criterion or practice applied in respect of a scheme or any physical features of premises occupied by the trustees or managers places a disabled person at a substantial disadvantage in comparison to non-disabled persons. One such adjustment is the alteration of the scheme's rules (*DDA 1995, s 4H*). Claims in relation to such schemes can be brought in the tribunal although the tribunal does not have the power to award compensation in relation to arrears of benefits or otherwise (although a sum can be awarded for injury to feelings) except where the trustees or managers fail to comply with any recommendations made by the tribunal (*DDA 1995, ss 4J(4), 17A(5)*).

Insurance services. It used to be the position that, where an insurer entered into an arrangement with an employer under which employees receive benefits in respect of the termination of service, retirement, old age, death, accident, injury, sickness, invalidity or any other prescribed matter, it was unlawful for the insurer to discriminate against a disabled employee in refusing to provide or deliberately not providing the disabled employee with such benefits or in the terms on which such benefits were provided to the disabled employee (*DDA 1995, s 18*). However, that provision is repealed as of 5 December 2005 (*DDA 2005, s 11(1)*). A disabled person is now not entitled to bring a claim that another person has discriminated against him in relation to the provision under a 'group insurance arrangement' (as defined by *DDA s 68(1)* as amended) of facilities by way of insurance or that (by virtue of *DDA 1995, s 57* or *58*) he is to be treated as having been so discriminated against (*DDA 2005, s 11(2)*).

10.21 Dismissal, harassment or subjection to any other detriment

It is unlawful for an employer to discriminate against a disabled employee by dismissing him, or by subjecting him to any other detriment (*DDA 1995, s 4(2)(d)*; cf DISCRIMINATION AND EQUAL OPPORTUNITIES – I (12)). *DDA 1995, s 4(5)* expressly provides that dismissal includes the termination of a person's employment by the giving of notice in circumstances such that he is entitled to terminate it without notice by reason of the employer's conduct (ie constructive dismissal). However, notwithstanding the absence of any express reference to constructive dismissal under the previous (pre-October 2004) provisions, case law had established (after some debate) that this was included within the meaning of dismissal under *s 4(2)(d)* (see *Catherall v Michelin Tyres plc* [2003] ICR 28, [2003] IRLR 61). A continuing failure to make reasonable adjustments can amount to a repudiatory breach of contract entitling the employee to resign and claim constructive dismissal (see *Miekle v Nottinghamshire County Council* [2004] EWCA Civ 859, [2004] IRLR 703).

Harassment. As with claims of harassment under other discrimination legislation, the absence of an express statutory prohibition prior to 1 October 2004 did not preclude claims of harassment being brought. These were generally brought on the basis that harassment falls within 'any other detriment' in the course of employment. As of 1 October 2004, however, *DDA 1995* contains an express prohibition on harassment by an employer of a disabled person whom he employs or who has applied to him for employment. A person will be taken to have subjected a disabled person to harassment where, for a reason which relates to the disabled person's disability, he engages in unwanted conduct which has the purpose or effect of:

(*a*)   violating the disabled person's dignity; or

(*b*)   creating an intimidating, hostile, degrading, humiliating or offensive environment for him.

(*DDA 1995, s 3B.*) Conduct is to be regarded as having such effect only if, having regard to all the circumstances, including in particular the perception of the disabled person, it should reasonably be considered as having that effect. Although the test is objective, the subjective experience of the victim is relevant (see *Code of Practice, para 4.39*).

10.22 Unfair dismissal and disability discrimination

Although a dismissal which is unlawful under *DDA 1995* will not necessarily be unfair under *ERA 1996*, it is thought unlikely that an employment tribunal would find that an employer who had discriminated against a disabled employee in dismissing him was not also acting unfairly in so doing. (See *British Sugar plc v Kirker* [1998] IRLR 624 in which it was conceded, properly so according to the EAT, that if the tribunal was entitled to find that unlawful disability discrimination caused the dismissal, then it would be highly exceptional for that dismissal not to be unfair.) However, it does not follow that if the dismissal of a disabled employee is unfair within the meaning of *ERA 1996*, then that dismissal must also be discriminatory. Much will depend on the reason for dismissal and whether that reason was one which related to the disabled person's disability. This issue is most likely to arise in the case of incompetence and ill-health dismissals.

10.23   *Incompetence and ill-health dismissals.* Where an employer dismissed an employee for the potentially fair reason of incapacity and that incapacity is related to disability, there is a risk that the dismissal will be discriminatory unless the discrimination can be justified. If an employee is said to be incompetent and that incompetence arises as a result of, for example, learning difficulties or impaired mobility, then the employer, as well as having to ensure that the normal procedural steps are followed to ensure that the dismissal is fair, may also be under a duty to make reasonable adjustments to enable the employee to become competent. Such adjustments might include the provision of additional training, or modified equipment or even the removal or reallocation of certain duties. If such adjustments would be reasonable ones for the employer to make but are not made, then the dismissal will be discriminatory unless the dismissal would have been justified even after making the adjustments.

Similarly, where an employer wishes to dismiss an employee for illness-related absences and the illness is such that it amounts to a disability within the meaning of *DDA 1995*, the employer will have to consider whether any adjustments could be made. Adjustments in this context could include the reduction of working hours or the reallocation of duties to enable the employee to resume work, allowing the employee to take more time off than other employees or even transferring him to another vacancy at a different grade. If it is reasonable to

167

make such adjustments, then the failure to make them would render the dismissal unlawful unless the dismissal could be justified even if the adjustments had been made.

Disability-related absences. There is no obligation on an employer to disregard disability-related absences in operating a sickness absence procedure although in some circumstances it might be reasonable to do so (*Royal Liverpool Children's NHS Trust v Dunsby* [2006] IRLR 351). In *O'Hanlon v Revenue and Customs Comrs* [2006] IRLR 840 (upheld by the Court of Appeal, [2007] IRLR 404), the EAT found that the employment tribunal had not erred in finding that it was not a reasonable adjustment to expect the employers to pay the claimant's salary in full when she was absent from work due to disability-related absence, in circumstances in which she had exhausted her entitlement to sick pay under the employer's sick pay rules.

Clearly, in cases of serious illness resulting in long-term absence, the employer may be justified in dismissing the employee even if the illness relates to a disability within the meaning of *DDA 1995*. Care should be taken, however, to ensure that proper information is available, that consideration is given to alternative employment which is more suited to the employee's health and that there is consultation before such a dismissal. Otherwise the dismissal will probably be unfair (see UNFAIR DISMISSAL – II (52)). It is to be noted, however, that there would appear to be no duty under *s 4A, DDA 1995* (the duty to make reasonable adjustments) to offer part-time employment as an alternative to dismissal in circumstances where the applicant had not asked to work part-time and where he was not fit for any form of work at the relevant time (*Callagan v Glasgow City Council* [2001] IRLR 724; cf *Archibald v Fife Council* [2004] UKHL 32, [2004] ICR 954 and *Southampton City College v Randall* [2006] IRLR 18).

10.24 EXCEPTIONS AND SPECIAL CASES

(a) Employment at an establishment in Great Britain

Discrimination in employment is only unlawful under the *Act* in respect of employment at an establishment in Great Britain (*DDA 1995, s 4(6)*). Where an employee does his work wholly or mainly outside Great Britain, his employment will be treated as being work at an establishment in Great Britain if the employer has a place of business at an establishment in Great Britain, the work is for the purposes of the business carried on at the establishment and the employee is ordinarily resident in Great Britain (*DDA 1995, s 68(2), (2A)*).

The former exclusion under *DDA 1995* in respect of employment on board a ship, aircraft or hovercraft was repealed on 1 October 2004 (*Amendment Regulations, reg 27*). Such employment may now be covered by *DDA 1995* when certain conditions (eg that the ship, aircraft or hovercraft is registered in the United Kingdom) are satisfied. Regulations may prescribe other kinds of employment which are to be regarded as not being employment at an establishment in Great Britain (*DDA 1995, s 68(4)*).

Employment in a private household would be employment at an establishment in Great Britain (cf *RRA 1976, s 4(3)*; see DISCRIMINATION AND EQUAL OPPORTUNITIES – I (12)).

(b) Facilities provided to public

Where an employer is concerned with the provision (whether or not for payment) of benefits (including facilities and services) of any description to the public or to a section of the public which includes the employee in question, the sections of the *Act* relating to discrimination against a disabled employee in respect of the provision of benefits (*DDA 1995, s 4(2)*) do not apply unless:

(i)   that provision differs in a material respect from the provision of benefits by the employer to his employees; or

(ii)   the provision of benefits to the employee in question is regulated by his contract of employment; or

(iii)   the benefits relate to training.

(DDA 1995, s 4(3), (4))

(*c*)   **Acts done under statutory authority**

The *Act* does not render unlawful any act done pursuant to any enactment or statutory instrument or in order to comply with a ministerial condition or requirement imposed pursuant to statute. In the employment context the Act does not render unlawful any act done for the purpose of safeguarding national security if the doing of that act was justified by that purpose (*DDA 1995, s 59(1), (2A), (3)*).

(*d*)   **Exemption for small businesses**

As of 1 October 2004, there is no exemption for small employers from the provisions of *DDA 1995* (*Amendment Regulations*), *reg 6*).

(*e*)   **Charities**

Any act done by a charity pursuant to any charitable purpose connected with categories of persons determined by reference to any physical or mental capacity will not be unlawful under the employment provisions of the *Act* (*DDA 1995, s 18C*)).

(*f*)   **Local Government employees**

All employees of a local authority, parish or community council must be appointed only on merit (*Local Government and Housing Act 1989, s 7*). This applies to disabled applicants as well, although the authority will remain under a duty to make reasonable adjustments in order to remove any substantial disadvantage suffered by the disabled applicant in the recruitment process. Thus, a local authority may be obliged to provide a partially sighted applicant with special application forms, but must not take into account the applicant's partial sightedness when deciding whether or not to appoint him to the job (see *Archibald v Fife Council* [2004] UKHL 32, [2004] ICR 954 and 9.14 above).

It should be noted that the duties of local authorities under *DDA 1995* have been expanded considerably with the coming into force of *DDA 2005*. It is now unlawful for local authorities to discriminate against a disabled person who is a member of the authority or to subject that person to harassment in connection with his carrying out of official business, and local authorities are (as of 4 December 2006) subject to a duty to make reasonable adjustments in relation to such members (*DDA 1995, ss 15A, 15B, 15C*; *DDA 2005, s 1*). Furthermore, public authorities are subject to a new general duty (under new *DDA 1995, s 49A*) as from 4 December 2006 in carrying out their functions to have due regard to the need to eliminate unlawful disability discrimination, the need to eliminate harassment, the need to promote equality of opportunity, the need to take steps to take account of disabled persons' disabilities (even where that involves treating disabled persons more favourably than other persons), the need to promote positive attitudes towards disabled persons and the need to encourage participation by disabled persons in public life (*DDA 2005, s 3*). A full analysis of these provisions is outside the scope of this book.

(*g*)   **School governors**

School governors are, as from 2 March 1998, deemed to be the employers of teachers at their schools for the purposes of *DDA 1995* (see *Education (Modification of Enactments Relating to Employment) Order 1998 (SI 1998/218)* and *Murphy v Slough Borough Council* [2005] EWCA Civ 122, [2005] ICR 721).

(*h*)   **Statutory office holders, police and prison officers, members of fire brigades**

Whereas these and other categories of worker were excluded from the employment provisions of *DDA 1995* prior to 1 October 2004, those provisions now apply to all employers in respect of people they employ to work wholly or partly at an establishment in Great Britain. The sole exception is in relation to the armed forces (*DDA 1995, ss 4(6), 64(7)*).

(i)   **Others**

DDA 1995 now also applies to partners in firms, barristers and advocates. (*DDA 1995, ss 6A to 7D.*)

10.25   **DISCRIMINATION AGAINST CONTRACT WORKERS**

It is unlawful for the hirer of contract labour to discriminate against a contract worker:

(*a*)   in the terms on which he allows him to do that work;

(*b*)   by not allowing him to work or continue working;

(*c*)   in the way he affords him access to any benefits or by refusing or deliberately omitting to afford him access to them; or

(*d*)   by subjecting him to any other detriment.

(*DDA 1995, s 4B(1)*.)

As of 1 October 2004, it is also unlawful to subject a contract worker to harassment in relation to his disability (*DDA 1995, s 4B(2)*). As with an employer, the hirer of contract labour is exempt from the provisions of the *Act* where he is concerned with the provision (whether or not for payment) of benefits (including facilities and services) of any description to the public or to a section of the public which includes the contract worker in question, unless the provision of such benefits differs in a material respect from the provision of benefits by the principal to contract workers (*DDA 1995, s 4B(3)*; see 10.24(B) above).

Contract workers and reasonable adjustments. The duty to make reasonable adjustments applies to the hirer of contract labour as it does to an employer. However, it might not be reasonable for a hirer of contract labour to make certain adjustments if the period for which the contract worker works for the hirer of contract labour is short (*Code of Practice, para 9.8*). The provider of contract labour may also have a duty to make a reasonable adjustment where a similar substantial disadvantage is likely to affect a contract worker as a result of the arrangements or premises of all or most of the hirers of contract labour to whom he might be supplied In such circumstances, the provider of contract labour would have to make any reasonable adjustment within his power which would overcome the disadvantage wherever it might arise. Thus, in a case of a blind word-processor operator working for an employment agency, it would be reasonable for the agency to provide her with a specially adapted computer to take with her to any temporary engagement to which she is sent because otherwise she would be suffering the same substantial disadvantage at all or most such engagements (*Code of Practice, para 9.10*).

In *Abbey Life Assurance Co Ltd v Tansell* [2000] IRLR 387, the applicant had set up his own company and was employed by it. That company supplied the applicant's services as a computer consultant to third parties under a contract with an employment agency, MHC. Abbey Life had an agreement with MHC to supply computer personnel. Abbey Life rejected the applicant's services and a complaint of disability discrimination was made to an employment tribunal. The tribunal held that the applicant was a contract worker for MHC within the meaning of what is now *s 4B, DDA 1995* and not Abbey Life. MHC appealed successfully to the EAT (see *MHC Consulting Services Ltd v Tansell* [1999] IRLR 677). The Court of Appeal dismissed Abbey Life's appeal against that decision, holding that Abbey Life was the 'principal' or the hirer of contract labour for the purposes of *DDA 1995*. The fact that Abbey Life's contract was with MHC and not the applicant's employer did not preclude the application of *s 4B, DDA 1995* as there was a chain of unbroken contracts between the applicant and the 'end user', namely, Abbey Life.

10.26 **DISCRIMINATION BY TRADE UNION ORGANISATIONS AND QUALIFYING BODIES**

Trade organisations, trade unions, organisations of workers or employers, or any other organisation whose members carry on a particular profession or trade for the purposes of which the organisation exists, may not discriminate against a disabled person:

(*a*)   in the terms on which they are prepared to admit him to membership; or

(*b*)   by refusing to accept or deliberately not accepting, his application for membership.

(*DDA 1995, s 13(1)*.)

Such organisations may not discriminate against a disabled member:

(i)   in the way they afford him access to any benefits or by refusing or deliberately omitting to afford him access to them;

(ii)   by depriving him of membership or varying the terms on which he is a member; or

(iii)   subjecting him to any other detriment.

(*DDA 1995, s 13(2)*.)

As of 1 October 2004, it is also unlawful to subject a disabled member to harassment relating to his disability (*DDA 1995, s 13(3)*). 'Discrimination' by a trade organisation bears the same meaning as discrimination by an employer, save that trade organisations are under a distinct duty to make adjustments similar to those to be made by an employer (*DDA 1995, ss 14*; see 10.12 above). Trade organisations occupying premises under a lease (or a sub-lease) will be entitled to make alterations to their premises, subject to the lessor's written consent, in the same circumstances as employers occupying leased (or sub-leased) premises (*DDA 1995, s 18A*); see 10.12 above).

Qualifying Bodies. New provisions at *DDA 1995, ss 14A* and *14B* (which came into force on 1 October 2004) render it unlawful for qualifying bodies to discriminate against disabled persons. Insofar as a qualifying body applies a competence standard to those seeking qualification and seeks to justify any disability-related discrimination against a disabled person, the application of the competence standard will only be justified if the same standard was applied to persons that did not have the particular disability and its application is a proportionate means of achieving a legitimate aim (*DDA 1995, s 14A(3)*).

Separate Code of Practice. The Disability Rights Commission has issued an entirely separate code of practice dealing with discrimination by Trade Organisations and Qualifying Bodies. Readers are advised to consult this code as well as the *Code of Practice* in addressing questions relating to the acts of such organisations and bodies.

10.27 OTHER UNLAWFUL ACTS

Any unlawful act (other than an offence under *DDA 1995, s 57(4)*; see 10.30 below) under *DDA 1995* committed by an employee in the course of his employment shall be treated as also done by his employer, whether or not it was done with the employee's knowledge or approval (*DDA 1995, s 58(1)*). The employer will have a defence if he can prove that he took such steps as were reasonably practicable to prevent the employee from doing that act, or from doing that kind of act in the course of his employment (*DDA 1995, s 58(5)*) (see VICARIOUS LIABILITY (56); and cf DISCRIMINATION AND EQUAL OPPORTUNITIES – I (12)). It is now also unlawful for a person to give instructions to another person to discriminate against a disabled person or to induce a person to do so (*DDA 1995, s 16C*). The new provisions mirror similar provisions already in existence under *SDA 1975* and *DDA 1995*. As with the EOC and CRE, respectively, in those cases, only the DRC will be able to take enforcement action in respect of breaches of *s 16C*. The question of whether *DDA 1995* should be interpreted so as to include within its scope associative discrimination (that is to say discrimination against a non-disabled person by reason of their connection to a disabled person) has been referred to the ECJ (*Attridge Law v Coleman* [2007] IRLR 88).

10.28 Liability for unlawful act of an agent

Any unlawful act (except an offence under *DDA 1995, s 57(4)*; see 10.30 below) committed by an agent with the express or implied authority of his principal (whether such authority was given before or after the act in question was done), shall be treated as also done by his principal (*DDA 1995, s 58(2)(3)*). (See 10.15 above in relation to an agent's knowledge of an employee's disability.)

10.29 Aiding unlawful acts

A person who knowingly aids another person to do an act made unlawful by the *Act* is to be treated as if he himself did the same kind of unlawful act. However, a person does not knowingly aid another to do an unlawful act if:

(*a*)   he acts in reliance upon a statement made to him by that person that the act would not be unlawful; and (*b*)   it is reasonable for him to rely on the statement.

(*DDA 1995, s 57*.)

10.30 **False or misleading statements**

A person who knowingly or recklessly makes a statement mentioned in 10.29(A) above, which is false and misleading in a material respect, is guilty of an offence and is liable on summary conviction to a fine not exceeding level 5 on the standard scale (*DDA 1995, s 57(4), (5)*; see also 1.10 INTRODUCTION).

10.31 **THE DISABILITY RIGHTS COMMISSION**

The Disability Rights Commission ('the DRC') was established by the *Disability Rights Commission Act 1999* ('the *DRCA 1999*'). As well as advising the Secretary of State on matters relevant to the *Act*, the DRC can:

(*a*)   undertake formal investigations into the activities of one or more named persons where it has reason to believe that a person has committed or is committing an unlawful act or, more generally, to find out what is happening in a particular sector of society or in relation to a particular kind of activity;

(*b*)   assist disabled people by offering information, legal advice and support in the form of arranging legal representation in taking cases forward;

(*c*)   issue non-discrimination notices;

(*d*)   obtain injunctions in respect of persons who are guilty of persistent discrimination;

(*e*)   prepare statutory codes of practice providing practical guidance on how to comply with the law; and

(*f*)   in lieu of other enforcement action, enter into a legally binding written agreement with a person who has committed or may be committing an unlawful act. Once such an agreement is entered into, the DRC will agree not to take any enforcement action in return for an undertaking that the named person will not commit any further unlawful acts of the same kind and will take any action specified in the agreement. This is a new power which is not available to the CRE or EOC. It is backed up by the courts' power to impose fines for infringements of the agreement.

The DRC also has exclusive enforcement powers in respect of provisions dealing with instructions and pressure to discriminate, discriminatory advertisements and certain other matters (*Amendment Regulations, reg 16*). The *DRCA 1999* also renders it a criminal offence (subject to a fine not exceeding level 5 on the Standard Scale) to make false or misleading statements in relation to any non-discrimination notice, agreement or order of the court (*DRCA 1999, ss 1–7 and 9; and Sch 3 paras 23 and 24*). *Section 36* of the *Equality Act 2006* gives the Secretary of State power to make an order for the dissolution of the DRC, and the DRC shall cease to exist by no later than the end of 31 March 2009. The DRC (along with the EOC and the CRE) will be replaced by the Commission for Equality and Human Rights.

The DRC has already supported a number of employment-related and other cases. Information on these cases and on the DRC's activities can be obtained from its website: www.drc-gb.org.

10.32 Disability Discrimination

The National Advisory Council on Employment of People with Disabilities ('NACEPD') is responsible for advising the Government on all issues related to the training of disabled people.

10.32 Codes of Practice

The *Code of Practice* and the Code of Practice relating to Trade Organisations and Qualifying Bodies issued by the DRC contain comprehensive practical guidance on matters relating to the application of the Act in employment. Decisions of the EAT, the Court of Appeal and the House of Lords have emphasised or demonstrated that employment tribunals should refer to relevant provisions of the *Code of Practice* in their decisions. (See *Ridout v TC Group* [1998] IRLR 628; *Goodwin v Patent Office* [1999] IRLR 4; and *Archibald v Fife Council* [2004] UKHL 32, [2004] ICR 954) The extensive nature of the most recent publications renders it essential that reference is made to them before considering any issue under *DDA 1995*.

If a provision of a code of practice appears to the tribunal to be relevant, it must take that provision into account (*DDA 1995, s 53A(8A)*). The Court of Appeal has also held that in determining whether there has been less favourable treatment, a proper self-direction in law would include taking into account those parts of the *Code of Practice* which a reasonable tribunal would regard as relevant to the determination of that question (see *Clark v Novacold Ltd* [1999] IRLR 318).

Non-compliance with the provisions of such Codes of Practice would not, of itself, render a person liable to any proceedings (*DDA 1995, s, 53A(8)*).

(Cf DISCRIMINATION AND EQUAL OPPORTUNITIES – I (12).)

10.33 ENFORCEMENT

Except as provided by the *Act*, no civil or criminal proceedings may be brought against any person in respect of unlawful acts of discrimination (*DDA 1995, Sch 3 para 2(1)*). However, this does not prevent an application for judicial review in respect of an act of a public body (*DDA 1995, Sch 3 para 2(2)*). As to the enforcement powers of the DRC, see 10.31 above.

10.34 Enforcement by an individual: application to an employment tribunal

A person may present a complaint to an employment tribunal that he has been discriminated against in relation to any of the provisions relating to employment (*DDA 1995, s 17A(1)*). For persons employed under a contract of employment where the complaint is not about dismissal, a grievance must first be submitted in writing to the employer and 28 days allowed to elapse before a complaint may be presented (*s 32, Employment Act 2002*). Complaints to the employment tribunal are to be drafted with care since tribunals should only deal with complaints of less favourable treatment as they are defined by the applicant and not as the tribunal subsequently chooses to define them (see *British Gas Services Ltd v McCaull* [2001] IRLR 60 and *Tarbuck v Sainsbury's Supermarkets Ltd* [2006] IRLR 664 where similar points were made in respect of claims alleging the failure to make reasonable adjustments). Where a reasonable adjustment requiring the consent of the employer's landlord is not made (for whatever reason), and a disabled person brings a complaint against the employer to the employment tribunal, the employer or the disabled person may ask the tribunal to make the landlord a party to proceedings (*DDA 1995, s 18A, Sch 4 para 2*). The time limit for the presentation of such a complaint is three months from the time that the act complained of was done (*DDA 1995, Sch 3 para 3(1)*). The tribunal may, however, consider a complaint which is out of time if, in all the circumstances of the case, it considers it just and equitable to do so (*DDA 1995, Sch 3 para 3(2)*). It is probable that in cases involving employees whose disabilities involve learning or communication difficulties, the tribunal will more readily extend time to consider late applications.

For the purposes of deciding the time of the act complained of:

(*a*)   where the act is attributable to a term in a contract, that act is to be treated as extending throughout the duration of the contract;

(*b*)   any act extending over a period shall be treated as done at the end of that period; and

(*c*)   a deliberate omission shall be treated as done when the person in question decided upon it.

(*DDA 1995, Sch 3 para 3(3)*.)

If the cause for complaint is an omission rather than an act, the omission will be taken to have been decided upon when a person does something inconsistent with the omitted act, or when the period within which he would reasonably have done the act has expired (*DDA 1995, Sch 3 para 3(4)*).

In *British Gas Services Ltd v McCaull* [2001] IRLR 60, the EAT confirmed that in cases of alleged discriminatory dismissals, time does not begin to run until the notice of dismissal expires and the employment ceases.

The approach which tribunals must adopt to the burden of proof is the same here as in other areas of discrimination law (*DDA 1995, s 17A(1C)* and see 14.3 DISCRIMINATION AND EQUAL OPPORTUNITIES – III). A tribunal shall, if it finds a complaint well-founded, take such of the following steps as it considers just and equitable:

(i)   make a declaration as to the rights of the complainant and the respondent in relation to the matters to which the complaint relates;

(ii)   order the respondent to pay compensation to the complainant. The amount of compensation shall be calculated on principles applicable to the calculation of damages in claims in tort. Compensation may include compensation for injury to feelings. There is no upper limit on the amount of such compensation. The award may include interest;

(iii)   recommend that the respondent take, within a specified period, action appearing to the tribunal to be reasonable in the circumstances for the purpose of obviating or reducing the adverse effect on the complainant of any matter to which the complaint relates. Failure, without reasonable justification, to comply with such a recommendation may lead to an increase in the amount of compensation to be paid, if such an increase is considered by the tribunal to be just and equitable.

(*DDA 1995, s 8(2)–(6)*.)

The EAT has provided important guidance on the management of remedies hearings in disability discrimination cases (see *Buxton v Equinox Design Ltd* [1999] IRLR 158). In particular, it was stated that the relatively brief and informal hearing on remedy appropriate in unfair dismissal cases may not be appropriate in this context.

In line with awards in sex and race discrimination cases, tribunals have not shirked from awarding large sums in disability discrimination cases where this is appropriate. Thus, a visually impaired chemist selected for redundancy was awarded £103,000 after the tribunal found that the selection was influenced by his disability (*British Sugar plc v Kirker* [1998] IRLR 624). This sum was made up largely of future loss because of the evidence of difficulties faced by visually impaired people in obtaining work. The award also included £3,500 for injury to feelings. (The DRC confirms that awards for future loss make up a substantial proportion of the compensation awarded by tribunals to disabled applicants.) In October 2005, a tribunal awarded a successful claimant £529,000 in a claim brought under *DDA*.

Restricted reporting orders in the employment tribunal. Employment tribunals are empowered to make restricted reporting orders in proceedings under the *DDA 1995* on the application of the complainant or of its own motion where evidence of a personal nature is likely to be heard by the employment tribunal hearing the complaint (*ETA 1996, s 12(1), (2)*). *SI 1993/2687, Sch 1, Rule 14(1A), (1B)*, inserted by *SI 1996/1757*). Evidence of a personal nature would be evidence of a medical, or other intimate nature, which might reasonably be assumed to be likely to cause significant embarrassment to the complainant if reported (*ETA 1996, s 12(7)*). Contravention of such a restricted reporting order would be an offence liable on summary conviction to a fine (*ETA 1996, s 12(3)*). There are similar provisions enabling the Employment Appeal Tribunal to make similar restricted reporting orders in respect of an appeal against a decision of the employment tribunal making or not making a restricted reporting order (*ETA 1996, s 32; EAT (Amendment) Rules 1996 (SI 1996/3216)*). For restricted reporting orders generally, see 20.36 EMPLOYMENT TRIBUNALS – I.

10.35   HELP AND ADVICE FOR PERSONS SUFFERING DISCRIMINATION

There are prescribed forms which the complainant can use to question employers about, or in relation to, an alleged act of discrimination (*DDA 1995, s 56(2); Disability Discrimination (Questions and Replies) Order 2004 (SI 2004/1168)*). Such forms, which correspond to the questionnaires currently available for use by complainants in race or sex discrimination cases, are admissible in evidence in proceedings before a tribunal (*DDA 1995, s 56(3)(a)*). If it appears to the tribunal that the respondent deliberately and without reasonable excuse omitted to reply to such forms within a period of eight weeks beginning with the day on which the question was served on him, or that the respondent's reply is evasive or equivocal, the tribunal may draw any inference which it considers just and equitable including an inference that the respondent discriminated unlawfully (*DDA 1995, s 56(3)(b)* as amended by *DDA 2005, s 17* with effect from 5 December 2005).

Disabled persons may also apply to the DRC for advice and support in taking their claims forward (see 10.31 above).

Specialist help and advice for both disabled people and employers is available from the Employment Service through its local Placing, Assessment and Counselling Teams ('PACTs'). PACTs can provide employers with a publication called *Sources of Information and Advice* produced by the Employment Service. This contains a list of some of the organisations which can provide help to employers on disability-related matters. PACTs themselves cannot, however, advise on an employer's specific legal obligations.

10.36 **NO CONTRACTING OUT**

Any term in a contract which, in relation to the employment provisions of the *Act*, purports to:

(*a*)   require a person to contravene any such provision;

(*b*)   exclude or limit the operation of any such provision; or

(*c*)   prevent the presentation of a complaint to an employment tribunal,

is void (*DDA 1995, s 9(1)*).

10.37 **SETTLEMENT OF A CLAIM**

Except where a complainant has received independent advice in relation to a written compromise agreement (see 20.27 EMPLOYMENT TRIBUNALS – I), an agreement to settle a complaint must be made with the assistance of a conciliation officer (*DDA 1995, s 9(2)(3)*).

11   Disclosure of Information

(See also ACAS Code of Practice No 2.)

11.1   An employer is under a duty to disclose certain information to his employees and their representatives, by virtue of the *Trade Union and Labour Relations (Consolidation) Act 1992* ('*TULRCA 1992*') (see 11.2–11.5 below), *the Transfer of Undertakings (Protection of Employment) Regulations 2006 (SI 2006/246)* replacing the previous *1981* Regulations (*SI 1981/1794*) (see 11.6 below) and the *Health and Safety at Work, etc Act 1974* (see 11.7–11.8 below). Information may also have to be disclosed for the purposes of consultation about forthcoming redundancies (see 39.2 REDUNDANCY – II). If the employer is a company it has to disclose or make available certain information by virtue of the *Companies Act 1985* (see 11.9 below). The trustees of occupational pension schemes are put under certain duties of disclosure by virtue of the *Occupational Pension Schemes (Disclosure of Information) Regulations 1986 (SI 1986/1046)* (see 11.10 below). Duties to afford access to certain records (as well as other obligations) arise from the *Data Protection Act 1988* (see 11.12 below), and the *Access to Medical Reports Act 1988* and *Access to Health Records Act 1990* (see 11.15 below).

Further, the employer is under a duty *not* to disclose certain types of information about his employees to third parties (see 11.16 below).

As to disclosures of information made by employees concerning their employer or its business, the law of breach of confidence is relevant. (See RESTRAINT OF TRADE, CONFIDENTIALITY AND EMPLOYEE INVENTIONS (41).) Specific protection is also afforded in certain circumstances to employees who disclose information to third parties relating to wrongdoing by the *Public Interest Disclosure Act 1998*. This Act is considered in outline at the end of this chapter. (See 11.17 below.)

11.2   INFORMATION FOR COLLECTIVE BARGAINING

TULRCA 1992, Part IV Chapter I imposes an obligation on an employer to disclose information necessary for collective bargaining. He can no longer be in the advantageous position of withholding information about such matters as profits and wages when negotiating. The right to enforce such an obligation is given to trade unions recognised for the particular group of employees in whose interests the information is sought (for recognition, see 50.11 TRADE UNIONS – I). The sanctions for non-disclosure are wide: if the information required for negotiation is not disclosed, the Central Arbitration Committee ('CAC') may order that the terms and conditions under negotiation become part of the individual employee's contract of employment. The CAC may order these terms to take effect as claimed or in a modified form. If the employer refuses to implement these terms the employees affected may bring an action for breach of contract in the county court or High Court.

11.3   Duty to disclose

If, at any stage of collective bargaining, a representative of a trade union which is recognised by the employer requests, either orally or, if required by the employer, in writing, information which is both:

(*a*)   information without which the trade union representative would be, to a material extent, impeded in carrying on with the employer such collective bargaining; and

(*b*)   information which it would be in accordance with good industrial relations practice that the employer should disclose for the purposes of collective bargaining,

the employer must (in writing, if requested by the representative) disclose such information, unless it falls within one of the exceptions below (*TULRCA 1992, s 181*).

Exceptions. The employer need not disclose the information where:

(i)   it would be against the interests of national security;

(ii)   it is information which he could not disclose without contravening a prohibition imposed by or under an enactment;

(iii)   it is information which has been communicated to the employer in confidence or which the employer has otherwise obtained in consequence of the confidence reposed in him by another person;

(iv)   it is information relating specifically to an individual and he has not consented to its being disclosed;

(v)   it is information the disclosure of which would cause substantial injury to the employer's undertaking for reasons other than its effect on collective bargaining; or

(vi)   it is information obtained by the employer for the purpose of bringing, prosecuting or defending any legal proceedings.

(*TULRCA 1992, s 182(1)*.)

In the performance of his duty under *TULRCA 1992, s 181*, an employer will not be required:

(A)   to produce, or allow inspection of, any document (other than a document prepared for the purpose of conveying or confirming the information) or to make a copy of, or extracts from, any document; or

(B)   to compile or assemble any information where the compilation or assembly would involve an amount of work or expenditure out of reasonable proportion to the value of the information in the conduct of collective bargaining.

(*TULRCA 1992, s 182(2)*.)

A union only has the right to information concerning matters which are relevant to collective bargaining for which it is recognised. Thus, although a union may have the right to represent a certain class of employee, unless it has a right to represent them *for the purpose of collective bargaining* it does not enjoy the statutory right to information (*R v Central Arbitration Committee, ex p BTP Tioxide Ltd* [1981] ICR 843).

Furthermore, information which would not assist collective bargaining need not be disclosed. Thus, the High Court refused to order the disclosure of figures obtained by the Ministry of Defence showing detailed tenders submitted by contract labour cleaners (*Civil Service Union v Central Arbitration Committee* [1980] IRLR 274).

11.4 Disclosure of Information

11.4 Code of Practice

ACAS issued its Code of Practice No 2, on 'Disclosure of Information', in 1977 (and subsequently revised in 1998: see *SI 1998/45*). The Code does not provide a complete list of items which should be disclosed, as these will vary according to the circumstances, but merely provides some examples of information which should be considered for disclosure (see also CODES OF PRACTICE (5)). Some of the categories of negotiations for which information may have to be disclosed are set out below.

(*a*)   Negotiations over pay and benefits.

(*b*)   Negotiations on conditions of service.

(*c*)   Negotiations over manpower.

(*d*)   Negotiations over performance.

(*e*)   Financial negotiations.

The extent of the duty, and the exceptions, will be matters for interpretation in individual cases. A common sense view of what information is necessary in all the circumstances will be taken.

11.5 Consequences of failure to comply with a request for information

Initial failure to give information. If an employer fails to comply with a request for information from an independent trade union, the union may present a complaint to the CAC. If conciliation seems a possibility, the CAC will refer the matter to ACAS. If ACAS fails in its attempt at conciliation, or if the complaint is not considered initially suitable for conciliation, the CAC will proceed to hear and determine the complaint. The trade union and employer concerned are entitled to be heard, as is any person whom the CAC considers to have a proper interest in the complaint (*TULRCA 1992, s 183(1)–(4)*).

If the CAC finds the complaint wholly or partly well-founded, it will make a declaration specifying the following:

(*a*)   the nature of the information which it considers should originally have been provided;

(*b*)   the date (or, if more than one, the earliest date) on which the employer refused or failed to disclose that information or to confirm it in writing; and

(*c*)   a period (not being less than one week from the date of the declaration) within which the employer must disclose the information or confirm it in writing.

(*TULRCA 1992, s 183(5).*)

Continued failure to give information. If the employer persists in failing to disclose the information specified in the CAC's declaration within the specified time limit, the trade union may present a further complaint to the CAC who will hear and determine the further complaint. The trade union and employer concerned are again entitled to be heard, as is any person whom the CAC considers has a proper interest in the complaint. If it finds the complaint well-founded, the CAC will issue a declaration specifying the information in respect of which it so finds (*TULRCA 1992, s 184*).

On or after presenting such a further complaint, the trade union may also present a claim relating to the terms and conditions of employment of employees of a description specified in the original claim for information (*TULRCA 1992, s 185(1)*). If the CAC finds or has found the further complaint well-founded, it may make an award that there be incorporated into those employees' contracts of employment:

(i)   the terms and conditions specified in the claim; or

(ii)   other terms and conditions which it considers appropriate.

The award may be back-dated to the date on which the CAC declared that the employer refused or failed to disclose (or confirm in writing) the information (see (*b*) above) (*TULRCA 1992, s 185(3)*). It may only be made in respect of a description of employees and shall comprise only terms and conditions relating to matters in respect of which the trade union making the claim is recognised by the employer (*TULRCA 1992, s 185(4)*).

However, if at any time after a trade union has presented a claim under *TULRCA 1992, s 185(1)* to the CAC, and before the CAC has made its award, the employer gives the union the required information, the claim is treated as withdrawn (*TULRCA 1992, s 185(2)*).

Terms incorporated by an award remain in force until they are superseded or varied:

(*a*)   by a subsequent award under this procedure;

(*b*)   by a collective agreement between the employer and the union; or

(*c*)   by express or implied agreement between the employees and the employer as far as it improves any terms and conditions awarded under this procedure.

(*TULRCA 1992, s 185(5)*.)

11.6   **TRANSFER OF UNDERTAKINGS REGULATIONS**

The *Transfer of Undertakings* (*Protection of Employment*) *Regulations 2006* (*SI 2006/246*) which apply to relevant transfers taking place after 6 April 2006 impose obligations from 19 April 2006 upon transferors to disclose to transferees 'employee liability information' (*reg 11*). Failure to make such disclosure is actionable in the employment tribunal by the transferee (*reg 12*). Transferor and transferee employers must also consult in relation to employees affected by a relevant transfer and disclose information to recognised trade unions or elected representatives when there is a transfer to which the *Regulations* apply. Both the transferor and transferee vendor must inform representatives of recognised trade unions, or elected representatives, of certain specified matters which arise on the transfer (*regs 13–16*). A failure to do so is actionable in the Employment Tribunal. The obligations of consultation and information provision relating to relevant transfers which took place prior to 6 April 2006 were set out in the predecessor Regulations, the *Transfer of Undertakings* (*Protection of Employment*) *Regulations 1981* (*SI 1981/1794*) (see *regs 10* and *11*, of the *1981 Regulations* as amended by *TURERA 1993, s 33* and *SI 1995/2587*). (See TRANSFER OF UNDERTAKINGS (52).)

11.7 Disclosure of Information

11.7 INFORMATION NECESSARY FOR HEALTH AND SAFETY PURPOSES

Employers are obliged by the *Health and Safety at Work, etc Act 1974* ('*HSWA 1974*') to provide their employees with information necessary to ensure, so far as is possible, their health and safety at work (*HSWA 1974, s 2(2)(c)*). An employer must prepare and, when appropriate, revise a written statement of his general policy with respect to the health and safety at work of his employees and the organisation and arrangements for the time being in force for carrying out that policy, and bring the statement and any revision of it to the notice of all his employees (*HSWA 1974, s 2(3)*; see also 27.18 HEALTH AND SAFETY AT WORK – I). Failure to provide such written information is an offence which carries a maximum fine of £20,000 on conviction in a magistrates' court, and an unlimited fine on conviction in the Crown Court (*HSWA 1974, s 33(1), (1A), (3)*; *Magistrates' Courts Act 1980, s 32(2)*; and see 1.10 INTRODUCTION).

11.8 Safety representatives, and representatives of employee safety

Safety representatives, appointed by a recognised trade union (see also 28.21 HEALTH AND SAFETY AT WORK – II), were given statutory powers to obtain certain information by the *Safety Representatives and Safety Committees Regulations 1977* (*SI 1977/500*), *reg 7*. They are entitled, after giving the employer reasonable notice, to inspect and take copies of any document which the employer is legally obliged to keep, except a document consisting of or relating to any health record of an identifiable individual (*reg 7(1)*). In addition, an employer is obliged to make available to safety representatives any information within his knowledge relating to health, safety or welfare, which is necessary to enable them to fulfil their functions, *except*:

(*a*) any information the disclosure of which would be against the interests of national security;

(*b*) any information which he could not disclose without contravening a prohibition imposed by or under an enactment;

(*c*) any information relating specifically to an individual, unless he has consented to its being disclosed;

(*d*) any information the disclosure of which would, for reasons other than its effect on health, safety or welfare at work, cause substantial injury to the employer's undertaking or, where the information was supplied to him by some other person, to the undertaking of that other person; or

(*e*) any information obtained by the employer for the purpose of bringing, prosecuting or defending any legal proceedings.

(*Regulation 7(2), (3)*.)

As from 1 October 1996, employees who are not covered by trade union-appointed safety representatives are entitled to be consulted by their employer on health and safety matters, by virtue of the *Health and Safety (Consultation with Employees) Regulations 1996* (*SI 1996/1513*). The consultation may be either with the employees directly or with representatives elected by the relevant employees (referred to in the *Regulations* as 'representatives of employee safety'). The employer must provide the necessary information to enable the employees or representatives to participate fully and effectively in the consultation. In the case of representatives, the information must also be sufficient to enable them to carry out their functions under the *Regulations*. Information within the categories (*a*) to (*e*) above need not be provided. (See also 28.22 HEALTH AND SAFETY AT WORK – II.)

11.9   COMPANIES ACT 1985

The *Companies Act 1985* contains several provisions requiring the disclosure of information which may concern employees. The most important of these are the requirements that the directors' report contain the following:

(*a*)   where the average number of persons employed in the financial year exceeded 250, information concerning the employment of disabled persons; and

(*b*)   where the average number of persons employed in the financial year exceeded 250, information about employee involvement.

For the information to be supplied, see *Companies Act 1985, s 234, Sch 7 paras 9 and 11*.

11.10   OCCUPATIONAL PENSION SCHEMES

Under the *Occupational Pension Schemes* (*Disclosure of Information*) *Regulations 1996* (*SI 1996/1655*) the trustees of such schemes must make available to members and prospective members and (in most instances) to their spouses and to beneficiaries and independent recognised trade unions, various categories of information. These include the constitution of the scheme (*reg 3*), basic information about the scheme (*reg 4* and *Sch 1*), information about entitlements (*reg 5* and *Sch 2*) and audited accounts and annual reports (*reg 6* and *Sch 3*). Each of these regulations details the categories of persons and (where applicable) trade unions to whom the information is to be furnished.

THE INFORMATION AND CONSULTATION OF EMPLOYEES REGULATIONS 2004 (SI 2004/3426)

11.11   On 11 June 2001, the EU Social Policy Council agreed a draft Directive on informing and consulting employees. In March 2002 *Directive 2002/14/EC* ('the *Information and Consultation Directive*') was adopted by the member states. The *Directive* gives employees a right to be informed about the undertaking's economic situation and employment prospects, and be informed and consulted with a view to reaching agreement about decisions likely to lead to substantial changes in work organisation or contractual relations. The *Directive* is implemented in the UK by the *Information and Consultation of Employees Regulations 2004, SI 2004/3426* ('the *Regulations*').

It is important to note that the *Regulations* are structured to come into force over a number of years depending upon the size of the undertaking in question. The *Regulations* came into force on 6 April 2005 in relation to undertakings with 150 or more employees and 6 April 2007 for undertakings with 100 or more employees. In the case of undertakings with 50 or more employees, the commencement date will be 6 April 2008 but the *Regulations* will not apply to undertakings employing fewer than 50 employees. It is particularly important to identify whether there is an undertaking employing the requisite number of employees for the provisions of the *Regulations* to apply. The definition of undertaking in the *Regulations* (taken from the Directive) is 'a public or private undertaking carrying out an economic activity whether or not operating for gain'. As to calculating the number of employees engaged in the undertaking, this is averaged over a twelve month period. Further, only 'employees' are to be counted and accordingly subcontractors and temporary workers may be excluded from the calculation insofar as they are not 'employees'. The *Regulations* provide two ways in which information and consultation procedures may be established: first, by employee request and second, by the employer deciding to commence negotiations. If there is no existing mechanism for information and consultation in the undertaking then, for an employees' request to initiate the procedure, there must be a written request to the employer (or to the Central Arbitration Committee (CAC)) by not less than 10 per cent of the employees employed in the undertaking. In cases where there is a pre-existing agreement, if a 10 per cent request is made the employer must either enter into negotiations or ballot the employees on the issue of the continuance of the existing agreement. If 40 per cent of the workforce (or a majority of those voting in the ballot) vote in favour of the request then the employer must enter into negotiations for a new agreement. Also, in the case of pre-existing agreements relating to information and consultation, it must in any event be determined if that agreement satisfies the requirements of the *Regulations* (*reg 8(1)*). To be valid the agreement must be in writing, cover all the employees in the undertaking, have been approved by the employees and set out how the employer is to give information to the employees or their representatives and how their views will be sought on the information provided. The EAT in *Stewart v Moray Council* [2006] IRLR 592 has for the first time considered the *Regulations* in determining whether pre-existing agreements which had been negotiated with trade unions satisfied the requirements of the Regulations. On the facts the trade union representatives had agreed and approved the agreements but the agreements had not been specifically put to non-unionist employees for approval. The CAC rejected an argument that in these circumstances employee approval had not been obtained. It was held that the approval of the representatives was sufficient to satisfy the requirements of the *Regulations*. On the facts, however, one of the agreements failed the statutory requirement of setting out adequately how the employer would give information to the employees and consult with them. The CAC's decision was upheld by the EAT which went on to give guidance on the issue of union involvement and the issue of coverage under *reg 8(1)(b)*. The EAT also found that the requirement of approval by the employees (*reg 8(1)(c)*) could be met by collective approval by trade unions so long as the *majority* of employees were union members.

If there is no valid pre-existing agreement or no agreement at all and there has been an appropriate request and ballot, then the employer must enter into negotiations for an agreement with employees' representatives. Negotiations may last for up to six months (extendable by agreement).

For a negotiated agreement to be valid it must cover all the employees in the undertaking, be in writing and dated and signed by the employer, set out the circumstances in which the employer will inform and consult the employees and provide for the appointment or election of information and consultation representatives or for information and consultation directly with the employees (*reg 16(1)*). To be valid a negotiated agreement must also be approved by the employees by being signed by all or a majority of the negotiating representatives *and* by at least 50 per cent of the employees in the undertaking *or* approved by 50 per cent of the employees who vote in a ballot (*reg 16(2)*).

If the employer and representatives fail to reach a negotiated agreement (or if the employer fails to enter into negotiations following a 10 per cent request) then the *Regulations* impose standard information and consultation procedures by default. In cases of a negotiated agreement, or where the standard procedures are imposed, the *Regulations* provide specific provisions in order to protect confidential information. By *reg 25* it will be a breach of statutory duty for an individual to disclosure confidential information subject to a right of challenge to the confidentiality in issue which will be heard by the CAC. In certain cases where the effect of disclosure would be potentially seriously prejudicial to the undertaking, the employer may be justified in withholding the information from employee representatives (*reg 26*). As to individual rights, the *Regulations* extend the standard rights to time off and protection against dismissal or detriment on the grounds of taking part in the activities of an information and consultation representative to the employees' representatives. The right to time off, however, does not apply to representatives who are exercising their functions pursuant to a pre-existing agreement. The enforcement of the Regulations on a collective level rests with the CAC which will be empowered to adjudicate on the issue of what is an 'undertaking', the number of employees employed in an undertaking, the employer's provision of data, validity of balloting and appointment or election of representatives and whether an employer has complied with obligations under a negotiated agreement or standard arrangement (as the case may be). The *Regulations* provide for substantial penalties for employers who default on their obligations: in cases of complaint of failure to comply with the terms of an agreement (which has been upheld by the CAC), there will be a right for employee representatives to apply to the Employment Appeal Tribunal for a penalty notice (of up to £75,000) to be issued against the employer. The time limit for such an application will be three months from the date of the CAC's determination.

Guidance on the operation of the Regulations is available from the DTI website at www.dti.gov.uk/er/consultation/proposal/htm. The DTI's detailed Guidance (published in January 2005) is available to download on the same page. Further Guidance (including an e-learning package) is available from ACAS: see http://www.acas.org.uk/services/ic.html. (See, further, on the provisions of the *Directive and Regulations*: 18.4 EMPLOYEE PARTICIPATION.)

11.12 DATA PROTECTION: THE BACKGROUND

The obligations in relation to the storage of personal data on a computer were originally governed by the *Data Protection Act 1984*, passed in response to the Council of Europe's Convention for the Protection of Individuals with regard to Automatic Processing of Personal Data. The *1984 Act* required those processing personal data to register with the Data Protection Registrar (*DPA 1984, s 5(1)*) and restrictions were imposed upon the use or disclosure of data (*DPA 1984, s 5(2)*). Those processing data in relation to employees were obliged to adhere to the 'data protection principles', which provided that the employee should be informed that he is the subject of personal data and be allowed access to such data, and that the data should be corrected or erased where appropriate (*DPA 1984, Sch 1 Part I, para 7*). In addition there were obligations to inform employees whether personal data was kept on them, and to supply a copy of the relevant information (*DPA 1984, s 21*). Finally, an employer could be required to pay compensation where damage was caused by reason of the inaccuracy, loss or unauthorised disclosure of data (*DPA 1984, ss 22, 23*). The current, and considerably more extensive and onerous, data protection obligations required by the *EU Data Protection Directive (95/46)* are now contained in the *Data Protection Act 1998*.

11.13 DATA PROTECTION ACT 1998

On 15 January 1998, the Government published a Data Protection Bill which was designed to implement the *EU Data Protection Directive (95/46)*. On 16 July 1998, the *Data Protection Act 1998* received Royal Assent. The *Data Protection Act 1998* repeals and replaces the *Data Protection Act 1984*. The *Directive* was required to be implemented by 24 October 1998 and, accordingly, it was expected that the *Act* would come into force by this date. However, it actually came into force on 1 March 2000. It is important to note that the *Act* contains transitional provisions which will give employers several years fully to comply with the new provisions relating to paper based records (see *DPA 1998, Sch 8*). The final provisions of the *Data Protection Act* are due to come into force on 24 October 2007. A full consideration of the law of data protection is beyond the scope of this work. There follows a short summary of the key features of the *Data Protection Act 1998*.

11.14 Data Protection Act 1998: an overview

Most significantly, the law of data protection is extended to cover paper files as well as information stored on computer (*DPA 1998, s 1(1)*). Information contained in a 'relevant filing system' is brought within the compass of the *Act*'s protection. A relevant filing system is defined as non-automated information relating to individuals which is 'structured either by reference to individuals or by reference to criteria relating to individuals, in such a way that specific information relating to a particular individual is readily accessible'. Personal data includes any expression of opinion about a person and indications of intention by the employer or any other person in relation to that individual (*DPA 1998, s 1(1)*). It follows that paper-based personnel records will clearly come within the data protection regime.

Schedule 1 to the *DPA 1998* sets out eight principles relating to the *processing* of personal data. 'Processing' includes collection, storage, organisation, retrieval, alternation, disclosure or destruction of data. The principles may be summarised as follows:

(*a*)   personal data shall be processed fairly and lawfully;

(*b*)   personal data shall be obtained only for specified and lawful purposes and shall not be processed in any manner incompatible with those purposes;

(*c*)   personal data shall be adequate, relevant and not excessive in relation to the purposes for which it is processed;

(*d*)   personal data shall be accurate and, where necessary, kept up to date;

(*e*)   personal data shall be kept for no longer than is necessary for the purposes for which it is processed;

(*f*)   personal data shall be processed in accordance with the rights of data subjects under the *Act*;

(*g*)   personal data shall be subject to appropriate technical and organisational measures to protect against unauthorised or unlawful processing and accidental loss, destruction or damage; and

(*h*)   personal data shall not be transferred to a country or territory outside the European Economic Area unless that country or territory ensures an adequate level of data protection.

Under *Part II* of the *Act* employees (as 'data subjects') have the right (by written request and upon payment of a fee) to be told by the employer whether personal data about them is being processed, to be given descriptions of the data and its recipients, and to have the data supplied in an intelligible form (*DPA 1998, s 7*).

The employer must comply with the request within 40 days. Put simply, employees will be entitled in relation to paper records to receive a copy of their personnel file. Confidential references, however, given by the employer for the purposes of education, training or employment are excluded from the right under *s 7*. References given by third parties and held in a file by the current employer are not so excluded.

An employee is given a right under *s 14* of the *DPA 1998* to apply to the High Court or the county court on the ground that personal data relating to him is inaccurate. The court may order the employer to rectify, destroy or erase, as the case may be, data containing expressions of opinion based on inaccurate information. Where the inaccurate data is disclosed to third parties, the court may order the employer to notify those persons that the inaccurate data has been corrected. By *s 10, DPA 1998*, an employee may issue written notice requiring an employer not to process personal data where it is likely to cause substantial and unwarranted damage and distress. By *DPA 1998, s 13*, data subjects may recover compensation not only for loss and damage as a result of inaccurate data processing or unauthorised disclosure but also, in certain cases, for distress caused thereby. *DPA 1998, s 12* limits the use of computers exclusively in certain forms of decision making and employees may issue notices requiring that employers do not take a decision that significantly affects the employee *solely* on the automatic processing of personal data. The Data Protection Commissioner has extensive powers of enforcement in relation to the *Act*.

Finally, it is significant to note that new restrictions are introduced in relation to the processing of 'sensitive personal data'. Such data is broadly defined as including ethnic or racial origins, political opinions, religious beliefs or other beliefs of a similar nature, trade union membership, physical or mental health and data relating to the commission or alleged commission of any offence or the sentence in relation to any such offence. In relation to sensitive personal data, in addition to the *Sch 1* data protection principles, at least one of the conditions found in *Sch 3* to the *DPA 1998* must be satisfied. These conditions include the express consent of the employee for the following:

(i)   that the processing is necessary for performing or exercising a right or obligation imposed by or in connection with employment;

(ii)   that the processing is necessary in connection with legal proceedings or for the purposes of obtaining legal advice;

(iii) that the processing is necessary for the administration of justice or statutory duty; or

(iv)   the processing of racial or ethnic origin information is necessary for the purposes of monitoring equality of opportunity or treatment.

The Information Commissioner has published the Employment Practices Data Protection Code. The purpose of this Code is to ensure that, in relation to data obtained by employers on their employees, the storage and use of that data complies with the obligations imposed by the *Data Protection Act 1998* and also the *Human Rights Act 1998* (see HUMAN RIGHTS (30)). The Code is in four parts, all of which have now been published by the Information Commissioner. The first part deals with the recruitment and selection of employees and the second part concerns records management. The third part deals with monitoring at work and covers issues such as recording workers' activities by CCTV cameras, automated checking software and recording of workers' telephone calls. The final part of the Code relates to medical information and is titled 'Information about workers' health'. Much of this part of the Code deals with processing of sensitive personal data and covers the following areas: general considerations, occupational health schemes, medical examination and testing, drug and alcohol testing and genetic testing. The text of the Code, together with supplementary guidance, can be found on the Information Commissioner's website at www.informationcommissioner.gov.uk.

11.15   ACCESS TO MEDICAL REPORTS

Medical reports obtained by an employer should obviously not be disclosed to third parties without the employee's consent.

The *Access to Medical Reports Act 1988* ('*AMRA 1988*') gives individuals a right of access to medical reports relating to them which are supplied by medical practitioners for employment purposes (*AMRA 1998, s 1*). An employer may not apply to a medical practitioner for such a report without the employee's consent (*AMRA 1998, s 3(1)*). The ACAS handbook 'Discipline at Work' includes a model letter of enquiry to an employee's doctor. The employee is entitled to see the report *before* it is supplied (*AMRA 1998, s 4*) and to withhold consent to the report being supplied (*AMRA 1998, s 5(1)*). There is also provision for the correction of errors (*AMRA 1998, s 5(2)*). If there is a failure to comply with the *Act*, an application may be made to the court (*AMRA 1998, s 8*).

The statutory definition of 'medical report' refers to a medical practitioner who is or has been responsible for the clinical care of the individual. Therefore, a report obtained from a company doctor after an examination carried out for a particular purpose is unlikely to be subject to the *Act*. Nor does an employer request a medical report within the meaning of the *Act* where he merely seeks confirmation of information already received (*McIntosh v John Brown Engineering Ltd*, IDS Brief No 441, p 3).

The *Access to Health Records Act 1990* came into force on 1 November 1991 and, in general, applies only to information recorded after that date. It applies to health records, other than those falling within the scope of the *Data Protection Act 1984* (see 11.12 above). Individuals have a right to apply for access to records relating to them to the health professional who holds those records (*AHRA 1990, s 3*). There is also a right to apply for inaccurate records to be corrected (*AHRA 1990, s 6*). The right of access is subject to certain exclusions (*AHRA 1990, ss 4, 5*). A 'health professional' as defined by *AHRA 1990, s 2* includes any registered medical practitioner, so that the *Act* may be expected to apply to company doctors. An application may be made to the court if the holder of a health record fails to comply with the *Act* (*AHRA 1990, s 8*).

11.16   CONFIDENTIAL INFORMATION RELATING TO EMPLOYEES

Apart from the specific statutory obligations referred to above, the employer will normally be under a common law duty not to disclose to third parties confidential information which he holds concerning his employees. In *Dalgleish v Lothian and Borders Police Board* [1991] IRLR 422, there was held to be a *prima facie* case that employees' names and addresses were confidential.

However, it may well be that in a competitive tendering situation in which it is expected that there will be a transfer of an undertaking to the successful contractor (see TRANSFER OF UNDERTAKINGS (52)), there is little option but to disclose details of the workforce to potential tenderers. In such a case, it will be preferable to disclose the information, so far as possible, in such a way as not to identify individual employees.

11.17 **DISCLOSURE OF INFORMATION BY EMPLOYEES: THE PUBLIC INTEREST DISCLOSURE ACT 1998**

The *Public Interest Disclosure Act 1998* (*'PIDA 1998'*) received the Royal Assent on 2 July 1998 and came into force on 2 July 1999. This somewhat complicated piece of legislation introduces specific rights into the *ERA 1996* for those who disclose information about alleged wrongdoings, including the right not to suffer detriment in employment (*PIDA 1998, s 2*, inserting *ERA 1996, s 47B*) and the right not to be unfairly dismissed for making such disclosures (*PIDA 1998, ss 5, 7*). Such a dismissal will be automatically unfair and there is no qualifying period of employment, nor upper age limit. (See UNFAIR DISMISSAL – I (53).) The provisions of *PIDA 1998* do not apply to employment in the Security Service, the Secret Intelligence Service or the Government Communications Headquarters (*PIDA 1998, s 11*) nor to police officers nor persons employed under a contract of employment in the police service (*PIDA 1998, s 13*).

11.18 **Protected disclosures by workers**

In order for the protection afforded by the *Act* to apply, the disclosure must be made by 'a worker'. This is broadly defined in a new *s 43K, ERA 1996* (as inserted by *PIDA 1998, s 1*) and includes contractors acting under the control of the employer, persons on training courses and doctors, dentists, opticians and pharmacists providing services under statutory schemes.

Second, the disclosure must be a 'qualifying disclosure' as defined in a new *ERA 1996, s 43B* (*PIDA 1998, s 1*). A qualifying disclosure is information which, in the reasonable belief of the disclosing worker, shows one or more of the following six categories of wrongdoing:

(*a*)   that a criminal offence has been committed, is being committed or is likely to be committed;

(*b*)   that a person has failed, is failing or is likely to fail to comply with any legal obligation to which he is subject;

(*c*)   that a miscarriage of justice has occurred, is occurring or is likely to occur;

(*d*)   that the health or safety of any individual has been, is being or is likely to be endangered;

(*e*)   that the environment has been, is being or is likely to be damaged; or

(*f*)   that information tending to show any matter falling within any one of the preceding paragraphs has been, is being or is likely to be deliberately concealed.

The geographical location of the wrongdoing (ie whether inside or outside the United Kingdom) is irrelevant (*ERA 1996, s 43B(2)* inserted by *PIDA 1998, s 1*). A disclosure is not a qualifying disclosure, however, if a person making the disclosure commits a criminal offence in so doing, or if the disclosure is made in breach of legal professional privilege (*ERA 1996, s 43B(3), (4)* inserted by *PIDA 1998, s 1*). The Court of Appeal has held that the requirements under *s 43B* are (i) that the employee believes that the information disclosed meets the requirements of the section (ii) that the employee's belief is objectively reasonable and (iii) that the disclosure is made in good faith (*Babula v Waltham Forest College* [2007] EWCA Civ 174, [2007] IRLR 346). There is no absolute requirement that the legal obligation *in fact* exists, the objective reasonableness of the employee's belief is what is in issue (*Kraus v Penna plc* [2004] IRLR 260 disapproved).

11.18 Disclosure of Information

Third, in order to be a 'protected disclosure', a qualifying disclosure must be made only to the category of persons contemplated in the *Act* and not to other persons (*ERA 1996, ss 43C-43H* inserted by *PIDA 1998, s 1*). There are six ways contemplated in which a worker may make a 'protected disclosure', the first four of which are as follows:

(i)   to the worker's employer or (in cases where the information relates to the conduct of another person or to matters for which a person other than the employer has legal responsibility) that other person (*ERA 1996, s 43C*);

(ii) to a legal adviser in the course of obtaining legal advice (*ERA 1996, s 43D*);

(iii) to a Minister of the Crown where the worker's employer is (*a*) an individual appointed under any enactment by a Minister of the Crown or (*b*) a body whose members are appointed by a Minister of the Crown (*ERA 1996, s 43E*);

(iv) to a person prescribed by order made by the Secretary of State for the purposes of receiving qualifying disclosure information of relevant categories (*ERA 1996, s 43F*). The details of those persons and the relevant matters in respect of which they are prescribed are set out at length in the *Public Interest Disclosure (Prescribed Persons) Order 1999 (SI 1999/1549)*.

The fifth category of protected disclosure will permit disclosures to be made to persons other than those contemplated in categories (i) to (iv) above but only if the worker makes the disclosure in good faith, reasonably believes the information to be substantially true, does not make the disclosure for the purposes of personal gain, one of a number of stringent conditions is satisfied, and in all the circumstances it is reasonable to make the disclosure (*ERA 1996, s 43G*). A disclosure is not made in good faith if an ulterior motive is the predominant purpose for making the disclosure even if the worker making the disclosure reasonably believed it was true (*Street v Derbyshire Unemployment Workers Centre* [2004] EWCA Civ 964, [2004] IRLR 687). The burden of proving bad faith in relation to an employee's disclosure rests on the employer (*Bachnak v Emerging Markets Partnership (Europe) Ltd* (EAT, 27.01.06 (0288/05)).

The conditions contemplated by this section are:

(A)   that the worker reasonably believes, at the time of making the disclosure, that he will be subjected to a detriment by the employer if the disclosure is made to the employer or a prescribed person (*ERA 1996, s 43G(2)(a)*); or

(B)   that, in cases where there is no prescribed person in relation to the relevant qualifying disclosure, the worker reasonably believes that evidence relating to the wrongdoing will be concealed or destroyed if a disclosure is made to the employer (*ERA 1996, s 43G(2)(b)*); or

(C)   that the worker has previously made a disclosure of substantially the same information to the employer or to a prescribed person (*ERA 1996, s 43G(2)(c)*).

Finally, in determining whether it was reasonable for the worker to make the disclosure under *s 43G, ERA 1996*, regard must be had to the identity of the person to whom the disclosure is made, the seriousness of the relevant failure, whether the relevant failure is continuing or likely to occur in the future, whether the disclosure is made in breach of a duty of confidence owed by the employer to another person, the action which the employer or person to whom a previous disclosure was made might reasonably have been expected to take as a result of the previous disclosure, and whether the worker complied with any procedure whose use by him was authorised by the employer (*ERA 1996, s 43G(3)–(4)*).

The final category of protected disclosure relates to disclosure of 'exceptionally serious failures' (*ERA 1996, s 43H*). In this situation the worker must make the disclosure in good faith, believing the information to be substantially true, not for personal gain in circumstances when the relevant failure is of an exceptionally serious nature and where in all the circumstances it was reasonable to make the disclosure. For an example of a disclosure to the local press being a protected disclosure see *Collins v the National Trust* (Employment Tribunal 17.01.06 (2507255/05)).

In determining reasonableness of the disclosure, particular regard shall be had to the identity of the person to whom the disclosure is made.

By *ERA 1996, s 43J* (inserted by *PIDA 1998, s 1*) a provision in an agreement (including a contract of employment) which purports to preclude a worker from making protected disclosures is rendered void.

In cases where an employee has made a protected disclosure as defined in the *Act* and is subjected to a detriment or dismissal as a result by the employer, the remedy will be by way of complaint to an employment tribunal (*ERA 1996, ss 47B, 103A* inserted by *PIDA 1998, ss 2, 5*). Dismissal on such grounds will be automatically unfair and there is no qualifying period of employment or upper age limit. For the application of the burden of proof in such cases see *Kuzel v Roche Products Ltd* [2007] UKEAT/516/06 [2007] IRLR 309. As enacted, the *PIDA 1998* contemplated that the compensation for unfair dismissal by reason of making a protected disclosure would be on the same basis as that applying to other categories of unfair dismissal. *Section 8, PIDA 1998* kept open the possibility of introducing a different basis for assessment of compensation by way of regulations to be introduced by the Secretary of State prescribing the manner of calculation of compensation in such cases (see *ERA 1996, s 127B*, inserted by *PIDA 1998, s 8(4)*). The relevant *Regulations* (*Public Interest Disclosure* (*Compensation*) *Regulations 1999* (*SI 1999/1548*)) remove the limit on an unfair dismissal compensatory award in relation to this category of dismissal (see *ERA 1996, s 124(1A)* and *s 103A*). Awards for injury to feelings as a result of subjection to a detriment will be calculated on the same basis as in discrimination cases (ie applying the guidance in *Vento v Chief Constable of West Yorkshire (No 2)* [2002] EWCA Civ 1871, [2003] IRLR 102). See *Virgo Fidelis Senior School v Boyle* [2004] IRLR 268, EAT.

In a careful and detailed judgment the Court of Appeal has decided that the principles outlined in *Rhys Harper v Relaxion Group plc* [2003] ICR 867, HL in relation to acts of victimisation occurring after the termination of the employment contract do apply to detriments suffered after the termination of the employment relationship, for example an unfavourable reference provided by reason of having made a protected disclosure (see *Woodward v Abbey National plc* [2006] EWCA Civ 822). *Fadipe v Reed Nursing Personnel* [2001] EWCA Civ 1885, [2005] ICR 1760 (Note) which had held that post employment victimisation under *s 44* of the *ERA* (health and safety cases) was not protected should not now be followed after *Woodward*.

The breadth of application of the protection afforded by the concept of a protected disclosure is illustrated by two cases involving dismissal occurring *after* the *PIDA 1998* came into force but in relation to disclosures of information made *before* the *PIDA 1998* came into force. In circumstances where the dismissal or other detriment imposed by the employer by reason of the disclosure occurred after 2 July 1999 an Employment Tribunal had jurisdiction to hear a complaint (see *Stolt Offshore Ltd v Miklaszewicz* [2002] IRLR 344 and *Meteorological Office v Edgar* [2002] ICR 149). In *Pinnington v City and Council of Swansea* [2005] ICR 685 (CA), however, the Court of Appeal held that a suspension from work which had commenced prior to the coming into force of the *PIDA 1998* but which continued for two days during which the Act was in force did not amount to a detriment under *ERA, s 47B* in relation to the final two days as there was no distinct act or omission by the employer on those two days on the grounds of the employee having made a protected disclosure.

The wide ambit of 'protected disclosure' is further illustrated by *Parkins v Sodexho Ltd* [2002] IRLR 109 in which case the EAT held that a complaint by an employee to his employer of a breach of the contract of employment could be a protected disclosure in relation to 'any legal obligation'. It followed that a dismissal by reason of making the complaint could be automatically unfair under the provisions of the *PIDA 1998* as contained in the *ERA 1996*.

The employer may be liable for detrimental treatment of an employee by work colleagues as a result of a protected disclosure on vicarious liability grounds if there is a sufficiently close connection between the breach of duty by the other employees and their employment (*Carlisle-Morgan v Cumbria County Council* [2007] IRLR 314, [2007] All ER (D) 248 (Jan), EAT).

The protection against detriment is not, however, without limits and does not extend to employees deciding to conduct an 'investigation' into possible misconduct by the employer by hacking into the employer's computer system or searching files for 'evidence'. Such activity does not amount to a 'disclosure'. See *Evans v Bolton School* [2006] EWCA Civ 1653, [2007] ICR 641, sub nom Bolton School v Evans [2007] IRLR 140 in which a disciplinary warning given to a teacher for hacking into a computer was held to be legitimate and not a detriment imposed by reason of a protected disclosure.

12   Discrimination and Equal Opportunities – I

12.1   THE SCOPE AND APPROACH OF THIS CHAPTER

Scope

Over the course of the last half-century, UK employment law has seen the ongoing and often vigorous development of a body of equal opportunities law. The underlying concept is a straightforward one: people should not be subject to disadvantage in the job market or in the workplace for reasons that have nothing to do with the skills they have to offer or their performance of their duties. There has been a steady incrementing of grounds upon which it is no longer accepted that an employer may base employment-related decisions. As the law stands they are: sex; marital or civil partnership status; racial grounds; disability; gender reassignment; religion or belief; sexual orientation; pregnancy or maternity leave; and age. These grounds are referred to below as the 'prohibited grounds'.

Protection against discrimination on each of the prohibited grounds has been introduced by a specific legislative measure. Whilst, for the most part, the scope, nature and language of the relevant provisions are very similar, there are some important differences. Three forms of unlawful discrimination have legislative regimes which are sufficiently distinctive to require separate treatment in this work: Disability Discrimination (see DISABILITY AND DISCRIMINATION (10)); Discrimination on Grounds of Sex in respect of contractual terms and conditions, which is known more familiarly as 'Equal Pay' (see EQUAL PAY (23)); and Age Discrimination (see AGE DISCRIMINATION (3)).

Approach

The approach taken below is first to explain the relevant general principle and immediately thereafter to indicate where particular issues arise in the context of its application to one or more of the prohibited grounds.

12.2   LEGAL SOURCES AND GUIDANCE MATERIAL

Each protection against discrimination has been introduced by a legislative instrument. Sometimes the Domestic law implements an obligation originally to be found in a European legislative measure. However, even those measures such as protection against discrimination on grounds of sex or race which have domestic origins have since been shaped by European Law. Set out immediately below is a summary of the legislative framework applicable to each of the prohibited grounds:

(1) Sex

Discrimination on grounds of sex is made unlawful by the *Sex Discrimination Act 1975* ('*SDA 1975*'). Only the provisions of the *SDA 1975* relating to employment are considered below. Although the provisions relating to sex discrimination are worded in terms of discrimination against women, they should be read as applying equally to the treatment of men (with the exception of the special treatment afforded to women in connection with pregnancy or childbirth) (*SDA 1975, s 2*).

12.2 Discrimination and Equal Opportunities – I

Equal treatment between the sexes in employment is within the scope of competence of the European Union. The *Equal Treatment Directive (76/207/EEC)* ('*ETD 76/207/EEC*') is vertically directly effective (see 24.2 EUROPEAN COMMUNITY LAW) which means that public sector workers are able to rely directly on its provisions. *SDA 1975* is interpreted, so far as possible, so as to be consistent with the requirements of the Directive. On 5 July 2006, the EU Commission adopted *Directive 2006/54/EC* on the implementation of the principle of equal opportunities and equal treatment of men and women in matters of employment and occupation. The new directive consolidates a number of measures including the *ETD 76/207/EEC*.

On 1 May 1999, the *Amsterdam Treaty* came into force. It amended *art 119* of the *Treaty of Rome* (now *art 141*) incorporating a principle of equal treatment into the Treaty itself. This, in turn, has opened up the possibility of a horizontally directly effective right to equal treatment conferred on both public and private sector employees.

(The EOC, CRE and NDC have published a guide to equal opportunities aimed at small businesses. It is entitled 'Equal Opportunities is Your Business Too' and is available on the CRE website at http://www.cre.gov.uk/downloads/eoiybt.pdf).

(2) Marital or Civil Partnership Status

Discrimination against married persons in the employment field is made unlawful by the *SDA 1975, s 3*. Note that it protects only married persons, it does not preclude discrimination against unmarried persons.

SDA 1975, s 3 was amended by *Civil Partnership Act 2004, s 251(1)* and (2) with effect from 5 December 2005 (see *SI 2005/3175, Art 2(1)* and *Sch 1*). The effect of the amendment it to make it unlawful to discriminate in the employment field against persons who are civil partners.

(3) Race

Discrimination on racial grounds is made unlawful by the *Race Relations Act 1976* ('*RRA 1976*') which repealed and replaced the *Race Relations Acts 1965* and *1968*.

The Commission for Racial Equality ('CRE') was established by the 1976 Act to replace the Race Relations Board. The purpose and powers of the Commission are considered in 14.11 below.

Article 13 of the *Treaty of Rome* (as amended by the *Treaty of Amsterdam*) confers a power on the European Union to legislate to combat discrimination on a variety of grounds including 'racial or ethnic origin'. On 29 June 2000, the European Council issued the *Race Discrimination Framework Directive* (*Council Directive 2000/43/EC*). The scope of the Directive is not identical to that of *RRA 1976*. For instance, the Directive does not apply to discrimination on grounds of nationality (*art 3, para 2*). Where a material difference exists between the domestic and European provisions, it is noted in the appropriate section below.

The Directive was implemented by the *Race Relations Act 1976* (*Amendment*) *Regulations 2003* (*SI 2003/1626*) which, with effect from 19 July 2003, amended *RRA 1976* in a number of significant respects.

(4) Gender Reassignment

On 1 May 1999, *SDA 1975* was amended to bring transsexuals within its protective scope (*SDA 1975, s 2A*). Protection against less favourable treatment on grounds of transsexuality was provided as a result of the ECJ's decision in *P v S and Cornwall County Council (Case C-13/94)* [1996] IRLR 347. The key issue was whether discrimination on grounds of transsexuality could be said to be discrimination on grounds of sex. The European Court of Justice adopted a broad test which rendered unlawful any discrimination based 'essentially if not exclusively on the sex of the person concerned'. The EAT subsequently held that the *SDA 1975* could be interpreted so as to be consistent with the broad European scope of protection (*Chessington World of Adventures Ltd v Reed* [1997] IRLR 556). Nevertheless, the Government issued regulations which amended *SDA 1975* expressly to prohibit discrimination on the grounds that a person intends to undergo, is undergoing or has undergone a gender reassignment (*The Sex Discrimination (Gender Reassignment) Regulations 1999 (SI 1999/1102)* and *SDA 1975, s 2A*). The Regulations came into force on 1 May 1999.

(5) Religion or Belief

Employees and certain others are protected against discrimination on grounds of religion or belief. The protection has its origins in *art 13(1)* of the *Treaty of Rome* (as amended by the *Treaty of Amsterdam*) which provides that 'the Council ... may take appropriate action to combat discrimination based on ... religion or belief ...'. On 27 November 2000, the Council issued *Directive 2000/78/EC* establishing a general framework for equal treatment in employment and occupation ('the *Framework Directive 2000/78/EC*').

The elements of the *Framework Directive 2000/78/EC* concerned with discrimination on grounds of religion or belief have been implemented in the United Kingdom by the *Employment Equality (Religion or Belief) Regulations 2003 (SI 2003/1660)* ('*RBR 2003*') which were made on 26 June 2003 and came into force on 2 December 2003.

The *RBR 2003* do not extend to Northern Ireland (*reg 1(2)*). Northern Ireland has its own legislation dealing with discrimination on grounds of religion or belief which is not dealt with in this work.

ACAS has issued guidance on putting the *RBR 2003* into practice. It was issued on 5 November 2003 and is available online at http://www.acas.org.uk/media/pdf/f/l/religion_1.pdf.

(6) Sexual Orientation

Discrimination on grounds of sexual orientation is made unlawful by the *Employment Equality (Sexual Orientation) Regulations 2003 (SI 2003/1661)* (as amended by the *Employment Equality (Sexual Orientation) (Amendment) Regulations 2003 (SI 2003/2827)*) which came into force on 1 December 2003 ('*SOR 2003*').

The origin of the protection is, once again, *art 13* of the *Treaty of Rome* and the *Framework Directive 2000/78/EC*. The *SOR 2003* implement the relevant elements of the *Framework Directive 2000/78/EC* into the law of Great Britain. They do not extend to Northern Ireland.

English courts and tribunals will, so far as possible, construe the regulations consistently with the directive. Where there are irreconcilable differences between the regulations and the directive, public sector workers may be able to rely on the directive itself under the principle of direct effect, provided the criteria for the application of that principle are met (cf 25.2 EUROPEAN COMMUNITY LAW).

(7) Pregnancy or Maternity Leave

Until 1 October 2005 discrimination on grounds of pregnancy or maternity leave was treated as a species of unlawful discrimination on ground of sex. From that date such discrimination is expressly and specifically prohibited by *SDA 1975, s 3A* (inserted by the *Employment Equality (Sex Discrimination) Regulations 2005 (SI 2005/2467)* ('*SDR 2005*') *reg 4*).

12.3   MEANING OF DISCRIMINATION

For the purposes of the legislative instruments that prohibit discrimination, there are four ways in which a person may discriminate against another:

(1)   by *directly* discriminating against them (12.4 below);

(2)   by *indirectly* discriminating against them (12.7 below);

(3)   by *victimising* them (12.10 below); or

(4)   by *harassing* them (12.11 below).

It should be borne in mind that a determination that a respondent has discriminated against an employee does not (save in cases of harassment) necessarily mean that they have acted unlawfully. Only certain specific forms of less favourable treatment fall within the protective scope of the relevant legislative instruments. This is explained in greater detail below.

12.4   DIRECT DISCRIMINATION

A person directly discriminates against an employee where, on a prohibited ground, he treats them less favourably than he treats or would treat another. Thus, there are two elements to the test: There must be less favourable treatment and that treatment must be on the relevant prohibited ground.

The relevant provisions in the respective legislative instruments are as follows:

Sex	*SDA 1975, s 1(2)(a)*
Marital and Civil Partnership Status	*SDA 1975, s 3(1)*
Race	*RRA 1976, s 1(1)(a)*
Gender reassignment	*SDA 1975, s 2A*
Religion or Belief	*RBR 2003, reg 3(1)(a)*
Sexual Orientation	*SOR 2003, reg 3(1)(a)*
Pregnancy or Maternity Leave	*SDA 1975, s 3A(1)(a) and (b), and (2)*

The account set out immediately below breaks the legislative tests into two elements: less favourable treatment and the reason for that treatment. Whilst that division reflects the manner in which a tribunal will usually approach the issue, in *Shamoon v Chief Constable of the Royal Ulster Constabulary* [2003] UKHL 11, [2003] ICR 337 a number of their Lordships opined that it may sometimes be appropriate to ask the latter question first. For an account of when it will be appropriate to do so, see 12.5(2) below.

12.5   Less Favourable Treatment

(1)   Unfavourable and Less Favourable treatment distinguished

The keys to understanding the concept of direct discrimination are to appreciate first that the legislation provides for a 'comparative' test (this is explained in greater detail below) and secondly that there is a distinction between *unfavourable* treatment (ie where an employee is treated badly) and *less favourable* treatment (ie where other employees receive better treatment even though their circumstances are not materially different). Thus, it is not an act of racial discrimination to dismiss an ethnic minority employee for a trivial act of misconduct, however disproportionate the penalty, if all employees would have been treated in that manner. An employer who treats all of his employees equally badly will not normally be found to have discriminated. For that reason, the House of Lords upheld a decision of the EAT in a racial discrimination case, to the effect that the conduct of a hypothetical reasonable employer is irrelevant:

> 'The fact that, for the purposes of the law of unfair dismissal, an employer has acted unreasonably casts no light whatsoever on the question whether he has treated an employee less favourably for the purposes of the [*RRA 1976*]'.

(*Glasgow City Council v Zafar* [1998] ICR 120, HL. See also *Martins v Marks & Spencer plc* [1998] IRLR 326.) Despite the House of Lords' robust rejection of the relevance of merely unreasonable treatment, other authorities have been prepared to recognise a limited and indirect relevance. Thus in *Law Society v Bahl* [2003] IRLR 640, EAT, the Employment Appeal Tribunal opined that the more unreasonable the treatment the more the credibility of any non-discriminatory explanation proffered may be called into question. The question was considered more closely by the Court of Appeal (*Bahl v Law Society* [2004] EWCA 1070; [2004] IRLR 799). Their Lordships reiterated that unreasonable behaviour cannot found an inference of discrimination. An employer is not obliged, therefore, to lead evidence that others have been treated equally unreasonably. However, if there is no explanation for the unreasonable treatment the absence of an explanation (as opposed to the unreasonableness of the treatment) might found an inference. The Court of Appeal has returned to the issue in another case in which no explanation was provided and held that whilst a tribunal should not be 'too ready' to infer unlawful discrimination from unreasonable conduct in the absence of evidence of other discriminatory behaviour, it was 'not wrong in law' to do so (*Wong v Igen Ltd* [2005] EWCA Civ 142, [2005] ICR 931).

Even in cases where employees have plainly been treated differently, it may still be difficult immediately to determine whether there has been less favourable treatment. Thus, where male and female employees are subject to different but comparably restrictive dress requirements there is no less favourable treatment on grounds of sex (*Schmidt v Austicks Bookshops Ltd* [1977] IRLR 360, EAT; and see *Smith v Safeway plc* [1996] ICR 868, CA and *Department for Work and Pensions v Thompson* [2004] IRLR 348 EAT).

The test of what amounts to less favourable treatment is an objective one (*Burrett v West Birmingham Health Authority* [1994] IRLR 7, EAT). However, there may be a limited role for the subjective preferences of the complainant. Thus, where a local education authority provided more places for boys than for girls in selective schools, the House of Lords held that it was not necessary for the complainant to demonstrate that selective education was, objectively, 'better' than non-selective education. It was enough that, by denying the girls the same opportunity as the boys, the council was depriving them of a choice which was valued by them (or at least by their parents) and which was a choice obviously valued, on reasonable grounds, by many others (*R (Birmingham City Council) v Equal Opportunities Commission* [1989] IRLR 173, HL).

It is the treatment itself rather than its consequences which must be different and less favourable (*Balgobin v Tower Hamlets London Borough Council* [1987] ICR 829, EAT).

(2) Comparators

As will be apparent from the examples given above, the legislative tests involve the making of a comparison. It is open to an employee either to demonstrate that another specific individual employee has been more favourably treated (in which case that other employee is known as the 'comparator') or to show that, absent any concrete examples, the tribunal may nevertheless still be sure that the employer would have treated another employee more favourably. In the latter case, the Tribunal considers what is known as a 'hypothetical comparator'. In either case it is the employee that has the burden of proof at this stage.

In certain specific contexts the authorities allow for the disapplication of the ordinary comparative approach. The principal example is discrimination on grounds of pregnancy which is discussed specifically below (see 12.5(3)(ii) below).

(i) Identifying a suitable comparator

In order to perform a valid comparison, it is necessary to compare like with like. With the exception of discrimination on ground of pregnancy or maternity leave, each of the legislative regimes makes specific provision to that effect by requiring that the 'relevant circumstances' of the complainant and comparator are 'the same' or 'not materially different':

Sex	*SDA 1975, s 5(3)*
Marital or Civil Partnership Status	*SDA 1975, s 5(3)*
Race	*RRA 1976, s 3(4)*
Gender Reassignment	*SDA 1975, s 5(3)*
Religion or Belief	*RBR 2003, reg 3(3)*
Sexual Orientation	*SOR 2003, reg 3(2)*

For guidance on the question of when circumstances will be materially different see *Dhatt v McDonalds Hamburgers Ltd* [1991] ICR 238: it was not discriminatory to treat potential employees differently according to whether they were or were not free to work in the United Kingdom without permission and, hence, it was legitimate to require evidence of such permission only from those who were not British or EU citizens (however, see discussion at 13.12(d) below on the *Asylum and Immigration Act 1996*). (See also *Wakeman v Quick Corpn* [1999] IRLR 424, CA: UK employees of a Japanese company could not complain about higher rates of pay enjoyed by colleagues seconded from Japan. The fact that they were secondees meant that their circumstances were materially different to those of the UK employees; but see *Spicer v Government of Spain* [2004] EWCA Civ 1046, [2005] ICR 213; *Bullock v Alice Ottley School* [1993] ICR 138: The comparator selected in a sex discrimination case concerned with a disparity in retirement ages was inappropriate because he performed a different job to that performed by the complainant; *Shomer v B & R Residential Lettings Ltd* [1992] IRLR 317, *Leeds Private Hospital Ltd v Parkin* [1992] ICR 571 and *Brook v Haringey London Borough Council* [1992] IRLR 478.) Where a female prison officer complained about being made to search male prisoners the appropriate comparator was a man required to search female prisoners and not a man required to search men (*Home Office v Saunders* [2006] ICR 318, EAT).

When dealing with hypothetical comparators it might be possible to construe the legislation so as to require the tribunal to construct a comparator who is 'in effect, a clone of the applicant in every respect (including personality and personal characteristics)' save that they are, for instance, of a different race. However, that approach was rejected in *Madden v Preferred Technical Group CHA Ltd* [2004] EWCA Civ 1178, [2005] IRLR 46 (*per* Wall LJ at paragraph 87). The effect of such an approach would be to run together the two relevant questions, namely whether the complainant was less favourably treated and whether they were less favourably treated on the prohibited ground. The reasoning would be that if the complainant and comparator are identical in all respects save, for instance, for their race any less favourable treatment must, logically, be on racial grounds. In practice it can be very difficult to keep the two issues distinct.

The selection of the comparator is the responsibility of the complainant. However, in some circumstances, a tribunal that determines that the complainant's chosen comparator is inappropriate may be required to go on to make the comparison with a hypothetical comparator (see *Balamoody v UK Central Council for Nursing, Midwifery and Health Visiting* [2001] EWCA Civ 2097, [2002] IRLR 288: the complainant was unrepresented. The Court of Appeal appears to have felt that the tribunal had a rather better grasp of the nature of the complainant's case than he did himself).

(ii) Performing the comparison

In most cases involving an actual comparator the comparison will be relatively straightforward. For instance, a complainant who has not been appointed to a particular post may seek to compare themselves to the person who was and evidence will centre on the selection process. Similarly, an employee who is made redundant may seek to compare themselves to someone who was retained in employment.

Matters are more complex when dealing with hypothetical comparators because the Tribunal will be asked to infer that the complainant has been less favourably treated. By definition one is dealing with a situation where there may be little direct evidence. In *Chief Constable of West Yorkshire v Vento* [2001] IRLR 124, the EAT suggested that a tribunal might look to see how 'unidentical but not wholly dissimilar cases' had been dealt with. Thus, someone whose circumstances differ sufficiently from those of the complainant to make them an inappropriate comparator may nevertheless have relevance in the context of the consideration of how a hypothetical comparator would have been treated.

In other cases a complainant may wish to lead evidence of, for instance, sexist comments made by the respondent on the basis that they tend to suggest a discriminatory attitude and thus that a male employee would have been treated differently. In such a case evidence principally relevant to the question whether less favourable treatment was on a prohibited ground may assist in establishing that the complainant would have been less favourably treated. Support for this approach may be found in *Shamoon v Chief Constable of the Royal Ulster Constabulary* [2003] UKHL 11, [2003] ICR 337, in which a number of members of the House of Lords opined that the constituent elements of the test could be approached in a different order to that described above where it was appropriate to do so. The decision in *Shamoon* was concerned with the law as it was before the enactment of *SDA 1975, s 63A*. That section formally reversed the burden of proof in sex discrimination cases. Provisions similar to *SDA 1975, s 63A* govern the burden of proof in the case of each of the other prohibited grounds (see 12.6 below). As the burden only shifts where a prima facie case of discrimination has been established an exploration of the employer's reasons for actions as a first step would seem to jump the gun. However, the EAT has stressed the particular suitability of the *Shamoon* guidance when dealing with cases involving hypothetical comparators (see *Laing v Manchester City Council* [2006] ICR 1519 EAT). The Court of Appeal has sought to allow tribunals the greatest flexibility, holding both that whilst it is generally good practice to follow the two stage test, there is no necessary error of law if a tribunal does not do so (*Brown v London Borough of Croydon* [2007] EWCA Civ 32, [2007] IRLR 259) and that it cannot be said to be an error of law in cases involving hypothetical comparators to deal first with the question of less favourable treatment (see *Madarassy v Nomura International plc* [2007] EWCA Civ 33, [2007] IRLR 246).

(3) Particular Cases

(i) Sex Discrimination: Is a comparison necessary where the conduct complained of is 'gender-specific'?

The short answer is 'yes'. At one point the courts and tribunals had come to accept that a comparative approach might not always be possible or appropriate in sex discrimination cases. The motivation for the departure from the ordinary approach had been that there existed a judicial concern that in two particular respects the Act failed to give sufficient protection to women. The first respect in which the Act was considered deficient was that it provided no express protection for women against discrimination on grounds of pregnancy. The second deficiency was in relation to sexual harassment. It is important to note that as from 1 October 2005, both deficiencies were remedied by amendments to *SDA 1975* introduced by *SDR 2005* (see 12.5(3)(ii)(B) and 12.11 below respectively). The account set out immediately below applies to acts of discrimination occurring on or before 30 September 2005.

In both cases the deficiency arose from the operation of the comparative test. In the case of discrimination on grounds of pregnancy, the UK courts had accepted an argument that an appropriate comparator was a man with an illness that would cause him to be absent for a period equivalent to that which would flow from pregnancy and maternity leave. If the employer would have dismissed the man he could safely dismiss the pregnant woman. The approach was considered by the ECJ in *Webb v EMO Air Cargo (UK) Ltd* [1994] ICR 770. The European Court rejected the UK courts' preferred comparator. The European Court's approach, in contrast, was that pregnancy was not sensibly comparable to illness. The discrimination was gender-specific and no comparison was necessary. Thus it came to be accepted that where a woman is treated unfavourably because she is pregnant a comparative exercise was no longer necessary as a matter of Domestic Law (*McGuigan v TG Boynes & Sons* (1999) 633 IDS Brief 6, EAT). A very considerable body of authority was then developed better to delineate the scope of this protection. That jurisprudence is outlined in section (ii) immediately below.

There have been attempts to extend the reasoning and to develop a general principle that no comparison is necessary where unfavourable treatment is 'gender-specific'. Arguments of this sort have been advanced with particular force in the context of claims concerned with harassment. Until the amendments made to the *SDA 1975* by *SDR 2005* (for which see 12.11 below) there was no express prohibition on sexual harassment. Harassment was brought within the scope of the Act on the basis that it constituted a form of direct discrimination which in turn required the employee to show that she had been less favourably treated. In some cases this can be straightforward. For instance, where a male employer makes a sexual advance to a female employee it will often be readily possible to demonstrate that he would not have made an advance to a member of his own sex. Equally, a female employer who only picks on and belittles her male employees would be likely to fall foul of the Act. However, much harassment is 'environmental'. It may consist of the display of pornographic images in a workplace or a culture of so-called 'banter'. It is possible that members of either sex would be offended but it may affect one more than the other. Pornographic posters might, for instance, offend a man but degrade a woman. These cases have caused the Tribunals consistent conceptual difficulty. In *Brumfitt v Ministry of Defence* [2005] IRLR 4 EAT a trainer's 'banter' offended all but was more offensive to women. The EAT determined that there could not be said to have been discrimination as the behaviour had not been 'directed' at the women. By contrast in *Moonsar v Fiveways Express Transport Ltd* [2005] IRLR 9 EAT the female claimant worked in an office where male colleagues were downloading pornographic images from the internet. That was found potentially to amount to less favourable treatment even though it could not be said to be 'directed' at her. To treat harassment as 'gender-specific' would escape many of these difficulties and courts have, correspondingly, been tempted to take that course. In *British Telecommunications plc v Williams* [1997] IRLR 668, the EAT stated that:

'Because the conduct which constitutes sexual harassment is itself gender-specific, there is no necessity to look for a male comparator.'

However, this approach was specifically disapproved by the House of Lords in *Macdonald v Advocate General for Scotland* [2003] UKHL 34, [2003] ICR 937) (see also *Smith v Gardner Merchant Ltd* [1998] IRLR 510, CA).

(ii) Sex Discrimination: Discrimination on grounds of pregnancy

(A) The Position Prior to 1 October 2005.

As indicated above, discrimination on grounds of pregnancy represents something of a special case. The UK courts had formerly sought to compare the treatment of pregnant women with the treatment received by men afflicted by an illness (see *Hayes v Malleable Working Men's Club and Institute* [1985] ICR 703, EAT and *Webb v EMO Air Cargo (UK) Ltd* [1993] ICR 175, HL). However, the consistent approach taken by the ECJ has been that pregnant women are in a unique and sex-specific position (see *Dekker v Stichting VJV-Centrum Plus* [1992] ICR 325, ECJ and *Webb v EMO Air Cargo (UK) Ltd* [1994] ICR 770, ECJ). In consequence, the comparative test in practice no longer applied (see *McGuigan v TG Boynes & Sons* (1999) 633 IDS Brief 6, EAT and *Smith v Gardner Merchant Ltd* [1998] IRLR 510 per Ward LJ obiter and *Fletcher v NHS Pensions Agency* [2005] ICR 1458, EAT). However, it should be noted that in *Webb v EMO Air Cargo (UK) Ltd (No 2)* [1995] IRLR 645, HL itself, the House of Lords sought to preserve a role for the comparative test. The reason why Ms Webb had been dismissed was that she had been unavailable for a period to fulfil her role, which was covering for a woman absent on maternity leave. She was not, however, employed purely as maternity cover; she was retained on a contract of indefinite duration. Lord Keith stated that, following the ECJ's ruling, *SDA 1975, ss 1(1)(a)* and *5(3)* were to be interpreted as meaning that in a case where a woman was engaged for an indefinite period, the fact that, at a time when to her knowledge her services would be particularly required, the reason why she would be temporarily unavailable for work was pregnancy, was a circumstance relevant to her case, being a circumstance that could not be present in the case of a hypothetical male comparator. This seems to amount, in practice, to applying the comparative test only to find that the circumstances of the complainant and comparator are incomparable. This rather complicated approach appears to have been taken first as a result of a concern as to whether *SDA 1975* might otherwise be capable of being interpreted as being consistent with Community Law and, second, because their Lordships wished to keep open the possibility that had Ms Webb been retained as temporary maternity cover, she could have been dismissed without recourse. That possibility has since been closed off by the ECJ (see the *TeleDanmark A/S* case below).

(1) *Unfavourable treatment on grounds of pregnancy*

As a result of the ECJ decisions referred to immediately above, it is clear that unfavourable treatment of a woman on the ground that she is pregnant will amount to an act of direct unlawful discrimination. The strictness of the principle is well illustrated by the case of *Mahlburg v Land Mecklenburg-Vorpommen* [2000] IRLR 276, ECJ. The ECJ considered the case of a pregnant woman who applied for and was refused a job intended to last for an indefinite period on the basis that, at the time at which she would otherwise have started the job, domestic law precluded her from working. Did the fact that the *ETD 76/207/EEC* was expressed to be without prejudice to such protective legislation mean that a refusal to appoint the applicant had not been discriminatory? The court decided that there had been an act of direct discrimination. The result pursued by the *ETD 76/207/EEC* was 'substantive, not formal, equality'. As a result, 'the application of provisions concerning the protection of pregnant women cannot result in unfavourable treatment regarding their access to employment'. Similarly, where an employee is prevented, by reason of her pregnancy, from performing her usual job tasks, a failure to consider alternative employment may be discriminatory on the basis that the employer has treated the employee less favourably in relation to access to opportunities for transfer within *SDA 1975, s 6(2)(a)* (*Iske v P&O European Ferries (Dover) Ltd* [1997] IRLR 401, EAT). A failure to comply with the obligation imposed by the *Management of Health and Safety Regulations 1999* (SI 1999/3242) to carry out a risk assessment in respect of a pregnant employee is an act of unlawful sex discrimination (see *Hardman v Mellon (t/a Orchard Lodge Nursing Home)* [2002] IRLR 517, EAT).

In *Ministry of Defence v Pope* [1997] ICR 296, EAT, the Employment Appeal Tribunal held that where an employee terminated her pregnancy in order to avoid being dismissed for pregnancy, she could bring a claim against her employer for damages for injury to feelings. In its decision in *Webb* the ECJ had expressly referred to preventing women feeling pressured into terminations as one of the policies underlying the maternity leave period.

In the light, in particular, of the ECJ decisions referred to above, it is clear that no comparator is required in cases of pregnancy discrimination. If a woman has been treated less favourable on pregnancy grounds it does not assist an employer to establish that a man in supposedly comparable circumstances would have been treated in the same way. However, in *Madarassy v Nomura International Plc* [2007] EWCA Civ 33, [2007] IRLR 246, the Court of Appeal indicated that even in pregnancy cases a comparator might still be of use. Their Lordships had in mind a case where there is real doubt as to whether pregnancy was the reason for the treatment. Thus, where a pregnant employee is dismissed for dishonesty and claims that the employer only took the step of dismissing her (rather than disciplining her) because she was pregnant, it might be relevant to ask what had happened to male employees who had behaved in the same way. Where, however, the reason is a matter directly connected with the pregnancy (such as absence) it will not be appropriate to ask how a man with a similar absence record would have been treated.

(2) *Unfavourable treatment for a reason connected with pregnancy*

Cases in which the reason for the employee being unfavourably treated is the pregnancy *per se* will be rare. More commonly, the employer points to a reason connected with the pregnancy. The ECJ has proven reluctant to draw any distinction between dismissals for pregnancy *per se* and dismissals for reasons connected with pregnancy. In *Dekker* (above), the complainant applied for a job as a teacher. Although suitable she was not appointed because the respondent would have had to pay her a maternity allowance, which, because she would have been pregnant on appointment, the respondent would have been unable to recover under their insurance policy. The reason for the refusal to appoint was thus not the pregnancy *per se* but the substantial irrecoverable costs of the appointment. However, the ECJ approached the case on the basis that the refusal to appoint was on ground of pregnancy. The domestic courts have adopted a similar approach. In *O'Neill v Governors of St Thomas More RCVA Upper School* [1997] ICR 33, EAT, the Employment Appeal Tribunal considered a case where a Roman Catholic school dismissed a religious education teacher who was pregnant by a priest. The school argued that it was not the pregnancy itself but the circumstances of the pregnancy that provided the dominant motive for the decision to dismiss. The EAT held that the dismissal had been discriminatory and rejected the concept of dismissal for pregnancy per se as misleading. Instead the tribunal should simply ask itself whether, on an objective basis, the dismissal was on the ground of pregnancy. Pregnancy did not need, in the EAT's opinion, to be the sole or even the main ground for the decision to dismiss. Thus, where an employer refused to allow an employee to return after her maternity leave because he thought her temporary replacement was better at the job, the EAT considered that the employee's dismissal was discriminatory. The 'effective cause' had been the pregnancy as, had the employee not been absent as a result of her pregnancy, the replacement would never have been employed (*Rees v Apollo Watch Repairs plc* [1996] ICR 466, EAT and cf *Abbey National plc v Formoso* [1999] IRLR 222, EAT; employee dismissed for gross misconduct whilst absent on maternity leave. The lack of an opportunity to explain herself at a disciplinary hearing meant that the dismissal was discriminatory as her pregnancy was the reason that she did not get a hearing).

The EAT seems to have gone further still in *Lewis Woolf Griptight Ltd v Corfield* [1997] IRLR 432, EAT. In the Lewis case, the tribunal found that the effective cause of the decision to dismiss was a breakdown in the relationship between the complainant and the respondent's Chief Executive. That reason was, of course, entirely gender-neutral. However, the respondent used an alleged failure by the complainant properly to exercise her right to return following maternity leave as a 'pretext' for the termination of her contract of employment. As this pretext was only available where the employee was a woman, the EAT reasoned, the dismissal was discriminatory.

There does, however, appear to be a limit to how remote the reason can be from the pregnancy. Thus in *Walter v Secretary of State for Social Security* [2001] EWCA Civ 1913, [2002] ICR 540, the *Jobseeker's Allowance Regulations 1996* (SI 1996/207) did not offend against the *Social Security Directive 79/7/EEC* (which prohibits sex discrimination in access to social security entitlements; see 25.5 EUROPEAN COMMUNITY LAW) where a student breaking her studies to have a child was precluded from claiming the allowance. Those taking breaks from studies are treated under the Regulations as retaining their status as a student, a status which disqualifies them from making a claim. The Court of Appeal decided that the complainant's ineligibility to claim derived from her student status and not from her pregnancy.

The most common reason relied upon by respondents in the case law is a reason related to absence. Those cases involving absence arising from a maternity-related illness have special features and are discussed separately below. In general terms, an employer may not use a maternity-related absence as either a reason for or (it would appear from the *Rees* and *Lewis Woolf* cases above) the occasion of treating a pregnant employee unfavourably. See by way of further example *Caisse Nationale D'Assurance Viellesse Des Travailleurs Salaries v Thibault* (Case C-136/95) [1999] ICR 160, ECJ: employees who had been present at work for at least six months in a particular year were entitled to a performance appraisal. A satisfactory appraisal would lead to a pay increase. Where the reason that an employee did not qualify for an appraisal was that she had been absent on maternity leave, it was an act of discrimination not to allow her an appraisal in any event. Contrast, however, *Hoyland v Asda Stores* [2005] ICR 1235, EAT (Sc); the claimant was not entitled to receive a bonus which had been earned by male colleagues during the period of her absence on maternity leave.

In *Land Brandenburg v Sass C-284/02* [2005] IRLR 147, the ECJ considered a different aspect of the effect of absence on benefits. Some benefits will be conditional on length of service. Should time spent absent on maternity leave count as service for those purposes? The ECJ held that the claimant should have been given credit for length of service for any period during which she had been on 'statutory maternity leave intended to protect women who have given birth'.

Webb was itself a case concerned with absence. It is significant that both the ECJ and the House of Lords placed considerable emphasis on the fact that Ms Webb had been employed for an indefinite period. The implication is that the case might have been decided differently had the contract of employment been for a fixed term over the whole or major part of which Ms Webb would have been unavailable. The distinction was further refined in *Caruana v Manchester Airport plc* [1996] IRLR 378, EAT where it was decided that a further distinction had to be drawn between cases where a woman is employed for a single 'one-off' fixed period, and cases where she is employed on a series of fixed-term contracts. The latter type of case should be treated in the same way as employment for an indefinite period. In previous editions, we have opined that even in cases where the engagement is to be for a single fixed term, it would nevertheless be an act of discrimination not to appoint a pregnant candidate by reason of her pregnancy. The basis of our view has been that it is not open to an employer to justify an act of direct discrimination. In *Tele Danmark A/S v Handels-og Kontorfunktion-aerernes Forbund i Danmark (HK)* [2004] ICR 610, ECJ, a woman was given a contract with a fixed maximum term of six months. The first two months of the contract would be spent being trained. The complainant was pregnant when she was offered the job. She did not tell the respondent. Her pregnancy had the effect that she was precluded from working for a substantial part of the fixed term. She was dismissed on the ground that she had failed to tell the respondent of her condition when applying for the job. The ECJ decided that the dismissal was contrary to *art 5(1)* of the *ETD 76/207/EEC* and *art 10* of the *Pregnant Worker's Directive 92/85/EC*. The former provision is a general prohibition of less favourable treatment on grounds of sex. The latter is a specific prohibition on dismissal of pregnant workers during the period from conception to the end of maternity leave, 'save in exceptional cases not connected with their condition, which are permitted under national legislation and/or practice'. The court held:

'Since the dismissal of a worker on account of pregnancy constitutes direct discrimination on grounds of sex whatever the nature and extent of the economic loss incurred by the employer as a result of her absence because of the pregnancy, whether the contract of employment was concluded for a fixed or an indefinite period has no bearing on the discriminatory character of the dismissal. In either case, the employee's inability to perform her contract of employment is due to pregnancy.'

The court pointed out that neither directive distinguishes between those employed on fixed terms and those employed pursuant to contracts of indefinite duration. The European Court of Justice gave further consideration to the *Pregnant Worker's Directive* in *Jimenez Melgar v Ayuntamiento de Los Barrios* [2004] ICR 610, ECJ. The court determined that:

(1)   The Directive has direct effect;

(2)   Where a member state wishes to enact legislation permitting dismissals in exceptional circumstances, it need not specify the particular grounds on which such workers may be dismissed; and

(3)   A refusal to renew a fixed-term contract is not a dismissal. However, such a refusal may breach the provisions of the *ETD 76/207/EEC*.

A common complaint made by employers is that an employee has 'deceived' them by not declaring that they are pregnant at a point at which an important decision is made. For example, in *Busch v Klinikum Neustadt GmbH & Co Betriebs-KG* C-320/01 [2003] IRLR 625, ECJ, an employee absent on parental leave applied to return early. Having been allowed to do so, she declared she was pregnant and sought to take maternity leave which would have been unavailable to her during a period of parental leave. The employers purported to rescind their consent to her return from parental leave. It was held that the employee was not obliged to declare her pregnancy and, in any event, the employer would not have been entitled to take her pregnancy into account even if she had told them about it. That being so, they had discriminated against her.

(3) *Unfavourable treatment for reasons relating to a maternity-related illness*

Cases where employees are treated less favourably as a result of their suffering maternity-related illnesses have proven to be a source of conceptual difficulty in what is an already very complex context. Almost invariably, the employer justifies the treatment on the basis that the illness has caused absence and that the absence, in turn, has had a deleterious effect on his business. Where, for instance, a man would have been dismissed for having been absent by reason of illness, should a woman be treated any differently merely because her illness is maternity-related? In *Hertz v Aldi Marked K/S* [1991] IRLR 31, [1992] ICR 332, the ECJ considered a case in which a woman was dismissed by reason of absences arising from a post-natal illness. The court decided that if her employer would have dismissed a male employee in comparable circumstances, there would be no discrimination on grounds of sex. In *Webb*, however, the court was careful to point out that in *Hertz* the illness had arisen only after the end of the period of maternity leave to which the woman had been entitled under domestic law. This idea that the period of maternity leave provided a special 'protected period' was developed further by the court in *Brown v Rentokil Ltd* [1998] IRLR 445.

The following principles are now established.

(a)   An employee may not be dismissed by reason of absence arising from a maternity-related illness at any point between conception and the end of her maternity leave period ('the protected period').

(b)   Where the maternity-related illness occurs after the end of the protected period, a dismissal will not be discriminatory if a man would have been dismissed had he been absent, because of illness, for a comparable period.

(c)   Where the illness arises during the protected period but persists thereafter, only days of absence which occur after the end of the protected period may be relied upon by an employer in deciding to dismiss (*William B Morrison & Son Ltd* (1999) 648 IDS Brief, EAT).

In a case decided before the ECJ's decision in *Brown*, the EAT went further still and held that a dismissal effected after the end of the protected period was contrary to *SDA 1975* if it was for a maternity-related illness that arose during the employee's period of maternity leave (*Caledonia Bureau Investment and Property v Caffrey* [1998] ICR 603).

(B)The Position after 1 October 2005

From 1 October 2005, the *SDA 1975* has been amended (by *SDR 2005, reg 4*) by addition of a new *s 3A*. The new provision is radically different in form if not effect to what went before.

(1)Discrimination on the ground of Pregnancy

The starting point is the concept of the 'protected period' (a concept ultimately derived from European Court jurisprudence – see e g *Brown v Rentokil* above). The 'protected period' relating to any particular pregnancy starts when the women becomes pregnant and ends in one of the following circumstances

(a)   if the woman is entitled to Ordinary Maternity Leave ('OML') **but not** Additional Maternity Leave ('AML') (for which see MATERNITY AND PARENTAL LEAVE (33)) either:

(i)   at the end of the period of OML connected with the pregnancy; or, if earlier

(ii)   when she returns to work after the end of her pregnancy;

(b)   if the woman is entitled to OML **and** AML either:

(i)   at the end of the period of AML connected with the pregnancy; or, if earlier

(ii)   when she returns to work after the end of her pregnancy; or

(c)   if she is not entitled to OML, at the end of a period of 2 weeks beginning with the end of her pregnancy.

(SDA 1975, s 3A (3)(a))

During the protected period a person must not treat a woman less favourably on the ground of her pregnancy than he would treat her had she not become pregnant (*SDA 1975, s 3A(1)(a)*). The historical difficulties associated with identifying a suitable male comparator are thus neatly avoided by requiring a comparison with a hypothetical version of the complainant. However, the neatness of the solution did not appeal to the Divisional Court in *Equal Opportunities Commission v Secretary of State for Trade and Industry* [2007] EWHC 483 (Admin), [2007] IRLR 327, which held that the statutory requirement for a comparator who is not pregnant or on maternity leave is incompatible with *ETD 2002/73/EC* and that the provision therefore requires re-drafting.

Discrimination on ground of pregnancy occurring outside the protected period may nevertheless qualify as discrimination on grounds of sex under the pre-existing regime as would discrimination on what might be called other pregnancy-related grounds such as dismissing a woman for having terminated her pregnancy. However, note that one form of 'pregnancy-related' ground; discrimination on grounds pregnancy-related illness, is treated as a form of discrimination on ground of pregnancy (*SDA 1975, s 3A (3)(b)*).

In *New Southern Railways Ltd v Quinn* [2006] IRLR 266, EAT, a case on the old provisions, an employer was found to have discriminated where it removed a pregnant employee from a trial position and returned her to her less senior and lower-paid position. The Tribunal was not prepared to treat the case as one of medical suspension.

(2)Discrimination on ground of Maternity Leave.

A person may not treat a woman less favourably on the ground that she 'is exercising or seeking to exercise, or has exercised or sought to exercise, a statutory right to maternity leave' (ie OML or AML)(*SDA 1975, s 3A (1)(b)*). As with discrimination on ground of pregnancy the complainant is her own comparator (but see *EOC v Secretary of State for Trade and Industry*, above). The tribunal should ask whether she would have been treated any differently had she not been exercising, seeking to exercise, exercised or sought to exercise a right to maternity leave. Where an employer discriminates against an employee because he believes that she wishes to start a family and anticipates that she may wish to take maternity leave in the future, his act is not, on the face of it, rendered unlawful by *SDA 1975, s 3A*. It is likely, however, that his act will nevertheless amount to an act of unlawful sex discrimination falling within *SDA 1975, s 1(2)(a)*. The same would likely be true of discrimination on ground of taking **contractual** maternity leave which is also not covered by *s 3A*.

The protection afforded by *SDA 1975, s 3A* is not limited to acts occurring within the protected period.

In addition to the rights to OML and AML (which are conferred by *ERA 1996, ss. 71(1)* and *73(1)* respectively) *ERA 1996, s 72(1)* creates a two week period of 'compulsory' maternity leave during which an employer must not permit an employee to work. It is unlawful for a person to treat a woman less favourably on ground that *ERA 1996, s 72(1)* has to be complied in respect of her than he would have treated her if that provision had not had to be complied with (*SDA 1975, s 3A(2)*).

In *Sarkatzis Herrero v Instituto Madrileño de la Salud* [2006] IRLR 296, C-294/04, the ECJ determined that an employer acts unlawfully where it counts continuous service only from the day on which an employee takes up her duties rather than on the date of her appointment where the reason for the delay was the taking of maternity leave.

(iii) Race Discrimination: Segregation

Segregating a person from others on racial grounds is treating him less favourably (*RRA 1976, s 1(2)*). Thus, it is not open to an employer to argue that the provision of segregated facilities for his black employees is not discriminatory even though the facilities provided for black workers are equal to, if not better than, those provided for his white employees.

(iv) Gender Reassignment: Absence due to undergoing a gender reassignment

There is specific provision to deal with how absence for the purpose of undergoing a gender reassignment is to be treated (*SDA 1975, s 2A(3)*). The employee must not be treated less favourably than someone who is absent through sickness or injury. There is an alternative catch-all provision which allows the tribunal to look at how people absent for reasons other than sickness or injury are (or would be) treated. If the tribunal thinks it is 'reasonable' that the employee should be treated no less favourably than those absent for a non-sickness reason, that may form the basis of a comparison upon which a finding of discrimination may be based.

(v) Gender Reassignment: Pre-operative transsexuals and toilet facilities

In the case of a pre-operative transsexual, avoiding less favourable treatment does not necessarily require that the complainant be treated as if their gender had already been changed. What is required in any case will depend on the particular circumstances (*Croft v Royal Mail Group plc* [2003] EWCA Civ 1045, [2003] IRLR 592: pre-operative male to female transsexual not treated less favourably when not allowed to use female toilets).

(vi) Positive discrimination

There is only a very limited role in UK law for so-called 'positive discrimination'. It involves treating one group of employees more favourably (and thus their colleagues less favourably) on a prohibited ground but for well-intentioned reasons. As explained below (see 12.6(a)), the UK law largely disregards such intentions and motives. Well-intentioned discrimination is still unlawful. However, the law does allow a limited scope for positive discrimination. The essence of exception is that, in certain defined circumstances, positive discrimination may be lawful where the purpose is to redress the effect of pre-existing discriminatory disadvantage. A full consideration of positive discrimination may be found at 13.19 DISCRIMINATION AND EQUAL OPPORTUNITIES – II below.

12.6   On the prohibited grounds

(a) General principles

It is not sufficient for a tribunal to be satisfied that a complainant has been less favourably treated than their chosen actual or hypothetical comparator. The tribunal will also want to consider *why* the complainant was less favourably treated. It is only if the reason for the less favourable treatment was a prohibited ground that liability will lie. Broadly, once less favourable treatment has been shown, it is for the employer to show that it was not on a prohibited ground.

Less favourable treatment will only amount to an act of racial discrimination where the complainant was less favourably treated 'on racial grounds' (*RRA 1976, s 1(1)(a)*). Other enactments adopt a similar formulation. In cases of sex discrimination less favourable treatment must be 'on ground of ... sex' (*SDA 1975, s 1(1)*), in religion or belief cases it must be 'on grounds of religion or belief' (*RBR 2003, reg 3(1)(a)*) and in cases of sexual orientation discrimination the treatment complained of should be 'on grounds of sexual orientation' (*SOR 2003, reg 3(1)(a)*).

The test for establishing whether or not someone has been treated less favourably is 'causal', ie one looks at what causes the less favourable treatment.

The question of causation is generally resolved in other areas of the law by reference to the so-called 'but for' test. One might ask, for instance, 'but for the complainant's sex would she have been less favourably treated?' If the answer is 'no', causation could then be said to have been made out. The 'but for' approach was adopted in *James v Eastleigh Borough Council* [1990] ICR 554, HL. In that case pensioners were entitled to use a swimming pool for free. As the state pension age was higher for men than for women, men were disadvantaged. The complainant was able to say that 'but for' his sex he would have had a lower pension age and have been able to use the swimming pool for free.

The advantage of the 'but for' test in *James* was that it meant that the complainant did not have to show any discriminatory intention or motive. However, in other cases appeal courts have preferred an approach which concentrates on what might be called 'reasons for action'. In *Martin v Lancehawk Ltd* (2004, 22 March, unreported), EAT the Appeal Tribunal considered a case where an employer dismissed a female employee when their affair concluded. It was argued that as the employer would not have slept with a man, it could be said that 'but for' the complainant's sex she would not have been dismissed. The EAT found that there had been no discrimination. They felt that the 'reason why' the complainant was dismissed was the end of the affair and not her sex. Her sex was a causally relevant but not causally determinative factor. The Appeal Tribunal also considered that the appropriate comparator was a homosexual lover and that such a lover would have been treated no differently. On that analysis the 'but for' test would not have been made out. However, the Appeal Tribunal went on, in any event, to reject the 'but for' test formulating instead a test based on 'the reason why' the employer has acted as he had, relying on dicta in chief *Constable of West Yorkshire Police v Khan* [2001] UKHL 48, [2001] IRLR 830 and *Shamoon* (above).

The best guidance is first to apply the 'but for' test and then to ask whether it can nevertheless be said that 'the reason why' the complainant was less favourably treated was a reason other than the prohibited ground, always bearing in mind that it is not necessary to take the still further step of showing a discriminatory 'motive' underpinning the discriminatory reason for action. This last point is dealt with immediately below.

Provided that the causal question points to unlawful discrimination, the Tribunal is not required to go on investigate the employer's motives or intention. Thus, unintentional direct discrimination is unlawful as are acts of direct discrimination performed for entirely non-discriminatory motives. On the other hand, the presence of a discriminatory motive or intention will plainly be compelling evidence pointing to a finding of unlawful discrimination (*Nagarajan v London Regional Transport* [2001] 1 AC 501 at 519).

Discrimination is on a prohibited ground if the substantial or effective, although not necessarily the sole or intended, reason for the discriminatory treatment was the prohibited ground (see *R v Commission for Racial Equality, ex p Westminster City Council* [1984] ICR 770; affd in part [1985] ICR 827 – a race case). In *Barton v Investec Henderson Crosthwaite Securities Ltd* [2003] ICR 1205, EAT, the Employment Appeal Tribunal went further in the context of sex discrimination holding that sex should not be 'any part of the reasons for the treatment in question' (approved by the Court of Appeal in *Igen v Wong* (above). Even so, it must be a significant factor in the sense of being more than trivial. See also *Villalba v Merrill Lynch & Co Inc* [2007] ICR 469, EAT).

(b) Meaning of 'on grounds of sex'

'Sex' is not defined in *SDA 1975*. 'Woman' and 'Man' are defined as being a female and male respectively of any age (*SDA 1975, s 5(3)*).

The *ETD 76/207/EEC* prohibits 'discrimination ... on grounds of sex either directly or indirectly by reference in particular to marital or family status'. It is not immediately clear why discriminating against a married person (of either sex) might be said to be discrimination on 'grounds of sex'. However, it is plain that the definition in the *ETD* is wide enough to cover it.

SDA 1975 makes separate provision for discrimination on grounds of marital status (see 12.6 (c) immediately below). It is unclear whether the words 'on the ground of her sex' in *SDA 1975, s 1(2)(a)* should be read as having the same broad meaning as the words 'on grounds of sex' have in the *ETD*. Strongly against such an interpretation is the fact that it would make the express prohibition against discrimination on grounds of marital status in *SDA 1975, s 3* nugatory. On the other hand, as from 1 October 2005, *SDA 1975* has included an express provision against harassment which only prohibits harassment 'on the ground of [the victim's] sex' (see *SDA 1975, s 4A(1)(a)* as added with effect from 1 October 2005 by *SDR 2005, reg 5*). Unless 'sex' is interpreted broadly enough to encompass discrimination on grounds of marital status, the changes introduced by *SDR 2005* will have had the unexpected and undesirable effect of making it lawful to harass someone on ground of their marital status. This effect is produced by *SDR 2005, reg 33* which amends the definition of 'detriment' in *SDA 1975, s 82(1)* so as to exclude harassment thereby making it impossible to argue that to harass a married person is to subject them to a detriment within the meaning of *SDA 1975, s 6(2)(b)* (that being how acts of harassment were previously brought within the scope of the Act).

Before the UK enacted specific protection for transsexuals, the European Court of Justice decided that discrimination against transsexuals was a form of sex discrimination. In *P v S and Cornwall County Council (Case C-13/94)* [1996] IRLR 347, the European Court adopted a broad test which rendered unlawful any discrimination based 'essentially if not exclusively on the sex of the person concerned'.

(c) Meaning of on ground of marital or civil partnership status

SDA 1975, s 3(1) prohibits less favourable treatment of married persons on 'the ground of [the complainant's] marital status'. The act does not define marriage. The provision has been amended by the *Civil Partnership Act 2004*. The new, somewhat lumpen, formulation makes it unlawful for a person to treat someone less favourably 'on the ground of the fulfilment of the condition [in subsection 3(2)]'. There are two conditions stipulated in *SDA 1975, s 3(2)*: that a person is married or that they are a 'civil partner'. A 'civil partner' is someone who has been registered as the civil partner of a person of the same sex (see *Civil Partnership Act 2004, s 1*).

For an example of direct discrimination on grounds of marital status see *Chief Constable of the Bedfordshire Constabulary v Graham* [2002] IRLR 239, EAT.

(d) Meaning of 'on racial grounds'

Meaning of 'racial grounds' and 'racial group'.

'Racial grounds' are defined in *RRA 1976, s 3(1)* as any of the following grounds: colour, race, nationality, or ethnic or national origins. A member of a particular race is referred to in the *Act* as belonging to a 'racial group'.

A distinction is drawn between racial origin and citizenship: *Ealing London Borough Council v Race Relations Board* [1972] AC 342; *Tejani v Superintendent Registrar for the District of Peterborough* [1986] IRLR 502.

The House of Lords in *Mandla v Dowell Lee* [1983] ICR 385 held that 'ethnic ... origins' in the definition of 'racial group' meant a group which was a segment of the population distinguished from others by a sufficient combination of shared customs, beliefs, traditions and characteristics derived from a common or pre-sumed common past, even if not drawn from what in biological terms was a common racial stock. On that basis, it held that Sikhs were a racial group entitled to the protection of the *RRA 1976*.

'National origins' means more than the legal nationality acquired at birth (*BBC Scotland v Souster* above). One may 'acquire' national origins by adherence.

Jews are members of a racial group (see, for example, *Seide v Gillette Industries* [1980] IRLR 427). So are gypsies in the sense of those who belong to the Romany race, although mere habitual wanderers are not (*Commission for Racial Equality v Dutton* [1989] IRLR 8). Rastafarians are not an ethnic group (*Crown Suppliers (PSA) v Dawkins* [1993] ICR 517). The Scots and the English are separate racial groups (*Northern Joint Police Board v Power* [1997] IRLR 610, EAT and *BBC Scotland v Souster* [2001] IRLR 150, Ct Sess).

Examples from authority.

In *Bradford Hospitals NHS Trust v Al-Shabib* [2003] IRLR 4, EAT, the tribunal decided that a grievance panel had treated the complainant less favourably on racial grounds when they formed an adverse impression of him as a result of his being 'difficult to control' and 'emotive'. The tribunal found that the respondent had erred by failing to take into account that, as an Iraqi, the complainant could not be expected to behave in a 'conventional Anglo-Saxon way'. However, the EAT found that it was not open to the tribunal to assume, in the absence of evidence, that there was a material difference in the manner in which 'Anglo-Saxons' and Iraqis might behave.

In *Simon v Brimham Associates* [1987] ICR 596, the Court of Appeal reached the somewhat surprising conclusion that an employment tribunal was entitled to find that a Jew who had withdrawn a job application when he learned that to be Jewish might preclude his selection was not discriminated against in circumstances in which the interviewer had merely asked him the same question about his religion as he would have asked any candidate, not knowing whether or not he was Jewish.

Where an employee was dismissed for fighting, he was not dismissed on racial grounds merely because his employer applied a policy of not taking into account acts of provocation and thus ignored the fact that he had been provoked by acts of racial abuse and violence. The policy was applied consistently to employees of all races: *Sidhu v Aerospace Composite Technology Ltd* [2001] ICR 167, CA.

The relevant race need not be the race of the employee that is the victim of the discrimination. For instance, in *Showboat Entertainment Centre v Owens* [1984] IRLR 7, EAT a white employee was dismissed for refusing to carry out a discriminatory instruction.

In *Redfearn v Serco Ltd* [2006] EWCA Civ 659, [2006] ICR 1367, the Court of Appeal refused to extend the approach taken in *Showboat* to a case in which a white bus driver whose passengers and colleagues were mainly Asian was dismissed, in essence, for being a member of the British National Party. It is a condition of membership of that party that one should be white. The employee contended that the race of his passengers and colleagues had substantially contributed to the decision to dismiss him. The Court of Appeal distinguished *Showboat* on the basis that whilst it was within the policy of *RRA 1976* that those affected by an employer's racist policies should be protected, it did not follow that racists should be protected from the anti-discriminatory policies of their employers.

(*e*) *Meaning of 'on ground of Gender Reassignment'*

Transsexual persons are protected where they intend to undergo, are undergoing or have undergone a gender reassignment (*SDA 1975, s 2A(1)*). Gender reassignment is defined by *SDA 1975, s 82* as:

'... a process which is undertaken under medical supervision for the purpose of reassigning a person's sex by changing physiological or other characteristics of sex and includes any part of such process.'

In *Ashton v Chief Constable of West Mercia Constabulary* [2001] ICR 67, EAT considered a case concerning a transsexual undergoing a gender reassignment. As part of her treatment she received medication, which caused her to be depressed. Her depression affected her ability to work and she was dismissed on grounds of incapability. The EAT upheld the tribunal's finding that the fact that the incapability was a result of the side-effects of her medication did not establish a *causal* link between the dismissal and her sex for the purposes of the *SDA 1975, s 1(1)* and thus that she had not been unlawfully discriminated against.

In *A v Chief Constable of the West Yorkshire Police* [2002] EWCA Civ 1584, [2003] ICR 161, the Court of Appeal considered that, for the purposes of employment law, post-operative transsexuals fall to be treated for all purposes as having their re-assigned sex. Thus a post-operative male to female transsexual is to be treated as a woman rather than as a transsexual. Their Lordships reasoning was as follows: Post-operative male to female transsexuals are to be treated as women for the purposes of the European Convention on Human Rights (see *Goodwin v United Kingdom* (2002) 35 EHRR 447). The *ETD 76/207/EEC* must be interpreted, so far as possible, as being compatible with the *ECHR*. *SDA 1975*, in turn, has to be interpreted, where possible, as being consistent with the *ETD 76/207/EEC*. However, the *Goodwin* case recognised that a departure from the normal rule may be required where 'significant factors of public interest ... weigh against the interests of the individual applicant in obtaining legal recognition of her gender reassignment'. The decision was affirmed by the House of Lords ([2004] UKHL 21, [2004] ICR 806).

(*f*) *Meaning of 'on ground of Religion or Belief'*

RBR 2003 protects both adherents to a religion and those who do not have a religion; those who hold a particular religious or philosophical belief and those who do not.

(i) Meaning of 'religion'

For the purposes of the *RBR 2003*, 'religion' is defined to mean 'any religion' (*RBR reg 2(1)(a)* as amended by *Equality Act 2006* ('*EA 2006*') *s 77(2)* with effect from 30 April 2007). A reference to religion in *RBR 2003* is also to be taken to encompass 'lack of religion' (*RBR 2003, reg 2(1)(c)* as amended by *EA 2006*, *s 77(2)* with effect from 30 April 2007) with the effect that an employer is no more free to discriminate against atheists than he is against Christians.

No more detailed definition is given in *RBR 2003*. This represents, it would appear, a deliberate decision on the part of the Government. The Government assumes that controversy about the scope of the definition will be rare and that in controversial cases it is best left to the courts and the tribunals to resolve the matter without further guidance.

It is tempting to suppose that it is the difficulty of defining 'religion' rather than the ease of doing so which has led the Government to avoid offering a more specific definition. The ACAS guidelines do not take matters very much further. The guidelines state that the tribunal is likely to 'consider things such as collective worship, a clear belief system and a profound belief affecting the way of life or view of the world'.

Although not a matter which the ACAS guidelines touch upon, it is suggested that a religion will be concerned with the supernatural and, in particular, is likely to be theistic, ie it will be a belief about a god or gods.

The present context is not the only one in which this difficult definitional question has been faced and some assistance can be gained from consideration of those other contexts.

One context in which the issue has arisen is the law pertaining to charities. The advancement of religion is recognised as a charitable purpose (see *Income Tax Special Purposes Comr v Pemsel* [1891] AC 531). In their decision of 17 November 1999 in relation to an application for charitable status made by the Church of Scientology, the Charity Commissioners reviewed the existing case law on the definition of religion and derived the following characteristics:

(1)   a belief in a god, deity or supreme being (*R v Registrar General, ex p Sergedal* [1970] 2 QB 697 – though Buddhism qualified as a religion despite there being some doubt as to whether it required a belief in a supreme being);

(2)   reverence and recognition of the dominant power and control of any entity or being outside their own body and life (*Sergedal* above); and

(3)   faith and worship: faith in a god and worship of that god (*South Place Ethical Society* [1980] 1 WLR 1565).

The Commissioners identified a further significant factor, absent from the *RBR 2003*; whilst the court will not consider the truth of the tenets of the relevant religion it will not treat as a religion everything which calls itself a religion. It seems likely that the tribunal will adopt a similar approach. Because Charity Law is concerned with the 'advancement of religion', if the court is satisfied that the tenets of a particular sect 'inculcate doctrines adverse to very foundations of all religion and/or subversive of all morality' it will not be treated as 'advancing religion'. The *RBR 2003* cover all religions whether or not they espouse morally repellent precepts. This is likely to lead to problems in which religious precepts conflict with the interests of other protected groups.

Another context in which the definition of religion arises as an issue is the *European Convention on Human Rights*. This second context has a more direct relevance because the *RBR 2003* implement a European Directive and European legislation has to be interpreted, wherever possible, so as to be compatible with the *European Convention on Human Rights. ECHR, art 9(1)* provides that 'everyone has the right to freedom of thought, conscience and religion'. The right also includes 'freedom to change ... religion or belief ... and freedom, either alone or in community with others and in public or in private, to manifest [one's] religion or belief, in worship, teaching, practice and observance'. However, whilst it might be hoped that a developed body of authority of the European Court of Justice would be available to assist in interpreting the scope of the words 'religion or belief', in fact there is remarkably little helpful case law. The Commission has assumed that Scientology is a religion (*X and Church of Scientology v Sweden* (1979) 16 DR 68) whereas the UK courts have consistently declined to confer that status upon them (though they would probably amount to a 'similar philosophical belief'). The court decided that 'Wicca' was not a religion on the ground that it had no clear structure or belief systems (*X v United Kingdom* (1977) 11 DR 55) (but note Wicca appears as an example of a religion in the *ACAS Code*).

(ii) Meaning of 'religious belief'

Belief is defined to mean 'any religious or philosophical belief' (*RBR 2003, reg 2(1)(b)* as amended, with effect from 30 April 2007 by *EA 2006, s 77(2)*). The *Regulations* distinguish, therefore, between religion and religious belief. The distinction arises from the fact that religious beliefs are not exclusively about a god or gods. Most religions profoundly affect what the *ACAS Code* describes as one's 'world view'. In other words, religious adherence affects what one believes about the world as well as what one believes about the supernatural (but see *R (on the application of Williamson) v Secretary of State for Education and Employment* [2001] EWHC Admin 960, [2002] ELR 214 where Elias J opined that a religious belief, for the purposes of the *ECHR* was not simply a belief which is 'in accordance with the religious faith' but which 'embod(ied) or define(d)' the belief or conviction itself).

The distinction is best illustrated by an example. Paragraph 2357 of Roman Catholic Catechism states that 'basing itself on Sacred Scripture, which presents homosexual acts as acts of grave depravity, tradition has always declared that homosexual acts are intrinsically disordered'. In 2003, the Roman Catholic Sacred Congregation for the Doctrine for the Faith published a document entitled 'Considerations regarding proposals to give legal recognition to unions between Homosexual Persons' at *para 5* of which it is proposed that 'allowing children to be adopted by persons living in such unions would actually mean doing violence to these children, in the sense that their condition of dependency would be used to place them in an environment that is not conducive to their full human development'. A Roman Catholic social worker refuses to co-operate with the placing of children for adoption by same-sex couples and is disciplined. In those circumstances, it is not the employee's religion that is at issue, but a belief which her church requires her to adopt about the world. In such circumstances, the employee may have been treated less favourably because of her religious belief.

(iii) Meaning of 'philosophical belief'

RBR 2003, reg 2(1) formerly protected those who held philosophical beliefs which could be said to be 'similar' to religious beliefs. The question how one identified a 'philosophical belief' which was sufficiently 'similar' to a religious belief as to fall within the scope of the legislation was harder to answer the more closely it was considered. Perhaps the defining characteristic of a religious belief is its theistic nature; it is a belief in a god or gods. If the belief is theistic it is a religious belief. If it is not it is difficult to see how it could be said to be in any way 'similar' because the defining characteristic is absent.

An alternative approach was to assume that the similarity with which the legislation is concerned arises not from the essence of the belief but rather its ancillary characteristics. This would seem to be the approach adopted in the *ACAS Code* which stresses the likely importance of there being a 'clear belief system' and the belief being one which is 'profound' and which affects the adherent's 'way of life or view of the world'. The *ACAS Code* offers Humanism as an example of the sort of belief that might qualify. Other examples would include Confucianism and some commentators have even suggested that Vegetarianism might qualify.

With effect from 30 April 2007, *RBR 2003, reg 2(1)* was amended (by *EA 2996, s 77(2)*). The requirement that the philosophical belief be 'similar' to a religious belief has now been removed. Holding a particular philosophical belief (or equally, not holding it) will now suffice. The logical consequence of the amendment must be that holding a belief that is philosophical but not similar to religious beliefs will now qualify for protection. However, it can scarcely be said that scope of protection has become any easier to define.

Guidance issued by the Department for Communities and Local Government on the implementation of *EA 2006* echoes the *ACAS Code* in identifying Humanism as an example of a philosophical belief that will qualify. It goes on to say that 'other philosophical beliefs similar to a religion' will also suffice, thereby apparently re-emphasising the notion of similarity to religious belief that has been specifically removed from the legislation.

The absence of a more helpful definition is likely to be problematic in two specific types of cases. The first concerns beliefs that might be classified as relating to moral philosophy or ethics. If a nurse refuses to perform abortions because she considers it to amount to the taking of a human life, would she be protected? Her belief would certainly be a philosophical one. A nurse who refused to perform abortions because of a religious belief could expect to be protected and it is difficult to see why someone who holds the same belief but on a philosophical rather than a religious foundation should expect any less. Once one admits ethical beliefs as protected beliefs a question arises as to whether all ethical beliefs are admitted or only some of them. What, for instance, of an employee that refuses to work with gay colleagues because he considers their sexuality to be 'immoral'? If the legislation does not intend to encompass all philosophical beliefs, it has provided no criterion with which to distinguish between those it wishes to protect and those it does not.

The second type of case which is likely to cause difficulties is political beliefs. The Bristol Employment Tribunal decided in *Baggs v Fudge* (Case No 1400114/05) that the political beliefs of members of the British National Party were not 'similar' to religious beliefs and the guidance issued by the DCLG specifically assumes that political beliefs will continue to be excluded. Despite the apparent confidence of the guidance, it is difficult, however, to see why that distinction should necessarily survive the removal of the requirement that the belief should be 'similar' to a religious belief. Many political beliefs, to adopt the language of the *ACAS Code*, can be 'profound' and can affect an adherent's way of life or view of the world. In fact, applying such a test has the effect that the more extreme the belief the more likely it is to qualify. It follows that, until matters are further clarified by authority, employers would be well-advised to tread with care when dismissing for reasons of political philosophy.

(g) *Meaning of on grounds of Sexual Orientation*

Sexual orientation is defined by *reg 2* as a sexual orientation towards:

(*a*)   persons of the same sex (ie lesbians and gay men);

(*b*)   persons of the opposite sex (ie heterosexual people); or

(*c*)   persons of the same sex and of the opposite sex (ie bisexual people).

No definition is given of 'sexual orientation' *per se*. The *Oxford English Dictionary* defines 'orientation' as 'the state of being oriented', 'a person's attitude or adjustment in relation to circumstances'. It follows that there is no requirement that a person be sexually active in order to be regarded as being of a particular sexual orientation.

The *SOR 2003* do not cover asexuals or sexual orientation towards anything other than persons (eg bestiality), nor do they cover (regardless of orientation) sexual conduct or particular sexual preferences (eg sadomasochism, paedophilia, etc) or the absence of such (eg celibacy).

Before the enactment of the *SOR 2003* there were a number of attempts made to establish that sexual orientation discrimination was a species of sex discrimination. However, the House of Lords ultimately determined that it is not an act of sex discrimination contrary to *SDA 1975* to treat an employee less favourably on grounds of their sexual orientation (*MacDonald v Advocate General for Scotland* [2003] UKHL 34, [2003] ICR 937).

However, if an employer were to treat gay men less favourably than lesbian women (or vice versa), that would constitute a breach of *SDA 1975* on ordinary principles.

Further, those employed by the State are able to argue that dismissal on grounds of sexual orientation may constitute a breach of their right to respect for their private lives under *art 8* of the *European Convention on Human Rights* (*Smith v United Kingdom* [1999] IRLR 734, ECtHR).

(*h*) *Meaning of on grounds of pregnancy or maternity leave*

(i) Meaning of 'pregnancy'

For the purposes of *SDA 1975, s 3A* the definition of 'pregnancy' is enlarged to include 'illness suffered by the woman as a consequence of a pregnancy of hers' (*SDA 1975, s 3A(3)(b)*). Thus, discrimination on ground of such an illness is treated as discrimination on grounds of pregnancy.

(ii) Meaning of 'Maternity Leave'

SDA 1975, s 3A(1) only prohibits discrimination on grounds of statutory maternity leave (as opposed to contractual maternity leave which may nevertheless be protected under *SDA 1975, s 1(2)(a)*). The term 'statutory right to maternity leave' is defined by *SDA 1975, s 3A (3)(c)* to mean 'a right conferred by *s 71(1)* or *73(1)* of the Employment Rights Act (ordinary and additional maternity leave)' (for which MATERNITY AND PARENTAL RIGHTS (33)).

SDA 1975, s 3A(2) additionally prohibits discrimination on the ground that *ERA 1996, s 72(1)* had to be complied with in respect of the woman. That provision creates a two week period of compulsory maternity leave during which it is an offence for an employer to allow a woman to work (see MATERNITY AND PARENTAL RIGHTS (33)).

(i) Cases where the member of the protected category is a third party

Most claims will be brought by people who are members of the relevant protected group. Thus, in most race discrimination cases, the complainant will be alleging that they have been less favourably treated on grounds of their own race. However, *RRA 1976,* uses the phrase 'on racial grounds' rather than 'on grounds of [the complainant's] race'. It follows that an employee may be discriminated against on racial grounds whether the racial characteristics in question are those of some other person. The only question in each case is whether the unfavourable treatment afforded to the claimant was caused by racial considerations (see *Showboat Entertainment Centre Ltd v Owens* [1984] ICR 65 at 71H, in which a white manager of an entertainment centre was dismissed for refusing to obey an instruction to exclude all black customers; *Weathersfield Ltd (t/a Van and Truck Rentals) v Sargent* [1999] ICR 425, CA, where an employee resigned rather than comply with the employer's policy of not hiring vehicles to members of ethnic minorities; and *Zarczynska v Levy* [1979] ICR 184).

RBR 2003, reg 3(1)(a) provides expressly that the less favourable treatment has to be on grounds of the religion or belief of someone other than the *respondent* . It does not, however, has to be the religion or belief of the *complainant* that founds the complaint. Less favourable treatment on the grounds of the religion or belief of any person other than the respondent will do. Thus, if an employee is treated less favourably when he intervenes on behalf of harassed adherents of a particular religion there will be an act of discrimination.

The *SOR 2003* protect employees from less favourable treatment 'on grounds of sexual orientation' (*reg 3(1)*). This reflects the wider formula found in *RRA 1976* and it is likely that the principles established in the *Showboat* case would apply by analogy.

By contrast *SDA 1975, s 1(2)(a)* only protects an employee against less favourable treatment 'on ground of her sex'. Similarly, a married person is only protected against discrimination on ground of 'his or her marital status' (*SDA 1975, s 3 (1)(a)*). The protection for transsexual person is similarly limited to cases where the ground for the less favourable treatment is their own gender reassignment (*SDA 1975, s 2A(1)*).

12.7 Indirect Discrimination

The concept of indirect discrimination has always been easier to define than to apply in practice. In essence, it is concerned with cases where employers treat all of their employees in the same way but there is a disparity in the effect of that treatment. For instance, to insist that all of one's employees are at least 6 foot tall will exclude more women than men from employment. Similarly, to require one's employees to work Saturday shifts will have a different effect on Christian employees to the effect that it would have on Jewish employees.

The dividing line between direct and indirect discrimination is not always an easy one to draw but the two forms of discrimination are distinct statutory torts and the distinction makes a material difference, particularly because a defence of justification is available in cases of indirect but not direct discrimination (*R v Secretary of State for Defence* [2006] EWCA Civ 1293, [2006] IRLR 934; For an account of the justification defence see 13.8 DISCRIMINATION AND EQUAL OPPORTUNITIES – II). To have a rule which requires that job applicants be white would plainly fall into the former category. An apparently neutral requirement, such as insisting that job applicants be graduates, may have an indirectly discriminatory effect because members of particular ethnic minorities are under-represented in tertiary education. It may be that the same broad set of facts may give rise both to a claim for direct and indirect discrimination. Thus, if a set of job requirements is indirectly discriminatory and, in addition, the interviewer favours members of one race over another, both claims may lie. However, in such a case the complainant will rely on different facts to make out each claim. A particular set of facts should normally (although not invariably) found one or other, but not both, sorts of claim (see *Jaffrey v Department of Environment Transport and the Regions* [2002] IRLR 688, EAT).

In the case of sex discrimination there are two potentially applicable definitions of indirect discrimination. The first applies to cases of indirect discrimination occurring prior to 1 October 2005 and was introduced by amendment to the *SDA 1975* made, with effect from 12 October 2001, by *SI 2001/2660*. The second applies to acts of indirect discrimination occurring on or after 1 October 2005 and was introduced by amendment to the *SDA 1975* by *SDR 2005, reg 3*.

The position in relation to *RRA 1976* is, unhelpfully, also somewhat complicated. 'Race' for the purposes of *RRA 1976* encompasses: colour, race, nationality, or ethnic or national origins. As from 19 July 2003 the *Race Relations Act 1976 (Amendment) Regulations 2003 (SI 2003/1626)* amended *RRA 1976* to provide a new test of indirect discrimination implementing the *Race Discrimination Framework Directive*. However, that new test (*RRA 1976, s 1(1A)*) only covers cases where the indirect discrimination is on grounds of 'race, ethnic or national origins'. It excludes, therefore, 'colour' and 'nationality'. In this it reflects the scope of the Directive but, bafflingly, means that there are two potentially applicable tests. The old test (*RRA 1976, s 1(1)(b)*) continues to apply where the new test does not (*RRA 1976, s 1(1)(c)*). In practice, it is difficult to envisage a case of indirect discrimination in which an employee is disadvantaged because of their colour which will not equally comfortably be analysable as a form of discrimination on grounds of 'race'. It follows that the old test's scope of application will be limited to cases concerned with nationality.

The tests, which are described below, may be found in the relevant legislation as follows:

Sex	*SDA 1975, s 1(2)(b)*
Marital and Civil Partnership Status	*SDA 1975, s 3(1)(b)*
Race	*RRA 1976, s 1(1A)* (with effect from 9 July 2003) and *s 1(1)(b)*
Gender Reassignment	No protection from indirect discrimination.
Religion or Belief	*RBR 2003, reg 3(1)(b)*
Sexual Orientation	*SOR 2003, reg 3(1)(b)*

The various tests have different formulations but achieve the same result.

The test: Sex Discrimination

(a) Cases before 1 October 2005

A person discriminates against a woman if he applies to her a 'provision, criterion or practice which he applies or would apply equally to a man but:

(1)   which is such that it would be to the detriment of a considerably larger proportion of women than of men;

(2)   which he cannot show to be justifiable irrespective of the sex of the person to whom it is applied; and

(3)   which is to her detriment.'

(b) Cases after 1 October 2005

A person discriminates against a woman if he applies to her a 'provision, criterion or practice' which he applies or would apply equally to a man but:

(1)   which puts or would put women at a particular disadvantage when compared with men,

(2)   which puts her at that disadvantage, and

(3)   which he cannot show to be a proportionate means of achieving a legitimate aim.

The test: Marital and Civil Partnership Status

The formulation is the same as that for sex discrimination save that the references to men are replaced with references to unmarried persons and the references to women to married persons.

The test has been amended with effect from 5 December 2005 by the *Civil Partnership Act 2004, s 251(1), (2)* so as include civil partners.

The test: Racial Discrimination

The test applicable in cases of 'nationality' and 'colour'

RRA 1976 provides that a person discriminates indirectly if he applies to one person a requirement or condition which he applies or would apply equally to persons not of the same racial group as that person but:

(1)   which is such that the proportion of persons in that racial group who can comply with it is considerably smaller than the proportion of persons not of that racial group who can comply with it; and

(2)   which he cannot show to be justifiable irrespective of the colour, race, nationality or ethnic or national origins of the person to whom it is applied; and

(3)   which is to the detriment of that other person because he cannot comply with it.

(*RRA 1976, s 1(1)(b)*.)

The test applicable in all other cases.

A person discriminates against another if he applies to that other a provision, criterion or practice which he applies or would apply equally to persons not of the same race or ethnic or national origins as that other, but:

(1)   which puts or would put persons of the same race or ethnic or national origins as that other at a particular disadvantage when compared with other persons;

(2)   which puts that other at that disadvantage; and

(3)   which he cannot show to be a proportionate means of achieving a legitimate aim.

12.8 Discrimination and Equal Opportunities – I

The test: Religion or Belief

A person ('A') discriminates against another person ('B') if A applies to B a provision, criterion or practice which he applies or would apply equally to persons not of the same religion or belief as B, but:

(*a*)   which puts or would put persons of the same religion or belief as B at a particular disadvantage when compared with other persons;

(*b*)   which puts B at that disadvantage; and

(*c*)   which A cannot show to be a proportionate means of achieving a legitimate aim.

(*Reg 3(1)(b)*.)

The comparison described at (a) above should be 'such that the relevant circumstances in the one case are the same, or not materially different, in the other' (*reg 3(3)*).

The test: Sexual Orientation

The test is the same as that for religion or belief (for which see immediately above) save that references to persons of the same religion or belief are replaced by references to people of the same sexual orientation.

12.8   Indirect Discrimination: Applying the test

(*a*) *The discriminatory measure*

With a single exception, the statutory tests each focus on a 'provision, criterion or practice' applied by the employer. These terms are not defined in the legislation itself.

The term 'provision' would be apt to include both contractual provisions and the provisions of non-contractual policies. It should be borne in mind that in cases of sex discrimination, unlawful discrimination in relation to contractual terms is combated by means of a separate legislative regime known, misleadingly, as 'Equal Pay' (see EQUAL PAY (24)). The term 'equal pay' is misleading because all discriminatory differences in contractual terms fall within the scope of that protective regime whether or not they are, strictly speaking, to do with pay. A provision may consist of a 'one-off decision' (*Starmer v British Airways plc* [2005] IRLR 862, EAT: decision not to allow an employee to reduce her work to 50% of normal hours constituted the application of a 'provision').

'Criterion' is self-explanatory and significant as many cases involving discrimination will be concerned with selection decisions whether for appointment, promotion or dismissal. There is no requirement (as there had been under the old sex and racial discrimination tests) for the discriminatory criterion to be an absolute bar to the member of the protected class. Thus a criterion that an applicant for a post should have English as a first language will be struck down if it disadvantages an employee of a particular race even if it appears on a list of desirable rather than required characteristics.

'Practice' naturally bears the widest of meanings. It enables the Tribunal to look past an employer's Human Resources policies and to look at the day to day experience of the employees.

In cases concerned with indirect racial discrimination on grounds of colour or nationality the complainant must establish that the employer applied a 'requirement or condition' to him. In order to constitute a 'requirement or condition' for the purposes of *RRA 1976*, the relevant provision must be mandatory so that failure to comply with it is either a complete bar to the complainant obtaining the desired benefit, or else makes it certain that he will suffer the disbenefit he had wished to avoid. Thus, in *Perera v Civil Service Commission* [1983] ICR 428, CA, although the selection criteria for applicants for the post of administrative trainee included a number which were to the disadvantage of members of ethnic minorities (including, for instance, 'experience in the UK' and 'ability to communicate in English'), Mr Perera's claim failed because he was unable to show that the apparently discriminatory criteria, taken together, constituted an 'absolute bar' to his becoming employed as a legal assistant. This principle was applied in *Meer v Tower Hamlets London Borough Council* [1988] IRLR 399, with the result that one criterion among several used in shortlisting for a job could not be relied upon to found a successful claim. However, the application of the *Act* is not avoided merely by describing a qualification as 'desirable' where, in fact, it is clear that it is a decisive factor in the selection process. In such a case, the qualification is classified as a 'requirement or condition' of the post and so could, therefore, be discriminatory (*Falkirk Council v Whyte* [1997] IRLR 560, EAT, Scotland). In some cases, the relevant requirement or condition may be expressly defined by the employer. In other cases, the tribunal may need to formulate a requirement or condition by analysing the employer's practice or behaviour. There may be a number of different formulations which are consistent with the underlying circumstances of the case. If a complainant can 'realistically identify a requirement or condition capable of supporting [their] case ... it is nothing to the point that [their] employer can with equal cogency derive from the facts a different and unobjectionable requirement or condition' (*Allonby v Accrington and Rossendale College* [2001] EWCA Civ 529, [2001] IRLR 364, CA).

(b) Disparity of Effect

At the heart of indirect discrimination is the notion that a single measure taken by an employer may affect different groups of employees very differently.

In cases of indirect discrimination on grounds of religion or belief, sexual orientation, race and national or ethnic origins, pregnancy or maternity leave, and, as from 1 October 2005, sex and marital status, the complainant must show that the provision, criterion or practice, puts persons of the same religion, belief, etc as the complainant at a 'particular disadvantage'. This term is not defined in the regulations. It is unclear whether the use of the word 'particular' is intended to convey something more than mere disadvantage. It is thought likely that it is intended to indicate a requirement for a disadvantage which is substantial and not merely trivial or theoretical.

Sex and Marital Status – the position prior to 1 October 2005

In case of discrimination on grounds of sex and marital status, the complainant must show that the provision, criterion or practice would be to the 'detriment of a considerably larger proportion of [women or married persons] than [men or unmarried persons]' (*SDA 1975, s 1(2)(b)*. This version of the test was introduced with effect from 12 October 2001 by the *Sex Discrimination (Indirect Discrimination and Burden of Proof) Regulations 2001 (SI 2001/2660), reg 3*). The test requires detriment rather than disadvantage (though in practice they will bear very similar meanings) but also that a 'considerably larger proportion' of the protected group be affected. This same threshold applied under the pre-2001 test and authorities on the meaning of 'considerably larger proportion', decided under the former provisions will continue to be useful. In approaching those authorities it must be recalled that whilst they talk of 'requirements' and 'conditions', the legislation is now concerned with provisions, criteria and practices. In the account below, the cases were all concerned with conditions and/or requirements. In summarising the cases the new formulation is used instead where appropriate.

Assessing disparity of impact is a comparative process. Whereas, in a case of direct discrimination, one compares the treatment received by an individual with that received or which would have been received by another, indirect discrimination cases require comparisons between groups of employees. Taking, by way of example, a case of indirect sex discrimination, the Tribunal looks at the impact of the relevant provision, criterion or practice on the men and women affected by it. The first task of the Tribunal is to determine which group or groups of employees it is going to look at in order to perform the comparison. This is known as selecting the 'pool' for comparison. The task of identifying the relevant pool can be difficult and is often, in practice, determinative of the case.

Because it may be possible in a particular case, to identify more than one potentially appropriate pool, the selection of the pool is, in the first instance, a matter for the claimant. However, the tribunal is not necessarily bound to adopt the pool suggested by the claimant and it may reject the claimant's pool where it considers that it is an artificial or arbitrary one (*Abbott v Cheshire and Wirral Partnership NHS Trust* [2006] EWCA Civ 523, [2006] ICR 1267). If the Tribunal determines to reject the claimant's proposed pool, it should explain its reasons for doing so in its decision (*Secretary of State v Rutherford (No 2)* at the EAT, reported at [2005] ICR 119 at 160). Once the Tribunal has resolved to determine the pool for itself, it does not have a broad discretion as to how the pool is identified. In most cases, the Court of Appeal suggested in *Allonby* ([2001] IRLR 364, CA), it should be a matter of logical deduction from the measure (ie the relevant provision, criterion or practice). The starting point, however, should be the whole of the group to which the provision, criterion or practice is applied, and the tribunal will be wary of any further sub-division (cf *London Underground Ltd v Edwards* [1995] IRLR 355, *Jones v University of Manchester* [1993] ICR 474, CA and *Rutherford v Secretary of State for Trade and Industry* [2006] UKHL 19, [2006] ICR 785 – provisions precluding claims for redundancy payments and unfair dismissal by those over 65 applied to the whole working population and not just those older employees for whom the 'retirement had some meaning'). Equally, an expansion of the pool to include those who were not even potentially subject to the provision, criterion or practice, would be inappropriate (cf *Briggs v North Eastern Education and Library Board* [1990] IRLR 181). However, where the provision, criterion or practice relates to recruitment criteria the relevant pool might be very large and in *Greater Manchester Police Authority v Lea* [1990] IRLR 372, the EAT held that the employment tribunal had not erred in accepting that the economically active population was an appropriate pool for the purpose of determining the proportion of men and women who could comply with a condition of not being in receipt of an occupational pension. In *Lord Chancellor v Coker* [2001] IRLR 116, the EAT considered a case where the Lord Chancellor had decided to appoint a particular individual to be his special adviser. The appointment was challenged by two complainants who alleged that the failure publicly to advertise the position had resulted in their having been the subjects of acts of indirect sex and race discrimination, respectively. As the criterion was, in effect, that the candidate should be the relevant specific individual, the EAT concluded that no pool could sensibly be identified. The EAT's decision was upheld by the Court of Appeal ([2001] EWCA Civ 1756, [2002] ICR 321). The relevant criterion was identified before their Lordships as being a friend of the Lord Chancellor. The Court of Appeal concluded that the necessary disparity of impact could not be established. Looking at the pool of those qualified to perform the role, the criterion excluded almost the entirety of its members. The criterion could only be said to have a disproportionate effect where a significant proportion of the pool were able to satisfy it. That was not the case on the facts. Lord Phillips went on to opine that:

'Making an appointment from within a circle of family, friends and personal acquaintances is seldom likely to constitute indirect discrimination.'

Once the appropriate pool had been identified, one had then to consider whether the provision, criterion or practice has a disparate impact. What constitutes a 'considerably smaller' proportion was not further explained in the legislation.

There has been little guidance on how one determines whether a particular disparate impact is sufficient. The issue was referred to the European Court of Justice in *R v Secretary of State for Employment, ex p Seymour-Smith* [1999] ICR 447. The guidance provided by the ECJ was disappointingly vague. The ECJ decision echoed the language of *SDA 1975* in requiring that a 'considerably smaller percentage' of women than men were able to satisfy the relevant condition. A mere statistically significant disparity was insufficient. However, the ECJ went on to hold that a 'lesser but persistent and relatively constant disparity over a long period' might suffice. It was hoped that the House of Lords might feel able to put a little meat on these bones when the matter came back for their further consideration in the light of the reference ([2000] ICR 244). The issue in *Seymour-Smith* was whether the requirement, introduced in 1985, that employees should have two years' continuous service before qualifying for protection against unfair dismissal indirectly discriminated against women. In 1985, 77.4% of men could comply with that requirement whereas only 68.9% of women could do so. In 1991, the year which their Lordships identified as being the critical one for the purposes of the particular case, the relevant percentages were 74.5% and 67.4%. None of their Lordships thought that those figures, on their own, suggested that a 'considerably smaller percentage' of women could comply. However, the majority felt that the disparity (which narrowed slowly to about 4.3% by 1993) fell into the category of the sort of 'persistent and relatively consistent' disparity that the ECJ had indicated might suffice. They determined, therefore, that the requirement was indirectly discriminatory although they went on to find that it was justified.

In practice, the tribunals are given a considerable margin of discretion in deciding when the percentages should be taken to indicate a sufficiently significant disparity. The courts had consistently rejected the adoption of a rule of thumb (see *McCausland v Dungannon District Council* [1993] IRLR 583 which was concerned with the construction of the *Fair Employment (Northern Ireland) Act 1976* which applies the same test of disparate impact to religious discrimination). In *Harvest Town Circle Ltd v Rutherford* [2002] ICR 123, EAT, the EAT expressed the pious (if rather faint) hope that 'as more cases of indirect discrimination are heard a more soundly based assessment of what is or is not properly regarded as a considerable or substantial disparity will develop'. In *London Underground Ltd v Edwards (No 2)* [1999] ICR 494, there was only one person in the pool of comparison who could not comply with the relevant requirement. 100% of the 2,023 men to whom the provision applied could comply. Of the 21 women affected, only the complainant could not comply. This meant that the proportion of women that could comply was 95.2%. Nevertheless, the Court of Appeal upheld the tribunal's decision that the proportion of women that could comply was considerably smaller.

The approach adopted in *Edwards* illustrates another general principle applicable to the assessment of disparate impact; one should not focus on the absolute numbers underlying the relevant proportions but on the percentages themselves. The principle was specifically endorsed by the ECJ in *Seymour-Smith* (but see *Harvest Town Circle Ltd* above, in which the EAT interpret *Seymour-Smith* as allowing a domestic court to look at either absolute numbers or relative proportions of those who could comply).

In many cases, the tribunal will look at the relevant proportions and simply subtract one from the other. In the *Edwards* case, for instance, one might say that 4.8% more men can comply than women. *McCausland* suggests taking a further mathematical step. Rather than subtracting the smaller percentage from the larger, one should calculate a ratio. In the *McCausland* case itself, 2.9% of Protestants could comply with the relevant requirement as compared with only 1.5% of Catholics. Simply subtracting one percentage from the other produces an unimpressive difference of only 1.4%. However, when one looks at the ratio of the two percentages one finds that the group of Catholics that could comply was only 71% of the size of the group of Protestants that could do so. A further variation was suggested by Lord Nicholls in *Barry v Midland Bank plc* [1999] ICR 859 at page 869. He suggested that having calculated what proportion of men and women fell within the advantaged and disadvantaged groups respectively one should then calculate a ratio of the proportions of those falling within the disadvantaged group. His approach is thus akin to the *McCausland* approach save that it focuses on those who cannot comply rather than those who can. However, in *Secretary of State for Trade and Industry v Rutherford* above, the Court of Appeal indicated that it would be wrong to focus only on the disadvantaged group. When *Rutherford* came before the House of Lords, Lord Walker of Gestingthorpe opined that, save where special circumstances justify it, attention should be focused on the 'advantaged' group (*Rutherford v Secretary of State for Trade and Industry* [2006] UKHL 19, [2006] ICR 785).

The EAT has sought to rely on *Seymour-Smith* as a basis for taking a much less mechanistic approach to the assessment of the sufficiency of disparity. In *Chief Constable of Avon and Somerset Constabulary v Chew* (2002) 701 IDS Brief 5, the EAT indicated that a 'flexible approach' could be adopted to assessing the sufficiency of any disparity. It was not always necessary to rely on statistics. Further, the tribunal was entitled to consider whether the objectionable provision was inherently more likely to produce a detrimental effect, which disparately affected a particular sex. Thus in *Chew*, a shift rota would likely be harder for those with childcare responsibilities to comply with, and women are more likely to have childcare responsibilities.

Colour and Nationality

In cases concerned with colour and nationality, the complainant must show that the proportion of those of his 'racial group' (as defined by reference to colour or nationality) that can comply with the relevant condition or requirement is considerably smaller than the proportion of those of a different racial group that can do so. The approach to identification of an appropriate pool is broadly as set out immediately above in relation to indirect sex discrimination. The importance of properly identifying the racial group for the purpose of ascertaining whether indirect discrimination has taken place was emphasised by the EAT in *Tower*

Hamlets London Borough Council v Qayyum [1987] ICR 729. Where 'racial group', is defined by 'colour' the group may comprise people of more than one ethnic origin (*Lambeth London Borough Council v Commission for Racial Equality* [1990] ICR 768).

Unique to this test of disparity of effect is the assessment of those who can and cannot 'comply' with the relevant condition or requirement. Whether a person 'can' comply with a condition or requirement is to be judged by what he can, in practice, do when the condition is invoked (*Commission for Racial Equality v Dutton* [1989] IRLR 8). The fact that someone does not wish to comply with a condition or requirement does not mean that they cannot do so (see *Turner v Labour Party* [1987] IRLR 101, a sex discrimination case).

(c) Personal disadvantage

The third element of the test is personal disadvantage. It does not matter if, for instance, persons of a particular religion or sex are disproportionately disadvantaged by a provision, criterion or practice, if the complainant is not. Thus a female employee cannot complain that she has been indirectly discriminated against as a result of an employer imposing a minimum height requirement if she is taller than the minimum requirement. Under the old test, inability to comply with the requirement or condition was not its own detriment (*Lord Chancellor v Coker* [2001] IRLR 116, EAT). It is thought that a similar principle applies under the new test. The disadvantage must be the consequence of the application of the provision, criterion or practice and not the imposition of the measure itself.

12.9   Indirect Discrimination: Particular Cases

(a) Sex discrimination and full-time work

Provisions, criteria or practices which result in the less favourable treatment of part-time employees are frequently found indirectly to discriminate against women (cf *Bilka-Kaufhaus GmbH v Weber von Hartz* [1987] ICR 110, ECJ; *Clarke and Powell v Eley (IMI Kynoch) Ltd* [1983] ICR 165; *R v Secretary of State for Employment, ex p Equal Opportunities Commission* [1994] ICR 317), although it cannot be assumed that such a condition would have a discriminatory effect (see, for example, *Sinclair, Roche & Temperley v Heard* [2004] IRLR 763, EAT). Each case turns on its own facts and applicants have to be prepared to lead evidence which establishes a disparate impact (*Kidd v DRG (UK) Ltd* [1985] ICR 405).

Because the effects of a requirement to work full time are often complex, it is by no means always immediately obvious that the complainant had been less favourably treated. See, for instance, *Kachelmann v Banhaus Hermann Lampe KG* [2001] IRLR 48, ECJ, in which the ECJ wrestled with the question of whether a bank's decision, following the deletion of a part-time post, to limit the selection pool for redundancy to part-time workers amounted to less favourable treatment or (as it ultimately decided) that to have included full-timers would be to have conferred an advantage on part-timers by effectively entitling them to be offered a full-time post if a full-timer were selected for redundancy.

Historically, the predominance of women in the part-time sector has been assumed to be related to the fact that they have traditionally been expected to be the providers of homecare to young children. This assumption underpins the reasoning of the EAT in the case of *Price v Civil Service Commission (No 2)* [1978] IRLR 3 which held that imposing a maximum age limit of 28 for appointment as an Executive Officer in the Civil Service was, in practice, to the disadvantage of women as they were more likely to have had career breaks in order to start a family. Similarly, in *Meade-Hill and National Union of Civil and Public Servants v British Council* [1995] IRLR 478, the Court of Appeal was persuaded that the exercise of a contractual mobility clause might be discriminatory as women were more likely than their partners to be the 'second earner' and thus less able to re-locate. Whilst it appears that the tribunals and courts are frequently comfortable making such assumptions, in practice it is dangerous for an employer to do so. In *Skyrail Oceanic Ltd v Coleman* [1981] ICR 864, it was held that selection of a woman for redundancy on the assumption that men are more likely than women to be the primary supporters of their spouses and children could itself amount to unlawful discrimination.

The same issue arises in circumstances where a woman wishes to make changes to her work patterns following the birth of her child. In *Clymo v Wandsworth London Borough Council* [1989] ICR 250, an employer declined to allow an employee to change to a job-sharing (ie part-time) arrangement. The EAT held that the employer, having merely declined to provide an advantage not proffered to any employees in that grade, had not 'subjected' the employee to anything, and that there was no detriment. By contrast, in *Robinson v Oddbins Ltd* [1996] 27 DCLD 1 an industrial tribunal held that the employee's request to job-share had not been properly considered and the company's reliance on a contractual clause requiring employees, when asked, to work hours over and above the standard working week had indirectly discriminated against women who were more likely to have childcare responsibilities (cf also *Puttick v Eastbourne Borough Council* (unreported, 1995, COIT 3106/2)). In another case, the EAT held that a refusal to allow a woman to job-share was not directly discriminatory in the absence of evidence that a man making a similar request would have had it granted; however, it did not consider the issue of indirect discrimination (*British Telecommunications plc v Roberts* [1996] IRLR 601). In practice, employers will need to be able to establish that there is a sensible justification for requiring that employees work full-time if they are to be safe from claims. In *Lockwood v Crawley Warren Group Ltd* (2001) 680 IDS Brief 9, EAT, this approach was extended still further. A female employee encountered difficulties with her childcare arrangements. She offered to work full-time from home or else to take up to six months' unpaid leave with a view to resolving the difficulties. She was offered two weeks of leave instead and resigned. The EAT decided that the refusal to allow her either to work from home or to take the leave she had asked for, amounted to the application of a condition or requirement. For an example of the circumstances in which a refusal to allow an employee to work flexibly was justified, see *Georgiou v Colman Coyle* (2002) 705 IDS Brief 12, EAT: the office was small; there was a need for two full-time solicitors; commercial clients expected a prompt and efficient service; the need to consult files and to be supervised meant that the complainant had to attend the respondent's premises; and reduced fee income would adversely affect the respondent's profitability.

(b) Sexual Orientation

An obvious source of indirect discrimination against lesbians and gay men are requirements and benefits dependent on marital status. However, prevention or restriction of access to *benefits* dependent on marital status is specifically excluded from the ambit of the *Regulations* by *reg 25* (see 12.13 below).

To bring a claim of indirect discrimination, it will be necessary for a complainant to identify himself as being of a particular sexual orientation, something that is not necessary for a complaint of direct discrimination, victimisation or harassment.

12.10 Victimisation

In the United States, this form of discrimination is sometimes known as 'retaliation' a word which perhaps more accurately captures the essence of this form of discrimination than our own term 'victimisation'. There is little point conferring equal opportunity rights upon employees if their employers are free to take action against them whenever they assert those rights. Thus the various legislative measures each attempt to protect those who rely on their provisions from being less favourably treated.

The relevant provisions are as follows:

Sex	*SDA 1975, s 4(1)*
Marital and Civil Partnership Status	*SDA 1975, s 4(1)*
Race	*RRA 1976, s 2(1)*
Gender Reassignment	*SDA 1975, s 4(1)*
Religion or Belief	*RBR 2003, reg 4(1)*
Sexual Orientation	*SOR 2003, reg 4(1)*

Though there are slight differences in the formulae adopted in certain of the legislative measures they all comprise the same essential elements: a protected act and a prohibition on treating an employee less favourably on grounds of their having performed the protected act. In *Lindsay v Alliance & Leicester plc* [2000] ICR 1234, the EAT advised tribunals to approach the question of liability for an act of victimisation in discrete stages. The first question is whether the complainant has performed a protected act (in *Lindsay* that was not in issue). The tribunal should decide whether the employee has been less favourably treated and then consider whether the disparity in treatment may be said to have been by reason of the protected act. The second and third stages are considered immediately below.

(a) Who is protected from victimisation?

The following people are protected:

(1)   Those who have brought proceedings under the relevant legislation either against the respondent or any other person.

(2)   Those who have given evidence or information in connection with proceedings brought under the relevant legislation against the respondent or any other person.

(3)   Those who have otherwise done anything under, or by reference to the relevant legislation in relation to the respondent or other persons.

(4)   Those who have alleged that the respondent or any other person has committed an act which (whether or not the allegation so states) would amount to a contravention of the relevant legislation.

The complainant will also be protected where the respondent knows or suspects that the complainant has done any of those things or intends to do any of them.

The protection extends to cover those who make complaints under the *Equal Pay Act 1970* as well as *SDA 1975* (*SDA 1975, s 4(1)*).

The actions set out above are commonly referred to as the 'protected acts'.

If what is alleged would not be unlawful under the relevant legislation there is no protected act. For example, in *Waters v Metropolitan Police Comr* [1997] IRLR 589 a police officer, who was harassed by a colleague whilst both were off-duty, complained. She was later less favourably treated by her employer and alleged victimisation. As her harasser had been off duty, the employer was not vicariously liable for his actions. For that reason, the harassment was not unlawful under *SDA 1975*. In those circumstances, the later act of less favourable treatment could not amount to victimisation.

Bringing an internal complaint does not constitute bringing proceedings (*British Telecommunications plc v Grant* (1994) 518 IDS Brief, EAT) although it may, nevertheless, involve alleging a breach of the Act on the part of the employer with the effect that it falls within category (4) above.

An employee performs a 'protected act' falling within category (2) above even where the evidence given is not in support of the complaint (*Kirby v National Probation Service for England and Wales (Cumbria Area)* [2006] IRLR 508, [2006] All ER (D) 111 (Mar), EAT obiter). Nor need the evidence be given orally; providing a witness statement would be sufficient (*National Probation Service* above, again obiter).

Participating in an interview into allegations of discrimination made by a third party would qualify as having done something by reference to the relevant anti-discrimination legislation for the purposes of the catch-all category (3) above (see *National Probation Service* above)

A person is not protected where it is established that the evidence or information given by him or, as appropriate, the allegation made by him was false and not made in good faith (*SDA 1975, s 4(2)*; *RRA 1976, s 2(2)*; *RBR 2003, reg. 4(2)*; *SOR 2003, reg 4(2)*).

It is important to note that the person doing the victimising need not be the person who was the subject of the original complaint of discrimination. Thus if a prospective employer decides not to appoint a candidate because he had brought or given evidence in proceedings against his former employer, that will amount to an act of victimisation.

(b)   What are they protected from?

Those who qualify for the protection are protected against 'less favourable treatment' (for which see 12.5 above) on grounds of their having performed a protected act.

As with a case of direct discrimination (see 12.4 above), the tribunal is required to perform a comparison, although not necessarily the sort of 'like for like' comparison required in direct discrimination cases by, for instance, *RRA 1976, s 3(4)* (*Hounslow London Borough Council v Bhatt* [2001] 692 IDS Brief 5, EAT). Two different approaches to the question of identifying the appropriate comparator may be found in the authorities. In the first, one compares the complainant with someone who has brought proceedings which are not discrimination proceedings. In the second, the comparator is simply someone who has not performed a protected act. The question of how someone who had brought another type of proceedings would have been treated is not irrelevant. It is considered when the tribunal turns to assess whether the complainant has been treated less favourably *by reason that* he has performed a protected act. In *Chief Constable of West Yorkshire Police v Khan* [2001] UKHL 48, [2001] IRLR 830, HL), the House of Lords endorsed the second approach.

Whilst it was formerly thought that the requirement that the act of victimisation should be 'by reason that' the complainant has performed a protected act required conscious motivation, it is now clear that an act of victimisation may occur even where the protected act forms part only of the respondent's sub- or unconscious motivations (*Nagarajan v London Regional Transport* [1999] ICR 877). In a case where the protected act is only part of the employer's motivations it must be significant in the sense of being more than trivial (see *Wong v Igen Ltd (Equal Opportunities Commission intervening) and conjoined cases* [2005] EWCA Civ 142, [2005] IRLR 258 and *Villalaba v Merrill Lynch & Co Inc* [2007] ICR 469 EAT). In *Chief Constable of West Yorkshire Police v Khan* (above), the House of Lords held that the identification of what might be termed the 'subjective reason for action' was not achieved by application of the objective 'but for' test of causation.

In *Aziz v Trinity Street Taxis Ltd* [1988] ICR 534, the Court of Appeal dealt with a number of points arising out of the construction of *RRA 1976, s 2(1)*, and held in particular that it was necessary for a complainant under *s 2(1)(c))* to show that it was the very fact that his act had been done under, or by reference to, the race relations legislation that had influenced the unfavourable treatment. On the facts, the respondent association would have expelled any member who covertly recorded conversations, irrespective of whether that was done to support an allegation of racial discrimination and, therefore, the complaint of victimisation failed.

There is no victimisation where the reason for the unfavourable treatment is the disruptive way in which complaints are made rather than the complaints as such (*Re York Truck Equipment Ltd*, IDS Brief 439, p 10).

In *Khan* above, the House of Lords held that it was open to an employer faced with discrimination proceedings (and thus a protected act) to take honest and reasonable steps to protect its position in the relevant litigation even if that led to less favourable treatment. Thus, in *Khan* itself an employer could decline to issue a reference until the outcome of proceedings were known where the reference might otherwise have had to deal with matters that were in dispute. There are, however, limits. In *St Helens Metropolitan Borough Council v Derbyshire* [2005] EWCA Civ 977, [2006] ICR 90, it was held that it was not open to an employer to write to claimants who had brought equal pay claims and to seek to persuade them to settle their claim by pointing out the possible negative consequences that the success of their claim might have for colleagues.

12.11 Harassment

(A)*Harassment*

A number of the equal opportunities regimes recognise harassment as a free-standing form of discrimination.

The domestic statutes provide that a person is unlawfully harassed where, *on a prohibited ground*, the harasser engages in unwanted conduct which has the purpose or effect of:

(*a*)   violating that other person's dignity; or

(*b*)   creating an intimidating, hostile, degrading, humiliating or offensive environment for him.

(*SDA 1975, s 4A(1)* (on ground of sex – as inserted with effect from 1 October 2005 by *SDR 2005, reg 5*), *SDA 1975, s 4A(3)* (on ground of gender reassignment

– as inserted with effect from 1 October 2005 by *SDR 2005, reg 5*), *RRA 1976, s 3A* (on grounds of race other than colour and/or nationality); *RBR 2003, reg 5(1)*; *SOR, reg 5(1)*.)

However, the Administrative Court determined, in the context of a consideration of *SDA 1975, s 4A(1)*, that the existing statutory formula failed properly to implement *ETD 76/207/EEC (as amended)*. *ETD 76/207/EEC, art 1.2.2* defines harassment as unwanted conduct 'related to' as opposed to 'on grounds of' sex. The domestic formulation suggests that there should be some causal link between sex and the harassment whereas the broader European definition does not (see *Equal Opportunities Commission v Secretary of State for Trade and Industry* [2007] EWHC 483 (Admin), [2007] IRLR 327). What is true of harassment on grounds of sex is equally true of harassment on grounds of gender reassignment, race, religion and sexual orientation. In each case the domestic legislation requires that harassment should be on the prohibited ground whereas the underlying European legislation merely requires that the harassment should relate to it. The Court recognised that one consequence, therefore, of its finding in relation to *SDA 1975, s 4A(3)* was that the other domestic tests must equally fail properly to implement the relevant directive underpinning them. What is the consequence of this broader test? Were it to be implemented by an amendment to *SDA 1975* a case like *MOD v Brumfitt* (above) would have been wrongly decided. In that case a trainer harassed both his female and male trainees. The former contended that the effect of the treatment had been worse in their case. The EAT found that there had been no unlawful discrimination as the female employees had not been targetted because of their sex. Following *EOC v Secretary of State for Trade and Industry* above, it might be concluded that, although the harassment in *Brumfitt* could not be said to have been 'caused' by the victim's sex, in the circumstances it might be said to 'relate' to it.

The test of whether conduct has the relevant effect is not subjective. Conduct is not to be treated, for instance, as violating a complainant's dignity merely because he says it does. It must be conduct which could reasonably be considered as having that effect. However, the tribunal is obliged to take the complainant's perception into account in making that assessment (*SDA 1975, s 4A(2)* (on ground of sex – as inserted with effect from 1 October 2005 by *SDR 2005, reg 5*), *RRA 1976, s 3A(2)*; *RBR 2003, reg 5(2)*; *SOR 2003, reg 5(1)*).

There are some prohibited grounds which do not have an express protection against harassment. They are:

(a) nationality;

(b) colour;

(c) marital status;

(d) pregnancy;

(e) maternity leave; and

(f) civil partnership status.

Before 1 October 2005, there was no express prohibition on harassing a person on the ground of their sex. However, as is explained in 12.12 (g) below, such behaviour was nevertheless unlawful. The basis for its unlawfulness was that to harass an employee on ground of their sex was treated as an act of less favourable treatment (falling within *SDA 1975, s 1*) consisting of subjecting them to a detriment (falling within *SDA 1975, s 6(2)(b)*). A similar analysis applied in relation to harassment on grounds of marital status. As from 1 October 2005, it has been expressly and specifically unlawful to harass someone on the ground of their sex. Significantly, *SDR 2005, reg 33* amended *SDA 1975, s 82(1)* with the effect that 'detriment' is defined so as 'not to include subjecting a person to harassment'.

A difficult question arises whether it is any longer unlawful to harass someone on ground of their marital status. On the face of it such discrimination is not on the ground of the victim's sex and it will no longer be possible to argue that to harass someone on ground of their marital status involves subjecting them to a detriment. A similar problem arises in relation to discrimination on grounds of pregnancy or maternity leave. The answer may be to interpret 'on the ground of sex' in *SDA 1975, s 4A(1)* as including discrimination on those other grounds. Such an argument would be founded on *ETD 76/207/EEC* which defines 'on grounds of sex' to include discrimination on grounds of marital status and (arguably) harassment on ground of pregnancy or maternity leave. The difficulty with such an interpretation is that it would arguably make those specific prohibited grounds nugatory as *SDA 1975, s 1* would then fall to be treated as encompassing them.

Such an approach will not assist civil partners as there is no warrant for reading *ETD 76/207/EEC* as having any application to them. This would leave civil partners disadvantaged when compared to married persons.

RRA 1976, s 78 also defines 'detriment' so as to exclude harassment but only harassment falling within *RRA 1976, s 3A*. As that section does not include discrimination on grounds of nationality or colour (see *RRA 1976, s 3A(1)*) it should still be possible to argue that it constitutes subjection to a detriment within *RRA 1976, s 4(2)(c)*.

(B)*Sexual Harassment*

SDA 1975, s 4A(b) (as added, with effect from 1 October 2005 by *SDR 2005, reg 5*) creates a distinct form of sexual harassment. The additional form is found where a person 'engages in any form of unwanted verbal, non-verbal or physical conduct of a sexual nature that has the purpose or effect of (i) violating [his or] her dignity; or (ii) of creating an intimidating, hostile, degrading, humiliating or offensive environment for [him or] her'.

As with the more conventional form of harassment described above, conduct will only be taken to violate the victim's dignity, etc. if the conduct may "reasonably be considered as having that effect". However, in assessing that issue, the tribunal must have regard to all circumstances including in particular the perception of the victim (*SDA 1975, s 4A(2)* as added, with effect from 1 October 2005, by *SDR 2005 reg 5*).

(C)*Less favourable treatment of those who reject or submit to harassment*

In the case of harassment on sex or gender reassignment, it is additionally unlawful for a person to treat a complainant less favourably on grounds that he or she has rejected or submitted to the relevant unwanted conduct (*SDA 1975, ss 4A(2) and (4)* as added, with effect from 1 October 2005) by *SDR 2005, reg 5*).

12.12 DISCRIMINATION IN EMPLOYMENT

Discrimination alone will not found liability. It is only certain forms of discrimination which are unlawful, principally discrimination in employment.

Discrimination and harassment is prohibited at every stage of employment: advertising vacancies, engagement of employees, promotion and other opportunities, dismissal. For discrimination against non-employees, such as contract workers, office holders, etc, see 13.21 FF DISCRIMINATION AND EQUAL OPPORTUNITIES – II.

(a) The meaning of 'employment'

Employment has a wider definition in equal opportunities law than it does in some other employment protection legislation. It is defined as '... employment under a contract of service or of apprenticeship, or a contract personally to ['execute any work or labour' (the formulation in *SDA 1975* and *RRA 1976*)] [or 'do any work' (the formulation in the *RBR 2003* and the *SOR 2003*)].'

(See *SDA 1975, s 82(1); RRA 1976, s 78(1); RBR 2003, reg 2(3); SOR 2003, reg 2(3).* See *Wippel v Peek and Cloppenburg GmbH & Co KG, C-313/02* [2005] ICR 1604 ECJ – the *ETD 76/207/EEC* protects workers who are engaged on an 'on demand' basis and who are not obliged to take on work offered. *SDA 1975* must, of course, be interpreted, wherever possible, to be consistent with the directive.)

In *Mirror Group Newspapers Ltd v Gunning* [1986] ICR 145, a case about the *SDA 1975* the Court of Appeal held that *s 82(1)* referred to a contract, the *dominant purpose* of which was the execution of personal work or services.

A sub-postmaster who was responsible for seeing that the work of the Post Office was carried out but was not obliged to carry out the work himself was also held not to be an employee even within the extended meaning of the *Act* (*Tanna v Post Office* [1981] ICR 374). A taxi driver was not employed under 'a contract personally to execute any work or labour' where there was no mutual obligation between himself and the cab firm to offer or to accept any work (*Mingeley v Pennock & Ivory* [2004] EWCA Civ 328, [2004] ICR 727).

A person working under the Youth Opportunities Programme was also held not to be employed within the meaning of *RRA 1976, s 78* (*Daley v Allied Suppliers Ltd* [1983] ICR 90). A special constable is not employed under a contract to execute work or labour but is deemed to be in employment by virtue of *RRA 1976, s 16(1)* and thus enjoys the protection of *RRA 1976* (*Sheikh v Chief Constable of Greater Manchester Police* [1989] ICR 373).

An associate minister in the Church of Scotland was employed under 'a contract personally to execute ... work' despite being an office holder. The House of Lords concluded that she was both an office holder and an employee (*Percy v Church of Scotland Board of National Mission* [2005] UKHL 73, [2006] ICR 134, HL(S))

The definition of employment is broad enough to cover the personal provision of services by a professional and even the retention of a firm of solicitors, instructions to a firm being, in reality, a contract entered into with each partner (*Loughran and Kelly v Northern Ireland Housing Executive* [1998] ICR 828, HL(NI), distinguished in *Patterson v Legal Services Commission* [2003] EWCA Civ 1558, [2004] ICR 312 where there was no obligation on the complainant to carry out the work personally).

In *Halfpenny v IGE Systems Ltd* [2001] ICR 73, the House of Lords determined that a woman absent on maternity leave was not a 'woman employed' for the purposes of *s 6*. It should be noted, however, that this was a decision concerned with the maternity leave regime as it was prior to the amendments introduced by the *ERA 1999*. Their Lordships make it clear that the question would have to be addressed afresh under the new scheme. The new scheme contains a provision (*Maternity and Parental Leave Regulations 1999 (SI 1999/3312), reg 17*) which expressly preserves the application of certain contractual rights and obligations during a period of additional maternity leave, including the obligation of trust and confidence. This makes it much more likely that a woman absent on AML would fall to be treated as a 'woman employed'.

A person discriminated against by being dismissed does not have to have been employed for a qualifying period before being entitled to bring a claim.

(b) The requirement that employment be at an establishment in Great Britain

Protection against discrimination is afforded only in relation to employment at an establishment in Great Britain (*SDA 1975, s 6(1); RRA 1976, s 4(1); RBR 2003, reg 6(2); SOR, reg 6(2)*).

Employment is to be regarded as being at an establishment in Great Britain where an employee does his work *wholly or partly* in Great Britain (*SDA 1975, s 10(1)* as amended with effect from 1 October 2005 by *SDR 2005, reg 11); RRA 1976, s 8(1); RBR 2003, reg 9(1); SOR, reg 9(1)*).

When assessing whether or not work is done wholly or partly in Great Britain one looks at the position by considering the period of appointment as a whole and not by focusing solely on the point in time at which the act of discrimination occurred (*Saggar v Ministry of Defence* [2005] EWCA Civ 413, [2005] ICR 1073 – the case concerned an earlier formulation but its principle remains applicable).

Even where the complainant does his work entirely outside Great Britain, his employment will nevertheless be regarded as being at an establishment in Great Britain if:

(1)   the employer has a place of business at an establishment in Great Britain;

(2)   the work is for the purposes of the business carried on at that establishment; and

(3)   the employee is ordinarily resident in Great Britain:

    (a)   at the time when he applies for or is offered the employment, or

    (b)   at any time during the course of the employment

(*SDA 1975, s 10(1) and (1A)* (as amended with effect from 1 October 2005 by *SDR 2005, reg 11); RRA 1976, s 8(1) and (1A); RBR 2003, reg 9(2); and SOR 2003, reg 9(2)*).

Where work is not done at an establishment, as in the case of plumbers who are sent out on assignments, it is treated as done at the establishment from which the workers are sent out. If employees neither work at nor from a particular establishment, such as market researchers who work from their homes, the work will be considered to be done at the establishment with which it has the closest connection (*SDA 1975, s 10(4); RRA 1976, s 8(4)*).

Employment on board a British registered ship, is to be considered employment at an establishment in Great Britain, unless the employee does his work wholly outside Great Britain (*SDA 1975, s 10(2); RRA 1976, s 8(3); RBR 2003, reg 9(3)(a); SOR 2003, reg 9(3)*).

The regimes each make specific provision in relation to those employed in energy exploration. *SDA 1975, s 10(5) and RRA 1976, s 8(5)* provide that those whose employment is concerned with the 'exploration of the sea bed or subsoil or the exploitation of their natural resources' should, in effect, be treated as if they are employed at an establishment in Great Britain if they work in an area designated under *s 1(7) of the Continental Shelf Act 1964*. The *Race Relations (Offshore Employment) Order 1987 (SI 1987/929)* and the *Sex Discrimination and Equal Pay (Offshore Employment) Order 1987 (SI 1987/930)* have been made pursuant to the power to designate.

Both *SDA 1975, s 10(5)* and *RRA 1976, s 8(5)* are prospectively amended from a day as yet to be appointed. The definition of the relevant activity will change so that protection will be afforded to those whose employment is concerned with 'any activity within *s 11(2)* of the *Petroleum Act 1998*' and in addition to designation under the *Continental Shelf Act 1964*, those employed in an area specified under *s 10(8)* of the *Petroleum Act 1998* will also be treated as if they worked at an establishment in Great Britain (see *Petroleum Act 1998, s 50, Sch 4, paras 8* and *11*). In each case the provision is displaced if the law of Northern Ireland applies to the area in question.

In the case of the *SOR 2003* and *RBR 2003*, employment on the continental shelf is deemed to be employment at an establishment in Great Britain if it is an area designated under *s 1(7)* of the *Continental Shelf Act 1964* or is an area within the Frigg Gas Field (provided in the latter case that the employer is a company registered under the *Companies Act 1985* or an overseas company with an established place of business in Great Britain) (*RBR 2003, reg 9; SOR 2003 regs 9(4)* and *(5)*).

RRA 1976, s 9 makes further provision in respect of seamen recruited abroad.

In *JP Barker v Service Children's Schools Case C-374/95* (unreported) an employee worked in an establishment belonging to the UK but located in another member state. The question whether the *Equal Treatment Directive (76/207/EEC)* allows the UK to exclude proceedings in such circumstances was referred to the European Court of Justice but seems not to have proceeded to decision. The provision may, in any event, be contrary to *art 48* of the *Treaty* (Free Movement of Workers) (*Bossa v Nordstress Ltd* [1998] IRLR 284).

(c) Advertisements

In the case of discrimination falling within *SDA 1975* and *RRA 1976* it is, put broadly, unlawful for a potential employer to publish an advertisement which might reasonably be understood as indicating an intention to discriminate unlawfully (*SDA 1975, s 38, RRA 1976, s 29*). There is no equivalent provision made in the *RBR 2003* or the *SOR 2003*.

'*Advertisement*' is defined by *SDA 1975, s 82(1)* and *RRA 1976, s, 78(1)* as including 'every form of advertisement, whether to the public or not, and whether in a newspaper or other publication, by television or radio, by display of notices, signs, labels, showcards or goods, by distribution of samples, circulars, catalogues, price lists or other material, by exhibition of pictures, models or films', or in any similar way. References to the publishing of advertisements will be interpreted accordingly.

If the discrimination would be lawful, for example on the grounds that being of a particular race is a genuine occupational qualification for the job, the advertisement may lawfully be placed. Therefore, a restaurateur may lawfully advertise for Chinese waiting staff for his Chinese restaurant.

The restrictions on racially discriminatory advertisements do not apply to an advertisement for employment outside Great Britain which discriminates otherwise than by reference to colour, race, or ethnic or national origin (*RRA 1976, s 29(3)*). Thus, an employer may not advertise for English applicants only for employment overseas, although he may lawfully advertise for applicants with a public school education (which might well be indirectly discriminatory) and may lawfully select only English applicants for such employment.

Use of a job description with a sexual connotation such as 'waiter', 'salesgirl', 'postman' or 'stewardess' will be taken to indicate an intention to discriminate unless the advertisement contains an indication to the contrary (*SDA 1975, s 38(3)*). Therefore, either a new word such as 'salesperson' will have to be used or the advertiser will have to insert a disclaimer such as 'applications are invited from men and women'.

Both the publisher and the advertiser, who cause a discriminatory advertisement to be printed, are guilty of an unlawful act (*SDA 1975, s 38(1)*; *RRA 1976, s 29(1)*).

The publisher of a discriminatory advertisement may escape liability if he proves:

(i)   that the advertisement was published in reliance on a statement made to him by the person who caused it to be published to the effect that the advertisement was not in breach of the relevant legislation; and

(ii)   that it was reasonable for him to rely on the statement (*SDA 1975, s 38(4); RRA 1976 s. 29(4)*).

An advertiser who knowingly or recklessly makes a statement regarding the legality of the advertisement which is in a material respect false or misleading, commits an offence and is liable on conviction in a magistrates' court to a fine not exceeding level 5 on the standard scale (*SDA 1975, s 38(5)*; *RRA 1976, s 29(5)* and see 1.10 INTRODUCTION). Thus, for example, an advertiser who falsely assures a publisher that the people of Outer Monrovia would not accept women salespeople is guilty of a criminal offence, and the publisher of such an advertisement is guilty of an unlawful act unless he can establish that it was reasonable for him to rely upon that assurance.

Where there is a breach of *RRA 1976, s 29*, proceedings may be brought in the employment tribunal by the Commission for Racial Equality (*RRA 1976, s 63*). In *Cardiff Women's Aid v Hartup* [1994] IRLR 390, a charity advertised for a 'black or Asian woman'. Mrs Hartup, who was white, brought proceedings in the employment tribunal alleging that the effect of the advertisement was that she had been discriminated against in the arrangements made for the purpose of determining who should be offered employment contrary to *RRA 1976, s 4(1)*. She had not applied for the post. The EAT decided that as an advertisement only indicates an 'intention' to discriminate, Mrs Hartup could not claim to have suffered any actual discrimination.

Similarly, where there is a breach of *SDA 1975, s 38* proceedings may only be brought by the Equal Opportunities Commission (*SDA 1975, s 72*).

(d) Engagement

An employer may not discriminate directly or indirectly:

(1)   in the arrangements he makes for the purpose of determining who should be offered employment; or

(2)   in the terms on which he offers employment; or

(3)   by refusing or deliberately omitting to offer employment.

(*SDA 1975, s 6(1)*; *RRA 1976, s 4(1)*; *RBR 2003*; *reg 6(1)*; *SOR 2003, reg 6(1)*.)

Thus, if an employer offers a woman three weeks' holiday, whereas a man doing the same job is entitled to five weeks, he is guilty of discrimination under the *SDA 1975*. Also, the woman's contract will be modified by the *Equal Pay Act 1970* to give her the same holiday entitlement as that of the man (see EQUAL PAY (24)).

In *Saunders v Richmond-upon-Thames London Borough Council* [1978] ICR 75, it was assumed that questions asked at an interview constituted 'arrangements' within the meaning of (*1*) above. Whether or not the questions were unlawful was held to be a question of fact to be determined in each case. In *Brennan v JH Dewhurst Ltd* [1984] ICR 52, the arrangements made for interviewing applicants were operated so as to discriminate against women, and were therefore unlawful.

A refusal to re-instate a former employee following a dismissal does not constitute 'refusing to offer employment' (*Post Office v Adekeye* [1997] ICR 110, CA).

Racial Discrimination: Engagement and Asylum and Immigration

The *Asylum and Immigration Act 1996* makes it an offence for an employer to employ those whose immigration status precludes them from working in the UK. The *Immigration (Restrictions on Employment) Order 2004* (*SI 2004/755*) specifies a number of documents ('statutory documents') which, if produced prior to engagement, the employer may rely upon as establishing that the job applicant is entitled to work in the UK. Provided the employer has examined the document prior to making the appointment (and retains a copy thereafter), it has a defence to any prosecution under the *Act*. There is a danger that in seeking to avoid liability under the *Act*, employers may treat job applicants from ethnic minorities differently. This in turn creates the risk of discrimination claims. The Home Office has produced a code of practice which includes guidance on avoiding discrimination (http://www.ind.homeoffice.gov.uk).

A failure to comply with the provisions of the code may be taken into account by an employment tribunal considering a claim of race discrimination.

The EAT has suggested that a foreign national complaining of discriminatory treatment may only be able to compare herself with other foreign nationals rather than with British citizens (*Sheiky v Argos Distributions Ltd* (1997) 597 IDS Brief 16).

Sex Discrimination: The ETD and Positive Discrimination

Whilst the *Equal Treatment Directive 76/207/EEC* generally prohibits discrimination in favour of either sex, it allows for measures which are intended to promote equal opportunity for men and women (in particular, by removing existing inequalities). In *Kalanke v Freie Hansestadt Bremen* [1996] ICR 314, the ECJ held that the exception in the *Directive* did not permit national rules which required that, all other things being equal, the women should be appointed. A similar clause was considered by the ECJ in *Marschall v Land Nordrhein-Westfalen* [2001] ICR 45, ECJ. The particular clause was concerned with the promotion of teachers. It provided that where there were fewer women than men at the level of the relevant post and both female and male candidates were equally qualified in terms of their suitability, competence and professional performance, priority should be given to the female candidate. However, there was a saving clause which provided that priority should not be given to the female candidate where 'reasons specific to an individual male candidate [tilted] the balance in his favour'. The ECJ held that the savings clause saved the rule. The rule was compatible with the requirements of the *Directive*.

Abrahamsson v Fogelqvist [2002] ICR 932, ECJ provides an example of a case in which the positive action was found to be incompatible with European equal opportunities legislation. The particular provision was a Swedish Regulation governing appointments within universities. It provided for the automatic appointment of less well-qualified members of the under-represented sex in preference to better-qualified applicants of the other sex. The provision was qualified in two respects. First, the employer had to be satisfied that the beneficiary of the positive discrimination met the relevant minimum qualification requirement. Second, the employer had to be satisfied that the difference in qualifications was not such that there would be a 'breach of the requirement of objectivity in making appointments'. These qualifications did not save the provision, which the court felt was disproportionate to the aim pursued. The court considered, in particular, that the second qualification was too vague to preclude appointments being made on the basis of the sex of the candidate alone, and was unhappy that the provision applied automatically and without consideration of the individual circumstances of the candidates. The seniority of the post was not a relevant factor in deciding whether the principle of equal treatment had been breached (see also *EFTA Surveillance Authority v Kingdom of Norway* [2003] IRLR 318).

Sex Discrimination: Terms Offered – Special Provisions for those on Maternity Leave

The prohibition on discrimination in the terms on which employment is offered does not, subject to certain exceptions, make it unlawful to deprive a woman who is on OML of any benefit from the terms and conditions of her employment relating to remuneration. The exceptions are: (1) benefit by way of maternity-related remuneration; (2) benefit by way of remuneration in respect of times when the woman is neither on OML nor on AML, including increase-related remuneration in respect of such times; and (3) benefit by way of maternity-related remuneration that is increase related (*SDA 1975, s 6A(1),(2) and (5)* as added by *SDR 2005, reg 8* with effect from 1 October 2005)

'Maternity-related remuneration' is 'remuneration to which [a woman] is entitled as a result of being pregnant or being on' OML or AML and 'remuneration means benefits: (a) that consist of the payment of money to an employee by way of wages or salary; and (b) that are not benefits whose provision is regulated by the employee's contract of employment' (*SDA 1975, s 6A(7)*). Remuneration is 'increase-related' 'so far as it falls to be calculated by reference to increases in remuneration that the woman would have received had she not been on OML or AML' (*SDA 1975, s 6A(6)*).

In *EOC v Secretary of State of Trade and Industry* [2007] EWHC 483 (Admin), [2007] IRLR 327, the Administrative Court held that, properly interpreted, *SDA 1975, s 6A(1)* has the effect of precluding a claim from an employee in relation to a discriminatory failure to pay non-contractual benefits such as discretionary bonuses during her period of compulsory maternity leave. The Court went on to decide that since the provision had that effect it was inconsistent with the *ETD 76/207/EEC* as interpreted by the ECJ in the case of *Lewen v Denda* C-333/97 [2000] IRLR 67 and would have to be recast (for an account of the *Lewen* case see 24.14 EQUAL PAY).

Similar provisions govern the position of those on AML. Again *SDA 1975, s 6(1)(b)* does not make it unlawful to deprive a woman taking AML of the benefit of terms and conditions relating to remuneration and again it is subject to exceptions. In addition to the three exceptions identified above in the passage dealing with OML the following are excepted: (1) the benefit of her employer's implied obligation to her of trust and confidence, or (2) any benefit of terms and conditions in respect of: (a) notice of the termination by her employer of her contract of employment; (b) compensation in the event of redundancy; (c) disciplinary or grievance procedures; or (d) membership of a pension scheme (*SDA 1975, s 6A(3) and (4)*).

SDA 1975, s 6A was also found to be non-compliant by the Administrative Court in the EOC case above, as it draws a distinction between the rights protected during AML and those protected during OML, which distinction was said to be contrary to the position adopted by the ECJ in the case of *Land Brandenberg v Sass* C-248/02 [2005] IRLR 147, ECJ.

(e) Opportunities in employment

Once a complainant is in a job, their employer may not discriminate against them in the way in which he affords them access to opportunities for promotion, transfer, training or to any other benefits, facilities or services, or by refusing or deliberately omitting to afford her access to them (*SDA 1975, s 6(2); RRA 1976, s 4(2)(b)); RBR 2003, reg 6(2); SOR, reg 6(2)*).

The 'benefits' referred to at (b) above do not include benefits 'of any description if the employer is concerned with the provision (for payment or not) of benefits of that description to the public, or to a section of the public which includes the employee in question, unless:

(a)   that provision differs in a material respect from the provision of the benefits by the employer to his employees; or

(b)   the provision of the benefits to the employee in question is regulated by his contract of employment; or

(c)   the benefits relate to training'.

(*SDA 1975, s 6(7); RRA 1976, s 4(4); RBR 2003, reg 6(4); SOR, reg 6(4).*) In cases where the complainant is a former employee rather than an existing employee, failure to provide a non-contractual benefit will only exceptionally constitute discrimination in an opportunity to receive a benefit (*Relaxion Group plc v Rhys Harper* [2003] UKHL 33, [2003] ICR 867).

References in the *SDA 1975* and *RRA 1976* to the granting of access to benefits, facilities or services are not limited to those provided by one person (who might be an employer), but include any means by which it is in that person's power to facilitate access to benefits, facilities or services provided by any other person ('the actual provider') (*SDA 1975, s 50(1); RRA 1976, s 40(1)*). Thus, if there are two companies within a group, A and B, and employees are employed by B, but are afforded training facilities by A, both A and B may be liable for discriminatory training by A.

There are special additional provisions dealing with the access to opportunities in employment afforded to those on Maternity Leave which are dealt with below

Sex Discrimination: Opportunities Afforded – Special Provisions for those on Maternity Leave

SDA 1975, 6(2), broadly, prohibits discrimination in the way in which an employer affords access to opportunities for promotion, transfer or training, or to any other benefits, facilities or services. It also prohibits dismissal and subjection to any other detriment. *SDA 1975, s 6A* (added with effect from 1 October 2005 by the *SDR 2005, reg 8*) qualifies that non-discrimination principle in so far as it applies to those on maternity leave in an manner identical to that set out above in relation to terms offered.

(f) Dismissal

A dismissal on any of the prohibited grounds is unlawful (*SDA 1975, s 6(2)(b)*; *RRA 1976, s 4(2)(b)*; *RBR 2003, reg 6(2)(d)*; *SOR 2003, reg 6(2)(d)*) as well as being unfair within the meaning of the *Employment Rights Act 1996* (see UNFAIR DISMISSAL – II (54)).

Each of the legislative measures provides for an extended definition of 'dismissal'. In particular, they provide that employees or partners whose employment or partnership comes to an end (and is not immediately renewed on the same terms) on the expiration of a certain period or the occurrence of a certain event are dismissed. So, too, are employees or partners who terminate their employment or partnership by acceptance of their employer's or fellow partners' repudiatory breach of contract (ie 'constructive' dismissal or termination) (*SDA 1975, s 2(3); RRA 1976, s 4(4A); RBR 2003, reg 6(5); SOR 2003, reg 6(5)*).

(g) Subjection to other detriment

In addition to the specific employment-related detriments (described above) to which it is unlawful to subject a complainant, there is a residual 'catch all' obligation not to subject employees to detriment on a prohibited ground (*SDA 1975, s 6(2)(b)*; *RRA 1976, s 4(2)(c)*; *Religion and Belief Regulations 2003, reg 6(2)(d)*; *SOR, reg 6(2)(d)*).

A complainant seeking to establish that he has been subjected to a 'detriment' need not demonstrate that he has suffered a physical or economic consequence as a result of having been less favourably treated. It is sufficient to show that a reasonable employee would or might take the view that they had been disadvantaged in the circumstances in which they had to work (*Shamoon v Chief Constable of the Royal Ulster Constabulary (Northern Ireland)* [2003] UKHL 11, [2003] ICR 337 and see *Ministry of Defence v Jeremiah* [1980] ICR 13, CA in which it was held that requiring only male supervisors to carry out dirty work an unlawful detriment; see also *BL Cars Ltd v Brown* [1983] ICR 143; *Jiad v Byford* [2003] EWCA Civ 135, [2003] IRLR 232).

In *De Souza v Automobile Association* [1986] ICR 514, the Court of Appeal held that the Employment Appeal Tribunal had correctly concluded that Mrs De Souza had not been subjected to a 'detriment' within the meaning of *RRA 1976, s 4(2)(c)* as a result of overhearing a manager say to another manager, about her, to get his typing done by 'the wog'. The EAT in *Barclays Bank plc v Kapur* [1989] ICR 142 (appeal allowed, [1989] ICR 753) suggested, in a passage which was not a necessary part of its decision, that the words 'any other detriment' related to acts in connection with dismissal or disciplinary proceedings and were not wholly general in their scope. The correctness of this construction is, with respect, doubted. It is also open to argument whether *De Souza* was correctly decided, bearing in mind more recent cases dealing with sexual harassment

Failure, after the termination of the employment contract, to confer a non-contractual benefit on a former employee will only exceptionally constitute a 'detriment' (*Relaxion Group plc v Rhys-Harper* [2003] UKHL 33, [2003] ICR 867).

Sexual Harassment as detriment

Until 1 October 2005, sexual harassment did not, of itself, constitute a breach of *SDA 1975*. However, the Scottish Court of Session had held, in effect, that sexual harassment which affects a woman's working conditions was contrary to *SDA 1975* (*Porcelli v Strathclyde Regional Council* [1986] ICR 564). See also *Bracebridge Engineering Ltd v Darby* [1990] IRLR 3, and the EC *Recommendation on the Dignity of Men and Women at Work* which was referred to with approval by the EAT in *Wadman v Carpenter Farrer Partnership* [1993] IRLR 374 (see 20.1 EMPLOYMENT TRIBUNALS – I and 25.6 EUROPEAN COMMUNITY LAW). For the new law see 12.11 above.

In *Reed and Bull Information Systems Ltd v Stedman* [1999] IRLR 299, the EAT gave guidance to tribunals dealing with three troublesome questions which commonly arise in harassment cases:

(*a*) *If a woman regards as harassment of a sexual nature words or conduct to which many women would not take exception or regard as harassment, has her claim been made out?*

Borrowing from the EC *Recommendation on the Dignity of Men and Women at Work*, the EAT emphasises that a key characteristic of sexual harassment is that it creates a 'hostile' and 'offensive' environment for the employee in the workplace. The difficult question is whether the behaviour has to be objectively offensive or whether it is sufficient that it should be offensive in the subjective opinion of the employee. The EAT tries to steer a middle course. The fact that, objectively, the behaviour is not offensive does not dispose of the issue. If a particularly sensitive employee has made it clear that the conduct is unwelcome, any repetition may amount to harassment. Other forms of conduct are objectively hostile or offensive, and these do not require the employee to indicate that they are unwelcome before they may constitute harassment.

(*b*) *If a man does not appreciate that his words or conduct are unwelcome, has her claim been proved?*

The EAT has restated the general principle that, as with all cases of direct discrimination, the motive and intention of the alleged discriminator is irrelevant. If the man should have known that conduct is unwelcome either because that risk was obvious or else because the woman has made it clear to him, he will be liable even if he did not intend to harass. It would seem to follow from what is said above that the claim may not be made out where the man's behaviour would not, looked at objectively, fall to be considered hostile or offensive.

(*c*) *Is a 'one-off act' sufficient to constitute harassment?*

A one-off act may be sufficient. The clearer it is that objectively the conduct was hostile or offensive, the more likely it is that a one-off act will suffice to establish harassment (see also *Insitu Cleaning Co Ltd v Heads* [1995] IRLR 4).

Further guidance was given in *Driskel v Peninsula Business Services Ltd* [2000] IRLR 151, EAT. First, where there are a number of alleged incidents, the tribunal should be careful to focus on their cumulative effect rather than concentrating upon whether individual incidents are trivial in nature. Second, simply because a male superior engages in vulgar behaviour with male colleagues does not mean that a woman is not treated less favourably when she is subjected to such behaviour. Behaviour of that kind directed at a woman is more likely to be intimidatory and to undermine her dignity than similar behaviour directed at a male colleague. (On the question of the objective nature of the test, the Administrative Court expressed a preference for the guidance given in *Driskel* over that given in *Reed*; *EOC v Secretary of State for Trade and Industry* [2007] EWHC 483 (Admin), [2007] IRLR 327 at para 33)

While it is clear that employers must not harass their employees and may be liable for acts of harassment committed by an employee on a colleague (see 12.13 below), there has been some doubt as to whether or not they will ordinarily be liable for acts of harassment committed against their employees by third parties. In *Burton v De Vere Hotels Ltd* [1997] ICR 1 it had been suggested that an employer might be liable for acts of harassment committed by third parties if it could have taken steps which would have prevented or reduced the extent of the harassment. *Burton* was disapproved by the House of Lords in *Macdonald v Advocate General for Scotland* [2003] UKHL 34, [2003] ICR 937. However, in *EOC v Secretary of State for Trade and Industry*, above, the Administrative Court determined that *SDA 1975* failed properly to implement *ETD 76/207/EEC* in that it imposed no liability on an employer where despite knowing of 'continuing and/or regular objectionable conduct' by a third party they failed to take any step to prevent it. The Court's reasoning was that the employer's omission to act itself constituted unwanted behaviour relating to the sex of the employee. By necessary implication the other domestic anti-discrimination measures must be taken to have failed properly to implement their respective underlying European measures and require amendment.

If the reason for the employer's failure to take steps to protect the employee was the employee's sex, the employer would be liable on ordinary principles. Thus, if employers allows both male and female employees to be subject to harassment by third parties, they do not discriminate. However, if they take steps to protect men but not women a liability will arise.

If an employer fails to investigate an allegation of harassment when it is raised with him, and the tribunal is satisfied that, but for the complainant's sex it would have been investigated, the employer may thereby commit a further act of discrimination. However, absent any suggestion of less favourable treatment on grounds of sex, a failure to investigate a complaint of harassment will not in and of itself constitute unlawful discrimination (*Home Office v Coyne* [2000] ICR 1443, CA).

The *Criminal Justice and Public Order Act 1994* created an offence of 'intentional harassment'. It is committed where a person 'with intent to cause a person harassment, alarm or distress' uses threatening, abusive or insulting language or behaviour, or disorderly behaviour, or displays any writing, sign or other visible representation which is threatening, abusive or insulting, so that another person feels harassment, alarm or distress. The maximum penalties for the offence are six months in prison or a fine of £5,000. A further offence was created by the *Protection from Harassment Act 1997* (which came into force on 16 June 1997 (*SI 1997/1418*)). In addition to providing for harassers to be subject potentially to a fine or up to six months in prison, the *Act* creates a number of civil remedies, including damages and restraining orders backed by powers of arrest.

(h) Post-employment Discrimination

Even though the employment relationship has terminated, former employees may, in certain circumstances, continue to be entitled to be protected from acts of discrimination by their former employers.

12.12   Discrimination and Equal Opportunities – I

It is unlawful for a former employer to discriminate against a former employee on grounds of sex, marital status (or, from a date to be appointed, civil partnership) status, race or ethnic or national origins, religion or belief, sexual orientation, or pregnancy or maternity leave by subjecting them to a detriment or by harassing them 'where the discrimination or harassment arises out of and is closely connected to ... [the former employment] relationship' (*SDA 1975, s 20A* as amended, with effect from 1 October 2005, by *SDR 2005, reg 21), RRA 1976, s 27A(2); RBR 2003, reg 21(2); SOR 2003, reg 21(2)*). The provisions should not be read as rendering unlawful acts of discrimination committed before they came into force (*South East Essex College v Abegaze* [2006] ICR 468, EAT).

Cases of discrimination on grounds of colour or nationality or acts of sex discrimination occurring before 1 October 2005.

There is no specific statutory extension of liability beyond the end of employment in these cases. Nevertheless, the courts and tribunals have established through case law a broadly equivalent protection.

The wording of *SDA 1975, s 6* was formerly thought to restrict the protection provided by the *Act* to current employees or applicants for employment. It seemed to allow employers to discriminate against former employees with impunity. However, the European Court of Justice decided that such a narrow scope of protection would act to deprive women of an effective remedy for acts of sex discrimination and contravened the *ETD 76/207/EEC (Coote v Granada Hospitality Ltd* [1998] IRLR 656). The EAT subsequently decided that *SDA 1975, s 6* was capable of an interpretation which was consistent with the Directive (*Coote v Granada Hospitality Ltd (No 2)* [1999] ICR 942, EAT) the result of which was that a former employee was able to complain that she had been victimised when her former employer declined to provide her with a reference. The scope of post-termination protection was considered by the House of Lords in *Relaxion Group plc v Rhys Harper* [2003] UKHL 33, [2003] ICR 867. Lord Nicholls, in common with each of his colleagues, thought it significant that the termination of employment often did not mean a complete termination of the relationship. For instance, a dismissed employee might have a contractual right to appeal even though the contract of employment has been terminated. Whilst each of the judges had much the same approach in mind, their formulations of the appropriate test differ. Until lower appellate courts create a synthetic test, it is useful to set out each of the tests. Lord Nicholls' view was that the prohibition on discrimination applies to 'all incidents of the employment relationship whenever precisely they arise'. Lord Hope considered that the *RRA 1976* continues to apply to transactions remaining to be completed on termination of the contract of employment which 'are attributable to a continuation of the ... relationship [of the parties] as employer and employee'. Lord Hobhouse required there to be a 'sufficiently close connection with [the] employment'. That requirement might be met, by way of example, in circumstances where the post-termination discrimination related to a benefit which, as a former employee, the complainant had a legitimate expectation she would receive. Lord Scott concluded that the obligations under the *Act* continued for so long as the employment relationship (as opposed to the employment contract) continued to subsist. The relationship would continue to subsist for such period as was reasonably required to allow for the performance of ongoing contractual entitlements or the fulfilment of reasonable expectations. Lord Rodger thought it was unlawful to discriminate against former employees if 'there is a substantive connection between the discriminatory conduct and the employment relationship' (see also *Metropolitan Police Service v Shoebridge* [2004] ICR 1690, EAT).

As *RRA 1976, s 27A* only applies to a subset of the grounds for discrimination that fall within the statutory definition of 'racial grounds'. It is unclear whether the House of Lords' approach in *D'Souza* will apply in cases where discrimination is, for instance, on grounds of colour, or whether the existence of the specific express extension in *s 27A* suggests that it would be inappropriate to interpret the act as providing for a broad implied extension.

Where a tribunal makes a reinstatement order as a remedy for unfair dismissal, a discriminatory failure to comply with the order was not 'discrimination in employment' for the purposes of *RRA 1976 (D'Souza v Lambeth London Borough Council* [2003] UKHL 33, [2003] ICR 867).

12.13 Other Unlawful Acts

(a) Discriminatory practices

The application of discriminatory practices, namely, any provision, criterion or practice which results in any act of discrimination made unlawful by the provisions of the *RRA 1976* relating to employment, is in itself unlawful (*RRA 1976, s 28* as amended with effect from 19 July 2003 by the *Race Relations Act 1976 (Amendment) Regulations 2003 (SI 2003/1626)*).

(b) Instructions to commit unlawful acts

It is unlawful for one person who has authority over another, or in accordance with whose wishes that other person is accustomed to act, to instruct him to do any act which is unlawful under the *Act*, or to procure or attempt to procure the doing by him of any such act (*SDA 1975, s 39; RRA 1976, s 30*). There is no equivalent provision in the *RBR 2003* or the *SOR 2003*.

An instruction to discriminate unlawfully, which is followed by dismissal for disobedience of the instruction, may give rise to two possible consequences. They are proceedings commenced in the county court by the EOC for breach of *SDA 1975, s 39* or by the CRE for breach of *RRA 1976, s 30*, and proceedings by the individual in an employment tribunal under *SDA 1975, 6(2)(b)* or *RRA 1976, s 4(2)(c)*. (See *Zarczynska v Levy* [1979] ICR 184 and *Weathersfield Ltd (t/a Van and Truck Rentals) v Sargent* [1999] ICR 425, CA.)

In *Weathersfield Ltd v Sargent*, the receptionist at a truck rental company was instructed to tell black or Asian enquirers that no vehicles were available. As a result, she found her position intolerable and resigned. The respondent argued that as any employee would have been given the same instruction, the complainant could not establish that she had been less favourably treated. The EAT concluded that the instruction affected employees 'differentially' in that some, but not all, would regard themselves as 'victims of mistreatment'. The appropriate comparator, therefore, was somebody who was prepared to go along with the employer's unlawful instruction. The EAT's decision was affirmed by the Court of Appeal.

(c) Pressure to commit unlawful acts

It is unlawful to induce, or attempt to induce, a person to do anything which is unlawful by virtue of *SDA 1975* or *RRA 1976 (SDA 1975, s 40; RRA 1976, s 31(1)*). An attempted inducement is not prevented from being unlawful because it is not made directly to the person in question, if it is made in such a way that he is likely to hear of it (*SDA 1975, s 40(2)* and *RRA 1976, s 31(2)*). Thus if A, a managing director, tells B, one of his employees, that another employee, C, will be promoted if C discriminates against X in selecting applicants for a job, A is guilty of an unlawful act. In *Commission for Racial Equality v Imperial Society of Teachers of Dancing* [1983] ICR 473, the Employment Appeal Tribunal held that a prospective employer was in breach of *RRA 1976, s 31* for telling the head of careers at a school that he would prefer that the school did not put forward any coloured applicants.

(d) Liability for unlawful act of employee

Any unlawful act (other than a criminal offence) under any of the relevant legislative instruments committed by an employee in the course of his employment is treated as also having been done by his employer, whether or not it was done with the employer's knowledge or approval (*SDA 1975, s 41(1)*; *RRA 1976, s 31(2)*; *RBR 2003, reg 22(1)*; *SOR, reg 22(1)*.). (See, for example, *Kingston v British Railways Board* [1982] ICR 392, and contrast *Irving and Irving v Post Office* [1987] IRLR 289, *Tower Boot Co Ltd v Jones* [1995] IRLR 529; and see VICARIOUS LIABILITY (56); cf DISCRIMINATION AND EQUAL OPPORTUNITIES – II (13).)

At common law, an employer is liable for acts of negligence committed by an employee 'in the course of his employment'. This term of art came to be interpreted narrowly so as only to cover cases where what the employee did was 'so connected with acts which [the employer] has authorised that they may rightly be considered as modes – although improper modes – of doing them' (*Salmond and Heuston on the Law of Torts* (21st edn, 1996), p 443). Although the equal opportunities legislation also makes the employer responsible for acts committed by an employee 'in the course of his employment', the narrow common law interpretation did not apply (*Jones v Tower Boot Co Ltd* [1997] ICR 254, CA). In effect, it is open to a tribunal to find that an employer is liable for acts of discrimination where they are committed 'at work' instead of merely where they are committed 'as work'. The common law test has now 'caught up' (see *Lister v Helsey Hall Ltd* [2001] UKHL 22, [2001] IRLR 472, HL at 46.7). Acts committed by colleagues away from the workplace are less likely to fall within the scope of the *Act* (eg cf *Waters v Metropolitan Police Comr* [1997] IRLR 589, CA: sexual assault by one off-duty police officer on another in a police section house. Cf also *Sidhu v Aerospace Composite Technology Ltd* [2000] IRLR 602, CA: acts committed during the course of a 'family day' organised by an employer and held at an amusement park were not in the course of employment; and *HM Prison Service v Davis* (2000) 666 IDS Brief 14, EAT: harassment not in course of employment where employee visited colleague at her home, even though employer had power to discipline employees for misconduct committed away from the workplace) although that will not always be so. In *Chief Constable of Lincolnshire Constabulary v Stubbs* [1999] ICR 547, EAT, the EAT upheld a finding that drinks after work and an organised leaving party were sufficiently work-related to be treated as 'extensions of work'.

A police officer is not an employee, nor is the Chief Constable his employer. However, *RRA 1976, s 16*, formerly deemed police officers to be employees for the purposes of *Part II* of the *Act*. The Chief Officer was deemed to be their employer as respects any act done by him in relation to the police officer. The net effect is that police officers enjoy substantially the same protection against acts of discrimination as employees. However, the Court of Appeal has held that the Chief Officer did not fall to be treated as an employer for the purposes of *RRA 1976, s 32(1)* (*Chief Constable of Bedfordshire Police v Liversidge* [2002] EWCA Civ 894 ([2002] ICR 1135)). That section is to be found in *Part IV* of the *Act* and there was no deeming provision equivalent to *s 16* applicable to that part. The situation has since been altered by the *Race Relations (Amendment) Act 2000* ('*RR(A)A 2000*'). With effect from 1 April 2001, *RR(A)A 2000* repealed *RRA 1976, s 16*. It added a new *RRA 1976, s 76A* which again deems officers to be employees for the purposes of *Part II* of *RRA 1976* but also specifically deems them to be employees for the purposes of *RRA 1976, s 32*.

Defence to vicarious liability

The employer will have a defence if he can prove that he took such steps as were reasonably practicable to prevent his employee from doing that act, or from doing that kind of act during the course of his employment (*SDA 1975, s 41 (3)*; *RRA 1976, s 32(3)*; *RBR 2003, reg 22(3)*; *SOR, reg 22(3)*. See *Balgobin v Tower Hamlets London Borough Council* [1987] ICR 829). In determining whether the defence is made out, the tribunal should focus on what the employer has done prior to the occurrence of the act and not how he reacts once it has occurred (*Haringey London Borough Council (Haringey Design Partnership Directorate of Technical and Environmental Services) v Al-Azzawi* (2002) 703 IDS Brief 7, EAT). An employment tribunal may have regard to such matters as whether the employer has issued a written policy to employees on equal opportunities, whether it has given its managers training in such matters and whether it has taken steps to discipline employees if they have been guilty of unlawful discrimination. Where there were steps which it would have been reasonably practicable to take, it seems that the respondent must take them if he is to escape liability even if it cannot be shown that those steps would have prevented the discriminatory acts from occurring (*Canniffe v East Riding of Yorkshire Council* [2000] IRLR 555, EAT).

Where an employee's discriminatory behaviour occurs outside the course of his employment, an employer may have a primary, as opposed to a vicarious, liability if he has a sufficient control over the circumstances in which the behaviour occurred to have prevented it from happening and the reason for not exercising that control is a prohibited ground. Where, however, an employer simply fails to do so and would have so failed regardless of the prohibited ground he will not be liable under existing domestic statutory principles (*Macdonald v Advocate General for Scotland* [2003] UKHL 34, [2003] ICR 937 disapproving *Burton v De Vere Hotels Ltd* [1997] ICR 1). Note, however, that in *EOC v Secretary of State for Trade and Industry* [2007] EWHC 483 (Admin), [2007] IRLR 327, the Administrative Court decided in the context of an analysis of *SDA 1975*, that the existing domestic provisions failed properly to implement *ETD 76/207/EEC* in that rather than precluding harassment 'related to sex' it only prohibited harassment 'on ground of sex'. The latter formulation required sex to be causal factor, where as the former did not. The domestic law should have adopted the wider formulation and, if it had, *Burton* would have been rightly decided.

(e) Liability for unlawful act of agent

Any unlawful act committed by an agent with the express or implied authority (whether precedent or subsequent) of his principal is treated (except as regards offences under *RRA 1976*) as also having been done by his principal (*SDA 1975, s 41(2)*; *RRA 1976, s 32(2)*; *RBR 2003, reg 22(2)*; *SOR, reg 22(2)*.)

It is no answer for the principal to say that it did not give the agent authority to discriminate. It will be enough if the agent has authority to do an act which may be carried out, whether in a lawful or a discriminatory manner (*Lana v Positive Action Training in Housing (London) Ltd* [2001] IRLR 501, EAT).

Investigating and supervisory officers appointed under the *Police (Discipline) Regulations 1985* and the *Police (Conduct) Regulations 1999* do not act on behalf of the Chief Officer when carrying out their obligations under the regulations. However, a civilian employed as a manager by a police authority does act as the agent of the Chief Officer when dealing disciplinary matters relating to civilian staff (*Yearwood v Commissioner of Police of the Metropolis* [2004] ICR 1660, EAT).

(f)   Liability for act of other third party

Until the decision in *EOC v Secretary of State* (above), it was clear that where a complainant is subjected to acts of discrimination by third parties, his employer will not be liable merely because he had a sufficient control over the circumstances in which the behaviour occurred to have prevented it from happening (*Macdonald v Advocate General for Scotland* [2003] UKHL 34, [2003] ICR 937 disapproving *Burton v De Vere Hotels Ltd* [1997] ICR 1. See also *Hussain v HM Prison Service* (2002) 713 IDS Brief 7, EAT: prison service not liable for racial abuse of prison officer by prison inmates.).

However, in the *EOC* case, the Administrative Court took the view, in respect of cases of harassment, that the language of the relevant underlying directive (*ETD 76/207/EEC*) was wide enough to require that an employer should be liable for acts of harassment by third parties of which he was aware and could have reasonably have been expected to prevent. The same analysis would apply to harassment claims based on other domestic measures that are underpinned by similarly-worded European directives. It would apply, for instance to anti-discrimination measures that have to be read consistently with the *Framework Directive 2000/78/EC*, such as *RBR 2003* and *SOR 2003*. The analysis would not apply, however, to cases of direct discrimination.

In any event, if the reason for the employer's failure to intervene is a prohibited ground, he will be liable for that failure rather than for the harassment itself.

(g)   Aiding unlawful acts

A person who knowingly aids another to do an act made unlawful by the *Act* is treated as if he himself did that unlawful act (*SDA 1975, s 42(1)*; *RRA 1976, s 33(1)*; *RBR 2003, reg 23(1)*; *SOR, reg 23(1)*).

It is a defence for a person to show that:

(*a*)   he acted in reliance on a statement made to him by that other person that the act would not be unlawful; and

(*b*)   it was reasonable for him to rely on that statement.

(*SDA 1975, s 42(3)*; *RRA 1976, s 33(3)*; *RBR 2003, reg 23(3)*; *SOR, reg 23(3)*.)

Knowingly to make a false statement is an offence punishable by a fine not exceeding level 5 on the standard scale (*SDA 1975, s 42(4)*; *RRA 1976, s 33(4)*; *RBR 2003, reg 23(4)*; *SOR, reg 23(4)*).

In *Anyanwu v South Bank Student's Union* [2001] IRLR 391, HL, two paid student executives of a student union were dismissed by the union after an investigation into their activities had resulted in the University expelling them. The complainants alleged that their dismissals had been discriminatory and that, as their expulsion had meant that dismissal was inevitable, the University should be treated as having aided the discriminatory dismissals. The majority of the Court of Appeal ([2000] ICR 221) decided that whilst the University might be said to have 'brought about' the dismissals, it could not be said to have 'aided' the union in dismissing the complainants. The concept of providing aid involves a secondary participant assisting a 'primary actor'. It was the University that was the primary actor and, thus, its actions fell outside the scope of *RRA 1976, s 33(1)*. However, the Court of Appeal's decision was overturned by the House of Lords. Lord Bingham opined that the adoption of a terminology of primary and secondary movers amounted to an unjustified gloss on an otherwise straightforward provision. The following guidance was offered. First, the word 'aids' in the statutory provision should be given its ordinary meaning. Second, a person may knowingly aid another to do an unlawful act without inducing the wrongdoer to act unlawfully or procuring the act of discrimination. Third, provided that the assistance given is not so insignificant as to be negligible, it does not matter whether the help is substantive or productive.

In *Hallam v Avery* [2001] ICR 408, HL, the House of Lords made it clear that showing that a respondent had been 'helpful' did not necessarily allow a court or tribunal to conclude that they had 'aided' a discriminator. On the particular facts, a local authority had agreed to hire out rooms to a gypsy couple for their wedding reception. The police warned the local authority that they had experienced problems with gypsy weddings in the past. The local authority sought to impose further conditions on the hiring of the room, which, it was found, amounted to an act of discrimination. The House of Lords considered that the judge at first instance had been entitled to find that the police had not aided the local authority in its act of discrimination. Lord Millet made the point succinctly, observing that the information with which the authority was provided had not assisted it in making its decision to impose fresh conditions. Aiding an act required a closer degree of involvement in it. It was thought significant that the policemen concerned had played no part in the making of the decision itself.

Hallam had been decided on a different basis by the Court of Appeal ([2000] ICR 583, CA). Whilst the imposition of further conditions was an act of discrimination, it was decided that there was insufficient evidence that the police had been aware that, as a result of their advice, the local authority would treat the couple less favourably on grounds of their race. That being so, they could not be said knowingly to have aided an act of discrimination. Recklessness was insufficient; the police had to know that they were aiding a discriminator. See also *Sinclair, Roche & Temperley v Heard* [2004] IRLR 763, EAT.

A person does not 'aid' discrimination merely by creating an environment in which discrimination could occur. Fostering and encouraging a discriminatory culture may, however, suffice (*Gilbank v Miles* [2006] EWCA Civ 543, [2006] ICR 1297).

In *Shepherd v North Yorkshire County Council* [2006] IRLR 190, EAT a council was accused of knowingly aiding a trade union to delay the implementation of a collective agreement. The agreement had the effect of prolonging a disparity in pay between male and female employees. The EAT decided that even if the Council had been aware that the union was discriminating, they could not be said to have knowingly aided the discrimination. There was a material difference between taking advantage of a failure by another and aiding that party to discrimination. The Council had had its own interests to protect in any collective negotiation. Further, the union had not needed the employer's assistance to discriminate.

Where, during the course of his employment, an employee commits an act of discrimination, his employer may be liable for it (see 12.13(D) above). The employee may also be liable in a personal capacity. *RRA 1976, s 33* treats the employee as having knowingly aided the employer to perform the discriminatory act. The employee may be liable on this basis even in circumstances where the employer has succeeded in establishing an *RRA 1976, s 32* defence (*Crofton v Yeboah* [2002] EWCA Civ 794, [2002] IRLR 634).

If a person found liable under the provision is an individual acting in the course of his employment, it may be proper for any award of compensation to be made only against the employer, who will generally be liable on the principles set out in 12.13(D) above (*Deane v Ealing London Borough Council* [1993] ICR 329).

13   Discrimination and Equal Opportunities – II: Exceptions, Defences and Non-Employers covered by the Employment Rules

13.1   The scope and application of the *Sex Discrimination Act 1975* ('SDA 1975'), the *Race Relations Act 1976* ('RRA 1976'), *Employment Equality (Religion or Belief) Regulations 2003* ('RBR 2003') and the *Employment Equality (Sexual Orientation) Regulations 2003* ('SOR 2003') is described in DISCRIMINATION AND EQUAL OPPORTUNITIES – I (12). This chapter deals with the exceptions to the scope, and defences to the application of that legislation ('the equality legislation'). It also covers the application of the equality legislation to non-employers covered by the employment rules, such as trade organisations, vocational training providers, partnerships, barristers, police officers, the crown etc. (see below 13.21FF). Finally, the chapter deals briefly with the equality duties imposed on public authorities by the *RRA 1976* and the new Gender Equality Duty inserted into the *SDA 1975* by the *Equality Act 2006* (below 13.33).

In summary, an employer (or non-employer covered by the rules) may have a defence to claims of both direct and indirect discrimination where he can show that being of a particular race, religion or belief, sex or sexual orientation is a genuine requirement or qualification for a particular job (see below 13.2FF). A defence of justification is also available, but only to claims of indirect discrimination (see below 13.8).

There are also a number of general exceptions (or limits) to the scope of the equality legislation, which (broadly speaking) does not prohibit discrimination where the employee is employed outside Great Britain (below 13.15), or works under an illegal contract (below 13.16), or where the discrimination relates to benefits that the employer also provides to the public (below 13.17), is authorised by another enactment (below 13.18), is necessary for the purposes of national security (below 13.19) or where the employer qualifies for immunity under the *State Immunity Act 1978* (below 13.20). In addition, there are a number of exceptions that are specific to each of the different grounds of discrimination, such as where communal accommodation is provided, or where the employment is for the purposes of an organised religion, or where a particular benefit is dependent on the employee having marital or civil partnership status (see below 13.10–13.13).

There are also circumstances in which a respondent is permitted to discriminate positively in favour of persons of a particular race, sex, etc (see below 13.9FF).

For enforcement of the equality legislation and remedies, see DISCRIMINATION AND EQUAL OPPORTUNITIES – III (14).

Note that because of their distinct legislative regimes, disability discrimination and age discrimination are dealt with in separate chapters (DISABILITY DISCRIMINATION (10) and AGE DISCRIMINATION (3)), as is discrimination on grounds of sex in respect of contractual terms and conditions (see EQUAL PAY (24)).

13.2   **GENUINE OCCUPATIONAL REQUIREMENT OR QUALIFICATION**

Broadly speaking, where being of a particular race, religion or belief, sex or sexual orientation can be shown to be a genuine requirement or qualification for a particular job, a respondent may have a defence to certain forms of both direct and indirect discrimination. The defence is not, however, a licence to discriminate. Thus, in general, and except where otherwise indicated below, the existence of a genuine occupational requirement or qualification is *not* a defence to a claim of unlawful discrimination in the terms of employment offered or afforded to the complainant, or discrimination taking the form of subjecting a complainant to a detriment other than dismissal, or to harassment.

However, the defence *is* (again except where otherwise indicated below) potentially available where the discrimination takes one of the following forms:

(*a*)   Discrimination in the arrangements made for the purpose of determining who should be offered employment;

(*b*)   Refusal or deliberate omission to offer the complainant employment;

(*c*)   Discrimination in the way in which the complainant is afforded access to opportunities for promotion, transfer or training, (or is not afforded access to such opportunities); or

(*d*)   Dismissal.

The nature and extent of the defence available depends on the ground for the discrimination.

13.3   Sex: genuine occupational qualification

The *Sex Discrimination Act 1975* (*'SDA 1975'*) provides that where being a man (or, as appropriate, being a woman: see 12.2(I) DISCRIMINATION AND EQUAL OPPORTUNITIES – I) is a genuine occupational qualification ('a GOQ') for a job, a respondent may have a defence to a complaint of discrimination taking the limited forms listed above at 13.2(a), (b) and (c). The defence is *not* available where the complainant's complaint is that he has been dismissed (ie 13.2(d) above).

Being a man is only capable of being a GOQ for a job in certain defined circumstances, namely:

(*a*)   Where the essential nature of the job calls for a man for reasons of physiology (excluding physical strength or stamina) or, in dramatic performances or other entertainment, for reasons of authenticity, such that the essential nature of the job would be materially different if carried out by a woman.

Thus a woman may not be discriminated against simply because a job is perceived to require the physical strength and stamina of a man, provided that she is actually capable of performing the duties (ie provided the essential nature of the job would not be materially different if carried out by her). However, employers may discriminate for other physiological reasons, in particular where seeking male models or actors.

(*b*)   Where the job needs to be held by a man to preserve decency or privacy because:

    (i)   it is likely to involve physical contact with men in circumstances where they might reasonably object to its being carried out by a woman; or

    (ii)   the holder of the job is likely to do his work in circumstances where men might reasonably object to the presence of a woman because they are in a state of undress or are using sanitary facilities.

If an employer required his employees to work stripped to the waist, then in order to establish that he was justified in refusing to offer employment to women, a court hearing a complaint against him would, it is thought, decide whether that requirement was necessary for the performance of the task, or a mere whim on the part of the employer.

(c)   Where the job is likely to involve the holder of the job doing his work, or living, in a private home and needs to be held by a man because objection might reasonably be taken to allowing a woman –

    (i)   the degree of physical or social contact with a person living in the home; or

    (ii)   the knowledge of intimate details of such a person's life which is likely, because of the nature or circumstances of the job or of the home, to be allowed to, or available to, the holder of the job.

(d)   Where the nature or location of the establishment makes it impracticable for the holder of the job to live elsewhere than in premises provided by the respondent and:

    (i)   the only such premises which are available for persons holding that kind of job are lived in, or normally lived in, by men and are not equipped with separate sleeping accommodation for women and sanitary facilities which could be used by women in privacy from men; and

    (ii)   it is not reasonable to expect the respondent either to equip these premises with such accommodation and facilities, or to provide other premises for women.

(See, eg, *Sisley v Britannia Security Systems Ltd* [1983] ICR 628.)

(e)   Where the nature of the establishment, or the part of it within which the work is done, requires the job to be held by a man because:

    (i)   it is, or is part of, a hospital, prison or other establishment for persons requiring special care, supervision or attention; and

    (ii)   those persons are all men (disregarding any woman whose presence is exceptional); and

    (iii)   it is reasonable, having regard to the essential character of the establishment or that part, that the job should not be held by a woman.

(f)   Where the holder of the job provides individuals with personal services promoting their welfare or education or similar personal services, and those services can most effectively be provided by a man.

(g)   Where the job needs to be held by a man because it is likely to involve the performance of duties outside the United Kingdom in a country whose laws or customs are such that the duties could not, or could not effectively, be performed by a woman.

(*h*)   Where the job is one of two to be held by a married couple or (with effect from 5 December 2005) civil partners: see *s 7, SDA 1975*, as amended by *s 251* of the *Civil Partnership Act 2004*. See also below 13.13 for further discussion of civil partnership.

(*SDA 1975, s 7(2)*), as amended by the *Sex Discrimination Act 1986, s 1(2)* and the *Employment Act 1989, s 3(2)*.)

These exceptions apply even where only some of the duties of the job fall within the above provisions, as well as where all of them do (*SDA 1975, s 7(3)*). However, where an employer already has female employees who are capable of carrying out the duties of a vacant post, and whom it would be reasonable to employ on those duties and whose numbers are sufficient to meet his likely requirements in respect of those duties without undue inconvenience, then he may not discriminate by filling the vacancy with another man, even if the vacancy falls within (*a*) to (*g*) above (*SDA 1975, s 7(4)*). (See, eg, *Etam plc v Rowan* [1989] IRLR 150 and also *Lasertop Ltd v Webster* [1997] IRLR 498, EAT.) It is existing employees that count. It is not open to a tribunal to find that the defence is defeated on the basis that it was open to the respondent to appoint new female employees capable of performing the relevant duties.

For the exception under the *SDA 1975* for ministers of religion see below 13.10(G).

13.4   Race: genuine occupational requirement or qualification

The *Race Relations Act 1976* ('*RRA 1976*'), as amended by the *Race Relations Act (Amendment) Regulations 2003* (*SI 2003/1626*) ('*Race Relations Amendment Regulations*'), provides for two different genuine occupational exceptions. The first, the exception for genuine occupational requirement (*RRA 1976, s 4A*: 'the GOR exception'), applies with effect from 19 July 2003 in relation to discrimination on grounds of race or ethnic or national origins. Note that these grounds are a subset of the definition of 'racial grounds' used in the *Act* (see 12.6(D) DISCRIMINATION AND EQUAL OPPORTUNITIES – I). The second, the exception for genuine occupational qualification (*RRA 1976, s 5*: 'the GOQ exception'), applies where the first does not, ie in relation to discrimination on grounds of colour or nationality and to all racial discrimination occurring before 19 July 2003.

The GOR exception is available only where the discrimination takes one of the specific forms listed above at 13.2(a), (b) and (d). The exception is *not* available for discrimination in the way in which the complainant is afforded access to other benefits, facilities or services (ie 13.2(c) above). Unlike the exception under the *SDA 1975*, however, it *is* available as a defence to a dismissal complaint.

The first exception (the GOR exception) applies where it is shown that:

'having regard to the nature of the employment or the context in which it is carried out:

(a)   being of a particular race or of particular ethnic or national origins is a genuine and determining occupational requirement;

(b)   it is proportionate to apply that requirement in the particular case; and

(c)   either –

(i)   the person to whom that requirement is applied does not meet it; or

(ii)   the respondent is satisfied, and in all the circumstances it is reasonable for him not to be satisfied, that the person meets it.' (*RRA 1976, s 4A(2)*).

The Department of Trade and Industry has suggested that, in relation to the equivalent provision in the regulations relating to discrimination on grounds of sexual orientation and religion or belief (as to which see below 13.7 and 13.6) that, in order to ensure compatibility with the governing European Directive (*Directive 2000/78/EC*), the word 'genuine' in *s 4A(2)(a)* should be interpreted in its primary sense of 'actual, true', rather than its secondary sense of 'honestly held belief'.

The second exception (the GOQ exception) is only available where the discrimination takes the specific forms listed above at 13.2(a), (b) and (c). It is not available where the complainant's complaint is that he has been dismissed (ie 13.2(d) above). In contrast to the general 'nature and context' principle that forms the basis of the GOR exception, the GOQ exception applies only in certain defined circumstances, namely where:

(*a*)   the job involves participation in a dramatic performance or other entertainment in a capacity for which a person of that racial group is required for reasons of authenticity; or

(*b*)   the job involves participation as an artist's or photographic model in the production of a work of art, visual image or sequence of visual images for which a person of that racial group is required for reason of authenticity; or

(*c*)   the job involves working in a place where food or drink is (for payment or not) provided to, and consumed by, members of the public or a section of the public in a particular setting for which, in that job, a person of that racial group is required for reasons of authenticity (thus, a respondent may lawfully discriminate in selecting waiters for an Indian or Chinese restaurant); or

(*d*)   the holder of the job provides persons of that racial group with personal services promoting their welfare, and those services can most effectively be provided by a person of that racial group (*RRA 1976, s 5(2)*).

The scope of the GOQ exception was discussed in *Tottenham Green Under-Fives' Centre v Marshall* [1989] ICR 214 and in *Lambeth London Borough Council v Commission for Racial Equality* [1990] ICR 768. In *Lambeth*, the Court of Appeal held that the use of the word 'personal' in *s 5(2)(d)* indicates that the identity of the giver and the recipient of the services is important. The Court of Appeal agreed with the Employment Appeal Tribunal that the *RRA 1976* appears to contemplate direct contact between the giver and the recipient – mainly face to face or where there would be susceptibility to personal, physical contact.

The GOQ exception applies where some of the duties fall within (*a*) to (*d*) above as well as where all of them do (*RRA 1976, s 5(3)*), and also where those duties are merely ones which it is desirable that the post-holder should carry out and are not fundamental to the post. However, it does not apply where the duties are too trivial to be taken into account or where they have been deliberately put into the job description as a sham or smokescreen (*Tottenham Green Under Fives' Centre v Marshall (No 2)* [1991] ICR 320).

It also does not apply where a respondent already has employees of a particular racial group who are capable of carrying out the duties of a vacant post and whom it would be reasonable to employ on those duties and whose numbers are sufficient to meet his likely requirements in respect of those duties without undue inconvenience, regardless of whether the vacancy falls within *s 5(2)* (*RRA 1976, s 5(4)*). As with cases of sex discrimination (see above 13.3), it will be existing employees who count.

13.5   Gender reassignment: genuine occupational qualification

Following the insertion of *ss 7A* and *7B* into the *SDA 1975* by the *Sex Discrimination (Gender Reassignment) Regulations 1999* (*SI 1999/1102*) ('*Gender Reassignment Regulations*') with effect from 1 May 1999 a genuine occupational qualification ('GOQ') defence is available in appropriate circumstances to allegations of sex discrimination brought by persons intending to undergo, undergoing or who have undergone gender reassignment ('transsexuals'). (See generally 12.6(E) DISCRIMINATION AND EQUAL OPPORTUNITIES – I.)

Broadly speaking, there are two circumstances where the GOQ defence may arise in relation to complaints by transsexuals. First, a gender reassignment may mean that the employee falls foul of a GOQ that the complainant be a man or, as appropriate, a woman. Second, there may be circumstances where the requirement is, in effect, not that the complainant should be a particular sex but that they should not be a transsexual.

(1)   Where the requirement is that a complainant be a man or a woman

Turning first to consider cases where the requirement is for a complainant of a specific sex, one finds that, for the most part, *SDA 1975, s 7A* simply extends the GOQ exception for sex discrimination (see above 13.3) to cases involving transsexuals. However, there are three differences between the scope of the defence in cases involving transsexuals and its scope in other cases of sex discrimination. First, there is a defence available to a respondent even in cases where a respondent discriminates:

(*a*)   in the terms in which he offers employment; or

(*b*)   by dismissing the complainant, or by subjecting him to any other detriment (*SDA 1975, s 7A(1)*).

Second, the defence is subject to an overarching requirement that treatment meted out to the complainant is reasonable in view of the circumstances giving rise to the GOQ (*SDA 1975, s 7A(1)(b)*).

Third, the limitation on the GOQ defence to a claim of sex discrimination imposed by *s 7(4)* (ie that a GOQ defence cannot be used where a respondent already has female employees who are capable of carrying out the duties of a vacant post whom it would be reasonable to employ on those duties) applies to the dismissal of transsexuals as it does to the filling of vacant posts (*SDA 1975, s 7A(3)*).

Note, however, that the defence is not available where the complainant's sex has become the acquired gender under the *Gender Recognition Act 2004* ('*GRA 2004*'): *SDA 1975, s 7A(4)*, as inserted by *GRA 2004, s 14* with effect from 4 April 2005. The *GRA 2004* provides for the application by transsexuals for "gender recognition certificates". Where a gender recognition certificate has been issued to a person, that person becomes 'for all purposes' the acquired gender (*GRA 2004, s 9*). In such circumstances, the GOQ exception does not apply at all.

(2) Where the requirement is that the complainant not be a transsexual

SDA 1975, s 7B sets out the variation of the defence which deals with circumstances where it is thought that not being a transsexual is a GOQ. Those circumstances are in addition to those described above in relation to sex discrimination and are referred to as 'supplementary general occupational qualifications' ('supplementary GOQs'). The supplementary GOQs are as follows:

(*a*)   the job involves the holder of the job being liable to be called upon to perform intimate physical searches pursuant to statutory powers;

(*b*)   the job is likely to involve the holder of the job doing his work, or living, in a private home and needs to be held otherwise than by a person who is undergoing or has undergone gender reassignment, because objection might reasonably be taken to allowing such a person:

    (i)   the degree of physical or social contact with a person living in the home; or

    (ii)   the knowledge of intimate details of such person's life, which is likely, because of the nature or circumstances of the job or of the home, to be allowed to, or available to, the holder of the job;

(*c*)   the nature or location of the establishment makes it impracticable for the holder of the job to live elsewhere than in premises provided by the respondent, and:

    (i)   the only such premises which are available for persons holding that kind of job are such that reasonable objection could be taken, for the purpose of preserving decency and privacy, to the holder of the job sharing accommodation and facilities with either sex whilst undergoing gender reassignment; and

    (ii)   it is not reasonable to expect the respondent either to equip those premises with suitable accommodation or to make alternative arrangements; or

(*d*)   the holder of the job provides vulnerable individuals with personal services promoting their welfare, or similar personal services, and in the reasonable view of the respondent those services cannot be effectively provided by a person undergoing gender reassignment.

The supplementary GOQs set out in paras (c) and (d) above only apply where an employee intends to undergo or is undergoing a gender reassignment. They are not available where the employee has already undergone the reassignment (*SDA 1975, s 7B(3)*). Further, the supplementary GOQs may not be relied upon as a defence to discriminating against the employee:

    (i)   in the terms on which they are offered employment (*SDA 1975, s 7B(1)(a)*);

    (ii)   in the way in which the employee is afforded access to opportunities for promotion, transfer or training, other than where there is a deliberate refusal or a deliberate omission to afford such access to a job; or

    (iii)   by subjecting him to any other detriment.

The case of *A v Chief Constable of West Yorkshire Police (No 2)* [2004] UKHL 21, [2004] ICR 806, HL was a case that concerned, in effect, a requirement that a police officer not be a transsexual. It was decided on the basis of the *SDA 1975* as it stood prior to the coming into force of the *Gender Reassignment Regulations* on 1 May 1999. However, the decision is relevant to the new GOQ defence. *A* was a male-to-female transsexual who applied for a position as a police constable. Her birth certificate recorded her sex as 'male', but she had undergone gender reassignment surgery and was also in outward appearance female. The Chief Constable refused her application because he considered that in order to be a police officer it was necessary to be either a man or a woman, both in appearance and by birth. The Chief Constable relied for the genuineness of that requirement on *s 54(9)* of the *Police and Criminal Evidence Act 1984* (*'PACE'*), which stipulates that intimate searches must be carried out by a police officer of the same sex as the person searched. The House of Lords held that the jurisprudence of the European Court of Human Rights and the European Court of Justice required transsexuals to be recognised in their reassigned gender. Accordingly, *s 54(9)* had to be interpreted as applying to a transsexual's reassigned gender, thereby depriving the Chief Constable of his GOQ defence.

Note, however, that since the coming into force of the *GRA 2004* on 1 July 2004, transsexuals may apply for a gender recognition certificate. Where a gender recognition certificate has been issued to a person, that person becomes 'for all purposes' the acquired gender (*GRA 2004, s 9*). Where a person has not applied for a gender recognition certificate, it will be a matter for argument as to whether the reasoning of the House of Lords in *A* should apply to any provisions similar to *PACE, s 54(9)*. On the one hand, if the decision in *A* is viewed as being driven by the ECJ's interpretation of the *Equal Treatment Directive*, it should make no difference where Parliament has chosen to draw the line on recognition, since EU law is supreme. On the other hand, if the decision in *A* is viewed as being driven by the jurisprudence of the European Court of Human Rights, it could be argued that, Parliament having now enacted the *GRA 2004* and determined the precise circumstances in which gender recognition should be accorded to transsexuals, that determination is to be respected as a matter that falls within the 'margin of appreciation' accorded to sovereign states.

Finally, it should be noted that, with effect from 1 October 2005, a further *caveat* to the supplementary GOQs is inserted into *SDA 1975, s 7B* by the *Employment Equality (Sex Discrimination) Regulations 2005* (SI 2005/2467) ("the 2005 Sex Discrimination Regulations"). That *caveat* is similar to provisions applying in respect of race (see above 13.4) and sex (see above 13.3): the supplementary GOQs do not apply where the employer:

(i)   already has transsexual employees who either have not undergone gender reassignment (and not undergoing or intending to undergo gender reassignment) or (having already undergone reassignment) have become the acquired gender under *GRA 2004*; and,

(ii)   those employees are capable of carrying out the duties in question, are sufficient in number to meet the employer's likely requirements in respect of those duties without undue inconvenience and whom it would be reasonable to employ on those duties.

13.6   Religion or belief: genuine occupational requirement

The *Employment Equality (Religion or Belief) Regulations 2003* (*SI 2003/1660*) (*'RBR 2003'*) provide an exception for genuine occupational requirement ('GOR') in two sorts of cases. The exception only applies where the discrimination takes one of the specific forms listed above at 13.2(a), (b), (c) and (d).

The first type of case is like the GOR exception under the *RRA 1976* (see above 13.4). In the first type of case the exception applies where, having regard to the nature of the employment or the context in which it is carried out, being of a particular religion or belief is 'a genuine and determining occupational requirement' (*reg 7(2)*).

The second type of case is where the respondent has an ethos based on a religion or belief and, having regard to that ethos as well as to the nature of the employment, or the context in which it is carried out, being of a particular religion or belief is a GOR (*reg 7(3)*).

In both types of case, the mere existence of a GOR does not take the complainant outside the protective scope of the *Regulations*. First, it must also be shown that the complainant does not meet the requirement. Where it is not immediately clear whether the complainant meets the requirement, it is sufficient that the respondent is not satisfied, on reasonable grounds, that the complainant meets the requirement (*reg 7(2)(c) and (3)(c)*). Second, it must be proportionate to apply the requirement in the particular case (*reg 7(2)(b) and (3)(b)*).

13.7   Sexual orientation: genuine occupational requirement

The *Employment Equality (Sexual Orientation) Regulations 2003 (SI 2003/1661)* ('*SOR 2003*') provide for two types of cases in which a respondent may rely on the genuine occupational requirement ('GOR') exception in defence to a claim of discrimination on grounds of sexual orientation. In both types of case the defence is only available in relation to the limited forms of discrimination described above at 13.2(a), (b), (c) and (d).

The first type of case is like the first type of case under the *RBR 2003* (see above 13.6), ie the exception applies where, having regard to the nature of the employment or the context in which it is carried out, being of a particular sexual orientation is a 'genuine and determining occupational requirement'. The respondent must show that it was proportionate to apply the requirement in that particular case and that either the complainant did not meet the requirement as to sexual orientation or that it was reasonable, in all the circumstances, for the respondent to be satisfied that the complainant did not (*reg 7(2)*). In the absence of an express admission by the complainant, this will involve the tribunal determining whether the respondent's conclusion or assumption about the complainant's sexual orientation was a reasonable one.

The second type of case is where the employment is for the purposes of an organised religion and the respondent applies 'a requirement related to sexual orientation' in order:

(*a*)   to comply with the doctrines of that religion, or

(*b*)   owing to the nature or context of that employment, to avoid conflicting with the strongly held religious convictions of a significant number of the religion's followers (*reg 7(3)(a) and (b)*).

As with the first type of case, the respondent must also show that either the person to whom the requirement was applied did not meet that requirement or that it was reasonable for the respondent to have been satisfied that he did not (*reg 7(3)(c)*).

It was argued in *R (Amicus-MSF) v Secretary of State for Trade and Industry* [2004] EWHC 860 (Admin), [2004] IRLR 430 that *regs 7(2)* and *(3)* were incompatible with the governing European Directive (*Directive 2000/78/EC*). However, the High Court held that the *Regulations* were compatible. With regard to *reg 7(2)* (the first type of case), Richards J noted that, although the exception applied not only where the complainant did not in fact meet the requirement as to sexual orientation, but also where it was 'reasonable' for the respondent 'not to be satisfied' that the complainant met that requirement, the need for the respondent's decision to be 'reasonable' ensured that the decision could not be based on mere assumptions or social stereotyping. With regard to *reg 7(3)* (the second type of case), Richards J noted that the exception, as a derogation from the principle of equal treatment, had to be construed strictly. He noted that 'for the purposes of an organised religion' was a narrower expression than 'for the purposes of a religious organisation' or 'an ethos based on religion or belief', as used in the *RBR 2003*. Thus, employment as a teacher in a faith school was, he considered, likely to fall outside the exception as being 'for the purposes of a religious organisation' rather than 'for the purposes of an organised religion'. Further, he observed that the condition that the employer apply the requirement 'so as to comply with the doctrines of the religion' was an objective test and very narrow in scope. Similarly, the alternative condition that the exception be applied where required 'to avoid conflicting with the strongly held religious convictions of a significant number of the religion's followers' was also an objective test that would be difficult to satisfy in practice. He also noted that, although the phrase used in *reg 7(3)* 'a requirement related to sexual orientation' was linguistically wider in scope than the phrase 'being of a particular sexual orientation' used in *reg 7(2)*, it was difficult to see a practical difference between the two since 'being of a particular sexual orientation' necessarily encompassed matters relating to sexual behaviour, etc.

Compare the exception for employment for purposes of an organised religion with the exception for ministers of religion in the *SDA 1975*: see below 13.10(G).

13.8   JUSTIFICATION

A respondent will have a defence to a claim of *indirect* discrimination if he is able to show that the application of the relevant requirement, condition, provision, criterion or practice is justified. No such defence is available to claims of *direct* discrimination on grounds of race, religion or belief, sex or sexual orientation. (See generally 12.7 DISCRIMINATION AND EQUAL OPPORTUNITIES – I.)

Until recently, the test for whether a provision, criterion or practice, was justified differed depending on whether the complaint fell under the *SDA 1975*, related to discrimination on grounds of race or ethnic or national origins under the *RRA 1976*, or discrimination on grounds of colour under that *Act*, or fell under the *RBR 2003* or the *SOR 2003*. With the exception of discrimination on grounds of colour under the *RRA 1976*, the test is now the same in each of the *Acts* and *Regulations*. Under the *RBR 2003*, the *SOR 2003*, the *RRA 1976* (with effect from 19 July 2003) and the *SDA 1975* (with effect from 1 October 2005) indirect discrimination will be justified where the respondent shows that the application of the relevant provision, criterion or practice to the complainant is a 'proportionate means of achieving a legitimate aim' (*SDA 1975, s 1(2)*, as amended by the *Sex Discrimination Regulations 2005, reg 3*; *RRA 1976, s 1(1A)(c)*, as inserted by the *Race Relations Amendment Regulations* with effect from 19 July 2003; *RBR 2003, reg 3(1)(b)(iii)*; *SOR 2003, reg 3(1)(b)(iii)*).

This contrasts with the 'old' test, which required respondents only to show that the application of the relevant provision, criterion or practice was 'justifiable irrespective' of the sex/race etc. of the person to whom it was applied. The 'old' test still applies to indirect race discrimination on grounds of colour (*RRA 1976, s 1(1)(b)(ii)*), indirect race discrimination on any ground occurring prior to 19 July

2003 (*RRA 1976, s 1(1)(b)(ii)*) and indirect sex discrimination occurring prior to 1 October 2005 (*SDA 1975, s 1(2)(b)(ii)*).

The reason for the change in the test is so that the domestic legislation conforms with the governing European Directives (*Directive 76/207/EEC, art 2, para 2,* as amended by *Directive 2002/73*; *Directive* 2000/43/EC, *art 2, para 2(b)* and *Directive 2000/78/EC, art 2, para 2(b)*). It will be noted that the governing European Directives each provide that a respondent must demonstrate that the relevant provision, criterion or practice is 'objectively justified by a legitimate aim *and* the means of achieving that aim are appropriate and necessary'. Although the domestic legislation makes no mention of the requirements that the measure be 'appropriate and necessary', it is likely that, in line with the general principles for the application and interpretation of EC law (see 25.2 EUROPEAN COMMUNITY LAW) tribunals will no longer accept that a measure is proportionate unless a respondent has shown that it is both appropriate and necessary.

The classic test for establishing whether or not indirect discrimination may be justified is found in *Bilka-Kaufhaus GmbH v Weber Von Hartz (Case 170/84)* [1986] IRLR 317. There the European Court of Justice said that the national court (or tribunal) must be satisfied that the measures having a disparate impact 'correspond to a real need ... are appropriate with a view to achieving the objectives pursued and are necessary to that end' (para 36). In more recent cases (see especially *R v Secretary of State for Employment, ex p Seymour-Smith and Perez* [1999] IRLR 253 and also *Kutz-Bauer v Freie und Hansestadt Hamburg C-187/00,* [2003] IRLR 368) the ECJ has expanded on this, ruling that is for the national court (or tribunal) to ascertain, firstly, whether the measure in question has a legitimate aim, unrelated to any discrimination based on any prohibited ground; secondly, whether the measure is capable of achieving that aim; and, thirdly, whether in the light of all the relevant factors, and taking into account the possibility of achieving by other means the aims pursued by the provisions in question, the measure is proportionate.

Although the test for justification has changed, the case law on the 'old' test has continued to be regarded as relevant by tribunals. Care should be taken, however, to ensure that the specific requirements of the 'new' test are always met. A number of principles emerge from the case law on both the 'old' and 'new' tests:

(*a*)   The burden of proof is on the respondent to satisfy the tribunal that the measure applied was objectively justified for economic, administrative or other reasons (*Rainey v Greater Glasgow Health Board* [1987] ICR 129, an equal pay case in which the House of Lords held that the same principles are applicable to the *SDA 1975* as to the *Equal Pay Act 1970*; see 23.12 EQUAL PAY). (cf DISCRIMINATION AND EQUAL OPPORTUNITIES – III (14) for general discussion of the burden of proof.)

(*b*)   The test to be applied by the tribunal is an objective one: while the tribunal should take into account the reasonable needs of the respondent's business, the tribunal has to make its own judgment as to whether the provision, criterion or practice applied by the respondent is reasonably necessary: there is no scope for 'margin of discretion' or 'range of reasonable responses' approach when considering whether an indirectly discriminatory provision, criterion or practice is justified: *Hardys & Hansons plc v Lax* [2005] EWCA Civ 846, [2005] IRLR 727 (applied in *British Airways plc v Grundy,* EAT/0676/04RN, unreported, judgment delivered 19 August 2005 and *Redfearn v Serco Ltd* [2005] IRLR 744, EAT).

(c)   In considering whether a requirement or condition is justifiable, employment tribunals have to balance the discriminatory effect of the requirement or condition against the reasonable needs of the respondent (see *Ojutiku v Manpower Services Commission* [1982] ICR 661; *Hampson v Department of Education and Science* [1989] ICR 179, overturned by the House of Lords ([1990] ICR 511) on grounds other than justification, which was not argued before their Lordships). In *Board of Governors of St Matthias Church of England School v Crizzle* [1993] ICR 401, the EAT held that there were three questions to be asked: (i) was the respondent's objective legitimate; (ii) were the means used to achieve it reasonable in themselves; and, (iii) were they justified when balanced against their discriminatory effect on principles of proportionality? The principle of proportionality means that if a respondent imposes a requirement that employees of his should be able to lift heavy weights, such a requirement may be discriminatory if applied to typists but probably not if applied to warehouse staff (cf *Hampson* and *Cobb v Secretary of State for Employment* [1989] ICR 506; though see above 13.3(A)). When determining whether or not a measure is proportionate, it will be relevant to consider whether or not any lesser form of the measure would nevertheless serve the employer's legitimate aim. Thus, in *Azmi v Kirklees Metropolitan Borough Council*, EAT, 30 March 2007 (in which the Muslim claimant complained that she had been unlawfully discriminated against on grounds of her religious belief because she was not allowed to wear the veil while teaching at a primary school), the EAT held that the tribunal was right to have taken into account, in finding the requirement imposed by the school to be proportionate, the facts that (i) the respondent school had, before insisting on the claimant not wearing a veil, observed her teaching both with and without the veil and taken the view that she was much more effective without the veil, and (ii) the school had permitted her to wear the veil when moving around the school premises and had only required her not to wear the veil while teaching.

(d)   It is open to a tribunal to find that cost is a factor justifying indirect discrimination, provided it is combined with other factors: *Cross v British Airways plc* [2005] IRLR 423, EAT; *R (Elias) v Secretary of State for Defence* [2006] EWCA Civ 1293, [2006] IRLR 934. However, budgetary requirements alone will not be capable of justifying a discriminatory measure: *Schönheit v Stadt Frankfurt, C-4/02 and C-5/02* [2004] IRLR 983, ECJ and *Kutz-Bauer v Freie und Hansestadt Hamburg C-187/00* [2003] IRLR 368, ECJ, applied in *British Airways plc v Grundy* above.

(e)   The question of whether indirect discrimination is justified is one of fact for the employment tribunal (*Singh v British Rail Engineering* [1986] ICR 22), but the tribunal must identify the standards by which it tests justification (*Hampson*). The tribunal should 'critically evaluate' the defence relied upon and should never find it made out where the respondent's aim is itself discriminatory, for instance, where the purpose of imposing the condition is to enable him to avoid a statutory protection against discrimination (*Allonby v Accrington and Rossendale College* [2001] EWCA Civ 529, [2001] IRLR 364). The tribunal must consider both the quantitative and the qualitative effects of the discrimination, ie how many women or people of a particular racial group will suffer in consequence of it, and how seriously they will suffer (cf *Jones v University of Manchester* [1993] ICR 474 and also *EC Commission v Belgium* [1991] IRLR 393). For cases concerning justification of indirectly discriminatory requirements in relation to working practices in the armed forces, see *Macmillan v Ministry of Defence* (11 November 2003, unreported, EAT) and *Boote v Ministry of Defence* (3 March 2004, unreported, ChD).

(*f*)   The tribunal must demonstrate that it has critically evaluated any defence of justification: its reasons for finding that a measure is a 'proportionate means of achieving a legitimate aim' must be apparent from the decision: *Redfearn v Serco Ltd*, above. In that case, the EAT held that the tribunal had not given sufficient reasons for finding that a requirement that no employee be a member of the British National Party was justified as a proportionate means of achieving the legitimate aim of protecting the health and safety of Asian passengers using the Respondent's services.

(*g*)   Where the requirement, condition, provision, criterion or practice complained about is itself 'inextricably linked to' the forbidden ground of discrimination, it will not be possible for justification to be established: see *Orphanos v Queen Mary College* [1985] IRLR 349, HL, applied in *R (Elias) v Secretary of State for Defence and Commission for Racial Equality* [2006] EWCA Civ 1293, [2006] IRLR 934. The latter case concerned the requirement in a non-statutory compensation scheme for persons interned by the Japanese during the Second World War that, in order to qualify for compensation, internees had to have been born in the UK or have a parent or grandparent born in the UK. The Court of Appeal held that although the Government's desire to limit the scheme to those with a close connection with Britain was a legitimate aim, and cost factors could potentially justify such a limitation, the actual criteria imposed by the Government were so closely connected with the unlawful ground of discrimination (national origins) that their use could not be justified.

(*h*)   It is not necessary as a matter of law for the alleged discriminator to have analysed the proportionality question at the time of adopting a rule or policy: see *Cadman v Health and Safety Executive* [2004] EWCA Civ 1317, [2004] IRLR 97 and the *Elias* case (above). It is always open to the alleged discriminator to justify the rule or policy by factors not expressly taken into account at the time of adopting the rule or policy: see *Schönheit v Stadt Frankfurt conjoined cases C-4/02 and C-5/02,* [2004] IRLR 983. However, where the alleged discriminator has not even considered questions of proportionality at the time of adopting a rule or policy, it may be more difficult for him to establish justification (cf *Hockenjos v Secretary of State for Social Security* [2004] EWCA Civ 1749, [2005] IRLR 471 and the *Elias* case, above).

(*i*)   Under the 'old' test, it was held that a measure may be justified even though the respondent has not produced detailed evidence to show that there was no other way of achieving his or her object (cf *Cobb* above). Under the 'new' test, it is much more likely that a failure to adduce cogent evidence of justification will result in a finding that justification is not made out: see *British Airways plc v Starmer* [2005] IRLR 862 and also the Court of Appeal's decision in *Hockenjos v Secretary of State for Social Security* [2004] EWCA Civ 1749, [2005] IRLR 471 (below). In every case respondents need to take care to ensure that evidence adduced is aimed at the right issue. In *Whiffen v Milham Ford Girls' School* [2001] EWCA Civ 385, [2001] IRLR 468, the respondent attempted to justify a policy of responding to a redundancy situation by first allowing the contracts of temporary staff to lapse without renewal. The respondent argued that it needed to make redundancies and that the policy was gender-neutral. The Court of Appeal pointed out that all indirect discrimination cases concerned provisions which were gender-neutral on their face and that, where it had been found that an apparently gender-neutral provision had a disparate effect on a particular group (here, women), it was no justification that the policy might have operated non-discriminatorily in another situation. What required justification was that redundancies were first visited on temporary employees.

For justification of requirements or conditions that Sikhs who wear turbans should wear safety helmets on construction sites see below 13.12.

For a consideration of the justification for a requirement to work on Sundays (which was indirectly discriminatory under *RBR 2003*), cf *Williams-Drabble v Pathway Care Solutions Ltd* (ET, 10 January 2005, IDS Brief 776, p 8).

Challenging domestic legislation

Where a complainant seeks to have a provision of domestic legislation disapplied on the basis that it has an indirectly discriminatory effect and is thus contrary to Community Law, it is open to the member state to seek to justify the provision. In *R v Secretary of State for Employment, ex p Seymour-Smith* [1995] ICR 889 the House of Lords, following a reference to the ECJ, laid down a three-part test for assessing whether or not a discriminatory legislative provision was justified:

(i) Did the measure reflect a legitimate aim of social policy;

(ii) Was the aim unrelated to any discrimination based on sex; and

(iii) Could the Government reasonably consider that the means chosen were suitable for attaining the aim?

The ECJ further considered the issue in *Jørgensen v Foreningen af Speciallaeger and Sygesikringens Forhandlingsudvalg (Case C-226/98)* [2000] IRLR 726 and held that in deciding whether a member state had succeeded in demonstrating that a provision was justified, reliance on mere budgetary constraints would not be sufficient (see also *Kutz-Bauer v Freie Und Hansestadt Hamburg C-187/00* [2003] IRLR 368, ECJ).

The burden of proof for establishing justification is on the state: *Hockenjos v Secretary of State for Social Security* [2004] EWCA Civ 1749, [2005] IRLR 471. In *Hockenjos* the Court of Appeal considered a provision of the *Jobseeker's Allowance Regulations 1996* which had a clear disproportionate impact on men. The Court, applying the *Seymour-Smith* three-stage test, stressed that it was not necessary, in order for the claimant to succeed, for him to show that there was an obviously better way of achieving the legitimate aim. On the contrary, the burden was on the Secretary of State and his failure to apply his mind to the question of whether or not there was an alternative to the discriminatory provision meant that the burden of establishing justification had not been discharged. Note, however, that it is not necessary as a matter of law for the alleged discriminator to have analysed the proportionality question at the time of adopting a rule or policy: see *R (Elias) v Secretary of State for Defence and Commission for Racial Equality* [2006] EWCA Civ 1293, [2006] IRLR 934 (a case on a non-statutory scheme).

The *Seymour-Smith* test was also applied by the EAT in *Secretary of State for Trade and Industry v Rutherford (No 2)* [2003] IRLR 858. That case concerned the statutory age limit on the right not to be unfairly dismissed (*ERA 1996, s 109*) and to receive redundancy pay (*ERA 1996, s 156*). The EAT held that the tribunal had erred in finding that the statutory age limit had a disparate impact on men and that, even if it did, the policy arguments advanced (that it enabled employers to create opportunities for younger employees without having to justify the dismissal of older employees) were legitimate aims, unrelated to sex, which the government was entitled to pursue. The EAT's decision on disparate impact was affirmed by the Court of Appeal ([2004] EWCA Civ 1186, [2005] ICR 119) and by the House of Lords ([2006] UKHL 19, [2006] ICR 785). However, both the Court of Appeal and the House of Lords found it unnecessary, in the light of that decision, to decide the question of justification. In the Court of Appeal, however, Mummery LJ observed that the EAT had adopted the correct approach in law, but that it was, properly speaking, a question of fact for the tribunal as to whether justification was made out in any particular case.

13.9   **POSITIVE DISCRIMINATION**

Domestic law

Broadly speaking, positive discrimination is not permitted under the domestic equality legislation because discriminating in favour of one group of people generally involves unlawful discrimination against another group who are treated less favourably in comparison (*Lambeth London Borough Council v Commission for Racial Equality* [1990] ICR 768; though compare *Arnold v Barnfield College* [2004] All ER (D) 63 (Jul), EAT: mere existence of a policy of attracting more ethnic minority candidates not sufficient to indicate that there had been unlawful discrimination).

The position under EC law is less straightforward (see below). However, there are a number of exceptions to the general rule on positive discrimination, which are set out below.

See also 13.33 below for discussion of the equality duties imposed on all public authorities which, while not specifically authorising positive discrimination, do authorise and oblige public authorities to take positive action to eliminate unlawful discrimination.

(*a*) *Access to training*

Employers may discriminate positively in favour of a particular racial group or in favour of female or male employees in order to afford that group access to training and to encourage the members of that group to take advantage of opportunities for doing particular work, provided that, at any time within the 12 months immediately preceding the positive discrimination:

(i)   there were no persons of that group among those doing that work at that establishment; or

(ii) the proportion of persons of that group among those doing that work at that establishment is comparatively small (*RRA 1976, s 38(1), (2); SDA 1975, s 48(1), (2)*).

The *RRA 1976* specifies that the proportion of persons of that group must be 'small in comparison to':

(i)   all those employed by the respondent at that establishment; or

(ii) the population of the area from which that respondent normally recruits persons for work in his employment at that establishment.

Other persons concerned with the provision of vocational training may also discriminate in favour of racial groups, men or women (as appropriate) where it reasonably appears to that person that there are no, or a comparatively small number, of members of that particular race, sex, etc. doing that work in Great Britain (*RRA 1976, s 37*; *SDA 1975, s 47*). This exception specifically does not apply to discrimination by employers (*RRA 1976, s 38(3)* and *SDA 1975, s 47(4)*).

Similar provision is also made for positive discrimination in favour of persons of a particular religion or belief or sexual orientation where it reasonably appears to the person discriminating that it will prevent or compensate for disadvantages, linked to religion or belief or sexual orientation respectively, suffered by persons of that religion or belief or sexual orientation (as appropriate) (*RBR 2003, reg 25(1)*; *SOR 2003, reg 26(1)*). The ACAS Guidance on the *SOR 2003* and *RBR 2003* suggests that the exception would allow advertisements encouraging applications from people of a particular sexual orientation, religion or belief, provided it is made clear that selection will be on merit without reference to sexual orientation, religion or belief. The *Regulations* do not permit quota systems.

In addition, the *Employment Act 1989, s 8* provides that the Secretary of State may by order make special provision for vocational training for lone parents. Where such an order is made, discrimination in favour of lone parents in accordance with the order will not be regarded as unlawful under the *SDA 1975, s 3* (discrimination against married persons).

For advice on positive discrimination under the *RRA 1976*, see the Commission for Racial Equality's website, www.cre.gov.uk.

(b) Membership, etc. of trade organisations

Positive discrimination is permitted under the *SDA 1975* and the *RRA 1976* to encourage both membership of and postholding in trade organisations (including discrimination in affording access to training for holding such posts) where, at any time during the previous 12 months, there were no or proportionally few postholders or members of the relevant racial group or sex in that organisation (*RRA 1976, s 38(3), (4), (5)*; *SDA 1975, s 48(2), (3)*).

Similar provision is made by the *RBR 2003* and the *SOR 2003* to allow positive discrimination by trade organisations where it reasonably appears to the organisation that the act prevents or compensates for disadvantages linked to religion, belief or sexual orientation suffered by those of that religion, belief or sexual orientation who are members of the organisation, or are eligible to become members, or hold, or are likely to hold, posts within that organisation (*RBR 2003, reg 25(2)*; *SOR 2003, reg 26(2)*). The exception extends to "encouraging" only people of a particular sexual orientation, religion or belief to become members of the organisation where it reasonably appears to the organisation that doing so would prevent or compensate for disadvantages suffered by people of that sexual orientation, religion or belief (*RBR 2003, reg 25(3)*; *SOR 2003, reg 26(3)*).

Under the *SDA 1975* (but not under the *RRA 1976*, *SOR 2003* or *RBR 2003*), trade organisations are also permitted to discriminate positively by setting quotas reserving a certain number of elected seats to men only or women only where in the opinion of the organisation the quotas are in the circumstances needed to secure a reasonable lower limit to the number of members of that sex serving on the body (*SDA 1975, s 49(1)*). However, discrimination in the arrangements for determining who is entitled to vote in an election of members of the body or in any arrangements concerning membership of the union or organisation itself is *not* permitted: *SDA 1975, s 49(2)*.

Note that although a set of barristers chambers is a 'trade organisation' within the meaning of the equivalent provisions of the *Disability Discrimination Act 1995* (see 10.26 DISABILITY DISCRIMINATION), a pupil is not a 'member' of that organisation (*Higham and ors v Horton* [2004] EWCA Civ 941, [2005] ICR 292). (However, see 13.24 below for the general provisions relating to barristers.)

(c) Special treatment in connection with pregnancy or childbirth

Special treatment afforded to women in connection with pregnancy or childbirth is permitted, and may not be taken account of when considering a claim of sex discrimination brought by a man: *SDA 1975, s 2(2)*.

(d) Special treatment of Sikhs in relation to the wearing of helmets on construction sites

See below 13.12.

(e) Acts done to meet education, training or welfare needs of particular racial groups

The *RRA 1976* contains a further general exception for acts done for the purposes of protecting a particular racial group or groups. *Section 35* of the *RRA 1976* provides that nothing done by any body will be unlawful if it is done in order to afford persons of a particular racial group ('the protected group') access to facilities or services to meet the special needs of persons of that group in regard to their education, training or welfare, or any ancillary benefits. While this may appear to be a broad provision permitting positive discrimination, it is submitted that *s 35* will not render lawful an act of (negative) discrimination against a particular person or racial group unless that act is specifically done in order to provide services for the protected group. For example, it is unlikely that a trade organisation would be able to rely on this provision in order to justify having a membership consisting of only one racial group (or excluding a particular racial group) since a refusal of membership would not be directly related to the provision of services to the protected persons (though, where funds were limited, it ought to justify a refusal to provide legal services to members of the organisation if that was a 'special need' of the protected persons). This is particularly so given the specific express (and limited) provision as to positive discrimination by trade organisations (see above).

Positive action under EC law

Broadly speaking, the position in relation to positive action under EC law is, as one would expect, parallel to that under domestic law. However, the ECJ has held that *art 2(4)* of the version of *Council Directive 76/207/EEC* that was in force until 5 October 2005 (ie before the amendments made by *Council Directive 2002/73/EC*) permitted certain positively discriminatory measures. Measures permitted are those to the effect that where 'all else is equal' a female should be preferred for an appointment or promotion, provided that the measure is qualified by a requirement that consideration is given to the individual circumstances of each applicant: *Marschall v Land Nordrhein-Westfalen* (Case C-409/95) [2001] ICR 45, ECJ. However, where a national measure is not so qualified (*Kalanke v Freie Hansestadt Bremen (Case C-450/93)* [1996] ICR 314, ECJ), or that qualification is too vague to prevent appointments being made on the basis of sex alone (*Abrahamsson v Fogelqvist* (C-407/98) [2002] ICR 932, ECJ), the ECJ has held it to be incompatible with the *Directive* (cf also *EFTA Surveillance Authority v Norway* E-1/02 [2003] IRLR 318, ECJ).

The wording of the old *art 2(4)* is wider than that of *art 2(8)*, which replaced it as from 5 October 2005 (compare 'measures to promote equal opportunity for men and women, in particular by removing existing inequalities' with the new version to be found in *art 2(8)* and *art 141(4)* of the Treaty: 'the principle of equal treatment shall not prevent any Member State from maintaining or adopting measures providing for specific advantages in order to make it easier for the under-represented sex to pursue a vocational activity or to prevent or compensate for disadvantages in professional careers'). However, it is likely that the type of positive discrimination permitted by *art 2(4)* will continue to be held by the ECJ to be permissible under the new wording of the *Treaty* and the *Directive*. Similarly, it is likely to be acceptable in relation to the other grounds of discrimination, as to which EC legislation currently provides that 'the principle of equal treatment shall not prevent any Member State from maintaining or adopting specific measures to prevent or compensate for disadvantages linked to' race, sexual orientation, etc. (*Council Directive 2000/43/EC, art 5*; *Council Directive 2000/78/EC, art 7*). Further, with positive action now enshrined in *art 141(4)* of the *Treaty*, it is likely to be permissible for both private and public sector organisations positively to discriminate in this manner.

13.10 **EXCEPTIONS SPECIFIC TO THE DIFFERENT GROUNDS OF DISCRIMINATION**

Exceptions to the Sex Discrimination Act 1975

(a) *Where communal accommodation is provided*

If a respondent provides communal accommodation for his employees, contract workers, etc (as appropriate) he may discriminate on grounds of sex in its provision if the accommodation is managed in a way which is as fair as possible to men and women (*SDA 1975, s 46(3)*). In deciding whether a respondent has made fair provision, account is taken of:

(i)   whether and how far it is reasonable to expect that the accommodation should be altered or extended, or that further alternative accommodation should be provided; and

(ii)   the frequency of the demand or need for use of the accommodation by men as compared with women (*SDA 1975, s 46(4)*).

If, for example, a company provided a holiday home for its employees but the sleeping arrangements were only suitable for men, then provided that it was only used occasionally and it was impractical to modify it for the use of the women or to build additional accommodation for them, such discrimination may be lawful.

Benefits dependent on communal accommodation

Sex discrimination is lawful in respect of the provision of any benefit, facility or service if:

(i)   the benefit, facility or service cannot be properly and effectively provided except for those using communal accommodation; and

(ii)   in the relevant circumstances a woman could lawfully be refused the use of the accommodation under the rules above (*SDA 1975, s 46(5)*).

Therefore, if a firm ran a residential training course in Northern Scotland and accommodation could only be provided for men and it was fair so to do, failure to make the course available to women would not be unlawful discrimination.

Arrangements to compensate for detriment

It should be noted that sex discrimination is only permitted in the above circumstances where such arrangements as are reasonably practicable have been made to compensate for any detriment caused by the discrimination (*SDA 1975, s 46(6)*). For example, training courses run by the ABC Company for a few days in the north of Scotland are not available to women employees because of the unsuitability of the accommodation: the company will *not* have a defence against a claim alleging discrimination unless it can show either that an alternative course had been provided or that, having been considered carefully, it was thought with good reason not to be practicable to provide it.

(*b*) *Pay*

For all grounds of discrimination other than sex, differences in pay fall to be considered under the general provisions on discrimination. Under the *SDA 1975, s 6(5) and (6)*, however, offering or paying a woman less remuneration than a man is not an act of unlawful discrimination. Instead, it will, if certain conditions are satisfied, be unlawful under the *Equal Pay Act 1970* ('*EqPA 1970*'). Thus, if a woman is engaged on like work or on work rated as equivalent to that of a man or on work of equal value to that of a man, a woman's contract will be modified by the *EqPA 1970* so that she can claim pay equal to that which the man receives (see EQUAL PAY (24)). Less favourable treatment in relation to pay will still be an act of unlawful discrimination under the *SDA 1975* if the victim is a transsexual (*SDA 1975, s 6(8)*).

(*c*) *Retirement, death and related benefits*

Sex discrimination in relation to death and retirement benefits is partially excluded from the scope of the *SDA 1975* by *s 6(4)*. Instead, such discrimination is dealt with primarily by the *Pensions Act 1995*. *Sections 62* and *64* of the *Pensions Act 1995* imply into the rules of every occupational pension scheme an 'equal treatment rule' which operates in the same way as the more familiar 'equality clause' in the *Equal Pay Act 1970* (cf 24.5 EQUAL PAY). The partial exclusion under *s 6(4)* applies to discrimination taking the following forms:

(i)   Discrimination in the terms on which the woman is offered employment;

(ii) Discrimination in the way the woman is afforded access to benefits etc.;

(iii) Discriminatory dismissals; and

(iv) Discriminatory subjection to any other detriment.

Where a person discriminates against a woman in one of those respects in relation to her membership of, or rights under, an occupational pension scheme, that discrimination will not be unlawful where, if provision had been made for that discrimination in the terms of the scheme, that term would have been compliant with the equal treatment rule in the *Pensions Act 1995*.

Note that it is unlawful to apply different compulsory retirement ages to men and women and that the *SDA 1975* still applies in relation to death and retirement benefits where the victim of the discrimination is a transsexual (*SDA 1975, s 6(8)*).

A fuller account of the equal opportunities issues relating to death or retirement benefits is set out in 24.6 EQUAL PAY.

(*d*) *Members of the armed forces*

Broadly speaking, since 1 October 1997, the equality legislation applies to service in the armed forces as it does to other employment: cf the *Sex Discrimination (Complaints to Employment Tribunals) (Armed Forces) Regulations 1997 (SI 1997/2163)*, the *Race Relations (Complaints to Employment Tribunals) (Armed Forces) Regulations 1997 (SI 1997/2161)*; *RBR 2003, reg 36*; *SOR 2003, reg 36*; and see below 13.32. Prior to 1 October 2005, there were still two exemptions for sex discrimination under the *SDA 1975*:

(i)   Any act done 'for the purpose of ensuring the combat effectiveness of the armed forces' was not unlawful (*SDA 1975, s 85(4)*); and

(ii) Sex discrimination in admission to the Army Cadet Force, Air Training Corps, Sea Cadet Corps, Combined Cadet Force, or any other cadet training corps for the time being administered by the Ministry of Defence was not unlawful (*SDA 1975, s 85(5)*).

The second of those exemptions has now (with effect from 1 October 2005) been deleted from the *SDA 1975* by *reg 34* of the *Sex Discrimination Regulations 2005*. The only remaining exemption is therefore that for 'combat effectiveness' which was inserted into the *SDA 1975* by the *Sex Discrimination Act 1975 (Application to Armed Forces, etc) Regulations 1994 (SI 1994/3276)*. Its introduction raised a question as to whether the provisions of the *SDA 1975* complied with the *Equal Treatment Directive (Directive 76/207/EEC)*. The exemption was relied upon by the Army Board in *Sirdar v Army Board* (Case C-273/97) [2000] ICR 130. A woman who had applied to work as a chef in the Royal Marines was refused a transfer on the grounds that chefs were expected, where necessary, to be capable of fighting as a member of a commando unit. The complainant argued that *SDA 1975, s 85(4)* was contrary to the *Directive 76/207/EEC*. The matter was referred to the European court, which decided that whilst it was true that there was no *Treaty* right to derogate from equality legislation on grounds of national security, *art 2(2)* of the *ETD* nevertheless allowed the Army Board to refuse the complainant her transfer. *Article 2(2)* provides that *Directive 76/207/EEC* is 'without prejudice to the right of Member States to exclude from [the Directive's] field of application those occupational activities and, where appropriate, the training leading thereto, for which, by reason of their nature or the context in which they are carried out, the sex of the worker constitutes a determining factor'. In effect, the ECJ seems to have decided that being male is a genuine occupational requirement for a Royal Marine.

(*e*) *Police officers*

Discrimination in height requirements and uniform or uniform allowances, which would otherwise constitute sex discrimination, is lawful in the employment of police constables (*SDA 1975, s 17(2), (3)*).

(*f*) *Prison officers*

Discrimination is lawful between male and female prison officers as to requirements relating to height (*SDA 1975, s 18(1)*). Men may be governors of women's prisons (*SDA 1975, s 18(2)*).

(*g*) *Ministers of religion*

Generally speaking, ministers of religion will be regarded as employees under employment legislation: see *Percy v Church of Scotland Board of National Mission*

[2005] UKHL 73, [2006] ICR 134. However, prior to 1 October 2005, there was an exception under the *SDA 1975* for employment for the purposes of an organised religion where a particular post-holder was required to be either male or female (or required not to be a transsexual) in order to comply with the doctrines of the religion or to avoid offending the religious susceptibilities of a significant number of its followers (*SDA 1975, s 19(1), (3), (4)*). That exemption has been preserved, but with some changes, by *reg 20* of the *Sex Discrimination Regulations 2005* (which amend *SDA 1975, s 19* with effect from 1 October 2005). The amended version of *s 19* provides an exemption for employment for purposes of an organised religion where a requirement is applied that:

(a)   the employee be of a particular sex;

(b)   the employee not be undergoing or have undergone gender reassignment;

(c)   the employee not be married, or not be a civil partner;

(d)   the employee not have a living former spouse or civil partner (or that the employee's spouse or civil partner not have a living former spouse or civil partner); or

(e)   as to how the person, or the person's spouse or civil partner as at any time ceased to be married or ceased to be a civil partner.

The exemption only applies if the requirement in question is applied either so as to comply with the doctrines of the religion or because of the nature of the employment and context in which it is carried out, so as to avoid conflicting with the strongly-held religious convictions of a significant number of the religion's followers.

Compare the exception for genuine occupational requirement for employment for purposes of an organised religion in the *SOR 2003*: see above 13.7.

(h) Sports and competitions

Section 44 of the *SDA 1975* excludes from the scope of the *SDA 1975* any act that relates to participation as a competitor in a sport, game or other competitive activity, provided that the activity has been confined to competitors of one sex because the physical strength, stamina or physique of the average woman puts her at a disadvantage to the average man in carrying out that activity.

13.11 Exceptions to the Race Relations Act 1976

(a) Skills to be exercised outside Great Britain

The equality legislation applies to training a person in skills intended to be exercised wholly outside Great Britain as it does to training for skills to be exercised in Great Britain, with one exception: discrimination on grounds of colour in the provision of such training falls outside the scope of the legislation: *RRA 1976, s 6*, as amended by the *Race Relations Act 1976 (Amendment) Regulations 2003 (SI 2003/1626)*).

(b) Private household

The equality legislation applies to employment for the purposes of a private household as it does to businesses, with one exception: discrimination on grounds of colour in relation to employment for the purposes of a private household is excluded from the scope of the *RRA 1976* by *s 4(3)*. The question is whether the employment is for the purposes of a private household 'to a substantial degree'.

Thus, an applicant for a job as a chauffeur whose primary task was to drive a car for a company chairman could bring a complaint of racial discrimination (*Heron Corpn Ltd v Commis* [1980] ICR 713).

(c) Seamen recruited abroad

Seamen (whether employees or contract workers) recruited abroad to work on any ship may lawfully be discriminated against on grounds of their nationality unless their work is concerned with exploration of the sea bed or subsoil (or the exploitation of their natural resources) on the continental shelf, save for those parts of the continental shelf to which the law of Northern Ireland applies (*RRA 1976, s 9(1)*, (3)). If the ground for the discrimination is any of the other 'racial grounds' (for which see 12.6(D) DISCRIMINATION AND EQUAL OPPORTUNITIES – I) they may lawfully be discriminated against in relation to their pay but not otherwise. 'Pay' includes retirement or death benefits (*RRA 1976, s 9(5)*, as amended by the *Race Relations Act 1976 (Amendment) Regulations 2003 (SI 2003/1626)*). There are no equivalent provisions in relation to sex discrimination or discrimination on grounds of religion, belief or sexual orientation.

(d) Sports and competitions

Discrimination on the basis of a person's nationality, place of birth, or length of time for which he has been resident in a particular area will not be unlawful if it is done in selecting a person to represent a country, place or area, or any related association, in any sport or game (*RRA 1976, s 39*).

Exception to the RBR 2003 protection of Sikhs from discrimination in connection with requirements as to wearing of safety helmets

13.12 Properly speaking, this is not an exception, but a limitation on the availability of the defence of justification. Thus, where:

(*a*)   any person applies to a Sikh any provision, criterion or practice relating to the wearing by him of a safety helmet while he is on a construction site; and

(*b*)   at the time when he so applies the provision, criterion or practice that person has no reasonable grounds for believing that the Sikh would not wear a turban at all times when on such a site,

the provision, criterion or practice is taken to be one which cannot be shown to be a proportionate means of achieving a legitimate aim. It follows that the act of indirect discrimination will not be justified (see 13.8 above) (*reg 26(1)*).

Any special treatment afforded to a Sikh in consequence of *s 11(1)* or *11(2)* of the *Employment Act 1989* (exemption of Sikhs from requirements as to wearing of safety helmets on construction sites) is not to be regarded as giving rise, in relation to any other person, to any direct or indirect discrimination (*reg 26(2)*).

For the purposes of *reg 26* 'construction site' means any place in Great Britain where any building operations or works of engineering construction are being undertaken, but does not include any site within the territorial sea adjacent to Great Britain unless there are being undertaken on that site such operations or works as are activities falling within *art 8(1)(a)* of the *Health and Safety at Work etc Act 1974 (Application outside Great Britain) Order 2001*. 'Safety helmet' means 'any form of protective headgear'. 'Sikh' means 'a follower of the Sikh religion' and any reference to a Sikh being on a construction site is a reference 'to his being there whether while at work or otherwise' (*reg 26(3)* and (*4*)).

13.13 **Exception to the SOR 2003: benefits dependent on marital or civil partnership status**

Any benefit to which access is dependent on marital status is likely to be indirectly discriminatory against homosexuals as homosexuals are not currently permitted to marry under national law. Prior to 5 December 2005, *reg 25* of the *SOR 2003* nevertheless provided expressly that nothing in the *SOR 2003* should make it unlawful for an employer to prevent or restrict access to a benefit by reference to marital status. It was argued in *R (Amicus-MSF) v Secretary of State for Trade and Industry* [2004] EWHC 860 (Admin), [2004] IRLR 430 that *reg 25* was incompatible with the governing European *Directive 2000/78/EC*). Richards J held that *reg 25* was compatible because it reflected the limitation in *Recital 2* of the *Directive* which says that 'this *Directive* is without prejudice to national laws on marital status and the benefits dependent thereon'.

The provision was nevertheless amended with effect from 5 December 2005. It now provides for a complete exclusion from the *SOR 2003* 'for anything which prevents or restricts access to a benefit by reference to marital status where the right to the benefit accrued or the benefit is payable in respect of periods of service prior to the coming into force of the Civil Partnership Act 2004' (ie prior to 5 December 2005). Where the right to the benefit accrues, or the benefit is payable, after that date, however, an employer is no longer permitted to make any distinction between married persons and civil partners. An employer may still, however, make a particular benefit available to, say, married persons and civil partners, but withhold the benefit from other employees, including those in long-term heterosexual or homosexual relationships.

Employers should note that 'civil partnership' is defined in detail in the *Civil Partnership Act 2004* ('*CPA 2004*'). It includes not only those couples who have registered their partnership in the UK since the coming into force of that *Act*, but also those couples who have registered their partnership overseas whether before or after the coming into force of the *CPA 2004*. A large number of partnerships registered overseas are automatically to be recognised as 'civil partnerships' under the *CPA 2004*. These are listed in *Sch 20* to the *Act*. Other partnerships may be recognised if the conditions in *ss 212* to *218* of the *CPA 2004* (readers are referred to the text of the *Act*). Where a 'civil partnership' is recognised under the *CPA 2004*, it must also be recognised by employers for the purposes of *reg 25* of the *SOR 2003*.

13.14 **GENERAL EXCEPTIONS TO THE EQUALITY LEGISLATION**

A number of other exceptions or defences are available to claims of both direct and indirect discrimination. As a matter of principle, these exceptions ought to be narrowly or strictly construed: *Lambeth London Borough Council v Commission for Racial Equality* [1989] IRLR 379; upheld on appeal ([1990] ICR 768) (although the principle of construction was not referred to in the judgments of the Court of Appeal).

13.15 **Employment outside Great Britain**

Broadly speaking, the equality legislation applies where a complainant does his work wholly or partly in Great Britain and does not apply where the complainant works wholly outside Great Britain (*RRA 1976, ss 4, 8(1), (1A); SDA 1975, ss 6(1), 10(1)*, both as amended; *RBR 2003, reg 9(1); SOR 2003, reg 9(1)*). The question is whether, viewing the complainant's employment as a whole, he does his work wholly outside Great Britain (*Saggar v Ministry of Defence* [2005] EWCA Civ 413,

[2005] ICR 1073). In setting out this test, the Court of Appeal in *Saggar* expressly disapproved the approach of the tribunal and the EAT, which had been to consider where the employee worked during the period in which the discrimination was alleged to have occurred. The tribunal and EAT had understood this to be the approach dictated by the Court of Appeal in *Carver v Saudi Arabian Airlines* [1999] ICR 991. However, in *Saggar*, the Court of Appeal considered that the Court of Appeal in *Carver* had not laid down such a test. The EAT in *Saggar* ([2004] ICR 1708) suggested that a one-day working visit to Great Britain would not be sufficient to bring an employee within the tribunal's jurisdiction. This is probably still correct, notwithstanding the Court of Appeal's decision in that case. Where discrimination occurs during recruitment, the tribunal must consider whether it was within the contemplation of the parties that the employee's duties would be performed wholly outside Great Britain (*Deria v General Council of British Shipping* [1986] ICR 172; cf also *Saggar* in the EAT).

However, there are exceptions or qualifications to the rule that the equality legislation does not apply where a complainant works wholly outside Great Britain:

(1)   The tribunal's jurisdiction will not be excluded where the employment is at an establishment in another European Union member state and applying the exclusion would involve a breach of *art 48* of the *Treaty* (which provides for the free movement of workers within the European Union): *Bossa v Nordstress Ltd* [1998] IRLR 284. (Note that where a worker is 'posted' temporarily to another Member State, national legislation relating to equality of treatment will apply by virtue of the *Posted Workers Directive* (*Dir EC/96/71*): see 26.3 FOREIGN EMPLOYEES.)

(2)   Where discrimination is on grounds of race or ethnic or national origins, sexual orientation, religion or belief or (with effect from 1 October 2005) sex (but not colour), the equality legislation will still apply if:

(i)   the respondent has a place of business at an establishment in Great Britain;

(ii)   the work performed by the complainant is for the purposes of the business carried on at that establishment; and

(iii) the complainant is ordinarily resident in Great Britain either at the time when he applies for or is offered the employment, or at any time during the course of the employment (*SDA 1975, s 10(1)*, as amended by the *Sex Discrimination Regulations 2005, reg 11*; *RRA 1976, s 8(1A)*; *RBR 2003, reg 9(2)*; *SOR 2003, reg 9(2)*).

(3)   The legislation applies to employment on board ships registered in Great Britain, except where the employee does his work wholly outside Great Britain. The ship is deemed to be the establishment at which the employee works for the purposes of the legislation (*RRA 1976, s 8(3)*; *SDA 1975, s 10(2)(a), (3)*; *RBR 2003, reg 9(3)(a)*; *SOR 2003, reg 9(3)(a)*).

(4)   The *SDA 1975*, the *RBR 2003* and the *SOR 2003* (but not the *RRA 1976*) apply to employment on aircraft or hovercraft registered in Great Britain and operated by a person who has his principal place of business, or is ordinarily resident, in Great Britain, except where the employee does his work wholly outside Great Britain. The aircraft or hovercraft is deemed to be the establishment at which the employee works for the purposes of the legislation (*SDA 1975, s 10(2)(b)*; *RBR 2003, reg 9(3)(b)*; *SOR 2003, reg 9(3)(b)*).

Note also that there are specific provisions relating to employment concerned with exploration or exploitation of the sea bed or subsoil, employment on the Frigg gas field and other parts of the Continental Shelf: *RRA 1976, s 8(5); SDA 1975, s 10(5); RBR 2003, reg 9(4), (5)* and *SOR 2003, reg 9(4), (5)*. The *Race Relations (Offshore Employment) Order 1987, SI 1987/929* and the *Sex Discrimination and Equal Pay (Offshore Employment) Order 1987, SI 1987/930* have been made pursuant to the powers in those provisions of the *SDA 1975* and *RRA 1975*.

See also 12.12(B) DISCRIMINATION AND EQUAL OPPORTUNITIES – I.

13.16 Employment under an illegal contract

The test for excluding a tribunal's jurisdiction on grounds of illegality in relation to discrimination claims is not as strict as that used in cases of breach of contract. In breach of contract cases, a court or tribunal will not enforce a claim where the employment is pursuant to an illegal contract, or if there was an intention at the time of the formation of the contract to perform it illegally, or if the complainant has to rely on his or her illegal conduct in order to found his claim (*Colen v Cebrian (UK) Ltd* [2003] EWCA Civ 1676, [2004] ICR 568; see generally 8.15 CONTRACT OF EMPLOYMENT). By contrast, in discrimination cases, the fact that a contract is illegal or tainted by illegality will not exclude the tribunal's jurisdiction, unless the complainant's claim is so closely connected or inextricably bound up or linked with the complainant's illegal conduct that to allow the complainant to recover compensation would be to appear to condone that conduct (*Hall v Woolston Hall Leisure Ltd* [2001] ICR 99, CA, approving *Leighton v Michael* [1995] ICR 1091, EAT). Where the complaint is concerned with a dismissal only, the fact of dismissal may not be sufficiently closely connected with the illegality as to preclude a claim. However, a claim in respect of discrimination relating to access to opportunities for promotion, transfer or training or any other benefits, facilities or services may be precluded: see *Governing Body of Addey and Stanhope School v Vakante* [2003] ICR 290, EAT, (though the tribunal at the remitted hearing in that case decided that both the dismissal and the manner in which the employer gave the employee access to training and other benefits were so inextricably linked with the employee's illegal conduct – obtaining employment in breach of immigration rules – that both claims were precluded: see [2004] EWCA Civ 1065, [2005] ICR 231). The burden of proof is on the party alleging illegality (*Colen v Cebrian (UK) Ltd*, above).

The Court of Appeal in *Woolston Hall Leisure* left undecided a question whether the limited grounds for derogation from the right not to suffer less favourable treatment conferred by *Directive 76/207/EEC* meant that illegality could not be used as a ground for refusing an employee a remedy. The point was also raised in *Vakante v Governing Body of Addey and Stanhope School (No 2)* [2004] ICR 279, EAT (in relation to the equivalent provision of the *Race Directive 2000/43/EC*). However, the Court of Appeal held that, since Directive 2000/43 only came into force after the claimant's cause of action arose and, since it was clearly not intended to have retrospective effect, it could not assist the claimant ([2004] EWCA Civ 1065, [2005] ICR 231).

13.17 Benefits provided to public

The provisions relating to discrimination with regard to access to benefits of any description (including facilities and services) (*RRA 1976, s 4(2)(b); SDA 1975, s 6(2)(a); RBR 2003, reg 6(2)(b); SOR 2003, reg 6(2)(b)*) do not apply if the respondent is concerned with the provision (for payment or not) of benefits of that description to the public, or to a section of the public comprising the complainant in question, unless:

(i)   that provision differs in a material respect from the provision of the benefits to his employees (or non-employees covered by the employment rules: see below 13.21FF); or

(ii)   the provision of the benefits to the complainant in question is regulated by his contract of employment (or equivalent for non-employees covered by the employment rules); or

(iii) the benefits relate to training (*RRA 1976, s 4(4); SDA 1975, s 6(7); RBR 2003, reg 6(4); SOR 2003, reg 6(4)*).

Thus, for example, a bank which provides loans to members of the public and to most employees on the same terms may not be taken to an employment tribunal by an employee who is denied a loan on grounds of race, sex, religion or belief or sexual orientation if the employee is not entitled to the loan under his contract of employment. However, where the grounds for discrimination are race or sex, it will be liable to an action by that employee in the county court under the provisions relating to discrimination in the provision of goods, facilities or services: see *RRA 1976, s 20* and *SDA 1975, s 29*.

13.18   **Discrimination in compliance with the law**

In certain circumstances, it is a defence to a claim of racial or sex discrimination that the act complained of was carried out in order to comply with, or pursuant to, a legal requirement. No such defence is available to claims of discrimination on grounds of religion or belief or sexual orientation.

Racial discrimination

Prior to the amendments introduced with effect from 19 July 2003 by the *Race Relations Amendment Regulations*, there was a general defence available where the relevant act of discrimination was carried out pursuant to any enactment, Order in Council or statutory instrument, or in order to comply with a ministerial condition or requirement imposed pursuant to statute (*RRA 1976, s 41(1)*).

The scope of that provision was considered by the House of Lords in *Hampson v Department of Education and Science* [1990] ICR 511. Their Lordships held that the application of the defence was restricted to acts done in the necessary performance of an express obligation contained in an instrument, and did not extend to discretionary acts carried out by the Secretary of State, even in circumstances where he had a positive public duty to exercise his discretion. (See also *Dhatt v McDonalds Hamburgers Ltd* [1991] ICR 238.)

From 19 July 2003, the position is as follows:

(*a*)   Where discrimination is on grounds of race, ethnic or national origins, no defence is available (*RRA 1976, s 41(1A)*);

(*b*)   Otherwise, discriminatory acts are not unlawful if performed:

(i)   in pursuance of any enactment or Order in Council;

(ii)   in pursuance of any instrument made under any enactment by a Minister of the Crown; or

(iii) in order to comply with any condition or requirement imposed by a Minister of the Crown by virtue of any enactment (*RRA 1976, s 41(1)* as amended);

(c) Where discrimination is on grounds of the complainant's nationality, place of ordinary residence or the length of time for which he has been present or resident in or outside the UK, the defence is available in the three circumstances set out in (b) immediately above but also:

(i) in pursuance of any arrangements made by or with the approval of, or for the time being approved by, a Minister of the Crown; or

(ii) in order to comply with any condition imposed by a Minister of the Crown (*RRA 1976, s 41(2)(d)* and (*e*)).

For the application of the exemption in *s 41(2)(d)* for acts done pursuant to arrangements made by or with the approval of a Minister of the Crown, see *R(Dost Mohammed) v Secretary of State for Defence* [2007] EWCA Civ 983, unreported.

Sex discrimination

A respondent is not guilty of an unlawful act if he discriminates in order to comply with a statute passed before the *SDA 1975*, or a statutory instrument made or approved (whether before or after the passing of the *SDA*) by or under an act passed before the *SDA*, if such provision is one concerning the protection of women (*SDA 1975, s 51*, as substituted by *EA 1989, s 3(3)*). Thus, discrimination in order to comply with college statutes enacted under a statute prior to *SDA 1975* was considered lawful in *Hugh-Jones v St John's College, Cambridge* [1979] ICR 848. Many such statutory requirements have been or will be removed as a result of *EA 1989*.

Discriminatory action taken by an employer to ensure the health and safety of his employees will not be considered unlawful if it is taken in compliance with his statutory obligations and in order to protect the complainant (or class of women to which the complainant belongs): *SDA 1975, s 51(1)(c)(ii)* and see *Page v Freight Hire (Tank Haulage) Ltd* [1981] ICR 299.

13.19 National Security

Discrimination on grounds of sexual orientation, religion or belief will not be unlawful if it is done for the purpose of safeguarding national security, and the discriminatory act is justified by that purpose (*RBR 2003, reg 24*; *SOR 2003, reg 24*). An act of sex discrimination done for the purpose of safeguarding national security is also permitted by the *SDA 1975, s 52(1)*. However, it should be noted that no such derogation is available for sex discrimination in Community law, though cf *Sirdar v Army Board* (Case C-273/97) [2000] ICR 130, ECJ and above 13.10(D). There is no national security defence available for complaints of race discrimination, either in the *RRA 1976*, or in the Community law on race discrimination.

Note also that, before the passing of the *Sex Discrimination (Amendment) Order 1988 (SI 1988/249)*, a certificate signed by, or on behalf of, a Minister of the Crown and certifying that an act specified in the certificate was done for the purpose of safeguarding national security was conclusive evidence that it was done for that purpose (*SDA 1975, s 52(2)*). However, following the amendments made by *SI 1988/249*, the defence no longer applies to discrimination in employment and related areas. This followed the decision of the European Court of

Justice in *Johnston v Chief Constable of the Royal Ulster Constabulary* (Case 222/84) [1987] ICR 83, ECJ whereby a provision in a Northern Ireland Order, similar to the unamended *SDA 1975, s 52(2)*, was held to be contrary to *art 6* of *Directive 76/207/EEC* (see 25.6 EUROPEAN COMMUNITY LAW).

See also 13.10(D) above for the exceptions relating to sex discrimination in the armed forces.

13.20 Employees working for those with State immunity

The immunity conferred by the *State Immunity Act 1978, s 16(1)(a)* extends to claims of discrimination. The provision does not infringe *art 6(1)* of the *European Convention on Human Rights*: *Fogarty v United Kingdom* [2002] IRLR 148, ECtHR.

13.21 NON-EMPLOYEES AND NON-EMPLOYERS COVERED BY THE EMPLOYMENT RULES

Contract workers

In recent times there has been a marked trend towards the use of contract workers. Contract workers are parties to a tri-partite arrangement. The first party is the person who has work which needs doing. He is known as the 'principal'. The principal enters into a contract with a second party who is obliged to supply employees to perform the work. The employees are known as 'contract workers' in relation to the principal.

It is unlawful for a principal, in relation to contract work at an establishment in Great Britain, to:

(*a*) discriminate against a contract worker:

  (i) in the terms on which he allows him to do that work;

  (ii) by not allowing him to do it or continue to do it;

  (iii) in the way he affords him access to any benefits or by refusing or deliberately not affording him access to them; or

  (iv) by subjecting him to any other detriment; or to

(*b*) subject a contract worker to harassment (*SDA 1975, s 9(2), (2A)*, as amended; *RRA 1976, s 7(1), (3A)*, as amended; *RBR 2003, reg 8(1), (2)*; and *SOR 2003, reg 8(1), (2)*).

The provisions relating to the meaning of 'at an establishment in Great Britain' (above 13.15) apply to principals as they do to employers. So, too, do the genuine occupational requirement exceptions (*SDA 1975, s 9(3), (3A)* and *(3B)*; *RRA 1976, s 7(3)*; *RBR 2003, reg 8(3)*; *SOR 2003, reg 8(3)*; see above 13.2FF) and the exceptions for benefits provided to the public (*SDA 1975, s 9(4)*; *RRA 1976, s 7(5)*; *RBR 2003, reg 8(4)*; *SOR 2003, reg 8(4)*; see above 13.17).

The provisions relating to contract workers are designed to prevent an employer from escaping its responsibilities under the equality legislation by bringing in workers on sub-contract and should therefore be given a broad construction so as to provide statutory protection to a wide range of workers (*Jones v Friends Provident Life Office* [2004] IRLR 783, NICA). In that case, Carswell LCJ held (para 17) that, in order to fall within the relevant provisions, it is necessary to show that: (i) the contract between the employer and the principal is one under which it is contemplated that employees will be supplied by the former to the latter; and, (ii) the principal is in a position to influence or control the conditions under which the employee worked.

The notion of a 'contract worker' extends to cover a case where the complainant works for a company operating a 'concession' within a department store. Thus, where a department store withdrew, on racial grounds, the necessary permission for the complainant to work in the store, the latter was entitled to bring proceedings against the former under *RRA 1976, s 7* (*Harrods Ltd v Remick* [1998] ICR 156, CA). However, it should be noted that the Northern Ireland Court of Appeal in *Jones v Friends Provident* considered that *Harrods Ltd v Remick* represented, possibly, too wide an interpretation of the relevant provisions. In particular, the Court in *Jones v Friends Provident* considered that it is unlikely to be sufficient for a complainant to establish merely that the principal benefited from the work done by them in order to bring that principal within the scope of the relevant provisions. Nevertheless, more complex contractual arrangements are probably covered by the provisions: see *MHC Consulting Services Ltd v Tansell* [2000] ICR 789, CA, a case under the *DDA 1995*. In that case the complainant contracted with a company that he had set up which company then contracted with a service provider, which in turn contracted with the ultimate beneficiary of the services. The beneficiary was a principal for the purposes of the *DDA 1995* notwithstanding the inclusion of an additional link in the contractual chain. In all cases, however, there must in fact be a *contractual* relationship: where arrangements take effect under statute (as, for example, the obligations placed on general practitioners and local health authorities under the *National Health Service* (*General Medical Services*) *Regulations 1992*) there may be no contractual relationship at all: *North Essex Health Authority v David-John* [2004] ICR 112.

A contract worker is not limited to comparing the treatment he has received with the manner in which the principal treats contract workers of different sexual orientation, racial group etc.; he may also compare himself to employees of the principal (*Allonby v Accrington and Rossendale College* [2001] EWCA Civ 529, [2001] IRLR 364). Thus, a company which refused to allow an agency worker to return to work for it after she had been on maternity leave discriminated against her on the grounds of her sex, contrary to *SDA 1975, s 9* (*BP Chemicals v Gillick* [1995] IRLR 128). Similarly, where a local authority appointed a permanent worker in place of a contract worker who had left to take maternity leave, it was argued on behalf of the principal that the contract worker could not rely upon the provisions of the equivalent Northern Irish legislation. The principal had not refused to allow her to continue to do the work (she had merely left to start maternity leave) and by the time that she wanted to return there was no work for a contract worker to do, a permanent worker having been appointed. Nevertheless, the NICA held that the principal was liable to the contract worker who had been subjected to 'other detriment' (*Patefield v Belfast City Council* [2000] IRLR 664, NICA).

13.22 Office holders

In addition to the general provisions applying the equality legislation to the Crown, etc (see below 13.32), specific provision is also made in relation to discrimination against office holders. Overwhelmingly, office holders are public sector appointees, often those with specific statutory powers or responsibilities. They are considered not to be employed in a post but, rather, as holding an office which exists independently of the terms of their appointment. An example would be Registrars of Births, Deaths and Marriages.

Scope of the provisions relating to office holders

Each of the discrimination statutes and statutory instruments has slightly different provisions relating to the protection of office holders. Essentially, two different types of office holder are covered by the legislation.

First, office holders appointed by a Minister of the Crown and government departments ('public office holders'). Prior to 1 October 2005 both the *SDA 1975* and the *RRA 1976* made provision in relation to such appointments (*SDA 1975, s 86; RRA 1976, s 76*). Section 86 of the *SDA 1975* is repealed, with effect from 1 October 2005, by the *Employment Equality (Sex Discrimination) Regulations 2005, reg 13*. Section 76 of the *RRA 1976* remains in force. With effect from 1 October 2005, the *SDA 1975* now contains a broader provision, in the same terms as those in the *RBR 2003* and *SOR 2003*, covering offices and posts to which appointments are made by (or on the recommendation of or subject to the approval of) a Minister of the Crown, a government department, the National Assembly for Wales or any part of the Scottish Administration (*SDA 1975, s 10B(1); RBR 2003, reg 10(8)(b); SOR 2003, reg 10(8)(b)*).

Second, office holders generally. The *RRA 1976*, the *RBR 2003*, the *SOR 2003* and (with effect from 1 October 2005) the *SDA 1975* define such offices as any office or post to which persons are appointed to discharge functions personally under the direction of another person, and in respect of which they are entitled to remuneration: (*SDA 1975, s 10A(1)*, as amended by the *Sex Discrimination Regulations 2005, reg 13*; *RRA 1976, s 76ZA(7)(b)* and (*c*); *RBR 2003, reg 10(8)(a); SOR 2003, reg 10(8)(a)*). The holder of an office or post is to be regarded as discharging his functions under the direction of another person if that other person is entitled to direct him as to when and where he discharges those functions. He is not to be regarded as entitled to remuneration merely because he is entitled to payments:

(i) in respect of expenses incurred by him in carrying out the functions of the office or post; or

(ii) by way of compensation for the loss of income or benefits he would or might have received from any person had he not been carrying out the functions of the office or post (*SDA 1975, s 10A(4); RRA 1976, s 76ZA(8); RBR 2003, reg 10(9); SOR 2003, reg 10(9)*).

Broadly speaking, political offices and posts are excluded from the scope of the legislation, and a list of specifically excluded posts is included in each of the *Acts* and *Regulations*, though there are differences between the *Acts* and *Regulations* as to how this exclusion is effected and the reader is referred to the provisions themselves: *SDA 1975, s 10A(3); RRA 1976, s 76ZA(7)* and (*9*)(*b*); *RBR 2003, reg 10(8)* and (*10*)(*b*); *SOR 2003, reg 10(8)* and (*10*)(*b*). Note also that each of the *Acts* and *Regulations* expressly excludes election to an office or post from the definition of 'appointment' to an office or post: *SDA 1975, s 10A(5); RRA 1976, s 76ZA(9)(a); RBR 2003, reg 10(10)(a); SOR 2003, reg 10(10)(a)*.

The provisions relating to both types of office holders are default provisions, applying only if the provisions relating to employees, contract workers, partnerships, etc., do not (*SDA 1975, s 86(1)* or, with effect from 1 October 2005, *s 10A(2); RRA 1976, s 7(2)(a); RBR 2003, reg 10(8); SOR 2003, reg 10(8)*).

Note that, prior to 1 October 2005, the *SDA 1975* made no provision for the second type of office holder and none of the detailed provisions discussed below applied in relation to sex discrimination. Thus, appointments to a non-public office did not fall within the scope of the *SDA 1975*. However, it was a very rare case where an appointment was not caught by one of the other provisions relating to employees, contract workers, police officers, etc. Following the amendments to the *SDA 1975* by the *Sex Discrimination Regulations 2005*, the scope of the *SDA 1975* is now broadly in line with that of the *RRA 1976* and the *Regulations* and the detailed provisions discussed below apply also in relation to sex discrimination.

Unlawful discrimination against applicants for an appointment

In relation to appointment to public office, the *RRA 1976* and the *SDA 1975* (prior to 1 October 2005) provide that it is unlawful for the relevant Minister or government department to do any act that would be unlawful if the appointment was a position of employment covered by the provisions relating to discrimination in employment: *RRA 1976, s76(2); SDA 1975, s 86(2)*. With effect from 1 October 2005, *section 86* of the *SDA 1975* has been repealed, but equivalent provisions have been inserted into the *Act* by *reg 13* of the *Sex Discrimination Regulations 2005*. Like the *RRA 1976, RBR 2003* and *SOR 2003*, the *SDA 1975* now provides in relation to appointment both to public office and to offices generally, that it is unlawful for a 'relevant person', in relation to an appointment to an office or post to discriminate against a person:

(*a*)   in the arrangements which he makes for the purpose of determining to whom the appointment should be offered;

(*b*)   in the terms on which he offers him the appointment; or

(*c*)   by refusing to offer him the appointment (*SDA 1975, s 10B(1)*, as amended with effect from 1 October 2005; *RRA 1976, s 76ZA(1); RBR 2003, reg 10(1); SOR 2003, reg 10(1)*).

The relevant person in relation to an office or post, means:

(i)   any person with power to make or terminate appointments to the office or post, or to determine the terms of appointment;

(ii)   any person with power to determine the working conditions of a person appointed to the office or post in relation to opportunities for promotion, a transfer, training or for receiving any other benefit; and

(iii)   any person or body on whose recommendation or subject to whose approval appointments are made to the office or post (*SDA 1975, s 10B(9)*, as amended with effect from 1 October 2005; *RRA 1976, s 76ZA(8)(c); RBR 2003, reg 10(10)(c); SOR 2003, reg 10(10)(c)*).

Unlawful discrimination in relation to recommendations for appointment

It is unlawful, in relation to an appointment to public office, for a relevant person on whose recommendation (or subject to whose approval) appointments to the office or post are made, to discriminate against a person:

(*a*)   in the arrangements which he makes for the purpose of determining who should be recommended or approved in relation to the appointment; or

(*b*)   in making or refusing to make a recommendation, or giving or refusing to give an approval, in relation to the appointment (*SDA 1975, s 10B(2)*, as amended with effect from 1 October 2005; *RRA 1976, s 76(3), (5); RBR 2003, reg 10(2); SOR 2003, reg 10(2)*).

In the *RRA 1976* this is extended to include recommendations and approvals in relation to a conferment by the Crown of a dignity or honour: *RRA 1976, s 76(4)*.

The same, or virtually the same, provisions apply to negative recommendations: see *SDA 1975, s 10B(11)*, as amended with effect from 1 October 2005; *RRA 1976, s 76(6)–(9)*; *RBR 2003, reg 10(10)(d)*; *SOR 2003, reg 10(10)(d)*.

Unlawful discrimination against holders of an appointment

It is unlawful for a relevant person, in relation to a person who has been appointed to an office or post to which this regulation applies, to discriminate against him:

(*a*)   in the terms of the appointment;

(*b*)   in the opportunities which he affords him for promotion, a transfer, training or receiving any other benefit, or by refusing to afford him any such opportunity;

(*c*)   by terminating the appointment; or

(*d*)   by subjecting him to any other detriment in relation to the appointment (*SDA 1975, s 10B(3)*, as amended with effect from 1 October 2005; *RRA 1976, s 76ZA(2)*; *RBR 2003, reg 10(3)*; *SOR 2003, reg 10(3)*.)

Note that 'termination of the appointment' is deemed to refer additionally:

(*a*)   to the termination of the appointment by the expiration of any period (including a period expiring by reference to an event or circumstance), not being a termination immediately after which the appointment is renewed on the same terms and conditions; and

(*b*)   to the termination of the appointment by any act of the person appointed (including the giving of notice) in circumstances such that he is entitled to terminate the appointment without notice by reason of the conduct of the relevant person (*SDA 1975, s 10B(8)*, as amended with effect from 1 October 2005; *RRA 1976, s 76ZA(6)*; *RBR 2003, reg 10(7)*; *SOR 2003, reg 10(7)*).

Unlawful harassment of applicants for appointment or holders of an appointment

It is unlawful for a relevant person, in relation to an office or post to which this regulation applies, to subject to harassment a person:

(*a*)   who has been appointed to the office or post;

(*b*)   who is seeking or being considered for appointment to the office or post; or

(*c*)   who is seeking or being considered for a recommendation or approval in relation to an appointment to an office or post (*SDA 1975, s 10B(4)*, as amended with effect from 1 October 2005; *RRA 1976, s 76ZA(3)*; *RBR 2003, reg 10(4)*; *SOR 2003, reg 10(4)*.)

Exceptions

The exceptions relating to genuine occupational requirements (*SDA 1975, 10B(5)* and (*6*), as amended with effect from 1 October 2005; *RRA 1976, s 76ZA(4)*; *RBR 2003, reg 10(5)*; *SOR 2003, reg 10(5)*: see above 13.2FF) and benefits provided to the public (*SDA 1975, s 10B(7)*, as amended with effect from 1 October 2005; *RRA 1976, s 76ZA(5)*, *RBR 2003, reg 10(6)*; *SOR 2003, reg 10(6)*: see above 13.17) apply to complaints of discrimination by office holders as they do to employees.

Note also that the provisions of the *RRA 1976* relating to office holders apply only to discrimination on grounds of race, ethnic or national origins and not to discrimination on grounds of colour.

13.23 **Police**

Police officers are office-holders and not employees. However, the equality legislation deems the relevant chief officer of police or police authority to be the employer of the complainant police officer as respects any act done by him or them in relation to that officer: *SDA 1975, s 17(1)*; *RRA 1976, s 76A(2)*; *RBR 2003, reg 11(1), (2)*; *SOR 2003, reg 11(1), (2)*. The requirement that the act should be done by the chief officer (or, similarly, by the police authority) is not to be interpreted literally and will include acts performed by those to whom the chief officer has delegated authority (see *Chief Constable of Cumbria v McGlennon* [2002] ICR 1156, EAT).

If the chief officer of police or police authority for the force to which the complainant police officer belongs does not in fact have direction and control of the force, then the relevant respondent will be the chief officer or authority which *does* have direction and control of the complainant police officer's force: *SDA 1975, s 17(9)*; *RRA 1976, s 76B(3)*; *RBR 2003, reg 11(8)*; *SOR 2003, reg 11(8)*.

Any proceedings which would lie against a chief officer of police should be brought against whoever holds the post of chief officer of police for the time being. If the post is vacant, proceedings should be brought against the person for the time being performing the functions of that office (*SDA 1975, s 17(5)*; *RRA 1976, s 76A(5)*; *RBR 2003, reg 11(4)*; *SOR 2003, reg 11(4)*).

The relevant chief officer of police is vicariously liable for the actions of those police officers for whom he is responsible and he is treated as the respondent for that purpose (see VICARIOUS LIABILITY (55)). The legislation specifies that anything done by a police officer in the performance, or purported performance, of his functions shall be treated as done in the course of his employment (*SDA 1975, s 17(1A)(b)*; *RRA 1976, s 76A(3)(b)*; *RBR 2003, reg 11(2)*; *SOR 2003, reg 11(2)*). Note that *s 76A* of the *RRA 1976* was inserted by the *Race Relations (Amendment) Act 2000* in response to the Court of Appeal's decision in *Chief Constable of Bedfordshire Police v Liversidge* [2002] ICR 1135. In that case, the Court of Appeal held that the Chief Officer did not fall to be treated as an employer for the purposes of *RRA 1976, s 32(1)* (i.e. the general provision relating to vicarious liability: see 12.13 DISCRIMINATION AND EQUAL OPPORTUNITIES – I). *Section 76A* reverses that decision.

Where proceedings are brought against a chief officer of police, any compensation, costs or expenses ordered against the chief officer are payable from the police fund. The chief officer can also recover the costs of successfully contesting proceedings from the fund in so far as they are not recovered from the complainant or other party. Finally, he can recover the cost of compromising proceedings against him, subject to his having obtained the approval of the relevant police authority for the settlement (*SDA 1975, s 17(4)*; *RRA 1976, s 76A(4)*; *RBR 2003, reg 11(3)*; *SOR 2003, reg 11(3)*).

Similarly, a police authority may, in such cases and to such extent as appear to it to be appropriate, pay out of the police fund any compensation, costs or expenses awarded by a court or tribunal against a person under the direction and control of the chief officer of police. It may also pay out of the police fund any costs or expenses incurred and not recovered by such a person, as well as any sum required in connection with the settlement of a claim that has or might have given rise to discrimination proceedings (*RRA 1976, s 76A(6)*; *SDA 1975, s 17(5A)*; *RBR 2003, reg 11(5)*; *SOR 2003, reg 11(5)*).

Further detailed provisions apply the legislation to cadets, employees and office holders of the National Criminal Intelligence Service, the National Crime Squad and other police bodies (*SDA 1975, s 17(6), (7), (9)*; *RRA 1976, s 76B*; *RBR 2003, reg 11(6), (7)*; *SOR 2003, reg 11(6), (7)*).

For circumstances in which police constables may lawfully be discriminated against see above 13.10(E).

13.24 Barristers and advocates

Unlawful discrimination against applicants for pupillage or tenancy

It is unlawful for a barrister or barrister's clerk, in relation to any offer of a pupillage or tenancy, to discriminate against a person on any of the unlawful grounds:

(*a*)   in the arrangements which are made for the purpose of determining to whom the pupillage or tenancy should be offered;

(*b*)   in respect of any terms on which it is offered; or

(*c*)   by refusing, or deliberately not offering, it to him (*SDA 1975, s 35A(1)*; *RRA 1976, s 26A(1)*; *RBR 2003, reg 12(1)*; *SOR 2003, reg 12(1)*).

Unlawful discrimination against pupils or tenants

It is unlawful for a barrister or barrister's clerk, in relation to a pupil or tenant in the set of chambers in question, to discriminate against him:

(*a*)   in respect of any terms applicable to him as a pupil or tenant;

(*b*)   in the opportunities for training or gaining experience, which are afforded or denied to him;

(*c*)   in the benefits which are afforded or denied to him; or

(*d*)   by terminating his pupillage, or by subjecting him to any pressure to leave the chambers or other detriment (*SDA 1975, s 35A(2)*; *RRA 1976, s 26A(2)*; *RBR 2003, reg 12(2)*; *SOR 2003, reg 12(2)*).

Unlawful harassment of pupils, tenants or applicants for pupillage or tenancy

It is unlawful for a barrister or barrister's clerk, in relation to a pupillage or tenancy in the set of chambers in question, to subject to harassment a person who is, or has applied to be, a pupil or tenant (*SDA 1975, s 35A(2A)*, as amended with effect from 1 October 2005; *RRA 1976, s 26A(3A)*; *RBR 2003, reg 12(3)*; *SOR 2003, reg 12(3)*; for the position prior to 1 October 2005 in relation to sexual harassment see 12.12(G) DISCRIMINATION AND EQUAL OPPORTUNITIES – I).

Unlawful discrimination by those instructing barristers

It is unlawful for any person, in relation to the giving, withholding or acceptance of instructions to a barrister, to discriminate against any person by subjecting him to a detriment, or to subject him to harassment (*SDA 1975, s 35A(3)*; *RRA 1976, s 26A(3)*; *RBR 2003, reg 12(4)*; *SOR 2003, reg 12(4)*).

'Barrister's clerk' includes any person carrying out any of the functions of a barrister's clerk. 'Pupil', 'pupillage', 'set of chambers', 'tenancy' and 'tenant' have the meanings commonly associated with their use in the context of barristers practising in independent practice, but 'tenancy' and 'tenant' also include reference to any barrister permitted to work in a set of chambers who is not a tenant (ie a 'squatter') (*SDA 1975, s 35A(4); RRA 1976, s 26A(4); RBR 2003, reg 12(5); SOR 2003, reg 12(5)*).

The exceptions for genuine occupational requirements (above 13.2FF) and benefits provided to the public (above 13.17) do not apply to barristers.

The provisions in respect of barristers extend to England and Wales only. Similar provision is made for advocates and their pupils in Scotland (*SDA 1975, s35B; RRA 1976, s 26B; RBR 2003, reg 13; SOR 2003, reg 13*).

13.25 Partnerships

Unlawful discrimination against partners and candidates for partnership

It is unlawful for a firm (or persons proposing to form a firm), in relation to a position as partner in the firm, to discriminate against a person on any of the unlawful grounds:

(*a*)   in the arrangements they make for the purpose of determining to whom they should offer that position;

(*b*)   in the terms on which they offer him that position;

(*c*)   by refusing to offer, or deliberately not offering, him that position; or

(*d*)   in a case where the person already holds that position:

    (i)   in the way they afford him access to any benefits or by refusing to afford, or deliberately not affording, him access to them, or

    (ii)   by expelling him from that position, or subjecting him to any other detriment (*SDA 1975, s 11(1), (2); RRA 1976, s 10(1), (2); RBR 2003, reg 14(1), (3); SOR 2003, reg 14(1), (3)*).

'Expulsion' of a person from a position as partner is (in the *RRA 1976, RBR 2003* and *SOR 2003*) defined additionally to refer:

(*a*)   to the termination of that person's position as partner by the expiration of any period (including a period expiring by reference to an event or circumstance), not being a termination immediately after which the partnership is renewed on the same terms; and

(*b*)   to the termination of that person's position as partner by any act of his (including the giving of notice) in circumstances such that he is entitled to terminate it without notice by reason of the conduct of the other partners (*RRA 1976, s 10(6); RBR 2003, reg 14(8); SOR 2003, reg 14(8)*).

Note that where one partner dissolves a two-person partnership the other partner is 'expelled' for the purposes of the provisions on partnerships and may sue the remaining partner (*Dave v Robinska* [2003] ICR 1248).

The legislation applies to limited partnerships and limited liability partnerships as it does to partnerships (with appropriate amendments of terminology) (*SDA 1975, s 11(5), (6); RRA 1976, s 10(4), (5); RBR 2003, reg 14(5), (6); SOR 2003, reg 14(5), (6)*). Note, however, that for discrimination on grounds of colour, the *RRA 1976* only applies to firms with six or more partners: *RRA 1976, s 10(1A)*.

Genuine occupational requirement

Genuine occupational requirement defences (see above 13.2FF) are available to partnerships. Under the *RBR 2003* and *SOR 2003*, an act falling into one of the categories set out above will not be unlawful if, had the complainant been an employee or applicant for employment, a genuine occupational requirement defence would have been available (*RBR 2003, reg 14(4)*; *SOR 2003, reg 14(4)*). Under the *RRA 1976* and the *SDA 1975* a genuine occupational requirement defence is only available where the discrimination takes the form of discrimination in the arrangements made for the purpose of determining who to offer a position as partner or a refusal to offer a position as partner ((a) and (c) in the categories set out above): *SDA 1975, s 11(3), (3A)*; *RRA 1976, s 10(3)*.

Special provision is made for a genuine occupational requirement defence to discrimination on grounds of gender reassignment (i.e. discrimination falling within *SDA 1975, s 2A*: see above 13.5). A partnership will have a defence to any form of discrimination on grounds of gender reassignment where, if it were employment, being a man (or being a woman) would be a genuine occupational qualification for the job and the firm can show that the treatment is reasonable in view of the circumstances (*SDA 1975, s 11(3A), (3B)*). Where the discrimination takes the form of discrimination in the arrangements made for the purposes of determining who should be offered a position as partner, refusing to offer a position as partner or expelling a partner, it is not necessary for the firm to show that the treatment was reasonable in the circumstances, provided that it is able to show that there would be a supplementary genuine occupational qualification for the position in question: see above 13.5 for supplementary genuine occupational qualifications.

Other exceptions

Prior to 1 October 2005 it was not unlawful to discriminate on grounds of sex against a partner (or potential partner) in relation to provision made for death and retirement. The exception applied to discrimination:

(*a*)   in the terms on which partnership is offered;

(*b*)   in a case where the person is already a partner:

    (i)   in the way he is afforded access to any benefits, etc.; or

    (ii)   by expelling him from that position, or subjecting him to any other detriment.

However, it did not apply to provision for expulsion (and the act of expulsion) in relation to retirement: discrimination in such matters remained unlawful except where a genuine occupational requirement applies (*SDA 1975, s 11(4)*).

The exception in relation to provision made for death and retirement in *s 11(4)* is repealed, with effect from 1 October 2005, by the *Sex Discrimination Regulations 2005, reg 9(3)*.

See 13.10(C) above for further discussion of the equality provisions relating to death and retirement benefits.

Unlawful harassment of partners and candidates for partnership

It is unlawful for a firm, in relation to a position as partner in the firm, to subject to harassment a person who holds or has applied for that position (*SDA 1975, 11(2A)*, as inserted with effect from 1 October 2005 by the *Sex Discrimination*

Regulations 2005; RRA 1976, s 10(1B); RBR 2003, reg 14(2); SOR 2003, reg 14(2); for the law relating to sexual harassment prior to 1 October 2005, see 12.12(G) DISCRIMINATION AND EQUAL OPPORTUNITIES – I).

13.26 **Trade organisations**

A 'trade organisation' is defined in the discrimination legislation as:

(i)   an organisation of workers,

(ii)   an organisation of employers, or

(iii) any other organisation whose members carry on a particular profession or trade for the purposes of which the organisation exists.

(*SDA 1975, 12(1); RRA 1976, s 11(1); RBR 2003, reg 15(4); SOR 2003, reg 15(4)*).

'Profession' is defined so as to include 'any vocation or occupation', and 'trade' to include 'any business': (*SDA 1975, s 82(1); RRA 1976, s 78(1); RBR 2003, reg 15(4); SOR 2003, reg 15(4)*.

The EAT has held that the National Federation of Self-Employed and Small Businesses Ltd is an 'employers' organisation': *National Federation of Self-Employed and Small Businesses Ltd v Philpott* [1997] IRLR 340. In *Medical Protection Society v Sadek* [2004] EWCA Civ 865, [2004] ICR 1263, the Court of Appeal considered the status of the Medical Protection Society, a membership organisation which had provided the claimant with advice and representation in relation to a claim he had brought against his employer, an NHS Trust. The Court held that the Society was 'an organisation of workers' within the first category of the definition of 'trade organisation' in *s 11(1)* of the *RRA 1976*, because medical and dental practitioners were properly classified as 'workers' even though they were 'members [of] a profession' within the third category of the definition of 'trade organisation' and even though some of them may be employees and others independent contractors. The Court considered that the EAT had been wrong to conclude that the Society fell within *both* the first and third categories of the definition: the third category was only a residual one.

Unlawful discrimination against applicants for membership of the organisation.

It is unlawful for a trade organisation to discriminate against a person:

(*a*)   in the terms on which it is prepared to admit him to membership of the organisation; or

(*b*)   by refusing to accept, or deliberately not accepting, his application for membership (*SDA 1975, s 12(2); RRA 1976, s 11(2); RBR 2003, reg 15(1); SOR 2003, reg 15(1)*).

Unlawful discrimination against members

It is unlawful for a trade organisation, in relation to a member of the organisation, to discriminate against him:

(*a*)   in the way it affords him access to any benefits or by refusing or deliberately omitting to afford him access to them;

(*b*)   by depriving him of membership, or varying the terms on which he is a member; or

(*c*)   by subjecting him to any other detriment (*SDA 1975, s 12(3); RRA 1976, s 11(3); RBR 2003, reg 15(2); SOR 2003, reg 15(2)*).

Note that, prior to 1 October 2005, *s 12* of the *SDA 1975* did not apply to provision made in relation to the death or retirement from work of a member (*s 12(4)*). This exception is repealed, with effect from 1 October 2005, by *reg 15(3)* of the *Sex Discrimination Regulations 2005*. (See 13.10(C) above for discussion of the equality provisions relating to death and retirement benefits.)

Unlawful harassment of members and applicants for membership

It is unlawful for a trade organisation, in relation to a person's membership or application for membership of that organisation, to subject that person to harassment (*SDA 1975, s 12(3A)*, as inserted with effect from 1 October 2005 by the *Sex Discrimination Regulations 2005*; *RRA 1976, s 11(4)*; *RBR 2003, reg 15(3)*; *SOR 2003, reg 15(3)*; for the law on sexual harassment prior to 1 October 2005, see 12.12(G) DISCRIMINATION AND EQUAL OPPORTUNITIES – I).

In *Fire Brigades Union v Fraser* [1998] IRLR 697 (Court of Session, Inner House), the union provided support and assistance for the alleged victim of the harassment, but refused to provide assistance to the alleged harasser. The Court of Session overturned a decision of the employment tribunal that the alleged harasser had been the victim of an act of discrimination on the part of the union. Whilst it was true that the union treated the alleged victims of harassment more favourably, the tribunal was making the wrong comparison in comparing harasser and harassee. The proper question was whether a female alleged harasser would have been treated differently.

13.27 Qualifications bodies

A qualifications body is an authority or body which can confer professional or trade qualifications. A 'professional or trade qualification' is an authorisation, recognition, enrolment, approval or certification, which is needed for, or facilitates, engagement in a particular profession or trade. 'Confer' is defined to include the renewal or extension of a qualification. (See *SDA 1975, s 13(1), (3)*; *RRA 1976, s 12(1), (2)*; *RBR 2003, reg 16(3)*; *SOR 2003, reg 16(4)*.) Establishments of further and higher education and schools are excluded from the definition. (Separate provision in relation to discrimination in education is made by both the *Acts* and the *Regulations*. Consideration of this is, however, outside the scope of this book.)

Note that the Labour Party is not a 'body' within this definition, at least in relation to the selection or nomination of candidates for elections: although being an MP is a 'profession', the selection or nomination of candidates is not an 'authorisation' or 'qualification' for that profession: *Triesman v Ali* [2002] EWCA Civ 92, [2002] ICR 1026 (disapproving the EAT's decision in *Sawyer v Ahsan* [1999] IRLR 609). In *Triesman*, the Court of Appeal did, however, hold that the Labour Party was an 'association' within *s 25* of the *RRA 1976* (which applies to any association of persons of 25 or more members, regulated by a constitution, that does not fall within *s 11* of the *RRA 1976*: *s 25* falls within Part III of the *RRA 1976*, is outwith the jurisdiction of the employment tribunal and the scope of this work).

It is unlawful for a qualifications body to discriminate against a person:

(a) in the terms on which it is prepared to confer a professional or trade qualification on him;

(b) by refusing or deliberately not granting any application by him for such a qualification; or

(c)   by withdrawing such a qualification from him or varying the terms on which he holds it (*SDA 1975, s 13(1)*; *RRA 1976, s 12(1)*; *RBR 2003, reg 16(1)*; *SOR 2003, reg 16(1)*.)

It is unlawful for a qualifications body, in relation to a professional or trade qualification conferred by it, to subject to harassment a person who holds or applies for such a qualification (*SDA 1975, s 13(1A)*, as inserted with effect from 1 October 2005 by the *Sex Discrimination Regulations 2005*; *RRA 1976, s 12(1A)*; *RBR 2003, reg 16(2)*; *SOR 2003, reg 16(2)* for the law on sexual harassment prior to 1 October 2005, see 12.12(G) DISCRIMINATION AND EQUAL OPPORTUNITIES – I).

Uniquely, the *SDA 1975* provides that, if the qualifications body has to consider an applicant's character, if there is evidence to show that an applicant has practised unlawful discrimination in connection with the carrying on of any profession or trade, that must be taken into account by the body (*SDA 1975, s 13(2)*).

The *SOR 2003* provides an exception equivalent to the genuine occupational requirement exception for discrimination in employment (see above 13.7). *SOR 2003, reg 16(3)* provides that the provisions relating to discrimination by qualifications bodies do not apply to 'professional or trade qualifications conferred for the purposes of an organised religion where a requirement related to sexual orientation is applied to the qualification so as to comply with the doctrines of the religion or to avoid conflicting with the strongly held religious convictions of a significant number of the religion's followers'. No equivalent exception is available under the *SDA 1975, RRA 1976* or *RBR 2003*.

In *British Judo Association v Petty* [1981] ICR 660, it was held that *SDA 1975, s 13* was to be widely construed so as to render unlawful a discriminatory restriction in a judo referee's certificate, since the certificate would in fact facilitate the holder's trade or profession. In *Patterson v Legal Services Commission* [2004] EWCA Civ 1558, [2004] ICR 312 the Court of Appeal held that the conferral of a franchise by the Legal Services Commission enabling the applicant's firm to receive public funds for the provisions of services in certain categories of legal work was an 'authorisation' that 'facilitates engagement in' the profession of solicitor for the purposes of *RRA 1976, s 12*. The authorisation was conferred on both the applicant's firm and the applicant personally. However, the provisions relating to qualifications bodies are not to be so widely construed as to extend to the mere awarding of a contract, even by a body or authority which has a *de facto* monopoly in the particular trade (*Malik v Post Office Counters Ltd* [1993] ICR 93). The provisions are aimed at discrimination by professional bodies and not individual businesses. Thus, where a private medical health insurer would only make payments in respect of treatment given by practitioners holding certain recognised qualifications, a plastic surgeon could not bring a claim where the insurer refused to recognise her Greek medical qualifications (*Tattari v Private Patients Plan Ltd* [1997] IRLR 586, CA). Being a Justice of the Peace is not 'engagement in a particular profession' (*Arthur v A-G* [1999] ICR 631). However, appointment as a Justice of the Peace would now be covered by the provisions relating to office holders (see above 13.22).

Note that it is not possible to complain to an employment tribunal under this provision if the act complained of is one in respect of which an appeal, or proceedings in the nature of an appeal, may be brought under any enactment (*SDA 1975, s 63(2)*; *RRA 1976, s 54(2)*; *RBR 2003, reg 28(2)*; *SOR 2003, reg 28(2))*. The scope and effect of this provision were considered in *R v Department of Health, ex p Gandhi* [1991] ICR 805 and *Khan v General Medical Council* [1994] IRLR 646, CA.

13.28 Providers of vocational training

A 'training provider' is any person who provides, or makes arrangements for the provision of, training or facilities for training which would help fit another person for any employment: *SDA 1975, s 14(1); RRA 1976, s 13(1); RBR 2003, reg 17(4); SOR 2003, reg 17(4)*. The *RBR 2003* and *SOR 2003* make clear that 'training' includes practical work experience provided by an employer to a person whom he does not employ; this is undoubtedly also within the meaning of 'training' in the *SDA 1975* (see especially *s 14(1B)*) and *RRA 1976*. In *Fletcher v NHS Pensions Agency* [2005] ICR 1458, the EAT held that the NHS Pensions Agency, which provides bursaries to trainee midwives combining academic study at universities with practical training through clinical placements in the community and hospitals, is a 'training provider' within the meaning of *SDA 1975, s 14(1)* since the bursaries are a 'facility' for training.

The definition of 'training provider' excludes employers in relation to training for their own employees and also education establishments: *SDA 1975, s 14(2); RRA 1976, s 13(2); RBR 2003, reg 17(4); SOR 2003, reg 17(4)*. This is because separate provision in relation to discrimination in education is made by both the *Acts* and the *Regulations*. Claims in relation to discrimination in education are excluded from the jurisdiction of the employment tribunals and are therefore outside the scope of this book. Note, however, that the mere fact that a provider of vocational training is acting as agent of an educational establishment does not mean that a claim against that provider is excluded from the jurisdiction of the employment tribunals, provided of course that the respondent otherwise falls within the definition of 'training provider' in the legislation: *Moyling v Homerton University Hospitals NHS Trust* (25 August 2005, unreported), EAT.

Unlawful discrimination against anyone undergoing or seeking to undergo vocational training

It is unlawful, in relation to a person seeking or undergoing training which would help fit him for any employment for any training provider to discriminate against him:

(a)   in the terms on which the training provider affords him access to any training (or any facilities concerned with such training);

(b)   by refusing or deliberately not affording him such access;

(c)   by terminating his training; or

(d)   by subjecting him to any other detriment during his training (*SDA 1975, s 14(1); RRA 1976, s 13(1); RBR 2003, reg 17(1); SOR 2003, reg 17(1)*).

With effect from 1 October 2005, the *SDA 1975* also applies expressly to 'arrangements' made 'for the purpose of selecting people to receive vocational training' (*SDA 1975, s 14(1)(a)*, as amended by the *Sex Discrimination Regulations 2005*).

In *Fletcher* the bursaries were stopped during the trainees' maternity leave: since the bursaries were a 'facilities concerned with training', which were stopped because the claimants were pregnant, this was unlawful sex discrimination. The EAT ruled that the tribunal had been wrong to conclude that there was no unlawful discrimination because employees absent for other reasons were treated the same way (see generally 12.5(3) DISCRIMINATION AND EQUAL OPPORTUNITIES – I).

All the exceptions that apply to discrimination by employers apply in relation to discrimination by providers of vocational training. The *RBR 2003* and *SOR 2003* provide that the training provider will have a defence where the alleged discrimination only concerns training for employment which, by virtue of the fact that the exception for genuine occupational requirement applies, the respondent could lawfully refuse to offer the person seeking training (*RBR 2003, reg 17(3); SOR 2003, reg 17(3)*). The exceptions in the *RBR 2003* and *SOR 2003* for national security, positive action and the protection of Sikhs from discrimination in relation to the wearing of safety helmets apply generally to Parts II and III of both sets of *Regulations* and therefore apply to training providers as they do to employers. The *SDA 1975* and *RRA 1976* provide, simply, that all the exceptions that apply in relation to discrimination by employers apply also to training providers (*SDA 1975, s 14(2); RRA 1976, s 13(2)*). (For exceptions see above 13.3, 13.9, 13.10, 13.11 and 13.14FF.)

Unlawful harassment of persons undergoing or seeking to undergo training

It is unlawful for a training provider, in relation to a person seeking or undergoing training which would help fit him for any employment, to subject him to harassment (*SDA 1975, s 14(1A)*, as inserted with effect from 1 October 2005 by the *Sex Discrimination Regulations 2005*; *RRA 1976, s 13(3)*; *RBR 2003, reg 17(2)*; *SOR 2003, reg 17(2)*; for the law relating to sexual harassment prior to 1 October 2005, see 12.12(G) DISCRIMINATION AND EQUAL OPPORTUNITIES – I).

13.29 **Employment agencies, careers guidance, etc**

Employment agencies are covered. The *RBR 2003* and *SOR 2003* define an employment agency as 'a person who, for profit or not, provides services for the purpose of finding employment for workers or supplying respondents with workers'. No definition is given in the *SDA 1975* or the *RRA 1976*, though both those *Acts*, like the *RBR 2003* and *SOR 2003*, state that references to the services of an employment agency include 'guidance on careers and any other services related to employment' (*SDA 1975, s 15(3)*; *RRA 1976, s 14(3)*; *RBR 2003, reg 18(6)*; *SOR 2003, reg 18(6)*). Education establishments are excluded from the definition of employment agencies (impliedly in the *SDA 1975* and the *RRA 1976*, expressly in the *RBR 2003* and *SOR 2003*: *reg 18(6)*). (Separate provision in relation to discrimination in education is made by both the *Acts* and the *Regulations*. Consideration of this is, however, outside the scope of this book.)

Note that users of employment agencies may also be able to bring claims against the employer to whom they are supplied, either under the provisions relating to contract workers (see above 13.21) or, in certain circumstances, as employees (see generally EMPLOYEE, SELF-EMPLOYED OR WORKER? (17)).

Unlawful discrimination against users and potential users of an employment agency

It is unlawful for an employment agency to discriminate against a person:

(*a*) in the terms on which the agency offers to provide any of its services;

(*b*) by refusing or deliberately not providing any of its services; or

(c)   in the way it provides any of its services (*SDA 1975, s 15(1); RRA 1976, s 14(1); RBR 2003, reg 18(1); SOR 2003, reg 18(1)*).

All the exceptions that apply to discrimination by employers apply in relation to discrimination by employment agencies. The *RBR 2003* and *SOR 2003* provide that the agency will have a defence where the alleged discrimination 'only concerns employment which, by virtue of ... (the) exception for genuine occupational requirement ... the employer could lawfully refuse to offer the person in question' (*RBR 2003, reg 18(3); SOR 2003, reg 18(3)*). The exceptions in the *RBR 2003* and *SOR 2003* for national security, positive action and the protection of Sikhs from discrimination in relation to the wearing of safety helmets apply generally to Parts II and III of both sets of *Regulations* and therefore apply to employment agencies as to employers. The *SDA 1975* and *RRA 1976* provide, simply, that the agency will have a defence where the alleged discrimination 'only concerns employment which an employer could lawfully refuse to offer the' person concerned (*SDA 1975, s 15(4); RRA 1976, s 14(4)*). (For circumstances in which an employer could lawfully refuse to offer employment see above 13.3, 13.9, 13.10, 13.11 and 13.14FF.)

A further defence is available that is peculiar to employment agencies. An employment agency will not be liable for unlawful discrimination where it proves that 'it acted in reliance on a statement made to it by the employer to the effect that, by reason of (the existence of a genuine occupational requirement) its action would not be unlawful', provided that it also proves that it was reasonable for it to rely on the statement (*SDA 1975, s 15(5); RRA 1976, s 14(5); RBR 2003, reg 18(4); SOR 2003, reg 18(4)*). Thus, if, for example, an employment agency relied on the statement of an employer who had been guilty of discrimination in the past, to the knowledge of the employment agency, it may be difficult for that agency to establish that it had acted reasonably in relying upon that statement.

If an employer knowingly or recklessly makes a statement to that effect which 'in a material respect is false or misleading', they thereby commit an offence punishable by a fine not exceeding level 5 on the standard scale (*SDA 1975, s 15(6); RRA 1976, s 14(6); RBR 2003, reg 18(5); SOR 2003, reg 18(5)*; see also 1.10 INTRODUCTION).

Unlawful harassment of users of an employment agency

It is unlawful for an employment agency, in relation to the provision of its services, to subject to harassment a person to whom it provides such services, or who has requested the provision of such services: *SDA 1975, s 15(1A)*, as inserted with effect from 1 October 2005 by the *Sex Discrimination Regulations 2005, reg 18; RRA 1976, s 14(1A); RBR 2003, reg 18(2); SOR 2003, reg 18(2)*; for the law relating to sexual harassment prior to 1 October 2005, see 12.12(G) DISCRIMINATION AND EQUAL OPPORTUNITIES – I.

13.30   State provision of employment-related services

The prohibitions on discrimination and harassment also apply to the provision of facilities or services by the Secretary of State under the *Employment and Training Act 1973, s 2* (arrangements for assisting persons to obtain employment) and by the Scottish Enterprise or Highlands and Islands Enterprise under the *Enterprise and New Towns (Scotland) Act 1990, s 2(3)* (the equivalent provision for Scotland) (*SDA 1975, s 16(1), (1A); RRA 1976, s 15(1), (1A); RBR 2003, reg 19(1), (2); SOR 2003, reg 19(1), (2)*).

Similarly, the prohibitions on racial and sex discrimination and harassment apply where a local authority provides services under the *Employment and Training Act 1973, s 10 (SDA 1975, s 15(2); RRA 1976, s 14(2))*.

The provisions relating to the provision of facilities or services under the *Employment and Training Act 1973, s 2* are default provisions, applying only where the Secretary of State would not be covered by the provisions relating to employment agencies (see above 13.29) or providers of vocational training generally (see above 13.28): *SDA 1975, 16(2); RRA 1976, s 15(2); RBR 2003, reg 19(3); SOR 2003, reg 19(3))*.

13.31 **Trustees and managers of occupational pension schemesss**

The *RBR 2003* and *SOR 2003* (as amended with effect from 2 December 2003 by *The Employment Equality (Religion or Belief) (Amendment) Regulations 2003 (SI 2003/2828)* and *The Employment Equality (Sexual Orientation) (Amendment) Regulations 2003 (SI 2003/2827)* respectively) apply to trustees and managers of occupational pension schemes.

'Occupational pension scheme' has the same meaning as in the *Pensions Act 1995 (RBR 2003, Sch 1A, para 1; SOR 2003, Sch 1A, para 1)*.

Unlawful discrimination against members and prospective members of occupational pension schemes

Except in relation to rights accrued or benefits payable in respect of periods of service prior to 2 December 2003, it is unlawful for the trustees or managers of an occupational pension scheme to discriminate against 'a member or a prospective member of the scheme in carrying out any of their functions in relation to it (including in particular their functions relating to the admission of members to the scheme and the treatment of members of it)' *(RBR 2003, reg 9A(1); SOR 2003, reg 9A(1))*.

Unlawful harassment of members and prospective members of occupational pension schemes

It is also unlawful for trustees or managers in relation to the scheme, to subject a member or prospective member to harassment *(RBR 2003, reg 9A(2); SOR 2003, reg 9A(2))*.

Inclusion of a 'non-discrimination rule' in the terms of the scheme

Sch 1A, para 2 of both the *RBR 2003* and *SOR 2003* provides that every occupational pension scheme should be treated as including a 'non-discrimination rule' (compare the provisions relating to sex discrimination, above 13.10(c)). The rule requires trustees or managers to refrain from 'doing any act which is unlawful by virtue of *reg 9A*'. All other provisions of the relevant pension scheme have effect subject to the non-discrimination rule *(RBR 2003, Sch 1A, para 3; SOR 2003, Sch 1A, para 3)*. The trustees or managers are given a power to alter the scheme by resolution so as to secure conformity with the non-discrimination rule where they either do not have an alteration power or else it is complex or dependent on the obtaining of consents which they are unable to obtain *(RBR 2003, Sch 1A, para 4; SOR 2003, Sch 1A, para 4)*. Resolutions may have a retrospective effect but cannot have effect in relation to any period prior to 2 December 2003 *(RBR 2003, Sch 1A, para 5; SOR 2003, Sch 1A, para 5)*.

Note, however, that benefits dependent on marital or civil partnership status are excluded from the scope of the *SOR 2003*: see above 13.13.

For remedies for breaches of *reg 9A* of the *RBR 2003* and *SOR 2003* see 14.8 DISCRIMINATION AND EQUAL OPPORTUNITIES – III.

For the rules relating to sex discrimination by trustees and managers of pension schemes see above 13.10(C).

There are no equivalent provisions relating to racial discrimination by trustees and managers of pension schemes.

13.32 **The Crown**

There are detailed provisions concerning the application of the legislation to:

(*a*) the Crown, government departments, service in the armed forces, etc. (*SDA 1975, s 85*; *RRA 1976, s 75*; *RBR 2003, reg 36*; *SOR 2003, reg 36*);

(*b*) House of Commons staff (*SDA 1975, 85A*; *RRA 1976, s 75A*; *RBR 2003, reg 37*; *SOR 2003, reg 37*); and

(*c*) House of Lords staff (*SDA 1975, s 85B*; *RRA 1976, s 75B*; *RBR 2003, reg 38*; *SOR 2003, reg 38*).

The effect of those provisions, broadly speaking, is that the equality legislation applies to the Crown, etc. 'as it does to an act done by a private person'. To achieve this, references in the legislation to a contract of employment are deemed to include references to the terms of service of Crown servants (*SDA 1975, s 85(2)*; *RRA 1976, s 75(2)*; *RBR 2003, reg 36(2)*; *SOR 2003, reg 36(2)*) and aircraft or hovercraft 'belonging to or possessed by Her Majesty in right of the Government of the United Kingdom' are deemed to be 'establishments' for the purposes of determining whether a person is employed at an establishment in Great Britain (*SDA 1975, s 85(7)*; *RRA 1976, s 75(4)*; *RBR 2003, reg 36(4)*; *SOR 2003, reg 36(4)*; and see above 13.15).

There are peculiarities specific to the different *Acts* and *Regulations*:

(*a*) 'Nothing' in the *SDA 1975* renders unlawful (i) an act done 'for the purpose of ensuring the combat effectiveness of the armed forces' (*SDA 1975, s 85(4)*) or (ii) discrimination in admission to the Army Cadet Force, Air Training Corps, Sea Cadet Corps, Combined Cadet Force, or any other cadet training corps for the time being administered by the Ministry of Defence.

(*b*) 'Nothing' in the *RRA 1976* invalidates 'any rules' (whether made before or after the passing of that *Act*) 'restricting employment in the service of the Crown or by any [prescribed] public body to persons of particular birth, nationality, descent or residence'; nor does it render unlawful 'the publication, display or implementation of any such rules, or the publication of advertisements stating the gist of any such rules' (*RRA 1976, s 75(5)*).

(*c*) In the *RBR 2003* and the *SOR 2003* the provisions relating to Crown employment etc. have effect subject to *reg 11* of each of those *Regulations*, which relates to the application of the *Regulations* to the police (see above 13.23).

Special provision is made in relation to the enforcement of complaints by members of the armed forces (*SDA 1975, s 85(9A)-(9E)*; *RRA 1976, s 75(8)–(9B)*; and regulations made under each of those provisions; *RBR 2003, reg 36(7)–(10)*;

SOR 2003, reg 36(7)–(10)). Broadly speaking, the effect of those provisions is that a member of the armed forces may only present a complaint to the employment tribunal if he has made a complaint in respect of the same matter to an officer under the service redress procedures and that complaint has not been withdrawn. A complaint will be treated as having been withdrawn if, having made the complaint to an officer, the complainant subsequently fails to submit that complaint to the Defence Council. However, presenting a complaint to the employment tribunal does not prevent the continuation of the service redress procedures. (See generally 14.2 DISCRIMINATION AND EQUAL OPPORTUNITIES – III.)

Detailed provisions also set out how the Crown Proceedings Act 1947 applies to proceedings under the SDA 1975 and the RRA 1976: SDA 1975, s 85(8), (9); RRA 1976, s 75(6), (7).

13.33 GENERAL EQUALITY DUTIES ON PUBLIC AUTHORITIES

Section 71 RRA 1976 has, since its amendment by the *Race Relations (Amendment) Act 2000* with effect from 2 April 2001, imposed a general duty on public authorities, when carrying out any of their functions, to have due regard to the need (a) 'to eliminate unlawful racial discrimination' and (b) 'to promote equality of opportunity and good relations between persons of different racial groups'. This new duty replaced an earlier, more limited, duty on public authorities contained in that section.

A similar duty has now been inserted into the *SDA 1975* by the *Equality Act 2006*. With effect from 6 April 2007, a new Gender Equality Duty ('GED') is imposed on all public authorities. By *s 76A(1) SDA 1975*, all public authorities are required, when carrying out their functions, to have due regard (a) 'to the need to eliminate unlawful discrimination and harassment', and (b) 'to promote equality of opportunity between men and women'.

'Public authority' is defined for the purposes of the *SDA 1975* in the same way as a 'public authority' under the *Human Rights Act 1998* as 'any person who has functions of a public nature'. Under the RRA 1976 a list of public authorities covered by the general duty is given in *Sch 1A* to the Act. However, broadly speaking both the *RRA 1976* and the *SDA 1975* cover all bodies who have functions of a public nature, apart from certain specific exceptions, which include the House of Commons, House of Lords, the Scottish Parliament, judicial functions and the government intelligence services.

Both the duties in the *SDA 1975* and those in the *RRA 1976* apply to all the functions of a public authority including their employment and procurement functions. They therefore have an impact on the employment field because public authorities are required to comply with the general equality duties in relation to their own employees (and applicants for employment). In addition, private companies who wish to win contracts to perform services for public authorities in turn have to demonstrate that they are taking steps to promote gender equality in order to be selected by the public authority.

The general duties are stated to be 'without prejudice' to other provisions of the *SDA 1975* and the *RRA 1976* (*SDA 1975, s 76A(5)* and *RRA 1976, s 71(7)*). The accompanying Codes of Practice, issued under *SDA 1975, s 76E* and *RRA 1976, s 71C*, explain that what is meant by this is that positive discrimination will be allowed (indeed, is required) insofar as it is designed to achieve equality of opportunity by, for example, targeting only men or only women when advertising a particular job or training opportunity. However, in relation to the actual appointment itself, positive discrimination remains prohibited.

The GED duty applies in relation to all discrimination rendered unlawful by the *SDA 1975* or the EqPA 1970, ie it applies not only to unlawful discrimination as between men and women, but also in relation to unlawful discrimination against transsexual persons and unlawful discrimination on grounds of maternity. The general duty under the *RRA 1976* applies in relation to all discrimination rendered unlawful by the *RRA 1976* (ie to discrimination on grounds of race, nationality, ethnic group, etc).

In addition to the general duties under the *RRA 1976* and the *SDA 1975*, certain specific duties are introduced by dint of subsidiary legislation made under *SDA 1975, s 76B* and *RRA 1976, s 71A*. These specific duties include obligations on the public authority:

(*a*)   to prepare and publish gender and racial equality schemes, showing how it will meet its general and specific duties under the Acts and setting out its gender equality objectives;

(*b*)   in formulating its overall objectives, to consider the need to include objectives to address the causes of any gender pay gap;

(*c*)   to gather and use information on how the public authority's policies and practices affect gender and racial equality in the workforce and in the delivery of services;

(*d*)   to consult stakeholders (ie employees, service users and others, including trade unions) and take account of relevant information in order to determine its gender and racial equality objectives;

(*e*)   to assess the impact of its current and proposed policies and practices on gender and racial equality;

(*f*)   to implement the actions set out in its scheme within three years, unless it is unreasonable or impracticable to do so; and,

(*g*)   to report against the scheme every year and review the scheme at least every three years.

13.34 Enforcement

Enforcement of the general duties under both *Acts* is via complaint to the Equal Opportunities Commission (*SDA 1975, s 76D* and *RRA 1976, ss 71D* and *71E*). *Section 76A(6) SDA 1975* further makes it clear that there is no 'cause of action at private law' in relation to an alleged breach of the GED. Theoretically, this leaves open the possibility of a judicial review claim by a private individual in relation to alleged breaches of these general duties. Permission to apply for judicial review may, however, be refused in such cases if the court considers that the option of complaint to the EOC constitutes an adequate alternative remedy for the individual.

14   Discrimination and Equal Opportunities – III: Enforcement

14.1   No civil or criminal proceedings may be taken against any person for a breach of any provision of the *Sex Discrimination Act 1975 ('SDA 1975'), Race Relations Act 1976 ('RRA 1976'), Employment Equality (Sexual Orientation) Regulations 2003 (SI 2003/1661) ('SOR 2003'),* or *Employment Equality (Religion or Belief) Regulations 2003 ('RBR 2003'),* except where such an action is expressly provided for by these *Acts* or *Regulations (SDA 1975, s 62(1); RRA 1976, s 53(1); SOR 2003, reg 27(1); RBR 2003, reg 27(1)).* This does not restrict the making of quashing, mandatory or prohibiting orders (which are remedies obtained against public bodies upon an application for judicial review) or a complaint to the Pensions Ombudsman *(SDA 1975, s 62(2); RRA 1976, s 53(2); SOR 2003, reg 27(2); RBR 2003, reg 27(2)).* The only means of direct enforcement open to an individual for discrimination, in relation to employment, is generally by application to an employment tribunal (see 14.2 below). In the case of sex and race discrimination the Equal Opportunities Commission ('EOC') and the Commission for Racial Equality ('CRE') have additional powers to hold formal investigations (see 14.27 below), issue non-discrimination notices (see 14.28 below) and may apply for an injunction in certain cases (see 14.29 – 14.30 below).

Following the enactment of the *Equality Act 2006 ('EqA 2006')* the EOC and CRE will in due course be abolished and their functions will be taken over by the Commission for Equality and Human Rights ('CEHR') (see 14.26 below). At the time of writing, the CEHR is in the process of formation and it is anticipated that it will become operational in October 2007. For the time being the EOC and CRE will remain in existence and continue to exercise their enforcement powers during the lifetime of the current edition of the book. Their powers are therefore considered below along with the powers that will be available to the CEHR.

Where *SDA 1975* does not confer the rights granted by *EEC Directive 76/207* ('the *Equal Treatment Directive'),* individuals may rely upon the *Equal Treatment Directive* in claims against state authorities (see 37.7 PUBLIC SECTOR EMPLOYEES and 12.2 DISCRIMINATION AND EQUAL OPPORTUNITIES – I). From 1 May 1999, the *Treaty of Rome* was amended to incorporate a principle of equal treatment which may allow, for the first time, private sector employees to rely directly upon European anti-discrimination law. Once the *Framework Directive 2000/78/EC* on equal treatment in employment comes fully into effect direct effect will extend to the forms of discrimination other than sex discrimination.

The provisions under the *SDA 1975, RRA 1976, SOR 2003* and *RBR 2003* are very similar and this chapter addresses the issue of enforcement in these four areas together, highlighting any relevant differences. Enforcement issues in age and disability discrimination cases are dealt with separately above at AGE DISCRIMINATION (3) and DISABILITY DISCRIMINATION (10).

Reference can also be made to *Harvey on Industrial Relations and Employment Law* (HARVEYS – DIVISION L.2 (SEX DISCRIMINATION), L.3 (RACIAL DISCRIMINATION) and L.5 (DISCRIMINATION ON THE GROUNDS OF SEXUAL ORIENTATION AND RELIGION OR BELIEF).

14.2   **APPLICATIONS TO AN EMPLOYMENT TRIBUNAL**

A person ('the complainant') may present a complaint to an employment tribunal that another person has committed an act of discrimination or harassment against them which is unlawful by virtue of any of the provisions relating to employment (*SDA 1975, s 63(1); RRA 1976, s 54(1); SOR 2003, reg 28(1); RBR 2003, reg 28(1)*). The principal or employer of the discriminator will *also* be treated as having committed the discrimination (*SDA 1975, ss 41, 42; RRA 1976, ss 32, 33; SOR 2003, reg 22, 23; RBR 2003, reg 22, 23*). In the case of sex and race discrimination members of the armed forces have also been able to bring claims in the employment tribunal since 1 October 1997 (the *Sex Discrimination (Complaints to Employment Tribunals) (Armed Forces) Regulations 1997 (SI 1997/2163)*; the *Race Relations (Complaints to Employment Tribunals)(Armed Forces) Regulations 1997 (SI 1997/2161)*). Previously, they were subject to a separate statutory regime. Similar provisions are now contained in *SOR 2003, reg 36* and *RBR 2003, reg 36*. A member of the armed forces may only present a complaint to the employment tribunal if he has made a complaint in respect of the same matter to an officer under the service redress procedures applicable to him and that complaint has not been withdrawn. A complaint will be treated as having been withdrawn if, having made the complaint to an officer the complainant subsequently fails to submit that complaint to the Defence Council. Presenting a complaint to the employment tribunal does not prevent the continuation of the service redress procedures.

An exception to the jurisdiction of the employment tribunals for employment-related claims exists for acts committed (or treated as committed) by qualifications bodies. It is not possible to complain to the employment tribunal if the act complained of is one in respect of which an appeal, or proceedings in the nature of an appeal, may be brought under any enactment (*SDA 1975, s 63(2); RRA 1976, s 54(2); SOR 2003, reg 28(2)(a); RBR 2003, reg 28(2)(a)*). The scope and effect of these provisions under the *RRA 1976* were considered in *R v Department of Health, ex p Gandhi* [1991] ICR 805; *Khan v General Medical Council* [1994] IRLR 646, CA; and *Chaudhary v Specialist Training Authority Appeal Panel (No 2)* [2005] EWCA Civ 282, [2005] ICR 1086). Tribunals also lack jurisdiction to hear complaints about discriminatory conduct in the course of judicial or quasi-judicial proceedings, and a police disciplinary board has been held to be a judicial body (*Heath v Metropolitan Police Comr* [2004] EWCA Civ 943, [2005] ICR 329). That immunity from suit does not extend to the decision to commence disciplinary proceedings nor to a chief constable's decision to dismiss (*Lake v British Transport Police* [2007] ICR 47, EAT). Moreover, a police disciplinary board's immunity from suit is not impeached so as to oust the employment tribunal's jurisdiction where the claimant merely seeks to advance before the employment tribunal a case that had been rejected by the board (*Lake v British Transport Police* [2007] EWCA Civ 424, reversing the EAT's decision on this issue).

Discrimination claims do not lapse on the death of the complainant. The deceased's estate may commence or continue proceedings (*Lewisham and Guys Mental Health NHS Trust v Andrews* [2000] ICR 707, CA). A discrimination claim is a 'hybrid' claim and a bankrupt has standing to bring such a claim provided that he limits the remedy sought to a declaration or compensation for injury to feelings (*Khan v Trident Safeguards Ltd* [2004] EWCA Civ 624, [2004] IRLR 961).

14.3   Burden of proof

The burden of proof in discrimination cases is now generally split. In order to understand the present burden of proof it is necessary to provide a brief account of how the burden worked prior to the more recent developments described below. *SDA 1975* and *RRA 1976* both originally had the effect that the complainant had the burden of showing both that they had been less favourably treated and also that the less favourable treatment had been on grounds of sex or race. In practice, the burden proved difficult to discharge. Discrimination was very rarely overtly sexist or racist and the complainant had instead to persuade the tribunal to draw an inference. Complainants were assisted by case law (most famously *King v Great Britain-China Centre* [1992] ICR 516, CA) in which the following approach was advocated. First, the complainant had to establish a difference in sex or race and that they had been less favourably treated. Once this prima facie case had been established the tribunal was entitled to turn to the employer and seek an explanation for this disparity in treatment. If the employer's explanation was unsatisfactory the tribunal was entitled but not obliged (see *Glasgow City Council v Zafar* [1998] ICR 120, HL) to draw an inference that the less favourable treatment was on the relevant prohibited ground. The advantage of the guidance allowing rather than compelling the drawing of an inference is that it makes allowance for the fact that humans are capable of acting inconsistently and unreasonably and yet not discriminatorily.

The old test continues to apply in cases of discrimination on grounds of colour or nationality, otherwise a new burden of proof is now applicable to all other discrimination and harassment claims under the *SDA 1975, RRA 1976, SOR 2003* and *RBR 2003*, including claims where the respondent is vicariously liable or knowingly aids a prohibited act. The relevant provisions are:

Sex	*SDA 1975, s 63A*
Marital status	*SDA 1975, s 63A*
Pregnancy or maternity leave	*SDA 1975, s 63A*
Gender reassignment	*SDA 1975, s 63A*
Race	*RRA 1976, s 54A*
Sexual orientation	*SOR 2003, reg 29*
Religion or belief	*RBR 2003, reg 29*

Where, on the hearing of the complaint, the complainant proves facts from which the tribunal could conclude in the absence of an adequate explanation that the respondent:

(*a*)   has committed an unlawful act against the complainant falling within the jurisdiction of the employment tribunal; or

(*b*)   is either vicariously liable for such an act or has knowingly aided the commission of such an act;

the tribunal should uphold the complaint unless the respondent proves that he did not commit, or as the case may be, is not to be treated as having committed, the act.

General guidance on the application of the new test was provided by the EAT in *Barton v Investec Henderson Crossthwaite Securities Ltd* [2003] ICR 1205, EAT at

1218F and by the Court of Appeal in *Wong v Igen Ltd* [2005] EWCA Civ 142, [2005] ICR 931. The guidance is set out below in full under the heading 'the revised *Barton* Guidance'.

The new statutory test is similar to the approach adopted in *King* in that the burden is initially on the complainant to make out what might be described as the '*prima facie* case'. The respondent must then give an explanation. However, the new test is stricter because once a *prima facie* case is established the respondent then has the burden of proving that he did not act unlawfully. If he fails to discharge the burden, the tribunal must find in favour of the complainant.

As indicated above, under the old test the tribunal would decide, once a *prima facie* case had been made out, whether the case was in truth one of discrimination on a prohibited ground or whether it was perhaps unreasonable or inconsistent but nevertheless non-discriminatory treatment. Because discretion is replaced with compulsion, it becomes particularly important to determine when the *prima facie* case has been made out. Recent case law indicates that it is now harder for the complainant to make out a *prima facie* case than it was under the old test.

In order to establish a *prima facie* case at stage one there must be something that raises a suggestion that a prohibited factor may have been at work. In *Igen v Wong* above, their Lordships addressed the issue in the context of the analysis of the *RRA 1976*:

'The relevant act is, in a race discrimination case ... that (a) in circumstances relevant for the purposes of any provision of the 1976 Act (for example in relation to employment in the circumstances specified in section 4 of the Act), (b) the alleged discriminator treats another person less favourably and (c) does so on racial grounds. All those facts are facts which the complainant, in our judgment, needs to prove on the balance of probabilities.'

The Court of Appeal confirmed in *Madarassy v Nomura International plc* [2007] EWCA Civ 33, [2007] IRLR 246, that a claimant must establish more than a difference in status (eg. sex) and a difference in treatment before a tribunal will be in a position where it 'could conclude' that an act of discrimination had been committed. See also *Adebayo v Dresdner Kleinwort Wasserstein Ltd* [2005] IRLR 514, [2005] All ER (D) 371 (Mar), EAT; *University of Huddersfield v Wolff* [2004] IRLR 534, EAT; *Fernandez v Office of the Parliamentary Commissioner* [2006] All ER (D) 460 (Jul), EAT; *Griffiths-Henry v Network Rail Infrastructure Ltd* [2006] IRLR 865, [2006] All ER (D) 15 (Jul), EAT; and *Fox v Rangecroft* [2006] EWCA Civ 1112 (unreported, 13 July 2006). However there does not have to be positive evidence that any difference in treatment was on a prohibited ground in order to establish a *prima facie* case (*Network Rail Infrastructure Ltd* above).

In deciding whether or not a *prima facie* case has been made out, the tribunal should ignore any explanation proffered by the employer for the treatment, turning to it only once the burden has shifted (*Igen* above). However this does not mean that at the first stage the tribunal should consider only evidence adduced by the claimant and ignore the respondent's evidence. The tribunal should have regard to all the facts at the first stage to determine what inferences can properly be drawn (*Laing v Manchester City Council* [2006] ICR 1519, [2006] IRLR 748, EAT; approved by the Court of Appeal in *Madarassy*, and in *Appiah v Governing Body of Bishop Douglass Roman Catholic High School* [2007] EWCA Civ 10, [2007] IRLR 264; see also *Mohmed v West Coast Trains Ltd* (2006) 814 IDS Brief 7, EAT, considering the *RBR, reg 29*). At this stage the tribunal will need to look at evidence that the act complained of occurred at all, evidence as to the actual comparator relied upon by the claimant, evidence as to whether the comparisons being made by the claimant were like with like, and available evidence as to the reasons for the differential treatment (*Madarassy* above). In *Madarassy* the Court of Appeal held that at the first stage the respondent may adduce evidence which: showed that the alleged acts did not occur; that, if they did, occur, there was not less favourable treatment of the claimant; that the comparators chosen by the claimant or the situations chosen by the claimant were not like the claimant or the situations with which comparison was sought to be made; and that even if there was less favourable treatment it was not on prohibited grounds. It is submitted that there may be some difficulty for tribunals in distinguishing this last category of evidence which the Court of Appeal has held that they are entitled to consider and accept at the first stage and any putative explanation from the respondent that would be considered at the second stage.

The complainant must establish on the balance of probabilities that the employer has committed the potentially discriminatory act. It would not be appropriate to require an explanation from the employer for something that the employer *may* have done. Thus where an act may have been committed by the employer or by a third party a *prima facie* case will not have been established (*Igen* above).

Logically the employer may offer one of a number of sorts of explanations at the second stage, if he offers one at all; those that confirm discrimination, those that explain the disparity in a manner which makes it clear that there was no unlawful discrimination but which, to use the words of the EAT in *Sinclair, Roche & Temperley v Heard* [2004] IRLR 763, EAT 'redound to the employer's discredit', and those which explain away discrimination and are themselves worthy reasons. It is not sufficient to establish discrimination that the tribunal considers that the explanation given is not one that is objectively justified or reasonable as unfairness is not sufficient to establish discrimination (see *Network Rail Infrastructure Ltd* above).

The explanation cannot simply be asserted, it must be proven. As the facts supporting the explanation will be in the respondent's knowledge cogent evidence is expected in support of any explanation proffered (see *Barton* above). The Court of Appeal has emphasised in *EB v BA* [2006] EWCA Civ 132, [2006] IRLR 471 that where the burden of proof has shifted the respondent must be required to adduce the evidence necessary to discharge that burden, otherwise the protection afforded to a claimant by (in that case) the *SDA 1975, s 63A* is negated. The weight of the burden imposed on the respondent at the second stage will depend on the strength of the *prima facie* case established by the claimant at the first stage (see *Network Rail Infrastructure Ltd* above).

Before the new test many authorities emphasised the importance of making clear findings of fact and explaining why inferences were (or were not) being drawn (see *Anya v University of Oxford* [2001] ICR 847, CA). The more recent authorities make the same point. There must be clear findings of fact in relation to less favourable treatment; a clear finding as to whether the burden has reversed (see *Wolff* above); clear findings of fact in relation to the explanation; and a clear finding as to whether the explanation offered has discharged the burden and, if not, why not (see *Sinclair, Roche & Temperley* above and *Bahl* below).

Where an employer advances an obviously non-discriminatory explanation, the tribunal's decision should show that it has recognised that an explanation has been provided and, if it still wishes to conclude that the act was unlawfully discriminatory, explain expressly why it is rejecting the explanation (*Bahl v Law Society* [2003] IRLR 640, EAT).

In a case where it is alleged that an act was on grounds of sex and/or on racial grounds and the evidence does not satisfy the tribunal that either ground, considered independently, is made out, it is not open to the tribunal to decide that 'taken together' the treatment was unlawful on both grounds (*Bahl* above). The same will hold true for any attempt to combine other prohibited grounds.

The Court of Appeal has now confirmed that it is not always necessary for a tribunal expressly to go through the two-stage test in sequence and instead can focus on the respondent's reasons for the treatment, for example where the comparator is hypothetical and the facts are not fundamentally in dispute (*Brown v London Borough of Croydon* [2007] EWCA Civ 32, [2007] IRLR 259; see also *Laing* above). Although it is generally good practice to go through the two-stage test there are cases where the claimant is not prejudiced by the tribunal omitting the first stage and going straight to the second stage and concluding that the respondent has discharged the burden of proving that the treatment was not on a prohibited ground.

The revised Barton Guidance

(1)   Pursuant to *SDA 1975, s 63A*, it is for the claimant who complains of sex discrimination to prove on the balance of probabilities facts from which the tribunal could conclude, in the absence of an adequate explanation, that the employer has committed an act of discrimination against the claimant which is unlawful by virtue of Part 2 or which, by virtue of *s 41* or *s 42* of *SDA 1975*, is to be treated as having been committed against the claimant. These are referred to below as 'such facts'.

(2)   If the claimant does not prove such facts he or she will fail.

(3)   It is important to bear in mind in deciding whether the claimant has proved such facts that it is unusual to find direct evidence of sex discrimination. Few employers would be prepared to admit such discrimination, even to themselves. In some cases the discrimination will not be an intention but merely based on the assumption that 'he or she would not have fitted in'.

(4)   In deciding whether the claimant has proved such facts, it is important to remember that the outcome at this stage of the analysis by the tribunal will therefore usually depend on what inferences it is proper to draw from the primary facts found by the tribunal.

(5)   It is important to note the word 'could' in the *SDA 1975*, s 63A(2). At this stage the tribunal does not have to reach a definitive determination that such facts would lead it to the conclusion that there was an act of unlawful discrimination. At this stage a tribunal is looking at the primary facts before it to see what inferences of secondary fact could be drawn from them.

(6)   In considering what inferences or conclusions can be drawn from the primary facts, the tribunal must assume that there is no adequate explanation for those facts.

(7)   These inferences can include, in appropriate cases, any inferences that it is just and equitable to draw in accordance with *SDA 1975, s 74(2)(b)* from an evasive or equivocal reply to a questionnaire or any other questions that fall within *SDA 1975, s 74(2)* (see *Dattani v Chief Constable of West Mercia Police* [2005] IRLR 327, EAT – *RRA 1976, s 65* (the equivalent provision to *SDA 1975, s 74(2)*) also covers evasive or equivocal pleading in a response to a claim).

(8)   Likewise, the tribunal must decide whether any provision of any relevant code of practice is relevant and, if so, take it into account in determining such facts pursuant to *SDA 1975, s 56A(10)*. This means that inferences may also be drawn from any failure to comply with any relevant code of practice.

(9)   Where the claimant has proved facts from which conclusions could be drawn that the employer has treated the claimant less favourably on the ground of sex, then the burden of proof moves to the employer.

(10)   It is then for the employer to prove that he did not commit, or as the case may be, is not to be treated as having committed, that act.

(11)   To discharge that burden it is necessary for the employer to prove, on the balance of probabilities, that the treatment was in no sense whatsoever on the grounds of sex, since 'no discrimination whatsoever' is compatible with the Burden of Proof Directive.

(12)   That requires a tribunal to assess not merely whether the employer has proved an explanation for the facts from which such inferences can be drawn, but further that it is adequate to discharge the burden of proof on the balance of probabilities that sex was not a ground for the treatment in question.

(13)   Since the facts necessary to prove an explanation would normally be in the possession of the respondent, a tribunal would normally expect cogent evidence to discharge that burden of proof. In particular, the tribunal will need to examine carefully explanations for failure to deal with the questionnaire procedure and/or a code of practice.

See also HARVEYS – DIVISION L.2.A(5)(A), L.3.B(9), L.5.E(1).

14.4   Time limit

A complaint must be presented to a tribunal before the end of the period of three months beginning when the act complained of was done (*SDA 1975, s 76(1); RRA 1976, s 68(1); SOR 2003, reg 34(1), (1A); RBR 2003, reg 34(1), (1A)*). A six month time limit applies to complaints by members of the armed forces. From 1 October 2004 the three month time limit may be extended by the 'extended period' under the *Employment Act 2002 (Dispute Resolution) Regulations 2004 (SI 2004/752)*, reg 15. See also HARVEYS – DIVISIONS L.2.B(7), L.3.B(8), L.5.E(1), T.A.5.

For the purposes of deciding when an act was done, in calculating the time limit:

(*a*)   where the inclusion of any term in any contract renders the making of the contract an unlawful act, that act shall be treated as extending throughout the duration of the contract;

(*b*)   any act extending over a period shall be treated as done at the end of that period (for an example, see *Calder v James Finlay Corpn Ltd* [1989] ICR 157);

(*c*)   a deliberate omission shall be treated as done when the person in question decided upon it; and

(*d*)   in the absence of evidence establishing the contrary, if the cause for complaint is an omission rather than an act, the omission will be treated as having been decided upon when a person does something inconsistent with the omitted act or when the period within which he would reasonably be expected to have done the act has expired.

(*SDA 1975, s 76(6); RRA 1976, s 68(7); SOR 2003, reg 34(4); RBR 2003, reg 34(4)*.)

14.5 *Omissions*

A difficulty of interpretation arose in cases where there was a delay between the point at which the discriminator decided upon a deliberate omission and the point at which he omitted to act. In *Swithland Motors plc v Clarke* [1994] ICR 231, EAT, the appellant decided, whilst negotiating the purchase of a car sales business from receivers, that in the event that its bid was successful it would follow its usual practice of employing only female sales staff. It would omit, therefore, to offer the existing male staff the opportunity to continue in employment. The purchase was completed more than three months after the decision to apply the policy had been taken. On its face *SDA 1975, s 76(6)(c)* would appear to suggest that the male employees were out of time to complain before they even knew that there was something to complain about. The EAT decided that the section had to be read as meaning 'decides at a time and in circumstances when he is in a position to implement that decision'. Time ran, therefore, from the date on which the business was purchased.

14.6 *Acts extending over a period*

Applications in discrimination cases will often make reference to a number of alleged instances of discrimination stretching back over a period, only part of which is within three months of the date of submission of the claim. The tribunal must then assess whether the individual allegations together constitute an 'act extending over a period' or else are to be treated as a series of discrete events.

In *Barclays Bank plc v Kapur* [1991] ICR 208, the House of Lords held that the bank's stipulation that service in Africa would not count for pension purposes, although originally made years before the complaints were brought, subjected the applicant employees to a continuing disadvantage which by virtue of *RRA 1976, s 68(7)(b)* was to be treated as an act done when the employees retired. It was necessary to distinguish a continuing rule such as this from an act which merely had continuing consequences. In *Sougrin v Haringey Health Authority* [1992] ICR 650, a pay re-grading was held to fall into the latter category, but in *Littlewoods Organisation plc v Traynor* [1993] IRLR 154 the failure to take the remedial measures promised after an earlier act of discrimination was held to be a continuing act. A number of apparently discrete acts may provide evidence of a policy, rule or practice. The existence of such a policy or practice may itself constitute a 'continuing act' (*Owusu v London Fire and Civil Defence Authority* [1995] IRLR 574). In *Cast v Croydon College* [1998] ICR 500, CA, an employee who was about to commence maternity leave asked to be allowed to return on a part-time basis. Her request was refused. She took her maternity leave, returned to work and repeated her request. When it was again refused she resigned, alleging that she was unable to comply with the requirement that she work full-time. She commenced proceedings in the tribunal. Only the second refusal was 'in time'. It was held that each refusal constituted a separate act of discrimination, because on each occasion the employer considered the matter afresh. Had it merely restated its earlier decision, the position might have been different. Further, the tribunal decided that the second refusal was merely a confirmation of the first and that the claim was out of time. However, the Court of Appeal determined, first, that the two refusals were discrete decisions and that the claim in relation to the second refusal was within time and, further, that the two refusals should have been treated as evidence of the existence of a 'policy' on the employer's part, the fact that the same decision was reached on each occasion was evidence of the existence of a discriminatory policy. The operation of such a discriminatory policy constituted an act 'extending over a period' within the meaning of *SDA 1975, s 76*. In contrast, in another case, the Court of Appeal has held that the time limit begins to run again on each occasion on which the policy is applied. Thus, where a complainant was refused the same request on a number of occasions, each refusal caused the three-month time limit to start afresh (*Rovenska v General Medical Council* [1998] ICR 85, CA). The EAT has held that an employment tribunal was entitled to conclude that a refusal by an employer to revoke a dismissal was entirely separate from the dismissal itself and not part of a continuing act (*Baynton v South West Trains Ltd* [2005] ICR 1730).

Other authorities have used terms such as 'rule', 'scheme', 'regime' or 'practice' as well as 'policy'. However, the Court of Appeal has stressed that such terms are merely examples of acts which may extend over a period. Their Lordships have adopted a broader description of what the tribunal should look for: an 'ongoing situation' or a 'continuing state of affairs' which may be contrasted with a 'a succession of unconnected or isolated specific acts' (*Hendricks v Metropolitan Police Comr* [2003] EWCA Civ 1686, [2003] ICR 530, CA). Leave to appeal to the House of Lords was refused ([2003] ICR 999). The Court of Appeal has confirmed the *Hendricks* approach in *Lyfar v Brighton and Sussex University Hospitals Trust* [2006] EWCA Civ 1548, [2006] All ER (D) 182 (Nov), emphasising the need to focus on the substance of the complaints when assessing whether they form a continuous act. However, in order to establish the existence of a policy or practice, the complainant must establish some degree of 'co-ordination' (*Metropolitan Police Comr v Hendricks* (2002) 707 IDS Brief 8, EAT). Following the House of Lords' decision in *Relaxion Group plc v Rhys-Harper* [2003] UKHL 33, [2003] ICR 867, the EAT has held that a serious of acts constituting an act extending over time can include an act taking place after the complainant has ceased to be an employee of the respondent (*BHS Ltd v Walker* (2005) 787 IDS Brief 11).

It will generally be an error of law for a tribunal to seek to determine whether there is an act extending over a period on the basis of legal argument alone without hearing any evidence and making findings of fact (see the 'protected disclosure' case of *Arthur v London Eastern Railways (t/a One Stansted Express)* [2006] EWCA Civ 1358, [2007] IRLR 58).

In *Tyagi v BBC World Service* [2001] EWCA Civ 549, [2001] IRLR 465, the complainant sought to allege that he had been discriminated against in relation to an application for promotion. His claim was lodged 15 months after he had failed to obtain the promotion and a year after he had ceased to be employed by the respondent. He contended that the respondent operated a discriminatory recruitment policy which was still in place at the date of his application. That being so, he argued, his application was not out of time. The Court of Appeal found against him drawing a distinction between those who remained in employment at the time of complaint and those who did not. The former group was entitled to complain about discriminatory policies which affected the way in which their employer afforded them 'access to opportunities for promotion'. They could, therefore, complain about the existence of the policy itself. The latter were only able to complain about the arrangements made for the purpose of determining who should be offered a particular job and, thus, could not complain about the policy.

In the case of a single act, time starts to run when the course of action is complete, that is when a complaint to a tribunal could first be made (*Clarke v Hampshire Electro-Plating Co Ltd* [1992] ICR 312; see also *Adekeye v Post Office* [1993] ICR 464). Where the alleged act of discrimination was the dismissal of an internal appeal relating to an unsuccessful promotion application time ran from the date of that decision, not the date that the claimant was notified of the decision (*Virdi v Metropolitan Police Comr* [2007] IRLR 24, EAT). In the case of a constructive dismissal which is alleged to be discriminatory, time runs from the complainant's resignation, not from the employer's repudiatory breach (*Meikle v Nottinghamshire County Council* [2004] EWCA Civ 859, [2005] ICR 1).

See also *Dimtsu v Westminster City Council* [1991] IRLR 450.

14.7   *Extension of time*

A tribunal may nevertheless consider a complaint or application which is out of time if, in all the circumstances of the case, it considers that it is just and equitable to do so (*SDA 1975, s 76(5); RRA 1976, s 68(6); SOR 2003, reg 34(3); RBR 2003, reg 34(3)*). One possible ground for doing so is that the complainant was unaware of his or her rights, another that she has received incorrect advice from her lawyer (*Hawkins v Ball and Barclays Bank plc* [1996] IRLR 258; *Chohan v Derby Law Centre* [2004] IRLR 685, EAT; *Virdi v Metropolitan Police Comr*, above; cf also *British Coal Corpn v Keeble* [1997] IRLR 336), or where a complainant has delayed because she was awaiting the outcome of an internal appeal or grievance procedure (*Aniagwu v London Borough of Hackney* [1999] IRLR 303). However exhausting internal procedures will not always justify a delay (*Robinson v Post Office* [2000] IRLR 804), and the Court of Appeal has since decided that *Aniagwu* is limited to its own facts (*Apelogun-Gabriels v Lambeth London Borough Council* [2001] EWCA Civ 1853, [2002] ICR 713). A tribunal is not required to accept a doctor's evidence that a claimant was unable due to psychiatric illness to present his claim in time where there was evidence that he had been fit enough to seek legal advice and had written coherent letters on unrelated matters within the limitation period (see *Chouafi v London United Busways Ltd* [2006] EWCA Civ 689 (unreported, 3 May 2006).

The tribunal may be assisted by considering the factors that the court is obliged to consider when extending time in personal injury cases (for which see the *Limitation Act 1980, s 33(3)*) or *CPR rule 3.9(1)*. However it is not obliged to do so. Its obligation is simply to ensure that no significant circumstance is left out of account (*Southwark London Borough Council v Afolabi* [2003] EWCA Civ 15, [2003] ICR 800). One of the most significant factors which the tribunal should consider is whether a fair trial of the issue is still possible (*DPP v Marshall* [1998] ICR 518). Whilst the fact that a fair trial is impossible will most likely preclude extension of time, it does not follow that merely because a fair trial is still possible time should be extended (*Simms v Transco plc* [2001] All ER (D) 1304, EAT). If a respondent wishes to establish that a fair trial is no longer possible, he should consider leading evidence to establish the point (*Southwark London Borough Council*, above). An employment tribunal will err if it fails to take account of the prejudice to the employer of allowing a claim out of time (*South East Essex College v Abegaze* [2006] ICR 468, EAT).Conversely, an employment tribunal will err if it fails to recognise the absence of any real prejudice to an employer when refusing to exercise its discretion to extend time (*Baynton v South West Trains Ltd* [2005] ICR 1730, EAT). In considering applications for extension, the correct approach for the tribunal to take is to bear in mind that employment tribunal time limits are generally enforced strictly and to ask whether a sufficient case has been made out to exercise its discretion in favour of extension. It is not a question of extending time unless a good reason can be shown for not doing so (*Robertson v Bexley Community Centre (t/a Leisure Link)* [2003] EWCA Civ 576, [2003] IRLR 434). Where time is extended an employee cannot rely on legislation that was not in force at the time of the act complained of if the act would not have been unlawful at the time that it was committed (see *Abegaze*, above).

In *Stevens v Bexley Health Authority* [1989] ICR 224, the EAT appeared to consider that the statutory time limits were not applicable to claims brought directly under European law, but more recent decisions have shown that view to be incorrect (see 24.18–24.19 EQUAL PAY, and 25.2 EUROPEAN COMMUNITY LAW).

See also HARVEYS – DIVISIONS L.2.B(7)(A), L.3.B(8), L.5.E(1), T.A.6(2), (3).

14.8   **Formulating the complaint**

Care must be taken in drafting the complaint. In *Chapman v Simon* [1994] IRLR 124, the Court of Appeal held that an employment tribunal is limited to considering those matters complained of in the originating application (see also, *Akinmolasire v Camden and Islington Mental Health Trust* [2004] EWCA Civ 1351). In the light of the Court of Appeal's decision it is also advisable, when specifying the detriments to which it is alleged that the complainant was subjected, specifically to recite that employees who are not members of the complainant's racial group, sex, sexual orientation or religion have not or would not be subjected to such detriments.

The Court of Appeal has now determined that direct and indirect discrimination are separate claims which must be separately identified in a claim form (*Ali v Office of National Statistics* [2004] EWCA Civ 1363, [2005] IRLR 201). The EAT had previously held, in *Quarcoopome v Sock Shop Holdings Ltd* [1995] IRLR 353, that where an originating application stated that the claim was one of 'race discrimination', it incorporated any claim of discrimination whether direct, indirect or by way of victimisation. The decision in *Quarcoopome* was in some doubt after the Court of Appeal's decision in *Housing Corporation v Bryant* [1999] ICR 123, in which it was held that the originating application must set out the 'causative link' on which a claim is based. Thus an application alleging unfair dismissal could not be read as including a claim for victimisation where there was no hint of this. *Quarcoopome* had been strongly criticised by the EAT in *Smith v Zeneca (Agrochemicals) Ltd* [2000] ICR 800, which held that a direct discrimination claim is different from, and does not include, either a claim for victimisation or indirect discrimination. It is therefore now essential fully to plead the facts on which different types of allegation of discrimination are based. Where a complainant believes that his dismissal was both discriminatory and unfair, it is essential that both are pleaded. If he first pursues a claim for unfair dismissal, he will not be entitled later to bring a fresh discrimination claim (*Divine-Bortey v London Borough of Brent* [1998] IRLR 525, CA, applying *Henderson v Henderson* (1843) 3 Hare 100).

Where a complainant relies on more than one alleged act of discrimination, it is up to the complainant to ensure that each of them is pursued at the hearing itself. The tribunal is not obliged to make a finding in relation to everything raised in pleadings, only in relation to those matters which the complainant pursues at the hearing (*Mensah v East Hertfordshire NHS Trust* [1998] IRLR 531, CA).

See also HARVEYS – DIVISION T.A.7.

14.9 Questionnaire and disclosure

The principle difficulty encountered by complainants is obtaining the information necessary to assess the strength of their case and to conduct it successfully once they are satisfied of its merits. To assist a person who considers that they may have been unlawfully discriminated against or subjected to harassment to decide whether to institute proceedings and, if they do so, to formulate and present the case in the most effective manner, such a person (whether an applicant or potential applicant) may serve, on the person against whom he or she has a complaint, a questionnaire in the form prescribed (under, respectively, *SDA 1975, s 74; RRA 1976, s 65; SOR 2003, reg 33; RBR 2003, reg 33*) to gather information about their complaint. The questionnaire and the replies to it should be in the prescribed form (under, respectively, the *Sex Discrimination (Questions and Replies) Order 1975 (SI 1975/2048), Sch 1; the Race Relations (Questions and Replies) Order 1977 (SI 1977/842), Sch 1; SOR 2003, Sch 2 and Sch 3; RBR 2003, Sch 2 and Sch 3*) or in a similar form adapted to the circumstances of the case.

A questionnaire and the replies to it are only admissible in evidence before an employment tribunal if it is served on the person (or company) questioned within the following time limits:

(a)   where it has been served before a complaint has been presented to a tribunal, within the period of three months beginning when the act complained of was done, or, from 1 October 2004, within the 'extended period' under *SI 2004/752, reg 15;* or

(b)   where it is served when a complaint has been presented to a tribunal, either within the period of 21 days beginning with the day on which the complaint was presented or later with the leave of the tribunal and within a period specified by a direction of the tribunal.

(*SDA 1975, s 74(2)(a),* and *SI 1975/2048, art 5; RRA 1976, s 65(2)(a),* and *SI 1977/842, art 5; SOR 2003, reg 33(4); RBR 2003, reg 33(4).*)

If the questionnaire is not served within the relevant time limit, it is not admissible as evidence before the tribunal.

The form for the reply is set out in *SI 1975/2048, Sch 2, SI 1977/842, Sch 2, SOR 2003, Sch 3,* or *RBR 2003, Sch 3.* If it appears to the tribunal that the respondent deliberately, and without reasonable excuse, omitted to reply within a reasonable period or that his reply is evasive or equivocal, the tribunal may draw any inference from that fact that it considers just and equitable to draw, including an inference that he committed an unlawful act (*SDA 1975, s 74(2)(b); RRA 1976, s 65(2)(b)*). In the case of sex discrimination or racial discrimination on grounds of race or ethnic or national origins or discrimination under the *SOR 2003* or *RBR 2003*, an omission to reply within eight weeks of service, may give rise to such an inference (*SDA 1975, s 74(2), (2A)* as amended by the *Employment Equality (Sex Discrimination) Regulations 2005 (SI 2005/2467); RRA 1976, s 65(2)(b)* as amended by the *Race Relations Act 1976 (Amendment) Regulations 2003 (SI 2003/1626); SOR 2003, reg 33(2); RBR 2003, reg 33(3)*). The EAT has held in *Dattani v Chief Constable of West Mercia Police* [2005] IRLR 327, EAT, that failure to answer, or evasive or late answers to, any question raised of the respondent by a complainant can justify the drawing of inferences. This might include information contained in the respondent's response to the claim or in further and better particulars.

A questionnaire may be obtained from the offices of the Department of Trade and Industry, or, in the case of sex discrimination, the EOC, or, in the case of racial discrimination, the CRE.

The EAT has suggested that, where a complainant wishes to obtain further information, an application for leave to serve a further questionnaire should be made to the tribunal (*Carrington v Helix Lighting Ltd* [1990] ICR 125).

The EAT has confirmed that, by virtue of the *Employment Act 2002* (*Dispute Resolution*) *Regulations 2004* (*SI 2004/752*), *reg 14*, the submission of a questionnaire does not constitute the submission of a grievance for the purposes of the *EA 2002, s 32, Sch 2* (*Horc-Gale v Makers UK Ltd* [2006] IRLR 178, [2006] ICR 462).

An employer may be asked by which criteria he chose an employee for a particular post, but he is not obliged to answer an unreasonable question such as the name and address of a successful applicant for a post (*Oxford v Department of Health and Social Security* [1977] ICR 884). He may also be asked, for example, for the numbers of men and women in particular posts and in the workforce as a whole and, if the case is one of failure to select for appointment or promotion, the breakdown by, for example, sex of applicants at the various stages of the selection process.

In pursuing a claim before an employment tribunal, an applicant may ask for the disclosure of documents by his employer or prospective employer. For the power of an employment tribunal to order the disclosure of documents which are relevant to the proceedings, see 21.11–21.12 EMPLOYMENT TRIBUNALS – II. However, in *Science Research Council v Nassé* [1979] ICR 921, the House of Lords held that tribunals should not order the disclosure of reports or references given and received in confidence, except when it is necessary for disposing fairly of the proceedings that the confidence should be overridden. In *West Midlands Passenger Transport Executive v Singh* [1988] ICR 614, the Court of Appeal upheld an employment tribunal's order for discovery of a schedule of statistics showing the ethnic origins of candidates for promotion and those actually promoted during the period preceding the alleged discrimination. The decision also gives guidance as to when discovery should be refused because, although relevant, it would be oppressive. The Court of Appeal further held that it might be possible, first, to infer from statistics that there had been discrimination against members of a racial group in general, and then to infer (in the absence of a satisfactory explanation in the particular case) that the applicant as a member of that group was discriminated against.

However, an employment tribunal does not have the power to require a schedule of statistics to be produced where the necessary information is not already in existence. In such circumstances, the questionnaire procedure should be used (*Carrington* above).

The Court of Appeal has held that, where a respondent claimed to be prohibited by law from disclosing the reasons why a claimant failed a security vetting, or indeed from disclosing the legal basis for that prohibition, a tribunal erred in law by ordering the respondent to disclose the reason why the claimant was not appointed to a post (*Barracks v Coles* [2006] EWCA Civ 1041, [2007] ICR 60, [2006] IRLR 73).

The EAT has held that evidence about a 'without prejudice' discussion with a complainant about bringing her employment to an end could be adduced as there was no dispute at the time attracting legal privilege and, in any event, the public interest in having discrimination allegations properly determined meant that it would be an abuse to apply the 'without prejudice' rule in that case (*BNP Paribas v Mezzotero* [2004] IRLR 508). In *Vaseghi v Brunel University* [2007] EWCA Civ 482, [2007] All ER (D) 377 (May) the EAT held that discussions with two employees about settlement of their discrimination claims took place in circumstances where the without prejudice privilege was waived and that the importance of establishing the truth in discrimination cases may tip the scales of justice against maintaining the privilege where the claimants' case would be severely prejudiced by not being able to refer to the discussions.

The Court of Appeal affirmed the EAT's judgment holding that in the particular and unusual circumstances of the case where the grievance procedure had in effect been a trial of the victimisation issue before an independent panel at which both parties gave evidence of the previous negotiations there was a waiver ([2007] EWCA Civ 482). The Court of Appeal also held that by pleading its response in the way it did and attaching a copy of the grievance report the university had confirmed its intention to waive privilege and it was too late to amend the response to withdraw that waiver.

See also HARVEYS – DIVISIONS L.2.B(5)(A), L.3.B(6)(A), T.A.14.

14.10 Conciliation

When a complaint has been presented to an employment tribunal, the conciliation officer must endeavour to promote a settlement of the complaint if:

(*a*)   he is requested to do so both by the complainant and the respondent; or

(*b*)   in the absence of requests by the complainant and the respondent, he considers that he could act with a reasonable prospect of success.

(*Employment Tribunals Act 1996* ('*ETA 1996*'), *s 18(1)*, *(2)*). His services may also be sought by a prospective party before the presentation of a complaint (*ETA 1996, s 18(3)*).

Information given to the conciliation officer in the performance of his duties is not admissible in evidence before the tribunal except with the consent of the giver of the information (*ETA 1996, s 18(7)*). Thus, frequently a conciliation officer will contact the employer to investigate the possibility of the removal of the cause of complaint. An employer is not obliged to give the conciliation officer information.

An ACAS conciliation officer has no responsibility to see that the terms of a settlement are fair to the employee and, indeed, a conciliation officer should not advise the parties on the merits of the case (see *Clarke v Redcar & Cleveland Borough Council* [2006] ICR 897, [2006] IRLR 324, EAT, for guidance on the role of a conciliation officer).

See also 2.4 ADVISORY, CONCILIATION AND ARBITRATION SERVICE (ACAS). For the validity of settlements, see 14.33 below.

See also HARVEYS – DIVISION T.A.20.

14.11 Restriction of publicity

EPCA 1978, Sch 9, para 1(5A), as inserted by *TURERA 1993, s 40*, empowered the Secretary of State to make regulations allowing for the restriction of publicity in cases where the commission of a sexual offence, or sexual misconduct, is alleged (this power is now contained in *ETA 1996, s 11*). Regulations were subsequently made which give powers to restrict publicity to both the employment tribunals and the Employment Appeal Tribunal. There are, broadly, two powers. The first is a power to ensure that the tribunal's own documents do not identify the parties concerned. The second power enables the tribunal to restrict others from reporting the identity of the parties or matters which might lead to them being identified. These powers are likely to be most relevant in some cases of sex discrimination, and now sexual orientation discrimination.

Where a case appears to involve allegations of the commission of a sexual offence, the tribunal is required to omit or delete from the register, and any judgment, document or record of proceedings which will otherwise be available to the public, any 'identifying matter which is likely to lead members of the public to identify any person affected by or making such an allegation' (*Employment Tribunals (Constitution and Rules of Procedure) Regulations 2004 (SI 2004/1861), Sch 1, rule 49*). The EAT is similarly required by the *Employment Appeal Tribunal Rules 1993 (SI 1993/2854), rule 23(2)*. A sexual offence means an offence of rape and related offences, and certain other offences including indecent assault, under-age intercourse, incest and buggery (*ETA 1996, s 11(6)*). A case will 'involve' such allegations even if they are not the basis of the claim or central to the decision-making; it is enough that they will fall to be considered (*X v Metropolitan Police Comr* [2003] ICR 1031, EAT).

Where a case appears to involve allegations of sexual misconduct the chairman of an employment tribunal may make a temporary restricted reporting order on application by one of the parties or of the tribunal's own motion (*SI 2004/1861, Sch 1, rule 50(1), (2), (3)*). The parties may apply to have the temporary restricted reporting order revoked or converted into a full restricted reporting order within 14 days of the temporary order being made, otherwise the order lapses after 14 days (*rule 50(4), (5)*). A full restricted reporting order can only be made if the parties are given the opportunity to advance oral argument at a pre-hearing review or a hearing as to whether the order should be made (*rule 50(6)*). A full restricted reporting order remains in force until the tribunal's judgment on liability and remedy is sent to the parties, unless revoked earlier (*rule 50(9), (11)*). Sexual misconduct is defined in *ETA 1996, s 11(6)* to mean the commission of a sexual offence, sexual harassment, or other adverse conduct related to sex (whether in its character or in its having reference to the sex or sexual orientation of the person at whom it is directed).

A restricted reporting order is one prohibiting the publication in Great Britain, in a written publication available to the public, of matter likely to lead members of the public to identify a person as one who is affected by or is the person making the allegation, or the inclusion of such matter in programs for reception in Great Britain. A corporate body is not a person for these purposes (*Leicester University v A* [1999] ICR 701). Contravention of a restricted reporting order is a criminal offence carrying a fine not exceeding level 5 on the standard scale (see 1.10 INTRODUCTION). The EAT has decided that the European Community law requirement that domestic procedural rules should not make enforcement of, *inter alia*, the directly effective right to equal treatment conferred on public sector workers by the *Equal Treatment Directive*, 'virtually impossible' or 'excessively difficult' (see 25.2 EUROPEAN COMMUNITY LAW) allows tribunals to make restricted reporting orders in cases other than where sexual misconduct is alleged. In that particular case, the EAT was satisfied that, without a restricted reporting order, the particular complainant would have been deterred from bringing her claim of discrimination on grounds of her transsexuality (*Chief Constable of the West Yorkshire Police v A* [2001] ICR 128, EAT).

The order should be no broader than is necessary to achieve the purpose of the legislation, which is to protect the identity of the alleged victim and perpetrator, and of any witness whose anonymity is essential to the proper conduct of the litigation. A restricted reporting order should not, therefore, conceal the identity of the complainant in circumstances where she does not wish to be anonymous (*Associated Newspapers Ltd v London (North) Industrial Tribunal* [1998] IRLR 569; see also *X v Metropolitan Police Comr*, above, for application of the same reasoning in the case of a claim brought by a transsexual).

The EAT is similarly empowered to make restricted reporting orders by *SI 1993/2854, rule 23(3), (5), (5A)* (as amended by the *Employment Appeal Tribunal (Amendment) Rules 2004 (SI 2004/2526), rule 15*).

For a more detailed consideration of restricted reporting orders, see 21.18 EMPLOYMENT TRIBUNALS – II, and also HARVEYS – DIVISION T.A.23(5), (6), T.B.8(1), (2).

14.12 Remedies

Where an employment tribunal finds that a complaint presented to it is well-founded, it must make such of the following orders as it considers just and equitable:

(*a*)   An order declaring the rights of the complainant and the respondent in relation to the act to which the complaint relates (*SDA 1975, s 65(1)(a); RRA 1976, s 56(1)(a); SOR 2003, reg 30(1)(a); RBR 2003, reg 30(1)(a)*). Such a declaration may state, for example, that the complainant is entitled to certain training facilities or should be considered for a certain position.

(*b*)   An order requiring the respondent to pay to the complainant compensation of an amount corresponding to any damages he could have been ordered by a county court to pay to the complainant if the complaint had fallen to be dealt with under the jurisdiction of the county court (*SDA 1975, s 65(1)(b); RRA 1976, s 56(1)(b); SOR 2003, reg 30(1)(b); RBR 2003, reg 30(1)(b)*). Once a tribunal has decided to award compensation the amount must be computed on the basis of what damages would be recoverable in a county court, and not on the basis of what the tribunal thinks is just and equitable (*Hurley v Mustoe (No 2)* [1983] ICR 422). If the complainant was barred from applying for a particular benefit, the tribunal must, in assessing compensation, consider the percentage chance that the application would have succeeded (*Calder v James Finlay Corpn Ltd* [1989] ICR 157).

(*c*)   A recommendation that the respondent take, within a specified period, action appearing to the tribunal to be practicable for the purpose of obviating or reducing the adverse effect on the complainant of any act of discrimination to which the complaint relates (*SDA 1975, s 65(1)(c); RRA 1976, s 56(1)(c); SOR 2003, reg 30(1)(c); RBR 2003, reg 30(1)(c)*).

See also HARVEYS – DIVISION L.2.B(6), L.3.B(7), L.5.E(1).

14.13 Compensation: general principles

Until the mid-1990s, awards of compensation in cases of sex or race discrimination were subject to a statutory maximum for compensatory awards for unfair dismissals. However, following the decision of the ECJ in *Marshall v Southampton and South West Hampshire Regional Health Authority (No 2)* [1993] IRLR 445, that capping compensation meant victims of discrimination did not have an 'effective remedy', the upper ceiling on the size of awards was removed by the *Sex Discrimination and Equal Pay (Remedies) Regulations 1993 (SI 1993/2798)*. These *Regulations* (now replaced by the *Employment Tribunals (Interest on Awards in*

Discrimination Cases) Regulations 1996 (SI 1996/2803) – see below) came into force on 22 November 1993 and apply to any award made by a tribunal on or after that date regardless of the date on which the alleged act of discrimination occurred (*Harvey v Institute of the Motor Industry (No 2)* [1995] IRLR 416). Prior to 3 July 1994, compensation for employment-related acts of race discrimination was also subject to the same statutory maximum (by the former *RRA 1976, s 56(2)*). The *Race Relations (Remedies) Act 1994*, which came into force on that date, removed the limit. For a case on the difficulties caused by the transition in the regime, see *Lambeth London Borough Council v D'Souza* [1999] IRLR 240, CA.

Where an employer is found to be vicariously liable for its employees' discriminatory acts, it will normally be required to make a payment in compensation. However, it does not follow that the individual discriminators should escape the consequences of liability. Where they have been named as individual respondents, it is open to the tribunal to make an order that they, too, should make a payment in compensation (see *Gbaja-Biamila v DHL International (UK) Ltd* [2000] ICR 730, EAT). Tribunals are entitled to order that liability be on a joint and several basis but, if doing so, must give their reasons and set the individual contributions at a level that is just and equitable taking into account the respondents' respective responsibility for the tort (*Way v Crouch* [2005] ICR 1362, EAT; see also *Miles v Gilbank* [2006] ICR 12, EAT). Exemplary damages may now be available in discrimination cases as a result of the decision of the House of Lords in *Kuddus v Chief Constable of Leicestershire Constabulary* [2001] UKHL 29, [2002] 2 AC 122.

For decisions relating to the assessment of compensation see *Alexander v Home Office* [1988] ICR 685, *North West Thames Regional Health Authority v Noone* [1988] ICR 813, *Sharifi v Strathclyde Regional Council* [1992] IRLR 259, and the cases summarised below. See also HARVEYS – DIVISION L.2.B(6)(A), (B), L.3.B(7).

14.14 Compensation: Indirect discrimination

In cases of indirect discrimination a tribunal's power to award compensation is more limited. Where the tribunal is satisfied that the respondent intended the discriminatory consequences of the provision, criterion or practice compensation can be ordered. Such an intention may be inferred where it is established that the employer was aware that discriminatory consequences would flow from its actions (*JH Walker Ltd v Hussain* [1996] ICR 291; and see *London Underground Ltd v Edwards* [1995] ICR 574 for the circumstances in which indirect discrimination may be said to have been intentional). If the respondent is able to prove that he had no intention of treating the complainant unfavourably on discriminatory grounds compensation may not be available. The *Sex Discrimination and Equal Pay (Miscellaneous Amendments) Regulations 1996 (SI 1996/438)*, which inserted a new s 65(1B) into the *SDA 1975*, gave tribunals, for the first time, a power to make awards of compensation in cases of unintentional indirect sex discrimination. The *SOR 2003, reg 30* and *RBR 2003, reg 30* contain similar provisions. Before awarding compensation for unintentional indirect discrimination the tribunal is required first to consider whether, if it had no power to order compensation it would make a declaration and/or recommendation. If it decides that it would not do so, it can move on to consider compensation. If it decides that it would do so, it should first make the declaration or recommendation and then ask itself whether it is just and equitable to make an award of compensation as well. In the case of race discrimination there is no such mechanism for awarding compensation for unintentional indirect discrimination (*RRA 1976, s 57(3)*).

14.15 **Compensation: pecuniary loss**

The measure of loss is tortious. In other words, a complainant must be put, so far as possible, into the position that he would have been in had the act of discrimination not occurred (*Ministry of Defence v Cannock* [1994] ICR 918, EAT). Thus, the tribunal must ask itself, 'If there had been no unlawful discrimination, what would have happened?'. Where the act complained of is a discriminatory dismissal, the tribunal will have to decide whether the complainant would have been dismissed in any event if there had been no discrimination (see *O'Donoghue v Redcar and Cleveland Borough Council* [2001] EWCA Civ 701, [2001] IRLR 615, CA). The tribunal often carries out a similar exercise when calculating compensation for unfair dismissal. However, in the context of discrimination proceedings, there is a significant difference of approach. In unfair dismissal cases, one asks whether a reasonable employer would have dismissed in any event. In discrimination cases, however, one asks whether the actual respondent would have dismissed (*Abbey National plc v Formoso* [1999] IRLR 222). In cases where the complainant alleges that her dismissal was both unfair and discriminatory, this difference may significantly complicate the process of calculation. Determining what would have happened in the absence of discrimination may involve the tribunal in assessing percentage chances. For instance, in cases of pregnancy dismissal, the tribunal will usually have to assess the chance that the complainant would, but for the dismissal, have returned to work. It is not necessarily perverse for the tribunal to conclude that there is a 100% chance that the relevant event would have occurred (*Ministry of Defence v Hunt* [1996] ICR 544, EAT). Where there are a number of contingent possibilities, the proper approach is to cumulate the percentages (eg where there is a 75% chance that a woman would have returned to work following the birth of her child had she not been dismissed and a 50% chance of her having received a pay rise thereafter, her loss should be assessed on the basis of the chance of her having earned at the higher rate, that is 50% × 75% – see *Hunt* above). Where an employer has made an *ex gratia* payment on dismissal or any other payment which falls to be deducted from the award, the proper approach is to make the deduction before applying the percentage chance (*Hunt* above; *Ministry of Defence v Wheeler* [1998] ICR 242; cf *Digital Equipment Ltd v Clements (No 2)* [1998] IRLR 134, CA). In assessing percentage prospects of particular events occurring, the tribunal is encouraged to rely upon statistical evidence. However, such evidence is simply one factor to take into account. Thus in *Vento v Chief Constable of West Yorkshire Police (No 2)* [2003] EWCA Civ 1871, [2003] ICR 318, the tribunal had been entitled to conclude that there was a 75% chance that the complainant would have remained in the police force until retirement (a period of 21 years of service) despite statistics suggesting that only 9% of female officers leaving the respondent's service had served for longer than 18 years. In *Brash-Hall v Getty Images Ltd* [2006] EWCA Civ 531, (2006) 811 IDS Brief 5, the Court of Appeal held that, where an employee had been dismissed constructively and in a discriminatory manner and the tribunal had decided that she would have been made redundant anyway, her compensation could only include the amount she would have received in contractual severance payment if she proved that she would have signed a severance agreement.

It is well established that a discriminator's motives are not relevant when it comes to deciding whether or not an act is discriminatory. However, a majority of the EAT (consisting of the two lay members) has decided that motives may be relevant when it comes to assessing compensation (*Chief Constable of Manchester v Hope* [1999] ICR 338). Upholding the tribunal's decision that the complainant had been the victim of an act of direct race and sex discrimination, it nevertheless went on to decide that, in the absence of discriminatory intent, the tribunal should have made a nil award of compensation.

Normal principles of mitigation apply. In *Cannock* (above), the EAT gave a strong indication that a woman dismissed by reason of pregnancy ought not to recover compensation relating to a period more than six months after the date of the birth of her child unless she is actively engaged in looking for work at that date. However, the tribunal is entitled to bear in mind the difficulties which a woman with a small child may face in obtaining work (*Hunt* above). Her personal characteristics and the state of the labour market at the relevant time would also be relevant considerations. As with unfair dismissal an employee can mitigate their loss by setting up in business, in which case the tribunal should consider when calculating compensation both lost remuneration and the costs incurred in setting up the business (if reasonably incurred) (*Dove v Aon Training Ltd* [2005] EWCA Civ 411, [2005] IRLR 891).

Where a complainant receives a sum in respect of future loss, a discount should be made for accelerated receipt unless the sums concerned are so small as to make it an unnecessary complication (*Bentwood Bros (Manchester) Ltd v Shepherd* [2003] EWCA Civ 380, [2003] ICR 1000).

Compensation should be calculated on the basis of net rather than gross loss of earnings (*Visa International Service Association v Paul* [2004] IRLR 42, EAT). In *Chan v Hackney London Borough Council* [1997] ICR 1014, the EAT decided that an employment tribunal had been right to deduct sums received by way of invalidity benefit from the compensatory award.

14.16 Compensation: injury to feelings

The amount of compensation awarded may include a sum for injury to feelings which results from the knowledge that it was an act of discrimination which brought about the employer's action (*SDA 1975, s 66(4); RRA 1976, s 57(4); Skyrail Oceanic Ltd v Coleman* [1981] ICR 864). See also *Wileman v Minilec Engineering Ltd* [1988] ICR 318; *Murray v Powertech (Scotland) Ltd* [1992] IRLR 257. It follows that in a case concerned with a discriminatory dismissal, the fact that the complainant would have been dismissed at a later date in any event is not a ground for reducing the award for injury to feelings. The purpose of the award is to compensate the complainant for the 'anger, upset and humiliation' caused by the fact that he knows that he has been discriminated against. That upset is not displaced by the prospect that he might have been dismissed lawfully at a later date (*O'Donoghue v Redcar and Cleveland Borough Council* [2001] IRLR 615, EAT). A tribunal erred in law in making no award at all for injury to feelings where it found that the claimant was merely angry and frustrated as a result of discrimination (*Assoukou v Select Services Partners Ltd* [2006] EWCA Civ 1442 (unreported, 11 October 2006).

The assessment of the appropriate sum to award in any case is a difficult one. General guidance on assessing compensation for injury to feelings where an act of harassment results in psychiatric or physical injury was given in *HM Prison Service v Johnson* [1997] ICR 275. Compensation for injury to feelings should be compensatory and not punitive, although it should not be set at so low a level as to 'diminish respect for the policy of the anti-discriminatory legislation'. It should also 'bear some similarity to the range of awards in personal injury cases and in exercising their discretion tribunals should remind themselves of the value in everyday life of the sum they had in mind' (*Johnson*, above). Subjecting the complainant to a disciplinary investigation, moving him to a different location and allowing a grievance procedure to drag on for 14 months were all factors a tribunal could take into account in awarding damages for injury to feelings (*British Telecommunications plc v Reid* [2003] EWCA Civ 1675, [2004] IRLR 327). The test of relevance was whether the matters arose from the act of discrimination and were consequential on it.

The Court of Appeal has identified three broad bands of compensation to assist the tribunals (*Vento v Chief Constable of West Yorkshire Police (No 2)* [2003] EWCA Civ 1871, [2003] ICR 318). The lowest band of awards runs from £500 to £5,000. The band is said to be appropriate for 'less serious' cases where the act of discrimination is an 'isolated' or 'one-off' incident. The middle band is £5,000 to £15,000 and should be used for 'serious cases which do not merit an award in the highest band'. Awards in the highest band fall between £15,000 and £25,000. The highest band is designed for use in the 'most serious' cases, e g where there has been a 'lengthy campaign of discriminatory harassment on the ground of sex or race'. Awards of less than £500 should be 'avoided altogether'. Awards of more than £25,000 should be made in only the 'most exceptional' cases.

In the *Johnson* case, the EAT had made reference to the Judicial Studies Board's guidelines on compensation for post-traumatic stress disorder as a useful source of guidance. The guidelines adopt a four-band classification of cases as 'minor', 'moderate', 'moderately severe' and 'severe'. In *Zaiwalla & Co v Walia* [2002] IRLR 697, EAT, the EAT found that the tribunal had erred by treating the injury to feelings suffered by the particular complainant as analogous to a 'moderately severe' stress disorder. The complainant had been belittled, bullied and harassed over a three-month period, and was left feeling despair and suffering from panic attacks and prolonged tearfulness. Nevertheless, a moderately severe disorder is one which promises 'some recovery with professional help' but with a 'significant disability' being experienced for the 'foreseeable future'. The EAT considered the case was more closely analogous to the 'moderate category' (the victim will have 'largely recovered and any continuing effects will not be grossly disabling'). The effect of this analogy being drawn was to decrease the award from £15,000 to £10,000.

The Court of Appeal in *Vento (No 2)* (above) itself made reference to the JSB guidelines suggesting that they continue to provide a useful source of assistance to a tribunal. As the JSB's four bands do not map precisely onto the Court of Appeal's three bands, reading them together may allow a more finely-tuned approach.

Reference to awards made in defamation proceedings as a guideline for assessing the appropriate award for injury to feelings has been deprecated by the EAT (*Vento v Chief Constable of West Yorkshire Police (No 2)* [2002] IRLR 177, EAT).

For the purpose of setting the size of the award, the tribunal should ignore the fact that the complainant will receive interest on the sums awarded (*Ministry of Defence v Cannock*, above). In *Orlando v Didcot Power Station Sports and Social Club* [1996] IRLR 262, the EAT considered statistics which indicated that the removal of the statutory cap on compensation had not resulted in a significant increase in the average size of awards made for injury to feelings.

In *Ministry of Defence v Anderson* [1996] IRLR 139, the EAT overturned an award of £250 on the grounds that it was perversely low, and stated that £500 was 'at or near the minimum' level of award which would ordinarily be appropriate. The EAT in *Moonsar v Fiveways Express Transport Ltd* [2005] IRLR 9 has found that an award of £1,000 was not too low in a case where the female complainant's colleagues had viewed pornography on the internet in her presence. In another case, where the discrimination was not directed at the complainant personally, there was no slur on his reputation or character and he was only marginally inconvenienced an award of £750 was appropriate (*Moyhing v Barts and London NHS Trust* [2006] IRLR 860, EAT).

In *Ministry of Defence v O'Hare (No 2)* [1997] ICR 306, the EAT considered two pregnancy discrimination cases where employees had been faced with a choice of losing their job or aborting their pregnancies. £2,000 was suggested as a guideline figure for cases where an employee was required to make such a choice. Where the employee actually opted to abort, matters were more difficult, but a bracket of £1,500 to £3,000 was suggested for cases where the injury to feelings was 'relatively transient' with a further bracket of £3,000 to £7,500 where the injury was 'more durable'. In *Vento (No 2)* above, the EAT overturned an award of £50,000 on the basis that it was 'manifestly excessive', substituting an award of £25,000. The complainant had suffered a 'moderate' psychiatric injury as a result of the discriminatory treatment received. The psychiatric injury had been compensated by an award of £9,000. For guidance on avoiding double recovery in cases where complainants suffer both injury to feelings and a psychiatric injury, see 'Compensation: personal injury' immediately below. In *Voith Turbo Ltd v Stowe* [2005] IRLR 228, EAT, the EAT observed, *obiter*, that a dismissal on grounds of race discrimination was always very serious and could not be regarded as one-off and suitable for a lower band award. In *Miles v Gilbank* [2006] ICR 12, the EAT upheld an award of £25,000 for injury to feelings resulting from the bullying and harassment of a pregnant employee repeatedly and consciously inflicted with total disregard for the welfare of the employee or her unborn child. This was affirmed by the Court of Appeal ([2006] EWCA Civ 543, [2006] ICR 1297, [2006] IRLR 538), which held that if the discrimination involved the well-being of the claimant's unborn child, this increased the seriousness.

For guidance on the circumstances in which the appeal tribunal will be prepared to interfere with the amount of an award under this heading, see *ICTS (UK) Ltd v Tchoula* [2000] IRLR 643, EAT. An appellate court will only interfere if the award is so much out of line that it amounts to an error of law through a misdirection in principle or is for some other reason, such as an erroneous evaluation of the facts, plainly wrong (*R (Elias) v Secretary of State for Defence* [2006] EWCA Civ 1293, [2006] IRLR 934). The EAT has demonstrated that it will overturn awards even if 'correctly categorised' so that its powers are not limited to correcting mis-categorisations (see *Doshoki v Draeger Ltd* [2002] IRLR 340, EAT).

There is no need for a tribunal to award compensation for injury to feelings on a grossed up basis as there is no authority that tax is payable on such an award (*Orthet Ltd v Vince-Cain* [2005] ICR 374, EAT).

14.17 Compensation: personal injury

Where the injury to feelings is such that it results in the onset of psychiatric illness, the complainant may recover compensation for personal injury in the tribunal (*Sheriff v Klyne Tugs (Lowestoft) Ltd* [1999] ICR 1170). It is thought that the same principle would apply where an employee is physically injured in the course of harassment. It may not always be easy to distinguish where injury to feelings stops and injury to mental health begins and there is consequently a danger of double recovery. In *HM Prison Service v Salmon* [2001] IRLR 425, the EAT suggested that in such cases it was open to a tribunal to make a single award for injury to feelings and to include an element for psychiatric harm. Tribunals should make it clear what they are doing.

Damages for personal injury are recoverable for any harm caused by the discriminatory act and not simply harm which was reasonably foreseeable (*Essa v Laing Ltd* [2003] ICR 1110, EAT). Although this decision was upheld on appeal by a majority of the Court of Appeal, there was some suggestion that the simple causation test may only apply to cases of racial abuse and not discrimination more widely ([2004] EWCA Civ 02, [2004] ICR 746).

14.18 **Compensation: aggravated and exemplary damages**

Aggravated damages may be awarded in discrimination cases where the complainant is able to establish a causal link between 'exceptional or contumelious conduct or motive' on the employer's part and her injury to feelings. Such damages may be appropriate, for instance, where an employer has failed properly to investigate the applicant's complaint of discrimination (*Johnson* above). The promotion of the alleged discriminator while he was still subject to disciplinary proceedings for his alleged discrimination was a matter a tribunal could take into account in awarding aggravated damages (see *British Telecommunications*, above). There has been some uncertainty over whether any sum awarded under this head should be incorporated into the award for injury to feelings. This approach was approved, *obiter*, by the EAT in *Gbaja-Biamila v DHL International (UK) Ltd* [2000] ICR 730, EAT (adopting the approach of the Northern Ireland Court of Appeal in *McConnell v Police Authority for Northern Ireland* [1997] IRLR 625, NICA). However, in *ICTS (UK) Ltd v Tchoula* [2000] IRLR 643, EAT, the EAT declined to find that the tribunal had erred by making a separate award of aggravated damages. The Court of Appeal has now confirmed the approach in *ICTS* and overruled *McConnell* by holding that aggravated damages should not be aggregated with damages for injury to feelings (*Scott v IRC* [2004] EWCA Civ 400, [2004] IRLR 713).

Exceptionally, an award of aggravated damages may be appropriate where the manner in which a respondent has conducted proceedings has aggravated the harm caused by the original act of discrimination (*Zaiwalla & Co* above).

The position regarding the availability of exemplary damages is less clear. The law had been that exemplary damages were not available in discrimination cases because these are statutory torts that did not exist at the time of the House of Lords decision in *Rookes v Barnard* [1964] AC 1129 (see *AB v South West Water Services Ltd* [1993] QB 507; *Deane v Ealing London Borough Council* [1993] ICR 329; *Ministry of Defence v Meredith* [1995] IRLR 539). However in *Kuddus v Chief Constable of Leicestershire Constabulary* [2001] UKHL 29, [2002] 2 AC 122 (a case of alleged misfeasance in public office) the House of Lords confirmed that the availability of exemplary damages depends on the nature of the tortious behaviour rather than whether or not the precise cause of action relied upon was recognised prior to 1964. There are two categories of case where exemplary damages may be awarded: (1) where there is oppressive, arbitrary or unconstitutional action by servants of the Government; or (2) where the tortfeasor's conduct was calculated to make a profit for himself that may exceed any compensation payable to the claimant (see *Rookes v Barnard*, above). The award of exemplary damages in discrimination cases will be rare and will occur only where the conduct falls into one of the two categories identified in *Rookes v Barnard* and the award of compensatory damages (including aggravated damages) will not sufficiently punish the respondent's conduct (*City of Bradford Metropolitan Council v Arora* [1991] IRLR 165, CA). Where the first limb of the *Rookes v Barnard* test is in issue careful consideration will need to be given to whether the respondent can be said to have acted as agent or servant of the Government, even at a local level.

In *Virgo Fidelis Senior School v Boyle* [2004] IRLR 268 the EAT held that the management of a voluntary-aided school were not agents or servants of the Government. In contrast, in *Arora* the Court of Appeal rejected the argument that the selection committee for a senior position in a college for which the respondent council had authority were exercising a private function of the council and could not be liable for exemplary damages. In *R (Elias) v Secretary of State for Defence*, above, the Court of Appeal held that on the facts the discrimination in that case was not of such a nature as to make aggravated or exemplary damages appropriate.

Exemplary damages will not be available in cases under the *EqPA 1970* as such claims are contractual, rather than tortious (see *Council of the City of Newcastle upon Tyne v Allan* [2005] IRLR 504, EAT).

14.19   Compensation: discrimination and unfair dismissal

Where a complainant has been the victim of a dismissal which is both discriminatory and unfair (ie contrary to the right not to be unfairly dismissed conferred on certain employees by the *ERA 1996*), the tribunal has a choice of two compensatory regimes. As compensation for unfair dismissal is subject to statutory maxima, whilst awards made under the anti-discrimination legislation are unlimited, the tribunal will almost invariably use the latter regime. However, the one clear advantage of the unfair dismissal regime is that it allows the tribunal to order the respondent to reinstate, or to re-engage, the complainant. If the respondent does not comply with a re-employment order, the matter is re-listed for a compensation hearing. A penal 'additional award' may be made (see 55.15 UNFAIR DISMISSAL – III). Although the statutory language states that where the matter returns for compensation issues to be considered, compensation should be awarded in accordance with the provisions of the *ERA 1996*, the EAT has now made it clear that the statute should not be taken to preclude the tribunal from using the *RRA 1976* regime (*D'Souza v London Borough of Lambeth* [1997] IRLR 677). The same principle will apply to other forms of discrimination. Making a re-employment order does not take away a complainant's right to unlimited compensation for the act of discrimination. However, if a tribunal orders re-employment and awards compensation for injury to feelings at the first remedies hearing, there is a risk that it will be taken to have made a final order in relation to compensation for discrimination, thereby precluding it from making a further award for loss arising from the discrimination where the re-employment order is not complied with. If the tribunal wishes to keep open the possibility of further compensation under the anti-discrimination regime, it should say so expressly (*London Borough of Lambeth v D'Souza* [1999] IRLR 240, CA).

This case also provides guidance in relation to the calculation of pension loss. Understandably reluctant to have to hear detailed and contested evidence from actuaries, tribunals more usually adopt the less precise but less complicated approach of awarding the complainant a sum equivalent to the contributions that the respondent would have made into the pension scheme had the employee not been dismissed. In *D'Souza* a complication arose from the fact that the respondent was at that time enjoying a contributions holiday. The EAT makes it clear that the contributions holiday should not result in the complainant's compensation being reduced. Compensation should be calculated on the basis of contributions at what would have been the ordinary rate. The complainant is not being compensated for the loss of contributions but for the loss of a pension. The contributions method is a way of approximating the loss and should not be followed slavishly if it is plainly not going to compensate the complainant for the loss of his pension. The EAT in *Clancy v Cannock Chase Technical College* [2001] IRLR 331has again stressed the need for accurate assessment of pension loss to ensure that complainants are fully compensated. In the light of this the Third Edition of the guidelines on pension loss for employment tribunals, *Compensation for Loss of Pension Rights – Employment Tribunals ('the Booklet')*, now sets out a 'substantial loss approach' better suited to the calculation of significant pension loss. This method will often be more appropriate in serious discrimination cases and should be adopted in cases where the loss is expected to last more than two years (*Orthet Ltd v Vince-Cain* [2005] ICR 374, EAT). In *Greenhoff v Barnsley Metropolitan Borough Council* [2006] ICR 1514 the EAT held that a tribunal should set out why it adopted a particular approach to pension loss and why other approaches, particularly those set out in the Booklet, were rejected. The EAT also gave guidance about the steps that tribunals should go through in considering pension loss.

Where a dismissal is fair, even though also an act of victimisation, the complainant will only be entitled to compensation for injury to feelings (*Lisk-Carew v Birmingham City Council* [2004] EWCA Civ 565, [2004] 20 LS Gaz R 35). Conversely, a respondent cannot rely upon a subsequent unfair dismissal to break the chain of causation in relation to a complainant's continuing losses (*HM Prison Service v Beart (No 2)* [2005] EWCA Civ 467, [2005] ICR 1206, upholding the EAT in *HM Prison Service v Beart (No 2)* [2005] IRLR 171).

14.20   Compensation: awards of interest

Interest is payable on any sums awarded pursuant to the *Employment Tribunals (Interest on Awards in Discrimination Cases) Regulations 1996 (SI 1996/2803)*). Interest should be awarded on the complainant's net and not gross loss (*Bentwood Bros (Manchester) Ltd v Shepherd* [2003] EWCA Civ 380, [2003] ICR 1000).

Where the tribunal is concerned with a sum other than an award for injury to feelings, it is required to identify a 'mid-point date'. This date is the halfway point between the date on which the act of discrimination complained of occurred and the date on which the interest is being calculated (*reg 4*). Interest is then awarded in respect of the period from the mid-point date to the date of calculation (*reg 6(1)(b)*). A different rule applies to the calculation of interest on awards for injury to feelings. By *reg 6(1)(a)*, interest is awarded for the whole period from the date of the act of discrimination through to the date of calculation.

Interest is simple interest and accrues from day to day (*reg 3(1)*). By *reg 3(2)*, the rate to be applied in England and Wales is that prescribed for the Special Investment Account by *rule 27(1)* of the *Court Funds Rules 1987 (SI 1987/821)*. In Scotland, the relevant rate is that fixed for the time being by the *Act of Sederunt (Interest in Sheriff Court Decrees or Extracts) 1975 (SI 1975/948)*. Where the rate has varied over the relevant period the tribunal may, in the interests of simplicity, apply a median or average of the rates (*reg 3(3)*).

If a respondent has made a payment to the complainant prior to the date of calculation, the date of payment is treated as if it were the date of calculation for the purposes of calculating the interest to be awarded (*reg 6(2)*).

The tribunal is given a discretion to calculate interest by reference to periods other than those set out above, or even to use different periods for different elements of the award. The discretion may be exercised only where the tribunal is of the opinion that:

(*a*)   there are exceptional circumstances, whether relating to the claim as a whole or to a particular element of the award; and

(*b*)   those circumstances have the effect that serious injustice would be caused if interest were to be awarded by reference to the period or periods specified in *reg 6(1)(a)* or (*b*) or *6(2)*.

14.21 Recommendations

A tribunal is empowered to make a recommendation that the respondent take, within a specified period, action appearing to the tribunal to be practicable for the purpose of obviating or reducing the adverse effect on the complainant of any act of discrimination to which the complaint relates. This does not give the tribunal power to recommend that an applicant for promotion who was discriminated against be promoted to the next open post (*British Gas plc v Sharma* [1991] ICR 19). Where statutory rules govern an appointment, a tribunal cannot recommend an applicant's appointment. It can merely recommend that the appointing body be made aware of the need to comply with the anti-discrimination legislation and of other relevant matters (*North West Thames Regional Health Authority v Noone* [1988] ICR 813).

In *Vento (No 2)* (see above), the respondent was held vicariously liable for the actions of certain of the complainant's colleagues. The colleagues were not themselves parties. The tribunal recommended that the respondent should meet with the colleagues and raise with them the adverse findings made by the tribunal's decision. This recommendation was endorsed by the EAT. However, the EAT, whilst acknowledging the very broad discretion conferred upon the tribunal, overturned a further recommendation that the respondent should suggest to the colleagues that they should make an apology in writing to the complainant. The EAT considered the recommendation was inappropriate because:

(1)   the complainant had already had an apology from her 'employer';

(2)   the colleagues were not parties and had not been given an opportunity to put their side of the case to the tribunal;

(3)   the recommendation could not be enforced and if the colleagues refused to apologise, that would aggravate the situation; and

(4)   an ordered apology would have little worth as it would not appear sincere.

Recommendations cannot be specifically enforced. However, if, without reasonable justification, the respondent to a complaint fails to comply with a recommendation made by an employment tribunal that he take certain action and it thinks it just and equitable to do so:

(i)   the tribunal may increase the amount of compensation required to be paid to the complainant in respect of the complaint by a compensation order; or

(ii)   if an order for compensation could have been made, but was not, the tribunal may make such an order.

(*SDA 1975, s 65(3)(a)*, (*b*); *RRA 1976, s 56(4)(a)*, (*b*); *SOR 2003, reg 30(3)*; *RBR 2003, reg 30(3)*.)

See also HARVEYS – DIVISION L.2.B(6)(C), L.3.B(7).

14.22 **Remedies in cases involving pension schemes**

The *SOR 2003* and *RBR 2003* contain specific provisions relating to discrimination or harassment involving pension schemes. The numbering of the relevant provisions is identical under both *Regulations,* so below the references to individual provisions apply to both. Under both *Regulations* claims alleging breaches of *reg 9A* should (subject to the availability of a complaint to the Pensions Ombudsman and any right, where appropriate, to commence judicial review proceedings (see *reg 27(2)*) be brought in the employment tribunal. This includes cases where the claim is based on *reg 21* (relationships which have come to an end), is a claim alleging vicarious liability, or is a claim alleging that a person has knowingly aided an unlawful act. The relevant employer is required to be a party to the proceedings (*Sch 1A, para 6*).

'Pensioner members' (for whom see *Pensions Act 1995, s 124(1)*) are not entitled to a remedy from the tribunal (*Sch 1A, para 7(1)(b)*).

Otherwise, where the tribunal concludes that a claim is well-founded, it has the following remedy options:

(1)   In cases concerned with admission to membership, the tribunal can make an order declaring that the complainant be admitted to the scheme. The tribunal may not order that the complainant be treated as being a member of the scheme prior to the *Regulations* coming into effect in December 2003 and can make such provision as it considers appropriate as to the terms on or the capacity in which the complainant is to be admitted.

(2)   In cases concerned with the terms on which members are treated, the tribunal can make an order declaring that the complainant should be entitled to membership without discrimination. Again, the order cannot have a retrospective effect and may make such provision as it considers appropriate as to the terms on or the capacity in which the complainant can enjoy membership.

(3)   The tribunal may make an order compensating the complainant for injury to feelings but may not otherwise compensate the complainant, whether in relation to arrears of benefits or otherwise, unless the respondent refuses to comply with a recommendation (though there is no specific power set out in the schedule to make a recommendation).

The right to seek an investigation or determination by the Pensions Ombudsman is specifically preserved (*reg 9A(4)* added by amendment in, respectively, the *Employment Equality (Sexual Orientation) (Amendment) Regulations 2003 (SI 2003/2827)*, and the *Employment Equality (Religion or Belief) (Amendment) Regulations 2003 (SI 2003/2828)*.

14.23 **ENFORCEMENT BY THE COMMISSIONS**

Until the creation of the CEHR, there had been three commissions created by statute to promote equality and eliminate discrimination. The EOC and CRE will be discussed below. The Disability Rights Commission ('DRC') is discussed above at 10.31–10.32 DISABILITY DISCRIMINATION. There were and are at present no corresponding bodies for sexual orientation and religious discrimination. However Part I of the *EqA 2006*, creates the single CEHR. This will in due course take over the functions of the DRC, CRE and EOC and will also have responsibility for fighting discrimination on the grounds of sexual orientation, religion or belief, and age. The CEHR will also be tasked with promoting human rights. At the time of writing only a limited number of enabling provisions in the *EqA 2006* relating to the CEHR have been commenced. Commissioners have now been appointed and the CEHR is in the process of formation. It is anticipated that it will become operational in October 2007. Therefore, for at least part of the lifetime of this edition of this work, the existing enforcement arrangements by the DRC, EOC and CRE will continue to apply. The current law relating to the EOC and CRE is therefore set out below. The prospective law in relation to the CEHR is also set out as this may well come into force during the lifetime of this edition.

14.24 The Equal Opportunities Commission

The *SDA 1975, s 53* and *Sch 3* established the EOC which has the following duties:

(*a*)   to work towards the elimination of discrimination;

(*aa*) to work towards the elimination of harassment that is contrary to any of the provisions of the Act;

(*b*)   to promote equality of opportunity between men and women generally;

(*c*)   to promote equality of opportunity in the field of employment and of vocational training, for persons who intend to undergo, are undergoing or have undergone gender reassignment; and

(*d*)   to keep under review the working of the *SDA 1975* and the *Equal Pay Act 1970* and when it is so required by the Secretary of State or otherwise thinks it necessary, to draw up and submit to the Secretary of State proposals for amending these *Acts*.

The EOC also has a duty to keep under review statutory provisions relating to health and safety at work which require men and women to be treated differently, to prepare reports on such matters and to prepare an annual report (*SDA 1975, ss 55, 56*).

The EOC has the power to issue codes of practice, giving practical guidance (*SDA 1975, s 56A*). It has issued a *Code of Practice – Sex Discrimination*. A breach of the Code does not of itself render a person liable to proceedings, but any relevant provision of the Code may be taken into account by an employment tribunal (*SDA 1975, s 56A(10)*).

In *R v Secretary of State for Employment, ex p Equal Opportunities Commission* [1994] ICR 317, the House of Lords considered that the EOC had *locus standi* to challenge by judicial review proceedings a refusal by the Secretary of State to accept that English law was sexually discriminatory in certain respects, and their Lordships also held (again by a majority) that the Divisional Court was a proper forum for the challenge in question.

For inquiries, copies of the Code, leaflets, etc, the address of the EOC is: Equal Opportunities Commission, Arndale House, Arndale Centre, Manchester M4 3EQ, tel: 0845 6015901.

See also HARVEYS – DIVISION L.2.B(9).

14.25 Commission for Racial Equality

The *RRA 1976* established the CRE to replace the old Race Relations Board. Its members are appointed by the Secretary of State to:

(*a*)   work towards the elimination of discrimination and harassment;

(*b*)   promote equality of opportunity, and good relations, between persons of different racial groups; and

(*c*)   keep under review the working of the *RRA 1976*.

(*RRA 1976, s 43(1)*.)

The CRE may issue codes of practice containing practical guidance for:

(*a*)   the elimination of discrimination and harassment in the field of employment; and/or

(*b*)   the promotion of equality of opportunity in that field for persons of different racial groups.

(*RRA 1976, s 47(1)*.)

The CRE has issued a code of practice on eliminating racial discrimination in the employment field entitled the *Statutory Code of Practice on Racial Equality in Employment* (http://www.cre.gov.uk/gdpract/employmentcode.2005.html). This version of the Code came into effect on 6 April 2006 pursuant to the *Race Relations Code of Practice relating to Employment (Appointed Day) Order 2006 (SI 2006/630)*. A breach of the *Code* does not of itself render a person liable to proceedings, but any relevant provision of the *Code* may be taken into account by an employment tribunal (*RRA 1976, s 47(10)*). Further information and assistance is to be found in various CRE publications.

The address of the CRE is: The Commission for Racial Equality, St Dunstan's House, 201–211 Borough High Street, London SE1 1GZ, tel: 020 7939 0000.

See also HARVEYS – DIVISION L.3.B(14)(A)–(C).

14.26 Commission for Equality and Human Rights

The *EqA 2006* received Royal Assent on 16 February 2006. Part 1 of the Act establishes the CEHR (*EqA 2006, ss 1, 2, Sch 1*). The CEHR will have a general duty to encourage and support the development of a society in which:

(*a*)   people's ability to achieve their potential is not limited by prejudice or discrimination,

(*b*)   there is respect for and protection of each individual's human rights,

(*c*)   there is respect for the dignity and worth of each individual,

(*d*)   each individual has an equal opportunity to participate in society, and

(*e*)   there is mutual respect between groups based on understanding and valuing of diversity and on shared respect for equality and human rights.

(*EqA 2006, s 3*).

The CEHR has a duty to prepare, and regularly review, a strategic plan of the activities that it will pursue in the exercise of its functions after it has consulted various parties (*EqA 2006, ss 4, 5*). *Sections 1* to *5* of the *EqA 2006* came into effect on 18 April 2006.

The CEHR will be required in exercising its powers to:

(*a*)   promote understanding of the importance of equality and diversity;

(*b*)   encourage good practice in relation to equality and diversity;

(*c*)   promote equality of opportunity;

(*d*)   promote awareness and understanding of rights under the equality enactments;

(*e*)   enforce the equality enactments;

(*f*)   work towards the elimination of unlawful discrimination; and

(*g*)   work towards the elimination of unlawful harassment.

(*EqA 2006, s 8(1)*).

'Unlawful' is defined as contrary to the equality enactments (*EqA 2006, s 34*). The equality enactments are the *EqPA 1970*, the *SDA 1975*, the *RRA 1976*, the *DDA 1995*, Part 2 of the *EqA 2006*, regulations made under Part 3 of the *EqA 2006*, the *SOR 2003*, and the *RBR 2003* (*EqA 2006, s 33(1)*). In fulfilling its duties under *s 8* the CEHR must take account of any relevant human rights (*EqA 2006, s 9(4)*). The CEHR will be required to monitor the effectiveness of the equality and human rights enactments and give advice and make recommendations to central government on changes to the law (*EqA 2006, s 11*). The CEHR will be required to monitor progress towards achieving its aims under *the EqA 2006, s 3*, and issue a report on this progress every three years (*EqA 2006, s 12*). The CEHR will also be required to issue an annual report on its performance (*EqA 2006, Sch 1, para 32*).

The CEHR may issue a code of practice in connection with a matter addressed by *EqPA 1970, SDA 1975, Pts 2–4, s 76A* and orders under *ss 76B, 76C*, the *RRA 1976, Pts 2–4* and *s 71, DDA 1995, Pts 2–4* and *5A, EqA 2006, Pt* 2 and regulations made under *Pt 3, SOR 2003, Pts 2, 3*, and *RBR 2003, Pts 2, 3* (*EqA 2006, s 14(1)*). Before issuing a code the CEHR must publish its proposals, consult such persons as it thinks appropriate and submit a draft to the Secretary of State for approval (*EqA 2006, ss 14(6), (7)*). A failure to comply with a code of practice does not make a person liable to criminal or civil proceedings but a code is admissible in evidence in such proceedings and shall be taken into account by a court or tribunal if it appears relevant (*EqA 2006, s 15(4)*).

The CEHR will have the power to institute or intervene in legal proceedings (including judicial review) if it appears to the Commission that the proceedings relate to a matter in connection with which it has a function (*EqA 2006, s 30*).

The Secretary of State has the power by order to dissolve or remove any of the functions of the EOC, CRE and DRC, and must dissolve these Commissions by 31 March 2009 at the latest (*EqA 2006, s 36*). The Secretary of State is empowered to order the transfer of the property, rights and liabilities from the existing Commissions to the CEHR and make directions to facilitate the implementation of such transfers (*EqA 2006, ss 37, 38*).

Consequential amendments set out in Sch 3 to the *EqA 2006* will repeal the provisions of the *SDA 1975* and *RRA 1976* setting up and giving powers to the EOC and CRE (*EqA 2006, s 40*).

The CEHR now has a website, http://www.cehr.org.uk.

The responsibilities of the CEHR will be wide-ranging and to a considerable extent fall outside the scope of this work, so the discussion below focuses on those aspects of the CEHR's enforcement powers that are relevant to discrimination in the employment field. As the enforcement regime of the CEHR will take a similar form to that of the EOC and CRE, the CEHR's powers are discussed below in relation to the different enforcement methods available to the Commissions.

14.27 Formal investigations

Apart from their general duties, the EOC and CRE may, if they think fit, and shall if required by the Secretary of State, conduct a formal investigation for any purpose connected with the carrying out of their duties (*SDA 1975, s 57(1); RRA 1976, s 48*). The EOC, CRE or the Secretary of State must draw up terms of reference (*SDA 1975, s 58(2); RRA 1976, s 49(2)*). These investigations may be general investigations or investigations into the activities of persons named in the terms of reference ('named persons investigations'). Before embarking on a named person investigation, the EOC or CRE must have already formed a suspicion that the persons named might have committed some unlawful act of discrimination and had at least some grounds for so suspecting. If they do not, the investigation and any non-discrimination notice based upon it may be challenged (*Commission for Racial Equality v Prestige Group plc* [1984] ICR 473; *Hillingdon London Borough Council v Commission for Racial Equality* [1982] AC 779). General notice of the holding of the investigation must be given unless the terms of reference are confined to the activities of named persons, in which case those persons must be given notice in the prescribed manner (*SDA 1975, s 58(3); Sex Discrimination (Formal Investigations) Regulations 1975 (SI 1975/1993); RRA 1976, s 49(3); Race Relations (Formal Investigations) Regulations 1977 (SI 1977/841)*).

If the EOC or CRE proposes, in the course of a formal 'named person' investigation, to investigate acts made unlawful by the *SDA 1975* or *RRA 1976* respectively which it believes such a person may have done, then it must inform that person accordingly. He will then have the opportunity to make oral or written representations, and to have legal or other representation if he makes oral representations (*SDA 1975, s 58(3A); RRA 1976, s 49(4)*).

The CEHR will be given an express power to conduct inquiries into any matter relating to its duties under the *EqA 2006, ss 8, 9* and *10* (*EqA 2006, s 16(1)*). If, during an inquiry the CEHR begins to suspect that a person has committed an unlawful act it must: (a) in continuing the inquiry, so far as possible, avoid further consideration of whether the person has committed an unlawful act, (b) commence an investigation, (c) may use information acquired during the inquiry in the investigation, and (d) ensure that any aspect of the inquiry which concerns the person investigated is not pursued while the investigation is in progress (*EqA 2006, s 16(2)*).

The CEHR will have the power to investigate whether a person has committed an unlawful act or has not complied with an unlawful act notice issued under *s 21* or an undertaking made in an agreement made under *s 23*, but may only investigate whether a person has committed an unlawful act if it suspects the person to have done so (such suspicion may, but need not arise as a result of an inquiry under *s 16*) (*EqA 2006, ss 20(1), (2), (3)*). Before settling the report of an investigation recording a finding that a person has committed an unlawful act or has failed to comply with an unlawful act notice or an undertaking, the CEHR will be required to send a draft to the person and specify a period of at least 28 days in which the person may make written representations, which the CEHR must consider (*EqA 2006, s 20(4)*). *Schedule 2* to the *EqA 2006* sets out supplemental provisions concerning investigations (*EqA 2006, s 20(5)*).

Where the CEHR conducts an inquiry it will be required to publish the terms of reference in a manner that it considers likely to bring the inquiry to the attention of persons whom it concerns or who might be interested in it, and in particular to the attention of any person specified in the terms of reference (*EqA 2006, Sch 2, para 2*). Before holding an investigation the CEHR will be required to prepare terms of reference specifying the person to be investigated and the nature of the alleged unlawful act, give the person the notice, give that person the opportunity to make representations about the terms of reference, and having considered such representations publish the terms of reference once settled (*EqA 2006, Sch 2, para 3*). The CEHR will be required to make arrangements for persons to make representations (which may, but need not, include oral representations) in relation to inquiries, investigations and assessments and must give any person specified in the terms of reference the opportunity to make representations (*EqA 2006, Sch 2, paras 6, 7*). The CEHR must consider any representations made but need not do so, if it considers it appropriate, where the representations are not made by a person specified in the terms of reference or by a barrister, advocate or solicitor on his behalf (*EqA 2006, Sch 2, para 8*).

Information. For the purposes of a formal investigation, the EOC and CRE may issue a notice requiring the production of written information or documents or the attendance of witnesses for examination. A notice requesting information may only be issued where:

(a)   an investigation is being made into compliance with a non-discrimination notice (*SDA 1975, s 69; RRA 1976, s 60*; and see 14.28 below); or

(b)   service of the notice was authorised by, or on behalf of, the Secretary of State (*SDA 1975, s 59(2)(a); RRA 1976, s 50(2)(a)*); or

(c)   the terms of reference of the investigation show that the EOC or CRE believes that a person may have been or may be:

    (i)   carrying out unlawful acts of discrimination or harassment;

    (ii)   applying discriminatory practices prohibited by, respectively, *SDA 1975, s 37*, or *RRA 1976, s 28*;

    (iii)   issuing discriminatory advertisements, or issuing instructions to discriminate or pressurising others to discriminate (ie breach of *SDA 1975, ss 38, 39 or 40*, or *RRA 1976, ss 29, 30 or 31*); or

    (iv)   (in the case of the EOC only) acting in breach of a term modified or included by virtue of an equality clause (see 24.5 EQUAL PAY).

(*SDA 1975, s 59(2)(b); RRA 1976, s 50(2)(b).*)

Such a notice cannot compel a person to disclose information or give evidence if he could not be compelled to do so in civil proceedings (*SDA 1975, s 59(3)(a); RRA 1976, s 50(3)(a)*). Thus, communications with a solicitor relating to advice or discussions about the EOC or CRE's action would be privileged. The *SDA 1975* and *RRA 1976* also state that necessary travelling expenses of persons required by notice to attend the EOC or CRE must be offered to them (*SDA 1975, s 59(3)(b); RRA 1976, s 50(3)(b)*). If a person fails to comply with a lawful notice or the EOC/CRE has reasonable cause to suspect that he intends not to comply with it, the EOC/CRE may apply to a county court for an order requiring him to comply with it. Witnesses who fail to attend may be fined up to £1,000 (*SDA 1975, s 59(4); RRA 1976, s 50(5); County Courts Act 1984, s 55(1), (2)*). The EOC/CRE may have reasonable cause to believe that a person does not intend to comply with the order if he expresses his intention of non-compliance and also if he neglects to respond to requests which are proved to have been sent to him.

If a person is convicted in a magistrates' court of:

(A) wilfully altering, suppressing, concealing or destroying a document required to be produced; or

(B) knowingly or recklessly making any statement which is false in a material particular,

he may be fined an amount not exceeding level 5 on the standard scale (*SDA 1975, s 59(6); RRA 1976, s 50(6)*; and see 1.10 INTRODUCTION).

The CEHR will have similar powers to require persons to provide information by issuing a notice in the course of an inquiry, investigation or assessment (*EqA 2006, Sch 2, para 9*). Such a notice may require a person to provide information in his possession, produce documents in his possession, or give oral evidence, and may specify the form of information, documents or evidence and the timing, but a notice may not require a person to provide information that he is prohibited from disclosing by an enactment, do anything that he could not be compelled to do in proceedings in the High Court or Court of Session, or require a person to attend at a place unless the CEHR undertakes to pay the expenses of his journey (*EqA 2006, Sch 2, para 10*). A recipient of a notice may apply to a county court (in England and Wales) or a sheriff (in Scotland) to have the notice cancelled on the grounds that the requirement imposed by it is unnecessary having regard to the purpose of the inquiry, investigation or assessment, or is unreasonable (*EqA 2006, Sch 2, para 11*). Where the CEHR believes that a person has failed, or is likely to fail, without reasonable excuse to comply with a notice it may apply to a county court (in England and Wales) or a sheriff (in Scotland) for an order requiring the person to take such steps as are specified in the order (*EqA 2006, Sch 2, para 12*). A person commits an offence if he fails to comply with a notice under *para 9* or an order under *para 12(2)*, falsifies any document provided in accordance with such a notice or order, or makes a false statement in giving oral evidence in accordance with a notice under *para 9*, and such an offence is punishable on summary conviction by a fine not exceeding level 5 on the standard scale (*EqA 2006, Sch 2, para 13*).

The Commission's report. The EOC or CRE may, as a result of its investigation, make recommendations to any person for changes in their procedures and to the Secretary of State for changes in the law or for other changes (*SDA 1975, s 60(1); RRA 1976, s 51(1)*). The report of such an investigation (other than one required by the Secretary of State) and its recommendations must be either published or made available for inspection.

The CEHR will be required to publish a report of its findings following an inquiry, investigation or assessment and may make recommendations as part of the report or in respect of a matter arising in the course of the inquiry, investigation or assessment, which may be addressed to any class of persons (*EqA 2006, Sch 2, paras 15, 16*). A tribunal or court may have regard to the findings of a report but shall not treat it as conclusive, and a person to whom a recommendation is addressed shall have regard to it (*EqA 2006, Sch 2, paras 18, 19*).

No information given to the EOC or CRE in connection with a formal investigation is to be disclosed by them or by their past or present Commissioners or employees except:

(*a*) on the order of any court; or

(*b*) with the informant's consent; or

(*c*)   in the form of a summary or other general statement published by the EOC or CRE, which does not identify the informant or any other person to whom the information relates; or

(*d*)   in a report of an investigation published by the EOC under *SDA 1975, s 60*, or CRE under *RRA 1976, s 51*; or

(*e*)   to the Commissioners, additional Commissioners or employees of the EOC/CRE or, so far as may be necessary for the proper performance of the functions of the EOC/CRE, to other persons; or

(*f*)   for the purpose of any civil proceedings under the *SDA 1975* to which the EOC is party or proceedings under the *RRA 1976* to which the CRE is a party, or any criminal proceedings.

(*SDA 1975, s 61(1); RRA 1976, s 52(1)*.)

Similar provisions will apply in relation to the CEHR to make it an offence for a Commissioner, Investigating Commissioner or employee of the CEHR to disclose any information acquired by the CEHR by way of representations made in relation to, or in the course of, an inquiry under the *EqA 2006, s 16*, an investigation under *s 20*, an assessment under *s 31* or a notice under *s 32*, or from a person with whom the CEHR enters into, or considers entering into, an agreement under *s 23* (*EqA 2006, ss 6(1)*, (2)). Disclosure of such information will be permitted only if the disclosure is:

(*a*)   for the purposes of a function of the CEHR under the *EqA 2006, ss 16, 20, 21, 24, 25, 31, 32*;

(*b*)   in a report of an inquiry, investigation or assessment published by the CEHR;

(*c*)   in pursuance of an order of a court or tribunal;

(*d*)   with the consent of the person to whom the disclosed information relates;

(*e*)   in a manner that ensures that no person to whom the disclosed information relates can be identified;

(*f*)   for the purposes of civil or criminal proceedings to which the CEHR is a party; or

(*g*)   if the information was acquired by the CEHR more than 70 years before the date of the disclosure.

(*EqA 2006, s 6(3)*).

Contravention of these rules is made an offence punishable on summary conviction with a fine not exceeding level 5 on the standard scale (*SDA 1975, s 61(2); RRA 1976, s 52(2); EqA 2006, s 6(6)*; and see 1.10 INTRODUCTION). The EOC and CRE are under a general duty when preparing a report for publication or inspection to exclude, so far as is consistent with its duties and the object of the report, any matter which relates to the private affairs of any individual or the business interests of any person where the publication of that matter might, in the opinion of the EOC/CRE, prejudicially affect that individual or person (*SDA 1975, s 61(3); RRA 1976, s 52(3)*).

See also HARVEYS – DIVISION L.2.B(9)(D), L.3.B(14)(D).

14.28 **Non-discrimination notices and other remedies**

The EOC or CRE may issue a non-discrimination notice if, during the course of a formal investigation, it is satisfied that a person has committed or is committing, or is vicariously liable, as principal or employer, for the actions of another who has committed or is committing:

(*a*)   an unlawful discriminatory act (including harassment);

(*b*)   a discriminatory practice;

(*c*)   a breach of the provisions relating to discriminatory advertising, instructions to discriminate or pressure to discriminate; or

(*d*)   (in the case of the EOC only) a breach of a term modified or included by virtue of an equality clause.

The non-discrimination notice may require the person:

(i)   not to commit any such acts; and

(ii)   where compliance involves changes in any of his practices or other arrangements:

(A)   to inform the EOC/CRE that he has effected those changes and what those changes are; and

(B)   to take such steps as may be reasonably required by the notice for the purpose of affording that information to other persons affected by those practices or arrangements.

(*SDA 1975, s 67(2); RRA 1976, s 58(2)*.)

The notice may require the person to supply information to show that the requirements of the EOC/CRE have been complied with. The time within which the notice must be complied with will be a date not later than five years from the date on which the notice became final (*SDA 1975, s 67(4); RRA 1976, s 58(4)*). A non-discrimination notice or a finding by a court or tribunal becomes final when an appeal against the notice or finding is dismissed, withdrawn or abandoned, or when the time for appealing expires without an appeal having been brought. An appeal against a non-discrimination notice will be taken to be dismissed if, notwithstanding that a requirement of the notice is quashed on appeal, a direction varying it is given under *SDA 1975, s 68* (*SDA 1975, s 82(4)*) or under *RRA 1976, s 59* (*RRA 1976, s 78(4)*).

The EOC/CRE may not issue a non-discrimination notice unless it has informed the relevant person of its intention and of the grounds of the notice, offered him an opportunity of making representations within a period of not less than 28 days specified in the notice and taken account of representations made by him (*SDA 1975, s 67(5); RRA 1976, s 58(5)*). The persons concerned are not entitled to cross-examine witnesses (*R v Commission for Racial Equality, ex p Cottrell and Rothon* [1980] 1 WLR 1580). Thus, for example, a company issuing an advertisement for male shop managers will be warned by the EOC of its intention of issuing a notice on the ground that it is contravening *SDA 1975, s 38*. If the company then expresses its regret at having contravened the section and submits its proposed non-discriminatory advertisement, a notice may not be issued. If, however, it makes no such proposals, a notice will probably be issued which should then be complied with. If it is not, the EOC may apply to a county court for the issue of an injunction (see 14.29–14.30 below) against the employer.

It is therefore in the best interests of employers that:

(1)   they ensure that they are not in contravention of any of the provisions of the *SDA 1975* or *RRA 1976*;

(2)   if they are in breach of any of the provisions and receive a notification of a proposal to issue a notice, they remedy the discrimination;

(3)   if a notice has been issued which they do not wish to challenge, they comply with it as soon as possible.

Appeal. If a person has any objection to a non-discrimination notice, he may appeal against any requirement of the notice. Such an appeal must be lodged within six weeks of the service of the notice. The appeal must be made to an employment tribunal or to a county court depending upon whether the acts to which the requirement relates are within the jurisdiction of the former or the latter (*SDA 1975, s 68(1); RRA 1976, s 59(1)*). The jurisdiction of employment tribunals is set out in *SDA 1975, s 63* and *RRA 1976, s 54*. The *Employment Tribunals (Constitution and Rules of Procedure) Regulations 2004 (SI 2004/1861)*, *Sch 5* regulates the procedure to be adopted upon the hearing of such appeals. For further procedural guidance from the EAT under the pre-1 October 2004 regime set out in the *Employment Tribunals (Constitution and Rules of Procedure) Regulations 1993 (SI 1993/2687), Sch 6*, see *Commission for Racial Equality v Amari Plastics Ltd* [1981] ICR 767, approved by the Court of Appeal at [1982] ICR 304. The EOC/CRE ought to state the facts on which they relied, and the employer, in answer, ought to say which of those findings of fact are challenged.

Where the court or tribunal considers a requirement in a non-discrimination notice, in respect of which an appeal is brought, to be unreasonable because it is based on an incorrect finding of fact or for any other reason, the court or tribunal will quash the requirement (*SDA 1975, s 68(2); RRA 1976, s 59(2)*). In addition to quashing the requirement, it may direct that a requirement be substituted in the terms specified in the direction (*SDA 1975, s 68(3); RRA 1976, s 59(3)*). There is no appeal from such a direction (*SDA 1975, s 68(4); RRA 1976, s 59(4)*). In appropriate cases a non-discrimination notice may be challenged by way of application for judicial review using the procedure under *Part 54* of the *CPR* (formerly *Order 53* of the *Rules of the Supreme Court* (*Hillingdon London Borough Council v Commission for Racial Equality* [1982] ICR 799; *R v Commission for Racial Equality, ex p Westminster City Council* [1984] ICR 770; affd [1985] ICR 827, CA).

Register of non-discrimination notices. A register is to be kept of non-discrimination notices which have become final (*SDA 1975, s 70; RRA 1976, s 61*). The register is available for inspection and for copying. The EOC and CRE have to give general notice of the place or places where, and the times when, the register or a copy of it may be inspected (*SDA 1975, s 70(4); RRA 1976, s 61(4)*).

The EOC and CRE may, in certain circumstances, serve notices to investigate a person's compliance with a non-discrimination notice, without the consent of the Secretary of State (*SDA 1975, s 69; RRA 1976, s 60*).

Remedies that will be available to the CEHR. The CEHR will have a wider range of remedies available than the EOC and CRE. Where, following investigation, the CEHR is satisfied that a person has committed an unlawful act it will have the power to issue a notice specifying the unlawful act and the provision of the equality enactments that has been infringed and the notice may require the person to prepare an action plan to avoid repetition or continuation of the unlawful act or recommend action to be taken for that purpose (*EqA 2006, s 21(1), (2), (4)*). A person in receipt of a notice may within six weeks beginning with the date on which the notice was given appeal to an employment tribunal or county court (depending on which of these would have jurisdiction to consider a claim in respect of the alleged unlawful act) on the grounds that either (a) the person did not commit the unlawful act specified in the notice or (b) the requirement to prepare an action plan was unreasonable (*EqA 2006, ss 21 (5), (7)*). On such an appeal the court or tribunal may affirm, annul or vary the notice, affirm, annul or vary the requirement, or make an order for costs or expenses (*EqA 2006, s 21(6)*).

Where the CEHR issues a notice under *s 21* requiring a person to prepare an action plan the notice must specify the time within which the person must give the CEHR a first draft plan (*EqA 2006, s 22(2)*). On the receipt of the first draft plan the CEHR may approve it or give the person notice that it is inadequate and require the person to submit a revised draft by a specified time, possibly with recommendations as to the content of the revised draft (*EqA 2006, s 22 (3), (4)*). The CEHR will be empowered to apply to a county court (in England and Wales) or (in Scotland) the sheriff for an order requiring a person to produce a first draft plan by a specified time, or a revised draft plan by a specified time and in accordance with any directions as to its contents (*EqA 2006, s 22(6)*). Where within six weeks of the person giving the draft plan to the CEHR it has not issued a notice that the draft plan is inadequate or applied for an order under *s 22(6)(b)*, or where such an order is refused, the action plan will come into effect (*EqA 2006, s 22(5)*). The CEHR may agree with the person who prepared it to vary an action plan (*EqA 2006, s 22(7)*).

The CEHR will also be empowered to seek an order from the county court or sheriff within five years of an action plan coming into force requiring a person to act in accordance with the plan or to take specified action for a similar purpose (*EqA 2006, s 22(6)(c)*). It will be a criminal offence punishable on summary conviction by a fine not exceeding level 5 on the standard scale to fail to comply with an order under *s 22(6)* without reasonable excuse (*EqA 2006, s 22(9); and see* 1.10 INTRODUCTION).

The CEHR will have another new remedy for potential unlawful acts contrary to the equality enactments. Under the *EqA 2006, s 23*, the CEHR may enter into an agreement with a person under which the person undertakes not to commit an unlawful act of a specified kind or to take, or refrain from taking, other specified action, and the CEHR agrees not to proceed against the person under *ss 20* or *21* in respect of any act of that specified kind (*EqA 2006, s 23(1)*). The CEHR will only be able to enter into an agreement if it believes that the person has committed an unlawful act but a person will not be taken to have admitted to the commission of an unlawful act only by virtue of entering into an agreement (*EqA 2006, ss 22(2), (3)*).

See also HARVEYS – DIVISION L.2.B(9)(D), L.3.B(14)(D).

14.29 INJUNCTIONS

Persistent discrimination

The EOC have certain powers to apply to the county court for an injunction where a person has been served with a non-discrimination notice or where a court or tribunal has found under *SDA 1975, s 63* (complaints relating to employment) or the *Equal Pay Act 1970, s 2* that he has done a discriminatory act or an act in breach of a term modified or included by virtue of an equality clause (see 24.5 EQUAL PAY) (*SDA 1975, s 71*). The CRE has similar powers regarding racially discriminatory acts (*RRA 1976, s 62*). If, within five years of the notice or of the court or tribunal finding becoming final, it appears to the EOC/CRE that unless restrained the person is likely to do an unlawful discriminatory act, breach an equality clause term or carry on a discriminatory practice made unlawful by *SDA 1975, s 37* or *RRA 1976, s 28*, the EOC/CRE may apply for an injunction to restrain him from doing so. If satisfied that the application is well-founded, the court may grant the injunction in the terms applied for or on more limited terms (*SDA 1975, s 71(1); RRA 1976, s 62(1)*).

The CEHR will be empowered, where it thinks that a person is likely to continue to commit an unlawful act, to apply (in England and Wales) to a county court for an injunction or (in Scotland) to the sheriff for an interdict to prevent the person from committing the act (*EqA 2006, s 24(1)*). The CEHR will also be able, if a person subject to an agreement under the *EqA 2006, s 23* has failed, or is likely to fail, to comply with an undertaking, to apply to a county court or sheriff for an order requiring the person to comply with the undertaking or such other order as the court or sheriff may specify (*EqA 2006, s 24((2), (3)*).

See also HARVEYS – DIVISION L.2.B(9)(D), L.3B(14)(D).

14.30 **Advertisements and instructions or pressure to discriminate**

Only the EOC and CRE may bring proceedings for breach of the provisions relating to advertisements and instructions or pressure to discriminate (*SDA 1975, ss 38–40, RRA 1976, ss 29–31*). They may make:

(*a*)   an application to an employment tribunal or a county court for a decision whether the alleged contravention occurred; and/or

(*b*)   an application to a county court for an injunction restraining continuance of such unlawful acts.

(*SDA 1975, s 72(1), (2), (4); RRA 1976, s 63(1), (2), (4).*)

In all proceedings for an injunction, the EOC or CRE may not allege that a person has done an unlawful act which is within the jurisdiction of the employment tribunal unless a finding of an employment tribunal relating to that act has become final (see above) (*SDA 1975, s 72(5); RRA 1976, s 63(5)*). An application must be made to a county court or to an employment tribunal within six months of the alleged act of discrimination within its jurisdiction, for a decision whether the alleged contravention occurred (*SDA 1975, ss 72(2), 76(3); RRA 1976, ss 63(2), 68(4)*).

Additionally, in employment cases the EOC or CRE may, before applying for an injunction under *SDA 1975 s 71(1)* or *s 72(4)* or *RRA 1976, s 62(1)* or *s 63(1)*, present a complaint to an employment tribunal that a person has done an act within the jurisdiction of the tribunal and, if the tribunal considers that the complaint is well-founded, it:

(i)   shall make a finding to that effect; and, if it thinks it just and equitable to do so, may

(ii)   make an order under, respectively, *SDA 1975, s 65(1)(a)* or *RRA 1976, s 56(1)* declaring the rights of the employer or person of whom the complaint is made, and the victim or the employee; and/or

(iii) make a recommendation under, respectively, SDA 1975, *s 65(1)(c)* or *RRA 1976, s 56(1)(c)* that the employer (or person of whom the complaint is made) take certain action within a specified period.

(*SDA 1975, s 73(1); RRA 1976, s 64(1).*)

Applications by the EOC and CRE under respectively SDA 1975, *s 73(1)* and *RRA 1976, s 64(1)* to an employment tribunal must be made before the end of the period of six months beginning when the act complained of was done (*SDA 1975, s 76(4); RRA 1976, s 68(5)*). Late applications may be considered if the tribunal considers that in all the circumstances it is just and equitable to do so (*SDA 1975, s 76(5); RRA 1976, s 68(6)*).

Applications by the EOC or CRE under *SDA 1975, s 72(4)* and *RRA 1976, s 63(4)* to a county court for an injunction must be made before the end of the period of five years beginning with the original discriminatory act (*SDA 1975, s 76(3); RRA 1976, s 68(4)*). A court may nevertheless consider any such complaint, claim or application which is out of time if, in all the circumstances of the case, it considers it just and equitable to do so (*SDA 1975, s 76(5); RRA 1976, s 68(6)*).

The CEHR will have similar powers to bring proceedings in relation to discriminatory advertising or instructions or pressure to discriminate contrary to the *SDA 1975, ss 38–40*, the *RRA 1976, ss 29–31*, the *DDA 1995, ss 16B* and *16C*, and the *EqA 2006, ss 54, 55* (religious discrimination: advertising and instructions or pressure to discriminate) (*EqA 2006, s 25(1)*). Only the CEHR will be able to bring such proceedings (*EqA 2006, s 25(2)*). Where the CEHR believes that a person has committed an act to which *s 25* applies it may present a complaint to an employment tribunal where the alleged act is unlawful by reference to the *SDA 1975, Pt 2*, the *RRA 1976, Pt 2*, the *DDA 1995, Pt 3*, or the *EqA 2006, Pts 3* (in so far as it relates to employment services), *2*, or otherwise in the county court (in England and Wales) or to a sheriff (in Scotland) (*EqA 2006, s 25(3)*). Such a complaint or application is to be made within the six month period beginning with the date (or last date) on which the alleged unlawful act occurred, or with the permission of the tribunal, court or sheriff (*EqA 2006, s 26(1)*). On an application under *s 25(3)* the court, sheriff or tribunal will determine whether the allegation is correct (*EqA 2006, s 25(4)*).

The CEHR will also be empowered to apply to a county court (in England and Wales) for an injunction or to a sheriff (in Scotland) for an interdict where a tribunal, court or sheriff has determined under *s 25(4)* that a person has done an act to which the section applies or the CEHR thinks that a person has done such an act, and the CEHR believes that if unrestrained the person is likely to do another such act (*EqA 2006, s 25(5), (6)*). A court or sheriff may not rely upon a determination under *s 25(4)* while an appeal against that determination is pending or may be brought (disregarding the possibility of an appeal out of time with permission) (*EqA 2006, s 26(2)*). Any application under the *EqA 2006, s 25(5), (6)* must be brought within five years of the unlawful acted occurring or with the permission of the court or sheriff (*EqA 2006, s 26(3)*).

See also HARVEYS – DIVISION L.2.B(9)(D), L.3.B(14)(D).

14.31   ASSISTANCE FOR PERSONS DISCRIMINATED AGAINST

The EOC and CRE may give assistance to claimants or prospective claimants (although not to respondents) if their case is of some complexity or raises a question of principle. That assistance may include obtaining or attempting to obtain a settlement, giving or arranging for the giving of advice or assistance, or representation by solicitor or counsel. The cost of this assistance constitutes a first charge for the benefit of the EOC/CRE on an award of costs made by the tribunal, or on any settlement whereby the respondent agrees to contribute to the complainant's costs (*SDA 1975, s 75; RRA 1976, s 66*). The addresses of both commissions can be found at 14.24–14.25 above.

The CEHR will be able to make grants to another person in pursuance of its duties under the *EqA 2006, ss 8, 9* and *10*, which may be subject to conditions (*EqA 2006, s 17*). The CEHR will be able to assist an individual who is, or may become, a party to legal proceedings where the proceedings relate to the equality enactments and the individual alleges that he has been the victim of behaviour contrary to those enactments (*EqA 2006, s 28(1)*). This assistance may take the form of legal advice, legal representation, facilities for settlement of a dispute, or any other form of assistance (*EqA 2006, s 28(4)*). Where the proceedings partly relate to matters other than the equality enactments the assistance may be given in relation to any aspect of the proceedings but must cease if the proceedings cease to relate to the equality enactments (*EqA 2006, s 28(6)*). The Lord Chancellor may by order disapply this restriction in specified kinds of cases (*EqA 2006, s 28(7)*). For these purposes the equality enactments are taken to include any provisions of EU law that confer rights on individuals and relate to discrimination on the grounds of sex (including gender reassignment), racial origin, ethnic origin, religion, belief, disability, age or sexual orientation (*EqA 2006, s 28(12), (13)*). Where an individual receives assistance from the CEHR under *s 28* and the individual becomes entitled to costs either as a result of settlement or an award by the court or tribunal the CEHR's expenses in providing assistance will be charged on any sum paid to the individual by way of costs (*EqA 2006, s 29*).

See also HARVEYS – DIVISION L.2.B(5)(B), L.3.B(6)(B).

14.32 EFFECT ON CONTRACTS

A term of a contract is void where:

(*a*)   its inclusion renders the making of the contract unlawful by virtue of the *Acts* or *Regulations*;

(*b*)   it is included in furtherance of an act rendered unlawful by the *Acts* or *Regulations*; or

(*c*)   it provides for the doing of an act which would be rendered unlawful by the *Acts* or *Regulations*.

(*SDA 1975, s 77(1); RRA 1976, s 72(1); SOR 2003, reg 35 and Sch 4, part 1, para 1(1); RBR 2003, reg 35 and Sch 4, part 1, para 1(1)*.)

Thus, a term in a contract for the provision of a discriminatory training program would be rendered void by these provisions. A term in a contract for an advertisement which provided for the inclusion of a discriminatory expression would similarly be void.

A term which constitutes (or is in furtherance of or provides for) unlawful discrimination against a party to a contract is not made void, but is unenforceable against that party (*SDA 1975, s 77(3); RRA 1976, s 72(3); SOR 2003, reg 35 and Sch 4, part 1, para 1(3); RBR 2003, reg 35 and Sch 4, part 1, para 1(3)*). For example, a term in a contract with a woman which states that she cannot use a smoking room normally reserved for men is not enforceable in a court of law. A party to the contract may apply to a county court in England and Wales or a sheriff court in Scotland which may remove or modify the discriminatory term, provided that all persons affected have been notified of the application (*SDA 1975, s 77(5); RRA 1976, s 72(5); SOR 2003, reg 35 and Sch 4, part 1, para 3(1); RBR 2003, reg 35 and Sch 4, part 1, para 3(1)*).

By the *Sex Discrimination Act 1986, s 6* (as amended), *SDA 1975, s 77* is made to apply to any term of a collective agreement (see COLLECTIVE AGREEMENTS (6)) (even if not intended to be legally enforceable) or to any rule made by an employer for application to his employees or to applicants for employment. Similar provisions are contained in *RRA 1976, s 72A, SOR 2003, reg 35 and Sch 4, part 2,* and *RBR 2003, reg 35 and Sch 4, part 2.* These provisions also apply to any rule made by an organisation of workers, an organisation of employers, or an organisation whose members carry on a particular profession or trade for whose purposes it exists, for application to its members and prospective members. They also apply to any rule made by an authority or body which can confer an authorisation or qualification needed for, or facilitating, engagement in a particular profession or trade, for application to those who have received or seek to receive such authorisation or qualification. Persons who are (as the case may be) employees, members or the recipients of authorisations or qualifications, or who are genuinely and actively seeking to become such, and who have reason to believe that the offending term or rule may at some future time have effect in relation to them may complain to an employment tribunal. If the tribunal finds the complaint well-founded, it will declare the term or rule void.

See also EQUAL PAY (24).

Local authorities may not insert clauses into their contracts obliging the other party to comply with the discrimination legislation, because these are 'non-commercial matters' (*Local Government Act 1988, s 17*; and see *R v Islington London Borough Council, ex p Building Employers Confederation* [1989] IRLR 382).

14.33 SETTLEMENT OF A CLAIM

There is one exception to the rule against contracting out of the anti-discrimination legislation. Contracts or agreements settling or compromising a complaint relating to discrimination in employment (and complaints relating to the *Equal Pay Act 1970, s 2* (see 24.21 EQUAL PAY)) are enforceable against the complainant only where the contract is made with the assistance of a conciliation officer (see 2.4 ADVISORY, CONCILIATION AND ARBITRATION SERVICE (ACAS)), or where the contract is a compromise contract meeting certain statutory conditions (see 21.33–21.35 EMPLOYMENT TRIBUNALS – II) (*SDA 1975, s 77(4)(aa)* as inserted by *TURERA 1993, Sch 6, para 1,* and *Employment Rights (Dispute Resolution) Act 1998, s 9; RRA 1976, s 72(4)* as amended by *TURERA 1993, Sch 6, para 2(4A)* and *Employment Rights (Dispute Resolution) Act 1998, s 9; SOR 2003, reg 35* and *Sch 4, part 1, para 2; RBR 2003, reg 35* and *Sch 4, part 1, para 2*). It is most important to comply with these provisions when settling such a complaint, otherwise, despite a sum to settle the complaint having been paid, a complainant may still pursue his application to an employment tribunal. However, the EAT has held that there is nothing in law that requires a tribunal to ensure that a compromise agreement is binding within the *SDA 1975* or *RRA 1976* before it permits a claim to be dismissed where the parties have reached what is otherwise a contractual agreement (*Mayo-Deman v University of Greenwich* [2005] IRLR 845).

The requisite conditions for a valid compromise agreement are the following:

(*a*)   the contract must be in writing;

(*b*)   the contract must relate to the particular complaint;

(*c*)   the complainant must have received advice from a relevant independent adviser as to the terms and effect of the proposed contract and in particular its effect on his ability to pursue a complaint before an employment tribunal;

(*d*)   there must be in force, when the adviser gives the advice, a contract of insurance, or an indemnity provided for members of a profession or professional body, covering the risk of a claim by the complainant in respect of loss arising in consequence of the advice;

(*e*)   the contract must identify the adviser; and

(*f*)   the contract must state that the conditions regulating compromise contracts are satisfied.

Item (*f*) must not be ignored as the failure to include all the conditions in the relevant statutes in a compromise agreement will invalidate the agreement even if the substance of the requirements is met (*Lunt v Merseyside TEC Ltd* [1999] ICR 17, CA; *Palihakkara v British Telecommunications plc* (2007) 823 IDS Brief 18, EAT). An employee was not precluded from bringing an equal pay claim despite signing a compromise agreement purporting to settle all claims that she 'believed' that she had which referred expressly to the *EqPA 1970*, where the employee was not aware that she had an equal pay claim when she signed the compromise agreement (*Hilton UK Hotels Ltd v McNaughton* [2006] All ER (D) 327 (May), EAT). An agreement that referred only to claims arising out of the termination of a claimant's employment did not cover discrimination claims arising prior to termination (*Palihakkara*, above). In *Bainbridge v Redcar and Cleveland Borough Council; Redcar and Cleveland Borough Council v Williams* (2007) 828 IDS Brief 11, EAT, a COT3 which covered 'all claims … in connection with the terms of [the claimants'] contracts of employment' was held to be unambiguous and enforceable (see *Clarke v Redcar and Cleveland Borough Council*, above).

A person is a 'relevant independent adviser' for the purposes of paragraph (*c*) immediately above if:

(*a*)   he is a qualified lawyer;

(*b*)   he is an officer, official, employee or member of an independent trade union who has been certified in writing by the trade union as competent to give advice and as authorised to do so on behalf of the trade union; or

(*c*)   he works at an advice centre (whether as an employee or a volunteer) and has been certified in writing by the centre as competent to give advice and as authorised to do so on behalf of the centre.

A person is *not* a 'relevant independent adviser':

(*a*)   if he is, is employed by or is acting in the matter for the other party or a person who is connected with the other party;

(*b*)   in the case of a person within paragraphs (*b*) or (*c*) immediately above, if the trade union or advice centre is the other party or a person who is connected with the other party; or

(*c*)   in the case of a person within paragraph (*c*) immediately above, if the complainant makes a payment for the advice received from him.

Any two persons are to be treated as connected if one is a company of which the other (directly or indirectly) has control, or else if both are companies of which a third person (directly or indirectly) has control.

'Qualified lawyer' means 'a barrister (whether in practice as such or employed to give legal advice), a solicitor who holds a practising certificate, or a person other than a barrister or solicitor who is an authorised advocate or authorised litigator (within the meaning of the *Courts and Legal Services Act 1990*). The definition of a 'qualified lawyer' has been extended, with effect from 1 October 2004, to include a Fellow of the Institute of Legal Executives employed by a solicitors' practice, who need not be supervised in giving the advice by a solicitor (see: for the purposes of the *SDA 1975* and *RRA 1976*, the *Compromise Agreements (Description of Person) Order 2004 (SI 2004/754)*, as amended by the *Compromise Agreements (Description of Person) Order 2004 (Amendment) Order 2004 (SI 2004/2515)*; for the purposes of the *SOR 2003*, the *Employment Equality (Sexual Orientation) Regulations 2003 (Amendment) Regulations 2004 (SI 2004/2519)*; and, for the purposes of the *RBR 2003*, the *Employment Equality (Religion or Belief) Regulations 2003 (Amendment) (No 2) Regulations 2004 (SI 2004/2520)*).

'Independent trade union' has the same meaning as in the *Trade Union and Labour Relations (Consolidation) Act 1992* (see 50.22 TRADE UNIONS – I).

See also HARVEYS – DIVISION T.A.21.

15   Dispute Resolution

15.1   INTRODUCTION

The *Employment Act 2002* (*'EA 2002'*), *Part 3*, and the *Employment Act 2002 (Dispute Resolution) Regulations 2004* (*SI 2004/752*) (*'Dispute Resolution Regulations'*), which came into force on 1 October 2004, introduced provisions designed to encourage employers and employees to resolve disputes without recourse to the employment tribunal. They lay down minimum procedures to be followed before taking disciplinary action or dismissing employees, and minimum procedures to be followed in the case of grievances. (For the purposes of the statutory procedures, the definition of 'employer' and 'employee' is the same as those used in the *ERA 1996*: see *EA 2002, s 40*.)The general purpose of the legislation has been described as 'to encourage conciliation, agreement, compromise and settlement rather than the precipitate issue of proceedings': *Shergold v Fieldway Medical Centre* [2006] IRLR 76, EAT (Burton J (President) at [26]). Breach of the statutory procedures does not give rise to a free-standing cause of action (see *Scott-Davies v Redgate Medical Services* [2007] ICR 348); rather, enforcement takes a number of forms: non-compliance with the statutory dismissal and disciplinary procedure renders a dismissal automatically unfair; non-compliance with the statutory grievance procedure may result in an employee being barred from presenting a complaint before an employment tribunal; and non-compliance with either procedure may result in an increase or decrease in compensation. By *s 30(1)* of *EA 2002* it was provided that every contract of employment shall have effect to require the employer and employee to comply, in relation to any matter to which a statutory procedure applies, with the requirements of the procedure, however, this provision has not yet been brought into force. In addition, the EAT in *Sahatciu v DPP Restaurants Ltd* (EAT/0177/06/RN: 27 March 2007) held that it was not permissible to imply a term into a contract of employment requiring an employer to comply with the statutory dismissal and disciplinary procedure by virtue of the implied trust and confidence obligation.

The Department of Trade and Industry published an independent review of these dispute resolution procedures in March 2007 ('Better Dispute Resolution: A review of employment dispute resolution in Great Britain', see, www.dti.gov.uk). A central recommendation of this review was for the repeal of the Dispute Resolution Regulations. In light of this, the DTI has issued a consultation paper, 'Resolving Disputes in the workplace', seeking views on the issues arising out of the review. In the meantime, the body of case law on these complex provisions has rapidly built up.

15.2   CONTENT OF DISMISSAL AND DISCIPLINARY PROCEDURES

There are two types of dismissal and disciplinary procedure: standard and modified.

The *standard* dismissal and disciplinary procedure is set out in *paras 1* to *3* of *Sch 2* to *EA 2002*. It follows a three stage process. The *first* stage requires the employer to set out in writing and send to the employee the grounds (ie alleged conduct, characteristics or circumstances) which lead him to contemplate dismissing or taking disciplinary action against the employee, and to invite him to a meeting to discuss the matter (*para 1*). The *second* stage requires the employer to hold a meeting. The meeting must take place before any disciplinary action (except suspension) is taken, and must not take place until the employer has explained the basis for the disciplinary proceedings and given the employee a reasonable opportunity to consider his response (*para 2(1)* and (*2*)). The employee must take all reasonable steps to attend the meeting (*para 2(3)*). After the meeting the employer must inform the employee of his decision and his right to appeal (*para 2(4)*). The *third* stage is appeal. If the employee wishes to appeal he must inform the employer, who must then invite him to a further meeting (*paras 3(1) and (2)*). There is no prescription about the form in which the appeal should be registered (see *Wilson v Mars UK (tla Masterfoods)* [2007] ICR 370). The appeal meeting may take place after the dismissal or disciplinary action has taken effect (*para 3(4)*). The employee must take all reasonable steps to attend the meeting (*para 3(3)*). After the appeal meeting, the employer must inform the employee of his final decision (*para 3(5)*).

In *Alexander v Bridgen* [2006] IRLR 422 the EAT (Elias J, President) gave guidance on the information that must be given by the employer during the standard disciplinary and dismissal procedure. At stage one, the employee need only be told in broad terms that he is at risk of dismissal and why ie lack of capability, redundancy or misconduct (in the case of misconduct, the type of misconduct should be identified). At stage two the employer must inform the employee in advance of the step two meeting of the matters which have led the employer to contemplate dismissing for the stated ground or grounds. This information need not be reduced into writing; it can be given orally. In a conduct case, while the detailed evidence need not be provided for compliance with the statutory procedure, sufficient detail should be given to enable the employee to properly put his or her side of the story (see also *Ingram v Bristol Street Parts* (UKEAT/0601/06/CEA: 23 April 2007). In a redundancy case, information should be provided as to both why the employer considers there to be a redundancy situation and why the employee is being selected. Thus, the employer should notify the employee of the redundancy selection criteria which have been used, and also the assessment of the employee. In order to comply with the statutory procedure, however, it is not necessary to provide the assessments of other employees.

Where a wholly new and distinct allegation arises in the course of a disciplinary proceeding it will be necessary for the employer to send a fresh statement in writing under stage one of the procedure with respect to that allegation; where there is merely a change in focus, however, it will not be necessary to do so: *Silman v ICTS (UK) Ltd* (EAT/0630/05: 6 March 2006).

In *YMCA Training v Stewart* [2007] IRLR 185 the EAT gave further guidance on various aspects of steps 1 and 2 of the standard procedure. First, in determining whether the requirements of step 1 are met, it is necessary to look beneath the parties' own labels and focus on whether the substantive terms of the statute are met. Second, the information regarding the basis for the grounds set out in the step 1 statement (which has to be provided in advance of the step 2 meeting) may be addressed in the step 1 letter itself. Third, if the step 2 meeting throws up a need for further investigation in respect of the grounds given in the step 1 statement, that does not impose any further obligation under the statutory procedure (see also *Sahatciu v DPP Restaurants Ltd* (EAT/0177/06/RN: 27 March 2007). Fourth, provided an employee has had an opportunity to put their case at the step 2 meeting the fact that the employer announces its decision at some later stage during the meeting itself, rather than after the conclusion of the meeting, does not necessarily mean that the employer has failed to comply with step 2.

The EAT in *Draper v Mears Ltd* [2006] IRLR 869 held that the Employment Tribunal was entitled to find that the employers had complied with step 1 of the standard procedure by providing the claimant with a letter which set out the complaint against him as 'conduct which fails reasonably to ensure health and safety of oneself and others', where the conduct referred to was that, contrary to the employer's rules, the claimant had consumed alcohol when intending to drive a company vehicle. Further, it was held that in considering whether a document complies with step 1, it is legitimate for a Tribunal to look at the whole context, including whether the employee knew what the allegations against him or her were. The EAT set out further guidance on the interrelationship between steps 1 and 2. It held that a Tribunal must consider whether there has been compliance with step 1 separately from whether the employer has informed the employee of the basis for the grounds included in the step 1 statement prior to the step 2 meeting. Thus, a defective document which does not comply with step 1 cannot be regarded as complying simply because the employers have fully complied with step 2. It was further noted that the information requirements under step 2 might be complied with before step 1 given that an investigatory meeting will often precede an employer's decision on what charges might be considered at a disciplinary meeting.

The *modified* dismissal and disciplinary procedure is set out in *paras 4* and *5* of *Sch 2* to *EA 2002*. The modified procedure applies where an employee has already been dismissed for gross misconduct (see further 15.3 below). The *first* stage is that the employer must set out in writing and send to the employee the alleged misconduct which has led to dismissal, the basis for thinking at the time of the dismissal that the employee was guilty of the alleged misconduct, and the employee's right of appeal against dismissal (*para 4*). The *second* stage is appeal. The employee, if he wishes to appeal, must inform his employer, who must then invite him to a meeting (*para 5(1)* and (2)). The employee must take all reasonable steps to attend the appeal meeting (*para 5(3)*). After the appeal meeting, the employer must inform the employee of his final decision (*para 5(4)*).

There are a number of general requirements which apply to both the standard and modified procedures: each step and action must be taken without unreasonable delay; the timing and location of meetings must be reasonable; meetings must be conducted in a manner that enables both employer and employee to explain their cases, and so far as reasonably practicable appeals against a decision should be heard by a more senior manager: *EA 2002, Sch 2, paras 11 to 13*. An employee has the right to be accompanied by a trade union representative or another of the employer's workers at any hearing under the statutory procedures: *EA 2002, Sch 2, para 14* and *s 10* of the *Employment Relations Act 1999*. In respect of the appeal stage, the EAT in *Khan & King v The Home Office* (EAT/0026/06/LA and EAT/0250/06/LA: 14–17 November 2006) held that since the standard time limit in respect of bringing an unfair dismissal claim was three months it followed that such a period with nothing happening in respect of an internal appeal was, without any explanation, unreasonable.

If it is not reasonably practicable for an employee, his representative or accompanying colleague, or the employer to attend a meeting for a reason which was not foreseeable when the meeting was arranged, the employee or employer will not be treated as having failed to comply with the procedure: *reg 13(1)*. In these circumstances, the employer remains under a duty to invite the employee to a meeting; if, however, a meeting is cancelled twice for a reason which was not foreseeable then the duty to invite to a meeting ceases, and the parties are deemed to have complied with the relevant statutory procedure: *reg 13(2), (3) and (4)*.

15.3 Dispute Resolution

Where a meeting has been cancelled because of the unavailability of an employee's representative or colleague, and the employee proposes an alternative time under *s 10(4)* of the *ERA 1999* (ie the time is reasonable and within 5 working days of the date suggested by the employer), the employer must arrange a meeting for that time: *reg 13(2)*.

There are two particular circumstances in which the parties are not required to comply with the appeal stage of the dismissal and disciplinary procedures. First, where an employee presents an application for interim relief to a tribunal under *s 128* of *ERA 1996* and the parties have complied with the modified or standard procedure up to but not including the appeal stage set out in *paras 3* and *5* of *Sch 2* to *EA 2002*, they will be treated as having complied with the appeal stage: *reg 5(1)*. Second, where there is in place an appropriate appeal procedure under which an employee may appeal against his dismissal instead of appealing to his employer, and he appeals under that procedure, both parties will be deemed to have complied with the appeal stage of the statutory procedure under *para 3* or *5* of *Sch 2* to *EA 2002*: *reg 5(2)*. An appeal procedure is 'appropriate' for these purposes if it (a) gives the employee an effective right of appeal against dismissal or disciplinary action taken against him, and (b) operates by virtue of a collective agreement made between two or more employers or an employers' association and one or more independent trade unions: *reg 5(3)*.

15.3 APPLICATION OF DISMISSAL AND DISCIPLINARY PROCEDURES

The *standard dismissal and disciplinary procedure* must be followed with certain exceptions, set out below, wherever an employer contemplates *dismissing* or taking *relevant disciplinary action* against an employee: *Dispute Resolution Regulations, reg 3(1)*. Dismissal in this context has the same meaning as in *s 95(1)(a)* and *(b)* of the *ERA 1996*, and therefore includes any termination by the employer of an employment contract with or without notice, and the expiry of a limited-term contract, but does not include constructive dismissal: *reg 2(1)*. It is important to note that the dismissal and disciplinary procedure is not therefore limited to cases where dismissal is contemplated on the ground of misconduct. 'Relevant disciplinary action' is defined in *reg 2(1)* to mean any action, short of dismissal, which the employer asserts to be based wholly or mainly on the employee's conduct or capability, except suspension on full pay or the issuing of oral or written warnings. It follows that suspension without pay is a form of 'relevant disciplinary action' (see *Wilson v Mars UK (t/a Masterfoods)* [2007] ICR 370). The EAT held in the case of *Brock v Minerva Dental Ltd* [2007] ICR 917 that where an employer commences disciplinary proceedings against an employee with a warning that dismissal may follow in the event that the disciplinary charge is found proven then the employer is 'contemplating' dismissal.

The *modified* procedure applies where: the employer is entitled to dismiss the employee by reason of his conduct without notice (ie the conduct must be gross misconduct which constitutes a repudiatory breach of contract); he does so at the time, or immediately after, he becomes aware of the conduct; and it was reasonable for him to dismiss before enquiring into the circumstances in which the conduct took place: *reg 3(2)(a)* to *(d)*. It is unlikely that an employer will be able to satisfy these requirements, in particular the requirement that it is reasonable to dismiss without first making enquiries, save in the most exceptional case. The procedure need not be followed, however, if an employee dismissed in these circumstances presents a complaint relating to the dismissal to an employment tribunal before the employer has complied with the first stage of the modified procedure (ie before the employer has notified the employee of the reason for his dismissal and his right to appeal): *reg 3(2)*.

Neither the standard nor modified dismissal and disciplinary procedure applies to dismissals where:

(*a*)　the employer has dismissed all the employees of a description or in a category to which the employee belongs, provided that the employer offers to re-engage all employees who have been dismissed either before or upon termination of their contracts of employment into the previous job or into a different job which would be suitable in the employee's case (with offers of re-engagement by a successor or associated employer of the dismissing employer being included) (*reg 4(1)(a)*);

(*b*)　the dismissal is one of a number of dismissals in relation to which the duty to consult employee representatives under *s 188* of *TULCRA 1992* arises (*reg 4(1)(b)*) (ie dismissal of 20 or more employees for redundancy);

(*c*)　the employee is dismissed whilst taking part in an unofficial strike or other unofficial industrial action, or a strike or other industrial action (being neither unofficial industrial action nor protected industrial action) unless the circumstances of the case bring it within *s 238(2)* of *TULRCA 1992* (*reg 4(1)(c)*);

(*d*)　the reason or principal reason for the dismissal is that the employee took part in protected industrial action and the dismissal would be regarded as automatically unfair by virtue *of s 238A(2)* of *TULRCA 1992* (*reg 4(1)(d)*);

(*e*)　the employer's business suddenly ceases to function, because of an event unforeseen by the employer, with the result that it is impractical for him to employ any employees (*reg 4(1)(e)*);

(*f*)　the reason or principal reason for the dismissal is that the employee could not continue to work in the position which he held without contravention by him or his employer of a duty or restriction imposed by or under any enactment (*reg 4(1)(f)*);

(*g*)　the employee is one to whom a dismissal procedures agreement designated by an order under *s 110* of the *ERA 1996* applies at the date of dismissal (*reg 4(1)(g)*).

The dismissal and disciplinary procedures will also not apply in certain circumstances where it is not practicable to commence the relevant procedure within a reasonable time or there is a reasonable belief that it will result in harassment or threat to life or property, or where compliance would be contrary to the interests of national security: see further 15.6 below.

15.4　CONTENT OF GRIEVANCE PROCEDURES

There are two types of grievance procedure: standard and modified.

The standard and modified procedures require as a first stage that the employee set out his or her grievance in writing and send a copy to the employer . Under step one of the modified procedure, the employee must also set out in writing 'the basis' for the grievance and send a copy to the employer. A grievance is defined in *Dispute Resolution Regulations, reg 2(1)* as 'a complaint by an employee about action which his employer has taken or is contemplating taking in relation to him'. 'Action' includes a failure to act: *Canary Wharf Management v Edebi* [2006]

IRLR 416. In determining whether a communication constitutes a grievance, it is irrelevant that it may also deal with some other matter: *reg 2(2)*.

The EAT has adopted a broad approach to the question of when a written communication constitutes a grievance under the statutory procedures. The communication must be in writing and must enable the employer to understand the general nature of the complaint made; it need not, however, set out the complaint in technical detail provided that the identified complaint is essentially the same complaint as is subsequently allowed before the Employment Tribunal; where the standard procedure applies, it is not necessary to set out the basis for the complaint (although the employee must inform the employer of this prior to the step two meeting: see below); it need not comply with the terms of any contractual grievance procedure; there is no need to make it plain that the document is a grievance or an invocation of the grievance procedure; and a grievance may take the form of a letter which also serves as a letter of resignation: *Shergold v Fieldway Medical Centre* [2006] IRLR 76. A letter before claim from an employee's solicitor to his employer's solicitor can in principle constitute a grievance; moreover, it is not necessary to show that the employee expressly intended by his written communication to raise a grievance: see *Mark Warner v Aspland* [2006] IRLR 87. There is no need in the grievance to indicate that the complainant wishes to proceed further to some discussion or resolution of the complaint; what is essential is that the substance of the complaint is raised: *Galaxy Showers Ltd v Wilson* [2006] IRLR 83. The principles established in *Shergold, Warner* and *Galaxy* were approved by the EAT (Elias J, President) in *Canary Wharf Management v Edebi* [2006] IRLR 416. While approving the succinct statement in *Shergold* that the grievance in question must relate to the subsequent claim, and the claim must relate to the earlier grievance, the EAT in *Canary Wharf* also held that the relevant approach should be whether on a fair reading of the written communication and having regard to the particular context in which it is made, the employer can be expected to appreciate that the relevant complaint is being raised.

On the facts of *Canary Wharf*, the EAT held that the Employment Tribunal was entitled to find that the employee's complaints about health and safety and conditions of work were not enough for the complaints to constitute a grievance under the standard procedure relating to a claim under the *Disability Discrimination Act 1995*.

In *Martin v Class Security Installations Ltd* (EAT/0188/06/D: 16 March 2006) the EAT (Elias J, President) held that a letter from an employee making plain that he was leaving due to the employer's conduct towards him and making reference to a particular incident as being the final straw was sufficient by way of grievance under the standard procedure to allow him to pursue a constructive unfair dismissal claim which might then rely on other additional matters not referred to in the grievance letter. This was because it was not necessary under the standard procedure (unlike the modified procedure) for the basis of the complaint of constructive dismissal to be identified in the grievance letter.

The EAT in *Odoemelam v The Whittington Hospital NHS Trust* (EAT/0016/06: 6 February 2007) held that an Employment Tribunal was correct to find that an employee's grievance complaint about less favourable treatment compared with another employee was not sufficient to allow the employee to pursue a claim of race discrimination since the grievance letter did not spell out that it was the employee's race which had resulted in the inconsistent treatment between her and the other employee.

In *Serco Group Plc v Wild* (EAT/0519/06: 19 December 2006) the EAT held that in respect of an equal pay claim the Employment Tribunal was entitled to hold that a grievance letter referring to the claimant not being paid fairly was sufficient to comply with the standard procedure when construed in the context of an unchallenged conversation between the claimant and the respondent's personnel officer during which the claimant raised concerns that she was not being paid on an equal basis to men in similar roles. Similarly, a letter sent to the claimant's employer referring to 'unlawful sex discrimination in relation' to pay and conditions was held to be sufficient to constitute a grievance in respect of a subsequent equal pay claim, although the absence of reasons for this grievance in sufficient detail to allow the employer to respond prevented it from complying with step 1 of the modified procedure which requires the basis for a grievance to be set out: see *City of Bradford Metropolitan District Council v Pratt* [2007] IRLR 192.

The flexibility about the form of a written grievance is illustrated by two further decisions of the EAT. In *Commotion Ltd v Rutty* [2006] IRLR 171 it was held that a request for flexible working may also be a grievance even where it does not expressly state that this is the position. Further, in *Arnold Clark Automobiles v Stewart* (EATS/0052/05/RN: 20 December 2005) it was held that a letter from a solicitor expressed to be 'without prejudice' may even be a grievance.

Whether a letter constituted compliance with step 1 of the standard procedure was considered to be an issue of fact by the EAT in *Commotion Ltd v Rutty*. However, the EAT in *Martin v Class Security Installations Ltd* (Elias J, President) cast doubt on this indicating that it was at least one of mixed fact and law.

There are some statutory limitations on what may constitute a grievance. The making of a protected disclosure under *Part 4A* of the *ERA 1996* is not to be treated as a grievance, unless the information relates to a matter which the employee could raise as a grievance, and the employee intends to raise the matter as a grievance: *EA 2002 Sch 2, para 15(2)*. Further, use of the questionnaire procedure by an employee under discrimination legislation does not constitute a statement of grievance under the grievance procedures: *Dispute Resolution Regulations, reg 14* and *Holc-Gale v Makers UK Ltd* [2006] ICR 462.

Also, the EAT held in *Gibbs (t/a Jarlands Financial Services) v Harris* (EAT 0023/07: 27 February 2007) that a claim form commencing litigation could not constitute a valid grievance complaint for the purpose of the statutory procedures. This was so because the statutory grievance procedure envisaged a grievance being raised prior to proceedings. Moreover, since the claim form was provided to the respondent employer by the Employment Tribunals Service it could not be said that the employee had 'sent' the grievance to the employer. This underlined the fact that the two procedures were distinct.

The EAT in *Kennedy Scott Ltd v Francis* (EAT/0204/07/DM:3 May 2007) held that the Employment Tribunal was entitled to find that where an employee was known by his employer to be attending a meeting with his line manager to explain a grievance complaint and during the meeting his explanation was seen to be written down contemporaneously by the manager and the written record of the employee's complaint accurately reflected what he had complained about, then the manager's note of the meeting could constitute a valid grievance complaint under the standard procedure.

The *standard* grievance procedure is set out in *paras 6 to 8* of *Sch 2* to *EA 2002*. It provides in substance for a three-stage process. The *first* stage requires the employee to set out the grievance in writing and send a copy to the employer (*para 6*). (As to the form and content of the grievance, see above). At the *second* stage the employer must invite the employee to a meeting to discuss the grievance (*para 7(1)*). The employee must take all reasonable steps to attend the meeting (*para 7(3)*). The meeting must not take place unless the employee has informed the employer of the basis for his grievance and the employer has had a reasonable opportunity to consider his response (*para 7(2)*). After the meeting the employer must inform the employee of his response to the grievance and notify him of his right of appeal (para 7(4)). The *third* stage is appeal. If the employee wishes to appeal, he must inform the employer, who must then invite him to a further meeting (*para 8(1)* and (*2*)). The employee must take all reasonable steps to attend the meeting (*para 8(3)*). After the appeal meeting, the employer must inform the employee of his final decision (*para 8(4)*).

The *modified* procedure is set out in *paras 9 to 10* of *Sch 2* to *EA 2002*. It provides that *first*, the employee must set out in writing the grievance, the basis for it and send a copy to his employer (*para 9*), and *second*, the employer must set out his response in writing and send a copy to the employee (*para 10*).

There are a number of general requirements which apply to both the standard and modified grievance procedures: each step and action must be taken without unreasonable delay; the timing and location of meetings must be reasonable; meetings must be conducted in a manner that enables both employer and employee to explain their cases, and so far as reasonably practicable appeals against a decision should be heard by a more senior manager: *EA 2002, Sch 2, paras 11 to 13*. An employee has the right to be accompanied by a trade union representative or another of the employer's workers at any hearing under the statutory procedures: *EA 2002, Sch 2, para 14* and *s 10* of the *Employment Relations Act 1999*.

The EAT in *Department for Constitutional Affairs v Jones* (EAT/0333/06/DM: 24 November 2006) held that while the Dispute Resolution Regulations should be construed to meet the purpose of the *EA 2002*, they should not be construed any more widely than is necessary to give effect to the intention of the statute because they have the potential to limit remedies for important rights.

15.5   APPLICATION OF GRIEVANCE PROCEDURES

The grievance procedures must be followed in relation to any grievance about action (or proposed action) by the employer that could form the basis of a complaint by an employee to an employment tribunal: *reg 6(1)*. The definition of grievance and the form it must take is considered at 15.4 above. The full list of possible complaints is set out in *Schs 3 and 4* of *EA 2002*; it includes complaints of equal pay, discrimination on the grounds of sex, race, disability, sexual orientation, religion or belief, age, detriment in relation to trade union membership and activities, detriment in relation to union recognition rights, unauthorised deductions from wages, detriment in employment, redundancy payments, detriment in relation to national minimum wage, breach of contract, breach of *Working Time Regulations*, and detriment relating to European Works Councils. The distinction between *Schs 3* and *4* of *EA 2002* relates to the form of enforcement arising from a failure to comply with procedures: thus, *Sch 3* complaints are where non-compliance results in an increase or decrease in award (see, *s 31 EA 2002*); and, *Sch 4* complaints are where non-compliance bars presentation of a claim (see *s 32 EA 2002*): This is considered at 15.10 and 15.11 below.

With effect from 6 April 2007, the *EA 2002* (*Amendment of Schedules 3,4 and 5*) *Order 2007* (*SI 2007/30*) adds three further specific complaints of detriment in employment to those complaints already set out in *Schs 3* and *4* to the *EA 2002*, namely, under the *European Public Limited-Liability Company Regulations 2004* (*SI 2004/2326*), the *Information and Consultation of Employees Regulations 2004* (*SI 2004/3426*) and the *Occupational and Personal Pension Schemes* (*Consultation by Employers and Miscellaneous Amendment*) *Regulations 2006* (*SI 2006/349*).

The *standard* procedure applies to all grievances unless (a) the employee has ceased to be employed by the employer, (b) the employer was unaware of the grievance before the employment ceased, or the standard procedure was not commenced or completed before the last day of the employee's employment; and (c) the parties have agreed in writing in relation to the particular grievance that the modified procedure should apply, in which case the *modified* procedure applies: *reg 6(3)*.

Neither the *modified* nor the *standard* grievance procedure need be followed where:

(*a*)   the grievance is that the employer has dismissed or is contemplating dismissing the employee (*reg 6(5)*) 'Dismissal' has the meaning given to it in *s 95(1)(a)* and (*b*) of the *ERA 1996*, and therefore includes any termination by the employer of an employment contract with or without notice, and the expiry of a limited-term contract, but does not include constructive dismissal: see, *reg 2(1)*. It follows that the grievance procedures apply in respect of constructive unfair dismissal claims (see *Pinkus v Crime Reduction Initiative* (EAT 0528–9/06: 31 January 2007; and *Brock v Minerva Dental Ltd* [2007] ICR 917). The EAT in *Department for Constitutional Affairs v Jones* (EAT/0333/06/DM: 24 November 2006) held that a grievance that an employer has dismissed or is contemplating dismissal includes a complaint about the manner in which the employer is contemplating dismissal so that *reg 6(5)* bites. Further, a complaint of unlawful discrimination in respect of a dismissal (ie a complaint in respect of the reason for dismissal) is also covered by the *reg 6(5)* exception (see *Lawrence v HM Prison Service* [2007] IRLR 468. Also, the EAT held in *London Borough of Lambeth v Corlett* [2007] ICR 88 that a complaint of wrongful dismissal is a complaint about dismissal, not a complaint that the employer has failed to pay notice pay, so that *reg 6(5)* bites (although a shorter route to the conclusion that the grievance procedures do not apply to a wrongful dismissal claim in respect of the *s 32* provisions would have been that breach of contract claims are not listed in *Sch 4*: see 15.11 below);

(*b*)   the grievance is that the employer has taken or is contemplating taking relevant disciplinary action against the employee (ie action short of dismissal other than suspension on full pay or the issuing of warnings (whether oral or written), see *reg 2(1)*) (*reg 6(6)*); in these circumstances, however, if the grievance is that the disciplinary action amounts to unlawful discrimination or that the grounds asserted for the action are not the true grounds, the standard or modified procedure applies but the parties will be deemed to have complied if the employee sets out the grievance in writing and sends it to the employer (i) before any appeal meeting if the dismissal and disciplinary procedure is being followed, or (ii) before presenting a complaint arising out of the grievance to the employment tribunal (*reg 7(1)* and (*2*));

(*c*)   the employee has ceased to be employed by the employer, neither procedure has been commenced and since the employment ceased it has not been reasonably practicable for him to set out his grievance in writing and send a copy to his employer (*reg 6(4)*). The question of reasonable practicability is one of fact for the Employment Tribunal: see *Brown v London Borough of Tower Hamlets* (EAT/0246/06: 17 November 2006)

The grievance procedures will also not apply in certain circumstances where it is not practicable to commence the relevant procedure within a reasonable time, where there is a reasonable belief that it will result in harassment or threat to person or property, or where compliance would be contrary to the interests of national security: see further 15.6 below.

Further, the EAT in *Smith v Network Rail Infrastructure Ltd* (EAT/0047/07/DA: 24 April 2007) held that where, in the context of a complaint of an alleged failure to make reasonable adjustments under the *Disability Discrimination Act 1995*, a written grievance complaint was properly construed as raising a continuing complaint that looked forward as well as back, there was no obligation to submit a further written grievance in respect of complaints of an alleged failure up until the date of presentation of the claim form.

Special provision is made for grievances which are raised collectively. If an appropriate representative of the employee has written to the employer setting out the grievance and specified in writing that the grievance is lodged on behalf of at least two employees, of whom one is the employee having the grievance, then there is no need for either party to follow the statutory grievance procedure: *reg 9(1)*. An 'appropriate representative' for these purposes is: (a) an official of an independent trade union recognised by the employer for the purposes of collective bargaining in respect of a description of employees that includes the employee having the grievance, or (b) an employee representative elected or appointed by employees consisting of or including employees of the same description as the employee having the grievance, who has the authority to represent employees under an established procedure for resolving grievances agreed between employee representatives and the employer: *reg 9(2)*. The parties are also treated as having complied with the applicable grievance procedure where an employee is entitled to and has raised a grievance under a procedure in operation under a collective agreement: *reg 10*. The collective agreement must be made between two or more employers or an employers' association and one or more independent trade unions, and provide for employees of the employer to raise grievances about the behaviour of the employer and have these considered (*reg 10(a)*).

15.6 DEEMED COMPLIANCE AND DISAPPLICATION OF STATUTORY PROCEDURES

In certain circumstances set out below, the *Dispute Resolution Regulations* make special provision for the statutory procedures not to apply, and for the parties to be treated as having complied with the relevant procedure.

15.7 Where the standard procedure is the applicable statutory procedure and the employee has ceased to be employed by the employer but a written grievance has been sent to the employer either before or after the end of employment and since then it has ceased to be reasonably practicable for the employee or the employer to comply with steps 2 or 3 under the procedure then the parties shall be treated as having complied with those steps, except that in the event that there has been a step 2 meeting the employer is obliged to communicate in writing its response to the grievance: *reg 8(1)* and *(2)*.

Where it is not practicable for a party to commence a statutory procedure within a reasonable period, that procedure does not apply: *reg 11(1)* and *(3)(c)*. Where having commenced the procedure it is not practicable for a party to comply with a subsequent requirement within a reasonable period, the parties will be treated as having complied with the requirement: *reg 11(2)* and *(3)(c)*.

In *Bainbridge v Redcar and Cleveland Borough Council; Redcar and Cleveland Borough Council v Williams* (EAT 0424/06;0031/07: 31 January 2007) the Respondent Council had argued that it was not practicable, pursuant to *reg 11*, to address in meetings the grievances raised by a number of employees since there were not enough managers to deal with the volume of grievances speedily; the employees were spread around many parts of the borough and only worked for a short number of hours per week, thus making meetings very difficult; and, in any event, the whole exercise would have been pointless given the terms of conditional fee agreements which prohibited the employees from negotiating a settlement independently of their solicitor (or bringing the services of the solicitor to an end without payment of a potentially significant sum) and given that attempts to resolve matters had already failed. The EAT held that 'practicable' meant no more than 'feasible' and that the Employment Tribunal had been entitled to find that it would have been practicable to hold grievance meetings under stage 2 of the standard procedure. (However, the EAT went on to hold that the pointlessness argument was well-made so that it was 'manifestly unjust and inequitable' to increase the compensation awarded by any amount under the uplift provisions: see 15.10 below).

Where: (a) a party has reasonable grounds to believe that commencing a statutory procedure or complying with a requirement in that procedure would result in a significant threat to himself, his property, or any other person or property, or (b) a party has been subjected to harassment and has reasonable grounds to believe that commencing the procedure or complying with the subsequent requirement would result in his being subjected to further harassment, then the relevant procedure if not yet commenced does not apply, and if commenced, the parties are deemed to have complied with it: *reg 11(1), (2)* and *(3)(a)* and *(b)*. Harassment for these purposes is defined in *reg 11(4)*. If, however, it is the behaviour of one of the parties which constitutes the harassment or threat to person or property under *reg 11(3)(a)* or *(b)*, then that party will be treated as having failed to comply with the relevant procedure: *reg 12(3)* and *(4)*.

There is no requirement to comply with a statutory procedure where it is not possible to comply without disclosing information where such disclosure would be contrary to the interests of national security: *reg 16*.

If one party fails to comply with a requirement under the statutory procedure, the non-completion of the procedure will be attributed to that party and neither party will be under any obligation to comply further with the procedure: *reg 12(1)*.

15.8   EFFECTS OF NON-COMPLIANCE

Failure to comply with a statutory procedure does not give an employee the right to raise a free-standing complaint before a Tribunal: see *Scott-Davies v Redgate Medical Services* [2007] ICR 348 . There are three main consequences for employers and employees if they fail to comply with the statutory disciplinary and grievance procedures: (a) failure to comply with the dismissal and disciplinary procedure will render a dismissal automatically unfair; (b) failure to comply with the dismissal and disciplinary or grievance procedure may lead to an increase or reduction in compensation, and (c) a failure by an employee to raise a grievance with his employer before presenting a complaint to the Tribunal about the same subject matter may bar him from presenting that complaint.

15.9 Dispute Resolution

15.9 Automatically unfair dismissal

Section 98A(1) of *ERA 1996*, inserted by *EA 2002*, provides that an employee (with the requisite 1 year's qualifying service) is automatically unfairly dismissed if the dismissal or disciplinary procedure applies to the dismissal, that procedure has not been completed, and the non-completion is wholly or mainly attributable to failure by the employer to comply with its requirements. The EAT held in *A to B Travel Ltd v Kennedy* (EAT/0341/06:11 October 2006) that the fact that there has been a failure in relation to a distinct disciplinary step, such as suspension without pay, ought not to have any bearing on the question of whether the statutory procedure has been completed in relation to the dismissal itself. See further UNFAIR DISMISSAL -I, II, III (53, 54, 55).

15.10 Increase or reduction in compensation

Where a statutory procedure is not completed wholly or mainly because the employee has failed to comply with it or to exercise a right of appeal under it, and he brings a claim before a Tribunal (within the category of claims listed in *EA 2002, Sch 3*) concerning a matter to which the procedure would have applied, then the Tribunal must reduce the employee's compensation by a minimum of 10%, and may, if it considers it just and equitable, reduce his compensation by a maximum of 50%: *EA 2002 , s 31(2)*. Conversely, where the failure to complete the procedure is wholly or mainly due to the failure of the employer, the Tribunal must increase the compensation payable to the employee by 10%, and may increase it on just and equitable grounds by up to 50%: *EA 2002, s 31(3)*. Although *s 31(2)* and *(3)* impose a duty on the Tribunal to reduce or increase compensation by 10%, the Tribunal may make a smaller or no reduction or increase if there are exceptional circumstances which would make a 10% increase or reduction unjust or inequitable: *s 31(4)*. In *Bainbridge v Redcar and Cleveland Borough Council; Redcar and Cleveland Borough Council v Williams* (EAT 0424/06;0031/07: 31 January 2007) the EAT held that it was indeed unjust and inequitable to increase any award in respect of a number of claims where the terms of a conditional fee agreement and an earlier unsuccessful attempt to resolve matters rendered pointless the holding of grievance meetings under stage 2 of the standard procedure.

Where the employer is at fault for non-compliance with the statutory procedures the degree of the employer's culpability is likely to be of high significance in determining the appropriate size of the uplift given that the underlying purpose of these provisions has been held to be 'more penal than compensatory in nature' (see *Metrobus Ltd v Cook* (EAT/0490/06: 9 January 2007). That said, in the context of an unfair dismissal claim the effect of any potential uplift of an award to a claimant could be limited by virtue of the fact that the uplift to a compensatory award, under *s 31* of *EA 2002*, is to be applied before the application of any deduction under the contributory fault provision governing the compensatory award: *ss 124A, 123(6) ERA 1996* (see *Ingram v Bristol Street Parts* (EAT/0601/06/CEA; 23 April 2007). See further UNFAIR DISMISSAL-III (55).

The basic award in an unfair dismissal claim is excluded from the effect of the *s 31* uplift by virtue of *s 124A ERA 1996* (see *Alexander v Bridgen Enterprises Ltd* [2006] IRLR 422), although where a dismissal is automatically unfair under *s 98A(1) ERA 1996*, and the amount of the basic award, before any reduction under *ERA 1996, s 122(3A)* or *(4)* is less than four weeks' pay, the Tribunal will increase the basic award to four weeks' pay, unless the increase would result in injustice to the employer (*ERA 1996, s 120(1A)* and (*1B*)) (see *Ingram v Bristol Street Parts* (EAT/0601/06/CEA: 23 April 2007). See further UNFAIR DISMISSAL-III (55).

15.11 **Grievance procedures: right to bring tribunal proceedings**

Section 32 of the *2002 Act* provides that an employee shall not present (ie is barred from presenting) a complaint to a tribunal if:

(*a*)   he has failed to lodge a grievance about the subject matter of the complaint under the statutory grievance procedures (*s 32(2)*);

(*b*)   he has lodged such a grievance, but has done so without allowing 28 days to pass before presenting his complaint to the Tribunal (*s 32(3)*). The requirement is for 28 clear days to elapse between a grievance and presentation of a claim: see *The Basingstoke Press Ltd (In Administration) v Clarke* (EAT/0375/06CEA and 0376/06/CEA: 9 January 2007); or

(*c*)   he has lodged such a grievance, but he has done so more than one month after the end of the original time limit for making a complaint (*s 32(4)*); the term 'original time limit' in this context refers to the relevant statutory time limit *including* any provision for extension of time, for example on just and equitable grounds: *Bupa Care Homes Ltd v Cann* [2006] IRLR 248.

The categories of complaint to which *s 32* applies are set out in *Sch 4* and include most complaints which the Tribunal has jurisdiction to determine. Note that there is no obligation to lodge a grievance about breach of contract for the purposes of *s 32* (because such claims are not listed in *EA 2002, Sch 4*). (However, the increase or decrease in compensation provisions may apply in respect of a breach of contract claim since such claims are listed in *EA 2002, Sch 3*)

There is no obligation to lodge a grievance about an express dismissal, because the grievance procedures do not apply to complaints about 'dismissal', where this includes any termination by the employment of an employment contract with or without notice and the expiry of a limited term contract (see *Dispute Resolution Regulations, reg 6(5)* and *reg 2(1)*; there is, however, an obligation to lodge a grievance about a constructive unfair dismissal (or indeed a constructive dismissal under discrimination legislation), because the exception in *reg 6(5)* does not apply to constructive dismissals (see, definition of 'dismissal' in *reg 2(1)* and see, *Pinkus v Crime Reduction Initiative* (EAT 0528–9/06: 31 January 2007) and *Brock v Minerva Dental Ltd* [2007] ICR 917 in respect of constructive unfair dismissal claims).

The question of what constitutes a valid grievance under the statutory procedures is considered at 15.4 above. In order to show that a grievance has been lodged 'about the subject matter of the complaint' under *s 32* it is necessary to show that the grievance in question relates to the subsequent claim, and the claim relates to the earlier grievance. Thus, for example, the fact that an employee may have lodged a grievance about holiday pay will not entitle him subsequently to bring a complaint of race discrimination. In *Shergold v Fieldway Medical Centre* [2006] IRLR 76 the EAT held that the grievance need not be identical with the subsequent claim – which may involve a much lengthier exposition, a different description, or vary in its particulars; provided that the general nature of the grievance in writing is substantially the same as the matter which then forms the subject matter of the claim, that is sufficient. See further *Canary Wharf Management v Edebi* [2006] IRLR 416.

The prohibition on presenting a claim in the circumstances set out in *s 32* goes to the jurisdiction of the Employment Tribunal, with the result that if the section applies, a Tribunal will have no discretion to permit a claim to proceed, for example on the ground of the overriding interest of justice: *Canary Wharf v Edebi* [2006] IRLR 416. That said, *s 32(6)* of the *EA 2002* provides that an Employment Tribunal shall be prevented from considering a complaint presented in breach of *s 32(2)* to *(4)* of the *Act* only if the breach is apparent to the tribunal from the information supplied to it by the employee in connection with the bringing of the proceedings, or the tribunal is satisfied of the breach as a result of the employer raising the issue of compliance in accordance with the ET rules of procedure (see *Petia Chickerova v Holovachuk* (EAT/0016/07/ZT: 21 February 2007). This raises the question as to whether or not a respondent employer might take the point in the event that it failed to do so in the response form. The EAT held in *Holc-Gale v Makers UK Ltd* [2006] ICR 462 that it was permissible for an ET to consider the point when raised by the respondent employer for the first time at a Case Management Discussion, notwithstanding the terms of *s 32(6)*, since it went to the Tribunal's jurisdiction and given that no point was taken that no formal application for leave to amend the response was made. Thus, it would seem to follow that in the event that a *s 32* point is not taken or is conceded in the response form, then the appropriate course for a respondent employer is to raise the matter by way of an application to amend the response (see *DMC Business Machines plc v Plummer* (EAT 0381/06: 13 October 2006).

The terms of *s 32* do not allow for a stay of a claim pending compliance with the requisite procedural steps under that provision (see *London Borough of Hounslow v Miller* (EAT/0645/06/DA: 20 March 2007).

The EAT held in *Bisset v Martins and Castlehill Housing Association Ltd* (EAT/0022/06: 18 August 2006) that the Dispute Resolution Regulations do not require grievances to be raised about fellow employees in order to enable a claim, such as a disability or other discrimination claim, to be brought against those employees. This was questioned by the EAT in *obiter* remarks in *London Borough of Lambeth v Corlett* [2007] ICR 88. However, the EAT in *Odoemerlam v The Whittington Hospital NHS Trust* (EAT/0016/06: 6 February 2007) agreed with the view expressed in *Bisset* (albeit for different reasons) that the statutory grievance procedures did not apply to claims against employees so that a failure to raise a grievance against a fellow employee would not block a claim against the employee.

15.12 **TIME LIMITS**

In terms of the timing of the grievance, there is no maximum time limit prior to the lodging of the claim to the Tribunal in which the grievance must have been raised. However, the act of raising a complaint months or years prior to lodging the Tribunal claim will not necessarily constitute the appropriate raising of the grievance. The grievance must be extant. If it can no longer properly be said to be an outstanding grievance, perhaps because it was apparently satisfactorily dealt with or because the employee has not pursued it in circumstances where it may properly be inferred that he no longer wishes to have it determined, then it will be necessary for the employee to raise the complaint again in written form: see, *Edebi v Canary Wharf Management Ltd* [2006] IRLR 416.

15.13 The normal time limits for lodging complaints are extended in certain circumstances where a statutory dismissal and disciplinary or grievance procedure applies. 'Normal time limit' is defined to mean the time limit which applies, disregarding any power or discretion the tribunal may have to extend time (e g on just and equitable grounds, or on grounds that it was not reasonably practicable to present a claim in time): see *reg 15(5)*.

Where one of the dismissal and disciplinary procedures applies, the normal time limit is extended by three months (beginning with the day after the day on which it would otherwise have expired) where: (a) an employee presents a complaint to a tribunal after the expiry of the normal time limit, and (b) he had reasonable grounds for believing when the time limit expired that a dismissal or disciplinary procedure, whether statutory or otherwise, was being followed in respect of matters that included the substance of the tribunal complaint: *reg 15(1)(a)* and (2). The issue under these provisions is obviously whether or not the employee reasonably held the necessary belief at the date when the normal time limit expired (see *Arnold Clark Automobiles Ltd v Glass* (EAT/0095/06/MT: 7 June 2007)). It was held by the EAT in *Piscitellia v Zilli Fish Ltd* (EAT/0638/05: 21 December 2005) that where an employer had no appeal procedure and upon the employee lodging an appeal the employer refused to entertain it, then the employee would not have reasonable grounds for believing that a disciplinary process was being followed so that a claim would have to be presented within the ordinary three month limitation period. However, the EAT in *Harris v Towergate London Market Ltd* (EAT/0090/07/DM: 21 March 2007) held that where an employee had not appealed against her redundancy dismissal under the employer's internal procedure but did have a meeting with her employer at which she questioned her dismissal and then, on the basis of incorrect advice from a trade union official, presented a written grievance complaint within the standard three months limitation period, the Employment Tribunal should, on the facts of the case, have found that she had reasonable grounds for believing that a dismissal process was being followed so as to extend time under *reg 15(1)(a)* and (2). (See also *Wong v Codemasters Software Company Ltd* (EAT/0639/06/DA: 14 December 2006.)

Where one of the grievance procedures applies, the normal time limit is extended by three months (beginning with the day after the day on which it would otherwise have expired) if the employee presents a complaint to the tribunal within the normal time limit, but in circumstances where *s 32(2)* or (3) of *EA 2002* does not permit him to present his complaint (ie he has failed first to lodge a grievance, or has lodged one without allowing 28 days to pass before presenting his complaint, see 15.10 above) (*reg 15(1)(b)* and *15(3)(a)*). Time for presentation of a complaint to the tribunal is also extended by three months (beginning with the day after the day on which it would otherwise have expired) if the employee lodges a grievance with his employer within the normal time limit (*reg 15(1)(b)* and *15(3)(b)*).

The statutory extension of time under *reg 15(1)(a)* or (b) of the *Dispute Resolution Regulations* means 3 months and not 3 months less a day: see *Singh (t/a Rainbow International) v Taylor* (EAT/0183/06/MAA: 27 June 2006). Thus, on the facts of the *Singh* case, where the normal time limit expired on 19 September 2005, time was extended until 20 December 2005 and a claim lodged by that date, that is, on 20 December 2005, was within time.

For the purposes of the extension of time afforded by *reg 15 (1)(b)* and *(3)(b)* of the *Dispute Resolution Regulations*, an employee's grievance is to be treated as sent within the normal time limit even if it is sent before the effective date of termination or other date from which time starts to run: see *London Borough of Lewisham v Colbourne* (EAT/0339/06: 15 November 2006 and *HM Prison Service v Dr Barua* [2007] IRLR 4.

15.14 TRANSITIONAL PROVISIONS

The Dispute Resolution Regulations apply in relation to dismissal and relevant disciplinary action where the employer first contemplates dismissing or taking such action against the employee after the Regulations came into force on 1 October 2004: *reg 18*. The test of whether the employer contemplated dismissal before 1 October 2004 (so as to disapply the *Regulations*) is a subjective one: see *Madhewoo v NHS Trust Direct* (EAT/0030/06/LA: 1 March 2006). The EAT held in *Patel v Clemence Hoare Cummings* (EAT 0214/06: 23 June 2006) that the disciplinary and dismissal procedure did not apply to an employee's redundancy dismissal because, although he did not receive notice of dismissal until 6 October 2004, the employer had first contemplated dismissing him on 13 September 2004. Further, the *Regulations* apply in relation to grievances where the action about which the employee complains occurs or continues after 1 October 2004, except where the action continues after this date and the employee raised a grievance about the action with the employer before 1 October 2004: *reg 18*. For the purposes of *reg 18* of the *Dispute Resolution Regulations*, the question whether the action of which an employee was complaining in a grievance letter was a single occurrence or continued over a period of time is not dissimilar from the 'continuing act' question which Tribunals have to decide under the time limitation provisions of the discrimination legislation: see *Odoemelam v The Whittington Hospital* (EAT/0016/06: 6 February 2007).

16   Education and Training

16.1   An employer has no obligation at common law to provide facilities for the education and training of his employees unless they are engaged under a contract of apprenticeship or their contract of employment provides otherwise. Similarly he does not have to allow employees time off for day-release or sandwich courses. However, with effect from 1 September 1999, young persons in employment have the right to take time off from work in order to undertake study or training leading to a 'relevant qualification' (see 4.7 CHILDREN AND YOUNG PERSONS).

In addition, an employer should not ask his employee to carry out a task requiring a special skill unless he has ensured that the employee possesses those skills or unless the employer has undertaken to train the employee. (If he does so and an accident occurs he may be liable, see 27.5–27.7 HEALTH AND SAFETY AT WORK – I.) For the income tax treatment of training costs, see *ICTA 1988, s 588*.

Various bodies and schemes have been created by the Government to encourage the education and training of employees and those seeking employment. Changes have occurred frequently in recent years. The most notable recent developments are the integration of regional Government offices in 1994, and the merger in July 1995 of the Department for Education ('DFE') with the employment and training functions of the Department of Employment, to become the Department for Education and Employment ('DfEE'). After the general election of June 2001, there was a further reorganisation whereby the education and skills responsibilities of the DfEE were transferred to the Department of Education and Skills ('DfES'), with the employment responsibilities of the DfEE being transferred to a new Department of Work and Pensions ('DWP').

Prior to this, in April 1990 a nationwide system of Training and Enterprise Councils was established in England and Wales; their Scottish equivalents are known as Local Enterprise Councils. Their remit is to foster economic growth and contribute to the local community they serve. The National Training Task Force was replaced by the National Council for Education and Training Targets ('NACETT') in March 1993. The Labour Government is committed to education and training and has introduced measures such as the 'New Deal' (see 16.6 below) as one of its priorities, as well as setting up the Learning and Skills Council for England, and the National Council for Education and Training for Wales (whose functions have now been transferred to the Welsh Assembly Government – see 16.9 below).

Up-to-date information may be obtained from Job Centres, Careers Offices and the Department for Education and Skills, and the Department of Work and Pensions. The DfES's enquiry point can be contacted as follows: tel: 0870 000 2288; e-mail: info@dfes.gsi.gov.uk. Further information can be obtained from the DfES's website at www.dfes.gov.uk and from the DWP's website at www.dwp.gov.uk (where a facility for sending an e-mail to the DWP's enquiry office is available).

16.2   **APPRENTICESHIPS**

Apprenticeships offer what must be the oldest form of training in skilled trades for young people.

The apprenticeship is normally for a fixed term of years or until a set qualification is achieved, the apprentice, his parent or guardian (if he is a minor), and the employer entering into a written agreement. The agreement will usually be in a form common to all apprenticeships for the trade concerned. In general the apprentice will have time off to attend college and take examinations.

A contract for apprenticeship may not be terminable for misconduct in the same way as an ordinary contract of employment; and in the event of wrongful termination, different principles apply to the assessment of damages (*Dunk v George Waller & Son Ltd* [1970] 2 QB 163).

In *Wallace v C A Roofing Services Ltd* [1996] IRLR 435, Sedley J in the High Court held that a contract of apprenticeship (unlike a contract of employment or training contract) cannot be terminated on the grounds of redundancy, falling short of closure or a fundamental change in the character of the employers' enterprise. He stated that a contract of apprenticeship remains a distinct entity at common law; its first purpose is training, and the execution of work for the employer is secondary. Thus, the ordinary law as to dismissal does not apply. The contract is for a fixed term and is not terminable at will, unlike a contract of employment at common law.

Wallace was applied in *Whitely v Marton Electrical Ltd* [2003] IRLR 197, in which the EAT held that a 'modern apprenticeship agreement', under which an employer agrees to employ an apprentice 'for the duration of the training plan', is different from an ordinary contract of employment and is not terminable on notice. The provision in the agreement requiring the apprentice to comply with the employer's terms and conditions of employment did not mean that the employer's terms as to notice of termination applied to the apprentice. Where any provision of the employer's terms and conditions were inconsistent with those of the agreement, the agreement must prevail because it was plainly the agreement which the parties intended should govern their relationship. However, in *Thorpe v Dul* [2003] ICR 1556, the EAT remitted the case for the employment tribunal to decide, as a question of fact, the legal status of the modern apprenticeship agreement in that case.

The cases referred to above were reviewed by the Court of Appeal in *Flett v Matheson* [2006] IRLR 277. Some eight months after commencing employment at the age of 16, the employee entered into a tripartite individual learning plan (ILP) with the employer and a training provider, which was stated to be carried out under advanced modern apprenticeship arrangements (see also 16.7 below). The employee was subsequently dismissed without notice, and claimed unfair dismissal and/or breach of contract of employment. The EAT held that the employee was employed under a contract of employment but not under a contract of apprenticeship; the employee appealed against the latter finding.

Allowing the appeal, the Court of Appeal held that a modern tripartite apprenticeship arrangement can constitute a common law contract of apprenticeship. In its view, the important issue is the nature and duration of the employer's obligations under the agreement. The fact that part of the training is provided by a third party is not crucial to the analysis of those obligations. In the present case, the ILP had the essential features of an apprenticeship. The contract of employment was varied or overlaid by the ILP, and that variation gave rise to additional obligations on the employer. The individual learning plan was called an 'apprenticeship' and provided for a combination of off and on the job training for a lengthy period. What occurred at the workplace was part of the training. While the employer did not provide the more academic part of the training, he was required to give the apprentice time off to obtain it and to fund the cost of attendance at classes. It was not open to the employer to dismiss on reasonable notice, subject to making reasonable efforts to find another employer willing and able to continue the training. If attempts to find another employer failed, the obligations on the employer remained and, save in certain specified circumstances, the apprentice could not be dismissed within the period of training.

If they satisfy the necessary qualifying conditions, apprentices enjoy the statutory employment protection rights (*Employment Rights Act 1996, s 230(2); Sex Discrimination Act 1975, s 82(1); Race Relations Act 1976, s 78(1); Disability Discrimination Act 1995, s 68(1)*).

The Employment Appeal Tribunal, on the basis of the evidence before it that the Law Society recommended the operation of a dual system whereby a clerk was articled to an individual partner in a firm of solicitors under a deed of articles but was employed by the firm under a contract of employment, held that an articled clerk was engaged under such a system (*Oliver v J P Malnick & Co* [1983] ICR 708).

In *Edmonds v Lawson* [2000] IRLR 391, the Court of Appeal (allowing an appeal from Sullivan J: [2000] IRLR 18) held that, although a pupil barrister was employed under a contract by the set of barristers' chambers where she was taken on as a pupil, the contract was not a contract of apprenticeship or an equivalent contract. The pupil was, therefore, not a 'worker' for the purposes of the *National Minimum Wage Act 1998*, and was not entitled to be paid the national minimum wage ('NMW'). (For the NMW, see generally 34.9 PAY – I, where it is also noted that workers under 26 years of age employed on the first 12 months of a contract of apprenticeship do not qualify for the NMW, by virtue of the *National Minimum Wage Regulations 1999* (*SI 1999/584), reg 12(2).*)

16.3 **RECOVERY OF TRAINING COSTS**

Problems are sometimes encountered in practice where an employer expends significant sums of money on training an employee, for example, by sending him on outside courses, and the employee then leaves his job shortly afterwards, in some instances without giving proper notice.

The wasted training costs will not usually be recoverable in the absence of an express agreement to that effect. That is so even if the employee leaves without giving proper notice, because the costs would have been incurred whether or not that breach of contract had occurred.

An agreement for the repayment of training costs in the event of an early departure will have to be very carefully drafted in order to be enforceable. If it applies where there is a breach of contract by the employee, it may be struck down as a 'penalty clause' unless it can be said to represent a genuine pre-estimate of loss suffered by the employer (*Giraud UK Ltd v Smith* [2000] IRLR 763). This will usually mean, for example, that the proportion of the costs to be repaid must depend upon how long the employee remains after being trained (a clause meeting that requirement was upheld in *Neil v Strathclyde Regional Council* [1984] IRLR 14). Another possible argument against an agreement to repay training costs is that it is in restraint of trade, although the contention in *Neil* that the clause in that case was also illegal and unenforceable as an unlawful restrictive covenant or, alternatively, as being contrary to public policy because it was an undue restraint on the employee's liberty, was rejected at first instance (*Strathclyde Regional Council v Neil* [1984] IRLR 11; the point was not pursued on appeal).

16.4   **INDUSTRIAL TRAINING BOARDS**

Industrial Training Boards were established by the Secretary of State for Employment under the *Industrial Training Act 1982* ('*ITA 1982*'), as amended (most recently by *EA 1989*), which repealed and replaced the *Industrial Training Act 1964*, as amended. The Boards' role is to ensure that the quantity and quality of training are adequate to meet the needs of the industries for which they are established, and they may:

(*a*)   provide or secure the provision of such courses and other facilities (which may include residential accommodation) for the training of those persons as the Board considers adequate, having regard to any alternative courses or facilities available;

(*b*)   approve alternative courses and facilities;

(*c*)   publish recommendations regarding the length and nature of courses and standards to be attained in training;

(*d*)   make tests for ascertaining the standards recommended and award certificates of the attainment of those standards;

(*e*)   assist persons in finding facilities for being trained for employment in the industry;

(*f*)   carry out, or assist others to carry out, research into any matter relating to training for employment in the industry; and

(*g*)   provide advice about training connected with the industry.

(*ITA 1982, s 5(1)*.)

An Industrial Training Board may enter into contracts of service or apprenticeship with persons who intend to be employed in the industry and to attend courses or avail themselves of other facilities provided or approved by the Board (*ITA 1982, s 5(2)*).

Industrial Training Boards may provide advice on training. They may also:

(i)   pay maintenance and travelling allowances to persons attending courses provided or approved by the Board;

(ii)   make grants or loans to persons providing courses or other facilities approved by the Board, to persons who make studies for the purpose of providing such courses or facilities, and to persons who maintain arrangements to provide such courses or facilities which are not for the time being in use;

(iii)   pay fees to persons providing post-school education in respect of persons who receive it in association with their training in courses provided or approved by the Board; and

(iv)   make payments to persons in connection with arrangements under which they or employees of theirs make use of courses or other facilities provided or approved by the Board.

(*ITA 1982, s 5(4)*.)

An Industrial Training Board ('ITB') may make grants to persons in connection with arrangements under which they or employees of theirs make use of courses or other facilities provided or approved by the Board. Forms are available from the relevant Industrial Training Board for the employer to provide the information enabling him to claim such a grant (*ITA 1982, s 5(4)(d)*).

An Industrial Training Board, with the approval of the Secretary of State, may require employers in the industry to furnish returns and other information, to keep certain records and to produce them for examination by the Board (*ITA 1982, s 6(1)*). Penalties may be imposed for the infringement of any of these provisions. Penalties also exist for knowingly or recklessly furnishing false records or information.

Two statutory Boards remain: the Construction Industry Training Board ('CITB') and the Engineering Construction Industry Training Board ('ECITB').

Provision is made for the imposition of a levy from time to time on employers in the industry, for the purpose of raising money towards meeting the expenses of each Board (*ITA 1982, s 11*). A levy is imposed by means of a 'levy order' made by the Secretary of State. The most recent levy orders took effect on 1 March 2007 (*Industrial Training Levy (Construction Industry Training Board) Order 2007 (SI 2007/607)* and *Industrial Training Levy (Engineering Construction Industry Training Board) Order 2007 (SI 2007/609)*).

Where ITBs have been abolished, their place has been taken by independent employer-led Industry Training Organisations ('ITOs'). ITOs are now having to meet searching new criteria, which will result in a smaller number of more effective and strategic bodies. Those who meet the criteria will be known as National Training Organisations.

16.5 SERVICES FOR SCHOOL-LEAVERS

The *Trade Union Reform and Employment Rights Act 1993* substituted new *ss 8–10A* in the *Employment and Training Act 1973* so as to place a duty on the Secretary of State to secure the provision of careers guidance and placing services ('relevant services') for people attending schools and colleges. The Secretary of State is also given power to arrange for the provision of relevant services for other people, and may direct local education authorities to provide (or arrange for the provision of) relevant services. The *1973 Act* requires the providers of relevant services to provide them in accordance with the directions given by the Secretary of State. The Chief Inspector of Education, Children's Services and Skills in England must inspect and report on the provision of services in England in pursuance of *s 8* or *s 9* by any person or institution, when requested to do so by the Secretary of State; he may also undertake other inspections of the provision of those services as he thinks fit. However, any such inspection may not relate to services provided for persons who are over 20 years old. (*ETA 1973, s 10B*, inserted by the *Learning and Skills Act 2000* and amended by the *Education Act 2005* and the *Education and Inspections Act 2006*).

16.6 NEW DEAL

The Government has introduced a New Deal, which is the collective name for a number of schemes to assist people who are seeking employment. The New Deal is broadly divided into the following categories:

(*a*)   New Deal for Young People (for 18–24 year-olds);

(*b*)   New Deal 25 Plus (for persons aged 25 or over);

(*c*)   New Deal for Lone Parents;

(*d*)   New Deal for Disabled People;

(*e*)   New Deal for Partners; and

(*f*)   New Deal 50 Plus (for persons aged 50 or over).

In addition, there is a New Deal for Musicians, which is intended to help aspiring unemployed musicians into a sustainable career in the music industry; it is also part of New Deal for Young People and New Deal 25 Plus.

Details of each of these categories are available on the Jobcentre Plus website (www.jobcentreplus.gov.uk).

16.7 WORK-BASED TRAINING FOR YOUNG PEOPLE

Work-based training opportunities for young people are currently provided through various types of apprenticeships (formerly known as Foundation Modern Apprenticeships and Advanced Modern Apprenticeships, and now known as Apprenticeships and Advanced Apprenticeships), and other training initiatives. Both types of apprenticeship are aimed at young people aged 16 to 24, and involve working and training with an employer, and studying for other qualifications with a training provider. An apprenticeship commenced before a person's 25th birthday may be completed.

Local Learning and Skills Councils in England and DELLS in Wales (see 16.9 below) (and Local Enterprise Companies in Scotland) are responsible for delivery of training through their network of training providers. Trainees can have employed status or non-employed status. Employed status trainees receive a wage from their employer whilst non-employed status trainees receive a training allowance. The minimum training allowance is £30 per week for 16-year-olds, and £35 per week for those aged 17 and over. Employers are free to top up this allowance and many choose to do so. For further information regarding apprenticeships, see www.apprenticeships.org.uk.

For the purposes of health and safety legislation, trainees are treated as the employees of the person whose undertaking is providing training (*Health and Safety (Training for Employment) Regulations 1990 (SI 1990/1380)*). For the application of discrimination laws see DISCRIMINATION AND EQUAL OPPORTUNITIES – I, II, III (12, 13, 14); an 'Equal Opportunities Toolkit' has also been produced for use in conjunction with training for young people.

Further information about the opportunities being planned for any particular area may be obtained from the local Learning and Skills Council or (in Wales) from DELLS (see 16.9 below).

16.8 WORK-BASED LEARNING FOR ADULTS

Work-based Training for Adults (now renamed Work-based Learning for Adults) replaced Training for Work in England and Wales in April 1998. Work-based Learning for Adults (WBLA) is delivered by Learning and Skills Councils in England and DELLS in Wales (see 15.9 below) (and Local Enterprise Companies in Scotland, where the scheme is known as Training for Work (TFW)). The objective of Work-based Learning for Adults is to help long-term unemployed people aged over 25 (although certain younger people are eligible) to improve their employability and chances of sustained employment through training and/or work experience.

Each person joining WBLA or TFW agrees a training plan with the training provider. This contains details of the individual programme to be followed, which may include job-specific training, actual work experience, working towards a

National Vocational Qualification (NVQ) (or, in Scotland, a Scottish Vocational Qualification (SVQ)), or a mixture of all these. Participants receive a weekly allowance equivalent to their former benefit entitlement plus £10. They may also receive help towards travel expenses and childcare costs. For further details, see www.direct.gov.uk.

16.9   LEARNING AND SKILLS COUNCIL, AND DELLS

The *Learning and Skills Act 2000* received Royal Assent in July 2000, enabling the Government to begin establishing the new Learning and Skills Council (LSC) in England. (In Wales, the equivalent body, also established by the *Learning and Skills Act 2000*, was the National Council for Education and Training for Wales, known as Education and Learning Wales (ELWa), but with effect from 1 April 2006 (see *SI 2005/3238*) the Council was abolished and its functions transferred to the Welsh Assembly Government's Department for Education and Lifelong Learning and Skills (DELLS).)

In England, the LSC co-ordinates, promotes and plans all post-16 education and training below higher education. It became a legal entity in September 2000, and became fully operational from April 2001. It comprises a national office (based in Coventry) and nine regional offices. From April 2002, it took over the responsibilities of over 200 separate funding bodies across four different sectors. Further information about the LSC can be found on its website: www.lsc.gov.uk. Another relevant service is *learndirect*, which is a Government-sponsored initiative in flexible learning that provides courses (mainly on-line) and information through its network of learning centres; for further information, see www.learndirect-.co.uk. See also *nextstep*, which provides face-to-face information and advice to adults over 20 years old who wish to earn new skills, gain new qualifications, or retrain; further information can be found on its website, www.nextstep.org.uk.

For further details on post-16 education and training in Wales, see http:// new.wales.gov.uk/topics/educationandskills.

17   Employee, Self-Employed or Worker?

Cross-reference. See also CONTRACT OF EMPLOYMENT (8).

17.1   The prime focus of this chapter is the distinction between who is an employee and who is self-employed. This was described in *Montgomery v Johnson Underwood* [2001] IRLR 269, para 1 as a 'troublesome question'. The difference between an employee and a self-employed person is of great importance. The legal rights enjoyed by each differ in many ways. For example, an employee will enjoy many of the statutory employment protection rights discussed elsewhere in this book if he meets the necessary qualifying requirements. In particular, it is only employees who are entitled to brings claims of unfair dismissal or to recover redundancy payments.

Different treatment by the tax authorities is another important distinction. An employee's earnings are liable to tax under *Schedule E* to the *Income and Corporation Taxes Act 1988*, and tax is deducted under the PAYE system, whereas a self-employed person is liable to tax under *Schedule D*. The Inland Revenue publishes a booklet IR 56/N139 'Employed or Self-employed?'.

The question of whether a person is an employee or self-employed is determined by reference to the contract under which he works – is it a contract of employment or a contract 'for services'?

However, it is not necessary to be an employee in the legal sense discussed below in order to enjoy all statutory rights. Many statutory provisions, in particular those enacted in more recent years, either use a statutory definition of employment which is wider than being employed under a contract of service, or they confer protection on a class of person called 'workers'.

The *Equal Pay Act 1970, Sex Discrimination Act 1975, Race Relations Act 1976, Disability Discrimination Act 1995, Employment Equality (Religion or Belief) Regulations 2003* and *Employment Equality (Sexual Orientation) Regulations 2003* define employment as including not only work under a contract of service but also a contract 'personally to execute any work ...'.

The provisions of the Employment Rights Act prohibiting unlawful deductions from wages applies to 'workers' who are defined to include those employed under a contract of service but also any contract

> 'whereby the individual undertakes to do or perform personally any work or services for another party to the contracts whose status is not by virtue of the contract that of a client or customer of any profession or business undertaking carried on by the individual'

(*ERA s 230*).

The provisions of *ERA* dealing with protected disclosure apply to workers as so defined. There is also an extended definition of worker in *s 43K*.

Other legislation which applies to workers as defined above includes the *National Minimum Wage Act 1998* and the *Working Time Regulations 1998*.

There are therefore many occasions when it will be necessary to decide whether a person is a worker, even if not an employee.

This chapter will first consider the legal definition of employee before dealing with the concept of a 'worker'.

17.2   CONTRACT OF SERVICE AND CONTRACT OF EMPLOYMENT

The terms 'contract of service' and 'contract of employment' are identical in meaning. The former is the more archaic term which was used when the parties to the contract were known as 'master' and 'servant'. The term 'contract of employment' for the purposes of *ERA 1996* includes a contract of apprenticeship (*ERA 1996, s 230(2)*).

17.3   DISTINGUISHING A CONTRACT OF EMPLOYMENT FROM A CONTRACT FOR SERVICES

The question of who is an employee has proved to be a difficult and much litigated one. It is necessary to determine which workers are employees for a number of reasons. For example, many of the employment protection rights apply only to those employed under a contract of employment. Also, principals are vicariously liable for the acts of their employees but not for the acts of independent contractors hired by them.

Thus, the issue in law is how to distinguish between a *contract of employment* (also known as a *contract of service*) on the one hand, and a *contract for services* on the other. Some elements of the nature of the distinction between the two types of contract emerge from their names. Under a contract *of* service, a person agrees to serve another. Under a contract *for* services, a person agrees to provide certain services to another.

The starting point is to establish that there is a contract at all between the alleged employer and alleged employee. This may sound like stating the obvious, but there are contexts in which the analysis of the contracts will require some thought. For example, when a person works for another through an employment agency, there will usually be two contracts – between the agency and the worker and between the agency and the agency's client – the business for which the worker carries out his work. There will not ordinarily be an express contract between the worker and the client. In the absence of a contract between worker and client, the worker cannot be an employee of the client: *Hewlett Packard Ltd v O'Murphy* [2002] IRLR 4. The effect of this is that the worker has no employment protection rights as against the client business for which he or she works. This has been recognised in a number of cases to be unsatisfactory. However, it has also been held that even if there is no express contract between the worker and the client of the agency, it may be possible to *imply* a contract between those persons through their conduct. Thus if in fact the same person consistently works for and under the direction of the client of an employment business, it may be possible to imply a contract between the worker and the end client. See *Franks v Reuters Ltd* [2004] EWCA Civ 417, [2003] ICR 1166; *Dacas v Brook Street Bureau (UK) Ltd* [2004] EWCA Civ 217, [2004] IRLR 358; *Cable & Wireless plc v Muscat* [2006] EWCA Civ 220; and *James v London Borough of Greenwich* [2007] IRLR 168. The fact that a person has worked for another through an agency does not compel the conclusion that there is an implied contract. But such a contract is a possibility that must be considered. The *Muscat* case emphasises that a contract can be implied only where it is necessary to do so in order to give business efficacy to the arrangements.

Once the existence of a contract is established, the next question is whether the contract is a contract of employment or of some other sort. There are three elements which must be present in every contract of employment. These form the irreducible core of the contract of employment without which a contract cannot be regarded as a contract of employment:

(*a*)   the contract must impose an obligation on a person to provide work personally;

(*b*)   there must be a mutuality of obligation between employer and employee; and

(*c*)   the worker must expressly or impliedly agree to be subject to the control of the person for whom he works to a sufficient degree, to make that person master.

If any of these elements is not present, the contract cannot be a contract of employment. If each element is present, the contract may be a contract of employment. Whether or not it is will depend on an assessment of all the other circumstances.

Dealing with those elements which must be present in order for a contract to be a contract of employment, the first – that the person must be obliged to provide work personally – was made clear in *Express and Echo Publications Ltd v Tanton* [1999] IRLR 367. In that case, the contract provided that if the worker was unable or unwilling to do the work personally, he had to provide a substitute. The Court of Appeal held that the power to send a substitute meant that this could not be a contract of employment. The irreducible minimum of a contract of employment was an obligation on the worker to provide his services personally. The obligation to undertake work personally does not cease to exist where there is a power to send a substitute only where the worker is *unable* to do the work: *James v Redcats (Brands) Ltd* [2007] IRLR 296. The point about *Tanton* was that the worker could send a substitute if he did not want to do the work as well as if he could not. But where the employee must do the work personally if he is able, then the requirement of personal obligation is satisfied.

However, where a contract contains a limited power to delegate, that does not lead inescapably to the conclusion that the contract is not a contract of employment: *MacFarlane v Glasgow City Council* [2001] IRLR 7. According to the EAT in *MacFarlane,* the clause in *Tanton* allowing the worker to send a replacement was 'extreme'. The worker in *Tanton* was not under any personal obligation ever to attend work. He was always entitled to send a substitute. In the present case, the worker was entitled to send a replacement only in the event that the worker was unable to attend work. Therefore, the clause was of far more limited effect, and was not sufficient of itself to justify the conclusion that the contract was not a contract of employment.

In *Staffordshire Sentinel Newspapers Ltd v Potter* [2004] IRLR 752, the EAT provided further guidance on the application of *Tanton* and *MacFarlane.* If there is a clear express contractual term which does not impose personal obligations on the individual, effect must be given to that term unless it is a sham or there has, on the facts, been a variation of the contract. In that case what happened in practice is not relevant. Where there is no clear express term, it is necessary to consider both the written terms of the contract and what happened in practice in order to determine what was the true agreement between the parties.

The second requirement – that there be a mutuality of obligations – means that for the entire duration of the contract under consideration, both the employer and the employee must be under legal obligations to one another. Of course, without the presence of an obligation towards another party, there would not be a contract at all. Thus the requirement for mutual obligations is relevant to the question whether there is a contract at all: *Stephenson v Delphi Diesel Systems Ltd* [2003] ICR 471; *Cotswold Developments Construction Ltd v Williams* [2006] IRLR 181. In the ordinary case, the obligations in question will be an obligation on the employee to work and an obligation on the employer to pay for that work. It it may not be necessary in every case for there to be obligations to work and to provide work. It may be sufficient if there is an obligation on the employee to accept and do such work as is offered to him and on the employer to pay the employee for the work which is done and, if there are periods when there is no work for the employee to do, to pay a retainer. In the absence of such a retainer in periods where there is no work to be done, there will be no contract of employment between the parties. The clearest exposition of this principle is to be found in *Clark v Oxfordshire Health Authority* [1998] IRLR 125. However, see also *O'Kelly v Trusthouse Forte* [1983] ICR 728, *Nethermere (St Neots) v Gardiner* [1984] ICR 612 and *Hellyer Bros v McLeod* [1987] ICR 526.

The House of Lords has reiterated that the existence of mutual obligations between the parties is the irreducible minimum of a contract of employment (*Carmichael v National Power plc* [2000] IRLR 43). Hence, in a case where workers were engaged as power station guides on a 'casual as required' basis, there was no contract of employment. There was no obligation on the workers to work. Indeed, they had failed to attend on a number of occasions and had not been disciplined. Further, there was no obligation on the company to provide work.

Where the terms of a contract express negative mutuality of obligations, there cannot be a contract of employment: *Stevedoring and Haulage Services Ltd v Fuller* [2001] EWCA Civ 651, [2001] IRLR 627. In that case, the worker worked under a series of individual contracts, each of which recorded that there was no obligation to offer or accept any further contract. In those circumstances, it was impermissible to imply an over-arching or umbrella contract of employment pursuant to which each individual contract was issued.

The third element – that the employer must have control over the employee – does not mean that work must necessarily be carried out under the employer's actual supervision or control. In a more general sense, it requires that ultimate authority over the employee in the performance of his work resides in the employer, so that the employee is subject to the latter's orders and directions.

The necessity of control derives from the judgment of McKenna J in *Ready Mixed Concrete (South East) Ltd v Minister of Pensions and National Insurance* [1968] 2 QB 497 at 515. McKenna J's remarks on control have been cited with approval in the majority of subsequent important cases dealing with the essential ingredients of an employment contract. The Court of Appeal has re-affirmed that in the absence of sufficient control, there cannot be a contract of employment. What is sufficient control – and whether that means the imposition of a framework within which a person works or direct supervision of the performance of a person's functions – will vary from case to case. But control is a necessary condition of a contract of employment: *Montgomery v Johnson Underwood Ltd* [2001] EWCA Civ 318, [2001] IRLR 269. Once there is mutuality of obligation such that there is a contract, control is relevant for deciding whether the contract is a contract of employment: *Stephenson v Delphi Systems Ltd* [2003] ICR 471.

If the contract does not impose an obligation to provide services personally or if there is no mutuality of obligation throughout the period under consideration, or if there is no control present, then the contract in question cannot be a contract of employment. If all these elements are present, the contract may be one of employment. It will then be necessary to consider the surrounding circumstances to determine the nature of the relationship.

In order to determine, once the irreducible minimum requirements are present, whether the contract is a contract of employment, it is necessary to paint a picture from the accumulation of relevant details. This means not only looking at specific matters, but also standing back and considering the overall picture. This approach derives from *Hall v Lorimer* [1994] ICR 218. Matters which are relevant are too numerous to list. However, they might include payment by wages or salary; whether the worker provides his own equipment; whether he is subject to the employer's disciplinary and grievance procedures; receipt of sick pay or contractual holiday pay; provision of benefits traditionally associated with employment such as a pension scheme, health care or other perquisites; whether the worker is a part of the employer's business; whether there are restrictions on working for others.

Some cases have focused on factors which distinguish the employee from the person in business on his own account. The sorts of details which may be relevant include whether:

(*a*)   he is employed as part of the business of the employer and his work is done as an integral part of that business;

(*b*)   he provides his own equipment;

(*c*)   he hires his own helpers;

(*d*)   he takes a degree of financial risk;

(*e*)   he has responsibility for investment and management; and

(*f*)   how far he has the opportunity of profiting from sound management in performing his task.

This list is derived from *Market Investigations Ltd v Minister of Social Security* [1969] 2 QB 173, *per* Cooke J at 185. In *Lee v Chung* [1990] IRLR 236, the Privy Council said that the best expression of the test was that stated in the *Market Investigations* case: is the person concerned in business on his own account? This test was again applied in *Andrews v King* [1991] ICR 846, where the Vice-Chancellor went on to say that the essence of business was that it was carried on with a view to profit (whereas it was not open to the employee there to make an increased profit from the way in which he carried out his tasks). However, it is not a matter of running through these indicia as if they were an all-purpose checklist. Part of the function of painting the picture is to determine what are the significant details in the instant case and to look at the whole arrangement. Thus, in *Hall v Lorimer*, a vision mixer who supplied no tools, equipment or money to his business and did not hire staff was still self-employed. The key factor was that he was a professional person who worked for a variety of people for short periods and was not dependent on any one paymaster.

However, more recently it has been observed that one cannot reliably rely on a dichotomy between the employed and those on business on their own account. There are categories of person who are not in business on their own account but who are not, for that reason, necessarily to be regarded as employees. In particular, many statutory provisions either contain a wider definition of employee than that which is used in the common law (for example, the discrimination legislation) or extend protection to a category of persons called 'workers' who are not employed but not in business on their own account either: see *James v Redcats (Brands) Ltd* [2007] IRLR 296.

As a general rule, the greater the degree of personal responsibility an individual undertakes in any of the matters set out above, the more likely he is to be considered an independent contractor rather than an employee.

The way in which a person is treated for tax may be relevant but this is not decisive. The tax and employment regimes are separate and do not necessarily have to give the same answer as to a person's status.

In assessing all these factors, it is legitimate in a case where the contract is said to be based partly on oral exchanges and on conduct to consider evidence of the way in which the parties understood their relationship and the way in which they conducted themselves in practice (see *Carmichael v National Power plc* [2000] IRLR 43). However, the conduct of the parties cannot be relied upon for the purpose of implying a term which flatly contradicts its express terms: *Stevedoring and Haulage Services Ltd v Fuller* [2001] EWCA Civ 651, [2001] IRLR 627. In *Stevedoring and Haulage Services*, workers were engaged on terms that specifically negatived mutuality of obligation in that they made it clear that there was no obligation to offer or accept employment beyond the individual engagement which was the subject of the contract. The conduct of the parties (which remained the same throughout several renewals of the contract) could not override those express written terms by creating mutual obligations to offer and to accept work outside the individual engagement.

Where the nature of the relationship between the parties is in doubt or is ambiguous, it is open to the parties, by agreement, to stipulate what the legal situation between them is to be (*Massey v Crown Life Insurance Co Ltd* [1978] ICR 590). However, all the circumstances of the relationship must be considered, and the courts will look behind the parties' intentions, and labels, to ascertain the true nature of the agreement (*Young & Woods Ltd v West* [1980] IRLR 201). Where a person worked for an agency and the tribunal found that there were mutual obligations and considerable control, it was illegitimate to decide that there was no contract of employment on the basis that this is what the parties had originally intended. The label applied by the parties would only be decisive where all the other factors were evenly balanced: *Dacas v Brook Street Bureau (UK) Ltd* [2003] IRLR 190 (on appeal [2004] EWCA Civ 217, [2004] IRLR 358).

It is wrong to say that a person is an employee simply because he is not self-employed. There may also be intermediate categories of worker (*Dacas v Brook Street* [2004] IRLR 358). But to enjoy the statutory rights which apply only to employees (e g to claim unfair dismissal), the person must be an employee.

Note also that a full-time working director of his family firm (who drew fees rather than being paid a salary) was held to be self-employed (*Parsons v Albert J Parsons & Sons Ltd* [1979] ICR 271), as were musicians with a London orchestra (*Winfield v London Philharmonic Orchestra Ltd* [1979] ICR 726) and a sub-postmaster (*Hitchcock v Post Office* [1980] ICR 100, *Wolstenholme v Post Office Ltd* [2003] ICR 546). A police cadet was held not to be an employee or an apprentice (*Wiltshire Police Authority v Wynn* [1980] ICR 649). A Presbyterian minister was held not to be an employee, as was a Sikh priest (*Davies v Presbyterian Church of Wales* [1986] ICR 280; *Singh v Gurdwara* [1990] ICR 309). But in *Percy v Board of National Mission of the Church of Scotland* [2006] ICR 134 a minister of the Church of Scotland was held to be employed within the wider definition of that term in the Sex Discrimination Act. There is no rule of law that a person who provides services via a company cannot be an employee (*Catamaran Cruisers Ltd v Williams* [1994] IRLR 386). It has been held that a volunteer is not an employee because of the absence of consideration moving from the recipient of the volunteer's services. There is no obligation on that party to make payment and, in the absence of payment, there is no consideration and no contract: *Melhuish v Redbridge Citizens' Advice Bureau* [2005] IRLR 419, EAT.

The Court of Appeal considered the status of a modern apprenticeship agreement between a trainee, an employer and a Training and Enterprise Council or some other educational establishment in *Flett v Matheson* [2006] ICR 673. The Court of Appeal overturned the EAT's decision that such an arrangement created a contract of employment between the individual and the employer. The Court held that the purpose of the arrangement was to provide practical aspects of training. The apprentice was to be released from work to attend academic training. The Court approved the distinction which had been drawn between an employment contract and a contract for apprenticeship in *Whitely v Marton Electrical Ltd* [2003] ICR 495. In the event, the Court in *Flett* remitted the matter for the Tribunal to make further findings of fact.

A general practitioner is not employed by a health authority. GPs are under obligations in relation to the nature of the work they undertake. But since these obligations are imposed by statutory instrument and not by contract, those obligations do not make the GP an employee of the health authority: *North Essex Health Authority v David-John* [2004] ICR 112.

There may be contracts which are neither contracts of employment nor contracts for services but which fall into an intermediate category (*Construction Industry Training Board v Labour Force Ltd* [1970] 3 All ER 220; *Ironmonger v Movefield Ltd* [1988] IRLR 461). It is thought that a person who works under such a contract will, for most purposes, be in the same position as one who is self-employed. However, such persons may also be regarded as 'workers' for other statutory purposes such as the Working Time Regulations and the provisions in relation to unlawful deductions of wages.

In *O'Kelly v Trusthouse Forte plc* [1983] ICR 728, the majority of the Court of Appeal held that an appellate court could only interfere with a decision of an employment tribunal on the question of whether an individual was an employee if it could be shown that the employment tribunal had erred in law or reached a perverse conclusion. See also *Lee v Chung* [1990] IRLR 236; *Hall v Lorimer* [1994] ICR 218. However, when the issue whether a person is an employee or self-employed depends on the construction of a written document, this will involve questions of law (*Davies v Presbyterian Church of Wales*) but only to the extent that it appears that the parties intended all the express terms of their contract to be contained in the document. Whether or not that was their intention is a question of fact (*Carmichael v National Power plc* [2000] IRLR 43).

Can a controlling shareholder be an employee? A question sometimes arises as to whether a person who controls the shareholding in the employing enterprise can also be employed by that enterprise. The point is made that a person who can ultimately control whether or not he is dismissed, because he controls the shareholding, cannot be said to be under the control of the employing company. In *Secretary of State for Trade and Industry v Bottrill* [1999] IRLR 326, the Court of Appeal held that there was no rule of law which meant that such a person could not be an employee. It was a question of fact in each case. The court gave instances of factors which would be relevant. That the employee is also the controlling shareholder would be a relevant matter. However, since companies are generally controlled by their boards and not by shareholder voting, it would also be relevant to consider how often the majority shareholder exercised his powers. Was the contract of employment genuine or did it have the appearance of a sham?

If the contract was entered into only when insolvency loomed, that might suggest the latter. Was the company controlled by a board of directors? Was the majority shareholder also a member of that board? How many other directors were there? Was there any provision which precluded the majority shareholder from voting on matters in which he had a personal interest? The Court of Appeal has followed the line established in *Bottrill* in *Sellars Arenascene v Connolly* [2001] EWCA Civ 184, [2001] IRLR 222. The same approach was taken in *Gladwell v Secretary of State for Trade and Industry* [2007] ICR 264.

Specific engagements. When one asks whether a person was employed or self-employed, the question usually concerns the general relationship between the parties to the contract. The question – although rarely framed in these terms – is whether the 'general engagement' between the parties was a contract of employment or a contract for services. Often it will be necessary to consider whether, over a period, a person was an employee. This will be the case, for example, when one is concerned to determine whether a person has sufficient continuity to bring an unfair dismissal claim. However, in some cases it may be relevant to enquire whether a particular or specific engagement was a contract of employment or a contract for services. Thus, for example, in the case of a regular casual worker who is paid only when work is available but who is not paid in times when there is no work, it may be that the general engagement is not a contract of employment because of a lack of mutual obligations. However, it may be that, when the worker does actually work, the relationship is one of employment. Thus, it would be said that the worker was employed for each 'specific engagement' (for an example where the distinction was drawn, see *Clark v Oxfordshire Health Authority* [1998] IRLR 125). The process for analysing whether a specific engagement is a contract of employment is the same as that set out above. However, the focus is on each particular assignment when the worker does actually work and not on the general relationship.

There may be several ways in which it may be relevant to determine whether there was a contract of employment for each specific engagement. For example, the regular casual worker may wish to claim unfair dismissal. Because there is no mutuality of obligations, he cannot establish sufficient continuity of employment by relying on the general relationship. However, if each specific engagement was a contract of employment then it may be that he could establish sufficient continuity by relying on the statutory provisions which allow for gaps in employment to be bridged (see CONTINUOUS EMPLOYMENT (7)). This was the case in *Prater v Cornwall County Council v Prater* [2006] EWCA Civ 102, [2006] ICR 731 where a teacher was employed on a number of assignments. There was no overarching contract of employment because there were no mutual obligations between assignments. But the Court of Appeal held that this was irrelevant to determining the person's status when she was performing an assignment. If the conditions of employment were satisfied for each assignment, then the worker was an employee whilst undertaking them. The question then was whether gaps when there was no contract could be bridged. *James v Redcats (Brands) Ltd* [2007] IRLR 296 also supports the point that a person's status between engagements is irrelevant to that person's status when an assignment is being performed.

An example in the case law where the court focused on the specific engagement is *McMeechan v Secretary of State for Employment* [1997] IRLR 353. The case concerned a person who worked via an employment agency for a number of different companies. The last company for which he worked went into insolvent liquidation without having paid him for his assignment. He made a claim against the Secretary of State in respect of those payments under *ERA 1996, s 182 et seq.*

17.3 Employee, Self-Employed or Worker?

The question before the Court of Appeal was whether the worker could be regarded as an employee of the agency for the purposes of the *specific* engagement in respect of which he was not paid regardless of his status for the purpose of his *general* engagement by the agency. The Court of Appeal held that a person may be an employee for the purposes of specific engagements even though the general relationship between the parties is not one of employer and employee. It is then a question of assessing the person's status when he does in fact turn up for work regardless of the fact that there may be no general obligation on him to do so.

Employment agencies. Where a person is found work by an employment agency, there will be a contract between the worker and the agency (which may or may not be a contract of employment) and a separate contract between the agency and the person to whom the services are provided. But absent a further contract between the worker and the recipient of the services, the worker will not be an employee of that person (see *Costain Building and Civil Engineering Ltd v Smith* [2000] ICR 215, EAT). However, it may be possible to infer a contract between the worker and the recipient of services from the conduct of both those parties: *Dacas v Brook Street Bureau (UK) Ltd* [2004] EWCA Civ 217, [2004] IRLR 358; *Cable & Wireless plc v Muscat* [2006] EWCA Civ 220. In *Royal National Lifeboat Institute v Bushaway* [2005] IRLR 674, the EAT held that a tribunal had been entitled to ignore an entire agreement clause in finding that a person was employed by the client of an agency. See also 47.2 TEMPORARY AND SEASONAL EMPLOYEES).

In *Motorola Ltd v (1) Davidson and (2) Melville Craig* [2001] IRLR 4, the EAT was concerned to consider whether a person taken on by a recruitment agency, Melville Craig, to work for Motorola, was to be regarded as employed by Motorola for the purposes of a complaint of unfair dismissal. The EAT upheld the decision of the tribunal that there was sufficient control by Motorola over Mr Davidson in fact to mean that the relationship was one of employer-employee even though Motorola had no direct legal control over Mr Davidson. It was sufficient that Motorola had indirect control over Mr Davidson in that it could give directions to Melville Craig, including a direction no longer to send Mr Davidson to work for Motorola. Further, at the site, there was a sufficient degree of control in fact. The appeal was unusual in that the only issue argued was that of control. Hence, the case does not lay down any wider propositions about persons engaged by employment agencies becoming employees of the agency's clients. The importance of the case is in the stress which it lays on 'practical aspects of control that fall short of direct legal rights' and the recognition that an employment relationship may be created by a combination of practical control and indirect legal control.

The Court of Appeal has reiterated in *Montgomery v Johnson Underwood Ltd* [2001] IRLR 269 that the essential test to apply in judging whether a person is employed by a recruitment agency (or, indeed, by a hirer) is the existence of irreducible minima of mutual obligation and control. To the extent that Waite LJ in *McMeechan* appeared to reduce mutual obligation and control to mere factors to be taken into account, the absence of which would not necessarily be decisive, Buckley J indicated that he was wrong to do so.

In *Montgomery*, the courts below had already determined that the applicant was not an employee of the hirer (a finding which the applicant did not challenge). The result of the Court of Appeal's finding was that the applicant was held not to be an employee of the respondent agency either, since the agency had little or no control over her. The court indicated its unhappiness with this state of affairs, which left the applicant without a remedy and in a state of legal limbo. However, it stated that the solution to her dilemma lay with Parliament. The government has issued regulations governing the relationships between recruitment bureaux, work-seekers and hirers, *The Conduct of Employment Agencies and Employment Businesses Regulations 2003 (SI 2003/3319)*. The regulations require that recruitment businesses should be required to clarify whether their relation to work-seekers is one of an employment business or an agency (*reg 14*). (The distinction between agencies and employment businesses in the *Regulations* is derived from the *Employment Agencies Act 1973*. Under *s 13* of the *Act*, agencies find workers employment with employers; employment businesses supply persons to act for, or under the control of, other persons.) The Regulations also require that employment businesses must state in any agreement with work-seekers whether the work-seeker is engaged by them under a contract of service or contract for services (*reg 15*).

In *Bunce v Postworth (t/a Skyblue)* [2005] EWCA Civ 557, [2005] IRLR 557, the Court of Appeal held that an agency worker was not an employee of the agency either because of the general relationship between the parties or when the worker was engaged on a specific assignment. There were no mutual obligations as between agency and worker for the purposes of individual assignments nor was there sufficient control

In *Dacas v Brook Street* [2004] IRLR 358, the Court of Appeal analysed the circumstances in which a person provided to another by an agency could be employed by the end user. The analysis was approved in *Cable & Wireless v Muscat* [2006] IRLR 354, [2006] ICR 975. However, the Court of Appeal added the important qualification that a contract could only be implied between the worker and the end user when it was 'necessary' to do so in order to give the relationship business reality.

Later cases have indicated that it will be difficult to show that it is necessary to imply such a contract. In *James v Greenwich London Borough Council* [2007] ICR 577 the EAT observed that there were no mutual obligations between the worker and the end user: the end user was not obliged to pay the worker. The end user was also not able to insist on a particular worker being provided. It was the agency which was obliged to pay, but it did not control the worker. It would only be in exceptional circumstances that it was necessary to imply a contract. The express terms of the contract described the relationship and it would not be necessary to imply a contract. It might be possible to infer a contract from the parties' conduct if that departed from the express terms of the contracts. But the mere fact that an agency worker worked for an end user for a long time could not justify the implication of a contract.

In *Cairns v Visteon UK Ltd* [2007] IRLR 175, [2007] ICR 616, the EAT toyed with the idea that there could be two contracts of employment – one with the agency and one with the end user. However, this could not resolve the problem that it would only be possible to imply a contract where it was necessary to do so. Also, there would be enormous practical problems – would both employers have to follow the dismissal procedures in the event of a dismissal?

The present state of the law is thus that it will only be in exceptional circumstances that an agency worker will be held to have a contract of employment with the end user.

17.4 SOME LEGAL CONSEQUENCES OF THE DISTINCTION

(The lists set out below are not exhaustive.)

17.5 Employee, Self-Employed or Worker?

For the employee

Rights

An employee enjoys (subject to satisfaction of the qualifying conditions) the following rights:

(1) Unfair dismissal protection

(2) Redundancy payment entitlement

(3) Written particulars of terms of employment

(4) Statutory minimum period of notice

(5) Guarantee payment

(6) Medical suspension payment

(7) Protection from discrimination on grounds of race, sex, marital status, disability, gender reassignment, religion or belief or sexual orientation.

(8) Equal pay

(9) Maternity rights

(10) Time off for trade union activities, duties, etc

(11) Not to be refused employment because of membership or non-membership of a trade union

(12) To be employed for the agreed period or be given the agreed length of notice

(13) To be provided with a safe place of work and to have reasonable care taken of his safety

(14) To be paid statutory sick pay

(15) To be paid his wages free of any deductions not properly authorised

(16) In the case of those employed as shop workers or betting workers, the right to object to working on Sundays

(17) To limits on working time and the right to paid holidays under the Working Time Regulations 1998

Obligations

(1) To obey the employer's lawful orders

(2) To work faithfully and with due diligence

(3) To give the contractually agreed or statutory minimum period of notice to terminate the employment

(4) To pay income tax by way of deductions under the PAYE scheme

(5) To pay employee's National Insurance contributions

17.5 For the employer

Rights

(1) To benefit from the employee's obligations set out above

Obligations

(1) To observe the employee's rights set out above

(2) To deduct tax under the PAYE scheme

(3) To keep the necessary statutory sick pay records

(4) To make the appropriate National Insurance contributions

17.6 Self-employed – the self-employed person

Rights

(1) To benefit from all his contractual entitlements

(2) Not to be discriminated against on grounds of race, sex, marital status, disability, gender reassignment, religion or belief or sexual orientation and to the right to claim equal pay with a comparator of the opposite sex

(3) Where applicable, to be provided with a safe place and safe system of work

(4) To be paid his wages free of any deductions not properly authorised

(5) To limits on working time and to the benefit of annual leave in accordance with the *Working Time Regulations 1998*

Obligations

(1) To fulfil his contractual obligations

(2) To work with due skill and diligence

(3) To pay income tax under *Schedule D*

(4) To pay self-employed person's National Insurance contributions

17.7 Self-employed – the person who engages a self-employed person

Rights

(1) To benefit from the self-employed person's contractual obligations

Obligations

(1) To observe the self-employed person's rights set out above

17.8 Employees and office-holders

Another distinction may be identified between employees who are employed under a contract of employment and 'office-holders' who may not be employees or have the rights of employees (such as the right to complain of unfair dismissal). In *Johnson v Ryan* [2000] ICR 236, the worker was a local authority rent officer appointed pursuant to the *Rent Act 1977*. It was argued that, as an office-holder, the worker was not entitled to present a claim of unfair dismissal. The EAT identified three categories of 'office-holder'. First, those whose rights and duties are defined by the office they hold and not by any contract. An example is police officers. Second, persons who are called office-holders but who in reality are employed under contracts of service. Third, those who are both employees and office-holders. An example is company directors. In determining whether a worker who is described as an office-holder is an employee, the factual situation must be considered. Relevant matters include whether the worker receives a salary, whether the salary was fixed and whether the worker's duties

371

were subject to close control by the employer or whether the worker worked independently. The EAT held that a rent officer was an employee. In doing so, it noted that the recent approach of the appellate courts had been to take an inclusive approach to employee protection (see generally PUBLIC SECTOR EMPLOYEES (37)).

In *Percy v Board of National Mission of the Church of Scotland* [2006] ICR 134, the House of Lords held that a minister of the Church of Scotland was employed within the broader meaning of that term in the Sex Discrimination Act. Holding an office and being an employee were not mutually exclusive. To the same effect is *New Testament Church of God v Stewart* [2007] IRLR 178, sub nom Stewart v The New Testament of God [2006] All ER (D) 362 (Oct), EAT.

Workers

17.9

It has already been indicated that many of the provisions of employment legislation providing protection to individuals are not confined to those who are to be regarded in law as employees. Much protection is accorded to those who satisfy the definition of 'worker'.

That definition (found, for example, in s 230 of *ERA* and in similar form in the *Working Time Regulations* and elsewhere) is wider than the definition of employee because it includes those who undertake to 'do or perform personally any work or services for another party to the contracts whose status is not by virtue of the contract that of a client or customer of any profession or business undertaking carried on by the individual'.

This wider definition applies to a number of employment rights which are referred to in the start of this chapter. Reference should be made to each individual chapter for an explanation of the classes of person who benefit from the right. However, because there are now so many provisions which protect 'workers', this chapter seeks to provide an introduction to that concept.

The definition can be seen as comprising two elements. First the individual must be under an obligation personally to do work. Second, the person for whom the work is done must not be a client or customer of a business being run by the individual. The second limb is obviously necessary because otherwise the truly self-employed would be caught by a definition which required only that the person do work personally.

Several cases have considered what is meant by the definition of worker. The cases are decided under different provisions, but because the definition is the same, no distinction needs to be drawn based on the legal context of the decision. It is legitimate to consider decisions under the discrimination legislation and under other provisions which use the term worker, such as the *National Minimum Wage Act* and the *Working Time Regulations*.

The leading case is *James v Redcats (Brands) Ltd* [2007] IRLR 296. There the EAT held that one had to draw a careful distinction between employees, workers and those engaged in their own business. When a right extended to workers, it was only the last category who was excluded. The EAT referred to cases such as *Lee v Chung* (cited above) and said that the dichotomy suggested in those cases between employees and the self-employed could be too simple. It was necessary also to draw a further distinction between those in business on their own account and workers. The EAT suggested that it was useful to consider a 'dominant purpose' test, derived from discrimination cases. If the dominant feature of the arrangement was that the person was to provide personal service then, even if the prerequisites of employment were missing, the person was likely to be a worker.

Byrne Bros (Formworks) Ltd v Baird [2002] IRLR 96 was a case under the *Working Time Regulations*. The EAT concluded that labour-only sub-contractors had been correctly identified as workers notwithstanding that they had a limited power to send a substitute, the individuals were still under a personal obligation. Referring to the second part of the definition, the EAT said that the aim was to extend protection to an intermediate class of person between employees and those who are carrying on business on their own account. Such people, although not employees, are subordinate to the person for whom they work and hence in need of protection. The EAT said that a consideration of who was a worker would involve the same sorts of factors as are considered in deciding who is an employee 'but with the boundary pushed further in the putative worker's favour'.

In *Wright v Redrow Homes (Yorkshire) Ltd* [2004] EWCA Civ 469, [2004] IRLR 720 the Court of Appeal held that the question whether there was an obligation to undertake work personally depended on the terms of the contract and not what happened in practice. Pill LJ cautioned against relying too heavily on policy reasons when deciding who was a worker.

In dealing with the second part of the definition (that the person for whom the work is done is not a client or customer of a business undertaken by an individual), the EAT in *Cotswold Developments Construction Ltd v Williams* [2006] IRLR 181 suggested that the paradigm case of a person who did work for clients was a professional such as a solicitor or barrister. The paradigm case of a person who did work for customers was the owner of a shop or a tradesman such as a domestic plumber. The EAT suggested that a helpful test would be to consider whether the individual marketed his services to the public generally (in which case he would not be a worker) or whether he was integrated into the business of his principal (in which case he would be a worker).

The cases thus distinguish between those who are running their own business and those who, although not employed, are providing services as a part of another's business. In *Bacica v Muir* [2006] IRLR 35, the EAT suggested that factors such as working on the basis of a CIS certificate (in the construction industry), having accounts prepared for submission to the Inland Revenue, being free to work for others and in fact doing so, being paid a rate which included an overhead allowance and not being paid when not working were all factors indicating that a person was undertaking his own business.

18 Employee Participation

18.1 Until fairly recently there has been little statutory provision in the UK for the participation or involvement of employees in the affairs of the organisations in which they work. Some legislation in the 1970s (the *Health and Safety at Work, etc Act 1974* and the *Employment Protection Act 1975*) compelled employers with recognised trade unions to consult with their employees on such matters as health and safety, disclosure of information and on redundancies (see appropriate chapters for details). EC obligations then led to further legislation widening consultation requirements in the case of redundancies, transfers of undertakings, and health and safety. (For a brief summary see 18.12 below.)

The former Conservative Government chose to pursue participation by encouraging employee share ownership and profit-related pay. To that end, two specific legislative provisions were introduced (see 18.2 and 18.3).

The Labour Government has made a point of stressing its commitment to stakeholding and partnership at work. The *Employment Relations Act 1999, s 30* contains measures to enable the Government to make funding available to assist and develop 'partnerships at work' (see 18.14 below). More specifically, the *Act* requires employers to recognise trade unions where a majority of the relevant workforce wishes it (see TRADE UNIONS – I (50)). In a separate development, workforce consultation has been incorporated into the bidding process of the Private Finance Initiative.

The European Community is now the source of significant legislation in this area. The Social Protocol to the Maastricht Treaty on European Union gave the EC the power, *inter alia*, to adopt directives concerning the information and consultation of workers. The Treaty came into force on 1 November 1993. At the time, the United Kingdom 'opted out' of the Social Protocol. However, the Labour Government which came to power in 1997 ended the opt-out. On 1 May 1999 the Treaty of Amsterdam came into effect, incorporating the Social Protocol into the EC Treaty (see further EUROPEAN COMMUNITY LAW (25)). One effect of this will be to give increased emphasis to securing framework agreements on social legislation through negotiation between European-level trade union and employer bodies (the 'social partners'). One such agreement resulted in the *Directive on Parental Leave (96/34)* (see generally MATERNITY AND PARENTAL RIGHTS (33)).

The first employment measure adopted under the Social Protocol was the *European Works Council Directive (94/45)*, adopted in September 1994. This places obligations on companies with more than 1,000 employees, including at least 150 employees in a second European member state, and was implemented in national legislation by the *Transnational Information and Consultation of Employees Regulations 1999 (SI 1999/3323)* (see below 18.2). This was followed by *Directive 2002/14/EC* 'establishing a general framework for informing and consulting employees in the European Community'. This places obligations on smaller, national companies and was implemented into domestic law by the *Information and Consultation of Employees Regulations 2004 (SI 2004/3426*, as amended by *SI 2006/514)*(see below 18.2). Finally, the European Company Statute ('ECS') (consisting of EU Council *Regulation 2157/2001* and *Directive 2001/86/EC*), which enables companies operating in more than one member state to be established as a single company under Community law, has been implemented domestically by the *European Public Limited-Liability Company Regulations 2004 (SI 2004/2326)*. Information and consultation with employees is a pre-requisite for the registration of European Companies under the ECS (see below 18.2).

18.2   DIRECTORS TO HAVE REGARD FOR INTERESTS OF EMPLOYEES

By the *Companies Act 1985*, the directors of a company are to have regard to the interests of the employees as well as of the shareholders (*CA 1985, s 309(1)*). However, by *s 309(2)* that duty is owed not to the employees but to the company alone, and the employees cannot thus complain if the directors give greater priority to the interests of the shareholders.

18.3   DIRECTORS' REPORT

The directors' report of any company employing an average number of 250 employees in the United Kingdom in the financial year must now contain a statement describing the action that has been taken during the financial year to introduce, maintain or develop arrangements aimed at:

(a)   providing employees systematically with information on matters of concern to them as employees;

(b)   consulting employees or their representatives on a regular basis so that the views of employees can be taken into account in making decisions which are likely to affect their interests;

(c)   encouraging the involvement of employees in the company's performance through an employees' share scheme or by some other means;

(d)   achieving a common awareness on the part of all employees of the financial and economic factors affecting the performance of the company.

(*CA 1985, s 234(4), Sch 7 para 11*, as amended by *CA 1989*.)

18.4   GENERAL EC FRAMEWORK FOR EMPLOYEE INVOLVEMENT

Implementation in the UK

In February 2002 member states adopted *Directive 2002/14/EC* 'establishing a general framework for informing and consulting employees in the European Community'. The Directive is the national-level counterpart to the *European Works Council Directive (94/45)* (see above 18.2). It provides for employees of undertakings with at least 50 employees in any one member state to be provided with information and consulted by their employer over a wide range of issues concerning the operation of the organisation. The Directive has been implemented into domestic law by the *Information and Consultation of Employees Regulations 2004 (SI 2004/ 3426*as amended by *SI 2006/514)* ('the *ICE Regulations*'). From 6 April 2005, employees in organisations with 150 or more employees have a right to be informed and consulted on a regular basis about issues in the organisation they work for. Organisations with 100 or more employees will come within the scope of the legislation in April 2007 and ones with 50 or more employees in April 2008 (see *reg 3* and *Sch 1* to the *ICE Regulations*). The number of employees is to be calculated by taking the average number of employees employed by the employer over the preceding twelve-month period (*reg 4(1), (2)*). Employees who work for less than 75 hours in each month count as 'half' an employee for this purpose (*reg 4(3)*).

18.5 Employee Participation

The *ICE Regulations* apply to 'undertakings'. An undertaking is defined as a 'public or private undertaking carrying out an economic activity, whether or not operating for gain' (*reg 2*). This will cover almost all employers. However, there is uncertainty about whether particular parts of the public sector are carrying out economic activities: see *Henke v Gemeinde Schierke* (C-298/94) [1996] IRLR 701, *Mayeur v Association Promotion de l'Information Messine* (C-175/99) [2002] ICR 1316, *Collino v Telecom Italia SpA* (C-343/98) [2002] ICR 38 and cf the definition of 'undertaking' in the *Transfer of Undertakings* (*Protection of Employment Regulations 1981* (*SI 1981/1794*) (52.3 TRANSFER OF UNDERTAKINGS). The DTI Guidance on the *ICE Regulations*, issued in January 2005, suggests that the definition of an undertaking covers, in the case of a company, a separately incorporated legal entity, rather than organisational entity such

The DTI has issued guidance dated January 2006 on the *ICE Regulations* which is available on the DTI website.

18.5 Employee requests and employer notifications

Employees or their representatives have the right to request data from the employer for the purpose of ascertaining the number of people employed by the employer in the UK (and therefore whether or not the *ICE Regulations* apply): *reg 5*. A complaint that an employer has failed to provide the data requested, or that the data is false or incomplete in a material particular, may be presented to the Central Arbitration Committee ('CAC') up to one month after the date of the request: *reg 6*.

Even once it is ascertained that the employer has sufficient employees and the *ICE Regulations* in principle apply, the obligations under the *ICE Regulations* to inform and consult do not apply automatically, but have to be initiated either by the employer or the employees.

In the case of employees, at least 10% of the workforce (subject to a minimum of 15 and a maximum of 2,500 employees) must have requested that the employer negotiate an agreement in respect of information and consultation (*reg 7(1)–(3)*), Requests must be sent to the registered office, head office or principal place of business of the employer, or the CAC, A request must be in writing and must specify the names of the employee(s) making it and the date on which it is sent (*reg 7(4)*). Where the request is sent to the CAC, the CAC is then required to notify the employer of the request, request from the employer such information as it needs to verify the number and names of the employees who have made the request, and inform the employer and the employees who have made the request how many employees have made the request (*reg 7(5)*).

Employers may initiate negotiations under the *ICE Regulations* by giving notice in writing (*reg 11(1)*). Notice must be published in such a manner as to bring it to the attention of all the employees of the undertaking, so far as is reasonably practicable (*reg 11(2)*).

As a general rule, no employee may request negotiation (or renegotiation) of any agreement, and no employer may give notice of an intention to negotiate (or renegotiate) any agreement within three years of:

(*a*) the date of the conclusion of any negotiated agreement under the *ICE Regulations* (see below 18.6); or

(*b*) the date when the standard information and consultation provisions began to apply (see below 18.7, but note the provision in *reg 18(2)* for the renegotiation of the standard provisions 'at any time'); or (*c*)   where the employer has held a ballot following an employee request which has resulted in endorsement of a pre-existing agreement (see below 18.8), from the date of the employee request (*reg 12(1)*).

There is an exception to the general rule where there are material changes in the undertaking during the three-year period having the result that the agreement in force no longer covers all the employees of the undertaking, or, if it is a pre-existing agreement (as to which see below 18.8) can be said to have been approved by all the employees of the undertaking (*reg 12(2)*).

If the employer considers that there was no valid employee request, or an employee (or employee's representative) considers that an employer notification was not valid, a complaint may be presented to the CAC (*reg 13(1), (2)*). Complaints must be presented to the CAC within one month of the date of the employee request or the date of the employer notification (*reg 13(3)*). If the CAC finds the complaint made out, it may make a declaration to that effect.

Note that it is necessary, in order to initiate negotiations for an agreement in relation to more than one undertaking, for there to be a valid employee request or employer notification in relation to each undertaking: *reg 14(6)*.

18.6   Negotiated agreements

Where a valid employee request has been made (see above 18.5), the employer is obliged to initiate negotiations by taking the steps set out in *reg 14*. The employer must, as soon as reasonably practicable:

(*a*)   make arrangements for the employees of the undertaking to elect or appoint negotiating representatives;

(*b*)   inform the employees in writing of the identity of the negotiating representatives;

(*c*)   invite the negotiating representatives to enter into negotiations to reach a negotiated agreement (*reg 14(1), (2)*).

There are only two requirements in relation to the election or appointment of negotiating representatives: (i) the election or appointment must be arranged in such a way that all employees of the undertaking are represented by one or more representatives; and (ii) all employees of the undertaking must be entitled to take part in the election or appointment of the representatives and, if there is a ballot, all employees must be entitled to vote in the ballot (*reg 14(2)*).

Complaints about the election or appointment of negotiating representatives may be made to the CAC within 21 days of the election or appointment (*reg 15(1)*). If the CAC finds the complaint well-founded it must make an order requiring the employer to arrange for the process of election or appointment to take place again (*reg 15(2)*).

Once negotiating representatives have been appointed, the *ICE Regulations* are designed to encourage employers, employees and their representatives to agree information and consultation arrangements which suit their particular circumstances. Thus, the *ICE Regulations* specifically require employer and employee representatives to work in a spirit of co-operation (*reg 21*).

The *ICE Regulations* are, however, notably non-prescriptive with respect to the substance of the arrangements for information and consultation, for example as to the subjects, method, timing or frequency of any information provision or consultation. Guidance as to the possible content of an agreement may be gained from the standard information and consultation provisions, which will apply in default if the parties fail to reach a negotiated agreement (see below 18.8).

There are, however, some express requirements with which any negotiated agreement must comply. Any agreement must:

(a) Cover all employees of the undertaking (either in a single agreement or in different parts);

(b) Set out the circumstances in which the employer must inform and consult the employees to which it relates;

(c) Be in writing;

(d) Be dated;

(e) Be approved by the employees in accordance with the *ICE Regulations* (see below);

(f) Be signed by or on behalf of the employer; and either—

    (i) provide for the appointment or election of information and consultation representatives to whom the employer must provide the information and whom the employer must consult; or

    (ii) provide that the employer must provide information directly to the employees to which it relates and consult those employees directly.

(*Regulation 16(1)*)

In addition, to be valid, a negotiated agreement must have been signed by all the negotiating representatives, or, if it is only signed by a majority of the negotiating representatives, it must have been approved by at least 50% of the employees in the undertaking either: (i) in writing, or (ii) in a ballot (*reg 16(3), (4)*).

If a ballot is held the employer must make such arrangements as are reasonably practicable to ensure that the ballot is fair, all employees must be entitled to vote, and the ballot must be conducted so as to secure that (again so far as is reasonably practicable) those voting do so in secret and the votes given in the ballot are accurately counted (*reg 16(5)*). The employer must inform all employees entitled to vote of the result of the ballot as soon as is reasonably practicable (*reg 16(6)*).

A complaint may be presented to the CAC in circumstances where an employee representative considers that the ballot for approval of a negotiated agreement has not complied with the *ICE Regulations* (*reg 17(1)*). Complaints may only be made by a negotiating representative (and not by an employee). They must be made within 21 days of the date of the ballot. If the CAC finds the complaint well-founded it must order the employer to re-run the ballot (*reg 17(2)*).

A time limit is set on negotiations: they may last (in the first instance) for no more than six months commencing at the end of the period of three months beginning with the date on which the valid employee request was made or the valid employer notification was issued (*reg 14(3)*). However, time spent holding a ballot to determine whether or not to use a pre-existing agreement rather than negotiate a new one (see below 18.8) or on making an application to the CAC is ignored when calculating the six-month negotiating period (see *reg 14(3), (4)* for the detailed provisions on the calculation of time). If the employer and a majority of the negotiating representatives agree, before the end of the six-month period to extend the period for negotiation, it may be extended by such further period(s) as the parties agree (*reg 14(5)*).

18.7   **Standard information and consultation provisions**

Where no arrangements are agreed, standard provisions on information and consultation will apply automatically from six months after the date on which negotiations should have started (if they did not start) or on which the negotiating period ended (if agreement was not reached): *reg 18(1)*. The standard provisions are set out in *reg 20*. In summary, they require the employer:

(a)   to provide information and consultation representatives (as to the election and appointment of which, see below) with information on:

(i)   the recent and probable development of the undertaking's activities and economic situation;

(ii)   the situation, structure and probable development of employment within the undertaking and on any anticipatory measures envisaged, in particular, where there is a threat to employment within the undertaking; and

(iii)   decisions likely to lead to substantial changes in work organisation or in contractual relations, including those referred to in *ss 188–192* of the *Trade Union and Labour Relations (Consolidation) Act 1992* (see generally REDUNDANCY – II: PRACTICE AND PROCEDURE (39)) and *regs 10* to *12* of the *Transfer of Undertakings (Protection of Employment) Regulations 1981* (see 52.18 TRANSFER OF UNDERTAKINGS) (*reg 20(1)*);

(b)   to consult the information and consultation representatives as to developments, threats and changes to employment within the undertaking (*reg 20(3)*); and

(c)   to ensure that the timing, method and content of the consultation are appropriate, that it takes place with the appropriate level of management and that a reasoned response is given by the employer to any opinion expressed by the representatives (*reg 20(4)*).

Note that although there is an obligation to inform and consult on developments, threats and changes to employment within the undertaking, the obligation under the *ICE Regulations* ceases once either of the duties in *s 188* of *TULR(C)A 1992* or *reg 10* of *TUPE* applies (*reg 20(5)*).

Whenever the standard provisions are going to apply, there is an obligation on the employer to arrange for the holding of a ballot of its employees to elect information and consultation representatives (*reg 19(1)*). There must be one representative for every fifty employees (or part thereof), provided that there are always at least two and not more than 25 representatives (*reg 19(3)*). The requirements for the holding of ballots under *reg 19* are set out in *Sch 2* to the *ICE Regulations*.

Complaints in relation to the conduct of a ballot for the election of information and consultation representatives may be made by any employee or employee's representative to the CAC (*reg 19(4)*). Where the CAC finds the complaint well-founded, it must order the employer to arrange, or re-arrange, the ballot (*reg 19(5)*). If such an order is made, the complainant employee or employee's representative may also make an application to the Employment Appeal Tribunal, within three months of the CAC's decision, for a penalty notice to be issued against the employer (*reg 19(6)*: see 18.11 below for the award of penalty notices).

18.8 Employee Participation

18.8 Pre-existing agreements

If a valid employee request to negotiate an agreement under the *ICE Regulations* is made (see above 18.5), but there is a pre-existing agreement which:

(*a*)   is in writing;

(*b*)   sets out how the employer is to give information to the employees or their representatives and seek their views on such information;

(*c*)   covers all the employees of the undertaking; and

(*d*)   has been approved by the employees,

the employer may, instead of initiating negotiations (see above 18.6), hold a ballot to seek the endorsement of the employees for the employee request (*reg 8(1)*, *(2)*), ie to determine whether or not it is necessary to negotiate a new agreement, or whether the old agreement may continue in force. The option is only open to the employer where the employee request has been made by fewer than 40% of the employees employed in the undertaking. Where the pre-existing agreement covers more than one undertaking, the employer may hold a combined ballot for all the undertakings so covered if the employee request either alone or aggregated with any requests made by employees in the other undertakings is made by fewer than 40% of the employees in all the undertakings (*reg 9(1)*, *(2)*). However, even if the pre-existing agreement covers more than one undertaking, it is still open to the original undertaking to ballot only its own employees (*reg 9(3)*).

If the employer wishes to hold a ballot, he must inform the employees in writing within one month of the date of the employee request and arrange for the ballot to be held as soon as reasonably practicable thereafter (but no less than 21 days after the employer has informed the employees of its intention to hold a ballot): *reg 8(3)*. The requirements for the ballot are the same as for the ballot for employee approval of a negotiated agreement where only a majority of the negotiating representatives have signed the agreement (see above 18.6), save that the employees are only to be regarded as having endorsed the employee request if at least 40% of the employees employed in the undertaking and the majority of the employees who vote in the ballot have voted in favour of endorsing the request (*reg 8(4)*, *(6)*).

If the employees endorse the employee request, the employer is under a duty to initiate negotiations as described in 18.7 above (*reg 8(5)(b)*). If the employees do not endorse the employee request, the employer is not under such an obligation (*reg 8(5)(c)*) and the pre-existing agreement will continue to govern information and consultation within the undertaking.

An employee or employees' representative who believes that the employer has not complied with the requirements of the *ICE Regulations* in relation to the holding of a ballot to endorse an employee request may complain to the CAC (*regs 8(7)–(8)* and *10*). There is a time limit of 21 days for the bringing of complaints, which runs from the date the employer informed the employees of its intention to hold a ballot (if it is the employer's entitlement to hold a ballot that is disputed) or from the date of the ballot (if it is alleged that the employer has failed to comply with a ballot requirement): *reg 10(1)*, *(2)*. There is no time limit for complaints that an employer has failed to inform employees that it intends to hold a ballot, or (having announced that it intends to hold a ballot) fails to hold it within the requisite time period (*reg 8(7)*, *(8)*). Where the CAC finds the complaint well-founded, it may (as appropriate) order the employer to hold the ballot (*regs 8(9)* and *10(3)(c)*) or commence negotiations in accordance with the procedure described at 18.7 above: *reg 10(3)(a)*, *(b)* and *(c)(i)*.

18.10 **Confidential information**

An employer cannot be required by any agreement to disclose any information or document where the nature of the information or document is such that, according to objective criteria, its disclosure would seriously harm the functioning of, or would be prejudicial to, the undertaking (*reg 26(1)*). Any dispute between an employer and employee representatives in relation to the nature of any document that an employer has refused to disclose may also be referred to the CAC (*reg 26(2)*). The CAC has power to order the disclosure of the document or information where it considers that disclosure would not be seriously harmful or prejudicial and to prescribe the terms on which it should be disclosed (*reg 26(3), (4)*).

If an employer discloses any information or document, pursuant to its obligations under the *ICE Regulations*, and requires that information or document to be held in confidence and not to be disclosed to others except, where terms permit him to do so, in accordance with those terms, then any disclosure by the recipient in breach of those terms will be actionable by the employer as a breach of statutory duty (*reg 25(1)–(3)*). This is in addition to any right which any person might have in relation to that disclosure otherwise than under the *ICE Regulations* (*reg 25(4)*). The employer will not, however, have any right of action for breach of statutory duty under the *ICE Regulations* if the recipient reasonably believed the disclosure to be a 'protected disclosure' within the meaning of *s 43A* of the *Employment Rights Act 1996* (see 11.17–11.18 DISCLOSURE OF INFORMATION).

There is a right for a recipient to apply to the CAC for a declaration if the recipient believes that it was unreasonable for the employer to require him to hold the information or document in confidence (*reg 25(6)*). If the CAC considers that the disclosure of the information or document by the recipient would not, or would not be likely to, harm the legitimate interests of the undertaking, it must make a declaration to that effect (*reg 25(7)*).

18.11 **Complaints**

In addition to the various rights to bring complaints to the CAC mentioned above, a complaint may be presented to the CAC where an employee representative considers that an employer is not acting in accordance with an agreement negotiated under the ICE Regulations or with the standard arrangements. The time limit for presenting complaints is three months from the date of the failure. If the complaint is upheld, CAC may make a declaration and order the employer to take such steps as are reasonable for it to take in order to comply with the terms of the negotiated agreement or the standard arrangements (*reg 22(1)–(5)*).

If the CAC makes such a declaration (whether with or without order) an application may be made to the Employment Appeal Tribunal for a penalty notice to be issued, under which the employer may be required to pay up to £75,000 (*regs 22(6), (7)* and *23*). The time limit for such applications is three months from the date of the CAC's declaration. Matters to be taken into account by the EAT when setting the amount of the penalty include: the gravity of the failure; the period of time over which the failure occurred; the reason for the failure; the number of employees affected by the failure; and the number of employees employed by the undertaking or, where a negotiated agreement covers employees in more than one undertaking, the number of employees employed by both or all of the undertakings (*reg 23(3)*).

18.12 **Employment protection**

Employee representatives have the right to reasonable paid time off during working hours for the purpose of performing their functions as representatives (*regs 27, 28*). A complaint that an employer has refused to permit the employee representative a reasonable amount of paid time off, or has failed to pay the whole or part of any amount to which the employee is entitled, may be presented to an employment tribunal (*reg 29(1)*). The time limit for bringing a complaint is 'three months beginning with the day on which the time off was taken or on which it is alleged the time off should have been permitted' (*reg 29(1)(2)(a)*). If the tribunal is satisfied that it was not reasonably practicable for the complaint to be presented before the end of the period of three months, then it may extend time for such further period as it considers reasonable (*reg 29(2)*). Where a tribunal finds a complaint well-founded, it must make a declaration and order the employer to pay the employee an amount equivalent to the amount of time off it should have allowed the employee, or the amount it should have paid the employee (as appropriate): *reg 29(3)–(5)*. In relation to the right to time off work, see generally TIME OFF WORK (49).

An employee who is dismissed is to be regarded as unfairly dismissed if the reason or (if more than one) the principal reason for dismissal is that the employee:

(*a*)   performed or proposed to perform any functions or activities as an employee's representative, a negotiating representative, an information and consultation representative or stood or proposed to stand as a candidate in an election to be such a representative;

(*b*)   exercised or proposed to exercise an entitlement to reasonable paid time off for performing any of those functions;

(*c*)   made or proposed to make a request to exercise such an entitlement;

(*d*)   exercised, or proposed to exercise, (in good faith) any entitlement to complain (or appeal) to an employment tribunal, the CAC or the EAT in connection with any rights conferred by the *ICE Regulations*;

(*e*)   requested, or proposed to request data in accordance with *reg 5* (above 18.5);

(*f*)   took any action in relation to, or indicated that he supported, or did not support, the negotiation of an agreement, the application of the standard information and consultation provisions;

(*g*)   influenced or sought to influence by lawful means the way in which votes were to be cast by other employees in a ballot arranged under the *ICE Regulations*;

(*h*)   voted in a ballot;

(*i*)   expressed doubts as to whether such a ballot had been properly conducted; or

(*j*)   proposed to do, failed to do, or proposed to decline to do, any of the things mentioned above (*reg 30*).

There is an exception where and employee has, in the performance of any of his functions or activities as a representative or candidate disclosed any confidential information in breach of the provisions of the *ICE Regulations* (see 18.10). Such dismissals will be potentially fair, unless the employee reasonably believed the disclosure to be a 'protected disclosure' within the meaning of *s 43A* of the *Employment Rights Act 1996* (see 11.17–11.18 DISCLOSURE OF INFORMATION). See also generally 54.3 UNFAIR DISMISSAL- II: THE FAIRNESS OF THE DISMISSAL.

An employee also has the right not to be subjected to a detriment for any of the above actions (or inactions): *reg 32*. This is subject to an identical exception for protected disclosures (*reg 32(4)*). A complaint that an employee has been subjected to a detriment in contravention of *reg 32* may be presented to an employment tribunal in the same manner as complaints under the *Employment Rights Act 1996* for subjection to a detriment on other grounds (*reg 33*): compare 50.37 TRADE UNIONS – I: NATURE AND LIABILITIES.

18.13 EUROPEAN COMPANIES

Longstanding proposals for a European Company Statute ('ECS'), which allows European Companies or 'Societas Europaea' (SEs) to be formed under EC law, came to fruition on 8 October 2001 with the adoption by the EU Council of Ministers of *Regulation 2157/2001*. The ECS gives companies operating in more than one member state, with a share capital of more than 120,000 Euro, the option of being established as a single company under Community law and so able to operate throughout the EU with one set of rules and a unified reporting system. The regulation is accompanied by a Directive on worker involvement (*Directive 2001/86/EC*). The *Directive* and *Regulation* have been implemented domestically by the *European Public Limited-Liability Company Regulations 2004* (*SI 2004/2326*) ('the *EPLC Regulations*').

Under the *EPLC Regulations*, before an SE can be registered, the various companies or establishments involved in its creation must have complied with the *EPLC Regulations'* requirements in relation to the information, consultation and participation of employees (*reg 12*). All SEs must have such employee involvement arrangements. *Part 3* of the *EPLC Regulations* deals specifically with employee involvement. The requirements of *Part 3* apply whenever a company intends to establish an SE whose registered office is to be in Great Britain, or whenever an SE has its registered office in Great Britain (*reg 17(1)*). In relation to the election or appointment of members of the 'special negotiating body' (below 18.15) or employee representatives, the requirements apply whenever there are employees of the relevant company in Great Britain (*reg 17(2)*). In relation to matters of enforcement and employee protection, *Part 3* also applies where any subsidiary or establishment of a relevant company or SE, or an employee or employees' representative, is registered or situated in Great Britain (*reg 17(3)*).

18.14 Employer's duty to provide information

Regulation 18 places a duty on the participating company (or companies) to provide information to employee representatives (or, if there are no such representatives, the employees themselves) whenever they propose to form an SE. The company must, as soon as possible after publishing the terms of any draft merger, or creating a holding company, or agreeing a plan to form a subsidiary or to transform into an SE, provide information to employees which, at least:

(*a*)   identifies the participating companies, concerned subsidiaries and establishments,

(b)   gives the number of employees employed by each participating company and concerned subsidiary and at each concerned establishment, and

(c)   gives the number of employees employed to work in each EEA State in each of those companies (*reg 18(1), (2)*).

Complaints that a company has failed to provide information, or has provided information that is false or incomplete in a material particular may be presented to the CAC by an employee's representative or (if there is no such representative) an employee (*reg 19(1)*). If the CAC finds the complaint well-founded, it must order the disclosure of the information in question (*reg 19(2)*).

There is a continuing obligation on the company to provide information as to progress in establishing an SE (*reg 18(3)*). The obligation is to provide that information to the 'special negotiating body' (see below 18.15).

18.15 The special negotiating body

The company or companies proposing to form an SE are obliged to set up a 'special negotiating body' ('SNB') (*reg 21(1)*). The function of the SNB is to reach an 'employee involvement agreement' with the participating companies (see below 18.16). The SNB consists of employee representatives elected from the employees in each member state. The employees from each member state have the right to elect one representative if they make up 10% of the total workforce, two representatives if they make up 20% of the total workforce, etc. (*reg 21(2)*). Where more than one company is involved there must be at least one representative from each company (*reg 21(3)*). Employees must be informed of the identity of the members of the SNB within one month of the election (*reg 21(5)*). There is provision for appointing additional members and for changing members in certain circumstances (*reg 21(4), (6)*).

Complaints in relation to the establishment of (or failure to establish) an SNB may be presented to the CAC by a person elected or appointed to the SNB, an employees' representative (or, if there is no such representative, the employee) or a participating company (*reg 22(1)–(2)*). Complaints must be made within one month of the last date on which the participating companies complied or should have complied with the obligation to inform employees of the identity of members of the SNB (*reg 22(3)*). Where the CAC finds an application well-founded it must make a declaration to that effect and the participating companies will continue to be under an obligation to comply with their duties under the *EPLC Regulations* (*reg 22(4)*).

The requirements of the ballot for the election of representatives are set out in *regs 23* and *24*. Any UK employee or UK employees' representative who believes that the arrangements for the ballot of the UK employees do not comply with the requirements of the *EPLC Regulations* may present a complaint to the CAC (*reg 23(4)*). Complaints must be presented within a period of 21 days beginning on the date on which the management published the final arrangements for the ballot. Where the CAC finds the complaint well-founded it must make a declaration to that effect and may make an order requiring the management to modify the arrangements it has made for the ballot of UK employees so as to comply with the requirements of the *EPLC Regulations* (*reg 23(5)*).

Where there is already a 'consultative committee' within the organisation concerned, the company is relieved of the obligation to arrange a ballot and instead the 'consultative committee' is permitted to appoint one or more of its own members to the SNB (*reg 25(1)*). A 'consultative committee' is defined as a body of persons which represents all the employees of the participating company, consists wholly of persons who are employees of the participating company or its concerned subsidiaries, whose normal functions include carrying out 'an information and consultation function', and which is able to carry out its functions without interference from the management of the participating company (*reg 25(3)*). 'Information and consultation function' is defined in *reg 25(4)* as 'receiving, on behalf of all the employees of the participating company, information which may significantly affect the interests of the employees of that company, but excluding information which is relevant only to a specific aspect of the interests of the employees, such as health and safety or collective redundancies; and being consulted by the management of the participating company on that information'. Most trade unions will be 'consultative committees' within the *EPLC Regulations*.

Where such a consultative committee exists, it is entitled to appoint so many of its number (which may include trade union representatives who are not employees of the company) to the SNB as that company would be entitled to elect under a ballot (*reg 25(2)*). The consultative committee must then publish the names of those it has appointed to the SNB in such a manner as to bring them to the attention of the management of the participating company, employees and employees' representatives (and those of its concerned subsidiaries (*reg 25(5)*).

Where the management of a participating company, an employee or an employee's representative believes that a 'consultative committee' does not fulfil the requirements of *reg 25*, or that the representative appointed by that committee is not entitled to be appointed, they may complain to the CAC (provided they do so within 21 days of the publication of the names of the representatives purportedly appointed by the consultative committee): *reg 25(6)–(8)*. If the CAC finds the complaint well-founded, it must make a declaration. Any appointment made by the consultative committee will then be of no effect and appointment of representatives must thereafter be by ballot (*reg 25(8)*).

18.16   Negotiated employee involvement agreement

The task of the SNB is to reach an employee involvement agreement with the (proposed) SE (*reg 20*). The parties are under a duty to negotiate in a spirit of co-operation (*reg 27(2)*). An initial six-month time limit is set within which to reach agreement, but with provision for extension for up to 12 months by agreement between the parties (*reg 27(3)*).

There are no specific requirements as to the substance of the agreement to be reached on employee involvement, save that the elements of employee involvement at all levels must be at least as favourable as those which exist in the company to be transformed into an SE (*reg 28(4)*). However, to be valid, the agreement must be in writing and must specify the agreement reached on certain key points:

(*a*)   the scope of the agreement;

(*b*)   the composition, number of members and allocation of seats on the representative body;

(*c*)   the functions and the procedure for the information and consultation of the representative body;

(*d*)   the frequency of meetings of the representative body;

(e)   the financial and material resources to be allocated to the representative body;

(f)   if, during negotiations, the parties have decided to establish one or more information and consultation procedures instead of a representative body, the agreement must specify the arrangements for implementing those procedures;

(g)   if, during negotiations, the parties have decided to establish arrangements for participation in the board of the SE, the agreement must record the substance of those arrangements including (if applicable) the number of members in the SE's administrative or supervisory body which the employees will be entitled to elect, appoint, recommend or oppose, the procedures as to how these members may be elected, appointed, recommended or opposed by the employees, and their rights; and

(h)   in all cases, the date of entry into force of the agreement and its duration, the circumstances, if any, in which the agreement is required to be re-negotiated and the procedure for its re-negotiation (*reg 28*).

There are specific rules as to how decisions must be taken by the SNB, and what level of majority is required for each sort of decision (an absolute majority generally, but two thirds where a decision would result in a reduction of participation rights): *reg 29(1)–(3)*).

For the purpose of negotiations, the SNB may be assisted by experts of its choice (*reg 29(5)*). The participating company or companies must pay for any reasonable expenses of the SNB, though the company is not required to pay for the expenses of more than one expert (*reg 29(6)*).

The details of any decision taken by the SNB must be published to the employees represented on the body as soon as reasonably practicable and, in any event no later than 14 days after the decision has been taken (*reg 29(4)*).

Complaints in relation to decisions of the SNB may be presented to the CAC by a member of the SNB, an employees' representative, or where there is no such representative in respect of an employee, that employee (*reg 31(1)*). Complaints may only be presented on the grounds that (a) the decision was not taken by the requisite majority, or (b) that the SNB failed to publish a decision as required by the *EPLC Regulations*. The time limit for presentation of complaints is 21 days from the date the SNB did or should have published their decision. Where the CAC finds the complaint well-founded it must make a declaration that the decision was not taken properly and that it is to have no effect (*reg 31(2)*).

18.17 Standard rules on employee involvement

Where no employee involvement agreement has been reached within the six-month (or twelve-month extended) time limit in *reg 27(3)*, or the parties have so agreed, the 'standard rules on employee involvement' will apply (*reg 32*). These are detailed and complex and are set out in *Sch 3* to the *EPLC Regulations*. In summary, however, the standard rules provide as follows:

(a)   The management of the SE must arrange for the establishment of a 'representative body' that will receive information from management on behalf of the employees and act on behalf of the employees in consultations;

(b)   The representative body must be composed of employees of the SE and its subsidiaries and establishments (one member for each 10% or fraction thereof of employees of the SE, its subsidiaries and establishments employed for the time being in each Member State). Its members must be elected or appointed by the members of the SNB, by whatever method the SNB decides;

(c)   Once the representative body has been established for four years, it must decide whether to open negotiations with the management of the SE to reach an employee involvement agreement or whether the standard rules should continue to apply. If a decision is taken to open negotiations the procedure described at 18.16 above will apply, save that references to the SNB should be read as being references to the representative body;

(d)   For the purpose of informing and consulting on questions which concern the SE and any of its subsidiaries or establishments, the management is obliged to:

    (i)   prepare and provide to the representative body regular reports on the progress of the business of the SE and the SE's prospects;

    (ii)   provide the representative body with the agenda for meetings of its administrative, management or supervisory committees and copies of all documents submitted to any general meeting of the SE's shareholders.

    (iii)   Inform the representative body when there are exceptional circumstances affecting the employees' interests to a considerable extent, particularly in the event of relocations, transfers, the closure of establishments or undertakings or collective redundancies;

(e)   If the representative body so desires, the management must meet with it at least once a year to discuss the reports on the progress of the business. Such meetings should relate, in particular, to the structure, economic and financial situation, the probable development of business and of production and sales, the situation and probable trend of employment, investments and substantial changes concerning organisation, introduction of new working methods or production processes, transfers of production, mergers, cutbacks or closures of undertakings, establishments or important parts thereof and collective redundancies;

(f)   Where there are exceptional circumstances affecting the employees' interests, the representative body must be permitted to meet with the most appropriate level of management and, if the SE does not act in accordance with the representative body's opinion as to what should be done in the circumstances, the representative body may request a further meeting to seek agreement;

(g   The members of the representative body must inform the employees' representatives or, if no such representatives exist, the employees of the SE and its subsidiaries and establishments, of the content and outcome of the information and consultation procedures;

(h)   The representative body may be assisted by experts of its choice;

(i)   The costs of the representative body must be borne by the SE. However, again, where the representative body or the select committee is assisted by more than one expert the SE is not required to pay the expenses of more than one of them.

18.18   Employee Participation

18.18 Alternative arrangements

The members of the SNB may 'opt out' of any sort of employee involvement, in which case the usual national rules on employee involvement will apply, and the obligations to agree employee involvement procedures under the *EPLC Regulations* will fall away (*reg 30(3)*). The 'opt out' may be exercised by the SNB deciding, by a two thirds majority vote, not to open negotiations for an employee involvement agreement or to terminate any such negotiations (*reg 30(1)*). The SNB cannot, however, 'opt out' if the SE is to be formed by way of transformation of an existing company, and the existing company is one in which any of the employees have the right to participate in the board of that company (*reg 30(2)*). Procedures for agreeing employee involvement under the *EPLC Regulations* may, provided at least two years have past since the decision to 'opt out' be 'reactivated' by an employee request that is:

(*a*)   in writing; and

(*b*)   made by at least 10% of the employees of, or by employees' representatives representing at least 10% of the total number of employees employed by the participating companies and its concerned subsidiaries, or (where the SE has been registered) the SE and it subsidiaries (*reg 30(4)*).

Where the SE has been registered, the SE may agree to the SNB being reconvened earlier than the specified two years.

18.19 Disputes and complaints

Disputes about the operation of an employee involvement agreement or the standard rules on employee involvement may be referred to the CAC (*reg 33(1)*). There is a three-month time limit, running from the date on which the defaulting party failed to comply with the agreed procedure (*reg 33(2)*). If the CAC finds a complaint well-founded it may make a declaration and an order requiring the defaulting party to take requisite steps to remedy the default (*reg 33(4)–(5)*). In the event of the CAC making such a declaration, the aggrieved party then has three months in which to apply to the Employment Appeal Tribunal for a penalty notice to be awarded against the defaulting party (*reg 33(6)*). Matters to be taken into account by the EAT when setting the amount of the penalty include: the gravity of the failure; the period of time over which the failure occurred; the reason for the failure; the number of employees affected by the failure; and the number of employees employed by the undertaking or, where a negotiated agreement covers employees in more than one undertaking, the number of employees employed by both or all of the undertakings (*reg 34(3)*).

18.20 Employment protection

Similar provisions apply in relation to rights to reasonable paid time off (*regs 39 and 40*), protection from dismissal (*reg 40*) and protection from other detriment (*reg 42*) as apply under the *ICE Regulations* (see above 18.12),

18.21 EUROPEAN WORKS COUNCILS

Implementation in the UK

The *European Works Council (EWC) Directive (94/45)* applied in EEA states except the UK from 22 September 1996. For the purposes of informing and consulting employees, the *Directive* requires the establishment of a European-level information and consultation procedure or works council in all undertakings (or groups) employing at least 1,000 workers in the EEA with at least 150 in each of at least two member states. (The EEA comprises the member states of the European Union plus Norway, Iceland and Liechtenstein.) The *Directive* was extended to the UK by *Directive 97/74* and has now been implemented in national legislation by the *Transnational Information and Consultation of Employees Regulations 1999* (*SI 1999/3323*) ('the *TICE Regulations*') from 15 January 2000.

The *TICE Regulations* do not apply to undertakings which had pre-existing voluntary agreements made before 23 September 1996 under the original directive and which cover the entire workforce, or to voluntary agreements made prior to 16 December 1999 by undertakings which are subject to the 15 January 2000 implementation date (*regs 44, 45*).

18.22 Number of employees

In order to determine whether an undertaking has the necessary number of employees to qualify as a Community-scale undertaking (or group of undertakings) for the purposes of the *Directive* and *TICE Regulations*, an average is taken of the two years preceding the relevant date (*reg 6*). For UK employees this means adding together monthly numbers over a two-year period and dividing by 24 (*reg 6(2)*). For employees elsewhere, calculations are to be made according to the law and practice of the member state concerned (*reg 6(1)(b)*). Further, for the purpose of calculating the number of employees in the UK, employees who are contracted to work 75 hours or less in a normal month without overtime may be counted as half an employee for that month if the UK management so decides (*reg 6(3)*). When an employee or employees' representative seeks information to establish whether the organisation is part of a Community-scale undertaking (or group), management must provide details of numbers employed in the UK and in each of the other member states in the past two years (*reg 7*). The Central Arbitration Committee ('CAC') may order disclosure where the employer has failed to comply (*reg 8*).

In *Betriebsrat der Bofrost Josef H Boquoi Deutschland West GmbH & Co KG v Bofrost Josef H Boquoi Deutschland West GmbH & Co KG* [2001] IRLR 403, the ECJ stated, in relation to the interpretation of *Directive 97/74*, that an undertaking which is part of a group is required to supply information on number of employees, etc to workers' representatives, even where it has not yet been established that the management to which the request for information is addressed is the management of a controlling undertaking within the group (see also *Betriebsrat der Firma ADS Anker GmbH v ADS Anker GmbH* (2004) 763 IDS Brief 11 ('*ADS Anker*')). Workers are entitled to have access to information enabling them to ascertain whether they have the right to request that negotiations on an EWC be opened with central management. The sorts of information that the group may be obliged to supply includes information on the average total number of employees, their distribution across the Member States, the establishments of the undertaking and the group undertakings, and on the structure of the undertaking and of the undertakings in the group, as well as the names and addresses of the employee representation which might participate in the setting up of an EWC (*Gesamtbetriebsrat der Kühne & Nagel AG & CoKG v Kühne & Nagel AG & Co KG* [2004] IRLR 332, ECJ ('*Kühne & Nagel*')). The group's obligation to supply information extends only to such information as is 'essential' (*Kühne & Nagel*, paras 64 and 69) to the opening of negotiations for establishing an EWC. In *ADS Anker* (above), the ECJ ruled that it was for the national court to determine what information was 'essential'.

18.23 Employee Participation

Where the central management of a Community-scale group of undertakings is not located in an EU Member State, then the management ('the deemed management') that is required to provide information to employees and employees' representatives is the management of the undertaking employing the greatest number of employees in any Member State (*art 4(2)* and see *Kühne & Nagel*). In order to fulfil its obligations under *Directive 97/74*, the deemed management must request the information from other undertakings in the group and the other undertakings must supply that information to the deemed management.

18.23 Requests for EWC

Central management situated in the UK is required to initiate negotiations for the establishment of a European Works Council ('EWC') or an information and consultation procedure if it receives either:

(*a*)   a valid request from 100 employees or from employees' representatives who represent at least that number in at least two undertakings or establishments in at least two different member states; or

(*b*)   separate requests by employees or employees' representatives which, taken together, mean that 100 employees or employees' representatives representing that number have made requests in at least two undertakings or establishments in at least two different member states.

(*Regulation 9(1), (2)*.)

Such requests must be in writing, dated and sent to central or local management (*reg 9(3)*). Central management may initiate negotiations on its own initiative (*reg 9(5)*). Disputes over the validity of requests to set up an EWC are to be referred to the CAC within three months, and undertakings which consider that they have a valid voluntary agreement but which receive a request to establish an EWC may also apply to the CAC to decide the point (*reg 10*).

These requirements also apply where the central management is not situated in a member state and the representative agent of central management is located in the UK and, in other cases, where a UK-based establishment or group has more employees than other establishments or groups in member states (*reg 5(1)*).

18.24 Special negotiating body

A 'special negotiating body' ('SNB') is to represent employees in their negotiations with management on the setting up of an EWC or arrangements for implementing an information and consultation procedure. It consists of representatives of employees from all EEA states in which the organisation operates. The number of representatives for each member state is decided by a formula set by the state in which the central management (or representative agent if the central management is outside the EEA) is located. For a UK-based undertaking there must be at least one representative for each of the member states in which the organisation operates plus:

(a)   one additional member from a country where 25% but under 50% of the workforce are employed;

(b)   two additional members from countries where 50% but under 75% are employed; and

(c)   three additional members from countries employing 75% or more of the EEA workforce.

(*Regulation 12.*)

UK members of the SNB are to be elected by a ballot of UK employees. Requirements for the ballot are set out in *regs 13* and *14*. There is no need for a ballot where there already exists a consultative committee carrying out an information and consultation function whose members were elected by a ballot of UK employees. In these circumstances the committee may nominate UK representatives for the SNB (*reg 15*).

In order to reach an EWC agreement, central management must convene a meeting with the SNB, informing local managements. SNBs are to take decisions by majority vote except that two-thirds of the votes are needed on a decision not to open, or to terminate, negotiations. The SNB may be assisted in these negotiations by experts. The reasonable expenses of the SNB are to be borne by central management, including the expenses of one expert where applicable (*reg 16*).

18.25 Setting up an EWC

Where the SNB and central management agree to establish an EWC, the agreement must specify:

(a)   the undertakings or establishments covered;

(b)   composition of the EWC, number of members, allocation of seats and term of office of the members;

(c)   functions and procedure for information and consultation;

(d)   venue, frequency and duration of meetings;

(e)   financial and material resources allocated to the EWC;

(f)   duration of the agreement and procedure for its renegotiation.

(*Regulation 17(4).*)

An agreement to establish an information and consultation procedure instead of an EWC is also subject to certain requirements. It must specify a method by which the representatives can meet to discuss the information provided; and that information is to relate in particular to transnational questions affecting significantly the interests of employees (*reg 17(5)*).

A statutory EWC is to be set up if:

(a)   the parties agree;

(b)   central management refuses to start negotiations within six months of the date on which a valid request was made; or

(c)   no agreement has been concluded within three years of the request being made, provided the SNB has not taken a decision to terminate (or not to start) negotiations.

(*Regulation 18.*)

Central management and the EWC or information/consultation representatives are under a duty to work in a spirit of co-operation with due regard to their reciprocal rights and obligations (*reg 19*).

18.26   Employee Participation

The *Schedule* to the *TICE Regulations* sets out a 'statutory model' comprising a standard set of rules for the constitution of a statutory EWC governing its competence, composition, meetings and procedures. In particular, it lists topics about which the EWC is to be informed and consulted (*Sch, para 7(3)*).

The Employment Appeal Tribunal ('EAT') will rule on disputes about the operation of an EWC or the failure to establish an EWC. If a complaint is well-founded, the EAT must make a decision to that effect and may make an order requiring central management to take appropriate steps by a specified date. In addition, the EAT will, in appropriate cases, issue a penalty notice requiring central management to pay an amount to the Secretary of State (*regs 20, 21*). The maximum penalty to be imposed is £75,000 (*reg 22(2)*). The EAT also hears appeals on points of law from the CAC (*reg 38(8)*).

Both the EAT and CAC may refer cases to ACAS if they believe that a dispute is reasonably likely to be settled by conciliation (*reg 39(1)*).

18.26   Confidential information

Members of SNBs, EWCs, information/consultation representatives or experts assisting them must not disclose information which central management requires to be kept confidential. Civil action may be taken for breach of this statutory duty of confidence except where the individual reasonably believed disclosure to be a protected disclosure within the meaning of *s 43A* of the *Employment Rights Act 1996*, as inserted by the *Public Interest Disclosure Act 1998*. Members or representatives can appeal to the CAC for a declaration if they believe management is imposing confidentiality unreasonably. A declaration will be made if the CAC considers that disclosure would not, or would not be likely to, 'prejudice or cause serious harm to the undertaking' (*reg 23*).

Management may withhold any information which, according to objective criteria, would seriously harm the functioning of, or be prejudicial to, the undertaking. The CAC will rule on disputes over whether a document or information should be disclosed and will order disclosure where it considers, on objective criteria, that no serious harm or prejudice would result (*reg 24*).

18.27   Employment protection

Members of SNBs, EWCs, information/consultation representatives and candidates for election are entitled to take reasonable time off work, with pay, to carry out their functions (*regs 25–27*). See TIME OFF WORK (49).

Such employees also have the right not to be subjected to a detriment by the employer on the grounds that they performed their functions or activities or made a request for statutory time off or payment for time off (*reg 31(1)–(4)*). Additional rights not to be victimised apply to any employee whether or not he or she falls within the above categories. It is unlawful to subject an employee to a detriment on grounds connected with:

(a)   bringing proceedings in tribunal to enforce a right or entitlement under the TICE Regulations (provided any claim is made in good faith);

(b)   applications to the EAT or CAC;

(c)   requesting information under reg 7;

(d)   acting to secure (or not secure) the setting up of an SNB, an EWC or information/consultation procedure;

(e)   supporting (or failing to support) the setting up of an SNB, an EWC or information/consultation procedure;

(f)   standing as a candidate for election, seeking to influence how votes are cast, voting in a ballot or questioning the conduct of the ballot; or

(g)   proposing to do, or declining to do, any of the above.

(*Regulation 31(5), (6)*.)

It is also automatically unfair under *reg 28* to dismiss an individual on any of the above grounds (see UNFAIR DISMISSAL – II (54)).

Complaints of detrimental treatment may be made to an employment tribunal within three months of the act or failure to act or, if that is not reasonably practicable, within such further period as the tribunal considers reasonable (*reg 32*). Compensation may be awarded if the complaint is well-founded (*ERA 1996, s 49*). Complaints may be settled by ACAS conciliation or by valid compromise agreements (*reg 41*).

18.28   CONSULTATION RIGHTS

EC influence may be seen in the recent development of other legislation on employee consultation.

Employers' obligations to consult representatives over collective redundancies and on the transfer of an undertaking were originally confined to organisations which recognised trade unions. Following two ECJ rulings in 1994 (*Commission v United Kingdom* [1994] IRLR 392 and 412), the UK was required to provide for employees' representatives to be informed and consulted over the transfer of an undertaking and where a large number of redundancies are planned, irrespective of whether the employer recognises trade unions. This adjustment was made by the *Collective Redundancies and Transfer of Undertakings (Protection of Employment) (Amendment) Regulations 1995 (SI 1995/2587)* which amended relevant provisions of *TULRCA* and the *Transfer of Undertakings (Protection of Employment) Regulations 1981 ('TUPE')*. Further amendments were made by the *Collective Redundancies and Transfer of Undertakings (Protection of Employment) (Amendment) Regulations 1999 (SI 1999/1925)*, which came into effect on 28 July 1999.

Employers must consult with trade union representatives if they recognise a trade union in respect of the affected employees. (For recognition of trade unions, see 48.19FF TRADE UNIONS – I: NATURE AND LIABILITIES.) In non-unionised situations, they must consult with 'employee representatives' appointed or elected by affected employees. Employee representatives are accorded similar rights and protection to those of union representatives. In the case of redundancies, the consultation provisions do not come into play until there is a proposal for 20 or more redundancies within a 90-day period. For transfers of businesses, the rules apply regardless of the number of employees involved. Further regulations are expected which will incorporate certain amendments to the *Acquired Rights Directive (77/187)*. Various amendments made over the years to *Directive 77/187* have now been incorporated into *Directive 2001/23* of 12 March 2001. Between September and December 2001, the Government consulted on reforms to *TUPE*.

Further details of these consultation measures are contained in REDUNDANCY – II (39) and 52.18 TRANSFER OF UNDERTAKINGS.

Employers in both unionised and non-unionised workplaces are obliged to consult over health and safety under the *Safety Representatives and Safety*

Committees Regulations 1977 (SI 1977/500) and the Health and Safety (Consultation with Employees) Regulations 1996 (SI 1996/1513). For further details see 28.20–28.22 HEALTH AND SAFETY AT WORK – II.

18.29 **CONSULTATION ON TRAINING**

The *Employment Relations Act 1999, s 1* and *Sch 1*, which came into effect on 6 June 2000, contains statutory procedures for the recognition of a trade union for collective bargaining purposes where the union has achieved a specified level of support and the union and employer are unable to reach agreement voluntarily. (For further details, see TRADE UNIONS – I (50).) Under the statutory procedure the employer is not obliged to bargain on training matters but has a duty to consult (*TULRCA 1992, s 70B*, as inserted by *ERA 1999, s 5*). Representatives of the union must be invited to a meeting at least every six months for the purpose of:

(a)   consulting on the employer's policy for training workers in the bargaining unit;

(b)   consulting on the employer's plans for training those workers in the following six months; and

(c)   reporting on training provided since the previous meeting.

Relevant information must be provided by the employer to the union at least two weeks before the meeting. Enforcement is through employment tribunals.

18.30 **PARTNERSHIP FUND**

Employment Relations Act 1999, s 30 gives statutory authority to the Secretary of State to provide money for the purpose of encouraging and helping employers (or their representatives) and employees (or their representatives) to improve the way they work together. Money may be provided as grants or otherwise, on such terms as the Secretary of State thinks fit.

The Partnership at Work Fund was created in 1999. The stated purpose of the Fund was to encourage the development of industrial relations by encouraging employers and employees to work together effectively. During the period of its operation, the Fund funded 249 workplace projects and committed over £12.5 million up to 31 March 2004. However, following a review which took place in 2004, the Fund was closed.

19   Employee's Past Criminal Convictions

19.1   SPENT CONVICTIONS

The *Rehabilitation of Offenders Act 1974* ('*ROA 1974*') provides that, after a period of time, people who have been convicted of criminal offences and who have served their sentences are, with some exceptions (see 19.4 below), not obliged to disclose those convictions. The length of time which must elapse before a person's conviction becomes 'spent' in this way depends upon the nature of the sentence imposed and runs from the date of sentence. Certain sentences, such as imprisonment or custody for life, sentences of imprisonment, youth custody or detention in a young offender institution, or corrective training for a term exceeding 30 months, and detention during Her Majesty's pleasure, can never become spent (*ROA 1974, s 5(1)*; as amended by *Criminal Justice Act 1982, ss 77, 78, Sch 14 para 36, Sch 16*). An offender whose conviction has become spent is known as a 'rehabilitated person' (*ROA 1974, s 1(1)*).

19.2   Non-disclosure of spent convictions

Subject to certain exceptions, a rehabilitated person is to be treated for all purposes in law as a person who has not committed or been charged with or convicted of the offence in question. Evidence of such matters may not be adduced in judicial proceedings and questions should not be asked in such proceedings which cannot be answered without revealing such matters; if asked, they need not be answered (*ROA 1974, s 4(1)*). This also applies to employment tribunal proceedings (*ROA 1974, s 4(6)*).

Further, if questions about past convictions and related matters are put in other circumstances (such as at a job interview or on an application form), they may be answered on the basis that they do not refer to spent convictions, and the person questioned shall not be subjected to any liability or otherwise prejudiced in law by failing to acknowledge or disclose his spent convictions (*ROA 1974, s 4(2)*). Any obligation imposed on a person, by a rule of law or an agreement or arrangement (which would include a contract of employment), to disclose any matters does not require the disclosure of spent convictions or ancillary matters (*ROA 1974, s 4(3)(a)*).

A person who reveals another's spent criminal convictions may raise the defence of justification (ie truth) in any subsequent action for libel or slander, provided that the revelation was not made with malice (*ROA 1974, s 8(3), (5)*).

19.3   Spent convictions and dismissal

A spent conviction or a failure to disclose such a conviction are not proper grounds for dismissing or excluding a person from any office, profession, occupation or employment or for prejudicing him in any way in any occupation or employment (*ROA 1974, s 4(3)(b)*). Thus, an employer may not dismiss an employee merely because he discovers that the employee has a conviction which has become spent. In *Hendry v Scottish Liberal Club* [1977] IRLR 5, a Scottish employment tribunal held that a spent conviction for possession of cannabis had to some extent influenced the club's decision to dismiss the employee. Therefore, the reason for the dismissal could not fall within the range of permitted reasons and the dismissal was unfair (see 54.2 UNFAIR DISMISSAL – II). A security officer is not an occupation excluded from the benefit of the *ROA 1974* (see 19.4 below) and, consequently, an employer who dismissed two security officers for failing to disclose a spent conviction was held to have dismissed them unfairly (*Property Guards Ltd v Taylor and Kershaw* [1982] IRLR 175).

Furthermore, the fact that a person has a spent conviction is not a proper ground for an employer to refuse to engage that person, unless the person falls within a category to which the *Exceptions Order* applies (see below) (*ROA 1974, s 4(3)(b)*). However, it is not clear what remedy there would be for such a refusal: possibly it would be an action for breach of statutory duty.

19.4 EXCEPTIONS

The *Rehabilitation of Offenders Act 1974* (*Exceptions*) *Order 1975* (*SI 1975/1023*) provides that people following certain occupations and professions are obliged (despite the provisions of *ROA 1974, s 4(2)*) to disclose any spent convictions and may be dismissed or excluded from employment because of such a conviction (despite the provisions of *ROA 1974, s 4(3)*). Those professions and occupations include: doctors, nurses, midwives, dentists, barristers, solicitors, accountants, teachers, police officers and (by virtue of *SI 1986/2268*, which amends the (*Exceptions*) *Order 1975*) directors or other officers of building societies. The *Rehabilitation of Offenders Act 1974* (*Exceptions*) (*Amendment*) *Order 1986* (*SI 1986/1249*) also amends the (*Exceptions*) *Order 1975* by substituting, for a number of specific excepted occupational groups, a general exception covering any office or employment which is concerned with the provision of accommodation, care, leisure and recreational facilities, schooling, social services, supervision or training to persons under 18 years, where the holder of the office or employment would have access to such minors in the normal course of his duties or if the duties are carried out wholly or partly on the premises where such provision takes place. Further amendments to the (*Exceptions*) *Order 1975* are made by the *Osteopaths Act 1993, s 39(2)*, *(4)*, by the *Chiropractors Act 1994, s 40(2)*, *(4)*, and by the *Insurance Companies* (*Third Insurance Directives*) *Regulations 1994* (*SI 1994/1696*). The application of the (*Exceptions*) *Order 1975* to work 'in connection with the provision of social services' was considered by the EAT in *Wood v Coverage Care Ltd* [1996] IRLR 264.

By virtue of the *1975 Order*, as amended, an applicant for, or candidate for admission to, any profession or occupation specified in the *Order*, or which falls within the general exception referred to above, is not statutorily excused from the obligation to disclose spent convictions where a question is asked in order to assess his suitability for any profession, occupation, office or employment in the circumstances described, if the question relates to the applicant for such a post or (where applicable) if it relates to a person who lives in the same household as the applicant, and the provision of the services mentioned would normally take place in that household.

The *Rehabilitation of Offenders Act 1974* (*Exceptions*) *Order 1975* has been further amended by the *Rehabilitation of Offenders Act 1974* (*Exceptions*) (*Amendment*) *Order 2002* (*SI 2002/441*), which came into force (in part) on 29 February 2002. The professions to which the rehabilitative provisions of the *ROA 1974* do not apply are extended to include chartered psychologists, actuaries, registered foreign lawyers, legal executives and receivers appointed by the Court of Protection. Further employments subject to exemption from some of the provisions of the *ROA 1974* will now include the Crown Prosecution Service, Customs and Excise, the National Crime Squad, the National Criminal Intelligence

Service, those working with vulnerable adults and certain employments in the RSPCA. Further exceptions relate to National Lottery Commission personnel, air traffic workers, and to the licensing of taxi drivers and National Lottery licences.

A further exception to the *Act* is set out in the *Financial Services Act 1986, s 189*, which provides that convictions for offences involving fraud or dishonesty, or for offences under legislation relating to companies (including insider dealing), various financial institutions, insolvency, consumer credit and consumer protection, shall not be regarded as spent for the purposes of certain proceedings, questions and actions specified in *FSA 1986, Sch 14*.

19.5 EFFECT OF PROVISIONS FOR REHABILITATION

If, for example, at an interview, an applicant is asked whether he has any criminal convictions, a negative answer may mean:

(i) that he has no previous convictions;

(ii) that he has convictions but they are spent; or

(iii) that he has convictions which are not spent and he is not telling the truth.

If the employer subsequently discovers, after engaging the applicant, that he has previous convictions:

(*a*) if these are not spent, he may consider the applicant for dismissal if such a dismissal would be fair in all the circumstances (see 54.4 UNFAIR DISMISSAL – II); or

(*b*) if these are spent, he may not take any action, unless there are other reasons which justify him in doing so.

If the applicant reveals at an interview that he has previous convictions:

(A) if the convictions are spent, they do not form a good reason for refusing the applicant the job; or

(B) if they are not spent, they may form good grounds for refusing the applicant the job (and there will be no legal redress if the applicant is refused the job on such grounds).

Any agreement or arrangement that an applicant must reveal past convictions is ineffective so far as spent convictions are concerned (see 19.2 above).

Applicants for any position in a profession or occupation excluded from the protection of the *Act* (see 19.4 above) must answer questions relating to previous convictions and may be refused or dismissed from such employment for a conviction or for failing to disclose such a conviction.

19.6 REHABILITATION PERIODS

The period of rehabilitation is related to the length of the sentence which was passed on the offender. The main rehabilitation periods are set out below.

Sentence	Rehabilitation period
Imprisonment, custody, or detention for life, or detention at Her Majesty's pleasure.	Not applicable

19.7   Employee's Past Criminal Convictions

Sentence	Rehabilitation period
Imprisonment, youth custody, detention in a young offender institution for a term exceeding 30 months.	Not applicable
Imprisonment, youth custody, detention in a young offender institution or corrective training for between 6 and 30 months.	10 years
Imprisonment, youth custody or detention in a young offender institution for 6 months or less.	7 years
Fine, or (in the case of adults) probation.	5 years
Detention under the Children and Young Persons Act 1933, s 53 for between 6 and 30 months.	5 years
Detention under above Act for 6 months or less.	3 years
Probation (in the case of minors).	2½ years from conviction, or (if later) when the probation order ceases to have effect
Conditional discharge, binding over, care or supervision order.	1 year or the duration of the order, if longer
Disqualification from driving.	Period of disqualification
Absolute discharge.	6 months

(*ROA 1974, s 5* as amended. Note that for those placed on probation prior to 3 February 1995, the rehabilitation period is one year (*Criminal Justice and Public Order Act 1994, Sch 9 para 11(2)*; *Criminal Justice and Public Order Act 1994 (Commencement No 5 and Transitional Provisions) Order 1995 (SI 1995/127)*).)

19.7   REFORM OF ACCESS TO PAST CRIMINAL CONVICTIONS: PART V OF THE POLICE ACT 1997

Part V of the *Police Act 1997* ('*PA 1997*'), which received Royal Assent on 27 March 1997, contains a number of provisions for access to the records of employees' past convictions. The *Act* provides for the issue of a number of certificates which may be sought by the employee or provided to an employer in order to satisfy a prospective employer of the accuracy of the employee's disclosure of criminal convictions (*PA 1997, ss 112–127*).

An applicant may apply to the Secretary of State upon payment of a fee for a 'criminal conviction certificate' ('CCC') which records all convictions of the applicant (as defined in the *Rehabilitation of Offenders Act 1974* but excluding spent convictions) or states that there are no such convictions, as the case may be (*PA 1997, s 112*). This provision is not yet in force but the Criminal Records Bureau's Code of Practice (see below), referring to this as 'Basic Disclosure', provides at paragraph 1.2.2: 'Any employer will be able to request a potential employee to apply for a BD'. See also *s 56* of the *Data Protection Act 1998* (similarly, not yet in force) prohibiting *requiring* provision of certain information in relation to recruitment or for the purposes of continued employment.

An application may be made for a 'criminal record certificate' ('CRC') in cases where *s 4(2)(a)* or (*b*) of the *Rehabilitation of Offenders Act 1974* have been excluded by order of the Secretary of State. The application must be counter-signed by a 'registered person' within the meaning of the *Act* (*PA 1997, s 120*) who confirms that the information is sought in relation to a matter which is exempt from the provisions of the *Rehabilitation of Offenders Act 1974 (PA 1997, s 113(2))*. The CRC is broader than the CCC in that it includes details of *all* convictions (including spent convictions) and also details of all cautions administered, or confirms the absence of any convictions or cautions, as the case may be (*PA 1997, s 113(3), (5)*). The certificate will be sent to the registered person and copied to the applicant (*PA 1997, s 113(4)*). Similarly, in the case of application for Crown employment, a CRC may be issued in cases of exempted questions concerning an applicant's suitability for Crown appointment (*PA 1997, s 114*).

An 'enhanced criminal record certificate' ('ECRC') may be obtained in relation to applications for certain sensitive employments (*PA 1997, s 115*). The application must be countersigned by a registered person who confirms that the certificate is sought in relation to considering the applicant's suitability for employment in a number of positions defined in the *Act* or for the purpose of considering the applicant for a number of licences as defined (*PA 1997, s 115(2)*). The positions covered are:

(*a*)   training, caring, supervising or being in sole charge of persons under 18 (*PA 1997, s 115(3)*); and

(*b*)   training, caring supervising or being in sole charge of persons over 18 if the position is one specified in regulations made by the Secretary of State (*PA 1997, s 115(4)*).

The other matters in relation to which an ECRC may be sought are gaming and gaming licences (*PA 1998, s 115(5)(a), (b)*), lottery management and promotion (*PA 1998, s 115(5)(c), (d)*), child minding (*PA 1998, s 115(5)(e)*) and foster placement and the approval of persons as foster carers (*PA 1998, s 115(5)(f), (g)*).

The ECRC (as in the case of the CRC) gives details of all convictions and cautions (or their absence) but, in addition, the Secretary of State will request the Chief Officer of every relevant police force to provide any information which the Chief Officer considers relevant to the issue of the applicant's suitability for such a position; this information will be included in the certificate (*PA 1997, s 115(7)*). The application, meaning and effect of *s 115(7)* has been considered authoritatively in *R (X) v Chief Constable of the West Midlands Police* [2004] EWCA Civ 1968, [2005] 1 WLR 65. It was held that the Chief Constable was under a duty to disclose if the information might be relevant, unless there was some good reason for not making such a disclosure, and that he was not required to afford the subject of the information a right to make representations. Further *s 115* has been held to engage *Art 8* of the European Convention for the Protection of Human Rights and Fundamental Freedoms but has been held to be compliant with that Article (see *R(X) v Chief Constable of the West Midlands Police* (above). See also *R (L) v Metropolitan Police Comr* [2006] EWHC 482 (Admin) and *R v Local Authority and Police Authority in the Midlands, ex p LM* [2000] 1 FLR 612).

Additionally, the Chief Officer may provide further information which ought not to be included in the certificate on the grounds that its disclosure may hamper detection or prevention of crime but which may be disclosed directly to the registered person signing the application (*PA 1997, s 115(8), (9)*). The discretion afforded is broad and extends to any information which may, in the opinion of the Chief Officer, be relevant. It has been explained judicially that 'any' means just what it says and is not limited in its scope to information relating to criminal conduct: see *R (L) v Metropolitan Police Comr* [2006] EWHC 482 (Admin). By *s 116*, the issuing of ECRCs are extended to Crown employment.

19.8 Employee's Past Criminal Convictions

In the case of each certificate outlined above, the Secretary of State may refuse to issue a certificate unless satisfied of the applicant's identity, which may involve the provision of fingerprints to confirm identity (*PA 1997, s 118*). If the applicant believes that any of the information contained in any certificate is inaccurate, he may apply in writing to the Secretary of State for a new certificate (*PA 1997, s 117*). On the utilisation of *s 117* see *R(B) v Secretary of State for Home Department and Metropolitan Police Comr* [2006] EWHC 579 (Admin). It will be an offence to falsify or alter certificates or use certificates belonging to another (*PA 1997, s 123*). It will also be an offence for employees of registered bodies or recipients of CRC or ECRC information to disclose the information contained in the certificates otherwise than in the course of their duties (*PA 1997, s 124*). The Secretary of State has issued a code of practice in relation to the provision of information under the *Act (PA 1997, s 122(1), (2))*. The Code, titled 'Code of Practice and Explanatory Guide for Registered Persons and other recipients of Disclosure Information', is available from www.crb.gov.uk.

The majority of the provisions of *Part V* of the *Police Act 1997* (contained in *ss 112–127*) have gradually come into force by a complicated series of commencement orders and regulations made under the *PA 1997*. The principal statutory instruments are as follows: *Police Act 1997 (Criminal Records) Regulations 2002 (SI 2002/233); Police Act 1997 (Enhanced Criminal Record Certificates) (Protection of Vulnerable Adults) Regulations 2002 (SI 2002/446); Police Act 1997 (Criminal Records) (Registration) Regulations 2001 (SI 2001/1194); Police Act 1997 (Criminal Records) (Registration) (Amendment) Regulations 2001 (SI 2001/2498)* (in force 13 August 2001); and the *Police Act (Commencement No 9) Order 2002 (SI 2002/413)* bringing into force on 1 March 2002 *Part V* of the *PA 1997 (ss 112–127)* except *s 112*. The effect of this mass of commencement orders is that criminal record certificates ('CRC') and enhanced criminal record certificates ('ECRC') may, since March 2002, be obtained from the Criminal Records Bureau by appropriate bodies that are registered with the Criminal Records Bureau because of the nature of the specific employment which is in issue (e g caring for children).

The more basic and general criminal conviction certificate ('CCC') which may be sought by individual application by any employee or prospective employee and which applies to any employment whatsoever will not, however, be available until the provisions of *s 112* of *Part V* of the *Police Act 1997* are brought fully into force. There is no indication at present of the date of expected introduction of the basic, generally applicable ('CCC') certificate.

19.8 RECORDING EMPLOYEES' CRIMINAL CONVICTIONS

The *Data Protection Act 1998* limits the right of an employer to process data on employees' criminal convictions without the express consent of the employee, save for limited purposes specified in the *Act (DPA 1998, Sch 3)*. (See further 11.12 DISCLOSURE OF INFORMATION.)

20   Employment Tribunals – I

20.1   HISTORY

Employment tribunals (known until 1998 as 'industrial tribunals') are the principal forum for adjudicating disputes between employees (and prospective or former employees, and in some cases other workers) and employers. The tribunals, which were originally created in 1964 to decide disputes about liability to pay Industrial Training Levy, have over the years been given significant additional jurisdiction, increasingly so in recent years.

The workload of the employment tribunals has, unsurprisingly, fluctuated over the 40 years of their operation. In recent years the number of cases rose from a low of 29,304 applications registered in 1988/89, to 103,935 in 1999/2000. Since then, the underlying trend of numbers of individual cases has been relatively stable, with a slight downward trend, whilst significant variations in the number of multiple cases instituted have created an overall picture of considerable increases and decreases in numbers of claims from year to year. Thus in 2003/4 there were 115,042 new cases registered, falling in 2004/5 to 86,181 and in 2005/6 (the latest year for which figures are available) rising again to 115,039; the variation is almost entirely attributable to fluctuations in the number of multiple cases, the figure for individual claims in each year being between 50,000 and 55,000. A slight but steady downward trend in individual cases appears to have been reversed during the first months of 2006/7.

The Department of Trade and Industry (DTI) anticipated a considerable drop in tribunal claims as a result of reforms introduced with effect from October 2004 requiring the use of internal procedures prior to the making of tribunal claims, but it is not clear from these statistics whether that has proved to be the case. The ETS annual report for 2005/6 reveals that 12,258 claims submitted during that year were initially rejected, and of those only 4,897 were successfully resubmitted. If, as is probable, most of the rejected claims were single rather than multiple claims, this suggests that up to one in eight such claims are excluded at the initial stage for procedural reasons, indicating in turn an underlying increase in the number of individuals wishing to pursue claims.

Statistics of numbers of cases do not give the full picture of the increase in the volume and complexity of the tribunals' case load in recent years. The number of individual claims under separate jurisdictions raised in each case has been steadily rising and now averages nearly 1.8 per case. The trend to more complex cases and lengthier hearings has been reinforced by the recent extension of the tribunals' jurisdiction to cover discrimination on grounds of religion or belief, sexual orientation and age.

The increase in workload through the 1990s, which was not matched by increases in resources, put a considerable strain on the tribunal system. A number of changes were made to jurisdiction and procedures by the *Trade Union Reform and Employment Rights Act 1993* (*'TURERA 1993'*) and new rules of procedure were made the same year. Further reforms were enacted by the *Employment Rights (Dispute Resolution) Act 1998* (*'ERDRA 1998'*). Although more controversial proposals for reform were dropped following consultation, a number of the substantive changes *ERDRA 1998* makes were not implemented, and have effectively been overtaken by later reforms.

20.2   In response to these pressures of workload and concerns about the working of employment tribunals (and the tribunal system generally) several further initiatives have been taken.

(*a*)   A major review of the tribunal system generally, under Sir Andrew Leggatt, a former Lord Justice of Appeal, was established in May 2000. The Leggatt report (*Tribunals for Users*, TSO) was published in August 2001. The principal recommendation of the Report was the creation of a unified tribunal system, with a transfer of responsibility for employment tribunals from the DTI to the Lord Chancellor's Department (subsequently renamed the Department for Constitutional Affairs and since May 2007 the Ministry of Justice), but with the employment tribunals retaining their separate identity, and the existing tripartite structure of membership. A recommendation for limited legal assistance for representation in cases where there are particular difficulties for an unrepresented party did not find favour with the Government. A further recommendation, for the regulation of organisations providing representation in tribunals but not otherwise not subject to professional regulation, has been implemented by the *Compensation Act 2006.*

In its response to the Leggatt Report in March 2003, and a subsequent White Paper in June 2004, the Government announced that a unified tribunals service would be established under the auspices of the Department for Constitutional Affairs, which would include the employment tribunals. The unified tribunal structure was implemented with effect from 1 April 2006, as an administrative measure without specific enabling legislation. Enabling legislation, the *Tribunals, Courts and Enforcement Bill 2006*, is currently (May 2007) before Parliament. The legislation expressly preserves the separate identity of employment tribunals and the EAT, but not their administrative independence from the rest of the new tribunal system. The newly created Tribunals Service, an Executive Agency of the Ministry of Justice, now has responsibility for the administration of employment tribunals and the Employment Appeal Tribunal, with the DTI retaining responsibility for the Rules of Procedure.

(*b*)   The scheme for voluntary arbitration through ACAS in unfair dismissal cases, foreshadowed by the *ERDRA 1998*, came into operation in 2001 for England and Wales and early 2004 in Scotland. It has subsequently been extended to cover disputes about the right to request flexible working arrangements. However, the scheme has had a very limited impact, with only 55 cases referred to it in the period up to 31 March 2006, (*ACAS Annual Report, 2005–6*). Details of the scope and main features of the scheme are in 20.37 below. Despite the limited impact of the voluntary arbitration service, there is increasing interest in alternative dispute resolution schemes for employment disputes, and initiatives in this area include the development of mediation services by ACAS (which handled 85 cases in 2005–6) and proposals for a scheme within the employment tribunals themselves.

(*c*)   New Rules of Procedure were introduced as from July 2001 (the *Employment Tribunals* (*Constitution and Rules of Procedure*) *Regulations 2001* (*SI 2001/1171*) and their Scottish counterpart (*SI 2001/1170*)). The new rules embodied a number of changes, of which the most significant were:

(i)   The introduction of an Overriding Objective for tribunals, which must be taken into account in interpreting the rules of procedure and in deciding issues affecting the conduct of the proceedings. The Overriding Objective is 'to deal with cases justly', which includes so far as practicable ensuring that the parties are on an equal footing, saving expense, dealing with cases in ways proportionate to their complexity, and ensuring that they are dealt with expeditiously and fairly. The parties are required to assist in the achievement of this objective.

(ii)   Tribunals were given powers to order a claim (or defence) to be struck out on the ground that it was 'misconceived', a term defined as including having 'no reasonable prospects of success'. This was intended to assist tribunals in weeding out hopeless claims, and effectively reversed a decision of the Court of Appeal (*Care First Partnership Ltd v Roffey* [2001] IRLR 85) that there was no such power under the previous rules.

(iii)   The power to award costs was extended to cases where the bringing or conducting of proceedings was 'misconceived' (defined as above), and the amount that could be awarded on a summary assessment by the tribunal was raised from £500 to £10,000. In addition the deposit that could be required on a pre-hearing review was increased to a maximum of £500; previously it had been £150.

These changes have been retained and built on in the further reform of the rules in 2004 (see below).

(*d*)   In the autumn of 2001, the Government announced the creation of a special Task Force to reassess the workings of the employment tribunal system as a whole. The Task Force, chaired by a prominent employment solicitor, Janet Gaymer, issued its report in July 2002. Its numerous recommendations concentrate on the avoidance of employment disputes, and their settlement through internal procedures, as a preferable alternative to litigation in the tribunal, and pilot schemes for mediation to settle employment disputes, together with improved access to information for tribunal users, and earlier disclosure of information by the parties in tribunal proceedings.

In November 2002, the Government announced its broad acceptance of the recommendations in the Task Force report, and the general approach is reflected in the 2004 revision of the *Rules of Procedure* discussed below. The Task Force itself has been reconstituted as a permanent strategic body charged with monitoring progress on the implementation of its recommendations.

(*e*)   As a separate exercise, the DTI instituted a review of the employment tribunal system which resulted, following consultations in the summer of 2001, in a number of provisions affecting the procedure of tribunals in what subsequently became the *Employment Act 2002*. The principal changes introduced by the *Employment Act 2002 have* been implemented through a new set of Regulations, the *Employment Tribunals* (*Constitution and Rules of Procedure) Regulations 2004* (*SI 2004/1861*), which (unlike previous such *Regulations*), apply to England and Wales and to Scotland (with some minor differences of terminology and practice identified within the *Regulations*). *Schedule 1* to the *Regulations* contains the rules of procedure for the principal tribunal jurisdictions and is known as the *Employment Tribunals*

Rules of Procedure 2004. The *Regulations* are referred to in this and the two following chapters as the *2004 Regulations*, and the *Rules of Procedure* as the *ET Rules.* The *ET Rules* have applied as from 1 October 2004 to all claims first presented on or after that date, and (with the exception of the rules as to costs, for which the *2001 Rules* still apply to cases where the claim was presented before 1 October 2004) to all aspects of continuing cases not finally disposed of before that date. The *Regulations* were subsequently amended to add, as *Sch 6,* complementary rules of procedure for Equal Value claims (see *SI 2004/2351*), and were further amended subsequently, mainly to correct a number of minor errors of drafting (see *SI 2005/1865*) and to delay the introduction of a requirement to use prescribed Claim and Response Forms until 1 October 2005 (see *SI 2005/435*); the text in this and the following chapter refers to the *Regulations* as amended.

20.3   The Employment Act 2002 and Rules of Procedure 2004

The principal changes affecting the powers and procedure of employment tribunals which were introduced by the *Employment Act 2002*, with effect from 1 October 2004, can be summarised as follows.

(*a*)   a requirement for claimants to go through workplace grievance procedures where relevant, before a claim can be made to a tribunal, with power to reduce compensation if the claimant does not do so (and increase it if the employer did not provide a procedure, or dismissed or took disciplinary action without following the statutory procedure) (*s 31*);

(*b*)   changes in the time limits for commencing tribunal claims to allow time for internal procedures to be concluded without the necessity to present a claim to preserve the employee's rights; the employee is not permitted to present his or her claim to the tribunal in certain cases until after the employer has been given the opportunity to resolve it under the grievance procedure and in certain circumstances the time limit for claiming is automatically extended by three months (*ss 32, 33*);

(*c*)   provision for a limited conciliation period for ACAS to attempt to secure a settlement; if the case is not settled within that period (or any extension of it), ACAS ceases be under a duty to offer its assistance in any further attempts at settlement (*s 24*);

(*d*)   further changes in the rules on the awarding of costs (expenses in Scotland), to permit tribunals to award costs against a representative, or disallow the representative's costs as against his or her client; to permit tribunals to award compensation for time spent in preparing a case, as an alternative to an award of the costs of professional representation; and to allow tribunals to take into account the means of a party in determining what costs to award against him or her (reversing the decision of the Court of Appeal in *Kovacs v Queen Mary and Westfield College* [2002] EWCA Civ 352, [2002] IRLR 414 that this cannot be taken into account) (*s 22*);

(*e*)   new powers conferred on the Secretary of State to prescribe the forms used in tribunal proceedings;

(*f*)   an extension of the powers of tribunals conducting a pre-hearing review to permit the tribunal to strike out a claim or response (or part of either) if it finds it to be scandalous, vexatious or misconceived (*s 28*);

(*g*)   a new power for the Presidents of tribunals (for England and Wales and for Scotland) to issue Practice Directions regulating tribunal procedures (*s 27*; as at May 2007 this power had only been used for Scotland).

A number of proposals canvassed in the consultation exercise or included in the original Bill were not proceeded with, including a proposal for charging a fee to bring proceedings in the tribunal, and changes in the statutory provisions on compromise agreements.

The implementation of the first two sets of provisions referred to above was by way of supplementary *Regulations* under the *2002 Act*, the *Employment Act 2002 (Dispute Resolution) Regulations 2004 (SI 2004/752)*, which came into force on 1 October 2004, subject to transitional provisions (the *Dispute Resolution Regulations*). The remainder have been implemented by the *2004 Regulations* and *ET Rules*. In March 2007 the DTI instituted a consultation exercise on whether the procedures introduced by the *2002 Act* should be scrapped, as recommended by a Review commissioned by the Department; however any such action would require primary legislation and it is understood that this could not be brought into force before 2009 at earliest.

20.4   The *2004 Regulations* contain the provisions for the appointment and tenure of office of the Presidents of the Tribunals (one for England and Wales and one for Scotland), the Vice-President (for Scotland only), Regional Chairmen (in England and Wales only) and Chairmen and members. The *Regulations* also cover the composition of tribunals for particular cases, special rules for cases involving issues of national security, and a number of ancillary provisions which are referred to at relevant points in the text below. *Schedule 1* contains the rules of procedure applicable to most claims, and is referred to as the *Employment Tribunals Rules of Procedure 2004* ('the *ET Rules*'). The other Schedules cover the following:

(*a*)   *Schedule 2:*   Complementary rules for National Security cases;

(*b*)   *Schedule 3:*   Training levy appeals;

(*c*)   *Schedule 4:*   Appeals against improvement and prohibition notices issued under the *Health and Safety at Work, etc Act 1974*;

(*d*)   *Schedule 5:*   Appeals against non-discrimination notices issued by the Equal Opportunities Commission, Commission for Racial Equality or Disability Rights Commission.

(*e*)   *Schedule 6:*   Complementary rules for Equal Value cases (added by *SI 2004/2351*).

The *2004 Regulations* and *ET Rules* made considerable changes in the substance of the procedure to be applied by tribunals. The *Rules* have been written in what is intended to be simpler language more readily understandable by litigants without legal training. As part of the simplification, a number of changes in terminology were introduced:

(i)   Those applying to a tribunal are now known as 'claimants' rather than 'applicants'; however there is no change to the term 'respondent'.

(ii)   The document by which an application is made to the tribunal is now a 'Claim Form' instead of an 'originating application'.

(iii)   The response by a respondent is now a 'Response Form' rather than a 'notice of appearance'.

(iv)   What were known as either directions hearings or interlocutory hearings are now referred to as Case Management Discussions ('CMDs').

(v)   What was formerly called a Decision is now a Judgment.

20.5   Alongside the changes of terminology are changes of substance. Below is a brief summary of the principal changes of substance effected by the *2004 ET Rules*.

(*a*)   New Claim Forms (known as Form ET1) and Response Forms (Form ET3) have been introduced, together with electronic equivalents available on the tribunals' website. Use of the paper or electronic version of the prescribed forms became compulsory on 1 October 2005. Separately, the information required to be given on the Claim Form is prescribed in more detail.

(*b*)   A screening process applies by which the tribunal secretariat weed out claims not containing the required information or which appear to have been brought in breach of the requirements of *s 32 Employment Act 2002* to make use first of the statutory grievance procedure, or otherwise to be outside the tribunal's jurisdiction. Such cases are referred to a Chairman for decision whether to refuse to accept and register the claim. (Such refusals are open to review, or appeal.) Claims not submitted on the prescribed form are returned to the claimant by the secretariat with a copy of the form for completion and resubmission. A proposal for 'pre-acceptance hearings' at this stage was dropped after consultations on the draft Rules.

(*c*)   Response Forms must be received by the tribunal within 28 days following the date that the Claim Form was sent to the respondent (not, as previously, 21 days from the date of *receipt*). Unless an extension of time has been requested before the period for responding has elapsed, and subsequently granted, if no Response Form has been received in due time a Chairman may issue a default judgment in favour of the claimant; the respondent may apply to have the default judgment reviewed, but this application will only be granted if the Chairman hearing the review application is satisfied that there are reasonable prospects of successfully defending the claim, and may still be refused if there were no good reasons for failing to submit the Response Form in time. Late or incomplete responses may simply be rejected by a Chairman, in which case the respondent will be treated as not having responded, and if the prescribed form has not been used, the Response will be rejected by the secretariat and returned to the respondent.

(*d*)   The *Rules* implement the provisions of the *Employment Act 2002* providing for a limited period of conciliation, after which ACAS will not normally assist parties to settle their cases. There are three categories of case, for which the conciliation period is either 7 weeks or 13 weeks from the date of presentation of the claim, or is unlimited. During either fixed conciliation period the substantive hearing of the claim cannot take place, but other preliminary steps in the case including Case Management Discussions and Pre-hearing Reviews, the making of Case Management Orders, and listing the case for a full Hearing after the conciliation period has expired, are permitted. There is a limited power to extend the conciliation period if a case appears to be likely to settle.

(*e*)   The types of hearing of a case that can be held have been rationalised. The possible categories are:

(i)   Case Management Discussions (CMDs), conducted by a Chairman sitting alone, and in private, and which cannot deal with substantive issues in the claim, or applications to strike out a claim or response. CMDs are used to make any of a large range of possible case management directions to prepare the case for a full hearing.

(ii)   Pre-hearing Reviews (PHRs), which are held in public, normally by a Chairman sitting alone (but a party may request a full tribunal). PHRs can deal with preliminary issues such as whether the claim was presented in time or whether the Claimant had sufficient service to complain of unfair dismissal, claims for interim relief and applications to strike out all or part of a claim or response, in addition to the former function, retained under the new *ET Rules,* of considering whether a claim or response has reasonable prospects of success and, if not, giving a costs warning and ordering a deposit as a condition of continuing to pursue it. Evidence can now be given at a PHR (except where the only issue is whether a deposit should be ordered).

(iii)   Hearings, which may be of the entire case or a preliminary issue (if not dealt with at a PHR) or just on liability or remedy. A Hearing (capitalised in the *Rules* to distinguish it from other types of hearings) must normally be in public and before a full tribunal, unless the claim is one which under *s 4 Employment Tribunals Act 1996* can be determined by a Chairman sitting alone (in such cases there is, as previously, a discretion to refer the matter to a full tribunal).

(iv)   Review hearings, which will be before a Chairman alone if the review is of a refusal to accept a Claim Form or Response Form, but otherwise normally before the tribunal or Chairman, as the case may be, whose decision is the subject of an application for a review.

(*f*)   Decisions of tribunals which represent the final determination (subject to any appeal or review) either of the whole of a case or a specific issue (such as jurisdiction), are now renamed Judgments; tribunals may also issue 'orders' (formerly referred to as 'directions') in relation to any requirements imposed the parties at an interim stage in the proceedings or dealing with other case management issues. All Judgments must be made or confirmed in writing and signed by the Chairman. Reasons (the distinction between summary and extended reasons has been discontinued) may be given orally or in writing, and if given orally will not automatically be followed by written reasons unless this is requested by a party within 14 days of the issuing of the Judgment. Reasons for orders will be given if requested at the time, but not necessarily in writing.

(*g*)   New powers to award costs have been introduced (but only apply to cases presented on or after 1 October 2004). These enable a tribunal to make an award in favour of a party who is not legally represented, to cover the costs of his or her time in preparing for the hearing (a 'preparation time order'), covering such hours as the tribunal assesses as reasonable at a fixed rate of £27 an hour (the rate was increased to this amount from 6 April 2007 and will increase thereafter by a further £1 an hour each year). Preparation time orders cannot be made if a costs order is also made (or vice versa) and can only be made under the same conditions as a costs order. The second new type of order, a wasted costs order, can be made against a representative, provided the representative is acting for profit, and is either an order to pay costs to the other party, or an order disallowing the representative's charges to his or her client in whole or in part.

(*h*)   Tribunals may have regard to the means of the paying party in deciding whether, and if so how much, to award by way of costs.

(*i*)   A number of changes of detail have been made, including the procedure for making restricted reporting orders, and wider powers to conduct hearings by telephone or video link. New powers are given to Chairmen to order a non-party to produce documents in his or her possession relevant to the issues in the case, and to join any person the Chairman considers has an interest in the outcome of the case as a party.

(*j*)   The public register of applications has been closed. The register of decisions (now a register of judgments) is retained, and judgments and written reasons remain available for public inspection.

The *Regulations* also confer power on the Presidents to issue Practice Directions regulating the procedure of tribunals and the manner of exercise of the powers conferred on tribunals and Chairmen by the *Regulations* and *Rules*. The first Practice Directions issued under this power, which apply in Scotland only, were issued in December 2006; they cover lists of documents, sists (the Scots Law term for stays) for mediation and the procedure for counterclaims in contract cases.

20.6   ADMINISTRATION

The employment tribunals are constituted under the *Employment Tribunals Act 1996* ('*ETA 1996*') (a consolidating Act replacing equivalent earlier legislation) and the *Regulations* and *Rules of Procedure* made under the powers conferred by the *ETA 1996*. (The changes effected by the *Employment Act 2002* were made by way of amendments to the enabling provisions of the *1996 Act*.) The overall responsibility for the running of the tribunals in England and Wales is vested in the President of the Employment Tribunals, a judicial officer appointed by the Lord Chancellor (*2004 Regulations, reg 4*). The tribunal system is divided into 12 regions, each with a Regional Chairman also appointed by the Lord Chancellor (*2004 Regulations, reg 6*). There is a separate President of the Tribunals for Scotland, and a Vice-President, both appointed by the Lord President of the Court of Session (*2004 Regulations, regs 4, 7*). Tribunals sit at all the regional centres and at a further 13 permanent centres and a number of *ad hoc* centres.

The administration of tribunals (and of the EAT) is the responsibility of the Tribunals Service ('TS'), which came into existence on 1 April 2006 as an executive agency of the Department for Constitutional Affairs, now the Ministry of Justice. The Tribunals Service is responsible for the administration of some twenty separate statutory tribunals, including the provision of premises, staff and facilities such as computing, and has instituted a programme intended to rationalise premises and support arrangements. It has not been publicly stated whether the administrative staff assigned to the employment tribunals will retain a separate identity as such

There is a Central Office of Employment Tribunals (COET) at Bury St Edmunds, which maintains the public Register of Judgments. Formerly, all applications had to be sent to the Central Office but, since 1996, applications (now called claims) have been required to be lodged at local offices. The relevant office is determined by the postcode of the claimant's place of work or former place of work, and claims presented electronically are automatically routed to the appropriate office based on the postcode given by the claimant for his or her (former) workplace. There is a separate Central Office of Tribunals for Scotland, in Glasgow, and separate offices for the Presidents of the Tribunals in England and Wales and for Scotland (in Croydon and Glasgow, respectively).

20.7   **COMPOSITION**

Tribunals are drawn from three panels (*2004 Regulations, reg 8*):

(*a*)   Chairmen, who are appointed by the Judicial Appointments Commission (a body established by the *Constitutional Reform Act 2005*), or in Scotland by the Lord President of the Court of Session, and must have a seven-year legal qualification – appointments are both full-time and part-time (Chairmen are to be redesignated 'Employment Judges' under the *Tribunals, Courts and Enforcement Bill*: see below).

(*b*)   Persons appointed by the Secretary of State for Trade and Industry after consulting organisations representative of employees.

(*c*)   Persons so appointed after consultation with organisations representative of employers.

The members drawn from panels (*b*) and (*c*) (variously referred to as 'lay members', 'wing members' and 'the industrial jury') all serve part-time. One of the changes proposed to be effected when the unified Tribunals Service was brought into being was that tribunal Chairmen would be given the title Employment Judge. As the Tribunals Service was created by administrative action rather than legislation, this was not possible at that stage but provision for this change has been included, by way of an amendment to the *ETA 1996*, in the *Tribunals, Courts and Enforcement Bill*.

The Presidents are required to maintain separate panels of Chairmen, and of each of the two categories of lay members, who are considered suitable to hear cases involving issues of national security, and the tribunal assigned to such a case will be composed of a member of each special panel (*2004 Regulations, regs 10, 11*). There is also a power to establish panels of Chairmen and members with specialist knowledge to hear particular categories of proceedings for which such knowledge would be beneficial (*reg 8(5)*). This power has been used to create specialist panels to hear equal pay cases, but there are no plans at present for other specialist panels.

The Department of Trade and Industry has in recent years attempted with some success to recruit more women, members of ethnic minorities, and younger people to the panels of lay members. In 1999, a further initiative to this end was announced and, for the first time, the option of self-nomination of lay members was made available. Lay members are paid a daily fee for sitting.

The composition, and methods of appointment and reappointment to membership, of the employment tribunals have in the past given rise to a potential difficulty under the *Human Rights Act 1998* ('*HRA 1998*'). *Article 6* of the *European Convention on Human Rights*, which the *HRA 1998* incorporates into UK law, confers the right to a determination of issues relating to civil rights (which includes most if not all issues brought before employment tribunals) at a fair and public hearing before an independent and impartial tribunal. The issue was raised whether employment tribunals could satisfy this requirement in cases where the Secretary of State for Trade and Industry was a party to the proceedings, as where claims were made against the Secretary of State because the employer was insolvent. Changes in the method of appointment of Chairmen and lay members in 2000 largely removed the potential conflicts of interest, and the creation of the Tribunals Service, together with the transfer of responsibility for appointments of Chairmen to the Judicial Appointments Commission, is thought to have resolved the problem, but this must remain open to possible judicial determination.

20.8   A full tribunal consists of one member from each panel. Decisions may be by majority. A tribunal may sit with only one lay member if both or all parties agree (*2004 Regulations, reg 9(3)*); in that event the Chairman has a casting vote. If one party is neither present nor represented at a hearing, the tribunal cannot proceed to sit with only two members. This anomaly was intended to be rectified by *s 4* of *ERDRA 1998*; however, as of May 2007 this provision has still not been brought into force. If agreement is sought to the tribunal sitting with only one lay member, the parties must be informed as to whether the lay member is from the employers' or employees' panel: *Rabahallah v British Telecommunications plc* [2005] ICR 440 (following *De Haney v Brent Mind* [2003] EWCA Civ 1637, [2004] IRLR 348, a case about the equivalent situation in the EAT). In *Rabahallah*, the EAT recommended that the parties be asked to sign a standard form to confirm that informed consent has been given to the tribunal sitting or continuing with only one lay member.

Tribunals normally sit in public; the circumstances in which they may sit in private or reporting of proceedings may be restricted are explained below (see 20.18–20.19 below). The importance of a public hearing was reiterated in *Storer v British Gas plc* [2000] IRLR 495, where the Court of Appeal set aside a decision on a preliminary issue reached at a hearing held in the private office of the Regional Chairman because no tribunal room was available. The court dismissed as irrelevant the argument that no members of the public had been prevented from attending the hearing.

20.9   **Chairmen sitting alone**

A full tribunal is required for the Hearing of most claims: however, certain categories of proceedings must be heard by a tribunal consisting of a Chairman sitting alone, unless a Chairman (not necessarily the same person who hears the case) directs to the contrary (*ETA 1996, s 4*). The principal categories of case covered by these provisions are:

(*a*)   applications for interim relief in relation to dismissal in health and safety and public interest disclosure cases (*ERA 1996, ss 128–132*) or for trade union reasons (*TULRCA 1992, ss 161, 165* and *166*);

(*b*)   applications against the Secretary of State under *ERA 1996, ss 170* and *188* or *Pension Schemes Act 1993, s 126* (where the former employer is insolvent);

(*c*)   applications under the *ERA 1996, s 23* or *TULRCA 1992, s 68A* (unlawful deductions from wages, etc);

(*d*)   applications under the following provisions of *ERA 1996: s 11* (particulars of employment terms and itemised pay statements), *s 34* (guarantee payments), *s 70* (remuneration during suspension on medical grounds), *s 163* (redundancy payments), and *s 206(4)* (appointment of 'appropriate person' in proceedings, following the death of an employee);

(*e*)   applications under *TULRCA 1992, s 192* or *reg 11(5)* of the *Transfer of Undertakings (Protection of Employment) Regulations 1981 (SI 1981/1794)* (failure to pay a protective award);

(*f*)   claims for breach of contract under the *Employment Tribunals Extension of Jurisdiction (England and Wales) Order 1994 (SI 1994/1623)* or the equivalent Scottish order;

(*g*)   proceedings where both or all parties have given their written consent to a hearing before a Chairman alone (whether or not consent has been subsequently withdrawn);

(*h*)   proceedings where the claimant has given written notice withdrawing the claim; and

(*i*)   proceedings where the respondent (or all respondents if more than one) does not contest the claim, or no longer does so.

(*ETA 1996, s 4(2)*.)

In addition, CMDs are always heard before a Chairman sitting alone, regardless of the type or complexity of the claim, and this is generally the case for PHRs. In the latter case there is a discretion to order a hearing before a full tribunal, but only if this has been requested at least 10 days in advance by one of the parties, and the Chairman considering the request considers that there will be one or more substantive issues of fact to be determined at the PHR, and that it is desirable that the matter be heard by a full tribunal (*ET Rules, rule 18(3)*). The requirement for Chairmen to sit alone for a PHR unless a party has requested a full tribunal may result in cases which would formerly have been regarded as suitable for a full tribunal being finally determined without the participation of lay members (as to this see the comments of the EAT in *Sutcliffe v Big C's Marine Ltd* [1998] ICR 913), and this has resulted in a significant reduction in the proportion of cases in which lay members participate. The Chairman who orders a PHR has no direct power to stipulate a full tribunal, and can at most only encourage the parties to ask for one. This makes it particularly important that a party whose case has been referred to a PHR should consider whether to ask for a full tribunal, and to make any application in good time.

One omission from the list of claims which can be heard by a Chairman sitting alone is claims under the *Working Time Regulations 1998 ('WTR'), reg 30,* which must therefore be heard by a full tribunal of three. Following the ruling of the Court of Appeal in *IRC v Ainsworth* [2005] EWCA Civ 441, [2005] IRLR 465 that claims for unpaid holiday pay under the *WTR* could only be brought under *reg 30,* and not as a complaint of unlawful deductions under *Part II* of the *ERA 1996,* any claim for arrears of pay which includes a statutory holiday pay claim must now be heard by a full tribunal. This in turn has somewhat restricted the use of a recent innovation in the listing of cases whereby claims for unpaid wages (which are often for relatively small amounts, and often uncontested) are 'fast tracked', with a hearing date given immediately the claim is registered, and the hearing listed for one hour only before a chairman sitting alone. The Court of Appeal's decision has been appealed to the House of Lords, but this part of the appeal was stayed in November 2006 pending a reference to the ECJ of another issue in the case, and no final decision on the point is likely before early 2009. Subject to that appeal succeeding, it will require primary legislation amending *s 4* of the *ETA 1996* to enable holiday pay cases to be dealt with in the same way.

An order for a Hearing before a full tribunal of a case falling within *ETA 1996, s 4(2)* may be given, having regard to whether there is a likelihood of a dispute of fact making this desirable; whether there is a likelihood of a point of law arising making a Hearing before a Chairman alone desirable; the views of the parties; and the existence of any concurrent proceedings which have to be heard by a full tribunal (*ETA 1996, s 4(5)*).

There have been conflicting authorities on the extent of the obligation to consider ordering a hearing before a full panel in cases within *s 4(2)*. The EAT has revisited its previous decisions, and the position, based on *Gladwell v Secretary of State for Trade and Industry*, EAT/0337/06 and *Sterling Developments (London) Ltd v Pagano*, EAT/0511/06, is as follows:

(*a*)   Listing, including a decision whether to list a case before a Chairman sitting alone or a full tribunal, is a judicial function, but it is permissible for a Regional Chairman to lay down a general policy on listing, subject to the consideration of individual cases.

(*b*)   There is a discretion to refer a case that may be heard by a Chairman alone to a full panel, and the exercise or non-exercise of this discretion is open to challenge by an appeal. In the event of an appeal, if the chairman has not given reasons for the way the discretion was exercised, the EAT may ask for reasons.

(*c*)   The parties should be told of their right to request a full panel, either at a CMD, if one is held, or in the Notice of Hearing; any request for a full panel should be judicially considered.

(*d*)   The Chairman responsible for the hearing should consider whether a full panel is needed, having regard to any developments in the case (such as that it has become clear that there are significant disputes of fact), but also having regard to the desirability of not creating delay or expense.

(*e*)   It may be necessary to canvass the views of the parties on whether the hearing should go ahead before the chairman alone, but it is not an error of law to fail to do so or to fail to give reasons for declining to order a full tribunal, and the Chairman is not bound to accede to the wishes of the parties.

(*f*)   It may be necessary to at least consider ordering a full panel even if neither party asks for one, since unrepresented litigants may not appreciate the possibility of a full panel or why that would be desirable in the particular case .

The EAT in *Gladwell* declined to decide whether (as had been held in the earlier case of *Sogbetun v London Borough of Hackney* [1998] ICR 1264), a failure to exercise the discretion given by *s 4(5)* made the subsequent proceedings a nullity. It is this point in particular on which earlier cases differ, but in the light of the more recent guidelines the question has become largely academic, as a failure to follow the points indicated is likely to provide the basis for a successful appeal by the aggrieved party.

It should be noted that a Chairman sitting alone has no jurisdiction to decide a claim which is not in the list of claims in *ETA 1996, s 4* authorising determination by a Chairman alone, and any such determination will be a nullity: *British Bakeries Ltd v Nascimento*, EAT/0888/04.

20.10   There is provision in the *ETA 1996, ss 4(6A)* and *7(3A)* (added respectively by the *ERDRA 1998, s 2* and the *Employment Act 2002, s 26*) to allow for certain proceedings to be disposed of by a Chairman alone and without a hearing. These powers have been partly implemented by the new *ET Rules*, which permit a Chairman to issue a default judgment in favour of a Claimant either on liability only or including awarding the remedy claimed, if the respondent has failed to submit a Response Form within the time limit (*ET Rules, rule 8*). A Judgment can also be issued without a hearing if all parties have agreed in writing as to its terms (*rule 28(2)*), and a Judgment dismissing the claim can be issued without the need for a hearing if it has been withdrawn by the claimant and the respondent requests such an order within 28 days of the notice of the withdrawal being sent to him or her (*rule 25(4)*, replacing the former practice that a claim would be dismissed automatically on the applicant notifying the tribunal that the claim was withdrawn). In certain circumstances also, a claim may be struck out for non-compliance by the claimant with an order of the tribunal without the right to a further hearing: see *Sodexho plc v Gibbons* [2005] IRLR 836 (striking out for non-payment of a deposit ordered at a PHR), but such a step is a judicial act and therefore a Judgment within the meaning of *rule 28*, and therefore open to review in certain circumstances: see further 20.15–20.16 and 20.75–20.76.

In addition, there is provision for a case to be heard in the absence of a party who fails to attend (and is not represented) at the Hearing (*ET Rules, rule 27(5)*) or in the absence of a respondent who has been excluded from participating in the proceedings by virtue of *rule 9* for failure to submit a valid Response Form in time.

20.11 JURISDICTION

Tribunals have jurisdiction both under English and Scots law, and under EU law. The jurisdiction under English and Scots law is entirely statutory. The total number of separate jurisdictions is now in excess of 70, albeit many of these arise extremely infrequently in practice. The principal statutory provisions, which all apply equally to Scotland, are:

(a) *Employment Rights Act 1996 ('ERA 1996')*, as amended (unfair dismissal, redundancy payments, disputes over written particulars of employment and itemised pay statements, unlawful deductions from wages or requirements to make payments to employers (formerly under the *Wages Act 1986*), breaches of the *National Minimum Wage Act 1998*, guarantee payments, rights to time off for public duties, protection from detriment in certain health and safety (and other) cases and as a result of a protected disclosure under the *Public Interest Disclosure Act 1998*, time off for family emergencies, maternity, paternity, adoption and parental leave issues, issues over requests for flexible working arrangements, written reasons for dismissal, claims (other than pension claims) against the Secretary of State in insolvency cases, interim relief in certain unfair dismissal cases and a number of minor and ancillary matters);

(b) *TULRCA 1992* (unfair dismissal or action short of dismissal for trade union reasons or for participation in industrial action; time off for union and other duties; failure to consult recognised unions or employee representatives over proposed redundancies; failure to consult recognised unions over training; and union membership disputes);

(c) *Equal Pay Act 1970, ss 2, 2A* (including claims relating to pension rights under the *Act* as extended and modified by the *Pensions Act 1995, ss 62–66* and relevant regulations);

(*d*)   *Sex Discrimination Act 1975* (*'SDA 1975'*), *ss 63, 68* and *72* (individual claims of unlawful discrimination, harassment or victimisation in employment and training and related matters, appeals against non-discrimination notices and enforcement proceedings brought by the Equal Opportunities Commission);

(*e*)   *Race Relations Act 1976* (*'RRA 1976'*), *ss 54, 59, 63* (the equivalent jurisdictions to those under the *Sex Discrimination Act 1975*);

(*f*)   *Employment Tribunals Extension of Jurisdiction* (*England and Wales*) *Order 1994* and the equivalent Scottish Order (claims in contract and employers' counterclaims, subject to a maximum jurisdiction of £25,000);

(*g*)   *Disability Discrimination Act 1995* (*'DDA 1995'*), *s 17A* and *Sch 3* (individual claims by disabled and formerly disabled persons alleging discrimination, harassment or victimisation in recruitment or employment and related fields);

(*h*)   *Disability Rights Commission Act 1999* (appeals against non-discrimination notices made by the Commission under *s 4* in employment cases);

(*i*)   *Working Time Regulations 1998* (*SI 1998/1833*), *regs 30–32* (complaints of dismissal or subjection to detriment for insisting on entitlements to breaks or rest periods, or refusing to agree to work hours in excess of the maximum, and of refusal to permit the exercise of rights to annual leave, rest breaks or rest periods conferred on workers by the *Regulations* or to pay for annual leave or in lieu of accrued leave rights on termination of employment; also complaints of detrimental treatment or dismissal of those elected as representatives to negotiate workforce agreements, or standing as candidates for election);

(*j*)   *Employment Relations Act 1999* (*'ERA 1999'*), *s 11* (failure to permit workers to be accompanied at grievance or disciplinary hearing or to postpone hearing for that purpose);

(*k*)   *Part-time Workers* (*Prevention of Less Favourable Treatment*) *Regulations 2000* (*SI 2000/ 1551*), *reg 8* (infringement of right not to be less favourably treated; subjection to detriment for assertion of rights);

(*l*)   *Fixed-term Employees* (*Prevention of Less Favourable Treatment*) *Regulations 2002* (*SI 2002/2034*), *reg 7* (infringement of right not to be less favourably treated; subjection to detriment for assertion of rights) and *reg 9(5)* (application for declaration of status as permanent employee);

(*m*)   *Employment Equality* (*Religion or Belief*) *Regulations 2003* (*SI 2003/1660*), *reg 28, Sch 4 para 5* (individual claims of unlawful discrimination, harassment or victimisation in employment or vocational training, and complaints regarding discriminatory collective agreements or rules);

(*n*)   *Employment Equality* (*Sexual Orientation*) *Regulations 2003* (*SI 2003/1661*), *reg 28, Sch 4 para 5* (individual claims of unlawful discrimination, harassment or victimisation in employment or vocational training, and complaints regarding discriminatory collective agreements or rules);

(*o*)   *Transfer of Undertakings* (*Protection of Employment*) *Regulations 2006* (*SI 2006/246*), *regs 12* (failure to notify employee liability information to transferee) and *15* (failure to inform or consult with trade unions or employee representatives, and associated claims for non-payment of protective awards);

(*p*)   *Employment Equality (Age) Regulations 2006 (SI 2006/1031), reg 36* (individual complaints of unlawful discrimination, harassment or victimisation in employment or vocational training, and complaints regarding discriminatory collective agreements or rules) and *Sch 6, para 11* (failure to give notice of retirement and of right to request extension) or *12* (denial of right of accompaniment at meetings to discuss requests for extensions);

(*q*)   miscellaneous legislation (including claims arising from failure to consult recognised union over application to contract out of occupational pension scheme and certain other claims under the *Pension Schemes Act 1993*; appeals against industrial training levies; appeals against improvement and prohibition notices; disputes over time off for safety representatives and union learning representatives; proceedings against employment agencies under the *Deregulation and Contracting Out Act 1994*).

On the coming into force of the *Equality Act 2006* (expected to be on 1 October 2007), the Commission for Equality and Human Rights will assume the enforcement functions of the Equal Opportunities Commission, the Commission for Racial Equality and the Disability Rights Commission, and any appeals against such enforcement action will be to an employment tribunal.

The EAT has held in relation to complaints of unlawful deduction from wages under *ERA 1996 Part II* that tribunals have no jurisdiction to hear complaints of non-payment or under-payment of Statutory Sick Pay, where the employer disputes liability to pay, as such disputes are reserved to the Inland Revenue: *Taylor, Gordon & Co Ltd v Timmons* [2004] IRLR 180. The reasoning applies equally to disputes about entitlement to Statutory Maternity Pay, Statutory Paternity Pay and Statutory Adoption Pay.

It should be noted that tribunals in England and Wales, and in Scotland respectively, only have jurisdiction over cases with the required territorial connection with the respective part of Great Britain. The requirements for jurisdiction are set out in the *2004 Regulations, reg 19*; this confers jurisdiction where the respondent resides or carries on business in England and Wales, or Scotland, as the case may be. (This may allow for a claim to be brought in either jurisdiction if the respondent carries on business in both.) In addition, for England and Wales, there is jurisdiction if the County Court would have had jurisdiction had the remedy been by way of an action in that court. In Scotland there is jurisdiction if the place of execution or performance of the contract of employment concerned was in Scotland; the second limb of this test will only be satisfied if the place of performance is wholly or substantially in Scotland (*Prescription Pricing Authority v Ferguson* [2005] IRLR 464). The *ET Rules, rule 57*, give powers to transfer cases between jurisdictions, provided that the tribunal receiving the claim has jurisdiction, and otherwise by reference to the balance of convenience in the proceedings. It should be noted that all of these points are separate from the jurisdictional issues which arise in relation to whether legislation conferring a substantive employment right applies to the particular circumstances of employment with an extra-territorial element; these issues are discussed in the context of the particular rights concerned.

20.12   Jurisdiction over EU law

Tribunals' jurisdiction is statutory but there is no statutory provision giving the tribunal power to determine claims under EU law. The basis for tribunals hearing such claims has therefore been a source of legal difficulty.

There is clear authority recognising tribunals' jurisdiction where a claimant relies on *art 141* of the *Treaty of Rome* (equal pay claims – formerly *art 119*): *Pickstone v Freemans plc* [1987] ICR 867, CA. Claims relying on the *Equal Treatment Directive 76/207* (see now the consolidating *Directive 2006/54*) against state authorities have been acknowledged to be within the jurisdiction of tribunals since the principle of 'horizontal direct effect' was established by the European Court of Justice in *Marshall v Southampton and S W Hampshire Area Health Authority* [1986] ICR 335 and are now relatively common. However, the Court of Appeal has ruled that tribunals have no jurisdiction to hear 'freestanding' claims under EU law. Any such claims must be made under the relevant statute with the offending provision disapplied (*Biggs v Somerset County Council* [1996] ICR 364; *Staffordshire County Council v Barber* [1996] ICR 379). These decisions have two main effects.

(*a*)   Procedural provisions, particularly those relating to time limits for making claims, contained in the relevant national legislation apply equally where that legislation is used as a basis for a claim relying on EU law. (The same principle applies to other procedural rules; for an example, see *Livingstone v Hepworth Refractories Ltd* [1992] ICR 287.)

(*b*)   Claims against the Government for damages for failure to implement EU Directives cannot be brought in the tribunal; the claim must be made in the High Court against the Attorney-General, or in Scotland the Lord Advocate (*Secretary of State for Employment v Mann* [1997] ICR 209, CA; for an example of such a claim, see *R v A-G for Northern Ireland, ex p Burns* [1999] IRLR 315).

However, there are still considerations of EU law which may affect how any discretion under the national legislation has to be exercised (e g to extend time), whether time limits run against the claimant and whether restrictions on remedies available under the national statute are compatible with EU law (*Marshall v Southampton and S W Hampshire Area Health Authority (No 2)* [1993] ICR 893 and *Levez v T H Jennings (Harlow Pools) Ltd* [1999] ICR 521 (both decisions of the ECJ)). For an interesting example see *Chief Constable of West Yorkshire Police v A* [2000] IRLR 465 (tribunal has power under EU law to make restricted reporting order protecting identity of transsexual applicant; see further 20.18 below).

The ECJ has endorsed the principle of the application of national time limits to cases reliant on EU law, provided that the time limits are no less favourable than for those for similar claims in domestic law and do not render the exercise of rights under EU law impossible in practice: *Fisscher v Voorhuis Hengelo BV* [1995] ICR 635. For a case where a limit was held to infringe this principle, see *Magorrian v Eastern Health and Social Services Board* [1998] IRLR 86, ECJ.

20.13 Human Rights Act 1998

Proceedings under the *HRA 1998, s 7* can only be brought in those courts or tribunals designated as 'appropriate'. As no designation has been made for employment tribunals, it follows that no 'freestanding' claims can be brought in the tribunal under that *Act*. (See on this *Whittaker v P & D Watson* [2002] ICR 1244, confirming that the EAT is in the same position, and cannot therefore issue a declaration that a statutory provision is incompatible with the *HRA 1998*.) However, tribunals are 'public authorities' within *s 6* of the *Act*, and thus are required not to act in a way which is incompatible with rights secured by the *European Convention on Human Rights* unless compelled to do so by legislation.

This means that issues of alleged infringement of a party's human rights may be raised in the course of tribunal proceedings, and the tribunal may find it necessary to take the *Convention* into account in the course of deciding substantive or procedural issues in the case. To that extent the position is similar to that under EU law, but the power to overrule primary legislation incompatible with a directly applicable EU obligation does not have a direct parallel. For guidance on how the *Convention* affects the application of the general law of unfair dismissal see *X v Y* [2004] EWCA Civ 662, [2004] IRLR 625, CA.

As a separate point, the right under *art 6* of the *Convention* to a fair trial in the determination of one's civil rights imposes obligations on tribunals as the forum in which that right is afforded in most employment cases. In addition to the obligations of independence and impartiality, discussed at 20.17 above, tribunals are required to afford a determination 'within a reasonable time' in order to satisfy *art 6*. Even the relatively generous timescale applied by the European Court of Human Rights in its jurisprudence under *art 6* was held to have been exceeded in *Somjee v United Kingdom* [2002] IRLR 886, where a series of applications to the tribunal and appeals to the EAT, with lengthy delays at a number of stages, had led to a nine year delay between the initial application and its final determination. However delay is not in itself a ground of appeal: rather the question in any appeal where there has been serious delay, whether in issuing the tribunal's judgment or more generally, is whether there is a real risk that the party appealing has in substance been deprived of the right to a fair trial in accordance with *art 6*: *Bangs v Connex South Eastern Ltd* [2005] EWCA Civ 14, [2005] IRLR 389, where the Court of Appeal laid down guidance on the correct approach to such appeals. The earlier decision of the EAT in *Kwamin v Abbey National plc* [2004] ICR 841, in which a broader approach was taken, was disapproved by the Court. In more mundane situations, compliance with the timeliness requirement of *art 6* is a relevant factor for a tribunal in deciding whether to grant an adjournment, if the effect of doing so would be to create any significant delay or further delay in the proceedings.

In *Woodrup v Southwark London Borough Council* [2002] EWCA Civ 1716, [2003] IRLR 111, the Court of Appeal considered an argument that employment tribunals are engaged in the provision of services to the public within *Part III* of the *Disability Discrimination Act 1995,* which would entail a duty to make reasonable adjustments in favour of disabled parties in the conduct of the proceedings. Without formally ruling on the point, both members of the Court (Simon Brown and Clarke LJJ) expressed strong doubts as to the suggestion that there is such a legal duty on tribunals. This view is now reflected in the express exclusion of judicial acts, including things done on the instructions a person exercising judicial authority, from the general duty of public bodies not to discriminate against disabled persons in the exercise of any of their functions: *DDA 1995, ss 21B(1), 21C(1)).* In practice tribunals do their best to accommodate to the needs of disabled litigants, provided the tribunal staff are made aware of the particular disability.

20.14 THE OVERRIDING OBJECTIVE

Regulation 3 of the *2004 Regulations* provides that the Overriding Objective of the *Regulations* and the *ET Rules* is to enable tribunals and Chairmen to deal with cases justly. This objective is spelt out as including, so far as practicable, ensuring that the parties are on an equal footing; dealing with cases in ways that are proportionate to the complexity or importance of the issues (there is no reference to the amounts at stake, but this may be reflected in the importance of the issues);

ensuring that the case is dealt with expeditiously and fairly; and saving expense. It is the duty of tribunals, and Chairmen, to seek to give effect to the Overriding Objective when exercising any power under the *Regulations* or the *Rules* and in interpreting any provision of them, and the duty of the parties to assist the tribunal to further the objective.

The extent to which the conduct of tribunal proceedings will be influenced by these overarching provisions will vary according to the circumstances, but it can generally be said that it would not be consistent with the Overriding Objective, or the parties' duty of co-operation, for a party who is legally represented or otherwise well resourced to seek to exploit technical or procedural points against an unrepresented litigant, or to drive up costs by excessive applications for additional disclosure or information. Deliberate delaying tactics, the concealment until the last minute of relevant evidence, or attempting to overload the tribunal with excessive and marginally relevant documentation are examples of behaviour that would be judged unreasonable by reference to the Objective, and which could result in an award of costs against the offending party.

Case law on the provisions of pre-2001 rules equivalent to the *ET Rules* should now be read subject to the effect of the Overriding Objective (which was introduced in 2001). An example of the impact of the Objective on previous interpretations of comparable provisions in previous versions of the *ET Rules* is *Williams v Ferrosan Ltd* [2004] IRLR 607, where the EAT held that the power of a tribunal to review its decisions 'in the interests of justice' (now contained, in the same terms, in *rule 34(3)* of the *2004 ET Rules*) should not be restricted to cases where new facts had arisen subsequently or there had been a procedural mishap, but should be applied more widely to give effect to the Objective, effectively overruling the earlier and narrower approach taken by the EAT in *Trimble v Supertravel Ltd* [1982] ICR 440. This approach has been strongly endorsed in a case under the *2004 ET Rules*: *Sodexho plc v Gibbons* [2005] IRLR 836.

20.15 COMMENCING PROCEEDINGS

A person who wishes to bring a claim ('the claimant') commences proceedings by presenting a Claim Form to the appropriate tribunal office. The information accompanying the official Claim Form gives details of how to identify the correct office (depending on the postcode of the claimant's (former) place of work). The claim is presented when it is received rather than when it is sent. For further details see 20.21 below. Applications may be presented by personal delivery, by post or fax, or electronically. (The electronic version of the Claim Form can be accessed via the tribunals' website at www.employmenttribunals.gov.uk, and can either be completed and submitted online, or downloaded for separate completion.)

In conjunction with the introduction of the *2004 Regulations*, a new Claim Form, Form ET1, was prescribed by the Secretary of State under the powers conferred by *reg 14*; a modified version, with different formats for single and multiple claims, was introduced in 2005. The use of the current version of this form (which is obtainable from Jobcentres and CABx as well as tribunal offices and online) is mandatory for any claim presented since 1 October 2005. In addition, certain information must be given in the completed form:

(*a*)   the name and address of the claimant, or of each claimant if more than one person is making a claim on the same form;

(*b*)   the names and addresses of each respondent;

(*c*)   details of the claim;

(*d*)   whether or not each claimant is or was an employee of the respondent;

(*e*)   if so, whether or not the claim includes a complaint that the respondent has dismissed the claimant or contemplated doing so;

(*f*)   whether or not the claimant has raised the subject matter of the claim with the respondent in writing at least 28 days prior to presenting the claim to the tribunal;

(*g*)   if not, why not.

(*Rule 1(4)*.)

The information in (*e*), (*f*) and (*g*) is not required if the claimant is not and was not an employee of the respondent; if the claimant is complaining solely about his or her dismissal, the information at (*f*) and (*g*) is not required. However if the complaint is of constructive dismissal, the additional information *is* required. Where two or more claimants claim using the same form (which is specifically permitted by *rule 1(7)* where the claims arise out of the same facts) the required information must be given for each claimant, and if there is more than one respondent it must be given in relation to each respondent.

The purpose of the required information under (*d*) to (*g*) is to enable the tribunal to assess whether the requirements to make use of the statutory grievance procedure laid down by the *Dispute Resolution Regulations* apply, and if so whether the claimant has complied with them.

20.16   The consequence of not using the prescribed form is that the tribunal secretariat will return the claim to the claimant and not register it. A standard letter explaining the need to use the prescribed form is sent, with a blank form enclosed (*ET Rules, rule 3(1)*). It will then be open to the claimant to resubmit the claim in the correct form, but it will only be recorded as presented when this is done. If that is outside the time limit for the claim, the tribunal will have no jurisdiction to consider the claim unless it can be persuaded to extend time (for the law on extension of time see 20.25-20.33).

The position is a little more complex if a claimant presents a claim using the prescribed Claim Form but does not give all the required information. The power to prescribe includes the power to stipulate which sections of the form must be completed (*ET Regulations 2004, reg 14(1)(c)*). However the administrative power to refuse to register the form only applies where the prescribed Claim Form has not been used, not where it has been used but not all the mandatory sections have been completed (*ET Rules, rules 1(3), 2(1)*). A separate power to refuse to accept the form if it is incomplete, or the tribunal does not have the power to consider the particular complaint, or it appears that the claimant has not complied with *s 32* of the *2002 Act* (see below for this) is given by *rule 2(2)*; but under this provision the matter must be referred to a Chairman for determination.

The purpose of these provisions is to ensure that the claim is made in the proper manner, and that the time of the tribunal is not wasted in obtaining adequate information from the claimant. However concerns that strict application of the requirements could lead to a claimant being deprived of the right to have his or her case heard, especially if the incomplete form was submitted at the very end of the applicable limitation period, have led the EAT to interpret these provisions broadly in favour of claimants. In *Grimmer v KLM Cityhopper UK Ltd* [2005] IRLR 596, the claimant appealed against the rejection of a Claim Form in which she had given as the details of her complaint the phrase 'Flexible working', with a sentence setting out why she believed the employer had rejected her request to work flexibly. The EAT held that sufficient information had been given; the correct test was:

> 'Whether it can be discerned from the claim as presented that the claimant is complaining of an alleged breach of an employment right which falls within the jurisdiction of the employment tribunal.'

A similarly benevolent approach was taken by the EAT in *Richardson v U Mole Ltd* [2005] IRLR 668, where the employee had not ticked the box to indicate that he was an employee of the respondent, but it was apparent from other material on the completed form that he did so claim (and the point was in any event not in dispute). Burton P held the refusal to accept this Claim Form to be perverse, and indicated that in general, minor or immaterial omissions should not be penalised in this way.

In two further decisions, the EAT has held that there is a right of appeal against the refusal of the secretariat to register the claim (*Grant v In 2 Focus Sales Development Services Ltd*, EAT/0310/06) and that a claim should not be rejected because of an immaterial irregularity or omission (*Hamling v Coxlease School Ltd* [2007] IRLR 8; in *Grant* this was that the claim form had been submitted by fax, and as received and printed out it was smaller than the size of the prescribed form; in *Hamling* it was that the Claimant's address had been omitted, her solicitors' address having been given instead as the address for correspondence). In *Grant* the President of the EAT, Elias J, commented that it would be 'a constitutional outrage' if a public official could take a decision with the effect of blocking a citizen's recourse to law, without any means of challenge to the decision, and endorsed the point made in *Grimmer* that the rules of procedure were, and should be applied as, subordinate to the statutory rights the tribunals are empowered to enforce (*Butlins Skyline Ltd v Beynon* [2007] ICR 121 shows a similar approach to administrative rejection of responses).

These cases are helpful to unrepresented claimants. Their effect is that in practice, the Chairman considering a claim which does not strictly comply with the requirements to provide information is likely to direct that it should be accepted, but the claimant directed to supply the missing particulars; but it would be unwise for a claimant to assume that this will happen. In any event, there are potentially serious consequences if inadequate details of the claim are given; see 20.17 below.

There is a further screening process which may lead to a claim not being accepted and registered, arising from the procedural requirements introduced by the *Employment Act 2002*. If it appears to a Chairman considering a claim that it has been presented in breach of *s 32*, either because the claimant did not submit a written grievance about the matter at least 28 days before presenting his or her complaint to the tribunal, or because the grievance had already been stale (defined as having been raised more than a month after the original time limit for presenting a complaint about the matter would have expired, but for the effects of the provisions of *ss 32* and *33*), the Claim Form will be rejected and treated as not having been received. This is subject to rights to apply for a review, or to appeal, and to the claimant's right to resubmit the claim having correctly followed the grievance procedure. However the last option may not be possible within the applicable time limit for the complaint, or for the submission of the grievance. The consequences of not having complied with *s 32* are therefore potentially extremely serious. (See further 20.19 below.) As to the requirements of the statutory Grievance procedures see further 15.11 DISPUTE RESOLUTION.

The provisions of the *ET Rules* relating to non-acceptance of claims apply equally to parts of a claim. This may entail separate consideration not just of claims made under different statutory provisions, but of each of a number of separate complaints of discrimination. The result may be that a claim under one jurisdiction is permitted to proceed, but not that under another, or that part but not all of a complaint of discrimination is permitted to proceed, with the possibility in either case of the rejected claim or part being resubmitted later. It should be emphasised that the preconditions to presenting a claim set down by *s 32* of the *2002 Act* are mandatory, and the tribunal has no jurisdiction if it is established that the requirements of *s 32* have not been met. The tribunal has no power to stay a claim brought in breach of *s 32* to enable the claimant to submit a grievance and the required 28 days thereafter to elapse: *London Borough of Hounslow v Miller*, EAT/0645/06.

The initial screening described above will not necessarily prevent all claims presented in breach of the requirements introduced by the *2002 Act* from proceeding. However, the point that a claim was presented prematurely, or without the Claimant first having instituted the statutory grievance procedure, can also be raised by the respondent in its response. The EAT has however somewhat limited the possibility of a respondent raising the issue of the claimant's compliance with *s 32* late in the proceedings (by which time it may not be possible to rectify the error). In *DMC Business Machines v Plummer*, EAT/0381/06, the EAT held that a respondent can only put in issue the claimant's compliance with the statutory requirements either by raising the point in its Response, or subsequently by an amendment to the response (for which the permission of the tribunal is required). However, a tribunal (or Chairman) is not bound by an initial decision to allow the claim to proceed (*ET Rules, rule 3(9)*) – necessarily so, since it would have been taken without hearing the respondent's reasons for challenging its admissibility.

20.17 It is also important for other reasons for claimants to complete the Claim Form carefully, and as completely and accurately as possible. Apart from any possibility that a defectively completed form could be rejected and not registered, if the Claim Form does not specify each of the particular claims being asserted, difficulties may arise if the claimant subsequently seeks to rely on a further claim, depending in part on whether the new claim arises out of the same factual allegations already set out in the Claim Form, and/or on whether the time limit for bringing the new claim has expired by the time the further claim is first raised with the tribunal. Whilst claimants acting without legal representation are accorded more leeway by tribunals, it is important to ensure that all claims the claimant is able to advance are properly identified in the Claim Form. In particular, in discrimination cases the tribunal has no power to determine specific allegations of acts alleged to be discrimination which are not made in the Claim Form (or added by amendment with the leave of the tribunal): *Chapman v Simon* [1994] IRLR 124; *Nagarajan v London Regional Transport* [1998] IRLR 73, CA. The Court of Appeal has held that a complaint of race discrimination does not, as such, encompass a complaint of *indirect* discrimination; this must be separately pleaded, or added by amendment: *Ali v Office of National Statistics* [2004] EWCA Civ 1363, [2005] IRLR 201.See further 21.10 below. In addition to possible difficulties over amendment, if the grounds are not sufficiently particularised, an order to provide further information may be made. Moreover, if a claimant gives evidence which differs from the narrative in the Claim Form, he or she may be challenged to explain the inconsistency.

20.18 **TIME LIMITS FOR CLAIMS**

General

All applications to employment tribunals must be presented within a certain time limit, which varies according to the particular statutory provision relied on. The statutory provisions as to time limits are relatively complex, as they differ according to the particular statutory provisions relied on, and have become considerably more complex as a result of the provisions in *ss 32* and *33* of the *Employment Act 2002*. It is important to appreciate a number of basic points about time limits.

(*a*)   Time limits go to the jurisdiction of the tribunal. A claim presented after the time limit has expired cannot be considered at all on its merits, however strong these may be, unless the tribunal can be persuaded to extend time under the limited discretionary powers to do so conferred by the relevant statute. There is power to extend time in relation to almost all the statutory jurisdictions of the tribunals, but the criteria vary according to the particular type of claim; full details are given in 20.25-20.33 below.

(*b*)   Time limits do not only lay down the latest date for bringing a claim. In relation to some (though not all) jurisdictions, the tribunal is precluded from hearing a claim because it was brought prematurely, *before* the relevant time period began to run. In addition, it may not be permissible in some cases to present a claim until the employee has made use of the employer's internal grievance procedure, although this will often mean that time is extended under the *Dispute Resolution Regulations* for a period to compensate for the time taken in pursuing the grievance procedure. See 20.20 for details.

(*c*)   Time limits apply to the *presentation* of a claim, that is, its delivery (physically or electronically) to the relevant office of the tribunal (see (*e*) below for further details on how the date of presentation is calculated in marginal situations).

(*d*)   Time runs from a particular event, the nature of which varies depending on the particular jurisdiction. It may be both important and difficult to determine what is the relevant date in a particular case – notoriously so where it is the 'effective date of termination' that is in issue, as in an unfair dismissal claim. Normally it is the date of the event which starts the clock running, not the date (if later) on which the individual becomes aware of the event (eg an unlawful deduction from wages which the employee does not spot on first receiving the relevant payslip). However some events, such as termination of employment, may require communication to the employee to be effective (cf *McMaster v Manchester Airport plc* [1998] IRLR 112). See further 20.22 below. (This point may be important not just in determining when time starts to run for presenting a claim, but also whether there is a claim at all, as where legislation comes into force after the first point in time at which the right to complain arises: see for a good example *Coutts & Co plc v Cure* [2005] ICR 1098.)

(*e*)   The usual formulation of the time limit in employment legislation is that the complaint must be presented within a period (usually of three months) beginning with the date of the relevant event, such as the dismissal. This means that that date is the first day of the three-month period, which therefore ends one day earlier in the month. The correct way of calculating the three-month period is to take the day of the month of the day immediately prior to the date (eg of dismissal) and go forward three months. Thus if the employee is dismissed on 1 June, the last date for presentation is 31 August, but if the date of dismissal was 30 April, the correct last date is 29 July; some anomalies may arise from months of different lengths. See further *Pruden v Cunard Ellerman Lines Ltd* [1993] IRLR 317 and *University of Cambridge v Murray* [1993] ICR 460.

(*f*)   The principal exceptions to the three-month time limit are claims for a statutory redundancy payment (six months from the 'relevant date', usually the date of dismissal) and equal pay (during, or within six months following the termination of, the relevant employment). One category of claims, for interim relief in certain categories of unfair dismissal claim (see *ERA, ss 128–132; TULRCA 1992, ss 161–163*), has a time limit of only seven days from the effective date of termination.

(*g*)   It is not necessarily possible to circumvent time limits for a particular claim by presenting an application under one jurisdiction and then applying to add further claims. The rules on amendment of claims (see 21.30 below) require tribunals balance the prejudice or hardship that would be suffered by each party if the amendment is, or is not, allowed, taking into account, if it be the case, that the new claim has been raised for the first time after the time limit has expired. This may result in the application to amend being refused, particularly if made at the last minute before the Hearing (see *Lehman Brothers Ltd v Smith*, EAT/0486/05).

(*h*)   Since time points are a matter going to the jurisdiction of the tribunal, they may be raised at any time in the proceedings. The point may be (and quite frequently in practice is) raised by the tribunal itself, and in such cases it must be considered and decided on although the respondent is content to have the matter adjudicated on its merits. It is even possible (as an exception to the normal practice) for the issue of time to be raised for the first time in the course of an appeal: for an example see *Landon v Lill*, EAT/1486/00.

(*i*)   The time point is often considered as a preliminary issue separately from the substantive hearing; as it may raise questions of fact, evidence can be called by either or both parties. Under the *2004 ET Rules*, the time point can be dealt with at a PHR (*Rule 18(2)*). Sometimes it is inappropriate to determine the issue of jurisdiction separately, for example where it involves the same factual issues as have to be determined on the merits of the case: see *Lindsay v Ironsides, Ray and Vials* [1994] IRLR 318. The general approach of the EAT before the introduction of the *2004 ET Rules was* to discourage the separation of preliminary points unless they were clearly distinct from other issues arising in the case: see eg *Wellcome Foundation v Darby* [1996] IRLR 538 and *Sutcliffe v Big C's Marine Ltd* [1998] ICR 913. The *2004 Rules* have given more weight to the PHR procedure, and the practice of ordering PHRs to determine time issues has again become more common, at least in unfair dismissal cases; however in discrimination cases, where evidence of alleged discrimination over a relatively extended period may be admissible, tribunals are markedly more reluctant to deal separately with time points.

(*j*)   The further question may arise whether the running of any applicable time limit is delayed by the effect of a failure of the UK Government properly to implement the relevant provisions of EU law. In relation to directives this question received an affirmative answer from the ECJ in *Emmott v Minister for Social Welfare*: C-208/90, [1993] ICR 8; but the ECJ has since held that *Emmott* should be regarded as limited to its own special facts. The position on the Treaty itself is that time runs from the date prescribed by the domestic statute concerned: *Biggs v Somerset County Council* [1996] ICR 364.

(*k*)   Special provisions apply to the presentation of claims by members or former members of the armed forces; see 30.2 for details.

20.19   Changes following the Employment Act 2002

In cases where the *Employment Act 2002, s 32* and the grievance provisions of the *Dispute Resolution Regulations* apply, it is in principle a prerequisite to the presentation of a claim that the claimant has first submitted a grievance in writing to the employer, and has done so no later than a month after the original time limit applicable to the complaint to the tribunal expired, and that 28 days have elapsed since it was submitted (to allow the employer time to attempt to resolve the grievance internally) before the claim is presented. The (somewhat complex) provisions of *s 32* and of the supplementing provisions of the *Dispute Resolution Regulations* apply only if the claimant is or was an employee (in the narrow sense of a person employed under a contract of employment), and if the complaint falls within one of the categories listed in *Sch 4* to the *2002 Act*, and do not apply if the complaint is that the claimant was dismissed (but the provisions *do* apply if it is a case of alleged constructive dismissal).

There are limited circumstances in which the requirements do not apply because it is inappropriate to expect the employee to pursue a grievance; the exceptions are set out in the *Dispute Resolution Regulations,* and are summarised below. *Section 32* applies to claims under any of the jurisdictions listed in *Sch 4* to the *Act*, which include unfair dismissal, redundancy payments, unlawful deductions from wages, all the principal discrimination provisions and equal pay claims, but not a number of other jurisdictions, including contract claims, disputes about written particulars or claims in relation to time off or maternity rights. (Breach of contract claims are however within the scope of *s 33,* which provides for an extension of time in certain cases where the statutory procedures have been engaged – see further below.) (There is power to amend the list of jurisdictions in *Sch 4* (*s 32(8)*), which was used in early 2007 to add certain complaints of victimisation for acting as an employee representative; see *SI 2007/30* for details.).

The context of these complex provisions is the introduction by *s 29* of a new statutory grievance procedure. (*Section 30* of the *Act* gives contractual force to the new procedure, but this section was not brought into force pending an assessment by the Government of the working of the statutory procedures; there are no plans (as of May 2007) to bring the section into force.) The circumstances in which it is necessary to make use of the grievance procedure, and what constitutes compliance with the requirement to notify a grievance in writing to the employer, are the subject of more detailed provisions contained in the *Dispute Resolution Regulations* (see DISPUTE RESOLUTION (15)). These provisions relieve employees from the obligation to submit a written grievance where:

(i)   the subject of the grievance applies to at least two employees of the employer, and has been taken up on behalf of those employees in writing by an appropriate employee representative (either an official of a recognised independent trade union, or an authorised elected employee representative) (*reg 9*);

(ii)   the grievance is raised instead under a procedure operated under a collective agreement to which at least two employers, or an employers' association, and at least one independent trade union are party (*reg 10*);

(iii) the employee has reasonable grounds to believe that using the statutory grievance procedure would result in a significant threat to him or herself or to any other person, or to his or her property or that of any other person (*reg 11(3)(a)*);

(iv)   the employee has been subjected to harassment (defined broadly as in the various Discrimination Acts) and has reasonable grounds to believe that using the procedure would result in his or her being subjected to further harassment (*reg 11(3)(b)*); or

(v)   it is not practicable for him or her to submit the grievance within a reasonable period (*reg 11(3)(c)*).

In addition, the requirement to use the statutory procedure only applies to grievances about matters occurring, or continuing, on or after 1 October 2004 (and in the latter case not if the employee had already raised a grievance under the employer's procedure before 1 October 2004) (*reg 18(b)*). A number of further points regarding the requirement to submit a written grievance should be noted:

(*a*)   The question what constitutes the submission of a written grievance, or more precisely whether the employee has complied with Step 1 of the statutory procedures in the *Employment Act 2002, Sch 2,* has been the subject of considerable case law. See for details DISPUTE RESOLUTION (15). The cases indicate that a flexible approach should be taken; see in particular *Shergold v Fieldway Medical Centre* [2006] IRLR 76; *Galaxy Showers Ltd v Wilson* [2006] IRLR 83, *Rutty v Commotion Ltd* [2006] IRLR 171 and *Edebi v Canary Wharf Management Ltd* [2006] IRLR 416. Note that the service of a statutory questionnaire under the *Equal Pay Act* or any of the discrimination statutes does not count, for the purposes of *s 32*, as the submission of a written grievance (*reg 14*; *Holc-Gale v Makers (UK) Ltd* [2006] IRLR 178). The EAT has also held that presentation of a claim to the tribunal cannot constitute sending a written statement of a grievance to the employer (and so a claim cannot be relied on as the grievance for the purpose of later proceedings): *Gibbs v Harris,* EAT/0023/07.

(*b*)   The grievance must be notified to the employer in writing no later than a month after the date on which the original time limit for presenting a complaint about the issue the subject of the grievance expired (*s 32(4)*). The Secretary of State may by regulations direct that the time limit for having notified the grievance does not apply in a particular case (*s 32(5)*); however this power has not been exercised. The EAT has however held that the 'original time limit' encompasses any extension of time justified in the particular case: *BUPA Care Homes (BNH) Ltd v Cann* [2006] IRLR 248. It is also sufficient that the claimant has submitted a grievance *before* the time limit began to run (eg before the employee resigned, in a constructive dismissal case): *HM Prison Service v Barua* [2007] IRLR 4.

(*c*)   It is often the case in complaints of discrimination that more than one incident is raised in the claim. Each incident the subject of a claim must have been raised in writing by the employee in accordance with the statutory procedure, and issues may arise as to whether this was done, and if so whether the matter was raised within the time limit referred to in (*a*). This in turn may depend on whether the matters complained of (eg failure to promote the complainant on a number of successive occasions) are parts of an act continuing over a period (as to which see 20.29 below). A case where a grievance about working conditions was held not to amount to a grievance about disability discrimination is *Canary Wharf Management Ltd v Edebi* [2006] IRLR 416. The tribunal has no power to hear those claims which were not raised by the grievance (or one of the grievances, if the employee has made multiple complaints).

(d)   The exclusion of jurisdiction only applies if the breach of *s 32* is apparent from the information supplied to the tribunal by the employee, or the tribunal is satisfied that *s 32* has not been complied with as a result of the employer raising the issue (*s 32(6)*). The prescribed Claim Form contains a section requiring information to be given as to whether, and if not why not, the claimant submitted a written grievance about the matter the subject of the claim, the answers to which will assist Chairmen in weeding out claims where jurisdiction is excluded by the effect of *s 32* and the supporting *Regulations*, but it will also be possible for the respondent to challenge the jurisdiction of the tribunal on the ground that the claimant had not in fact complied with the statutory requirements, or did not (as claimed) fall within one of the exemptions, notwithstanding that the claim has been accepted. Any such challenge must however be raised in the Response, or subsequently by way of an amendment to the Response, for which the permission of the tribunal will be needed: *DMC Business Machines plc v Plummer*, EAT/0381/06. If the respondent's challenge is successfully maintained at a PHR, it may by then be too late for the claimant to rectify matters by submitting a written grievance, waiting 28 days and then resubmitting the claim. For that reason it may be to the advantage of the claimant that claims are checked rigorously for compliance with *s 32* at a stage in the proceedings when non-compliance can be rectified. It is also open to a claimant to re-present his or her claim as a precaution if an issue of admissibility has been raised in relation to the first claim.

(e)   The requirements for submitting a grievance in writing are relatively undemanding where the standard grievance procedure applies, but where the parties have agreed in writing that the modified procedure applies, it is necessary for the claimant, in order to have complied with Step 1 of the procedure, to set out not only the grievance itself but also the *basis* of the grievance, and failure to do so will deprive the tribunal of jurisdiction: *City of Bradford Metropolitan District Council v Pratt* [2007] IRLR 192.

20.20 The converse of the postponement of the time when a claimant is allowed to present his or her claim is the extension of the time limits for presenting claims which fall within the statutory procedure. This is dealt with by *s 33* and regulations thereunder. The applicable regulation giving effect to *s 33* is the *Dispute Resolution Regulations, reg 15*. This extends the otherwise applicable time limit by 3 months where:

(a)   either of the statutory dismissal and disciplinary procedures applies and at the date when the original time limit would have expired the employee had reasonable grounds for believing that the procedure (or any equivalent procedure) was still being followed in relation to the issue about which he or she is complaining to the tribunal; or

(b)   in a case where *s 32* applies, the employee presented the claim within the normal time limit, but it was not accepted by the tribunal because he or she had not complied with the requirement to submit a grievance in writing, or

28 days had not elapsed since he or she did so, or the employee presents the claim after the normal time limit has expired, having complied within that time limit with the requirement to submit a written grievance.

In each case there is a single, automatic three month extension to the applicable time limit. The provisions permitting the tribunal to extend time continue to apply if a claim is presented after the expiry of the period of extension. However, and somewhat confusingly, if the employee submits a grievance after the original time limit has expired, there is no automatic extension of time: the employee will have to wait 28 days after the grievance is submitted before presenting the claim and then seek an extension of time.

An extension of time under (*a*) above on the ground that there is a pending appeal only applies if the employee has in fact lodged an appeal, and reasonably believes that it has not been determined. A letter before action threatening tribunal proceedings if the employer did not agree to pay compensation was held not to be an appeal for these purposes in *Piscitelli v Zilli Fish Ltd,* EAT/0638/05. There is no extension if the employee is notified of the outcome of his or her appeal before the end of the original period for claiming, since he or she cannot thereafter have reasonable grounds for believing that the appeal is outstanding; this is so even if the notification is given the day before the time period expires, as in *Royal Bank of Scotland plc v Theobald,* EAT/0444/06. However it is not a bar to the employee having an extension of time that an appeal against dismissal was only submitted towards the end of the three month period, and after the time for appealing under the employer's disciplinary procedure had expired: *Codemasters Software Co Ltd v Wong,* EAT/0639/06.

In *Singh v Taylor*, EAT/0183/06, the issue was how the three month extension is calculated. The EAT held that it runs from the day immediately following the last day of the initial time limit; however it should be noted that there is an apparent error in the way the duration of the extension was calculated by the EAT, and the case should not be relied on for that purpose.

It should be noted that under transitional provisions in *reg 18* of the *Dispute Resolution Regulations,* the statutory procedures do not apply (and therefore no extension of time is given) in cases where the subject matter of a claim had been raised by way of a grievance before 1 October 2004. There are conflicting decisions of the EAT on whether the requirement to submit a grievance applies in relation to claims against individual respondents other than the claimant's employer: see *Bissett v Martins*, EATS/0022/06 (yes); *London Borough of Lambeth v Corlett,* [2007] ICR 88 (doubted); and *Odoemelam v The Whittington Hospital NHS Trust*, EAT/0016/06 (probably, but with reservations). The practical implication of the point is that unless the grievance procedures do apply, no extension of time can apply, even if the claimant in fact submitted a grievance.

20.21   PRESENTATION OF A CLAIM

A claim is presented by sending a completed Claim Form to the Secretary of the Employment Tribunals at the appropriate local office for the claimant's (former) place of work. Which office is the correct one is determined by the postcode of the relevant workplace. Technically, the Claim Form can be sent to any office in England and Wales (for a case arising in either country) or Scotland (where the claimant is or was employed in that country) (*ET Rules, rule 1(1)*, (*2*); see 19.11 above as to the limits on the jurisdiction of tribunals in England and Wales and Scotland respectively and the transfer of cases between the two). If a Claim Form

427

is sent to the wrong office it will simply be forwarded to the correct office; the date of presentation will be the date it reaches the first office.

If the Claim Form arrives at a tribunal office before midnight on the last day of the three-month limitation period, it is presented in time (*Post Office v Moore* [1981] ICR 623). Claims sent by fax are accepted; there is as yet no case law indicating the position if a fax transmission is not received, or what the position is when a fax is transmitted after working hours on the last permissible day. In the former case it is thought that, by analogy with cases on electronic presentation (see below), the claim would simply be regarded as not having been presented (so that an extension of time would have to be sought); in the latter, it is submitted that the claim should be regarded, by analogy with *Moore,* as having been presented in time. Claimants submitting claims by fax are discouraged from sending a second copy by post. The Court of Appeal has given general guidance about presentation by post: *Sealy v Consignia plc* [2002] EWCA Civ 878, [2002] 3 All ER 801, and this has in part been applied by analogy to presentation by e-mail. The guidance is set out at 20.25(VI) below.

In November 2002, the Employment Tribunals Service introduced a facility for presenting what are now Claim Forms and Responses electronically; the templates can be accessed via the tribunals' website (www.employmenttribunals.gov.uk) and the claim is automatically routed to the correct office by reference to the postcode given for the claimant's (former) place of work.

Since a Claim Form is presented if it is placed through a letter-box or dealt with in some way held out by a Tribunal Office as a means whereby it will accept communications, when the limitation period ends on a non-working day the time limit is not automatically extended to the next working day (*Swainston v Hetton Victory Club Ltd* [1983] ICR 341; *Sealy v Consignia plc, above*). It was formerly the position that where there was no letter-box or other authorised means by which a complaint could have been presented on a day when the tribunal office was closed, the time for presenting the complaint would be extended to the next working day (*Ford v Stakis Hotels and Inns Ltd* [1987] ICR 943). However widespread availability of fax facilities, and since November 2002 the facility to present a Claim Form electronically, make it difficult to see how there is room for this possibility in the great majority of cases. Brooke LJ in *Sealy v Consignia plc* considered that this was not a ground for extending the time limit to the next working day, but rather a situation where a tribunal would need to consider whether it was not reasonably practicable to present the claim in time.

It is the claimant's responsibility to ensure that the Claim Form is in fact received by the tribunal. Generally, acknowledgements of receipt of applications are sent out on the same day as the claim is received, or the following working day, and if an acknowledgement is not received it is important to check the position with the tribunal office as soon as practicable, if necessary by telephoning the tribunal office to confirm receipt. See further 20.25(VI) below.

The EAT has had to consider what constitutes presentation when a claim is submitted by e-mail. In one case, *Mossman v Bray Management Ltd,* EAT/0477/04. it was held that where the claimant had clicked the 'submit' button for the completed form, but it had not been received on the tribunal website, it had not been presented. However in *Tyne and Wear Autistic Society v Smith* [2005] IRLR 336, the opposite conclusion was reached on the basis of only slightly different facts, and additional information. The claimant in that case had received an acknowledgement of receipt, and the claim form had reached the server of the company hosting the tribunals' website, but had not reached the tribunal office, for unknown reasons.

It is submitted that the *Tyne and Wear* case is the more likely to be followed, but the position remains unclear pending a further ruling, since the two cases were each decided without reference to the other. If transmission is successful, an e-mail receipt is generated, and unless such a receipt is received, the claimant should contact the tribunal office to check whether the Claim Form has in fact been received, and if necessary resubmit it. The website contains a warning that receipt cannot be guaranteed, and it is prudent to take the warning at face value. For the position on extension of time if a claim submitted electronically is not received, see 20.25(VI) below.

20.22 EXTENSION OF TIME

Different statutes have provided different criteria for the extension of time. It is important to appreciate that the tribunal cannot extend time unless the relevant condition is satisfied; in addition, in relation to the first category of criteria noted below, even if it is satisfied, the tribunal must decide the further question whether the length of extension sought to validate the claim is reasonable. The principal categories of criteria, and the jurisdictions to which each applies, are as follows:

(i)   that it was not reasonably practicable to present the Claim Form within time: unfair dismissal; unlawful deduction from wages; subjection to a detriment for a reason within *ERA 1996* and *TULRCA 1992*; most other claims within *ERA 1996* and *TULRCA 1992*; claims under the *Working Time Regulations 1998*; claims for breach of contract;

(ii)   that it would be just and equitable to extend time: unlawful discrimination under *SDA 1975, Part II, RRA 1976, Part II, DDA 1995 Part II*, the *2003 Regulations* on religion and sexual orientation and the *Employment Equality (Age) Regulations 2006*, and less favourable treatment or subjection to detriment under the *Part-time Workers (Prevention of Less Favourable Treatment) Regulations 2000, reg 8* or the *Fixed-term Workers (Prevention of Less Favourable Treatment) Regulations 2002, reg 7*; redundancy payments (subject to a maximum extension of six months: *ERA 1996, s 164*);

(iii) no provision for extension (except in cases of concealment of the information on which the claim is based): *Equal Pay Act 1970*. See further 20.27 below.

The tests to be applied by the tribunals in relation to each of the first two criteria are considered below, at 20.25-20.26 and 20.29-20.30 respectively.

20.23 Establishing the Effective Date of Termination

In claims alleging unfair dismissal, time starts to run from and including the 'effective date of termination' ('EDT'). If an employee is summarily dismissed, with or without a payment in lieu of notice, the EDT is the date on which he is dismissed or ceases to work (*ERA 1996, s 97(1); Dedman v British Building and Engineering Appliances Ltd* [1974] ICR 53). However, if the employer gives notice to terminate a contract of employment but does not require the employee to work during the notice period, the EDT is not the date on which the employee ceases work but the date on which the notice expires. In a constructive dismissal case, where an employee resigns with notice, the EDT is the date on which the notice takes effect, not when it is given (and see *Peterborough Regional College v Gidney*, IDS Brief 644). This was applied in a case where the employee sent notice of resignation by fax as the date on which the fax was received by the employer, not the (later) date when it was read: *Potter v R J Temple plc (in liquidation)* [2003] All ER (D) 327 (Dec). Similarly, where the employer terminates the employment, the termination is only effective when communicated to the employee. In *McMaster v Manchester Airport plc* [1998] IRLR 112, the employee was dismissed by letter sent by post to his home. He was away when it was delivered; as a result he did not read it until the following day. The EAT held that time did not begin to run until the employee was informed of his dismissal by reading the letter. Thus, the latter date was the EDT and the date from which the time limit under *ERA 1996, s 111* ran.

The determination of the EDT is a question of fact which should be decided in a practical and common sense manner having regard to what the parties understood at the time: *Newman v Polytechnic of Wales Students Union* [1995] IRLR 72. However, the applicable date is a matter of law, and a date other than that derived from a correct application of legal principles to the facts cannot simply be agreed by the parties: *Fitzgerald v University of Kent at Canterbury* [2004] EWCA Civ 143, [2004] IRLR 300. If the employee invokes an internal appeal procedure to appeal against his dismissal (whether this is a contractual appeal or the statutory appeal stage of the dismissal and disciplinary procedure prescribed by *Sch 2* to the *2002 Act*), time normally starts to run from the date of the original dismissal, *not* the date of the dismissal of the appeal, unless the contract provides for the employment to continue until the appeal is determined (*J Sainsbury Ltd v Savage* [1981] ICR 1); for an example of a situation where the EDT was held to be the date of dismissal of the appeal, see *Drage v Governors of Greenford High School* [2000] IRLR 314, CA For a case where the EDT was held to be affected by a decision to reinstate the employee following an appeal, which in turn was overruled, see *London Probation Board v Kirkpatrick* [2005] IRLR 443; see also UNFAIR DISMISSAL–I (53).

For some purposes, the EDT is extended by a period equivalent to the employee's statutory notice entitlement, if the dismissal is summary; however, this does *not* apply for the purposes of computing the time limit for presenting a claim. See further 20.20 above for the effects of *ss 32* and *33* of the *Employment Act 2002* on the applicable time limit in a case where the employee exercises a right of appeal.

20.24 Applications in respect of dismissal with notice may be presented during the period the notice is running (*ERA 1996, s 111(3)*). Subject to the possible application of *Employment Act 2002, s 32*, this applies equally in a case of a claim of constructive dismissal where the employee *resigns* with notice: *Presley v Llanelli Borough Council* [1979] ICR 419. However an ultimatum to an employee who was absent from work that if he did not return by a stated deadline, his employment would be treated as terminated, was held by the EAT not to be a sufficiently unequivocal notice of dismissal to be effective as such, so that a complaint presented before the deadline had expired was premature and outwith the tribunal's jurisdiction: *Rai v Somerfield Stores Ltd* [2004] ICR 656. The subsequent summary dismissal of an employee who has presented a claim during the notice period does not affect the validity of the claim (*Patel v Nagesan* [1995] IRLR 370).

20.25 'Not reasonably practicable' to present in time

An extension of time may be granted by the tribunal to validate a late complaint of unfair dismissal if, but only if, it is satisfied (the onus of proof being on the claimant) that it was 'not reasonably practicable for the complaint to be presented before the end' of the three-month period: *ERA 1996, s 111(2)*. The complaint must nevertheless have been presented 'within such further period as the tribunal considers reasonable' in order for an extension to be granted. The wording quoted is repeated in virtually identical terms in several other statutory provisions conferring jurisdiction on the tribunal: see 20.22 above. The EAT has confirmed that the principles and case law in relation to unfair dismissal claims apply equally to such other categories of claim: *GMB v Hamm*, IDS Brief 682. The comments which follow in this section accordingly apply equally to such claims.

What follows is a summary of the law as it had developed prior to the changes introduced by *ss 29* and *32* of the *2002 Act,* and the *Dispute Resolution Regulations.* In principle, the criteria for an extension of time should not be affected by the fact that the primary limitation period may in some cases be extended automatically; that will affect whether the claim is in time, but if it is not, the issues to be considered in dealing with an application for an extension remain the same. However the clear parliamentary indication of the desirability of exhausting internal procedures before a matter is taken to a tribunal may influence the approach of tribunals to the continuation of such procedures (e g by the hearing of a final appeal against dismissal) being used as an explanation for further delay in presenting the claim.

A separate point (which will arise most often in practice in relation to claims of constructive dismissal and unlawful deductions from wages) is what approach a tribunal should take where a claim is presented without the claimant having first submitted a grievance in accordance with *s 32* of the *2002 Act,* the claim is then refused by the tribunal, and the claimant fails to re-present the claim, having complied with the statutory requirement to submit a grievance in writing and allow time for its resolution, until after the expiry of the time limit (as extended by *reg 15* of the *Dispute Resolution Regulations*).

A decision of the EAT is likely to be needed to clarify the correct approach to each of these situations; pending such decisions it is suggested that it should be assumed that the principles set out below will apply to the facts as arising.

It is a question of fact in each case whether it was reasonably practicable to present a claim in time. This question has generated extensive reported authority, but the Court of Appeal and EAT have repeatedly stressed that particular decisions should not be taken as laying down hard and fast rules (particularly as to the effect of the employee receiving advice). Following a review of the authorities, the Court of Appeal in *Palmer v Southend-on-Sea Borough Council* [1984] ICR 372 was able to offer no more specific test than that the tribunal should ask whether it was 'reasonably feasible' to present the claim in time – a test which May LJ acknowledged was easier to state than to apply. The general approach to be adopted was stated by the Court of Appeal in *Marks & Spencer plc v Williams-Ryan* [2005] EWCA Civ 470, [2005] IRLR 562 to be that the statute should be given a liberal interpretation in favour of the employee, but it has since been suggested that this is against the weight of other authority: see *Royal Bank of Scotland plc v Theobald*, EAT/0444/06..

Some examples of the application of the test of whether it was reasonably practicable for the applicant to present his or her complaint in time are set out below. These should be treated as indicative rather than decisive.

(i) It is not reasonably practicable for an employee to bring a complaint of unfair dismissal until he or she has knowledge of the facts giving him or her grounds to apply to the tribunal (*Machine Tool Industry Research Association v Simpson* [1988] ICR 558; *James W Cook (Wivenhoe) Ltd v Tipper* [1990] ICR 716; *Marley (UK) Ltd v Anderson* [1996] IRLR 163). An extreme example of the point is *Howlett Marine Services Ltd v Bowlam*

431

[2001] IRLR 201, where the three-month time limit for claiming payment under a protective award had expired before the award was actually made by the tribunal.

(ii)   With the passage of time since unfair dismissal legislation was introduced and the publicity given to unfair dismissal cases, a claimant is unlikely to be able to show that it was not reasonably practicable for him or her to present a complaint because of ignorance of the right to claim for unfair dismissal. If the claimant ought reasonably to have known of his or her right to claim, then it will probably be held that it was reasonably practicable to present a complaint within the time limit, whether he or she in fact knew of the right or not (see *Porter v Bandridge Ltd* [1978] ICR 943). However it is always necessary for the tribunal to consider what the claimant knew, and whether his or her lack of relevant knowledge was reasonable.

(iii) Where an employee has knowledge of his or her rights to claim unfair dismissal, there is an obligation upon him or her to seek information or advice about the enforcement of those rights (*Trevelyans (Birmingham) Ltd v Norton* [1991] ICR 488). In *Norton*, the EAT also held that a decision to await the outcome of related criminal proceedings did not render the presentation of a complaint within the three-month time limit not reasonably practicable.

(iv)   The fact that the employee has been re-employed as a consultant by the employer and is reluctant to jeopardise this arrangement by making a claim does not necessarily render it not reasonably practicable to claim in time (*Birmingham Optical Group plc v Johnson* [1995] ICR 459). Similarly, in *London Underground Ltd v Noel* [1999] IRLR 621, CA, the fact that the employer had offered the dismissed employee another job but then withdrew the offer did not affect the question whether it was reasonably practicable for the employee to present her claim in time, since from the outset she had knowledge of the facts giving rise to a claim for unfair dismissal.

(v)   By analogy with these cases, the fact that an internal appeal is pending (after the extension of time automatically given by *reg 15* of the *Dispute Resolution Regulations*) does not render it not reasonably practicable to present the complaint before the final resolution of the appeal. This view was confirmed by the EAT in *Bodhu v Hampshire Area Health Authority* [1982] ICR 200, and later confirmed by the Court of Appeal in *Palmer*. However as indicated above, this view is potentially open to reconsideration following the coming into force of the *Dispute Resolution Regulations* and the related provisions of the *2002 Act*.

(vi)   The principles applicable where an application is posted immediately before the deadline were fully reviewed by the Court of Appeal in *Sealy v Consignia plc* [2002] EWCA Civ 878, [2002] 3 All ER 801. Brooke LJ, with the concurrence of the other members of the court, set out guidance which can be summarised as follows:

(1)   A complaint is 'presented' when it arrives at the tribunal office.

(2)   If it is proved that it was impossible to present the complaint in time, for example because the office was locked and did not have a letter-box, it is possible to argue that it was not reasonably practicable for the complaint to be presented in time.

(3)   If the complaint is presented by post, it will be assumed, unless the contrary is proved, to have been received at the time that a letter would have been delivered in the ordinary course of post.

(4)   If the letter was sent by first-class post it is legitimate to assume that this would be the second day after it was posted (excluding Sundays, Bank Holidays, Christmas Day and Good Friday: see on this point *Coldridge v HM Prison Service,* IDS Brief 788).

(5)   If the letter does not arrive at the expected time, but is delayed in the post, a tribunal may conclude that it was not reasonably practicable to present it in time.

(6)   If a form is date-stamped on a Monday by a tribunal office but the time limit expired on the preceding Saturday or Sunday, and it is found by the tribunal that it was posted by first-class post not later than the Thursday, it will be open to the tribunal to find as a fact that it arrived on the Saturday (and thus was in time), or alternatively to extend time as a matter of discretion.

(7)   There is no room for any unusual subjective expectation by the claimant that a letter may arrive earlier than the second working day after it is posted. The test is objective.

(8)   If despite being posted the day before the final day, the application arrives on the final day of the relevant period, it is in time.

If the application of the points set out above results in a finding that the claim would but for some unusual or unforeseen event have been received by the tribunal office in time, it does not matter that the claimant could have avoided the problem by sending the claim in earlier: see per Hart J at para 19. However, the risk of additional delay and cost being incurred in securing an extension of time for a claim that is delayed in the course of post makes it prudent to present claims earlier if possible. For an example of a case where delay in the post was accepted as justifying an extension of time, see *Lancaster v DEK Printing Machines Ltd* (EAT/623/99: application sent by Royal Mail special delivery).

In relation to appeals to the EAT, there is express provision in the *EAT Rules 1993* that where time for the service expires on a non-working day, time is extended to the next working day (*rule 37(2)*), but there is no equivalent provision in the *ET Rules*, with the consequence that if the last day for presenting a claim is a Sunday, and it is posted on Friday, the presumed date of receipt will be too late to assist a claimant if the Claim Form is not in fact delivered until the Monday: *Coldridge v HM Prison Service,* IDS Brief 788. Burton P suggested in that case an amendment to the *ET Rules* to extend the time limit automatically to the next working day, but this has not as yet been implemented.

The guidelines at (4) and (5) were applied by analogy to presentation by e-mail in *Initial Electronic Security Systems Ltd v Avdic* [2005] IRLR 671, where the Claim Form had been submitted by e-mail at 2.30 pm on the last day, but had not been received. The EAT held that there was a presumption that an e-mail will be received in the ordinary course of transmission within 30–60 minutes of being sent, and if it is not, the sender can argue that it was thereby not reasonably practicable to present the claim in time. (It would still be necessary in such a case to show that he or she had acted promptly in following up the matter when no acknowledgement was received, and had resubmitted the claim expeditiously.)

(vii)   Where the employee is prevented by serious illness from claiming in time, it will normally be held not to have been reasonably practicable to present the claim in time. In *Schultz v Esso Petroleum Ltd* [1999] IRLR 488, the employee became ill some six weeks before the time limit expired and was unable to instruct solicitors. The Court of Appeal rejected an argument that an extension of time should be refused since he could have claimed before he fell ill: the court held that although the whole period of three months is relevant, it is necessary to focus particularly on the latter part of the period of three months. This decision was applied by the EAT in *Agrico UK Ltd v Ireland*, EATS/0042/05, in support of a finding that it had been perverse of a tribunal to hold that it had not been reasonably practicable to present the claim in time where the Claim Form had been left by the claimant's solicitor for his secretary to complete and send in on the last day for presentation, but she fell ill and was absent that day, and the matter was not attended to until she returned to work the following day. The tribunal's error was to focus exclusively on the end of the three months, and not consider the practicability of the claim having been presented earlier. It is difficult to reconcile this approach and that in the *Avdic* case, above, and it would be helpful to have further clarification from the Court of Appeal of the position where an intention to submit at the last moment goes wrong for unforeseen reasons.

(viii) If the claimant instructs solicitors or advisers to act on his or her behalf and through their default the Claim Form is not presented in time, the tribunal will consider that it was reasonably practicable for the application to be presented in time and will not entertain the application. As Lord Denning MR said in *Dedman v British Building and Engineering Appliances Ltd* [1974] ICR 53 (at 61):

> 'I would suggest that in every case the tribunal should inquire into the circumstances and ask themselves whether the man or his advisers were at fault in allowing [the time limit] to pass by without presenting the complaint. If he was not at fault, nor his advisers – so that he had just cause or excuse for not presenting his complaint within [the time limit] – then it was "not practicable" for him to present it within that time.'

(See also *Wall's Meat Co Ltd v Khan* [1979] ICR 52, *Riley v Tesco Stores Ltd* [1980] ICR 323 and *Croydon Health Authority v Jaufurally* [1986] ICR 4.) In *Harvey's Household Linens v Benson* [1974] ICR 306 it was held that Department of Employment officials were not 'advisers' for this purpose, so their error ought not to be attributed to a claimant who followed their advice; this was followed in *Dixon Stores Group v Arnold*, EAT/772/93. The same applies to advice given by tribunal employees (*Rybak v Jean Sorelle Ltd* [1991] ICR 127; and see *London International College v Sen* [1993] IRLR 333). In *Alexanders Holdings Ltd v Methven*, EAT/782/93, the EAT upheld a finding in the case of a claimant who believed, as a result of ambiguous advice from the Department of Social Security, that he was not permitted to present his claim for three months following dismissal, that it was not reasonably practicable for him to do so in time.

In *Marks & Spencer plc v Williams-Ryan* [2005] EWCA Civ 470, [2005] IRLR 562, the Court of Appeal upheld a finding that it was not reasonably practicable for the claimant to claim in time where she had been led by misleading information provided by the employer to understand that she could not present a tribunal claim until her internal appeal against dismissal had been concluded (and that process was in turn delayed beyond the three month limit).

Royal Bank of Scotland plc v Theobald EAT/0444/06 makes the distinction between instructing an adviser to act on the employee's behalf, in which case it will usually be held to have been reasonably practicable to present the claim in time, and taking advice from an adviser but retaining control over the submission of the claim, where the fault of the adviser in giving erroneous advice will not count against the claimant; however the position depends in each case on the precise facts.

(ix) A rather stricter view of ignorance of rights may be taken where the rights are based on principles of European law overriding restrictions in domestic law. Thus, in *Biggs v Somerset County Council* [1996] ICR 364, the Court of Appeal held as a matter of law that it was reasonably practicable for Ms Biggs to present a claim for unfair dismissal at a time when (as a part-time employee) she was expressly debarred by statute from the right to complain and the statute was only held to infringe EU law many years later.

20.26 If it is not reasonably practicable to present a claim in time, the tribunal may allow an extension of time of such further period as it considers reasonable. There is no fixed limit, and each case must be considered on its facts in the light of the employee's explanation for the delay: *Marley (UK) Ltd v Anderson* [1996] IRLR 163. The EAT has commented that the tribunal has an unfettered discretion as to how long an extension of time to allow in the light of all the circumstances, albeit the discretion must be exercised judicially: *Howlett Marine Services Ltd v Bowlam* [2001] IRLR 201. In practice, however the starting point is that there is an obligation on claimants to act expeditiously in asserting their rights in the tribunal, so that even a relatively short delay beyond the point when it became reasonably practicable to present the claim may be more than is reasonable in the absence of an explanation for the further delay; in *Royal Bank of Scotland plc v Theobald* EAT/0444/06, a delay of 13 days was held on the facts to be too long. For the practical application of the process of assessing a reasonable time, see *James W Cook (Wivenhoe) Ltd v Tipper* [1990] ICR 716, at 724–725.

A claimant who loses the opportunity to have his or her case heard by the tribunal because of the negligence of professional advisers is able to sue them in the ordinary courts. The claim is for the loss of a chance of making a successful claim, so that an assessment of the prospects of success in the tribunal would have to be made when calculating damages.

If a claimant wishes to pursue his or her claim in another forum (eg in proceedings for wrongful dismissal (see WRONGFUL DISMISSAL (58)) but also wishes to preserve the right to proceed in the tribunal, he or she should submit a Claim Form, using Box 10 to explain the position, and seek to have the tribunal proceedings stayed (*Warnock v Scarborough Football Club* [1989] ICR 489; and see 21.22 below).

20.27 Redundancy payments

A time limit of six months applies. This period runs from the 'relevant date', which is defined in *ERA 1996, s 145* and is in most cases (where there has not been a trial period in alternative employment) the same as the EDT. In order to preserve the right to institute tribunal proceedings, it is sufficient that within the six-month period the employee has made a claim by notice in writing to the employer; or referred the claim to a tribunal; or presented a claim of unfair dismissal to the tribunal; or that a payment (not necessarily the full entitlement) has been agreed and paid. The effect of any of these actions is to preserve the right to claim indefinitely (*ERA 1996, s 164(1)*). The six-month time limit may be extended by up to a further six months if the tribunal is persuaded that it is just and equitable to do so (*ERA 1996, s 164(2)*, *(3)*). See 20.30 below for the principles applicable to a 'just and equitable' extension of time. There is no jurisdiction to extend time beyond the further period of six months: *Crawford v Secretary of State for Employment* [1995] IRLR 523.

20.28 **Equal pay**

The standard time limit laid down by the *Equal Pay Act 1970* is six months from the date the employee ceased to be employed by the respondent employer (*ss 2(4), 2ZA(3), (4)*). A claim may, of course, be made whilst the applicant is still employed. The time limit provisions are modified in cases about pension rights by the *Pensions Act 1995, s 63(4)*. The validity of the six-month time limit was challenged as contrary to EU law in *Preston v Wolverhampton Healthcare NHS Trust* [2001] UKHL 5, [2001] ICR 217, but was upheld, subject to qualifications (see below) by the House of Lords.

Following amendments made by the *Equal Pay Act 1970 (Amendment) Regulations 2003 (SI 2003/1656)*, there are three categories of case in which the time limit may be extended. First, whilst normally the limit applies to each contract where an employee is employed under a number of contracts, even if the contracts are immediately consecutive, where there is a succession of contracts at regular intervals forming part of a stable employment relationship (a 'stable employment case'), time only runs from the end of the last such contract (*s 2ZA(2),(4)*). Second, where the employer deliberately concealed from the claimant a fact relevant to his or her claim and without knowledge of which he or she could not reasonably have been expected to institute the proceedings, and the claimant did not discover and could not with reasonable diligence have discovered the fact until after the end of the period of employment (a 'concealment case') time is extended to 6 months from the day on which the claimant discovered, or could with reasonable diligence have discovered, the fact (*s 2ZA(2), (5)*). Third, if at the date of the ending of his or her employment (or any later date from which time would otherwise run by virtue of either of the other exceptions) the claimant is under a disability, i.e. is a minor (or under 16 in Scotland) or is of unsound mind (a 'disability case'), time runs from the date that he or she ceases to be under such a disability (*ss 2ZA(2), (6), (7), 11(2A)*).

Subject to these exceptions, the tribunal has no jurisdiction to extend time. However, provided that a claim is presented in time, i.e. (usually) within six months following the termination of the employment, an equal pay claim relating to a job in which the employee had ceased to be employed some time previously may be pursued: *Young v National Power plc* [2001] ICR 328, CA: see further on this *Newcastle upon Tyne City Council v Allan* [2005] IRLR 504.

The House of Lords has ruled that where an employee's employment has been transferred under the *Transfer of Undertakings (Protection of Employment) Regulations 1981* time for making a claim in respect of employment with the previous employer runs from the date of the transfer, not the eventual end of the employment with the transferee employer: *Powerhouse Retail Ltd v Burroughs*

[2006] UKHL 13, [2006] IRLR 381. The same principle would apply to a transfer under the replacement *2006 Regulations*.

20.29 **Unlawful discrimination**

A claim must be presented to the tribunal within the period of three months 'beginning when the act complained of was done': *Sex Discrimination Act 1975, s 76(1), Race Relations Act 1976, s 68(1), Disability Discrimination Act 1995, Sch 3, para 3, Employment Equality (Religion or Belief) Regulations 2003 (SI 2003/1660), reg 34(1), Employment Equality (Sexual Orientation) Regulations 2003 (SI 2003/1661), reg 34(1), Employment Equality (Age) Regulations 2006 (SI 2006/1031), reg 42(1)*. There are specific provisions to deal with discrimination by omission, which is to be treated as occurring when the person in question decided upon it; and an act extending over a period is to be treated as done at the end of that period: see *SDA 1975 s 76(6), RRA 1976, s 68(7), DDA 1995, Sch 3 para 3(2), reg 34(4)* of each of the *Religion or Belief* and *Sexual Orientation Regulations* and *reg 42(4)* of the *Age Regulations*. The latter provision covers the maintenance of a continuing policy or state of affairs, as well as a continuing course of discriminatory conduct such as harassment: see *Barclays Bank plc v Kapur* [1991] IRLR 136. The line between a continuing policy or course of conduct and a single act with continuing consequences is illustrated by cases on each side of the line in *Owusu v London Fire and Civil Defence Authority* [1995] IRLR 574. The leading case on what it is necessary to show to establish an act continuing over a period is now *Hendricks v Metropolitan Police Comr* [2002] EWCA Civ 1686], [2003] ICR 530. In this case the Court of Appeal emphasised that whilst a policy or practice of discrimination will normally provide a basis for a claim that there was a discriminatory act continuing over a period, it is not a necessary precondition, as earlier cases had appeared to indicate. The correct test is whether the acts complained of are linked, and are evidence of a continuing discriminatory state of affairs. In *Lyfar v Brighton and Sussex University Hospitals Trust* [2006] EWCA Civ 1548, [2006] All ER (D) 182 (Nov), the Court of Appeal confirmed that its decision in *Hendricks* was to be followed, in preference to *Robertson v Bexley Community Centre* [2003] EWCA Civ 576, [2003] IRLR 434, a case decided after *Hendricks* but which does not refer to it, and applies the requirement of a policy or practice; and see further *Spencer v HM Prison Service,* EAT/0812/02 and *Pugh v National Assembly for Wales* EAT/0251/06, on the test to be applied where a tribunal is deciding whether to extend time at a preliminary hearing.

Where a discriminatory policy is operated by a respondent, time begins to run afresh each time the policy is operated to the detriment of the applicant: *Rovenska v General Medical Council* [1998] ICR 85. However, if the complainant is an employee, the continued existence of the policy or practice, or state of affairs evidenced by the specific acts, postpones the running of time until the policy is discontinued or rescinded or (if earlier) the employment ends: *Cast v Croydon College* [1998] ICR 500. This is not necessarily the case, however, where a claimant complains of repeated rejections of job applications: cf *Tyagi v BBC World Service* [2001] EWCA Civ 549, [2001] IRLR 465. Time does not start to run in respect of an act of discrimination until the discriminator is in a position to put into effect his discriminatory intention: *Swithland Motors plc v Clarke* [1994] IRLR 275.

A particular difficulty in relation to when time starts to run is cases where the complaint is of discrimination by way of, or leading to, dismissal. It is now clearly established (after earlier conflicting case law) that time runs from the date of the dismissal (rather than (if earlier) the date on which notice was given): see the cases cited in *British Gas Services Ltd v McCaull* [2001] IRLR 60 at para 25. In *Derby Specialist Fabrications Ltd v Burton* [2001] ICR 833 this principle was followed in a race discrimination case where the claim was for constructive dismissal. The EAT held that this constituted a 'dismissal' within *s 4(2)* of the *RRA 1976* and it was not therefore necessary to rely on the discriminatory acts which had led to the employee's resignation as 'detriments' (in which case the claim would have been out of time). The same conclusion has now also been reached by the Court of Appeal in relation to the *DDA 1995*: *Nottinghamshire County Council v Meikle* [2004] EWCA Civ 859, [2004] IRLR 703, following *Catherall v Michelin Tyres plc* [2003] ICR 28, EAT, and disapproving the earlier contrary view expressed by a different division of the EAT in *Metropolitan Police Comr v Harley* [2001] ICR 927.

20.30 'Just and equitable' extension of time

A tribunal has discretion to extend time where it would be 'just and equitable' to do so: *SDA 1975, s 76(5), RRA 1976, s 68(6), DDA 1995, Sch 3 para 3(2), Religion or Belief Regulations 2003, reg 34(3), Sexual Orientation Regulations 2003, reg 34(3), Age Regulations 2006, reg 42(3)*. This is a broader discretion than the 'not reasonably practicable' test and the EAT has (albeit with limited success) discouraged the development of authorities on the application of the test: see *Hutchison v Westward Television Ltd* [1977] ICR 279.

The Court of Appeal has emphasised that there is no presumption in favour of the extension of time. The onus is on the claimant to convince the tribunal that it is just and equitable to extend time, in the context that time limits in employment cases are intended to apply strictly: *Robertson v Bexley Community Centre* [2003] EWCA Civ 576, [2003] IRLR 434. However, if there are circumstances which otherwise render it just and equitable to extend time, the length of the extension required is not of itself a limiting factor, unless the delay would prejudice the possibility of a fair trial: *Southwark London Borough Council v Afolabi* [2003] EWCA Civ 15, [2003] ICR 800, where the Court of Appeal upheld an extension of time of nearly nine years where the claimant had without fault on his part been unaware of the facts relied on to support his claim, and had acted reasonably promptly when those facts came to his knowledge. However it will be exceptional that a delay of or approaching that order would not render a fair trial impossible, especially where facts are disputed and there is no clear contemporaneous documentation.

Case law prior to the implementation of the *Dispute Resolution Regulations* had established that a decision by the employee to delay presenting a claim whilst an internal grievance procedure or appeal was being pursued would not necessarily be a sufficient reason to extend time under the 'just and equitable' principle, even if the delay had not prejudiced the employer. It was only one of the relevant factors to be taken into account, and the weight to be attached to it was a matter for the tribunal in the light of the facts of each case: *Apelogun-Gabriels v London Borough of Lambeth* [2001] EWCA Civ 1853, [2002] ICR 713, overruling *Aniagwu v London Borough of Hackney* [1999] IRLR 303 and affirming *Robinson v Post Office* [2000] IRLR 804.

Under the *Employment Act 2002, ss 32* and *33* and the *Dispute Resolution Regulations,* in most cases the employee will be required to submit a written statement of his or her grievance and allow 28 days thereafter for the employer to attempt to resolve it, before presenting a claim to the tribunal. In such cases, provided the grievance has been submitted within the normal time limit fro bringing a claim, or within a month thereafter, time will be extended by 3 months from the date on which the limit would otherwise have expired. However, the possibility of an extension of time may still arise if the presentation of the claim is further delayed whilst the grievance is being considered, and this leads to the claim being presented after the extended time limit has expired. It remains to be determined what attitude a tribunal should take to the reason for the delay in such cases, but it is suggested that it would be consistent with the statutory policy of promoting the internal resolution of disputes, and compatible with the broad discretion to extend time if it is just and equitable to do so, for tribunals to give particular weight to the reason for the delay in such cases, and to look critically at the reasons for the delay in completing the internal procedure.

Other factors which a tribunal should take into account in the exercise of its discretion will depend on the facts of each case, and cannot be exhaustively listed. They will however include the reason for the delay, whether the claimant was aware of his or her rights to claim, and/or of the time limit, the conduct of the employer, the length of the extension sought, and the prejudice that would be suffered by the employer if the claim were permitted to proceed (necessarily balanced against the prejudice to the claimant if he or she is refused an extension of time). Tribunals are encouraged to consider by analogy the checklist of factors listed in the *Limitation Act 1980, s33* (which confers discretion to extend time for personal injury claims in the courts), but the EAT has stated that this process is not mandatory (*Chohan v Derby Law Centre* [2004] IRLR 685). There is authority for the proposition that the most important factor in whether to extend time is whether the delay has affected the ability of the tribunal to conduct a fair trial of the issues: *DPP v Marshall* [1998] ICR 518. However it is suggested that this should not be relied on as a reason not to attach weight to other factors such as serious and avoidable delay by the claimant in claiming, or in obtaining advice about a possible claim.

The EAT has held that where delay in presenting a claim is attributable to incorrect legal advice from the claimant's solicitor, this should not be visited on the claimant by refusing an extension of time, notwithstanding that the claimant may have a valid claim in negligence against the solicitor, since this would confer a windfall on the respondent: *Chohan v Derby Law Centre*, above. This does not mean that time *should* be extended in all such cases, but that all other factors must also be considered. See also *Hawkins v Ball* [1996] IRLR 258 for a more cautious approach to this point.

The principle established in relation to unfair dismissal claims by the Court of Appeal in *Biggs v Somerset County Council* [1996] ICR 364, that a failure to appreciate that European law confers a right to claim apparently excluded by the UK statute does not make it 'not reasonably practicable' to claim in time, does not apply to discrimination claims. The 'just and equitable' test is wider, and an understandable misapprehension as to the state of the law is a relevant factor in deciding whether to extend time: *British Coal Corpn v Keeble* [1997] IRLR 336. It has been suggested that a change in the law could render it just and equitable to extend time to allow a claim which could not have been brought as the law had previously been understood to be: *Foster v South Glamorgan Health Authority* [1988] ICR 526.

Whilst it is open to a tribunal to consider as a preliminary point whether a discrimination claim is out of time, and if so whether it is just and equitable to extend time, in most cases tribunals will not accede to applications for a PHR, unless there is a clear point which would potentially dispose of the entire case. Discrimination cases are usually 'fact-sensitive', and it is therefore preferable to hear all the evidence before deciding issues as to the ambit of the tribunal's jurisdiction, particularly where at least part of the complaint is clearly in time. Matters which in themselves may be out of time may still be evidentially relevant, and the tribunal will in such cases have to hear evidence about the earlier matters, at least as background, in any event. In such cases there is little potential to save time or cost by holding a preliminary hearing, and indeed there may be a duplication of evidence over two hearings.

Unlawful deductions from wages and claims arising from a failure to pay holiday pay or the National Minimum Wage

20.31   A complaint of unlawful deduction from wages must be presented within the period of three months beginning with the date of the deduction or enforced payment complained of, or such further period as the tribunal considers reasonable if it is satisfied that it was not reasonably practicable to present the claim within the three-month period: *ERA 1996, s 23(4)*. Claims under *s 23* are amongst those to which *s 32* of the *2002 Act* applies, with the consequence that time may be automatically extended by 3 months under *reg 15* of the *Dispute Resolution Regulations:* see 20.20 above for details. See 20.25 and 20.26 above for the application of the 'not reasonably practicable' test.

For the purpose of calculating the time limit, a failure to pay is not treated as an unlawful deduction until the last date on which the employer was contractually permitted to make the payment concerned, even if part payment was made earlier: *Group 4 Nightspeed Ltd v Gilbert* [1997] IRLR 398. It follows that a claim presented *before* the last date for payment may be outside the jurisdiction of the tribunal because it is premature: *Hyde v Lehman Bros* [2004] All ER (D) 40 (Aug). Where the complaint is of a series of deductions or payments, time runs from the last such deduction or payment (*ERA 1996, s 23(3)*) and the tribunal can order repayment in respect of the entire series: see *Reid v Camphill Engravers* [1990] ICR 435. It would appear that this includes deductions continuing after the claim is presented: *Arthur H Wilton Ltd v Peebles*, EAT/835/93. Guidance as to the application of the time limits both to single deductions and to a series of deductions was given by the EAT in *Taylorplan Services Ltd v Jackson* [1996] IRLR 184.

Complaints by workers of a failure by their employer to pay the National Minimum Wage can be brought as claims for unlawful deductions from wages under *Part II* of the *ERA 1996* by virtue of the *National Minimum Wage Act 1998, ss 17,18*, and the foregoing comments therefore apply equally to such claims. However the Court of Appeal has ruled that claims for holiday pay or payment in lieu for accrued but untaken holidays under the *Working Time Regulations 1998* can only be brought by way of a complaint under *reg 30* of the *1998 Regulations: IRC v Ainsworth* [2005] EWCA Civ 440, [2005] IRLR 465. The practical consequences of this include that the claim must be heard by a full tribunal of three; in relation to time limits, the consequence is that effectively the same time limit provisions apply as for a complaint of unlawful deductions, with the exception of the 'series of deductions' provision in *ERA 1996, s 23(3)*. This prevents employees from claiming in respect of non-payment for holidays where the payment was due more than three months before the claim was presented, unless an extension of time can be obtained. (An appeal to the House of Lords in the *Ainsworth* case has been delayed in consequence of the reference of another issue raised in the appeal to the ECJ fro a preliminary ruling, and is unlikely to be decided by the Lords until 2009.)

20.32 **Contract claims**

Claims in contract brought under the *Employment Tribunals Extension of Juris-diction (England and Wales) Order 1994 (SI 1994/1623)* or the equivalent Scottish Order may only be made if the claim arises out of, or is outstanding at the date of termination of, the employment concerned. The time limit for presentation is the same as in unfair dismissal cases and subject to the same 'not reasonably practicable' extension. The automatic extension of time provisions of *reg 15* of the *Dispute Resolution Regulations* apply in part to breach of contract claims. The *1994 Orders* are not listed in *Sch 4* to the *2002 Act,* but are listed in *Sch 3.* Because they are not included under *Sch 4,* claims presented without a grievance having first been submitted will not be rejected for that reason, but if a grievance has been submitted within the three month time limit, there is an automatic extension of time.

Time runs from the EDT where the employee has been dismissed, and in other cases from the employee's last day of work in the employment concerned (*art 7*). There is no provision equivalent to that for unfair dismissal cases permitting the claim to be presented during the notice period (*ERA 1996, s 111(3)*), and a breach of contract claim presented before the EDT is premature, with the result that the tribunal has no jurisdiction to determine it (*Capek v Lincolnshire County Council* [2000] IRLR 590, CA). The EAT has held (in *Miller Bros and F P Butler Ltd v Johnston* [2002] ICR 744) that the tribunal has no jurisdiction to consider a claim for breach of contract where the contract was only concluded after the employ-ment had terminated (in that case a compromise agreement which the employer had failed to implement).

Contract claims are the only class of claim in respect of which an employer may counterclaim. A counterclaim may only be brought if presented at a time when the employee's claim is before the tribunal (ie it has been presented but neither settled nor withdrawn) and is subject to a time limit of six weeks beginning with the day the employer received from the tribunal a copy of the employee's originating application (*Employment Tribunals Extension of Jurisdiction (England and Wales) Order 1994, art 8*). The same 'not reasonably practicable' test applies to any application for an extension of time. The validity of the counterclaim is not, however, affected by whether the claim itself was brought in time: all that is relevant is that a claim has been brought and a counterclaim is presented within the time limit running from the date of presentation of the claim (*Patel v RCMS Ltd* [1999] IRLR 161).

The counterclaim must contain the information specified in *rule 7* of the *ET Rules,* ie the respondent's name and address, the name and address of each claimant against whom a counterclaim is made, and details of the counterclaim. There is no prescribed form for counterclaims (and no space on the Response Form for making one), and the *ET Rules* do not specify any requirements as to the claimant's response to the counterclaim. These are therefore matters which have to be dealt with in each case by Case Management Orders (see 21.2 below). A Practice Direction issued by the President of the employment tribunals in Scotland (No 3 of December 2006) requires that respondents making a counter-claim should if reasonably practicable state in the counterclaim the amount being claimed, and that claimants must, if they intend to resist the counterclaim, notify the tribunal office of this within 28 days of receiving it, and give their reasons for so doing. This Practice Direction does not apply in England and Wales but its requirements are likely to be reflected there in case management orders.

20.33 Other claims

For details of time limits for other classes of claim, and provisions as to extension of time, the relevant statutory provisions should be consulted. Three points of importance merit mention here:

(a)   Claims under the *Part-time Workers* (*Prevention of Less Favourable Treatment*) *Regulations 2000* and the *Fixed-term Employees* (*Prevention of Less Favourable Treatment*) *Regulations 2002*, alleging either less favourable treatment or subjection to a detriment by way of victimisation, are subject to provisions as to the applicable time limit, when time runs and extensions of time which are substantially the same as those in the anti-discrimination statutes: see 20.29 and 20.30 above. By contrast an application under *reg 9* of the *Fixed-term Employees* (*Prevention of Less Favourable Treatment*) *Regulations 2002* for a declaration that the employee is a permanent employee may be made at any time provided that the employee has requested a statement to that effect from the employer, and that he or she is still employed by the employer when the tribunal application is made: *reg 9(6)*.

(b)   Complaints by trade unions or employee representatives, or in certain circumstances individual employees, under the *Transfer of Undertakings* (*Protection of Employment*) *Regulations 2006* (*'TUPE'*), *reg 15*, of a failure to inform or consult over a relevant transfer, are subject to a three-month time limit, time running from the date of the transfer, and any extension is subject to the 'not reasonably practicable' criteria. However the EAT has held that a complaint may also be presented before the transfer has occurred, where it is alleged that there has been a material breach of the duty to inform or to consult: *South Durham Health Authority v UNISON* [1995] ICR 495. A similar position arises in relation to complaints of failure to consult recognised trade unions or employee representatives about proposed redundancies (*TULRCA, s 188*): a complaint must be presented either before the last of the dismissals the subject of the complaint takes effect or within the period of three months beginning with that date (*s 189(5)*) but there is no restriction on earlier presentation, provided that the employer is subject to an obligation to consult (i e the employer *proposes* redundancies).

(c)   Complaints of failure to pay sums due under a protective award made under either of the two above provisions are subject to separate time limits. In a case under *TUPE,* the time limit is three months beginning with the date of the order for a protective award (with the possibility of an extension if presentation in time was not reasonably practicable: *reg 15(12)*). In redundancy cases, the period of three months runs from the last day in respect of which the protective award was made, again with the possibility of extension. However, it is possible that the protective award is not made (or confirmed on appeal) until after the time limit has expired. In such a case the claimant must rely on the 'not reasonably practicable' extension, and should therefore not delay in presenting his or her claim: *Howlett Marine Services Ltd v Bowlam* [2001] IRLR 201.

20.34 ACTION FOLLOWING PRESENTATION

Upon receipt of a Claim Form, the Secretary of the Tribunals is required to determine whether the claim or part of it should be accepted. The circumstances in which a claim may be rejected are set out in *ET Rules, rule 3*, and are as follows:

(*a*)   If the claim is not on the prescribed Claim Form, the Secretary is required to refuse to accept it, and it will simply be returned to the claimant with a letter explaining the need to use the correct form and a copy of the form. If the claimant then submits the prescribed form, the date of presentation will be the date of resubmission.

(*b*)   In any case, the Secretary will not accept a claim or part thereof if the Claim Form does not include all the required information (as to which, see 20.15 above), or if he or she considers that the tribunal does not have the power to consider the claim (or part), or it appears that it has been presented without prior compliance with the requirement to submit a written grievance, or less than 28 days after the written grievance was submitted. In any such case, the Claim Form must be referred to a Chairman for a decision whether to accept the claim (in whole or in part). This procedure may be used to weed out at the outset claims where there is a clear jurisdictional bar to an otherwise permissible claim (e g the claimant lacks the service required to make an unfair dismissal claim, but not where the claim is out of time, since this might be overcome by a successful application for an extension of time).

The Chairman's decision to reject a Claim Form, or any part of it, must be recorded in writing, together with the reasons for the decision, and sent to the claimant as soon as reasonably practicable, together with information as to how the decision may be reviewed (*ET Rules, rule 3(5)*). Unless the claimant successfully applies for a review of the decision, it is treated as not having been received. The same applies to a part of the Claim Form which has been rejected.

If the claimant applies for a review, this will normally be conducted by the Chairman who took the decision in issue, unless he or she refuses the application for review on the ground that it has no reasonable prospects of success (*ET Rules, rule 34(3)*). An application for a review must be made in writing within 14 days of the date the decision not to accept the claim was sent to the Claimant, and must set out the grounds of the application (*rule 35(1), (2)*). The time limit may be extended by a Chairman if he or she considers it just and equitable to do so.

The permissible grounds for a review are that the decision was wrongly made as a result of an administrative error, or that the interests of justice require such a review (*rule 34(3), (4)*). The *ET Rules* are silent as to whether, if the application is not summarily rejected, there must be a formal hearing, but it appears to be implicit that this is the case (by the combined effect of *rules 14* and *36*). The possible outcomes of a review are that the original decision is confirmed, varied or revoked, in which case it must be taken again, by a Chairman and without a (further) hearing (*rule 36(3)*). The EAT has held that 'administrative error' includes an error by a party (*Sodexho Ltd v Gibbons* [2005] IRLR 836), and this would be sufficient to cover accidental omission of the prescribed information, or putting the wrong dates of employment on the form so as to make it appear that the claimant lacked the required service to claim. The same case holds that the 'interests of justice' ground of review is to be interpreted to give effect to the Overriding Objective.

There is no power to review a refusal by the secretariat to accept a claim because it was not submitted on the prescribed form. However the EAT has held that such a decision is open to appeal: *Grant v In 2 Focus Sales Development Services Ltd*, EAT/0310/06. Similarly, where the claim was rejected by a Chairman, the prospective claimant may appeal to the EAT as an alternative to, or in addition to, an application for a review: *Richardson v U Mole Ltd* [2005] IRLR 668. However the grounds for an appeal would usually be limited to perversity (as in that case), and in the light of the broad approach to powers of review taken by the *Sodexho* case, that is the preferable recourse for a disappointed claimant who is too late simply to put in a correctly completed Claim Form. A more recent example of a successful appeal is *Hamling v Coxlease School Ltd* [2007] IRLR 8, where the claim form did not give the claimant's address, but did give the address of the solicitors acting for her.

If the Secretary or a Chairman decides to accept a claim, a copy must be sent to each respondent, together with information about how to respond, the time limit for doing so, and the consequences of not responding within the time limit. Information must also be given about any applicable provision for conciliation, and the time limit for conciliation if the case is subject to a fixed conciliation period (see 21.29 and 21.30 for details of conciliation periods). Information is also required to be given about which parts of the claim have been accepted and which rejected, in any case where the claim has been accepted only in part. (*ET Rules, rule 2(2)*). The parties are also notified of the case number and address for correspondence. The papers are also copied at this point to the relevant ACAS office if (as in almost all cases) there is provision for conciliation in the relevant legislation. The tribunal has no power under *rule 34* to review the decision to accept the claim, as this is expressly limited to reviewing decisions not to accept a claim or part. If the respondent wishes to assert that the claim should not have been accepted, it is necessary to appeal (by analogy with the claimant's appeal in *Richardson v U Mole Ltd*, above), or, more practically, to apply for a PHR to determine the jurisdictional issue on which the acceptance is challenged.

Prior to the introduction of the *2004 Regulations,* all originating applications were entered into a public register. This register was discontinued and closed on 1 October 2004, principally in response to concerns that it was being abused by largely unregulated organisations which used the information about applicants and respondents contained in it to cold call the parties offering representation in the proceedings. There is now no public record of claims, or claimants or respondents, other than the register of judgments.

20.35 **RESPONSE BY THE RESPONDENT**

If a respondent wishes to defend a claim, he or she must complete and return a written response within 28 days of the date that the Claim Form was sent to him or her (*ET Rules, rule 4(1)*). This is a slightly longer period than under the previous rules, but it runs from the date the Claim Form was sent to the respondent not, as previously, the date it was received (this point was expressly confirmed by the EAT in *Bone v Fabcon Projects Ltd* [2006] IRLR 908).

A response must contain the required information, which is the respondent's full name and address, and a statement as to whether the respondent intends to resist the claim (in whole or in part) and if so, on what grounds, and must be on the prescribed Response Form. If it is not, it will not be accepted, and the respondent will be treated as not having presented a response unless and until the correct form is submitted (*ET Rules, rules 4(2), 6(1)*). A blank Response Form is sent to respondents with the notification of the claim; the electronic version may be used if the respondent wishes (it is accessed via the tribunals' website, www.employmenttribunals.gov.uk).

A respondent may submit the response to two or more claimants' claims on the same Response Form, provided that the claims each arise out of the same set of facts, and either the grounds for resisting the claims are the same in each case, or the respondent does not resist the claims. There is a separate version of the form for use in responding to multiple claims. Similarly, two or more respondents to the same claim may respond using the same Response Form, provided that the grounds of resistance are the same for each respondent or the claim is not resisted (*ET Rules, rules 4(5), (6)*). There is no apparent sanction against a joint response being submitted in a case where the respondents' grounds of resistance differ, provided that the prescribed form is used and all required information given.

The respondent should set out with some care the grounds upon which he or she wishes to resist the claim, because if he or she omits a ground and wishes to raise it at any subsequent tribunal hearing, the claimant may successfully resist an application to amend the response or apply for an adjournment, possibly at the respondent's expense, to consider the additional matter (see also *Hotson v Wisbech Conservative Club* [1984] IRLR 422). Also, as with the claimant's Claim Form, any statement made by a respondent in the response may be challenged at the hearing. The degree of detail is a matter of judgment, but it needs to be remembered that the claimant may apply for an order for further particulars of the grounds set out by the respondent; further information may also be required by order of the tribunal of its own motion.

20.36 **Failure to respond in time and extensions of time**

If the response is not presented in time, in general the respondent is not entitled to take any further part in the proceedings, and a default judgment may be issued in favour of the claimant (see 20.38 below). He or she may, however, apply to the tribunal for an extension of time for submitting the response. An application for an extension of time may only be granted if it is just and equitable to do so. Such an application must be made *before* the expiry of the 28 day limit for submitting the response, in writing, and must explain why the time limit cannot be complied with. If the respondent is legally represented, there is an additional requirement to notify all other parties to the proceedings of the application and the reasons for it, and to inform them of their right to object to the application within 7 days of receiving the copy, and confirm to the tribunal that this has been done (*ET Rules, rules 4(4)* and *11*). If the respondent does not notify the claimant of the application, the tribunal will do so (thereby somewhat delaying consideration of the application, although it may require an immediate reply if the matter is urgent).

Although the rules do not say so in terms, it appears to follow from the notification requirements that in practice an application for an extension of time needs to be made well before the time limit for presenting the reply will expire, since otherwise the tribunal cannot decide the application, having given the other party or parties time to submit objections, and notify the respondent of the decision, before the deadline has passed. Whilst there is nothing to prevent an extension of time from being granted retrospectively, the respondent takes a grave risk if he or she relies on such an extension being granted and fails to present a response within the time limit.

There is as yet no direct judicial guidance on when it will be just and equitable to grant an extension of time for a response. Since the consequence of refusal of an extension may be to prevent the respondent from defending the claim at all, there is a strong argument for the exercise of discretion in the respondent's favour, at least in any case where there is no objection from the claimant, or no prejudice to the claimant is likely to be occasioned if the requested extension is granted. In other cases, the reasons for the respondent's inability to submit a response will need to be scrutinised with care.

One obvious situation in which extensions will be sought is where the respondent did not receive the Claim Form until some time after it was sent (either because of postal delays, or the respondent's absence, or because the claimant had given an incorrect address). If genuine, these reasons are likely to be compelling factors in favour of an extension of time: compare *Bone v Fabcon Projects Ltd,* above, where the claim was not received from the tribunal until, having heard of the claim through ACAS, the employer contacted the tribunal office and had it re-sent. However, as an alternative to applying for an extension, the respondent may be in a position to submit a response with the bare minimum of reasons for resisting the claim, and an offer to provide full particulars as soon as the necessary information can be obtained. This approach may also need to be adopted if there is insufficient information about the subject matter of the complaint in the Claim Form; however in most cases this will not be regarded as a compelling reason for an extension of time, since the respondent will normally be fully aware of the point in dispute because it will have been considered under the statutory grievance procedure or have been the subject of disciplinary proceedings.

20.37 In addition to the requirement, from 1 October 2005, to use the prescribed Response Form, if a response does not contain all the required information, or is received by the tribunal after the time limit (plus any extension) has expired, it will be referred to a Chairman to decide whether to accept or reject it (*ET Rules, rules 6(2), (3)*). There appears to be no discretion under the terms of the *rule* to accept a response at this stage if it is late or incomplete, but it is clear from the cases referred to below that the *rule* is to be interpreted as permitting a discretion not to reject a response for trivial or immaterial omissions of required information, or where there is good reason for lateness. The same conclusion follows by parity of reasoning from the cases on the acceptance of claims despite immaterial errors or omissions (see **20.16** above).

The respondent will be notified of any decision to reject a response, and the reasons for it, in writing, and is entitled to apply for a review of the rejection of the response in accordance with *rule 34,* but only on the grounds of an administrative error or that a review is in the interests of justice; see further *Butlins Skyline Ltd v Beynon* [2007] ICR 121, which holds that an administrative decision to reject a response is also open to appeal. Failing a successful review or appeal, the respondent cannot take any part in the proceedings other than by way of appearing as a witness or applying for a review of a default judgment (see 20.38 below); the respondent has the very limited comfort that he or she will be sent a copy of any judgment in the proceedings (*ET Rules, rule 9*).

The scope for review of the non-acceptance of a response has been clarified by the EAT in *Moroak (t/a Blake Envelopes) v Cromie* [2005] IRLR 535. The EAT rejected the argument that there could be no power to review non-acceptance because there was no right under *rule 4(4)* to apply for an extension of time to present the response once the 28 day limit had expired. Non-acceptance was itself a decision open to review, and if it was in the interests of justice to extend time and admit a late response, the tribunal should do so. The test to be applied was that set out (in relation to previous *Rules of Procedure*) by the EAT in *Kwik Save Stores Ltd v Swain* [1997] ICR 49, which requires the tribunal to balance all relevant factors, with particular weight being given to whether the respondent would suffer greater prejudice by being denied relief than the claimant would suffer if relief were granted to the respondent. The merits of the defence, so far as readily ascertainable at this stage in the proceedings, may also be relevant. (The *Moroak* case concerned a response sent in 44 minutes late following a malfunction of the respondent's representative's computer, which the EAT understandably regarded as causing no prejudice to the claimant.) Review on the ground of administrative error is wide enough to include an error by the respondent, such as in omitting necessary information from the response, or (possibly) sending it to the wrong address: see *Sodexho Ltd v Gibbons* [2005] IRLR 836.

In the alternative, non- acceptance of a response is a decision open to appeal, although as the grounds for review are significantly less rigorous, that is the more appropriate route. A further reason for review being the more appropriate alternative is that the respondent is entitled to apply for written reasons for the rejection of the response if this is done for the purposes of a review application, but not (because of an apparent defect in the drafting of the Rules) for the purposes of an appeal: *Leefe v NSM Music* EAT/0663/05, (2005) Sol Jo LB 400.

20.38 DEFAULT JUDGMENTS

A default judgment in favour of the claimant can be issued at any time after the date for presenting a response (as extended, if applicable) has passed without a response having been accepted (*rule 8(1)*). There is an exception where a response has been submitted but not accepted, and a Chairman's decision whether to accept the response is pending. Subject to this, a default judgment will normally be issued as soon as a Chairman can consider the file, unless the claimant has asked that a default judgment should not be issued, or the tribunal is informed that the case has settled (*rule 8(2)*). If a case is settled on the day that a default judgment is issued, the judgment is ineffective and will be set aside on request: *rule 8(5)*, (6).

A default judgment may deal solely with liability, or also with remedy. There is no provision in the *ET Rules* restricting the Chairman's discretion as to whether to issue a judgment, and if so which type. In practice default judgments on liability are issued relatively readily, unless the claimant has asked that this not be done or the Claim Form itself raises doubts as to whether the claimant has a valid claim (eg he or she has claimed unfair dismissal but appears to have had insufficient service). A default judgment on remedy would only be appropriate where it is clear from the papers what the claimant is claiming, and this is unlikely except in claims for unlawful deductions or redundancy payments (and it may not be clear in many such cases what amount is being claimed). A claimant who wishes to have a default judgment covering remedy made may submit additional information, preferably by way of a Schedule of Loss; the Chairman will determine what remedy is appropriate in the light of the information available to him or her at the time of deciding (*rule 8(3)*).

If the default judgment is for liability only, there is no provision in the rules for a second default judgment dealing with remedy. A Hearing will therefore be necessary for this purpose. However, the respondent will not normally be permitted to participate in the Hearing unless he or she has successfully challenged the non-acceptance of the Response Form by way of review. The limits to this approach are shown by *Foster v D & H Travel Ltd* [2006] ICR 1537, where the respondent failed to serve a response in time, and a default judgment on liability was issued. The respondent attended at the remedy hearing, but the tribunal declined to hear it; the EAT held that this was an error. The respondent's attendance was an implied application to review the rejection of its late response, and it would have been proportionate as between the parties to have allowed the review and permitted the respondent to take part in the remedy hearing.

If a default judgment is issued, it will be sent to the parties and entered in the register of judgments (*rule 8(4)*). There is no requirement that reasons for the judgment be given. Either party may apply for a review of the judgment in accordance with *rule 33*. In the case of the claimant, this is likely to arise only in relation to remedy, as where the tribunal has awarded less than he or she considers should have been awarded. Application must be made within 14 days of the date on which the default judgment was sent to the parties; the time limit can be extended by the chairman if it is just and equitable to do so (an example would be where the respondent only became aware of the proceedings, or the judgment, after the time limit for review had expired, because an incorrect address had been given by the claimant) (*rule 8(1)*). The application must state the reasons for seeking the review. If it is the respondent who is applying, the application must also attach the proposed response to the claim, and include an application for an extension of time for the response to be accepted, and an explanation for the failure to present it in time and/or with all the required information (*rule 33(2)*).

A review is conducted in public by a Chairman sitting alone (not necessarily the same Chairman who issued the default judgment). The Chairman may reject the application for a review, or grant it but affirm the default judgment, or the default judgment may be varied or revoked in whole or in part (*rule 33(2), (3)*). If it is the respondent who has applied for the review, the effect of a successful application is likely to be that the response will be accepted, and the respondent will be able to defend the claim in the normal way, but this is not automatic (*rule 33(7)*).

There are no criteria in the *ET Rules* as to when an application by a claimant should be granted; this will therefore be a simple question of whether there are good grounds for varying the original award. The respondent, however, faces further hurdles. The Chairman may vary or revoke the judgment if, but only if, the respondent can show that there are reasonable prospects of successfully defending the claim (or, as the case may be, successfully disputing the amount of compensation, or any other remedy, awarded). In addition the Chairman is required to have regard to whether there was good reason for the respondent not having presented his or her response in time (*rule 33(5), (6)*). Thus a failure to submit a complete and timely response may lead to even a meritorious defence being excluded from consideration. However the EAT has held that the absence of good reason for failing to submit a valid response in time is not as such a bar to review of the default judgment: *Pendragon plc v Copus* [2005] IRLR 1671; and see *The Pestle and Mortar v Turner*, EAT/0652/05, where the default judgment was revoked despite a finding that there was no good reason for the respondent's failure to present its response on time.

There are at a number of unresolved points arising from the EAT's decisions in *Moroak* and *Pendragon,* clarification of which will need to await further decisions of the EAT.

(*a*)   Whether different criteria apply to a review where a default judgment has not been issued, as against the criteria where one has, which require the tribunal to consider the respondent's prospects of successfully defending the claim; this is not expressed in terms as a consideration relevant to the general power of review in the interests of justice, but if it is not required to be taken into account, the position of the respondent will differ for no obviously relevant reason. The adoption by the EAT in both *Moroak* and *Pendragon* of the approach mandated in the *Kwik Save* case may remove the substance of this point.

(*b*)   What test has to be applied in determining whether the respondent has reasonable prospects of successfully defending the claim (or part of it). There is as yet no appellate authority on this point.

(*c*) A subsidiary point is whether it is enough that the respondent has reasonable prospects of disputing the amount of compensation claimed or likely to be claimed, even if there is no reasonable prospect of defending on the issue of liability. It would not make sense to deny a respondent the right to contest remedy where there are real issues in dispute, merely because liability will probably be established.

(*d*) Whether the respondent has the right to be heard at any review of a default judgment initiated by the claimant; it appears that he or she is not entitled to appear, unless the tribunal has in the meantime accepted the response, since *rule 9,* which specifies the extent to which such a respondent may participate in the case, only provides for him or her to *apply* for a review. This may create anomalies, e g where both parties apply for a review, and the applications are heard together.

As an alternative to a review application, a party may appeal against a default judgment. However, in practice it is difficult to envisage circumstances in which it would be preferable to appeal rather than apply for a review. Since permissible grounds of appeal are limited to points of law, it would be much more likely in the majority of cases that grounds for a review could be identified.

21 Employment Tribunals – II

21.1 THE OVERRIDING OBJECTIVE AND CASE MANAGEMENT

The traditional approach to litigation in Britain was that it was for the parties to prepare and present their respective cases, with relatively little management of the proceedings by the court. That approach, which was to a considerable extent followed in the early years of the operation of employment tribunals, was superseded in the civil courts by the requirements of the *Civil Procedure Rules 1998* for the active management of cases to ensure that the principles embodied in the Overriding Objective are achieved in practice. The move towards much more active management of cases has been followed in employment tribunals, particularly since the introduction by the *2001 Regulations* of the Overriding Objective of dealing with cases justly. The revision of the *Regulations* in 2004 developed the process further.

It is important to appreciate that the various powers of case management given to the tribunal, as described below, are required to be interpreted and exercised so as to give effect to the Overriding Objective, which is now set out in *reg 3* of the *2004 Regulations*. This requires that the tribunal should, so far as practicable, ensure that the parties are on an equal footing, deal with issues in a way that is proportionate to the complexity and importance of the issue and expeditiously and fairly, and save expense.

21.2 CASE MANAGEMENT POWERS OF THE TRIBUNAL

The case management powers of the tribunal are primarily exercised by the making of orders (the term the *ET Rules* use to cover what were formerly either directions or orders). Orders may be issued by a Chairman on his or her own initiative, having reviewed the case file, or on the application of one of the parties without a hearing, or at a hearing. Hearings intended solely to deal with case management issues are now termed Case Management Discussions ('CMDs'), and are held in private with a Chairman sitting alone (*ET Rules, rule 17(1)* as amended by *SI 2005/1865*); such hearings may be conducted by telephone, or by video link if facilities are available, by prior arrangement; telephone CMDs are increasingly common in practice. However case management orders may be made at any type of hearing, and certain orders may not be made at a CMD.

The principal types of case management orders which may be made at a CMD are set out in *ET Rules, rule 10(2)*. The list is not intended to be exhaustive, but no order which determines the civil rights or obligations of a party may be made at a CMD, since this would not be a determination at a public hearing for the purposes of *art 6* of the *European Convention on Human Rights* (see the *ET Rules, rule 17(2)* requiring CMDs to be held in private). It should be noted that the term 'order' in this context has a wider meaning than in the definition given in *rule 28* ('which may be issued in relation to interim matters and ... will require a person to do or not to do something'): see *Hart v English Heritage* [2006] IRLR 915, paras 29, 30; but for present purposes the difference has no obvious practical consequences.

The types of order listed in *rule 10(2)* are as follows:

(*a*)   General orders as to how the proceedings are to be conducted, including orders laying down time limits;

(*b*)   Orders that a party provide further information;

(*c*)   Orders requiring the attendance of any person in Great Britain to give evidence, or to produce documents or information ('witness orders');

(*d*)   Orders (against any person in Great Britain, not just a party to the proceedings) requiring that person to give disclosure of documents to a party and to allow the party to inspect the documents, provided that such an order could be made by the County Court (or in Scotland by a Sheriff); if such an order is sought against a non-party to the proceedings it can only be made if the disclosure sought is necessary in order to dispose fairly of the claim or to save expense (*rule 10(5)*);

(*e*)   Orders extending a time limit, whether or not it has already expired, but subject to a number of limitations made by the rules applicable to the particular time limits which specify either that the time limit can only be extended if the Chairman considers it just and equitable to do so, or specify the required manner and timing of an application to extend time;

(*f*)   Orders requiring the provision of written answers to questions put by the tribunal;

(*g*)   Orders converting a short conciliation period which has not yet expired into a standard period (see 21.29–21.30 for conciliation periods);

(*h*)   Orders staying (or in Scotland sisting) the proceedings or part thereof;

(*i*)   Orders that part of the proceedings (e g the issue of liability, or one of the claims) be dealt with separately;

(*j*)   Orders that different claims be heard together (whether or not the same parties are involved in each claim); such orders may only be made if all affected parties have had the opportunity to make oral or written representations as to whether it should be made: *ET Rules, rule 10(7);*

(*k*)   Orders joining as a respondent any person who the Chairman considers may be liable for the remedy claimed in the proceedings;

(*l*)   Orders dismissing the claim against a respondent who is no longer directly interested in the claim (e g because the part of the claim affecting that respondent has been struck out or withdrawn);

(*m*)   Orders postponing or adjourning any hearing;

(*n*)   Orders varying or revoking other orders;

(*o*)   Orders giving notice to the parties of a Pre-hearing Review or Hearing;

(*p*)   Orders giving notice under *rule 19* (requiring a party to show cause at a later hearing why that party's case or part thereof should not be struck out on one or more of the grounds given in *rule 18(7)* (below));

(*q*)   Orders giving leave to amend a claim or response;

(*r*)   Orders permitting the joining as a party of any person the Chairman or tribunal considers has an interest in the outcome of the proceedings;

(*s*)   Orders for the preparation and/or exchange of witness statements;

(*t*)   Orders regarding the use of expert witnesses in the proceedings.

The scope and use of the principal categories of orders listed above is discussed further below at 21.7–21.14. It is important to emphasise that the list is illustrative not exhaustive. The types of order listed above may, if required, be made at any stage in the proceedings, and either at a CMD or other hearing, or on the written application of a party or on the Chairman's own initiative. There are however a number of provisions as to the status and effect of different types of order, and as to the procedure for applying for such orders.

21.3 Applying for orders

A party can apply at any stage of the proceedings for an order (in the wider sense of any order, decision or ruling under *rule 10*), and can ask that the application be dealt with on paper, or at a CMD or other type of hearing. The appropriate forum for considering the application will depend on when it is made and how far the case has progressed. As a general rule, the earlier in the proceedings an application is made, the more likely it is to be granted.

The requirements for applications for orders are contained in *ET Rules, rule 11*. This provides that any application for an order, unless it is made during the course of a hearing, must be made in writing, and contain an explanation of how the order sought would help the tribunal to deal with the proceedings efficiently and fairly.

In addition, if the party applying is legally represented, the representative must send details of the application to all other parties, and advise them that they may object to the application, in writing, within 7 days of receiving the notification, or (if earlier) before the date of the hearing. The notice must also explain that if a party does object, he or she must send a copy of the objection to all other parties as well as to the tribunal itself. The party applying must confirm to the tribunal that the required notifications have been sent (*rule 11(4)*). Compliance with this requirement is important since if the applicant for an order omits to confirm that the other party has been notified, the tribunal will require this to be done before the application is considered. There is no equivalent obligation of notification imposed on parties who are not legally represented, and if the party making the application has not done so, the tribunal will itself inform all other parties of the application and their right to object. However, since this may delay consideration of the application, it is advisable for a party who is not legally represented to follow the procedure in *rule 11(4)*.

An application which is to be considered at a hearing must be made, in writing, at least 10 days before the hearing is due to take place, unless this is not reasonably practicable, or the Chairman permits a shorter notice period in the interests of justice (*ET Rules, rule 11(1)*).

There is one exception to the requirement to notify all parties of an application, which is where the application is for a witness order (*rule 11(4)*). This is because it may be inappropriate for a party to be aware that a witness order has been sought or granted in certain cases.

The outcome of an application for an order will be notified to all the parties in writing if the matter is not dealt with at a CMD or other hearing. (In the case of a witness order or an order against a non party for disclosure, the normal practice is for the tribunal to leave it to the party in whose favour the order was made to notify the person subject to the order, but in the latter case the other parties will also be notified of the order by the tribunal). Any order made, whether at a hearing or not, must be recorded in writing and signed by the Chairman (*rule 10(8)*). There is no requirement for reasons for the order to be given. If a case management order is made at a hearing, and reasons are requested at the time, they must be given, either orally or subsequently in writing; if the order is made on the Chairman's initiative or following a written application, reasons may be given, and will usually be provided if this is requested by a party, but there is no obligation on the Chairman to give reasons unless requested to do so by the EAT (see *rule 30(1)–(3)*).

If an order is made against a party who has not had an opportunity to make representations before the order is made (as when the order is made of the chairman's own initiative, or is an order against a non-party), the order is subject to the right of the person subject to the order to apply to the tribunal to revoke or vary it. Any such application must be made in writing, before the date for compliance with the order, and giving reasons for objecting to the order. The provisions above as to informing all other parties apply to such applications if made by a party, but would appear not to apply to applications to set aside made by a non-party. The application to set aside may be considered on the papers or at a hearing ordered for the purpose. (*ET Rules, rule 12(2), (3);* and see *Reddington v S Straker& Sons Ltd* [1994] ICR 172).

In addition to applications to set aside orders, it is possible to apply for an order to be varied or revoked. The availability of the general power to vary or revoke orders made under *rule 10* has been confirmed by the EAT: see *Onwuka v Spherion Technology UK Ltd* [2005] ICR 567 and *Hart v English Heritage* [2006] IRLR 915. This is distinct from the power of review, which that case also confirms is not available for orders. However it is important to note that as a matter of practice a tribunal or chairman will not vary or revoke an order unless there has been a material change of circumstances: *Goldman Sachs Services Ltd v Montali* [2002] ICR 1251, a decision affirmed in relation to the *2004 ET Rules* in *Hart v English Heritage* (above).

21.4 Sanctions for non-compliance with Orders

Any person (whether a party to the proceedings or not) who without reasonable cause fails to comply with a witness order or an order for disclosure commits a criminal offence punishable on summary conviction with a fine not exceeding £1,000 (*ET Act 1996, s 7(4)*). This fact must be conveyed by a penal notice attached to any order made under *ET Rules, rule 10(2)(c)* or (*d*) (para (*c*) or (*d*) in 21.2 above). In practice the procedure for prosecution of offenders is so complex that the sanction is all but unenforceable; this has given added weight to the sanctions available to the tribunal itself (as distinct from being dependent on other agencies for enforcement), but these are of necessity only available where the default is that of a party to the proceedings.

The sanctions available to the tribunal if a party fails to comply (or is late in complying) with an order, or with any requirement laid down by a Practice Direction, are that the tribunal may make an order for costs, or a preparation time order, against the offending party, or, in more serious cases, order that the party's claim or part thereof be struck out, or that a response or part thereof be struck out and/or that the respondent be debarred from defending the claim (*ET Rules, rule 13(1)*). The potentially drastic consequences for a party of the powers to strike out a claim or response necessitate that such powers are used sparingly and only for extreme cases of disregard of orders or cases where the consequences for the possibility of a fair trial are significant. See further 21.16 below.

Rule 13(2) introduces an intermediate option, long available to the courts, of the making of an 'unless' order: unless the party complies with an order by a stated date, his or her case is to be struck out on the date for compliance without further consideration or notice (*Rule 13(2)*). In practice such an order will only normally be made after there has been a failure to comply with an earlier order, and the general power to vary or revoke orders, or to review the consequential judgment striking out the claim or response, can be used to relieve the party concerned of the consequences of an 'unless' order if it is shown that the party would otherwise suffer serious injustice.

21.5   **Orders which cannot be made at a Case Management Discussion**

In addition to the general provision that no order may be made at a CMD which determines the civil rights or liabilities of a party (*rule 17(2)*), the *ET Rules* provide that certain specific categories of order cannot be made at a CMD. These are:

(*a*)   A judgment as to the entitlement of any person to bring or contest particular proceedings;

(*b*)   An order striking out all or part of a claim or response, or part thereof, on any of the grounds on which such an order may be made at a PHR or substantive Hearing;

(*c*)   A restricted reporting order (other than a temporary order under *rule 50* pending a decision whether to make a full order, which must be taken at a PHR or Hearing);

(*d*)   An order that a party must pay a deposit as a condition of continuing to pursue or defend a claim.

The first three are specifically excluded by the terms of *rule 17(2)*; the fourth is an order which by *Rule 18* may only be made at a PHR. In addition, the effect of the general prohibition on orders determining a person's civil rights or obligations is probably wide enough to exclude the making of an order for costs or a preparation time order at a CMD.

21.6   **Pre-hearing Reviews**

The *ET Rules* have conferred a much more significant role in the case management process on Pre-hearing Reviews (PHRs). Formerly, such a hearing could only be used for a consideration, on the papers and with the benefit of the parties' submissions but without hearing any evidence, of whether a claim or response, or some particular part of either, had little reasonable prospect of success, in which case the tribunal could order the payment of a deposit of up to £500 as a condition for that party being permitted to continue to pursue or (as the case might be) defend the point. In practice it was almost always the claim that was subjected to this scrutiny, in the relatively small proportion of cases that were referred to a PHR.

This procedure remains available through a PHR, and is discussed further below (see 21.15). However the 2004 *ET Rules* have significantly enlarged the role of PHRs, with the consequence that the making of a deposit order is now a much less frequent feature of these hearings. PHRs may now be used to determine any preliminary issue in a case, even if it results in the effective determination of the whole proceedings (eg because the claim is dismissed for lack of jurisdiction: *rule 18(5)*). Preliminary issues may include such matters as whether a claim was presented in time (and if not, whether time should be extended); whether the claimant is or was an employee or a worker, where the status of the claimant is in dispute; whether he or she had sufficient service to qualify for the right claimed;

whether the claimant is or has been disabled; or whether a transfer amounted to a relevant transfer for the purposes of the *Transfer of Undertakings (Protection of Employment) Regulations 2006.*

PHRs are conducted in public (unless the provisions of *rule 16* permitting a hearing in private apply – see 21.51), and are conducted by a Chairman sitting alone, unless a hearing before a full panel is ordered. However this can *only* be done if a party applies in writing for a full panel at least 10 days before the hearing, and the Chairman considering the application considers that it would be desirable to have a full panel because of the substantive issues of fact to be determined at the PHR. There is no power for the Chairman on the day to convert the hearing to one before a full panel, and any application for an adjournment to enable a party to make the necessary application is likely to be viewed with disfavour and may result in an application for the costs thrown away (*ET Rules, rule 18(1), (3)*). It is therefore essential for a party wishing to have any preliminary issue decided by a full tribunal to apply promptly for an order to that effect. The fact that normally a PHR will be heard by a Chairman sitting alone has not prevented tribunals from ordering the determination of factually complex preliminary points in this way.

The hearing of a PHR may be conducted by telephone or video link, provided that suitable arrangements are in place for members of the public to hear or see the proceedings: *rule 15;* however in practice this facility is very rarely used (as distinct from the practice of telephone CMDs, which has become relatively common).

In addition to the determination of preliminary issues, PHRs are used to decide applications to strike out a claim or response, or part thereof. The power to strike out may be exercised on any of the following grounds:

(*a*)   That the claim or response, or part to be struck out, is scandalous or vexatious, or has no reasonable prospect of success;

(*b*)   That the manner in which the proceedings have been conducted by or on behalf of the party whose case is to be struck out has been scandalous, unreasonable or vexatious;

(*c*)   That there has been non-compliance by the party whose case is to be struck out with an order or practice direction;

(*d*)   That the claim has not been actively pursued (this applies only to claims, not responses);

(*e*)   That it is no longer possible to have a fair hearing of the claim (this also applies only to a claim).

(*ET Rules, rule 18(7)*).

Applications to strike out can in most cases only be considered if a notice has been sent by the tribunal to the party concerned informing him or her of the order being sought or proposed, and giving him or her the opportunity to give reasons why such an order should not be made; the party affected may then request that the matter be decided at a hearing, and if such a request is made, the order can only be made at a PHR or full Hearing; if no request is made, the matter may be dealt with without any hearing (*ET Rules, rules 18(6), 19(1)*).

Prior notice is not required, however, if the party has been given an opportunity to 'show cause' orally (*rule 19(1)*). This makes it possible to deal with an application to strike out a claim or response, for instance because of conduct in the face of the tribunal, without having to adjourn to a separate hearing in order to enable the notice to be sent.

However the normal practice is for written notice to be given to the parties of the fact that a strike-out order is to be considered. A similar procedure for prior notification to the parties applies to the making of a restricted reporting order at a PHR.

Where the reason for striking out is failure to comply with an 'unless' order made under *rule 13*, notice is not required at all, and is not normally given; if the Chairman reviewing the papers is satisfied that there has been non-compliance, the order is made without further inquiry. However, an order striking out a claim or response is technically (somewhat confusingly) a judgment within the definition of that term in *rule 28*, and thus open to review, as well as appeal, at the instance of the aggrieved party (see *Sodexho Ltd v Gibbons* [2005] IRLR 836).

Rule 14 of the *ET Rules* makes general provisions about hearings which apply equally to PHRs. The provisions of *rule 14(2)* and *(3)*, which deal with the way in which hearings are to be conducted, are considered below at 21.52. In addition it should be noted that there is a general requirement, which applies equally to PHRs, that notice of any hearing (other than a CMD, which may be called on 'reasonable' notice, which may be very short if necessary), must be sent to the parties at least 14 days before the date of the hearing, unless the parties all agree to shorter notice (*rule 14(4)*). 'Sent' refers to the date of despatch, not receipt, so the notice may be received less than 14 days before the hearing date. The notice of the PHR must say that the parties have the right to submit written representations (which must be received by the tribunal at least 7 days before the hearing, unless the Chairman agrees to consider representations received nearer to the hearing: *rule 14(5)*), and to advance oral argument at the hearing. Although the notice is not required to draw attention to this, evidence can be called at a PHR as at a Hearing, except when the PHR is only for the purpose of considering whether to make a deposit order.

For more detailed consideration of the powers to make orders at PHRs and the grounds on which they may be made, see 21.15–21.18 below.

21.7   CASE MANAGEMENT POWERS IN PRACTICE

In the following paragraphs under this heading, consideration is given to the scope of the more important case management powers of the tribunal, and the criteria for their exercise. The following paragraphs should be read subject to the caution that many of the cases referred to were decided before the introduction of the *2004 Rules*. It should in particular be remembered that many of the cases were decided at a time when there was no general duty on the tribunal to have regard in the interpretation or application of the rules to the Overriding Objective. The extent to which earlier authorities can be relied on will only become clear as the issues arise for reconsideration under the *2004 Rules*.

A consequence of the greater emphasis on case management by the tribunal is the greater use of CMDs, particularly in the more complex kinds of cases. The Court of Appeal had previously stressed the desirability of a directions hearing (the predecessor of the CMD) in discrimination cases to enable the tribunal to deal with preliminary matters, identify the issues in dispute and establish a realistic time estimate for the hearing so that the case can be listed for long enough to avoid adjournments and delays in the substantive hearing: *Martins v Marks and Spencer plc* [1998] IRLR 326. Its comments were reiterated, specifically in relation to claims based on the *Public Interest Disclosure Act 1998,* in *ALM Medical Services Ltd v Bladen* [2002] EWCA Civ 1085, [2002] ICR 1444. Despite this, there is no uniform practice on the ordering of CMDs, and it is often left to the parties to identify the need for a CMD, even in discrimination cases and some relatively complex claims.

The tribunal has power to vary orders made under *rule 10;* this power is given by *rule 10(2)(n)* (see also *Onwuka v Spherion Technology UK Ltd* [2005] ICR 567). However the EAT has held that the power to vary an order (unless it was originally made without the party affected having had an opportunity to make representations before the order was made) should not be exercised unless there has been a material change in circumstances (*Goldman Sachs Services Ltd v Montali* [2002] ICR 1251, where a preliminary hearing had been ordered on the issue of whether some of the applicant's complaints were out of time, but the tribunal appointed to hear the preliminary point instead directed that the issue should be determined at the substantive hearing; this decision was set aside by the EAT; see now *Onwuka,* above, *Sodexho Ltd v Gibbons* [2005] IRLR 836) and *Hart v English Heritage* [2006] IRLR 915, where the comment was made that there are stronger objections to reopening a decision taken after argument on the point than where the basis of the application is a point which had not been considered when the order was first made.

21.8   Further information about parties' cases

Additional information about a claim or response may be required because it fails to give sufficient details to enable the other party to know the case he or she has to meet; or the grounds stated may be ambiguous as to the facts or the basis in law of the claim. Orders to give additional information (previously referred to as 'further particulars') are designed primarily to spell out or clarify the party's case. The criterion which the applicant for an order for additional information is required to address in making the application is how the provision of that information will assist *the tribunal* in dealing with the proceedings efficiently and fairly (*ET Rules, rule 11(3)*). However this is wide enough to embrace the need for the applicant for the order to know the case he or she has to meet, since if that is not achieved it is difficult for the tribunal to deal with the proceedings fairly. A tribunal will not normally order the provision of additional information unless a written request has been made and either refused or ignored; the main exception is where a Chairman on reviewing the file considers that particulars or clarification are needed for the tribunal's own benefit as well as the parties'.

The EAT in *Byrne v Financial Times Ltd* [1991] IRLR 417 set out general principles governing the ordering of further particulars, which it is thought remain applicable to orders to provide additional information. These include the principle that the parties should not be taken by surprise at the last minute; that particulars should only be ordered when necessary to do justice in the case or to prevent adjournment; that the order should not be oppressive; that particulars are for the purposes of identifying the issues not for the production of evidence; and that complicated pleadings battles should not be encouraged. Particulars of generalised allegations of discrimination will usually be ordered because of the potential seriousness of such allegations.

Additional information may be ordered not only in relation to the claim or response as served, but in relation to any other matter relevant to the proceedings – for instance the claimant's losses or attempts to find alternative work, or, in equal pay or discrimination cases, the kind of information that is commonly sought by way of statutory questionnaires (see further 21.9 for these).

21.9 Employment Tribunals – II

21.9 An alternative procedure for obtaining information from the respondent, or from a prospective respondent before proceedings are started, applies in discrimination cases. The claimant or prospective claimant can serve a statutory questionnaire on the respondent under the *Equal Pay Act 1970, s 7B,* the *SDA 1975, s 74,* the *RRA 1976, s 65,* the *DDA 1995, s 56,* the *Employment Equality (Religion or Belief) Regulations 2003 (SI 2003/1660), reg 33,* the *Employment Equality (Sexual Orientation) Regulations 2003 (SI 2003/1661), reg 33* or the *Employment Equality (Age) Regulations 2006, reg 41.* A questionnaire must normally be served within 21 days following presentation of the Claim Form, or before proceedings have been started but within three months following the alleged discrimination.

There is no obligation on respondents to reply to such questionnaires and the tribunal has no power to order answers. Its only direct power is to grant an extension of the time limit laid down in each case for serving a questionnaire or to grant leave to serve a further questionnaire. The sanction for not answering within a reasonable time (this is now set as 8 weeks in each of the statutory provisions on questionnaires)), or answering inadequately or evasively, is that in certain circumstances the tribunal hearing the case may draw adverse inferences against the respondent: *EqPA 1970 s 7B(4), SDA 1975, s 74(2)(b), RRA 1976, s 65(2)(b), DDA 1995, s 56(3)(b), Religion or Belief Regulations 2003, reg 33(2)(b), Sexual Orientation Regulations 2003, reg 33(2)(b), Age Regulations 2006, reg 41(2)(b):* see AGE DISCRIMINATION (3), DISCRIMINATION AND EQUAL OPPORTUNITIES – I, II AND III (12, 13, 14), DISABILITY DISCRIMINATION (10), and EQUAL PAY (24). The EAT has held that the same power to draw adverse inferences from equivocal or evasive responses, or failure to respond, applies equally in discrimination cases in relation to questions outside the statutory questionnaire procedure; this would therefore cover replies to requests for information framed as questions (*Dattani v Chief Constable of West Mecia Police* [2005] IRLR 327).

Similar procedures have been provided for part-time workers by the *Part-time Workers (Prevention of Less Favourable Treatment) Regulations 2000, reg 6,* and for fixed-term employees under the *Fixed-term Employees (Prevention of Less Favourable Treatment) Regulations 2002, reg 5,* to enable workers to ask their employers to explain the reasons for apparently less favourable treatment than that given to comparable full-time or, as the case may be, permanent workers. The consequences of failing to reply or deficient replies are also as under the *Discrimination Acts.*

21.10 Adding new claims

In practice it is not uncommon that 'additional information' raises new allegations or heads of claim: in such cases the principles applicable to amendments apply. These are summarised below. The points apply equally where there is a direct application by a party to amend his or her case.

(a) A party may only amend his or her claim or response with the permission of the tribunal. If permission is given on a written application without the other party having an opportunity to oppose the application, or without the amendment having been directly considered by the tribunal (as where permission to amend is given in general terms) the permission is provisional and the other party may apply to have it set aside: *Reddington v S Straker & Sons Ltd* [1994] ICR 172. This is expressly confirmed by *rule12(2)* in relation to orders made without any opportunity for the opposing party to make representations; it is implicit that this also applies to a general permission to amend, where the opposing party has not had the opportunity to object to the particular amendment.

(*b*)   An important distinction is made between amendments which add a new or different claim, and those which merely amend the factual or legal basis of an existing claim, for instance by adding further facts in support of a claim that a dismissal was unfair. The latter are admissible whenever application is made, subject to the discretion of the tribunal, which is exercised in accordance with principles restated in *Selkent Bus Co Ltd v Moore* [1996] ICR 836. These are that the tribunal must take into account all the relevant circumstances and balance the hardship and injustice to each party of either allowing or refusing the amendment. The timing of the amendment as well as its nature is likely to be of importance, but it is possible (and not uncommon in practice) for amendments to be allowed up to or even during the hearing, where no prejudice is caused to the other party. The same principles apply to an application by a respondent to amend the response: *Chadwick v Bayer plc* [2002] All ER (D) 88 (Jun) (a case involving an application to withdraw an admission of liability).

(*c*)   Before the introduction of the *2004 ET Rules*, it was generally understood that an amendment to add a new claim could not be made outside the applicable time limit for the claim (subject to the tribunal's discretion to extend time in accordance with the relevant statutory criteria for the particular new claim). The position is now less clear following two decisions of the EAT, *Lehman Brothers Ltd v Smith,* EAT/0486/05, which holds that the principles in *Selkent Bus Co* (above) apply equally in this situation, and *Hart v English Heritage* [2006] IRLR 915, where the decision is based on the traditional distinction referred to above; *Lehman Brothers* was not cited in *Hart*. However on either view the weight given to the competing considerations in each case will make it more difficult to persuade a tribunal to permit an amendment to be made after the time limit for a new claim has expired, if it would add a new claim, not least because in a case where the time limit has not yet expired, it is open to the claimant simply to present a second claim.

(*d*)   There is a fine line between a new claim and a claim implicit in the facts already pleaded, but not expressly identified as a claim. Examples of what is a new claim can be found in *Housing Corpn v Bryant* [1999] ICR 123, CA (victimisation in addition to a claim of direct sex discrimination); *Harvey v Port of Tilbury (London) Ltd* [1999] ICR 1030 (applicant alleging unfair dismissal seeking amendment to add claim that dismissal was disability discrimination); and *Ali v Office of National Statistics* [2004] EWCA Civ 1363, [2005] IRLR 201 (complaint of direct racial discrimination does not cover indirect discrimination). A case on the other side of the line is *Eltek (UK) Ltd v Thomson* [2000] ICR 689, where an amendment to a claim of pregnancy-related discrimination against an employee was permitted to base the claim on her status as a contract worker; the distinction was based on the same pleaded facts and was still an allegation of sex discrimination. However, this decision is difficult to reconcile with the decisions cited above, and should be regarded as confined to its own facts. The earlier EAT decision of *Quarcoopome v Sock Shop Holdings Ltd* [1995] IRLR 353, that an allegation of discrimination encompassed both direct and indirect discrimination and victimisation was strongly criticised in *Smith v Zeneca (Agrochemicals) Ltd* [2000] ICR 800, and has effectively been overruled by *Ali* (above).

(*e*)   It is important in discrimination cases to appreciate that the tribunal only has jurisdiction to adjudicate on the acts complained of, so that it is necessary to amend the Claim Form to refer specifically to any further complaints (and to obtain permission to do so) if they are to be relied on: see the *Smith* case, above.

(*f*)   The general view of practitioners was until recently that only matters which could have been the subject of a claim at the time of presentation of the originating application could be added by an amendment to the original claim: allegations of matters occurring *after* the claim was presented could not be added (since they could not have been included at the time), and a fresh application would be needed to pursue such matters as substantive claims. This view now appears to be incorrect in the light of the EAT's decision in *Prakash v Wolverhampton City Council,* EAT/0140/06, that an amendment could be made to a claim of unfair dismissal to add a complaint of dismissal occurring after the original claim had been presented. It was also suggested by the EAT that this reflected the practice in discrimination cases. Independently of this decision, in discrimination cases subsequent events may, if relevant, be relied on as *evidence* supporting the inference of discrimination sought to be made in relation to the substantive allegations, and an amendment to this effect may be permitted.

(*g*)   The question whether an application to amend the claim to add a new claim should be granted has become more complicated as a result of the implementation of *ss 32* and *33* of the *Employment Act 2002* and the *Dispute Resolution Regulations 2004.* These provisions may extend the applicable time limit, in which case the tribunal will need to take into account whether the application for permission to add the claim was made within the extended, rather than the original, time limit. Alternatively, if the case is one within the ambit of *s 32*, the answer to the question whether or not the claimant could have presented the new claim at all on the date the application to amend was made will usually depend on whether he or she had submitted a written grievance in relation to the matter the subject of the new claim at least 28 days beforehand. If not, and if the tribunal concludes that a fresh claim could not have been presented at that time because of the failure to raise a grievance, the amendment would have to be refused. (The less rigorous attitude to amendments to add claims out of time shown in the *Lehman Brothers* case, above, is thought not to apply to the procedural requirements of *s 32*; the issue will usually be whether the 'new' claim was in fact raised in the employee's grievance preceding the original claim: for an example see *Canary Wharf Management Ltd v Edebi* [2006] IRLR 416.)

(*h*)   One other category of amendment requiring mention is an amendment to add a party or alter the name of a party. The discretion of the tribunal in dealing with such amendments is governed by similar principles to those set out above, summarised in *Cocking v Sandhurst (Stationers) Ltd* [1974] ICR 650; and see *Drinkwater Sabey Ltd v Burnett* [1995] ICR 328. A party may be added or substituted even at the hearing in an appropriate case, e g where a manager rather than the employing company had been identified as the employer in an unfair dismissal case: *Linbourne v Constable* [1993] ICR 698.

21.11 Disclosure of documents

Disclosure (formerly known as discovery) is the process in civil litigation where each party discloses to the other all documents relevant to the proceedings and not protected from disclosure. The tribunal's power to order disclosure is the same as that of the civil courts under *Part 31* of the *Civil Procedure Rules 1998 ('CPR')*

(*ET Rules, rule 10(2)(d)*). An important consequence of this is that the scope of disclosure should be consistent with the Overriding Objective of civil litigation (see 21.1 above).

There is no automatic disclosure in tribunals – unless given voluntarily or ordered by the tribunal it must be specifically asked for. However it has increasingly become the practice of tribunals to order mutual disclosure at an early stage of the proceedings, and this practice has been encouraged by the relatively short period available for conciliation in most cases, since disclosure is likely to assist the conciliation process. In Scotland a Practice Direction issued in December 2006 requires the mutual notification by the parties of the documents each intends to rely on at least 14 days before the Hearing.

The formal process of disclosure involves supplying a list of all the documents in a party's possession and allowing the other party to inspect and take copies. In practice the parties may agree simply to supply copies of all the documents concerned.

An increasingly important element in disclosure of documents is the retrieval of e-mails. These are equally documents, and are disclosable not only if paper copies have been put on a file, but also if retained electronically within the party's computer system (this extends to deleted or archived e-mails, if they can still be accessed).

Disclosure may be either general (ie covering the case as a whole) or specific (ie covering identified documents or classes of documents). Parties ordered to disclose documents need only undertake a reasonable search for relevant documents. A party giving voluntary disclosure need not disclose all documents; however, a document cannot properly be kept back if its non-disclosure would render a disclosed document misleading: *Birds Eye Walls Ltd v Harrison* [1985] ICR 278, where the claimant was permitted to amend his claim to add new grounds part way through the hearing after coming into possession of a relevant document in the possession of the employer that had not been included in its earlier disclosure. The same point probably applies to documents the concealment of which would render oral evidence misleading.

The obligation to disclose documents is a continuing one, so that if further documents come to light, or come into existence, during the course of the proceedings, they must be disclosed if they are relevant to material already disclosed, or within the terms of an order for disclosure. This principle was applied by the Court of Appeal in *Scott v IRC* [2004] EWCA Civ 400, [2004] IRLR 713 in relation to a new policy on permitting employees to continue to work beyond the normal retirement age, which was adopted whilst the claim was proceeding and which affected the basis on which the claimant's claim for compensation for future loss of earnings would fall to be calculated.

The normal and recommended practice, where either disclosure has not been ordered by the tribunal at an early stage in the proceedings or the disclosure given appears to be incomplete, is for disclosure, or additional specific disclosure, to be requested by correspondence in the first instance. If this request is refused, ignored or not fully complied with, an application should be made to the tribunal for an order.

21.12 The test for whether disclosure of a particular document or class of documents should be granted is whether disclosure is necessary for disposing fairly of the proceedings. This involves more than just relevance; an application for disclosure of a large quantity of documents of marginal relevance is likely to be refused on the ground of excessive burden on the other party, in accordance with the Overriding Objective, which includes the requirement to act proportionately to the importance and complexity of the case. A good example of a refusal of excessive disclosure is *British Aerospace plc v Green* [1995] ICR 1006, CA where in a substantial redundancy selection exercise disclosure of assessment records of several hundred employees was refused. (See also *King v Eaton Ltd* [1996] IRLR 199.)

The ambit of disclosure is likely to be widest in discrimination cases, because of the need to show evidence from which inferences can be drawn (*West Midlands Passenger Transport Executive v Singh* [1988] ICR 614). However, even in discrimination cases a test of relevance still applies; further guidance is given in *Ministry of Defence v Meredith* [1995] IRLR 539.

Confidentiality is not as such a reason for refusing disclosure. In a doubtful case the tribunal may inspect the documents before deciding whether they are sufficiently relevant to overcome the need to respect confidentiality (see *Science Research Council v Nasse* [1979] ICR 921). However if disclosure is ordered, it must be disclosure to the other party or parties; the tribunal cannot order disclosure to itself alone: *Knight v Department of Social Security* [2002] IRLR 249. If necessary in order to preserve confidentiality, the tribunal can order disclosure subject to anonymising the document and/or deleting passages which would or might reveal the identity of the author or source of a statement, a procedure known as redaction: *Asda Stores Ltd v Thompson* [2002] IRLR 245 (a case concerning disclosure of witness statements taken under terms of confidentiality in an investigation of alleged drug dealing). Further guidance as to the procedure to be followed where a party wishes to disclose documents subject to redaction is given in *Asda Stores Ltd v Thompson (No 2)* [2004] IRLR 598. The tribunal also has power to restrict disclosure to the party him or herself and his or her representative, and to limit the purpose for which disclosure is given to the conduct of the particular case (see the *Knight* case, above; this is in any event an implied condition of any non-voluntary disclosure of documents that are not subsequently put into the public domain by being referred to in the course of a public hearing).

If, exceptionally, a party cannot disclose a document without acting unlawfully, it is wrong in principle to order disclosure: *Barracks v Coles* [2006] EWCA Civ 1041, [2007] ICR 60, a case about a police officer refused security clearance for reasons the police force was unable lawfully to disclose.

Disclosure can only be ordered of existing documents; it cannot be used to require the creation of a document (e g by compiling statistics): *Carrington v Helix Lighting Ltd* [1990] ICR 125. The restricting effect of this point is considerably eased by the tribunal's general power to order a party to provide additional information, which can include in an appropriate case a table, chart or schedule containing relevant information (including a Schedule of Loss or a table giving numbers of staff classified by grade and ethnic origin – the issue in the *Carrington* case), and by the availability of the questionnaire procedure in discrimination cases: see 21.9 above.

21.13 Documents privileged from disclosure

Certain documents are immune from disclosure. These include those subject to legal professional privilege and (with qualifications) public interest immunity. However, legal professional privilege applies only to communications with and from professional legal advisers, not, for instance, a trade union official or lay adviser (including a professional but not legally qualified consultant): *New Victoria Hospital v Ryan* [1993] ICR 201. Public interest immunity is a specialised area of law outside the scope of this work; the leading recent cases relevant to its application in tribunal proceedings are *Balfour v Foreign and Commonwealth Office* [1994] ICR 277 and *R v Chief Constable of West Midlands, ex p Wiley* [1995] 1 AC 274 (overruling *Halford v Sharples* [1992] ICR 583).

'Without prejudice' communications between the parties are in a slightly different category, as they are in their nature already known to the parties. They are, however, not admissible as evidence before the tribunal unless both parties agree, or to prove the contents of an agreement subsequently reached. The same principle applies to evidence of oral communications conducted without prejudice.

However, the privilege against disclosure to the tribunal only applies to genuinely 'without prejudice' communications, ie those generated as or forming part of an attempt to settle a dispute. By contrast, a meeting called by an employer to put proposals to the employee for a severance package was held by the EAT in *BNP Paribas v Mezzotero* [2004] IRLR 508 not to be within the privilege (with the result that the employee could rely on what was said at the meeting to support a complaint of sex discrimination), despite the fact that she was pursuing a grievance at the time, both because there was no dispute to which the proposals were directed, and also because it would be wrong to allow the employer to rely on the privilege when the status of the meeting was first raised unilaterally after it had begun, and had not been agreed in advance.

In addition, the privilege attached to without prejudice discussions may be waived by the conduct of a party (in a case where the other party also seeks to rely on the discussions): see *Vaseghi v Brunel University* [2007] EWCA Civ 482, [2007] All ER (D) 377 (May) (privilege waived by making reference to discussions during grievance hearing before independent panel, and by referring to them in response form).

It is possible to restrict the 'without prejudice' nature of communications by adding the qualification 'save as to costs', to the effect that such communications may be relied on in any issue as to costs, after the tribunal has determined the claim itself. See further 21.36 below.

21.14 Witness orders

An order for the attendance of a witness can be sought if the witness is believed to have relevant knowledge or information to give and the party seeking the order believes he or she may not attend voluntarily. A witness order is in practice often needed where an employer would otherwise not be cooperative in releasing the witness. Orders are almost invariably required to secure the attendance of police officers. As indicated above (21.3) an ordered witness may apply before the hearing to set aside the order; however, there is no minimum period of notice of the order that has to be given to the witness. It is normally for the party obtaining the order to ensure it is served on the intended witness, although some tribunal offices undertake the service of witness orders.

The granting of witness orders is a matter of discretion; the tribunal must consider whether the witness is likely to be able to give relevant evidence and whether the giving of that evidence is necessary, and may refuse unjustified requests as a part of the general power to control and manage the proceedings and in the interests of proportionality to the issues in dispute. In particular, the tribunal may properly limit the number of witnesses who are to be heard on a particular issue of fact, especially where the issue is not central to case: *Noorani v Merseyside TEC Ltd* [1999] IRLR 184.

Evidence is generally relevant only if it relates to issues which are in dispute between the parties, and where issues of fact are agreed (for instance a note of a meeting is agreed by both parties) it is not necessary to call a witness to 'prove' that which is not in dispute. This may apply equally to issues of character: claimants often assume, for instance, that evidence of their good character is an important part of their case, but it would only be relevant in practice if good character is disputed by the employer.

The use of genuinely reluctant witnesses is a matter requiring considerable care. The party calling the witness cannot normally prompt him or her, dispute what he or she says or cross-examine him or her, and so may be faced with an unsympathetic witness giving unhelpful or damaging evidence that cannot effectively be challenged. There is no guarantee that the tribunal will intervene to probe the witness to rectify this. It may also be difficult to establish in advance what evidence a reluctant witness is in a position to give. For these reasons an application by a claimant for witness orders in respect of managers of the employer are likely to be refused.

One way around this difficulty is for the tribunal to be asked to call the witness concerned itself; the witness can then be offered for cross-examination by both parties. The EAT has confirmed that tribunals have this power: *Clapson v British Airways plc* [2001] IRLR 184, a case where the claimant himself was called by the tribunal after his representative indicated that he would not be called. However, this power is used very sparingly, and in general it remains the responsibility of the parties to put evidence before the tribunal and call any witnesses they rely on.

The use of expert witnesses in tribunal proceedings is still relatively rare, but has become somewhat more common, especially in cases where a claim that the applicant is disabled is disputed, or there is a claim for compensation for personal injury in a discrimination claim. In unfair dismissal cases there may be technical issues affecting the computation of compensation, the calculation of pension loss in particular, which may on occasion require an expert witness. (In such cases it is advisable to apply to the tribunal for an order for issues of remedy to be heard separately, to avoid unnecessary costs being incurred on experts' fees.) Separate procedures apply in equal value cases, where the tribunal may be required to appoint an independent expert; details of the applicable rules are in *Sch 6* to the *2004 Regulations*.

The EAT has given detailed guidance on the procedures to be adopted when expert evidence is required: *de Keyser Ltd v Wilson* [2001] IRLR 324. The main points are that there is no presumption that expert evidence will be allowed merely because one party wishes to call an expert; where appropriate the parties should use a joint expert, or at least if one party is calling an expert the other party should have an opportunity to agree to the terms of the instructions to the expert, and where there are experts on both sides, the tribunal should give directions setting out a timetable for the experts to meet to attempt to agree or at least define the issues in dispute.

An expert witness, even if instructed by one party and not jointly, has an overriding duty to the tribunal, which takes precedence over his or her duty to the paying party. In practice, the use of joint experts may be inhibited by difficulties in agreeing who pays for the expert; as noted by the EAT in *de Keyser*, the tribunal has no power, beyond its general powers to award costs, to order the parties to share the cost, or for one party to bear the cost, of an expert witness.

It would be a serious matter, quite possibly amounting to contempt of court, for an employer to seek to prevent one of his or her employees from being called to give evidence or to influence his or her evidence (*Peach Grey & Co v Sommers* [1995] IRLR 363). Any such attempt could also be regarded as scandalous or unreasonable conduct, entitling the tribunal to strike out the response in a sufficiently clear case. The employer may, however, seek to obtain a statement from such a witness as part of the preparation for the case; as a general principle, which applies to both parties, there is no 'property' in a witness.

21.15 **DEPOSIT ORDERS AND STRIKING OUT**

One of the case management powers available to the tribunal is the making of a deposit order, which is an order (in principle against either party, but in practice it is used most often against claimants) that the party will not be permitted to continue to take part in the proceedings unless that party pays a deposit of an amount ordered by the tribunal, and subject to a warning that if the party persists in maintaining the relevant claim or contention, the tribunal may make an order for costs against him or her. The criterion for issuing a costs warning and making a deposit order is that the party's case, or a particular contention put forward by the party 'has little reasonable prospect of success'.

The question whether to make a deposit order must be dealt with at a PHR. This may be on the application of the other party or as a result of an order made by the tribunal of its own initiative. All parties to the proceedings may submit written representations and/or appear and present oral argument, but evidence may not be adduced. The tribunal (comprising a Chairman sitting alone unless there has been a successful application for a full tribunal – see 21.6) considers the Claim Form and Response, the representations (which may include relevant documents) and argument.

If it determines that a party's case or part thereof has little reasonable prospect of success, the tribunal may make an order against that party requiring him or her to deposit a sum not exceeding £500 as a condition of being permitted to continue to take part in the proceedings (*ET Rules, rule 20(1)*). The tribunal must have regard to the party's means in fixing the sum, so far as they are reasonably ascertainable (*rule 20(2)*)). If the tribunal orders a deposit, the order and the grounds for it must be recorded in a document signed by the Chairman; copies of the document must be sent to each party with a note explaining that, if the party against whom the order is made persists in participating in proceedings relating to the relevant issue, he or she may have an order for costs or a preparation time order made against him or her and/or could lose his or her deposit (*rule 20(3)*). The decision will be available to the tribunal which hears the substantive case; however, the Chairman who conducted the PHR is disqualified from hearing the main case, whether or not a deposit was ordered (*rule 18(9)*).

If a deposit is ordered it must be paid within 21 days (extendable on cause shown for 14 days) from the date the order was sent to the party; if it is not so paid, the claim or, as the case may be, response is struck out (*ET Rules, rule 20(4)*). *Regulation 15(6)* of the *2004 Regulations* makes it clear that 'sent' refers to despatch not receipt, overruling case law to the contrary on the previous *Regulations*. The deposit paid by a party is refundable unless at the main hearing an order for costs is made against that party (*Rule 20(5)*). As to the effect of an order for a deposit under *rule 20* in relation to orders for costs, see 21.71.

Guidance as to the correct approach to whether a claim or response 'has little reasonable prospect of success' is given (in relation to the similarly worded test in *Part 24* of the *CPR 1998*) by the Court of Appeal decision in *Swain v Hillman* [2001] 1 All ER 91.The utility of the deposit order procedure in weeding out unmeritorious claims and responses is in practice limited by the fact that no evidence can be given. If there are serious conflicts of fact on the pleadings, a tribunal cannot properly judge what the prospects are. The value of the procedure is that many claimants who are made to realise that they are at risk of a costs order do not pursue their claim. Until relatively recently, tribunals were reluctant to order PHRs and they were held in only a very small percentage of cases, but as concern about the tribunals' apparent inability to weed out hopeless claims at an early stage has grown, the willingness of tribunals to direct a PHR for the purpose of considering the making of a deposit order has increased. Such applications can be considered as a lesser alternative to the striking out of a claim or response as misconceived, if the order for the holding of a PHR provides for this.

There is no power to review a deposit order under *rule 34,* but there is power to vary or revoke the order under *rule 10(2)(n)*. In *Sodexho Ltd v Gibbons* [2005] IRLR 836, the EAT upheld the use of this power to restart the time for payment of the deposit where it had transpired that the claimant had not received the order, having put an incorrect address for his solicitor on the Claim Form. The same case holds that the striking out of a claim or response if the deposit is not paid is technically a judgment, and therefore can be reviewed under *rule 34* (and was reviewable for 'administrative error' on the facts referred to). An appeal is also possible, but less likely to be appropriate given the much more limited grounds of appeal. In principle it is possible for a party to make a second application for a deposit order if the first is unsuccessful, but this is only likely to be entertained if the material circumstances have changed.

21.16 **Striking out**

The tribunal has power to strike out the claim or response, or a part or parts of either, or order that a respondent be debarred from defending a claim altogether, as a sanction for failure to comply with an order made under any of the tribunal's case management powers (*ET Rules, rule 13(1)(b)*). This power includes, but only for cases presented on or after 1 October 2004, power to strike out for failure to pay costs the party has been ordered to pay: *Criddle v Epcot Leisure Ltd,* EAT/0275/05 (cases in progress on 1 October 2004 are governed by the previous costs regime, which has no equivalent sanction).

The power to strike out is subject to the important safeguard that the tribunal must first send a notice in writing to the party concerned giving him or her the opportunity to show cause why the tribunal should not do so (unless the party has already been given an opportunity to show cause orally): *rule 19(1)*. In practice any decision to strike out for non-compliance with an order is likely to be taken at a PHR (although it may arise at the Hearing). The significant exception to the requirement to give an opportunity to show cause is where an 'unless' order has been made and not complied with, in which case striking out can follow without more ado.

The requirement to give the offending party an opportunity to show cause was held, in relation to the equivalent provision under the former *ET Rules* then in force, to be mandatory, and a 'show cause' notice sent before the deadline for compliance was held to be ineffective and invalid, in *Beacard Property Management and Construction Ltd v Day* [1984] ICR 837. It is thought that this remains the position under the 2004 *ET Rules.*

The striking out of a claim or response has been described by the Court of Appeal as a 'draconic power', not to be too readily exercised: *James v Blockbuster Entertainment Ltd* [2006] EWCA Civ 684, [2006] IRLR 630. The guiding principle in deciding whether or not to strike out a party's case for non-compliance with an order is the requirements of the Overriding Objective. This requires the tribunal to consider all relevant factors, including in particular what prejudice the other party has suffered, whether a lesser sanction could cure the prejudice, and as an overriding consideration, whether a fair trial remains possible. These points were articulated by the EAT in *Armitage v Weir Valves & Controls (UK) Ltd* [2004] ICR 371, where the employers successfully appealed against the striking out of their notice of appearance because they had been 10 days late in complying with a direction to exchange witness statements. (See also *National Grid Co plc v Virdee* [1992] IRLR 555, where it was indicated that the power should not be used punitively except in serious cases of deliberate non-compliance with an order, and where any judgment ultimately obtained could not be considered fair between the parties.)

The Court of Appeal has twice ruled that striking out as a sanction should only be applied where it is proportionate to the offence: *Bennett v Southwark London Borough Council* [2002] EWCA Civ 223, [2002] IRLR 407, where the issue was a party's conduct during the Hearing, and *Blockbuster Entertainment Ltd v James* (above), where it was failure to comply with orders. An additional consideration in favour of the sparing use of the power to strike out for non-compliance with orders is that the tribunal now has the power to make an 'unless' order where there has been a failure to comply with an earlier order (*rule 13(2)*). Striking out is not, of course, available for default by a non-party such as a witness failing to attend the hearing as ordered.

In *Blockbuster*, the Court of Appeal held that striking out could only be justified if *either* the offending party has been guilty of deliberate and persistent disregard of required procedural steps, *or* the unreasonable conduct of the case by that party (not necessarily deliberately so) has made a fair trial impossible. These are gateways to the exercise of the power; they do not necessitate the exercise of the power. Thus in *Premium Care Homes Ltd v Osborne*, EAT/0077/06, the sanction of debarring the respondent from defending the case on liability but permitting it to defend itself at the remedy stage was held to be a proper and proportionate response to breaches of orders that had made a fair trial on liability impossible (compare the similar sanction applied by the EAT where a response had not been submitted in time in *D & H Travel Ltd v Foster* [2006] ICR 1537).

In *Maresca v Motor Insurance Repair Research Centre* [2005] ICR 197, a case concerning the striking out of a claim for failure to comply with a case management order for mutual disclosure of documents, the EAT held that in considering whether to strike out a party's case, the tribunal should have regard to the factors listed in the *CPR 1998, rule 3.9*. These are the criteria to be taken into account by a Court in deciding whether to grant relief from sanctions imposed for non-compliance with an order, and include whether the application for relief was made promptly, whether the default was intentional, and whether the expected hearing date can still be met if the original order is now complied with.

Further guidance has also been given by the EAT on the exercise of the power to strike out for partial failure to provide particulars ordered by the tribunal. This power should not be used, even in discrimination cases, where the replies given could fairly be described as 'particulars' given in good faith, even if not all the demands for particulars had been substantially met; and in any event not if a fair trial of the claim remained possible: *Sanni v SmithKline Beecham Ltd*, EAT/656/98; *Green v Hackney London Borough Council*, EAT/182/98.

The incorporation of *art 6* of the *European Convention on Human Rights*, through the *Human Rights Act 1998*, provides a possible basis for challenges to striking-out decisions on the ground that the party (particularly a claimant) is deprived of the right to a determination of his or her civil rights by way of a fair and public hearing. However the case law of the European Court of Human Rights (which guides the decision-making of UK courts and tribunals) indicates that the proper judicial use of powers to control litigants, including striking out, does not in principle offend the *Convention*. (See also *Soteriou v Ultrachem Ltd* [2004] EWHC 983 (QB), [2004] IRLR 870 (striking out where contract of employment tainted by illegality not contrary to *art 6*).)

21.17 There are a number of other grounds on which a party's case may be struck out, in whole or in part. The tribunal may make such an order, if it thinks fit:

(*a*)   on the grounds that the offending case or part is scandalous or vexatious, or has no reasonable prospect of success;

(*b*)   on the grounds that the manner in which the proceedings have been conducted by the offending party has been scandalous, unreasonable or vexatious;

(*c*)   in relation to a claim, if it has not been actively pursued;

(*d*)   also in relation to a claim, if the Chairman or tribunal considers that it is no longer possible to have a fair hearing of the claim.

(*Rule 18(7)(b), (c), (d) and (f).*)

In relation to each of these powers, the requirement to send a 'show cause' notice to the party affected referred to above applies, unless the party has had the opportunity to make oral submissions against the order. Striking out orders can only be made at a PHR or a Hearing.

The last of the four grounds for striking out listed above was introduced by the *2004 Regulations*. The occasions when it would be appropriate to use this power will be very rare, where for instance a case has been adjourned on several occasions over such a period that witnesses are either no longer available or liable to have no recollection of relevant events. To this extent it overlaps with the power to strike out a claim which has not been actively pursued; it is also unlikely that such a claim would be struck out whilst there the possibility of a fair trial remains, unless the claimant has clearly indicated that he or she no longer intends to pursue the claim.

The power to strike out a party's case as having no reasonable prospect of success was introduced by the *2001 Regulations*. The power mirrors the power of the High Court under *Part 24* of the *CPR 1998* to give summary judgment where a case has no reasonable prospect of success, as to which there is helpful guidance in *Swain v Hillman* [2001] 1 All ER 91, CA. A tribunal is unlikely to entertain an application to strike out the claim or response at a PHR in factually contentious cases, since tribunals are reluctant to deny a party the opportunity to put his or her case to the tribunal except on the strongest grounds. The drastic nature of the power justifies caution in its exercise; the tribunal has a discretion to strike out, and is not required automatically to do so merely because it determines that the claim (or defence) has no reasonable prospects of success. The importance of not striking out discrimination cases in particular in any but the clearest of cases has been reinforced by dicta in the House of Lords: *Anyanwu v South Bank Students' Union* [2001] UKHL 14, [2001] IRLR 305 (see Lord Steyn at para 24, Lord Hope at para 39). See also *Balamoody v UK Central Council for Nursing, Midwifery and Health Visiting* [2002] EWCA Civ 2097, [2002] ICR 646, paras 31–50 and *HM Prison Service v Dolby* [2003] IRLR 694 and, for a similar approach to whistle-blowing cases, *Boulding v Land Securities Trillium Ltd*, EAT/0023/06.

One consequence of changes introduced by the *2004 Regulations* is that the questions whether a deposit should be ordered or an order made to strike out all or part of a claim or response can both be dealt with at a PHR. The grounds for the former are now virtually identical to the 'no reasonable prospects' ground for the latter (the difference is that in the latter case the test is 'no' rather than 'little' reasonable prospect of success). As striking out is a more drastic remedy – what has been described as showing the 'Red card' (as compared to the 'Yellow card' of a deposit order and costs warning: see *HM Prison Service v Dolby* [2003] IRLR 694) – tribunals can be expected to consider the merits of the case more rigorously. One important difference between the two powers is that evidence can be called in support of or in opposition to a strike-out application under *rule 18* but not where the only issue is whether to make a deposit order and give a costs warning. It is open to a party (and advisable in practice) to apply for both orders in the alternative.

The conduct of a representative, as well as a party, may be grounds for striking out the party's case under (*b*) above, and it is not open to the party to 'disown' the representative: *Harmony Healthcare plc v Drewery* EAT/886/00 (respondent's representative assaulting claimant's representative in waiting room). However, the tribunal should only use the drastic sanction of striking out a claim or defence if this is a proportionate response to the offence: *Bennett v Southwark London Borough Council* [2002] EWCA Civ 223, [2002] IRLR 407, a case with helpful guidance on what constitutes 'scandalous' conduct. See also *Bolch v Chipman* [2004] IRLR 140, where guidance was given by the EAT both as to the procedure to be followed and the basis for making a strike-out order, in a case where the unreasonable conduct alleged was a threat of violence. The EAT stressed that the ground for striking out is not simply unreasonable *behaviour* but *conducting the proceedings* in an unreasonable manner.

In *Ganase v Kent Community Housing Trust* [2001] All ER (D) 07 (Jul), the EAT held that a tribunal had erred in law in striking out the originating application for unreasonable conduct where the claimant, having failed to obtain an adjournment on medical grounds, attended the hearing with a letter dated the previous day from her GP certifying her ill-health, which resulted in the proceedings having to be adjourned. The Court of Appeal has commented that it will only be in a very unusual case that it would be justified to strike out on procedural grounds a claim which has reached the point of trial: *James v Blockbuster Entertainment Ltd* [2006] EWCA Civ 684, [2006] IRLR 630.

The question what amounts to unreasonable or vexatious conduct may arise in relation to the claimant's persistence in a claim when the respondent is prepared to concede all or part of the claim. In this connection it is important to remember that the remedies available to the claimant may include a declaration (that he or she has been unlawfully discriminated against, or unfairly dismissed) as well as compensation. Thus it has been held not to be vexatious for a claimant to pursue his or her claim for unfair dismissal even after the respondent has offered to pay the maximum sum which the tribunal could award, so long as the respondent has not admitted that the dismissal was unfair (*Telephone Information Services Ltd v*

Wilkinson [1991] IRLR 148). On the other hand, a claimant who decides at the last moment to withdraw a claim, thereby causing the respondent unnecessary work and expense in preparing for the case, may be held to have acted unreasonably in delaying the withdrawal: *McPherson v BNP Paribas (London Branch)* [2004] EWCA Civ 569, [2004] IRLR 558.

Where *res judicata* or issue estoppel (see 21.26 below) does not apply, the party seeking an order to strike out the other party's case must show that there is a special reason why relitigation of the issue would be an abuse of process and therefore vexatious (*Department of Education and Science v Taylor* [1992] IRLR 308; and see *Blaik v Post Office* [1994] IRLR 280 and *Staffordshire County Council v Barber* [1996] ICR 379 on the principles applicable where a claimant who has failed in, or withdrawn, a claim under domestic law attempts to pursue the same point by way of a claim based on EU law).

21.18 RESTRICTED REPORTING ORDERS

In recent years some employment tribunal cases involving allegations of sexual misconduct have attracted considerable publicity in the media, all too often prurient and embarrassing to those involved. In order to diminish the adverse effect on the parties of such publicity, *TURERA 1993* introduced new powers for tribunals and the EAT to restrict publication of material identifying those involved in such cases. These were implemented in the *1993 ET Regulations* and *EAT Rules*, which introduced the power to make restricted reporting orders and register deletion orders. Equivalent powers were introduced by the *Disability Discrimination Act 1995* for cases where evidence of a personal nature is to be given (see now the *ETA 1996, ss 12* and *32*). The relevant provisions are now contained in *rules 50* and *51* of the *ET Rules*, and *rules 23* and *23A* of the *EAT Rules.*

A restricted reporting order may be made by the tribunal of its own motion or on the application of a party. The precondition is that the case involves allegations of sexual misconduct. This is not limited to claims of discrimination by sexual harassment; it may include cases where the applicant's dismissal was for an alleged sexual offence (see e g *Securicor Guarding Ltd v R* [1994] IRLR 633) or any other proceedings in which allegations of sexual misconduct are expected to form part of the evidence, and regardless of whether or not the allegations can be substantiated: *X v Stevens* [2003] IRLR 411. 'Sexual misconduct' means a sexual offence, sexual harassment or other adverse conduct, of whatever nature, related to sex: *ETA 1996, s 11(6)*. The criterion in disability discrimination cases is whether 'evidence of a personal nature' is likely to be given (*ET Rules, rule 50(1)(b)*).

A restricted reporting order prohibits, subject to criminal penalty, the publication in Great Britain of any matter likely to lead members of the public to identify a person as the person making, or a person affected by, the allegations of misconduct or, in a disability case, to identify the complainant or any other person named in the order (*ETA 1996, ss 11(2), 12(3)*). The scope of the order would appear to be wide enough to cover not only the alleged miscreant in a sexual misconduct case, but also the employer and employee parties to the claim, if not directly covered otherwise. However, the EAT has ruled (departing from a previous decision) that a body corporate cannot be the subject of a restricted reporting order (*Leicester University v A* [1999] IRLR 352, following *R v London (North) Industrial Tribunal, ex p Associated Newspapers Ltd* [1998] ICR 1212 in preference to *M v Vincent* [1998] ICR 73). The tribunal must specify the persons who must not be identified (*ET Rules, rule 50(8)(a)*).

A restricted reporting order (other than a temporary order, for which see below) may only be made either at a PHR or at a Hearing, after the parties have been given an opportunity to make oral submissions as to whether an order should be made and as to the terms of any order; it is one of the categories of order that may not be made at a Case Management Discussion (*ET Rules, rules 17(2), 18(7)(g), 50(2), (6)*). Because of the wider public interest in justice being dispensed publicly, tribunals should not automatically order a restriction on publication simply – indeed especially – because both parties seek it: *X v Z Ltd* [1998] ICR 43, CA. The point was followed in *R v London (North) Industrial Tribunal, ex p Associated Newspapers Ltd* (above), in which Keene J stated that the words 'a person affected by the allegations of misconduct' should be interpreted narrowly, having regard to the principle of the freedom of the press to report court and tribunal proceedings fully and contemporaneously. The wider interest in public justice is reflected in a new provision in the 2004 *ET Rules* giving interested parties (in practice this will almost always be media representatives) the right to make representations at the hearing at which the decision is made whether to impose an order (*rule 50(7)*).

A new power is given by the 2004 *ET Rules* enabling a Chairman to make a temporary restricted reporting order, either on application by a party or of his or her own motion, and either without any hearing, or at a CMD. The parties must be notified of a temporary order and informed of their right to apply for the continuance of the order; if no party applies within 14 days, the order lapses, but if an application to continue it is made, the order remains in force until the question whether it should be continued can be determined, either at a PHR or at the full Hearing (*ET Rules, rule 50(2)–(5)*). This is a useful provision to deal with the situation where a party anticipates media interest in the case and seeks emergency protection from publicity.

A restricted reporting order remains in force until the promulgation of the judgment in the case, unless revoked earlier. Where the judgment is given separately on liability and the tribunal will need to hold a further hearing to decide on remedy, the order remains in force until the final remedy judgment is issued: *ET Rules, rule 50(8)(b)*, confirming the effect of *A v Chief Constable of West Yorkshire Police* [2001] ICR 128. This has the consequence that if the claim is settled after liability has been determined but before a remedy hearing is concluded, the order will remain in force indefinitely.

A notice drawing attention to the existence of the order must be placed on the tribunal door (*ET Rules, rule 50(8)(c)*). Guidance as to the scope and dissemination of orders has also been given by the High Court in *R v Southampton Industrial Tribunal, ex p INS News Group Ltd* [1995] IRLR 247.

The relatively narrow category of cases in which orders can be made may result in individuals who would be embarrassed, or might be subjected to harassment, if their identity was publicised, being deterred from bringing claims by the lack of protection available. Considerations of this kind led the tribunal in the *West Yorkshire* case, above, to hold that there is a further power to order restrictions on reporting tribunal proceedings in any case where this is necessary to ensure that a claimant seeking to assert enforceable rights under EU law (in this case a remedy for refusal to engage the claimant as a police officer because she was a transsexual) is not deterred from doing so by fear of publicity. The basis for this decision was the requirement of *art 6* of the *Equal Treatment Directive 1976* for member states to afford access to effective remedies for victims of unlawful sex discrimination. This point was expressly left open by the EAT in the *West Yorkshire* case, but in *X v Stevens*, above, it held that both the EAT under its inherent jurisdiction, and tribunals using their powers under *ET Rules 2001, rule 15(1)* (now *ET Rules, rule 60(1)*) to regulate their own procedure, could make restricted reporting orders where this was necessary in order to prevent a claimant from being deterred from pursuing a claim, and regardless of whether the statutory conditions for a restricted reporting order or register deletion order were met and whether the respondent was or was not a state authority.

The equivalent provisions governing appeals to the EAT are reviewed in *A v B, ex p News Group Newspapers Ltd, Chief Constable of West Yorkshire Police v A* and *X v Stevens,* above (see 22.13 below).

21.19   Where allegations of a sexual offence are involved, there was prior to 2004 a separate power to make a 'register deletion order'. This had the effect of requiring that the public register of judgments and any other public documents generated in the proceedings were modified so as to prevent identification of persons making or affected by the allegation (*ETA 1996, s 11(1)(a)*). Under the *2004 Regulations* (*ET Rules, rule 49*), it is no longer necessary to have an order of the tribunal; the rule simply imposes a requirement on the Chairman, and the Secretary in preparing judgments and reasons for placing on the register, to delete any matter likely to identify persons making or affected by the allegations in any case where it appears that there are allegations of a sexual offence. This provision applies indefinitely, and is mandatory. In practice, in any doubtful case the matter is likely to be referred to the Chairman who heard the case for a ruling. Following the abolition of the register of applications in October 2004, the principal importance of *rule 49* is that the identity of affected parties remains concealed after the promulgation of the final judgment in the case.

21.20 MISCELLANEOUS POWERS OF THE TRIBUNAL

In addition to the general power of the tribunal to issue orders, and to regulate its own procedure (as to which see respectively *ET Rules, rules10(1), 60(1)*), there are a number of specific powers given to the tribunal, which can be exercised in most cases by a Chairman rather than a full tribunal (see *rule 10(1)*)).

21.21 Extension of time

A Chairman may extend the time appointed by or under the *ET Rules* for doing any act, whether or not the time has expired (*rule 10(2)(e)*). However this is subject to the qualification that time may only be extended for certain purposes if the Chairman considers that it is just and equitable to do so; this qualification applies to the extension of time for submitting a response, for applying for a review or a costs or preparation time order, and for applying for written reasons for a judgment where reasons were given orally. In addition, time may only be extended for the purpose of submitting a response to the claim if an application has been made before the time limit expired: *rule 4(4)*; see however *Moroak (t/a Blake Envelopes) v Cromie* [2005] IRLR 535, holding that there is a power to review the non-acceptance of a late response, which may effectively circumvent this provision where the interests of justice so require.

21.22 Stay of proceedings

The power to order a stay (or sist in Scotland) of proceedings is conferred by *ET Rules, rule 10(2)(h)*. A stay operates to suspend the proceedings, not to end them. Applications to stay tribunal proceedings are often made, and frequently granted, where there are concurrent proceedings in the High Court (or Court of Session) and the employment tribunal arising out of the same employment. Tribunal proceedings may also be stayed pending the outcome of foreign litigation (*JMCC Holdings Ltd v Conroy* [1990] ICR 179). In such cases, the EAT should only interfere with the tribunal's decision to postpone or continue with the proceedings before it if that decision resulted from an error of law or if it was perverse (*Carter v Credit Change Ltd* [1979] ICR 908; *Automatic Switching Ltd v Brunet* [1986] ICR 542). For a discussion of the factors to be taken into consideration, see *First Castle Electronics Ltd v West* [1989] ICR 72, *Bowater plc v Charlwood* [1991] ICR 798 and *Chorion plc v Lane*, IDS Brief 642 (where the High Court proceedings had been brought by the former employer).

A different reason for seeking a stay of the proceedings is that the parties wish to attempt to settle their dispute by alternative means, such as through mediation (see further **21.31**). Tribunals encourage the use of such alternatives to litigation. In Scotland this encouragement has been formalised into a Practice Direction on the sisting of cases for mediation, issued in December 2006.

One reason for staying tribunal proceedings in such cases is that the doctrine of *res judicata* (ie that issues decided in one set of proceedings cannot be relitigated) may apply so as to bind the High Court later. This will only be true if precisely the same issue arises in both sets of proceedings (see *Munir v Jang Publications Ltd* [1989] ICR 1; *Crown Estate Comrs v Dorset County Council* [1990] Ch 297; *Soteriou v Ultrachem Ltd* [2004] EWHC 983 (QB), [2004] IRLR 870). A claimant who wishes to bring both High Court (or county court) and tribunal proceedings, and to pursue the former first, should present his or her claim to the tribunal within the statutory time limit and immediately apply for a stay pending the outcome of the other proceedings, explaining that the tribunal claim has been made at that time to ensure the claim is not time-barred (*Warnock v Scarborough Football Club* [1989] ICR 489).

Where the proceedings are for unfair dismissal of participants in industrial action, there is specific power for the tribunal to adjourn the proceedings where certain civil proceedings have been brought in relation to the industrial action (effectively a claim for an injunction or interdict) until those proceedings, including any appeal, have been determined (*ET Rules, rule 55*).

21.23 Joining additional parties and dismissing a party

It is sometimes necessary for a claimant to apply to join one or more additional respondents to the claim. This may arise, for instance, where the respondent originally named disputes that it is or was the employer, or an issue arises as to whether the claimant's employment was transferred to a third party following a transfer of the former employer's undertaking.

The powers of the tribunal to add parties have been widened by the *ET Rules*. A tribunal may at any time, on the application of any person or of its own motion, order that any person the Chairman or tribunal considers may be liable for the remedy claimed be joined as a party to the proceedings (*Rule 10(2)(k)*). Joinder may be ordered by a Chairman alone or by a full tribunal. An important limitation on the power of joinder under the previous *ET Rules* was that a party could not be joined unless relief was sought against him or her by another party. In practice this was the claimant, since there was (and still is), except in the special cases referred to in the following paragraph, no power for the tribunal to make orders for contribution between respondents, and orders for disclosure of documents or further particulars are not 'relief'. The *ET Rules* meet this difficulty by giving the Chairman power to join any person he or she considers has an interest in the outcome of the proceedings. The new power (contained in *Rule 10(2)(r)*) is also wide enough to permit an interested third party such as a trade union to be joined where a claim is in the nature of a test case with implications for its members generally.

When either the employer or the complainant claims that dismissal was due to union pressure (see UNFAIR DISMISSAL – III (53)) a tribunal must grant an application to join the union as a party to proceedings if it is made before the hearing of the complaint, and may do so if the application is made after the commencement of the hearing but before an award is made (*TULRCA 1992, s 160(1), (2)*); the tribunal then has the power to order that the party joined pay some or all of any compensation awarded. A similar procedure operates under the *Transfer of Undertakings (Protection of Employment) Regulations 2006, reg 15(5)*), where a transferor facing a complaint of failure to inform employee representatives of measures envisaged by the transferee, who intends to allege that this was due to the default of the transferee in breach of *reg 13(4)*), must notify the transferee of this intention; in this case, notification automatically makes the transferee a party and no order of the tribunal is necessary (but it must be advised of the joinder so that the transferee can be informed of the hearing, etc).

Analagous issues can arise in discrimination cases, where a claim is brought against more than one respondent (typically the employer or former employer, and one or more individual managers said to have committed the acts of discrimination for which the employer is vicariously liable); the tribunal has power to apportion any compensation between the respondents, and in exceptional cases to make an award against the respondents jointly and severally (*Way v Crouch* [2005] IRLR 603; *Gilbank v Miles* [2006] EWCA Civ 543, [2006] IRLR 538). It is therefore important for a claimant alleging discrimination to consider whether to claim against individuals in addition to the employer. An application to add an individual respondent after the proceedings have been started is subject to the considerations referred to in 21.10(*g*) above.

There is a corresponding power to dismiss from the proceedings a respondent who is no longer directly interested in the proceedings: *rule 10(2)(l)*. Usually, the powers to join and dismiss parties will be exercised by a Chairman on the papers or at a CMD, but they may if necessary be exercised by the full tribunal at a Hearing, or by the Chairman at a PHR. Any dispute about the right of a party joined by the tribunal to contest the claim can be decided at a PHR (*rule 18(7)(a)*).

21.24   Powers in relation to multiple claims

Representative claimants or respondents. Where many people have the same interest in defending a claim, one or more of them may be cited as the person or persons against whom relief is sought, or may be authorised by the tribunal, before or at the hearing, to defend on behalf of all the persons so interested. This was formerly expressly provided for by the *ET Rules (ET Rules 2001, rule 19(3))*. There is no equivalent express provision in the 2004 *Rules,* but the general case management powers of the tribunal are sufficiently wide to cover the point (and see *Affleck v Newcastle Mind* [1999] IRLR 405 (claim against one member of a committee of unincorporated association on behalf of all the members of the committee)).

Consolidation. A tribunal may order that two or more applications be heard together, often, but technically incorrectly, referred to as consolidation of the proceedings. The relevant power is not subject to express restrictions on the circumstances of its use (see *rule10(2)(j)*). In practice an order is likely to be made if the same question of law or fact arises in each case, or if the remedy claimed in them arises out of the same set of facts, such as if several workers claim redundancy payments on the closure of a business, or if for some other reason it is desirable to hear the claims together; consolidation will normally be appropriate if a claimant has brought more than one claim against the same respondent. The parties must have an opportunity to make representations before such an order is made (*rule 10(7)*).

Test cases. If there are a large number of originating applications raising the same question, some may be selected as lead, or test, cases, and attempts to reopen the issues thus determined in later cases may be struck out as an abuse of process (*Ashmore v British Coal Corpn* [1990] ICR 485; contrast *Department of Education and Science v Taylor* [1992] IRLR 308). The power to order test cases is not contained in a specific rule, but is part of the tribunal's general powers to regulate its own proceedings and to give directions.

21.25 Transfer of proceedings

Where a claim is pending before an employment tribunal in England or Wales which could be determined by a tribunal in Scotland, and it is more convenient to do so, the claim can be transferred to Scotland, and vice versa (*rule 21*).

21.26 Estoppel and prevention of abuse of process

One important aspect of preventing abuse of the tribunal's process is the prevention of the relitigation of issues previously decided, or which could have been decided by the tribunal in earlier proceedings between the parties. The wider form of issue estoppel (sometimes referred to as the rule in *Henderson v Henderson* (1843) 3 Hare 100) applies in employment tribunal proceedings; this lays down that parties to litigation must bring forward their whole case and, except in special circumstances, will not be permitted to bring fresh proceedings in a matter which could and should have been litigated in earlier proceedings, but was omitted through negligence, inadvertence or accident. It is not a 'special circumstance', so as to displace that rule, that parties in employment tribunal proceedings are encouraged not to be legally represented (*Divine-Bortey v London Borough of Brent* [1998] ICR 886). For a recent example of the operation of the rule in *Henderson v Henderson*, see *Sheriff v Klyne Tugs (Lowestoft) Ltd* [1999] IRLR 481 (action for personal injury allegedly caused by racial harassment struck out by the Court of Appeal, as this claim could and should have been pursued as part of the claimant's tribunal claim of racial discrimination against the same employers, which had been settled).

A related but equally venerable doctrine, of the merger of causes of action, arose in *Fraser v HLMAD Ltd* [2006] EWCA Civ 738, [2006] IRLR 687, where it was held that a successful claim under the tribunal's contractual jurisdiction precluded the claimant from then bringing High Court proceedings to recover the balance of the damages for wrongful dismissal. His claim had been valued by the tribunal at some £80,000, but its power to make an award under the *Extension of Jurisdiction Order 1994* is limited to £25,000, and the merger of his claim prevented him from pursuing the balance through separate proceedings.

21.27 The doctrine of issue estoppel has been the subject of three decisions of the Court of Appeal, which are not easily reconciled.

    (1)   In *Lennon v Birmingham City Council* [2001] IRLR 826, the claimant had brought tribunal proceedings alleging sex discrimination resulting in a stress-related illness. She withdrew the proceedings before the hearing, and

they were dismissed by the tribunal at her request. She then commenced county court proceedings in respect of stress-related ill health based on the same allegations (of offensive and intimidatory behaviour by fellow employees). The Court of Appeal, following *Barber v Staffordshire County Council* [1996] IRLR 209, held that the county court claim was rightly struck out as an attempt to relitigate matters which had been judicially determined by the tribunal's decision dismissing her earlier claim.

(2)   However in *Sajid v Sussex Muslim Society* [2002] IRLR 113, a contrary conclusion was reached where the claimant had initially brought a breach of contract claim in the tribunal which he quantified well in excess of the maximum the tribunal could award, and then withdrew that claim specifically in order that he could pursue it in the High Court. *Barber* was distinguished because the withdrawal and subsequent dismissal of the claim was done with a view to pursuing the dispute elsewhere and not intended to determine the dispute.

(3)   Finally in *Ako v Rothschild Asset Management Ltd* [2002] EWCA Civ 236, [2002] ICR 899, on facts materially indistinguishable from *Lennon*, the court nevertheless held that it was necessary and permissible to look at the surrounding circumstances; tribunals, unlike courts, did not have a procedure for discontinuance of proceedings (which does not trigger an issue estoppel), and if in substance the withdrawal was a discontinuance it should not bar fresh proceedings based on the same facts.

It is likely that *Ako* will be followed in preference to *Lennon*, as the later authority and which considered all the recent case law including *Sajid*. However, in any case where rights of future action may need to be preserved it is important for a claimant to make clear to the respondent and the tribunal why he or she is withdrawing his or her claim. Mummery LJ in *Ako* also recommends that tribunals ask claimants to state the reason for withdrawal before making an order. Changes introduced by the *2004 ET Rules* affecting such cases are described in 21.28 below.

21.28   Withdrawal and dismissal of claims

The claimant may withdraw his or her claim at any stage in the proceedings. This may be done because a settlement has been reached, or because the claimant does not want to proceed with the claim, or wishes to pursue the issue through other proceedings. Prior to the coming into force of the 2004 *ET Rules*, the practice if a claimant withdrew the claim was for the tribunal to issue a formal order dismissing it. Some of the potential difficulties that this could cause are set out at 21.27 above. The *ET Rules* introduced a new procedure (*Rule 25*), but this rule is drafted in terms described by the Court of Appeal as 'lamentable'. The claimant must notify the tribunal in writing of his or her wish to withdraw the claim or a particular part of it, and as against which respondent or respondents, if there are more than one, it is withdrawn. Alternatively, a claim or part thereof may be withdrawn orally at a hearing. The withdrawal is then notified by the tribunal to the other parties, and this brings the proceedings to an end automatically, to the extent of the withdrawal. (As to withdrawal of part of a claim, see *Verdin v Harrods Ltd*, below.)

Once notice of withdrawal of the claim has been given, it cannot be revoked by the claimant: *Khan v Heywood and Middleton Primary Care Trust* [2006] EWCA Civ 1087, [2006] IRLR 793. However the claim will only be *dismissed* if the respondent applies for an order to that effect. The application must be made within 28 days of the notice of withdrawal being sent to the respondent; the time limit can be extended if a Chairman considers it just and equitable to do so (*ET Rules, rule 25(3), (4), (5)*).

The effect of withdrawal of a claim has been explained by the EAT in *Verdin v Harrods Ltd* [2006] IRLR 339. The consequence of withdrawal, without more, is that the proceedings automatically come to an end, but the claimant is not precluded from pursuing the claim in other proceedings (including further proceedings in the tribunal, subject to the applicable time limits); if the tribunal claim has been dismissed, however, the bringing of further proceedings (in the tribunal or elsewhere) is likely to be regarded as an abuse of process.

Because of the consequences for a claimant of dismissal of the claim, there is no automatic right to an order dismissing the claim; indeed the claimant has the right to apply for a review of such an order, or to appeal against it (*rule 25(4)*). In this way, the potential difficulties of withdrawal for claimants discussed in 21.27 above should be avoided. However, in order to avoid the possibility of an order for dismissal of the claim being made in such circumstances, a claimant should explain to the tribunal when withdrawing the claim the basis on which it is being withdrawn, and whether there is any reason not to dismiss the claim.

Where a claim is withdrawn but not dismissed, the file will be closed and retained for a year before being destroyed; however it is open to any party to make an application for costs or a preparation time order.

21.29 CONCILIATION AND SETTLEMENT OF CLAIMS

The majority of tribunal claims are either withdrawn (often after a private settlement between the parties) or settled through the auspices of an ACAS conciliation officer. Almost all employment disputes within the jurisdiction of the tribunal are within the scope of ACAS conciliation, including breach of contract claims and claims for statutory redundancy payments (*ETA 1996, s 18(1)*). ACAS has a *duty* to attempt to conciliate if so requested; its services may also be requested, and there is then a like duty to act, where a claim is being considered or threatened, but has not yet been presented: *ETA 1996, s 18(2), (3)*. However, for cases presented since the coming into force of the *Employment Act 2002, s 24* (on 1 October 2004), the duty only applies, in the majority of cases, during an initial conciliation period (which may be extended); once this period has passed it is a matter of *discretion* for ACAS officers whether to provide any further assistance: *ETA 1996, s 18(2A)*. The practice is that ACAS will normally decline to intervene once the fixed period has expired.

The purpose of this change is to encourage early settlement. Past experience suggests that many parties do not consider settlement until a hearing is imminent, not least because the strength of the other party's case often does not emerge clearly until documents have been disclosed and witness statements prepared and exchanged. It is unlikely that this habit has been significantly affected by the new arrangements. However tribunals may list cases for hearing immediately after the expiry of the fixed conciliation period, which may assist settlement by ensuring that ACAS's services remain available during the run up to the hearing. In March 2007 the DTI initiated consultations on whether the fixed conciliation periods should be scrapped.

The functions of conciliation officers are discussed in some detail in *Clarke v Redcar & Cleveland Borough Council* [2006] IRLR 324. It is not the conciliation officer's responsibility to ensure that the terms of any settlement are fair to the employee (or employer), and the conciliation officer must never advise a party as to the merits of the case, or advise the employee whether he or she could expect to get more compensation from the tribunal. The primary function is to promote a settlement by whatever legitimate means the officer thinks appropriate in the circumstances. These limitations are considered important to protect the impartiality of the conciliation service.

Anything said to a conciliation officer is confidential and cannot be disclosed to the tribunal without the consent of the communicator (*ETA 1996, s 18(7)*, and equivalent provisions in the discrimination statutes). If a settlement is reached with the aid of the conciliation officer it is recorded on a Form COT3. It is the policy of ACAS not to be involved in settlements where it has no conciliation role, ie the conciliation officer is merely asked to record a settlement reached privately.

The fixed conciliation periods do not apply if the claim is made under the *Equal Pay Act 1970*, the *SDA 1975*, the *RRA 1976*, the *DDA 1995*, the *Employment Equality (Sexual Orientation) Regulations 2003*, the *Employment Equality (Religion or Belief) Regulations 2003*, the *Employment Equality (Age) Regulations 2006* or the *ERA 1996 ss 47B, 103A* or *105(6A)* (which cover subjection to detriment, dismissal or selection for redundancy for having made a protected disclosure). It is sufficient to exclude the whole claim from the fixed conciliation period regime that it includes a claim under any of these provisions, regardless of whether it also includes claims which would ordinarily be subject to a fixed period; but all claims not including one of the listed categories are subject to the fixed conciliation period regime (*ET Rules, rule 22(1), (2)*).

There are two fixed conciliation periods, the 'short period', which is seven weeks from the date on which the Claim Form is sent by the tribunal to the respondent concerned, and the standard period, which is 13 weeks (*rules 22(2), (3), (5), (6)*); in each case the period is calculated separately for each respondent (since a respondent may be joined to the proceedings at a later date, and only served the papers at that stage) (*rule 22(4)*). The short period applies to claims which consist only of one or more of the following:

(*a*)   A complaint of breach of contract;

(*b*)   A claim under *Part II* of the *ERA 1996* (unlawful deduction from wages);

(*c*)   A claim under the *ERA 1996, ss 163* or *164* (failure to pay a redundancy payment);

(*d*)   A claim under the *ERA 1996, s 28* (failure to pay a guarantee payment);

(*e*)   A claim under any of *ss 50, 52, 53, 55, 56, 64* or *68* of the *ERA 1996* (provisions relating to time off and remuneration in respect thereof, and remuneration during suspension on medical or maternity grounds);

(*f*)   A claim under any of *ss 168, 169* or *170* of the *TULRCA 1992* (rights to time off and remuneration for trade union duties, and to time off for trade union activities);

(*g*)   A claim under *s 68* of the *TULRCA 1992* (unlawful deductions from trade union subscriptions);

(*h*)   A claim for non-payment of a protective award under *TULRCA s 192* or *reg 11(5)* of the *Transfer of Undertakings (Protection of Employment) Regulations 1981*;

(*i*)   A claim under *reg 13, 14(2)* or *16* of the *Working Time Regulations 1998* (right to paid annual leave).

(*ET Rules, rule 22(5)*); claims under para (i) were added as from 1 October 2005 by *SI 2005/1865.*)

21.30 The short conciliation period may be converted by a Chairman into a standard period (thus extending it by six weeks) if he or she considers that the latter would be more appropriate on the basis of the complexity of the proceedings. Such an order may be made on the Chairman's own initiative or on the application of one or both parties; in the latter case the normal procedure for making and determining applications under *rules 10* and *11* applies. The extension can only be ordered if the short period has not already expired; it is therefore necessary to make any application promptly so that it can be determined in time (*rule 22(8)*). A standard period can only be extended by two weeks, and only if ACAS notifies the tribunal that there is a proposal for settlement of the case, that it is probable that it will be settled within the extended period, and that all parties agree to an extension (*rule 22(7)*; this does not apply to the short conciliation period). There is no power for the tribunal to disapply the short or standard conciliation period altogether. The conciliation period is suspended during any period that the proceedings are stayed (or sisted in Scotland) (*rule 24*). This does not mean that conciliation cannot take place during a stay, but the unexpired part of the conciliation period is available once the stay is lifted.

The Hearing of a claim cannot take place during a fixed conciliation period, but the Hearing can be listed, and case management powers can be exercised (including by way of a CMD) and a PHR can be held, before the conciliation period has expired (*rule 22(3)*).

There are a number of circumstances in which a fixed conciliation period comes to an end against a particular respondent before it would otherwise have done so. The conciliation period ends on:

(*a*)   The date on which a default judgment (whether for liability and remedy, or for liability only) is signed;

(*b*)   The date on which a claim or response is struck out, or the claimant notifies the tribunal that the claim is withdrawn;

(*c*)   The date on which a settlement of the claim is concluded through ACAS, or a settlement reached privately by way of a compromise agreement is notified to the tribunal;

(*d*)   Where either party has notified ACAS in writing that they do not wish to make use of its services, the date on which ACAS notifies the tribunal of this;

(*e*)   Where no response has been received from the respondent, but no default judgment is issued (e.g. because the claimant has asked for a Hearing), 14 days after the time limit for a response expires.

(*Rule 23(1)*.)

If a default judgment is subsequently revoked, or the respondent's right to defend the proceedings is re-established in some other way by the tribunal, after the conciliation period has terminated, the tribunal may also order that there be a fresh conciliation period. In that event the conciliation period runs from the date of the order, and is of the length appropriate to the category of claim (*rule 23(2)(3)*).

21.31 An alternative to ACAS conciliation or private negotiations is mediation. This method of dispute resolution, which is increasingly favoured by the courts, and increasingly commonly used in civil litigation, has not yet become common in employment tribunal cases. However it is becoming less unusual, particularly in relatively high value claims, and cases where there is the prospect of related civil litigation. Mediation is a method of structured negotiations led by an independent mediator, who meets with both parties in the course of the mediation and attempts to guide each to common ground and to make concessions to facilitate settlement. Unlike an arbitrator, a mediator cannot impose a decision on the parties. A number of organisations now offer the services of trained mediators, and mediation has a relatively high rate of success. It also has advantages of privacy, and often of speed.

Generally, mediations are set up as private arrangements between the parties and the mediator. The major disadvantage of this is that the parties must bear the cost of engaging the mediator, as well as their own costs of representation and attendance at the mediation, and this usually makes the option less attractive, and may make it impracticable, in claims for modest compensation, or where the employee is not in a position to meet his or her share of the mediation cost and the employer is not willing to meet the whole cost. A pilot scheme within the tribunal system offering the (free) services of a chairman to mediate between the parties if they so wish has been established at the London Central, Birmingham and Newcastle tribunals; it is also possible within the framework of ACAS conciliation for the parties to have the claim referred to a mediator nominated by ACAS, and this service has been used in a number of cases (85 in the year 2005–6, according to the *ACAS Annual Report*).

21.32 **Conciliated settlements**

Normally, an agreement not to pursue a claim in the tribunal is void and unenforceable as an attempt to contract out of statutory rights (*ERA 1996, s 203(1)* and equivalent provisions in other statutes). An exception to the general principle is claims for breach of contract; but see further on this 21.35 below. (For the position where the parties agree a settlement subject to a consent judgment by the tribunal, and the tribunal subsequently issues the judgment, see *Carter v Reiner Moritz Associates Ltd* [1997] ICR 881, and *Mayo-Deman v University of Greenwich* [2005] IRLR 845.) An agreement reached where a conciliation officer has taken action under one of the relevant statutes is a statutory exception: the agreement will, subject to its terms, be binding on the parties.

Endorsing an agreement on a Form COT3 is sufficient 'action': *Duport Furniture Products Ltd v Moore* [1982] ICR 84. Technically a conciliated settlement can be reached orally (see *Duru v Granada Retail Catering Ltd*, EAT/281/00, IDS Brief 697) but it is strongly advisable to reduce the terms of the agreement to writing as soon as possible, to avoid later disputes about the terms of the agreement (as occurred in that case). It is important that the agreement is properly worded to compromise all claims intended to be covered by the agreement.

Issues may arise subsequently as to the scope or application of a COT3 agreement. The ordinary principles of law for the interpretation of contracts apply to such agreements. Unlike compromise agreements (see below) a settlement reached through ACAS conciliation may in principle cover any disputes between the parties, including disputes that have not arisen at the time of the settlement. However, as a matter of construction, a court or tribunal will expect very clear words to convey the parties' intention to compromise future disputes: *Royal National Orthopaedic Hospital Trust v Howard* [2002] IRLR 849. In an extreme case a conciliated settlement agreement may be set aside, eg if the conciliation officer acted in bad faith or adopted unfair methods to procure a settlement, but it would not be enough to justify setting aside the agreement that the conciliation officer had not adopted best practice, provided that he or she had acted in good faith: *Clarke v Redcar & Cleveland Borough Council* [2006] IRLR 324 (an unsuccessful attempt to set aside agreements to settle a large number of equal pay claims).

A party will normally be bound by a settlement signed by his or her authorised representative, even if not a lawyer: *Freeman v Sovereign Chicken Ltd* [1991] ICR 853. However this is only so if the party has held out the representative as being his or her representative (as by including his details on the Claim Form or Response Form). If a representative merely holds him or herself out as having the requisite authority, an agreement reached by the opposing party with the representative will not bind the 'client': *Gloystarne & Co Ltd v Martin* [2001] IRLR 15.

21.33 **Compromise agreements**

In the absence of ACAS conciliation, before 1993 the only option to secure an effective compromise of a tribunal claim, in practice, was to include a term in the agreement that the applicant would apply to the tribunal to have his or her claim dismissed on withdrawal; or if the parties were at the tribunal when a settlement was reached, an application could be made to the tribunal for an appropriate order. The former procedure has the disadvantage that the claimant can change his or her mind before making the application; the practice therefore is to make any payment conditional on the application to withdraw being made. (It is important that the respondent also applies to have the claim dismissed, not merely withdrawn or stayed, since in the latter case – in the absence of a binding agreement to the contrary – the case can subsequently be reopened: see 21.28 above.)

Both of the procedures referred to above are still available, but *TURERA 1993* added a further and potentially more effective avenue of binding settlement, namely, a compromise agreement. The scope for compromise agreements was extended by *ERDRA 1998*. The principal relevant statutory provisions are now in *ERA 1996, s 203(2)(f),(3),(4), SDA 1975, s 77(4)(aa),(4A), RRA 1976, s 72(4)(aa),(4A), DDA 1995, Sch 3A, para 2, TULRCA 1992, s 288(2A),(2B), Working Time Regulations 1998, reg 35(2)(b),(3), National Minimum Wage Act 1998, s 49(3),(4), Employment Equality (Religion or Belief) Regulations 2003, Sch 4, para 2, Employment Equality (Sexual Orientation) Regulations 2003, Sch 4, para 2,* and *Employment Equality (Age) Regulations 2006, Sch 5, para 2.* The *Part-time Workers (Prevention of Less Favourable Treatment) Regulations 2000, reg 9* provides that *ERA 1996, s 203* applies as if the *Regulations* were contained in that *Act*, and there is a similar provision in the *Fixed-term Employees (Prevention of Less Favourable Treatment) Regulations 2002, reg 8* and in the *Transfer of Undertakings (Protection of Employment) Regulations 2006, reg 18* (rectifying the anomaly that there was no equivalent provision in the predecessor *1981 Regulations*). The discrimination statutes refer to compromise contracts rather than compromise agreements, but are otherwise in the same terms.

21.34 A compromise agreement is an agreement to refrain from issuing or continuing proceedings under one of the statutes or regulations listed in 21.33, or the *Equal Pay Act 1970*. In order for a compromise agreement to be binding, the following conditions must now be satisfied:

(*a*)   The agreement must be in writing;

(b)   It must relate to the particular complaint or proceedings (see further below);

(c)   The claimant must have received advice from a relevant independent adviser as to the terms and effect of the proposed agreement and in particular its effect on his or her ability to pursue his or her rights before an employment tribunal;

(d)   There must be in force, when the adviser gives the advice, a contract of insurance, or an indemnity provided for members of a profession or professional body, covering the risk of a claim by the claimant in respect of loss arising in consequence of the advice;

(e)   The agreement must identify the adviser; and

(f)   The agreement must state that the conditions regulating compromise agreements under the relevant Act or Regulations are satisfied.

A provision in the Bill which became the *Employment Act 2002* removing the requirement at (b) above was withdrawn during the Bill's passage through Parliament because of fears that it could facilitate the misuse of the compromise agreement procedure. As a consequence it is not possible to compromise potential future disputes or claims under this procedure.

The requirements at (e) and (f) are applied strictly. It is not sufficient that there is an independent adviser and that the statutory requirements have been satisfied; it is essential that this be stated. In *Lunt v Merseyside TEC Ltd* [1999] ICR 17, the EAT upheld a decision that a compromise agreement which did not contain the statement required at (f) above was therefore void; this must apply equally to (e). In *Palihakkara v British Telecommunications plc*, EAT/0185/06, the EAT went further and held that a statement that the conditions under *ERA 1996, s 203* were satisfied was not effective to validate the agreement so far as it related to complaints of sex and race discrimination, although the requirements for such complaints are the same as those set out in *s 203* for complaints under *ERA 1996*. It is therefore necessary to state that the requirements for compromise agreements under the particular statute or statutes applicable for *each claim* intended to be compromised are satisfied; it is not clear following this decision whether it would be enough to say that the conditions under *s 203* 'and all similar statutory provisions' are satisfied.

The following are the categories of 'relevant independent advisers' who may act in compromise agreements:

(i)   Qualified lawyers;

(ii)   Fellows of the Institute of Legal Executives;

(iii)   Officers, officials, employees or members of an independent trade union; or

(iv)   Employees or volunteer workers at advice centres,

in each of the last two categories subject to the individual being certified in writing by the union or advice centre as competent and authorised to give advice. A 'qualified lawyer', means a barrister (or in Scotland an Advocate) in practice as such or employed to give legal advice, or a solicitor holding a practising certificate.

In addition:

(A)   The adviser must not be, or be employed by, or be acting in the matter for, the employer or an associated employer;

(B)   In the case of a trade union or advice centre, that organisation must not be the employer or an associated employer; and

(C)   Advice from an advice centre worker must be free (but a union may apparently charge for its services).

A compromise agreement may be used to compromise more than one complaint, provided it clearly identifies each of the complaints being compromised and the relevant statutory provisions: *Lunt v Merseyside TEC Ltd* [1999] ICR 17. This case also confirms that claims can be validly compromised without the need to commence tribunal proceedings; but there must be an actual complaint: as noted above, a compromise agreement cannot settle potential disputes which have not yet arisen. This last point is a significant restriction on the utility of compromise agreements where the parties wish to ensure a 'clean break'. Moreover, compromise agreements are likely to be strictly construed, and any ambiguity resolved against the employer, as in *Palihakkara v British Telecommunications plc,* above, where an agreement to compromise all claims arising out of the termination of the employment was held not to cover claims of discrimination against the claimant whilst she had been employed.

The effective scope of compromise agreements was clarified and restricted by the Court of Appeal in *Hinton v University of East London* [2005] EWCA Civ 532, [2005] IRLR 552, and advice on the framing of agreements was also offered. The agreement must specifically identify the 'particular proceedings' (or the complaints which could lead to proceedings) being compromised. This entails for tribunal proceedings that the actual case be identified, and the agreement should identify complaints by a brief description of the complaint and a reference to the statutory provision under which the claim is asserted. A bare reference to the relevant statute is unlikely to be sufficient, especially if the statute is the *ERA 1996,* since this covers a wide range of separate types of complaint.

Mummery LJ added the advice that it is good practice to include a summary of the factual and legal basis of the complaint or proceedings to identify the subject matter of the compromise more clearly. It is also generally unwise to rely on standard form compromise agreements or simply include a list of all the statutory provisions in relation to which compromise agreements may be required under the statute. The policy underpinning these points is that compromise agreements are a device to protect employees when agreeing to relinquish their statutory rights, and the statutory provisions should be construed to give effect to that policy.

A further restriction on the scope of compromise agreements was shown by the EAT's decision in *Hilton UK Hotels Ltd v McNaughton,* EAT/0059/04. This case decides that a compromise agreement will not be interpreted as compromising a claim referred to in the agreement if at the time of the agreement the claimant did not appreciate that she had a possible claim, even though the independent adviser should have advised on the possibility. (The case concerned a part-time pension claim, and the adviser had not appreciated that the claimant had previously worked part-time.)

21.35 An agreement to refrain from instituting or continuing proceedings in a contract claim brought in the tribunal will be binding without the need for any special requirements to be satisfied. The position where an agreement compromises both statutory and contractual claims is more complex. If it meets the requirements for a statutory compromise agreement it is clearly valid, but the position if it does not is the subject of conflicting authorities in the EAT: *Sutherland v Network*

Appliance Ltd [2001] IRLR 12 holds that the contractual claim is validly compromised but *Hoeffler v Kwik Save Stores Ltd*, EAT/803/97 holds the opposite (in a case where one of the issues settled by the agreement was the parties' respective rights of appeal to the EAT, which it was held are outside *ERA 1996, s 203*).

A compromise agreement settling a prospective unfair dismissal claim, under which the employer agrees to make a payment to the employee, is a 'contract connected with employment' for the purposes of the tribunal's contract jurisdiction, so that the employee can bring a claim in the tribunal (subject to the relevant time limits) for money due under the agreement: *Rock-It Cargo Ltd v Green* [1997] IRLR 581. However, if the compromise agreement is not reached until after the employment has terminated, the tribunal's contractual jurisdiction is not available to enforce it, since the claim is not outstanding on the termination and does not arise on termination: *Miller Bros and FP Butler Ltd v Johnston* [2002] IRLR 386.

21.36 **'Calderbank' offers**

Attempts to settle tribunal claims by negotiation are not always successful, and parties are sometimes inhibited from entering into negotiations by the fear that if the case is not settled, disclosure of offers made will weaken their case at the tribunal. However, such negotiations, conducted on a 'without prejudice' basis, are not normally admissible in the tribunal without the consent of both parties. This is so even if the term 'without prejudice' was not used, if it is clear that the parties intended the negotiations to be confidential. A limited exception to this is that the party making an offer may reserve the right to rely on the offer in support of an application for costs, if he or she is successful at the tribunal. Correspondence conducted 'without prejudice save as to costs' (known as 'Calderbank' correspondence after the case in which its use was first sanctioned by the Court of Appeal) is admissible in support of an application for costs after the tribunal has made its substantive decision. There has, however, been considerable doubt as to how far such offers may be taken into account by the tribunal. The point was expressly left open by the Court of Appeal in *Kovacs v Queen Mary and Westfield College* [2002] ICR 919. The EAT has since held that although the mere fact that the employer made an offer to settle for more than the tribunal awarded (or the claimant offered to accept less than he or she subsequently secured from the tribunal) is not a reason to award costs, the fact of rejecting a reasonable offer to settle *may* amount to unreasonable conduct, for which costs can be awarded, and Calderbank letters are admissible to establish that offers were made but not accepted in support of the claim of unreasonable conduct: *Kopel v Safeway Stores plc* [2003] IRLR 753. See further 21.71 as to the circumstances in which a costs order may be made.

21.37 **ACAS ARBITRATION SCHEMES**

Section 7 of the *ERDRA 1998* provides for the making of a scheme by ACAS, subject to the approval of the Secretary of State, for the determination of unfair dismissal claims by private arbitration. The process of establishing a scheme proved unexpectedly protracted, but it was finally brought into effect, for England and Wales only, in May 2001. It was extended to Scotland in 2004. The *ACAS Annual Report* for 2005–6 records a disappointingly small take-up of the scheme, with only 55 cases registered up to 31 March 2006.

The Scheme is now contained in a Schedule to the *ACAS Arbitration Scheme (Great Britain) Order 2004* (*SI 2004/753*) ('the *ACAS Order*'), and is given effect by *TULRCA 1992, s 212A*, as inserted by *ERDRA 1998, s 7*. The Scheme is lengthy (running to 227 paragraphs, including some containing separate provisions for England and Wales and for Scotland) and is supported by a separate Guide published by ACAS, which should be consulted by any party considering the submission of a dispute to arbitration under the Scheme. The Arbitration Scheme is entirely voluntary, in the sense that it requires the agreement of both parties, and it is available only for unfair dismissal claims.

The *Employment Act 2002* amended *s 212A* to provide for a similar arbitration scheme in relation to disputes over requests for flexible working arrangements raised under the provisions of the *ERA 1996* (as added by the *2002 Act*) conferring the right to make such requests. A Scheme (for England and Wales only) was made by the *ACAS* (*Flexible Working*) *Arbitration Scheme* (*England and Wales*) *Order 2003* (*SI 2003/694*). This was extended to Scotland by the *ACAS* (*Flexible Working*) *Arbitration Scheme* (*Great Britain*) *Order 2004, SI 2004/2333*.

The principal features of the unfair dismissal Scheme are as follows (a similar structure has been adopted for the flexible working scheme):

(i)   The terms of reference of every reference to arbitration will be as set out in *para 17:*

'In deciding whether the dismissal was fair or unfair, the arbitrator shall:

    (i)   have regard to general principles of fairness and good conduct in employment relations (including for example, principles referred to in any relevant ACAS "Disciplinary and Grievance Procedures" Code of Practice or "Discipline at Work" Handbook), instead of applying legal tests or rules (e g court decisions or legislation);

    (ii) apply EC Law.

The arbitrator shall not decide the case by substituting what he or she would have done for the actions taken by the Employer.

If the arbitrator finds the dismissal unfair, he or she shall determine the appropriate remedy under the terms of this Scheme.'

(ii)   The Scheme is limited to the determination of whether a dismissal was unfair and, if so, the remedy. Any other matter in dispute (such as whether there was a dismissal or whether there is a jurisdictional bar to the claim) and any other claim (such as unlawful deduction of wages) must be dealt with by the employment tribunal. Jurisdictional matters will therefore either have to be settled between the parties or decided by the tribunal before a matter can be referred to arbitration, since the parties will be required to waive their rights to dispute jurisdictional issues as a condition of the arbitration agreement; the existence of separate outstanding claims is not a bar to arbitration, but the arbitrator will have discretion to postpone the arbitration proceedings pending their determination by the tribunal (*paras 18–24*).

(iii)   Access to the Scheme will be by agreement in writing in the form either of an ACAS-conciliated agreement or a compromise agreement (referred to as an 'Arbitration Agreement': see 21.33–21.35) (*paras 25–28*). The agreement must be notified to ACAS within two weeks; if it is not, ACAS will not appoint an arbitrator unless notification in time was not reasonably practicable (*paras 29–32*).

(iv)   Once an agreement to arbitrate has been made, the employer cannot unilaterally withdraw from it, although the ex-employee is free to withdraw his or her claim; there are provisions for settlement and consent awards equivalent to those for tribunals (*paras 34–40*).

(v) ACAS will appoint an arbitrator for the case; the parties will have no say in the choice of arbitrator (but there are safeguards for any objection on grounds of lack of impartiality or incapacity, which may be dealt with by ACAS or if necessary by the High Court: *paras 42–59S*).

(vi) There is no power to order the production or disclosure of documents or the attendance of witnesses, but both parties are under a duty to cooperate to secure the 'proper and expeditious conduct' of the proceedings, including complying with any directions of the arbitrator to that end (*para 65*), and non-cooperation can be taken into account by the arbitrator in his or her decision (*para 81*).

(vii) Arbitrations can be held at any venue, except that they may only be held at the employer's premises with the consent of all parties (*para 73*). ACAS will meet the cost of hiring premises but the parties must meet their own travelling costs; if compensation is awarded such costs may be included in the total award (*paras 76–77*). There is no other power for the arbitrator to award costs.

(viii) Written statements of case and supporting documentation must be submitted at least 14 days before the hearing (and will be copied to the other party); *para 85* lists types of documentation that may be relevant, including witness statements.

(ix) The hearing will be in private, attended only by the arbitrator, the parties, their representatives (if any) and any witnesses; representatives may include a party's legal adviser (*para 67*). No special status is accorded to legal advisers (*para 100*).

(x) The conduct of the hearing is to be as determined in each case by the arbitrator, whose general duty is to adopt suitable procedures for the fair disposition of the case, avoiding unnecessary delay or expense (*para 63*). Evidence may not be given on oath and there is a prohibition on cross-examination of witnesses (*para 97*); instead the arbitrator may be asked to put questions to witnesses.

(xi) In some cases issues may arise of EC law or the applicability of the *Human Rights Act 1998*. In such cases the arbitrator will be able to appoint a legal adviser (who will attend the hearing); in addition or alternatively such legal questions may be referred by one or other party to the High Court or Central London County Court under the *Arbitration Act 1996*, or in Scotland to the Court of Session (*paras 106–112S*).

Most of the remaining paragraphs of the Arbitration Scheme deal in detail with the form of awards and the remedies available if the claimant's claim succeeds. The provisions on remedy follow closely, with necessary modifications, the statutory provisions applicable to employment tribunals in *ss 111–124* of the *ERA 1996*.

The Scheme also deals with the issuing of awards, which are confidential (*para 170*), save that summary information about awards which does not identify parties may be published from time to time. There is of course nothing to prevent the parties from agreeing to publicise an award, but for one party to do so unilaterally might be in breach of the original arbitration agreement, depending on its terms. The final section of the Scheme provides for limited grounds of challenge to the conduct of an arbitration, or an award, by application to the High Court under the *Arbitration Act 1996*, modified to meet the particular features of the Scheme. The two permissible grounds of challenge are lack of jurisdiction and serious irregularity causing substantial injustice to the complainant. In Scotland, there is a right of appeal to the Court of Session under conditions set out in *paras 201S-204S, 206S-208S* and *210S*.

21.38 PREPARING FOR THE HEARING

The length of time from presentation of a claim to a Hearing varies considerably. The Tribunals Service and its predecessor, the ETS, have for several years set performance targets for tribunals, one of which is that 75% of single cases will receive a first hearing within 26 weeks of receipt of the Claim Form. The percentage achieved has ranged in recent years between 69% in 2001–02 and 82% in 2004–5; in 2005–6 it was 79%. The overall performance conceals variations for particular offices, with some regions still experiencing delays particularly in listing lengthier cases; the worst performing region achieved only 57% in 2005–6, whilst the best-performing region achieved 95% (details are contained in the *ETS Annual Report 2005–6* (TSO)). For relatively simple cases many tribunal regions are now able to list cases to be heard almost immediately after the fixed conciliation period ends, but it is not unusual for there to be a delay of several months if a case needs to be listed for more than one day. It is expected that delays in listing will increase following budget cuts in 2006.

The tribunal must give the parties at least 14 days' notice of the date of the Hearing, or of any PHR, unless shorter notice is agreed (*ET Rules, rule 14(4)*)). The 14 day period is calculated from the date the notice is sent out, not the date it is received (see *reg 15(5)*). In practice, longer notice is usually (but not always) given. The usual practice for simple cases is to issue a notice of hearing without first checking with the parties whether the date is suitable. In cases involving only claims for unlawful deductions or breach of contract, the practice in most tribunal regions is now to issue a notice of hearing at the same time that the Claim Form is sent to the respondent, with a hearing date as early as possible after the short fixed conciliation period has expired.

If a date is given which causes problems, application can and should be made as soon as possible, and if possible within 14 days, to change the date. Such applications are matters of discretion for the tribunal but are much more likely to be granted if made promptly giving clear reasons. The standard notice of a Hearing date indicates that applications for postponement made more than 14 days after notification of the hearing date will be allowed only in exceptional cases. There is no automatic right to postponement of a hearing even if *both* parties request a postponement, and it is difficult on appeal to dispute a refusal to postpone (*Employment Service v Nathan*, EAT/1316/95, IDS Brief 568; *London Fire and Civil Defence Authority v Samuels*, EAT/450/00, IDS Brief 669); it is therefore important to apply as early as possible and with full reasons for the request.

21.39 Listing arrangements

Cases are usually listed in the first instance for one day, and if a case is likely to take longer than a day it is important to apply at an early stage for a longer listing; otherwise the tribunal will have to reconvene, possibly months later, if the case is not completed within the allotted day (it is very rare indeed that the case would be continued the following day in those circumstances). For apparently complex cases, particularly those to be listed for more than a day, most regions write to the parties advising them of the intention to list the case and requiring notification to the tribunal if a party considers the proposed time allocation to be inappropriate. It is important to respond to such an invitation, since the tribunal may hold the parties to a time allocation even if at the hearing they suggest that the time allowed is insufficient, and this is also an opportunity to give the tribunal dates to be avoided because e g a witness will not be available. The basis on which cases are listed is that sufficient time should be allowed not only to hear the evidence and submissions of the parties, but also for the tribunal to reach and announce its decision, and to deal if appropriate with remedies. Parties are now generally warned of this, and are advised also of the tribunal's power to set a timetable to ensure that the case is completed within the time available.

Special priority is given to hearings of applications for interim relief (see 55.21 UNFAIR DISMISSAL – III). However the former rule that notice of the hearing of such an application need only be given seven days in advance has been dropped in the 2004 revision of the *ET Rules*, and 14 days' notice of the hearing is therefore now required (see *rule 14(4)*). Interim relief applications are dealt with at PHRs. Where a CMD is held prior to the substantive Hearing, the 14-day notice provision does not apply to the CMD (*ibid.*), and much shorter notice is sometimes given to deal with urgent applications. Where a CMD is held it is usual to deal with the listing of the main Hearing at that time, and parties or representatives are expected to have with them the dates of availability of witnesses to facilitate this.

There are several steps a party should take prior to the hearing – preferably earlier rather than later. These are addressed in the following sections.

21.40 A decision should be taken whether a legal or other representative is to be engaged; if so, this should be done in good time to enable the representative to prepare for the hearing and take any necessary interlocutory steps. There is no restriction on who may represent a party in the tribunal (see *Bache v Essex County Council* [2000] IRLR 251) and no legal aid for such representation (except in limited circumstances in Scotland) although legal assistance for the preparation of the case may be available to claimants of limited means. Employers are often represented by an appropriate manager or a trade association official, employees by a union officer or a Citizens' Advice Bureau or advice centre worker. The fact that no representative is given on the Claim Form or Response Form by no means necessarily indicates that the party concerned will not be represented. Whoever is to represent a party, it is desirable that the representative be consulted in good time before the hearing.

A number of organisations offer their services as representatives in tribunal proceedings, either as consultants offering a package of advice and representation to employers, or on a no-win no-fee basis for claimants. Concerns about the quality of representation offered by some of these organisations, and the lack of any professional or statutory regulation of their professional conduct, have led to the introduction of a requirement, under the *Compensation Act 2006, Part 2,* for claims management services (including those providing representation in employment tribunals for reward) to be regulated. Before engaging a representative on a no win no fee basis, a prospective claimant needs to appreciate that the representative will normally have to be paid out of whatever compensation is awarded if the claim succeeds, since costs are not usually awarded, but compensation is assessed without regard to this liability.

In an extreme case the conduct of a representative may lead to sanctions being imposed by the tribunal on the party represented, including striking out that party's case (see *Bennett v London Borough of Southwark* [2002] EWCA Civ 223, [2002] IRLR 407). In cases where the claim was presented on or after 1 October 2004, the tribunal has the power to make a wasted costs order against a representative acting for profit, ie an order that the representative must pay the other party's costs, or debarring the representative from recovering costs incurred from his client. See further 21.73 below.

For those, particularly claimants, who cannot afford to pay for legal representation, free representation may be available through one or other of a number of organisations including the Citizens' Advice Bureaux (CABx) and the Free Representation Unit (6th Floor, 289–293 High Holborn, London WC1V 7HZ, tel. 020 7611 9555), and in discrimination cases application may be made for legal assistance to the relevant Commission, although the Commissions' budgets for legal assistance are almost invariably insufficient to meet all claims on them. Most trade unions provide a free representation service for members, either through union officials or union appointed solicitors, and usually subject to being satisfied that the claim has some merit. An increasing number of claimants are represented by lawyers paid for under legal expenses insurance (often provided as an optional addition to household insurance). Further advice on possible sources of free professional representation can be obtained through CABx.

21.41 Consideration should be given to whether an application for any case management orders, or a CMD, is needed. Orders may be any of those listed in 21.2 above or other orders such as for a PHR (see 21.15 above) or the joinder of parties (see 21.23 above) or for a restricted reporting order (see 21.18 above). A CMD may be listed by the tribunal of its own motion; most commonly this happens in discrimination cases; where the issues appear complex; or where a party's application for an order has been opposed. It may also be necessary to apply to the tribunal for a PHR to determine a particular preliminary point (such as whether it has jurisdiction over the claim).

A party may wish to apply for permission to amend the claim or response. An application which is likely to be contested should not be granted by the tribunal without the opposing party being given an opportunity to resist the application (in writing or, if the tribunal so orders, at a CMD) and if an amendment is allowed *ex parte*, without such an opportunity, the opposing party may apply to the tribunal to have the order set aside (see *Reddington v S Straker & Sons Ltd* [1994] ICR 172, and *ET Rules, rule 12(3)*). The practice in relation to applications to amend was restated by the EAT in *Selkent Bus Co Ltd v Moore* [1996] ICR 836. A tribunal should not normally decide an application to amend a Claim Form which raises an issue of substance, without giving the parties an opportunity to make representations at a CMD (*Smith v Gwent District Health Authority* [1996] ICR 1044). As to the considerations relevant to the tribunal's decision, see 21.10 above.

21.42 It is sometimes necessary for a party to apply for an adjournment of the hearing, either because a witness becomes unavailable or for a variety of other reasons. Any application to adjourn should if possible be made with the agreement of the other party. However even agreed applications are not necessarily granted by the tribunal. It is important to give full reasons for the application, especially if it is opposed. The earlier the application is made, the more likely it is to be granted. In deciding applications, tribunals are entitled to have regard to the public interest in cases being heard as promptly as reasonably practicable, now reinforced by the incorporation into domestic law of the right under *art 6* of the *European Convention on Human Rights* to have a dispute decided within a reasonable time.

If a hearing was listed at a CMD, it is particularly difficult to persuade the tribunal to change the listing because a witness is not available: *London Fire and Civil Defence Authority v Samuels*, EAT/450/00.

21.43 The relevant documentary evidence should be identified. Documentation likely to be relevant will include the contract of employment or letter of engagement, statutory statement of particulars of employment, relevant parts of any staff handbook (such as a disciplinary procedure), any written warnings, records of performance or attendance (if these are relevant issues), the letter of dismissal, notes or minutes of any relevant meetings, appeal documents if applicable, documents demonstrating the need for a redundancy, and documents relevant to quantification of the claim, such as payments made to the employee and pension documentation. The employee may need to produce documentation showing his or her attempts to mitigate his or her loss and any earnings since dismissal, as well as evidence of pay and benefits prior to dismissal, and social security benefits received after termination.

It is desirable if possible for the parties to agree a bundle of documents including those to be relied on by both sides; it is now standard practice for the tribunal to make an order to this effect. Such a bundle may be referred to as an 'agreed' bundle; this means that the authenticity of the documents is not disputed, but not that their relevance or accuracy is necessarily conceded. The bundle should be paginated (ie each page should be consecutively numbered) and, if substantial, indexed. Six copies will be needed for the hearing (three for the tribunal, or one if the Chairman is sitting alone, and one for each party and for the witnesses). In Scotland, documents produced to the tribunal are referred to as 'productions'.

As the rules of evidence do not apply fully in tribunals, it is not necessary formally to prove the documents in the tribunal bundle, unless the genuineness or accuracy of a document is disputed (eg in the latter case, minutes of a meeting). If there is a dispute, a witness who can confirm the accuracy of the document from personal knowledge should be called or the document should not be used. Originals of any documents where there may be issues of authenticity should wherever possible be available at the hearing.

There are no formal rules as to who should produce the bundles of documents needed for the hearing. The usual practice is for the party advancing a case to take this responsibility (ie the claimant in discrimination or breach of contract cases, but the employer in unfair dismissal cases where the dismissal is admitted). However, it has in recent years become increasingly common for the respondent to accept the burden (and cost) of preparing the bundles, and the requirement of the Overriding Objective that the parties should so far as possible be put on an equal footing has led to it becoming part of the common practice of tribunals, at least in cases with substantial documentation, to require respondents to undertake this task.

21.44 One category of documents is not normally admissible before a tribunal; this is 'without prejudice' correspondence. This means correspondence conducted in an attempt to reach a settlement of a dispute; it is only admissible either to prove an agreement reached as a result or if *both* parties agree. For further details of the limits of the 'without prejudice' privilege see 21.13 above. Correspondence is sometimes conducted under the heading 'Without prejudice save as to costs'. This preserves the right of the party putting forward proposals to refer to the correspondence after the substantive issues have been decided by the tribunal, solely in support of an application for costs – see further 21.36 above.

21.45 The relevant witnesses should be identified and their statements taken. An employer in an unfair dismissal case will need to call at least the manager who took the decision to dismiss the employee and, if applicable, the manager who decided the appeal. In a redundancy case, evidence of the redundancy situation, of the decision to select the claimant, of consultation with the claimant and any recognised union, and of attempts to redeploy, may all be required. Where there has been a disciplinary hearing and the reason for the dismissal was that the manager decided on the evidence that the employee was guilty of misconduct, it is not the tribunal's function to re-try the case or decide for itself as to the employee's guilt; it should not therefore normally be necessary to call all those persons who were involved in the disciplinary hearing (apart from the manager conducting the hearing) or any earlier investigation. It may, however, be necessary to call the manager conducting any separate investigation prior to the disciplinary hearing if there is any dispute as to the sufficiency or fairness of the investigation. As to the employee, whether any additional witness is to be called depends on the availability (and sometimes willingness) of those who have knowledge of relevant events.

21.46 Witnesses should be asked to prepare written statements of their evidence (legal representatives will normally prepare drafts themselves following an interview with each witness). These should be typed or legibly written, using short, numbered paragraphs. It is important that all relevant matters of which the witness has knowledge are covered. Whilst the practice as to timing is not consistent between tribunal regions, the common practice is that the tribunal will direct the parties to prepare witness statements, and to exchange them prior to the hearing. Sometimes the tribunal will also direct that the witness statements will be taken as the evidence-in-chief of the witness. This means that the party calling the witness will not be able to ask him or her additional questions without the permission of the tribunal. If there is good reason why a statement cannot be produced for a particular witness, it is advisable to apply to the tribunal for an order exempting that witness from the general requirement for statements to be exchanged in advance.

In most cases the tribunal will invite the witnesses to give their evidence by reading the statement; sometimes the tribunal will pre-read the statements and simply ask the witnesses to confirm the truth of their contents. If a witness would have difficulty reading out his or her statement, the clerk should be advised before the start of the Hearing.

If it will not be possible to call a witness, evidence can be given by way of a signed statement. Such evidence should be sent to the tribunal and the other party at least seven days before the hearing; it is then admissible as of right as a written representation (see *ET Rules, rule 14(5)* and 21.47 below). If tendered late, the tribunal may decline to consider it. In any case, however, the weight to be attached to evidence in this form is affected by the unavailability of the witness (for however cogent a reason) for cross-examination. Accordingly, unless the evidence is not in dispute, great caution should be used in relying on written evidence instead of a live witness.

The practice in Scotland is still that witness statements are not normally used as a means of giving evidence, or exchanged before the hearing.

21.47 It is open to any party to submit representations in writing to the tribunal; they must be submitted (and sent to each other party) at least seven days before the hearing date, unless the tribunal consents to a shorter period (*ET Rules, rule 14(5), (6)*). Written representations may be made by a party attending the hearing, or in lieu of attendance. However, the latter course is extremely hazardous, since the absent party cannot deal with questions from the tribunal, points that arise unexpectedly or assertions made in evidence by the other party. In all but the simplest cases, attendance in person or by a representative is essential.

21.48 The current practice of tribunals in straightforward cases is to deal with all questions including, if appropriate, remedy, at one hearing. Accordingly, and unless the tribunal has directed that remedy will be dealt with subsequently, parties should come to the hearing prepared accordingly. This means that the claimant should include in his or her statement details of the earnings lost, any income received from new employment or state benefits, and information relevant to any claim that he or she has failed to take reasonable steps to mitigate his or her loss. In most regions the standard orders issued in unfair dismissal and discrimination cases include a requirement for the claimant to serve a Schedule of Loss detailing the amounts claimed, benefits received etc. The respondent should have the necessary information to put before the tribunal to establish take home pay (if disputed) and the value of any employment benefits. If there is likely to be a dispute about this, relevant documentation should be in the bundle. (It does not follow that the tribunal will have the time to deal with remedy, and it will often agree to give the parties time to attempt to agree the remedy; however cases are listed on the basis that time is allowed for the tribunal to hear the case, reach and deliver its decision, and then deal with remedy if necessary.)

21.49 **THE HEARING**

Tribunal hearings are usually conducted in modern rooms with the three members of the tribunal sitting at a table on a slightly raised dais and the claimant and respondent sitting at tables facing the tribunal. There is a table at which the witness sits to give evidence. The tribunal is composed of a legally qualified Chairman, one member with management experience and one member with trade union experience; as to cases where the Chairman may sit alone or with just one other member, see 20.8 and 20.9 above. The proceedings are public (although in practice members of the public not connected with the proceedings attend relatively infrequently). For the power of the tribunal to sit in private, see 21.51 below. The provisions for holding hearings by telephone or video link do not extend to Hearings: *rule 15*.

The Chairman is addressed as 'Sir' or 'Madam'. Proceedings are formal but considerably less so than in an ordinary court. Witnesses (including a party if giving evidence) are required to give their evidence on oath or affirmation (*rule 27(3)*).

Before the hearing starts, the clerk will speak to both parties and make a list of names of representatives and witnesses, and will collect copies of documents each party intends to rely on to give to members of the tribunal.

21.50 **Bias or conflict of interest**

If any tribunal member has any connection with either of the parties, or the events in issue in the case, that fact should be made known to all concerned at the outset, and the case relisted before a fresh tribunal if necessary (see e g *University College of Swansea v Cornelius* [1988] ICR 735 and 22.12 below). If a party raises an objection to the composition of the tribunal before the hearing commences, then unless that objection is irresponsible or frivolous it is preferable to reconstitute the tribunal if possible (*Halford v Sharples* [1992] ICR 146 at 171, a point not considered in the Court of Appeal). See further on the circumstances in which participation by a particular tribunal chairman or member in a hearing may be regarded as creating an appearance of bias *Locabail (UK) Ltd v Bayfield Properties Ltd* [2000] IRLR 96 and *Jones v DAS Legal Expenses Insurance Co Ltd* [2003] EWCA Civ 1071, [2004] IRLR 218.

The *Jones* case makes the important point that if the Chairman discloses an interest and invites the parties to indicate whether they agree to the case proceeding before him or her, and a party makes no objection, then provided that sufficient disclosure of the potential conflict of interest has been given, the party will be taken to have waived any right to challenge the fairness of the hearing on appeal by reference to the Chairman's declared interest. The Court of Appeal also stressed the importance of giving the parties, particularly if unrepresented, a full explanation of the options available to them and time to consider their position, and of taking a full note of what the parties are told.

The fact that an accusation of bias has previously been made against a Chairman by one of the parties, or that the Chairman has in previous proceedings made adverse comments about a party or witness, is not of itself a reason for the Chairman to recuse him- or herself: *Ansar v Lloyds TSB Bank plc* [2006] EWCA Civ 1462, [2007] IRLR 211, a case in which the Court of Appeal sets out detailed guidance on the relevant principles to be applied. As to the circumstances in which a tribunal should withdraw from hearing a case (in technical language, 'recuse itself') where an allegation of bias in the conduct of the case is made by a party or his or her representative, see *Bennett v London Borough of Southwark* [2002] EWCA Civ 223, [2002] IRLR 407.

In sex discrimination cases, both sexes will normally be represented on the tribunal, and in race discrimination cases at least one member should have special knowledge of race relations; however, these are not mandatory requirements.

21.51 **When hearing may be in private**

Tribunal hearings are generally conducted in public and may be reported in the media. The requirement to sit in public applies to a Hearing and to a PHR, but not to a CMD, which must be held in private (*ET Rules, rules 17(1), 18(1), 26(3)*). The tribunal has power under *rule 16(1)* to direct that evidence or representations be heard in private which in the opinion of the tribunal would be likely to consist of information which could not be disclosed without a breach of a statutory prohibition or which had been communicated to or obtained by the person concerned in confidence, or which if publicly disclosed could cause substantial damage to that person's undertaking or the undertaking in which he or she works, for reasons other than the effect of disclosure on collective bargaining. The reference to information obtained in confidence may allow for medical evidence to be given in private. The EAT has held that the relevant statutory provisions include the tribunal's duty under *s 6* of the *Human Rights Act 1998,* so that there may be a duty to sit in private for the reception of evidence if the public reception of the evidence would be an impermissible violation of the right of privacy of an individual under *Art 8* of the *Human Rights Convention (XXX v YYY* [2004] IRLR 137 (reversed by the Court of Appeal on other grounds [2004] IRLR 471), a case involving a video recording containing pictures of a young child).

If the tribunal decides to hold a hearing or part thereof in private, it must give reasons for doing so (*ET Rules, rule 16(2)*). In addition, the tribunal may sit in private if directed to do so by a Minister of the Crown for reasons of national security (*ET Rules, rule 54(1)(a); rule 54* also contains more general powers to control the conduct of tribunal proceedings in national security cases. An example of such an order under equivalent provisions in previous *ET Rules* is *Fry v Foreign and Commonwealth Office* [1997] ICR 512 (order did not extend to excluding claimant's husband who was assisting the presentation of her case)).

Subject to the provisions permitting a hearing in private, failure to hold the hearing at a place made accessible to the public renders any resulting judgment a nullity, even if no members of the public wished to attend the hearing: *Storer v British Gas plc* [2000] IRLR 495. There is no general power to exclude the press or public from a hearing where the power to sit in private does not apply but the evidence is of a sensitive or salacious nature: *R v Southampton Industrial Tribunal, ex p INS News Group Ltd* [1995] IRLR 247; and see as to the importance attached to tribunal hearings being conducted in public *R v London (North) Industrial Tribunal, ex p Associated Newspapers Ltd* [1998] ICR 1212.

The reporting of proceedings in cases involving allegations of sexual misconduct or evidence of a personal nature in disability discrimination cases is subject to special procedures for the restriction of reports identifying the parties concerned: see 21.18 above.

21.52 Conduct of the hearing

The general principle is that the tribunal is free to regulate its own procedure within the framework of the *Rules of Procedure* (*ET Rules, rule 60(1)*). This is subject to general legal principles designed to ensure fairness to the parties, and to the specific rules of procedure, including the Overriding Objective. The *Rules* place a general obligation on the Chairman or tribunal 'so far as it appears appropriate to do so, [to] seek to avoid formality in his or its proceedings' (*rule 14(2)*). The tribunal is not bound by the rules of evidence which apply in a court of law and is enjoined by *rule 14(3)* to 'make such inquiries of persons appearing before him or it and witnesses as he or it considers appropriate', and to conduct the hearing:

> 'in such manner as he or it considers most appropriate for the clarification of the issues and generally for the just handling of the proceedings.'

This broad discretion results in considerable variation in the extent to which particular tribunals conduct cases in an inquisitorial way or leave it to the parties to present their case as they think best; much depends on the style of individual Chairmen. The provision that a party is entitled to give evidence, call witnesses, question witnesses and address the tribunal (*rule 27(2)*) is subject to the general power given to the tribunal by *rule 14(3)*.

The EAT has, however, stressed that a degree of formality and structure is necessary; informality can be counter-productive and tribunals should normally adhere to the generally recognised rules of procedure (*Aberdeen Steak Houses Group plc v Ibrahim* [1988] ICR 550). Although this case pre-dates the revisions of the *Rules* in 2001 and 2004, it is still relevant. In particular, tribunals are required to observe such basic rules of fair conduct or natural justice as the rules against bias on the part of a Chairman (*Laher v London Borough of Hammersmith and Fulham*, EAT/215/91, IDS Brief 531; for a recent example of a case where there was found to be an appearance of bias on the part of the Chairman see *Diem v Crystal Services plc*, EAT/0398/05 (comment on colour of claimant's skin)).

The Chairman should alert the parties before taking a point on which they have not addressed the tribunal (*Laurie v Holloway* [1994] ICR 32; and see also *Albion Hotel (Freshwater) Ltd v Maia e Silva* [2002] IRLR 200 (tribunal should not rely on cases discovered through its own researches without giving the parties an opportunity to make submissions on them; but see also *Sheridan v Stanley Cole (Wainfleet) Ltd* [2003] EWCA Civ 1046, [2003] IRLR 885, adopting a less strict view on this point)).

The Chairman and members must also, unsurprisingly, remain attentive throughout the hearing: thus the Court of Appeal in *Stansbury v Datapulse Ltd* [2004] EWCA Civ 1951, [2004] IRLR 466 set aside the judgment of a tribunal reached after a hearing during which one of the lay members had fallen asleep after allegedly drinking alcohol during the lunch break.

The Court of Appeal has recently emphasised that despite the relative informality accorded to tribunal proceedings, employment tribunals are not inquisitorial bodies, so that where the burden of proof rests on a particular party, the onus is on that party to put evidence before the tribunal enabling that burden to be discharged: *McNicol v Balfour Beatty Rail Maintenance Ltd* [2002] EWCA Civ 1074, [2002] ICR 1498, a case where the claimant's status as a disabled person was in dispute. However, the Court indicated that the tribunal should use its case management powers to ensure that a claimant appreciated the kind of medical evidence that might be needed to establish disability. More generally, tribunals are not under a duty to ensure that every allegation in a Claim Form is dealt with, regardless of whether the claimant puts forward evidence or argument in support of it (*Mensah v East Hertfordshire NHS Trust* [1998] IRLR 531, CA). This point is particularly important because of the general rule that arguments and points not taken at the tribunal hearing cannot be raised for the first time by way of appeal: see 22.15 below.

21.53 Order of presenting the parties' evidence

In preparing for the hearing, a representative needs to consider whether he or she, or the other party's representative, will be required to open the case. The party bearing the burden of proof normally opens: in an unfair dismissal case this is the employer if dismissal is admitted, as he or she must show the reason; if dismissal is disputed (as often happens in constructive dismissal claims) the employee normally opens. The employee also normally opens in discrimination cases and claims for breach of contract or unlawful deduction of wages. Tribunals do not normally permit the party who starts to make an opening statement, and if one is permitted it should be a reasonably brief introduction to the parties, the facts, the issues in dispute, the key documents and the principal contentions on any points of law that arise.

21.54 Non-attendance of parties and applications to adjourn

Applications are sometimes made at the start of the hearing for an adjournment on the ground of the claimant's ill health. Guidance has been given by the Court of Appeal in two cases – *Teinaz v London Borough of Wandsworth* [2002] EWCA Civ 1040, [2002] IRLR 721 and *Andreou v Lord Chancellor's Department* [2002] EWCA Civ 1192, [2002] IRLR 728 – as to how a tribunal should apply the conflicting considerations of justice when such an application is made on or immediately before the date of the hearing. The tribunal should generally grant an adjournment if there is medical evidence which satisfies it that a party is unfit to attend the hearing, but it is entitled to require clear medical evidence to satisfy it that the impediment to attendance is genuine, the burden being on the party (in practice usually the claimant) making the application.

It is also not uncommon in practice that one party or the other does not attend. In this event the *Rules* give the tribunal the power to dismiss or dispose of the proceedings in the absence of the party concerned, or to adjourn the Hearing; however the tribunal must, before proceeding to dismiss or dispose of the proceedings consider any information which has been made available by the parties (*rule 27(5), (6)*). If a representative for the party attends, the representative is entitled to be heard even though the party has not attended (see *Astles v A G Stanley Ltd*, IDS Brief 588).

The Court of Appeal has ruled that the tribunal has a very wide discretion in the light of the available evidence whether to dismiss the claim, proceed in the claimant's absence or adjourn to another date: *Roberts v Skelmersdale College* [2003] EWCA Civ 954, [2003] ICR 1127. If the respondent fails to appear without good reason having been given, the tribunal will normally hear the claimant's case and give a decision in the respondent's absence. If the case is determined in the absence of a party and it later transpires that that party had not received notification of the hearing date, the tribunal may review its decision: see 21.74–21.75 below.

Since the decision in *Roberts*, the matter has been considered further on two occasions by the EAT (*Southwark London Borough Council v Bartholomew* [2004] ICR 358 and *Cooke v Glenrose Fish Co* [2004] ICR 1188). The effect of these decisions is that, at least if the circumstances suggest that the non-attendance is in any way unexpected, inquiries should be made of the absent party by telephone, and if the party in attendance is represented, inquiries should also be made of that representative, before any decision to dismiss the case or proceed in a party's absence is taken. An alternative option often adopted in practice in cases involving a claim of unfair dismissal, where the respondent has the initial burden of proof, is for the tribunal to hear the respondent's evidence and submissions before deciding the case on its merits, in the absence of the claimant.

21.55 Rights of representation

The right of a party to be represented at a hearing by whoever he or she chooses (whether or not professionally qualified) is expressly given by *s 6, ETA 1996*. In *Bache v Essex County Council* [2000] IRLR 251, the Court of Appeal ruled that the tribunal therefore has no power to 'sack' a party's representative under its general power to control the proceedings. If it does so, this is a ground of appeal notwithstanding the acquiescence of the party at the time. However, denial of representation by the chosen person did not render the hearing a nullity, and on the facts the decision was upheld.

The EAT has applied the principle in *Bache* in a case where the employers unsuccessfully sought an order forbidding the claimant from using a particular firm of solicitors to represent him at the hearing because of a conflict of interest: *Dispatch Management Services (UK) Ltd v Douglas* [2002] IRLR 389. However, if the party's chosen representative behaves inappropriately, the tribunal's powers to act in response to the misbehaviour of a party (in an extreme case extending to the striking out of the claim or defence, provided that this is a proportionate response: see *Bennett v London Borough of Southwark* [2002] EWCA Civ 223, [2002] IRLR 407) are equally available in respect of conduct of the representative acting on behalf of the party: *rule 18(7)*. If the representative is acting for profit, the further sanction of a wasted costs order (see 21.73 for this) is available to the tribunal.

21.56 Tribunal's powers to control the procedure

The tribunal has a considerable discretion as to the management of the proceedings before it. A party does not have the right to cross-examine come what may. The tribunal has a duty to keep the inquiry before it within reasonable bounds, and it does not have to allow lengthy and detailed cross-examination on matters that do not appear to it to be of assistance. These points were emphasised by the EAT in *Zurich Insurance Co v Gulson* [1998] IRLR 118.

Although not in issue in that case, it is an increasingly common practice for tribunals to set time limits on stages in the proceedings, such as cross-examination of a particular witness or the making of a closing submission. Such restrictions should not be so restrictive as to deny a party the opportunity to put his or her case, but can be justified in many cases by reference to the requirement of proportionality in the Overriding Objective. However, if the tribunal reaches a flawed conclusion because it disabled itself from receiving relevant and significant evidence, that may be a ground for appeal.

In his judgment in *Bache*, Mummery LJ made the following statement of the principles governing the conduct of tribunal hearings:

'(1) At the hearing the tribunal must follow a procedure which is fair to both sides. It must normally allow each party to call relevant evidence, to ask relevant questions of the other side's witnesses and to make relevant submissions on the evidence and the law.

(2) The tribunal is responsible for the fair conduct of the hearing. It is in control. Neither the parties nor their representatives are in control of the hearing.

(3) Procedural fairness applies to the conduct of all those involved in the hearing. Just as the tribunal is under a duty to behave fairly, so are the parties and their representatives. The tribunal is accordingly entitled to require the parties and their representatives to act in a fair and reasonable way in the presentation of their evidence, in challenging the other side's evidence and in making submissions. The rulings of the tribunal on what is and is not relevant and on what is the fair and appropriate procedure ought to be respected even by a party and his representative who do not agree with a ruling. If the party and his representative disagree with a ruling, an appeal lies against it if the tribunal has made an error of law.'

The Court of Appeal has expressed the view that it is always desirable that any irregularity in procedure such as the Chairman or a member falling asleep, or the making of inappropriate comments, should be raised at the time, but failure to do so (particularly if the party subsequently complaining was not represented at the time) is not necessarily a bar to raising the point on appeal: *Stansbury v Datapulse plc* [2003] EWCA Civ 1951, [2004] IRLR 466, para 23; Peter Gibson LJ acknowledged the difficulty that even a legal representative may have in raising such a point, since if the objection is unsuccessful the person complained about will continue to sit in the case.

The procedure in practice is that the Chairman (who, along with the lay members, will have read the Claim Form and Response Form) will first seek to clarify what issues are, or remain, in dispute between the parties. He or she will deal at the start of the hearing with any preliminary points such as correcting the name of the respondent, considering any applications to amend the Claim Form or Response

Form and ruling on any disputes about disclosure of documents or attendance of witnesses either party wishes to raise. The usual procedure thereafter is as follows:

(*a*)   the party upon whom the burden of proof rests normally opens (the claimant in a discrimination case, the employer in an unfair dismissal claim where dismissal is conceded; if there are issues on which there is a burden of proof on both parties in turn, the tribunal is likely to hear submissions from the parties before deciding who should go first);

(*b*)   the party called upon to open:

    (i)   may sometimes make an opening statement giving an outline of the case (but this is increasingly rare except in the most substantial and complex cases: see 21.53 above); and

    (ii)   calls his or her evidence, each witness giving evidence on oath or under affirmation and being open to cross-examination by the other party, and questions by the members of the tribunal;

(*c*)   the other party:

    (i)   calls his or her evidence; and

    (ii)   makes a closing speech; and

(*d*)   the party who opened the case then makes a closing speech.

21.57 Witnesses

Witnesses are examined on oath or affirmation. They give their evidence seated at a table and should address the Chairman of the tribunal as 'Sir' or 'Madam'. If, as is almost always required, a written witness statement has been prepared, the tribunal will normally ask the witness to read this out, or will read the statement themselves. Additional questions may then be asked if necessary. It is increasingly common for case management orders to include a provision that the witness statements are to stand as evidence-in-chief; in that case additional questions can only be asked with the permission of the tribunal. Where a claimant is unrepresented, the Chairman may ask more questions to elicit relevant matters.

When the representative of one party cross-examines a witness of the other party, he or she should put questions to the witness and not make comments or statements. It must be remembered that there is a dual purpose to cross-examination. One is to test the truth and the reliability of the witness; the other is to put the questioner's version of the facts to the witness so far as it concerns him or her, so that he or she has an opportunity of commenting on it. A failure to do this may prejudice the cross-examiner's case. It is a general principle that a party or representative may not cross examine his or her own witness; the concept of a 'hostile witness' is in practice almost unknown.

Witnesses will not normally be permitted to refer to notes whilst giving evidence, unless these are agreed documents or a note taken by the witness at the time of an event or very soon thereafter; the witness may refer to such notes to refresh his or her memory of the event.

The *ET Rules* give a general power to the tribunal to exclude a person who is to appear as a witness from the Hearing until that person gives evidence, if it considers it to be in the interest of justice to do so (*rule 27(4)*). In Scotland it is the practice to require witnesses to wait outside the tribunal room until they are called to give their evidence; however, this is very infrequently done in English or Welsh proceedings.

The powers of the tribunal extend to a power to call witnesses of its own initiative (or at the request of a party who is for some good reason unable or unwilling to call the witness): *Clapson v British Airways plc* [2001] IRLR 184.

21.58 Other points of procedure

The Chairman is required to keep a full note of the evidence given; this is normally done in longhand, or occasionally on a laptop computer; the taking of notes sometimes results in a speed of proceedings which many observers not used to tribunal proceedings find rather slow. The notes are important not only to assist the tribunal in reaching its judgment (especially if the hearing is adjourned part-heard, or judgment is reserved) but also for the benefit of the EAT, if necessary, on any subsequent appeal.

Documents should be introduced in the evidence in chronological or other systematic order and explained by the witness who can best deal with them. It is desirable, if possible, to cross refer in the written witness statements to the page numbers of any relevant documents, and to invite the tribunal to read the documents or relevant parts at the point in the witness statement that the document is referred to.

In a closing speech, the representative of each party should sum up the relevant facts and the law, answering any points raised by the opposing party or the Chairman or members of the tribunal. Tribunals sometimes ask the parties to make their final submissions in writing, when there is not enough time to complete the case without an adjournment, or in addition to oral submissions in complex cases. The parties' representatives may sometimes suggest this. The EAT has given guidance to tribunals as to the procedure for written submissions, where these are in place of, rather than in support of, oral submissions: *London Borough of Barking and Dagenham v Oguoko* [2000] IRLR 179. The procedure should only be implemented with the consent of both parties, and each party must be served a copy of the other's submissions and given time to comment on them (comments being limited to correction of factual errors and responses to any new points of law not previously raised) before the tribunal proceeds to reach its decision. In a lengthy or legally complex case, the tribunal may ask for written submissions in addition to oral submissions. In such cases, adequate time must be allowed for the other party's representative, and the tribunal, to read and digest the written submissions before oral submissions are made: *Sinclair Roche & Temperley v Heard* [2004] IRLR 763.

21.59 It is open to a party to submit at the conclusion of the other party's evidence that there is no case to answer. This should be done without prejudice to the right to call evidence if the submission is rejected. However, the making of such submissions has increasingly been discouraged by the higher courts, especially in discrimination cases where it is necessary to weigh the circumstantial evidence of discrimination with the employer's explanation in assessing whether the evidence justifies an inference of discrimination: see *British Gas plc v Sharma* [1991] ICR 19, where it was described as 'exceptional' for such a submission to be appropriate in a discrimination case. The principles were restated in *Clarke v Watford Borough Council*, EAT/43/99, in terms expressly approved by the Court of Appeal in *Logan v Customs and Excise Comrs* [2003] EWCA Civ 1068, [2004] IRLR 63, as follows:

'(1)   There is no inflexible rule of law and practice that a tribunal must always hear both sides, although that should normally be done.

(2)   The power to stop a case at "half-time" must be exercised with caution.

(3)   It may be a complete waste of time to call on the other party to give evidence in a hopeless case.

(4)   Even where the onus of proof lies on the [claimant], as in discrimination cases, it will only be in exceptional or frivolous cases that it would be right to take such a course.

(5)   Where there is no burden of proof, as under *s 98(4)* of the *Employment Rights Act*, it will be difficult to envisage arguable cases where it is appropriate to terminate the proceedings at the end of the first party's case.'

It should be noted that the reference above to the burden of proof in discrimination cases pre-dates changes in the burden introduced from 2001 onwards.

21.60 For the sake of certainty, it is best to obtain, at the commencement of the hearing, a clear indication from the employment tribunal of whether it will consider liability and remedy separately, and when it will consider evidence and argument on contributory fault and/or on whether a *Polkey* reduction in compensation should be made if a dismissal is found to be procedurally unfair. The EAT has held that it is an error of law for the tribunal to deal with the *Polkey* point without giving the parties an opportunity to make submissions on it: *Market Force (UK) Ltd v Hunt* [2002] IRLR 863. By analogy this would apply equally to the issue of contribution.

The usual practice, in the absence of a direction to the contrary, is that the tribunal will proceed to deal with remedy, if time permits, immediately following its decision on liability (and assuming that that decision is in the claimant's favour). However, it is unusual for a tribunal to hear evidence relating solely to compensation before it has reached a decision on liability. In *Iggesund Converters Ltd v Lewis* [1984] ICR 544, the EAT suggested ways in which employment tribunals could deal with evidence and argument on the reduction of an award for contributory fault, and in *Ferguson v Gateway Training Centre Ltd* [1991] ICR 658 it suggested that the Chairman should restate which issues are being considered prior to final submissions. The EAT has also emphasised that it is important that the tribunal gives the parties a chance to be heard on any issue of remedy before deciding the point: *Duffy v Yeomans & Partners Ltd* [1993] ICR 862.

21.61 Sometimes in the course of the hearing the Chairman will give an indication to the parties of the tribunal's provisional view as to the merits of the case, or more commonly a particular issue in the case. This may be done for a number of reasons: to encourage the parties to settle, or give them assistance to settle by giving an indication as to the likely outcome on a particular point or the case as a whole; to identify which issues should be focused on in evidence or cross-examination; or to identify the issues on which submissions are particularly sought. Caution is needed in giving any kind of preliminary indication of the tribunal's view, since this may be interpreted as indicating that the decision has already been reached, or provide a basis for a later appeal on grounds of apparent bias. However the Court of Appeal has confirmed that, provided that it is made quite clear that any views expressed are provisional, there is no objection in principle to the Chairman expressing a view in the course of the case: *Jiminez v London Borough of Southwark* [2003] EWCA Civ 502, [2003] IRLR 477. By contrast, in *Gee v Shell UK Ltd* [2002] EWCA Civ 1479, [2003] IRLR 82, the Court of Appeal held that there had been procedural unfairness where the Chairman had warned the claimant (who was acting in person) that she was at risk of an award of costs against her, in circumstances where there was no real basis for an award of costs, and she felt obliged to withdraw her claim to avoid the costs sanction.

21.62 THE JUDGMENT AND REASONS

The *2004 Regulations* made significant changes to the way in which the final determination of the tribunal after a Hearing (or a PHR to determine a preliminary point) is conveyed to the parties. What was formerly called a decision is now termed a judgment, and the former distinction between summary and extended reasons has been abolished.

The position now, by virtue of *rule 30,* is that a judgment may either be given orally at the conclusion of the Hearing or PHR, in which case it must subsequently be reduced to writing and signed by the Chairman, and is then sent to the parties; or it may be reserved, in which case the written judgment will be sent to the parties in due course. If the judgment is reserved, reasons in writing will be sent at the same time as the judgment itself. However if the judgment is pronounced at the hearing, and reasons are given orally at the time, written reasons are no longer given unless a party specifically requests that they be supplied, at the time the judgment is given or within 14 days thereafter (this period is extendable if the Chairman considers it just and equitable to do so: *rule 30(5)*). In addition, the Chairman may be required to provide written reasons if the EAT so requests for the purpose of an appeal. The written reasons will normally be required as a prerequisite to an appeal against a judgment.

The provisions of *rule 30* governing written reasons have the somewhat surprising consequence that if neither party chooses to ask for reasons in writing, there will be no formal record of the reasons available to the press or other interested parties. Even in a case raising issues of wider public interest, there appears not only to be no duty, but even no *power* to give the reasons in writing, provided they have been given orally and none of the parties makes a request for written reasons and the matter is not appealed.

The Chairman or tribunal must also give reasons for orders made under case management powers if so requested before or at the hearing (which can be a CMD or PHR as well as a Hearing) at which the order is made: *ET Rules, rule 30(1)(b)*. The reasons may be given orally or in writing, and there is no right for a party to require that the reasons be given in writing; in practice if such a request is made, it would be unusual for the Chairman to refuse it, not least because the request may be a prelude to an appeal, and if the order is appealed without the benefit of written reasons, these can be requested by the EAT. The *Rules* make no provision as to reasons for orders that are made on paper; this means that it is a matter for the Chairman making the order to decide whether to provide reasons, but the giving of reasons cannot be compelled, except possibly by way of an appeal.

The tribunal may reach a unanimous or majority judgment (*rule 28(4)*). In the rare cases in which the tribunal is composed only of two members (eg because of the illness of a member part-way through the proceedings) the Chairman has a casting vote. *Rule 31* makes provision for judgments, orders or written reasons to be signed on behalf of a Chairman who is unavailable through death, incapacity or absence, either by the President, Vice President or Regional Chairman if the judgment etc was of a Chairman alone, or by the other members of the tribunal. The Court of Appeal in *Anglian Home Improvements Ltd v Kelly* [2004] IRLR 763 gave guidance that a tribunal should if at all possible avoid a majority decision, if necessary reserving its decision to give the members time to reflect and the Chairman an opportunity to prepare reasons which accurately reflect the majority view (especially if he or she is in the minority).

The ETS sets a target for the promulgation of written judgments and reasons, which is currently that they must be promulgated within 4 weeks of the conclusion of the Hearing in 85% of cases; this target has been met consistently in recent years, although some tribunal offices have in some years fallen below the target. However occasionally there have been instances of serious delays in issuing the judgment in cases where the judgment was reserved at the end of the hearing. In one such case, *Bangs v Connex South Eastern Ltd* [2005] EWCA Civ 14, [2005] IRLR 389, the Court of Appeal, in the course of refusing to overturn the tribunal's decision, gave guidance as to how such delay is to be considered in the context of an appeal. Delay in issuing a judgment is not of itself an error of law and therefore not as such a ground of appeal. The key question, the Court held, is whether due to the delay there was a real risk that a party had been denied or deprived of the right to a fair trial. In the related case of *Kwamin v Abbey National plc* [2004] IRLR 516, the EAT had taken a broader approach, which was disapproved by the Court of Appeal; it had also given strong guidance, which was implicitly approved by the Court of Appeal, as to the need to avoid lengthy delays in reaching and issuing reserved judgments. Three and a half months is the longest acceptable time for the delivery of judgment following the conclusion of the Hearing (or the delivery of written submissions, if later), and except in the most complex cases, longer delay without proper explanation (such as illness) would be regarded as culpable; it does not however follow that such delay justifies an appeal.

21.63 Adequacy of reasons

The *2004 Rules* set out for the first time in detail what matters must be covered in the reasons given for a judgment (but not an order): *rule 30(6)*, which lists the required information as:

(*a*)   The issues identified as relevant to the claim;

(*b*)   If some of the issues were not determined, which, and why not;

(*c*)   The findings of fact relevant to the issues determined;

(*d*)   A concise statement of the applicable law;

(*e*)   How the relevant findings of fact and the applicable law have been applied;

(*f*)   An explanation of how any compensation awarded has been calculated (which may be by way of a table).

There is an additional and specific duty to give an explanation of an award of interest, and reasons for any decision not to award interest, in discrimination and equal pay cases (*Employment Tribunals (Interest on Awards in Discrimination Cases) Regulations 1996 (SI 1996/2803), reg 7*).

These statutory requirements reflect and to some extent consolidate requirements increasingly emphasised by the appellate courts as a necessary part of the judicial process: see in particular *English v Emery Reimbold & Strick Ltd* [2002] EWCA Civ 605, [2003] IRLR 710.

The following statement by Bingham LJ in *Meek v Birmingham District Council* [1987] IRLR 250 is generally regarded as the leading statement of principle on inadequacy of reasons as a ground of appeal, and is regularly referred to for this purpose:

> 'It has on a number of occasions been made plain that the decision of an [Employment] Tribunal is not required to be an elaborate formalistic product of refined legal draftsmanship, but it must contain an outline of the story which has given rise to the complaint and a summary of the Tribunal's basic factual conclusions and a statement of the reasons which have led them to reach the conclusion which they do on those basic facts. The parties are entitled to be told why they have won or lost. There should be sufficient account of the facts and of the reasoning to enable the EAT ... to see whether any question of law arises; and it is highly desirable that the decision of an [Employment] Tribunal should give guidance both to employers and trade unions as to practices which should or should not be adopted.'

Whilst the tribunal must reach a conclusion on all the issues required by the statute concerned to be decided, and at least consider all the relevant facts, its decision need only refer to the important and/or controversial points: *High Table Ltd v Horst* [1997] IRLR 513. It is, however, important that the tribunal properly identifies the legal rules and tests it has applied in reaching its decision: *Conlin v United Distillers* [1994] IRLR 169, para 6.

Further guidance on the adequacy of reasons was given by the Court of Appeal in *Tran v Greenwich Vietnam Community Project* [2002] EWCA Civ 553, [2002] IRLR 735. Reasons need not be lengthy, but should be sufficient to explain to the parties how the tribunal got from its findings of fact to its conclusions. In addition, whilst the reasons are primarily addressed to those already familiar with the context of the case, it is desirable that the reasoning can be ascertained from the face of the decision; in any case it is necessary that the decision is sufficiently reasoned to enable an appellate court or tribunal to ascertain what the tribunal's findings of fact and reasons for its conclusions were. The decision of the Court of Appeal in *Anya v University of Oxford* [2001] EWCA Civ 405, [2001] IRLR 377 contains important comments on the need for tribunals in discrimination cases to set out the findings reached on the issues of primary fact, and an explanation why the tribunal does or does not draw inferences of discrimination from the facts as found.

The appellate courts will generally be slow to overturn a tribunal's judgment on the grounds that the reasons given are inadequate, and no detailed analysis of the facts by the tribunal is required. The Court of Appeal in the *English* case stressed that it is not a good ground of appeal that the reasons for a judgment are inadequate if it is clear from reading the judgment with knowledge of the evidence given and submissions made why the point in question was decided as it was. However a rather stricter approach has more recently been taken by the Court of Appeal in *Bahl v Law Society* [2004] IRLR 799 (a discrimination case), emphasising that only in a limited class of cases will it be possible to make good on appeal inadequate reasons given by the tribunal.

The EAT has adopted a practice, in cases where an appeal is brought on the ground of inadequate reasons, to remit the case to the tribunal for it to clarify or amplify its reasons, prior to the hearing of the substantive appeal, although this is not done in all such cases. The legality of the practice (which had been in doubt because of conflicting decisions of the Court of Appeal on the EAT's powers) was initially confirmed by the EAT in *Burns v Consignia plc (No 2)* [2004] IRLR 425, and subsequently (but on a different basis) by the Court of Appeal itself in *Barke v SEETEC Business Technology Centre Ltd* [2005] EWCA Civ 578, [2005] IRLR 633. The power is to be found in the *ET Rules, rule 30(3)(b)*, which requires the tribunal to provide reasons for any order or judgment if requested by the EAT. This power can equally be used where reasons were either not given at all (in the case of an order) or only given orally (for either an order or a judgment). The EAT also has the power under a general provision giving it the power to regulate its own procedure (*ETA 1996, s 30(1)*). The Court added that the procedure should not be used in cases where the reasons were fundamentally deficient, or there is an allegation of bias, or a danger that the tribunal will tailor its response to shoring up the original decision rather than give its true reasons.

21.64 Changing and correcting the decision

A judgment given orally at the end of the hearing is a final decision. The powers of a tribunal to change its judgment subsequently, prior to promulgation in writing (e g where there is a subsequent change in the relevant case law), are very limited. In *Lamont v Fry's Metals Ltd* [1985] ICR 566 the Court of Appeal assumed, without deciding the point, that a tribunal can recall its judgment before it is entered in the Register. However, it should then give both parties an opportunity of addressing further argument to the tribunal (see also *Arthur Guinness Son & Co (GB) Ltd v Green* [1989] ICR 241; *Gutzmore v J Wardley (Holdings) Ltd* [1993] ICR 581). More recent EAT decisions have emphasised the limits on the power of recall, and suggest that there is no power on recall to change the substantive judgment (*Spring Grove Services Group plc v Hickinbottom* [1990] ICR 111; *Casella London Ltd v Banai* [1990] ICR 215). There is a power to correct clerical errors in a judgment by a certificate signed by the Chairman, or the Regional Chairman, President or Vice President (*ET Rules, rule 37(1)*). The power of review is considered at 21.74–21.75 below.

21.65 Register of judgments

There is a public register of tribunal judgments and written reasons. All such judgments and reasons are entered in it and available for public (and press) scrutiny, except in cases of national security or where the tribunal has sat in private and it so orders (*ET Regulations, reg 17, ET Rules, rule 31(1)* and (2)); in a case appearing to involve allegations of a sexual offence, material identifying individuals making or affected by the allegations is deleted from the public copy (*rule 49*)). Necessarily only written reasons can be included in the Register, a factor which parties should consider before deciding whether to ask for written reasons where the reasons have been given orally.

21.66 REMEDIES AND ENFORCEMENT

The remedies available in the tribunal depend on the particular jurisdiction covering the case, and are discussed together with the substantive law elsewhere in this book. A number of additional points require mention.

A judgment ordering the payment of money made by a tribunal is enforceable as if it was a judgment of the county court. It must first be registered with the court: *ETA 1996, s 15*. The fact that an appeal is pending does not itself suspend the remedy awarded, but if an application to enforce it is made to the County Court, the other party will usually be granted a stay of execution pending the appeal.

Tribunals have no power to enforce their own non-monetary judgments except by awards of compensation; the best examples are an additional award for failure to comply with an order for re-employment in an unfair dismissal case (*ERA 1996, s 117(3)–(5)*), and power to increase compensation if the employer has failed without reasonable justification to comply with a recommendation in a discrimination case (*SDA 1975, s 65(3), RRA 1976, s 56(4), DDA 1995, s 8(5), Religion or Belief Regulations 2003, reg 30(3), Sexual Orientation Regulations 2003, reg 30(3), Age Regulations 2006, reg 38(3)*).

The absence of any enforcement machinery other than the County Court has led in a significant number of cases to real difficulties in the successful claimant recovering the compensation awarded, even disregarding cases where the employer is insolvent (in which case there may be a claim against the Secretary of State: see INSOLVENCY OF EMPLOYER (31)). Difficulties in enforcing awards of compensation have led the National Association of Citizens' Advice Bureaux to propose that awards of compensation should be paid by the state, with the right to recover the money from the employer passing to the government (*Hollow Victories,* March 2005). This proposal has not been accepted by the Government, but the *Tribunals, Courts and Enforcement Bill,* which is before Parliament at the date of writing (May 2007) will, when implemented, significantly improve procedures for enforcing tribunal judgments.

Where the tribunal has given judgment in favour of the claimant on liability but adjourned the question of remedy, it is open to the parties to reach a private agreement as to the remedy, subject to a formal consent judgment being made by the tribunal. Such an agreement, embodied in a judgment, is binding without the need to comply with the requirements for a compromise agreement (as to which, see 21.33–21.35 above): *Carter v Reiner Moritz Associates Ltd* [1997] ICR 881.

21.67 **Interest on awards**

Interest is payable on any compensation ordered by a tribunal which has not been paid within 42 days of the issue of the written decision. Interest starts to run at the end of the 42-day period and is payable at the rate fixed from time to time under the *Judgments Act 1838* applicable at the date it starts to accrue. The current rate is 8%. If compensation is subsequently increased or decreased on appeal, the new amount is subject to interest from the original date (*Employment Tribunals (Interest) Order 1990 (SI 1990/479)*). Awards of costs or expenses do not carry interest.

Normally, tribunals cannot award interest as a remedy in its own right, however long the delay since the matters giving rise to the remedy. The exception to this is in discrimination and equal pay cases. The relevant regulations (which originate from regulations in sex discrimination and equal pay cases introduced in 1993 to give effect to a decision of the ECJ (*Marshall v Southampton and SW Hampshire Health Authority (No 2)* [1993] ICR 893)) are currently the *Employment Tribunals (Interest on Awards in Discrimination Cases) Regulations 1996 (SI 1996/2803)* (the '*1996 Interest Regulations*'). There is no automatic right to interest under the *1996 Interest Regulations,* but the tribunal is required to consider the question even if not asked to do so (*reg 2(1)(b)*). In practice, in any case where there is a significant time lag between the discrimination and the decision, a tribunal may be expected to award interest unless there are special reasons for not doing so.

The rate of interest is that laid down from time to time under *rule 27(1)* of the *Court Funds Rules 1987 (SI 1987/821)* as the rate of interest for the Special Investment Account (*reg 3(2)*); this is currently (since 1 March 2002) 6%. Where the calculation period covers periods of varying rates of interest, an average rate can be taken (*reg 3(3)*). There are detailed rules as to the period in respect of which interest should be awarded (*reg 6*) and the normal rules as to interest on the total sum (including interest) awarded by the tribunal are varied, so that interest on the sum awarded runs from the day after the day on which the decision on remedy is issued, unless the respondent pays in full within 14 days (*reg 8*).

In an attempt to remedy the injustice to claimants that may arise from the lack of any power to award interest in, for instance, unfair dismissal cases, the Court of Appeal in *Melia v Magna Kansei Ltd* [2006] IRLR 117 held that compensation may be increased to reflect delay in receipt, by analogy with the reduction that may be made in calculating future loss to reflect accelerated payment. The latter is usually set at $2\frac{1}{2}\%$ a year, and the Court ruled that compensation could be increased at that rate for the delay between the date of dismissal and the date of the award. This principle applies primarily where there is also a discount for accelerated payment for future loss, but it is submitted that it is not limited to such cases, and thus amounts to a limited general power to award interest, at least where there has been significant delay between the dismissal and the decision on remedy.

21.68 **Recoupment of benefits received**

Where an employee has received Jobseeker's Allowance or Income Support between the date of dismissal and the date of the award of compensation for unfair dismissal (and certain other forms of compensation such as a protective award in redundancy consultation cases, but not compensation for loss of earnings in discrimination cases), there is a liability for *recoupment*, and the tribunal must apply the *Employment Protection* (*Recoupment of Jobseeker's Allowance and Income Support*) *Regulations 1996* (*SI 1996/2349*). Recoupment only applies to Jobseeker's Allowance and Income Support; other social security benefits are not affected. For details of how they may be taken into account in assessing compensation see 55.6 UNFAIR DISMISSAL – III.

The system of recoupment is that the tribunal identifies the proportion of its award that relates to loss of income between dismissal and the date of the award; this is known as 'the prescribed element', and must be separately identified in the judgment and reasons. The employer should withhold this amount from any payment to the employee until notified by the Department for Work and Pensions how much it wishes to recoup from the award; notification must be given within 21 days, and the amount recoupable will be the amount of benefits paid, up to the maximum of the prescribed element. The employer must then pay the amount recouped to the DWP instead of the employee. If an award is made by the tribunal for future loss, the employee may lose relevant benefits during the period covered by the award, but this does not affect the amount or payment of the actual award.

The recoupment system applies only to an award by the tribunal. Whilst it ensures that neither the employer nor the employee benefits from the social security benefits paid to the employee, it may reduce quite considerably the value in the employee's hands of the tribunal's award. This does not apply to a payment agreed by the parties – a significant incentive to settle the amount of any compensation. Since recoupment does not apply to awards in discrimination cases, social security benefits have to be taken into account (subject to rather complex rules affecting particular benefits) in calculating the employee's net losses.

21.69 **COSTS**

Costs (referred to in Scotland as 'expenses') are awarded to a successful party only in relatively limited circumstances. However the range of circumstances was somewhat broadened by changes in the relevant provisions of the *ET Regulations* made in 2001. Further changes in the powers of the tribunal to award costs came into effect on 1 October 2004, under the *2004 Regulations,* but these only apply in cases where the claim was presented on or after that date (*reg 20(2)–(5)*). Claims already in the pipeline before 1 October 2004 continue to be governed by the *2001 ET Rules.* The legal provisions set out below are those which apply under the new rules; the principal differences for the diminishing number of cases to which the former rules continue to apply are as follows:

(*a*)   There is no power to make a preparation time order; the EAT has also held that tribunals do not have jurisdiction under the *2001 ET Rules* to award costs or expenses to a party to compensate for time spent by the party (or his or her employees, if applicable) in preparing for the case: *Kingston upon Hull City Council v Dunnachie (No 3)* [2004] ICR 227.

(*b*)   There is no power to make a wasted costs order.

(*c*)   The tribunal is not permitted to take into account the means of the party against whom an order for costs is made in assessing the amount of the costs or expenses to be awarded to the other party: *Kovacs v Queen Mary and Westfield College* [2002] EWCA Civ 352, [2002] IRLR 414

(*d*)   There is no power to make an 'unless' order requiring the payment of costs, or to strike out the paying party's case if the costs are not paid accordingly (this point was decided by the EAT in *Criddle v Epcot Leisure Ltd,* EAT/0275/05).

It should however be noted that the grounds on which an order for costs may be made in pre October 2004 cases are the same as for cases determined under the *2004 Regulations.*

21.70   The powers available to a tribunal under the *ET Rules* are to award costs or expenses to be paid by one party to the other (or in limited circumstances to the Secretary of State: a 'costs order' or 'expenses order'), to order the payment of a sum to compensate for time spent preparing the case (a 'preparation time order') and make a wasted costs order against a party's representative. A number of general points need to be made about these powers:

(*a*)   The party against whom an order is made is referred to as the 'paying party', and the party in whose favour the order is made as the 'receiving party' (*rule 38(1)(a)*). Orders may be made against or in favour of a respondent who has not had his or her response accepted, in relation to any part the respondent has taken in the proceedings (eg applying for a review of a default judgment). However if the respondent has not participated in the proceedings because it was prevented from doing so, having failed to have a response accepted, no costs can be awarded against it: *Sutton v The Ranch Ltd* [2006] ICR 1170; this is so even though the claimant may have incurred costs, eg in proving losses at a remedies hearing.

(*b*)   A costs or expenses order can only be made in favour of a receiving party who was legally represented (ie by a barrister, advocate or solicitor) at the Hearing, or if the proceedings are determined without a Hearing, is legally represented at the time the proceedings are determined (*rule 38(2), (5)*).

(c)   It is not possible to make both a costs or expenses order and a preparation time order in the same proceedings and in favour of the same party (*rule 46(1)*). This may cause difficulties if a party obtains orders on more than one occasion during the proceedings, and either becomes or ceases to be legally represented between the making of the orders. To meet this potential difficulty, *rule 46(2)* gives the tribunal power to make an order part way through the proceedings but to defer until the conclusion of the proceedings determining which category of order it should be. This will necessitate also deferring the decision as to the amount of the award.

(d)   A costs order cannot be made at a CMD, since it is an order determining the paying party's civil rights or obligations: see *rule 17(2)*. In practice, apart from a provisional order made under *rule 46(2)*, the requirement referred to in (b) above prevents the making of a costs order before at least the hearing on liability has been concluded, or the case has come to an end without a hearing.

(e)   It is probable that a costs order cannot be made in respect of costs incurred before the claim or (in favour of the respondent) the response was presented. This was the view of the EAT in *Health Development Agency v Parish* [2004] IRLR 550. This decision appears to have been doubted in the later Court of Appeal decision in *McPherson v BNP Paribas (London Branch)* [2004] EWCA Civ 569, [2004] IRLR 558, where Mummery LJ stated that the *Parish* case was not authority for limiting the costs recoverable to those which resulted from the paying party's unreasonable behaviour, but costs were in fact limited to those so arising. See also *Sutton v The Ranch Ltd*, above.

The award of costs is still relatively unusual. Following the broadening of the grounds on which costs could be awarded under the *2001 Regulations*, the frequency and amount of orders has increased somewhat, but in 2005–6 the number of awards fell to 580 (from 1036 the previous year) following almost 30,000 hearings. Of these awards, 432 were in favour of respondents; the median sum awarded was £1,136, and only 34 awards were of more than £8,000, whilst 51 were for £200 or less. It should be noted that these figures do not include cases where costs were ordered to be assessed in the County Court, a category which includes any case where more than £10,000 is claimed, full costs are awarded and the receiving party is not willing to limit their claim to £10,000.

The sections below set out the provisions as to each of the three categories of orders available to the tribunal. For simplicity, references to costs and costs orders are intended to encompass expenses and expenses orders in Scottish proceedings.

21.71   Costs orders

The relevant provisions of the *ET Rules* governing the power to make, and the making and terms of, costs orders are briefly as follows:

(a)   If the paying party has, in the opinion of the tribunal, acted vexatiously, abusively, disruptively or otherwise unreasonably in bringing or conducting proceedings, or his or her representative has so acted in conducting them, or if the bringing or conducting of the proceedings by that party has in the tribunal's opinion been 'misconceived', the tribunal may make an order. 'Conducting' proceedings applies equally to a respondent as to a claimant. 'Misconceived' is defined by *reg 2(2)* as including 'having no reasonable prospect of success'. For the meaning of 'vexatiously', see 21.72 below.

Note that the tribunal is *required* to consider the award of costs, but has a discretion whether actually to *make* the award, and as to the amount (*rule 40(2), (3)*).

(*b*)   Costs may be awarded against a party if a hearing has to be postponed or adjourned through that party's fault (*rule 40(1)*). In respect of certain complaints of unfair dismissal, costs *must* also be awarded where the claimant has expressed a wish to be reinstated or re-engaged which has been communicated to the respondent at least seven days before the hearing of the complaint, and a postponement or adjournment of the hearing has been caused by the respondent's failure, without good reason, to adduce reasonable evidence as to the availability of the job from which the claimant was dismissed, or of comparable or suitable employment.

(*c*)   A costs order may require the paying party to pay the whole or part of the other party's costs or expenses as assessed (by a County Court Costs Judge under the *CPR 1998*) if not otherwise agreed, or be for an agreed amount, or for a stated sum (not exceeding £10,000) fixed by the tribunal (*ET Rules, rule 41(1)*). The limit of £10,000 on fixed costs was introduced by the *2001 Regulations* (it had previously been £500); it does not apply to costs agreed between the parties or assessed by the County Court.

(*d*)   If the conditions in (*a*) or (*b*) above are satisfied, the paying party may also (or as an alternative) be ordered to pay to the Secretary of State the whole or a part of witness allowances paid by the Secretary of State to witnesses for their attendance at the tribunal (*rule 38(1)(b)*).

(*e*)   In deciding whether to make an order for costs, and if so in determining the amount to be awarded, the tribunal is permitted but not required to have regard to the means of the party against whom the order is made (*rule 41(3)*, reversing the decision of the Court of Appeal in *Kovacs,* above). It was observed by Simon Brown LJ in *Kovacs* that logically, the discretion to have regard to the paying party's means would require the tribunal also to consider the means of the receiving party (para 10), and by Chadwick LJ that if means are a relevant factor, it would not be reasonable for a tribunal to make an award that it was satisfied the paying party could not meet (para 32). This in turn highlights the point that the tribunal has no specific powers to inquire into the means of a party for this purpose. Neither of the points raised in *Kovacs* is reflected in the *ET Rules,* and it is therefore unclear how far they can be taken as surviving the reversal of the substantive decision in *Kovacs.*

(*f*)   If there has been a PHR, and a party was ordered to pay a deposit, and that party loses, the tribunal must consider whether to make a costs order on the ground of the losing party's unreasonable conduct in persisting in having the matter determined. However the tribunal is not required to make such an order solely on this ground unless, having considered the reasons given for the making of the deposit order, it considers that the reasons given were substantially the same as the reasons for finding against the party at the Hearing. If costs are awarded, the deposit is used to pay, or in part payment of, the costs; if not, or if the costs awarded are less than the deposit, the deposit or balance is refunded to the party concerned (*rule 47*).

(*g*)   An application for costs may be made at any time, either at a CMD or PHR, or at the conclusion of a Hearing, or subsequently in writing. However if made after judgment is given finally determining the claim, it must be received by the tribunal no later than 28 days from the issuing of the judgment, unless a Chairman can be persuaded to grant an extension of time because he or she considers it to be in the interests of justice to do so. Note that the date of issue of the judgment is the date on which it is given orally, in the case of an unreserved judgment, not the date on which the written judgment is subsequently sent to the parties (*rule 38(7), (8)*).

(*h*)   If an application for costs is made at the hearing, the other party will be given an opportunity to oppose the application orally. In any other case, an order cannot be made unless the intended paying party has been given an opportunity to give reasons why the order should not be made. This may be by way of a further hearing, or on paper, as the Chairman may direct (*rule 38(9)*). The party claiming costs should, if the sum claimed is more than nominal, prepare a schedule showing the costs incurred.

(*i*)   If within 14 days of the date of the order either party requests written reasons for a costs order, reasons must be given in writing (*rule 38(10)*). This codifies the Court of Appeal's comments in *Lodwick v London Borough of Southwark* [2004] EWCA Civ 306, [2004] IRLR 554 as to the importance of a tribunal giving sufficient reasons for both the fact and the amount of an award of costs.

(*j*)   There is in principle a power under *rule 13(1)*, which was not available under previous rules on costs, for the tribunal to make an 'unless' order for the payment of costs (*Criddle v Epcot Leisure Ltd*, EAT/0275/05). The effect of this is that if the costs are not paid by the date required, the party's case is automatically struck out; for a claimant this means that the proceedings are at an end, whilst a respondent in that position is debarred from further participation in the case. In practice it is difficult to see how this power could ever be exercised, since no order can be made (except on the provisional basis permitted by *rule 46(2)*, which precludes the fixing of the amount awarded), until it is known whether the receiving party was legally represented at the hearing, or the proceedings have ended.

21.72   There have been several decisions on the scope of the power to award costs, and when and how the discretion to do so should be exercised. A number of points can usefully be drawn from these cases.

It is important to bear in mind that costs orders are relatively rare, but a tribunal is not obliged to refer to that fact in its reasoning, provided that it follows the statutory, two-stage procedure of first determining whether there has been unreasonable conduct etc, and then exercising a discretion whether to make an award, and if so of what amount or proportion of costs incurred: *Power v Panasonic (UK) Ltd*, EAT/0439/04, following *Salinas v Bear Stearns International Holdings Inc* [2005] ICR 1117.

The bringing or maintaining of a claim which has no reasonable prospect of success (and is therefore in the terms of the ET Rules 'misconceived') is a sufficient reason for the tribunal to conclude that the party should be made liable for costs; this is equally so for a respondent which has presented, or maintained through the proceedings, a defence which had no reasonable prospect of success. It is a factor relevant to the exercise of the tribunal's discretion whether to award costs on this ground that the tribunal has warned the party concerned that he or she is at risk of a costs order, but such a warning is not a prerequisite to the making of an order.

It has been accepted by the Court of Appeal that deliberately delaying notification of a decision to withdraw a claim can constitute unreasonable behaviour

(*McPherson v BNP Paribas (London Branch)* [2004] IRLR 558); the same would be true of unjustifiable delay in conceding liability, or an issue in the claim such as whether the claimant is disabled. This should not be relied on to penalise a party who, perhaps in the light of disclosure of documents or seeing the other party's witness statements, or the failure of settlement negotiations, takes a pragmatic decision to abandon a claim or defence. The unreasonable behaviour lies in then failing to inform the other party and the tribunal of the decision promptly, thereby allowing the other party to incur further costs (and possibly preventing the tribunal from listing another case for the date listed for the hearing).

A party may also be found to have acted unreasonably if he or she has rejected an offer to settle the proceedings, either made openly or 'without prejudice save as to costs', but it is not unreasonable behaviour to reject an offer simply because the tribunal's decision is more favourable to the party making the offer (eg the claimant is awarded less than the respondent had offered, or even nothing at all): *Kopel v Safeway Stores plc* [2003] IRLR 753. This decision has the effect that the tribunal may take into account offers made without prejudice save as to costs (often referred to as 'Calderbank' offers; see 21.36 above), but costs do not automatically follow in the way that would be the case in equivalent situations in the High Court. See also *Power v Panasonic (UK) Ltd*, above, where a costs order was upheld on appeal in circumstances where the claimant was found by the tribunal to have put an unrealistically high value on her claims, rejected offers substantially in excess of what she was eventually awarded, and acted intransigently in negotiations.

In a case involving a claim of unfair dismissal or discrimination, one of the remedies is a declaration by the tribunal that the claimant was unfairly dismissed or discriminated against. It will not necessarily be unreasonable conduct for a claimant to refuse a reasonable monetary offer where he or she is seeking such a declaration and the respondent is not prepared as part of the terms of settlement to admit liability: cf *Telephone Information Systems Ltd v Wilkinson* [1991] IRLR 148.

Awards of costs on the basis that the paying party has acted vexatiously in the bringing or conduct of the proceedings are rare, since it is not necessary to show such extreme conduct in order to make a case for an award of costs. However a tribunal would be much more likely to exercise its discretion in favour of such an order if it found vexatious conduct. The essential difference between vexatious and merely unreasonable conduct is that the party concerned need not be aware that his or her claim has no reasonable prospect of success in order for it to be misconceived (and therefore the bringing of it to be unreasonable), but if a party pursues a claim knowing it has no reasonable prospect of success, or depends on false evidence, or pursues the claim out of malice towards the other party or for some other ulterior reason, his or her conduct may be found to be vexatious. See further *E T Marler Ltd v Robertson* [1974] ICR 72.

21.73 **Preparation time orders**

Preparation time orders are intended to compensate a party who is not legally represented at the Hearing (or the conclusion of proceedings which do not reach a Hearing) for time spent preparing the case. This covers time spent by the receiving party personally, or (where applicable) by his or her employees, by a representative who is not a practising lawyer, or by a legal representative who was engaged at an earlier stage in the proceedings. Paragraphs (*a*), (*b*) and (*e*) to (*k*) in 21.71, and the points in 21.72 about when a costs order should be made, apply equally, with appropriate modifications in terminology, to preparation time orders (see *rules 42–44*). The paying party may also be ordered to make a payment to the Secretary of State as referred to in 21.71(*d*).

The amount to be awarded by way of a preparation time order is assessed by the tribunal by applying an hourly rate to a notional number of hours allowed as preparation time. The hourly rate is fixed by *rule 45(2)* and (*4*) at £27 an hour from 6 April 2007; it will increase by £1 an hour in each succeeding year (the *Rule* does not make it clear whether the increase applies to awards *made* after the relevant date, or only to *work done* after the date of the increase). The same hourly rate applies regardless of whose time is being compensated; it will thus be the same for a claimant who had been dismissed from a job paid at the National Minimum Wage as for a solicitor engaged to prepare the case for hearing but not used to conduct the case at the Hearing.

The time allowed is what the tribunal assesses to be a reasonable and proportionate amount of time to spend on preparation having regard to such matters as the complexity of the case, the number of witnesses and the amount of documentation involved. Only time spent in preparation for the hearing will be compensated, not time spent attending the hearing itself. Awards for preparation time are limited to a maximum of £10,000 (*rule 45(2)*).

The principle referred to at 21.71(*e*), that the tribunal may have regard to the paying party's means in deciding whether to make an order and if so the amount, applies equally to preparation time orders (*rule 45(3)*); however it is not clear how this principle is to be applied in determining the amount – in particular whether the tribunal can reduce the hourly rate, or make an award for fewer hours' preparation time, or both. The points made at 21.71(*e*) as to the uncertainty surrounding certain observations in *Kovacs* apply equally here.

21.74 Wasted costs orders

The power to make wasted costs orders is entirely new within the tribunal system (it has also been introduced, for the first time, in the *Employment Appeal Tribunal (Amendment) Rules 2004*, for appeals instituted on or after 1 October 2004). However the equivalent provisions have existed for many years in the civil courts, where experience has been that they are rarely made, no doubt in considerable part because of the necessary procedural safeguards for representatives potentially subject to such orders. It appears that there has, initially at least, been similar circumspection in the use of this power in employment tribunals; there is as yet (May 2007) no appellate guidance on the use of the power.

A wasted costs order is an order against a party's representative, which may be either that the representative pay to the receiving party the whole or part of any wasted costs, or repay to his or her client any costs already paid to the representative by the client, or disallowing the representative from recovering such costs not yet paid, or any combination of these (*rule 48(1)*, (*2*)). In addition or alternatively, the representative may be ordered to meet personally any allowances paid by the Secretary of State for the attendance of any person at the hearing.

The term 'representative' is defined to exclude any representative who is not acting for profit, such as a trade union official or CAB adviser, or a representative who is employed by the party, such as a manager of the employing company. However the term is not limited to legal representatives, and is expressly applied to a representative acting under a conditional fee agreement (*rule 48(4)*, (*5*)). 'Wasted costs' are defined as costs incurred by a party (who may be the representative's own client, or may not be represented at all) as a result of any improper, unreasonable or negligent act or omission on the part of the representative, or, where there has been improper, negligent or unreasonable conduct after the costs were incurred, costs that are such that the tribunal considers it unreasonable for the party who incurred those costs to have to pay (*rule 48(3)*).

There is a requirement that the tribunal must give the representative a reasonable opportunity to make oral or written representations before making a wasted costs order. In addition the tribunal may (but is not obliged to) take into account the representative's ability to pay (*rule 48(6)*); it is probable that where the representative is a company or firm, it is the means of that entity, not the individual representative, that is to be considered, and that it is the company or firm against which any order should be made, but these points are not made clear by the *Rules*. As with costs orders, reasons must be given if requested within 14 days of the order; unusually, *rule 48(9)*, which contains this requirement, expressly prohibits any extension of time for requesting written reasons.

There are a number of potential practical difficulties in this procedure. The first and most basic is that there may be a conflict of interest between a representative and his or her client. In these circumstances (e g where the tribunal is considering disallowing the representative's fees), the client will have to be advised to consider obtaining separate representation, and the representative will have to be given the opportunity to engage his or her own advocate; this will of course necessitate an adjournment of the hearing. Second, the question whether a representative was negligent may turn on what instructions were given by the client, and/or what advice was given by the representative. In the case of legal representatives (but not others), such matters are covered by legal professional privilege, which can only be waived by the client. The client will be deemed to have waived privilege if he or she claims wasted costs against the representative, but not in other cases, such as where the other party has made the application. The tribunal will not be able to draw inferences against the representative from the refusal of the client to waive privilege.

21.75 REVIEW

The powers of a tribunal to review a judgment have been enlarged by the *2004 Regulations*. Powers to review a decision to refuse to accept a Claim Form or Response, or a default judgment, are considered at 20.34, 20.37 and 20.38 respectively, and are not considered further here.

Those provisions apart, a tribunal only has power to review a judgment, or an order for costs, expenses, preparation time or wasted costs (*ET Rules, rule 34(1)(b)*). A judgment for these purposes is defined to include any decision, including a determination of a preliminary point, which finally disposes of a particular issue, as well as a judgment on liability or remedy, or both (*rule 28(1)(a)*). This has been held to include the striking out of a claim when a deposit ordered at a PHR was not paid (*Sodexho Ltd v Gibbons* [2005] IRLR 836), and would also include striking out for other reasons such as unreasonable conduct (*rule 18*) and the formal dismissal of a case on the application of a respondent following withdrawal by the claimant (*rule 25*). It is not clear whether the striking out of a case automatically because an 'unless' order has not been obeyed is a judgment, but it is thought that this is so. There is no power to review any other order; in particular case management orders are not open to review. (This will not normally present a problem, since there is a general power to vary or revoke such orders, which can be exercised without the formality of a review; but the tribunal will not normally vary an order unless there has been a change of circumstances or new facts have become available; *Onwuka v Spherion Technology UK Ltd* [2005] ICR 567; *Hart v English Heritage* [2006] IRLR 915.)

A judgment can be reviewed on any of the following grounds:

(*a*)   the decision was wrongly made as a result of an administrative error; it should be noted that this is not limited (as under the previous *Rules*) to errors on the part of the tribunal staff – an error on the part of a party, including the party seeking a review, will suffice in an appropriate case: *Sodexho Ltd v Gibbons* [2005] IRLR 836;

(*b*)   a party did not receive notice of the proceedings leading to the decision;

(*c*)   the decision was made in the absence of a party;

(*d*)   new evidence has become available since the conclusion of the hearing which could not have been reasonably known of or foreseen; or

(*e*)   the interests of justice require such a review.

(*Rule 34(3)*.)

An application for a review must be made to the Secretary of Tribunals in writing within 14 days from the date the judgment or order was sent to the parties, unless it has been made orally at the hearing; time may be extended by a Chairman if he or she considers it just and equitable to do so (*rule 35(1), (2)*). If made in writing, the application must identify the grounds for review in accordance with the list above.

An application for a review must be considered (without a hearing being required, although it would appear that a hearing *may* be ordered for the purpose) by the Chairman of the tribunal which issued the judgment, or if that is not practicable, by a Regional Chairman or the Vice President or a Chairman nominated by one of those office holders, or (exceptionally) by the President. The application must be rejected if in the opinion of the Chairman or other office holder considering it, there is no reasonable prospect of the judgment or order being varied or revoked (*rule 35(3)*). Prior to the *2004 Regulations*, there was a right of appeal against a refusal to permit a review.

There is a separate power for the Chairman or tribunal who or which issued the judgment concerned to review it of his or her or their own initiative. This power can only be exercised on one or more of the grounds listed above, and only on the condition that a notice is sent to the parties informing them of the intention to review the judgment or order, and explaining in summary form the grounds for the proposed review, within 14 days of the date on which the original judgment or order was sent to the parties. The notice must also offer the parties an opportunity to give reasons why there should not be a review (*rules 34(5), 36(2)*). However the rules are silent as to how any reasons given in opposition to the proposal to review are to be considered, and it appears that they will in practice be considered within the review hearing rather than as a separate and prior process.

If an application by a party for a review is not refused under *rule 35(3)*, the review will be conducted either by the Chairman or tribunal who or which decided the case or, if that is not practicable, by a different Chairman or tribunal appointed either by a Regional Chairman, the Vice President or the President. If the review has been directed on the Chairman's or tribunal's own initiative, it may *only* be heard by the Chairman who issued the judgment, or by the tribunal as originally constituted.

A review is a formal oral hearing at which if necessary evidence can be called. If the application is granted, the tribunal will either vary the decision or revoke it and order a re-hearing (*rule 36(3)*). If, on the review, the tribunal concludes that the original decision was wrong, the power to vary is wide enough to allow variation by substitution of the opposite result, e g unfair rather than fair dismissal: *Stonehill Furniture Ltd v Phillippo* [1983] ICR 556. On the other hand, if the previous judgment is revoked, the matter must be decided, either without a hearing, if the judgment was originally issued without a hearing having been held, or at a fresh hearing (*rule 36(3)*).

21.76 The criteria for a review were previously relatively narrow, but have in one important respect been widened by recent judicial authority. The test for whether fresh evidence should be admitted on a review is that laid down by the EAT in *Wileman v Minilec Engineering Ltd* [1988] ICR 318; see 22.16 below. The interests of justice include justice to the party which was successful at the hearing, and the public interest in the finality of litigation.

The review procedure enables errors which occur in the course of the proceedings to be corrected regardless of whether the error is major or minor (*Trimble v Supertravel Ltd* [1982] ICR 440), but until recently it was considered that it ought not to be invoked when an error of law was alleged after the parties have had a fair opportunity to present their case without procedural mishap. The EAT has however held in several recent decisions that the introduction into the *ET Rules* of the Overriding Objective justifies a significantly less strict approach.

Where there is an obvious advantage in a mistake being addressed through a review rather than requiring a party to appeal, it is in the interests of justice to permit a review: *Williams v Ferrosan Ltd* [2004] IRLR 607 (a case where compensation had been awarded on a mistaken view on the part of both parties' representatives, and the Chairman, as to whether it would be taxable); and see also *Sodexho Ltd v Gibbons* [2005] IRLR 836, in which *Williams* was strongly endorsed, and *Maresca v Motor Industry Repair Research Centre* [2005] ICR 197. A broad and non-technical approach to the power to review a judgment in the interests of justice was also shown in the case of *Southwark London Borough Council v Bartholomew* [2004] ICR 358.

In a decision prior to the introduction of the Overriding Objective into the *ET Rules*, the EAT held that the incompetence of a party's representative is not a sufficient reason for a review of the decision: *Ironsides, Ray and Vials v Lindsay* [1994] ICR 384 (failure to argue that it was just and equitable to extend time in a discrimination case); but it must now be doubted whether that view would be followed in the light of the more recent authority referred to above.

There is a separate power for the Chairman to correct clerical errors or accidental slips (*rule 37*). This power is sometimes used to correct errors in the computation of compensation.

21.77   VEXATIOUS LITIGANTS

The EAT has power, upon an application by the Attorney General, to make a restriction of proceedings order against a person who has habitually and persistently and without any reasonable ground either instituted vexatious proceedings in an employment tribunal or before the EAT (whether against the same person or against different persons), or made vexatious applications in tribunal or EAT proceedings. The effect of such an order, which may be for a limited or an indefinite period, is that employment tribunal and EAT proceedings may not be commenced or continued, and applications in such proceedings may not be made, without the leave of the EAT. The EAT may not give leave unless satisfied that the proceedings or application are not an abuse of process and that there are reasonable grounds for them; there is no appeal from a refusal of leave (*ETA 1996, s 33*).

The first order made under *s 33* was made in *A-G v Wheen* [2000] IRLR 461; the decision gives guidance as to the scope of the power and how the EAT should exercise the discretion conferred by it. The order was subsequently upheld by the Court of Appeal ([2001] IRLR 91); the court rejected an argument that an order was in breach of the litigant's rights under *art 6* of the *ECHR*.

In addition, a person who has been held to be a vexatious litigant by the High Court making an order under the *Supreme Court Act 1981, s 42(1A)* is prohibited from instituting proceedings in an employment tribunal without the leave of the High Court (*Vidler v UNISON* [1999] ICR 746).

21.78   PROCEDURE IN CERTAIN SPECIALIST JURISDICTIONS

The procedures described above apply to proceedings covered by *Sch 1* to the *ET Regulations*. Other Schedules set out complementary rules of procedure in claims involving national security (*Sch 2*) and claims for equal pay for work of equal value (*Sch 6*; see EQUAL PAY (24)), and certain specialist jurisdictions (see 20.4 above for details). These rules of procedure should be consulted if relevant; the jurisdictions concerned are either too specialised to justify a detailed discussion here, or are outside the scope of this book.

22   Employment Tribunals – III: Appeals

22.1   THE EMPLOYMENT APPEAL TRIBUNAL

An appeal from the decision of an employment tribunal is heard by the Employment Appeal Tribunal ('EAT'), save for appeals to the High Court or Court of Session in health and safety cases involving appeals against improvement and prohibition notices, and in certain special jurisdictions outside the scope of this book. An appeal can only be brought on a point of law (see further below).

The EAT is a tribunal created by statute, and its substantive jurisdiction is statutory: *ETA 1996, s 21*. It also has both statutory (by *s 30(3) ETA 1996*) and (limited) inherent jurisdiction to regulate proceedings before it, as a superior court of record (ie of equivalent status to the High Court): see *A v B, ex p News Group Newspapers Ltd* [1998] ICR 55 at 67 and *X v Stevens* [2003] IRLR 411.

In addition to its appellate functions the EAT has certain limited jurisdictions as a court of first instance, in relation to information and consultation of employees; these rarely arise in practice and are not considered in detail in this chapter.

The EAT is not a 'court' within the meaning of *s 4* of the *Human Rights Act 1998*, and it therefore does not have the power to make a declaration that a statutory provision is incompatible with a Convention right guaranteed by the *Human Rights Act 1998:* see *Whittaker v P & D Watson* [2002] ICR 1244, where it was suggested that in a case where there was a serious issue of compatibility the EAT should dispose of the appeal on paper, giving permission to appeal to the Court of Appeal.

The status and effect of decisions of the EAT was the subject of a public statement by its then President, Morison J, on 3 April 1998 ([1998] IRLR 435). The EAT is a single appellate court which sits in divisions and may sit anywhere in Great Britain (in fact, it normally sits in London and Edinburgh and has facilities to sit in Cardiff, but does so only occasionally). Both judicial and lay members may, and occasionally do, sit in both principal centres. In the past commentators have referred to apparent differences in approach of the EAT in Scotland on particular issues, and raised questions as to how far a decision given in Scotland binds English tribunals, and vice versa. The statement makes it clear that all tribunals are equally bound by decisions of any division of the EAT wherever given.

Despite the foregoing, the EAT sitting in England or Wales is not formally bound by decisions of the Court of Session on appeals from the EAT sitting in Scotland, and the EAT sitting in Scotland is not bound by decisions of the Court of Appeal on appeals from the EAT in England or Wales. The consequences of this were starkly demonstrated in *Marshalls Clay Products Ltd v Caulfield* [2003] IRLR 552, a case on 'rolled up' holiday pay under the *Working Time Regulations 1998,* where the EAT refused to follow a decision of the Court of Session (*MPB Structures Ltd v Munro* [2002] IRLR 601); the Court of Appeal ([2003] IRLR 350) held that it had been entitled to do so, and that its decision was right, thereby raising the prospect of a different interpretation of the same legislation binding tribunals north and south of the border. The only way to resolve such differences is by way of further appeal to the House of Lords (a United Kingdom Court, whose decisions are binding in both jurisdictions) or, as happened in this case, by a reference to the ECJ (see *Robinson-Steele v R D Retail Services Ltd, Case C-131/04* [2006] IRLR 386).

Decisions of the EAT are not formally binding on the EAT itself. They are normally followed but a number of inconsistent decisions have been reported, and on occasion the EAT itself has overruled a previous decision; a good recent example is *Woodward v Abbey National plc* [2005] IRLR 782, overruling *Clark v Midland Packaging Ltd* [2005] 2 All ER 266, on the question when a Notice of Appeal is taken as received by the EAT. The range of representation means that the EAT's attention is not always drawn to relevant reported decisions; this problem has become greater since the unreported decisions of the EAT have become publicly available on its website (www.employmentappeals.gov.uk); in addition, all final judgments of the EAT issued since 1992 are now available on www.bailii.org.

The statutory nature of the EAT's jurisdiction and the proliferation of statutes and regulations conferring additional jurisdictions on employment tribunals has led on occasions to errors of drafting being found to have failed to confer jurisdiction on the EAT over a particular class of appeal; most recently this was held to be so in relation to appeals concerning the statutory right of accompaniment under the *Employment Relations Act 1999, s 10* (*Refreshment Systems Ltd v Wolstenholme*, EAT/608/03). This oversight was corrected by the *Employment Relations Act 2004, s 38*. However the opportunity was not taken to fill the equivalent gap in relation to complaints concerning the right to be accompanied at meetings to consider requests for flexible working: see the *Flexible Working (Eligibility, Complaints and Remedies) Regulations 2002 (SI 2002/3236), reg 15*.

22.2   The composition of the EAT mirrors that of the employment tribunals. The judicial members are High Court or Circuit Judges, with one High Court Judge appointed as President for three years at a time. One Court of Session judge is also allocated to the EAT and presides over most Scottish appeals. The lay members are formally appointed by the Queen on the recommendation of the Lord Chancellor and the Secretary of State (*ETA 1996, s 22(1)(c)*), and are selected for their experience in employment matters. They are generally very senior and experienced in their respective fields. Since April 2006, the Judicial Appointments Commmission has become responsible for selection of candidates for lay membership.

The practice adopted by the Lord Chancellor in 2002 of appointing a number of eminent practising QCs, who also sat as part-time Recorders, as additional part-time judicial members of the EAT, was effectively brought to an end by comments by the House of Lords in *Lawal v Northern Spirit Ltd* [2003] UKHL 35, [2003] IRLR 538, that the practice tended to undermine public confidence in the judicial system and should be discontinued. The reason for this was that the part-time judicial members also regularly appeared as advocates, and an appearance of bias could be created when they appeared in front of lay members of the EAT with whom they had previously sat judicially.

The EAT normally sits in divisions of three, although there is provision for a panel of five (one judicial member and two from each of the panels of lay members). There is power for appeals to be heard by a judicial member sitting alone, where the decision appealed from was taken by a Chairman sitting alone (*ETA 1996, s 28(4)*); this power is also used for appeals against interlocutory decisions such as non-acceptance of a claim or response. In addition, issues arising after a notice of appeal has been lodged but prior to the full hearing of an appeal are determined by a judicial member (often the President) sitting alone. Such matters include hearings for directions (when held) and appeals from decisions of the Registrar on preliminary points taken under *rule 20* (eg on extending time for a Notice of Appeal). References under *rule 3(10)* arising from a decision of the Registrar or a Judge that an appeal should not be admitted at the preliminary sift (see below for this) are required to be heard by a Judge alone.

Where an appeal is required to be heard by a panel of three, the hearing may proceed in the absence of one of the lay members, but only with the agreement of all parties to the appeal (*ETA 1996, s 28(3)*). The Court of Appeal has ruled that it is a prerequisite to proceeding under this rule that the parties are informed as to which of the panels (employer or employee) the missing member belongs to: *De Haney v Brent Mind* [2003] EWCA Civ 1637, [2004] ICR 348. There is no facility for the EAT to sit with only one member at a preliminary hearing, even with the consent of the appellant, unless the respondent also consents, but the respondent is usually not entitled to be heard, and will therefore usually not be present to give consent if a lay member is unexpectedly prevented from attending.

Legal aid is available to individuals for appeals from employment tribunals, subject to the normal conditions. (One exception in favour of the legally aided party in the EAT is that the statutory charge on money awarded to or preserved in favour of a party for the Legal Services Commission's costs does not apply in proceedings in the EAT.)

22.3   The case-load of the EAT grew significantly during the 1990s, although not at the same rate as the employment tribunals, but the number of appeals has been declining somewhat in recent years. The number of potential appeals received in 2001–2 was 1,843; this increased to 1,938 in 2002–3 and 2,084 in 2003–4, but fell back to 1,876 in 2004–5 and 1,728 in 2005–6. A significant and growing proportion of these potential appeals are screened out by the Registrar and are never registered as full appeals; the number actually registered as appeals was 1,170 in 2002–3 and 1,235 in 2003–4, but there was a significant drop to 885 in 2004–5 and a further drop to 836 in 2005–6.

Serious delays in the hearing of appeals in England and Wales (but not in Scotland) occurred in the early 1990s, and again in the early 2000s. However, following the appointment of Burton J as President in 2002, the number of courts sitting was increased, and various procedural reforms were adopted to ensure the more expeditious hearing of appeals. The ETS set a target for the EAT for 2003–4 for 75% of appeals to reach a first hearing within 39 weeks of first being received; in the event 97% did so. The target for 2004–5 was tightened to 75% of appeals reaching first hearing within 26 weeks; in the event the percentage achieved was 93%; this rose to 97% in 2005–6. It can thus be seen that improved administrative arrangements, increased judicial resources and a more rigorous screening of potential appeals have together brought the problems of delay under control.

As part of the process of regulating its own procedure, and also as a means to improve the appellate process, the EAT has from time to time issued Practice Directions. The current Direction is the *Practice Direction* of 9 December 2004 ([2005] IRLR 94), referred to below as the '*Practice Direction*'. The *Practice Direction* replaces the previous Practice Direction of 2002. The text of the *Practice Direction* is available on the EAT website (www.employmentappeals.gov.uk), and it is strongly advised that this be read carefully by anyone involved as a party to an appeal or as a representative.

The *Practice Directions* of 2002 and 2004 have introduced significant changes in procedure, including the adoption of the Overriding Objective (see 20.14 and 21.1 above) and a duty for parties to co-operate with the EAT in achieving it, new obligations on the parties (rather than, as hitherto, the staff of the EAT) to prepare and submit the documentation to be considered at each appeal, and new 'tracks' to which different categories of appeal are allocated. The Overriding Objective was formally incorporated into the *EAT Rules,* along with other amendments to bring the *Rules* into harmony with the *2004 ET Regulations,* and changes in the power to award costs, by the *Employment Appeal Tribunal (Amendment) Rules 2004, SI 2004/2526.*

22.4 APPEALS

The procedure for appeals to the EAT is governed by the *Employment Appeal Tribunal Rules 1993 (SI 1993/2854)* (the *'EAT Rules')* as amended by the *Employment Appeal Tribunal (Amendment) Rules 2001 (SI 2001/1128)* and the *2004 Amendment Rules* referred to above. The *2004 Amendment Rules* contain transitional provisions for appeals where a decision was issued by the employment tribunal before 1 October 2004, and the new power to make wasted costs orders (*EAT Rules, rule 34C*) only applies to appeals instituted on or after 1 October 2004, but in other respects the *Rules* as amended have applied in full as from 1 October 2004.

The *EAT Rules* also contain modifications to the procedure for appeals in the (very infrequent) cases where the modified procedure for national security cases in *Sch 2* to the *ET Regulations* applies. These modifications are too specialised to be covered in this chapter.

As part of the consultation preceding the making of the *2004 Amendment Rules,* the DTI solicited views on whether a statutory requirement should be introduced that permission would be required to appeal to the EAT; however this proposal was widely opposed and was not pursued. There has however been a further strengthening of the procedures for weeding out obviously hopeless appeals without a hearing, by means of the amended *EAT Rules* and associated changes introduced by the *2004 Practice Direction.*

Any party to the proceedings in an employment tribunal may appeal against an adverse decision. This includes a respondent to the original claim who has not presented a response, or whose response was not accepted by the tribunal (e g because it was out of time) and who has therefore not been permitted to take part in the proceedings: *Atos Origin IT Services Ltd v Haddock* [2005] IRLR 20; *Butlins Skyline Ltd v Beynon* [2007] ICR 121 (and see the *Practice Direction, para 16,* for the procedural steps required of such an appellant); it also includes a claimant whose Claim Form has been rejected, either by a Chairman or by the secretariat, and who wishes to appeal against its rejection: see respectively for appeals against rejection by a Chairman and by the secretariat *Richardson v U Mole Ltd* [2005] IRLR 668 and *Grant v In 2 Focus Sales Development Ltd,* EAT/0310/06.

22.5 Institution and content of Appeals

Appeals to the EAT must be instituted by presenting a Notice of Appeal in or substantially in accordance with the prescribed form (Form 1) to the EAT within 42 days from the date on which the written reasons were sent to the parties or, in a case where the reasons for the judgment were not reserved and written reasons were not requested when the judgment and reasons were given orally, or within 14 days thereafter, within 42 days of the judgment being sent to the parties. An appeal from an order must be presented within 42 days of the date of the order (*rule 3(3)*).

The requirement for presentation means that the Notice of Appeal must be received by the EAT within the prescribed time. *Rule 37(1A)* requires that any act required to be done on or before a particular day must be done before 4 pm on that day; this includes the lodging of a Notice of Appeal: *Woodward v Abbey National plc* [2005] IRLR 782. It was also held in this case that the whole of the documentation required as part of a Notice of Appeal must be received by the EAT office by the deadline; this means that an appeal submitted by fax is only in time if the whole of the fax has been received on the EAT machine by 4 pm on the final day. With this important proviso, service may be by fax as well as by post or personal delivery; however there is as yet no facility to lodge a Notice of Appeal by e-mail.

The date from which time starts to run is the day after the judgment or reasons is or are sent (ie despatched, not received) to the parties or, in the case of an order, the day following the date of the order; this date is recorded on the document containing the judgment, reasons or order itself. The date on which a judgment or order is sent or made does not count in calculating the 42 days. Previous and somewhat conflicting case law led to suggestions that 'sent' meant 'received' or the date on which receipt in the ordinary course of post would be presumed, but following changes in the *ET Regulations* to make clear that 'sent' refers to the date of sending (see *reg 15(6)*), the basis for these decisions no longer applies. This has now been confirmed by the Court of Appeal: *Gdynia America Shipping Lines Ltd v Chelminski [2004] EWCA Civ 871, [2004] ICR 1523*, and is reiterated by the *Practice Direction (paras 1.8.1, 1.8.2, 3.2 and 3.3)*. The 42 day period for lodging an appeal is automatically extended if it expires on a day on which the offices of the EAT are closed; in practice this will only apply to public holidays, since it is not the practice of tribunals to make orders or send out judgments on a Saturday or Sunday.

Form 1 is set out in the *Schedule* to the *EAT Rules;* it was replaced with an updated version by *SI 2004/2526, rule 24;* confusingly, a slightly differently worded version is appended to the *2004 Practice Direction.*. The Notice of Appeal must be accompanied by (i) a copy of the judgment or order which is the subject of the appeal; (ii) a copy of the written reasons for that judgment or order, if any; (iii) in the case of an appeal against a judgment, if written reasons are not enclosed, an explanation of why not; and (iv) also in the case of an appeal against a judgment, copies of the claim and response forms or an explanation of why they are not included (*EAT Rules, rule 3(1)*). If there are no written reasons for the judgment being appealed, the appellant must include in the Notice of Appeal an application for the EAT to exercise its discretion to hear the appeal without written reasons, or to request the tribunal to supply them (*Practice Direction, para 2.3*).

A *Practice Statement* issued by the President in February 2005 ([2005] IRLR 189) makes it clear that all the required documentation must be received by the EAT in order for an appeal to be treated as lodged; so, for instance, if the judgment under appeal and any written reasons are not submitted by the deadline, the Notice of Appeal will be treated as out of time. This is very strictly applied: in *Woods v Suffolk Mental Health Partnership NHS Trust* UKEATPA/0360/06, an extension of time was refused where the Notice of Appeal was submitted on the last day with an incomplete copy of the claim form, and the missing pages were not received until after the time for appealing had expired. If there has been an application for a review, the application, and if available the judgment or order determining it, must be included with the Notice of Appeal (*Practice Direction, para 2.2*), but it appears from the wording of the *Practice Direction* that failure to do so will not lead to the appeal being treated as not validly lodged. It has been stated that the use of a document other than the prescribed form will be permitted only in exceptional cases (*Martin v British Railways Board* [1989] ICR 24); however, in practice this requirement is not enforced, particularly not against unrepresented appellants, provided at least that the document contains the information required to complete Form 1 (in either of its current versions) and is accompanied by the required documents.

It is important that the grounds for the appeal are fully and clearly set out. The *Practice Direction* makes it clear (*para 2.7*) that there is no automatic right to add to or amend grounds of appeal, and permission to pursue a ground of appeal may be refused if it has not been set out in the original Notice of Appeal; even if permission to amend is given, there may be adverse costs consequences for the appellant. Delay in applying to amend a Notice of Appeal is likely to lead to permission to amend being refused; for a detailed review of considerations affecting applications to amend see *Khudados v Leggate* [2005] IRLR 540.

22.6   Time limits are very strictly enforced (see e g *Mock v IRC* [1999] IRLR 785: last minute failure of computer of counsel preparing the Notice of Appeal not sufficient excuse for appeal being lodged one day late; *Woodward v Abbey National plc* [2005] IRLR 782: last page of faxed Notice not received until 4.06 pm on final day for appealing; extension only allowed because previous authority had suggested it was sufficient if the *first* page arrived in time). Every appeal lodged out of time must be accompanied by an application for an extension of time under *EAT Rules, rule 37* setting out the reasons for the delay. The time limit for an appeal applies even though there may be a pending application to the tribunal to review its decision (*Practice Direction, paras 3.4, 3.5*). Nor is the fact that an application for legal aid or other public funding is pending a reason for exceeding the time limit: *Marshall v Harland and Wolff Ltd (Practice Note)* [1972] ICR 97; *Practice Direction, para 3.8*.

The strict approach to the time limit adopted by the EAT has been upheld by the Court of Appeal, notwithstanding that a less rigorous approach applies to appeals to that court: *Aziz v Bethnal Green City Challenge Co Ltd* [2000] IRLR 111.

General guidance as to the criteria for allowing appeals out of time has been given in *United Arab Emirates v Abdelghafar* [1995] ICR 65 (and see *Practice Direction, para 3.7*)). For an example of exceptional circumstances justifying an extension of time, see *Dodd v Bank of Tokyo-Mitsubishi Ltd*, EAT/0480/05 (tribunal judgment not received by appellant's solicitor until the 42nd day following its issue). In *Peters v Sat Katar Co Ltd* [2003] IRLR 574, the Court of Appeal allowed an appeal against a refusal to extend time where a litigant in person had posted her Notice of Appeal 14 days before the deadline but it had been lost in the post. It was, in the Court's view, not reasonable to expect an unrepresented party to realise the need to check with the EAT that the Notice had been received. However, an appeal out of time will not necessarily be permitted merely because a decision of a higher court has changed what was generally understood to be the law in favour of the intending appellant: *Setiya v East Yorkshire Health Authority* [1995] ICR 799.

The Registrar of the EAT will determine any application for an extension of time to validate the Notice of Appeal on the basis of written representations from the parties (*Practice Direction, para 3.6*). Any party aggrieved by the Registrar's decision (including a respondent to the appeal, if the decision is to extend time) may appeal to a judge of the EAT within five days of the date the Registrar's decision is sent to the parties (*EAT Rules, rule 21; Practice Direction, para 4.3*).

A respondent to an appeal who wishes to resist the appeal must set out his or her grounds of resistance, and cross-appeal where applicable (see below), in or substantially in accordance with Form 3 (this is referred to as a 'Respondent's Answer') and deliver it to the EAT within the time specified by the Registrar (*EAT Rules, rule 6;* the form is set out in the *Schedule*). The respondent may rely on the reasons given by the tribunal, or (alternatively or additionally) other grounds put forward to the tribunal but not relied on by it in support of its findings. These should be set out fully at the outset; the same considerations as to amendments to the Notice of Appeal apply equally to any application to amend the Respondent's Answer.

If an appeal is registered, the respondent is given the opportunity to cross-appeal, that is, to appeal against any elements of the judgment or order under appeal that are adverse to him or her. Directions as to the time for filing the cross-appeal will be notified to the respondent at the same time that he or she is directed to file a Respondent's Answer. If there is a cross-appeal, the procedure applicable to appeals under *rule 3(7)* applies equally to the cross-appeal (*rule 6(12), (14)–(16)*); see 22.8 below for details. If the cross-appeal is accepted following scrutiny under *rule 3(7)*, it will be dealt with in accordance with directions given by a Judge or the Registrar; these can be expected to follow broadly the same procedures as for the appeal; further details are given in the *Practice Direction*.

22.7   Grounds of appeal

The EAT's jurisdiction is limited to appeals on points of law. In practice, the most common ground of appeal is 'perversity'. This is recognised to be a separate head of appeal but is narrowly construed and rarely successful. See *Piggott Bros & Co Ltd v Jackson* [1992] ICR 85, *East Berkshire Health Authority v Matadeen* [1992] ICR 723 and *Yeboah v Crofton* [2002] EWCA Civ 794, [2002] IRLR 634. It is not acceptable for an appellant to contend that 'the decision was contrary to the evidence' or that 'there was no evidence to support the decision', or to advance similar contentions, unless full and sufficient particulars identifying the particular matters relied upon are set out in the Notice of Appeal (*Practice Direction, para 2.6*). It is not a valid ground of appeal that the decision appealed against was a majority decision (even where the Chairman was the minority): *Chief Constable of the Thames Valley Police v Kellaway* [2000] IRLR 170. However a serious procedural irregularity, leading to a hearing which was unfair to the appellant, may be the subject of an appeal on that ground, as may a failure to give adequate reasons for the tribunal's conclusions.

22.8   Preliminary sifting of appeals

All Notices of Appeal are subject to a preliminary sift by either the Registrar or a Judge, in accordance with *rule 3(7)*. If it appears to the Registrar or Judge reviewing the Notice that it discloses no reasonable grounds for bringing the appeal, or is an abuse of the EAT's process or otherwise likely to obstruct the just disposal of proceedings, the prospective appellant is notified that no further action will be taken on the appeal. When such a notice is served, the appellant may serve a fresh Notice of Appeal within the time limit remaining for serving a Notice of Appeal, or within 28 days from the date on which the notification was sent to him or her, whichever is the later (*EAT Rules, rule 3(8)*). Such a notice is treated as if it were the original Notice of Appeal and had been lodged in time (and is therefore open to rejection under the same procedure) (*EAT Rules, rule 3(9)*). Where an appellant expresses dissatisfaction in writing with the reasons given by the Registrar or Judge for his or her opinion that the grounds of appeal stated in the Notice of Appeal do not disclose any reasonable grounds for bringing the appeal, etc, the Registrar will refer the case for a hearing before a Judge sitting alone (*EAT Rules, rule 3(10)*).

The Registrar also deals with interim applications, which must be made by notice in writing (*EAT Rules, rules 19, 20*). She disposes of such applications herself or refers them to a Judge, who may him or herself refer them for hearing before the EAT. An appeal lies against a decision of the Registrar (*EAT Rules, rule 21*). There are separate procedures for applications for restricted reporting orders; see further below for these.

22.9   In October 1997, the practice was introduced of referring all appeals (other than urgent interlocutory appeals) to *ex parte* preliminary hearings at which the appellant would be required to demonstrate that the appeal raised an arguable point of law, and any directions (eg for production of the Chairman's notes of evidence) would be dealt with. Normally, only the appellant would be required to attend a preliminary hearing, although a respondent might be invited to appear in exceptional cases, eg to deal with an application by the appellant for fresh evidence to be admitted, or where there was a cross-appeal. Experience showed, however, that this practice added to the EAT's workload, and in an increasing number of cases where it was clear from the papers that there was an arguable point of law in the appeal, the requirement of a preliminary hearing was dispensed with. The *2002 Practice Direction* adopted a new approach (retained in the *2004 Practice Direction*) by which (except in Scotland) each appeal is allocated to one of four tracks:

(*a*)   action by the Registrar under *rule 3(7)*;

(*b*)   reference to an *ex parte* preliminary hearing (for cases where there is doubt whether the Notice of Appeal discloses an arguable point of law);

(*c*)   reference to a full hearing;

(*d*)   a fast track, used for cases of importance and urgency, where a decision will determine the outcome of other pending cases, for cases involving reinstatement or interim relief, and for interlocutory appeals.

(*Practice Direction, para 9.*)

Directions are now dealt with on paper, and a party seeking particular directions should therefore apply as soon as practicable by letter. It is open to the parties to make a reasoned application for an appeal to be allocated to the fast track.

Where a preliminary hearing is to be held, it is now the practice to order or invite the respondent to the appeal to make concise written submissions as to why the appeal should not be allowed to proceed to a full hearing (*Practice Direction, para 9.8*). At this stage of the proceedings the respondent is also required to lodge any cross-appeal, which will then also be considered at the preliminary hearing (with the consequence that both parties will have the opportunity to put their respective cases). In any case, the appellant is required to submit a skeleton argument in support of the appeal in advance of the preliminary hearing.

The outcome of a preliminary hearing may be that the appeal is dismissed, referred to a full hearing, or permitted to proceed but only on some of the grounds advanced in the Notice of Appeal. In the latter category of case, the EAT may not consider any other ground of appeal at the substantive hearing of the appeal, unless there are exceptional reasons to do so, but the appellant may seek permission to appeal to the Court of Appeal against what is effectively the dismissal of part of the appeal: *Miriki v General Council of the Bar* [2001] EWCA Civ 1973, [2002] ICR 505. Permission may also be given at this stage to amend the Notice of Appeal, but the respondent (unless present at the hearing and thus given an opportunity to object to the proposed amendment) will in such cases have the opportunity to apply to have the amendment set aside (see generally *Practice Direction, para 9.14*).

Hearings for directions may also be held under *EAT Rules, rule 24*, and there is a general power to give directions under *EAT Rules, rule 25* and to waive compliance with the normal rules under *EAT Rules, rule 39*.

22.10 Notes of evidence

An issue often arising on an appeal is what evidence the tribunal had heard on a particular point. Normally, the only admissible evidence of this is the Chairman's note of the evidence given. These notes are not produced automatically or on the direct request of a party to the tribunal but only if ordered by the EAT. Reasons must be given in support of any application for an order for the production of the Chairman's notes. The *Practice Direction, para 7*, sets out the procedure to be followed in, and the criteria applicable to, an application for production of the Chairman's notes. Applications must be made promptly, giving reasons in accordance with the criteria set out in the *Practice Direction*. Appellants should make their application together with the Notice of Appeal; if this is not done, and the case is referred to a preliminary hearing, the application for notes must be made at that hearing. In other cases, applications will be considered on paper by the Registrar or a Judge. The parties will normally be given 21 days to endeavour to agree a note of the evidence in question, and any further application for the Chairman's notes must be accompanied by evidence of the steps taken to agree the evidence (such as relevant correspondence).

There is no automatic right to production of the Chairman's notes simply because the appellant alleges that the decision was perverse: *Hawkins v Ball* [1996] IRLR 258. 'Fishing expeditions' are specifically disapproved by the *Practice Direction* (see *para 7.7*), with a warning that unreasonable applications may lead to an order for costs against the offending party.

22.11 Reference back to tribunal for clarification of reasons

A relatively recent innovation in the EAT's procedure is the reference back of appeals which are based on the inadequacy of the tribunal's reasons, for amplification or clarification of the reasons under challenge. It had been thought that there was no power for the EAT to refer a case back to the tribunal, whether for reconsideration of its findings or to clarify or amplify its reasons, except as part of the disposition of the case after hearing and deciding the appeal; this view was based on obiter comments by the Court of Appeal in *Kien Tran v Greenwich Vietnam Community Project* [2002] EWCA Civ 533, [2002] IRLR 735 on the ambit of *ETA 1996, s 35(1)*. However a different view was expressed, in relation to civil appeals generally, in the later case of *English v Emery Reimbold & Strick Ltd* [2002] EWCA Crim 605, [2003] IRLR 710, and following that decision, the EAT held in *Burns v Consignia (No 2)* [2004] IRLR 425 that there is such a power. This view was subsequently endorsed by the Court of Appeal, but on different grounds, in *Barke v SEETEC Business Technology Centres Ltd* [2005] EWCA Civ

578, [2005] IRLR 633. The view expressed in *Tran* was held to be correct, but it was held that there is power to remit derived from the provision (newly introduced in 2004) in the *ET Rules, rule 30(3)(b)*, for tribunals to be required to provide reasons if requested by the EAT; alternatively, the inherent jurisdiction of the EAT allowed this course to be adopted. The power may be exercised on a Judge's initiative or at a preliminary hearing; the appeal then proceeds on the reasons as clarified or amplified. In a case where there is an appeal against a judgment or order for which the tribunal has not given written reasons, *rule 30(3)(b)* gives the EAT power to ask the tribunal or Chairman to supply written reasons for the purpose of the appeal.

The practice has also been adopted, since 2002, of staying the appeal in some cases to enable the appellant to apply for a review of the tribunal's decision, where it is thought that a review decision might obviate the need for an appeal (see now *Practice Direction, para 9.5*).

22.12   Allegations of bias

The EAT will not normally consider complaints of bias or of the conduct of an employment tribunal unless full and sufficient particulars are set out in the grounds of appeal. In any such case the Registrar may inquire of the party making the complaint whether it is the intention to proceed with the complaint, in which case the Registrar will give directions. Such directions may include the filing of affidavits dealing with the matters upon the basis of which the complaint is made or for giving further particulars. The Chairman of the tribunal (and in appropriate cases the other members) will be given the opportunity of commenting upon the complaints made against him or her (*Practice Direction, para 11*). It has been held that this procedure should also be followed where a ground of appeal is that the tribunal refused or failed to adjourn the proceedings: *Knight v Central London Bus Co Ltd*, EAT/443/00.

The Court of Appeal has confirmed that the EAT has jurisdiction to hear an appeal based on an allegation of bias, unless the allegation was on its face so lacking in substance that it could not be said to amount to a real challenge: *Lodwick v Southwark London Borough Council* [2004] EWCA Civ 306, [2004] ICR 884, a case where the appellant had objected to the Chairman but the latter had declined to recuse himself. Further detailed guidance as to how appeals alleging bias by the tribunal should be conducted, particularly where there is a dispute of fact as to what occurred at the hearing, has been given in *Facey v Midas Retail Security* [2001] ICR 287.

Where there is an allegation of bias based on the conduct of one of the members of a tribunal at a hearing, the test is an objective one: whether, having regard to the relevant circumstances 'a fair minded and informed observer who had considered the facts would conclude that there was a real possibility that the tribunal was biased' (*Porter v Magill* [2002] UKHL 67, [2002] 1 All ER 465. Bias of this kind on the part of one tribunal member is sufficient (*Lodwick v Southwark London Borough Council*, above; and see *Zahedi v McGee*, EAT/465/94, IDS Brief 551: Chairman had previously acted as solicitor for appellant in a criminal matter). An example of a case where the EAT found that there was an appearance of bias was *Diem v Crystal Services plc*, EAT/0398/05, where, in a claim of race discrimination, the Chairman made comments about the colour of the claimant's skin.

In *Ansar v Lloyds TSB Bank plc* [2006] EWCA Civ 1462, [2007] IRLR 211, the Court of Appeal gave guidance on when the fact that a complaint of bias had been made against a Chairman makes it inappropriate for the Chairman to continue to hear the case, or to deal with any later application by the person complaining. The mere fact of an allegation of bias having been made is not in itself a reason for the Chairman to stand aside (the technical term is recusal). See also *Bennett v Southwark London Borough Council* [2002] EWCA Civ 223, [2002] IRLR 407 (allegations made against Chairman during course of hearing).

For the position where a tribunal member is directly associated with a body with an interest in the outcome of the proceedings (such as a pressure group) see *R v Bow Street Metropolitan Stipendiary Magistrate, ex p Pinochet Ugarte (No 2)* [2000] 1 AC 119, HL.

There have been conflicting decisions of the EAT as to whether any issue arising in the course of the proceedings, such as improper conduct by a member, had to be raised at the time of its occurrence if it was to be the subject of an appeal (see *Peter Simper Ltd v Cooke* [1986] IRLR 19 and *Red Bank Manufacturing Co Ltd v Meadows* [1992] ICR 204). The Court of Appeal has reviewed the position and given general guidance (*Stansbury v Datapulse plc* [2003] EWCA Civ 1951, [2004] IRLR 466, a case where the original decision was set aside for procedural irregularity on evidence that one of the lay members had fallen asleep during the proceedings after having consumed alcohol during the lunch break). The test where the issue was not raised with the tribunal at the time is one of reasonableness, recognising in particular that while it is desirable that the matter should be raised at the time, so that if possible corrective action can be taken, it is difficult even for a legal representative, let alone an unrepresented party, to raise a complaint against a member of the tribunal who, if the complaint is not accepted, will proceed to adjudicate on the case.

Where it is claimed that there was procedural unfairness as a result of a ruling of the tribunal in the course of the hearing, the failure of the disadvantaged party to object at the time does not necessarily prevent the point from being taken on appeal, especially if the appellant had not been professionally represented: *Bache v Essex County Council* [2000] IRLR 251, CA. On the other hand, if a declaration of interest is made by the Chairman or a member and the parties agree that the hearing may proceed despite this, the parties will be taken to have waived their rights to pursue the issue as a ground of appeal, provided that there was full disclosure and a proper opportunity to decide whether to consent to the hearing proceeding: *Jones v DAS Legal Expenses Insurance Ltd* [2003] EWCA Civ 1071, [2004] IRLR 218.

22.13 Miscellaneous preliminary points

Where a separate hearing or PHR is held on a preliminary issue and the tribunal gives a judgment, it is open to the losing party to appeal, and time for appealing runs from the date the reasons for the judgment on the preliminary issue are sent to the parties (or the date the written judgment is sent, if reasons have not been given in writing). However, the EAT has stated that it is only in exceptional cases that such an appeal will be heard before the final determination of the case by the tribunal: *Sutcliffe v Big C's Marine Ltd* [1998] ICR 913. (Appeals against *interlocutory* case management orders, by contrast, often need to be, and are, heard very speedily.)

Rule 23 of the *EAT Rules* contains provisions which closely follow those of *rules 49* and *50* of the *ET Rules* conferring powers on tribunals to make restricted reporting orders and for the exclusion from public documents of matter identifying affected parties in the case of allegations of a sexual offence. The latter is treated as an administrative responsibility of the Registrar, and does not require an application by a party (*rule 23(2)*). In other cases, a restricted reporting order may only be made either on a temporary basis or, on the application of a party or of the EAT's own motion, having given the parties an opportunity to be heard on the matter (*rule 23(3), (5)*). A temporary order lasts for 14 days unless a party applies for it to be extended, in which case the order continues in force until that application has been heard and determined (*rule 23(5A)–(5C)*). There is however no equivalent provision in *rule 23* to the provision in *rule 50* of the *ET Rules* providing for interested third parties such as press representatives to be given an opportunity to make representations before an order is made. For further details of the scope of and case law relating to restricted reporting orders see 21.18 – 21.19.

22.14 CONDUCT OF THE APPEAL

As in employment tribunals, there is no restriction as to the persons who may represent a party to an appeal (*ETA 1996, s 29(1)*). In the nature of the proceedings, legal representation is more common, but by no means universal. A scheme known as ELAAS has existed since 1996 for the provision of professional advice for, and, if desired, representation of, unrepresented appellants at preliminary hearings. This is operated with the active encouragement of the EAT by experienced barristers and solicitors who provide free representation on a rota basis. The Free Representation Unit and the Bar Pro Bono Unit also provide free representation in a number of cases.

The EAT will have before it at the substantive hearing the Notice of Appeal, the respondent's answer, the decision of the employment tribunal and any documents which were before the employment tribunal and which are relied on by the parties as relevant to the appeal. It is the responsibility of the appellant to lodge copies of a core bundle of documents (if possible this should be an agreed bundle, and it should be in the format set out in *para 6* of the *Practice Direction*). Irrelevant documents should not be included. Permission is required for the submission of a core bundle exceeding 100 pages. The Chairman's notes should be included in the appeal papers if their production was ordered. A party seeking to show that no reasonable tribunal could have reached the conclusion it reached on the evidence will almost certainly require the notes of evidence, or a jointly agreed note supplied by the parties (*Piggott Bros & Co Ltd v Jackson* [1992] ICR 85 at 96). (This view was qualified by the EAT in *Hawkins v Ball* [1996] IRLR 258, where the evidence was clearly recorded in the tribunal's decision and the issue was whether the conclusions reached from that evidence were perverse.) Any application for an order to produce all or part of the notes must be made in accordance with *para 7* of the *Practice Direction*; see 22.10 above

Most cases are listed for a fixed date. It is the practice of the EAT that the listing office consults the parties or as appropriate their representatives over dates to avoid, and as a consequence once a hearing is listed, cogent reasons will be needed to secure a postponement. It is the duty of the parties to advise the EAT if for any reason the time estimate given for the hearing is likely to be inadequate or too long. Parties are also required to notify the EAT immediately of any settlement which results in the appeal being withdrawn; the Court of Appeal has stated that it is a strict professional duty of legal representatives to avoid waste of judicial time by notifying settlements of cases under appeal immediately, particularly if a settlement is achieved in the immediate run up to the hearing of the appeal: *Yell Ltd v Garton* [2004] EWCA Civ 87, IDS Brief 753. Shorter, and urgent, appeals may be called on at short, sometimes very short, notice

In accordance with *para 13* of the *Practice Direction*, skeleton arguments are required to be lodged with the EAT and exchanged between the parties' representatives, normally 21 days in advance of the hearing (precise timing varies depending on the length of notice of the hearing and type of hearing); appellants may lodge a skeleton argument with the Notice of Appeal, and should prepare an agreed chronology of relevant events. Skeleton arguments are also required for preliminary hearings, and should be lodged 10 days in advance. The format and content of skeleton arguments are prescribed in some detail in *para 13* of the *Practice Direction*. The requirements for skeleton arguments do not apply in Scotland unless specifically directed.

It is the practice of the EAT to read the papers, and skeleton arguments, in advance and representatives can expect to be asked questions arising from their and the other party's skeleton arguments as well as points arising in the course of their oral submissions.

The hearing before the EAT consists of legal argument; it is not the practice to hear evidence again, and therefore witnesses who attended at the tribunal do *not* need to attend the appeal. If fresh evidence is put forward this is by way of affidavit or witness statement with a signed Statement of Truth.

22.15 Raising points not taken at the tribunal hearing

A party is not normally permitted to raise points of law which were abandoned or never raised before the employment tribunal, especially where such points would require further investigation of the facts. The law and practice on this issue was reviewed by the EAT in *Glennie v Independent Magazines (UK) Ltd* [1999] IRLR 719, following the decision of the Court of Appeal in *Jones v Governing Body of Burdett Coutts School* [1998] IRLR 521, which established that the EAT's discretion to allow a new point of law to be raised, or a conceded point to be reopened, should be exercised only in exceptional circumstances, for compelling reasons. This was especially so if the result would be to open up fresh issues of fact which, because the point was not in issue, were not sufficiently investigated before the employment tribunal. The facts that the point is of wider importance, or that the amount at stake in the claim is very significant, are not reasons to depart from the general practice: *Unison v Leicestershire County Council* [2006] EWCA Civ 825, [2006] IRLR 810 (where the tribunal had made a protective award totalling several million pounds). An example of an exceptional case is *Lipscombe v Forestry Commission* [2007] EWCA Civ 428, [2007] All ER (D) 132 (May), where a litigant in person was permitted by the Court of Appeal to rely on a point not taken at the hearing, which involved undisputed facts and was decisive of whether the tribunal had jurisdiction.

The position now is that the EAT will not normally allow an appellant to rely on a point not taken at the original hearing, where that hearing had proceeded on one factual basis and it is now sought to argue the appeal on a different factual basis which could have been put forward at the first hearing. Where the issue sought to be raised goes to the jurisdiction of the tribunal a less rigorous practice applies, but leave to raise the point will only be given in an exceptional case. If the point raised is an argument that, on the evidence already given, the decision was a nullity, leave may be given; on the other hand, if the point would require fresh evidence, and particularly if a legal representative had deliberately chosen not to rely on the point at the tribunal, leave will be refused. The inexperience of a party's advocate is not a sufficient reason, nor is the importance of the point to be raised; and nor is the confused state of the relevant law at the time of the tribunal hearing: *Harrison v Boots the Chemist Ltd*, EAT/1098/97. The somewhat less restrictive approach adopted by the EAT in *Barber v Thames Television plc* [1991] ICR 253 should not now be relied on.

22.16 Fresh evidence

A party will not be permitted to adduce factual matters before the EAT which it chose not to put before the employment tribunal (*Bingham v Hobourn Engineering Ltd* [1992] IRLR 298). The test for the admission of fresh evidence is as set out in *Wileman v Minilec Engineering Ltd* [1988] ICR 318, adopting the established formula applied in appeals from the civil courts to the Court of Appeal, as set out in *Ladd v Marshall* [1954] 1 WLR 1489. The three requirements, which are cumulative, are set out in the *Practice Direction, para 8.2,* as follows

'8.2.1 the evidence could not have been obtained with reasonable diligence for use at the Employment Tribunal hearing;

8.2.2 it is relevant and would probably have had an important influence on the hearing;

8.2.3 it is apparently credible.'

The procedure is that the evidence sought to be admitted should be put before the EAT in the form of one or more sworn affidavits or witness statements with a signed Statement of Truth, normally together with the Notice of Appeal or Respondent's Answer (*Practice Direction, para 8*). If leave to admit the evidence is given, the case will usually be remitted for a rehearing. The same test of admissibility applies to fresh evidence as a ground of review of the tribunal's decision under *rule 34(3)(d)* of the *ET Rules.*

22.17 Errors of law and perversity

The EAT can only overturn the decision of an employment tribunal if the tribunal can be shown to have erred in law. Where an appeal succeeds, the point of law on which the tribunal erred should be identified in the EAT's decision (*British Gas plc v McCarrick* [1991] IRLR 305). The error of law may be an express misdirection or it may be inferred from the fact that the conclusion of the tribunal was one which no reasonable employment tribunal, properly directing itself, could have reached; in other words, that the decision of the tribunal was perverse. Even if the EAT would have come to a different conclusion, it must not interfere with the decision of the employment tribunal unless an error of law is identified (*Retarded Children's Aid Society Ltd v Day* [1978] ICR 437). Misunderstanding or misapplication of the facts does not of itself amount to an error of law unless the tribunal proceeds upon a basis contrary to the undisputed or indisputable facts (*British Telecommunications plc v Sheridan* [1990] IRLR 27).

Unless an employment tribunal has misdirected itself in law, neither the EAT nor the Court of Appeal should disturb its decision on the fairness of a dismissal under *ERA 1996, s 98(4)* on the ground of perversity unless the decision under appeal was not a permissible option (*Piggott Bros & Co Ltd v Jackson* [1992] ICR 85). In *Piggott*, the Court of Appeal held (at 92) that in concluding that the decision under appeal was not a permissible option, the EAT will almost always have to be able to identify a finding of fact which was unsupported by *any* evidence or a clear self-misdirection in law by the employment tribunal (see also *Hough v Leyland DAF Ltd* [1991] ICR 696, in which the EAT pointed out that a finding of fact was not perverse merely because the tribunal had reached it by way of inference and without any direct evidence). However, the EAT in *East*

Berkshire Health Authority v Matadeen [1992] ICR 723 held that a conclusion drawn from unassailable facts could be attacked as perverse. The approach adopted in *Piggott* represented a departure from the test of whether one could say of a decision, 'My goodness, that was certainly wrong', formulated in *Neale v Hereford and Worcester County Council* [1986] ICR 471. Subsequently, Mummery J has categorised perversity as including a decision that on the evidence before the tribunal is 'irrational', 'offends reason', 'must be wrong', 'is not a permissible option', or 'flies in the face of properly informed logic': *Stewart v Cleveland Guest (Engineering) Ltd* [1994] IRLR 440 at 443. The Court of Appeal has given further guidance as to the correct approach to deciding perversity appeals in *Yeboah v Crofton* [2002] EWCA Civ 794, [2002] IRLR 634:

> 'Such an appeal ought only to succeed where an overwhelming case is made out that the employment tribunal reached a decision which no reasonable tribunal, on a proper appreciation of the evidence and the law, would have reached.' (Mummery LJ at para 93).

The court also warned of the danger of turning an appeal on a point of law into a rehearing of parts of the evidence.

A failure by an employment tribunal to give adequate (or any) reasons for a judgment or order, or a substantive finding in the proceedings, may amount to an error of law rendering the decision liable to be set aside on appeal (as to the adequacy of reasons, see the citation from *Meek v Birmingham District Council* [1987] IRLR 250 in 21.63 above and the cases cited there). The EAT may also, if inadequacy of reasons is given as a ground of appeal, remit the case to the tribunal for it to clarify or amplify its reasons, prior to hearing the substantive appeal: see 22.11 above.

22.18 A separate category of error of law is a failure by the tribunal to afford the parties a fair hearing, whether through some serious procedural failure or through bias, or where the circumstances have created a real danger, or a perception, of bias. Cases falling within this general categorisation would include, for instance, those where relevant evidence was unjustifiably excluded or a party was prevented from putting forward part of his or her case, or the tribunal failed to invite the parties to deal with a particular point before deciding it or relied on a point of law not canvassed at the hearing; the Chairman or a member sitting despite a potential conflict of interest; and inappropriate conduct by the Chairman or a member in the course of the hearing (see generally as to these potential grounds 22.12 above). Excessive delay in delivering judgment following the hearing is not of itself an error of law, and will only provide grounds for appeal if in the circumstances there is a real risk that the appellant was deprived of the right to a fair trial: *Bangs v Connex South Eastern Ltd* [2005] EWCA Civ 14, [2005] IRLR 389.

22.19 **Disposition of the appeal**

There are essentially two possible outcomes if an appeal is successful. Either the matter may be remitted (to the original tribunal or a fresh tribunal), to be considered further in the light of the EAT's judgment or for a complete rehearing; or the EAT may substitute a decision in favour of the appellant, eg that the dismissal was fair, rather than unfair. In cases not involving a specific point of statutory construction, which may necessarily determine the result, the EAT is careful not to usurp the tribunal's role as arbiter of facts. It will therefore not substitute a decision unless there is only one decision that a tribunal correctly directing itself in law could have reached (*Morgan v Electrolux Ltd* [1991] ICR 369).

Where an error of law is identified, the EAT must allow the appeal unless the conclusion of the employment tribunal was plainly and unarguably right, notwithstanding the misdirection (*Dobie v Burns International Security Services (UK) Ltd* [1984] ICR 812). Equally, unless the decision was plainly and arguably *wrong*, the EAT should not substitute a different decision but should remit the matter for rehearing; see below. The same principles apply to appeals from interlocutory orders or judgments as to appeals from final judgments (*Adams and Raynor v West Sussex County Council* [1990] ICR 546). The EAT in *Sinclair Roche & Temperley v Heard* [2004] IRLR 763 gave guidance as to when a case should or should not be remitted to the same tribunal.

If a case is ordered by the EAT to be remitted (to the same or a fresh tribunal) following a successful appeal, the tribunal which hears the case on remission only has jurisdiction by reason of the remission. It cannot, therefore, even with the agreement of the parties, reopen or deal with issues other than those remitted for its consideration. This conclusion was reached by the Court of Appeal in *Aparau v Iceland Frozen Foods Ltd (No 2)* [2000] IRLR 196, where (in a constructive dismissal case) the issue remitted to the tribunal was whether a term had been incorporated in the contract of employment. This was then conceded, with the consequence that the constructive dismissal claim was made out, but the employers persuaded the tribunal to deal with the fairness of the dismissal, which had not been disputed at the original hearing. The Court of Appeal held that its decision on that point was a nullity. These principles would not, however, prevent the tribunal from dealing with a point affecting its jurisdiction to deal with the matters remitted.

22.20 Where both the parties to an application to an employment tribunal agree that the decision of the tribunal was in error and reach a proposed settlement, the parties may not themselves reverse that decision but must refer the matter to the EAT. The parties should draw up a formal order and request the EAT to accept it, ratify it and make it part of the order of the Appeal Tribunal. However, unless the consent order is part of an overall settlement of the proceedings (in which case the EAT will usually agree to the order without hearing full argument – see *British Publishing Co Ltd v Fraser* [1987] ICR 517) a consent order will not be granted unless the EAT is persuaded by argument at a hearing that the decision appealed against was wrong in law; and if the effect of the proposed order is to remit the case to the tribunal for further consideration, the EAT will give a reasoned judgment on the appeal: *J Sainsbury plc v Moger* [1994] ICR 800. (See also *Practice Direction, para 15.3*.)

22.21 **OTHER POWERS OF THE APPEAL TRIBUNAL**

For the purpose of disposing of an appeal, the EAT may exercise any powers of the body or officer from whom the appeal was brought (*ETA 1996, s 35*). It also has the same general powers as the High Court in relation to production of documents, attendance of witnesses, contempt of court and other matters incidental to its jurisdiction (*ETA 1996, s 29(2)*). As to the EAT's powers to make restricted reporting orders, see 22.13, and 21.18 and 21.19, above.

The *2002 Practice Direction* introduced new procedures regarding the transcription of judgments of the EAT, and these have been retained in the 2004 revision. Unless the decision is reserved or the EAT so directs as part of its judgment given orally, or, in the case of a preliminary hearing, the judgment is given in the absence of the appellant, a transcript will only be drawn up if requested by one or both parties within 14 days (*Practice Direction, para 18*). Transcripts of judgments given after full hearings are posted on the EAT website. The *Practice Direction* gives more detailed information about the arrangements for handing down reserved judgments and any consequential applications (for permission to appeal, for costs etc). In Scotland the practice is that judgments are normally reserved.

22.22   COSTS

The powers of the EAT to award costs were significantly recast by the *2004 Amendment Rules.* The provisions are now contained in *rules 34–34D.* The scheme of the new provisions follows that of the *ET Rules* in providing separately for the costs incurred by unrepresented parties, and in introducing wasted costs orders (but only in appeals instituted on or after 1 October 2004).

A party may apply for a costs order at any stage during the appeal, or within 14 days of the date the order finally disposing of the proceedings is sent to the parties *(rule 34(4))*. However, unless the paying party is given an opportunity at the hearing to make representations against the making of an order, it can only be made after an opportunity to make such representations has been afforded by notice to the party concerned *(rule 34(5))*. The representations will normally be dealt with on the papers, but if it is considered appropriate, they can be referred for a further hearing. Written reasons must be given for a costs order if a party so requests within 21 days of the date of the order *(rule 34(6))*.

The principal circumstances in which a costs order can be made against a party are that the paying party has brought proceedings that were unnecessary, improper, vexatious or misconceived, or that there has been unreasonable delay or other unreasonable conduct by the paying party. Without prejudice to the general application of those criteria, costs may be ordered in three specific cases, namely where the paying party has not complied with a direction of the EAT, or has amended a Notice of Appeal, Respondent's Answer or similar document, or has caused an adjournment of the proceedings *(rule 34A(1), (2))*. The most important of these conditions is the bringing of an appeal which is misconceived (ie has no reasonable prospect of success), and unreasonable conduct by a respondent, which may include resisting an appeal on misconceived grounds. In practice, however, there will rarely be grounds for an award of costs under either head, since misconceived appeals are likely to be screened out, at latest at the preliminary hearing, before the respondent to the appeal needs to incur significant costs in resisting it; and it will only very rarely be the case that it can be said that defending a decision of a tribunal against an appeal is as such unreasonable conduct.

There are limits on the making of an order for costs against the respondent to an appeal who has not had an answer accepted by the EAT: in such a case *rule 34(3)* allows for a costs order (in favour of, as well as against, the respondent) in relation to his or her conduct of any part of the proceedings in which he or she has taken part; the necessary limitation implied by this is that if the respondent takes no part in the appeal, there is no power to award costs against that respondent (compare in relation to costs in the employment tribunal *Sutton v The Ranch Ltd* [2006] ICR 1170).

Further guidance on when the bringing or pursuit of an appeal can be categorised as unreasonable is given in *Iron and Steel Trades Confederation v ASW Ltd (in liquidation)* [2004] IRLR 926. An example of a case where costs were awarded against a successful appellant because the proceedings were 'unnecessary' is *British School of Motoring v Fowler*, EAT/0059/06, where the appellant employer had failed for no good reason to present its response in time, and successfully appealed against the tribunal's refusal to review a decision that it should not be permitted to take part in the proceedings. The appeal was 'unnecessary' because the appellant could and should have submitted its response in good time.

The fact that the preconditions for an award of costs exist does not *entitle* the receiving party to an order. The EAT has a discretion whether to award costs. If it decides to do so, it has a further discretion to take into account the means of the paying party (*rules 34A(3), 34B(2)*). The powers available subject to this discretion are to award a sum determined by the EAT itself by summary assessment, or an agreed sum, or to award costs subject to a detailed assessment by the High Court or taxation by the Auditor of the Court of Session (*rule 34B(1)*).

22.23 There are separate rules as to the amount that may be awarded where the receiving party is a litigant in person or party litigant, equivalent to the powers of the tribunal to make a preparation time order. It should however be noted that, in contrast to the position in employment tribunals, the general power to award costs is not confined to an award to legally represented parties; any party who does not fall within the definition of a litigant in person or (in Scottish appeals) a party litigant is eligible for an award of costs in accordance with *rule 34B*. A litigant in person is defined to include a company or corporation which is acting without a legal representative, or a solicitor, barrister, advocate or other person qualified to conduct litigation, who is appearing for him or herself (*rule 34D(7)*). This does not cover a company represented by an in-house lawyer, or an individual represented by a non-legal representative, including a relative or friend, or a professional consultant who is not a lawyer; the latter are therefore eligible for ordinary costs orders under *rule 34A*.

The conditions for an award of costs in favour of a litigant in person are the same as for any other party. The costs recoverable may not exceed two thirds of the costs that would be payable if the party had had legal representation (with an exception for any disbursements, such as a payment for legal advice, which may be recovered in full if a full award is made and the payment was of a reasonable amount) (*rule 34D(2)*). Within this overall restriction, the costs recoverable are payments for advice, and for expert assistance in assessing the claim for costs, and expenses incurred in the proceedings (eg for photocopying or travel to the hearing), and compensation for time spent preparing the case and attending the hearing (*rule 34D(3)*). In relation to this head, the rate of payment will either be the amount the party can prove he or she has lost (eg lost wages) or a flat rate of £27 an hour (from 6 April 2007; this will increase in the same way as the equivalent rate for preparation time orders: see 21.72 for further details) (*rule 34D(4), (5)*). The amount awarded will be subject to the EAT's assessment of what was a reasonable and proportionate amount of time to spend preparing for the hearing.

22.24 The powers to make wasted costs orders and the procedures to be followed are set out in new *rule 34C*. This is for all practical purposes in exactly the same terms, with necessary modifications of terminology, as *rule 48* of the *ET Rules*, and reference should therefore be made to the discussion of that *Rule* at 21.73 above for details.

22.25 **REVIEW**

The EAT may review any order made by it on the grounds that:

(*a*) the order was wrongly made as the result of an error on the part of the EAT or its staff;

(*b*)   a party did not receive proper notice of the proceedings leading to the order; or

(*c*)   the interests of justice require such review.

(*EAT Rules, rule 33.*)

The circumstances in which the review procedure can be invoked are rare (see *Stannard & Co (1969) Ltd v Wilson* [1983] ICR 86). In *Jenkins v P & O European Ferries Ltd* [1991] ICR 652, the EAT on its own initiative was prepared to review its earlier decision on the ground that it recognised that there was a fundamental error of law in that decision, but in *Blockleys plc v Miller* [1992] ICR 749 it appeared to prefer a narrower approach. In *Digital Equipment Co Ltd v Clements (No 2)* [1997] ICR 237 the EAT reviewed, and reversed, its initial decision in circumstances where that decision had been given in ignorance of another decision on essentially the same point of law; the review thus enabled the EAT to resolve the law on a point on which there would otherwise have been conflicting authorities. There is as yet no reported decision of the EAT on whether its powers of review in the interests of justice have been enlarged by the addition to the *EAT Rules* of the Overriding Objective, but this would be consistent with the view taken by the EAT of the equivalent change in the *ET Rules* (see e g *Williams v Ferrosan Ltd* [2004] IRLR 607).

Where the EAT has not formally drawn up and issued the order embodying its decision, it has a wider power of review based on its inherent jurisdiction as a superior court of record, and need not confine itself to the *Blockleys* approach: *Bass Leisure Ltd v Thomas* [1994] IRLR 104 at 108–109. Exceptionally, the EAT may reach a provisional decision, notify the parties accordingly and invite further submissions before pronouncing final judgment; this was done in *Rubenstein v McGloughlin* [1996] IRLR 557.

22.26   FURTHER APPEALS

A further appeal may be taken to the Court of Appeal (or in Scotland, the Court of Session) on a point of law, but only with permission from the EAT or the Court of Appeal or Court of Session (*ETA 1996, s 37(1), (2)*). Permission should be sought initially from the EAT. If the EAT refuses permission, an application may be made to the Court of Appeal. The principles to be applied upon such an application were considered by the Court of Session in *Campbell v Dunoon and Cowal Housing Association Ltd* [1992] IRLR 528. The restrictions on 'second appeals' to the Court of Appeal introduced by the *Access to Justice Act 1999, s 55* do not apply to appeals from the EAT, and the introduction of more restrictive criteria in relation to other areas does not appear significantly to have affected the Court of Appeal's practice in granting permission to appeal in employment cases. The Leggatt Report included a recommendation that the more restrictive test in *s 55* be applied to appeals from the EAT. This, if implemented, could result in a significant reduction in the number of appeals heard by the Court of Appeal in employment cases, and arguably greater uncertainty owing to conflicting reported decisions of the EAT, but no steps to implement it have yet been put forward. It should nevertheless be emphasised that compelling reasons are needed to persuade the Court to give permission to appeal.

In appeals from the EAT, the Court of Appeal is a second-tier appellate court and is concerned with whether the decision of the employment tribunal was right, not with whether the EAT was right (*Hennessy v Craigmyle & Co Ltd* [1986] ICR 461; *Campion v Hamworthy Engineering Ltd* [1987] ICR 966). However, the Court of Appeal itself has recently expressed serious reservations about the correctness of this approach (*Gover v Propertycare Ltd* [2006] EWCA Civ 286, per Buxton, Lloyd and Richards LJJ), and it may fairly be regarded as arguable in the light of these reservations. Where the EAT has allowed an appeal from the original decision of the tribunal, the focus of a further appeal to the Court of Appeal is inevitably directed more to whether there was sufficient basis for that decision.

The time limit for lodging an appeal to the Court of Appeal with the permission of the EAT is 14 days from the date on which the order or judgment of the EAT was drawn up, unless the EAT gives a longer period; if permission is refused, an appellant's notice must be served on the court, by way of application for permission to appeal, within the same 14-day period (*Civil Procedure Rules 1998, r 52.3*).

A further appeal lies to the House of Lords if the Court of Appeal or the House of Lords gives permission. A number of special rules govern House of Lords appeals.

In Scotland, the appeal from the EAT is to the Inner House of the Court of Session, and thence to the House of Lords. In Northern Ireland, appeals lie directly from the tribunal to the Northern Ireland Court of Appeal, and thence to the House of Lords. Leave to appeal to the Inner House and the House of Lords is required.

22.27 **ISSUES OF EU LAW**

Where the outcome of an application or an appeal turns on a question of European Community law, the answer to which is unclear, the tribunal or court may, or if it is a court of final appeal must, refer the question to the European Court of Justice under *art 234* of the *Treaty of Rome* (formerly *art 177*). The parties to the application or appeal can request a reference in these circumstances. In *Enderby v Frenchay Health Authority and Secretary of State for Health* [1991] ICR 382, the EAT suggested that national appeals procedures ought normally to be exhausted before a reference was made, but the Court of Appeal ([1992] IRLR 15) decided to refer the case to the ECJ before making any order itself. A number of cases have been referred to the ECJ by employment tribunals, both before and after *Enderby*: see e g *Neath v Hugh Steeper Ltd*, C-152/91 [1994] 1 All ER 929, *Smith v Avdel Systems Ltd*, C-408/92 [1995] ICR 596, *P v S and Cornwall County Council*, C-13/94 [1996] IRLR 347 and *Robinson-Steele v R D Retail Services Ltd*, C-131/04 [2006] IRLR 386. The tribunal, and the EAT, should not refer a matter to the ECJ unless its ruling is 'necessary' for the determination of the case; if the case may turn on questions of fact, these should first be determined by the tribunal. However, in *Attridge Law v Coleman* [2007] IRLR 88, the EAT held, rejecting an appeal against an order of the tribunal referring an issue to the ECJ at a preliminary stage in the case, that a reference could be 'necessary' even if the point would not be determinative of the case, if the ruling sought was necessary to do justice. The *ET Regulations 1996* contained provisions to prevent an employment tribunal from referring a case to the ECJ until any appeal against its order for reference has been determined, but this restriction was omitted in the *2004 Regulations.*

23   Engagement of Employees

Cross-reference. See REFERENCES (36) for employment made conditional on references.

23.1   ADVERTISING

When advertising for prospective employees, an employer must be careful not to infringe the provisions of the *Sex Discrimination Act 1975*, the *Race Relations Act 1976* (see 14.12 DISCRIMINATION AND EQUAL OPPORTUNITIES – III), the *Disability Discrimination Act 1995* (see 10.18 DISABILITY DISCRIMINATION), the *Employment Equality (Religion or Belief) Regulations 2003* or the *Employment Equality (Sexual Orientation) Regulations 2003*. An advertisement indicating that a job is open only to persons who are or who are not union members will lead to a conclusive presumption that work has been refused on union membership grounds and thus, in general, unlawfully (see 23.2(D) below, and the reference there cited).

23.2   INTERVIEWING AND SELECTION

An employer may use any interviewing and selection procedures he wishes, provided that they are not discriminatory within the meaning of the *Sex Discrimination Act 1975*, the *Race Relations Act 1976*, the *Disability Discrimination Act 1995*), the *Employment Equality (Religion or Belief) Regulations 2003* or the *Employment Equality (Sexual Orientation) Regulations 2003* (see DISABILITY DISCRIMINATION (10), DISCRIMINATION AND EQUAL OPPORTUNITIES – I, II, III (12, 13, 14)). In arranging an interview for a disabled person, it may be necessary for the employer to make reasonable adjustments to enable that person to attend. He is free to select whomsoever he chooses, subject to the following:

(*a*)   the restrictions on the employment of CHILDREN AND YOUNG PERSONS (4);

(*b*)   the restrictions on the employment of FOREIGN EMPLOYEES (26);

(*c*)   the restriction on excluding a person from any office, profession, occupation or employment by reason of a spent conviction (see EMPLOYEE'S PAST CRIMINAL CONVICTIONS (19));

(*d*)   the bar on refusing a person employment because he is or is not a trade union member (see TRADE UNIONS – I (50)).

23.3   ENGAGEMENT

An employer should inform a new employee of the terms and conditions under which he is to work and his commencement date and time. This should be done by letter (if not by a formal signed agreement). He is obliged by law to give the employee written particulars of those terms and conditions within two months of the commencement of his employment (see 8.4 CONTRACT OF EMPLOYMENT).

The *actual day* on which employment commences has importance under the rules for computing continuity of employment (see 7.3 CONTINUOUS EMPLOYMENT) irrespective of whether the employee actually performs any duties on that day (see *General of the Salvation Army v Dewsbury* [1984] ICR 498).

23.4 **EMPLOYMENT AGENCIES**

For the law regulating employment agencies, and the status of those recruited through such agencies, see 47.2 TEMPORARY AND SEASONAL EMPLOYEES.

23.5 **WITHDRAWAL OF OFFERS OF EMPLOYMENT**

Once an offer of employment has been made and accepted, a valid contract exists even though the date when the employee is due to start work may be delayed. If in these circumstances the employer retracts the offer or terminates the contract prior to the actual commencement of work, the employee will not be without a remedy. There are three remedies which may potentially be available to the employee depending on the circumstances. First, there may be a claim for wrongful dismissal (see WRONGFUL DISMISSAL (58)). That claim may be brought before the employment tribunal or the county court. Second, if the reason for the dismissal is an inadmissible reason, there may be a claim of unfair dismissal. No period of qualifying employment is necessary when the reason for dismissal is an inadmissible reason (see 54.3 UNFAIR DISMISSAL – II). Third, it may be possible to bring a claim alleging that the dismissal was discriminatory on grounds of sex or race or disability or religion or belief or sexual orientation (see DISCRIMINATION AND EQUAL OPPORTUNITIES – I, II, III (12, 13, 14), DISABILITY DISCRIMINATION (10)). The authority for these propositions is *Sarker v South Tees Acute Hospitals NHS Trust* [1997] IRLR 328.

24   Equal Pay

Cross-reference. See DISCRIMINATION AND EQUAL OPPORTUNITIES – I (12) for the rules forbidding discrimination on grounds of sex in matters other than the terms and conditions of employment and also 13.4 DISCRIMINATION AND EQUAL OPPORTUNITIES – II.

24.1   Since the coming into force on 29 December 1975 of the *Equal Pay Act 1970* (*'EqPA 1970'*), women have been able to claim equal pay with men. The accession of Great Britain to the *Treaty of Rome* on 1 January 1973 also affected women's rights to equal pay since *art 141* (formerly *art 119*) provides that 'Each Member State shall during the first stage ensure and subsequently maintain the application of the principle that men and women should receive equal pay for equal work'. *Article 141* and *Directive No 75/117* ('the *Equal Pay Directive*') provide a European underpinning of the domestic rights to equal pay (see below 24.3).

24.2   **THE LEGISLATIVE FRAMEWORK**

Domestic legislation

The *EqPA 1970* provides the domestic legal framework for the elimination of discrimination between the sexes in the terms of their contracts of employment.

The *EqPA 1970* has been amended by subsequent legislation including: the *Sex Discrimination Act 1975* ('*SDA 1975*'), the *Equal Pay (Amendment) Regulations 1983 (SI 1983/1794)* ('the *1983 EqP Regulations*'), the *Sex Discrimination Act 1986*, the *Pensions Act 1995* ('*PA 1995*'), the *Armed Forces Act 1996*, the *Employment Rights (Dispute Resolution) Act 1998*, the *Equal Pay Act 1970 (Amendment) Regulations 2003 (SI 2003/1656)* and the *Equal Pay (Questions and Replies) Order 2003 (SI 2003/722)*. Further provision relating to equal pay is made by the *Social Security Act 1989*, the *Sex Discrimination and Equal Pay (Remedies) Regulations 1993 (SI 1993/2798)*, the *Armed Forces Act 1996*, the *Sex Discrimination (Gender Reassignment) Regulations 1999 (SI 1999/1102)* ('the *Gender Reassignment Regulations*') and the *Employment Equality (Sex Discrimination) Regulations 2005*.

The *1983 EqP Regulations* were introduced in an attempt to bring the United Kingdom into conformity with EU requirements. They introduced for the first time the right to claim equal pay for work of equal value in circumstances in which the jobs of the claimant and the comparator have not been rated as equivalent under a job-evaluation scheme.

The *EqPA 1970* and the examples set out below are framed with reference to women but they are to be read as applying equally to men.

Part-time workers. Discrimination against part-time workers was for some time (and is still to a certain extent) dealt with by way of the protection against indirect sex discrimination in the *SDA 1975* (see 12.7 DISCRIMINATION AND EQUAL OPPORTUNITIES – I). However, since 1 July 2000, part-time workers have been protected in relation to pay and other detriments by the *Part-time Workers (Prevention of Less Favourable Treatment) Regulations 2000 (SI 2000/1551)* ('*Part-time Workers Regulations*') (LESS FAVOURABLE TREATMENT OF PART-TIME WORKERS (32); see also 24.18 below).

Transsexuals. In 1996, the European Court of Justice decided that discrimination against transsexual employees constituted sex discrimination (*P v S and Cornwall County Council: C-13/94* [1996] IRLR 347). The *Sex Discrimination (Gender Reassignment) Regulations 1999 (SI 1999/1102)* inserted into the *SDA 1975* provisions relating to discrimination against those who intend to undergo, are undergoing or have undergone a gender reassignment (see, in particular *SDA 1975, ss 2A* and *4*). Matters relating to pay discrimination are ordinarily excluded from the scope of *SDA 1975* by *s 4(4)–(6)* (see 13.10 DISCRIMINATION AND EQUAL OPPORTUNITIES II). However, those subsections are specifically disapplied in relation to transsexuals by *sub-s 4(8)*. It is important to note that although a right not to suffer pay discrimination is very closely related to a right to equal pay, there are significant differences. For instance, transsexuals do not rely upon an equality clause to underpin their right to receive the same pay as their comparators. The rules relating to claims by transsexuals are set out at 24.13 below.

Code of Practice. Note that a code of practice prepared by the EOC came into force on 26 March 1997 and is admissible as evidence in *EqPA 1970* and *Sex Discrimination Act 1975 ('SDA 1975')* proceedings: see the re-issued *Equal Opportunities Commission Code of Practice on Equal Pay (2003)*.

24.3   EU Provisions

The foundation of the right to equal pay in EU law is contained in *art 141* of the *Treaty of Rome* (the *'Treaty'*) which provides:

'Each Member State shall ensure that the principle of equal pay for male and female workers for equal work or work of equal value is applied.

For the purposes of this Article, "pay" means the ordinary basic or minimum wage or salary and any other consideration, whether in cash or in kind, which the worker receives, directly or indirectly, in respect of his employment from his employer.

Equal pay without discrimination based on sex means:

(*a*)   that pay for the same work at piece rates shall be calculated on the basis of the same unit of measurement;

(*b*)   that pay for work at time rates shall be the same for the same job.'

Article 141 and *Directive No 75/117* ('the *Equal Pay Directive*') provide a European underpinning to domestic rights to equal pay. These provisions have been relied upon as an aid to construction of domestic law and, increasingly, as a basis for disapplying inconsistent provisions of domestic legislation (cf *Scullard v Knowles* [1996] IRLR 344 and below). However, it is not possible in all circumstances to enforce *art 141* claims directly before the domestic courts (see EUROPEAN COMMUNITY LAW (25)).

The Council of the EU has also adopted *Directive 86/378/EEC* on the progressive implementation of the principle of equal treatment for men and women in occupational social security schemes, including pension schemes. *Directive 96/96/EC* (which came into effect on 1 July 1997) amended *Directive 86/378/EC* to take account of the ECJ's decision in *Barber v Guardian Royal Exchange Assurance Group* [1990] ICR 616 (see 24.27 below).

Directive No 76/207 (the *'Equal Treatment Directive'*) provides by *art 5.1*:

'Application of the principle of equal treatment with regard to working conditions, including the conditions governing dismissal, means that men and women shall be guaranteed the same conditions without discrimination on grounds of sex.'

See also 12.2 DISCRIMINATION AND EQUAL OPPORTUNITIES – I and generally EUROPEAN COMMUNITY LAW (25).

The meaning of 'work' in EU law

Article 141 enshrines the right to equal pay for equal work. The appropriate definition of 'work' for this purpose has proven to be wider than might initially be imagined. In *Davies v Neath Port Talbot County Borough Council* [1999] ICR 1132, EAT, the issue was whether attending a union-organised course for elected health and safety representatives constituted 'work' for the purposes of *art 141*. Relying on an analogy with the ECJ cases of *Botel (Case C-360/90* [1992] ECR I-3589 and *Lewark (Case C-457/93)* [1996] ECR I-243, the EAT determined that:

'Attending a training course organised by a recognised trade union is still related to the employment relationship and is safeguarding staff interests which is ultimately beneficial to the employer.'

The effect of this finding was that the complainant, who ordinarily worked part-time, was able to claim full-time pay as she was attending the course on a full-time basis. Reliance on *art 141* enabled the EAT to avoid applying *TULRCA 1992, s 169* which would otherwise have required her to be paid her normal part-time pay. *Section 169* has had an indirectly discriminatory effect and was thus contrary to *art 141* and was not applied.

The meaning of 'pay' in EU law

It is now well established that 'pay' in *art 141* is to be given a broad meaning. In *Barber v Guardian Royal Exchange Assurance Group: C-262/88* [1990] ICR 616, it was held that a benefit is in the nature of pay if the worker is entitled to receive it from his employer by reason of the existence of the employment relationship. Thus, it included benefits paid by the employer upon compulsory redundancy, even where they consisted of pension payments made after the termination of employment. It did not matter that the payment was received only indirectly from the employer (eg through the trustees of a pension scheme). The ECJ reached a similar decision in *Kuratorium Für Dialyse und Nierentransplantation eV v Lewark* [1996] IRLR 637, ruling that compensation paid pursuant to a German statute for loss of earnings whilst attending training sessions for participants in staff councils is pay. (Contrast, however, *Manor Bakeries Ltd v Nazir* [1996] IRLR 604, EAT: employee entitled to paid time off pursuant to a collective agreement to attend a trade union conference. The paid time-off was not 'pay' for the purposes of *art 141* as attending the conference was not 'work' and pay is remuneration for work.) In *Barber*, the ECJ also observed that pensions from both contributory and non-contributory schemes were 'pay' within *art 141*. (See also *Bilka-Kaufhaus GmbH v Weber von Hartz: 170/84* [1987] ICR 110.) The ECJ, unusually, specifically limited the effect of its decision by stating that it could not be relied upon to claim entitlement to a pension prior to 17 May 1990 (the date of the decision). This matter is considered in greater detail at 24.15 *et seq* below.

A long-standing controversy over whether compensation for unfair dismissal is pay for the purposes of *art 141* was resolved by the decision of the ECJ in *R v Secretary of State for Employment, ex p Seymour-Smith and Perez: C-167/97* [1999] ICR 447. The ECJ decided that the basic and compensatory awards (for which see 55.7 and 55.10 UNFAIR DISMISSAL – III) are deferred pay to which the worker is entitled (ultimately) by reason of his employment. The fact that the compensation consisted of a judicial award did not invalidate that conclusion. However, neither an order for reinstatement nor for re-engagement (for which see 55.2 and 55.3 UNFAIR DISMISSAL – III) is 'pay'. The ECJ does not seem to have considered the status of the monetary award made in cases where re-employment is ordered.

Pay includes sums paid in lieu of notice and also covers payments made by the Secretary of State on the insolvency of an employer in respect of the employee's contractual entitlement to notice (*Clark v Secretary of State for Employment* [1997] ICR 64, CA).

Further, 'pay' within *art 141* includes a statutory redundancy payment or an *ex gratia* payment upon redundancy (see *McKechnie v UBM Building Supplies (Southern) Ltd* [1991] ICR 710 for entitlement to equal statutory and contractual redundancy payments).

In *Rinner-Kühn v FWW Spezial-Gebäudereinigung GmbH & Co KG: 171/88* [1989] IRLR 493, 'pay' was held to include the statutory sick pay which an employee was entitled to receive from her employer; see also *EC Commission v Belgium: C-173/91* [1993] IRLR 404.

The ECJ has, in recent times, been expanding the definition of 'pay' to cover contractual terms which relate to the calculation of entitlements or to requirements imposed as prerequisites to the granting of entitlements. In *Hill v Revenue Comrs and Department of Finance: C-243/95* [1999] ICR 48, ECJ, the ECJ considered the employment conditions of certain Irish civil servants. Salary was dependent on length of service. Employees who worked half-time earned half of the full-time rate. However, when they moved to full-time employment their pay did not double. Instead, they were placed on the full-time pay spine at a level that gave them credit for only half of the actual period that they had worked for their employer. In other words, their length of service was pro-rated to reflect their previous part-time status. The ECJ decided that the method adopted by the employer for converting part-timers to full-time status constituted 'pay' within *art 141* and that it was, in the particular circumstances, discriminatory and not justified. However, terms with a less direct connection to pay rates may be treated differently. In *Gerster v Freistadt Bayern (C-1/95)* [1998] ICR 327, Bavarian civil service regulations, which required that periods of part-time service should (depending on the number of hours worked) either be entirely or partly discounted when assessing eligibility for consideration for promotion, were held not to offend *art 141*. The ECJ distinguished *Nimz (C-148/89)* [1991] IRLR 222, in which a complainant had successfully challenged a similar rule which gave part-time workers only partial credit for their periods of service. In *Nimz* promotion was practically automatic on completion of the relevant period of service. As the provision in *Gerster* was only concerned with eligibility for promotion, the connection to pay was insufficiently direct to bring the case within the scope of *art 141* which was not concerned with inequalities relating to 'access to career advancement'. The ECJ opined, however, that the rule was potentially contrary to the *Equal Treatment Directive (EEC/76/207)*. It was left to the national court to decide whether or not the respondent's contention that the requirement was intended to ensure that employees had sufficient experience (and was therefore objectively justified) was made out.

The dividing line between what constitutes 'pay' and what is a 'working condition' that falls to be considered under the *Equal Treatment Directive* has been addressed by the ECJ in a number of cases. *Kording v Senator für Finanzen (C-100/95)* [1997] IRLR 710 concerned German legislation which exempted employees with sufficient length of service from having to take certain examinations. Part-time workers had to work a longer period which was pro-rated to the proportion of full-time hours that they worked. The ECJ considered that the provision was not 'pay', but that it was nevertheless indirectly discriminatory (though capable of objective justification). Similarly, the provision of subsidised nursery places to female staff only is to be regarded as a 'working condition' within the meaning of the *Equal Treatment Directive* rather than 'pay' within *art 141*: *Lommers v Minister van Landbouw Natuurbeheer en Visserij Case C-476/99* [2002] IRLR 430. The ECJ held that the fact that the fixing of certain working conditions may have pecuniary consequences is not sufficient to bring such conditions within the scope of *art 141*, which is a provision based on the close connection between the nature of the work done and the amount of pay. However, the ECJ went on to hold that measures giving a specific advantage to women with a view to eliminating inequality (such as providing nursery places for working mothers only) was not contrary to the *Equal Treatment Directive*, in particular, where male single parents were given places on the same conditions. (See also *Steinicke v Bundesanstalt für Arbeit: C-77/02* [2003] IRLR 892: schemes of membership that may have pecuniary consequences not 'pay', though they were indirectly discriminatory contrary to the *Equal Treatment Directive*).

24.4   THE RIGHT TO EQUAL PAY IN THE EQUAL PAY ACT 1970

The right to equal pay applies:

(a)   to women employed in an establishment in Great Britain whether they are British or not and regardless of the law governing their contract of employment (*EqPA 1970, s 1(1)*, *(11)*);

(b)   to men as well as women (*EqPA 1970, s 1(13)*).

'Employed' in equal pay legislation is defined as 'employed under a contract of service or of apprenticeship or a contract personally to execute any work or labour' (*EqPA 1970, s 1(6)(a)*). The definition therefore includes contracts personally to perform services (cf 17.3 EMPLOYEE, SELF-EMPLOYED OR WORKER?).

Office-holders. Statutory office-holders were formerly excluded from the provisions of the *Act*. However, with effect from 1 October 2005, office-holders (with the exception of holders of political office) are expressly brought within the scope of the *Act: s 1 (6A)-(6C) EqPA 1970* as amended by *reg 35* of the *Employment Equality (Sex Discrimination) Regulations 2005*. *Section 1 (6A)* of the *Act* extends the right to equal pay to those holding an office or post to which persons are appointed to discharge functions personally under the direction of another person, and in respect of which they are entitled to remuneration, or any office or post to which appointments are made by (or on the recommendation of or subject to the approval of) a Minister of the Crown, a government department, the National Assembly for Wales or any part of the Scottish Administration. This amendment followed the decision of the Northern Ireland Court of Appeal in *Perceval-Price v Department of Economic Development* [2000] IRLR 380, holding that an identically worded provision in the *Equal Pay Act (Northern Ireland) 1970* was incompatible with *art 141* as the right to equal pay conferred by the *EC Treaty* extends to all 'workers' as defined by the ECJ in *Lawrie-Blum v Land Baden-Wurttemberg: 66/85* [1986] ECR 2121 (a case about *art 48* of the *EC Treaty*). In *Lawrie-Blum*, the ECJ identified the 'essential feature' of an employment relationship as being that 'for a certain period of time a person performs

543

services for and under the direction of another person in return for which he receives remuneration'. The NICA concluded that the tribunal chairmen fell within that definition despite their status as statutory office-holders, and disapplied the exclusion.

Employees posted abroad. Employment in an establishment in Great Britain formerly required that the employee should not work 'wholly or mainly outside Great Britain'. However, the *Equal Opportunities (Employment Legislation) (Territorial Limits) Regulations 1999 (SI 1999/3163)* remove the words 'or mainly' from the relevant provision. The effect is that the legislation now covers workers posted abroad. The *Regulations* came into effect on 16 December 1999. With effect from 1 October 2005, employment is regarded as being at an establishment in Great Britain if (a) the employee does her work wholly or partly in Great Britain, or (b) if she does her work wholly outside Great Britain but her employer has a place of business at an establishment in Great Britain, her work is for the purposes of the business carried on at that establishment, and she is ordinarily resident in Great Britain at the time when she applies for or is offered the employment, or at any time during the course of the employment: *SDA 1975, s 10* as amended by the *Employment Equality (Sex Discrimination) Regulations 2005, reg 11(2)* .

(See generally 13.15 DISCRIMINATION AND EQUAL OPPORTUNITIES – II.)

Women suspended on maternity grounds. Women whose pay is reduced when they are suspended on maternity grounds may not seek to challenge the reduction by bringing claims under *EqPA 1970. ERA 1996, ss 66–70* represent a complete code governing the contractual entitlements of such women (*British Airways (European Operations at Gatwick) Ltd v Moore* [2000] IRLR 296, EAT). However, there are circumstances in which women absent on maternity leave may bring challenges in relation to pay and benefits paid to them while on maternity leave: see further below 24.14 and 24.21.

Members of the armed forces. Members of the armed forces were formerly expressly excluded from the scope of the *Act.* However, *EqPA 1970* was amended by the *Armed Forces Act 1996, s 24* to allow claims to be brought. This was brought into force on 1 October 1997 by the *Armed Forces Act 1996 (Commencement No 3 and Transitional Provisions) Order 1997 (SI 1997/2164)* and the *Equal Pay (Complaints to Employment Tribunals) (Armed Forces) Regulations 1997 (SI 1997/2162)*.

24.5   **The equality clause**

The *EqPA 1970* does not straightforwardly prohibit direct and indirect discrimination in matters of contractual entitlement. Instead, it adopts a rather oblique and artificial approach. It implies an 'equality clause' into any contract of employment that does not already include one (*EqPA 1970, s 1(1)*). The clause modifies the woman's contract in any situation where she is engaged:

(*a*)   on *like work* to a man (see below 24.6); or

(*b*)   on *work rated as equivalent* to work done by a man (see below 24.7); or

(*c*)   on work of *equal value* to that done by a man (see below 24.8)

and her employer does not seek to, or fails to, establish that the difference between the woman's contract and the man's is genuinely due to a material factor which is not the difference of sex (*EqPA 1970, s 1(3)*) (see 24.11 below).

An equality clause operates so that:

(i)   if any term of a woman's contract is, or becomes, less favourable to the woman than a term of a similar kind in a contract under which a man is employed, that term in the woman's contract is modified to become as favourable as the corresponding term in the man's contract; or

(ii)   if at any time a woman's contract does not include a beneficial term which is in a man's contract, the woman's contract will be modified so as to include that term.

(*EqPA 1970, s 1(2)(a)*, (*b*), (*c*).)

Thus, for example, if a man and a woman are engaged on like work and the man is paid £500 per week for that work, but the woman only £400, the equality clause will operate so as to entitle the woman to £500 per week. Also, if the man's contract contains a clause which entitles him to be paid during absence from work due to sickness, but the woman's contract contains no such clause, the woman's contract will be deemed by law to include such a clause. (For appropriate comparators see below 24.9.)

The equality clause applies to all terms and conditions of employment and not only to pay (e g *Sun Alliance and London Insurance Ltd v Dudman* [1978] ICR 551, relating to a contractual term granting a mortgage interest allowance). The provisions of the *SDA 1975* and the *EqPA 1970* contain an interlocking but mutually exclusive prohibition on discrimination on grounds of sex: *s 6(6) SDA 1975* and *Peake v Automotive Products Ltd* [1977] ICR 480. The *EqPA 1970* applies where the contract regulates the provision of benefits in the form of money: *Grundy v British Airways* (EAT/0676/04RN) (unreported, judgment delivered 19 August 2005). It is not necessary for the payment in question to be expressly provided for in the contract. Provided that the contract 'regulates' the payment it will fall under *EqPA 1970* and not under the *SDA 1975*: thus a so-called 'discretionary' bonus scheme will fall to be considered under *EqPA 1970* if the discretionary element of it is in fact only as to the amount paid in any one year and not as to whether or not the employee is entitled to a bonus at all: *Hoyland v Asda Stores Ltd* [2006] IRLR 468. In that case the Court of Session expounded a 'but for' test in order to determine whether or not the payment fell to be considered under *EqPA 1970* or the *SDA 1975*, ruling that if the payment would not have been made 'but for' the existence of the contract of employment, then *EqPA 1970* applied. It is questionable whether this ruling will prove to be generally applicable, since on a 'but for' test, almost any monetary gift or benefit bestowed on an employee *qua* employee by an employer *qua* employer must be regarded as only having been paid because of the contract of employment, even if wholly discretionary.

It is however clear that the equality clause cannot operate so as to give the complainant a more favourable term than that contained in her comparator's contract. Where, for instance, qualified female employees are paid at the same rate as male trainees, the employee cannot rely on the clause to secure a premium over the rate paid to a trainee selected as a comparator (see *Enderby v Frenchay Health Authority (No 2)* [2000] ICR 612, CA).

In *Hayward v Cammell Laird Shipbuilders Ltd* [1988] ICR 464, the House of Lords rejected the argument that the 'total remuneration package' must be taken into account when making the comparison between a woman's pay and a man's. What must be compared is each distinct provision of the contract dealing with pay and benefits in kind. The applicant was thus entitled to the same rate of basic pay and overtime pay as her male comparator even if she was more favourably treated in other respects, in this case paid meal breaks, additional holidays and better sickness benefits. However, it can be difficult to determine what constitutes a distinct provision or term of the contract. In *Degnan v Redcar & Cleveland Borough Council* [2005] EWCA Civ 726, [2005] IRLR 615, the Court of Appeal held that attendance allowances paid to male employees were all part of a single term of the contract together with their hourly rate and fixed bonuses for the purposes of the comparison of the terms in the woman's contracts. This approach was held to be consistent with *Hayward* in that it did not lump together different terms but instead looked at the reality of the situation by classifying all these payments which related to the same subject-matter as coming under the same contractual term, being 'provision for monetary payment for the performance of the contract by employees during normal working hours'. All monetary payments received by the men should be aggregated and divided by the number of hours in the working week to give an hourly rate which, if lower for women than men, should be increased for women to eliminate the difference. This approach, of treating different payments as different elements of a single contractual term, does sit uneasily with the prohibition on taking a 'swings and roundabouts' approach in *Hayward*. This approach is also difficult to reconcile with the ECJ's decision in *Elsner-Lakeberg v Land Nordrehein-Westfalen* [2005] IRLR 209 in which it held that, in order to determine whether the principle of equal pay is being complied with, genuine transparency permitting an effective review is assured only if that principle applies to each aspect of remuneration, excluding any general overall assessment of the consideration paid. In that case, the ECJ held that it was necessary for there to be separate comparison in respect of the pay for regular hours and the pay for additional hours. *Redcar (No 1)* reconciled this case by analysing the attendance allowance as pay for the same subject-matter, being remuneration for normal working hours. The difficulty post-*Redcar No 1* will be in deciding when it is permissible to aggregate different elements of remuneration which relate to the same subject-matter and when this is impermissible 'lumping together' of different contractual terms relating to different subject-matter.

It was suggested in *Hayward* that the 'material factor' defence under *EqPA 1970, s 1(3)* (see 24.11 below) might be available to an employer who could show that the unfavourable character of the term in the woman's contract was due to the more favourable character of the other terms. Broadly, the same approach is taken by the ECJ in relation to claims based upon *art 141* (see *Barber v Guardian Royal Exchange Assurance Group: C-262/88* [1990] ICR 616 and *Jamstalldhetsombudsmannen v Orebro Lans Lansdsting: C-236/98* [2001] ICR 249, ECJ).

Note, however, that once it has been established that there is a 'genuine material factor' (see 24.11 below) that justifies a difference in pay the equality clause will not operate so as to 'correct' a particular term of an employee's contract simply because that employee is, by the date of the hearing, a member of a group of women who are being paid less than a group of men: see *Armstrong v Newcastle Upon Tyne NHS Hospital Trust* [2005] EWCA Civ 1608, [2006] IRLR 124.

For indirect discrimination under the *EqPA 1970*, see below 24.10.

24.6   Like work

A woman is regarded as employed on like work with men if, but only if, her work and theirs is of the same or of a broadly similar nature and the differences (if any) between the things she does and the things they do are not of practical importance in relation to the performance of her contract of employment. In comparing her work with theirs, the nature and extent of the differences will be considered, as will the frequency or otherwise with which such differences occur in practice (*EqPA 1970, s 1(4)*).

Thus, although the job descriptions of male and female employees or their written job specifications may be different, if the differences in their duties are of no practical importance, the women will be considered to be employed on like work with the men. The question of what is or is not a difference of practical importance will always be one of fact and degree depending upon the particular circumstances of the case. If, for example, male guillotine operators in a paper mill are required once in two weeks to lift reams of paper whereas women are not, the lifting is purely incidental to their main employment and is not of practical importance. Accordingly, it is not a difference which would prevent the women's right to equal pay.

The EAT has stated in *Capper Pass Ltd v Lawton* [1977] ICR 83, that 'in deciding whether the work done by a woman and the work done by a man is "like work" within the meaning of *s 1(4)* of the *EqPA 1970* the employment tribunal has to make a broad judgment. The intention is that the employment tribunal should not be required to undertake too minute an examination, or be constrained to find that work is not like work merely because of insubstantial differences. In order to be like work within the *Act*'s definition the work need not be of the same nature; it need only be broadly similar.' In that case, a cook in the directors' dining room was held to be engaged on like work with the assistant chefs of the company's factory canteen. The fact that women do their work at a different time of the day from men may not prevent them from claiming that they are engaged upon like work (*Dugdale v Kraft Foods Ltd* [1977] ICR 48; *National Coal Board v Sherwin* [1978] ICR 700; contrast with *Thomas v National Coal Board* [1987] ICR 757 in which the EAT held that a male canteen worker on permanent night-shift was not employed on like work with female day-shift canteen workers).

However, the duties actually performed are not the only considerations to be taken into account in deciding whether a woman is engaged on like work. In *Eaton Ltd v Nuttall* [1977] ICR 272, the EAT held that 'In considering whether there is like work, though the most important point is what the man does and what the woman does, the circumstances in which they do it should not be disregarded. One of the circumstances properly to be taken into account is the degree of responsibility involved in carrying out the job.'

Article 141 uses the term 'same work' rather than 'like work' (see above 24.3). However, the case law on the European provision suggests that a tribunal should not simply confine its consideration to the duties actually performed. In *Angestelltenbetriebsrat der Wiener Gebeitskrankenkasse v Wiener Gebeitskrankenkasse* [1999] IRLR 804, the ECJ considered a case concerning psychotherapists. Whilst the psychotherapists were all engaged in 'seemingly identical activities', they could be divided into those who had had training in psychology to graduate level and those who had been trained as general practitioners. The graduate psychologists, the majority of whom were women, were paid less. The ECJ decided that training and qualifications could be matters which were relevant to the determination whether the work and/or job were the same and were not merely relevant to a possible material factor defence. It should be noted, however, that although the ECJ purported to proceed on the basis that the applicants and their comparators were engaged in the same activity, it also observed that the former general practitioners, who were better qualified, could be called on to perform 'different tasks or duties'. It is not a case, therefore, where it could be said that the applicants and their comparators necessarily performed identical tasks. The ECJ seems to have had a broader notion in mind when it referred to the 'activity' in which both groups were engaged. In *Brunnhofer v Bank der Osterreichischen Postsparkasse AG: C-381/99* [2001] IRLR 571, ECJ, the ECJ followed *Angestelltenbetriebsrat*, to draw the conclusion that the existence of an identical collective agreement governing the employment of two employees was not in itself sufficient to show that they performed the same work, or work of equal value.

If a woman's work is more onerous or more responsible than a man's, she may not be considered to be engaged on like work, even though less well paid (*Waddington v Leicester Council for Voluntary Service* [1977] ICR 266). However, she may now be able to obtain equal pay on the basis described in *Murphy v Bord Telecom Eireann* [1988] ICR 445 (see also 24.8 below).

24.7 Work rated as equivalent

A woman may claim equivalence with a man even though she is not engaged on like work, if a job-evaluation study has been carried out in respect of his work and hers, and her job has been rated as equivalent to the man's in terms of the demand made on a worker under various headings (ie effort, skill, decision), or would have been rated as equivalent but for the evaluation being made on a system setting different values for men and women on the same demand under any heading (*EqPA 1970, s 1(5)*).

The principal methods of job evaluation are set out in ACAS Advisory Booklet No 1, 'Job evaluation'. These methods are known as job ranking, paired comparison, job classification, points assessment and factor comparison. See also the EOC's Equal Pay Review Kit (and Guidance Notes) at http://www.eoc.org.uk/EOCeng/EOCcs/advice/equalpay.asp. For the purposes of *s 1(5)*, the comparison of jobs must be done by reference to the same job-evaluation study (*KD Paterson v London Borough of Islington*, EAT, 23 April 2004, unreported). A job evaluation must be carried out on an objective basis. The principles were set out in *Eaton Ltd v Nuttall* (see above 24.6). The job of each worker covered by the study must be valued in terms of the demand made on the worker under the various headings (eg effort, skill, responsibility) in the study (*Bromley v H & J Quick Ltd* [1988] ICR 623). Thus, it will not suffice simply to compare 'whole jobs'. The assessment should be qualitative, not quantitative – matters such as a difference in the number of hours worked go to the defence of material factor (see 24.11 below), not to evaluation of the job (*Leverton v Clwyd County Council* [1989] ICR 33). Whilst the study as a whole must be objective, it is permissible for it to contain certain subjective elements, so long as they are not themselves inadvertently discriminatory. It is for the employer to explain how any job-evaluation study worked and what was taken into account at each stage (see also *Rummler v Dato-Druck GmbH* [1987] ICR 774). The validity of a job-evaluation study which is not impartial or which is not conducted on a scientific basis may be challenged if reliance is placed on such a study to claim or to resist a claim for equal pay.

In determining whether two jobs have been given an equal value by a job-evaluation study, it is necessary to look at the full results of the study, including the allocation to grade or scale at the end of the evaluation process. Thus, in *Springboard Sunderland Trust v Robson* [1992] ICR 554, the EAT held that the applicant and a male comparator were employed on work rated as equivalent because each of their scores resulted in an allocation of the same grade, albeit their scores in a job-evaluation study had been different.

If no job-evaluation study has been carried out, there is no legal requirement for an employer to conduct one. However, once a job-evaluation study has been undertaken and has resulted in a conclusion that the job of a woman is of equal value to that of a man, the woman may claim equal pay, despite the fact that the employers may not have implemented the scheme (*O'Brien v Sim-Chem Ltd* [1980] ICR 573). Where a valid job-evaluation study has been carried out and a woman's job has been rated as slightly lower than her male comparator, it is not permissible for a tribunal, by reliance on extraneous expert evidence, to find that the difference is insignificant: *Home Office v Bailey* [2005] IRLR 757. But, for work to be rated as equivalent under the *EqPA 1970* there must be a *completed* job-evaluation study, and there is no complete job-evaluation study unless and until the parties who have agreed to the carrying out of the study have accepted its validity (*Arnold v Beecham Group Ltd* [1982] ICR 744).

24.8   Work of equal value

Where a woman is employed on work which is not like work or work which has been rated as equivalent to that of a male comparator, she may claim equal pay with a man if her work is of equal value to his, in terms of the demands made on her, eg under such headings as effort, skill and decision (*EqPA 1970, s 1(2)(c)*). Relying upon EU law, she may also claim equal pay where she is doing work of *greater* value (*Murphy v Bord Telecom Eireann (Case 157/86)* [1988] ICR 445 and *Redcar & Cleveland Borough Council v Bainbridge* [2007] IRLR 91, EAT). Employees of one sex may use *s 1(2)(c)* to claim equal pay with those of the other sex doing a quite different job. Using this provision, a female cook employed as a canteen assistant succeeded in a claim for equal pay with male skilled tradesmen (see *Hayward v Cammell Laird Shipbuilders Ltd* [1988] ICR 464). The fact that one man is being paid the same as a woman for doing like work to hers is no longer a bar to the woman claiming equal pay with another man doing a different job of equal value to hers (see *Pickstone*). In that case, the House of Lords held that the construction of *EqPA 1970* which enabled them to achieve this result was consistent with EU law. (For the procedure to be adopted on claims based on work of equal value see 24.22 below.)

A woman will not be able to succeed in an equal value claim if a valid job-evaluation study has concluded that she and her male comparator do work which is *not* of equal value (*EqPA 1970, s 2A(2)*). It was suggested by the EAT in *Dibro Ltd v Hore* [1990] ICR 370 at 377 that a job-evaluation study carried out at the request of the employer after the institution of proceedings which evaluates the jobs of the applicants and the comparator may be relied upon for the purposes of *s 2A(2)* (see also *Avon County Council v Foxall* [1989] ICR 407). In *McAuley v Eastern Health and Social Services Board* [1991] IRLR 467, the Northern Ireland Court of Appeal held that an employment tribunal had correctly concluded that the work of the applicants and that of their comparator could not be regarded as having been given different values under a job-evaluation study so as to preclude their equal value claim, in circumstances in which the job-evaluation study was prepared in respect of health boards in Great Britain and its results applied in Northern Ireland only through a policy of maintaining parity of remuneration with Great Britain.

24.9   Persons with whom an employee may claim equivalence

The man with whom a woman seeks to compare herself is known as the 'comparator'. In contrast to cases brought under *SDA 1975*, the orthodox position is that an employee cannot use a 'hypothetical' comparator. In other words, she cannot base a claim on an allegation that if a man were employed, for instance, on like work, he would be paid more (cf 12.5 DISCRIMINATION AND

EQUAL OPPORTUNITIES – 1). A woman absent on maternity leave cannot rely on an actual male comparator to bring a claim under the *EqPA 1970* since there is no appropriate comparator for a pregnant woman. In a claim for a pay increase received before the beginning of maternity leave to be taken into consideration when calculating statutory maternity pay, it is appropriate to disapply those parts of *s 1* of the *EqPA 1970* which impose a requirement for a male comparator: *Alabaster v Barclays Bank plc and Secretary of State for Social Security* [2005] EWCA Civ 508, [2005] IRLR 576. A claim for unlawful deduction from wages under *s 13 ERA 1996* would not comply with the EC principles of equality, equivalence and effectiveness in these circumstances. In *Allonby v Accrington and Rossendale College: C-256/01* [2004] IRLR 224, the ECJ was asked to decide whether a male comparator with the right to join a pension scheme was necessary in a claim brought by part-time employees who had been dismissed and re-engaged as self-employed contractors to lecture at their former college. The complainant could not identify a male comparator who, like herself, was not an employee. The question was whether the statutory requirement that, in order to join the pension scheme, a teacher be employed under a contract of employment, should, if found to have a differential impact on women, be set aside. The ECJ set out the orthodox position that a worker cannot rely on *art 141* in order to claim pay to which she could be entitled if she belonged to the other sex unless, now or in the past, there were workers in the undertaking concerned who perform or performed comparable work. However, where national legislation was the cause of the differential impact (the statutory requirement to be an employee in order to join the pension scheme being a provision of domestic law) there is no need to point to a comparator: it will be sufficient to show a statistical disadvantage. In the absence of objective justification for the national legislation, the requirement to be an employee should be set aside where it is shown that, among the teachers who are workers within *art 141* and fulfil all other conditions for membership of the pension scheme, a much lower percentage of women than men is able to fulfil that condition. In short, where it is the national legislation that is the sole source of the different treatment, there is no need to identify a particular comparator, as the comparison can be done by examining the position nationally using statistics.

Where a comparator is required, selection of an appropriate comparator is a matter for the employee (*Ainsworth v Glass Tubes and Components Ltd* [1977] ICR 347). She may select more than one individual, although tribunals have been warned by the House of Lords to be alert to prevent abuse of the procedure by applicants who 'cast their net over too wide a spread of comparators' (*Leverton v Clwyd County Council* [1989] ICR 33). The comparator must be in the 'same employment' (*EqPA 1970, s 1(6)*). This concept is explained in greater detail below.

The *Act* does not expressly require that the comparator should be in any way a 'typical' of his class (although the Court of Appeal in *North Yorkshire County Council v Ratcliffe* [1994] IRLR 342 considered that such a requirement might be thought to be implicit in the *EqPA 1970*. The issue was not considered by the House of Lords when it heard the subsequent appeal.)

There is nothing to prevent a complainant from selecting as a comparator a male employee whom she believes is engaged in work of a lesser value than her own. However, if she is successful in her claim she will only receive the pay awarded to her comparator. A complainant cannot use the *Act* to establish a salary differential in her favour (*Enderby v Frenchay Health Authority (No 2)* [2000] ICR 612, CA).

It is now well-established that there is no requirement for contemporaneous employment between the complainant and her chosen comparator. Lindsay P, giving the judgment of the EAT in *Kells v Pilkington plc* [2002] IRLR 693, held that the effect of the ECJ's decision in *Macarthys Ltd v Smith* was that there was no requirement for contemporaneous employment and once the need for that has gone, there was, on the face of things, no specified period under the *EqPA 1970* within which comparisons can or cannot be made. The six-year period of limitation in *s 2(5), EqPA 1970* (see 24.19 below) is concerned with the period of default which can be compensated for, rather than the period during which comparison is acceptable. Although considerable difficulties may arise in claims based on comparisons with predecessors or successors from many years ago, these are difficulties of fact and evidence and not difficulties of law: see *Kells v Pilkington* at paras 8–15.

EqPA 1970, s 1(6) allows a complainant to compare herself with others in the 'same employment' which is defined as follows:

' ... men shall be treated as in the same employment with a woman if they are men employed by her employer or any associated employer at the same establishment or establishments in Great Britain which include that one and at which common terms and conditions of employment are observed either generally or for employees of the relevant classes.'

Thus, where an employer operates more than one establishment a woman employed at one of them may compare herself with a man employed at another provided that 'common terms and conditions' apply to the relevant classes of employees at both establishments (*EqPA 1970, s 1(6)*).

Challenges made under European Community law to the requirement that comparators be in the 'same employment' have resulted in a 'single source' test for equal pay comparisons: *Lawrence v Regent Office Care Ltd* [2003] ICR 1092. The ECJ held that although there was nothing in the wording of *art 141* to suggest that its application was limited to situations in which men and women worked for the same employer, where, as in *Lawrence,* the differences in pay of workers of different sex performing equal work or work of equal value could not be attributable to a single source, such as a collective agreement, there was no one body responsible for the inequality which could restore equal treatment. Such a situation did not come within the scope of *art 141* and the work and pay of the different sets of workers could not be compared on the basis of *art 141*. See also *South Ayrshire Council v Morton* [2001] IRLR 28. This approach has been confirmed by the ECJ in *Allonby v Accrington and Rossendale College: C-256/01* [2004] IRLR 224, ECJ. In *Allonby*, the applicant worked as a lecturer in the respondent college, but was a self-employed worker, hired by the college through an agency holding a database of lecturers. She claimed comparison with a named, salaried teacher at the college. The issue was whether working in the same establishment or service, for the benefit of a single employer, but under different contracts with different employers, was nevertheless working in the same employment for the purposes of *art 141*. The Court of Appeal ([2001] EWCA Civ 529, [2001] IRLR 364) referred the issue to the ECJ. The ECJ ruled that, except where the terms of employment arise directly from legislative provisions or collective agreements, a woman is not working in the 'same employment' as a man for the purposes of *art 141* where she is not employed by the same person as the man. This is so even though she may provide the same services as the man and for the benefit of the man's employer. The 'single source' test was considered by the Court of Appeal in *Robertson v Department for Environment, Food and Rural Affairs* [2005] EWCA Civ 138, [2005] ICR 750. In that case, the complainant and her comparator were both civil servants in common employment (all employed by the Crown) this was neither a necessary nor sufficient basis for an equal pay comparison. The bare fact of common employment is not enough: it is necessary in all circumstances to consider whether the terms and conditions were traceable to one source. The relevant body is the one which is responsible for the inequality and which could restore equal treatment. This will often but not always be the same employer. As responsibility for negotiating civil servant pay had been delegated down to the individual departments, an inter-department comparison did not involve comparison of pay from a single source and was not permissible. See also *Armstrong v Newcastle upon Tyne NHS Hospital Trust* [2005] EWCA Civ 1608, [2006] IRLR 124: in that case, although both sets of employees were employed by the same NHS Trust, which had endeavoured to a certain extent to harmonise terms and conditions across the hospitals for which it was responsible, the Court of Appeal held that the tribunal was right to find that the Trust had not assumed responsibility for the setting of terms and conditions of employment across all its hospitals and that therefore female employees in one hospital could not compare themselves with male employees in another. It remains to be seen what approach will be taken to employers hiving off their pay negotiations for different departments to different decision-making bodies or companies in order to avoid a 'single source' for cross-departmental comparison.

For the purpose of comparison where 'common terms and conditions' apply to the relevant class of employees, the relevant class is the class of employee which includes the comparator. It is not necessary that there should be common terms and conditions applied at both establishments to the complainant's class of employee (*North Yorkshire County Council v Ratcliffe* [1994] IRLR 342, CA). In order to establish that terms are 'common', the employee does not need to go so far as to show that they are identical. Terms which are 'broadly similar' will suffice (*British Coal Corpn v Smith* [1996] IRLR 404). In *Leverton v Clwyd County Council* [1989] ICR 33, the Court of Appeal suggested that a case where two establishments were covered by the same collective agreement would be a simple example of the sort of circumstances in which terms and conditions could be said to be 'common'. The fact that the particular term to which the woman purports to be entitled is common to those employed in the comparator's class at both establishments does not, of itself, mean that the requirements of *s 1(6)* are satisfied.

If two or more employers are associated (ie if one is a company of which the other directly or indirectly has control or if both are companies of which a third person directly or indirectly has control; see 7.9 CONTINUOUS EMPLOYMENT) a woman working in a factory owned by Company A can claim equivalence with a man working in another factory owned by an associated company, Company B, provided that the same terms and conditions of employment apply either generally or for employees of the class of which the comparator is a member (*EqPA 1970, s 1(6)(c)*). Because the statutory language requires one of the allegedly associated employers to be a 'company', it appeared to exclude the possibility of two public sector employers being associated. However, in *Scullard v Knowles* [1996] IRLR 344 the EAT held that such an exclusion would be contrary to *art 141* and should be treated as 'displaced' by the broader European approach.

24.10   Indirect Discrimination

The model adopted by the *EqPA 1970*, in which an employee compares her terms and conditions with those of a specific comparator, works well enough in relation to cases of direct discrimination. Indeed, it favours the complainant in that, once she has established that her male colleague enjoys different and more favourable terms, the employer must then establish that the difference is due to a material factor which is not a difference in sex. In effect, to use the language of *SDA 1975*, the employee need only establish that she has been 'less favourably treated'. She need not show that the less favourable treatment is 'on the ground of her sex'; it is for the employer to show that the difference in sex is not the ground of the difference in treatment (see 24.11 below). However, the *EqPA 1970* is much less obviously suited to dealing with cases of indirect discrimination. (For the concept of indirect discrimination see 12.7 DISCRIMINATION AND EQUAL OPPORTUNITIES – I.)

In cases of alleged indirect discrimination the employee's terms will often be identical to those of her male comparator. In such cases, the issue will centre instead on a benefit which, whilst theoretically available to the complainant, is contingent on her satisfying a condition or requirement which fewer women than men are able to satisfy. For instance, the contracts of both employees may provide that they are entitled to join their employer's pension scheme only if they work full-time. It is difficult to apply the equality clause to such cases. What is needed in order to eliminate the discrimination is not the addition to the complainant's contract of a clause already present in her comparator's, but the replacement of the term common to both contracts with one which does not have a discriminatory effect. For this reason, there was initially some doubt as to whether or not *EqPA 1970* prohibited indirect discrimination at all although it has now long been established that indirect discrimination is contrary to both UK and European law (*Jenkins v Kingsgate (Clothing Productions) Ltd* [1981] ICR 715, EAT, *Bilka-Kaufhaus GmbH v Weber von Hartz: C-170/84* [1986] ICR 110, ECJ).

EU law may be relied upon in an equal pay claim in order to overcome indirect discrimination (*Bilka-Kaufhaus* and *Rinner-Kühn*, above). If pay criteria are adopted which apparently tend to favour men, it is for the employer to justify those criteria. Such criteria would include ones less favourable to part-time workers (see, e g *Arbeiterwohlfahrt der Stadt Berlin eV v Botel: C-360/90* [1992] IRLR 423 and *Vroege v NCIV Instituut voor Volkshuisvesting BV: C-57/93* [1995] ICR 635 and generally 24.18 below).

What remains unclear, despite extensive consideration in the domestic and ECJ case law, is precisely what constitutes a prima facie case of indirect discrimination so as to require justification by the employer and, in particular, how a complainant must prove a prima facie case of indirect discrimination. When it made its reference to the ECJ in *R v Secretary of State for Employment, ex p Seymour-Smith and Perez* [1999] ICR 447, the House of Lords asked for guidance on the circumstances in which a court is entitled to conclude that a provision has an indirectly discriminatory effect. It is well settled that there must be a disparity in the impact of the provision as between men and women; but how does one judge whether the disparity is great enough to allow the court to conclude that there is a discriminatory effect? Will any statistically significant difference do, or is something more required? Characteristically, in giving guidance, the ECJ posed as many questions as it answered.

The ECJ declined to give any precise guidance as to the assessment of disparate impact; it merely observed that the national court must be satisfied that the proportion of women that can comply must be 'considerably smaller' than the proportion of men who can do so. In that case, which was concerned with the upper age limit on the availability of the right to claim unfair dismissal, the particular period with which the court was concerned was 1985, the date on which the former requirement of one year's service was increased to two years. At that point, the proportion of men who could comply with the requirement was 77.4%, whereas the proportion of women who could comply was 68.9%. Since that time the gap has narrowed. The ECJ observed that these figures did not suggest a sufficient disparity of impact to result in a discriminatory effect. However, the Court also observed that a small but persistent difference may result in a finding of discrimination. No guidance was given as to how this new, alternative test will operate. The majority of the House of Lords found the relevant provision to be discriminatory on the basis of this 'alternative' test. They do not appear to have seen it as an alternative, however (see 12.8(B) DISCRIMINATION AND EQUAL OPPORTUNITIES – I). A failure by a tribunal to make a finding that the employer's arrangements have a 'considerable' impact on women prior to concluding that an arrangement is discriminatory will be an error of law: see *Armstrong v Newcastle Upon Tyne NHS Hospital Trust* [2005] EWCA Civ 1608, [2006] IRLR 124.

Further guidance on the proper test to be applied can be gleaned from *Barry v Midland Bank* [1999] ICR 859, HL. Lord Nicholls remarked at 869 that a comparison between the proportions of men and women disadvantaged by a particular provision could *on its own* be misleading, because those proportions would be affected by the comparative sizes of the disadvantaged and non-disadvantaged groups. (For an example of a case where the tribunal was so misled, see *Best v Tyne & Wear Passenger Transport Executive (t/a) Nexus)* [2007] ICR 523, [2006] All ER (D) 362 (Dec), EAT in which the EAT ruled that the tribunal had been wrong to find that a disparate impact had been established in circumstances where the disadvantaged group was mainly male, albeit that there were more women in the disadvantaged group than there were women in the advantaged group – in such circumstances there was no disparate impact on women generally.) In *Barry v Midland Bank*, Lord Nicholls suggested that the better guide would often be found by expressing the proportions of men and women in the disadvantaged groups as a ratio of each other. Moreover, the absolute size of numbers of those disadvantaged remains relevant, since a low ratio may be of little significance in a small company, but of considerable significance in a large company.

The proper approach to statistical evidence was considered in *Secretary of State for Trade and Industry v Rutherford (No 2)*. This concerned a challenge to the upper age limit of 65 for unfair dismissal claims in *ss 109* and *156 ERA 1996* on the basis that it had a disparate impact on men which could not be objectively justified. The tribunal selected a pool consisting of those employees for whom retirement at 65 had 'some real meaning', being those aged 55 to 74. The Court of Appeal ([2004] EWCA Civ 1186, [2005] ICR 119) held that the tribunal had erred in law in concentrating on the 'disadvantaged group'. The Court of Appeal considered that the tribunal should have based its assessment of adverse impact on the statistics for the entire workforce to which the requirement of being under 65 applied and then primarily compared the respective proportions of men and women who could satisfy that requirement. Adopting this approach, the statistics clearly established that the difference in the working population between the proportion of men aged under 65 who could comply and the proportion of women under 65 who could comply was very small indeed. Accordingly, the complainants had failed to establish that there was any indirect sex discrimination against men in the imposition of the upper age limit. The Court of Appeal rejected the submission that the *Burden of Proof Directive* (97/80/EC) (which provides that '... indirect discrimination shall exist where an apparently neutral provision, criterion or practice disadvantages a substantially higher proportion of the members of one sex unless that provision, criterion or practice is appropriate and necessary and can be justified by objective factors unrelated to sex') altered the guidance given in *Seymour-Smith*. The Court observed that the definition of indirect sex discrimination in the *Burden of Proof Directive* describes when indirect discrimination exists and does not prescribe the methodology for assessing the statistical evidence in order to determine whether or not that state of affairs exists. That problem has been left to the courts and tribunals to work out from case to case a satisfactory method for assessing whether or not there is disparate adverse impact in any case. The Court of Appeal's approach to the issue of disparate impact had what might be termed an 'attractive simplicity'. On appeal, the House of Lords ([2006] UKHL 19, [2006] IRLR 551) disagreed with the Court of Appeal's approach, but the judgments of their Lordships are not models of clarity as to the approach that is to be preferred. A majority of their Lordships rejected the classification of the case as one of (even potential) indirect discrimination. They each considered that this was not a case where one could speak coherently of a those who are 'able to satisfy' a rule or requirement and those who are not. Since the rule in question simply imposes a disadvantage on those who stay in employment after the age of 65, there was therefore no comparison to be made since all men and all women over the age of 65 were equally disadvantaged. Lord Nicholls and Lord Walker, however, took a statistical approach as the Court of Appeal had done. However, unlike the Court of Appeal, they focused on the disadvantaged group (ie on the percentage of the workforce over 65), but emphasised how small this group was in comparison to the workforce as a whole. They noted that the proportion of the entire workforce affected by the age limit was 1.2%. 1.4% of the male workforce was affected, and 1% of the female workforce. Lords Walker and Nicholls considered that those proportions were simply too small to indicate a 'substantial' disadvantage to the male workforce.

One difficult question has been the extent to which an employee who is alleging indirect pay discrimination must in every case follow the familiar steps of identifying a provision, criterion or practice, choosing a pool for comparison and establishing a disparate impact. In *Ratcliffe v North Yorkshire County Council* [1995] IRLR 439, the House of Lords refused to draw a distinction between cases of direct and indirect discrimination. In *Staffordshire County Council v Black* [1995] IRLR 234, the EAT decided that where an employee alleged that she had been indirectly discriminated against in relation to matters of pay contrary to *art 141* she must identify a condition or requirement that could be shown to have a disparate impact. In *Enderby v Frenchay Health Authority: C-127/92* [1994] ICR 112, ECJ, another *art 141* case, the ECJ adopted a different approach to the determination of the question of whether there was a *prima facie* discriminatory difference in contractual entitlement. The court decided that the employer could be called upon objectively to justify a difference in pay once the complainant had demonstrated that 'significant statistics disclosed an appreciable difference in pay between two jobs of equal value, one of which was carried out almost exclusively by women and the other predominantly by men'. Whilst this approach focuses on disparities in pay, it plainly does not require the identification of any condition or requirement. In *Nelson v Carillion Services Ltd* [2003] EWCA Civ 544, [2003] IRLR 428, the Court of Appeal rejected the argument that, in a case of alleged indirect discrimination under *s 1(3)* of the *EqPA 1970*, the complainant need only advance a 'credible suggestion' of disproportionate impact. In *Nelson,* Simon Brown LJ decided that tribunals should approach the burden of proof in indirect discrimination cases in the same way irrespective of whether they are brought under *art 141*, under the *SDA* or under the *EqPA 1970*, but did not in terms decide whether this required the complainant to identify a condition or requirement in order to establish a disparate impact.

In *Ministry of Defence v Armstrong* [2004] IRLR 672, the EAT favoured the *Enderby* approach, holding that there is no need for a tribunal always to adopt the formulaic approach of the *SDA 1975* when considering whether there is a disparate impact for the purposes of *EqPA, s 1(3)*. Cox J stressed (para 46) that the question in all cases is 'whether there is a causative link between the applicant's sex and the fact that she is paid less than the true value of her job as reflected in the pay of her named comparator'. Tribunals should 'focus on substance, rather than form and on the result, rather than route taken to arrive at it'.

An attempt to reconcile these competing approaches and to focus on substance rather than form was made by the Court of Appeal in *Bailey v Home Office* [2005] EWCA Civ 327, [2005] IRLR 369. The Court of Appeal held that the tribunal's attempt to fashion a condition or requirement out of the circumstances of the case had led it into error. It rejected the EAT's attempt to distinguish between condition and requirement cases on the one hand and cases which did not have an obvious condition or requirement but which involved a disparity of pay between two groups on the other. In each case, the tribunal is concerned to determine whether what on its face is a gender-neutral practice may be disguising the fact that female employees are being disadvantaged as compared with male employees to an extent that signifies that the disparity is prima facie attributable to a difference of sex. The Court of Appeal held that the statistical approach in *Seymour-Smith* could be used in either case. A common approach to both types of cases has the merit of ensuring that the *Act* is applied consistently to all forms of indirect discrimination. On the facts of *Bailey,* the Court of Appeal held that the tribunal could sufficient disparate impact requiring justification where there was one group of employees which contained a significant number, even though not a clear majority, of female workers whose work is rated as equal to that of another group of employees who are predominantly male and who receive greater pay. The fact that the disadvantaged group contained a significant number of men was not a bar to a claim.

Care must also be taken in selecting the appropriate pools for comparison. In *Abbott v Cheshire & Wirral Partnership NHS Trust* [2006] EWCA Civ 523, [2006] IRLR 546 the Court of Appeal ruled that, while it was for the claimant in the first instance to select a pool for comparison, it was open to the employer to dispute the appropriateness of that pool, and it was for the tribunal to determine the appropriate pool for comparison purposes. In that case, claims were brought by hospital domestic workers (almost entirely female) whose terms and conditions did not include a right to a bonus. They sought to compare themselves to hospital porters (entirely male) whose terms and conditions included a right to a bonus. The employers had argued that the proper comparator pool was not just the porters, but the porters and the catering staff. The catering staff were predominantly female and had also received bonuses. The Court of Appeal ruled that the tribunal had been wrong to reject the employer's argument as to pool: the three groups were plainly comparable. However, the Court of Appeal considered that the right result had been reached in any event because the porters and catering staff together were still 65% male in comparison to the domestic staff who were almost exclusively female: that was sufficient to establish a *prima facie* case of discrimination. The Court of Appeal also rejected an argument (based on *Specialarbejderforbundet i Danmark v Dansk Industri, acting for Royal Copenhagen A/S C-400/93* [1995] IRLR 648, ECJ) that the comparator group (of 37) was too small in order to establish a valid statistical difference in the proportions of male and female workers. The Court of Appeal considered that it would be wrong to set minimum numerical requirements because that would mean that indirect discrimination could never be established for small employers.

The introduction of equal pay questionnaires under the *Equal Pay (Questions and Replies) Order 2003* (see 24.22 below) should, however, assist complainants with gathering appropriate statistics if required to show disparate impact and to enable complainants to pierce the culture of secrecy. The importance of transparency is also emphasised at paras 39–41 of the EOC Code of Practice in Equal Pay (2003).

Justification. Indirect discrimination (and possibly also direct discrimination: see below 24.12) may be justified under EU law. Under domestic law, justification is dealt with by way of the defence of 'material factor' (see below 24.11).

24.11 Defence of 'material factor'

Although a woman may establish that she is engaged on like work, work rated as equivalent to that of a man or work of equal value, she will not be able to claim equivalence with that man if the employer can show that the variation between the woman's contract and the man's contract is genuinely due to a material factor which is not the difference of sex (*EqPA 1970, s 1(3)*). In the case of equality claimed on the basis of *like work* or *work rated as equivalent*, that factor *must* be a material difference between the woman's case and the man's (*EqPA 1970, s 1(3)(a)*). In the case of equality claimed on the basis of *work of equal value*, that factor *may* be a material difference between the woman's case and the man's (*EqPA 1970, s 1(3)(b)*). Thus, in establishing a defence to a claim based on like work or work rated as equivalent, any difference in terms must be justified by a difference between the woman's case and the man's case. In a claim based on work of equal value the defence includes but is not limited to such differences. In *Davies v McCartneys* [1989] ICR 705, the EAT held that a defence was made out under *s 1(3)* despite the fact that some of the matters relied upon, such as circumstances in which the job was performed, were relevant to an assessment of whether the jobs were of equal value. In *Christie v John E Haith Ltd* [2003] IRLR 670, the EAT held that the mere fact that a particular factor may be relevant in the evaluation exercise to determine the question of equal value was not a ground for excluding it as part of a *s 1(3)* defence: the principle in *Davies v McCartneys* was not limited to cases where there had not actually been a determination of equal value taking into account the factors in question. Once an employee has shown that she is engaged on like work, work rated as equivalent to that of a man, or work of equal value to that of a man it is for the employer to prove that he has a defence under *s 1(3)* (*Financial Times Ltd v Byrne (No 2)* [1992] IRLR 163).

The House of Lords in *Rainey v Greater Glasgow Health Board* [1987] ICR 129 resolved earlier doubts upon the matters which may be taken into account in considering a defence of 'material difference' under *s 1(3)*. At 140, Lord Keith stated:

> 'The difference must be "material", which I would construe as meaning "significant and relevant", and it must be between "her case and his". Consideration of a person's case must necessarily involve consideration of all circumstances of that case. These may well go beyond what is not very happily described as "the personal equation", ie the personal qualities by way of skill, experience or training which the individual brings to the job. Some circumstances may on examination prove to be not significant or not relevant, but others may do so, though not relating to the personal qualities of the employee. In particular, where there is no question of intentional sex discrimination whether direct or indirect (and there is none here) a difference which is

connected with economic factors affecting the efficient carrying on of the employer's business or other activity may well be relevant.'

He held that the defence available in *EqPA 1970, s 1(3)* is equivalent in scope to the defence of justification held by the European court in *Bilka-Kaufhaus Gmbh v Weber von Hartz (Case 170/84)* [1987] ICR 110 to be available under *art 141.*

The Court of Appeal in *Cadman v Health and Safety Executive* [2004] EWCA Civ 1317 has reiterated that 'after the event' justification is permissible so that an employer may rely on matters which did not consciously and contemporaneously feature in its decision making at the time. The ECJ adopted the same approach in *Schonheit v Stadt Frankfurt Am Main* [2004] IRLR 983.

The ECJ has held that differences in seniority and length of service are generally material differences (not requiring special justification), at least where the employer is distinguishing between full-time workers (*Handels-Og Kontorfunktionaererernes Forbund i Danmark v Dansk Arbejdsgiverforening ('Danfoss')* [1991] ICR 74. In two subsequent cases, however, the ECJ appeared to doubt the correctness of *Danfoss* or at least have second thoughts as to its general application in cases such as *Nimz v Freie und Hansestadt Hamburg: C-184/89* [1991] ECR 1–297and *Gerster Freistaat v Bayern: C-1/95* [1998] ICR 327. In *Cadman v Health and Safety Executive* the Court of Appeal therefore referred the issue to the ECJ again. The ECJ (Case C-17/05, [2006] IRLR 969 affirmed that, as a general rule, an employer may rely on seniority and length of service as being genuine material differences not requiring special justification or (at least where pay is based on a job evaluation system) evidence that the individual in question has indeed acquired experience during his or her years in service. However, the ECJ made clear that, if the complainant provides evidence capable of giving rise to serious doubts as to whether the criterion of length of service is, in the circumstances, appropriate to attain the legitimate objective of rewarding experience which enables the worker to perform his duties better, then the burden will shift to the employer to justify in detail reliance on the criterion of length of service by proving, as regards the job in question, that length of service goes hand in hand with experience and that experience enables the worker to perform his duties better.

If there is evidence that women are systematically disadvantaged, it will not be acceptable to say simply that pay awards are based on the quality of work – it would be plain from the result that the system was being abusively applied (*Danfoss*). The ECJ in that case also held that where an undertaking applies a system of pay which is totally lacking in transparency, it is for the employer to show that his practice concerning wages is not discriminatory. The Court of Appeal in *Calder v Rowntree Mackintosh Confectionery Ltd* [1993] IRLR 212 apparently accepted that the transparency principle applied in English law, but held that it did not require the employer to explain exactly how a figure for shift premium was achieved. By contrast, in an important decision on City bonus payments, *Barton v Investec Henderson Crosthwaite Securities Ltd* [2003] IRLR 332, the EAT held that the tribunal erred in appearing to condone the lack of transparency in the employer's bonus system on the basis of its 'industrial knowledge' that the City 'bonus culture' was one of secrecy. Although the bonus claim was brought under the *SDA*, the lack of transparency was also relevant to the material factor defence in the *EqPA* claim: see paras 30 and 37.

A relevant material difference for the purposes of *s 1(3)* may relate to circumstances other than the personal qualifications or merits of the male and female workers who are the subject of comparison. The House of Lords disapproved the restrictive approach adopted to *s 1(3)(a)* by the Court of Appeal in *Fletcher v Clay*

Cross (Quarry Services) Ltd [1979] ICR 1, which held that the wording of the section required an analysis of 'the personal equation of the woman as compared with the man, to what appertained to her in her job and to him in his', and considered that extrinsic factors such as market forces could not justify a pay differential.

One 'extrinsic factor' which may, in certain circumstances, justify a difference in pay is the scarcity of suitably qualified employees to fill a particular post. In such circumstances, an employer may be able to justify a resultant difference in pay as consisting of a necessary premium paid to obtain the scarce skills which the more highly paid employee has to offer (*Enderby v Frenchay Health Authority* [1994] ICR 112). In *Ratcliffe v North Yorkshire County Council* (above) the women concerned, who were catering assistants, had been the subject of a job-evaluation exercise. Their job had been rated as equivalent to that of certain other employees engaged in very different jobs and they had received the same pay. Their function was subject to competitive tendering. A competing company had much lower overheads as it paid its (largely female) staff lower wages than those paid by the Council. In order properly to compete, the Council believed it needed to reduce the pay of its own catering assistants. The majority of the tribunal found that whilst there was a material difference between the circumstances of the women and their comparators, namely that the women were employed in functions which had to be subjected to the market, the market itself was not sexually neutral and therefore the material difference was 'due to [a] difference in sex'. The catering sector was regarded as 'women's work' and the pay of those employed by the competing company, was discriminatorily low. The Court of Appeal disagreed ([1994] IRLR 342). It found that the defence was made out on the controversial basis that even if the competing company's pay rates were discriminatory it did not follow that the Council discriminated if it lowered its own rates in order to compete. The decision of the House of Lords in *Ratcliffe* ([1995] IRLR 439) is not a model of clarity. What is clear is that their Lordships found that the tribunal was entitled to reach the view that the defence had not been made out. It does not appear, however, that the basis of the decision was that the pay reduction was tainted by the competing company's discrimination. Lord Slynn noted (ibid, at 442): 'The fact, if it be a fact, that [the competing company] discriminated against women in respect of pay and that the [Council] had to pay no more than [the competing company] in order to be competitive does not however conclude the issue'. Unfortunately, it is not clear, from what follows, what their Lordships considered to be the conclusive factor. 'The basic question is whether the [Council] paid women less than men for work rated as equivalent. The reason they did so is certainly that they had to compete ... The fact, however, is that they did pay women less than men engaged on work rated as equivalent. The employment tribunal found and was entitled to find that the employers had not shown that this was genuinely due to a material difference other than a difference of sex.' The decision does not, in the view of the author, mean that the need to establish or maintain a difference in pay will never found a successful *s 1(3)* defence, merely that the employer had not discharged the burden in the particular case.

The House of Lords held in *Leverton v Clwyd County Council* [1989] ICR 33 that, if there was no significant difference between the hourly rates of pay of the applicant and her male comparator, it would be a legitimate, if not a necessary, inference that the difference between their total salaries was due to, and justified by, the difference in the number of hours worked. This approach was adopted by the ECJ in *Stadt Lengerich v Helmig* [1995] IRLR 216 which held that, *prima facie*, there is unequal treatment wherever the overall pay of full-time employees is higher than that of part-time employees for the same number of hours worked.

The ECJ determined that there was no discrimination where part-time employees only received pay at overtime rates once they had worked the equivalent of a full-time worker's ordinary weekly hours rather than once they had completed the number of hours which they themselves ordinarily worked each week.

The material difference or factor relied upon must be one which exists throughout the period during which there is a difference in pay. For example, where a woman was appointed at a lower rate of pay than existing male employees because of financial constraints, there was no defence to her equal pay claim after those constraints had ceased to exist (*Benveniste v University of Southampton* [1989] ICR 617). 'Red-circling' of existing pension entitlements will not amount to a genuine material factor where, although justifying an initial difference in pension entitlement, it does not provide justification for maintaining the differential over twenty years: *Home Office v Bailey* [2005] IRLR 757. In some cases where an employer has identified that there is an 'equal pay issue' as between two groups of employees, the employer has sought to equalise pay over the course of a number of years, by gradually reducing the pay of the highest-paid group, but in the meantime offering 'pay protection' to existing employees within that group. In *Redcar & Cleveland Borough Council v Bainbridge* [2007] IRLR 91, EAT, the Council sought to justify a four-year 'pay protection' scheme introduced in the aforementioned circumstances on grounds that may broadly described as cost (ie because it would have been too expensive to pay the predominantly female group more) and employee relations (ie in relation to the predominantly male group). However, the EAT approved the Tribunal's finding that the Council had failed to establish the genuine material factor defence because the 'pay protection' policy was irredeemably tainted by sex discrimination: the EAT found that the primary reason why 'pay protection' was afforded to one group of employees was because they were male. Nevertheless, the EAT was keen to stress that this decision did not rule out all such 'pay protection' policies: 'If the employer can show a carefully crafted and costed scheme negotiated for the purpose of cushioning the effects of a drop in pay and without any reason to suppose when it is implemented that this would have discriminatory effects, then it may be that he could demonstrate objective justification. The argument would potentially be reinforced if the costs of retrospectively conferring these additional benefits on the women were significant. But that is not this case; it is an argument for another day' (ibid, [163], *per* Elias P).

Moreover, an initial difference in pay between male and female employees performing the same work cannot be justified on the basis of factors, such as a difference in performance levels, which become known only after the employees concerned have taken up their duties and which can only be assessed during the employment relationship (*Brunnhofer v Bank der Österreichischen Postsparkasse AG: C-381/99* [2001] IRLR 571, ECJ). However, such factors will obviously be relevant when what is complained about is the level of an annual bonus which is based on an assessment of an employee's performance during the year: *Villalba v Merrill Lynch & Co* [2006] IRLR 437. Of course, the material difference must not itself be the result of sex discrimination (*Re Equal Opportunities Commission for Northern Ireland's Application* [1989] IRLR 64) and the rules as to the burden of proof in proving discrimination under the *SDA 1975* apply also to *EqPA 1970*: it is for the employee to prove facts from which the Tribunal could conclude, in the absence of an adequate explanation from the employer, that unlawful discrimination had occurred: see *Villalba* and, generally, DISCRIMINATION AND EQUAL OPPORTUNITIES – III (14).

In equal value claims, differences in contractual entitlements sometimes arise from the complainant and her comparator having been represented by different negotiating bodies. The justificatory force of this factor was considered by the European Court of Justice in *Enderby v Frenchay Health Authority* ([1994] ICR 112). In *Enderby* a woman employed as a speech therapist sought to establish an inequality of pay by comparing herself with two men – a clinical psychologist and a pharmacist. It having been established that the woman was engaged in work of equal value to that of the comparators, the employer sought to justify the difference in pay by showing that the pay rates had resulted from different collective bargaining processes, each of which was free from any sex bias. The ECJ found, in effect, that whilst this explained the difference in pay it did not, where the complainant's job was 'carried out almost exclusively by women and the [comparator's] ... predominantly by men', objectively justify it and in those circumstances the employer did not have a defence.

This 'almost exclusively by women' formula has given rise to a number of difficulties of interpretation. It was subjected to close consideration by the Court of Appeal in *British Road Services Ltd v Loughran* [1997] IRLR 92, CA. Their Lordships made it clear that the *Enderby* decision does not decide that the factor can never justify a difference in pay. They also rejected an argument that the mere fact of there being different bargaining structures would always justify a disparity in pay, provided that the group of employees engaged to perform the complainant's job is not comprised 'almost exclusively' of women. Instead, they decided that if there is a 'significant proportion of women' in the claimant's group, the tribunal is obliged to look carefully at the bargaining structures in order to satisfy itself that there was no discriminatory effect. The EAT in *KD Paterson v London Borough of Islington* (23 April 2004, unreported) considered both those decisions and held that the broader underlying principle of *Enderby* 'must be, and is, that there will be cases in which, having regard to the relative sizes of the proportions of women in the disadvantaged group and men in the advantaged group, a prima facie case of direct sex discrimination in relation to pay will arise that is sufficient to place on to the employer the burden of proving that the pay difference is objectively justifiable' (ibid, para 67). It could not, however, be said, as the tribunal had held, that the *Enderby* principle applied only to cases in which the disadvantaged group was 'almost exclusively' comprised of women. See also *Home Office v A Bailey* (27 July 2004, unreported), EAT.

As to what might constitute a material factor, it is useful to note the approach adopted by the EAT in *Redcar & Cleveland Borough Council v Bainbridge* [2007] IRLR 91, EAT. There the EAT considered whether or not a difference in pay between two groups of employees that resulted principally from the fact that the predominantly male group of employees received an attendance allowance in addition to their salary was objectively justified. The attendance allowance had been introduced in order to improve attendance rates among that group of employees. However, the Tribunal had found that there was no longer a need for this and so the predominantly male group was receiving more cash without any particular additional benefit accruing to the employer. In those circumstances, the EAT approved the Tribunal's decision that the differential factor was not objectively justified. The EAT contrasted this with the position of another group of employees in the same case who were paid more as a result of productivity agreements. The EAT ruled (overturning the decision of the Tribunal) that, since a direct benefit accrued to the employer as a result of this productivity agreement, the additional payments made to the male group as a result of the implementation of this agreement were justified. The EAT found that the Tribunal had erred in finding that the difference in pay that resulted from this agreement was not objectively justified because a similar agreement could have been introduced in relation to the predominantly female group of employees. The EAT ruled that it was not for the Tribunal to make that finding or leap: if the productivity agreement brought a benefit to the employer that was untainted by sex discrimination, then it was an objectively justifiable factor differentiating the position of the predominantly male group from that of the predominantly female group. (Note, though, that such speculation by employers about alternative schemes is relevant to remedies in *EqPA 1970* claims: see below 24.19). However, it is permissible for the Tribunal to consider, when determining whether or not a factor put forward by the employer is a material factor, whether there are other (less discriminatory) ways by which the employer may achieve the same end. This, the EAT observed, is what the principle of proportionality requires. Thus, in the case of the attendance allowance, the EAT pointed out that there were other (equally good) ways of managing attendance which did not involve paying the predominantly male group more than the complainants. The scheme was thus not a proportionate way for the employer to achieve what was otherwise a legitimate aim and the employer's defence in that respect failed.

Note also that there have been *obiter* indications in UK authorities that, in cases where there is a challenge to a pay system which is alleged to be indirectly discriminatory, the clarity and simplicity of the system may amount to a material factor. Put another way, the material factor may consist of the 'administrative convenience' of operating a simple and straightforward system, or equally, the administrative inconvenience of having to alter it (cf Dillon and Hirst LJJ in *R v Secretary of State for Employment, ex p EOC* [1993] ICR 251, CA, and *Barry v Midland Bank plc* [1999] ICR 319, CA; the Court of Appeal's decision in *Barry* was upheld by the House of Lords ([1999] ICR 859), but on a different basis: their Lordships looked at the 'primary object' of the redundancy scheme in considering whether it was discriminatory, rather than reserving such issues to a consideration of whether the scheme could, if it had a disparate impact, be justified).

The question whether an employer may succeed in a defence by relying upon a factor which does not objectively justify the difference in pay between the employee and her comparator remains vexed. There was for some time a marked difference in the approach taken to the scope of the defence at European and domestic levels. The European approach is set out in *Enderby*, above: it requires that a difference in pay be objectively justified. Further, *Enderby* requires, subject to a *de minimis* principle, that the *whole* of the difference must be justified.

The approach taken by the UK courts has been, traditionally, less demanding. The domestic approach has been simply to require the employer to be able to account for the difference by reference to a factor which is material but is not the sex of the employee. Thus, in *Yorkshire Blood Transfusion Service v Plaskitt* [1994] ICR 74, the employer succeeded in establishing a defence in circumstances where the disparity in pay was due to a mistake. Whilst an error may explain an unlawful disparity, it clearly cannot be said to justify it. Nevertheless, if a factor provides no sensible basis for justifying the disparity, domestic tribunals have tended to conclude that the factor is not 'material'. In *Tyldesley v TML Plastics Ltd* [1996] ICR 356, the EAT made an ambitious attempt to reconcile the domestic and European approaches. The principle which the EAT developed may be summarised as follows: if the factor relied upon by the employer is one which may itself be tainted by sex discrimination, it must be shown that the factor objectively justifies the difference; however, if it is not tainted by sex discrimination, the factor need only explain the difference. The EAT decision in *Tyldesley* was approved by the House of Lords in *Strathclyde Regional Council v Wallace* [1998] ICR 205, HL and *Glasgow City Council v Marshall* [2000] ICR 196, HL) and applied by the EAT in *Parliamentary Comr for Administration and Health Service v Fernandez* [2004] ICR 123; *King's College London v Clark* (2003) IDS Brief 747, p 11 (in which the EAT held that a mistake and a TUPE transfer adequately explained the difference in pay); and *Armstrong v Newcastle Upon Tyne NHS Hospital Trust* [2005] EWCA Civ 1608, [2006] IRLR 124. In *Sharp v Caledonia Group Services Ltd* [2006] IRLR 4, the EAT, having cited this author's view that the issue 'remains vexed', then proceeded to eschew the *Tyldesley* approach in favour of the more stringent European approach in the *Enderby* and *Brunnhofer* cases, the latter of which the EAT considered 'provides clear guidelines in equal pay cases as to the need for objective justification in all cases'. However, in *Armstrong* Lord Justice Buxton warned that, 'once the House of Lords has determined the meaning of [European Community rules] it is not open to domestic courts to resort to the decisions of the Court of Justice on which the House of Lords based its analysis in order to find a different or wider meaning'. Although Lord Justice Buxton does not appear to have been referred to the *Sharp* case, this would appear to be a condemnation of the approach taken by the EAT in that case and a reaffirmation that *Tyldesley* should continue to be applied unless and until the issue is reconsidered by the House of Lords or the ECJ.

Nevertheless, there must be very considerable doubt about whether the *Tyldesley* approach can be sustained in the light of the more recent decisions of the ECJ. In particular, it is clear from a number of the ECJ's decisions (and most recently that in *Cadman v Health and Safety Executive, Case C-17/05* [2006] IRLR 969) that, where a factor relied upon by an employer is tainted by, or 'related to', sex discrimination, then it *cannot* form the basis of a material factor defence. This undermines the distinction sought to be made in *Tyldesley* between cases where the factor is and is not tainted by sex discrimination. Moreover, most recent decisions of the EAT have (notwithstanding Lord Justice Buxton's warning) followed the strict ECJ approach: for a very recent example, see *Redcar & Cleveland Borough Council v Bainbridge* [2007] IRLR 91, EAT. Others have, however, accepted that, once an employer has established that a difference in pay was owing to factors other than sex, the employer will not be required to go further and objectively justify the difference in pay: see *Villalba v Merrill Lynch & Co Inc* [2006] IRLR 437. In that case, which concerned bonus payments based on performance assessments, it was sufficient that the employer had shown that sex was not a factor in its decision-making. (Or, rather, as the case in fact concerned a complaint of victimisation and not sex discrimination, all the employer had to show was that the claimant's previous complaint of sex discrimination was not a 'significant influence' on its decision-making, as *per* Lord Nicholls in *Nagarajan v London Regional Transport* [1999] IRLR 572, HL.)

In determining when a factor relied on by the employer as justifying a difference in pay is 'tainted by sex discrimination', some care should be taken. In the *Armstrong* case (above) the tribunal had determined that the Trust's explanation for the difference in pay (essentially that a decision had been taken not to 'contract out' the portering contracts because portering was not subject to Compulsory Competitive Tendering and any decision to do so might therefore attract more controversy) was tainted by sex discrimination. The tribunal relied on its own experience to the effect that male workforces were more likely to be unionised and to object to contracting out and on that basis held the employer's explanation to be 'tainted by sex discrimination'. The Court of Appeal ruled that it had not been open to the tribunal so to hold in the light of its findings of fact as to the Trust's reasons. The Court distinguished the *Ratcliffe* case (above) on the basis that in that case the tribunal had made an express finding as to the Council's reason for its decision to contract-out the domestic ancillary services and it was that express reason (rather than a further reason inferred by the Tribunal from its own experience) that the tribunal found was tainted by sex discrimination. Buxton LJ further observed that in the *Ratcliffe* case the House of Lords appeared to have been satisfied that the employer had failed to show any material difference between the comparator groups other than the difference in sex. In *Armstrong*, however, there were a number of differences between the two groups.

For other cases on *EqPA 1970, s 1(3)* see: *Snoxell and Davies v Vauxhall Motors Ltd* [1977] ICR 700; *National Vulcan Engineering Insurance Group Ltd v Wade* [1978] ICR 800; *Methven v Cow Industrial Polymers Ltd* [1980] ICR 463; *Jenkins v Kingsgate (Clothing Productions) Ltd* [1981] ICR 715; *Montgomery v Lowfield Distribution Ltd* (1996) 576 IDS Brief, p 16 (where the difference in pay was justified by the need to reward those working flexible shifts).

Budgetary factors alone cannot justify discrimination against one of the sexes (*Schonheit v Stadt Frankfurt Am Main* [2004] IRLR 983), but cost considerations may be prayed in aid where the difference in pay is objectively justified by some other factor (*Cross v British Airways plc* [2006] EWCA Civ 549, [2006] ICR 1239 and *Redcar & Cleveland Borough Council v Bainbridge* [2007] IRLR 91, EAT).

Guidance is given in the *Danfoss* case (C-109/88, above) as to the factors which the ECJ has considered to be relevant to the objective justification of differences in pay under *art 141*.

24.12 Direct discrimination and the 'material factor' defence

There is some doubt as to whether the distinction between 'direct' and 'indirect' discrimination is relevant to cases under the *EqPA 1970* (see above 24.10). The inappropriateness of the distinction becomes particularly apparent when considering the 'material factor' defence. Thus, it would appear to be impossible to succeed on a *s 1(3)* 'material factor' defence where the inequality of pay is the result of direct rather than indirect sex discrimination. In direct discrimination the difference in sex will be the reason for the difference in pay and the *s 1(3)* defence, which requires that the employer show the difference in pay is 'genuinely due to a material factor which is not the difference of sex ...', will inevitably fail. However, there is still no authority which decides the point (although the EAT in *Parliamentary Comr for Administration and Health Service v Fernandez* [2004] IRLR 22 noted (*obiter*) that as a matter of logic direct sex discrimination cannot be justified and Mummery LJ observed, when considering the Disability Discrimination Act 1995 in *Clark v Novacold Ltd* [1999] ICR 951 at 963H, that direct discrimination cannot be justified 'in any of the discrimination statutes').

Further, the issue has been confused by European authority. In *Birds Eye Walls Ltd v Roberts* [1994] IRLR 29, the ECJ considered the position in European law. Advocate-General Van Gerven's view was that there might be circumstances in which it would be possible to justify an act of direct discrimination in relation to pay. The ECJ notes the views of those who made submissions on the issue but does not address it directly in the judgment. Instead, it merely finds that the question of whether the circumstances of the woman and her comparator are materially different is central to the determination of whether there has been any discrimination in the first place.

In *Strathclyde Regional Council v Wallace* [1998] IRLR 146, Lord Browne-Wilkinson noted that although the ECJ had not held that direct discrimination could be objectively justified, such a position could not be ruled out.

24.13 TRANSSEXUALS

In order to take advantage of the right to equal pay conferred on transsexuals, a person must:

(*a*)   intend to undergo, be undergoing or have undergone a gender reassignment (*SDA 1975, s 2A*) (for the definition of gender reassignment see 12.6(E) DISCRIMINATION AND EQUAL OPPORTUNITIES – I);

(*b*)   be engaged under a 'contract of service or of apprenticeship, or a contract personally to execute any work or labour' (*SDA 1975, s 82(1)*); and

(*c*)   not do their work wholly outside Great Britain (*SDA 1975, ss 6(1), 10(1)*) (for exceptions, see 13.5 DISCRIMINATION AND EQUAL OPPORTUNITIES – II).

Certain ministers of religion are also excluded (see 13.10(G) DISCRIMINATION AND EQUAL OPPORTUNITIES – II).

An employer must not, in relation to matters of pay, discriminate directly against a transsexual (see 12.4 et seq DISCRIMINATION AND EQUAL OPPORTUNITIES – I). There is no prohibition on indirect discrimination against transsexuals. This limited the effectiveness of the protections for transsexuals prior to the coming into force of the *Gender Recognition Act 2004* ('*GRA 2004*') on 1 July 2004. Thus, where, for example, an occupational pension scheme provided for benefits payable to be dependent on marital status, that was indirectly discriminatory against transsexuals who could not marry in their reassigned gender. However, such discrimination was not unlawful under the *SDA 1975*. In *KB v National Health Service Pensions Agency: C-117/01* [2004] ICR 781, ECJ, the European Court of Justice considered whether this situation was contrary to *art 141* of the *Treaty*. It noted that a failure to recognise a transsexual's reassigned gender and to permit them to marry was a breach of the *European Convention on Human Rights* (*Goodwin v United Kingdom* (2002) 35 EHRR 447, ECtHR) and went on to rule that the situation was also incompatible with *art 141* of the *Treaty*. However, also in line with the ECtHR, the ECJ held that it was for the member states to determine the conditions under which legal recognition is given to a change of gender. Accordingly, the court ruled that it was for the national court to determine whether a transsexual was able to rely on *art 141* in order to gain recognition of her right to nominate her partner as the beneficiary of a survivor's pension. Under the *GRA 2004*, transsexuals are now able to apply for a gender recognition certificate, and may marry in their reassigned gender. The decision in *KB* will still be relevant for transsexuals who have not obtained such a certificate. (For claims relating to pension entitlements generally, see 24.16 below.)

The normal time limits for a sex discrimination claim apply to claims of discrimination by transsexuals. The claim must be lodged with the tribunal within three months of the date on which the last act of discrimination occurred (*SDA 1975, s 76(1)*). In this respect, the limitation is less generous than that applicable to claims brought under the *EqPA 1970* which allow claims to be made within six months of the termination of the complainant's employment (*EqPA 1970, s 2(4)*). However, the *SDA 1975* time limit may be disapplied where the tribunal considers it just and equitable that it should do so (*SDA 1975, s 76(5)*). The complainant is also spared the cumbersome tribunal procedure applicable to equal pay claims (for which see 24.21 below). Compensation may include an award for injury to feelings. Further, where an award of compensation is made, interest is payable pursuant to the *Employment Tribunals* (*Interest on Awards in Discrimination Cases*) *Regulations 1996* (*SI 1996/2803*). (See generally DISCRIMINATION AND EQUAL OPPORTUNITIES – III (14).)

24.14 MATERNITY PAY

(See generally MATERNITY AND PARENTAL RIGHTS (33).)

The *Act* has been amended (with effect from 1 October 2005) to expressly provide for the equality clause to apply to maternity-related pay in certain circumstances: reg 36 of the *Employment Equality* (*Sex Discrimination*) *Regulations 2005*. *Section 1(2) EqPA 1970* now provides for the equality clause to apply to pay increases and bonus in the following circumstances. *Section 1(2)(d)* of the *EqPA 1970* now provides for the calculation of maternity-related pay as follows, where:

   (i)   any term of the woman's contract regulating maternity-related pay provides for any of her maternity-related pay to be calculated by reference to her pay at a particular time,

   (ii)   after that time (but before the end of the statutory maternity leave period) her pay is increased, or would have increased had she not been on statutory maternity leave, and

   (iii)   the maternity-related pay is neither what her pay would have been had she not been on statutory maternity leave nor the difference between what her pay would have been had she not been on statutory maternity leave and any statutory maternity pay to which she is entitled,

if (apart from the equality clause) the terms of the woman's contract do not provide for the increase to be taken into account for the purpose of calculating the maternity-related pay, the term mentioned in sub-paragraph (i) above shall be treated as so modified as to provide for the increase to be taken into account for that purpose.

'Maternity-related pay' is defined in *s 5A* of the *EqPA 1970* as follows:

pay (including pay by way of bonus) to which she is entitled as a result of being pregnant or in respect of times when she is on statutory maternity leave, except that it does not include any statutory maternity pay to which she is entitled.

Statutory maternity leave includes ordinary maternity leave, additional maternity leave and compulsory maternity leave: *s 5B* of the *EqPA 1970* (as amended).

Pay increases following a return from statutory maternity leave are governed by *s 1(2)(f)* of the *EqPA 1970* (as amended) as follows:

if (apart from the equality clause) the terms of the woman's contract regulating her pay after returning to work following her having been on statutory maternity leave provide for any of that pay to be calculated without taking into account any amount by which her pay would have increased had she not been on statutory maternity leave, the woman's contract shall be treated as including a term providing for the increase to be taken into account in calculating that pay.

Again, with effect from 1 October 2005, *s 1(2)(e)* of the *EqPA 1970* (as amended) provides for contractual bonuses to be paid as follows:

if (apart from the equality clause) the terms of the woman's contract as to—

(i)   pay (including pay by way of bonus) in respect of times before she begins to be on statutory maternity leave,

(ii)   pay by way of bonus in respect of times when she is absent from work in consequence of the prohibition in section 72(1) of the Employment Rights Act 1996 (compulsory maternity leave), or

(iii) pay by way of bonus in respect of times after she returns to work following her having been on statutory maternity leave,

do not provide for such pay to be paid when it would be paid but for her having time off on statutory maternity leave, the woman's contract shall be treated as including a term providing for such pay to be paid when ordinarily it would be paid.

The ECJ held in *Gillespie v Northern Health and Social Services Board: C-342/93* [1996] IRLR 214, that women whose pay is reduced when they are suspended on maternity grounds may not seek to challenge the reduction by bringing claims under *EqPA 1970*. This position was compatible with *art 141*: a woman absent on maternity leave is not entitled to full pay. Women taking maternity leave are in a unique position which is not comparable with that of a man actually at work (see 12.5 DISCRIMINATION AND EQUAL OPPORTUNITIES – I). However, that does not mean that a woman is excluded from all equal pay rights while on maternity leave. The following case-law will remain relevant for pre-1 October 2005 cases and any cases not covered by the amendments to the *EqPA 1970*.

Any increases in pay awarded during a woman's maternity leave must be taken into account when calculating the amount of maternity pay to which a woman is entitled, regardless of whether that increase is backdated to the reference period for calculating statutory maternity pay (as it was in *Gillespie*) or is awarded with only prospective effect at any time up until the end of the maternity leave (*Alabaster v Woolwich plc and Secretary of State for Social Security*: C-147/02 [2004] IRLR 486, ECJ). This principle has now been given statutory force in the amended *EqPA 1970*.

In *Edwards v Derby City Council* [1999] ICR 114, the EAT considered an unusual case in which the male comparator was in receipt of full pay even though he was not at work. The complainant was a teacher absent on maternity leave and in receipt of half-pay. Her maternity leave overlapped with a half-term holiday. Had she not been absent on maternity leave, she would have received full pay without having to attend work. The EAT rejected her claim that she should have received full pay during the half-term period, relying on *Gillespie* as authority for the proposition that a woman absent on maternity leave was in a unique position which could not be compared with that of those working normally even if, in the particular circumstances, that might include periods in which no actual duties were performed. The decision was made, however, before the ECJ gave its ruling in *Boyle v EOC (C-411/96)* [1999] ICR 360, ECJ. In that case, EOC employees absent on maternity leave were entitled to three months' full pay and thereafter a period at a reduced rate. Those absent as a result of sickness were entitled to six months' full pay. In the fourth month of an absence, therefore, an employee absent through sickness would receive more than an employee absent on maternity leave. An employee fell sick during her maternity leave and wished to be put on sick leave. The EOC's contract of employment allowed the employee to move onto sick leave but only on the basis that the maternity leave was terminated. The ECJ decided that the provision was discriminatory. The employee had to be allowed to swap into a period of sick leave and then to swap back. *Boyle* is an example of a case where it has been decided, in effect, that though a pregnant woman is not comparable to a man with an illness, a pregnant woman with an illness may be treated as being comparable (see also *Handels-og Kontorfunktio-naernes Forbund I Danmark, acting on behalf of Hoj Pederson v Faelesforeninger for Danmarks Brugsforninger, acting on behalf of Kvickly Skive* [1999] IRLR 55 (C-66/760): national legislation providing that men who are unfit to work through illness should receive full pay but women absent from work as a result of a pregnancy-related condition should not, is contrary to *art 141*; *Osterreichischer Gewerkschaftsbund v Wirtschaftskammer Osterreich* (2004) 760 IDS Brief, p 9: period of voluntary parental leave not comparable to compulsory military or civilian service; cf also *P & O European Ferries (Dover) Ltd v Iverson* (1999) IDS Brief 640, p 6).

In *Abdoulaye v Regie National des Usines Renault SA Case C-218/98* [1999] IRLR 811, the ECJ had to consider a provision in a collective agreement which governed the terms and conditions of Renault employees. Female employees not only continued to receive their full salary whilst on maternity leave but also received a lump sum to compensate them for the 'occupational disadvantages' that arose from their absence. Male employees argued that new fathers should receive the same bonus. However, the court decided that men were not subject to the same disadvantages. Unlike the women, they did not lose the chance of promotion or the right to performance-related pay for the period of maternity leave, nor did they suffer the resulting loss in the length of service.

The European Court considered yet another variation on the theme of payments due or refused to those on maternity leave in *Lewen v Denda Case C-333/97* [2000] IRLR 67. A firm paid Christmas bonuses to those in 'active' employment on 1 December each year. The complainant was absent on maternity leave on the relevant date. She was refused a bonus and claimed that her employers had breached *art 141*. The court felt that the result hinged upon the nature of the payment. A requirement that an employee should be in active employment was not discriminatory if the purpose of the payment was to encourage those at work to be loyal and to work hard in the following year. If, on the other hand, the purpose of the payment was to reward the employees for having worked hard in the previous year, it would be discriminatory to refuse to make any payment at all to those absent on parental leave. An employer could legitimately pro-rate the bonus to take account of the employee's absence from work, provided no account was taken of any period during which, by reason of her pregnancy, the employee was prohibited from attending work. For an example of a permissible proportion-ate reduction in bonus paid in recognition of work undertaken by the workforce during a period of ordinary maternity leave, see also, *Hoyland v Asda Stores Ltd* [2006] IRLR 468 (Court of Session).

Gruber v Silhouette International Schmeid GmbH & Co KG Case C-249/97 (1999) IDS Brief 647, p 8 was a case concerned with termination payments. In Austria, those who simply resign from employment receive no payment. However, those who resign for 'important reasons' and who have been employed for more than three years receive a payment. The European court determined that the 'impor-tant reasons' justifying payments had in common that they were all either concerned with poor working conditions or with misconduct on the part of the employer. Those who work for longer than five years and resign within a certain period after childbirth receive smaller payments. The complainant, who resigned after having had a child, argued that she should be entitled to compare herself with those who resigned for 'important reasons' and to pay her a reduced sum resulted in discrimination contrary to *art 141*. The court rejected her argument. Her situation was not analogous to that of someone who resigned because of poor working conditions or employer misconduct. That being so, her proposed comparison, and thus her claim, was ill-founded.

The suggestion in *Gillespie* that women absent on maternity leave are not entitled to receive pay is subject to an important qualification. The ECJ did suggest in *Gillespie* that 'the amount payable [to a woman absent on maternity leave] could not ... be so low as to undermine the purpose of maternity leave, namely the protection of women before and after giving birth'. The *Pregnant Workers Directive EEC/92/85* requires member states to provide that women absent from work on maternity leave receive an 'adequate allowance' (*art 11(2)(b)*). An allowance will be adequate provided that it is at least equivalent to what the employee would receive if she were absent through illness. In effect it requires that SMP should be at least as generous as SSP. A number of cases have since raised claims that sums received by the complainants during maternity leave did not amount to an 'adequate allowance'. In *Iske v P&O European Ferries (Dover) Ltd* [1997] IRLR 401, the EAT was asked to consider the adequacy of SMP. It declined to do so, although it suggested that it might have been prepared to consider the issue had the respondent been an emanation of the state. In *Gillespie v Northern Health and Social Services Board (No 2)* [1997] IRLR 410, the Northern Ireland Court of Appeal rejected a complaint that an employee's contractual maternity payments were less generous than contractual sick pay on the ground that the *Directive* merely required the payment to be more than SSP. In *Banks v Tesco Stores Ltd* [1999] ICR 1141, the EAT considered a case where an employee received no SMP at all. This was because, as her previous earnings were less than the lower earnings limit, she did not qualify for SMP. Notwithstanding that she was receiving nothing at all, the EAT declined to conclude that this was a case in which the amount received was so low as to undermine the purpose of maternity leave. The EAT relied on the fact that *art 11* of the *Pregnant Worker's Directive* allows member states to impose conditions upon entitlement to maternity pay. If the *Directive* allowed it, reasoned the EAT, it could not be read as contravening *art 141*. Where the maternity pay received by the employee is determined by reference to full pay, pay rises should be reflected in the level of maternity pay, even where the rises take place while the woman is away on maternity leave and after the reference period used to calculate the level of maternity pay (*Alabaster v Woolwich plc and Secretary of State for Social Security: c-147/02* [2004] IRLR 486; though cf *Clark v Secretary of State for Employment* [1997] ICR 64, CA).

24.15 EQUAL PAY AND PENSIONS

The principles applicable to retirement and pensions have evolved slowly and continue to evolve. Prior to the decision in *Barber v Guardian Royal Exchange Assurance Group: C-262/88* [1990] ICR 616 domestic legislation on the matter was piecemeal. Following *Barber* (and the flurry of ECJ decisions which followed it: see above 23.3) the UK was forced to rethink its approach. The fruits of this re-consideration have been the *Occupational Pension Schemes (Equal Access to Membership) Amendment Regulations 1995 (SI 1995/1215)* and, subsequently, the *Pensions Act 1995*.

The greater part of this section is devoted to describing the statutory regime currently in force. However, an account is also given below of the progress of the enormous number of cases currently within the employment tribunal system which, because they relate to periods of service before either *SI 1995/1215* or *PA 1995* came into force, are based instead, like *Barber*, on *art 141:* see 24.18 below.

24.16   Equal Pay

24.16 The statutory regime

The first respect in which there has, traditionally, been an inequality between men and women is the age at which they are expected to retire. The State pension is payable to women who are aged 60 or older, whereas men do not receive corresponding benefits until aged 65. *PA 1995* provides for the progressive implementation of a common age of entitlement to State retirement benefits of 65 over a period of 10 years beginning on 6 April 2010 (*PA 1995, s 126*). Employers, however, have been prohibited from discriminating, either directly or indirectly, in relation to the age at which employees are required to retire since 7 February 1987 (*SDA 1986, s 2(1)*). An employer is not obliged to have a common retiring age for all its employees. It can provide for different ages to apply to different jobs (*Bullock v Alice Ottley School* [1993] ICR 138), but it should be aware that if the employees performing a particular job are predominantly of one sex, there is a risk of a claim of indirect discrimination.

Where an employer provides its employees with access to an occupational pension scheme (see RETIREMENT (42)), further rules prohibit discrimination in relation to access to membership of the scheme and to the benefits payable thereunder. Protections are set out in three different statutes.

The first of the three relevant statutes is *PA 1995* which is principally concerned with the rules of the occupational pension scheme itself. The current provisions came into force on 1 January 1996 (the *Pensions Act 1995 (Commencement No 2) Order 1995 (SI 1995/3104)*) and replaced the regime only recently established by *SI 1995/1215* which had prohibited indirect discrimination in relation to access to membership from 31 May 1995. The *Act* has a limited retrospective effect (see below).

By *Pensions Act 1995, s 62(1)* and (2) occupational pension schemes are deemed to include an 'equal treatment rule' which relates to the terms on which persons become members of the scheme and are treated thereafter. The provisions have a limited retrospective effect. Where the relevant term of the scheme is one which applies to the manner in which members are treated (as opposed to the terms on which employees are admitted as members) the provisions have effect in relation to any pensionable service on or after 17 May 1990 (the date of the *Barber* decision) (*PA 1995, s 63(6)*). The temporal limitation mirrors the one stipulated in the *Barber* case itself. However, the ECJ has made it clear that the temporal limitation does not apply to a 'benefits' claim which is made ancillary to an 'admissions' claim (*Dietz v Stichting Thuiszorg Rotterdam (C-435/93)* [1996] IRLR 692). In the light of this decision, a question arises as to whether *PA 1995* has fully implemented the relevant EU law. *Section 63(1)* provides that terms which have effect for the benefit of dependants of members should be subject to the equal treatment rule.

It is usual for a scheme to confer on the trustees or managers certain discretions. *Section 62(6)* subjects the exercise of those discretions to the same principle of equal treatment.

As with the familiar equality clause, a woman may only take advantage of an equal treatment rule if she is employed on like work, work rated as equivalent or work of equal value to that of a male comparator in the same employment (*PA 1995, s 62(3)*). If the scheme distinguishes between married and unmarried members, the comparator selected should have the same marital status (*PA 1995, s 63(2)*). The equal treatment rule operates to modify less favourable terms in the woman's scheme to ensure that they are 'not less favourable' than those which apply to the comparator.

The question of what constitutes the 'same employment' for the purposes of *PA 1995, s 62(3)* arose in *Allonby v Accrington and Rossendale College* [2001] EWCA Civ 529, [2001] IRLR 364. In *Allonby*, the applicant's contract with the first respondent college was terminated, and she was told that she had to register with an agency supplying lecturing services if she wished to continue working at the college. The agency was not a contributing employer to the Government's occupational scheme for teachers. Mrs Allonby therefore argued that for the purposes of *s 62(3)*, in order to conform to the non-discrimination requirements of *art 141*, the agency and the college should be regarded as 'the same employment'. This raises issues identical to those raised with regard to the meaning of the 'same employment' for the purposes of the *EqPA* (see 24.9 above), although, as noted by Gage J in *Allonby*, the language of *s 62(3)* differs from the language of the parallel provision in the *EqPA 1970*, which requires a comparator to be employed '*by her employer at the same establishment*'. The Court of Appeal referred the matter to the ECJ, which ruled ([2004] IRLR 224) that, except where the terms of employment arise directly from legislative provisions or collective agreements, a woman is not working in the 'same employment' as a man for the purposes of *art 141* where she is not employed by the same person as the man. This is so even though she may provide the same services as the man and for the benefit of the man's employer (see further 24.9 above).

A 'material factor' defence is available (*PA 1995, s 62(4)*). Consistent with the jurisprudence of the ECJ, men and women may be paid different sums under the scheme if the difference is attributable to differing entitlements to State retirement benefits (*PA 1995, s 64(2)*) (ie a 'bridging' pension) or because of actuarial factors (*PA 1995, s 64(3)*).

The statutory scheme under *PA 1995* has an unusual interrelation with the *EqPA 1970*. By *PA 1995, s 63(4)*, *s 62* of that *Act* should be construed 'as one' with *EqPA 1970, s 1*. The *PA 1995* did not introduce any new enforcement mechanism. Instead, it extends the existing *EqPA 1970* measures (*ss 2* and *2A*) to cover the enforcement of the equal treatment rule.

The provisions were supplemented by the *Occupational Pension Schemes (Equal Treatment) Regulations 1995 (SI 1995/3183) ('OPS(ET) Regulations 1995')*. The *Regulations* provide that, save in cases where a claim is made by a retired employee (*reg 7*), the tribunal has no power to make any award of compensation in relation to an alleged breach of an equal treatment rule (*reg 3*). Instead, the tribunal is given a power to declare that the equal treatment rule has been breached. Where the complaint relates to access to membership of the scheme, the tribunal may make a declaration that the employee is or was entitled to membership of the scheme (*reg 5*). The declaration of entitlement to join has to specify a 'deemed entry date' which may not be more than two years before the institution of proceedings (*reg 5*). Declarations that the rule has been breached in relation to terms on which members are treated may not relate to any period of service prior to 17 May 1990 (*reg 6*). In any case in which it is declared that the equal treatment rule has been breached, the employer may be required to provide additional resources so as to give effect to the declaration or, in the case of pensioner members, to provide the necessary funds for an award of compensation. The additional resources must be provided without recourse to additional contributions either from the complainant herself or any other member of the scheme (*regs 5–7*). Perhaps for this reason the employer is entitled to appear and be heard in any case in which it is alleged that the equal treatment rule has been breached whether or not it is specified as a respondent by the employee (*reg 4*).

The second relevant statute is *SDA 1975* (as amended by *PA 1995*) which prohibits discrimination against a woman in relation to her membership of, or rights under, an occupational pension scheme:

(*a*)   in the arrangements which an employer makes for the purpose of determining who should be offered employment;

(*b*)   in the terms on which it offers her employment;

(*c*)   by refusing or deliberately omitting to offer her employment;

(*d*)   in the way it affords her access to opportunities for promotion, transfer or training, or any other benefits, facilities or services, or by refusing or deliberately omitting to afford her access to them; or

(*e*)   by dismissing her, or subjecting her to any other detriment.

Otherwise, pension-related matters are excluded from the scope of *SDA 1975* by s 6(*4*) and (*4A*) save in relation to acts of pension-related discrimination against transsexuals (see above 24.13).

The final element in the statutory scheme is *EqPA 1970* (again, as amended by *PA 1995*). *Section 6(1B)* extends the operation of the equality clause to cover any term in the contract relating to a person's membership of, or rights under, an occupational pension scheme, unless the term is one in relation to which the equal treatment rule would be excluded. The clause and the rule, therefore, have co-extensive scopes of operation. *OPS(ET) Regulations 1995* established a new enforcement regime. The regime is substantially identical to that applicable to claims based on an alleged breach of the equal treatment rule (see above). Again, unless the complainant is already retired (*reg 12*) no award of compensation may be made (*reg 9*). The relief available is declaratory, but the declaration may have the effect of requiring the employer to allocate resources to the pension scheme in order to give effect to the declaration (*regs 10–12*).

SSA 1989, Sch 5 paras 5 and *6* also make provision for the protection of rights of access to, and to benefits under, a pension scheme for employees absent on maternity or family leave.

Note that the Pensions Ombudsman's decision that a pension rule excluding those who earn less than the lower earnings limit was indirectly discriminatory and infringed *art 141* (*Shillcock v Uppingham School* [1997] Pens LR 207) has been overturned on appeal (*Trustees of Uppingham School Retirement Benefits Scheme v Shillcock* [2002] EWHC 641 (Ch), [2002] IRLR 702) where it was held that: (1) there was no difference in treatment where the purpose of the rule was to achieve a broad integration between benefits under the scheme and the provision of the state pension; and (2) in any event, the rule could be objectively justified where its purpose was to achieve integration with the state scheme (see *Birds Eye Walls Ltd v Roberts* [1994] IRLR 29). (As to claims based on *art 141*, see 24.18, 24.19 and 24.22 below.)

(For pension claims by transsexuals see also 24.13 above.)

24.17 Barber and claims based on art 141

The impetus for the statutory scheme described above came from Europe. *Directive 86/378/EEC* required member states to introduce measures providing for equal rights to membership of occupational pension schemes by 1 January 1993. The UK had drafted legislation which was set out at *Social Security Act 1989, Sch 5* but before it could be brought into force it was overtaken by events, specifically the decision of the ECJ in *Barber*. The ECJ decided that pensions from both contributory and non-contributory schemes were 'pay' within the meaning of *art 141*. The effect of the decision was that an obligation not to discriminate in relation to access to, or benefits under, a pension scheme was found already to exist without the need for implementing domestic legislation.

The potential consequences of the decision were so great that the ECJ took the unusual step of specifically limiting the effect of its decision by stating that it could not be relied upon to claim entitlement to a pension with effect from a date prior to 17 May 1990 (the date of the decision) unless the applicant had already commenced proceedings by that date. It was not initially clear whether the limitation excluded all claims relating to periods of service before the stipulated date or only those where the benefits arising out of such service were also payable prior to 17 May 1990. The precise scope of the limitation was later clarified in *Ten Oever v Stichting Bedrijfspensionfonds Voor Het Glazenwassers En Schoon-maakbedrijf: C-109/91* [1995] ICR 74, in which the ECJ determined that *Barber* only applied to benefits payable in respect of periods of service after 17 May 1990 (but cf *Dietz v Stichting Thuiszord Rotterdam: C-435/93* [1996] IRLR 692 below). This interpretation corresponds with the Protocol to the Maastricht Treaty on European Union which reads as follows:

> 'Benefits under occupational pension schemes shall not be considered as remuneration if and insofar as they are attributable to periods of employment prior to 17 May 1990.'

The *Barber Protocol* applies only to claims relating to the level of benefit provided and not to claims alleging denial of access to benefits. For instance, the formerly commonplace refusal of pension schemes to admit part-time workers was indirectly discriminatory on grounds of sex. Where a former part-time employee complains that she was refused access to membership, the *Protocol* does not apply and her claim may, subject to any other domestic limitations, go back as far as 8 April 1976, that being the date on which the ECJ gave its decision in *Defrenne* (*Schroder v Deutsche Telekom (C-50/96)* [2000] IRLR 353) (see also below 24.19).

In *Quirk v Burton Hospitals NHS Trust* [2002] EWCA Civ 149, [2002] IRLR 353, the Court of Appeal had to consider the effect of a provision in the *National Health Service Pension Scheme Regulations 1995* (*SI 1995/300*). Formerly, female members of the NHS Pension scheme could, in certain circumstances, retire early at 55. Men could only take early retirement once they were 60. The *1995 Regulations* corrected this discriminatory situation by providing that both men and women could retire at 55. However, whereas a woman retiring at 55 received a pension calculated by reference to her whole period of service, a man doing the same would receive a pension calculated by reference only to his service since 17 May 1990. Unsurprisingly, the woman's pension would be greater than that of a man with a comparable length of service. A male complainant sought to argue that the *1995 Regulations* were incompatible with *art 141*. He contended that the provision had the effect of precluding him from access to benefits in respect of his pre-1990 service. The Court of Appeal decided that, properly analysed, the case was not an 'access to benefits' case at all. The complainant was a member of the scheme. The contentious provision simply resulted in his receiving less money. It was, therefore, a 'level of benefit' case and the *Barber Protocol* applied. Lord Justice Buxton opined that the 'access'/'level of benefit' dichotomy was an unhelpful basis for analysis. The tribunal should ask itself whether the alleged discrimination relates to an age condition which varies according to sex. If it does, it is a case to which the *Barber Protocol* applies.

Following the *Barber* decision, a number of cases were referred to the ECJ with the intention of clarifying the difficult issues left unresolved by the *Barber* decision itself. The following matters have now been settled. Benefits payable to survivors fall within *art 141* (*Ten Oever v Stichting Bedrijfspensioenfonds voor het Glazenwassers en Schoonmaakbedrijf: C-109/91* [1995] ICR 74) as do benefits payable under non-contracted out supplementary schemes (*Moroni v Collo GmbH: C-110/91* [1995] ICR 137). Benefits payable under schemes which have at all times been 'single sex' are not, nor are benefits payable as a result of contributions made by employees on a voluntary basis, covered (*Coloroll Pension Trustees Ltd v Russell: C-200/91* [1995] ICR 179).

Where a member state provides for men and women to become entitled to a State pension at different ages (eg in the UK women become so entitled at 60 whereas men become entitled at 65, although the *Pensions Act 1995* provides for progressive implementation of a common age of entitlement of 65 over a period of 10 years beginning on 6 April 2010), occupational pension schemes sometimes provide for payment of a 'bridging pension', the purpose of which is to ensure that employees, of whichever sex, receive the same total sum by way of pension when their State entitlements are aggregated to their entitlements under the scheme. Between the ages of 60 and 65 in the UK male and female employees would, under such a scheme, receive the same total sum but the male employees would receive substantially more from their employers. It follows, therefore, that under a 'bridging pension' male employees will receive more 'pay' than their female colleagues over the period. However, the State pension is not 'pay' for the purposes of *art 141* (see further 24.3 above). In *Roberts v Birds Eye Walls Ltd: C-132/92* [1994] ICR 338 the ECJ held that it is not contrary to *art 141* to take account of an employee's entitlement to a State pension when calculating benefits payable under a bridging pension; see also *Trustees of Uppingham School retirement Benefits Scheme v Shillcock* [2002] EWHC 641 (Ch), [2002] IRLR 702. Inequality of employer's contributions to a scheme (as opposed to the benefits payable to the employee under the scheme) which result from the use of different actuarial factors for men and women is not contrary to *art 141* (*Neath v Hugh Steeper Ltd: C-152/91* [1995] ICR 158 and *Coloroll Pension Trustees Ltd v Russell: C-200/91* [1995] ICR 179).

Claims made in relation to pension inequality may be made against the trustees of the scheme as well as against the employer (*Coloroll* above). Claims may, of course, be made in respect of exclusion from membership of the scheme as well as in relation to the benefits payable under it. Where the employee has been excluded from the scheme, the *Barber* temporal limitation does not apply to the claim. That is true both in relation to the straightforward exclusion claim and, surprisingly, to any ancillary claim for non-payment of benefits (*Dietz v Stichting Thuiszorg Rotterdam: C-298/94* [1996] IRLR 692). A woman seeking a remedy in respect of such a denial of access to membership must pay the contributions which she would have paid had she been admitted to membership at the appropriate time if she is to be entitled to any benefits under the scheme in respect of the period of her exclusion (*Fisscher v Voorhuis Hengelo BV: C- 128/93* [1995] ICR 635).

The ECJ has also given guidance on how a scheme should approach the task of modifying its rules so as to provide for equality. No action need be taken in relation to benefits payable in respect of periods of service prior to 17 May 1990 by reason of the temporal limitation established in *Barber*. Benefits payable in respect of the period between 17 May 1990 and the date on which the scheme is amended to provide for equality should be rounded up to the higher of the differential rates. After entitlements have been equalised, however, the scheme may reduce benefits overall provided that it is done in a way which involves no discrimination and which is consistent with the obligations of the employer and/or trustees under national laws and the contract of employment or rules of the scheme. Equalisation must be done in one step; it is not lawful for the employer or trustee to equalise benefits progressively over a transitional period (*Smith v Advel Systems Ltd: C- 409/92* [1995] ICR 596). Schemes which reduced male entitlements to match female entitlements between 17 May 1990 and the date on which the discriminatory scheme was actually amended ('the *Barber* window') will be unlawful for that period, and male employees will be entitled to claim the difference in pension benefits attributable to any difference in pension entitlement arising during the *Barber* window: *Harland & Wolff Pension Trustees Ltd v Aon Consulting Financial Services Ltd* [2006] EWHC 1778 (Ch), [2007] ICR 529.

The decision of the ECJ in *Bestuur van het Algemeen Burgerlijk Pensioenfonds v Beune: C-7/93* [1995] IRLR 103 settled a long-running controversy over whether benefits payable under schemes established by statute and applicable to State employees are 'pay' for the purposes of *art 141*. There was domestic authority to the effect that they were not (*Griffin v London Pensions Fund Authority* [1993] ICR 564, which concerned a Local Government Superannuation Scheme). In *Beune* benefits payable under the statutory scheme applicable to the Dutch civil service were held to fall within *art 141* on the basis that they complied with what the ECJ termed the 'only possible decisive criterion', namely, whether the pension is paid to the worker by reason of the employment relationship between himself and his former employer. Whilst being 'decisive' the criterion is not, according to the court, 'exclusive'. Some consideration of the balance between the relative importance to the determination of the benefits payable of social policy on the one hand, and employment-related questions on the other may still be necessary. Employment-related questions will include whether the scheme applies to a particular category of worker only and whether the benefits are directly related to length of service.

On 1 July 1997, *Directive 96/96/EC* came into force. It amends *Directive 86/378* to take account of the *Barber* decision and a number of the subsequent authorities.

24.18   The part-time workers litigation

The *Preston* litigation concerned claims brought by many thousands of part-time workers before employment tribunals alleging that they have been indirectly discriminated against as a result of having been refused membership of their occupational pension scheme on the ground that they worked part-time. Until it was amended by *PA 1995*, the *EqPA 1970* only prohibited directly discriminatory exclusion from membership. In the circumstances, each applicant relies upon *art 141* and the *Barber* decision to found his or her claim.

The cases raised many questions about whether employees may enforce rights based on European legislation in the domestic courts and tribunals and, if so, as to the appropriate procedural rules which apply to such claims. Such questions are dealt with in greater detail at 24.17 above in the context of a more general consideration of the application of *art 141* in the UK. In the *Preston* litigation, two points have now been resolved: firstly, the claims are brought in the employment tribunal on the basis that the incompatible domestic legislation should be disapplied rather than as a 'free standing' *art 141* claim (see further 24.22 below); and, secondly, the claimant's remedy is limited to a declaration of entitlement to membership of the relevant scheme and to benefits whilst a member.

The first series of test cases was considered by the Birmingham Employment Tribunal, and appeals from those decisions were decided by the EAT (*Preston v Wolverhampton Healthcare NHS Trust* [1996] IRLR 484), the Court of Appeal ([1997] IRLR 233), the House of Lords ([1998] ICR 227), the ECJ on a referral from the House of Lords ([2000] IRLR 506) and the House of Lords on its return from the ECJ ([2001] IRLR 237).

The ECJ in *Preston* held that the two-year limitation period for arrears of pay contained in *EqPA 1970, s 2(5)* was incompatible with Community law. On return to the House of Lords, their Lordships concluded that due to this incompatibility, the respondent employers could not rely on that section to defeat a claim for periods prior to the two years to be taken into account, subject to the employee paying contributions owing in respect of the period for which membership was claimed retroactively. Future pension benefits therefore had to be calculated by reference to full and part-time periods of service subsequent to 8 April 1976 as the date when the ECJ held in *Defrenne v Sabena: C-43/75* [1976] ICR 547 that *art 141* had direct effect.

In respect of the six-month limitation period formerly contained in *EqPA 1970, s 2(4)*, the ECJ held that the requirement to bring proceedings within six months of the termination of employment was not incompatible so long as such limitation period was not less favourable for actions based on Community law than for those based on domestic law. The ECJ decided that an action alleging a breach of the *1970 Act* was not a domestic action 'similar' to a claim for infringement of *art 141*. The House of Lords on return held that the claim in Community law was to establish the right of retroactive access to the pension schemes. That was not similar in form to a claim in contract for damages but in substance the eventual benefit to the employee was sufficiently similar for the purposes of testing equivalence. Although the limitation period for a claim in contract was six years, that period did not run from the termination of employment. Since a claim in contract could only go back six years, whereas a claim brought within six months of termination could go back to the beginning of employment or 1976, it could not be said that the provisions of *EqPA 1970, s 2(4)* were less favourable than those applying to a claim in contract despite the apparent difference in length of the limitation periods. Therefore the provisions of *s 2(4)* did not violate Community law as to effectiveness and equivalence.

In relation to employees on successive short-term contracts, the House of Lords held that it was clear from the ECJ's judgment that where there were intermittent contracts of service without a 'stable employment relationship' the period of six months ran from the end of each contract, but where such contracts were concluded at regular intervals in respect of the same employment in a stable employment relationship the period ran from the end of the last contract. Their Lordships referred the question of which applicants were in stable employment relationships back to the employment tribunal.

After the employment tribunal's decisions in the test cases, a second round of appeals has now reached the Court of Appeal (*Preston v Wolverhampton Healthcare NHS Trust (No 3)* [2005] ICR 222 (*'Preston (No 3)'*). Three issues on appeal to the EAT related to the circumstances in which there would be a breach of the equality clause. The EAT held:

(1) The equality clause is breached where part-time employees are excluded from a pension scheme that is available to full-time employees, irrespective of whether the part-time employee would have joined the scheme if it had been made available to her.

(2)   However, there is no breach of the equality clause where membership of the scheme is obligatory for full-time employees but only optional for part-time employees.

(3)   Although it had been (rightly) accepted before the tribunal that the imposition of a qualifying hours threshold in relation to membership of occupational pension scheme was a breach of the equality clause, where an employer removed that threshold but failed to inform his employees that was not itself either a breach or a continuing breach of the equality clause. It may well, however, be a breach of an implied term of the employment contract (see *Scally v Southern Health and Social Services Board* [1991] ICR 771 and 8.9, 8.13 CONTRACT OF EMPLOYMENT).

A fourth issue concerned the limitation period: the EAT held that a 'stable employment relationship' consisting of a succession of short term contracts (see further below 24.19) ceased, and the six-month limitation period began to run, where one of the two essential features of the relationship was no longer present, i.e. the same employment or periodicity of employment. These features will not be present where there is no longer an intention to employ, or to work, on a regular basis.

A fifth issue concerned the point at which the time limit begins to run where an employee's employment has been transferred from one employer ('the transferor') to a new employer ('the transferee') under the *Transfer of Undertakings (Protection of Employment) Regulations 1981* ('*TUPE*'; see TRANSFER OF UNDERTAKINGS (52)). The EAT held that time begins to run against the transferor from the end of the employee's employment with the transferee, and not from the date of the transfer. Only this last issue was appealed to the Court of Appeal in *Powerhouse Retail Ltd v Burroughs* [2004] EWCA Civ 1281. The Court of Appeal (affd [2006] UKHL 13, [2006] IRLR 381) reversed the EAT's decision and held that time runs for the purposes of a pensions claim from the date of the transfer, pensions being the one element of the contract of employment that does not transfer under *TUPE*.

A further limitation issue was determined by the tribunal, but not appealed to the EAT or Court of Appeal. The tribunal held that, where a series of employments are covered by an overarching pensions scheme, time starts to run from the end of each employment and not from the end of the series (unless, of course, they are *TUPE* transfers, in which case they count as a single employment).

It should also be noted that it was conceded before the tribunal that a male part-time worker could bring a claim if he could identify a female comparator with the right to join the pension scheme by operation of her equality clause. One of the questions referred to the ECJ in *Allonby v Accrington and Rossendale College* [2004] IRLR 224 was whether or not the requirement for a comparator was incompatible with EU law. The ECJ limited its ruling to the facts of that particular case, which concerned access to the statutory Teachers' Superannuation Scheme. It ruled that, where state legislation (such as the Teachers' Superannuation Scheme) was at issue, there is no need for an employee to point to a comparator: it will be sufficient to show statistical disadvantage. It seems that a comparator will still be necessary where state legislation is not in issue.

Information Bulletins and up-to-date information on the case management of the part-time pension claims can be found on the part-time worker pension cases section of the tribunal service website (www.employmenttribunals.gov.uk).

24.19 **REMEDIES FOR UNEQUAL PAY**

Under the Equal Pay Act 1970

Any claim brought by virtue of the *EqPA 1970*, whether for arrears of remuneration or damages, may be brought before an employment tribunal (*EqPA 1970, s 2(1)*).

A tribunal may hear a case in the following circumstances:

(*a*)   An employee may claim the benefit of the *Act* (*EqPA 1970, s 2(1)*).

(*b*)   An employer may apply to the tribunal for an order declaring his and the employee's rights in relation to an equality clause (*EqPA 1970, s 2(1A)*).

(*c*)   The Secretary of State may refer a question to the tribunal on behalf of an aggrieved employee where it is not reasonable to expect the parties to take steps to have the question determined (*EqPA 1970, s 2(2)*).

(*d*)   A court in which any proceedings are pending may direct that a claim or counter-claim in respect of the operation of an equality clause may be struck out where it appears that it would more conveniently be disposed of separately by an employment tribunal. Alternatively, a court may on application of any party or of its own motion refer a question to an employment tribunal and stay the proceedings meanwhile (*EqPA 1970, s 2(3)*).

Prior to 19 July 2003, no claim in respect of an equality clause could be referred to an employment tribunal otherwise than by virtue of (*d*) above, unless the woman had been employed in the employment within the six months preceding the date of the reference. The question of the compatibility of this limitation period was referred to the ECJ by the House of Lords in *Preston v Wolverhampton Healthcare NHS Trust* [1998] ICR 227. The ECJ decided ([2000] IRLR 506) that the limitation was not, in principle, contrary to Community law. However, that decision was qualified in two respects. First, the ECJ stated that the national court would have to be satisfied that the limitation was not less favourable than the limitations applied to comparable domestic law claims. Second, the ECJ addressed the application of this limitation period to circumstances where an employee has been employed pursuant to a series of discrete contracts of employment. In *Preston* the ECJ held that the limitation should not apply from the date of termination of each employment contract in a case where the employee is engaged pursuant to a series of such contracts so that it can be said that a 'stable employment relationship' existed across the period of time covered by the individual contracts. On return to the House of Lords ([2001] IRLR 237), the six-month limitation period was held to be compatible with Community law but the issue of what constitutes a 'stable employment relationship' was remitted back to the employment tribunal: see 24.18 above for the progress of the *Preston* part-time workers pensions litigation.

With effect from 19 July 2003, *EqPA 1970* was amended by the *Equal Pay Act 1970 (Amendment) Regulations 2003* so that no claim in respect of an equality clause may be referred to an employment tribunal otherwise than by virtue of (*d*) above unless the proceedings are instituted on or before the 'qualifying date' (*EqPA 1970, s 2(4)*). The 'qualifying date' before which a claim must be brought varies depending on which of the following five categories applies to the circumstances of the claim (*EqPa 1970, s 2ZA*):

A stable employment case

(*a*)   A 'stable employment case' means a case where the proceedings relate to a period during which a stable employment relationship subsists between the woman and the employer, notwithstanding that the period includes any time after the ending of a contract of employment when no further contract of employment is in force. In a stable employment case, the qualifying date is the date falling six months after the date on which the stable employment relationship ended.

A concealment case

(*b*)   A 'concealment case' is a case where the employer deliberately concealed from the woman any fact (referred to as a 'qualifying fact') which is relevant to the contravention to which the proceedings relate, and without knowledge of which the woman could not reasonably have been expected to institute the proceedings, and the woman did not discover the qualifying fact (or could not with reasonable diligence have discovered it) until after the last day on which she was employed in the employment, or the day on which the stable employment relationship between her and the employer ended (as the case may be). In a concealment case, the qualifying date is the date falling six months after the day on which the woman discovered the qualifying fact in question (or could with reasonable diligence have discovered it).

A disability case

(*c*)   A 'disability case' means a case where the woman was under a disability at any time during the six months after the last day on which she was employed in the employment, the day on which the stable employment relationship between her and the employer ended, or the day on which she discovered (or could with reasonable diligence have discovered) the qualifying fact deliberately concealed from her by the employer (if that day falls after the day(s) referred to above, as the case may be). In a disability case, the qualifying date is the date falling six months after the day on which the woman ceased to be under a disability.

A case which is both a concealment and a disability case

(*d*)   In such a case, the qualifying date is the later of the two dates which would otherwise apply if it were just disability or just a concealment case.

A standard case

(*e*)   A 'standard case' is a case which is not a stable employment case, a concealment case, a disability case or a case which is both a concealment and a disability case. In a standard case, the qualifying date is the date falling six months after the last day on which the woman was employed in the employment.

See *Degnan v Redcar and Cleveland Borough Council* [2005] IRLR 504 for consideration of what constitutes 'stable employment'.

The tribunal has no discretion to extend time in a claim under *EqPA 1970*. In this respect the *SDA* is more generous as it allows for an extension of time where the tribunal considers it to be just and equitable: see 14.3 DISCRIMINATION AND EQUAL OPPORTUNITIES – III.

If the claim is successful, the amount awarded will be the difference in pay between that of the claimant and the 'equal' or 'equivalent' employee. In certain cases, such as those involving performance-related pay or bonuses, that may require the tribunal to engage in the speculative exercise of devising an equivalent performance-related bonus scheme to apply to the group of workers to which the claimant belongs in order to determine the appropriate level of award: see *South Tyneside Metropolitan Borough Council v Anderson* UKEAT/0684/05/ZT and UKEAT/0525/06/ZT, 26 March 2007, unreported.

Compensation for non-economic loss is not recoverable in a claim under the *EqPA 1970*: *Degnan v Redcar and Cleveland Borough Council* [2005] IRLR 504.

The two-year limitation period in respect of arrears of pay formerly contained in *EqPA 1970, s 2(5)* was held by the ECJ in *Preston v Wolverhampton Healthcare NHS Trust* to be incompatible with Community law. On return to the House of Lords ([1998] ICR 227, HL), it was held that the respondent employers could not rely on this two-year limitation which must be disapplied. The respondent employers could not therefore defeat a claim for periods prior to the two years to be taken into account, subject to the employee paying contributions owing in respect of the period for which membership was claimed retroactively. Future pension benefits had to be calculated by reference to full and part-time periods of service subsequent to 8 April 1976 as the date when the ECJ held in *Defrenne v Sabena: 43/75* [1976] ICR 547 that *art 141* had direct effect. See now the *Equal Pay Act 1970 (Amendment) Regulations 2003*.

Following the ECJ's declaration of incompatibility in *Preston*, with effect from 19 July 2003, *EqPA 1970, s 2ZB* provides that arrears of pay may be recovered up to six years back from the 'arrears date': see *Bainbridge v Redcar & Cleveland Borough Council* UKEAT/0424/06/LA and

UKEAT/0031/07/LA, 23 March 2007. As with the qualifying date under *s 2ZA*, the arrears date depends upon whether the case is a standard case, a concealment case, a disability case or both a concealment and a disability case. In a standard case, the arrears date is the date falling six years before the date on which proceedings were instituted. In all other cases, the arrears date is the date of the contravention of *EqPA 1970*.

The *Sex Discrimination and Equal Pay (Remedies) Regulations 1993 (SI 1993/2798)* (now replaced by the *Employment Tribunals (Interest on Awards in Discrimination Cases) Regulations 1996 (SI 1996/2803)*) conferred on the employment tribunal a power to award interest on sums awarded under the *EqPA 1970*.

The tribunal is required to identify a 'mid-point date'. This date is the halfway point between the date on which the act of discrimination complained of occurred and the date on which the interest is being calculated (*reg 4*). Interest is then awarded in respect of the period from the mid-point date to the date of calculation (*reg 6(1)(b)*), except that interest on any sum for injury to feelings is to be awarded for the whole of the period from the date of the act of discrimination to the date of calculation (*reg 6(1)(a)*). Interest is simple interest and accrues from day to day (*reg 3(1)*). By *reg 3(2)* the rate to be applied in England and Wales is that prescribed for the Special Investment Account by *rule 27(1)* of the *Court Funds Rules 1987 (SI 1987/821)*. In Scotland the relevant rate is that fixed for the time being by the *Act of Sederunt (Interest in Sheriff Court Decrees or Extracts) 1975 (SI 1975/948)*.

If a respondent has made a payment to the complainant prior to the date of calculation, the date of payment is treated as if it were the date of calculation for the purposes of calculating the interest to be awarded (*reg 6(2)*).

The tribunal is given a discretion to calculate interest by reference to periods other than those set out above, or even to use different periods for different elements of the award (*reg 6(3)*). The discretion may be exercised only where the tribunal is of the opinion that:

(*a*)   there are exceptional circumstances, whether relating to the claim as a whole or to a particular element of the award; and

(*b*)   those circumstances have the effect that serious injustice would be caused if interest were to be awarded by reference to the period or periods specified in *reg 6(1)(a)* or (*b*) or 6(2).

Note that it will not necessarily be an abuse of process (and nor will a claim necessarily be *res judicata* or otherwise precluded by the rule in *Henderson v Henderson*) where a claimant, having been successfully in one claim under the *EqPA 1970*, subsequently brings a second claim identifying a different (and more highly paid) comparator in respect of the same period of employment: *Bainbridge v Redcar & Cleveland Borough Council* UKEAT/0424/06/LA and UKEAT/0031/07/LA, 23 March 2007.

24.20 **Agricultural Wages Orders**

If such an order contains any discriminatory term, it may be referred by the Secretary of State to the Central Arbitration Committee ('CAC') for amendment. He may be requested to do so by employer or worker representatives on the Agricultural Wages Board, or may do so on his own motion. If the CAC decides that the amendments should be made, the Agricultural Wages Board must make an order giving effect to those amendments not later than five months from the date of the decision (*EqPA 1970, s 5*).

24.21 **PROCEDURE IN EQUAL PAY CLAIMS**

The *Employment Tribunals (Constitution and Rules of Procedure) Regulations 2004 (SI 2004/1861)* ('the *ET Regulations*') govern the procedure relating to all claims before employment tribunals with effect from 1 October 2004 (see EMPLOYMENT TRIBUNALS – I (20)). For transitional provisions applicable to claims commenced before this date, see *reg 20* of the *ET Regulations*.

Proceedings in equal pay claims are started in the same way as all proceedings before employment tribunals, by the filing of a Claim (*ET Regulations, Sch 1, rule 1*). The respondent enters a Response (*ET Regulations, Sch 1, rule 4*). The tribunal has power to order the discovery and inspection of documents, and the attendance of witnesses (*ET Regulations, Sch 6, rule 3*).

Note that the statutory grievance and disciplinary procedures in Schedule 2 to the *Employment Act 2002* apply to claims under the *EqPA 1970*. Accordingly, an employee must have set out her complaint in writing and sent a copy of it to her employer at least 28 days prior to commencing proceedings in the employment tribunal: see generally DISPUTE RESOLUTION (15) for the requirements of the statutory grievance and disciplinary procedures. Note, however, that the completion and submission to the employer of an *EqPA* questionnaire does not count as a 'grievance' for these purposes: *reg 14* of the *EA 2002 (Dispute Resolution) Regulations 2004* and *Holc-Gale v Makers UK Ltd* [2006] IRLR 178.

Like work or work rated as equivalent. If a claim for equal pay is brought asserting that the claimant is employed on like work or work rated as equivalent with a male comparator, the issues to be determined by the tribunal are whether the work is like work, or has been rated as equivalent under a valid job evaluation study. If it is raised, the tribunal will then decide whether the claimant has a genuine material factor defence under *s 1(3)*. These claims are determined under the ordinary rules of procedure in schedule 1 to the *ET Regulations*.

Work of equal value. Under the predecessor to the 2004 *ET Regulations*, equal pay claims in which it was alleged that the work done was work of equal value were the subject of complementary rules of procedure contained in *Sch 3* to the regulations. The 2004 *ET Regulations*, as originally enacted, made no reference to equal value claims. This omission was rectified by *Employment Tribunals (Constitution and Rules of Procedure) (Amendment) Regulations 2004 (SI 2004/2351)* which inserts schedule 6 to the *ET Regulations* to provide for a new procedure to be adopted in equal value claims which is intended to reduce the costs and delay in equal value claims.

By s 2A of the *EqPA 1970* as amended by *Equal Pay Act 1970 (Amendment) Regulations 2004 (SI 2004/2352)* with effect from 1 October 2004, where a dispute arises as to whether any work is of equal value, the Tribunal may proceed to determine that question itself or appoint an independent expert on this basis (*EqPA 1970, s 2A(1)(b)*). This amendment removes the defence that there are no reasonable grounds for determining that the work was of equal value so that the Tribunal is left with a straight choice between deciding the question for itself or appointing an expert.

In a case where there has already been a job evaluation study which has given different values to the work of the claimant and the comparator, the employment tribunal must determine that the work is not of equal value unless it has reasonable grounds for suspecting that the study discriminated on the grounds of sex, or there are other reasons why it is not suitable to be relied upon: *s 2A(2)* and *2A(2A)* of the *EqPA 1970* as amended.

In response to widespread concerns about the costs and delay involved in the independent expert procedure, the new *Sch 6* to the *ET Regulations* makes provision for a two-stage procedure with an 'indicative timetable'. In cases not involving an independent expert, the indicative timetable takes a total of 25 weeks and allows for a Stage 1 equal value hearing within 3 weeks of the Response with the merits hearing to follow within 18 weeks. In cases where an expert is appointed, the indicative timetable takes 37 weeks and provides for a Stage 1 equal value hearing within 3 weeks of the Response, a Stage 2 hearing within 10 weeks of Stage 1, the expert's report within 4 weeks of Stage 2, written questions to the expert 4 weeks after his or her report and the merits hearing within a further 8 weeks. However, the requirement to hold a Stage 1 or a Stage 2 equal value hearing does not preclude holding more than one of each of those types of hearing or other hearings from being held in accordance with the ordinary Tribunal rules of procedure in *Sch 1* to the *ET Regulations: rule 13 (2)* of *Sch 6* to the *ET Regulations*.

The new procedure for equal value claims provides as follows.

Stage 1 Equal Value Hearing. At the stage 1 equal value hearing the tribunal shall (*rule 4* of *Sch 6* to the *ET Regulations*):

(a)   where *s 2A(2)* of the *EqPA 1970* applies, strike out the claim (or the relevant part of it) if, in accordance with *s 2A(2A)* of that *Act*, the tribunal must determine that the work of the claimant and the comparator are not of equal value. The Claimant must be given notice and the opportunity to make representations before a claim is struck out on this basis: *rule 4 (4)* of *Sch 6*;

(*b*)   decide, in accordance with *s 2A(1)* of the *EqPA 1970*, either that the tribunal shall determine the question of whether the work is of equal value itself, or to require a member of the panel of independent experts to prepare a report with respect to the question of equal value. The tribunal may, on the application of a party, hear evidence upon and permit the parties to address it upon the defence of a genuine material factor before determining whether to require an independent expert to prepare a report;

(*c*)   make the standard orders according to the 'indicative timetable';

(*d*)   if the Tribunal has decided to appoint an independent expert, to order disclosure to the expert and fix a date for the Stage 2 hearing;

(*e*)   if no expert is to be appointed, to fix a date for the hearing; and

(*f*)   to make consequential orders, having regard to the indicative timetable.

The tribunal shall, unless it considers it inappropriate, make the following 'standard orders' at the Stage 1 hearing (*rule* 5 of *Sch 6*):

(*a*)   before the end of the period of 14 days after the date of the Stage 1 hearing the claimant shall:

　　(i)   disclose in writing to the respondent the name of any comparator, or, if the claimant is not able to name the comparator he shall instead disclose such information as enables the comparator to be identified by the respondent; and

　　(ii)   identify to the respondent in writing the period in relation to which he considers that the claimant's work and that of the comparator are to be compared;

(*b*)   before the end of the period of 28 days after the date of the Stage 1 hearing:

　　(i)   where the claimant has not disclosed the name of the comparator to the respondent, if the respondent has been provided with sufficient detail to be able to identify the comparator, he shall disclose in writing the name of the comparator to the claimant;

　　(ii)   the parties shall provide each other with written job descriptions for the claimant and any comparator;

　　(iii)   the parties shall identify to each other in writing the facts which they consider to be relevant to the question;

(*c*)   the respondent is required to grant access to the claimant and his representative (if any) to his premises during a period specified by the tribunal or chairman in order for him or them to interview any comparator;

(*d*)   the parties shall before the end of the period of 56 days after the date of the stage 1 equal value hearing present to the tribunal a joint agreed statement in writing of the following matters:

　　(i)   job descriptions for the claimant and any comparator;

　　(ii)   facts which both parties consider are relevant to the question;

　　(iii)   facts on which the parties disagree (as to the fact or as to the relevance to the question) and a summary of their reasons for disagreeing;

(e)   the parties shall, at least 56 days prior to the hearing, disclose to each other, to any independent or other expert and to the tribunal written statements of any facts on which they intend to rely in evidence at the hearing; and

(f)   the parties shall, at least 28 days prior to the hearing, present to the tribunal a statement of facts and issues on which the parties are in agreement, a statement of facts and issues on which the parties disagree and a summary of their reasons for disagreeing.

Where the Tribunal has decided to appoint an independent expert to prepare a report on the question, the Tribunal or a Chairman may if it or he considers it appropriate (for example where a party is not legally represented etc) at any stage of the proceedings order an independent expert to assist the tribunal in establishing the facts on which the independent expert may rely in preparing his report: *rule 6 (2) of Sch 6.*

Stage 2 Equal Value Hearing. At the Stage 2 hearing the Tribunal shall make a determination of facts on which the parties cannot agree which relate to the question and shall require the independent expert to prepare his report on the basis of facts which have (at any stage of the proceedings) either been agreed between the parties or determined by the tribunal (referred to as 'the facts relating to the question'): *rule 7(3) of Sch 6.* The facts relating to the question shall be the only facts on which the tribunal shall rely at the hearing, subject to an application by the independent expert for some or all of the facts relating to the question to be amended, supplemented or omitted: *rule 7(5) and (6) of Sch 6.*

At the Stage 2 hearing the Tribunal shall, unless it considers it inappropriate to do so, make the following 'standard orders' having regard to the indicative timetable (*rule 7(4) of Sch 6*):

(a)   make any orders which it considers appropriate;

(b)   fix a date for the hearing, having regard to the indicative timetable.

(c)   order, by a date specified by the Tribunal (with regard to the indicative timetable) the independent expert to prepare his report on the question and shall (subject to *rule 14*) have sent copies of it to the parties and to the tribunal; and

(d)   order the independent expert to prepare his report on the question on the basis of the facts relating to the question and no other facts which may or may not relate to the question.

The merits hearing. In proceedings in relation to which an independent expert has prepared a report, unless the Tribunal determines that the report is not based on the facts relating to the question, the report of the independent expert shall be admitted in evidence in those proceedings: *rule 9(1) of Sch 6.* If the Tribunal does not admit the report of an independent expert, it may determine the question itself or require another independent expert to prepare a report on the question: *rule 9(2) of Sch 6.* The Tribunal may refuse to admit evidence of facts or hear argument as to issues which have not been disclosed to the other party as required by these rules or any order made under them, unless it was not reasonably practicable for the party to have so complied: *rule 9(3) of Sch 6.*

The role of the independent expert. When a Tribunal requires an independent expert to prepare a report with respect to the question or to assist in establishing the facts, the secretary shall inform that independent expert of the duties and powers he has under this rule: *rule 10(1) of Sch 6.* The independent expert shall have a duty to the Tribunal to:

(a)   assist it in furthering the overriding objective in *reg 3* of the *ET Regulations*;

(b)   comply with the requirements of the rules in *Sch 6* and any orders made by the Tribunal or a chairman in relation to the proceedings;

(c)   keep the Tribunal informed of any delay in complying with any order in the proceedings with the exception of minor or insignificant delays in compliance;

(d)   comply with any timetable imposed by the Tribunal or chairman in so far as this is reasonably practicable;

(e)   inform the Tribunal or a chairman on request by it or him of progress in the preparation of the independent expert's report;

(f)   prepare a report on the question based on the facts relating to the question and (subject to the provisions for national security cases in *rule 14*) send it to the Tribunal and the parties; and

(g)   make himself available to attend hearings in the proceedings.

An expert is under a duty to assist the Tribunal on matters within his expertise and this duty overrides any obligation to the person from whom he has received instructions or by whom he is paid: *rule 11(2)* of *Sch 6*. The independent expert may make an application for any order or for a hearing to be held as if he were a party to the proceedings: *rule 10(3)* of *Sch 6*. An independent expert shall be given notice of all hearings, orders or judgments in those proceedings as if a party to those proceedings and when a party is required to provide information to another party, such information shall also be provided to the independent expert: *rule 10(6)* of *Sch 6*. At any stage of the proceedings the Tribunal may, after giving the independent expert the opportunity to make representations, withdraw the requirement on the independent expert to prepare a report. If it does so, the Tribunal may itself determine the question, or it may determine that a different independent expert should be required to prepare the report: *rule 10(4)* of *Sch 6*. When a Tribunal determines that an independent expert is no longer required, the expert shall provide the Tribunal with all documentation and work in progress relating to the proceedings by a date specified by the Tribunal in a form which the tribunal is able to use: *rule 10(5)* of *Sch 6*. Such documentation and work in progress may be used in relation to those proceedings by the Tribunal or by another independent expert.

Use of expert evidence Expert evidence shall be restricted to that which, in the opinion of the tribunal, is reasonably required to resolve the proceedings: *rule 11(1)* of *Sch 6*. No party may call an expert or put in evidence an expert's report without the permission of the Tribunal and no expert report shall be put in evidence unless it has been disclosed to all other parties and any independent expert at least 28 days prior to the hearing: *rule 11(3)* of *Sch 6*. In proceedings in which an independent expert has been required to prepare a report on the question, the Tribunal shall not admit evidence of another expert on the question unless such evidence is based on the facts relating to the question. Unless the Tribunal considers it inappropriate to do so, any such expert report shall be disclosed to all parties and to the Tribunal on the same date on which the independent expert is required to send his report to the parties and to the Tribunal: *rule 11(4)* of *Sch 6*. If an expert (other than an independent expert) does not comply with these rules or an order made by the Tribunal or a chairman, the Tribunal may order that the evidence of that expert shall not be admitted: *rule 11(5)* of *Sch 6*. Where two or more parties wish to submit expert evidence on a particular issue, the Tribunal may order that the evidence on that issue is to be given by one joint expert only. When such an order has been made, if the parties wishing to instruct the joint expert cannot agree who should be the expert, the Tribunal may select the expert: *rule 11(6) of Sch 6*.

Written questions to experts. Rule 12 of *Sch 6* makes provision for written questions to be put to experts (including an independent expert) on their report. The question must be: put once only; put within 28 days of the date on which the parties were sent the report; for the purpose only of clarifying the factual basis of the report; copied to all other parties and experts involved in the proceedings at the same time as they are sent to the expert who prepared the report; and answered within 28 days of receiving the question. An expert's answers to questions shall be treated as part of the expert's report: rule 12(4) of Sch 6. Where a party has put a written question to an expert instructed by another party and the expert does not answer that question, or does not do so within 28 days, the Tribunal may order that the party instructing the expert may not rely on the evidence of that expert: *rule 12(5) of Sch 6*.

The burden of proving a claim under *EqPA 1970* is on the Claimant. The burden does not in law become heavier if the independent expert's report is against the Claimant. Nor is the transferred to the employer if the report is in favour of the claimant (see *Tennants Textile Colours Ltd v Todd* [1989] IRLR 3).

An employer may commission a job-evaluation study in order to obtain material with which to resist an equal pay claim. However, the fact that an employer was initiating and would implement an independent job evaluation was not considered sufficient grounds for granting a stay of proceedings on an equal pay claim in *Avon County Council v Foxall* [1989] ICR 407.

With effect from 6 April 2003, claimants or potential claimants in equal pay claims may serve questionnaires in the same manner as under the other discrimination statutes. The *Equal Pay (Questions and Replies) Order 2003 (SI 2003/722)*, provides for such questionnaires to be served before a claim is presented to a tribunal or within 21 days after such a claim or such longer period as the tribunal may on application allow. The tribunal may draw adverse inferences, including an inference that the equality clause has been breached, where an employer deliberately and without reasonable cause fails to reply in the eight-week period specified by *reg 4* of the *Order* or where an employer's reply is evasive or equivocal: *EqPA 1970, s 7B*. Such questionnaires will be particularly useful to complainants who bear the burden of establishing a disparate impact by reference to statistics: see *Nelson v Carillion Services Ltd* [2003] EWCA Civ 544, [2003] ICR 1256, CA.

24.22 EFFECT ON CONTRACTS

A term in a contract which purports to exclude or limit any provision of the *EqPA 1970* is unenforceable by any person in whose favour the term would operate (*Sex Discrimination Act 1975, s 77(3)*; and see 14.17 DISCRIMINATION AND EQUAL OPPORTUNITIES – III). However, a contract settling a complaint to an employment tribunal will be upheld if it was made with the assistance of a conciliation officer (*Sex Discrimination Act 1975, s 77(4)*; and see 2.3 ADVISORY, CONCILIATION AND ARBITRATION SERVICE). It will also be upheld if it meets the statutory conditions for a compromise agreement entered into after the employee has had independent advice (*SDA, s 77(4)(aa), (4A)*; and see 20.27 EMPLOYMENT TRIBUNALS). In other circumstances, an agreement by a woman that she will not bring a claim for equal pay will be void, and the payment of any sum to compromise such a claim will not prevent her from continuing with her complaint. In *Nimz v Freie und Hansestadt*

Hamburg [1991] IRLR 222, the ECJ held that where there is indirect discrimination in a provision of a collective agreement, the national court is required to disapply that provision, without requesting or awaiting its prior removal by collective negotiation (see also *Kowalska v Freie und Hansestadt Hamburg: C-33/69* [1992] ICR 29).

24.23 **Collective agreements**

Prior to the coming into force of *SDA 1986* a collective agreement containing differing provisions for men and women could by *EqPA 1970, s 3* be referred (at the request of any party to the agreement or the Secretary of State) to the Central Arbitration Committee ('CAC') which had jurisdiction to modify contracts governed by the collective agreement. *EqPA 1970, s 3* is now repealed by *SDA 1986* which provides that collective agreements (whether they would otherwise be legally enforceable or not) are deemed automatically unenforceable and void insofar as they provide for the inclusion in a contract of employment of a provision which contravenes *EqPA 1970, s 1*. Discriminatory collective agreements which are contracts can be referred to a county court by a person interested in the agreement. The court may remove or modify any unenforceable term (*SDA 1975, s 77; SDA 1986, s 6*). Actual or potential employees have certain rights to complain to employment tribunals about discriminatory collective agreements (*SDA, s 6(4A)*), as inserted by *TURERA 1993, s 32*; see 14.17 DISCRIMINATION AND EQUAL OPPORTUNITIES – III). Declarations made by the CAC prior to the repeal of *EqPA 1970, s 3* continue in force (*SDA 1986, s 9*). In *Nimz v Freie und Hansestadt Hamburg: C-184/89* [1991] IRLR 222, the ECJ held that where there is indirect discrimination in a provision of a collective agreement, the national court is required to disapply that provision, without requesting or awaiting its prior removal by collective negotiation (see also *Kowalska v Freie und Hansestadt Hamburg: C-33/69* [1992] ICR 29).

25 European Community Law

25.1 THE EUROPEAN COMMUNITY AND ITS LAW

European Community ('EC') law has applied to the United Kingdom since its accession to the European Community on 1 January 1973 (*European Communities Act 1972; European Communities (Amendment) Acts 1986* and *1993*). There are three basic sources of EC law:

(i)   the provisions of the principal *EC Treaty* itself;

(ii) EC legislation;

(iii) decisions of the European Court of Justice ('ECJ').

The constitutional underpinning of the EC is the Treaty establishing the European Economic Community. Often known as the *Treaty of Rome*, it is referred to below as the *EC Treaty*. The *EC Treaty* was made in 1957. It has been substantially amended since. The *Single European Act* in 1986, the *Maastricht Treaty* of December 1991 (which came into force on 1 November 1993) and the *Treaty of Amsterdam* which was signed on 1 October 1997 and which came into force on 1 May 1999, have all introduced significant changes. The *Treaty of Amsterdam* resulted in a renumbering of the articles of the *EC Treaty*. The new numbering is used below though, where applicable, the old numbering is included in brackets for ease of reference. The *EC Treaty* sets out the fundamental principles of the EC. The provisions particularly relevant to the EC's powers in the employment law field are *Arts 13, 94(100), 95(100A), 136(117), 137(118), 138(118A), 139(118B), 140(118C), 141(119), 251(189B)* and *302(235)*.

EC legislation takes the form of regulations and directives. Regulations are the closest equivalent to an Act of Parliament (in that they are 'directly applicable', ie they do not need to be implemented by national legislation) whereas directives are instructions to Member States to bring their national legislation into conformity with EC requirements.

The EC also promulgates 'recommendations'. Recommendations have no legal effect, but ought, as a matter of European law (although not necessarily national law) to be taken into account when construing national legislation adopted in order to implement them or where they are designed to supplement binding Community measures (*Grimaldi v Fond des Maladies Professionelles: 322/88* [1990] IRLR 400). The EAT adopted this approach to the *Recommendation on the Dignity of Men and Women at Work* (see 25.6 below) in *Wadman v Carpenter Farrar Partnership* [1993] IRLR 374.

The EC has its own court, the European Court of Justice ('ECJ'), which sits in Luxembourg, and is not to be confused with the European Court of Human Rights in Strasbourg (see HUMAN RIGHTS (30)). In deciding a particular case, the ECJ is assisted by an Advocate General, who gives an opinion upon the issues for decision after the ECJ has heard the arguments of the parties. There is also a Court of First Instance ('CFI'), but its role in employment matters is limited to dealing with disputes between the EC and its own employees (see 37.7 PUBLIC SECTOR EMPLOYEES). The rules of procedure of the ECJ and the CFI are to be found set out at [1991] 3 CMLR 745 and 795 respectively.

In *Mangold v Helm Case C-144/04* [2006] IRLR 143, the ECJ adopted a novel approach by identifying a 'general principle' of Community law (in that case a general principle of non-discrimination on grounds of age), the source of which was held to be found in various international instruments and in the constitutional traditions common to the Member States. It remains to be seen whether this approach, of identifying general principles of Community law based on common traditions, will become embedded in the jurisprudence of the ECJ.

25.2 **THE EFFECT OF EC LAW**

The wellspring of European law is the *EC Treaty*. Historically, UK law has been reluctant to accept that obligations arising from treaties have any substantive effect on domestic law. British jurists have insisted that for a treaty to produce rights or obligations within the domestic legal context there must be some implementing domestic legislation (for example see *Civilian War Claimants Association Ltd v R* [1932] AC 14). A doorway into the domestic law was created by *European Communities Act 1972, s 2(1)* which provided:

> 'All such rights, powers, liabilities, obligations and restrictions from time to time created or arising by or under the Treaties, and all such remedies and procedures from time to time provided for by or under the Treaties, as in accordance with the Treaties are without further enactment to be given legal effect or used in the United Kingdom shall be recognised and available in law, and be enforced, allowed and followed accordingly; and the expression "enforceable Community right" and similar expressions shall be read as referring to one to which this subsection applies.'

Where a directive is issued it is, of course, anticipated that some further act of enactment will normally be required.

Numerous domestic statutes and statutory instruments have been introduced or amended so as to give effect to EC obligations. These include, for example, the *Transfer of Undertakings (Protection of Employment) Regulations 2006* (*SI 2006/246*) (see TRANSFER OF UNDERTAKINGS (52)), and changes made to the law on the CONTRACT OF EMPLOYMENT (8), MATERNITY AND PARENTAL RIGHTS (33) and REDUNDANCY — II (39) by the *Trade Union Reform and Employment Rights Act 1993*.

It may be that the implementing legislation clearly and unequivocally implements the relevant European law. Such legislation will usually define the right conferred, state the remedy available for breach and identify the jurisdiction in and procedures by which the right may be enforced. However, all too often the legislation does not clearly and unequivocally implement the relevant law.

In such circumstances the principle that European law has primacy is expressed first through a principle of interpretation. Courts and tribunals are required, so far as possible, to interpret national law in the light of the wording and purpose of any relevant EC Directive (*Marleasing SA v La Comercial Internacional de Alimentacion SA: C-106/89* [1992] 1 CMLR 305). The House of Lords has been prepared to go so far as to read additional words into the statute (*Litster v Forth Dry Dock and Engineering Co Ltd* [1989] ICR 341). There is, however, a limit to how far the court or tribunal is able to go. The House of Lords has held that *Marleasing* only applies where the wording of the domestic provision is capable of being interpreted consistently with the directive, and not where consistency could be achieved only by distorting the meaning of the domestic legislation. (*Webb v EMO Air Cargo (UK) Ltd* [1993] ICR 175; see also *Duke v GEC Reliance Systems Ltd* [1988] ICR 339, *Re Hartlebury Printers Ltd* [1992] ICR 559, *Porter v*

Cannon Hygiene Ltd [1993] IRLR 329). In some circumstances, the court will be required to interpret a piece of legislation which, though it deals with the same subject matter as a directive, was not intended to implement European law. Whilst there had been controversy as to whether, in those circumstances, the principle of interpretation described above should be applied, *Marleasing* decided that it should.

R v Secretary of State, ex p EOC [1994] ICR 317, HL marked the beginning of a new approach. The House of Lords held that a provision of *EPCA 1978* which indirectly discriminated against women was contrary to the *Equal Treatment Directive 75/117/EEC* and should be disapplied in cases where the employee was entitled to rely on the direct effect of the European provisions (see below). The approach has since been used to disapply a number of the provisions of *EqPA 1970* including, by way of example, the provisions which excluded complaints by those indirectly discriminated against in relation to access to occupational pension schemes (*Preston v Wolverhampton Healthcare NHS Trust* [1997] IRLR 233, CA) and which provided that two employers could only be treated as 'associated' for the purposes of determining whether a complainant and her comparator are in the same employment where one of the two employers was a company (*Scullard v Knowles and Southern Region Council for Education and Training* [1996] IRLR 344). The latter case indicates the broad scope of the *EOC* principle. The provision disapplied in the *EOC* case was one which was discriminatory in itself. The provision in *Scullard*, on the other hand, is merely narrower in scope than the European provision (*art 141(119)*). See also *Perceval-Price v Department of Economic Development* [2000] IRLR 380, NICA, *Allonby v Accrington and Rossendale College: C-256/01* [2004] IRLR 224, *Alabaster v Barclays Bank plc and Secretary of State for Social Security* [2005] EWCA Civ 508, [2005] IRLR 576 and *R (on the application of) Finian Manson v Ministry of Defence* [2005] EWCA Civ 1678, (2006) ICR 355 (see below).

A directive enters into force in the sense of producing legal effects in the member states from the date of its publication in the Official Journal of the European Communities or from the date of its notification to Member States, *Adeneler v Ellinikos Organismos Galaktos: C-212/04* [2006] IRLR 716. During the period prescribed for transposition of a directive, member states must refrain from taking any measure liable seriously to compromise the attainment of the result prescribed by it, whether or not the national measure is concerned with transposition of the directive: *Mangold v Helm* (above) and *Adeneler v Ellinikos Organismos Galaktos*. During this period, domestic courts must refrain as far as possible from interpreting domestic law in a manner which might seriously compromise, after the period for transposition has expired, attainment of the objective pursued by that directive: *Adeneler v Ellinikos Organismos Galaktos*. Where the relevant provisions of the directive do not have direct effect, the general obligation owed by national courts to interpret domestic law in conformity with the directive exists once the period for its transposition has expired.

What if the State has failed to introduce legislation which properly and fully implements the European law by the date specified in the Directive? In those circumstances the Commission is empowered by *art 226 (169)* to bring enforcement proceedings against the defaulting Member State (see for example *Commission v United Kingdom: C-382/92* [1994] IRLR 392). *Article 227(170)* contains a related but rarely used power for other Member States to bring similar proceedings. In addition, there are three mechanisms by which European legislation which has not yet been implemented (or properly implemented) may be given effect to in British courts and tribunals: (1) a *Francovich* claim against the government for failure to implement; (2) reliance on the direct effect of the European legislation to bring a claim to enforce a European right; and (3) reliance on the direct effect of the European legislation to disapply an inconsistent domestic provision.

(1)Francovich claims

Firstly, the landmark decision of *Francovich v Italy: C- 6, 9/90* [1992] IRLR 84 decided that an individual may have an EC law claim for damages against the State for failure properly to implement a directive. *Francovich* claims should be brought in the High Court; the tribunal does not have jurisdiction to hear such claims (*Secretary of State for Employment v Mann* [1996] ICR 197, EAT, affirmed by the Court of Appeal [1997] ICR 209. The point was not considered by the House of Lords ([1999] ICR 898)). The appropriate defendant is the Attorney General (*Mann; R v Secretary of State, ex p EOC* above). In order to bring a claim, the claimant will have to show that the unimplemented European provision is intended to confer rights on individuals. She must also establish that the breach is sufficiently serious and that the failure to implement the European provision is causally connected to the loss incurred (*Francovich* above). The ECJ's decision in *Brasserie du Pêcheur SA v Germany: C-46/93* [1996] IRLR 267 provides useful guidance as to the scope of the substantive and procedural rights of an individual wishing to bring a *Francovich* claim. Where the relevant provision is enacted in an area of policy in relation to which a wide discretion is reserved to the Member State the breach must be 'manifest' and 'grave'. Factors relevant to deciding whether a particular failure to implement is sufficiently serious include: the clarity and precision of the European provision, the breadth of the discretion reserved to the Member State and the question whether the default was intentional. A breach will almost certainly be 'sufficiently serious' where a Member State fails to implement a provision in circumstances where the ECJ has already ruled that there is an infringement or where it fails to take any steps to implement the Directive before the date specified for implementation (*Dillenkofer v Germany C-178/94* [1997] IRLR 60, ECJ).

The Member State cannot:

(a)   restrict the right to damages to cases where intentional or negligent default can be established;

(b)   adopt procedural rules governing the bringing of *Francovich* claims which are less favourable than those applying to analogous domestic claims or which have the effect of making it impossible or excessively difficult for individuals to obtain damages;

(c)   impose limits on the amount of damages recoverable which would have the effect that the compensation available was not commensurate with the loss suffered.

Provided the breach is sufficiently serious, damages are available whether or not the ECJ has ruled that there is an infringement: *Robins v Secretary of State for Work and Pensions: C-278/05* [2007] IRLR 270.

Within our own jurisdiction legislation purporting to implement EC law has been successfully challenged using judicial review (for instance *R v Secretary of State for Employment, ex p Equal Opportunities Commission* [1994] ICR 317, HL and *Equal Opportunities Commission v Secretary of State for Trade and Industry* [2007] IRLR 327).

(2)claims to enforce a directly effective European right

Secondly, the ECJ's doctrine of 'direct effect' means that, in some circumstances, an enforcement right may be conferred on an individual whether or not there has been any implementing legislation. There are two sources of directly effective rights: articles of the Treaty and Directives. An example of the former is the right to equal pay conferred by *art 141 (119)*. The ECJ decided that this particular provision was directly effective in the case of *Defrenne v Sabena: 43/75* [1976] ICR 547.

A directly effective provision may be either horizontally or vertically directly effective. A provision which has vertical direct effect is one which creates rights which an individual may enforce against the State but not against other individuals. A provision which has horizontal direct effect creates a right which may be enforced against other individuals.

Some, though not all, directly effective Treaty provisions have horizontal direct effect. An example of the application of horizontal direct effect is the case of *Barber v Guardian Royal Exchange Insurance Group: C-262/88* [1990] ICR 616. Existing domestic anti-discrimination legislation excluded, broadly speaking, matters relating to pensions. In *Barber* the ECJ decided that occupational pensions were 'pay' within the meaning of *art 141 (119)*. As a result, individuals were able to bring a claim if they suffered sexual discrimination in relation to the benefits paid under that scheme. European law filled the gap left by the domestic legislation.

Where a Member State fails properly to implement a directive by the due date, a directive may be the source of directly effective rights. However, these rights only have vertical direct effect (*Faccini Dori v Recreb Srl: C-91/92* [1995] All ER (EC) 1; but cf *CIA v SA Signalson: C-194/94* [1996] All ER (EC) 557 in which a defendant to a counterclaim was entitled to have the domestic provision upon which the counterclaim was based disapplied on the basis that it had not been notified to the European Commission as required by *Directive 83/189/EEC* thus arguably giving some limited horizontal effect to the directive). The rationale is that the State cannot rely on its own failure to implement the right to defend itself against those who might have been able to exercise the right against it. Direct effect can only arise where the Member State concerned has failed to implement the directive properly within the time allowed for such implementation (*Suffritti v Istituto Razionale della Previdenza Sociale (INPS)* [1993] IRLR 289), although it is immaterial that the factual situation relied upon by the individual arose before the implementation deadline (*Verholen v Sociale Verzekeringsbank Amsterdam* [1992] IRLR 38). But for this purpose the 'State' includes any body, whatever its legal form, which has been made responsible by the State for providing a public service under the control of the State, and which has special powers for that purpose (*Foster v British Gas plc* [1991] ICR 84 and 463 and see *National Union of Teachers v Governing Body of St Mary's Church of England (Aided) Junior School* [1997] ICR 334, CA – a voluntary aided school is an emanation of the State; see further 37.7 PUBLIC SECTOR EMPLOYEES). Finally, the individual seeking to rely upon the directive must be a citizen of an EC Member State (*Bernstein v Immigration Appeal Tribunal* [1988] Imm AR 449, and must be a person of a kind within the scope of the directive (*Verholen*, above).

Not all treaty provisions or directives are directly effective. The precise requirements for direct effect to be established are complex, but the provision concerned must be clear, unconditional and precise.

A directly effective right may, in theory, operate in one of two main ways. The right may be used in order to disapply a bar to an existing domestic remedy, or it may create a 'free-standing' right to a remedy. In many cases both rationales may be appropriate. For instance, in a case similar to *Barber* (above) a claimant may argue either that the Community right works to disapply the exclusion of pension-related discrimination from the existing domestic legislation or that there is a free-standing right to an equal pension under *art 141* (*119*) which, being horizontally directly effective, may be enforced against other individuals. The distinction between the two affects the question of what court or tribunal may consider cases based on European law, and what time limits apply to them.

At one point it seems to have been assumed that the employment tribunal had jurisdiction to hear claims based directly upon *art 141* (*Stevens v Bexley Health Authority* [1989] IRLR 240; *Secretary of State for Scotland v Wright and Hannah* [1991] IRLR 187). The problem with that assumption is that the employment tribunal has a statutory jurisdiction. In other words, it can only hear the cases which a statute has specifically conferred jurisdiction upon it to hear. No statute has ever conferred jurisdiction on the employment tribunal to hear cases which are directly based upon *art 141*. In two cases (*Biggs v Somerset County Council* [1996] IRLR 203 and *Barber v Staffordshire County Council* [1996] IRLR 209) the Court of Appeal stated very clearly that the tribunal does not have a jurisdiction to hear 'free-standing' *art 141* claims.

The question of what time limits apply to such claims based directly on *art 141* has proved vexed (see the detailed discussion in 24.24 and 24.25 EQUAL PAY). Broadly speaking, European law has left the question of time limits to the Member State subject to the following general principles:

(1)   the time limits applied to the enforcement of EC law rights should be no more restrictive than those which apply to analogous domestic claims (see *Preston v Wolverhampton Healthcare NHS Trust* [2000] IRLR 506, ECJ and [2001] UKHL 5, [2001] IRLR 237);

(2)   the time limits should not make the enforcement of the rights impossible in practice (see *Rewe-Zentralfinanz GmbH v Landwirtschaftskammer für Saarland: 33/76* [1977] 1 CMLR 533 and *Fisscher v Voorhuis Hengelo BV: C-128/93* [1994] IRLR 662); and

(3)   provisions which seek to limit the amount of compensation recoverable by restricting the extent to which a claim may be back-dated are less likely to be considered to make enforcement of rights impossible than more straight-forward time limits (*Steenhorst-Neerings v Bestuur van de Bedrijfsvereniging voor Detailhandel, Ambachten en Huisvrouwen: C-410/92* [1994] IRLR 244; *Johnson v Chief Adjudication Officer (No 2): C-338/91* [1995] IRLR 157 and *Preston v Wolverhampton Healthcare NHS Trust* [2001] IRLR 237).

There was formerly thought to be a fourth principle, namely that where the right which the claimant seeks to enforce is a vertically directly effective right, time will not begin to run until the directive has been properly implemented (*Emmott v Minister for Social Welfare: C-208/90* [1993] ICR 8). But in *Fantask A/S v Industrieministeriet (Ehrvervsministeriet) Case C-188/95* [1998] All ER (EC) 1 the ECJ decided that *Emmott* was restricted to its own facts and applied the *Rewe* criteria.

(3)reliance on directly effective European legislation to disapply a domestic bar to a claim

The third mechanism by which unimplemented European legislation may be given effect to in domestic courts and tribunals derives from the decision in *Biggs v Somerset County Council* [1995] IRLR 452 (affirmed by the Court of Appeal at [1996] IRLR 203) which concerned a woman who did not qualify for protection against unfair dismissal because she worked part-time. The application was prompted by the decision of the House of Lords in the *EOC* case (above) that the hours thresholds contained in *EPCA 1978* were discriminatory, contrary to the *Equal Treatment Directive*, and could not be justified. The application was submitted many years after the relevant dismissal. An issue arose, therefore, as to what the relevant time limit was. The claimant argued, *inter alia*, that her claim was for equal pay under *art 141 (119)*. The 'pay' in question was compensation for unfair dismissal. Though once a matter of considerable controversy, the ECJ has now decided that unfair dismissal compensation is pay for the purposes of *art 141 (119)* (*Seymour-Smith* [1999] ICR 447, ECJ). The applicant relied upon *Rankin v British Coal Corpn* [1993] IRLR 69 to support an argument that there was no time limit for EC rights other than a requirement that they be brought within a reasonable time. In her submission this meant within a reasonable time of the decision in *EOC* which was the point at which it first became clear that they might have a claim.

The decision of the EAT in *Biggs* was to the effect that the claim was not brought under *art 141 (119)* but rather under the domestic legislation. The significance of the EC right was that it operated to override and disapply what would otherwise have been a bar to the bringing of proceedings under the domestic law. As the claim was under domestic law the domestic time limit (three months from the date of dismissal) applied unless it was itself inconsistent with EC law which it was not. A radically 'free-standing' European right of the sort argued for by the claimant would not have been enforceable in the employment tribunal as its jurisdiction is strictly defined by statute. No statute has conferred on the industrial tribunal any jurisdiction to consider claims based solely on EC law, which are independent of the operation of any domestic legislation (cf also *McManus v Daylay Foods Ltd* (unreported) EAT/82/95 and *Preston v Wolver-hampton Healthcare NHS Trust* [1997] IRLR 233, CA for the application of the same reasoning to claims for a redundancy payment and in relation to the indirectly discriminatory exclusion of part-timers from access to membership of occupational pension schemes respectively). The decision was expressly limited to a consideration of cases based upon *art 141 (119)*. The EAT accepted that as a result of *Emmott*, cases based on a directive might fall to be treated differently.

The obligation of English courts and tribunals to determine questions of EC law in accordance with the decisions of, and the principles laid down by, the ECJ is to be found in the *European Communities Act 1972, s 2(1)*. The national court is entitled to take a point of EC law of its own motion (*Verholen*, above, where the Advocate General suggested that it was under a positive obligation to do so). *Article 234 (177)* of the *Treaty of Rome* provides a mechanism whereby national courts may, and sometimes must, refer questions to the ECJ for a preliminary ruling (see 20.47 EMPLOYMENT TRIBUNALS – I). The jurisdiction of employment tribunals to determine whether a domestic provision is in fact incompatible with EC law was confirmed by the Court of Appeal in *R (on the application of) Finian Manson v Ministry of Defence* [2005] EWCA Civ 1678, (2006) ICR 355. In reliance on the approach taken by the EAT in *Biggs,* the Court of Appeal rejected the argument that the tribunal's role was limited to determining whether or not the domestic bar applied on the facts and questions of compatibility with EC law were to be left to another forum, such as in a judicial review claim.

In a potentially very far-reaching judgment, the ECJ in *Mangold v Helm Case C-144/04* [2006] IRLR 143 held that domestic courts are obliged to set aside provisions of national legislation which are incompatible with a Directive even before the expiry date for implementation of the EC legislation had passed. The ECJ held that provisions of German domestic law relating to fixed-term workers over the age of 52 were incompatible with EC law even before the date for German implementation of the Directive prohibiting age discrimination had passed (2006). The ECJ relied on two grounds for such a finding. First and less controversially, the ECJ referred to *Inter-Environnement Wallonie ASBL v Region Wallonie* ECJ, 7.2.98 (C-129/96) for the principle that, during the period prescribed for implementing a directive, Member States must 'refrain from taking any measures liable seriously to compromise the result prescribed by that directive' and held that the German provisions were liable to compromise the end result of prohibiting age discrimination by 2006. Second, and in a novel approach to constitutional principle, the ECJ held that the Equal Treatment Directive did not itself lay down the principle of equal treatment; it simply laid down a framework for combating discrimination on the grounds of religion or belief, disability, age or sexual orientation. The source of the actual principle underlying the prohibition of those forms of discrimination in the Directive was found in various international instruments and constitutional traditions common to Member States. The principle of non-discrimination on the ground of age was accordingly a general principle of Community law. As a result, domestic courts are required to set aside domestic legislation adopted during the period for implementing a directive which is incompatible with general principles of Community law, even before the date for implementation of the relevant directive.

25.3 EC REQUIREMENTS AFFECTING EMPLOYMENT LAW

The area of employment law, and in particular its place within the more general framework of EC social policy, has proved to be both controversial and problematic.

In 1989 the Commission produced a draft Community Charter of the Fundamental Social Rights of Workers, generally known as the Social Charter. In the form adopted by the majority of Member States in the European Council at Strasbourg in December 1989, it deals *inter alia* with freedom of movement, the right to an 'equitable wage' (ie sufficient to enable a decent standard of living), the right to a weekly rest period and to paid annual leave, the freedom to join or not to join trade unions, the right to strike, access to vocational training, equal treatment for men and women, information, consultation and worker participation (especially in relation to technological changes, restructuring and mergers, collective redundancy procedures and employment policies affecting trans-frontier workers), health and safety, the minimum employment age and protection of young people (by limiting the duration of work and prohibiting nightwork under the age of 18) and disabled persons.

The Charter is expressed in fairly general terms and does not itself create legal rights and obligations. However, the European Council in adopting it invited the Commission to submit initiatives as soon as possible pursuant to its powers under the *EC Treaty*, 'with a view to the adoption of legal instruments for the effective implementation, as and when the internal market is completed, of those rights which come within the Community's area of competence'. This led to the formulation of a Social Action Programme which to date has comprised about 50 measures, some legally binding and others not (see 25.1 above) of which the majority have been adopted. However, other measures foundered on the opposition of certain Member States. The UK strongly opposed certain measures, notably legislation on works councils and working hours. Certain measures made their way through to becoming law by an alternative route; the Social Protocol, which is discussed below.

595

On 29 April 1998, the Commission produced a new Social Action Programme setting out the Commission's initiatives for the next three years. The new programme reflects the broader scope of responsibility created by the *Amsterdam Treaty* (see below). A wide variety of potential measures is envisaged including, for the first time, measures aimed at combating racial discrimination.

In December 1991 the European Council, meeting at Maastricht, agreed a new *European Treaty*, which came into force on 1 November 1993. The original intention was that this should include a Social Chapter, which would provide the means of implementing many of the ideas in the Social Charter, both by extending the scope of majority voting on proposals, in place of a requirement of unanimity among Member States, and by extending the areas in which the EC had competence to act. However, the United Kingdom was strongly opposed to the Social Chapter, and negotiated the right to 'opt out'. As a result, the relevant provisions took the form of a Social Protocol to the *Maastricht Treaty*, which did not bind the United Kingdom. Accordingly, EC measures adopted thereafter in the employment law field only formed part of English law if they were agreed pursuant to the existing Treaty provisions, and not if they were adopted by the other eleven Member States under the Social Protocol.

This alternative mechanism, as indicated above, allowed certain specific measures to which the United Kingdom was implacably opposed, to be adopted. One example was *Directive 94/45/EC*, the *Works Councils Directive* which deals with employee participation in multinational companies of a certain size. The UK has since implemented the *Directive* (see 25.12 below). See also EMPLOYEE PARTICI-PATION (18).

The Social Protocol procedure is notable for the role that it gives to the 'Social Partners'. These are the ETUC (representing employees), the UNICE (representing private sector employers) and the CEEP (representing public sector employers). Where the Commission is proposing to adopt legislation pursuant to the Social Protocol it must consult with the Social Partners. The Partners then have up to nine months in which to seek to reach an agreement between themselves as to the content of the legislation. If they succeed in agreeing, they can then ask the Commission to put the matter before the Council in order to seek a decision or directive giving the agreement legislative force (this process was followed in relation to the *Parental Leave Directive* and the *Directive on fixed-term contracts* (*1999/70/EC*)).

The election, on 1 May 1997, of a Labour Government significantly altered the UK's attitude to the Social Chapter. The Labour Party had campaigned on the basis that it would 'opt into' the European measures.

On 1 October 1997, a new Treaty on European Union ('the *Amsterdam Treaty*') was signed. It was ratified on 1 May 1999. The *Amsterdam Treaty* incorporates the Social Chapter into the main body of the EC Treaty. The Council adopted directives to extend the three measures previously adopted under the Social Protocol (ie the *Works Councils, Parental Leave* and *Burden of Proof Directives*) to cover the UK. The first two have been implemented by the *Transnational Information and Consultation with Employees Regulations 1999* (*SI 1999/3323*) and the *Maternity and Parental Leave etc. Regulations 1999* (*SI 1999 /3312*). The last has been implemented by the *Sex Discrimination* (*Indirect Discrimination and Burden of Proof*) *Regulations 2001* (*SI 2001/2660*), which came into force on 12 October 2001.

The new Treaty contains a specific chapter on employment, though this is concerned with the promotion of high levels of employment within the Community rather than employment protection measures. A new *art 13* is incorporated into the *EC Treaty* which enables the Council to 'take appropriate action to combat discrimination based on sex, racial or ethnic origin, religion or belief, disability, age or sexual orientation' (see *Council Directive establishing a general framework for equal treatment in employment and occupation* 2000/78/EC and *Council Directive implementing the principle of equal treatment between persons irrespective of racial or ethnic origin* 2000/43/EC and the amendments made to the *Equal Treatment Directive 76/207/EEC by Directive 2002/73/EC*).

Community law requirements have been enacted or proposed in relation to a wide variety of different areas, notably to the following:

(*a*)   free movement of labour;

(*b*)   equal access to social security benefits;

(*c*)   equal pay and equal treatment;

(*d*)   other individual employment rights, including rights on the insolvency of the employer;

(*e*)   redundancy procedure;

(*f*)   rights on the transfer of an undertaking;

(*g*)   health and safety at work;

(*h*)   information and consultation.

These are examined in the following paragraphs.

Other EC requirements affect specific employments such as that of transport drivers. Information about relevant EC legislation may be obtained from the office of the Commission of the EC at 8 Storey's Gate, London SW1.

25.4 FREE MOVEMENT OF LABOUR

Articles 39–42 (48–51) of the *EC Treaty* require Member States to permit the free movement of workers between Member States. No discrimination based on nationality may be exercised against EC nationals in relation to employment, remuneration or other conditions of work and employment. Free access to employment is a fundamental right, and there must be a judicial remedy against decisions which refuse the benefit of that right to EC nationals. (*UNECTEF v Heylens: 222/86* [1989] 1 CMLR 901). Directives and regulations relating to these Articles have been passed. Great Britain has complied with these requirements so that EC nationals have a right to enter the country to take or seek work without the necessity of obtaining a work permit.

Article 39(48) of the *EC Treaty*, as a directly enforceable provision, was relied upon by the EAT in its decision in *Bossa v Nordstress Ltd* [1998] IRLR 284 to disapply *ss 4* and *8(1)* of the *Race Relations Act 1976*. These sections exclude those whose work is wholly or mainly outside Great Britain from bringing claims in the employment tribunal.

Directives regulate the mutual recognition of qualifications in Member States for professions such as medicine and dentistry. The *First and Second Diploma Directives (Directives 89/48/EEC and 92/51/EEC)* deal with the equivalence of degree-level qualifications and other higher education and vocational qualifications respectively. The former has already been implemented by the United

Kingdom, and the latter was due for implementation by June 1994 but has only been partially implemented. Community nationals employed or seeking work here have the right to remain and to bring their families with them (see also FOREIGN EMPLOYEES (26)). On 4 June 1998 political agreement was reached at the Social Affairs Council with respect to a proposed directive aimed at safeguarding the supplementary pension rights of employed and self-employed workers who move within the EU.

25.5   EQUAL ACCESS TO SOCIAL SECURITY BENEFITS

EC art 10(5) provides for the passing by the Council of the EC of measures to ensure the aggregation of social security benefits which may have been paid in different Member States, and for the payment of benefit in one Member State where contributions have been made in another member State. Such regulations have been passed (*Regulation 1408/71*, as amended; *Regulation 574/72*). The regulations also ensure that the rules about liability to pay national insurance in the UK while working elsewhere in the EC are in line with the rules applied by the other Member States. (See generally DSS leaflet SA 29 'Your social security and pension rights in the European Community'.) Equal treatment between men and women in matters of social security, including occupational social security schemes, is largely dealt with by *Directive 79/7/EEC* and *Directive 86/378/EEC*; however, the ECJ has also held domestic social security provisions to be contrary to the *Equal Treatment Directive 76/207/EEC* (*Meyers v Adjudication Officer: C-116/94* [1995] IRLR 498, a UK case about 'Family Credit'). A detailed account of this area is beyond the scope of this book.

25.6   EQUAL PAY AND EQUAL TREATMENT

From 1 May 1999, the *EC Treaty* has had equality between men and women as an explicit objective of the community (*art 2*). In all its activities, the EC must aim to eliminate inequalities, and to promote equality between men and women (*art 3(2)*). *EC art 141(119)* obliges each Member State to ensure and maintain the principle that men and women should receive equal pay for equal work. (*Article141(3)(119)* empowers the Council using the qualified majority procedure provided for in *art 251(189b)* to adopt measures to ensure the application of the principle of equal opportunities and equal treatment of men and women in matters of employment (see *art 1* of *Council Directive 75/117/EEC*.) Further, *Council Directive 76/207/EEC* requires Member States to take the measures necessary to implement the principle of equal treatment for men and women in relation to the following stages of employment: engagement, training, promotion, working conditions and dismissal. *Directive 2002/73/EC* amends *Directive 76/207/EEC* and, as implemented in domestic legislation by the *Employment Equality (Sex Discrimination) Regulations 2005, SI 2005/2467,* makes sexual harassment a form of direct sex discrimination in and of itself. The definition of indirect discrimination is also reformulated as covering situations where: 'an apparently neutral provision, criterion or practice disadvantages a substantially higher proportion of the members of one sex unless that provision, criterion or practice is appropriate and necessary and can be justified by objective factors unrelated to sex': as implemented by *s 1 SDA 1975* (as amended by the *Employment Equality (Sex Discrimination) Regulations 2005, SI 2005/2467*). A number of other amendments are made so as to incorporate the effect of the ECJ's jurisprudence in matters of equal treatment.

The UK sought to comply with the requirements imposed by *art 141* and *Council Directives 75/117/EEC* and *76/207/EEC*. However, in a number of cases, the ECJ has held that the UK had failed to comply fully with its EC obligations and further legislation has had to be introduced. See eg *Commission v United Kingdom: 61/81* [1982] ICR 578; *Commission v United Kingdom:165/82* [1984] ICR 192; *Marshall v Southampton and South West Hampshire Area Health Authority (Teaching): 152/84* [1986] ICR 335 (and now see *Marshall (No 2): C-271/91* [1993] IRLR 445); and *Johnston v Chief Constable of the Royal Ulster Constabulary: 222/84* [1987] ICR 83. The domestic courts have also proven to be willing to find, without a reference to the ECJ, that domestic legislation is incompatible with European provisions. See eg *R v Secretary of State for Employment, ex p EOC* [1994] ICR 317, *Scullard v Knowles* [1996] IRLR 344 and *Equal Opportunities Commission v Secretary of State for Trade and Industry* [2007] IRLR 327. The Government has accepted that the exclusion of members of armed forces from the scope of the protection of the *SDA 1975* was contrary to EC law. The *Sex Discrimination Act 1975 (Application to Armed Forces etc) Regulations 1994 (SI 1994 No 3276)* amended the *SDA 1975* with effect from 1 February 1995. See also EQUAL PAY (24) and DISCRIMINATION AND EQUAL OPPORTUNITIES – I (12).

Directive 86/378/EEC provides for equal treatment in occupational social security schemes (or pensions as they are more familiarly known in the UK). It has been amended by *Directive 96/96/EC* which came into effect on 1 July 1997 and which is intended to formalise the principles established by the ECJ in *Barber* and subsequent cases (cf EQUAL PAY (24)).

In October 1992 a *Directive on the Protection of Pregnant Women at Work (Directive 92/85/EEC)* was adopted, which has led to the inclusion of a number of new and improved maternity rights provisions in *ERA 1996*. See also MATERNITY AND PARENTAL RIGHTS (33).

Parental leave. The Government has sought to implement the *Parental Leave Directive (Directive 96/34/EC)* by bringing into force the *Maternity and Parental Leave Regulations 1999 (SI 1999/3312)*. The domestic provisions only confer a right to leave on parents of children born on or after 15 December 1999. The compatibility of this restriction with Community law was referred to the ECJ (*R v Secretary of State for Trade and Industry, ex p Trades Union Congress* [2000] IRLR 565). Consequent amendments were made to ensure compliance with the *Directive*: see the *Maternity and Parental Leave (Amendment) Regulations 2001 (SI 2001/4010)*.

Part-timers. The *Part-time Workers (Prevention of Less Favourable Treatment) Regulations 2000 (SI 2000/1551)* came into force on 1 July 2000 and implement the *EU Part-time Work Directive (97/81/EEC)*.

In December 1991 a *Recommendation on the Dignity of Men and Women at Work* was adopted, which is not legally binding, but will be taken into account by courts and tribunals (see 25.1 above). It may be especially relevant to complaints of sex discrimination founded upon incidents of sexual harassment (see DISCRIMINATION AND EQUAL OPPORTUNITIES – I (12)). A further *Recommendation on Child Care* was adopted in March 1992.

The *Sex Discrimination (Indirect Discrimination and Burden of Proof) Regulations 2001 (SI 2001/2660)* came into force from 12 October 2001. The *Regulations* implement the provisions of the *EC Directive on the burden of proof in cases of discrimination based on sex (EEC/97/80)* by inserting a new *s 63A* and *s 1(2)* into the *Sex Discrimination Act 1975* (see DISCRIMINATION AND EQUAL OPPORTUNITIES – I (12)).

Discrimination on grounds other than sex. Article 13 of the *EC Treaty* confers a power on the EU to legislate against discrimination on grounds of racial or ethnic origin, religion or belief, disability, age and sexual orientation. The European Council has adopted two directives which are intended to give effect to the broad anti-discrimination principles found in *art 13* of the *Treaty*.

The first is *Council Directive 2000/43/EC* of 29 June 2000 implementing the principle of equal treatment between persons irrespective of racial or ethnic origin'. The *Directive* prohibits direct and (unless it is objectively justified) indirect discrimination on grounds of racial or ethnic origin in both the public and private sectors. It does not prohibit discrimination on grounds of nationality. Harassment is expressly to be treated as an act of direct discrimination. Victimisation is also prohibited. There is a genuine occupational requirement defence. The provisions of the *Directive* have been implemented, so far as the UK considered necessary, by the *Race Relations Act 1976 (Amendment) Regulations (SI 2003/1626)*.

The second directive is *Council Directive 2000/78/EC* of 27 November 2000 establishing a general framework for equal treatment in employment and occupation. The *Directive* prohibits direct and unjustified indirect discrimination on grounds of 'religion or belief, disability, age or sexual orientation'. Like the *Race Discrimination Framework Directive* described above, it applies to both public and private sectors, prohibits harassment and victimisation, and includes an 'occupational requirements' defence. *Article 5* of the *Directive* introduces a duty to take proportionate and appropriate measures to enable disabled persons to have access to, participate, or advance, in employment or to undergo training which is analogous to the obligation imposed to by the *Disability Discrimination Act 1995, s 6* to make reasonable adjustments, see *Chacón Navas v Eurest Colectividades SA: C-13/05* [2006] IRLR 706. *Article 6* creates a defence of objective justification in cases of direct age discrimination. The *Directive* has been implemented in Great Britain by the *Employment Equality (Religion or Belief) Regulations 2003 (SI 2003/1660)*, and the *Employment Equality (Sexual Orientation) Regulations 2003 (SI 2003/1661)* and the *Employment Equality (Age) Regulations 2006 (SI 2006/1031)* which came into force on 1 October 2006.

25.7   OTHER INDIVIDUAL EMPLOYMENT RIGHTS

Directive 91/353/EEC (the *Proof of Employment Directive*) was adopted in October 1991. As a result of this *Directive*, the United Kingdom, with effect from 30 August 1993 and by means of amending the *EPCA 1978* (now *ERA 1996*), extended the rights which already existed for employees to receive written particulars of the terms of their employment (see 8.4 CONTRACT OF EMPLOYMENT).

Minimum rights for the employees of insolvent employers were specified by *Directive 80/987/EEC*, amended by *Directive 2002/74/EC* (see 31.1 INSOLVENCY OF EMPLOYER).

In September 1996, the Council adopted a *Directive on the Posting of Workers (96/71/EC)*, which deals with cross-border sub-contracting. It was implemented by means of the *Equal Opportunities (Employment Legislation) (Territorial Limits) Regulations 1999 (SI 1999/3163)*. EqPA 1970, SDA 1975, RRA 1976 and DDA 1995 are all subject to territorial limitation. The complainant has to be employed at an establishment on Great Britain and was not formerly treated as being so employed if he worked 'wholly or mainly outside Great Britain'. As from

16 December 1999, the *Regulations* delete the words 'or mainly' from the various statutory provisions and thereby extend their scope of application to those posted overseas.

On 18 March 1999, a framework agreement was reached between the Social Partners in relation to those employed on fixed-term contracts. The agreement has twin aims, namely, to:

(*a*)   improve the quality of fixed-term work by ensuring the application of the principle of non-discrimination; and

(*b*)   establish a framework to prevent abuse arising from the use of successive fixed-term employment contracts or relationships.

The principle of non-discrimination requires employers not to treat those employed on fixed-term contracts less favourably than those employed permanently unless the less favourable treatment can be objectively justified. The agreement seeks to tackle abuse by introducing rules requiring objective reasons for renewal, a maximum duration and a limit on the number of times that a contract can be renewed.

On 28 June 1999, the Council adopted a *Directive* transposing the framework agreement into European Law (*1999/70/EC*). The *Directive* was implemented in the UK by the *Fixed-term Employees* (*Prevention of Less Favourable Treatment*) *Regulations 2002* (*SI 2002/2034*) which came into force on 1 October 2002.

25.8   REDUNDANCY PROCEDURE

Directive 75/129/EEC contains requirements for the approximation of the laws of Member States relating to collective redundancies. This was complied with by the enactment of provisions now to be found in *TULRCA 1992, ss 188–198*. A new directive, *Directive 92/56/EEC*, was adopted in June 1992 so as to amend the previous legislation. This was implemented by amendments made to the *TULRCA 1992*. See 39.2–39.6 REDUNDANCY – II.

The ECJ found that by restricting the obligation to consult prior to collective redundancies to circumstances where the employer recognises a trade union in respect of the class of employees affected, the UK had failed properly to implement *Directive 75/129/EEC* (*Commission v United Kingdom: Case C-383/92* [1994] ICR 664). In order to remedy this, the *Collective Redundancies and Transfer of Undertakings* (*Protection of Employment*) (*Amendment*) *Regulations 1995* (*SI 1995/2587*) were enacted (see also 25.9 below).

The two Directives (*75/129/EEC* and *92/56/EEC*) were consolidated in a new *Directive 98/59/EC* which was adopted on 20 July 1998.

25.9   RIGHTS ON TRANSFER OF BUSINESS

The *Transfer of Undertakings* (*Protection of Employment*) *Regulations 1981* (*SI 1981/1794*) (now repealed by the *Transfer of Undertakings* (*Protection of Employment*) *Regulations 2006* (*SI 2006/246*) were intended to implement the requirements of *Directive 77/187/EEC* (the *Acquired Rights Directive*). In fact, the *1981 Regulations* proved to be defective in several respects, and various amendments were made by the *Trade Union Reform and Employment Rights Act 1993* in an attempt to bring them into line with the *Directive*. However, subsequent to those amendments being made, a further failure properly to comply was identified in *Commission v United Kingdom: Case C- 382/92* [1994] ICR 664 the ECJ found that by restricting the obligation to consult prior to a transfer to circumstances where the employer recognises a trade union in respect of the class of employees affected, the UK had failed properly to implement *Directive 77/187/EEC*. In order to remedy this, the *Regulations* mentioned in 25.8 above (*SI 1995/2587*) were enacted.

On 4 June 1998, amendments to the *Acquired Rights Directive*, designed to reduce uncertainty about the *Directive*, were agreed at the Social Affairs Council. The amendments (which were published in the OJ on 17 July 1998):

(*a*)   establish that the *Directive* applies to subcontracting operations;

(*b*)   specify that the *Directive* applies to transfers made from the public to the private sector;

(*c*)   enable the *Directive* to be applied to pension rights;

(*d*)   detail the requirements for a consultation under the *Directive*; and

(*e*)   enable employee representatives to negotiate to save jobs when a business which is insolvent is transferred.

On 12 March 2001, a new *Transfers Directive* (*2001/23/EC*) came into force. It is intended to codify the *Acquired Rights Directive* (*77/187/EEC*) and the amendments thereto adopted in 1998 (which are described in the main text). The *Transfer of Undertakings* (*Protection of Employment*) *Regulations 2006* (*SI 2006/246*) came into force with effect from 6 April 2006 and are intended to implement the *Transfers Directive*.

(See TRANSFER OF UNDERTAKINGS (52).)

25.10 HEALTH AND SAFETY

Between 1977 and 1986, the EC adopted directives on various aspects of health and safety, including safety signs, lead, asbestos and noise. A framework Directive was adopted in 1989, and five further directives (relating to minimum standards for safety and health, the use of machines and equipment, personal protective equipment and visual display units, and the handling of heavy loads) were subsequently adopted. Regulations were made by statutory instrument towards the end of 1992 to implement these later *Directives*, with effect from 1 January 1993. The *1989 Directive* on use of work equipment has been amended by *Directive 95/63/EC* and *Directive 2001/45/EC*. The amendments made by *Directive 95/63/EC* were implemented by *The Construction* (*Health, Safety and Welfare*) *Regulations 1996*. New regulations implementing *Directive 2001/45/EC* are currently being drafted by the Health and Safety Executive. A *Directive* concerned with the protection of workers from risks relating to chemical agents was adopted by the Council on 7 April 1998. (See 27.25 HEALTH AND SAFETY AT WORK – I.)

25.11 WORKING TIME

One *Directive* which managed to be adopted despite the objections of the UK is the *Working Time Directive 93/104/EEC*. It provides, with certain exceptions, for a maximum 48-hour week including overtime, averaged over four months (but for seven years, Member States will be able to allow employees to agree to work for longer, although they cannot be compelled to do so). There is also provision for a minimum daily rest period of 11 consecutive hours, for a weekly break of not less than 35 consecutive hours, and for restrictions upon the length of night shifts. Finally there is provision for a minimum of four weeks' paid holiday per annum.

Whilst the Directive was adopted under the provisions of the *EC Treaty* relating to Health and Safety at Work, the view of the UK Government was that, in substance, it was an attempt to regulate conditions of employment, a matter which is outside the EC's competence. The UK brought a challenge to the *Directive* in the European Court of Justice. Advocate General Leger delivered his opinion on 12 March 1996. He recommended that the UK's objections be rejected. His view was upheld by the ECJ on 12 November 1996 (*United Kingdom v EU Council, Case C-84/94* [1997] ICR 443).

Following the change of Government in May 1997, draft regulations for implementing the *Working Time Directive* were published for consultation in April 1998. These were subsequently issued (with certain modifications) as the *Working Time Regulations 1998 (SI 1998/1833)*, and came into force on 1 October 1998. The provisions of the *Regulations* relating to annual leave are summarised in HOLIDAYS (29); as to the provisions relating to hours of work and rest breaks, see 28.15 HEALTH AND SAFETY AT WORK – II. On 25 May 1999, the Council agreed measures which will have the effect of extending the provisions of the *Working Time Directive* to transport workers, offshore oil and gas workers, sea-fishermen and junior doctors.

In *R (on the application of the Broadcasting, Entertainment, Cinematographic and Theatre Union) v Secretary of State for Trade and Industry: C-173/99* [2001] IRLR 559 the ECJ held that *reg 13* of the *Regulations*, restricting entitlement to paid annual leave to workers continuously employed for 13 weeks by the same employer, constituted an impermissible restriction on the rights conferred by the *Working Time Directive*. Consequential alterations to the *Regulations* were made by the *Working Time (Amendment) Regulations 2002 (SI 2002/3128)* with effect from 6 April 2003: see HOLIDAYS (29). In *Commission v UK: C-484/04* [2006] IRLR 888, the ECJ held that the UK had failed to fulfil its obligations under the *Working Time Directive* by issuing guidance on the *Regulations* which advised employers that they must make sure that workers can take their rest, but were not required to make sure they do take their rest.

The *Working Time Directive (93/104/EEC)* excluded employment in certain sectors from its scope. The sectors were: road, rail, air, inland waterway and lake transport, sea fishing, other work at sea, and doctors in training. *Directive 2000/34/EC* extended the application of the *Directive* to non-mobile workers in the excluded sectors (with a special transitional period for its application to doctors in training). A consolidating *Directive 2003/88/EC* was adopted on 4 November 2003 and this is now the *Directive* governing this area (see WORKING TIME (57)).

A specific Directive covering the organisation of the working time of seafarers (*EC/99/63*) was adopted on 21 June 1999 and must be implemented within three years. A further proposed Directive dealing with the enforcement of seafarers' hours of work on board non-EU flagged ships using Community ports was the subject of an agreement on a common position by the European Parliament on 16 November 1999.

25.12 INFORMATION AND CONSULTATION

The UK's implacable opposition to the *European Works Councils Directive (Directive 94/45/EC)* led to its having to be adopted under the Social Protocol procedure. See EMPLOYEE PARTICIPATION (18). Following the election of the Labour Government, the UK sought to 'opt into' the scope of the *Directive*. The

Directive was implemented with effect from 15 January 2000 by the *Transnational Information and Consultation of Employees Regulations 1999* (*SI 1999/3323*).

On 4 June 1997, the Commission commenced a period of consultation with the Social Partners with a view to devising a framework for Community legislation on the provision of information to and consultation with workers. This resulted in the *Directive of the European Parliament and of the Council 2002/14/EC establishing a general framework for informing and consulting employees in the European Community.* This Directive has been implemented in the UK by the *Information and Consultation of Employees Regulations 2004, SI 2004/3426.*

26   Foreign Employees

26.1   The first issue which arises in respect of employees who are not nationals of the UK is whether they are lawfully entitled to work in this country. Under the existing regime, a distinction has to be drawn between nationals of Member States of the European Economic Area ('EEA'), which now comprises 27 Member-States, and others. With the exception of Switzerland, individuals who are not nationals of a Member State of the EEA must have a valid work permit in order to be able to work lawfully in the UK. Swiss nationals have been exempted from this requirement since 1 June 2002 and are accordingly free to work in the UK. 'Applying for a work permit – guidance for employers' (WP1 (notes)), published by Work Permits (UK), sets out the procedure governing work permit applications. There are six separate sets of work permit arrangements which include, for example, arrangements in respect of business and commercial sector recruitments; arrangements in respect of sportspeople and entertainers and arrangements in respect of individuals seeking to gain access to work-based training schemes. Under the work permit scheme, it is easier for permits to be obtained in respect of senior employees, employees transferring within companies, and employees whose skills are in short supply (see 26.5–26.8 below). Employees who are nationals of countries within the EEA do not require work permits (see further the *Immigration (European Economic Area) Regulations 2006 (SI 2006/1003)* which came into force on 30 April 2006). However, under the *Accession (Immigration and Worker Registration) Regulations 2004 (SI 2004/1219* as amended by SI *2006/1003)*, individuals who are nationals of recently acceded Member-States (apart from Cyprus and Malta) and who want to work more than one month are required to register with the home office 'Worker Registration Scheme' as soon as they find work. Once registered persons have been working legally in the UK for 12 months without a break they obtain full rights of free movement and will no longer need to register on the Worker Registration scheme. Maltese and Cypriot nationals are exempted from the scheme. Details on the Worker Registration Scheme and the Work Permit Scheme can be found on the Home Office website: www.working-intheuk.gov.uk. Information for EEA nationals on working in another EEA country is available through the EURES network at www.europa.eu.int.

26.2   NATIONALS OF THE EUROPEAN ECONOMIC AREA

The principle of free movement of labour, which is now applicable to all members of the EEA, is derived principally from *art 39* (formerly *art 48*) of the Treaty of Rome as amended, and *Regulation 1612/68*. Other relevant pieces of legislation include *Directive 68/360, Regulation 1251/70 Directive 90/365* and *Directive 90/364*. On 30 April 2006, the *Immigration (European Economic Area) Regulations 2006 (SI 2006/1003)* came into force in the UK. These regulations govern the freedom of movement of citizens of EU states and their families (including civil partners). Although Turkey and certain other states have Association Agreements with the EU, these confer no general right of free movement upon individuals (*R v Secretary of State for the Home Department, ex p Narin* [1990] 2 CMLR 233; but see also *Sevince v Staatssecretaris van Justitie: C-192/89* [1992] 2 CMLR 57).

The family of an EEA worker may also come to this country without any restriction on their right of entry. EEA nationals are entitled to the same treatment as UK nationals with regard to pay, working conditions, access to housing and property, training, social security and trade union rights. They are free, if unemployed but seeking work, to claim jobseeker's allowance for up to three months if they have been claiming benefit in their own country for at least four weeks. There is also a considerable body of EU legislation directed towards establishing equivalence of mutual recognition of professional qualifications by member states (see 25.4 EUROPEAN COMMUNITY LAW).

Pursuant to the *Immigration (European Economic Area) Regulations 2006*, EEA nationals (and Swiss nationals) may, along with their families, reside in the UK for an initial period of three months, provided that they have a valid passport or identity card and do not become an unreasonable burden on the domestic social security system. After the initial three month period has expired, the EEA/Swiss national may continue to reside in the UK along with their family for so long as they continue to be a 'qualified person'. A person will be a 'qualified person' for the purposes of the Regulations if he or she is: a job-seeker, a worker, a self-employed person, a self-sufficient person or a student. EEA and Swiss nationals will acquire a permanent right of residence if they have both resided and worked in the UK for more than five years.. These rules do not apply to nationals of the recently acceded States (apart from Cyprus and Malta). Such individuals may apply for a residence permit only after they have worked in the UK continuously for 12 months,

Member states are entitled to except employment in the public service from the general requirement of free movement, and to reserve such employment for their own nationals (*EC Treaty, art 39(4)*); see also PUBLIC SECTOR EMPLOYEES (37). These provisions have given rise to a substantial number of reported cases in national courts and in the ECJ, a detailed discussion of which is beyond the scope of this book.

Collective agreements must take account of comparable employment completed in the public service of another member state for the purposes of seniority and promotion (*Schöning-Kougebetopoulou v Freie und Hansestadt Hamburg: C-15/96* [1998] All ER (EC) 97). A clause in a collective agreement which treats foreign nationals differently in this respect breaches *art 39* of the Treaty of Rome and *Regulation 1612/68* on freedom of movement. For an ECJ ruling concerning the relationship between *art 39* and national legislation denying termination payments to a worker who left employment in order to take up work in another member state, see *Graf v Filzmoser Maschinenbau GmbH (Case C-190/98)* [2000] All ER (EC) 170.

See also EUROPEAN COMMUNITY LAW (25).

26.3   **EUROPEAN UNION: POSTED WORKERS**

Measures have been taken to implement in the UK the *Posting of Workers Directive (96/71)* which came into force on 16 December 1999. The *Directive* now applies to all EEA states. Broadly, it provides that minimum terms and conditions laid down by national laws, regulations or collective agreements should apply to workers posted temporarily by their employer to work in another State.

Article 1 provides that the *Directive* applies to undertakings which:

(*a*)   post workers to another member state on their account and under their direction under a contract concluded between the undertaking and a party in the other state for whom the services are intended;

(*b*)   make intra-company postings; or

(c)   are temporary employment undertakings or agencies which hire out workers to undertakings established or operating in an EU member state.

A further requirement in each case is that there must be an employment relationship between the undertaking making the posting and the worker during the period of posting. The terms and conditions of employment covered by the *Directive* are set out in *art 3*, as follows:

(i)   maximum work periods and minimum rest periods;

(ii)   minimum paid annual holidays;

(iii)   minimum rates of pay, including overtime rates (but not supplementary occupational pension schemes);

(iv)   conditions of hiring out workers, in particular the supply of workers by temporary employment undertakings;

(v)   health, safety and hygiene at work;

(vi)   measures to protect at work pregnant women, new mothers, children and young people; and

(vii)   equality of treatment between men and women and other provisions on non-discrimination.

Various flexibilities are permitted under the *Directive*, such as not applying the minimum rate of pay to postings of less than one month. However, the UK Government has decided not to take advantage of any of the exemptions.

Workers may enforce their rights under the *Directive* in the territory of the member state to which they were posted without prejudice to their rights in the country where they are normally employed (*art 6*).

In *Mazzoleni, Case C-165/98* [2001] ECR I-2189, the ECJ ruled (15 March 2001) that the principle of freedom of movement did not preclude one member state from requiring an undertaking established in another State which provides services in the territory of the first state to pay its workers the minimum remuneration fixed by the national rules of that state. However, application of these rules might prove to be disproportionate where the workers operate in a frontier region and are required to carry out their work, on a part-time basis and for brief periods, in more than one member state. It is for the host member state to decide the extent to which the imposition of a minimum wage is necessary and proportionate to protect the workers in question. For two cases in which the ECJ has examined the compatibility of German law governing posted workers with the principle of freedom of movement, see *Finalarte Sociedade de Construcao Civil Lda v Urlaubs- und Lohnausgleichskasse der Bauwirtschaft, Case C-49/98* [2001] ECR I-7831; *Proceedings against Portugaia Construcoes Lda, Case C-164/99* [2003] 2 CMLR 1093 and *Commission v Germany (Re Minimum Wages for Posted Construction Workers)* [2005] Case C-341/02).

Most existing UK legislation relevant to the *Directive* applies to all workers, whether they are employed on a temporary or permanent basis in the UK (eg the *Working Time Regulations 1998*, the *National Minimum Wage Act 1998*, and health and safety legislation). For a discussion of the effect of the Directive on the application of the *Employment Rights Act 1996* see the Court of Appeal's decision in *Lawson v Serco Ltd* [2004] EWCA Civ 12, [2004] ICR 204..

26.4   Foreign Employees

26.4 NON-EEA NATIONALS

Non-EEA nationals who are subject to immigration control must obtain work permits in order to be able to take up employment in the UK, unless the Immigration Rules provide otherwise. Certain limited categories of persons do not require work permits. These include business visitors, Gibraltarians, Commonwealth citizens given leave to enter or remain in the UK on the basis that at least one grandparent was born in the UK, persons with indefinite leave to remain in the UK (which may be granted after four continuous years in approved or permit-free employment), and persons wishing to engage in certain specified occupations (eg ministers of religion and representatives of overseas firms with no UK branch or subsidiary). Subject to certain conditions, non-EEA students studying at UK institutions are no longer required to obtain permission from a jobcentre to take up spare time and vacation work. They may also do work placements as part of a sandwich course without obtaining permission from the Home Office.

Various proposals for improving freedom of movement for third-country nationals have been tabled by the European Commission and are being considered by the European Parliament and member states.

A person who wishes to take up employment for which he believes a permit may not be needed should first make enquiries of a UK representative overseas and obtain entry clearance if appropriate. Commonwealth citizens must obtain UK immigration clearance before travelling to the UK.

26.5 WORKERS ELIGIBLE FOR PERMIT

Permits are normally issued only in respect of individuals who have the following specified qualifications or skills:

(*a*)   a UK equivalent degree level qualification;

(*b*)   an HND level occupational qualification which is relevant to the post;

(*c*)   a general HND level qualification plus one year's relevant work experience; or

(*d*)   high level or specialist skills acquired through doing the type of job for which the permit is sought for at least three years. This type of job should be at NVQ level 3 or above. (Examples of those who would qualify in this category include: head or second chefs; specialist chefs with skills in preparing ethnic cuisine; and those with occupational skills and language or cultural skills not readily available in the EEA.)

In addition, permits are issued for:

(i)   established entertainers, including self-employed entertainers coming to fulfil engagements;

(ii)   sportsmen and sportswomen who meet the appropriate skills criteria (professional sportsmen and sportswomen taking part in competitions of international standing do not normally require permits);

(iii)   people coming for a limited period of approved training or work experience (see Form WP2 and accompanying notes). Training and Work Experience applications should now be made on Form WP1; and

608

(iv)   from 28 January 2002 the Highly Skilled Migrant Programme ('HSMP') allows highly skilled people who meet certain criteria – high level qualifications and specialist skills – to come to the UK to seek employment without having a specific job offer, provided they can support themselves until they find work.

26.6   APPLICATIONS FOR WORK PERMITS

Work permit application forms and guidance notes are available on the Work Permits (UK) website at www.workingintheuk.gov.uk or by telephoning 0870 6067766. A major review of the work permit arrangements is under way. Among the measures planned or already in force are:

(*a*)   more effective identification of skills shortages;

(*b*)   revision of work permit skills criteria;

(*c*)   changes to criteria for hotel and catering posts;

(*d*)   a pilot scheme to streamline intra-company transfers;

(*e*)   abolition of the labour market test for extensions and changes of employment;

(*f*)   an increase in the maximum period for which a work permit can be issued from four to five years;

(*g*)   introduction of a facility to submit applications by email.

As the changes are implemented they will be announced through the Work Permits (UK) website.

Subject to the principles set out above with respect to EEA nationals and nationals of Accession states, if an employer wishes to employ a foreign national he must first apply for a work permit on his behalf. There are two main types of application: Tier 1 and Tier 2. (The separate 'keyworker' category was merged into the main work permit arrangements from 2 October 2000.) Applications should be made on Form WP1. Guidance notes WP1 (notes) explain the supporting documentation required in each case. A simplified procedure applies to Tier 1 applications.

General criteria to be satisfied before a work permit can be issued are that:

(*a*)   the employment falls within the categories set out in 26.5 above;

(*b*)   a genuine vacancy exists;

(*c*)   there is no suitable resident labour available to fill the post offered;

(*d*)   the employer has made adequate efforts to find a worker from suitable resident labour or from other member states of the EEA;

(*e*)   the application is for a named worker for a specific post; and

(*f*)   the person is suitably qualified or experienced.

The worker will also normally be expected to have an adequate command of the English language.

The procedure for Tier 1 applications is to be used if the post meets the skills criteria and one of the following conditions applies:

(i)   intra-company transfers: an employee of a multinational company is transferring to a skilled post in Great Britain;

    (ii)   the post is at board level;

    (iii)   the post is new and is essential to inward investment; or

    (iv)   the post is in an occupation recognised by Work Permits (UK) as being in short supply (for current details of such occupations, telephone 0114 259 4074).

Tier 1 applications do not need to be supported by evidence of educational qualifications and references, and need not be advertised in advance (see 26.7(I) below). Other documentation required is listed in WP1 (notes).

Tier 2 applications are standard work permit applications, requiring proof of qualifications and experience, evidence of employment history and details of recruitment search.

Since November 2001, multiple entry work permits allow workers who are based overseas to enter the country for short periods of time on a regular basis to work, rather than obtaining a permit each time they enter the country. Multiple entry work permits can be issued for a minimum of six months and up to two years.

26.7   Procedure

    (i) *Proving no suitable resident labour.* In order to satisfy condition 26.6(C) above, an employer should:

        (A)   consider carefully whether the vacancy can be filled by the promotion or transfer of an existing worker, perhaps after suitable training;

        (B)   advertise the vacancy in the most appropriate medium, normally national newspapers or professional journals which are readily available throughout the EEA (but in Tier 1 cases (see 26.6 above) this will not be required if it can be shown that it would not be appropriate or productive). Internet advertising may be accepted where it is the most appropriate means of advertising the post;

        (C)   send copies of any such advertisements with the application for the permit and give full details of the results of such advertising.

    A full explanation must be given if the prospective employer considers that it would be unproductive to search the resident and/or EEA labour market.

    (ii) *Making an application.* The employer should submit an application on Form WP1 for a work permit no more than six months before the permit is required. Applications may be made by post or email. Work Permits (UK) aims to decide at least 90% of applications submitted with all the relevant information within one week of receiving them. Applications for permits for entertainers and sportspersons must be made on Form WP3. The forms should be returned, when completed, to the appropriate address given on the form together with specified documentation. A company which has not made a work permit application in the previous four years is required to send specified documentation to show that it is a trading company.

    (iii) *Issue of permit.* When an application is approved the work permit is issued to the employer, who is responsible for forwarding it to the worker concerned. From 1 November 2000, permits are issued for up to five years, instead of the previous maximum of four years.

(iv) *Arrival of worker*. When workers arrive in the UK, they must present the permit together with a valid passport (not an identity card) to the immigration authorities. Nationals of certain foreign countries also require visas. Without these documents they may be refused entry. Leave to enter will usually be given for the period specified on the work permit.

(v) *Change of job*. If a permit holder wishes to change his job, he will usually only be permitted to take up employment of a type similar to that for which the permit was originally issued. Application must be made on his behalf to Work Permits (UK) for permission for the change of job, the application being made by the new employer on Form WP1. From May 2000 individuals' passports and police registration certificates, together with those of any dependants, should wherever possible be submitted with the change of employment application. For changes of employment, employers do not need to carry out a recruitment search when the person is going to do the same type of job as he or she is doing for the current employer. The existing employer also needs permission if it wants the permit holder to change jobs within the organisation. Work Permits (UK) must be informed in writing if the overseas worker is transferred to different premises while doing the same job.

(vi) *Registering with police*. Certain overseas workers who are not Commonwealth citizens are required to register with the police or the Central Aliens' Registration Office (for London).

Since 11 May 1998, the requirement to register with the police has been restricted to the nationals of certain countries. Among those no longer required to register are Japanese and United States nationals. The scope of the registration scheme is limited, from that date, to those given limited leave to enter or remain for longer than six months.

(vii) *Permit extension applications* must be made on Form WP1X before the original permit expires, and supporting material supplied. From May 2000 individuals' passports and police registration certificates, together with those of any dependants, should wherever possible be submitted with the extension application.

(viii) *Extensions of stay* may be granted by the Home Office to permit holders who remain in approved employment. After four years in approved employment they may apply to the Home Office for the removal of the time limit on their stay. If the time limit is removed, there will be no conditions attached to their stay and they are free to take any employment without reference to the authorities.

26.8 Further information

More detailed information about the work permit scheme can be obtained be sending an e-mail to indpublicenquiries@ind.homeoffice.gsi.gov.uk or by writing to:

Border and Immigration Agency
Lunar House
40 Wellesley Road
Croydon,
CR9 2BY

or by telephoning 0870 606 7766.

26.9   **ASYLUM AND IMMIGRATION ACT**

Since 27 January 1997 it has been an offence to employ a person who is not entitled, under the Immigration Rules, to work in the UK. This is so pursuant to *s 8* of the *Asylum and Immigration Act 1996* ('*AIA 1996*'). From a date yet to be appointed *AIA 1996, s 8* will be repealed and replaced by provisions in the recently enacted *Immigration Asylum and Nationality Act 2006*. The effect of this new legislation is dealt with separately below.

Under the regime established under *AIA 1996, s 8*, in respect of any employment which began prior to 1 May 2004, employers will have a statutory defence if they have checked that a potential employee is in possession of one of a range of documents verifying his or her status. Acceptable documents include: a documented National Insurance number; a passport confirming that the person is a British citizen; a passport or identity card of an EEA national or which otherwise shows entitlement to live and work in the UK; a birth certificate of the UK or Republic of Ireland; a letter from the Home Office confirming that the person is allowed to work. The complete list of permissible documentation is contained in the *Immigration (Restrictions on Employment) Order 2004 (SI 2004/755))*. As a result of an amendment to *s 8* effected by *s 147* of the *Nationality, Immigration and Asylum Act 2002*, with respect to employment commencing after 1 May 2004, the statutory defence will only be available in circumstances where the employer can prove that, before the employment began, it complied with the requirements contained in the *Immigration (Restrictions on Employment) Order 2004 (SI 2004/755)*. Under the Order, the employer is obliged both to require the employee to produce the documents identified in *para 4* and the Schedule of the Order and, further, to copy or record the content of the documents produced. The following website contains useful guidance on the applicable principles: www-.workingintheuk.gov.uk. The Home Office has a helpline for employers: 0845–0106677

Checks must be made, before individuals start work on all applicants aged 16 or over to be employed under a contract of service or apprenticeship. In order to avoid contravening race discrimination legislation, it is necessary to carry out identical checks for all applicants.

Irrespective of when the employment commenced, the statutory defence will not be available if the employer has actual knowledge that it would be an offence under *s 8* to employ the individual concerned. An organisation found guilty of an offence under *s 8* is liable, on summary conviction, to a fine not exceeding level 5 (see 1.10 INTRODUCTION). As for the criminal liability of individuals responsible for the unlawful employment of a person subject to immigration control, see further subsections 8(4)–(6B) *AIA 1996*.

In complying with their obligations under s *8 AIA 1996* to refrain from employing a person who is not entitled under immigration rules to work in the UK, employers may run the risk of unlawful discrimination under the *Race Relations Act 1976*. The *Immigration and Asylum Act 1999 (s 22)* inserts a new *s 8A* in the *Asylum and Immigration Act 1996* requiring the Home Secretary to issue a code of practice as to the measures which employers are expected to take (or not to take) in order to comply with their obligations both under *s 8* of the *AIA 1996* (ie not to employ someone who is not entitled to work in the UK) and to avoid unlawful race discrimination under the *Race Relations Act 1976*. In May 2001, the Home Office issued a code of practice for all employers 'on the avoidance of race discrimination in recruitment practice while seeking to prevent illegal working'. The code explains the steps that employers need to take in order to ensure that they do not act in a discriminatory fashion when complying with their obligation to employ only workers who are entitled to work in the UK. Failure to observe the code is admissible in evidence in employment tribunal proceedings. The current version of the Code is available on the Home Office website: www.ind-.homeoffice.gov.uk. (See further the Comprehensive Guidance for UK Employers on Changes to the Law on Preventing Illegal Working which can be found on the Home office website.)

In *Vakante v Governing Body of Addey & Stanhope School* [2004] EWCA Civ 1065, [2004] 4 All ER 1056, the Court of Appeal considered the question of whether an claimant could pursue complaints of race discrimination against the respondent in circumstances where, as a person who was subject to immigration control, he had entered into an employment with the respondent knowing that the employment was unlawful. The Court of Appeal found that the claims of race discrimination could not be pursued because they were inextricably bound up with the claimant's own illegal acts and any other conclusion would create the impression that the Tribunal was condoning the illegal conduct.

26.10 Immigration, Asylum and Nationality Act 1996

From a date yet to be appointed, *AIA, ss 8 and 8A* will be repealed and replaced by provisions in the recently enacted *Immigration, Asylum and Nationality Act 1996* ('*IAN*'). In particular, *ss 15–26* of *IAN* will constitute a new statutory scheme governing the treatment of employers who employ persons not lawfully entitled to work in the UK. Under *s 15*, the Secretary of State may issue a penalty notice to employers who employ persons: (a) who have no leave to enter or remain in the UK; or (b) whose leave is invalid, has ceased to have effect or does not entitle them to work in the UK. The penalty notice will require the employer to pay a specific amount subject to a statutory maximum. The employer will be excused from paying the penalty if he complied with certain 'prescribed requirements' relating to the employment, unless he knew at the time that the employment was unlawful despite his having complied with the requirements; the 'prescribed requirements' are to be enacted under secondary legislation but may include requiring the employer to obtain particular documents. Under *s 16*, the employer has a right to object to the notice by sending an objection to the Secretary of State. *Section 17* provides that the employer also has a right of appeal to the court against the penalty notice. The introduction of a penalty notice regime is one of the key novelties of the scheme introduced under *IAN*. Under *s 19*, the Secretary of State must issue a Code of Practice relating to the giving of penalties. Pursuant to s *21*, a person who employs a person who is subject to immigration control knowing that he or she is either in the UK unlawfully or is not lawfully entitled to work in the UK will be guilty of an offence and liable, on conviction, to imprisonment and/or a fine. *Section 22* provides that an employer (whether corporate or not) shall be treated as knowing a fact about an employee for the purposes of *s 21* if a person within the employing body has responsibility for an aspect of the employment and knows that fact. *Section 22(2)* makes provision for officers of the employer to be liable to conviction along with the employer itself in circumstances where the offence is committed with the consent or connivance of the officer. Under *s 23*, the Secretary of State is required to issue a code of practice to assist employers in avoiding racially discriminatory behaviour in the context of their complying with their obligations under *IAN*.

SYSTEM OF LAW GOVERNING CONTRACTS OF EMPLOYMENT AND JURISDICTION OF COURTS AND TRIBUNALS IN EMPLOYMENT DISPUTES

26.11 Where an employer and employee are both English, and the work is done in England, it will generally be clear that the contract of employment is governed by English law, and there will normally be no doubt as to the jurisdiction of the English courts to deal with disputes which may arise. However, where there is a foreign element of some kind, difficult questions may arise concerning the system of law which governs the contract, and as to where any proceedings may be brought. This is an extremely complicated area of law, and what follows is intended only as a simplified outline guide.

The *Contracts (Applicable Law) Act 1990* was enacted to give force in the United Kingdom to the *Rome Convention on the Law Applicable to Contractual Obligations* of 1980. That was a treaty between the EC member states, and provision is made for the ECJ to be given jurisdiction to determine questions concerning its interpretation (see EUROPEAN COMMUNITY LAW (25)). However, the Act applies to all contracts, not merely to those with an EC connection.

Under the *Convention*, a contract is governed by the system of law chosen by the parties, such choice being either expressed or demonstrated with reasonable certainty by the terms of the contract or the circumstances of the case (*art 3(1)*). However, in the case of a contract of employment, a choice of law made by the parties cannot deprive an employee of the protection afforded to him by the mandatory rules of the system of law which would apply if no such choice had been made (*art 6(1)*). Mandatory rules are those which cannot be derogated from by contract in the law of the country concerned (*art 3(3)*). Hence, for example, if an English employee works in Great Britain for an English employer, it is not possible to deprive him of the right to claim UNFAIR DISMISSAL (53, 54, 55) by providing that the contract shall be governed by, say, Hong Kong law (see further *Base Metal Trading Ltd v Shamurin* [2003] EWHC 2419 (Comm), [2004] 1 All ER (Comm) 159).

Even if one system of law applies (eg English law), effect *may* be given to the mandatory rules of the law of another country with which the contract has a close connection (eg France), provided that they would be applied under French law whatever system of law governed the contract, and depending upon the nature and purpose of those rules and the consequences of their application or non-application (*art 7(1)*). However, *art 7(1)* does not have the force of law in the United Kingdom (*Contracts (Applicable Law) Act 1990 Act, s 2(2)*).

If the parties to a contract of employment have not chosen the system of law which is to govern the contract, then it is governed by:

(*a*)   the law of the country in which the employee habitually carries out his work in performance of the contract, even if he is temporarily employed in another country; or

(*b*)   if the employee does not habitually carry out his work in any one country, the law of the country in which the place of business through which he was engaged is situated,

unless it appears from the circumstances as a whole that the contract is more closely connected with another country, in which case the contract shall be governed by the law of that country (*art 6(2)*).

The *Convention* does not have retrospective effect upon contracts already in existence when the *Convention* entered into force in the relevant state (*art 17*). In the United Kingdom, that occurred on 1 April 1991.

For the common law rules governing a claim in tort by an employee against an employer, see, eg *Sayers v International Drilling Co NV* [1971] 3 All ER 163; *Johnson v Coventry Churchill International Ltd* [1992] 3 All ER 14. From 1 May 1996 the common law rules are abolished and superseded by provisions contained in the *Private International Law (Miscellaneous Provisions) Act 1995* ('*PILMPA*'). Under this *Act* the general rule is that the applicable law is the law of the country in which the events constituting the tort in question occur (*s 11(1)*). However, the general rule is displaced where, viewed overall, it appears that the tort is more closely connected to a country other than that which would be appropriate if the general rule were applied (*s 12(1)*). See further *Harding v Wealands* [2006] UKHL 32, [2006] 3 WLR 83 where the House of Lords decided, in respect of an accident which took place in New South Wales, that the provisions of PILMPA did not operate to enable the capping provisions contained in New South Wales personal injury legislation to apply to quantification by the UK courts of personal injury damages.

26.12 JURISDICTION

Common Law Claims

Where an employee brings a claim based on breach of the contract of employment or, alternatively, a claim in tort against his employer and the events about which the employee complains have a connection with more than one country, questions may arise as to whether the defendant can properly be served with proceedings and, further, whether the UK is the appropriate country in which the claims should be brought.

In the context of claims brought against foreign defendants in the ordinary courts, reference must be made to *Part 6* of the *CPR* which contains detailed provisions on the question of when a foreign defendant may be served with proceedings. Service out of the jurisdiction will require the permission of the courts, save where the requirements of *CPR 6.19* have been met. If permission is required, the court will only consider granting permission in circumstances where the requirements contained in *CPR 6.20* have been met. Under *CPR 6.21(2A)*, the courts will not grant permission where the domestic courts are clearly not the most appropriate forum for the claim. For an example of a case in which the domestic courts were considering whether they were the proper forum for tortious claims brought by foreign employees see *Schalk Willem Burger Lubbe v Cape plc* [2000] 2 Lloyd's Rep 383, HL.

Where a breach of contract claim is brought in the Employment Tribunal, *rule 61(4)(h)* of *Sch 1* to the Employment *Tribunals (Constitution & Rules etc) Regulations 2004*, will apply. The proper application of *rule 61(4)(h)*, which does not on its face expressly mirror the requirements as to service contained in the *CPR*, has yet to be considered in any detail by the appellate courts or tribunals.

Where the defendant is domiciled in an EC member state, the *Civil Jurisdiction and Judgments Act 1982* applies. This *Act* originally gave effect to the *Brussels Convention*. More recently, it has given effect to *Regulation 44/2001* (the '*Brussels I Regulation*'), which is a new regulation that came into force on 1 March 2002. (The regulation covers all member states except Denmark, in respect of which the *Brussels Convention* still applies. Changes to the existing law in the UK required by the *Brussels I Regulation* are contained in the *Civil Jurisdiction and Judgments*

Order 2001 (SI 2001/3929).) The *Act* deals not only with jurisdiction, but also with the enforcement of judgments in other member states. Questions of interpretation arising under the *Convention* or the *Brussels I Regulation* may be referred to the ECJ (see EUROPEAN COMMUNITY LAW (25)). Similar provisions apply under the *Lugano Convention* where the defendant is domiciled in an EFTA member state (*Civil Jurisdiction and Judgments Act 1991*). For a decision on jurisdiction concerning proceedings which involve the same cause of action brought in two different EU member states where one action commenced before the *Brussels Convention* came into force between those states, see *Von Horn v Cinnamond, Case C-163/95* [1998] QB 214, ECJ.

Under the *Brussels I Regulation* the normal rule is that the defendant must be sued in the state in which he is domiciled (*art 2*). However, in matters relating to a contract, he may also be sued in the courts for the place of performance of the obligation in question. In matters relating to individual contracts of employment, the place of performance will be (a) the place where the employee habitually carries out his work; or (b) if the employee does not habitually carry out his work in any one country the place where the business which engaged the employee was or is now situated (*art 5(1)*). (*Weber v Universal Ogden Services Ltd: C-37/00* [2002] IRLR 365 is a case concerned with jurisdiction where an employee has been engaged in more than one EU member state. The ECJ held that the relevant criterion for establishing the employee's habitual place of work was, having regard to the whole duration of employment, the place where he or she has worked the longest on the employer's business. See also: *Rutten v Cross Medical Ltd* [1997] IRLR 249, ECJ and *Mulox IBC Ltd v Geels: C-125/92* [1994] IRLR 422, ECJ.) In *Harada Ltd (t/a Chequepoint UK) v Turner* (EAT/516/99), the EAT held that an employment tribunal had jurisdiction to hear a wrongful dismissal claim made by an English employee working in Spain for an Irish offshore company since the central management and control of the company was exercised in England. In matters relating to tort, the defendant may also be sued in the courts for the place where the harmful event occurred (*art 5(3)*).

Under *art 18(2)* of the *Brussels I Regulation* an employer will be 'deemed to be domiciled' in a member state if it has a branch, agency or other establishment in that member state and the dispute arises out of the operations of that branch, agency or establishment.

The parties may agree that the courts of a particular member state are to have exclusive jurisdiction (*art 17*). However, in matters relating to individual contracts of employment, an agreement conferring jurisdiction has legal force only if it is entered into after the dispute has arisen or if it is the employee who invokes it.

Where proceedings involving the same cause of action and between the same parties are brought in the courts of different contracting states, a court other than the court 'first seised' is to stay proceedings and where the jurisdiction of the court first seised is established, other courts are to decline jurisdiction (*art 21*). In the case of *Turner v Grovit (Case C-159/02)* [2004] All ER (EC) 485, the ECJ was called upon to decide whether it was possible under the *Brussels Convention* for the English courts to grant restraining orders in respect of proceedings in another Convention country on the ground of abuse of process. The ECJ concluded that the functioning of the Convention was underpinned by the necessity for the contracting state to place trust in the judicial systems and institutions of other states and that, accordingly, it did not permit the jurisdiction of a court to be reviewed by a court in another contracting state other than in the special cases enumerated in article 28.

The employment tribunals have no jurisdiction to hear common law tortious claims brought by employees, whether foreign or domestic. However, they do have jurisdiction to hear breach of contract claims brought in respect of particular contracts of employment under the *Employment Tribunals Extension of Jurisdiction (England and Wales) Order 1994*. Article 3 of that Order provides that the tribunal will have jurisdiction to hear the particular claim in circumstances where, had the claim been brought in the ordinary courts, the courts would have been jurisdiction to hear and determine the claim. For a recent case on the effect and scope of Article 3 in respect of foreign employment see further *Crofts v Cathay Pacific* [2005] EWCA Civ 599, [2005] ICR 1436.

It is important to note that the new *Employment Tribunal Regulations*, which came into force on 1 October 2004, contain new regulations as to jurisdiction. In particular, *reg 19* provides that the tribunal will 'only have jurisdiction to deal with proceedings' where certain pre-conditions are met. Materially, under *reg 19*, if the cause of action did not arise in England or Wales, then the question of whether the tribunal has jurisdiction to hear the claim will turn on whether the respondent or one of the respondents resides or carries on business in England or Wales. This provision could potentially operate to exclude certain claims brought against foreign employers. It remains to be seen whether this regulation, which is contained in secondary legislation, can be effectively relied upon to ensure that employees who have rights under primary enactments are prevented from prosecuting those claims in the tribunal.

A common law claim which is brought by an employee in the ordinary courts will usually be subject to the doctrine of *forum non conveniens* with the result that claim will not be allowed to proceed before the domestic courts if there is another more appropriate (foreign) forum for the claim (see further *Spiliada Maritime Corpn v Cansulex Ltd* [1987] AC 460, HL). It would seem that following a change in the Employment Tribunal Rules of Procedure wrought by the *Employment Tribunals (Constitution & Rules etc) Regulations 2004*, the doctrine can be applied equally by the Employment Tribunals in the context of breach of contract claims which are brought before them (see further *Crofts v Cathay Pacific* [2005] EWCA Civ 599, [2005] ICR 1436).

26.13 Statutory Claims

The question whether foreign employees can avail themselves of the protection afforded by the various domestic anti-discrimination enactments is not a simple one to answer. This is because those enactments do not adopt a consistent approach on the issue. For the relevant provisions in the individual enactments see further: *s 1* of the *Equal Pay Act 1970; ss 6* and *10* of the *Sex Discrimination Act 1975* (as amended by the *Employment Equality (Sex Discrimination) Regulations 2005 (SI 2005/2467)*; *ss 4* and *8* of the *Race Relations Act 1976*; *ss 4(6)* and *68* of the *Disability Discrimination Act 1995*; and *reg 9* of the *Employment Equality (Religion and Belief) Regulations 2003* and of the *Employment Equality (Sexual Orientation) Regulations 2003*.

In the case of *Saggar v Ministry of Defence* [2005] EWCA Civ 413, [2005] IRLR 618, the Court of Appeal was asked to consider whether the Race Relations Act 1976 applied to complaints of racial discrimination brought by an MOD employee who had initially been based in the UK for 16 years but had then been permanently stationed abroad. The Court of Appeal found that the Employment Appeal Tribunal had erred when it concluded that the Act only applied if the claimant was employed in the UK at the time when the discrimination occurred. It went on to find that the employment as a whole, from its beginning to its end, must be considered in order to determine whether the Act applied to the employment in question. The Court of Appeal remitted the case to the Tribunal for a decision on whether the Act applied to the claimant's employment.

The question whether foreign employees enjoy the rights afforded under the *Employment Rights Act 1996* ('*ERA 1996*') has recently been addressed by the House of Lords in the joined cases of *Lawson v Serco Ltd, Botham v MOD and Crofts v Veta Ltd* [2006] UKHL 3, [2006] ICR 250 ('*Lawson v Serco*'). The following principles were enunciated by the House of Lords in *Lawson v Serco*:

(*a*)   the question whether a particular claim falls within the territorial ambit of the unfair dismissal provisions contained in the Employment Rights Act 1996 will depend on the nature of the particular employment arrangements in issue in the case;

(*b*)   in 'standard cases' (ie cases where the employee works in Great Britain), the employee will be able to pursue their claim of unfair dismissal if they were 'working in Great Britain at the time of the dismissal';

(*c*)   international travelling salespersons), the employee will be able to pursue their claim of unfair dismissal if they were 'based in Great Britain' during the employment;

(*d*)   in cases involving 'expatriate employees' (ie employees who work and live abroad), the employee will not be able to pursue their claim of unfair dismissal in the absence of 'exceptional circumstances'. Those exceptional circumstances could include, for example: where the employee was posted abroad by a British-based employer to work on behalf of or as a representative of that employer (such a situation might arise in the case of a foreign correspondent posted to a foreign country by a British newspaper); or where the employee is working abroad but within a 'political or social enclave' (for example a British military base).

However, it is important to note that their Lordships declined to opine on whether these principles would apply equally to rights afforded under the *Employment Rights Act 1996* other than the right not to be unfairly dismissal. In the circumstances, there continues to be uncertainty as to the territorial scope of provisions within the *Employment Rights Act 1996* apart from the unfair dismissal provisions. It is also important to note that the judgment in *Lawson v Serco* does not provide any easy answers, in particular, in cases involving the secondment of employees. Following the judgment of the House of Lords in *Lawson v Serco*, it would seem that domestic employment tribunals cannot apply the doctrine of *forum non conveniens* in the context of statutory claims which come before it (see in particular per Lord Hoffmann at para 24.

When bringing a claim against a foreign respondent in the Employment Tribunal, the rules of service as set out *in rule 61(4)(h)* of the *Employment Tribunals (Constitution & Rules etc) Regulations 2004* will apply, No authoritative guidance as to how this rule should be applied in the case of a foreign respondent has yet been provided by the appellate courts or tribunals.

27   Health and Safety at Work – I: The Legal Framework

The law relating to health and safety is both long-established and rapidly developing. To that end, keeping track of it is difficult, like most other legal subject-matter. However, the Health and Safety Executive ('HSE') produces a wide range of free and priced information on health and safety in the workplace. See also www.hse.gov.uk.

Cross-reference. See HEALTH AND SAFETY AT WORK – II (28) for specific legislation and health and safety issues.

27.1   THE LEGISLATIVE FRAMEWORK

An employer is under a common law duty to have regard to the safety of his employees. He is also liable at common law for accidents caused by acts of his employees where the employees were acting in the course of their employment. The assessment of damages in personal injury actions is beyond the scope of this book. In addition to these common law duties, statutory obligations have been imposed upon employers in certain circumstances by such enactments as the *Occupiers' Liability Act 1957*, the *Occupiers Liability Act 1984* (see 27.12 below) and the *Health and Safety at Work, etc Act 1974* (see 27.16 below). An employer owes specific statutory duties to his own employees, members of the public who are affected by the activities of the employer, and other people's employees working on the employer's premises. A breach of an employer's statutory duties under the *Health and Safety at Work, etc Act 1974* ('*HSWA 1974*') imposes only criminal liability, although a breach of health and safety regulations made thereunder, insofar as damage is caused, will give rise to civil liability unless the regulations provide otherwise (see 27.43 below).

Under provisions in the *Employment Rights Act 1996*, employees are protected from dismissal or victimisation by the employer in health and safety cases (see 54.3 UNFAIR DISMISSAL – II and 28.9 HEALTH AND SAFETY AT WORK – II). In addition, an employer who fails to fulfil his legal duties may face a claim for constructive dismissal should an employee resign as a result of an alleged breach of the employer's duty of care. For example, in *British Aircraft Corpn v Austin* [1978] IRLR 332, an employer's obstinate and unjustified refusal to deal with a safety grievance was held to justify a complaint of constructive dismissal when the employee resigned (see 28.11 HEALTH AND SAFETY AT WORK – II).

27.2   THE COMMON LAW DUTY

An employer is obliged to take such steps as are reasonably necessary to ensure the safety of his employees. The definition of 'employee' is given a wide interpretation by the courts (*Lane v Shire Roofing (Oxford) Ltd* [1995] IRLR 493). The duty is not an absolute one and the mere occurrence of an accident does not of itself necessarily impose liability on the employer (see *McCook v Lobo* [2002] EWCA Civ 1760, [2003] ICR 89). All the circumstances of the accident will be investigated in deciding whether the employer acted reasonably or not. If an accident occurs as a result of the employer's failure to comply with his duty to his employees, he is liable for any resulting injury or damage.

Where a job has inherent risks to health and safety which are not commonly known but of which the employer is or ought to be aware, and if the employer cannot guard against those risks by taking precautionary measures, then he has a duty to inform prospective employees of the risks if knowledge of them would be likely to affect a sensible and level-headed person's decision on whether or not to accept the job (*White v Holbrook Precision Castings* [1985] IRLR 215). The employer must keep abreast of contemporary knowledge in the field of accident prevention (*Baxter v Harland and Wolff plc* [1990] IRLR 516; *Bowman v Harland and Wolff plc* [1992] IRLR 349).

The employer's compliance with his common law duty of care is usually tested under the following headings:

(*a*)   providing a safe place of work;

(*b*)   providing a safe means of access to the place of work;

(*c*)   providing a safe system of work;

(*d*)   providing safe plant and equipment;

(*e*)   employing competent fellow employees; and

(*f*)   protecting employees from unnecessary risk of injury.

However, these are simply specific aspects of the employer's overall general duty not to be negligent, and so should be viewed as examples of ways in which employers can take steps to ensure that their employees are reasonably safe at work.

27.3   Safe place of work

An employer is obliged to see that the place where his employees work is reasonably safe in all the circumstances. A place of work must be safely constructed and adequately maintained in a reasonable state of repair. An employer would be as guilty of failing to provide a safe place of work if, for example, a platform high above the ground on which men were required to stand was not adequately fenced as if one of the planks provided for the platform were rotten and liable to give way.

So far as construction of the workplace is concerned, it is not sufficient to show that the employer engaged a competent contractor to provide a safe place (*Paine v Colne Valley Electrical Supply Co Ltd and British Insulated Cables Ltd* [1938] 4 All ER 803, *per* Goddard LJ at 807). This reflects the general principle that the employer's duty of care to his employees is non-delegable. If, however, an employer maintains an adequate system of inspection of the workplace and despite inspection, a part of the workplace becomes inadequate or defective, the employer will probably not have been in breach of his common law duty. (He may nevertheless be in breach of a statutory provision which imposes a stricter duty.)

Temporary conditions affecting the workplace. A place of work which is intrinsically safe may become unsafe by the occurrence of certain events. Liquid may be spilt on a workshop floor making it slippery, a fence may be temporarily removed or an object placed in an unfamiliar position. All these events could cause accidents. The employer's liability will depend upon whether a reasonable employer would in the particular circumstances have taken measures to avoid the accident or different measures from those in fact taken. What is reasonable will vary according to the facts of the case. If a man slips on an oil slick at his workplace and thereby injures himself, his employer's potential liability may well vary according to how long the oil had been present (or according to the frequency with which such spillages occur, as in *Bell v Department of Health and*

Social Security (1989) Times, 13 June). If the oil had been spilt just a few minutes before the accident there may well be no liability, whereas if it had been there for half a day, the position would be different. In *Thomas v Bristol Aeroplane Co Ltd* [1954] 2 All ER 1, an employer was held not to be in breach of the common law duty of care in failing to take steps to remove from the entrance to the factory frozen snow which had fallen about a quarter of an hour before the factory opened.

Employee working on other premises. An employer owes a general duty to his employee to provide him with a safe place of work whether he is employed on the employer's own premises or elsewhere; see the House of Lords judgment in *McDermid v Nash Dredging Ltd* [1987] AC 906. However, the extent of that duty when the employee is on other premises may well be less than when he is on his employer's premises. The test again is: did the employer in question act as a reasonable employer would have acted in the circumstances? Thus, if an employer sends a window-cleaner to premises he knows to be unsafe, he may well be held liable for any accident caused as a result of the state of the premises. If he does not know whether the premises are safe or not, then, depending on the convenience of inspection and the degree of risk involved, he may be held negligent in failing to inspect and, if necessary, make those premises safe (*General Cleaning Contractors Ltd v Christmas* [1953] AC 180).

The extent of an employer's duty in relation to employees working on other premises was considered by the Court of Appeal in *Square D Ltd v Cook* [1992] IRLR 34. An employer must take all reasonable steps to ensure the safety of his staff and this includes the premises where the staff are required to work (whether occupied by the employer or by a third party). This duty cannot be delegated. However, the duty is not an absolute one and considerations such as the place where the work is to be done, the nature of the building on the site concerned, the experience of the employee who is sent to work at such a site, the nature of the work he is required to do, the degree of control that the employer can reasonably be expected to exercise in the circumstances and the employer's own knowledge of the defective state of the premises are all factors to be taken into account. These considerations apply whether the third party's premises are in the UK or abroad. However, the court may take a different view of the employer's duty where staff are sent to work abroad for a considerable period of time. The Court of Appeal suggested that in such an instance, the employer may be expected to inspect the site personally and satisfy himself that the occupiers are conscious of their obligations concerning the safety of people working there.

27.4   Safe means of access

It is the duty of every employer to provide his employees with a safe means of access to their place of work. Thus, if access to a factory is by means of a footpath, that footpath should be kept in a reasonable state of repair.

Sometimes it is hard to distinguish the means of access to the place of work from the place of work itself. A painter may use a ladder to reach a position from where to carry on his decorating. The ladder may in certain circumstances be considered the means of access and in others the place of work. In any event the common law duty of care in relation to both is the same.

27.5   Safe system of work

A system of work is the method used for carrying out the work, the sequence of events followed. It includes such things as manning of operations, provision of equipment, and supervision. It may be that the system used by an employer is intrinsically unsafe or it may be that there is in existence a suitable system of work but that the system itself is applied unsatisfactorily. For example, an employer who provides insufficient workers to carry out a task may be held liable for any accident caused thereby.

One defect in an otherwise unimpeachable system may render the whole system unsafe. If, for example, the procedures for carrying out blasting in a quarry were adequate but the warning given to workers in the quarry to leave was too short, the whole system would thereby be rendered unsafe. Similarly, it would be considered an unsafe system to require men who had insufficient training or supervision to carry out a task which would otherwise be considered safe.

Where an operation is so inherently dangerous that it should not be performed at all, the employer must provide explicit instructions banning employees from carrying it out (*King v Smith* [1995] ICR 339).

Employers who require their workers to carry out manoeuvres which involve several actions should first check to see whether there are any relevant statutory requirements relating to the procedure. Before devising a system of working they should consult the employees who are to work the system or their representatives. Where the workforce is unionised, the employer has a duty to consult with union-appointed safety representatives. Non-unionised groups of workers or their representatives must also be consulted (see 28.20 HEALTH AND SAFETY AT WORK – II). If the procedure is at all complicated, employers should consult the Health and Safety Executive (see 27.26).

Duty based on reasonable steps. The duty to provide a safe system of work is not an absolute one. The duty is to take reasonable steps to provide a system which will be reasonably safe, having regard to the dangers necessarily inherent in the operation. In deciding what is reasonable, long-established practice in the trade (although not necessarily conclusive) is generally regarded as strong evidence in support of reasonableness (*General Cleaning Contractors Ltd v Christmas* [1953] AC 180 *per* Lord Tucker at 195). Nevertheless, acceptable standards of safety change over the years and the courts will have regard to current best practice. In deciding the extent of the duty the courts will take into account: (i) the size of the danger; (ii) the likelihood of an accident occurring; (iii) the possible consequences of the occurrence of an accident; and (iv) the steps needed to eliminate all risk and the cost of doing so (*Edwards v National Coal Board* [1949] 1 KB 704).

Ensuring implementation of safety measures. It is not sufficient to provide a safe system of work. An employer should take such steps as are reasonably practicable to see that the system is implemented. If it is within his knowledge that a piece of safety equipment is persistently not used, he should take reasonable steps to encourage his workers to use it (*Bux v Slough Metals* [1974] 1 All ER 262). However, this duty is not so onerous as the duty to provide the safety equipment, etc in the first place. As Lord Radcliffe said in *Qualcast (Wolverhampton) Ltd v Haynes* [1959] AC 743 at 753: 'the courts should be circumspect in filling out that duty with the much vaguer obligation of encouraging, exhorting or instructing workmen or a particular workman to make regular use of what is provided'. In *Crouch v British Rail Engineering Ltd* [1988] IRLR 404 it was held to be insufficient on the facts merely to make safety goggles available for collection from a point about five minutes away. The failure to have them available where they were needed encouraged the taking of risks.

27.6   Safe equipment and materials

An employer is under a common law duty to provide equipment, materials and clothing to enable his workmen to carry out their duties in safety. As with the system of work, the duty is not an absolute one. It may be, for example, that goggles costing £300 per pair are marginally safer than those costing £50 per pair. In deciding whether an employer was in breach of his duty in failing to provide his employees with the more expensive goggles, the court would have regard to the difference in effectiveness between the cheaper and the more expensive goggles, the degree of risk involved, and the additional cost.

When an employer bought materials from a reputable supplier, and injury was caused by an undetected defect in those materials, his failure to examine the materials would not render him liable for the accident at common law. However, under the *Employers' Liability (Defective Equipment) Act 1969*, if an employee is injured by reason of a defect in the equipment, the injury is by statute deemed to be attributable to the fault of the employer. This does not affect the employer's right to allege that the accident was wholly or partly due to negligence on the part of the employee; nor does it affect any remedy the employer may have against his supplier. Thus, if an employee is injured by a piece of metal flying from a defective high-pressure hose, supplied to him by his employer, he could succeed in a claim against the employer for his injury. The employer could only seek to reduce the damages awarded against him by showing that the accident was caused or contributed to by the fault of the employee and/or by claiming against the supplier of the hose.

Under s *1(3)* of the *Employers' Liability (Defective Equipment) Act 1969* 'equipment' includes any plant, machinery, vehicle, aircraft and clothing. A ship is 'equipment' for the purposes of s *1(3)* (*Coltman v Bibby Tankers Ltd, The Derbyshire* [1988] ICR 67). 'Equipment provided by the employer' includes materials (in this case a flagstone) which an employee is given by the employer to do the job (*Knowles v Liverpool City Council* [1993] IRLR 588).

27.7   Fellow workers

An employer is under a duty to provide competent fellow workers. Thus, if an employee of his is injured because of the known inadequacy of a fellow worker, the employer is liable to that employee in damages for the injury caused by the fellow worker. Even if the employee's action is untypical, the employer may nevertheless be held liable by reason of his VICARIOUS LIABILITY (54). This principle also applies to the employer's duty not to engage or continue to employ employees who are known to indulge in dangerous 'horseplay' (*Hudson v Ridge Manufacturing Co Ltd* [1957] 2 QB 348).

An employer may not contract out of his liability to his employees for the negligence of fellow workers. The *Law Reform (Personal Injuries) Act 1948, s 1(3)* renders void any agreement to that effect.

27.8   Protection from risk of injury

An employer is under a duty to take reasonable care to see that his employees are not subjected to any unnecessary risks of injury. In *Charlton v Forrest Printing Ink Co Ltd* [1980] IRLR 331, the Court of Appeal held that an employer has a duty to take steps to eliminate a risk which he knows or ought to know is a real risk and not a mere possibility which would never influence the mind of a reasonable man. The Court of Appeal in *Coxall v Goodyear Great Britain Ltd* [2002] EWCA Civ 1010, [2003] ICR 152, considering whether or not an employer was under a duty to prevent an employee from doing work which he was willing to do because of a risk to his health, depended largely on the actual nature and extent of the risk. Consequently, if on the facts the employer were negligent in failing to either move the employee from the job in question or dismiss him in order to protect him from the danger, the employer would become liable.

Where a risk is not obvious, the employee will succeed only if he can show that the state of knowledge in the relevant industry at the relevant time was such that the employer knew or ought to have known of that risk. But an employer must keep reasonably abreast of developing knowledge, and if he has greater than average knowledge of the risks, he may have to take greater than average precautions (*Stokes v Guest Keen & Nettlefold (Bolts and Nuts) Ltd* [1968] 1 WLR 1776).

An employer may also be liable in certain circumstances for psychiatric illness caused by work if it is reasonably foreseeable (see *Page v Smith* [1996] AC 155 for the principles involved, and *Walker v Northumberland County Council* [1995] IRLR 35 and *Cross v Highlands and Islands Enterprise* [2001] IRLR 336 at 28.24 HEALTH AND SAFETY AT WORK – II). The House of Lords in *White v Chief Constable of South Yorkshire Police* [1999] IRLR 110 overturned the ruling of the Court of Appeal in *Frost v Chief Constable of South Yorkshire Police* [1997] IRLR 173 relating to an employer's liability for work-related psychiatric illness. The case concerned police officers who sustained psychiatric damage as a result of tending to victims of the Hillsborough football stadium disaster which was caused by the employer's admitted negligence. Compensation for physical injury caused by negligence was recoverable if it was reasonably foreseeable that the conduct would cause such injury. Where this situation does not apply (ie the claimant is not within the range of foreseeable physical injury), individuals are 'secondary victims' and, in order to recover compensation for psychiatric injury, it was necessary that the conditions set out in *Alcock v Chief Constable of South Yorkshire Police* [1992] 1 AC 310 should be satisfied:

(*a*)   there must be a close tie of love and affection between the claimant and the victim;

(*b*)   the claimant must have been present at the accident or its immediate aftermath; and

(*c*)   the psychiatric injury must have been caused by direct perception of the accident or its immediate aftermath and not by hearing about it from someone else.

Since the officers did not have sufficiently close ties to the victims, their claim failed. The House of Lords concluded that the employment relationship did not put the officers in a special position in this regard. See also *Robertson and Rough v Forth Road Bridge Joint Board* [1995] IRLR 251, *Young v Charles Church (Southern) Ltd* (1997) 33 BMLR 101, CA and *Hunter v British Coal Corpn* [1999] QB 140, CA.

In cases of industrial disease, it may often be difficult to determine whether the employee's illness was *caused* by the employer's breach of duty. The decision of the House of Lords in *Fairchild v Glenhaven Funeral Services Ltd* [2003] 1 AC 3240 contains a comprehensive review of the relevant authorities. In cases of mesothelioma only, s 3 of the *Compensation Act 2006* enables a claimant to recover in full from any culpable employer even though the victim was exposed to asbestos in more than one job.

27.9 **Vicarious liability for acts of employees**

An employer is liable for the acts of his employee if they are committed in the course of the employee's employment. This is known as vicarious liability. The modern test is whether the incident was job related or job connected. An incident can be job related even if it forms no part of the employee's authorised work. In *Lister v Hesley Hall Ltd* [2001] 2 WLR 1311 it was found that a teacher who abused a pupil was acting in the course of employment even though what he did was criminal ,unauthorised and something that no teacher should ever have done. Thus, if a van delivery driver drives negligently while in the normal course of his duties and causes an accident, his employer is held liable for the resulting damage or injury. This question is dealt with in more detail in VICARIOUS LIABILITY (56).

27.10 **Employee working under direction of third party**

The primary employer remains liable for the safety of an employee who is working under the direction of a third party. However, where the employee suffers an accident which is wholly due to the third party's negligence in breach of its duty of care, the primary employer may be able to recover full indemnity from the third party in accordance with the *Civil Liability (Contribution) Act 1978* (*Nelhams v Sandells Maintenance Ltd* (1995) Times, 15 June, CA).

27.11 **Independent contractors**

With the exception of the statutory occupier's liability (see 27.12 below), in general an employer is not liable for acts of an independent contractor engaged by him, provided that he exercised due diligence in selecting the contractor for the task. (For criminal liability in respect of the negligence of an independent contractor, see 27.19 below.)

27.12 **OCCUPIERS' LIABILITY ACT 1957**

Apart from the common law duties of an employer to provide his employees with a safe place of work, as an occupier of premises he owes his employees, and other visitors, the common duty of care imposed by the *Occupiers' Liability Act 1957* ('*OLA 1957*'). The extent of the duty which is owed to trespassers is defined by the *Occupiers' Liability Act 1984*. An outline is given below of the duties imposed on an employer, as the occupier of premises, to employees and other visitors by the *OLA 1957*.

27.13 **Meaning of 'occupier'**

An occupier of premises may be the owner, the lessor, or the licensee (a person who merely has permission to occupy). An occupier need not have exclusive control over premises in order to have a duty to persons who visit those premises; more than one person may owe a duty in respect of the same premises. For example, both an employer and an independent contractor may be held to be occupiers of premises where the employer has engaged the independent contractor to carry out work on the premises.

27.14 **Duty of occupier**

The extent of the duty of care is defined in *OLA 1957, s 2(2)* as:

'a duty to take such care as in all the circumstances of the case is reasonable to see that the visitor is reasonably safe in using the premises for the purposes for which he is invited or permitted by the occupier to be there.'

In defining the extent of the duty, the courts will take into account the *degree of control over the premises actually enjoyed* by the occupier and, if applicable, the division of duties between the two occupiers of the same premises. Thus, if a harbour authority leases a certain wharf to a shipping company and an employee of that company suffers an accident due to the state of repair of the wharf, the apportionment of blame will depend on the actual degree of control exercised by the harbour authority and the shipping company.

Children and persons pursuing a calling. OLA 1957, s 2(3) provides a little help in defining the extent of the duty of care to be exercised in relation to children and to persons on the premises in pursuance of a particular calling.

'The circumstances relevant for the present purpose include the degree of care, and of want of care, which would ordinarily be looked for in such a visitor, so that (for example) in proper cases:

(*a*)   an occupier must be prepared for children to be less careful than adults; and

(*b*)   an occupier may expect that a person, in the exercise of his calling, will appreciate and guard against any special risks ordinarily incident to it, so far as the occupier leaves him free to do so.'

The duty under *OLA 1957, s 2(2)* is to see that the visitor is reasonably safe in using the premises for the purpose for which he or she is there. This covers the static state of the premises and does not extend to dangers occurring to employees of contractors as a result of activities they are performing on the premises. The House of Lords, in its landmark ruling in *Fairchild v Glenhaven Funeral Services Ltd* [2002] UKHL 22, [2002] IRLR 533, overruled the Court of Appeal's decision ([2002] EWCA Civ 1881, [2002] IRLR 129) that claimants were not entitled to recover damages from their former employers in relation to mesothelioma, a form of cancer which develops as a result of negligent exposure to asbestos.

Unanimously, their Lordships held that the victim, on grounds of so-called 'justice', should not be deprived of a remedy because it cannot be established which of a series of different employers caused the alleged harm. As Lord Nicholls put it: '*Any other outcome would be deeply offensive to instinctive notions of what justice requires and fairness demands.*' Consequently, employers may now be held liable for damage which they did not cause. The House of Lords established a right to damages by departing from the orthodox test of causation where justice so requires, by establishing a notion of joint liability. For instance, on the facts of this case, it was sufficient that the employer's breach of duty materially increased the risk that the claimants would contract mesothelioma. Therefore, the *Fairchild* ruling presupposes negligence by all employers. Clearly, the impact of this historic ruling is that once a breach of duty can be established, then each employer becomes liable for the full damages.

27.15 Faulty work by independent contractor

If an accident occurs as a result of faulty work by an independent contractor employed at the premises which the employer occupies, *OLA 1957, s 2(4)(b)* provides that:

'the occupier is not to be treated without more ["without more" in the sense of "on those facts alone"] as answerable for the danger if in all the circumstances he had acted reasonably in entrusting the work to an independent contractor and had taken such steps (if any) as he reasonably ought in order to satisfy himself that the contractor was competent and that the work had been properly done.'

Thus, if injury is caused to a visitor to the premises by the fault of an independent contractor, the occupier will not be held liable for the injury or damage so caused if he can show that:

(*a*)   he acted reasonably in entrusting the work to the independent contractor (it may be held to be reasonable to employ an independent contractor where the work to be done is of a skilled or specialist nature and is beyond the capabilities of the employer);

(*b*)   he exercised a reasonable degree of care in selecting the independent contractor to see that he was competent to do the task entrusted to him; and

(*c*)   he checked so far as was possible to see that the work was properly carried out.

For example, an employer may need to have his factory rewired. He may have no electricians in his employ and, therefore, need to engage an outside firm. If he has reasonable grounds for regarding that firm as competent, he will not ordinarily be expected to supervise the firm's activities in order to ensure that a safe system of work is being used. But if he knows or has reason to suspect that the firm is using an unsafe system of work, it may well be reasonable for him to take steps to see that it is made safe. If he does not, he might be liable to one of his own or the firm's employees injured, eg by receiving an electric shock (*Ferguson v Welsh* [1988] IRLR 112, on different facts). He may also be liable to the employee for breach of other statutory provisions.

27.16 THE HEALTH AND SAFETY AT WORK, ETC ACT 1974

The *Health and Safety at Work, etc Act 1974* ('*HSWA 1974*') lays down general principles to be followed by employers governing the health and safety at work of employees. It also establishes the Health and Safety Commission ('the Commission') and the Health and Safety Executive ('the Executive'); gives powers to inspectors to issue improvement notices and prohibition notices; and imposes certain civil and criminal liabilities upon employers. The Executive publishes many explanatory guides and booklets.

27.17 Health, safety and welfare

The provisions of *HSWA 1974, Part I* (as expressed in s *1(1)*) are designed to have the effect of:

(*a*)   securing the health, safety and welfare of persons at work;

(*b*)   protecting persons other than persons at work against risks to health or safety arising out of, or in connection with, the activities of persons at work; and

(*c*)   controlling the keeping and use of explosive or highly flammable or otherwise dangerous substances, and generally preventing the unlawful acquisition, possession and use of such substances.

Regulations and codes of practice are issued under *HSWA 1974* to give effect to the general principles set out and also to enforce the provisions of a large body of health and safety legislation which is set out in *Sch 1* to the *Act*. Among the more important regulations made under *HSWA 1974* are the *Health and Safety (First-Aid) Regulations 1981* (*SI 1981/917*), the *Reporting of Injuries, Diseases and Dangerous Occurrences Regulations 1995* (*SI 1995/3163*) and the *Electricity at Work Regulations 1989* (*SI 1989/635*). There are also many regulations dealing with specific problems such as asbestos at work. From 1 October 1989 a large number of outdated Statutory Instruments were replaced upon the coming into force of the *Control of Substances Hazardous to Health Regulations 1988* ('*COSHH*'). The *1988 Regulations* were subsequently amended and replaced by the *2002 Regulations* (*SI 2002/2675*) of the same name. *COSHH* has been described as 'the most far-reaching health and safety legislation since 1974'. Further important changes have taken place with the implementation of EC Directives on health and safety issues by regulations made under *HSWA 1974*. These regulations cover, *inter alia*, noise at work, management of health and safety, display screen equipment (VDUs), manual handling, work equipment, and workplace health, safety and welfare.

Further details of regulations made under *HSWA 1974* are contained in HEALTH AND SAFETY AT WORK – II (27) under specific subject headings.

As will be seen below, inspectors appointed under the *Act* have powers to enforce the legislation set out in *Sch 1* as well as the provisions of the *Act* itself, and health and safety regulations.

The protection of *HSWA 1974* is extended by *Health and Safety (Training for Employment) Regulations 1990* (*SI 1990/1380*) to those receiving work experience provided pursuant to a training course or programme, or training for employment, or both, except if the training is received on a course run by an educational establishment.

27.18   Employer's obligations under HSWA 1974

HSWA 1974 contains provisions broadly equivalent to the common law duty of care of an employer to his employees (see 27.2 above) (*HSWA 1974, s 2(1), (2)*). Criminal liability under *HSWA 1974* can arise even where senior management has taken all reasonable steps to protect employees. A failure at local management level may be attributable to the employing organisation (*R v Gateway Foodmarkets Ltd* [1997] IRLR 189). A failure by an employer to comply with the requirements relating to the safety of his employees may also in certain circumstances constitute a fundamental breach of contract entitling the employee to resign and claim that he was constructively dismissed (*British Aircraft Corpn Ltd v Austin* [1978] IRLR 332).

Health and safety policy statement. Employers are obliged to prepare (and, if necessary, revise) a written statement of their general policy with respect to the health and safety at work of their employees and the organisation and arrangements for carrying out that policy. In addition, employers must bring such information to the notice of all of their employees (*HSWA 1974, s 2(3)*). The length and complexity of the notice required will depend on the nature of the employer's undertaking. Such information should in all cases be placed on an easily accessible notice board. In addition, information relating to health, safety and welfare must be given to employees by means of posters and leaflets approved and published by the Health and Safety Executive. From 1 July 2000 employers are required to use a revised version of the poster; additional detail is provided on aspects of the *Management of Health and Safety at Work Regulations 1999* (*SI 1999/3242*) and new sections have been incorporated for the insertion of the names and locations of safety representatives and competent persons together with their health and safety responsibilities. Copies of the form of approved poster or leaflet may be obtained from HSE Books (see the *Health and Safety Information for Employees Regulations 1989 (SI 1989/682)*). Alternative health and safety posters may be approved by the HSE provided certain criteria are met (the *Health and Safety Information for Employees (Modifications and Repeals) Regulations 1995 (SI 1995/2923)*).

Employers who carry on undertakings in which for the time being they employ fewer than five employees are exempted from the requirement of *s 2(3)* by the *Employers' Health and Safety Policy Statements (Exception) Regulations 1975 (SI 1975/1584)*.

27.19 Employers and the self-employed

Employers and self-employed people are obliged to conduct their undertakings, so far as is reasonably practicable, in a way which will ensure that persons who may be affected, not being their employees, are not exposed to risks to health or safety (*HSWA 1974, s 3(1)*, *(2)*). The conduct of the undertaking extends to the manner in which equipment is made available for use by employees outside business hours (*R v Mara* [1987] ICR 165). The Court of Appeal has ruled that it is not necessary to prove actual danger to members of the public for criminal liability to arise. It is sufficient to show that there is a risk which might be run (*R v Board of Trustees of the Science Museum* [1994] IRLR 25).

Subject to reasonable practicability, s *3(1)* creates an absolute prohibition on exposing non-employees to risk. It is no defence to argue that the employer is not liable because senior management was not involved in the incident (*R v British Steel plc* [1995] IRLR 310). It may not be sufficient to show that the employer has issued a code of instructions on a safe system of work. In certain circumstances tangible technical equipment may be necessary to ensure safety (*R v Rhône-Poulenc Rorer Ltd* [1996] ICR 1054, CA).

Nevertheless, employers should not necessarily be held criminally liable under s *3(1)* for an isolated act of negligence by the employee performing the work (*R v Nelson Group Services (Maintenance) Ltd* [1999] IRLR 646). It is a sufficient obligation to require the employer to show that everything reasonably practicable was done to see that the person doing the work had the appropriate skill and training, was adequately supervised and provided with safe equipment, and that a safe system of work was laid down.

In February 1997 Port Ramsgate, together with others, was convicted of a breach of *s 3(1)* and heavily fined following the collapse of a ferry passenger walkway which caused the death of six people. The port had employed highly reputable contractors and designers and made arrangements for safety checks but, according to the judge, it had not ensured that proper quality assurance provisions were included in the contract or given detailed thought to its own responsibilities for the design, construction and installation of the walkway.

In *R v Associated Octel Co Ltd* [1997] IRLR 123 the House of Lords held that an employer was criminally liable under s *3(1)* for the negligence of an independent contractor in respect of injuries sustained by an employee of the contractor while undertaking maintenance and repair work for the employer. The conduct of the employer's undertaking could cover ancillary activities carried out by independent contractors, particularly when the activity was carried out on the employer's premises.

Regulations may be introduced compelling employers and self-employed people to give information relating to health and safety to people (not being their employees) who may be affected by the way in which they conduct their undertakings (*HSWA 1974, s 3(3)*).

27.20 **Duties of occupiers**

Obligations are imposed on occupiers of 'non-domestic' premises in respect of persons who are not their employees but who are working on their premises or using plant or substances provided for use on the premises (*HSWA 1974, s 4*). They must take such measures as are reasonable for persons in their position to ensure, so far as is reasonably practicable, that the premises, plant and machinery are safe and without risks to the health of the non-employees working there. These provisions would apply to protect workers who were sent by their employer, for example, to re-decorate a client's factory. The nature of the duties imposed by *HSWA 1974, s 4* was considered by the House of Lords in *Austin Rover group Ltd v HM Inspector of Factories* [1990] ICR 133.

Operators in control of an establishment or installation which involves the use of dangerous substances are required to take all measures necessary to prevent major accidents and to limit their consequences to people and the environment, under the *Control of Major Accident Hazards Regulations 1999 (SI 1999/743)*, which came into force on 1 April 1999. Known as '*COMAH*', the *1999 Regulations* (which primarily affect the chemical industry) revoke and replace the *Control of Industrial Major Accident Hazards Regulations 1984 (SI 1984/1902)*. Under the *1999 Regulations*, operators are obliged to notify the competent authority about their activities and prepare a major accident prevention policy.

27.21 **Duties of manufacturers**

Manufacturers, designers, importers and suppliers of articles or substances for use at work are placed under a duty to ensure so far as is reasonably practicable that the design of their product is safe, to carry out necessary tests for so ensuring and to provide adequate information about the use of the product and the conditions necessary for its safe use (*HSWA 1974, s 6*, as amended by the *Consumer Protection Act 1987, s 36* and *Sch 3*). The manufacturers, designers, importers or suppliers of articles for use at work are exempt from such duties if they obtain a written undertaking from their customers that the customer will take specified steps sufficient to ensure, so far as is reasonably practicable, that the article will be safe and without risk to health when properly used (*HSWA 1974, s 6(8)*). This exemption is qualified where the goods are imported (*HSWA 1974, s 6(8A)*).

27.22 **Duties of employees**

Every employee while at work has the duty:

(*a*)   to take reasonable care for the health and safety of himself and of other persons who may be affected by his acts or omissions at work; and

(*b*)   to co-operate with his employer, or any other person, in ensuring that requirements or duties imposed by the relevant statutory provisions (including those specified in *Sch 1*) are complied with.

(*HSWA 1974, s 7.*)

Thus, if an employer is required to provide his workers with goggles, supervisors should, if that task is delegated to them, ensure that adequate goggles are available. Also, the workers themselves are under an obligation to wear them.

27.23 Interference with safety measures

No person may intentionally or recklessly interfere with or misuse anything provided in the interests of health, safety or welfare in pursuance of any of the relevant statutory provisions (*HSWA 1974, s 8*). Thus, an employee who removes a safety guard provided by his employer, in breach of the regulations, is in breach of *s 8* and is guilty of an offence for which in a magistrates' court he may be fined up to level 5 on the standard scale and in the Crown Court there may be an unlimited fine (*HSWA 1974, s 33(1)(b), (3)(b)*; see 1.10 INTRODUCTION).

Such conduct may also justify dismissal, provided the employee was properly instructed about the safety measures and had been made aware that interference could lead to dismissal (*Martin v Yorkshire Imperial Metals Ltd* [1978] IRLR 440).

27.24 No charge for safety measures

An employer may not charge any employee of his for anything done or supplied in compliance with any specific requirement of the relevant statutory provisions (*HSWA 1974, s 9*). If, for example, an employer is required to provide an employee of his with a mask, he may not require that employee to contribute towards the cost of that mask.

27.25 EU LEGISLATION

The influence of European-derived legislation in the health and safety field is substantial. The original *Treaty of Rome*, as amended by the subsequent Treaties of Maastricht, Amsterdam and Nice (see 25.1 EUROPEAN COMMUNITY LAW), provides in *art 137* (formerly *art 118A*) for the adoption of Directives in connection with improvements to the working environment to protect workers' health and safety. Such Directives are subject to the co-decision procedure whereby the European Parliament jointly adopts proposals with the Council of Ministers. Health and safety directives are normally implemented in UK law by means of regulations made under *HSWA 1974*.

A surge in EU health and safety legislation occurred following the adoption of the so-called *Framework Directive (89/391)*, implemented on 1 January 1993. The *Directive* imposes a number of general obligations upon both employers and employees. Whereas much English legislation uses the standard of what is 'reasonably practicable', the EC approach is to set absolute standards and to permit a defence of *force majeure* for non-compliance (see *art 5(4)* of the *Directive*).

Five further Directives, laying down detailed requirements, were initially adopted pursuant to the Framework Directive. They relate to minimum requirements for safety and health in the workplace (*89/654*), the use of machines and equipment (*89/655*), the use of personal protective equipment (*89/656*), the use of visual display units (*90/270*) and the handling of heavy loads (*90/269*).

In addition, Directives have been adopted on, *inter alia*: carcinogens (*90/394, 97/42, 99/38*), biological agents (*90/679*), construction sites (*92/57*), health and safety signs (*92/58*), and protection of pregnant workers (*92/85*).

Regulations have been made by statutory instrument to implement the EC Directives referred to above. For further details of Regulations within the scope of this book, see HEALTH AND SAFETY AT WORK – II (8) under the specific subject heading.

27.26 THE HEALTH AND SAFETY COMMISSION AND EXECUTIVE

HSWA 1974, s 10 establishes the Health and Safety Commission and the Health and Safety Executive. The Commission is made up of both employer and employee representatives and the Executive is made up of three of the Commission's appointees approved by the Secretary of State for the Environment, one of whom is first chosen as the director of the Executive and who is consulted as to the appointment of the other two members. The Commission's chief function is to advise, authorise research and make suggestions for the implementation of the provisions of the *HSWA 1974*. It may make suggestions for the passing of regulations. The Executive also has the duty of providing information and advice to any government minister who requests it.

The Commission may either direct the Executive or authorise any other person to investigate and make a special report on any accident, occurrence, situation or other matter that the Commission thinks is necessary or expedient to investigate, or (with the consent of the Secretary of State) direct an inquiry to be held into any such matter (*HWSA 1974, s 14(1)(2)*). The *Health and Safety Inquiries (Procedure) Regulations 1975*, as amended.

(*SIs 1975/335; 1976/1246*) lay down the procedure for the conduct of such inquiries. Since civil or criminal liability for an accident may depend on the outcome of such an inquiry, proper representation is essential.

27.27 Information

HSWA 1974, s 27 enables the Commission to obtain information necessary for the discharge of its functions, or for provision to an enforcing authority (eg the Executive or an inspector) of information necessary to discharge its duties.

27.28 Codes of Practice

The Commission is empowered by *HSWA 1974, s 16* to approve and issue Codes of Practice for the enforcement of ss *2–7* or of health and safety regulations introduced under the *Act*, or any other existing statutory provisions. Approved Codes give guidance on methods of complying with regulations and on what is considered reasonably practicable.

27.29 ENFORCING AUTHORITIES AND INSPECTORS

The Health and Safety Executive and local authorities are responsible for the enforcement of the *Health and Safety at Work Act 1974*. From 1 April 1998 the *Health and Safety (Enforcing Authority) Regulations 1998* (*SI 1998/494*) re-enact, with amendments, the *1989 Regulations* of the same name (*SI 1989/1903*) which are revoked. *Schedule 1* sets out the main activities which determine whether local authorities will be enforcing authorities.

The enforcement powers under *HSWA 1974* cover all the 'relevant statutory provisions', which comprise the provisions of *HSWA 1974, Part I*, all the enactments specified in *HSWA 1974, Sch 1* and regulations made under them, and any health and safety and agricultural health and safety regulations (*HSWA 1974, s 53(1)*).

In January 2002 the Health and Safety Commission published its revised enforcement policy statement which, for the first time, sets out specific criteria to enable enforcement officers to decide when to investigate health and safety incidents, and to prosecute breaches of the law. The statement may be viewed on the HSE's website at www.hse.gov.uk/pubns/. This policy provides clarity on offences and the penalties available, as well as the HSE's role in investigations and inquiries. Since 2001 the HSC has published a list of health and safety offenders convicted and a prosecutions database.

27.30 Powers of inspectors

Every enforcing authority has the power to appoint inspectors. An inspector has many powers to enforce the statutory provisions for which his enforcing authority has responsibility. He may enter premises, if necessary accompanied by a police constable, take measurements and photographs and make other records, and take samples of articles or substances found in any premises which he has power to enter and of the atmosphere in or near such premises. If he fears that an article or substance found on premises which he has power to enter has caused or is likely to cause danger to health or safety, he may have it dismantled or subjected to any process or test. He may not destroy it unless that action is necessary for the performance of his duties. The inspector may take possession of a dangerous or potentially dangerous article or substance to examine it, to ensure that it is not tampered with or to ensure that it is available for use as evidence in any proceedings under the *HSWA 1974*. When he takes possession of any article, the inspector must fix, in a conspicuous position, a notice giving particulars of the article or substance and stating that he has taken possession of it (*HSWA 1974, s 20(2)(a)–(i), (4)*).

An inspector may require persons to answer questions in the course of his investigations and to sign a declaration of the truth of their answers. He may require the production of books and documents and take copies of them. If he requires any facilities or assistance in the course of his investigations, he may require the person able to do so to provide him with such facilities (*HSWA 1974, s 20(2)(j)–(l)*). No answer given by a person to an inspector is admissible in evidence against that person or the husband or wife of that person (*HSWA 1974, s 20(7)*). The section does not compel a person to disclose a document which could be withheld on grounds of legal professional privilege in High Court proceedings (such as an opinion of counsel) (*HSWA 1974, s 20(8)*).

Where an inspector has reasonable cause to believe that an article or substance on premises he is empowered to enter is a cause of imminent danger of serious personal injury, he may seize it and cause it to be rendered harmless (*HSWA 1974, s 25(1)*).

27.31 IMPROVEMENT AND PROHIBITION NOTICES

Improvement notices

If an inspector is of the opinion that a person:

(*a*)   is contravening one or more of the relevant statutory provisions (see 27.29 above); or

(*b*)   has contravened one or more of those provisions in circumstances that make it likely that the contravention will continue or be repeated,

he may serve on that person a notice (referred to as 'an improvement notice') (*HSWA 1974, s 21*).

An improvement notice must: (i) state that he is of that opinion; (ii) specify the provisions which in his opinion are being or have been contravened; (iii) give particulars of the reasons for his opinion; and (iv) require that person to remedy the contravention within a specified period.

The specified period in (iv) above is not to be shorter than that allowed for an appeal to an employment tribunal (which is 21 days from the date of the service on the appellant of the notice appealed against; see *Employment Tribunals (Constitution and Rules of Procedure) Regulations 2001, Sch 5 (SI 2001/1171)*).

27.32 Prohibition notices

If an inspector regards any activities as involving or potentially involving *a risk of serious personal injury*, he may serve on the person in control of those activities a notice known as 'a prohibition notice' (*HSWA 1974, s 22*).

A prohibition notice must:

(*a*) state the opinion of the inspector;

(*b*) specify the matters which in his opinion give or, as the case may be, will give rise to the risks;

(*c*) where in his opinion any of those matters involves or will involve a contravention of any of the relevant statutory provisions, state that he is of that opinion, specify the relevant provision or provisions, and give particulars of the reasons why he is of that opinion; and

(*d*) direct that the activities to which the notice relates shall not be carried on by or under the control of the person on whom the notice is served unless the matters specified in the notice and any associated contraventions so specified have been remedied.

A direction given in pursuance of (*d*) above takes effect immediately if the inspector is of the opinion, and states it, that the risk of serious personal injury is or will be imminent. For example, in *BT Fleet Ltd v McKenna* [2005] EWHC 387 (Admin), QBD, Evans-Lombe J. held that an improvement notice served by a health and safety Inspector, pursuant to s. 21 HSWA 1974, should be clear and easily understood for it to be operative.

Improvement and prohibition notices may make reference to any approved Code of Practice (see 27.28 above) (*HSWA 1974, s 23(2)(a)*).

27.33 Withdrawal of notices

Where an improvement notice or a prohibition notice which is not to take immediate effect has been served, the notice may be withdrawn by an inspector at any time before it takes effect and the period before it takes effect may be extended or further extended by an inspector at any time when an appeal against the notice is not pending (*HSWA 1974, s 23(5)*).

27.34 APPEALS AGAINST THE NOTICES

A person on whom an improvement or prohibition notice is served may, within 21 days, appeal to an employment tribunal (*Employment Tribunals (Constitution and Rules of Procedure) Regulations 2001 (SI 2001/1171), Sch 5, rule 2(1)*). A tribunal may extend the period for lodging an appeal (on an application made in writing to the Secretary of the Tribunals either before or after the expiration of the time limit) if it is satisfied that it is not or was not reasonably practicable for an appeal to be brought within that time (*rule 2(2)*).

One or more assessors may be appointed for the purposes of any such appeals brought before an employment tribunal (*HSWA 1974, s 24(4)*).

The tribunal may either cancel or affirm the notice and, if the tribunal affirms it, may do so either in its original form or with such modifications as the tribunal may in the circumstances think fit (*HSWA 1974, s 24(2)*).

27.35 Suspension of notices pending appeal hearing

Where an appeal is brought within the time limit allowed:

(a)   *Improvement notice*: the bringing of the appeal has the effect of suspending the operation of the notice until the appeal is finally disposed of or, if the appeal is withdrawn, until the withdrawal of the appeal (*HSWA 1974, s 24(3)(a)*); and

(b)   *Prohibition notice*: the bringing of the appeal will not affect the notice unless, on application by the appellant, the tribunal so directs, in which case the prohibition notice will be suspended from the time that the tribunal gives its direction (*HSWA 1974, s 24(3)(b)*).

27.36 Cost of remedy required

In deciding whether an improvement notice which required the cleaning and repainting of walls should be cancelled or not, an employment tribunal sitting at Shrewsbury held that the company's financial position was irrelevant and evidence relating to its financial position would not be admitted (*T C Harrison (Newcastle-under-Lyme) Ltd v K Ramsey (HM Inspector)* [1976] IRLR 135). It may therefore be no ground for appeal against such notices that the company cannot afford to remedy the defects.

27.37 CRIMINAL PROCEEDINGS

The HSE publishes an annual report naming companies and individuals convicted in the previous 12 months of flouting health and safety law. The names of those convicted are also listed on the HSE's website.

HSWA 1974, s 33 lists various offences including:

(a)   failure to discharge a duty under *ss 2–7* (see 27.18–27.22 above) (*HSWA 1974, s 33(1)(a)*);

(b)   contravention of any health and safety regulations or any requirement or prohibition imposed under such a regulation (*HSWA 1974, s 33(1)(c)*);

(c)   contravention of any requirement or prohibition imposed by an improvement notice or a prohibition notice (including any such notice as modified on appeal) (*HSWA 1974, s 33(1)(g)*);

(d)   intention to obstruct an inspector in the exercise or performance of his powers or duties (*HSWA 1974, s 33(1)(h)*).

Criminal offences are triable either summarily (ie in the magistrates' court) or on indictment (ie in the Crown Court) or 'either way' (ie where the defendant may normally elect the mode of trial). In respect of offences committed on or after 6 March 1992, *HSWA 1974, s 33(1A) and (2A)* (inserted by *Offshore Safety Act 1992, s 4*) empowers a magistrates' court to impose a fine of up to £20,000 for breaches of *HSWA 1974, ss 2–6* (see (*a*) above), failure to comply with an improvement or prohibition notice (see (*c*) above), and failure to comply with a court remedy order under *HSWA 1974, s 42* (see 27.39 below).

On indictment the penalty may be a fine unlimited in amount and/or, for certain offences, imprisonment for up to two years (*HSWA 1974, s 33(2)–(4)*; see 1.10 INTRODUCTION).

In two cases, the courts have emphasised that where a company is convicted of offences under the *HSWA 1974* the financial penalties imposed should reflect the seriousness of the case. In *R v F Howe & Son (Engineers) Ltd* [1999] IRLR 434, the Court of Appeal indicated that the general level of fine for health and safety offences was too low and outlined some of the factors which should be taken into account by the courts when setting the level of fines. These observations were subsequently given unqualified support by the Court of Appeal in *R v Rollco Screw and Rivet Co Ltd* [1999] IRLR 439.

More recently, in *R v Davies (David Janway)* [2003] ICR 586, an employer was convicted and fined for being in breach of *ss 3(1)* and *33(1)* of the *HSWA 1974*, having failed to discharge the duty to conduct his undertaking in such a way as to ensure that he did not expose his employees to risks to their health and safety. The Court of Appeal, dismissing the employer's appeal, ruled that the *HSWA 1974* was regulatory and designed to protect and that the defence of 'reasonably practicable' was not incompatible with the *Human Rights Act 1998*. Consequently, £15,000 fine and £22,544.32 costs were upheld.

Current maximum penalties for offences specified in the Health and Safety at Work etc Act 1974, section 33 (HSWA)

HSWA SECTION	HSW(O)B, Schedule 6A, Item	*CURRENT MAXIMUM*
33(1)(a) Sections 2, 3, 4 and 6 – the general duties on employers and others	1	**Summary** - a fine not exceeding £20,000 **Indictment** - an unlimited fine
33(1)(a) Section 7 – duty on employees	2	**Summary** - a fine not exceeding £5,000 **Indictment** - an unlimited fine

HSWA SECTION	HSW(O)B, Schedule 6A, Item	*CURRENT MAXIMUM*
33(1)(b) Section 8 – duty not to interfere with or misuse things provided for health and safety	3	**Summary** - a fine not exceeding £5,000 **Indictment** - an unlimited fine
33(1)(b) Section 9 – duty not to charge employees for things done to meet requirements of relevant statutory provisions	4	**Summary** - a fine not exceeding £5,000 **Indictment** - an unlimited fine
33(1)(c) Contravening requirements of health and safety regulations, licences or authorisations	5	**Summary** - a fine not exceeding £5,000 **Indictment** - an unlimited fine
33(1)(d) Contravening requirements imposed specifically in relation to public inquiries or special investigations	6	**Summary only** - a fine not exceeding £5,000

HSWA SECTION	HSW(O)B, Schedule 6A, Item	*CURRENT MAXIMUM*
33(1)(e) Contravening any requirement imposed by an inspector under section 20 (e g to give information for an investigation, or to leave premises undisturbed after an incident) or under section 25	7	**Summary** - a fine not exceeding £5,000 **Indictment (section 25 breaches only)** - an unlimited fine
33(1)(f) Preventing another person from appearing before an inspector, or from answering an inspector's question	7 (continued)	**Summary only** - a fine not exceeding £5,000
33(1)(g) Contravening an improvement or prohibition notice	7 (continued)	**Summary** - 6 months' imprisonment, or a fine not exceeding £20,000, or both **Indictment** - 2 years' imprisonment or an unlimited fine or both
33(1)(h) Obstructing an inspector	8	**Summary only** - a fine not exceeding £5,000

HSWA SECTION	HSW(O)B, Schedule 6A, Item	*CURRENT MAXIMUM*
33(1)(i) Contravening any notice issued under section 27(1) (general powers of HSC/E to obtain information)	9	**Summary** - a fine not exceeding £5,000 **Indictment** - an unlimited fine
33(1)(j) Disclosing information in breach of HSWA section 27(4) or 28	10	**Summary** - a fine not exceeding £5,000 **Indictment** - 2 years' imprisonment, an unlimited fine, or both
33(1)(k), (l) and (m) Offences relating to deception	11	**Summary** - a fine not exceeding £5,000 **Indictment** - an unlimited fine
33(1)(n) Falsely to pretend to be an inspector	11	**Summary only** - a fine not exceeding £5,000
33(1)(o) Failure to comply	13	**Summary** - 6 months'

HSWA SECTION	HSW(O)B, Schedule 6A, Item	*CURRENT MAXIMUM*
with a court remedy order (section 42)		imprisonment, or a fine not exceeding £20,000, or both **Indictment** - 2 years' imprisonment or an unlimited unlimited fine or both
33(3) (in so far as no other penalty is specified) Penalties for health and safety offences arising from 'existing statutory provisions' (pre-1974 enactments) set out in HSWA Schedule 1	14	**Summary** - a fine not exceeding £5,000 **Indictment** - an unlimited fine
33(4)(a), (b) and (c) Offences of breaching licensing or explosives requirements	Covered under Bill items above	**Summary** - a fine not exceeding £5,000 **Indictment** - 2 years' imprisonment or an unlimited fine or both

Any explosive article or substance may be forfeited by order of the court and may be destroyed (*HSWA 1974, s 42(4)*).

Breaches of Codes of Practice approved by the Health and Safety Commission (see 27.28 above) are not in themselves criminal offences. However, if in a prosecution for a contravention of the *Act* or the Regulations, it is shown that there was a failure to observe any relevant Code, then that contravention will be considered proven unless the court is satisfied that the requirement or prohibition was complied with in an alternative, acceptable manner (*HSWA 1974, s 17(2)*).

27.38 Personal liability of directors and other company officers

Under *HSWA 1974, s 37*, personal liability is imposed on any director, manager, secretary or other similar officer of a company (or any person who was purporting to act in that capacity) if an offence is committed by the company under

HSWA 1974, or any of the other health and safety legislation specified in *HSWA 1974, Sch 1*, with the consent or connivance, or due to the neglect, of any such person.

In practice, such prosecutions are rare. However, several successful prosecutions of directors and senior managers have resulted, for example, in *Armour v Skeen* [1977] IRLR 310 (the director of roads and bridges for a Scottish regional council) and *R v Mara* [1987] IRLR 154 (the director of a cleaning company).

Defining who is responsible. In *Tesco Supermarkets Ltd v Nattrass* [1972] AC 153, in a prosecution of a company for a breach of the *Trade Descriptions Act 1968*, Lord Reid observed that:

' ... a board of directors can delegate part of their functions of management so as to make their delegate an embodiment of the company within the sphere of delegation.'

In that case, the company was held not to have delegated any of its functions, so that the acts or omissions of the store manager were not acts of the company itself; the House of Lords therefore quashed the company's conviction. However, the Court of Appeal decision in *R v British Steel plc* [1995] IRLR 310 has cast doubt on whether the approach of the House of Lords in a consumer protection case is sufficiently stringent for health and safety legislation.

In *R v Boal* [1992] IRLR 420, the Court of Appeal defined 'manager' in relation to personal liability under the *Fire Precautions Act 1971*. The court held that the relevant provision was intended:

' ... to fix with criminal liability only those who are in a position of real authority, the decision-makers within the company who have both the power and responsibility to decide corporate policy and strategy. It is to catch those responsible for putting proper procedures in place; it is not meant to strike at underlings.'

Where directors have been convicted of offences under the *HSWA 1974*, the Court of Appeal has said that the penalties imposed should make it clear that directors had a personal responsibility which could not be shuffled off to the company (*R v Rollco Screw and Rivet Co Ltd* [1999] IRLR 439). See also, *R v Transco* [2006] All ER (D) 416 (Mar), CA, where in assessing the level of fine, the Court takes account of the employer's knowledge regarding their responsibility for any breach of health and safety.

Company Directors Disqualification Act 1986. A director found guilty of an indictable offence under *HSWA 1974* (whether on indictment or summarily) may be disqualified from holding office as a director under the *Company Directors Disqualification Act 1986, s 2(1)*. The first such disqualification occurred in 1992 when a director was disqualified for two years after being found guilty of serious breaches of *HSWA 1974*. The director had been fined £5,000 for refusing to comply with a prohibition notice in relation to dangerous rock falls where men were working. In September 1998, the managing director of a recycling company was disqualified under the *Company Directors Disqualification Act 1986* following a breach of the *Provision and Use of Work Equipment Regulations 1992* (see 28.12 HEALTH AND SAFETY AT WORK – II) which had resulted in a serious injury to an employee operating an unguarded machine.

In July 2001 the HSC published guidance on health and safety responsibilities for company directors and board members (IND(G) 343, HSE) of public sector and voluntary organisations. In particular, the guidance specifies that Boards need to:

(*a*)   accept joint responsibility and leadership for their organisations' health and safety performance;

(*b*)   appoint one Board member as a health and safety director;

(*c*)   ensure that each Board member accepts his or her individual role in providing health and safety leadership;

(*d*)   ensure that all Board decisions reflect their health and safety intentions;

(*e*)   encourage the active participation of workers in improving health and safety; and

(*f*)   keep up-to-date with all health and safety issues affecting the organisation and review performance regularly.

27.39 Order to remedy default

If a person is convicted of an offence and it appears to the court that the matter is one which it is in his power to remedy, the court may, in addition to or instead of imposing any punishment, order him (within such time as may be fixed by the order) to take such steps as may be specified in the order to remedy the situation. The time fixed by such an order may be extended or further extended by order of the court on an application made before the end of the time originally fixed or as extended (*HSWA 1974, s 42(1)*, (*2*)). Failure to comply with an order under *HSWA 1974, s 42* is an offence (*HSWA 1974, s 33(1)(o)*), which is punishable: (i) on summary conviction, by up to six months' imprisonment and/or a fine of up to £20,000; and (ii) on indictment, by up to two years' imprisonment and/or an unlimited fine (*HSWA 1974, s 33(2A)*, inserted by *Offshore Safety Act 1992, s 4*).

27.40 Time for bringing proceedings

Summary proceedings may be brought at any time within six months from the date on which there comes to the knowledge of an enforcing authority evidence to justify a prosecution (*HSWA 1974, s 34(3)*). A failure to do something required by the Act is treated as continuing until the requirement is complied with, so that the six-month period runs from the last day on which the requirement was not complied with (*HSWA 1974, s 34(2)*). The time limit is extended in cases where there is a special report under *s 14(2)(a)*, a report of an inquiry under *s 14(2)(b)*, a coroner's inquest, or a public inquiry (in Scotland) into a death, to three months from the making of the report or three months from the conclusion of the inquest or inquiry (*HSWA 1974, s 34(1)*).

27.41 Defence

Many of the statutory provisions contain the modification 'so far as is reasonably practicable', or 'practicable' or to use 'the best practicable means to do something'. In those cases the onus is on the accused to prove that it was not practicable or not reasonably practicable to do more than was in fact done to satisfy the duty or requirement, or that there was no better practicable means than was in fact used to satisfy the duty or requirement (*HSWA 1974, s 40*). However, where proceedings are brought under *HSWA 1974, s 33(1)(g)* for contravention of an improvement notice, the offence is established if there has been a non-compliance with a requirement of the notice irrespective of whether compliance was reasonably practicable (*Deary (HM Inspector of Factories) v Mansion Hide Upholstery Ltd* [1983] IRLR 195).

In addition, since 11 July 2001 the defence that UK health and safety provision did not apply in the part of the business outside the jurisdiction (ie not situated in the UK) was abolished by the *Health and Safety at Work etc Act 1974* (*Application outside Great Britain*) *Order* (*SI 2001/2127*). This Order primarily sought to ensure health and safety regulation on offshore installations outside British waters.

27.42 **Corporate killing**

The successful prosecution for manslaughter following the death of 23 cocklers on Morecambe Bay in February 2004, and consequential sentencing on 21 counts of manslaughter, re-emphasises the need to tighten up existing laws on corporate manslaughter. Under the current state of the law a conviction for corporate manslaughter is obtainable only where a senior individual in a company (the 'controlling mind') is shown to have been grossly negligent and thereby responsible for the fatal accident. This is difficult to prove where managerial responsibilities are shared. In February 2000 the Court of Appeal confirmed the principle, in relation to a finding of corporate manslaughter by gross negligence, that a corporation cannot be convicted unless there is evidence which establishes the guilt of an identified human individual for the same crime (*A-G's Reference* (*No 2 of 1999*) [2000] IRLR 417). See also *R v DPP, ex p Jones* [2000] IRLR 373. The first conviction for corporate manslaughter occurred in 1994 where the managing director who personally controlled an activity centre was held responsible for the deaths of four children in his company's care while on a canoeing trip. This was followed, in 1996, by the conviction for corporate manslaughter of a medium-sized transport company and the jailing of its former managing director, after an employee was killed while cleaning chemical residues from a road tanker without protective equipment.

In a consultation document issued in May 2000, the Government proposed the introduction of a new offence of corporate killing and two offences of reckless killing and killing by gross carelessness. The offence of corporate killing would arise where an undertaking's management failure causes death and the undertaking's conduct fell far below what could reasonably be expected in the circumstances. There will be a 'management failure' if the way in which the undertaking's activities are managed or organised fails to ensure the health and safety of persons employed in or affected by those activities. No guidance has been given as to what 'falling far below what could reasonably be expected' means. The Government has proposed that the new offence will apply to any employing organisation consisting of any trade or business or other activity providing employment. It is further proposed that prosecutions should be capable of being undertaken by the Health and Safety Executive. The punishment for the new offence is intended to be an unlimited fine, together with orders to take remedial action. The Government has expressed concern that companies will devolve the riskier parts of their undertakings to subsidiary companies to enable holding companies to escape any liability. It therefore proposes that the holding company will be liable to prosecution if it can be shown that its own managerial failings were a cause of the death concerned. Furthermore, individuals shown to have had some influence on or been responsible for such management failure could be disqualified from acting in a managerial capacity in any undertaking in Great Britain. Directors and employees could also be charged with reckless killing or killing by gross carelessness.

At last the fruits of this long consultation have come to fruition, when on 23 March 2005 the Home Secretary set out new laws to prosecute companies and organisations whose gross failure at senior management level results in a fatality. In the proposed Corporate Manslaughter Bill, existing laws are updated and a new criminal offence of corporate manslaughter is created. This new offence will apply when someone has been killed because the senior management of a corporation has grossly failed to take reasonable care for the safety of employees or others. This seeks to address the key problem with the current law: the need to show that a single individual at the very top of a company is personally guilty of manslaughter before the company can be prosecuted. Under this newly proposed offence the courts will be able to examine a wider range of management conduct than at present. It focuses responsibility on the working practices of the organisation, as set by senior managers, rather than limiting investigations to questions of individual gross negligence by company directors. This Bill is to be put to parliament during its session 2006–07.

27.43 CIVIL LIABILITY

Breaches of *HSWA 1974, ss 2–8* cannot form the basis of a civil action (*HSWA 1974, s 47(1)(a)*) but breach 'of a duty imposed by health and safety regulations … shall, so far as it causes damage, be actionable except in so far as the regulations provide otherwise' (*HSWA 1974, s 47(2)*). In other words, a civil action can be brought where a breach of the health and safety regulations causes damage, unless the regulations prevent such an action from being brought.

Any provision in any agreement to contract out of liability for such breaches is void unless the health and safety regulations provide otherwise (*HSWA 1974, s 47(5)*).

27.44 CONTRIBUTORY NEGLIGENCE

In any successful action against the employer for breach of duty at common law or under some enactment, the amount of damages may be reduced in proportion to the degree to which the employee failed to take reasonable steps for his own safety (*Law Reform (Contributory Negligence) Act 1945, s 1(1)*). The *Act* applies where both the employer and employee have contributed to the damage. For example, in *Bux v Slough Metals Ltd* [1974] 1 All ER 262 the employee's failure to use the goggles with which he was provided contributed to the extent of the injury he suffered and reduced his damages by 40%. Yet, as in the case of *Anderson v Newham College of Further Education* [2002] EWCA Civ 505, [2003] ICR 212, Sedley LJ noted that a high standard of proof was required to shift the entire blame from a breach of statutory duty to an injured employee. For a case on the interrelationship between the principle of contributory negligence and disciplinary action taken against an employee following an accident at work, see *Casey v Morane Ltd* [2001] IRLR 166, CA.

27.45 CORONER'S INQUESTS

In some health and safety incidences, interaction with the coroner is necessary. A coroner enquires into reported deaths. It is the coroner's duty to find out the medical cause of the death, if it is not known, and to enquire about the cause of it if it was due to violence or otherwise appears to be unnatural. In most cases the deceased's own doctor, or a hospital doctor who has been treating him or her, is able to give a cause of death. However, there are a number of circumstances under which a death will be reported to the coroner. For example, when no doctor has treated the deceased during his or her last illness or when the death was sudden or unexpected or unnatural. Yet deaths are usually reported to the coroner by the police or by a doctor called to the death if it is sudden. A doctor will also report a patient's death if unexpected. In other cases, the local registrar of deaths may make the report. Whenever the death has been reported to the coroner the registrar must wait for the coroner to finish his or her enquiries before the death can be registered.

27.46 CORONER'S FINDINGS

The coroner may decide that death was natural and that there is a doctor who can sign a form saying so. In this case the coroner will advise the registrar. The coroner may ask a pathologist to examine the body. If so, the examination must be done as soon as possible. The coroner or his or her staff will, unless it is impracticable or cause undue delay, give notice of the arrangements to, amongst others, the usual doctor of the deceased and any relative who may have notified the coroner of his or her wish to be medically represented at the examination. If the examination shows the death to have been a natural one, there may be no need for an inquest and the coroner will send a form to the registrar of deaths so that the death can be registered by the relatives and a certificate of burial issued by the registrar. If the person is to be cremated, the certificate may be issued by the coroner.

27.47 INQUESTS

An inquest is not a trial. It is a limited inquiry into the facts surrounding a death. It is not the job of the coroner to blame anyone for the death, as a trial would do. The inquest is an inquiry to find out who has died, and how, when and where they died, together with information needed by the registrar of deaths so that the death can be registered. Most inquests are held without a jury. There are particular reasons when a jury will be called, including if the death occurred in prison or in police custody or if the death resulted from an incident at work. In every inquest which is held with a jury, it is the jury, and not the coroner, which makes the final decision.

27.48 'INTERESTED PERSONS'

An 'interested person' is someone who can question a witness at an inquest. They can be:

(*a*)   a parent, spouse, child and anyone acting for the deceased;

(*b*)   anyone who gains from a life insurance policy on the deceased;

(*c*)   any insurer having issued such a policy;

(*d*)   anyone whose actions the coroner believes may have contributed to the death, accidentally or otherwise;

(*e*)   the chief officer of police (who may only ask questions of witnesses through a lawyer);

(*f*)   any person appointed by a government department to attend the inquest;

(*g*)anyone else who the coroner may decide also has a proper interest.

28 Health and Safety at Work – II: Specific Legislation and Health and Safety Issues

Cross-reference. See HEALTH AND SAFETY AT WORK – I (27) for safety duties at common law and the general legislative framework.

28.1 ACCIDENT REPORTING

Notification of accidents, diseases and dangerous occurrences. The current regulations governing the notification and recording of accidents are the *Reporting of Injuries, Diseases and Dangerous Occurrences Regulations 1995 (SI 1995/3163)*. These supersede *1985 Regulations* of the same name. A newly revised HSE guide on 'RIDDOR Reporting: what the Incident Contact Centre (ICC) can do for you!' is now available (HSE, 2002 (MISC310 (rev1); Tel. 0845 300 9924) describing the reporting process under the *1995 Regulations* and aiming to raise duty holder awareness of the existence of the new reporting arrangements, including the promotion of telephone reporting.

An employer must notify the Health and Safety Executive ('HSE') or local authority, whichever is in the circumstances the enforcing authority (see 27.29 HEALTH AND SAFETY AT WORK – I), of:

(*a*)   an accident arising out of or in connection with work resulting in:

    (i)   the death of any person;

    (ii)   a 'major injury' (specified in *Sch 1*) to any person at work;

    (iii)   hospital treatment of a person not at work; or

    (iv)   major injury to a person not at work as a result of an accident in connection with work at a hospital;

(*b*)   a dangerous occurrence (specified in *Sch 2*);

(*c*)   an accident connected with work as a result of which a person at work is incapacitated for work for more than three days;

(*d*)   the death of an employee within one year of being injured as the result of a notifiable accident or notifiable dangerous occurrence (this applies whether or not the accident was reported at the time it occurred);

(*e*)   any person suffering from one of the reportable work-related diseases specified in *Sch 3*;

(*f*)   any 'gas incident' as specified in *reg 6*.

(*Regulations 3–6.*)

In cases under (*a*) and (*b*) the enforcing authority must be notified by the fastest practicable means in the first instance, and a report on the prescribed form must be sent to that authority within 10 days (*reg 3*).

In cases under (*c*) a report must be sent on an approved form within 10 days of the accident. Category (*d*) requires notification in writing as soon as the employer becomes aware of the death. Under (*e*) a report on an approved form must be made forthwith and for cases falling within (*f*) notification is required immediately, followed by a report within 14 days. Accident reports must be made on Form F2508 and disease reports on Form F2508A. For notification to the HSE, a central reporting system for the whole of the UK is in operation. Users have the choice of contact by telephone, by emailing electronic copies of the report forms or via a website, or continuing to complete Form F2508 and sending them by normal post or fax. See www.riddor.gov.uk.

Road accidents are not covered by the *Regulations*, except where they result from exposure to a substance which is being transported, the loading or unloading of vehicles, specified roadworks or where a train is involved (*reg 10*). See *Road Safety Act 2005*.

The definition of 'accident' includes acts of non-consensual physical violence done to a person at work.

Examples of 'major injuries' are: amputations, fractures (other than to fingers or toes), certain dislocations, loss of sight, chemical or hot metal burns or penetrating injury to the eye and injuries requiring hospital attendance for more than 24 hours (*Sch 1*).

Records must be kept of all notifiable accidents, dangerous occurrences and reportable diseases, containing the necessary particulars set out in *Sch 4*. They must be kept at the place of work to which they relate, or at the usual place of business of the responsible person as defined in the *Regulations*, for a period of three years from the date the details were entered in the records (*reg 7*).

Accidents to self-employed persons are covered if they were working under the control of someone else, in which case the obligations attach to the person in control of the premises where the accident occurred.

Special rules within *RIDDOR 1995* are applied specifically to mines, quarries, railways and pipe-lines.

A consultation exercise was conducted in 2001 on the HSC's proposal to introduce a compulsory duty on companies and other organisations to investigate all reportable workplace accidents, ill health or incidents which could have resulted in serious injury.

Major accident hazards. Operators of premises liable to major accident hazards are, in addition, subject to a special regime under the *Control of Major Accident Hazards Regulations 1999* (*SI 1999/743*) from 1 April 1999 (see 27.20 HEALTH AND SAFETY AT WORK – I).

Notification of industrial injuries. An employee who suffers an 'industrial injury' must report the accident to his employer. Notice of the accident may be given orally or in writing, and may be given by someone else on the employee's behalf. It is sufficient notice if the accident is recorded in the accident book (see below). The employer is required to take reasonable steps to investigate the accident and must, on request, provide all information uncovered to the Department for Work and Pensions. Failure by an employee to notify an accident may jeopardise his entitlement to industrial injury benefits.

Accident book. Every employer who normally employs 10 or more persons on or about the same premises in connection with a trade or business must keep an accident book (Form BI 510) in which specified particulars of accidents may be recorded, as must (however few employees they have) all employers who are owners or occupiers of a mine or quarry or of a 'factory' within the meaning of the *Factories Act 1961, s 175* (*Social Security* (*Claims and Payments*) *Regulations 1979* (*SI 1979/628*), *reg 25*). *Part 3* of the *Data Protection Code of Practice* (*Employment*), issued on 11 June 2003, sets out basic rules for employers to follow in relation to monitoring employee activities. Such activities may include accidents. Hence, accident books kept by employers will fall within these provisions. Since accident books contain personal details and information which can be seen by anyone making an entry in the book, such practices may well not comply with the *Data Protection Act 1998*.

28.2 **ALCOHOL AND DRUG MISUSE**

Problems arising from consumption of alcohol and misuse of drugs are seen as an increasing problem in the workplace. Employers have a duty of care, both at common law and under *HSWA 1974, s 2*, to ensure, so far as reasonably practicable, the health, safety and welfare at work of their employees. In addition, they are required to assess risks to health and safety under the *Management of Health and Safety at Work Regulations 1992* (see 28.17). An employer who allows a person under the influence of drink or drugs to continue working could be in breach of its duty of care by putting the employee or others at risk.

Under the *Transport and Works Act 1992* it is a criminal offence for certain transport workers in safety-sensitive posts, primarily in the railway industry, to be unfit through drink or drugs while working. Transport system operators are required to show all due diligence in order to prevent an offence being committed.

It is an offence for occupiers of premises (such as employers) knowingly to allow the production or supply of controlled drugs on their premises or to permit the smoking of cannabis (*Misuse of Drugs Act 1971, s 8*).

Dependency on alcohol or drugs is an illness. Where an employee's performance or misconduct is found to be a result of alcohol dependency this should normally be handled as a capability issue (see 54.6 UNFAIR DISMISSAL – II). ACAS advises that drug dependency should be treated in the same way. However, the fact that use of non-prescription drugs is illegal may justify disciplinary action depending on the circumstances. One-off incidents of excessive consumption of alcohol by employees who are not alcohol-dependent would normally be dealt with according to disciplinary procedures. Off-duty use of alcohol or drugs is not normally the legitimate concern of the employer unless it has a connection with the workplace, damages the reputation of the employer's business or undermines trust and confidence in the employee.

As part of an overall health and safety policy, employers are advised to have a written policy on alcohol and drug misuse. Once a policy is in place, it should be applied consistently (*Angus Council v Edgley* EAT/289/99).

28.3 **Drug testing**

Drug testing is a controversial and sensitive issue. The HSE warns that testing is only likely to be acceptable if it is part of an organisation's health policy and is clearly designed to prevent risks to the misuser and others. Testing programmes should be introduced only with the consent of existing employees. Otherwise this may be seen as a breach of the implied term of trust and confidence, leading to constructive dismissal (see 53.7 UNFAIR DISMISSAL – I). Pre-employment testing where applicants are asked to take a test voluntarily raises fewer legal problems. In all cases individuals need to be assured of the integrity of the screening process and medical confidentiality. Company policies should indicate the action which will be taken if testing yields a positive result.

The draft code of practice for employers on data protection, published by the Information Commissioner, says that drug testing (except in highly safety-critical areas) is unlikely to be justified unless there is a reasonable suspicion of drug use that has an impact on safety. Employers should also bear in mind the effect on protection of privacy of the *1950 European Convention on Human Rights* and the *Human Rights Act 1998* (see 30.6 HUMAN RIGHTS).

28.4   CONSTRUCTION SITE MANAGEMENT

Some 2.2 million workers make up the UK's construction industry. The *Construction (Design and Management) Regulations 1994 (SI 1994/3140)* gave effect to the EC Directive on temporary or mobile construction sites (*92/57*). The *Regulations* impose detailed requirements with respect to design and management aspects of construction work, placing new obligations on all parties involved in construction projects. The *1994 Regulations* were amended by the *Construction (Design and Management) (Amendment) Regulations 2002 (SI 2002/2380)*. A revised Approved Code of Practice ('ACOP') and guidance on the *Construction (Design and Management) Regulations 1994 (SI 1994/3140)* have been published by the Health and Safety Commission and came into force on 1 February 2002. The revised ACOP is designed to clarify roles and responsibilities, placing emphasis on managing health and safety throughout the life of a project.

Further effect has been given to *Directive 92/57* by the *Construction (Health, Safety and Welfare) Regulations 1996 (SI 1996/1592* as amended by *SI 1999/3242)* which also incorporate three sets of existing Regulations which have been modernised and simplified.

Note that no statutory provision or rule of law is to be taken as imposing, upon a Sikh on a construction site, any requirement to wear a safety helmet at any time when he is wearing a turban (*EA 1989, s 11*). However, a Sikh who does not comply with a requirement that would otherwise have been imposed, and is injured, may recover damages in tort only to the extent that he would have suffered injury even if wearing a helmet (*EA 1989, s 11(5)*). A person who does require a Sikh to wear a safety helmet on a construction site will probably be guilty of indirect racial discrimination, and if he has no reasonable grounds to believe that the Sikh would not wear a turban at all times when on site, he will not be permitted to justify that requirement (*EA 1989, s 12(1)*). Nor will special treatment afforded to a Sikh in consequence of s *11* constitute racial discrimination against anyone else (*EA 1989, s 12(2)*). See *Construction (Head Protection) Regulations 1989 (SI 1989/2209)*.

28.5   DISPLAY SCREEN EQUIPMENT

The *Health and Safety (Display Screen Equipment) Regulations 1992 (SI 1992/2792)* give effect to the EU Directive relating to the use of display screen equipment (e g VDUs) (*90/270*). Broadly, the *Regulations* require every employer, after making a suitable and sufficient analysis of each workstation (ie display screen equipment, its accessories and the surrounding work environment) to ensure that it meets the detailed requirements set out in the *Schedule* to the *Regulations*. Users of display screen equipment must: (i) be provided with eye and eyesight tests on request, both initially and at regular intervals thereafter; (ii) be provided with adequate health and safety information relating to the equipment; and (iii) have their daily work routine planned in such a way that they have periodical interruptions from using the equipment. See also 28.29 on work-related upper limb disorders.

The ECJ has given a ruling on the application of *Directive 90/270* in *Dietrich v Westdeutscher Rundfunk, Case C-11/99* [2000] ECR I-5589. *Article 2(a)* of the *Directive* and *reg 1(2)* of the *Health and Safety (Display Screen Equipment) Regulations 1992* provide that 'display screen equipment' means 'an alphanumeric or graphic display screen, regardless of the display process involved'. The court concluded that the term 'graphic display screen' had to be interpreted broadly and therefore included screens that display film recordings, whether in analogue or digital form. A film cutter in a television production studio was therefore entitled to the protection of the provisions of the Directive.

Regulation 3 of the *Health and Safety (Miscellaneous Amendments) Regulations 2002 (SI 2002/2174)*, by removing the limitation in relation to workstation users and operators, so as to widen the remit to all users, amends *reg 3* of the *DSE Regulations 1992*.

28.6   ELECTRICITY AT WORK

The *Electricity at Work Regulations 1989 (SI 1989/635)* place a duty on employers to assess all foreseeable risks associated with work activities involving electricity which might give rise to personal injury or danger. Electrical equipment covers everything from power lines to electric kettles.

Employers are required to install safe systems of working with well-maintained equipment (*reg 4*). Steps must be taken to avoid danger in the use of equipment where it is reasonably foreseeable that it will be exposed to adverse or hazardous environments (*reg 6*). Specific precautions are laid down with regard to the insulation and protection of conductors (*regs 7–9*).

Regulations 12 and *13* lay down requirements for cutting off the supply, isolation and for working on dead equipment. No person should be engaged in work near a live conductor except where it is reasonable in all the circumstances and suitable precautions are taken to prevent injury (*reg 14*). Special attention should be paid to adequate working space, means of access and lighting where work is to be done on electrical equipment (*reg 15*), and no person should work on electrical equipment unless he or she possesses appropriate technical knowledge or is adequately supervised (*reg 16*).

The *Regulations* were extended to offshore workers from 21 February 1998 by virtue of the *Offshore Electricity and Noise Regulations 1997 (SI 1997/1993)*.

A *Memorandum of Guidance* on the Regulations is published by HSE. See ww.hse.gov.uk/electricity/information/law.htm

28.7   EMPLOYMENT PROTECTION

The *Employment Rights Act 1996 ('ERA 1996')* provides that certain dismissals in health and safety cases are to be deemed automatically unfair (see 54.3 UNFAIR DISMISSAL – II below), and confers protection on employees in such cases from unfavourable treatment.

28.8   Detriment in health and safety cases

ERA 1996, s 44 confers on an employee the right not to be subjected to any detriment by any act (short of dismissal), or any deliberate failure to act, by his employer done on the ground that:

(a)   having been designated by the employer to carry out activities in connection with preventing or reducing risks to the health and safety of employees at work, he carried out, or proposed to carry out, any such activities;

(b)   being a health and safety representative or member of a safety committee, in accordance with any statutory arrangements or by reason of being acknowledged as such by the employer, he performed or proposed to perform any functions as such a representative or member;

(c)   he took part (or proposed to take part) in consultation with the employer in accordance with the *Health and Safety* (*Consultation with Employees*) *Regulations 1996* (*SI 1996/1513*) or in an election for representatives of employee safety;

(d)   where there is no representative or it is not possible to raise the matter by this means, he brought to his employer's attention, by reasonable means, circumstances which he reasonably believed were harmful or potentially harmful to health and safety;

(e)   in circumstances of serious or imminent danger which he could not reasonably be expected to avert, he left, or proposed to leave, his place of work or any dangerous part of his place of work; or

(f)   in circumstances of serious or imminent danger, he took, or proposed to take, appropriate steps to protect himself or other persons from the danger. 'Other persons' includes members of the public (*Masiak v City Restaurants (UK) Ltd* [1999] IRLR 780).

'Circumstances of danger' is not confined to dangers arising out of the workplace itself. It can include dangers caused by the misbehaviour of fellow employees (*Harvest Press Ltd v McCaffrey* [1999] IRLR 778). For the purposes of (f) above, whether the steps which the employee took, or proposed to take, were appropriate will be judged by reference to all the circumstances including, in particular, his knowledge and the facilities and advice available to him at the time (*ERA 1996, s 44(2)*). An employee will not be regarded as having suffered any detriment on the ground specified in (f) above if the employer shows that it was, or would have been, so negligent for the employee to take the steps which he took, or proposed to take, that a reasonable employer might have treated him as the employer did (*ERA 1996, s 44(3)*).

Provided a safety representative acts in good faith when pursuing a genuine health or safety matter, there is no duty to act reasonably (*Shillito v Van Leer (UK) Ltd* [1997] IRLR 495). In *Goodwin v Cabletel UK Ltd* [1997] IRLR 665 the Employment Appeal Tribunal held that the manner in which designated employees carry out health and safety activities can fall within the statutory protection. Tribunals must consider whether the way in which such employees approach their concerns about safety takes them outside the scope of health and safety activities.

28.9 Whistleblowing on safety

The *Public Interest Disclosure Act 1998* (*'PIDA 1998'*), which came into force 2 July 1999, provides further protection against victimisation by employers in specified circumstances if workers who ordinarily work in Great Britain raise concerns about, *inter alia*, health and safety issues (*ERA 1996, s 47B*, inserted by *PIDA 1998, s 2*). The legislation protects not only direct employees but also most other workers including, specifically, agency workers, homeworkers, NHS practitioners and trainees on vocational or work experience schemes (*ERA 1996, s 43K* inserted by *PIDA 1998, s 1*). Provided certain conditions are met workers will be protected against detrimental treatment (or dismissal, see 54.3 UNFAIR DISMISSAL – II) if they reveal information about the workplace relating to: a criminal offence; failure to comply with a legal obligation; a miscarriage of justice; endangering health and safety; or damage to the environment. Information disclosed which tends to show that any of the above matters is being deliberately concealed would also qualify for protection (*ERA 1996, s 43B* inserted by *PIDA 1998, s 1*). Workers are required to raise their concerns initially with the employer or prescribed regulator. External disclosures are protected only if stringent conditions are met; an exception is made for 'exceptionally serious cases' (*ERA 1996, ss 43C–43H*, inserted by *PIDA 1998, s 1*).

'Detrimental treatment' under *PIDA 1998* covers the victimisation short of dismissal of workers, any deliberate failure to act and the termination of contract of non-employees. *See Pinnington v Swansea City Council* [2005] EWCA Civ 135, [2005] ICR 685 and *Street v Derbyshire Unemployed Workers' Centre* [2004] EWCA Civ 964, [2005] ICR 97.

28.10 The remedy

An employee has the right to complain to an employment tribunal for a declaration and compensation if he has suffered a detriment by an act, or failure to act, done on any of the grounds specified in (*a*) to (*f*) in 28.9 above. On such a complaint it is for the employer to show the ground on which any act, or deliberate failure to act, was done (*ERA 1996, s 48(1), (2)*). Workers who have suffered detrimental treatment for making a protected disclosure are able to make a complaint to an employment tribunal (*ERA 1996, s 48(1A)*, inserted by *PIDA 1998, s 3*).

The employee may make a complaint within three months of the act, or failure to act, complained of (or the last act or failure, where that act or failure is part of a series of similar acts or failures). Where the tribunal is satisfied that it was not reasonably practicable for the complaint to be presented within three months, it may be presented within such further period as the tribunal considers reasonable (*ERA 1996, s 48(3)*; as to the meaning of 'the date of the act' and 'a deliberate failure to act', see *ERA 1996, s 48(4)*).

If the tribunal finds the complaint well-founded it will make a declaration to that effect and order compensation to be paid to the employee. The compensation will be such amount as it considers just and equitable in the circumstances, having regard to the right infringed and any loss which is attributable to the act or failure which infringed his right (*ERA 1996, s 49*). In the case of workers penalised for making a protected disclosure the tribunal may award such compensation as it considers just and equitable.

28.11 Breach of safety regulations and unfair dismissal

A failure by an employer to have regard for the safety of his employees can be considered a fundamental breach of contract entitling the employee to resign and claim that he has been constructively dismissed. In *British Aircraft Corpn Ltd v Austin* [1978] IRLR 332, the Employment Appeal Tribunal held that the employer's failure to give consideration to the employee's request that she should be provided with protective goggles incorporating the prescription lenses of her spectacles amounted to conduct entitling the employee to resign and, when she did resign, to claim that she had been constructively dismissed under what is now *ERA 1996, s 95(1)(c)*.

Where employees refuse to work with materials which in the past have adversely affected their health, and as a consequence are dismissed, the dismissals will be held to be unfair if the employer has not taken adequate steps to remedy the danger (*Piggott Bros & Co Ltd v Jackson* [1991] IRLR 309).

An employer may fairly dismiss an employee for breach of safety regulations if he brought the regulations to the attention of the employee and made clear to him the fact that such a breach would lead to dismissal (*Martin v Yorkshire Imperial Metals* [1978] IRLR 440).

28.12 EQUIPMENT FOR WORK

Three main sets of EU-derived Regulations set minimum standards for the provision and use of equipment at work:

The *Provision and Use of Work Equipment Regulations 1998* (*SI 1998/2306*) (*PUWER*) give effect to the EC Directive relating to the use of machines and equipment (*89/655*) and amending *Directive 95/63*. The *Regulations* came into force on 5 December 1998, replacing *1992 Regulations* of the same name (*SI 1992/2932*). *Regulations 4–10* set out general requirements with which employers must comply, for example in relation to suitability, maintenance and inspection. The requirement contained in *reg 5(1)* of the *1998 Regulations* for work equipment to be maintained in an efficient state and working order and in good repair imposes an absolute duty on employers (*Stark v Post Office* [2000] ICR 1013, CA). The very purpose of the *Regulations* is to make the employer liable for the unexplained and indeed inexplicable incident held the Court of Appeal in *Ball v Street* [2005] EWCA Civ 76, [2005] All ER (D) 73 (Feb).

More specific requirements, concerning, for example, specific hazards, extremes of temperature, lighting, maintenance operations and dangerous parts are set out in *regs 11–24* (see *Horton v Taplin Contractors Ltd* [2002] EWCA Civ 1604, [2003] ICR 179). In *Horton* the Court of Appeal emphasised that the target of achieving suitability of work equipment for its purpose was to be measured by reference to such hazards to anyone's health and safety as were reasonably foreseeable (Bodey J). In addition the *1998 Regulations* impose requirements relating to mobile work equipment and power presses. The provisions relating to mobile work equipment do not apply until 5 December 2002 to equipment provided for use in an undertaking before 5 December 1998. Since 14 April 1999, certain duties set out in the *Regulations* are modified by the *Police (Health and Safety) Regulations 1999* (*SI 1999/860*). The effect is to take account of the special circumstances in which police officers sometimes have to work. For provisions applying to UK ships and to others when in UK waters, see the *Merchant Shipping and Fishing Vessels (Personal Protective Equipment) Regulations 1999* (*SI 1999/2205*), in force since 25 October 1999.

Since 5 December 1998 the *Lifting Operations and Lifting Equipment Regulations 1998* (*SI 1998/2307*) (LOLER) gather together requirements relating to lifting equipment formerly contained in industry-specific legislation, and implement certain provisions of EC *Directives 89/655* and *95/63*. *Directive 2001/45* of 27 June amends *Directive 89/655* concerning the minimum health and safety requirements for the use of work equipment, so that it covers worker safety when using equipment to carry out work at height.

The *Personal Protective Equipment at Work Regulations 1992* (*SI 1992/2966*) (*PPE*) give effect to the EC Directive relating to the use of personal protective equipment (*89/656*). Personal protective equipment is defined as all equipment (including clothing giving protection against the weather) which is intended to be worn or held by a person at work and which protects the employee against health and safety risks. Broadly, the *Regulations*, which came into force on 1 January 1993, require employers to ensure that suitable personal protective equipment is provided for their employees and impose various other requirements, for example in relation to maintenance and storage of the equipment. Personal protective equipment supplied from 1 July 1995 must bear the 'CE' marking. Under *HSWA 1974, s 9* employers are barred from charging employees for equipment provided in accordance with a specific statutory requirement. Recently, the House of Lords clarified in *Fytche v Wincanton Logistics plc* [2004] UKHL 31, [2004] ICR 975, a majority (3:2) ruling (Lady Hale and Lord Hope dissenting), that *reg 4* of the *1992 Regulations* required employers to provide suitable equipment to protect employees against an identified risk. Such a duty was further maintained by repairs required under *reg 7(1)*. Yet the latter duty only extended to repairs for the purposes of ensuring that assessed risks under *reg 4* are met.

For further details, see www.hse.gov.uk/equipment/legilsation.htm

28.13   FIRE PRECAUTIONS

Fire safety requirements at work are governed by the *Fire Precautions Act 1971* ('*FPA 1971*'), as amended by the *HSWA 1974* and the *Fire Safety and Safety of Places of Sport Act 1987*, and by the *Fire Precautions (Workplace) Regulations 1997 (SI 1997/1840)* as amended from 1 December 1999 by the *Fire Precautions (Workplace) (Amendment) Regulations 1999 (SI 1999/1877)*.

It is an offence under the *FPA 1971* not to have a fire certificate in respect of work premises covered by the Act. Before granting a certificate the fire authority will inspect the premises to satisfy itself as to the means of escape, securing the means of escape, fire-fighting equipment and warning methods. Breaches of a fire certificate may result in prosecution of a body corporate and of 'any director, manager, secretary or other similar officer' if the offence was attributable to neglect on their part (*s 23*). In *R v Boal* [1992] IRLR 420 the Court of Appeal ruled that 'manager' in this context meant a person in a position of real authority, a decision-maker with the power and responsibility to decide corporate policy and strategy.

Under the *Fire Precautions (Workplace) Regulations 1997 (SI 1997/1840)*, in force from 1 December 1997, employers are required to comply with specific requirements in relation to: fire-fighting equipment; fire detectors and alarms; measures for fire-fighting; emergency routes, exits and evacuations; and maintenance of equipment and devices. Enforcement is the responsibility of the fire authorities. From 1 December 1999 the exemption from the *Regulations* for workplaces with a current fire certificate issued under the *1971* and *1987 Acts* is revoked. Updated guidance for employers on the Regulations was issued by the Stationery Office and the HSE in July 1999.

28.14   FIRST AID

First aid requirements are contained in the *Health and Safety (First Aid) Regulations 1981 (SI 1981/917)*, supplemented by an Approved Code of Practice (revised 1997). Employers are placed under a duty to make adequate and appropriate provision for first aid (*reg 3*). The *1997 Code of Practice* and accompanying notes stress the duty of the employer to make an assessment of first aid needs appropriate to the circumstances of each workplace. A checklist is included for evaluating first aid requirements and guidance given on criteria for deciding on the extent of first aid equipment, first aid boxes and facilities which are necessary and on the number of first aiders required. The guidance notes explain how first aid provision should be related to the level of risk. Employers must inform their employees of the arrangements that have been made in connection with the provision of first aid, including the location of equipment, facilities and personnel (*reg 4*). *Regulation 2* of the *Health and Safety* (*Miscellaneous Amendments*) *Regulations 2002* (*SI 2002/2174*) amends *reg 2* of the existing *1981 Regulations* so as to require that a first-aid room must be easily accessible and sign-posted. This amendment gives effect to *Annex II* of *Directive 89/654/EEC* (OJ L393 30.12.1989).

28.15 HOURS OF WORK

The *Working Time Directive* (*93/104*), as amended 2000/34, imposes requirements relating to hours of work, night work, breaks and holidays. Provisions restricting the working hours of children and young persons are contained in the *Young Workers' Directive* (*94/33*). From 1 October 1998 the *Working Time Regulations 1998* (*SI 1998/1833*) implement the *Working Time Directive* together with aspects of the *Young Workers' Directive* which relate to young persons (ie those who have reached minimum school leaving age but are under 18). For details of provisions relating to working hours, night work and breaks, see WORKING TIME (57). For statutory holiday provisions, see HOLIDAYS (29). The *Working Time Regulations 1998* were amended in 2006 by the *Working Time* (*Amendment*) *Regulations 2006* (*SI 2006/99*), in order to comply with EU proposals to remove the opt-out. Consequently, since 6 April 2006, *reg 20(2)*, unmeasured working time, has been revoked.

28.16 INSURANCE AGAINST LIABILITY

The *Employers' Liability* (*Compulsory Insurance*) *Act 1969*, as amended, obliges every employer carrying on a business in Great Britain to maintain insurance, under one or more approved policies with an authorised insurer, against liability for bodily injury or disease sustained by employees and arising out of and in the course of their employment in Great Britain. An employer is not obliged to insure members of his family (*s 2(2)(a)*). Insurance companies issue annual certificates which must be displayed at every place where the employer carries on business so that they may be easily seen and read by every person employed there. From 1 January 1999 the *Employers' Liability* (*Compulsory Insurance*) *Regulations 1998* (*SI 1998/2573*) fix the limit of the sum to be insured at not less than £5m in respect of any one occurrence. The *Regulations* require employers to keep certificates for 40 years and give powers to inspectors to inspect past certificates.

There is generally no duty upon the employer to protect his employees from economic loss as opposed to physical injury. Hence it was not a breach of duty to fail to arrange or advise insurance for an employee sent to work in a country without compulsory motor insurance (*Reid v Rush & Tompkins Group plc* [1990] ICR 61).

28.17 MANAGEMENT OF HEALTH AND SAFETY AT WORK

The *Management of Health and Safety at Work Regulations 1999* (*SI 1999/3242*) came into effect on 29 December 1999, re-enacting *1992 Regulations* of the same name, with modifications. The Regulations give effect to the EC 'Framework Directive' (*89/391*), the 'Temporary Workers' Directive' (*91/383*), and certain provisions of the 'Pregnant Workers' Directive' (*92/85*) and 'Young Workers' Directive' (*94/33*).

The *1999 Regulations* are accompanied by an Approved Code of Practice and guidance issued in March 2000.

The *Health and Safety (Miscellaneous Amendments) Regulations 2002 (SI 2002/2174)* which came into force on 17 September 2002 amended various long-established regulations, including the *1981 First Aid, 1992 Display Screen Equipment, 1992 Manual Handling Operations, 1992 Protective Personal Equipment, 1992 Workplace, 1998 Lifting Operations and Lifting Equipment,* and *1999 Quarries Regulations.* Whilst many of these amendments are minor, they seek to ensure full European compliance with their requisite Directives.

Every employer (and self-employed person) must make a risk assessment relating to his premises, so as to identify the measures he needs to take to comply with the health and safety and fire precautions requirements applicable to him; the assessment must be reviewed when necessary and (where there are more than five employees) recorded. Assessment of the risks to young people must be made before they start work, taking their immaturity and other specified factors into account (*reg 3*). When an employer implements any preventive and protective measures, it is to be done on the basis of the following principles:

(*a*) avoiding risks;

(*b*) evaluating the risks which cannot be avoided;

(*c*) combating the risks at source;

(*d*) adapting the work to the individual, especially as regards the design of workplaces, the choice of work equipment and the choice of working and production methods, with a view in particular to alleviating monotonous work and work at a predetermined work rate and to reducing their effect on health;

(*e*) adapting to technical progress;

(*f*) replacing the dangerous with the non-dangerous or the less dangerous;

(*g*) developing a coherent overall prevention policy which covers technology, organisation of work, working conditions, social relationships and the influence of factors relating to the working environment;

(*h*) giving collective protective measures priority over individual protective measures; and

(*i*) giving appropriate instructions to employees.

(*Regulation 4, Sch 1.*)

Every employer must also make, and give effect to, adequate health and safety arrangements, including the effective planning, organisation, control, monitoring and review of the preventive and protective measures. Where there are five or more employees, these arrangements must be recorded in writing (*reg 5*).

Every employer must ensure that his employees are provided with appropriate health surveillance (*reg 6*), and must appoint one or more competent persons to assist him in undertaking the preventive and protective measures. Where there is a 'competent person' in the employer's employment then that person must be appointed as the competent person to assist in undertaking health and safety measures, in preference to a competent person from another source (*reg 7*).

Every employer must, *inter alia*:

(*a*)   establish (and where necessary, give effect to) procedures to be followed in the event of serious and imminent danger to persons working in his undertaking; and

(*b*)   nominate a sufficient number of competent persons to implement such procedures in relation to the evacuation of the premises.

The procedures referred to in (*a*) above must:

(i)   so far as is reasonably practicable, require persons at work who are exposed to serious and imminent danger to be informed of the nature of the hazards and the steps to be taken to protect them from it;

(ii)   enable the persons concerned to stop work and proceed to a place of safety in the event of being exposed to serious, imminent and unavoidable danger; and

(iii)   require the persons concerned to be prevented from resuming work where there is still a serious and imminent danger.

(*Regulation 8.*)

Employers are required to ensure that any necessary contacts with external services are arranged, particularly as regards first aid, emergency medical care and rescue work (*reg 9*).

Employees must be provided with comprehensible and relevant health and safety information (*reg 10*), as must non-employees working in the employer's undertaking (*reg 12*) and temporary workers (*reg 15*). When employing school-age children, employers must inform their parents or guardians of the risks and control measures introduced (*reg 10*). Where two or more employers share a workplace, they must co-operate as necessary to enable them to comply with the applicable health and safety and fire precautions requirements, and co-ordinate measures they are taking to comply with such requirements (*reg 11*).

Employers must take into account employees' capabilities as regards health and safety in entrusting tasks to them. Employees must be provided with adequate health and safety training within working hours, which must be repeated where appropriate (*reg 13*). Employees must use all machinery and equipment in accordance with the training they have received. They must inform the employer of: (i) any work situation which represents an immediate danger to health and safety; and (ii) any shortcoming in the employer's protection arrangements for health and safety (*reg 14*).

An assessment must be made of workplace risks to new and expectant mothers, and measures must be taken to avoid any risk by altering working conditions or hours of work. Where it is not practicable to take these steps the woman should be suspended from work (subject to *ERA 1996, s 67*). Where it is necessary for her health and safety, a new or expectant mother must be removed from night work (*regs 16, 17*). (See also the *Suspension from Work (on Maternity Grounds) Order 1994 (SI 1994/2930)*.) In *Day v T Pickles Farms Ltd* [1999] IRLR 217, the EAT emphasised that employers must undertake an assessment of the workplace risks to pregnant women as soon as a woman of child-bearing age is employed. It is not sufficient to wait until an employee becomes pregnant.

Young persons must not be employed in certain dangerous or harmful work activities unless it is necessary for their training, the risks are reduced to the minimum, and they are competently supervised. Children must never be permitted to do such work (*reg 19*).

In criminal proceedings employers have no defence for a contravention of their health and safety obligations by reason of any act or default caused by an employee or by a person appointed to give competent advice (*reg 21*).

Since October 2003, the *Management of Health and Safety at Work Regulations 1999* (*SI 1999/3242*) have been amended to allow employees to claim damages from their employer if they suffer illness or injury as a result of a breach of the *Regulations*. Amending *reg 22*, the lifting of the civil liability exclusion will ensure full compliance with the *Health and Safety Framework Directive 89/391*.

Manual handling of loads

28.18 The HSE estimates that some 12.3 million working days have been lost due to work-related musculoskeletal disorders. As a result, some 1.1 million people a year are affected, making manual handling the most common cause of occupational illness in the UK. According to HSE statistics, some 37% of reported accidents are related to manual handling incidents. The *EU Manual Handling Operations Regulations 1992* (*SI 1992/2793*) as amended by *SI 2002/2174*, give effect to the EU Directive relating to the manual handling of loads (*90/269*). Broadly, the *Regulations* require each employer, so far as reasonably practicable, to avoid the need for his employees to undertake manual handling operations involving a risk of injury. That is a real risk, a foreseeable possibility of injury, not a probability (see *O'Neill v DSG Retail Ltd* [2002] EWCA Civ 1139, [2003] ICR 222). It is important to be able to show that consideration has been given to ways of avoiding such operations. Where it is not reasonably practicable, the employer is required to assess such operations and reduce the risk of injury arising from them to the lowest practicable level. For a case interpreting 'reasonably practicable' in this context, see *Hawkes v London Borough of Southwark* (20 February 1998, unreported), CA. Emphasising the importance of providing, where practicable, information to employees on the weight of loads they are required to handle was noted in *Swain v Denso Marston Ltd* [2000] ICR 1079, CA.

Regulation 4 of the *Health and Safety* (*Miscellaneous Amendments*) *Regulations 2002* (*SI 2002/2174*) amends the *1992 Regulations* by adding *reg 4(3)* by specifying factors to be taken account of, in determining whether operations involve risk, particularly of back injury to workers. The new regulation adds that particular regard should be given to: (a) the physical suitability of the employee to carry out the task; (b) the clothing and footwear the person is wearing; (c) the person's knowledge and training; and (d) the results of any relevant risk assessments. This amendment gives full effect to *Annex II* of *Directive 90/269/EEC* (OJ L156 26.6.90).

The *Regulations* also contain, in *Sch 1*, a list of the factors to which an employer must have regard (tasks, loads, working environment, individual capability and other factors) and the relevant questions which must be considered in each case when making an assessment of manual handling operations. Guidance on the *Regulations* has been published by the HSE (revised November 1998).

Since 31 December 1998, the *Merchant Shipping and Fishing Vessels* (*Manual Handling Operations*) *Regulations 1998* (*SI 1998/2857*) give effect to *Directive 90/269* in respect of shipping activities in the UK. The *Regulations* apply to UK-registered ships and, in part, to ships registered outside the UK when they are in UK waters.

The HSE has developed an online manual handling chart tool (MAC Tool) to help identify high risk workplace manual handling activities.

28.19 **NOISE AT WORK**

According to the HSE, over 170,000 people in the UK suffer deafness, tinnitus or other ear conditions as a result of exposure to excessive noise at work. The *Control of Noise at Work Regulations 2005* (the *Noise Regulations*), in force since 6 April 2006 (except for the music and entertainment sectors where they come into force on 6 April 2008), replace the long-standing *Noise at Work Regulations 1989* (*SI 1989/1790*) which came into force on 1 January 1990. The aim of these new *Noise Regulations* is to ensure that workers' hearing is protected from excessive noise at their place of work, which could cause them to lose their hearing and/or to suffer from tinnitus (permanent ringing in the ears).

The level at which employers must provide hearing protection and hearing protection zones is now 85 decibels (daily or weekly average exposure) and the level at which employers must assess the risk to workers' health and provide them with information and training is now 80 decibels. There is also an exposure limit value of 87 decibels, taking account of any reduction in exposure provided by hearing protection, above which workers must not be exposed.

There is a general duty upon the employer to reduce the risk of damage to the hearing of his employees from exposure to noise to the lowest level reasonably practicable.

The *Schedule* to the *Regulations* contains formulae for calculating an employee's 'daily personal noise exposure' and its weekly average. These are to be applied without taking into account the effect of ear protectors. If any employees are likely to be exposed to noise or sound pressure in excess of certain specified levels, the employer must ensure that a competent person makes a noise assessment identifying which employees are so exposed and providing such information with regard to the noise to which they may be exposed as will facilitate compliance with various duties imposed by the *Regulations*. Noise assessments must be reviewed if there is reason to suspect that they are no longer valid, or if there has been a significant change in the relevant work.

Where any employees are likely to be exposed to certain specified noise or sound pressure levels, their exposure to noise must so far as is reasonably practicable be reduced, other than by the provision of personal ear protection), and also so far as practicable be provided with suitable personal ear protectors to keep the risk of damage to below that arising from exposure to those levels. Employers must also, so far as reasonably practicable, identify by signs 'ear protection zones' where such exposure is likely and prevent employees from entering them without personal ear protectors.

At certain specified lower levels of noise, an employee must so far as practicable be provided with suitable and efficient personal ear protectors at his request.

There are also duties relating to ensuring the proper use and maintenance of equipment provided and to informing and training employees.

The HSE may grant exemptions from certain requirements where average weekly exposure does not exceed given levels.

Employees themselves are under a duty to use personal ear protectors and other protective measures and to report defects to the employer, and the self-employed are brought within the scope of the *Regulations*.

28.20 SAFETY REPRESENTATIVES

Employers are obliged to consult with employees over health and safety matters. Two different régimes operate: one for groups of workers in respect of which a union is recognised and the other where there is no union recognition.

As a result of responses to its discussion document on improving worker consultation on health and safety matters, the HSC has confirmed that it proposes to replace the *1977* and *1996 Regulations*, relating to the rights of safety representatives in unionised and non-unionised workplaces, with harmonised arrangements based on the principles of the *1977 Regulations*.

28.21 Union-appointed safety representatives

Employers must recognise, afford facilities and allow time off for the training of safety representatives appointed in accordance with the *Safety Representatives and Safety Committees Regulations 1977* (*SI 1977/500* as amended by *SI 1992/2051, SI 1996/1513, SI 1999/860*) made under the *HSWA 1974, s 2(4)*. Safety representatives are appointed by a trade union recognised by an employer from among the employees of a unionised workforce, with certain exceptions, eg members of the British Actors' Equity Association or of the Musicians' Union who need not be employees (*regs 3(1), 8(2)*). The representative should, if possible, either have been employed by his employer throughout the preceding two years or have had at least two years' experience in similar employment (*reg 3(4)*).

Safety representatives represent the employees in consultations with the employer over arrangements for their health and safety at work. Every employer is under a duty to consult safety representatives regarding such arrangements (*HSWA 1974, s 2(6)*); without prejudice to that general duty, employers are now required to consult safety representatives with regard to a number of specified health and safety matters, and to provide safety representatives with such facilities and assistance as they may reasonably require for the purposes of carrying out their functions under *HSWA 1974, s 2(4)* and the *Regulations* (*reg 4A*, inserted by the *Management of Health and Safety Regulations 1992* (*SI 1992/2051*)). See also the Code of Practice and guidance notes, *Safety representatives and safety committees* (third edition 1996).

In addition, safety representatives have other functions, including the investigation of potential hazards and complaints about health, safety or welfare. They can make representations about such matters and attend meetings of safety committees (*reg 4(1)*). (See also 11.8 DISCLOSURE OF INFORMATION.) Employers must allow safety representatives time off with pay to perform these functions (*reg 4(2)*). An employer must also permit safety representatives time off with pay to undergo training to fulfil these duties. (See 49.9–49.10 TIME OFF WORK and the *Code of Practice on Time off for the Training of Safety Representatives*.) A safety committee must be established if two or more safety representatives request one in writing (*reg 9*). Safety representatives and others enjoy special protection from dismissal and action short of dismissal (see 28.9 above, 54.3 UNFAIR DISMISSAL – II).

28.22 Non-unionised workers

From 1 October 1996 the obligation on employers to consult over health and safety matters was extended to employees who are not covered by trade union-appointed safety representatives (*Health and Safety (Consultation with Employees) Regulations 1996* (*SI 1996/1513*)).

Employers may consult either with their employees directly or through elected representatives (*reg 4*). Employees will be entitled to receive such information as is necessary to participate fully and effectively in the consultation process (*reg 5*). The functions of elected representatives are to make representations to the employer on health and safety issues and to represent employees in consultations with inspectors (*reg 6*). Elected representatives are entitled to time off with pay for training and to carry out their duties, and are protected against dismissal and victimisation (*regs 7, 8*).

28.23 SMOKING AT WORK

Restrictions on smoking are, of course, essential in certain environments for safety and hygiene reasons. Elsewhere, in general, the law has not intervened to regulate smoking at work although it can be argued that the employer's duty of care contained in s *2(2)(e)*, *HSWA 1974* may be relevant to the issue of passive smoking. The EAT, in *Waltons and Morse v Dorrington* [1997] IRLR 488, held that there is a term implied into employment contracts that 'the employer will provide and monitor for his employees, so far as is reasonably practicable, a working environment which is reasonably suitable for the performance by them of their contractual duties'. In this particular case, a non-smoker was held to have been constructively dismissed when she was required, despite her protests, to work in a smoke-affected atmosphere. One specific piece of legislation relating to smoking is contained in the *Workplace (Health, Safety and Welfare) Regulations 1992*. Under *reg 25* all employers are required to make arrangements so that non-smokers using rest areas are protected from discomfort caused by tobacco smoke.

The main difficulty likely to be encountered by employers who wish to withdraw smoking facilities is that smokers regard this as unacceptable victimisation, causing them to resign and claim unfair constructive dismissal. Provided the employer has introduced restrictions in a reasonable manner, it is unlikely that such a claim would succeed (*Dryden v Greater Glasgow Health Board* [1992] IRLR 469).

A reasonable procedure will include: a survey of workplace opinion; provision of information on smoking and health issues; consultation with representatives and individuals; help to enable smokers to adapt; introduction of the restrictions and/or ban over a reasonable period. Once the restrictions are in place, it should be made clear that failure to adhere to the smoking policy is a disciplinary offence.

A Scottish ban has been in place since March 2006. The *Health Act 2006* prohibits smoking in the workplace from 2nd April 2007 in Wales, from 30th April in Northern Ireland and from 1st July in England.

28.24 STRESS

Stress-related illness connected with work remains a controversial and topical issue for employers. According to the HSE, nearly 1 in 3 of workers across the EU (some 40 million people, estimated 5 million Britons) report that they are affected by stress at work (see www.hse.gov.uk), losing some 12.8 million working days lost in 2004–2005. Consequently, DTI has issued new guidance '*Work-related stress: a guide*' (2005).

28.25   'Many, alas, suffer breakdowns and depressive illnesses and a significant proportion could doubtless ascribe some at least of their problems to the strains and stresses of their work situation: be it simply overworking, the tension of difficult relationships, career prospect worries, fears or feelings of discrimination or harassment, to take just some examples. Unless, however, there was a real risk of breakdown which the claimant's employers ought reasonably to have foreseen and they ought properly to have averted there can be no liability.' This statement from Simon Brown LJ in *Garrett v Camden London Borough Council* (2001) EWCA Civ 395 at para 63, [2001] All ER (D) 202 (Mar) sets out the relevant legal test to be applied by the Court when considering a common law action in negligence.

In *Sutherland v Hatton* [2002] EWCA Civ 76, [2002] IRLR 263 the Court of Appeal has set out guidelines for determining employer liability for psychiatric injury caused by stress at work, summarised below.

The ordinary principles of employers' liability apply. First, the kind of harm to the particular employee must be reasonably foreseeable. Foreseeability depends on what the employer knows (or ought reasonably to know) about the individual. It may be harder to foresee mental conditions than physical injury, but may be easier in a known individual. Unless the employer knows of a particular problem or vulnerability, it is usually entitled to assume that the employee can withstand normal job pressures. No occupations should be regarded as intrinsically dangerous to mental health. The court listed a number of factors likely to be relevant in establishing foreseeability, such as the nature and extent of the work done by the employee. In general, an employer does not need to make detailed inquiries of the employee or his or her medical adviser.

To trigger the employer's duty to take steps, the indications of likely harm to the employee's health must be obvious enough for the reasonable employer to realise that something should be done. An employer will only be in breach of duty if it fails to take steps which are reasonable in the circumstances. Where an employer offers a confidential advice service with referral to counselling, it is unlikely to be in breach of its duty. It will not amount to a breach of duty to allow a willing employee to continue in a job if the only reasonable step involves dismissal or demotion.

The steps an employer could and should have taken need to be identified. For the employee, it must be shown that the breach of duty caused or materially contributed to the harm suffered. Employers should pay only for that proportion of the harm suffered which is attributable to their wrongdoing unless the harm is indivisible. Defendants should raise the question of apportionment. When assessing damages, the court will take account of pre-existing disorders or vulnerability and of the possibility that the employee would have succumbed to a stress-related disorder in any event.

Where stress risks are a feature of a particular job, a risk assessment should be made under the *Management of Health and Safety at Work Regulations 1992* (see 28.17 above) in the same way as for the risk of physical injury. It is important that complaints of working conditions or workloads causing stress are dealt with quickly and thoroughly and efforts made to reduce the risk of future health problems.

In cases of bullying the claimant might be able to rely on the civil cause of action established by s 3 of the *Protection from Harassment Act 1997* as was the case in *Green v Deutsche Bank* [2006] EWHC 1898. A secretary bullied by fellow employees established both negligence and breach of duty under the *1997 Act*. A significant advantage of the Act is that it provides for a 6 year limitation period .The common law time limit to institute proceedings is 3 years.

As well as claims for damages, it is also possible that employees whose complaints of excessive stress have gone unheeded could resign and claim constructive dismissal on the basis that the employer failed in the duty of care or breached the implied term to maintain the relationship of trust and confidence.

See www.hse.gov.uk/stress/index.htm

28.26 SUBSTANCES HAZARDOUS TO HEALTH

References in this section are to provisions of the *Control of Substances Hazardous to Health Regulations 2002* (*SI 2002/2677*), now in force, which replaced the *1999 Regulations* of the same name (except for *regs 4* and *20*, which are due in force in 2004). Employers' duties remain unaffected. The main change in the *1999 Regulations* is the removal of the *Schedule* listing maximum exposure limits ('MELs') from the *Regulations*. These appear instead in the HSE's publication *EH40* which is revised annually.

The definition of a substance hazardous to health is contained in *reg 2(1)*, and includes:

(*a*)   substances listed as dangerous for supply and whose specified nature of risk is very toxic, harmful, corrosive or an irritant;

(*b*)   substances for which the HSC has approved a maximum exposure limit or an occupational exposure standard;

(*c*)   a biological agent;

(*d*)   dust of any kind, when present at specified concentrations in air of total inhalable dust or respirable dust;

(*e*)   other substances which create a comparable hazard to the health of any person.

Employers owe duties under *COSHH Regulations 2002* to their employees and, so far as reasonably practicable and with certain exceptions, to other persons who may be affected by the work which they carry on (*reg 3*). The Executive has powers to grant exemption certificates (*reg 14*).

An employer may not carry on any work liable to expose any employees to any substance hazardous to health unless he has made a suitable and sufficient assessment of the risks to their health and of the steps necessary to meet the requirements of *COSHH* (*Dugmore v Swansea NHS Trust* [2002] EWCA Civ 1689, [2003] ICR 574). The assessment must be reviewed forthwith if there is reason to suspect that it is no longer valid or if there has been a significant change in the work to which it relates (*reg 6*).

The employer must ensure that the exposure of his employees to hazardous substances is either prevented or, where this is not reasonably practicable, adequately controlled (*reg 7(1)*). So far as reasonably practicable, that objective is to be secured by measures *other* than the provision of personal protective equipment, although that is also to be provided where necessary. Special measures apply to exposure to carcinogens (*reg 7(2), (3), (4)*).

Employers are under a duty to take all reasonable steps to ensure that control measures, protective equipment etc. are properly used or applied, and employees are under a duty to make full and proper use of such facilities, to return them after use and to report any defects to their employer (*reg 8(1), (2)*). The employer must maintain control measures and equipment in an efficient state, in efficient working order and in good repair, and keep records of tests carried out on them (*reg 9*).

In appropriate cases the employer must ensure that the exposure of employees to hazardous substances is monitored (*reg 10*) and/or that the relevant employees are under suitable health surveillance. In certain specified cases that must include medical surveillance, as a result of which the employer may be barred from engaging an employee for the work concerned (*reg 11*).

Employees whose work may expose them to hazardous substances are to be provided with suitable and sufficient information, instruction and training to enable them to know the risks of exposure and the precautions which should be taken (*reg 12*).

The Health and Safety Commission has approved a number of relevant Codes of Practice: 'Control of Substances Hazardous to Health', 'Control of Carcinogenic Substances' and 'Control of Biological Agents' are published in a single volume (revised 1999). Codes of Practice on the control of vinyl chloride at work, control of substances hazardous to health in pottery production, prevention or control of legionellosis and on the safe use of pesticides for non-agricultural purposes are also available. The Executive has published 'COSHH assessments: a step by step guide to assessment and the skills needed for it' and 'Health Surveillance under COSHH'. EH40, which lists the occupational exposure limits for use in complying with *COSHH*, is updated annually.

The *COSHH Regulations 2002* do not cover asbestos or lead which are subject to specific legislation, including the *Control of Asbestos at Work Regulations 1987* (*SI 1987/2115*) and the *Control of Lead at Work Regulations 1998* (*SI 1998/543*), both revised in 2002.

The *COSHH Regulations* have been extended in Northern Ireland – see *COSHH* (*Amendment*) *Regulations* (*NI*) *2005, SI 2005/165*.

Additional requirements are applied to particularly dangerous substances by the *Chemicals* (*Hazard Information and Packaging for Supply*) *Regulations 1994* (*SI 1994/3247* as amended by *SI 1996/1092, SI 1997/1460, SI 1998/3106, SI 1999/197, SI 1999/3165; SI 2000/2381; SI 2000/2897*), the *Dangerous Substances* (*Notification and Marking of Sites*) *Regulations 1990* (*SI 1990/304*) and the *Notification of New Substances Regulations 1993* (*SI 1993/3050*).

Seven sets of Regulations on the carriage of dangerous goods by road and rail came into force on 1 September 1996. These are accompanied by six 'Approved Documents' and a Code of Practice. However, following the Cullen Inquiry, rail safety regulation has been overhauled, as previously noted, in the newly enacted (since 10 July 2003), *Railways and Transport Safety Act 2003*.

Rails safety has been enhanced under *Sch 3* to the *Railways Act 2005*, providing standards and regulations in relation to the transfer of safety functions connected with railways.

In addition, the *Control of Major Accident Hazards Regulations 1999* (*COMAH*) which came into force on 1 April 1999 and are amended by the *Control of Major Accident Hazards* (*Amendment*) *Regulations 2005* from 30 June 2005. They implement *Council Directive 96/82/EC*, as amended by *Directive 2003/105/EC* and replaced the *Control of Industrial Major Accident Hazards Regulations 1984* (*CIMAH*).

28.27 VIBRATION AT WORK

The new *Control of Vibration at Work Regulations 2005* came into force on 6 July 2005. These new regulations will help both employers and employees to take preventive action from vibration risks in the workplace. These Regulations comply with *European Physical Agents (Vibration) Directive (Directive 2002/44)* which seeks to deal with the control of diseases caused by vibration at work from equipment, vehicles and machines.

Hand Arm Vibration (HAV) is a major cause of occupational ill health and it is estimated around five million workers are exposed to HAV in the workplace. Two million of these workers are exposed to levels of vibration where there are clear risks of developing disease. Each year, approximately 3,000 new claims for Industrial Injury Disability Benefit are made in relation to vibration white finger and vibration related carpal tunnel syndrome.

See www.hse.gov.uk/vibration/index.htm. Also, see the HAV Health Surveillance scheme and vibguide.

28.28 VIOLENCE AND BULLYING AT WORK

The employer's duty of care at common law and under *HSWA 1974, s 2* means that an employer needs to provide adequate security precautions where it is reasonably foreseeable that employees may suffer violence in the course of their work (which, given the escalation of violent incidents at work, probably covers every workplace). When making the risk assessment required under the *Management of Health and Safety at Work Regulations 1992*, as amended in 1999, (see 28.17 above) the possibility of violence to employees must be evaluated. When an employee has been the victim of an attack and the employer has taken inadequate safety measures, the employee may resign and claim constructive dismissal (*Dutton & Clark Ltd v Daly* [1985] IRLR 363), or claim damages for negligence.

The HSE leaflet *Violence at Work: a guide for employers* sets out a strategy for the effective management of violence.

Employees must also be safeguarded against bullying or harassment at work either by members of the public or fellow employees. Such behaviour, if not causing actual physical harm, may have a detrimental effect on an employee's morale and health. Where insufficient action is taken to stamp out the problem it is possible that the employer may be held liable for personal injury even if psychological damage only is caused. Intentional harassment is a criminal offence under the *Public Order Act 1986, s 4A* (as inserted by the *Criminal Justice and Public Order Act 1994*). From 16 June 1997, the *Protection from Harassment Act 1997* creates two new criminal offences of harassment and provides a civil remedy whereby an individual can apply for an injunction and damages against the harasser. Racially aggravated harassment constitutes a separate offence from 30 September 1998 (*Crime and Disorder Act 1998, ss 31, 32*). In July 1999, ACAS published two advisory leaflets (one for employers and one for employees) on *Bullying and harassment at work*.

It is imperative that all complaints from employees of violence, bullying or harassment are investigated fully and prompt action taken where necessary.

28.29 WORKPLACE STANDARDS

The *Workplace (Health, Safety and Welfare) Regulations 1992* (*SI 1992/3004*) give effect to the EC Directive concerning the minimum health and safety requirements for the workplace (*89/654*). The *Regulations* came into force on 1 January

1993 in respect of any new workplace, and apply to any modification, extension or conversion of an existing workplace on or after that date. In respect of any other existing workplace, the requirements came into effect on 1 January 1996. *Regulation 6* of the *Health and Safety (Miscellaneous Amendments) Regulations 2002 (SI 2002/2174)* amends the *1992 Regulations* to give complete or clearer effect to the technical definitions of its key terms, such as the meaning of 'workplace'. These requirements supersede provisions in the *Factories Act 1961 (ss 1–7, 18, 28, 29, 57–60* and *69), Offices, Shops and Railway Premises Act 1963 (ss 4–16)*, and *Agriculture (Safety, Health and Welfare Provisions) Act 1956 (ss 3, 5, 25(3)* and *(6))*.

The requirements under the Regulations are imposed on employers, persons having control of a workplace, and any person who is deemed to be the occupier of a factory by virtue of s *175(5)* of the *Factories Act 1961* (*reg 4*). The requirements relate to the following matters:

(*a*)   maintenance of workplaces, and of equipment, devices and systems (*reg 5*);

(*b*)   ventilation of enclosed workplaces (*reg 6*);

(*c*)   temperature in indoor workplaces (including provision of thermometers) (*reg 7*);

(*d*)   lighting (*reg 8*);

(*e*)   cleanliness and waste materials (*reg 9*);

(*f*)   room dimensions and space (*reg 10*);

(*g*)   workstations and seating (*reg 11*);

(*h*)   conditions of floors and traffic routes, and organisation of traffic routes (*regs 12, 17*);

(*i*)   falls or falling objects (*reg 13*);

(*j*)   windows, doors, gates, walls, skylights and ventilators (*regs 14–16, 18*);

(*k*)   escalators and moving walkways (*reg 19*);

(*l*)   sanitary conveniences (*reg 20*);

(*m*)   washing facilities (*reg 21*);

(*n*)   drinking water (*reg 22*);

(*o*)   accommodation for clothing, and facilities for changing clothing (*regs 23, 24*); and

(*p*)   facilities to rest and to eat meals (*reg 25*).

Regulation 24 requires facilities to be provided for changing clothes when workers have to wear special clothing for work and, for reasons of health or propriety, cannot be expected to change in another room. 'Special clothing' in this context means any clothing which would not ordinarily be worn other than for work, such as a distinctive uniform (*Post Office v Footitt* [2000] IRLR 243).

28.30 **Safety signs**

The *Health and Safety (Safety Signs and Signals) Regulations 1996 (SI 1996/341)* implements the EC Directive on safety signs and signals (*92/58*). All workplace safety signs are required to be of a type referred to within the Regulations.

28.31 WORK-RELATED UPPER LIMB DISORDERS ('WRULDS')

Work-related upper limb disorders or 'RSI' (repetitive strain injury) as they are commonly known, are becoming an increasingly worrying issue for employers, particularly in relation to keyboard users. Although there have only been a small number of claims successfully pursued through the courts, a number of employers have settled claims for large sums of money.

In 1996 a secretary who had developed 'writer's cramp' (a WRULD disorder) as a result of an excessive typing workload succeeded before the Court of Appeal in a claim that her employer had been negligent in allowing her to type for long periods on a word processor without breaks. The court held that it was reasonably foreseeable that a WRULD condition could occur with the amount of typing involved and that the company had negligently failed to warn the employee of the need to take breaks. This ruling was overturned by the House of Lords in *Pickford v Imperial Chemical Industries plc* [1998] IRLR 435, primarily because of inconclusive medical evidence. In addition the employer was held not to be in breach of the duty of care in failing to warn of the need to take breaks because, unlike a typist, a secretary could organise the workload to avoid continuous working on a word processor. (A statutory requirement to provide information to workers on health and safety risks associated with VDUs is now contained in the *Health and Safety (Display Screen Equipment) Regulations 1992 (SI 1992/2792)* (see 28.6 above).)

In July 1999 the Court of Appeal rejected an appeal against an award of £60,000 made to five former bank employees who developed diffuse RSI after being required to attain high speeds on keyboards while encoding cheques. There was evidence that the bank was aware of the risk of injury but that insufficient precautions had been taken (*Alexander v Midland Bank plc* [1999] IRLR 723).

The possibility of contracting WRULDs can be minimised by paying attention to posture, ergonomics, job design and working methods and conditions.

29 Holidays

29.1 The right of an employee to a period of paid holiday is regulated by his contract (see 29.9 below) and, since 1 October 1998, by the *Working Time Regulations 1998* (*SI 1998/1833*) (see 29.2–29.6 below). In addition, in certain fields of employment, separate statutory provision is made (see **29.7–29.8** below).

29.2 STATUTORY RULES

Working Time Regulations 1998

The *Working Time Regulations 1998* (*SI 1998/1833*) came into force on 1 October 1998. They implemented the *Working Time Directive 93/104/EC* which has now been replaced by the *Working Time Directive 2003/88/EC*. The *Regulations* confer a right on workers to take paid annual leave (*reg 13(1)*). There is no continuous service requirement to qualify for paid annual leave. Initially, *reg 13(7)* did specify that only workers with 13 weeks' continuous service qualified. However, this limitation was ruled contrary to European law by the ECJ in *R (on the application of the Broadcasting, Entertainment, Cinematographic and Theatre Union) v Secretary of State for Trade and Industry: C-173/99* ('*BECTU*') [2001] IRLR 559. The ECJ stated that the right to paid leave is an important social right which does not permit of derogation by member states. As a consequence of this decision, *regs 13(7)* and *13(8)* were revoked by the *Working Time (Amendment) Regulations 2001* (*SI 2001/3256*) with effect from 25 October 2001.

'Worker' is defined in the *Regulations* to include employees and those employed under a contract pursuant to which they undertake personally to provide services, but excludes those who are in business on their own account and whose 'employer' is in reality their customer or client (*reg. 2(1)*). In *James v Redcats (Brands) Ltd* [2007] IRLR 296 the EAT suggested (in a case under the National Minimum Wage Act 1998 which adopts the same definition of worker) that for a person to be a worker the obligation personally to provide services must be the dominant feature of the contract, an approach borrowed from the test for whether someone is 'employed' for the purposes of the discrimination statutes. The exclusion of those in business on their own account was considered in *Bacica v Muir* [2006] IRLR 35 in which the EAT concluded that the fact that Mr Muir, a painter, provided his services personally to Mr Bacica over an extended period did not make him a 'worker'. By contrast the fact that Mr Muir worked on the basis of a Construction Industry Scheme (CIS) certificate, had his own business accounts prepared and submitted to the Inland Revenue, was free to work for others and in fact did so, was paid at a rate which included an overheads allowance and was not paid if not working, all supported the conclusion that he was running a business and that Mr Bacica was a customer of that business. See also, on the definition of worker under the *Regulations*, *Byrne Brothers (Formwork) Ltd v Baird* [2002] ICR 667, [2002] IRLR 96; *Wright v Redrow Homes (Yorkshire) Ltd* [2004] ICR 1126, [2004] IRLR 720; *Cotswold Developments Construction Ltd v Williams* [2006] IRLR 181; and WORKING TIME (57.3).

Children under the age for compulsory schooling are not workers and, therefore, are not entitled to holiday pay: *Ashby v Addison* [2003] ICR 667, [2003] IRLR 211, EAT.

In *Gibson v East Riding of Yorkshire Council* [2000] IRLR 598 the Court of Appeal, overturning the decision of the EAT, held that *art 7* of the *Working Time Directive*, which sets out a right to paid holiday, does not have direct effect. This means that employees may not rely directly on *art 7* of the *Directive* before the domestic courts, but may only rely on their equivalent rights under the *Regulations*. The decision in *Gibson* has been applied by the EAT in *South Tyneside Metropolitan Borough Council v Toulson* [2003] 1 CMLR 867 and *Voteforce Associates Ltd v Quinn* [2002] ICR 1. In both cases the EAT concluded that the claimants were not entitled to paid annual leave as they did not have 13 weeks' continuous employment (as required at that time by *reg 13(7)*). The fact that the ECJ had decided in *BECTU* that the 13 week requirement was unlawful could not assist the claimants as the *Directive* did not have direct effect and, therefore, employment tribunals were obliged to apply the *Regulations* that were in force at the relevant time.

For further discussion of the *Working Time Regulations* and *Directive* see WORKING TIME (57), EUROPEAN COMMUNITY LAW (25) and HEALTH AND SAFETY AT WORK – II (28).

29.3 **Period of leave**

A worker is entitled to four weeks' annual leave in each leave year (*reg 13(1)*). The *Regulations* set only minimum requirements: more generous provisions relating to annual leave may be made in the contract of employment. Public holidays (of which there are 8 each year) may count towards the employee's annual leave entitlement. The DTI has just concluded a consultation exercise which included a government proposal to increase the annual leave entitlement to 5.6 weeks which, for a person working 5 days a week, would increase the entitlement to 28 days. The proposal is that the leave entitlement will increase in stages from 4 to 4.8 weeks from 1 October 2007 and to 5.6 weeks from 1 October 2008. Where a worker is part way through his leave year (see below) when (or if) these proposed increased entitlements come into force, he will receive a proportionate additional holiday entitlement in that leave year.

A leave year commences on the date set out in a relevant agreement. In the absence of such an agreement, the leave year commences on 1 October 1998 and on the anniversary of that date for those workers already in employment on that date, and, for workers who start work after 1 October 1998, on the date their employment commences (*reg 13(3)*).

A worker may take the leave to which he is entitled under the *Regulations* in instalments, but currently he may not carry forward untaken leave from one leave year to the next (*reg 13(9)*). The DTI has, however, proposed to amend the *Regulations* to enable employers and workers to agree to carry over a limited amount of holiday to the following holiday year, provided that the worker remains entitled to at least 4 weeks' annual leave each year.

In addition, an employer may not pay a worker in lieu of permitting him to take annual leave except on termination of his employment (*reg 13(9)*). The prohibition of payment in lieu of annual leave is intended to remove any incentive for workers to accept additional payment rather than taking leave as this would undermine the health and safety objectives of the *Directive*: see *Federatie Nederlandse Vakbeging v Netherlands* [2006] ICR 962, [2006] IRLR 561, ECJ. As part of its recent consultation exercise the DTI considered but rejected a proposal to allow payment in lieu of taking the leave entitlement.

On average, bearing in mind the current annual entitlement to four weeks' leave, the *Regulations* allow a third of a week's leave for each month worked. However, save for workers in their first year of employment, the *Regulations* do not make provision for leave to be accrued incrementally on a month by month basis. So, for example, subject to agreement with the employer (which is discussed at 29.5 below), a worker would be entitled under the *Regulations* to take all four weeks' leave in the first month of the leave year. By contrast, workers in their first year of employment accrue entitlement to leave at the rate of one-twelfth of four weeks on the first day of each month and leave under the *Regulations* may only be taken after it has been accrued.

The question of how entitlement to leave is accrued is particularly relevant to workers who do not work for the entire leave year. How is leave entitlement calculated in these cases? Three particular scenarios are commonly encountered in the workplace. First, a worker may commence employment part-way through the leave year. Where this happens, in that leave year he is entitled to the proportion of the four week annual leave equal to the proportion of the leave year for which he is employed (*reg 13(5)*).

The second scenario is that the worker leaves the employment part way through the leave year. In this situation, *reg 14* provides a mechanism to compare the amount of leave taken by a worker in that part of the leave year which he worked with the amount of leave accrued during that part. So, for example, if a worker left the employment exactly 6 months through the leave year, he would have accrued two weeks' annual leave; this can be compared to the amount of leave actually taken. *Regulation 14* then sets out procedures for dealing with any difference between leave accrued and leave taken. These procedures are discussed at **29.4** below.

The third scenario occurs where, although the worker remains employed through-out the leave year, he is absent for much or all of the year due to, for example, illness. The *Regulations* do not expressly address this situation and, therefore, it has been left to the courts to seek a solution. Originally the EAT decided in *Kigass Aero Components Ltd v Brown* [2002] ICR 697, [2002] IRLR 312 that holiday entitlement under *reg 13(1)* continues to be accrued when an employee is on long-term sick leave. This decision had the benefit of simplicity in that the same rule could be applied to all employees, whether at work, on long term sick leave, or occasionally sick: all were entitled to four weeks' paid annual leave. However, on its facts, *Kigass* lead to an unusual result as a worker on long term sick leave who had exhausted all sick pay entitlements could nonetheless claim payment for four weeks' 'holiday' even though he was not fit to work. In *Ainsworth v IRC* [2005] ICR 1149, [2005] IRLR 465 the Court of Appeal concluded that the interpretation in *Kigass* was incorrect and overturned the EAT's decision.

The workers in *Ainsworth* had all been off sick for the entire leave year and were claiming either (i) paid annual leave even though they were not actually able to work or (ii) payment in lieu of untaken annual leave following the termination of employment. The Court of Appeal decided that the claimants were not entitled to four weeks' paid annual leave under the *Regulations* in these circumstances. At the heart of the case was the question (left open by the text of the *Regulations*) of how the entitlement to leave accrues in cases of absence during the leave year. On the one hand, it would seem ridiculous (and contrary to the *Regulations*) to link leave entitlement closely to attendance at work with the result that leave entitlement was reduced proportionally with every absence, regardless of length. On the other hand, the decision in *Kigass* could be seen as granting sick workers a windfall outside the scope of entitlements to sick pay. In the end the Court of

Appeal in *Ainsworth* did not give a definitive answer to the broader question of how leave should be treated as accruing during absence. Instead it confined its decision to the facts of the cases before it in which the workers had done no work during the leave year. In view of the limited scope of the Court of Appeal's decision, it would be prudent to assume that the decision in *Ainsworth* does not lay down a rule that holiday entitlement is only accrued when the worker attends work. On this approach, an employer would not be entitled to reduce a worker's holiday entitlement simply because he has been absent for part of the leave year. This interpretation could still result in some unusual situations: for example, a worker, absent due to illness for 10 or 11 months, only to recover and return to work, would appear to be entitled to claim 4 weeks annual leave. However, following *Ainsworth* there is no entitlement, as previously permitted in *Kigass*, to claim leave even though the worker has been unable to work throughout the leave year.

The Court of Appeal decision in *Ainsworth* has been appealed to the House of Lords, now under the name *Her Majesty's Revenue & Customs v Stringer*. On 13 December 2006, the Lords referred the case to the ECJ to consider whether a worker can take paid holiday leave during a period when the worker would otherwise be on sick leave and whether an allowance in lieu of holiday entitlement should be paid at the termination of employment even if the worker has been absent on sick leave for all or part of the holiday year. The ECJ hearing is expected to take place in late 2007 or 2008.

29.4 Payment

A worker is entitled to be paid for any period of leave at the rate of a week's pay for each week of leave. In *British Airways plc v Noble* [2006] EWCA Civ 537, [2006] ICR 1228, the Court of Appeal reiterated that pay while on holiday should be the same as pay while at work. The application of this simple principle to various employment situations is not, however, as straightforward as it sounds.

A week's pay under the *Regulations* is calculated in accordance with the rules in *ERA 1996, ss 221–224 (reg 16)*. Under *ERA 1996, ss 221–224 and 234*, where an employee has normal working hours, overtime only qualifies as part of a week's pay where the overtime is fixed under the contract of employment. The effect is that only contractual hours are included and, for example, non-contractual overtime hours are not. This can lead to situations where, although the employee regularly works substantial periods of overtime, pay while on holiday is based upon the lower number of contractual hours. For example, in *Bamsey v Albion Engineering* [2004] ICR 1083, [2004] IRLR 457 the employee worked on average 58 hours per week. However as his contractual hours were only 39 this formed the basis of his entitlement to holiday pay. He argued that this was contrary to the *Working Time Directive* which required workers to be paid during holiday periods at the same or similar level to their normal income when actually at work and that *WTR reg 16* should be interpreted purposively to ensure that this was achieved. The Court of Appeal rejected this argument and confirmed that non-contractual overtime did not form a part of a week's pay for workers. It also concluded that this interpretation was not contrary to the purpose of the Directive which did not require member states to guarantee more pay during a holiday period than a worker was contractually entitled to even if the worker regularly worked periods of non-contractual overtime. Where, however, a worker does not have normal working hours a week's pay is calculated under *ERA 1996, s 224,* by averaging his pay over the last 12 weeks in which he worked. A further impact of the application of the rules in *ERA 1996, ss 221–224* is that commission payments are not normally taken into account when determining a week's pay: see *Evans v Malley Organisation Ltd* [2003] ICR 432, [2003] IRLR 156. For further discussion on the calculation of a week's pay, see REDUNDANCY – I (38) and PAY– I (34)).

The right to annual paid holiday does not affect the right of a worker to remuneration under his contract. However, any contractual remuneration paid during a period of leave will be offset against leave payments due under the *Regulations*, and similarly any payment for a period of leave under the *Regulations* will be offset against a claim for contractual remuneration for the same period (*regs 16(4)* and (*5*)).

For some time there was debate and dispute about whether an employer could 'roll up' holiday pay: ie whether the *Regulations* allowed the rate of pay while actually working to be enhanced to include an element referable to holiday pay so that no additional pay was due when the worker took leave. The ECJ decided in *Robinson-Steele v RD Retail Services Ltd* [2006] ICR 932, [2006] IRLR 386 that the *Directive* required that workers were paid for annual leave at the time they took it. Accordingly 'rolling up' holiday pay is contrary to the *Regulations* and *Directive*. The ECJ explained this decision on the basis that, although the *Directive* did not expressly lay down when payment for leave should be made, the purpose of the requirement of payment for annual leave is to put the worker, during annual leave, in a position which is, as regards remuneration, comparable to periods of work. Therefore, the entitlements to annual leave and to payment for that leave are two aspects of a single right. The rationale which underlies this conclusion is that workers may be discouraged from taking leave if they will receive no remuneration during that period of leave.

The ECJ's decision resolves the previous inconsistent decisions in England and Scotland in favour of the approach of the Court of Session in Scotland which had concluded that rolled up holiday pay was unlawful: see *Munro v MPB Structures Ltd* [2003] IRLR 350. By contrast the Court of Appeal and the EAT in England had held that, subject to certain restrictions, rolling up holiday pay into pay for periods when the worker was actually working did comply with the *Regulations*: see, as background, *Marshalls Clay Products v Caulfield* [2004] ICR 1502, [2004] IRLR 564, CA and *Smith v AJ Morrisroes & Sons Ltd* [2005] ICR 596, [2005] IRLR 72, EAT.

Bearing in mind that, prior to the ECJ decision in *Robinson-Steele*, rolled up holiday pay was thought to be lawful (at least in England and Wales), it is unsurprising that the practice had been commonly adopted in a number of industries where working patterns are irregular and/or unpredictable (for, example, industries with certain shift patterns and recruitment businesses providing temporary staff). It is now clear that this will not comply with the *Regulations*. However this does not necessarily mean that any workers who have benefited from rolled up holiday pay can gain a windfall by claiming payment for leave at the time they take it notwithstanding that they have already been paid for that leave through rolled up holiday pay. In this regard, the ECJ held that the *Directive* did not preclude sums paid transparently and comprehensibly as rolled up holiday pay being set off against the payment due for specific leave which is actually taken by a worker.

Payment on Termination of Employment

Where a worker's employment is terminated and he has accrued but untaken leave to which he is entitled under the *Regulations*, the employer must pay him in lieu of that untaken leave (*reg 14*). The amount payable to the worker in these circumstances may be specified in a relevant agreement. A relevant agreement may not, however, specify that no sum is to be paid: see *Witley and District Men's Club v Mackay* [2001] IRLR 595, EAT, in which an agreement that no sum was to be paid for accrued holiday where the employee was dismissed on grounds of dishonesty was void under *reg 35(1)(a)*. In the absence of such an agreement, it is to be calculated by determining the amount he would have been paid under *reg 16* for the period of leave accrued but untaken (ie the period of leave which, in proportion to the leave year, he is entitled to take), less the period of leave he has in fact taken (*reg 14(3)*). Compensation for failure to pay for accrued but untaken holiday on termination of employment is not limited by principles of justice and equity under *reg 30(4)*; *reg 30(5)* requires a tribunal to make an award for the actual sum due: *Witley and District Men's Club v Mackay* (above). An employer may specify in a relevant agreement that, where a worker has at the date of his dismissal taken more than his accrued leave entitlement, he reimburse his employer, for example, by making a payment or undertaking additional work (*reg 14(4)*). In the absence of a relevant agreement, the employer will not be entitled to claw back payment for holidays taken but not accrued and no term can be implied which would allow such a claw back: see *Hill v Chapell* [2003] IRLR 19, EAT.

29.5 **Notice requirements**

The procedures which must be complied with when a worker requests, or an employer refuses, annual leave, may be specified in a relevant agreement (*reg 15(5)*). In the absence of such an agreement, the provisions of *reg 15(1)–(4)* apply as follows. A worker must give notice of the dates he intends to take leave. The notice period must be equivalent to at least twice the period of leave he is proposing to take. An employer may refuse leave on the requested dates by serving a counter-notice on the employee at least as many days before the proposed leave commences as the number of days' leave refused. The employer may also require an employee to take all or part of his leave on certain dates by giving him notice of that requirement; the length of notice must be at least twice the period of leave he requires the worker to take. The right of an employer to require leave to be taken at certain times may, however, be restricted in cases of maternity leave: in *Merino Gomez v Continental Industrias del Caucho SA: C-342/01* [2004] IRLR 407, the ECJ concluded that a worker returning from maternity leave had to be allowed to take her statutory leave entitlement even though it meant that she would take the leave outside the established periods for leave set out in a workforce agreement.

29.6 **Remedies**

A worker may complain to an employment tribunal that his employer has refused to allow him to take annual leave (*reg 30(1)(a)*) or has failed to pay him sums due in respect of leave which he has taken (*reg 30(1)(b)*). A complaint must be presented to the Tribunal within three months of the date of the act complained of. This time limit is extended by a further 3 months under the Employment Act 2002 when the statutory grievance procedures apply (see EMPLOYMENT TRIBUNALS – I (20.19) above). The tribunal may also extend time where it considers it was not reasonably practicable for the worker to submit his claim within three months (*reg 30(2)*).

If the employment tribunal finds that a claim under *reg 30(1)(a)* (refusal to allow a worker to take annual leave) is well-founded, the tribunal must make a declaration to that effect and, in addition, may order payment of such compensation as it considers just and equitable in all the circumstances, having regard to the employer's default in refusing to permit the worker to exercise his right, and any loss sustained by the worker as a consequence of that refusal (*regs 30(3) and 30(4)*). If the complaint is made under *reg 30(1)(b)* (failure to make a payment for leave taken during employment or leave accrued but untaken on termination), and the tribunal finds that the complaint is well-founded it must order payment of the sum due for that period of leave (*reg 30(5)*).

In *IRC v Ainsworth* [2005] ICR 1149, [2005] IRLR 465 the Court of Appeal ruled that *reg 30* was intended to provide a single and exclusive regime for the enforcement of the statutory rights in the *Regulations*. In doing so it overruled earlier decisions of the EAT which had concluded that a claim in respect of unpaid holiday pay could also be brought under Part II, ERA 1996; ie unlawful deduction of wages (the EAT cases were *List Design Group v Douglas* [2002] ICR 686, [2003] IRLR 14 and *Canada Life Ltd v Gray* [2004] ICR 673). In reaching its conclusion in *Ainsworth* the Court of Appeal reasoned that *Part II, ERA 1996* cannot have been intended as a remedy for breach of a subsequently created statutory right which had its own enforcement regime. The impact of the decision in *Ainsworth* is that a claim for unpaid holiday pay must be brought under *reg 30* within three months of the date when paid leave was refused. It will no longer be open for a worker to seek to show that several refusals to allow paid leave were part of a series of deductions under *s 23(3) ERA 1996* and that the claim was brought within three months of the last deduction in that series. *Ainsworth* has been appealed to the House of Lords who referred certain issues to the ECJ (see 29.3 above) but not the remedies issue. The Lords, however, will not decide the remedies issue until after the decision of the ECJ.

Notwithstanding *Ainsworth*, an employee may still be entitled to bring a claim for unlawful deduction of wages or breach of contract on the basis that, under his contract of employment, he was entitled to holiday pay or payment in lieu of accrued but untaken holiday. This will depend on the interpretation of the contract of employment and is discussed at paragraph **28.9** below.

29.7   Agricultural workers

Under the *Agricultural Wages Act 1948, s 3*, as substituted by *EPA 1975, s 97(1), Sch 9 Pt 1*, the Agricultural Wages Board may direct that holidays be allowed and that certain rates of pay be given for holidays. An agreement inconsistent with the order is void (*s 11*). Failure to allow holidays or give holiday pay specified in the order gives rise to a right to claim by the employee as well as liability for a criminal offence and a fine of level 3 on the standard scale (*s 4*). Special provisions are applicable to agricultural workers under the *Working Time Regulations 1998, Sch 2*.

Civil Aviation Workers

29.8

Statutory leave entitlements for crew members employed in civil aviation are governed by the *Civil Aviation (Working Time) Regulations 2004*. *Regulation 4* provides that 'a crew member is entitled to paid annual leave of at least four weeks, or a proportion of four weeks in respect of a period of employment of less than one year'. As with the *Working Time Regulations*, this leave may be taken in installments and may not be replaced by a payment in lieu, except where the crew member's employment is terminated, and the right is enforceable through a claim to the Employment Tribunals.

However the *Civil Aviation* (*Working Time*) *Regulations 2004* do not contain any of the detailed mechanisms in the *Working Time Regulations* for determining when annual leave may be taken and the rate of pay during leave. These lacunas have been the source of a number of claims.

29.9   **CONTRACT**

The *Working Time Regulations 1998* lay down a minimum paid annual holiday entitlement. The contract of employment may, however, make more generous provision than provided for by the *Regulations*. In such circumstances, the contract will determine the employee's rights in respect of that more generous provision. Authorities on the common law on employee's rights to holidays which were decided before the *Regulations* came into force must now be read subject to those *Regulations*.

Particulars of holiday entitlement are among those the employer is obliged by the *Employment Rights Act 1996, s 1(4)(d)(i)* to supply in writing to the employee (see 8.5(G) CONTRACT OF EMPLOYMENT). In the absence of express provisions, certain terms relating to holidays have been implied by the courts.

It is thought likely that in most industries, in the absence of express provision, it will be held to be an implied term of the contract of employment that bank holidays may be taken as paid holiday: see *Tucker v British Leyland Motor Corpn Ltd* [1978] IRLR 493 at 496, in which a county court judge decided that ' ... if no express contractual provision or regular usage to the contrary is established an hourly paid employee is entitled to a day's holiday on recognised public holidays without fear of dismissal as an absentee; and that if he is entitled to a guaranteed minimum weekly wage he is entitled to be paid for that day without having to work additional hours in that week.'

It was held in *Hurt v Sheffield Corpn* (1916) 85 LJKB 1684, that the right to a holiday accrued only at the end of the year in the absence of any express provision to the contrary. Although this does not accord with the normal modern practice, the Court of Appeal in *Morley v Heritage plc* [1993] IRLR 400 declined to disapprove the decision in *Hurt.*

In *Morley*, above, it was held that there was no implied term of the contract that the employee should be paid for accrued but untaken when he left part-way through the year. However, in an appropriate case it might be possible to imply such a term as a matter of custom and practice. The decision of the EAT in *Janes Solicitors v Lamb-Simpson* (1996) 541 IRLB 15 suggests that in the case of an oral contract where there is nothing in writing, there is a wide area over which terms could be implied on the basis of business efficacy, including one as to accrued holiday pay. Payment for accrued but untaken leave may, however, be payable under the *Working Time Regulations* (see 29.4 above).

Where there is a contractual entitlement to pay due under the contract for accrued but untaken holiday the contract may also make express provision as to how that entitlement is calculated. In the absence of such provision, there is inconsistent EAT authority as to how the rate of a day's pay should be calculated where the worker is paid an annual salary. The two approaches adopted have been to divide annual salary by 365 or to divide it by the actual number of working days. Obviously the former calculation will mean that the worker is entitled to lower payment for each untaken day of accrued holiday. In *Thames Water Utilities v Reynolds* [1996] IRLR 186 the EAT concluded that the *Apportionment Act 1870* applied with the result that a day's pay was to be calculated by dividing annual salary by 365. In *Taylor v East Midlands Offender Employment Consortium* [2000]

29.9   Holidays

IRLR 760 the EAT accepted that the *Apportionment Act* did apply in calculating a day's pay. However on the facts of the case, the pay for the employee's 10 days accrued but untaken holiday were 'grossed up' to 14 days pay to take account of weekends necessarily included in the 10-day holiday period. Subsequently (at a preliminary hearing) in *Leisure Leagues UK Ltd v Maconnachie* [2002] IRLR 600 the EAT concluded that the approach in *Thames Water* was wrong for two reasons. First, the approach was at odds with the virtually universal practice in industry in respect of the calculation of holiday pay in respect of holiday entitlement which is by reference to a day's work rather than calendar days per year. Second, *Thames Water* predated the *Working Time Regulations*. It is submitted that the approach in *Leisure Leagues UK Ltd* is to be preferred. But, in any event, the decision in *East Midlands Offender Employment Consortium* illustrates that the EAT had already found a way to mitigate the apparent harshness of the decision in *Thames Water*.

30   Human Rights

30.1   INTRODUCTION

The employment relationship may give rise to issues involving human rights law. At the individual level, human rights law may give an employee important protection against acts of discrimination or protect the employee's privacy or right to a fair hearing. Similarly, in relation to collective labour relations, human rights law is relevant to the right of members of a trade union to associate, to join a trade union of their choice and to take part in industrial action.

From 2 October 2000, with the coming into force of the *Human Rights Act 1998*, the domestic courts have been required to interpret United Kingdom law in accordance with the provisions of the European Convention on Human Rights and Fundamental Freedoms ('the Convention'). Prior to the *Act* coming into force, the Convention did not form part of the domestic law of the UK but was an international obligation which could, in appropriate cases, be used as an aid to the interpretation of unclear UK statutory provisions. An aggrieved individual seeking to rely upon the Convention was required to seek to present a case to the European Court of Human Rights for the determination of that court. This process could be expensive and very slow. Whilst the right of petition to the European Court remains as the final source of determination and jurisprudence on Convention Rights, issues of Convention rights may now be determined directly in the UK domestic courts.

This chapter presents an overview of the Convention and the historical development of the rights most relevant to the employment relationship, identifying some of the key decisions of the European Court of Human Rights and instances where Convention principles have assisted the UK courts in interpreting statutory provisions. The chapter goes on to consider, in outline, the key provisions of the *Human Rights Act* and its application and recent UK decisions in the employment sphere raising issues under the *Act*.

30.2   THE CONVENTION

Effect of the Convention

The European Convention on Human Rights and Fundamental Freedoms is an international treaty which was drawn up in 1950 and came into force in 1953. The Convention sets out in broad terms a number of fundamental rights and freedoms. It also established the European Commission of Human Rights and the European Court of Human Rights, both based in Strasbourg. It should be emphasised that the Convention and its institutions are entirely separate from the law and institutions of the European Community. The subscribing states are the members of the Council of Europe. Also, unlike European Community Law, the provisions of the Convention are not part of domestic law; they only bind the Government. The main text of the Convention, which has been amended by several protocols, can be found in Command Paper *Cmd 8969* (1953), published by the Stationery Office.

If a state which is a party to the Convention interferes with or abrogates any of the rights or freedoms enshrined in the Convention, a complaint may be made by any other party state. More importantly, the Convention allows for a right of direct complaint by an *individual* affected by an alleged breach of the Convention (such an individual right of complaint is very rare in international law). The Government of the United Kingdom ratified the Convention in 1950. However, it was not until 1966 that the UK Government recognised the jurisdiction of the European Court of Human Rights and accepted the right of an individual in the UK to petition the court.

30.3 Procedure for petition by an individual

In outline the procedure is as follows. The aggrieved individual must pursue every remedy available under UK law. When he has exhausted these 'domestic' remedies, without having his complaint satisfactorily resolved, he may present his petition to the European Commission of Human Rights. The Commission investigates the complaint. If it decides that there is, or may be, a breach of the Convention and that the complaint is admissible, it will endeavour to obtain a settlement between the parties. If no settlement is reached, the Commission will refer the case, together with its report, to the European Court of Human Rights. The court will then proceed to decide on the complaint.

UK legal aid is not available for petition, but limited legal aid is available from the Council of Europe. ECHR cases are now also among the limited categories of litigation in which English lawyers are now permitted to work on a conditional fee basis.

30.4 KEY DECISIONS OF THE ECHR ON FREEDOM OF ASSOCIATION AND OTHER RELEVANT PROVISIONS

One of the most significant cases concerning UK collective employment law to reach the European Court of Human Rights was the British Rail closed shop case, *Young, James and Webster v United Kingdom* [1981] IRLR 408, [1983] IRLR 35.

Article 11 of the Convention provides:

'1. Everyone has the right to ... freedom of association with others, including the right to form and to join trade unions for the protection of his interests.

2. No restrictions shall be placed on the exercise of these rights ... [certain exceptions permitted].'

In the *Young, James and Webster* case, the court held that the requirement on the applicants to join one of the unions specified in the closed shop agreement between British Rail and the railway unions, in circumstances where there had been no such requirement at the time when they were engaged, amounted to a restriction on the freedom guaranteed by *art 11* because the alternative to their joining was that they would lose their jobs ([1981] IRLR 408 at 409). The court made substantial monetary awards to the applicants.

The decision left the general question of the consistency of closed shop agreements with *art 11* unclear. Now that the right of individuals not to join a specified trade union has been entrenched and the pre-entry closed shop has been outlawed (see TRADE UNIONS – I (48)), it has become less important to resolve that issue. However, in *Sibson v United Kingdom* (1993) 17 EHRR 193, the court held that there was no breach of *art 11* where the complainant had no objection based on conviction to being a member of the union concerned, and where non-membership would not lead to dismissal (but rather to a move to another depot at which he could be required to work under his contract); contrast *Sigurjonsson v Iceland* (1993) 16 EHRR 462.

In a further important decision of collective employment rights (*Wilson and NUJ v United Kingdom; Palmer, Wyeth and RMT v United Kingdom; Doolan v United Kingdom* [2002] IRLR 568) the ECHR ruled that the UK was in breach of the right of freedom of association under *art 11* by permitting employers to use financial incentives to persuade employees to surrender trade union rights (see *s 146(1)(a), TULRCA 1992*). This is the first case in which the ECHR has upheld a claim relating to trade union rights under *art 11*. (For example, in the past, a complaint by workers at GCHQ that they were not permitted to belong to trade unions was not referred to the court by the Commission, which accepted the Government's argument based upon national security.) The *Wilson* decision prompted the introduction of *s 29* of the *Employment Relations Act 2004* which introduces new sections into *TULRCA 1992* conferring a right upon workers not to have an offer made by the employer for the purpose of inducing the worker not to be a member of a union or to take part in the activities of the union.

The corollary of the right to associate is the right to disassociate, which arose for consideration in *Associated Society of Locomotive Engineers and Firemen v United Kingdom (Application No 11002/05)* [2007] IRLR 361, ECtHR. The case involved the expulsion of a trade union member who was a member of the BNP. The Court held that the issue was the balance between the individual's right to associate and the right of the union to disassociate. Article 11 did not place an obligation on the union to admit anyone who wished to join, particularly as an individual's livelihood was not dependent upon membership of a union and collectively bargained benefits would apply to all employees whether union members or not. Accordingly, the expulsion did not breach the ECHR (see, further, 51.18 TRADE UNIONS – II).

Another area of employment law to which the Convention might be relevant is picketing (see STRIKES AND INDUSTRIAL ACTION (45)), given that *arts 10* and *11* protect freedom of expression and assembly (see *Middlebrook Mushrooms Ltd v TGWU* [1993] IRLR 232 at para 25). More recently, in *Unison v United Kingdom* [2002] IRLR 497, the ECHR dismissed an application in relation to an alleged breach of *art 11* rights by the imposition of an injunction restraining a strike which fell outside the definition of a 'trade dispute' (see STRIKES AND INDUS-TRIAL ACTION (45)). The ECHR concluded that a prohibition upon a strike was a restriction on the freedom of association right in *art 11(1)*. The restraint was, however, in compliance with *art 11(2)* as a proportionate measure necessary in a democratic society for the protection of others (in this case, the employer). The point of significance in the case is the recognition that restraint upon the right to strike may, in appropriate circumstances, be a breach of *art 11*.

Article 10 has also been invoked (unsuccessfully) as part of a challenge to the statutory restrictions upon the political activities of certain local government employees (*NALGO v Secretary of State for the Environment* (1992) 5 Admin LR 785 and see 37.2 PUBLIC SECTOR EMPLOYEES). However, in *Vogt v Germany* (1995) 21 EHRR 205, the court held that the dismissal of a teacher employed in a state school on the grounds of membership of the German Communist Party breached *arts 10* and *11* of the Convention.

Article 14 provides that the rights conferred by the Convention are to be exercised without any discrimination on grounds of *inter alia* race or sex (see, e g *Schuler-Zgraggen v Switzerland* (1993) 16 EHRR 405).

In *Halford v United Kingdom* [1997] IRLR 471, *art 8* of the Convention which protects private and family life was successfully invoked by a United Kingdom employee before the European Court of Human Rights. The court held that the applicant, a former Police Assistant Chief Constable, had been subjected to telephone tapping by her employer in an attempt to gather material to be used against her in a sex discrimination claim she was pursuing against her employer. The court in an important judgment held that such recording, without the knowledge of the employee, was a breach of the right to private life and correspondence. The applicant was awarded £10,000 compensation for non-pecuniary loss.

Further, in the important case of *Smith and Grady v United Kingdom* [1999] IRLR 734, the European Court of Human Rights has concluded that a ban on homosexuals in employment contravenes the right to respect for private life (*art 8*). As is well known, the UK armed forces did not permit homosexual men or women to serve. Persons known to be homosexual were the subject of an 'administrative discharge' from the armed services. The applicants brought test cases challenging their discharges by way of judicial review in the UK courts, alleging that the policy banning homosexuals was a breach of the *ECHR* and the *EC Equal Treatment Directive*. The domestic challenges were ultimately unsuccessful. Before the European Court of Human Rights, however, the applicants were successful, the court finding that the investigation into their homosexuality and their subsequent discharge from the armed forces violated *art 8*. The court concluded that such investigations were not 'necessary in a democratic society' (*art 8(2)*). The court further found that there was an infringement of *art 13* in that there was 'no effective remedy' before a national authority in relation to the violation of the right to respect for their private lives. A supplementary alleged violation of *art 3* ('degrading treatment or punishment') was not, however, made out on the facts. The court stated, nevertheless, that treatment on the basis of a bias against a homosexual minority could, in principle, fall within the scope of *art 3* but a minimum level of severity of treatment was required to bring such action within the scope of that article. The court held that it was not necessary to examine an alleged violation of *art 10* (right to freedom of expression) but commented that the silence imposed on the applicants in relation to their sexual orientation could not be ruled out as a potential interference with freedom of expression. In a further case, *Saligueiro da Silva Moula v Portugal* [2001] 1 FCR 653, ECHR, the ECHR found that denial of the right to visit the child by a male homosexual was a breach of *arts 8* and *14*. In *Goodwin v United Kingdom* [2002] IRLR 664, the ECHR held that the UK's failure to give legal recognition to gender reassignment was a breach of *arts 8* and *12* (the right to marry). The decision may have implications for employment in relation, say, to the provision of pensions and certain fringe benefits. *Goodwin* was considered by the House of Lords in *A v Chief Constable of West Yorkshire Police* [2004] UKHL 21, [2004] IRLR 573, a case involving discrimination by the police against a transsexual. The House of Lords held that such discrimination was contrary to the provisions of the *EC Equal Treatment Directive* and, accordingly, recourse was not needed to reliance upon human rights law.

Denial of access to the courts and the rights conferred by *art 6* have also arisen in the employment context before the ECHR. In *Fogarty v United Kingdom* [2002] IRLR 148 an employee of the US Embassy in London had successfully brought a sex discrimination claim. In relation to subsequent victimisation proceedings following non-appointment to other posts, the US claimed immunity under the *State Immunity Act 1978*. The complainant complained of a breach of *art 6(1)* on the grounds of denial of access to the courts. The ECHR held that the claim fell within *art 6(1)* but that sovereign immunity was an aspect of international law and within the margin of appreciation allowed to states to limit access to the courts. In *Devlin v United Kingdom* [2002] IRLR 155 the ECHR held that, in the context of a discrimination claim, the issue by the Secretary of State of a national security certificate blocking proceedings in the tribunal was a disproportionate restriction on the applicant's right of access to the courts and, accordingly, a breach *of art 6(1)*. Damages of £10,000 were awarded. See also *Devenney v United Kingdom* (2002) Times, 11 April where a similar judgment was given by the ECHR and the same sum awarded by way of damages.

In *Somjee v United Kingdom* [2002] IRLR 886 the judicial process in the Employment Tribunal and the Employment Appeal Tribunal was found wanting. At the end of various hearings it had taken eight years for Ms Somjee's discrimination and unfair dismissal complaints to be fully dealt with and more than seven years in the case of her victimisation claim. The ECHR held that a significant proportion of the blame for the delay rested with the Employment Tribunal and the Employment Appeal Tribunal and that such delay constituted a violation of the right to a fair hearing 'within a reasonable time' under *art 6* of the Convention. Ms Somjee was awarded 5,000 euros plus costs.

THE POSITION PRIOR TO THE HUMAN RIGHTS ACT 1998: THE CONVENTION AS AN AID TO INTERPRETATION

30.5   Prior to the coming into force of the *Human Rights Act 1998*, as the Convention was not incorporated in UK law, it could not be relied upon directly in domestic courts and tribunals. However, it was, like other treaties, cited on the basis that Parliament is presumed to have intended to legislate consistently with the UK's international obligations unless the contrary intention appears. But there was no scope for such a presumption to operate where the statutory words were clear. The position was reviewed by the House of Lords in *R v Secretary of State for the Home Department, ex p Brind* [1991] 1 AC 696 and in *Derbyshire County Council v Times Newspapers Ltd* [1993] AC 534.

In a number of cases the UK courts showed a willingness to apply Convention principles as an aid to interpretation of domestic law. By way of example, in *Camelot Group plc v Centaur Communications Ltd* [1998] IRLR 80 the Court of Appeal upheld an order for the delivery up to the plaintiff of confidential information sent to a journalist (employed by the defendant) by an employee of Camelot. The purpose of Camelot seeking the order was to identify their disloyal employee. The Court of Appeal in applying *s 10* of the *Contempt of Court Act 1981* (which gives certain protections to journalists from disclosure of their sources of information) held that the domestic court would give the greatest weight to the judgments of the European Court of Human Rights in cases where the facts are similar to the case before the domestic court, and considered in detail the ECHR's decision in *Goodwin v United Kingdom* (1996) 22 EHRR 123. Under the *Human Rights Act 1998*, the courts are required to adopt such an approach where issues of Convention rights are raised (see 30.6 and 30.7 below). The influence of the decisions of the ECHR on the domestic courts is further illustrated by the decision of the Scottish EAT, in *MacDonald v Ministry of Defence* [2000] IRLR 748. *Macdonald v Ministry of Defence* is now reported at [2002] ICR 174 (Court of Sessions). In that case the EAT relied upon *Smith and Grady* and *Saligueiro* (see 30.4 above) to reach the conclusion that discrimination on grounds of sexual orientation is discrimination on grounds of sex for the purposes of the *SDA*. In *obiter dicta*, the EAT stated that it was not clear if the *Human Rights Act 1998* applied only to discriminatory acts committed after commencement on 2 October 2000 or whether it also applied to proceedings pending in relation to discriminatory acts before that date.

It is also material to note that the jurisprudence of the European Court of Justice, applying EUROPEAN COMMUNITY LAW (25) (which *is* part of English law), is heavily influenced by the Convention (see e g *R v Kirk*: 63/83 [1984] 3 CMLR 522). See also *Grant v South-West Trains Ltd: C-249/96* [1998] IRLR 206, ECJ, a case on discrimination against homosexual persons brought under *art 141* (formerly *art 119*) of the EC Treaty in which the ECJ considered some of the jurisprudence on, and relevant articles of, the European Convention on Human Rights.

30.6   HUMAN RIGHTS ACT 1998

The *Human Rights Act 1998* (which received the Royal Assent on 9 November 1998) came into force on 2 October 2000 and is a radical reform of the status of the Convention in domestic law. The *Act* requires that the courts interpret United Kingdom law in accordance with the Convention. *Section 1* of the *HRA 1998* lists those articles of the Convention to which the *Act* is to apply and those articles are set out as *Sch 1* to the *Act*. By *HRA 1998, s 2* a court or tribunal determining a question in connection with a Convention right must take into account relevant judgments, decisions, declarations and opinions made or given by the Commission and Court of Human Rights and the Committee of Ministers of the Council of Europe. Primary and subordinate legislation are to be read, wherever possible, as being compatible with Convention rights but are not rendered void if incompatible (*HRA 1998, s 3*). Certain courts will be given the power to make a declaration of incompatibility when satisfied that the provision of primary legislation is incompatible with a Convention right (*HRA 1998, s 4*). This power does not, however, extend to an employment tribunal or the EAT. Accordingly, a detailed consideration of the *Act* is beyond the scope of this work.

The effect of the *Act*, as more cases are brought in domestic law relying upon Convention rights, is likely to be considerable in many fields; not least employment law, where *art 6* (the right to a fair hearing), *art 8* (the right to respect for private and family life), and also *arts 10, 11* and *14* (considered in 25.4 above) are likely to be of the greatest importance. The *Act* makes it unlawful for a 'public authority' to act in contravention of the Convention (*HRA 1998, s 6*). Those aggrieved will be able to bring proceedings against the authority in question (*HRA 1998, s 7*). The definition of 'public authority' is broad and includes any body whose function is of a public nature (*HRA 1998, s 6(3)*) and includes, expressly, courts and tribunals. The definition would appear to be sufficiently broad to apply to, for example, privatised public utilities.

The *Act* provides for remedies including an award of damages analogous to the principles applied by the European Court of Human Rights in relation to compensation (*HRA 1998, s 8*). Ministers of the Crown are given the power to amend offending legislation following a declaration of incompatibility (*HRA 1998, s 10*). Finally, in relation to any new legislation, a Minister of the Crown is required in either House prior to the second reading of the Bill to make a statement that the provisions of the Bill are compatible with the Convention rights or to state that, despite incompatibility, the Government wishes the House to proceed with the Bill in any event (*HRA 1998, s 19*).

30.7   THE APPLICATION OF THE HUMAN RIGHTS ACT 1998 IN EMPLOYMENT CASES

A number of cases have arisen in employment law raising issues under the *Human Rights Act 1998* particularly in relation to the right to a fair hearing (*art 6*) and the right to private and family life (*art 8*). The paragraphs below provide illustrations. As a point of procedure, it is to be observed that recently the Court of Appeal has sought to discourage a perceived tendency for Employment Tribunals to treat EC and human rights issues as appropriate for determination as preliminary issues (see *Barracks v Coles (Secretary of State for the Home Department intervening)* [2006] EWCA Civ 1041, [2007] ICR 60). In the light of this, it is likely that such arguments will have to be raised as part of the full hearing of the claim rather than at a preliminary point.

(a) Article 6

A-G v Wheen [2001] IRLR 91 concerned *s 33* of the *Employment Tribunals Act 1996* which permitted the Attorney General to make a restriction of proceedings order against a litigant barring him from bringing further proceedings without the leave of the EAT on the grounds of vexatious institution of proceedings. The Court of Appeal held that *s 33* did not conflict with the right to a fair hearing under *art 6(1)* of the *Convention*. The Court of Appeal stated that the right under *art 6(1)* was not an absolute right but was to be balanced between the rights of the citizen to use the courts and the rights of others (and the court) to avoid wholly unmeritorious claims. Further, the order made *did* provide for access to the Employment Tribunal system but required permission first. As access was not prohibited, but was provided on terms, there could be no breach of *art 6(1)*.

In *Tehrani v United Kingdom Central Council for Nursery, Midwifery and Health Visiting* [2001] IRLR 208, the issue was to what extent *art 6* of the *Convention* (namely, the entitlement 'to a fair and reasonable public hearing within a reasonable time by an independent and impartial tribunal established by law') applied to disciplinary proceedings other than in a court of law. Whilst *art 6* may not apply to purely internal disciplinary inquiries, it was held in *Tehrani* that, when disciplinary proceedings determine the right to practice a profession, *art 6* may apply, as the decision of the Council's Professional Conduct Committee fell within a 'determination' of 'civil rights and obligations' for the purposes of *art 6*. It followed that there was an entitlement to a hearing before an independent and impartial tribunal. However, the Court of Session held that a professional disciplinary tribunal was not required to meet all the requirements of an independent and impartial tribunal if the disciplinary procedures provided for a right of appeal to a court of law. The Court of Session, following a review of relevant authorities, concluded that the case law of the ECHR established that there was no breach of the Convention if the disciplinary tribunal is subject to the control of a court of full jurisdiction, which court complies with the requirements of *art 6(1)*. This case raises important questions in relation to professional disciplinary bodies which do not have a statutory right of appeal to a court. If the disciplinary body is not sufficiently independent or important to satisfy *art 6(1)*, it is not clear whether a right to present subsequent complaints in an Employment Tribunal will be sufficiently akin to a statutory right of appeal to satisfy the exception recognised in the jurisprudence of the ECHR.

As to the Employment Tribunal system itself and *art 6(1)*, it had been suggested in *Smith v Secretary of State for Trade and Industry* [2000] IRLR 6 that the Employment Tribunals may not be independent when determining matters on redundancy payments from the DTI as the DTI appointed lay members of the tribunals. The case was not appealed. In *Scanfuture UK Ltd v Secretary of State for Trade and Industry* [2001] IRLR 416, the EAT revisited the question of whether the mechanism of appointment of lay members to the Employment Tribunal breached *art 6(1)* of the *Convention*. It is significant to note that the procedures for the appointment of lay members have changed since the procedures which were in place in 1999 (the time of the Employment Tribunal decision in *Scanfuture*). The EAT found that the new procedures complied with the

ECHR. As to the position in 1999, the EAT concluded that the procedures for the appointment of lay members breached *art 6(1)* of the *Convention*. The application of *art 6* has also led to successful appeals against decisions of the employment tribunal which have been issued after a lengthy period of delay. See also the consideration of *art 6* in the context of allegations of bias in relation to an employment tribunal in *Jones v DAS Legal Expenses Insurance Co Ltd* [2003] EWCA Civ 1071, [2004] IRLR 218. In *Kwamin v Abbey National plc* [2004] IRLR 516 the EAT emphasised that it is a fundamental principle of natural justice that a fair trial includes the absence of excessive or avoidable delay by the tribunal and that the same principle is enshrined in the right to a fair trail within a reasonable period in *art 6*. In *Kwamin* the decisions under appeal had been delivered 7.5, 12 and 14.5 months after the end of the hearings respectively. The EAT gave guidance that, whilst it remained for an appellant to show that the result was unfair as a consequence of delay, employment tribunal decisions must be delivered within 3.5 months (after which there would, in the view of the EAT be 'culpable delay'). The issue of whether *arts 6* and *8* may require certain tribunal hearings to be conducted in private (beyond the categories of cases for which statutory provision for the tribunal sitting in private is already made) has been raised in *XXX v YYY*. The EAT had held that *arts 6* and *8* required the tribunal to sit in private. On appeal (*XXX v YYY* [2004] EWCA Civ 231, [2004] IRLR 471) the Court of Appeal reached its decision on different grounds relating to relevance of the evidence in issue. Accordingly the *art 6* and *8* points on the need for a tribunal to sit in private (outside the existing categories of claims) remain undecided at Court of Appeal level.

In *R v Securities and Futures Authority, ex p Fleurose* [2002] IRLR 297, the Court of Appeal held, in relation to disciplinary proceedings of the SFA (which could result in a fine and/or suspension), that such proceedings were not a criminal charge or offence for the purposes of *art 6* of the Convention. Nevertheless, the SFA were required to prove the allegations, to permit the accused to prepare a defence in the knowledge of the 'charges' and to allow a proper opportunity to give evidence and call evidence and to question witnesses giving evidence in support of the allegations.

In *Dispatch Management Services (UK) Ltd v Douglas* [2002] IRLR 389, the EAT considered the situation where an application was made to remove representatives in Employment Tribunal proceedings on the grounds of conflict of interest. The Court of Appeal in *Bache v Essex County Council* [2000] IRLR 251 had held that there was no power in an Employment Tribunal to interfere with a party's choice of representative. In *Douglas*, the EAT held that this principle of non-interference was not inconsistent with the right to a fair hearing under *art 6* of the Convention.

In *Whittaker v P & D Watson (t/a P and M Watson Haulage)* [2002] ICR 1244 the EAT confirmed that it was not a 'court' for the purposes of hearing a submission that domestic legislation was incompatible with Convention rights. Referring to the definition of 'court' in *s 4(5)* of the *Human Rights Act 1998*, the EAT held that the conclusion was clear but puzzling (not least when the EAT was composed of a High Court judge sitting with lay members) and was, perhaps, a result which had not been intended in the drafting of the legislation.

On the issue of adjournment of hearings, the Court of Appeal held in *Teinez v Wandsworth London Borough Council* [2004] EWCA Civ 1040, [2002] IRLR 721 that, in order to comply with the right to a fair trial under *art 6*, a litigant whose presence is needed for the fair trial of a case and who is unable to attend through no fault of his own will usually have to be granted an adjournment regardless of the inconvenience of such adjournment to the court or other parties (see also *Andreou v Lord Chancellor's Department* [2002] EWCA Civ 1192, [2002] IRLR 728).

The practice of part-time EAT judges appearing as counsel before lay members of the EAT with whom they had previously sat in a judicial capacity and the compatibility of that practice with *art 6* reached the House of Lords in *Lawal v Northern Spirit Ltd* [2003] UKHL 35, [2003] IRLR 538. Overturning the decision of the Court of Appeal (which had upheld the decision of the EAT), the House of Lords held that such a practice tended to undermine confidence in the judicial system and ought to be discontinued. In determining whether there is bias in terms of the right to a hearing before an impartial tribunal under *art 6(1)* or the common law test of bias, the principle to be applied was that stated by the House of Lords in *Porter v Magill* [2001] UKHL 67, [2002] 2 AC 357 namely whether a fair minded and informed observer, having considered the given facts, would conclude that there was a real possibility that the tribunal was biased. The key to this test is public perception of the possibility of unconscious bias.

The principle that illegal contracts will not be enforced by the Courts was the subject of an *art 6* challenge in *Souteriou v Ultrachem Ltd* [2004] EWHC 983 (QB), [2004] IRLR 870. A claim of wrongful dismissal was struck out by reason of illegality. The Claimant contended that this contravened the right to a fair hearing and also that the strike out was contrary to *art 1* of the *First Protocol* to the *Convention*. These arguments were rejected. The Court held that art 6 was not breached as the issue of illegality was part of the substantive law of contract and not a mere procedural bar and that, in any event, the strike out would have been legitimate under *art 6(2)*. As to the claim based upon the *First Protocol* right (in relation to 'possessions'), it was held that, although a claim of breach of contract could indeed be a 'possession', there was no deprivation of a possession here as the contract was unenforceable (on the grounds of illegality) and therefore conferred no 'possession' which the claimant could complain that he was deprived and that the claimant had had his case considered substantively as part of the strike out application.

(b) Article 8

In relation to the right to private life, in the context of employment litigation, this right must be balanced with the right of the parties to have a fair trial of the issues between them. In *De Keyser Ltd v Wilson* [2001] IRLR 324, the EAT considered the *art 8* right to respect for private and family life in the context of an unfair dismissal claim in which the applicant alleged she suffered from a depressive illness caused by stress at work. In the course of the proceedings, the applicant agreed to be seen by the employer's medical expert and a letter of instruction was drafted on behalf of the employer to the expert which letter included certain details of the applicant's private life. The employment tribunal struck out the employer's notice of appearance on the basis that the employer's conduct of the proceedings was scandalous and in breach of the applicant's Convention right to privacy. Allowing the employer's appeal, the EAT held that there was no breach of *art 8* and that in relation to the need, in the context of the case, for a medical examination, the right to privacy was qualified as far as necessary by the right of both parties to have a just trial of the issues between them. In judicial review proceedings, the provisions of the *Employment Equality (Sexual Orientation) Regulations 2003* were found to be compatible with the convention rights in *art 8* and *art 14* (see *R (on the application of Amicus –MSF section v Secretary of State for Trade and Industry* [2004] EWHC 860 (Admin), [2004] IRLR 430).

In *Whitefield v General Medical Council* [2002] UKPC 62, [2003] IRLR 39 the Privy Council considered the extent to which *art 8* was engaged in circumstances where the respondent, the General Medical Council, made it a condition of the applicant's continued practice as a doctor that he 'abstain absolutely from the consumption of alcohol'. The Privy Council held that the condition was not a breach of *art 8(1)* and in any event would, in the circumstances, have been justified under *art 8(2)*.

The provisions of the Human Rights Act are only directly applicable against public authorities. However, in the context of proceedings before the employment tribunal, Convention rights (and in particular the rights contained in *art 8*) may nonetheless be relevant in proceedings before the employment tribunal even where the employer is in the private sector. This is illustrated by the decision of the Court of Appeal in *X v Y* [2004] EWCA Civ 662, [2004] IRLR 625. The case concerned a dismissal by the employer for the employee's failure to disclose a caution. The employee contended that the dismissal was unfair as breaching the Convention right to respect for family life. While the claim failed on the facts, the Court of Appeal accepted that, if a dismissal was on grounds of an employee's private conduct within *art 8*, and was an interference with the right to respect for private life, that fact would be relevant to the determination of a claim of unfair dismissal whether the employer was a public authority or not. This is because the employment tribunal must, under *s 3* of the *Human Rights Act* read and give effect to relevant legislation (in this case the general provisions as to fairness of dismissal in *s 98* of the *ERA*) in a way which is compatible with Convention Rights such as *art 8*. In such circumstances there is no basis to treat a public employer differently from a private employer. Accordingly, say the Court of Appeal, it would not normally be fair to dismiss an employee for a reason which was an unjustified interference with the employee's private life. For a consideration of the role of *art 8* in relation to the fairness of the dismissal of a employee employed by a public sector employer see *Pay v Lancashire Probation Service* [2004] IRLR 129, EAT where the EAT held that a tribunal should effect consideration of Convention rights in the context of the fairness or otherwise of a dismissal by interpreting the words 'reasonably or unreasonably' in *s 98(4)* of the *ERA* as including the words 'having regard to the applicant's Convention rights'. Accordingly, in assessing the fairness in all the circumstances, consideration must be given to whether there had been an interference with the applicant's Convention rights and also any matters advanced by the employer as justification for such an interference. On the facts of *Pay*, the applicant was unsuccessful in establishing that the *art 8* right to private life was engaged and, in relation to the *art 10* right of freedom of expression, the interference in issue was found to be justified in the circumstances. Notwithstanding the outcomes on the facts of both *X v Y* and *Pay*, the cases provide important indications of the likely relevance of Convention rights to the issue of the substantive fairness of dismissals both in the private and public sector.

Issues of surveillance of employees arose in *McGowan v Scottish Water* [2005] IRLR 167, EAT. The employee, suspected of falsely claiming on time sheets, was put under surveillance by private investigators engaged by the employer. The employee was dismissed in the light of evidence obtained on the surveillance. In an unfair dismissal claim the employee alleged the surveillance was a breach of *art 8*. This was rejected by the Scottish EAT on the facts of the case. The EAT held that *art 8* was indeed engaged in circumstances of covert surveillance but the central issue was that of proportionality. In the circumstances of suspected serious fraud, the surveillance was undertaken for legitimate reasons and was held to be proportionate. The case is significant in illustrating that, where employers do engage in covert surveillance of employees by whatever means, *art 8* is engaged and a 'strong presumption' (per Lord Johnston) of invasion of the right to family life will arise. Accordingly, it will be of central importance for an employer to be able to show that the interference arising was for a legitimate purpose and also 'proportionate' in all the circumstances which will involve consideration of the seriousness or gravity of the issue which prompted the surveillance and the extent of the surveillance exercise undertaken. The admissibility of covert recordings of a disciplinary hearing was considered in *Chairman and Governors of Amwell View School v Dogherty* [2007] IRLR 198. On the facts the EAT held that an employment tribunal had not, in allowing some of the covert recordings to be admitted in evidence, breached the school's governors' *art 8* rights. Recording of the private deliberations of the panel were, however, excluded on public policy grounds.

Closely related to the right to family and private life is the right to peaceful enjoyment of possessions. In *Nerva v United Kingdom* [2002] IRLR 815 the ECHR held that the decision of the UK High Court and the Court of Appeal that tips included in cheque and credit card payments were the property of the employer and could be used by them to discharge their statutory obligations to pay the applicant waiters a minimum level of remuneration did not amount to a breach of the applicants' rights under *art 1* of the *First Protocol to the Convention* to the peaceful enjoyment of their possessions (see 34.21 PAY – I). See also *Legal & General Assurance Ltd v Kirk* [2001] EWCA Civ 1803, [2002] IRLR 124 in which the Court of Appeal held that a right to seek a particular employment cannot constitute a possession for the purposes of *art 1* of the *First Protocol to the Convention*. In *R (Malik) v Waltham Forest Primary Care Trust* [2006] IRLR 526, however, in a judicial review application which related to the unlawful suspension of a general practitioner by the relevant Primary Care Trust, it was held that the right to practice a profession can be regarded as a 'possession' for the purposes of *art 1* of the *First Protocol* and hence the suspension an interference with the right of peaceful enjoyment.

(c) Other Convention rights in the employment context

Article 9 protects freedom of thought, conscience and religion and the right to manifest religion or belief in worship, teaching, practice and observance. Its application to the requirement of Sunday working was considered in *Copsey v WWB Devon Clays Ltd* [2005] EWCA Civ 932, [2005] IRLR 811. In that case a change in shift pattern giving rise to an obligation to work on a Sunday led to the dismissal of the claimant for whom Sunday working was incompatible with his religious beliefs. The claimant brought a claim for unfair dismissal and alleged a breach of *art 9*. His claim was dismissed by the employment tribunal. On appeal to the Court of Appeal the decision of the Tribunal was upheld. Mummery LJ held that *art 9* was not in any event engaged as the employee was not compelled to work on a Sunday – he could always leave and get alternative employment (*Stedman v UK* [1997] 23 EHHR CD 168 applied). Rix and Neuberger LJJ held that *art 9* might be engaged but, applying the test of reasonableness and *s 98(4)* of the *ERA*, reasonable steps had been taken to accommodate the employee and accordingly the employment tribunal had not erred in reaching the decision which it did. This approach to human rights issues being engaged at the level of the general fairness of a dismissal under *s 98(4)* of the *ERA* is consistent with the approach adopted in relation to *art 8* in *Pay v Lancashire Probation Service* [2004] IRLR 129 and in *X v Y* [2004] EWCA Civ 662, [2004] IRLR 625 (see 30.7(b) above).

Articles 10 and *11* on freedom of expression and association respectively were engaged in *Gate Gourmet London Ltd v Transport and General Workers Union* [2005] EWHC 1889 (QB), [2005] IRLR 881. This case involved applications for injunctions restraining picketing at Heathrow Airport. Fulford J held that in deciding whether to grant such an injunction appropriate weight must be given to the 'right to picket' (as a consequence of the a*rt 10* and a*rt 11* rights). On the facts of the case an order was granted limiting the number of pickets but the decision is significant in its express recognition in the domestic courts of effectively the right to picket in relation to an employment dispute (see also *Unison v United Kingdom* [2002] IRLR 497 above at 30.4). *Redfearn v Serco Ltd (t/a) West Yorkshire Transport Service)* [2006] EWCA Civ 659, [2006] IRLR 623 involved the dismissal of an employee because of him standing as a candidate for the British National Party. The claim was brought under the *Race Relations Act 1976* (the claimant having insufficient continuous employment to bring an unfair dismissal claim) raising claims of direct and indirect discrimination which were both rejected. Issues of freedom of expression were raised under the *Human Rights Act* relying upon a*rt 10* but these were rejected on the basis of applying *art 17* of the Convention which provides that nothing in the Convention gives a right to engage in activities which themselves are aimed at destroying Convention rights and freedoms.

30.8 OTHER INTERNATIONAL OBLIGATIONS RELEVANT TO HUMAN RIGHTS

The Council of Europe has also promulgated, and the United Kingdom has ratified, the *European Social Charter*, which contains provisions relating to, for example, annual holidays and the right to strike. This should not be confused with the Social Charter and the Social Chapter to the Maastricht Treaty agreed by the EC (see 25.3 EUROPEAN COMMUNITY LAW). There is an Additional Protocol which has not been signed by the UK.

The International Labour Organisation ('ILO') is a specialist body of the United Nations. It has issued a number of conventions, some of which have been ratified by the United Kingdom. They deal with matters such as health and safety, freedom of association and racial discrimination. UK law has been held by the ILO to infringe these conventions in a number of respects. However, there is no remedy for any such breaches in English courts or tribunals.

31   Insolvency of Employer

31.1   In the event of insolvency, an employer is likely to have limited funds which are insufficient to pay all its debts. These debts may include sums due to employees, for example payment of wages. Some statutory protection is afforded to employees in this situation.

First, under the *Insolvency Act 1986*, employees' rights to payment of certain sums due to them from their employer take precedence over payment of debts to other creditors. Second, under the *ERA 1996* (which in part implements the *EC Directive on Insolvency Protection 80/987* as amended by *EC Directive 2002/74/EC*), the Secretary of State offers a limited guarantee to pay certain sums due to employees from their employers, and to make up unpaid employer pension contributions, out of the National Insurance Fund. Third, statutory maternity, paternity, adoption and sick payments may be claimed from HM Revenue and Customs. Fourth, under the *Pensions Act 2004*, compensation for loss of pension entitlements following insolvency of an employer may be payable from the Pension Protection Fund. Finally, in certain circumstances, an administrative receiver of a company may take on liability under an employee's contract of employment.

A detailed analysis of the law of insolvency is beyond the scope of this book. See *Tolley's Company Law* for a detailed treatment of corporate insolvency. A brief outline of the provisions affecting employees is set out below. Government guidance on this topic is set out in the Insolvency Service booklets 'Redundancy and Insolvency: A Guide for Employees' (2006) and 'Redundancy and Insolvency – A Guide for Insolvency Practitioners to Employees' Rights on the Insolvency of their Employer' (2005).

31.2   **CLAIMS GIVEN PRECEDENCE BY THE INSOLVENCY ACT 1986**

Under the *Insolvency Act 1986, s 386* and *Sch 6* any claim to remuneration payable to an employee, in respect of the four-month period immediately preceding the insolvency of the employer, is treated as a preferential debt and given precedence over other creditors' claims. 'Remuneration' is defined to include:

(*a*)   wages or salary (including commission);

(*b*)   a guarantee payment under *Part III, ERA 1996* (see PAY– I (34));

(*c*)   a payment for time off work under *ERA 1996, ss 53* (time off to look for work or training in the event of redundancy), and *56* (time off for ante-natal care) or *TULRCA 1992, s 169* (time off for trade union activities) (see generally TIME OFF WORK (49));

(*d*)   a payment on medical suspension or on maternity grounds under *Part VII* of *ERA 1996* (see MATERNITY AND PARENTAL RIGHTS (33) and PAY – I (34));

(*e*)   a protective award made under *s 189* of *TULR(C)A 1992* (see REDUNDANCY – II (39));

(*f*)   accrued holiday pay (see HOLIDAYS (30)); and

(*g*) remuneration payable in respect of a period of holiday or absence from work through sickness or good cause.

(*Insolvency Act 1986, Sch 6, paras 9–15.*)

The maximum total sum which may be treated as a preferential debt under *s 386* is £800 (save that remuneration for accrued holiday pay under *para 10* of *Sch 6* is not subject to this cap) (*Insolvency Proceedings (Monetary Limits) Order 1986 (SI 1986/1996), art 4*). If the employers' assets are insufficient to pay claims for remuneration, each individual claim ranks equally and is to be paid in equal proportions to other such claims.

The test whether an employee is an employee for the purposes of *s 386* and *Sch 6* falls to be determined by whether the employee has a contract for services or a contract of employment: see *Eaton v Robert Eaton Ltd* [1988] ICR 302 and EMPLOYEE, SELF-EMPLOYED OR WORKER? (17).

An employee may have other contractual or statutory claims against his employer which are not treated as preferential debts under *s 386* and *Sch 6* (including any claim for sums in excess of £800 which are owed as remuneration, etc). Such claims must be proved in the normal way under the *Insolvency Rules 1986 (SI 1986/1925)* as amended.

31.3 PAYMENTS OUT OF THE NATIONAL INSURANCE FUND: EMPLOYMENT RIGHTS ACT 1996

Where their employer is insolvent employees may claim redundancy payments from the Secretary of State for Trade and Industry under *ERA 1996, Part XI* and certain other debts owed to employees under *ERA 1996, Part XII*. Payments are made by the Redundancy Payments Office from the National Insurance Fund on behalf of the Secretary of State. The statutory provisions, in part, implement the *Insolvency Protection Directive* (as amended by *EC Directive 2002/74/EC*). Under the *Directive* where an employer has its registered office in one member state but also employs workers in another member state, it is the guarantee institution of the member state in which the employee is employed which must pay out in the event of an insolvency (*Everson and Barrass v Secretary of State for Trade and Industry and Bell Lines Ltd: C-198/98* [2000] IRLR 202, ECJ).

Any debts which fall outside the scope of these statutory provisions (or any excess above the statutory maximum payable) may be claimed by the employee as a creditor against his employer's insolvency.

31.4 Redundancy payments

Where an employer is insolvent, and has failed to pay in whole or in part:

(*a*) a statutory redundancy payment;

(*b*) a payment under a formal compromise agreement made in respect of a claim to a statutory redundancy payment; or

(*c*) a redundancy payment under a collective agreement approved under the collective contracting out provisions (*ERA 1996, s 157*),

to which an employee is entitled, the employee may apply to the Redundancy Payments Office for payment (*ERA 1996, ss 166–167*).

'Insolvency' for these purposes is defined in *ERA 1996, s 166(5)* to (*8*). *Section 166(6)* defines insolvency where the employer is an individual. Where the employer is a partnership, the test as to whether or not the employer is insolvent will only be satisfied if every partner has been adjudged bankrupt (*Secretary of State for Trade and Industry v Forde* [1997] ICR 231). Where the employer is a company, insolvency is defined in *s 166(7)* and *s 166(8)* applies where the employer is a limited liability partnership. In each case, the employee seeking payment out of the National Insurance Fund must show that the employer falls within the relevant definitions of insolvency. If he fails to do so, there is no discretion to make a payment and the employee will not be entitled to payment (*Secretary of State for Trade and Industry v Walden* [2000] IRLR 168). The same definitions of insolvency are used to determine whether the Secretary of State is obliged to make a payment under *ERA 1996, Part XII*: see **31.5** below.

An individual who is a controlling shareholder of the company he works for may be an employee of that company for the purposes of obtaining a redundancy payment from the Secretary of State: see *Secretary of State for Trade and Industry v Bottrill* [1999] IRLR 326, in which the Court of Appeal disapproved the earlier decision of the EAT in *Buchan v Secretary of State for Employment* [1997] IRLR 80; see also *Smith v Secretary of State for Trade and Industry* [2000] ICR 69, [2000] IRLR 6 and *Sellers Arenascene Ltd v Connolly (No 2)* [2001] ICR 760; [2001] IRLR 222 and *Gladwell v Secretary of State for Trade and Industry* [2007] ICR 264.

There is no express time limit for making an application to the Secretary of State for a redundancy payment, but if the employee is out of time to claim the payment from his employer (see *ERA 1996, s 164*), he may not claim it from the Secretary of State (*Crawford v Secretary of State for Employment* [1995] IRLR 523).

Where an employee applies for a payment under *s 166*, the amount payable is determined in accordance with *s 168*. This will normally be the amount of a statutory redundancy payment. However, where there is a compromise agreement or collective agreement under *s 157* in relation to the redundancy payment, the Secretary of State will pay out whichever is the less of a statutory redundancy payment or the amount payable under the compromise agreement/ collective agreement.

The Secretary of State, where an employee applies for a payment under s 166, has the power to request in writing that the employer provide information and documents to allow the Secretary of State to decide whether the application is well founded. Failure to comply with such a request without reasonable excuse is a criminal offence (*ERA 1996, s 169*). In addition, in cases where the Secretary of State makes a payment, he will assume the rights of the employee as against the employer, and any monies recovered from the employer pursuant to this right are paid into the National Insurance Fund (*ERA 1996, s 167(3)* and *(4)*).

Disputes relating to payments by the Redundancy Payments Office are to be referred to the employment tribunal under *ERA 1996, s 170*. The employee may refer a dispute to a tribunal without joining his employer as a party to the proceedings (*Jones v Secretary of State for Employment* [1982] ICR 389). However, the EAT has suggested that it may be proper on such occasions to join the company in liquidation for the purposes of discovery (*Bradley v Secretary of State for Employment* [1989] ICR 69).

31.5   **Other guaranteed debts: arrears of pay, notice and holiday pay etc**

If, on an application made to him in writing by an employee, the Secretary of State is satisfied:

(*a*)   that the employer of that employee has become insolvent;

(*b*)   that the employment of the employee has been terminated; and

(*c*)   that on the appropriate date the employee was entitled to be paid the whole or part of any debt set out in (i) to (v) below,

the Secretary of State must pay him his entitlement out of the National Insurance Fund (*ERA 1996, s 182*).'Insolvency' for these purposes is defined in *ERA 1996, s 183* in the same terms as the definition in *s 166* relating to the Secretary of State's obligation to pay redundancy payments in the event of an employer's insolvency: see **31.4** above.

This right applies to the following debts:

(i)   any arrears of pay in respect of one or more (but not more than eight) weeks; arrears of pay are deemed to include the following statutory payments: a guarantee payment under *Part III, ERA 1996* (however, this will not include contractual guarantee payments in excess of the statutory scheme: *Benson v Secretary of State for Trade and Industry* [2003] ICR 1082, [2003] IRLR 748, EAT), any payment for time off for trade union duties, remuneration for suspension on medical or maternity grounds, and remuneration under a protective award (*ERA 1996, s 184(2)*));

(ii)   any amount which the employer is liable to pay the employee for the statutory minimum period of notice under *ERA 1996, s 86*, or for any failure of the employer to give the period of notice required;

(iii)   any holiday pay due for a period or periods of holiday not exceeding six weeks in all, both for holidays already taken and holiday entitlement accrued but not taken, and to which the employee became entitled during the 12 months ending with the appropriate date;

(iv)   any basic award of compensation for unfair dismissal (see 55.7 UNFAIR DISMISSAL – III);

(v)   any reasonable sum by way of reimbursement of the whole or any part of any fee or premiums paid by an apprentice or articled clerk.

(*ERA 1996, s 184(1)*.)

'Appropriate date' in relation to arrears of pay and holiday pay means the date on which the employer becomes insolvent. An employee may therefore only claim unpaid wages and holiday pay which accrued before the insolvency of his employer. In relation to a protective award and to a basic award of compensation for unfair dismissal, the appropriate date is the latest of:

(1)   the date on which the employer became insolvent;

(2)   the date of the termination of the employee's employment; and

(3)   the date on which the award was made.

In relation to any other debt, the appropriate date is the later of the dates mentioned in (1) and (2) above (*ERA 1996, s 185*).

The total amount payable to an employee in respect of any debt referred to above, where that debt is calculated according to a period of time, may not exceed £310 for any one week (or proportionately less for a period less than one week) (*ERA 1996, s 186* as amended by *SI 2006/3045* with effect from 1 February 2006; where the appropriate date falls between 1 February 2006 and 31 January 2007 the maximum weekly sum will be £290). The House of Lords have held that this cap is not contrary to *EC Directive 87/164*. Assessment of the amount due to the employee for arrears of pay and holiday should be made on the basis of salary net of tax and National Insurance contributions. When applying the statutory cap, tax and National Insurance contributions should be deducted from the sum payable *after* it has been capped, rather than deducting them from the total sum owing to the employee and then applying the cap (*Morris v Secretary of State for Employment* [1985] ICR 522, [1985] IRLR 297, EAT, followed in *Titchener v Secretary of State for Trade and Industry* [2002] ICR 225, [2002] IRLR 195, EAT).

The eight-week limit in respect of which an employee may claim arrears of pay under *s 184(1)(a)* is a permitted derogation to the *EC Directive* and, as a derogation, it must be interpreted restrictively, so as to afford maximum benefit to the employee. Accordingly, it must be construed as permitting an employee to choose the eight weeks in respect of which his claim is most valuable: see *Mann v Secretary of State for Employment* [1999] IRLR 566, HL and *Regeling v Bestuur van de Bedrijfsvereniging voor de Metaalnijverheid: C-125/97* [1999] IRLR 379, ECJ (a case on the meaning of the *EC Directive* which *ERA 1996, s 182* partly implements). See further *Mau v Bundesanstaltfur Arbeit: C160/01* [2004] 1 CMLR 34.

Where an employee claims notice pay under *s 184(1)*, the amount he may recover depends on whether he worked out his notice or was unlawfully dismissed without notice. In the former case, he may recover his arrears of pay from the Secretary of State as a liquidated sum. In the latter case, he is subject to the normal rules on mitigating his loss. Thus, the Secretary of State may in those circumstances, in assessing the amount he is liable to pay, take into account any earnings of the employee during the notice period, or, where the employee has failed to mitigate his loss properly, any earnings he should have received (*Secretary of State for Employment v Cooper* [1987] ICR 766, EAT; *Secretary of State for Employment v Stewart* [1996] IRLR 334, EAT). He may also deduct from the amount payable the amount of state benefits the employee has received during the notice period, which he would not have received but for his dismissal (see *Westwood v Secretary of State for Employment* [1985] ICR 209, HL).

The liability of the Secretary of State to make payments under *s 182* cannot exceed that of the insolvent employer. Thus, where the insolvent employer would be entitled to set-off against the debt owed by him to the employee sums owed by the employee to him, the Secretary of State is entitled to deduct from the amount he pays the employee the amount of the employer's set-off (see *Secretary of State for Employment v Wilson* [1997] ICR 408, [1996] IRLR 330, EAT).

Where an insolvency practitioner such as a trustee in bankruptcy, liquidator, administrator or receiver has been (or is required by law to be) appointed, the Secretary of State will not normally make any payment from the National Insurance Fund until the insolvency practitioner sends the Secretary of State a statement of what is due to the employee. The Secretary of State may, however, at his discretion, satisfy himself that the employee's claim is valid and that he does not need a statement before paying the claim (*ERA 1996, s 187*). Once payment has been made to the employee by the Secretary of State, the employee's rights to claim the debt against his employer are transferred to the Secretary of State. In addition, any sums payable as the result of a subsequent decision of an employment tribunal requiring an employer to pay the debt to the employee must be paid to the Secretary of State (*ERA 1996, s 189*). Following an application under *s 183*, the Secretary of State has the power to request in writing that the employer provide information and documents to allow the Secretary of State to decide whether the application is well founded. Failure to comply with such a request without reasonable excuse is a criminal offence (*ERA 1996, s 190*).

31.6   Remedy under ERA 1996 Part XII

A person who has applied for payment of other guaranteed debts may, within the period of three months beginning with the date on which the decision of the Secretary of State on that application was communicated to him (or if that is not reasonably practicable, within such further period as is considered reasonable), present a complaint to an employment tribunal that:

(*a*)   the Secretary of State has failed to make any such payment; or

(*b*)   any such payment by him is less than the amount which should have been paid.

(*ERA 1996, s 188.*)

If the employment tribunal finds the complaint well-founded, it will make a declaration to that effect and state the amount due from the Secretary of State. See *Secretary of State for Employment v Reeves* [1993] ICR 508 for the law relating to interest upon the tribunal's award in such a case (for interest generally, see 20.33 EMPLOYMENT TRIBUNALS – I).

31.7   Unpaid contributions to occupational pension schemes

The Secretary of State may make payments out of the National Insurance Fund into an occupational pension scheme if he is satisfied that an employer has become insolvent and that, at the time he became insolvent, there remained unpaid relevant contributions falling to be paid by him to the scheme. Application for payment is to be made by the person competent to act in respect of the pension scheme (*Pension Schemes Act 1993 ('PSA 1993'), s 124(1)*). 'Relevant contributions' are defined as contributions to be paid by the employer on his own behalf or on behalf of an employee from whose pay a deduction has been made for that purpose (*PSA 1993, s 124(2) and 124(6)*).

The amount payable in respect of contributions of an employer on his own behalf is the least of the following:

(*a*)   the balance of relevant contributions remaining unpaid on the date when the employer became insolvent and payable by the employer on his own account to the scheme in respect of the 12 months immediately preceding that date;

(*b*)   the amount certified by an actuary to be necessary for the purpose of meeting the liability of the scheme on dissolution to pay the benefits provided by the scheme to or in respect of the employees of the employer;

(*c*)   an amount equal to 10% of the total amount of remuneration paid or payable to those employees in respect of the 12 months immediately preceding the date on which the employer became insolvent.

Where the scheme is a money purchase scheme, the sum payable is the lesser of the amounts in (*a*) and (*c*) above.

(*PSA 1993, ss 124(3) and (3A)* (as inserted by the *Pensions Act 1995*).)

The sum payable in respect of unpaid contributions on behalf of an employee may not exceed the amount deducted from the pay of the employee in respect of the employee's contributions to the occupational pension scheme during the 12 months immediately preceding the date on which the employer became insolvent (*PSA 1993, s 124(5)*).

The liquidator, receiver or trustee in bankruptcy (or other 'relevant officer', as defined) must make a statement to the Secretary of State of the amounts so owing before any payment out of the National Insurance Fund may be made (*PSA 1993, s 125(3), (4)*). However, the Secretary of State may make a payment from the National Insurance Fund if he is satisfied that he does not require such a statement in order to determine the relevant amounts (*PSA 1993, s 125(5)*).

The rights and remedies of the persons competent to act in respect of the scheme will be transferred to the Secretary of State (*PSA 1993, s 127(1)*).

A person who has applied to the Secretary of State for payment of pension contributions may present a complain to the Employment Tribunal that the Secretary of State has failed to make any such payment or that any such payment by him is less than the amount which should have been paid (*PSA 1993, s 126*). The provisions in relation to remedy are the same as those for claims for payment of guaranteed debts under Part XII *ERA 1996:* see **31.6** above.

31.8   Statutory maternity, paternity, adoption and sick pay

An employee who, due to the insolvency of his or her employer, is unable to obtain statutory maternity pay, paternity pay, adoption pay or sick pay may claim such payment from HM Revenue and Customs: see *Statutory Maternity Pay (General) Regulations 1986 (SI 1986/1960), regs 7* and *30, the Statutory Paternity Pay and Statutory Adoption Pay (General) Regulations 2002 (SI 2002/2822), reg 43* and *the Statutory Sick Pay (General) Regulations 1982 (SI 1982/894), reg 9B* respectively. See also MATERNITY AND PARENTAL RIGHTS (33) and SICKNESS AND SICK PAY (44).

Pensions Act 2004

31.9   The *Pensions Act 2004* provides new protections for employees of employers who become insolvent. The Act established a new body corporate, the Pensions Regulator, together with the Pension Protection Fund, the Board of the Pension Protection Fund and the Pension Protection Fund Ombudsman.

Chapter 3 of *Part 2* to the *Act (ss 126–181)* provides for pension protection for 'eligible' pension schemes in the event that the employer suffers an 'insolvency event'. The complex details of the protection offered are set out in detail in the Act and also in the *Pension Protection Fund (Compensation) Regulations 2005 (SI 2005/670)*. However, in summary the Board of the Pension Protection Fund will, in defined circumstances, be under a duty to assume responsibility for eligible schemes following an insolvency event. The Board may pay compensation to members of the pension scheme whose pensions are affected by the insolvency pursuant to the pension compensation provisions set out in *Sch 7*.

The *Pension Protection Fund (Pension Compensation Cap) Order 2007 (SI 2007/989)* caps the relevant compensation. The cap as of 1 April 2007 was £29,928.56.

31.10 OTHER CONSEQUENCES OF INSOLVENCY AND RELATED EVENTS

Insolvency frequently necessitates the dismissal of the employees formerly engaged by the insolvent business. Insolvency itself does not absolve employers from the duty to have consultation with the unions and employees before the dismissal notices are sent out (see the cases cited in 39.6 REDUNDANCY – II).

31.11   Insolvency of Employer

The *Transfer of Undertakings (Protection of Employment) Regulations 2006* (*SI 2006/246*), *regs 8 and 9* make special provision with regard to employee rights where at the time of a relevant transfer the transferor is subject to relevant insolvency proceedings. Note that the old *Transfer of Undertakings (Protection of Employment) Regulations [1981 (SI 1981/1794), reg 4* (as amended by *SI 1987/442* and *SI 1999/1925*)] still apply in relation to transfers taking place before 6 April 2006 (see 52.11 TRANSFER OF UNDERTAKINGS).

Subject to the application of the *Transfer of Undertakings (Protection of Employment) Regulations* (see TRANSFER OF UNDERTAKINGS (52)), the effect of a winding-up order is to terminate the contracts of employment made by the company (*Re General Rolling Stock Co* (1866) LR 1 Eq 346; *Measures Bros Ltd v Measures* [1910] 2 Ch 248). The same occurs where a receiver is appointed by the court (*Reid v Explosives Co Ltd* (1887) 19 QBD 264; *Midland Counties District Bank Ltd v Attwood* [1905] 1 Ch 357), and if employees continue to work for the business they will be deemed to have entered into new contracts of employment with the receiver.

However, a voluntary winding-up does not terminate contracts of employment, because the liquidator is an officer of the company and the personality of the employer does not change (*Midland Counties District Bank*, above). Nor does the appointment of a receiver who is an agent of the company otherwise than by the court (e.g. under a loan security agreement) have that effect, at any rate unless the employees concerned are directors or managers who could not continue to perform their functions without a conflict with the exercise of the receiver's powers (*Re Foster Clark Ltd's Indenture Trusts* [1966] 1 WLR 125; *Re Mack Trucks (Britain) Ltd* [1967] 1 WLR 780; *Griffiths v Secretary of State for Social Services* [1974] QB 468; *Nicoll v Cutts* [1985] PCC 311; *Re Ferranti International plc* [1994] 4 All ER 300). See also *Deaway Trading Ltd v Calverley* [1973] 3 All ER 776; and *Pambakian Ltd v Brentford Nylons* [1978] ICR 665.

31.11   Liability of administrative receivers and administrators

An administrative receiver is, essentially, a receiver or manager of substantially the whole of a company's property appointed on behalf of the holders of debentures secured by a floating charge (*Insolvency Act 1986, s 29(2)*). By contrast, a person may be appointed as the administrator of a company by an administration order of the court, by the holder of a floating charge or by the company or its directors (*Insolvency Act 1986, Sch B1 paras 10, 14* and *22* respectively). The administrative receiver or administrator will be treated as adopting the contract of employment of an employee if he continues the employment relationship for 14 days after appointment (*Insolvency Act 1986, s 44(2)* and *Sch B1, para 99(5)(a)*). An administrative receiver or administrator will not be able to avoid adoption of the contract simply by writing to employees expressly to state that he is not adopting the contracts. If he takes advantage of the services of existing employees without negotiating new contracts of employment for more than 14 days he will be regarded as having adopted their contracts (*Powdrill v Watson* [1995] 2 AC 394; see also *Re Antal International Ltd* [2003] EWHC 1338, [2003] 2 BCLC 406).

An administrative receiver will be personally liable on any contract of employment adopted by him on or after 15 March 1994 in carrying out his functions. Any such liability is limited to payment of a sum by way of wages or salary or contribution to an occupational pension scheme where that liability is incurred while the administrative receiver is in office and in respect of services rendered wholly or partly after the adoption of the employment contract. However, the administrative receiver is entitled to be indemnified out of the company's assets (*Insolvency Act 1986, s 44* as amended by *Insolvency Act 1994*). The liability of administrative receivers on contracts of employment adopted before 15 March 1994 is not restricted to the liabilities identified above and may, for example, include the liability to pay wages in lieu of notice of termination (see *Powdrill v Watson* [1995] 2 AC 394). However any claims relating to the period before 15 March 1994 are now, almost certainly, time-barred under the *Limitation Act 1980*.

An administrator does not undertake a personal liability. However liabilities for wages, salary and pension contributions after the adoption of the contract are charged on the company's property in their custody or control in priority to most other charges and securities including the fees and expenses of the administration (*Insolvency Act 1986, Schedule B1, para 99*; see also *Re Allders Department Stores Ltd (in administration)* [2005] ICR 867). In *Krasner v McMath* [2005] EWCA Civ 1072, [2006] ICR 205 the Court of Appeal concluded that an administrator's liabilities to employees of a company in administration for protective awards and payments in lieu of notice were not payable in priority to the expenses of the administration (save that any payments in lieu of notice where an employer did not require an employee to work during his notice period and paid his wages attributable to that period in a lump sum would be payable in priority as such payments constitute wages as set out in *Delaney v RJ Staples (t/a De Montford Recruitment)* [1992] 1 AC 687).

In *Larsen v Henderson* [1990] IRLR 512 an important suggestion was made that a receiver owes a duty of care to the employees of a company in receivership to adopt such method of achieving his desired end as will have the least adverse effect upon them. There is some doubt as to whether this suggestion is, in fact, correct.

32 Less-Favourable Treatment of Part Time Workers

32.1 LEGAL SOURCES AND GUIDANCE MATERIAL

Protection for part-time workers has traditionally been provided by laws on indirect sex discrimination and equal pay. Since most part-time workers are, and traditionally have been, women, the unequal treatment of such workers is likely to affect far more women than men. The differential treatment of part-time workers could amount to indirect sex discrimination contrary to *s 1(1)(b)* of the *Sex Discrimination Act 1975* or a breach of the principle of equal pay for equal work contrary to the *Equal Pay Act 1970*. However, the anti-discrimination legislation is complex and requires part-time workers to show that there has been a gender bias in the treatment received (see 12.7–12.9 DISCRIMINATION AND EQUAL OPPORTUNITIES – I and 24.10 EQUAL PAY).

Council Directive 97/81/EC concerning the Framework Agreement on part-time work, was adopted on 15 December 1997. The Framework Agreement was concluded by the European Social Partners (*'the Framework Agreement'*) and is aimed at eliminating discrimination against part-time workers and contributing to the encouragement and development of part-time work. The Directive was made to apply to the United Kingdom by *Directive 98/23/EC*. The *Part Time Workers (Prevention of Less Favourable Treatment) Regulations 2000 (SI 2000/1551)* ('the *Part Time Workers Regulations*') were designed to implement the *Directive*, and were made pursuant to the *Employment Relations Act 1999, s 19*. The effect of the *Part Time Workers Regulations* is that part-time workers have rights as part-timers, rather than as members of a particular gender group, and they will no longer have to resort to the complex anti-discrimination legislation in order to argue that they are suffering from indirect sex discrimination. The *Part Time Workers Regulations* provide a simpler, gender-neutral route for tackling discrimination against part-time workers.

Sections 20 and *21* of the *Employment Relations Act 1999* allow the Secretary of State to issue a code of practice containing guidance for the dual purposes set out in the *Framework Agreement*, being both the elimination of discrimination in the field of employment against part-time workers and the more aspirational aspect of the *Framework Agreement*, which is concerned with facilitating the development of opportunities for part-time work and the flexible organisation of working time. To date, no code has been issued. However, the DTI has issued Guidance Notes to accompany the *Part Time Workers Regulations*. It has also issued a detailed 'Law and Best Practice' guide which provides advice on how to comply with the law as well as how employers can widen access to part-time work. Both documents are available at http://www.dti.gov.uk/employment/employment-legislation/employment-guidance/page19479.html.

A claimant may frequently still have a claim in the alternative under the *Sex Discrimination Act 1975* or *Equal Pay Act 1970*. This chapter is concerned with the *Part Time Workers Regulations* only. For details of how sex discrimination legislation continues to apply to part-time workers, see DISCRIMINATION AND EQUAL OPPORTUNITIES I-III (12, 13, 14) and EQUAL PAY (24).

32.2 WHO HAS THE RIGHT?

The majority of the rights laid down by the *Part Time Workers Regulations* are granted to 'workers'. The definition of 'worker' is identical to the definition in *s 230(3)* of the *Employment Rights Act 1996*. It covers individuals who work or worked under a contract of employment or any other contract, whether express or implied and whether oral or in writing, whereby the individual undertakes to do or perform personally any work or services for another party to the contract, whose status is not by virtue of the contract that of a client or customer of any profession or business undertaking carried on by the individual: *reg 1(2)* (SEE EMPLOYEE, SELF-EMPLOYED OR WORKER? (17)).

The *Part Time Workers Regulations* apply to those in Crown employment and to House of Lords and House of Commons staff: *regs 12, 14* and *15*. They also apply to members of a police force, special constables or police cadets, who are treated as employed under a contract of employment: *reg 16*. The *Part Time Workers Regulations* broadly apply to members of the armed forces: *reg 13(1)*. However, they do not apply to service as a member of the reserve forces in so far as that service consists of undertaking training obligations or voluntary training or duties under *s 27* of the *Reserve Forces Act 1996*: *reg 13(2)*. No complaint concerning the service of any person as a member of the armed forces may be presented to an employment tribunal unless that person has made a complaint in respect of the same matter to an officer under the service redress procedures, and that complaint has not been withdrawn: *reg 13(3)*. The *Part Time Workers Regulations* do not apply to any individual in his capacity as the holder of a judicial office if he is remunerated on a daily fee-paid basis: *reg 17*.

Clause 2(2) of the *Framework Agreement* permits Member States to exclude from protection part time workers who work on a casual basis. The view has been expressed in *R (on the application of Manson) v Ministry of Defence* [2005] EWHC 427 (Admin), [2005] All ER (D) 270 (Feb) that the exclusion in *reg 13(2)* is compatible with the Directive. In *Wippel v Peek & Cloppenburg GmbG & Co KG* [2005] ICR 1604, the ECJ considered whether 'framework contracts of employment' or 'work on demand' contracts, which set out applicable rates of pay, but provide that there are no fixed working hours, no guarantee of income, and the worker can accept or refuse the job offered to her each week without having to give any reason for doing so, fell within the scope of the Directive. The ECJ considered that they did, provided the following conditions were met: (a) such workers have a contract or employment relationship as defined by the law, collective agreement or practices in force in the Member State, (b) they work 'part-time', ie their normal working hours are less than those of a comparable full time worker; and (c) in regard to part-time workers working on a casual basis, the Member State has not excluded them from the benefit of the terms of the Framework Agreement, pursuant to *cl 2.(2)*. Under UK law, a framework contract would lack the mutuality of obligation necessary to amount to a contract of employment (see EMPLOYEE, SELF-EMPLOYED OR WORKER? (17)). Depending on the precise terms of the framework contract, an individual may also fall outside the domestic definition of a 'worker' if she has not 'undertaken to perform any work or services', eg if the individual is not obliged to accept any work offered to her under the framework contract.

It is also important to note that *reg 7(1)* applies only to employees (see 32.18). Applicants for employment are not within the scope of the *Regulations*.

32.3   QUALIFYING PERIOD

There is no qualifying period for entitlement to the rights conferred by the *Part Time Workers Regulations*.

32.4   DISCRIMINATION

Less Favourable Treatment

A part time worker has the right not to be treated by his employer less favourably than a comparable full time worker as regards the terms of his contract: *reg 5(1)(a)*. The DTI Guidance Notes and the Law and Best Practice Guide indicate that the *Part Time Workers Regulations* apply to

(a)   rates of pay;

(b)   contractual sick pay and maternity pay;

(c)   access to occupational pension schemes;

(d)   access to training;

(e)   annual leave, maternity leave, parental leave and career breaks;

(f)   fringe benefits, such as staff discounts, subsidised mortgages, health insurance and company cars

A part time worker also has the right not to be treated by his employer less favourably than a comparable full time worker by being subjected to any other detriment by any act, or deliberate failure to act, of his employer: reg 5(1)(b). It has been accepted that 'any other detriment' includes a dismissal: *Hendrickson Europe Ltd v Pipe* UKEAT/0272/02. It is likely that the same approach will be taken to 'detriment' as has been adopted in relation to other anti-discrimination provisions: see 12.12(G), DISCRIMINATION AND EQUAL OPPORTUNITIES – I. Asserting pressure on an individual to work full time, issuing an ultimatum to a part-time worker that she will have to work full-time if she wishes to remain in employment, and selecting the individual for redundancy are examples of less favourable treatment. Requiring a part time worker to work a higher proportion of 'standby' to rostered hours than a full time worker can also constitute a detriment: *Gibson v Scottish Ambulance Service* EATS/0052/04.

32.5   *The Pro Rata Principle*

In determining whether a part time worker has been treated less favourably than a comparable full time worker, the pro rata principle shall be applied unless it is inappropriate: *reg 5(3)*. The pro rata principle means that where a comparable full time worker receives or is entitled to receive pay or any other benefit, a part time worker is to receive or be entitled to receive not less than the proportion of that pay or other benefit that the number of his weekly hours bears to the number of weekly hours of the comparable full time worker: *reg 1(2)*. 'Weekly hours' is defined as the number of hours a worker is required to work under his contract of employment in a week in which he has no absences from work and does not work any overtime or, where the number of such hours varies according to a cycle, the average number of such hours.

A tribunal addressing *reg 5* should always consider whether it is 'appropriate' to apply the pro rata principle. The fundamental purpose of the pro rata principle is to enable a valid comparison to be made between the remuneration of a part-time worker and his full time counterpart, so as to identify whether a part-time worker is being treated less favourably, and if so, to what extent. It is a tool for determining whether a part-time worker has been treated less favourably than a full time worker. It will usually be appropriate to use the pro rata principle where the claim is based on a difference in the remuneration for hours worked in the ordinary course of events: *James   v   Great   North   Eastern   Railway*

UKEAT/0496/04/SM. In *Matthews v Kent and Medway Towns Fire Authority* [2004] EWCA Civ 844, [2005] ICR 84, the Tribunal held that it was inappropriate to apply the pro rata principle over the whole range of a financial package for fire fighters which included pension benefit, sick pay and pay for additional duties. This conclusion was not challenged in the EAT or the Court of Appeal.

In *McMenemy v Capita Business Services Ltd* [2006] IRLR 761 employees at a call centre which operated seven days a week were all entitled to public holidays when they 'fell on your normal working day'. The claimant worked part-time, Wednesday to Friday. He was not allowed time off in lieu when public holidays fell on a Monday, although full time workers in his team who normally worked on Mondays were given the day off. The claimant argued that he had a stand-alone right to pro rata treatment as regards holidays, and that he could demonstrate that he received less holidays than a comparable full time worker. The EAT held that the pro-rata principle is related only to the question of whether or not a part-time worker has received less favourable treatment than a full-time worker. It is not an independent right, and it was not something that a tribunal had to have in mind when considering whether or not any less favourable treatment is on the ground that the employee is a part-time worker (see 32.14 below).

32.6 *Overtime*

Where part-time workers only receive overtime rates of pay once they have worked the equivalent of a full time worker's weekly hours, and not once they have completed the number of hours which they themselves ordinarily work each week, there is no less favourable treatment: *reg 5(4)*. This reflects the orthodox position with regards to equal pay: *see Stadt Lengerich v Helmig* [1996] ICR 35, ECJ and 24.11 EQUAL PAY. This does not affect the right of a part-time worker to receive, for example, unsocial hours payments, weekend payments or other forms of enhanced pay on comparable terms to full-time workers. *In James v Great North Eastern Railways* UKEAT/0496/04/SM, the EAT held that the *reg 5(4)* exception did not apply to an 'additional hours payment' made to full time workers. Full time employees were contractually obliged to work a 40 hour week judged over the length of an 8-week roster cycle. Employees could also be required to work overtime. Pay for the first 35 hours was paid at basic rate; they then received an 'additional hours payment' for the next five hours, being 1¼/ times basic pay. Any overtime over and above the 40 hours was paid at 1¼/ times basic pay. Pay for the set hours for part-time workers was at the same basic rate as full-time equivalent posts, with pay for any overtime up to 35 hours being at the same basic rate. Pay for additional hours over 35 hours was at 1¼/ times basic pay. Part-time workers did not receive an 'additional hours payment'. The EAT held that the payment in question must amount to a 'true' overtime payment to fall within the statutory disregard. The 'additional hours payment' made to full time workers was pay for the contractual rostered hours that they worked, and the statutory disregard in *reg 5(4)* was not applicable.

32.7 **Comparators**

Identifying 'part time' and 'full time' workers

As with other anti-discrimination provisions, the legislation involves the making of a comparison. The comparison is between a part-time worker and a 'comparable' full time worker.

The first step is to identify 'full time workers' and 'part time workers'. A worker is a part time worker if he is 'paid wholly or in part by reference to the time he works and, having regard to the custom and practice of the employer in relation to workers employed by the worker's employer under the same type of contract, is not identifiable as a full-time worker': *reg 2(2)*. By contrast, a worker is a full time worker if he is 'paid wholly or in part by reference to the time he works and, having regard to the custom and practice of the employer in relation to workers employed by the worker's employer under the same type of contract, is identifiable as a full-time worker': *reg 2(1)*.

For the purpose of comparing the treatment of full-time and part-time workers, and for the purpose of determining whether a worker is full time or part-time in the first place, *reg 2(3)* states that each of the following shall be regarded as being employed *under different types of contract* – (a) employees employed under a contract that is not a contract of apprenticeship; (b) employees employed under a contract of apprenticeship; (c) workers who are not employees; (d) any other description of worker that it is reasonable for the employer to treat differently from other workers on the ground that workers of that description have a different type of contract.

Previously, the *Part Time Workers Regulations* stated that those working under fixed term contracts were employed under different types of contract to those who worked under permanent contracts. However, the distinction between fixed-term and permanent contracts was removed by the *Part Time Workers (Prevention of Less Favourable Treatment) Regulations 2000 (Amendment) Regulations 2002* with effect from 1 October 2002 in order to give effect to the *Fixed Term Employees (Prevention of Less Favourable Treatment) Regulations 2002*, which prohibit discrimination between fixed term employees and comparable permanent employees.

32.8   *Identifying a 'comparable full time worker'*

The second stage is to determine whether the part-time workers' full time colleagues are 'comparable full time workers' within the meaning of *reg 2(4)*. A comparable full time worker is one who is employed by the employer under the same type of contract and is engaged in the same or broadly similar work who has a similar level of qualifications, skills and experience: *reg 2(4)(a)*. The comparable full time worker must also work or be based at the same establishment as the part-time worker. If there are no full-time workers who satisfy these requirements, full time workers who are based at a different establishment may be considered: *reg 2(4)(b)*.

32.9   'Same type of Contract'

Matthews v Kent and Medway Towns Fire Authority [2004] ICR 257, EAT,[2004] EWCA Civ 844, [2005] ICR 84 and [2006] UKHL 8, [2006] ICR 365 is a test case brought by part-time firefighters (traditionally known as 'retained' firefighters) under the *Part Time Workers Regulations*. The retained firefighters claimed that they were treated less favourably in that they were denied access to statutory pension arrangements, they were denied increased pay for additional responsibilities and their sick pay arrangements were calculated on a less favourable basis. The employment tribunal held that the retained firefighters were employed under a different type of contract from fulltime firefighters, as it was reasonable for the employer to treat them differently. This was because they had a different type of contract, as there were many differences and many special features of the working patterns as between both groups. The EAT agreed with this conclusion, but the Court of Appeal took a different view. Both retained firefighters and full time firefighters properly belonged to category (a), being employees employed under a contract that is not a contract of apprenticeship. The Court of Appeal held that it would unduly complicate eligibility and would run counter to the purpose of the legislation if it was open to an employer to remove an employee from what are now categories (a)-(c) because it is reasonable to treat him differently on the ground that alleged comparators have a different type of contract. Instead, *reg 2(3)(d)* is aimed at providing a residual category of 'other' descriptions of worker who fall outside categories (a)-(c). A majority of the House of Lords (Lord Nicholls, Lord Hope, Baroness Hale and Lord Carswell, Lord Mance dissenting) upheld the approach of the Court of Appeal: [2006] UKHL 8, [2006] ICR 365. The requirement that the part time worker and the full time worker proposed as a comparator had to be employed under the same type of contract was directed to comparable types of employment relationship rather than comparable terms and conditions of employment. The categories set out in *reg 2(3)* are defined broadly in a way that allows for a wide variety of different terms and conditions within each category. The categories are mutually exclusive. Under reg. 2(3)(d) the courts are asked to examine a type of worker who is different from any of those previously mentioned in *reg 2(3)(a)-(c)*. While it is difficult to think of a type of contract which is different to those mentioned in *reg 2(3)(a)-(c)*, a contract will only fall within *reg 2(3)(d)* if a worker does not fall into one of the other categories. It is a long-stop or residual category. It is not designed to allow employers to single out particular kinds of part-time working arrangements and treat them differently from the rest.

In *Wippel v Peek & Cloppenburg GmbG & Co KG* [2005] ICR 1604 (see 32.2 above) the ECJ held that as there was no full-time worker who worked according to need under a framework contract, there was no comparable full time worker who worked under the same type of employment contract or relationship. The employment relationship of a full time worker, who worked under a 'traditional' contract, and the claimant, who worked under a framework agreement, was different as to subject matter and basis.

32.10 'The same or broadly similar work'

In *Matthews v Kent and Medway Towns Fire Authority* the employment tribunal also held that retained firefighters and full time firefighters were not engaged in the same or broadly similar work, and this finding was upheld by the EAT and the Court of Appeal: [2004] EWCA Civ 844, [2005] ICR 84. The argument that firefighting was the central role of all operational fire fighters, such that retained and full time firefighters must be engaged in broadly similar work was rejected. Full time firefighters carried out measurable additional job functions, such as educational, preventive and administrative tasks which were not carried out by retained firefighters. There were differences in entry standards, probationary standards and on-going training, which led to differences in the level of qualification and skills between retained firefighters and full time firefighters. Differences in recruitment procedures and promotion prospects also served to illustrate the different work carried out by full time firefighters, as they are recruited to do a job with measurable additional functions and are overwhelmingly the recruitment pool for promotion to higher grades.

The House of Lords overturned this conclusion: [2006] UKHL 8; [2006] ICR 365. The majority (Lord Nicholls, Lord Hope and Baroness Hale) held that the tribunal erred in concentrating on the differences between the work rather than the weight to be given to the similarities. They emphasised that tribunals are conducting a different exercise from that required by *s 1(4)* of the *Equal Pay Act 1970*: see 24.6 EQUAL PAY). The Equal Pay Act test is employed in the context of a scheme which imposes an equality clause upon the contracts of employment of women who are employed on like work with men. The test in the *Part Time Workers Regulations* is a threshold condition which is the precursor to considering whether there has been less favourable treatment which cannot be objectively justified. The question is not whether the work is different, but whether it is the same or broadly similar. This question has to be approached in the context of the *Part Time Workers Regulations* which are inviting a comparison between two types of workers whose work will almost inevitably be different to some extent. In carrying out the assessment, particular weight should be given to the extent to which the work of part-time and full-time workers is exactly the same. If a large component of the work is exactly the same, the question is whether any differences are of such importance as to prevent their work being regarded overall as 'the same or broadly similar'. Where both full- and part-timers do the same work, but the full-timers have extra activities with which to fill their time, their work is not prevented from being regarded as the same or broadly similar overall. The importance of the work which they do to the work of the enterprise as a whole is also of great importance in this assessment. If full-timers do the more important work and part-timers are brought in to do the more peripheral tasks, it is unlikely that the work is the same or broadly similar. However, where full-timers and part-timers spend much of their time on the core activity of the enterprise, the fact that full-timers may do some extra tasks will not prevent their work being the same or broadly similar.

The case was remitted to the employment tribunal for reconsideration of whether the retained and full-time firefighters are engaged in the same or broadly similar work.

32.11 Actual Comparator

Questions have arisen as to whether there is a need for an 'actual' comparator (as is ordinarily required by the *Equal Pay Act 1970*: see 24.9 EQUAL PAY) or whether a hypothetical comparator can be constructed (as occurs under the *Sex Discrimination Act 1975 and Race Relations Act 1976*: see 12.5(2) DISCRIMINATION AND EQUAL OPPORTUNITIES – I). The wording of the Regulations suggests that a narrow comparison is all that is envisaged, and if there is no full-time comparator employed by the same employer, any claim will fail. The wording of the Directive is somewhat wider, and states that 'where there is no comparable full-time worker in the same establishment, the comparison shall be made by reference to the applicable collective agreement or, where there is no applicable collective agreement, in accordance with national law, collective agreements or practice'. Initially, the EAT observed that it was arguable that *the Part Time Workers (Prevention of Less Favourable Treatment) Regulations 2000* do not permit the construction of a hypothetical comparator if no actual comparator can be identified: *Tyson v Concurrent Systems Incorporated Ltd* EAT/0028/03 and *Royal Mail Group plc v Lynch* UKEAT/0426/03. However, in *Wippel v Peek & Cloppenburg GmbH & Co KG* [2005] ICR 1604 the ECJ held that a particular part-time contract was not in breach of the *Directive* in circumstances where there was no full-time worker in the establishment with the same type of contract or employment relationship as the part-time worker for comparison purposes. The ECJ did not go on to construct a hypothetical comparator. The effect of this limitation suggests that the Regulations will not provide protection for the many part-timer workers who are doing jobs only done by part-timers. Following *Wippel,* in *McMenemy v Capita Business Services Ltd* [2006] IRLR 761, the EAT observed (without concluding) that the approach of constructing a hypothetical comparator was probably 'not apposite' under the *Part Time Workers Regulations*. The prohibition is confined to treatment on the proscribed ground that is less favourable than that actually afforded to a full time comparator and is not extended to treatment that 'would' be afforded to a comparable full time worker. The EAT noted that this approach was supported by that of the ECJ in *Wippel* (above).

32.12 The Scope of the Comparison

The EAT has rejected the argument that a 'broad brush' comparison be carried out, and followed the approach of the House of Lords in *Hayward v Cammell Laird Shipbuilders Ltd* [1988] ICR 464 in holding that what must be compared is each specific term of the contract: see *Matthews v Kent and Medway Towns Fire Authority* [2004] ICR 257, EAT. This argument was repeated in *Matthews* in the House of Lords, where the appellants argued that less favourable treatment and objective justification should be considered term by term, whereas the respondents contended that both should be looked at overall. Baroness Hale (with whom Lord Nicholls and Lord Hope agreed) did not rule out the possibility that a less favourable term might be so well balanced by a more favourable one that it could not be said that part timers were treated less favourably overall. Nor did she rule out the possibility that more favourable treatment on one point might supply justification for less favourable treatment on another. On the facts of *Matthews,* however, the majority found it difficult to see how a differently structured pay package for retained fire-fighters could justify total exclusion from the pension scheme or a sick pay scheme, which was unrelated to the hours actually worked.

32.13 *Specific Circumstances where a comparator is not required*

In certain specific contexts, the *Part Time Workers Regulations* allow for the disapplication of the comparative approach.

If an individual becomes a part time worker having previously worked in a job on a full-time basis, he can compare his part-time conditions with his previous full time contract: *reg 3*. Regulation 3 applies where the worker was a full-time worker but, following a termination or variation of his contract, he continues to work under a new or varied contract, whether of the same type or not, that requires him to work for a number of weekly hours that is lower than the number he was required to work immediately before the variation. *Regulation 5* applies to such a worker as if he were a part-time worker and as if there were a comparable full time worker employed under the terms that applied to him immediately before the variation or termination.

If an individual returns to a part-time role after a period of absence, such as maternity leave, which does not exceed twelve months, she can compare her part-time conditions with her previous full time contract: *reg 4*. This regulation applies where the worker was a full time worker immediately before a period of absence (whether the absence followed a termination of the worker's contract or not), and where that worker returns to work for the same employer within 12 months of the date on which the absence started. The worker must return to the same job or a job at the same level under a contract where she is required to work for a number of weekly hours that is lower than the number she was required to work immediately before the period of absence, regardless of whether the new contract is a different contract or a varied contract, or whether it is of the same type as the original contract or not. *Regulation 5* applies to such a worker as if she were a part-time worker and as if there were a comparable full time worker employed under (a) the contract under which the returning worker was employed immediately before the period of absence; or (b) where it is shown that, had the returning worker continued to work under the original contract, a variation would have been made to its term during the period of absence, the original contract including that variation.

32.14   'On the ground that the worker is a part-time worker'

It is not sufficient for a tribunal to be satisfied that a claimant has been less favourably treated than his comparator. It is only if the less favourable treatment is on the ground that the worker is a part-time worker that liability will lie: *reg 5(2)(a)*. The EAT *in Matthews v Kent and Medway Towns Fire Authority* [2004] ICR 257 applied the 'but for' test (as used in race and sex discrimination) to this provision in the *Part Time Workers Regulations*: ie 'but for' a claimant's part time status, would he have been treated as he was? However, there is some doubt whether the traditional 'but for' test is sufficient in race and sex discrimination cases. The correct test in deciding whether a causal link has been made out is to ask 'why' the treatment complained of had taken place, and not to ask whether 'but for' the claimant's part-time status he would have been treated as he had been. A tribunal is to ask what, consciously or unconsciously, was the employer's reason for acting as he did: see *Chief Constable of West Yorkshire Police v Khan* [2001] UKHL 48, [2001] 1 WLR 1947; *Shamoon v Chief Constable of the Royal Ulster Constabulary* [2003] ICR 337. This approach was adopted by the Scottish EAT in *Gibson v Scottish Ambulance Service* EATS/0052/04 and was followed by the same Tribunal in *McMenemy v Capita Business Services Ltd* [2006] IRLR 761. It is submitted that the *Gibson* and *McMenemy* approach should be followed in preference to that in *Matthews*. In *Gibson*, the EAT held that the 'real reason' for the less favourable treatment was the issue of demand in the local area, with the result that the claimant was not being discriminated against on the ground that he was a part time worker per se. The EAT also had regard to the fact that part-time workers in other areas did not fail to meet the pro-rata principle, and therefore it could not be said to be a sole question that the issue was determined by part-time status and nothing else.

In *McMenemy,* the tribunal found that the reason that the claimant was receiving the treatment complained of was not because he was a part-time worker, but because he did not work on a Monday. The EAT held that the tribunal was entitled to construct a hypothetical employee when considering the 'reason why' question. The tribunal was entitled to consider how a hypothetical comparator would have been treated, and so was entitled to ask what would have happened if there had been, at the time, a full-time employee in the claimant's team who did not work on Mondays. There was evidence that the respondents' business operated on a basis which meant that full-time workers might not work on a Monday, that the terms of their contract regarding the availability of Monday holidays was identical to those in the claimant's contract, that there had been a full-time employee in the claimant's team who had until recently worked Tuesday to Saturday, that when he had been doing so, the respondents had made it clear to him that he was not entitled to take days off in lieu when there was a Monday public holiday and that had an employee worked part-time on days that included Mondays, they would have been able to take every Monday holiday. In those circumstances, the EAT held that the tribunal was entitled to conclude that that ground for the respondent's decision to refuse the claimant's request for days off in lieu of Monday holidays was not that he was a part-time worker, but that he did not work on a Monday (see 12.6 DISCRIMINATION AND EQUAL OPPORTUNI-TIES – I for application of the 'on the prohibited grounds' test in other contexts).

32.15 **Objective Justification**

Any less favourable treatment may be justified on objective grounds: *reg 5(2)(b)*. The concept of objective justification is likely to be treated in the same way as in the context of the anti-discrimination legislation (see 13.8 DISCRIMINATION AND EQUAL OPPORTUNITIES – II and 24.11 EQUAL PAY). Less favourable treatment will be justified on objective grounds only if it can be shown that the treatment (1) aims to achieve a legitimate objective, for example, a genuine business objective; (2) is necessary to achieve that objective; and (3) is an appropriate way of achieving that objective.

32.16 **Direct Effect**

In *R (on the application of Manson) v Ministry of Defence* [2005] EWHC 427 (Admin), [2005] All ER (D) 270 (Feb), the court observed, albeit obiter, that *cl 4* of the *Framework Agreement* (the non discrimination provision) has direct effect. This is likely to be followed, allowing a claimant to rely on *cl 4* and contend that provisions excluding its operation are incompatible with *cl 2(2)* of the Framework Agreement (see 32.2 above).

32.17 **RIGHT TO RECEIVE A WRITTEN STATEMENT OF REASONS FOR LESS FAVOURABLE TREATMENT**

Part time workers can make a request in writing to their employer for a written statement of reasons if they believe that the employer has treated them less favourably than a comparable full time worker: *reg 6*. The employer must respond to the request within 21 days and such statements on the part of the employer will be admissible as evidence in any proceedings under the *Part Time Workers Regulations*. Inferences may be drawn from a refusal to answer or an evasive or equivocal response.

Regulation 6 does not apply where the treatment in question consists of the dismissal of an employee, and that employee is entitled to a written statement of reasons for his dismissal under *s 92* of the *Employment Rights Act 1996* (see 46.14, 46.15 TERMINATION OF EMPLOYMENT).

32.18 **VICTIMISATION**

A part-time worker has the right not to be subjected to any detriment by an act, or deliberate failure to act, by his employer done on the grounds that:

(i) he has brought proceedings under the *Part Time Workers (Prevention of Less Favourable Treatment) Regulations 2000*;

(ii) he has requested a written statement;

(iii) he has given evidence or information in connection with any proceedings under the *Regulations*;

(iv) he has done anything under the *Regulations* relating to his employer or any other person;

(v) he has alleged that his employer has infringed the *Regulations*;

(vi) he has refused or proposed to refuse to forego any rights under the *Regulations*; or

(vii) the employer believed or suspected that the worker had done or intended to do any of the things mentioned above: see *reg 7(3)(a)* and (*b*).

32.19   Less-Favourable Treatment of Part Time Workers

An employee who is dismissed shall be regarded as unfairly dismissed if the reason or principal reason for the dismissal is a reason set out in (i)- (vii) above: *reg 7(1)*.

32.19 RELATIONSHIP WITH UNFAIR DISMISSAL

A breach of the *Part Time Workers Regulations* does not make any dismissal automatically unfair: *Henderickson Europe Ltd v Pipe* UKEAT/0272/02. A tribunal must ascertain the reason for the dismissal, and then determine whether the dismissal was unfair within the terms of *s 98(4)* of the *Employment Rights Act 1996* (see UNFAIR DISMISSAL – II (54)). The act of discrimination may be an important factor for the tribunal to take into account when carrying out this evaluation, but it does not automatically follow that the dismissal is unfair.

32.20 APPLICATIONS TO AN EMPLOYMENT TRIBUNAL

A worker may present a complaint to an employment tribunal that his employer has infringed a right conferred on him by *reg 5* or *reg 7(2)*. A claim for breach of the *Part Time Workers Regulations* that includes an allegation that the *Regulations* themselves are incompatible with Directive 97/81 cannot be brought by way of judicial review, and must be brought in the tribunal: *R (on the application of Manson) v Ministry of Defence* [2006] EWCA 1678; [2006] ICR 355,.

Under *reg 8(1)* of the *Part Time Workers Regulations*, the Employment Tribunal has jurisdiction over a private law complaint that an employer has infringed a part-time worker's right not to be treated less favourably than a comparable full-time worker. This jurisdiction includes jurisdiction to dis-apply a restriction on that right contained in the *Part Time Workers Regulations* if that restriction is incompatible with European Community law. However, as the employment tribunal has no inherent jurisdiction, it cannot determine claims based on a freestanding right found only in Community law (for the Tribunal's jurisdiction over EU law, see 20.12 EMPLOYMENT TRIBUNALS – I).

In cases where the *Employment Act 2002, s.32* applies, it is in principle a prerequisite to the presentation of a claim that the claimant has first submitted a grievance in writing to the employer (see DISPUTE RESOLUTION (15)). However, there is no requirement to grieve in respect of claims under the *Part Time Workers Regulations,* as *s 32* only applies to the jurisdictions listed in *Sch 4* of that *Act*. The *Part Time Workers Regulations* are not included in that list.

32.21 TIME LIMITS

A claim must be presented to a tribunal before the end of the period of three months beginning with the date of the less favourable treatment or detriment to which the complaint relates. Where an act or failure to act is part of a series of similar acts or failures comprising the less favourable treatment, the time runs from the last of those acts. A six month time limit applies to complaints by members of the armed forces: *reg 8(2)*. For the purposes of calculating the date of the less favourable treatment or detriment, *reg 8(4)* provides:

(a)   where a term in the contract is less favourable, that treatment shall be treated, subject to paragraph (b), as taking place on each day of the period during which the term is less favourable;

(b)   where an application relies on *reg 3* or *4* the less favourable treatment shall be treated as occurring on, and only on, in the case of *reg 3*, the first day on which the applicant worked under the new or varied contract and, in the case of *reg 4*, the day on which the applicant returned; and

(c)   a deliberate failure to act contrary to *reg 5* or *7(2)* shall be treated as done when it was decided on. In the absence of evidence establishing the contrary, a person shall be taken for these purposes to decide not to act when he does an act inconsistent with doing the failed act, or if he has done no such inconsistent act, when the period expires within which he might reasonably have been expected to have done the failed act if it was to be done: *reg 8(5)*.

The extension of the 'normal' time limit for bringing a claim provided in *reg 15* of *the Employment Act 2002 (Dispute Resolution) Regulations 2004* does not apply to claims under the *Part Time Workers Regulations,* as the *Regulations* are not listed in either *Sch 3* or *4* of *the Employment Act 2002* (see DISPUTE RESOLUTION (15)). The absence of the *Regulations* from the *Schedules* to the *Employment Act 2002* is curious, and appears to have been an oversight. It results in the anomalous position that a claimant will be required to grieve if she wishes to bring an equal pay claim or a claim for indirect sex discrimination, and the normal time limit for bringing such a claim will be extended by three months. However, she is not required to grieve in respect of a claim under the *Regulations*, even though it may be based on identical facts, and the time limit will not be extended for such a claim.

A tribunal may nevertheless consider a complaint which is out of time if, in all the circumstances of the case, it considers that it is just and equitable to do so: *reg 8(3)*. Where a worker presents a complaint to the tribunal under the *Regulations*, it is for the employer to identify the ground for the less favourable treatment or detriment: *reg 8(6)*.

32.22 REMEDIES

Where an employment tribunal finds that a complaint presented to it is well-founded, it shall take such of the following steps as it considers just and equitable:

(a)   making a declaration as to the rights of the complainant and the employer in relation to the matters to which the complaint relates: *reg 8(7)(a)*;

(b)   ordering the employer to pay compensation to the complainant: *reg 8(7)(b)*. Where a tribunal orders compensation, the amount of the compensation awarded shall be such as the tribunal considers just and equitable in all the circumstances having regard to (a) the infringement to which the complaint relates, and (b) any loss which is attributable to the infringement having regard, in the case of an infringement of the right conferred by *reg 5*, to the pro rata principle, except where it is inappropriate to do so: *reg 8(9)*. The loss shall be taken to include any expenses reasonably incurred by the complainant in consequence of the infringement and loss of any benefit which he might reasonably be expected to have had but for the infringement: *reg 8(10)*. Unlike compensation awards under other anti-discrimination provisions, compensation in respect of less favourable treatment on the grounds of part-time status will not include compensation for injury to feelings: *reg 8(11)*. In *Tyson v Concurrent Systems Incorporated Ltd* EAT/0028/03, the appellant sought to argue that stigma damages and stigma compensation were not excluded by *reg 8(11)*. The EAT doubted whether stigma damages which did not include loss of earnings produced by the stigma could be brought within the provisions of *reg 8*. Normal principles of mitigation apply: *reg 8(12)*. Where the tribunal finds that the act, or failure to act, to which the complaint relates was to any extent caused or contributed to by the action of the complainant, it shall reduce the amount of the compensation by such proportion as it considers just and equitable having regard to that finding: *reg 8(13)*;

(c)   recommending that the employer take, within a specified period, action appearing to the tribunal to be reasonable, in all the circumstances of the case, for the purpose of obviating or reducing the adverse effect on the complainant of any matter to which the complaint relates: *reg 8(7)(c)*.

If the employer fails, without reasonable justification, to comply with a recommendation made by an employment tribunal under *reg 8(7)(c)* the tribunal may, if it thinks it just and equitable to do so, increase the amount of compensation required to be paid to the complainant in respect of the complaint where an order for compensation has already been made, or may make such an order for the first time: *reg 8(14)*.

(for a more detailed discussion of these rules in relation to other anti-discrimination legislation, see DISCRIMINATION AND EQUAL OPPORTUNITIES – III (14))

32.23   RESTRICTION ON CONTRACTING OUT

The restriction on contracting out of employment rights contained in *s 203* of the *Employment Rights Act 1996* applies in relation to the *Part Time Workers Regulations* as if they were contained in the *1996 Act* (see 53.19, 53.20 UNFAIR DISMISSAL – I). The requirements for a valid compromise agreement which satisfies the statutory conditions is addressed at 21.33–21.35 EMPLOYMENT TRIBUNALS – II).

32.24   LIABILITY OF EMPLOYERS AND PRINCIPALS

As in other anti-discrimination provisions, any unlawful act under the *Part Time Workers Regulations* committed by a person in the course of his employment is treated as also having been done by his employer, whether or not it was done with the employer's knowledge or approval. Anything done by a person as agent for the employer with the authority of the employer shall be treated as also done by the employer. It shall be a defence for any person in respect of an act alleged to have been done by a worker of his to prove that he took such steps as were reasonably practicable to prevent the worker from (a) doing that act, or (b) doing, in the course of his employment, acts of that description: *reg 9*. See 12.13(*D*) AND (*E*) DISCRIMINATION AND EQUAL OPPORTUNITIES – I).

33   Maternity and Parental Rights

Cross-references. See UNFAIR DISMISSAL – I and II (51, 52) for the general rules on unfair dismissal; EQUAL PAY (24) and DISCRIMINATION AND EQUAL OPPORTUNITIES – I (12) for the rules prohibiting discrimination against women.

33.1   The *Employment Protection Act 1975* created new statutory rights for female employees. These provisions were re-enacted in the *Employment Protection (Consolidation) Act 1978* (*'EPCA 1978'*). An additional right, the right to paid time off for ante-natal care, was conferred by the *Employment Act 1980*, which also amended the existing provisions, and statutory rights were further extended by the *Trade Union Reform and Employment Rights Act 1993* (*'TURERA 1993'*). With the exception of the law relating to statutory maternity pay (which is contained in the *Social Security Contributions and Benefits Act 1992*), all the relevant legislation was consolidated into the *Employment Rights Act 1996* (*'ERA 1996'*). Most of the rights and principles set out in the *ERA 1996* which relate to maternity leave have found their way into the *Employment Relations Act 1999* (*'ERA 1999'*), or appear in the regulations made under the *ERA 1999*. *The Maternity and Parental Leave, etc Regulations 1999* (*SI 1999/3312*) made under the *ERA 1999*, extended the period of ordinary maternity leave from 14 to 18 weeks; and reduced the service requirement before an employee earned the right to extended maternity leave of 29 weeks from two years to one year. The *Employment Act 2002* (*'EA 2002'*) and accompanying regulations ushered in some significant changes to the law on maternity and paternity rights, extending the period of ordinary maternity leave from 18 weeks to 26 weeks, and the period of additional maternity leave to 26 weeks from the date when ordinary maternity leave has ended. The *Work and Families Act* 2006, and accompanying regulations, have introduced further changes for those whose employees whose children were born on or after 1 April 2007 (see *Maternity and Parental Leave etc Regulations 1999*, as amended).

Female employees who can satisfy the relevant qualifying conditions enjoy the following statutory rights:

(*a*)   paid time off to receive ante-natal care;

(*b*)   26 weeks' ordinary maternity leave and 26 weeks' additional maternity leave;

(*c*)   protection from dismissal by reason of pregnancy or childbirth;

(*d*)   protection from detriment by reason of pregnancy, childbirth or maternity;

(*e*)   maternity pay;

(*f*)   return to work after ordinary maternity leave or additional maternity leave;

(*g*)   offer of alternative work before being suspended on maternity grounds;

(*h*)   remuneration on suspension on maternity grounds.

The *Social Security Act 1989, Sch 5 paras 2, 5, 6*, contains provisions which deal with unfair maternity and family leave provisions in employment-related benefits schemes. These provisions are intended to implement *Directive 86/378/EEC* (see

711

25.5 EUROPEAN COMMUNITY LAW) and were brought into force to a limited extent on 23 June 1994 (*Social Security Act 1989 (Commencement No 5) Order 1994 (SI 1994/1661)*).

The law as to sex discrimination (see DISCRIMINATION AND EQUAL OPPORTUNITIES – I, II, III (12, 13, 14)) is also extremely important in defining the extent of the protection which the law confers on women in connection with pregnancy or childbirth (see 33.6 below).

33.2   **TIME OFF FOR ANTE-NATAL CARE**

An employee who is pregnant and who has, on the advice of a registered medical practitioner, registered midwife or registered health visitor, made an appointment to attend at any place for the purpose of receiving ante-natal care, has the right not to be unreasonably refused time off during her working hours to enable her to keep the appointment (*ERA 1996, s 55(1)*), and to be paid for the period of absence at the appropriate hourly rate (*ERA 1996, s 56(1)*).

33.3   **Qualifying requirements**

Except for the first appointment for ante-natal care, the employee must, if requested by the employer, produce for his inspection:

(*a*)   a certificate from a registered medical practitioner, registered midwife or registered health visitor stating that the employee is pregnant; and

(*b*)   an appointment card or some other document showing that the appointment has been made.

(*ERA 1996, s 55(2)(a), (b)*.)

There is no minimum qualifying period of employment for the enjoyment of this right. If an employer could reasonably refuse to allow an employee time off to attend an ante-natal appointment – for example, if she was a part-time employee and could arrange to attend during her time off – yet he allows her time off, it is thought that he is not obliged to pay her during the period of her absence provided that he obtains her agreement and makes it clear that the time is not being given in satisfaction of a statutory obligation. The reason for this qualification is that if an employee is entitled to take time off in accordance with the provisions of *ERA 1996, s 55(1)*, she is automatically entitled to be paid for the time taken (*ERA 1996, s 56(1)*). (See *Gregory v Tudsbury Ltd* [1982] IRLR 267.)

33.4   **Amount**

The employee is entitled to payment from the employer for the period of absence at the appropriate hourly rate. That is the amount of one week's pay divided by:

(*a*)   the number of normal working hours in a week for that employee when employed under the contract of employment in force on the day when the time off is taken;

(*b*)   where the number of such normal working hours differs from week to week or over a longer period, the average number of such hours, calculated by reference to the hours worked during the period of 12 weeks ending with the last complete week before the day on which the time off is taken; or

(*c*)   where the number of hours worked in a week differs, but the employee has not been employed long enough for the 12-week calculation to be made, a number which fairly represents the number of normal working hours in a week taking into account the employee's contract and the average number of hours worked by other employees of the same employer in comparable employment.

(*ERA 1996, s 56(2)–(4)*; and see PAY – I (32).)

33.5 Remedies

An employee may present a complaint to an employment tribunal to the effect that her employer has unreasonably refused her time off as required by *ERA 1996, s 55(1)* or has failed to pay her the whole or part of any amount to which she is entitled under *ERA 1996, s 56(1)* (*ERA 1996, s 57(1)*). Such a complaint must be presented within the period of three months beginning with the date of the appointment concerned, or within such further period as the tribunal considers reasonable in a case where it is satisfied that it was not reasonably practicable for the complaint to be presented within the period of three months (*ERA 1996, s 57(2)*; for reasonable practicability see 20.7 EMPLOYMENT TRIBUNALS – I). By analogy with the time limit in unfair dismissal cases, it is thought that it will not be considered to be reasonably practicable for an employee to present a claim until she is aware or ought reasonably to be aware of her rights (see *Nu-Swift International Ltd v Mallinson* [1979] ICR 157). Where an employment tribunal finds a complaint well-founded, it will make a declaration to that effect and make an order for payment of the amount of money due under the statutory provisions (*ERA 1996, s 57(3)–(5)*). The employee's statutory right to remuneration does not affect her contractual right, but any contractual remuneration will go to discharge her statutory entitlement, and vice versa (*ERA 1996, s 56(5), (6)*).

33.6 PROTECTION FROM DISMISSAL BY REASON OF PREGNANCY

A woman will automatically be held to be unfairly dismissed if the reason or principal reason for her dismissal is connected with any of the following:

(*a*)   her pregnancy;

(*b*)   the fact that she has given birth to a child, where her ordinary or additional maternity leave period is ended by the dismissal;

(*c*)   where her contract of employment was terminated after the end of her ordinary or additional maternity leave period;

(*d*)   the fact that she took, sought to take or availed herself of the benefits of ordinary or additional maternity leave;

(*e*)   the fact of a requirement or recommendation such as is referred to in *ERA 1996, s 66(1), (2)* (suspension from work on maternity grounds; see 33.23 below);

(*f*)   she is made redundant and the circumstances of the redundancy apply equally to other employees and the reason for her selection is (*a*), (*b*) or (*d*) above;

(*g*)   she failed to return to work after a period of ordinary or additional maternity leave in circumstances where her employer did not notify her of the date on which the period in question would end or gave her less than 28 days' notice of the relevant end date, and she reasonably believed that the period had not ended, or the period in question had ended but it was not reasonably practicable for her to return on that date;

(h) she undertook, considered undertaking or refused to undertake work during her statutory maternity leave period (that is, ordinary maternity leave and/or additional maternity leave periods).

(*Regulation 20.*)

In addition, a woman will be treated as having been automatically unfairly dismissed even if there is a genuine redundancy situation, and even if she was not selected for redundancy on any of the grounds (*a*), (*b*) or (*d*) above, if the employer fails to comply with the requirements set out in *reg 10* for dealing with redundancies during ordinary or additional maternity leave (see para 33.19 below) (*reg 20(1)(b)*). The dismissal for redundancy must, however, end the maternity leave period.

There is no longer a small employers' exemption for automatically unfair dismissal. However, there is an exemption in non-redundancy situations, if the employer can show that it is not reasonably practicable to permit the employee to return to a job which is both suitable for her and appropriate for her to do in the circumstances; and an associated employer offers her a job of that kind, and she accepts or unreasonably refuses that offer (*reg 20(7)*). It is for the employer to establish that he has satisfied this statutory defence (*reg 20(8)*).

Even though the dismissal may not be treated as automatically unfair, however, it may still be unfair according to ordinary principles of the law of unfair dismissal. If she is dismissed because another employee has been engaged in her position, that will not be an acceptable reason for her dismissal (*McFadden v Greater Glasgow Passenger Transport Executive* [1977] IRLR 327).

Under the previous legislation, it was held that the words 'or any other reason connected with her pregnancy' were to be interpreted broadly (*Clayton v Vigers* [1989] ICR 713). This included a pregnancy-related illness, such as post-natal depression arising in the period of maternity leave following childbirth (*Caledonia Bureau Investment Property v Caffrey* [1998] ICR 603). The same broad interpretation is likely to apply under the present legislation.

In *Ramdoolar v Bycity Ltd* [2005] ICR 368, the EAT held that for a dismissal to be automatically unfair for a reason connected with pregnancy, the employer must know, or believe in the existence, of the pregnancy. It is not sufficient that symptoms of pregnancy existed which the employer ought to have realised meant that the employee was pregnant. The EAT left open the possibility, however, that a dismissal may be automatically unfair if an employer, detecting the symptoms of pregnancy and fearing the consequences, dismisses the employee before his suspicion could be proved right.

A dismissal in connection with pregnancy and the taking of maternity leave may also amount to sex discrimination (see *The Employment Equality* (*Sex Discrimination*) *Regulations 2005 SI 2005/2467*).

33.7 **Qualifying period**

There is no qualifying period for a complaint of unfair dismissal where the dismissal is for any of the reasons set out in 33.6(*a*)-(*e*) above, nor (although less common!) is there any upper age limit (*ERA 1996, ss 108(3), 109(2)*). See also 48.14 TERMINATION OF EMPLOYMENT for the obligation to give reasons for dismissal of pregnant employees.

33.8   **PROTECTION FROM DETRIMENT BY REASON OF PREGNANCY**

Regulation 19 introduces a new statutory right protecting women from being subject to any detriment (other than dismissal) by any act, or any deliberate failure to act, by her employer if it is done for the reason that:

(*a*)   she is pregnant;

(*b*)   she has given birth to a child, if the act or failure to act takes place during the employee's ordinary or additional maternity leave period;

(*c*)   she is the subject of a relevant requirement, or a relevant recommendation, as defined by s *66(2)* of the *ERA 1996*;

(*d*)   she took, sought to take or availed herself of the benefits of, ordinary maternity leave; or

(*e*)   she took or sought to take additional maternity leave;

(*f*)   she failed to return to work after a period of ordinary or additional maternity leave in circumstances where her employer did not notify her of the date on which the period in question would end or gave her less than 28 days' notice of the relevant end date, and she reasonably believed that the period had not ended, or the period in question had ended but it was not reasonably practicable for her to return on that date;

(*g*)   she undertook, considered undertaking or refused to undertake work during her statutory maternity leave period (that is, ordinary maternity leave and/or additional maternity leave periods).

A woman is treated as availing herself of the benefits of ordinary maternity leave if, during her ordinary maternity leave period, she avails herself of the benefit of any of the terms and conditions of her employment preserved by *s 71* of *ERA 1996* during that period.

The failure of an employer to pay a woman on maternity leave wages, salary or a bonus which she would have earned had she been at work cannot be a 'detriment' within the meaning of *reg 19*: see *Hoyland v Asda Stores Ltd* [2005] ICR 1235.

33.9   **Remedies**

Where an employee has suffered such a detriment, she may claim to an employment tribunal pursuant to *ERA 1996, s 48*. On such a complaint, it is for the employer to show the ground on which any act, or deliberate failure to act, was done. The complaint must be presented within the period of three months beginning with the date of the act or failure to act, or the last of the series of such acts. Time for presenting a complaint can be extended where (as in the case for unfair dismissal) the employment tribunal is satisfied that it was not reasonably practicable for the complaint to be presented within the period of three months.

If the complaint is well-founded, the employment tribunal shall make a declaration to that effect, and may make an award of compensation. The amount of compensation shall be such as the tribunal considers to be just and equitable in all the circumstances, having regard to the infringement to which the complaint relates, and any loss attributable to the act in question (*ERA 1996, s 49*).

33.10   **STATUTORY MATERNITY PAY**

The statutory provisions relating to the system of statutory maternity pay ('SMP'), first introduced by the *Social Security Act 1989,* were consolidated into the *Social Security Contributions and Benefits Act 1992* ('*SSCBA 1992*'). The relevant provisions of the *SSCBA 1992* have been the subject of significant amendments due to the *Pregnant Workers Directive* (*Directive 92/85/EEC*).

There may also be a contractual right to maternity pay under the contract of employment. If the employee fails to return to work and contractual maternity pay becomes repayable to the employer pursuant to a term of the contract, either the employer or the employee may be able to recover the National Insurance contributions on such pay from the Secretary of State (*Social Security* (*Refunds*) (*Repayment of Contractual Maternity Pay*) *Regulations 1990* (*SI 1990/536*)).

33.11 Qualifying requirements

An employee must normally satisfy the following conditions before she can qualify for SMP:

(*a*)   she must have been continuously employed by her employer for at least 26 weeks ending with the week immediately preceding the 14th week before the expected week of confinement (see CONTINUOUS EMPLOYMENT (7));

(*b*)   her normal weekly earnings, for the period of eight weeks ending with the week immediately preceding the 14th week before the expected week of confinement, must be not less than the lower limit for the payment of National Insurance contributions (currently £84);

(*c*)   she must have become pregnant and reached, or been confined before reaching, the start of the 11th week before the expected week of confinement.

(*SSCBA 1992, s 164(1), (2)*.)

'Confinement' is defined as labour resulting in the issue of a living child, or labour after 24 weeks of pregnancy resulting in the issue of a child whether alive or dead (*SSCBA 1992, s 171(1)*).

There are certain exceptions to the above requirement of continuous employment. Thus, the employer remains liable if the period of continuous employment was not less than eight weeks and he brought the contract of employment to an end solely or mainly for the purpose of avoiding his liability for SMP (*SI 1986/1960, reg 3*). The right to SMP survives if the woman is confined more than 14 weeks before the expected date of confinement, and would, but for her confinement, otherwise have qualified (*SI 1986/1960, reg 4* as amended by *SI 1994/1367, reg 3*).

For the purpose of calculating continuity of employment, it is the existence of the contract of employment which is crucial, and not whether the employee is in fact working. In *Secretary of State for Employment v Doulton Sanitaryware Ltd* [1981] ICR 477 (a case decided under the previous law relating to maternity pay) it was held on the facts that the parties intended the contract to continue even though the employee had stopped working (she had been put on a list of 'prolonged absentees').

It is clearly intended that the right to SMP should not be conditional upon an intention to return to work after the confinement.

There is no entitlement to SMP in respect of any week in which the employee is in legal custody or sentenced to a term of imprisonment, other than a suspended sentence, or in respect of any subsequent week within the maternity pay period (*SI 1986/1960, reg 9*).

Members of Her Majesty's forces are excluded from the right to SMP (*SSCBA 1992, s 161(2)*). The right extends to persons working within the EC, to employees who are absent from Great Britain on holiday or for business purposes at any time during the maternity pay period, as well as to certain mariners (*Statutory Maternity Pay (Persons Abroad and Mariners) Regulations 1987 (SI 1987/418)*, as amended by *Social Security Contributions, Statutory Maternity Pay and Statutory Sick Pay (Miscellaneous Amendments) Regulations 1996 (SI 1996/777), reg 4*).

SSCBA 1992, s 164(6) provides that any agreement is void in so far as it purports to exclude or limit the right to SMP.

33.12 Period of entitlement

SMP is payable in respect of each week during the 'maternity pay period'. The maternity pay period will be a period of 39 consecutive weeks. In general, when it starts depends upon when the employee gives notice and stops work. However, the first day of the period will not be earlier than the 11th week before the expected week of confinement, nor later than the day immediately following the day of confinement.

33.13 Procedure for making a claim

The employee must give her employer (or the person liable to make payments of SMP) 28 days' prior notice of her absence from work because of her pregnancy, or if that is not reasonably practicable, such notice as is reasonably practicable. That notice must be in writing if the liable person so requests (*SSCBA, s 164(4)*).

The employee must also provide a maternity certificate signed by a doctor or midwife as evidence of her pregnancy and of the expected date of confinement, and there is a prescribed form for such certificates (*Social Security Administration Act 1992, s 15; Statutory Maternity Pay (Medical Evidence) Regulations 1987 (SI 1987/235)*).

33.14 Amount of payments

SSCBA 1992, s 166 provides for two rates of payment. (The application of *s 166* is modified by *SI 1986/1960, reg 4(3)* (as amended by *SI 1994/1367, reg 3*) where the employee is confined more than 14 weeks before the expected date of confinement, and would, but for her confinement, otherwise have qualified; see 33.11 above.)

For the first six weeks of the maternity pay period, the rate is calculated as being 9/10ths of the employee's normal weekly earnings for the period of eight weeks immediately preceding the 14th week before the expected week of confinement (there is no minimum rate of payment).

Where a woman receives or is entitled to receive a backdated pay increase which includes a sum in respect of that eight-week period, the employee's normal weekly earnings should be calculated as if such sum was paid in that period (*Statutory Maternity Pay (General) Amendment Regulations 1996 (SI 1996/1335), reg 2*). (These *Regulations* were designed to give effect to the decision of the ECJ in *Gillespie v Northern Health and Social Services Board: C-342/93* [1996] IRLR 214.) In *Alabaster v Woolwich plc* [2000] ICR 1037 the EAT held that the *1996 Amendment Regulations* did not give proper effect to the decision of the ECJ in *Gillespie v Northern Health and Social Services Board: C-342/93* [1996] IRLR 214. It held that in calculating maternity pay, a woman was entitled to the benefit of all increases in her basic salary which took effect between the start of the 'relevant period' (the period of eight weeks immediately preceding the 14th week before the expected week of confinement) and the end of her maternity leave, and not just backdated pay increases. The EAT also held that the proper remedy for failure to make appropriate payments of maternity pay was an action for unlawful deduction of wages. The matter was referred to the ECJ, which has recently held ([2005] ICR 695) that a woman who receives a pay increase before the start of her maternity leave is entitled to have the increase taken into consideration even though the pay rise was not backdated to the relevant reference period for the purposes of the *1996 Amendment Regulations*. New regulations have been introduced to give effect to the ECJ's decision: *Statutory Maternity Pay (General) Amendment Regulations 2005 (SI 2005/729)*. (For the conclusion to this story, and to see how the 'remedy' was made available to the employee, see *Alabaster v Barclays Bank (No 2)* [2005] EWCA Civ 508, [2005] ICR 1246).

After the first six weeks, the payment for the remaining 33 weeks is set at the lesser of £112.75 per week or 90% of the woman's average weekly earnings.

SMP should be paid in the like manner and at the same time as the employee would normally be paid, or if there is no agreement as to a pay day, or no normal pay day, on the last day of a calendar month (*SI 1986/1960, regs 27, 29*). It does not exclude any contractual benefits to which the employee may be entitled, but the employer is entitled to set off SMP against contractual remuneration in respect of the same period and vice versa (*SSCBA, Sch 13 para 3*). In other words, the employer has to meet the more onerous of the contractual and statutory burdens, but not both of them. Similarly, tax, National Insurance contributions and any other regular deductions fall to be deducted from SMP.

33.15   Remedy for non-payment

If the employer fails to make payments of SMP to which the employee believes herself to be entitled, the employee may first of all require the employer within a reasonable time to supply her with a written statement of the position which he is adopting (*Social Security Administration Act 1992, s 15(2)*). Where an employer decides that he has no liability to pay SMP or further SMP, he must also furnish her with the details of and reasons for his decision, and with other information in connection with the making of a claim by her for a maternity allowance or incapacity benefit (*SI 1986/1960, reg 25A* (inserted by *SI 1990/622*)). If the dispute is not resolved, either the employee or the DWP may refer the matter to the Board of the Inland Revenue (*Statutory Sick Pay and Statutory Maternity Pay (Decisions) Regulations 1999 (SI 1999/776)*. An employer's continued refusal to pay after an adverse determination is an offence.

If the employee is unable to obtain her entitlement from the employer (which may be because he has become insolvent), she is entitled to look to the Commissioners of Inland Revenue for payment (*SI 1986/1960, regs 7, 30*).

33.16   Recoupment by employer

The system whereby the employer recoups payments of SMP made by him is similar to that which used to apply to statutory sick pay (see SICKNESS AND SICK PAY (44)). In short, the relevant moneys are deducted by the employer from National Insurance contributions which would otherwise fall to be remitted by him. Apart from 'small employers' (broadly, those whose contributions payments for the qualifying tax year do not exceed £45,000), employers will be able to recover only 92% of each payment of SMP. Small employers are entitled to recover an 'additional payment', equal to 4.5% of each payment of SMP, which is intended to recoup the National Insurance contributions payable on such payments.

The system of recoupment is governed by regulations made under *SSCBA 1992, s 167* (substituted by *EA 2002, s 21(1)*). These are the *Statutory Maternity Pay (Compensation of Employers) and Miscellaneous Amendment Regulations 1994 (SI 1994/1882)*, as amended.

Under the new statutory regime, employers can, in certain circumstances, obtain advance recovery of SMP from the Board of the Inland Revenue (*EA 2002, s 21(2); SI 1994/1882, reg 5* (as amended by *SI 2003/672*)).

33.17 THE RIGHT TO TAKE MATERNITY LEAVE AND RETURN TO WORK

ERA 1996, ss 71–75 and regulations made thereunder provide for a statutory right to maternity leave and modify the right to return to work to take account of that right. It is necessary to distinguish between the different types of maternity leave: 'ordinary maternity leave', 'additional maternity leave' and 'compulsory maternity leave'.

33.18 Right to ordinary maternity leave

An employee who is absent from work at any time during her ordinary maternity leave period is entitled to the benefit of the terms and conditions of employment which would otherwise have been applicable to her, such as holiday entitlement even if they do not arise under her contract of employment, although this does not confer any entitlement to remuneration (*ERA 1996, s 71*). The *Regulations* define 'remuneration' as wages or salary only (*reg 9*). The employee is also bound during this period by any obligations arising under these same terms and conditions.

In *Merio Gomez v Continental Industries Del Caucho: C-342/01* [2004] IRLR 407, the ECJ held that a worker must be able to take the paid annual leave to which she is entitled under the *Working Time Directive* during a period other than the period of her maternity leave.

The maternity leave period commences with the date which the employee notifies as the date on which she intends her absence to commence (see below), or if earlier, the first day on which she is absent from work wholly or partly because of pregnancy or childbirth after the beginning of the fourth week before the expected week of childbirth, or if earlier, the day after the day on which childbirth occurs (*reg 6*). 'Childbirth' is defined as the birth of a living child or the birth of a child whether living or dead after 24 weeks of pregnancy (*ERA 1996, s 235(1)*). The maternity leave period continues for 26 weeks or until the end of the compulsory maternity leave period if later, or if later until the expiry of any period during which there is any statutory prohibition on the employee working by reason of her recently having given birth, or if earlier upon the dismissal of the employee (*reg 7*). The period of 'ordinary maternity leave' is 26 weeks.

In order to enjoy the right to ordinary maternity leave, the employee must either:

(a)   notify her employer of the date on which she intends her period of ordinary maternity leave to commence (which must be no earlier than the beginning of the 11th week before the expected week of childbirth), and do so no later than the end of the 15th week before the expected week of childbirth or, if that is not reasonably practicable, as soon as is reasonably practicable notify her employer of her pregnancy, the expected week of childbirth, and the date on which she intends her ordinary maternity leave period to start.

If requested to do so by her employer, she must produce for his inspection a certificate from a registered medical practitioner, or a registered midwife, stating the expected week of childbirth. The notification of the date on which she intends her ordinary maternity leave period to start shall be given in writing, if the employer so requests, and shall not specify a date earlier than the beginning of the 11th week before the expected week of childbirth; or

(b) where the period of ordinary maternity leave commences the day following the first day after the beginning of the fourth week before the expected week of childbirth, notify her employer as soon as is reasonably practicable that she is absent wholly or partly because of pregnancy; or

(c) where childbirth occurs before the notified leave date or before she has notified such a date, notify her employer that she has given birth as soon as is reasonably practicable after the birth.

Any such notice must be given in writing if the employer so requests (*reg 4*).

The date upon which the employee commences the period of ordinary maternity leave may be varied if she gives 28 days' notice before the date that is being varied, or 28 days' notice before the new date, whichever is earlier; or if those dates cannot be complied with she gives notice to the employer as soon as it is reasonably practicable to do so.

Apart from a redundancy situation (see 32.19 below), an employee returning after an isolated period of ordinary maternity leave is entitled to return to the job in which she was employed before her absence. This carries with it the right to return on terms and conditions no less favourable than those that she would have enjoyed had she not been absent (*reg 18A*).

An employee who has a contractual or other right to maternity leave may not exercise both that and the statutory right separately, but may take advantage of whichever right is in any particular respect more favourable. The provisions of *ERA 1996* and of the *Regulations* then apply, modified as necessary, to the exercise of the composite right (*reg 21*).

33.19 Redundancy during ordinary maternity leave

If, during the maternity leave period (ordinary or additional), redundancy makes it impracticable to continue to employ an employee under her existing contract, she is entitled to be offered alternative employment with her employer, his successor (as defined by *ERA 1996, s 235(1)*) or an associated employer (see 7.9(*a*) CONTINUOUS EMPLOYMENT) if a suitable available vacancy exists. The offer must be made before the old employment ends, and the new employment must commence immediately the old employment ends. It must involve work of a kind suitable in relation to the employee and appropriate for her to do in the circumstances, and the terms and conditions as to capacity, place of employment and otherwise must not be substantially less favourable than under the old contract (*reg 10*).

33.20 Compulsory maternity leave

An employee entitled to ordinary maternity leave in accordance with *ERA 1996* shall not be permitted by her employer to work for a period of two weeks commencing with the day on which childbirth occurs. (This is described as 'compulsory maternity leave' (*ERA 1996, s 72; reg 8*). Failure to comply with this prohibition renders the employer liable on summary conviction to a fine (*ERA 1996, s 72(5)*.)

At present, a woman who exercises her right to take ordinary maternity leave is entitled to return from that leave to the job in which she was employed before her absence (*ERA 1996, s 71(4)(c)*). Under the new statutory regime, she will only be entitled to return from leave to a 'job of a prescribed kind' (*EA 2002, s 17(1)*).

33.21 Additional maternity leave

An employee who qualifies for ordinary maternity leave now qualifies automatically for additional maternity leave as well. (There is no longer any qualifying period of employment to access this right). The right to additional maternity leave continues until the end of the period of 26 weeks from the date upon which it commences (*reg 7(4)*). The additional maternity leave period commences on the day after the last day of the employee's ordinary maternity leave period (*reg 6(3)*). Where the employer has been notified by the employee of the date on which the ordinary maternity leave period will commence, or has commenced, the employer must notify the employee of the date on which the additional maternity leave period ends (*reg 7(6)(7)*).

An employee who is entitled to additional maternity leave might be able to return to work before the end of the additional maternity leave period. To do so, she has to give her employer not less than 8 weeks' notice of the date on which she intends to return. If she does give this notice, then it would appear that her employer cannot seek to postpone her return date.

Where an employee does not give 8 weeks' notice of her intended return date and attempts to return to work earlier than the end of her additional maternity leave period, then her employer is entitled to postpone her return to a date such as will secure that he has 8 weeks' notice of her return. The only exception to this is that the postponement cannot extend beyond the date of the end of the additional maternity leave period. During the period of postponement, the employer is under no contractual obligation to pay any remuneration until the date to which her return was postponed, save where the employer has failed to notify the employee of when the additional maternity leave period was due to end.

An employee is now entitled to change her mind as to when to return to work during the additional maternity leave period, if she has already given notice of return before the end of that period or if the employer has (in line with the procedure above) postponed her return date. If the employee wishes to return to work later than the original return date, she must give her employer not less than 8 weeks' notice ending with the original return date. If she wishes to return earlier than the original return date, she must give at least 8 weeks' notice of the new return date.

Unlike the situation under the earlier legislative provisions, the employee does not need to inform her employer that she intends to exercise her right to return at the end of the additional maternity leave period unless she is specifically requested to do so by her employer. In addition, an employer is no longer entitled to request confirmation that the employee will be returning to work at the end of the additional maternity leave period (the former *reg 12* has been revoked).

The right on redundancy is the same as for employees seeking to return after ordinary maternity leave (see 33.18 above).

The returning employee has the right to return on terms and conditions no less favourable than would have applied if she had not been absent. She is entitled to the same seniority, pension rights and similar rights as she would have enjoyed if she had not taken any additional maternity leave (*reg 18A*). There is no right to return to work on a part-time basis, or on terms preferable to the returning employee. Nevertheless, an employer's refusal to permit an employee to job share or return part-time might constitute indirect sex discrimination (*Hardys & Hansons plc v Lax* [2005] EWCA Civ 846, [2005] ICR 1565). Employees taking additional maternity leave are entitled, during the period of that leave, to the benefit of the implied obligation of trust and confidence and any terms and conditions of employment applicable to notice of termination of the employment contract; compensation in the event of redundancy; or disciplinary or grievance procedures (*reg 17(a)*). These employees are similarly bound by the obligation of good faith to the employer and any terms and conditions of employment relating to notice of termination of the employment contract; the disclosure of confidential information; the acceptance of gifts or other benefits; or the employee's participation in any other business (*reg 17(b)*).

The new legislation has nothing to say about the vexed question of women who fail to return to work on the return date. It may well be that the law under the previous legislation will prevail. It is useful therefore to consider the recent decision of the House of Lords in *Halfpenny v IGE Medical Systems Ltd* [2001] ICR 73, construing the former legislation.

The facts of *Halfpenny* are relatively straightforward. The employee failed to return to work on the notified return date for reasons of ill-health, supported by a medical certificate. As she had not exhausted her contractual entitlement to sick leave and had a good reason for her absence, her employer was found to have dismissed her wrongfully by refusing to extend her period of leave. In addition, the employer was found to have discriminated against the employee on grounds of her sex as it would have allowed a male employee to continue sick leave with pay.

In the Court of Appeal ([1999] IRLR 177), it was held (confirming the earlier decision of *Crees v Royal London Mutual Insurance Society Ltd* [1998] IRLR 245) that to avail herself of the right not to be unfairly dismissed following maternity leave, an employee need not physically return to work on the notified day of return. An employee was held to have exercised the right to return to work following maternity leave (and also preserved her continuity of employment) merely by giving the appropriate notice of return before the notified date of return.

This aspect of the decision was overturned by the House of Lords, where it was held that an employee did not avail herself of the 'return to work' merely by giving the appropriate notice of return if she did not actually return to work on the notified day. Rather, the employee had to give the appropriate notice and also demonstrate that, on the notified date for return, she had done something consistent with the due performance by her of her revived contract of employment. Normally, this would mean that she actually returned to work physically. If, however, under the contract she would not be bound to return on that day (eg as a result of an accident, a strike, or poor weather conditions) she merely had to have done something to demonstrate that she would have returned to work otherwise. If she were ill, she would have to provide the necessary certificates that would be required of her under the contract.

The House of Lords went on to decide that where the employee had demonstrated the appropriate conduct for a 'return to work', she would be treated as having been 'dismissed' by her employer if he refused to let her return, for the purposes of the law of unfair dismissal only. She had no right, however, to claim that she had been wrongfully dismissed as the contract of employment would be treated as having been suspended until her actual return. Nor would she have any right to claim sex discrimination, as she would not be treated for the purposes of the *Sex Discrimination Act 1975* as being 'a woman employed by' the employer at the relevant time.

An employee who has both a statutory and a contractual right to return to work may not exercise the two rights separately, but may take advantage of whichever right is the more favourable in any particular respect (*reg 21*).

33.22   Dismissal of replacement

Where an employer engages an employee to take the place of one who is absent due to pregnancy, the subsequent dismissal of that employee upon the resumption of work by the original employee will be considered to be a dismissal for a substantial reason (see 54.14 UNFAIR DISMISSAL – II) only if the employer informs the employee in writing, on engaging her, that her employment will be terminated on the resumption of work by another employee who is, or will be, absent wholly or partly because of pregnancy or childbirth (*ERA 1996, s 106*). However, this fact does not, in itself, make the dismissal fair. The employment tribunal will consider whether the dismissal was fair in all the circumstances (see further 52.4 UNFAIR DISMISSAL – II).

33.22A Work during statutory maternity leave

The *Maternity and Parental Leave etc and the Paternity and Adoption Leave (Amendment) Regulations 2006 (SI 2006/2014)* have introduced a new right for an employee to work for her employer for up to 10 days during her 'statutory maternity leave' period (that is, ordinary maternity leave and additional maternity leave periods) without bringing her maternity leave to an end. This 'work' may include training or other activity undertaken for the purposes of keeping in touch with the workplace. The employee will continue to be paid statutory maternity pay for this period of 'work' (if she is still entitled to it), although the parties may agree a greater level of remuneration. Where 'work' is carried out, this does not extend the maternity leave periods. There is no corresponding right for an employer to insist that an employee 'work' during her maternity leave.

33.23   SUSPENSION FROM WORK ON MATERNITY GROUNDS

An employee will be taken to be suspended from work on maternity grounds if her employer suspends her on the ground that she is pregnant, has recently given birth, or is breastfeeding a child, and he does so in consequence either of a statutory requirement, or of a recommendation contained in a relevant provision of a *Health and Safety at Work Act 1974* code of practice (see 28.17 HEALTH AND SAFETY AT WORK – II), which means a provision specified in an order made by the Secretary of State (*ERA 1996, s 66*).

The *Suspension from Work (on Maternity Grounds) Order 1994 (SI 1994/2930)* specified the following provisions of the *Management of Health and Safety at Work Regulations 1992 (SI 1992/2051)*, both inserted by the *Management of Health and Safety at Work (Amendment) Regulations 1994 (SI 1994/2865)*:

(*a*)   *reg 13A(3)* (suspension from work of new or expectant mother to avoid risk from any processes or working conditions, or physical, biological or chemical agents)(now set out at *reg 16* of the *Management of Health and Safety at Work Regulations 1999, SI 1999/3242*); or

(*b*)   *reg 13B* (suspension from work of new or expectant mother working at night).

For a recent discussion of the concept of 'suspension' see *New Southern Railways Ltd v Quinn* [2006] IRLR 266.

33.24 Right to alternative work

Before being suspended on maternity grounds, the employee must be offered suitable alternative work if the employer has it available. This means work which is of a kind both suitable in relation to her and appropriate for her to do in the circumstances, and to which terms and conditions not substantially less favourable than her own apply (*ERA 1996, s 67(1)*, *(2)*).

If the employer fails to offer the employee such work which is available, she may complain to an employment tribunal, which has power, if it finds the complaint well-founded, to award such compensation as is just and equitable having regard to the infringement of the employee's right and to any loss which she has sustained because of it (*ERA 1996, s 70(4)*, *(6)*, *(7)*). The complaint must be presented before the end of the period of three months beginning with the first day of the suspension, or within such further period as the tribunal considers reasonable where it is satisfied that it was not reasonably practicable to present the complaint within three months (*ERA 1996, s 70(5)*; see 20.7 EMPLOYMENT TRIBUNALS – I).

A recent example of a claim brought under *ERA 1996, s 67(2)* involved airline cabin crew members who were employed on ground-based work only during their pregnancy: *British Airways (European Operations At Gatwick) Ltd v Moore* [2000] ICR 678. The Employment Appeal Tribunal upheld a finding of an employment tribunal that the employees had not been offered suitable alternative work while they were pregnant as the terms and conditions offered to them were substantially less favourable. The women were given their basic pay only, but did not receive the flying allowances which they would normally have received had they been airborne.

33.25 Right to remuneration

If an employee is suspended on maternity grounds, she is entitled to remuneration at the rate of a week's pay for each week of suspension, unless she has been offered suitable alternative work which she has unreasonably refused (see 33.24 above; 38.12 REDUNDANCY – I) (*ERA 1996, ss 68, 69(1)*).

This statutory right does not affect any contractual rights to remuneration during her suspension which the employee may have, and any contractual payments which are made go towards discharging the statutory obligation and vice versa (*ERA 1996, s 69(2)*, *(3)*).

If the employer fails to pay the whole or part of the remuneration which is due under *ERA 1996, s 68*, the employee may complain to an employment tribunal. If it finds the complaint well-founded, the tribunal will order payment of the amount due (*ERA 1996, s 70(1)*, *(3)*). The complaint must be presented before the end of the period of three months beginning with the unremunerated day to which it relates, or within such further period as the tribunal considers reasonable where it is satisfied that it was not reasonably practicable to present the complaint within three months (*ERA 1996, s 70(2)*; 20.7 EMPLOYMENT TRIBUNALS – I).

33.26 PARENTAL/PATERNITY LEAVE

Parental Leave

Parliament introduced the right of unpaid parental leave in respect of children born or adopted on or after 15 December 1999: *The Maternity and Parental Leave, etc Regulations 1999 (SI 1999/3312)*. The *Regulations* were designed to give effect to provisions contained in the *EU Parental Leave Directive (96/34)*. Amendments have been made to the original scheme to ensure compliance with the *Directive*: see the *Maternity and Parental Leave (Amendment) Regulations 2001 (SI 2001/4010);* see also the *Maternity and Parental Leave (Amendment) Regulations 2002 (SI 2002/2789)*.

At present, the right to parental leave is exercisable by any employee with one year's continuous service who has, or expects to have, responsibility for a child. This means 'parental responsibility' or registration as the child's father (*reg 13*).

The period of parental leave is set at 13 weeks for each child (*reg 14(1)*); parents of disabled children may take up to 18 weeks' leave. Ordinarily, this entitlement must be exercised before the child's fifth birthday (*reg 15(1)(a)*). Exceptions include parents of disabled children (those qualifying for disability living allowance), where parental leave can be taken until the 18th birthday. Also, where a child was born before 15 December 1999, and his fifth birthday was or is on or after that date, parental leave can be taken up until 31 March 2005: see *reg 15(2)*. Leave can only be taken, however, in blocks of one week at a time. It is not open to an employee to take one day's parental leave (unless this is agreed to by his employer as part of a Workforce Agreement): see *New Southern Railways Ltd (formerly South Central Trains Ltd) v Rodway* [2005] EWCA Civ 443, [2005] ICR 1162.

The *Regulations* set out 'conditions of entitlement' for the taking of parental leave. These include the provision of evidence of responsibility if required, notice to the employer of the leave dates, the ability of the employer to postpone leave in certain circumstances and maximum leave entitlement of four weeks per child in any given year (*Sch 2 to the 1999 Regulations*). These 'conditions of entitlement' are described as 'Default Provisions in Respect of Parental Leave' (the 'Default Provisions'). It is envisaged that Workforce Agreements will govern parental leave arrangements in most workplaces.

The *Regulations* provide a mechanism to protect employees who are victimised for taking parental leave. They are protected against suffering any detriment by reason of taking or seeking to take parental leave (*reg 19(2)(e)(ii)*), and can claim that they have been automatically unfairly dismissed if dismissed by reason of taking or seeking to take parental leave (*reg 20(2)(e)(ii)*).

In *New Southern Railways Ltd (formerly South Central Trains Ltd) v Rodway* [2005] EWCA Civ 443, [2005] ICR 1162, an employee sought to take one day's leave to look after his son. This was refused by the employer. The employee took the day off anyway, and was subsequently issued with a disciplinary warning for being absent without permission. He successfully argued before an employment tribunal that he had been victimised because the disagreement as to whether or not he was entitled to take one day's parental leave was for 'a reason related to parental leave'. This finding was rejected by the EAT, and more recently the Court of Appeal, which found that victimisation by the employer must be 'done for a prescribed reason', which is one prescribed by the parental leave regulations. As the employee could not lawfully take one day of parental leave under the 'Default Provisions', the disciplinary action was not for a prescribed reason, and was therefore lawful.

As with mothers availing themselves of 'additional maternity leave', certain contractual provisions continue to apply during the parental leave period (*reg 17*). There is also a right to return to work after parental leave.

An employee who takes parental leave for a period of four weeks or less, other than immediately after taking additional maternity leave, is entitled to return from leave to the job in which he or she was employed before the absence. An employee who takes parental leave for a period of more than four weeks is entitled to return from leave to the job in which he or she was employed before her absence or, if it is not reasonably practicable for the employer to permit the employee to return to that job, to another job which is both suitable and appropriate to do in the circumstances. The returning parent should be provided with the same terms and conditions as enjoyed previously. The provisions are analogous to those for mothers returning after additional maternity leave (see 33.21 above).

33.27 Paternity Leave

The *Employment Act 2002* introduced an entitlement to 'paternity leave'. The details are set out in the *Paternity and Adoption Leave Regulations 2002* (*SI 2002/2788*).

The entitlement to paternity leave for the purpose of caring for a child or supporting the child's mother is available on both the birth and adoption of a child. With respect to birth, an employee is entitled to paternity leave if he has been continuously employed for a period of not less than 26 weeks ending with the week immediately preceding the 14th week before the expected date of the child's birth, and he is either the child's father or is married to or is the partner of the child's mother and he has or expects to have responsibility for bringing up the child. The employee does not get additional rights if there are multiple births.

The employee may take either one week's leave, or two weeks' consecutive leave. This leave may be taken during the period commencing with the child's birth and either 56 days' later or, if the child is born before the first day of the expected week of its birth, 56 days after that date.

Before taking this leave, the employee must give notice of the expected week of childbirth, the length of leave, and the date on which the leave is to be taken. Notice must be given in or before the 15th week before the expected week of the child's birth or as soon as reasonably practicable if notice could not have been given sooner. Also, if requested by the employer, the employee must sign a declaration that he is taking leave for the proper purpose (caring for the child or supporting the child's mother) and satisfies the eligibility requirements.

During the course of paternity leave, the employee is entitled to the benefit of all the terms and conditions that would have applied to him had he not been absent save for remuneration (wages or salary), and is also bound by the obligations that arise out of those terms and conditions. The employee is entitled to return to the same job at the end of the period of paternity leave or, if that is not reasonably practicable, to another job which is suitable and practicable for him to do. The employee's return to work carries with it the same seniority, pension and other rights that he would have enjoyed had he not taken leave (*reg 13*).

As with employees taking maternity leave, employees taking paternity leave are protected against suffering detriment as a result of taking or seeking to take paternity leave (*reg 28*). It will be an automatically unfair dismissal if an employee is dismissed for taking or seeking to take paternity leave (*reg 29*).

Adoption leave can be taken for a period of 26 weeks (*reg 18*). The rules applying to adoption leave are similar to those applying to ordinary maternity leave.

33.28 **Statutory Paternity and Adoption Pay**

Employees who satisfy certain qualifying conditions (the eligibility conditions are: relationship to child and mother; employed earner's employment for a continuous period of at least 26 weeks; normal weekly earnings for the period of 8 weeks ending with the 'relevant week' at or above the lower earnings limit (£87 per week); and continued employed earner's employment beginning with the end of the 'relevant week') shall be entitled to statutory paternity pay or statutory adoption pay for up to two weeks in the sum of £112.75 per week or 90% of his normal weekly earnings, whichever is the lesser: *Statutory Paternity Pay and Statutory Adoption Pay (Weekly Rates) Regulations 2002 (SI 2002/2818)*, as amended. See also *Statutory Paternity Pay and Adoption Pay (General) Regulations 2002 (SI 2002/2822)*.

34   Pay – I: Payments, Pay Statements and Miscellaneous Statutory Pay Rights

(See also the following DTI Guidance documents 'Pay Statements: what they must itemise' (PL 704 (Fifth Revision)), 'Contracts of Employment: changes, breach of contract and deduction from wages' (PL 810 (6th Rev)) and 'Guarantee payments' (PL 724 (2nd Revision)). See also 'Suspension from work on medical or maternity grounds under Health and Safety Regulations' (PL 705, 4th revision) and 'Continuous Employment and a Week's Pay: Rules for Calculation' (PL 711 8th Revision).

Each of these guides is available to download on the DTI website (www.dti.gov.uk/er/regs.htm).

Cross-references. See PAY – II (35) for statutory deductions from pay; EQUAL PAY (24) for the rules against sex discrimination in pay; TRADE UNIONS – II (51) for deduction of trade union subscriptions.

34.1   INTRODUCTION

An employee's right to payment for his services is, of course, fundamental to the employment relationship and is principally governed by the particular terms of the contract of employment between the individual employee and employer. For example, the rate of pay and the intervals at which payment is made are governed by the individual employee's contract of employment, which also provides for any bonuses, commission, overtime, holiday pay or sick pay which may be payable (see also 34.22 below). Such matters must be included in the written particulars of the contract of employment given by the employer to the employee (see 8.4 CONTRACT OF EMPLOYMENT). There is, however, a substantial overlay of statutory rights and protection afforded to employees in relation to payment for their services in the form of the right not to suffer unauthorised deductions from wages, the right to a National Minimum Wage (from April 1999) and the right to itemised pay statements. These important rights are considered below.

Various other statutory rights to payment, such as statutory sick pay (see SICKNESS AND SICK PAY (44)) and statutory maternity pay (see MATERNITY AND PARENTAL RIGHTS (33)) are considered in other chapters in this work. Certain miscellaneous statutory rights to payment, namely, guarantee payments and medical suspension payments are outlined towards the end of this chapter. In addition there is an overview of the principles applicable to the calculation of 'a week's pay' – a statutory concept relevant to calculation of the sums payable under a number of the statutory employment rights such as the right to a redundancy payment and the payment of a basic award in a claim for unfair dismissal.

34.2   PAYMENT OF WAGES AND DEDUCTIONS FROM WAGES

Deductions from employees' pay were originally regulated by the *Wages Act 1986* ('*WA 1986*'). The *WA 1986* had replaced the *Truck Acts*, which had formerly restricted payment of wages other than in cash (but see 34.3 below). The *WA 1986* made special provision for employees in retail employment affording them greater protection against deductions from their wages. The provisions of the *WA 1986* are all consolidated in *Part II* of the *Employment Rights Act 1996*. In this section of this chapter, references below are to the *Employment Rights Act 1996* (*'ERA'*) unless otherwise stated. In very rare cases, involving contracts of employment predating 1987, it may be necessary to have regard to the previous law as set out in 34.3 and 34.4 below. In the vast majority of cases the position will be governed exclusively by the provisions of *Part II* of the *ERA* as discussed in 34.6 *et seq* below.

34.3   PAYMENT OF WAGES

WA 1986, s 11 (now repealed) removed restrictions on the way in which payment of wages to manual and other workers may be made. The method of payment is now to be determined solely by the terms of the contract. It will be either the subject of express agreement or determined by an implied term. If no express agreement is reached it is likely that the method of payment impliedly agreed will be that which is customary in the industry.

The provisions of *WA 1986* replaced the old restrictions on the payment of wages contained in the *Truck Acts* and the *Payment of Wages Act 1960*. *Section 11* came into force on 1 January 1987 (*The Wages Act 1986 (Commencement) Order 1986 (SI 1986/1998)*). However, because *s 1* of the *Truck Act 1831* operated by implying into the contract of employment a term that wages were payable in coin and not otherwise, it would appear that the contractual terms thus created survived the repeal of the *Act*. In other words, where the worker was employed before 1 January 1987, it remains necessary to refer to the provisions set out in 34.4 and 34.5 below, but the requirement is now contractual rather than statutory and may be varied by consent. Such consensual variation may no doubt be implied if payment has in fact been other than in coin for a lengthy period.

34.4   PAYMENT OF WAGES: PRE-1987 POSITION

Until 1 January 1987, all wages payable to a manual labourer for work done by him, with certain exceptions, had to be paid to him in current coin of the realm or, if he so requested, by payment into a bank account or by cheque, postal order or money order (*Truck Act 1831, s 3; Payment of Wages Act 1960, s 1*). Any agreement to the contrary was illegal, null and void. If an employer acted in breach of the *Truck Acts*, for example, by payment in kind by the delivery of goods, or by payment by cheque against the employee's wishes:

(*a*)   the employee could sue for the wages due, no allowance being made for the value of the goods supplied; and

(*b*)   the employer was guilty of an offence.

(*Truck Act 1831, s 9.*)

A foreman did not fall within the protection of the *Truck Acts* (*Brooker v Charrington Fuel Oils Ltd* [1981] IRLR 147).

34.5   Exceptions

(i)   The provision of medicine or medical attendance, fuel materials, tools and accommodation could form part of the consideration for the employee's services (*Truck Act 1831, s 23*).

(ii)   Payments to domestic servants did not need to comply with the requirements as to payment in coin (*Truck Act 1831, s 20*).

(iii)   Contracts for the provision for agricultural workers of food, non-intoxicating drink, a cottage or other similar allowances or privileges were not illegal if money wages were paid in addition to these benefits (*Truck Amendment Act 1887, s 4*).

34.6 DEDUCTIONS FROM WAGES: THE CURRENT PROVISIONS

No deduction from a worker's wages may be made unless either:

(*a*)   it is required or permitted by a statutory or contractual provision; or

(*b*)   the worker has given his prior written consent to the deduction.

(*ERA 1996, ss 13(1), 15(1)*.)

It is extremely important that deductions are not made in breach of this provision. Not only may sums wrongfully deducted be ordered to be repaid, but the employer may lose the right to recover the sums which he was seeking to deduct by any means at all (see 34.8 below).

If the deduction is made pursuant to a contractual provision, the terms of the contract must have been shown to the worker or, if not in writing, its effect notified in writing to the worker before the deduction is made (*ERA 1996, ss 13(2), 15(2)* and see *Kerr v Sweater Shop (Scotland) Ltd; Sweater Shop (Scotland) Ltd v Park* [1996] IRLR 424, EAT). In *Mennell v Newell & Wright (Transport Contractors) Ltd* [1997] IRLR 519 the Court of Appeal held that, although a complaint could be presented where the employee had been employed for less than two years (now one year), an employment tribunal had no jurisdiction to deal with *threatened* deductions from wages as this *Act* stated that a tribunal could only hear complaints where an employer had actually made a deduction. Accordingly, a threat of dismissal in order to impose a variation of the contract of employment so as to enable an employer to make deductions from wages did not amount to a breach of the relevant wages provisions of the *ERA 1996*. In *Discount Tobacco and Confectionery Ltd v Williamson* [1993] ICR 371, it was held that for there to be prior written consent, the consent must precede not only the deduction itself, but also the event or conduct giving rise to the deduction. What has to appear in writing in either case is not merely provision for repayment of the sum concerned but for it to be deducted *from wages* (*Potter v Hunt Contracts Ltd* [1992] ICR 337).

The above provisions do not apply to deductions:

(i)   made in order to reimburse the employer for any overpayment of wages or expenses made for any reason;

(ii)   made pursuant to any statutory disciplinary proceedings;

(iii)   which are statutory payments due to a public authority;

(iv)   payable to third parties, for example, trade union dues, made either pursuant to a contractual term to the inclusion of which the worker has agreed in writing, or otherwise with his prior written agreement or consent (but as to union dues, see 49.1 TRADE UNIONS – II for restrictions on the deduction of union dues);

(v)   made from a worker's wages for taking part in a strike or other industrial action; or

(vi)   made, with the worker's prior written agreement or consent, for the purpose of satisfying an order of a court or tribunal for the payment of an amount by the worker to the employer.

(*ERA 1996, ss 14, 15.*)

It is irrelevant whether deductions made for a purpose falling within these exceptions are in fact lawful and justified. Such issues are outside the jurisdiction of the tribunal under the *ERA 1996* in any event (*Sunderland Polytechnic v Evans* [1993] ICR 392, in which the EAT disapproved its own earlier reasoning in *Home Office v Ayres* [1992] ICR 175; see also *SIP (Industrial Products) Ltd v Swinn* [1994] ICR 473). In an important clarification, however, in *Gill v Ford Motor Co Ltd; Wong v BAE Systems Operations Ltd* [2004] IRLR 840, the EAT held that where an exception provided by *s 14* is relied upon by an employer, the employment tribunal must make findings of fact as to whether the *s 14* ground is actually engaged on the facts of the case. This does not, however, oblige the tribunal to make findings as to whether, as a matter of contract, such deductions are lawful as the enquiry is limited to whether the factual basis for reliance upon a *s 14* exception is made out.

Equivalent restrictions apply to the receipt of payments by an employer, from a worker employed by him, in his capacity as the worker's employer (*ERA 1996, s 15(1), (5)*).

The scope of the wages provisions of the *ERA 1996* is dependent upon the meaning given to the crucial terms 'wages', 'deduction' and 'worker'.

Wages. Wages are defined by *ERA 1996, s 27(1)* to mean any sums payable to the worker by his employer in connection with his employment, including:

(A)   any fee, bonus, commission, holiday pay or other emolument referable to his employment (or unpaid commission; see *Robertson v Blackstone Franks Investment Management Ltd* [1998] IRLR 376, CA below);

(B)   sums payable pursuant to orders for reinstatement or re-engagement (see UNFAIR DISMISSAL – III (55));

(C)   sums payable pursuant to interim orders for the continuation of a contract of employment (see 53.21 UNFAIR DISMISSAL – III);

(D)   PAY – I (34), guarantee payments, medical suspension payments (see further below), remuneration on suspension on maternity grounds (see MATERNITY AND PARENTAL RIGHTS (33)), certain payments for TIME OFF WORK (47) and remuneration under protective awards (see 39.6 REDUNDANCY – II);

(E)   statutory sick pay (see SICKNESS AND SICK PAY (44)); and

(F)   statutory maternity pay, paternity pay and adoption pay (see MATERNITY AND PARENTAL RIGHTS (33)).

A non-contractual bonus also counts as wages when payment is made (*ERA 1996, s 27(3)*). The EAT in *Kent Management Services Ltd v Butterfield* [1992] ICR 272 appeared to suggest that the *WA 1986* extended to any sums of the relevant kinds which would normally be expected to be paid, even if there was no strict contractual entitlement to receive them (see also *Farrell Matthews & Weir v Hansen* [2005] IRLR 160 below). Further, an employment tribunal has no jurisdiction, in relation to a claim of unlawful deduction from wages, to determine an applicant's *entitlement* to statutory sick pay where that entitlement was disputed by the employer. In relation to statutory sick pay, the exclusive juris-diction for the determination of disputes as to entitlement rests with the Inland

Revenue and, on appeal, the Inland Revenue Commissioners. The employment tribunal only has jurisdiction in relation to statutory sick pay where the employer admitted entitlement to statutory sick pay but had withheld all or part of that pay. The same limitation will apply in relation to statutory maternity, paternity or adoption pay. See *Taylor Gordon & Co Ltd v Timmons* [2004] IRLR 180, EAT.

However, the following payments are excluded from the definition of wages by *s 27(2)*:

(I)   advances under loan agreements or by way of an advance of wages;

(II)   payments in respect of expenses incurred in carrying out the employment (for example a car mileage allowance; see *Southwark London Borough v O'Brien* [1996] IRLR 420, EAT);

(III)   payments by way of pension, allowance or gratuity in connection with the worker's retirement or as compensation for loss of office;

(IV)   any payment referable to the worker's redundancy; and

(V)   any payment otherwise than in his capacity as a worker.

Benefits in kind are not treated as wages unless they are vouchers, stamps or similar documents of a fixed monetary value capable of being exchanged for money, goods or services (*ERA 1996, s 27(5)*). This would embrace, for example, luncheon vouchers.

Particular doubts arose as to whether a payment in lieu of notice amounts to wages. However, the House of Lords in *Delaney v Staples* [1992] ICR 483 held that it did not. Wages were payments in respect of the rendering of services during the employment, so all payments in respect of the termination of the contract are excluded, save to the extent that they are expressly caught by *s 27(1)*.

In *Robertson v Blackstone Franks Investment Management Ltd* [1998] IRLR 376, the Court of Appeal, upholding the decision of the EAT, held that commission payments which become payable after the termination of employment are 'wages' within the definition of *ERA 1996, s 27* and, accordingly, are protected against unauthorised deductions made by the employer. The statutory requirement was that the sum was payable 'in connection with the employee's employment' but it did not require the sum to be payable *during* the currency of the employee's contract. The Court of Appeal further held that the employer was entitled to set off sums paid as an advance against future commission in assessing the amount payable. To hold to the contrary would contravene *ERA 1996, s 25(3)* which obliges a tribunal to take into account sums 'already paid or repaid' by the employer to the worker. In *New Century Cleaning Co Ltd v Church* [2000] IRLR 27, the Court of Appeal held that the employer did not breach the provisions of *Part II* of the *ERA 1996* in reducing the amount of money paid to teams of employees for each job done by the team. On the facts of the case, which concerned a window-cleaning business, there was no express or implied contractual term for identifying the amount of money which each team would be paid nor any such term relating to the distribution of the money among the team. Accordingly, there was no breach of *ERA 1996, s 13(3)* which relates to the amount of wages 'properly payable' to each employee. The amount payable to each member of the team was not sufficiently certain to allow the wages to be ascertained prior to allocation of the money to each individual.

In *Farrell Matthews & Weir v Hansen* [2005] IRLR 160 the issue of discretionary bonuses as 'wages' was further considered. In that case a solicitor was paid an annual discretionary bonus in instalments. The claimant left her employer in circumstances where £9,000 of the bonus was still outstanding. The EAT held that a deductions from wages claim under s 13 had been rightly allowed. The employer's argument relying upon *ERA s 27(3)* that non-contractual bonus could only become wages when actually paid was rejected by the EAT which held that once the bonus payable had been declared by the employer the sum became payable and amounted to wages within the meaning of *ERA s 27(1)*.

The issue of quantification of the sum in issue is crucially relevant to whether a claim may be brought under the deduction from wages provisions of the *ERA*. In *Adcock v Coors Brewers Ltd* [2007] EWCA Civ 19, [2007] All ER (D) 190 (Jan), sub nom *Coors Brewers Ltd v Adcock*, the Court of Appeal considered whether a claim in relation to an *unquantified* discretionary bonus could be advanced under the provisions of *Part II* of the *ERA*. While such claims could be brought under the Employment Tribunal's *contractual* jurisdiction after termination of employment (by analogy with the discretionary bonus cases such as *Clark v Nomura plc* [2000] IRLR 766 which had been brought as a contractual claim in the High Court) that jurisdiction is limited to £25,000 whilst the jurisdiction under the provisions of *Part II* of the *ERA* is unlimited. The Court of Appeal held (applying *Delaney v Staples* [1992] ICR 483 HL) that the jurisdiction under *Part II* of the *ERA* is limited to claims brought on the premise that a *specific amount of money* by way of wages is owing. Accordingly, the jurisdiction does not extend to an unquantified claim in relation to an unidentified sum (such as a claim to a discretionary bonus). Such claims will remain limited to the contractual jurisdiction and, in relation to claims with a potential value of in excess of £25,000, or whether the employee remains in the employer's employment, will still have to be brought in the Courts rather than the employment tribunal.

Deductions. A broad definition of deductions is contained in *ERA 1996, s 13(3), (4)*. Where the total amount of any wages that are paid on any occasion by an employer to any worker employed by him is less than the total amount of the wages properly payable on that occasion (after deductions), the amount of the deficiency counts as a deduction, unless it is attributable to an error of computation as defined by *s 13(4)*. A conscious decision not to pay a particular sum which is caused by the employer's mistaken interpretation of the contract of employment is not such an error of computation (*Yemm v British Steel plc* [1994] IRLR 117; *Morgan v West Glamorgan County Council* [1995] IRLR 68).

It is clear that the tribunal may have to resolve disputes about the facts and about the construction and application to the facts of the worker's contract in order to determine what sums are in fact properly payable on a particular occasion (*Greg May (Carpet Fitters and Contractors) Ltd v Dring* [1990] ICR 188), and what deductions are in fact authorised (*Fairfield Ltd v Skinner* [1992] ICR 836). Again, there were originally doubts as to whether *s 13(3), ERA 1996* applies only to cases where there is some amount due as wages and the employer has sought to recover some *other* sum allegedly due to him by setting it off against those wages, or whether it also extends to the case where the employer has simply refused to pay the wages allegedly due or some part of them (usually because he denies that they are due at all). In *Delaney v Staples* [1991] ICR 331, the Court of Appeal held that a total non-payment *was* a deduction. The House of Lords ([1992] ICR 483) did not have to consider this point on appeal. In *Francis v Elizabeth Claire Care Management Ltd* [2005] IRLR 858 the EAT held that 'deduction' had a wide meaning and can include a case of failure to pay wages on time (rejecting robustly the employer's argument that there was no right to be paid on time). In that case, the employee was dismissed for complaining about the late payment. Unsurprisingly, that dismissal was held to be automatically unfair as a dismissal for asserting a statutory right (ie the right not to suffer deductions from wages. See also *s 104* of the *Employment Rights Act 1996* and 54.3(D) UNFAIR DISMISSAL – II.).

In *Bruce v Wiggins Teape (Stationery) Ltd* [1994] IRLR 536, the *WA 1986* (as it then was) was held to cover a situation in which the employer, in breach of contract, reduced the employee's wages. In *Morgan* (above), the wages provisions of the *ERA 1996* were similarly applied where the employer had demoted the employee without having power to do so. In *Hussman Manufacturing Ltd v Weir* [1998] IRLR 288, the employer had a contractual right to change the employee's working hours. After the employee was moved from night shift he was worse off as a result of loss of unsocial hours pay. The EAT held that a reduction in income which is the result of a lawful act by the employer is not a deduction. The EAT acknowledged, however, that in exceptional cases the unilateral exercise of such a contractual right by the employer might breach the implied term of mutual trust and confidence. In a situation where there is no contractual right to change the hours of work, a unilateral change by the employer, without the consent of the workers, to short-time working and, consequently, a reduction in remuneration, will amount to an unlawful deduction from wages: *International Packaging Corpn (UK) Ltd v Balfour* [2003] IRLR 11. In *Beveridge v KLM UK Ltd* [2000] IRLR 765, the EAT considered whether it was an unlawful deduction from wages to fail to pay any salary to an employee (who, following a period of sickness absence, claimed to be fit and willing to return to work) during a six-week period when the employer wished to satisfy itself that the employee was in fact fit to return. The EAT held that, in the absence of express provision to the contrary, an employee who offers his services is entitled to be paid wages. Accordingly there was an unlawful deduction for wages for the purposes of *Part II* of *ERA 1996* (see 53.7 UNFAIR DISMISSAL – I.).

An illustration of the sometimes complicated exercise of contractual construction in relation to determining entitlement to payment for the purposes of *s 13* of the *ERA 1996* is the Court of Appeal decision in *Dunlop Tyres v Blows* [2001] EWCA Civ 1032, [2001] IRLR 629 which involved the construction of ambiguous contractual terms in a collective agreement as to rates of pay. The Court of Appeal concluded that, on the proper construction of the agreement, the employees were entitled to triple pay for public holidays and, accordingly, the claim for unlawful deduction of wages was well founded. See also *Henry v London General Transport Services Ltd* [2002] EWCA Civ 488, [2002] IRLR 472. An example of the requirement of employee consent to variations to the rate of remuneration is provided by *Davies v MJ Wyatt (Decorators) Ltd* [2000] IRLR 759. In that case, the employer, in an attempt to meet its obligations to provide paid holiday under the *Working Time Regulations*, unilaterally reduced the employees' hourly pay in order to fund the holiday payment. Unsurprisingly, this amounted to an unlawful deduction from wages. In relation to holiday pay to which an employee is entitled under the *Working Time Regulations*, there may be an overlap between the right to recover these sums (in the event of non payment) under the *Working Time Regulations* and under the *ERA 1996, s 13*. In *List Design Group Ltd v Douglas* [2003] IRLR 14 it was held that even though the claim to holiday pay was out of time under the relevant provisions of the *Working Time Regulations*, it was recoverable pursuant to the *ERA 1996* as an unauthorised deduction from wages. Finally, the fact that the government declares a public holiday does not necessarily give rise to a right to additional payment for that day. In *Campbell and Smith Construction Group Ltd v Greenwood* [2001] IRLR 588, the EAT held that the failure by an employer to pay an additional day's pay for the Millennium public holiday (which, on the facts, the employees were already contractually entitled to take as holiday) was not an unlawful deduction from wages. The EAT stated that a government declaration of an additional so-called public holiday does not, of itself, entitle employees to an additional day's paid holiday.

Worker. By *s 230(3)*, *ERA 1996* those entitled to the protection from deductions from wages include persons working under contracts of apprenticeship and contracts for services as well as contracts of employment (see EMPLOYEE, SELF-EMPLOYED OR WORKER? (17)). The contract for services must be one whereby the individual undertakes to do or perform personally any work or services for another party to the contract whose status is not, by virtue of the contract, that of a client or customer of any profession or business undertaking carried on by the individual.

34.7   **Deductions from wages of, and receipt of payments from, workers in retail employment**

Special provisions apply to deductions from the wages of workers in retail employment and to payments by such workers, on account of cash shortages or stock deficiencies. Retail employment is defined as employment involving the carrying out by workers of retail transactions – the sale or supply of goods, or the supply of services (including financial services) – directly with members of the public (*ERA 1996, s 17(1)–(3)*).

The employer of a worker in retail employment may not deduct for cash shortages or stock deficiencies more than one-tenth of gross wages payable to the worker on a particular pay day (*ERA 1996, s 18(1)*). The employer must make such a deduction not more than 12 months after the date when he discovered or ought reasonably to have discovered the shortage or deficiency (*ERA 1996, s 18(2), (3)*).

If such a worker's pay is calculated by reference to cash shortages or stock deficiencies, the difference between the payment made when there are shortages and when there are not is treated as a deduction and the difference may not be more than one-tenth on any pay day (*ERA 1996, s 19(1)*).

In addition, the employer of a worker in retail employment may not receive from the worker any payment on account of a cash shortage or stock deficiency, unless certain requirements are met. The employer must:

(*a*)   notify the worker in writing of his total liability to him in respect of that shortage or deficiency; and

(*b*)   make a demand for payment which is:

    (i)   in writing; and

    (ii)   on a pay day.

(*ERA 1996, s 20(1), (2)*.)

The demand must be made not earlier than the first pay day on or after the date of the written notification and not later than 12 months after the date when the employer discovered or ought reasonably to have discovered the shortage or deficiency (*ERA 1996, s 20(3)*).

The amount demanded on a particular pay day must not exceed one-tenth of the gross wages payable to the worker on that day, or the balance of that one-tenth remaining after any deductions on account of cash shortages or stock deficiencies (*ERA 1996, s 21(1)*).

The restriction of deductions and payments to one-tenth of gross wages (and the requirements referred to in (*a*) and (*b*) above) do not apply to deductions or payments made from the final payment of wages. Nor do *ss 20* and *21* apply to payments made after the final payment of wages (*ERA 1996, ss 20(5), 21(3), 22(1)–(4)*). However, after the 12-month time limit referred to above has expired, the employer may neither receive payments (even after the final payment of wages), nor bring legal proceedings for recovery unless he has made a demand in accordance with *ss 20* or *21* within that time limit (*ERA 1996, ss 21(3), 22(4)*).

Even if legal proceedings are taken against a worker still in retail employment, a court which finds him liable to pay sums in respect of a shortage or deficiency must make provision so that the rate of payment does not exceed that which the employer could recover under *s 20* or *s 21* (*ERA 1996, ss 21(3), 22(4)*).

34.8   Remedies

The worker's exclusive remedy for breach by his employer of the statutory provisions outlined above is to present a complaint to an employment tribunal (*ERA 1996, s 23(1)*). The remedy of a worker for any contravention of *ss 13(1), 15(1), 18(1)* or *21(1)* is by way of a complaint to an employment tribunal under *s 23(1)* and not otherwise (*ERA 1996, s 205(2)*). However, the Court of Appeal has held in *Rickard v PB Glass Supplies Ltd* [1990] ICR 150 that what is now *s 205(2)* was not intended to prevent an employee from pursuing a claim in contract before the county court or High Court for moneys due to him where the non-payment is alleged by the employer to be due to the fact that no payment is due at all. Such a claim may now also be brought in the employment tribunal, within certain limits (see 8.23 CONTRACT OF EMPLOYMENT).

A complaint may be made that:

(*a*)   an unauthorised deduction has been made contrary to *s 13(1)* or *s 15(1)*;

(*b*)   an unauthorised payment has been received by the employer contrary to *ss 15(1)* or *20(1)*;

(*c*)   deductions exceeding the limit set by *s 18(1)* have been made; or

(*d*)   the employer has received more than the limit set by *s 21(1)*.

(*ERA 1996, s 23(1)*.)

The time limit for presenting a complaint to an employment tribunal under these provisions is three months beginning with the date of the deduction or the receipt of which complaint is made. The tribunal has jurisdiction to extend the time limit where it is satisfied that it was not reasonably practicable for the complaint to be presented within the relevant period of three months (see 20.8 EMPLOYMENT TRIBUNALS). Guidance on dealing with limitation points arising under those provisions was given by the EAT in *Taylorplan Services Ltd v Jackson* [1996] IRLR 184.

Where a series of deductions or payments are made, in certain circumstances, the time limit runs from the date of the last payment (*ERA 1996, s 23(3)*). A complaint may then be made about the entire unlawful series (*Reid v Camphill Engravers* [1990] IRLR 268). See also *Group 4 Nightspeed Ltd v Gilbert* [1997] IRLR 398, EAT. In *Arora v Rockwell Automation Ltd* (EAT 21.04.06 (0097/06)) the EAT held (applying *Group 4 Nightspeed Ltd v Gilbert*) that, in relation to an unlawful deductions claim, time starts to run, not from the date of termination of the contract, but from the date of the payment of wages containing the shortfall.

Where an employment tribunal finds that a complaint under *s 23(1)* is well-founded, it will make a declaration to that effect and, where an unlawful deduction or payment has been made, will order the employer to pay (or, as the case may be, repay) to the worker the amount of the deduction or payment (*ERA 1996, s 24*).

If the wages provisions of the *ERA 1996* have been satisfied in respect of an amount less than the deduction, the employer will be ordered to pay the worker the difference between the amount actually deducted and that which could lawfully have been deducted (*ERA 1996, s 25(1), (2)*).

In making the order, the tribunal will take into account payments or repayments already made to the worker (*ERA 1996, s 25(3)*). *Section 25(3)* applies to any payment made by an employer in respect of a deduction at any time prior to the date on which the tribunal makes its order and is not limited to amounts paid *before* the deduction (see *Robertson v Blackstone Franks Investment Management Ltd* [1998] IRLR 376).

Where a tribunal has ordered an employer to pay or repay a worker any amount (the relevant amount), the amount which the employer is entitled to recover by whatever means in respect of the matter which gave rise to the deduction or payment (including cash shortages or stock deficiencies) is reduced by the relevant amount (*ERA 1996, s 25(4), (5)*). In other words, sums wrongfully deducted cannot later be recovered at all, even if they were properly owing to the employer. The correctness of this far-reaching proposition was confirmed by the EAT in *Potter v Hunt Contracts Ltd* [1992] ICR 337.

Where an order is made under *ERA 1996, s 11* and *ss 23–25* (see 34.20 below) the aggregate of the amount ordered to be paid by the employer to the worker will not exceed the amount of the deduction (*ERA 1996, s 26*).

Parties cannot, by agreement, exclude or limit the operation of *ERA 1996, ss 23–25* except where agreement has been reached to refrain from presenting or continuing with a complaint where a conciliation officer has taken action in accordance with *s 18(2)* or *(3)* of *ERA 1996* or where the employee has entered into a compromise agreement which meets certain conditions, principally that legal advice has been taken (*ERA 1996, s 203(1), (2)*; for compromise agreements, see 20.27 EMPLOYMENT TRIBUNALS – I).

These provisions do not apply to employment where under his contract the person employed ordinarily works outside Great Britain (*ERA 1996, s 196(2), (3)*; and see 53.15 UNFAIR DISMISSAL – I).

34.9 **THE NATIONAL MINIMUM WAGE ACT 1998**

The *National Minimum Wage Act 1998* ('*NMWA 1998*') received the Royal Assent on 31 July 1998 and came fully into force on 1 April 1999. Many of the detailed provisions as to the operation of the National Minimum Wage ('NMW') are contained in the *Regulations*. The *National Minimum Wage Regulations 1999* (*SI 1999/584*) were issued in March 1999 and also came into force on 1 April 1999. In addition, the government has issued 'A detailed guide to the National Minimum Wage' (URN 99/662) which runs to some 112 pages and which helpfully contains worked examples. (See also *Tolley's National Minimum Wage: A Practical Guide* (ISBN: 075450 226–0).)

All 'workers' (see *NMWA 1998, s 54* and below) are to be paid at a rate which is not less than the NMW. As to the level of the NMW, the main points as now enacted in the *Regulations* are as follows:

(*a*)   with effect from 1 October 2006 the NMW is at the rate of £5.35 per hour (an increase from £5.05 in 2005) (*reg 11*) and see *National Minimum Wage Regulations 1999 (Amendment) Regulations 2006 (SI 2006/2001)*;

(*b*)   workers under 18 who have ceased to be of 'compulsory school age' will be entitled to £3.30 per hour with effect from 1 October 2006 (up from £3.00);

(*c*)   workers under 26 employed on the first 12 months of a contract of apprenticeship or who are under 19 do not qualify for the NMW (*reg 12(2)*). Moreover, trainees on Government training schemes ('National Traineeships') are similarly excluded from entitlement (*reg 12*, as amended by the *National Minimum Wage Regulations 1999 (Amendment) Regulations 2001 (SI 2001/1108)*);

(*d*)   with effect from 1 October 2006 the rate of the NMW for workers between 18 and 21 inclusive is £4.45 per hour (an increase from £4.25 in 2005) (*reg 13(1)*) and see the *National Minimum Wage Regulations 1999 (Amendment) Regulations 2006 (SI/2006/2001)*. The same rate applies to workers over 22 who are in the first six months of accredited training with a new employer.

Guidance and up to date information on the MNMW including proposals for forthcoming reforms may be found on the on the DTI website (www.dti.gov.uk/er/nmw).

Detailed provisions are contained in the *Regulations* for the purpose of calculating whether a worker has been paid the NMW. Thus, the individual's hourly rate of pay must be determined by reference to total remuneration over a 'relevant pay reference period' and the hours worked during that period. The pay reference period is one month or a shorter period if the worker is paid by reference to such shorter period (e g a week) (see *reg 10*). Regulations exist for allocation of pay to relevant periods (*reg 30*). As to determining the actual remuneration received in the relevant period, *regs 30–37* set out in detail the treatment of various types of payment. Gross pay must be determined and the following payments will be included for the purpose of calculation:

(i)   incentive payments including commission;

(ii)   bonuses; and

(iii)   tips and gratuities paid through the payroll system. (In *Nerva v United Kingdom* [2002] IRLR 815, the European Court of Human Rights (see 30.7 HUMAN RIGHTS) held that an employer could use such gratuity payments in discharge of the *NMWA 1998* remuneration obligations to employees and that such a practice did not amount to a breach of the applicants' rights (under Article 1 of Protocol No 1 to the European Convention on Human Rights) to peaceful enjoyment of their possessions).

Certain deductions are ignored for the purpose of calculating the remuneration in the relevant period (e g tax and National Insurance deductions, deductions in respect of the worker's conduct in relation to which he is contractually liable, deductions in respect of loans or overpayment, deductions in relation to accidental overpayment and deductions in relation to the purchase of shares, options or other securities (*reg 33*)). The general principle is that benefits in kind are not to be included for the purpose of calculating the remuneration (*reg 9*). The exception to this is living accommodation provided by the employer. The 'value' of the accommodation is set by *reg 36* and cannot exceed, with effect from 1 October 2006, £4.15 for each day the accommodation is provided giving a maximum of

£29.05 per week. See *National Minimum Wage Regulations 1999 (Amendment) Regulations 2006 (SI/2006/2001), reg 5.* The previous maximum was £3.90 per day for employment prior to 1 October 2006. *Regulations 31* and *36* in relation to accommodation and deductions have been considered by the Court of Appeal in *Leisure Employment Services Ltdv HM Revenue & Customs Comrs* [2007] EWCA Civ 92, [2007] IRLR 450. Upholding the decision of the EAT, the Court of Appeal held that, in relation to holiday resort workers living on site in accommodation provided by the employer, it was not permissible to count a £6 sum per fortnight which they had agreed to pay for gas and electricity as counting towards the minimum wage as the total permitted by *reg 36* in relation to accommodation had already been exhausted by their rent payments. Accordingly, the employer was in breach of the NMW.

The provisions for the calculation of the number of hours worked by the worker in the relevant pay reference period are similarly complicated. There are four types of work which can be carried out:

(A)   time work (*reg 3*) which is paid by reference to the time which a worker works;

(B)   salaried hours work (*reg 4*) which deals with the situation where a worker is paid under the contract for a fixed number of hours a year and is paid an annual salary in instalments;

(C)   output work (*reg 5*) which covers piece-work and commission-related working (as amended by the *National Minimum Wage Regulations 1999 (Amendment) Regulations 2004 (SI 2004/1161)* with effect from 1 October 2004 with further amendments coming into force on 6 April 2005); and

(D)   unmeasured work (*reg 6*) which provides a residual category.

The hours worked must be calculated in accordance with the *Regulations*. A detailed consideration of these provisions is beyond the scope of this work. For the detail of the provisions and the methods of calculation the reader is referred to *Tolley's National Minimum Wage: A Practical Guide* (ISBN: 075450 226–0).

34.10 Coverage of the Act

Section 54(3) defines 'worker' for the purpose of the *NMWA 1998* as 'an individual who has entered into or works under (or where employment has ceased worked under):

(*a*)   a contract of employment;

(*b*)   or any other contract, whether express or implied and (if it is express) whether oral or in writing, whereby the individual undertakes to do or perform personally any work or services for another party to the contract whose status is not by virtue of the contract that of client or customer of any profession or business undertaking carried on by the individual.'

Regulation 12 of the *National Minimum Wage Regulations 1999 (SI 1999/584)* and *s 54* (the definition of Worker) of the *National Minimum Wage Act 1998* were considered recently by the Court of Appeal in the context of a pupil barrister in *Edmonds v Lawson* [2000] IRLR 391. The applicant was a pupil in the defendant's chambers and was over the age of 31. Accordingly, she did not fall within *reg 12(2)* which excludes workers under the age of 26 on the first 12 months of a contract of apprenticeship from the NMW. At first instance Sullivan J held that the applicant was entitled to the NMW on the basis that during her pupillage there was a contract of apprenticeship between the applicant and the barristers' chambers (see [2000] IRLR 18). On appeal, the Court of Appeal held that the pupillage arrangement between the applicant and the chambers had the essential characteristics of an intention to create legal relations and, accordingly, there was a legally binding contract between the applicant and the chambers. The Court of Appeal held, however, allowing the appeal, that the contract was not a contract of apprenticeship and did not fall within the definition of a contract of employment within *s 54(3)* of the *NMWA 1998*. In relation to *s 54(3)(b)* (which relates to any other contract whereby the individual undertakes to do or perform personally any work or services for another party) the Court of Appeal held that the pupil did not undertake to perform work or services for the members of the chambers and in the event that the pupil did any work for which she was paid, the person for whom the work was done was the pupil's professional client. Accordingly, the pupil was not entitled to the benefit of the National Minimum Wage.

Prisoners, share fisherman and voluntary workers working for no remuneration are expressly not covered (*NMWA 1998, ss 43–45*). Persons who are covered by the Act include Crown employment (*NMWA 1998, s 36*), most work on board ships registered in the United Kingdom (*NMWA 1998, s 40*), work in the armed services (*NMWA 1998, s 37*) and in the House of Commons and House of Lords (*NMWA 1998, ss 38, 39*). Additionally (and importantly), home workers are expressly included in the coverage of the *Act* (*s 35*) as are agency workers (*NMWA 1998, s 34*). The definition of 'home worker', in *s 35* of the *NMWA 1998*, is intended to cover persons whose place of work is not materially under the control of the person for whom the work is being done: *IRC v Post Office* [2003] IRLR 199.

The coverage of the *NMWA* was further considered in *James v Redcats (Brands) Ltd* [2007] UKEAT/475/06 in which the EAT had to determine if a parcel courier was a 'worker' or a 'home worker' or not covered by the *NMW* at all (as had been held by the employment tribunal). The decision of the EAT provides important and helpful guidance on the issue of 'worker' generally, the requirement of mutuality of obligation, and emphasises that in marginal cases a person is *presumed* to qualify for the *NMW* unless the contrary is established (*NMWA s 28*). As to the issue of 'homeworker', a submission that to qualify a person must have some identified 'place' from which they work (albeit not necessarily their own home) was rejected in the light of the general policy of the *NMWA*. Thus a person engaged in delivery or distribution of items could nevertheless be a 'homeworker' for the purposes of the *NMWA*.

The Secretary of State is afforded an additional power to make regulations applying the minimum wage to persons not otherwise covered (*NMWA 1998, ss 41* and *42*). By the *National Minimum Wage (Offshore Employment) Order 1999* (*SI 1999/1128*) the operation of the *NMWA 1998* has been extended to workers in offshore employment, defined as employment in United Kingdom territorial waters, exploring or exploiting natural resources in the UK sector of the continental shelf or (in a foreign sector) a cross boundary petroleum field. *Section 22* of the *Employment Relations Act 1999* inserts a new *s 44A* into the *NMWA 1998*. By this section the exclusion from the entitlement to the NMW (see *ss 43–45*) is extended to cover residential members of religious communities. Accordingly, it would appear that nuns and monks will be excluded from entitlement to the NMW. The relevant provisions came into force on 25 October 1999.

The power to set the rate is conferred by *NMWA 1998, s 2* (for the current rates, see above). *NMWA 1998, s 3* gives the power to the Secretary of State to exclude persons under 26 from the operation of the National Minimum Wage or to apply a different hourly rate to such persons. The statutory role of the LPC and the obligations of the Secretary of State to refer matters to the LPC are set out in *ss 5–8* and *Sch 1*.

34.11 Written records and pay statements

In addition to the fixing of the minimum wage, the *Act* casts further obligations upon employers of maintaining records in relation to hours worked and payments made to workers in a manner to be prescribed by the regulations (*NMWA 1998, s 9*). By *reg 38(1)* the employer is obliged to keep records 'sufficient to establish that [the worker] is remunerated at a rate at least equal to the national minimum wage'. The records must be kept in such a way that the information about a worker in respect of a pay reference period may be produced in a single document (*reg 38(2)*). Workers may require the employer to produce the records and the worker may take a copy in order to determine if the worker is in fact being paid the minimum wage (*NMWA 1998, s 10*). Failure to comply with such a request may lead to a complaint being made to an employment tribunal (*NMWA 1998, s 11*). If the tribunal upholds the complaint it shall make a declaration to that effect and order that the employer pay the worker a sum equivalent to 80 times the relevant National Minimum Wage (*NMWA 1998, s 11(2)*). The Act in *s 12* provides a power for regulations to be made to provide workers with a National Minimum Wage statement which would be similar to the right an itemised statement under the provision of *ERA 1996* (see below). Following widespread opposition to this proposal the *Regulations* contain no obligation to provide a National Minimum Wage statement.

34.12 Failure to pay the National Minimum Wage: individual remedies

A failure to pay to an employee the National Minimum Wage will entitle the employee to commence proceedings in the employment tribunal or the county court to recover the difference between what has been paid and what ought to have been paid under the National Minimum Wage. The claim may be brought either as a breach of *Part II* of the *ERA 1996* as an unlawful deduction from wages or as a breach of contract claim. In relation to workers (as defined in *NMWA 1998, s 54(3)*) who are not covered by the provisions of *Part II* of the *ERA 1996* (see above) because they do not satisfy the particular definition of worker in *s 230(3), ERA 1996*, they are deemed to be covered by the provisions by *s 18* of the *National Minimum Wage Act 1998*. An employee has a right not to suffer a detriment (*NMWA 1998, s 23*) nor to be dismissed by reason of bringing proceedings relating to the enforcement of the National Minimum Wage (*NMWA 1998, s 25* which inserts *ERA 1996, s 104A*). (See also 52.3 UNFAIR DISMISSAL – II.) As to proceedings in the employment tribunal, claims relating to non-payment of the NMW, may be heard by an employment tribunal chairman sitting alone (*NMWA 1998, s 27* amending *ETA 1996, s 4*). The burden of proof in such cases will be unusual: it will be presumed that the employee is paid less than the minimum wage unless the employer establishes the contrary (*NMWA 1998, s 28*). This principle applies whether the proceedings are brought in the employment tribunal under *Part II* of the *ERA 1996* or for breach of contract claims whether in the county court or in the employment tribunal. Accordingly, this will be an added incentive for employers to keep proper records as required in order to be able to establish that a worker has in fact been paid, at least, the National Minimum Wage. The worker's right to present a complaint that he has been subjected to a detriment in contravention of *s 23* is contained in *s 24* which extends the powers in *ss 48* and *49* of the *ERA 1996* to detriment cases arising in relation to the National Minimum Wage. On a related point, the EAT has held in

Paggetti v Cobb [2002] IRLR 861 that, in assessing a compensatory or basic award for unfair dismissal, calculations pursuant to *ss 221–229* of the *ERA 1996* were automatically subject to the NMW. This principle applies even if the applicant has not made a specific NMW claim as it is sufficient if, prior to the dismissal, he was remunerated at a rate less than the NMW. On the facts of the instant case, the applicant was only paid £120 for a 63-hour week. Compensation was, accordingly, to be assessed based upon the NMW rate.

Devices adopted by employers to attempt to meet the minimum wage obligation without additional expenditure are unlikely to succeed in practice. In *Laird v AK Stoddart Ltd* [2001] IRLR 591, the EAT considered whether there was a breach of the *NMWA 1998* or an unlawful deduction from wages contrary to *s 13(1)* of *ERA 1996* in circumstances where the employer consolidated part of an employee's attendance allowance into the basic hourly rate for the job in order to comply with the NMW requirement (at that time £3.60 per hour). By *reg 31* of the *National Minimum Wage Regulations 1999 (Amendment) Regulations 2000 (SI 2000/1989)*, certain payments are not to be taken into account in calculating the total remuneration. This exclusion includes an attendance allowance. Accordingly, the employer sought to reduce the attendance allowance and increase the basic pay to comply with the NMW. The employees were not consulted. The EAT held that there was no breach of the *NMWA 1998*. The EAT went on, however, to hold that the reduction in the attendance allowance was an unlawful deduction from wages for the purposes of *s 13* of the *ERA 1996* as there was no consent to the change and *s 27* of the *ERA 1996* required attendance allowances to be taken into account in determining whether there was any unlawful deduction from wages. Moreover, an employer cannot minimise his obligations by attempting to exclude certain work time from the calculation of hours worked. By way of example, in *British Nursing Association v Inland Revenue (National Minimum Wage Compliance Team)* [2002] IRLR 480, the Court of Appeal upheld the decision of the EAT ([2002] EWCA Civ 494, [2001] IRLR 659) that nurses providing a night service by telephone from home were working throughout the shift period for the purposes of the *NMWA 1998*, although free to do whatever they wanted between telephone calls. The fact that there was an obligation to be ready to answer the call throughout the night shift meant that the nurses were working throughout the shift and were engaged on 'time work' within the meaning of the *NMWA 1998* (see 34.9 above). It is also worthy of note that this case was an appeal from an enforcement notice served by the Inland Revenue – an example of a State as opposed to individual remedy in relation to the *NMWA 1998* (see below).

The *British Nursing Association* case was followed by the Court of Session in *Scottbridge Construction Ltd v Wright* [2003] IRLR 21. That case concerned a nightwatchman, who was permitted by his employer to sleep on the employer's premises whilst at work. It was held that he was engaged on 'time work' for the purposes of the *NMWA 1998* and, accordingly, was entitled to the NMW for all the hours he was required to be on the premises, including time asleep as, even if asleep, he could respond to an alarm when he awoke and was thus liable to perform functions at every stage during the night. Conversely, in *Walton v Independent Living Organisation Ltd* [2003] IRLR 469 the Court of Appeal held that a live-in carer, required to be on the client's premises for a consecutive period of 72 hours each week, was only entitled, under the *NMWA 1998*, to payment in respect of the time that she was actually carrying out her duties as her work was properly characterised as 'unmeasured work' (with a daily average agreement falling within *reg 28*) and not 'time work' and, accordingly, *British Nursing Association* and *Scottbridge Construction* (above) were distinguished (see 33.9

above). In *McCartney v Oversley House Management* [2006] ICR 510 (EAT) *British Nursing Association* was applied in relation to 'on-call' work holding that a manager at a residential home with 'on call' obligations was engaged on 'salaried hours work' with the result that it was found that the employee was remunerated at a rate below that permitted by the *NMW*.

34.13 **Failure to pay the National Minimum Wage: state remedies**

The *Act* also provides a system whereby the right to minimum wage may be enforced by state officials rather than individuals. The relevant officers will be the Inland Revenue and in the agricultural sector, the agricultural wages inspectors (see *NMWA 1998, s 13*). Officers will be able to carry out enforcement activities, including the requirement that an employer produce records, allow access to premises and provide information in order to determine an issue under the *Act* (*NMWA 1998, s 14*). Information which is so obtained may be used only for the purposes of the *Act* or for criminal or civil proceedings relating to the *Act* if authorised by the Secretary of State (*NMWA 1998, s 15*). In cases where it appears that an employer is paying less than the National Minimum Wage there is a power to issue enforcement notices requiring an employer to comply with the obligation to pay the minimum wage and to pay back pay for a specified period (*NMWA 1998, s 19*). An employer so served will have the right of appeal to an employment tribunal within four weeks of the issue of the enforcement notice (*NMWA 1998, s 19(4)–(9)*). If the amount specified in an enforcement notice under the *NMWA 1998* is incorrect, an employment tribunal has a duty to rectify the notice by inserting the appropriate sum by making the best estimate the tribunal can on the information available: *IRC v St Hermans Estate Co Ltd* [2002] IRLR 788, EAT. Failure to comply with an enforcement notice has two possible consequences: an officer may act on behalf of workers and issue civil proceedings including proceedings in the employment tribunal for recovery of the sums that ought to have been paid (*NMWA 1998, s 20*). Alternatively, *s 21* provides for the employer to be served with a penalty notice for non-compliance with the National Minimum Wage. The penalty is at the rate of twice the hourly rate of the minimum wage for each day of non-compliance and is paid to the Secretary of State (*NMWA 1998, s 21(3)*) and is recoverable by county court order of execution or otherwise as if it were payable under an order of that court (*NMWA 1998, s 21(5)*). There is a right of appeal to the employment tribunal against a penalty notice (*NMWA 1998, s 22*) within four weeks of being served. Further, if an appeal against an enforcement notice is pending, a penalty notice may still be served but shall not be enforced until the appeal has been determined or withdrawn (*NMWA 1998, s 21(6), (7)* and *s 19(4)*). See, by way of example of a state remedy, *British Nursing Association v Inland Revenue (National Minimum Wage Compliance Team)* [2002] IRLR 480.

In *IRC v Bebb Travel plc* [2002] IRLR 783 the EAT had held that, on a proper construction of the legislation, compliance officers were not entitled, pursuant to *s 19* of the *NMWA 1998*, to serve an enforcement notice on the respondent employer requiring it to pay arrears of wages in respect of employees who had ceased employment before the notice was issued. This unsatisfactory result was reversed by the passage of the *National Minimum Wage (Enforcement Notices) Act 2003* which came into force on 8 July 2003. The new *Act* amended *s 19* of the *NMWA 1998* to ensure that an enforcement notice may be served on an employer who has not paid an employee a rate of pay at least equal to the NMW whether or not the worker is still employed.

The DTI has issued a document 'National minimum wage enforcement: penalty notice policy' (January 2007) which sets out the enforcement powers and how they will be used in practice. It is available on the DTI website: www.dti.gov.uk/files/file36381.pdf.

Finally, if the preceding enforcement measures are to no avail, there is a new criminal offence created for employers who wilfully breach their obligations to workers under the Act. It is an offence:

(i)   to fail to refuse or wilfully neglect to pay the minimum wage (*NMWA 1998, s 31(1)*);

(ii)   to fail to keep records as required by *s 9* (*NMWA 1998, s 31(2)*);

(iii) to falsify *s 9* records (*NMWA 1998, s 31(3)*);

(iv)   to knowingly provide false information to an officer (*NMWA 1998, s 31(4)*); or

(v)   to obstruct or delay an officer or to refuse to answer questions or furnish information (*NMWA 1998, s 31(5)*).

Each offence under *s 31* is punishable on summary conviction with a fine not exceeding level 5 on the Standard Scale (see 1.10 INTRODUCTION) (*NMWA 1998, s 31(9)*). In the case of a body corporate, if an offence is committed with the consent, connivance or by the neglect of an officer of the company, that officer, as well as the body corporate, is guilty of the offence (*NMWA 1998, s 32*). Proceedings for offences under the *Act* will be in the Magistrates Court (*NMWA 1998, s 33(1)*).

The ability to effectively police whether employers are abiding by their obligations to pay the NMW is enhanced by the provisions of *s 39* of the *Employment Relations Act 1999* which permits revenue officials to disclose information which comes into their possession in the course of carrying out the function of Commissioners of the Inland Revenue to other agencies for the purposes of the *National Minimum Wage Act 1998*. The information may be disclosed to the Secretary of State for any purpose relating to the *National Minimum Wage Act 1998*. That information may be supplied by the Secretary of State for any purpose relating to the *National Minimum Wage Act 1998*. That information may be supplied by the Secretary of State to any person acting under *s 13(1)(b)* of the *NMWA 1998* or to the agricultural wages inspectors. The provisions of *s 39* came into force on 25 October 1999.

34.14   OTHER DEDUCTIONS FROM WAGES

In *Sim v Rotherham Metropolitan Borough Council* [1986] ICR 897, it was held that the principle of equitable set-off applied to contracts of employment. In other words, where an employee's breach of contract has caused the employer loss, the employer is in principle entitled to retain for himself sums representing the amount of that loss when he pays the employee's wages. This saves the employer from paying the full wage and suing for damages for breach of contract. However, the court retains a discretion to disallow the set-off. Further, if there is no contractual provision or written consent permitting a deduction by way of set-off, for the employer to make such a deduction may contravene the wages provisions of the *ERA 1996* (see 34.6 above; this will not be an obstacle where the deduction is made for taking part in industrial action).

The leading authority on the employer's right to pay less than the full contractual wage where the employee refuses to carry out all his contractual duties is now the decision of the House of Lords in *Miles v Wakefield Metropolitan District Council* [1987] ICR 368. A superintendent registrar with a normal working week of 37 hours, including three hours on Saturday mornings, took industrial action and refused to conduct weddings on Saturdays. He worked normally during the rest of the week. It was held that the council was entitled to deduct 3/37ths from his normal salary, even though the registrar would have been willing to perform duties other than the conduct of weddings on Saturdays (in fact, the council instructed him to work normally or not at all).

Lord Brightman and Lord Templeman took the view that a worker not performing the full range of his contractual duties was not entitled to his full wages but to a *quantum meruit* payment based upon the value of the work actually done. An employer placed in such a position must make it clear to the employee that he is not waiving that employee's breach of contract in failing to perform the full range of his contractual duties. He should state that, whilst the breach continues, he will make a specified adjustment to the employee's wages. However, an employer cannot be *compelled* to accept and pay for something significantly less than the efficient performance of all the employee's contractual duties (*MacPherson v London Borough of Lambeth* [1988] IRLR 470). In *Wiluszynski v Tower Hamlets London Borough Council* [1989] IRLR 259 the Court of Appeal, dealing with a council employee who had refused to perform a material part of his duties, held that the council was entitled to withhold the whole of his pay. This decision was arrived at only because the council had clearly informed the employee that if he attempted to undertake limited work, he would not be paid for it. See also *British Telecommunications plc v Ticehurst* [1992] ICR 383.

Where an employee is actually required to work only on, say, 245 days in the year, and that employee participates in a one-day strike, the question frequently arises as to whether the employer is entitled to deduct 1/245 or only 1/365 of the annual salary in respect of that day. It is thought that this may depend upon the precise terms of the contract of employment, and upon the nature of the work done (e g does it require extensive preparation outside actual working hours?). In *Smith v Bexley London Borough Council,* IDS Brief 448, p 5, a county court judge took the approach more favourable to the employer. However, in *Re BCCI SA* [1994] IRLR 282, Evans-Lombe J, although approving this approach where the question was what a lost day had cost the employer, held that, when considering what part of a monthly salary had accrued by the date of a dismissal, the total number of days in that month had to be taken into account, and not merely working days; this point was not considered on appeal. (See also *Thames Water Utilities v Reynolds* [1996] IRLR 186, EAT applying *Re BCCI SA.*) In *Leisure Leagues UK Ltd v Maconnachie* [2002] IRLR 600, however, in the context of holiday pay, the EAT held that the correct denominator was the number of working days in the year (in this case, 233 days) and the *Thames Water* decision was distinguished on the basis it predated the *Working Time Regulations.* Clearly, this is an area which would benefit from a clear and exhaustive judicial statement of the principles to be applied.

The court will not normally make mandatory interlocutory orders for the payment of wages; in clear cases, the employee's remedy is to apply for summary judgment (*Jakeman v South West Thames Regional Health Authority and London Ambulance Service* [1990] IRLR 62).

34.15 **OVERPAYMENT**

Payments made under a mistake of fact (as opposed to a mistake of law) are in principle recoverable by the party who made the payment. This would extend to a mistaken overpayment of wages. However, if the employee in good faith changes his position by incurring expenditure which he would not otherwise have incurred, he may have a defence in whole or part to any subsequent claim to recover the overpayment (*Lipkin Gorman v Karpnale Ltd* [1991] 2 AC 548; see also *Avon County Council v Howlett* [1983] 1 WLR 605).

34.16 ITEMISED PAY STATEMENTS

An employer must give any employee of his, at or before the time at which any payment of wages or salary is made to him, a pay statement in writing containing the following particulars:

(*a*)   the gross amount of the wages or salary;

(*b*)   the amounts of any variable and any fixed deductions from that gross amount and the purposes for which they are made, unless a statement of fixed deductions has been given to the employee (see 34.17 below);

(*c*)   the net amount of wages or salary payable; and

(*d*)   where different parts of the net amount are paid in different ways, the amount and method of payment of each part payment.

(*ERA 1996, s 8.*)

Tips paid by customers to a waiter in a restaurant were held not to be wages within the meaning of *EPCA, s 8* (now *ERA 1996, s 8*), and his employers were therefore not required to give particulars of such tips or of payments from them to the manager of the restaurant (*Cofone v Spaghetti House Ltd* [1980] ICR 155).

34.17 Statement of fixed deductions

Provided that the employer has given in writing a standing statement of fixed deductions, there is no need to itemise fixed deductions on an employee's pay statement, but simply to state the total amount of the deductions. This standing statement should give the following information:

(*a*)   the amount of each deduction;

(*b*)   the intervals at which the deduction is to be made; and

(*c*)   the purpose for which it is made.

(*ERA 1996, s 9(1)–(3).*)

A statement of fixed deductions may be amended, whether by the addition of a new deduction or by a change in the particulars or cancellation of an existing deduction, by notice in writing containing particulars of the amendment given by the employer to the employee (*ERA 1996, s 9(3)*).

It must be remembered that a standing statement of fixed deductions only remains effective for 12 months from the date on which it is given to the employee. Before the expiry of the 12-month period, the employer must re-issue the statement, together with any amendments, in consolidated form (*ERA 1996, s 9(4)*).

34.18 Exclusions

The requirement for an employer to provide an employee with a pay statement does not apply:

(*a*)   to persons engaged in police service (*ERA 1996, s 200(1)*);

(b)   to employment as a merchant seaman, or as a master or member of the crew of a fishing vessel where the employee is remunerated only by a share in the profits or gross earnings of the vessel (*ERA 1996, s 199(2)(4)*); or

(c)   where the employee ordinarily works outside Great Britain (*ERA 1996, s 196(2), (3)*).

34.19 Application to an employment tribunal

If an employer does not give any employee of his a pay statement, the employee may refer the matter to an employment tribunal to determine what particulars ought to have been included in a statement so as to comply with the requirements in 34.11 above (*ERA 1996, s 11(1)*). An employee may also apply to a tribunal, as may an employer, to determine provisions which should have been included in a pay statement or a standing statement of fixed deductions, but which have been omitted (*ERA 1996, s 11(2)*).

Any application concerning a pay statement must be brought while the employee is still employed by the relevant employer, or within three months of the date on which the employment ceased (*ERA 1996, s 11(4)*). Unlike in the case of most other applications, the tribunal has no power to extend this time limit.

34.20 Tribunal order

Where, on a reference under these provisions, an employment tribunal finds that an employer has failed to give an employee a pay statement or that a pay statement or standing statement of fixed deductions does not, in relation to a deduction, contain the particulars required to be included in that statement, the tribunal will make a declaration to that effect.

Where the tribunal further finds that any unnotified deductions have been made from the pay of the employee during the period of 13 weeks immediately preceding the date of the application (whether or not such deductions were made in breach of the contract of employment), the tribunal may order the employer to pay the employee a sum not exceeding the aggregate of the unnotified deductions so made (*ERA 1996, s 12(3)–(5)*; see 34.8 above for the relationship between *ERA 1996, s 11* and *ss 23–25*).

For example, an employee may be required by his contract of employment to pay subscriptions to a sports club of £1 per week. If the employer does not notify the employee of this deduction, either in a note with his pay packet or in a statement of fixed deductions, then, on an application to an employment tribunal, the tribunal may order the employer to repay the employee a sum of up to £13, which is equivalent to the employee's subscriptions for the previous 13 weeks.

In *Milsom v Leicestershire County Council* [1978] IRLR 433, an employment tribunal held that an employer was in breach of the requirement to give an itemised pay statement. A sum had been deducted from the employee's wages, the only explanation being that it was a 'miscellaneous deduction/payment'. The tribunal ordered the employer to pay £25 to the employee for the failure to give a proper statement, despite the fact that the employee was well aware of the reason for the deduction and that the employer was entitled under the contract between the parties to make such a deduction.

However, in *Scott v Creager* [1979] ICR 403, the EAT held that where an employer had made unnotified deductions, an employment tribunal had not erred in awarding a sum to the employee equal to the amount by which the pay she actually received fell short of the net pay she should have received.

34.21 **GRATUITIES AND TRONCS**

The authorities relating to a system whereby customers' gratuities are pooled in a 'tronc' and distributed among employees (typically, restaurant staff) were reviewed by the Court of Appeal in *Nerva v RL & G Ltd* [1996] IRLR 461. This was a case dealing with whether payments out of a tronc counted towards the minimum remuneration required under a Wages Council order; it establishes that a gratuity left by a customer as a cash tip is normally held on trust for the benefit of the restaurant's employees, whereas payments received by those employees in respect of such a gratuity added to a customer's cheque or credit-card payment are not held on trust, but instead form part of their remuneration. (As to whether such payments are counted for the purpose of calculating the minimum wage, see 34.9 above.) The case, under the name *Nerva v United Kingdom* [2002] IRLR 815, went to the European Court of Human Rights (see 30.7 HUMAN RIGHTS). The ECHR upheld the decision of the Court of Appeal concluding that an employer could use such payments in discharge of remuneration obligations to the waiter employees and that such a practice did not amount to a breach of the applicants' rights (under Article 1 of Protocol No 1 to the European Convention on Human Rights) to peaceful enjoyment of their possessions.

34.22 **PAY ON TERMINATION OF EMPLOYMENT**

Upon termination of employment, an employer should pay to the former employee any of the following sums which may be due, depending upon the circumstances: wages in lieu of notice (see 48.9 TERMINATION OF EMPLOYMENT); accrued holiday pay (see 29.4 HOLIDAYS); reimbursement of expenses; other contractual payments; and redundancy pay (see REDUNDANCY – I (38)).

If the employee is paid weekly or monthly and the employment has terminated part-way through the week or month, he will be taken to have earned a rateable proportion of his wages or salary for that period. This is the result of applying the *Apportionment Act 1870*, which provides by *s 2* that (*inter alia*) all annuities and other periodical payments in the nature of income shall be considered as accruing from day to day, and shall be apportionable in respect of time accordingly. 'Annuities' are defined by *s 5* to include salaries and pensions. It is possible to exclude apportionment by an express stipulation to the contrary (*Apportionment Act 1870, s 7*). The *Act* is also capable of being applied to a payment such as an annual bonus when the employee leaves part-way through the year (see, on the application of the *Apportionment Act 1870, Thames Water Utilities v Reynolds* [1996] IRLR 186, EAT and *Re BCCI SA* [1994] IRLR 282) and compare *Leisure Leagues UK Ltd v Maconnachie* [2002] IRLR 600 at 34.14 above. See also *Item Software (UK) Ltd v Fassihi* [2004] EWCA Civ 1244, [2004] IRLR 928.

34.23 **GUARANTEE PAYMENTS FOR WORKLESS DAYS**

(See also DTI guidance 'Guarantee payments' (PL 724 2nd Revision).)

The *Employment Protection Act 1975* created certain rights to payment when no work is done owing to circumstances beyond the control of the employee. These provisions are now contained in the *Employment Rights Act 1996* ('*ERA 1996*'). These are of benefit, chiefly, to hourly paid employees and to workers on piece rates.

34.24 RIGHT TO GUARANTEE PAYMENT

Workless day

Where any employee, throughout a day during any part of which he would normally be required to work in accordance with his contract of employment, is not provided with work by his employer by reason of:

(*a*)   a diminution in the requirements of the employer's business for work of the kind which the employee is employed to do; or

(*b*)   any other occurrence affecting the normal working of the employer's business in relation to work of the kind which the employee is employed to do,

he is, subject to certain exceptions, entitled to a guarantee payment (*ERA 1996, s 28(1)–(3)*).

A threatened power cut is such an occurrence (*Miller v Harry Thornton (Lollies) Ltd* [1978] IRLR 430).

If a worker can turn down work given to her she is not normally 'required to work' within the meaning of the section and is not entitled to a guarantee payment when not provided with any work (*Mailway (Southern) Ltd v Willsher* [1978] ICR 511).

If an employer provides some although not the usual amount of work during a day, that is not considered a 'workless day' for which an employee is entitled to a guarantee payment. Examples of situations which may cause a day to be 'workless' are a lack of orders, under (*a*), or any other occurrence such as a power cut affecting the normal working of the employer's business in relation to work of the kind which the employee is employed to do, under (*b*).

Where employment begins before midnight and extends into the next day, the period of employment for the purpose of deciding which is the workless day is defined as follows:

(i)   if the employment before midnight is, or would normally be, of longer duration than that after midnight, that period of employment is treated as falling wholly on the first day; and

(ii)   in any other case, that period of employment is treated as falling wholly on the second day.

(*ERA 1996, s 28(4), (5)*.)

34.25 Qualifying period

In order to qualify for the entitlement, an employee must have been continuously employed for one month ending with the day before the workless day (*ERA 1996, s 29(1)*). (See CONTINUOUS EMPLOYMENT (7).)

An employee who is employed:

(*a*)   under a contract for a fixed term of three months or less; or

(*b*)   under a contract made in contemplation of the performance of a specific task which is not expected to last for more than three months,

is not entitled to a guarantee payment unless he has been continuously employed for a period of more than three months ending with the day before that in respect of which the guarantee payment is claimed (*ERA 1996, s 29(2)*).

34.26 Exclusions

Trade disputes. An employee is not entitled to a guarantee payment in respect of a workless day if the failure to provide him with work occurs in consequence of a strike, lock-out or other industrial action involving any employee of his employer or of an associated employer (*ERA 1996, s 29(3)*; for 'associated employer' see 7.9(A) CONTINUOUS EMPLOYMENT). Thus, a dispute with his employer involving members of another union at his workplace or of employees of his employer at a factory in another part of the country, which causes a halt in production, disentitles an employee from receiving a guarantee payment.

Offer of suitable alternative work. An employee is not entitled to a guarantee payment in respect of a workless day if:

(a)   his employer has offered to provide alternative work for that day which is suitable in all the circumstances (whether or not it is work which the employee is employed to perform under his contract) and the employee has unreasonably refused that offer; or

(b)   he does not comply with reasonable requirements imposed by his employer with a view to ensuring that his services are available.

(*ERA 1996, s 29(4), (5)*.)

Both objective and subjective tests are involved in deciding what is 'suitable' and 'reasonable' within the meaning of (a) above. No general rules can be laid down, but what tribunals will have in mind are pay, hours, geographical location and skill required. So far as (b) is concerned, clearly, if an employer asked an employee to telephone to find out whether work was available, that would be considered a reasonable requirement.

34.27 Amount of payment

The amount of the guarantee payment payable in respect of any day is the sum produced by multiplying the *number of normal working hours* in that day by the *guaranteed hourly rate* (*ERA 1996, s 30(1)*).

The 'guaranteed hourly rate' is the amount of one week's pay (see below 33.34) divided by the number of normal working hours in that week. In calculating 'normal working hours' where the number of working hours in a week fluctuate, one takes the average number of working hours over the 12 weeks ending with the last complete week before the day in respect of which the guarantee payment is payable. If the employee has not been employed for 12 weeks, a calculation is made having regard to:

(a)   the average number of normal working hours in a week which the employee could expect in accordance with the terms of his contract; and

(b)   the average number of such hours of other employees engaged in relevant comparable employment with the same employer.

(*ERA 1996, s 30(2)–(4)*.)

If any employee's contract has been varied or a new contract has been entered into for short-time working, the calculation is made by reference to the last day that the original contract was in force (*ERA 1996, s 30(5)*).

The amount of a guarantee payment payable to an employee in respect of any day will not exceed £19.60 (with effect from 1 February 2007: *Employment Rights (Increase of Limits) Order 2005* (*SI 2006/3045*); previously the maximum was

£18.90) and such payments cannot exceed five days in any period of three months. The present maximum annual liability is therefore £392 (*ERA 1996, s 31*). Any contractual remuneration paid to an employee in respect of a workless day goes towards discharging any statutory liability of the employer to pay a guarantee payment in respect of that day and, conversely, any guarantee payment paid in respect of a day goes towards discharging any liability of the employer to pay contractual remuneration in respect of that day (*ERA 1996, s 32*). Thus, if any employee is paid on a weekly or monthly basis, irrespective of the work actually done, these payments will go towards discharging any statutory liability. Contractual payments made in respect of any workless days are to be taken into account when calculating the maximum number of days within the three-month period for which the employee is entitled to a payment (*Cartwright v G Clancey Ltd* [1983] ICR 552).

The Secretary of State may by order exempt certain industries from these provisions where there is in force a collective agreement or an agricultural wages order which complies with certain conditions (*ERA 1996, s 35*).

34.28 Remedy for failure to make payment

An employee may present a complaint to an employment tribunal that his employer has failed to pay the whole or any part of a guarantee payment to which he is entitled. The tribunal, if it finds the complaint well-founded, will order the employer to pay the complainant the amount of guarantee payment which it finds due to him (*ERA 1996, s 34(1), (3)*). Such a complaint must be presented to a tribunal before the end of the period of *three months* beginning with the workless day (or within such further period as the tribunal considers reasonable, when it is satisfied that it was not reasonably practicable for the complaint to be presented within the period of three months; see 19.7 EMPLOYMENT TRIBUNALS – I) (*ERA 1996, s 34(2)*).

34.29 MEDICAL SUSPENSION PAYMENTS

(See also 'Suspension from work on medical or maternity grounds under Health and Safety Regulations' (PL 705, 4th revision).)

Statutes and regulations safeguard workpeople from exposure to health hazards. They may provide, for example, that a factory be closed when the atmosphere in it becomes contaminated. At common law, if a factory closed down in compliance with regulations relating to the health of the factory workers, the workers were not entitled to be paid for the time lost unless their contracts provided otherwise. However, now where an employee is suspended from work by his employer on medical grounds in compliance with any law or regulation concerning the health and safety of workers, he may be entitled to be paid remuneration by his employer while he is so suspended for a period not exceeding 26 weeks. The provision which leads to him being suspended must be one of those for the time being specified in *ERA 1996, s 64(3)*. At present only the *Control of Lead at Work Regulations 1980* (*SI 1980/1248*), *reg 16*, the *Ionising Radiations Regulations 1985* (*SI 1985/1333*), *reg 16* and the *Control of Substances Hazardous to Health Regulations 1988* (*SI 1988/1657*), *reg 11*, are so specified. (See also 31.25 MATERNITY AND PARENTAL RIGHTS for an employee's right to remuneration when suspended on maternity grounds.)

34.30 **Qualifying conditions**

An employee will be regarded as suspended from work only if, and so long as, he continues to be employed by his employer but is not provided with work or does not perform the work he normally performed before the suspension (*ERA 1996, s 64(5)*).

In order to be entitled to claim a medical suspension payment, the employee must have been continuously employed for a period of one month ending with the day before that on which the suspension begins (*ERA 1996, s 65(1)*).

An employee who is employed:

(*a*)   under a contract for a fixed term of three months or less; or

(*b*)   under a contract made in contemplation of the performance of a specific task which is not expected to last for more than three months,

is not entitled to a medical suspension payment unless he has been continuously employed for a period of more than three months ending with the day before that on which the suspension begins (*ERA 1996, s 65(2)*).

For continuity of employment, see CONTINUOUS EMPLOYMENT (7).

34.31 **Exclusions from right to payment**

(*a*)   An employee will not be entitled to a medical suspension payment in respect of any period during which he is incapable of work by reason of disease or bodily or mental disablement (*ERA 1996, s 65(3)*).

(*b*)   An employee is not entitled to a medical suspension payment in respect of any period during which:

(i)   his employer offered to provide him with suitable alternative work, whether or not it was work the employee was engaged to perform; and

(ii)   the employee unreasonably refused to perform that work.

(*ERA 1996, s 65(4)(a)*.) If, for example, a man is engaged as a machine operator in the toolroom of a factory and the toolroom has to be closed for medical reasons for a few weeks, it may be considered unreasonable for the operative to refuse to work on a similar type of machine in a different part of the factory, provided he is offered the same rate of pay as that which he had previously received.

(*c*)   An employee is not entitled to a medical suspension payment in respect of any period during which he did not comply with reasonable requirements imposed by his employer with a view to ensuring that his services were available (*ERA 1996, s 65(4)(b)*).

Therefore, if an employer sent a man home because his workplace was medically unsafe but asked him to telephone each day to find out whether his services were required, and the employee failed to do so, he may be deprived of his right to a medical suspension payment.

34.32 **Amount of payment**

The employee is entitled to a week's pay in respect of every week of suspension (with proportionate reduction for part of a week) (*ERA 1996, s 69(1)*). A week's pay is calculated in accordance with *ERA 1996, ss 220–229* (see below 33.34). If an employee is entitled to payment during suspension on medical grounds by a term of his contract, he will only be able to claim from the employer the additional amount by which his statutory entitlement exceeds the contractual entitlement. Any payment under a contract goes to discharge the statutory liability and vice versa (*ERA 1996, s 69(2), (3)*). Thus, if an employee's week's pay is £310 (the same as the statutory week's pay) and on suspension from work on medical grounds he is contractually entitled to £200, he can claim £110 as a statutory medical suspension payment. If, however, the week's pay is £400 and the contractual entitlement £200, the statutory medical suspension payment will still be capped at £110.

34.33 Remedy for failure to make payment

If an employer fails to make a medical suspension payment, an employee may present a complaint to an employment tribunal in respect of that payment (*ERA 1996, s 70(1)*).

The complaint must be presented to the tribunal within three months beginning with the day in respect of which the claim is made (or within such further period as the tribunal considers reasonable, in a case where it is satisfied that it was not reasonably practicable for the complaint to be presented within the period of three months) (*ERA 1996, s 70(2)*; for reasonable practicability, see 20.7 EMPLOYMENT TRIBUNALS – I).

Where an employment tribunal finds a complaint well founded, it will order the employer to pay the complainant the amount of remuneration which it finds is due to him (*ERA 1996, s 70(3)*).

34.34 'A WEEK'S PAY'

(See also the DTI Guidance 'Continuous Employment and a Week's Pay: Rules for Calculation' (PL 711 8th Revision).)

The amount of money payable under several of the statutory employment protection rights depends upon a calculation based on the week's pay of the employee concerned. For example, a week's pay is the basis for the calculation of a redundancy payment and of the basic award in a claim for unfair dismissal.

The calculation of a week's pay differs according to whether the employee is in employment for which there are normal working hours or whether he is in employment for which there are no normal working hours.

The statutory rules governing 'a week's pay' are set out in *ERA 1996, ss 221–229,* formerly *EPCA 1978, Sch 14.*

34.35 EMPLOYMENT FOR WHICH THERE ARE NORMAL WORKING HOURS

If the employee's normal working hours are the same every week and his remuneration for employment in normal working hours does not vary with the amount of work done in the period, the amount of a week's pay is the amount which is payable by the employer under the contract of employment in force on the calculation date if the employee works throughout his normal working hours in a week (*ERA 1996, s 221(2)*).

Where the amount of the remuneration varies with the amount of work done but the number of normal working hours does not vary, the amount of a week's pay is the amount of remuneration for the number of normal working hours in a week calculated at the *average* hourly rate of remuneration payable by the employer to the employee in respect of the period of 12 weeks:

(*a*)   where the calculation date is the last day of a week, ending with that week;

(*b*)   in any other case, ending with the last complete week before the calculation date.

(*ERA 1996, s 221(3)*.) This is the provision which must be applied even where the variation may be attributable to the amount of work done by other employees (*Keywest Club Ltd v Choudhury* [1988] IRLR 51).

Where the employee is required under his contract to work during normal working hours on days of the week or at times of the day which differ from week to week or over a longer period so that the remuneration payable for or apportionable to any week varies, the amount of a week's pay is based upon the average remuneration paid and the average number of hours worked in the last 12 weeks before the calculation date (*ERA 1996, s 222*).

For the purposes of these calculations, weeks in which the employee was not paid because he was not working are excluded, and a previous working week is brought into account (*ERA 1996, s 223(1), (2)*).

34.36 **Overtime**

In a case where remuneration for employment in normal working hours is unaffected by any variable element in the pay structure, overtime hours and payment for them only fall within the calculation if the employer is obliged to provide, and the employee is obliged to work, the overtime (*Tarmac Roadstone Holdings Ltd v Peacock* [1973] ICR 273; *Gascol Conversions Ltd v Mercer* [1974] ICR 420). Thus, where overtime is voluntary and there is no such variable element, a week's pay is simply the contractual amount payable for the normal working hours in a full week, excluding overtime (*ERA 1996, ss 221(2), 234(1), (2)*). The same definition of a week's pay applies where a minimum number of hours of overtime is fixed by the contract of employment except that, in such a case, 'normal working hours' include that minimum number of hours of compulsory overtime (*ERA 1996, s 234(3)*).

However, where there is a variable element in the employee's remuneration dependent on results, eg piece rates, productivity bonus, or commission, the amount of a week's pay is to be calculated in accordance with *ERA 1996, s 221(3)* and *223(3)*. *Section 223(3)* provides as follows:

'Where, in arriving at the (average) ... hourly rate of remuneration, account has to be taken of remuneration payable for, or apportionable to, work done in hours other than normal working hours, and the amount of that remuneration was greater than it would have been if the work had been done in normal working hours (or, in a case within *s 234(3)* falling within the number of hours without overtime), account shall be taken of that remuneration as if –

(*a*)   the work had been done in normal working hours, falling within the number of hours without overtime in a case within *s 234(3)*; and

(*b*)   the amount of that remuneration had been reduced accordingly.'

In *British Coal Corpn v Cheesbrough* [1990] ICR 317, the House of Lords had to consider the situation where there was a variable element, namely, a weekly bonus paid to the employee for work done during normal working hours. The employee also regularly worked voluntary overtime, which was paid at time and a half, but no additional bonus was paid in respect of overtime. In such a case, the effect of *ERA 1996, s 223(3)* was that the total hours worked in the relevant weeks (including overtime) had to be taken into account, but the overtime premium was to be disregarded, and the overtime was to be treated as having been worked in normal working hours. The House of Lords held that the overtime was to be treated as having been paid at the basic hourly rate, without the addition of an amount to reflect the employee's weekly bonus. On the particular facts, this worked against the employee because his bonus had to be spread over more hours, thereby reducing his average rate of remuneration and the amount of his 'week's pay'.

34.37 EMPLOYMENTS FOR WHICH THERE ARE NO NORMAL WORKING HOURS

The amount of a week's pay is the amount of the employee's average weekly remuneration in the period of 12 weeks:

(*a*)   where the calculation date is the last day of a week, ending with that week;

(*b*)   in any other case, ending with the last complete week before the calculation date.

In arriving at the average weekly rate of remuneration no account shall be taken of a week in which no remuneration was payable by the employer to the employee, and remuneration in earlier weeks is brought in so as to bring the number of weeks of which account is taken up to 12 (*ERA 1996, s 224*).

34.38 THE CALCULATION DATE

In ascertaining the 'calculation date' for the purpose of the calculations described above, it is necessary to look to *ERA 1996, ss 225, 231*. Different calculation dates apply for the various purposes for which it may be necessary to ascertain the amount of a week's pay.

34.39 THE AMOUNT OF A WEEK'S PAY

For the purposes of calculating the amount of a week's pay, remuneration includes wages, salaries and expenses insofar as they represent profit in the employee's hands (*S & U Stores Ltd v Wilkes* [1974] 3 All ER 401). It also includes an incentive bonus, irrespective of whether the bonus is identifiably related to the particular employee's efforts (*British Coal Corpn v Cheesbrough* [1990] ICR 317). The amount of remuneration without deduction of tax is taken into account for the purposes of calculating a basic award and a redundancy payment (*Secretary of State for Employment v John Woodrow & Sons (Builders) Ltd* [1983] ICR 582). In *W A Armstrong & Sons v Borril* [2000] ICR 367, the EAT held that a week's pay for the purpose of a redundancy payment payable to an agricultural worker was the amount specified in the *Agricultural Wages Order* without deduction of board and lodging.

The amount of a week's pay for certain calculations is subject to statutory maxima. The present limit on the amount of a week's pay for the purpose of calculating a basic award of compensation for unfair dismissal and for calculating a redundancy payment is, with effect from 1 February 2007, £310 (*Employment Rights (Increase of Limits Order 2006 (SI 2006/3045)*; the previous limit was £290).

35 Pay – II: Attachment of Earnings

35.1 An *attachment of earnings order* is a means of enforcing a court order that a person must pay a sum of money. The order is made by the court and operates as an instruction to that person's employer to deduct sums from his earnings and pay them directly to the court office. The employer must also notify the court of certain matters. The *Attachment of Earnings Act 1971* ('*AtEA 1971*'), as amended, sets out the obligations of employers and the methods of calculating the deductions. Similar systems for attachment of earnings have been introduced in order to assist with the enforcement of the council tax (see 35.10 below) and of child support maintenance under the *Child Support Act 1991* (see 35.11 below).

An attachment of earnings order may be made by a court if it appears to it that a person has failed, or is likely to fail, to pay in a satisfactory way sums due from him. Orders may be made for the payment of:

(*a*) **maintenance:**

    (i)   if under a High Court maintenance order, an attachment of earnings order may be made in the High Court or the county court;

    (ii)   if under a county court maintenance order, an order may be made in the county court;

    (iii)   if under a magistrates' court maintenance order, an order may be made in a magistrates' court;

(*b*) **judgment debts exceeding £5**, including the balance remaining payable under a judgment for not less than £5 – county court;

(*c*) **payments under an administration order** (dealing with a number of debts owed by the same person) – county court;

(*d*) **payment of any sum ordered to be paid on conviction** or treated as so ordered to be paid, e g a fine or compensation order – magistrates' court;

(*e*) **payment under a legal aid contribution order** – magistrates' court.

(*AtEA 1971, s 1(1)–(3)*; *County Court Rules 1981, Order 27 r 7(9)* as amended; now contained *in Sch 2* to the *Civil Procedure Rules*; *Civil Procedure Act 1997, ss 1–4.*)

Where a county court makes an administration order in respect of a debtor's estate, it may also make an attachment of earnings order to secure the payments required by the administration order (*AtEA 1971, s 5(1)*).

The person who is obliged to make the deduction is the employer. No obligation rests on someone who as servant or agent makes payments to the employee (*AtEA 1971, s 6(2)*).

35.2 EARNINGS FROM WHICH THE DEDUCTIONS ARE MADE

Earnings, for the purposes of attachment of earnings, include wages or salary together with bonuses, commission, overtime pay and other emoluments payable under a contract of employment in addition to wages or salary. Pensions, annuities and compensation for loss of office are also included as is statutory sick pay (*AtEA 1971, s 24(1)* as amended by, *inter alia, Social Security Act 1985, s 21, Sch 4 para 1; Social Security Act 1986, Sch 10 para 102; Pension Schemes Act 1993, s 190, Sch 8 para 4*).

The following payments are not taken into account:

(*a*)   income payable by any public department of a territory outside the United Kingdom;

(*b*)   pay or allowances payable to the debtor as a member of Her Majesty's forces;

(*c*)   pensions, allowances or benefits payable under any social security enactment (including, in particular, statutory maternity pay);

(*d*)   pensions or allowances payable in respect of disablement or disability;

(*e*)   except in relation to a maintenance order, wages payable to a person as a seaman, other than wages payable to him as a seaman of a fishing boat;

(*f*)   guaranteed minimum pension within the meaning of the *Pensions Schemes Act 1993*;

(*g*)   a tax credit within the meaning of the *Tax Credits Act 2002*.

(*AtEA 1971, s 24(2)* as amended by, inter alia, *Social Security Pensions Act 1975, s 65; Merchant Shipping Act 1979, s 39; Merchant Shipping Act 1995, s 314(2), Sch 13 para 46; Pension Schemes Act 1993, s 190, Sch 8 para 4; Tax Credits Act 2002, s 47, Sch 3, para 1*).

In order to determine whether payments made by him are earnings, an employer may apply to the court which made the order (*AtEA 1971, s 16(1), (2)*). While such an application, or an appeal from the finding on such an application, is pending, an employer will not incur any liability for non-compliance with the order to which the application relates (*AtEA 1971, s 16(3)*).

35.3   DEDUCTIONS FROM PAY

Where an employer receives an attachment of earnings order which relates to one of his employees, he must make such deductions from his employee's pay as are specified in the order (*AtEA 1971, s 6 as amended by Courts and Legal Services Act 1990, Sch 17 para 5; Access to Justice Act 1999, s 90, Sch 13 paras 64, 66*).

The court may use the following terms.

'*Attachable earnings*': that part of the employee's earnings to which an attachment of earnings order applies (usually income after statutory deduction).

'*Normal deductions*': the sum to be deducted from the employee's income on each pay day.

'*Protected earnings*': the earnings below which no deduction may be made.

35.4   Calculating the deduction

If an attachment of earnings order is made, then the employer must, on pay day:

(*a*)   if the attachable earnings are greater than the protected earnings:

　　(i)   deduct the lesser of the normal deduction and the amount of the excess; and

(ii)   in the case of orders *not* made to secure the payment of a judgment debt or payments under an administration order, deduct any *arrears* still outstanding, insofar as the excess allows;

(b)   if the attachable earnings are equal to or less than the protected earnings, take no action (but the arrears are increased by the amount due).

(*AtEA 1971, Sch 3 Pt I; ERA 1996, s 240, Sch 1 para 3.*)

Example. Bill Jones earns, on average, £90 per week after tax, National Insurance, etc but because he is on piece-work his weekly earnings may vary. The court has ordered him to pay £300 at a *normal deduction rate* of £15 per week, and has decided that his *protected earnings rate* is to be £60 (in other words, he will always be allowed to take home £60, provided that he earns that much). The order does not relate to a judgment debt or an administration order.

The following table shows his pay, and the deductions over a five-week period.

Week no.	Attachable earnings	Deductions under the order	Take home	Comments
	£	£	£	
1	90	15	75	Normal deduction
2	95	15	80	Normal deduction
3	70	10	60	Only £10 deducted, Jones takes home his protected earnings
4	95	20	75	Normal deduction plus £5 of arrears
5	100	15	85	Normal deduction

See also *Pepper v Pepper* [1960] 1 WLR 131.

35.5 Priority of orders

Where there are two or more orders in existence, which are not to secure either the payment of judgment debts or payments under an administration order, then the employer must deal first with the first in time and apply the residue of the debtor's earnings over and above his protected earnings to subsequent orders, dealing with them in date order. Where there are several types of orders in existence, those to satisfy judgment debts or administration orders must be dealt with after the rest (*AtEA 1971, Sch 3 Pt II paras 7, 8*).

35.6 Time limits

It should be noted that the following notices should be complied with, within seven days:

(a)   an attachment of earnings order (*AtEA 1971, s 7(1)*);

(b)   a variation (*AtEA 1971, s 9(2)*);

(*c*)   a notice of cessation or discharge (*AtEA 1971, s 12(3)*).

35.7 EMPLOYER'S OBLIGATIONS TO NOTIFY COURT

An employer must notify the relevant court as follows.

(*a*)   Where a person is served with an attachment of earnings order directed to him and the debtor is not in his employment, *or* subsequently ceases to be in his employment, he must within 10 days give notice of that fact to the court (*AtEA 1971, s 7(2)*).

(*b*)   If the court orders him to do so, the employer must give the court, within a specified period, a statement signed by him or on his behalf of the debtor's earnings and anticipated earnings (*AtEA 1971, s 14(1)(b)*).

(*c*)   If he becomes the debtor's employer and knows that the order is in force and by what court it was made, he must within seven days of his becoming the debtor's employer or acquiring that knowledge (whichever is the later) notify that court in writing that he is the debtor's employer and include in his notification a statement of the debtor's earnings and anticipated earnings (*AtEA 1971, s 15(c)*).

35.8 PENALTIES FOR NON-COMPLIANCE

If an employer, required to comply with any of the above provisions relating to deductions or notice, fails to do so, he may be liable on conviction in a magistrates' court to a fine of not more than level 2 on the Standard Scale (see 1.10 INTRODUCTION) or he may be fined up to £250 by a judge of the High Court or the county court (*AtEA 1971, s 23, as amended*). Furthermore, if he gives a notice or makes any statement on these matters which he knows to be false in a material particular then, in addition to being fined, he may be imprisoned for not more than 14 days.

It will be a defence for an employer to prove:

(*a*)   that he took all reasonable steps to comply with the attachment of earnings order; or

(*b*)   that he did not know and could not reasonably be expected to know that the debtor was not in his employment, or had ceased to be so, and that he gave the required notice as soon as reasonably practicable after that fact came to his knowledge.

(*AtEA 1971, s 23(5)*.)

35.9 OTHER MATTERS

Clerical costs. When an employer makes a deduction in compliance with an order from an employee's earnings, he is entitled to deduct £1 (or such sum as is currently applicable) for clerical and administration costs (*AtEA 1971, s 7(4)(a); Attachment of Earnings (Employer's Deduction) Order 1991 (SI 1991/356), art 2*). The employer must give the employee a statement in writing of the deduction (*AtEA 1971, s 7(4)(b)*).

Pay statements. The employee must be given a pay statement showing, among other things, deductions from his pay. An employer need not, on each occasion upon which a payment of wages is made, give separate particulars of a fixed deduction. It is sufficient if he supplies a statement of the aggregate amount of fixed deductions having supplied a standing statement in writing of each fixed deduction stating:

(*a*)   the amount of the deduction; and

(*b*)   the intervals at which the deduction is to be made; and

(*c*)   the purpose for which it is made.

Any such standing statement is valid for 12 months. It may be amended (by adding a new deduction or altering or cancelling an existing one) by a written notice to the employee, detailing the amendment. If the employer wishes to continue to rely on the statement, it must be reissued in a consolidated form, incorporating any amendments previously notified to the employee, at intervals not exceeding 12 months.

(*ERA 1996, ss 8, 9.*) (See further 34.16 PAY – I.)

If an employer requires advice or information concerning an attachment of earnings order or subsequent procedures he should contact the court where the order was made.

35.10 COUNCIL TAX

Attachment of earnings for failure to pay the council tax is provided for by the *Council Tax (Administration and Enforcement) Regulations 1992 (SI 1992/613)*, as amended (by, inter alia, the *Local Government Changes for England (Community Charge and Council Tax, Administration and Enforcement) Regulations 1995 (SI 1995/247)*, the *Local Authorities (Contracting Out of Tax Billing, Collection and Enforcement Functions) Order 1996 (SI 1996/1880)*, the *Community Charge and Council Tax (Administration and Enforcement) (Amendment) (Jobseeker's Allowance) Regulations 1996 (SI 1996/2405)*). There must first be an outstanding sum in respect of which the relevant billing authority (in general, a district or borough council) has obtained a liability order from magistrates pursuant to *reg 34*. The authority is then itself empowered by *reg 37(1)* to make an attachment of earnings order to secure the payment of any outstanding sum covered by the liability order.

The attachment order is directed to the debtor's employer, and is in a prescribed form (*reg 37(2)*). A duty to comply with an order served upon him is imposed on the employer by *reg 37(3)*. Non-compliance is an offence unless the employer proves that he took all reasonable steps to comply with the order, and is punishable by a fine not exceeding level 3 on the Standard Scale (*reg 56(2)*; and see 1.10 INTRODUCTION).

The amount to be deducted under the order is regulated by *reg 38* and *Sch 4*. An amount is specified for any given level of net earnings. 'Earnings' has the same meaning as in the *AtEA 1971* (see 34.2 above), and the net earnings are arrived at by the deduction of income tax, primary class 1 contributions under the *Social Security Act 1975* and certain amounts deductible for the purposes of a superannuation scheme (*reg 32(1)*).

The employer must notify the debtor of the total sum deducted up to the date of each notification (*reg 39(2)*). He may deduct £1 towards administrative costs for each deduction made (*reg 39(1)*).

While such an order is in force, the debtor is under a duty to notify the authority of changes in his employment pursuant to *reg 40*. The ex-employer is under a similar duty (*reg 39(4)*), as is the new employer if he knows of the order (*reg 39(6)*).

If two or more orders are made under these provisions (or such an order is made following the making of an order under the *AtEA 1971*), the priority between them is governed by *reg 42*.

35.11 CHILD SUPPORT MAINTENANCE

A similar system to that under the *AtEA 1971* operates in relation to the enforcement by the Child Support Agency of the payment of child support maintenance by an absent parent, under the *Child Support Act 1991* ('*CSA 1991*'). An order under the *CSA 1991* is referred to as a 'deduction from earnings order', and the procedure is set out in the *Child Support* (*Collection and Enforcement*) *Regulations 1992 (SI 1992/1989)*, as amended. It is similar to that under the *AtEA 1971* and is therefore not dealt with separately in this chapter. Priority between deduction from earnings orders, and between one or more such orders and one or more attachment of earnings orders, is governed by *reg 24*.

36   Probationary Employees

36.1   LEGAL STATUS

Many employers when engaging new employees state that they will initially be employed for a 'probationary' period. It is a commonly held but mistaken belief that giving a new employee the status of probationer enables the employer to dispense with that employee's services, if he is found to be unsatisfactory, without the normal hazards of dismissal, such as a claim for unfair dismissal. The labelling of an employee as a 'probationer' has virtually no effect on the employer/employee relationship. Claims by probationary employees remain fairly rare despite the reduction of the qualifying period to one year (see 53.11 UNFAIR DISMISSAL – I). If a probationer with the necessary length of service is dismissed, he may bring a claim for unfair dismissal as may any other employee in a similar situation. The fact that he only had probationer status will not automatically make the dismissal fair. It is merely a circumstance which the tribunal will take into account in deciding whether the dismissal was fair or unfair. If the probationer's contract is not renewed after the expiry of a fixed term, provided he has the necessary qualifying period of employment, he can claim for unfair dismissal unless he has contracted out of his right to claim. An agreement to contract out of the right to claim for unfair dismissal is enforceable only in certain circumstances (see 53.19 UNFAIR DISMISSAL – I).

In the case of dismissals for certain impermissible reasons (including trade union activities, union membership or non-membership, health and safety activities, pregnancy or childbirth, refusal of a protected shop worker or betting worker or opted-out shop worker or betting worker to do shop work on a Sunday, the assertion of a statutory right) there is no qualifying period (see UNFAIR DISMISSAL – I (53)). Further, employees who are dismissed on the grounds of their sex or race or disability can bring claims under *SDA 1975*, *RRA 1976* or *DDA 1995* without establishing any qualifying period of employment.

Unless his employment continues for less than a month, a probationer will have to be given written particulars of the main terms of his employment (see 8.4 CONTRACT OF EMPLOYMENT).

36.2   EAT guidelines

In *Post Office v Mughal* [1977] ICR 763 at 768, the Employment Appeal Tribunal laid down guidelines for employment tribunals considering the fairness of the dismissal of an employee during a probationary or trial period. They considered that the following question should be asked: 'Have the employers shown that they took reasonable steps to maintain appraisal of the probationer throughout the period of probation, giving guidance by advice or warning when such is likely to be useful or fair; and that an appropriate officer made an honest effort to determine whether the probationer came up to the required standard, having informed himself of the appraisals made by supervising officers and any other facts recorded about the probationer?'.

However, in *Anandarajah v Lord Chancellor's Department* [1984] IRLR 131, the EAT cautioned against reliance on previous authority – in that case *Mughal* – in assessing the fairness of a dismissal. The preferred approach was to apply the statutory test now set out in *Employment Rights Act 1996, s 98(4), (6)* to the circumstances of each case.

However, it is thought that the matters referred to in *Mughal* remain useful considerations to take into account in assessing the fairness of the dismissal of a probationer.

37   Public Sector Employees

37.1   Many people are employed in the public sector, either in the Civil Service, or by local authorities, or by other agencies or in areas such as the National Health Service. Alternatively, they may work in industries which are publicly owned. Much of the law described in other chapters of this book applies equally to such people. However, there may sometimes be special factors to bear in mind when dealing with or advising upon public sector employment. Indeed, in *Dyke v Hereford and Worcester County Council* [1989] ICR 800 the EAT held that the contract of employment, which included the articles of a college of education, had to be read against the then statutory background relating to the authority's relevant functions, and that it was in this way that a residual power to dismiss could at that time be found.

37.2   **Special statutory provisions**

In many cases, there are specific statutory provisions which affect employment in particular areas of the public sector. The provisions set out below are among the most important, but it will be important to look carefully at all the relevant statutes and Statutory Instruments when dealing with an individual case.

Civil Service. Crown servants enjoy most of the normal statutory rights by virtue of *ERA 1996, s 191.* The main exceptions are the right to a minimum notice period (because of the doctrine that employment by the Crown is terminable at will), and the right to a statutory redundancy payment (although redundancy payments are in fact made to civil servants when appropriate); see also 37.6 below. For continuity of employment see *ERA 1996, s 191.* The legislation governing racial discrimination and sex discrimination (see DISCRIMINATION AND EQUAL OPPORTUNITIES – I, II, III (12, 13, 14)) and disability discrimination (see DISABIL-ITY DISCRIMINATION (10)) is applied to Crown servants by *RRA 1976, s 75* (with exceptions for rules restricting the nationality or residence of civil servants), by *SDA 1975, s 85* and by *DDA 1995, s 64.* The *Employment Equality (Religion or Belief) Regulations 2003 (SI 2003/1660)* and the *Employment Equality (Sexual Orientation) Regulations 2003 (SI 2003/1661)* are also applied to Crown servants (*reg 36* in each case), as will be the *Employment Equality (Age) Regulations 2006 (SI 2006/1031)* (see *reg 44*). For the status of Crown servants at common law, and the question of whether they have contracts of employment, see 37.3 below.

Armed forces. When *ERA 1996, s 192* comes into force, on a date to be fixed by regulations (*ERA 1996, Sch 2 para 16*), most of the rights enjoyed by other Crown servants, eg unfair dismissal, will be extended to members of the armed forces, although not any rights associated with trade union membership. Members of the armed forces have the protection of the racial discrimination, equal pay, and sex discrimination legislation by virtue of respectively *RRA 1976, s 75* and the *Race Relations (Complaints to Employment Tribunals) (Armed Forces) Regulations 1997 (SI 1997/2161),* the *EqPA 1970, s 7A* the *Equal Pay (Complaints to Employment Tribunals) (Armed Forces) Regulations 1997 (SI 1997/2162),* the *SDA 1975, s 85* and the *Sex Discrimination (Complaints to Employment Tribunals) (Armed Forces) Regulations 1997 (SI 1997/2163).* The main statutory provisions specific to service in the armed forces include the *Army Act 1955, Air Force Act 1955, Naval Discipline Act 1957* and the *Armed Forces Acts 1966, 1991* and *1996.* In *Quinn v*

Ministry of Defence [1998] PIQR P387, the Court of Appeal held that the plaintiff, who had enlisted in the Royal Navy in the 1950s had not entered into a contract of employment because there was no intention to create legal relations (*R v Lord Chancellor's Department, ex p Nangle* [1991] ICR 743 (distinguished)).

Police. The main statute is the *Police Act 1996* (a consolidating statute), which includes provisions barring membership of trade unions other than the Police Federation (*s 64*), and making it a criminal offence to induce or attempt to induce breaches of discipline, which would include the taking of industrial action (*s 91*). *Section 64* is extended to members of the National Criminal Intelligence Service and of the National Crime Squad, partly as from a date to be appointed (*s 64(4A) and (4B)*). *Section 15* enables a police authority to employ persons to assist the police force and requires the authority to exercise its powers in relation to arrangements for the discharge of its functions so as to secure that (broadly) any person employed by the authority is under the direction and control of the Chief Constable. Police officers are excluded from the benefit of various statutory rights, including the right to complain of UNFAIR DISMISSAL – I, II, III (53, 54, 55) and the right to complain for an unlawful deduction of wages (see *Metropolitan Police Comr v Lowrey-Nesbitt* [1999] ICR 401), by *ERA 1996, s 200(1)*. They may, however, claim in relation to detriment on the ground that, or dismissal by reason that, they made a protected disclosure: *ERA 1996,s 43KA* (and see *Lake v British Transport Police* [2007] EWCA Civ 424).This also applies to other persons having the powers or privileges of a constable, subject to s *126* of the *Criminal Justice and Public Order Act 1994* (prison staff not to be regarded as in police service) (*ERA 1996, s 200(2)*; for the previous status of prison staff, see *Home Office v Robinson and the Prison Officers' Association* [1982] ICR 31). However, police officers have the protection of the discrimination legislation by virtue of *RRA 1976, s 76A* and *SDA 1975, s 17*; *Employment Equality (Religion or Belief) Regulations 2003, reg 11*; *Employment Equality (Sexual Orientation) Regulations 2003, reg 11*; *Employment Equality (Age) Regulations 2006, reg 13*; *see* also *Sheikh v Chief Constable of Greater Manchester Police* [1989] ICR 373. As to the duty of care owed to an officer see *Waters v Metropolitan Police Comr* [2000] ICR 1064.

Local government. Local authorities have the power to appoint staff under *Local Government Act 1972, s 112* and to take steps to maintain good staff relations (see *R v Greater London Council, ex p Westminster City Council* (1984) Times, 27 December, and limited powers to grant indemnities (see *Burgoine v Waltham Forest London Borough Council* (1996) 95 LGR 520). By s *116* of the *Local Government Act 1972*, members of an authority may not be appointed to any paid office with that authority. Further restrictions are contained in the *Local Government and Housing Act 1989*: certain posts are 'politically restricted', which means that their holders may not be members of *any* local authority without express exemption (*ss 1–3*); with certain exceptions, all appointments must be made on merit (*s 7*); authorities must ensure so far as practicable that they are not represented in negotiations about terms and conditions of employment by members of the authority who are also in local authority employment or who are officials or employees of trade unions whose members include local authority employees (*s 12*). The *Local Government Officers (Political Restrictions) Regulations 1990* have been held not to contravene the European Convention on Human Rights (*Ahmed v United Kingdom* [1999] IRLR 188, European Court of Human Rights). As to the law on the transfer of undertakings in the context of local government reorganisation, see *Henke v Gemeinde Schierke* [1996] IRLR 701, *Directive 2001/23, art 1(1)(c)*; *Collino v Telecom Italia SpA* [2002] ICR 38; *Viggásdóttir v Íslandspóstur hf* [2002] IRLR 425 (EFTA Court); and 52.5 TRANSFER OF UNDERTAKINGS. The power of local authorities to make payments to their staff is restricted by what is reasonable and by the wording of the relevant statutory provisions (see *Allsop v North Tyneside Metropolitan Borough Council* [1992] ICR 639 and now the *Local Government (Discretionary Payments) Regulations 1996 (SI 1996/1680)*). An authority which decides to seek fresh tenders for works which have already been awarded to its own workforce is not thereby in breach of its public law duties to its employees (*R v Walsall Metropolitan Borough Council, ex p Yapp* [1994] ICR 528). An authority cannot, however, rely on a need to cut wages for competitive purposes as a defence to an equal pay claim, unless the reduction can be shown to be gender-neutral (*North Yorkshire County Council v Ratcliffe* [1995] ICR 833). Nor can it give women who have the same qualifications as men applying for the same post priority in sectors and or grades where women are underrepresented (*Kalanke v Freie Hansestadt Bremen: C-450/93* [1995] IRLR 660).

Health Service. There are provisions to secure continuity of employment on changes of employer within the National Health Service. See *ERA 1996, s 218(8)–(10)* and *R v North Thames Regional Health Authority, ex p L (an infant)* [1996] 7 Med LR 385.

Education. Schools are divided into three categories: community schools, voluntary aided schools or foundation schools. In the second two categories, the employment position is relatively straightforward and staff are employed by the LEA. However, the position is more complicated in community schools which have delegated budgets since the LEA is the employer, but many of the normal powers of an employer are exercised by the governing body (*Schools Standards and Framework Act 1998*; and see the *Education (Modification of Enactments relating to Employment) Order 2003 (SI 2003/1964)*). The complicated interrelationship of the employment responsibilities of the LEA and the governing body was considered by the Court of Appeal in *Murphy v Slough Borough Council* [2005] EWCA Civ 122, [2005] IRLR 382 and (in relation to comparators under the *EqPA*) by the EAT in *Dolphin v Hartlepool Borough Council* (9 August 2006) (a decision of the CA is awaited). School teachers' pay and conditions of employment are subject to control by the Secretary of State for Education and Employment by virtue of the *Education Act 2002, ss 119–130*; and compensation for redundancy is subject to regulations made under the *Superannuation Act 1972*, now the *Teachers (Compensation for Redundancy and Premature Retirement) Regulations 1997 (SI 1997/311)*.

Industrial action. In relation to industrial action in the public sector, there is an extension to the statutory immunity from claims in tort for action taken in contemplation or furtherance of a trade dispute (see 45.3 STRIKES AND INDUSTRIAL ACTION). Whereas the dispute must normally be between the workers concerned and their employer in order to attract the immunity, a dispute between a Minister of the Crown and any workers is treated as a dispute between those workers and their employer if the dispute relates to matters which:

(*a*)   have been referred for consideration by a joint body on which statutory provision is made for the Minister to be represented, or

(*b*)   cannot be settled without the Minister exercising a statutory power.

(*TULRCA 1992, s 244(2)*.)

This provision was considered at first instance, but not on appeal, in *Wandsworth London Borough Council v NASUWT* [1994] ICR 81.

37.3 Status of Crown servants

Crown servants have a special status in the eyes of the law. The term includes civil servants.

At common law, the Crown servant is employed at the pleasure of the Crown. That is, he can be dismissed at will – without notice and without the need to show cause or to follow any particular procedure (see *Dunn v R* [1896] 1 QB 116; *Council of Civil Service Unions v Minister for the Civil Service* [1985] AC 374). However, the effect of *ERA 1996, s 191* is to extend to Crown servants the right of an ordinary employee to pursue a claim for UNFAIR DISMISSAL – I (53).

There has for many years been a controversy as to whether Crown servants in fact have a CONTRACT OF EMPLOYMENT (8) at all. By *TULRCA 1992, s 245*, they are deemed to have one for certain purposes (principally, for the purpose of liability for torts involving the inducement or threatened inducement of a breach of contract (see 43.2 STRIKES AND INDUSTRIAL ACTION), and of certain provisions of *TULRCA 1992*). The question was considered by the Divisional Court in *R v Civil Service Appeal Board, ex p Bruce* [1988] ICR 649 (the Court of Appeal did not express an opinion when it considered the case). It was suggested that there was nothing unconstitutional in a Crown servant having a contract of employment: the question was whether that was the intention of the Crown when the employment began. In *Bruce*, it was said that the evidence suggested no such intention in relation to civil servants prior to 1985 (which was the case in question), but a likelihood that future civil service appointments *would* be on the basis of contract. However, in *R v Lord Chancellor's Department, ex p Nangle* [1991] ICR 743, the Divisional Court upon similar facts concluded that *Bruce* was wrong and that a contract *did* exist. See also *McClaren v Home Office* [1990] ICR 824.

In *Department of Health v Bruce* (1992) Times, 31 December the majority of EAT considered that an industrial tribunal had been entitled to make an order for re-engagement (see 55.3 UNFAIR DISMISSAL – III) against the Department of Health, even though the employee had been unfairly dismissed by the Department of Social Security.

37.4 Availability of judicial review

Those who work in the public sector may sometimes seek to assert their rights, not simply in an industrial tribunal or in an action for tort or breach of contract in the ordinary courts, but by way of an application for judicial review. This is a means of challenging the unlawful actions and decisions of public authorities and bodies exercising statutory power. The possible grounds for such challenge include failure to observe natural justice or a statutorily prescribed procedure, the taking into account of irrelevant considerations (or the failure to consider all matters which ought to be considered), acting for an improper purpose, and extreme irrationality. Applications are heard in the Administrative Court, and the procedure is governed by *Civil Procedure Rules, Part 53* (note also the *Practice Direction* and the *Pre-Action Protocol*). Its features include a need to obtain leave to proceed from the court, and a strict time limit (applications must be brought promptly, and *in any event* within three months of the action challenged).

However, the courts have held that the judicial review procedure *must* be used when a *public* right is being asserted, but *must not* be used when the subject matter is a *private* right (*O'Reilly v Mackman* [1983] 2 AC 237; *Davy v Spelthorne Borough Council* [1984] AC 262). This distinction between public and private rights, which is often difficult to draw, applies to employment-related cases. If the claim is really founded upon a contract, in the sense that that is the sole basis of the relationship between the parties, judicial review will not be appropriate (*R v East Berkshire Health Authority, ex p Walsh* [1984] ICR 743; see also *R v BBC, ex p Lavelle* [1983] 1 WLR 23; *R v Crown Prosecution Service, ex p Hogg* [1994] 6 Admin LR 778; *R v Secretary of State for the Home Department, ex p Moore* [1994] COD 67; and *R v Secretary of State for Education and Science, ex p Prior* [1994] COD 197).

The most helpful statement of the position is to be found in the judgment of Woolf LJ in *McClaren v Home Office* [1990] ICR 824. He concluded that judicial review was generally an unnecessary and inappropriate remedy for public sector employees, but that there were two types of case where it might be available. One was where the decision impugned was that of a tribunal or other body (such as the Civil Service Appeal Board) which had a sufficient public law element and was not wholly domestic or informal. The other was where the employee was adversely affected by a decision of *general* application which was alleged to be flawed (the decision to bar trade union membership at GCHQ was an example of this). Even if judicial review was unavailable, it might be possible to seek a declaration or injunction to ensure that disciplinary proceedings were conducted fairly. Similarly, the Court of Appeal held in *R v Derbyshire County Council, ex p Noble* [1990] ICR 808 that what mattered was not so much the status of the employee as whether judicial review was appropriate given the subject matter of the challenged decision. (It was not an appropriate way to challenge the termination of a police surgeon's appointment.) See also *R v Liverpool City Corpn, ex p Ferguson and Ferguson* [1985] IRLR 501; *R v Home Secretary, ex p Attard* [1990] COD 261; *Nangle*, above; *Secretary of State for Scotland and Greater Glasgow Health Board v Wright and Hannah* [1991] IRLR 187; *Roy v Kensington and Chelsea and Westminster Family Practitioner Committee* [1992] IRLR 233.

It should also be remembered that the court hearing an application for judicial review has an overriding discretion as to whether any relief should be granted. One possible reason for refusing relief is that some alternative remedy was available and should have been pursued. Thus in *Bruce* (see 37.3 above) the Divisional Court accepted that there was a sufficient public law element for an unsuccessful appeal against dismissal to the Civil Service Appeal Board to be judicially reviewable, but held that only in exceptional cases would it be right not to confine the applicant to his remedy in an industrial tribunal. The Court of Appeal upheld the refusal of relief on the facts without expressing a view on the general proposition. In *R v Hammersmith and Fulham London Borough Council, ex p NALGO* [1991] IRLR 249, it was held that a local authority's redundancy selection policy should be tested by way of cases brought in the tribunal alleging unfair dismissal or discrimination, and not by way of judicial review. See also *R v Secretary of State for Employment, ex p Equal Opportunities Commission* [1995] 1 AC 1, where the House of Lords held that an individual employee did not have standing to apply for judicial review, but the Equal Opportunities Commission did.

However, if available, judicial review can provide a powerful remedy to the employee, as it did in *R v Civil Service Appeal Board, ex p Cunningham* [1992] ICR 816, where a decision of the Board was struck down because of the Board's failure to give adequate reasons. See also *R v Civil Service Appeal Board, ex p Chance* [1993] COD 116.

In public law there is a doctrine of 'legitimate expectation', which means that, where a public authority has given the impression, by its words or by its consistent past practice, that it will follow a particular course of action, it may not be permitted to go back on that, at least without consulting those who are affected. For a successful attempt to invoke this doctrine in the employment field, see the Northern Ireland case *Re NUPE and COHSE's Application* [1989] IRLR 202, in which it was held that the health service unions whose members were affected by proposed hospital closures had a legitimate expectation of consultation before such decisions were taken. See also *Council of Civil Service Unions v Minister for the Civil Service* [1985] AC 374; *R v Director of Government Communications Headquarters, ex p Hodges* [1988] COD 123; *R v British Coal Corpn and Secretary of State for Trade and Industry, ex p Vardy* [1993] IRLR 104; and *R v British Coal Corpn and Secretary of State for Trade and Industry, ex p Price* [1994] IRLR 72.

37.5 Exemplary damages

It is possible in principle for exemplary damages to be available in claims brought by employees against public bodies. This is a category of damages which goes beyond the normal rule that a plaintiff may only recover such damages as will compensate him for the loss which he has actually suffered. In *Cassell & Co Ltd v Broome* [1972] AC 1027 the House of Lords held that exemplary damages could be awarded, *inter alia*, where the plaintiff had suffered from oppressive, arbitrary or unconstitutional action by servants of the Government, and that 'Government' was to be interpreted broadly in this context. This applies to all torts which satisfy the tests in *Rookes v Barnard* [1964] AC 1129, irrespective of the date on which the tort was created: *Kuddus v Chief Constable of Leicestershire Constabulary* [2002] 2 AC 122. There is, therefore, no reason why exemplary damages should not be available in cases of discrimination. Earlier authorities to the contrary (for example *Deane v Ealing London Borough Council* [1993] ICR 329) were based on a line of authority now overruled.

37.6 Public interest immunity and national security

In litigation against public authorities, in particular government departments, attempts to obtain documents by way of an order for discovery (see 20.16 EMPLOYMENT TRIBUNALS – I) may sometimes be met by a claim that those documents should not be disclosed because they are subject to public interest immunity. This means that the interest in preventing the disclosure of such documents outweighs the interest in the court or tribunal having all the relevant evidence. The court may itself examine the documents in order to decide whether they ought to be disclosed. See in particular *Conway v Rimmer* [1968] AC 910, *Air Canada v Secretary of State for Trade* [1983] 2 AC 394 and *R v Chief Constable of West Midlands Police, ex p Wiley* [1995] 1 AC 274, now the leading civil case.

The question of public interest immunity in the employment law context was considered in *Metropolitan Police Comr v Locker* [1993] ICR 440. The Court of Appeal has also indicated that a tribunal should not normally regard itself as qualified to pass judgment upon the view expressed in a Minister's certificate that disclosure would be contrary to the public interest (*Balfour v Foreign and Commonwealth Office* [1994] 1 WLR 681).

Occasionally employment disputes will also raise questions of national security (see, e g *Council of Civil Service Unions v Minister for the Civil Service* [1985] AC 374). For this reason, the *Employment Tribunals Act 1996 ('ETA 1996'), ss 4* and *28* provide for Ministers to have power on grounds of national security to direct that tribunal and EAT hearings should be conducted by the President of Employment Tribunals or the President of the EAT sitting alone. Provision is also made for requiring or enabling tribunals and the EAT to sit in private in cases involving national security (*ETA 1996, s 10*). See also 20.29 EMPLOYMENT

TRIBUNALS – I, *Employment Tribunals (Constitution and Rules of Procedure) Regulations 2004 (SI 2004/1861), rule 54*, and *Employment Appeal Tribunal Rules 1993 (SI 1993/2854), rule 30A.*

Where in the opinion of any Minister of the Crown the disclosure of any information would be contrary to the interests of national security, disclosure of that information will not be required by certain provisions of *ERA 1996*, and no person may disclose that information in any court or tribunal proceedings relating to any of those provisions (*ERA 1996, s 202*). A Minister may also certify that certain categories of Crown employment require to be exempted from certain statutory employment rights for the purpose of safeguarding national security (*ERA 1996, s 193*).

37.7 European Community law

All employment relationships are now affected by EUROPEAN COMMUNITY LAW (25). However, public sector employees may find themselves in a special position because of the way in which the doctrine of 'direct effect' is applied. Some categories of EC legislation (the Treaties themselves, and regulations) become applicable once promulgated without any need for further action by member states. In the case of *Directives*, however, the intention is that member states should, within a given time, take such steps as they consider appropriate to implement the *Directive* in their territory. The European Court of Justice has frequently held that, if a member state fails to comply with its obligation (either because it does nothing or because what it does is held not to achieve all that the *Directive* requires), then, although that *Directive* cannot be relied upon in proceedings against private persons, provided that the *Directive* is clear and unconditional, it may be relied upon against that State. The State may not take advantage of its own wrong in failing to introduce measures to implement the *Directive*. In order for a person to be able to rely on a *Directive* against the State, the terms of the *Directive* must be clear and it must be unconditional, ie it must require no further implementing measures or time before it is intended to have effect.

It was this doctrine which enabled the applicant in *Marshall v Southampton and South West Hampshire Area Health Authority (Teaching)* [1986] ICR 335 to succeed in her claim of unlawful sex discrimination based on discriminatory retiring ages at a time before the *Sex Discrimination Act 1986* was passed. The health authority which employed her was agreed to be an organ of the state, so that she could rely directly upon *Directive 76/207/EEC* (see 25.6 EUROPEAN COMMUNITY LAW).

The question of whether a nationalised industry (since privatised) is the state for these purposes fell to be considered in *Foster v British Gas plc*. The House of Lords referred the question to the European Court of Justice, which held ([1991] ICR 84) that the doctrine applies to 'a body, whatever its legal form, which has been made responsible, pursuant to a measure adopted by the state, for providing a public service under the control of the state and has for that purpose special powers beyond those which result from the normal rules applicable in relations between individuals'. The House of Lords ([1991] ICR 463) went on to hold that British Gas before privatisation fell within this definition. However, mere control by the state is not enough, and so the doctrine did not apply to a manufacturing company which was wholly owned by the state but which did not provide a public service and possessed no special powers (*Doughty v Rolls-Royce plc* [1992] ICR 538). The doctrine did apply to a water company privatised under the *Water Act 1989* and *Water Industry Act 1991* (*Griffin v South West Water Services Ltd*

[1995] IRLR 15), and to the governing body of a voluntary aided school (*National Union of Teachers v St Mary's Church of England Junior School* [1997] IRLR 242, CA). In *Hillman v London General Transport Services Ltd* (14 April 1999, unreported), the EAT held that the respondent company was simply a commercial concern and was not an emanation of the state, applying *Foster v British Gas plc.*

The general right of free movement of labour and the bar on discrimination against EC nationals in relation to employment contained in *art 39* of the EC Treaty (see 25.4 EUROPEAN COMMUNITY LAW, 26.2 FOREIGN EMPLOYEES) is subject to an exception in the case of employment in the public service, to which *art 48* does not apply (*art 39(4)*). The definition of public service in this context has been the subject of several cases. The ECJ has held in *Re Employees of the Consiglio Nazionale Ricerche* [1988] 3 CMLR 635 that the question is not one of the status of the employee or of his or her legal relationship with the national administration, but depends upon whether the employee is one who exercises powers conferred by public law or is responsible for safeguarding the general interests of the state. See also *Anker v Germany* [2003] ECR I-10447. The relevant UK legislation has been amended by the *European Communities* (*Employment in the Civil Service*) *Order 1991* (*SI 1991/1221*) in order to secure compliance with *art 48.*

37.8 European Community employees

Since the merger of the EEC, the Coal and Steel Community and Euratom in 1965, the officials of the European Communities have belonged to a unified civil service. Their employment is governed by Staff Regulations contained in *EEC Council reg 31* and *Euratom Council reg 11* of 18 December 1961 as subsequently amended on numerous occasions. Thus the terms and conditions of EC officials are governed essentially by EC legislation rather than by individually negotiated contracts. Similar provisions are made for temporary, auxiliary and local staff and special advisers by the Conditions of Employment of Other Servants of the Communities.

The Staff Regulations provide *inter alia* for appointment, for termination by resignation, retirement or dismissal, for remuneration and for disciplinary procedures. An official may be required to make good damage suffered by the EC as a result of serious misconduct on his part. Conversely, the EC is obliged under the *Regulations* to assist officials, in particular in proceedings against persons who threaten, insult or attack such officials, their families or property by reason of their position or duties. The scope of that obligation was discussed in *Hamill v EC Commission: 180/87* [1990] 1 All ER 982.

In addition to their internal effects, the Staff Regulations are binding upon member states insofar as their co-operation is necessary in order to give effect to those rules (*Re Family Benefits: EC Commission v Belgium: 186/85* [1988] 2 CMLR 759).

Disputes between the EC and its servants, which were formerly adjudicated upon by the ECJ, now fall within the jurisdiction of the Court of First Instance of the European Communities, with an appeal to the ECJ being available on points of law (*Council Decision 88/591*).

For a decision upon the right of EC staff to engage in trade union activities, including time off and proper facilities for trade union representatives, see *Maurissen v Court of Auditors of the European Communities* [1989] ECR 1045.

37.8 Public Sector Employees

For a decision on alleged sex discrimination within the EC civil service, see *Delauche v EC Commission* [1989] 2 CMLR 565.

See also EUROPEAN COMMUNITY LAW (25).

38   Redundancy – I: The Right to a Redundancy Payment

(See also DTI booklet 'Redundancy Payments' (URN 98/85); 'Offsetting Pensions against Redundancy Payments' (RPL1); 'Time Off for Job Hunting or to Arrange Training when Facing Redundancy' (PL703).)

Cross-references. TRANSFER OF UNDERTAKINGS (52). See 54.11 UNFAIR DISMISSAL – II for dismissal on grounds of redundancy, and PAY – I (34) for details of the calculation of the employee's weekly pay.

38.1   The *Redundancy Payments Act 1965* (*'RPA 1965'*) introduced the right of employees who lost their jobs in certain circumstances to a payment from their employers irrespective of whether they had another job to go to. The *RPA 1965* was amended by the *Employment Protection Act 1975* (*'EPA 1975'*) and the provisions, as amended, were re-enacted in the *Employment Protection* (*Consolidation*) *Act 1978* (*'EPCA 1978'*). The provisions are now contained in the *Employment Rights Act 1996* (*'ERA 1996'*).

38.2   **PRE-CONDITIONS FOR PAYMENT**

The conditions which must be fulfilled for a person to be entitled to a redundancy payment are:

(*a*)   that he was an employee;

(*b*)   that he had been continuously employed for the requisite period;

(*c*)   that he was dismissed (as defined); and

(*d*)   that the dismissal was by reason of redundancy.

(*ERA 1996, ss 135, 155.*)

Certain employees are excluded from the right to a redundancy payment (see 38.10 below).

38.3   **APPLICANT MUST HAVE BEEN AN EMPLOYEE**

Only 'employees' are entitled to claim a redundancy payment. Thus, those engaged under a contract for services are not entitled to make such a claim. 'Employee' is defined as:

'... an individual who has entered into or works under (or, where the employment has ceased, worked under) a contract of employment.' (*ERA 1996, s 230(1)*)

See EMPLOYEE, SELF-EMPLOYED OR WORKER? (17).

If the respondent to an application for a redundancy payment (ie the employer) disputes the fact that the applicant was an employee, it is for the applicant to prove that he was.

38.4 **Continuous employment for the requisite period**

In order to be entitled to a redundancy payment, an applicant must have been *continuously employed for a period of two years ending with the relevant date* (see below for 'relevant date') (*ERA 1996, s 155*).

Formerly, different rules of continuity applied to full-time and part-time employees. A challenge to the rules of continuity as they affected part-timers, on the basis that they were sexually discriminatory and contrary to EC law, was successful in *R v Secretary of State for Employment, ex p EOC* [1994] ICR 317. As a result, the *Employment Protection (Part-time Employees) Regulations 1995 (SI 1995/31)* were introduced, which amended *EPCA 1978, Sch 13* so that all part-time employment counts towards continuity in the same manner as full-time employment. Accordingly, there are no special rules relating to continuity for part-timers in the *ERA 1996*.

The rules for computing continuous employment are dealt with in detail in CONTINUOUS EMPLOYMENT (7).

The relevant date. The relevant date in relation to the dismissal of an employee:

(*a*) where his contract of employment is terminated by notice, whether given by his employer or by the employee, means the date on which that notice expires;

(*b*) where his contract of employment is terminated without notice, means the date on which the termination takes effect; and

(*c*) where he is employed under a contract for a fixed term and that term expires without being renewed under the same contract, means the date on which that term expires.

(*ERA 1996, s 145.*)

This provision corresponds to the definition of the 'effective date of termination' for the purposes of unfair dismissal contained in *ERA 1996, s 97(1)*; for a discussion of its application see 53.13 UNFAIR DISMISSAL – I.

If an employee is dismissed with no notice or less than the statutory minimum period of notice, for the purposes, *inter alia*, of calculating the qualifying period of employment, the relevant date will be the date upon which the statutory minimum period of notice would have expired had it been given (*ERA 1996, s 145(5)*). (See 48.7 TERMINATION OF EMPLOYMENT.) However, this provision does not affect the employer's right to dismiss without notice for an employee's gross misconduct (*ERA 1996, s 86(6)*). In the event of such a dismissal, the statutory minimum period of notice will not be added on for the purpose of computing the length of continuous employment.

38.5 **Changes in the ownership of the business**

The *Transfer of Undertakings (Protection of Employment) Regulations 2006 (SI 2006/246)* are discussed fully in TRANSFER OF UNDERTAKINGS (52). By virtue of the *Regulations*, on a 'relevant transfer' of an undertaking, the existing employees' contracts of employment are not terminated. On completion of such a transfer all the transferor's rights, powers, duties and liabilities under or in connection with any such contract are transferred to the transferee (*Transfer of Undertakings Regulations, reg 4(2)(a)*). Therefore, such an employee will be deemed not to have been dismissed by the transferor and the continuity of his employment will be preserved.

38.6   **The employee must have been 'dismissed'**

There is no presumption of dismissal and, if the employer disputes the fact, it is for the employee to prove it. For redundancy payments purposes, dismissal has a statutory meaning instead of merely meaning termination of the contract by the employer. Sub-paragraph (*a*) below reflects the common law position (see 48.5 TERMINATION OF EMPLOYMENT), and occurs most frequently in practice, while (*b*) would not be a dismissal at common law. In addition, certain forms of termination of the contract at common law are disregarded for redundancy payments purposes (see below).

An employee will be taken to be dismissed by his employer if, but only if:

(*a*)   the contract under which he is employed by the employer is terminated by the employer, whether it is terminated by notice or without notice;

(*b*)   where under that contract he is employed for a fixed term, that term expires without being renewed under the same contract; or

(*c*)   the employee terminates that contract with or without notice in circumstances such that he is entitled so to terminate it without notice by reason of the employer's conduct (not being termination by reason of a lock-out).

(*ERA 1996, s 136(1), (2).*)

The statutory definition of dismissal for redundancy payments purposes is the same as for the purposes of unfair dismissal (see UNFAIR DISMISSAL – I (53)).

Where in accordance with any enactment or rule of law any act on the part of an employer, or any event affecting an employer, operates so as to terminate a contract of employment, that is treated for redundancy payments purposes as a termination by the employer, even if it would not otherwise amount to such a termination (*ERA 1996, s 136(5)*; and see *Pickwell v Lincolnshire County Council* [1993] ICR 87).

Situations where no dismissal occurs. An employee is deemed not to have been dismissed in certain circumstances where a dismissal by reason of redundancy has in fact taken place. Two examples are given below.

(i)   *Renewal or re-engagement.* If an employee's contract is renewed or he is re-engaged under a new contract of employment and:

(A)   the offer, whether in writing or not, is made before the ending of the existing contract; and

(B)   it is to take effect either immediately on the ending of the original employment or within a period of not more than four weeks thereafter (if the contract ends on Friday, Saturday or Sunday, the new employment must take effect four weeks from the following Monday),

no dismissal will be deemed to have taken place in respect of the termination of the original contract (*ERA 1996, s 138(1)*).

If the terms and conditions of the new employment differ wholly or in part from the original contract, the employee has a trial period of four weeks from the ending of the original employment, or such longer period as may be agreed in writing, within which to decide whether to accept or reject the offer (see 38.12 below). If he rejects the offer or if the employer terminates or gives notice to terminate the contract for a reason connected with the change in contractual terms, within that period, the employee will be taken to have been dismissed on the date of termination of the original contract for the reason that contract was terminated (*ERA 1996, s 138(2)–(6)*).

(ii)   *Offers of employment by associated companies.* It should be noted that where the employer is a company, any reference to re-engagement by the employer is construed as including a reference to re-engagement by *that company or by an associated company*, and any reference to an offer made by the employer is construed as including a reference to an offer made by an associated company (*ERA 1996, s 146(1)*). For the meaning of 'associated company', see 7.9(A) CONTINUOUS EMPLOYMENT.

Employee who leaves prematurely. An employee who leaves his employment before his employer's notice of dismissal expires may lose his right to a redundancy payment. If the employee gives written notice to terminate his employment on a date earlier than that given by his employer, he will not lose his right to a redundancy payment if the employer does not object to his premature departure. If, however, the employer does object and serves on the employee a written request to withdraw his notice, warning him that if he does not do so the employer will contest any liability to make a redundancy payment, he may lose the right to such a payment. If the employer withholds the redundancy payment, the employee may apply to an employment tribunal which will decide whether the employee is entitled to the full payment, or no payment, or part of the payment. The tribunal will consider whether the employee's action in leaving prematurely was reasonable or unreasonable in the circumstances (*ERA 1996, ss 136(3), 142(1), (2)*). If, however, the parties agree by mutual consent to substitute some other date of termination for the date specified by the employer, no such question arises (*CPS Recruitment Ltd v Bowen and Secretary of State for Employment* [1982] IRLR 54).

38.7   Redundancy must be the reason for dismissal

In order to be entitled to a redundancy payment, the employee must be dismissed by reason of redundancy. An employee who has been dismissed by his employer is, unless the contrary is proved, presumed to have been dismissed by reason of redundancy for the purposes of any claim for a redundancy payment (*ERA 1996, s 163(2)*). It is therefore for the employer to prove that the reason for the dismissal was other than redundancy or that for some reason the employee is not entitled to the payment.

'Redundancy' is defined as follows:

'For the purposes of this Act an employee who is dismissed shall be taken to be dismissed by reason of redundancy if the dismissal is wholly or mainly attributable to –

(*a*)   the fact that his employer has ceased or intends to cease:

  (i)   to carry on the business for the purposes of which the employee was employed by him, or

  (ii)   to carry on that business in the place where the employee was so employed, or

(*b*)   the fact that the requirements of that business:

  (i)   for employees to carry out work of a particular kind, or

  (ii)   for employees to carry out work of a particular kind in the place where the employee was employed by the employer, have ceased or diminished or are expected to cease or diminish.'

(*ERA 1996, s 139(1)*; note that a different definition applies for the purposes of the redundancy consultation provisions of *TULCRA 1992* (see 39.3 REDUN-DANCY – II).)

Sub-paragraph (*a*) covers the closure of the employer's business as a whole, or, alternatively, just at the place where the employee is employed. The test for determining 'the place where the employee was employed' is primarily a factual one, although the employee's contractual terms may provide evidence of the place of work where the employee did go from place to place (see *High Table Ltd v Horst* [1998] ICR 409, CA). Thus, if an employee had as a matter of fact worked in only one location, then the existence of a contractual mobility clause (entitling the employer to transfer him) will not widen the definition of the place where the employee was employed under *ERA 1996, s 139(1)* (see also *Bass Leisure Ltd v Thomas* [1994] IRLR 104).

Under sub-para (*b*) it must be considered whether the business requires so many employees to carry out certain work. In deciding whether there has been a cessation or diminution in the requirements of the business for employees to carry out 'work of a particular kind', it was uncertain whether the work is defined by what is required under an employee's contract of employment ('the contract test'), or by what an employee is actually doing ('the function test'), or by a blend of the two. Until 1997, it was assumed that the Court of Appeal in *Cowen v Haden Ltd* [1983] ICR 1 had established that the proper test was the contract test. However, the EAT in *Safeway Stores plc v Burrell* [1997] ICR 523 disagreed with this interpretation of *Cowen v Haden* and stated that the terms of an employee's contract of employment were irrelevant when determining whether there was a redundancy situation within the meaning of *ERA 1996, s 139(1)*. The House of Lords confirmed in the case of *Murray v Foyle Meats Ltd* [1999] ICR 827 that both the 'contract test' and the 'function test' are an unnecessary gloss on the plain wording of the statute. Further, the Court of Appeal held in *Shawkat v Nottingham City Hospital NHS Trust (No 2)* [2001] EWCA Civ 954, [2001] IRLR 555 that whether there was less need for employees to carry out work of a particular kind was always a question of fact for a tribunal to decide.

The House of Lords in *Murray* approved the reasoning of the EAT in *Safeway Stores v Burrell* (see above), one of whose conclusions was that 'bumped employ-ees' will be dismissed by reason of redundancy. A 'bumping' situation will exist where Smith, whose job is no longer required, is put by his employer into Brown's position, so that Brown is dismissed instead of Smith. The reasoning in *Safeway Stores v Burrell* would mean that Brown was redundant, because the employer's requirement for work of a particular kind had diminished, and because Brown was dismissed as a result. It is not necessary that any reduction in the employer's requirements for work of a particular kind should be a reduction in the type of work that Brown himself carried out. *Safeway Stores v Burrell* follows earlier authority (see *W Gimber & Sons Ltd v Spurrett* (1967) 2 ITR 308; applied by the EAT in *Elliott Turbomachinery Ltd v Bates* [1981] ICR 218) in reaching this conclusion. The EAT decision in *Church v West Lancashire NHS Trust* [1998] ICR 423 created some uncertainty as to whether *Safeway Stores* was correct, but those doubts have now been dispelled by *Murray*, and more recently, by the EAT in *Stankovic v Westminster City Council* (17 October 2001, unreported). Indeed, the EAT specifically stated in *Stankovic* that *Church* was no longer good authority on the point.

38.8 Redundancy – I: The Right to a Redundancy Payment

Where an employee is employed on a succession of fixed-term contracts this can, in principle, give rise to a dismissal by reason of redundancy on the expiration of each fixed-term contract (*Pfaffinger v City of Liverpool Community College* [1997] ICR 142).

38.8 Redundancy payments for lay-off and short time

Special provisions relating to redundancy claims by piece-workers who are laid off or put on short time are contained in *ERA 1996*. An employee is considered to be *laid off* during a particular week if under his contract he gets no pay of any kind from his employer for that week because there is no work for him to do although he is available for work (*ERA 1996, s 147*). An employee is considered to be on short time for a week if during that week he gets less than half a week's pay (*ERA 1996, s 147(2)*).

A redundancy payment may only be claimed by a worker laid off or on short time if he gives notice in writing to his employer of his intention to claim and the claim is submitted within four weeks of:

(*a*)   the end of a continuous period of lay-off or short time of four or more weeks' duration; or

(*b*)   the end of a period of six weeks' lay-off or short time out of 13 weeks (where not more than three weeks were consecutive).

(*ERA 1996, s 148.*)

He must then terminate his contract of employment by giving the contractual period of notice or one week's notice, whichever is the greater (*ERA 1996, s 150(1)*).

The notice to terminate must be given within the following time limits:

(*a*)   if the employer does not give a counter-notice (see 38.9 below) within seven days after the service of the notice of intention to claim, that period is three weeks after the end of those seven days;

(*b*)   if the employer gives a counter-notice within those seven days, but withdraws it by a subsequent notice in writing, that period is three weeks after the service of the notice of withdrawal; and

(*c*)   if the employer gives a counter-notice within those seven days and does not so withdraw it, and a question as to the right of the employee to a redundancy payment in pursuance of the notice of intention to claim is referred to a tribunal, that period is three weeks after the tribunal has notified to the employee its decision on that reference.

(*ERA 1996, s 150(3).*)

Even if an employee fails to comply with these statutory requirements, he may claim that he has been constructively dismissed for redundancy if he is laid off in fundamental breach of his contract of employment (*A Dakri & Co Ltd v Tiffen* [1981] ICR 256; cf *Kenneth McRae & Co Ltd v Dawson* [1984] IRLR 5).

38.9 Counter-notice

An employee who gives a notice of intention to claim pursuant to *ERA 1996, s 148* will not be entitled to a redundancy payment if, on the date of service of that notice, it was reasonably to be expected that he would (if he continued to be employed by the same employer), not later than four weeks after that date, enter upon a period of employment of not less than 13 weeks during which he would not be laid off or kept on short time (*ERA 1996, s 152(1)*).

However, an employer cannot take advantage of this rule unless, within seven days after service of the notice of intention to claim, he gives the employee notice in writing that he will contest liability to make a redundancy payment (*ERA 1996, s 152(1)(b)*). If the employee wishes to pursue his claim after the service of a counter-notice, an employment tribunal must be asked to determine whether he is entitled to a redundancy payment (*ERA 1996, s 149*).

38.10 Exclusions from right to payment

The following are excluded from the right to a redundancy payment.

(*a*)　Masters or crew of a fishing vessel who are not remunerated otherwise than by a share of the profits or gross earnings of the vessel (*ERA 1996, s 199(2)*) (see *Goodeve v Gilsons (a firm)* [1985] ICR 401)).

(*b*)　Civil servants and other public employees (*ERA 1996, s 159*).

(*c*)　Persons employed in any capacity under the Government of any territory or country outside the United Kingdom (*ERA 1996, s 160*).

(*d*)　Domestic servants in a private household where the employer is the parent (or step-parent), grandparent, child (or step-child), grandchild or brother or sister (or half-brother or half-sister) of the employee. References to step-parent or step-child include relationships arising through civil partnership: see the *Civil Partnership Act 2004, ss 246, 247, Sch 21* (*ERA 1996, s 161*).

(*e*)　Employees who have been offered employment on the same terms and conditions as their original employment or offered *suitable alternative employment* and in either case have *unreasonably refused the offer* (see 38.12 below) (*ERA 1996, s 141(1)–(3)*).

(*f*)　Employees who have been offered suitable alternative employment, and have unreasonably terminated their contracts during the statutory trial period (see 38.12 below) (*ERA 1996, s 141(4)*).

(*g*)　Employees who are dismissed for misconduct. If notice is given for this reason it must be accompanied by a statement in writing that the employer would, because of the employee's conduct, be entitled to terminate the contract without notice. If the employee is dismissed without notice, there is no need to give any statement in writing that dismissal was on the ground of misconduct (*ERA 1996, s 140(1)*). The employer is entitled to terminate when the employee has been in fundamental breach of his contract of employment (*Bonner v H Gilbert Ltd* [1989] IRLR 475). This provision does not apply where the dismissal is for taking part in a strike (*ERA 1996, s 140(2)*). The tribunal, in any event, has a discretion to award the whole or part of a redundancy payment to the dismissed employee where it is just and equitable to do so (*ERA 1996, s 140(3)*).

(*h*)　Employees who are dismissed if an *exemption order* is in force (*ERA 1996, s 157*). An exemption order is an order made by the Secretary of State for Trade and Industry exempting an employer or a group of employers from liability to make redundancy payments under the *Act* where they have similar or more advantageous agreements with their employees for making payments on redundancy.

38.11 Redundancy – I: The Right to a Redundancy Payment

38.11 Time limit for claims

Employees are not entitled to a redundancy payment unless, before the end of the period of six months beginning with the relevant date:

(*a*)   the payment has been agreed and paid;

(*b*)   the employee has made a claim for the payment by notice in writing given to the employer;

(*c*)   a question as to the right of the employee to the payment, or as to the amount of the payment, has been referred to an employment tribunal; or

(*d*)   a complaint of unfair dismissal has been presented by the employee to a tribunal.

(*ERA 1996, s 164(1)*.) (For the meaning of 'relevant date', see 38.4 above.)

If, however, within the *next* six months, the employee takes the action in (*b*), (*c*) or (*d*), a tribunal may award a redundancy payment if it considers it just and equitable to do so having regard to the reason for the delay (*ERA 1996, s 164(2)*).

An application for a redundancy payment is 'referred' to an employment tribunal when it is received by the tribunal office and not when it is sent by the employee (*Secretary of State for Employment v Banks* [1983] ICR 48).

See also 38.14 below.

38.12 UNREASONABLE REFUSAL OF SUITABLE ALTERNATIVE EMPLOYMENT

An employee who is dismissed by reason of redundancy loses his right to a redundancy payment if he unreasonably refuses an offer of suitable alternative employment. The offer of alternative employment:

(*a*)   must be made by his original employer or an associated employer (*ERA 1996, s 141(1)*; and see 7.9(A) CONTINUOUS EMPLOYMENT);

(*b*)   must be made before the ending of his employment under his previous contract (*ERA 1996, s 141(1)*);

(*c*)   may be oral or in writing;

(*d*)   must take effect either immediately on the ending of the employment under the previous contract or after an interval of not more than four weeks thereafter (*ERA 1996, s 141(1)*). The alternative employment will be treated as taking effect immediately on the ending of the employment under the previous contract if that employment ends on a Friday, Saturday or Sunday, and the alternative employment is to commence on or before the next Monday. The interval of four weeks is calculated accordingly (*ERA 1996, s 146(2)*). An offer which is not ongoing and which would take effect prior to the dismissal will not satisfy *ERA 1996, s 141(1)* (*McHugh v Hempsall Bulk Transport Ltd*, IDS Brief 480, p 6); and

(*e*)   must be either:

(i)   on the same terms and conditions as the previous contract; or

(ii)   suitable employment in relation to the employee.

(*ERA, s 141(3)*.)

If the terms and conditions of the renewed or new contract of employment differ (wholly or in part) from the corresponding provisions of his previous contract, the employee has a statutory trial period of four weeks, beginning with the ending of his previous employment, in which to decide whether the alternative employment is suitable for him. The four-week trial period means four calendar weeks. Thus, 11 days when the factory was closed over Christmas had to be taken into account (*Benton v Sanderson Keyser Ltd* [1989] ICR 136). This four-week period may be extended by agreement, for the purpose of retraining the employee for employment under the new or renewed contract. Such an agreement must:

(i)   be made before the employee starts work under the renewed or new contract;

(ii)   be in writing;

(iii) specify the date of the end of the trial period; and

(iv)   specify the terms and conditions of employment which will apply in the employee's case after the end of that period.

(*ERA 1996, s 138(6)*.)

Although the employer is no longer required, in making the offer, to give the employee details of the changes in terms and conditions in writing, where applicable, employers may still find it useful to do so. The employer, however, remains obliged to give written particulars of the main terms of an employee's employment within one month of the change (*ERA 1996, s 4(1)*). (See 8.7 CONTRACT OF EMPLOYMENT.)

An employee whose contract was repudiated by his employers was held to be entitled, in accordance with the common law, to a reasonable period in which to decide whether to enter into a new contract or to treat himself as dismissed (see TERMINATION OF EMPLOYMENT (46)). It was only after that period had expired and a new contract, or the old contract with variations, was in force that the statutory trial period began to run (*Turvey v C W Cheney & Son Ltd* [1979] ICR 341).

If the employee accepts the alternative employment, which was offered before the termination of his original employment and which takes effect not more than four weeks thereafter, he is deemed not to have been dismissed on the termination of the original employment for the purposes of determining any liability of the employer for redundancy payments (*ERA 1996, s 138(1)*; see *Jones v Burdett Coutts School* [1997] ICR 390, cf *Ebac Ltd v Wymer* [1995] ICR 466). If, during the trial period, the employee terminates the contract or gives notice to terminate it, or if the employer, for a reason connected with or arising out of any difference between the renewed or new contract and the previous contract, terminates the contract or gives notice to terminate it, the employee is treated as having been dismissed on the date on which his original contract came to an end (*ERA 1996, s 138(2), (4)*).

If, during the trial period, the employer dismisses the employee for a reason unconnected with or not arising out of the change, the employee can bring an unfair dismissal claim on the basis of the fairness of the dismissal in the trial period (*Hempell v W H Smith & Sons Ltd* [1986] ICR 365).

If the terms of the new contract are suitable and the employee unreasonably terminates the contract during the trial period, he will not be entitled to a redundancy payment by reason of his dismissal under the original contract (*ERA 1996, s 141(4)*).

38.13   Redundancy – I: The Right to a Redundancy Payment

The question of the suitability of an offer of alternative employment is an objective matter, whereas the reasonableness of the employee's refusal depends on factors personal to him and is a subjective matter to be considered from the employee's point of view. So, for example, the offer to a butcher's shop manager of a job as a supermarket butchery department manager may be suitable alternative employment, but his perceived loss of status may make it reasonable for him to refuse it (*Cambridge & District Co-operative Society v Ruse* [1993] IRLR 156). The Court of Appeal in *Spencer and Griffin v Gloucestershire County Council* [1985] IRLR 393 has said that in evaluating the separate questions of suitability of employment and reasonableness of refusal, the employment tribunal is entitled to look at factors which may prove, on analysis, to be common to both. In that case, the Court of Appeal, in upholding a decision of an employment tribunal, considered that a refusal by an employee to do work of a lower standard than the employee considered reasonable, may be a reason for holding that the work offered is not suitable or has been reasonably refused.

38.13 AMOUNT OF THE PAYMENT

The amount of the redundancy payment is based upon the employee's age, length of continuous employment and gross average wage.

The calculation of continuity is made in accordance with rules set out in *ERA 1996, ss 210 to 219*, formerly *EPCA 1978, Sch 13*; see 38.4 above and CONTINUOUS EMPLOYMENT (7).

Contractual agreements relating to continuity of employment cannot affect an employer's statutory liability to make a redundancy payment (*Secretary of State for Employment v Globe Elastic Thread Co Ltd* [1979] ICR 706). Therefore, if an employer agrees to preserve an employee's continuity of employment where there is no continuity in accordance with the statutory provisions, he will be contractually liable to make a redundancy payment calculated in accordance with his agreement, but not liable to make any payment under statute.

The amount of the redundancy payment is calculated by reference to the period, ending with the relevant date, during which the employee has been continuously employed. (For the meaning of 'relevant date' see 38.4 above.) There is then allowed:

(*a*)   one and a half week's pay for each such year of employment which consists wholly of weeks in which the employee was not below the age of 41;

(*b*)   one week's pay for each such year of employment (not falling within (*a*) above) which consists wholly of weeks in which the employee was not below the age of 22; and

(*c*)   half a week's pay for each such year of employment not falling within either of the preceding sub-paragraphs.

(*ERA 1996, s 162(1), (2)*.) The maximum number of years to be taken into account in calculating a redundancy payment is 20 (*ERA 1996, s 162(3)*). A previous redundancy payment breaks continuity for this purpose (*ERA 1996, s 214(2)*).

A week's pay is calculated in accordance with *ERA 1996, ss 221–229*, formerly *EPCA 1978, Sch 14*. The calculation is based on average wages without deduction of tax, not taking into account overtime, unless the employer is contractually bound to provide and the employee to work such overtime. (See PAY – I (34) for full details.)

With effect from 1 February 2007, the maximum amount of a week's pay allowed in computing a statutory redundancy payment is £310 (*ERA 1996, s 227* and the *Employment Rights (Increase of Limits) Order 2006 (SI 2006/3045)*). Thus, the current maximum redundancy payment is £9,300.

Following the promulgation of the *Employment Equality (Age) Regulations 2006, SI 2006/1031*, the tapering of the amount of a redundancy payment after an employee's 64th birthday, and the lower age limit of 18 in relation to computing a period of continuous employment for the purposes of redundancy payments, no longer apply as from 1 October 2006. Employees under the age of 18, and over the age of 64, who are dismissed for redundancy, are entitled to redundancy payments calculated on the same basis as payments to employees between those ages. An employer's right under *ERA 1996, s 158* and the *Redundancy Payments Pensions Regulations 1965 (SI 1965/1932)* to pay a pension instead of a redundancy payment in certain specified circumstances has also been removed with effect from 1 October 2006 by the *Employment Equality (Age) Regulations 2006, Sch 8*.

38.14 REFERENCES TO EMPLOYMENT TRIBUNAL AND RESTRICTION ON CONTRACTING OUT

Any question arising as to the right of an employee to a redundancy payment, or as to the amount of a redundancy payment, is to be referred to and determined by an employment tribunal (*ERA 1996, s 163(1)*).

Any provision in any agreement (whether a contract of employment or not) is *prima facie* void insofar as it purports to exclude or limit any provisions relating to redundancy, or to preclude any person from bringing any proceedings in respect of a redundancy payment before an employment tribunal (*ERA 1996, s 203(1)*).

However, an employee will be bound by a settlement agreement reached following action by a conciliation officer, or by a compromise contract which satisfies the statutory conditions, including that the employee should have had independent advice (*ERA 1996, s 203(2)*; and see 2.4 ADVISORY, CONCILIATION AND ARBITRATION SERVICE and 20.27 EMPLOYMENT TRIBUNALS – I).

39 Redundancy – II: Practice and Procedure

(See DTI booklet 'Redundancy Consultation and Notification' (PL833) and ACAS advisory booklet No 12 'Redundancy handling'.)

Cross-reference. See REDUNDANCY – I (38) for the right to a redundancy payment.

39.1 If an employer dismisses an employee by reason of redundancy, he has a number of statutory obligations in addition to that of making the employee a redundancy payment.

He may be liable in a claim of unfair dismissal unless he acts fairly. He must allow the employee reasonable time off work to look for alternative employment. If the proposed dismissal is of 20 or more employees at one establishment within 90 days, the employer must consult 'appropriate representatives' of the employees concerned. For the meaning of 'appropriate representatives' in this context, see 39.4 below.

This chapter considers the following.

(a) The requirements for consultation before making an employee redundant (see 39.2–39.6 below).

(b) The basic 'fair dismissal' considerations relating to proposed redundancies (see 39.8 below).

The chapter ends with a checklist of redundancy dismissal procedure.

39.2 CONSULTATION AND NOTIFICATION REQUIREMENTS

The Trade Union and Labour Relations (Consolidation) Act 1992 ('TULRCA 1992'), as amended by the Trade Union Reform and Employment Rights Act 1993 ('TURERA 1993') and relevant regulations, impose far-reaching obligations on employers to notify and consult appropriate employee representatives about proposed redundancies. TULRCA 1992, s 193 also imposes obligations on employers to notify the Secretary of State for Employment about proposed redundancies. The statutory provisions give effect to the EC Collective Redundancies Directive 98/59/EC, amending Directive 75/129/EEC and Directive 92/56/EEC (see 25.8 EUROPEAN COMMUNITY LAW). For the use of the Directive as an aid to construction of the statute, see *Hough v Leyland DAF Ltd* [1991] ICR 696; but cf *Re Hartlebury Printers Ltd* [1992] ICR 559.

39.3 Meaning of 'redundancy'

In *TULRCA 1992, Part IV Chapter II*, which contains the statutory consultation and notification requirements, references to 'dismissal as redundant' are references to dismissal for a reason not related to the individual concerned or for a number of reasons all of which are not so related (*TULRCA 1992, s 195(1)* as substituted by *TURERA 1993, s 34(5)*). This is a substantially different definition from that which applies for redundancy payments purposes (see 38.7 REDUNDANCY – I). For the purposes of any proceedings under *TULRCA 1992*, where an employee is or is proposed to be dismissed, it shall be presumed that he is or is proposed to be dismissed as redundant unless the contrary is proved (*TULRCA 1992, s 195(2)* as substituted by *TURERA 1993, s 34(5)*). It follows from the definition of 'dismissal as redundant' in *TULRCA 1992, s 195(1)* that the collective consultation and notification provisions in *TULRCA 1992* can apply to proposed dismissals, notwithstanding the fact that there is no intention to lose jobs or workers. Thus, where an employer seeks to change the terms and conditions of employment of a part or group of the workforce by giving notice of termination to the employees concerned and offering them re-engagement on new terms, the employer may be under a duty to consult in accordance with *TULRCA 1992, s 188* (*GMB v MAN Truck & Bus UK Ltd* [2000] IRLR 636).

39.4   Notification to appropriate representatives

Where an employer is proposing to dismiss as redundant at least 20 employees at an establishment within a period of 90 days or less, he must consult about the dismissals 'appropriate representatives' of the affected employees (*TULRCA 1992, s 188(1)* as amended by the *Collective Redundancies and Transfer of Undertakings* (*Protection of Employment*)(*Amendment*) *Regulations 1999* (*SI 1999/1925*)). The class of 'affected employees' includes not only those who may be dismissed, but also any employee affected by the proposed dismissals or who may be affected by measures taken in connection with those dismissals (*TULRCA 1992, s 188(1)* as amended by *SI 1999/1925*) An employer has to include employees whom it is hoped to redeploy in calculating the number it proposes to dismiss as redundant, if what is proposed amounts to a termination of the employee's existing contract of employment (*Hardy v Tourism South East* [2005] IRLR 242, EAT). This is because the applicable definition of dismissal for the purposes of *TULRCA s 188* (that in *ERA 1996, s 95*) refers to the termination of an employee's contract, with or without notice.

The 'appropriate representatives' of any affected employees are:

(*a*)   if the employees are of a description in respect of which an independent trade union is recognised, representatives of the trade union; or

(*b*)   in any other case, either:

    (i)   employee representatives appointed or elected by the affected employees for other purposes but who have authority to receive information and to be consulted about the proposed dismissals on their behalf; or

    (ii)   employee representatives elected by the affected employees for the purposes of *TULRCA 1992, s 188* and in accordance with the statutory procedure set out in *TULRCA 1992, s 188A*.

(*TULRCA 1992, s 188(1B)* as amended by *SI 1999/1925*.)

'Representatives of a trade union' are officials or other persons authorised by the union to carry on collective bargaining with the employer (*TULRCA 1992, s 196(2)* as substituted by the *Collective Redundancies and Transfer of Undertakings* (*Protections of Employment*)(*Amendment*) *Regulations* (*SI 1995/2587*)). 'Recognition', in relation to a trade union, is defined by *TULRCA 1992, s 178(3)* as meaning the recognition of the union by an employer, or two or more associated employers, to any extent, for the purpose of collective bargaining (as defined by *TULRCA 1992, s 178(1)*). In *National Union of Gold, Silver and Allied Trades v Albury Bros Ltd* [1979] ICR 84, the Court of Appeal held that recognition should not be held to be established unless there was clear and unequivocal evidence of an express agreement, or conduct from which recognition should be inferred which involved not a mere willingness to discuss but a positive decision to negotiate on one or more of the issues specified in what is now *TULRCA 1992, s 178(2)*.

It has long been understood that, in order to comply with the requirements of *TULRCA 1992, s 188*, the employer must begin consultations before giving individual notices of dismissal (*National Union of Teachers v Avon County Council* [1978] IRLR 55). However, the ECJ has now ruled that, for the purposes of Directive 92/58/EC, consultation must in fact already have been completed before employees are given notice of dismissal (*Junk v Kühnel (C-188/03)* [2005] IRLR 310). This is because a 'redundancy' for the purposes of the Directive means the declaration of an employer of its intention to terminate the contract of employment (ie the giving of notice), rather than actual dismissal on the expiry of notice.

Consultation must not be a sham exercise; there must be time for the representatives, who are consulted, to consider properly the proposals that are being put to them (*Transport and General Workers' Union v Ledbury Preserves (1928) Ltd* [1985] IRLR 412). Fair consultation involves giving the body consulted a fair and proper opportunity to understand fully the matters about which it is being consulted, and to express its views on those subjects, with the consulting employer thereafter considering those views properly and genuinely. The process of consultation is not one in which the employer is obliged to adopt any or all of the views expressed by the person or body whom he is consulting (*R v British Coal Corpn and Secretary of State for Trade and Industry, ex p Price* [1994] IRLR 72). Further, the consultation envisaged by *s 188* cannot begin until the information required by the section, as set out below, has been given (*E Green & Son (Castings) Ltd v Association of Scientific, Technical and Managerial Staffs* [1984] ICR 352; see also *GEC Ferranti Defence Systems Ltd v MSF* [1993] IRLR 101 and [1994] IRLR 104).

The employer does not 'propose' to dismiss until he has reached the stage of having formulated a specific proposal (*Hough v Leyland DAF Ltd* [1991] ICR 696). Thus, the word 'propose' connotes an intention in the mind of the employer (*Scotch Premier Meat Ltd v Burns* [2000] IRLR 639). Significantly, the EAT held in the *Burns* case that where an employer had determined a plan of action which had two alternative scenarios only one of which necessarily included redundancies then this was capable of amounting to the employer 'proposing to dismiss' employees. It was, however, emphasised that this was essentially a question of fact for the employment tribunal to determine. In addition, a 'proposal' to dismiss does not necessarily have to be made by the person with power to carry out the dismissal (*Dewhirst Group v GMB Trade Union* EAT/486/03). For further consideration of what is meant by a 'proposed' dismissal, and for the application of *TULRCA 1992, s 188* where administrators have been appointed, see *Re Hartlebury Printers Ltd* [1992] ICR 559, *R v British Coal Corpn, ex p Vardy* [1993] ICR 720 and *MSF v Refuge Assurance plc* [2002] IRLR 324. In *MSF* the EAT held that *s 188* did not have the same meaning as *Directive 75/129*, which requires consultation when collective redundancies are first 'contemplated'. 'Contemplation' means 'having a view', and refers to a relatively early stage in the decision-making process, whereas 'proposes' relates to a state of mind which is much more certain (see also *Scotch Premier Meat Ltd v Burns* [2000] IRLR 639 and *R v British Coal Corpn, ex p Vardy* [1993] ICR 720). Following the *Junk* case, however, the EAT has held in *Unison v Leicestershire County Council v Unison* [2006] EWCA Civ 825, [2005] IRLR 920 that the phrase 'proposing to dismiss' should be construed purposively as meaning 'proposing to give notice of dismissal', approving the tribunal's finding that a 'proposal' meant 'something less than a decision that dismissals are to be made and more than a possibility that they might occur'. While not inconsistent with *Vardy* or *MSF*, this ruling suggests that an employer may "propose" to dismiss employees at an earlier stage of the decision-making process than previously understood. Of course, insofar as there is any difference between the requirements of the *Directive* and that of *TULRCA 1992*, employees of 'the State' may be able to rely directly on the *Directive* (cf *Griffin v South West Water Services Ltd* [1995] IRLR 15) (see 25.2 EUROPEAN COMMUNITY LAW; 37.7 PUBLIC SECTOR EMPLOYEES).

Where a consultation is required, it must begin 'in good time', and in addition:

(*a*)   if an employer is proposing to dismiss *at least 100* employees at any one establishment within a period of 90 days or less, the consultation must begin at least *90* days before the first of the dismissals takes effect; and

(*b*)   in any other case in which consultation is required, consultation must begin at least 30 days before the first of the dismissals takes effect.

(*TULRCA 1992, s 188(1A)*, as substituted by *SI 1995/2587.*)

The phrase 'before the first of the dismissals takes effect' obviously refers to the proposed date of the first dismissal, not the actual date, otherwise the provisions would be unworkable (see *E Green & Son (Castings) Ltd v ASTMS* [1984] IRLR 135, following *GKN Sankey Ltd v National Society of Motor Mechanics* [1980] IRLR 8). Following *Junk v Kühnel (C-188/03)* [2005] IRLR 310, consultation for the purposes of *Directive 92/58/EC* must occur before notice of dismissal is given (suggesting that *TULRCA s 188(1A)* may be out of line with European law). However, *Junk v Kühnel* does not state that the full consultation period of 90 or 30 days, as the case may be, would necessarily have to elapse before notice was given in any particular case: only that consultation would in substance have to be completed before that point. Whether consultation has begun 'in good time' is a matter of fact and degree for the employment tribunal: see *Leicestershire County Council v UNISON* [2006] IRLR 810, CA.

The ECJ held in *Rockfon A/S v Specialarbejderforbundet i Danmark (C-449/93)* [1996] ICR 673 that the word 'establishment' under *Directive 75/129* referred to the local employment unit, that is the unit to which the workers made redundant are assigned to carry out their duties. Although the term 'establishment' connotes a distinct entity assigned to perform particular tasks, an 'establishment' need not have any legal, economic, or administrative autonomy, nor have a management that can independently effect collective redundancies, nor be geographically separate from other units of the undertaking in question: see *Athinaiki Chartopoiia AE v Panagiotidis (C-270/05)* [2007] IRLR 284, interpreting *Directive 98/59* (the successor to *Directive 75/129*). The question as to what constitutes 'one establishment' is essentially a question of fact for the employment tribunal (*Bulwick v Mills & Allen Ltd* (8 June 2000, unreported), EAT).

For the purposes of the consultation, the employer must disclose in writing to the appropriate representatives:

(i)   the reasons for his proposals;

(ii)   the number and descriptions of employees whom it is proposed to dismiss as redundant;

(iii)   the total number of employees of any such description employed by the employer at the establishment in question;

(iv)   the proposed method of selecting the employees who may be dismissed;

(v)   the proposed method of carrying out the dismissals with due regard to any agreed procedure, including the period over which the dismissals are to take effect; and

(vi)   the proposed method of calculating the amount of any redundancy payments otherwise than in compliance with a statutory obligation.

(*TULRCA 1992, s 188(4)* as amended by *TURERA 1993, s 34(2)(a)* and *SI 1995/2587.*)

Where the employer has invited affected employees to elect representatives, but the affected employees fail to do so within a reasonable time, then the employer must give the requisite information to each affected employee individually (*TULRCA 1992, s 188(7B)* as inserted by *SI 1999/1925*).

The information must be provided in proper form: it will not do to say that it may be gleaned from the surrounding circumstances and from a number of documents (*Sovereign Distribution Services Ltd v TGWU* [1990] ICR 31).

The consultation must include consultation about ways of avoiding the dismissals, reducing the number of employees to be dismissed and mitigating the consequences of the dismissals, and must be undertaken by the employer with a view to reaching agreement with the appropriate representatives (*TULRCA 1992, s 188(2)* as substituted by *SI 1995/2587*). The fact that consultation must be undertaken with a view to reaching agreement means that it is tantamount to negotiation (*Junk v Kühnel (C-188/03)* [2005] IRLR 310). An employer must consult on all the matters set out in *s 188(2), TULRCA 1992*, which are to be viewed disjunctively. Furthermore, it is not open to an employer to argue that consultation would, in the circumstances, be futile or useless (*Middlesbrough Borough Council v TGWU* [2002] IRLR 332). Consultation does not extend to the economic background or context in which the proposal for redundancy arises. Thus, an employer is not in breach of *TULRCA 1992 s 188* because he determines to close a plant or branch, before commencing consultation about the consequences of that decision (*Securicor Omega Express Ltd v GMB* [2004] IRLR 9). Note, however, that specified employers may be obliged to inform and consult appropriate representatives about economic decisions likely to lead to changes in work organisation or contractual relations under the *Information and Consultation of Employees Regulations 2004, SI 2004/3426.*

Failure to consult with the appropriate representatives, or to do so within the stipulated time when it was reasonably practicable to do so, may lead to the employer being held liable to pay each redundant employee a protective award (see 39.6 below). Such a failure is also highly likely to render the dismissals unfair (*Kelly v Upholstery and Cabinet Works (Amesbury) Ltd* [1977] IRLR 91; *North East Midlands Co-operative Society Ltd v Allen* [1977] IRLR 212; *Polkey v AE Dayton Services Ltd* [1988] ICR 142; but cf *Hough*, above).

39.5   **Election of employee representatives**

If elections are held for employee representatives they must be held in accordance with the provisions of *TULRCA 1992, s 188A* (as inserted by *SI 1999/1925*). This provides that:

(*a*)   the employer shall make such arrangements as are reasonably practical to ensure that the election is fair;

(*b*) the employer shall determine the number of representatives to be elected so that there are sufficient representatives to represent the interests of all the affected employees having regard to the number and classes of those employees;

(*c*) the employer shall determine whether the affected employees should be represented either by representatives of all the affected employees or by representatives of particular classes of those employees;

(*d*) before the election the employer shall determine the term of office as employee representatives so that it is of sufficient length to enable information to be given and consultations under this section to be completed;

(*e*) the candidates for election as employee representatives are affected employees on the date of the election;

(*f*) no affected employee is unreasonably excluded from standing for election;

(*g*) all affected employees on the date of the election are entitled to vote for employee representatives;

(*h*) the employees entitled to vote may vote for as many candidates as there are representatives to be elected to represent them or, if there are to be representatives for particular classes of employees, may vote for as many candidates as there are representatives to be elected to represent their particular class of employee; and

(*i*) the election is conducted so as to secure that:

  (i) so far as is reasonably practicable, those voting do so in secret; and

  (ii) the votes given at the election are accurately counted.

(*TULRCA 1992, s 188A(1).*)

Further, if after an election held in accordance with this procedure, an elected representative ceases to act as a representative so that employees are no longer represented then they shall elect another representative by an election held in accordance with the requirements at (*a*), (*e*), (*f*) and (*i*) above (*TULRCA 1992, s 188A(2)*).

39.6 Protective award

If an employer fails to comply with any of the statutory requirements for consultation or fails to do so within the appropriate time, a complaint may be made to an employment tribunal by the trade union where the failure relates to trade union representatives, or by any of the affected employees or by any of the employees who have been dismissed as redundant where the failure relates to the election of employee representatives, or in the case of any other failure relating to employee representatives, by any of the employee representatives to whom the failure related and, in any other case, by any of the affected employees or by any of the employees who have been dismissed as redundant (*TULRCA 1992, s 189* as amended by *SI 1999/1925*). A protective award can only be made in favour of those in respect of whom a complaint of breach has been proved. So, where a claim is made by a trade union, the protective award will benefit only those employees who are represented by the trade union: *TGWU v Brauer Coley Ltd* (*in administration*) [2007] IRLR 207.

If a question is raised on any such complaint as to whether or not any employee representative was an appropriate representative for the purposes of *s 188*, the burden of proof will be on the employer to show that the employee representative had the authority to represent the affected employees (*TULRCA 1992, s 189(1A)* as inserted by *SI 1999/1925*). Also, where the alleged failure relates to the election of employee representatives, the burden will be on the employer to show that the statutory election procedure in *s 188A* has been complied with.

The complaint must be presented before the date on which the last of the dismissals to which the complaint relates takes effect, or during the period of three months beginning with that date, or within such further period as the tribunal considers reasonable in a case where it is satisfied that it was not reasonably practicable for the complaint to be presented during the period of three months (*TULRCA 1992, s 189(5)* as amended by *SI 1995/2587*; and see 20.7 EMPLOYMENT TRIBUNALS – I).

It is a defence to such an application for an employer to show that there were special circumstances which rendered it not reasonably practicable for him to comply with the requirements, and that he took all such steps as were reasonably practicable in those circumstances (*TULRCA 1992, s 188(7)* as amended by *TURERA 1993, s 34(2)(c)*). For example, an unforeseen financial crisis may make it necessary to close down a plant at short notice so that consultations can only take place during a shorter period than that prescribed by law.

In *Clarks of Hove Ltd v Bakers' Union* [1978] ICR 1076, the Court of Appeal held that insolvency is not on its own a special circumstance and that it depends entirely on the course of the insolvency whether the circumstances can be described as special or not. (See also *Angus Jowett & Co (in liquidation) v NUTGW* [1985] ICR 646; *Re Hartlebury Printers Ltd* [1992] ICR 559.) The employer may not neglect his duty under *TULRCA 1992, s 188* merely because he considers that consultation will achieve nothing (*Sovereign Distribution Services Ltd v TGWU* [1990] ICR 31).

Section 188(7) precludes the employer from relying upon a failure to provide information by the person whose decision led to the proposed dismissals if that person directly or indirectly controls the employer. The meaning of this provision was considered in *GMB and Amicus v Beloit Walmsley Ltd* [2004] IRLR 18. The EAT determined that: (i) the mischief at which this provision is aimed is a controlling entity's delay in providing the employer with information. Any period of delay in providing information must therefore count against the employer, for the purposes of determining whether or not the duty under *TULRCA 1992, s 188* could have been complied with; (ii) there must be a causal link between the decision, and the proposed dismissals. However, it is not necessary that the person making the decision contemplates any particular number of dismissals, at any particular establishment; (iii) the 'information', required to be provided by *TULRCA s 188(7)*, is not confined to the 'information' required to be disclosed by *TULRCA s 188(4)*. It includes information necessary to begin the process of consultation.

An employer would appear to escape its information and consultation obligations under *s 188* if he invites any affected employees to elect representatives and has given enough time to allow for an election but such election is not organised (*TULRCA 1992, s 188(7A)*; and see *R v Secretary of State for Trade and Industry, ex p UNISON* [1996] IRLR 438).

Where a tribunal finds the complaint well-founded it makes a declaration to that effect and may also make a protective award (*TULRCA 1992, s 189(2)*). A protective award is an order that an employer make payments for the protected period in respect of specified employees who have been dismissed, or whom it is proposed to dismiss, as redundant without complying with the statutory requirements for consultation. The length of the period will be what is considered to be just and equitable by the tribunal in the circumstances having regard to the seriousness of the employer's default and will be up to 90 days, beginning on the date on which the first of the dismissals to which the complaint relates was proposed to take effect, or the date of the award, whichever is the earlier (*TULRCA 1992, s 189(4)*, as amended by *SI 1999/1925*). See *Transport and General Workers' Union v Ledbury Preserves (1928) Ltd* [1986] ICR 855; *E Green & Son (Castings) Ltd v Association of Scientific, Technical and Managerial Staffs* [1984] ICR 352. The purpose of the award is to provide a sanction for breach by the employer of the obligations in *TULRCA s 188*, not to compensate employees for any loss suffered: hence the futility of consultation is not relevant to the making of a protective award (*Susie Radin Ltd v GMB* [2004] EWCA Civ 180, [2004] IRLR 400, reversing *Spillers-French (Holdings) Ltd v USDAW* [1979] IRLR 339, EAT). Nor is the employer's insolvency relevant to the size of any protective award: the employment tribunal should focus simply upon the seriousness of the employer's default in failing to comply with its statutory duty (*Smith v Cherry Lewis Ltd* [2005] IRLR 86). In the *Susie Radin* case, the Court of Appeal stated that how the length of the protected period is assessed is a matter for the tribunal, but a proper approach in a case where there has been no consultation is to start with the maximum period and reduce it only if there are mitigating circumstances justifying a reduction. Mitigating circumstances may, however, include any steps taken by the employer before proposals have crystallised in relation to keeping employees informed or consulted, even if there has been no consultation under *TULRCA s 188* itself (*AMICUS v GBS Tooling Ltd (in administration)* [2005] IRLR 683). A union's obstructive approach to statutory consultation may also be taken into account when assessing the correct level of a protective award: see *GMB v Lambeth Service Team; TGWU v Lambeth Service Team* UKEAT 0127/05 and 0129/05.

Where a tribunal has made a protective award, every employee to whom it relates is entitled to be paid remuneration by the employer for the protected period at the rate of a week's pay PAY – I (28) for each week of the period (*TULRCA 1992, s 190(1), (2), (5)*). There is no upper limit on the amount of a week's pay for this purpose.

If an employee, specified in the award, receives payments under his contract of employment during the protected period, those payments no longer go to discharge his employer's liability under the protective award, nor vice versa (*TURERA 1993, s 34(3)*, which repealed *TULRCA 1992, s 190(3)*).

Liability for protective awards will transfer as a result of a transfer of an undertaking under the *Transfer of Undertakings (Protection of Employment) Regulations 1981 (SI 1981/1794)* (*Alamo Group (Europe) Ltd v Tucker* [2003] ICR 829, following *Kerry Foods Ltd v Creber* [2000] ICR 556 and not following *TGWU v McKinnon* [2001] ICR 1281 – see also TRANSFER OF UNDERTAKINGS (52)).

Disallowance of payment under award. If an employee remains employed during a protected period and:

(i)   he is fairly dismissed by his employer for a reason other than redundancy;

(ii)   he unreasonably terminates the contract of employment; or

(iii)   he unreasonably refuses an offer of suitable alternative employment made to take effect before or during the protected period,

he will not be entitled to payment under the protective award in respect of any period during which he would have been employed but for the dismissal, termination or refusal of employment (*TULRCA 1992, s 191(1)–(3)*). If the offer of alternative employment embodies terms which differ from those under which he previously worked, the employee has a trial period of four weeks beginning with the commencement date of the new contract (or by agreement in writing, a longer period) (*TULRCA 1992, s 191(4)–(6)*; see also 38.6 REDUNDANCY – I). If during the trial period, the employment is terminated by the employer for a reason connected with the change to the new or renewed employment, or by the employee, the employee remains entitled to his protective award unless he acted unreasonably in terminating or giving notice to terminate the contract (*TULRCA 1992, s 191(7)*).

Remedy for non-payment of award. If an employer fails to pay a protective award, the employee concerned may present a complaint to an employment tribunal which will order the employer to make the payment (*TULRCA 1992, s 192(1), (3)*). The time limit for the presentation of a complaint by an individual employee for failure to pay a protective award is three months from the day or last day of the failure to make the payment, or such further period as the tribunal considers reasonable in a case where it is satisfied that it was not reasonably practicable for the complaint to be presented within the period of three months (*TULRCA 1992, s 192(2)*; and see 20.7 EMPLOYMENT TRIBUNALS – I).

The Employment Appeal Tribunal held in *Howlett Marine Services Ltd v Bowlam* [2001] IRLR 201 that the three months' time limit for bringing a complaint in respect of non-payment of a protective award under *TULRCA 1992, s 192(2)* runs from the last day of the protected period. Moreover, this remains the case even when the protective award was made by a tribunal well after the expiry of the protective period. However, the EAT held in *Howlett* that in these circumstances it would obviously not have been 'reasonably practicable' to present a complaint within the three months' time limit so that the tribunal would still have jurisdiction to hear it provided that it was presented in such further period of time as was reasonable.

39.7   NOTIFICATIONS TO THE DTI

An employer must send written notification of certain redundancies to the Department of Trade and Industry ('DTI'). If he proposes to make 100 or more employees redundant at one establishment within a period of 90 days or less, the employer must give at least 90 days' notice before the first of those dismissals takes effect (*TULRCA 1992, s 193(1)*). If he proposes to make 20 or more employees redundant at one establishment within a period of 90 days or less, the employer must give at least 30 days' notice (*TULRCA 1992, s 193(2)*, as amended by *SI 1995/ 2587*). The notice must be in a prescribed form and sent to the specified office. Forms are available from the local DTI office. If consultation with appropriate representatives is required, the representatives concerned must be identified and the date when consultations began must be stated (*TULRCA 1992, s 193(4)*, as amended by *SI 1995/2587*). Where consultation with appropriate representatives is required, he must give a copy of the notice to those representatives (*TULRCA 1992, s 193(6)*, as amended by *SI 1995/2587*). If there are special circumstances which make it impossible for the employer to comply with any of the requirements of notifying the DTI or the representatives concerned, he must take such steps to comply as are reasonably practicable in the circumstances

(*TULRCA 1992, s 193(7)* as amended by *TURERA 1993, s 34(4)*). Ignorance of the statutory obligation to notify the DTI cannot constitute such special circumstances (*Secretary of State for Employment v Helitron Ltd* [1980] ICR 523); see also 39.5 above.

In *Vauxhall Motors Ltd v TGWU* [2006] IRLR 674, the employer sent written notification of proposed redundancies to the DTI twice in respect of a single redundancy exercise, because the length over which redundancy proposals were considered (approximately two years) meant that the first notification had expired. The union argued that following the second notification, fresh consultation should have occurred under *TULRCA 1992, s 188*. The EAT disagreed, stating that the lodging of notification was immaterial to the question of whether the employers were in breach of *TULRCA 1992*.

Failure to notify the DTI may lead to a conviction and fine of up to level 5 on the Standard Scale in a magistrates' court (*TULRCA 1992, s 194(1);* and see 1.10 INTRODUCTION).

39.8   FAIRNESS OF THE DISMISSAL

Where redundancy is the reason for a dismissal the employer will be liable in a claim for unfair dismissal in addition to the redundancy payment if he fails to act fairly. The principles governing the fairness of dismissals for redundancy are set out in full in UNFAIR DISMISSAL – II (52), and in particular in 52.11. The main points to bear in mind are that the dismissal may either be automatically unfair, or unfair because the employer has failed to act reasonably in all the circumstances.

Automatic unfairness arises, subject to certain exceptions, where an employee is selected for an inadmissible reason, or where an employer has failed to comply with an applicable statutory dismissal procedure under the *Employment Act 2002, Sch 2* (note, however, that the statutory dismissal procedures do not apply to collective redundancy dismissals falling within *TULRCA s 188*: see the *Employment Act 2002 (Dispute Resolution) Regulations 2004 (SI 2004/752) reg 4*). Circumstances where the employer may be held to have acted unreasonably include where he has failed to consult the trade unions or individuals involved (his obligations in this respect may go beyond the express statutory obligations dealt with in 39.4 above), where selection criteria are inadequate or have been improperly applied, or where inadequate efforts have been made to find alternative employment for those whose jobs have disappeared.

39.9   CHECKLIST OF REDUNDANCY DISMISSAL PROCEDURE

In practical terms, the first step in the redundancy dismissal procedure is the business decision on the necessity of making one or more employees redundant. Thereafter the following actions should be considered and undertaken as necessary.

(*a*)   *Preliminary procedure* (not necessarily in chronological order)

    (i)   Where the proposal is to make at least 20 employees redundant within 90 days or less, consult with the appropriate representatives of the employees concerned within the appropriate time limits on the measures to be taken which are set out below. Provide them with all necessary information. (Provide each affected employee with the necessary information where the affected employees fail to elect representatives within a reasonable time.)

(ii)   Decide on the number of employees to be made redundant.

(iii) Invite volunteers for redundancy.

(iv)   Consider whether alternative jobs are available within the organisation or group. If it should be necessary to retrain employees for those jobs, consider the practicability of doing this.

(v)   Select employees to be made redundant in accordance with any customary arrangement or agreed procedure. If no such arrangement or procedure exists, establish, if possible with the agreement of the relevant unions or employee representatives, objective criteria for selection, and apply them.

(vi)   Consult with individuals affected before a final decision is taken.

(vii) Inform those employees as soon as possible of their impending redundancies.

(viii) Allow them time off to look for other employment.

(ix)   Notify the DTI of impending redundancies within the appropriate time limits.

(*b*)   *Dismissal notices* (taking due note of the time limits – see below)

NB Consultations must be completed before notices of dismissal are sent out.

Time limits. The date on which the dismissal is to take effect should be fixed having regard to the obligations of the employer as regards notice (see TERMINATION OF EMPLOYMENT (48)) and with an eye on the following time limits.

For step (*a*)(i):

(A)	'in good time'	in all cases in which consultation is required and in any event:
(B)	90 days before first dismissal	100+ employees in one establishment to be dismissed within 90 days
(C)	30 days before first dismissal	20–99 employees in one establishment to be dismissed within 90 days

For step (*a*)(ix), as (B) and (C) for step (*a*)(i) above.

40 References

40.1 An employer may be requested to provide a general reference or specific details about an employee or ex-employee of his by that employee, by a prospective employer or by any other person interested in obtaining such information. (For example, the employee may need a reference in order to obtain a mortgage or a lease of residential premises.) The request may be for a reference to be given over the telephone, but more usually it will be for a written document.

40.2 **THE EMPLOYER'S OBLIGATION**

An employer is not obliged to provide such a reference but, as the consequences of a failure to do so may be grave for an employee, the circumstances in which an employer or ex-employer will refuse to supply a reference are probably rare. However, as one of the terms of settlement of a claim or a potential claim before an employment tribunal, an employer may agree to provide a reference, and he will then be bound to do so, assuming the agreement to be enforceable (see 40.8 below).

40.3 **CONTENTS**

If the enquiry for a reference poses certain questions, then clearly those issues should be dealt with. If, however, the request is a general one, for example, from a prospective employer, an employer should consider dealing with the following matters.

(*a*) Length of service.

(*b*) Positions held.

(*c*) Competence in the job.

(*d*) Honesty.

(*e*) Time-keeping.

(*f*) Reason for leaving.

(*g*) Any other particular remarks about the employee, such as long periods of absence due to sickness.

(*h*) Any relevant remarks of a more personal nature about the employee.

For references relating to a certain level of employee, some employers complete a form dealing with these matters. However, for a more senior employee such a form may give an inadequate picture and a full letter should be written.

40.4 **EMPLOYER'S LIABILITIES**

To the employee

References given by one employer to a prospective employer may not be made the grounds for a libel action by the employee even if the information given proves to be inaccurate, provided that the employer believes the information to be correct and gives it without malice. This is because the employer (or ex-employer) and the prospective employer have a common interest in the statement made about the

795

employee, and the statement is protected by what is known as 'qualified privilege'. As Lord Ellenborough CJ said in 1818: 'In the case of master and servant, the convenience of mankind required that what is said in fair communication between man and man, upon the subject of character, should be privileged, if made *bona fide* and without malice. If, however, the party giving the character knows what he says to be untrue, that may deprive him of the protection which the law throws around such communications' (*Hodgson v Scarlett* (1818) 1 B & Ald 232; see also *Sutherland v British Telecommunications plc* (1989) Times, 30 January). The defence of qualified privilege may, however, be lost if the statement is not merely passed between people having a mutuality of interest in the subject matter but falls into the hands of a third person. Thus, all references should be carefully marked 'private and confidential'.

In *Spring v Guardian Assurance plc* [1994] ICR 596, the House of Lords (Lord Keith dissenting) held that an employer owes a duty of care to an employee about whom he writes a reference. The employer's duty is to take reasonable care in the preparation of the reference, and he will be liable to the employee in negligence if he fails to do so and the employee thereby suffers damage.

The obligation on the employer is to provide a true, accurate and fair reference. The reference must not give a misleading impression. However, as long as the reference is accurate and does not tend to mislead, there is no obligation on the employer to set great detail or to be comprehensive. In *Bartholomew v London Borough of Hackney* [1999] IRLR 246, the employer stated that the employee had been suspended and was subject to disciplinary action, which action ceased upon an agreed termination of the employee's employment. The employee complained that a reference was negligent because it failed to say that he strongly disputed the charges. The reference was held not to be negligent. It was accurate and fair and did not cease to be so simply because it did not recite chapter and verse.

In *Kidd v Axa Equity and Law Life Assurance Society plc* [2000] IRLR 301, the High Court held that the duty of care on an employer did not require the employer to provide a reference which was fair full and comprehensive. The duty is to take reasonable care. That means not giving misleading information whether by selective provision of information or by the inclusion of information in a manner that would lead a reasonable recipient to draw a false or mistaken inference. However, there is no duty to give a full or comprehensive reference, nor to refer to all material facts.

Subsequent to *Bartholomew*, the Court of Appeal has further considered the requirements of accuracy and fairness in a reference for an employee who has resigned while under investigation, so that the investigation was never completed: *Cox v Sun Alliance Life Ltd* [2001] EWCA Civ 649, [2001] IRLR 448. In *Cox*, the employer provided an inaccurate and unfair reference, suggesting that it would have had a reasonable basis for dismissing the employee on the grounds of dishonesty amounting to corruption. Mummery LJ drew an analogy between the principle to be applied and the proper approach of a tribunal to dismissal for misconduct, as set out in *British Home Stores Ltd v Burchell* [1978] IRLR 379. If an employee is to be fairly dismissed for misconduct, the employer must genuinely believe in the employee's guilt, must have reasonable grounds for that belief, and must have carried out a reasonable investigation. The same principles will render negligent a reference that alludes to an employee's misconduct, when the employer has not carried out an investigation, and does not have reasonable grounds for believing in his misconduct.

In order to succeed in an action based on an allegedly negligent reference, a claimant will have to show first that the information contained in the reference is misleading, second, that it would be likely to have a material effect on a reasonable recipient and, third, that the defendant was negligent in compiling the reference.

The EAT has held that the implied term of trust and confidence in a contract of employment requires the employer to provide a reference that is 'fair and reasonable'. If the employer fails to do so, the employee may resign and claim constructive dismissal (see *TSB Bank plc v Harris* [2000] IRLR 157). However, that case was decided prior to *Kidd*, and *Bartholomew* was not referred to.

A former employee who is refused a reference or given a bad reference because he or she had made a complaint of discrimination or done some other protected act under the *Sex Discrimination Act 1975*, *Race Relations Act 1976* or *Disability Discrimination Act 1995*, the *Employment Equality (Religion or Belief) Regulations 2003* or the *Employment Equality (Sexual Orientation) Regulations 2003* would be entitled to sue for victimisation provided that the claim arose out of the incidents of the employment relationship or was sufficiently proximate to the employment or that there was a substantive connection between the complaint and the employment. This entitlement was first recognised in the context of sex discrimination law by the decision of the European Court of Justice in *Coote v Granada Hospitality Ltd: C-185/97* [1999] ICR 100. It was there held that an employer who refused to provide a reference to an ex-employee on the grounds that the employee had brought legal proceedings to enforce the right to equal treatment of men and women would be liable for victimisation. At the time of this decision the position under domestic law was that the discrimination legislation only applied to events occurring during employment and not afterwards: *Adekeye v Post Office (No 2)* [1997] IRLR 105. The EAT has held that the *Sex Discrimination Act 1975* (*'SDA 1975'*) can be construed consistently with this decision (*Coote v Granada Hospitality Ltd (No 2)* [1999] IRLR 452). More recently the House of Lords has overturned *Adekeye* and held that the protection afforded to employees by the discrimination legislation is not coterminous with the existence of a contractual relationship. Therefore claims may be brought by former employees so long as there is a substantive connection between the discriminatory conduct alleged and the employment relationship, whenever the discriminatory conduct arises: *Rhys-Harper v Relaxion Group plc* [2003] UKHL 33, [2003] IRLR 484. See also *Metropolitan Police Service v Shoebridge* UKEAT/0234/03.

An employee who was refused a reference after employment had ended or who was provided with a poor reference because he had made a protected disclosure under *Part IVA* of the Employment Rights Act 1996 (see DISCLOSURE OF INFORMATION (11)) would be able to allege that that the failure to provide the reference to or the content of it involved the employee being subjected to a detriment on the ground that the employee had made a protected disclosure, contrary to *s 47B*: *Woodward v Abbey National plc* [2006] IRLR 677, CA.

40.5   **To the recipient**

The recipient of a negligent reference may also be able to sue the person giving the reference for any loss suffered. It is reasonably foreseeable that the recipient of a reference will act on its contents and if he relies on a reference which is inaccurate because it was carelessly drawn up and thereby suffers loss, the giver of the reference may be held liable to pay the recipient damages on account of his negligence (cf *Hedley Byrne & Co Ltd v Heller & Partners Ltd* [1964] AC 465).

40.6 References

There is no sure way of avoiding the possibility of liability for negligent mis-statements in references since the *Unfair Contract Terms Act 1977* (*'UCTA 1977'*). Disclaimers such as 'The above information is given in confidence and in good faith. No responsibility, however, can be accepted for any errors, omissions or inaccuracies in the information or for any loss or damage that may result from reliance being placed upon it' may have been effective to exclude liability before the *UCTA 1977* came into force, but now such a disclaimer will only be effective insofar as it 'satisfies the requirement of reasonableness' (*UCTA 1977, s 2(2)*). The 'explanatory provisions' of the *Act* state that such a notice of disclaimer will satisfy this requirement of reasonableness where it is 'fair and reasonable to allow reliance upon it, having regard to all the circumstances obtaining when the liability arose or (but for the notice) would have arisen' (*UCTA 1977, s 11(3)*). If the reference purports to give facts which are ordinarily within the knowledge of an employer, it is thought that liability cannot now be excluded for negligent mis-statement of those facts. If, however, it contains an opinion as to the employee's suitability for a certain post which he has not filled in the past, it may be considered reasonable to insert a disclaimer for such a statement of opinion.

40.6 Data Protection Act 1998

If information about an employee is stored on a computer, the provisions of the *Data Protection Act 1998* must be complied with (see 11.13 *et seq* DISCLOSURE OF INFORMATION).

40.7 LIABILITY OF PERSONS OTHER THAN THE EMPLOYER

It is frequently the case that employment will be dependent on a satisfactory medical report being presented to the prospective employer. In *Kapfunde v Abbey National plc and Daniel* [1998] IRLR 583, the claimant was refused employment on the basis of a medical report. She sought to sue the author of the report alleging that it was negligent. The Court of Appeal dismissed the claim holding that a medical practitioner who compiles a report about a prospective employee does not owe a duty of care to the prospective employee. There is insufficient proximity between the author of the report and the prospective employee. It may well be, however, that the medical practitioner owes a duty of care to the prospective employer.

40.8 REFERENCES AND EMPLOYMENT PROTECTION RIGHTS

Although employees do not have a statutory right to a reference, references may affect proceedings in employment tribunals. A good reference may be powerful evidence against an employer who tries to justify the dismissal of an employee on grounds of misconduct or incompetence. Similarly, a reference which is inconsistent with written reasons for a dismissal supplied to an employee may be persuasive in enabling the employee to show that those written reasons were inadequate or untrue, thus entitling him to an award under *ERA 1996, s 93* (see 48.15 TERMINATION OF EMPLOYMENT).

A reference may sometimes be used to compromise a claim for unfair dismissal. If a reference is given in such circumstances, care should be taken to ensure that the reference is accurate and complete and the compromise reached with the assistance of a conciliation officer (see 2.4 ADVISORY, CONCILIATION AND ARBITRATION SERVICE).

40.9 EMPLOYMENT CONDITIONAL UPON REFERENCES

Sometimes, a contract of employment may be offered 'subject to satisfactory references'. In *Wishart v National Association of Citizens' Advice Bureaux Ltd* [1990] ICR 794, the Court of Appeal was strongly of the opinion that such a provision was satisfied only if the references supplied were subjectively satisfactory to that particular employer. However, it recognised that it was arguable that the requirement was an objective one.

41   Restraint of Trade and Confidential Information

41.1   INTRODUCTION

Considerations of restraint of trade operate in employment law in two distinct ways: first, there is the common law doctrine of restraint of trade comprising a body of rules under which certain contractual restraints must be justified before the court will enforce them. Secondly, a court will have regard to the impact of restraints on trade in any form in situations where the common law doctrine does not apply, or cannot be applied in accordance with its rules, as a factor influencing its discretion to grant or withhold the remedy of an injunction and in framing the terms of any injunction granted. The latter operation of what may be called 'considerations' of restraint of trade is seen most clearly in so-called 'garden leave' and 'springboard' injunction cases. Confusion between restraint of trade as a narrow doctrine of the law of contract and as a factor in the exercise of judicial discretion as to whether or not to grant an injunction, has lead to considerable confusion in the law and, on occasion, to judicial error: see *J A Mont (UK) Ltd v Mills* [1993] IRLR 172.

Obligations of confidentiality that arise in the employment situation are also apt to cause confusion and, again, a clear distinction must be drawn between those obligations which underpin, in part, the doctrine of restraint of trade and those which give rise to relief and remedies which lie outside that doctrine altogether.

It is impossible in a work of this nature to do more than briefly sketch the main principles of these large and partially interlocking fields of law which apply specifically to the employment relationship. Hence we do not deal in this chapter with restraint of trade principles as they apply to business sale agreements, shareholder agreements or partnerships, etc, even where there may be partial overlaps of principle. It should, however, be noted that the statutory regulation of competition in the United Kingdom has recently undergone major changes to bring it into line with European models: see *Competition Act 1998* and *Enterprise Act 2002*. These reforms affect the common law doctrine of restraint of trade and, in certain circumstances, displace it altogether: see *Days Medical Aids Ltd v Pihsiang Machinery Manufacturing Co Ltd* [2004] EWHC 44 (Comm), [2004] 1 All ER (Comm) 991. The new statutory controls, however, apply to individuals only if they may be treated as 'undertakings'. The vast majority of employees will not therefore fall within the provisions of Part I of the *Competition Act 1998* or *Art 81* of the *Treaty of Rome*. For this reason, we do not attempt a review of competition law in this chapter. However, although the principles of competition law do not apply directly to most employees, they may have an indirect impact in shaping public policy, from which the common law doctrine itself springs (see below 41.2 and 41.5).

Proceedings in relation to the enforcement or breach of covenants in restraint of trade must in almost all cases be brought in the ordinary courts, and not in the employment tribunals. This is because most disputes in relation to the enforcement or breach of such covenants will fall outside the jurisdiction of the employment tribunals, since any claim in respect of such a covenant will not (as a general rule) be one that 'arises or is outstanding' on the termination of the employee's employment so as to bring it within the scope of the *Employment Tribunals Extension of Jurisdiction (England and Wales) Order 1994*. (This Order

800

extended the jurisdiction of the employment tribunals so as to encompass, for the first time, breach of contract claims by employees and, where the employee has brought such a claim, counterclaims for breach of contract by the employer: see *Peninsula Business Services Ltd v Sweeney* [2004] IRLR 49 and generally 8.23 and 8.24 CONTRACT OF EMPLOYMENT)). Further, the employment tribunals' contractual jurisdiction (as set out in the *Extension of Jurisdiction Order*) only extends to the power to award damages for breach of contract: the employment tribunals have no power to issue injunctions, which is the usual remedy sought by the claimant in restraint of trade cases (see below 41.16).

There have been a handful of cases in which the question of the enforceability of covenants in restraint of trade has been raised as part of a claim falling within the jurisdiction of the employment tribunals, for example where an employee's refusal to sign up to covenants in restraint of trade is relied on by an employer as a reason for dismissing an employee, or where sums deducted pursuant to a covenant in restraint of trade are claimed as an unlawful deduction from wages. However, the Court of Appeal has now confirmed that, in both those situations, the employment tribunal need not determine whether or not the covenant in question is reasonable and enforceable. Thus in *Willow Oak Developments Ltd (t/a Windsor Recruitment) v Silverwood* [2006] EWCA Civ 660, [2006] IRLR 607 the Court of Appeal confirmed previous authority to the effect that a refusal on the part of an employee to sign up to new terms and conditions of employment that included covenants in restraint of trade was capable (whether or not the restraints were reasonable) of being a potentially fair reason for dismissing an employee. However, the Court of Appeal observed that the reasonableness (or otherwise) of the restraints was a (non-determinative) factor which the employment tribunal could take into account when determining whether or not it was in fact fair to dismiss the employee for that reason under *ERA 1996, s 98(4)* (see generally 54.14 UNFAIR DISMISSAL – II). The Court of Appeal disapproved the earlier decision of the EAT in *Forshaw v Archcraft Ltd* [2006] ICR 60 in which it was held that, if the new term sought to be imposed by the employer was in fact an unreasonable restraint of trade, then an employee dismissed for failing to sign up to that term had been unfairly dismissed. As to unlawful deductions from wages claims under *s 23* of the *Employment Rights Act 1996*, the EAT in *Peninsula Business Services* (above) confirmed that deductions pursuant to clauses in restraint of trade are to be treated in the same way as deductions pursuant to any other clause in the employee's contract: provided the covenant is set out in writing, and the employee has agreed to it in writing, the employer will have a defence to any such claim in the employment tribunal. The employee's remedy in such circumstances lies in a claim for breach of contract in the ordinary courts: see generally PAY – I: PAYMENTS, PAY STATEMENTS AND MISCELLANEOUS STATUTORY PAY RIGHTS (32).

We propose to review first the law in relation to the common law doctrine of restraint of trade (below 41.2), then to review confidential information (below 41.13) and to consider restraint of trade as a discretionary element in granting injunctive relief outside of the narrow common-law doctrine of restraint of trade (including so-called 'garden leave' and 'springboard' injunctions) (below 41.14, 41.15). Finally, we consider procedural issues and remedies (below 41.16).

41.2   **THE COMMON LAW DOCTRINE OF RESTRAINT OF TRADE**

Although of ancient origin the doctrine in its modern form may be traced to the speech of Lord McNaghten in *Nordenfelt v Maxim Nordenfelt Guns and Ammunition Co Ltd* [1894] AC 535, 565:

> 'All interference with individual liberty of action in trading, and all restraints of trade of themselves, if there is nothing more, are contrary to public policy, and therefore void. That is the general rule. But there are exceptions: restraints of trade and interference with individual liberty of action may be justified by the special circumstances of a particular case. It is a sufficient justification, and indeed it is the only justification, if the restriction is reasonable – reasonable, that is, in reference to the interests of the parties concerned and reasonable in reference to the interests of the public, so framed and so guarded as to afford adequate protection to the party in whose favour it is imposed, while at the same time it is in no way injurious to the public.'

It follows that in applying the common law doctrine of restraint of trade it is necessary to consider the following fundamental issues:

(1)   what restraints of trade are covered by the doctrine?

(2)   what are the legitimate interests of the parties?

(3)   is the restraint injurious to the public interest?

41.3   What restraints are covered?

A very large number of contracts or contractual provisions will impose some limits on a person's freedom to trade (for example, a contract to sell specific goods or a lease of a property prohibiting the use of the premises for business purposes). Such contracts or provisions are not subject to the restraint of trade doctrine: see *Esso Petroleum Co Ltd v Harper's Garage* [1968] AC 269.

Various tests have been propounded as to restraints which do, or do not, fall within the doctrine. The best of these tests, it is submitted, is contained in the speech of Lord Pearce in the *Esso* case:

> 'The doctrine does not apply to ordinary commercial contracts for the regulation and promotion of trade during the existence of the contract, provided that any prevention of work outside the contract, viewed as a whole, is directed towards the absorption of the parties' services and not their sterilisation. Sole agencies are a normal and necessary incident of commerce and those who desire the benefits of a sole agency must deny themselves the opportunities of other agencies. So, too, in the case of a film star who may tie herself to a company in order to obtain from them the benefits of stardom ... parties habitually fetter themselves to one another.

> When a contract only ties the parties during the continuance of the contract and the negative ties are only those which are incidental and normal to the positive commercial arrangements at which the contract aims, even though those ties exclude all dealing with others, there is no restraint of trade within the meaning of the doctrine and no question of reasonableness arises. If, however, the contract ties the trading activities of either party after its determination, it is a restraint of trade and the question of reasonableness arises. So, too, if *during* the contract one of the parties is too unilaterally fettered so that the contract loses its character of a contract for the regulation and promotion of trade and acquires the predominant character of a contract in restraint of trade. In that case ... the question whether it is reasonable arises.'

Applying this to a contract of employment, it is clear that the doctrine will apply to restraints imposed on the employee's working activities or fields of work after the original contract has ended. It is also clear from that test, however, that the doctrine can apply to some employment contracts, or provisions within those contracts, intended to operate during the currency of the employment relationship. Thus extravagantly oppressive and one-sided employment contracts may be held unenforceable during their lifetime: see *Young v Timmins* (1831) 1 Cr & J 331. The doctrine may also apply where, for example, other contractual provisions may be imposed which have the substantive effect of restraining the freedom of the employee to move jobs (for example, provisions clawing back bonuses if an employee goes to work for a rival or depriving an employee of commission which he has earned during the currency of his employment if he leaves to work for a rival). The courts are by no means consistent in their treatment of these kind of provisions and the application of the restraint of trade doctrine to them. In *Sadler v Imperial Life Assurance Co of Canada Ltd* [1988] IRLR 388, HC the doctrine was held to apply to a covenant depriving an employee of commission payable post-termination on the condition that he did not go to work for a rival. The provision in question was held unenforceable and severed from the agreement, thereby entitling the employee to recover the commission payments (see also *Marshall v NM Financial Management Ltd* [1997] IRLR 449, CA). However, in *Peninsula Business Services Ltd v Sweeney* [2004] IRLR 49 the EAT held that a provision in an employee's contract denying him post-termination commission was not a restraint of trade since it did not impose any restraint on him as to whom he might work for or what he might do: it was merely an 'economic disincentive' to discourage the employee from leaving his employment. The EAT's decision in *Peninsula* seems far too restrictive in its refusal to apply the doctrine of restraint of trade to the provision in question. The doctrine is not based upon the form of the contractual restraint, but upon its substantive effect: 'whether a particular provision operates in restraint of trade is to be determined not by the form the stipulation wears but ... by its effect in practice. ... The clause in question here contains no direct covenant to abstain from any kind of competition or business, but the question to be answered is whether, in effect, it is likely to cause the employee to refuse business which otherwise he would take or, looking at it in another way, whether the existence of this provision would diminish his prospects of employment' (*per* Lord Wilberforce, *Stenhouse Australia Ltd v Phillips* [1974] AC 391, PC at 402F-H). In the *Stenhouse* case the clause held to be unenforceable as an unreasonable restraint of trade was a profit-sharing clause imposed on an employee of an insurance broker as part of a settlement agreement entered into on the termination of his employment. The clause provided that, in the event that any client of the employer within a period of five years from the date of termination of the employment placed any insurance business (of the type transacted by the employer) with the departing employee, the departing employee would be entitled to a one-half share of the commission received in respect of such transaction.

An exclusive services provision intended to operate during the currency of the employment relationship will not have the doctrine apply to it. Nonetheless, if, during the currency of the employment contract, the employer puts the employee on garden leave and seeks an injunction to prevent the employee, during that notice period, from working for a competitor, the court will pay heed to the restrictive effect of the exclusive services provision in determining whether to grant such an injunction and, if so, for what period. This is not the application of the doctrine of restraint of trade but the application of considerations of restraint of trade in the exercise of a judicial discretion: see *Symbian Ltd v Christensen* [2001] IRLR 77 and *Provident Financial Group plc v Hayward* [1989] ICR 160.

It is a cardinal principle of the application of the common law doctrine of restraint of trade that the court must determine the enforceability of the contract or contractual provision concerned as at the date the contract was entered into, not at the date when it comes to be enforced (see *Gledhow Autoparts Ltd v Delaney* [1965] 1 WLR 1366, *Home Counties Dairies Ltd v Skilton* [1970] 1 WLR 526 and *Commercial Plastics Ltd v Vincent* [1965] 1 QB 623 and *Allan Janes LLP v Balraj Johal* [2006] EWHC 286 (Ch), [2006] ICR 742). It is accordingly apparent that the restraint of trade doctrine in its pure form may be readily applied to an employee's post-termination restraints, but cannot in its 'pure' form be applied to disputes which arise in relation to garden leave injunctions. In the case of exclusive service provisions in contracts of employment their reasonableness at the date the contract is entered into is obvious: they are there to provide the employer with the means of ensuring that the employee's skills and endeavours are fully absorbed. Thus they satisfy Lord Pearce's test at that stage. It is only when they are deployed during notice periods as the basis for seeking injunctive relief to enforce garden leave that they cease to have the character of a provision to absorb skills and endeavours and take on the character of a provision aimed at sterilising the employee.

There is one area of potential difficulty in applying this rule as to the date when the court must consider the reasonableness of any covenant in restraint of trade, namely that caused by the effect of the *Transfer of Undertakings (Protection of Employment) Regulations 2006* ('the *2006 TUPE Regulations*', which replace the *1983 TUPE Regulations* with effect from 6 April 2006: see generally TRANSFER OF UNDERTAKINGS (52)). The effect of those *Regulations* is that, where there is a 'relevant transfer' of an undertaking or part of one, employees whose contracts would otherwise be terminated by that transfer are instead subject to a statutory novation of their existing employment contract so that the transferee company is substituted for the transferor company. *Regulation 4(1)* of the *TUPE Regulations* provides that, following a transfer, an employee's contract of employment 'shall have effect after the transfer as if originally made between the person so employed and the transferee'. If *reg 4(1)* were to be applied literally then it would have the effect of rendering certain restrictive covenants (which prohibit dealing with customers of a specified business) imposed by the specified business (the transferor) upon its employees nugatory if the transfer that takes place had the result of substituting in every respect (and at all material times) the transferee for the transferor. In *Morris Angel & Son Ltd v Hollande* [1993] IRLR 169 the court considered the effect of *reg 5(1)* of the *1983 TUPE Regulations* (now *reg 4(1)* of the *2006 TUPE Regulations*) on a restrictive covenant in the employee's contract of employment which prohibited him, for a period of one year after the contract came to an end, from seeking 'to procure orders from or do business with any person, firm or company who has, at any time during the one year immediately preceding the cesser done business with [Group Y]'. The business of Group Y was sold to X Ltd and on the date of sale the employee's contract of employment with Group Y was terminated. The employee sought to contend that the effect of the transfer was to substitute in the restrictive covenant for clients of Group Y the clients of X Ltd. Accordingly, the employee contended that he could not be in breach of the covenant by canvassing or soliciting persons who had been clients of group Y during the period one year prior to the termination of his contract because the effect of the old *reg 5(1)* was to alter the wording of the covenant 'clients of X Ltd' which, as a matter of fact, he had not solicited or dealt with after the termination of his employment. At first instance, it was held that the old *reg 5(1)* applied so that, although the transferee company could enforce the covenant, the customers with whom he was prohibited from doing business with after termination were those of the transferee X Ltd. It followed that there was no breach of the covenant in question. On appeal, the Court of Appeal preferred a construction of the rules under which the transferee company was deemed to have been the owner of the transferor's business during the relevant 12-month period (i.e. the 12 months prior to the termination of the employment contract). Thus, the customers with whom the employee was prohibited from dealing with under the covenants were those of the part of the business transferred (i.e. those of Group Y prior to the transfer). It followed that the employee was in breach and an interim injunction was ordered.

Any attempt to impose a new restrictive covenant upon employees following a TUPE transfer was, prior to 6 April 2006, almost bound to fail. Such variations to an employee's contract of employment were unenforceable under *reg 5(1)* of the *1983 TUPE Regulations* even if they formed part of a 'package' which was to the overall benefit of the employee (see *Credit Suisse First Boston (Europe) Ltd v Lister* [1998] IRLR 700). However, under the *2006 TUPE Regulations* variations to an employee's contract that are implemented for 'economic, technical or organisational' reasons entailing changes in the workforce will be valid even if the reason for the variation is connected to the transfer: see generally TRANSFER OF UNDERTAKINGS (51).

41.4 The interests of the parties

In order to justify a contract or provision in restraint of trade it must be proved that it is reasonable in the interests of the parties. This does not mean that the provision in question must support the interests of both parties equally. Rather, it means: 'For a restraint to be reasonable in the interests of the parties it must afford *no more than* adequate protection of the party in whose favour it is imposed ... though in one sense no doubt it is contrary to the interests of the covenantor to subject himself to any restraint, still it may be for his advantage to be able so to subject himself in cases where, if he could not do so, he would lose other advantages, such as ... the possibility of obtaining employment or training under competent employers' (*Herbert Morris Ltd v Saxelby* [1916] 1 AC 688, 707 *per* Lord Parker). It is now firmly established that the burden of proof in relation to this first step in the justification process is on the party seeking to enforce that covenant: see *Mason v Provident Clothing and Supply Co Ltd* [1913] AC 724 *per* Viscount Haldane, LC at 733 and Lord Shaw at 741 and *Herbert Morris*, above, at 700, 707 and 715. This will normally, but not invariably, be the employer (see, for example, *Wyatt v Kreglinger and Fernau* [1933] 1 KB 793, where it was the employee who sought to enforce the covenant in question).

The courts will not enforce any provision against mere competition (such covenants are generally referred to as 'covenants in gross'). It is of the essence that an employer demonstrates that he has a legitimate interest to protect. Preventing competition *per se* is not a legitimate interest. Covenants in restraint of trade are upheld not on the ground that the employee 'would, by reason of his employment or training, obtain the skill and knowledge necessary to equip him as a possible competitor in the trade, *but that he might obtain such personal knowledge of and influence over the customers of his employer or such an acquaintance with his employer's trade secrets as would enable him, if competition were allowed, to take advantage of his employer's trade connection or utilise information confidentially obtained*' (*per* Lord Parker in *Herbert Morris*, above, 709). This quotation from Lord Parker demonstrates that, historically, the courts had recognised two legitimate interests of the employer justifying the imposition of a reasonable restraint: (a) trade secrets (and confidential information); and, (b) customer connection.

The categories of legitimate interest that may be protected by an employer are not, however, confined to the two interests mentioned by Lord Parker. The modern approach to the identification of interests justifying provisions in restraint of trade is not based on a narrow categorisation: '... the employer's claim for protection must be based upon the identification of some advantage or asset inherent in the business which can properly be regarded as, in a general sense, his property and which it would be unjust to allow the employee to appropriate for his own purposes, even though he, the employee, may have contributed to its creation. For while it may be true that an employee is entitled and is to be encouraged to build up his own qualities of skill and experience, it is equally his duty to develop and improve his employer's business for the benefit of his employer. These two obligations interlock during his employment: after its termination they diverge and mark the boundary between what the employee may take with him and what he may legitimately be asked to leave behind to his employers' (per Lord Wilberforce *Stenhouse v Phillips*, ibid at p 400). Thus, in recent years new interests of an employer have been identified by the courts as justifying the protection of provisions in restraint of trade. In *Office Angels Ltd v Rainer-Thomas* [1991] IRLR 214, CA the court recognised as a legitimate interest of an employment agency the pool of workers on the agency's books. In *Dawnay, Day & Co Ltd v de Braconier d'Alphen* [1997] IRLR 285, affd [1998] ICR 1068, CA the court recognised as a legitimate interest the stability of an employer's workforce, holding that a covenant imposed on an employee prohibiting him from soliciting his former colleagues to leave their employment was a reasonable restraint. Nevertheless, some caution needs to be exercised in framing contractual provisions in restraint of trade. Client connection is an important aspect of the goodwill of any business, but it is not the exclusive component of that goodwill. A competent and hard-working employee who does not have any dealings with clients may enhance the reputation of his employer's business, and the reputation of the business is part of its goodwill, but an employer cannot prohibit an employee from going to work for a competitor upon termination of his employment merely to protect the enhanced reputation of his business to which the employee has contributed: the employee is entitled to take with him his own skills and knowledge, even where those skills and knowledge have contributed to the reputation enjoyed by the employer (see *Countrywide Assured Financial Services Ltd v Smart* [2004] EWHC 1214, Ch, unreported).

Having identified a legitimate interest to protect, the contract or contractual provision in question must be no more than adequate to protect that interest. Clearly the reasonableness of the ambit or duration of any restraint is tied to the nature of the interest in question. If it is sought by an employer to protect his customer connection, that may be achieved by post-termination restraints which prohibit for a reasonable period of time the ex employee from soliciting or dealing with those customers with whom the employee had contact during the course of his employment. *Prima facie* there would be no justification for imposing on that employee a post-termination restraint which prohibited him from entering into employment with a competitor. However, if an employer wishes to protect trade secrets or confidential information he may be justified in imposing a post-termination restraint prohibiting the employee from joining a competitor for a reasonable period of time. It is dangerous for an employer to seek too wide a protection for a limited interest because a court is entitled to look at the nature of the restraints imposed with a view to determining whether a lesser restraint would have been adequate to protect the employer's interest: see *Office Angels*, above. We return to the various forms of restraint and issues of reasonableness in more detail below.

41.5 **The public interest**

Much confusion has arisen about the second step in the justification process enunciated by Lord McNaghten in the *Nordenfelt* case (see above, 41.2). Problems arise for two reasons: first, the doctrine of restraint of trade is a creation of public policy which collides head on with another public policy, namely the sanctity of contract; secondly, in some cases (particularly those decided in the early part of the 20th century) judges tend to use the expressions 'public policy' and 'public interest' interchangeably (see for example Cozens-Hardy MR in *Sir WC Leng & Co Ltd v Andrews* [1909] 1 Ch 763). This confusion has led in more recent times to judicial debate about whether the doctrine of restraint of trade has been properly applied in the past in distinguishing between the private interest of the parties and public policy in the sense of public interest (see, for example, *per* Lord Reid in the *Esso Petroleum* case (above, at p300E)). It is submitted that the true analysis of the doctrine is as follows:

(*a*)   It is contrary to public policy for parties to a contract to enter into restraints which go beyond the reasonable protection of legitimate private interests (the first limb of Lord McNaghten's test).

(*b*)   It is also contrary to public policy for parties to a contract to enter into restraints which are no more than adequate to protect a private legitimate interest recognised by the law, if those restraints are contrary to the public interest (the second limb of Lord McNaghten's test).

(*c*)   It follows that, in theory at least, a covenant which satisfies public policy to the extent that it is no more than adequate to protect a private legitimate interest may fail to satisfy public policy because it is not in the public interest.

Unfortunately, it is not possible to identify any cases in the employment field which clearly illustrate proposition (c). In a number of cases, eg *Sir WC Leng* (above), *Herbert Morris v Saxelby* (above), *Strange (SW) Ltd v Mann* [1965] 1 WLR 629, *Countrywide Assured Financial Services Ltd v Smart* (above) and *Commercial Plastics Ltd v Vincent* [1965] 1 QB 123, the courts have held covenants to be against 'public policy' (and sometimes against the 'public interest') where, it is submitted, the real basis for the decisions in those cases is that there is no legitimate interest of the covenantee to protect or, alternatively, that the restraints go beyond what is reasonable to protect that interest. This is against public policy in the sense set out in (a) above, but is not illustrative of the principle in (c) above. (The only exception in these cases would appear to be the, (perhaps) *obiter*, statement of Farwell LJ in the *Sir WC Leng* case above at p 334.)

In a number of cases the public interest (as distinct from public policy) has been raised as a discrete ground of attack on contractual restrictions, but with a marked lack of success. Although Lord Denning MR in *Oswald Hickson Collier & Co v Carter-Ruck* [1984] AC 720 appeared to hold that it was contrary to 'public policy' that a fiduciary (a solicitor) should be precluded by a restrictive covenant from acting for a client who wanted him to act, that decision was swiftly departed from: see *Edwards v Warboys* [1984] AC 724; *Bridge v Deacons* [1984] AC 705 and *Allan Janes LLP v Balraj Johal* [2006] EWHC 286 (Ch), [2006] ICR 742. See also, in relation to the medical profession, *Kerr v Morris* [1988] 3 All ER 217.

Probably the real reason why issues of public interest do not generally arise for decision, at least in employment cases, is because restraints which customarily appear in employment contracts normally have no impact on the public at large and hence the public interest. Moreover the onus of proving that a restraint is injurious to the public interest is upon the person (normally the employee) who is making that allegation. The burden is a heavy one: *A-G Commonwealth of Australia v Adelaide Steamship Co Ltd* [1913] AC 781 at 797 *per* Lord Parker. It is, however, submitted that one area in which the issue of public interest is of great significance in the employment field is where an employee challenges an indirect restraint upon his freedom. These kind of restraints arise where the employee has no direct restraint imposed upon him in his contract of employment but nonetheless is fettered by contractual restraints which his employer has entered into with other parties. In these cases the private interests of the parties are not in issue because the parties are not challenging the enforceability of the restraints: a third party (the employee) is challenging the restraints in so far as they affect him and not the parties to the contract. (See *Eastham v Newcastle United Football Club Ltd* [1964] Ch 413 and *Greig v Insole* [1978] 3 All ER 349 and compare *Kores Manufacturing Co Ltd v Kolok Manufacturing Co Ltd* [1957] 1 WLR 1072 which involved an agreement between two employers not to employ each other's employees for a period of five years after their leaving the employment of the respective parties. In fact, however, in that case, the challenge to the agreement was not made by an employee but by one of the parties. Nonetheless, the Court of Appeal opined, *obiter*, that such an agreement could not be justified under the restraint of trade doctrine because of its indirect effect upon employees.)

It was suggested by Lord Hodson in the *Esso* case that issues of the burden of proof in relation to the interests of the parties and the public interest will seldom arise because, once the agreement is before the court, it is open to the scrutiny of the court in all its surrounding circumstances 'as a question of law': *Esso*, above, 319. It is submitted that this is not right. In the employment situation the employer must (if he seeks to enforce a restraint) establish that the covenant is in the interests of the parties in the narrow sense required by the doctrine. If the employee wishes to challenge the restraint on the ground that it is injurious to the public interest he cannot rely on the employer to furnish the court with the evidence required to prove injury to the public: the onus is on him to do that. The evidence which would require the court to consider the impact of a restraint upon a particular market is likely to be voluminous and to require expert opinion. Most employees would lack the financial means to undertake the provision to the court of that kind of evidence themselves. It is therefore extremely improbable that a court will have furnished to it in an employment case all the evidence that is required to deal properly with the issue of the public interest. It may be, however, that restraint of trade law is entering into a new era where issues of public interest will become more prominent. In the case of *Dranez Anstalt v Zamir Hayek* [2002] EWCA Civ 1729, [2003] FSR 32 restrictive covenants entered into by the inventor of a new ventilator for use in hospitals were held to constitute unreasonable restraints of trade by the Court of Appeal amongst other grounds on the basis that they offended against the public interest in restricting the inventor from making further developments which would be of great benefit to the public. There are, too, the recent developments in competition law to which reference has already been made (see above 41.1). The current guidance both from the Commission in Brussels and from the Office of Fair Trading limits ancillary restraints taken upon the merger or acquisition of businesses ('concentrations' in the vocabulary of competition law) to a period of two years where goodwill only is sold and three years where both goodwill and know-how are involved. (The Guidance is available on the OFT website: http://www.oft.gov.uk/Business/Mergers+EA02/ publications.htm.) Thus, an undertaking selling a business and being subject to a restraint on competing with the business sold may complain if that restraint exceeds the guidelines mentioned. However, an employee who owns less than a controlling interest of the shares in the business sold, and whose employment is transferred to the purchaser, and who has a covenant imposed on him not to compete with the business sold for a period of, say, five years cannot invoke directly either European or UK competition law to strike down the covenant. This is because competition law regulates agreements between undertakings. Unless an employee holds a controlling interest in the business sold, he will not be an 'undertaking' and cannot therefore rely on competition law. The position is therefore anomalous. Nevertheless, it is conceivable that the employee selling his share in the business could invoke the Brussels and OFT guidelines indirectly as representing public policy in relation to the duration of ancillary restraints. This would not require the employee to devote huge resources to producing evidence as to the state of any particular market for the purpose of judging the impact of ancillary restraints upon the public and it is to be anticipated that such arguments may be deployed by individuals seeking to escape restraints undertaken by them in the course of a business sale or merger.

41.6 **Judging the reasonableness of restraints**

Construction of covenants in restraint of trade

In *Clarke v Newland* [1991] 1 All ER 397 the Court of Appeal reviewed the approach to construction that ought to be adopted in construing contracts for the purpose of the application of the doctrine of restraint of trade. The Court concluded that the following approach should be adopted. First, the court should consider the construction of the term in question without having regard to the issue of validity or invalidity of the covenant, ie the court must decide what the contractual provision means before it decides whether the provision is reasonable or not. Second, the court must have regard to the object of such restraints, namely the protection of one of the parties against trade rivalry. Finally, the court must construe the provision in context, that is to say, having regard to the factual matrix at the date when the contract was made. By following this approach, a court ought to avoid the worst excesses of an over literal construction or an over purposive approach. The vice inherent in the over-literal construction of a covenant in restraint of trade is that the court ignores the intent of the parties and construes the covenant so that it extends to situations not contemplated by the parties:

> 'Another matter which requires attention is whether a restriction on trade must be treated as wholly void because it is so worded as to cover cases which may possibly arise, and to which it cannot be reasonably applied ... Agreements in restraint of trade, like other agreements, must be construed with reference to the object sought to be obtained by them. In cases such as the one before us, the object is the protection of one of the parties against rivalry in trade. Such agreements cannot be properly held to apply to cases which, although covered by the words of the agreement, cannot reasonably be supposed ever to have been contemplated by the parties, and which on a rational view of the agreement are excluded from its operation by falling, in truth, outside and not within its real scope.' *Haynes v Doman* [1899] 2 Ch 13, CA, *per* Lindley LJ at 24–25.

In this respect much criticism has been levelled at the decision in *Commercial Plastics v Vincent* [1965] 1 QB 123. A purposive approach to construction is well illustrated by the following cases. In *Moenich v Fenestre* (1882) 67 LT 602 the expression 'any trade or business' in a restrictive covenant was held to mean, contextually, 'any trade or business as commission merchant'. In *G W Plowman & Son Ltd v Ash* [1964] 1 WLR 568 a covenant requiring an employee after termination of the employment 'not [to] canvass or solicit for himself or any other person ... any farmer or market gardener who shall ... have been a customer of the employers' was construed by the court as meaning, in the context of the employment agreement read as a whole, 'not to canvass or solicit with respect to the goods which the employee dealt with during his employment'. In *Home Counties Dairies Ltd v Skilton* [1970] 1 WLR 526 the words 'dairy produce' were construed by the court as being limited to only that sort of dairy produce with which the employee had been concerned whilst in employment. (See also *Hollis & Co v Stocks* [2000] IRLR 712.) In *TFS Derivatives Ltd v Morgan* [2004] EWHC 3181 (QB), [2005] IRLR 246 'business' was held to refer to a particular business activity of the investment company in question, and not to the whole of the 'business entity' that was the company: see also *Dyson Technology Ltd v Strutt* [2005] EWHC 2814 (Ch).

However, the Court can be guilty of, in effect, re-writing a covenant by an over-purposive approach (see *Littlewoods v Harris* [1977] WLR 1472). The court ought not to be over indulgent when faced with ill-drafted and ambiguous provisions in restraint of trade. In *J A Mont (UK) Ltd v Mills* [1993] IRLR 172, CA a sales and marketing director of a paper mill entered into a severance agreement with his employer to terminate his employment. Under this agreement the employee received one year's remuneration although he was not required to work for the employer during that period. The severance agreement contained the following restraint: 'This total payment is made on condition that you do not join another company in the tissue industry within one year of leaving our employment'. The Court of Appeal held that the wording of the covenant was too wide because it operated worldwide and restrained the defendant from working in any capacity whatsoever in any sector of the tissue industry. The employer argued that the court should apply a purposive construction to the covenant to cut down its ambit. The Court of Appeal refused to do so, holding that it was clear that the employer had made no attempt whatever 'to formulate the covenant so as to focus upon the particular restraint necessary to guard against [the employee's] possible misuse of confidential information, the only legitimate target for imposing any restraint on his future employment'. The Court of Appeal relied heavily on the consideration that if covenants, *ex facie* too wide, could always be 'rescued' by the court implying restrictions to the restraint in order to render it enforceable then employees would be trapped into accepting excessive restraints or facing expensive litigation. This vice has long been recognised by the courts:

> 'It would in my opinion be *pessimi exempli* if, when an employer had exacted a covenant deliberately framed in unreasonably wide terms, the courts were to come to his assistance and, by applying their ingenuity and knowledge of the law, carve out of this void covenant the maximum of what he might validly have required. It must be remembered that the real sanction at the back of these covenants is the terror and expense of litigation, in which the servant is usually at a great disadvantage, in view of the longer purse of his master. It is sad to think that in this present case this appellant, whose employment is a comparatively humble one, should have had to go through four courts before he could free himself from such unreasonable restraints as this covenant imposes, and the hardship imposed by the exaction of unreasonable covenants by employers would be greatly increased if they could continue the practice with the expectation that, having exposed the servant to the anxiety and expense of litigation, the Court would in the end enable them to obtain everything which they could have obtained by acting reasonably.' (*Mason v Provident Clothing and Supply Co Ltd* [1913] AC 724, *per* Lord Moulton at 745.)

Accordingly, in construing provisions in restraint of trade the courts must establish a balance between extreme literalism and extreme liberalism. However, the approach to construction enunciated in *Clark v Newland* leads to one difficulty. It is a principle of contractual construction that in resolving ambiguities a court must strive to render the contractual term in question legal rather than illegal. Faced with an ambiguity which on one construction would render it too wide to be enforceable under the restraint of trade doctrine (thereby rendering the contractual provision 'illegal') and an alternative construction which would render the provision of narrower impact (and therefore legal), the court must choose the latter. It is not clear how, if the court, is not permitted to have regard to the consequences of its construction exercise, it is able at the same time to comply with this principle (see *Mills v Dunham* [1891] 1 Ch 576). This principle has been confirmed in more recent cases where the courts have accepted that if, having examined the restrictive covenant in the context of the relevant factual matrix, there remains an element of ambiguity, the court should adopt the construction that would render the covenant lawful under the restraint of trade doctrine: see *Turner v Commonwealth and British Minerals Ltd* [2000] IRLR 114 at para 14 *per* Waller LJ and *TFS Derivatives Ltd v Morgan* [2004] EWHC 3181 (QB), [2005] IRLR 246 at para 43 *per* Cox J.

41.7   *Severance*

An English court is not permitted to uphold a covenant in restraint of trade by reducing its ambit or duration for that is to impose a new bargain upon the parties: see *Mont v Mills* (above). (In many foreign jurisdictions courts do have this power.) Under English law, the covenant either satisfies the test of reasonableness as drawn and properly construed or it does not. Any provision in a contract (and one frequently sees them) stating that the covenants in question 'if held to be unenforceable, but would be enforceable if the ambit or duration of them were reduced, may be reduced accordingly' are of no effect and probably constitute an unlawful attempt to oust the jurisdiction of the court (see *Living Design (Home Improvements) Ltd v Davidson* [1994] IRLR 69). Moreover, a covenant imposing restraints of trade: 'so far as the law would allow' will be held too vague to be enforceable (see *Davies v Davies* (1887) 36 Ch D 359, CA.

Nonetheless, the English court does have the power of severance. That is to say, to sever parts of contractual provisions too wide to be enforceable leaving in place those parts which the court considers reasonable. A contractual provision imposing a restraint of trade may be in simple or compound form. Very frequently seen in employment contracts are covenants which proscribe a number of separate activities thus: '[the employee] shall not, for a period of twelve months after termination of this contract, solicit, or canvas, or entice away, or deal with any client of the employer' (or words to that effect). A court may take the view that in the circumstances of any particular case it would be reasonable for an employer to protect himself against solicitation of his clients, but that, for example, it is unreasonable for the employer to require protection against the employee dealing with his clients. The common law, as part of the exercise of construction of a provision in restraint of trade, permits the court to uphold part of the restrictions imposed whilst holding invalid other restrictions in such composite clauses. The process by which the court does this is colloquially referred to as 'blue-pencilling' in respect of those parts of a covenant struck out as unreasonable. The following conditions must be satisfied in order for the court to be able to blue-pencil parts of provisions:

(*a*)   as a matter of construction the court must be able to discern within the composite provision a number of independent restraints;

(*b*)   the court must be able to excise one or more of these independent restraints without having to add words to the agreement, or modify the wording of what remains;

(*c*)   there must remain adequate consideration to support that or those part(s) of the covenant which remain after the blue-pencilling of the unreasonable parts;

(*d*)   the severance exercise must be conducted in accordance with public policy.

These propositions may be drawn from the cases of *Attwood v Lamont* [1920] 3 KB 571, CA and *Marshall v N M Financial Management Ltd* [1997] ICR 1065. (See also *TFS Derivatives*, above.) It used to be considered, in employment cases, that there was an additional requirement, namely that the part of the covenant excised should be no more than trivial in nature. This no longer represents the law: see *T Lucas & Co Ltd v Mitchell* [1974] Ch 129, CA.

It follows from this approach to severance that if the entire consideration to support a covenant (for example, to pay to a retiring employee a pension) is constituted by an unenforceable obligation in restraint of trade then the obligation to pay the pension is likewise unenforceable. The blue-pencilling of the one obligation not to compete with the employer results in the disappearance of the obligation to pay the pension: see *Wyatt v Kreglinger* and cf *Marshall v N M Financial Management Ltd* (above). (In the latter case the Court of Appeal held that the obligation to pay monies was sufficiently supported by other consideration to enable to the court to strike out the offending obligation in restraint of trade whilst preserving the obligation to pay the employee the monies in question.) The draughtsman of restrictive covenants must exercise some caution. The mere insertion of the word 'or' may not be sufficient to render one part of the covenant in restraint of trade disjunctive or 'independent' of another part: see, for example, *British Reinforced Concrete Engineering Co Ltd v Schelff* [1921] 2 Ch 563, Ch D (though note that *British Reinforced Concrete* was a case of a business sale agreement restraint) and *Scully UK Ltd v Lee* [1998] IRLR 259, CA. It is very far from clear what the fourth condition for severance (which emerged from the *Marshall* case) means. It may be that in these cases the court had in mind the restrictions on severance referred to in the *British Reinforced Concrete* case (above). However, that was case on business sale agreements and, moreover, it is difficult to see how the limitations there referred to survive the decision (specifically in relation to employment contracts) in *T Lucas and Co Ltd v Mitchell* (above). Certainly in employment cases the first three conditions are likely to be the only consideration to which the court need pay heed in using its blue pencil.

41.8   *Testing reasonableness*

General approach

The court's approach to enforcement of restraints in employment contracts is far less sympathetic than its approach to restraints arising in commercial transactions such as business sale agreements, agency agreements, distribution agreements and agreements between equity partners (see *Herbert Morris Ltd v Saxelby* [1916] 1 AC 688, *Systems Reliability Holdings plc v Smith* [1990] IRLR 377 and *Allied Dunbar (Frank Weisinger) Ltd v Weisinger* [1988] IRLR 60). However, see the apparently contradictory approach taken by the court in *Beckett Investment Management Group Ltd v Hall* [2007] EWHC 241 (QB), [2007] All ER (D) 178 (Mar). It is frequently suggested that the reason for the closer scrutiny paid by English courts to employment contracts than to other forms of commercial bargain is because employees are by and large not in a strong bargaining position when compared to employers. Whereas this may no doubt have some veracity, it is not a full explanation of the rigour with which the court approaches covenants in restraint of trade in employment contracts. Indeed, the courts recognise that not all employees are in an unequal bargaining position: 'Managing directors can look after themselves' (see *M&S Drapers (a Firm) v Reynolds* [1957] 1 WLR 9; see also *Hanover Insurance Brokers Ltd v Schapiro* [1994] IRLR 82 and *TFS Derivatives*, above). The principal reason why courts are more generous towards restraints between equity partners, for example, is because those restraints are <u>mutual</u> and because a partnership resembles (to some extent, at least) a 'business' sale agreement: see *Bridge v Deacons* [1984] AC 705, PC. A business sale agreement creates intrinsically different interests for protection than those that exist between employer and employee (see *Herbert Morris v Saxelby*). In addition, the vendor of the business will receive an enhanced consideration if he is prepared to undertake not to compete with the business he sells. In employment contracts there is no mutuality of obligation: an employer does not undertake not to compete with the employee if the employee were to set up a rival business on the termination of his employment. Neither is there any enhancement, necessarily, of the remuneration that an employee receives during the currency of the employment contract because he assumes obligations under a restrictive covenant operative only post termination of his employment. In this latter respect, an employer who pays a sum of money to an employee in consideration of the latter accepting provisions in restraint of trade as part of a settlement for the termination of his contract of employment, is not absolved from having to justify the restraints imposed on the employee under the ordinary principles of the restraint of trade doctrine (see *J A Mont (UK) Ltd v Mills* [1993] IRLR 172 and *Turner v Commonwealth and British Minerals Ltd* [2000] IRLR 114). The court may, however, have regard to the additional payment made to the employee on the settlement as one factor in considering reasonableness: *Turner* (above).

Having ascertained what the proper meaning of the provisions imposing restraints may be (see above 41.6) the court must next determine whether on that proper construction the covenants are reasonable in the sense of being no more than adequate to protect that legitimate interest.

Covenants may be unreasonable in the following respects:

(*a*)   the nature of the restraint;

(*b*)   the ambit of the restraint;

(*c*)   the duration of the restraint.

Nature of the restraint

The approach of the court is first to identify the legitimate interest or interests which the employer is seeking to protect by the restraints in question. Restraints can take a wide variety of forms, but broadly fall into two categories:

(*a*)   Restraints against conducting or being engaged or interested in a competing business (whether specifically identified or not in the covenant) for a period of time; and

(*b*)   Restraints which prohibit a limited kind of competitive activity, such as soliciting or dealing with customers.

The former category of restraint (a non-compete restraint) may be in a wide form prohibiting an employee from joining a competitor's business regardless of the field of that business in which he is proposing to work, or it may be limited to prohibiting him working for a competitor in the particular field in which the employee has been engaged by the former employer imposing the covenant. The more limited form of non-compete provision is now more frequently encountered in modern contracts of employment.

The court, having identified an interest of the employer justifying protection, is entitled to look at the nature of the restraint deployed to determine whether the legitimate interest could have been protected by a narrower restraint than, for example, either a wide or narrow non-compete provision (see *Office Angels Ltd v Rainer-Thomas* [1991] IRLR 214, CA). In identifying the legitimate interest to be protected the court is entitled to look at any express words in the contract which may identify that interest (*Office Angels*). If the employer has identified the interest he seeks to protect (for example, client connection) he cannot, when the covenant comes to be tested in court, claim that the restraint in fact is aimed at protecting a different interest (for example, confidential information: see *Office Angels*). Again, if the interest to be protected is, for example, client connection or the stability of the employer's workforce a covenant in the nature of a non-compete provision risks being held to be disproportionate for such interests may be protected by a covenant directed at the prohibition of specific competitive acts, such as the soliciting or dealing with customers, or the soliciting or enticing away of staff. It follows that the nature of the interest to be protected will dictate the nature of the restraint which should be employed by the employer to protect the interest. Non-compete provisions are generally only justifiable if the nature of the interest to be protected is trade secrets and confidential information: see *per* Simon Brown LJ in *J A Mont (UK) Ltd v Mills* [1993] IRLR 172. This is because it is notoriously difficult to police covenants which merely restrain the disclosure or use of confidential information. Moreover, it is notoriously difficult for a covenantee to know what information is truly confidential and which he cannot use or disclose and what information is merely part of his stock of accumulated knowledge and experience which he is entitled to disclose or use. Accordingly an employer may protect his trade secrets and confidential information by imposing on an employee a covenant restraining that employee for a reasonable period of time from joining a competitor, at least in the same field of activity in which he was engaged for the former employer (see *Littlewoods Organisation Ltd v Harris* [1977] 1 WLR 1472, CA; *Printers & Finishers Ltd v Holloway* [1965] RPC 239; and *David (Lawrence) Ltd v Ashton* [1991] 1 All ER 385, [1989] ICR 123, CA).

In some cases the court has upheld non-compete provisions where the interest to be protected is client connection. The basis for this is that in some instances it may be impossible, or, at least, very difficult for the employer to 'police' a more limited covenant restraining soliciting or dealing with clients (see *Scorer v Seymour-Johns* [1966] 1 WLR 1419, *per* Salmon LJ, p 1427C-E, *Turner v Commonwealth and British Minerals Ltd* [2000] IRLR 114, *per* Waller LJ at para 18 and *TFS Derivatives Ltd v Morgan* [2004] EWHC 3181, QB, [2005] IRLR 246).

It is, however, submitted that the courts should be suspicious of assertions that it is difficult to police non-solicitation and non-dealing covenants. If it is difficult to do so, it is likely to be because there is no firm connection between the client and the employer in the first place, and the justification sometimes advanced for area non-compete restraints (namely that they are intended to protect what is in effect passing trade) is surely, for that reason, wrong in principle. If trade is passing it is difficult to see how the employee can gain any material knowledge of, or influence over, such clientele. In the *TFS Derivatives* case the court appeared to assume that it would be difficult to police non-solicitation and non-dealing covenants in circumstances in which the only evidence proffered by the employer to support this assertion was their experience of losing clients when an employee had previously left their employment. However, the employer did not at the same time suggest that that other employee had surreptitiously breached his non-solicitation and non-dealing covenants. If clients leave an employer in circumstances in which the employer is not asserting that their departure is consequent upon breaches of restrictive covenants by a former employee, it is difficult to see how the conclusion may be drawn that the covenants in question cannot be effectively policed. It is equally, if not more, plausible that the covenants were simply ineffective to achieve their purpose.

In a recent decision (*Thomas v Farr Plc* [2007] EWCA Civ 118, [2007] IRLR 419) the Court of Appeal held that it was 'self-evident' that a non-solicit provision could not be policed. It is respectfully submitted that no such assumption can be made without evidence of some sort to that effect. The fact is that breaches of non-solicitation/-dealing covenants are regularly uncovered by covenantees: see, for example, *Allan Janes LLP v Balraj Johal*, above.

The court also held in the *TFS Derivatives* case that a non-compete provision was justified to protect confidential information. However, the court does not appear to have fully analysed the restraint in question to determine whether its duration was in fact commensurate with the length of time in which such information may have been of continuing use to a competitor.

The ambit of the restraint

The ambit of a restraint will comprise the following elements:

(a)   the geographical area within which the restraint is to operate;

(b)   the proscribed actions (eg non-solicitation or non-dealing with clients and the class of client not to be solicited or dealt with).

Geography

Restraints may be worldwide (and will be so construed) if they contain no express or, perhaps, implied geographical limitation (see *Commercial Plastics Ltd v Vincent*, above). Worldwide non-compete restraints may be justifiable on the basis that they are necessary to protect trade secrets or confidential information: see *Scully v Lee*, above. Conversely, a restraint against soliciting or dealing with clients will not require an express geographical limitation (see *G W Plowman & Son Ltd v Ash* [1964] 1 WLR 568), even if clients may be located throughout the world, because the restraint is limited by the class of proscribed person. In many employment contracts radial or other area restraints are frequently employed. These are extremely clumsy instruments and appear to be a hang-over from the old common-law 18th and 19th-century rules about 'general' and 'partial' restraints. Area restraints must have a functional correspondence with the legiti-mate interest to be protected (see *Office Angels*). Thus, a local business whose customers are drawn exclusively or substantially from a radius of, say, five miles from the place of that business cannot justify a radial restraint of ten miles. Equally, the area in which a restraint is to operate will be considered carefully by the court. Thus, a radial restraint of five miles, for example, may be justifiable in rural or lightly populated areas, but could not be justified in a major conurbation where it may cover populations of a million or more: see *Fellowes & Son v Fisher* [1976] QB 122 and *Spencer v Marchington* [1988] IRLR 392. The real difficulty with radial or area restraints is that they are unnecessary if the protection is sought for the purposes of, say, customer connection because a non-solicit or non-compete covenant will suffice. It is difficult to see how they can be justified on the basis that they are necessary to protect confidential information or trade secrets since such interests are not confined to territorial boundaries (see *Scully UK Ltd v Lee*, above). Neither can radial restraints be justified on the basis of an interest in the stability of the workforce because solicitation of employees can readily be conducted from outside the radius imposed and, again, a more focused form of protection is afforded by a non-solicitation/non-enticement of staff covenant. The only practical effect of an area restraint, over and above that of a more limited non-solicitation or non-dealing covenant, is that it will prevent an ex employee from competing with his ex employer for new customers, ie customers who have not dealt with the former employer before (see *Allan Janes LLP v Balraj Johal*, above). Accordingly, radial restraints of the non-compete provision variety extend the protection afforded to an employer beyond that element of good will, namely existing client connection which he is entitled to protect. In business sale agreements it may be legitimate for the purchaser to protect himself against the vendor acquiring future business which ought otherwise to go to the business sold (see *Allied Dunbar (Frank Weisinger) Ltd v Weisinger* [1988] IRLR 60). The acquisition of new clients by reason of recommendation of existing clients is, however, based on the reputation of the business which, although it forms part of the goodwill on a business sale, forms no part of a legitimate interest to protect in the case of employer/employee covenants (see *Countrywide Assured Financial Services Ltd v Smart* [2004] EWHC 1214 (Ch), unreported).

The proscribed actions

If the proscription is against conducting, or joining, or being employed in (or being otherwise interested in) another business then the covenant will be too wide if the proscribed business is described as 'a similar business' to that of the employer. An employer may be entitled to protect himself from unfair competition by the employee, but he is not permitted to prohibit the ex employee from joining or setting up a business which is merely 'similar' and not competitive (see *Scully v Lee* [1998] IRLR 259, CA, but cf *Spafax Ltd v Harrison* [1980] IRLR 442, CA, where the court reached the opposite conclusion). It is sometimes held by the courts that it is not legitimate to bar an employee from working in a competitive business in an area of work in which he has not been engaged in the employer's business (see, for example, *Commercial Plastics v Vincent*, above) or in a part of a competitor's business which does not compete with the former employer. Given, however, that a non-compete covenant may generally only be justified on the basis that it protects trade secrets or confidential information, it is difficult to see the logic behind such decisions: a former employee may impart confidential information of his former employer to a competing business after he leaves his employment and joins that competing business, regardless of the capacity in which he is working with the competitor or the department in which he may be engaged: see *Symbian Ltd v Christensen* [2001] IRLR 77.

Lesser forms of restraint, such as non-solicitation or dealing with customers, may be too wide if the class of customer with which the ex employee may not deal is drawn too widely. For example, covenants which prohibit soliciting or dealing with any client of the employer will be too wide if the employer has many hundreds or thousands of customers and the employee covenantor has dealt with only a limited number of them whilst employed: see *Marley Tile Co Ltd v Johnson* [1982] IRLR 75 and *Office Angels*, above. However, courts have upheld covenants that are not limited to dealings with clients which the employee has dealt with whilst employed: see *Gilford Motor Co. Ltd v Horne* [1933] Ch 935, CA, *Plowman v Ash* (above) and *Business Seating (Renovations) Ltd v Broad* [1989] ICR 729 and *Allan Janes LLP v Balraj Johal*, above. The better view is, however, that proscribed classes of customers should be limited to those that the employee has dealt with or, at least, may have knowledge about because the employee in question has overseen the work of other employees dealing with them (see *Spafax v Harrison*, above). Similarly, the class of customer ought to be limited to those persons who were clients of the employer for a defined period of time prior to the termination of the employee's contract of employment. In this way the covenant will not embrace persons who may have been clients prior to the employment of the employee, but were not clients of the employer at any time during the period of the employee's employment. It would seem that an employer is entitled to protect customers who have ceased to deal with him. However, in *Plowman v Ash* (above) the Court of Appeal held that an employer is entitled to protect by a non-dealing covenant customers who have ceased to deal with that employer during the currency of the employment contract in which that restraint appeared. This seems contrary to principle. It is of the essence of a reasonable restraint that it should protect the employer only against unfair competition by the employee, which means the exploitation by the employee of his knowledge about, and influence over customers that he has acquired during his employment (see *per* Lord Parker in *Herbert Morris v Saxelby*, above). A covenant will be too wide in its ambit if it purports to prohibit the ex employee from soliciting or dealing with persons who only become customers of the employer after the employee has left his employment (see *Konski v Peet* [1915] 1 Ch 530). There is a limited exception to this, namely prospective customers. An employer is entitled to protect himself against solicitation or dealing with prospective customers, at least where those prospective customers have been in negotiation with the employer prior to the employee leaving his employment and the employee has had contact with that prospective customer in the course of the negotiations (see *International Consulting Services (UK) Ltd v Hart* [2000] IRLR 227). The problem posed by the existence of contradictory authorities on whether the class of clients not to be solicited or dealt with ought to be closed by reference to clients actually dealt with by the employee remains to be resolved, the Court of Appeal having failed to grapple with the issue in *Dentmaster (UK) Ltd v Kent* [1997] IRLR 636.

Difficulty can arise even with limited restraints on dealing with customers where the market may be small and the customers therefore limited in number. This difficulty may be exacerbated by the use of ambiguous phraseology (see *Austin Knight (UK) Ltd v Hinds* [1994] FSR 52). The courts regard the non-solicitation covenant as being the least form of restraint and therefore more readily justifiable (see *Stenhouse v Phillips*, above, and *Scully v Lee*, above). There is remarkably little authority on what constitutes 'solicitation'. The only clear authority appears to be the case of *Wessex Dairies Ltd v Smith* [1935] 2 KB 80 where a milkman, prior to the termination of his employment contract, informed his customers, that he was leaving his existing employment, but would be available to do business with them again after a specified date in the future. Other forms of solicitation less direct than that involve advertising. In *Trego v Hunt* [1896] AC 7 it was held that an advertisement not directed specifically to the clients of the business concerned, but more generally, did not constitute 'solicitation'.

Further difficulties arise where, in addition to a prohibition on 'solicitation', a draughtsman of a restrictive covenant adds other expressions such as: 'enticing away' or 'interfering with' the clients or customers of the employer. In such cases, it is difficult for the court to know whether the covenant merely prohibits solicitation in the sense of making the first approach or whether acts beyond making the first approach are also prohibited such as to render the covenant a prohibition against dealing with customers even if those customers make the first approach to the employee: see *Austin Knight (UK) Ltd v Hinds* [1994] FSR 52 and *Hanover Insurance Brokers v Schapiro*, above, *per* Dillon LJ, but *cf* Nolan LJ. In

Hydra plc v Anastasi [2005] EWHC 1559 (QB) Royce J held in respect of a covenant 'not to solicit or entice away any employee of the employer for a period of twelve months following the termination of the covenantor's employment' that the word 'entice' meant 'tempt, lure, persuade and inveigle'. In that case the facts established were that the covenantee employer company was a small business with few employees and it was therefore entitled to protect the entirety of its employees from poaching by a former employee and, further, on the facts the employee who had left to join the covenantee's rival business had himself approached the covenantor and sought to persuade him to let him join the new venture. In those circumstances, there was no breach of the covenant not to entice away an employee. It seems therefore that, even in the extended meaning of the word 'entice' given by Royce J, the essential ingredient of that term is making the first approach.

It is to be observed that the views of the client cannot affect or influence the court in determining whether to enforce a non-solicitation or non-dealing covenant. In *John Michael Design plc v Cooke* [1987] ICR 445 a client intervened in an application by a claimant employer for interim injunctive relief against former employees to restrain them from dealing with former clients of the employer. The client protested that the interim injunction should not extend to prohibit the former employees from dealing with the intervenor because the intervenor had no intention whatsoever of doing any further business with the claimant. At first instance, the judge acceded to the intervenor's argument. The Court of Appeal, however, held that there should be no qualification of the interim injunction to enforce the restrictive covenants in question so as to exclude from its ambit an individual client. Rather, the Court of Appeal held that the restrictive covenant was most necessary to the claimant in the cases of clients refusing to do future business because, manifestly, if a client proposed to remain loyal to the claimant employer there was no need for the protection of the restrictive covenant.

Until the case of *Dawnay, Day & Co Ltd v de Braconier d'Alphen* [1998] ICR 1068 there was conflicting authority at Court of Appeal level as to whether an employer could justify a restraint on soliciting his employees to leave his employment. In the *Dawnay, Day* case it was held that an employer had a legitimate interest in the stability of his workforce, at least so far as senior employees were concerned. However, in *Dawnay, Day* there were two restraints relating to the protection of the workforce in the employment contracts in question. The first restraint prohibited soliciting senior employees to leave their employment. The second restraint prohibited the covenantor employing the covenantee's senior employees. The claimants sought relief only in respect of the first of these covenants which the judge held to be reasonable. The judge, however, opined *obiter* that the second form of restraint would be too wide to be enforceable. The objection to any form of restraint prohibiting an ex employee from employing in his business, or in a business that he has joined, a colleague of his at his former employers is that it amounts to a restraint on that colleague from seeking or obtaining work with whom he pleases. In *Kores v Kolok* (above) two employers in the same industry entered into an agreement that they would not employ members of each other's staff for a period of time after those employees had left their respective employment. The Court of Appeal held that this provision was unenforceable because it was not limited to senior employees who might carry away trade secrets or confidential information to the competitor. However, the Court of Appeal also opined, *obiter*, that the covenant was against public policy because it would prevent employees of each of the parties from seeking employment with the other in circumstances in which those individual employees did not have in their employment contracts any restraint prohibiting them from joining a competitor. The effect of the covenant in *Kores v Kolok* was to enable the two employers to achieve through the back door what they had failed to achieve through the front.

However, in *TFS Derivatives* (above) one of the restrictive covenants in the employee's contract was as follows: '[you will not] for six months employ, engage or work with an employee for the purpose of the supply of relevant services or a business which competes, or which plans to compete with, or is similar to a relevant business'. The learned judge held that this covenant went 'no further than is reasonably necessary in all the circumstances to protect [a legitimate interest] of the employer'. The judge did not, however, grant an injunction to enforce this restraint on the grounds that there was no evidence of breach. However, the judge's attention does not appear to have been drawn to the decision in *Dawnay, Day* (above) or to *Kores v Kolok* (above). Employers seeking to impose restrictions on the solicitation of their staff should be cautious about distinguishing for the purposes of such protection those staff occupying positions of importance to the covenantor's business or have training or business or technical knowledge and experience from those members of staff who do not: see *TSC Europe (UK) Ltd v Massey* [1999] IRLR 22. In small organisations, however, it may be that all the staff will have the necessary qualities or importance to justify protection against solicitation by an ex employee.

Duration

Whether the length of any restraint renders it unreasonable is a matter of impression for the judge. In *Stenhouse Australia Ltd v Phillips* [1974] AC 391 (above) Lord Wilberforce stated that the question of a reasonable duration for a covenant in restraint of trade could not 'advantageously form the subject of direct evidence. It is for the judge, after informing himself as fully as he can of the facts and circumstances relating to the employer's business, the nature of the employer's interest to be protected, and the likely effect on this of solicitation, to decide whether the contractual period is reasonable or not. An opinion as to the reasonableness of elements of it, particularly of the time during which it is to run, can seldom be precise, and can only be formed on a broad and commonsense view' (*Stenhouse*, 402). The question that the court must ask itself is: 'what is a reasonable time during which the employer is entitled to protection against solicitation of clients with whom the employee had contact and influence during employment and who were not bound to the employer by contract or by stability of association' (ibid). So far as the protection of confidential information is concerned acute problems are likely to arise in relation to fixing a reasonable duration for a post-termination covenant restraining an employee from engaging in competition with the employer. Logically, if the covenant is designed to protect trade secrets or equivalent confidential information in the sense of information that would never be disclosed by the employer and could not be 'reverse engineered' by a rival then it would be reasonable to impose a lifetime prohibition on the employee working for a competitor. Yet the courts constantly refer to the necessity, even when protecting trade secrets and equivalent confidential information, of keeping the non-compete provision to a reasonable duration: see, for example, *per* Cross J in *Printers and Finishers Ltd v Holloway (No 2)* [1965] 1 WLR 1. Where a covenant over a limited geographical area is taken to protect confidential information, the courts have, in the past, accepted a non-compete provision of unlimited duration: *Haynes v Doman* [1899] 2 Ch 13, CA. But, as the Court of Appeal has recently observed in *Scully v Lee* (above), confidential information knows no territorial boundaries and, accordingly, the imposition of an area blanket restraint to protect confidential information is, in itself, illogical.

41.9 Restraint of Trade and Confidential Information

All that can be said about the duration of covenants to protect confidential information is that it must be an issue of fact in every case as to the reasonableness of the duration of the covenant and it is submitted that the covenant's duration must necessarily be a function of how long the information to be protected is likely to remain confidential. Thus, if the confidential information to be protected is information relating to a proposed business strategy the covenant cannot endure for longer than the period during which the strategy is to remain confidential before being implemented (in effect, made public) by the employer. This, however, does not resolve the essential problem presented by extremely confidential technical information (for example, the secret of the recipe for the manufacture of Coca-Cola – anecdotally the most treasured and most protected trade secret in the world). Would it be permissible for that company to impose a lifetime ban on an employee who knew what the recipe was from joining a competitor like Pepsi-Cola? The law has yet to grapple with this problem. It is, however, clear that a judge is not bound by precedent to uphold as reasonable a restraint of the same duration and in the same field as a previous judge: see *Dairy Crest Ltd v Pigott* [1989] ICR 92, CA. It is equally clear that the more limited the ambit of the restraint, the greater the period of duration that will be upheld: see *Stenhouse v Phillips*, above, and *Fitch v Dewes* [1921] 2 AC 158. However, it must be doubtful that the latter case would, on the same facts, nowadays be followed (see, for example, *Allan Janes LLP v Balraj Johal*, above).

(Subject always to the caveat that judges should not slavishly follow precedent in restraint of trade cases, but rather examine the reasonableness of covenants in the light of the facts of each case, for a convenient compendium of cases where covenants have been upheld, or not, see *Restrictive Covenants Under Common and Competition Law* (4th edn, Sweet & Maxwell), Kamerling & Osman, p 381ff.)

41.9 *What is the consequence of a finding of unreasonableness?*

Many judges (see, for example, Lord McNaghten in *Nordenfelt*, above, and Cox J in *TFS Derivates*, above) have erroneously described a covenant in restraint of trade which is not justifiable as being 'void'. This is not correct. A covenant in unreasonable restraint of trade is merely unenforceable. The significance of this distinction is that a covenant in restraint of trade is not illegal in the sense of it being a criminal offence to enter into or perform the obligations so imposed: *Apple Corpns Ltd v Apple Computer Inc* [1992] FSR 431, Ch D. Accordingly, covenants in restraint of trade, the proper law of which is English law will be enforced by an English court by, for example, a worldwide injunction even if the restraint may be invalid under the law of other jurisdictions. Equally, whole contracts may be found to be in restraint of trade (see, for example, *A Schroeder Music Publishing Co Ltd v Macaulay* [1974] 1 WLR 1308), but rights which may have accrued to the respective parties under the contract before it is challenged as an unreasonable restraint will not be overridden.

41.10 Other Elements

Consideration

There is considerable debate as to whether a court is permitted to look at the adequacy of the consideration which supports any contract or provision in restraint of trade as part of the court's investigation into the reasonableness of the covenant. Authorities against the court considering adequacy of consideration include: *M and S Drapers v Reynolds* [1957] 1 WLR 9 *per* Hodson LJ and *Allied Dunbar (Frank Weisinger) Ltd v Weisinger* [1988] IRLR 60, paras 30–32 *per* Millett J. Contradicting these authorities are: Lord McNaghten in *Nordenfelt* (above) at 565, Lord Hodson (apparently dissenting from his own earlier judgment in *M and S Drapers*) in *Esso Petroleum v Harper's Garage* (above) at 318D-F and Lord Pearce in the same case at 323E-F. The better view, it is submitted, is that the court cannot look to the adequacy of the consideration in the sense of determining whether the value of the bargain to the party restrained is the same as the value imparted to the covenantee. The court does not ask 'whether the consideration is equal in value to that which the party gives up or loses by the restraint under which he has placed himself ... it is impossible for the court ... to say whether, in any particular case, the party restrained has made an improvident bargain or not'. Rather the test is whether 'the restraint of a party from carrying on a trade is larger and wider than the protection of the party with whom the contract is made can possibly require': (*per* Tindale CJ, *Hitchcock v Coker* (1837) 6 Ad & El 959). It is therefore submitted that the issue of consideration has become confused because in many cases the courts have elided the issue of consideration in the technical sense of the contractual rule that there must be adequate consideration to support a bargain enforceable by the courts with consideration in the sense of a balance of benefit between the parties bestowed under a contract. The latter form of consideration may be considered only to the extent that the covenantee does not under the bargain struck extract more protection from the covenantor than is reasonable to protect the covenantee's legitimate interests. Extreme cases do, however, arise in which the courts will indulge in balancing the benefit and burden as between the two parties: see *Schroeder v Macaulay* (above) and *M and S Drapers v Reynolds* [1957] 1 WLR 9. There must be some consideration to support the restraint and it should be noted that in this respect a deed will not be sufficient if it is a seal alone: see *Hutton v Parker* (1839) 7 Dowl. 739.

41.11 *Repudiatory breach*

An employer in repudiatory breach of an employment contract, where that breach is accepted as terminating the same by the employee, cannot enforce any post-termination restraints: *General Billposting Co Ltd v Atkinson* [1909] AC 118. However, the fact that a restrictive covenant purports to apply upon termination of the contract of employment, 'howsoever caused, whether lawfully or unlawfully', does not itself render the covenant too wide and unenforceable: cf *Rock Refrigeration v Jones and Seward Refrigeration Ltd* [1996] IRLR 675. There was a period when this proposition was doubted by the courts and it was held that restrictive covenants purporting to apply upon termination of the contract of employment 'howsoever caused, whether or lawfully or unlawfully' were held to be too wide. However, in the *Rock Refrigeration* case this argument was resolved in favour of upholding covenants expressed to apply even to a termination of the employment contract occasioned by a repudiatory breach by the employer. The Court of Appeal held that the doctrine of restraint of trade does not become engaged unless and until the contract of employment containing the restraints is lawfully terminated. Thus, if the employer repudiates the contract, which is then terminated by the acceptance of that repudiation by the employee, the restrictive covenant does not fall to be considered at all under the restraint of trade doctrine because both parties to the contract which has been repudiated are discharged from future performance of their express contractual obligations: see *Photo Production Ltd v Securicor Transport Ltd* [1980] AC 827. The principle of *Securicor* is that upon acceptance of repudiatory breach express future obligations upon both parties (the innocent and the guilty) to a contract are discharged, whereupon implied secondary obligations (such as the obligation to pay damages for breach) come into force. However, despite the (minority) views expressed by

Phillips LJ in *Rock Refrigeration* (above), it is submitted that the court cannot at this stage <u>imply</u> obligations in restraint of trade because they are, *prima facie*, contrary to public policy and unenforceable (see *Wallace Bogan & Co v Cove* [1997] IRLR 453). (To this principle there are the very narrow exceptions of an implied obligation in business sale agreements on the part of the vendor not to solicit customers of the business sold (see *Trego v Hunt*, above) and an implied obligation on the part of employees not to make use of or disclose trade secrets or equivalent confidential information of their employers after the termination of the employment contract (see *Faccenda Chicken v Fowler*, above).) It is inconceivable beyond these two implied obligations that a court will impose by implication any other provisions in restraint of trade because it is contrary to public policy in the broad sense to do so. The decision in *Rock Refrigeration* does, however, reveal a real danger for employers (identified by Phillips LJ). If an employer accepts a repudiatory breach by an employee as terminating the contract of employment he will (under the principle in the *Securicor* case) be in danger of losing the protection of any post-termination restraints in the contract of employment. It should be noted, however, that the majority of the court in *Rock Refrigeration* considered that a repudiatory breach did not discharge an employee from his obligations of confidentiality (see also *Naomi Campbell v Vanessa Frisbee* [2002] EWHC 328). It is for this reason that it is crucial for employers to provide expressly in any contract of employment for a right to terminate the contract (ie in accordance with its terms) in the event of any conduct of the employee which would constitute a repudiatory breach (for example, gross misconduct). If the contract of employment is terminated in accordance with an express term of that kind then the rules relating to repudiatory breach do not apply because the employer will have terminated the contract in accordance with its express terms and will not have to rely on any implied obligation arising under common law but can rely instead on the obligations expressed in the contract of employment as applying post-termination of the same.

41.12   Conflict of laws

Because the law of restraint of trade arises as a matter of public policy, foreign law, even if it is the proper law of the contract, cannot dictate the validity or invalidity of a provision in restraint of trade. Contracts of employment the proper law of which is a foreign law will not be enforced by an English court if the restraints in question are unenforceable under the public policy of England and Wales: see *Rousillon v Rousillon* (1880) 14 Ch D 351.

41.13   TRADE SECRETS AND CONFIDENTIAL INFORMATION

The courts have long recognised that trade secrets are a legitimate interest which an employer may protect by imposing a covenant limiting the field of activity in which an ex employee may engage after leaving his employment (see, for example, Lord Parker in *Herbert Morris v Saxelby*, above, and *Printers and Finishers Ltd v Holloway* [1965] RPC 239). In this respect, therefore, obligations of confidentiality that an employee owes his employer have an important role to play in the doctrine of restraint of trade. However, obligations of confidentiality, if breached by an employee either during or after the employment contract has ended, may give rise to claims for relief which lie outside any claim for breach of restrictive covenants in employment contracts, specifically the so-called 'springboard injunction'. In recent years, decisions of the court have lead to much confusion in these areas, such that discussions of the principles of the law of confidentiality now resemble medieval theological debates about how many angels can dance on pinheads.

It is necessary, therefore, to identify certain basic principles relating to the obligations of confidence owed by employees to their employers. The obligation of good faith and fidelity (now transmuted into an obligation of trust and confidence: see GENERALLY 8.13 CONTRACT OF EMPLOYMENT) implied into all contracts of employment has as an incident of that larger duty a specific obligation that the employee shall not make use of, or disclose, for the benefit of a competing business information acquired by the employee about his employer's business in the course of his employment (see *Robb v Green* [1895] 2 QB 1). In that case an employee during his contract of employment made a list of the names and addresses of his employer's clients and, following the termination of his employment, used that list to canvas the clients of the former employer for a rival business established by the employee. The employee was held to have breached the implied duty of good faith and fidelity in so acting and was ordered by injunction to hand over the list he had made to his former employer and to pay damages. The decision was affirmed on appeal ([1895] 2 QB 315). It is of the greatest significance to observe that the defendant contended that the information contained on the list which he had made was information that could be obtained from sources within the public domain. The trial judge (Hawkins J) did not accept that all the information could have been so sourced, but added (p 18) that even were that true the employee had nonetheless acted in breach of his duty in creating a convenient compilation of material for the purpose of assisting an intended competitor. (For a more recent case on the scope of the employee's obligations of good faith and fidelity while in employment, see *Helmet Integrated Systems Ltd v Tunnard* [2006] EWCA Civ 1735, [2007] IRLR 126, in which the Court of Appeal accepted that the employee had not breached his obligations to his employer by taking, during his employment and unbeknownst to his employer, steps preparatory to competing with his employer. Note, however, that the position is otherwise for company directors and very senior employees: see 8.16 DIRECTORS.)

Some ninety years after *Robb v Green* [1895] 2 QB 1 the Court of Appeal embarked on an analysis of the duties of confidentiality owed by an employee: see *Faccenda Chicken Ltd v Fowler* [1986] ICR 297, CA. At first instance in that case, Goulding J had analysed the position thus ([1984] ICR 589 at 598–599):

'Let me now deal with the alleged abuse of confidential information. I must make it clear that anything I say about the law is intended to apply only to cases of master and servant. In my view information acquired by an employee in the course of his service, and not the subject of any relevant express agreement, may fall as regards confidence into any of three classes. First, there is information which, because of its trivial character or its easy accessibility from public sources of information, cannot be regarded by reasonable persons or by the law as confidential at all. The servant is at liberty to impart it during his service or afterwards to anyone he pleases, even his master's competitor. An example might be a published patent specification well known to people in the industry concerned ... Secondly, there is information which the servant must treat as confidential (either because he is expressly told it is confidential, or because from its character it obviously is so) but which once learned necessarily remains in the servant's head and becomes part of his own skill and knowledge applied in the course of his master's business. So long as the employment continues, he cannot otherwise use or disclose such information without infidelity and therefore breach of contract. But when he is no longer in the same service, the law allows him to use his full skill and knowledge for his own benefit in competition with his former master; and ... there seems to be no established distinction between the use of such information where its possessor trades as a principal, and where he enters the employment of a new master, even though the latter case involves disclosure and not mere personal use of the information. If an employer wants to protect information of this kind, he can do so by an express stipulation restraining the servant from competing with him (within reasonable limits of time and space after the termination of his employment). Thirdly, however, there are, to my mind, specific trade secrets so confidential that, even though they may necessarily have been learned by heart and even though the servant may have left the service, they cannot lawfully be used for anyone's benefit but the master's. An example is the secret process which was the subject matter of *Amber Size & Chemical Co Ltd v Menzel* [1913] 2 Ch 239.'

Goulding J went on to hold that the information that had been used by the defendants upon leaving the plaintiff company's employment and setting up a rival business fell into the second of the three categories and, accordingly, there was no breach of duty involved in its use by the defendants. This was not a case in which there were any post-termination restraints in the defendants' contract of employment with Faccenda limiting their business activities in any way. Goulding J, however, opined (above, 599E) that an employer can protect the use of information in the second category, even though it does not include any information in the third category (ie a trade secret or its equivalent) by means of a restrictive covenant. The Court of Appeal held:

(1)   That in contracts of employment confidentiality obligations of the employee are to be determined by that contract.

(2)   Absent any express term relating to confidential information in an employment contract, the obligations of the employee in respect of the use and disclosure of information are the subject of implied terms.

(3)   During the currency of the employment relationship the obligations in relation to the use and disclosure of information are included in the implied term imposing a duty of good faith and fidelity (or trust and confidence) on the employee. The Court of Appeal declined to consider the precise limits of the confidentiality obligation arising out of that implied term during the currency of the employment contract, but observed:-

(a)   that the extent of the duty of good faith will vary according to the nature of the contract; and

(b)   that that duty would be broken if an employee makes a list of customers, or memorises such a list, for use after his employment ends, even though there is no legal impediment on the employee soliciting or doing business with those customers after he leaves his employment. For this proposition the Court of Appeal returned to and relied on *Robb v Green* (above).

(4)   The implied term imposing an obligation on the employee not to use or disclose information learnt during his employment after the determination of the same is more restricted in its scope than the obligation during the currency of the employment contract and arising from the general duty of good faith and fidelity. Specifically, the implied post-termination obligation does not extend to all information given to, or acquired by, the employee while in his employment, and may not cover information which is only 'confidential' in the sense that it falls within the broader category of information that is protected during the currency of the employment contract as an incident of the obligation of good faith and fidelity. For this

proposition the Court of Appeal relied upon the judgment of Cross J in *Printers and Finishers Ltd v Holloway* [1965] RPC 239 at 253:

> 'In this connection one must bear in mind that not all information which is given to a servant in confidence and which it would be a breach of his duty for him to disclose to another person during his employment is a trade secret which he can be prevented from using for his own advantage after the employment is over, even though he has entered into no express covenant with regard to the matter in hand. For example, the printing instructions were handed to Holloway to be used by him during his employment exclusively for the plaintiffs' benefit. It would have been a breach of duty on his part to divulge any of the contents to a stranger while he was employed, but many of these instructions are not really 'trade secrets' at all. Holloway was not, indeed, entitled to take a copy of the instructions away with him; but in so far as the instructions cannot be called 'trade secrets' and he carried them in his head, he is entitled to use them for his own benefit or the benefit of any future employer.'

(See also *E Worsley & Co Ltd v Cooper* [1939] 1 All ER 290.)

Accordingly, the Court of Appeal (*obiter*) disagreed with Goulding J's judgment where he stated that an employer can protect 'category 2' information (not also falling within 'category 3') by means of an express post-termination restraint. The Court said:

> 'In our view the circumstances in which a restrictive covenant would be appropriate and could be successfully invoked emerge very clearly from the words used by Cross J in *Printers & Finishers Ltd v Holloway* [ibid]... If the managing director is right in thinking that there are features in the plaintiffs' process which can fairly be regarded as trade secrets and which their employees will inevitably carry away with them in their heads, then the proper way for the plaintiffs to protect themselves would be by exacting covenants from their employees restricting their field of activity after they have left their employment, not by asking the court to extend the general equitable doctrine to prevent breaking confidence beyond all reasonable bounds.'

> On this analysis, as the Court of Appeal pointed out, it is impossible to provide a comprehensive list of those things which constitute trade secrets, or equivalent confidential information, that will be protected by the implied obligation of confidence operating post-termination and which would therefore form a legitimate interest justifying an express post-termination restraint limiting the fields of activity in which the ex employee may work for a period of time. Secret processes of manufacture are an obvious example of such information but 'innumerable other pieces of information are capable of being trade secrets, though the secrecy of some information may be only short lived ... the fact that the circulation of certain information is restricted to a limited number of individuals may throw light on the status of the information and its degree of confidentiality'.

(5) The Court of Appeal went on to hold that in order to determine whether any particular item of information falls to be protected under the implied obligation of confidentiality operative after the termination of the employment contract a court must consider all the circumstances of the case, including the following matters:-

(a)   the nature of the employment (ie was the employee engaged in a capacity where confidential material was habitually handled by him and he might, accordingly, be expected to realise its sensitivity);

(b)   the nature of the information itself (ie only information which is a 'trade secret' or the equivalent of a trade secret is protected by the post-termination implied obligation);

(c)   whether the employer impressed on the employee the confidentiality of the information;

(d)   whether the relevant information can be easily isolated from other information which the employee is free to use or disclose.

The decision by the Court of Appeal in *Faccenda Chicken* has been criticised by some judges and by some textbook writers. In *Balston Ltd v Headline Filters Ltd* [1987] FSR 330 Scott J doubted the Court of Appeal's opinion that information falling within Goulding J's second category which did not also fall within his third category (termed by some textbook writers as 'mere confidential information') could not be protected by an express post-termination restraint. Similarly, in *Systems Reliability Holdings plc v Smith* [1990] IRLR 377, Harman J refused to follow this part of the Court of Appeal's judgment in *Faccenda*. See also *Lancashire Fires Ltd v SA Lyons & Co Ltd* [1997] IRLR 113 CA, per Bingham LF, para 16 and *A T Poeten Ltd v Horten* [2000] ICR 208.

It is respectfully submitted that these doubts are erroneous. First, it is unquestionably a matter of principle that it is against public policy to restrain the use by an ex employee of knowledge and skills that he has acquired in the course of his employment: see *Herbert Morris v Saxelby*, above, per Lord Parker and *Commercial Plastics Ltd v Vincent* [1965] 1 QB 623. If the employer is to have a legitimate interest to protect in confidential information that information must fall into a special category of sensitivity beyond the mass of more mundane information that an employee will necessarily accumulate during his employment. Second, the Court of Appeal's decision in *Faccenda* does not warrant the criticism that has been levelled against it that it constitutes an excessively narrow view of the obligations of confidentiality in employment contracts or the class of information that may legitimately be protected by an express post-termination restraint or by the implied obligation of confidence operating after the contract of employment has come to an end. As the Court of Appeal pointed out, innumerable other pieces of information besides secret processes of manufacturing may constitute trade secrets, or their equivalent, and thus fall within the protection of express or implied post-termination obligations. Thus in one industry the identity of clients or customers may constitute the equivalent of a trade secret, as will information about the prices charged to those customers by the employer. In other businesses (as in *Faccenda* itself) the same kind of information will constitute only information protectable during the currency of the employment contract, but not afterwards. To an extent, confusion that has arisen since *Faccenda* is the product of quibbles about vocabulary: the expression 'trade secrets' is no doubt more apt to describe information relating to secret processes of manufacture than it is to describe information such as the identity of customers, but there is no sensible reason why one should not describe the latter information as 'information the equivalent of a trade secret' where it is treated as so equivalent in certain industries or businesses. It would, perhaps, be better if the use of the expression 'trade secrets' was abandoned altogether and replaced with the expression 'protectable confidential information'. It was certainly the view of Staughton LJ in *Lansing Linde Ltd v Kerr* [1991] 1 WLR 251, 260B that the problem was one of vocabulary: 'It appears to me that the problem is one of definition: what are trade secrets, and how do they differ (if at all) from confidential information? [It has been] suggested that a trade secret is information which, if disclosed to a competitor, would be liable to cause real (or significant) harm to the owner of the secret. I would add, first, that it must be information used in a trade or business and, secondly, that the owner must limit the dissemination of it or at least not encourage or permit widespread publication.'

There are reasons to doubt the test there propounded by Staughton LJ for identifying protectable confidential information, not least because it appears to place too much emphasis on the subjective view of the employer as to the status of information as distinct from the correct test which must needs be based upon the objective view of the court, but Staughton LJ, nonetheless, correctly identified the confusion that can arise from the terminology that abounds in these cases.

A second area of confusion arises from the difference between the implied obligation of confidentiality which survives after the employment contract has come to an end and the protection that may be afforded by an express post-termination restraint. The implied obligation is limited to an obligation not to disclose or make use of 'protectable confidential information'. This obligation does not prohibit an employee who possesses such information from going to work for a competitor of his former employer. It merely restrains him, when working for that competitor, from disclosing or using, the protectable confidential information. As has been pointed out above (41.8), such an obligation is virtually impossible to police. Accordingly, employers frequently resort to an express post-termination restraint limiting the fields of activity in which the former employee may be involved for a period following the termination of the employment (ie a non-compete provision or, at least, an obligation not to join that part of a competitor's business which competes with the former employer). It is respectfully submitted that Scott J's reservations in *Balston* about the Court of Appeal's decision in *Faccenda* were based on confusion between the scope of the implied obligation of confidentiality and the more practical protection that can be afforded by post-termination non-compete restraints. Equally, in the *Systems Reliability* case, it should be observed that the learned judge had characterised the restraints that he was dealing with as having arisen with respect to a business sale agreement, and <u>not</u> an employment contract. As has also been pointed out above (41.8), the court's approach to business sale agreements and the restraint of trade doctrine is very different to the approach adopted to restraints in employment contracts.

In conclusion, it is submitted that the law on an employee's obligations of confidentiality may be stated as follows:

(*a*)   During the currency of the employment contract the employee is bound as an incident of his implied obligation of trust and confidence not to disclose or make use of the mass of information he acquires about his employer's business. The information covered by that obligation is limited so as to exclude only information which is trivial or in the public domain. However, it should be noted that if the employee draws up lists of customers from the records of his employer the identity of which might otherwise have been sourced in the public domain he will nonetheless have breached the implied obligation of confidentiality during his employment contract.

(*b*)   After the contract of employment comes to an end the employee is subject to an implied obligation not to disclose to, or make use for the benefit of, a competitor information which constitutes protectable confidential information, ie information which has the status of a trade secret or its equivalent. It is an issue of fact, in every case, depending on all the circumstances and applying the various guidelines, whether or not information falls into this category. Certain information, such as the identity of clients or customers is capable of falling into this category, but not necessarily in all businesses. The same is true of price information and many other kinds of information. No comprehensive list can therefore be drawn up of this kind of information. It is, however, clear that technical information regarding manufacturing processes and high level strategic business plans (for example, whether and, if so, when old models are to be replaced by new) will be likely to fall into this third category of protectable confidential information regardless of the nature of the business concerned.

(c) The protection afforded by the implied confidentiality obligation operating after the employment contract has come to an end is limited to disclosing or making use of the information concerned. This implied obligation is therefore of limited practical use to an employer because it does not prevent the employee from going to work for a rival and, once within a rival's business, it is impossible for the employer to monitor whether or not the employee is disclosing or making use of the concerned information.

(d) Accordingly, an employer who rightly considers that an employee may in the course of his employment acquire information falling within the class of protectable confidential information (ie a trade secret or equivalent confidential information) has a legitimate interest to protect under the doctrine of restraint of trade and may justify imposing a covenant restricting the field of activity of that employee when he leaves his employment. The covenant must, however, be reasonable as to its ambit and duration. Although 'category 3' confidential information can, in certain circumstances, justify worldwide restraints because confidentiality knows no territorial limitations (see *Scully v Lee*, above), in other cases, the evidence may show that a worldwide restraint will be held to be too wide to be enforceable (see *Lansing Linde Ltd v Kerr*, above and *Commercial Plastics Ltd v Vincent*, above). It may also be the case that a non-compete provision, ie one prohibiting an employee who possesses confidential information in the third category from working in any capacity for a competitor will also be held to be too wide in its ambit: see *Commercial Plastics v Vincent*. The contrary argument, however, is that it is legitimate to restrain an employee with 'category 3' confidential information from working in any capacity for a competitor because he is still in a position, at the very least, to reveal that information to the competitor that he joins even where he may be employed by that competitor in the part of its business which does not compete with the former employer or he joins it in a capacity in which he does not need to make use of or disclose that information in order to perform his new duties. These are difficult considerations which the court must weigh in considering the reasonableness of any post-termination restraint taken to protect 'category 3' confidential information.

(e) An express restrictive covenant in an employment contract not to make use of the employer's confidential information during or after the employment will be construed so as to apply to 'Faccenda Category 2' information during the contract but only 'Faccenda Category 3' information after the contract has ended: see *S&J Stephenson Ltd v Mendy* [2000] IRLR 233.

41.14 RESTRAINT OF TRADE AS A DISCRETIONARY ELEMENT IN GRANTING INJUNCTIVE RELIEF

Garden leave injunctions

It is now clear (see *Symbian v Christensen*, above) that considerations of restraint of trade play an important part in influencing the court's discretion to grant injunctive relief to enforce express or implied negative obligations of employees during notice periods. This is not the application of the 'classic' doctrine of restraint of trade. It differs in the following fundamental respects from the classic doctrine:-

(a)   the court is enforcing contractual rights which at the time the contract is made would not be subject to the restraint of trade doctrine in its classic form because those rights of the employer (namely the right to exclusive service by the employee) would not, under the classic doctrine, be considered a restraint of trade;

(b)   the court looks to the position as at the date when garden leave is imposed rather than the position when the contract was first entered into;

(c)   the court is able to temper the relief granted, both as to the ambit of any injunction and as to its duration; the court is not obliged to impose injunctive relief which exactly mirrors the contractual provisions in question (see *GFI Group Inc v Eaglestone* [1994] IRLR 119);

(d)   it would seem that the court can take into account interests of the employer which go beyond the legitimate interests that the court would uphold in enforcing post-termination restraints under the restraint of trade doctrine. In *Provident Financial* Dillon LJ considered it legitimate, in principle, to grant garden leave injunctions not only when there was a risk to the employer's confidential information or client connection from the departing employee, but also where the employee would merely enhance a competitor's business if he joined it during his notice period. This appears to come perilously close to supporting covenants in gross (ie covenants against mere competition).

Thus, the court can impose injunctions restraining an employee on garden leave from joining or assisting a competitor of the employer for a period less than the notice period stipulated in the contract of employment (*GFI v Eaglestone*, above). Equally, the court may limit the injunctive relief granted – and will so limit it – to restrain the employee only from working for a competitor during the whole or part of the notice period, but will not restrain an employee during his notice period from working for a new employer not in competition with the existing employer: see *Provident Financial Group plc v Hayward* [1999] ICR 160. There is no principle which requires a court to refuse to enforce a covenant in restraint of trade operating post termination of a contract of employment where a court has, during the notice period of the employee under that contract, granted a 'garden leave' injunction: see *Credit Suisse Asset Management Ltd v Armstrong* [1996] ICR 882, CA. However, the Court of Appeal in that case opined that the position might be different, and the post-termination restraint not enforced, in circumstances where it was preceded by a very lengthy period of garden leave, ie of a year or more. Nevertheless, it should not be supposed that a period of garden leave is to be regarded as a desirable alternative to post-termination restraints: in *TFS Derivatives Ltd v Morgan* [2004] EWHC 3181 (QB), [2005] IRLR 246, counsel for the employee sought to argue that a three-month non-compete clause was unlawful because the interest to be protected (client connection) could more appropriately and reasonably have been protected by a 'garden leave' clause of six months. He invited Cox J to make general observations as to the reasonableness and greater attraction of garden leave clauses generally. Cox J declined, observing that a six-month garden leave clause could legitimately be regarded as more onerous for the employee than a three-month non-compete because it prevented the employee from working at all. She also noted that the employer may understandably not wish to pay the employee for six months of no work and, further, that such a clause may not, in any case, be adequate to protect the employer's interests because it would not operate on summary termination of the contract by either party.

41.15   Restraint of trade and springboard relief

Employees who commit breaches of duty to their employer whilst employees by copying or removing customer lists or other confidential information for use in a rival business either during or after the termination of their employment contracts may be restrained by 'springboard injunction' from dealing with the customers whose details they have filched from their employer (see *Roger Bullivant Ltd v Ellis* [1987] ICR 464 and *PSM International Ltd v Whitehouse* [1992] IRLR 279). Recent developments suggest that springboard injunctions will no longer be limited to breaches of obligations of confidence. In *Midas IT Services Ltd v Opus Portfolios Ltd* (21 December 1999, unreported), Ch D springboard relief injuncting a company which it was alleged had procured breaches of the duty of trust and confidence by a senior employee of the claimant for a period of six months from acquiring a licence to distribute software was granted. The breaches of duty allegedly induced by the enjoined company were not breaches of the obligations of confidentiality.

The ambit and duration of springboard injunctions will be influenced by considerations of restraint of trade. A springboard injunction necessarily interferes with the enjoined parties' right to do certain kinds of business with certain people and judges appreciate that the effect of imposing such injunction will be to impose restraints of trade in circumstances in which an employee may not have any express post-termination restraints in his contract of employment:

'I am acutely conscious of the fact that competition should be encouraged and I am acutely conscious of the fact that it must be quite wrong to impose a restraint which is effectively only going to operate to stop a man using his acquired skills rather than to stop him using confidential information which he ought never to have taken into use at all.' *Fisher-Karpark Industries Ltd v Nichols* [1982] FSR 351.

Nonetheless, the judge granted the springboard injunction in that case against employees who it was alleged had misused confidential information of their employer in a rival business.

'Interim injunctions can be granted to prevent defendants ... from obtaining an unjust headstart in, or a springboard for, activities detrimental to the person who provided them with confidential information. ... However, in relation to that type of information, as distinct from that concerning real trade secrets, the court should be concerned that it does not, in granting such an injunction, give the injured party more protection than he realistically needs and, in particular, discourage or prohibit what in the course of time becomes legitimate competition.' *per* May LJ in *Bullivant v Ellis*, above, at 481G-H.

'The [springboard] injunction is directed to fairness of competition. Because the policy of the law is to encourage and certainly not to restrain fair competition the injunction is limited in duration to that period in which, in the court's estimation, the person injuncted could reasonably be expected to have assembled the confidential information using lawful means if earlier the assembled information comes as such into the public domain' *per* Blackburn J in *Midas IT Services Ltd v Opus Portfolios Ltd* (unreported, Ch D, 21 December 1999, pp 13–14)

In one springboard case at least (*Bullivant v Ellis*, above), the Court of Appeal considered that the appropriate duration of springboard relief in respect of an employee who had removed a card index of clients from his employer prior to the termination of his contract which he afterwards used in a rival business ought to be limited to the same period of a post-termination restraint in his contract of employment prohibiting dealing with his former employer's customers. It is submitted, however, that this direct correlation between springboard relief and the period of any post-termination restraint will not be invariably be adopted by the courts. Some forms of activity by employees in breach of their duties of trust and confidence whilst employed either in respect of the removal or misuse of confidential information or in respect of other wrongdoings, such as the canvassing or soliciting of the employer's customers during their employment for a rival business will cause serious harm requiring periods of restraint by springboard injunction of a longer duration than any post-termination restraint in the employment contract. After all, post-termination restraints are framed at the outset of a contract to protect a limited class of interests and in the expectation that the employee will abide by his contractual duties during his employment. The employer cannot, in framing covenants which are no more than adequate to protect his interests, anticipate and build into such covenants protection against any possible breach of trust and confidence which might be committed by the employee during his contract of employment.

A recent and valuable extension of the springboard principle to grant injunctive relief to cancel out wrongs (other than breach of confidence) committed during employment by an employee, those wrongs being induced by a third party, is similarly subject to restraint of trade considerations (see *Midas*, above).

41.16 PROCEDURAL MATTERS

Pleading

Because the common law doctrine of restraint of trade requires contractual provisions falling within it to be justified before they are enforceable, employers seeking to enforce such provisions ought to plead in their particulars of claim the grounds justifying the restraint. Equally, a defendant who wishes to attack a covenant as unenforceable should raise in his defence the grounds upon which he claims the covenant is unenforceable. It would appear that a court cannot of its own motion raise issues of unenforceability of covenants under the restraint of trade doctrine: see *Petrofina (Great Britain) Ltd v Martin* [1966] Ch 146. Accordingly, the parties must raise these issues themselves. It is to be observed, however, that there have been instances in which a court has, of its own volition, taken the point that a covenant is in unlawful restraint of trade: see *Marion White Ltd v Francis* [1972] 1 WLR 1423.

In cases which raise issues of confidential information (whether as justifying a covenant in restraint of trade or otherwise) the information claimed to be confidential must be properly and fully particularised in any statement of case and as early as possible (see *Ocular Sciences Ltd v Aspect Vision Care Ltd* [1997] RPC 289). In order to protect highly confidential information from public disclosure in the course of proceedings orders should be sought from the court at the earliest possible stage that particulars of confidential information contained in any statement of case should not be available on the court file for public inspection. The best practice is to plead the details of any confidential information at issue between the parties in a confidential annexure to the statement of case.

41.17   Injunctions

It has long been recognised by the courts that the proof of loss and damage arising from a breach of a post-termination restraint in an employment contract is a difficult, if not impossible, matter. Accordingly, in the vast majority of cases, the covenantee will seek to enforce restraints by way of injunction. However, it must be remembered that an injunction is a discretionary remedy and, even where a court holds a restraint to be valid, it will retain a residual discretion as to whether to enforce that contractual restraint by injunction or not. Thus, if an employer delays before seeking an injunction, such that a substantial part of the period of the restraint sought to be enforced has elapsed before injunctive relief is sought, then the court may not grant an injunction at all: see *Wincanton Ltd v Cranny* [2000] IRLR 716, CA. The personal circumstances of the defendant in injunction cases may also be relevant in that the court will weigh any hardship that might be occasioned by the imposition of an injunction (see *Corporate Express Ltd v Lisa Day* [2004] EWHC 2943, QB). It is, however, submitted that injunctions should not be refused merely because the defendant is likely to be impoverished by them for that would create a licence to breach contractual duties based upon a means test.

For the purposes of interim injunction, there is no special rule applicable to restrictive covenants in employment contracts. The principles in *American Cyanamid Co v Ethicon Ltd* [1975] AC 396 will apply and if the covenantee raises serious issues to be tried as to the enforceability of that covenant an interim injunction will almost invariably be granted: see *Lawrence David Ltd v Ashton* [1989] ICR 123. The court will, if requested by the defendant against whom an interim injunction has been granted, generally order a 'speedy trial'. In the event that a 'speedy trial' is not possible before the period of the restraint in question elapses, however, a different approach will be taken by the court to the grant of an interim injunction. In such a case, the court must go beyond deciding whether there is a serious issue to be tried and attempt some assessment of the claimant's prospect of success at trial: see *Lansing Linde Ltd v Kerr* [1991] 1 WLR 251, *per* Staughton LJ at 258. The court should not, however, allow the hearing of an application for interim injunctions in these circumstances to degenerate into a prolonged battle based upon evidence which cannot be tested at that stage by cross-examination. It is to be noted that issues as to the proper construction of a restrictive covenant (see above 41.6) should normally be resolved at the interlocutory stage, unless the construction of the covenant depends on disputed facts that cannot properly be resolved without a trial: see *Arbuthnot Fund Managers Ltd v Nigel Rawlings* [2003] EWCA Civ 518, para 20.

For the procedure on obtaining interim injunctions see *Parts 23* and *25* of the *Civil Procedure Rules*. Injunctions can also be sought as final relief at trial.

41.18   Declaration

It is, of course, open to a covenantor (employee) to challenge the enforceability of a covenant in restraint of trade by initiating legal proceedings seeking a declaration that the covenant in question is unenforceable. It is not clear, and must be open to doubt, whether a defendant could obtain an interim declaration to this effect pending trial, even a speedy trial. Alternatively, where a court refuses a claimant an injunction on the basis that there is only a very short period left for the restraint to run, it may nonetheless grant the claimant a declaration that the covenant in question is reasonable and enforceable (see *Corporate Express Ltd v Day* [2004] EWHC 2943 (QB), [2004] All ER (D) 290 (Dec)).

41.19 Damages where confidential information or trade secrets are involved

As for damages, there is a dearth of reported cases upon how damages for breach of a post-termination restraint are to be calculated. On ordinary principles, however, an employer can only recover for loss of any profit that he might have made had the covenant not been breached rather than his loss of revenue. In the event that customers have been filched by an ex employee in breach of a restraint against soliciting or dealing with them, the court may be able to assess at trial the loss of profits incurred by the employer up to the date of trial, but will be faced with the difficult task of assessing future loss which must be based on the employer's chance of retaining those customers: see *SBJ Stephenson Ltd v Mandy* [2000] IRLR 233.

41.20 Accounts of profits

Where an employee has breached a post-termination restraint prohibiting him from joining a competitor and it can be demonstrated that he has revealed to that competitor confidential information or trade secrets of the employer, an account of profits may be ordered by the court. This will, however, be an account of profits for breach of confidence rather than for breach of the negative covenant not to join a competitor. Despite the House of Lords' decision in *A-G v Blake* [2001] 1 AC 268 that accounts of profits can, in certain circumstances, be ordered against an employee for breach of a negative restraint, it is submitted that this principle cannot and should not be applied in the case of ordinary employees outside government security services.

42 Retirement

42.1 RETIREMENT AGE

The age at which an employee must retire was, until recently, a matter solely to be determined by the contract of employment. In the past, employers and employees were free to agree a contractual retirement age, in which case employment would terminate without the need for further action by the parties at the date the employee reaches the relevant age. But if the contract was silent as to retirement, and there was no established custom or practice sufficient to found a contractual term, the employee was free to continue working until the employer terminated the contract or until he or she chose to retire.

However, following the coming into force of the *Employment Equality (Age) Regulations 2006* ('*2006 Regulations*') on 1 October 2006, the situation is somewhat more complicated. Now, any retirement age lower than 65 is unlawful unless it can be objectively justified. The details of the new position are considered further below.

The state pension age is not of itself a contractual retiring age. Indeed it would be unlawful sex discrimination for an employer to require employees to retire at state pension age, since this disadvantages women whilst pension age differs according to sex. Under the *Pensions Act 1995*, the state pension age is to be equalised at age 65. This change is to be phased in over a 10-year period commencing on 6 April 2010.

In practice contracts do commonly specify retirement ages, which may differ according to the nature of the occupation. Increasingly, a maximum age is specified coupled with an entitlement for the employee to retire at an earlier age without loss of pension benefits. It is also not unusual for employers to stipulate a normal retirement age but that employees may remain in post thereafter on a discretionary basis. For a case arising from such an arrangement see *Taylor v Secretary of State for Scotland* [2000] IRLR 502, HL.

Under the *2006 Regulations*, employees now have the right to request to work beyond their retirement age. Employers are under a duty to consider any such request.

Pensionable age under an occupational pension scheme is distinct from both the contractual retirement age and the state pension age (although each may be the same). It is unlawful to provide different pensionable ages for men and women in an occupational pension scheme following the decision of the ECJ in *Barber v Guardian Royal Exchange Assurance Group: C-262/88* [1990] ICR 616 that pension benefits were 'pay' within *art 141* of the *Treaty of Rome* (formerly *art 119*): see further EQUAL PAY (24) for the UK legislation giving effect to this decision; note that this does not affect pensions earned by service prior to 17 May 1990 (the date of the *Barber* decision). It follows that, so long as pensionable age under the statutory provisions is different according to sex, (ie 60 for women and 65 for men), an employer cannot simply use the state pension age for an occupational pension scheme.

The question whether an individual has retired (e g for the purposes of a pension scheme) is one of fact and degree; thus the House of Lords has held that a managing director who withdrew from active involvement in the running of a company but remained in office as an unpaid non-executive director had retired: *Venables v Hornby* [2003] UKHL 65, [2004] ICR 42. The Court of Appeal has held that a provision in a pension scheme conferring enhanced benefits on employees who 'retire at the request of' the employer applies to those employees who take voluntary redundancy or early retirement, but not those who are made compulsorily redundant: *Agco v Massey Ferguson Works Pension Trust Ltd* [2003] EWCA Civ 1044, [2004] ICR 15.

42.2 EMPLOYMENT PROTECTION AND RETIRING AGE

The enforced retirement of an employee is often a source of resentment, and may provoke a claim for unfair dismissal and, since October 2006, for age discrimination. (If there is no provision in the contract for retirement and contractual notice is not given, there could also be a claim for wrongful dismissal.)

Until October 2006, most employees were unable to bring claims for unfair dismissal if, on or before the effective date of termination, they had attained the 'normal retiring age' for an employee holding the position they held or, if there was no 'normal retiring age', the age of 65 (pursuant to the now repealed *ERA 1996, s 109(1)*). A body of case law considered the meaning of 'normal retiring age' and there were exceptions for most dismissals which were deemed automatically unfair.

The *2006 Regulations* removed the age ceiling on the right to complain of unfair dismissal as of 1 October 2006. They added 'retirement' as a fair or potentially fair reason for dismissal in certain circumstances. The effect of these provisions is discussed further below.

Similarly, the *2006 Regulations* have revoked a similar provision which previously restricted the right to a redundancy payment to those who had attained the 'normal retiring age' or, where there was no such age, the age of 65.

A number of claims were brought in employment tribunals on the basis that the provision in *ERA 1996, s 109(1)* whereby jurisdiction to hear claims of unfair dismissal was excluded where there was no normal retiring age and the employee is over 65, is unlawful indirect sex discrimination, a breach of *art 141* (formerly *art 119*) of the *Treaty of Rome*, and therefore must be disapplied. The essence of the argument is that a higher proportion of men continue in employment after 65 than women. Accordingly, it has been claimed, the cut-off age fixed by the employment legislation has a disparate impact on men. Similar considerations might also apply with regard to the 'National Default Retirement Age' of 65, introduced by the *2006 Regulations*.

In *Secretary of State for Trade and Industry v Rutherford* [2006] UKHL 19, the House of Lords considered the argument. The first applicant, a man aged 67, had been dismissed on grounds of redundancy and wished to claim that his dismissal was unfair. A second applicant, a man aged 73, complained on a similar basis of his exclusion from the right to a redundancy payment. The two men argued that the *ERA 1996, s 109(1)* amounted to indirect discrimination.

The Lords rejected this argument, albeit giving different reasons. Lord Scott, Lady Hale and Lord Rodger held that the statistics brought before the House were irrelevant. This was essentially because there was no indirect discrimination as men over 65 were treated in the same way as women over 65 and any disadvantage was purely because it so happened that more men than women *wanted* to work over 65. By contrast, Lord Nicholls and Lord Walker considered that the statistics, focusing on those who were advantaged, did not reveal an adverse effect on a substantially higher proportion of men than women.

An employee required to retire in breach (or in the absence) of a contractual retirement age will be able to make a claim for breach of contract. However, if the employer gives the notice required under the contract, the fact that the reason for giving notice is to enforce retirement will not render an otherwise lawful dismissal a breach of contract. This is so even where the employer has an equal opportunity policy which includes provisions excluding age discrimination: *Taylor v Secretary of State for Scotland*, above.

42.3   THE EMPLOYMENT EQUALITY (AGE) REGULATIONS 2006

The separate chapter on age discrimination (AGE DISCRIMINATION (3)) sets out further detail of the provisions of the *2006 Regulations*. In particular, that chapter addresses questions such as objective justification. The following section summarises the key provisions in so far as they relate to retirement. The *2006 Regulations* came into force on 1 October 2006. The principal changes are that:

(*a*)   Dismissing an employee by reason of retirement is now a potentially discriminatory act, unless the employee is at or over the age of 65. Retirement of an employee below the age of 65 amounts to age discrimination, unless the retirement is a proportionate means of achieving a legitimate aim (*reg 30(2)* read with *reg 3(1)*). (The question of when a dismissal is 'by reason of retirement' is discussed further below.)

(*b*)   Employers are obliged to give employees written notice of the date upon which it is intended that they will retire. This notice must be given not more than one year and not less than six months before dismissal: *para 2(1), Sch 6, 2006 Regulations*. Employers are also required to notify employees of the right to make a request not to retire on that date. If an employer fails to give such notice, an employment tribunal may make an award of compensation of up to 8 week's pay subject up to the limit on a week's pay set out in *s 227(1)(b)* of the *Employment Rights Act 1996* (*para 11* of *Sch 6*).

(*c*)   An employer who has failed to give notice is under a continuing duty to do so until the 14th day before dismissal (*para 4* of *Sch 6*).

(*d*)   Employees have a statutory right to make a request to their employers not to retire on the intended retirement date. A request must be in writing and must be stated to be such a request. In any request, the employee must propose that his employment should continue indefinitely, for a stated period, or until a stated date. An employee is only be able to make one request. The request must be made within time limits. If the employer has given notice in accordance with (*c*) above, the employee must make the request more than three months but not more than six months before the intended date of retirement. If the employer has not complied with (*c*), then the employee may make a request not more than six months before the intended date of retirement (*para 5* of *Sch 6*).

(*e*)   Employers are under a duty to consider any such request (*para 6* of *Sch 6*). The employer is required to hold a meeting to discuss the request with the employee within a reasonable period after receiving it. Both the employer and the employee must take all reasonable steps to attend the meeting. The duty to hold a meeting does not apply if the employer and the employee agree that the employment will continue indefinitely, or for an agreed period, and the employer has given notice of this to the employee. If it is not practicable to hold a meeting within a reasonable period, the employer may consider the request without holding a meeting provided that he considers any representations made by the employee. The employer is then required to give the employee written and dated notice of the decision. If the employer decides to refuse the request, the notice must also confirm that the employer wishes to retire the employee, the date on which the dismissal shall take effect and how the decision might be appealed (*para 7* of *Sch 6*).

(*f*)   Employees are entitled to appeal in writing against a refusal to a request. If an employee appeals, the employer is required to hold a meeting with the employee to discuss the appeal (unless the appeal is upheld or this is not reasonably practicable). The employer must then notify the employee in writing of the decision on the appeal. There are fairly strict time limits for each of these stages (*para 8* of *Sch 6*).

The *Regulations* have removed the age limit on the right to complain of unfair dismissal. Instead, retirement is now a potentially fair reason for dismissal (see *s 98(2)(ba), ERA 1996*). In order for a 'retirement' dismissal to be fair, the employer must show that retirement is the reason for the dismissal and also that the dismissal was fair. These are not questions of fact which a tribunal may determine in all the circumstances. Instead, there are specific provisions determining when these conditions are met.

Is retirement the reason for the dismissal?

It is only when specified criteria are met that retirement is taken to be the reason for a dismissal. The specification relies on the concept 'normal retirement age'. This is defined to mean the age at which employees in the employer's undertaking who hold, or have held, the same kind of position as the employee are normally required to retire (*ERA, s 98ZH*). A body of case law had built up around the meaning of the slightly different phrase 'normal retiring age'. These authorities may be helpful in the context of the normal retirement age, although they are unlikely to be binding in the new context. For a helpful restatement of the principles concerned in determining the 'normal retiring age' by the Court of Appeal, see *Barclays Bank plc v O'Brien* [1994] IRLR 580

Retirement is taken to be the reason for a dismissal in the following circumstances:

(*a*)   the employee has no 'normal retirement age', the date of termination falls after the employee's 65th birthday, the employer has properly notified the employee of the intended retirement in accordance with *para 2* of *Sch 6* to the *2006 Regulations*, and the employment contract terminates on the intended date;

(*b*)   there is a 'normal retirement age', that age is 65 or higher, the date of termination falls after the employee reaches the normal retirement age, the employer has properly notified the employee and the employment contract terminates on the intended date; or

(*c*)   there is a 'normal retirement age' of under 65, this retirement age is justified, the date of termination is on or after the date when the employee reached this age, the employer has properly notified the employee, and the employment terminates on the intended date.

(See ERA 1996, ss 98ZA to 98ZE as inserted.)

42.3 Retirement

Retirement is not the reason for the dismissal if:

(*a*) the employee has no 'normal retirement age' and the date of termination falls before the date when the employee reaches the age of 65;

(*b*) the contract of employment terminates before the intended date of retirement (regardless of whether or not there is a 'normal retirement age', what that age is, whether or not the employee is over 65 or over the 'normal retirement age' and whether the employer has properly notified the employee.);

(*c*) there is a 'normal retirement age', and the date of termination falls before the date on which the employee reaches that age; or

(*d*) there is a 'normal retirement age' of under 65 and it constitutes unlawful discrimination under the *Regulations* for the employee to have that normal retirement age (ie it cannot be justified).

(See ERA 1996, ss 98ZA to 98ZE as inserted.)

It should be noted that, on the face of these provisions, if there is an unjustified normal retirement age of under 65, then an employer will *never* be able to retire an employee, even when that employee has reached the age of 65.

In other cases, the Tribunal (or court) is required to consider whether or not retirement was the reason for the dismissal more generally. In so doing, the Tribunal will have particular regard to:

(*a*) whether the employer informed the employee of the intended retirement more than 14 days before the intended date of retirement;

(*b*) how long before the notified retirement date the notification was given; and

(*c*) whether or not the employer followed the procedures relating to the duty to consider a request to work beyond retirement

(the *s 98ZF* of *ERA 1996* as inserted).

Was the dismissal fair?

If the reason or principal reason for a dismissal is retirement, the employee is regarded as unfairly dismissed if and only if there has been a failure on the part of the employer to comply with one or more of the following provisions of *Sch 6* to the *2006 Regulations*:

(*a*) the continuing duty to notify the employee of the retirement until 14 days before the intended date of retirement (*para 4*, if not already given under *para 2*);

(*b*) the duty to consider the employee's request not to be retired (*para 6* and *7*); and

(*c*) the duty to consider an appeal against the decision to refuse a request not to be retired (*para 8*).

In all other circumstances, a retirement dismissal will be fair.

As will be clear from these provisions, employers are now obliged to follow a precise and fairly rigorous procedure before retiring an employee. However, so long as the employer properly follows the procedure, it is unlikely that a retired employee will be able to bring a successful claim for unfair dismissal (or age discrimination).

See further AGE DISCRIMINATION (3).

42.4   **EARLY RETIREMENT**

There is no legal impediment to employees voluntarily retiring early, subject only to the giving of any notice required under the contract of employment. Where there is a pension scheme, of which the employee is a member, the scheme may provide for the drawing of a pension on early retirement, generally with the consent of the employer. Occupational pension schemes which meet the requirements for Inland Revenue approval (the vast majority do, since this is a condition for favourable tax treatment) are precluded from paying a pension earlier than age 50 except where retirement is on grounds of ill-health. For employees over 50, early retirement may be used as an inducement to accept redundancy, and pension scheme rules typically offer one or more of the following benefits:

(*a*)   immediate payment of the pension that would have been payable at pensionable age, without reduction for early payment;

(*b*)   commutation of part of the pension to a lump sum;

(*c*)   conferment of additional years of service in computing the pension; and

(*d*)   permitting the employee to divert all or part of a severance payment into the pension scheme to purchase added years.

The position of individuals depends on the detail of usually complex scheme rules, operating within limits defined by Inland Revenue requirements. The European Court of Justice has ruled (*Beckmann v Dynamco Whicheloe Macfarlane Ltd: C-164/00* [2002] IRLR 578) that benefits by way of payment of an immediate and/or augmented pension on termination of employment for redundancy are not 'old age, invalidity or survivors' benefits' within the meaning of the *Acquired Rights Directive 1977*, and accordingly the right to such benefits is preserved when an employee is transferred to a new employer as a result of a relevant transfer of the former employer's undertaking, or part thereof. The ECJ has reiterated these conclusions, in relation to voluntary early retirement, and confirmed their application to public sector pension schemes regulated by statutory provisions, in *Martin v South Bank University: C-4/01* [2004] IRLR 74. See also *reg 10* of the *Transfer of Undertakings* (*Protection of Employees*) *Regulations 2006*, in force from 6 April 2006 and TUPE (see TRANSFER OF UNDERTAKINGS (52)). This has particular practical significance where employees transfer from such public sector employers as the NHS as a result of the contracting out of services, since the responsibility for funding often very expensive early retirement or redundancy terms will fall on the transferee employer.

Ill-health retirement is frequently provided for in pension scheme rules. There is no standard set of criteria or procedures. Rules typically require medical evidence sufficient to satisfy the employer, the trustees or both that the employee is incapacitated from either performing any work or from his usual occupation. The requirement may be that the incapacity is expected or likely to be permanent, and rules may provide for the suspension of the payment of a pension (during the period until the employee reaches pensionable age) on evidence that he or she is again capable of work. For guidance as to the interpretation and application of criteria in scheme rules determining eligibility for ill-health retirement, see *Derby Daily Telegraph Ltd v Pensions Ombudsman* [1999] IRLR 476.

The benefits provided under the rules of pension schemes also vary considerably, but typically include immediate payment of an unreduced pension, sometimes with added years. The statutory pension schemes for police officers and firefighters provide for enhanced benefits, known as 'injury awards', where members retire on ill-health grounds as a result of an injury sustained in the course of duty. There are defined procedures for assessing the degree of incapacity (beyond incapacity for active police or fire service) and elaborate rights of appeal under each set of regulations.

Despite the pension advantages of ill-health retirement, if the employee objects to retiring, and if he or she has a disability within the *Disability Discrimination Act 1995*, the possibility that enforced retirement constitutes disability discrimination needs to be considered. See further DISABILITY DISCRIMINATION (10). Following 1 October 2006, ill-health retirement may now constitute age discrimination as discussed above and in AGE DISCRIMINATION (3).

Decisions whether to grant or refuse an ill-health pension are subject to limited control by the courts; good examples are *Harris v Lord Shuttleworth* [1994] ICR 991 on the correct interpretation of the definition of incapacity and *Mihlenstedt v Barclays Bank International Ltd* [1989] IRLR 522 on the employer's duty to act in good faith in assessing medical evidence of incapacity (discussed further at 42.11 below) and the *Derby Daily Telegraph* case (above) on the duty to construe the rules in a purposive and practical way.

42.5   **CHANGING THE RETIREMENT AGE**

Where the contract provides for a particular retirement age, the legal principles governing changes in terms of the contract of employment apply equally to any attempt to change the retirement age. In the absence of consent by the employees, or incorporation of an agreement reached through collective bargaining, a change cannot be unilaterally imposed through the contract. The failure of an employee to object to a change notified to him, as by a new statement of particulars of terms, does not amount to acceptance of the change by silence. This is most clearly so where the change has no immediate practical effect on the employee: *Aparau v Iceland Frozen Foods plc* [1996] IRLR 119.

This may have no practical consequences where the employer seeks to increase the retirement (as distinct from pension) age, since this would be no more than a promise to defer enforced retirement. Nor would a lowering of the age by unilateral notification, not accepted by the employee, prevent the employer from retiring an employee at the lower age by giving the contractual notice of termination. However, such a dismissal would in all probability be open to challenge as unfair, since the principal test of what is 'normal retirement age' within *ERA 1996, s 109(1)* is what the contract provides but see *Cross v British Airways*, above. From October 2006 onwards, it could also amount to unlawful age discrimination.

A unilateral reduction in the contractual retirement age imposed in breach of contract would not be effective to displace the presumption that the normal retirement age is the contractual retirement age. This is the effect of *Bratko v Beloit Walmsley Ltd* [1995] IRLR 629, where the EAT reviewed conflicting *dicta* in earlier Court of Appeal decisions. The recent EAT decision of *Royal Sun Alliance Insurance Group v Payne* [2005] IRLR 848, upheld *Bratko v Beloit Walmsley* and also rejected the arguments of an employer that it was an implied term of the claimant's employment contract that his contractual retirement age would be governed by the terms of the pension scheme.

It should also be noted that a term of a contract (including a contractual retirement age) is unenforceable against a person if it would otherwise constitute unlawful age discrimation against that person: see *para 1, Sch 5* of the *2006 Regulations.* Age discriminatory terms which discriminate against someone who is not a party to the contract are void.

Different considerations apply to changes in pensionable age under an occupational pension scheme. In relation to past service, such changes may be precluded by the rules of the scheme unless they are in all respects advantageous to the members affected. Changes designed to equalise pension ages between men and women following the ECJ's decision in *Barber v Guardian Royal Exchange Assurance Group: C-262/88* [1990] ICR 616 are, in addition, subject to restrictions arising from principles of EU law: *Smith v Avdel Systems Ltd: C-408/92* [1995] ICR 596; see further EQUAL PAY (24). Whilst these requirements do not prohibit a change that would have the effect, as regards future service, of 'levelling down' rights as a matter of European law, this is subject to the requirements of national law as to the validity of any change. The consent of individual employees would be required for a change in the pensionable age, even for benefits derived from future service, where that age is expressly or impliedly a term of the contract.

42.6 BENEFITS AFTER RETIREMENT

Employers may provide certain benefits to employees which continue beyond retirement. Even if the benefits are expressly provided to be discretionary they will nevertheless almost certainly be 'pay' in EU law: *Garland v British Rail Engineering Ltd* [1982] ICR 420, ECJ (concessionary travel facilities for families of retired employees); such benefits must therefore be provided without discrimination on grounds of sex.

If a benefit is contractual it must be provided, even if it becomes unduly expensive to continue its provision: *Baynham v Philips Electronics (UK) Ltd* (1995) IDS Brief 551 (private medical insurance during retirement). As there is no basis for compelling a former employee, who cannot be dismissed, to agree to abandon a continuing contractual right, the employer has no option but to 'buy out' the benefit or continue to provide it. The inclusion of such provisions in the contract of employment is therefore a matter requiring great caution.

42.7 PENSIONS

The law of pensions is outside the scope of this book. It is a large and complex area which it would not be practicable fully to summarise here. Pensions law rests mainly on the principles of the law of trusts (most pension schemes are administered, and the funds held, by trustees) and increasingly detailed statutory regulation. The principal legislation governing pension schemes is the *Pension Schemes Act 1993*, a consolidating Act, together with the *Pensions Act 1995*, a major reform implementing recommendations of the Goode Committee which was set up in the wake of the Maxwell scandal. In addition, stakeholder pension schemes, which became available from April 2001, are the subject of *Part I* of the *Welfare Reform and Pensions Act 1999* and supporting Regulations: see 42.8 below for brief details.

Following a review by the Department for Work and Pensions of the structure of pensions legislation, a major new piece of legislation, the *Pensions Act 2004* was introduced. The Act established a new Pensions Regulator (replacing the Occupational Pensions Regulatory Authority) with a remit including the prevention of fraud and ensuring the proper funding of pension schemes and a Board of the Pension Protection Fund. The Board has responsibility for administering a compensation scheme for employees in private sector pension schemes, who risk losing accrued pension rights if their employer becomes insolvent and the pension scheme is insufficiently funded. Other provisions include a requirement for the transferee employer following a transfer within the *Transfer of Undertakings (Protection of Employment) Regulations 2006* to provide those employees who have transferred with pension benefits for future service broadly comparable with those previously enjoyed.

Six areas of particular relevance to employment are dealt with below: stakeholder pensions; sex discrimination and pension benefits; the application of the *Disability Discrimination Act 1995* to pension rights; the rights of members to elect trustees under the *Pensions Act 1995* and the legal protection of employee trustees; employers' duties in respect of pension schemes; and the machinery available to resolve employees' disputes and grievances about pension rights. Brief notes about some of the principal features of pension schemes, and pension terminology are given first. A helpful summary of the various types of state and occupational pensions is given in the booklet *'Compensation for loss of Pension Rights'* (D Sneath, C Sara, C Daykin and A Gallop, 3rd edn, TSO 2003).

Pension schemes may be described as occupational or personal. The growth of personal pension schemes for employees followed the statutory prohibition on compulsory membership of occupational pension schemes for employees introduced by the *Social Security Act 1986.*

Personal pension schemes are money purchase funds invested by the pension provider on behalf of the individual and used to purchase an annuity at retirement. Within statutory limits employee contributions are tax deductible. Employers may agree to make contributions, but are under no obligation to match contributions they would have made on the employee's behalf to the *occupational pension scheme.*

Occupational pension schemes may be *statutory* (the major public sector schemes covering a quarter of the employed workforce, principally the civil service and armed forces, local government and NHS workers, teachers and the police and fire service, under the *Superannuation Act 1972* and specific statutory regulations) or established by trust deed, to which the scheme rules are usually appended. They may be either *defined benefit*, also referred to as *final salary*, schemes, or *money purchase* schemes. The former provide benefits based on pensionable salary and years of service, normally either 1/60 or 1/80 of pensionable salary for each year of pensionable service. A lump sum retirement benefit may be provided, in addition to pension based on 1/80 of salary, or by commuting the capital value of part of the pension in 1/60 schemes (subject to limits imposed by the Inland Revenue). All the principal statutory public sector schemes are final salary schemes.

All major public sector schemes and most private sector schemes also provide for a (usually reduced) pension to be payable to a surviving spouse, often referred to as *survivor's benefit*. Some schemes extend the coverage of survivors' benefits to unmarried partners. In such cases, it would be unlawful to limit the benefit to partners of the opposite sex to the member concerned (see the *Employment Equality (Sexual Orientation) Regulations 2003, reg 9A* and *Sch 1A*); but the restriction of benefits to the deceased member's spouse remains lawful by virtue of *reg 25*. The European Court has confirmed that the 'spouse only' limitation on survivors' benefits is compatible with EU equal pay requirements, provided that special provision is made for the rights of transsexuals, who cannot marry in their acquired gender: *KB v National Health Service Pensions Agency: C-117/01* [2004] IRLR 240.

Money purchase schemes (also referred to as *defined contribution* schemes) have fixed rates of contribution, and benefits are purchased according to market conditions from the investment yield of the contributions.

Defined benefit schemes are funded by employer and employee contributions. Employees contribute a fixed percentage of salary and other pensionable earnings. Some schemes are non-contributory. The employer contributes the balance required to fund the scheme sufficiently, in accordance with an actuarial review of the liabilities of the scheme conducted at regular intervals. If the scheme is in surplus, the employer's contributions may be temporarily suspended (a 'pensions holiday'). There are complex rules, largely outside the scope of this book, as to the permissible uses of pension fund surpluses; see 41.12 for the most important cases on this.

Pensionable salary is the reference point for the calculation both of benefits under a defined benefit scheme and employee contributions. What earnings fall to be treated as pensionable is primarily a matter for the rules of the particular scheme; normally this will cover basic salary, but the position may be more complex where total pay is made up of a number of additional components such as shift allowances, production bonuses and other allowances. In *Newham London Borough Council v Skingle* [2003] EWCA Civ 280, [2003] ICR 1008, the Court of Appeal held that pensionable salary for the purpose of the *Local Government Pension Scheme Regulations 1997* included overtime payments, but only where, as in the instant case, the overtime was in effect obligatory on the employee, a school caretaker, who had been required to perform duties out of normal working hours by the nature of his job.

Schemes generally provide for employees to purchase additional years of pensionable service, up to the scheme maximum, by making *additional voluntary contributions* ('AVCs') up to the overall permitted maximum of 15% of pensionable earnings. (These are distinct from *free-standing additional voluntary contributions* ('FSAVCs') which are either single payment or periodic contribution personal pension schemes marketed by pension companies and purchased direct by employees, using the balance of tax relief available to the employee and not used up by contributions to the employer's occupational scheme.)

Pension schemes may provide additional benefits, including (as well as survivors' benefits as described above) pensions for surviving children or other dependants. Death in service benefit, in effect life insurance, of up to a maximum of four times pensionable salary, is commonly provided. The availability of these benefits, and of increases in benefits provided, is a matter primarily for the rules of the particular scheme, but increasingly the statutory framework of approved pension schemes lays down not only maximum benefits permitted within the framework of a favourable tax regime, but minimum standards that must be met.

Contributions to personal pension schemes attract tax relief up to limits which vary with age and salary (or taxable profits for the self-employed) and according to the type of pension scheme. A major simplification of the legal framework for pension contributions has been introduced by the *Finance Act 2004*, to take effect from 6 April 2006. Under this legislation, individuals will be able to accumulate a pension fund totalling up to £1.5 million without tax liability, and a maximum of £215,000 of contributions in any one tax year will attract tax relief. The ceiling on tax exempt funds (which will be indexed to inflation) will apply also to the value attributed to any rights in a defined benefit scheme.

The value of pension funds is necessarily dependent on the underlying value of investments in which the funds are held, and the amount of pension that can be bought from a fund of a given value depends on current annuity rates, which are lower for women than for men owing to differences in life expectancy (it is understood that a proposal by the European Commission to extend the *Equal Treatment Directive,* which would have the effect of prohibiting such gender-based differentiation, is not to be proceeded with).

Recent sharp falls in the values of equities, following a steady decline in the rate of annuities which can be purchased on the realisation of pension fund investments, have led many major employers to conclude that the provision of defined benefit pension schemes has become too expensive. Accordingly employers have, in significant numbers, adopted policies of closing their defined benefit schemes to new entrants, offering instead to contribute to new defined contribution schemes. Less commonly but more controversially, some employers have sought the closure of their defined benefit schemes in relation to future service of current members. The legality of such a step may be open to challenge, but whether it is challengeable in any particular case will depend on the precise terms of the employees' contracts, and of the pension scheme rules. A further distinction is that the rights earned by past service are likely to be protected by the rules of the Scheme from any retrospective adverse change, whereas rights to be accrued by future service are likely only to be protected (if at all) as a matter of contract. There is a general consensus that the benefits available under a defined benefit scheme are of greater value to employees than the alternative of money purchase scheme membership.

A different but related matter of concern has arisen in a number of cases where a pension scheme has been wound up following the insolvency of the employer. The rules of each scheme determine the order in which claims on the scheme must be met in such circumstances; typically these require that the claims of those already in receipt of a pension must be met first. If the scheme is in deficit (which is possible up to a permitted margin, and more likely at a time of declining share prices) this may leave a serious shortfall for employees who were active (ie contributing) members of the scheme at the date of its closure, whose pensions may be dramatically reduced as a result. The Pensions Act 2004 addressed this problem in two ways, by changing the priorities required to be followed in distributing the scheme assets, and by creating a compensation scheme for employees who lose accrued pension rights. This compensation scheme applies with a degree of retrospectivity.

The *members* of a pension scheme are those employees who, being eligible, have elected to join the scheme, retired employees in receipt of a pension, and those former employees who have retained the right to a deferred pension payable at pensionable age. Employees who leave the service of the employer may withdraw their contributions, but only if pensionable service is under two years, or transfer the value to another employer's scheme or a personal pension. In either case the employee ceases to be a member of the first scheme. *Transfer values* are calculated by reference to actuarial valuations, but actual criteria depend on the rules of each scheme. A lump-sum payment is made to the new scheme which gives credit for years of service depending on its own advisers' computations of the cost of purchasing service. *Transfer values* may not therefore fully reflect accrued service. Further, the actuarial factors used include mortality tables reflecting the different life expectancy of, and therefore different cost of providing pensions for, each sex, so that transfer values may differ according to sex. The ECJ has held that this does not contravene *art 141* (formerly *art 119*) of the *Treaty of Rome* (*Coloroll Pension Trustees Ltd v Russell: C-200/91* [1995] ICR 179). This exception is preserved by the UK legislation giving effect to EU law (see 24.17 EQUAL PAY for details). The same consequences, and legal exceptions, apply to the value attributed, in terms of additional years of service, to AVCs. (The proposed changes to the *Equal Treatment Directive* which would affect the use of gender-based actuarial factors now appear unlikely to be adopted: see above.)

The *State Earnings Related Pension Scheme* ('SERPS'), established in 1975, was designed as a fallback for employees who do not benefit from occupational pensions. Pension schemes which met prescribed minimum standards could apply to be *contracted out* of SERPS. *Contracting out* was the norm for larger schemes, not least because both employer and employee paid lower rates of National Insurance if the employee was in a contracted-out scheme. In place of the SERPS pension the scheme was required to assure a *Guaranteed Minimum Pension,* protected by more stringent rules as to indexation and preservation where benefits are transferred or commuted. With effect from April 2002, SERPS has been replaced, but for future earnings only, by the *State Second Pension.* Because the change is not retrospective, rights under SERPS will exist, in preserved form, for very many years. The State Second Pension accrues at different rates on banded earnings between the National Insurance lower earnings limit (£4,368) and £12,500, £12,501 and £28,764, and £28,765 and the National Insurance upper earnings limit (£33,500). The figures quoted are for 2006–2007, and are reviewed annually. Additionally, there are some credits for earnings for people with a long-term illness or disability.

42.8 Stakeholder pensions

The legislation for this relatively new form of pension is *Part I* of the *Welfare Reform and Pensions Act 1999* (which is largely enabling) and the *Stakeholder Pensions Scheme Regulations 2000 (SI 2000/1403)* as amended. The intention behind these pensions (which became available in April 2001) was to encourage individuals, particularly those with modest earnings, and who are not members of occupational pension schemes, to make provision for their retirement. Stakeholder pensions are private sector schemes but subject to registration, minimum standards of performance and approved schemes of governance. Schemes are required to be flexible, so that contributions can be suspended or varied, and any individual who is not contributing to a contracted out occupational pension scheme, including minors and those not in employment, can contribute up to a fixed amount per year. Contributions are made net of standard rate income tax, which is made up by the State, even if the individual is not a taxpayer. If earnings are sufficient, contributions in excess of the fixed amount a year gross can be made, with corresponding tax relief.

Employers may, but cannot be obliged to, contribute to individual employees' pensions. However, employers with five or more employees who do not have a contracted-out occupational pension scheme for which all employees (with very limited exceptions) are eligible must designate a stakeholder scheme as, effectively, the preferred scheme: *s 3, Welfare Reform and Pensions Act 1999.* The obligations on employers in relation to a designated scheme (which must be one available to all the employer's employees) include:

(*a*) consulting the employees or their representatives as to the choice of scheme;

(*b*) supplying all employees with information about the scheme;

(*c*) affording representatives of the scheme provide reasonable access to employees to provide information about the scheme; and (*d*) agreeing on request to collect employees' contributions from pay and remit them to the scheme.

There are limited exemptions, principally for employers with fewer than five employees, and in respect of some short-term employment. Contravention of any of these obligations renders the employer liable to civil penalties under *s 10* of the *Pensions Act 1995* of up to £5,000 in relation to an individual or £50,000 in other cases: such penalties are imposed by the Pensions Regulator (see 42.14 below).

Employers designating a particular stakeholder scheme are exempted from any duty to investigate or assess the performance of the scheme (*s 3(8) Welfare Reform and Pensions Act 1999*).

The absence of any requirement for employers to contribute to employees' stakeholder pensions has contributed to a disappointing take-up of the new facility, and possible further reforms in this area include an obligation on employers to contribute, or match employee contributions up to, a fixed percentage of pensionable salary.

42.9 Sex discrimination and pension benefits

Pension schemes are subject to important restrictions on discrimination in the provision of benefits and terms of membership. In addition to the application of rules of sex equality and equal pay between the sexes, the *Social Security Act 1989* ('*SSA 1989*'), *Sch 5*, gives protection to women who take paid maternity leave, and members of both sexes who take paid parental leave. Periods of paid maternity leave since 23 June 1994 must count as pensionable service. 'Paid' includes receipt of flat-rate Statutory Maternity Pay. However, contributions by employees may not be required to exceed the relevant percentage of pensionable salary applicable to employees generally, assessed on actual pay. The Pensions Act 2004 extends the provisions of *SSA 1989* to periods of statutory paid paternity and adoption leave. The *SSA 1989* does not provide for employer contributions; in a defined benefit scheme the employer is likely to pay the applicable percentage of actual pay, but a significant additional pension burden would affect the overall requirements certified by the actuary on a scheme valuation. In a money purchase scheme the position appears to be that the employer must make up any shortfall.

See generally DISCRIMINATION AND EQUAL OPPORTUNITIES – I (12) and EQUAL PAY (24).

The *SSA 1989* does not require unpaid maternity or parental leave to count as pensionable service. It is therefore a matter for the scheme rules as to whether any such periods are counted, and if so how they are funded. The effect of the decision of the ECJ in *Gillespie v Northern Health and Social Services Board* [1996] IRLR 214 is that exclusion of unpaid leave from service does not contravene either *art 141* or the EU *Equal Pay* or *Equal Treatment Directives*.

However, the ECJ has ruled in *Boyle v Equal Opportunities Commission: C-411/96* [1998] IRLR 717 that it is a breach of the *Pregnant Workers Directive* (*92/85*) to exclude from pensionable service any part of the core 14 weeks' maternity leave conferred by the *Directive*, whether it is paid or unpaid. The statutory framework for ordinary maternity leave, which is (since April 2003) a maximum of 26 weeks, requires the continuation of all contractual terms and conditions except those concerning remuneration (*ERA 1996, s 71(4),(5)*); 'remuneration' is defined by the *Maternity and Parental Leave, etc Regulations 1999* (*SI 1999/3312*), *reg 9(3)* as limited to sums payable by way of wages or salary, and therefore not including contributions by the employer to the pension fund. This achieves the implementation of the *Boyle* decision, but for a longer period of maternity leave. All periods of statutory paid paternity and adoption leave which began on or after 6 April 2005 are treated in the same way as maternity leave (*ss 5A* and *5B* of the *Social Security Act 1989* as inserted by the *Pensions Act 2004*).

The ECJ has also ruled that a reduction in the pension of civil servants who have worked part time contravened *art 141* since it affected a considerably higher proportion of women than men, if the reduction in the pension was greater than the proportion of the reduction of working hours: *Schönheit v Stadt Frankfurt Am Main* [2004] IRLR 983.

42.10 **Disability discrimination and pension benefits**

The *Disability Discrimination Act 1995* (*'DDA 1995'*) was extensively amended with effect from 1 October 2004. Under the provisions of the *DDA* as amended, *s 4G* applies the prohibition on discrimination against disabled persons and those who have had a disability to occupational pension schemes. All occupational pension schemes are made subject to an overriding 'non-discrimination rule' prohibiting the trustees and managers from discriminating against disabled (or formerly disabled) members or prospective members of the scheme. This provision applies only in relation to rights accruing from service on or after 1 October 2004; less stringent but broadly equivalent provisions which applied under the unamended Act continue to govern the position for earlier periods of service. *Section 4G* also enables trustees to amend scheme rules by simple resolution in order to remove any provisions which would have a discriminatory effect contrary to the non-discrimination rule. The employer is in turn prohibited from unlawful discrimination in relation to terms of employment, opportunities for or access to benefits, and subjecting an employee to any detriment (*DDA 1995, s 4(1), (2)*).

Discrimination is defined by *DDA 1995, s 3A(1)* as less favourable treatment of a person for a reason related to his or her disability (or former disability) which the discriminator cannot justify. In relation to the application of justification to pensions, the *Disability Discrimination (Employment) Regulations 1996* (*SI 1996/1456*), which made specific provisions for deemed justification, were revoked as from 1 October 2004. This has the effect of removing the automatic justification of provisions excluding disabled employees from access to pension-related benefits on health grounds (eg the greater risk of the employee qualifying for benefits such as death in service payments). Justification of such exclusions on a case by case basis would still be possible.

The *DDA 1995* also imposes a duty on employers in certain circumstances to make reasonable adjustments, in favour of a disabled employee, to any arrangements made by or on behalf of the employer (*DDA 1995, s 4A(1)*). A similar requirement is imposed on trustees of pension schemes by *s 4H*, which gives as an example of possible adjustments the alteration of a provision in the scheme rules.

Sections 4I and *4J* make provision for employees alleging a breach of the non-discrimination rule or a failure to make reasonable adjustments to institute proceedings against the trustees in an employment tribunal. The relevant employer has a right to be joined as a party to the proceedings. The tribunal has power to make a declaration as to the claimant's rights (eg to membership of the scheme, or to be given access to particular benefits under the scheme), and to award compensation for injury to feelings. It can also make recommendations for remedial action, but cannot award compensation for financial loss, except by way of an award of further compensation if the trustees fail to implement the recommendations: see *ss 4I, 4J, 17A(5)*.

(See generally DISABILITY DISCRIMINATION (10).)

42.11 **Age discrimination and pension benefits**

As stated above, the *Employment Equality (Age) Regulations 2006* ('*2006 Regulations*') came into force on 1 October 2006. Under *reg 11*, it is unlawful for the trustees or managers of an occupational pension scheme to discriminate against a member or prospective member of the scheme in carrying out any of their functions in relation to it. In particular, it will be unlawful to discriminate in their functions relating to the admission of members to the scheme and the treatment of members of it. However, this does not apply in relation to rights accrued or benefits payable in respect of periods of service prior to 1 October 2006. It is also be unlawful for the trustees or managers, in relation to the scheme, to subject members or prospective members to harassment.

Schedule 2 to the *2006 Regulations* sets out detailed provisions in relation to pensions including a list of practices that are apparently exempted. It should be noted that it is not certain that the exemptions are lawful in the light of United Kingdom's duties under the *Equality Directive*. This is a difficult question of European and domestic law which is not addressed here in full. The *2006 Regulations* themselves state that the inclusion of a practice in the list of exemptions does not mean that it would otherwise be unlawful.

The following are, in summary, the practices which are exempted by *Sch 2* and so are lawful on the face of the *2006 Regulations* in the case of occupational pensions (personal pensions are not addressed here):

(*a*)   provisions which treat members or potential members of a scheme differently on the grounds of their length of service with an employer so long as that length of service is less than five years (*para 3A, Sch 2*);

(*b*)   length of service criteria of greater than five years, if it reasonably appears to the employer that this meets a business need (with regard to action by trustees or managers, they may rely on a confirmation by the employer-)(*para 3A(2) , Sch 2*);

(*c*)   setting minimum or maximum ages for admission, including different ages for different groups or categories of worker (*para 7(a), Part 2, Sch 2*);

(*d*)   setting a minimum level of pensionable pay for admission (provided this is not above one and a half times the lower earnings limit in *s 5(1)* of the *Social Security Contributions and Benefits Act 1992*, does not exceed an amount calculated by reference to the lower earnings limit where the aim is more or less to reflect the amount of the basic state retirement pension; or an amount calculated more or less to reflect the amount of the basic statement retirement pension plus the additional state retirement pension-)(*para 7(b), Part 2, Sch 2*);

(*e*)   the use of age criteria in actuarial calculations (*para 8*);

(*f*)   differences in contributions attributable to differences in pensionable pay (*para 9*);

(*g*)   under money purchase arrangements, different rates of contributions according to age where the aim is to equalise, or make more nearly equal, the amount of benefit to which members of different ages who are otherwise in comparable situations will become entitled (*para 10(a)*);

(*h*)   under money purchase arrangements, equal rates of contributions irrespective of age (*para 10(b)*);

(*i*)   under money purchase arrangements, any limitation on any employer contributions in respect of a member or member contributions by reference to a maximum level of pensionable pay (*para 10(c)*);

(*j*)   under defined benefits arrangements, different rates of contributions according to age to the extent that each year of pensionable service entitles members in a comparable situation to accrue the right to defined benefits based on the same fraction of pensionable pay, and the aim of setting the different rates is to reflect the increasing cost of providing the defined benefits in respect of members as they get older (*para 11*);

(k)   under defined benefit arrangements, any limitation on employer contributions in respect of a member or member contributions by reference to a maximum level of pensionable pay (*para 11A*);

(*l*)   a minimum age for entitlement to or payment of any age related benefit to a member, provided that, in the case of any age-related benefit paid under a defined benefits arrangement before any early retirement pivot age, this benefit is subject to actuarial reduction for early receipt, and the member is not credited with additional periods of pensionable service (except where certain other exemptions for minimum ages for entitlement apply) (*para 12*);

(*m*)   a minimum age for entitlement to or payment of any age-related benefits under a defined scheme where it is not made subject to actuarial reduction for early receipt and/or it results from crediting the member with additional period of pensionable service, where a worker is an active or prospective member of the scheme as at 1 December 2006, the benefit may be paid at a minimum age with or without consent and the age related benefit is enhanced in a specified manner (*para 13*);

(*n*)   a minimum age for payment or entitlement to a particular age related benefit on grounds of redundancy where it is enhanced in a specified manner and paid either with or without consent (*para 13B*);

(*o*)   an early retirement or late retirement pivot age, including different ages for different groups or categories and any early retirement pivot age or later retirement pivot age for deferred members which is different than for active members (*para 14*);

(*p*)   a minimum age for any member of a scheme for payment or entitlement to a particular age related benefit on grounds of ill health where the age related benefit is enhanced in a specified manner and paid with or without consent (*para 15*);

(*q*)   the calculation of any death benefit payable in respect of a member by reference to some or all of the years of prospective pensionable service a member would have completed if he had remained in service until normal pension age or by reference to a fixed number of years of prospective pensionable service, death benefits calculated by reference to the period remaining in a pension guarantee period and any difference between death benefits between those who die before, on or after normal pension age in respect of deferred members (*para 15A*);

(*r*)   reducing a rate of pension to which a pensioner member is entitled at any time between age 60 and 65 by an amount not exceeding the relevant state retirement pension rate or the rate of the pension on payment where the relevant state retirement pension is greater (*para 16(1)*);

(*s*)   entitling a member, from the date he is entitled to present payment of a pension from a scheme, to an additional amount of pension which does not exceed the amount of the basic state retirement pension plus the additional state retirement pension that would be payable at state pension age (*para 16(1)*);

(*t*)   disentitling a member on reaching state pension age from being able to receive an additional amount of pension which does not exceed the amount of the basic state retirement pension plus the additional state retirement pension that would be payable at state pension age (*para 16(1)*);

(*u*)   the actuarial reduction of any pension payable from a scheme in consequence of a member's death to any dependent of the member where the dependent is more than a specified number of years younger than the member (*para 17*);

(*v*)   discontinuing life assurance to pensioner members who have retired from the scheme on ill health grounds once they reach the normal retirement age or, if none, at the age of 65 (*para 18*);

(*w*)   differences in the amount of any age-related benefit or death benefit attributable to differing lengths of service, so long as members in a comparable situation are entitled to accrue rights based upon the same fraction of pensionable pay (*para 19*);

(*x*)   certain differences in the fraction of pensionable pay at which any age related benefit accrues, or the amount of death benefit, or age related benefits, where the aim is to give members in a comparable situation the right to the same fraction proportion or multiple of pensionable pay without regard to pensionable service, and provided that each continues in pensionable service until normal pension age (*para 19A*);

(*y*)   where the aim is as in (s) above, setting a maximum amount of age related benefits or death benefit equal to a fraction, proportion or multiple of the member's pensionable pay, or a minimum period of pensionable service (*para 19A(1) and (4)*);

(*z*)   where the aim is as in (s) above, setting different rates of member or employer contributions according to the age of the members where, for each year of pensionable service, members in comparable situations accrue different fractions of pensionable pay (*para 19B*);

(*aa*)   differences in the amount of age-related benefits or death benefits payable so far as this is attributable to differences in pensionable pay (*para 20*);

(*bb*)   limiting the amount of a benefit where this results from imposing a maximum number of years of service by reference to which the benefit is calculated and/or where it arises from imposing a maximum amount on the age related benefit or death benefit equal to a fraction, proportion or multiple of pensionable pay (*para 21*);

(*cc*)   limiting age related benefits or death benefits to those entitled to short service benefit (*para 22*);

(*dd*) excluding from a calculation of pensionable pay an amount which does not exceed one and a half times the lower earning limit, aimed to reflect the basic state retirement pension, or calculated to reflect the basic state retirement pension plus the additional state retirement pension (*para 23*);

(*ee*) differences in age related or death benefits attributable to accrual of age related benefit at a higher fraction for pensionable pay over the upper limit to reflect the additional state retirement pension (*para 23A*);

(*ff*) limiting the amount of a benefit where this relates to all members joining or eligible to join on, after or before a particular date and which results from imposing a maximum level of pensionable pay by reference to which such benefit is calculated (*para 24*);

(*gg*) closing a scheme, or a section of a scheme to workers who have not already joined it (*paras 25* and *25A*);

(*hh*) increases of pensions in payment which are made only to members over 55 (*para 26*);

(*ii*) different rates of increase of pensions for members of different ages (or of members who have contributed for different period) to maintain the relative value of members' pensions (*paras 27* and *28*);

(*jj*) applying an age limit for transfer of the value of accrued rights, provided that this is not more than one year before the normal pension age (*para 29*); and

(*kk*) where necessary to secure any tax relief or exemption available under *Part 4* of the *Finance Act 2004* or to prevent any charge to tax arising.

Part 3 of *Sch 2* sets out exceptions relating to contributions by employers to personal pension schemes. In particular, it will be lawful for employers to pay different rates of contributions according to the age of the workers in respect of whom contributions are made where this is done to equalise, or make more nearly equal, the amount of benefit to which workers of different ages who are otherwise in a comparable situation will become entitled. It is also lawful to make different rates of contribution in respect of different workers to the extent that this is attributable to differences in remuneration payable to the workers.

Pursuant to *para 2(1)* of *Sch 2*, every occupational pension scheme will be treated as including a non-discrimination rule. Further, trustees or managers of occupational pension schemes are given powers to alter the scheme so as to secure conformity with the non-discrimination rule (*para 2(2), Sch 2*).

Discrimination is defined by *reg 3(1)* as less favourable treatment on the grounds of age which cannot be justified. Indirect discrimination is defined as the application of a provision, criterion or practice which is equally applied to all age groups but puts someone in a particular age group at a particular disadvantage which cannot be justified.

Finally, *Sch 2* makes provision in relation to the procedures by which certain complaints relating to occupational pension schemes can be presented to an employment tribunal. Where a member or prospective member of a pension scheme presents a complaint to the employment tribunal, the employer is treated as a party and is entitled to be heard by the tribunal (*para 5, Sch 2*). The tribunal, if it finds a complaint well-founded, may make an order declaring that the complainant has a right to be admitted to the scheme or to membership of the scheme without discrimination (*para 6 of Sch 2*). In such cases, the tribunal may not make an order for compensation for age discrimination except for injury to feelings or where a respondent fails to comply with a recommendation (*para 6(4), Sch 2*).

For more on age discrimination, see AGE DISCRIMINATION (3)

42.12 **Employee pension trustees**

Most pension schemes provide for the appointment by the employer of the trustees of the scheme. Many schemes provide for the appointment of a trustee company as sole trustee; its directors are in such cases usually nominated by the employer. Despite the stringent legal obligations of trustees to the members of the scheme, concern that in practice trustees are often vulnerable to pressure from the employer to take decisions in the employer's interest led to a significant change in the law.

The *Pensions Act 1995, ss 16–21* required the majority of occupational pension schemes established under a trust ('trust schemes' – see *s 124*) to have at least a prescribed minimum number of trustees elected by members of the scheme. *Sections 16 to 21* of the *Pensions Act 1995,* and the associated *Occupational Pension Schemes (Member-nominated Trustees and Directors) Regulations 1996 (SI 1996/1216)* were repealed as from 6 April 2006.

The new *ss 241–242* of the *Pensions Act 2004* require a pension scheme established under a trust to have at least one third of its trustees to be member-nominated, and the same minimum proportion of member-nominated directors where a trust company is the sole trustee. Further, the Secretary of State now has the power (by order) to increase the proportion to a half. New regulations, the *Occupational Pension Schemes (Member-nominated Trustees and Directors) Regulations 2006 (SI 2006/714)* also came into force on 6 April 2006. These Regulations set out detailed exceptions to the requirement for member-nominated trustees and member-nominated directors of corporate trustees for certain schemes, including small schemes and those that have few members.

The *Pensions Act 2004* also contains provisions requiring all individual trustees and corporate trustees to have knowledge and understanding of key documents and legal principles. These too came into force on 6 April 2006.

Member-nominated trustees need not all be employees, but in practice most will be. Those who are employees have the right to be permitted to take reasonable time off for training in their duties and for the performance of those duties, and to be paid for such time off (*ERA 1996, ss 58–60,* consolidating provisions introduced by the *Pensions Act 1995*). There is no equivalent right for candidates for election. Employee trustees are also protected from suffering detriment short of dismissal by reason of their performance or proposed performance of their functions as such (*ERA 1996, s 46*) and from dismissal for that reason (*ERA 1996, s 102*). The ambit of these provisions is similar to, but not identical to, the statutory rights and protection given to officials of an independent trade union and to statutory safety representatives and representatives of employee safety; see 47.2 and 47.9 TIME OFF WORK.

Member-nominated trustees have the same duties in law to the beneficiaries of the trust funds as other trustees. Where (as will often be the case in practice) the nominated trustees have been put forward as candidates by trade unions there is a potential for conflict between their obligations as trustees and advocacy of union policy on such matters as ethical investment of funds or non-investment in competitor industries: see for a good practical example *Cowan v Scargill* [1984] ICR 646 (resolving the conflict in favour of the trustee obligations).

42.13   Employers' duties in respect of pension schemes

The obligations of pension trustees in relation to the management of funds, the alteration of rules and decisions as to individual cases are outside the scope of this book. A helpful judicial discussion of the position is to be found in *Stannard v Fisons Pension Trust Ltd* [1992] IRLR 27 (and see *Hillsdown Holdings plc v Pensions Ombudsman* [1997] 1 All ER 862, where the employer was ordered to return to the pension fund a surplus improperly paid out by the trustees). However, there have also been a number of important recent decisions dealing with the rights and obligations of employers as opposed to trustees.

In *Mihlenstedt v Barclays Bank International Ltd* [1989] IRLR 522, the Court of Appeal held that, where a contract of employment provides for membership of a pension scheme, there is an implied obligation upon the employer to discharge his functions under the scheme in good faith and, so far as lies within his power, to procure the scheme's benefits for the employee.

In *Mettoy Pension Trustees Ltd v Evans* [1991] 2 All ER 513, it was held that, where an employer was given a discretion under the rules of the scheme as to how certain surplus funds were to be applied, that was to be treated as a fiduciary power: the employer was under a duty to the objects of the power (the beneficiaries under the scheme) to consider whether and how to exercise it, and (presumably) to do so fairly and in good faith. Similarly, it was held in *Imperial Group Pension Trust Ltd v Imperial Tobacco Ltd* [1991] ICR 524 that an employer's power under the rules of the scheme to give or withhold consent to an amendment of the rules had to be exercised in good faith, and the employer could only have regard to his own financial interests to the extent that to do so was consistent with that obligation of good faith. Thus the employer's rights had to be exercised with a view to the efficient running of the scheme, and not for the collateral purpose of forcing its members to give up their accrued rights. The Vice-Chancellor based this conclusion upon the employer's implied obligation to maintain the trust and confidence of its employees (see 8.13 CONTRACT OF EMPLOYMENT). However, in *British Coal Corpn v British Coal Trustees Ltd* [1994] ICR 537 Vinelott J held that whilst the duty to act in good faith in relation to amendments was related to the duty applicable in cases of distribution of a surplus, it was not a fiduciary duty in the full sense. He found that it could not be said that *any* exercise of the relevant power of amendment had to be invalid if and insofar as the amendment might benefit the employer directly or indirectly.

The most recent decision on the question of recovery by the employer of surplus pension funds is *National Grid Co plc v Mayes* [2001] UKHL 20, [2001] ICR 544, upholding the right of the employer to appropriate a substantial surplus in the pension fund to meet debts owed by it to the fund. This case turned principally on the construction of the particular rules, and does not lay down any new general principles.

Where the pension scheme rules afford a benefit to employee members which is only available subject to the employee making an application or taking steps which necessitate being aware of the availability of and conditions for the benefit, the employer is under an applied contractual duty to draw to employees' attention the benefit and the necessity to take action to obtain or preserve it: *Scally v Southern Health and Social Services Board* [1991] ICR 771. An extension of this approach was shown in *Aspden v Webbs Poultry and Meat Group (Holdings) Ltd*

[1996] IRLR 521, where the High Court held that an express term permitting dismissal on notice was subject to an implied term that it would not be used so as to defeat the employee's claim to disability benefits also provided for by the contract. This reasoning would apply equally to ill-health pension benefits. The implied term applied in *Aspden* received support, *obiter*, in the Court of Appeal in *Brompton v AOC International Ltd* [1997] IRLR 639 at 643, but was given a more limited construction in *Hill v General Accident Fire and Life Assurance Co plc* [1998] IRLR 641. See also *Villella v MFI Furniture Centres Ltd* [1999] IRLR 468.

The limits to the principle established by *Scally* are shown in *University of Nottingham v Eyett* [1999] IRLR 87: where an employee is aware of his entitlement to a benefit and is taking a decision as to how to maximise it, the employer is not under a positive duty to warn him that he has not chosen the most advantageous way. *Eyett* was approved and applied in the Court of Appeal in *Outram v Academy Plastics* [2000] IRLR 499, where a claim that employers owed a duty of care to an employee who had resigned after 20 years' service and later re-joined the employer, to advise him to re-join the employer's pension scheme, was struck out as having no prospect of success. Two points were emphasised: the established law that trustees of a pension scheme do not owe a duty of care to advise scheme members faced with choices about pension matters; and the principle (confirmed in *Scally*) that there cannot be any wider duty owed by an employer to an employee in tort than that owed in contract.

An employer answering queries from pension scheme trustees about a former employee's work record owes no duty of care to that employee which could make him liable for damages in negligence (*Petch v Customs and Excise Comrs* [1993] ICR 789; but cf *Spring v Guardian Assurance plc* [1994] ICR 596, referred to in 40.4 REFERENCES).

42.14 Claims and disputes over pension rights

Some employees' claims in relation to pension rights may be taken to an employment tribunal. These include claims in respect of membership or benefits made under the *Equal Pay Act 1970*, as applied to pensions by the *Pensions Act 1995, s 62* and the *Occupational Pension Schemes (Equal Treatment) Regulations 1995 (SI 1995/3183)* and claims under the *DDA 1995 and the Employment Equality (Age) Regulations 2006* (in force from 1 October 2006) . Such claims may be made in appropriate cases against the trustees as well as (or instead of) the employer (see 42.9 above).

In addition, employees' rights against employers in relation to pensions are in their nature contractual, and the Court of Appeal has held this to be so in principle also for the member's relationship to the trustees (*Harris v Lord Shuttleworth* [1994] ICR 991). Accordingly, pension disputes may be taken to an employment tribunal by an aggrieved employee, if they arise on or are outstanding at the termination of his employment, under the *Employment Tribunals Extension of Jurisdiction (England and Wales) Order 1994 (SI 1994/1623)* or the parallel Scottish Order. Claims against the trustees based on the contract of membership are permissible because the Order applies to claims under contracts connected with employment, and does not limit claims to those against the former employer. (This jurisdiction may not apply where the scheme is a statutory public sector scheme with the right to membership conferred, and benefits prescribed, by statute.)

However, there are important limitations to the tribunal's contractual jurisdiction. The only remedy it can award is damages, with a statutory maximum of £25,000.

Claims can also be brought only following termination of employment, and within a three-month time limit. Claims must arise out of, or be outstanding on, the termination of the employment. In pension claims remedies such as a declaration of rights or a direction to the employer or trustees to determine a claim in accordance with law are often of importance, and claims may have a value considerably in excess of £25,000 where a pension payable for the rest of the claimant's life is in issue. Such claims must be brought in the ordinary courts and are in consequence rare.

However, there are other avenues to pursue claims and disputes, of increasing practical importance. The *Pensions Act 1995, s 50* created a statutory requirement for all occupational pension schemes (except those with only one member or where all the members are trustees) to establish a procedure for the internal resolution of all disputes raised by or on behalf of members or their dependents or prospective members. (This requirement applies equally to stakeholder pension schemes.) The procedures must meet requirements prescribed by the *Occupational Pension Schemes* (*Internal Dispute Resolution Procedures*) *Regulations 1996* (*SI 1996/1270*). Use of the procedures does not preclude subsequent resort to external channels of complaint. Section 50 of the Pensions Act 1995 will be substituted by a new *s 273* of the *Pensions Act 2004* from a date to be appointed.

A remedy of growing importance is a complaint to the Pensions Ombudsman (11 Belgrave Road, London SW1V 1RB, tel: 020 7834 9144; www.pensions-ombudsman.org.uk). The Pensions Ombudsman is a statutory body constituted under *ss 145–151* of the *Pension Schemes Act 1993* (as amended by the *Pensions Act 1995*), and his decisions are enforceable in law, subject to a right of any aggrieved party to appeal on a point of law to the High Court. The Pensions Ombudsman may determine any question of fact or law, or claim of maladministration raised by or on behalf of a scheme member, against either the employer or the scheme trustees, or (since 1 July 1996) the managers or administrators of a pension scheme. There are limited exceptions to this jurisdiction in relation to public sector schemes and he cannot normally act where the complainant has instituted court or tribunal proceedings (but the fact that such proceedings could be brought has no bearing on his jurisdiction). The High Court has held that the sanctions available to him include the award of compensation for distress and inconvenience, but the Court of Appeal expressly left this point open: *Westminster City Council v Haywood* [1998] ICR 920.

There is a time limit of three years for lodging complaints (extendable at his discretion in limited circumstances): *Personal and Occupational Pension Schemes* (*Pensions Ombudsman*) *Regulations 1996* (*SI 1996/2475*). Complaints should first be referred to the Pensions Advisory Service (TPAS) for possible informal resolution, and this step needs to have been completed, so that the complaint can be lodged before the expiry of the three-year time limit. TPAS can be contacted at 11 Belgrave Road, London SW1V 1RB, tel 0845 6012923; further information is available on its website (www.opas.org.uk).There is a right of appeal to the High Court against final, but not preliminary, decisions of the Pensions Ombudsman. (However, in cases where there is no right of appeal an application for judicial review may be possible: see on both these points *Legal & General Assurance Society Ltd v Pensions Ombudsman* [2000] 2 All ER 577.) The Pensions Ombudsman is not automatically a party to an appeal, but may apply to appear in the appeal; in that event, if his decision is not upheld, the successful party may obtain an order for the Ombudsman to pay its costs on the appeal (*Moores (Wallisdown) Ltd v Pensions Ombudsman (Costs)* [2002] 1 All ER 737).

42.14 Retirement

The Pensions Ombudsman has issued a number of determinations of far-reaching significance, particularly in relation to the use by employers of surpluses in pension funds; this has been accompanied by an increase in the number of appeals against his determinations, which have highlighted restrictions in the powers conferred by the *1993 Act* on the Ombudsman: see, e g *Westminster City Council v Haywood* (above) and *Edge v Pensions Ombudsman* [1999] 4 All ER 546, holding that the Pensions Ombudsman cannot entertain complaints which could only be remedied by steps which would adversely affect the interests of third parties not party to the determination. (See also on this point *Marsh & McLennan Companies UK Ltd v Pensions Ombudsman* [2001] IRLR 505.)

The Pensions Regulator is the principal regulatory body controlling the activities of pension funds and trustees. It was established under the *Pensions Act 2004*, replacing the Occupational Pensions Regulatory Authority. Individual complaints continue to be dealt with by the Pensions Advisory Service.

43   Service Lettings

43.1   Some employers provide residential accommodation for their employees. They may do so because the nature of the work is such that the job can be done more efficiently if the employee is close at hand. Another reason may be that the work is in a part of the country in which there is a shortage of accommodation, and the only way in which the employer can attract workers is to provide them with somewhere to live.

The provision of such accommodation poses a dilemma for both employee and employer when the employment relationship comes to an end. The interest of the employee in retaining security of tenure in his home conflicts with the interest of the employer in regaining the accommodation so that he can use it for the employee's replacement. Another question is the extent to which rent controls apply.

It is not possible to give more than a broad outline of this area of law in a book on employment law, and those wishing to find more detailed discussion should consult such works as *Woodfall's Landlord and Tenant* or *Hill and Redman's Law of Landlord and Tenant*. That is particularly true of some of the complex transitional provisions associated with the change from the regime of the *Rent Act 1977* ('*RA 1977*') to that of the *Housing Act 1988* ('*HA 1988*'). Nor have we sought to deal here with matters such as the scope of the landlord's and the tenant's respective repairing obligations. A summary of the law as it affects employees is set out below. It has been assumed that situations such as that of a resident landlord are unlikely to arise in the employment context.

43.2   NATURE OF THE OCCUPANCY

It is of the greatest importance to distinguish between a *service tenancy* and a *service licence*. The grounds on which possession may be recovered from a tenant as opposed to a licensee are limited by statute (see below).

The test for distinguishing between a tenancy and a licence has been re-stated by Lord Templeman, giving the decision of the House of Lords in *Street v Mountford* [1985] AC 809 (see also *Bruton v London and Quadrant Housing Trust* [2000] 1 AC 406, HL). In *Street v Mountford*, Lord Templeman also gave guidance about the position of service occupiers.

'To constitute a tenancy the occupier must be granted exclusive possession for a fixed or periodic term certain in consideration of a premium or periodical payments' (p 818E).

'A service occupier is a servant who occupies his master's premises in order to perform his duties as a servant. In those circumstances the possession and occupation of the servant is treated as the possession and occupation of the master and the relationship of landlord and tenant is not created; see *Mayhew v Suttle* (1854) 4 E & B 347. The test is whether the servant requires the premises he occupies in order the better to perform his duties as a servant:

"Where the occupation is necessary for the performance of services, and the occupier is required to reside in the house in order to perform those services, the occupation being strictly ancillary to the performance of the duties which the occupier has to perform, the occupation is that of a servant";

per Mellor J in *Smith v Seghill Overseers* (1875) LR 10 QB 422, 428'. (p 818G–H)

A requirement that the employee live in certain accommodation for the better performance of his duties (so that he is a licensee and not a tenant) may be expressed in his contract of employment or may be implied. A chauffeur who is given a flat above the garage, or a housekeeper who is given accommodation in the premises she is charged with looking after, would, save in exceptional circumstances, be considered to be occupying that accommodation for the better performance of his or her duties. Employers may consider it wise to state expressly in any contract of employment or letter of offer of employment (where it is the case) that the employee will be required to occupy certain premises for the better performance of his duties and that his occupation is to cease upon the termination of the employment. But such a statement will not avail the employer if it does not accurately reflect the reality of the situation: cf *Aslan v Murphy* [1989] 3 All ER 130. An employee will be a licensee rather than a tenant where he exclusively occupies an employer's residential accommodation in anticipation that, at a reasonable time in the future, the employment will benefit from that occupation; this applies notwithstanding that at the time when the employee entered into occupation, the occupation was irrelevant to his existing duties (*Norris v Checksfield* [1991] 4 All ER 327).

If the employee is not a service licensee in this sense, he may still be a lodger and not a tenant if the employer provides attendance or services which require him or his servants to exercise unrestricted access to, and use of, the premises. Otherwise, however, the agreement to grant exclusive possession for a term at a rent points to the creation of a tenancy. Indeed, in *Ashburn Anstalt v Arnold* [1989] Ch 1, the Court of Appeal held that even a rent was not an essential constituent of a lease (although this case was overruled by the House of Lords in *Prudential Assurance Co Ltd v London Residuary Body* [1992] 2 AC 386; and cf *Bostock v Bryant* (1990) 61 P & CR 23. Two cases illustrate the application of these principles in employment cases.

In *Postcastle Properties Ltd v Perridge* [1985] 2 EGLR 107, the plaintiffs brought a possession action for an estate cottage. The occupant, a man of 80 years, had been employed by the plaintiffs' predecessor in title. He remained in occupation, and continued to work for and to pay £1.50 per week rent to the plaintiffs after they purchased the premises. He was held to have a tenancy. Strong evidence was needed to rebut the presumption of tenancy, which was not forthcoming in that case.

In *Royal Philanthropic Society v County* [1985] 2 EGLR 109, the defendant was employed as a houseparent at the plaintiff's school. Initially he was provided with furnished accommodation in the school building. He was a licensee of the room. On marrying, he was provided with a house some miles from the school. Approximately one year later his employment came to an end, whereupon a notice to quit was served. Possession was successfully claimed in the county court. This was overturned on appeal, the Court of Appeal holding that the defendant was a tenant. Fox LJ said:

'The overall effect of *Street v Mountford* as we understand it is that an occupier of residential accommodation at a rent for a term is either a lodger or a tenant ...' (p 1071).

'The employment, it seems to us, is material only if there is a true service occupancy, ie where the servant requires the premises for the better performance of his duties as a servant ...' (p 1072).

Referring to a variety of factors put forward by counsel for the plaintiffs in his attempt to show that no tenancy was created, such as the informality of the paperwork, the relationship of the parties, and the fact that the previous occupancy was that of lodger, Fox LJ said:

' ... it seems to us that they amount really to an attempt to go back to the approach, disapproved by the House of Lords in *Street v Mountford*, of examining the circumstances with a view to ascertaining the intention of the parties. The only intention that is relevant under the law as it now stands "is the intention demonstrated by the agreement to grant exclusive possession for a term at a rent" (*Street v Mountford* at p 891).' (p 1072)

These decisions serve to demonstrate that, although the employment relationship continues as before, the nature of the employee's occupancy of premises may change.

Somewhat different considerations may apply in cases of joint occupation (see, eg *Mikeover Ltd v Brady* [1989] 3 All ER 618; *Stribling v Wickham* [1989] 2 EGLR 35).

43.3   RECOVERY OF POSSESSION

In order to recover possession from an occupying employee or ex-employee, the employer/landlord will first have to ensure that the employee's *contractual* right to occupy, whether under a licence or a tenancy, is brought to an end. If the employee does not leave voluntarily, it will then be necessary to obtain an order for possession, generally in the county court. In the case of a tenancy, the court's powers to make such an order are restricted by statute.

It is important that the employer does not seek to regain possession, whether by forcible eviction or by harassment without recourse to court proceedings. Such a course of action will contravene the *Protection from Eviction Act 1977* ('*PFEA 1977*').

Where premises are let as a dwelling, even under a tenancy which is not statutorily protected, it is not lawful for the owner to exercise a right of re-entry or forfeiture under the lease, or to enforce his right to recover possession, otherwise than by court proceedings (*PFEA 1977, ss 2, 3(1)*). 'Let as a dwelling' means 'let wholly or partly as a dwelling', so *PFEA 1977 s 2* applies to premises which were let for mixed residential and business purposes (*Pirabakaran v Patel* [2006] All ER (D) 380 (May)). However, premises let for such mixed purposes are not 'let as a separate dwelling' within *Rent Act 1977, s 1* (*Tan v Sitkowski* [2007] EWCA Civ 30, [2007] All ER (D) 16 (Feb)).

There is a deemed tenancy for these purposes whenever a person has exclusive possession of any premises under the terms of his employment (*PFEA 1977, s 8(2)*).

It is a criminal offence unlawfully to deprive the employee of his occupation (*PFEA 1977, s 1(2)*). It is also an offence if a person, with the intention of causing the residential occupier to give up occupation or to refrain from exercising any rights or pursuing any remedy open to him, does acts which are likely to interfere with the peace and comfort of the occupier, or his family, or persistently withdraws or withholds services normally required for the occupation of the premises as a residence (*PFEA 1977, s 1(3)*, as amended by *HA 1988, s 29*). Where that intent cannot be shown, an offence is nonetheless committed if the employer or his agent, without reasonable grounds, does acts likely to interfere with the peace or comfort of the residential occupier or members of his household or persistently withdraws or withholds services reasonably required for the occupation of the premises as a residence, knowing or having reasonable cause to believe that that conduct is likely to cause the occupier to give up occupation or to refrain from exercising a right or remedy (*PFEA 1977, s 1(3A),(3B)*, as inserted by *HA 1988, s 29*). The offence of harassment under *PFEA 1977, s 1(3)* may be committed even if the actions complained of do not otherwise amount to a civil wrong (*R v Burke* [1991] 1 AC 135).

Further, a right to damages for unlawful eviction (in addition to any existing rights to claim in tort or for breach of contract) is created by *HA 1988, s 27* (see *Tagro v Cafane* [1991] 2 All ER 235 and *Sampson v Wilson* [1996] Ch 39). Where a landlord obtained an order for possession from the court and applied for a warrant for possession against a tenant, the tenant remained protected under *PFEA 1977, s 3(1)* (see above) until the warrant had been executed and was therefore entitled to damages for unlawful eviction under *HA 1988, s 27* when the landlord forcibly evicted the tenant before such execution (*Haniff v Robinson* [1993] 1 All ER 185).

Once the licence or tenancy has been brought to an end and the employer is seeking to recover possession, the employer ought not to accept further payments of rent (at least without making clear in writing the basis on which he does so), because the acceptance of such payments may lead to the creation of a fresh tenancy. If the employee continues to occupy the premises after he should have left, compensation will eventually be recoverable by order of the court (called 'mesne profits').

43.4   Service licence

A true *service licence* can be determined on termination of the relevant employment contract, with the notice period provided for in the contract. If the contract is silent on this point, then reasonable notice should be given. It is unlikely that a period of less than four weeks would be reasonable. If the licence is a *periodic licence* (ie one which continues from week to week or month to month, rather than for a fixed term), a minimum of four weeks' notice to terminate it must be given in the prescribed form (*PFEA 1977, s 5(1A)* as inserted by *HA 1988, s 32*; *Notices to Quit, etc* (*Prescribed Information*) *Regulations 1988* (*SI 1988/2201*)). The termination of a licence which is expressed to come to an end with the termination of the employee's employment need not comply with the requirements of *PFEA 1977, s 5(1A)* as to notice, because such a licence is not a 'periodic licence' for the purposes of that provision (*Norris v Checksfield* [1991] 4 All ER 327).

On the termination of a *service licence* the employer can take proceedings for possession. He will have to show:

(*a*)   that the premises were occupied by the employee for the duration of his employment (or for some agreed lesser period), and for the better performance of his duties;

(*b*)   that the employment (or the lesser period) has ended, or that proper notice to determine the licence has been given;

(c)   that either the agreed notice has been given or the former employee has been given an adequate period in which to vacate the premises;

(d)   that no new arrangement has been created since the contract ended (therefore it is unwise to accept further payments of rent without specifying the basis on which this is done).

In *Whitbread West Pennines Ltd v Reedy* [1988] ICR 807, the former employee sought to argue that possession should not be ordered against him because there was pending an unfair dismissal claim in which he sought reinstatement (see 55.2 UNFAIR DISMISSAL – III). The argument failed. The Court of Appeal held that for the replacement employee to move into the accommodation would not make reinstatement any less practicable, and that in any event the employer could elect not to reinstate but to pay enhanced compensation instead. In a case where the licence to occupy terminates along with the employment, it does so notwithstanding that the dismissal is wrongful (*Ivory v Palmer* [1975] ICR 340) or contractually lawful but statutorily unfair (*Carroll v Manek*, All England Transcripts, 12 July 1999).

43.5 Service tenancy

Tenancies in existence prior to 15 January 1989 continue to be governed by *RA 1977* or *Housing Act 1980* ('*HA 1980*'). Tenancies entered into on or after that date, however, are governed by *HA 1988*. Tenancies entered into on or after 28 February 1997 are affected by amendments made to *HA 1988* by the *Housing Act 1996* ('*HA 1996*'). Various kinds of tenancy therefore fall to be considered.

(i)   *Protected tenancies under RA 1977.* These are automatically converted into *statutory tenancies* when the original, contractual tenancy expires through effluxion of time or a notice to quit is served.

(ii)   *Protected shorthold tenancies under HA 1980.* These arose where, before the grant of the tenancy, the landlord served a prescribed notice indicating that this was the nature of the tenancy. The term must have been between one and five years, with the landlord having no right to end it sooner whilst the tenant complied with his obligations (*HA 1980, s 52*).

(iii)   *Assured tenancies under HA 1988.* This will now be the normal basic type of tenancy (but see (v) below). The tenant must be an individual who occupies the dwelling as his only or principal home, and the letting must not be one which is specifically excluded from protection (*HA 1988, s 1*).

(iv)   *Assured shorthold tenancies under HA 1988 (pre-HA 1996 tenancies).* These are similar in concept to the old protected shorthold tenancies, but their scope is less restricted. They must be for a fixed term of not less than six months, contain no landlord's right to terminate during the first six months if the tenant complies with his obligations, and the grant must be preceded by service of a notice in the prescribed form (*HA 1988, s 20*). The notice may be served on the tenant's authorised agent (*Yenula Properties Ltd v Naidu* [2002] EWCA Civ 719, [2003] HLR 229). A notice not in the prescribed form nor 'substantially to the same effect' is invalid (*Manel v Memon* (2000) 33 HLR 235), as is a notice which fails to state correctly the landlord's name (*Gill v Cremadez* [2000] CLY 3876); see also *Ravenseft Properties v Hall* [2001] EWCA Civ 2034, [2002] HLR 624 and *Osborn & Co Ltd v Dior* [2003] HLR 645.

(v)   *Assured shorthold tenancies under HA 1988 (post-HA 1996 tenancies).* Any assured tenancy which is entered into on or after 28 February 1997 (otherwise than pursuant to a contract entered into before that date) will be an assured shorthold tenancy, unless it falls within one of the exceptions set out in *HA 1988, Sch 2A* (*HA 1988, s 19A*, inserted by *HA 1996, s 96*). Unlike pre-*HA 1996* assured shorthold tenancies, no notice need be served by the landlord on the tenant prior to the grant, and the tenancy need not be for a fixed term. However, if requested to do so in writing, a landlord under a post-*HA 1996* assured shorthold tenancy has a duty to provide a tenant with a written statement of the principal terms of the tenancy where these are not evidenced in writing (*HA 1988, s 20A*, inserted by *HA 1996, s 97*).

In order to recover possession from a service tenant, the contractual tenancy must be terminated. This will occur if (in the case of a fixed-term tenancy) the term of the tenancy expires without being renewed, if the landlord claims to forfeit the lease where the lease makes provision for forfeiture for breach of certain terms in it, or (in the case of a periodic tenancy) if the landlord serves a notice to quit.

Expiry of term. If the tenancy is for a fixed term of, for example, two years, the contractual tenancy will automatically terminate on the expiry of the two-year period and it is not necessary for a notice to quit to be served.

Forfeiture for breach of a term of the lease. Except in the case of forfeiture for the non-payment of rent, the landlord must serve a notice under the *Law of Property Act 1925, s 146* on the tenant, specifying the breaches complained of and requesting him to remedy the same within a reasonable period of time and to pay reasonable compensation.

Notice to quit. A notice to quit should be in writing and some acknowledgement of receipt should be asked for. If sent by post, it should be sent by recorded delivery. To be valid the notice to quit must expire on the proper day. The notice to quit must expire at the end of the period of the tenancy. Because specifying a wrong date is fatal to a notice to quit, landlords should add the following saving clause in the notice to quit after the specified date: 'or at the expiration of the (week/month) of your tenancy which shall expire next after the expiration of four weeks from the service upon you of this notice'. The notice to quit must be served not less than four weeks before the date on which it is to take effect (*Protection from Eviction Act 1977, s 5*). Information prescribed by the *Notices to Quit, etc* (*Prescribed Information*) *Regulations 1988* (*SI 1988/2201*) must be included in the notice to quit; otherwise it will be invalid.

No rent must be accepted after discovery of a breach of a term in the lease which gives the landlord the right to forfeit, such as unlawful sub-letting. Accepting rent may be construed as waiving the breaches complained of or creating a new tenancy.

43.6   Situations in which possession may be claimed from tenant

Where a *protected shorthold tenancy* or an *assured shorthold tenancy* comes to an end, the court *must* grant the landlord possession if the proper procedure is followed. In the case of an assured shorthold tenancy, this involves giving the tenant not less than two months' notice in writing that possession is required. The notice must specify a date that is the last date of a period of the tenancy (*Fernandez v McDonald* [2003] EWCA Civ 1219, [2003] 4 All ER 1033; see also *Notting Hill Housing Trust v Roomus* [2006] All ER (D) 432 (Mar)). In the case of a post-*HA 1996* assured shorthold tenancy (see category (v) in 43.5 above), a possession order may not be made so as to take effect earlier than six months after the beginning of the tenancy (where the tenancy is a replacement tenancy, the six-month period runs from the beginning of the *original* tenancy) (*HA 1988, s 21,* as amended by *HA 1996, ss 98, 99*). The procedural requirements in relation to the old protected shorthold tenancy were somewhat more complex: see *HA 1980, s 55; RA 1977, s 98(2), Sch 15 Case 19.* Possession of properties let on shorthold tenancies can also be recovered on the same grounds as are available in the case of ordinary tenancies.

In the case of a *protected tenancy* under *RA 1977,* the landlord must bring himself within one of a number of specified 'Cases' set out in *Sch 15.* Those Cases in *Sch 15 Part I* are 'discretionary' grounds, in that they require the court to be satisfied also that it is reasonable to grant possession; they include grounds such as arrears of rent or the causing of a nuisance. Those Cases in *Sch 15 Part II* constitute mandatory grounds for possession. In addition, the court may make an order, if it is reasonable to do so, where suitable alternative accommodation is or will be available for the tenant. See generally *RA 1977, s 98.*

The ground particularly relevant to pre-1989 service lettings is *Case 8* (a discretionary ground): this arises if the landlord requires the premises for a whole-time employee, the existing tenant was granted a tenancy in consequence of his employment, and he has ceased to be in that employment.

A similar approach governs recovery of possession under *assured tenancies* under *HA 1988.* Again, there are both mandatory and discretionary grounds, and where one of the latter is established the court will have to be persuaded that it is reasonable to order possession (*HA 1988, s 7, Sch 2*). *Ground 16* is a discretionary ground which applies where the dwelling-house was let to the tenant in consequence of his employment by the landlord or a previous landlord, and the tenant has ceased to be in that employment. It will be seen that this is less stringent, from the landlord's point of view, than *Case 8* under *RA 1977* (see above), because it is not necessary to show that the accommodation is required for another employee. However, to do so would obviously assist the argument that it was reasonable to order possession. The availability of suitable alternative accommodation is another discretionary ground (*Ground 9*).

As in the case of *RA 1977* (see *s 100*), the court has a wide discretion under *HA 1988, s 9* to adjourn possession proceedings and to suspend the execution of orders.

43.7 **Tenants of public authorities**

Under *HA 1985,* security of tenure was conferred upon tenants of local authorities and of certain other public bodies. However, various categories are excluded from security of tenure. Those which are pertinent to employment include:

(*a*) Cases where the tenant is an employee of the landlord; or of:

    (i) a local authority;

    (ii) a new town corporation;

    (iii) the governors of an aided school;

    (iv) an urban development corporation;

    (v) a housing action trust;

and his contract of employment requires him to reside in the dwelling for the better performance of his duties. (In *Surrey County Council v Lamond* [1999] 1 EGLR 32 (see also [1999] 2 CLY 3736), the Court of Appeal held that in deciding whether for this reason a tenancy was not a secure tenancy, the court needed to ascertain what duties the employee was to perform and then determine whether it was genuinely practicable for the employee to perform them if he did not occupy the dwelling concerned; see also *Hughes v Greenwich London Borough Council* [1994] 1 AC 170, HL, *Elvidge v Coventry City Council* [1993] 4 All ER 903, CA and *Brent London Borough Council v Charles* (1997) 29 HLR 876, CA.)

(*b*) Where the tenant is a member of the police force, and the dwelling is provided rent-free by regulations made under the *Police Act 1996*.

(*c*) Where the tenant is employed by a fire and rescue authority; and

(i) he is contractually bound to live close to a particular fire station; and

(ii) the dwelling-house was let to him by the authority so that he could comply with the condition.

(*d*) Cases where temporary accommodation is granted in order to assist employees who are new to an area to find permanent accommodation there, provided that it is linked to an offer of employment to a person who was not resident in the district immediately before the grant, that it does not exceed one year and that the tenant is informed, in writing, of the circumstances in which the exception applies and that the landlord is of the opinion that it falls within that exception.

(*Housing Act 1985, Sch 1 paras 2(1), (2), (3), 5(1),* as amended.)

43.8 RENT CONTROL

Occupation under a *licence* is not subject to rent control.

Where the employee went into occupation under a *RA 1977 protected tenancy* or a *protected shorthold tenancy*, he could apply under *Part IV* of that *Act* for a fair rent to be registered, and the landlord was not then entitled to charge a greater rent (*RA 1977, s 44*). Now that new protected tenancies cannot be created, that provision will be of diminishing importance, although the possibility of such an application remains.

A tenant under an *assured tenancy* under *HA 1988* has no right to challenge the contractual rent which he has agreed to pay, whether the rent demanded of him is that originally agreed upon, or has subsequently been varied pursuant to a rent review clause. However, if the contractual tenancy comes to an end and the landlord wishes to increase the rent, he must serve notice of the proposed increase upon the tenant in a prescribed form (*HA 1988, s 13*). The tenant may then go before a Rent Assessment Committee and seek a determination that the proposed new rent exceeds that which might reasonably be expected to be obtained in the open market, by a willing landlord, on the same terms of letting (*HA 1988, s 14*). There are strict time limits within which any reference by the tenant to the Rent Assessment Committee must be made.

A tenant under an *assured shorthold tenancy* may refer the rent charged to the Rent Assessment Committee, during the initial fixed term of the tenancy (in the case of a pre-*HA 1996* assured shorthold tenancy) or during the first six months of the tenancy (in the case of a post-*HA 1996* assured shorthold tenancy). However, the Committee may reduce the rent only if:

(i) there is a sufficient number of similar dwelling-houses in the locality let on assured tenancies (whether shorthold or not) for a proper determination to be possible; and

(ii)   the rent charged is *significantly* higher than the rent which the landlord might reasonably be expected to obtain having regard to the rents payable under other assured tenancies in the locality.

(*HA 1988, s 22*, as amended by *HA 1996, s 100.*)

43.9   AGRICULTURAL TIED HOUSES

Where the employee is or was engaged in agriculture or forestry, special rules may apply. A discussion of these rules is beyond the scope of this book. They are to be found in the *Rent (Agriculture) Act 1976* as amended by *HA 1988*, and in *HA 1988, ss 24, 25* (as amended by *HA 1996, s 103*).

44   Sickness and Sick Pay

Cross-references. See TERMINATION OF EMPLOYMENT (48) for sickness and frustration of contract of employment; for sickness and unfair dismissal, see 54.8 UNFAIR DISMISSAL – II.

44.1   In relation to pay for periods of sickness, the following may apply:

(*a*)   contractual provisions for sick pay (see 44.2 below);

(*b*)   the statutory right to a specified level of sick pay ('statutory sick pay', see 44.3–44.8 below).

As in many areas of employment law, statutory payments are offset against contractual payments and vice versa. This 'offsetting' of payments during sickness is considered in 44.9–44.11 below.

Employers may now opt out of the statutory sick pay scheme, so long as they provide the same minimum level of remuneration as an employee would be entitled to as a matter of statute. (See 44.3 below.)

Persistent illness may constitute such incapacity for work as to warrant dismissal (see 54.8 UNFAIR DISMISSAL – II).

In rare circumstances, sickness may render performance of the contract so radically different from that contemplated by the parties as to amount to a frustration of the contract (see 48.3 TERMINATION OF EMPLOYMENT).

44.2   CONTRACTUAL PROVISIONS FOR SICK PAY

An employer may agree to pay his employees while they are absent due to ill-health. Such payments commonly run for a specified period of time and are subject to conditions.

The written particulars given to an employee setting out the terms and conditions of his employment must state whether or not the employer makes payments for periods of absence due to sickness and, if so, upon what terms (see 8.4 CONTRACT OF EMPLOYMENT). In *Mears v Safecar Security Ltd* [1982] ICR 626, the Court of Appeal held that where such a term is not specified or agreed, the tribunal must consider all the facts and circumstances to ascertain the term to be implied. There is no presumption of a contractual right to sick pay. An employment tribunal must look to all the facts and circumstances, and to the conduct of the parties since the contract began.

Where there is a contractual right to sick pay, but no provision as to its duration, the court will imply a reasonable term (*Howman & Son v Blyth* [1983] ICR 416).

For the failure to comply with the statutory duty to specify in the written particulars of terms of employment what provisions for sick pay apply, see 8.9 CONTRACT OF EMPLOYMENT.

44.3   STATUTORY SICK PAY

(For further details see HMRC's booklet 'What to do if your employee is sick' (E14) (2007)).

Since 1983, all employees, subject to certain specified exceptions (see 44.4 below), have been entitled to receive statutory sick pay ('SSP') from their employers, who until recently were able to recover the greater part of it from National Insurance contributions (see 44.6 below). The entitlement limit is, generally, 28 weeks in a three-year period. The basic provisions are now consolidated into the *Social Security Contributions and Benefits Act 1992* ('*SSCBA 1992*'). The main set of regulations is the *Statutory Sick Pay (General) Regulations 1982 (SI 1982/894)* as amended, principally by the *Statutory Sick Pay (General) Amendment Regulations 1986 (SI 1986/477)*, the *Statutory Sick Pay (General) Amendment (No 2) Regulations 1987 (SI 1987/868)* and the *Social Security Contributions, Statutory Maternity Pay and Statutory Sick Pay (Miscellaneous Amendments) Regulations 1996 (SI 1996/777)*.

The essential requirements for qualification are that an employee must:

(*a*)   have four or more consecutive days of sickness (including Sundays and holidays) during which he is too ill to be capable of doing his work (see further 44.5 below); and

(*b*)   notify his absence to his employer, subject to certain statutory requirements and any agreement between them; and

(*c*)   supply evidence of incapacity – this is also a matter for the employer: a common example of an employer's requirement would be:

    (i)   a 'self-certificate' for periods of four to seven days;

    (ii)   a doctor's certificate or other evidence of sickness for periods after the first seven days.

(*SSCBA 1992, ss 151, 152, 156; Statutory Sick Pay (General) Regulations 1982, reg 7.*)

Employers cannot require employees to contribute towards payments (*SSCBA 1992, s 151(2)*).

Employees may still be entitled to SSP even if they are absent from Great Britain on holiday or for business purposes at any time during the incapacity (*SI 1996/777, reg 3*).

For days of incapacity for work on or after 6 April 1997, an employer may choose to opt out of the statutory sick pay scheme, provided that he continues to pay contractual remuneration to his employees at or above the SSP rate and does not make his employees contribute to the cost of their sick pay up to that rate. Such employers still have to comply with certain documentary and record keeping requirements (see 44.7 below).

44.4   Excluded employees

The following categories of employee are not entitled to receive SSP. These are an employee:

(*a*)   over the age of 65 on the first day of sickness;

(*b*)   having average weekly earnings less than the weekly lower earnings limit for National Insurance ('NI') contribution liability (currently £84 per week);

(*c*)   going sick within 57 days of having previously received one of a number of social security benefits;

(*d*)   who has done no work for his employer under the contract of service;

(e)   going sick during a stoppage of work at his place of employment due to a trade dispute, unless he proves that at no time has he had a direct interest in that dispute;

(f)   who is pregnant and goes off sick during the maternity pay period (see 33.11 MATERNITY AND PARENTAL RIGHTS);

(g)   who has already been due 28 weeks' SSP from his employer in any one 'period of incapacity for work' (or any two or more 'linked' periods) (see 44.5 below);

(h)   who, subject to certain provisions, has already been due 28 weeks' SSP from his former employer, and the gap between the first day of incapacity with the new employer and the last day on which SSP was paid by the former employer is eight weeks or less;

(i)   who is in legal custody at any time on the first day of incapacity.

(*SSCBA 1992, Sch 11*, as amended by the *Statutory Sick Pay Act 1994, s 1; Social Security Act 1985, s 18(2)(d); Statutory Sick Pay (General) Regulations 1982 (SI 1982/894); Statutory Sick Pay (General) Amendment Regulations 1986 (SI 1986/477)*.)

Where the employer is notified that an excluded employee has been absent for four consecutive days or more, he is legally bound to send a form to the employee not later than seven days after being so notified (or, where this is impracticable, not later than the first pay day in the following tax month). This form provides the explanation to the employee and the DWP of why SSP is not being paid, and allows the employee to claim state sickness benefit instead (*Statutory Sick Pay (General) Regulations 1982 (SI 1982/894), reg 15*, as amended).

44.5   The payment period

The period of four or more days of sickness (see 44.3 above) is called a 'period of incapacity for work' ('PIW'). Two or more PIWs which are separated by eight weeks or less are said to be 'linked' and are counted as one PIW (*SSCBA, s 152; Statutory Sick Pay (General) Amendment Regulations 1986 (SI 1986/477)*).

During a PIW, SSP is payable *only*:

(a)   while there is a 'period of entitlement', as defined (e g payment will cease, in the normal case, if the employment ends); *and*

(b)   for days within the PIW which are 'qualifying days'.

The intention behind the idea of 'qualifying days' was that they would be the days on which the employee would normally be required to work, but it is open to employers in all cases to specify the pattern of qualifying days by agreement with the employees concerned. Each week must have at least one qualifying day, and qualifying days must not be defined by reference to the days of sickness (*Statutory Sick Pay (General) Regulations 1982 (SI 1982/894); Statutory Sick Pay (General) Amendment Regulations 1985 (SI 1985/126)*).

SSP is not payable for the first three qualifying days in a PIW (*SSCBA 1992, s 155(1)*). It is paid for the fourth qualifying day onwards until either the employee becomes well again or the maximum payment period is reached (*SSCBA 1992, s 155(2)*).

The maximum entitlement to SSP is now 28 weeks in any period of entitlement. A period of entitlement, as between an employee and his employer, is a period beginning with the commencement of a period of incapacity for work and ending with the earliest of:

(i)   the termination of that period of incapacity for work;

(ii)   the day on which the employee reaches, as against the employer concerned, his maximum entitlement to statutory sick pay;

(iii) the day on which the employee's contract of service with the employer concerned expires or is brought to an end;

(iv)   in the case of an employee who is, or has been, pregnant, the day immediately preceding the beginning of the disqualifying period (as defined by *SSCBA 1992, s 153(12)*) (*SSCBA 1992, s 153(2)*).

A period of entitlement ends after three years if it has not otherwise ended (*Statutory Sick Pay (General) Regulations 1982 (SI 1982/894), reg 3(3)*, inserted by *SI 1986/477*).

Day-to-day workers. The Court of Appeal recently held in *Brown v Chief Adjudication Officer* [1997] IRLR 110, that an employee who had been employed on a daily contract for nine months was entitled to receive SSP during her period of incapacity from work due to a neck injury. The court rejected the ruling of the social security commissioner that there was no period of entitlement for an employee engaged on a day-to-day basis as the contract ended with the last day worked before the period of incapacity. Instead, the Court of Appeal held that as the employee had been continuously employed for a period of at least three months, she was entitled by law to receive at least one week's notice of termination of her contract of employment (see *ERA 1996, s 86(1)(a), (4)*), and so the general principles governing the period of entitlement applied (see *SSCBA 1992, s 153(2)*). On the facts, the employer's failure to give the employee notice of termination meant that the contract of employment subsisted throughout her period of incapacity. The period of entitlement to sick pay, therefore, extended until her period of incapacity came to an end.

Days of entitlement to SSP from a previous employer, in a previous period of entitlement, will be taken into account in calculating whether maximum entitlement has been reached if:

(A)   the period of entitlement, as between the employee and his new employer, arose not more than eight weeks after the last day in respect of which his previous employer had been liable to pay him SSP, and either

(B)   the employee had provided the new employer with a leaver's statement (see 44.12 below), or

(C)   the employer has himself issued such a statement to the employee.

(*Statutory Sick Pay (General) Amendment Regulations 1986 (SI 1986/477)*.)

Employees who are still sick when their entitlement to SSP terminates may be entitled to state benefits, including incapacity benefit (*Social Security (Incapacity for Work) Act 1994*). Employers of such employees must inform them in a prescribed form of the reason for the termination of SSP (*Social Security Administration Act 1992, s 130; Statutory Sick Pay (General) Regulations 1982 (SI 1982/894), reg 15*, as amended by *Statutory Sick Pay (General) Amendment Regulations 1986 (SI 1986/477)*). *SSCBA 1992, Sch 12* deals with the relationship between statutory sick pay and other benefits and payments.

44.6   Sickness and Sick Pay

44.6 The amounts payable and recoverable

Employees who earn less than the lower weekly earnings limit for NI liability (£84) are excluded from SSP (*SSCBA 1992, Sch 11 para 2(c)*). In all other cases, the amount of SSP payable is £72.55. Thus, the maximum amount payable over 28 weeks is £1,961.40 (*SSCBA 1992, s 157(1)*, as amended by the *Social Security (Incapacity for Work) Act 1994, s 8(1)*).

SSP is considered as earnings for PAYE, income tax and NI contribution purposes (*SSCBA 1992, s 4(1); Income and Corporation Taxes Act 1988, s 150*).

Right of recovery. The right of employers to recover from their NI contributions amounts paid by way of SSP was abolished by the *Statutory Sick Pay Act 1994*. Small employers are no longer granted relief on payments of SSP above a certain threshold. Instead, any employer may recover an amount paid out as SSP if, and to the extent that, it exceeds 13% of his liability to pay NI contributions in the income tax month in question (*Statutory Sick Pay Percentage Threshold Order 1995 (SI 1995/512)*, which revoked the *Statutory Sick Pay (Small Employers' Relief) Regulations 1991 (SI 1991/428)* with effect from 6 April 1995). The same principles apply to employers who opt out of the SSP scheme if and to the extent that the amount which he would have paid out in SSP exceeds the percentage threshold.

44.7 Records

Employers are obliged to keep records for SSP purposes. In particular, the following *minimum* information must be recorded by the employer and retained for at least three years.

(*a*)   Dates of each employee's PIWs.

(*b*)   Any payment of SSP made in respect of any day within a PIW, except where the payment is by way of contractual remuneration which equals or exceeds the SSP payable in respect of that day.

(*Statutory Sick Pay (General) Regulations 1982 (SI 1982/894), reg 13; Statutory Sick Pay (General) Amendment Regulations 1986 (SI 1986/477), reg 5; Social Security Contributions, Statutory Maternity Pay and Statutory Sick Pay (Miscellaneous Amendments) Regulations 1996 (SI 1996/777), reg 2; Statutory Sick Pay (General) Amendment Regulations 1996 (SI 1996/3042), reg 2.*)

The statutory records must be retained for at least three years, and must be stored in such a way that inspectors can have access to them.

In addition, accounting records must be kept showing, *inter alia*, details of all SSP payments made, along with those of pay, NIC and PAYE income tax. Revenue records must be retained for seven years.

Employers may find it useful to keep fuller records, e g self-certification forms, medical certificates, dates of all absences and the reasons for them. Such records can be used for the purposes of audit, and may also help to identify personnel problems.

Where personnel records are stored electronically, the provisions of the *Data Protection Act 1984* should be borne in mind (see 11.12 *et seq* DISCLOSURE OF INFORMATION, where the *Data Protection Act 1998* is also discussed).

Where employers opt out of the SSP scheme, they will still need to keep basic records of sickness absence and amounts paid so that the NI inspector can check that the employees are receiving their full entitlement. The employer will need to record the following details:

(i)   the first day for which SSP liability arises;

(ii)   the last day for which SSP liability arises;

(iii)   the number of weeks and days of SSP entitlement; and

(iv)   the number of SSP qualifying days (see 44.5 above).

See 'Employer's Manual on Statutory Sick Pay' (CA 30).

44.8   Disputes

If an employer does not pay an employee SSP, the employee may ask him to give written reasons for the decision, and the employer must comply within a reasonable time (*Social Security Administration Act 1992, s 14(3)*).

If the employee wishes to challenge the employer's decision, he may ask for a determination of the issue by the Board of the Inland Revenue (*Statutory Sick Pay and Statutory Maternity Pay (Decisions) Regulations 1999 (SI 1999/776)*). An employment tribunal does not have jurisdiction to determine whether an employee is entitled to statutory sick pay, although it would have jurisdiction to determine a claim of unlawful deduction from wages if the employer admitted entitlement but withheld payment of SSP: *Taylor Gordon & Co Ltd v Timmons* [2004] IRLR 180.

As far as evidence of incapacity is concerned, the employer cannot require the employee to produce a medical certificate from a doctor for the first seven days of sickness. With that qualification, he can request the employee to provide reasonable evidence of incapacity, such as a self-certificate for absences of up to seven days (*Social Security Administration Act 1992, s 14; Statutory Sick Pay (Medical Evidence) Regulations 1985 (SI 1985/1604)*).

44.9   OFFSETTING PAYMENTS MADE DURING SICKNESS AGAINST SSP

Any contractual remuneration paid to an employee for a day of sickness is to be offset against the SSP due for the *same day* (*SSCBA 1992, Sch 12 para 2*). An employer can never pay the employee an amount in total which is *less* than the SSP due.

In personal injury actions, any special damages claimed will be subject to a deduction for SSP paid (*Palfrey v Greater London Council* [1985] ICR 437). The same principle was applied to payments under a non-contributory permanent health insurance scheme in *Hussain v New Taplow Paper Mills Ltd* [1987] ICR 28.

44.10 Contributory sickness schemes

An employee must not contribute to his own SSP. Thus, in the case of a jointly funded, ie 'contributory', sickness scheme, the amount of sick pay which will be offset against SSP must be in the proportion that the employer's contribution bears to the joint contributions to the scheme.

44.11 Contributory pension schemes

In the case of contributory pension schemes, offsetting will depend on how the pension scheme defines salary for calculation purposes: if salary is defined as 'earnings subject to PAYE income tax', then any SSP paid should be included in earnings for pension purposes. In that case the employee's pension contribution would be deducted from his full gross sick pay, i e including the SSP element. (See, in particular, the *Occupational Pensions Board Announcement No 2 (March 1983)*.)

44.12   ACTION WHEN EMPLOYEES LEAVE

If when an employee leaves there is a PIW which is separated from the date of termination by eight weeks or less, and SSP was payable for one week or more during the PIW, the employer must (if the employee so requests) issue the employee with one or more statements relating to the payment of SSP. Any such statement must be provided within seven days of the employee's request (or where it is not practicable, not later than his first pay day which would have fallen within the next income tax month), and must state:

(*a*)   the date of the first day of the period of entitlement;

(*b*)   the number of weeks of SSP payable (odd days of three will round down and four will round up to the nearest whole week) in that period of entitlement;

(*c*)   the last day for which SSP was payable;

(*d*)   the date the statement was made by the employer; and

(*e*)   the full name, address and, if there is one, telephone number of the employer making the statement.

(*Statutory Sick Pay (General) Regulations 1982 (SI 1982/894), reg 15A*, as amended).

44.13   PENALTIES

Non-compliance with the SSP provisions can amount to a criminal offence (*Social Security Administration Act 1992, s 113; Statutory Sick Pay (General) Regulations 1982 (SI 1982/894); Statutory Sick Pay (General) Amendment Regulations 1986 (SI 1986/477)*.)

44.14   PERMANENT HEALTH AND SALARY CONTINUANCE BENEFITS

It is increasingly common for employers to provide their employees with permanent health or salary continuance benefits during periods of long-term sickness or incapacity, lasting usually more than six or twelve months. Employers will normally provide these benefits by taking out insurance coverage for the benefit of their employees.

The right of an employee to receive permanent health or salary continuance benefits will usually depend on the terms of the insurance policy entered into by the employer, as the contract of employment will probably state that the benefits payable to the employee in the event of long-term incapacity are 'subject to' or 'governed by' the rules of the insurance policy. However, where the employer makes no reference to its insurance policy in documents provided to an employee, then the employer cannot rely upon the terms of the policy as against the employee. The employer will be bound by the words of its own contractual documentation with the employee: see *Jowitt v Pioneer Technology (UK) Ltd* [2003] EWCA Civ 411, [2003] ICR 1120. Also, where the insurance policy provides for significant exemptions to the payment of benefits (e g disentitling employees to benefits on leaving service), the employer will not be able to rely on these exemptions as against the employee if the employee was not shown the policy itself or was not told that he should read it (*Villella v MFI Furniture Centres Ltd* [1999] IRLR 468).

In *Briscoe v Lubrizol Ltd* [2002] EWCA Civ 508, [2002] IRLR 607, the Court of Appeal held that the claimant's entitlement to disability benefit depended upon his satisfying the definition of 'disablement' contained in the employer's insurance policy ('totally unable ... to perform his normal occupation'), rather than the definition set out in the company information handbook ('unable to follow any occupation'). The court referred to the decision in *Villella*, and held that 'the court looks unfavourably upon an employer who seeks to restrict his contractual obligation as described in a handbook in reliance upon a policy which he has not brought to the attention of his employee; but that does not mean, by way of corollary, that where the handbook expressly or by implication refers to such a policy and purports to summarise its effect upon the employee's rights in a manner which is disadvantageous to the employee, the court will similarly regard the handbook as definitive of those rights'. The court looked at all the facts and determined that it was the clear contractual intention of the parties to bestow upon the employee the benefits provided for in the insurance policy, rather than the handbook.

As the employee will not be a party to the insurance policy, he will ordinarily not be entitled to enforce his rights to receive these benefits directly against the insurer. Rather, he will have to enforce those rights against the employer, who in turn will probably seek to join the insurer as a third party (*Rutherford v Radio Rentals Ltd* 1993 SLT 221). Where, under the contract of employment, the employer is obliged to pay over to the employee such sums as it receives from the insurer, then the employer will be under a duty to take all reasonable steps to secure that the insurance benefits are paid. This may include the pursuit of litigation against the insurer if necessary (*Marlow v East Thames Housing Group Ltd* [2002] IRLR 798).

An employee is not automatically deprived of his entitlement to receive salary continuance benefits from his employer merely because the employer ceases to pay his insurance premiums or terminates the policy (*Bainbridge v Circuit Foil UK Ltd* [1997] IRLR 305).

44.15   Effect on the right to terminate the contract of employment

The existence of these benefits may restrict the employer's ability to terminate the contract of employment. In circumstances where the insurance policy provides that benefits will only be paid in respect of employees who continue to be employed by the policy-holder (ie the employer), the courts will probably imply a term into the contract of employment to the effect that the employer cannot bring the contract to an end solely with a view to terminate those benefits, or for a specious or arbitrary reason or for no reason at all, while the employee was incapacitated for work (see *Hill v General Accident Fire and Life Assurance Corpn plc* [1998] IRLR 641; compare *Aspden v Webbs Poultry & Meat Group (Holdings) Ltd* [1996] IRLR 521) (see 8.10 CONTRACT OF EMPLOYMENT).

In *Briscoe* [2002] EWCA Civ 508, [2002] IRLR 607, the Court of Appeal had to determine whether the employer was justified in terminating a contract of employment, the effect of which would be to deprive the employee of his entitlement to disability benefit. The Court of Appeal reviewed the case law and held that 'the employer ought not to terminate the employment as a means to remove the employee's entitlement to benefit but the employer can dismiss for good cause whether that be on the ground of gross misconduct or, more generally, for some repudiatory breach by the employee'. On the facts, the Court of Appeal held that the employer was entitled to treat the contract as having come to an end: the employee, who had been off work for a prolonged period of time, had disobeyed the employer's lawful instruction to attend so as to discuss his long-term absence; he was in breach of an instruction to return the employer's calls to re-arrange that appointment; and his continued absence from work was unexplained by any current medical report. In the circumstances, he was held to have been in breach of the duty of trust and confidence, which justified the employer in treating the contract of employment as having been terminated.

44.16 Effect of permanent health benefits on the calculation of damages

Payments made by an employer under a permanent health insurance plan are not treated as remuneration or earnings from employment within the meaning of the *Administration of Justice Act 1982, s 10(i)*. Rather, they are to be regarded as a 'contractual' pension or benefit and are therefore not taken into account so as to reduce damages to an employee suing in respect of injuries sustained as a result of an accident at work (*Lewicki v Brown & Root Wimpey Highland Fabricators Ltd* [1996] IRLR 565).

44.17 'Unable to follow any occupation'

Permanent health insurance schemes often require the employee to show that he is unable to follow his own occupation for a period of time and thereafter that he is 'unable to follow any occupation' if he is to obtain long-term benefits. In *Walton v Airtours plc* [2002] EWCA Civ 1659, [2003] IRLR 161, the Court of Appeal held that the words 'unable to follow any occupation' had to be read in a common sense practical way and any inability must be assessed realistically. It was held that the phrase connoted being engaged in regular work for a substantial or indefinite period. It was enough that an employee could work on a temporary basis, or was able to start a new job for a few days but not continue thereafter to earn income. See also *Jowitt* [2003] EWCA Civ 411, [2003] IRLR 356.

45   Strikes and Industrial Action

(See DTI Guidance available online at www.dti.gov.uk/employment/index.htm, 'Industrial Action and the Law: A Guide for Employees, Trade Union Members and Others' (URN No 06/551), 'Industrial Action and the Law: Guidance', (URN No 06/551), 'Industrial Action and the Law: Citizen's Right to Prevent Disruption' (URN No 06/553).)

Cross-references. See TRADE UNIONS – I (50) for the liability of unions for industrial action and HUMAN RIGHTS (29).

45.1   LIABILITY FOR INDUSTRIAL ACTION – BACKGROUND

The right to take industrial action takes the form, in this country, of statutory *immunity* for action which would otherwise attract legal liability at common law. The statutory immunity first appeared in something like its present form in the *Trade Disputes Act 1906, s 3*, and its scope has varied frequently since then. The future development of this area of the law is likely to be influenced by the right to freedom of association embodied in *art 11* of the *ECHR* which was incorporated into domestic law by the *Human Rights Act 1998*. The current basic immunity and the qualifications upon it are contained in the *Trade Union and Labour Relations (Consolidation) Act 1992 ('TULRCA 1992')* as amended.

In deciding whether legal proceedings can be taken against individuals (or unions) carrying on industrial action, it first must be ascertained whether a tort is being committed, for example, inducing a breach of contract (see 45.2 below). Then it must be ascertained whether the act amounting to the commission of that tort attracts the immunity conferred by *TULRCA 1992*.

This will involve consideration of whether the act was done in contemplation or furtherance of a trade dispute, whether the industrial action has the support of a ballot, whether the industrial action has been properly initiated, and whether the immunity has been lost because the action is unlawful secondary action or for some other reason.

The law relating to trade disputes is extremely complex. What appears below is an outline of the principles involved.

45.2   LIABILITY AT COMMON LAW

The law relating to the so-called 'economic torts' has developed gradually over the years; it is a difficult area which in many respects is still unclear. The most frequently encountered of the torts relate, broadly, to interference with contractual relations (note that *TULRCA 1992, s 245* deems Crown servants to have contracts of employment for these purposes). They include:

(a)   direct inducement of a breach of contract. A union which calls a strike will almost always induce the relevant employees to breach their contracts of employment;

(b)   the indirect inducement or procurement of a breach of contract by unlawful means. For example, A may be able to sue the union if his contract to obtain goods from B is breached by B when the union induces B's employees to go on strike in breach of their contracts of employment;

(*c*)   interference with business by unlawful means. This may include the case where the performance of contracts is impeded but there is no actual breach;

(*d*)   intimidation. This is designed to deal with the situation where the harm results, directly or indirectly, not from the actual using of unlawful means, but from the threat of such use;

(*e*)   conspiracy, ie an agreement either to do an unlawful act or to do a lawful act by unlawful means. The effect of the second limb is that an act done by two or more people may be unlawful even though it would have been lawful if done by one person acting alone.

Apart from the usual requirements of causation and foreseeability, it will usually be necessary to show that the defendant knows of the relevant contract and intends to procure its breach or the interference with its performance. Conspiracy is made out only where the agreement is to do an unlawful act, or where the defendant's predominant purpose is to injure the plaintiff, and not to further his own legitimate interests (see most recently *Lonrho plc v Fayed* [1992] 1 AC 448).

Some of the most important of the many authorities on the economic torts are *D C Thomson & Co Ltd v Deakin* [1952] Ch 646, *J T Stratford & Son Ltd v Lindley* [1965] AC 269, *Torquay Hotel Co Ltd v Cousins* [1969] 2 Ch 106, *Merkur Island Shipping Corpn v Laughton* [1983] ICR 490, *News Group Newspapers Ltd v SOGAT '82 (No 2)* [1987] ICR 181, *Middlebrook Mushrooms Ltd v TGWU* [1993] ICR 612; *Timeplan Education Group Ltd v National Union of Teachers* [1997] IRLR 457; and *OBG Ltd v Allan* [2007] 2 WLR 920.

Although it is usually a breach of contract which is ultimately at the root of liability, that is by no means necessarily the case. See, e g *Lonrho plc v Fayed*, above (allegation of interference with business by unlawful means based upon fraudulent misrepresentation made to, but not causing loss to, third party). Doubt surrounds the extent to which breach of a statutory duty or a penal statute may be relied upon as unlawful means if the breach is not itself actionable. See *Lonrho Ltd v Shell Petroleum Co Ltd (No 2)* [1982] AC 173; *Barretts & Baird (Wholesale) Ltd v Institution of Professional Civil Servants* [1987] IRLR 3; *Associated British Ports v TGWU* [1989] 1 WLR 939 (point not argued in the House of Lords); and *OBG Ltd v Allan* [2007] 2 WLR 920.

Any successful picket will almost certainly involve the *prima facie* commission of the tort of inducing a breach of contract or of interference with contract by unlawful means (see *Union Traffic Ltd v TGWU* [1989] ICR 98). Picketing may also involve the torts of nuisance and intimidation (especially if it is mass picketing), or of trespass (see *Mersey Dock and Harbour Co v Verrinder* [1982] IRLR 152, *Thomas v National Union of Mineworkers (South Wales Area)* [1985] ICR 886, *News Group Newspapers Ltd v SOGAT (1982)* [1987] ICR 181) (see 45.9 below).

45.3 THE IMMUNITY FOR LIABILITY

TULRCA 1992, s 219 provides as follows:

'(1)   An act done by a person in contemplation or furtherance of a trade dispute shall not be actionable in tort on the ground only:

(*a*)   that it induces another person to break a contract or interferes or induces any other person to interfere with its performance; or (*b*)   that it consists in his threatening that a contract (whether one to which he is a party or not) will be broken or its performance interfered with, or that he will induce another person to break a contract or to interfere with its performance.

(2)   An agreement or combination by two or more persons to do or procure the doing of any act in contemplation or furtherance of a trade dispute shall not be actionable in tort if the act is one which, if done without any such agreement or combination, would not be actionable in tort.'

This formula provides immunity from actions based upon the most common of the economic torts. However, it is possible to formulate a cause of action which falls outside *s 219* (see, e g *Prudential Assurance Co Ltd v Lorenz* (1971) 11 KIR 78 (inducing breach of fiduciary duty); *Associated British Ports v TGWU* [1989] 1 WLR 939 (inducing breach of statutory duty; the point was not argued in the House of Lords)). In such cases it is probably irrelevant that the act complained of may also constitute an inducement to breach of contract which does fall within the immunity.

The statutory immunity does not protect employees from actions by their employers for breach of contract. However, in practice it is unlikely to be worthwhile for an employer to sue individual employees for losses arising from industrial action (see 45.16(D) below).

45.4   'A TRADE DISPUTE'

'Trade dispute' is given a statutory definition for this purpose by *TULRCA 1992, s 244(1)*, namely:

'... a dispute between workers and their employer which relates wholly or mainly to one or more of the following, that is to say:

(*a*)   terms and conditions of employment, or the physical conditions in which any workers are required to work;

(*b*)   engagement or non-engagement, or termination or suspension of employment or the duties of employment, of one or more workers;

(*c*)   allocation of work or the duties of employment as between workers or groups of workers;

(*d*)   matters of discipline;

(*e*)   a worker's membership or non-membership of a trade union;

(*f*)   facilities for officials of trade unions; and

(*g*)   machinery for negotiation or consultation, and other procedures, relating to any of the above matters, including the recognition by employers or employers' associations of the right of a trade union to represent workers in any such negotiation or consultation or in the carrying out of such procedures.'

In *s 244* 'employment' includes any relationship whereby one person personally does work or performs services for another (*TULRCA 1992, s 244(5)*).

'Worker', in relation to a dispute with an employer, means:

(*a*)   a worker employed by that employer; or

(*b*)   a person who has ceased to be employed by that employer where:

    (i)   his employment was terminated in connection with the dispute; or

    (ii)   the termination of his employment was one of the circumstances giving rise to the dispute.

(*TULRCA 1992, s 244(5).*)

The test of whether there is a trade dispute is an *objective* test (*NWL Ltd v Woods* [1979] ICR 867). A dispute for political reasons which is unconnected with terms and conditions of employment is not considered to be a trade dispute. One such case involved a refusal by broadcasting technicians to make a broadcast to South Africa during the apartheid era (*BBC v Hearn* [1977] IRLR 273). Similarly, a proposed strike intended as a protest against Government policies was held not to be in contemplation or furtherance of a trade dispute (*Express Newspapers v Keys* [1980] IRLR 247). In *Mercury Communications Ltd v Scott-Garner* [1984] ICR 74, an injunction was granted to restrain industrial action since the court held that the risk to jobs did not appear to be the major factor in the dispute. However, if the union genuinely wishes to achieve its demands relating to terms and conditions of employment (or any other matter falling within *TULRCA 1992, s 244(1)*, it is not relevant to establish whether those demands are realistic (*Associated British Ports v TGWU* [1989] 1 WLR 939, a point not argued on appeal). See also *Newham London Borough Council v NALGO* [1993] ICR 189.

If workers take industrial action in this country in order to further a trade dispute abroad, then, provided that the outcome of the dispute relating to matters occurring outside the UK is likely to affect them in one or more of the aspects specified in *s 244(1)*, it will be considered to be a trade dispute for the purpose of the immunity conferred by *s 219* (*TULRCA 1992, s 244(3)*).

Although the dispute must be between workers (not merely the union) and their employer, it will be sufficient to show that it results from the breakdown of negotiations in which the union was acting on behalf of those workers; and in any event a 'Yes' vote in the strike ballot will amount to an adoption of the dispute by the workers (*Associated British Ports v TGWU* [1989] I WLR 939, a point not argued on appeal).

Where a dispute relates to terms and conditions, a strike will be treated as 'in furtherance of a trade dispute' even if some of those balloted and who may be called out are not themselves affected by the terms and conditions in dispute: see *British Telcommunications plc v Communications Workers Union* [2003] EWHC 937 (QB), [2004] IRLR 58. However, in *University College London Hospitals NHS Trust v Unison* [1999] ICR 204, the Court of Appeal upheld an injunction granted against the defendant union following a dispute relating to the future terms and conditions of the employees of a number of private companies which it was proposed should take over the activities of the claimant hospital trust. It was held that a dispute about the terms and conditions of employees of third party employers, who had never been employed by the subject of the proposed strike action, was not a trade dispute within the meaning of *TULRCA 1992, s 244(1)*. Nor was a dispute that was mainly concerned with the terms and conditions of existing employees with an unidentified future employer a trade dispute within the meaning of the section. This approach was held by the European Court of Human Rights to be in accordance with the right to freedom of association contained in *art 11(1)* of the European Convention of Human Rights in *Unison v United Kingdom* [2002] IRLR 497. Interestingly, however, the European court accepted for the first time that the prohibition on the right to strike was an interference with the *art 11(1)* right which required justification under *art 11(2)*, albeit the restriction was justified in that case.

In contrast with the approach in the *University College London Hospitals NHS Trust* case, in *Westminster City Council v Unison* [2001] EWCA Civ 443, [2001] ICR 1046, the Court of Appeal held that a dispute which was predominantly about the change in the identity of the employer consequent on the transfer of employees from a local authority to a private company did fall within the definition of trade dispute.

In *P (a minor) v National Association of School Masters/Union of Women Teachers* [2003] UKHL 8, [2003] ICR 386, the House of Lords held that a dispute as to the reasonableness of an order by the head teacher of a school that the staff should teach an excluded pupil, who had subsequently been reinstated, did amount to a trade dispute as to the teachers' terms and conditions of employment. The dispute related to the teachers' terms and conditions in the sense that it concerned the nature and extent of their contractual obligation to teach the pupil.

Thus, subject to the limits outlined above and to the further restrictions considered below, a person or a trade union may take part in industrial action so long as it is in contemplation or furtherance of a trade dispute as defined.

45.5 'In contemplation or furtherance ...'

If there is a trade dispute, the question whether a particular act is in contemplation or furtherance of it is to be judged *subjectively*. In *Express Newspapers Ltd v McShane* [1980] ICR 42, the House of Lords held that 'If the party who does the act honestly thinks at the time he does it that it may help one of the parties to the trade dispute to achieve their objectives and does it for that reason, he is protected by the section' (*per* Lord Diplock at 57). The House of Lords reversed the decision of the Court of Appeal which had applied a more objective test. The subjective test was also applied by the House of Lords in *Duport Steels Ltd v Sirs* [1980] IRLR 116. It is sufficient if one purpose of the strike is the furtherance of the dispute, even though there may be other purposes not within the immunity (*Associated British Ports v TGWU* [1989] 1 WLR 939, a point not argued on appeal).

45.6 LIMITS IMPOSED ON SECONDARY ACTION

In non-legal language, 'secondary action' is the term used to describe industrial action taken by workers where the real dispute is not between themselves and their own employer. The typical example is the 'sympathy strike'.

Nothing in *TULRCA 1992, s 219* prevents an act from being actionable in tort where one of the facts relied upon for the purpose of establishing liability is that there has been secondary action which is not lawful picketing (*TULRCA 1992, s 224(1)*). Lawful picketing means acts done in the course of such attendance as is declared lawful by *TULRCA 1992, s 220* by a worker employed or last employed by the employer who is party to the dispute, or by a trade union official whose attendance is lawful by virtue of *s 220(1)(b)*. There is secondary action in relation to a trade dispute when, and only when, a person:

(a) induces another to break a contract of employment or interferes with or induces another to interfere with its performance, or (*b*)   threatens that a contract of employment under which he or another is employed will be broken or its performance interfered with, or that he will induce another to break a contract of employment or to interfere with its performance,

and the employer under the contract of employment is not the employer party to the dispute (*TULRCA 1992, s 224(2)*). An employer cannot be party to a dispute between another employer and his workers, and if more than one employer is in dispute with his workers, each dispute is to be treated as separate (*TULRCA 1992, s 224(4)*). A contract of employment is defined to include any contract for personal service, and is thus not confined to the contracts of those who are employees in the strict sense (*TULRCA 1992, s 224(6)*; cf EMPLOYEE, SELF-EMPLOYED OR WORKER? (17)).

The effect of *TULRCA 1992, ss 220* and *224(1)* is that it will not be actionable if, for example, strikers in dispute with their own employer and picketing their workplace induce a lorry-driver not to cross the picket-line, and thus to breach his contract of employment with his own employer who is not a party to the dispute. Subject to this limited type of exception, however, it will be tortious to organise any form of secondary action, including secondary picketing. Unlike under earlier legislation, there is no exception where the aim of the secondary action is to disrupt the supply of goods and services to or from the employer who is party to the dispute or an associated employer of that party.

However, if a particular act constitutes primary action in relation to a trade dispute, the same act may not be relied upon as constituting secondary action so as to evade the immunity in tort. Primary action means the same as secondary action but where the employer under the contract of employment *is* party to the dispute (*TULRCA 1992, s 224(5)*).

45.7   PRESSURE TO IMPOSE UNION MEMBERSHIP OR RECOGNITION

Under *TULRCA 1992, ss 222* and *225*, certain industrial action taken to impose union membership or recognition requirements does not have the protection of *s 219* and will therefore be unlawful. Specifically, there is no immunity from actions in tort for individuals who induce or attempt to induce another:

(*a*)   to incorporate in a contract to which that other person is a party, or proposed contract to which that other person intends to be a party, a term or conditions which would require that a party to the contract should recognise one or more trade unions for the purpose of negotiating on behalf of workers employed by him, or that he should negotiate with or consult with an official of one or more trade unions;

(*b*)   on grounds of union exclusion (that is, that the supplier or prospective supplier does not or is not likely to recognise, negotiate or consult as set out in (*a*) above), to:

(i)   exclude a person from a list of approved suppliers of goods and services or persons from whom tenders for the supply of goods or services are invited;

(ii)   exclude a person from the group of persons from whom tenders for the supply of goods or services are invited;

(iii)   fail to permit a particular person to submit such a tender; or

(iv)   terminate or determine not to enter into a contract with a particular person for the supply of goods or services.

(*TULRCA 1992, ss 186, 187, 225.*)

Nor is there any immunity where the act concerned is done because, or partly because, a particular employer is employing, has employed or might employ a person who is not a member of any, or any particular, trade union, or because a particular employer refrains from discriminating against such a person, or because it is believed that any of these things has occurred (*TULRCA 1992, s 222(1)*).

Nor is there any immunity where the act concerned is, or is part of, an inducement or an attempted inducement of a person:

(*a*)   to incorporate in a contract to which that person is party or intends to be party a term or condition which would require that the whole, or some part, of the work done for the purposes of the contract be done only by persons who are or are not members of trade unions or a particular trade union; or

(*b*)   on union membership grounds (that is, that if the proposed contract were entered into with the person concerned, work for the purposes of the contract would be or would be likely to be done by persons who were or were not members of trade unions or a particular trade union; or in the case of the termination of a contract that such work has been or is likely to be done by such persons), to

(i)   exclude a person from a list of approved suppliers of goods and services or persons from whom tenders for the supply of goods and services may be invited;

(ii)   exclude a person from the group of persons from whom tenders for the supply of goods or services are invited;

(iii)   fail to permit a particular person to submit such a tender;

(iv)   determine not to enter into a contract with a particular person for the supply of goods or services; or

(v)   terminate a contract with a particular person for the supply of goods or services.

(*TULRCA 1992, ss 144, 145, 222(3).*)

See also 49.20 TRADE UNIONS – II.

45.8   **Action in response to dismissal of unofficial strikers**

The immunity under *TULRCA 1992, s 219* is lost where the reason, or one of the reasons, for doing the act in question (such as an inducing of breaches of contract by organising a strike) is the fact or belief that an employer has dismissed one or more employees in circumstances such that by virtue of *TULRCA 1992, s 237* they have no right to complain of unfair dismissal (*TULRCA 1992, s 223*).

TULRCA 1992, s 237, which is discussed in detail in 51.18 UNFAIR DISMISSAL – I, provides that an employee has no right to complain of unfair dismissal if at the time of dismissal he was taking part in an unofficial strike or other unofficial industrial action.

45.9   PICKETING

As noted above, any successful picket will be liable to involve the commission of a tort. The statutory immunity for picketing is contained in *TULRCA 1992, s 220*. A person acts lawfully if he attends:

(*a*)   in contemplation or furtherance of a trade dispute; *and*

(*b*)   at a specified place, namely:

    (i)   at or near his own place of work; or

    (ii)   if he is unemployed and either his last employment was terminated in connection with a trade dispute or if the termination was one of the circumstances giving rise to a trade dispute, at or near his former place of work; or

    (iii)   if he does not work or normally work at any one place or if the place where he works or normally works is in a location such that attendance there for picketing is impracticable, at any premises of his employer from which he works or from which his work is administered; or

    (iv)   if he is an official of a trade union, at or near the place of work or former place of work of a member of that union whom he is accompanying and whom he represents; and

(*c*)   for the purpose only of peacefully obtaining or communicating information or peacefully persuading any person to work or abstain from working.

Any person who pickets outside these limits will lose the immunity from actions in tort. By reason of *TULRCA 1992, s 219(3)* he cannot rely upon the general immunity conferred by *s 219* upon acts done in contemplation or furtherance of a trade dispute unless *s 220* is also satisfied. Accordingly, he will be liable to a claim for an injunction and/or damages if, in the course of such picketing, he commits a tort.

The purpose of condition (*b*) above is to remove the immunity from 'flying pickets'. The Court of Appeal considered its effects in *Union Traffic Ltd v Transport and General Workers Union* [1989] ICR 98 in which it was held that lorry drivers were not entitled to picket depots at which they frequently called for deliveries, repairs and the like, because they were not the bases from which the drivers worked. In *Rayware Ltd v Transport and General Workers Union* [1989] ICR 457 a gate leading to a private trading estate but some way from the employer's premises on that estate was held to be 'near' the place of work since it was the nearest the pickets could get to their place of work without committing a trespass.

Further, *s 220* only serves to give immunity from actions in tort where the tort arises out of the mere act of attendance at the place concerned. If the picket commits further torts, such as inducing breaches of the contracts of employment of those whom he seeks to dissuade from crossing the picket line, he will be liable unless he has the protection of *s 219*, which is discussed more fully elsewhere in this chapter.

One of the circumstances in which the protection of *TULRCA 1992, s 219* is lost is where one of the facts relied on for the purpose of establishing liability is that there has been secondary action which is not lawful picketing (*TULRCA 1992, s 224(1)*) (see 45.6 above). Any picket is liable to involve secondary action, because the pickets will try to turn back the employees of third parties, hence the exception in *s 224(1)* for lawful picketing. Lawful picketing is defined in *TULRCA 1992, s 224(3)* as acts done, in the course of attendance declared lawful by *s 220*, by a worker employed (or, if not in employment, last employed) by the employer party to the dispute or by a trade union official whose attendance is lawful by virtue of *TULRCA 1992, s 220(1)(b)*. The effect of these provisions is to remove the immunity from secondary picketing whilst retaining it for direct picketing of the employer who is a party to the dispute, even if that involves pickets trying to turn back the employees of third parties.

45.10 Broome's case

In *Broome v DPP* [1974] ICR 84, the defendant, a picket during an industrial dispute, stood holding a placard in front of a vehicle on a highway, urging the driver not to go to a nearby site and preventing him from so doing for some nine minutes. The Divisional Court reversed the decision of the Stockport magistrates acquitting the defendant and convicted him of obstructing the highway. The House of Lords affirmed the conviction. The law which their Lordships had to consider was *Industrial Relations Act 1971, s 134* (which was framed, for these purposes, in similar terms to the present *TULRCA 1992, s 220*). Lord Reid said of the defendant's conduct (at 89):

' … his attendance there is only made lawful by subsection (2) if he attended only for the purpose of obtaining or communicating information or "peace-fully persuading" the lorry driver. Attendance for that purpose must I think include the right to try to persuade anyone who chooses to stop and listen, at least in so far as this is done in a reasonable way with due consideration for the rights of others. A right to attend for the purpose of peaceful persuasion would be meaningless unless this were implied.

But I see no ground for implying any right to require the person whom it is sought to persuade to submit to any kind of constraint or restriction of his personal freedom.'

Lord Salmon made similar observations.

Thus, police officers acted within their powers when they prevented pickets from approaching a lorry carrying 'strike breakers' during an industrial dispute because they feared an obstruction or a breach of the peace (*Kavanagh v Hiscock* [1974] ICR 282).

45.11 Code of Practice

The Secretary of State for Employment has issued a Code of Practice on picketing under his statutory powers (see 5.4 CODES OF PRACTICE). The original Code was revised and reissued by virtue of the *Employment Code of Practice (Picketing) Order 1992 (SI 1992/476)*.

The most notable provisions of the *Code* include the recommendation that there should not generally be more than six pickets at any one entrance (*para 51*), recommendations as to the functions of the picket organiser (*paras 54 to 57*), and recommendations concerning avoiding impediments to the movement of essential supplies, services and operations (*paras 62 to 64*).

45.12 CRIMINAL LIABILITY

Action taken by pickets may give rise to criminal liability. For example, they may be prosecuted under *TULRCA 1992, s 241(1)(d)*, which provides that a person who:

' ... with a view to compelling another person to abstain from doing or to do any act which that person has a legal right to do or abstain from doing, wrongfully and without legal authority ... watches or besets the house or other place where that person resides, or works, or carries on business, or happens to be, or the approach to such house or place',

shall, on summary conviction, be liable to a fine not exceeding level 5 on the Standard Scale, or up to six months' imprisonment, or both (*TULRCA 1992, s 241(2)*; see 1.10 INTRODUCTION).

However, compulsion of the other person, and not mere persuasion of him, must be the object of the watching and besetting (*DPP v Fidler* [1992] 1 WLR 91). The watching and besetting is not wrongful unless tortious (*Thomas v National Union of Mineworkers (South Wales Area)* [1985] ICR 886), but it appears that it may be wrongful even if no action in tort could be brought because of the statutory immunity (*Galt v Philp* [1984] IRLR 156). Other criminal charges for assault, criminal damage and offences under the *Public Order Act 1986* (especially *ss 1–5*) may arise if the pickets behave unlawfully. In such cases *TULRCA 1992, s 220* cannot provide them with a defence. *Public Order Act 1986, Part II* gives the police certain powers to impose conditions upon public processions and assemblies, in addition to their common law powers to take such action as may be necessary to prevent a breach of the peace.

The House of Lords held in *DDP v Jones* [1999] 2 AC 240 that the public have the right to use the highway for such reasonable and usual activities, including peaceful assembly, as are consistent with the primary right of passage. This important decision was plainly influenced by *art 11* of the European Convention on Human Rights (the right to freedom of peaceful assembly).

Any action which does not fall within the provisions of *TULRCA 1992, s 220* constitutes an offence if the obstruction takes place on the public highway, since the *Highways Act 1980, s 137(1)* provides:

'If a person, without lawful authority or excuse, in any way wilfully obstructs the free passage along a highway he is guilty of an offence ... '.

For the definition of obstruction, see *Cooper v Metropolitan Police Comr* (1985) 82 Cr App Rep 238. However, picketing may take place outside factory gates which are on private property. In such a case, the pickets cannot be guilty of obstructing the highway but may be liable for a private trespass or nuisance.

45.13 THE LIABILITY OF TRADE UNIONS

Trade unions are no longer, as they once were, immune from all proceedings in tort arising from industrial action. They are now liable for tortious acts which they are taken to have authorised or endorsed (see 50.16 TRADE UNIONS – I). They enjoy the same statutory immunity as individuals, but only if they fulfil the ballot requirements of *TULRCA 1992*. The liability of trade unions in actions in tort is subject to statutory financial limits (see 50.17 TRADE UNIONS – I).

45.14 BALLOTS BEFORE INDUSTRIAL ACTION

In order to enjoy immunity from actions in tort for acts inducing persons to take part or continue to take part in industrial action, trade unions must be supported by a ballot (*TULRCA 1992, s 226(1)*). The following are the prerequisites of a ballot before industrial action.

(*a*)   All of those members whom it is reasonable for the union to believe will be called upon in the industrial action, and no others, must be balloted (*TULRCA 1992, s 227(1)*). However, since 18 September 2000, this requirement has been mitigated by a new *TULRCA 1992, s 232B* which provides that a failure to comply which is accidental and on a scale which is unlikely to affect the result of the ballot will be disregarded. By virtue of *TULRCA 1992, s 232A*, industrial action will not be regarded as having the support of a ballot if any member whom it was reasonable at the time of the ballot for the union to believe would be induced to take part in the action is induced to take part. It was held by the Court of Appeal in *London Underground Ltd v National Union of Rail, Maritime and Transport Workers* [1996] ICR 170 that the defendant union could induce members who had not been balloted to take part in industrial action if those members had joined the union since the ballot. It was also recognised that a union may induce non-members to participate, even though they will not have been balloted. In *P (a minor) v National Association of School Masters/Union of Women Teachers* [2003] UKHL 8, [2003] ICR 386 the House of Lords held that the union's failure to send ballot papers to two teachers who had recently joined the staff did not invalidate the ballot. In particular, the failure to send those teachers ballot papers did not necessarily mean that they had not been accorded entitlement to vote within the meaning of *TULRCA 1992, s 232A(c)*. The requirement to send out ballot papers to those defined as entitled to vote in *s 227(1)* is subject to the caveat 'so far as is reasonably practicable' in *s 230(2)*. Further, *s 232B* makes the requirement to send out ballot papers subject to the disregard of small accidental errors. Accordingly, the ballot was valid. By contrast, in *Midline Mainline Ltd v National Union of Rail, Maritime and Transport Workers* [2001] EWCA Civ 1206, [2001] IRLR 813 the failure to ballot 25 union members in a ballot of 91 members was held by the Court of Appeal to be too significant to be disregarded.

If the persons balloted have different places of work, *TULRCA 1992, s 228* requires a separate ballot for each workplace, unless those balloted share a common feature of terms and conditions of employment or occupational description which is not shared by other members with the same employer who are not balloted and, in a case where there are such other members, is not a factor which employees of that employer have in common by virtue of having the same place of work. A new *TULRCA 1992, ss 228* and *228A*, enable unions to hold a ballot across separate workplaces if the dispute affects at least one member of the union in each workplace, or if the ballot is limited to all members whom the union reasonably believes to have particular kinds of occupation and are employed by a particular employer or employers with whom the union is in dispute, or if entitlement to vote is given to only to members of the union who are employed by an employer or employers with whom the union is in dispute. 'Workplace' is defined as the premises at which an employee works or, where an employee does not work at a particular premises, the premises with which his employment has the closest connection (*TULRCA 1992, s 228(4)*). Where separate workplace ballots are not required, the ballot may legitimately include employees of more than one employer, if a number of employers are party to the dispute (*University of Central England v NALGO* [1993] IRLR 81). Employees of different employers may be held to have the same place of work even if their respective employers each have only a licence over the premises at which they work (*Intercity West Coast Ltd v National Union of Rail, Maritime and Transport Workers* [1996] IRLR 583).

(*b*)   So far as is reasonably practicable, every person entitled to vote must have a voting paper sent to him by post at his home address (or other address which he has requested the union to treat as his postal address), and must be given a convenient opportunity to vote by post (*TULRCA 1992, s 230(2)*). Special provisions apply to merchant seamen. It was held in *British Railways Board v National Union of Railwaymen* [1989] ICR 678 that the words 'reasonably practicable' mean that inadvertent errors such as missing some members off the list will not necessarily invalidate the ballot. This principle was given statutory force by *TULRCA 1992, s 232B* which provides for small-scale, accidental failures to be disregarded (see (*a*) above).

(*c*)   The voting paper must contain at least one of the following questions –

   (i)   a question which requires the voter to say, by answering 'Yes' or 'No' whether he is prepared to take part, or to continue to take part, in a strike;

   (ii)   a question which requires the voter to say, by answering 'Yes' or 'No', whether he is prepared to take part, or as the case may be to continue to take part, in industrial action falling short of a strike.

(*TULRCA 1992, s 229(2)*.)

This means that a strike and action short of a strike must be the subject of separate questions on the ballot paper (*Post Office v Union of Communications Workers* [1990] ICR 258).

TULRCA 1992, s 229 provides that an overtime ban and a call-out ban constitute action short of a strike for the purposes of the strike ballot provisions.

(*d*)   The following statement must appear without comment on every voting paper:

   'If you take part in a strike or other industrial action, you may be in breach of your contract of employment.

   However, if you are dismissed for taking part in strike or other industrial action which is called officially and is otherwise lawful, the dismissal will be unfair if it takes place fewer than eight weeks after you started taking part in the action, and depending on the circumstances may be unfair if it takes place later.'

(*TULRCA 1992, s 229(4)*.)

(*e*)   The voting paper must clearly specify the address to which, and the date by which, it is to be returned, and must be numbered (*TULRCA 1992, s 229(1A)*).

(*f*)   The voting paper must specify who, in the event of a vote in favour of action, is authorised for the purposes of *TULRCA 1992, s 233* (see 45.15 below) to call upon members to take part or continue to take part in the industrial action (*TULRCA 1992, s 229(3)*). The specified person need not be authorised under the rules of the union, but must be within *TULRCA 1992, s 20(2)* (ie a person empowered by the rules to call for the action, or the principal executive committee, president or general secretary, or any other committee or official of the union; see also TRADE UNIONS – I (48)). It is thought that the voting paper may specify alternative persons as having the authority to call for action. Further, in a case where an independent scrutineer is required (see (*k*) below), the ballot paper must state his name (*TULRCA 1992, s 229(1A)(a)*).

(*g*)   So far as is reasonably practicable those voting must vote in secret (*TULRCA 1992, s 230(4)(a)*). They must be allowed to vote without interference from the union, and so far as reasonably practicable, without incurring direct costs to themselves (this presumably means that reply-paid envelopes must be used for the postal ballot) (*TULRCA 1992, s 230(1)*). For reasonable practicability, see (*b*) above.

(*h*)   The votes must be fairly and accurately counted, although an inaccuracy in counting is to be disregarded if it is accidental and on a scale which could not affect the result of the ballot (*TULRCA 1992, s 230(4)*).

(*j*)   The majority of those voting in the ballot must have answered 'Yes' to the appropriate question (*TULRCA 1992, s 226(2)(b)*). Where a ballot poses two separate questions, one relating to strike action and the other to industrial action short of a strike, the relevant majority is a majority of those voting on the specific question. It is not necessary that the majority voting 'Yes' in response to the particular question also comprise a majority of those taking part in the ballot (*West Midlands Travel Ltd v Transport and General Workers' Union* [1994] ICR 978).

(*k*)   In a case where the number of members entitled to vote in the ballot (the aggregated number is taken where there are separate workplace ballots in accordance with (*a*) above) exceeds 50, a qualified scrutineer must be appointed. The union must ensure that he duly carries out his functions without interference, and must comply with all his reasonable requests. The scrutineer will make a report as soon as reasonably practicable after the ballot, and in any event within four weeks, stating whether he is satisfied that there are no reasonable grounds for believing that there was any contravention of statutory requirements, that the ballot arrangements included all reasonably practicable security arrangements to minimise the risk of unfairness or malpractice, and that he has been able to carry out his functions without interference from the union. Any person entitled to vote in the ballot, and the employer of any such person, is entitled (upon request made within six months of the ballot and upon payment of any reasonable fee specified by the union) to be provided with a copy of the report (*TULRCA 1992, ss 226B, 226C, 231B*). The persons qualified to be scrutineers are those satisfying the requirements of the *Trade Union Ballots and Elections (Independent Scrutineer Qualifications) Order 1993* (*SI 1993/1909*).

(*l*)   The union must take such steps as are reasonably necessary to secure that every person whom it is reasonable for the union to believe will be the employer of persons entitled to vote in the ballot receives both notice that the ballot will take place, and a sample voting paper. In *English, Welsh & Scottish Railway Ltd v National Union of Rail, Maritime and Transport Workers* [2004] EWCA Civ 1539, 148 Sol Jo LB 1246 the Court of Appeal held that, where a notice of intention to hold an industrial action ballot was addressed to only one of two very closely related employers involved in an industrial dispute with the union, the notice should be treated as having been given to both companies. The notice must be received not later than the seventh day before the opening of the ballot, and must specify the anticipated opening day and identify the categories of employees of that employer whom the union believes will be entitled to vote. The sample voting paper must be received not later than the third day before the opening day (*TULRCA 1992, s 226A*). Under the legislation prior to its amendment, in *Blackpool and the Fylde College v National Association of Teachers in Further and Higher Education* [1994] ICR 648, it was held that the notice must enable the employer readily to ascertain which individual employees were to be balloted, and so in some cases would require individuals to be named in the notice. However, this requirement was amended by *ERA 1999, Sch 3* with effect from 18 September 2000, by virtue of which the union was required to provide such information as is in its possession as would help the employer to make plans and bring information to the attention of the employees. The Court of Appeal considered the new requirements for identification of employees to be balloted in a notice to the employer in *London Underground Ltd v National Union of Rail, Maritime and Transport Workers* [2001] EWCA Civ 211, [2001] ICR 647. The amendments contained in *ERA 1999, Sch 3* would appear to have had less of an impact in this area than was perhaps intended. Although those amendments made it clear that a union cannot be compelled to produce a list of names, the Court of Appeal held that there had been no significant change to the underlying legislative policy. That policy was that employers should know which part or parts of their workforce are being asked to participate in industrial action, in order that they can try to dissuade them and, if unsuccessful, make plans to minimise disruption. It was not sufficient, therefore, for the union simply to state that the ballot would be of all members, employed in all categories at all workplaces. If the union knew the numbers in particular grades and at particular workplaces, it was bound to give that information. With effect from 1 October 2005, the notice provisions contained in *TULRCA 1992, s 226A* were amended yet again by *s 22* of the *Employment Relations Act 2004*. A valid notice must now contain lists of the categories of employee whom the union reasonably believes will be entitled to vote in the ballot and the workplaces at which they work. The notice must also state the total number of employees to be balloted and the number in each category. Unions are expressed not to be under a duty to supply an employer with the names of the employees concerned.

(*m*)   As soon as is reasonably practicable after the holding of the ballot, the union must take such steps as are reasonably necessary to ensure that all persons entitled to vote, and their employers, are informed of the number of votes cast, the number of 'Yes' and 'No' votes, and the number of spoiled voting papers (*TULRCA 1992, s 231, s 231A*).

Where there are separate ballots for different workplaces, paras (*b*) to (*m*) are to be tested in relation to the ballot for the workplace of the person whose inducement to take part in the action is relied upon to found the liability in tort (*TULRCA 1992, s 226(3)*). This means in particular that a 'Yes' vote is required at every workplace where the members are to be called upon to take action.

If there is a suspension of industrial action for negotiations, a further ballot need not be held before industrial action is resumed, provided that the terms of the original ballot cover the reason for the resumed action (*Monsanto plc v Transport and General Workers Union* [1987] ICR 269). However, this will not apply where there is a substantial interruption of the action as opposed to a mere suspension; where the action is irregular and spasmodic, it is a question of fact and degree whether it is sufficiently continuous and self-contained to be covered by a single ballot (*Post Office v Union of Communications Workers* [1990] ICR 258).

In *London Underground Ltd v National Union of Railwaymen* [1989] IRLR 341 it was held that at the time of the ballot there must be a genuine, definite, substantial dispute (actual or reasonably foreseeable) between the parties, and that the ballot question must relate wholly to matters capable of constituting a trade dispute. However, in *Associated British Ports v TGWU* [1989] 1 WLR 939 it was held that there was no need for the ballot information to describe or define every issue with which the dispute was concerned, provided that it was possible to identify the strike which was called with the strike which was voted for (the point was not argued on appeal).

Special provisions apply to overseas members and to members in Northern Ireland (*TULRCA 1992, s 232*). A union which is a federation, and which does not have individual members whom it will call out on strike, cannot comply with the relevant provisions of *TULRCA 1992* and therefore will enjoy no immunity from action when calling a strike (*Shipping Co Uniform Inc v International Transport Workers Federation* [1985] ICR 245).

The Secretary of State is empowered by *TULRCA 1992, ss 203, 204* to issue codes of practice relating to the conduct by trade unions of ballots and elections (see CODES OF PRACTICE (5)). The original *Code on Trade Union Ballots on Industrial Action* has been revised and reissued (*Employment Code of Practice (Industrial Action Ballots and Notice to Employers) Order 2005 (SI 2005/2420)*). The *Code* deals with, among other things, the situations in which an industrial action ballot is appropriate, establishment of the balloting 'constituency', preparation and distribution of voting papers, and the conduct and counting of the ballot.

45.15 CALLING FOR INDUSTRIAL ACTION

In order for the action to be treated as supported by the ballot, there must have been no call by the union to take part in or continue to take part in the action to which the ballot relates, or any authorisation or endorsement of such action (see 50.16 TRADE UNIONS – I), *before* the date of the ballot (*TULRCA 1992, s 233(3)(a)*).

The call for industrial action must be made by the person specified on the ballot paper (see 45.14(*f*) above). It is permissible for the specified person to call for action subject to some condition whose fulfilment is a matter for the judgment of local officials, although he may not simply delegate his authority (*Tanks and Drums Ltd v TGWU* [1992] ICR 1).

The call for action must be made, and the action must commence, before the end of the period of four weeks beginning with the date of the ballot (*TULRCA 1992, ss 233, 234(1)*). However, *TULRCA 1992, s 234(1)* provides that this period may be extended up to a maximum of eight weeks by agreement between the union and the employers. There are provisions which enable the union to apply to the court for an extension of time, up to a maximum of 12 weeks from the date of the ballot, where for the whole or part of that period action is prohibited by a court order or an undertaking given to the court which subsequently ceases to have effect (*TULRCA 1992, s 234(2)–(6)*).

The union must take such steps as are reasonably necessary to give notice to an employer whose employees it reasonably believes will be or have been induced to take part in the action, describing the categories of employees concerned and specifying whether the action is intended to be continuous (in which case it must state the intended commencement date for any of those employees) or discontinuous (in which case it must state the intended dates for any of them to take part). As with the notice of ballot, until 18 September 2000 it was necessary for the notice to enable the employer readily to ascertain which individual employees were to be called upon to take industrial action, and this in some cases required individuals' names to be given (*Blackpool and the Fylde College v National Association of Teachers in Further and Higher Education* [1994] ICR 648). However, again, as with the notice of ballot, this latter requirement was amended by *ERA 1999, Sch 3*, pursuant to which the union was required to provide only such information as would help the employer to make plans and bring information to the attention of the employees. With effect from 1 October 2005, these notice provisions were amended yet again by section 25 of the *Employment Relations Act 2004*. A valid notice must now contain lists of the categories of employee whom the union reasonably believes will be induced to take part in industrial action. The notice must also state the total number of employees to be induced to participate and the number in each category. Unions are expressed not to be under a duty to supply an employer with the names of the employees concerned. The notice must be received within the period beginning with the day when the requirement to notify employers of the ballot result is satisfied (see 45.14(M) above) and ending with the seventh day before the first day specified in the notice (*TULRCA 1992, s 234A*). Thus the union is effectively required to give an employer at least a week's notice of industrial action.

45.16 EMPLOYER'S RIGHTS AND REMEDIES

The withdrawal of labour will usually amount to a breach of the contracts of employment of the individuals concerned. A strike notice may however, at least in theory, be construed as due notice to *terminate* the contracts of employment of the strikers. Whether this is so depends upon the words used and on the circumstances (*Boxfoldia Ltd v National Graphical Association* [1988] ICR 752). Action taken in a go-slow or work-to-rule may also be considered a breach by each individual participant of his contract of employment. In *Secretary of State for Employment v Associated Society of Locomotive Engineers and Firemen* [1972] ICR 7 at 56 Lord Denning MR said:

> 'If [an employee] with ... others, takes steps wilfully to disrupt the undertaking, to produce chaos so that it will not run as it should, then each one who is a party to those steps is guilty of a breach of his contract. It is no answer for any one of them to say "I am only obeying the rule book", or "I am not bound to do more than a 40-hour week". That would be all very well if done in good faith without any wilful disruption of services; but what makes it wrong is the object with which it is done.'

See also *British Telecommunications plc v Ticehurst* [1992] ICR 383.

The courses of action open to an employer, and others affected by industrial action, include the following:

(*a*)   An employer may try to conciliate, if necessary with the assistance of the ADVISORY, CONCILIATION AND ARBITRATION SERVICE (2).

(*b*)   If employees are on strike or their work is disruptive within the meaning of Lord Denning's statement above, they do not have to be paid for the period during which industrial action persists. If employees are refusing to perform part of their contractual duties, employers may deduct an appropriate sum from their salaries (*Sim v Rotherham Metropolitan Borough Council*

[1986] ICR 897; *Miles v Wakefield Metropolitan District Council* [1987] ICR 368; *Wiluszynski v Tower Hamlets London Borough Council* [1989] ICR 493; and see PAY – I (33)).

(*c*)   If employees or unions are taking disruptive industrial action which is not in contemplation or furtherance of a trade dispute or is unprotected secondary action or action for a purpose not within the statutory immunities, or is action by trade unions taken without a ballot, an employer affected may apply to the High Court for an *injunction* to prevent them from continuing such action. He may sue either the individuals involved or the union responsible, or both. Note that *TULRCA 1992, s 221(1)* requires that any application for an injunction must be brought to the attention of the other party if it seems likely that he may claim that he is acting in contemplation or furtherance of a trade dispute. Unless the court is satisfied that all reasonable steps have been taken, an injunction will not be granted. However, it is important to apply to the court speedily.

In deciding whether or not to grant the injunction, a court must have regard to the likelihood of the defendant succeeding in establishing a defence under *TULRCA 1992, s 219* or *s 220* (*TULRCA 1992, s 221(2)*). Although the likelihood of establishing the defence is only one factor to be considered in deciding where the 'balance of convenience' lies (that being the test of whether to grant an interim injunction if the plaintiff has an arguable case and an ultimate award of damages would not be an adequate remedy for either party), the injunction will normally be refused if it appears more likely than not that the statutory defence will be made out (*NWL Ltd v Woods* [1979] ICR 867). The court will also have regard to whether it is likely that in practice the grant or refusal of the injunction will be decisive in determining the legal proceedings for an injunction (if so, it becomes more important to try to form a view of the ultimate chances of success); it will compare the disadvantage to the workers in being unable to strike while the iron is hot with the potential losses to the employer. In a proper case it may have regard to the public interest, and if all other considerations are evenly balanced it will usually attempt to preserve the status quo (see, e g *Dimbleby & Sons Ltd v NUJ* [1984] ICR 386; *Union Traffic Ltd v TGWU* [1989] ICR 98; *Associated British Ports v TGWU* [1989] 1 WLR 939 (point not argued in the House of Lords)). The court will, however, under no circumstances grant an injunction if its effect would be to compel the employees to work (*TULRCA 1992, s 236*).

In proceedings arising out of an act which is by virtue of *TULRCA 1992, s 20* taken to have been one by a trade union (as to which see 50.16 TRADE UNIONS – I), the court's power to grant an injunction includes power to require the union to take such steps as the court considers appropriate for ensuring that there is no, or no further, inducement of persons to take part in industrial action or to continue to do so, and that no person engages in any conduct after the granting of the injunction by virtue of such inducement prior to the injunction (*TULRCA 1992, s 20(6)*). This represents a statutory development of the decision in *Solihull Metropolitan Borough v National Union of Teachers* [1985] IRLR 211, that where industrial action was called without a ballot, union leaders could be required to rescind the instruction.

If the union or the individuals against whom a court order is obtained act in breach of the order, proceedings may be taken for contempt of court (see, e g *Richard Read (Transport) Ltd v National Union of Mineworkers*

(South Wales Area) [1985] IRLR 67; *Express and Star Ltd v NGA* [1986] ICR 589;*Kent Free Press v NGA* [1987] IRLR 267). The penalties which a court may impose if it finds a contempt proved are a fine, sequestration and imprisonment. A writ of sequestration will not affect the separate funds of a branch which is an unincorporated association (see *News Group Newspapers Ltd v Society of Graphical and Allied Trades 1982* [1986] ICR 716). Note that the union will not be able to use its funds to indemnify individuals penalised for contempt of court, nor for certain criminal offences (*TULRCA 1992, s 15*; and see 50.18 TRADE UNIONS – I).

(*d*)   The employer may also claim damages against those taking part in or organising the industrial action, or against the union (see 50.16 TRADE UNIONS – I). A claim in *tort* for inducing breaches of contract (the most common cause of action) will only succeed if the statutory immunity does not apply. However, the immunity does not extend to straightforward actions for *breach of contract*, and individual strikers may be sued on that basis. In practice, this is rarely likely to be worthwhile for an employer. Notwithstanding the absence of a statutory immunity for breach of contract, an employer is precluded from obtaining an injunction to restrain a breach of contract where the effect of the order would be to compel the employee to work (*TULRCA 1992, s 236*). Damages are limited to the loss actually caused by the individual striker (*National Coal Board v Galley* [1958] 1 WLR 16), which may be difficult to prove, or confined to the extra cost of hiring a substitute; and to seek to enforce a substantial award of damages against ordinary employees, even if practicable, will clearly have industrial relations implications. In certain circumstances it may also be possible to recover money which the employer has been forced to pay under duress in the form of unlawful industrial action (see, e g *Dimstal Shipping Co SA v ITWF* [1992] IRLR 78).

(*e*)   If necessary, an employer may in limited circumstances dismiss all employees on strike (or taking other industrial action) and try to engage a new labour force. In the case of unofficial action, he may dismiss selectively. The employment tribunal's unfair dismissal jurisdiction is also *prima facie* excluded in respect of workers dismissed during official industrial action (subject to the significant exception contained in *s 238A* – see below) if two conditions are met: *first*, all the employees in the employer's establishment who were taking part in the industrial action at the date when the complainant was dismissed must also be dismissed; *second*, none of those employees can be offered re-engagement by the employer until *after* the expiry of the period of three months beginning with the date of the dismissal, or else all of them must be offered re-engagement within that period (see further 53.17 UNFAIR DISMISSAL – I) (*TULRCA 1992, ss 237, 238*).

However, the exclusion from the right to claim unfair dismissal contained in *TULRCA 1992, s 238* does not apply where the employee is taking part in 'protected industrial action' and if certain other conditions are satisfied (*TULRCA 1992, s 238A*). 'Protected industrial action' is defined as action which was induced by an act protected by *TULRCA 1992, s 219*. An employee will be treated as having been automatically unfairly dismissed if the reason or principal reason for his dismissal was that the employee has taken part in protected industrial action and:

(*i*)   the dismissal took place within twelve weeks of the start of the protected industrial action by the employee (or within such further period as falls to be added to the twelve weeks to reflect any period during which the employee was locked out by his employer); or

(ii)   the dismissal took place more than twelve weeks (or such longer period as results from a lock-out period) after the start of the protected industrial action and the employee had ceased taking part in the industrial action within the twelve-week period; or

(*iii*)   the dismissal took place more than twelve weeks (or such longer period as results from a lock-out period) after the start of the protected industrial action, the employee had not ceased to take part in the industrial action within the first twelve weeks but the employer had failed to take such procedural steps as would have been reasonable for the purposes of resolving the dispute.

(See further 54.3 UNFAIR DISMISSAL – II.)

45.17 UNION MEMBERS' RIGHT TO A BALLOT

TULRCA 1992, s 62 gives a remedy to a trade union member whose union seeks to involve him in industrial action without the support of a ballot. This includes all those members who work under contracts for personal services, and not merely those who are employees in the strict sense (*TULRCA 1992, s 62(8)*). Such a person may apply to the High Court (or the Court of Session in Scotland), which will make an order (see below) if he can demonstrate that:

(*a*)   the union has, without the support of a ballot, authorised or endorsed any industrial action; and

(*b*)   that members of the union, including the applicant, have been or are likely to be induced by the union to take part in or continue to take part in that action.

Again, any application should be made without undue delay.

For the purpose of deciding whether the members are induced by the union and whether action is authorised or endorsed by the union, reference is made to the test of liability of unions for official action contained in *TULRCA 1992, s 20* (*TULRCA 1992, s 62(5)* and see 50.16 TRADE UNIONS – I). The fact that the inducement is ineffective is immaterial (*TULRCA 1992, s 62(6)*).

The action is authorised or endorsed without the support of a ballot unless, not more than four weeks (or such longer period as may be agreed in accordance with *TULRCA 1992, s 234(1)*) before the commencement of the action, there has been a ballot complying with *TULRCA 1992, ss 226B to 233* (see 45.14 and 45.15 above) in respect of the action, in which the applicant was entitled to vote. The majority of those voting must have answered 'Yes' to a question asking them whether they are prepared to strike or take part in the industrial action concerned (*TULRCA 1992, s 62(2)*).

If the court upholds the complaint, it will make such order as it considers appropriate for requiring the union to take steps to ensure that there is no further inducement of members to take part in the action and that no member engages in any further conduct resulting from the prior inducement. The steps so required may include the withdrawal of any relevant authorisation or endorsement (*TULRCA 1992, s 62(3)*). Disobedience to such an order will, of course, be a contempt of court.

45.18 THIRD PARTIES' RIGHTS AND REMEDIES

At common law, parties whose contracts were interfered with by unlawful industrial action could apply to the High Court for an injunction and damages, provided that the loss caused was not too remote or unforeseeable. The holder of a train ticket was able to recover damages from the rail unions for wrongfully interfering with his contract with British Rail (*Falconer v ASLEF and NUR* [1986] IRLR 331).

There is a statutory right under *TULRCA 1992, s 235A*, for an individual to apply to the High Court where he claims that any trade union or other person has done or is likely to do an unlawful act to induce any person to take part or continue to take part in industrial action, if a likely effect of the industrial action is to prevent or delay the supply of goods or services to the applicant, or to reduce the quality of goods or services supplied to him (*TULRCA 1992, s 235A(1)*). For these purposes an act is unlawful if it is actionable in tort by any one or more persons (which need not include the applicant himself), or in the case of an act by a trade union, if it could form the basis of an application by a member under *TULRCA 1992, s 62* (see 45.17 above) (*TULRCA 1992, s 235A(2)*). It is immaterial whether the applicant has any entitlement to be supplied with the goods or services in question (*TULRCA 1992, s 235A(3)*).

If the court is satisfied that the claim is well-founded, it must make such order as it considers appropriate for requiring the person by whom the act of inducement has been or is likely to be done to take steps for ensuring that no or no further act of inducement is done by him, and that no person engages in further conduct by virtue of his prior inducement (cf 45.16(*c*) above) (*TULRCA 1992, s 235A(4)*). The court also has power to grant interlocutory relief (*TULRCA 1992, s 235A(5)*).

45.19 CONSEQUENCES FOR EMPLOYEES

For any industrial action, whether or not in contemplation or furtherance of a trade dispute:

(*a*)   the employee loses his right to pay during the industrial action (see 45.16(B) above and PAY – I (34));

(*b*)   he is not entitled to receive jobseeker's allowance or income support, although his family may in some circumstances receive income support (see *Cartlidge v Chief Adjudication Officer* [1986] ICR 256) subject to the deduction of a prescribed sum in respect of notional strike pay (see *Tolley's Social Security and State Benefits Handbook* for further details);

(*c*)   he is not entitled to any guarantee payment in respect of the days on which he is engaged in industrial action;

(*d*)   if dismissed during a strike, a participant in that strike may not be able to claim compensation for unfair dismissal (although he will be treated as automatically unfairly dismissed in the circumstances outlined in 45.16(E) above);

(*e*)   so far as the computation of periods of continuous employment is concerned (for example, for redundancy and unfair dismissal claims), absence due to participation in a strike will not break continuity, but the period of absence is not counted in the computation. The start of the period of employment will be deemed to be postponed by the appropriate number of days (see 7.10 CONTINUOUS EMPLOYMENT).

45.20 **EMPLOYEES WHO MAY NOT STRIKE**

Some employees are forbidden by law to strike. These include members of the armed services and police officers. In a few cases employees, especially in industries which are or were within the public sector, may be under certain statutory duties. Attempts have been made to argue that, given that inducement of a breach of statutory duty does not fall within the *TULRCA 1992, s 219* immunity (see 45.3 above), such provisions effectively prohibit organised strike action. But the decisions of the House of Lords in *Associated British Ports v TGWU* [1989] 1 WLR 939 at 970 and of Mantell J in *Wandsworth London Borough Council v NASUWT* [1994] ICR 81 (the point was not argued on appeal), suggest that the courts will be reluctant to construe the relevant statutes so as to reach such a result.

It is a criminal offence for a person 'wilfully and maliciously [to break] a contract of service or of hiring, knowing or having reasonable cause to believe that the probable consequences of his so doing, either alone or in combination with others, will be to endanger human life, or cause serious bodily injury, or to expose valuable property whether real or personal to destruction or serious injury' (*TULRCA 1992, s 240(1)*). The penalty is a fine not exceeding level 2 on the Standard Scale (see 1.10 INTRODUCTION) or imprisonment for not more than three months (*TULRCA 1992, s 240(3)*).

46 Taxation

46.1 OUTLINE

ITEPA 2003

The employment tax legislation is contained in the main in the *Income Tax (Earnings and Pensions) Act 2003* which is referred to in this chapter as *ITEPA 2003*. The Act superseded the former legislation contained in the *Income and Corporation Taxes Act 1988*. The legislation was rewritten as part of the tax law rewrite project. Changes were made to the language used and to align the rules with existing HM Revenue and Customs' practice.

46.2 Employment income

For income tax purposes, income from employment includes 'general earnings' and 'specific employment income'.

(*a*) General earnings include (in each case, excluding exempt amounts):

  (i) earnings which are defined by *ITEPA 2003, s 62* as including any salary, wage or fee, gratuities or other profit or benefit obtained if it is money or money's worth, or anything else constituting an emolument of employment ('money's worth' means something of direct monetary value to the employee or capable of being converted into money or something of direct monetary value to the employee); and

  (ii) amounts treated as earnings which include amounts paid to agency workers (*ss 44–47*), amounts paid through intermediaries (*ss 48–61*), benefits in kind (*ss 63–220*), sickness and disability pay (*s 221*), payments of tax by the employer (ss *222, 223*), payments to non-approved personal pension arrangements (*ss 44–47*), payments or valuable consideration given for restrictive undertakings (*ss 225, 226*), or balancing charges treated as earnings (*Capital Allowances Act 2001, s 262*).

(*b*) Specific employment income includes (in each case, excluding exempt amounts):

  (i) other non-share related income including payments to and benefits from non-approved pension schemes (*ss 386–400*) or payments on termination of employment (*ss 401–416*);

  (ii) share related payments and benefits (*ss 417–554*); and

  (iii) payments which count as employment income under any other enactment.

(*ITEPA 2003, s 7.*)

General earnings include 'benefits in kind' as per (*a*)(ii) above (see 46.21 et seq below). Such benefits are taxable where they are received by employees or directors but there are certain exclusions in the case of 'lower-paid' employees (see 45.3 and 45.23 below). In general terms, the amount assessable in respect of a benefit is its cash equivalent value. Unless specific rules apply to determine the calculation of the cash equivalent value of the benefit (as, for example in the case of company cars and fuel, living accommodation etc), cash equivalent value is simply the cost to the employer less any amount made good by the employee (*ITEPA 2003, ss 203–206*) (see 46.28 below).

46.3 'Directors and lower-paid employees'

The rules governing the taxability of benefits in kind recognise two categories of employers – directors and employees earnings at the rate of at least £8,500 a year and lower-paid employees.

As far as directors are concerned, the rules for directors apply to all 'directors', irrespective of the level of their earnings unless they:

(*a*)   earn less than £8,500 per year (including all benefits in kind and before deduction of any necessary expenses of the employment); and

(*b*)   have no material interest (ie the interest does not exceed 5% with or without associates) in the company; and

(*c*)   are either working full-time as a director or the company is non-profit making and does not hold investments, or is a charity.

The charging provisions apply equally to employees with specific exclusions for 'lower-paid' employees. These are employees whose earnings are at the rate of less than £8,500 per year, including all benefits in kind and before deduction of any necessary expenses of the employment.

The charging provisions also cover the provision of benefits to the family or household of the employee or director.

(*ITEPA 2003, ss 63, 67, 68, 216–220.*)

For the purpose of this chapter, a director who is not excluded by virtue of (*a*)–(*c*) above or an employee who is not a 'lower-paid employee' is referred to as a 'P11D employee'.

46.4 PAY AS YOU EARN (PAYE)

Definition and earnings limits

PAYE is the statutory system of deducting income tax from the employment income (see 46.2 above) of an employee at the time they are paid by the employer so as to secure, as far as possible, that the income tax liability in respect of the employment income is satisfied by the deductions made. The employer effectively acts as a tax collector for HM Revenue and Customs. In addition, the PAYE system collects National Insurance contributions of both employee and employer. It is also used for the operation of Statutory Sick Pay (SSP). Statutory Maternity Pay (SMP), Statutory Paternity Pay (SPP) and Statutory Adoption Pay (SAP), to collect student loan repayments and to collect charitable donations under Payroll Giving (see 46.33 below). Prior to 31 March 2006, the system was also used to pay Working Tax Credit (see 46.34). However, since 31 March 2006, this has been paid direct to all claimants by HM Revenue and Customs.

The PAYE system applies to all payments of employment income assessable to income tax in excess of certain defined limits. These limits (the 'PAYE thresholds') are as laid down from time to time by HM Revenue and Customs. For a person with one employment only, the PAYE threshold is broadly aligned with the weekly/monthly equivalent of the personal allowance for income tax.

46.5 Taxation

The regulations governing the operation of PAYE are the *Income Tax (Pay As You Earn) Regulations 2003 (SI 2003/2682)*. These replaced the predecessor regulations (*SI 1993/744*) from 6 April 2004. The regulations were rewritten as part of the tax law rewrite project. References in this chapter to the regulations are to the rewritten regulations. References to the predecessor regulations are to *SI 1993/744*.

(*ITEPA 2003, ss 684, 686, 708; Income Tax (Pay As You Earn) Regulations (SI 2003/2682*, as amended by *SI 2004/85* (before 6 April 2004, *Income Tax (Employments) Regulations (SI 1993/744*)).)

46.5 Sources of information

Detailed instructions on the operation of PAYE are contained in the HM Revenue and Customs booklet 'Employer's Further Guide to PAYE and NICs' (CWG2) and supplements issued from time to time. This guide is provided to all operators of PAYE and National Insurance contributions as a matter of course, but additional copies may be obtained from any tax office or from the employer's orderline. Copies can also be downloaded from the HM Revenue and Customs' website (see www.hmrc.gov.uk). The guide complements the general PAYE instructions and documents (see 46.6 below) that are sent to employers prior to 6 April each year. In addition, HM Revenue and Customs publish various 'Employer Help Books' (E10 to E16), which contain all the relevant information most employers will need to operate PAYE and National Insurance contributions. HM Revenue and Customs also operates 'Employer Helplines' and provides support services including one-to-one visits.

Guidance on the operation of PAYE is also contained in the HM Revenue and Customs guidance manuals – PAYE Instructions (collection) manual and PAYE Online Manual. Guidance on employment income generally is found in the Employment Income Manual.

A wealth of guidance is also available in the employer area of the HM Revenue and Customs' website (see www.hmrc.gov.uk/employers/index.htm) and on the Employer CD-ROM sent to employers by HM Revenue and Customs as part of the annual pack. See also the *Payroll Management Handbook 2007* (or later edition).

46.6 Method of deduction

Employers must maintain (among other documents) a deductions working sheet (P11 or equivalent) for each employee known to be earning amounts above the PAYE threshold. Special arrangements can be made instead for employers with computerised payrolls etc, by providing a list of employees and their codes. The code shown on the deductions working sheet (or list) determines the appropriate amount of tax to be deducted from that employee's wages. A code will vary to reflect the circumstances of the employee and will be the appropriate amount of personal allowances less the final digit. For example, an allowance of £5,225 would result in a code of 522. A suffix or prefix is then added to the code.

The suffix code letter indicates how the code should be updated to reflect changes announced in the Budget. The suffix code letters in use are as follows:

L = Personal allowance

P = Personal allowance (age 65–74)

Y = Personal allowance (age 75 or over)

V = Personal and married couple's allowance (age 65–74)

T = Specific notification required from HM Revenue and Customs.

Sometimes a code will have a prefix instead of a suffix:

D0 = Higher rate tax (week 1 or month 1 basis)

K = Where state pension or benefits in kind exceed personal allowances

BR = Basic rate tax and no personal allowances

0T = No personal allowances

NT = No tax to be deducted

A K code requires an addition to be made to the employee's pay (or to a pension) in order to arrive at taxable pay. This enables the correct amount of tax to be deducted where emoluments such as benefits in kind exceed personal allowances. There is an overriding regulatory limit to ensure that the maximum amount deducted from emoluments in any pay period does not exceed 50% of cash pay after allowing for deductions such as pension contributions and payroll giving.

The calculation of tax due is made on the deductions working sheet from tax tables provided by HM Revenue and Customs; alternatively, such computations can be done by and stored in computer installations where computerised payrolls are in operation. Approved superannuation contributions and charitable donations through Payroll Giving (see 46.33 below) are deducted from the gross pay before calculation of tax due.

46.7   Employees joining after 6 April

(*a*)   *Employees holding form P45 from previous employer.* The form P45 will show details of total pay and tax paid to the date of leaving the last employment, and the employee's code. These figures are entered on a deductions working sheet for the employee and the normal procedure is followed from the first pay day in the new employment with these figures incorporated into the totals on that day.

(*b*)   *New employees, with no form P45, earning in excess of the PAYE threshold (including existing employees earning over this threshold for the first time).* The employer must operate the code specified for Emergency use on the non-cumulative (Week or Month 1) basis until he is notified by the tax office of the correct code. The employer must notify the tax office as soon as possible after taking on such new employees. Employees taking up employment for the first time following full-time education are dealt with on a cumulative, rather than non-cumulative, Emergency coding basis. On the other hand, employees having other employment should have basic rate tax deducted from earnings. In either case, deductions must continue to be made on the appropriate basis until the correct code is notified. Any pension received by such employees must be brought to HM Revenue and Customs' attention to ensure the correct code is used.

46.8   Employee leaving or dismissed

The employer must send to the tax office part 1 of form P45, giving details of the employee's total pay to date and tax deducted therefrom. The employee is given parts 1A, 2 and 3 of this form of which he should pass over to his new employer parts 2 and 3 or if unemployed, parts 2 and 3 to the Unemployment Benefit Office dealing with his benefit claim.

Where payments are made to the former employee after the form P45 has been issued, tax must be deducted at the basic rate and not by reference to the tax code and no further form P45 should be issued. If the amount of the payment made after the leaving date is known before the employee leaves, it must be entered on the deductions working sheet by reference to the date of the future payment and the amount therefore included in the form P45.

Pay in lieu of notice. Where an employee is dismissed with pay in lieu of notice, the taxation treatment is dependent on whether there was any contractual entitlement to such a payment. The tax treatment of pay in lieu of notice is complex. However, HM Revenue and Customs accepts that where a contract makes no reference to pay in lieu of notice and the employee has no expectation of receiving pay in lieu of notice, a payment of such compensation would generally be for an employer's breach of contract. In that case, the payment will come within the charging provisions relating to termination payments (*ITEPA 2003, ss 401–403*) and so the first £30,000 of the payment would be exempt from tax. HM Revenue and Customs' views on whether or not a payment is contractual is set out in HM Revenue and Customs' Employment Income Manual EIM 12975ff.

In *Delaney v Staples* [1992] 1 All ER 944 it was held that *non-contractual* payments in lieu of notice were not to be regarded as wages for the purposes of what is now *ERA 1996, s 27*. However, HM Revenue and Customs takes the view that 'what constitutes wages under employment law is not the same as what constitutes emoluments under tax law'.

In *EMI Group Electronics Ltd v Coldicott* [1999] STC 803 the Court of Appeal confirmed the HM Revenue and Customs' long-standing practice that *contractual* payments in lieu of notice are assessable as employment income but it was accepted that payments made to junior employees were not taxable since those employees had no contractual right to them. See HM Revenue and Customs' Employment Income Manual EIM 12977

Care should be taken when drafting termination letters and ambiguous language can cause confusion as to the correct tax treatment. This was illustrated in the decision in *Ibe McNally (Inspector of Taxes)* [2005] EWHC 1551 (Ch), [2005] STC 1426.

46.9 Employee retiring on pension from employer

The employer must notify the tax office within 14 days and continue operating the code but on the non-cumulative basis until revised instructions are received from the tax office. However, if the pension is to be paid by the trustees of a pension scheme etc, the employee should be treated as leaving (see 46.8 above).

46.10 Death of employee

The employer must send to the tax office all four copies of form P45, completed as in 46.8 above (writing 'D' in the box at the bottom of the form), and in addition tell the tax office the name and address of the deceased employee's personal representative, if known. From 6 April 2004, the same rules apply in the case of payments made after the date of death as for payments made after the date an employee leaves (see 46.8 above). (Previously, where payments were made after the date of death, deductions and refunds were to be made on a cumulative basis as though the employment (or pension) had continued.)

46.11 **Students employed during vacation**

The general rules apply, except that under certain arrangements the tax office may notify the employer that tax need not be deducted. These arrangements require a signed statement from the student and a declaration on form P38(S) by the employer, following which the tax office will notify the employer that a deductions working sheet need only be prepared for National Insurance purposes. If form P38(S) has been completed and no tax has been deducted, there is no requirement to fill in a form P45 when the student leaves the employment.

46.12 **Employees working abroad**

Where an employee who is resident and ordinarily resident in the UK works abroad, PAYE should be operated in the normal way (except for seafarers in certain cases). Where the employee is not UK resident, UK tax is not chargeable on earnings paid for work performed abroad. Where the worker is resident but not ordinarily resident in the UK, earnings for work performed in the UK will be taxable and earnings for work performed abroad will be taxable but only on a remittance basis. There are special provisions regarding the operation of PAYE in respect of payments made for work performed either in or outside the UK where the employee is not UK resident, or if so resident, not ordinarily resident. In that case, the employer may apply to HM Revenue and Customs for a direction that only a proportion of earnings in a given tax year is assessable to tax and subject to PAYE.

An employer who has a place of business in the UK must pay Class 1 National Insurance contributions on all earnings paid during the first 52 weeks that an employee is working abroad where the employee is ordinarily resident in the UK and was resident in the UK immediately before starting the employment abroad.

Guidance can be found in HM Revenue and Customs leaflets IR 20 'Residents and Non-residents – Liability to Tax in the UK' and NI138 'Social Security Abroad – National Insurance contributions, Social Security benefits, Health care in certain overseas countries. Both leaflets are available on the HM Revenue and Customs' website (www.hmrc.gov.uk).

Because of the complexities involved, reference to the Tax Office is essential, and it may often be advisable to obtain professional advice in particular cases. When an employer sends an employee to work abroad, he should provide him with a letter giving details of the date sent abroad and the gross pay and tax deducted whilst employed in the UK.

46.13 **Refunds of tax when employee is away from work**

Because of the cumulative nature of the PAYE system, periods during which no emoluments are received may give rise to a right to repayments of tax. In the case of such an absence, e g unpaid leave, a repayment may be made by the employer to the employee. This procedure is unlikely to apply to short absences caused by sickness since the statutory sick pay (see 44.6 SICKNESS AND SICK PAY) required to be paid by an employer is taxable in the usual way. Tax is also chargeable on any payment made by the employer (or by a third party under arrangements made by the employer) through a sick pay scheme.

An employer must not refund tax to an employee who is absent from work in consequence of a trade dispute in which the employee is involved, until the dispute has ended unless the employer is authorised to make a tax refund on form P48, or the employee leaves during a trade dispute.

901

46.14 Taxation

Where an employee becomes unemployed (see 46.8 above) and claims jobseekers' allowance or income support, any tax refund due to him will be made by the Jobcentre Plus. However, because these benefits are taxable, payment of any refund will be withheld until the person obtains a new job or, if earlier, until the end of the tax year. Where the employee does not claim either jobseekers allowance or income support and sends Part 2 and 3 of form P45 to HM Revenue and Customs with a declaration that he/she will remain unemployed for the rest of the tax year, any tax refund due will be paid by HM Revenue and Customs.

46.14 PAYE – PAYMENT OF TAX BY EMPLOYER

The employer must pay to the Collector of Taxes, within 14 days of the end of every tax month (ie by the 19th of each month), or within 17 days (ie by the 22nd of each month) where the payment is made by an approved method of electronic communication: all tax and National Insurance contributions deducted together with the employer's National Insurance contributions; plus any student loan deductions; less any recoveries of statutory sick pay, statutory maternity pay, statutory paternity pay and statutory adoption pay (see 33.15 MATERNITY AND PARENTAL RIGHTS and 44.6 SICKNESS AND SICK PAY) (where applicable including an amount to compensate for employer's National Insurance contributions thereon); and prior to 31 March 2006, less any working tax credits paid to employees (see 46.35 below). A single remittance is sufficient although a breakdown of the payment, as between income tax and National Insurance contributions, is required. Failure to remit amounts due may result in proceedings for recovery against the employer.

Employers with 250 or more employees must make monthly payments of PAYE electronically from 6 April 2004. Penalties are charged for failure to comply with compulsory electronic payment.

Employers who have reasonable grounds for believing that the average monthly total tax and National Insurance to be paid to the Collector will be less than £1,500 (£1,000 before 6 April 2000) may make payments quarterly instead of monthly (*reg 70* (before 6 April 2004, *regs 41, 42*)). New employers must notify HM Revenue and Customs if they wish to make quarterly payments, but existing employers need not do so unless a demand is received from HMRC.

HM Revenue and Customs has the power under *reg 80* (before 6 April 2004, *reg 49*) to determine the amount of tax payable where it appears to it that tax may have been payable but has not been paid; and interest at the prescribed rate on unpaid tax in respect of *reg 80* determinations can be charged under *reg 82* (before 6 April 2004, *reg 50*).

Interest at the prescribed rate will be charged automatically on late payments of PAYE where tax is outstanding by more than 14 days after the end of the tax year, or by more than 17 days where the payment is made by an approved method of electronic communication. A repayment supplement at the prescribed rate is also available where overpaid deductions are later refunded (*regs 82, 83* (before 6 April 2004, *regs 47–53*)).

46.15 PAYE – END OF YEAR PROCEDURE

(*a*) *Employee's certificates.* By 31 May following the end of the tax year, the employer must give each employee in office on 5 April a certificate (P60 or P60 (substitute)) showing the following details: the tax year to which the certificate applies, total taxable emoluments, net tax deducted, the code in use on 5 April, the employer's PAYE reference, the employee's name and National Insurance number, and the employer's name and address.

In the case of an employee engaged after 6 April, the certificate should include details of pay and tax of the previous employment, insofar as they were taken into account in computing the tax due under this employment.

(*b*)   *Returns.* By 19 May following the end of the tax year, the employer must give to HM Revenue and Customs the End of Year Return (P14 or substitute) which for each employee (including any employee who has left during the year) gives details of the total earnings, total net tax deducted, and National Insurance contributions together with amounts of any statutory sick pay, maternity pay, paternity pay or adoption pay (see 46.13 and 46.14 above) included in total earnings and details of any student loan deductions or payments of tax credits (see 46.35 below). This form must be accompanied by the employer's end of year return, form P35, containing a declaration and statement by the employer. Employers with 50 or more employees must file 2005–2006 and subsequent returns electronically. Incentive payments are available to small employers (fewer than 50 employees) who file electronically ahead of time. Employers with fewer than 50 employees are required to file year-end returns online from 2009–10.

46.16 Forms P11D and P9D

In addition to the returns noted in 46.15 above, forms P11D (or substitute form) must be submitted by 6 July after the end of the tax year for all directors and employees (other than 'lower-paid' employees – see below) to whom the employer (or a third party) provides benefits for or reimburses expenses. The employer must also submit form P11D(b) by 6 July following the end of the tax year to which it relates. Form P11D is a return of 'Expenses and Benefits' (see 15.20 and 15.23 above) and return P11D(b) is a 'Return of Class 1A National Insurance Contributions' which declares the total amount of Class 1A contributions due to be paid on P11D benefits (see 46.17 below) and includes a declaration that all the required forms P11D and P11D(b) have been completed and submitted to HM Revenue and Customs.

Forms P9D (or substitute forms) must also be submitted by 6 July after the end of the tax year for employees in an excluded employment (formerly known as 'lower-paid employees') who earn at a rate of less than £8,500 per annum (including expenses payments and benefits). Directors who have no material interest in the company (ie an interest not exceeding 5% control) are treated solely as employees if either they are full-time working directors or the company is non-profit-making or a charity (see 46.3 above) and so fall within this category where they earn less than £8,500 per annum. Certain benefits are not taxable in the case of P9D employees (see 46.22 below) and Class 1A National Insurance contributions are not payable on P9D benefits.

For self-assessment purposes, employers must provide to each employee or director either a copy of the form P11D or P9D or a statement of their benefits by 6 July after the end of the tax year.

See 46.28 below with respect to dispensations not to subject expenses payments to PAYE or to include expenses and benefits on the employees' form P11D for both tax and Class 1A National Insurance contributions purposes.

46.17 Class 1A National insurance contributions

Class 1A National Insurance contributions must be paid by 19 July following the end of the tax year and must be reported on form P11D(b) (see 45.16 above). Returns P11D(b) not submitted by that date attract a penalty. From 6 April 2000, Class 1A National Insurance contributions were extended to cover most benefits in kind. Before then, they were only chargeable on the provision by employers of cars and fuel for private use by employees (*Social Security Contributions and Benefits Act 1992, ss 10, 10ZA; Child Support, Pensions and Social Security Act 2000, ss 74, 75*). For further details of Class 1A contributions, see *Tolley's National Insurance Contributions 2006/07* (or later edition).

46.18 PAYE Settlement Agreements

Employers may enter into PAYE Settlement Agreements whereby they can settle, in a single payment, the income tax and National Insurance liability on certain expenses payments and benefits provided to employees. Such expenses payments and benefits do not then need to be processed through the PAYE system or recorded on forms P11D or P9D. A formal written agreement to make such a payment must be made with HM Revenue and Customs by 6 July following the end of the tax year.

The benefits which are covered by the agreement are subject to tax and Class 1B National Insurance contributions which must be paid by 19 October following the end of the tax year. Class 1B National Insurance contributions are payable on the benefits that would otherwise be subject to Class 1 or Class 1A contributions if they were not included in the agreement. The tax payable must be 'grossed-up' at either the basic or higher rate of tax depending on the liability of the employees concerned since the payment of the tax liability is itself a benefit subject to tax.

Class 1B National Insurance contributions are payable on the aggregate of the total value of the benefits and the grossed-up amount of income tax due.

46.19 PAYE ONLINE

Large employers (ie those with 250 or more employees) were required to file their year-end returns P14s and P35 by an approved electronic method from the 2004–2005 returns, which were due by 19 May 2006. Approved methods are the PAYE online service and electronic data interchange (EDI)

Medium-sized employers (50 to 249 employees) were brought within compulsory electronic filing of year end returns from 2005–2006 returns, due 19 May 2006.

Small employers are not required to file returns electronically until the 2009–2010 returns, due 19 May 2010. However, to encourage earlier electronic filing, incentives payments are made to small employers who file electronically ahead of time. Small employers who file their P14s and P35 online from 2004–2005 can earn £825 tax-free in incentive payments.

From 6 April 2009 employers with 50 or more employees will also be required to file certain in-year information online. Compulsory filing will apply from this date to the following:

(*a*)   P45(1): details of employee leaving;

(*b*)   P45(3): new employee details;

(*c*)   P46: employee without a form P45; and

(*d*)   similar information for people receiving a pension.

Small employers (fewer than 50 employees) will be required to send the above information electronically from 6 April 2011.

The PAYE online service can be used to send and receive payroll information. It can be used by employers, agents and payroll bureaux alike. The use of the service is not limited to year-end returns. It can also be used for P11Ds, P9Ds, P11D(b)s and a range of other forms, notices and reminders.

Before using the service, employers and agents must register on the HMRC web page and then activate the service using the activation PIN that is sent through the post.

HM Revenue and Customs is keen that the PAYE service is widely used and are keen to publicise the benefits. See also www.hmrc.gov.uk.

46.20 RECORDS

All records which the PAYE regulations require the employer to maintain, but not to send to HM Revenue and Customs, must be retained for not less than three years after the end of the year to which they relate. Under self-assessment, regulations require employees to keep records to enable them to make a correct and complete return.

46.21 TAXABLE BENEFITS – GENERAL RULES

Detailed information on the tax treatment of benefits in kind is to be found in *Tolley's Income Tax 2005/06* (or later edition). Concise factual information, in tabular form, is contained in *Tolley's Tax Data 2005/06* (or later edition). A brief account of general principles in relation to those benefits most commonly derived from employment is given in this paragraph and in 46.22–46.28 below. Special rules applying to employee share schemes are outlined briefly in 46.29–46.33 below.

The main taxable benefits are as follows.

(*a*)   Expense payments and allowances – taxable subject to relief for actual expenses; see 46.28 below (*ITEPA 2003, ss 70–72*).

(*b*)   Cash vouchers – taxed on their redemption value.

Non-cash vouchers and transport vouchers – taxed on the cost to the employer of providing them less any contribution from employee (unless used to obtain certain non-taxable benefits).

Credit tokens – taxed on the cost to the employer of the money, goods or services obtained less any contribution from employee (unless used to obtain certain non-taxable benefits).

(*ITEPA 2003, ss 73–96.*)

(*c*)   'Living accommodation' – taxed on the annual value (as defined) or the actual rent paid by the employer if greater, subject to exemptions (e g where the employee is a representative occupier). For accommodation costing in excess of £75,000, a higher value is attributed to the excess (*ITEPA 2003, ss 97–113*).

(*d*)   Cars, vans and related expenses – tax based on cash equivalent values, see 46.24 to 46.27 below (ITEPA 2003, ss 114–172). For cars the cash equivalent depends on the level of CO2 emissions and the list price, for car fuel, the determinant is the level of CO_2 emissions and vans are taxed by reference to a scale charge. From 6 April 2007 a separate fuel charge applies to vans.

(e)   Interest-free or reduced interest loans – the taxable benefit is the difference between the interest paid (if any) and the 'official rate' of interest at a rate prescribed by the Treasury. There are certain reliefs for loans made at fixed rates not below market value when made, and loans for some specified purposes. No tax charge arises on loans made to employees on commercial terms where the employer lends to the general public. Nor is there any charge where the aggregate value of beneficial loans does not exceed £5,000 at any time in the tax year.

Loans written off are taxed on the amount written off.

(*ITEPA 2003, ss 173–191.*)

(f)   Shares and securities – an employee who is given shares or securities or options over shares and securities, or is allowed to acquire them on terms more favourable than those available to the public, is taxed on the value of the benefit he receives. Tax and National Insurance advantages are available in relation to certain share option and share incentive schemes (*ITEPA 2003, ss 192–200*).

(g)   Assets gifted – if new, charged at cost to employer and if used, generally taxed at market value. See 46.22(F) below in the case of P9D employees (*ITEPA 2003, ss 203, 204*).

(h)   Mileage allowances – taxed on excess over tax-free rates (before 2002/03 also on excess over actual business expenditure) (*ITEPA 2003, ss 229–232, 235, 236*).

(i)   Medical treatment or insurance premiums, unless for treatment outside the UK while the employee is working abroad (*ITEPA 2003, s 325*).

(j)   Relocation expenses – non-qualifying expenses and benefits and qualifying expenses and benefits exceeding £8,000 per move (*ITEPA 2003, ss 271–289*).

(k)   Use of employer's assets – land taxable at annual value, other assets at 20% of market value when first lent or rental charge if higher (*ITEPA 2003, ss 203–205*). Exemptions for computers loaned prior to 6 April 2006 (costing up to £2,500) and bicycles and special rules for company cars, company vans, and living accommodation.

(l)   Services supplied by employer, such as in-house goods or services provided at less than cost – taxed on the direct extra (marginal) cost the employer incurs, less any payments made by the employee or director. This was found to be the correct way of computing such benefits in *Pepper v Hart* [1993] 1 All ER 42.

46.22 Benefits taxable on employees in an excluded employment

A number of the benefits noted in 46.21 above are not taxable on those employees in an excluded employment, ie employees who earn at a rate of less than £8,500 per annum including expenses payments and benefits. The benefits taxable for such employees are as follows:

(a)   Vouchers and credit tokens – as per 46.21(B) above.

(*b*)   'Living accommodation' – as per 46.21(C) above.

(*c*)   Loans written off – taxed on amount written off.

(*d*)   Non-business related expenses and personal expenses paid on the employee's behalf – expenses under £25 can be ignored.

(*e*)   Relocation expenses – as per 46.21(J) above.

(*f*)   Assets gifted to employee – taxed at second hand value.

46.23 Tax-free benefits

The main tax-free benefits are as follows.

(*a*)   Meals provided in a canteen – not assessable, but taxable on directors and P11D employees if not provided for the staff generally (*ITEPA 2003, s 317*). Meals and refreshments provided to employees who participate in 'cycle to work' days are not assessable. (For 2002/03 when first introduced, it was limited to six occasions a year.)

(*b*)   Luncheon vouchers – not taxable up to 15 pence per day.

(*c*)   Approved superannuation or pension schemes – contributions by an employer are not taxable.

(*d*)   Medical insurance premiums or medical treatment outside the UK where the employee performs duties abroad but not including the cost of an air ambulance back to or treatment in the UK (*ITEPA 2003, s 325*).

(*e*)   Childcare facilities, such as workplace nurseries, for employees' children under 18 provided by the employer alone or with other employers, local authorities etc. From 6 April 2005 the exemption also applies (subject to qualifying conditions) to the provision of childcare at or away from the workplace at registered, non-residential facilities provided by the employer (either alone or in partnership with other parties but financed and managed wholly by the employer). The provision can also be provided to employees of other employers working at the same location. Also from 2005/06, the exemption is available (subject to qualifying conditions) in respect of the provision of certain other registered or approved childcare contracted by the employer, the benefit being wholly tax-free for 'lower paid' employees and otherwise tax-free up to a maximum of £55 per week (£50 per week before 6 April 2006) (regardless of the number of children) for other employees. The exemption applies (subject to similar conditions) to the provision of childcare vouchers up to £55 per week (£50 per week prior to 6 April 2006) (plus the cost of supplying the vouchers) used to obtain qualifying childcare. (*ITEPA 2003, ss 84(2A), 270A, 318–318D; FA 2004, s 78, Sch 13*). Prior to 6 April 2005, the childcare exemption only applied for tax purposes to care provided in a workplace nursery meeting the qualifying conditions.

(*f*)   Work-related training (*ITEPA 2003, ss 250–260*) and outplacement counselling services for employees who are or become redundant. Also welfare counselling (*SI 2000/2080*).

(*g*)   For employees starting a new job or moving with their existing employer, qualifying relocation expenses and benefits up to the value of £8,000 per move (*ITEPA 2003, ss 271–289*).

(*h*) In-house workplace sports and recreational facilities provided by employers for use by the staff generally, provided overnight accommodation is not available and the facilities are not on domestic premises. The exemption does not cover the use of assets such as yachts, cars and aircraft for private use (*ITEPA 2003, ss 261–263*).

(*i*) The provision of living accommodation for employees (but not directors) in certain circumstances where it is necessary for their job. This exemption extends to the employer's payment of employees' council tax. Accommodation provided as a result of a security threat is also exempt (*ITEPA 2003, ss 99, 100*).

(*j*) The provision of accommodation, supplies or services used by the employee in performing the duties of the employment, provided that any private use is insignificant, and that the sole purpose of providing the benefit is to enable the employee to perform the duties (from 6 April 2000) (*ITEPA 2003, s 316*).

(*k*) Alterations and additions to premises of a structural nature or landlord's repairs to premises of living accommodation which is provided by reason of a person's employment (*ITEPA 2003, s 313*).

(*l*) The provision of parking facilities at or near the workplace for a car, cycle or motorcycle (*ITEPA 2003, s 237*).

(*m*) Provision of travel, accommodation and subsistence during public transport disruption caused by industrial action (*ITEPA 2003, s 245*).

(*n*) Provision of transport between home and place of employment or the provision of cars for severely disabled employees (*ITEPA 2003, ss 246, 247*).

(*o*) Provision of transport for occasional late night journeys from work to home (*ITEPA 2003, s 248*).

(*p*) Private use of mobile phones provided by the employer (from 6 April 1999) – limited to one phone per employee from 6 April 2006 (*ITEPA 2003, s 319*).

(*q*) The loan of certain computer equipment provided prior to 6 April 2006 with a value not exceeding £2,500 (equating to a cash equivalent of £500) by the employer to the employee (providing that loans are not restricted to senior employees) (from 6 April 1999). From 2004/05, computer equipment provided as above is also exempt from the general charge under *ITEPA 2003, s 62* on earnings (see 45.2 above), thus avoiding a charge where the employee is given the choice of the loan of computer equipment or additional salary. (*ITEPA 2003, s 320; FA 2004, s 79*).

(*r*) Provision of works buses with a seating capacity of nine or more, provided for employees to travel to and from work (reduced from 12 which applied from 6 April 1999 to 5 April 2002). Additionally, (from 6 April 2002) where employees benefit from their employer's subsidy of a bus service by receiving free or reduced-price travel, there is no tax charge on this benefit (*ITEPA 2003, ss 242, 243*). Also (from 6 April 2002) there is an exemption for the provision of buses for local shopping services (*SI 2002/205*).

(*s*) The loan of bicycles and cycling safety equipment provided for employees to travel from home to work (from 6 April 1999) (*ITEPA 2003, s 244*).

(*t*)   The cost of an annual Christmas party or similar event, providing that it is open to all staff generally and the cost per person attending does not exceed £150 (£75 before 2003/04) (*ITEPA 2003, s 264*).

46.24 COMPANY CARS, VANS AND FUEL

The provision of company cars, vans and fuel are taxable benefits for directors and 'P11D' employees (ie they are not taxable on 'lower-paid employee's as defined, see 46.3 above).

46.25 Company cars

From 2002/03, the cash equivalent of the benefit derived from the private use of a company car is based on a percentage of the car's list price, graduated according to the level of the vehicle's carbon dioxide (CO2) emissions. The scale begins at 15% for cars emitting (for 2005/06, 2006/07 and 2007/08) 140 grams per kilometre or less, increasing by 1% for each extra 5 grams per kilometre, to a maximum of 35% of the list price. This is reduced to 135g/km from 2008/09

Diesel cars have an additional 3% charge but are still subject to the 35% maximum. For cars registered after 31 December 1977 with no approved CO2 emissions figure, the tax charge is 15% of the list price for engines up to 1,400 cc, 25% for engines of 1,401–2,000 cc and 35% for engines above 2,000 cc or without a cylinder capacity. Electric cars are charged to tax on 9% of the car's list price.

For cars registered before 1 January 1998, the tax charge is 15% of the list price for engines up to 1,400 cc, 22% for engines of 1,401–2,000 cc and 32% for engines above 2,000 cc. Cars without a cylinder capacity are taxed on 32% of the car's price (or 15% for electric cars).

A system of discounts applies in relation to certain environmentally friendly cars, whereas certain diesel cars attract a supplement.

Diesel cars attract a 3% supplement. However, the supplement does not apply for 2005–2006 and earlier years to cars registered prior to 1 January 2006 that meet the Euro IV emissions supplement. The diesel supplement is capped such that the maximum charge cannot exceed 35 per cent of the car's list price.

From 2006–2007, a 2% discount is available for bi-fuel gas and petrol cars manufactured and converted before type approval. A 3% discount is given to hybrid electric and petrol cars and a 6% discount to electric only cars. A 2% discount is to be introduced for cars that run on E85 fuel.

From 6 April 2008 a new category of environmentally-friendly cars is introduced. Qualifying low emissions cars (QUALECS) are cars with CO2 emissions (unrounded) that do not exceed the statutory figure, set at 1209/km for 2008–09. The appropriate percentage is 10% regardless of fuel used. The 30% supplement still applies to diesel cars that are QUALECS).

For 2005–2006 and earlier years, the cost of conversion was disregarded in determining the list price of bi-fuel gas and petrol cars converted after type approval and a 1% discount was given. Bi-fuel gas and petrol cars manufactured or converted before type approval benefited from a 1% discount plus a further 1% for each 20g/km that the car's emissions fall below the level of CO2 qualifying for the minimum petrol percentage charge of 15% (140g/km for 2005–2006). Hybrid petrol and electric cars benefited from a 2% discount plus a further 1% for each 20g/km by which the car's emissions fall below the level of CO2 qualifying for the minimum petrol percentage. Electric cars were subject to a 6% discount.

The 'list price' (subject to an overall limit of £80,000) is the price published by the manufacturer, importer or distributor (inclusive of delivery charges and taxes) at the time of registration. It is important to note that this is unlikely to be the price actually paid by the employer for the car. The list price for the car includes any standard accessories provided with the car, but the price of any optional extras supplied with the car when first made available to the employee, together with any further accessory costing £100 or more must be added in. Where an employee makes a capital contribution to the initial cost of the car, the price of the car for the year of contribution and subsequent years is reduced by that contribution or £5,000 if less.

The value of the benefit is reduced proportionately if the car is 'unavailable' for part of the year. The benefit is further reduced (or extinguished) by the amount of contributions which an employee is required to make for private use. Cars more than 15 years old and worth over £15,000 are taxed by reference to their open market value in accordance with special rules for classic cars.

(*ITEPA 2003, ss 114–148.*)

46.26 Car fuel

From 2003/04, the benefit on car fuel provided for private motoring in a company car is calculated by applying the car benefit appropriate percentage ascertained in 46.25 above to a figure of £14,000. Before 2003/04 the benefit was calculated by applying a system of scale rates dependent on the cylinder capacity of the car.

The value of the benefit is proportionately reduced if the car is not available for part of the year. No charge applies if the employee is required to, and does, make good to the employer the cost of all fuel used for private purposes (including travel between home and work). The charge is proportionately reduced if the employee begins to meet the cost of the fuel provided for private use, or fuel ceases to be provided for private use, from a date part way through the year, provided this condition continues to be met for the rest of the year.

HM Revenue and Customs has published 'advisory' fuel rates for company cars which can be used to negotiate dispensations for mileage payments for business motoring in company cars. The figures may also be used for reimbursement by employers of fuel used for private motoring. The advisory rates will not be binding where the employer can demonstrate that the cost of business motoring is higher than the advisory rates. With effect from 1 February 2007, the rates are as follows:

Engine size	Petrol	Diesel	LPG
1,400cc or less	9p	9p	6p
1,401 to 2,000cc	11p	9p	7p
Over 2,000cc	16p	12p	10p

The rates are reviewed if prices vary by more than 10%.

(*ITEPA 2003, ss 149–153.*)

46.27 Vans

The provision of a company van weighing no more than 3.5 tonnes for the private use of employees is taxed by reference to an annual scale charge. From 6 April 2007, the charge is £3,000, regardless of the age of the van. For 2005/06 and earlier years the charge was £500 for vans less than four years' old at the end of the tax year and £350 for vans at least four years old. The charge is reduced proportionately if the van is not available for the whole year, or is unavailable for 30 consecutive days or more. Payments by an employee towards private use of the van will also reduce the tax charge. Special provisions apply where vans are shared between several employees. From 6 April 2005, no charge applies to employees who have to take their van home and are not allowed, and do not make, any private use of the van (insignificant use being disregarded).

From 6 April 2007, a separate fuel scale charge of £500 applies where fuel is provided for private mileage in the company van. Prior 6 April 2007 there was no additional charge to the provision of fuel. The charge applies unless the employee is required to make good the full cost of fuel provided for private use and does, in fact, do so (*ITEPA 2003, ss 155–170*).

Since 6 April 2004, no charge has applied where emergency service workers in the fire, police and ambulance services have to take their emergency vehicle home when on call (*ITEPA 2003, s 248A*).

46.28 RELIEF FOR ASSESSABLE BENEFITS

In many of the above cases, the assessable benefit may be reduced by payments made by the employee to the employer and/or by a claim for relief for expenses incurred wholly, exclusively and necessarily in the performance of the duties. The latter is an especially difficult test to satisfy and it must be shown that the employee is obliged to incur and pay the expense as the office holder. Similarly, reimbursements to employees (other than employees in an excluded employment, as defined in 46.3 above) in respect of expenses, or any sum put at their disposal to cover expenses (such as for business travel and subsistence), are treated as earnings and relief can be claimed for the allowable part (*ITEPA 2003, ss 333–336*, previously *ICTA 1988, s 198*).

To avoid unnecessary administration, where expenses payments or benefits do no more than cover expenses incurred wholly, exclusively and necessarily in the performance of the duties, the employer can obtain a dispensation from HM Revenue and Customs. Such a dispensation would avoid the employer having to include the expenses payments and benefits on the employee's form P11D for tax and Class 1A National Insurance purposes or the expenses payments in the employee's gross pay for tax and Class 1 National Insurance purposes.

46.29 EMPLOYEE SHARE SCHEMES

Savings-related share option schemes

Savings-related share option schemes are tax-advantaged schemes established in accordance with *ITEPA 2003 ss 516–520, Sch 3* (amended by *FA 2003, Schs 21, 22*) whereby a company may establish a scheme for its employees to obtain options to acquire the company's shares without charge to income tax either on the value of the options or on any subsequent increase in the value of the shares before the options are exercised. The scheme must be linked to an approved savings scheme (subject to a monthly limit of £250) to provide the funds for the acquisition of the shares when the option is exercised. For capital gains tax purposes, the market value is not substituted for the consideration given so the base cost is the amount paid for both the shares and the option. Taper relief runs from the date of exercise. For further details of the scheme rules, see *Tolley's Income Tax 2005/06* (or later edition).

46.30 Company share option schemes

A company share option plan (CSOP) is a tax-advantaged share option plan set up in accordance with *ITEPA 2003, ss 521–526, Sch 4* (as amended by *FA 2003, Sch 21 para 16*). The scheme applies to options granted from 17 July 1995 (before that date, options were granted under what was known as the 'executive share option scheme' which provided more generous tax relief). The aggregate market value of shares acquired under the option and any other approved options held by the employee (other than savings-related schemes) must not exceed £30,000. There is no tax charge when the options are granted, if all the conditions have been complied with. Options under the scheme have to be exercised between three and ten years after being granted but may be exercised within three years of the grant where the individual ceases to be an employee due to injury, disablement redundancy or retirement. Options granted before 9 April 2003 must be exercised between three and ten years after being granted (without exception), and not more frequently than once in every three years. For capital gains tax purposes, the base cost is the amount paid for both the shares and the option and taper relief runs from the date the option is exercised. For further details of the plan rules, see *Tolley's Income Tax 2005/06* (or later edition).

46.31 Share incentive plans

Share incentive plans were introduced by *FA 2000, s 47, Sch 8*, then known as the all-employee share ownership plan. The legislation is now found in *ITEPA 2003, ss 418, 488–515, Sch 2* (amended by *FA 2003, Schs 21, 22*). Share Incentive Plans (SIPs) are intended to be available to all employees, and were designed to replace profit-sharing schemes. Employees can receive up to £3,000 worth of free shares per year, with the option of purchasing shares up to £1,500 per year by deductions from salary. For every share purchased, the employee can be given two free shares. To remain free of tax and National Insurance, all shares acquired must be held in the plan for a specified period of time, normally at least three years. Dividends of up to £1,500 per employee per tax year can be reinvested tax-free in additional shares in the company. Withdrawals of shares from the plan are not subject to capital gains tax and they are treated as acquired by the employee at their market value at that time. Taper relief applies from the date the shares are withdrawn. For further details of the plan rules, see *Tolley's Income Tax 2005/06* (or later edition).

46.32 Enterprise management incentives

The 'enterprise management incentive scheme' was introduced by *FA 2000, s 62, Sch 14* and amended by *FA 2001, s 62, Sch 14*. The legislation is now contained within *ITEPA 2003, ss 527–541, Sch 5*. The scheme allows small independent trading companies to reward employees with tax-advantaged share options worth up to £100,000 per employee. (The original legislation provided that no more than 15 employees could hold such options at any one time but this limit was removed by *FA 2001*.) Any gain on the sale of such shares is chargeable to capital gains tax but the shares qualify for business assets taper relief. The company must be an independent UK company carrying on a qualifying trade, and its gross assets must not exceed £15,000,000. For further details, see *Tolley's Income Tax 2005/06* (or later edition).

For a thorough discussion of the schemes outlined in 46.29–46.32 above, see *Tolley's Tax Planning 2005/06* (or later edition).

46.33 **PAYROLL GIVING SCHEME**

Employees can authorise their employers to deduct charitable donations from their earnings before tax, for passing on to nominated charities approved through agency charities with which the employer has made arrangements. Deductions must be made under a scheme authorised by HM Revenue and Customs and subject to regulations made by Statutory Instrument. Before 6 April 2000, the amount that could be donated in this way was limited to £1,200. The Government added a 10% supplement to donations made in this way until 5 April 2004 (*ITEPA 2003, ss 713–715; SI 1986/2211; FA 2000, s 38*). National Insurance contributions remain payable on the gross earnings.

46.34 **WORKING TAX CREDIT**

Child Tax Credit ('CTC') and Working Tax Credit ('WTC') were introduced with effect from 6 April 2003, replacing the Children's Tax Credit, the Working Families Tax Credit and the Disabled Person's Tax Credit. They also replaced the child-related elements of a number of other state benefits. The credits are not taxable and the amount payable is related to the claimant's income or joint income in the case of a couple.

WTCs were originally paid to employees by their employers through the payroll and the payment is funded by deducting the credits from the monthly (or quarterly) remittances of PAYE payments (see 45.14 above). However, from 31 March 2007 they are paid direct to all claimants by HM Revenue and Customs.

46.35 **PROVISION OF SERVICES THROUGH AN INTERMEDIARY**

Provisions were introduced with effect from 6 April 2000 by *FA 2000, Sch 12* which are designed to counter what the Government considers to be tax avoidance where services are provided through an intermediary, ie typically single workers contracting out their services to a client via their own company. The provisions are generally referred to as IR35 after the Budget Press Release in which they were announced. The legislation is now found within *ITEPA 2003, ss 48–61* (as amended by *FA 2003, s 136*).

The measures were introduced following 'concern about the hiring of individuals through their own service companies so that they can exploit the fiscal advantages offered by a corporate structure'. The rules were extended from 10 April 2003 so they not only apply to services provided for another person's business but now also to those engaged in a domestic capacity, such as nannies. For an example of a case where, before the enactment of these provisions, personal service companies were used to avoid PAYE, see *Sports Club v HM Inspector of Taxes (and related appeals)* (Sp C 253) [2000] STC (SCD) 443.

The provisions are designed to ensure that PAYE is payable on contractors' income in circumstances where, if the service company did not exist, the worker would be an employee of the client. There are corresponding NIC provisions, contained in the *Welfare Reform and Pensions Act 1999, s 75* (*SI 1999/3420*) and the *Social Security Contributions (Intermediaries) Regulations 2000*.

The provisions apply to 'relevant engagements'. To be a relevant engagement, the terms of all the contracts applying to the engagement will be reviewed, including the contract between an agency and the client, and between the worker's personal service company and the agency. If the terms of the contracts would have created a contract of employment had they been entered into directly between the client and the worker, the IR35 rules apply. The provisions do not introduce any statutory definition of employment or self-employment, so the existing case law will still apply to decide employment status.

For further details of the provisions, see *Tolley's Income Tax 2005/06* (or later edition). HM Revenue and Customs has a substantial library of information about these provisions on its website at www.hmrc.gov.uk/ir35/index.htm.

The Court of Appeal confirmed the legality of the provisions in the judicial review case of *R (on the application of Professional Contractors Group Ltd) v IRC* [2001] EWCA Civ 1945, [2002] STC 165. A group of contractors had applied for judicial review of the provisions, contending that, by reclassifying contractors who worked through personal service companies as employees, they were a breach of the *EC Treaty* and the European Convention on Human Rights. The CA reviewed the evidence in detail, rejected these contentions, and dismissed the application. Robert Walker LJ held that the provisions did not constitute a 'state aid' within the meaning of *art 87EC* of the *EC Treaty*. They also did not breach the provisions of the *EC Treaty* concerning freedom of movement or freedom to provide services. On the evidence, they did not involve a 'direct and demonstrable inhibition' on the establishment of a business within the UK, or on the provision of services without establishment. Genuine self-employed activities would not be affected and 'a business of providing employee-like services will be taxed as if there was a real employment situation'.

The corresponding NIC provisions (contained in the *Social Security Contributions (Intermediaries) Regulations 2000 (SI 2000/727)*) were held to apply in *Battersby v Campbell* (Sp C 287) [2001] STC (SCD) 189 and *FS Consulting Ltd v McCaul* (Sp C 305) [2002] STC (SCD) 138.

46.36 MANAGED SERVICE COMPANIES

Managed service companies are intermediary companies through which the services of a worker are provided to an end client. They are not the same as personal service companies and in contrast to a personal service company the worker is not usually in business on his own account and does not exercise control over the business. The control is with the provider of the managed service company.

With effect from April 2007 legislation is being introduced to target the use of managed services companies to avoid tax and National Insurance contributions. The legislation does not apply to personal service companies. Under the provisions, from 6 April 2007, all payments received by individuals providing their services through a managed service company will be subject to PAYE. From the same date, the cost of travel from the individual's home to work will not be an allowable tax expense for workers within managed service companies.

It is intended that from 6 August 2007, National Insurance contributions will also be due on all payments received by individuals working through managed service companies.

Also from August, where the PAYE and NIC debts of a managed service company cannot be recovered from the company, HMRC may transfer the debt personally to the company director or to the managed service company provider. Debts may be transferred to third parties from 6 January 2008.

47   Temporary and Seasonal Employees

(See also DTI Guidance: Fixed Term Work: A Guide to the Regulations PL 512)

Cross-references. See 17.3 EMPLOYEE, SELF-EMPLOYED OR WORKER? for the distinction between a contract for services and a contract of service/employment. See TAXATION (46) for vacation employment of students. See also ENGAGEMENT OF EMPLOYEES (23) and PROBATIONARY EMPLOYEES (36).

47.1   An employer may sometimes engage workers on a temporary basis. This might be to take over work while a permanent employee is away or to cope with fluctuating work loads (eg due to seasonal work requirements). In this chapter, the description 'temporary' is applied to a worker who is referred to an employer by an employment agency (the kind of worker commonly referred to as a 'temp') and also to an employee who is employed for a limited period. 'Seasonal worker' is applied to a person who enters into the direct employment of the employer for a limited period at a busy time of the year. Employees who are engaged for a limited period (including seasonal workers) may be fixed-term employees and accordingly will qualify for protection under the provisions of the *Fixed-Term Employees (Prevention of Less Favourable Treatment) Regulations 2002 (SI 2002/2034)* (these *Regulations* are considered below at 47.9).

As to employment of part-time workers or job-sharers, their employment rights are not dependent on their working a specified number of hours in a week: see CONTINUOUS EMPLOYMENT (7). See also the *Part-time Workers (Prevention of Less Favourable Treatment) Regulations 2000 (SI 2000/ 1551)* as amended by *SI 2002/2035* (see 24.15 EQUAL PAY).

47.2   **TEMPORARY WORKERS**

Employment agencies

Employment agencies fulfil two main functions: they effect introductions of permanent staff to employers and they supply temporary staff for a short period of time. So far as the first category is concerned, after the introduction has been made, the employment agency drops out of the picture, and the employer enters into a direct relationship with the employee with all the attendant duties and responsibilities of a normal employment contract. If, however, the worker is supplied on a temporary basis – the agency charging its client a weekly fee out of which it pays the worker – the client is more accurately to be regarded in most circumstances as a user of that worker's services and not his employer (here called the 'quasi employer'). Because the quasi employer controls not only what the agency worker does but how he does it, the quasi employer may be vicariously liable for any wrong done by the worker while working for him (see VICARIOUS LIABILITY (56)) and be liable to the worker for any claim by him for damages for personal injuries (*Mersey Docks and Harbour Board v Coggins and Griffiths (Liverpool) Ltd* [1947] AC 1; *Denham v Midland Employers' Mutual Assurance Ltd* [1955] 2 QB 437). However, it was for a considerable period doubtful whether the quasi employer would be liable to the worker for unfair dismissal or redundancy if the employment agency could be regarded as the primary employer who lends the worker's services to other employers (*Cross v Redpath Dorman Long (Contractors) Ltd* [1978] ICR 730). In *Ironmonger v Movefield Ltd* [1988] IRLR

461, it was held that the contract with the employment agency was one *sui generis*, somewhere between a contract of employment and a contract for services. A similar approach was taken in *Wickens v Champion Employment* [1984] ICR 365 where there was held to be no contract of employment between a worker and an employment agency.

In *McMeechan v Secretary of State for Employment* [1997] IRLR 353 the Court of Appeal held that an agency worker *may* have the status of an employee in relation to a *particular engagement* actually worked even if there is no such status as an employee under the *general terms of engagement* between the worker and the employment agency. In this case, the appellant's claim to employee status was limited to a specific contract in relation to which he was owed money. The Court of Appeal held, despite an express term describing the appellant as 'a self-employed worker' that he was in fact an employee in relation to the specific engagement under consideration. It was, accordingly, unnecessary for the Court of Appeal to determine whether the appellant was to be considered an employee under the general terms of the engagement with the employment agency. In a series of recent decisions, however, the Court of Appeal, has developed the law relating to the employment status of agency workers on the basis that a contract of employment could, in appropriate cases, be *implied* between the temporary worker and the client (or quasi employer) for whom they are executing work (see *Franks v Reuters Ltd* [2003] EWCA Civ 417, [2003] IRLR 423; *Dacas v Brook Street Bureau (UK) Ltd* [2004] EWC Civ 217, [2004] IRLR 358; *Cable & Wireless plc v Muscat* [2006] EWCA Civ 220 [2006] IRLR 354). This difficult issue of the employment status of temporary and agency workers is considered further below with the key cases developing the applicable principles outlined.

In *Costain Building and Civil Engineering Ltd v Smith* [2000] ICR 215, the EAT had reversed a finding by an Employment Tribunal that a worker supplied by an agency and appointed by a trade union as a safety representative was an employee. The worker was paid without deduction of tax or National Insurance. The EAT held that the only contracts were between the employment agency and the worker and between the employment agency and the company. By way of contrast, in *Motorola Ltd v Davidson* [2001] IRLR 4, the EAT held that a worker supplied by an agency was an employee of the hiring company (Motorola) and could, accordingly, present a complaint of unfair dismissal. The EAT held that Motorola exercised sufficient control in reality over the worker to give rise to employee status, rejecting Motorola's argument that the worker was controlled by the agency. This was a significant decision in that there was no express contract between the worker and Motorola, a factor which had previously been fatal to the contention that the worker was an employee of the quasi employer. The facts of the case should also be noted in that the employee was *specifically selected* to work at Motorola and had done so *permanently* for *over two years*.

While each case may turn upon its own facts, in the area of employment status of agency workers even on similar facts, wholly different conclusions have been reached by different courts. This left agency workers in a very unsatisfactory and uncertain position with regard to employment protection rights. A clear illustration of the problem was provided by *Montgomery v Johnson Underwood Ltd* [2001] EWCA Civ 318, [2001] IRLR 269. In that case the claimant had worked for the client of the employment business for some two and a half years. Upon the termination of her 'employment' she presented a claim for unfair dismissal. The issue of who was the employer arose as a preliminary issue. The case eventually reached the Court of Appeal which concluded, applying the tests of control and mutuality of obligation, that, on the particular facts, the claimant was not an employee of the employment business. The unfortunate consequence of this decision was that the claimant was left without a remedy as the original employment tribunal decision (to the effect that she was not an employee of the client business at which she had worked for two and a half years) had not been appealed. A striking example of very long term agency workers being found not to have employment status was provided by *Esso Petroleum Co Ltd v Jarvis* (EAT/0831/00). In that case, agency workers who had worked for the same client for 9 and 11 years, respectively, were found not to be employees of the client on the basis of the absence of a contractual relationship between the workers and the client. This may be contrasted with the *Motorola* decision above. In *Hewlett Packard Ltd v O'Murphy* [2002] IRLR 4 it was held that there was no contractual nexus between the worker (who had worked for six years) and the appellant client. Accordingly, he was not an employee. *Motorola* was not, however, referred to in the *Hewlett Packard* case.

The lack of certainty in this area of the law and the apparently conflicting decisions at EAT level has lead to a trilogy of decisions of the Court of Appeal which develop the concept of an *implied contract of employment* arising between the worker and the client using his services. In *Franks v Reuters Ltd* [2003] EWCA Civ 417, [2003] IRLR 423 the claimant entered into a temporary worker agreement with an employment agency and was supplied to Reuters where he worked for five years working hours fixed by Reuters but paid by the employment agency. The Court of Appeal held that the worker was an employee of Reuters. The question to be addressed by an employment tribunal was whether a contract of employment could be implied between the worker and Reuters from the circumstances of his work and what was said by the parties at the time work commenced and subsequently. The Court of Appeal explained that although a person cannot become an employee simply by reason of length of the time which they have worked, the length of 'service' was not irrelevant evidence in the context of a person who was allowed to stay working in the same place for the same client for over five years because dealings between parties over a period of years, as distinct from weeks or months, are capable of generating implied contractual relationships.

The principles in *Franks* were further developed in *Dacas v Brook Street Bureau (UK) Ltd* [2004] EWCA Civ 217, [2004] IRLR 358.In *Dacas* the applicant had worked exclusively as a cleaner at a hostel run by Wandsworth Council for at least four years until the engagement was terminated. Mrs Dacas brought proceedings for unfair dismissal against the supplying agency and, alternatively, the Council. In a striking illustration of the unsatisfactory nature of the law in this area the Employment Tribunal concluded that she was employed by neither the agency not the council. This result – that Mrs Dacas was employed by nobody – was described in the Court of Appeal (by Sedley LJ) as 'simply not credible'. The Court of Appeal concluded that the agency was not the employer of the claimant as the necessary mutuality of obligation or control was not present. As to the Council, Mummery LJ concluded that employment by that body would accord with 'practical reality and commonsense' and in Sedley LJ's view there was an inference to be drawn that the Council was the employer. The decision represents an important shift in relation to the employment of agency workers *by the client* to whom the services are provided so long as the elements of control and mutuality of obligation are satisfied in relation to the client and regardless of the precise terms of the contractual relationship between the client and the agency or the agency and the worker. Indeed, the Court of Appeal in *Dacas* stressed that, in proceedings before an Employment Tribunal where the status of a claimant is in issue, the Tribunal is required as a matter of law to consider whether there is an *implied* contract between the parties who are not in an express contractual relationship with each other. (On the facts of *Dacas* there was a contract between Mrs Dacas and the agency and between the agency and the Council. The relationship between Mrs Dacas and the Council was considered by the majority (Munby J dissenting) to be an *implied* contract of employment.) Thus, a cautious approach would suggest that, in the light of *Dacas*, clients who avail themselves of the services of agency workers on a exclusive basis for one year or more (the qualifying period for unfair dismissal) will be likely, in the event of termination of the worker's engagement (whether by the client or the agency), to be considered by the Employment Tribunals to be the employer of the worker in question and thus liable for any unfair dismissal. As to other rights which are not dependent upon one year's service, *Dacas* does not lay down a hard and fast rule for when a worker will become an employee of the client on the basis of continued service, but it should not be assumed that continuous service for less than one year will inevitably lead to the conclusion that the worker is not an employee. On this point, Sedley LJ in *Dacas* stated that conduct which was maintained over 'weeks or months' as opposed to 'a brief time' might give rise to a finding that there was an implied contract of employment between the client and the worker.

In *Cable & Wireless plc v Muscat* [2006] EWCA Civ 220 [2006] IRLR 354 the implied contract approach was considered further. In that case the Court of Appeal held for the first time that there was *in fact* an implied contract of employment between the worker and the client end-user (in *Franks* the issue had been remitted to the Employment Tribunal and the observations in *Dacas* as to implied contract status of the claimant were, on the particular facts of that appeal, *obiter*). The facts of *Muscat* were complicated and somewhat unusual. The worker had originally been an employee who was then required to go to agency provided services followed by a TUPE transfer. As such, the case did not illustrate the more common factual circumstances of a worker providing services to a client consistently through an agency for a period of time in excess of, say, one year. Further the Court held that the guidance of the majority in *Dacas* was to be applied and followed by Employment Tribunals in future cases. On the issue of the fact that payment of the worker was made by the agency rather than the client end user (which factor was one of the main reasons for Munby J's dissent in *Dacas*), the Court held that this is not a particularly strong factor against employee status if the other factors point to employment by the end user client.

In *James v Greenwich London Borough Council* [2007] ICR 577, [2007] IRLR 168 the issue has been revisited by the EAT following the *Muscat/Dacas* guidance. On the facts the claimant was an agency worker who had worked for the local authority for a number of years acting under the direction of the council without intervention from the employment agency. She was treated like a permanent member of staff on the staff rota. When she went off work by reason of sickness the agency replaced her with another worker. On her return the claimant was informed her services were no longer required and she brought a claim for unfair dismissal. So far this looks to be a strikingly similar set of facts to *Dacas* leading to an implied contract of employment, the reader might (reasonably) think. No, says the EAT in *James*. The core issue, explains the EAT, is whether it is '*necessary*' to imply a contract of employment between the worker and the end-user. The EAT (Elias P) held that it was not sufficient that the arrangements are *consistent* with a contract of employment as in order to imply such a contract it must be necessary in that the way in which the contract is performed is only consistent with an implied contact between the worker and the end-user and not consistent with another contractual relationship. The EAT held that mere passage of time will not justify such an implication but that there must be some words or conduct after commencement of the working relationship entitling the Tribunal to conclude that the agency relationship no longer adequately reflects the reality of the relationship. The EAT observed that 'we suspect that it will be a rare case where there will be evidence entitling the tribunal to imply a contract between the worker and end user'. While this is a powerful decision for employment agencies and end-users keen to avoid workers being granted employee status, it appears somewhat at odds with the *obiter dicta* in the factually similar *Dacas* and it is unlikely that this will be the last word on the issue and further Court of Appeal guidance may be expected. The case is a further example in this area of different courts reaching opposite conclusions on very similar facts whilst applying the same guidance. For atypical workers (and those advising them) the issue of their status, and the prediction of the likely judicial determination if the matter were to be litigated, remains as difficult as ever.

The *Dacas* line of cases consider the possibility of employment by the client end-user. The issue of employment by the employment agency was revisited by the Court of Appeal in *Bunce v Postworth Ltd (t/a Skyblue) [2005] EWCA Civ 490,* [2005] IRLR 557. In that case the Court of Appeal held that an agency welder was not employed by the agency who supplied him. In this case the worker did not work for only one end user and a claim against the end user was not pursued. The absence of control exercised by the agency was held to be fatal to the claim against the agency and the Court of Appeal distinguished its earlier decision in *McMeechan* (above) in relation to the possibility of an overall contract with the agency and separate contracts in relation to each assignment. The legal position of such workers remains uncertain and unsatisfactory with a large number of people not enjoying the full range of employment rights solely because of their agency work arrangements as opposed to more typical 'employment'; a point stressed by Keene LJ in the Court of Appeal. The answer, however, was said to lie in the need for new legislation and not judicial creativity. In *Cairns v Visteon UK Ltd* [2007] IRLR 175 the facts engaged were somewhat unusual in that there *was* a contract of employment between the worker and the employment agency. The issue before the EAT was whether, in such circumstances, a contract of employment could nevertheless also be implied between the worker and the end-user client as well. The EAT held that there was no business necessity to make such an implication (nor any policy reason) to extend parallel protection under the *ERA* to an employee who was already protected by the employment relationship between the employer and the employment agency employer. In *Royal National Lifeboat Institution v Bushaway* [2005] IRLR 674, the EAT held that a written agreement, which defined the claimant as a 'temporary worker' supplied by an employment agency, was not conclusive as to the relationship between the parties notwithstanding a provision that the written agreement constituted the entire agreement between the parties. The EAT considered that as the relationship was not accurately reflected in the contractual document it was permissible to go beyond the terms of the document and examine the employment status of the claimant. On the facts the claimant was found to be an employee even though engaged on quite different terms and conditions to those of other employees.

47.3 **Statutory control of employment agencies**

Persons who carry on employment agencies or employment businesses had formerly to be licensed by the Secretary of State. The licensing provisions have now been replaced by a system under which the Secretary of State may apply to an Employment Tribunal for an order prohibiting a person from carrying on, or being concerned with the carrying on, of any employment agency or employment business or any specified description of such agency or business. The Tribunal may make the order if it is satisfied that the person concerned is unsuitable, on account of misconduct or for other sufficient reason, to do what the order prohibits; there are detailed provisions concerning the application of this test to companies and partnerships. There is an appeal on a question of law to the Employment Appeal Tribunal (see 20.40 EMPLOYMENT TRIBUNALS – I).

The prohibition, which may be for a maximum period of 10 years, may be absolute or it may be on carrying on the business otherwise than in accordance with specified conditions. Non-compliance with a prohibition order without reasonable excuse is a summary offence punishable with a fine not exceeding level 5 on the Standard Scale (see 1.10 INTRODUCTION). The person to whom the order applies may apply to the tribunal to have it varied or revoked where there has been a material change in circumstances.

(*Employment Agencies Act 1973, ss 3–3D*, as inserted by *Deregulation and Contracting Out Act 1994, Sch 10 para 1*.)

It is a criminal offence, punishable by a fine not exceeding level 5 on the Standard Scale (see 1.10 INTRODUCTION) to charge a person a fee for finding or seeking to find him employment, save in such cases as the Secretary of State prescribes (*Employment Agencies Act 1973, s 6*). The classes which have been prescribed relate to occupations in the entertainment industry, to modelling and to *au pairs*.

In *First Point International Ltd v Department of Trade and Industry* (1999) 164 JP 89 the Court of Appeal, for the first time, considered the scope of *s 6*. The section provides that a person 'shall not demand or directly or indirectly receive from any person a fee for finding him employment or seeking to find him employment'. The facts of *First Point International* were as follows. A person interested in work in Thailand contacted First Point International which sent him promotional materials and details of a 'personal client appraisal service' which required payment of almost £100 for an 'appraisal pack' containing appraisal questionnaires to be completed by the potential employee. The potential employee duly paid the fee, completing the questionnaires. First Point International then offered to identify suitable employment for him, for which service they would charge £3,150. The potential employee did not avail himself of this opportunity but First Point International was convicted of two offences under *s 6*. The £100 payment was found to be a fee for seeking to find employment; the £3,150 was found to be a 'demand' for payment for seeking to find employment. On appeal, the Court of Appeal upheld the convictions concluding that the fee for the appraisal documents was, as a matter of law, part of the 'seeking of employment'. As to the invitation to pay £3,150, the Court of Appeal concluded that *s 6* was not limited to cases where there was an enforceable legal right to payment but extended to invitations to make payments.

The *Employment Relations Act 1999* clarifies the application of *s 6* by providing that the prohibition on the charging of fees will extend to 'requests' for payment or the provision of information. The relevant amendments came into force on 25 October 1999.

The conduct of employment agencies was further regulated by the *Conduct of Employment Agencies and Employment Businesses Regulations 1976* (*SI 1976/715*). These Regulations have now been replaced with the *Conduct of Employment Agencies and Employment Businesses Regulations 2003* (*SI 2003/3319*) with effect from 6 April 2004 (see below 47.5).

47.4   **Statutory control of employment agencies: the 2003 reforms**

As far back as 1999, the Government published a consultation paper, 'Regulation of the Private Recruitment Industries', proposing the replacement of, *inter alia*, the *Conduct of Employment Agencies and Employment Businesses Regulations 1976* (*SI 1976/715*). The key proposals in that document sought to clarify the legal rights and obligations of agencies, their workers and clients, to require checks to be made upon the relevant qualifications of workers and, in certain cases, to require references and to prevent workers engaging in hazardous work for which they were not qualified. Consultation of the proposed changes had a lengthy history continuing into 2002–2003. From 6 April 2004 the *Conduct of Employment Agencies and Employment Business Regulations 2003* (*SI 2003/3319*) ('the *Regulations*') have been in force.

This area continues to be one likely to be the subject of further reform. A Private Member's Bill (The Temporary and Agency Workers (Prevention of Less Favourable Treatment) Bill) was introduced in Parliament on 13 December 2006 but is unlikely to become law absent support from the Government. The Department for Trade and Industry has however commenced consultation on proposals to introduce new measures to protect vulnerable agency workers. The present proposals do not go as far as providing analogous protection to that provided to part time workers or fixed term employees (see below 47.9) but propose certain protections against detriment and limit fees for finding work in areas of particularly vulnerability such as those seeking work through talent agencies. The consultation closed on 31 May 2007 but at the time of publication the results of that consultation are not available.

In the meantime the *2003 Regulations* remain the governing legislative provisions and, accordingly, the key features of the *Regulations* are outlined below. In addition the DTI has published guidance on the *Regulations* which is available from the DTI website (ww.dti.gov.uk/er/agency/conduct.pdf).

The Conduct of Employment Agencies and Employment Businesses Regulations 2003 (SI 2003/3319)

47.5   The majority of provisions of the *Regulations* came into force with effect from 6 April 2004 with certain provisions relating to workers providing services through limited companies coming into force on 6 July 2004. Transitional provisions deal with engagements which were in place prior to the coming into force of the *Regulations*.

At the outset it is important to identify the precise terminology used by the *Regulations*. Under the *Regulations* a person seeking work through an agency or employment business is a 'work-seeker'. The client to whom the services are supplied is the 'hirer' (*reg 2*). As to the agencies, the relevant definitions are found in the *Employment Agencies Act 1973* as follows. An 'employment agency' finds work-seekers employment with hirers or supplies hirers with work-seekers for employment (*s 13(2)*). An 'employment business' engages work seekers directly and supplies them on a temporary basis to the hirer (*s 13(3)*). Thus in ordinary usage headhunters are employment *agencies* and temping agencies are employment *businesses*.

Under the *Regulations*, written terms of business must be agreed between the employment agency or business (as the case may be) and the work-seeker and the hirer. The terms must identify whether the service is that of an employment agency or an employment business (see *regs 14* and *17*). In relation to a work-seeker, terms must be agreed in advance of provision of services in one document or a number of documents given at the same time (*reg 14(2)*). The terms of engagement can only be varied with the work-seeker's consent and the variation must be agreed in writing (*reg 14(4),(5)*). When terms have been agreed, the employment agency/business cannot threaten to withdraw its services in order to induce the work-seeker to accept a variation to the terms of business (*reg 14(6)*). Specifically in the case of employment businesses, the written terms must state whether the work-seeker is to be an employee of the business (*reg 15*). The terms must also specify the terms of employment including notice periods, holidays and holiday pay and remuneration intervals. There must be an undertaking from the employment business to pay the agreed rate of pay (even if the hirer does not pay) and the level of remuneration must be specified (or at least the minimum rate expected to be obtained) (*reg 15*).

In relation to the hirer, the written terms with the agency or employment business are governed by *reg 17*. The terms must be agreed in advance and included in a single document. Variations must be recorded in writing and details of fees payable, refund provisions and refund scales must be set out. For employment businesses a procedure to cover the situation of unsatisfactory workers must be provided and in the case of employment agencies the scope of the agency's authority must be expressly specified (*reg 17*).

The Regulations contain detailed provisions in relation to the charging for the services of an employment agency or employment business. In general, employment agencies and businesses are prohibited from charging a fee to work-seekers for finding a job. Under the *Employment Agencies Act 1973* it is not unlawful to charge for certain services such as training or assistance with CV drafting and the like. By *reg 5* it is, however, unlawful to insist that a work-seeker avails themselves of such additional services as a condition for the provision of employment business services. Limited exceptions to the general principles apply in relation to employment agencies who deal with actors, musicians, models and sportspersons (see *Sch 3* to the *Regulations*). Even in these categories the practice of demanding payment of fees in advance of securing an engagement is, in the main, prohibited (see *regs 26(3),(5)* and *(6)*) along with the practice of charging both the work-seeker and the hirer a fee.

The *Regulations* permit charges to be made to hirers on a more broad basis. One important area of limitation is, however, in relation to 'transfer fees' (ie where a hirer wishes to permanently engage a temporary worker supplied by an employment business or where the hirer wishes to re-engage the worker through a different employment business). In the light of concerns about such fees being an unhelpful restriction on the provision of labour, the *Regulations* limit transfer fees as follows. In cases of workers becoming permanent employees, transfer fees may only be charged if the hirer employs the worker within eight weeks of the end of the engagement or within 14 weeks of the start of the assignment. Further, the contract between the employment business and the hirer must provide the option for the hirer to extend the period of the original hire on no less favourable terms.

The *Regulations* also impose minimum obligations on the employment agency or employment business to take steps to ensure that the work-seeker is suitable and also that the hirer is suitable (see *reg 20*). In relation to the work-seeker the employment business or agency must obtain confirmation of identity and willingness to perform the role (*regs 19, 21(1)(a)(i)*). Where an employment business receives information relevant to the suitability of a worker supplied it must inform the hirer or terminate the engagement (*reg 20(2), (3), (4)*). Similar provisions apply in relation to an employment agency (*reg 20(5), (6)*). Further obligations arise in relation to checking professional qualifications (*reg 22*) and in relation to suitability for working with vulnerable persons (*reg 22*). Information about the post, health and safety risks, qualifications required and rates payable and other terms of engagement must be obtained by the agency or employment business from the hirer (*reg 18*) and the employment business or agency should ensure that the hirer has carried out an adequate risk assessment for health and safety purposes.

Further, a employment business or agency must not withhold pay due to a work-seeker in a number of circumstances (including that the hirer has not paid the employment business) (see *reg 12*) and must not disclose information relating to the work-seeker without prior consent, save for the purposes of providing the job finding services or for legal proceedings or to professional bodies relevant to the work-seeker (*reg 28*). An employment agency or business may not subject a work-seeker to any detriment on the ground that the work-seeker has terminated the contract or given notice to terminate the contract and cannot require a work-seeker to provide information as to the identity of future employers (*reg 6*).

As to work-seekers who provide their services via limited companies, the provisions of the *Regulations* were, by *reg 32(1)*, extended to this category of work-seeker with effect from 6 July 2004. The work-seeker is the limited company providing the individual's services and the individual is termed the 'person supplied by the work-seeker to carry out the work'. In this category the worker with a service company may opt out of the application of the *Regulations*. Any such opt out must be signed by the individual and the company before any assignment starts (*reg 32(9)*) but does not apply to engagements which involve working with vulnerable groups such as children and the elderly (*reg 32(12)*).

Breach of the *Regulations* (or breach of the *Employment Agencies Act 1973*) resulting in damage is actionable in the civil courts (*reg 30(1)*) and an employment agency or employment business which breaches the *Regulations* may be liable to prosecution and a fine (*Employment Agencies Act 1973, s 5(2)*). By *reg 31(1), (2)* contractual terms in agreements with work-seekers or hirers which are prohibited by the *Regulations* are unenforceable and transfer fees which are in breach of the *Regulations* are liable to be repaid.

Guidance on the operation of the *Regulations and the Employment Agencies Act 1973* has been issued by the DTI and can be found on the DTI website at www.dti.gov.uk/er/agency/conduct.pdf.   and   www.dti.gov.uk/er/agency/ShorterGuidanceFinal.htm.

47.6   **The application of the National Minimum Wage**

The *National Minimum Wage Act 1998*, applies to all workers (as defined in *s 54(3)*). By *s 34* of the *National Minimum Wage Act 1998*, agency workers shall have the right to the National Minimum Wage in relation to whichever of the parties (agent or principal) is responsible for paying or actually pays the worker (see further PAY – I (34)).

47.7   **Employees**

A temporary employee may accrue sufficient qualifying employment to present a complaint of unfair dismissal. If at the outset of his employment it was made clear to him that he was only engaged on a temporary basis, the employer's refusal to renew his temporary contract should be considered to be for a substantial reason falling within *ERA 1996, s 98(1)(b)* and may well be considered fair. (See *Fay v North Yorkshire County Council* [1986] ICR 133 approving *Terry v East Sussex County Council* [1977] 1 All ER 567.) The dismissal of replacement employees, taken on in place of permanent employees on medical suspension or absent because of pregnancy or confinement, will be considered to be for a reason falling within *s 98(1)(b)* provided that the dismissal is effected so as to allow the permanent employee to resume his original work, and provided that the dismissed employee was informed in writing at the time of the engagement that the employment was temporary and would be terminated when the permanent employee returned (*ERA 1996, s 106*). The Tribunal will then go on to decide whether the dismissal was fair within the meaning of *ERA 1996, s 98(4)(b)*. See also the provisions of the *Fixed-Term Employees (Prevention of Less Favourable Treatment) Regulations 2002 (SI 2002/2034)* (below at 46.9).

47. 8 SEASONAL WORKERS

Workers taken on for a limited period of time, such as seasonal sales staff or extra staff taken on to deal with the tourist season, are considered to be employees for all purposes. They enjoy all the normal employment protection rights provided that they have the necessary qualifying periods of employment.

Where such an employee is dismissed when the seasonal demand has ended, the fact that he was only taken on as a seasonal worker will not automatically make the dismissal fair. It is merely one of the circumstances which must be taken into account by an Employment Tribunal in deciding whether the employer acted reasonably (see UNFAIR DISMISSAL – II (54)). Also, a seasonal worker must be given at least the statutory minimum period of notice to terminate his contract of employment, unless the contract was for a fixed term (see 48.7 TERMINATION OF EMPLOYMENT).

If the period of unemployment between seasons is short and the employee is habitually re-engaged, his continuity of employment may be preserved during the period of his absence due to the temporary cessation of work (*ERA 1996, s 212(3)(b)*). (See 7.6 CONTINUOUS EMPLOYMENT, *Fitzgerald v Hall, Russell & Co Ltd* [1970] AC 984, *Ford v Warwickshire County Council* [1983] ICR 273 *Sillars v Charringtons Fuels Ltd* [1989] ICR 475, *Cornwall County Council v Prater* [2006] EWCA Civ 102, [2006] IRLR 362 and see also *Hellyer Bros Ltd v McLeod* [1987] ICR 526.)

Employers should therefore take just as much care to comply with all the applicable employment rules regarding seasonal staff as they do in the case of their permanent staff. See also the provisions of the *Fixed-Term Employees (Prevention of Less Favourable Treatment) Regulations 2002 (SI 2002/2034)* (below at 47.9).

Fixed-Term Employees (Prevention of Less Favourable Treatment) Regulations 2002 (SI 2002/2034)

47.9   In the case of employees who are engaged for a fixed period or for a particular task the *Fixed-Term Employees (Prevention of Less Favourable Treatment) Regulations 2002 (SI 2002/2034)* ('*the Regulations*') provide important rights to ensure that these employees are not less favourably treated than employees who are permanent or employed for an unlimited duration. The provisions of the Regulations came into force on 1 October 2002 and are derived from the *Fixed-Term Work Directive 99/70/EC*. DTI Guidance on the application of the Regulations is available: Fixed Term Work: A Guide to the Regulations PL 512 and may be found on the DTI website (www.dti.gov.uk).

A fixed term contract is defined under the *Regulations (reg 1)* as a contract of employment that under its provisions will terminate (a) on the expiry of a specific term (b) on the completion of a particular task or (c) on the occurrence or non occurrence of any other specific event other than the attainment by the employee of any normal and bona fide retirement age. Thus (a) covers, say, an engagement for six months, (b) covers engagement to undertake a specific task (cf 47.7 above) and (c) is apt to cover the situation where an employee is engaged to cover for an absent employee until their return to work (eg following, say, a period of maternity absence). If a contract is to terminate on expiry of a specific term then the fact that there is also provision for earlier termination by notice does not prevent the contract being a fixed term contract for the purpose of the Regulations (*Allen v National Australia Group Europe Ltd* [2004] IRLR 847, EAT).

Certain employments are excluded from the protection afforded by the *Regulations* including apprentices, those on work experience and the armed forces (*regs 14, 18, 20*). The most significant exclusion, perhaps, is contained in *reg 19* whereby 'agency workers' are excluded from the protection of the *Regulations*. Agency worker means any person who is supplied by an employment business to do work for another person under a contract or other arrangements made between the employment business and the other person. 'Employment Business' for the purpose of the *Regulations* means 'the business ... of supplying persons in the *employment* of the person carrying on the business, to act for, and under the control of, other persons in any capacity' (emphasis added (*reg 19(3)*). In the light of the complexity of the law relating to the issue of when an agency worker is employed by the agency (see 47.2 above) it appears likely that the ambit of this exclusion will be uncertain and highly likely to lead to continued litigation of the issue of who in fact employs an agency worker.

The *Regulations* introduce the concept of a 'comparable permanent employee' (*reg 2*) who is, in relation to the fixed term employee, employed by the same employer and engaged in the same or broadly similar work having regard, where relevant, to whether they have a similar level of qualification or skill. The comparable permanent employee is to be employed at the same establishment as the fixed term employee or, if no suitable comparator exists at the establishment at which the fixed term employee is engaged, at another of the employer's establishments.

By *reg 3* the fixed term employee has the right not to be treated less favourably than a comparable permanent employee as regards terms of the contract or by being subjected to any detriment by the employer. The right includes the right not to be less favourably treated in relation to any period of service qualification relating to any particular condition of service, any opportunity to receive training or the opportunity to secure any permanent position in the establishment (*reg 3(2)*). The Court of Appeal in *Department of Work and Pensions v Webley* [2004] EWCA Civ 1745, [2005] IRLR 288 held that the non-renewal of a fixed-term contract, of itself, is not capable of involving less favourable treatment for the purpose of the Regulations. In that case fixed term workers had their contracts terminated after 51 weeks as a matter of policy regardless of whether there was an ongoing need for work or not.

In relation to the opportunity to secure permanent positions, the fixed term employee has the right to be informed of available vacancies in the establishment by the employer (*reg 3(6), (7)*). The protection against less favourable treatment applies only if the treatment in issue is on the grounds that the employee is a fixed term employee and the treatment is not justified on objective grounds (*reg 3(3)*). Thus, for example, if an employer pays a fixed term employee at a lower rate than comparable permanent employees by reason of the fixed term status, this may (but not must) be less favourable treatment which the employer may have to objectively justify. Similarly, if, say, the employer limits certain facilities to permanent staff such as health care or other benefits, this may (but not must) be less favourable treatment of the fixed term employee which may require objective justification if it is to be permissible. It is not every difference in treatment, however, that will amount to less favourable treatment. *Regulation 3(5)* is an important provision which provides that, in order to determine whether a fixed term employee has been treated less favourably than a comparator, the 'pro rata' principle shall be applied unless it is inappropriate. The pro rata principle is defined in *reg 1* as follows:

> 'where a comparable permanent employee receives or is entitled to pay or any other benefit, a fixed term employee is to receive or be entitled to such proportion of that pay or other benefit as is reasonable in the circumstances having regard to the length of his contract of employment and to the terms on which the pay or other benefit is offered.'

Regulation 4 provides an important gloss on objective justification providing that, in the event of less favourable treatment of a fixed term employee as regards any term in his contract, that treatment is to be regarded as objectively justified if the terms of the fixed term employee's contract 'taken as a whole' are at least as favourable as the comparator's contract of employment. Thus it is appropriate to look at the whole employment package afforded to the fixed term employee and not to concentrate on any single term when considering objective justification of contractual differences.

By *reg 5* a fixed term employee has the right to request in writing a statement from the employer setting out the reasons for any treatment in issue. That statement is to be provided within 21 days of the request (*reg 5(1)*). The statement is admissible in evidence before an employment tribunal (*reg 5(2)*) and failure to provide a statement without reasonable excuse or provision of an evasive or equivocal statement permits the tribunal to draw such inferences as appear just and equitable including an inference that the right in question has been infringed (*reg 5(3)*).

By *reg 6* a fixed term employee who is dismissed by reason of (i) bringing proceedings or (ii) giving evidence in relation to proceedings under the *Regulations*, or (iii) requesting a statement of reasons or (iv) alleging that the employer had contravened the *Regulations* or (v) doing anything under the *Regulations* or (vi) refusing forego a right conferred by the *Regulations,* is to be regarded as having been unfairly dismissed for the purposes of *Part 10* of the *ERA*. (See *reg 6(3)*). If the fixed term employee is dismissed in contravention of *reg 6*, then no qualifying period of service applies for the purposes of the *ERA*: see *ERA s 108(3)(j)*. By *reg 6(2)* a fixed term worker has the right not to be subjected to any detriment for like reasons to those applying to dismissal (see *reg 6(3)*).

The right to present complaints to the employment tribunal is set out in *reg 7* and the normal three month time limit subject to just and equitable extension applies (*reg 7(2), (3)*). By *reg 7(6)* it is for the employer to identify the ground for the less favourable treatment or detriment. If an employment tribunal finds a complaint well founded it may provide a declaration as to the claimant's right and may award compensation assessed on the just and equitable basis including compensation for any loss suffered by the claimant (*reg 7(8), (9)*). Infringement of *reg 3* (Less favourable treatment) shall not, however, include an injury to feelings award (*reg 7(10)*). The employment tribunal also has power to make recommendations for the purpose of obviating or reducing the adverse effect on the complainant (*reg 7(7)(c)*). Failure without reasonable justification to comply with such recommendations may lead to an increase in the award of compensation (*reg 7(13)*).

An important right arises under *reg 8* to deal with the situation of persons employed on a succession of purported fixed-term contracts or a lengthy fixed term contract which is renewed. *Regulation 8* provides that, where a fixed term employee has been continuously employed under (i) a single fixed-term contract which is renewed or (ii) a number of fixed term contracts for a total period of four years or more and where continuity of employment is preserved, then the employee will become a permanent employee unless the employer can show objective justification (*reg 8(2)*). For the purposes of determining continuous employment *Chapter 1* of *Part 14* of the *ERA* is applied (*reg 8(4)*) (See also CONTINUOUS EMPLOYMENT (7)).

It should be noted, however, that any period of continuous employment prior to 10 July 2002 does not count for the purposes of *reg 8*. The effect is that from 10 July 2006 and thereafter those who have been employed on two or more successive fixed term contracts for four or more years will be deemed to be permanent employees absent objective justification. On objective justification see the judgment of the ECJ in *Adeneler v Ellinikos Organismos Galaktos* [2006] IRLR 716 in which the compatibility of Greek legislation on fixed–term work with the *Fixed-Term Work Directive 99/70/EC* and Framework Agreement was considered. The ECJ held that 'objective reasons' requiring the use of fixed-term contacts required justification by specific factors relating to the particular activity carried out and the conditions under which it is carried out. What is required is 'precise and concrete circumstances characterising a given activity, which are therefore capable in that particular context of justifying the use of successive fixed term contracts'. The ECJ explained that these 'circumstances' may arise from the specific nature of the tasks undertaken or their inherent characteristics or from the pursuit of a legitimate social policy objective of a Member State.

Regulation 8 may be modified or excluded by a collective agreement or workforce agreement (*reg 8(5)*). A fixed term worker, however, may not individually contract out of his rights under the Regulations save as is permitted under *s 203* of the *ERA*.

By *reg 9* an employee who considers that by application of *reg 8* he is a permanent employee may request a written statement from the employer confirming his permanent employee status. Such a statement is to be provided within 21 days and must either confirm the change in status or provide reasons why it is said the employee remains a fixed term employee (*reg 9(1), (2)*). If the employer intends to rely upon objective justification the grounds must be specified in the statement (*reg 9(2)*). The statement is admissible in any court proceedings (*reg 9(3)*) and failure to provide a statement or evasive or equivocal replies permit adverse inferences to be drawn (*reg 9(4)*). An employee who considers himself to be a permanent employee by virtue of *reg 8* may apply to the employment tribunal for a declaration to that effect (*reg 9(5)*) but prior to making an application for the declaration the employee must have sought or obtained a statement pursuant to *reg 9(1)* (*reg 9(6)(a)*). Finally, at the time of the application for the declaration the employee must be employed by the employer and accordingly 'historical' applications for a declaration by former employees are not to be entertained (*reg 9(6)(b)*).

The *Regulations* make provision for vicarious liability of the employer for the acts of its employees and agents (*reg 12(1), (2)*) subject to a defence for the employer to prove that it took such steps as were reasonably practicable to prevent the employee doing the act or acts of that description in the course of his employment (*reg 12(3)*).

48 Termination of Employment

48.1 A contract of employment may be terminated in several ways: by mutual agreement; by frustration; by expiry; by dismissal by the employer; by notice given by the employee; or by acceptance of a fundamental repudiatory breach of contract by the employer or the employee. The distinction between these different modes of termination may be of importance in determining whether the employee may bring a claim for UNFAIR DISMISSAL (53), WRONGFUL DISMISSAL (58) or REDUNDANCY (38).

The death of either party terminates the contract of employment, unless the contract expressly or impliedly provides otherwise. The bankruptcy of the employer does not operate as a dissolution of the contracts of employment between himself and his employees, but in general the winding-up of a company and the dissolution of a partnership do operate to terminate the contract (see, eg *Briggs v Oates* [1990] ICR 473, holding that the expiration of the partnership represented a breach of the employee's contract, but suggesting that mere departures from, and additions to, a body of partners would not have such an effect). This is subject to the effect of the *Transfer of Undertakings* (*Protection of Employment*) *Regulations 1981* (*SI 1981/1794*) (see TRANSFER OF UNDERTAKINGS (52)).

It may be held in a particular case that, where an employee starts to work for his old employer in a new capacity, then the old contract has come to an end and has been replaced by a new one. Whether or not this is so is a question of degree (*Hogg v Dover College* [1990] ICR 39; *Alcan Extrusions v Yates* [1996] IRLR 327).

48.2 MUTUAL AGREEMENT

Termination by agreement between employer and employee may be effected either orally or in writing. The agreement to terminate may take effect on any day in the month or year, and does not have to coincide with a pay-day.

The courts will scrutinise an apparent agreement to terminate if the employee alleges that he was given no choice but to consent to the ending of his employment. The general principle which the courts will apply is that if the sole cause of the employee's willingness to agree to the termination of his employment is the threat of dismissal, he will be held to have been dismissed. If, however, other additional factors, such as financial inducements, affected his decision he will be taken to have resigned by mutual agreement. He will then not be entitled to bring any claim for unfair or wrongful dismissal.

In *Sheffield v Oxford Controls Co Ltd* [1979] ICR 396, the employee was told that if he did not resign he would be dismissed. He signed an agreement to resign in return for certain financial benefits. The Employment Appeal Tribunal found that he had resigned and had not been dismissed because his resignation had been brought about not by the threat of dismissal but by other factors such as the offer of financial benefits. See also *Birch v University of Liverpool* [1985] ICR 470, *Scott v Coalite Fuels and Chemicals Ltd* [1988] ICR 355 and *Hellyer Bros Ltd v Atkinson and Dickinson* [1992] IRLR 540. But in *Caledonian Mining Co Ltd v Bassett* [1987] ICR 425, an employer who dishonestly persuaded his employees to resign was treated as having dismissed them. The dishonesty in that case was held by the employment tribunal to consist of a preconceived arrangement designed by the employers to avoid liability for redundancy payments.

An agreement for the automatic termination of a contract of employment on the occurrence of a certain event may be ineffective to exclude entitlement to statutory employment protection rights because of *ERA 1996, s 203(1)* (see 53.19 UNFAIR DISMISSAL – I).

48.3   FRUSTRATION

Frustration occurs where the performance of the contract of employment becomes impossible or substantially different from that which the parties contemplated at the time of entering into the agreement by reason of an unforeseen and unprovided for event which has occurred without the fault or default of either party to the contract (*Paal Wilson & Co A/S v Partenreederei Hannah Blumenthal* [1983] 1 AC 854 at 909). A contract will be terminated by frustration if performance becomes unlawful (eg by the passing of a statute after the contract is made). The question of termination of a contract of employment by reason of frustration most frequently arises in cases of absence of the employee because of illness or imprisonment. Where the contract is frustrated, there is no dismissal (the essence of frustration is that in law termination is *automatic*), and hence no possible claim for wrongful or unfair dismissal or redundancy. The employee will be able to recover for services rendered prior to the frustrating event, relying if necessary upon *Law Reform (Frustrated Contracts) Act 1943, s 1(3)*.

In *Williams v Watsons Luxury Coaches Ltd* [1990] ICR 536, the EAT drew together the principles of the doctrine of frustration as they apply to contracts of employment. At 541, Wood J held that the following principles applied to cases of frustration by reason of illness:

'First, that the court must guard against too easy an application of the doctrine, more especially when redundancy occurs and also when the true situation may be a dismissal by reason of disability. Secondly, that although it is not necessary to decide that frustration occurred on a particular date, nevertheless an attempt to decide the relevant date is far from a useless exercise as it may help to determine in the mind of the court whether it really is a true frustration situation. Thirdly, that there are a number of factors which may help to decide the issue as they may each point in one or other direction. These we take from the judgment of Phillips J in *Egg Stores (Stamford Hill) Ltd v Leibovici* [1977] ICR 260, 265:

" ... Among the matters to be taken into account in such a case in reaching a decision are these: (1) the length of the previous employment; (2) how long it had been expected that the employment would continue; (3) the nature of the job; (4) the nature, length and effect of the illness or disabling event; (5) the need of the employer for the work to be done, and the need for a replacement to do it; (6) the risk to the employer of acquiring obligations in respect of redundancy payments or compensation for unfair dismissal to the replacement employee; (7) whether wages have continued to be paid; (8) the acts and the statements of the employer in relation to the employment, including the dismissal of, or failure to dismiss, the employee; and (9) whether in all the circumstances a reasonable employer could be expected to wait any longer."

To these we would add the terms of the contract as to the provisions for sickness pay, if any, and also, a consideration of the prospects of recovery. Fourthly – see *FC Shepherd & Co Ltd v Jerrom* [1986] ICR 802 – the party alleging frustration should not be allowed to rely upon the frustrating event if that event was caused by that party – at least where it was caused by its fault.'

For earlier cases of frustration of the contract due to illness, see *Marshall v Harland and Wolff Ltd* [1972] ICR 101; *Hart v AR Marshall & Sons (Bulwell) Ltd* [1977] ICR 539; *Egg Stores (Stamford Hill) Ltd v Leibovici* [1977] ICR 260; and *Notcutt v Universal Equipment Co (London) Ltd* [1986] ICR 414. For frustration of the contract of employment due to imprisonment, see *FC Shepherd & Co Ltd v Jerrom* [1986] ICR 802, in which the Court of Appeal held that a contract of employment was capable of being frustrated by the imposition of a custodial sentence.

In *Four Seasons Healthcare Ltd v Maughan [2005] IRLR 324, on the other hand, the EAT held that bail conditions which effectively prevented a registered mental nurse from attending work at a care home did not constitute a 'frustrating event'. The EAT noted that it was unaware of similar cases which supported an argument for 'frustration', and further that the employer had the opportunity, of dismissing the employee, if it so wished.*

The rule that frustration could not be induced by a party's own default applied only to the party alleging that frustration had occurred.

The doctrine of frustration was recently analysed by Gray J in *Gryf-Lowczowski v Hinchingbrooke Healthcare NHS Trust* [2005] EWHC 2407 (QB), [2006] IRLR 100. The case concerned a consultant general and colorectal surgeon who, following a referral to the National Clinical Assessment Authority, had been on special leave from work for almost two years and could not resume his duties at the employing trust until he had undergone a period of training at another trust. The employer sought to argue that the contract of employment had been frustrated. This was rejected by Gray J who stressed that, in looking at point (9) (in the *Leibovici*) case, where the employment was of such a nature that its termination by frustration would have a 'catastrophic' effect on the employee of making it highly unlikely that he would find work again as a medical practitioner within the NHS, it would be reasonable to expect an employer to wait rather longer than might be the case in other circumstances before the contract was held to be frustrated.

On the facts of that case, Gray J held that the crucial question for the Court was whether there remained a realistic possibility that a placement could be found to enable the employee to be re-skilled and thereafter to resume his former duties with the employer. Gray J held that there was such a possibility, and so the contract was not frustrated.

Where a contract of employment has been brought to an end by reason of 'frustration' (ie performance of the contract becomes impossible or substantially different from that contemplated by the parties at inception without fault on either side), the parties cannot thereafter agree that the contract continues to subsist: see *G F Sharp & Co Ltd v McMillan* [1998] IRLR 632. In that case, a joiner lost the use of his left hand and could never work for his employer in that capacity again. Although the parties agreed to keep the employee 'on the books' so that he could gain access to greater pension benefits, the EAT held that this did not amount to a continuation of the contract of employment. The contract had been nullified by the employee's injury. As a consequence, the employee was not entitled to notice of termination of his employment or payment in lieu.

48.4   EXPIRY

If a contract is for a fixed period, it will automatically terminate at the end of that period. No notice need be given. It should be noted that, for the purposes of a claim for redundancy pay or in respect of unfair dismissal, the expiry of a fixed-term contract may nevertheless constitute a dismissal (see 34.6 REDUN-DANCY – I and 51.4–51.6 UNFAIR DISMISSAL – I). If an employee remains in his employment after the expiry of the term, he will be considered to be working under the same terms and conditions as before, save only that his employment is subject to an implied term that it can be terminated by either party upon giving reasonable notice (see 48.6 below).

48.5   DISMISSAL BY THE EMPLOYER

'Dismissal' is here used in its popular sense, to mean termination of a contract of employment by the employer. For the purposes of the unfair dismissal and redundancy payments legislation, the concept of dismissal is given a special statutory meaning which includes both the expiry of a fixed-term contract without its renewal and 'constructive dismissal' (see 38.6 REDUNDANCY – I and 53.4 UNFAIR DISMISSAL – I).

Sometimes there may be a dispute as to whether the words used by the employer (or the employee in the case of a resignation) in fact amount to a dismissal. Where those words are ambiguous, the court or tribunal should ask how they would have been understood by a reasonable listener in the circumstances (*Sothern v Franks Charlesly & Co* [1981] IRLR 278). A party who has used unambiguous words cannot normally be heard to say that he did not mean what he appeared to mean. However, it seems that there may be exceptions to this rule. In *Barclay v City of Glasgow District Council* [1983] IRLR 313 the EAT, dealing with a purported resignation by a mentally handicapped employee, held that there might be circumstances where words are spoken, for example, under emotional stress, which the other party ought to know are not meant to be taken seriously. This approach was upheld in relation to words spoken in the heat of the moment by the Court of Appeal in *Sovereign House Security Services Ltd v Savage* [1989] IRLR 115. See also *Kwik-Fit (GB) Ltd v Lineham* [1992] ICR 183.

Dismissal may be either *summary* or with *notice*. At common law, either party to the contract of employment is always free to terminate the relationship by giving the proper notice provided that the contract is one which, whether expressly or impliedly, is terminable upon giving notice. Thus, if such notice is given, there can be no claim for WRONGFUL DISMISSAL (58). To be effective in law, the notice must expire on a certain specified day (*Morton Sundour Fabrics Ltd v Shaw* (1966) 2 ITR 84), or upon the occurrence of a specified event (*Burton Group Ltd v Smith* [1977] IRLR 351). There is no dismissal on notice where an employer informs an absent employee that if he does not return to work by a particular date he will be treated as having terminated his employment, even if the employee does not turn up on that date and the employer treats the employment as having been terminated (*Rai v Somerfield Stores Ltd.* [2004] ICR 656).

For the date at which termination takes effect, see 53.13 UNFAIR DISMISSAL – I. The parties may by agreement either advance or postpone the date of termination (*Mowlem Northern Ltd v Watson* [1990] ICR 751; and see also *Palfrey v Transco plc* [2004] IRLR 916).

The contract of employment may provide for summary termination in certain circumstances. Summary dismissal in other circumstances is *prima facie* a breach of contract, unless the employee is in fundamental breach of the contract (see

48.13 below). Whether the dismissal is or is not fair is an entirely separate question. A dismissal may be fair even though proper notice is not given, and a dismissal on notice may nonetheless be unfair (see *Treganowan v Robert Knee & Co Ltd* [1975] ICR 405; *BSC Sports and Social Club v Morgan* [1987] IRLR 391; and UNFAIR DISMISSAL – II (54)).

48.6   Termination on notice – the contractual notice period

The contract of employment will usually specify the period of notice to be given to terminate the contract; indeed, the written particulars given to the employee must include the length of notice which the employee is obliged to give or entitled to receive (see 8.5 CONTRACT OF EMPLOYMENT).

If the contract is not for a fixed term and the notice period has not been expressly agreed, there is an implied term that it may be terminated upon reasonable notice (see *Reda v Flag Ltd* [2002[UKPC 28, [2002] IRLR 747). The court will determine what amounts to reasonable notice. Factors taken into account include the seniority and remuneration of the employee, his age, his length of service and what is usual in the particular trade. As a very rough guide, a period of two weeks or one month might be appropriate in the case of a manual worker, three months in the case of senior skilled workers or middle management, and between three months and one year in the case of more senior managers. However, the period of notice must be determined on the particular facts of each case. (For a discussion of the factors, see *Clarke v Fahrenheit 451 (Communications) Ltd (EAT 591/99)* (1999) IDS Brief 666, p 11.)

48.7   Termination on notice – statutory minimum notice

Whatever may be the contractual provisions – whether express or implied – for termination of the contract, the notice actually given must not be less than the statutory minimum period of notice. The contractual notice must be given if that is longer. The statutory rules are as follows:

(*a*)   an employee who has been continuously employed for one month or more but less than two years is entitled to not less than one week's notice;

(*b*)   an employee who has been continuously employed for two years or more but less than 12 years is entitled to one week's notice for each year of continuous employment;

(*c*)   any employee who has been employed for 12 years or more is entitled to not less than 12 weeks' notice.

(*ERA 1996, s 86(1)*.)

This results in the following:

Table of statutory minimum notice

Period of continuous employment (years)	Minimum period (weeks)
Less than 2 (but 1 month or more)	1
At least 2 but less than 3	2
At least 3 but less than 4	3
At least 4 but less than 5	4
At least 5 but less than 6	5
At least 6 but less than 7	6

Period of continuous employment (years)	Minimum period (weeks)
At least 7 but less than 8	7
At least 8 but less than 9	8
At least 9 but less than 10	9
At least 10 but less than 11	10
At least 11 but less than 12	11
12 or more	12

For example, if a clerk has been employed for 12 years under a contract which does not specify the period of notice to which he is entitled, a term of reasonable notice would be implied which in his case may well be one month. However, his length of service entitled him to 12 weeks' notice and that is the minimum notice he must be given.

An employee cannot contract out of his right to the statutory minimum period of notice (*ERA 1996, s 203*). However, he may waive his right to notice on a particular occasion, or accept a payment in lieu of notice (*ERA 1996, s 86(3)*; *Trotter v Forth Ports Authority* [1991] IRLR 419).

In *Cerberus Software Ltd v Rowley* [2000] ICR 35, the former President of the Employment Appeals Tribunal (Morrison J) cast doubt on the lawfulness of including 'payment in lieu' clauses in a contract of employment at the outset of the employment relationship. He queried whether this practice was compatible with the statutory right to minimum notice. This observation is not sustainable following the decision of the Court of Appeal, which upheld the employer's use of the 'payment in lieu' clause: [2001] ICR 376.

48.8 Exceptions

The following employees do not have the right to be given the statutory minimum period of notice:

(*a*) employees engaged in work wholly or mainly outside Great Britain, unless the employee ordinarily works in Great Britain and the work outside Great Britain is for the same employer (*ERA 1996, s 196(1)*; cf 53.15(B) UNFAIR DISMISSAL – I);

(*b*) employees in employment under a contract made in contemplation of the performance of a specific task which is not expected to last for more than three months, unless they have been continuously employed for more than three months (*ERA 1996, s 86(5)*);

(*c*) certain seamen (*ERA 1996, s 199*).

48.9 Pay in lieu of notice

An employer who intends to dismiss an employee may consider it desirable that the employee should cease work immediately and not work out his notice period. For example, some employers consider it unwise to let a sales representative, who knows that he is to be dismissed, have any further contact with the employer's customers, for fear of endangering their goodwill. If an employee is dismissed without notice or with short notice it is usual to give him pay in lieu of notice. It would be possible, although unusual, to give an employee notice to expire halfway through the contractual or statutory notice period and to make a payment in lieu of notice in respect of the remainder of the period. Another possibility is to continue to pay the employee as usual, but to ask him to remain at home. This will not normally represent a breach of contract by the employer (but see 8.12 CONTRACT OF EMPLOYMENT). Even if he makes a payment in lieu of notice, an employer will nevertheless in theory be guilty of a breach of contract (unless the contract provides for this possibility – as, for example, in *Marshall (Cambridge) Ltd v Hamblin* [1994] ICR 362). However, the employee will not normally have a right of action in damages unless, through the premature determination of his contract, he has been deprived of valuable statutory rights. (See observations in *Robert Cort & Son Ltd v Charman* [1981] ICR 816; *Delaney v Staples* [1992] IRLR 191; and *Abrahams v Performing Rights Society* [1995] IRLR 487.) However, in certain circumstances, the employee may be able to obtain an injunction to restrain a termination before the expiry of the contractual notice period. Such relief may be obtained where, by the employer's breach, the employee will suffer loss for which he cannot be compensated in damages, as where during the notice period the employee would have been able to exercise a share option in respect of which a claim in damages has been excluded.

The practice of giving pay in lieu of notice is virtually universal, but it does not fit easily into the traditional legal framework. Two connected problem areas are:

(*a*)   whether pay in lieu of notice is taxable (see 48.10 below);

(*b*)   if tax-free, whether it should be paid gross or net (see 48.11 below).

48.10 *Taxation of pay in lieu of notice.* The contract of employment may expressly empower the employer to dismiss the employee summarily on making a payment in lieu of notice. If the contract does set out such a right then the payment in lieu constitutes an 'emolument' of the employment, and tax should be deducted under PAYE in the usual way (see *EMI Group Electronics Ltd v Coldicott (Inspector of Taxes)* [1999] IRLR 630). The employee is not entitled to the benefit of the £30,000 exemption referred to below. It is probable that any appropriate National Insurance contributions should be paid as well.

Normally, there is no express contractual term relating to the making of payments in lieu of notice, but the employer may have an almost invariable custom of giving pay in lieu of notice. The House of Lords has held that such a payment is a payment of compensation for the employer's breach of contract in not giving due notice (*Delaney v Staples* [1992] ICR 483). Accordingly, the payment escapes the general Schedule E charge. It follows that neither the frequency with which such payments are made nor any expectation on the part of the employee would affect this. Since a non-contractual payment in lieu of notice falls to be regarded as compensation, it will be tax-free under the general rules. It may nevertheless be taxable under the special rules on compensation payments for loss of office (eg 'golden handshakes'), but only if the *total* amount paid to the employee, including any redundancy payment and any other termination payments, exceeds £30,000 (*Income and Corporation Taxes Act 1988, ss 148, 188(4); FA 1988, s 74*). A non-contractual payment in lieu of notice is not subject to National Insurance contributions.

Where the employer and employee genuinely negotiate an agreement to terminate the employment contract, and no question of breach of contract by the employer arises, then any lump sum payable as part of the agreement will be treated as an 'emolument' from employment and will be taxable under Schedule E. The £30,000 exemption will not apply: see *Richardson (HM Inspector of Taxes) v Delaney* [2001] IRLR 663.

48.11 *Payment gross or net?* Most employers who make a payment in lieu of notice which is tax-free, pay over to the employee his full gross wages or salary. Legally, however, if pay in lieu of notice is to be regarded as compensation for breach of contract (see above), it would follow that the employer is only liable to pay the net amount that the employee would have received after deduction of tax and National Insurance. This is because the measure of damages for breach of contract is calculated on the basis of *the amount lost* by the employee in not being allowed to work his notice. However, there is nothing to prevent an employer from paying the gross amount and there may be sound reasons for doing so, eg to maintain good industrial relations or public relations. It is also conceivable, although unlikely, that an employer who had a consistent practice of making payments gross might be held liable to pay the gross amount to an employee on the ground that the consistent practice had given rise to an implied contractual term (see, eg *Gothard v Mirror Group Newspapers Ltd* [1988] ICR 729). (To avoid the tax charge it would be necessary to establish that this term related only to the manner of calculating pay in lieu and not to the employer's liability to make the payment.) Pay in lieu of notice does not amount to wages for the purposes of the provisions relating to protection of wages which were formerly found in the *Wages Act 1986* and have now been consolidated in *ERA 1996, ss 13–27* (see 34.6 PAY – I).

48.12 **Employee's rights during period of notice**

Where an employee has been continuously employed for one month or more (see CONTINUOUS EMPLOYMENT (7)), and his employment is terminated either by the employer giving notice, or by notice given by himself, the employee is given certain rights during the statutory minimum notice period, ie the period shown in 48.7 above where the employer gives notice, and one week where the employee gives notice (*ERA 1996, s 87(1), (2)*). This does not apply, however, where notice is given by the employer and the contractual notice period exceeds the statutory minimum by at least one week (*ERA 1996, s 87(4)*), as illustrated in the recent case of *Scotts Co (UK) Ltd v Budd* [2003] IRLR 145.

The rights in question are set out in *ERA 1996, ss 87–91*, formerly *EPCA 1978, Sch 3*. Although it will not be possible to rely upon them directly if the statutory minimum notice is not given by the employer, they are to be taken into account in assessing damages in a WRONGFUL DISMISSAL (58) action (*ERA 1996, s 91(5)*).

The principal right conferred is to be paid in cases where the employee is ready and willing to work, but no work is provided for him by his employer, or where the employee is incapable of work because of sickness or injury, or where the employee is absent from work wholly or partly because of pregnancy or childbirth, or is absent in accordance with the terms of his employment relating to holidays. Where there are normal working hours, the amount payable is arrived at by taking the number of hours covered by the above situations and applying to them the hourly rate of remuneration produced by dividing a week's pay by the number of normal working hours (*ERA 1996, s 88*). Where there are no normal working hours, the employer must pay a week's pay in each week of the notice period, provided that the employee is ready and willing to do work of a reasonable nature and amount to earn a week's pay (*ERA 1996, s 89*). In each case, any payments in fact made (including holiday pay and sick pay) go towards meeting the employer's liability.

Accordingly, an employee who has been dismissed on account of prolonged sickness absence is entitled to receive full salary during his notice period if his sickness continues during that period. This is the case even if the employee had by the time of his dismissal exhausted his rights to sick pay, and would have received no payment from his employer if his contract had not been terminated.

The employer is not liable to make payments in respect of a period during which the employee is on leave at his own request (*ERA 1996, s 91(1)*), nor where the employee has given notice and thereafter takes part in a strike (*ERA 1996, s 91(2)*).

Where the employer breaks the contract during the notice period, payments made under *ERA 1996, ss 87–91* go to mitigate the damage suffered (*ERA 1996, s 91(3)*). Where the employer terminates the contract during the notice period and is entitled to do so because of the employee's breach of contract (see 48.13 below), there is no liability under *ERA 1996, s 88* or *s 89* in respect of the subsequent part of the full notice period (*ERA 1996, s 91(4)*).

48.13 Summary dismissal

If the employee acts in a way which is incompatible with the faithful discharge of his duty to his employer he may be dismissed instantly, without notice or wages in lieu of notice. Examples of misconduct which can in certain circumstances give rise to the right to dismiss summarily are wilful disobedience of a lawful order from the employer, theft of the employer's property, and drunkenness such as to impair the performance of his duties. The misconduct must be gross or grave, seen in the light of all the circumstances of the case. In general, employees should be given a clear indication of the type of conduct which the employer regards as warranting summary dismissal (*ACAS Code No 1, para 8*).

Summary dismissal for misconduct which is not gross is a breach of contract rendering the employer liable in damages for WRONGFUL DISMISSAL (58).

For a discussion of the exact moment when a dismissal without notice takes effect, see *Octavius Atkinson & Sons Ltd v Morris* [1989] ICR 431.

48.14 Written statement of reasons for dismissal

An employee is entitled to be provided by his employer, on request, within 14 days of that request, with a written statement giving particulars of the reasons for his dismissal if:

(*a*)   he is given by his employer notice of termination of his contract of employment; or

(*b*)   his contract of employment is terminated by his employer without notice; or

(*c*)   where he is employed under a contract for a fixed term, that term expires without being renewed under the same contract.

(*ERA 1996, s 92(1)*.)

The reasons given by an employer are admissible in evidence in any proceedings. The employer's reply to a request may refer to full reasons given in an earlier written communication, a copy of which should be sent with the reply. Where a legal adviser is appointed by the employee, as a duly authorised agent to receive the information, it is sufficient to communicate the information to the legal adviser (*Kent County Council v Gilham* [1985] ICR 227).

An employee is not normally entitled to written reasons unless he has been continuously employed for a period of one year ending with the effective date of termination (*Unfair Dismissal and Reasons for Dismissal (Variation of Qualifying Period) Order 1999 (SI 1999/1436)*).

Special rules apply if an employee is dismissed at any time while she is pregnant, or after childbirth in circumstances in which her maternity leave period ends by reason of her dismissal (for the maternity leave period, see 33.23 MATERNITY AND PARENTAL RIGHTS). She is entitled to a written statement of reasons for the dismissal, irrespective of the length of her employment, and without having to make any request (*ERA 1996, s 92(4)*).

48.15 Remedy for failure to give reasons

A complaint may be made by the employee to an industrial tribunal on the grounds:

(*a*)   that his employer unreasonably failed to provide a written statement under *ERA 1996, s 92* of the reason for dismissal; or

(*b*)   that the particulars given in purported compliance with that section are inadequate or untrue.

(*ERA 1996, s 93(1)*.)

The obligation is, of course, to give the actual reason for dismissal; the question is not whether that reason is in fact well-founded.

In *Daynecourt Insurance Brokers Ltd v Iles* [1978] IRLR 335, the company failed to answer an employee's request for written reasons for his dismissal. Its justification for doing so was a general request by the police officer who investigated the alleged theft of company funds by the employee, that the company should not answer any correspondence or deal with any matter that related to the police investigations of the company's records. The EAT held that the industrial tribunal's finding, that the company should not have simply ignored the employee's statutory request but should have sought further advice of the police officer, was not wrong in law. A failure to provide written reasons may be unreasonable even if the employee knows perfectly well why he has been dismissed, since one purpose of the provision is that the employee should be able to show the reasons to third parties (*McBrearty v Thomson*, IDS Brief 450, p 15).

Except in maternity cases (see 48.14 above), there cannot be a complaint to the tribunal that the reasons given are inadequate if there has been no request for proper reasons by the employee pursuant to *ERA 1996, s 92(1)* (*Catherine Haigh Harlequin Hair Design v Seed* [1990] IRLR 175).

In *Banks v Lavin*, IDS Brief 410, p 6, the EAT held that the statement 'many jobs not being done' was an inadequate reason, because it was not sufficiently specific.

The time limit for presentation of the complaint is three months from the effective date of termination of employment. This period can be extended if the industrial tribunal is satisfied that it was not reasonably practicable to present it within the three-month period (*ERA 1996, s 93(3)*; and see 17.7 EMPLOYMENT TRIBUNALS).

If the tribunal finds the complaint well-founded, it will make an award that the employer pay to the employee a sum equal to the amount of two weeks' pay. It may also make a declaration as to what it finds that the employer's reasons were for dismissing the employee (*ERA 1996, s 93(2)*). A week's pay is calculated in accordance with the provisions of *ERA 1996, ss 221–229*, formerly *EPCA 1978, Sch 14* and the calculation date is:

(i) where the dismissal was with notice, the date on which the employer's notice was given; or

(ii) in any other case, the effective date of termination.

(*ERA 1996, s 226(2)*.)

(See further REDUNDANCY – I (38).)

The amount of a week's pay is not subject to a statutory maximum for this purpose.

48.16 RESIGNATION BY THE EMPLOYEE

As in the case of dismissal by the employer, the employee may resign with or without notice. For the question of whether the words used will amount to a resignation, see 48.5 above. No particular terms of art are required for resignations (*Walmsley v C&R Ferguson Ltd* [1989] IRLR 112). A failure to give due notice is *prima facie* a breach of contract, but may be justified where the employee resigns in response to a repudiatory breach of contract by the employer (see 48.18 below).

A failure by an employee to give proper notice of resignation is *prima facie* a breach of contract. The more difficult question will usually be what, if any, are the damages payable by the employee. In *Giraud UK Ltd v Smith* [2000] IRLR 763, the Employment Appeal Tribunal struck down a clause in an employment contract which provided that 'failure to give the proper notice and work it out will result in a reduction from your final payment equivalent to the number of days short'. This was held to be an unlawful penalty clause rather than a lawful liquidated damages clause. There was evidence to suggest that the employer could easily find replacements for the employee in question (he worked as a driver), so that it was not a genuine pre-estimate of loss. Furthermore, the clause was oppressive, as there was no limitation on the right of the employers to recover damages for actual loss if this was greater than that specified in the clause. Therefore, the employee was in a position where if the actual loss turned out to be nil, he would be liable for the sum set out in the clause, but if the actual loss was greater than the sum set out in the clause, he could face an unlimited claim for the balance. The clause enabled the employer to say, 'Heads I win, tails you lose'.

48.17 Termination by the employee giving notice

The statutory minimum period of notice to be given by an employee, who has been continuously employed for one month or more, is one week (*ERA 1996, s 86(2)*). However, the contractual period of notice to be given will, in many cases, be longer. The contractual notice may be either expressly agreed upon or implied. If it is implied, the notice to be given is that which is a reasonable period in all the circumstances (see 48.6 above).

48.18 Summary termination by the employee

If an employer is in breach of a fundamental term of the contract of employment, the employee is entitled to leave the employment forthwith. Leaving the employment in these circumstances is known as 'constructive dismissal' for redundancy payments and unfair dismissal purposes, since although the employee takes the initiative in leaving his employment he will be considered to have been dismissed within the meaning of *ERA 1996, s 136(1)* (see 38.6 REDUNDANCY – I) and *ERA 1996, s 95(1)* (see 53.4 UNFAIR DISMISSAL – I). In such circumstances, the employee would also be able to claim damages for WRONGFUL DISMISSAL (58).

48.19 REPUDIATORY CONDUCT

It has already been seen (see 48.13 and 48.18 above) that a repudiatory breach of contract by either the employer or the employee entitles the other party to terminate the relationship without giving notice or by giving short notice. A dismissal in such circumstances is not necessarily fair, nor a constructive dismissal following the employer's breach necessarily unfair, although they often will be.

The courts have sometimes gone further, and suggested that a repudiatory breach *automatically* brings a contract of employment to an end (see, e g *Marriott v Oxford and District Co-operative Society Ltd (No 2)* [1970] 1 QB 186). Such a principle would be contrary to the normal rule in the law of contract, which is that the 'innocent' party always has the option whether to accept the breach (and thus bring the contract to an end) or to 'affirm' the contract.

More recently, however, the courts have taken the view that a contract of employment is no exception to the general rule: see *Thomas Marshall (Exports) Ltd v Guinle* [1978] ICR 905; *Gunton v Richmond-upon-Thames London Borough Council* [1980] ICR 755; *London Transport Executive v Clarke* [1981] ICR 355; *Rigby v Ferodo Ltd* [1988] ICR 29; *Boyo v Lambeth London Borough Council* [1994] ICR 727; *Villella v MFI Furniture Centres Ltd* [1999] IRLR 468. This means that (leaving aside questions of frustration and expiry at a specified time or upon the occurrence of a specified event) there is no such thing as an automatic termination because of one party's conduct. There must always be an acceptance of the breach constituting a dismissal by the employer or a resignation by the employee.

However, it is of the nature of the employment relationship that, where one party is unwilling to perform the contract, it will be very difficult for the other party to say that the relationship remains alive. An acceptance of the breach by the innocent party will readily be inferred from his conduct. See also *Marsh v National Autistic Society* [1993] ICR 453.

The Court of Appeal in *Weathersfield Ltd v Sargent* [1999] IRLR 94 overruled the decision of the EAT in *Holland v Glendale Industries Ltd* [1998] ICR 493 that an employee must make plain to his employer the reason for leaving if he is to rely upon his employer's repudiatory conduct as justifying his resignation and subsequent claim of constructive dismissal. The court held that whether there has been an 'acceptance' of the employer's repudiatory conduct is for the employment tribunal (or court) to determine on the facts and evidence in each case. On the facts of that case (where an employee had been instructed to discriminate against black and Asian customers), the employee had been put in 'an outrageous and embarrassing position', and so did not want to confront her employers with the reason for leaving. She just left the job a few days after being issued with the instruction. This did not prevent her from claiming successfully that she had been constructively dismissed on the grounds of the instruction.

It is always a question of fact for the court or tribunal as to whether the employee resigned in consequence of the employer's repudiatory breach of contract. In *TSB Bank plc v Harris* [2000] IRLR 157, the Employment Appeal Tribunal upheld a finding of constructive dismissal where the employee was considering leaving her job in any case before the repudiatory breach of contract occurred (the breach arose out of the contents of a reference supplied to a prospective employer). See also *White v Bristol Rugby Ltd* [2002] IRLR 204.

48.20 RETRACTION OF RESIGNATION OR DISMISSAL

The general rule is that words of resignation or dismissal, once communicated to the other party and accepted by him, cannot unilaterally be withdrawn (*Riordan v War Office* [1959] 3 All ER 552). However, the EAT has suggested that good industrial relations practice requires that an employer should be able to withdraw words of dismissal provided that he does so almost immediately (*Martin v Yeoman Aggregates Ltd* [1983] ICR 314). If this view is correct, it should apply equally to a case of resignation by the employee.

48.21 REMEDIES FOR WRONGFUL TERMINATION

An employee who has been dismissed, or who has resigned in circumstances amounting to a constructive dismissal, may complain of UNFAIR DISMISSAL (53) to an employment tribunal, whether or not proper notice was given to him. If proper notice was not given, or if he resigned summarily in response to the employer's repudiatory breach, he may bring a claim for WRONGFUL DISMISSAL (58) in the ordinary courts. Where the employee fails to give proper notice, the employer may also in principle sue for damages. Also, either party may in certain, limited circumstances be able to obtain an injunction restraining an unlawful termination. See further 8.22 CONTRACT OF EMPLOYMENT.

49   Time Off Work

(See also DTI website http://www.dti.gov.uk/employment/employment-legislation/
employment-guidance/time-off-maternity-parental/page22251.html.

49.1   There are several distinct rights in exercise of which an employee may take time
off work in specific circumstances.

— Trade union officials and members may take time off work for certain
duties and activities (see 49.2–49.5 below).

— Employees have the right to take time off work to perform certain public
duties (see 49.5–49.6 below).

— An employee under notice of redundancy may take time off to look for
work, etc (see 49.7–49.8 below).

— Safety representatives, and elected representatives, must be given time off to
perform their duties (see 49.9–49.10 below).

— A pregnant woman has a right to take time off for ante-natal care (see
49.11 below).

— Employees who are trustees of occupational pension schemes have a right
to time off for performing their duties (see 49.12–49.13 below).

— Employee representatives must be given time off to perform their functions
(see 49.14–49.15 below).

— Employees have the right to time off for European Works Council duties
(see 49.16 below).

— Employees have the right to time off to care for dependants (see 49.17–
49.18 below).

— Employees have the right to time off to care for their children (see 49.19
below).

This chapter also considers the obligation to reinstate members of the reserve
forces in employment after military service (see 49.20 below).

49.2   TRADE UNION OFFICIALS

An employer is obliged to permit an employee, who is an official of an independent trade union recognised by the employer, to take time off during working hours
to:

(*a*)   carry out duties as such an official which are concerned with –

(i)   negotiations with the employer that are related to or connected with
any matters that fall within *TULRCA 1992, s 178(2)* (see 45.4
STRIKES AND INDUSTRIAL ACTION) and in relation to which the
trade union is recognised by the employer, or

(ii)   the performance, on behalf of employees of the employer, of any
functions that are related to or connected with any matters falling

within *TULRCA 1992, s 178(2)* that the employer has agreed may be so performed by the trade union, or

(iii)   receipt of information from the employer and consultation with the employer under *TULRCA 1992, s 188* or under the *Transfer of Undertakings (Protection of Employment) Regulations 2006 (SI 2006/246)* (see REDUNDANCY – II (39) and TRANSFER OF UNDERTAKINGS (52));

(*b*)   undergo training in aspects of industrial relations which is –

(i)   relevant to the carrying out of any such duties as are mentioned in (*a*); and

(ii)   approved by the Trades Union Congress or by the independent trade union of which he is an official.

(*TULRCA 1992, s 168(1), (2).*)

An employee who is a member of an independent trade union recognised by the employer and who is a learning representative of the trade union is entitled to time off under *s 168A, TULRCA 1992*. An employee who is a learning representative is entitled to time off in order to undertake, in relation to qualifying members of the trade union, the analysis of learning and training needs, the provision of information and advice on learning and training matters, the promotion of the values of learning and training, the consultation of the employer on learning and training activities, and preparation for the learning representative's activities. The right to time off arises only where the trade union has provided the employer with written notice that the employee is a learning representative and that he or she has undergone sufficient training within the last six months. The employer's obligation to permit time off is subject to a reasonableness test.

The Court of Appeal in *British Bakeries (Northern) Ltd v Adlington* [1989] ICR 438 held that it was a question of fact, dependent on the particular circumstances of the case, whether a preparatory meeting was sufficiently proximate to carrying out duties concerned with (at that time) industrial relations to come within the statutory predecessor of *s 168, TULRCA 1992*. Although the section has been amended since *Adlington*, it is thought that the decision is equally applicable to whether attendance at a meeting is sufficiently proximate to carrying out the duties now specified in *s 168*. See also *London Ambulance Service v Charlton* [1992] ICR 773.

The amount of time a trade union official is permitted to take off in the exercise of his statutory right, the purposes for which, the occasions on which, and any conditions subject to which, time off may be so taken are those that are reasonable in all the circumstances, having regard to any relevant provisions in the ACAS Code of Practice (*TULRCA 1992, s 168(3)*).

It is to be noted that the right accrues only to officials of independent trade unions recognised by the employer (see 50.20 TRADE UNIONS – I). There is no right to time off if, for example, the purpose is to attend a demonstration in support of a dispute with another employer or to carry out internal union duties. Nor would *s 168* extend to, say, taking part in a course on pension schemes if the employer does not consult or bargain with the union about pensions and has not agreed to it performing any pension-related functions on behalf of his employees.

In *Ashley v Ministry of Defence* [1984] ICR 298, the EAT held that unless it can be shown that the recognised union expressly or impliedly required the attendance of its official at a meeting, the attendance of the official at such a meeting cannot constitute the carrying out by the official of a duty within the meaning of *s 168*. The EAT further held that attendance at an advisory meeting could be a duty within the meaning of *s 168*; whether it is, is a question of fact.

In deciding whether the right to time off is being exercised reasonably within the meaning of *s 168(3)*, the EAT in *Depledge v Pye Telecommunications Ltd* [1981] ICR 82, considered that where comprehensive arrangements existed for the discussion of industrial relations matters it would be reasonable for trade union officials to use them.

In considering whether the request for time off is reasonable in all the circumstances, tribunals will take into account such matters as the nature, extent and purpose of time off already being taken by that employee (*Wignall v British Gas Corpn* [1984] ICR 716; *Borders Regional Council v Maule* [1993] IRLR 199). *Section 168(3)* assumes that a request for time off has been made and that such request has come to the notice of the employer. It is only if these two conditions are satisfied that the employee can have a remedy for an employer's failure to permit him to take time off (see *Ryford Ltd v Drinkwater* [1996] IRLR 16 and 49.6 below).

The trade union official who is entitled to take time off work to perform his duties is entitled to be paid for the period of his absence. Where his pay does not vary with the amount of work done, he is paid as if he had worked during the period of absence. Where his pay does vary according to the amount of work done, the amount he is to be paid during his absence is calculated by reference to the average hourly earnings for that work. The average hourly earnings are those of the employee concerned unless they cannot fairly be estimated, in which case the tribunal will take the average earnings of persons in comparable employment with the same employer or (if there are no such persons) a reasonable figure (*TULRCA 1992, s 169*). The employee is entitled to paid time off only at a time when he would otherwise be working, and not to paid time off in lieu if the trade union duties are performed at a time when he would not otherwise be working (*Hairsine v Kingston upon Hull City Council* [1992] IRLR 211).

If an employer is obliged under a contract of employment to pay an employee for time off taken to perform trade union duties, then those payments will go to discharge any statutory liability he may have to make such payments, and vice versa (*TULRCA 1992, s 169(4)*). For example, Bill Jones is entitled to receive £5 per hour under his contract of employment for time taken off on union business. His statutory entitlement (ie his normal pay) is £6 per hour. Since the *contractual payment* goes to discharge the employer's *statutory liability*, he will receive £6 per hour and not £6 plus £5.

Trade union officials are statutorily entitled to a reasonable amount of paid time off to accompany a worker at a disciplinary or grievance hearing, provided that they are certified by the union as being capable of acting as the worker's companion (*ERA 1999, s 10(6)*). This right applies whether or not the union is recognised by the employer, but the worker must be employed by the same employer as the union official.

An employee who is an official of an independent trade union recognised by his employer may present a complaint to an employment tribunal that his employer has failed to permit him to take the time off, or to pay him the whole or part of any amount to which he is statutorily entitled (and see 49.6 below) (*TULRCA 1992, ss 168(4), 169(5)*). (See *Ryford*, above.)

See also the ACAS Code of Practice 3: Time off for trade union duties and activities (*SI 2003/1191*) which lays down guidelines. The Code is to be taken into account in determining what is reasonable and the current version came into force on 27 April 2003.

49.3 TRADE UNION ACTIVITIES

An employer is obliged to permit an employee of his, who is a member of an independent trade union recognised by him, to take part in certain trade union activities during working hours. The activities are defined as:

(*a*) any activities of the trade union of which the employee is a member; and

(*b*) any activities in relation to which the employee is acting as a representative of such union;

excluding activities which themselves consist of industrial action whether or not in contemplation or furtherance of a trade dispute (*TULRCA 1992, s 170(1), (2)*).

TULRCA 1992, s 170(2A)-(2C) permits an employee to take time off in order to access the services of a trade union learning representative.

In *Luce v Bexley London Borough Council* [1990] ICR 591, the EAT held that whether trade union activity concerned fell within the definition was a matter of fact and degree, but that it must in a broad sense be linked to the employment relationship; the tribunal had been entitled to hold that teachers were not entitled to time off to lobby Parliament against the *Education Reform Bill*. See also 54.3(A) UNFAIR DISMISSAL – II.

The amount of time that may be taken, and the purposes for which and the occasions on which it may be taken, are those that are reasonable in all the circumstances; the same test applies to the imposition of conditions by the employer (*TULRCA 1992, s 170(3)*). The employee is not entitled to be paid for time he takes off to participate in trade union activities unless he is a trade union official and the time is taken in accordance with 49.2 above.

An employee who is a member of an independent trade union recognised by his employer may present a complaint to an employment tribunal that his employer has failed to permit him to take time off to which he is entitled (and see 49.6 below) (*TULRCA 1992, s 170(4)*).

49.4 Article 141 and pay for time off

Where a collective agreement provides for a right to pay for time off to attend the union's annual conference, it is not indirectly discriminatory to pay a female part-time employee less for such time off than a male full-time employee even though both attend the conference for the same length of time. This is because, according to the EAT, attendance at a union conference is not 'work' within the meaning of *art 119* (now *art 141*) of the *Treaty of Rome* which provides for the right to equal pay for equal work (see *Manor Bakeries Ltd v Nazir* [1996] IRLR 604 and 25.6 EUROPEAN COMMUNITY LAW). This decision of the EAT does not, however, sit easily with a decision of the ECJ in which it was held that compensation received for loss of earnings due to time taken off for attendance at staff council training courses must be regarded as 'pay' within the meaning of *art 119* (now *art 141*) as it constitutes a benefit paid indirectly by the employer by reason of the existence of an employment relationship (see *Kuratorium für Dialyse und Nierentransplantation eV v Lewark* [1996] IRLR 637).

49.5 **PUBLIC DUTIES**

An employer is obliged to permit an employee of his who is:

(*a*)   a justice of the peace;

(*b*)   a member of a local authority, a National Park Authority or the Broads Authority;

(*c*)   a member of a police authority or the Service Authority for the National Criminal Intelligence Service, or the National Crime Squad;

(*d*)   a member of any statutory tribunal;

(*e*)   a member of a National Health Service Trust, an NHS foundation trust, a strategic health authority, a health authority, a special health authority, a Primary Care Trust, or a health board;

(*f*)   a member of the managing or governing body of an educational establishment maintained by a local education authority, the governing body of a further education corporation or higher education corporation, a school council, a school board, a board of management of a college of further education, a governing body of a central institution, a governing body of a designated institution, or the General Teaching Council for England or Wales; or

(*g*)   a member of, in England and Wales, the Environment Agency or, in Scotland, the Scottish Environment Protection Agency; or

(*h*)   a member of Scottish Water or a water customer consultation panel; or

(*i*)   a member of a board of prison visitors in England and Wales, or of a visiting committee in Scotland,

to take time off work to perform his duties (*ERA 1996, s 50*).

In deciding when and how much time is to be taken off, regard will be paid to:

(i)   how much time off is required for the performance of the duties of the office, or as a member of the body in question, and how much time off is required for the performance of the particular duty;

(ii)   how much time off has already been permitted for the performance of any relevant public duty, union duty or activity;

(iii)   the circumstances of the employer's business and the effect of the employee's absence on the running of that business;

and these considerations will be applied in deciding what is reasonable in the circumstances (*ERA 1996, s 50(4)*). (See *Borders Regional Council v Maule* [1993] IRLR 199.)

Local authorities may not allow their employees more than 208 hours' paid time off in any financial year for the purpose of performing duties as councillors (other than council chairmen) (*Local Government and Housing Act 1989, s 10*).

Although there is no statutory provision entitling an employee to time off for jury service, prevention of a person from attending as a juror is a contempt of court. Thus, it is probable that there is an implied term that an employee should be allowed time off to attend court for jury service. The same reasoning would imply a right to time off to attend court as a witness. The *Criminal Justice Act 2003* (*s 321, Sch 33*) dramatically increased from 5 April 2004 the category of workers who are obliged to perform jury service. A worker may, however, obtain one deferral or even be excused from jury service if he can show 'good reason' for being excused. The guidance to summoning officers recognises that valid business reasons may exist in support of a worker's request for excusal from jury service and that small businesses may be able to show the requisite unusual hardship; however, every application for excusal or deferral will depend upon its own merits. The circumstances in which business needs will be sufficient to outweigh the obligation to perform jury service will be rare.

49.6   EMPLOYEE'S REMEDIES IN RESPECT OF TIME OFF FOR TRADE UNION AND PUBLIC DUTIES

An employee may present a complaint to an employment tribunal that he has not been allowed time off to carry out (*a*) trade union duties or activities, or (*b*) public duties and (in the case only of a trade union official's duties) that he has not been paid for time he has been permitted to take off (*ERA 1996, s 51(1); TULRCA 1992, ss 168(4), 169(5), 170(4)*). An employee can only bring a complaint under *TULRCA 1992, s 168(4)*, that an employer has failed to permit him to take time off, in circumstances where a request for time off has been made by the employee and that request has come to the notice of the employer (see *Ryford Ltd v Drinkwater* [1996] IRLR 16).

If it finds such a complaint well-founded, the tribunal will make a declaration to that effect and may order the employer to pay the employee compensation for the default and for any loss caused thereby (*ERA 1996, s 51(3); TULRCA 1992, s 172(1), (2)*). In the case of a union official who has not been paid for time taken off, the tribunal will order the employer to make the appropriate payment (*TULRCA 1992, s 172(3)*; see 49.2 above). In *Skiggs v South West Trains Ltd* ([2005] IRLR 459) a union official was prevented by his employer from attending meetings in the capacity of union representative pending the outcome of a grievance investigation into his behaviour. The EAT held that although he had suffered no financial loss nor injury to feelings, he was entitled to recover compensation to reflect the fact that a wrong was done to him, because *TULRCA 1992, s 172(2)* makes reference to both the employer's default and any loss sustained by the employee.

An employment tribunal does not have the power to impose conditions upon the parties as to the way in which the time off shall be taken or to specify the amount of time off which should be allowed (*Corner v Buckinghamshire County Council* [1978] IRLR 320).

The time limit for presenting such complaints is three months from the date of the failure complained of. If the tribunal is satisfied that it was not reasonably practicable for the complaint to be presented within the period of three months (see 20.7 EMPLOYMENT TRIBUNALS – I), then this time limit may be extended (*ERA 1996, s 51(2); TULRCA 1992, s 171*).

49.7   TIME OFF TO LOOK FOR WORK OR MAKE ARRANGEMENTS FOR TRAINING

An employee who has been given notice of dismissal by reason of redundancy must be allowed, before the expiry of the notice, reasonable time off by his employer, during his working hours, to look for new employment or to make arrangements for training for future employment (*ERA 1996, s 52(1)*). In order to qualify for this right, the employee must have been continuously employed for a period of at least two years, by the date on which (*a*) the notice is due to expire, or (*b*) the date on which it would expire had the statutory minimum period of notice been given, whichever is the longer (*ERA 1996, s 52(2)*). (See CONTINUOUS EMPLOYMENT (7).)

An employee who is so allowed time off is entitled to be paid for the time taken off at the appropriate hourly rate, which is calculated by the amount of one week's pay divided by the number of normal working hours in a week, or where the number of those hours varies, by taking the average of the 12 weeks ending with the last complete week before the notice was given (*ERA 1996, s 53(1)–(3)*). The maximum amount payable cannot exceed 40% of a week's pay (*ERA 1996, s 53(5)*). The right to be paid is dependent upon the right to take time off. Thus, if an employee with less than two years' continuous service is given time off to seek other employment, there is no statutory obligation on the employer to pay him for time so taken.

An employee who is under notice of redundancy is entitled to time off to look for work irrespective of whether he has an appointment to attend a specific interview (*Dutton v Hawker Siddeley Aviation Ltd* [1978] IRLR 390).

If an employer unreasonably refuses to allow an employee time off work when statutorily obliged to do so, the employee is entitled to be paid the remuneration to which he would have been entitled if he had been allowed time off, in addition to his normal pay (*ERA 1996, s 53(4)–(6)*).

49.8   **Remedy**

If an employer has unreasonably refused the employee time off or has failed to pay him, the employee may present a complaint to an employment tribunal (*ERA 1996, s 54(1)*). The time limit for the presentation of such a complaint is three months beginning with the day on which it is alleged that time off should have been allowed. If the tribunal is satisfied that it was not reasonably practicable for the complaint to be presented within the period of three months (see 20.7 EMPLOYMENT TRIBUNALS – I), then this time may be extended (*ERA 1996, s 54(2)*).

The employer may be made liable to pay (i) remuneration for the period of absence or (ii) remuneration for the period during which he should have allowed time off, or both. The maximum amount, where both these provisions are applicable together, cannot exceed 40% of a week's pay (*ERA 1996, s 54(4)*).

Any contractual remuneration paid to an employee for a period of time which he takes off to seek or train for new employment when he is under notice of dismissal for redundancy goes towards discharging the employer's statutory liability, and vice versa (*ERA 1996, s 53(7)*).

49.9   **SAFETY REPRESENTATIVES AND ELECTED REPRESENTATIVES**

The *Safety Representatives and Safety Committees Regulations 1977* (*SI 1977/500*), as amended, impose a duty upon employers to allow safety representatives time off with pay for the performance of their duties as safety representatives, and to undergo training in health and safety matters. There are guidelines for the exercise of the latter right; the 1978 Code of Practice approved by the Health and Safety Commission on time off for the training of safety representatives remains in force.

The *Health and Safety (Consultation with Employees) Regulations 1996* (*SI 1996/1513*) impose a similar duty upon employers who, pursuant to those *Regulations* (see 28.22 HEALTH AND SAFETY AT WORK – II), consult with elected employee representatives. In addition to the duty to allow such representatives time off with pay to perform their duties as such and to undergo training, an employer must also permit a candidate for election as such a representative time off with pay to perform his functions as such a candidate.

49.10 **Remedy**

If an employer refuses a safety representative or elected representative time off for these purposes or if he does not pay him for the time taken, the safety representative or elected representative may present a complaint to an employment tribunal (*1977 Regulations, reg 11(1); 1996 Regulations, Sch 2 para 2*). The time limit within which a complaint must be presented is three months from the date where the failure occurred, or within such further period as the tribunal considers reasonable in a case where it is satisfied that it was not reasonably practicable for the complaint to be presented within the period of three months (*1977 Regulations, reg 11(2); 1996 Regulations, Sch 2 para 3*; see 20.18 EMPLOY-MENT TRIBUNALS – I). Where an employment tribunal finds the complaint well-founded, it may make an award of such an amount as the tribunal considers just and equitable in all the circumstances, having regard to the employer's default in failing to permit time off to be taken by the employee and to any loss sustained by the employee which is attributable to the employee's complaint (*1977 Regulations, reg 11(3); 1996 Regulations, Sch 2 para 4*). Where the complaint is based upon the failure of the employer to pay remuneration due, the employment tribunal will order that sum to be paid to the employee (*1977 Regulations, reg 11(4); 1996 Regulations, Sch 2 para 5*).

49.11 **TIME OFF FOR ANTE-NATAL CARE**

ERA 1996, s 55 provides a statutory right for pregnant women not to be unreasonably refused time off with pay during working hours to keep an appointment for ante-natal care prescribed by a doctor, midwife or health visitor. There is no minimum qualifying period for this right. A complaint may be made to an employment tribunal if such time off is unreasonably refused. (This right is considered in detail 33.2–33.5 MATERNITY AND PARENTAL RIGHTS.)

49.12 **TIME OFF FOR OCCUPATIONAL PENSION SCHEME TRUSTEES**

The *Pensions Act 1995* introduced a right to time off during working hours for employees who are also trustees of an occupational pension scheme; the relevant provisions are set out in *ERA 1996, ss 58–60* and came into force on 6 October 1996. Such employees will have a right to time off for the purpose of performing any of their duties as trustees or undergoing training relevant to such perform-ance (*ERA 1996, s 58(1)*). This right is not subject to a period of continuous employment which an employee may have with an employer. The amount of time off which an employee is to be permitted to take and the conditions under which time off may be taken are those that are reasonable in all the circumstances having regard, in particular, to (*a*) the amount of time off required for the performance of the duties of a trustee of the scheme and undergoing training, and (*b*) the circumstances of the employer's business and the effect of the employee's absence on the running of that business (*ERA 1996, s 58(2)*).

An employee who is so allowed time off is entitled to be paid for the time taken off. The amount to be paid is the amount which he would have been paid if he had worked during the time taken off or, if his remuneration varies with the amount of work done, an amount calculated by reference to his average hourly earnings (*ERA 1996, s 59(1)–(3)*). If the work is such that no fair estimate can be made of the employee's average hourly earnings, then the amount to be paid will be calculated by reference to the average hourly earnings of similar work of a person in comparable employment with the same employer as the employee in question, or if there are no such persons, a figure of average hourly earnings which is reasonable in the circumstances (*ERA 1996, s 59(3)(4)*).

49.13 Remedy

If an employer has failed to permit the employee to take time off, or has failed to pay him, the employee may present a complaint to an employment tribunal (*ERA 1996, s 60(1)*). The time limit for the presentation of such a complaint is three months beginning with the date when the failure occurred. If the tribunal is satisfied that it was not reasonably practicable for the complaint to be presented within the period of three months (see 20.7 EMPLOYMENT TRIBUNALS), then this period may be extended (*ERA 1996, s 60(2)*).

Where an employment tribunal finds the complaint as to failure to permit time off to be well-founded, it will make an order to that effect and may award such an amount as the tribunal considers just and equitable in all the circumstances, having regard to the employer's default in so failing and any loss sustained by the employee which is attributable to the complaint (*ERA 1996, s 60(3), (4)*). Where the complaint is that the employer has failed to pay the employee for time taken off, the employment tribunal will order the employer to pay the sum found to be due (*ERA 1996, s 60(5)*).

Any contractual remuneration paid to an employee for a period of time off for the purpose of performing his duties as a trustee of an occupational pension scheme or for related training, goes towards discharging the employer's statutory liability, and vice versa (*ERA 1996, s 59(6)*).

49.14 TIME OFF FOR EMPLOYEE REPRESENTATIVES

An employee who is an employee representative for the purposes of *TULRCA 1992, Part IV Chapter II* (see 39.4 REDUNDANCY – II) or *Transfer of Undertakings (Protection of Employment) Regulations 2006 (SI 2006/246), regs 13–16* (see TRANSFER OF UNDERTAKINGS (52)), or a candidate in an election for such an employee representative, has the right to reasonable time off during working hours in order to perform his functions as such an employee representative or candidate, or in order to undergo training to perform such functions (*ERA 1996, s 61*).

This right is not subject to a period of continuous employment which the employee may have with an employer. The employee is entitled to be paid for time taken off during working hours. The amount of pay is calculated in accordance with the provisions governing a week's pay and *Part XIV of ERA 1996* (*ERA 1996, s 62(1)*) (see PAY – I (34)).

An employee who is a negotiating representative or an information and consultation representative is entitled to take reasonable time off during his working hours in order to perform his representative functions (*Information and Consultation of Employees Regulations 2004, reg 27 (SI 2004/3426)*). He is entitled to be paid remuneration for the time off at the appropriate hourly rate (*reg 28*).

An employee who is a member of a special negotiating body, a member of a representative body, an information and consultation representative, an employee member on a supervisory or administrative organ, or a candidate in an election in which any person elected will, on being elected, be such a member or representative, is entitled to take reasonable time off during working hours in order to perform the functions of member, representative or candidate (*European Public Limited-Liability Company Regulations 2004, reg 39*). Where an employee takes time off in this way, he is entitled to be paid remuneration at the appropriate hourly rate (*reg 40*).

The *Occupational and Personal Pension Schemes* (*Consultation by Employers and Miscellaneous Amendment*) *Regulations 2006* (*SI 2006/349*) provide (*para 2, Sch*) that an employee who is a representative falling within *reg 12(2)(a)* or (*3*) or *13(2)*, and is consulted under the *Regulations* about a listed change by a relevant employer is entitled to be permitted by his employer to take reasonable time off during the employee's working hours in order to perform his functions as such a representative. He is entitled to be paid for such time off at the appropriate hourly rate (*para 3*).

The *European Cooperative Societies* (*Involvement of Employees*) *Regulations 2006, SI 2006/2059* give under *reg 28* a right to reasonable time off to an employee who is a member of a special negotiating body or representative body, an information and consultation representative, an employee member of a supervisory or administrative organ, an election candidate or meeting participant under *reg 17(2)(h)* or *para 11(2)(h)* of *Sch 1* or *para 7(4)* of *Sch 2*. *Regulation 29* entitles the employee to payment at the appropriate hourly rate and *reg 30* gives the employee the right to present an employment tribunal claim where time off or payment are denied.

49.15 Remedy

If an employer unreasonably fails to allow an employee to take time off or fails to pay him for time off, the employee may complain to an employment tribunal. The claim must be presented within three months of the day on which time off was taken, or which it is alleged time off should have been allowed. The tribunal may extend time if it was not reasonably practicable to present the claim within three months. Where the complaint is that time off has unreasonably been denied, the tribunal may order payment at the appropriate rate for the period which should have been allowed.

49.16 TIME OFF FOR EUROPEAN WORKS COUNCIL DUTIES

An employee who is a member of a European Works Council, a member of a special negotiating body, an information and consultation representative, or a candidate for election to be such a representative, is entitled to paid time off in order to carry out his or her duties (*Transnational Information and Consultation of Employees Regulations 1999, regs 25 and 26* (*SI 1999/3323*)). An employee who is unreasonably refused such time off, or denied payment in accordance with the formula contained in *reg 26*, may bring a complaint to an employment tribunal under *reg 27*. The complaint is subject to a three-month time limit, which may be extended where the employment tribunal is satisfied that it was not reasonably practicable for the application to have been made within the three-month period.

49.17 TIME OFF FOR DEPENDANTS

Under *ERA 1996, s 57A* employees are entitled to be permitted by their employer to take a reasonable amount of time off during working hours in order to take action which is necessary:

(*a*)   to provide assistance when a dependant falls ill, gives birth, is injured or assaulted;

(*b*)   to make arrangements for the provision of care for a dependant who is ill or injured;

(*c*)   in consequence of the death of a dependant;

(*d*)   because of the unexpected disruption or termination of arrangements for the care of a dependant; or

(*e*)   to deal with an incident which involves the employee's child which occurs unexpectedly in a period during which an educational establishment which the child attends is responsible for him.

(*ERA 1996, s 57A(1)*.)

Sick leave taken because of a bereavement reaction does not qualify as time off in consequence of the death of a dependant (*Forster v Cartwright Black* [2004] IRLR 781).

An employee must inform his employer as soon as reasonably practicable of the reason for his absence, and, where he is able to inform his employer in advance of his absence, how long he expects to be absent (*ERA 1996, s 57A(2)*).

'Dependant' is defined as a spouse, child or parent of the employee, or a person who lives in the same household as the employee (excluding tenants, lodgers and boarders). Civil partners are included within the definition of 'dependant'. In addition, for the purposes of (*a*), (*b*) and (*d*) above, a dependant includes any person who reasonably relies on the employee to assist him if ill or injured, or who reasonably relies on the employee to make arrangements to provide care for him (*ERA 1996, s 57A(3), (4)* and *(5)*). Illness and injury are defined to include mental illness and injury (*ERA 1996, s 57A(6)*).

49.18   Remedy

An employee who has unreasonably been refused permission to take time off in accordance with his right under *s 57A* may complain to an employment tribunal (*ERA 1996, s 57B(1)*). The time limit for such complaints is three months beginning with the date the refusal occurred. The tribunal has a discretion to extend time where it was not reasonably practicable for the employee to present his claim in the three-month period (*ERA 1996, s 57B(2)*). If a tribunal finds the complaint well-founded, it may make a declaration to that effect, and may award such compensation as it considers just and equitable, having regard to the employer's default in refusing to permit time off to be taken by the employee, and any loss sustained by the employee (*ERA 1996, s 57B(3)* and *(4)*).

49.19   TIME OFF TO CARE FOR CHILDREN

The *Employment Act 2002* introduced significant changes to the statutory leave scheme for the carers of children. In summary, there were amendments to maternity leave and pay with effect from 24 November 2002, the introduction of entitlements to paid paternity leave and adoption leave with effect from 8 December 2002, and the introduction of provisions to promote 'flexible working', including the right for an employee to request 'flexible working' with effect from 6 April 2003. Further important changes have been made in respect of babies due on or after 1 April 2007. Rights to maternity and parental leave are considered fully in MATERNITY AND PARENTAL RIGHTS (33)

Maternity Leave

There are three types of maternity leave: compulsory leave, ordinary leave and additional leave. A compulsory maternity leave of at least two weeks must be taken in all cases (*ERA 1996, s 72* and *Maternity and Parental Leave Regulations 1999, reg 8*) from the day on which childbirth occurs.

All female employees, irrespective of length of service and hours of work, are entitled to ordinary maternity leave (*ERA 1996, s 71* and *Maternity and Parental Leave Regulations 1999, reg 4*) of up to 26 weeks.

Additional maternity leave is a further period of leave of up to 26 weeks, which is taken immediately after ordinary maternity leave (*ERA 1996, s 73* and *Maternity and Parental Leave Regulations 1999, reg 5*). The right to take additional maternity leave has now been extended to cover all pregnant employees.

Unlike the right to time off in the form of maternity leave, the right to receive statutory maternity pay is limited to 39 weeks and is due only to pregnant employees who meet the qualifying conditions.

Parental Leave

Under the *Maternity and Parental Leave Regulations 1999* (*SI 1999/3312*), made under *ERA 1996, s 76*, an employee, whether full-time or part-time, who has one year's continuous service and who has or expects to have responsibility for a child, is entitled to be absent from work on parental leave for the purpose of caring for that child (*reg 13(1)*). 'Parental responsibility' is a legal concept, defined in *s 3* of the *Children Act 1989*. Both male and female employees have the right to take parental leave and each parent has a separate entitlement. The *Regulations* implement *Council Directive 96/34/EC*.

Parental leave may normally only be taken to care for a child who is under five years old, although special provisions apply to disabled and adopted children.

An employee may take up to a total of 13 weeks' leave to care for any one child (*reg 14(1)*) but no more than four weeks' leave may be taken in respect of any one child in any one year (*Sch 2, para 8*). During the period of parental leave, an employee is not entitled to be paid, but the implied duty of trust and confidence under the contract of employment remains in force for the benefit of both employee and employer, as do any terms and conditions relating to notice, compensation in the event of redundancy, and disciplinary and grievance procedures (*reg 17*). A collective or workforce agreement incorporated into an employee's contract of employment may set out the procedure an employee must follow when taking parental leave: in default of such agreement, the provisions set out in *Sch 2* to the *Regulations* apply (*reg 16*). (The term 'workforce agreement' is defined in *Sch 1*.) Under *Sch 2*, parental leave may not be taken other than in periods of a week or multiples of a week (also see *Rodway v South Central Trains Ltd* [2005] EWCA Civ 443, [2005] IRLR 583). An employer may require an employee to produce evidence of responsibility for the child, the child's date of birth and, where appropriate, evidence of the date of adoption placement or disability living allowance. An employee must give at least 21 days' notice of intention to take leave and the notice must specify the date on which the period of leave is to begin and end. Where an employer considers that the parental leave would unduly disrupt the operation of his business, he may postpone the leave for up to six months (*Sch 2, para 6*).

An employee who takes parental leave for a period of four weeks or less is entitled to return to the job he or she was employed in before his or her absence; an employee who takes a longer period of leave is entitled to return to his or her job or, if that is not reasonably practicable, a job which is suitable and appropriate to the circumstances (*reg 18*). On return, an employee's rights to remuneration, seniority, pension rights and other similar rights must be no less favourable than before the absence (*reg 18(5)*). Special provisions apply where parental leave is taken in conjunction with maternity leave (see *reg 18(3), (5)*).

An employee is entitled not to suffer a detriment by reason that he or she took parental leave (*reg 19(2)(e)*; *ERA 1996, s 47C*). It is automatically unfair to dismiss an employee if the reason for the dismissal is connected to the fact that he or she took or sought to take parental leave (*reg 20(2) and (3)*).

Where the contract of employment provides a right to take parental leave, the employee may not take leave under both the contract and the *Regulations* but may take advantage of whichever right is more favourable (*reg 21*).

Paternity Leave

Paternity leave is a period of either one week's or two weeks' leave taken within 56 days of the date on which the baby was born (*ERA 1996, ss 80A–80E* and *Paternity and Adoption Leave Regulations 2002* (*SI 2002/2788*), *regs 4–14*). The purpose of paternity leave is to care for the child or to support the child's mother. It is available to the partner of the child's mother or adopter, who lives with the mother in an enduring family relationship, and is not the mother's parent, grandparent, sibling, aunt or uncle. If he is the father of the child, he must have parental responsibility for the upbringing of the child, but if he or she is simply the mother's partner, then he or she must have the main responsibility (other than the mother's responsibility) for the upbringing of the child. In order to qualify for paternity leave, an employee must have at least 26 weeks' continuous employment ending with the week immediately preceding the fourteenth week before the expected week of childbirth. The entitlement to paternity leave is unaffected by the mother's death at the time of or within 56 days of the birth. Paternity leave may be taken where a baby is stillborn after 24 weeks of pregnancy or dies within 56 days of birth. Where more than one child is born as a result of the same pregnancy there is no entitlement to extra paternity leave.

Complex rules govern the employee's duty to give his or her employer notice of intention to take paternity leave (*Paternity and Adoption Leave Regulations 2002, reg 6*) and notice must be given in or before the fifteenth week before the expected week of childbirth wherever reasonably practicable. The employee may chose to begin paternity leave on the date on which the child is born, or on a date falling a specified number of days after the date on which the child is born, or on a pre-determined date later than the first day of the expected week of childbirth. Where an employee has chosen to begin his or her leave on the date on which the child is born and he or she is at work on that day, the paternity leave begins on the next day. The employee may vary the date for commencement of paternity leave on giving at least 28 days' notice before the relevant day (which is not the day on which the child is born), or, where it is not reasonably practicable to give 28 days' notice, as soon as is reasonably practicable.

An employee also has a right to paternity leave for the purpose of caring for an adopted child or supporting the child's adopter (*Paternity and Adoption Leave Regulations 2002, regs 8–11*).

During paternity leave an employee is entitled to enjoy all his or her terms and conditions of employment as if he or she had not been absent and is bound by his or her contractual obligations (*Paternity and Adoption Leave Regulations 2002, reg 12*). He or she is entitled to return to the same job, where he or she took an isolated period of paternity leave or where the paternity leave was the last of two or more consecutive periods of statutory leave which did not include any period of additional maternity leave, additional adoption leave, or parental leave in excess of four weeks (*Paternity and Adoption Leave Regulations 2002, reg 13*). In other cases, the entitlement to return is to the same job only where reasonably practicable, failing which the employee is entitled to return to a job that is both suitable for the employee and appropriate for the employee to do in the circumstances.

An employee may be entitled to receive statutory paternity pay (*Statutory Paternity Pay and Statutory Adoption Pay (Weekly Rates) Regulations 2002; Statutory Paternity Pay and Statutory Adoption Pay (Administration) Regulations 2002;* and *Statutory Paternity Pay and Statutory Adoption Pay (General) Regulations 2002*). Statutory paternity pay is administered by employers in a similar way to statutory maternity pay.

An employee is protected against detriment or dismissal in connection with his or her taking or seeking to take paternity leave (*Paternity and Adoption Leave Regulations 2002, regs 28* and *29*).

Adoption Leave

An employee who adopts a child has an entitlement to ordinary adoption leave and additional adoption leave which mirror the entitlements to ordinary maternity leave and additional maternity leave (*Employment Rights Act 1996, ss 75A–75D; Paternity and Adoption Leave Regulations 2002, regs 15–27; Statutory Paternity Pay and Statutory Adoption Pay (Weekly Rates) Regulations 2002; Statutory Paternity Pay and Statutory Adoption Pay (Administration) Regulations 2002;* and *Statutory Paternity Pay and Statutory Adoption Pay (General) Regulations 2002*). The right to adoption leave arises only with the adoption of a new child into the family, and not, for example, where a step-parent or foster carer adopts a child in law for whom he or she has already been caring. An employee may commence ordinary adoption leave either on the date on which the child is placed with him or her for adoption, or on a pre-determined date which has been notified to the employer, and is no earlier than 14 days before the date on which the placement is expected and no later that the expected date of placement.

An employee is protected against detriment or dismissal in connection with his or her taking or seeking to take adoption leave (*Paternity and Adoption Leave Regulations 2002, regs 28* and *29*). This protection extends to the situation in which the employee suffers detriment or dismissal because of the employer's belief that the employee was likely to take adoption leave (regardless of whether the placement eventually occurs) and, like the protection given to pregnant women, provides a protection for an employee who is expecting to receive the placement of an adopted child.

Flexible Working

An employee may formally apply in writing to his or her employer to request a change in hours, times or location of work for the purpose of enabling the employee to care for a child (*Employment Rights Act 1996, ss 80F–I; Flexible Working (Procedural Requirements) Regulations 2002;* and *Flexible Working (Eligibility, Complaints and Remedies) Regulations 2002*). An employee is eligible to request flexible working if he or she is, or is the partner of, the mother, father, adopter, guardian or foster parent of the child, and expects to have responsibility for the upbringing of the child. The employer may refuse such an application only on grounds of the burden of additional costs, detrimental effect on the ability to meet customer demand, inability to re-organise work among existing staff, inability to recruit additional staff, detrimental impact on quality, detrimental impact on performance, insufficiency of work during the periods during which the employee proposes to work, or planned structural changes.

An employer must hold a meeting with the employee to discuss the request for flexible working within 28 days from the making of the application. The employer must notify the employee in writing of the decision on the application within 14 days of the meeting. An employee has a right of appeal against the decision within 14 days of the decision. An appeal meeting must be held within 14 days of the employee's notice of appeal and the employer must notify the employee of the appeal decision within 14 days of the appeal meeting. The employee has a right to be accompanied at the meetings to discuss flexible working and is protected against detriment or dismissal on the ground that he or she exercised or sought to exercise the right to be accompanied or to accompany in such a situation. An employee is protected against detriment (*Employment Rights Act 1996, s 47E*) and dismissal (*Employment Rights Act 1996, s 104C*) on the ground that he or she exercised or sought to exercise the rights to apply for, take, or enforce the right to request flexible working.

An employee may complain to an employment tribunal that an employer has failed to deal with his or her request for flexible working properly or has rejected the application on the basis of incorrect facts (see e g *Commotion Ltd v Rutty* [2006] IRLR 171). If the complaint is upheld the employment tribunal may order the employer to reconsider the application and may award compensation of up to eight weeks' pay. The employment tribunal may not order the employer to implement the employee's request for flexible working.

49.20 REINSTATEMENT AFTER MILITARY SERVICE

Where a person has entered upon a period of whole-time service in the armed forces of the Crown, and has done so in pursuance of a notice or directions for the calling out of reserve or auxiliary forces, or for the recall of service pensioners, or in pursuance of an obligation or undertaking to serve as a commissioned officer, then he has certain rights to be reinstated in employment by his former employer under the *Reserve Forces (Safeguard of Employment) Act 1985*. The following is a short summary of the main provisions of the *Act*.

The former employee must apply in writing to his former employer after the period of military service ends and not later than the third Monday after the end of that period, or as soon afterwards as reasonably possible (*s 3*). He must also notify the employer of a date, not later than 21 days after the latest date allowed for the application, when he will be available for employment (*s 4*).

The employer must then reinstate the former employee in his old occupation on terms no less favourable than would have applied but for the military service, or (if that is not reasonable and practicable – as to which, see *s 5*), in the most favourable occupation and on the most favourable terms and conditions which are reasonable and practicable in his case (*s 1(2)*). The person concerned must then be employed for at least 13, 26 or 52 weeks, depending on the length of his continuous employment prior to the military service, or for so much of that time as is reasonable and practicable (*s 7*; see *Slaven v Thermo Engineers Ltd* [1992] ICR 295).

Complaints that a person's statutory rights have been infringed may be made to a Reinstatement Committee, which may order employment to be made available to the applicant, and order the payment of compensation to him (*s 8*). There are rights of appeal in certain circumstances to an umpire sitting with assessors (*s 9*). Non-compliance with an order is a criminal offence (*s 10*). The procedure upon applications and appeals is governed by the *Reinstatement in Civil Employment (Procedure) Regulations 1944 (SR & O 1944/880)*.

50   Trade Unions – I: Nature and Liabilities

(See DTI Guidance available online at www.dti.gov.uk/employment/index.html 'Trade union executive elections' (URN No 06/555), 'Trade union funds and accounting records' (URN No 06/556) and 'Trade union political funds' (URN No 06/557).)

Cross-references. See also STRIKES AND INDUSTRIAL ACTION (43); TIME OFF WORK (49) for time off for trade union duties or activities; TRADE UNIONS – II (51) for individual rights and union membership; 54.3 UNFAIR DISMISSAL – II for dismissal for participation in union activities.

50.1   **THE STATUS OF A TRADE UNION**

The present law on the status and liability of trade unions is governed by the *Trade Union and Labour Relations (Consolidation) Act 1992 ('TULRCA 1992')*. 'Trade union' is statutorily defined in *TULRCA 1992, s 1* as an organisation (whether permanent or temporary) which either –

(*a*)   consists wholly or mainly of workers of one or more descriptions and is an organisation whose principal purposes include the regulation of relations between workers of that description or those descriptions and employers or employers' associations; or

(*b*)   consists wholly or mainly of ⸺

　　(i)   constituent or affiliated organisations which fulfil the conditions specified in para (*a*) above (or themselves consist wholly or mainly of constituent or affiliated organisations which fulfil those conditions), or

　　(ii)   representatives of such constituent or affiliated organisations;

and in either case is an organisation whose principal purposes include the regulation of relations between workers and employers or between workers and employers' associations, or include the regulation of relations between its constituent or affiliated organisations.

In *British Association of Advisers and Lecturers in Physical Education v National Union of Teachers* [1986] IRLR 497, the Court of Appeal construed this definition broadly so as to include an association 'concerned with the professional interests of its members'.

Several of the larger trade unions are made up of a number of constituent sections. The definition in *TULRCA 1992, s 1* ensures that both the conglomerate organisation and its constituent parts are considered to be trade unions. The National Union of Mineworkers is made up of a number of areas such as the National Union of Mineworkers (South Wales area), all of which are, under *TULRCA 1992*, to be considered trade unions. Similarly, a branch of a trade union may be held to be a trade union (see *News Group Newspapers Ltd v SOGAT 1982* [1987] ICR 181).

50.2   **Legal capacity**

Unless a trade union is a special registered body as defined by *TULRCA 1992, s 117* (such bodies are mostly incorporated professional associations), it is not, nor to be treated as if it were, a corporate entity (*TULRCA 1992, s 10*). However, *TULRCA 1992, s 10(1)* gives a trade union a statutory legal personality which it would otherwise lack so that it can:

(*a*)   make contracts;

(*b*)   sue or be sued in its own name (see 50.16 and 50.17 below for certain immunities enjoyed by trade unions); and

(*c*)   be a defendant in criminal proceedings.

All property belonging to a trade union must be vested in trustees in trust for the union (*TULRCA 1992, s 12(1)*).

50.3   CERTIFICATION OFFICER

The Secretary of State appoints a Certification Officer in consultation with ACAS under *TULRCA 1992, s 254*. He makes an annual report to the Secretary of State, who presents it to Parliament and publishes it (*TULRCA 1992, s 258*). His functions include:

(*a*)   dealing with complaints relating to the keeping of the register of a union's members (see 50.13 below);

(*b*)   dealing with complaints relating to trade union internal elections (see 50.14 below);

(*c*)   dealing with complaints relating to political fund ballots (see 50.15 below);

(*d*)   maintaining a list of trade unions (see 50.21 below);

(*e*)   certifying whether trade unions are independent (see 50.22 below);

(*f*)   certain supervisory functions in relation to trade union amalgamations (see 50.39 below); and

(*g*)   administering the scheme for financial contributions towards trade union ballots.

The Certification Officer may at any time, if he thinks there is good reason to do so, require a trade union (or any person who appears to be in possession of the documents) to produce specified documents which are accounting documents or which may be relevant in considering the union's financial affairs (*TULRCA 1992, s 37A*). He may also appoint inspectors to investigate and report upon a union's financial affairs if there are circumstances suggesting fraud, misconduct or a breach of statutory obligations or union rules in relation to those affairs, and all past and present officials and agents of the union and other persons appearing to be in possession of relevant information must then co-operate with the investigation, including by producing documents and attending before the inspectors (*TULRCA 1992, s 37B*). Reports made will be published by the Certification Officer, and there are various other administrative provisions, as well as criminal sanctions for contravention of statutory requirements (*TULRCA 1992, ss 37C–37E; TULRCA 1992, ss 45, 45A*).

The Certification Officer has jurisdiction to consider applications by members or former members of a trade union claiming that there has been a breach or threatened breach of the union's rules, pursuant to a new *TULRCA 1992, s 108A*. The Certification Officer may consider such a claim only if it relates to:

(*a*)   the appointment or election of a person to, or their removal from, any office;

(b)   disciplinary proceedings (including expulsion);

(c)   the balloting of members on any issue other than industrial action;

(d)   the constitution or proceedings of any executive committee or of any decision-making meeting; and

(e)   such other matters as the Secretary of State may specify.

In *Unison v Gallagher* (2005) IDS Brief No 791 the Employment Appeal Tribunal found that the Certification Officer had exceeded his jurisdiction in holding that the appellant union had breached its disciplinary rules by excluding a member, who had been previously been disciplined and debarred from holding office for five years, from is annual delegate conference. The exclusion followed a decision by the union that all those who had been expelled or debarred from holding office should no longer be allowed to attend the conference. Although the exclusion was consequent upon the previous disciplinary determination, it was held to be administrative in nature, and therefore fell outside the Certification Officer's jurisdiction.

The complaint must be made within six months of either the alleged breach or threatened breach, the conclusion of an internal complaints procedure relating to the breach or the expiry of one year from such a complaints procedure being invoked. *TULRCA 1992, s 108B* provides that the Certification Officer must accept an application only if satisfied that the applicant has taken all reasonable steps to resolve the claim through internal complaints procedures. If he accepts an application, he may make a declaration and an enforcement order requiring steps to be taken to remedy the breach. By *TULRCA 1992, s 108C* an appeal lies on points of law to the Employment Appeal Tribunal.

50.4   CENTRAL ARBITRATION COMMITTEE

The Central Arbitration Committee ('CAC') was established pursuant to the *Employment Protection Act 1975* and continues by virtue of *s 259* of the *Trade Union and Labour Relations (Consolidation) Act 1992 ('TULRCA 1992')*.

50.5   Constitution

The Secretary of State for Trade and Industry is responsible for appointing members of the CAC whom he selects from persons nominated by ACAS as being experienced in industrial relations and who include both employers' and workers' representatives. In addition, the Secretary of State appoints a chairman and may appoint one or more deputy chairmen after consultation with ACAS (*TULRCA 1992, s 260*).

50.6   Functions

(a)   Arbitration in trade disputes (see 50.7 below).

(b)   Resolution of complaints that an employer has failed to disclose information which he was required to disclose by *TULRCA 1992, s 181* (*TULRCA 1992, s 183*) (see 50.8 below).

(c)   Determination of questions previously referred to the Industrial Arbitration Board (*TULRCA 1992, Sch 3 para 7*). (The Board was the successor of the Industrial Court created by the *Industrial Courts Act 1919*, to which trade disputes of various kinds could be referred.)

(d)   Union recognition disputes (see 50.11 below).

(*e*)   Resolution of complaints that an employer has failed to comply with its duty to provide data requested under the *Information and Consultation of Employees Regulations 2004* (*SI 2004/3426*) (see EMPLOYEE PARTICIPATION (18)).

50.7   Arbitration

The CAC may arbitrate on trade disputes at the request of one or more parties to the dispute, provided that all parties consent to the arbitration. The request for arbitration is made to ACAS in the first instance, which may refer the matter to the CAC (*TULRCA 1992, s 212(1)(b)*; and see 2.6 ADVISORY, CONCILIATION AND ARBITRATION SERVICE).

50.8   Complaint of failure to disclose information

The CAC may hear and determine complaints made by an independent trade union recognised for collective bargaining purposes that the employer by whom it is recognised has not disclosed information to which the union is statutorily entitled (see 11.3 DISCLOSURE OF INFORMATION) (*TULRCA 1992, ss 181, 183*). The CAC is only empowered to make a declaration if the union is recognised by the employer for the particular purpose to which the information relates (*R v Central Arbitration Committee, ex p BTP Tioxide Ltd* [1981] ICR 843). The CAC will refer the complaint for conciliation by ACAS if it considers that it is reasonably likely to be settled in that way (*TULRCA 1992, s 183(2)*). Any person with a proper interest in the complaint is entitled to be heard by the CAC (*TULRCA 1992, s 183(4)*). If the CAC finds the complaint well-founded, it will make a declaration specifying the information which must be disclosed, the date upon which the employer refused or failed to disclose it and the period within which it must be disclosed (*TULRCA 1992, s 183(3), (5)*).

If the employer fails to comply with the order of the CAC, the union may present a further complaint which may be coupled with, or followed by, a claim that certain terms and conditions should be included in the contracts of one or more descriptions of employees in respect of whom the union is recognised by the employer (*TULRCA 1992, ss 184, 185*).

If the CAC finds the further complaint wholly or partly well-founded, it may make an award that, in respect of any description of employees specified in a claim for the inclusion of terms and conditions, the employer shall from a certain date observe either the terms and conditions specified in the claim or other terms and conditions which the CAC considers appropriate (*TULRCA 1992, ss 184(2), (4), 185(3)*). These terms and conditions have effect as part of the contract of employment of any such employee, unless superseded or varied by a further award, a collective agreement, or an agreement with the employee which improves those terms (*TULRCA 1992, s 185(5)*).

An award may only be made in respect of a description of employees, and may only comprise terms and conditions relating to matters in respect of which the trade union making the claim is recognised by the employer (*TULRCA 1992, s 185(4)*). The right to present a claim for terms and conditions expires if the employer discloses, or confirms in writing, the information specified in the declaration, and a claim presented shall be treated as withdrawn if the employer does so before the CAC makes an award on the claim (*TULRCA 1992, s 185(2)*).

50.9 **No contracting out**

Any provision in an agreement is void insofar as it purports to prevent a person from bringing proceedings before the CAC, unless a conciliation officer has taken action pursuant to his statutory duties or unless the agreement varies or supersedes an award under *TULRCA 1992, s 185* (*TULRCA 1992, s 288*).

50.10 **Appeal**

There is no appeal against an award of the CAC, but its decision may be challenged by judicial review proceedings in the High Court (or, in Scotland, the Court of Session) and set aside if it can be shown that the CAC:

(*a*)   misdirected itself in law or exceeded its jurisdiction;

(*b*)   failed to take into account relevant considerations or took into account irrelevant ones; or

(*c*)   acted unreasonably or in breach of natural justice.

For an example of the very limited basis on which the Court of Session was prepared to intervene in a decision of the CAC, see *Fullarton Computer Industries Ltd v Central Arbitration Committee* [2001] IRLR 752.

50.11 **Statutory trade union recognition**

With the coming into force of *s 70A* and *Sch A1* of *TULRCA 1992*, introduced by the *Employment Relations Act 1999* ('*ERA 1999*'), the role of the CAC was considerably expanded and enhanced. With effect from 6 June 2000, trade unions gained a statutory right to be recognised by employers for collective bargaining purposes. See further 50.19–50.38.

The CAC, under the chairmanship of Sir Michael Burton, plays a central role in relation to the recognition procedures. Applications to the CAC in relation to recognition are heard by a panel of three members, including the chairman or a deputy chairman.

50.12 **OBLIGATIONS**

Trade unions have statutory obligations to keep accounting records (for members' rights of inspection, see 51.2 TRADE UNIONS – II), to make annual returns, to appoint auditors and to make arrangements for the inspection of their members' superannuation schemes (*TULRCA 1992, ss 28, 32, 32A, 33, 40*). They must keep an up-to-date register of members (see 50.13 below), hold periodic elections for membership of the principal executive committee and for certain other positions (see 50.14 below), and hold ballots on the continued application of trade union funds for political purposes (see 50.15 below) (*TULRCA 1992, ss 24, 46, 71*). In *Paul v NALGO* [1987] IRLR 43 the Certification Officer considered several of these obligations. A trade union must, at the request of any person, supply him with a copy of its rules either free or on payment of a reasonable charge (*TULRCA 1992, s 27*).

50.13 **Register of members**

Every trade union is obliged by *TULRCA 1992, s 24* to compile and keep up to date a register of members. A member has a right to a copy of any register entry relating to him (*TULRCA 1992, s 24(3)*).

A member of the union may apply to the Certification Officer, or to the High Court in England or the Court of Session in Scotland, for a declaration that these requirements have not been complied with (*TULRCA 1992, ss 25, 26*). The court or (since 25 October 1999) the Certification Officer may also make an enforcement order requiring the union to compile or update the register (*TULRCA 1992, ss 25(5A), 26(4)*). There is a right of appeal against this Certification Officer's decisions under this section to the Employment Appeal Tribunal on any question of law pursuant to *TULRCA 1992, s 45D*.

50.14 Elections and disqualification from office

Trade unions are obliged to secure that, with certain exceptions, all members of its principal executive committee, and its president and general secretary, stand for election at least every five years (*TULRCA 1992, ss 46(1), 119*). Members of the principal executive committee are those who, under the rules or practice of the union, may attend at some or all of its meetings (other than merely to provide factual information or professional advice) (*TULRCA 1992, s 46(3)*). The position of president or general secretary is exempted from the election requirement if its holder is not an employee of the union, is not a voting member of the executive and holds the position for not more than 13 months (*TULRCA 1992, s 46(4)*). The position of president is also exempted if the incumbent was appointed or elected in accordance with the union's rules, at the time of such appointment or election he or she held a designated executive position by virtue of having been elected in accordance with the election requirements under the section and continues to hold such a designated position, and has held such a position for no more than five years (*TULRCA 1992, s 46(4A)*).

The ballot must, as far as is reasonably practicable, be secret. An independent scrutineer must be appointed to oversee the ballot, and his name must appear on the voting paper. Among his other duties, the scrutineer is obliged to make a report on the ballot to the union which must send it or notify its contents to members. Handling of voting papers and counting of votes must also be independently undertaken. Candidates must, so far as reasonably practicable, be enabled to distribute election addresses without cost to themselves. The members entitled to vote must, so far as is reasonably practicable, be given a convenient opportunity to vote by post. Members may not be unreasonably excluded from standing as candidates, and may not be required, directly or indirectly, to belong to a political party. There are detailed provisions governing the circumstances in which particular classes of members may be excluded from voting (*TULRCA 1992, ss 47–52; Trade Union Ballots and Elections (Independent Scrutineer Qualifications) Order 1993 (SI 1993/1909)*).

Although *TULRCA 1992, s 51(6)* requires the election result to be determined solely by counting the number of votes cast, this did not invalidate a rule limiting the number of members of the National Executive Council ('NEC') who could be elected from any one geographical division (*R v Certification Officer, ex p Electrical Power Engineers' Association* [1990] ICR 682). The House of Lords took the view that the statutory provision was intended only to exclude weighted or block votes and electoral colleges.

The Certification Officer has held that it is permissible for ballot papers to contain information, such as the names of nominating branches, other than that prescribed by the statute (*Decision D/3/89*).

A person who claims that his union is in breach of the election provisions may apply to the Certification Officer, or to the High Court in England or to the Court of Session in Scotland. He must have been a member of the union at the date of the election, and at the date of the application. The application must be made within one year of the date on which the result of the election was announced (*TULRCA 1992, s 54*). The Certification Officer or the court may make a declaration specifying the provisions with which the trade union has failed to comply (*TULRCA 1992, ss 55(2), (3), 56(3)*). If it makes a declaration, the court or the Certification Officer must also, unless it is considered that to do so would be inappropriate, make an enforcement order to secure the holding of an election specified in the order (*TULRCA 1992, ss 55(5A), 56(4)*). There is a right of appeal to the Employment Appeal Tribunal against a decision of the Certification Officer, or a question of law, under *TULRCA 1992, s 56A*.

The Secretary of State is empowered by *TULRCA 1992, ss 203* and *204* to issue a Code of Practice relating to the conduct by trade unions of ballots and elections (see CODES OF PRACTICE (5)). Codes of Practice have been issued, which deal with ballots on industrial action (see STRIKES AND INDUSTRIAL ACTION (45)) and access to workers during recognition and derecognition ballots.

In the event that the executive council of a union seeks to breach the union's election rules, individual members of the union have a contractual right by virtue of their contracts of membership to challenge the validity of the council's decision (*Wise v Union of Shop Distributors and Allied Workers* [1996] ICR 691). It was held by the High Court in *Ecclestone v National Union of Journalists* [1999] IRLR 166 that a union's exclusion of a candidate for election on the basis that he did not have the confidence of the NEC was both a breach of the union's rules and contrary to the prohibition on unreasonably excluding candidates within *TULRCA 1992, s 47*.

Persons who have previously been convicted of certain offences under *TULRCA 1992, s 45* as amended (which deals in particular with failure to comply with statutory obligations, and with dishonest falsification or destruction of documents) are disqualified from membership of the principal executive committee and from being president or general secretary (subject to the same exemptions as set out above). The disqualification is for five or ten years, depending upon the offence committed (*TULRCA 1992, s 45B*). If a union allows a disqualified person to hold office, a member of the union may apply to the Certification Officer or to the court for a declaration to that effect. They have the power to require the union to take steps to remedy the position (*TULRCA 1992, s 45C, 45C(5A)*). There is a right of appeal against the Certification Officer's decisions under this section to the Employment Appeal Tribunal on any question of law, under *TULRCA 1992, s 45D*.

In *AB v CD* [2001] IRLR 808, the Court of Appeal considered the appropriate mechanism for resolving a tied vote in the second round of the election, by single transferable vote, of a regional union representative. The rules of the union, the RMT, were silent as to how such a tie should be resolved. In the absence of any express rule, the candidate who had received the most votes in the first round was declared elected.

The Court of Appeal upheld this decision. A term was to be implied into the union rules that a tie would be resolved in this way, in order to give efficacy to the contract, as an obvious inference from the express terms of the rules and in order to complete the contract between the members. However, such a term was not to be implied from custom and practice. In order for custom and practice to warrant the implication of a contractual term in the rules of a trade union, the relevant custom must be known, or at least readily ascertainable, by all members.

50.15 **Political levy**

A trade union may not apply its ordinary funds in the furtherance of political objects as defined by *TULRCA 1992, s 72*, which deals mainly with support for political parties and with attempts to influence the outcome of elections. Payments for such purposes may only be made out of a separate political fund, and then only if there is a political resolution in force approving the furtherance of those objects (*TULRCA 1992, s 71*). Union members have a right to apply to the Certification Officer for a decision that funds have been applied in breach of *s 71* (*TULRCA 1992, s 72A*). Such a resolution must be passed at least every 10 years by a ballot held in accordance with union rules which have been approved by the Certification Officer as complying with the relevant statutory requirements (*TUL-RCA 1992, ss 73, 74*). Those requirements, found in *TULRCA 1992, ss 75–78* are very similar to those which apply to ballots for union elections (see 50.14 above). Complaints of non-compliance with the ballot requirements may be made either to the Certification Officer or to the court within a year after the announcement of the result (*TULRCA 1992, ss 79–81*).

A union member is entitled to give notice that he objects to contributing to the political fund, and he is then to be exempted from making such contributions, and must not be put at any disadvantage or excluded from the union as a result (*TULRCA 1992, s 82*). A member who complains of a breach of these requirements may complain to the Certification Officer, who may make such order for remedying the breach as he thinks just under the circumstances (*TULRCA 1992, s 82(2), (3)*). A notice of objection should be in the form set out in *TULRCA 1992, s 84(1)* or to like effect. When a political resolution is adopted, members must be notified of their right to object and be given the opportunity to obtain exemption notice forms from union offices or from the Certification Officer (*TULRCA 1992, s 84(2)*).

If a union member certifies to his employer that he is exempt from making political contributions, the employer must ensure that they are not deducted from his wages (*TULRCA 1992, s 86*). There is a right to apply to an employment tribunal for a declaration that the employer has breached this obligation, and for an order that the employer repay sums deducted and, if considered appropriate, require the employer to take specified steps in relation to emoluments payable to the union member. If the member considers that the employer has failed to comply with an order to take such specified steps, he may present a further complaint to the tribunal (*TULRCA 1992, ss 86, 87*; and see PAY – I (34)).

50.16 **LIABILITY IN TORT**

The immunity of trade unions in proceedings in tort arising out of strikes or industrial action is now similar to that of individuals (see STRIKES AND INDUS-TRIAL ACTION (45)). Such immunity only applies to action taken in contemplation or furtherance of a trade dispute. With certain narrowly defined exceptions, it does not protect secondary action or action taken to enforce trade union membership. Further, a trade union does not enjoy immunity from liability in tort for inducing breaches of contracts of employment unless its action has the support of a ballot (see 45.14 STRIKES AND INDUSTRIAL ACTION). However, where proceedings in tort are brought against a trade union:

(*a*)   for a reason specified in *TULRCA 1992, s 219* (inducing breach of, and interference with, contracts; see 45.2 STRIKES AND INDUSTRIAL ACTION); or (*b*)   in respect of an agreement or combination by two or more persons to induce or do an unlawful act;

then that act will only be taken to have been done by the union if it is taken to have been authorised or endorsed by the union (*TULRCA 1992, s 20(1)*). An act will only be taken to have been authorised or endorsed if it was done, authorised or endorsed by one of the following:

(i)   the principal executive committee; or

(ii)   any person who is empowered by the rules to do, authorise or endorse acts of the kind in question; or

(iii)   the president or general secretary as defined in *TULRCA 1992, s 119*; or

(iv)   any other official of the union (whether employed by it or not), or by any member of a group to which such an official belongs and whose purposes include organising or co-ordinating industrial action; or

(v)   any other committee of the union, by which is meant any group of persons constituted in accordance with the rules of the union.

(*TULRCA 1992, s 20(2), (3)*).

An act will not be taken to have been endorsed by a person in category (iv) or (v) above if it was repudiated by the principal executive committee or the president or general secretary as soon as reasonably practicable after coming to the knowledge of any of them (*TULRCA 1992, s 21(1)*).

In order to be effective, written notice of the repudiation must be given without delay to the committee or official in question, and the union must also do its best to give individual written notice without delay to every member who it has reason to believe is taking part in, or might otherwise take part in, industrial action as a result of the repudiated act, and to the employer of every such member. The written notice must contain a statement in statutorily prescribed form (*TULRCA 1992, s 21(2)–(4)*).

The union will not be able to rely upon such a repudiation if the principal executive committee, or president or general secretary, has subsequently behaved in a way which is inconsistent with the purported repudiation (*TULRCA 1992, s 21(5)*). They will be treated as so behaving if, upon a request made within three months of the purported repudiation by a party to a commercial contract whose performance has been or may have been interfered with by the repudiated act and to whom written notice of the repudiation has not been given, they do not forthwith confirm in writing that the act has been repudiated (*TULRCA 1992, s 21(6)*). (See also *Express and Star Ltd v NGA* [1985] IRLR 455; upheld on other grounds, [1986] ICR 589.)

The liability of trade unions in such actions in tort is subject to financial limits, considered below.

Limits on damages awarded against a trade union, enforcement of judgments and protected property

50.17   With the exception of amounts awarded in actions for personal injury or for breach of duty in connection with the ownership, occupation, possession, control or use of property, the amount of damages awarded (not including interest; see *Boxfoldia Ltd v National Graphical Association* [1988] ICR 752) in any proceedings in tort brought against a trade union must not exceed the following limits:

  (i)   £10,000, if the union has fewer than 5,000 members;

 (ii)   £50,000, if it has 5,000 or more members but fewer than 25,000 members;

(iii)   £125,000, if it has 25,000 or more members but fewer than 100,000 members;

(iv)   £250,000, if it has 100,000 or more members.

(*TULRCA 1992, s 22(2)*.)

The Secretary of State may by order vary any of these sums (*TULRCA 1992, s 22(3)*).

A judgment, order or award made in proceedings of any description brought against a trade union is enforceable against any property held in trust for the union (see 50.2 above) to the same extent and in the same manner as if it were a body corporate (*TULRCA 1992, s 12(2)*). However, no award of damages, costs or expenses is recoverable by enforcement against protected property (*TULRCA 1992, s 23(1)*). Protected property includes the property of individual members, officials and trustees, the contents of a political fund which cannot, under the rules, be used to finance industrial action (see 50.15 above), and the contents of separate provident benefit funds (*TULRCA 1992, s 23(2)*).

50.18 LIABILITY OF INDIVIDUAL MEMBERS

The individual participants in industrial action have the same immunity as trade unions. Such immunity only applies to action taken in contemplation or further-ance of a trade dispute. There is, however, no limit on the damages which may be awarded if an individual is found liable. With certain narrowly defined exceptions, secondary industrial action is not protected. (See 45.6 STRIKES AND INDUSTRIAL ACTION.)

TULRCA 1992, s 15 renders unlawful the application of the property of a trade union towards the payment of any penalty imposed upon an individual for an offence or for contempt of court, or towards any indemnity in respect of such liabilities. This applies to all kinds of offences unless designated otherwise by order made by the Secretary of State (*TULRCA 1992, s 15(5)*). However, the prohibition does not extend to civil liabilities, provided that the indemnity or contribution is otherwise lawful and *intra vires* the union. The union is given the right to recover property or its value applied in contravention of these provisions from the individual concerned (*TULRCA 1992, s 15(2)*), and in the event of its unreasonable failure to take proceedings to this end, the court may order, upon application by a union member, that that member shall be authorised to do so in the union's name and at its expense (*TULRCA 1992, s 15(3)*).

50.19 RECOGNITION, INDEPENDENCE AND RIGHTS

Arguably the most far-reaching change in the law brought about by the *Employment Relations Act 1999* was the new recognition machinery for collective bargaining purposes contained in *Sch 1* to that *Act*. The relevant provisions, which are now contained in *Sch A1* to *TULRCA 1992*, confer a right upon trade unions to be recognised by employers for collective bargaining purposes, provided various (extremely complex) conditions are fulfilled. Thus, whilst the new proce-dures encourage employers and unions to agree on recognition wherever possible, they bring about a fundamental change in the law in providing for compulsory recognition in certain circumstances. The new provisions came into force on 6 June 2000. The principal features of the new recognition machinery are summarised at 50.25–50.38 below. The *Employment Relations Act 2004* has amended the recognition provisions in a number of respects.

The European Court of Human Rights held in *Wilson v United Kingdom* [2002] IRLR 568 that *art 11* of the European Convention of Human Rights did not impose a requirement for compulsory collective bargaining.

Previous provisions in the *Employment Protection Act 1975* ('*EPA 1975*'), covering the statutory procedure by which independent trade unions could refer recognition issues to ACAS, were repealed in 1980.

Although the previous statutory recognition machinery in the *EPA 1975* was repealed, the concepts of 'independence' and 'recognition' discussed below continue to be relevant for some purposes. One is the procedure for handling redundancies laid down in *TULRCA 1992, Part IV* (see 39.2 REDUNDANCY – II). Others are disclosure of information for collective bargaining purposes under *TULRCA 1992, s 181* (see 11.2 DISCLOSURE OF INFORMATION), the information and consultation requirements contained in the *Transfer of Undertakings* (*Protection of Employment Regulations 2006* (*SI 2006/246*) (see 52.18 TRANSFER OF UNDERTAKINGS) and the right to time off for trade union duties and activities (see 49.2, 49.3 TIME OFF WORK). In addition, the concept of 'independence' is central to the new procedures for recognition for collective bargaining purposes (see below).

50.20 Voluntary recognition

The recognition provisions contained in *TULRCA 1992, Sch A1* provide specifically for voluntary recognition. Even before those provisions came into effect, however, an employer could voluntarily agree to recognise a trade union. Recognition can be express or implied. An employer need not have entered into a formal recognition agreement in order to be considered to have recognised a particular trade union. 'Recognition' is defined in *TULRCA 1992, s 178(3)* as 'the recognition of the union by an employer ... to any extent, for the purpose of collective bargaining', and 'collective bargaining' means negotiations relating to or connected with: terms and conditions of employment; physical conditions of work; recruitment, dismissal and suspension; allocation of work; matters of discipline; union membership; facilities for officials of trade unions; and bargaining machinery and other procedures (*TULRCA 1992, s 178(1)(2)*). A different definition of collective bargaining applies under the new recognition machinery (see below).

If management, in fact, consult a trade union about some or all of these matters they may be taken to have recognised that trade union (*Joshua Wilson & Bros Ltd v Union of Shop, Distributive and Allied Workers* [1978] IRLR 120). In *National Union of Gold, Silver and Allied Trades v Albury Bros Ltd* [1979] ICR 84, the Court of Appeal held that an act of recognition is such an important matter that it should not be held to be established unless the evidence is clear, either by actual agreement for recognition or clear and distinct conduct showing an implied agreement to recognise the trade union for the purposes of collective bargaining. In that case, the Court of Appeal held that an attempt by the union to negotiate with the management increased wages for one man did not establish recognition by the employer. Recognition will not be inferred from the fact that a union has been given a right of representation in pay bargaining where that right is given by a third party over whom the employer has no control (*Cleveland County Council v Springett* [1985] IRLR 131).

50.21 Listing

A list of trade unions is maintained by the Certification Officer (*TULRCA 1992, s 2*). Any trade union whose name is entered on the list may apply to the Certification Officer for a certificate that it is independent (*TULRCA 1992, s 6(1)*). A union which is not on the list maintained by the Certification Officer will automatically be refused a certificate of independence (*TULRCA 1992, s 6(3)*).

50.22 Independence

If the union is listed, the Certification Officer will proceed to determine whether the applicant is an independent trade union. An independent trade union is defined in *TULRCA 1992, s 5* as:

' ... a trade union which –

(*a*)   is not under the domination or control of an employer or a group of employers or of one or more employers' associations; and

(*b*)   is not liable to interference by an employer or any such group or association (arising out of the provision of financial or material support or by any other means whatsoever) tending towards such control.'

In *Squibb (UK) Staff Association v Certification Officer* [1979] ICR 235, the Certification Officer refused to grant a certificate of independence to a staff association which relied to a considerable extent upon facilities provided by the employers. He considered that the association could not be said to be free from liability to interference by the employers. The Court of Appeal upheld the refusal of the grant of the certificate. For a more recent example, see *Government Communications Staff Federation v Certification Officer* [1993] ICR 163.

50.23 Factors implying independence

In *Blue Circle Staff Association v Certification Officer* [1977] 1 WLR 239, some of the principles upon which the Certification Officer acts are set out (at 245–246):

'1   *Finance*: If there is any evidence that a union is getting a direct subsidy from an employer, it is immediately ruled out.

2   *Other assistance*: The Certification Officer's inspectors see what material support, such as free premises, time off work for officials, or office facilities a union is getting from an employer, and attempt to cost them out.

3   *Employer interference*: If a union is very small and weak and gets a good deal of help, then on the face of it its independence will be considered to be in danger and liable to employer interference.

4   *History*: The recent history of a union ... is considered. It was not unusual for a staff association to start as a "creature of management and grow into something independent".

5   *Rules*: The applicant union's rule book is scrutinised to see if the employer can interfere with or control it, and if there are any restrictions on membership. If a union is run by people near the top of a company it could be detrimental to rank and file members.

6   *Single company unions*: While they are not debarred from getting certificates, because such a rule could exclude unions like those of

miners and railwaymen, they are considered to be more liable to employer interference. Broadly based multi-company unions are considered more difficult to influence.

7   *Organisation*: The Certification Officer's inspectors then examine the applicant union in detail, its size and recruiting ability, whether it is run by competent and experienced officers, the state of its finance, and its branch and committee structure. Again, if the union was run by senior men in a company, employer interference was a greater risk.

8   *Attitude*: Once the other factors have been assessed, inspectors looked for a "robust attitude in negotiation" as a sign of genuine independence, backed up by a good negotiating record ... '

Before making a determination on the question of independence, the Certification Officer makes such inquiries as he sees fit and takes into account any relevant information submitted to him (*TULRCA 1992, s 6(4)*). In general, he should not be cross-examined upon his reasons for his decision (*Squibb* at 50.22 above).

Withdrawal of certificate of independence and appeals against Certification Officer's decision

50.24 The Certification Officer may at any time withdraw a certificate, after giving notice to the trade union affected and determining the relevant questions, if he is of the opinion that the trade union in question is no longer independent (*TULRCA 1992, s 7(1)*).

A trade union aggrieved by the refusal of the Certification Officer to issue it with a certificate, or by a decision of his to withdraw its certificate, may appeal to the Employment Appeal Tribunal. If the appeal is successful the Employment Appeal Tribunal will give directions to the Certification Officer to act according to its findings (*TULRCA 1992, s 9*).

50.25 RECOGNITION FOR COLLECTIVE BARGAINING PURPOSES

The current procedure for the recognition of trade unions by employers for the purposes of collective bargaining was introduced by *ERA 1999, Sch 1*. This recognition machinery came into effect on 6 June 2000 and is contained in *TULRCA 1992, Sch A1*. The new law represented a fundamental change in industrial relations in the United Kingdom, since it conferred upon trade unions a right to be recognised by employers for collective bargaining purposes, provided various conditions are satisfied. The new regime does, however, seek to promote voluntary recognition wherever possible. Also significant is the enhanced role for the Central Arbitration Committee ('CAC') (see 50.4) in determining a range of issues relating to recognition. In carrying out these functions, the CAC is under a duty to have regard to the object of encouraging and promoting fair and efficient practices in the workplace. The provisions relating to the membership of the CAC contained in *TULRCA 1992, s 260* were amended by *ERA 1999, s 24* so as to require the Secretary of State to appoint only persons experienced in industrial relations, having first consulted with ACAS and such other persons as he may choose to consult (*TULRCA 1992, Sch A1 para 171*) (see 50.11 above). The new recognition procedures are extremely complex. Below is set out a summary of the principal provisions. It should be noted that the *Employment Relations Act 2004* has amended the recognition provisions in a number of respects.

50.26 **The scope of the new procedure**

The recognition procedures apply only to employers which, taken with any associated employers, employ either at least 21 workers on the day on which a request for recognition is received, or have employed an average of at least 21 workers in the 13 preceding weeks (*TULRCA 1992, Sch A1 para 7(1)*). For this purpose, the definition of 'worker' contained in *TULRCA 1992, s 296(1)* applies. In *R (on the application of the BBC) v Central Arbitration Committee* [2003] EWHC 1375 (Admin), [2003] ICR 1542 it was held that an application for recognition should not have been entertained by the CAC in respect of freelance cameramen and women working for the BBC, since they were excluded from the definition of 'workers' as 'professionals'. The CAC had erred in finding that the cameramen and women were not 'professionals' merely because they had no regulatory body.

Only unions which have been certified as independent under *TULRCA 1992, s 6* may make a request for recognition.

50.27 **Collective bargaining**

The definition of collective bargaining contained in *TULRCA 1992, s 178* does not apply to the new recognition provisions. Instead, collective bargaining is defined as negotiations relating to pay, hours and holidays, subject to the parties agreeing that additional matters may also be the subject of collective bargaining (*Sch A1, paras 1–4*). For the purposes of this provision, the CAC has held that pension benefits fall within the definition of pay (see *UNIFI v Union Bank of Nigeria* [2001] IRLR 713).

50.28 **The request for recognition**

A union or unions seeking recognition must apply first to the employer. The request must be made in writing, identify the relevant unions and bargaining unit and state that it is made under *TULRCA 1992, Sch A1 para 8*. If the parties agree within 10 working days on the appropriate bargaining unit and further agree that the union is (or unions are) to be recognised to conduct collective bargaining on behalf of that unit, then the union is (or unions are) deemed to be recognised, and no further steps need be taken. If the employer does not accept the request, but agrees to negotiate, then the union will be deemed to be recognised if the parties are able to agree within a further 20-day period. The parties may request ACAS to assist in conducting such negotiations (*Sch A1, para 10*).

50.29 **Reference to the CAC**

If the employer either rejects or fails to respond to the request within 10 days, or if negotiations break down during the subsequent 20-day period, the union may apply to the CAC to decide on the appropriate bargaining unit and whether the union has the support of a majority of workers within that unit. The union may ask the CAC to determine the question of majority support if the parties have agreed on the appropriate bargaining unit, but have not agreed on whether the union should be entitled to conduct collective bargaining on its behalf. However, the union may not apply to the CAC if it has rejected or failed to respond to a proposal by the employer that ACAS be requested to assist in negotiations (*Sch A1, paras 11, 12*).

TULRCA 1992, Sch A1 sets out a detailed procedure for the various sequential steps that must be taken by the CAC once it has received an application for union recognition. This procedure is subject to a relatively strict timetable, with the CAC generally being given 10 days to reach a determination at each stage of the procedure. The time limits within the recognition procedure are subject to extension by the CAC in most cases, although in some circumstances the CAC is under a duty to give reasons for such an extension to the parties.

The CAC must decide whether any application for recognition is 'valid' within the meaning of *TULRCA 1992, Sch A1 paras 5–9* and 'admissible' within the meaning of *TULRCA 1992, Sch A1 paras 33–42*, having considered any evidence provided by the employer or the union (*Sch A1, para 15*). The criteria of 'validity' are essentially the requirements as to union independence and number of workers employed referred to above. An application may be 'inadmissible' if there is already in force a collective agreement under which a union is recognised for collective bargaining purposes (*Sch A1, para 35*). This exclusion can have far-reaching consequences. In *R (on the application of National Union of Journalists) v Central Arbitration Committee* [2005] EWCA Civ 1309, [2006] ICR 1 the Court of Appeal upheld the decision of the High Court that the NUJ's application to the CAC was inadmissible, because the employer already had a recognition agreement with another union. This was the case notwithstanding that that agreement had not been used to determine the terms and conditions of workers within the bargaining unit and the other union had at most one member working in the relevant division of the employer's business. Similarly, in *Transport and General Workers' Union v Asda* [2004] IRLR 836 the CAC held the union's application inadmissible because the employer had a 'partnership agreement' in place with another union. This was despite the fact that the 'partnership agreement' provided for only limited representational rights, and specifically excluded collective bargaining on terms and conditions of employment, including pay

An application will be inadmissible unless members of the relevant union (or unions) constitute at least 10% of workers within the bargaining unit and a majority of the workers within that unit are likely to favour recognition (*Sch A1, para 36*). Further, where an application is made by more than one union, the application will be inadmissible unless they show that they will co-operate with each other so as to secure and maintain a stable and effective collective bargaining arrangement, and further that they will act together for collective bargaining purposes if the employer wishes (*Sch A1, para 37*). An application will also be inadmissible if brought within three years of a previous application by the same union or unions in respect of the same or substantially the same bargaining unit (*Sch A1, paras 39–40*). If the application does not fulfil the criteria of 'validity' and 'admissibility', it must not be accepted by the CAC.

If the CAC accepts an application, it must first try to assist the parties in seeking to agree on the appropriate bargaining unit within a period of 20 working days (which may be extended). In the absence of agreement, the CAC must decide on the appropriate bargaining unit (*Sch A1, paras 18, 19*).

In *Prison Officers' Association and Securicor Custodial Services Ltd* (Central Arbitration Committee, 21 August 2000) (IDS Brief 670), the CAC accepted that the employer's recognition of a non-independent staff association precluded the application by an independent trade union for recognition pursuant to *Sch A1, para 35*. Where such an association is recognised, therefore, the independent union may well have to seek to initiate derecognition proceedings.

50.30 **The appropriate bargaining unit**

In deciding on the appropriate bargaining unit, the CAC must take into account the need for the unit to be compatible with effective management and, in so far as they do not conflict with that primary need, the following additional factors:

(*a*)   the views of the parties;

(*b*)   existing national and local bargaining arrangements;

(*c*)   the desirability of avoiding small fragmented bargaining units within an undertaking;

(*d*)   the characteristics of the workforce falling within and outside of the unit; and

(*e*)   the location of workers (*Sch A1, para 19*).

In *R (on the application of Kwik-Fit (GB) Ltd) v Central Arbitration Committee* [2002] EWCA Civ 512, [2002] ICR 1212, the Court of Appeal considered the approach to be adopted by the CAC when considering competing contentions by the union and employer as to the appropriate bargaining unit. Buxton LJ rejected the employer's contention that the CAC has a duty to treat on equal terms the unit proposed by the union and any alternative proposed by the employer. The recognition machinery is put in motion by a request from the union. Provided the CAC finds that the unit put forward by the union is 'appropriate', it need not go further and consider whether there is a more appropriate unit that might be identified. It must take into account the employer's views, but should not weigh up whether an alternative unit put forward by the employer might be better than that proposed by the union, provided that that proposed by the union meets the requirement of being 'appropriate'. The decision highlights the way in which the recognition process is essentially union-driven.

In *Re Benteler Automotive UK and ISTC* (Central Arbitration Committee, 17 October 2000) (IDS Brief 677), the CAC broadly accepted the union's argument that the relevant bargaining unit was shop-floor employees only. Although the employer argued that supervisory, technical and administrative staff should be included, so as to reflect their 'whole company' ethos, the CAC noted that this did not reflect the existing management organisation and practice at the company. Although the CAC did not wish to impede the employers in achieving a 'whole company' approach, existing economic realities determined the appropriate bargaining unit.

In *Graphical Paper and Media Union v Derry Print Ltd* [2002] IRLR 380, the CAC considered the proper approach to determining the appropriate bargaining unit where a single business was run through two separate companies, with members of the workforce being allocated to one business or the other. The CAC concluded that, under the recognition machinery in *TULRCA 1992, Sch A1*, a bargaining unit could not include the employees of more than one employer. The language and scheme of the recognition provisions envisaged the determination of a bargaining unit by reference to a single employer.

However, the CAC went on to hold that, on the facts of the case, it was permissible to treat the two companies in question as a single employer. A more liberal approach to lifting the corporate veil in this way was appropriate here than in some other legal contexts. The CAC accordingly determined that the appropriate bargaining unit comprised the production workers of both companies. The CAC thereby recognised the importance of determining the bargaining unit by reference to the economic realities on the shop floor.

If the parties have agreed, or the CAC has decided on, a bargaining unit which differs from that originally proposed, the CAC must consider whether the application is valid by reference to further criteria of 'validity' set out in *paras 43–50* (*Sch A1, para 20*). These further criteria of validity closely mirror those of 'admissibility' set out above (see *paras 33–42*). Where there is no such disparity, and where the CAC is satisfied that the criteria of validity are satisfied, the CAC must proceed with the application for union recognition.

50.31 **Union recognition**

The central provisions of the new recognition procedure are those which provide for the compulsory recognition of unions for collective bargaining purposes. Such recognition may or may not be preceded by a secret ballot of the workers within the relevant bargaining unit. Where the CAC is satisfied that a majority of the workers within the bargaining unit are members of the union, it must issue a declaration that the union is recognised as entitled to conduct collective bargaining on behalf of the workers within the bargaining unit, unless:

(a)   it is satisfied that a ballot should be held in the interests of good industrial relations; or

(b)   there is credible evidence from a significant number of union members within the bargaining unit that they do not want the union to conduct collective bargaining on their behalf; or

(c)   evidence about the circumstances in which members joined the union or about the length of time they have been members is produced, which leads the CAC to conclude that there are doubts about whether a significant number of members wish the union to conduct collective bargaining on their behalf.

If any of those circumstances apply, the CAC must give notice that it intends to arrange for the holding of a secret ballot in which the workers will be asked whether they want the union to be recognised. Equally, the CAC must give notice of its intention to arrange for the holding of a secret ballot if it is not satisfied that a majority of workers within the bargaining unit are members of the union. The CAC must then arrange for the holding of a ballot unless it receives notification within 10 working days (or such longer period as the CAC specifies) from the union (or from the union and employer jointly) that they do not want a ballot to take place (*Sch A1, paras 20–24*).

In *Fullarton Computer Industries Ltd v Central Arbitration Committee* [2001] IRLR 752, the Court of Session upheld the CAC's decision that a trade union should be recognised without a ballot on the grounds that a ballot would not be in the interests of good industrial relations. The Court of Session approached the case on the basis that the CAC was under no obligation to give reasons for its decision. (The CAC is obliged by the statute to give reasons for some of its decisions, particularly those relating to the extension of time limits within the recognition procedure, but not, ironically, for those substantive decisions, such as this one, which are likely to be determinative of the outcome of the recognition application.) If reasons were given, the decision could be set aside only if they disclosed some manifest error or flaw on the face of the record. This case highlights the difficulty inherent in challenging the CAC's decision as to whether a ballot is likely to be in the interests of good industrial relations.

50.32 **The recognition ballot**

The recognition ballot, which must be conducted by a qualified independent person appointed by the CAC, may be conducted in the workplace, by post or, exceptionally, by some combination of the two. A 'qualified independent person' is defined for these purposes as someone who fulfils the conditions of either being a practicing solicitor or being eligible for appointment as a company auditor. In addition, a number of organisations providing electoral services are specified by name to be such persons (*Recognition and Derecognition Ballots (Qualified Persons) Order 2000 (SI 2000/1306)*).The costs of the ballot are divided equally between the employer on the one hand and the union (or unions) on the other. In deciding on the appropriate method, the CAC must take into account the risk of unfairness or malpractice if the ballot is conducted in the workplace, costs and practicality, and such other matters as it considers appropriate (*Sch A1, paras 25, 28*).

The employer is placed under five duties in relation to a recognition ballot:

(*a*)   it must co-operate generally with both the union and the person appointed to conduct the ballot;

(*b*)   it must give the union such reasonable access to the workers within the bargaining unit as will enable it to inform the workers of its object and seek their support and opinions;

(*c*)   it must give the CAC the names and home addresses of the workers within the bargaining unit, including any workers who join the unit after the initial list has been provided, and must further inform the CAC if any such workers have ceased to be within the unit. The CAC passes this information on to the person appointed to conduct the ballot;

(*d*)   it must refrain from unreasonably seeking to induce workers to refrain from attending meetings with a union regarding recognition;

(*e*)   it must refrain from taking or threatening action against a worker because he has attended or intends to attend a meeting with a union regarding recognition

A new code of practice on access to workers during recognition and derecognition ballots came into effect on 1 October 2005 pursuant to *TULRCA 1992, ss 203–204* and the *Employment Code of Practice (Access to Workers during Recognition and Derecognition Ballots) Order 2005 (SI 2005/2421)*.

It the employer fails to comply with any of these duties, the CAC may order the employer to take remedial steps. If the employer fails to comply with such an order, the CAC may cancel the ballot (or ignore it if it has taken place) and make a declaration of recognition (*Sch A1, paras 26, 27*).

The person appointed to conduct the ballot must send all relevant workers any information supplied by the union, provided that the union bears the cost of sending such information.

The most important (and controversial) provision in the union recognition procedure is that which determines the effect of the outcome of the recognition ballot. If union recognition for collective bargaining purposes is supported by:

(*a*)   a majority of the workers voting, and

(*b*)   at least 40% of the workers within the bargaining unit,

then the CAC must issue a declaration that the union is recognised for collective bargaining purposes. If those conditions are not satisfied, then the CAC must declare that the union is not so recognised. The Secretary of State may by order amend this provision so as to specify a different degree of requisite support (*Sch A1, para 29*). It follows that, even if a majority of those voting support recognition, the union will not be recognised if a low turnout entails that those in favour constitute less than 40% of the workforce within the bargaining unit.

In *R (on the application of Ultraframe (UK) Ltd) v Central Arbitration Committee* [2005] EWCA Civ 560 [2005] ICR 1194 the Court of Appeal upheld a decision of the CAC directing a re-run of a recognition ballot. Although a majority of those voting had supported recognition, the 40% requirement had not been achieved by four votes. The unions complained that a number of employees had not received ballot papers, and the CAC concluded that five employees, who would have voted in favour of recognition, had not been given a reasonable opportunity to vote. The Court of Appeal concluded that the CAC had jurisdiction to investigate and, if appropriate, to annul the ballot, and so had acted within its powers in ordering a re-run.

All parties informed by the CAC of a recognition ballot must refrain from using unfair practices in relation to such a ballot (*Sch A1, para 27A*). 'Unfair practices' are defined so as to include; making inducements to vote in a particular way; coercion; undue influence; and dismissal, disciplinary action or detriment, or threats of such actions, aimed at influencing the outcome of the ballot. A party may complain to the CAC if it believes that unfair practices have been used (*Sch A1, para 27C*). If the CAC finds a complaint well-founded, it must make a declaration to that effect, and may order the party concerned to take specified action, or give notice that it intends to arrange a secret ballot in which the workers are asked whether they want the union to conduct collective bargaining on their behalf (*SchA1, para 27C*). The CAC's further powers upon such a finding also include a power in certain circumstances to cancel or annul a ballot.

50.33 The method of collective bargaining

Once a declaration of recognition has been made, the parties may seek to negotiate an agreement as to the method by which they will conduct collective bargaining during a 30-day period or such longer period as they agree. If no agreement is reached, the parties may apply to the CAC for assistance. The CAC must try to help the parties to reach an agreement. If after a further 20 days (or such further period as the CAC agrees with the parties) still no agreement has been reached, the CAC must specify the method by which the parties will conduct collective bargaining. A detailed 'specified method' is set out in the *Trade Union Recognition (Method of Collective Bargaining) Order 2000 (SI 2000/1300)*. This must be taken into account by the CAC when specifying a method of collective bargaining for the parties. In those circumstances, unless the parties agree otherwise, the specified method has effect as if made in a legally enforceable contract between parties. However, specific performance will be the only remedy available for any breach of the specified method. If the parties have agreed the method by which they will conduct collective bargaining, but one or more of the parties fails to carry it out, the parties may apply to the CAC for assistance (*Sch A1, paras 30–32*).

50.34 Voluntary recognition

TULRCA 1992, Sch A1 Part II contains additional provisions relating specifically to voluntary recognition. These provisions apply where the parties reach agreement that the union should be recognised as entitled to conduct collective bargaining at some point before the compulsory recognition procedure summarised above has been exhausted. Agreement may have been reached either before or after an application to the CAC has been made (*Sch A1, para 52*). Any party to such an agreement may apply to the CAC for a decision whether or not the agreement is indeed an 'agreement for recognition' as defined (*Sch A1, para 55*).

If the CAC decides that the agreement is an 'agreement for recognition', the employer may not terminate the agreement for a period of three years. The union, however, may terminate such an agreement at any time, with or without the consent of the employer. It follows that an employer, but not a union, who enters into a recognition agreement may be bound by that agreement for up to three years (but see below for the provisions relating to changes in the bargaining unit and derecognition) (*Sch A1, para 56*).

Where the parties have entered into a recognition agreement, but have failed to agree on a method for conducting collective bargaining, they may apply to the CAC for assistance. Equally, if the parties have agreed on a method, but one or more of the parties fails to carry it out, they may apply to the CAC for assistance. The CAC must not accept either type of application unless the requirements as to number of workers employed and union certification are satisfied. Once it has decided that an application is admissible, the CAC must try to help the parties to reach an agreement. If after a period of 20 days (or such further period as the parties agree) still no agreement has been reached, the CAC must specify the method by which the parties will conduct collective bargaining, taking into account the 'specified method' set out in the *Trade Union Recognition* (*Method of Collective Bargaining*) *Order 2000* (*SI 2000/1300*). As in the case of compulsory recognition, unless the parties agree otherwise, the specified method has effect as if made in a legally enforceable contract between parties. Again, however, specific performance is the only remedy available for any breach of the specified method (*Sch A1, paras 58–63*).

50.35   Changes in the bargaining unit

If either party believes that the original bargaining unit is no longer appropriate, it may apply to the CAC for a decision as to the appropriate bargaining unit. Such an application is admissible only if the CAC decides that the original unit is likely to be no longer appropriate, either because the organisation or structure of the employer's business or the employer's business activities have changed, or because there has been a substantial change in the number of workers employed in the original unit (*Sch A1, paras 64–68*). Once the CAC has accepted the application, the parties may agree on a new bargaining unit. If no such agreement is reached, the CAC must decide whether the original unit is appropriate and, if not, decide on a new unit or units. Again, in deciding whether the original unit is appropriate, the CAC must take into account only changes in the organisation or structure of the employer's business or the employer's business activities, or any substantial change in the number of workers employed in the original unit. In deciding what new unit might be appropriate, the CAC must adopt similar criteria to those outlined above in respect of an initial application for recognition (*Sch A1, paras 69–73*).

If an employer believes that the original bargaining unit has ceased to exist and wishes the collective bargaining arrangements to cease to have effect, it must give notice to the union, copied to the CAC. Provided proper notice is given, the collective bargaining arrangements will cease to have effect unless the union applies to the CAC within 10 days for a decision on whether the original unit has ceased to exist and whether it is no longer appropriate in any event. If such an application is made, the CAC must determine these questions, having given the employer and the unions an opportunity to put forward their views on whether the unit has ceased to exist or is no longer appropriate. Again, in deciding whether the original unit is no longer appropriate, the CAC must take into account only any changes in the organisation or structure of the employer's business or the employer's business activities, or any substantial change in the number of workers employed in the original unit. If the CAC decides that the original unit has ceased to exist, the collective bargaining arrangements cease to have effect. If it decides that it has not ceased to exist and remains an appropriate bargaining unit, the collective bargaining arrangements remain in place. If, however, the CAC decides that the original unit has not ceased to exist, but that it is no longer an appropriate unit, it must decide what other bargaining unit is (or units are) appropriate by reference to the same criteria as apply when initially deciding on the appropriate bargaining unit (see above) (*Sch A1, paras 74–81*).

The CAC must further decide whether the difference between the original unit and the new unit is such that the level of support for the union within the new unit needs to be assessed. If not, then the CAC simply issues a declaration that the union is recognised as entitled to conduct collective bargaining on behalf of the new unit. If, however, the CAC decides that the level of support needs to be assessed, it must carry out a procedure similar to that in respect of an initial application for recognition before determining whether to make a recognition declaration. This procedure may require the holding of a secret ballot. The threshold for recognition is the same as in the case of an initial application for recognition (ie a majority of those voting and 40% of workers within the unit voting in favour of union recognition) (*Sch A1, paras 85–89*).

50.36 Derecognition

The procedure set out in *TULRCA 1992, Sch A1* also contains detailed provisions relating to the derecognition of unions for collective bargaining purposes. Following the expiry of three years from a declaration of recognition by the CAC, the employer may apply for derecognition if he believes that he (taken with any associated employers) has employed an average of fewer than 21 workers over a period of 13 weeks (*Sch A1, paras 99–103*). Further, an employer may issue a request to the unions to agree to end the collective bargaining arrangements, again following the expiry of three years from a declaration of recognition. If the union rejects or fails to respond to such a request, or the parties enter negotiations but fail to reach agreement, the employer may apply to the CAC with a view to a secret ballot being held to decide whether the bargaining arrangements should be ended (*Sch A1, paras 104–111*). A specific derecognition procedure applies where a declaration of recognition has been made automatically by the CAC on the basis that it is satisfied that a majority of the workers within the bargaining unit are members of the union, and the basis of the employer's request for an end to the bargaining arrangements is that fewer than half of the workers within the unit are, in fact, union members (*Sch A1, paras 122–133*).

Any worker falling within the bargaining unit similarly may apply to the CAC to have collective bargaining arrangements ended once three years have expired after a declaration of recognition. However, such an application is inadmissible unless the CAC decides that at least 10% of the workers within the bargaining unit favour ending the collective bargaining arrangements *and* that a majority of the workers within the unit would be *likely* to favour ending the arrangements. In the absence of agreement through negotiation (or withdrawal of the application), the CAC must arrange for the holding of a secret ballot to decide whether the bargaining arrangements should be ended (*Sch A1, paras 112–116*). A specific derecognition procedure applies where an employer and a union which has not been certified as independent have agreed that the union should be recognised as entitled to conduct collective bargaining purposes and a worker wishes to apply to the CAC to have the bargaining arrangements ended (*Sch A1, paras 134–147*).

The provisions relating to the conduct of a derecognition ballot mirror closely the provisions summarised above in relation to a recognition ballot (*Sch A1, paras 117–121*).

If a union which the CAC has declared to be recognised as entitled to conduct collective bargaining has its certificate of independence withdrawn (or, where, several unions are parties, they all have their certificates withdrawn), the relevant bargaining arrangements shall cease to have effect and the parties shall be taken to have agreed that the union is entitled to conduct collective bargaining on behalf of the bargaining unit concerned. However, if the union (or one of the unions) succeeds in an appeal against the decision to withdraw its certificate, the bargaining arrangements are reinstated (*Sch A1, paras 149–153*).

50.37 Detriment

TULRCA 1992, Sch A1 Part VIII creates a right on the part of workers not to be subjected to a detriment on union recognition-related grounds. In particular, a worker has a right not to be subjected to a detriment by any act, or any deliberate failure to act, by his employer on grounds that the worker:

(*a*)   sought to obtain or prevent recognition of a union;

(*b*)   indicated support for, or opposition to, recognition;

(*c*)   sought to secure or prevent the ending of collective bargaining arrangements;

(*d*)   indicated support for, or opposition to, the ending of collective bargaining arrangements;

(*e*)   influenced or sought to influence the way in which votes would be cast in a recognition ballot;

(*f*)   influenced or sought to influence other workers to vote or abstain in such a ballot;

(*g*)   voted in such a ballot;

(*h*)   proposed to do, failed to do, or proposed to decline to do, any of the matters set out above.

However, an unreasonable act or omission by the worker is not capable of falling within these grounds. If subjected to such a detriment, the worker may complain to an employment tribunal (*Sch A1, para 156*).

There is a parallel right not to be dismissed on union recognition-related grounds. Such dismissal will be automatically unfair (see 54.3 UNFAIR DISMISSAL – II) (*Sch A1, paras 161–165*).

The worker may make a complaint to an employment tribunal within three months of the act or failure to act complained of, or within such further period as the tribunal considers reasonable in a case where it is satisfied that it was not reasonably practicable for the complaint to be presented within three months (*Sch A1, para 157*).

It is for the employer to show the ground on which he acted or failed to act (*Sch A1, para 158*). If the tribunal finds the complaint well-founded, it will make a declaration to that effect and may order compensation to be paid. The compensation will be such amount as it considers just and equitable in all the circumstances, having regard to the infringement complained of and any loss sustained by the complainant. Compensation may be reduced on account of a failure to mitigate, or on account of the applicant's contributory fault (*Sch A1, para 159*). By analogy with the principles applied to action short of dismissal on trade union grounds (see 51.18 TRADE UNIONS – II), it is likely that such compensation may include an award in respect of injury to feelings (compare *Adams v Hackney London Borough Council* [2003] IRLR 402).

50.38 **Training**

The *Employment Relations Act 1999* also imposed training obligations upon employers where a union is recognised for collective bargaining purposes in accordance with *TULRCA 1992, Sch A1* in circumstances where the CAC has specified to the parties the method for conducting collective bargaining (*ERA 1999, s 5*). In those circumstances, an employer is under a duty to invite trade union representatives to meetings, to be held at least once every six months, for the purpose of:

(*a*)   consulting about the employer's policy on training workers within the bargaining unit;

(*b*)   consulting about the employer's plans for such training in the following six months; and

(*c*)   reporting about training provided since the previous meeting.

The employer must provide to the union any information without which the union representatives would be materially impeded in participating, and which it would be in accordance with good industrial relations practice to provide, at least two weeks before such a meeting. The employer must also take into account any written representations submitted by the union within four weeks of a meeting (*TULRCA 1992, s 70B*).

A trade union may complain to an employment tribunal if an employer fails to comply with the obligation to consult on training. Such a complaint must be presented within three months of the alleged failure complained of, or within such further period as the tribunal considers reasonable in a case where it is satisfied that it was not reasonably practicable for the complaint to be presented within three months. Where a complaint is upheld, the tribunal shall make a declaration to that effect and may award compensation to each person who was, at the time when the failure occurred, a member of the bargaining unit. The maximum amount of compensation is two weeks' pay per worker (subject to the limit on a week's pay set out in *ERA 1996, s 227(1)*, currently £290).

50.39 **AMALGAMATIONS AND TRANSFERS OF ENGAGEMENTS**

One trade union may amalgamate with or transfer its engagements to another trade union. However, it may not do so unless a resolution which approves the amalgamation or transfer, in a form approved by the Certification Officer, has been passed by a vote of members. The right to be balloted may not extend to members who are not full members of the union (see *National Union of Mineworkers (Yorkshire Area) v Millward* [1995] ICR 482). *TULRCA 1992, ss 97–105* and the *Trade Unions and Employers' Associations (Amalgamations, etc) Regulations 1975 (SI 1975/536)*, as amended, regulate amalgamations and specify the information which must be given to union members and the manner in which the ballot must be taken. *TULRCA 1992, s 103* provides a remedy, by way of complaint to the Certification Officer, to a union member dissatisfied with the way in which the vote on the resolution was taken.

51 Trade Unions – II: Individual Rights and Union Membership

(See DTI Guidance available online at www.dti.gov.uk/employment/index.html 'Union membership: rights of members and non-members'(URN No 06/558) and 'Unjustifiable discipline by a trade union' (URN No 06/559).)

51.1 RIGHTS OF UNION MEMBERS IN RELATION TO EMPLOYER

An employee who is a member of a trade union has the following rights in relation to his employer.

(a) He may not be refused employment because of his membership of a trade union (see 51.3 below).

(b) Dismissal for membership of, or for taking part in the activities of, an independent trade union is automatically unfair, as is dismissal on union recognition-related grounds (see 54.3 UNFAIR DISMISSAL – II).

(c) Subjection to detriment by his employer for membership of, or for taking part in the activities of, or using the services of, an independent trade union, or on union recognition-related grounds, gives the employee the right to complain to an employment tribunal which may award him compensation (see 51.18 below).

(d) The right to time off from work to take part in trade union activities (see 49.3 TIME OFF WORK).

(e) The right not to suffer the deduction of unauthorised or excessive union subscriptions from his wages (see 51.21 below).

(f) Where a trade union is recognised for collective bargaining purposes within *TULRCA 1992, Sch A1, TULRCA 1992, s 70B* imposes upon the employer a duty to consult with trade union representatives on training for workers within the bargaining unit (see TRADE UNIONS – I (50));

(g) A worker who is required or invited to attend a disciplinary or grievance hearing by his employer has the right to be accompanied by a trade union official (see 51.22 below).

In addition, a trade union *official* has the right to take time off with pay for his trade union duties (see 49.2 TIME OFF WORK).

51.2 RIGHTS OF UNION MEMBERS OR INTENDING MEMBERS IN RELATION TO UNION

A trade union member or would-be member has the following rights in relation to his union.

(a) The right not to be excluded or expelled save on certain specified grounds and in accordance with the rules of the union (see 51.11 to 51.14 below).

(b) The right under *TULRCA 1992, s 69* to terminate his membership with the union on giving reasonable notice and complying with any reasonable conditions.

(c) The right not to have disciplinary action taken against him by the union save in accordance with the rules of the union and to be protected from disciplinary action taken on certain grounds (see 51.15 and 51.16 below).

(d) The right under *TULRCA 1992, s 62* to apply to the High Court (or, in Scotland, the Court of Session) if members of his union, including himself, have been called on to take industrial action which has not received prior ballot approval (see 45.18 STRIKES AND INDUSTRIAL ACTION).

(e) The right under *TULRCA 1992, s 30* to inspect the union's accounting records, in the company of an accountant if he so desires.

(f) The right under *TULRCA 1992, s 16* to apply for relief to the High Court (or, in Scotland, the Court of Session) where the trustees of the union's property permit it to be applied unlawfully or comply with unlawful directions from the union.

He or she is also protected against racial discrimination and sex discrimination (see 13.26 DISCRIMINATION AND EQUAL OPPORTUNITIES – II) and DISABILITY DISCRIMINATION (10). Nationals of other EU member states are entitled to equal rights as members of trade unions (*Regulation 1612/68/EEC, art 8*; and see EUROPEAN COMMUNITY LAW (25)).

An attempt to bring a common law claim against a union which had not achieved a result favouring a particular member was struck out as having no prospect of success in *Iwanuszezak v General Municipal Boilermakers and Allied Trades Union* [1988] IRLR 219. The union had to put the collective interests of its whole membership first.

51.3   CLOSED SHOP

The *Industrial Relations Act 1971* gave the right to employees to belong to the trade union of their choice or not to belong to a trade union at all. That *Act* was repealed by the *Trade Union and Labour Relations Act 1974* ('*TULRA 1974*'), which enabled an employer lawfully to enforce a closed shop by a 'union membership agreement' made with a trade union or trade unions. The *Employment Acts 1980* and *1982* subsequently imposed certain restrictions and conditions on the closed shop. The *Employment Act 1988* effectively outlawed dismissals to enforce a closed shop. Dismissals to enforce a union membership agreement are automatically unfair. The *Employment Act 1990* made it unlawful to refuse a person employment on grounds of membership or non-membership of a trade union. The relevant provisions are now all to be found in the *Trade Union and Labour Relations (Consolidation) Act 1992* ('*TULRCA 1992*').

(See also 30.4 HUMAN RIGHTS.)

51.4   The pre-entry closed shop

Where an employer has a policy of offering employment only to members of a particular trade union, this is known as a pre-entry closed shop. Until 1991 such a policy remained lawful.

TULRCA 1992, s 137(1) now provides that it is unlawful to refuse a person employment because he is, or is not, a member of a trade union. The refusal is also unlawful if it is because the person is unwilling to accept a requirement to become or remain (or to cease to be or not to become) a member, or to make payments or suffer deductions in the event of his not being a member. References in this context to being or not being a member of a trade union are to being or not being a member of any trade union, of a particular trade union or of one of a number of particular trade unions, or of a particular branch or section of a trade union (*TULRCA 1992, s 143(3)*). In *Harrison v Kent County Council* [1995] ICR 434, it was held that an employer's refusal to employ an applicant because of his previous union *activities* could amount to an unlawful refusal of employment on grounds of union membership.

These provisions do not apply where the employee would ordinarily work outside Great Britain (*TULRCA 1992, s 285(1)*; 53.15(B) UNFAIR DISMISSAL – I). Nor do they apply to cases where a person may not be considered for appointment to an office in a trade union unless he is a member of the union, even though as a holder of the office he would be employed by the union (*TULRCA 1992, s 137(7)*). For the meaning of 'office', see *TULRCA 1992, s 137(7)(a), (b)*.

A deliberate omission to offer employment is considered to be a refusal for these purposes, as are a refusal or deliberate omission to deal with the application or the causing of its withdrawal, a spurious offer of employment (that is, one the terms of which are such as no reasonable employer who wished to fill the post would offer and which is not accepted) and an offer of employment which is withdrawn or which the offeror causes the prospective employee not to accept, or an offer which is not accepted because it includes a requirement of union membership or non-membership (*TULRCA 1992, s 137(5), (6)*).

There are two situations where the refusal of employment is deemed to have been on union membership grounds:

(*a*)   where an advertisement is published which indicates or might reasonably be understood as indicating that the employment is only open to union members or non-members, or that a requirement of the sort referred to in *s 137(1)(b)* will be imposed, and a person who does not satisfy that condition or is unwilling to accept that requirement is refused employment to which the advertisement relates (*TULRCA 1992, s 137(3)*); or

(*b*)   where there is an arrangement or practice under which employment is offered only to persons put forward or approved by a union which puts forward or approves only its members, and a person who is not a member of the union is refused employment in pursuance of the arrangement or practice (*TULRCA 1992, s 137(4)*).

A person who is refused employment on unlawful grounds has a right of complaint to an employment tribunal, and no other remedy (*TULRCA 1992, s 143(4)*). The complaint must be presented within three months of the refusal or other conduct complained of, unless the tribunal considers that it was not reasonably practicable to do so (*TULRCA 1992, s 139(1)*; and see 20.7 EMPLOY-MENT TRIBUNALS – I). Where the respondent has acted under pressure from a third party such as a trade union, there is provision for that third party to be joined into the proceedings and to be ordered to pay all or part of any compensation awarded (*TULRCA 1992, s 142*).

If the tribunal finds the complaint well-founded, it will make a declaration to that effect, and may (if it considers it just and equitable to do so) order the respondent to pay compensation assessed on the same basis as damages for breach of statutory duty, which may include compensation for injury to feelings (*TULRCA 1992, s 140(1), (2)*). The tribunal will presumably ask itself whether the applicant would have obtained the job had it not been for his membership or non-membership of a union, or the percentage chance of his doing so, and will compensate him for lost earnings if so. The maximum award of compensation is the same as for unfair dismissal, currently £60,600 (*ERA 1999, s 34*; *Employment Rights (Increase of Limits) Order 2006 (SI 2006/3045*.

The tribunal may also, or alternatively, make a recommendation that the respondent take within a specified period action appearing to the tribunal to be practicable for the purpose of obviating or reducing the adverse effect on the applicant of the conduct complained of, and may make or increase an award of compensation (up to the statutory maximum) if the respondent fails without reasonable justification to comply (*TULRCA 1992, s 140(1)(b), (3)*).

An appeal on a question of law lies from the decision of the tribunal to the Employment Appeal Tribunal (*TULRCA 1992, s 291(2)*).

Any agreement purporting to exclude the right to complain under these provisions is void, unless reached as part of a settlement after a conciliation officer has taken action, or where the statutory conditions governing compromise contracts have been satisfied, including that the complainant should have had advice from a relevant independent advisor (*TULRCA 1992, s 288*; and see 2.4 ADVISORY, CONCILIATION AND ARBITRATION SERVICE and 20.27 EMPLOYMENT TRIBUNALS – I).

There are also provisions dealing similarly with cases where an employment agency acts on behalf of an employer, or where such an agency refuses its services on unlawful grounds (*TULRCA 1992, s 138*; see also *TULRCA 1992, ss 141* and *143(2)*).

51.5   Dismissal and the closed shop

The dismissal of an employee or his selection for redundancy will automatically be regarded as unfair if the principal reason for the dismissal or selection was that he was not a member of any trade union, or of a particular trade union, or of one of a number of particular trade unions, or had refused or proposed to refuse to become or remain a member (*TULRCA 1992, ss 152(1)(c), 153*) (see 54.3 UNFAIR DISMISSAL – II). References to trade union membership include membership of any trade union, or of a particular trade union or one of a number of particular trade unions, or of a particular branch or section of a trade union (*TULRCA 1992, s 152(4)*).

'Proposing to refuse to remain a member' covers the situation where the proposed refusal is contingent upon a particular event (*Crosville Motor Services Ltd v Ashfield* [1986] IRLR 475).

For the relevance of the employer's belief in the employee's membership or non-membership, see *Leyland Vehicles Ltd v Jones* [1981] ICR 428.

Compensation for the dismissal is assessed as described in 51.7 below.

Note that there is no minimum qualifying period of employment before an employee is entitled to make such a complaint of unfair dismissal, nor is there any upper age limit (*TULRCA 1992, s 154*).

51.6   FAILURE TO MAKE PAYMENTS

Instead of being a member of a trade union, an employee may be subject to a requirement to make a payment, e g to a charity. If such an employee who is not or ceases to be a union member refuses, in breach of a requirement, to make such a payment and is dismissed for that reason, he will be treated as dismissed for failure to become or remain a member of a trade union. The same is true if he is dismissed for objecting to a provision which entitles his employer to deduct such a payment from his wages (*TULRCA 1992, s 152(3)*). A dismissal for failure to make such a payment or for objecting to such a provision will be regarded as automatically unfair, and will be compensated as described in 51.7 below.

An employer may only deduct a trade union subscription from an employee's pay if certain statutory requirements are complied with (see 51.21 below).

51.7   COMPENSATION FOR CLOSED SHOP DISMISSALS

For the detailed rules on compensation, see 55.6–55.19 UNFAIR DISMISSAL – III. Note in particular, however, that *in addition* to the general rules governing unfair dismissal awards, the following apply to 'automatically' unfair dismissals to enforce a closed shop.

(*a*)   There is a minimum basic award of £4,200, although the compensatory award is calculated in the normal way.

(*b*)   There is provision that conduct of the employee in refusing to join a union or to make payments in lieu of joining, or in objecting to such payments, should be disregarded in assessing contributory fault for possible reduction of any part of the award (*TULRCA 1992, s 155*). However, it seems that confrontational conduct by the employee could form the basis for a finding of contributory fault provided that the immediate circumstances constituting the principal reason for dismissal are excluded from consideration (*TGWU v Howard* [1992] ICR 106).

(*c*)   The employee may request that a third party (eg a union) be joined in the unfair dismissal proceedings if pressure by it has induced the dismissal and the award may be made wholly or partly against that third party.

(*TULRCA 1992, ss 155–156, 160.*)

51.8   DETRIMENT

Every worker has the right not to be subjected to detriment by his employer for the purpose of compelling him to be or become a member of a trade union or a particular trade union, or for the purpose of enforcing a requirement that in the event of his failing to become or ceasing to be a member he must make one or more payments (*TULRCA 1992, s 146(1)(c), (3)*). Infringement of this right entitles the employee to complain to an industrial tribunal and seek a declaration and compensation (*TULRCA 1992, s 146(5)*; and see 51.18, 51.19 below).

51.9   INDUSTRIAL ACTION, TRADE UNION DISCIPLINE AND THE CLOSED SHOP

The statutory immunity for industrial action is inapplicable where the purpose of the action is to impose union membership requirements or to enforce a closed shop. For a more detailed account of the relevant provisions, see 45.7 STRIKES AND INDUSTRIAL ACTION.

An individual member of a trade union may not be disciplined either for proposing to resign from the union, or for working with non-union members or for an employer who employs non-union labour (*TULRCA 1992, s 65(2)* as amended; for further details, see 51.16 below).

51.10   TRADE UNION 'BLACKLISTS'

The *ERA 1999* contains provisions to prohibit the compilation of trade union 'blacklists'. The Secretary of State is empowered to make regulations prohibiting the making of lists which relate to trade union members or those who have taken part in trade union activities with a view to such lists being used by employers or employment agencies for discriminating in relation to recruitment or treatment of workers. The Secretary of State may further make regulations prohibiting the use, sale and supply of such lists. Such regulations may provide for a variety of remedies and penalties for breach of the prohibition, including the creation of criminal offences (*ERA 1999, ss 3, 4*). No relevant regulations have yet been made.

51.11   EXCLUSION OR EXPULSION FROM A UNION – GENERAL

TULRCA 1992, s 174 confers upon persons seeking or in employment, in respect of which a closed shop agreement is in force, the right not to be unreasonably excluded or expelled from a trade union. However, since it is unlawful for an employer to refuse employment on grounds of non-membership of a trade union, this provision is of little practical importance. *TURERA 1993, s 14* introduced a new right not to be excluded or expelled, save on certain grounds, which is not dependent upon the existence of a closed shop. This right is considered in 51.13 below.

The common law also provides a remedy for members expelled from a trade union in breach of an express or implied provision of the rules (see 51.12 below).

51.12   The common law

Since there is no contract in existence between an applicant for membership and a trade union, the only right he may have in certain circumstances at common law is not to have his application rejected arbitrarily or capriciously (see *Nagle v Feilden* [1966] 2 QB 633). However, this right was developed in cases where a closed shop or the equivalent was in force (which is no longer likely to be a practical problem, for the reasons given in 51.3 above), and there may be little need to invoke it in future in view of the new statutory right discussed in 51.13 below.

Once a person has been accepted as a member of a union he may not be expelled except in accordance with the rules (see, for example, *Edwards v Society of Graphical and Allied Trades* [1971] Ch 354). In *Goring v British Actors Equity Association* [1987] IRLR 122, the court took the view that the sole common law rights of a union member against the union were those conferred by its rules (including the implied obligation not to act capriciously or arbitrarily). Further, in *Hamlet v General Municipal Boilermakers and Allied Trades Union* [1987] ICR 150, the court held that where a member of a union complained of the decision of a union, the court's function was not to review that decision but merely to ensure that the internal procedures of the union had been complied with. However, in addition to any implied term that a member is not to be expelled arbitrarily or capriciously, a member whose expulsion is being considered is entitled to be dealt with in accordance with the rules of natural justice (*Lee v Showmen's Guild of Great Britain* [1952] 2 QB 329 and see also *Hudson v GMB* [1990] IRLR 67). See also 51.15 below.

The common law remains important in relation to expulsions because, unlike the statutory right (see 51.13 below) it provides a means of controlling the procedure which is followed. Further, the common law right may be used, by means of an application for an injunction, to prevent the expulsion taking place at all.

51.13 **The statutory right**

A union member has a statutory right not to be excluded or expelled from a trade union except on certain specified grounds (*TULRCA 1992, ss 174–177*) (see 51.3 above).

The exclusion or expulsion of an individual from a union is only permissible in the following circumstances:

(*a*)   he does not satisfy an enforceable membership requirement contained in the rules (ie one which restricts membership solely by reference to one or more of the following criteria: employment in a specified trade, industry or profession; occupational description; or possession of specified qualifications or work experience);

(*b*)   he does not qualify for membership because the union only operates in particular parts of Great Britain;

(*c*)   the union's purpose is to regulate relations between its members and a particular employer (or particular associated employers; for associated employers see 7.9(A) CONTINUOUS EMPLOYMENT), and he is not employed by such an employer;

(*d*)   the exclusion or expulsion is entirely attributable to his conduct, provided such conduct does not include either conduct consisting of being, ceasing to be or having been or ceased to be a member of another trade union or employed by a particular employer or at a particular place or conduct to which *TULRCA 1992, s 65* applies (see 51.16 below); and the conduct to which his exclusion or expulsion is wholly or mainly attributable is not conduct consisting of being or ceasing to be or having been or ceased to be a member of a political party.

(*TULRCA 1992, s 174(1)–(4)*.)

The provision in *s 174* preventing a trade union from excluding or expelling a member for being or ceasing to be a member of a political party has been held by the European Court of Human Rights in *Associated Society of Locomotive Engineers and Firemen v United Kingdom (Application No 11002/05)* [2007] IRLR 361, ECtHR to infringe the right to freedom of association under Article 11 of the European Convention. The Court found that the UK law did not strike the right balance between the member's rights and those of the union in so far as it prevented the union from expelling the member on grounds of his membership of the British National Party. It is likely that it will be necessary to amend *s 174* as a result.

For these purposes, if an application for membership of a trade union is neither granted nor rejected, it will be treated as having been refused on the expiry of the period within which it might reasonably have been expected to have been granted or refused. In addition, if under the rules of a trade union any person ceases to be a member of the trade union on the happening of an event specified in the rules, he will be treated as having been expelled from the union (*TULRCA 1992, s 177(2)*).

An employee, who had voluntarily surrendered his membership of a union, could not make a complaint under the predecessor of *s 174* on the basis that his resignation had been forced on him by the conduct of union officials, although there might be cases where the resignation was not truly voluntary (*McGhee v Midlands British Road Services Ltd* [1985] ICR 503). Furthermore, an employee who had been suspended from a union beyond the six-month period allowed in the union's rule book was held to have been neither excluded nor expelled within the meaning of *s 174* (*NACODS v Gluchowski* [1996] IRLR 252).

These rights are additional to common law rights in relation to expulsion or exemptions (see 51.12 above) (*TULRCA 1992, s 177(5)*).

51.14   **The remedy**

TULRCA 1992 provides for a two-stage remedy for an employee who complains that he has been expelled or excluded in breach of *s 174*. He must begin by presenting a complaint to an employment tribunal against the union in question, within the period of six months from the refusal or expulsion. Applications outside this time limit can only be heard if the tribunal is satisfied that it was not reasonably practicable to present the complaint in time and the complaint was presented within such further period as the tribunal considers reasonable (*TULRCA 1992, ss 174(4), 175*; and see 20.7 EMPLOYMENT TRIBUNALS – I).

At the first stage, the tribunal's function is limited to rejecting the application or finding that it is well-founded, and, if the latter, making a declaration to that effect (*TULRCA 1992, s 176(1)*).

Where the tribunal declares that the applicant has been wrongly refused or expelled from union membership, he will be entitled to compensation. However, he cannot apply for compensation until four weeks have elapsed after the declaration. This four-week period is designed to give the trade union an opportunity of admitting or readmitting the applicant to membership. The application must be made to an employment tribunal, however, within six months of the declaration. (*TULRCA 1992, s 176(2), (3)*).

Amount of compensation. Compensation will be of such amount as is considered just and equitable in all the circumstances, but the minimum award is £6,600. The maximum award of compensation is equal to the aggregate of:

(a)   30 times the current limit on the amount of a week's pay for the purposes of calculating the basic award in unfair dismissal cases, which is at present £310; and

(b)   the current maximum compensatory award in unfair dismissal cases, which is at present £60,600.

(See UNFAIR DISMISSAL – III (55).) Thus the present maximum award is £69,900. Since it will now be unusual, because the closed shop has been outlawed, for the inability to belong to a union to cause financial loss, it is unclear how the assessment of compensation should be approached. In *Bradley v NALGO* [1991] ICR 359, the EAT indicated that, assuming compensation for injury to feelings to be available, it should be on a modest scale. However, in *Adams v Hackney London Borough Council* [2003] IRLR 402 the EAT held, in the context of action short of dismissal by an employer on trade union grounds, that in principle awards for injury to feelings should not be approached any differently whatever the ground of discrimination relied upon, although each case will depend on its own facts. (See also *Beaumont v Amicus MSF* (2004) 148 Sol Jo LB 1063 in which an award for injury to feelings was made in a claim for unjustifiable discipline by a trade union).

Compensation may be reduced where the exclusion or expulsion was, to any extent, caused or contributed to by the action of the applicant (*TULRCA 1992, s 176(5)*). It appears that this step should precede the application of the statutory maximum or minimum.

Where a complaint of expulsion under *s 174* succeeds, the applicant cannot also complain of the expulsion under *TULRCA 1992, s 66* (unjustifiable disciplining; see 51.16 below).

51.15 DISCIPLINING BY A TRADE UNION – COMMON LAW

A member of a trade union has a right to be dealt with in accordance with the rules of his union and in accordance with natural justice (see also 51.12 above). If a union acts in breach of the rules or in breach of natural justice, the member affected may apply to the High Court for an injunction and a declaration of his rights. Members of the National Union of Mineworkers ('NUM'), disciplined for breach of a union instruction given in breach of the rules, were held to be entitled to a declaration of the invalidity of the instruction and the unlawfulness of the disciplinary action (*Taylor v National Union of Mineworkers (Derbyshire Area)* [1984] IRLR 440). Injunctions were granted to NUM members to restrain their union from instructing or seeking to persuade them or others not to work. The NUM had described the strike as official, where it had been called without a ballot as required by the rules, and had threatened disciplinary action. However, the courts will not review a decision of a trade union which is taken in accordance with the rules but which is attacked on the basis that it is one which no reasonable trade union could have reached in the circumstances (*Hamlet v General Municipal Boilermakers and Allied Trades Union* [1987] ICR 150). Nevertheless, the rules may be subject to an implied obligation not to act capriciously or arbitrarily (*Goring v British Actors Equity Association* [1987] IRLR 122). For examples of the courts intervening where there has been a breach of natural justice (ie the right to a fair hearing before an unbiased decision-maker), see *Roebuck v National Union of Mineworkers (Yorkshire Area)* [1977] ICR 573 and *Stevenson v United Road Transport Union* [1977] ICR 893. However, the rules of natural justice are not generally applicable in the context of a union's contractual relations with its officials, in its capacity as an employer (*Meacham v Amalgamated Engineering and Electrical Union* [1994] IRLR 218). The court may imply into a union's rule-book a power to discipline its members where no express power exists (*McVitae v UNISON* [1996] IRLR 33).

The court will ignore any provision of the union's rules which purports to provide that his only remedy is by way of some form of determination or conciliation in accordance with the rules (*TULRCA 1992, s 63(1)*). It will also ignore any provision which requires or permits such determination or conciliation, provided that the member has made a valid application to the union for determination or conciliation more than six months before bringing court proceedings (*TULRCA 1992, s 63(2)*), unless the member has himself unreasonably delayed matters (*TULRCA 1992, s 63(4)*). Applications are deemed valid unless the union informs the member of invalidity within 28 days of receipt (*TULRCA 1992, s 63(3)*).

51.16 DISCIPLINING BY A TRADE UNION – STATUTORY PROVISIONS

TULRCA 1992, s 64(1) confers an important right 'not to be unjustifiably disciplined' by a union of which a person is or has at any time been a member. This right is conferred in addition to any existing rights and the only remedies for any infringement are those conferred by *ss 66 and 67* (*TULRCA 1992, s 64(4), (5)*).

A person is unjustifiably disciplined if the conduct or supposed conduct for which he is disciplined falls within, or is believed by the union to amount to conduct which falls within, any of the 12 categories which may be summarised as follows:

(*a*)   failing to participate in or support, or opposing, any industrial action;

(*b*)   failing to break a contract of employment or other agreement with the employer for the purposes of industrial action;

(*c*)   asserting, including by bringing proceedings, that the union or any of its officials or representatives is in breach of its obligations under the general law, its rules or any agreement (although false assertions made in bad faith are excluded by *s 65(6)*);

(*d*)   encouraging or assisting another person to fulfil obligations to the employer or to make or to attempt to vindicate assertions of the kind described in para (*c*);

(*e*)   failing to comply with any requirement imposed as a result of unjustifiable disciplinary action taken against himself or another;

(*f*)   failing to agree to the deduction of union dues from his wages;

(*g*)   resigning or proposing to resign from the union or another union, or being or becoming, or proposing or refusing to become, a member of another union;

(*h*)   working or proposing to work with individuals who do not belong to the union, or who are or are not members of another union;

(*j*)   working or proposing to work for an employer of such individuals;

(*k*)   requiring the union to do an act which any provision of *TULRCA 1992* requires it to do on a member's requisition;

(*l*)   consulting or requesting assistance from the Certification Officer (see 49.3 TRADE UNIONS – I), or from any other person in relation to assertions of the kind described in para (*c*);

(*m*)   proposing to do any of these things, or doing acts which are preparatory or incidental to them,

unless that conduct would independently and justifiably lead to disciplinary action (*TULRCA 1992, s 65(2)–(5)*).

The disciplinary action against which members are protected includes expulsion, fines, deprivation of benefits or facilities, encouragement to another union not to accept him as a member, or subjection to any other detriment (*TULRCA 1992, s 64(2)*). This extends to suspension from membership, and to naming a strike-breaker in a branch circular with the intention of causing embarrassment (*NALGO v Killorn and Simm* [1991] ICR 1).

Complaints of unjustifiable disciplinary action are to be made to an employment tribunal within three months of the determination complained of (*TULRCA 1992, s 66(1), (2)*). A mere recommendation is not a determination (*TGWU v Webber* [1990] ICR 711). Time may be extended for such period as the tribunal considers reasonable, either where it was not reasonably practicable to present the complaint within three months (see 20.7 EMPLOYMENT TRIBUNALS – I), or where any delay is wholly or partly attributable to a reasonable attempt to pursue an appeal or otherwise to have the decision reconsidered (see *NALGO v Killorn and Simm*, above). If the complaint is well-founded, the tribunal will make a declaration to that effect (*TULRCA 1992, s 66(3)*). If such a declaration is made, the complainant may make an application to the employment tribunal to seek compensation and/or the repayment of any sums paid by him as the result of the disciplinary action (*TULRCA 1992, s 67(1)*). Applications for compensation are to be made not less than four weeks or more than six months after the disciplinary action is declared unjustifiable (*TULRCA 1992, s 67(3)*).

The compensation awarded will be that sum which is just and equitable in all the circumstances, taking account of the duty to mitigate loss and of any contributory fault (*TULRCA 1992, s 67(5)–(7)*). Before dealing with mitigation or contribution, however, the tribunal is required by *TULRCA 1992, s 67(9)* to apply the statutory maxima and minima contained in *s 67(8)*. The maximum is the aggregate of (*a*) 30 times the maximum week's pay for calculating the basic award in unfair dismissal cases (*ERA 1996, s 227*), and (*b*) the maximum compensatory award in such cases (*ERA 1996, s 124*). These figures are at present £310 and £60,600, respectively, giving a maximum award under *s 67(8)* of £69,900. The minimum is the amount for the time being specified in *TULRCA 1992, s 156(1)*, which is at present £6,600. (See also 55.14 UNFAIR DISMISSAL – III.) The compensation awarded may include a sum in respect of injury to feelings: see *Beaumont v Amicus MSF* (2004) 148 Sol Jo LB 1063, EAT.

51.17 **DETRIMENT ON GROUNDS OF UNION MEMBERSHIP OR ACTIVITIES**

TULRCA 1992, s 146 concerns detriment caused by an employer against a worker as an individual:

(*a*)   to prevent or deter him from, or to penalise him for, belonging to an independent trade union; or

(*b*)   to prevent him or deter him from taking part in the activities of an independent union at an appropriate time (ie a time outside working hours or a time when the employer has consented to him taking part in union activities), or to penalise him for doing so; or

(*c*)   from 1 October 2004, to prevent him or deter him from making use of trade union services at an appropriate time, or to penalise him for doing so; or

(*d*)   to compel him to join any trade union.

There was previously considerable doubt as to whether omissions could constitute 'action' for those purposes. In *Associated Newspapers Ltd v Wilson; Associated British Ports v Palmer* [1995] ICR 406, a majority of the House of Lords held that withholding a salary increase from employees who refused to sign personal contracts and give up collectively bargained terms and conditions did not amount to a breach of *s 146*.

However, the *ERA 1999, Sch 2* had the effect of reversing this aspect of the House of Lords' decision in *Wilson/Palmer* with effect from 25 October 1999. In particular, *TULRCA 1992, s 146(1)* now prohibits subjecting an individual to a detriment by any act, or any deliberate failure to act, by the employer on grounds of trade union membership or activities.

Wilson/Palmer subsequently went to the European Court of Human Rights in *Wilson v United Kingdom* [2002] IRLR 568. The Court held that, by permitting employers to use financial incentives to induce employees to surrender the right to union representation (as opposed to deterring union membership altogether), the United Kingdom had failed in its positive duty to secure the enjoyment of the right to freedom of association under *art 11* of the *European Convention on Human Rights*. In response to that decision, *s 29* of the *Employment Rights Act 2004* has inserted new *ss 145A-145F* into *TULRCA 1992* which from

1 October 2004 conferred upon workers a right not to have an offer made to them by their employer for the sole or main purpose of inducing the worker:

(*a*)   not to be or seek to become a member of a trade union;

(*b*)   not to take part, at an appropriate time, in trade union activities;

(*c*)   not to make use, at an appropriate time, of trade union services; or

(*d*)   to be or become a member of a trade union (*s 145A*).

In addition, a worker who is a member of an independent trade union which is recognised, or is seeking to be recognised, by his employer, has the right not to have an offer made to him by his employer if:

(a)   acceptance of that offer, together with other workers' acceptance of similar offers, would result in the workers' terms and conditions no longer being determined by collective bargaining with the union; and

(b)   the employer's sole or main purpose in making the offers is to achieve that result (*s 145B*).

In *Davies v Asda Stores Ltd* (IDS Brief 801) an employment tribunal held that the employer had breached *s 145B* of *TULRCA 1992* by offering new terms and conditions to union members provided they relinquished collective bargaining. The 340 members were each awarded £2,500.

In *Department of Transport v Gallacher* [1994] ICR 967, the Court of Appeal held that an employer's advice that an employee's prospects of promotion would be improved if he returned to a line management position, instead of engaging in full-time trade union duties, was not given for the purpose of deterring the employee from taking part in union activities within the meaning of *TULRCA 1992, s 146*. The relevant purpose is the object which the employer desires or seeks to achieve – in *Gallacher*, his purpose was to assist the employee in obtaining promotion.

In *FW Farnsworth Ltd v McCoid* [1998] IRLR 362, it was held that the derecognition of a shop steward by an employer could amount to action taken against the shop steward as an individual for the purpose of preventing or deterring him from taking part in trade union activities or penalising him for doing so within the meaning of *TULRCA 1992, s 148*.

A worker also has the right not to be subjected to a detriment in order to require him to make payments in lieu of union subscriptions when he is not (or is no longer) a union member (*TULRCA 1992, s 146(3)*). In addition, *ERA 1999, Sch 1* introduced a new right not to be subjected to a detriment on union recognition-related grounds with effect from 6 June 2000 (see 48.37 TRADE UNIONS – I).

See also 52.3 UNFAIR DISMISSAL – II.

51.18 **The remedy**

The employee may make a complaint to an employment tribunal within three months of the action complained of, or within such further period as the tribunal considers reasonable in a case where it is satisfied that it was not reasonably practicable for the complaint to be presented within three months (see 20.7 EMPLOYMENT TRIBUNALS – I) (*TULRCA 1992, ss 146(5), 147*).

It is for the employer to show the purpose for which action was taken against the employee (*TULRCA 1992, s 148(1)*). If the tribunal finds the complaint well-founded, it will make a declaration to that effect and may order compensation to be paid. The compensation will be such amount as it considers just and equitable in all the circumstances, having regard to the right infringed and any loss sustained by the complainant. Compensation may be reduced on account of the applicant's contributory fault (*TULRCA 1992, s 149*). It would appear that compensation for an action short of dismissal may include an award in respect of injury to feelings (*Cleveland Ambulance NHS Trust v Blane* [1997] ICR 851). In *Adams v Hackney London Borough Council* [2003] IRLR 402 the EAT held that in principle awards for injury to feelings should not be approached any differently in cases of discrimination on trade union grounds than in other cases of discrimination. However, the level of award will depend on the individual applicant. Some may feel deeply hurt by trade union discrimination, whilst other more robust characters may suffer little, if any, distress. Since the aim is to compensate and not to punish, the compensation ought not to be the same in each case.

Joinder of third parties. Where the employer was induced to take the action complained of by industrial action or threat of such action, although no account is to be taken by the tribunal of such pressure when deciding the complaint, the union (or unions) may be joined as a third party to the proceedings and may be ordered to pay all or part of the compensation as the tribunal considers just in the circumstances (*TULRCA 1992, ss 148(2), 150*).

PROHIBITION ON UNION MEMBERSHIP AND UNION RECOGNITION REQUIREMENTS IN CONTRACTS FOR GOODS OR SERVICES

51.19 Any term or condition of a contract for the supply of goods or services is void insofar as it purports:

(*a*)   to require that the whole, or some part, of the work done for the purposes of the contract is to be done only by persons who are or who are not members of trade unions or of a particular trade union (*TULRCA 1992, s 144*);

(*b*)   to require any party to the contract to recognise one or more trade unions (whether or not named in the contract) for the purpose of negotiating on behalf of workers, or any class of worker, employed by him or to negotiate or consult with, or with any official of, one or more trade unions (whether or not so named) (*TULRCA 1992, s 186*).

The power of local authorities to have regard to non-commercial considerations in awarding contracts is limited by the *Local Government Act 1988, Part II.*

(For the prohibition of industrial action to impose union membership or recognition requirements, see 45.7 STRIKES AND INDUSTRIAL ACTION.)

Further, it is unlawful for a person to refuse to deal with a supplier or prospective supplier of goods or services on union membership grounds (*TULRCA 1992, s 145(1)*). Refusing to deal with a person means excluding that person's name from a list of approved suppliers or of persons from whom tenders may be or are invited, or if he fails to permit that person to submit a tender, decides not to enter into a contract with that person, or terminates an existing contract (*TULRCA 1992, s 145(2), (3), (4)*). Such a refusal is on union membership grounds if the ground or one of the grounds for it is that work done for the purposes of any contract would be done, or would be likely to be done, by persons who were or were not members of a trade union or of a particular union (*TULRCA 1992, s 145(2)*).

It is also unlawful to refuse to deal with such a person on the ground that he does not, or is not likely to, recognise one or more trade unions for negotiating purposes or negotiate or consult with one or more trade unions or their officials (*TULRCA 1992, s 187*).

In the case of an unlawful refusal to deal, an action for breach of statutory duty may be brought by the person with whom the defendant has refused to deal or by any other person adversely affected (*TULRCA 1992, ss 145(5), 187(3)*).

51.20 DEDUCTION OR SUBSCRIPTIONS: THE 'CHECK-OFF'

The following provisions are to be found in *TULRCA 1992, ss 68* and *68A* as amended by the *Deregulation (Deduction from Pay of Union Subscriptions) Order 1998 (SI 1998/1529)*.

Where arrangements exist between an employer and a union relating to the making of deductions from wages in respect of union subscriptions (commonly known as the 'check-off'), the employer must ensure that deductions are only made in accordance with an authorisation signed and dated by the worker concerned (*TULRCA 1992, s 68(1), (2)*). A worker has the same meaning as in *Part II* of the *Employment Rights Act 1996* (see PAY – I (28)), and is thus not confined to employees in the strict sense (*TULRCA 1992, s 68(4)*). If the worker subsequently withdraws the authorisation in writing, the employer must cease to make deductions as soon as is reasonably practicable (*TULRCA 1992, s 68(2)*).

The signing of an authorisation does not oblige the employer to maintain or continue to maintain the arrangements for making deductions (*TULRCA 1992, s 68(3)*).

If the employer makes a deduction in contravention of these provisions, the worker may present a complaint to an employment tribunal within the period of three months beginning with the date of payment of the wages from which the deduction (or the last deduction, if the complaint relates to more than one) was made (*TULRCA 1992, s 68A(1)*). If the tribunal is satisfied that it was not reasonably practicable for the complaint to be presented within that period, it may extend time for such further period as it considers reasonable.

Where the tribunal finds a complaint well-founded, it will make a declaration to that effect, and will order the employer to repay the amount improperly deducted and not already repaid (*TULRCA 1992, s 68A(2)*). Provision is made to avoid double recovery where the same deduction also contravenes other statutory provisions (*TULRCA 1992, s 68A(3)*). It is not clear whether, if the sums deducted had already been paid by the employer to the union, the employer would be able to recover them from the union in a common law claim for restitution.

Prior to 23 June 1998, the 'check-off' provisions further required that the worker's authorisations must have been signed within the last three years. They also required that an increased subscription could only be deducted if the employer had given the worker at least one month's written notice. These requirements were removed by the *Deregulation (Deduction from Pay of Union Subscriptions) Order 1998 (SI 1998/1529)* made under the *Deregulation and Contracting Out Act 1994* which came into force on 23 June 1998.

The repealed requirements continue to apply to authorisations given before 23 June 1998 (*reg 3(1)*). However, by *reg 3(2), (3)*, an employer may give a worker notice in a form prescribed in the *Schedule* to the *Regulations* that such an authorisation is to be treated as having been given under the new provisions (and so will be treated as of unlimited duration until withdrawal, and as not requiring advance notice of any increase in the amount deducted). Provided the worker does not object by written notice within 14 days, the new provisions will apply.

51.21 THE RIGHT TO BE ACCOMPANIED

A new right to be accompanied by a trade union official (or a fellow employee) was introduced by *s 10* of the *Employment Relations Act 1999*, which came into force on 18 September 2000. Any worker who is required or invited to attend a disciplinary or grievance hearing by his employer is now entitled to be accompanied either by a trade union official (as defined in *TULRCA 1992, ss 1, 119*) or fellow worker of his choice. The employer must permit the companion to put the worker's case, respond to any views expressed and confer with the worker during the hearing. However, the employer is not required to permit the companion to answer questions on the worker's behalf (*ERA 1999, s 10(2B), (2C)*). If the worker's chosen companion is not available at the time of the hearing, and the worker proposes a reasonable alternative time within the subsequent period of five working days, the employer must postpone the hearing to the time proposed (*ERA 1999, s 10(4), (5)*). The employer must also give the worker's companion time off for the purpose of accompanying the worker to the meeting (*ERA 1999, s 10(6)*). Guidance on the application of this right is given in the ACAS Code of Practice on Disciplinary and Grievance Procedures (2000).

A 'disciplinary hearing' is defined for these purposes so as to include a hearing which could result in a formal warning (*ERA 1999, s 13(4)*). For these purposes, the test of whether a warning is 'formal' is one of substance. If the warning will become part of the worker's disciplinary record, then the right to be accompanied applies (*Ferenc-Batchelor v London Underground Ltd* [2003] ICR 656). However, the right is confined to disciplinary or grievance matters. It therefore did not apply to a meeting which led to an employee's dismissal on grounds of redundancy: see *Heathmill Multimedia ASP Ltd v Jones* [2003] IRLR 856. The EAT held in *Skiggs v South West Trains Ltd* [2005] IRLR 459 that an investigative interview regarding a grievance raised by another employee against the claimant was not a disciplinary hearing at which the claimant had a right to be accompanied.

This new statutory right does not require a union to provide representation to an employee. However, a member may have a contractual right to representation deriving from the union rule-book. In *English v Unison* (2000) IDS Brief 668, the county court held that a qualified right to representation arose as a matter of contract from the union's guide to disciplinary hearings.

A worker denied the right to be accompanied may complain to the employment tribunal within three months of the employer's failure (or such further period as is considered reasonable where it was not reasonably practicable to present the complaint within three months) (*ERA 1999, s 11(1), (2)*). Where a complaint is upheld, the tribunal may make an award of up to two weeks' pay, subject to the statutory maximum contained in *ERA 1996, s 227(1)*, currently £310. In addition, a worker has a right not to be subjected to a detriment or dismissed for seeking to exercise the right to be accompanied. Dismissal on this ground will be automatically unfair (*ERA 1999, s 12*).

51.22 ADVICE BY TRADE UNIONS TO MEMBERS

The scope of a trade union's duty of care towards its members in giving advice was considered by the High Court in *Friend v Institute of Professional Managers and Specialists* [1999] IRLR 173. It was held that a trade union advising or acting for a member in an employment dispute owed the member a duty of care in tort to use ordinary skill and care. However, once solicitors had been engaged on the member's behalf, any duty there might previously have been on the union to advise on the dispute came to an end.

52   Transfer of Undertakings

52.1   Far-reaching rules for the protection of employees' rights on the transfer of an undertaking are contained in the *Transfer of Undertakings (Protection of Employment) Regulations 2006 (SI 2006/246)* ('the *Regulations*'). These came into force on 6 April 2006. They replace entirely the previous legislation, the *Transfer of Undertakings (Protection of Employment) Regulations 1981 (SI 1981/1794)* as amended by the *Transfer of Undertakings (Protection of Employment) (Amendment) Regulations 1987 (SI 1987/442)*, by the *Trade Union Reform and Employment Rights Act 1993*, by the *Collective Redundancies and Transfer of Undertakings (Protection of Employment) (Amendment) Regulations 1995 (SI 1995/2587)* and by the *Collective Redundancies and Transfer of Undertakings (Protection of Employment) (Amendment) Regulations 1999 (SI 1999/1925.)*

The purpose of the original 1981 Regulations was to fulfil the United Kingdom's obligations under European Community law to give effect to *EC Council Directive 77/187*, generally known as the *Acquired Rights Directive*. A new *Directive* was adopted on 29 June 1998 which amends *Directive 77/187* by wholly replacing the texts of *arts 1–7*. Member states had three years within which to bring into force measures which implement the amended *Directive*. See *Official Journal, 17 July 1998 (L201/88)*. The provisions of the original and the amending *Directive* have been consolidated in a further *Directive* adopted on 12 March 2001: *Directive 2001/23/EC*, Official Journal, 22 March 2001 (L82/16). It was the need to transpose the new provisions into UK law which prompted the introduction of the *Regulations*. However, the *Regulations* go further than is required by European law and introduce an additional concept, that of 'a service provision change'. That they go further than European law is emphasised by the fact that the *Regulations* are made not only under *s 2(2)* of the *European Communities Act 1972* but also under *s 38* of the *Employment Relations Act 1999*, which empowered the Secretary of State to make regulations in circumstances other than those to which the Community obligation applies. In addition, the *Regulations* seek to clarify the meaning of certain terms by incorporating concepts developed by the courts.

Historically, English courts and tribunals have so far as possible construed the *Regulations* consistently with the *Directive*, even to the extent of reading in additional words (see 52.10 below, and 25.2 EUROPEAN COMMUNITY LAW). However, when considering the meaning of a service provision change, they may not feel obliged so to do, although the concepts of 'service provision change' and 'transfer of an undertaking' are not mutually exclusive.

References below are to provisions of the *Regulations* unless stated otherwise.

52.2   Where there is a 'relevant transfer', that is either where there is a 'service provision change' (see 52.3 below) from person *A* to person *B*, or where an 'undertaking' (see 52.4 below) is 'transferred' (see 52.5 below) from person *A* to person *B*:

    (*a*)   individuals who are employed by *A* 'immediately before the transfer' (see 52.12 and 52.11 below) automatically become the employees of *B* from the time of the transfer, on the terms and conditions they previously held with *A* (see 52.10 below);

(b)   *B* inherits *A's* rights and liabilities in relation to those individuals (see 52.15 below);

(c)   collective agreements, made by or on behalf of *A* with a trade union recognised by *A*, are inherited by *B* (see 52.17 below);

(d)   where *A* recognises a union in respect of employees in the undertaking to be transferred and, following the transfer, the undertaking transferred maintains an identity distinct from any other undertaking owned by *B*, *B* must recognise the union in respect of those employees (see 52.18 below);

(e)   *A* must inform recognised trade unions about the consequences of the transfer, and *B* must provide *A* with sufficient information in this regard (see 52.19 below);

(f)   in certain circumstances, it may be necessary for *A* or *B* to consult with recognised trade unions or elected employee representatives concerning the transfer (see 52.19 below); and

(g)   dismissal of any employee (whether before or after the transfer) for any reason connected with the transfer is automatically unfair unless the reason is 'an economic, technical or organisational reason entailing changes in the workforce' in which case the dismissal is fair if reasonable in the circumstances (see 52.21 below).

52.3   WHAT IS A 'RELEVANT TRANSFER'?

Service provision change

There are three situations which may amount to a service provision change (*reg 3(1)(b)*):

(a)   Activities cease to be carried out by a person ('a client') on his own behalf and are carried out instead by another person on the client's behalf ('a contractor'). This situation is sometimes referred to as contracting out or outsourcing.

(b)   Activities cease to be carried out by a contractor on a client's behalf (whether or not those activities had previously been carried out by the client on his own behalf) and are carried out instead by another person ('a subsequent contractor') on the client's behalf. This situation is sometimes referred to as reassigning.

(c)   Activities cease to be carried out by a contractor or a subsequent contractor on a client's behalf (whether or not those activities had previously been carried out by the client on his own behalf) and are carried out instead by the client on his own behalf. This situation is sometimes referred to as contracting in or insourcing.

In any of these three situations there will be a relevant transfer if immediately before the service provision change:

(a)   There is an organised grouping of employees situated in Great Britain which has as its principal purpose the carrying out of the activities concerned on behalf of the client; and

(b)   The client intends that the activities will, following the service provision change, be carried out by the transferee other than in connection with a single specific event or task of short-term duration (*reg 3(3)(a)*).

However, a service provision change will not be a relevant transfer if the activities concerned consist wholly or mainly of the supply of goods for the client's use (*reg 3(3)(b)*).

Where there is a service provision change which is a relevant transfer, 'the transferor' means the person who carried out the activities prior to the service provision change and 'the transferee' means the person who carries out the activities as a result of the service provision change (*reg 2(1)*).

52.4   Transfer of an undertaking or business

Undertaking or business

The *Regulations* apply to the transfer of an undertaking or of a business situated immediately before the transfer in the United Kingdom.

The *Regulations* also cover the transfer of part of an undertaking or business. A 'part' of an 'undertaking' means a unit which is to some extent separate and self-contained from the remainder of the enterprise such as an operating division which is autonomous from the remainder of the business by virtue, for example, of having its own accounts, management structure, and product specialisation. In *Fairhurst Ward Abbotts Ltd v Botes Building Ltd* [2004] ICR 919 the Court of Appeal ruled that, provided that there is an identifiable stable economic entity before the transfer takes place, the law does not require that the particular part transferred should itself, before the date of the transfer, exist as a discrete and identifiable economic entity: it is sufficient if a part of the larger entity becomes identified for the first time as a separate economic entity on the occasion of the transfer separating a part from the whole.

'Undertaking' would appear to include a professional practice, such as that of an NHS doctor (see *Jeetle v Elster* [1985] ICR 389), the activities of a charitable foundation (*Stichting v Bartol* [1992] IRLR 366), and the carrying out of an activity pursuant to a contract (see 52.5 below). An undertaking which is carried out on a non-profit making basis but is contracted out to be carried out on a commercial basis may still transfer where all the other characteristics of the activity remained the same before and after the alleged transfer: *Alderson v Secretary of State for Trade and Industry* [2003] EWCA Civ 1767, [2004] ICR 512.

However, an economic entity is not defined only by the employment status of a group of employees, but also by the function which that group undertakes: *Wynnwith Engineering Co Ltd v Bennett* [2002] IRLR 170. In *Wain v Guernsey Ship Management Ltd* [2007] EWCA Civ 294, [2007] All ER (D) 35 (Apr) the Court of Appeal rejected the contention that a group of short-term contract employees comprised an economic entity.

52.5   *Transfer*

A relevant transfer occurs where there is a transfer of an economic identity which retains its identity (*reg 3(1)(a)*).

Thus, in deciding whether there has been a transfer of an undertaking, the critical question is whether the undertaking retains its identity and is carried on by the transferee. In answering that question, all the factual circumstances must be considered, but particular factors include: the type of undertaking or business concerned; whether tangible assets such as buildings and moveable property are transferred; the value of intangible assets at the time of the transfer; whether the majority of employees are taken over by the new employer; whether customers are transferred; the degree of similarity between the activities carried on before and after the alleged transfer; and the period, if any, for which those activities are suspended (*Spijkers v Gebroeders Benedik Abbatoir CV*: 24/85 [1986] 2 CMLR 296; *Stichting v Bartol*: C-29/91 [1992] IRLR 366; *Rask v ISS Kantineservice A/S*: C-209/91 [1993] IRLR 133).

The ECJ has considered the application of this test in a number of cases involving the contracting out of services and changes of contractors. The importance within the UK of this line of authority is likely to be limited in the future since such cases are likely to constitute service provision changes, whether or not there is a transfer of an undertaking.

In *Schmidt v Spar und Leihkasse der Früheren Ämter Bordersholm, Kiel und Cronshagen*: C-392/92 [1995] ICR 237 it was held that there could be a transfer of contracted-out cleaning services, even where the services are performed by a single employee and there is no transfer of tangible assets; and *Merckx v Ford Motors Co Belgium SA*: C-171/94 and C-172/94 [1996] IRLR 467. The ECJ held in *Rygard v Stro Molle Akustik* [1996] IRLR 51, however, that the transfer of an undertaking must involve the transfer of a 'stable economic entity' and went on to hold in *Süzen v Zehnacker Gebäudereingung GmbH Krankenhausservice*: C- 13/95 [1997] ICR 662 that an activity does not, in itself, constitute such an entity. It follows, the ECJ stated, that the mere fact that a similar activity is carried on before and after a change of contractors does not mean there is a transfer of an undertaking. In the case of a labour-intensive undertaking with no significant assets (eg contract cleaning), there will generally be no transfer unless the new contractor takes on a majority of the old contractor's staff. This approach was reinforced in *Francisco Hernández Vidal SA v Pérez Gomez*: C-127/96, C-129/96 and C-74/97 [1999] IRLR 132 and in *Sánchez Hidalgo v Asociación de Servicios Aser*: C-173/96 [2002] ICR 73. The ECJ again emphasised the requirement for a stable economic entity, adding that 'an organised group of wage earners who are specifically and permanently assigned to a common task may, in the absence of other factors of production, amount to an economic entity'. The most recent application of this approach was in *Oy Liikenne Ab v Liskojarvi*: C-172/99 [2002] ICR 155 (the absence of a transfer of assets conclusive where the activity required substantial tangible assets).

The importance of the distinction between a labour-intensive undertaking and an asset reliant undertaking was crucial in *Abler v Sodexho MM Catering Gesellschaft mbH*: C-340/01 [2004] IRLR 168, in which the ECJ found that the catering sector was based essentially on equipment. Thus, where a new contractor took over the use of that equipment then there was a transfer, even though the equipment was in fact owned by neither the transferor nor the transferee but by the party contracting out the activity. The ECJ specifically held that the degree of importance to be attached to each factor will vary according to the activity carried on. (See also *Güney-Görres v Securicor Avidation*: C-232/04 [2006] IRLR 305.)

The Court of Appeal has emphasised that the correct approach is 'multi-factorial': *Balfour Beatty Power Networks Ltd v Wilcox* [2006] EWCA Civ 1240, [2007] IRLR 63. No single aspect need determine the question. All factors must be balanced before a decision is reached. The CA considered that there could be a relevant transfer even in an industry which was asset reliant and where there was no transfer of tangible assets: the ECJ had not, the CA considered, laid down any stark rule to the contrary in *Oy Liikenne*. On the facts, the assets were in any event leased and so they could be better characterised as tools and equipment. The CA also observed that an enterprise may be 'stable' as a matter of practical and industrial reality, even though its long-term future is not assured. A similar, multi-factorial approach had been followed by the EAT in *P&O Trans European Ltd v Initial Transport Services Ltd* [2003] IRLR 128 and in *NUMAST v P&O Scottish Ferries Ltd* [2005] ICR 1270.

A number of cases involving contracting out and changes of contractors have also come before the UK courts, many arising out of local government compulsory competitive tendering. The courts have held in this context that if similar activities are carried on before and after a change of service provider, there can be a transfer of an undertaking notwithstanding that no assets are transferred (*Dines v Initial Health Care Services Ltd* [1995] ICR 11) or that neither assets nor staff are transferred (*BSG Property Services v Tuck* [1996] IRLR 134). See also *Kenny v South Manchester College* [1993] IRLR 265, *Isles of Scilly Council v Brintel Helicopters Ltd* [1995] ICR 249 and *Kelman v Care Contract Services Ltd* [1995] ICR 260. The reasoning of these cases must now, however, be reconsidered in the light of *Betts v Brintel Helicopters Ltd* [1997] IRLR 361, in which the Court of Appeal followed *Süzen* (see above) and held that there was no transfer on a change of contractor providing helicopter services to a company, where the new contractor took over no staff, and only a limited part of the old contractor's assets. The court distinguished labour intensive undertakings, where the key factor is whether the majority of employees are taken over by the new employer, and other types of undertaking, where a broader range of factors must be considered.

The Court of Appeal reconsidered the scope of *Süzen* (with express reference to *Sánchez Hidalgo*) in *ECM (Vehicle Delivery Service) v Cox* [1999] IRLR 559. The court stated that the importance of *Süzen* had been overstated: the ECJ had not overruled its previous interpretive rulings. It is for the national court to make the necessary factual appraisal, considering in particular the factors identified in *Spijkers*. One relevant factor is whether the majority of employees are taken over by the new employer to enable it to carry on the activities of the undertaking on a regular basis. The mere loss of a service contract to a competitor does not of itself indicate the existence of a transfer. This appeal was followed by Lindsay J in *RCO Support Services Ltd v Unison* [2000] ICR 1502 and in *Cheesman v R Brewer Contracts Ltd* [2001] IRLR 144.

The Court of Appeal's judgment in *RCO Support Services Ltd v Unison* [2002] EWCA Civ 464, [2002] ICR 751 appeared to accept that *Süzen* represented a shift on the previous position, such that a mere similarity in the activities of the entity before and after the transfer cannot be enough to establish a transfer. However, the additional factors required need not amount to a transfer of a majority of the workforce (in terms of numbers and skills) as had been the case in *Süzen*. On the facts of *RCO* a similarity in operating methods and training within the activities was found to be enough, even where the location of the activity had moved.

As to the question of the relevance of an intention of the transferee to avoid the application of TUPE, the Court of Appeal in *RCO* stated that a subjective motive of the putative transferee to avoid the application of TUPE is not the real point. However, in deciding whether or not there is a transfer, it may be relevant to take into account the objective circumstances surrounding a decision not to take on the workforce. It is far from clear how that distinction will be drawn in practice. Some guidance is to be found in the decision in *Astle v Cheshire County Council* [2005] IRLR 12. The EAT held that if a tribunal finds that the reason or principal reason of the transferee was to avoid the application of TUPE then it is a relevant factor to take into account in the *Spijkers* exercise, and may be decisive.

In *RCO* the Court of Appeal made reference to its earlier decision in *ADI (UK) Ltd v Willer* [2001] EWCA Civ 971, [2001] IRLR 542 in which it had recognised that *Süzen* represented something of a retreat by the ECJ from its earlier decisions. In *ADI* it concluded that, in a labour-intensive operation, the absence of a transfer of staff from the outgoing contractor to the incoming contractor should lead to the conclusion that there is no transfer of an undertaking, even though the work, the equipment used, the location and the ultimate customers are the same. However, in such cases, the balance would be tipped the other way if the reason why there was no transfer of staff was that the parties wished to avoid the application of the *Regulations*. If such an intention is established, then there will be deemed to have been a transfer. This ruling substantially supersedes the decisions in *Whitewater Leisure Management Ltd v Barnes* [2000] ICR 1049, EAT and *Lightways (Contractors) Ltd v Associated Holdings Ltd* [2000] IRLR 247, Ct of Sess.

In *Rygaard v Stro Molle Akustik* [1996] IRLR 51, the ECJ held that existing authorities presuppose that the transfer relates to a stable economic entity whose activity is not limited to one specific works contract. However, the scope of this ruling was restricted to its facts (ie single contracts for building works) by the EAT in *Argyll Training Ltd v Sinclair* [2000] IRLR 630, in which it stated that there is no basis for automatically excluding all single-contract undertakings from the possibility of being transferred. Indeed, it is possible (though not common) for a single employee to constitute a stable economic entity, provided that the entity can be said to be sufficiently structured and autonomous: *Dudley Bower Building Services Ltd v Lowe* [2003] ICR 843.

52.6   Other concepts defining 'relevant transfer'

General

The *Regulations* apply to public and private undertakings engaged in economic activities, whether or not they are operating for gain (*reg 3(4)(a)*).

The *Regulations* apply even if the transfer is governed or effected by foreign law, or if the employees in the undertaking, business or activities work outside the UK or if their employment is governed by foreign law (*reg 3(4)(b)*).

In *Allen v Amalgamated Construction Co Ltd* [2000] ICR 119, the ECJ held that the *Acquired Rights Directive* can apply to a transfer between two subsidiary companies in the same group, provided that they are distinct legal persons each with specific employment relationships with their employees. This was so even though the two companies had the same management, were in the same premises, and were engaged in the same works.

In *Foreningen af Arbejdsledere i Danmark v Daddy's Dance Hall A/S*: 324/86 [1988] IRLR 315 the European Court of Justice held that there was a relevant transfer where a lessee of restaurant premises gave notice to its employees upon the determination of the lease, and the lessor then granted a new lease to a third party which continued to run the business without any interruption. Where the identity of the economic unit was retained, it did not matter that the transfer took place in two phases. The same result was reached on similar facts in *Litster v Forth Dry Dock and Engineering Co Ltd* [1989] ICR 341 and in *P Bork International A/S v Foreningen af Arbejdsledere i Danmark*: 101/87 [1989] IRLR 41 (owner of leased undertaking repossessed it after forfeiture of the lease and then sold it on to a third party who resumed operation of the business). These decisions will be important where businesses are operated on a franchise (see also *LMC Drains Ltd v Waugh* [1991] 3 CMLR 172).

If the agreement pursuant to which the transfer occurred is rescinded, there may be a relevant 'retransfer' back to the original transferor (*Berg and Busschers v Besselsen*: 144/87 and 145/87 [1990] ICR 396).

52.7   *More than one transaction*

A relevant transfer may be affected by a series of two or more transactions (*reg 3(6)(a)*). In construing the *1981 Regulations* purposively, it has been held that the court will seek to identify whether there is in truth a single transfer and will look beyond an 'ingenious device' whereby an intermediary company is introduced for the sole purpose of achieving the contracting parties' mutual wish to transfer an undertaking between them which is stripped of liability to the employees (see *Re Maxwell Fleet and Facilities Management Ltd (No 2)* [2000] ICR 717). In *Temco Service Industries SA v Imzilyen*: C-51/00 [2002] IRLR 214 the ECJ confirmed that the absence of a contractual link does not in itself prevent the application of the *Directive*; it was enough if the transferor and transferee were part of the web of contractual relations.

52.8   *Transfer of property*

A transfer may take place whether or not any property is transferred to the transferee by the transferor (*reg 3(6)(b)*).

52.9   *Administrative functions carried out by a public body*

'A relevant transfer' does not include an administrative reorganisation of public administrative authorities, or the transfer of administrative functions between public administrative authorities (*reg 3(5)*). This limited exclusion was originally explained by the European Court of Justice in *Henke v Gemeinde Schierke*: C-298/94 [1996] IRLR 701 and was then recognised in *art 1(1)(c)* of *Directive 2001/23*. It was further clarified in two subsequent decisions of the European Court of Justice: *Mayeur v Association Promotion de l'Information Messine*: C-175/99 [2002] ICR 1316 (transfer where the work of a non-profit making tourist agency was taken over by the municipality); and *Collino v Telecom Italia SpA*: C-343/98 [2002] ICR 38 (transfer on a reorganisation of telephone service providers). In *Viggásdóttir v Íslandspóstur hf* [2002] IRLR 425, the EFTA Court held that the *Directive* could apply to the conversion of a state entity into a wholly state-owned limited liability company, and that it is for the national court to decide whether the individuals fall under the protection of national employment law in accordance with the principles set out by the ECJ in *Collino*.

52.10   *Share transfers*

The *Regulations* apply only to the transfer of an undertaking from one legal person to another. They do not apply, for example, to the transfer of shares in a company which carries on the undertaking (*Initial Supplies Ltd v McCall* 1992 SLT 67). This is so even though this form of transaction was adopted with the purpose of avoiding the *Regulations* (*Brookes v Borough Care Services* [1998] IRLR 636).

In *Millam v Print Factory (London) 1991 Ltd* [2007] EWCA Civ 322, [2007] All ER (D) 160 (May) the Court of Appeal reiterated this principle, but went on to uphold a tribunal's conclusion that the business nevertheless transferred to the acquiring company. The CA also rejected the EAT's analysis that it could pierce the corporate veil. An issue of piercing the corporate veil arises only when it is established that activity X is carried on by company A, but for policy reasons it is sought to show that in reality the activity is the responsibility of the owner of company A, company B; to pierce the corporate veil it must generally be shown that the subsidiary company is a sham or façade. In the present case, the activity was in fact carried on by company B, and so there was a relevant transfer from A to B.

52.11   *Insolvency*

The ECJ held in *Abels v Bedriifsveereniging voor de Metaalindustrie en de Electrotechnische Industrie*: 135/83 [1985] ECR 469 that the *Directive* does not apply to the transfer of an undertaking, business or part of a business in the course of insolvency proceedings. In *Jules Dethier Equipment SA v Dassy*: C-319/94 [1998] ICR 541, it ruled that it does apply in the event of the transfer of an undertaking which is being wound up by a court if the undertaking continues to trade. It also applies where the undertaking transferred is being wound up voluntarily (*Europieces SA v Saunders* IDS Brief 627, P10, ECJ). The distinction drawn in *Donaldson v Perth & Kinross Council* [2004] ICR 667 was between an 'irretrievable insolvency and cessation of business' and 'the sale of the business as a going concern'.

Clarification is now given in *reg 8(7)*, which provides that *reg 4* (effect of relevant transfer on contracts of employment) and *reg 7* (dismissal of employee because of relevant transfer) do not apply to any relevant transfer where the transferor is the subject of 'bankruptcy proceedings or any analogous insolvency proceedings which have been instituted with a view to the liquidation of the assets of the transferor and are under the supervision of an insolvency practitioner'.

Furthermore, *regs 8(1)* to (*6*) apply to 'relevant insolvency proceedings', that is insolvency proceedings which have been opened in relation to the transferor not with a view to the liquidation of the assets of the transferor and which are under the supervision of an insolvency practitioner. They extend the statutory regimes for payments by the Secretary of State (under chapter VI of *Part XI* and *Part XII* of the *Employment Rights Act 1996*) to transfers in such cases.

52.12   **Time of the transfer**

It may be important to identify the precise time of the transfer, because of the requirement (see 51.10 below) that the employee be employed by his old employer immediately before the transfer. However, following the decision of the House of Lords in *Litster v Forth Dry Dock and Engineering Co Ltd* [1989] ICR 341, a gloss is effectively put on that requirement if the employee is dismissed for a reason connected with the transfer, and some of the reported cases would now be decided differently as a result (a principle now enshrined in *reg 4(3)*; see 52.14 below).

A number of cases have arisen where, for example, the employee has been dismissed between the exchange of contracts for the sale of the business and the completion date (*Wheeler v Patel* [1987] ICR 631), or joined the new employers after they were let into possession under a deed of assignment but before completion (*Brook Lane Finance Co Ltd v Bradley* [1988] ICR 423). In these cases it was held that the contract of employment was not automatically continued by virtue of the *Regulations*. In both *Wheeler* and *Brook Lane* the EAT considered that it was bound by the decision of the Court of Appeal in *Secretary of State for Employment v Spence* [1986] ICR 651 to hold that a transfer was only capable of taking place at a particular moment, and not over a period of time. However, after the judgment of the House of Lords in *Litster*, the EAT in *Macer v Abafast Ltd* [1990] ICR 234 did not follow the approach adopted in *Brook Lane*.

In *Celtec Ltd v Astley* C-478/03 [2005] ICR 1409 the ECJ considered a reference from the House of Lords which raised this issue. It recognised that a transfer may take place over a period of time. However, there is a 'date of a transfer' and this must be understood a referring to the date on which responsibility as employer for carrying on the business of the unit in question moves from the transferor to the transferee. The ECJ was clear that the date of the transfer cannot be postponed to another date at the will of either party. This judgment was applied by the House of Lords at [2006] ICR 992.

52.13 **THE AUTOMATIC ASSIGNMENT OF CONTRACTS OF EMPLOYMENT AND ASSOCIATED RIGHTS AND LIABILITIES**

The most drastic consequences of a transfer of an undertaking are specified in *reg 4*. Those of the transferor's employees:

(i)   who were employed by the transferor immediately before the transfer; and

(ii)   whose contracts would otherwise have been terminated by the transfer,

automatically become, from the moment of the transfer, employed by the transferee on the terms and conditions which they enjoyed with the transferor. This is subject only to an employee's right of objection (see 52.16 below); it cannot be prevented by an intention on the part of the transferor and transferee, or agreement between them, to the contrary (*Hertaing v Benoidt*: C-305/94 [1997] IRLR 127), nor by ignorance on the part of the employee of the transfer or identity of the transferee (*Secretary of State for Trade and Industry v Cook* [1997] ICR 288) disapproving the decision of the EAT to the contrary in *Photostatic Copiers (Southern) Ltd v Okuda* [1995] IRLR 11. With certain specified exceptions, all the transferor's rights and liabilities connected with their contracts of employment are likewise assigned to the transferee, and anything done by the transferor prior to the transfer in relation to those employees or their contracts is deemed to have been done by the transferee.

Under the *Regulations*, an 'employee' covers an individual who works for another person under a contract of employment or apprenticeship, or otherwise, but does not include an independent contractor (*reg 2(1)*). The words 'or otherwise' in the definition do not exclude the fact that there must be a contract between the individual and the transferor. Thus, the *Regulations* did not apply on the reorganisation of a school by its governing body since the teacher was employed by the local education authority and not the governing body (*Governing Body of Clifton Middle School v Askew* [2000] ICR 286, CA). In *Morris Angel & Son Ltd v Hollande* [1993] ICR 71 Dillon LJ queried whether the unique nature of a managing director's position might mean that employment in that capacity was incapable of being transferred, but the correctness of this suggestion is doubted.

52.14 **Immediately before the transfer**

Regulation 4(1) applies to a person employed in an undertaking or part of one transferred, provided that he is so employed immediately before the transfer or would have been so employed if he had not been dismissed in the circumstances described in *reg 7*, that is for a reason which is the transfer itself or a reason connected with the transfer (*reg 4(3)*). This enshrines the approach adopted by the House of Lords in *Litster v Forth Dry Dock and Engineering Co Ltd* [1989] ICR 341: if the dismissal in fact took place solely or principally because of the prospective transfer, then the employee would be deemed to have been employed immediately before the transfer. Their Lordships accepted the reasoning of the

European Court of Justice in *P Bork International A/S v Foreningen af Arbejdsle-deren i Danmark*: 101/87 [1989] IRLR 41, namely, that the fact that *Directive 77/187* prohibited dismissal because of a transfer (see 52.25 below) meant that a dismissal in breach of that prohibition could not effectively exclude the operation of the *Regulations*. See also *Macer v Abafast Ltd* [1990] ICR 234, where the EAT warned in a similar context that the courts would lean against artificial attempts to break continuity; and *Harrison Bowden Ltd v Bowden* [1994] ICR 186 and *A & G Tuck Ltd v Bartlett* [1994] ICR 379. However, contrast *Longden v Ferrari Ltd* [1994] ICR 443, where the EAT held that a succession of events over a period of a few weeks, causally connected to one another, were not a series of transactions by which a transfer of the employers' undertaking was 'effected' and that the transfer was effected only by the final act, a single agreement for sale. As a consequence, the employees (dismissed nearly two weeks before the agreement) were not employed 'immediately before the transfer', even though they were dismissed after the agreement had been submitted in draft.

Regulation 4(3) also deals with cases where there is more than one transaction by which the transfer is effected, and provides that *reg 4* catches any person employed immediately before any of the transactions in question.

Where an employee has been dismissed at the time of the transfer but is subsequently reinstated on appeal, he is deemed to have been employed immediately before the transfer and so transfer to the transferee: *G4S Justice Services v Anstey* [2006] IRLR 575.

52.15 **'Would otherwise have been terminated'**

Regulation 4 transfers the contracts of employment of those, and only those, whose contracts of employment would otherwise have been terminated by the transfer. The contracts of employment of individuals employed in a part of the undertaking which is not being transferred will not be assigned by the *Regulations* to the transferee. It may be that an employee will also not be transferred if his contract contains a clause whereby he may be required to work in a part of the undertaking which is not being transferred.

A difficult question may arise if the employee divides his time between two or more parts of the undertaking, some but not all of which are transferred. In *Botzen v Rotterdamsche Droogdok Maatschappij BV*: 186/83 [1986] 2 CMLR 50 the Advocate General of the ECJ suggested that an employee could only be transferred if he worked wholly or almost wholly in the part transferred, but it is also possible that the court would apply a test of where the employee was predominantly employed. See also *Northern General Hospital NHS Trust Ltd v Gale* [1994] ICR 426; *Sunley Turriff Holdings Ltd v Thomson* [1995] IRLR 184; *Michael Peters Ltd v Farnfield* [1995] IRLR 190; *Duncan Web Offset (Maidstone) Ltd v Cooper* [1995] IRLR 633; and *Buchanan-Smith v Schleicher & Co International Ltd* [1996] ICR 613. In *CPL Distribution Ltd v Todd* [2002] EWCA Civ 1481, [2003] IRLR 28, the Court of Appeal upheld a decision that a personal assistant was not assigned to the part of an undertaking transferred, even though the majority of her work related to the contract transferred. The employee was effectively assigned to a particular manager and there was no evidence that the manager was assigned to the undertaking transferred since a substantial part of his time was involved in other activities.

52.16 **The employee's right of objection**

In *Katsikas v Konstantinidis* [1993] IRLR 179 the ECJ held that an employee could not be transferred to the employment of a new employer against his will. As a result, *reg 4(7)* provides that the transfer of the contract of employment and rights, powers, duties and liabilities under and in connection with it will not occur if the employee informs the transferor or the transferee that he objects to becoming employed by the transferee. In that event, the transfer will terminate the employee's contract of employment with the transferor, but he will not be treated for any purpose as having been dismissed by the transferor (*reg 4(8)*).

The ECJ held, however, in *Merckx v Ford Motors Co Belgium* [1997] ICR 352 that where an employee resigns prior to a transfer because the transferee refuses to guarantee his level of remuneration after the transfer, his 'employer' is to be treated, under *art 4(2)* of the *Directive*, as having dismissed him. In *P & O Property Ltd v Allen* [1997] ICR 436 the EAT held that the 'employer' responsible for the dismissal in these circumstances is the transferee. The EAT has held that an employee objects to his employment being transferred if he refuses to give his consent to the transfer, and that refusal is communicated to the transferor or transferee prior to the transfer (*Hay v George Hanson (Building Contractors) Ltd* [1996] IRLR 427).

In *Senior Heat Treatment Ltd v Bell* [1997] IRLR 614 an employee who 'opted out' of the transfer and accepted a severance payment from the transferor was found not to have objected within the meaning of the *Regulations*. He had accepted employment with the transferee from the date of transfer and so his contract of employment had not terminated.

Under the *Regulations*, where a relevant transfer involves or would involve a substantial change in the working conditions to the material detriment of a person whose employment contract is or would be transferred, such an employee may treat the contract as having been terminated. If he does so, the employee shall be treated for any purpose as having been dismissed by the employer, although no damages are payable by the employer in respect of wages otherwise payable in respect of a notice period which the employee has failed to work (*reg 4(9)* and (*10*)).

In any event, an employee retains the right to resign in response to a repudiatory breach of contract by his employer (*reg 4(11)*).

Relying upon the decision in *Merckx*, the Court of Appeal in *University of Oxford v Humphreys* [2000] ICR 405 emphasised that it is necessary to distinguish the case where an employee objects to his transfer under what is now *reg 4(7)* and will not then be able to claim that he has been dismissed, from the case where an employee treats his contract as terminated by the employer. In the latter case, the employee could seek compensation.

52.17 **What the transferee acquires**

As noted above, the transferee inherits those employees employed by the transferor immediately before the transfer on their existing terms and conditions, assuming that they do not object in accordance with 52.16 above. He has no power to impose, without the agreement of the individual employee (see 52.28 below), any different terms and conditions from those he has inherited from the transferor (see 52.26 below). Equally, the transferred employee has no right to insist that he be given the benefit of any superior terms and conditions enjoyed by the transferee's existing staff (except possibly by means of a claim for EQUAL PAY (24)).

For the effect of a transfer upon restrictive covenants expressed in terms of the transferor's customers, see *Morris Angel & Son Ltd v Hollande* [1993] ICR 71; see also 52.29 below and RESTRAINT OF TRADE, CONFIDENTIALITY AND EMPLOYEE INVENTIONS (41). For the effect of a transfer on the question whether employees are redundant, see *Chapman and Elkin v CPS Computer Group plc* [1987] IRLR 462. For the effect of a transfer on an employee's normal retiring age, see *Cross v British Airways* [2006] EWCA Civ 549, [2006] ICR 1239.

52.18 The transferee inherits all accrued rights and liabilities connected with the contract of employment of the transferred employee. This includes liability for negligence and breach of statutory duty (*Taylor v Serviceteam Ltd* [1998] PIQR P201). If, for example, the transferor was in arrears with wages at the time of the transfer, the employee can sue the transferee as if the original liability had been the transferee's. The transferor is relieved of his former obligations without any need for the employee's consent (*Berg and Busschers v Besselsen* [1990] ICR 396). Equally, the transferee can sue an employee for a breach of contract committed against the transferor prior to transfer. The transferee will also inherit all the statutory rights and liabilities which are connected with the individual contract of employment. The transferred employee's period of continuous employment will date from the beginning of his period of employment with the transferor, and the statutory particulars of terms and conditions of employment, which every employer is obliged to issue, must take account of any continuity enjoyed by virtue of the *Regulations*. (As to continuity of employment when a school transfers to grant-maintained status, see *Pickwell v Lincolnshire County Council* [1993] ICR 87.)

Liability for (for example) sex discrimination transfers to the transferee, even though the employee was employed part-time at the time of the transfer and the discrimination concerned the termination of a previous full-time contract (*DJM International Ltd v Nicholas* [1996] IRLR 76). In *Bernadone v Pall Mall Services Group* [2001] ICR 197, the Court of Appeal held that an employee's claim for personal injuries against his former employer was transferred to the new employer, together with the right of the former employer to an indemnity from its insurers: it was an implied term of the employee's contract of employment that he would be protected by insurance, as required by statute and that right to an indemnity fell within *reg 4(2)*. It did not matter whether the employee's claim was pleaded in contract, tort or breach of statutory duty.

Where a contract provides that nationally agreed pay rates will normally be paid by an employer, it is an implied term that the employer must give notice if it intends to depart from that normal situation. That implied term will transfer, so that if a transferee employer fails to give such notice it will be bound to pay a nationally agreed pay increase, even though it is not itself part of the transferor's bargaining structure: *Glendale Managed Services v Graham* [2003] EWCA Civ 773, [2003] IRLR 465.

However, in *Mitie Managed Services Ltd v French* [2002] ICR 1395 the EAT accepted the transferee's argument that the employees' right to benefit from a profit sharing or share option scheme required only that the transferee provide the right to participate in a scheme of 'substantial equivalence, but one which is free from unjust, absurd or impossible features'.

52.19 **Rights and liabilities which are not assigned under the Regulations**

The *Regulations* do not have the effect of assigning:

(*a*)   criminal liabilities (*reg 4(6)*); or

(*b*) rights and liabilities relating to provisions of occupational pension schemes which relate to benefits for old age, invalidity or survivors (*reg 10*).

In *Walden Engineering Co Ltd v Warrener* [1993] ICR 967, the EAT rejected arguments that employees should be entitled to equivalent pension benefits after the transfer. Moreover, it was held by the Court of Appeal in *Adams v Lancashire County Council* [1997] ICR 834 that the *Regulations* and the *Directive* do not cover transfer of future pension rights, that the exclusion of pension rights from the *Regulations* is consistent with the *Directive*, and that therefore there was no duty on a private contractor to provide an occupational pension scheme for former local government catering workers; see *Eidesund v Stavanger Catering A/S*: C-2/95 [1996] IRLR 684. Since the term relating to pension does not transfer under the *Regulations*, time to bring a claim under the *Equal Pay Act 1970* starts to run from the time of the transfer: *Preston v Wolverhampton Healthcare NHS Trust (No 3); Powerhouse Retail Ltd v Burroughs* [2004] EWCA Civ 1281, [2005] ICR 222.

Nor will every liability owed by the transferor to his employee pass on the transfer. If the liability arises from breach of a duty owed to the union – for example, to consult over redundancy under *TULRCA 1992, s 188* (see 37.3 REDUNDANCY – II) – it is not sufficiently connected with the individual's contract and therefore does not pass to the transferee (see *Angus Jowett & Co Ltd v NUTGW* [1985] ICR 646).

However, these exceptions are to be interpreted strictly: *Beckmann v Dynamco Whicheloe Macfarlane Ltd*: C-164/00 [2003] ICR 50. The ECJ ruled that early retirement benefits and benefits intended to enhance the conditions of such retirement did not fall within the meaning of rights to old-age pension schemes and so the obligation to pay such benefits did transfer to the new employer. These principles were applied by the ECJ in *Martin v South Bank University*: C-4/01 [2004] IRLR 74.

Moreover, *ss 257* and *258* of the *Pensions Act 2004* (together with the *Transfer of Employment (Pension Protection) Regulations 2005 (SI 2005/649)*) require a transferee to provide certain pension benefits to employees for whom there was an occupational pension scheme with the transferor.

52.20 TRANSFER OF AN UNDERTAKING AND THE TRADE UNION

Collective agreements

Under *reg 5*, a collective agreement, which:

(*a*) is made between the transferor and a union recognised by the transferor; and

(*b*) applies to an employee whose contract has become automatically assigned to the transferee by virtue of the transfer,

is automatically transferred to the transferee in its application to that employee. Further, anything done by or under or in connection with that agreement by the transferor before the transfer is deemed to have been done by the transferee.

The practical effect of this provision is probably minimal, since collective agreements are in English law presumed to be unenforceable (see *TULRCA 1992, s 179* and 6.2 COLLECTIVE AGREEMENTS) unless, which is rare, the contrary is stated in the agreement. It is only in this rare case where a binding agreement is entered into that *reg 5* will pass any legal obligation to the transferee. If the terms of a collective agreement are incorporated into the contract of employment of an individual, whose service is automatically assigned on the transfer, then its terms will bind the transferee simply by virtue of the general rule that the transferee inherits the rights and liabilities in the individual's contract: *Whent v T Cartledge Ltd* [1997] IRLR 153. However, a contract which incorporates a collective agreement may not necessarily also incorporate the mechanism for incorporating subsequent agreements: *Ackinclose v Gateshead Metropolitan Borough Council* [2005] IRLR 79. Indeed, the ECJ has recently ruled that any changes made after the transfer are not binding on the transferee if it is not itself a part of the collective bargaining machinery: *Werhof v Freeway Traffic Systems GmbH & Co KG*: Case C-499/04 [2006] IRLR 400.

Regulation 5(b) provides that any order made in respect of a collective agreement transferred under *reg 5* takes effect as if the transferee were a party to the agreement. In effect, this means that awards of the Central Arbitration Committee ('CAC') made against the transferor are binding against the transferee to the extent that they previously bound the transferor.

52.21 Recognition

Where the transferor recognises a union in respect of employees in the undertaking or part of the undertaking to be transferred and, following the transfer, the undertaking or part of the undertaking transferred maintains an identity distinct from the rest of the transferee's business or businesses, the transferee must recognise the union in respect of those employees (*reg 6*).

Although machinery for enforcing trade union recognition has now been repealed and there is no penalty under the *Regulations* for refusal to recognise, or for withdrawal of recognition, the transfer of recognition may be significant when a transferred employee seeks to invoke against the transferee a right which is dependent on the existence of a recognised union, eg the right to take time off for trade union activities under *TULRCA 1992, s 170* (see 49.3 TIME OFF WORK).

52.22 Information and consultation

Employee Liability Information

Regulations 11 to 16 provide an important code for the provision of information by the transferor to the transferee, and by employers to affected employees.

Regulation 11 imposes a duty on the transferor to notify the transferee of certain information relating to any person employed by him who is assigned to the activity which is the subject of the relevant transfer. The information must be in writing or some other readily accessible form.

That information, defined as 'employee liability information' is:

(*a*)   the identity and age of the employee;

(*b*)   the information specified in *s 1* of the *Employment Rights Act 1996* (see 8.5 CONTRACT OF EMPLOYMENT);

(*c*)   information of any disciplinary action taken against the employee and of any grievance raised by them within the previous two years to which the *Employment Act 2002 (Dispute Resolution) Regulations 2004* apply (see DISPUTE RESOLUTION (15));

(*d*)   information relating to actual or potential claims against the transferor;

(*e*)   information of any collective agreement which will apply to the employee pursuant to *reg 5*.

This information must also be provided in relation to an employee who has resigned because of the transfer (or for a reason connected to it): *reg 11(4)*.

This information must be provided not less than fourteen days before the relevant transfer, unless there are special circumstances which mean that this is not reasonably practicable, in which case it must be given as soon as reasonably practicable thereafter: *reg 11(6)*.

If the transferor fails to comply with this obligation, the transferee may present a complaint to an employment tribunal. If successful, the tribunal may make an award of compensation to the transferee, such as is just and equitable in particular having regard to any loss sustained by the transferor which is attributable to the breach and the terms of any contract between transferor and transferee which provide for the payment of such a sum in any event. The minimum level of such an award is, however, fixed at £500 per employer (subject to a discretion to award a lower figure if the tribunal considers that just and equitable).

52.23 *Information and consultation of employees*

Under *reg 13*, the employer of employees affected by the transfer, whether he is the transferor or transferee, must inform all the appropriate representatives of any of the affected employees, long enough before the transfer to enable consultations to take place between the employer and those representatives, of the following:

(*a*)   the fact that a relevant transfer is to take place;

(*b*)   when it is to take place;

(*c*)   the reasons for it;

(*d*)   the legal, economic and social implications of the transfer for affected employees;

(*e*)   the measures which he envisages taking in relation to those employees (and if no measures are envisaged, that fact);

(*f*)   if the employer is the transferor, the measures which the transferee envisages that he will take in relation to those employees who are to be automatically assigned to him on the transfer (or if no measures are envisaged, that fact).

Appropriate representatives are representatives of an independent trade union recognised by the employer for employees of that description. If there is no such union then the appropriate representatives are, at the employer's choice, either (i) employee representatives elected by the affected employees for this purpose in an election complying with the requirements of *reg 14*, or (ii) employee representatives appointed or elected by the affected employees for some other purpose but who have authority from those employees to receive information and to be consulted about the proposed dismissals on their behalf (*reg 13(3)(b)*). If there are no appropriate representatives at the relevant time, the employer is under a positive duty to invite the affected employees to elect employee representatives for this purpose: *Howard v Millrise Ltd* [2005] ICR 435.

If a question arises as to whether or not any employee representative was an appropriate representative, it is for the employer to show that the employee representative had the necessary authority to represent the affected employees (*reg 15(3)*).

Regulation 14 sets out the requirements for the election of employee representatives under *reg 13(3)*. In particular, all affected employees on the date of the election are entitled to vote for employee representatives and so far as reasonably practicable the vote should be in secret. It is for the employer to show that the requirements of *reg 14* have been satisfied (*reg 15(4)*). If the employer has invited affected employees to elect representatives and they fail to do so within a reasonable time, then the employer must give the information required by *reg 13(2)* to each affected employee (*reg 13(11)*).

Employee representatives are afforded special protection in certain circumstances. They have the right not to be subjected to any detriment on the ground that they perform or propose to perform any function or activity as an employee representative (*ERA 1996, s 47*, as amended by *SI 1999/1925*) and any dismissal of an employee representative on that ground is automatically unfair (*ERA 1996, s 103*, as amended by *SI 1999/1925*). They have the right to take reasonable time off (which is paid) in order to perform their functions as an employee representative (*ERA 1996, ss 61–63*).

These provisions (as enacted in another context) were extensively discussed in *Institution of Professional Civil Servants v Secretary of State for Defence* [1987] IRLR 373, which is authority for several of the propositions referred to below, although not all of them were essential to the decision.

The transferee must give the transferor the information necessary to enable him to comply in time with sub-para (*f*) above (*reg 13(4)*). But the transferee is under no *obligation* to envisage any measures, and sometimes he may envisage them too late for there to be compliance with sub-para (*f*).

The information to be given to the representatives is to be delivered to them personally or (in the case of union representatives) sent by post to the union's head office or other address notified by the representatives (*reg 13(5)*).

If either the transferor or the transferee envisages that he will take measures in relation to any of the affected employees, he must enter into consultation with their appropriate representatives with a view to seeking their agreement to measures to be taken. (This is the only *obligation* to consult. Although, as stated above, there are other obligations to give information in time for consultation, consultation itself is voluntary in those cases.) The measures referred to must be definite plans or proposals, not mere hopes or possibilities, and must be such as would not have happened but for the transfer. The information to be disclosed does not include the calculations and assumptions underlying those plans. Consultation involves considering and replying to representations made by the representatives and, insofar as representations are rejected, stating the reasons for the rejection. Reasons need not be given in writing, though this may be advisable. It is as yet unclear how the content of the obligation has been affected by the addition of the stipulation that the consultation must be with a view to seeking agreement (*reg 13(6)*).

If an employer fails to inform or consult, then a complaint may be made to an employment tribunal by the trade union (where the failure relates to trade union representatives) or by the employee representatives or any of them (where the failure relates to employee representatives) or by any of his employees who are affected employees (where the failure relates to the election of employee representatives and in any other case) (*reg 15(1)*). If it is not reasonably practicable to bring the complaint within three months, it may be presented within a reasonable time thereafter (*reg 15(12)*; and see 20.7 EMPLOYMENT TRIBUNALS – I). There is no need to wait for the transfer to take place before presenting the complaint

(*South Durham Health Authority v Unison* [1995] ICR 495), and it appears that the complaint may proceed even if in fact the transfer never takes place (*Banking Insurance and Finance Union v Barclays Bank plc* [1987] ICR 495).

Where a complaint succeeds, the tribunal must make a declaration to this effect and may order the employer to pay compensation to affected employees (*reg 15(7)*). The maximum payable is 13 weeks' pay for each employee affected (*reg 16(3)*).The transferee is jointly and severally liable with the transferor in respect of compensation payable (*reg 15(9)*). In determining the amount of an award, the tribunal must apply the same approach as it does to protective awards in redundancy cases and in particular follow the guidance of the Court of Appeal in *Susie Radin Ltd v GMB* [2004] IRLR 400 (see *Sweetin v Coral Racing* [2006] IRLR 252; and see 39.6 REDUNDANCY – II).

It is a defence for the employer to show that there were special circumstances which rendered it not reasonably practicable to perform the duty in question, provided that he took whatever steps to perform that duty as were reasonably practicable in the circumstances (*reg 13(9)*). By analogy with the case law on *TULRCA 1992, s 188* (see 39.5 REDUNDANCY – II), an employer is unlikely to show that a failure to inform or consult was due to 'special circumstances' unless the transfer has to be arranged or expedited because of a sudden and unforeseen emergency. However, the tribunal should look at the matter broadly, and ought not ordinarily to grant relief unless the employer has plainly been recalcitrant or neglectful of his obligations.

If a transferor wishes to allege that the reason for his default is the failure of the transferee to supply him with information, he must give the transferee notice of that fact and the transferee must be made a party to the proceedings (*reg 15(5)*).

If an employer fails to pay compensation ordered to be paid by the tribunal, the employee concerned may present a complaint to an employment tribunal (*reg 15(10)*). This is subject to the same time limits as the original complaint under *reg 15(12)*.

52.24 DISMISSAL ON THE TRANSFER OF AN UNDERTAKING

If an individual employed in an undertaking is dismissed:

(*a*)   by the transferor in advance of the transfer of that undertaking; or

(*b*)   by the transferee after the transfer,

he may wish to bring a claim for unfair dismissal, a redundancy payment or wrongful dismissal.

52.25 Unfair dismissal and transfer of an undertaking

Dismissal

In order to complain of unfair dismissal the individual must first show that he has been dismissed within the statutory definition, that is to say:

(*a*)   that his contract of employment has been terminated by the employer (direct dismissal);

(*b*)   that he was employed for a fixed term which has expired and not been renewed; or

(c)   that he resigned in circumstances where he was entitled to do so without notice on account of his employer's conduct (constructive dismissal).

(*ERA 1996, s 95.*)

(For a discussion of the statutory definition of dismissal see 53.4–53.10 UNFAIR DISMISSAL – I.)

The *Regulations* affect the operation of this definition in a number of ways.

First, the transfer itself cannot be treated as a dismissal. As can be seen from 52.9 above, the transfer operates to assign to the transferee the contracts of employment of those who would otherwise have been dismissed upon the transfer. An employee who exercises his right of objection to the transfer (see 52.12 above) will not be treated as having been dismissed. Nor is a transfer a repudiatory breach of contract by the transferor which the employee can obtain an injunction to restrain, at least where the transferor is acting in good faith (*Newns v British Airways plc* [1992] IRLR 575); and see *Sita (GB) Ltd v Burton* [1998] ICR 17.

Second, if the transferor refrains from dismissing employees before the transfer so that they are automatically assigned to the transferee, but the transferee indicates – before the transfer – that he is unwilling to employ them, it appears that the employees will be treated as dismissed by the transferee immediately after the transfer (see *Premier Motors (Medway) Ltd v Total Oil (Great Britain) Ltd* [1984] ICR 58).

Third, if the transferee substantially changes the terms and conditions of employment previously enjoyed by the transferred staff to their detriment, the staff may resign and treat themselves as constructively dismissed. For this purpose, the change must amount to a repudiatory breach of contract (*reg 4(11)*).

Where an employee treats himself as constructively dismissed on the grounds that the transfer will involve a substantial and detrimental change in his terms and conditions of employment the employee's right lies against the transferor (*University of Oxford v Humphreys* [2000] ICR 405). In that case, the Court of Appeal said that it would be inconsistent with the scheme of the *Directive* and the *1981 Regulations* for existing rights and liabilities to pass to the transferee when existing contracts of employment did not.

Fourth, where a relevant transfer involves or would involve a substantial change in working conditions to the material detriment of a person whose contract of employment is or would be transferred, such an employee may treat the contract as having been terminated and the employee shall be treated for any purpose as having been dismissed by the employer (*reg 4(9)*). However, no damages are payable by the employer in respect of any failure by the employer to pay wages to an employee in respect of a notice period which the employee has failed to work.

52.26 *The fairness of the dismissal*

If an employee has been dismissed by either the transferee or the transferor and the reason for the dismissal is he transfer, the dismissal is automatically unfair (*reg 7(1)(a)*).

If an employee has been dismissed by either the transferee or the transferor and the reason for the dismissal is a reason connected with the transfer, the dismissal is automatically unfair unless it qualifies as an 'economic, technical or organisational reason entailing changes in the workforce' of either the transferor or the transferee (*reg 7(1)(b)*). If the reason falls within this category ('an ETO reason') it will be held to be fair and either by reason of redundancy or for some other substantial reason justifying dismissal (*reg 7(3)* and see UNFAIR DISMISSAL – II (54)). The employee's remedy for a breach of *reg 7(1)* is to complain of unfair dismissal. Both transferee and transferor may dismiss employees for an economic, technical or organisational reason (*Jules Dethier Equipement v Dassy* [1998] ICR 541).

Regulation 7(1) must be read in sequence. Consider first whether the transfer was the reason for the dismissal. If so, the dismissal is unfair. Then consider whether the reason for the dismissal was connected with the transfer. If not, there is no need to enquire further; if so, it may be necessary to consider whether the reason for dismissal was an economic, technical or organisational reason. See *Warner v Adnet Ltd* [1998] IRLR 394 and *Collins v John Ansell & Partners Ltd*, IDS Brief 659.

In *Kerry Foods Ltd v Creber* [2000] ICR 556, receivers dismissed all of the employees of an undertaking prior to its transfer. The employment tribunal found that the reason for this dismissal was the transfer. The EAT ruled that the tribunal should then have concluded that (by reason of the *Litster* principle – see 52.10 above) the employees were employed in the undertaking immediately before the transfer, that their employment was transferred and the transferee was then treated as having dismissed them. However, if the main reason for the dismissal is an ETO reason within *reg 7(1)(b)*, then the employee is not deemed to have been employed immediately before the transfer, his employment does not transfer and his only remedy for unfair dismissal is against the transferor. If the dismissal is in fact effected by the transferee, then the employee's remedy lies against the transferee, which may itself invoke an ETO reason.

In *Wilson v St Helens Borough Council* [1999] 2 AC 52 the House of Lords (reversing the decision of the Court of Appeal) held that an actual dismissal before, on or after the transfer is effective, even where the transfer (or a reason connected with it) was the reason for the dismissal. The dismissal is not a nullity and the employee cannot compel the transferee to employ him on the same terms and conditions as those on which the transferor employed him.

For the transfer or a reason connected with it to be the reason for dismissal within *reg 7(1)*, it is not necessary that the employer had in mind a specific transferee at the time of the dismissal (*Morris v John Grose Group Ltd* [1998] ICR 655).

The passage of time may increase the chances that the chain of causation between the transfer and the reason for the dismissal has been broken; however, the mere passage of time without anything happening does not in itself constitute a weakening to the point of dissolution of the chain of causation: *Taylor v Connex South Eastern Ltd*, IDS Brief 670, p 10.

The reason for dismissal may be connected with the transfer, even though the employee dismissed was never employed in the undertaking or part transferred (*reg 7(4)*). If, for example, the transferee dismisses his existing staff to accommodate the employees he is to inherit from the transferor, or if the job of an existing employee disappears following a reorganisation consequent upon the transfer, the dismissal will nonetheless be connected with the transfer.

It appears that a transferor may not invoke the defence of an 'organisational' or 'economic' reason where a transferee is willing to acquire the undertaking only on terms that the transferor's staff are first dismissed, because the reason must relate to the conduct of the business for those words to apply (*Wheeler v Patel* [1987]

ICR 631 and *Gateway Hotels Ltd v Stewart* [1988] IRLR 287, not following *Anderson v Dalkeith Engineering Ltd* [1986] ICR 66. See also *Ibex Trading Co Ltd v Walton* [1994] ICR 907).

Whitehouse v Blatchford & Sons Ltd [2000] ICR 542 concerned a transfer following the award of a new contract for the provision of services to a hospital. It was a stipulation of that contract that the number of employees be reduced. The applicant was dismissed following the transfer. The Court of Appeal held that the employment tribunal had been entitled to find that the applicant's dismissal was for an economic, technical or organisational reason. If the trans-feree had not complied with the stipulation then it would not have won the contract. The court followed *Wheeler v Patel*: the reason must be connected with the future conduct of the business as a going concern. See also *Thompson v SCS Consulting Ltd* [2001] IRLR 801. A transferor cannot dismiss and then rely upon the future conduct of the business by the transferee after the transfer in an attempt to establish an ETO reason; the transferor itself has no intention of continuing the business and so the reason for the dismissal does not relate to its future conduct of the business: *Hynd v Armstrong* [2007] CSIH 16, [2007] IRLR 338 (Court of Session, Inner House).

The EAT has held that when a transferor gives notice of termination to employees before a transfer takes place and the notice expires after the transfer, it is the transferor's reasons for the dismissals which should be examined in determining whether the transferee can be held to have unfairly dismissed the employees (*BSG Property Services v Tuck* [1996] IRLR 134).

The words 'entailing changes in the workforce' impose important limitations on the defence of 'economic, technical or organisational reason'. It is only when the employer sets out to change the structure of his workforce, by reducing numbers or changing the functions which individuals perform, that the reason will entail a change in the workforce. Hence, the employer cannot fairly dismiss transferred employees who will not agree to changes in their old terms and conditions of employment (see *Berriman v Delabole Slate Ltd* [1985] ICR 546; *Crawford v Swinton Insurance Brokers Ltd* [1990] ICR 85; *Porter and Nanayakkara v Queen's Medical Centre (Nottingham University Hospital)* [1993] IRLR 486).

There is, however, no limitation on the defence of 'economic, technical or organisational reason' that the dismissal would have been made in any case, for instance pursuant to a decision taken before there was any question of transfer-ring the undertaking (*Trafford v Sharpe & Fisher (Building Supplies) Ltd* [1994] IRLR 325, not following Advocate-General Van Gerven in *D'Urso v Ercole Marelli Elettromeccanica Generale SpA*: C-362/89 [1992] IRLR 136).

If an employer brings the case within the category of economic, technical or organisational reason entailing changes in the workforce, it will remain to be considered whether he acted reasonably in the circumstances. The considerations which will be relevant must vary with the circumstances of the individual case. It is fair to assume, however, that a failure to offer the employee an available job in some part of the business not affected by the economic technical or organisa-tional problem in question, or a failure to consult the employee, will be grounds on which such dismissals may sometimes be considered unfair.

52.27 Redundancy payments

An employee dismissed by reason of redundancy is, subject to various qualifying conditions, entitled to a redundancy payment (see REDUNDANCY – I (38)). He is dismissed by reason of redundancy if the principal reason is that his employer has ceased or intends to cease carrying on business in the place where the employee was employed or if there is a diminution in the requirements of the employer's business for the work of the particular kind for which the employee is employed.

An employee whose contract is automatically assigned under the *Regulations* will not be dismissed by the transferor and cannot therefore become entitled to a redundancy payment unless and until he is dismissed by the transferee by reason of redundancy.

If, however:

(*a*)   an employee is dismissed by the transferor in advance of the transfer by reason of the fact that the transferor is to go out of business in the place where the employee was employed or no longer requires work of the particular kind done by the employee; or

(*b*)   following the transfer, the transferee dismisses the employee for either of these reasons,

the employee is, on the face of it, entitled to a redundancy payment.

Despite decisions of the EAT in Scotland to the contrary, the Employment Appeal Tribunal in England has now confirmed that the employee will, in these circumstances, qualify for a redundancy payment even though the reason for his dismissal may qualify as an economic, technical or organisational reason entailing changes in the workforce. In *Gorictree Ltd v Jenkinson* [1985] ICR 51, it was held that the dismissal does not cease to be by reason of redundancy merely because it also qualifies as an economic, technical or organisational reason under the *Regulations*. It is likely that this decision, and not the earlier Scottish decisions, will be followed in future.

52.28   AVOIDING THE REGULATIONS AND THEIR CONSEQUENCES

An agreement to exclude or limit the application of the *Regulations* is invalid (*reg 18*). The transferor and transferee may, however, validly agree that one shall indemnify the other for sums payable in consequence of the operation of the *Regulations*. In practice, it is quite common for transferees to take such indemnities from transferors.

The principle of automatic transfer may not be derogated from by a collective agreement with a trade union (*D'Urso v Ercole Marelli Elettromeccanica Generale SpA* [1992] IRLR 136), nor on account of the business being in critical difficulties (*Spano v Fiat Geotech SpA*: C-472/93 [1995] ECR I-4321, ECJ).

Where an employee's employment contract is brought to an end, a compromise agreement will be effective and is not an agreement which purports to exclude or limit the operation of the *Regulations*: *Solectron Scotland Ltd v Roper* [2004] IRLR 4.

52.29   Variation of employees' contracts after transfer of an undertaking

Although an employee cannot waive the benefit of the *Regulations*, there may be an agreed variation to the terms and conditions of employment following the transfer provided that the reason for the change is not the transfer itself or is a reason connected with the transfer that is an economic, technical or organisation reason entailing changes in the workforce (*reg 4(4)* and (*5*) developing principles established in *Martin v South Bank University*: C-4/01 [2004] IRLR 74; *Foreningen af Arbejdsledere i Danmark v Daddy's Dance Hall A/S*: 324/86 [1988] IRLR 315);

cf the judgment of the EAT in *Power v Regent Security Services Ltd* [2007] IRLR 226, applying the *1981 Regulations*, which did not have provisions equivalent to *reg 4(4)* and (*5*)).

The ECJ has ruled that the *Directive* does not preclude a public body, as a transferee, from reducing the pay of its incoming staff where it is necessary to do so in order to comply with national rules in force for public employees. However, if the variation is sufficiently detrimental, then the employees will be entitled to resign and claim that the employer was responsible for their dismissal (under *art 4(2)*).

In *Cornwall County Care Ltd v Brightman* [1998] ICR 529, employees were dismissed by the transferee after the transfer and re-employed on less favourable terms and conditions. The EAT held that they had been unfairly dismissed since the reason for the dismissals had been the transfer. However, the employees had 'accepted' the new terms and conditions by continuing to work for the transferee. They were unable to continue to claim a right to their original terms and conditions – that claim was 'bought out' by the compensation for unfair dismissal. A change in terms and conditions brought about merely because of the expiry of employees' fixed-term contract may be effective: *Ralton v Havering College of Further and Higher Education* [2001] IRLR 738. The tribunal had been right to apply the test of whether the variation was solely by reason of the transfer.

53   Unfair Dismissal – I: The Right to Make a Claim

(See also DTI website http://www.dti.gov.uk/employment/Resolving_disputes/unfair-dismissal/index.html.)

Cross-references. See TERMINATION OF EMPLOYMENT (48) for the various ways of terminating the contract at common law; UNFAIR DISMISSAL – II (54) for whether the dismissal was fair; UNFAIR DISMISSAL – III (55) for remedies for unfair dismissal; WRONGFUL DISMISSAL (58) for dismissals in breach of contract.

53.1   The *Employment Protection (Consolidation) Act 1978* (*'EPCA 1978'*) re-enacted a right originally created by the *Industrial Relations Act 1971* – the right not to be unfairly dismissed. The right not to be unfairly dismissed has been re-enacted in the *Employment Rights Act 1996* (*'ERA 1996'*). *ERA 1996* is a consolidation Act, so the rights thereunder are exactly the same as those which previously existed under *EPCA 1978* and the old case law remains relevant.

An employer who dismisses an employee without good reason or without following a fair procedure lays itself open to a claim for unfair dismissal. When such a claim is brought, the employer has to establish the reason for the dismissal. The employment tribunal will then consider whether the dismissal was fair in all the circumstances, neither party having the evidential burden in this enquiry. If the dismissal is held to be unfair, the employer can be ordered to re-engage, reinstate or to pay compensation to the ex-employee. The parties to a claim for unfair dismissal are known as the *claimant* (employee) and the *respondent* (employer). The claimant was formerly called the applicant.

53.2   PRE-CONDITIONS OF A CLAIM

A complaint of unfair dismissal must be presented to an employment tribunal before the end of the period of three months beginning with the effective date of termination of the employment (or within such further period as the tribunal considers reasonable in a case where it is satisfied that it was not reasonably practicable for the complaint to be presented within the period of three months) (*ERA 1996, s 111(2)*). In certain circumstances, an employee benefits from a limitation period of six months from the effective date of termination of the employment (*EA 2002, s 32* and *Employment Act 2002 (Dispute Resolution) Regulations 2004, reg 15*). (See further 20.19–20.20 EMPLOYMENT TRIBUNALS – I; DISPUTE RESOLUTION (15) and 53.13 below for effective date of termination.)

A claimant must also satisfy the conditions set out below if he wishes to bring a claim for unfair dismissal. If these conditions are not disputed by the respondent, no evidence need be brought by the claimant to establish them. If, however, there are grounds for suspecting that any of those necessary prerequisites is absent, the employment tribunal will inquire into the matter, as it affects their jurisdiction to hear the case. The burden is on the claimant to show that he satisfies those conditions. The conditions are:

(*a*)   that the claimant was employed by the respondent under a contract of employment (see 53.3 below);

(*b*)   that the claimant was dismissed, as defined (see 53.4 below);

(c)   in most cases, that the claimant was employed for the necessary qualifying period (see 53.11 below). (The employer may sometimes argue that a claim cannot be brought because the employee did not work for the qualifying period under a *lawful* contract (see 53.16 below).); and

(d)   that the claimant has met the requirements of *s 32* of the *Employment Act 2002*.

In addition, certain employees are excluded from the right not to be unfairly dismissed:

(i)   certain specified classes of employees (see 53.15 below);

(ii)   those dismissed in connection with a lock-out or unofficial strike and, in some cases, persons dismissed in connection with an official strike, provided certain conditions are satisfied (see 53.17, 53.18 below).

Note that from 1 October 2006 employees over retirement age are no longer excluded from the right to complain of unfair dismissal. Special rules apply to dismissals by reason of retirement (see 53.14 below and 3.47–3.48).

In addition, certain employees are excluded from the right not to be unfairly dismissed:

(i)   certain specified classes of employees (see 53.15 below);

(ii)   those dismissed in connection with a lock-out or unofficial strike and, in some cases, persons dismissed in connection with an official strike, provided certain conditions are satisfied (see 53.17, 53.18 below).

53.3   EMPLOYMENT BY THE RESPONDENT

In order to bring a claim for unfair dismissal, a claimant must show that he was employed by the respondent under a contract of employment (*ERA 1996, ss 94(1), 230(1)*). Therefore, sub-contractors or consultants under contracts for services are not protected by the unfair dismissal provisions even though they may work regularly for one person or organisation. See EMPLOYEE, SELF-EMPLOYED OR WORKER? (17).

The *Employment Relations Act 1999, s 23* gives the Secretary of State the power to extend the right not to be unfairly dismissed to individuals who do not fit the current definition of 'employee'.

53.4   DISMISSAL BY THE RESPONDENT

An employee is treated as having been dismissed if, but only if:

(a)   the contract under which he is employed by the employer is terminated by the employer, whether it is so terminated by notice or without notice;

(b)   where under that contract he is employed for a fixed term, that term expires without being renewed under the same contract; or

(c)   the employee terminates that contract with or without notice in circumstances such that he is entitled to terminate it without notice by reason of the employer's conduct (usually called 'constructive dismissal').

(*ERA 1996, s 95(1)*.)

The contract of employment of an employee who is on ordinary or additional maternity leave or parental leave is deemed to continue whilst he or she is on leave, with appropriate amendments (*ERA 1996, s 71* and *Maternity and Parental Leave, etc Regulations 1999 (SI 1999/3312), reg 17)*. It follows that if an employer does not permit the employee to return at the end of the leave or acts in repudiatory breach of contract during the leave period (and the employee accepts the repudiation), the employee will be treated as having been dismissed (see further 33.20 MATERNITY AND PARENTAL RIGHTS).

53.5   Termination by the employer

Notice of dismissal, once accepted, cannot generally be withdrawn (*Riordan v War Office* [1959] 1 WLR 1046). Thus, an employer who gives notice to an employee which is accepted cannot thereafter withdraw that notice without the consent of the employee. The same principle applies to notice of resignation given by the employee. For possible exceptions to the general rule, see 53.10(B) below.

Where an employer gives notice to an employee to terminate his contract of employment and, at a time within the period of that notice, the employee gives notice to the employer to terminate the contract of employment on a date earlier than the date on which the employer's notice is due to expire, the employee will nevertheless be taken to have been dismissed by his employer for the purposes of an unfair dismissal claim. The reasons for the dismissal are then taken to be the reasons for which the employer's notice was given (*ERA 1996, s 95(2)*). According to the EAT, an employer may vary the notice of dismissal which determines the effective day of termination, with the effect of bringing forward that date (*Palfrey v Transco plc* [2004] IRLR 916). If an employee gives notice to terminate his employment and, during that period of notice, the employer summarily dismisses him, the employee will be considered to have been dismissed despite the fact that he first gave notice to terminate his contract (*Harris and Russell Ltd v Slingsby* [1973] 3 All ER 31). However, if, after the employee has given notice, the employer takes advantage of a contractual right to make a payment in lieu of notice, there is no dismissal (even if the employee is thereby deprived of commission income) (*Marshall (Cambridge) Ltd v Hamblin* [1994] ICR 362, [1994] IRLR 260).

A contract of employment is only terminated by an employer if there is a specified or ascertainable date on which the contract is to cease (*Haseltine Lake & Co v Dowler* [1981] ICR 222). Dismissal, to be effective, must be communicated to the employee (*Hindle Gears Ltd v McGinty* [1985] ICR 111).

An employer is not entitled to deny that there was a dismissal merely because the individual who dismissed the employee did not in fact have the authority to do so (*Warnes v Trustees of Cheriton Oddfellows Social Club* [1993] IRLR 58).

A very substantial departure by an employer from an original contract of employment may amount to termination of that contract of employment and its replacement by the offer of a different and inferior contract. In such cases, there is a termination by the employer, rather than a constructive dismissal (see 53.7 below; *Alcan Extrusions v Yates* [1996] IRLR 327).

53.6   Expiry of a fixed-term contract

It used to be thought that a fixed-term contract was one which did not contain a provision for prior determination by notice. However, in *Dixon v BBC* [1979] ICR 281, the Court of Appeal held that the words 'a fixed term' include a specified stated term even though the contract is determinable by notice within its term. A contract which is expressed to terminate on the occurrence of a specified event at some uncertain future time is not a contract for a fixed term within the meaning of the *ERA 1996* (*Wiltshire County Council v National Association of Teachers in Further and Higher Education* [1980] ICR 455). Thus, the termination of the contract when that event occurs is not a dismissal (see also 53.10(D) and 53.15(C) below). *Regulation 1* of the *Fixed-term Employees* (*Prevention of Less Favourable Treatment*) *Regulations 2002* (*SI 2002/2034*) provides that a fixed-term contract is a contract of employment that, under its provisions determining how it will terminate in the normal course, will terminate – (a) on the expiry of a specific term, (b) on the completion of a particular task, or (c) on the occurrence or non-occurrence of any other specific event other than the attainment by the employee of any normal and *bona fide* retiring age in the establishment for an employee holding the position held by him. (see LESS FAVOURABLE TREATMENT OF PART-TIME WORKERS (32)).

53.7 Constructive dismissal

In order to establish that he has been constructively dismissed, an employee must show the following:

(i) His employer has committed a serious breach of the contract – this is known as a repudiatory breach (*Western Excavating (ECC) Ltd v Sharp* [1978] ICR 221). It is not enough to show merely that the employer has behaved unreasonably. However, the line between serious unreasonableness and a breach of the implied term of trust and confidence (see 8.12 CONTRACT OF EMPLOYMENT) is a fine one (see eg *Sheridan v Stanley Cole (Wainfleet) Ltd* [2003] ICR 297, [2003] IRLR 52). Every breach of the implied term of trust and confidence is a repudiatory breach of contract (*Morrow v Safeway Stores* [2002] IRLR 9). The breach of contract may be an *anticipatory* rather than an *actual* one, ie even though no breach has yet occurred, it is sufficient if the employer has indicated a clear intention not to fulfil the terms of the contract in the future, and the employee accepts that intention to commit a breach as bringing the contract to an end (*Norwest Holst Group Administration Ltd v Harrison* [1985] ICR 668; *Greenaway Harrison Ltd v Wiles* [1994] IRLR 380). However, in *Kerry Goods Ltd v Lynch* [2005] IRLR 680 the EAT held that an employee had resigned prematurely in response to his employer's notice that it intended to terminate his employment and re-engage him on varied terms to which he had refused to agree. The EAT considered that the giving of lawful notice of termination could not by itself constitute a repudiatory breach of contract. In *Brown v Merchant Ferries Ltd* [1998] IRLR 682, the Northern Ireland Court of Appeal said that, although the correct approach to constructive dismissal is to ask whether the employer was in breach of contract and not whether the employer acted unreasonably, if the employer's conduct is seriously unreasonable, that may provide sufficient evidence that there has been a breach of contract.

(ii) He has left because of the breach (*Walker v Josiah Wedgwood & Sons Ltd* [1978] ICR 744; *Holland v Glendale Industries Ltd* [1998] ICR 493). It was also suggested in *Walker* that the employee must make clear when he resigns that he regards himself as having been constructively dismissed.

(iii) He has not waived the breach (also known as 'affirming' the contract). In other words, he must not delay his resignation too long, or do anything else which indicates acceptance of the changed basis of his employment. See the discussion in *WE Cox Toner (International) Ltd v Crook* [1981] ICR 823, [1981] IRLR 443. Merely to protest at the time will not prevent such acceptance being inferred, although an express reservation of rights may in certain circumstances be effective (see *Bliss v South East Thames Regional Health Authority* [1987] ICR 700; *Waltons & Morse v Dorrington* [1997] IRLR 488).

Examples of breaches of contract upon which a complaint of constructive dismissal might be founded include: a reduction in pay (*Industrial Rubber Products v Gillon* [1977] IRLR 389); a complete change in the nature of the job (*Ford v Milthorn Toleman Ltd* [1980] IRLR 30; *Pedersen v Camden London Borough Council* [1981] ICR 674; *Land Securities Trillium Ltd v Thornley* [2005] IRLR 765); a failure to follow the prescribed disciplinary procedure (*Post Office v Strange* [1981] IRLR 515). See also CONTRACT OF EMPLOYMENT (8).

A complaint of constructive dismissal may be based upon the conduct of a fellow employee even though that employee would not have had the authority to dismiss the complainant; the test is whether the employer is vicariously liable for the conduct complained of (*Hilton International Hotels (UK) Ltd v Protopapa* [1990] IRLR 316; see also *Warnes v Trustees of Cheriton Oddfellows Social Club* [1993] IRLR 58; and VICARIOUS LIABILITY (56)).

The employer may be held to be in repudiatory breach of contract not only if he breaks an express term but also if he infringes an implied term. Thus, an employer will be held guilty of a breach which entitles an employee to resign and claim that he has been constructively dismissed if the employer behaves in a way which destroys the relationship of trust and confidence with his employee (*Bliss*, above) (see also *Wigan Borough Council v Davies* [1979] ICR 411; *Woods v WM Car Services (Peterborough) Ltd* [1982] ICR 693; *Morrow v Safeway Stores* (above); see also *Horkulak v Cantor Fitzgerald International* [2004] IRLR 756 and 942). Even if the employer's act which was the proximate cause of an employee's resignation was not by itself a fundamental breach of contract, the employee may be able to rely upon the employer's course of conduct considered as a whole in establishing that he was constructively dismissed. The 'last straw' must contribute, however slightly, to the breach of trust and confidence (*Waltham Forest London Borough Council v Omilaju* ([2005] IRLR 35). Glidewell LJ conveniently summarised some of the relevant principles in *Lewis v Motorworld Garages Ltd* [1986] ICR 157 at 169D–170A:

> 'If the employer is in breach of an express term of a contract of employment, of such seriousness that the employee would be justified in leaving and claiming constructive dismissal, but the employee does not leave and accepts the altered terms of employment, and if subsequently a series of actions by the employer might constitute together a breach of the implied obligation of trust and confidence, the employee is entitled to treat the original action by the employer which was a breach of the express terms of the contract as a part – the start – of the series of actions which, taken together with the employer's other actions, might cumulatively amount to a breach of the implied terms.'

In *BG plc v O'Brien* [2001] IRLR 496, the EAT rejected an argument that the implied duty of trust and confidence could not impose a positive obligation upon an employer; it held that the employer in that case had breached the duty of trust and confidence by failing to offer him a revised contract of employment when all his colleagues were offered a revised contract. This is a somewhat surprising decision, because it means that the duty of trust and confidence can impose a contractual obligation to vary a contract, but it has been upheld by the Court of Appeal ([2002] IRLR 441). In *Visa International v Paul* [2004] IRLR 42 the duty of trust and confidence was breached by a failure to notify an employee on maternity leave of a new post, for which she was not shortlistable but for which she would have applied.

There is a line of demarcation, however, between an employee's common law cause of action for breach of contract through destroying the relationship of trust and confidence and the employee's statutory complaint of unfair dismissal (see further *Eastwood v Magnox Electric plc* [2004] UKHL 35, [2004] IRLR 733 and 8.13 CONTRACT OF EMPLOYMENT).

Where there is a genuine dispute between parties about the terms of a contract of employment, it is not an *anticipatory breach* of the contract for one party to do no more than argue his point of view (*Financial Techniques (Planning Services) Ltd v Hughes* [1981] IRLR 32; see also *Bridgen v Lancashire County Council* [1987] IRLR 58).

However, there can be a constructive dismissal even where the employer acts on a genuine, although mistaken, belief. So, for example, an employer's action in appointing a replacement for the claimant and in telling customers that the claimant was no longer employed is capable of amounting to a constructive dismissal, even in circumstances where the employer genuinely, although mistakenly, believed that the employee had left (*Brown v JBD Engineering Ltd* [1993] IRLR 568).

The offer of a new contract on less favourable terms upon the expiry of a fixed-term contract cannot amount to a constructive dismissal, because when the offer is made, there is no contract in existence (*Pfaffinger v City of Liverpool Community College* [1997] ICR 142).

A constructive dismissal is not necessarily unfair (*Savoia v Chiltern Herb Farms Ltd* [1982] IRLR 166). The tribunal will look at the conduct of the employer which amounted to the breach of contract and ask whether he acted reasonably, in the usual way (see UNFAIR DISMISSAL – II (54)). However, in practice, it will be harder to demonstrate that a particular action is reasonable where it contravenes the contract of employment.

It is vital to note the statutory dismissal and disciplinary and grievance procedures contained in *EA 2002, Sch 2, paras 6–9* and *EA (Dispute Resolution) Regulations 2004, regs 6–10*. In nearly all cases, it is relevant to ask whether and to what extent an employee has invoked the statutory grievance procedure, and to what extent the employer has complied, when assessing whether or not there has been a constructive dismissal and whether or not such a dismissal was unfair.

53.8   Forced resignation

If an employee resigns in circumstances where he is given no alternative but to resign or be dismissed, he will be considered to have been dismissed for the purposes of unfair dismissal. The question of whether the conduct of the employer caused the employee to leave is one of fact for the employment tribunal (*Martin v MBS Fastenings (Glynwed) Distribution Ltd* [1983] ICR 511). However, telling an employee that he will be dismissed at some unspecified date in the future does not give the employee the right to resign and claim that he has been constructively dismissed if the employer is guilty of no anticipatory breach of contract – the employer may intend to give due notice, and a dismissal giving contractual notice is not, of course, a breach of contract (*Haseltine Lake & Co v Dowler* [1981] ICR 222; see also *Norwest Holst Group Administration Ltd v Harrison* [1985] ICR 668).

If an employee decides to leave because he has negotiated satisfactory terms for his departure, he will be considered to have resigned. In *Sheffield v Oxford Controls Co Ltd* [1979] ICR 396, Arnold J said, at 402:

'It is plain, we think, that there must exist a principle ... that where an employee resigns and that resignation is determined upon by him because he prefers to resign rather than to be dismissed (the alternative having been expressed to him by the employer in the terms of the threat that if he does not resign he will be dismissed), the mechanics of the resignation do not cause that to be other than a dismissal. The cases do not in terms go further than that. We find the principle to be one of causation.'

Sheffield v Oxford Controls was endorsed by the Court of Appeal in *Jones v Mid-Glamorgan County Council* [1997] ICR 815.

The Court of Appeal in *Birch v University of Liverpool* [1985] ICR 470 held that an employee who took advantage of an early retirement scheme was not dismissed. Dismissal does not include termination by mutual consent, however, special rules now apply to dismissal by reason of retirement.

53.9 Repudiatory conduct by the employee

Employers sometimes consider that an employee has 'dismissed himself' by breaching some fundamental term of his contract of employment, such as failing to attend work. This is almost certainly not a correct approach. In *Thomas Marshall (Exports) Ltd v Guinle* [1978] ICR 905, Megarry VC held that an employee's repudiation of his contract of employment had to be accepted by the employer to bring the contract to an end. This 'acceptance' view was approved by a majority of the Court of Appeal in *Gunton v Richmond-upon-Thames London Borough Council* [1980] ICR 755, and by a majority of the Court of Appeal in *London Transport Executive v Clarke* [1981] ICR 355. Similarly, in *Boyo v Lambeth London Borough Council* [1994] ICR 727, the Court of Appeal endorsed the 'acceptance' view of the termination of a contract of employment (see TERMINATION OF EMPLOYMENT (48)).

53.10 Situations of no dismissal

There is *no dismissal* in the following cases.

(a)   *Termination of the contract of employment by consent of both parties* (see 53.8 above).

(b)   *Termination by the employee whether with or without notice* in the absence of 'constructive dismissal' or forced resignation (see 53.7 and 53.8 above). A valid notice given by an employee cannot usually be withdrawn without the employer's consent (*Riordan v War Office* [1959] 3 All ER 552, [1960] 3 All ER 774; *Sothern v Franks Charlesly & Co* [1981] IRLR 278). However, it may be that words of resignation (or dismissal) spoken in the heat of the moment can be regarded as not being a true resignation, or else can be withdrawn if this is done very quickly (*Martin v Yeoman Aggregates Ltd* [1983] ICR 314; *Barclay v City of Glasgow District Council* [1983] IRLR 313).

(c)   *Termination of employment by 'frustration'.* If the contract of employment cannot be performed or if its performance becomes radically different from that contemplated when the contract was entered into, it may be considered to have been terminated by frustration (see further 48.3 TERMINATION OF EMPLOYMENT).

(d)   *Termination on the occurrence of an external event.* A contract for a voyage may be terminated 'automatically' when the voyage is completed (*Ryan v Shipboard Maintenance Ltd* [1980] ICR 88). An appointment for 'as long as sufficient funds are provided either by the Manpower Services Commission or by other firms/sponsors to fund it' was held to come to an end automatically when the specified event took place (*Brown v Knowsley Borough Council* [1986] IRLR 102). See also 53.6 above.

53.11 EMPLOYMENT FOR QUALIFYING PERIOD

From 1 June 1999, the qualifying period for claims of unfair dismissal was reduced from two years to one year (*ERA 1996, s 108(1)* and the *Unfair Dismissal and Statement of Reasons for Dismissal (Variation of Qualifying Period) Order 1999 (SI 1999/1436)*).

In *Seymour-Smith* (*R v Secretary of State for Employment, ex p Seymour-Smith and Perez* [2000] IRLR 263), the applicants had argued that the two-year qualifying period for unfair dismissal claims then in force had a disproportionately adverse effect on women and was inconsistent with the *EC Treaty, art 119*, now *art 141* (equal pay). The European Court of Justice had held that the two-year qualifying period for unfair dismissal claims could be struck down only if there was a considerable difference in the ability of men and women to comply with it, and if the period could not be justified by the Government. The House of Lords in the light of the guidance (such as it was) given by the ECJ ([1999] IRLR 253) decided that the date by reference to which the comparison should be made was the date of the applicants' dismissal in 1991. At that time, 74.5% of men could comply, as against 67.4% of women. Notwithstanding the hint given by the European court that the statistics provided to the court did not, on the face of it, show that a considerably smaller percentage of women than men were able to comply, the House of Lords, by a 3–2 majority, held that, since there had been a constant disparity since the two-year limit was introduced in 1985, the necessary disparate impact existed. However, the House of Lords held that the Government had justified the discriminatory effect of the limit, because it had been entitled to decide that the requirement was a suitable method of achieving its stated end of increasing employment opportunities in 1985, and six years was a reasonable period to wait to see if the policy was working. Accordingly, the appeals of Mrs Seymour-Smith and Mrs Perez failed.

The qualifying period is calculated from the beginning of the employee's employment under the relevant contract of employment. This could be earlier than the date the employee starts performing duties under the contract (*General of the Salvation Army v Dewsbury* [1984] ICR 498; but in *Wood v Cunard Line Ltd* [1991] ICR 13 the Court of Appeal expressed some doubt as to whether *Dewsbury* was correctly decided). The first day on which the employee started work is included, so that an employee who has worked 365 days is protected against unfair dismissal (*Pacitti Jones v O'Brien* [2005] CSIH 56, [2005] IRLR 888).

If an employee is dismissed on medical grounds in compliance with any law, regulation or code of practice providing for health and safety at work, the qualifying period for a claim is only one month (*ERA 1996, s 108(2)*).

An employee who is wrongfully dismissed in breach of the contractual notice entitlements and whose dismissal has the effect of preventing him or her from attaining the qualifying period for a complaint of unfair dismissal may not in an action for wrongful dismissal recover damages representing the loss of the chance to bring unfair dismissal proceedings (*Harper v Virgin Net Ltd* [2004] EWCA Civ 271, [2004] IRLR 390).

In certain other cases, no qualifying period is necessary. These are where the reason or principal reason for the dismissal:

(a)   was that the employee was summoned for jury service or was absent from work because he attended at any place in pursuance of being summoned for jury service, unless the employee's absence was likely to cause substantial injury to the employer's undertaking, the employer brought those circumstances to the employee's attention, and the employee unreasonably refused or failed to apply to the appropriate officer for excusal from or deferral of the obligation to attend (*ERA 1996, s 108(3)(aa)*);

(b)   was a prescribed reason in connection with leave for family reasons (*ERA 1996, s 108(3)(b)* and see 33.6 MATERNITY AND PARENTAL RIGHTS);

(c)   was a health and safety-related reason (*ERA 1996, s 108(3)(c)*; and see 54.3(B) UNFAIR DISMISSAL – II);

(d)   was a reason connected with the refusal of Sunday work by a shop worker or betting worker (*ERA 1996, s 108(3)(d)*; see 54.3(G) UNFAIR DISMISSAL – II);

(e)   was a reason related to working time (*ERA 1996, s 108(3)(dd)*; and see 54.3(H) UNFAIR DISMISSAL – II);

(f)   was a reason connected with the performance by an employee who is a pension scheme trustee of his functions as such a trustee (*ERA 1996, s 108(3)(e)*; see 54.3(E) UNFAIR DISMISSAL – II);

(g)   was a reason connected with the performance by an employee representative (see 39.4 REDUNDANCY – II and 52.18 TRANSFER OF UNDERTAKINGS), or a candidate in an election for such an employee representative, or of his functions as such an employee representative or candidate in a redundancy or transfer of undertakings context (*ERA 1996, s 108(3)(f)*; see 54.3(F) UNFAIR DISMISSAL – II),

(h)   was a reason connected with the making of a protected disclosure under *ERA 1996, ss 43A–43L* (*ERA 1996, s 108(3)(ff)*; see 54.3(N) UNFAIR DISMISSAL – II);

(i)   was the assertion of a statutory right (*ERA 1996, s 108(3)(g)*; and see 54.3(C) UNFAIR DISMISSAL – II);

(j)   was a reason connected with the assertion of rights under the *National Minimum Wage Act 1998* (*ERA 1996, s 108(3)(gg)*; see 54.3(M) UNFAIR DISMISSAL – II);

(k)   was that the worker took, or proposed to take, action with a view to enforcing or securing the benefit of a right under the *Tax Credits Act 2002*, or a penalty was imposed upon the employer as a result of action taken by, or on behalf of, the employee for the purpose of enforcing his or her rights under the *Act* (*ERA 1996, s 108(3)(gh)*, under the *Tax Credits Act 1999* and substituted by the *Tax Credits Act 2002*);

(l)   was a prescribed reason in connection with flexible working (*ERA 1996, s 108(3)(gi)*);

(m)   was a selection for redundancy for a reason which would have been automatically unfair if it had been the reason for dismissal (*ERA 1996, s 108(3)(h)*);

(n)   was that the worker had carried out activities as a member of a special negotiating body, a European Works Council, as an information and consultation representative, or as a candidate in an election for such a position, or that the employee exercised the specific rights relevant to the above bodies which are listed in the *Transnational Information and Consultation of Employees Regulations 1999, reg 28 (ERA 1996, s 108(3)(hh)*, and see 54.3(U), UNFAIR DISMISSAL – II);

(*o*) was that the worker has brought proceedings against his employer under the *Part-time Workers (Prevention of Less Favourable Treatment) Regulations 2000* or has otherwise done anything under the *Regulations* in relation to the employer or any other person (*ERA 1996, s108(3)(i)*);

(*p*) was that the employee brought proceedings against his employer under the *Fixed-term Employees (Prevention of Less Favourable Treatment) Regulations 2002* or has otherwise done anything under the *Regulations* in relation to the employer or any other person (*ERA 1996, s 108(3)(j)*);

(*q*) was the performance or attempted performance by an employee representative or election candidate in the context of the *European Public Limited-Liability Company Regulations 2004 (ERA 1996, s 108(3)(k)*);

(*r*) was the performance or attempted performance by an employee representative or election candidate in the context of the *Information and Consultation of Employees Regulations 2004 (ERA 1996, s 108(3)(l)*);

(*s*) was the performance or attempted performance of functions or activities as a representative or candidate under the *Occupational and Personal Pension Schemes (Consultation by Employers and Miscellaneous Amendment) Regulations 2006 (ERA 1996, s 108(3)(m)*);

(*t*) was that the employee exercised or sought to exercise his right to be accompanied at a meeting to consider his request not to retire, or that the employee accompanied or sought to accompany another employee who sought to exercise the right to be accompanied at such a meeting (*ERA 1996, s 108(3)(n)*);

(*u*) was that the employee performed or proposed to perform any functions or activities as a member, representative, candidate or participant under the *European Cooperative Society (Involvement of Employees) Regulations 2006 (SI 2006/2059)* or that the employee or a person on his behalf made or proposed to make a request for time off or remuneration for time off under the Regulations (*ERA 1996, s 108(3)(o)*);

(*v*) was a union-related reason (or where selection for redundancy was for a union-related reason) (*TULRCA 1992, s 154*; and see 54.3(A) UNFAIR DISMISSAL – II);

(*w*) was a reason connected with trade union recognition or bargaining arrangements (*TULRCA 1992, Sch A1, para 162* inserted by *Employment Relations Act 1999, s 1(2)* and *Sch 1*: see 54.3(O) UNFAIR DISMISSAL – II);

(*x*) was that the employee exercised or sought to exercise the right, pursuant to *Employment Relations Act 1999, s 10*, to be accompanied to a disciplinary or grievance hearing or that the employee accompanied or sought to accompany another worker to such a hearing (*Employment Relations Act 1999, s 12(4)*). see 54.3(P) UNFAIR DISMISSAL – II);

(*y*) was that the employee was dismissed for taking part in protected industrial action in the circumstances set out in *TULRCA 1992, s 138A*, introduced by *Employment Relations Act 1999, s 16* and *Sch 5*. See 53.17 below.

53.12 Calculation of period of continuous employment

The detailed provisions relating to the calculation of a period of continuous employment are set out in *ERA 1996, ss 210–219*. They are considered fully in CONTINUOUS EMPLOYMENT (7). They provide, for example, that there is continuity of employment when the business in which an employee works is transferred from one owner to another, when the employee is incapable of work because of sickness or injury, or absent from work wholly or partly because of pregnancy or childbirth or family-related leave.

53.13 Effective date of termination

The qualifying period is calculated up to and including the effective date of termination. The effective date of termination is defined as:

(a)   in relation to an employee whose contract of employment is *terminated by notice*, whether given by his employer or by the employee, the date on which that notice expires;

(b)   in relation to an employee whose contract of employment is terminated *without notice*, the date on which the termination takes effect; and

(c)   in relation to an employee who is employed under a *contract for a fixed term*, where that term expires without being renewed under the same contract, the date on which that term expires.

(*ERA 1996, s 97(1)*.)

The effective date of termination is an objectively determined statutory construct, which it is not open to the employer and employee to agree between themselves (*Fitzgerald v University of Kent at Canterbury* [2004] EWCA Civ 143, [2004] IRLR 300). In most cases, the effective date of termination is the date on which the employee ceases work. If an employer makes it clear to an employee that he is terminating his employment forthwith and pays him a sum of money in lieu of notice, the effective date of termination is the actual date of termination of the employment whether or not the employee was dismissed in breach of contract (*Dedman v British Building and Engineering Appliances Ltd* [1974] ICR 53; *Robert Cort and Son Ltd v Charman* [1981] ICR 816; see also *Stapp v Shaftesbury Society* [1982] IRLR 326; *Leech v Preston Borough Council* [1985] ICR 192; *Batchelor v British Railways Board* [1987] IRLR 136; *Octavius Atkinson & Sons Ltd v Morris* [1989] ICR 431). If, however, the contract continues although the employee stays away from work, the effective date of termination will be the date upon which the contract comes to an end in accordance with the notice.

In *West v Kneels Ltd* [1987] ICR 146, the EAT held that 'seven days' notice', used on dismissal, meant seven *clear* days. The contract cannot be terminated until the employee receives notification of the dismissal (*Brown v Southall and Knight* [1980] IRLR 130 and *McMaster v Manchester Airport plc* [1998] IRLR 112). Where an employee exercises a right of appeal against his dismissal but his appeal is not allowed, in the absence of any contrary contractual provision the effective date of termination will be the date of the original dismissal (*J Sainsbury Ltd v Savage* [1981] ICR 1, approved in *West Midlands Co-operative Society Ltd v Tipton* [1986] ICR 192).

For the purpose of deciding whether the employee had the necessary qualifying period of employment, if an employer dismisses an employee giving him no notice or less notice than that required by *ERA 1996, s 86*, the effective date will be the date on which the statutory minimum period of notice would have expired had it been given (*ERA 1996, s 97(2)*). Thus, if an employer dismisses an employee without notice after 51 weeks, the effective date of termination will be taken to be one week later, as the minimum period of notice after more than one month's employment is one week (see 48.7 TERMINATION OF EMPLOYMENT). The employee will thus be entitled to claim compensation for unfair dismissal. However, the extra time will not be added where an employee is summarily dismissed in circumstances where the employer is entitled to dismiss summarily, eg for gross misconduct (see 48.13 TERMINATION OF EMPLOYMENT). An employer is not entitled simply to define a dismissal as being for gross misconduct without the tribunal investigating whether that description is justified (*Lanton Leisure Ltd v White and Gibson* [1987] IRLR 119). The statutory extension of the effective date of termination applies even where the employee waives his right to notice (*Secretary of State for Employment v Staffordshire County Council* [1989] IRLR 117, the Court of Appeal holding that the fact that an employee has waived his right to notice or has accepted a payment in lieu of notice under *ERA 1996, s 97(4)* is relevant only to his rights in contract).

For the purpose of calculating the qualifying period of employment where an employee terminates his contract of employment in circumstances in which he is entitled to do so by reason of his employer's conduct, the effective date of termination will be considered to be the date on which the statutory minimum notice required of the employer would have expired (*ERA 1996, s 97(4)*).

53.14 RETIRING AGE

The *Employment Equality (Age) Regulations 2006 (SI 2006/1031)* came into force on 1 October 2006. See AGE DISCRIMINATION (3).

The upper age limit for complaining of unfair dismissal, contained in *ERA 1996, s 109*, has been removed.

In respect of dismissals prior to 1 October 2006, an employee could not normally complain of unfair dismissal if, on or before the effective date of termination, he had attained the age which, in the undertaking in which he was employed, was the normal retiring age for an employee holding the position which he held and the retiring age was the same for men and for women (*ERA 1996, s 109(1)*). 'Normal retiring age' was to be ascertained from the reasonable expectation of the group of employees holding the position of the claimant at the date of dismissal. The relevant expectation was that of members of the group generally as to what would eventually happen to them, and not the expectation of those currently nearing retirement (*Brooks v British Telecommunications plc* [1992] IRLR 66). However, it was sometimes possible to divide employees doing the same job into different groups by virtue of their being subject to different terms and conditions concerning retiring age (*Barber v Thames Television plc* [1992] IRLR 410).

The contractual retiring age (if any) was *prima facie* the normal retiring age but it could be departed from in practice, with the result either that there was some other normal retiring age, or that there was no such normal age at all. Administrative policies communicated to the employees may give rise to such expectations, but when those policies are changed so too are those expectations (*Waite v Government Communications Headquarters* [1983] 2 AC 714; *Hughes Coy and Jarnell v Department of Health and Social Security* [1985] AC 776; *Whittle v Manpower Services Commission* [1987] IRLR 441). However, it was not possible to lower the normal retirement age below the contractual retiring age unless the employees agreed to a contractual variation (*Bratko v Beloit Walmsley Ltd* [1995] IRLR 629). A policy as to retirement at a particular age did not cease to define the normal retiring age merely because limited exceptions were made to it on compassionate grounds (*Barclays Bank plc v O'Brien* [1994] IRLR 580). An employee whose position in the undertaking was unique could have a normal retiring age, which could be the contractual retiring age and require no comparators (*Wall v British Compressed Air Society* [2003] EWCA Civ 1762, [2004] IRLR 147).

Where there was no normal retiring age, employees aged 65 and over could not normally bring an application for unfair dismissal (*ERA 1996, s 109(1)*).

An employee over normal retiring age or over the age of 65 was able to bring a claim for unfair dismissal if it is shown that the reason (or, if more than one, the principal reason) for the dismissal was one of a number of 'inadmissible' reasons. These were the same reasons as made it unnecessary to have been employed for a qualifying period. See 53.11 above.

In *Harvest Town Circle Ltd v Rutherford* ([2001] IRLR 599) the EAT rejected an argument that the upper age limit of 65 in *ERA 1996, s 109(1)* was incompatible with *art 141* (formerly *art 119*) of the *Treaty of Rome* as being indirectly discriminatory against men. The EAT held that there was no adequate basis in law, on the statistics presented to the employment tribunal, for its conclusion that the upper age limit contravened *art 141* and so should be disapplied. The EAT held that the tribunal had looked at the wrong statistics and should not have ruled upon the arguments raised relating to objective justification for the exclusion without giving the Secretary of State the opportunity to participate in the proceedings.

The case was remitted to the employment tribunal and on appeal the EAT and CA held that the age limits in the *ERA 1996* which apply to redundancy payments and unfair dismissal protection do not have a disparate impact upon men (*Rutherford v Secretary of State for Trade and Industry* [2003] IRLR 858; on appeal [2004] EWCA Civ 1186, [2004] IRLR 892). The CA held that the correct pool for analysis was the entire workforce, which showed that almost identically high proportions of men and women qualified for the statutory unfair dismissal and redundancy rights and met the test of being under 65 in 2001 (men 98.88% and women 99.0%). According to the CA, the statistics demonstrated that the disadvantaged group of older workers was very small and in borderline territory which did not justify a finding of disparate impact. It was also held by the CA that the Secretary of State had objectively justified the default age limit of 65, in regard to both unfair dismissal and redundancy payments.

The House of Lords considered these issues in *Rutherford v Secretary of State for Trade and Industry (No 2)* [2006] UKHL 19, [2006] IRLR 551 and agreed with the EAT and CA that the upper age limit was not discriminatory, because, in essence, it applied to those aged over 65 of both sexes, so that the disadvantage applied to all those over 65, and not disproportionately to men.

53.15 EXCLUDED CLASSES OF EMPLOYEES

Certain classes of employment are excluded from the protection of the unfair dismissal provisions. If a respondent wishes to show that an claimant falls within an excluded class, the burden of proof is on him to do so (*Kapur v Shields* [1976] ICR 26). The excluded cases are defined by *ERA 1996, ss 199* and *200*.

(*a*)   Dismissal from any employment as a master or as a member of the crew of a *fishing vessel* where the employee is not remunerated otherwise than by a share in the profits or gross earnings of the vessel (*ERA 1996, s 199(2)*).

(*b*)   Dismissal from employment in respect of which the employee has validly contracted out of his right to claim compensation for unfair dismissal (*ERA 1996, s 203(2)* and see 53.19, 53.20 below).

(*c*)   Dismissal from employment under a contract of employment in police service or to persons engaged in such employment (*ERA 1996, s 200*), except for unfair dismissals on health and safety grounds (contrary to *ERA 1996, s 100*), or because the employee has made a protected disclosure (contrary to *ERA 1996, s 103A*).

(*d*)   Dismissal from employment in circumstances in which the employee has failed to make use of the statutory grievance procedure (*Employment Act 2002, s 32* and *Sch 2*).

An employee or ex-employee is barred from bringing a claim for unfair dismissal in three circumstances:

(i)   the grievance concerns a matter to which the requirement in *Sch 2* to set out the grievance in writing applies and the requirement has not been complied with; or

(ii)   the employee has not waited 28 days after serving his or her grievance in writing; or

(iii) the employee does not set out and serve the grievance in writing until more than one month after the end of the original time limit for making the tribunal complaint in question (*s 32(2)– (4)*).

In each of the three cases, the tribunal will be prevented from considering the complaint only if the breach is apparent to the tribunal from the information supplied to it by the employee in connection with the bringing of the proceedings, or the tribunal is satisfied of the breach as a result of the employer raising the matter in accordance with the *Rules of Procedure Regulations* (*s 32(6)*).

(*e*)   *Section 196* of the *ERA 1996* was repealed in its entirety by s *32(3)* of the *Employment Relations Act 1999* and so, with effect from 25 October 1999, the territorial limits were removed. For those dismissed before 25 October 1999, any employment where under his contract of employment *the employee ordinarily worked outside Great Britain* was an excluded case.

The House of Lords has now given guidance in *Lawson v Serco Ltd* ([2006] UKHL 3, [2006] IRLR 289) on the circumstances in which the right not to be unfairly dismissed applies. A claimant will generally be protected if he was working in Great Britain at the time of his dismissal and peripatetic employees are subject to a 'base' test. It is a question of law where an employee is based.

The factual examples within the case law on *ERA 1996, s 196* therefore remain of relevance to cases where it is asserted that an employment tribunal has jurisdiction over certain employment, even though the legal test for jurisdiction over unfair dismissal claims has changed with the repeal of *s 196*. Where an employee worked both inside and outside Great Britain, one would look at the terms of the contract, express or implied, and how the contract operated in practice, in order to ascertain where the employee's base was (cf *Wilson v Maynard Shipbuilding Consultants AB* [1978] ICR 376, and *per* Lord Denning MR and Sir David Cairns in *Todd v British*

Midland Airways Ltd [1978] ICR 959). See also *Jackson v Ghost Ltd* [2003] IRLR 824 and *Crofts v Cathay Pacific Airways Ltd* ([2005] EWCA Civ 599, [2005] IRLR 624).

The contract to be considered is that subsisting at the time of dismissal, and not any previous contract between the parties (*Weston v Vega Space Systems Engineering Ltd* [1989] IRLR 429). Where the contract of employment is of little assistance, the tribunal should go by the conduct of the parties and the way they have operated the contract (*per* Lord Denning MR in *Todd* at 964).

The relevant location used to be the employer's operational base, not the actual place of work (*Addison v Denholm Ship Management (UK) Ltd* [1997] IRLR 389).

A person employed to work on board a ship registered in the United Kingdom (not being a ship registered at a port outside Great Britain) was regarded as a person who under his contract ordinarily worked in Great Britain unless:

(i)   the employment was wholly outside Great Britain; or

(ii)   the employee was not ordinarily resident in Great Britain.

(*ERA 1996, s 196(5)*; see, e g *Wood v Cunard Line Ltd* [1991] ICR 13.)

Employees engaged upon certain activities connected with offshore drilling were given employment protection rights by the *Employment Protection (Offshore Employment) Order 1976 (SI 1976/766)*. See *Addison*, above, and *ERA 1996, s 201*.

(*f*)   Section 197 of the *ERA 1996* was repealed in its entirety by the *Fixed-term Employees (Prevention of Less Favourable Treatment) Regulations 2002 (SI 2002/2034)*, reg 11, Sch 2, Pt 1, para 3(1) and (15), (subject to Sch 2, Pt 2, para 5) with effect from 1 October 2002.

Formerly, with effect from 25 October 1999, *s 18(1)* of the *Employment Relations Act 1999* had repealed the parts of *ERA 1996, s 197* which permitted agreements to exclude unfair dismissal provisions in fixed-term contracts, and so such agreements were no longer effective (subject to the transitional provisions in *para 2* of *Sch 3* to the *ERA 1999* (*Commencement No 2 and Transitional and Saving Provisions) Order 1999 (SI 1999/2830*)).

For those dismissed before 25 October 1999, an excluded case was dismissal from employment under a contract for a fixed term of one year or more, where the dismissal consisted only of the expiry of that term without it being renewed if before the term so expires the employee had agreed in writing to exclude any claim in respect of rights to claim for unfair dismissal in relation to that contract (*ERA 1996, s 197*). It was immaterial whether or not the fixed-term contract contained a provision for early termination by notice. However, it was not permissible to aggregate successive fixed terms so as to amount to one year or more (*Housing Services Agency v Cragg* [1997] ICR 1050). In *BBC v Kelly-Phillips* [1998] IRLR 294, a contract for a fixed term of one year had been extended by four months. The Court of Appeal held that on the facts of the case, the contract had been varied and was a single contract for 16 months, rather than two separate contracts for one year and for four months, respectively. Therefore, the employer could take advantage of the exclusion of *ERA 1996, s 197(1)* at the end of the four-month extension. See also *Bhatt v Chelsea and Westminster Health Care NHS Trust* [1997] IRLR 660.

53.16 EMPLOYEE CANNOT ENFORCE RIGHTS IF CONTRACT ILLEGAL

The courts will not enforce an illegal contract. Thus, if it appears to an employment tribunal that, for example, a contract of employment was entered into with an agreement that no tax be paid on some part or all of the remuneration, the tribunal may consider the agreement to be a fraud on the Inland Revenue and may dismiss the claim. The position will normally be different if the employee was innocent of any wrongdoing, or if he merely performed some unlawful act in the course of an otherwise lawful employment. For a fuller discussion, see 8.14 CONTRACT OF EMPLOYMENT.

53.17 DISMISSAL IN CONNECTION WITH A LOCK-OUT OR STRIKE

Official action

The law relating to unfair dismissals in the context of official industrial action was changed substantially by *Employment Relations Act 1999, s 16 and Sch 5*, which introduced a new *TULCRA 1992, s 238A* from 24 April 2000. (See *Employment Relations Act 1999 (Commencement No 5 and Transitional Provision) Order 2000, art 3 (SI 2000/875)) (TULRCA 1992, s 238*, as amended by *TURERA 1993, Sch 8 para 77* and *ERA 1996, Sch 1 para 56). Section 238A* was amended further by the *Employment Relations Act 2004.*

Prior to the changes introduced by *Sch 5* and the *Employment Relations Act 2004*, employees who took part in lawful industrial action lost their right to claim unfair dismissal if they were dismissed whilst the industrial action was taking place and all other employees who were taking part in the industrial action were similarly dismissed. The main consequences of the changes were that:

(*a*)   the right to claim unfair dismissal is restored for many employees who are taking part in lawful, official, industrial action, provided that the reason for their dismissal is their participation in the industrial action; and

(*b*)   dismissal for such a reason will, in such cases, be automatically unfair.

TULRCA 1992, s 238, as amended by *Sch 5*, provides that the exclusion from the right to claim unfair dismissal if dismissal takes place during industrial action will not apply where the employee is regarded as unfairly dismissed by reason of *TULRCA 1992, s 238A*. An employee will be treated as being unfairly dismissed by reason of *s 238A* if the employee is taking part in protected industrial action and if certain other conditions (set out below) are satisfied.

Section 238A defines 'protected industrial action' as meaning action which was induced by an act protected by *TULRCA 1992, s 219* (see 45.3 STRIKES AND INDUSTRIAL ACTION). In effect, 'protected industrial action' is official industrial action in respect of which the trade union concerned and its officials enjoy immunity from suit.

An employee will be treated as having been automatically unfairly dismissed if the reason or principal reason for dismissal was that the employee has taken part in protected industrial action and:

(i)   the date of dismissal is within the protected period; or

(ii)   the date of dismissal is after the end of protected period and the employee had stopped taking protected industrial action before the end of that period; or

(iii)   the date of dismissal is after the end of the protected period, the employee had not stopped taking protected industrial action before the end of that period, and the employer had not taken such procedural steps as would have been reasonable for the purposes of resolving the dispute to which the protected industrial action relates.

An employee may be taking part in industrial action even though he is not in breach of his contract of employment, eg by refusing to work overtime (*Power Packing Casemakers Ltd v Faust* [1983] ICR 292). Industrial action will generally exist where there is concerted action involving the application of pressure in the search for some advantage (*Glenrose (Fish Merchants) Ltd v Chapman*, IDS Brief 438, p 5). One person may be involved in industrial action on his own (*Lewis and Britton v E Mason & Sons* [1994] IRLR 4).

In deciding whether the employer has taken reasonable procedural steps, the tribunal must consider whether the employer complied with procedures set out in any relevant collective bargaining agreement, whether the employer or the union agreed to take part in negotiations after the industrial action had commenced, and whether the employer or the union had unreasonably refused to take part in conciliation or mediation. *TULCRA 1992, s 238A(7)* provides that in deciding whether the employer has taken reasonable procedural steps, the tribunal should take no account of the merits of the dispute which gave rise to the industrial action.

The above provisions represented a major change in the law relating to unfair dismissal in the context of official industrial action. It should be emphasised that not that every employee who is dismissed whilst taking part in official industrial action will be deemed to be unfairly dismissed. It is only if the reason for dismissal is that the employee was taking part in the protected industrial action that the dismissal will be automatically unfair. If the employee is dismissed for some other reason, such as misconduct or redundancy, during the relevant period, the dismissal will not be automatically unfair; rather, the tribunal will consider whether the dismissal was fair applying normal principles. Similarly, if the employee is dismissed for inducing the industrial action, rather than being induced, the dismissal will not be automatically unfair under s *238A*.

There may still be cases in which the right to claim unfair dismissal will be excluded, namely, if the whole of the part of the workforce which is taking part in industrial action is dismissed and the conditions set out in *s 238A* are not satisfied, for example because the industrial action has lasted for more than the protected period and the employer has taken reasonable procedural steps to resolve the dispute. In practice, however, *TULRCA 1992, s 238A* is likely to deter employers from dismissing all employees who are taking part in industrial action, because of the risk that this will lead to a finding that each of the employees concerned has been automatically unfairly dismissed.

TULRCA 1992, s 239(4) provides that if a claim for unfair dismissal arising out of protected industrial action succeeds, a tribunal should not consider the question of reinstatement or re-engagement until after the end of the employee's participation in the protected industrial action.

53.18 Unofficial action

The changes to the law relating to dismissals in the context of official industrial action, introduced by *Employment Relations Act 1999, Sch 5* and *Employment Relations Act 2004*, do not affect the law relating to unofficial industrial action.

TULRCA 1992, s 237 provides that an employee has no right to complain of unfair dismissal if at the time of dismissal he was taking part in an unofficial strike or other unofficial industrial action. This bar to jurisdiction is different from that contained in *TULRCA 1992, s 238*. The effect of the change is that, where the employees take part in unofficial industrial action, the employer can dismiss selectively without the tribunal thereby acquiring jurisdiction to hear a complaint of unfair dismissal. It is immaterial whether participation in the unofficial action was in fact the reason for the dismissal.

The time of dismissal means:

(*a*)   where the employee's contract is terminated by notice, when the notice is given;

(*b*)   where the contract is terminated without notice, when the termination takes effect; and

(*c*)   where the employee is employed under a fixed-term contract which expires without renewal, when that term expires.

(*TULRCA 1992, s 237(5)*.)

The test of whether a person is taking part in unofficial action at a particular time will presumably be the same as in cases under *TULRCA 1992, s 238* (see 53.17 above).

Industrial action will be unofficial in relation to the dismissed employee unless:

(i)   that employee is a member of a union which has authorised or endorsed the action;

(ii)   the employee is not a union member, but those taking part in the action include members of a union which has authorised or endorsed it; or

(iii) none of those taking part in the action are union members.

(*TULRCA 1992, s 237(2)*.)

Thus, if the employee is a union member, his own union *must* have authorised or endorsed the action if it is not to be unofficial. If he is not, then if there are *any* union members among the participants, at least one union whose members are involved must have authorised or endorsed the action if it is not to be unofficial.

For the purposes of determining whether industrial action is to be taken to have been endorsed by a union, *TULRCA 1992, s 20(2)* is to be applied, by reference to the facts as at the time of dismissal (see 48.16 TRADE UNIONS – I). However, a repudiation under *TULRCA 1992, s 21* does not make action unofficial before the end of the next working day (*TULRCA 1992, s 237(3), (4)*).

For the purposes of *s 237*, membership of a union for purposes unconnected with the employment in question shall be disregarded. But an employee who is a union member when he starts to take part in action will be treated as such throughout the action even if he ceases to be a member (*TULRCA 1992, s 237(6)*).

Again, the exclusion of jurisdiction does not apply if the reason for the dismissal is one specified in *ERA 1996, ss 98B, 99, 100, 101A(d), 103, 103A, 104, or 104C* (jury service, family, health and safety, working time or redundancy or transfer of undertaking employee representative, protected disclosure cases, or assertion of statutory right to take time off work for dependants).

53.19 **NO CONTRACTING OUT**

With certain exceptions (see 53.20 below), any agreement to prevent any person from presenting or pursuing a complaint of unfair dismissal is void (*ERA 1996, s 203(1)*). A clause in a contract of employment purporting to exclude this right will be ineffective, leaving the employee free to pursue a claim for unfair dismissal in the employment tribunal. In *Igbo v Johnson Matthey Chemicals Ltd* [1986] ICR 505, the Court of Appeal held that a variation of an employment contract which provided that if an employee failed to return from a period of leave on a certain date, her contract would be automatically terminated, converted a right not to be unfairly dismissed into a conditional right not to be dismissed; accordingly, it was void by reason of *EPCA 1978, s 140(1)* (the predecessor section of *ERA 1996, s 203(1)*). However, in *Scott v Coalite Fuels and Chemicals Ltd* [1988] ICR 355, an employee who had agreed to accept voluntary retirement as an alternative to redundancy was not successful in putting forward a similar argument. In *Logan Salton v Durham City Council* [1989] IRLR 99, a case where an employee under threat of dismissal agreed terms for termination, *Igbo* was distinguished on the grounds that this was a separate contract from the contract of employment, entered into without duress, after proper advice and for good consideration, and that termination was not contingent upon the happening of future events in circumstances which the parties might not have envisaged.

Similarly, any agreement to pay an ex-employee money in consideration for his refraining from presenting or pursuing a complaint in an employment tribunal is normally unenforceable, subject to the exceptions considered in 53.20 below.

53.20 **Exceptions**

An agreement restricting the right to claim for unfair dismissal is enforceable if it is contained in the following agreements:

(*a*)   a valid compromise contract satisfying the statutory conditions, including that the employee should have taken independent legal advice (see 20.27 EMPLOYMENT TRIBUNALS – I and note *Hinton v University of East London* [2005] EWCA Civ 532, [2005] IRLR 552) (*ERA 1996, s 203(2)*);

(*b*)   a dismissal procedure agreement reached between employers and one or more independent trade unions which has been approved by the Secretary of State;

(*c*)   any agreement to refrain from presenting a complaint that he was unfairly dismissed where the conciliation officer has taken action in accordance with his statutory duties (see 2.3 ADVISORY, CONCILIATION AND ARBITRATION SERVICE (ACAS));

(*d*)   any agreement to refrain from proceeding with a complaint where the conciliation officer has taken action in accordance with his statutory duties (see 2.3 ADVISORY, CONCILIATION AND ARBITRATION SERVICE (ACAS)). Where there has been a transfer of an undertaking for the purposes of the *Transfer of Undertakings (Protection of Employment) Regulations 1981 (SI 1981/1794)* or, from 6 April 2006, the *2006 Regulations (SI 2006/246)*, such an agreement if made by the transferor and not finalised until after the transfer will not prevent an employee from claiming against the transferee (*Thompson v Walon Car Delivery* [1997] IRLR 343).

54   Unfair Dismissal – II: The Fairness of the Dismissal

(See also DTI website http://www.dti.gov.uk/employment/Resolving_disputes/unfair-dismissal/index.html).

Cross-references. See UNFAIR DISMISSAL – I (53) for the right to make a claim; UNFAIR DISMISSAL – III (55) for remedies for unfair dismissal.

54.1   REASONS FOR DISMISSAL

Once the fact of dismissal has been established, it is for the employer to show:

(*a*)   what was the reason (or, if there was more than one, the principal reason) for the dismissal; and

(*b*)   that it was one of the reasons set out in 54.2 below.

(*ERA 1996, s 98(1)*.)

An employment tribunal will investigate the real reason for the dismissal of the employee. The fact that an employer told an employee that the reason for his dismissal was redundancy will not preclude the tribunal from deciding that, for example, the real reason for dismissal was lack of capability (*Abernethy v Mott, Hay and Anderson* [1974] ICR 323). However, the tribunal should not find for the employer on a ground not argued if the employee will be prejudiced in that he might have put his case differently if aware of that argument (*Hannan v TNT-Ipec (UK) Ltd* [1986] IRLR 165). The facts which cause the employer to act as he does are to be treated as the reason for the dismissal even if the employer does not realise that his actions amount to a dismissal (*Ely v YKK Fasteners (UK) Ltd* [1994] ICR 164).

If there is a dispute over the reason for the dismissal, the burden of proving which one of the competing reasons for the dismissal was the principal reason is on the employer (*Maund v Penwith District Council* [1984] ICR 143). Also, the employer will only be allowed to rely upon facts known to him at the time of the dismissal to establish what the reason for the dismissal was. Thus, facts which come to light after the dismissal cannot be relied upon to justify the dismissal, although they may affect the level of compensation (*W Devis & Sons Ltd v Atkins* [1977] ICR 662; and see 55.13 UNFAIR DISMISSAL – III).

When a dismissal is by notice, the employer's reason for the dismissal must be determined both by reference to the reason for giving the notice to terminate and by reference to the reason when dismissal occurs (*Parkinson v Marc Consulting Ltd* [1998] ICR 276).

54.2   Acceptable reasons for dismissal

The following are acceptable reasons for dismissal:

(*a*)   reasons related to the capability or qualifications of the employee for performing work of the kind which he was employed to do;

(*b*)   reasons related to the conduct of the employee;

(*c*)   retirement of the employee;

(d) that the employee was redundant (for the definition of 'redundancy' see 34.7 REDUNDANCY – I);

(e) that the employee could not continue to work in the position which he held without contravention (either on his part or on that of his employer) of a duty or restriction imposed by or under an enactment; or

(f) some other substantial reason of a kind such as to justify the dismissal of an employee holding the position which that employee held.

(ERA 1996, s 98(1), (2).)

It is a question of law for the tribunal to determine under which one of these acceptable reasons ((a)–(f)) the reason, in fact, given by the employer falls. For example, where the reason for dismissal put forward by the employer was 'incapability by reason of unsatisfactory attendance record' but it was clear that the reason for the dismissal was the claimant's poor attendance and not the ill health which caused this attendance, the tribunal erred in law in characterising the reason for the dismissal as 'capability' rather than 'some other substantial reason' (*Wilson v Post Office* [2000] IRLR 834).

If the employer fails to establish that the reason for the dismissal was an acceptable one, the tribunal *must* find the dismissal unfair (*Earl v Slater and Wheeler (Airlyne) Ltd* [1973] 1 All ER 145, observation of Sir John Donaldson *obiter* at 149).

After a consideration of the *unacceptable* reasons for dismissal (see 54.3 below) and the criteria for assessment of the fairness of a dismissal where the reason is acceptable (see 54.4 below), this chapter considers each of the acceptable reasons listed above in turn.

54.3 DISMISSALS WHICH ARE DEEMED UNFAIR

Most of the following automatically unfair reasons for dismissal will also render the dismissal unfair if they were the reason why an employee was selected to be dismissed for redundancy (see 54.11(A) below). In most cases, they will also make it possible for the tribunal to investigate the complaint and pronounce the dismissal unfair, when it would not normally have jurisdiction to do so because the employee lacked sufficient continuous service (see UNFAIR DISMISSAL – I (53)). In union-related cases, some health and safety cases, and cases where there has been a breach of the statutory dismissal and disciplinary and/or grievance procedures, special rules apply in calculating the compensation for UNFAIR DISMISSAL – III (55).

(a) Employer's failure to follow statutory dismissal and disciplinary procedures

EA 2002, s 34 inserted a new *s 98A* into the *Employment Rights Act 1996*. *Section 98A(1)* provides that a dismissal will automatically be unfair if one of the statutory disciplinary procedures set out in *Sch 2* applies in relation to the dismissal, the procedure has not been completed and the non-completion of the procedure is wholly or mainly attributable to failure by the employer to comply with its requirements. The *Employment Act 2002 (Dispute Resolution) Regulations 2004 (SI 2004/752)* describe the circumstances and manner in which the statutory dismissal and disciplinary procedures apply. These *Regulations* deal with questions about the application of procedures, the question whether a procedure has been completed, and matters relating to whether an employer should be regarded as having failed to comply with the procedure. The *EA 2002, s 30,* is still not in force. It provides that it will be a term of every contract of employment that the statutory procedures will be complied with, although it will be possible for the parties to agree more elaborate procedures. No regulations have been made, under *s 30(3)*, to make provision about the application of the statutory procedures in relation to contracts of employment and there is no implied term that the statutory procedures will be followed by the parties to the employment contract. (See DISPUTE RESOLUTION (15).)

The statutory dispute resolution procedures provide only a bare minimum of protection for employees. There is no requirement that the procedure be adversarial, or about the use of witnesses or statements. It is very different, therefore, from the *ACAS Code of Practice*.

The standard dismissal and disciplinary procedure applies when an employer contemplates either dismissing the employee or taking action short of dismissal (being action which the employer asserts to be based wholly or mainly on the employee's conduct or capability, other than suspension on full pay or the issuing or oral or written warnings) against the employee (*Dispute Resolution Regulations, regs 2(1)* and *3(1)*). The modified procedure is relevant only to dismissal (and not to action short of dismissal) and applies where the employer dismissed the employee by reason of his conduct without notice, the dismissal took place as soon as the employer became aware of the conduct or immediately afterwards, the employer was entitled to dismiss the employee summarily in the circumstances by reason of the employee's conduct, and it was reasonable for the employer to dismiss in the circumstances before enquiring into the circumstances in which the conduct took place (*reg 3(2)*).

Although procedures set out in *Sch 2* are not very onerous it is important that employers have regard to the statutory procedures and do not assume that their own contractual or non-contractual disciplinary procedure will suffice. The standard procedure consists of three steps (see *Alexander v Bridgen* [2006] IRLR 422 on the information which must be given). Step 1 is that the employer must set out in writing the employee's conduct or characteristics, or other circumstances, that have led the employer to contemplate dismissal or disciplinary action. The statement must be copied to the employee and the employee must be invited to a meeting to discuss the matter.

Step 2 is the dismissal meeting itself. The meeting must take place before the action is taken, unless the action consists of suspension (normally, of course, suspension is not of itself disciplinary action, but is intended to preserve the *status quo* before action is taken). The meeting must not take place until the employer has explained the reason for the disciplinary proceedings or dismissal and the employee has had a reasonable opportunity to consider his response to that information.

A number of general requirements for all the statutory procedures are set out in *Part 3* of *Sch 2*. These are that each step and action is taken without unreasonable delay, and the timing and location of meetings must be reasonable. Meetings must be conducted in a manner that enables both employer and employee to explain their cases.

The employee must take all reasonable steps to attend the meeting. After the meeting, the employer must inform the employee of the decision and notify him of the right to appeal against the decision if he is not satisfied with it. The right to be accompanied by a colleague or union representative, under *Employment Relations Act 1999, s 10* applies to the meeting, as it does to all meetings under the statutory procedures (*Sch 2, para 14*).

Step 3 is the appeal stage. The responsibility lies with the employee to tell the employer that he wishes to appeal. If the employee does so, the employer must arrange for another meeting, which the employee must take all reasonable steps to attend. After the appeal meeting, the employer must inform the employee of his final decision. The appeal meeting need not take place before the dismissal takes place. At an appeal meeting, the employer should, if reasonably practicable, be represented by a more senior manager than attended the first meeting.

The modified procedure is very limited indeed and is designed to take place where an employee has already been dismissed on the spot, which generally happens in a case of gross misconduct.

Effectively, the employee is granted a right of appeal. There are two stages. Step 1 is that the employer must set out in writing a description of the alleged misconduct which has led to the dismissal, what the basis was for thinking that the employee was guilty of the misconduct, and the employee's right of appeal. A copy must be sent to the employee. Step 2 replicates the appeal stage which is Step 3 in the standard procedure, as described in the preceding paragraph.

The dismissal and disciplinary procedures do not apply to dismissals where:

(*a*)   an employee who has been summarily dismissed presents his or her complaint relating to the dismissal to the employment tribunal at a time when the employer has not complied with the duty under the modified procedure (*EA, Sch 2, para 4*) to send to the employee a written statement of the alleged misconduct, the basis for thinking that the employee was guilty, and giving the employee a right of appeal against the dismissal (*Dispute Resolution Regulations, reg 3(2)*); or

(*b*)   the employer has dismissed all the employees of a description or in a category to which the employee belongs, provided that the employer offers to re-engage all the employees who have been dismissed either before or upon termination of their contracts of employment (with offers of re-engagement by successor or associated employer of the dismissing employer into the previous job or into a different job which would be suitable in the employee's case being included) (*Dispute Resolution Regulations, reg 4(1)(a)*); or

(*c*)   the dismissal is one of a number of dismissals in relation to which the duty to consult employee representatives under *s 188* of *TULRCA 1992* arises (*Dispute Resolution Regulations, reg 4(1)(b)*); or

(*d*)   the employee is dismissed whilst taking part in an unofficial strike or other unofficial industrial action, or a strike or other industrial action (being neither unofficial industrial action nor protected industrial action) unless the circumstances of the case bring it within *s 238(2)* of *TULRCA 1992* (dismissals in connection with other industrial action the fairness of which the employment tribunal is entitled to consider if certain facts are shown) (*Dispute Resolution Regulations, reg 4(1)(c)*); or

(*e*)   the reason, or the principal reason, for the dismissal is that the employee took protected industrial action and the dismissal would be regarded as automatically unfair by virtue of *s 238A* of *TULRCA 1992* (*Dispute Resolution Regulations, reg 4(1)(d)*); or

(*f*)   the employer's business suddenly ceases to function because of an event unforeseen by the employer with the result that it is impracticable for it to employ any employees (*Dispute Resolution Regulations, reg 4(1)(e)*); or (*g*)   the reason or principal reason for the dismissal is that the employee could not have continued to work in the position which he or she held without contravention on either the employer or employee's part of a duty or restriction imposed by or under any enactment (*Dispute Resolution Regulations, reg 4(1)(f)*); or

(*h*)   at the date of dismissal the employee is one to whom a dismissal procedures agreement designated by order under *ERA 1996, s 110* applies (*Dispute Resolution Regulations, reg 4(1)(g)*); or

(*i*)   it would not be possible to comply with an applicable statutory procedure on national security grounds (*Dispute Resolution Regulations, reg 16*).

The parties are to be treated as having fully complied with the dismissal and disciplinary procedures where either the standard or modified procedure applies, the employee presents an application for interim relief under *ERA 1996, s 128*, and at that date the employer has complied with either the standard or modified procedures (as appropriate) to the extent of providing the employee with a written statement of the conduct or characteristics giving rise to the risk or fact of dismissal, holding the meeting (if the standard procedure applies), informing the employee in writing of the employer's decision, and giving written notification of the employee's right of appeal, but the appeal stage has not been completed (*Dispute Resolution Regulations, reg 5(1)*).

The parties are to be treated as having complied with the appeal requirements under the either the standard or modified dismissal and disciplinary procedures (as applicable) where at the time of the dismissal or the taking of action short of dismissal by the employer an appropriate procedure exists, the employee is entitled to appeal under the appropriate procedure against the dismissal or action short of dismissal instead of appealing to the employer, and the employee has appealed under that procedure (*Dispute Resolution Regulations, reg 5(2)*). A procedure is appropriate for the purposes of *reg 5(2)* if it gives the employee an effective right of appeal against the dismissal or disciplinary action and the procedure operates by virtue of a collective agreement made between two or more employers or an employers' association and one or more independent trade unions (*Dispute Resolution Regulations, reg 5(3)*).

The statutory disciplinary and dismissal procedures do not apply (and, where commenced, failure to compete shall not be treated as a failure to have complied) where the party failing to commence or to comply with the statutory procedure has reasonable grounds to believe that commencing or complying with the procedure would result in a significant threat to him- or herself, his or her property, another other person, or any other person's property, or where the party has been subjected to harassment and has reasonable grounds to believe that commencing or complying with the procedure would result in further harassment, or where it is not practicable for the party to commence or comply with the subsequent requirement under the statutory procedure within a reasonable period (*Dispute Resolution Regulations, reg 11*). The definition of harassment is consistent with that now contained in the discrimination legislation (*reg 11(4)*).

If either the employer or employee fails to comply with a requirement of statutory dismissal or disciplinary procedure, where a procedure applies, including the general requirements, then the non-completion of the statutory procedure will be attributed to that party, and neither party remains under any obligation to persist with the statutory procedure (*Dispute Resolution Regulations, reg 12(1)*). Where the employer or employee fails to commence or continue the statutory procedure in exercise of the right under *reg 11* to refrain from the statutory procedure out of fear of harm to people or property or harassment, then the party giving rise to that fear shall be treated as if the statutory procedure had not been disapplied but there had been a failure to comply attributable to that party (*reg 12(3) and (4)*). An employer or employee shall not be treated as having failed to comply with a requirement of the applicable statutory disciplinary and dismissal procedure where it is not reasonably practicable for him or her to attend a meeting under the statutory procedure (or for the employee's companion under the *ERelA 1999, s 10*) for a reason which was not foreseeable when the meeting was arranged (*Dispute Resolution Regulations, reg 13(1)*). In such circumstances, the employer remains under the duty to invite the employee to a meeting and if the employee proposes another time and date under *ERelA 1999, s 10(4)* then the employer is obliged to invite the employee to meeting at that time. Once, however, the employer has invited the employee to attend two meeting and each of them has been cancelled because of circumstances within *reg 13(1)*, then the employer ceases to be under a duty to continue inviting the employee to meetings (*reg 13(3)*) and both parties shall be treated as having complied with the applicable statutory procedure (*reg 13(4)*).

Where an employee, on the date on which the time limit for his complaint of unfair dismissal would normally expire, has reasonable grounds for believing that a dismissal or disciplinary procedure, whether statutory or otherwise, was being followed in respect of matters that consisted of or included the substance of the employment tribunal complaint, then the time limit will be extended for a period of three months beginning with the day after the day on which the normal time limit would have expired (*Dispute Resolution Regulations, reg 15*).

(b) Union-membership, participation and non-membership dismissals

The dismissal of an employee will automatically be regarded as unfair if the reason or principal reason for it was that the employee:

(i)   was, or proposed to become, a member of an independent trade union;

(ii)   had taken part, or proposed to take part, in the activities of an independent trade union at an appropriate time;

(iii)   had made use, or proposed to make use, of trade union services at an appropriate time;

(iv)   had failed to accept an inducement contrary to *TULRCA 1992, s 145A* or *145B;* or

(v)   was not a member of any trade union, or of a particular trade union, or of one of a number of particular trade unions, or had refused, or proposed to refuse, to become or remain a member.

(*TULRCA 1992, s 152.*) (Note that there is no need for an employee to have been employed for any qualifying period to present a complaint on this ground. Further, employees over the normal retiring age or over the age of 65 are not barred from pursuing such a complaint (*TULRCA 1992, s 154*).)

The burden of proving that the reason for dismissal was union-related is upon the employee where he would otherwise lack sufficient qualifying service to complain of unfair dismissal. In other cases, it is for the employer to prove the reason for dismissal in the usual way (*Smith v Hayle Town Council* [1978] ICR 996; *Maund v Penwith District Council* [1984] ICR 143).

An 'independent trade union' is defined as any union which is not under the control or domination of an employer (see 51.22 TRADE UNIONS – I) (*TULRCA 1992, s 5*).

'Membership of a trade union' within the meaning of *TULRCA 1992, s 152* was construed broadly by the EAT in *Discount Tobacco and Confectionery Ltd v Armitage* [1990] IRLR 15 to include approaching a trade union officer to enlist his help in elucidating and attempting to negotiate terms and conditions of employment. *Discount Tobacco v Armitage* was followed by the EAT in *Speciality Care plc v Pachela* [1996] IRLR 248.

Such action may, alternatively, be considered to be taking part in the activities of a trade union (*Dixon and Shaw v West Ella Developments* [1978] ICR 856; see also *British Airways Engine Overhaul Ltd v Francis* [1981] ICR 278). For an employee to be taking part in the activities of a trade union, the activity must be that of the union and not merely that of an individual who happens to belong to a union (*Drew v St Edmundsbury Borough Council* [1980] ICR 513, holding also that trade union activity within *s 152* did not include the taking of industrial action). The dismissal of an employee because of union activities with a previous employer can come within *s 152*, although dismissing an employee for failing to tell the truth about past activities would not (*Fitzpatrick v British Railways Board* [1992] ICR 221).

'An appropriate time', in relation to an employee taking part in the activities of a trade union, means a time which either:

(A)   is outside his working hours; or

(B)   is a time within his working hours at which, in accordance with arrangements agreed with or consent given by his employers, it is permissible for him to take part in those activities or make use of trade union services.

(*TULRCA 1992, s 152(2)*.)

'Working hours', in relation to an employee, means any time when, in accordance with his contract of employment, he is required to be at work. In *Marley Tile Co Ltd v Shaw* [1980] ICR 72, the Court of Appeal held that such consent could be express or implied.

It is not necessary for the employee to show that the employer's actions were motivated by malice or anti-union hostility (*Dundon v GPT Ltd* [1995] IRLR 403).

Dismissal for conduct which on its own would justify dismissal, such as assault, may not become automatically unfair simply because it took place in the course of union activities (but see *Bass Taverns v Burgess* [1995] IRLR 596 in which the Court of Appeal held a dismissal to be automatically unfair under *s 152* even though the employee had gone 'over the top' in making critical remarks about the employer).

Closed shop. Under the relevant provisions of *TULRCA 1992*, all dismissals to enforce a closed shop are now automatically unfair (see TRADE UNIONS – II (51)).

(c) Health and safety-related dismissals

TURERA 1993, s 28 and *Sch 5* (now repealed and re-enacted within the *ERA 1996, s 100*) introduced new protection against dismissal for a health and safety-related reason. This followed the more limited special protection conferred by the *Offshore Safety (Protection against Victimisation) Act 1992*, now repealed.

The dismissal of an employee will automatically be regarded as unfair if the reason or principal reason for it was that the employee:

(i)   having been designated by the employer to carry out activities in connection with preventing or reducing risks to health and safety at work, carried out, or proposed to carry out, any such activities;

(ii) being a representative of workers on matters of health and safety at work, or a member of a safety committee in accordance with arrangements established under or by virtue of any enactment, or by reason of being acknowledged as such by the employer, performed or proposed to perform any functions as such a representative or a member of such a committee;

(iii) took part (or proposed to take part) in consultation with the employer pursuant to the *Health and Safety (Consultation with Employees) Regulations 1996 (SI 1996/1513)* (see 28.22 HEALTH AND SAFETY AT WORK – II) or in an election of representatives within the meaning of those *Regulations*, whether as a candidate or otherwise;

(iv) being an employee at a place where there was no such representative or safety committee, or where it was not reasonably practicable for the employee to raise the matter by means of the representative or safety committee, brought to his employer's attention by reasonable means circumstances connected with his work which he reasonably believed were harmful or potentially harmful to health or safety;

(v)   in circumstances of danger which he reasonably believed to be serious and imminent and which he could not reasonably have been expected to avert, left or proposed to leave or (while the danger persisted) refused to return to his place of work or any dangerous part of his place of work; or

(vi) in circumstances of danger which he reasonably believed to be serious and imminent, took or proposed to take appropriate steps to protect himself or other persons from the danger.

(*ERA 1996, s 100(1)*, as amended.)

In the case of (vi) above, whether the steps in question were appropriate will be judged by reference to all the circumstances, including in particular the employee's knowledge and the facilities and advice available to him at the time. The dismissal will not be unfair if the employer shows that it was or would have been so negligent for the employee to take those steps that a reasonable employer might have dismissed him for taking or proposing to take them (*ERA 1996, s 100(2), (3)*).

In *Goodwin v Cabletel UK Ltd* [1998] ICR 112, the EAT applied by analogy the approach adopted by the Court of Appeal in *Bass Taverns Ltd v Burgess* [1995] IRLR 596 (see above) to rule that the manner in which an activity is carried out may be protected, as well as the actual doing of it. The protection afforded to the way in which a protected employee carries out his health and safety activities must not be diluted too easily by finding that acts done for that purpose in fact justify dismissal. On the other hand, not every act should be treated as a protected act, however malicious or irrelevant to the task in hand.

Since 25 October 1999, there has been no statutory maximum upon compensation in automatically unfair health and safety unfair dismissal cases (*ERA 1996, s 124(1A)*, as introduced by *Employment Relations Act 1999, s 37*).

For safety representatives and safety committees, see 28.20 HEALTH AND SAFETY AT WORK – II. For the right not to suffer detriment short of dismissal on these grounds, see 28.9 HEALTH AND SAFETY AT WORK – II.

In *Harvest Press Ltd v McCaffrey* [1999] IRLR 778, a night-shift worker walked out because he was frightened of the abusive behaviour of his co-worker and was dismissed for leaving his post. The EAT upheld the finding of the tribunal that Mr McCaffrey was automatically unfairly dismissed because he was dismissed for leaving his post in circumstances of danger (*s 100(1)(d), ERA 1996*), even though the danger was caused by his co-worker and did not arise from the workplace itself.

In *Masiak v City Restaurants (UK) Ltd* [1999] IRLR 780, a chef left his employment after refusing to cook food which he considered to be a hazard to public health. The EAT held that Mr Maziak was automatically unfairly dismissed, under *s 100(1)(e)*, because he had been dismissed for 'taking steps to protect other persons from danger' and it was not necessary, for *s 100(1)(e)* to apply, that the 'other persons' were co-workers.

(d) Dismissals for asserting statutory rights

The dismissal of an employee will automatically be regarded as unfair if the reason or principal reason for it was that the employee brought proceedings against the employer to enforce a right of his which is a relevant statutory right, or alleged that the employer had infringed a right of his which is a relevant statutory right (*ERA 1996, s 104(1)*). (This protection was introduced by *TUR-ERA 1993, s 29*, which inserted the relevant provisions into *EPCA 1978*, now repealed and re-enacted within *ERA 1996*.)

The relevant statutory rights are:

(i) any right conferred by the *ERA 1996* for which the remedy for its infringement is by way of complaint or reference to an employment tribunal;

(ii) the right to statutory minimum notice under *ERA 1996, s 86* (see 48.7 TERMINATION OF EMPLOYMENT);

(iii) the rights conferred by *ss 68, 86, 145 A, 145B, 146, 168, 168A, 169* and *170* of *TULRCA 1992* (deductions from pay, union activities and time off); and

(iv) the rights conferred by the *Working Time Regulations 1998* or the *Merchant Shipping (Working Time: Inland Waterways) Regulations 2003* or the *Fishing Vessels (Working Time: Sea-fishermen) Regulations 2004*.

Provided that the employee's claim is made in good faith, it does not matter whether he in fact had the right or whether it was in fact infringed (*ERA 1996, s 104(2)*; and see *Mennell v Newell & Wright (Transport Contractors) Ltd* [1997] ICR 1039). The employee need not have specified the right concerned if he made it reasonably clear to the employer what the right claimed to have been infringed was (*ERA 1996, s 104(3)*).

The statutory rights whose assertion is protected under *ERA 1996, s 104* do not include the rights protecting against unlawful discrimination, however, the various anti-discrimination statutes and regulations contain their own anti-victimisation provisions (see 12.3 et seq DISCRIMINATION AND EQUAL OPPORTUNITIES – I); in any event, the dismissal of an employee who had asserted such rights would probably be unfair on normal principles (see 54.4 below).

(e) Family-related dismissals

ERA 1996, s 99 provides that an employee's dismissal will automatically be unfair if the reason or principal reason for the dismissal was a reason relating to:

  (i)   pregnancy, childbirth or maternity;

  (ii)   ordinary, compulsory or additional maternity leave;

  (iii) ordinary or additional adoption leave;

  (iv) parental leave;

  (v)   paternity leave; or

  (vi) time off for dependants.

and which reason has been prescribed by the Secretary of State in regulations (*Maternity and Parental Leave, etc Regulations 1999* (*SI 1999/3312*), *reg 20* and *Paternity Leave and Adoption Leave Regulations 2002* (*SI 2002/2788*), *reg 29*). A reason is of a prescribed kind if it is the employee's pregnancy, the fact that she has given birth, the application of a relevant health and safety requirement or recommendation because of maternity, the fact that the employee has taken (or sought to take) ordinary or additional maternity leave, parental leave or time off for dependants under *ERA 1996, s 57A*, the fact that she failed to return to work after ordinary or additional maternity leave where either the employer failed to notify her of the return date and she reasonably believed her maternity leave had not ended or the employer gave her less than 28 days' notice of the return date and it was not reasonably practicable for her to return on that date, the fact that she has declined to sign a workforce agreement for the purposes of the regulations, or that the employee has performed any functions or activities as an employee representative (or candidate for employee representative) under a workforce agreement, or the fact that the employee took, or sought to take, paternity or adoption leave, that the employer believed that the employee was likely to take ordinary or additional adoption leave, or that the employee failed to return after a period of additional adoption leave in a case where either the employer failed to notify the employee in accordance with the relevant regulations of the date on which the leave period would end and the employee reasonably believed that the period had not ended or the employer gave him less than 28 days' notice of the date on which the leave period would end and it was not reasonably practicable for him to return on that date.

A full discussion of these provisions appears 33.6 MATERNITY AND PARENTAL RIGHTS.

(f) Pension scheme trustees

This provision was introduced by the *Pensions Act 1995, s 46(5)* and is now contained in *ERA 1996, s 102*. An employee's dismissal will automatically be regarded as unfair if the reason or principal reason for it is that, being a trustee of a trust scheme which relates to his employment, the employee performed (or proposed to perform) any functions as such a trustee.

(g) Employee representatives

This provision was introduced by the *Collective Redundancies and Transfer of Undertakings* (*Protection of Employment*) (*Amendment*) *Regulations 1995*

(*SI 1995/2587*), and is now contained in *ERA 1996, s 103*. An employee's dismissal will automatically be regarded as unfair if the reason or principal reason for it is that the employee, being:

(i) an employee representative for the purposes of *TULRCA 1992, Part IV Chapter 2* (see 39.4 REDUNDANCY – II) or *Transfer of Undertakings (Protection of Employment) Regulations 1981 (SI 1981/1794)*, and from 6 April 2006 the *2006 Regulations (SI 2006/246)* (see 52.18 TRANSFER OF UNDERTAKINGS); or

(ii) a candidate in an election for such an employee representative,

performed, or proposed to perform, any functions or activities as such an employee representative or candidate. A dismissal will also be automatically unfair if the reason or principal reason is the employee's participation in an election for employee representatives in a redundancy or transfer of undertakings context.

Similarly, dismissals of employee representatives contrary to the *Occupational and Personal Pension Schemes (Consultation by Employers and Miscellaneous Amendment) Regulations 2006 (SI 2006/349) (para 5, Sch)* are automatically unfair, as are dismissals contrary to the *European Cooperative Society (Involvement of Employees) Regulations 2006 (SI 2006/2059) (reg 31)*.

(h) Shop workers and betting workers who refuse Sunday work

These provisions were introduced by the *Sunday Trading Act 1994* (shop workers) and the *Deregulation and Contracting Out Act 1994* (betting workers) and are now contained in *ERA 1996, s 101* (see 8.23 CONTRACT OF EMPLOYMENT). The dismissal of an employee who is a shop worker or betting worker will automatically be regarded as unfair if the reason or principal reason for the dismissal is that the employee:

(i) being a protected shop worker or an opted-out shop worker, or a protected betting worker or an opted-out betting worker, refused (or proposed to refuse) to do shop work, or betting work, on Sunday or on a particular Sunday, except (in the case of an opted-out shop worker or an opted-out betting worker) in respect of any Sunday or Sundays falling before the opting-out notice expired; or

(ii) gave (or proposed to give) an opting-out notice to the employer.

(j) Working time cases

This provision was inserted into *ERA 1996* by the *Working Time Regulations 1998 (SI 1998/1833), reg 32*. An employee's dismissal will automatically be regarded as unfair if the reason or principal reason for the dismissal is that the employee:

(i) refused (or proposed to refuse) to comply with a requirement which the employer imposed (or proposed to impose) in contravention of the *Working Time Regulations 1998* or the *Merchant Shipping (Working Time: Inland Waterways) Regulations 2003*;

(ii) refused (or proposed to refuse) to forgo a right conferred on him by those regulations;

(iii) failed to sign a workforce agreement for the purposes of those regulations, or to enter into, or agree to vary or extend, any other agreement with his employer which is provided for in those *Regulations*; or

(iv)   being a representative of members of the workforce for the purposes of *Sch 1* to those regulations, or a candidate in an election for such a representative, performed (or proposed to perform) any functions or activities as such a representative or candidate.

(*ERA 1996, s 101A.*)

(k) Unfair selection for redundancy

A dismissal for redundancy will be unfair if the selection was made upon any of the grounds which would render a dismissal automatically unfair (*ERA 1996, s 105*).

(l) Dismissals on a transfer of an undertaking

Where either before or after a relevant transfer, any employee of the transferor or transferee is dismissed, that employee shall *prima facie* be treated as unfairly dismissed if the transfer or a reason connected with it is the reason or principal reason for his dismissal (*Transfer of Undertakings* (*Protection of Employment*) *Regulations 2006* (*SI 2006/246*), *reg 7(1(a))*). However, the dismissal is not *automatically* unfair if the reason for it falls within *reg7(1)(b)*, ie if it is for an economic, technical or organisational reason entailing changes in the workforce. See TRANSFER OF UNDERTAKINGS (52).

(m) Spent convictions

A spent conviction or a failure to disclose it is not a proper ground for dismissal (see 19.3 EMPLOYEE'S PAST CRIMINAL CONVICTIONS).

(n) National Minimum Wage cases

This provision was inserted into *ERA 1996* by the *National Minimum* Wage *Act 1998, s 25* (see 34.9 PAY – I). An employee's dismissal will automatically be regarded as unfair if the reason or principal reason for the dismissal is that:

(i)   any action was taken, or was proposed to be taken, by or on behalf of the employee with a view to enforcing, or otherwise securing the benefit of, specified rights granted under the *National Minimum Wage Act 1998*;

(ii)   the employer was prosecuted for any offence under the *National Minimum Wage Act 1998, s 31*, by reason of any action taken by or on behalf of the employee; or

(iii)   the employee qualifies, or will or might qualify, for the National Minimum Wage or for a particular rate of the National Minimum Wage.

It is immaterial whether the employee in fact has the right to the National Minimum Wage or that right has been infringed, provided that the claim made by or on behalf of the employee was made in good faith.

(*ERA 1996, s 104A.*)

(o) Public interest disclosure cases

This provision was inserted into *ERA 1996, ss 103A and 105(6A)* by the *Public Interest Disclosure Act 1998, s 5* (the 'Whistleblowers' Act', see 11.17 DISCLOSURE OF INFORMATION). An employee's dismissal will automatically be regarded as unfair if the reason or principal reason for the dismissal is that the employee made a protected disclosure as defined in *ERA 1996, ss 43A–43L* (inserted by the

Public Interest Disclosure Act 1998, s 1). There is no statutory maximum cap upon compensation in public interest disclosure cases (*ERA 1996, s 124(1A)*, as introduced by *Employment Relations Act 1999, s 37*). In *Stolt Offshore Ltd v Miklaszewicz* [2002] IRLR 344, the Scottish Court of Session upheld the EAT's ruling that it was possible to bring a claim under *ERA 1996, ss 103* and *105(6A)* even if the disclosure itself took place many years before the *Public Interest Disclosure Act 1998* came into force, provided that the dismissal itself took place after 2 July 1999.

(*ERA 1996, s 103A.*)

(p) Dismissals connected with union recognition

Dismissals connected with union recognition are automatically unfair (*TULRCA 1992, Sch A1, para 161*, inserted by *Employment Relations Act 1999, s 1(2)* and *Sch 1*). This applies to dismissals where the reason or principal reason is that the employee acted with a view to obtaining or preventing recognition; indicated that he supported or did not support recognition; acted with a view to securing or preventing the ending of bargaining arrangements; indicated that he supported or did not support the ending of bargaining arrangements; influenced or sought to influence whether other employees voted or how they voted; voted in such a ballot; or proposed to do or failed to do or proposed to decline to do, any of the above acts. A dismissal for one of the above reasons will not be automatically unfair, however, if the reason was an unreasonable act or omission by the employee.

(q) Right to be accompanied at disciplinary and grievance hearings

This set of automatically unfair dismissals consists of dismissals of employees because they exercised or sought to exercise the right under *s 10* of the *ERA 1999* to be accompanied at disciplinary and grievance hearings, or because they accompanied a fellow worker to such a hearing (*Employment Relations Act 1999, s 12*). *Sections 10–12* do not apply only to employees in the normal sense used for the purposes of the *ERA 1996* (*ERA 1996, s 230(3)*), but to a wider group of workers set out in *Employment Relations Act 1999, s 13* and include agency workers and home workers.

(r) Protected industrial action

Employment Relations Act 1999, s 16 and *Sch 5* provide that the dismissal of employees who are taking part in protected (ie official) industrial action will be automatically unfair if the conditions set out in the new *TULRCA 1992, s 238A* are satisfied.

(s) Dismissals for asserting the rights of part-time workers

Regulation 7 of the *Part-time Workers (Prevention of Less Favourable Treatment) Regulations 2000* provides that an employee who is dismissed for any of the following reasons will automatically be regarded as having been unfairly dismissed:

(i)   if the employee has brought proceedings against his employer under the *Regulations* or requested a written statement of reasons under the *Regulations*;

(ii) if the employee has given evidence or information in connection with such proceedings brought by a worker or otherwise done anything under the

> *Regulations* in relation to the employer or any other person, or alleged that the employer had infringed the *Regulations*;

(iii)   if the employee refused (or proposed to refuse) to forgo a right conferred on him by the *Regulations*; or

(iv)   if the employer believes or suspects that the employee has done or intends to do any of the above things.

(t)   Action to enforce rights under the Tax Credits Act 1999

ERA 1996, s 104B provides that a dismissal will be automatically unfair if the reason, or principal reason, is that the employee took, or proposed to take, action with a view to enforcing or securing the benefit of a right under the *Tax Credits Act 1999*, or that a penalty was imposed upon the employer as a result of action taken by or on behalf of the employee for the purpose of enforcing his or her rights under the *Act*, or that the employee is entitled, or will or may be entitled to working families' tax credit or disabled persons tax credit.

(u)   Activities as member of special negotiating body, European Works Council, etc

The *Transnational Information and Consultation of Employees Regulations 1999, reg 28* provides that a worker will be automatically unfairly dismissed if the reason or principal reason for the employee's dismissal was that:

(i)   the employee had performed any functions or activities as a member or representative of, or a candidate for, a special negotiating body, a European Works Council, or as an information and consultation representative or as a candidate for such a position; or

(ii)   the employee or a person acting on his behalf asked for time off in relation to such activities; or

(iii)   the employee took specific steps in relation to such activities specified in *reg 28(6)*, including taking proceedings before the Employment Tribunal, the Employment Appeal Tribunal or the CAC, acting with a view to securing that a relevant body did or did not come into existence, voting in a ballot, or seeking to influence others' votes.

The *European Public Limited-Liability Company Regulations 2004, reg 42* and the *Information and Consultation of Employees Regulations 2004, reg 30* create similar protections for employee representatives and candidates.

(v)   Dismissals for asserting the rights of fixed-term employees

Regulation 6 of the *Fixed-term Employees (Prevention of Less Favourable Treatment) Regulations 2002* provides that a dismissal will be automatically unfair if the reason or principal reason was that:

(i)   the employee brought proceedings against his employer under the *Regulations* or requested a written statement of reasons under the *Regulations;*

(ii)   the employee gave evidence or information in connection with such proceedings brought by an employee or otherwise did anything under the *Regulations* in relation to the employer or any other person, or alleged that the employer had infringed the *Regulations*;

(iii)   the employee refused (or proposed to refuse) to forgo a right conferred on him by the *Regulations*;

(iv) the employee declined to sign a workforce agreement for the purpose of the *Regulations;*

(v)   the employee, being a workforce representative or candidate for the purpose of the *Regulations*, performed (or proposed to perform) any functions or activities in that capacity; or

(iv) the employer believes or suspects that the employee has done or intends to do any of the above things.

(w) Dismissals for asserting the right to request flexible working

Section 104C of the *ERA 1996* renders a dismissal automatically unfair where the reason (or if more than one, the principal reason) was that the employee:

(i)   made (or proposed to make) an application for a contract variation (see *ERA 1996, s 80F*);

(ii) exercised (or proposed to exercise) a right conferred on him by *ERA 1996, s 80G* (procedural entitlements);

(iii) brought proceedings against his employer to enforce the right to request flexible working under *ERA 1996, s 80H*; or

(iv) alleged the existence of any circumstance which would constitute a ground for bringing such proceedings against his employer.

(x) Jury Service

ERA 1996, s 98B makes a dismissal automatically unfair where the reason or principal reason was that the employee was summoned to do jury service, or was absent from work because he attended at any place in pursuance of being called to perform jury service. The dismissal is not unfair if the employer shows that the circumstances were such that the employee's absence in pursuance of being summoned was likely to cause substantial injury to the employer's undertaking, that the employer brought those circumstances to the attention of the employee, and the employee unreasonably failed or refused to apply to the appropriate officer for excusal from or deferral of the obligation to attend in pursuance of being so summoned.

54.4 FAIRNESS IN THE CIRCUMSTANCES

If the employer establishes that the reason for the dismissal is an acceptable reason other than retirement, the tribunal will proceed to determine whether the dismissal was fair or unfair in the circumstances (including the size and administrative resources of the employer's undertaking), having regard to equity and the substantial merits of the case (*ERA 1996, s 98(4)*). Where an employer shows that the reason for the dismissal is retirement, the fairness of the dismissal will be considered under *ERA 1996, s 98ZG* (*ERA 1996, s 98(3A)* (see 3.48 AGE DISCRIMINATION).

Whereas the burden of establishing the reason for the dismissal is on the employer, the burden on this second limb of the tribunal's inquiry has been placed neutrally where the reason for dismissal is capability or qualifications, conduct, redundancy or some other substantial reason. The presumption of fairness in respect of a dismissal by reason of retirement which is contained in *ERA 1996, s 98ZG* is unique. The analysis of fairness below does not apply to dismissals by reason of retirement.

The tribunal will consider whether the employer acted reasonably or unreasonably in treating the reason for the dismissal as a sufficient reason for dismissing the employee. If *part* of the reason or principal reason was not reasonably relied upon, the dismissal will be unfair (*Smith v Glasgow City District Council* [1987] ICR 796). The EAT has traditionally held that the correct approach for an employment tribunal, when applying *ERA 1996, s 98(4)*, is to consider whether the employer's decision to dismiss fell within the band of reasonable responses to the employee's conduct which a reasonable employer could adopt (*Iceland Frozen Foods Ltd v Jones* [1983] ICR 17; *British Leyland (UK) Ltd v Swift* [1981] IRLR 91, CA; *Gilham v Kent County Council (No 2)* [1985] ICR 233; and *Neale v Hereford and Worcester County Council* [1986] ICR 471). In other words, the tribunal must not ask itself whether it thinks the employer did the right thing, but must recognise that different employers may reasonably react in different ways to a particular situation.

Until the EAT decision of *Haddon v Van den Bergh Foods Ltd* [1999] ICR 1150, it was considered trite law that, when deciding whether a dismissal was fair, it was not for the tribunal to substitute its own view for that of the employer. Instead, the tribunal should consider whether the dismissal fell within the range of reasonable responses open to a reasonable employer. This test had been approved by the Court of Appeal in *Neale v Hereford and Worcester County Council* [1986] IRLR 168.

In *Haddon*, however, the EAT (Morison J) disapproved the 'range of reasonable responses test' and held that it was the duty of tribunals both to exercise their own judgment about the dismissal and to substitute it on occasions. Morison J stressed that the test of reasonableness in *s 98* of the *ERA 1996* was not a perversity test. In *Wilson v Ethicon* [2000] IRLR 4, the Scottish EAT followed *Haddon* and held that a tribunal had erred in law in applying the 'range of reasonable responses test', instead of directing itself in accordance with the language of *s 98(4)*.

Morison J was replaced as President of the EAT by Lindsay J. Lindsay J considered *Haddon* in *Midland Bank Ltd v Madden* [2000] IRLR 288. The EAT in *Madden* held that:

(*a*)   in a misconduct case, a tribunal must consider whether, looked at objectively, there were reasonable grounds for the employer's conclusion that the employee was guilty of the offence for which he or she was dismissed, and must decide whether it was reasonable to dismiss in the circumstances. To that extent the tribunal can substitute its own view for the employer;

(*b*)   however, the tribunal is not free to substitute its own view as to whether dismissal was merited, if the tribunal is satisfied that the employer's actions were reasonable; and

(*c*)   in the light of the doctrine of precedent, no court below the Court of Appeal can discard the 'range of reasonable responses' test. However, tribunals must guard against confusing the 'range of reasonable responses' test with a perversity test. Until the Court of Appeal rules definitively on the 'range of reasonable responses' test, therefore, tribunals' application of the test should always be accompanied by a reminder to themselves of the language of *s 98(4)*.

Yet another division of the EAT, presided over by HHJ Clark, in *Beedell v West Ferry Printers Ltd* [2000] IRLR 650, applied the old 'range of reasonable responses' test, notwithstanding *Haddon* and *Madden*, pointing out that the test had been approved on many occasions by the Court of Appeal.

The 'range of reasonable responses' test was then emphatically reinstated by the Court of Appeal in *Foley v Post Office and HSBC Bank (formerly Midland Bank) v Madden* [2000] IRLR 827. The Court of Appeal held that tribunals were not to approach the issue of the reasonableness or unreasonableness of a dismissal by reference to their own judgment of what would have been done if they had been the employer. In the light of the decision in *Foley*, *Haddon* and *Madden* (in the EAT) should be regarded as having been wrongly decided.

In *Ulsterbus Ltd v Henderson* [1989] IRLR 251, the Northern Ireland Court of Appeal applied the 'range of reasonable responses' test to the procedure adopted, concluding that a reasonable employer could decide not to permit the confrontation and cross-examination of witnesses. The 'band of reasonable responses' test has been applied to the procedural process by which an employer arrives at the decision to dismiss for misconduct, even in circumstances where the employee has admitted the misconduct: *Whitbread plc v Hall* [2001] ICR 699. In *Hall*, the Court of Appeal held that the requirement of reasonableness applies not only to the outcome in terms of the penalty imposed by the employer but also to the process by which the employer arrived at that decision.

Before deciding to dismiss, the employer must have investigated all the relevant facts adequately. The reason for, and the fairness of, the action taken is determined by examining the circumstances known to the employer at the time of the dismissal or when he maintains that decision at the conclusion of an internal appeal (*West Midlands Co-operative Society Ltd v Tipton* [1986] ICR 192). See also 54.10, 54.15 below. An employer cannot be criticised for failing to have regard to material which came to light for the first time as evidence during the tribunal hearing (*Dick v Glasgow University* [1993] IRLR 581).

Fair procedure. The tribunal will take into account not only whether the employer had grounds for dismissing the employee, but also whether he adopted a fair procedure in dismissing him. Even if the employer has complied with the statutory dispute resolution procedures, the tribunal may nevertheless consider that the employer did not adopt a fair procedure in dismissing him. It is therefore important to consider in each case what procedural requirements fairness called for. In this context, the paragraphs in the *ACAS Code of Practice No 1 (2000)* relating to disciplinary practice and procedures provide useful guidelines (*Lock v Cardiff Rly Co* [1998] IRLR 358). The main point of these provisions is that *there should be a known disciplinary procedure which should be followed.* If there is a complaint against an employee, he should be informed in detail and preferably in writing of the complaint, and be given an opportunity to make representations, if necessary through, or in the presence of, an employee representative. (If the employee is a union member, his representative may be his shop steward.) In *Clark v Civil Aviation Authority* [1991] IRLR 412 at para 20, the EAT gave guidance as to how a disciplinary hearing should be conducted.

The employee should also be given the opportunity, where practicable, to appeal to a level of management not previously involved (although cf *Robinson v Ulster Carpet Mills Ltd* [1991] IRLR 348). A dismissal may be held to be unfair when the employer has refused to entertain an appeal to which the employee was contractually entitled. In general, whether a dismissal has been carried out in breach of contract is a relevant factor in assessing its fairness, but is not conclusive either way (*Hooper v British Railways Board* [1988] IRLR 517; *Post Office v Marney* [1990] IRLR 170; and see *Stoker v Lancashire County Council* [1992] IRLR 75). Nor will every procedural defect make a dismissal unfair; the seriousness of the defect must be considered in deciding whether the overall result was unfair (*Fuller v Lloyds Bank plc* [1991] IRLR 336).

The most common procedural failings in practice include: a failure to give warnings when shortcomings in an employee's performance first emerge, or to record them properly in writing; failure to give adequate advance notice of a disciplinary hearing, or to inform the employee before the hearing of the substance of the complaint to be considered or the fact that, if the complaint is found proved, the employee may be dismissed; failure to inform the employee of or to permit him to exercise the right to be accompanied to a disciplinary hearing; managers acting on evidence on which the employee has had no chance to comment; decisions being taken or influenced by persons other than those who have considered what the employee has to say; and appeals being determined by persons with a prior involvement in the matter. Procedural requirements in particular contexts are dealt with in more detail in 54.6–54.14 below.

For several years it was thought that if an employer had adopted an unfair procedure in dismissing an employee, but established that if he had adopted a fair procedure the employee would still have been dismissed, the dismissal could be held to be fair. However, in *Polkey v AE Dayton Services Ltd* [1988] ICR 142, the House of Lords reaffirmed that the sole question for the tribunal was whether the employer acted reasonably at the time. In the vast majority of cases, there was no scope to consider what might have happened if the employer had acted differently, except at the stage of assessing compensation (see 55.13 UNFAIR DISMISSAL – III). However, the House of Lords also stated that where the employer could reasonably have concluded in the light of circumstances known to him at the time of dismissal that it would have been utterly useless to follow the normal procedure, he might well have acted reasonably if he did not follow the procedure. In *Duffy v Yeomans & Partners Ltd* [1994] IRLR 642, the Court of Appeal said that it was not necessary, in order to come within this exception, that the employer actually applied his mind to the question whether normal procedures would be utterly useless. (The EAT in Scotland had reached a contrary view in *Robertson v Magnet Ltd (Retail Division)* [1993] IRLR 512.)

EA 2002, s 34, introduced a new *s 98A(2)* into *ERA 1996* which has the effect of overturning *Polkey*. Failure to follow a procedure in relation to the dismissal of an employee shall not be regarded – by itself – as making the employer's action unreasonable if he shows that he would have decided to dismiss the employee if he had followed the procedure.

The President of the EAT, Elias J, has in *Kelly-Madden v Manor Surgery* [2007] IRLR 17 indicated that (as the EAT had held in *Alexander v Bridgen Enterprises Ltd* [2006] IRLR 422) *s 98A(2)* applies to any procedure which the employment tribunal considers in fairness the employer should have complied with. The *Kelly-Madden* judgment rejected the analysis adopted by a differently-constituted EAT in *Mason v Governing Body of Ward End Primary School* [2006] IRLR 432 that *s 98A(2)* referred to the employer's own procedures only. The aim of *s 98A(2)*, plainly, is to deter employees from bringing unfair dismissal claims if they are relying upon a technical breach of procedure by the employer, which had no effect on the outcome.

In *White v South London Transport Ltd* [1998] ICR 293, the EAT held that the date at which the reasonableness of an employer's reason to dismiss was to be assessed was the effective date of termination rather than the date on which notice of termination was given, following *Stacey v Babcock Power Ltd* [1986] ICR 221 (see also *Alboni v Ind Coope Retail Ltd* [1998] IRLR 131 and 54.11 below).

Although a failure to follow the *ACAS Codes of Practice*, or internal procedures, is not determinative of the fairness of a dismissal, it is important to bear in mind that with the shift of the burden of proof in discrimination cases, a failure to follow a relevant Code of Practice or internal procedure may lead an employment tribunal to infer unlawful discrimination (see 12.6 DISCRIMINATION AND EQUAL OPPORTUNITIES – I).

54.5 GROUNDS FOR DISMISSAL – LACK OF CAPABILITY OR QUALIFICATIONS

Capability means capability assessed by reference to skill, aptitude, health, or any other physical or mental quality. *Qualifications* means any degree, diploma or other academic, technical or professional qualification, *relevant to the position which the employee held* (*ERA 1996, s 98(3)*).

54.6 Capability

In cases of lack of capability, it is essential for the employer to show what was required of the employee, that the employee was informed of, or must have been aware of, those requirements, and that he fell short of them.

Procedure for capability dismissals(see also 54.10 below)

Since the statutory dismissal procedure is very basic, employers would be well-advised to adopt their own capability procedures in order to reduce the likelihood of subsequent disputes. Employers should follow procedures agreed with or notified to their employees. Such procedures may include the following steps.

(i)   If an employee falls short of the performance required of him, a meeting (of which the employee is given prior written notice containing an outline of the matters to be considered) should be arranged with him and his representative at which he is informed of:

  (*a*)   the respects (in detail) in which he falls short of the required standards;

  (*b*)   the time within which his performance must improve; and

  (*c*)   the fact that if he fails to improve he will receive a written warning and if he still fails to improve within a reasonable time he may be dismissed.

  If possible, a witness should attend this meeting and take a contemporaneous note of what is said. If this cannot be done, a written record of what was said should be made as soon as possible after the meeting. The employee and his representative should be sent a letter setting out a brief summary of the meeting and of the conclusions reached, including any warning given.

(ii)   If the employee's performance fails to improve, he should be sent a letter:

  (*a*)   setting out the respects in which he has failed to improve; and

  (*b*)   inviting him and his representative to another meeting to explain this failure.

(iii)   At the second meeting, at which again there should be a witness and a record kept:

  (*a*)   the complaints against the employee should be reiterated; and

  (*b*)   he should be given an opportunity to explain.

If he has no satisfactory explanation for his failure to improve, he should be informed that:

(c)   he has a further time in which to improve; and

(d)   failure to improve within this time will result in dismissal.

The employee and his representative should again be sent a summary of the meeting.

(iv)   If there is no improvement, repeat step (ii), warning him that his dismissal will be considered.

(v)   At the third meeting, repeat steps (iii)(a) and (b) and if no satisfactory explanation is given, give notice of dismissal if the circumstances warrant such a sanction.

(vi)   If practicable, and in any event if the contract or any disciplinary or grievance procedure requires it, if the employee wishes to challenge his dismissal, a manager or managers not involved in the original decision to dismiss should conduct an appeal hearing.

Other steps which may be taken are the offer of training to assist the employee's performance, and consultation with his union representative. Consideration should be given to whether the employer has other work available to which the employee would be better suited.

The importance of these steps will vary according to the circumstances. For example, it may be that a senior employee ought to be well aware of what is required of him and the consequences of failing to perform his duties adequately. However, it is best to give warnings in cases of incapability, irrespective of the seniority of the employee.

54.7   Qualifications

Dismissal for lack of qualifications is not common since an employer will have difficulty in convincing a tribunal that an employee whom he engaged with full knowledge of his qualifications is not qualified for the job. If, however, the employee misled the employer into believing that he possessed certain qualifications which were essential for the performance of the task to which he was appointed, he may be dismissed for his lack of qualifications. Some of the cases on lack of qualifications have arisen where a man employed as a driver is disqualified from driving and therefore is no longer able to perform his duties (*Appleyard v Smith (Hull) Ltd* [1972] IRLR 19). Consideration should be given to offering a disqualified employee suitable alternative employment.

54.8   Lack of capability due to ill-health

In cases of ill-health which make future performance of the contract of employment impossible, the contract may be considered to have been frustrated and the employee not to have been dismissed (see 46.3 TERMINATION OF EMPLOYMENT). However, instances of frustration of the contract of employment are extremely rare.

Before dismissing an employee for reasons of ill-health, an employer should find out the current medical position. This will involve obtaining, with the employee's consent, a report from the employee's general practitioner and, if appropriate, his consultant (see 11.15 DISCLOSURE OF INFORMATION for the *Access to Medical Reports Act 1988* and the *Access to Health Records Act 1990*). In many cases, it may be thought necessary to have the employee examined, with his consent, by a doctor appointed by the employer. Once the employer has properly informed himself of the employee's state of health and the prognosis, he should consider the requirements of his business, the employee's past sickness record and whether the employee could be offered an alternative position more suitable to his state of health (*Spencer v Paragon Wallpapers Ltd* [1977] ICR 301). The employer should also consider whether the employee should be regarded as disabled and, if so, whether any reasonable adjustments should be made for the employee (see DISABILITY DISCRIMINATION (10)). The employer should consult the employee and any representative before dismissing him (*East Lindsay District Council v Daubney* [1977] ICR 566; *Merseyside and North Wales Electricity Board v Taylor* [1975] ICR 185) but an employer will not act unreasonably if he offers the employee alternative employment at a reduced rate of pay where this is the only suitable alternative employment which is available for him (*British Gas Services Ltd v McCaull* [2001] IRLR 60). The employee, on the other hand, has no duty to volunteer information about his prospects of recovery to his employer (*Mitchell v Arkwood Plastics (Engineering) Ltd* [1993] ICR 471).

Where the problem consists not of a long absence but of persistent short absences caused by unconnected minor ailments, a medical examination has little purpose. The employee should be told what level of attendance he is expected to attain, the period within which that is to be achieved and that dismissal may follow if there is no sufficient improvement. The situation should then be monitored to see whether absence is reduced below a reasonable level. A second warning would be appropriate in borderline cases (see *International Sports Co Ltd v Thomson* [1980] IRLR 340; *Rolls-Royce Ltd v Walpole* [1980] IRLR 343; *Lynock v Cereal Packaging Ltd* [1988] ICR 670).

In deciding whether a dismissal on grounds of ill-health is fair or unfair, the tribunal will not be interested in whether the ill health was caused by the employer's actions. The issue of responsibility for the illness or injury is irrelevant to the question of fairness (*London Fire and Civil Defence Authority v Betty* [1994] IRLR 384).

In *HJ Heinz Co v Kenrick* [2000] IRLR 144, the EAT held that it would be an error of law for a tribunal to proceed on the basis that a disability-related dismissal which is not 'justified' under the *Disability Discrimination Act 1995* is, without more, automatically unfair under the *ERA 1996*. Separate consideration must be given to the question of unfairness. On disability discrimination, see DISABILITY DISCRIMINATION (10).

54.9   **GROUNDS FOR DISMISSAL – CONDUCT**

In order to warrant dismissal, misconduct must be extremely serious, or if not extremely serious, repeated on more than one occasion. However fair the procedure adopted, a single incident of, for example, bad timekeeping, will not in most cases be considered sufficiently serious to justify a dismissal. Equally, the fact that an employee has recently been given a disciplinary warning (especially if it was for a similar offence) may make it more reasonable to dismiss. The EAT in *Auguste Noel Ltd v Curtis* [1990] ICR 604 confirmed that previous warnings for dissimilar conduct may also be relevant. Where an appeal against a prior warning is pending, the employer should take into account both the warning and the fact that it is subject to an undetermined appeal in considering whether to dismiss, although he is not precluded from dismissing before the appeal is heard (*Tower Hamlets Health Authority v Anthony* [1989] ICR 656). In *Diosynth Ltd v Thomson* [2006] CSIH 5, [2006] IRLR 284, however, the Court of Session concluded that it had been unreasonable for an employer to dismiss an employee for breaches of safety procedures after a fatality, because the employer had treated an expired warning for breach of safety procedures as a determining factor in the decision to dismiss. For the dismissal to be held fair, it must be a reasonable sanction for the offence and other possible penalties should be considered. It is important to consider the circumstances of the individual case, and not simply to apply an inflexible policy (*Post Office v Marney* [1990] IRLR 170; *Rentokil Ltd v Machin* [1989] IRLR 286). For example, even where an employee is dismissed for misconduct such as dishonesty which is referred to in the employer's disciplinary code as being misconduct which would normally lead to dismissal, the duty on an employer to act fairly and reasonably requires that they should investigate the seriousness of the offence in the particular case (*John Lewis plc v Coyne* [2001] IRLR 139).

Where an employer relies upon the employee's conduct in refusing to obey an instruction, the lawfulness of that instruction was not decisive when considering the reasonableness of the dismissal under *ERA 1996, s 98(4)*, although it is relevant: *Farrant v Woodroffe School* [1998] ICR 184.

The conduct for which an employee is dismissed usually relates to behaviour during working hours, but in certain cases an employee may be dismissed for other behaviour, if it is likely to affect the performance of his contract. If, for example, a playgroup leader is convicted of an indecent assault on a child outside his hours of work, his conviction for such an offence may make him unsuitable for carrying on his employment (eg *Nottinghamshire County Council v Bowly* [1978] IRLR 252, in which the EAT held to be fair the dismissal of a teacher after his conviction for an offence of gross indecency with a man and similarly the Court of Appeal in *X v Y* [2004] EWCA Civ 662, [2004] IRLR 625 including consideration of *art 8* of the *ECHR*).

Even in a case of misconduct justifying dismissal from the employee's existing job, it may sometimes be necessary to consider whether the employee could still be employed in some other capacity. However, it may be reasonable to leave investigation of that possibility until after the time when notice is given (*P v Nottinghamshire County Council* [1992] ICR 706).

Length of service is a factor which an employment tribunal may properly take into account in deciding whether the decision of an employer to dismiss in reaction to the employee's conduct was an appropriate one (*Strouthos v London Underground Ltd* [2004] EWCA Civ 402, [2004] IRLR 636).

In certain circumstances, even where the employee has committed misconduct, an employment tribunal may consider the dismissal unfair because the misconduct was not in fact the real reason for the dismissal, as in *Brady v Associated Society of Locomotion Engineers and Firemen* [2006] IRLR 576, [2006] All ER (D) 14 (Apr), EAT.

Sometimes a dismissal may be held unfair on the ground of inconsistency, in that the employer has on other occasions dealt more leniently with similar misconduct (*Cain v Leeds Western Health Authority* [1990] ICR 585). However, this should only be the case if the circumstances were strongly similar in the two cases (see *Post Office v Fennell* [1981] IRLR 221; *Hadjioannou v Coral Casinos Ltd* [1981] IRLR 352; *Paul v East Surrey District Health Authority* [1995] IRLR 305; *London Borough of Harrow v Cunningham* [1996] IRLR 256). See also *Procter v British Gypsum Ltd* [1992] IRLR 7.

The Court of Appeal in *W Weddel & Co Ltd v Tepper* [1980] ICR 286 approved the approach to cases of misconduct formulated by Arnold J in *British Home Stores Ltd v Burchell* [1980] ICR 303n. At 304 he stated:

> 'What the tribunal have to decide every time is, broadly expressed, whether the employer who discharged the employee on the grounds of misconduct in question (usually, though not necessarily, dishonest conduct) entertained a reasonable suspicion amounting to a belief in the guilt of the employee of that misconduct at that time. That is really stating shortly and compendiously what is in fact more than one element. First of all, there must be established by the employer the fact of that belief; that the employer did believe it. Secondly, that the employer had in his mind reasonable grounds upon which to sustain that belief. And thirdly, we think, that the employer, at the stage at which he formed that belief on those grounds, at any rate at the final stage at which he formed that belief on those grounds, had carried out as much investigation into the matter as was reasonable in all the circumstances of the case.'

However, in *Boys and Girls Welfare Society v McDonald* [1997] ICR 693, the EAT pointed out that *Burchell* had been decided when the burden of proof rested with the employer and warned that a simplistic application of the *Burchell* test in every case involves the danger of the employment tribunal falling into error by placing the onus of proof on the employer to prove reasonableness. The EAT added that (i) in any event, *Burchell* may not be appropriate where there is no real conflict on the facts; and (ii) *Burchell* does not mean that an employer who fails one or more of the three tests is, without more, guilty of unfair dismissal. The employment tribunal should focus upon the question whether the employer's action fell within the range of reasonable responses open to a reasonable employer. The 'range of reasonable responses' test was also applied to procedural questions by the Northern Ireland Court of Appeal in *Ulsterbus Ltd v Henderson* [1989] IRLR 251. Since *McDonald*, the *Burchell* test has been approved by the Scottish Court of Session in *Scottish Daily Record and Sunday Mail (1986) Ltd v Laird* [1996] IRLR 665, and by the Court of Appeal in *Foley v Post Office, HSBC Bank (formerly Midland Bank) v Madden* [2000] IRLR 827.

For other general discussions, see *ILEA v Gravett* [1988] IRLR 497, and also *Whitbread & Co plc v Mills* [1988] ICR 776. The more serious the allegation of misconduct, generally, the greater the scope required in a fair investigation. Where the investigation is unfair, the dismissal will be unfair, even if a fair investigation would have made no practical difference to the outcome (*A v B* [2003] IRLR 405). Note the importance of framing the disciplinary charge carefully in order to ensure that a misconduct dismissal is for a matter charged (see *Strouthos* above). However, if the employer reasonably believes that one of a number of employees is guilty of dishonesty and, despite proper investigation, cannot identify the culprit, it may be reasonable to dismiss all those who could have been responsible (*Monie v Coral Racing Ltd* [1981] ICR 109; *Whitbread & Co plc v Thomas* [1988] ICR 135; *Parr v Whitbread & Co plc* [1990] ICR 427; *Frames Snooker Centre v Boyce* [1992] IRLR 472). In *John Lewis v Coyne* [2001] IRLR 139, the EAT gave useful guidance on what type of misconduct can be said to amount to 'dishonesty'. The EAT held that the best working test of what amounts to dishonesty is that set out in *R v Ghosh* [1982] QB 1053. In summary, there are two aspects to dishonesty – the objective and the subjective – and judging whether or not there has been dishonesty involves going through a two-stage process. First, it must be decided whether according to the ordinary standards of reasonable and honest people, what was done was dishonest. If so, then second, consideration must be given to whether the person concerned must have realised that what he or she was doing was by those standards dishonest. See also *Panama v Hackney London Borough Council* [2003] EWCA Civ 278, [2003] IRLR 278 on proof of fraudulent conduct.

Cases in which an employee is arrested by the police and charged with theft of his employer's property pose particular difficulties. Is it proper for the employer to conduct his own investigation and question the employee whilst the police investigations are proceeding? In *Harris v Courage (Eastern) Ltd* [1982] ICR 530, the Court of Appeal approved the decision of the EAT that there is no absolute rule that once an employee had been charged with an offence and advised to say nothing until his criminal trial, an employer could not dismiss him for the alleged offence. Because of the long delay before a criminal prosecution is finally disposed of, it will often be necessary or desirable for the employer to act before its conclusion. Employers frequently carry out their own investigations and dismiss for dishonest conduct before a prosecution is concluded. If the employer awaits the outcome of a criminal trial and the employee is acquitted, he may find it harder to justify a subsequent dismissal, although the burden on the prosecution at the criminal trial is heavier than upon the employer in showing that he acted reasonably. The evidence which it is permissible for the employer to rely upon is less restricted than that which is admissible in the criminal trial, but how far it is reasonable for the employer to rely upon evidence which has been ruled inadmissible in a criminal trial depends on the facts in each case (*Dhaliwal v British Airways Board* [1985] ICR 513).

Even if the employee may be charged with a criminal offence, he must be given an opportunity by his employer to state his case (*Read v Phoenix Preservation Ltd* [1985] ICR 164).

54.10 **Procedure for misconduct dismissals**

Whilst employers are under a legal obligation to follow only the statutory dismissal procedures they are advised to adopt and use more rigorous internal procedures. The *ACAS Code of Practice No 1* stresses the importance of having a known disciplinary procedure. Paragraph 12 lays down guidelines for disciplinary action. ACAS has also published a handbook, 'Discipline at Work' (see 54.4 above). The EAT emphasised the need for tribunals to have regard to the *ACAS Code* in *Lock v Cardiff Rly Co Ltd* [1998] IRLR 358.

The statutory dismissal and disciplinary procedures are described at 54.3(A), above (see also DISPUTE RESOLUTION (15)). The new procedures, unlike the *ACAS Code*, are not intended to be a guide to the procedures that should be followed if a dismissal for misconduct is to be fair. Rather, they are intended to lay down the bare minimum procedure that all employers should follow. Failure to comply with the statutory procedures may result in the dismissal being automatically unfair (see 54.3(A) above).

It should be noted, in particular, that an employer has no right to suspend an employee without pay unless this is expressly provided for in the contract of employment. A suspension without pay in the absence of a contractual right to do so may be a serious breach of contract enabling the employee to resign and claim constructive dismissal (*Morrison v Amalgamated Transport and General Workers Union* [1989] IRLR 361).

If an employee is suspected of misconduct, the employer should investigate the matter fully and give the employee an opportunity to explain himself. The extent of the investigation will depend on the circumstances. In *Royal Society for the Protection of Birds v Croucher* [1984] ICR 604, the EAT held that in a case in which an employee admitted offences of dishonesty there was very little scope for the kind of investigation referred to in *Burchell* (see 54.9 above). The employer does not have to prove beyond reasonable doubt that the employee was guilty of the misconduct, but merely that he had acted reasonably in treating the misconduct as sufficient for dismissing the employee in the circumstances known to him (or which he ought reasonably to have known) at the time. It does not matter if the employer's view, if reasonable at the time, is subsequently found to be mistaken (*St Anne's Board Mill Co Ltd v Brien* [1973] ICR 444; *British Home Stores Ltd v Burchell* [1980] ICR 303n). Equally, if the employer did not have reasonable grounds to dismiss at the time, the dismissal will be considered to be unfair even if evidence subsequently comes to light which proves him right (*W Devis & Sons Ltd v Atkins* [1977] ICR 662). In such a case, however, the employee may be awarded little or no compensation (see UNFAIR DISMISSAL – III (55)).

The reasonableness of the employer's decision will be scrutinised at the time of the final decision to dismiss, namely, at the conclusion of any appeal hearing (*West Midland Co-operative Society Ltd v Tipton* [1986] ICR 192). Defects in the original procedure may be capable of being cured by a fair appeal, depending upon the seriousness of any allegations made against the employee, how bad the initial unfairness was and whether the appeal takes the form of a complete rehearing (*Whitbread & Co plc v Mills* [1988] ICR 776; *Byrne v BOC Ltd* [1992] IRLR 505). See also 54.15 below. The Court of Appeal has emphasised that there is no rule of law that earlier unfairness can be cured only by an appeal by way of a rehearing and not by way of a review, because the examination should be of the fairness of the disciplinary process as a whole (*Taylor v OCS Group Ltd* [2006] EWCA Civ 702, [2006] IRLR 613).

It is important in considering the reasonableness of a dismissal that an employer's disciplinary procedures should follow the principles of natural justice, although a breach of the rules of natural justice does not automatically make a dismissal unfair (*Slater v Leicestershire Health Authority* [1989] IRLR 16). The degree to which an employment tribunal will scrutinise such procedures depends, to a certain extent, upon the size and resources of the employer's undertaking. In *Khanum v Mid-Glamorgan Area Health Authority* [1979] ICR 40, it was held that natural justice required that the employee should know the accusations made against her, that she should be given an opportunity to state her case and that the members of the management team and the appeals panel should act in good faith. Further, in *Bentley Engineering Co Ltd v Mistry* [1979] ICR 47, the EAT held that natural justice required not merely that a man should have a chance to state his own case but that he must know sufficiently what was being said against him so that he could put forward his own case properly. This principle was reaffirmed in *Louies v Coventry Hood and Seating Co Ltd* [1990] ICR 54: if heavy reliance is placed upon the statements of witnesses, the dismissal will almost always be unfair unless the employee has sight of the statements or is told exactly what is in them. However, in *Hussain v Elonex plc* [1999] IRLR 420, the Court of Appeal stressed that there is no hard and fast rule that in all cases an employee must be shown copies of witness statements obtained by an employer about the employee's conduct. Nor is there a rule obliging an employer to make witnesses available for cross examination by the employee (*Santamera v Express Cargo Forwarding* [2003] IRLR 273). It is a matter of what is fair and reasonable in each case. For guidance in cases where an informant does not wish to be identified, see *Linfood Cash and Carry Ltd v Thomson* [1989] ICR 518 and *Asda Stores Ltd v Thompson (No 2)* [2004] IRLR 598. The EAT has held that unjustifiable delay in carrying out disciplinary proceedings can render unfair a dismissal which would otherwise have been held fair (*Royal Society for the Prevention of Cruelty to Animals v*

Cruden [1986] ICR 205). If possible, the employer should avoid a situation where the same members of management act as witnesses or complainants and as judges (*Slater*, above, but the Court of Appeal recognised that avoidance of this might sometimes prove impracticable).

Other points to bear in mind are: that the employee should be given reasonable advance warning of the hearing and that disciplinary action is under consideration; that the employee should be given the opportunity to call witnesses if appropriate; and that the decision to dismiss should preferably be taken by those who conduct the hearing, and not by someone who had only received a report of the disciplinary hearing. (This was held to be an essential requirement of fairness by the EAT in *Budgen & Co v Thomas* [1976] ICR 344.) A failure to keep adequate notes of a disciplinary hearing may amount to a procedural defect (*Vauxhall Motors Ltd v Ghafoor* [1993] ICR 376). A clandestine recording of a disciplinary hearing may be admissible evidence during an unfair dismissal claim, as in *Chairman and Governors of Amwell View School v Dagherty* [2007] IRLR 198, although the EAT held that those parts of the secret recording which contained the disciplinary panel's private deliberations were not admissible.

In *Bailey v BP Oil (Kent Refinery) Ltd* [1980] ICR 642, the Court of Appeal held that the failure by employers to comply with a disciplinary procedure agreement was a factor to be taken into account, but that the weight to be given to it depended upon the circumstances; see also *Stoker v Lancashire County Council* [1992] IRLR 75. Similarly, in *Westminster City Council v Cabaj* [1996] ICR 960, the Court of Appeal held that failure by an employer to follow its own contractually enforceable disciplinary procedure does not inevitably mean that the dismissal was unfair.

Section 10 of the *Employment Relations Act 1999* gives an employee a right to be accompanied at a disciplinary hearing by a trade union official or another of the employer's workers. If the employee is denied this right, he may present a claim to the employment tribunal and may be awarded up to two weeks' pay (*ERA 1999, s 11*).

54.11 GROUNDS FOR DISMISSAL – REDUNDANCY

Redundancy is a potentially fair reason for dismissal, but where the reason or the principal reason for the dismissal of an employee was that he was redundant (see REDUNDANCY – I (38)), the dismissal may nevertheless be considered unfair under *ERA 1996, s 105*. *Section 105* protects a wide range of cases and must be read carefully.

(*a*)   The dismissal will be automatically unfair if the circumstances constituting the redundancy applied equally to one or more employees in the same undertaking who held positions similar to that held by the dismissed employee and who have not been dismissed by the employer, and the reason for dismissed employee's selection was an automatically-unfair reason for dismissal (see 53.3 above). The automatically-unfair reasons for redundancy selection are:

    (i) the reason (or if more than one, the principal reason) for which he was selected for dismissal was union-related (see *Dundon v GPT Ltd* [1995] IRLR 403); or

    (ii) the reason (or, if more than one, the principal reason) for which he was selected for dismissal was health and safety-related contrary to *ERA 1996, s 100*; or

(iii) the reason (or, if more than one, the principal reason) for which he was selected for dismissal was the assertion by him of a statutory right contrary to *ERA 1996, s 104*; or

(iv) the reason (or, if more than one, the principal reason) for which he or she was selected for dismissal was family-related contrary to *ERA 1996, s 99* or *s 104C*; or

(v) the reason (or, if more than one, the principal reason) for which he was selected for dismissal was that, being a trustee of a trust scheme which related to his employment, the employee performed (or proposed to perform) any functions as such a trustee (see *ERA 1996, s 102*); or

(vi) the reason (or, if more than one, the principal reason) for which he was selected for dismissal was that, being an employee representative (see 39.4 REDUNDANCY – II and 51.18 TRANSFER OF UNDERTAKINGS), or a candidate in an election for such an employee representative, the employee performed, or proposed to perform, any functions or activities as such an employee representative or candidate (see *ERA 1996, s 103*; *European Public Limited-Liability Company Regulations 2004, reg 42*; and *Information and Consultation of Employees Regulations 2004, reg 30*); or

(vii) the reason (or, if more than one, the principal reason) for which he was selected for dismissal was contrary to *ERA 1996, s 101* in that either:

  (*a*)   being a protected or opted-out shop worker or betting worker, he refused (or proposed to refuse) to do shop work or betting work on a Sunday or a particular Sunday (except where the refusal relates to a Sunday before the end of the notice period); or

  (*b*)   being a shop worker or betting worker he gave (or proposed to give) his employer an opting-out notice; or

(viii) the reason (or, if more than one, the principal reason) for which he was selected for dismissal was) contrary to *ERA 1996, s 101A* (assertion of rights under the *Working Time Regulations 1998* or the *Merchant Shipping (Working Time: Inland Waterways) Regulations 2003*) or the *Fishing Vessels (Working Time: Sea-fishermen) Regulations 2004*; or

(ix) the reason (or, if more than one, the principal reason) for which he was selected for dismissal was the assertion of his rights under the *National Minimum Wage Act 1998* (see *ERA 1996, s 104A*); or

(x) the reason (or, if more than one, the principal reason) for which he was selected for dismissal was that he made a protected disclosure, as defined in *ERA 1996, ss 43A–43L* (see *ERA 1996, s 103A*); or

(xi) the reason (or, if more than one, the principal reason) for which he was selected for dismissal was connected with union recognition (*TULRCA 1992, s 152*; *ERA 1996, s 105* and (for (xi)), *TULRCA 1992, Sch A1, para 162*, inserted by *Employment Relations Act 1999, s 1(2) and Sch 1*); or

(xii) the reason (or, if more than one, the principal reason) for which he was selected for dismissal was the assertion of rights under the *Tax Credits Act 2002*, contrary to *ERA 1996, s 104B*; or

(xiii) the reason (or, if more than one, the principal reason) for which he was selected for dismissal was one specified in *reg 7(3)* of the *Part-time Workers* (*Prevention of Less Favourable Treatment*) *Regulations 2000;* or

(xiv) the reason (or, if more than, the principal reason) for which he was selected for dismissal was one specified in *reg 6(3)* of the *Fixed-term Employees* (*Prevention of Less Favourable Treatment*) *Regulations 2002*;

(xv) the reason (or, if more than one, the principal reason) for which he was selected for dismissal was that the employee was summoned for or was absent from work in pursuance of being summoned for jury service, contrary to *ERA 1996, s 98B*;

(xvi) the reason (or, if more than one, the principal reason) for which he was selected for dismissal was one specified in *para 5(3)* or *(5)* of the *Schedule* to the *Occupational and Personal Pension Schemes* (*Consultation by Employers and Miscellaneous Amendment*) *Regulations 2006* (read with *para 5(6)* of that *Schedule*);

(xvii) the reason (or, if more than one, the principal reason) for which the employee was selected for dismissal was that he—(a) exercised or sought to exercise his right to be accompanied in accordance with *para 9* of *Sch 6* to the *Employment Equality* (*Age*) *Regulations 2006*, or (b) accompanied or sought to accompany an employee pursuant to a request under that paragraph; or

(xviii) the reason (or, if more than one, the principal reason) for which the employee was selected for dismissal was one specified in paragraph (3) or (6) of regulation 31 of the *European Cooperative Society* (*Involvement of Employees*) *Regulations 2006* (read with *paras* (4) and (7) of that *Regulation*).

An employer should not, however, give preferential consideration to an employee in a redundancy selection process on the ground that he or she is a health and safety representative (*Smiths Industries Aerospace and Defence Systems v Rawlings* [1996] IRLR 656).

(b) Even if a redundancy dismissal is not automatically unfair for the reasons set out in (*a*) above, it may be automatically unfair for breach of the statutory dismissal procedures. A redundancy dismissal which is not automatically unfair may nevertheless be unfair 'in all the circumstances' within the meaning of *ERA 1996, s 98(4)* as amended, although the Northern Ireland Court of Appeal suggested in *Robinson v Ulster Carpet Mills Ltd* [1991] IRLR 348 that a tribunal should be cautious in finding a dismissal unfair if an agreed or customary procedure had been followed.

Among the circumstances which will be taken into account is the duty imposed by *TULRCA 1992, s 188* (as amended by *TURERA 1993, s 34* and *SI 1995/2587*) to consult appropriate representatives of the employees concerned. A failure to comply with that requirement will probably – although not necessarily – render the dismissal unfair (*Kelly v Upholstery and Cabinet Works (Amesbury) Ltd* [1977] IRLR 91; *North East Midlands*

Co-operative Society Ltd v Allen [1977] IRLR 212; *Hough v Leyland DAF Ltd* [1991] ICR 696). In order to comply with the requirements of *s 188*, the employer must begin consultations before giving individual notices of dismissal (*National Union of Teachers v Avon County Council* [1978] ICR 626). See also 39.2–39.5 REDUNDANCY – II.

The EAT in *Williams v Compair Maxam Ltd* [1982] ICR 156 listed the principles which, in the experience of the two lay members, reasonable employers adopt when dismissing for redundancy employees who are represented by an independent trade union recognised by them. The EAT stressed that the principles would not stay unaltered forever, and that they are not principles of law, but standards of behaviour. However, the principles outlined in *Williams* have been adopted by employment tribunals and the EAT as standards by which to judge the fairness of dismissals for redundancy where a trade union is recognised by an employer. They are, therefore, of some importance and are set out below. (Following the changes made by *SI 1995/2587*, these principles will be equally relevant where the employees being dismissed for redundancy are represented by employee representatives rather than by an independent trade union, and should be read accordingly.)

(i)   The employer will seek to give as much warning as possible of impending redundancies so as to enable the union and the employees who may be affected to take early steps to inform themselves of the relevant facts, consider possible alternative solutions and, if necessary, find alternative employment in the undertaking or elsewhere.

(ii) The employer will consult the union as to the best means by which the desired management result can be achieved fairly and with as little hardship to the employees as possible. In particular, the employer will seek to agree with the union the criteria to be applied in selecting the employees to be made redundant. When a selection has been made, the employer will consider with the union whether the selection has been made in accordance with those criteria.

(iii) Whether or not an agreement as to the criteria to be adopted has been agreed with the union, the employer will seek to establish criteria for selection which so far as possible do not depend solely upon the opinion of the person making the selection but can be objectively checked against such things as attendance record, efficiency at the job, experience, or length of service.

(iv) The employer will seek to ensure that the selection is made fairly in accordance with these criteria and will consider any representations the union may make as to such selection.

(v)   The employer will seek to see whether instead of dismissing an employee he could offer him alternative employment.

(*Williams*, as above, at 162.) However, the extent to which any one or more of these principles apply depends on the circumstances of the particular case, and an employer's failure to adopt any one or more of these practices will not necessarily lead to a finding of unfair dismissal (*Grundy (Teddington) Ltd v Plummer* [1983] ICR 367). Moreover, the principles set out in *Williams* should not be treated as if they were a statute (*Rolls-Royce Motors Ltd v Dewhurst* [1985] ICR 869). In particular, it is now a common and accepted practice for employers to adopt a system of selection for redundancy which relies upon managerial assessment of employees' ability and performance as well as upon more purely objective criteria. However, it is still the case that a simple subjective judgement by line managers about 'who should stay and who should go' is unlikely to be a fair method of selection.

The position was summarised by Lord Bridge in *Polkey v A E Dayton Services Ltd* [1988] ICR 142 at 162–163:

> ' ... in the case of redundancy, the employer will normally not act reasonably unless he warns and consults any employees affected or their representative, adopts a fair basis on which to select for redundancy and takes such steps as may be reasonable to avoid or minimise redundancy by redeployment within his own organisation ... It is quite a different matter if the tribunal is able to conclude that the employer himself, at the time of dismissal, acted reasonably in taking the view that, in the exceptional circumstances of the particular case, the procedural steps normally appropriate would have been futile, could not have altered the decision to dismiss and therefore could be dispensed with.'

The question to be asked in the exceptional case contemplated by *Polkey* is not whether the employer in fact made a conscious decision not to consult, but whether a reasonable employer could have decided not to consult in the light of the facts that were known at the time (*Duffy v Yeomans & Partners Ltd* [1993] IRLR 368; cf *Dick v Boots the Chemists Ltd* IDS Brief 451, p 12; see also *Heron v Citylink – Nottingham* [1993] IRLR 372).

It is important to note, however, that the *Polkey* principle was overturned on 1 October 2004 by *EA 2002, s 34*, which introduced a new *s 98A(2)* into *ERA 1996*. *Section 98A(2)* provides that failure to follow a procedure in relation to the dismissal of an employee shall not be regarded as, by itself, making the employer's action unreasonable if he shows that he would have decided to dismiss the employee if he had followed the procedure. The purpose of this new subsection is to deter employees from bringing unfair dismissal claims if they are relying upon a technical breach of procedure by the employer, which had no effect on the outcome (see further *Kelly-Madden* above).

Even where no trade union is recognised for bargaining purposes, in respect of dismissals taking effect on or after 1 March 1996, employers must (by virtue of *SI 1995/2587*) consult with employee representatives before deciding which employees should be made redundant, where at least 20 or more employees are proposed to be made redundant at one establishment within 90 days or less (see 35.2 *et seq* REDUNDANCY – II). It has been held that where an employee has no representative, good industrial relations practice requires consultation with the employee before dismissing him as redundant, except in special circumstances (*Freud v Bentalls Ltd* [1983] ICR 77; *Ferguson v Prestwick Circuits Ltd* [1992] IRLR 266). A tribunal may hold a redundancy dismissal to be unfair for lack of consultation with individual employees even where their union has been consulted (*Walls Meat Co Ltd v Selby* [1989] ICR 601; *Rolls-Royce Motor Cars Ltd v Price* [1993] IRLR 203). However, a dismissal may be fair where there was consultation with a trade union, even if there was no consultation with the individual employees: *Mugford v Midland Bank plc* [1997] ICR 399. It is not enough for an employer to warn of impending redundancies and then to announce the result; the employer must consult and consider the employees' views properly and genuinely (*Rowell v Hubbard Group Services Ltd* [1995] IRLR 195).

Consultation may be necessary at a number of separate stages: when the overall need for redundancies is being considered; when the *s 188* notice is issued (see 39.4 REDUNDANCY – II); when employees are being selected for redundancy; and upon the giving of notice or during the notice period (*Dyke v Hereford and Worcester County Council* [1989] ICR 800). The fact that the employer is a small company does not remove the obligation to consult, although it may affect the nature or formality of the consultation process required (*De Grasse v Stockwell Tools Ltd* [1992] IRLR 269). However, if a company is in dire financial straits and in desperate need of a purchaser, the normal requirement of consultation does not apply (*Warner v Adnet Ltd* [1998] IRLR 394).

Although individual consultation is not always necessary, employees should have the opportunity to contest their selection, either by themselves or through their trade unions. This may involve showing employees the marks given to them in the selection process (*John Brown Engineering Ltd v Brown* [1997] IRLR 90).

A dismissal of an employee may be considered unfair if no consideration is given to finding him another job within that company, or if the company is a member of a group, within that group (*Vokes Ltd v Bear* [1974] ICR 1; *Euroguard Ltd v Rycroft*, IDS Brief 498, p 2). The redundant employee should be offered an available vacancy even if it is at a lower salary or is of lower status than the post from which he is being made redundant (*Avonmouth Construction Co Ltd v Shipway* [1979] IRLR 14). In some cases, it may be necessary to consider dismissing some other (perhaps less long-serving) employee to make way for the employee whose job has disappeared (*Thomas and Betts Manufacturing Ltd v Harding* [1980] IRLR 255). This is known as 'bumping'. It is permissible to take 'spent' convictions into account when considering whether a redundant employee is suitable for alternative positions (*Wood v Coverage Care Ltd* [1996] IRLR 264).

The fairness of a dismissal for redundancy will be judged not simply at the date on which notice is given but also with regard to events up to the date on which it takes effect (*Stacey v Babcock Power Ltd* [1986] ICR 221; see also *Dyke*, above, and *White v South London Transport Ltd* [1998] ICR 293). Hence, if a suitable vacancy arises during the notice period it should be offered to the otherwise redundant employee.

In *Lloyd v Taylor Woodrow Construction* [1999] IRLR 782, the EAT held that, as with conduct and capability cases, a defect in a redundancy consultation process could be cured on appeal, provided that the appeal is a rehearing and not merely a review of the original decision. The Court of Appeal, however, has ruled that the appeal need not take the form of a rehearing (see *Taylor v OCS Group Ltd* above).

If the employer can establish that had he taken reasonable steps to consult with the employee or find him other employment, he would still have been dismissed, an employment tribunal may find the dismissal to be unfair but award no compensation, or compensate only for the wages and benefits which would have been received while consultation was taking place. (See also 54.4 above; and 53.13 UNFAIR DISMISSAL – III.)

A tribunal will not investigate the commercial merits of an employer's decision that redundancies were required (*James W Cook and Co (Wivenhoe) v Tipper* [1990] ICR 716; *Campbell v Dunoon and Cowal Housing Association* [1993] IRLR 496). Nor should an employment tribunal review the markings of employees for redundancy selection purposes (*British Aerospace v Green* [1995] ICR 1006; *King v Eaton Ltd* [1996] IRLR 199).

54.12 Unfair Dismissal – II: The Fairness of the Dismissal

54.12 Dismissal procedure

From decided cases (see 54.11 above) the following guidelines emerge, in addition to the statutory dismissal and disciplinary procedures (see DISPUTE RESOLUTION (15)):

(*a*)   consult with employee representatives;

(*b*)   consider possible alternatives to redundancies, e g short-time working, work sharing, other costs savings, etc;

(*c*)   if redundancy becomes necessary, in consultation with employee representatives, agree objective criteria for selection for redundancy;

(*d*)   apply the criteria objectively;

(*e*)   inform the employees affected at the earliest opportunity and give the employees an opportunity to contest the scores they are given;

(*f*)   investigate the possibilities of offering them alternative employment within the company or group, continuing the investigation until the employment has come to an end;

(*g*)   give them time off to seek employment;

(*h*)   pay all moneys due;

(*i*)   conduct an appeal; and

(*j*)   keep careful records and minutes of these steps. .

54.13 GROUNDS FOR DISMISSAL – CONTRAVENTION OF ANY ENACTMENT

If an employer dismisses an employee because the employee could not continue to work in the position which he held without contravention (either on his part or on that of his employer) of a duty or restriction imposed by or under an enactment, the reason for the dismissal falls within *ERA 1996, s 98(2)(d)*.

The fact that an employer genuinely but erroneously believes that he would be breaking the law by continuing to employ an employee does not make the reason for the dismissal of that employee a reason falling within *ERA 1996, s 98(2)(d)*, but it could be 'some other substantial reason' justifying the dismissal within *ERA 1996, s 98(1)(b)* (see 54.14 below) (*Bouchaala v Trusthouse Forte Hotels Ltd* [1980] ICR 721).

Procedure. In these cases employers should:

(*a*)   arrange a formal meeting at which the employee (ideally with an accompanying person) should be informed of the situation and invited (himself or through a representative) to express his views; and

(*b*)   in appropriate cases, find out if the company or an associated company has a suitable vacancy which the employee can be offered instead.

54.14 GROUNDS FOR DISMISSAL – 'SOME OTHER SUBSTANTIAL REASON'

These reasons need not be of the same type as those that are specified in the *Act*. If the reason for dismissal is not one of those set out in *ERA 1996, s 98(2)* (see 54.2 above), it may nevertheless be an acceptable reason if the employer can show that it was 'some other substantial reason of a kind such as to justify the dismissal of an employee holding the position which that employee held' (*ERA 1996, s 98(1)(b)*). Examples of such reasons are the following.

(a) *Necessary re-organisation of the business* (*Hollister v National Farmers' Union* [1979] ICR 542; *Richmond Precision Engineering Ltd v Pearce* [1985] IRLR 179; *Catamaran Cruisers Ltd v Williams* [1994] IRLR 386; *Cobley v Forward Technology Industries plc* [2003] EWCA Civ 646, [2003] IRLR 706). This may also apply in cases where changes in terms and conditions have led the employee to claim constructive dismissal (*Genower v Ealing, Hammersmith and Hounslow Area Health Authority* [1980] IRLR 297). But note that the employee must be fairly considered for any new job created by the reorganisation (*Oakley v Labour Party* [1988] ICR 403).

(b) *Economic, technical or organisational reasons entailing changes in the workforce* of the transferor or the transferee before or after a relevant transfer within the meaning of the *Transfer of Undertakings* (*Protection of Employment*) *Regulations 1981* (*SI 1981/1794*), *reg 8(2)(b)* (see 52.20 TRANSFER OF UNDERTAKINGS).

(c) Reasons of *necessary economies* such as in *Durrant and Cheshire v Clariston Clothing Co Ltd* [1974] IRLR 360 in which a tribunal held that it was reasonable for a company to dismiss two employees who were earning £25.87 per week each but for whom they had to provide transport costing the company £24 per week each.

(b) *Protection of the interest of the business* such as in *RS Components Ltd v Irwin* [1974] 1 All ER 41 in which the company was held to have fairly dismissed an employee for refusing to sign a reasonable restrictive covenant which was considered necessary. In considering the fairness of a dismissal for a refusal to accept new terms and conditions, it is material to consider what proportion of the workforce had accepted the change when the decision to dismiss was taken (*St John of God (Care Services) Ltd v Brooks* [1992] ICR 715). The Court of Appeal has now gone further in *Willow Oak Developments Ltd (t/a Windsor Recruitment) v Silverwood* [2006] EWCA Civ 660, [2007] IRLR 607 and held a dismissal lawful for refusal to sign restrictive covenants, where the new covenants were provided to the employee earlier on the same day and were unreasonably wide, on the basis that the employer's reliance on the refusal to sign was lawful because the reliance was on a reason of the 'kind' capable of justifying dismissal.

(c) *An employee's personality* cannot, by itself, be a fair reason for dismissal, however, in certain circumstances the manifestations of that personality can give rise to 'some other substantial reason' for dismissal (*Perkin v St George's Healthcare NHS Trust* [2005] EWCA Civ 1174, [2005] IRLR 934).

(e) *Expiry of a fixed-term contract* when it is shown that the contract was adopted for a genuine purpose and that fact was known to the employee, and it is also shown that the specific purpose for which the contract was adopted has ceased to be applicable (*North Yorkshire County Council v Fay* [1986] ICR 133. See also *Terry v East Sussex County Council* [1976] ICR 536). Note, however, the *Fixed-term Employees* (*Prevention of Less Favourable Treatment*) *Regulations 2002*.

(f) The imposition of a *sentence of imprisonment* (*Kingston v British Railways Board* [1984] ICR 781). In some cases, this may have the effect of *frustrating* the contract, thus bringing it to an end without a dismissal (see 48.3 TERMINATION OF EMPLOYMENT).

(g)   *Dismissal of the replacement of an employee suspended on medical or maternity grounds (ERA 1996, s 106(3))*. Where an employer suspends an employee on medical grounds in compliance with a statutory requirement and engages another in his place, he should inform the replacement employee in writing when engaging him that his employment will be terminated at the end of the suspension of the original employee. If he dismisses the replacement employee in order to allow the original employee to resume work, the dismissal will be regarded as having been for a reason falling within *ERA 1996, s 98(1)(b)*.

(h)   *Dismissal of the replacement of an employee absent due to pregnancy or childbirth (ERA 1996, s 106(2))*. Where an employer engages an employee to replace another employee who is absent due to pregnancy and on engaging the replacement employee the employer informs him in writing that his employment will be terminated on the return to work of the pregnant employee, a dismissal of the replacement employee to give work to the original employee will be considered as a dismissal for a reason falling within *ERA 1996, s 98(1)(b)*.

As usual, dismissal for such a reason will be fair if it was within the 'range of reasonable responses' (see 54.4 above) and a fair procedure was followed. In *Alboni v Ind Coope Retail Ltd* [1998] IRLR 131, the Court of Appeal held that an employment tribunal is bound to have regard to events between notice of dismissal and the date that dismissal took effect, both in determining the reason for dismissal and whether the employers acted reasonably in the circumstances in treating it as a sufficient reason for dismissal.

54.15 **DISMISSAL FOLLOWING AN INTERNAL APPEAL**

If an employee uses an internal appeal procedure to challenge a decision to dismiss him, and his appeal is rejected, he will be regarded as having been dismissed from the date of his original dismissal, unless his contract provides otherwise (see, e g *J Sainsbury Ltd v Savage* [1981] ICR 1, approved in *West Midlands Co-operative Society Ltd v Tipton* [1986] ICR 192).

The House of Lords in *West Midlands Co-operative Society* decided that the fairness of a dismissal is to be judged at the time of the final decision to dismiss, which, if there is an internal appeal, will be at the conclusion of such an appeal. Lord Bridge said at 204D:

'A dismissal is unfair if the employer unreasonably treats his real reasons as a sufficient reason to dismiss the employee, either when he makes his original decision to dismiss, or when he maintains that decision at the conclusion of an internal appeal.'

In other words, facts and matters that come to light during the appeal hearing, whether in favour of the employee or against him, ought to be taken into account. However, if after an appeal the employer thinks that the employee ought to be dismissed not for the original reason but for some completely different reason, the best course is to recommence the disciplinary procedure. In *Post Office v Marney* [1990] IRLR 170, the EAT warned tribunals against losing sight of the fundamental question of whether the *dismissal* was unfair; unfairness ought not to be found as a result of flaws in the appeal procedure unless a properly conducted appeal could and should have demonstrated a flaw in the original decision. Some flaws in the appeal procedure, for example, a defect in the composition of the appeals tribunal, are so serious as to render the dismissal unfair. See also 54.10 above.

Note that an employee's failure to appeal against a dismissal may exclude him from benefiting from an extension of time for presenting his employment tribunal claim of unfair dismissal (*Employment Act 2002 (Dispute Resolution) Regulations 2004, reg 15(2)*). Nevertheless, an extension of time flows from his having reasonable grounds for believing that, when the normal time limit expired, a dismissal procedure was being followed, and not from the fact that he has appealed against the dismissal. A failure to appeal may also result in a reduction in his award of compensation (*Employment Act 2002, s 31(2)(c)(ii)*).

54.16   PRESSURE ON AN EMPLOYER TO DISMISS UNFAIRLY

In determining the reason for a dismissal, or whether it was fair in the circumstances, no account is taken of any pressure which by calling, organising, procuring or financing a strike or other industrial action, or threatening to do so, was exercised on the employer to dismiss the employee. Any question relating to dismissal will be determined as if no such pressure had been exercised (*ERA 1996, s 107*).

However, a trade union or an individual who induced the employer to dismiss an employee may, in certain circumstances, be joined in the proceedings and be ordered to pay all or part of any compensation awarded for unfair dismissal (*TULRCA 1992, s 160*). (See 55.20 UNFAIR DISMISSAL – III.)

55   Unfair Dismissal – III: Remedies

55.1   When an employment tribunal finds that a complaint of unfair dismissal is well-founded, it may make an order for the reinstatement or re-engagement of the complainant, or an order for compensation. This chapter deals with the remedies for unfair dismissal and the settlement of claims, as follows.

— Reinstatement (see 55.2 below) and re-engagement (see 55.3 below) and related rules (see 55.4, 55.5 below).

— Awards of compensation (see 55.6–55.19 below), comprising the following:

   ● Basic award (see 55.7–55.9 below).

   ● Compensatory award (see 55.10–55.13 below).

   ● Maximum awards (see 55.14 below).

   ● Additional award in case of non-compliance with order for reinstatement or re-engagement (except union-related, health and safety, pension scheme trustee and employee representative cases) (see 55.15 below).

   ● Union-related, health and safety, pension scheme trustees and employee representative dismissals – special award (see 55.16–55.18 below) and reduction of total award (see 55.19 below).

— Joinder of parties (see 55.20 below).

— Interim relief (see 55.21 below).

— Settlement (see 55.22 below).

For the enforcement of, and interest upon, tribunal awards, see 21.66 and 21.67 EMPLOYMENT TRIBUNALS – II.

In practice, a successful complainant will in most cases receive an award of compensation which is made up of a basic award and a compensatory award. Orders for reinstatement and re-engagement are rare. Other payments are restricted to special circumstances as indicated in the relevant paragraphs.

The tribunal's first step on finding a dismissal to be unfair should be to explain to the employee the possibility of an order for reinstatement or re-engagement, and to ask him whether he wishes such an order to be made (*ERA 1996, s 112(1)*). This question should be asked even if the employee has indicated his preferred remedy in his originating application. Although the tribunal's failure to ask the claimant whether he wishes to be reinstated or re-engaged does not render its decision on remedies a nullity, at least where the claimant was legally represented (*Cowley v Manson Timber Ltd* [1995] ICR 367), an appeal tribunal should be very ready to remit a case for further consideration of remedy in these circumstances (*Constantine v McGregor Cory Ltd* [2000] ICR 938).

Even where an employer has offered to pay the maximum possible award of compensation, but has not admitted that the dismissal was unfair, the employee is entitled to proceed with his complaint (*Telephone Information Services Ltd v Wilkinson* [1991] IRLR 148; see also *NRG Victory Reinsurance Ltd v Alexander* [1992] ICR 675).

55.2   REINSTATEMENT

An order for reinstatement is defined as *an order that the employer shall treat the complainant in all respects as if he had not been dismissed*. In deciding whether to make such an order, the tribunal must consider:

(*a*)   whether the complainant wishes to be reinstated;

(*b*)   whether it is practicable for an employer to comply with an order for reinstatement; and

(*c*)   (in a case where the complainant wholly or partially caused or contributed to the dismissal) whether it would be just to order his reinstatement.

(ERA 1996, s 116(1).)

In deciding whether to make an order for reinstatement, the tribunal will consider the effect that such an order would have on the respondent's business. If, as in *Coleman and Stephenson v Magnet Joinery Ltd* [1974] ICR 25, such an order would inevitably lead to industrial unrest, it should not be made. Nor should it be considered practicable where it would lead to a redundancy situation or to significant overmanning (*Cold Drawn Tubes Ltd v Middleton* [1992] ICR 318; see also *Port of London Authority v Payne* [1994] ICR 555). A finding on the practicality or otherwise of ordering re-employment is one which is obviously within the tribunal's exclusive territory as an 'industrial jury' and an appeal against such a finding on grounds of perversity alone was described as 'virtually impossible' in *Clancy v Cannock Chase Technical College* [2001] IRLR 331. If the tribunal orders reinstatement, it must specify:

(i)   any amount payable by the employer in respect of any benefit which the complainant might reasonably be expected to have received but for the dismissal, including arrears of pay, for the period between the date of termination of employment and the date of reinstatement;

(ii)   any rights and privileges, including seniority and pension rights, which must be restored to the employee; and

(iii)   the date by which the order must be complied with.

(ERA 1996, s 114(1).)

Moreover, if the complainant would have benefited from an improvement in his terms and conditions of employment had he not been dismissed, the order for reinstatement will require him to be treated as if he had benefited from that improvement from the date on which he would have done so had he not been dismissed. Thus, if an order for reinstatement is made, the claimant must be restored to his original job and receive back pay and benefits from the date of his dismissal (*ERA 1996, s 114(3)*).

Where an employee's appeal against dismissal is successful and he is reinstated, he cannot pursue any claim of unfair dismissal which he has already presented (*Roberts v West Coast Trains Ltd* [2004] EWCA Civ 900, [2004] IRLR 788).

Where there is a breakdown in trust and confidence, the remedy of reinstatement of re-engagement has very limited scope and will only be practicable in the rarest of cases. In *Wood Group Heavy Industrial Turbines Ltd v Crossan* [1998] IRLR 680, the Scottish EAT overturned an order for re-engagement made by a tribunal in a case in which the employee had been unfairly dismissed for dealing in drugs in the workplace and the employer genuinely believed in the guilt of the employee.

55.3 RE-ENGAGEMENT

If an employment tribunal decides not to order reinstatement, it must go on to consider re-engagement (*ERA 1996, s 116(2)*). An order for re-engagement is defined as *an order that the complainant be engaged by the employer*, or by a successor of the employer or by an associated employer, *in employment comparable to that from which he was dismissed or other suitable employment* (ie not in the same job) (*ERA 1996, s 115(1)*). For associated employers, see 7.9(A) CONTINUOUS EMPLOYMENT. 'Successor' is defined by *ERA 1996, s 235(1)*.

In deciding whether to order re-engagement, the tribunal will take into consideration the same factors as for reinstatement above. The tribunal must specify the terms on which re-engagement will take place and, unless it considers that the complainant contributed to the dismissal, the terms of the re-engagement must be, as far as is reasonably practicable, as favourable as if reinstatement had been ordered (*ERA 1996, s 116(4)*).

In particular, the tribunal will specify:

(*a*)   the identity of the employer;

(*b*)   the nature of the employment;

(*c*)   the remuneration for the employment;

(*d*)   any amount payable by the employer in respect of any benefit which the complainant might reasonably be expected to have received but for the dismissal, including arrears of pay, for the period between the date of termination of employment and the date of re-engagement;

(*e*)   any rights and privileges including seniority and pension rights which must be restored; and

(*f*)   the date by which the order must be complied with.

(*ERA 1996, s 115(2)*.)

An employment tribunal may not, however, order re-engagement on terms substantially more favourable than the terms of the former job (*Rank Xerox (UK) Ltd v Stryczek* [1995] IRLR 568). In *Stryczek*, the EAT added that it was generally inadvisable for the employment tribunal to order re-engagement to a specific job, as distinct from identifying the nature of the proposed employment.

55.4 GENERAL RULES ON REINSTATEMENT AND RE-ENGAGEMENT

For the purpose of deciding whether it is practicable to make an order for reinstatement or re-engagement, the tribunal will not take into account the fact that the employer has engaged a permanent replacement for the dismissed employee unless he can show *either* that it was not practicable for him to arrange for the dismissed employee's work to be done without engaging a permanent replacement, *or* that he engaged the replacement after the lapse of a reasonable period of time, without having heard from the dismissed employee that he wished to be reinstated or re-engaged, and that when the employer engaged the replacement it was no longer reasonable for him to arrange for the dismissed employee's work to be done except by a permanent replacement (*ERA 1996, s 116(5), (6)*).

Where the employee has indicated at least seven days before the hearing of his complaint of unfair dismissal that he will seek such an order, the employer must come ready with evidence as to the availability of the old job or comparable or suitable employment, or else bear the costs of any adjournment in the absence of a special reason for the failure (*Employment Tribunals (Constitution and Rules of Procedure) Regulations 2004 (SI 2004/1861), rule 39*).

The continuity of employment of the employee is preserved, and any week falling between the effective date of termination and his re-employment counts towards his period of continuous employment (*ERA 1996, s 219; Employment Protection (Continuity of Employment) Regulations 1996 (SI 1996/3147)*). The *Regulations* deal not only with cases where the tribunal orders reinstatement or re-engagement, but also where that is part of an agreed settlement (see 20.26 EMPLOYMENT TRIBUNALS – I).

In calculating the amount payable on account of arrears of pay and benefits, the tribunal will take into account, so as to reduce the employer's liability, any sums received by the complainant in respect of the period between the date of termination of employment and the date of reinstatement or re-engagement by way of:

(*a*)   wages in lieu of notice or *ex gratia* payments paid by the employer;

(*b*)   remuneration paid in respect of employment with another employer;

and such other benefits as the tribunal thinks appropriate in the circumstances (*ERA 1996, ss 114(4), 115(3)*). It is not permissible to reduce the award of arrears on the ground of delay in asserting the employee's rights in relation to re-engagement (*City and Hackney Health Authority v Crisp* [1990] ICR 95).

If an order for reinstatement or re-engagement is made but the terms of the order are not fully complied with, the tribunal will make an award of compensation of such an amount as it thinks fit having regard to the loss sustained by the complainant as a result of the employer's failure to comply with the particular terms in question (*ERA 1996, s 117(1), (2)*). This is subject to the same statutory maximum as the compensatory award, save that the usual maximum may be exceeded to the extent necessary to enable the award fully to reflect any sums which ought to have been paid pursuant to the original order (*ERA 1996, s 124(3)*; and see 55.10 below). A purported reinstatement which is on much inferior terms will be treated as a refusal to reinstate at all, so that additional compensation may be awarded in accordance with *ERA, s 117(3), (4)* (see 55.5 below) (*Artisan Press Ltd v Srawley and Parker* [1986] IRLR 126).

55.5   REFUSAL TO REINSTATE OR RE-ENGAGE

If an order for reinstatement or re-engagement is made but the employer refuses to comply with it, the tribunal will award the complainant additional compensation over and above the basic and compensatory awards (see 55.15 below), unless the employer can satisfy the tribunal that it was not practicable to comply with the order (*ERA 1996, s 117(3), (4)*). Although the tribunal should carefully scrutinise the reasons advanced by the employer, it should give due weight to the commercial judgment of the employer unless the employer was to be disbelieved. The tribunal should not set the standard of proof too high, since the test is practicability, not possibility (*Port of London Authority v Payne* [1994] ICR 555).

For the purpose of deciding whether it was practicable for the employer to comply with the order, the tribunal will not take into account the fact that he has engaged a permanent replacement unless the employer can show that it was not practicable for the dismissed employee's work to be done without engaging a permanent replacement (*ERA 1996, s 117(7)*).

The employee's only remedy for the employer's failure to reinstate or to re-engage in breach of an order to do so is to obtain compensation under *s 117(3)*, comprising a compensatory, basic and additional award (see 55.7–55.15 below). The employee cannot ask for a renewed order that he be reinstated or re-engaged (*Mabrizi v National Hospital for Nervous Diseases* [1990] ICR 281). However, in awarding the additional compensation, the tribunal will be able to reflect any amounts which should have been paid to the employee under the reinstatement or re-engagement order (see *Selfridges Ltd v Malik* [1998] ICR 268 and 55.10 below). The employer will not be permitted to obtain a financial advantage through non-compliance with an order for reinstatement. The statutory cap on compensation for unfair dismissal may be disapplied, if the amount of back pay due to an employee exceeds that cap and the employer has refused to comply with an order for reinstatement (*Parry v National Westminster Bank plc* [2004] EWCA Civ 1563, [2005] IRLR 193).

If the employer reinstates or re-engages an employee following an order, but the terms of the order are not fully complied with, then, subject to the upper limit on compensatory awards (see 55.14 below), the employee will be awarded compensation of such amount as the tribunal thinks fit having regard to the loss sustained by the complainant in consequence of the failure to comply fully with the terms of the order (*ERA 1996, s 117(2)*).

Under the *EA 2002, s 34(3), (4)* (in force from 1 October 2004) if an employee has been automatically unfairly dismissed, pursuant to *ERA 1996, s 98A*, because of his employer's failure to comply with the statutory disciplinary procedures and an order for reinstatement or re-engagement is made, the claimant will also be awarded a sum equivalent to four weeks' pay, unless the tribunal considers that this would result in injustice (*ERA 1996, s 112(5)*). If, however, the employer refuses to reinstate or re-engage, the award of four weeks' pay is deducted from the compensation ((*ERA 1996, ss117(2A)* and *123(8)*). This award will be made whether or not the employer agrees to reinstate. In practice, the employee rarely desires reinstatement or re-engagement and, even if he does, it is rarely ordered. If no such order is made, the amount of compensation will be calculated as set out below.

On the other hand, the employee's duty to mitigate encompasses reasonable acceptance of an offer of reinstatement or re-engagement (*Wilding v BT plc* [2002] EWCA Civ 349, [2002] IRLR 524).

55.6 COMPENSATION

When a tribunal makes an award of compensation for unfair dismissal, the award must consist of a *basic award* and a *compensatory award* (*ERA 1996, s 118(1)*). These awards are the most common and are often the only categories of award. They are considered first (see 55.7–55.13 below). There are statutory maxima for nearly all the awards and these are set out for reference in 55.14 below.

Some awards are made only in certain circumstances: these are the 'additional award' where there has been non-compliance with an order for reinstatement or re-engagement (see 55.15 below) and, in similar circumstances for union-related dismissals, health and safety-related dismissals, pension scheme trustee dismissals and employee representative dismissals only, the 'special award' (see 55.16–55.18 below).

Recoupment provisions. Where the claimant has received statutory benefits, the respondent will be ordered to pay part of the compensation awarded not to the claimant but to the authority which paid the benefit, so that it recovers the money paid. This procedure, known as 'recoupment', is initiated by the service on the respondent of a 'recoupment notice' issued pursuant to the *Employment Protection* (*Recoupment of Jobseeker's Allowance and Income Support*) *Regulations 1996* (*SI 1996/2349*). It does not apply where a sum is paid by way of settlement of a dispute, before or after a finding of unfair dismissal is made.

A recoupment order will be made only in respect of that period before the hearing for which the tribunal concludes that the claimant has suffered loss. So, where the hearing took place ten months after dismissal, but compensation for loss of earnings was restricted to six months, recoupment should be ordered only in respect of six months' benefits (*Homan v A1 Bacon Co Ltd* [1996] ICR 721).

55.7 BASIC AWARD

Amount

The amount of the basic award will, in most cases, be the same as that of a statutory redundancy payment (see REDUNDANCY – I (38) and the ready reckoner at the end of that chapter; the principal difference is that in the case of redundancy payments, employment prior to the 18th birthday is not counted). It depends upon basic weekly pay, length of service and age.

The maximum amount of a week's pay for the purpose of the calculation is £310 (for dismissals taking place after 1 February 2007) and the maximum number of years to be taken into account is 20 (*ERA 1996, s 119(3)* and *s 227(1)*; (*SI 2006/3045*)). A week's pay is calculated in accordance with *ERA 1996, ss 221–229* and is based on gross pay. The *Employment Relations Act 1999* provides that the maximum amount of a week's pay will be revised annually and linked to the retail prices index (see a week's pay). Subject to the exceptions set out below, the amount of the basic award is calculated by reference to the period, ending with the effective date of termination, during which the employee was continuously employed, by starting at the end of that period and reckoning backwards the number of complete years of employment falling within that period and allowing:

(*a*)   one and a half week's pay for each year of employment in which the employee was not below the age of 41;

(*b*)   one week's pay for each year of employment not falling within (*a*) in which the employee was not below the age of 22; and

(*c*)   half a week's pay for each such year of employment not falling within either (*a*) or (*b*).

(*ERA 1996, s 119(2)*.)

Where an employer is obliged but fails to give the statutory minimum period of notice, the effective date of termination for the purposes of calculating the basic award is taken as that upon which the notice would have expired had it been given (*ERA 1996, s 92(7)*). Similarly, if the employee is constructively dismissed, and the employer has not given notice, the effective date of termination for the purposes of calculating the basic award is taken as that upon which the statutory minimum period of notice would have expired had it been given by the employer (*ERA 1996, s 97(4)*).

Where an employee is unfairly dismissed both by the transferor and then (after being re-engaged) again by the transferee of a business, the transferee may be liable to pay two basic awards because of the provisions of the *Transfer of*

Undertakings (*Protection of Employment*) *Regulations 2006* (*Fenton v Stable-gold Ltd* (*t/a Chiswick Court Hotel*) [1986] ICR 236) (see also TRANSFER OF UNDERTAKINGS (52)).

55.8   Exceptions

The amount of the basic award is *two weeks' pay* where the tribunal finds that the reason or the principal reason for the dismissal of the employee was that he was redundant and that:

(*a*)   he unreasonably refused or left suitable alternative employment (contrary to *ERA 1996, s 141*); or

(*b*)   his employment was renewed or he was re-engaged and he was therefore not considered dismissed under *ERA 1996, s 138(1)*.

(*ERA 1996, s 121.*)

The above provision has the curious effect that an employee is entitled to a basic award of compensation notwithstanding the fact that he is not considered as dismissed for the purposes of claiming a redundancy payment (see 39.6 REDUN-DANCY – I).

Where a dismissal is to be regarded as unfair by virtue of:

(i)   *TULRCA 1992, s 152* or *153* (ie for a 'union-related' reason); or

(ii)   *ERA 1996, s 100(1)(a)* or (*b*) (health and safety activities as a representative, committee member or designated employee; note that this does not apply to all the circumstances in which a health and safety dismissal is automatically unfair); or

(iii)   *ERA 1996, s 101A(1)(d)* (activities as a workforce representative in a 'working time' case; note that this does not apply to all the circumstances in which a 'working time' dismissal is automatically unfair); or

(iv)   *ERA 1996, s 102(1)* (activities as a pension scheme trustee); or

(v)   *ERA 1996, s 103* (activities as an employee representative),

then the amount of any basic award (before any reduction) will be not less than £4,200 (TULRCA 1992, s 156(1); ERA 1996, s 120(1)).

Where the dismissal is automatically unfair because of *ERA 1996, s 98A* , and the amount of the basic award, before any reduction under *ERA 1996, s 122(3A)* or (*4*) (see 55.9, below) is less than four weeks' pay, the tribunal will increase the basic award to four weeks' pay, unless the increase would result in injustice to the employer (*ERA 1996, s 120(1A)* and (*1B*), introduced by *EA 2002, s 34(6)*).

55.9   Reduction of basic award

Where the tribunal considers that any conduct of the complainant before the dismissal (or, where the dismissal was with notice, before the notice was given) was such that it would be just and equitable to reduce or further reduce the amount of the basic award to any extent, the tribunal will so reduce the award (*ERA 1996, s 122(2); TULRCA 1992, s 156(2)*). See also 55.13 below. However, a basic award can never be reduced on the basis of a failure to mitigate (*Lock v Connell Estate Agents* [1994] IRLR 444).

The amount of the basic award will not be reduced by virtue of the above provisions where the reason or principal reason for the dismissal was that the employee was redundant, unless the dismissal is to be regarded as unfair (*a*) by virtue of *TULRCA 1992, s 153* (selection for redundancy for a 'union-related' reason), or (*b*) because the reason for selecting the employee for dismissal was one of those specified in *ERA 1996, s 100(1)(a)* or (*b*), *101A(1)(d)*, *102(1)* or *103* (see (ii)–(v) in 55.8 above). In that event, the reduction will apply only to so much of the basic award as is payable because of *TULRCA 1992, s 156(1)* or *ERA 1996, s 120* (see 55.8 above) (*ERA 1996, s 122(3); TULRCA 1992, s 156(2)*).

Where the tribunal finds that the complainant has unreasonably refused an offer by the employer which, if accepted, would have the effect of reinstating the complainant in his employment in all respects as if he had not been dismissed, the tribunal will reduce or further reduce the amount of the basic award to such extent as it considers just and equitable having regard to that finding (*ERA 1996, s 122(1)*).

The basic award may also be reduced where the employee has been awarded any amount in respect of the dismissal under a designated dismissal procedures agreement, to such extent as the tribunal considers it just and equitable having regard to that award (*ERA 1996, s 122(3A)*) inserted by the *Employment Rights (Dispute Resolution) Act 1998, s 15, Sch 1, para 22*).

The amount of the basic award will be reduced or, as the case may be, further reduced, by the amount of any redundancy payment awarded by the tribunal in respect of the same dismissal or of any payment made by the employer to the employee on the ground that the dismissal was by reason of redundancy, whether in pursuance of statutory provisions or otherwise (*ERA 1996, s 122(4)*). No reduction of the basic award will be made, however, when the employer makes a payment in respect of redundancy but, objectively viewed, the employee was not redundant (*Boorman v Allmakes Ltd* [1995] IRLR 553).

Note that, where an employee had received an *ex gratia* payment from his former employers which included his statutory entitlement and which was sufficient to cover any basic or compensatory award, the EAT held that an employment tribunal was not obliged to make a basic award (*Chelsea Football Club and Athletic Co Ltd v Heath* [1981] ICR 323; cf *Barnsley Metropolitan Borough Council v Prest* [1996] ICR 85).

See also 54.19 below for reduction in union-related cases.

55.10 COMPENSATORY AWARD

The compensation recoverable on a complaint of unfair dismissal increased dramatically in 1999, but, in the current job market, the maximum award is often criticised as being unrealistically low. There are some calls to increase or even remove the cap. For dismissals before 25 October 1999, the maximum amount of the compensatory award was £12,000. With effect from 25 October 1999, the maximum amount of the compensatory award was increased to £50,000, and was abolished altogether in a small number of cases (*Employment Relations Act 1999, ss 34(4)* and *37(1); SI 1992/2830*). For dismissals after 1 February 2007, the maximum compensatory award has been increased to £60,600 (*SI 2006/3045*). There is no maximum compensatory award in health and safety cases (*ERA 1996, s 100*), protected disclosure cases (*ERA 1996, s 103A*), selection for redundancy on health and safety grounds (*ERA 1996, s 105(3)*), and selection for redundancy on protected disclosure grounds (*ERA 1996, s 105(6A)*). In the case of a refusal to reinstate or re-engage (see 55.5 above), the tribunal may exceed the normal maximum to the extent necessary fully to reflect the sums which would have been payable under its original order (*ERA 1996, s 124(4)*).

The application of the statutory limit is the last step in the calculation, applied after assessing the amount of loss and after taking into account any payments made by the respondent to the claimant and after any increase or reduction required by any statute or rule of law (*ERA 1996, s 124(5)*). For example, if a claimant's loss was assessed at £90,000 after making an adjustment under the *Employment Act 2002*, and the tribunal found that he was 50% to blame for the dismissal, he would be awarded £45,000 and not 50% of the statutory maximum (*Walter Braund (London) Ltd v Murray* [1991] ICR 327). Similarly, an employment tribunal must first deduct an *ex gratia* payment and then apply the statutory maximum (*McCarthy v British Insulated Callenders Cables plc* [1985] IRLR 94).

The order in which deductions should be made is further considered at 55.13 below.

For the relationship between compensation for unfair and wrongful dismissal, see 58.10 WRONGFUL DISMISSAL.

55.11 Amount

The amount of compensation is such amount as the tribunal considers just and equitable in all the circumstances, having regard to the loss sustained by the complainant in consequence of the dismissal insofar as that loss is attributable to action taken by the employer (*ERA 1996, s 123(1)*).

The loss shall be taken to include:

(*a*) any expenses reasonably incurred by the complainant in consequence of the dismissal; and

(*b*) loss of any benefit save for the contingent right to a redundancy payment which he might reasonably be expected to have had but for the dismissal.

(*ERA 1996, s 123(2), (3).*)

55.12 Assessment of compensatory award

Since the decision in *Norton Tool Co Ltd v Tewson* [1972] ICR 501, the tribunal has a duty to show how compensation is made up. The most common heads of compensation are those set out below. Whereas the basic award is based upon *gross* pay, the compensatory award depends upon the *net* value of wages and other benefits.

Immediate loss of wages. This is the sum of the loss of wages from the date of termination until the date of the hearing. Account will be taken of wages paid in lieu of notice and earnings in other employments (see also 55.13 below). If the employee has obtained new permanent employment, but has then lost it again, the original employer should not be taken as having caused the loss of earnings after the second dismissal (*Mabey Plant Hire Ltd v Richens*, IDS Brief 495, p 13).

In *Burlo v Langley* [2006] EWCA Civ 1178, [2007] IRLR 145 the Court of Appeal confirmed that *Norton Tool* is authority only for the proposition that compensation for unfair summary dismissal should include full pay for the notice period, without any requirement for the claimant to mitigate his loss during the notice period or to give account of earnings from other employers during the notice period. The observation in *Norton Tool* that it was good industrial relations practice to pay full notice pay whenever an employee was dismissed without notice had to be considered in the light of the House of Lords judgment in *Dunnachie v Kingston-Upon-Hull City Council* [2004] UKHL 26, [2005] 1 AC 226, and a claimant was only entitled to receive compensation for his actual losses.

This meant that the claimant nanny was not entitled to receive full pay in respect of the notice period following her unfair dismissal during which she was in fact unable to work after accidental injury; her loss during the notice period was her sick pay entitlement only.

Future loss of earnings. If the claimant is unemployed at the time of the hearing or is in less remunerative employment than that from which he was dismissed, he will be awarded a sum for future loss of earnings. The award will be based upon the claimant's net loss of earnings for such period as the tribunal considers reasonable, bearing in mind such matters as the length of time he may be unemployed. Compensation must be assessed on the basis of what has actually occurred by the time of the hearing, rather than what might have been expected to occur at the time of the dismissal (*Gilham v Kent County Council (No 3)* [1986] ICR 52). Nevertheless, the exercise of assessing future loss involves predicting what might have happened if the Claimant had not been dismissed and what might happen in the future, and the tribunal will have to make an assessment based on uncertainties and sometimes speculation (*Scope v Thornett* [2006] EWCA Civ 1600, [2007] IRLR 155). Future loss of earnings does not necessarily cease when an employee obtains employment of a permanent nature at an equivalent or higher salary than he previously enjoyed. If the employee obtains another job but then loses the new job within a short time with no right to compensation, the loss from the first dismissal may continue (*Dench v Flynn & Partners* [1998] IRLR 653, overruling *Whelan v Richardson* [1998] IRLR 114).

The award will take into account any increase in salary or any other benefit the claimant would have enjoyed had he not been dismissed, even beyond his contractual entitlements (*York Trailer Co Ltd v Sparkes* [1973] ICR 518). It will take account not only of regular wage or salary payments but also, for example, commission or bonus payments.

If the employee has obtained new employment which is more remunerative than the original job, it may be that the overall result by the time of the hearing is that he has suffered no loss at all (*Ging v Ellward Lancs Ltd* [1991] ICR 222). But where there has been a great delay in assessing the loss suffered, it may not be just and equitable to apply *Ging* (*Fentiman v Fluid Engineering Products Ltd* [1991] ICR 570; *Lytlarch Ltd v Reid* [1991] ICR 216).

The tribunal may award damages for loss of earnings in relation to a period in which the claimant is unfit for work and in receipt of invalidity benefit, if the inability to work is itself attributable to the actions of the employer in unfairly dismissing him. So, for example, if the claimant is receiving invalidity benefit because of depression caused by unemployment, which in turn was caused by the unfair dismissal, the claimant may receive compensation for the period in which he was unfit to work (*Hilton International Hotels (UK) Ltd v Faraji* [1994] ICR 259; *Devine v Designer Flowers Wholesale Florists Sundries Ltd* [1993] IRLR 517). The invalidity benefit received will, however, be taken into account (*Puglia v C James & Sons* [1996] ICR 301).

Loss of use of a company car. If the employee had the use of a company car not only for the purposes of his employment but also for private use, he will be compensated for the loss of that benefit. The tribunal will take into account whether or not the employer paid for the petrol for private motoring. The incidence of tax will be taken into account as it is in the assessment of loss of all benefits in kind. In assessing the value of a car, petrol and running costs, reference is sometimes made to annual estimates published by the AA (*Shove v Downs Surgical plc* [1984] ICR 532).

Loss of benefits in kind. In assessing compensation, the tribunal will take into account other benefits in kind such as free accommodation, medical insurance and subsidised meals. It may do so even where there was no strict contractual entitlement to such benefits. A claimant is not entitled to receive compensation in respect of life insurance (and, logically, any other insurance) for a period following dismissal during which he did not take out replacement cover and the risks insured did not occur (*Knapton v ECC Card Clothing Ltd* [2006] IRLR 756). This is because to make a payment in respect of that period would give the claimant a windfall.

Loss of reputation. It had long been believed that the claimant is not entitled to damages for the loss to his reputation which has resulted from the dismissal (*Addis v Gramophone Co Ltd* [1909] AC 488). However in *Malik v BCCI* [1997] ICR 606, the House of Lords held that the claimant will be entitled to 'stigma damages' to compensate for difficulties in finding work which may result from the poor reputation of the employer at the time of dismissal, on the basis that the employer breached its duty of trust and confidence to the employee by acting in a manner which gave rise to its poor reputation. A claimant may not receive damages for the stress or injury to feelings resulting from the manner of dismissal (*Bliss v South-East Thames Regional Health Authority* [1987] ICR 700, *French v Barclays Bank plc* [1998] IRLR 646, CA and *Dunnachie v Kingston-Upon-Hull City Council* [2004] UKHL 36, [2004] IRLR 727 in which the HL ended the uncertainty created by Lord Hoffman's comments in *Johnson v Unisys Ltd* [2001] UKHL 13, [2001] IRLR 279 and the CA's decision [2004] EWCA Civ 84, [2004] IRLR 287). If an employee suffers from a reactive depression following a dismissal, which renders him unfit for employment between the date of dismissal and the date on which compensation is determined, the employment tribunal must ask what caused his loss. It may be just and equitable to compensate him for all or part of his loss of earnings, despite his unfitness for work, depending on the degree to which the dismissal caused his loss (*Dignity Funerals v Bruce* [2005] IRLR 189).

Pension rights. If, prior to his dismissal, the complainant was a member of a company pension scheme, and fails to obtain new employment, or obtains new employment where there is no company pension scheme, he will almost certainly suffer financial loss because any deferred pension payable will be based on the employee's salary at the date of dismissal (subject to statutory uplifting) instead of on the salary he would have received at normal retiring age. Even if he has obtained employment in another company which operates such a scheme, so that he is able to transfer his accrued rights under the previous scheme to the new scheme, it is likely that this will still involve a degree of loss because the transfer value will only reflect the value of those accrued rights at the date of leaving rather than reflecting the enhanced value which would have been added to those accrued rights, had the complainant remained with the previous company until retirement age instead of being dismissed. In any of these circumstances, the task of assessing compensation for loss of pension rights is a hard one. Some guidance is provided by a booklet prepared by a committee of employment tribunal chairmen in consultation with the Government Actuary's Department ('Industrial Tribunals – Compensation for Loss of Pension Rights', HMSO, 1991), although it is now very out of date. The booklet is not binding upon tribunals (*Bingham v Hobourn Engineering Ltd* [1992] IRLR 298; see also *Manpower Ltd v Hearne* [1983] ICR 567; *Tradewinds Airways Ltd v Fletcher* [1981] IRLR 272; *Willmont Bros Ltd v Oliver* [1979] ICR 378; *Mono Pumps Ltd v Froggatt and Radford* [1987] IRLR 368). An alternative approach may be for the tribunal to assess the period for which the employee should be compensated for loss of pension rights, and to make an award based upon the cost of purchasing a policy to make up the difference between the pension which he will receive and the amount he would have received had he remained in employment until the end of the period. An award for loss of pension rights which is based solely on the value of the employer's contributions is not appropriate in assessing loss of pension rights under a scheme which yields not only an income benefit but also a lump sum arising as of right rather than by commutation. In *Clancy v Cannock Chase Technical College* [2001] IRLR 331, Lindsay J, giving judgment for the EAT, held that such an award was not just and equitable compensation since it produced an amount which could not begin to replace the reduction in the lump sum and annual pension that the claimant would suffer as a result of his dismissal. The *1991 Guidelines* provide no yardstick for the compensation of pension loss in such a case and Lindsay J noted in *Clancy* (above) that careful consideration should be given to whether the *1991 Guidelines* ought to be revised, in particular, now that the maximum compensatory award has been greatly increased and full pension compensation is more likely to require to be accurately computed than in the past. In *Bentwood Bros (Manchester) Ltd v Shepherd* [2003] EWCA Civ 380, [2003] IRLR 364 the Court of Appeal held that an employment tribunal had erred in applying only a 5% discount for accelerated receipt, even though the sum represented two and a half years' future earnings and ten years' pension payments.

Payments received by an employee under an occupational or private pension scheme, whether contributory or not, should not be offset against compensation awarded for unfair dismissal. This is because pensions are deferred pay and a decision by an employee to take an early pension after unfair dismissal is a personal decision about money management, rather than a factor which reduces the loss suffered in consequence of the unfair dismissal (*Knapton v ECC Card Clothing Ltd* [2006] IRLR 756).

Loss of statutory rights. The tribunal will assess a nominal figure for loss of protection from unfair dismissal for the first two years (the period for acquiring unfair dismissal protection) of any new employment. A few years ago, the appropriate figure was normally £100 (*SH Muffett Ltd v Head* [1987] ICR 1). It is now common for tribunals to award £250.

It will also award compensation for loss of the accrued right to the statutory minimum period of notice. The loss was assessed in *Daley v AE Dorsett (Almar Dolls) Ltd* [1982] ICR 1 as half the wages due during that period, but it is thought that this may be too high in the ordinary case. See also *Arthur Guinness Son & Co (Great Britain) Ltd v Green* [1989] ICR 241.

Frequently, employment tribunals will award just one sum for loss of statutory rights, commonly in the region of £250, to cover loss of protection from unfair dismissal and loss of accrued right to statutory notice.

55.13 FACTORS REDUCING OR INCREASING THE COMPENSATORY AWARD

Just and equitable. The tribunal has a discretion to make an award which is less than the full amount of the claimant's loss if the tribunal considers it just and equitable to do so (*ERA 1996, s 123(1)*). Thus, if the employee has been guilty of misconduct which was only discovered after the dismissal, and therefore could not be relied upon to establish contributory fault (see below), a reduced award or no award may be made (*W Devis & Sons Ltd v Atkins* [1977] ICR 662; *Tele-Trading Ltd v Jenkins* [1990] IRLR 430; *Chaplin v H J Rawlinson Ltd* [1991] ICR 553). See *Slaughter v C Brewer & Sons Ltd* [1990] ICR 730 for reductions under *s 123(1)* in cases of ill-health.

The fact that an employer could have dismissed an employee fairly for poor attendance when he dismissed her unfairly for ill-health was held by the Court of Appeal not to justify a reduction in the compensatory award on just and equitable grounds where the employer, in full knowledge of the facts, chose not to dismiss her on grounds of poor attendance (*Devonshire v Trico-Folberth Ltd* [1989] ICR 747).

It is only events which took place before dismissal which can render it just and equitable to reduce the compensatory award. A tribunal may not, for example, take account of a breach of a duty of confidentiality which took place after dismissal (*Soros v Davison* [1994] ICR 590).

In *Simrad Ltd v Scott* [1997] IRLR 147, the EAT held that it was not just and equitable to assess the compensatory award by reference to the lower rate of pay which the applicant was receiving because of her decision to change career and train as a nurse. The change of career was too remote to be linked to the dismissal.

Contributory fault. Where the tribunal finds that the dismissal was to any extent caused or contributed to by any action of the complainant, it will reduce the amount of the compensatory award by such proportion as it considers just and equitable having regard to that finding (*ERA 1996, s 123(6)*). The same percentage of deduction will usually apply to both basic and compensatory awards.

If, therefore, an employee was guilty of misconduct which was grave, but did not justify dismissal, or if the procedures used to dismiss him were unfair, but his own conduct to a certain extent contributed to his misfortune, the amount of compensation may be reduced. The reduction may be as much as 100% in an appropriate case (*W Devis & Sons Ltd v Atkins* [1977] ICR 662). See also 55.19 below for reduction in union-related cases.

In order for a deduction for contributory fault to be made for the employee's misconduct, that conduct must be culpable or blameworthy in the sense that, whether or not it amounted to a breach of contract or tort, it was foolish or perverse or unreasonable in the circumstances (*Nelson v BBC (No 2)* [1980] ICR 110).

Where the tribunal has jurisdiction in the case of a dismissal for taking part in industrial action (see 53.17 UNFAIR DISMISSAL – I), it is not open to the tribunal to hold that participation in the industrial action in itself amounts to contributory fault: *Crossville Wales Ltd v Tracey* [1997] ICR 862, overruling *TNT Express Ltd v Downes* [1994] ICR 1.

Lack of capability is unlikely to be blameworthy in the *Nelson* sense unless it involves, for example, laziness or obstructive behaviour. However, in a case, say, of incapability due to ill-health, it may be appropriate to make a reduction under the general 'just and equitable' formulation referred to above (*Slaughter*, above).

A reduction for contributory fault may be made in the case of constructive dismissal and where the employer has failed to establish an acceptable reason for the dismissal (*Morrison v Amalgamated Transport and General Workers Union* [1989] IRLR 361; *Polentarutti v Autokraft Ltd* [1991] ICR 757).

In *Optikinetics Ltd v Whooley* [1999] ICR 984, the EAT held that where a tribunal found that there was contributory fault on the part of a claimant, it was obligatory for the tribunal to make a reduction in the compensatory award by such proportion as it considered just and equitable, but there was no similar obligation in respect of the basic award.

The Court of Session in Scotland has held that it is an error of law for a tribunal to fail to give reasons for a reduction in an award for contributory fault (*Nairne v Highlands and Islands Fire Brigade* [1989] IRLR 366).

Failure to follow statutory procedures: reduction or increase in compensation. The *EA 2002* introduced statutory minimum disciplinary and grievance procedures (see 54.3(A) UNFAIR DISMISSAL – II, 8.5 CONTRACT OF EMPLOYMENT and 20.18 EMPLOYMENT TRIBUNALS – I) with effect from 1 October 2004. The employee's failure to comply with the procedures may result in the compensatory award being reduced, and the employer's failure to comply may result in the compensatory award being increased.

(A) Reduction in compensation: *EA 2002, s 31(2)* provides that an award to an employee may be reduced if the claim to which the proceedings relate concerns a matter to which one of the statutory procedures applies, the statutory procedure was not completed before the proceedings were begun and the non-completion of the statutory procedure was wholly or mainly attributable to a failure by the employee to comply with a requirement of the procedure or to exercise a right of appeal under it.

Section 31(2) says that the tribunal must reduce the award in such circumstances by 10% and may, if it considers it just and equitable to do so, reduce it by a further amount, up to a total of 50%. *Section 31(4)* provides that the tribunal has a discretion not to make a reduction, or to make a reduction of less than 10% if there are exceptional circumstances which would make a larger deduction unjust or inequitable.

The reduction in the compensatory award is made before both the reduction for contributory fault and the reduction to take account of the extent to which a contractual or *ex gratia* redundancy payment exceeds the statutory redundancy payment (*ERA 1996, s 124A*).

(B) Increase in compensation: *Section 31(3)* provides that if the non-completion of the statutory procedure was wholly or mainly attributable to the failure by the employer to comply with a requirement of the procedure, the tribunal may increase the award by the same percentages as it may reduce the award if the fault lies with the employee.

The Secretary of State has made regulations in relation to the circumstances in which compensation should be increased or reduced, such as specifying what constitutes compliance with a requirement of a statutory procedure (*EA 2002, s 31(6)* and *EA 2002 (Dispute Resolution) Regulations 2004 (SI 2004/752)*).

Under *EA 2002, s 38*, an employment tribunal which finds in favour of an employee after hearing a complaint of unfair dismissal but makes no award to the employee, and which has noticed that when the proceedings began the employer was in breach of its duty to provide the employee with a written statement of initial employment particulars or particulars of change, must make an award of at least two weeks' pay (up to £620) and may, if it considers it just and equitable in all the circumstances, make an award of four weeks' pay (*EA 2002, s 38(2)*) (up to £1,240). Where the employment tribunal makes an award to the employee for unfair dismissal in such a case, that award must be increased by at least two and up to four weeks' pay (*EA 2002, s 38(3)*). The duty to award at least two and up to four week's pay in such a case does not arise if there are exceptional circumstances which would make the award or increase unjust or inequitable (*EA 2002, s 38(5)*).

Whether the unfairness made any difference. It was initially thought that, if the employee would have been dismissed even if the employer had done all that he ought to have done, the dismissal ought not to be regarded as unfair. That approach was held to be wrong in *Polkey v AE Dayton Services Ltd* [1988] ICR 142 (see 52.4 UNFAIR DISMISSAL – II) which introduced an approach requiring the tribunal to reduce compensation by a percentage to take account of the possibility that the employee would have been dismissed even if a fair procedure had been followed.

Now *ERA 1996, s 98A* (as introduced by *EA 2002, s 34*) is in force, it is unlikely that there will be many cases in which a tribunal will find a dismissal to be procedurally unfair but go on to award no compensation because the unfairness made no difference. If an employer fails to comply with the statutory dismissal procedures, the dismissal will be automatically unfair under *s 98A(1), ERA* 1996. *Section 98A(2)* will statutorily overrule *Polkey* to the extent that if the employer shows that failure to follow a procedure made no difference to the outcome, the dismissal will be fair, and the question of compensation will not arise. The Scottish Court of Session in *King v Eaton (No 2)* [1998] IRLR 686 said that it was open to a tribunal to decline to permit an employer at a remedies hearing to lead additional evidence to show that the result would have been the same even if fair procedures had been followed. If it is not realistic or practicable to embark upon such an exercise or the exercise would be highly speculative, the tribunal should not do so. The EAT held in *Kelly-Madden v Manor Surgery* [2007] IRLR 17 that *s 98A(2)* applies to the failure to follow any procedure with which the employment tribunal considers that the employer should in fairness have complied. To ask what would have happened if the employer had acted fairly is still relevant to compensation. For example, if the company shut down and all the employees were made redundant a few weeks after the claimant was unfairly dismissed, his compensatory award ought not to run beyond that date (see *James W Cook & Co (Wivenhoe) Ltd v Tipper* [1990] ICR 716, holding also that the tribunal cannot investigate the commercial and economic reasons behind the closure). The tribunal may take account of the fact that an employee with a short period of service is more at risk of being selected for redundancy if job losses occur (*Morris v Acco Co Ltd* [1985] ICR 306). Again, it may be that the tribunal considers that an employee dismissed for misconduct without a hearing could not, in fact, have said anything effective in his own defence, or that an employee dismissed without warning for lack of capability was not capable of improvement in any event. In a different context, it has been suggested that it ought not to be assumed too readily that a failure to observe the principles of natural justice made no difference to the result (*John v Rees* [1970] Ch 345 at 402).

In *O'Donoghue v Redcar and Cleveland Borough Council* [2001] EWCA Civ 701, [2001] IRLR 615, the Court of Appeal made it clear that it was not always necessary or appropriate to make a percentage assessment as to whether the claimant would have been dismissed fairly if there had been no unfair dismissal. This was especially the case if the tribunal was assessing the likelihood that the claimant might have been fairly dismissed, not at the time of dismissal, but at some time in the future. In such circumstances, it may not be possible to identify an overall percentage risk, because there may be, say, a 20% chance of dismissal in six months but a 30% chance in a year. In Miss O'Donoghue's case the tribunal concluded that her divisive and antagonistic approach was such that she would have been bound to be dismissed fairly within six months, and so the tribunal limited compensation for future loss to the six-month period. The Court of Appeal held that the tribunal had approached the matter correctly and that it had been appropriate to assess a safe date by which the tribunal was certain that that dismissal would take place and then to make an award of full compensation in respect of the period prior thereto. See also *Scope v Thornett* [2006] EWCA Civ 1600, [2007] IRLR 155.

The tribunal ought also to consider *when* that dismissal would have taken place, e g even if it is certain that a fair procedure would have led to the same result, it may be that its adoption would have prolonged the period of earning for a number of weeks (see *Mining Supplies (Longwall) Ltd v Baker* [1988] ICR 676) or perhaps not at all (*Robertson v Magnet Ltd (Retail Division)* [1993] IRLR 512). If the employee could only have hoped for continued employment in a different and less well-paid job, the calculation of his loss ought to be based upon those lower earnings (*Red Bank*, above).

The approach taken by the EAT in *Mining (Longwall) v Baker* was not followed by the EAT in *Elkouil v Coney Island Ltd* [2002] IRLR 174. In *Elkouil*, the tribunal held that redundancy consultation should have begun some 10 weeks before dismissal, and that consultation would have prolonged employment by two weeks. The tribunal made a compensatory award of two weeks' pay. The EAT held that the tribunal should have awarded 10 weeks' pay, because if consultation had taken place at the right time, the applicant would have had the opportunity of looking for another job some 10 weeks earlier than he could. Accordingly, he lost the chance of being re-employed substantially earlier than he was.

If a percentage reduction is being made on the basis that employment may have terminated fairly during the period for which compensation is being assessed and also on account of contributory fault, the two reductions should be applied sequentially (*Rao v Civil Aviation Authority* [1994] ICR 495). Thus, if there was a 50% chance that the employee would have been dismissed in any event, and he was 30% to blame for his dismissal, he should be awarded only 35% of his actual loss (ie half of 70%). If the employee receives a termination payment, the payment should be deducted after this process has been carried out (*Digital Equipment Co Ltd v Clements (No 2)* [1998] ICR 258; *Heggie v Uniroyal Englebert Tyres Ltd* [1998] IRLR 425).

In *Steel Stockholders (Birmingham) Ltd v Kirkwood* [1993] IRLR 515, the EAT held that it was only where the defect was procedural rather than substantive that a percentage reduction may be made. The distinction between procedural and substantive defects was however easier to state than to apply and in *O'Dea v ISC Chemicals Ltd* [1996] IRLR 599, the Court of Appeal held that employment tribunals should not attempt to categorise defects in this manner.

Mitigation of loss. The employee is under a duty to mitigate his loss. He must take reasonable steps to obtain alternative employment. A compensatory award is intended to compensate the employee for loss and is not a penal award against the employer. What employment he will be under a duty to accept is a matter to be determined by the tribunal. He must be realistic in his job expectations. He may not demand a salary or status higher than that which he previously enjoyed, and may have to accept some reduction. If the employee has not made reasonable efforts to find other work, his compensation will be reduced to reflect the tribunal's view of what would have happened if he *had* mitigated his loss. However, the burden of proving a failure to mitigate is on the employer, and the standard of what is reasonably required of the employee should not be set too high (*Fyfe v Scientific Furnishings Ltd* [1989] ICR 648).

Where an unfairly dismissed employee had unreasonably refused an employer's offer of reinstatement, he was rightly held only to be entitled to a basic award (*Sweetlove v Redbridge and Waltham Forest Area Health Authority* [1979] ICR 477). In *Wilding v BT plc* [2002] EWCA Civ 349, [2002] IRLR 524, the Court of Appeal held that the duty to mitigate which is imposed on an employee requires him when considering an offer of re-employment to act as a reasonable person unaffected by the prospect of compensation, that the onus is on the employer to show that the employee had failed in that duty, that the test of reasonableness was objective, that the circumstances in which an offer of re-employment was made and refused, the attitude of the employer, the way in which the employee had been treated, and all the surrounding circumstances should be taken into account by the tribunal, and that the tribunal must not be too stringent in its expectations of the injured party.

There is no duty to mitigate until the dismissal has actually taken place (*Trimble v Supertravel Ltd* [1982] IRLR 451). Failure by the employee to activate the internal appeals procedure after the dismissal cannot, as a matter of law, amount to a failure to mitigate (*Lock v Connell Estate Agents* [1994] IRLR 444, not following *Hoover Ltd v Forde* [1980] ICR 239). Under *EA 2002, s 31(2)* a claimant will be penalised by a reduction in compensation if he fails to exhaust internal procedures (see '*Failure to follow statutory procedures: reduction or increase in compensation*' above).

In *Daley v AE Dorsett (Almar Dolls) Ltd* [1982] ICR 1, the EAT did not interfere with an employment tribunal's finding that an employee's decision not to accept full-time employment at a rate of earnings less than the amount of unemployment benefit was reasonable. It stressed, however, that employment tribunals should be very slow indeed in finding reasonable a decision of a dismissed employee not to accept subsequent employment because he would be receiving less than unemployment benefit.

Expenses incurred in seeking to mitigate the loss suffered (e g the cost of travelling to job interviews) are recoverable as part of the compensatory award. That could include the cost of starting up a business of the employee's own, if that was a reasonable thing to do (see *Aon Trading Ltd v Dove* [2005] EWCA Civ 411, [2005] IRLR 891; *Gardiner-Hill v Roland Beiger Technics Ltd* [1982] IRLR 498). Legal expenses incurred in pursuing the unfair dismissal claim are not recoverable (for the award of costs see 20.35 EMPLOYMENT TRIBUNALS – I).

Payments made by the employer. Payments made by the claimant's former employer, whether under a contractual liability or *ex gratia*, will generally be taken into account (*Rushton v Harcros Timber and Building Supplies Ltd* [1993] ICR 230). In *Simrad Ltd v Scott* [1997] IRLR 147, however, the EAT held that a loan which was to be repaid by way of work need not be taken into account for these purposes as it would not be just and equitable to do so since the employee had been deprived of the opportunity to carry on working.

It was formerly understood that the employee must give credit for pay in lieu of notice and other benefits received from the old employer during the notice period (*Addison v Babcock FATA Ltd* [1987] ICR 805) and for earnings from any new employment during the notice period, because the contractual right to notice pay does not create a debt owed by the employer which must be paid irrespective of the employee's real loss, but gives rise merely to a claim in damages or compensation where the employer breaches his contractual or statutory notice obligations

(*Rowley v Cerberus Software Ltd* [2001] EWCA Civ 78, [2001] IRLR 160). Similarly, neither pension payments (*Hopkins v Norcros plc* [1994] ICR 11), nor an educational grant received in connection with a course embarked upon after dismissal (*Justfern Ltd v D'Ingerthorpe* [1994] ICR 286) were taken into account. The full amount of invalidity benefit was deducted in *Puglia v James & Sons* ([1996] IRLR 70), which did not follow *Hilton International Hotels (UK) Ltd v Faraji* ([1994] ICR 259). *Puglia v James* was itself not followed in *Rubenstein v McGloughlin* [1996] IRLR 557, in which the EAT deducted only half the amount of invalidity benefit.

There were subsequently conflicting decisions at EAT level concerning the deductibility from the compensatory award of monies which the employee earns or receives during the notice period. In *Hardy v Polk (Leeds) Ltd* [2004] IRLR 420 the EAT held that the same duty to mitigate arises as there is at common law and account should be taken of earnings from new employment. A differently-constituted EAT in *Voith Turbo Ltd v Stowe* ([2005] IRLR 228) held that it was open to an employment tribunal not to deduct earnings from new employment from the pay in lieu of notice, in accordance with good industrial practice. A more recent EAT decision, however, in *Morgans v Alpha Plus Security* [2005] IRLR 234, held that incapacity benefit received following a dismissal was properly deducted from the compensatory award, in order to ensure that the employee was compensated for his actual loss only. The Court of Appeal has now concluded that an employee is not required to give credit against his unfair dismissal compensatory award for earnings from another employer during the notice period, when unfairly dismissed without pay in lieu of notice, but that his entitlement for compensation in respect of the notice period is limited to his actual loss (see *Burlo v Langley* above [2006] EWCA Civ 1178, [2007] IRLR 145).

Jobseeker's allowance received will not be taken into account (but see 55.6 above for the rules on recoupment).

The payments made by the employer are deducted by the employment tribunal from the gross sum after compensation has been reduced to take account of contributory fault and/or the fact that dismissal might have taken place anyway: *Digital Equipment Co Ltd v Clements (No 2)* [1998] ICR 242.

Delayed Payment. In *Melia v Magna Kansei Ltd* [2005] EWCA Civ 1547, [2006] IRLR 117, the Court of Appeal held that when assessing a claimant's loss, an employment tribunal may make an allowance for delayed payment. According to the Court, this is distinct from a tribunal awarding interest, which it may not do.

The order in which deductions should be made. The Court of Appeal in *Digital Equipment v Clements (No 2)* [1998] IRLR 134 and the Scottish Court of Session in *Leonard v Strathclyde Buses Ltd* [1998] IRLR 693 have considered the order in which deductions should be made from the compensatory award. The position is now clear, except where non-statutory redundancy payments are concerned. The order of deduction is as follows:

(a)   calculate the total loss actually suffered by the claimant;

(b)   deduct amounts received in mitigation and any payment made by the former employer (other than a non-statutory redundancy payment);

(c)   make any adjustment for failure on the part of the employee or employer to follow statutory procedures ;

(d)   make any reduction for contributory fault;

(e)   apply the statutory maximum.

The controversy as regards non-statutory redundancy payments is as to whether the effect of *ERA 1996, s 123(7)* is that such payments should be deducted after the reduction for contributory fault but before the statutory maximum is applied, or whether they should only be deducted after the statutory maximum is applied. It is not clear from the judgments in *Digital Equipment v Clements (No 2)* which of the two alternative approaches should be followed. In *Leonard v Strathclyde Buses*, however, the Court of Session held that non-statutory redundancy payments should be deducted before the statutory maximum is applied and said that there was nothing in *Digital Equipment v Clements (No 2)* which points to any different view.

The approach taken by the Court of Appeal in *Digital Equipment v Clements (No 2)* was adopted once again by the Scottish Court of Session in *Heggie v Uniroyal Englebert Tyres Ltd* [1999] IRLR 802.

55.14   ADDITIONAL AWARD – NON-COMPLIANCE WITH AN ORDER

Additional compensation in cases where an order for reinstatement or re-engagement is made but not complied with (see 55.5 above) consisting of not less than 26 weeks' and not more than 52 weeks' pay (except union-related, health and safety, pension scheme trustee and employee representative cases where a special award may be made, see 55.16 below) (*ERA 1996, s 117*).

The tribunal may not simply make the maximum award in order to force compliance with its order. It must consider factors such as the employer's conduct and the extent to which the compensatory award has met the actual loss suffered (*Morganite Electrical Carbon Ltd v Donne* [1988] ICR 18).

Where the employer has made an *ex gratia* payment which exceeds the amount of any loss suffered, it may be possible to set off the surplus against any additional award (*Darr v LRC Products Ltd* [1993] IRLR 257).

55.15   REDUCTION OF AWARD – 'UNION-RELATED' CASES

Where an award of compensation is made in respect of a dismissal which is to be regarded as unfair by virtue of *TULRCA 1992, s 152* or *s 153*, a tribunal, in considering whether it would be just and equitable to reduce or further reduce the amount of *any part* of the award, will disregard any conduct or action which constitutes:

(*a*)   a breach or proposed breach of a requirement that the complainant should:

    (i)   be or become a member;

    (ii)   cease to be or refrain from becoming a member; or

    (iii)   not take part in the activities; or

    (iv)   not make use of the services which are made available to him

    of any trade union or a particular trade union or one of a number of particular trade unions;

(*b*)   acceptance of or failure to accept an offer by the employer made to induce the employee not to become a member or participate in activities of a trade union (contrary to *TULRCA 1992, s 145A*) or not to participate in collective bargaining (contrary to *TULRCA 1992, s 145B*); or

(c)   an objection or proposed objection (however expressed) to the operation of a provision for the deduction of union subscriptions from his remuneration (under *TULRCA 1992, s 152(3)*).

(*TULRCA 1992, s 155.*)

However, it seems that confrontational conduct by the employee could form the basis for a finding of contributory fault provided that the immediate circumstances constituting the principal reason for dismissal are excluded from consideration (*Transport and General Workers' Union v Howard* [1992] ICR 106).

55.16   MAXIMUM AWARDS

(i)   The maximum amount of a 'week's pay', which determines the maximum amount of a basic award, is reviewed annually and linked to the RPI (*ERelA 1999, s 34(1)*) (see PAY– I (32)). The current maximum is £310.

(ii)   The minimum basic award in a case of dismissal unfair under *TULRCA 1992, s 152* or *s 153* or *ERA 1996, s 100(1)(a)* and *(b)*, *101A(d)*, *102(1)* or *103* is £4,200.

(iii)   The maximum basic award is $20 \times 1\frac{1}{2} \times £310 = £9,300$.

(iv)   An employee may also receive an award in respect of unfair dismissal which is increased by £620-£1,240 under *EA 2002, s 38* (see 55.13 above).

(v)   The maximum compensatory award is £60,600 (see 55.10 above).

(vi)   Note the exceptions in which the ceiling on compensation does not apply (*ERA 1996, s 124(1A)*). There is no statutory maximum compensatory award in cases in which a person is regarded as automatically unfairly dismissed by reason of *ERA 1996, s 100* (health and safety cases), *s 103A* (public interest disclosure cases), *s 105(3)* (selection for redundancy on grounds of health and safety activity) or *s 105(6A)* (selection for redundancy on the ground of public interest disclosure) (*ERelA 1999, s 37(1)*).

(vii)   The additional award will, in all cases, be not less than 26 and not more than 52 weeks' pay, giving a maximum of £16,120 (see 55.15).

55.17   JOINDER OF THIRD PARTIES

If, in any proceedings before an employment tribunal on a complaint of unfair dismissal, either the employer or the complainant claims:

(a)   that the employer was induced to dismiss the complainant by the actual or threatened calling, organising, procuring or financing of a strike or other industrial action; and

(b)   that such pressure was exercised because the complainant was not a member of any trade union or of a particular trade union or of one of a number of particular trade unions,

the employer or the complainant may request the tribunal to direct that the person whom he claims exercised the pressure, be joined as a party to the proceedings (*TULRCA 1992, s 160(1)*).

A tribunal must grant such a request if it is made before the hearing of the complaint begins, but it may be refused if it is made after that time. The tribunal will refuse to hear such a request if it is made after the tribunal has made an award of compensation (*TULRCA 1992, s 160(2)*).

If the tribunal makes an award of compensation and considers that the complaint of pressure is well-founded, it may make an order that the third party (joined according to the procedure outlined above) pay all or such part of the award as the tribunal may consider just and equitable in the circumstances (*TULRCA 1992, s 160(3)*).

55.18 INTERIM RELIEF IN RESPECT OF CERTAIN DISMISSALS

An employee who complains that he has been dismissed for:

(*a*)   being or proposing to become a member of an independent trade union;

(*b*)   taking part or proposing to take part in the activities of an independent trade union at an appropriate time;

(*c*)   not being a member of any trade union, or of a particular trade union, or of one of a number of particular trade unions, or refusing or proposing to refuse to become or remain a member;

(*d*)   carrying out, or proposing to carry out, activities which he has been designated by the employer to carry out in connection with preventing or reducing risks to health and safety at work;

(*e*)   performing or proposing to perform any functions as a representative of workers on matters of health and safety at work, or as a member of a safety committee;

(*f*)   performing or proposing to perform any functions or activities as (i) a representative of members of the workforce for the purposes of *Sch 1* to the *Working Time Regulations 1998* or (ii) a candidate for election as such a representative;

(*g*)   performing or proposing to perform any functions as a trustee of a relevant occupational pension scheme which relates to his employment;

(*h*)   performing or proposing to perform any functions as (i) an employee representative for the purposes of *TULRCA 1992, Part IV, Chapter II* (redundancies) or *regs 10* and *11* of *Transfer of Undertakings (Protection of Employment) Regulations 1981* or (ii) a candidate for election as such a representative;

(*j*)   activities relating to union recognition or bargaining arrangements; or

(*k*)   exercising his or her right to be accompanied to disciplinary or grievance hearings, or to accompany a fellow employee to such a hearing; or

(*l*)   making a protected disclosure;

may apply to an employment tribunal for an order for interim relief (*TULRCA 1992, s 161(1)*; *ERA 1996, s 128*; and see 52.3 UNFAIR DISMISSAL – II). Note that this does not apply to all the cases where a health and safety dismissal or 'working time' dismissal is automatically unfair.

An order for interim relief may be made pending a substantive hearing where the tribunal considers that the complainant will succeed. The order is either for reinstatement or re-engagement, or for continuation of the terms of the contract.

An application for interim relief will only be entertained if it is presented to the tribunal within seven days following the effective date of termination and (where the complainant relies on (*a*) or (*b*) above) if there is also presented within that time a certificate from an authorised official of the union that the complainant was, or proposed to become, a member of the union and that there are good grounds for supposing that the reason or principal reason for the dismissal was one alleged in the complaint (*TULRCA 1992, s 161(2),(3); ERA 1996, s 128(2)*). The tribunal should deal with the interim application as soon as possible (*TULRCA 1992, s 162(1); ERA 1996, s 128(3)*). Both parties may be present at the hearing, the employer having had at least seven days' notice of the application (*TULRCA 1992, s 162(2); ERA 1996, s 128(4)*). A party who has been joined to the proceedings in accordance with a request made under *TULRCA 1992, s 160* made at least three days before the hearing (see 55.20 above), must have as much notice as is reasonably practicable (*TULRCA 1992, s 162(3)*). The hearing may only be postponed in special circumstances (*TULRCA 1992, s 162(4); ERA 1996, s 128(5)*). Guidance as to the procedure to be followed in interim relief cases was given by the EAT in *Derby Daily Telegraph Ltd v Foss*, IDS Brief 471, p 15.

If it appears likely to the tribunal that the complaint is well-founded (in *Taplin v C Shippam Ltd* [1978] ICR 1068, the EAT said that the test should be whether there was 'a pretty good chance' of success), it will ask the employer, if he is present, whether he is willing to reinstate or re-engage the complainant pending the full hearing or settlement of the matter. If the employer states that he is willing to reinstate the employee, the tribunal will make an order to that effect.

If the employer states that he is willing to re-engage the employee in another job and specifies the terms and conditions on which he is willing to do so, the tribunal will ask the employee whether he is willing to accept the job on those terms and conditions, and:

(i)   if he is willing, make an order to that effect; and

(ii)   if he is unwilling to accept the job on those terms and conditions, then if the tribunal is of the opinion that the refusal is reasonable, it will make an order for the *continuation* of his contract of employment (a 'continuation order').

If the employer has failed to attend the hearing before the tribunal or states that he is unwilling either to reinstate the employee or re-engage him, the tribunal will make a continuation order.

(*TULRCA 1992, s 163; ERA 1996, s 129.*)

A continuation order is an order that, until the complaint has been dealt with, the employee's contract will be treated as continuing for the purposes of his entitlement to benefits, including pay, and for the purposes of determining the length and continuity of his employment. If an employer fails to comply with a continuation order, compensation for such non-compliance may also be awarded if the complainant has thereby suffered loss, and the employer will be ordered to pay any amount of wages due under the continuation order (*TULRCA 1992, ss 164, 166; ERA 1996, ss 130, 132*).

At any time between the making of an order by an employment tribunal under these interim provisions and the determination or settlement of the complaint to which it relates, the employer or the employee may apply to the tribunal for the revocation of the order on the ground of a relevant change of circumstances which has occurred since the making of the order (*TULRCA 1992, s 165; ERA 1996, s 131*).

Where the employee presents an application for interim relief under *ERA 1996, s 128* in relation to a dismissal and at the time at which the application is presented the applicable dismissal and disciplinary statutory procedure has been complied with save for the appeal stage, then the parties shall be treated as having complied with the appeal stages of the applicable statutory procedure (*Dispute Resolution Regulations, reg 5(1)(b)*).

55.19 **SETTLEMENT**

Employers may wish to settle a claim or a potential claim for unfair dismissal rather than proceed to a hearing. The tribunals have a duty to encourage settlement and may do so at the hearing. If settlement is reached, one of two courses must be followed for any agreement reached with the employee to be binding. Either a conciliation offer must be involved (see 2.4 ADVISORY, CONCILI-ATION AND ARBITRATION SERVICE and note *BNP Paribas v Mezzoterro* [2004] IRLR 508 and *Hinton v University of East London* [2005] EWCA Civ 532, [2005] IRLR 552) or the conditions of a statutorily valid compromise agreement must be fulfilled, including that the employee has had independent advice (*ERA 1996, s 203*).

If this is not done, an employee will be free to bring a claim notwithstanding that he has received a sum in settlement. Although this amount may be taken into account in assessing compensation (as in the example at 55.10 above), neverthe-less it may not be sufficient to extinguish the employer's liability. If a compromise is reached after a tribunal has held a dismissal to be unfair but before making an award of compensation, the same is required in order for the agreement to be binding (see *Courage Take Home Trade Ltd v Keys* [1986] ICR 874). It was also held in *Courage* that where a settlement was fairly reached, but was not binding because of what is now *ERA 1996, s 203*, it might well not be 'just and equitable' to award any further compensation.

In the light of the increasing exercise of the employment tribunal's power to award costs, note *Kopel v Safeway Stores plc* [2003] IRLR 753 with regard to 'Calderbank' letters in the tribunal context, and see further 21.36 EMPLOYMENT TRIBUNALS – II.

Sums paid by an employer to an employee under a compromise of tribunal proceedings may be subject to different tax liabilities and recoupment rules from sums payable by order of a tribunal or sums payable under the contract of employment itself, therefore care is needed in negotiating and concluding settle-ments (see e g *Wilson (HM Inspector of Taxes) v Clayton* [2004] EWHC 898 (Ch), [2004] IRLR 611).

56 Vicarious Liability

56.1 'Vicarious liability' describes the principle of law which allows an employer to be held liable for the tortious acts of his employees committed in the course of their employment. Such liability would extend, for example, to the case of a van driver who drives negligently in the normal course of his duties and causes an accident: his employer will be held liable for any resulting injury. The employer may also be held vicariously liable where one employee injures another at work, or where an employee steals from a customer, again providing that the act is done in the course of employment.

There are some instances of vicarious liability imposed by statute, eg by *SDA 1975, s 41(1)* and *RRA 1976, s 32(1)* (see 13.35–13.38 DISCRIMINATION AND EQUAL OPPORTUNITIES – II), by *DDA 1995, s 58(1)* (see 10.27 DISABILITY DISCRIMINATION), by the *Sexual Orientation Regulations, reg 22*, by the *Belief Regulations, reg 22* and by the *Age Discrimination Regulations, reg 25* and by *Police Act 1996, s 88*. Notably, in the case of *EOC v Secretary of State for Trade and Industry* [2007] EWHC 483 (Admin), the Administrative Court decided that *s 4A(1)* of the *SDA*, as amended by the *Employment Equality (Sex Discrimination) Regulations 2005*, did not properly implement the provisions of the *Equal Treatment Directive* because it was structured in such a way that employers were not vicariously liable for acts of harassment directed by third parties against the employer's employees. Subject to any appeal, the effect of the judgment is that *s 4A(1)* must be recast to allow for such a claim.

The common law tests (see below) for vicarious liability are not applicable where there is express statutory provision in relation to vicarious liability (*Jones v Tower Boot Co Ltd* [1997] IRLR 168). However, the common law tests remain relevant to whether or not an employer may be vicariously liable for an employee's contravention of a statute that does not make any express provision as to vicarious liability: *Majrowski v Guys and St Thomas' NHS Hospital Trust* [2006] UKHL 34, [2006] 3 WLR 125, [2006] ICR 1199. In that case, the House of Lords held that an employer may be vicariously liable for harassment committed by its employee that was unlawful by virtue of s 3 of the Protection from Harassment Act 1997 (a provision that on its face only applies to individuals).

In general, there is no vicarious liability for the torts of persons other than employees, such as independent contractors engaged by the employer (but see 55.3 below). Provided that the employer has exercised due care in the choice of the contractor, he should not be held liable for acts of negligence committed by that contractor. However, where the employer owes a personal duty to safeguard others from harm (as he does in relation to the safety of his employees), he may not escape responsibility by delegating that duty, and will thus have to answer for harm caused by the negligent act of a contractor engaged for the purpose of discharging the duty (see, eg *McDermid v Nash Dredging and Reclamation Co Ltd* [1987] ICR 917); although, this is a case not so much of vicarious liability as a failure to discharge the employer's own primary duty. In the case of *Hawley v Luminar Leisure Ltd* [2006] EWCA Civ 18, [2006] IRLR 817, the Court of Appeal decided that the owners of a nightclub could be held vicariously liable for an assault carried out by a doorman on a member of the public, even though the doorman had been supplied to the nightclub by a third party company. Though the doorman was not directly employed by the nightclub, he could properly be deemed to be an employee of the nightclub for the purposes of vicarious liability principles. See also on the question of dual vicarious liability, *Viasystems v Thermal Transfer* [2006] EWCA Civ 1151, [2006] 2 WLR 428, [2006] ICR 327. In this case, the Court of Appeal held that both the employer and the third party exercising day-to-day control over the employee could be vicariously liable for the employee's negligence. The *Viasystems* decision was considered by the Court of Appeal in *Hawley*. The Court of Appeal concluded that, on the facts of the *Hawley* case, only the nightclub and not the doorman's employer should be liable for the assault on the basis that there had been a total transfer of control to the nightclub. See also the statutory occupier's liability for independent contractors (27.15 HEALTH AND SAFETY AT WORK – I) and statutory liability under *HSWA 1974* (27.16 HEALTH AND SAFETY AT WORK – I).

For a case in which a town council was held vicariously liable for the behaviour of a councillor towards a council employee, see *Moores v Bude Stratton Town Council* [2000] IRLR 676.

An employer which is liable to a third party for damages resulting from the negligence of its employee may seek to recover those damages from the negligent employee. See for example: *Lister v Romford Ice and Cold Storage* [1955] AC 555.

56.2   'In the course of his employment'

The essential precondition of vicarious liability is that the act complained of should have been done in the course of the employment. This concept extends beyond, although it will almost invariably include, acts which the employee is in fact instructed or authorised to perform. In 2001, the principle was refined by the House of Lords in *Lister v Hesley Hall Ltd* [2001] UKHL 22, [2002] 1 AC 215, [2001] IRLR 472 (see below).

In *Aldred v Nacanco* [1987] IRLR 292, the Court of Appeal approved the following test (taken from *Salmond on Torts*, 18th edn, p 437):

'If a servant does negligently that which he was authorised to do carefully, or if he does fraudulently that which he was authorised to do honestly, or if he does mistakenly that which he was authorised to do correctly, his master will answer for that negligence, fraud or mistake. On the other hand, if the unauthorised and wrongful act of the servant is not so connected with the authorised act as to be a mode of doing it, but is an independent act, the master is not responsible; for in such a case the servant is not acting in the course of his employment but has gone outside of it.'

Thus there may be vicarious liability for the consequences of an act which has been expressly forbidden, e g *Rose v Plenty* [1976] 1 WLR 141 (milk roundsman allowing boy to help with deliveries despite contrary instruction, and boy injured through roundsman's negligence), or which is clearly unauthorised, e g *Morris v CW Martin & Sons Ltd* [1966] 1 QB 716 (dry-cleaning company held liable to owner of fur coat stolen by employee to whom the goods had been entrusted). The employer may be vicariously liable for fraud even where the employee acts purely for his own benefit and not to advance the interests of the employer, if the employee is ostensibly authorised to act on the employer's behalf (*Lloyd v Grace, Smith & Co* [1912] AC 716).

In *Lister v Hesley Hall Ltd* [2001] UKHL 22, [2002] 1 AC 215, [2001] IRLR 472, the House of Lords pointed out that the *Salmond* test also states that an employer:

' ... is liable even for acts which he has not authorised, provided they are so *connected* with acts which he has authorised that they may rightly be regarded as modes – although improper modes – of doing them.'

The *Lister* case concerned acts of sexual abuse committed by a school warden on boys in his care. Previously, in *Trotman v North Yorkshire County Council* [1999] IRLR 98, a case with similar facts, the Court of Appeal had held that acts of indecent assault on a pupil were too far removed from being an unauthorised mode of carrying out a teacher's duties as to make the employer vicariously liable. This had been followed by the lower courts in *Lister*. However, the House of Lords in *Lister* held that this was the wrong approach. The correct test is to ask whether the employee's torts were so closely connected with the employment that it would be fair and just to hold the employer vicariously liable. On the facts in *Lister* the answer was that they were. See also *Fennelly v Connex South Eastern Ltd* [2001] IRLR 390, CA; *Mattis v Pollock (t/a Flamingo Nightclub)* [2003] EWCA Civ 887, [2003] 1 WLR 2158, CA and *Bernard v A-G of Jamaica* [2004] UKPC 47, [2005] IRLR 398. *Lister* indicates that the details of the relationship between employer and victim, not the precise terms of the tortfeasor employee's employment, will determine whether vicarious liability exists. If the employee's torts took place in the discharge of the employer's duties to the victim, the employer will be vicariously liable: see *Balfron Trustees Ltd v Peterson* [2001] IRLR 758.

There may be vicarious liability for acts done even whilst the employee is not working, if at the time that employee is being paid for his time, is carrying out the instructions of his employer or is subject to the employer's directions. In *Smith v Stages* [1989] ICR 272, the House of Lords held an employer vicariously liable for injuries sustained in a crash caused by the negligent driving of an employee driving his workmate (the injured claimant) home to Staffordshire after completing a job in Pembroke. The speeches of Lord Goff and Lord Lowry contain extensive analyses of vicarious liability for the acts of employees travelling to and from work. Generally, an employer will not be held vicariously liable for any accident caused by the negligent driving of an employee travelling between his home and his regular place of work, because such a journey is not 'in the course of employment'. However, liability for an accident may be established where the employee is travelling in the employer's time in the course of the employer's business (as in *Smith v Stages*). This will depend on the employee's status, and the nature of his occupation; employees in peripatetic occupations (such as engineers or sales representatives) are likely to come within this category.

It is a different matter if the tortious act is so far removed from what the employee is in fact authorised to do that he can be said to be on 'a frolic of his own'. Thus, there was no vicarious liability where firemen pursuing a go-slow drove at a snail's pace to a fire (*General Engineering Services Ltd v Kingston and St Andrew Corpn* [1989] ICR 88: their act was not a mere mode of performance, but was the very antithesis of what they were engaged to do). Nor was a contract cleaning company vicariously liable when its employee made international telephone calls from the offices of clients (*Heasmans v Clarity Cleaning Co Ltd* [1987] ICR 949: there was not sufficient nexus with the employment, which had merely provided the opportunity for the criminal act).

In two cases involving police officers, the courts have found the relevant authority to be vicariously liable for the acts of police officers on the basis that the officers in question had, at the time of the unlawful act, held themselves out to the complainant as being police officers. The first of those cases, *Weir v Chief Constable of Merseyside Police* [2003] EWCA Civ 111, [2003] ICR 708, concerned the vicarious liability of the Chief Constable under *s 88* of the *Police Act 1996.* In that case an off-duty police officer had told the claimant he was a police officer before violently assaulting him and locking him in a police van (taken by the officer without authority). The Court of Appeal held that the Chief Constable was vicariously liable: at the time of the incident the police officer was 'apparently acting as a constable, albeit one behaving very badly'. The second case, *Bernard v A-G of Jamaica* [2004] UKPC 47, [2005] IRLR 398, concerned the Attorney General's vicarious liability at common law. Applying the principles enunciated in *Lister*, the Privy Council held that the Attorney-General was vicariously liable for the acts of a police officer who, after announcing that he was a policeman, shot the claimant and subsequently purported to arrest the claimant for interfering with his duties as a policeman. Compare *Hartnell v A-G of the British Virgin Islands* [2004] UKPC 12, [2004] 1 WLR 1273 in which the Privy Council held that the Attorney-General was not vicariously liable where a police officer had used his police gun to open fire, without warning, in a bar. The Privy Council did, however, hold that the Attorney General was primarily liable in negligence for entrusting someone of Mr Hartwell's character and disposition with a gun. See also *N v Chief Constable of Merseyside* [2006] EWHC 3041 (QB), [2006] All ER (D) 421 (Nov), the Chief Constable was not vicariously liable where a police officer wearing his uniform and holding himself out as a police officer took an intoxicated woman to his home and raped her. The fact that the officer had used his uniform and position to secure the trust of the woman in question did not by itself render the Chief Constable vicariously liable. The Chief Constable was not liable from the point where the officer put the woman in his car. The judge made clear that the circumstances as whole must be looked at and that the result may have been different if he had been exercising a police functions such as making an arrest.

As will be seen from the above examples, the dividing line between what is and what is not within the course of employment is a fine one, and will often depend upon what the court considers that justice requires in the particular case.

56.3   'Pro hac vice' employment

Sometimes an employer (the general employer) may lend or hire his employee to another employer (the special employer) for a particular task or transaction. Although the employee continues to be employed by the general employer under his contract of employment, he may in certain circumstances be treated as the employee of the special and not of the general employer for the purposes of establishing vicarious liability. One term for this situation is *pro hac vice* ('for this occasion') employment.

Whether the potential liability has in fact been transferred from the general to the special employer must depend upon the arrangements that exist between them, and in particular upon which of them has the right to control the way in which the work is done. It will not be easy to show such a transfer (see, eg *Mersey Docks and Harbour Board v Coggins and Griffith (Liverpool) Ltd* [1947] AC 1), but it was established in the case of *Sime v Sutcliffe Catering Scotland Ltd* [1990] IRLR 228 where the special employer had complete control over day-to-day management and the way the work was carried out. The question of whether potential liability has transferred from the general employer to the special employer was recently considered by the Court of Appeal in *Hawley v Luminar Leisure Ltd* [2006] EWCA Civ 18, [2006] IRLR 817. In that case, a company which owned a nightclub ('L') contracted with a third party supplier of personnel ('S') for the supply of a doorman. The doorman went on to assault a member of the public whilst working at the nightclub. The Court of Appeal found that the doorman should be deemed to be a temporary employee of L for the purposes of determining vicarious liability. The Court of Appeal went on to find that vicarious liability should be attributed to L rather than S even though S employed the doorman. The Court of Appeal concluded that L, and not S, should be held vicariously liable for the assault, first, because, in obtaining the doorman's services, L had not been seeking to gain access to trained specialists on whose skill and expertise it depended and, second, because control of the doorman had rested with L; thus, there had been an effective transfer of both control and responsibility from S to L. Note, however, that while control is the paramount test, 'entire and absolute control' is not a necessary precondition of vicarious liability in such cases: *Viasystems (Tyneside) Ltd v Thermal Transfer (Northern) Ltd* [2005] EWCA Civ 1151, [2006] 2 WLR 428, [2005] IRLR 983.

Where it is the subcontracted employee himself who is injured, the 'pro hac vice' doctrine does not apply and there is a right of action against the main employer. The question of who controls the subcontracted employee is only relevant to the issue of liability if the subcontracted employee injures a third party (*Morris v Breaveglen Ltd* [1993] IRLR 350).

It was, until the decision of the Court of Appeal in the *Viasystems* case, generally assumed that it was not possible for both the general employer and the special employer to be vicariously liable for the same act of the same employee. *Viasystems* concerned the installation of air conditioning in a factory. The first defendants were engaged to do the work. They subcontracted ducting work to the second defendants, who in turn contracted with the third defendants for the provision of fitters and fitters' mates. A fitters' mate (Mr S) negligently damaged part of the ducting system, causing the factory to flood. At the time he was under the supervision of both the fitter (employed, like Mr S, by the third defendants) and the second defendants' supervisor. At first instance, the County Court found the third defendants alone to be vicariously liable for the negligence of Mr S. It was assumed (apparently by all parties) that it was not possible to have dual vicarious liability. On appeal to the Court of Appeal, however, the Court reviewed the authorities that were said to support that assumption. They found that, in most of those cases, the possibility of dual vicarious liability had not been argued or considered (as, indeed, it had not in *Viasystems* at first instance). May LJ (with whom Rix LJ, with greater reservation, agreed) observed that 'the core question is who was entitled, and in theory obliged, to control the employee's relevant negligent act so as to prevent it'. He concluded that, if there were (as there were in *Viasystems*) genuinely two 'employers' who could have controlled the employee, then both could be vicariously liable. However, the Court noted that such situations would be rare, and that dual vicarious liability would be redundant where one of the 'employers' was itself primarily liable. The Court determined that the second and third defendants were equally responsible and that the second and third defendants should each contribute 50% of the damages awarded to the claimant pursuant to *ss 1(1)* and *2* of the *Civil Liability (Contribution) Act 1978* (which provide, respectively, that 'any person liable in respect of any damage suffered by another person may recover contribution from any other person liable in respect of the same damage (whether jointly with him or otherwise)' and that the amount of recoverable contribution 'shall be such as may be found by the court to be just and equitable having regard to the extent of the person's responsibility for the damage in question'.

57 Working Time

57.1 INTRODUCTION

Until relatively recently working hours were not regulated by statute for the vast majority of workers in the UK. Special provisions have applied to specific groups in the past but most were swept away by the last Conservative Government. For example, restrictions on the employment of retail workers contained in the *Shops Act 1950* were repealed by the *Deregulation and Contracting Out Act 1994*, although some protection against enforced Sunday working has remained (now contained in *ss 36–43, Employment Rights Act 1996*).

This situation changed in 1998 as a result of European legislation, but only after a protracted battle. In November 1993 *EC Directive 93/104* 'concerning certain aspects of the organisation of working time' ('the *Working Time Directive*') was adopted; it came into force in member states on 23 November 1996. The legal basis for the *Directive* was as a health and safety measure under *art 118A* (now *art 137*) of the *Treaty of Rome*, which requires only qualified majority voting. Hence it could be, and was, adopted without the assent of the UK Government. However, the Conservative Government of the day refused to accept the legitimacy of the *Directive* on the grounds that it could not be categorised as health and safety legislation. No attempt was made by the UK to comply with the 1996 deadline for implementation, pending the outcome of a challenge to the *Directive* in the ECJ. In the event the Court ruled, in *United Kingdom v EU Council: C-84/94* [1997] ICR 443, that (with one minor exception) the UK's objections should be rejected. Following a change of government, implementation of the *Directive* eventually took place on 1 October 1998, by means of the *Working Time Regulations 1998* (*SI 1998/1833*). The *1998 Regulations* have been supplemented by guidance published by the Department of Trade and Industry, in accordance with a duty imposed on the Secretary of State by *reg 35A* (a provision added in 1999). It should, however, be noted that this guidance has no formal legal status as an interpretation of the *Regulations*. The guidance can be accessed on the DTI website at www.dti.gov.uk/employment.

The delayed implementation of the *Working Time Directive* led to a case in which a local authority employee argued that she had the right to statutory annual leave for the period from 23 November 1996 (when the *Directive* should have been implemented) until 1 October 1998, when the *Directive* came into force in Great Britain. The employee's argument was that *art 7* of the *Directive*, concerning annual leave, was directly enforceable against the local authority as an emanation of the state. However, the Court of Appeal ruled that the provisions were not sufficiently precise to have direct effect and the employee could not rely on the Directive (*Gibson v East Riding of Yorkshire Council* [2000] IRLR 598). See also 29.2 HOLIDAYS.

The *Directive*, which covers working hours, rest breaks and holidays, initially did not apply to a number of sectors of activity. The exceptions were: air, rail, road, sea, inland waterway and lake transport, sea fishing, other work at sea and the activities of doctors in training. (For the scope of these exceptions see further 57.3 below.)

However, agreement was reached in 2000 on the extension of the *Directive* to excluded sectors and activities. The *Working Time Directive* was amended by

Directive 2000/34 to cover all non-mobile workers in the excluded sectors, doctors in training, and offshore and railway workers (including mobile railway workers). The deadline for implementation of the *Directive* was 1 August 2003. It was duly implemented with effect from that date, but the application of the limits on working hours to doctors in training is subject to phased implementation (as permitted by the *Directive*), so that the 48-hour working week will not apply in full until 1 August 2009. Details of the scope of the *Regulations* are given below. The *Directive,* as amended by the *2000 Directive,* has since been replaced by *Directive 2003/88/EC,* a purely consolidating measure, which came into force on 2 August 2004. References in this chapter to the *Directive* apply equally to the 2003 version.

In addition to this general extension of the original *Directive*, further *Directives* have been adopted for specific groups still not covered by the principal provisions. The working time of seafarers engaged on merchant ships was covered in *Directive 99/63,* which was given effect in the UK by the *Merchant Shipping (Hours of Work) Regulations 2002;* see 57.31 below for more details. A further *Directive, 2002/15* 'on the organisation of working time of persons performing mobile road transport activities', which applies to drivers covered by *Regulation EEC 3820/85* (now *Regulation 561/2006*) or the AETR agreement, was adopted in February 2002, with a deadline for implementation of 23 March 2005. In the event, it was implemented slightly late, by the *Road Transport (Working Time) Regulations 2005, SI 2005/639,* with effect from 4 April 2005. Self-employed owner-drivers are not covered by the *Regulations;* this is in accordance with a specific provision in the *Directive* permitting deferment of its application to this category until 2009. For further details see 57.34 and 57.35 below. Comparable provisions covering workers on sea fishing vessels, in inland waterway and lake transport and in aviation respectively, are summarised at 57.31, 57.32 and 57.33.

The provisions of the original *Directive* permitting derogations from its provisions, in relation to the reference period for calculating the average number of weekly hours worked and permitting individual opt-outs from the 48 hour week, were expressly made subject to a review by the European Council on a report from the Commission. The Commission's initial report was issued in December 2003. This was open to comment by Member States and the social partners (employer and employee representative bodies), and a separate round of consultation was subsequently undertaken by the Commission with the social partners, whilst in the UK, the DTI instituted its own consultation process to inform its stance in negotiations over any proposals to amend the *Directive.*

The Commission's proposals following these consultations were issued in September 2004 in the form of a draft amending Directive (*COM (2004) 607 final*). If implemented (which would require a qualified majority vote in the Council of Ministers), the proposals would have preserved the possibility of individual opt-outs, but with significant restrictions on their use; in particular it would not be possible for an opt out to be signed at the same time as the contract of employment or during any probationary period; consent would only be valid for a maximum of a year at a time; and there would be a new maximum limit on working time for opted out workers of 65 hours a week, unless a collective agreement provided otherwise. More controversially, opt-outs would only be permitted at all with the sanction of a collective agreement or an agreement with employee representatives, with limited exceptions. The Commission also proposed to amend the definition of 'working time' to exclude periods of time on call during which the worker is not actually working (the 'inactive part' of on-call time).

The Commission's proposals were considered by the European Parliament, which in May 2005 adopted a number of amendments to the draft, including the removal altogether of the facility for individual opt-outs, the deletion of the Commission's proposed relaxation of the status of inactive on-call time, and the introduction of a requirement to count work for all employers of an individual worker in applying the 48 hour limit on the working week. The Commission immediately responded with amended proposals intended as a compromise between its original proposals and those of the Parliament (*COM (2005) 246 final*); however these proposals were in turn blocked by the UK Government at the June 2005 meeting of the Social Affairs Committee of the Council, with support from several other member states. Subsequent attempts to find a consensus amongst member states' governments, and with the Commission and the Parliament, have to date (April 2007) been unsuccessful, and the resulting stalemate has meant that no further progress has been made with the issue of revision of the *Directive*. It remains to be seen whether, and if so when and in what terms, a compromise can be reached under the Co-decision procedure which governs the making of Directives on health and safety matters.

57.2   WORKING TIME REGULATIONS 1998

As noted above, the *Working Time Directive* was implemented in Great Britain by the *Working Time Regulations 1998* (*SI 1998/1833*), which came into force on 1 October 1998. The *1998 Regulations* also brought into force certain provisions in the EC *Directive on the Protection of Young People at Work (94/33)* relating to rest periods, breaks and night work in respect of young people. See also 4.6 CHILDREN AND YOUNG PERSONS. The *1998 Regulations* have subsequently been amended several times; details are given below. The *1998 Regulations*, as amended, govern hours of work, night work, breaks and holidays.

Since the *1998 Regulations* (as amended) are the domestic implementation of the *Directive*, courts and tribunals will approach the interpretation of the *Regulations* on the basis that they should so far as possible be so interpreted as to give effect to the stated purposes of the *Directive*. In this context it is important to appreciate that the *Directive* was adopted as a health and safety measure, as one of the 'daughter' directives under the 1989 *Framework Health and Safety Directive*. It should therefore be interpreted so as to promote the protection of workers' health and safety whenever such an interpretation is possible. As the EAT in *Gallagher v Alpha Catering Services Ltd* [2004] ICR 1489 commented: 'Firmly in the minds of anyone dealing with these Regulations must be the ultimate source of the Regulations which is a measure to protect the health and safety of individual workers'. In addition, of course, the case law of the ECJ on the interpretation and application of the *Directive* is likely to be a decisive guide to the interpretation of equivalent provisions in the *1998 Regulations*.

An example of the approach of the ECJ is its decision in *European Commission v United Kingdom, Case C-484/04* [2006] IRLR 888. In this case, the European Commission had issued a Reasoned Opinion that the United Kingdom had failed fully to implement the *Working Time Directive* in two respects. The first complaint related to *reg 20(2)*, which gave exemptions from the *Regulations* for the unmeasured part of partly unmeasured working time. The second related not to the wording of the *Regulations* themselves but to the accompanying Guidance issued by the Department of Trade and Industry, which (at that time) stated that 'employers must make sure that workers *can* take [rest breaks and rest periods], but are not required to make sure that they *do* take their rest'. The UK

Government declined to act on the Reasoned Opinion, and enforcement proceedings were brought before the ECJ by the Commission in November 2004.

The United Kingdom formally conceded the first point, on partly unmeasured working time, at the hearing of the case in January 2006, and subsequently introduced the *Working Time (Amendment) Regulations 2006 (SI 2006/99)*, which removed the offending provision as from 6 April 2006. The Court however addressed the issue in its decision, finding that there was no room in the *Directive* for partial exemptions for those whose working time was partly unmeasured. On the second point, the Court also found against the UK. Whilst accepting that the *Directive* did not require member states to go so far as requiring employers to force their workers to take rest entitlements, the Guidance was 'liable to render the rights [to rest periods and rest breaks] meaningless' and was thus incompatible with the objective of the directive, which required minimum rest periods to be treated as 'essential for the protection of workers' health and safety'. The Court added that 'Member States are under an obligation to guarantee that each of the minimum requirements laid down by the directive is observed'. The DTI has now amended the passage in the Guidance criticised by the Court.

57.3 **Coverage**

Workers covered by the *1998 Regulations* include employees working under a contract of employment and other individuals who personally perform work or provide services for the 'employer' (except for people genuinely in business on their own account who are in a client or customer relationship with the 'employer') (*reg 2(1)*). *Regulation 36* provides that an agency worker who would not otherwise fall within the definition of a worker under these provisions will be treated as being employed by whichever of the agent or principal is responsible for paying him or her or, if that is not ascertainable, by whichever in fact pays the worker. The extended definition of 'worker' has been held to include self-employed building subcontractors who in practice worked exclusively for one employer: *Byrne Bros (Formwork) Ltd v Baird* [2002] IRLR 96. (See further on this *Wright v Redrow Homes (Yorkshire) Ltd* [2004] EWCA Civ 469, [2004] IRLR 720.) The EAT has held that sub-postmasters and postmistresses are not 'workers' within the definition in *reg 2(1)*: *IRC v Post Office Ltd* [2003] IRLR 199. The *Regulations* also apply, by express provision, to those in Crown service and the armed forces, and to police officers (who have been held to fall outside a comparable definition of 'workers'): *regs 37–41*. Certain non-employed trainees, such as those on the New Deal, are also covered by the *Regulations* (*reg 42*).

Those requirements of the *Young Workers' Directive* which were not implemented by the *1998 Regulations* were implemented, with effect from 6 April 2003, by amendments to the *1998 Regulations* introduced by the *Working Time (Amendment) Regulations 2002*. The principal changes are the imposition of a maximum working day of 8 hours, and a maximum working week of 40 hours (neither of which is subject to averaging over a longer period) for workers below the age of 18 (but above compulsory school age: see below). See further 57.6.

In addition, the *2002 Regulations* restrict the employment of a young worker during the 'restricted period', which is normally 10 pm to 6 am, but 11 pm to 7 am if the worker is contractually required to work later than 10 pm: for details of these restrictions see 57.10 below.

There are separate provisions in the *Children and Young Persons Act 1933, s 18(1)*, as amended in compliance with *Directive 94/33*, which regulate the working hours and holiday entitlements of children below the maximum compulsory school age.

(For Scotland, the equivalent provisions are in the *Children and Young Persons (Scotland) Act 1937*.) The EAT has held, by reference to these provisions, that such children are not 'workers' for the purposes of the *1998 Regulations,* and accordingly not covered by them: *Addison v Ashby* [2003] ICR 667, a case involving a claim for holiday pay by a 15 year old paper boy.

Following further amendments to the *1998 Regulations* made by the *Working Time (Amendment) Regulations 2003,* which were made to give effect to amendments to the parent *Directive,* the *1998 Regulations* now apply to all workers (with the exclusion of school age children) other than those mobile workers in certain transport sectors, who are now all covered by separate legislation, and, for a transitional period, doctors in training. The *Regulations* do not apply to 'certain activities of the armed forces, police or other civil protection services', but only to the extent that certain characteristics of the particular service concerned 'inevitably conflict' with the *Regulations: reg 18.* This exception mirrors a provision in *art 1(3)* of the *Directive,* which was narrowly construed by the European Court in *Pfeiffer v Deutsches Rotes Kreuz,* Cases C-397–401/01, [2005] IRLR 137 as applying to the emergency services only in the context of the provision of services essential for the protection of public health, safety or order in situations of exceptional gravity, and thus not excluding from the *Directive* the routine operation of a public ambulance service. This interpretation is very likely to be followed in the construction of the exception in the *1998 Regulations.*

With regard to the former exclusion of transport workers, there was initially some debate whether all workers in the sector, whether they are mobile or not, are excluded from the *Working Time Directive* and *1998 Regulations.* This point was referred to the ECJ by the EAT in *Bowden v Tuffnells Parcels Express Ltd* [2000] IRLR 560. The Court subsequently ruled ([2001] IRLR 838) that all workers, whether mobile or non-mobile, within undertakings in the excluded sectors, were excluded from the *Directive.* This almost certainly applies equally to the *1998 Regulations,* as in force prior to their amendment in 2003, and is still relevant to the exclusion of mobile workers in the civil aviation and road transport sectors referred to at (i) and (iii) below. The Court in *Pfeiffer,* above, held that emergency ambulance services were outside the road transport sector. It was accepted that bus drivers engaged in the provision of scheduled services fall within the provisions of the *1998 Regulations,* rather than the *Road Transport (Working Time) Regulations 2005,* in *First Hampshire & Dorset Ltd v Feist,* UKEAT/0510/06.

In summary, the position as to the coverage of the *1998 Regulations* is now as follows:

(a)   all workers in Great Britain are covered save for those in exempted categories listed below (but with a limited exception to the 48 hour working week for doctors in training, which will not be fully phased out until 2009);

(b)   the *Regulations* do not apply to those of compulsory school age;

(c)   the *Regulations* do not apply to merchant seafarers to whom *Directive 99/63* applies;

(d)   the *Regulations* do not apply to workers on board sea-going fishing vessels or ships or hovercraft operating inland waterway or lake transport (of goods or passengers); see further below.

In addition, the provisions of the *Regulations* limiting working time and night work, relating to monotonous work, and conferring rights to rest periods and rest breaks, do not apply:

(i)   to mobile workers in the civil aviation sector who are covered by the legislation implementing *Directive 2000/79;*

(ii)   to the extent that characteristics peculiar to the armed forces, the police and civil protection services inevitably conflict with any such provisions;

(iii)   to mobile workers in the road transport sector, who are covered by legislation under *Directive 2002/15.*

(For those in categories (i) and (ii), but not (iii), entitlements regarding health assessments and paid annual leave are also excluded.)

For the specific application of the *1998 Regulations* to mobile workers on railways see 57.29; for seafarers see further 57.31, for mobile workers in the lake and inland waterway transport sectors see further 57.32, for the aviation sector see further 57.33 and for mobile workers in road transport see 57.34 AND 57.35.

The *1998 Regulations* apply to Great Britain. The territorial scope of the *Regulations* was extended by the *Working Time (Amendment) Regulations 2003 (SI 2003/1684)* to 'offshore work', as defined, and from 1 October 2006 their territorial scope was further extended to cover workers on oil and gas rigs in UK territorial waters and the UK and cross-border oil and gas fields within the UK sector of the Continental Shelf (see the *Working Time (Amendment No 2) Regulations 2006, SI 2006/2389*); the EAT has since confirmed the view of the DTI that this amendment was simply declaratory of the effect of the *2003 Regulations*: *Transocean International v Russell* EATS/0072/05.

57.4   Agreements: definition

Where flexibility and modifications are permitted under the *Working Time Regulations*, employers may conclude agreements to cover the situation. Depending on the circumstances, these may take the form of a collective agreement, a workforce agreement or a relevant agreement.

Regulation 2(1) provides that a *collective agreement* is an agreement or arrangement made by or on behalf of one or more independent trade unions and one or more employers or employers' associations relating to matters set out in *TULRCA 1992, s 178(2)*. This may include an award made under a collective agreement providing for binding third party arbitration: *Bewley v HM Prison Service* [2004] ICR 422.

A *workforce agreement* means an agreement between an employer and its workers or their elected representatives in respect of which certain conditions are satisfied as set out in *Sch 1*:

(*a*)   the agreement is in writing;

(*b*)   it has effect for a specified period of five years or less;

(*c*)   it applies to all the relevant members of the workforce or to all of the relevant members who belong to a particular group (eg who undertake a particular function, work at a particular workplace or belong to a particular department);

(*d*)   it is signed by representatives of the workforce (or particular group, as applicable). If the employer has 20 or fewer workers, the agreement may be signed either by appropriate representatives or by the majority of workers employed by the employer;

(*e*)   before the agreement was signed, the employer provided all workers to whom the agreement applies with copies and such guidance as is reasonable to understand it fully.

Requirements concerning the election of representatives are set out at *Sch 1 para 3*.

A *relevant agreement* includes both collective and workforce agreements and, in addition, any other agreement in writing which is legally enforceable as between worker and employer. This definition may therefore include the written terms of a contract of employment.

Where a provision of the *Regulations* is modified or excluded by a workforce or collective agreement and a worker is thereby required to work during what would be a rest period or break, the employer must allow, where possible, an equivalent period of compensatory rest. In exceptional cases where it is not possible for objective reasons to grant compensatory rest, the employer must provide appropriate protection to safeguard the worker's health and safety (*reg 24*). The *Regulations* do not specify when compensatory rest must be given, or whether it must consist of time off what would otherwise be contractual hours. However in *Landeshauptstadt Kiel v Jaeger: C-151/02* [2003] IRLR 804, the European Court of Justice has ruled that periods of compensatory rest must be accorded 'at times immediately following the corresponding periods worked'. Whilst this ruling applies directly only to the *Directive*, it is likely that a Court in the UK would give a similar interpretation to the *1998 Regulations* in order to avoid a conflict between the *Regulations* and the *Directive*.

57.5   WORKING TIME

In relation to a worker, 'working time' is defined in *reg 2(1)* as:

(*a*)   any period during which the individual is working, at the employer's disposal and carrying out his or her activity or duties;

(*b*)   any period during which he or she is receiving 'relevant training'; and

(*c*)   any additional period which is to be treated as working time for the purpose of the *Regulations* under a relevant agreement.

'Relevant training' means work experience or training provided on a training course or programme of training for employment, other than courses run by educational institutions or organisations whose main business is the provision of training.

According to the DTI Guidance, the definition of working time includes: working lunches, business travel time, job-related training, and time spent abroad working for an employer in Great Britain. It does not include: home-to-work travel, rest breaks when no work is done, time spent travelling outside normal working time or non-job-related training.

One important issue as to the ambit of the definition of working time is the status of time 'on call'. This has been the subject of two decisions of the ECJ, to the effect that 'on-call' time constitutes working time where the worker is required to be at his or her place of work during this period. If the worker is away from the workplace when on call and can pursue leisure activities, on-call time is not working time (*Sindicato de Médicos de Asistencia Pública (SIMAP) v Conselleria de Sanidad y Consumo de la Generalidad Valenciana: C-303/98* [2001] IRLR 845). The Court has subsequently confirmed that time spent on call and at the workplace, but not actually performing the worker's duties, was to be regarded as working time in circumstances where the worker (a hospital doctor) was permitted to rest when his services were not required, and rest facilities were provided for this purpose by the employer: *Landeshauptstadt Kiel v Jaeger*, above.

In a further decision on this issue in 2005 (*Dellas v Premier Ministre*: C-14/04 [2006] IRLR 225) the ECJ held to be incompatible with the *Directive* a French law which provided for time spent on call and at the employer's premises, but not actually working, to count at the rate of only a half or a third of actual time; the principal objection of the Court was that it was (at least theoretically) possible for workers subject to this law to work in excess of the 48 hour week, although France has adopted a lower maximum of 44 hours.

These decisions of the ECJ have been controversial for their implications for the staffing of emergency medical services in particular, and would be affected by the implementation of the Commission's proposals for revision of the *Directive*, discussed at 57.1 above (but the amendments to these proposals proposed by the Parliament would retain the effects of the ECJ decisions). It remains to be seen whether, and if so in what terms, any revision of the *Directive* will be adopted. Clearly, if a worker is actually called out to perform work, the time spent working (but probably not travel time) is working time.

The EAT has held that the effect of the decision in *Jaeger* is that a warden employed at a sheltered housing complex on 24 hour call is to be regarded as working throughout the period on call although she was provided with a flat to occupy at the premises, and was free to use her time as she pleased subject to remaining in the vicinity to be available for call-outs. Accordingly the employer was in breach of the requirement to permit a daily rest period for the warden: *MacCartney v Oversley House Management* [2006] ICR 510, EAT, not following the earlier case of *South Holland District Council v Stamp*, EAT/1097/02, which the EAT regarded as inconsistent with the reasoning and decision in *Jaeger.*

The Court of Appeal has also considered the application of the definition of 'working time' to 'down time': *Gallagher v Alpha Catering Services Ltd* [2004] EWCA Civ 1559, [2005] IRLR 102. The employees delivered catering supplies to aircraft at Gatwick airport. They often had to wait for an aircraft to be ready for servicing; during these periods they had to remain at the airport and in radio contact with the employer, but could use the time eg to take refreshment. It was held that all three limbs of the definition of 'working time' were satisfied on these facts, and the down time or waiting time counted as working time.

The issue of what constitutes 'working time' may also arise as a matter of contract. An example is *Alexander v Jarvis Hotels plc* EATS/0062/05, where the EAT held that time spent by a hotel manager overnight at the hotel was working time, although he was free to sleep. His work consisted of being present at the hotel to respond to any emergency, an arrangement required of the hotel for health and safety reasons. There have also been a number of cases about what constitutes time for which payment is due under the *National Minimum Wage Act 1998*, but these relate to different definitions and do not necessarily assist in interpreting the definition of 'working time' in the *1998 Regulations*.

57.6   Maximum weekly working time

An employer is required to take all reasonable steps, in keeping with the need to protect health and safety, to ensure that each adult worker works no more than 48 hours on average in each working week, averaged over reference periods of 17 weeks. Such periods are extended to 26 weeks for certain workers – see 'special case' exemptions at 57.29 below. The reference period may be extended to a maximum of 52 weeks where a collective or workforce agreement so provides, on the basis of objective or technical reasons concerning the organisation of work (*regs 4(1)*, *(2)*, *(5)*, *23(b)*). The possible extension to 52 weeks is the technical basis on which 'annualised hours' agreements are most appropriately made. *Regulations 25A* and *25B* of the *1998 Regulations* make specific provision for the reference periods applicable respectively to doctors in training (26 weeks) and offshore workers (52 weeks).

A relevant agreement may stipulate when the reference period begins. Otherwise, the reference period will be a rolling 17-week (or 26 or up to 52 week) period (*reg 4(3)*). Where a worker has been employed for less than 17 weeks, the reference period will be the number of weeks which have elapsed since he or she started work (*reg 4(4)*).

Average working time is calculated according to the formula:

$$\frac{A + B}{C}$$

where:

'A' is the total number of hours of working time in the reference period;

'B' is the total number of hours worked immediately after the reference period during extra days equivalent to the number of 'excluded days' (see below for this) in the reference period; and

'C' is the number of weeks in the reference period (*reg 4(6)*).

For the purpose of calculating average hours, certain days are to be excluded: days taken as statutory annual leave under the *1998 Regulations* (but not days of annual leave taken under a contractual provision over and above the statutory entitlement); periods of sick leave and maternity, paternity, adoption or parental leave; and any hours in respect of which an individual opt-out agreement (see 57.7 below) is in force (*reg 4(7)*).

The weekly limit is disapplied in the case of workers whose time is 'unmeasured' (see 57.28 below). Following the revocation of *reg 20(2)*, this only applies to workers the *whole* of whose working time is unmeasured.

Transitional provisions apply to the extension of the 48-hour maximum working week to doctors in training. By virtue of *reg 25A(1)* of the *1998 Regulations,* until 31 July 2007 the maximum is 58 hours; from 1 August 2007 until 31 July 2009 it will be 56 hours; the limit of 48 hours will apply from 1 August 2009. The extended averaging provisions referred to above apply equally to the transitional maximum hours.

Young workers (ie those under 18 but above compulsory school age) are subject to stricter limits on working hours. There is a maximum working day of 8 hours, and a maximum working week of 40 hours; in neither case is there provision for averaging over a longer period: see *reg 5A*.

The restrictions on the working week for adult workers apply in relation to a particular employer. There is no provision in the *1998 Regulations* imposing any specific duty on employers to limit the aggregate working hours of those workers who work for more than one employer, and no mechanism for enabling employers to police such arrangements. The sole exceptions to this are the provisions relating to young workers: see *reg 5A(2)*, which specifically limits the total working time which may be undertaken for *all* employers; and *reg 12(5)*, which requires the aggregation of working time for different employers in calculating young workers' rest break entitlements. Whilst the absence of any equivalent provisions for adult workers is a significant weakness in the protection of workers from excessive hours, it is not considered to be contrary to the *Working Time Directive*. One of the amendments to the *Directive* proposed by the Parliament in May 2005 would have applied the 48 hour maximum to the aggregate time worked for all employers, but this amendment is strongly opposed by the UK and some other member states.

57.7   Opt-out agreements

It is permissible to disapply the 48-hour weekly maximum if the employer obtains the worker's written agreement to exceed these hours (*reg 4(1)*). Any such opt-out agreement may relate to a specified period or apply indefinitely. Agreements are to be terminable by the worker giving not less than seven days' notice in writing. The employer may not require more than three months' notice (*reg 5(2)*, *(3)*). Employers are required to maintain up-to-date records of all workers who have signed an opt-out agreement (*reg 4(2)*). However, following amendment of the *1998 Regulations* in 1999 it is no longer necessary to maintain records of hours actually worked by a worker who has opted out; this was raised by the Commission as a potential breach of the *Directive* in 2002, but the point has not been pursued further. Opt-outs must be made voluntarily. It is unlawful to victimise or dismiss a worker for refusing to sign an opt-out.

The consent of each individual worker to an opt-out agreement is required. Consent given by trade union representatives in the context of a collective agreement is not equivalent to that given by the worker (*SIMAP* [2000] IRLR 845). There is no specific provision in either the *1998 Regulations* or the *Directive* restricting the way in which consent may be recorded, and in practice it is not uncommon for employers to incorporate a requirement for consent in the offer of employment, so that agreement to opt out is tied in to the acceptance of the job offered. The validity of such agreements may be open to challenge on the basis that, giving effect to the approach of the ECJ to construe exemptions from the Directive narrowly, such an arrangement does not ensure that genuine consent is freely given. As at April 2007, there is no reported authority on this point.

As noted at 57.1 above, the *Directive* requires the provision for opt-outs to be reviewed by the European Council; for discussion of the various proposals for revision or abolition of the opt-out facility, see 57.1 above.

57.8   Records

In addition to recording opt-outs (see 57.7 above), employers are required to keep records for two years to show that they have complied with the provisions on maximum weekly working time (*reg 9*). The *Regulations* do not specify the format of such records; in particular, there is no requirement for records of the working hours of opted-out workers (as distinct from records of opt-out agreements, which are required to be kept by *reg 4(2)*) to be maintained.

57.9   NIGHT WORK

In the *1998 Regulations* 'night time' means a period of not less than seven hours which includes the period between midnight and 5am (*reg 2(1)*). The precise period may be determined by a relevant agreement (see 57.4 above). Where it has not been so agreed, the period will be 11pm to 6am. A 'night worker' is an individual who, as a normal course, works at least three hours of daily working time during night time or who is likely during night time to work at least such proportion of annual working time as may be specified for these purposes in a collective or workforce agreement. The definition provides that someone works hours 'as a normal course' if he or she works those hours on the majority of his or her working days, but this does not mean that other patterns of work do not qualify as being 'in the normal course'. In *R v A-G for Northern Ireland, ex p Burns* [1999] IRLR 315, the Northern Ireland High Court held that 'as a normal course' means simply that night work should be a regular feature of employment. Therefore, a worker who spent one week in three of a rotating shift working at least three hours during the night was a night worker for the purposes of the *Directive*.

57.10   **Length of night work**

Employers are required to take all reasonable steps, in keeping with the need to protect workers' health and safety, to ensure that night workers' normal hours of work do not exceed an average of eight in each 24 hours during a 17-week reference period (*reg 6(1), (2)*). This will be a rolling 17-week period unless a relevant agreement specifies successive periods (*reg 6(3)*). For individuals who have worked for less than 17 weeks, the average is calculated over the period since they started work for the employer (*reg 6(4)*).

Regulation 6(5) provides that average normal hours of work for a night worker are calculated according to the formula:

$$\frac{A}{B - C}$$

where:

'A' is the number of normal working hours during the reference period;

'B' is the number of days during the reference period; and

'C' is the total number of hours during the reference period spent by the worker in statutory weekly rest periods (see 57.17 below) divided by 24. The effect of the formula is to create a maximum of 48 hours a week (8 hours in each of the 6 days a week, excluding one weekly rest day).

Normal hours of work do not include overtime hours unless overtime is guaranteed; therefore it is not a breach of the *Regulations* if a night worker exceeds the permissible maximum hours only by virtue of working voluntary overtime (subject to compliance with the general 48-hour week, if the worker has not opted out of this limit). Further restrictions on working hours for night work involving special hazards or heavy mental or physical strain are summarised in **57.11** below.

Limits on the length of night work and the 17-week reference period may be excluded or modified by collective or workforce agreement (*reg 23*). Exclusions also apply to workers whose working time is 'unmeasured' and those covered by the 'special case' exceptions (see 57.28, 57.29 below).

The foregoing restrictions on night work apply to adult workers. For young workers under 18, there are much stricter restrictions, introduced by the *2002 Regulations*. Young workers are prohibited from working at all between midnight and 4 am, with very limited exceptions applicable to workplaces such as hospitals, or in connection with cultural, artistic, sporting or advertising activities, where the work is required to provide continuity of service, and no adult worker is available to perform the work. For most young workers there is a restricted period, which is either 10 pm to 6 am, or, if the worker is contractually required to work later than 10 pm, 11 pm to 7 am. Young workers are not permitted to work at all during this period, except as mentioned above, and subject to further exceptions in relation to work in agriculture, retail trading, postal and newspaper delivery, catering, hotels, restaurants and similar establishments, and bakeries; workers in these sectors are permitted to work during the restricted period, but not between midnight and 4 am, in the same limited circumstances of necessity mentioned above. These provisions are contained in *regs 6A* and *27A* of the *1998 Regulations*.

57.11 Special hazards

Where a night worker's job involves special hazards or heavy physical or mental strain, no averaging of hours is permitted. The employer must ensure that the worker does not work for more than eight hours in any 24-hour period which includes night work (*reg 6(7)*). This maximum applies separately to each 24-hour period, without averaging, and includes all hours actually worked.

Regulation 6(8) provides that work will be regarded as involving special hazards or heavy strain if it is identified as such in a collective or workforce agreement which takes account of the specific effects and hazards of night work, or alternatively if it has been recognised as involving significant risk in a risk assessment made under the *Management of Health and Safety at Work Regulations 1999* (*SI 1999/3242*): see 28.17 HEALTH AND SAFETY AT WORK – II. A collective or workforce agreement may modify or exclude the application of *reg 6(7)* (*reg 23*). Exceptions apply as for length of night work (see 57.10 above).

57.12 Health assessments

Before assigning an adult worker to night work, the employer must ensure that the worker has the opportunity of a free health assessment (*reg 7(1)*). However, if the worker has previously had an assessment and there is no reason to believe that it is no longer valid, a further assessment is not necessary. Free assessments must also be offered at regular intervals thereafter. The length of time between assessments should be whatever is appropriate to the particular circumstances. The DTI Guidance suggests that a yearly assessment will often be appropriate.

Young persons are to have the opportunity for a free assessment of health and capacities before being assigned to work during the restricted period (see 57.10) and at regular intervals (*reg 7(2)*). It is not necessary to offer a further assessment if the young person has previously had an assessment and there is no reason to believe that it is no longer valid. The DTI advises that special consideration should be given to young workers' suitability for night work, taking account of physique, level of maturity and experience. The requirement to offer an assessment to a young worker does not apply where the work is of an exceptional nature (*reg 7(4)*).

An assessment, whether of an adult or young worker, does not necessarily entail a full medical examination. The DTI suggests that employers ask workers to complete a questionnaire which asks about health issues which are relevant to the particular type of night work. If the employer is then unsure about a worker's fitness for night work, he or she should be asked to undergo a medical examination.

Regulation 7(5) provides that the assessment may not be disclosed, except to the worker in question, unless he or she has given consent in writing to the disclosure. This may cause difficulties for the employer if a medical adviser identifies that a worker has a medical condition which could expose him or her to a risk to health.

It would be the duty of the employer to safeguard the worker against such a risk, but the employer has no practical means of knowing of the risk unless the information is volunteered by the worker or there is consent to disclosure of the medical assessment. The medical adviser who has evaluated the information supplied or conducted the examination can however make a simple statement (if applicable) to the effect that the assessment shows the worker to be fit, or not fit, to take up, or continue, a night work assignment.

57.13 **Transfer to day work**

If an employer is advised by a registered medical practitioner that a worker is suffering from health problems which are connected with night working, the employer is required to transfer the worker, if possible, to work which does not qualify as 'night work' (see 57.9 above) (*reg 7(6)*). Normally this will be day work but could involve some night work, provided this is less than 3 hours in any 24 hours. Such work must be work 'to which the worker is suited'. Unlike the comparable provisions in relation to pregnant employees (under *s 67, ERA 1996* and *reg 17* of the *Management of Health and Safety at Work Regulations 1999*), there is no provision for the protection of enhanced rates of pay for night work for a worker who is transferred to other work under *reg 7(6)*. However, employers may also need to take into consideration their obligations under the *Disability Discrimination Act 1995* where a worker's lack of fitness amounts to a disability.

Employers are required to maintain, and retain for two years, records which are adequate to show compliance with the provisions on length of night work and health assessments (*reg 9*).

57.14 **REST PERIODS AND REST BREAKS**

Under the *1998 Regulations* workers are entitled to daily and weekly rest periods totalling 90 hours per week and to rest breaks during the working day. A 'rest period' is defined in *reg 2(1)* as a period which is not working time, other than a rest break or statutory annual leave. It therefore includes time spent in travelling between a worker's home and the normal workplace. However it does not include time spent on call at the employer's premises, even if the worker is in fact able to rest between times when his or her services are required, and is provided with facilities for resting: *Landeshauptstadt Kiel v Jaeger: C-151/02* [2003] IRLR 804, ECJ.

57.15 **Daily rest periods**

Adult workers are entitled to a rest period of at least 11 consecutive hours in each 24-hour working period (*reg 10(1)*). It is not necessary for the 11 hours to fall within the same calendar day provided they are consecutive.

The 11-hour rule does not apply to shift workers when they change shifts and cannot take a daily rest period between the end of one shift and the start of the next (*reg 22(1)(a)*). Similarly it does not apply to workers whose activities involve periods of work split up over the day, such as cleaning or catering staff working split shifts (*reg 22(1)(c)*). 'Shift work' means 'any method of organising work in shifts whereby workers succeed each other at the same workstations according to a certain pattern, including a rotating pattern, and which may be continuous or discontinuous, entailing the need for workers to work at different times over a given period of days or weeks'.

Compensatory rest must normally be offered to shift workers who have to work during what would otherwise be a rest period. If this is not possible, 'appropriate protection' is required to safeguard health and safety (*reg 24*). (For a judicial interpretation of 'compensatory rest', see the *Jaeger* case, above, 57.4. The Commission's proposals in 2005 for revision of the *Directive* included the introduction of a requirement that compensatory rest be taken within 72 hours of the work for which it is compensatory.)

There is a separate provision in *reg 24A* for those mobile workers not excluded from the right to rest periods generally (see as to this 57.33–57.36 below), excluding the right to rest periods provided that 'adequate rest' is afforded, the requirements of which are defined in *reg 24A(3)*. The right to adequate rest in such cases is in substitution for, not cumulative with, the right to compensatory rest under *reg 24: First Hampshire & Dorset Ltd v Feist* UKEAT/0510/06.

Adult workers whose time is 'unmeasured' (see 57.28 below) and those who are considered 'special case' exceptions (subject to certain conditions, see 57.29 below) are not covered by the entitlement to daily rest. The entitlement may also be modified or excluded by collective or workforce agreement (*regs 20, 21, 23*).

For young workers (ie those over compulsory school age but under 18) the requirement is to provide not less than 12 consecutive hours' rest in any 24-hour period (*reg 10(2)*). Where activities involve periods of work that are split up over the day or are of short duration, the 12-hour rest period may be interrupted (*reg 10(3)*). In addition a *force majeure* clause applies, which gives the employer leeway to require a young worker to work during the 12-hour minimum where work has to be done which no adult worker is available to do and the requirement:

(*a*)   is due to unusual and unforeseeable circumstances beyond the employer's control or exceptional events which could not have been avoided despite all due care by the employer;

(*b*)   is of a temporary nature; and

(*c*)   must be carried out straight away.

An equivalent period of compensatory rest must be allowed within the following three weeks (*reg 27*). This concession is designed to cope with exceptional circumstances which cannot be handled in any other way.

Entitlement to breaks entails at the least that the employer must *allow* employees who wish to do so to take their rest period. The extent to which it also entails an obligation on the employer to *ensure* that rest periods are *taken* is more contentious. The DTI view, as expressed in the Guidance on the *Regulations*, was that it does not. This view was, however, successfully challenged by the Commission in proceedings before the European Court (*European Commission v United Kingdom Case C-484/04* [2006] IRLR 888). For further details see 57.2 above.

57.16 Weekly rest periods

Adult workers are normally entitled (as to the meaning of this see the final paragraph of 57.15) to an uninterrupted rest period of at least 24 hours in each seven-day period of working. This may be arranged as two uninterrupted rest periods of not less than 24 hours in each 14-day period, or one uninterrupted period of not less than 48 hours in each 14-day period (*reg 11(1), (2)*). The minimum weekly rest period must not run concurrently with any part of a daily rest period (see 57.15 above) except where this is justified by objective or technical reasons, or reasons 'concerning the organisation of work' (*reg 11(7)*). Thus the combined effect of the daily and weekly rest entitlements is to create a minimum entitlement of 35 consecutive hours each week, or 59 hours in each 14-day period.

For young workers the minimum weekly rest period is 48 hours. This may be interrupted where activities involve periods of work that are split up over the day or are of short duration, and may be reduced where this is justified by technical or organisational reasons. However the period may not be reduced to less than 36 consecutive hours (*reg 11(3), (8)*).

A seven or 14-day period for these purposes begins on the day provided for in a relevant agreement (see 57.4 above) or, failing this, at the start of each week (or every other week, as the case may be). A 'week' for this purpose starts at midnight between Sunday and Monday (*reg 11(4), (6)*).

In the case of shift workers, the weekly rest requirement in respect of adults does not apply when workers change shift and cannot take a weekly rest period between the end of one shift and the start of another. Neither does it apply to workers whose activities involve periods of work split up over the day (*reg 22(1)*). Cleaning and catering staff may provide an example. For the definition of 'shift working' see 57.15 above. Compensatory rest must normally be offered to shift workers who have to work during what would otherwise be a rest period. If this is not possible, 'appropriate protection' is required to safeguard the worker's health and safety (*reg 24*).

The right to rest periods may also be modified or excluded by a collective or workforce agreement, but subject to the workers concerned being afforded compensatory rest: *regs 23, 24*. The position for mobile workers not excluded from the *Regulations* altogether is the same in relation to weekly rest periods as for daily rest periods: see *reg 24A* and 57.15 above.

Adult workers whose time is 'unmeasured' (see 57.28 below) and those who fall within the 'special case' exceptions (subject to certain conditions, see 57.29 below) are not subject to the weekly rest requirements.

57.17 Rest breaks

After a working period of six hours, an adult worker is entitled to a rest break (*reg 12(1)*). The length of the break and any conditions which apply to it are to be determined by collective or workforce agreement. In the absence of such an agreement, the break is to be at least an uninterrupted period of 20 minutes which the worker is entitled to take away from the workstation where applicable (*reg 12(2), (3)*).

Regulation 12(1) may be modified or excluded by collective or workforce agreement, subject to the provision of compensatory rest (*regs 23, 24*). The position of mobile workers not excluded altogether from the *1998 Regulations,* as summarised in 57.16 above, applies equally in relation to rest breaks. Adult workers whose time is 'unmeasured' or who fall within the 'special case' exceptions (subject to certain conditions) are not subject to the rest break requirements (see 57.28, 57.29 below).

It has been held that for a period to count as a rest period, the worker must be able to know at the beginning of the period that it will not be interrupted by the demands of work. Accordingly, 'down time', and periods during time on call, cannot be counted as a rest period, even if it transpires that there was a continuous period of at least 20 minutes during which the worker was not called on to perform any work: *Gallagher v Alpha Catering Services Ltd* [2004] EWCA Civ 1559, [2005] IRLR 102; *MacCartney v Oversley House Management* [2006] ICR 510, EAT. As to the meaning of 'entitled', see the final paragraph of 57.15.

In the case of young workers, there is an entitlement to a break of at least 30 minutes, consecutive if possible, if the individual's daily working time exceeds four and a half hours. The worker is entitled to take the break away from the workstation if applicable. When a young worker has more than one employment, the daily working time must be calculated by aggregating the number of hours worked for each employer (*reg 12(4)*, *(5)*). There is an exception to the entitlements of young workers under a *force majeure* clause (*reg 27*). This specifies that *reg 12(4)* does not apply where work has to be done which no adult worker is available to do and:

(*a*)   the requirement is due to unusual and unforeseeable circumstances beyond the employer's control or exceptional events which could not have been avoided despite all due care by the employer;

(*b*)   is of a temporary nature; and

(*c*)   must be carried out straight away.

An equivalent period of compensatory rest must be allowed within the following three weeks.

57.18 Monotonous work

Apart from the specific obligations to provide rest breaks described in 57.17, an employer is required to ensure that workers are given adequate rest breaks where the work pattern puts workers' health and safety at risk, in particular because the work is monotonous or the work rate pre-determined (*reg 8*). This appears to be a requirement which is additional to the basic entitlement to rest breaks set out in *reg 12*. The wording of the regulation is a paraphrase of *art 13* of the *Directive,* and it has not to date been the subject of judicial interpretation. Apart from those in excluded sectors to whom the *Regulations* do not apply at all, there are no exceptions to the application of *reg 8*.

57.19 ANNUAL LEAVE

Workers within the *1998 Regulations* are entitled to four weeks' statutory holiday in respect of each leave year (*reg 13*). The *Regulations* also cover statutory holiday pay, notice requirements in respect of taking annual leave, and pay in lieu on termination. Proposals to increase the entitlement to 4.8 weeks from 1 October 2007, and to 5.6 weeks from 1 October 2008, have been announced by the Government. Full details of the annual leave provisions in the *1998 Regulations* are set out in HOLIDAYS (29). Special rules apply to agricultural workers (*reg 43, Sch 2*).

57.20 ENFORCEMENT AND REMEDIES

Different enforcement arrangements operate according to the nature of the breach of the *1998 Regulations*. Working time limits are enforced by the Health and Safety Executive ('HSE') and local authorities, and within their areas of responsibility the Civil Aviation Authority ('CAA') and the Vehicle and Operator Services Agency ('VOSA') and the Office of Rail Regulation ('ORR'). The HSE enforces the limits in factories, building sites, mines, farms, fairgrounds, quarries, chemical plants, nuclear installations, schools and hospitals. Local authority officers have the same role in respect of shops and retailing, offices, hotels and catering, sports, leisure and consumer services. The enforcement powers of the various agencies are essentially the same as those provided for in the *Health and Safety at Work etc Act 1974*. For technical reasons the addition of the CAA and

VOSA to the list of enforcing authorities was considered to necessitate the restatement of the enforcement powers within the *1998 Regulations*, and these can be found in *regs 28–29E* and *Sch 3*. These provisions were then applied to the ORR when it was given enforcement responsibilities in relation to rail staff by the *Railways Act 2005* and regulations made under that Act. For further details of enforcement powers and penalties see 57.21 below and 27.29–27.41 HEALTH AND SAFETY AT WORK – II.

The other method of enforcement is that workers who are not receiving their entitlements or are penalised for insisting on their rights can pursue claims in employment tribunals: see 57.22–57.24 below.

57.21 Health and safety

Regulation 28 provides that the relevant enforcing authority, ie the HSE, local authority or the CAA, VOSA or ORR, is responsible for enforcing the following provisions: weekly working time (*reg 4(2)*); length of night work (*reg 6(2), (7)*); health assessments for night workers (*reg 7(1), (2)*) and transfers to day work (*reg 7(6)*); rest breaks for monotonous work (*reg 8*); record-keeping (*reg 9*); and compensatory rest in relation to night work (*reg 24*). Enforcing authorities are also responsible for the enforcement of the additional restrictions on working hours and night work for young workers in *regs 5A(4)* and *27A(4)(a)*, and for the provisions on adequate rest for mobile workers under *reg 24A*.

An employer who fails to comply with any of these requirements commits an offence (*reg 29*). The offences are punishable on summary conviction by a fine not exceeding £5,000. On conviction on indictment the punishment is an unlimited fine. *Regulations 29A–29E* contain provisions equivalent to those in the *Health and Safety at Work etc Act 1974* in relation to offences due to the default, etc of another person, offences by bodies corporate, powers to prosecute and powers of courts to require the remedying of causes of offences. Provisions as to the appointment and powers of inspectors, including the making of improvement and prohibition notices and rights of appeal against such notices, and restrictions on disclosure of information, are contained in *Sch 3*.

Additionally, the High Court has held that *reg 4(1)*, which specifies that a worker's average hours per week should not exceed 48, imposes a contractual obligation on an employer. Contracts should therefore be read as providing that an employee should work no more than an average of 48 hours during the reference period (*Barber v RJB Mining (UK) Ltd* [1999] IRLR 308). Consequently, employees who are asked to work over the 48-hour limit without their agreement may be able to bring proceedings in the civil courts for a declaration of rights and seek an injunction barring the employer from requiring them to work additional hours. However, this does not confer any right to claim compensation in an employment tribunal for being required to work more than 48 hours a week: the jurisdiction of the tribunals does not extend to claims for breach of *reg 4* (see 57.22 below).

There is as yet no reported case in which a worker has successfully claimed damages for personal injury resulting from being made to work hours in excess of those permitted under the *Regulations*, but in two recent cases in which the Court of Appeal upheld awards of damages for psychiatric injury, the fact that the employee had worked well in excess of the 48 hour limit without his agreement was regarded as an evidentially relevant factor in favour of the point that the damage ought to have been foreseen by the employer: *Hone v Six Continents Retail Ltd* [2005] EWCA Civ 922, [2006] IRLR 49; *Pakenham-Walsh v Connell*

Residential [2006] EWCA Civ 90, [2006] 11 LS Gaz R 25. In *Sayers v Cambridgeshire County Council* [2006] EWHC 2029 (QB), [2007] IRLR 29 (a case where a claim for damages for personal injury failed on the facts) the High Court held that a breach of *reg 4* by the employer does not confer a right for the worker to sue for damages for breach of statutory duty.

57.22 **Individual remedies**

Under *reg 30(1)(a)* a complaint may be made to an employment tribunal that the employer has refused to permit a worker to exercise his or her rights in connection with: daily rest (*reg 10(1)*, *(2)*); weekly rest (*reg 11(1)*, *(2)*, *(3)*); rest breaks (*reg 12(1)*, *(4)*); entitlement to annual leave (*reg 13(1)*); entitlement to compensatory rest (except in relation to night work) (*regs 24, 25, 27*) or to adequate rest (*reg 24A*).

Reg 30(1)(b) makes similar provision for complaints of failure to pay any sums due as payments in respect of annual leave entitlement or accrued holiday pay on termination under *reg 16(1)* or *14(2)* respectively, and it has been held that such claims can only be brought under *reg 30(1)(b)*, and not as complaints of unlawful deductions from wages (for which the time limit is in some cases less restrictive): *IRC v Ainsworth* [2005] EWCA Civ 441, [2005] IRLR 465, a case currently (April 2007) pending on appeal in the House of Lords following a reference of other issues in the case to the ECJ.

It should be noted that (apart from complaints of failure to pay sums due), the basis for complaints is of a refusal to permit the worker to exercise a relevant right. It is not enough that the right was not in fact exercised, unless this was attributable to the employer.

Tribunals have no express jurisdiction to hear claims by individuals for breach of the 48-hour limit on weekly working time. Following the lead given by the High Court in *Barber v RJB Mining (UK) Ltd* [1999] IRLR 308 (see 57.21), tribunals may accept that a term is implied into a contract of employment that the employer must not require the employee to work more than 48 hours a week in the reference period. The effect of this is, however, limited. An employee complaining of constructive dismissal could rely on being required to work excessive hours as a breach of contract, but the tribunal has no power to award compensation for excessive hours as such, unless overtime is required under the terms of the employee's contract to be paid, in which case a claim for unlawful deductions could be made (*Forbuoys Ltd v Rich*, EAT/144/01), or there is a claim under the *National Minimum Wage Act 1998*.

Claims must normally be presented within three months of the date on which the right should have been permitted or the payment should have been made. This period is extended to six months for complaints by members of the armed forces (who are required to utilise internal redress procedures before commencing tribunal proceedings). Where a tribunal is satisfied that it was not reasonably practicable to present a claim within the time limit, it may extend the period to a date it considers reasonable. Complaints to a tribunal pursuant to *reg 30(1)* are amongst those listed in *Schs 3* and *4* to the *Employment Act 2002*. Accordingly, by the combined effect of *ss 31* and *32* of the *2002 Act* and the *Employment Act 2002 (Dispute Resolution) Regulations 2004 (SI 2004/752)*:

(i)   subject to limited exceptions, if the complainant is an employee, he or she must submit a grievance in writing to the employer about the breach of the *1998 Regulations* at least 28 days before presenting a claim to the tribunal;

claim forms presented in circumstances where there appears not to have been compliance with this requirement will not be accepted by the tribunal;

(ii)   in certain circumstances the time limit for presenting a complaint to the tribunal is extended by three months; the cases in which there is an extension are where a grievance has been submitted by the employee in writing before the initial time limit expires, and where a claim has been presented to the tribunal within the original time limit but rejected because the employee had not submitted a written statement of grievance; and

(iii)   if the complaint is upheld, and it is determined by the tribunal that the statutory grievance procedure established by *Sch 2* to the *2002 Act* has not been completed, the tribunal must, except in certain exceptional cases, either increase or decrease any compensation awarded to the complainant, depending on to whom the non-completion of the procedure is attributable, by at least 10%, or up to a maximum of 50%.

For full details of these provisions see DISPUTE RESOLUTION (15) and EMPLOYMENT TRIBUNALS – I (20).

Where a complaint is considered to be well-founded, the tribunal will make a declaration to that effect and may make an award of such compensation (if any) as it considers to be just and equitable in all the circumstances, having regard to the employer's default and any loss sustained by the worker. Where the complaint involves failure to pay holiday pay (the issue arising in the vast majority of claims under the *1998 Regulations*), the tribunal will order the employer to pay the amount owed.

57.23 Victimisation

ERA 1996, s 45A (as inserted by *reg 31* of the *1998 Regulations*) provides that a worker has the right not to be subjected to any detriment by any act, or any deliberate failure to act, by his or her employer on the ground that the worker:

(*a*)   refused (or proposed to refuse) to comply with a requirement of the employer imposed in contravention of the *Regulations*;

(*b*)   refused (or proposed to refuse) to forgo a right conferred by the *Regulations*;

(*c*)   failed to sign a workforce agreement, or to enter into or agree to vary or extend any other agreement provided for in the *Regulations*;

(*d*)   being a representative of members of the workforce for the purposes of *Sch 1* or a candidate in an election for such a representative, performed (or proposed to perform) any functions or activities as such a representative or candidate;

(*e*)   brought proceedings against the employer to enforce a right conferred by the *Regulations*; or

(*f*)   alleged that the employer had infringed such a right.

So far as (*e*) and (*f*) are concerned, it is immaterial whether or not the worker has the right or whether or not the right has been infringed, but the claim must be made in good faith. In respect of (*f*), it is sufficient for the worker to make it reasonably clear to the employer what the right was that he or she alleges has been infringed.

There is separate protection, for employees only, from unfair dismissal (see 57.24 below) and dismissal is excluded from the definition of detriment for employees; for a worker who is not an employee, a complaint of subjection to detriment can be brought to cover the comparable situation of termination of his or her contract. It is at least arguable that *s 45A* covers detriments suffered after the termination of employment, by analogy with the Court of Appeal's reasoning in *Woodward v Abbey National plc* [2006] EWCA Civ 822, [2006] ICR 1436 on the equivalent provision in relation to 'whistleblowers' (*ERA 1996, s 47B*).

The remedy for a contravention of *s 45A* is a complaint to an employment tribunal. Normally the complaint must be presented within three months of the act or failure to act the subject of the complaint but tribunals have discretion to extend the time limit where it was not reasonably practicable to present the claim in time. In well-founded cases, the tribunal will make a declaration to that effect and may also award such compensation as it considers just and equitable. Compensation may include compensation for injury to feelings. The same additional points as are set out at 57.22 above in relation to grievances and time limits arising from the application of the *2002 Act* and *2004 Regulations* apply also to complaints of breaches of *s 45A*.

The amount of compensation which may be awarded is unlimited, except that where the detrimental action suffered by a worker (who is not working under a contract of employment) is termination of contract, the compensation must not exceed the maximum amount which could be awarded to an employee who has been unfairly dismissed for a similar reason (*ERA 1996, s 49*).

For workers in sectors covered by specific regulations, and who are either wholly or partially excluded from the application of the *1998 Regulations*, the position is inconsistent. *Section 45A* also applies in the same way in relation to the equivalent provisions of the *Merchant Shipping (Working Time: Inland Waterways) Regulations 2003* and the *Fishing Vessels (Working Time: Sea-fishermen) Regulations 2004*, but not (it appears through legislative oversight) to the comparable provisions for workers in civil aviation and road transport: see further 57.33 and 57.34. Merchant seamen (see 57.31) are also not covered by the provisions of *s 45A*.

57.24 Unfair dismissal

It is automatically unfair to dismiss an employee for certain reasons connected with rights and entitlements under the *1998 Regulations* (*ERA 1996, s 101A*, as inserted by *reg 32(1)*). Employees may present a claim under this provision regardless of length of service. For further details see 54.3(H) UNFAIR DISMISSAL – II.

It is also automatically unfair to dismiss an employee for 'asserting a statutory right' (*ERA 1996, s 104*). The rights conferred by the *1998 Regulations* are included within the definition of 'statutory rights' under *s 104* (as amended by *reg 32(2)*). Therefore where an employee has been dismissed for bringing proceedings to enforce a working time right or for alleging that the employer has infringed such a right, this will be considered automatically unfair. Employees may present a claim under this provision also regardless of length of service. See also 54.3(C) UNFAIR DISMISSAL – II. The points made in 57.23 above about the application of *s 45A* to workers covered by equivalent legislation for particular sectors apply equally to protection from unfair dismissal.

57.25 Restrictions on contracting out

A provision in an agreement which purports to exclude or limit the operation of any part of the *1998 Regulations* or to prevent a person from making a tribunal claim connected with the *Regulations* will be void, except, of course, where the *Regulations* themselves permit exclusion or modification (*reg 35*). The general rule does not apply where worker and employer have entered into an ACAS-conciliated settlement or a compromise agreement. For comments on the potential breadth of the restrictions on contracting out, see the contrasting reasoning of the Court of Session in *MPB Structure Ltd v Munro* [2003] IRLR 350 and the Court of Appeal in *Caulfield v Marshalls Clay Products Ltd* [2004] EWCA Civ 422, [2004] IRLR 564, and the views of the ECJ in *Robinson-Steele v RD Retail Services Ltd* [2006] IRLR 386, broadly endorsing the approach of the Court of Session.

57.26 GUIDANCE

The Secretary of State for Trade and Industry is responsible for arranging publication of information and advice on the *1998 Regulations* after consultation with both sides of industry (*reg 35A*). The DTI *Guide to the Working Time Regulations* is obtainable by calling 0845 6000 925 or can be accessed from the DTI website (www.dti.gov.uk/employment). The Guidance was updated in August 2003 to reflect the changes made in the *Regulations* by the *2003 Amendment Regulations,* and was further amended following the decision of the ECJ in *European Commission v United Kingdom, Case C-484/04* [2006] IRLR 888 that the guidance on workers' rights to rest periods and rest breaks put the UK in breach of its obligations to implement the *Directive* (see 57.2).

57.27 EXCEPTIONS

In addition to sectors of activity wholly excluded from the ambit of the *1998 Regulations* (see 57.3 above) various categories of worker are excepted from the full scope of the *Regulations.*

57.28 Unmeasured working time

The limit on the average working week, requirements as to daily and weekly rest periods and breaks for adults, and hours of work for night workers are disapplied for workers whose working time is not measured or pre-determined or can be determined by the workers themselves, on account of the specific characteristics of their job (*reg 20(1)*). *Regulation 20* suggests that this may be the case for:

(*a*) managing executives or other persons with autonomous decision-taking powers;

(*b*) family workers; or

(*c*) workers officiating at religious ceremonies in churches and religious communities.

(Annual leave entitlements nevertheless apply to workers within the exemptions created by *reg 20*.)

Following the enforcement proceedings by the Commission described in 57.2 above, the partial exemption from *reg 20* for those whose working time is partially unmeasured (*reg 20(2)*) was revoked by the *Working Time (Amendment) Regulations 2006 (SI 2006/99*) with effect from 6 April 2006.

57.29 **Special cases**

Regulation 21 provides that in certain specified situations or types of activity, the *Regulations* relating to daily and weekly rest periods and breaks (in respect of adults only) and hours of work for night workers are disapplied. This is subject to workers being permitted to take compensatory rest or, if that is not possible, being provided with appropriate health and safety protection. The following groups fall within the *reg 21* exception:

(*a*)   where the worker's activities are such that the place of work and home are distant from one another or different places of work are distant from one another, including cases where the worker is involved in offshore work;

(*b*)   where the worker is engaged in security and surveillance activities requiring a permanent presence in order to protect property and persons, as may be the case for security guards and caretakers or security firms;

(*c*)   where the worker's activities involve the need for continuity of service or production, as may be the case in relation to:

  (i)   services relating to the reception, treatment or care provided by hospitals or similar establishments (including the activities of doctors in training), residential institutions and prisons;

  (ii)   work at docks or airports;

  (iii)   press, radio, television, cinematographic production, postal and telecommunications services and civil protection services;

  (iv)   gas, water and electricity production, transmission and distribution, household refuse collection and incineration;

  (v)   industries in which work cannot be interrupted on technical grounds;

  (vi)   research and development activities;

  (vii)   agriculture;

  (viii)   the carriage of passengers on regular urban passenger services;

(*d*)   where there is a foreseeable surge of activity, as may be the case in relation to agriculture, tourism and postal services;

(*e*)   where the worker's activities are affected by:

  (i)   an occurrence due to unusual and unforeseeable circumstances, beyond the control of the worker's employer;

  (ii)   exceptional events, the consequences of which could not have been avoided despite the exercise of all due care by the employer; or

  (iii)   an accident or the imminent risk of an accident;

(*f*)   where the worker works in railway transport and –

  (i)   his or her activities are intermittent;

  (ii)   he or she spends his working time on board trains; or

  (iii)   his or her activities are linked to transport timetables and to ensuring the continuity and regularity of traffic.

Additionally, for workers falling within these categories the reference period for the weekly working time limit is extended from 17 weeks to 26 weeks (*reg 4(5)*).

The list of exclusions, which with one notable exception (see below) the regulation has copied verbatim from the *Directive*, is open to differences of interpretation. In particular, it should be noted that the categories listed in (*c*) are neither necessarily within the exemption (the wording is 'as may be the case for') nor exhaustive of possible exempt activities.

The application of these exceptions was considered for the first time at appellate level by the Court of Appeal in *Gallagher v Alpha Catering Ltd* [2004] EWCA Civ 1559, [2005] IRLR 102, a case concerning workers engaged in delivering and uplifting catering supplies to and from aircraft at Gatwick Airport, whose complaint was that they were refused rest breaks during the working day in breach of *reg 12*. The employers relied on two points in *reg 21* as providing exemption from their liability to afford rest breaks. These points were (*c*)(ii) and (*d*) above. As to the first, the Court emphasised that in the *Regulations*, in contrast to the *Directive*, the emphasis in (*c*) was placed squarely on the activity of the worker, not of the employer, so that the test was not whether the employer had to maintain continuity of service but whether the particular worker's activity involved such continuity; on the facts it did not. The Court also rejected an argument that the variations in the numbers of aircraft requiring servicing at different times of the week, and increases in numbers during holiday periods, amounted to a 'foreseeable surge of activity'. The requirement that equivalent compensatory rest should be afforded must now be read subject to the decision of the ECJ in *Jaeger* (see 57.4 above) that compensatory rest must be accorded immediately following the period worked.

The exception for the carriage of passengers on urban bus services was considered in *First Hampshire & Dorset Ltd v Feist* UKEAT/510/06, where it was held that the entitlement to compensatory rest attaching to the exemptions under *reg 21* applied only where the workers concerned were excluded from the right to rest solely by *reg 21*. In the case of bus drivers, who are also excluded as mobile workers by the effect of *reg 24A*, the corresponding right is limited to the right to 'adequate' rest conferred by *reg 24A*; the rights are not cumulative.

57.30 Exception: domestic service

Workers who are employed as domestic servants in a private household are excluded from the scope of the *Regulations* relating to: the 48-hour week; length of night work; health assessments and transfers to day work; and breaks for monotonous work. Such domestic workers are, however, covered by provisions on rest periods, breaks and annual leave (*reg 19*). The basis in the *Directive* for this exclusion is not clear.

57.31 SEAFARERS AND WORKERS ON INLAND WATERWAYS

A separate set of rules regulating the working time of seafarers on sea-going United Kingdom flagged vessels is laid down by the *Merchant Shipping (Hours of Work) Regulations 2002*. These implement EC *Directive 99/63*, which was adopted to fill one of the gaps in the coverage of the *Working Time Directive*. (Equivalent legislation is required of other member states in relation to the crews of ships flying their respective flags, but the inspection and enforcement provisions of the *2002 Regulations* extend to such vessels whilst in a UK port or UK waters: *reg 3(1)*). The *2002 Regulations* do not apply to fishing vessels, pleasure vessels, static offshore installations or most tug boats, or their respective crews. The *1998 Regulations* do not apply at all to those seafarers covered by *Directive 99/63*, or to the crews of fishing vessels: *reg 18(1)*.

The principal features of the *Merchant Shipping Regulations* are:

(*a*)   a minimum of 10 hours' daily rest (divided into not more than two periods);

(*b*)   a minimum of 77 hours' rest in any seven-day period;

(*c*)   provision for (*a*) and/or (*b*) to be made subject to exceptions by way of a collective or workforce agreement;

(*d*)   provision for the suspension of scheduled working hours and rest periods in an emergency;

(*e*)   maintenance of records of hours worked;

(*f*)   a prohibition on night work for those under 18;

(*g*)   entitlement to four weeks' paid annual leave (which may be taken in instalments);

(*h*)   powers of inspection and enforcement, including penalties.

Directive 99/95 provides a mechanism for the verification and enforcement of compliance with *Directive 99/63* by ships calling at ports of member states.

Separate regulations, the *Fishing Vessels* (*Working Time: Sea-fishermen*) *Regulations 2004* (*SI 2004/1713*) apply to the crews of UK registered fishing vessels; these *Regulations* came into force on 16 August 2004. The *1998 Regulations* do not apply at all to those workers covered by the *2004 Regulations: 1998 Regulations, reg 18(1)(b)*.

The *2004 Regulations* apply to those employed on sea fishing vessels registered in the UK, wherever the vessel may be, and also (but in relation only to rights to rest periods and certain enforcement provisions) to those working on vessels registered in an EU member state whilst in UK waters. They apply only to those employed under a contract of employment, not to workers in the wider sense; that point apart, the definitions used are essentially the same as those used in the *1998 Regulations*. The principal rights conferred are:

(i)   a maximum 48 hour working week (averaged over 52 weeks, but with no facility for individual opt-outs);

(ii)   adequate rest (with minimum entitlements of 10 hours in 24, in no more than two separate periods, and 77 hours in any week);

(iii)   health assessments, and transfer from night work if the health assessment discloses health problems associated with night work;

(iv)   paid annual leave; and

(v)   to make a complaint to an employment tribunal if denied adequate rest or paid leave.

The rights not to be subjected to detriment, or dismissed, for asserting rights under the *Regulations,* are conferred by amendments to the *ERA 1996.* Other enforcement provisions include powers for the Maritime and Coastguard Agency to inspect records and detain vessels. The Secretary of State has a limited power to grant exemptions from the limits on working time and the minimum required periods of rest, and there is a general exemption for emergencies.

57.32 Workers employed on UK vessels operating under certificates limiting the vessel to inland waterways and lakes, or not requiring to be certificated, or on non-UK registered vessels operating solely within such waters, are covered by the *Merchant Shipping (Hours of Work: Inland Waterways) Regulations 2003 (SI 2003/3049)*, made under *s 85* of the *Merchant Shipping Act 1995*. In summary, these *Regulations* provide for a maximum of 48 hours working time a week, averaged in the same way as under the *1998 Regulations*, rights for night workers to free health assessments and to be transferred to other work if available if the worker's health is prejudiced by night working, rights to adequate rest, which must be of at least 77 hours in total in any week, and to four weeks' paid annual leave in each leave year. Other rights conferred by the *1998 Regulations* are however not mirrored in these *Regulations*. There are limited exceptions for workers whose working time is unmeasured, and in certain cases the averaging period for the 48 hour week is extended to 26 weeks and may be further extended by a collective or workforce agreement. Employers are under a duty to maintain records. Breach of the provisions relating to maximum working time, health assessments and record keeping are offences, whilst the remedy for breaches of the provisions on rest periods and annual leave is by way of complaint to an employment tribunal. The *2003 Regulations* contain the usual prohibition on contracting out, except by way of a compromise agreement. The *2003 Regulations* mirror the *1998 Regulations* very closely in terminology; the *1998 Regulations* are excluded completely for those workers covered by the *2003 Regulations: 1998 Regulations, reg 18(1)(c)*.

57.33 **AVIATION SECTOR**

In November 2000 the Social Affairs Council formally adopted a *Directive* implementing the social partners' agreement on working time in the aviation sector, *Directive 2000/79 on the organisation of working time of mobile workers in civil aviation*. The domestic implementation of this *Directive* has been effected by the *Civil Aviation (Working Time) Regulations 2004 (SI 2004/756)*, which came into force on 13 April 2004. The *2004 Regulations* apply to crew members of civil aircraft flying for the purposes of public transport, and confer the following rights:

(*a*)   paid annual leave of at least four weeks;

(*b*)   free health assessments;

(*c*)   right of transfer from night work to day work where possible if health problems are caused by night work;

(*d*)   appropriate health and safety protection;

(*e*)   maximum working time of 2,000 hours a year, calculated on a rolling basis;

(*f*)   a maximum of 900 hours block flying time in any one (rolling) year;

(*g*)   at least seven local days (ie days at the crew member's home base) each month and at least 96 local days each year free of all duty and standby.

Infringements of the rights at (*a*), (*b*) and (*c*) may be made the subject of a complaint to an employment tribunal; however there is no equivalent to the protection from detriment or dismissal for asserting rights under the *1998 Regulations* for workers covered by the *Civil Aviation Regulations*; this appears to be an oversight. In other respects the *Regulations* are enforceable by the Civil Aviation Authority, following the model of the *1998 Regulations*.

Workers covered by *Directive 2000/79* are excluded from the operative provisions of the *1998 Regulations* governing adult workers: *reg 18(2)(b)*. However, unlike those in the sectors discussed in 57.31 and 57.32 above, this is not an exclusion of the *Regulations* in their entirety; the principal practical difference appears to be that specific provisions on young workers' hours in the *1998 Regulations* and the provisions for their enforcement by the CAA, do apply to the civil aviation sector.

57.34 MOBILE WORKERS IN ROAD AND RAIL TRANSPORT

Mobile workers are defined as 'any worker employed as a member of travelling or flying personnel by an undertaking which operates transport services for passengers or goods by road or air': *1998 Regulations, reg 2(1)*.

Most such mobile workers are excluded from the application of the *1998 Regulations* by *reg 18*, by virtue of their falling within the terms of either *Directive 2000/79* (as to which, see 57.32 above) or *Directive 2002/15,* which requires member states to enact parallel provisions as to working time, etc for mobile workers in road transport. Any mobile workers (as defined above) who fall outside these categories are subject to *reg 24A*, which excludes the provisions of the *Regulations* as to night work, rest breaks and rest periods, but not those relating to the working week, health assessments, monotonous work, or paid annual leave. The exclusions are subject to rights to periods of adequate rest, which are required to be sufficiently long and continuous to ensure that the worker's health is protected. The EAT has held that the right to adequate rest is in effect in substitution for rights under *reg 24* to compensatory rest, rather than cumulative with that right: *First Hampshire & Dorset Ltd v Feist* UKEAT/0510/06.

57.35 *Directive 2002/15* applies to mobile workers employed in the road transport industry who are covered by the *Drivers' Hours Regulations* (*Regulation 3820/85*), which cover maximum driving hours for drivers of most commercial freight and passenger vehicles within the EU or the European Economic Area, or by the AETR Agreement 1970, which makes equivalent provisions covering road transport across the outer boundaries of the EU and EEA. (Note that following the introduction of *Directive 2002/15*, the *Drivers' Hours Regulations* have been replaced by an updated equivalent, *Regulation 561/2006,* which came into force on 11 April 2007.) The *Directive* was required to be implemented by 23 March 2005, and its provisions are required to be extended to self-employed drivers from 23 March 2009. The *Directive* covers maximum working hours, breaks, rest periods and restrictions on night work, and the maintenance of records. It does not cover annual leave entitlement or rights to health assessments, or the rights in relation to working time, daily rest periods and rest breaks of young workers, in respect of which the *1998 Regulations* apply equally to workers otherwise governed by the *2002 Directive* (insofar as those provisions affecting only young workers are capable of applying to mobile workers in road transport).

The implementation of this *Directive* was effected, with effect from 4 April 2005, by the *Road Transport (Working Time) Regulations 2005 (SI 2005/639)*. The *2005 Regulations* apply to those mobile workers who in the course of their work drive, or travel in vehicles to which either the *Drivers' Hours Regulations* or the AETR agreement apply. They are thus not limited in their application to drivers as such, but may cover, for instance, attendants on long distance coaches. However, in line with the *Directive,* self employed drivers are not covered.

The *Regulations* impose a limit on working time of an average of 48 hours a week, averaged over either rolling or fixed periods of 17 weeks, with an absolute limit of 60 hours in any week. In limited circumstances the averaging period may be extended to 26 weeks. Working time is broadly defined to include all working time, not just the time spent driving or travelling, but excluding breaks and certain periods on standby (referred to as 'periods of availability'). In addition to limits on working hours, there are provisions for rest breaks and rest periods, and additional limits on night working. However the *Regulations* do not confer entitlements to paid annual leave; this is because the *1998 Regulations* apply in this respect; enforcement of rights to paid leave is by way of individual complaint to an employment tribunal under *reg 30* of the *1998 Regulations*.

Employers are required to ensure compliance with the *Regulations,* and enforcement is by inspectors appointed by the Department for Transport, using sanctions similar to those under the equivalent provisions of the *1998 Regulations.* The *2005 Regulations* do not make provision for individual workers to complain to an employment tribunal if not afforded the required rest breaks or rest periods, or dismissed or subjected to detriment for asserting their rights. The reasons for this omission are not clear, and it is thought to be a legislative oversight.

57.36 Mobile workers in the rail sector are covered by the *1998 Regulations*, and fall outside the exclusions applied by *reg 24A*, as they are outside the definition of 'mobile workers' quoted above; however they are subject to the effects of *reg 21*: see 57.29 above for this.

58   Wrongful Dismissal

58.1   INTRODUCTION

A wrongful dismissal occurs when an employer dismisses an employee in a way which is in breach of the employee's contract of employment. Most commonly, this arises when the employer dismisses the employee summarily (ie without any notice at all) or with short notice, and has no sufficient justification for doing so. However, there may also be a wrongful dismissal in other situations: for example, if the employer terminates the employment without following some procedure prescribed by the contract. Further, if the employee resigns in response to some repudiatory breach of contract by the employer, that will give rise to a claim which is in effect for wrongful dismissal.

Thus, wrongful dismissal is a common law cause of action based upon a breach of contract. The right not to be wrongfully dismissed, unlike the right not to be unfairly dismissed, is not one which depends upon statute. A dismissal which is wrongful need not necessarily be unfair, and vice versa. This is because an employer may behave unreasonably in dismissing an employee even though he has observed the letter of their contract, whilst a decision to dismiss may be reasonable even if it involves a breach of contract (although failure to comply with contractual procedures is one factor to be taken into account in deciding whether a dismissal is unfair). See *Treganowan v Robert Knee & Co Ltd* [1975] ICR 405; *BSC Sports and Social Club v Morgan* [1987] IRLR 391 and *Westminster City Council v Cabaj* [1996] ICR 960.

The primary remedy for an employee who is wrongfully dismissed is an action for damages for breach of contract. In certain circumstances, however, the employee may seek the assistance of the court in keeping the contract of employment alive.

58.2   Contracts whose breach may give rise to wrongful dismissal claims

The wrongful termination of any normal contract of employment will give rise to an action for wrongful dismissal. Certain special categories of employment are dealt with below (see 58.43 and 58.44). Where the contract pursuant to which a self-employed person provides services is wrongfully terminated, the action for breach of contract is not strictly speaking one for wrongful dismissal but similar principles will apply.

58.3   WHAT CONSTITUTES A DISMISSAL

The fundamental precondition for a wrongful dismissal claim is that the employee should have been dismissed. This will usually occur in one of the following ways:

(a)   dismissal upon notice by the employer (see 58.5 below), although there will normally be no wrongful dismissal if full notice has been given;

(b)   summary dismissal by the employer; and

(c)   constructive dismissal (see 58.6 below).

However, there may also be a deemed dismissal in certain other circumstances (see 58.8–58.10 below).

58.4 Wrongful Dismissal

58.4 Dismissal contrasted with other modes of termination

The employee will have no right to claim damages if the contract is brought to an end by mutual agreement or by his own resignation (unless in response to the employer's repudiatory breach), by frustration, or through the automatic operation of provisions in the contract (for example, expiry of a fixed term contract, or a provision that the employment will end as soon as the employee reaches a certain age).

For a fuller discussion of these possible modes of termination, see UNFAIR DISMISSAL – I (53). Note that expiry of a fixed term contract without renewal constitutes a deemed dismissal for the purposes of unfair dismissal but not for the purposes of wrongful dismissal.

58.5 Dismissal upon notice

Unless the contract otherwise provides, an effective notice may be given either orally or in writing. However, a notice is of no effect unless and until it is communicated to the employee (*Brown v Southall and Knight* [1980] ICR 617; *Hindle Gears Ltd v McGinty* [1985] ICR 111).

A purported notice is ineffective unless it is expressed to expire on a certain specified or ascertainable day, or upon the occurrence of a specified event (*Morton Sundour Fabrics Ltd v Shaw* (1966) 2 ITR 84; *Burton Group Ltd v Smith* [1977] IRLR 351). Accordingly, there will be no dismissal if the employee is merely warned that his job will come to an end at some point in the future (*Devon County Council v Cook* [1977] IRLR 188; *International Computers Ltd v Kennedy* [1981] IRLR 28), or if it is not possible to tell from the notice when the employment will end (*Haseltine Lake & Co v Dowler* [1981] ICR 222).

Usually, the employer's intention to dismiss will be clear. Sometimes, however, the language of a letter or conversation may leave room for doubt as to whether the employer is actually dismissing the employee, or whether he is merely warning or threatening that he may do so, or indeed whether he is simply expressing frustration or anger. In such circumstances, the court will consider, not the employer's subjective intention, but rather the objective meaning of the words used, considered against the background of the circumstances in which they are used. The ultimate question is how the words should reasonably have been regarded by the other party to the contract (*Tanner v DT Kean Ltd* [1978] IRLR 110; *Sovereign House Security Services Ltd v Savage* [1989] IRLR 115).

In order to decide whether due notice has been given, or whether the employee has been wrongfully dismissed, it may be important to decide on what date the notice takes effect. The day on which the notice is given will not normally be counted in calculating any period to which the notice refers (*West v Kneels Ltd* [1987] ICR 146).

Once notice has been given by one party to the contract, it may not be withdrawn except by mutual consent (*Riordan v War Office* [1959] 1 WLR 1046). Therefore, if an employer gives short notice to an employee, and later realises his mistake and seeks to retract that notice, the employee is entitled to refuse to agree to the retraction and to sue for wrongful dismissal (although the employer might then argue that the employee had failed to mitigate his loss).

58.6 Constructive dismissal

The employee will be treated as having been constructively dismissed if he resigns in response to a repudiatory breach of contract by the employer. This means that the employer must have breached some term of the contract, whether express or implied (or have indicated a clear intention to do so – see 58.22 below), and the breach must be sufficiently serious to 'go to the root of the contract'. (This will be the case if, for instance, the employer has breached the duty of trust and confidence: see *Morrow v Safeway Stores plc* [2002] IRLR 9). The employee must accept the breach by resigning, and he must not take so long to do so that he is deemed to have affirmed the contract or waived the employer's breach.

For a full discussion of the different factual circumstances which may amount to a constructive dismissal, see UNFAIR DISMISSAL – I (53). Note, however, that in the unfair dismissal context it has been held to be necessary for the employer's breach of contract to be the true cause of the resignation. It is not thought that this applies to an action for wrongful dismissal (cf *Boston Deep Sea Fishing and Ice Co v Ansell* (1888) 39 Ch D 339).

58.7   Need for employer's breach of contract to be accepted

Where one party commits a repudiatory breach of contract, it is normally necessary for that breach to be 'accepted' by the other, innocent party before the contract can be brought to an end. That is because the innocent party may instead choose to keep the contract in existence, and simply to sue for damages if the breach of contract has caused him loss.

There is no doubt that this normal rule applies to a contract of employment where the employer's breach of contract consists of some act or omission falling short of a purported dismissal. For instance, if the employer persists in withholding some significant benefit in kind, the employee may choose whether to resign and bring the contract to an end (thereafter suing for wrongful dismissal), or whether to remain in employment and simply sue for damages for the loss of the benefit.

However, some doubt remains as to the position where the employer purports to dismiss the employee in breach of contract (for example, in breach of a contractual procedure, or by purporting to dismiss summarily where there is no justification for doing so). In such a situation, the employee will normally simply accept his dismissal and sue for damages for wrongful dismissal. However, in some cases, the employee may wish to keep the contract alive — perhaps because there is an advantage to him in still being employed at a particular date (eg to receive a bonus or to invoke the benefits of an insurance policy), or because he hopes for a different outcome if the employer is obliged to go through a proper disciplinary procedure.

In relation to such cases, it has been suggested that a contract of employment is different from a normal contract, and that the act of wrongful dismissal brings the employment to an end without any need for acceptance of the breach by the employee (see eg *London Transport Executive v Clarke* [1981] ICR 355; *BMK Ltd v Logue* [1993] IRLR 477). However, the better view is that there is no exception to the normal rule, and that acceptance is indeed required (see eg *Thomas Marshall Ltd v Guinle* [1978] ICR 905; *Gunton v Richmond-upon-Thames London Borough Council* [1980] ICR 755; *Dietman v Brent London Borough Council* [1987] ICR 737; affd [1988] ICR 842, CA; *Marsh v National Autistic Society* [1993] ICR 453; see also *Rigby v Ferodo Ltd* [1988] ICR 29; *Boyo v Lambeth London Borough Council* [1994] ICR 727; *Brompton v AOC International Ltd* [1997] IRLR 639). Nonetheless, it is clear that in the employment context such acceptance will be readily inferred from the employee's words or conduct. For instance, an employee who seeks other work, or signs on for jobseeker's allowance, or even one who simply does not return to work and says nothing, will very probably be held to have ceased to be employed. (However, see *Brompton v AOC International Ltd* (above) where, on the facts of that case, the employee's request for his P45 did not amount to acceptance of the repudiatory breach.) An employee who wishes to argue that his employment continues will have to assert clearly and quickly that he regards himself as still employed, and that he is available for work if required.

58.8 Employer changing identity or ceasing to exist

If the employer is an individual, the death of that individual will bring the contract to an end. However, it appears that this will be regarded as a case of termination pursuant to an implied term of the contract, and not of wrongful dismissal (see *Farrow v Wilson* (1869) LR 4 CP 744).

If the employer is a partnership, then the dissolution of that partnership or a major change in its composition amounts to a dismissal of the employee (*Tunstall v Condon* [1980] ICR 786; *Briggs v Oates* [1990] ICR 473). It was held in *Brace v Calder* [1895] 2 QB 253 that the same applied when there was any change in the identity of the partners. However, it is not thought that this approach would be taken by the courts in modern cases of large partnerships whose membership frequently fluctuates. Firms should insert appropriate express terms into their contracts of employment to deal with this situation.

The permanent closure of the workplace amounts to a termination of the contracts of those employed there (*Glenboig Union Fireclay Co Ltd v Stewart* (1971) 6 ITR 14). This is not true of a temporary shutdown, although that might, depending upon the circumstances, amount to a repudiatory breach of contract.

58.9 Insolvency

Where the employer is a company, then an order for the compulsory winding up of that company has the immediate effect of terminating the contracts of employment of the company's employees (*Re General Rolling Stock Co* (1866) LR 1 Eq 346; *Measures Brothers Ltd v Measures* [1910] 2 Ch 248). However, contracts of employment continue during a voluntary winding up (*Midland Counties District Bank Ltd v Attwood* [1905] 1 Ch 357).

Again, contracts of employment are treated as coming immediately to an end if the employing company is put into receivership by an order of the court (*Reid v Explosives Co Ltd* (1887) 19 QBD 264; *Re Foster Clark Ltd's Indenture Trusts* [1966] 1 WLR 125). By contrast, the employment continues if the receiver is appointed otherwise by the court and as agent for the company, as typically occurs under, say, a creditor bank's debenture (*Hopley-Dodd v Highfield Motors (Derby) Ltd* (1969) 4 ITR 289; *Griffiths v Secretary of State for Social Services* [1974] QB 468). However, even a receivership of this latter kind may have the effect of terminating the contract of employment of a senior manager, if there is a fundamental inconsistency between the continuation of that individual's employment and the receiver's power and duty to conduct the business of the company (*Re Mack Trucks (Britain) Ltd* [1967] 1 WLR 780).

(See INSOLVENCY OF EMPLOYER (31).)

58.10 Removal from board of directors

In principle, a person's status as a director of the company and his status as an employee of that company are separate and distinct. Accordingly, the employee may cease to be a director without any impact upon his contract of employment.

Sometimes, however, it may be an express or implied term of the contract of employment that the employee is to be a director, either of the employing company itself, or of some associated company. In such a case, removal from the board will amount to a repudiation of the contract of employment, allowing the employee to sue for wrongful dismissal (*Shindler*, below).

However, even in a case where removal from the board brings the employment to an end, it may be contended that the company's articles of association were incorporated into the contract of employment when it was made, and have the effect of ending the employment without any breach on the company's part (see e g *Read v Astoria Garage (Streatham) Ltd* [1952] Ch 637; cf *Southern Foundries (1926) Ltd v Shirlaw* [1940] AC 701; *Shindler v Northern Raincoat Co Ltd* [1960] 1 WLR 1038).

(See DIRECTORS (9).)

58.11 DISMISSAL WITHOUT DUE NOTICE

Express notice periods

There will usually be a written contract of employment which stipulates expressly the period of notice to which the employee is entitled. Indeed, in most cases, the employer will be under a statutory obligation to provide this information as part of the written particulars of employment (see CONTRACT OF EMPLOYMENT (8)).

58.12 Fixed term contracts

Where the contract is for a fixed term, rather than one which contains a provision for the employer to give notice, damages for early termination will be awarded so as to put the employee in the same position as if the contract had continued until the end of that term. There is no need for the employer to give any advance notice that the contract will terminate at the end of the fixed term (although it may be sensible to do so), because it will do so automatically.

A contract which is for a fixed term, in that it will expire automatically on a given date, may also include provisions enabling either party to give notice to take effect at some earlier date.

Analogous to the fixed term contract is the contract which is expressed to terminate upon the occurrence of a specified event, such as the completion of a particular task.

58.13 Rolling contracts

A 'rolling contract' is not a precisely defined legal concept. However, the term is in general used to describe a contract which is of a length (say, two years) generally associated with a fixed term contract, but where the unexpired term always remains the same unless notice has been given. There is no difference in substance between a two-year rolling contract and a contract incorporating a two-year notice period.

58.14 Directors' notice periods

A restriction upon the length of notice periods in directors' contracts of employment is contained in *s 319* of the *Companies Act 1985*. Save with the prior approval of the company in general meeting, a company cannot validly enter into contracts with its directors which it cannot terminate by notice, or which it can terminate only in specified circumstances, for a period exceeding five years. The same applies to shadow directors, and to directors of holding companies employed within the group. For the purpose of calculating the period within which the company can terminate the contract, the unexpired period of any preceding contract will be added to the term of the new contract if the latter is concluded more than six months before the expiry of the former.

Any term which infringes this rule is void, and is replaced by a deemed term entitling the company to terminate the director's employment upon reasonable notice (see 58.15 below).

For other relevant principles, see DIRECTORS (9).

58.15 Implied notice periods

If the contract does not contain any expressly agreed notice period, and it is not a fixed term contract, then the court will generally imply a term that either party may bring the contract to an end by giving reasonable notice (*Richardson v Koefod* [1969] 1 WLR 1812. Cf *Reda v Flag Ltd* [2002] UKPC 38, [2002] IRLR 747,in which case the Privy Council held that there was no need to imply a term giving reasonable notice into a fixed term contract). It is most unusual for a contract to be construed as giving a right to a 'job for life', although in *McClelland v Northern Ireland Health Services Board* [1957] 1 WLR 594 the contract was held to be terminable only in the limited circumstances specified within it.

What constitutes a reasonable notice period must be decided by the court having regard to all the circumstances of the case. Such circumstances include the seniority and remuneration of the employee, his age and length of service, and what is usual in the particular trade. Very broadly speaking, the courts tend to approach such questions by adopting in most cases a period of one, three or six months or one year, with manual employees at one end of the range and senior executives at the other. The reasonable notice required to be given by the employer is not necessarily the same as that required to be given by the employee (cf *Libyan Arab Foreign Bank v Bankers Trust Co* [1989] QB 728 at 756G).

Where there is a training component to a contract of employment (eg in a Modern Apprenticeship type situation), then this will affect the period of notice that would be implied by the Courts. In *Flett v Matheson* [2005] ICR 1134, the EAT observed that reasonable notice would be geared towards the time in which it would be reasonable for arrangements to be made to place the apprentice with another employer.

58.16 Statutory minimum notice periods

Whatever the parties may have agreed in the contract, an employee who has worked for over a month is normally entitled at least to the statutory minimum period of notice prescribed by *s 86* of the *ERA 1996* (essentially, one week for each year's completed service up to a maximum of twelve weeks; see further CONTRACT OF EMPLOYMENT (8)) (see eg *Masiak v City Restaurants (UK) Ltd* [1999] IRLR 780). It is not possible to override this statutory right by a provision in the contract of employment, but the employee may waive his right to notice on any given occasion or accept a payment in lieu of notice (*ERA 1996, s 86(3)*). The Employment Appeal Tribunal has recently questioned whether waiver of statutory notice rights can take place at the outset of a contract by means of a contractual payment in lieu clause (*Cerberus Software Ltd v Rowley* [2000] ICR 35). This point was not specifically addressed by the Court of Appeal [2001] EWCA Civ 78, [2001] ICR 376. However, it must be doubted, as the Court did not find that a payment in lieu clause was invalid.

The existence of the statutory minimum period does not prevent the implication of some longer reasonable period as a term of the contract (see 58.15 above).

58.17 **Justification for summary dismissal**

An employee may be summarily dismissed if he is guilty of a repudiatory breach of the contract of employment. As in the converse case of constructive dismissal, this means a breach which is sufficiently fundamental (see eg *Laws v London Chronicle (Indicator Newspapers) Ltd* [1959] 1 WLR 698; *Jupiter General Insurance Co Ltd v Shroff* [1937] 3 All ER 67).

The most frequent example of a repudiatory breach of contract by the employee is misconduct sufficiently serious to be regarded as gross misconduct. There is no rigid definition of what amounts to gross misconduct but, by way of example, the courts would normally be expected to treat summary dismissal as justified in any case of dishonesty, in cases of deliberate and inexcusable failure to comply with lawful instructions, and in cases where the misconduct is repeated or otherwise particularly flagrant. See the discussion in *Wilson v Racher* [1974] ICR 428 and the decision of Lord Jauncey in the Westminster Abbey organist case (*Neary v Dean of Westminster* [1999] IRLR 288). See also the curious case of *Briscoe v Lubrizol Ltd* [2002] EWCA Civ 508, [2002] IRLR 607, where an employee's behaviour in refusing to adhere to his employer's instructions during a lengthy period of sickness absence was held to justify his summary dismissal.

If the misconduct occurs outside the scope of the employment (eg an employee caught stealing from his local shop), it may still in principle be such as to justify summary dismissal. However, this will be so only if it is so serious as to strike at the root of the confidence which must exist for the contract of employment to be effective (*Jackson v Invicta Plastics Ltd* [1987] BCLC 329).

Sometimes the contract of employment will give a list of cases in which the employee may be summarily dismissed. Subject to the possible effect of the *Unfair Contract Terms Act 1977* (see 57.37 below), the court should probably uphold a dismissal carried out pursuant to such a clause, even if the conduct in question would not otherwise be considered sufficiently gross to merit summary dismissal. However, the danger which the employer runs in including such a clause in the contract is that the court may hold that it is intended as a complete and exhaustive list of the situations in which summary dismissal may be justified (see eg *Dietman v Brent London Borough Council* [1987] ICR 737, affirmed [1988] ICR 842; but see *Macari v Celtic Football & Athletic Co Ltd* [1999] IRLR 787, where the failure to follow a contractual dismissal procedure did not prevent the employer from relying on his common law right to dismiss summarily). Accordingly, from the employer's point of view, any clause of this kind must always be carefully drafted so as to make clear that it does not prejudice any right to dismiss summarily that would otherwise exist.

It is possible in principle to dismiss an employee summarily (and lawfully) for incompetence. This is because there is an implied term in the contract of employment that the employee is reasonably competent to do the job (*Harmer v Cornelius* (1858) 5 CBNS 236). However, *Jackson* (above) suggests that a summary dismissal on grounds of competence will be justified only in fairly extreme cases. A summary dismissal may also be justified on grounds of extreme carelessness (*Savage v British India Steam Navigation Co Ltd* (1930) 46 TLR 294). Mere illness disabling the employee from performance through no fault of his own is not a breach of contract.

All-out strike action will almost certainly amount to a repudiatory breach of contract entitling the employer to dismiss summarily (see *Simmons v Hoover Ltd* [1977] ICR 61), although it is possible that a very short walk-out might be considered insufficiently serious to have this consequence. Lesser forms of industrial action may or may not amount to a breach of contract at all (for example, an overtime ban is only a breach of contract if the contract provides for compulsory overtime) and may or may not be fundamental enough to be considered repudiatory.

58.18 **DISMISSAL IN BREACH OF OTHER CONTRACTUAL REQUIREMENTS**

Dismissal procedures

If the contract of employment stipulates that a particular procedure must be followed before an employee is dismissed, then a dismissal which is carried out without that procedure having been followed is necessarily wrongful (see, e g *Gunton v Richmond-upon-Thames London Borough Council* [1980] ICR 755; *R v BBC, ex p Lavelle* [1983] ICR 99; and *Dietmann v Brent London Borough Council* [1988] ICR 842; but c f *Boyo v Lambeth London Borough Council* [1994] ICR 727).

However, it will be a question of fact in every case as to whether any disciplinary or similar procedure has in fact been incorporated into the contract of employment, or whether it merely represents a statement of the employer's current policy. If it is the latter, then breach of the procedure may well have the effect of making the dismissal unfair but it will not render it wrongful so far as the law of contract is concerned.

In *Johnson v Unisys Ltd* [2001] UKHL 13, [2001] ICR 480, the House of Lords rejected the contention that there could be implied into a contract of employment a provision that the employer would not dismiss save for good cause, and after giving the employee a reasonable opportunity to demonstrate that no such cause existed, in circumstances where there was an express term entitling the employer to dismiss on notice without any cause. In other words, the courts will not readily imply any procedural safeguards against dismissal into a contract of employment.

58.19 **Other requirements**

A dismissal might also be wrongful because, for example, it was carried out in contravention of a contractual term concerning the manner in which employees would be selected for redundancy. Such an argument was rejected on the facts in *Alexander v Standard Telephones and Cables Ltd (No 2)* [1991] IRLR 286.

Also, where the contract of employment contains the right to receive benefits under a permanent health insurance scheme, the court may imply a term preventing an employer from dismissing the employee (in the absence of conduct amounting to a repudiatory breach or for other cause, such as redundancy) during the period in which that employee is incapacitated from work. Dismissal in breach of this implied term would be wrongful, and may entitle the employee to recover damages reflecting the loss of permanent health benefits to which he would otherwise have been entitled (compare *Aspden v Webbs Poultry and Meat Group (Holdings) Ltd* [1996] IRLR 521 and *Hill v General Accident Fire and Life Assurance Corpn plc* [1998] IRLR 641; see also *Villella v MFI Furniture Centres Ltd* [1999] IRLR 468).

58.20 **RELEVANCE OF ACTUAL REASON FOR DISMISSAL**

In a complaint of unfair dismissal, the reason for which the employer actually chose to dismiss the employee is of central importance. But in an action for wrongful dismissal, it is possible to justify the dismissal by reference to conduct of the employee of which the employer was unaware at the time of the dismissal, and which may have happened a considerable time prior to the dismissal (*Boston Deep Sea Fishing and Ice Co v Ansell* (1888) 39 Ch D 339; *Cyril Leonard & Co v Simo Securities Trust Ltd* [1972] 1 WLR 80; *Item Software (UK) Ltd v Fassihi* [2003] IRLR 769).

In principle, it should also be possible for the employer to rely upon conduct of which he was aware at the time of the dismissal, but was not in fact his reason for dismissing the employee. However, unless that conduct occurred or was discovered only a short time prior to the dismissal, the employer is likely to be held to have waived his right to terminate the contract on account of it.

58.21 WAIVER OF NOTICE, PAY IN LIEU OF NOTICE AND GARDEN LEAVE

Frequently, an employer who has resolved to dismiss an employee will not wish that employee to continue working for him until the notice period has expired. It may, for example, be thought that the disgruntled employee's presence will be disruptive or bad for morale, or that there is a threat to confidential information, or simply that the employee will be unproductive and that a replacement should start work at the earliest opportunity.

In this situation, there are three principal options open to the employer (assuming that there are no grounds for a summary dismissal). The first is to negotiate an early termination with the employee. Some financial incentive may be offered, or the employee may simply be happy to be released from his obligations sooner rather than later. There is no legal obstacle to this course, because s 86(3) of the *ERA 1996* permits the employee to waive his right even to the statutory minimum period of notice (or to accept a payment in lieu of notice).

The second option is for the employer to pay the employee wages in lieu of notice. This course is frequently adopted. However, it should be borne in mind that to dismiss an employee with pay in lieu rather than to give due notice is in fact to dismiss wrongfully. The true legal analysis of this situation is that there is a summary dismissal carried out in breach of contract, and the wages paid in lieu in fact represent a payment of damages for that breach of contract (see *Gothard v Mirror Group Newspapers Ltd* [1988] IRLR 396). In some cases, the fact that the dismissal is theoretically wrongful may be of no practical significance. But that will not always be so. For instance, the dismissed employee may have a residual claim for the value of lost benefits in kind during the notice period. (See, for example, *Silvey v Pendragon plc* [2001] EWCA Civ 784, [2001] IRLR 685, where the early termination deprived an employee of enhanced pension rights. Even though the employee had accepted pay in lieu of notice, the Court of Appeal held that the loss of these pension rights was recoverable as damages for wrongful dismissal). The wrongful dismissal may also prevent the employer from relying upon restrictive covenants in the contract of employment (see 58.34 below).

An employee has no statutory or common law right to be paid in lieu of notice (*Rowley v Cerberus Software Ltd* [2001] EWCA Civ 78, [2001] ICR 376; *Hardy v Polk (Leeds) Ltd* [2004] IRLR 420, [2004] All ER (D) 282 (May). However, provision may be made by contract. In order to avoid the problems of the 'theoretically wrongful' dismissal described above, many service agreements now incorporate a clause which gives the employer the option of terminating the contract lawfully by making a payment in lieu of notice instead of actually giving notice. Such a clause ought to define clearly whether the payment is to be based upon basic pay only, or whether the calculation is also to have regard to other elements of the remuneration package, and whether the payment is to be made gross or net of tax. Summary termination pursuant to a provision of this kind does not constitute a breach of contract (*Rex Stewart Jeffries Parker Ginsberg Ltd v Parker* [1988] IRLR 483).

Where the employer exercises the right to terminate the contract with a payment in lieu of notice, the employee is under no obligation to give credit for actual or imputed earnings during what would have been the notice period. In other words, there is no duty on the employee to mitigate loss (as to which, see 58.30 below). He is entitled to claim for the full sum due to him under the contract as a debt (*Abrahams v Performing Rights Society* [1995] ICR 1028).

The sum paid to the employee in lieu of notice will be taxable in his hands under Schedule E (*EMI Group Electronics Ltd v Coldicott (Inspector of Taxes)* [1999] IRLR 630).

Merely because a contract of employment contains a payment in lieu clause, however, does not mean that every termination will be treated as if the employer exercised the right to dismiss and then make the payment in lieu without any deduction for mitigation. Much will depend on the precise wording of the contract. In *Gregory v Wallace* [1998] IRLR 387, the Court of Appeal held that, on the facts, the employer did not exercise the right to make a payment in lieu, where notice of termination had to be in writing and termination had been oral. Instead, the employer was treated as having dismissed the employee wrongfully and in breach of contract.

In *Cerberus Software Ltd v Rowley* [2001] ICR 376, on the other hand, where the contract stated that the employer 'may' make a payment in lieu of notice to the employee. The Court of Appeal held that this gave the employer the choice whether or not to make the payment.

There is no breach of contract even if it is the employee who has originally given notice, and the employer who then brings the employment to an immediate end with a payment in lieu (*Marshall (Cambridge) Ltd v Hamblin* [1994] IRLR 260). In *Hamblin* it was also held that the employment could be lawfully terminated with a payment in lieu of salary only, notwithstanding that the employee typically received a high proportion of his remuneration from commission; however, the EAT's reasoning is hard to follow and may depend upon the fact that the payment of commission was held to be discretionary and not a contractual right.

The third option is for the employee to be put on so-called 'garden leave'. This means that notice is duly given and the employee continues to be paid and to receive his full contractual benefits but he is not required or permitted to attend for work. This may be achieved by an express garden leave clause or, in certain circumstances, by 'implying' such a clause into the contract.

The power to place an employee on garden leave will not be implied if the refusal to provide work would constitute a repudiatory breach of contract. There will be a repudiatory breach if the contractual consideration moving from the employer includes an obligation to permit the employee to perform work but not if the contractual consideration is confined to payment of remuneration only (*Collier v Sunday Referee Publishing Co Ltd* [1940] 2 KB 647).

The Court of Appeal has acknowledged that employees increasingly regard work itself as important to them, and not just remuneration (*William Hill Organisation Ltd v Tucker* [1999] ICR 291). Moreover, it held that whether there is an obligation to provide work, rather than merely pay, will depend on a careful construction of the contractual arrangements. Of particular importance will be whether the position of the employee was 'specific and unique'; and whether the employee has some skill which will be lost if not practised. Other factors may be whether the contractual remuneration consists in part of a commission which depends upon work actually done (see e g *Devonald v Rosser & Sons* [1906] 2 KB 728). See also *Langston v AUEW* [1974] ICR 180, 510; *Breach v Epsylon Industries Ltd* [1976] ICR 316; *Spencer v Marchington* [1988] IRLR 392; *SBJ Stephenson Ltd v Mandy* [2000] IRLR 233 (no obligation to provide work to a divisional director of an insurance brokerage).

It should be borne in mind, however, that the existence of an express garden leave clause may be taken into account by a court in determining the validity of any post-termination restraints on the employee (*Credit Suisse Asset Management Ltd v Armstrong* [1996] ICR 882; see further RESTRAINT OF TRADE (41)).

58.22 ANTICIPATORY BREACHES OF CONTRACT

It is important to remember that a breach of contract, in this as in other contexts, may be either *actual* or *anticipatory*. An anticipatory breach of contract occurs where there has not yet been any actual breach, because the time for performance of the relevant obligation has not yet arrived, but one party has indicated a clear refusal to perform the contract, or has made it impossible for himself to fulfil his obligations when the time comes. In the case of an employment contract, this might occur, for example, if the employer announced that the employee's salary would be unilaterally reduced by a significant amount the following month.

Where an anticipatory breach of contract occurs, and it is sufficiently serious to be repudiatory, the innocent party is faced with a choice. First, he may immediately accept the breach as bringing the contract to an end, and sue for damages. Secondly, he may keep the contract alive, and continue to call for performance by the other party. Thus, in the example above, the employee could immediately resign and sue for damages for wrongful dismissal. Alternatively, he could continue to assert his right to be paid a full salary the following month, which would give the employer an opportunity to change his mind; if the salary was indeed reduced, then the employee would at that point have to choose between resigning and affirming the contract, as discussed in 58.6 above. In the latter event, he might also be able to sue in debt for arrears of salary, as discussed in 58.24 below.

It has been suggested that an anticipatory breach, as opposed to an actual breach of contract, will not be repudiatory if it stems from an innocent mistake on the part of the party in breach as to what the contract requires of him (see *Frank Wright (Holdings) Ltd v Punch* [1980] IRLR 217; *United Bank Ltd v Akhtar* [1989] IRLR 507; and *Brown v JBD Engineering Ltd* [1993] IRLR 568).

58.23 REMEDIES FOR WRONGFUL DISMISSAL

Remedies other than claims for damages

Injunctions

If the employee moves swiftly, he may be able to obtain an injunction restraining the employer from dismissing him wrongfully. However, it is unusual for the court to agree to insist upon performance of a contract of employment, because of the personal relationship between employer and employee without which the contract cannot properly function. Nevertheless, the breakdown of the relationship of trust and confidence will not automatically prevent an employee from obtaining injunctive relief (see *Jan Gryf-Lowczowski v Hinchinbrooke Healthcare NHS Trust* [2005] EWHC 2407 (QB), [2006] IRLR 100 (see further CONTRACT OF EMPLOY-MENT (8)).

58.24   *Claims in debt*

If the employer's breach of contract consists of the failure to pay a sum of money that is due, for example by imposing a reduction in salary, the employee's sole choice is not between resigning and claiming to have been wrongfully dismissed on the one hand, and accepting the reduced salary on the other. Rather, he may choose to affirm the contract of employment despite the employer's breach, yet continue to assert his entitlement to the unpaid moneys, and sue in debt for those moneys if they remain unpaid. For examples, see the decisions of the House of Lords in *Rigby v Ferodo Ltd* [1988] ICR 29 and the EAT in *Bruce v Wiggins Teape (Stationery) Ltd* [1994] IRLR 536.

58.25   **Actions for damages for wrongful dismissal**

General approach to assessment of damages

The basic principle in assessing the damages payable for wrongful dismissal is that the employee must be put into the same position as if the employer had properly performed the contract. However, it is to be assumed for these purposes that the employer would have performed the contract in the way least burdensome to himself, and would have minimised his obligations to the employee by giving due notice to terminate the contract at the earliest opportunity (see *Lavarack v Woods of Colchester Ltd* [1967] 1 QB 278 and *Clark v BET plc* [1997] IRLR 348, though see *Horkulak v Cantor Fitzgerald International* [2005] ICR 402. In that case, the Court of Appeal held that the rule did not apply to the failure to make discretionary bonus payments where the employer is contractually obliged to exercise his discretion rationally and in good faith. In those circumstances, the Court will look to see what bonus the employee probably would have received if he had continued in employment, rather than the minimum sum that his employer might have awarded him consistent with his contractual obligation to act rationally and in good faith).

Two main consequences follow from this basic principle. First, the court will have to ask itself how much better off the employee would have been if he had been given proper notice on the date when he was wrongfully dismissed (or if notice which had already been given had been allowed to run its course). This will normally mean that the *prima facie* measure of the damages is the net amount of the employee's salary and benefits for the notice period. In the case of a fixed term contract, the equivalent period is of course the unexpired portion of the term remaining as at the date of dismissal.

Second, the court (unlike an employment tribunal assessing compensation for unfair dismissal) will only compensate the employee for the loss of benefits to which he was contractually entitled, and not for those which he would probably have received in practice but to which he had no legal right (*Laverack*, above). It may also be necessary to consider questions of causation arising upon the particular facts of a given case. For example, the employer may be able to prove upon a balance of probabilities that the employee would have left his job voluntarily within the notice period in any event, or that an employee dismissed because of long-term absence through sickness would have remained off work throughout the notice period and would therefore have earned nothing during that period.

Where the wrongfulness of the dismissal stems from a failure to follow a proper procedure (see 57.18 above), damages should be awarded on the basis that notice could lawfully have been given on the day when the necessary procedures, if followed, could have been concluded (*Gunton v Richmond-upon-Thames London Borough Council* [1980] ICR 755; see also *Alexander v Standard Telephones and Cables Ltd (No 2)* [1991] IRLR 286 and *Boyo v Lambeth London Borough Council* [1994] ICR 727). The court will not speculate as to whether or not the employee would have remained in employment if the disciplinary procedure had been followed (*Focsa Services (UK) Ltd v Birkett* [1996] IRLR 325; *Janciuk v Winerite Ltd* [1998] IRLR 63; *Wise Group v Mitchell* [2005] ICR 896).

58.26 *'Liquidated damages' clauses and other provisions for termination payments*

Sometimes a service agreement may contain a provision that the employer is to pay a specified sum, or a sum calculated in a specified way, to the employee if the employment comes to an end in particular circumstances.

If the employee seeks to enforce such a provision, a basic question which may arise is whether the clause is a penalty clause. If so, the court will not give effect to it, and the employee will simply have to sue for damages in the normal way (assuming that he has been wrongfully dismissed). In order to decide whether a particular provision is indeed a penalty clause, it is necessary to apply a two-stage test.

First, does the clause apply where there has been a breach of contract? A provision which provides for a particular sum to be payable upon an occurrence which does *not* amount to a breach of contract cannot be a penalty clause. If the triggering event may or may not amount to a breach of contract depending upon the circumstances, the court will ask whether there was a breach of contract in the case in question. Thus, a provision in a contract of employment that, if the employer gave due notice to terminate the contract, he would pay £1,000 to the employee could not be a penalty clause, because there would be no breach of contract in circumstances to which it applied. If the contract provided for the employer to pay £1,000 if he dismissed *without* due notice, then that could be a penalty clause, depending upon the application of the second stage of the test (see below). If the provision was for £1,000 to be paid in any case in which the employee was dismissed, then that might amount to a penalty clause, but only in a case in which the dismissal was in fact wrongful. For these somewhat anomalous distinctions, see *Export Credit Guarantee Department v Universal Oil Products Co* [1983] 1 WLR 399.

Assuming that the provision operates upon a breach of contract (as will be the case if one is dealing with a wrongful dismissal), the second stage of the test is to ask whether it represents a genuine pre-estimate of the loss suffered (in which case it is a valid liquidated damages clause, and will be enforced), or whether it is in effect designed to terrorise the other party into performing the contract (see *Dunlop Pneumatic Tyre Co Ltd v New Garage and Motor Co Ltd* [1915] AC 79). A comparison between the amount that would be payable on breach with the loss which might be sustained is, however, merely a 'guide' as to whether the clause is penal. Thus, in *Murray v Leisureplay plc* [2005] EWCA Civ 963, [2005] IRLR 946, the Court of Appeal overturned the trial judge's finding that a clause requiring the payment of one year's gross salary in the event of wrongful termination was a 'penalty', emphasising Lord Dunedin's approach in *Dunlop* that a clause 'will be held to be a penalty if the sum stipulated for is extravagant and unconscionable in amount in comparison with the greatest loss that could conceivably be provided to have followed from the breach.' On the facts of the case, the Court held that the clause was 'generous' but 'not unconscionable', and did not meet the test of 'extravagance'. The Court held that it was appropriate for the remuneration package to provide 'generous reassurance against the consequences of dismissal.'

The difference between a liquidated damages clause and a penalty clause was considered in *Giraud UK Ltd v Smith* [2000] IRLR 763, a case that illustrates that an employee may be liable for damages if he gives short notice. In that case, the contract of employment provided that if an employee failed to give his contractual notice when resigning, it would result in a deduction from his wages equivalent to the number of days short. The EAT upheld the decision of the employment tribunal that this was a penalty clause (and thus invalid). It was not a liquidated damages clause because it was not a genuine pre-estimate of the loss to the employer if the employee failed to give proper notice. Further, it did not prohibit the employer from seeking further damages through the courts greater than that specified in the clause. There was evidence to suggest that the employer could easily find replacements for the employee in question (he was a lorry driver). In the circumstances, therefore, the clause enabled the employer to say 'Heads I win, tails you lose!'

The advantage of a valid liquidated damages clause is that, in a case where liability for wrongful dismissal is accepted, it may enable the parties to avoid costly and lengthy litigation involving disputes about the precise valuation of benefits and the adequacy of attempts at mitigation (cf *Abrahams* above).

58.27 *Rights of employee in period of notice*

As set out in 58.16 above, s 86 of the *ERA 1996* provides for statutory minimum notice periods. *Section 87(1), ERA 1996* provides that, if an employer gives notice of dismissal to an employee who has been continuously employed for at least one month, then during the statutory minimum period, the employee will enjoy the rights conferred by *ss 88 to 91, ERA 1996*.

The importance for present purposes of the rights conferred by these provisions is that they are to be taken into account in assessing any claim for damages for wrongful dismissal (*ERA 1996, s 91(5)*). In other words, when assessing what the employee would have received if the employer had performed his minimum obligations, it is necessary to take account not only of his contractual obligations, but of these statutory obligations as well.

The principal right conferred by these statutory provisions is for the employee to be paid in cases where he is ready and willing to work, but no work is provided for him by his employer, or where the employee is absent from work through sickness, pregnancy or being on holiday. This would include employees absent on long-term ill-health grounds. The precise qualifications for payment, and the amount to which the employee is entitled, are the subject of detailed provisions.

Where sums which should have been payable pursuant to these provisions fall to be taken into account in assessing damages, they are subject to reduction for mitigation in the usual way (*Westwood v Secretary of State for Employment* [1985] ICR 209).

It is significant to note that these rights do not apply where the contractual period of notice exceeds the statutory minimum period by at least one week (*ERA 1996, s 87(4)*). This point was highlighted in *Budd v Scotts Co (UK) Ltd* [2003] IRLR 145, where the employee's contractual notice period exceeded the statutory period. The EAT held that the employee was not entitled to be paid for his contractual notice period as he was sick throughout and was not capable of working. By contrast, he would have been paid for the entire period if the contractual notice period had been the same or less than the statutory period.

58.28 *Valuation of particular benefits*

Salary. This will normally be straightforward to calculate, since it will simply be a question of applying the rate of pay enjoyed by the claimant at the date of dismissal to the length of the notice period. Sometimes the employee is entitled to an annual increase either of a set amount, or related to the prevailing rate of inflation, and such an entitlement must of course be built into the calculation if the notice period extends beyond the date upon which the next increase was due (*Re Crowther & Nicholson Ltd* (1981) Times, 10 June).

Where the contract provides for an annual increase but the amount of the increase is in the absolute discretion of the employer, the employer will be obliged to exercise that discretion in good faith and not capriciously (*Clark*, above). Perhaps more commonly, the contract may stipulate that salary will be reviewed on an annual basis. However, in *Runciman v Walter Runciman plc* [1992] BCLC 1084 the court refused to award any damages to represent the loss of a chance that such a review would have led to a salary increase.

Bonuses and commission. Where the employee was entitled to receive a bonus or commission as part of his remuneration, the court will have to assess what the value of that entitlement would have been if the employee had remained employed through the notice period. Sometimes an exact figure will be readily ascertainable, as where the bonus depends upon the pre-tax profits of a large company, whose profits for the relevant period have already been declared and cannot have been significantly affected by the absence of the claimant. In other cases, such as where the employee was entitled to a percentage of the value of sales which he himself achieved, the court will have to make the best estimate possible of what would have happened if due notice had been given. It will consider, for example, evidence of past performance by that employee, and performance by other employees during the relevant period as compared with their own past performance. In yet other cases, the court may be required to assess the employer's likely profits in years which are yet to come, in which case expert evidence is likely to be required if the claim is of any size. Where an employer operates a discretionary bonus scheme an employee who has a contractual entitlement to participate in that scheme is entitled to a bona fide and rational exercise of discretion by his employer as to whether or not he receives his bonus and in what sum (*Clark v Nomura International plc* [2000] IRLR 766, EAT; *Horkulak v Cantor Fitzgerald International* [2005] ICR 402). In deciding how much compensation to award an employee where his employer has failed to exercise its discretion rationally and in good faith, the court may take into account the range of bonus payments made to other employees. The court is not obliged to award the employee the minimum bonus that the employer could lawfully have paid if it is not fair and reasonable to do so (see *Horkulak*).

Share options. The effect of dismissal may be that the employee loses the right to exercise share options which he holds, or that he is compelled to exercise them within a shorter timescale than would otherwise have been the case, with adverse implications for the differential between the exercise price and the market price of the shares. Where this is so, and where there is no valid exclusion clause in respect of liability for such loss (see 58.37 below), the court will have to assess the value of the shares which the employee could otherwise have obtained, less what it would have cost him to acquire them.

Cars. Company cars often represent a substantial head of loss, although for any damages to be recoverable it is obviously essential that the claimant should have been permitted to make some personal use of the car.

There are a number of possible ways in which the loss may be assessed. If the employee has actually had to hire a replacement car, and has acted reasonably in doing so, then the hire charges should be recoverable. Alternatively, a fairly rough and ready lump sum may be awarded.

More commonly, however, the court will be invited to have regard either to the value which the Inland Revenue places upon the car for tax purposes, or to the AA's estimated running costs. The Revenue scales, which are based on size or value, age and mileage, were formerly not much relied upon by employees, because the tax treatment of such benefits was generous, and did not reflect their true value. More recently, changes in policy have made the Revenue scales a better and fairer guide.

The AA estimates provided the basis of valuation adopted by the court in *Shove v Downs Surgical plc* [1984] ICR 532. They are annual figures comprising standing charges and running costs per mile for various sizes of car and a given annual mileage.

Clearly, whatever basis of valuation is adopted, it is necessary to examine the terms of the contract (either express, or implied through practice) as to what costs associated with running the car were to be met by the employer, and which by the employee. In particular, it is necessary to know which party was responsible for meeting the cost of petrol for private use.

Pensions. The loss of pension contributions, or pension rights, is also in many cases an extremely important head of damages.

Insurance cover. It is commonplace for employees to be contractually entitled to the benefit of free medical insurance, permanent health insurance and the like, both for themselves and for their families.

The value of such benefits is frequently assessed as if it could be equated with the cost to the employer of providing the insurance cover, and this may be convenient when the sums at stake are small. However, it is not a strictly accurate approach. If the employee has in fact obtained replacement cover, then the loss suffered is the reasonable cost to him of doing so (and an individual may have to pay more than a company purchasing the same cover on a group basis). However, if the employee has chosen not to take out such insurance himself, then he suffers no loss (save, perhaps for the 'peace of mind' which the employee previously enjoyed, knowing that insurance coverage was in place) unless during the relevant period some event occurs which would have led to the making of a payment under the policy, had it still been in force. In that event, there may be arguments as to whether the whole amount of the lost payment is recoverable, or whether the employee should have mitigated his loss by obtaining replacement cover.

It is also necessary to bear in mind that, depending upon the basis on which the insurance is arranged and paid for, the period for which cover is lost through the wrongful dismissal (or replacement cover has to be purchased) may not exactly correspond to the period between the dismissal and the date when due notice would have expired.

Holidays. The conventional view is that the right to paid holiday is not a separate compensatable head of loss, since the pay which would have been received is covered by the claim for lost salary. However, it is at least arguable that the opportunity to receive that salary, without having to work for it, is itself a valuable benefit, and that the salary payable in respect of the relevant period is the appropriate measure of that value. The counter-argument is that the wrongfully dismissed employee in effect finds himself enjoying a good deal of holiday time, whether he likes it or not. On the other hand, he is not truly on holiday (because he has a continuing duty to look for ways of mitigating his loss), and he may find other employment which offers the same pay but less generous holiday arrangements.

Accommodation. If it was a contractual benefit that the employee should be provided with free or cheap accommodation, and the employee has had to vacate that accommodation as a result of the dismissal, then the cost of finding alternative accommodation for the duration of the notice period is a recoverable head of loss.

Sometimes employees who have lost accommodation seek to claim for their removal expenses. However, it is unlikely that such expenses are properly recoverable in most cases, since the employee would have had to leave the accommodation in due course even if proper notice had been given.

Miscellaneous. In advising employees with wrongful dismissal claims, it is important to ensure that all contractual benefits have been identified and claims made for their value. Other than the common and valuable benefits discussed above, benefits in kind may include, for example, meals, payment of telephone bills and the use of a mobile phone, discounts on particular products (such as mortgages for bank employees), and personal use of credit cards offering preferential interest rates. See also 58.33 below for loss of the right to complain of unfair dismissal.

However, a right to reimbursement of expenses only represents a head of loss if the expenses in question were not confined to expenditure incurred for the purposes of the job (the point being that such expenditure will cease to be incurred once the job is lost).

In all cases, it is wise to be sure that benefits have been properly declared to tax before they are introduced into the calculation of loss, lest an argument be put forward that the contract is void for illegality (see 58.35 below).

A claim for damages for wrongful dismissal will often be combined with a claim in debt for wages accrued to the date of dismissal, and for accrued holiday pay if that is a contractual right. Claims in debt are not subject to the obligation to mitigate. Nor can the employer avoid paying accrued wages even if there was misconduct prior to the dismissal which justified summary termination (*Healey v Francaise Rubestic SA* [1917] 1 KB 946). Wages accrue on a daily basis and an employee will normally be entitled to claim an apportionment of wages for a period worked even where he has been summarily dismissed before his salary became due under the terms of his contract: *Item Software (UK) Ltd v Fassihi* [2002] EWHC 3116 (Ch), [2003] IRLR 769.

58.29 *Compensation for distress and other intangible loss*

The normal rule is that in an action for breach of contract, including an action for wrongful dismissal, it is not possible to recover damages for distress or injured feelings for the manner of the breach (*Addis v Gramophone Co Ltd* [1909] AC 488; *Johnson v Unisys Ltd* [2001] UKHL 13, [2001] ICR 480).

Further, while an employee may recover damages at common law for a breach of the implied term of trust and confidence occurring prior to a dismissal, the House of Lords has held that such a claim cannot be made in respect of the dismissal itself, for this would impinge on the statutory right not to be unfairly dismissed, the jurisdictional and compensatory limits for which have been determined by Parliament (*Johnson*, ibid). Their Lordships considered this boundary, which they called 'the *Johnson* exclusionary area', again in *McCabe v Cornwall County Council* [2004] UKHL 35; [2004] IRLR 733. Their Lordships affirmed the decision in *Johnson*, but expressed dissatisfaction with the boundary line drawn. Lord Steyn, noting that the reasoning of a number of their Lordships in *Johnson* had been underpinned by an assumption that compensation for non-pecuniary loss was available in unfair dismissal, suggested that the issue ought to be revisited in the light of the decision of the House in *Dunnachie v Kingston-Upon-Hull City Council* [2004] UKHL 36, [2004] IRLR 727. (In *Dunnachie*, their Lordships ruled that compensation for unfair dismissal was strictly limited to compensation for pecuniary loss: see generally 55.12 UNFAIR DISMISSAL – III.) Lord Nicholls, however, observed (at para 33) that the whole issue required the 'urgent attention' of Parliament.

It is possible, however, to recover damages for loss of reputation or future prospects on the labour market (in actions for wrongful dismissal or breach of contract – where the breach is not known until after termination) where the employer is in breach of the duty of trust and confidence: so-called 'stigma damages' (*Malik v BCCI SA* [1997] ICR 606). Recovery of stigma damages will probably be rare, however, as the employee is required to establish not only that there was a breach of the duty, but that the requirements of causation and remoteness are also satisfied. In the *Malik* case it was assumed for the purposes of argument that the employer bank operated its business in a corrupt and dishonest way; that its corruption and dishonesty were widely known; and that the employees were at a handicap on the labour market as they were tainted by their connection with the employer. At trial, however, none of the former employees were able to establish that the employer's breach caused them any financial loss, as they could not demonstrate that the bank's wrongdoing blighted their job prospects (*Bank of Credit and Commerce International SA v Ali* [1999] IRLR 508).

Damages for the loss of future employment prospects may be more readily available where the contract is one of apprenticeship (*Dunk v George Waller & Son Ltd* [1970] 2 QB 163), or where (as with the engagement of an actor) part of its purpose is to provide publicity for the employee (*Clayton and Waller Ltd v Oliver* [1930] AC 209).

58.30 *Mitigation and collateral benefits*

An employee who has been wrongfully dismissed is under a duty to mitigate his loss by seeking alternative sources of income. Any other income received during the notice period in relation to which the employee is being compensated will normally have to be taken into account so as to reduce the loss suffered.

The dismissed employee's obligation is to act reasonably. The principles applied in wrongful dismissal cases are very similar to those applicable in assessing compensation for unfair dismissal, and reference should also be made to the discussion in UNFAIR DISMISSAL – III (55).

The claimant's obligation to mitigate ought not to be treated as imposing too heavy an obligation upon him, and the burden of proving a failure to mitigate is upon the defendant (*Fyfe v Scientific Furnishings Ltd* [1989] ICR 648). In the first instance, it will probably (depending upon all the circumstances) be reasonable for the employee to seek to find employment of a status and at a salary commensurate with that which he lost upon being dismissed. However, if time goes by without other work being found, the court will expect him to lower his sights. Employees must certainly expect to provide cogent justification for refusing any jobs which are actually offered to them. How far afield in geographical terms a dismissed employee must seek for work in order to be acting reasonably will depend upon his age, the nature of his work, and his personal and domestic circumstances.

It is often advisable for the claimant employee to be able to show that he has pursued all the available avenues of job-seeking, such as registration with agencies and Jobcentres, perusal of job advertisements in general and specialist publications, and use of consultants or outplacement services; not all these possibilities will be appropriate in all cases, however. Copies of all letters written and other relevant documents should be retained, and a record kept of relevant telephone conversations.

It has become increasingly common in large wrongful dismissal claims for expert evidence to be given by recruitment consultants, who use their experience of the relevant industrial sectors to estimate when, and with what remuneration package, a person in the claimant's position should have been able to obtain alternative employment (see, for example, *Clark*, above).

Seeking employment is not the only reasonable means by which a dismissed employee may seek to mitigate his loss. In an appropriate case he may seek to set up his own business or to work in a self-employed or freelance capacity (*Gardiner-Hill v Roland Beiger Technics Ltd* [1982] IRLR 498). Only in an exceptional case, however, would it be held that a claimant had acted unreasonably in *failing* to go into business on his own account. It is more doubtful that there has been proper mitigation where a claimant chooses to undertake further education or retraining instead of seeking work, unless his or her existing skills are very unlikely to lead to a new job.

If the circumstances of the dismissal have been acrimonious, or have involved bad faith or unreasonable conduct on the part of the employer, it is unlikely that the employee will be held to have acted unreasonably if he rejects an offer of new employment made by that employer (see e g *Shindler v Northern Raincoat Co Ltd* [1960] 1 WLR 1038). Nor, it appears, is it an unreasonable failure to mitigate if the employee fails to invoke an internal appeal procedure (*Lock v Connell Estate Agents* [1994] IRLR 444). However, a failure to complete the statutory grievance procedure in *Sch 2* to the *Employment Act 2002* will mean that a tribunal will reduce any damages awarded (*s 31*) or even prevent the employee from bringing a claim altogether (*s 32*). See generally 54.10 UNFAIR DISMISSAL – II.

Expenses reasonably incurred in attempting to mitigate loss may be deducted from the fruits of the mitigation or added to the loss suffered as the case may be.

Moneys received during the notice period which have to be deducted from wrongful dismissal damages include not only income from a new job, but also any payments already made by the defendant on account of the dismissal, and state benefits (*Parsons v BNM Laboratories Ltd* [1964] 1 QB 95; but it was held in *Westwood v Secretary of State for Employment* [1985] ICR 209 that unemployment benefit should not be taken into account if the entitlement to it runs out whilst the employee is still out of work after the end of the notice period). However, the employee does not have to give credit for any benefits received from insurance policies which pay out in the event of unemployment, or for a pension which becomes payable upon the dismissal (*Hopkins v Norcros plc* [1994] ICR 11).

Nor does the employee have to give credit for the fact that he works shorter hours in his new job, or receives longer holidays than beforehand (*Potter v Arafa* [1995] IRLR 316).

58.31   *Interest and accelerated receipt*

Depending upon the length of the notice period or fixed term contract, and how long it takes for the wrongful dismissal claim to be brought to trial, the claimant may find either that he has suffered a loss through being deprived of the use and benefit of his salary for the period between the dismissal and the trial, or that he gains because the award of damages is in his pocket much sooner than the salary which it represents would have been paid.

Accordingly, that part of the award of damages which represents salary which ought to have been paid in the past will normally carry an award of interest. The discretionary power of the High Court to award interest is found in *s 35A* of the *Supreme Court Act 1981*, and that of the county court in *s 69* of the *County Courts Act 1984*. The rate and period of interest, as well as whether to award it at all, are in the court's discretion. However, the award will always be of simple interest; it will generally run from the date when payment should have been made until the date of judgment, unless the claimant has been culpably slow in prosecuting the proceedings; and it will frequently reflect the judgment rate of interest over the relevant period (currently 8%).

Where damages are being received earlier than the payments for whose loss they compensate were due, it is normal for a percentage discount to be applied on account of accelerated receipt, generally reflecting the anticipated rate of inflation over the relevant period.

Sometimes, where the award of damages covers a very long period, the percentage discount may be increased (or a further discount applied) to take account of the so-called 'vicissitudes of life' – in other words, the intangible chance that the claimant might never have served the full notice period because he fell ill, chose to depart, or encountered the proverbial number 57 bus. It is not thought that any very large discount is generally appropriate on this score.

58.32   *Taxation of damages*

The ultimate objective of the award of damages, as explained above, is to put the claimant into exactly the same position as if the contract had been duly performed. In that event, he would of course have been paid his salary net of tax and national insurance contributions, and would have had to pay tax upon most benefits in kind. However, simply to deduct tax and national insurance from the gross loss would be too simplistic an approach, because the award of damages will itself be subject to tax in the hands of the employee. A further complication is that the damages will only be taxed insofar as they exceed the tax-free allowance of £30,000 which applies to compensation payments for loss of office. The principal relevant taxing provisions are contained in *Part 6* of the *Income tax (Earnings and Pensions) Act 2003*. Employers are required to report to the Inland Revenue details of any award of payment and/or benefits upon termination of an employment contract where the total amount of the award exceeds £30,000 (*Income Tax (Pay as You Earn) Regulations 2003 (SI 2003/2682), regs 91 to 93*).

In *Richardson (Inspector of Taxes) v Delaney* [2001] IRLR 663, the court held that payments made by way of a negotiated settlement after proper notice of termination had been given were taxable in full, and that the £30,000 exemption did not apply. The exemption only applies where there has been a breach of contract and the sum payable to the former employee is referable to that breach.

The correct approach is therefore for the court to ascertain the net sum which the employee ought ultimately to receive, and to gross that amount up until it has arrived at a grossed-up sum which, when the damages are taxed, will reduce again to the correct net sum. Authority for this grossing-up procedure is to be found in *Stewart v Glentaggart* 1963 SLT 119 and *Shove v Downs Surgical plc* [1984] ICR 532. In order to ensure the correct application of tax rates, bands and allowances, it may be necessary to have details of the employee's income from all sources.

Similar principles should apply where one is calculating a settlement figure rather than an award of damages. However, an employer who pays a grossed-up sum by way of settlement should first ensure either that the Inland Revenue is content for moneys to be paid gross and taxed in the employee's hands, or that the employee has agreed as part of the settlement to reimburse the employer for any demand for tax upon the sums paid which may subsequently be made.

58.33 *Relationship with compensation for unfair dismissal*

An employee who has been both wrongfully and unfairly dismissed cannot be compensated twice for the same loss. However, there are a number of important respects in which the rules governing the compensatory award for unfair dismissal differ from those governing damages for wrongful dismissal. In particular: damages for wrongful dismissal are essentially limited to the notice period, whereas compensation for unfair dismissal may in principle extend indefinitely; in wrongful dismissal only strict contractual rights are taken into account, whereas the employment tribunal may allow for other benefits and heads of loss (e g likely future pay increases, discretionary bonuses, loss of statutory rights); and the compensatory award in unfair dismissal may not exceed a statutory maximum.

Therefore, if an employee who has already received damages for wrongful dismissal goes on to obtain a ruling from an employment tribunal that he has been unfairly dismissed, he may ask for compensation (up to the statutory maximum) representing his loss beyond the notice period and his non-contractual benefits within the notice period.

If an employee who has already been compensated for unfair dismissal brings an action for wrongful dismissal, the court must examine the way in which that compensation has been calculated, and deduct from the wrongful dismissal damages those elements already covered by the tribunal award. The same will apply where the unfair dismissal claim has been settled by payment of a sum to the former employee (*Aspden* — see 58.19 above). However, if the sum actually awarded by the tribunal has been capped at the statutory maximum, it will frequently not be possible to say whether the award actually received represents one sort of loss rather than another. In that situation, the court will therefore not make any deduction from the damages which it awards (*O'Laoire v Jackel International Ltd (No 2)* [1991] ICR 718).

A summary dismissal, albeit wrongful, is nonetheless effective to terminate the employment at once (subject to the question of acceptance of the breach, as to which see 58.7 above). It is not generally possible for an employee to complain of unfair dismissal unless he has been continuously employed for one year prior to the effective date of termination (see UNFAIR DISMISSAL – I (53)). Hence it is possible that the effect of a wrongful dismissal may be to deprive the employee of an unfair dismissal claim, if the absence of due notice or proper application of contractual disciplinary procedures makes the difference to whether there is the necessary period of service prior to termination. However, an employee cannot claim that lost right of complaint as a head of damages in the wrongful dismissal proceedings (*Harper v Virgin Net Ltd* [2004] EWCA Civ 271, [2005] ICR 921; applied in *Wise Group v Mitchell* [2005] ICR 896).

58.34   EFFECT OF A WRONGFUL DISMISSAL UPON OTHER CONTRACTUAL OBLIGATIONS

If the employee is wrongfully dismissed, the effect will normally be to release him from any further performance of his own contractual obligations, even those which are expressed to continue after the termination of the employment. In particular, this means that the employer will be unable to enforce any restrictive covenants contained in the contract of employment (*General Billposting Co Ltd v Atkinson* [1909] AC 118; *Rock Refrigeration Ltd v Jones* [1996] IRLR 675).

However, an arbitration clause will normally remain enforceable even after a wrongful dismissal.

58.35   POSSIBLE DEFENCES TO A WRONGFUL DISMISSAL CLAIM

Illegality

No action may be brought upon a contract which is treated as illegal upon grounds of public policy. In the employment context, this most frequently applies to situations where the employer and employee have colluded to evade the payment of income tax. For a fuller account, see CONTRACTS OF EMPLOYMENT (8) and UNFAIR DISMISSAL – I (53).

58.36   Invalidity of contract

The employer may seek to argue that the contract, or some of its terms, were never validly entered into. This might arise, for example, if the employer was a local authority, and contended that entry into the contract had for some reason been *ultra vires*. Alternatively, a limited company might contend that a director's contract of employment had been concluded in a way which was not in accordance with the company's articles of association, or that the contract had been concluded for an improper purpose (for example, if members of the board of directors voted to grant each other long fixed term contracts in order to protect their own positions in advance of an anticipated takeover). See *Re W and M Roith Ltd* [1967] 1 WLR 432; *Guinness plc v Saunders* [1990] 2 AC 663; and *Runciman v Walter Runciman plc* [1992] BCLC 1084.

58.37   Exclusion clauses

It is not common to find in a contract of employment provisions purporting to exclude or limit the employer's liability for wrongful dismissal (although share option schemes often provide that no sum in respect of lost opportunities under the scheme is to be awarded by way of compensation for dismissal). Although no such provision could effectively exclude compensation for statutory rights (see UNFAIR DISMISSAL – I (53)), there is no reason in principle why a contract should not seek to exclude or limit liability for wrongful dismissal or other possible contractual claims.

An employee faced with such an exclusion clause, however, might seek to argue that it was subject to the controls laid down by the *Unfair Contract Terms*

Act 1977 (UCTA). If *UCTA* applied, then the clause would be upheld only insofar as it satisfied the requirement of reasonableness at the time when the contract was made.

For a discussion of the applicability of *UCTA* to contracts of employment, and the reasons why it does not apply to share option exclusions of the kind mentioned above, see CONTRACTS OF EMPLOYMENT (8). It is unclear in what circumstances a clause excluding or limiting liability for wrongful dismissal might be considered reasonable. The most promising situation would be one where a senior executive with an opportunity to take his own advice freely chose to accept a limitation clause as part of an otherwise generous contract. In the context of a claim for wrongful dismissal, it is necessary to consider the case of *Brigden v American Express Bank Ltd* [2000] IRLR 94. In that case, it was held that a clause in a contract of employment under which an employee could be dismissed by notice and/or payment in lieu of notice during the first two years of employment without implementation of the employer's contractual disciplinary procedure did not contravene *UCTA*, albeit it was held that *UCTA* applied to the contract.

58.38   **PROCEDURAL ASPECTS OF WRONGFUL DISMISSAL CLAIMS**

Choice of court

Until recently, and subject to the possibility of arbitration, it has been necessary to bring an action for wrongful dismissal in the ordinary courts – that is, the High Court (in London or in a district registry) or the county court. Those courts remain the primary forum for such actions, certainly those of substantial value. However, as discussed below, employment tribunals also now have a contractual jurisdiction which extends to wrongful dismissal claims.

The choice of whether to proceed in the High Court or county court depends principally upon the value of the claim. In a wrongful dismissal action, there is no absolute bar to commencing proceedings in either court. However, the trial of the action will normally take place in the county court if the value of the action (ie the amount, exclusive of interest, which the claimant reasonably expects to recover) is less than £50,000, and will normally take place in the High Court if that value is £50,000 or more.

Employees are also able to bring proceedings in the employment tribunal in respect of claims for (inter alia) damages for breach of a contract of employment arising or outstanding on the termination of employment, which would of course include claims for wrongful dismissal (*Employment Tribunals Act 1996, s 3*; *Employment Tribunals Extension of Jurisdiction (England and Wales) Order 1994 (SI 1994/1623)* – see *SI 1994/1624* in relation to Scotland). However, the tribunal is not empowered in such proceedings to order the payment of an amount exceeding £25,000. Nor does the tribunal have any jurisdiction to award interest (although the award once made will carry interest if not satisfied within 42 days). Employees should bear in mind that where wrongful dismissal (or any breach of contract) proceedings are issued in the employment tribunal, the employer is entitled to counterclaim for any breach of contract committed by the employee which arises or is outstanding on the termination of employment (*art 4* of the *1994 Order*).

Occasionally, a contract of employment may contain an arbitration clause capable of applying to a wrongful dismissal claim. In such a case, the employee is entitled to refer the claim to arbitration rather than commencing proceedings in the ordinary courts or the employment tribunal. If the employee instead chooses to begin proceedings in the High Court or county court, the employer may seek to have those proceedings stayed under *s 4* of the *Arbitration Act 1950* so that the matter can be referred to arbitration. Except in cases with an international element falling within *s 1* of the *Arbitration Act 1975*, the court will have a discretion as to whether such a stay should be granted, but will normally accede to the application unless there is some good reason why arbitration is inappropriate (this would include a case where it can be seen that there is no genuine defence to the claim, so that it can be seen that there is no true dispute falling within the arbitration clause).

It would appear that wrongful dismissal proceedings brought in the employment tribunal could also be stayed so as to give effect to an arbitration clause. Although any provision in an agreement purporting to preclude the presentation of a complaint to a tribunal is normally void, this does not apply where (as here) the tribunal's jurisdiction is founded upon an order made under *s 3* of the *Employment Tribunals Act 1996*.

58.39   Relationship with tribunal proceedings

Where a claim for wrongful dismissal is commenced in the High Court or county court, and at the same time a complaint of unfair dismissal is presented to an employment tribunal, an application may be made for one or other set of proceedings (usually the tribunal claim) to be stayed pending the outcome of the other litigation.

Where the claim of wrongful dismissal has been brought in the employment tribunal and judgment has been reached by the tribunal, it is not open to the employee to recover damages in excess of the tribunal's jurisdiction (£25,000) by proceedings in the county court or High Court. The common law doctrine of merger of causes of action will be held to apply (see *Fraser v HLMAD Ltd* [2006] IRLR 687). Therefore, where the employee's potential recovery is greater than £25,000, the appropriate forum in which to proceed with an action must be thought through with some care.

An employee may be able to withdraw an employment tribunal claim for wrongful dismissal, however, and proceed instead in the county court or High Court without being barred by the operation of the principle of cause of action estoppel, if it is made clear that the withdrawal from the employment tribunal is for this very purpose (see *Sajid v Sussex Muslim Society* [2001] EWCA Civ 1684, [2002] IRLR 113).

58.40   Limitation periods

A wrongful dismissal action in the High Court or county court is a claim for breach of contract, and as such is subject to a limitation period of six years from the accrual of the cause of action (*Limitation Act 1980, s 5*). Hence, proceedings must be commenced before the sixth anniversary of the dismissal.

In the employment tribunal, the complaint will have to be presented within the period of three months beginning with the effective date of termination of the contract of employment, or (where the tribunal is satisfied that it was not reasonably practicable for the complaint to be presented within that period) within such further period as the tribunal considers reasonable (*Employment Tribunals Extension of Jurisdiction (England and Wales) Order 1994 (SI 1994/1623), art 7* – see *art 7* of *SI 1994/1624* in relation to Scotland). The time limit may be extended by up to one month to enable the statutory grievance procedure in *Sch 2* to the *Employment Act 2002* to be complied with (*s 32(4)*).

Claims may not be presented to the tribunal before the employee has set out his grievance to his employer in writing and at least 28 days have passed since that was done (*s 32(2)* and (*3*)). See generally 54.10 UNFAIR DISMISSAL – II.

58.41   Summary judgment, interim payments, payments into court, and hearings on liability and quantum

In the High Court and county court, although not the employment tribunal, the claimant employee who considers that the defendant employer has no real prospect of successfully defending the claim may apply for summary judgment on written evidence alone (*Civil Procedure Rules 1998, Part 24*). This is particularly important in wrongful dismissal claims, where the true issue between the parties is often not whether the employer was entitled to dismiss without due notice, but what loss the employee has suffered, and in particular the extent to which that loss could or should have been mitigated. In such a case the court may be persuaded to enter judgment for damages to be assessed, or at least to make the granting of leave to defend the action conditional upon the defendant making a payment into court (which will act as an incentive to settlement of the claim, and should ensure that the claimant is able to enforce any judgment ultimately obtained).

The application for summary judgment will often be combined with an application for an interim payment (*CPR 1998, rule 25.6*), which will also be appropriate in a case where the employer has admitted liability but contests the amount of damages.

If the defendant employer believes that the claimant is likely to succeed on the issue of whether he was wrongfully dismissed, but that he is claiming damages substantially in excess of those to which he is truly entitled, then it may be appropriate for that defendant to make a payment into court in satisfaction of the claimant's cause of action (*CPR 1998, Part 36*). If the claimant accepts the payment in within a specified period, the proceedings will come to an end, and the claimant will automatically be entitled to his costs up until the date of payment in. If the claimant does not do so, and ultimately recovers less at trial than the sum paid in, then he will have to pay the defendant's costs since payment in.

Where both liability and quantum are in dispute, the parties will wish to consider (especially where the calculation of loss raises complex points of detail) whether liability should be tried as a preliminary issue, with a hearing on quantum to follow only if the claimant establishes that he has been wrongfully dismissed and the parties are still unable to compromise their differences at that point.

Save for the possibility of separate hearings on liability and quantum, none of these procedural opportunities will be available if the claim is brought in the employment tribunal.

58.42   Compromise of claims

The various statutory restrictions, which prescribe that an employee may compromise claims based upon his statutory rights only in certain specified ways, do not apply to wrongful dismissal claims (*Sutherland v Network Appliance Ltd* [2001] IRLR 12). Any compromise contained in a binding contract will do, and a binding contract requires only offer and acceptance, an intention to create legal relations and consideration. There is good consideration for a contract of compromise even if the claimant's claim is in fact ill-founded, because the defendant is spared the expense and vexation of resisting it. However, it may in certain circumstances be possible to set aside a compromise on the grounds of mistake or misrepresentation (see e g *Bell v Lever Bros Ltd* [1932] AC 161).

Once High Court or county court proceedings have actually been commenced, it is not unusual for terms of settlement to be incorporated into an order of the court. In particular, the order may give the parties liberty to apply to the court for the purpose of enforcing those terms.

58.43 **SPECIAL CATEGORIES OF EMPLOYMENT**

Crown servants

This category covers, principally, civil servants and (probably) NHS employees. Although Crown servants have the right to complain of unfair dismissal (*ERA 1996, s 191*), it does not appear that it is possible for them to bring an action for wrongful dismissal. This is because it is a rule of law that Crown service is determinable by the Crown at will (*Riordan v War Office* [1959] 1 WLR 1046). Consistently with this principle, Crown servants do not enjoy the right to a statutory minimum period of notice.

58.44 **Apprentices**

The employer's right of summary dismissal is more restricted in a contract of apprenticeship than in a normal contract of employment. It appears that nothing short of conduct which makes it impossible for the employer to carry out the essential purpose of the contract (to teach the apprentice his trade) will justify termination without notice (see *Learoyd v Brook* [1891] 1 QB 431; *Newell v Gillingham Corpn* [1941] 1 All ER 552).

By the same token, an employer will generally be precluded from terminating a contract of apprenticeship solely on the ground of redundancy where the business is not closed down, or there is no change in the character of the business (*Wallace v CA Roofing Services Ltd* [1996] IRLR 435).

For special considerations applying to the assessment of damages for wrongful dismissal of an apprentice, see 58.29 above.

Index

[all references are to paragraph number]

A

Abuse of process
tribunal procedure, and, 21.26

ACAS
advisory function, 2.7
arbitration function
generally, 21.37
introduction, 2.6
Codes of Practice
introduction, 2.9
legal effect, 5.3
power to issue, 5.2
revision, 5.15
revocation, 5.15
compromise agreements, and, 20.27
conciliation function
CAC complaints, in, 2.5
employment tribunal complaints,
in, 2.4
generally, 21.29–21.32
introduction, 2.3
constitution, 2.2
contact details, 2.11
Dispute Resolution Scheme, 2.10
functions
advice, 2.7
arbitration, 2.6
conciliation, 2.3–2.5
inquiry, 2.8
inquiry function, 2.8
introduction, 2.1

Acceptance of employer's breach
wrongful dismissal, and, 58.7

Access to medical reports
disclosure of information, and, 11.15

Access to records
criminal convictions, and, 19.7

Access to training
positive discrimination, and, 13.9

Accident reporting
health and safety, and, 28.1

**Accompanied at disciplinary hearings,
right to be**
generally, 51.21
unfair dismissal, and, 54.3

Account of profits
restraint of trade covenants, and,
41.20

Accounts and records
trade unions, and, 50.12

Action short of dismissal
trade union members, and
generally, 51.17
remedy, 51.18
summary, 51.8

Addition of new claims
tribunal procedure, and, 21.10

Additional award
unfair dismissal, and, 55.14

Additional maternity leave
generally, 33.21

Adjournment application
tribunal procedure, and, 21.54

Adjustments by employer
generally, 10.12
knowledge, 10.15

Administrative receivers, liability of
insolvency of employer, and, 31.11

Adoption leave
generally, 49.19
payments from National Insurance
Fund, and, 31.8
statutory pay, 33.28
unfair dismissal, and, 54.3

Advertisements
disability discrimination, and, 10.18
discrimination, and
employment, in, 12.12
generally, 13.34
injunctions, 14.30
generally, 23.1

**Advisory, Conciliation and Arbitration
Service (ACAS)**
advisory function, 2.7
arbitration function
generally, 21.37
introduction, 2.6
Codes of Practice
introduction, 2.9
legal effect, 5.3
power to issue, 5.2
revision, 5.15

Index

**Advisory, Conciliation and Arbitration
Service (ACAS)** – *contd*
Codes of Practice – *contd*
  revocation, 5.15
compromise agreements, and, 20.27
conciliation function
  CAC complaints, in, 2.5
  employment tribunal complaints,
    in, 2.4
  generally, 21.29–21.32
  introduction, 2.3
constitution, 2.2
contact details, 2.11
Dispute Resolution Scheme, 2.10
functions
  advice, 2.7
  arbitration, 2.6
  conciliation, 2.3–2.5
  inquiry, 2.8
inquiry function, 2.8
introduction, 2.1
Advocates
discrimination, and, 13.24
Age
see also Age discrimination
retirement, and
  change, 42.5
  discrimination regulations, 42.3
  employment protection, and, 42.2
  generally, 42.1
  unfair dismissal, 53.14
unfair dismissal, and, 53.14
Age discrimination
aiding unlawful acts, 3.43
applicants, against
  employment, for, 3.12
  office, for, 3.30
  partnerships, by, 3.35
  pupillage, for, 3.33
  trade organisations, by, 3.36
"at an establishment in Great
  Britain", 3.11
background, 3.2
barristers, 3.33
benefits provided to the public, 3.18
burden of proof, 3.44
careers guidance agencies, 3.39
collective agreements, and, 3.45
contract terms, and, 3.45
contract workers, 3.29
Crown servants, 3.46
direct discrimination, 3.4

Age discrimination – *contd*
disparity of effect, 3.5
employees, against
  discrimination, 3.13
  harassment, 3.14
employer's liability, and, 3.42
employment agencies, 3.39
employment, in
  applicants, against, 3.12
  "at an establishment in Great
    Britain", 3.11
  employees, against, 3.13
  "employment", 3.10
  exceptions, 3.16–3.27
  former employees, against, 3.15
  introduction, 3.9
employment outside Great Britain,
  3.19
employment tribunal proceedings
  burden of proof, 3.44
  introduction, 3.44
  jurisdiction of employment
    tribunals, 3.44
  proof, 3.44
  questionnaire, 3.44
  remedies, 3.44
  time limits, 3.44
enhanced redundancy benefits, 3.26
exceptions
  benefits provided to the public, 3.18
  employment outside Great Britain,
    3.19
  enhanced redundancy benefits, 3.26
  genuine occupational requirement,
    3.17
  introduction, 3.16
  length of service benefits, 3.25
  life assurance cover to retired
    workers, 3.27
  national minimum wage, 3.24
  national security, 3.21
  positive action, 3.22
  retirement, 3.23
  statutory authority, 3.20
fairness of dismissal, 3.48
former employees, against
  generally, 3.41
  introduction, 3.15
genuine occupational requirement,
  3.17
harassment
  employees, against, 3.14

Age discrimination – *contd*
  harassment – *contd*
    employment agencies, by, 3.39
    generally, 3.8
    office-holders, against, 3.30
    partnerships, by, 3.35
    pupil barristers, against, 3.33
    trade organisations, by, 3.36
    vocational training providers, by,
      3.38
  Houses of Parliament staff, 3.46
  indirect discrimination, 3.5
  instructions to discriminate, 3.6
  introduction, 3.1
  jurisdiction of employment tribunals,
    3.44
  life assurance cover to retired
    workers, 3.27
  long service benefits, 3.25
  less favourable treatment, 3.4
  merchant seamen, 3.17
  national minimum wage, 3.24
  national security, 3.21
  non-employees covered
    barristers, 3.33
    contract workers, 3.29
    introduction, 3.28
    office-holders, 3.30
    police, 3.31
    pupillage, 3.33
    SOCA staff, 3.32
  non-employers covered
    careers guidance agencies, 3.39
    employment agencies, 3.39
    occupational pension scheme
      trustees, 3.34
    partnerships, 3.35
    qualifications bodies, 3.37
    Secretary of State, 3.40
    trade organisations, 3.36
    vocational training providers, 3.38
  occupational pension scheme
    trustees, 3.34
  office-holders, 3.30
  "on grounds of age", 3.4
  overview, 12.1–12.2
  Parliamentary staff, 3.46
  partnerships, 3.35
  pension scheme trustees, 3.34
  pensions, 3.49
  personal disadvantage, 3.5
  persons instructing barristers, 3.33

Age discrimination – *contd*
  police, 3.31
  positive action, 3.22
  principal's liability, 3.42
  proof, 3.44
  "proportionate means of achieving a
    legitimate aim"
    direct discrimination, 3.4
    indirect discrimination, 3.5
  pupillage, 3.33
  qualifications bodies, 3.37
  questionnaire, 3.44
  redundancy payments, and
    generally, 3.26
    introduction, 38.10
  remedies, 3.44
  retirement dismissals
    appeals, 3.47
    duty to consider request, 3.47
    employers' duty to notify, 3.47
    generally, 3.47, 42.2
    introduction, 3.23
    request to continue working, 3.47
    summary of regulations, 42.3
    transitional provisions, 3.47
  revision of discriminatory contract
    terms, 3.45
  seafarers, 3.11
  Secretary of State, 3.40
  Serious Organised Crime agency
    staff, 3.32
  statutory authority, 3.20
  time limits, 3.44
  trade organisations, 3.36
  unlawful acts
    direct discrimination, 3.4
    harassment, 3.8
    indirect discrimination, 3.5
    instructions to discriminate, 3.6
    introduction, 3.3
    office-holders, against, 3.30
    victimisation, 3.7
  unfair dismissal, 3.48
  unwanted conduct, 3.8
  validity of discriminatory contract
    terms, 3.45
  vicarious liability, 3.42
  victimisation, 3.7
  vocational training providers, 3.38

Agencies
  see also Agency workers
  draft Conduct Regulations, 47.5

Index

Agencies – *contd*
engagement of employees, and, 23.4
generally, 47.2
reform proposals, 47.4
statutory control, 47.3
Agency workers
see also Agencies
introduction, 47.2–47.5
less favourable treatment, 47.9
national minimum wage
generally, 47.6
introduction, 34.10
unfair dismissal, 47.7
working time, and, 57.3
Agents, discrimination by
disability discrimination, and, 10.28
generally, 12.12
persons responsible, 13.38
Aggravated damages
discrimination compensation, and,
14.18
Agricultural tied houses
service lettings, and, 43.9
Agricultural workers
equal pay, and, 24.21
holidays, and, 29.7
Aiding unlawful acts
age discrimination, and, 3.43
disability discrimination, and, 10.29
generally, 12.12
persons responsible, 13.36
Air crew
holidays, and, 29.8
working time, and, 57.33
Alcohol misuse
health and safety, and, 28.2
Alterations
contract of employment, and, 8.22
written particulars, and, 8.7
Alternative employment, refusal of
redundancy payments, and, 38.12
Amalgamations
trade unions, and, 50.39
Amendment of claims
tribunal procedure, and, 20.15
Annual Christmas party
tax-free benefits, and, 46.23
Annual leave
working time, and, 57.19
Ante-natal care, time off for
amount, 33.4
generally, 33.2

Ante-natal care, time off for – *contd*
insolvency of employer, and, 31.2
introduction, 49.11
qualifying requirements, 33.3
remedies for refusal, 33.5
Anticipatory breach of contract
wrongful dismissal, and, 58.22
Any other substantial reason
generally, 54.14
summary, 54.2
Appeals
Central Arbitration Committee, and,
50.10–50.11
Court of Appeal, to, 22.26
EAT, to
bias allegation, 22.12
conduct of, 22.14–22.20
content, 22.5
costs, 22.22–22.24
disposition of, 22.19–22.20
EAT, 22.1–22.3
error of law, 22.17
EU law issues, 22.27
fresh evidence, 22.16
generally, 22.4
grounds, 22.7
institution, 22.5
miscellaneous points, 22.13
notes of evidence, 22.10
other powers, 22.21
perverse decision, 22.17
preliminary sifting, 22.8–22.9
raising points not taken at tribunal
hearing, 22.15
reference back for clarification of
reasons, 22.11
review of order, 22.25
time limits, 22.6
improvement notices, and
cost of remedy required, 27.36
effect, 27.35
introduction, 27.34
prohibition notices, and
cost of remedy required, 27.36
effect, 27.35
introduction, 27.34
Applications to Employment Tribunal
abuse of process, 21.26
ACAS, and
arbitration schemes, 21.37
conciliation, 21.29–21.32
introduction, 2.4

Applications to Employment Tribunal – *contd*
adding new claims, 21.10
adjournment application, 21.54
administration, 20.6
bias, 21.50
breach of contract of employment, and, 8.23
'Calderbank' offers, 21.36
case management
case management discussions, 21.2–21.5
powers in practice, 21.7–21.14
overriding objective, and, 21.1
pre-hearing reviews, 21.6
tribunal's powers, 21.2
case management discussions
application for orders, 21.3
introduction, 21.2
non-compliance with orders, 21.4
orders not available, 21.5
claims
default judgments, 20.38
extension of time, 20.22–20.33
post-presentation action, 20.34
presentation, 20.21
response by respondent, 20.35–20.37
time limits, 20.18–20.20
commencing proceedings, 20.15–20.17
composition
Chairmen sitting alone, 20.9–20.10
generally, 20.7–20.8
compromise agreements, 21.33–21.35
conciliation
'Calderbank' offers, 21.36
compromise agreements, 21.33–21.35
discrimination complaints, 14.10
generally, 21.29–21.31
settlements, 21.32
conduct of hearing, 21.52
conflict of interest, 21.50
costs
generally, 21.69–21.70
orders, 21.71
preparation time orders, 21.72
wasted costs orders, 21.73
costs warning, 21.15
default judgments, 20.38
deposit orders, 21.15
disability discrimination, and, 10.34

Applications to Employment Tribunal – *contd*
disclosure
discrimination complaints, 14.9
generally, 21.11–21.12
privileged documents, 21.13
discrimination complaints
compensation, 14.13–14.20
conciliation, 14.10
disclosure, 14.9
extension of time, 14.7
formulation of complaint, 14.8
generally, 14.2
publicity, 14.11
questionnaire, 14.9
recommendations, 14.21
remedies, 14.12–14.22
time limits, 14.4–14.7
discrimination questionnaires, 14.9
dismissal of claims, 21.28
dismissal of party, 21.23
estoppel, 21.26
extension of time
contract claims, 20.32
discrimination complaints, 14.4
effective date of termination, 20.23–20.24
equal pay, 20.28
generally, 20.22
introduction, 21.21
'just and equitable, 20.30
'not reasonably practicable' to present in time, 20.25–20.26
other claims, 20.33
redundancy payments, 20.27
unlawful deductions from wages, 20.31
unlawful discrimination, 20.29
further information, 21.8–21.9
hearing
adjournment application, 21.54
bias, 21.50
conduct, 21.52
conflict of interest, 21.50
control of procedure, 21.56
generally, 21.49
non-attendance of parties, 21.54
order of evidence, 21.53
other procedural points, 21.58–21.61
private hearing, 21.51
representation, 21.55

Index

Applications to Employment Tribunal – *contd*
hearing – *contd*
  witnesses, 21.57
historical background, 20.1–20.2
interest, 21.67
introduction, 20.1–20.2
itemised pay statements, and
  generally, 34.19
  order, 34.20
joinder of parties, 21.23
judgments
  adequacy of reasons, 21.63
  corrections and changes, 21.64
  generally, 21.62
  register, 21.65
jurisdiction
  breach of contract of
    employment, 8.23
  EU law, over, 20.12
  generally, 20.11
  Human Rights Act, under, 20.13
listing arrangements, 21.39–21.48
miscellaneous powers, 21.20
multiple claims, 21.24
non-attendance of parties, 21.54
order of evidence, 21.53
overriding objective
  case management, 21.1
  generally, 20.14
part-time workers, and,
  introduction, 32.20
  remedies, 32.22
  time limits, 32.21
post-presentation action, 20.34
pre-hearing reviews, 21.6
preparation for hearing
  general, 21.38
  listing arrangements, 21.39–21.48
preparation time orders, 21.72
presentation of claim, 20.21
private hearing, 21.51
reasons for decision
  adequacy, 21.63
  generally, 21.62
recoupment of benefits, 21.68
references, and, 40.8
register of judgments, 21.65
remedies
  costs, 21.69–21.73
  generally, 21.66
  interest, 21.67

Applications to Employment Tribunal – *contd*
remedies – *contd*
  recoupment of benefits, 21.68
representation, 21.55
response by respondent, 20.35–20.37
restricted reporting orders, 21.18–21.19
review of judgment, 21.74–21.75
Rules of Procedure, 20.4–20.5
settlement
  conciliation, 21.32
  generally, 21.29–21.31
specialist jurisdictions, 21.77
statutory provision, 20.3
stay of proceedings, 21.22
striking out, 21.16–21.17
time limits for claims
  contract claims, 20.32
  discrimination complaints, 14.4–14.7
  equal pay, 20.28
  generally, 20.18
  'just and equitable, 20.30
  'not reasonably practicable' to
    present in time, 20.25–20.26
  other claims, 20.33
  post-EA 2002, 20.19–20.20
  redundancy payments, 20.27
  unlawful deductions from wages, 20.31
  unlawful discrimination, 20.29
transfer of proceedings, 21.25
vexatious litigants, 21.76
wasted costs orders, 21.73
withdrawal of claims, 21.28
witness orders, 21.14
witnesses, 21.57

Appointment of directors
introduction, 9.2
relationship between articles and
  contracts, 9.3
scope of employment, 9.5
status, 9.4
terms, 9.4
written particulars, 9.6

Apprenticeships
education and training, and, 16.2
payments from National Insurance
  Fund, and, 31.5
wrongful dismissal, and, 58.44

Appropriate bargaining unit
collective bargaining, and, 50.30
Appropriate representatives
election, 39.5
generally, 39.4
Arbitration
ACAS, and, 2.6
Central Arbitration Committee, and, 50.7
Armed forces
equal pay, and, 24.4
European law, 37.7
exemplary damages, 37.5
introduction, 37.1
judicial review as to rights, 37.4
national minimum wage, and, 34.10
national security, 37.6
public interest immunity, 37.6
sex discrimination, and, 13.10
special provisions, 37.2
status, 37.3
strikes, and, 45.20
working time, and, 57.3
Arrangements for training
generally, 49.7
remedies, 49.8
Arrears of pay
payments from National Insurance
Fund, and, 31.5
Articles of association
directors, and, 9.3
Assertion of statutory rights
unfair dismissal, and, 54.3
Assistance
discrimination, and, 14.31
Association, freedom of
human rights, and, 30.4
Associated company, offer by
redundancy payments, and, 38.6
Assured tenancies
generally, 43.5
recovery of possession, 43.6
rent control, 43.8
Assured shorthold tenancies
generally, 43.5
recovery of possession, 43.6
rent control, 43.8
Asthma
disability discrimination, and, 10.2
Attachment of earnings
attachable earnings
deductions, 35.3

Attachment of earnings – *contd*
attachable earnings – *contd*
generally, 35.2
child support maintenance, 35.11
clerical costs, 35.9
Council Tax, 35.10
deduction from attachable earnings
calculation, 35.4
introduction, 35.3
priority of orders, 35.5
time limits, 35.6
employer's obligations, 35.7
introduction, 35.1
itemised pay statements, 35.9
other issues, 35.9
penalties for non-compliance, 35.8
priority of orders, 35.5
protected earnings, 35.3
Attendance of witnesses
tribunal procedure, and, 20.17
Aviation sector
holidays, and, 29.8
working time, and, 57.33

B
Ballots before strike action
generally, 45.14
members' right, 45.1
Barristers
age discrimination, and, 3.33
discrimination, and, 13.24
Basic award
amount, 55.7
exceptions, 55.8
maximum award, 55.16
reduction, 55.9
Beginning of employment
generally, 7.3
postponement, 7.11
Belief
and see Religious and belief
discrimination
meaning, 12.5
Benefits in kind
disability discrimination, and, 10.20
meaning of 'wages', and, 34.6
taxation, and, 46.2
unfair dismissal, and, 55.12
Benefits provided to the public
age discrimination, and, 3.18
discrimination, and, 13.17

Index

Bias
EAT procedure, and, 22.12
tribunal procedure, and, 21.50
Bicycles, loans for
tax-free benefits, and, 46.23
'Blacklists'
trade union members, and, 51.10
'Blue pencil' test
restraint of trade covenants, and, 41.7
Breaks
children, and, 4.6
Bullying
health and safety, and, 28.28
Burden of proof
age discrimination, and, 3.44

C
'Calderbank' offer
tribunal procedure, and, 21.36
Calls for action
strike action, and, 45.15
Capability
generally, 54.6
ill-health, 54.8
introduction, 54.5
procedure, 54.6
qualifications, 54.7
summary, 54.2
Car fuel
taxation, and, 46.26
Care for children
time off work, and, 49.19
Careers guidance
age discrimination, and, 3.39
discrimination, and, 13.29
Cars
taxation, and, 46.25
Case management
addition of new claims, 21.10
case management discussions
application for orders, 21.3
introduction, 21.2
non-compliance with orders, 21.4
orders not available, 21.5
overview, 20.5
disclosure
discrimination complaints, 14.9
generally, 21.11–21.12
privileged documents, 21.13
dismissal of party, 21.23
further information, 21.8–21.9

Case management – *contd*
powers in practice, 21.7
overriding objective, and, 21.1
pre-hearing reviews
generally, 21.6
overview, 20.5
tribunal's powers, 21.2
witness orders, 21.14
Cash vouchers
taxable benefits, and, 46.21–46.22
Central Arbitration Committee (CAC)
ACAS's role, 2.5
appeals against awards, 50.10–50.11
arbitration, 50.7
collective bargaining, and, 50.29
complaint of failure to disclose
information, 50.8
constitution, 50.5
contracting out, and, 50.9
establishment, 50.4
functions, 50.6–50.9
Certification officer
trade unions, and, 50.3
Change of employer
continuous employment, and, 7.9
redundancy payments, and, 38.5
wrongful dismissal, and, 58.8
Charities
disability discrimination, and, 10.24
'Check-off'
deduction of union subscriptions,
and, 51.20
Child care facilities
tax-free benefits, and, 46.23
Child support maintenance
attachment of earnings, and, 35.11
Childbirth
and see Pregnancy
positive discrimination, and, 13.9
unfair dismissal, and, 54.3
Children, employment of
breaks, 4.6
contracts of employment, 4.10
definitions, 4.1
health and safety
breaks, 4.6
introduction, 4.5
night work, 4.6
rest periods, 4.6
local authority powers, 4.3
night work, 4.6
rest periods, 4.6

Children, employment of – *contd*
  restrictions
    generally, 4.2
    local authority powers, 4.3
    other provisions, 4.4
  time off for study or training
    introduction, 4.7
    remedy for refusal, 4.8
    right not to suffer detriment, 4.9
  working time, and, 57.3
Christmas party
  tax-free benefits, and, 46.23
Chronic fatigue syndrome (ME)
  disability discrimination, and, 10.2
Civil aviation workers
  holidays, and, 29.8
Civil liability
  health and safety, and, 27.43
Civil partnership status
  and see Discrimination
  direct discrimination, 12.4
  discrimination in employment, 12.12
  generally 12.2
  harassment, 12.11
  indirect discrimination, 12.7
  'on ground of', 12.6
  sexual orientation, and, 13.13
Civil servants
  European law, 37.7
  exemplary damages, 37.5
  introduction, 37.1
  judicial review as to rights, 37.4
  national security, 37.6
  public interest immunity, 37.6
  redundancy payments, and, 38.10
  special provisions, 37.2
  status, 37.3
Clerical costs
  attachment of earnings, and, 35.9
Closed shop
  dismissal, and
    compensation, 51.7
    generally, 51.5
  industrial action, and, 51.9
  introduction, 51.3
  pre-entry, 51.4
Codes of Practice
  ACAS
    introduction, 2.9
    legal effect, 5.3
    power to issue, 5.2
    revision, 5.15

Codes of Practice – *contd*
  ACAS – *contd*
    revocation, 5.15
  collective bargaining, 11.4
  Commission for Racial Equality
    legal effect, 5.7
    power to issue, 5.6
  Department for Education and
    Employment
    legal effect, 5.13
    power to issue, 5.12
    revision, 5.15
    revocation, 5.15
  Disability Rights Commission
    generally, 10.32, 5.14
    power to issue, 5.12
    revision, 5.15
    revocation, 5.15
  Department of Trade and Industry
    legal effect, 5.5
    power to issue, 5.4
    revision, 5.15
  Equal Opportunities Commission
    legal effect, 5.9
    power to issue, 5.8
    equal pay, and, 24.2
  Health and Safety Commission
    introduction, 27.28
    legal effect, 5.11
    power to issue, 5.10
  Industrial Relations Code
    generally, 5.2
    legal effect, 5.3
    introduction, 5.1
    picketing, and, 45.11
Collective agreements
  age discrimination, and, 3.45
  amendments, 6.4
  contracts of employment, and, 6.3
  equal pay, and, 24.24
  introduction, 6.1
  legal effect, 6.2
  miscellaneous, 6.6
  'no strike' clauses, 6.5
  transfer of undertakings, and, 52.20
  working time, and, 57.4
Collective bargaining
  Code of Practice, 11.4
  derecognition for, 50.36
  duty to disclose information, 11.3
  failure to comply with request, 11.5
  introduction, 11.2

Index

Collective bargaining – *contd*
recognition for
  appropriate bargaining unit, 50.30
  ballot, 50.31–50.32
  changes in bargaining unit, 50.35
  'collective bargaining', 50.27
  introduction, 50.25
  method of bargaining, 50.33
  reference to CA, 50.29
  request for recognition, 50.28
scope of procedure, 50.26
Commencement of proceedings
tribunal procedure, and, 20.15–20.17
Commission for Equality and Human Rights (CEHR)
formal investigations, 14.27
generally, 14.26
introduction, 14.23
non-discrimination notices, 14.28
Commission for Racial Equality (CRE)
Code of Practice
  legal effect, 5.7
  power to issue, 5.6
formal investigations, 14.27
generally, 14.25
introduction, 14.23
non-discrimination notices, 14.28
Communal accommodation
discrimination, and, 13.10
Company cars
taxation, and, 46.25
unfair dismissal, and, 55.12
Company share option schemes
generally, 46.30
Comparators
discrimination, and, 12.5
equal pay, and, 24.9
part-time workers, and,
  actual comparator, 32.11
  circumstances where comparator not required, 32.13
  'comparable full time worker', 32.8–32.12
  'full time worker', 32.7
  'part time worker', 32.7
  'same or broadly similar work', 32.10
  'same type of contract', 32.9
  scope of comparison, 32.12
Compensation
aggravated damages, 14.18
discrimination, 14.19

Compensation – *contd*
exemplary damages, 14.18
general principles, 14.13
indirect discrimination, 14.14
injury to feelings, 14.16
interests, 14.20
introduction, 14.12
pecuniary loss, 14.15
personal injury, 14.17
unfair dismissal, 14.19
Compensation for unfair dismissal
additional award, 55.14
basic award
  amount, 55.7
  exceptions, 55.8
  maximum award, 55.16
  reduction, 55.9
compensatory award
  amount, 55.11
  heads of loss, 55.12
  increase, 55.13
  introduction, 55.10
  maximum award, 55.16
  reduction, 55.15
  union-related cases, 55.15
introduction, 55.6
maximum amounts, 55.16
recoupment of statutory benefits, 55.5
union-related cases, 55.15
Compensatory award
amount, 55.11
heads of loss, 55.12
increase, 55.13
introduction, 55.10
maximum award, 55.16
reduction, 55.15
union-related cases, 55.15
Competent fellow workers
health and safety, and, 27.7
Compliance with the law
discrimination, and, 13.18
Composition of tribunals
Chairmen sitting alone, 20.9–20.10
generally, 20.7–20.8
Compromise agreements
tribunal procedure, and, 21.33–21.35
Compromise of claims
wrongful dismissal, and, 58.42
Computation of periods of employment
beginning of period
  generally, 7.3
  postponement, 7.11

Computation of periods of employment – *contd*
end of period, 7.3
generally, 7.2
Conciliation
CAC complaints, in, 2.5
'Calderbank' offers, 21.36
compromise agreements, 21.33–21.3
discrimination complaints, and, 14.10
employment tribunal complaints, in, 2.4 5
generally, 21.29–21.31
introduction, 2.3
settlements, 21.32
Conditional employment
references, and, 40.9
Conduct, dismissal on grounds of
generally, 54.9
procedure, 54.10
summary, 54.2
Confidential information
disclosure of information, and, 11.16
European Works Councils, and, 18.10
information and consultation rights, and, 18.10
restraint of trade covenants, and
generally, 41.13
remedies, 41.19
Confinement
statutory maternity pay, and, 33.11
Conflict of interest
tribunal procedure, and, 21.50
Conflict of laws
restraint of trade covenants, and, 41.12
Consideration
restraint of trade covenants, and, 41.10
Conspiracy
strike action, and, 45.1
Construction site management
health and safety, and, 28.4
Constructive dismissal
dismissal by employer, and, 48.5
summary termination by employee, and, 48.18
unfair dismissal, and, 53.7
wrongful dismissal, and, 58.6
Consultation
disclosure of information, and, 11.11
employee participation, and, generally, 18.28

Consultation – *contd*
employee participation, and – *contd*
training, on, 18.29
European law, and, 25.12
ICE Directive and Regulations, and,
complaints, 18.11
confidential information, 18.10
employment protection, 18.12
generally, 11.11
introduction, 18.4
negotiated agreements, 18.6
re-existing agreements, 18.8
requests and notifications, 18.5
standard provisions, 18.7
transfer of undertakings, and, 52.22
redundancy, and,
appropriate representatives, 39.4–39.5
introduction, 39.2
meaning of 'redundancy', 39.3
protective award, 39.6
time off for representatives, and,
generally, 49.14
remedies, 49.15
transfer of undertakings, and, 52.22
Continuous employment
beginning of employment,
generally, 7.3
postponement, 7.11
change of employer, 7.9
computation of periods of employment,
beginning and end of period, 7.3
generally, 7.2
end, 7.3
events affecting,
change of employer, 7.9
introduction, 7.4
preliminary points, 7.5
weeks which count, 7.6–6.8
weeks which do not count, 7.10–6.11
events breaking continuity, 7.12
introduction, 7.1
presumption, 7.5
qualifying periods, 7.13
redundancy payments, and
changes in ownership, 38.5
generally, 38.4
start of employment
generally, 7.3
postponement, 7.11

Continuous employment – *contd*
statutory concept, 7.5
unfair dismissal, and, 53.12
'week', 7.5
weeks which count
introduction, 7.6
'no employment' periods, 7.7
part timers, 7.8
weeks which do not count
introduction, 7.10
postponement of start of
employment, 7.11
Contract claims
time limits for claims, and, 20.32
Contract for services
generally, 17.3
Contract of employment
alterations, 8.22
children, and, 4.10
collective agreements, and, 6.3
contract for services, distinction from
distinction from contract for
services, 17.3–17.8
generally, 17.2
contracting out of certain provisions,
8.17
discriminatory terms, 8.18
employer handbooks and policies,
8.11
express terms, 8.12
form, 8.3
freedom to employ, and, 8.2
generally, 8.1
holidays, and, 29.9
implied terms, 8.12–7.13
industrial action restrictions, 8.20
introduction, 1.3
remedies for breach
employee, for, 8.23
employer, for, 8.24
restraint of trade, 8.19
sources of law, and, 1.5
Sunday trading, and, 8.25
terms
contrary to public policy, 8.15
employer handbooks, 8.11
express, 8.12
freedom to agree, 8.10
implied, 8.12–7.13
unenforceable, 8.16–7.21
unlawful, 8.15
variation by statute, 8.14

Contract of employment – *contd*
unenforceable terms
contracting out of certain
provisions, 8.17
discriminatory terms, 8.18
industrial action restrictions, 8.20
introduction, 8.16
restraint of trade, 8.19
UCTA 1977, and, 8.21
unfair terms, 8.21
unlawful terms, 8.15
variation by statute, 8.14
written particulars
alternatives to inclusion, 8.6
changes, 8.7
excepted employees, 8.8
introduction, 8.4
remedies fro failure to provide, 8.9
requirements, 8.5
Contract of service
and see Contract of employment
generally, 17.2
Contract workers
age discrimination, and, 3.29
disability discrimination, and, 10.25
discrimination, and, 13.21
Contracting out
Central Arbitration Committee, and,
50.9
disability discrimination, and, 10.36
part time workers, and, 32.23
redundancy payments, and, 38.14
unfair dismissal, and
exceptions, 53.20
generally, 53.19
working time, and, 57.25
Contractual notice period
dismissal, and, 48.6
Contrary to public policy, terms
contract of employment, and, 8.15
**Contravention of any enactment, dismissal
for**
generally, 54.13
summary, 54.2
Contributory fault
unfair dismissal, and, 55.13
Contributory negligence
health and safety, and, 27.44
Coroner's inquests
findings, 27.46
generally, 27.47
"interested persons", 27.48

Coroner's inquests – *contd*
introduction, 27.45
Corporate killing
health and safety, and, 27.42
Corrected impairment
disability discrimination, and, 10.7
Costs
EAT procedure, and, 22.22–22.24
generally, 21.69–21.70
orders, 21.71
preparation time orders, 21.72
warning, 21.15
wasted costs orders, 21.73
Council Tax
attachment of earnings, and, 35.10
Credit tokens
taxable benefits, and, 46.21
Criminal convictions
access to records, 19.7
effect of provisions, 19.5
recording of, 19.8
rehabilitation periods, 19.6
spent convictions
dismissal, and, 19.3
exceptions, 19.4
introduction, 19.1
non-disclosure, 19.2
Criminal liability
strike action, and, 45.12
Criminal proceedings
health and safety, and
corporate killing, 27.42
defence, 27.41
directors' liability, 27.38
generally, 27.37
order to remedy default, 27.39
time for commencing proceedings,
27.40
strike action, and, 45.12
Crown
discrimination, and, 13.32
Crown servants
age discrimination, and, 3.46
European law, 37.7
exemplary damages, 37.5
introduction, 37.1
judicial review as to rights, 37.4
minimum wage, and, 34.10
national security, 37.6
public interest immunity, 37.6
special provisions, 37.2
status, 37.3

Crown servants – *contd*
wrongful dismissal, and, 58.43

D
Daily rest periods
working time, and, 57.15
Damages
breach of contract of employment, and
employee's remedies, 8.23
employer's remedies, 8.24
wrongful dismissal, and
accelerated receipt, 58.31
accommodation, 58.28
assessment approach, 58.25
bonuses, 58.28
cars, 58.28
collateral benefits, 58.30
commission, 58.28
distress, 58.29
holidays, 58.28
insurance cover, 58.28
intangible loss, 58.29
interest, 58.31
'liquidated damages' clauses, 58.26
mitigation, 58.30
pensions, 58.28
rights in period of notice, 58.27
salary, 58.28
share options, 58.28
taxation, 58.32
unfair dismissal compensation,
and, 58.33
valuation of benefits, 58.28
Data protection
background, 11.12
generally, 11.13
overview, 11.14
references, and, 40.6
Death of employee
pay as you earn, and, 46.10
sex discrimination, and, 13.10
Deduction from wages
attachment of earnings, and
calculation, 35.4
introduction, 35.3
priority of orders, 35.5
time limits, 35.6
breach of contract of employment,
and, 8.24
generally, 34.6
minimum wage, and, 34.9–34.13

Index

Deduction from wages – *contd*
  other, 34.14
  remedies, for breach, 34.8
  retail employment, 34.7
  time limits for claims, and, 20.31
  trade union members, and
    generally, 51.20
    introduction, 34.6
Deemed disabled
  disability discrimination, and, 10.8
Default judgments
  tribunal procedure, and, 20.38
Defences
  wrongful dismissal, and
    exclusion clauses, 58.37
    illegality, 58.35
    invalidity of contract, 58.36
Defined benefit pension schemes
  generally, 42.7
**Department for Education and
  Employment Code of Practice**
  legal effect, 5.13
  power to issue, 5.12
  revision, 5.15
  revocation, 5.15
**Department of Trade and Industry Code
  of Practice**
  legal effect, 5.5
  power to issue, 5.4
  revision, 5.15
Dependants, time off work for
  generally, 49.16
  remedies, 49.17
  unfair dismissal, and, 54.3
Deposit orders
  tribunal procedure, ands, 21.15
Depression
  disability discrimination, and, 10.2
Detriment
  disability discrimination, and, 10.21
  discrimination, and, 12.12
  trade unions, and, 50.37
Direct discrimination
  age discrimination, and, 3.4
  disability discrimination, and
    generally, 10.10
    knowledge, 10.15
  generally, 12.4
  less favourable treatment, 12.5
  prohibited grounds, 12.6
Direction of third party
  health and safety, and, 27.10

Directors
  appointment
    introduction, 9.2
    relationship between articles and
      contracts, 9.3
    scope of employment, 9.5
    status, 9.4
    terms, 9.4
    written particulars, 9.6
  Companies Act 2006, and
    duties, 9.17
    introduction, 9.1
  duties
    Companies Act 2006, and, 9.17
    general, 9.15
    good faith, 9.16
    indemnity, 9.18
    introduction, 9.14
    reforms, 9.17
    relief from liability, 9.19
  duration of service contracts
    introduction, 9.11
    recommendations, 9.13
    section 319 restrictions, 9.12
  good faith, 9.16
  indemnity, 9.18
  introduction, 9.1
  pensions, 9.25
  property transfer, 9.30
  relief from liability, 9.19
  remuneration
    disclosure, 9.22
    introduction, 9.20
    Listing Rules requirements, 9.24
    pensions, 9.25
    recommendations, 9.21
    small company provisions, 9.23
  service contracts
    disclosure, 9.7
    duration, 9.11–8.13
    inspection, 9.8
    Listing Rules requirements, 9.9
    Take-over Code requirements, 9.10
  takeovers, 9.31
  taxation, and, 46.3
  termination of office payments
    generally, 9.27
    introduction, 9.26
    Listing Rules requirements, 9.29
    property transfer, 9.30
    recommendations, 9.28
    takeovers, 9.31

Directors – *contd*
transfer of undertakings, 9.32
written particulars, 9.6
Directors' liability
health and safety, and, 27.38
Directors' obligation
employee participation, and, 18.2
Directors' report
disclosure of information, and, 11.9
employee participation, and, 18.3
Disability discrimination
adjustments by employer
generally, 10.12
knowledge, 10.15
advertisements, 10.18
agents, 10.28
aiding unlawful act, 10.29
benefits, 10.20
charities, and, 10.24
company reports, 10.15
contract workers, 10.25
contracting out, 10.36
definitions
corrected impairment, 10.7
deemed disabled, 10.8
disability, 10.2
disabled person, 10.3
impairment, 10.2
normal day-to-day activities, 10.4
past disabilities, 10.5
progressive conditions, 10.7
relevant time, 10.6
severe disfigurement, 10.7
substantial adverse effect, 10.4
detriment, 10.21
direct discrimination
generally, 10.10
knowledge, 10.15
disability-related discrimination
generally, 10.11
knowledge, 10.15
Disability Rights Commission
Codes of Practice, 10.32
introduction, 10.31
discriminatory acts
advertisements, 10.18
benefits, 10.20
detriment, 10.21
dismissal, 10.21
engagement, 10.19
harassment, 10.21
introduction, 10.17

Disability discrimination – *contd*
discriminatory acts – *contd*
training, 10.20
unfair dismissal, 10.22–9.23
dismissal, 10.21
employer's obligations, 10.14
employment, in
adjustments by employer, 10.12
direct, 10.10
employer's obligations, 10.14
introduction, 10.9
knowledge of disability, 10.15
leased business premises, 10.13
victimisation, 10.16
employment outside GB, and, 10.24
enforcement
application to employment
tribunal, 10.34
introduction, 10.33
engagement, 10.19
exceptions, 10.24
facilities provided to public, and,
10.24
false statements, 10.30
fire brigade officers, and, 10.24
foreign employees, and, 26.13
harassment, 10.21
help and advice, 10.35
introduction, 10.1
leased business premises, 10.13
local government employees, and,
10.24
misleading statements, 10.30
other unlawful acts
agents, 10.28
aiding unlawful act, 10.29
false statements, 10.30
introduction, 10.27
misleading statements, 10.30
pensions, and, 42.10
police officers, and, 10.24
prison officers, and, 10.24
school governors, and, 10.24
settlement of claim, 10.37
small businesses, and, 10.24
statutory authority, and, 10.24
statutory office holders, and, 10.24
trade organisations, 10.26
training, 10.20
unfair dismissal
generally, 10.22
ill-health, 10.23

Index

Disability discrimination – *contd*
victimisation, 10.16
Disability-related absences
generally, 10.23
Disability-related discrimination
generally, 10.11
knowledge, 10.15
Disability Rights Commission
Codes of Practice,
generally, 10.32, 5.14
power to issue, 5.12
revision, 5.15
revocation, 5.15
introduction, 10.31
Disabled person
disability discrimination, and, 10.3
Disciplinary action against trade union members
common law, 51.15
right to be accompanied
generally, 51.21
unfair dismissal, and, 54.3
statutory provisions, 51.16
summary, 51.9
Disclosure
and see Disclosure of information
breach of contract of employment, and, 8.23
directors' remuneration, and
generally, 9.22
Listing Rules requirements, 9.24
small companies, 9.23
directors' service contracts, and
generally, 9.7
Listing Rules requirements, 9.9
Take-over Code, 9.10
discrimination complaints, and, 14.9
tribunal procedure, and
discrimination complaints, 14.9
generally, 21.11–21.12
privileged documents, 21.13
Disclosure of information
collective bargaining, for
Code of Practice, 11.4
duty to disclose, 11.3
failure to comply with request, 11.5
introduction, 11.2
confidential information, and, 11.16
data protection, and
background, 11.12
generally, 11.13
overview, 11.14

Disclosure of information – *contd*
directors' report, in, 11.9
economic situation of undertakings, 11.11
employees, by
generally, 11.17
protected disclosures, 11.18
employment prospects, 11.11
health and safety, for
introduction, 11.7
safety representatives, 11.8
ICE Regulations 2004, 11.11
introduction, 11.1
medical reports, and, 11.15
occupational pension schemes, by, 11.10
public interest, in
generally, 11.17
protected disclosures, 11.18
transfers of undertakings, for, 11.6
whistleblowing, and
generally, 11.17
protected disclosures, 11.18
Discrimination
advertisements
employment, in, 12.12
generally, 13.34
injunctions, 14.30
advocates, 13.24
age, and, 12.1
agent's acts
generally, 12.12
persons responsible, 13.38
aiding unlawful acts
generally, 12.12
persons responsible, 13.36
applications to Employment Tribunal
burden of proof, 14.3
compensation, 14.13–14.20
conciliation, 14.10
disclosure, 14.9
extension of time, 14.7
formulation of complaint, 14.8
generally, 14.2
publicity, 14.11
questionnaire, 14.9
recommendations, 14.21
remedies, 14.12–14.22
time limits, 14.4–14.7
assistance for persons discriminated against, 14.31
barristers, 13.24

Discrimination – *contd*
  benefits provided to public,   13.17
  burden of proof,   14.3
  careers guidance,   13.29
  civil partnership status,
    direct discrimination,   12.4
    discrimination in employment,
      12.12
    generally   12.2
    harassment,   12.11
    indirect discrimination,   12.7
    'on ground of',   12.6
  comparators,   12.5
  compensation
    aggravated damages,   14.18
    discrimination,   14.19
    exemplary damages,   14.18
    general principles,   14.13
    indirect discrimination,   14.14
    injury to feelings,   14.16
    interests,   14.20
    introduction,   14.12
    pecuniary loss,   14.15
    personal injury,   14.17
    unfair dismissal,   14.19
  compliance with law,   13.18
  conciliation,   14.10
  contract workers,   13.21
  Crown,   13.32
  detriment,   12.12
  direct discrimination
    generally,   12.4
    less favourable treatment,   12.5
    prohibited grounds,   12.6
  disability
    and see Disability discrimination
    generally,   10.1–10.37
  disclosure,   14.9
  discriminatory practices
    enforcement only by Commissions,
      13.40
    generally,   12.13
  dismissal,   12.12
  education needs,   13.9
  employment agencies,   13.29
  employment, in,   12.12
  employment outside Great Britain,
    13.15
  employment-related services,   13.30
  enforcement
    applications to Employment
      Tribunal,   14.2–14.22

Discrimination – *contd*
  enforcement – *contd*
    assistance for persons discriminated
      against,   14.31
    Commissions, by,   14.23–14.28
    injunctions,   14.29–14.30
    introduction,   14.1
    settlement,   14.33
    void contract terms,   14.32
  enforcement by the Commissions
    CEHR,   14.26
    CRE,   14.25
    EOC,   14.24
    formal investigations,   14.27
    generally,   14.23
    introduction,   13.40
    non-discrimination notices,   14.28
  engagement,   12.12
  equal opportunities, and
    advertising,   13.34
    enforcement only by Commissions,
      13.40
    general exceptions,   13.14–13.20
    genuine occupational requirement or
      qualification,   13.2–13.7
    introduction,   13.1
    justification,   13.8
    non-employees/employers covered,
      13.21–13.32
    persons responsible,   13.35–13.39
    positive discrimination,   13.9
    relationships terminated,   13.33
    specific exceptions,   13.10–13.13
  extension of time,   14.7
  foreign employees, and,   26.13
  formulation of complaint,   14.8
  gender reassignment,   12.2
  general exceptions
    benefits provided to public,   13.17
    compliance with law,   13.18
    employment outside Great Britain,
      13.15
    illegal contracts,   13.16
    introduction,   13.14
    national security,   13.19
    State immunity,   13.20
  genuine occupational requirement or
    qualification
    gender reassignment,   13.5
    generally,   13.2
    partnerships,   13.25
    race,   13.4

Index

Discrimination – *contd*
  genuine occupational requirement or
    qualification – *contd*
  religion or belief, 13.6
  sex, 13.3
  sexual orientation, 13.7
  grounds, 12.2
  harassment
    generally, 12.11
    partnerships, 13.25
    trade organisations, 13.26
  illegal contracts, 13.16
  indirect discrimination
    application of the test, 12.8
    generally, 12.7
    particular cases, 12.9
  injunctions
    advertisements, 14.30
    instructions to discriminate, 14.30
    persistent discrimination, 14.29
    pressure to discriminate, 14.30
  instructions to commit unlawful acts
    enforcement only by Commissions,
      13.40
    generally, 12.13
    injunctions, 14.30
  introduction, 12.1
  justification, 13.8
  legal sources, 12.2
  less favourable treatment, 12.5
  marital status,
    direct discrimination, 12.4
    discrimination in employment,
      12.12
    generally 12.2
    harassment, 12.11
    indirect discrimination, 12.7
    less favourable treatment, 12.5
    'on ground of', 12.6
  maternity leave,
    direct discrimination, 12.4
    discrimination in employment,
      12.12
    generally 12.2
    harassment, 12.11
    'on ground of', 12.6
  meaning
    direct discrimination, 12.4–12.6
    harassment, 12.11
    indirect discrimination, 12.7–12.9
    introduction, 12.3
    victimisation, 12.10

Discrimination – *contd*
  national security, 13.19
  non-discrimination notices, 14.28
  non-employees/employers covered,
    13.21–13.32
  occupational pension schemes, 13.31
  office holders, 13.22
  'one-off' act, 12.12
  opportunities in employment, 12.12
  other unlawful acts, 12.13
  part time workers, and,
    comparators, 32.7–32.13
    direct effect, 32.16
    less favourable treatment, 32.4–32.6
    objective justification, 32.15
    'on the ground that the worker is a
      part-time worker', 32.14
  partnerships, 13.25
  pensions, and,
    age discrimination, 42.2
    disability discrimination, 42.10
    introduction, 13.10
    sex discrimination, 42.9
  personal disadvantage, 12.9
  personal liability, 13.37
  persons responsible
    agents, 13.38
    aiding unlawful acts, 13.36
    employees, 13.37
    third party acts, 13.39
    vicarious responsibility, 13.35
  police, 13.23
  positive discrimination
    access to training, 13.9
    childbirth, 13.9
    EC law, under, 13.9
    generally, 13.9
    less favourable treatment, 12.5
    membership of trade organisation,
      13.9
    pregnancy, 13.9
    Sikhs on construction sites, 13.12
  post-employment, 12.12
  pregnancy,
    direct discrimination, 12.4
    discrimination in employment,
      12.12
    generally 12.2
    harassment, 12.11
    less favourable treatment, 12.5
    'on ground of', 12.6
    positive discrimination, 13.9

Discrimination – *contd*
pressure to commit unlawful acts
enforcement only by Commissions,
13.40
generally, 12.13
injunctions, 14.30
publicity, 14.11
pupillage, 13.24
qualifications bodies, 13.27
questionnaire, 14.9
race, 12.2
recommendations, 14.21
relationships terminated, 13.33
religion or belief, 12.2
remedies
compensation, 14.13–14.20
introduction, 14.12
pension rights, 14.22
recommendations, 14.21
segregation, 12.5
settlement of claim, 14.33
sex, 12.2
sexual orientation, 12.2
specific exceptions
civil partnership status, 13.13
marital status, 13.13
race, 13.11
religion or belief, 13.12
sex, 13.10
sexual orientation, 13.13
sports and competitions,
race discrimination, 13.11
sex discrimination, 13.10
State immunity, 13.20
state provision of facilities and
services, 13.30
third party acts
generally, 12.12
persons responsible, 13.39
time limits for claims, and
generally, 14.4–14.7
introduction, 20.29
trade organisations, 13.26
training needs, 13.9
transsexuals, 12.2
trustees of occupational pension
schemes, 13.31
unfavourable treatment, 12.5
unlawful acts, 12.12
unlawful instructions
enforcement only by Commissions,
13.40

Discrimination – *contd*
unlawful instructions – *contd*
generally, 12.13
injunctions, 14.30
unlawful pressure
enforcement only by Commissions,
13.40
generally, 12.13
injunctions, 14.30
vicarious liability
generally, 12.12
persons responsible, 13.35
victimisation, 12.10
vocational training providers, 13.28
welfare needs, 13.9
Discrimination questionnaires
generally, 14.9
tribunal procedure, and, 20.18
Discriminatory terms
unenforceable terms, and, 8.18
Dismissal
and see Redundancy
and see Unfair dismissal
and see Wrongful dismissal
disability discrimination, and, 10.21
discrimination, and, 12.12
dismissal and disciplinary procedures,
application, 15.3
content, 15.2
deemed compliance, 15.6–15.7
effects of non-compliance, 15.8–
15.10
increase in compensation, and,
15.10
introduction, 15.1
reduction in compensation, and,
15.10
time limits, 15.12–15.13
transitional provisions, 15.14
unfair dismissal, and, 15.9
grievance procedures,
application, 15.5
content, 15.4
deemed compliance, 15.6–15.7
effects of non-compliance, 15.8–
15.11
increase in compensation, and,
15.10
introduction, 15.1
reduction in compensation, and,
15.10

Index

Dismissal – *contd*
grievance procedures – *contd*
  right to bring tribunal
    proceedings, 15.11
  time limits, 15.12–15.13
  transitional provisions, 15.14
  unfair dismissal, and, 15.9
introduction, 48.5
notice, by,
  contractual notice period, 48.6
  employee, by, 48.17
  introduction, 48.5
  pay in lieu of notice, 48.9–48.10
  rights during notice period, 48.12
  statutory minimum notice, 48.7–
    48.8
pay as you earn, and, 46.8
retraction of, 48.20
spent convictions, and, 19.3
summary, 48.13
transfer of undertakings, and,
  introduction, 52.24
  redundancy, 52.27
  unfair dismissal, 52.25–52.26
written statement of reasons,
  generally, 48.14
  remedy for failure to give, 48.15
wrongful dismissal, and,
  acceptance of employer's breach,
    58.7
  cessation of existence of employer,
    58.8
  change of employer's identity, 58.8
  constructive dismissal, 58.6
  contrast with other modes of
    termination, 58.4
  dismissal with notice, 58.5
  dismissal without notice, 58.11–
    58.17
  insolvency of employer, 58.9
  introduction, 58.3
  removal of director from board,
    58.10

Dismissal and disciplinary procedures
application, 15.3
content, 15.2
deemed compliance, 15.6–15.7
effects of non-compliance,
  generally, 15.8
  increase in compensation, and,
    15.10

Dismissal and disciplinary procedures – *contd*
effects of non-compliance – *contd*
  reduction in compensation, and,
    15.10
  unfair dismissal, and, 15.9
increase in compensation, and, 15.10
introduction, 15.1
reduction in compensation, and, 15.10
time limits, 15.12–15.13
transitional provisions, 15.14
unfair dismissal, and, 15.9
Dismissal notices
redundancy, and, 39.9
Dismissal of claims
tribunal procedure, and, 21.28
Dismissal with notice
wrongful dismissal, and, 58.5
Dismissal without notice
directors' notice periods, 58.14
express notice periods, 58.11
fixed term contracts, 58.12
implied notice periods, 58.15
justification, 58.17
rolling contracts, 58.13
statutory minimum notice, 58.16
Display screen equipment
health and safety, and, 28.5
Dispute resolution
dismissal and disciplinary procedures,
  application, 15.3
  content, 15.2
  deemed compliance, 15.6–15.7
  effects of non-compliance, 15.8–
    15.10
  increase in compensation, and,
    15.10
  introduction, 15.1
  reduction in compensation, and,
    15.10
  time limits, 15.12–15.13
  transitional provisions, 15.14
  unfair dismissal, and, 15.9
DTI review, and, 15.1
grievance procedures,
  application, 15.5
  content, 15.4
  deemed compliance, 15.6–15.7
  effects of non-compliance, 15.8–
    15.11
  increase in compensation, and,
    15.10
  introduction, 15.1

Dispute resolution – *contd*
grievance procedures – *contd*
reduction in compensation, and,
15.10
right to bring tribunal
proceedings, 15.11
time limits, 15.12–15.13
transitional provisions, 15.14
unfair dismissal, and, 15.9
introduction, 15.1
sick pay, and, 44.8
Dispute Resolution Scheme
ACAS, and, 2.10
Disqualification from office
trade unions, and, 50.14
Doctors in training
working time, and, 57.3
Domestic legislation
sources of law, and, 1.6
Domestic servants
redundancy payments, and, 38.10
working time, and, 57.30
Drug misuse
generally, 28.2
testing, 28.3
Duration of directors' service contracts
introduction, 9.11
recommendations, 9.13
section 319 restrictions, 9.12
Duty of care for advice given
trade unions, and, 51.22
Dyslexia
disability discrimination, and, 10.2

E
Early retirement
generally, 42.4
Earnings limits
taxation, and, 46.4
Earnings, loss of
unfair dismissal, and, 55.12
EC law
consultation, 25.12
disclosure of information, and, 11.11
effect, 25.2
employment law requirements, 25.3
equal access to benefits, 25.5
equal pay, and, 24.3
equal treatment, 25.6
fixed-term contracts, 25.7
free movement of labour, 25.4

EC law – *contd*
health and safety, and
generally, 27.25
introduction, 25.10
information, 25.12
insolvent employers, 25.7
introduction, 25.1
posting of workers, 25.7
redundancy, 25.8
sources of law, and, 1.7
transfer of business, 25.9
working time, 25.11
works councils, 25.12
written particulars of terms, 25.7
Economic situation of undertakings
information and consultation, and,
11.11
Economic, technical or organisational reasons
unfair dismissal, and, 54.14
Economic torts
strike action, and, 45.1
Education and training
apprenticeships, 16.2
discrimination, and, 13.9
Industrial Training Boards, 16.4
introduction, 16.1
Learning and Skills Council, 16.9
New Deal, 16.6
recovery of costs, 16.3
school-leavers, for, 16.5
work-based learning for adults, 16.8
work-based training for young
people, 16.7
Education workers
continuous employment, and, 7.9
European law, 37.7
exemplary damages, 37.5
introduction, 37.1
judicial review as to rights, 37.4
national security, 37.6
public interest immunity, 37.6
special provisions, 37.2
status, 37.3
EEA nationals
foreign workers, and, 26.2
Effective date of termination
unfair dismissal, and, 53.13
Effluxion of time
termination, and, 48.4
Elections
trade unions, and, 50.14

Index

Electricity
health and safety, and,   28.6
Emoluments
taxation, and,   46.2
Employee participation
consultation
generally,   18.28
training, on,   18.29
directors' obligation,   18.2
directors' report,   18.3
EU law,   18.1
European companies,
alternative arrangements,   18.18
complaints,   18.19
disputes,   18.19
employer's duty to provide
information,   18.14
employment protection,   18.20
introduction,   18.13
negotiated agreements,   18.16
special negotiating body,   18.15
standard rules,   18.17
European Works Councils
confidential information,   18.26
employment protection,   18.27
establishment,   18.25
implementation,   18.21
introduction,   18.4
number of employees,   18.22
requests,   18.23
special negotiating body,   18.24
information and consultation rights,
application,   18.4
complaints,   18.11
confidential information,   18.10
employment protection,   18.12
introduction,   18.4
negotiated agreements,   18.6
overview,   11.11
re-existing agreements,   18.8
requests and notifications,   18.5
standard provisions,   18.7
introduction,   18.1
Partnership Fund,   18.30
Private Finance Initiative, and,   18.1
transfer of undertakings, and,   52.22
Employee representatives
generally,   49.14
remedies,   49.15
unfair dismissal, and,   54.3
Employee share schemes
company share option,   46.30

Employee share schemes – *contd*
enterprise management incentives,
46.32
incentive plans,   46.31
savings-related share option,   46.29
Employee trustees
pensions, and,   42.12
Employees
age discrimination, and
barristers,   3.33
contract workers,   3.29
introduction,   3.28
office-holders,   3.30
police,   3.31
pupillage,   3.33
SOCA staff,   3.32
disclosure, and,
generally,   11.17
protected disclosures,   11.18
excluded employment, and,   46.22
generally,   17.2–17.3
office-holders,   17.8
pension trustees, and,   42.12
rights and obligations,   17.4–17.5
taxable benefits, and,   46.22
Employee's certificates
pay as you earn, and,   46.15
Employer handbooks and policies
contract of employment, and,   8.11
Employer's liability
age discrimination, and,   3.42
Employment
meaning,   1.2–1.3
sources of law,   1.4–1.7
stages,   1.9
Employment agencies
age discrimination, and,   3.39
Conduct Regulations,   47.5
discrimination, and,   13.29
engagement of employees, and,   23.4
generally,   47.2
harassment, and,   13.29
reforms,   47.4
statutory control,   47.3
Employment agency workers
introduction,   47.2–47.5
national minimum wage
generally,   47.6
introduction,   34.10
unfair dismissal,   47.7
working time, and,   57.3

Employment Appeal Tribunal procedure
bias allegation, 22.12
conduct of,
  disposition, 22.19–22.20
  error of law, 22.17
  fresh evidence, 22.16
  introduction, 22.14
  raising points not taken at tribunal
    hearing, 22.15
content, 22.5
costs, 22.22–22.24
disposition of, 22.19–22.20
EAT, 22.1–22.3
error of law, 22.17
EU law issues, 22.27
fresh evidence, 22.16
generally, 22.4
grounds, 22.7
institution, 22.5
miscellaneous points, 22.13
notes of evidence, 22.10
other powers, 22.21
perverse decision, 22.17
preliminary sifting, 22.8–22.9
raising points not taken at tribunal
    hearing, 22.15
reference back for clarification of
    reasons, 22.11
review of order, 22.25
time limits, 22.6
Employment income
taxation, and, 46.2
Employment law, sources of
domestic legislation, 1.6
European law, 1.7
introduction, 1.4
terms of contract of employment, 1.5
Employment outside GB
age discrimination, and, 3.19
disability discrimination, and, 10.24
discrimination, and, 13.15
Employment prospects
information and consultation, and,
    11.11
Employment protection
European companies, and, 18.20
European Works Councils, and, 18.11
health and safety, and
  breach of safety regulations, 28.11
  detriment, 28.8
  introduction, 28.7
  remedy, 28.10

Employment protection – *contd*
health and safety, and – *contd*
  whistleblowing, 28.9
  information and consultation rights,
    18.12
Employment-related services
discrimination, and, 13.30
Employment status
employees
  generally, 17.2–17.3
  office-holders, 17.8
  rights and obligations, 17.4–17.5
introduction, 17.1
office-holders, 17.8
self-employed
  generally, 17.2–17.3
  rights and obligations, 17.6–17.7
workers, 17.9
Employment tribunals
abuse of process, 21.26
ACAS, and
  arbitration schemes, 21.37
  conciliation, 21.29–21.32
  introduction, 2.4
adding new claims, 21.10
adjournment application, 21.54
administration, 20.6
age discrimination, and
  burden of proof, 3.44
  introduction, 3.44
  jurisdiction of employment
    tribunals, 3.44
  proof, 3.44
  questionnaire, 3.44
  remedies, 3.44
  time limits, 3.44
appeals
  bias allegation, 22.12
  conduct of, 22.14–22.20
  costs, 22.22–22.24
  Court of Appeal, to, 22.26
  disposition of, 22.19–22.20
  EAT, 22.1–22.3
  error of law, 22.17
  EU law issues, 22.27
  fresh evidence, 22.16
  generally, 22.4
  grounds, 22.7
  institution, 22.5
  miscellaneous points, 22.13
  notes of evidence, 22.10
  other powers, 22.21

Index

Employment tribunals – *contd*
appeals – *contd*
 perverse decision, 22.17
 preliminary sifting, 22.8–22.9
 raising points not taken at tribunal
  hearing, 22.15
 reference back for clarification of
  reasons, 22.11
 review of order, 22.25
 time limits, 22.6
bias, 21.50
breach of contract of employment,
 and, 8.23
'Calderbank' offers, 21.36
case management
 case management discussions, 21.2–
  21.5
 powers in practice, 21.7–21.14
 overriding objective, and, 21.1
 pre-hearing reviews, 21.6
 tribunal's powers, 21.2
case management discussions
 application for orders, 21.3
 introduction, 21.2
 non-compliance with orders, 21.4
 orders not available, 21.5
claims
 default judgments, 20.38
 extension of time, 20.22–20.33
 post-presentation action, 20.34
 presentation, 20.21
 response by respondent, 20.35–
  20.37
 time limits, 20.18–20.20
commencing proceedings, 20.15–20.17
composition
 Chairmen sitting alone, 20.9–20.10
 generally, 20.7–20.8
compromise agreements, 21.33–21.35
conciliation
 'Calderbank' offers, 21.36
 compromise agreements, 21.33–
  21.35
 discrimination complaints, 14.10
 generally, 21.29–21.31
 settlements, 21.32
conduct of hearing, 21.52
conflict of interest, 21.50
costs
 generally, 21.69–21.70
 orders, 21.71
 preparation time orders, 21.72

Employment tribunals – *contd*
costs – *contd*
 wasted costs orders, 21.73
costs warning, 21.15
default judgments, 20.38
deposit orders, 21.15
disability discrimination, and, 10.34
disclosure
 discrimination complaints, 14.9
 generally, 21.11–21.12
 privileged documents, 21.13
discrimination complaints
 compensation, 14.13–14.20
 conciliation, 14.10
 disclosure, 14.9
 extension of time, 14.7
 formulation of complaint, 14.8
 generally, 14.2
 publicity, 14.11
 questionnaire, 14.9
 recommendations, 14.21
 remedies, 14.12–14.22
 time limits, 14.4–14.7
discrimination questionnaires, 14.9
dismissal of claims, 21.28
dismissal of party, 21.23
estoppel, 21.26
extension of time
 contract claims, 20.32
 discrimination complaints, 14.7
 effective date of termination,
  20.23–20.24
 equal pay, 20.28
 generally, 20.22
 introduction, 21.21
 'just and equitable, 20.30
 'not reasonably practicable' to
  present in time, 20.25–20.26
 other claims, 20.33
 redundancy payments, 20.27
 unlawful deductions from wages,
  20.31
 unlawful discrimination, 20.29
further information, 21.8–21.9
hearing
 adjournment application, 21.54
 bias, 21.50
 conduct, 21.52
 conflict of interest, 21.50
 control of procedure, 21.56
 generally, 21.49
 non-attendance of parties, 21.54

Employment tribunals – *contd*
  hearing – *contd*
    order of evidence, 21.53
    other procedural points, 21.58–
      21.61
    private hearing, 21.51
    representation, 21.55
    witnesses, 21.57
  historical background, 20.1–20.2
  interest, 21.67
  introduction, 20.1–20.2
  itemised pay statements, and
    generally, 34.19
    order, 34.20
  joinder of parties, 21.23
  judgments
    adequacy of reasons, 21.63
    corrections and changes, 21.64
    generally, 21.62
    register, 21.**65**
  jurisdiction
    breach of contract of
      employment, 8.23
    EU law, over, 20.12
    generally, 20.11
    Human Rights Act, under, 20.13
  listing arrangements, 21.39–21.48
  miscellaneous powers, 21.20
  multiple claims, 21.24
  non-attendance of parties, 21.54
  order of evidence, 21.53
  overriding objective
    case management, 21.1
    generally, 20.14
  post-presentation action, 20.34
  pre-hearing reviews, 21.6
  preparation for hearing
    general, 21.38
    listing arrangements, 21.39–21.48
  preparation time orders, 21.72
  presentation of claim, 20.21
  private hearing, 21.51
  reasons for decision
    adequacy, 21.63
    generally, 21.62
  recoupment of benefits, 21.68
  references, and, 40.8
  register of judgments, 21.65
  remedies
    costs, 21.69–21.73
    generally, 21.66
    interest, 21.67

Employment tribunals – *contd*
  remedies – *contd*
    recoupment of benefits, 21.68
  representation, 21.55
  response by respondent, 20.35–20.37
  restricted reporting orders, 21.18–
    21.19
  review of judgment, 21.74–21.75
  Rules of Procedure, 20.4–20.5
  settlement
    conciliation, 21.32
    generally, 21.29–21.31
  specialist jurisdictions, 21.77
  statutory provision, 20.3
  stay of proceedings, 21.22
  striking out, 21.16–21.17
  time limits for claims
    contract claims, 20.32
    discrimination claims, 14.4–14.7
    equal pay, 20.28
    generally, 20.18
    'just and equitable, 20.30
    'not reasonably practicable' to
      present in time, 20.25–20.26
    other claims, 20.33
    post-EA 2002, 20.19–20.20
    redundancy payments, 20.27
    unlawful deductions from wages,
      20.31
    unlawful discrimination, 20.29
  transfer of proceedings, 21.25
  vexatious litigants, 21.76
  wasted costs orders, 21.73
  withdrawal of claims, 21.28
  witness orders, 21.14
  witnesses, 21.57

End of year PAYE procedure
  certificates, 46.15
  Class 1A NICs, 46.17
  P9D, 46.16
  P11D, 46.16
  returns, 46.15

Enforcement
  Commission for Equality and Human
    Rights, by
    formal investigations, 14.27
    generally, 14.26
    introduction, 14.23
    non-discrimination notices, 14.28
  Commission for Racial Equality, by
    formal investigations, 14.27
    generally, 14.25

Index

Enforcement – *contd*
Commission for Racial Equality, by – *contd*
  introduction, 14.23
  non-discrimination notices, 14.28
disability discrimination, and
  application to employment tribunal, 10.34
  introduction, 10.33
discrimination, and
  applications to Employment Tribunal, 14.2–14.22
  assistance for persons discriminated against, 14.31
  Commissions, by, 14.23–14.28
  injunctions, 14.29–14.30
  introduction, 14.1
  settlement, 14.33
  void contract terms, 14.32
Equal Opportunities Commission, by
  formal investigations, 14.27
  generally, 14.24
  introduction, 14.23
  non-discrimination notices, 14.28
gender equality duty, 13.34
health and safety, and
  appeals against notices, 27.34–27.36
  enforcing authorities, 27.29
  improvement notices, 27.31
  inspectors, 27.31
  prohibition notices, 27.32
  withdrawal of notices, 27.33
working time, and
  health and safety authorities, by, 57.21
  individual, by, 57.22
  introduction, 57.20

Enforcing authorities
health and safety, and, 27.29

Engagement of employees
advertising, 23.1
agencies, and, 23.4
disability discrimination, and, 10.19
discrimination, and, 12.12
interview, 23.2
notification of terms and conditions, 23.3
selection, 23.2
withdrawal of offers, 23.5

Enhanced redundancy benefits
age discrimination, and, 3.26

Enterprise management incentives
generally, 46.32

Epilepsy
disability discrimination, and, 10.2

Equal access to social security benefits
European law, and, 25.5

Equal Opportunities Commission
Code of Practice
  legal effect, 5.9
  power to issue, 5.8
formal investigations, 14.27
generally, 14.24
introduction, 14.23
non-discrimination notices, 14.28

Equal pay
Agricultural Wages Orders, and, 24.21
armed forces personnel, 24.4
background, 24.1
Code of Practice, 24.2
collective agreements, 24.24
comparator, 24.9
contractual effect, 24.23
direct discrimination
  generally, 24.5
  'material factor' defence, and, 24.12
eligible employees, 24.4
equality clause
  comparator, 24.9
  introduction, 24.5
  like work, 24.6
  work of equal value, 24.8
  work rated as equivalent, 24.7
equivalence, 24.9
expert evidence, 24.22
foreign employees, and, 26.13
indirect discrimination, 24.10
introduction, 24.1
legislative framework
  domestic legislation, 24.2
  Equal Pay Act 1970, 24.4
  EU provisions, 24.3
like work, 24.6
'material factor' defence
  direct discrimination, and, 24.12
  generally, 24.11
maternity pay, 24.14
maternity suspension, and, 24.4
office-holders, 24.4
part-time workers
  generally, 24.15
  introduction, 24.2
  pensions, 24.19

Equal pay – *contd*
pensions, and
  Barber claims, 24.18
  introduction, 24.16
  part-time workers, 24.19
  statutory regime, 24.17
posted employees, 24.4
procedure, 24.22
remedies
  Agricultural Wages Orders, 24.21
  generally, 24.20
time limits for claims, and, 20.28
transsexuals, and
  generally, 24.13
  introduction, 24.2
work of equal value, 24.8
work rated as equivalent, 24.7
Equal treatment
European law, and, 25.6
time off work for trade union
  activities, and, 49.4
Equipment and materials
health and safety, and, 27.6
Equipment for work
health and safety, and, 28.12
Error of law
EAT procedure, and, 22.17
Estoppel
tribunal procedure, and, 21.26
European Community employees
generally, 37.8
European companies,
alternative arrangements, 18.18
complaints, 18.19
disputes, 18.19
employer's duty to provide
  information, 18.14
employment protection, 18.20
introduction, 18.13
negotiated agreements, 18.16
special negotiating body, 18.15
standard rules, 18.17
European Convention on Human rights
effect, 30.2
introduction, 30.1
pre-HRA 1998, 30.5
rights, 30.7
European law
consultation, 25.12
disclosure of information, and, 11.11
effect, 25.2
employment law requirements, 25.3

European law – *contd*
equal access to benefits, 25.5
equal pay, and, 24.3
equal treatment, 25.6
fixed-term contracts, 25.7
free movement of labour, 25.4
health and safety, and
  generally, 27.25
  introduction, 25.10
information, 25.12
insolvent employers, 25.7
introduction, 25.1
posting of workers, 25.7
public sector employees, and, 37.7
redundancy, 25.8
sources of law, and, 1.7
transfer of business, 25.9
working time, 25.11
works councils, 25.12
written particulars of terms, 25.7
European Social Charter
human rights, and, 30.8
European Works Councils
confidential information, 18.26
employment protection, 18.27
establishment, 18.25
European law, and, 25.12
implementation, 18.21
introduction, 18.4
number of employees, 18.22
requests, 18.23
special negotiating body, 18.24
time off work, and, 49.16
unfair dismissal, and, 54.3
Excluded employment, employees in
taxable benefits, 46.22
Exclusion and expulsion from trade union
common law, 51.12
introduction, 51.11
remedy, 51.14
statutory provisions, 51.13
Exemplary damages
discrimination compensation, and,
  14.18
public sector employees, and, 37.5
Expenses incurred in the performance of duties
generally, 46.21
relief, 46.28
Express terms
contract of employment, and, 8.12
contract claims, 20.32

Index

Express terms – *contd*
discrimination complaints, 14.4
effective date of termination, 20.23–20.24
equal pay, 20.28
generally, 20.22
introduction, 21.21
'just and equitable, 20.30
'not reasonably practicable' to present in time, 20.25–20.26
other claims, 20.33
redundancy payments, 20.27
unlawful deductions from wages, 20.31
unlawful discrimination, 20.29
Expression, freedom of
human rights, and, 30.7

F
Facilities provided to public
disability discrimination, and, 10.24
Failure to follow statutory disciplinary procedures
unfair dismissal, and, 54.3
Failure to make payments
trade union members, and, 51.6
Fair hearing, right to
human rights, and, 30.7
Fairness of dismissal
acceptable reasons for dismissal
any other substantial reason, 54.14
capability, 54.5–54.8
contravention of any enactment, 54.13
ill-health, 54.8
introduction, 54.1
misconduct, 54.9–54.10
qualifications, 54.7
redundancy, 54.11–54.12
summary, 54.2
age discrimination, and, 3.48
deemed unfair dismissals, 54.3
'in the circumstances', 54.4
redundancy, and, 39.8
transfer of undertakings, and, 52.26
False statements
disability discrimination, and, 10.30
Family and private life, right to
human rights, and, 30.7
Family-related dismissal
unfair dismissal, and, 54.3

Fines
standard scale, 1.10
Fire brigade officers
disability discrimination, and, 10.24
Fire precautions
health and safety, and, 28.13
First aid
health and safety, and, 28.14
Fixed-term contracts
European law, and, 25.7
dismissal on expiry of
generally, 53.6
some other substantial reason, 54.14
termination, and, 48.4
Fixed-term employees
less favourable treatment, and, 47.9
unfair dismissal, and, 54.3
Flexible working
generally, 49.19
unfair dismissal, and, 54.3
Forced resignation
unfair dismissal, and, 53.8
Foreign employees
EEA nationals, 26.2
employment-related offences, 26.9–26.10
governing law
generally, 26.11
jurisdiction, 26.12
introduction, 26.1
non-EEA nationals, 26.4
permits
applications, 26.6
eligible workers, 26.5
further information, 26.8
procedure, 26.7
posted workers, 26.3
statutory claims, 26.13
Forfeiture
service lettings, and, 43.5
Former employees
age discrimination, and
generally, 3.41
introduction, 3.15
Free movement of labour
European law, and, 25.4
Freedom of association
human rights, and, 30.4
Freedom to agree
terms of contract, and, 8.10

Freedom to employ
contract of employment, and, 8.2
Fresh evidence
EAT procedure, and, 22.16
Frustration
termination, and, 48.3
unfair dismissal and, 53.10
Further information
tribunal procedure, and, 21.8–21.9
Future loss of earnings
unfair dismissal, and, 55.12

G
'Garden leave'
restraint of trade covenants, and,
41.14
wrongful dismissal, and, 58.21
Gender equality duty
enforcement, 13.34
generally, 13.33
introduction, 13.1
Gender reassignment
and see Sex discrimination
generally, 12.2
General earnings
taxation, and, 46.2
**Genuine occupational requirement or
qualification**
age discrimination, and, 3.17
gender reassignment, 13.5
generally, 13.2
partnerships, 13.25
race, 13.4
religion or belief, 13.6
sex, 13.3
sexual orientation, 13.7
Gifted assets
taxable benefits, and, 46.21–46.22
Good faith
directors' duties, and, 9.16
Goods or services contracts
trade union members, and, 51.120
Governing law
generally, 26.11
jurisdiction, 26.12
Gratuities
national minimum wage, and, 34.9
pay, and, 34.21
Grievance procedures
application, 15.5
content, 15.4

Grievance procedures – *contd*
deemed compliance, 15.6–15.7
effects of non-compliance,
generally, 15.8
increase in compensation, 15.10
reduction in compensation, 15.10
right to bring tribunal
proceedings, 15.11
unfair dismissal, 15.9
increase in compensation, and, 15.10
introduction, 15.1
reduction in compensation, and, 15.10
right to bring tribunal proceedings,
15.11
time limits, 15.12–15.13
transitional provisions, 15.14
unfair dismissal, and, 15.9
Grounds of appeal
EAT procedure, and, 22.7
Guaranteed debts
insolvency of employer, and, 31.5
Guarantee payments
amount, 34.27
exclusions, 34.26
insolvency of employer, and, 31.2
introduction, 34.23
qualifying period, 34.25
remedy for failure to make payment,
34.28
'workless days', 34.24
Guidance
part time workers, and, 32.1
working time, and, 57.26

H
Handbooks and policies
contract of employment, and, 8.11
Harassment
age discrimination, and
employees, against, 3.14
employment agencies, by, 3.39
generally, 3.8
office-holders, against, 3.30
partnerships, by, 3.35
pupil barristers, against, 3.33
trade organisations, by, 3.36
vocational training providers, by,
3.38
barristers, 13.24
disability discrimination, and, 10.21
employment agencies, 13.29

Index

Harassment – *contd*
  generally, 12.11
  office holders, 13.22
  partnerships, 13.25
  trade organisations, 13.26
  trustees of occupational pension
    schemes, 13.31
Hazardous substances
  health and safety, and, 28.26
Health and safety
  accident reporting, 28.1
  alcohol misuse, 28.2
  appeals against notices
    cost of remedy required, 27.36
    effect, 27.35
    introduction, 27.34
  bullying, 28.28
  children, and
    breaks, 4.6
    introduction, 4.5
    night work, 4.6
    rest periods, 4.6
  civil liability, 27.43
  Codes of Practice, 27.28
  common law duty
    competent fellow workers, 27.7
    independent contractors, 27.11
    introduction, 27.2
    protection from risk of injury, 27.8
    safe equipment and materials, 27.6
    safe means of access, 27.4
    safe place of work, 27.3
    safe system of work, 27.5
    vicarious liability for acts of
      employees, 27.9
    working under direction of third
      party, 27.10
  competent fellow workers, 27.7
  construction site management, 28.4
  contributory negligence, 27.44
  coroner's inquests
    findings, 27.46
    generally, 27.47
    "interested persons", 27.48
    introduction, 27.45
  corporate killing, 27.42
  criminal proceedings
    corporate killing, 27.42
    defence, 27.41
    directors' liability, 27.38
    generally, 27.37
    order to remedy default, 27.39

Health and safety – *contd*
  criminal proceedings – *contd*
    time for commencing proceedings,
      27.40
  direction of third party, 27.10
  directors' liability, 27.38
  disclosure of information, and
    introduction, 11.7
    safety representatives, 11.8
  display screen equipment, 28.5
  drug misuse
    generally, 28.2
    testing, 28.3
  electricity, 28.6
  employment protection
    breach of safety regulations, 28.11
    detriment, 28.8
    introduction, 28.7
    remedy, 28.10
    whistleblowing, 28.9
  enforcement
    appeals against notices, 27.34–27.36
    enforcing authorities, 27.29
    improvement notices, 27.31
    inspectors, 27.31
    prohibition notices, 27.32
    withdrawal of notices, 27.33
  enforcing authorities, 27.29
  equipment and materials, 27.6
  equipment for work, 28.12
  European law, and
    generally, 27.25
    introduction, 25.10
  fire precautions, 28.13
  first aid, 28.14
  hazardous substances, 28.26
  Health and Safety Commission
    Codes of Practice, 27.28
    enforcement policy, 27.29
    establishment, 27.26
    information, 27.27
  hours of work, 28.15
  improvement notices
    appeals, 27.34–27.36
    generally, 27.31
    withdrawal, 27.33
  independent contractors
    faulty work by, 27.15
    generally, 27.11
  inspectors' powers, 27.31
  insurance against liability, 28.16
  introduction, 27.1

Health and safety – *contd*
management, 28.17
manual handling of goods, 28.18
means of access, 27.4
noise levels, 28.19
occupiers' liability
faulty work by independent
contractor, 27.15
introduction, 27.12
'occupier', 27.13
occupier's duty, 27.14
prohibition notices
appeals, 27.34–27.36
generally, 27.32
withdrawal, 27.33
place of work, 27.3
protection from risk of injury, 27.8
repetitive strain injury, 28.31
reporting of accidents, 28.1
safe equipment and materials, 27.6
safe means of access, 27.4
safe place of work, 27.3
safe system of work, 27.5
safety measures
charges for, 27.24
interference with, 27.23
safety representatives
disclosure of information, and, 11.8
introduction, 28.20
non-unionised workers, 28.22
time off work, and, 49.9–49.10
union-appointees, 28.21
safety signs, 28.30
smoking, 28.23
statutory provisions
employees' duties, 27.22
employer's obligations, 27.18
health, safety and welfare, 27.17
interference with safety measures,
27.23
introduction, 27.16
manufacturer's duties, 27.21
occupier's duties, 27.20
self-employed, 27.19
stress, 28.24—28.25
substances hazardous to health, 28.26
system of work, 27.5
time off work for safety
representatives, and
generally, 49.9
remedies, 49.10

Health and safety – *contd*
unfair dismissal
breach of safety regulations, 28.11
detriment, 28.8
generally, 54.3
introduction, 28.7
remedy, 28.10
vibration, 28.27
vicarious liability for acts of
employees, 27.9
violence, 28.28
whistleblowing, 28.9
working under direction of third
party, 27.10
workplace standards
generally, 28.29
safety signs, 28.30
work-related upper limb disorders,
28.31
Health and Safety Commission
Codes of Practice
introduction, 27.28
legal effect, 5.11
power to issue, 5.10
enforcement policy, 27.29
establishment, 27.26
information, 27.27
Health and safety representatives
disclosure of information, and, 11.8
introduction, 28.20
non-unionised workers, 28.22
time off work, and
generally, 49.9
remedies, 49.10
union-appointees, 28.21
Health assessment
night work, and, 57.12
Health service workers
European law, 37.7
exemplary damages, 37.5
introduction, 37.1
judicial review as to rights, 37.4
national security, 37.6
public interest immunity, 37.6
special provisions, 37.2
status, 37.3
Hearing
adjournment application, 21.54
bias, 21.50
conduct, 21.52
conflict of interest, 21.50
control of procedure, 21.56

Index

Hearing – *contd*
  generally,   21.49
  non-attendance of parties,   21.54
  order of evidence,   21.53
  other procedural points,   21.58–21.61
  private hearing,   21.51
  representation,   21.55
  witnesses,   21.57
Hearings on liability and quantum
  wrongful dismissal, and,   58.41
Help and advice
  disability discrimination, and,   10.35
Holidays
  agricultural workers,   29.7
  civil aviation workers,   29.8
  contractual entitlement,   29.9
  generally,   29.2
  insolvency of employer, and
    generally,   31.2
    payments from National Insurance
      Fund,   31.5
  introduction,   29.1
  notice requirements,   29.5
  payment,   29.4
  period of leave,   29.3
  remedies,   29.6
  statutory entitlement,   29.2
  termination of employment, and,   29.4
Home workers
  national minimum wage, and,   34.10
Hours of work
  agricultural workers,   29.7
  contract, under,   29.9
  health and safety, and,   28.15
  introduction,   29.2
  notice requirements,   29.5
  payment,   29.4
  period of leave,   29.3
  remedies,   29.6
Human rights
  European Convention
    effect,   30.2
    introduction,   30.1
    pre-HRA 1998,   30.5
    rights,   30.7
  European Social Charter,   30.8
  freedom of association,   30.4
  freedom of expression,   30.8
  freedom of thought, conscience and
    religion,   30.7
  Human Rights Act 1998,   30.6
  introduction,   30.1

Human rights – *contd*
  petition by individual,   30.3
  right to fair hearing,   30.7
  right to private and family life,   30.7

I
ICE Directive and Regulations
  information and consultation, and,
    11.11
Illegal contracts
  discrimination, and,   13.16
  unfair dismissal, and,   53.16
Ill-health dismissals
  disability discrimination, and,   10.23
  generally,   54.8
  introduction,   54.5
  retirement, and,   42.4
  summary,   54.2
Immunity from liability for strike action
  background,   45.1
  'in contemplation or furtherance',
    45.5
  introduction,   45.3
  'trade dispute',   45.4
Impairment
  disability discrimination, and,   10.2
Implied terms
  contract of employment, and,   8.12–
    7.13
Imprisonment
  unfair dismissal, and,   54.14
Improvement notices
  appeals
    cost of remedy required,   27.36
    effect,   27.35
    introduction,   27.34
  generally,   27.31
  withdrawal,   27.33
Incentive plans
  generally,   46.31
Incompetence dismissals
  disability discrimination, and,   10.23
Indemnity
  directors' duties, and,   9.18
Independence of trade unions
  factors,   50.23
  introduction,   50.22
  withdrawal of certificate,   50.24
Independent contractors
  health and safety, and
    faulty work by,   27.15

Independent contractors – *contd*
  health and safety, and – *contd*
    generally, 27.11
Indirect discrimination
  age discrimination, and, 3.5
  application of the test, 12.8
  compensation, 14.14
  disability discrimination, and, 10.9
  equal pay, and, 24.10
  generally, 12.7
  particular cases, 12.9
Inducement of breach of contract
  strike action, and, 45.2
Industrial action
  armed forces, 45.20
  ballots before action
    generally, 45.14
    members' right, 45.17
  calls for action, 45.15
  consequences for employers, 45.19
  criminal liability, 45.12
  deductions from wages, and, 34.6
  employer's rights and remedies, 45.16
  immunity from liability for
    background, 45.1
    'in contemplation or furtherance',
      45.5
    introduction, 45.3
    'trade dispute', 45.4
  liability for
    background, 45.1
    common law, at, 45.2
    statutory immunity, 45.3–45.5
  picketing
    case law, 45.10
    Code of Practice, 45.11
    generally, 45.9
  police officers, 45.20
  pressure to impose union membership
    or recognition, 45.7
  prohibited employees, 45.20
  public sector employees, and, 37.2
  remedies
    employers,' 45.16
    third parties', 45.18
  restricted employees, 45.20
  restrictions, 8.20
  secondary action, limits on
    dismissal of unofficial strikers, 45.8
    generally, 45.6
    pressure to impose membership or
      recognition, 45.7

Industrial action – *contd*
  third parties' rights and remedies,
    45.18
  time off work for trade union officials,
    and, 49.2
  trade union, liability of
    ballots before action, 45.14
    calls for action, 45.15
    generally, 45.13
    introduction, 51.9
  unenforceable terms, and, 8.20
  unfair dismissal, and
    introduction, 54.3
    official action, 53.17
    unofficial action, 53.18
Industrial Relations Act
  Codes of Practice, 5.2
Industrial Relations Code
  generally, 5.2
  legal effect, 5.3
Industrial Training Boards
  education and training, and, 16.4
Information
  see also Information, disclosure of
  European law, and, 25.12
  transfer of undertakings, and
    advance notification, 52.23
    employee liability information,
      52.22
Information and Consultation
  Regulations 2004
  and see Employee participation
  introduction, 18.4–18.12
  overview, 11.11
  transfer of undertakings, and, 52.22
Information, disclosure of
  collective bargaining, for
    Code of Practice, 11.4
    duty to disclose, 11.3
    failure to comply with request, 11.5
    introduction, 11.2
  confidential information, and, 11.16
  data protection, and
    background, 11.13
    overview, 11.14
  directors' report, in, 11.9
  employees, by
    generally, 11.17
    protected disclosures, 11.18
  economic situation of undertaking,
    11.11
  employment prospects, 11.11

Index

Information, disclosure of – *contd*
health and safety, for
introduction, 11.7
safety representatives, 11.8
introduction, 11.1
medical reports, and, 11.15
occupational pension schemes, by,
11.10
participation in company affairs,
11.11
public interest, in
generally, 11.17
protected disclosures, 11.18
transfer of undertakings, and
advance notification, 52.23
employee liability information,
52.22
introduction, 11.6
whistleblowing, and
generally, 11.17
protected disclosures, 11.18
Injunctions
breach of contract of employment, and
employee's remedies, 8.23
employer's remedies, 8.24
discrimination, and
advertisements, 14.30
instructions to discriminate, 14.30
persistent discrimination, 14.29
pressure to discriminate, 14.30
restraint of trade covenants, and,
41.17
wrongful dismissal, and, 58.23
Injury to feelings
discrimination compensation, and,
14.16
Inquests
findings, 27.46
generally, 27.47
"interested persons", 27.48
introduction, 27.45
Inspection
directors' service contracts, and, 9.8
Inquiries
ACAS, and, 2.8
Insolvency of employer
administrative receivers' liability,
31.11
European law, and, 25.7
introduction, 31.1
other consequences, 31.10

Insolvency of employer – *contd*
payments from National Insurance
Fund
adoption pay, 31.8
apprentices' fees, 31.5
arrears of pay, 31.5
guaranteed debts, 31.5
holiday pay, 31.5
introduction, 31.3
maternity pay, 31.8
notice pay, 31.5
paternity pay, 31.8
redundancy payments, 31.4
remedy for non-payment, 31.6
sick pay, 31.8
unfair dismissal compensation, 31.5
unpaid pension contributions, 31.7
pensions, and, 31.7
Pensions Act 2004, 31.9
unpaid contributions, 31.7
preferential debts, 31.2
transfer of undertakings, and
generally, 52.11
introduction, 31.9
wrongful dismissal, and, 58.9
Inspectors' powers
health and safety, and, 27.31
Instructions to discriminate
age discrimination, and, 3.6
enforcement only by Commissions,
13.40
generally, 12.13
injunctions, 14.30
Insurance against liability
health and safety, and, 28.17
Interest
discrimination, and, 14.20
generally, 21.67
Interest-free loans
taxable benefits, and, 46.21
Interests of the parties
restraint of trade covenants, and, 41.4
Interim payments
wrongful dismissal, and, 58.41
Interim relief
unfair dismissal, and, 55.21
Internal appeals
unfair dismissal, and, 54.15
Interviews
engagement of employees, and, 23.2
Intimidation
strike action, and, 45.1

Itemised pay statements
application to tribunal
generally, 34.19
order, 34.20
attachment of earnings, and, 35.9
exclusions, 34.18
fixed deductions, 34.17
generally, 34.16

J

Joinder of parties
tribunal procedure, and, 21.23
unfair dismissal, and, 55.20
Joining after 6 April
pay as you earn, and, 46.7
Judgments
adequacy of reasons, 21.63
corrections and changes, 21.64
generally, 21.62
register, 21.**65**
Jurisdiction of tribunals
age discrimination, and, 3.44
breach of contract of employment,
8.23
EU law, over, 20.12
generally, 20.11
Human Rights Act, under, 20.13
Judicial review
public sector employees, and, 37.4
Jury service
unfair dismissal, and, 54.3
Just and equitable
time limits for claims, and, 20.30
Justices of the Peace
time off work, and, 49.5
Justification
discrimination, and, 13.8

L

Lay-off
redundancy payments, and
counter-notice, 38.9
generally, 38.8
Learning and Skills Council
education and training, and, 16.9
Leased business premises
disability discrimination, and, 10.13
Legal capacity
trade unions, and, 50.2
Legal representation
tribunal procedure, and, 21.55

Less favourable treatment
age discrimination, and, 3.4
discrimination, and, 12.5
fixed-term employees, and, 47.9
part time workers, and,
introduction, 32.4
overtime, 32.6
pro rata principle, 32.5
written statement of reasons, and,
32.17
Licence
service lettings, and, 43.4
Life assurance cover to retired workers
age discrimination, and, 3.27
Like work
equal pay, and, 24.6
Limitation periods
and see Time limits on claims
wrongful dismissal, and, 58.40
Listing
trade unions, and, 50.21
Listing arrangements
tribunal procedure, and, 21.39–21.48
Listing Rules requirements
directors remuneration, 9.24
service contracts, 9.9
termination of office, 9.29
Living accommodation
and see Service lettings
taxable benefits, and, 46.21–46.23
Loans
taxable benefits, and, 46.21–46.22
Local authority powers
children, and, 4.3
Local government employees
disability discrimination, and, 10.24
European law, 37.7
exemplary damages, 37.5
introduction, 37.1
judicial review as to rights, 37.4
national security, 37.6
public interest immunity, 37.6
special provisions, 37.2
status, 37.3
Lock-outs
and see Strikes
unfair dismissal, and
official action, 53.17
unofficial action, 53.18
Long service benefits
age discrimination, and, 3.25

Index

Look for work, time off to
generally, 49.7
remedies, 49.8
Loss of earnings
unfair dismissal, and, 55.12
"Lower-paid" employees
generally, 46.3
taxable benefits, 46.22
Luncheon vouchers
tax-free benefits, and, 46.23

M
Managed service company
taxation, and, 46.36
Manual handling of goods
health and safety, and, 28.18
Marital status
and see Discrimination
direct discrimination, 12.4
discrimination in employment, 12.12
generally 12.2
harassment, 12.11
indirect discrimination, 12.7
less favourable treatment, 12.5
'on ground of', 12.6
sexual orientation, and, 13.13
'Material factor' defence
direct discrimination, and, 24.12
generally, 24.11
Maternity leave
additional leave, 33.21
discrimination, and,
    and see Discrimination
    direct discrimination, 12.4
    discrimination in employment,
        12.12
    generally 12.2
    harassment, 12.11
    'on ground of', 12.6
dismissal of replacement, 33.22
equal pay, and, 24.4
introduction, 33.17
ordinary leave
    generally, 33.18
    redundancy, and, 33.19
time off work, and, 49.19
unfair dismissal, and, 54.3
working during, 33.22A
Maternity pay
amount, 33.14
'confinement', 33.11

Maternity pay – *contd*
insolvency of employer, and, 31.8
introduction, 33.10
payments from National Insurance
    Fund, and, 31.8
period of entitlement, 33.13
qualifying requirements, 33.11
recoupment by employer, 33.16
remedy for non-payment, 33.15
sick pay, and, 44.4
Maternity rights
additional maternity leave, 33.21
ante-natal care, time off for
    amount, 33.4
    introduction, 33.2
    qualifying requirements, 33.3
    remedies for refusal, 33.5
equal pay
    generally, 24.14
    suspension, 24.4
insolvency of employer, and, 31.2
introduction, 33.1
leave
    additional leave, 33.21
    dismissal of replacement, 33.22
    introduction, 33.17
    ordinary leave, 33.18–33.19
    working during, 33.22A
ordinary maternity leave
    generally, 33.18
    redundancy, and, 33.19
pregnancy, detriment by reason of
    introduction, 33.8
    remedies, 33.9
pregnancy reasons, dismissal for
    generally, 33.6
    qualifying period, 33.7
statutory maternity pay
    amount, 33.14
    'confinement', 33.11
    insolvency of employer, and, 31.8
    introduction, 33.10
    period of entitlement, 33.13
    qualifying requirements, 33.11
    recoupment by employer, 33.16
    remedy for non-payment, 33.15
suspension on maternity grounds
    alternative work, 33.24
    introduction, 33.23
    remuneration, 33.25
unfair dismissal, and, 54.3
working during leave, 33.22A

Maximum weekly time
working time, and, 57.6
Meals in canteen
tax-free benefits, and, 46.23
Means of access
health and safety, and, 27.4
Medical insurance premiums
taxable benefits, and, 46.21
Medical reports
disclosure of information, and, 11.15
Medical suspension, pay during
amount, 34.32
equal pay, and, 24.4
exclusions, 34.31
generally, 34.29
insolvency of employer, and, 31.2
qualifying conditions, 34.30
remedy for failure to make payment,
34.33
Medical treatment
taxable benefits, and, 46.21
Merchant seamen
age discrimination, and, 3.17
working time, and, 57.31–57.32
Method of payment
generally, 34.3
Mileage allowances
taxable benefits, and, 46.21
Military service
time off work, and, 49.20
Minimum wage
age discrimination, and, 3.24
agency workers
generally, 47.6
introduction, 34.10
coverage, 34.10
introduction, 34.9
records, 34.11
relevant workers, 34.10
remedies for failure to pay, 34.12–
34.13
statements, 34.11
unfair dismissal, and, 54.3
Ministers of religion
sex discrimination, and, 13.10
Minors, employment of
breaks, 4.6
contracts of employment, 4.10
definitions, 4.1
health and safety
breaks, 4.6
introduction, 4.5

Minors, employment of – *contd*
health and safety – *contd*
night work, 4.6
rest periods, 4.6
local authority powers, 4.3
night work, 4.6
rest periods, 4.6
restrictions
generally, 4.2
local authority powers, 4.3
other provisions, 4.4
time off for study or training
introduction, 4.7
remedy for refusal, 4.8
right not to suffer detriment, 4.9
Misconduct dismissals
generally, 54.9
procedure, 54.10
redundancy payments, and, 38.10
summary, 54.2
Misleading statements
disability discrimination, and, 10.30
Mitigation of loss
unfair dismissal, and, 55.13
Mobile workers
working time, and, 57.34–57.36
**Modified dismissal and disciplinary
procedures**
application, 15.3
content, 15.2
deemed compliance, 15.6–15.7
effects of non-compliance,
generally, 15.8
increase in compensation, and,
15.10
reduction in compensation, and,
15.10
unfair dismissal, and, 15.9
increase in compensation, and, 15.10
introduction, 15.1
reduction in compensation, and, 15.10
time limits, 15.12–15.13
transitional provisions, 15.14
unfair dismissal, and, 15.9
Modified grievance procedures
application, 15.5
content, 15.4
deemed compliance, 15.6–15.7
effects of non-compliance,
generally, 15.8
increase in compensation, 15.10
reduction in compensation, 15.10

Index

Modified grievance procedures – *contd*
  effects of non-compliance – *contd*
    right to bring tribunal
        proceedings, 15.11
    unfair dismissal, 15.9
  increase in compensation, and, 15.10
  introduction, 15.1
  reduction in compensation, and, 15.10
  right to bring tribunal proceedings,
      15.11
  time limits, 15.12–15.13
  transitional provisions, 15.14
  unfair dismissal, and, 15.9
Money purchase pension schemes
  generally, 42.7
Money's worth
  taxation, and, 46.2
Monotonous work
  working time, and, 57.18
Multiple claims
  tribunal procedure, and, 21.24
Mutual agreement
  termination, and, 48.2

N
National Health Service
  continuous employment, and, 7.9
National insurance contributions
  pay as you earn, and, 46.17
National Insurance Fund, payments from
  adoption pay, 31.8
  apprentices' fees, 31.5
  arrears of pay, 31.5
  guaranteed debts, 31.5
  holiday pay, 31.5
  introduction, 31.3
  maternity pay, 31.8
  notice pay, 31.5
  paternity pay, 31.8
  redundancy payments, 31.4
  remedy for non-payment, 31.6
  sick pay, 31.8
  unfair dismissal compensation, 31.5
  unpaid pension contributions, 31.7
National minimum wage
  age discrimination, and, 3.24
  agency workers
    generally, 47.6
    introduction, 34.10
  coverage, 34.10
  introduction, 34.9

National minimum wage – *contd*
  records, 34.11
  relevant workers, 34.10
  remedies for failure to pay, 34.12–
      34.13
  statements, 34.11
  unfair dismissal, and, 54.3
National security
  age discrimination, and, 3.21
  discrimination, and, 13.19
  public sector employees, and, 37.6
Nationality
  and see Race discrimination
  generally, 12.7–12.8
Necessary economies
  unfair dismissal, and, 54.14
New Deal
  education and training, and, 16.6
Night work
  children, and, 4.6
  duration, 57.10
  health assessments, 57.12
  introduction, 57.9
  special hazards, 57.11
  transfer to day work, 57.13
'No employment' periods
  continuous employment, and, 7.7
'No strike' clauses
  collective agreements, and, 6.5
Noise levels
  health and safety, and, 28.19
Non-attendance of parties
  tribunal procedure, and, 21.54
Non-cash vouchers
  taxable benefits, and, 46.21–46.22
Non-competition covenants
  restraint of trade, and, 41.1
Non-contractual bonus
  meaning of 'wages', and, 34.6
Non-dealing covenants
  restraint of trade, and, 41.1
Non-discrimination notices
  discrimination, and, 14.28
Non-EEA nationals
  foreign workers, and, 26.4
Non-membership of union
  unfair dismissal, and, 54.3
Non-solicitation covenants
  restraint of trade, and, 41.1
Normal day-to-day activities
  disability discrimination, and, 10.4

'Normal retiring age'
retirement, and, 42.2

'Not reasonably practicable'
time limits for claims, and, 20.25–20.26

Notes of evidence
EAT procedure, and, 22.10

Notice, termination by
contractual notice period, 48.6
employee, by, 48.17
introduction, 48.5
pay in lieu of notice
generally, 48.9
gross or net, 48.11
taxation, 48.10
payments from National Insurance
Fund, and, 31.5
rights during notice period, 48.12
statutory minimum notice
exceptions, 48.8
generally, 48.7

Notice to quit
service lettings, and, 43.5

Notification requirements
redundancy, and, 39.7

Notification of terms and conditions
engagement of employees, and, 23.3

Nurseries
tax-free benefits, and, 46.23

O

Occupational pension scheme trustees
age discrimination, and, 3.34
introduction, 42.12
discrimination, and, 13.31
introduction, 42.12
time off work, and
generally, 49.12
remedies, 49.13
unfair dismissal, and, 54.3

Occupational pension schemes
see also Pensions
disclosure of information, and, 11.10
discrimination, and, 13.31
employee trustees
generally, 42.12
time off work, 49.12–49.13
generally, 42.7
retirement, and, 42.1

Occupiers' liability
faulty work by independent
contractor, 27.15
introduction, 27.12
'occupier', 27.13
occupier's duty, 27.14

Occurrence of external event
unfair dismissal, and, 53.10

Office-holders
age discrimination, and, 3.30
directors, and, 9.1
discrimination, and, 13.22
equal pay, and, 24.4
generally, 17.4

Offsetting sick pay
contributory pension schemes, 44.11
contributory sickness schemes, 44.10
introduction, 44.9

Offshore workers
national minimum wage, and, 34.10

'One-off' act
discrimination, and, 12.12

Opportunities in employment
discrimination, and, 12.12

Opt-out agreements
working time, and, 57.7

Order of evidence
tribunal procedure, and, 21.53

Ordinary maternity leave
generally, 33.18
redundancy, and, 33.19

Overpayment
deductions from wages, and, 34.6
pay, and, 34.15

Overriding objective
case management, 21.1
generally, 20.14

P

P9D
pay as you earn, and, 46.16

P11D
pay as you earn, and, 46.16

"P11D" employees
generally, 46.3

Parental leave
generally, 33.26
time off work, and, 49.19
unfair dismissal, and, 54.3

Parking facilities
tax-free benefits, and, 46.23

Index

Parliamentary staff
age discrimination, and, 3.46
Part time workers
applications to Employment Tribunal,
introduction, 32.20
remedies, 32.22
time limits, 32.21
comparators,
actual comparator, 32.11
circumstances where comparator not
required, 32.13
'comparable full time worker',
32.8–32.12
'full time worker', 32.7
'part time worker', 32.7
'same or broadly similar work',
32.10
'same type of contract', 32.9
scope of comparison, 32.12
continuous employment, and, 7.8
contracting out, 32.23
discrimination,
comparators, 32.7–32.13
direct effect, 32.16
less favourable treatment, 32.4–32.6
objective justification, 32.15
'on the ground that the worker is a
part-time worker', 32.14
employers' liability, 32.24
equal pay, and
generally, 24.15
introduction, 24.2
pensions, 24.19
generally, 47.1
guidance, 32.1
introduction, 32.1
legal sources, 32.1
less favourable treatment,
introduction, 32.4
overtime, 32.6
pro rata principle, 32.5
written statement of reasons, and,
32.17
pensions, and, 24.19
qualifying period, 32.3
relevant workers, 32.2
unfair dismissal, and,
generally, 32.19
introduction, 54.3
victimisation, 32.18
written statement of reasons, 32.17

Partnership Fund
employee participation, and, 18.30
Partnerships
age discrimination, and, 3.35
discrimination, and, 13.25
Past criminal convictions
access to records, 19.7
effect of provisions, 19.5
recording of, 19.8
rehabilitation periods, 19.6
spent convictions
dismissal, and, 19.3
exceptions, 19.4
introduction, 19.1
non-disclosure, 19.2
Past disabilities
disability discrimination, and, 10.5
Paternity leave
generally, 33.27
payments from National Insurance
Fund, and, 31.8
statutory pay, 33.28
time off work, and, 49.19
unfair dismissal, and, 54.3
Pay
and see Equal pay
attachment of earnings, and
attachable earnings, 35.2
child support maintenance, 35.11
Council Tax, 35.10
deductions, 35.3–35.6
employer's obligations, 35.7
introduction, 35.1
other issues, 35.9
penalties for non-compliance, 35.8
deductions from wages
generally, 34.6
minimum wage, and, 34.9–34.13
other, 34.14
remedies, for breach, 34.8
retail employment, 34.7
discrimination, and, 13.10
generally, 34.2
gratuities, 34.21
guarantee payments
amount, 34.27
exclusions, 34.26
introduction, 34.23
qualifying period, 34.25
remedy for failure to make
payment, 34.28
'workless days', 34.24

Pay – *contd*
holidays, and, 29.4
itemised statements
application to tribunal, 34.19–34.20
exclusions, 34.18
fixed deductions, 34.17
generally, 34.16
introduction, 34.1
medical suspension, and
amount, 34.32
exclusions, 34.31
generally, 34.29
qualifying conditions, 34.30
remedy for failure to make
payment, 34.33
method of payment, 34.3
national minimum wage
coverage, 34.10
introduction, 34.9
records, 34.11
relevant workers, 34.10
remedies for failure to pay, 34.12–
34.13
statements, 34.11
normal working hours, 34.35
overpayment, 34.15
overtime, 34.36
pre-1987 position
exceptions, 34.5
generally, 34.4
records, 34.11
termination of employment, and,
34.22
troncs, 34.21
'week's pay'
amount, 34.39
calculation date, 34.38
introduction, 34.34
no normal working hours, 34.37
normal working hours, 34.35
overtime, 34.36
'worker', 34.6
workless days, and, 34.23
Pay as you earn (PAYE)
death of employee, 46.10
definition, 46.4
dismissal, 46.8
earnings limits, 46.4
end of year procedure, 46.15–46.17
joining after 6 April, 46.7
method of deduction, 46.6
ONLINE SERVICES, 46.19

Pay as you earn (PAYE) – *contd*
payment by employer, 46.14
refunds, 46.13
retirement, 46.9
settlement agreements, 46.18
sources of information, 46.5
students during vacation, 46.11
working abroad, 46.12
Pay in lieu of notice
generally, 48.9
gross or net, 48.11
taxation, 46.8, 48.10
wrongful dismissal, and, 58.21
Payments into court
wrongful dismissal, and, 58.41
Payroll giving scheme
taxation, and, 46.33
Pecuniary loss
discrimination compensation, and,
14.15
Penalties for non-compliance
attachment of earnings, and, 35.8
Penalties for non-compliance
sick pay, and, 44.13
Pension contributions
insolvency of employer, and, 31.7
tax-free benefits, and, 46.23
Pension Protection Fund (PPF)
generally, 31.9
Pension rights
unfair dismissal, and, 55.12
Pension scheme trustees
discrimination, and, 13.31
introduction, 42.12
time off work, and
generally, 49.12
remedies, 49.13
unfair dismissal, and, 54.3
Pensions
age discrimination
generally, 42.2
introduction, 3.49
claims and disputes, 42.14
directors, and, 9.25
disability discrimination, 42.10
discrimination, and,
age discrimination, 42.2
disability discrimination, 42.10
introduction, 13.31
sex discrimination, 42.9
employee trustees
generally, 42.12

Index

Pensions – *contd*
  employee trustees – *contd*
    time off work, 49.12–49.13
  employers' duties, 42.13
  equal pay, and
    Barber claims, 24.18
    introduction, 24.16
    part-time workers, 24.19
    statutory regime, 24.17
  generally, 42.7
  insolvency, and,
    Pensions Act 2004, 31.9
    unpaid contributions, 31.7
  introduction, 42.5
  part time workers, and, 24.19
  sex discrimination, 42.9
  stakeholder, 42.8
  unfair dismissal, and, 55.12
Pensions Regulator
  generally, 31.9
Permanent health benefits
  effect, 44.15
  generally, 44.14
  'unable to follow any occupation',
    44.17
Permits for foreign workers
  applications, 26.6
  eligible workers, 26.5
  further information, 26.8
  procedure, 26.7
Personal disadvantage
  age discrimination, and, 3.5
  discrimination, and, 12.9
Personal injury
  discrimination compensation, and,
    14.17
Personal liability
  discrimination, and, 13.37
Perverse decision
  EAT procedure, and, 22.17
Petition by individual
  human rights, and, 30.3
Philosophical belief
  and see Religious and belief
    discrimination
  meaning, 12.5
Picketing
  case law, 45.10
  Code of Practice, 45.11
  generally, 45.9
Place of work
  health and safety, and, 27.3

Police officers
  age discrimination, and, 3.31
  disability discrimination, and, 10.24
  discrimination, and, 13.23
  European law, 37.7
  exemplary damages, 37.5
  introduction, 37.1
  judicial review as to rights, 37.4
  national security, 37.6
  public interest immunity, 37.6
  sex discrimination, and, 13.10
  special provisions, 37.2
  status, 37.3
  strikes, and, 45.20
  working time, and, 57.3
Political levy
  trade unions, and, 50.15
Positive action
  access to training, 13.9
  age discrimination, and, 3.22
  childbirth, 13.9
  EC law, under, 13.9
  generally, 13.9
  less favourable treatment, 12.5
  membership of trade organisation,
    13.9
  pregnancy, 13.9
  Sikhs on construction sites, 13.12
Posted abroad, employees
  equal pay, and, 24.4
  European law, and, 25.7
  foreign workers, and, 26.3
Postponement of start of employment
  continuous employment, and, 7.11
Post-traumatic stress disorder
  disability discrimination, and, 10.2
Pre-entry closed shop
  trade union members, and, 51.4
Preferential debts
  insolvency of employer, and, 31.2
Pregnancy
  detriment by reason of
    introduction, 33.8
    remedies, 33.9
  discrimination, and
    and see Discrimination
    direct discrimination, 12.4
    discrimination in employment,
      12.12
    generally 12.2
    harassment, 12.11
    less favourable treatment, 12.5

Pregnancy – *contd*
discrimination, and – *contd*
'on ground of', 12.6
positive discrimination, 13.9
dismissal for reasons of
generally, 33.6
qualifying period, 33.7
equal pay, and, 24.4
sick pay, and, 44.4
unfair dismissal, and, 54.3
written statement of reasons for
dismissal, and, 48.14
Pre-hearing reviews
and see Tribunal procedure
generally, 21.6
overview, 20.5
Pre-operative transsexuals
discrimination, and, 12.5
Preparation for tribunal hearing
general, 21.38
listing arrangements, 21.39–21.48
Preparation time orders
tribunal procedure, and, 21.72
Prerequisites
taxation, and, 46.2
Presentation of claim
tribunal procedure, and, 20.21
**Pressure to commit unlawful
discriminatory acts**
enforcement only by Commissions,
13.40
generally, 12.13
injunctions, 14.30
Pressure to dismiss unfairly
unfair dismissal, and, 54.16
**Pressure to impose union membership or
recognition**
secondary action, and, 45.7
Principal's liability
age discrimination, and, 3.42
Prison officers
disability discrimination, and, 10.24
sex discrimination, and, 13.10
Prisoners
national minimum wage, and, 34.10
sick pay, and, 44.4
Private Finance Initiative (PFI)
employee participation, and, 18.1
Private hearing
tribunal procedure, and, 21.51
Private households
race discrimination, and, 13.11

Private and family life, right to
human rights, and, 30.7
'Pro hac vice'
vicarious liability, and, 56.3
Probationary employees, status of
EAT guidelines, 36.2
introduction, 36.1
Progressive conditions
disability discrimination, and, 10.7
Prohibition notices
appeals
cost of remedy required, 27.36
effect, 27.35
introduction, 27.34
generally, 27.31
withdrawal, 27.33
Property transfers
directors, and, 9.30
**"Proportionate means of achieving a
legitimate aim"**
direct discrimination, 3.4
indirect discrimination, 3.5
Protected shorthold tenancies
generally, 43.5
recovery of possession, 43.6
rent control, 43.8
Protected tenancies
generally, 43.5
recovery of possession, 43.6
rent control, 43.8
Protection of interests of business
unfair dismissal, and, 54.14
Protective award
consultation on redundancy, and, 39.6
insolvency of employer, and, 31.2
Public authorities
gender equality duty
enforcement, 13.34
generally, 13.33
Public duties, time off for
generally, 49.5
remedies, 49.6
Public interest
disclosure, and,
generally, 11.17
protected disclosures, 11.18
unfair dismissal, 54.3
restraint of trade covenants, and, 41.5
Public interest immunity
public sector employees, and, 37.6
Public policy
contract of employment, and, 8.15

Public policy – *contd*
restraint of trade covenants, and, 41.1
Public sector employees
EC employees, 37.8
European law, 37.7
exemplary damages, 37.5
introduction, 37.1
judicial review as to rights, 37.4
national security, 37.6
public interest immunity, 37.6
redundancy payments, and, 38.10
special provisions, 37.2
status, 37.3
Public authority tenants
service lettings, and, 43.7
Publicity
discrimination complaints, and, 14.11
Pupillage
age discrimination, and, 3.33
discrimination, and, 13.24

Q
Qualifications bodies
age discrimination, and, 3.37
discrimination, and, 13.27
Qualifications-related dismissal
generally, 54.7
introduction, 54.5
summary, 54.2
Qualifying period of employment
calculation of continuous
employment, 53.12
effective date of termination, 53.13
introduction, 53.11
part time workers, and, 32.3
Questionnaires
age discrimination, and, 3.44

R
Race discrimination
advertisements
employment, in, 12.12
generally, 13.34
injunctions, 14.30
advocates, 13.24
age, and, 12.1
agent's acts
generally, 12.12
persons responsible, 13.38
aiding unlawful acts
generally, 12.12

Race discrimination – *contd*
aiding unlawful acts – *contd*
persons responsible, 13.36
applications to Employment Tribunal
burden of proof, 14.3
compensation, 14.13–14.20
conciliation, 14.10
disclosure, 14.9
extension of time, 14.7
formulation of complaint, 14.8
generally, 14.2
publicity, 14.11
questionnaire, 14.9
recommendations, 14.21
remedies, 14.12–14.22
time limits, 14.3
assistance for persons discriminated
against, 14.31
barristers, 13.24
benefits provided to public, 13.17
burden of proof, 14.3
careers guidance, 13.29
comparators, 12.5
compensation
aggravated damages, 14.18
discrimination, 14.19
exemplary damages, 14.18
general principles, 14.13
indirect discrimination, 14.14
injury to feelings, 14.16
interests, 14.20
introduction, 14.12
pecuniary loss, 14.15
personal injury, 14.17
unfair dismissal, 14.19
compliance with law, 13.18
conciliation, 14.10
contract workers, 13.21
Crown, 13.32
detriment, 12.12
direct discrimination
generally, 12.4
less favourable treatment, 12.5
prohibited grounds, 12.6
disclosure, 14.9
discriminatory practices
enforcement only by Commissions,
13.40
generally, 12.13
dismissal, 12.12
employment agencies, 13.29
employment, in, 12.12

Race discrimination – *contd*
employment outside Great Britain,
13.15
employment-related services, 13.30
enforcement
applications to Employment
Tribunal, 14.2–14.22
assistance for persons discriminated
against, 14.31
Commissions, by, 14.23–14.28
injunctions, 14.29–14.30
introduction, 14.1
settlement, 14.33
void contract terms, 14.32
enforcement by the Commissions
CEHR, 14.26
CRE, 14.25
EOC, 14.24
formal investigations, 14.27
generally, 14.23
introduction, 13.40
non-discrimination notices, 14.28
engagement, 12.12
equal opportunities, and
advertising, 13.34
enforcement only by Commissions,
13.40
general exceptions, 13.14–13.20
genuine occupational requirement or
qualification, 13.4
introduction, 13.1
justification, 13.8
non-employees/employers covered,
13.21–13.32
persons responsible, 13.35–13.39
positive discrimination, 13.9
relationships terminated, 13.33
specific exceptions, 13.11
extension of time, 14.7
foreign employees, and, 26.13
formulation of complaint, 14.8
general exceptions
benefits provided to public, 13.17
compliance with law, 13.18
employment outside Great Britain,
13.15
illegal contracts, 13.16
introduction, 13.14
national security, 13.19
State immunity, 13.20

Race discrimination – *contd*
genuine occupational requirement or
qualification
generally, 13.4
introduction, 13.2
grounds, 12.2
harassment
generally, 12.11
partnerships, 13.25
trade organisations, 13.26
illegal contracts, 13.16
indirect discrimination
application of the test, 12.8
generally, 12.7
particular cases, 12.9
injunctions
advertisements, 14.30
instructions to discriminate, 14.30
persistent discrimination, 14.29
pressure to discriminate, 14.30
instructions to commit unlawful acts
enforcement only by Commissions,
13.40
generally, 12.13
injunctions, 14.30
introduction, 12.1
justification, 13.8
legal sources, 12.2
less favourable treatment, 12.5
meaning
direct discrimination, 12.4–12.6
harassment, 12.11
indirect discrimination, 12.7–12.9
introduction, 12.3
victimisation, 12.10
national security, 13.19
non-discrimination notices, 14.28
non-employees/employers covered,
13.21–13.32
occupational pension schemes, 13.31
office holders, 13.22
'one-off' act, 12.12
opportunities in employment, 12.12
other unlawful acts, 12.13
partnerships, 13.25
personal disadvantage, 12.9
personal liability, 13.37
persons responsible
agents, 13.38
aiding unlawful acts, 13.36
employees, 13.37
third party acts, 13.39

Index

Race discrimination – *contd*
persons responsible – *contd*
vicarious responsibility, 13.35
police, 13.23
positive discrimination
access to training, 13.9
childbirth, 13.9
EC law, under, 13.9
generally, 13.9
less favourable treatment, 12.5
membership of trade organisation, 13.9
pregnancy, 13.9
Sikhs on construction sites, 13.12
post-employment, 12.12
pregnancy, 12.2
pressure to commit unlawful acts
enforcement only by Commissions, 13.40
generally, 12.13
injunctions, 14.30
publicity, 14.11
pupillage, 13.24
qualifications bodies, 13.27
questionnaire, 14.9
recommendations, 14.21
relationships terminated, 13.33
remedies
compensation, 14.13–14.20
introduction, 14.12
pension rights, 14.22
recommendations, 14.21
segregation, 12.5
settlement of claim, 14.33
specific exceptions, 13.11
sports and competitions, 13.11
State immunity, 13.20
state provision of facilities and services, 13.30
third party acts
generally, 12.12
persons responsible, 13.39
time limits, 14.4–14.7
trade organisations, 13.26
trustees of occupational pension schemes, 13.31
unfavourable treatment, 12.5
unlawful acts, 12.12
unlawful instructions
enforcement only by Commissions, 13.40
generally, 12.13

Race discrimination – *contd*
unlawful instructions – *contd*
injunctions, 14.30
unlawful pressure
enforcement only by Commissions, 13.40
generally, 12.13
injunctions, 14.30
vicarious liability
generally, 12.12
persons responsible, 13.35
victimisation, 12.10
vocational training providers, 13.28
Rail workers
working time, and, 57.36
Reasonableness
restraint of trade covenants, and, 41.6–41.9
Reasons for decision
adequacy, 21.63
generally, 21.62
Reasons for dismissal
wrongful dismissal, and, 58.20
Recognition of trade unions
collective bargaining, for
appropriate bargaining unit, 50.30
ballot, 50.31–50.32
changes in bargaining unit, 50.35
'collective bargaining', 50.27
introduction, 50.25
method of bargaining, 50.33
reference to CA, 50.29
request for recognition, 50.28
scope of procedure, 50.26
independence, 50.22–50.24
introduction, 50.19
listing, 50.21
transfer of undertakings, and, 52.21
unfair dismissal, and, 54.3
voluntary, 50.20
Recommendations
discrimination remedies, and, 14.21
Records
pay, and, 34.11
pay as you earn, and, 46.20
sick pay, and, 44.7
trade unions, and, 50.12
working time, and, 57.8
Recoupment of benefits
tribunal procedure, and, 21.68
unfair dismissal, and, 55.5

Recovery of costs
education and training, and, 16.3
Recovery of possession
generally, 43.3
grounds, 43.6
public authority tenants, 43.7
service licence, 43.4
service tenancy, 43.5
Recreational facilities
tax-free benefits, and, 46.23
Redundancy
and see Redundancy payments
checklist, 39.9
consultation requirements
appropriate representatives, 39.4–
39.5
introduction, 39.2
meaning of 'redundancy', 39.3
protective award, 39.6
dismissal notices, 39.9
European law, and, 25.8
fairness of dismissal, 39.8
introduction, 39.1
maternity leave, and, 33.19
notification to DTI, 39.7
preliminary procedure, 39.9
transfer of undertakings, and, 52.27
unfair dismissal, and
generally, 54.11
procedure, 54.12
summary, 54.2
unfair selection, 54.3
Redundancy payments
age discrimination, and
generally, 3.26
introduction, 38.10
amount, 38.13
continuous employment for requisite
period
changes in ownership, 38.5
generally, 38.4
contracting out, 38.14
excluded persons, 38.10
insolvency of employer, and, 31.4
introduction, 38.1
lay-off, and
counter-notice, 38.9
generally, 38.8
payments from National Insurance
Fund, and, 31.4
pension contributions, and, 31.6

Redundancy payments – *contd*
pre-conditions
applicant an employee, 38.3
continuous employment for requisite
period, 38.4–38.5
dismissal, 38.6
introduction, 38.2
reason for dismissal, 38.7–38.9
references to tribunal, 38.14
short time working, and
counter-notice, 38.9
generally, 38.8
time limits for claims, 20.27, 38.11
unreasonable refusal of alternative
employment, 38.12
Re-engagement
general rules, 55.4
generally, 55.3
redundancy payments, and, 38.6
refusal to reinstate, 55.5
References
conditional employment, and, 40.9
contents, 40.3
data protection, and, 40.6
employer's liabilities
employee, to, 40.4
recipient, to, 40.5
employer's obligation, 40.2
introduction, 40.1
third party's liabilities, 40.7
tribunals, and, 40.8
References to ECJ
tribunal procedure, and, 22.27
Refunds
pay as you earn, and, 46.13
Refusal of alternative employment
redundancy payments, and, 38.12
Refusal to work on Sunday
unfair dismissal, and, 54.3
Register of judgments
tribunal procedure, and, 21.65
Register of members
trade unions, and, 50.13
Rehabilitation periods
criminal convictions, and, 19.6
Reinstatement
general rules, 55.4
generally, 55.2
military service, and, 49.20
refusal to reinstate, 55.5
Relief for assessable benefits
taxation, and, 46.28

Index

Relief from liability
directors, and, 9.19

Religion or belief discrimination
advertisements
  employment, in, 12.12
  generally, 13.34
  injunctions, 14.30
advocates, 13.24
age, and, 12.1
agent's acts
  generally, 12.12
  persons responsible, 13.38
aiding unlawful acts
  generally, 12.12
  persons responsible, 13.36
applications to Employment Tribunal
  burden of proof, 14.3
  compensation, 14.13–14.20
  conciliation, 14.10
  disclosure, 14.9
  extension of time, 14.7
  formulation of complaint, 14.8
  generally, 14.2
  publicity, 14.11
  questionnaire, 14.9
  recommendations, 14.21
  remedies, 14.12–14.22
  time limits, 14.4–14.7
assistance for persons discriminated
  against, 14.31
barristers, 13.24
benefits provided to public, 13.17
careers guidance, 13.29
comparators, 12.5
compensation
  aggravated damages, 14.18
  discrimination, 14.19
  exemplary damages, 14.18
  general principles, 14.13
  indirect discrimination, 14.14
  injury to feelings, 14.16
  interests, 14.20
  introduction, 14.12
  pecuniary loss, 14.15
  personal injury, 14.17
  unfair dismissal, 14.19
compliance with law, 13.18
conciliation, 14.10
contract workers, 13.21
Crown, 13.32
detriment, 12.12

Religion or belief discrimination – *contd*
direct discrimination
  generally, 12.4
  less favourable treatment, 12.5
  prohibited grounds, 12.6
disclosure, 14.9
discriminatory practices
  enforcement only by Commissions,
    13.40
  generally, 12.13
dismissal, 12.12
employment agencies, 13.29
employment, in, 12.12
employment outside Great Britain,
  13.15
employment-related services, 13.30
enforcement
  applications to Employment
    Tribunal, 14.2–14.22
  assistance for persons discriminated
    against, 14.31
  Commissions, by, 14.23–14.28
  injunctions, 14.29–14.30
  introduction, 14.1
  settlement, 14.33
  void contract terms, 14.32
enforcement by the Commissions
  CEHR, 14.26
  CRE, 14.25
  EOC, 14.24
  formal investigations, 14.27
  generally, 14.23
  introduction, 13.40
  non-discrimination notices, 14.28
engagement, 12.12
equal opportunities, and
  advertising, 13.34
  enforcement only by Commissions,
    13.40
  general exceptions, 13.14–13.20
  genuine occupational requirement or
    qualification, 13.5
  introduction, 13.1
  justification, 13.8
  non-employees/employers covered,
    13.21–13.32
  persons responsible, 13.35–13.39
  positive discrimination, 13.9
  relationships terminated, 13.33
  specific exceptions, 13.12
extension of time, 14.7
foreign employees, and, 26.13

Religion or belief discrimination – *contd*
formulation of complaint, 14.8
general exceptions
  benefits provided to public, 13.17
  compliance with law, 13.18
  employment outside Great Britain,
    13.15
  illegal contracts, 13.16
  introduction, 13.14
  national security, 13.19
  State immunity, 13.20
genuine occupational requirement or
  qualification, 13.6
grounds, 12.2
harassment
  generally, 12.11
  partnerships, 13.25
  trade organisations, 13.26
illegal contracts, 13.16
indirect discrimination
  application of the test, 12.8
  generally, 12.7
  particular cases, 12.9
injunctions
  advertisements, 14.30
  instructions to discriminate, 14.30
  persistent discrimination, 14.29
  pressure to discriminate, 14.30
instructions to commit unlawful acts
  enforcement only by Commissions,
    13.40
  generally, 12.13
  injunctions, 14.30
introduction, 12.1
justification, 13.8
legal sources, 12.2
less favourable treatment, 12.5
meaning
  direct discrimination, 12.4–12.6
  harassment, 12.11
  indirect discrimination, 12.7–12.9
  introduction, 12.3
  victimisation, 12.10
national security, 13.19
non-discrimination notices, 14.28
non-employees/employers covered,
  13.21–13.32
occupational pension schemes, 13.31
office holders, 13.22
'one-off' act, 12.12
opportunities in employment, 12.12
other unlawful acts, 12.13

Religion or belief discrimination – *contd*
partnerships, 13.25
personal disadvantage, 12.9
personal liability, 13.37
persons responsible
  agents, 13.38
  aiding unlawful acts, 13.36
  employees, 13.37
  third party acts, 13.39
  vicarious responsibility, 13.35
police, 13.23
positive discrimination
  access to training, 13.9
  childbirth, 13.9
  EC law, under, 13.9
  generally, 13.9
  less favourable treatment, 12.5
  membership of trade organisation,
    13.9
  pregnancy, 13.9
  Sikhs on construction sites, 13.12
post-employment, 12.12
pressure to commit unlawful acts
  enforcement only by Commissions,
    13.40
  generally, 12.13
  injunctions, 14.30
publicity, 14.11
pupillage, 13.24
qualifications bodies, 13.27
questionnaire, 14.9
recommendations, 14.21
remedies
  compensation, 14.13–14.20
  introduction, 14.12
  pension rights, 14.22
relationships terminated, 13.33
segregation, 12.5
settlement of claim, 14.33
specific exceptions, 13.12
State immunity, 13.20
state provision of facilities and
  services, 13.30
third party acts
  generally, 12.12
  persons responsible, 13.39
time limits, 14.4–14.7
trade organisations, 13.26
trustees of occupational pension
  schemes, 13.31
unfavourable treatment, 12.5
unlawful acts, 12.12

Index

Religion or belief discrimination – *contd*
unlawful instructions
enforcement only by Commissions,
13.40
generally, 12.13
injunctions, 14.30
unlawful pressure
enforcement only by Commissions,
13.40
generally, 12.13
injunctions, 14.30
vicarious liability
generally, 12.12
persons responsible, 13.35
victimisation, 12.10
vocational training providers, 13.28
Religious communities
national minimum wage, and, 34.10
Relocation expenses
taxable benefits, and, 46.21–46.23
Remedies
age discrimination, and, 3.44
breach of contract of employment, and
employee, for, 8.23
employer, for, 8.24
compensation for discrimination
aggravated damages, 14.18
discrimination, 14.19
exemplary damages, 14.18
general principles, 14.13
indirect discrimination, 14.14
injury to feelings, 14.16
interests, 14.20
introduction, 14.12
pecuniary loss, 14.15
personal injury, 14.17
unfair dismissal, 14.19
costs, 21.69–21.73
deductions from wages, and, 34.8
detriment by reason of pregnancy,
and, 33.9
discrimination complaints, and
compensation, 14.13–14.20
introduction, 14.12
pensions chemes, 14.22
recommendations, 14.21
equal pay, and
Agricultural Wages Orders, 24.21
generally, 24.20
guarantee payments, and, 34.28
holidays, and, 29.6
interest, 21.67

Remedies – *contd*
medical suspension, and, 34.33
national minimum wage, and
individual remedies, 34.12
state remedies, 34.13
non-payment of statutory maternity
pay, and, 33.15
pension schemes, and, 14.22
recommendations, 14.21
recoupment of benefits, 21.68
restraint of trade covenants, and,
account of profits, 41.20
damages, 41.19
declaration, 41.18
injunctions, 41.17
pleading, 41.16
strike action, and
employers,' 45.16
third parties', 45.18
time off work, and
ante-natal care, 33.5
arrangements for training, 49.8
dependants, 49.18
employee representatives, 49.15
look for work, 49.8
pension scheme trustees, 49.13
public duties, 49.6
safety representatives, 49.10
trade union activities, 49.6
tribunal procedure, and
costs, 21.69–21.73
generally, 21.66
interest, 21.67
recoupment of benefits, 21.68
unfair dismissal, and
compensation, 55.6–55.16
interim relief, 55.18
introduction, 55.1
joinder of third parties, 55.17
re-engagement, 55.3–55.5
reinstatement, 55.2–55.5
settlement, 55.19
written statements of reasons for
dismissal, and, 48.15
wrongful dismissal, and
claims in debt, 58.24
damages, 58.25–58.33
injunctions, 58.23
wrongful termination, and, 48.21
Remuneration of directors
disclosure, 9.22
introduction, 9.20

Remuneration of directors – *contd*
Listing Rules requirements, 9.24
pensions, 9.25
recommendations, 9.21
small company provisions, 9.23
termination of office, on
generally, 9.27
introduction, 9.26
Listing Rules requirements, 9.29
property transfer, 9.30
recommendations, 9.28
takeovers, 9.31
transfer of undertakings, 9.32
Renewal of contract
redundancy payments, and, 38.6
Rent control
service lettings, and, 43.8
Reorganisation of business
unfair dismissal, and, 54.14
Repetitive strain injury (RSI)
health and safety, and, 28.31
Replacement employee
unfair dismissal, and, 54.14
Reporting of accidents
health and safety, and, 28.1
Representation
tribunal procedure, and, 21.55
Repudiatory conduct
restraint of trade covenants, and,
41.11
termination, and, 48.19
unfair dismissal, and, 53.9
Reputation, loss of
unfair dismissal, and, 55.12
Resignation
generally, 48.16
notice by employee, 48.17
retraction of resignation, 48.20
summary termination by employee,
48.18
Response by respondent
tribunal procedure, and, 20.35–20.37
Rest breaks
generally, 57.17
monotonous work, 57.18
Rest periods
children, and, 4.6
daily, 57.15
introduction, 57.14
weekly, 57.16
Restraint of trade covenants
ambit of restraint, 41.8

Restraint of trade covenants – *contd*
'blue pencil' test, 41.7
common law doctrine, 41.2
confidential information, 41.13
conflict of laws, 41.12
consequence of finding of
unreasonableness, 41.9
consideration, 41.10
construction, 41.6
coverage, 41.3
duration of restraint, 41.8
'garden leave' injunctions, and, 41.14
geographical restraint, 41.8
interests of the parties, 41.4
introduction, 41.1
nature of restraint, 41.8
procedural matters,
account of profits, 41.20
damages, 41.19
declaration, 41.18
injunctions, 41.17
pleading, 41.16
proscribed actions, 41.8
public interest, 41.5
reasonableness, 41.6–41.9
repudiatory breach, 41.11
severance, 41.7
'springboard' relief, and, 41.15
testing reasonableness, 41.8
trade secrets, 41.13
Restricted reporting orders
tribunal procedure, and, 21.18–21.19
Retail employment
deductions from wages, and, 34.7
Retirement
age discrimination, and,
appeals, 3.47
duty to consider request, 3.47
employers' duty to notify, 3.47
generally, 3.47, 42.2
introduction, 3.23
pension benefits, 42.11
request to continue working, 3.47
summary of regulations 42.4
transitional provisions, 3.47
age of,
change, 42.5
employment protection, and, 42.2
generally, 42.1
unfair dismissal, 53.14
benefits, 42.6

Index

Retirement – *contd*
discrimination, and,
  age discrimination, 42.2
  disability discrimination, 42.10
  introduction, 13.10
  sex discrimination, 42.9
early, 42.4
effect on protected rights, 42.2
introduction, 42.1
pensions,
  age discrimination, and, 42.11
  claims and disputes, 42.14
  disability discrimination, 42.10
  employee trustees, 42.12
  employers' duties, 42.13
  generally, 42.7
  sex discrimination, 42.9
  stakeholder, 42.8
post-retirement benefits, 42.5
pay as you earn, and, 46.9
sex discrimination, and, 13.10
unfair dismissal, and,
  generally, 53.14
  introduction, 42.2

Retirement age
age discrimination, and, 3.23
change, 42.5
employment protection, and, 42.2
generally, 42.1
unfair dismissal, 53.14

Retirement age, persons over
redundancy payments, and, 38.10
sick pay, and, 44.4
unfair dismissal, and, 53.12

Returns
pay as you earn, and, 46.15

Review of order
EAT procedure, and, 22.25
tribunal procedure, and, 21.74–21.75

Risk of injury, protection from
health and safety, and, 27.8

Road transport workers
working time, and, 57.34–57.35

S

Safe equipment and materials
health and safety, and, 27.6

Safe means of access
health and safety, and, 27.4

Safe place of work
health and safety, and, 27.3

Safe system of work
health and safety, and, 27.5

Safety measures
charges for, 27.24
interference with, 27.23

Safety representatives
disclosure of information, and, 11.8
introduction, 28.20
non-unionised workers, 28.22
time off work, and
  generally, 49.9
  remedies, 49.10
union-appointees, 28.21

Safety signs
health and safety, and, 28.30

Salary
attachment of earnings, and
  attachable earnings, 35.2
  child support maintenance, 35.11
  Council Tax, 35.10
  deductions, 35.3–35.6
  employer's obligations, 35.7
  introduction, 35.1
  other issues, 35.9
  penalties for non-compliance, 35.8
deductions from wages
  generally, 34.6
  minimum wage, and, 34.9–34.13
  other, 34.14
  remedies, for breach, 34.8
  retail employment, 34.7
generally, 34.2
gratuities, 34.21
guarantee payments
  amount, 34.27
  exclusions, 34.26
  introduction, 34.23
  qualifying period, 34.25
  remedy for failure to make
    payment, 34.28
  'workless days', 34.24
holidays, and, 29.4
insolvency of employer, and, 31.2
itemised statements
  application to tribunal, 34.19–34.20
  exclusions, 34.18
  fixed deductions, 34.17
  generally, 34.16
  introduction, 34.1
medical suspension, and
  amount, 34.32
  exclusions, 34.31

Salary – *contd*
medical suspension, and – *contd*
  generally, 34.29
  qualifying conditions, 34.30
  remedy for failure to make
    payment, 34.33
method of payment, 34.3
national minimum wage
  coverage, 34.10
  introduction, 34.9
  records, 34.11
  relevant workers, 34.10
  remedies for failure to pay, 34.12–
    34.13
  statements, 34.11
overpayment, 34.15
pre-1987 position
  exceptions, 34.5
  generally, 34.4
records, 34.11
termination of employment, and,
    34.22
troncs, 34.21
'week's pay'
  amount, 34.39
  calculation date, 34.38
  introduction, 34.34
  no normal working hours, 34.37
  normal working hours, 34.35
  overtime, 34.36
workless days, and, 34.23
Salary continuance benefits
effect, 44.15
generally, 44.14
Same work
equal pay, and, 24.6
Savings-related share option schemes
generally, 46.29
School governors
disability discrimination, and, 10.24
School-leavers
education and training, and, 16.5
School workers
continuous employment, and, 7.9
European law, 37.7
exemplary damages, 37.5
introduction, 37.1
judicial review as to rights, 37.4
national security, 37.6
public interest immunity, 37.6
special provisions, 37.2
status, 37.3

Seafarers
age discrimination, and, 3.11
working time, and, 57.31–57.32
Seamen recruited abroad
race discrimination, and, 13.11
Seasonal workers
generally, 47.8
unfair dismissal, and, 47.8
Secondary action, limits on
dismissal of unofficial strikers, 45.8
generally, 45.6
pressure to impose membership or
    recognition, 45.7
Secretary of State
age discrimination, and, 3.40
Segregation
discrimination, and, 12.5
Selection
engagement of employees, and, 23.2
Self-employed
generally, 17.2–17.3
rights and obligations, 17.6–17.7
Serious Organised Crime Agency staff
age discrimination, and, 3.32
SERPS
generally, 42.7
Service contracts for directors
disclosure, 9.7
duration, 9.11–8.13
inspection, 9.8
Listing Rules requirements, 9.9
Take-over Code requirements, 9.10
Service lettings
agricultural tied houses, 43.9
introduction, 43.1
licence, 43.4
nature of occupancy, 43.2
public authority tenants, 43.7
recovery of possession
  generally, 43.3
  grounds, 43.6
  public authority tenants, 43.7
  service licence, 43.4
  service tenancy, 43.5
rent control, 43.8
tenancy, 43.5
Service provision change
background, 52.1
introduction, 52.2
relevant activities, 52.3
Services through an intermediary
taxation, and, 46.35

Index

Settlement agreements
pay as you earn, and, 46.18
Settlement of claim
conciliation, 21.32
disability discrimination, and, 10.37
discrimination, and, 14.33
generally, 21.29–21.31
unfair dismissal, and, 55.22
Severance
restraint of trade covenants, and, 41.7
Severe disfigurement
disability discrimination, and, 10.7
Sex discrimination
advertisements
employment, in, 12.12
generally, 13.34
injunctions, 14.30
advocates, 13.24
age, and, 12.1
agent's acts
generally, 12.12
persons responsible, 13.38
aiding unlawful acts
generally, 12.12
persons responsible, 13.36
applications to Employment Tribunal
burden of proof, 14.3
compensation, 14.13–14.20
conciliation, 14.10
disclosure, 14.9
extension of time, 14.7
formulation of complaint, 14.8
generally, 14.2
publicity, 14.11
questionnaire, 14.9
recommendations, 14.21
remedies, 14.12–14.22
time limits, 14.4–14.7
assistance for persons discriminated
against, 14.31
barristers, 13.24
benefits provided to public, 13.17
burden of proof, 14.3
careers guidance, 13.29
comparators, 12.5
compensation
aggravated damages, 14.18
discrimination, 14.19
exemplary damages, 14.18
general principles, 14.13
indirect discrimination, 14.14
injury to feelings, 14.16

Sex discrimination – *contd*
compensation – *contd*
interests, 14.20
introduction, 14.12
pecuniary loss, 14.15
personal injury, 14.17
unfair dismissal, 14.19
compliance with law, 13.18
conciliation, 14.10
contract workers, 13.21
Crown, 13.32
detriment, 12.12
direct discrimination
generally, 12.4
less favourable treatment, 12.5
prohibited grounds, 12.6
disclosure, 14.9
discriminatory practices
enforcement only by Commissions,
13.40
generally, 12.13
dismissal, 12.12
employment agencies, 13.29
employment, in, 12.12
employment outside Great Britain,
13.15
employment-related services, 13.30
enforcement
applications to Employment
Tribunal, 14.2–14.22
assistance for persons discriminated
against, 14.31
Commissions, by, 14.23–14.28
injunctions, 14.29–14.30
introduction, 14.1
settlement, 14.33
void contract terms, 14.32
enforcement by the Commissions
EOC, 14.24
formal investigations, 14.27
generally, 14.23
introduction, 13.40
non-discrimination notices, 14.28
engagement, 12.12
equal opportunities, and
advertising, 13.34
enforcement only by Commissions,
13.40
general exceptions, 13.14–13.20
genuine occupational requirement or
qualification, 13.3
introduction, 13.1

Sex discrimination – *contd*
  equal opportunities, and – *contd*
    justification, 13.8
    non-employees/employers covered,
      13.21–13.32
    persons responsible, 13.35–13.39
    positive discrimination, 13.9
    relationships terminated, 13.33
    specific exceptions, 13.10
  extension of time, 14.7
  foreign employees, and, 26.13
  formulation of complaint, 14.8
  gender reassignment, 12.2
  general exceptions
    benefits provided to public, 13.17
    compliance with law, 13.18
    employment outside Great Britain,
      13.15
    illegal contracts, 13.16
    introduction, 13.14
    national security, 13.19
    State immunity, 13.20
  genuine occupational requirement or
    qualification
    generally, 13.3
    introduction, 13.2
  grounds, 12.2
  harassment
    generally, 12.11
    partnerships, 13.25
    trade organisations, 13.26
  illegal contracts, 13.16
  indirect discrimination
    application of the test, 12.8
    generally, 12.7
    particular cases, 12.9
  injunctions
    advertisements, 14.30
    instructions to discriminate, 14.30
    persistent discrimination, 14.29
    pressure to discriminate, 14.30
  instructions to commit unlawful acts
    enforcement only by Commissions,
      13.40
    generally, 12.13
    injunctions, 14.30
  introduction, 12.1
  justification, 13.8
  legal sources, 12.2
  less favourable treatment, 12.5
  marital status, 12.2

Sex discrimination – *contd*
  meaning
    direct discrimination, 12.4–12.6
    harassment, 12.11
    indirect discrimination, 12.7–12.9
    introduction, 12.3
    victimisation, 12.10
  national security, 13.19
  non-discrimination notices, 14.28
  non-employees/employers covered,
    13.21–13.32
  occupational pension schemes, 13.31
  office holders, 13.22
  'one-off' act, 12.12
  opportunities in employment, 12.12
  other unlawful acts, 12.13
  partnerships, 13.25
  personal disadvantage, 12.9
  personal liability, 13.37
  persons responsible
    agents, 13.38
    aiding unlawful acts, 13.36
    employees, 13.37
    third party acts, 13.39
    vicarious responsibility, 13.35
  police, 13.23
  positive discrimination
    access to training, 13.9
    childbirth, 13.9
    EC law, under, 13.9
    generally, 13.9
    less favourable treatment, 12.5
    membership of trade organisation,
      13.9
    pregnancy, 13.9
    Sikhs on construction sites, 13.12
  post-employment, 12.12
  pressure to commit unlawful acts
    enforcement only by Commissions,
      13.40
    generally, 12.13
    injunctions, 14.30
  publicity, 14.11
  pupillage, 13.24
  qualifications bodies, 13.27
  questionnaire, 14.9
  recommendations, 14.21
  relationships terminated, 13.33
  remedies
    compensation, 14.13–14.20
    introduction, 14.12
    pension rights, 14.22

Index

Sex discrimination – *contd*
  remedies – *contd*
    recommendations, 14.21
    segregation, 12.5
    settlement of claim, 14.33
    specific exceptions, 13.10
    sports and competitions, 13.10
    State immunity, 13.20
    state provision of facilities and
      services, 13.30
    third party acts
      generally, 12.12
      persons responsible, 13.39
    time limits, 14.4–14.7
    trade organisations, 13.26
    transsexuals, 12.2
    trustees of occupational pension
      schemes, 13.31
    unfavourable treatment, 12.5
    unlawful acts, 12.12
    unlawful instructions
      enforcement only by Commissions,
        13.40
      generally, 12.13
      injunctions, 14.30
    unlawful pressure
      enforcement only by Commissions,
        13.40
      generally, 12.13
      injunctions, 14.30
    vicarious liability
      generally, 12.12
      persons responsible, 13.35
    victimisation, 12.10
    vocational training providers, 13.28
Sexual harassment
  and see Sex discrimination
  generally, 12.12
Sexual orientation discrimination
  advertisements
    employment, in, 12.12
    generally, 13.34
    injunctions, 14.30
  advocates, 13.24
  age, and, 12.1
  agent's acts
    generally, 12.12
    persons responsible, 13.38
  aiding unlawful acts
    generally, 12.12
    persons responsible, 13.36

Sexual orientation discrimination – *contd*
  applications to Employment Tribunal
    burden of proof, 14.3
    compensation, 14.13–14.20
    conciliation, 14.10
    disclosure, 14.9
    extension of time, 14.7
    formulation of complaint, 14.8
    generally, 14.2
    publicity, 14.11
    questionnaire, 14.9
    recommendations, 14.21
    remedies, 14.12–14.22
    time limits, 14.4–14.7
  assistance for persons discriminated
    against, 14.31
  barristers, 13.24
  benefits provided to public, 13.17
  burden of proof, 14.3
  careers guidance, 13.29
  civil partnership status, 13.13
  comparators, 12.5
  compensation
    aggravated damages, 14.18
    discrimination, 14.19
    exemplary damages, 14.18
    general principles, 14.13
    indirect discrimination, 14.14
    injury to feelings, 14.16
    interests, 14.20
    introduction, 14.12
    pecuniary loss, 14.15
    personal injury, 14.17
    unfair dismissal, 14.19
  compliance with law, 13.18
  conciliation, 14.10
  contract workers, 13.21
  Crown, 13.32
  detriment, 12.12
  direct discrimination
    generally, 12.4
    less favourable treatment, 12.5
    prohibited grounds, 12.6
  disclosure, 14.9
  discriminatory practices
    enforcement only by Commissions,
      13.40
    generally, 12.13
  dismissal, 12.12
  employment agencies, 13.29
  employment, in, 12.12

Sexual orientation discrimination – *contd*
employment outside Great Britain,
13.15
employment-related services, 13.30
enforcement
applications to Employment
Tribunal, 14.2–14.22
assistance for persons discriminated
against, 14.31
Commissions, by, 14.23–14.28
injunctions, 14.29–14.30
introduction, 14.1
settlement, 14.33
void contract terms, 14.32
enforcement by the Commissions
EOC, 14.24
formal investigations, 14.27
generally, 14.23
introduction, 13.40
non-discrimination notices, 14.28
engagement, 12.12
equal opportunities, and
advertising, 13.34
enforcement only by Commissions,
13.40
general exceptions, 13.14–13.20
genuine occupational requirement or
qualification, 13.7
introduction, 13.1
justification, 13.8
non-employees/employers covered,
13.21–13.32
persons responsible, 13.35–13.39
positive discrimination, 13.9
relationships terminated, 13.33
specific exceptions, 13.13
extension of time, 14.7
foreign employees, and, 26.13
formulation of complaint, 14.8
general exceptions
benefits provided to public, 13.17
compliance with law, 13.18
employment outside Great Britain,
13.15
illegal contracts, 13.16
introduction, 13.14
national security, 13.19
State immunity, 13.20
genuine occupational requirement or
qualification, 13.7
grounds, 12.2

Sexual orientation discrimination – *contd*
harassment
generally, 12.11
partnerships, 13.25
trade organisations, 13.26
illegal contracts, 13.16
indirect discrimination
application of the test, 12.8
generally, 12.7
particular cases, 12.9
injunctions
advertisements, 14.30
instructions to discriminate, 14.30
persistent discrimination, 14.29
pressure to discriminate, 14.30
instructions to commit unlawful acts
enforcement only by Commissions,
13.40
generally, 12.13
injunctions, 14.30
introduction, 12.1
justification, 13.8
legal sources, 12.2
less favourable treatment, 12.5
marital status, 13.13
meaning
direct discrimination, 12.4–12.6
harassment, 12.11
indirect discrimination, 12.7–12.9
introduction, 12.3
victimisation, 12.10
national security, 13.19
non-discrimination notices, 14.28
non-employees/employers covered,
13.21–13.32
occupational pension schemes, 13.31
office holders, 13.22
'one-off' act, 12.12
opportunities in employment, 12.12
other unlawful acts, 12.13
partnerships, 13.25
personal disadvantage, 12.9
personal liability, 13.37
persons responsible
agents, 13.38
aiding unlawful acts, 13.36
employees, 13.37
third party acts, 13.39
vicarious responsibility, 13.35
police, 13.23
positive discrimination
access to training, 13.9

Index

Sexual orientation discrimination – *contd*
  positive discrimination – *contd*
    childbirth, 13.9
    EC law, under, 13.9
    generally, 13.9
    less favourable treatment, 12.5
    membership of trade organisation,
      13.9
    pregnancy, 13.9
  post-employment, 12.12
  pressure to commit unlawful acts
    enforcement only by Commissions,
      13.40
    generally, 12.13
    injunctions, 14.30
  publicity, 14.11
  pupillage, 13.24
  qualifications bodies, 13.27
  questionnaire, 14.9
  recommendations, 14.21
  relationships terminated, 13.33
  remedies
    compensation, 14.13–14.20
    introduction, 14.12
    pension rights, 14.22
    recommendations, 14.21
  segregation, 12.5
  settlement of claim, 14.33
  specific exceptions, 13.13
  State immunity, 13.20
  state provision of facilities and
    services, 13.30
  third party acts
    generally, 12.12
    persons responsible, 13.39
  time limits, 14.4–14.7
  trade organisations, 13.26
  transsexuals, 12.2
  trustees of occupational pension
    schemes, 13.31
  unfavourable treatment, 12.5
  unlawful acts, 12.12
  unlawful instructions
    enforcement only by Commissions,
      13.40
    generally, 12.13
    injunctions, 14.30
  unlawful pressure
    enforcement only by Commissions,
      13.40
    generally, 12.13
    injunctions, 14.30

Sexual orientation discrimination – *contd*
  vicarious liability
    generally, 12.12
    persons responsible, 13.35
  victimisation, 12.10
  vocational training providers, 13.28
Share fishermen
  national minimum wage, and, 34.10
  redundancy payments, and, 38.10
Share incentive plans
  generally, 46.31
Share options
  taxable benefits, and, 46.21
Share schemes
  company share option, 46.30
  enterprise management incentives,
    46.32
  incentive plans, 46.31
  savings-related share option, 46.29
Share transfers
  transfer of undertakings, and, 52.10
Ship-board workers
  national minimum wage, and, 34.10
Short time working
  redundancy payments, and
    counter-notice, 38.9
    generally, 38.8
Sick pay
  amount, 44.6
  contractual provisions, and
    generally, 44.2
    offsetting against SSP, 44.9–44.12
  disputes, 44.8
  excluded employees, 44.4
  generally, 44.3
  insolvency of employer, and
    generally, 31.2
    payments from National Insurance
      Fund, 31.8
  introduction, 44.1
  offsetting
    contributory pension schemes,
      44.11
    contributory sickness schemes,
      44.10
    introduction, 44.9
  payment period, 44.5
  penalties for non-compliance, 44.13
  permanent health benefits, and
    effect, 44.15
    generally, 44.14

Sick pay – *contd*
permanent health benefits, and – *contd*
'unable to follow any occupation',
44.17
records, 44.7
recoverable amount, 44.6
requirements, 44.3
salary continuance benefits, and
effect, 44.15
generally, 44.14
statutory framework, 44.3
termination, and, 44.12
Sikhs on construction sites
discrimination, and, 13.12
Small businesses
disability discrimination, and, 10.24
Smoking
health and safety, and, 28.23
"Some other substantial reason"
generally, 54.14
summary, 54.2
Sources of law
domestic legislation, 1.6
European law, 1.7
introduction, 1.4
terms of contract of employment, 1.5
Special hazards
night work, and, 57.11
Special negotiating body
European companies, and, 18.15
European Works Councils, and, 18.24
unfair dismissal, and, 54.3
Specific employment income
taxation, and, 46.2
Specific performance
employer's remedies, and, 8.24
Spent convictions
dismissal, and, 19.3
effect, 19.5
exceptions, 19.4
introduction, 19.1
non-disclosure, 19.2
rehabilitation periods, 19.6
unfair dismissal, and, 54.3
Sports and competitions
race discrimination, and, 13.11
sex discrimination, and, 13.10
Sports facilities
tax-free benefits, and, 46.23
Stakeholder pensions
generally, 42.8

**Standard dismissal and disciplinary
procedures**
application, 15.3
content, 15.2
deemed compliance, 15.6–15.7
effects of non-compliance,
generally, 15.8
increase in compensation, and,
15.10
reduction in compensation, and,
15.10
unfair dismissal, and, 15.9
increase in compensation, and, 15.10
introduction, 15.1
reduction in compensation, and, 15.10
time limits, 15.12–15.13
transitional provisions, 15.14
unfair dismissal, and, 15.9
Standard grievance procedures
application, 15.5
content, 15.4
deemed compliance, 15.6–15.7
effects of non-compliance,
generally, 15.8
increase in compensation, 15.10
reduction in compensation, 15.10
right to bring tribunal
proceedings, 15.11
unfair dismissal, 15.9
increase in compensation, and, 15.10
introduction, 15.1
reduction in compensation, and, 15.10
right to bring tribunal proceedings,
15.11
time limits, 15.12–15.13
transitional provisions, 15.14
unfair dismissal, and, 15.9
Start of employment
generally, 7.3
postponement, 7.11
**State earnings related pension scheme
(SERPS)**
generally, 42.7
State immunity
discrimination, and, 13.20
State provision of facilities and services
discrimination, and, 13.30
Statements of reasons for dismissal
generally, 48.14
remedy for failure to give, 48.15

Index

Status of employment
employees
generally, 17.2–17.3
office-holders, 17.8
rights and obligations, 17.4–17.5
introduction, 17.1
office-holders, 17.8
self-employed
generally, 17.2–17.3
rights and obligations, 17.6–17.7
workers, 17.9
Statutory authority
age discrimination, and, 3.20
disability discrimination, and, 10.24
Statutory adoption pay
generally, 33.28
Statutory maternity pay
amount, 33.14
'confinement', 33.11
insolvency of employer, and, 31.8
introduction, 33.10
payments from National Insurance
Fund, and, 31.8
period of entitlement, 33.13
qualifying requirements, 33.11
recoupment by employer, 33.16
remedy for non-payment, 33.15
sick pay, and, 44.4
Statutory paternity pay
generally, 33.28
Statutory minimum notice
exceptions, 48.8
generally, 48.7
Statutory rights, loss of
unfair dismissal, and, 55.12
Statutory office holders
disability discrimination, and, 10.24
Stay of proceedings
tribunal procedure, and, 21.22
Stoppage at work
sick pay, and, 44.4
Stress
health and safety, and, 28.24—28.25
Strike action
armed forces, 45.20
ballots before action
generally, 45.14
members' right, 45.17
calls for action, 45.15
consequences for employers, 45.19
criminal liability, 45.12
deductions from wages, and, 34.6

Strike action – *contd*
employer's rights and remedies, 45.16
immunity from liability for
background, 45.1
'in contemplation or furtherance',
45.5
introduction, 45.3
'trade dispute', 45.4
liability for
background, 45.1
common law, at, 45.2
statutory immunity, 45.3–45.5
picketing
case law, 45.10
Code of Practice, 45.11
generally, 45.9
police officers, 45.20
pressure to impose union membership
or recognition, 45.7
prohibited employees, 45.20
public sector employees, and, 37.2
remedies
employers,' 45.16
third parties', 45.18
restricted employees, 45.20
restrictions, 8.20
secondary action, limits on
dismissal of unofficial strikers, 45.8
generally, 45.6
pressure to impose membership or
recognition, 45.7
third parties' rights and remedies,
45.18
time off work for trade union officials,
and, 49.2
trade union, liability of
ballots before action, 45.14
calls for action, 45.15
generally, 45.13
introduction, 51.9
unfair dismissal, and
introduction, 54.3
official action, 53.17
unofficial action, 53.18
Striking out
tribunal procedure, and, 21.16–21.17
Students during vacation
pay as you earn, and, 46.11
Sub-lease of business premises
disability discrimination, and, 10.13
Substances hazardous to health
health and safety, and, 28.26

Substantial adverse effect
disability discrimination, and, 10.4
Suitable alternative employment
redundancy payments, and, 38.10
Summary dismissal
directors' notice periods, 58.14
express notice periods, 58.11
fixed term contracts, 58.12
implied notice periods, 58.15
justification, 58.17
rolling contracts, 58.13
statutory minimum notice, 58.16
termination, and, 48.13
Summary judgment
wrongful dismissal, and, 58.41
Sunday trading
contract of employment, and, 8.25
Sunday work
unfair dismissal, and, 54.3
Suspension on maternity grounds
alternative work, 33.24
introduction, 33.23
remuneration, 33.25
System of work
health and safety, and, 27.5

T
Take-over Code
directors' service contracts, and, 9.10
Takeovers
directors' compensation, and, 9.31
Tax credits
unfair dismissal, and, 54.3
Taxable benefits
car fuel, 46.26
company cars, 46.25
generally, 46.21
lower-paid employees, 46.22
vans, 46.27
Taxation
benefits in kind, 46.2
car fuel, 46.26
company cars, 46.25
company share option schemes, 46.30
death of employee, 46.10
directors, 46.3
dismissal of employee, 46.8
earnings limits, 46.4
employee share schemes
company share option, 46.30

Taxation – *contd*
employee share schemes – *contd*
enterprise management incentives, 46.32
incentive plans, 46.31
savings-related share option, 46.29
share incentive plans, 46.31
employment income, 46.2
end of year procedure
certificates, 46.15
Class 1A NICs, 46.17
P9D, 46.16
P11D, 46.16
returns, 46.15
enterprise management incentives, 46.32
expenses incurred in the performance of duties, 46.28
introduction, 46.1
joining after 6 April, 46.7
lower-paid employees
generally, 46.3
taxable benefits, 46.22
managed service company, 46.36
national insurance contributions, 46.17
online services, 46.19
pay as you earn
death of employee, 46.10
definition, 46.4
dismissal, 46.8
earnings limits, 46.4
end of year procedure, 46.15–46.17
joining after 6 April, 46.7
method of deduction, 46.6
online, 46.19
payment by employer, 46.14
refunds, 46.13
retirement, 46.9
settlement agreements, 46.18
sources of information, 46.5
students during vacation, 46.11
working abroad, 46.12
P9D, 46.16
P11D, 46.16
payroll giving scheme, 46.33
records, 46.20
refunds, 46.13
relief for assessable benefits, 46.28
retirement of employee, 46.9
savings-related share option, 46.29

Index

Taxation – *contd*
services through an intermediary,
46.35
settlement agreements, 46.18
share incentive plans, 46.31
students during vacation, 46.11
taxable benefits
car fuel, 46.26
company cars, 46.25
generally, 46.21
lower-paid employees, 46.22
vans, 46.27
tax-free benefits, 46.23
vans, 46.27
working abroad, 46.12
working tax credit, 46.34
Tax-free benefits
taxation, and, 46.23
Temporary employees
employment agencies
Conduct Regulations, 47.5
generally, 47.2
national minimum wage, 47.6
reforms, 47.4
statutory control, 47.3
unfair dismissal, 47.7
introduction, 47.1
less favourable treatment, 47.9
seasonal workers, 47.8
unfair dismissal, and, 47.7
Tenancy
service lettings, and, 43.5
Termination of employment
constructive dismissal, by, 48.18
contractual notice period, 48.6
dismissal, by
introduction, 48.5
notice, 48.6–48.12
retraction of dismissal, 48.20
summary, 48.13
written statement of reasons,
48.14–48.5
effluxion of time, by, 48.4
frustration, by, 48.3
holidays, and, 29.4
introduction, 48.1
mutual agreement, by, 48.2
notice, by
contractual notice period, 48.6
employee, by, 48.17
introduction, 48.5
pay in lieu of notice, 48.9–48.10

Termination of employment – *contd*
notice, by – *contd*
rights during notice period, 48.12
statutory minimum notice, 48.7–
48.8
pay, and, 34.22
pay in lieu of notice
generally, 48.9
gross or net, 48.11
taxation, 48.10
remedies, 48.21
repudiatory conduct, by, 48.19
resignation, by
generally, 48.16
notice by employee, 48.17
retraction of resignation, 48.20
summary termination by
employee, 48.18
sick pay, and, 44.12
statutory minimum notice
exceptions, 48.8
generally, 48.7
summary dismissal, by, 48.13
written statements of reasons for
dismissal
generally, 48.14
remedy for failure to give, 48.15
Termination of office
generally, 9.27
introduction, 9.26
Listing Rules requirements, 9.29
property transfer, 9.30
recommendations, 9.28
takeovers, 9.31
Terms of contract of employment
contrary to public policy, 8.15
employer handbooks, 8.11
express, 8.12
freedom to agree, 8.10
implied, 8.12–7.13
unenforceable
contracting out of certain
provisions, 8.17
discriminatory terms, 8.18
industrial action restrictions, 8.20
introduction, 8.16
restraint trade, 8.19
UCTA 1977, and, 8.21
unlawful, 8.15
variation by statute, 8.14
Terms of engagement
temporary workers, and, 47.2

Territorial scope
generally, 1.8
Third parties, discriminatory acts by
generally, 12.12
persons responsible, 13.39
Time limits for proceedings
age discrimination, and, 3.44
contract claims, 20.32
discrimination complaints, and, 14.4–14.7
EAT, and, 22.6
equal pay, 20.28
generally, 20.18
'just and equitable, 20.30
'not reasonably practicable' to present in time, 20.25–20.26
other claims, 20.33
post-EA 2002, 20.19–20.20
redundancy payments, 20.27
unlawful deductions from wages, 20.31
unlawful discrimination, 20.29
redundancy payments, and, 38.11
Time off work
adoption leave, 49.19
ante-natal care, and
amount, 33.4
generally, 33.2
introduction, 49.11
qualifying requirements, 33.3
remedies for refusal, 33.5
arrangements for training
generally, 49.7
remedies, 49.8
care for children, 49.19
consultation representatives
generally, 49.14
remedies, 49.15
dependants, for
generally, 49.16
remedies, 49.17
employee representatives
generally, 49.14
remedies, 49.15
European Works Council duties, 49.16
flexible working, 49.19
health and safety representatives
generally, 49.9
remedies, 49.10
insolvency of employer, and, 31.2
introduction, 49.1

Time off work – *contd*
look for work
generally, 49.7
remedies, 49.8
maternity leave, 49.19
military service, and, 49.20
parental leave, 49.19
paternity leave, 49.19
pension scheme trustees
generally, 49.12
remedies, 49.13
public duties
generally, 49.5
remedies, 49.6
safety representatives
generally, 49.9
remedies, 49.10
study and training, and
introduction, 4.7
remedy for refusal, 4.8
right not to suffer detriment, 4.9
trade union activities
equal treatment, and, 49.4
generally, 49.3
remedies, 49.6
trade union officials, 49.2
unfair dismissal, and, 54.3
Tips and gratuities
national minimum wage, and, 34.9
pay, and, 34.21
Tortious liability of trade unions
generally, 50.16
limits on damages, 50.17
Trade dispute
strike action, and, 45.4
Trade organisations
age discrimination, and, 3.36
disability discrimination, and, 10.26
discrimination, and, 13.26
Trade secrets
restraint of trade covenants, and, 41.13
Trade union activities
equal treatment, and, 49.4
generally, 49.3
insolvency of employer, and, 31.2
remedies, 49.6
unfair dismissal, and, 54.3
Trade union dues
deductions from wages, and, 34.6

Index

Trade union members

action short of dismissal
  generally, 51.17
  remedy, 51.18
  summary, 51.8
advice from unions, 51.22
'blacklists', 51.10
closed shop
  dismissal, and, 51.5
  industrial action, and, 51.9
  introduction, 51.3
  pre-entry, 51.4
closed shop dismissals
  compensation, 51.7
  generally, 51.5
deductions from wages
  generally, 51.20
  introduction, 34.6
disciplinary action
  common law, 51.15
  right to be accompanied, 51.21
  statutory provisions, 51.16
  summary, 51.9
exclusion from union
  common law, 51.12
  introduction, 51.11
  remedy, 51.14
  statutory provisions, 51.13
expulsion from union
  common law, 51.12
  introduction, 51.11
  remedy, 51.14
  statutory right, 51.13
failure to make payments, 51.6
goods or services contracts, 51.120
industrial action, 51.9
pre-entry closed shop, 51.4
rights
  employer, in relation to, 51.1
  union, in relation to, 51.2
time off work, and
  equal treatment, 49.4
  generally, 49.3
  remedies, 49.6
tortious liability. 50.18
unfair dismissal, and, 54.3

Trade union officials

time off work, and, 49.2
unfair dismissal, and, 54.3

Trade unions

accounts and records, 50.12
amalgamations, 50.39

Trade unions – *contd*

Central Arbitration Committee
  appeals against awards, 50.10–50.11
  constitution, 50.5
  establishment, 50.4
  functions, 50.6–50.9
certification officer, 50.3
collective bargaining, derecognition
  for, 50.36
collective bargaining, recognition for
  appropriate bargaining unit, 50.30
  ballot, 50.31–50.32
  changes in bargaining unit, 50.35
  'collective bargaining', 50.27
  introduction, 50.25
  method of bargaining, 50.33
  reference to CA, 50.29
  request for recognition, 50.28
  scope of procedure, 50.26
detriment, 50.37
disqualification from office, 50.14
duty of care for advice given, 51.22
elections, 50.14
independence
  factors, 50.23
  introduction, 50.22
  withdrawal of certificate, 50.24
legal capacity, 50.2
listing, 50.21
membership rights
  and see Trade union members
  generally, 51.1–51.22
obligations
  accounts and records, 50.12
  disqualification from office, 50.14
  elections, 50.14
  introduction, 50.12
  political levy, 50.15
  register of members, 50.13
political levy, 50.15
pressure to impose membership or
  recognition, and, 45.7
recognition
  collective bargaining, for, 50.25–
    50.35
  independence, 50.22–50.24
  introduction, 50.19
  listing, 50.21
  unfair dismissal, and, 54.3
  voluntary, 50.20
records, 50.12
register of members, 50.13

Trade unions – *contd*
status
generally, 50.1
legal capacity, 50.2
strike action, and
ballots before action, 45.14
calls for action, 45.15
generally, 45.13
tortious liability
generally, 50.16
limits on damages, 50.17
training, 50.38
transfers of engagements, 50.39
unfair dismissal, and, 54.3
voluntary recognition
collective bargaining, for, 50.34
generally, 50.20
Training and education
and see Time off
apprenticeships, 16.2
disability discrimination, and, 10.20
discrimination, and, 13.9
Industrial Training Boards, 16.4
introduction, 16.1
Learning and Skills Council, 16.9
New Deal, 16.6
positive discrimination, and, 13.9
recovery of costs, 16.3
school-leavers, for, 16.5
tax-free benefits, and, 46.23
time off from work, and
generally, 49.7
remedies, 49.8
trade unions, and, 50.38
generally, 50.20
work-based training, 16.7–16.8
Transfer of engagements
trade unions, and, 50.39
Transfer of proceedings
tribunal procedure, and, 21.25
Transfer of undertakings
administrative functions carried out by
public body, 52.9
applications to Employment
Tribunals, 21.25
avoidance of, 52.28
background, 52.1
collective agreements, and, 52.20
directors, and, 9.32
disclosure of information, and, 11.6
dismissal, and
introduction, 52.24

Transfer of undertakings – *contd*
dismissal, and – *contd*
redundancy, 52.27
unfair dismissal, 52.25–52.26
European law, and, 25.9
excluded rights and liability, 52.19
information and consultation
advance notification, 52.23
employee liability information,
52.22
introduction, 11.6
insolvency of employer
generally, 52.11
introduction, 31.9
introduction, 52.1–52.2
legislative background, 52.1
meaning
introduction, 52.2
"service provision change", 52.3
"transfer", 52.5
"undertaking", 52.4
more than one transaction, 52.7
payments from National Insurance
Fund, and
generally, 52.11
introduction, 31.9
recognition of trade unions, and,
52.21
redundancy, 52.27
redundancy payments, and, 38.5
"relevant transfer"
administrative functions carried out
by public body, 52.9
introduction, 52.2
more than one transaction, 52.7
other concepts, 52.6–52.10
service provision change, 52.3
share transfers, 52.10
transfer, 52.5
transfer of property, 52.9
undertaking or business, 52.4
rights and liabilities assigned
employee's right of objection, 52.16
exclusions, 52.19
'immediately before the transfer',
52.14
introduction, 52.13
nature of acquisition by
transferee, 52.17—52.18
'would otherwise have been
terminated', 52.15

Index

Transfer of undertakings – *contd*
rights and liabilities not assigned,
52.19
"service provision change"
background, 52.1
introduction, 52.2
relevant activities, 52.3
share transfers, and, 52.10
timing, 52.12
"transfer", 52.5
transfer of property, 52.9
"undertaking or business", 52.4
unfair dismissal, and
dismissal, 52.25
fairness of dismissal, 52.26
introduction, 54.3
variation of employees' contracts,
52.29
Transport vouchers
taxable benefits, and, 46.21
Transport workers
working time, and, 57.3
Transsexuals
and see Discrimination
direct discrimination, 12.5
equal pay, and
generally, 24.13
introduction, 24.2
generally, 12.2
Travel expenses
tax-free benefits, and, 46.23
Troncs
pay, and, 34.21
Trustees of pension schemes
discrimination, and, 13.31
introduction, 42.12
time off work, and
generally, 49.12
remedies, 49.13
unfair dismissal, and, 54.3
transsexuals, 12.2

U
Undertaking
and see Transfer of undertakings
meaning, 52.4
Unenforceable terms of contract
contracting out of certain provisions,
8.17
discriminatory terms, 8.18
industrial action restrictions, 8.20

Unenforceable terms of contract – *contd*
introduction, 8.16
restraint trade, 8.19
UCTA 1977, and, 8.21
Unfair Contract Terms Act 1977
unenforceable terms, and, 8.21
Unfair dismissal
acceptable reasons for dismissal
any other substantial reason, 54.14
capability, 54.5–54.8
contravention of any enactment,
54.13
ill-health, 54.8
introduction, 54.1
misconduct, 54.9–54.10
qualifications, 54.7
redundancy, 54.11–54.12
summary, 54.2
accompanied at disciplinary hearings,
and, 54.3
additional award, 55.14
adoption leave, and, 54.3
age discrimination, and, 3.48
agency workers, and, 47.7
any other substantial reason
generally, 54.14
summary, 54.2
assertion of statutory rights, 54.3
basic award
amount, 55.7
exceptions, 55.8
maximum award, 55.16
reduction, 55.9
capability
generally, 54.6
ill-health, 54.8
introduction, 54.5
procedure, 54.6
qualifications, 54.7
summary, 54.2
childbirth, and, 54.3
compensation
additional award, 55.14
basic award, 55.7–55.9
compensatory award, 55.10–55.13
introduction, 55.6
maximum amounts, 55.16
recoupment of statutory benefits,
55.5
union-related cases, 55.15
compensatory award
amount, 55.11

Unfair dismissal – *contd*
  compensatory award – *contd*
    heads of loss, 55.12
    increase, 55.13
    introduction, 55.10
    maximum award, 55.16
    reduction, 55.15
    union-related cases, 55.15
  conduct
    generally, 54.9
    procedure, 54.10
    summary, 54.2
  constructive dismissal, 53.7
  continuous employment, 53.12
  contracting out
    exceptions, 53.20
    generally, 53.19
  contravention of any enactment
    generally, 54.13
    summary, 54.2
  deemed unfair dismissals, 54.3
  disability discrimination, and
    generally, 10.22
    ill-health, 10.23
  disciplinary hearings, and, 54.3
  dismissal and disciplinary procedures,
    and, 15.9
  dismissal by respondent
    constructive dismissal, 53.7
    excepted terminations, 53.10
    expiry of fixed-term contract, 53.6
    forced resignation, 53.8
    introduction, 53.4
    repudiatory conduct by employee,
      53.9
    termination by employer, 53.5
  economic, technical or organisational
    reasons, 54.14
  effective date of termination, 53.13
  employee representatives, and, 54.3
  employment by respondent, 53.3
  European Works Council, and, 54.3
  excluded employees, 53.15
  expiry of fixed-term contract
    generally, 53.6
    some other substantial reason,
      54.14
  failure to follow statutory disciplinary
    procedures, 54.3
  fairness
    acceptable reasons for dismissal,
      54.1–54.2

Unfair dismissal – *contd*
  fairness – *contd*
    deemed unfair dismissals, 54.3
    'in the circumstances', 54.4
  family-related reasons, 54.3
  fixed-term employees, and, 54.3
  flexible working, and, 54.3
  forced resignation, 53.8
  frustration, and, 53.10
  grievance procedures, and, 15.9
  grounds
    capability, 54.5–54.6
    conduct, 54.9–54.10
    contravention of enactment, 54.13
    ill-health, 54.8
    qualifications, 54.7
    redundancy, 54.11–54.12
    some other substantial reason,
      54.14
  health and safety, and
    breach of safety regulations, 28.11
    detriment, 28.8
    generally, 54.3
    introduction, 28.7
    whistleblowing, 28.9
    remedy, 28.10
  illegal contracts, 53.16
  ill-health
    generally, 54.8
    introduction, 54.5
    summary, 54.2
  imprisonment, 54.14
  industrial action, and, 54.3
  insolvency of employer, and, 31.5
  interim relief, 55.21
  internal appeals, and, 54.15
  introduction, 53.1
  joinder of third parties, 55.20
  jury service, and, 54.3
  lock-outs, and
    official action, 53.17
    unofficial action, 53.18
  maternity leave, and, 54.3
  minimum wage, and, 54.3
  misconduct
    generally, 54.9
    procedure, 54.10
    summary, 54.2
  necessary economies, 54.14
  non-membership of union, 54.3
  occurrence of external event, and,
    53.10

Index

Unfair dismissal – *contd*

parental leave, and, 54.3

part-time workers, and,

generally, 32.19

introduction, 54.3

paternity leave, and, 54.3

payments from National Insurance Fund, and, 31.5

pension scheme trustees, and, 54.3

pre-conditions of claim

dismissal by respondent, 53.4–53.10

employment by respondent, 53.3

introduction, 53.2

qualifying period of employment, 53.11–53.13

pregnancy, and, 54.3

pressure on employer to dismiss unfairly, 54.16

protection of interests of business, 54.14

public interest disclosure, and, 54.3

qualifications

generally, 54.7

introduction, 54.5

summary, 54.2

qualifying period of employment

calculation of continuous employment, 53.12

effective date of termination, 53.13

introduction, 53.11

redundancy

generally, 54.11

procedure, 54.12

summary, 54.2

unfair selection, 54.3

re-engagement

general rules, 55.4

generally, 55.3

refusal to reinstate, 55.5

refusal to work on Sunday, and, 54.3

reinstatement

general rules, 55.4

generally, 55.2

refusal to reinstate, 55.5

remedies

compensation, 55.6–55.16

interim relief, 55.18

introduction, 55.1

joinder of third parties, 55.17

re-engagement, 55.3–55.5

reinstatement, 55.2–55.5

settlement, 55.19

Unfair dismissal – *contd*

reorganisation of business, 54.14

replacement employee, 54.14

repudiatory conduct by employee, 53.9

retirement, and

generally, 53.14

introduction, 42.2

seasonal workers, and, 47.8

settlement, 55.22

some other substantial reason

generally, 54.14

summary, 54.2

special negotiating bodies, and, 54.3

spent convictions, and, 54.3

strikes, and

official action, 53.17

unofficial action, 53.18

Sunday work, and, 54.3

tax credits, and, 54.3

temporary workers, and, 47.7

termination by employer, 53.5

time off for dependants, and, 54.3

transfer of undertakings, and

dismissal, 52.25

fairness of dismissal, 52.26

introduction, 54.3

union membership, and, 54.3

union recognition, and, 54.3

working time, and

generally, 57.24

introduction, 54.3

works councils, and, 54.3

Unfavourable treatment

discrimination, and, 12.5

Union membership

and see Trade unions

unfair dismissal, and, 54.3

Union recognition

and see Trade unions

unfair dismissal, and, 54.3

Unlawful acts

discrimination, and, 12.12

Unlawful deductions from wages

time limits for claims, and, 20.31

Unlawful instructions to discriminate

enforcement only by Commissions, 13.40

generally, 12.13

injunctions, 14.30

Unlawful pressure to discriminate
enforcement only by Commissions,
13.40
generally, 12.13
injunctions, 14.30
Unlawful treatment
discrimination, and, 12.5
Unlawful terms
contract of employment, and, 8.15
Unmeasured working time
working time, and, 57.28
Unofficial workers, dismissal of
strike action, and, 45.8
**Unreasonable refusal of alternative
employment**
redundancy payments, and, 38.12
Unwanted conduct
age discrimination, and, 3.8
Use of employer's assets
taxable benefits, and, 46.21

V
Vacation work
taxation, and, 46.11
Vans
taxation, and, 46.27
Variation of contract of employment
generally, 8.14
transfer of undertakings, and, 52.29
Vexatious litigants
tribunal procedure, and, 21.76
Vibration
health and safety, and, 28.27
Vicarious liability
age discrimination, and, 3.42
common law, and, 56.1
discrimination, and
generally, 12.12
persons responsible, 13.35
health and safety, and, 27.9
introduction, 56.1
meaning
generally, 56.1
'in the course of his employment',
56.2
part-time workers, and, 32.24
'*pro hac vice*' employment, 56.3
temporary workers, and, 47.2
Victimisation
age discrimination, and, 3.7
disability discrimination, and, 10.16
discrimination, and, 12.10

Victimisation – *contd*
part time workers, and, 32.18
working time, and, 57.23
Violence
health and safety, and, 28.28
Vocational training providers
age discrimination, and, 3.38
discrimination, and, 13.28
Voluntary recognition of trade unions
collective bargaining, for, 50.34
generally, 50.20
Voluntary workers
national minimum wage, and, 34.10
Vouchers
taxable benefits, and, 46.21–46.22

W
Wages
attachment of earnings, and
attachable earnings, 35.2
child support maintenance, 35.11
Council Tax, 35.10
deductions, 35.3–35.6
employer's obligations, 35.7
introduction, 35.1
other issues, 35.9
penalties for non-compliance, 35.8
breach of contract of employment,
and, 8.24
deductions from wages
generally, 34.6
minimum wage, and, 34.9–34.13
other, 34.14
remedies, for breach, 34.8
retail employment, 34.7
generally, 34.2
gratuities, 34.21
guarantee payments
amount, 34.27
exclusions, 34.26
introduction, 34.23
qualifying period, 34.25
remedy for failure to make
payment, 34.28
'workless days', 34.24
holidays, and, 29.4
insolvency of employer, and, 31.2
itemised statements
application to tribunal, 34.19–34.20
exclusions, 34.18
fixed deductions, 34.17

Index

Wages – *contd*
itemised statements – *contd*
generally, 34.16
introduction, 34.1
meaning, 34.6
medical suspension, and
amount, 34.32
exclusions, 34.31
generally, 34.29
qualifying conditions, 34.30
remedy for failure to make
payment, 34.33
method of payment, 34.3
national minimum wage
coverage, 34.10
introduction, 34.9
records, 34.11
relevant workers, 34.10
remedies for failure to pay, 34.12–
34.13
statements, 34.11
overpayment, 34.15
pre-1987 position
exceptions, 34.5
generally, 34.4
records, 34.11
termination of employment, and,
34.22
troncs, 34.21
'week's pay'
amount, 34.39
calculation date, 34.38
introduction, 34.34
no normal working hours, 34.37
normal working hours, 34.35
overtime, 34.36
workless days, and, 34.23
Waiver
wrongful dismissal, and, 58.21
Wasted costs orders
tribunal procedure, and, 21.73
Weekly rest periods
working time, and, 57.16
Weeks
continuous employment, and
meaning, 7.5
weeks which count 6.6–6.8
weeks which do not count, 7.10–
6.11
working time, and, 57.6
'Week's pay'
amount, 34.39

'Week's pay' – *contd*
calculation date, 34.38
introduction, 34.34
no normal working hours, 34.37
normal working hours, 34.35
overtime, 34.36
unfair dismissal, and, 55.7
Welfare
discrimination, and, 13.9
Whistleblowing
generally, 11.17
health and safety, and, 28.9
protected disclosures, 11.18
Withdrawal of claims
tribunal procedure, and, 21.28
Withdrawal of offer of employment
engagement of employees, and, 23.5
Withholding wages
breach of contract of employment,
and, 8.24
Witness orders
tribunal procedure, and, 21.14
witnesses, 21.57
Women suspended on medical grounds
equal pay, and, 24.4
Work-based learning
adults, and, 16.8
Work-based training
young people, and, 16.7
Work of equal value
equal pay, and, 24.8
Work permits
applications, 26.6
eligible workers, 26.5
further information, 26.8
procedure, 26.7
Work rated as equivalent
equal pay, and, 24.7
Workers
meaning, 17.9
Workforce agreement
working time, and, 57.4
Working abroad
taxation, and, 46.12
Working tax credit
taxation, and, 46.34
Working time
agency workers, 57.3
annual leave, 57.19
armed forces personnel, 57.3
aviation sector, 57.33
children, 57.3

Working time – *contd*
collective agreements, 57.4
contracting out, 57.25
daily rest periods, 57.15
definition, 57.5
doctors in training, 57.3
domestic service, 57.30
enforcement
health and safety authorities, by,
57.21
individual, by, 57.22
introduction, 57.20
European law, and, 25.11
exceptions
domestic service, 57.30
introduction, 57.27
special cases, 57.29
unmeasured working time, 57.28
Guidance, 57.26
holidays, and
agricultural workers, 29.7
introduction, 29.2
notice requirements, 29.5
payment, 29.4
period of leave, 29.3
remedies, 29.6
introduction, 57.1
maximum weekly time, 57.6
merchant seamen, 57.31–57.32
mobile workers, 57.34–57.36
monotonous work, 57.18
night work
duration, 57.10
health assessments, 57.12
introduction, 57.9
special hazards, 57.11
transfer to day work, 57.13
offshore workers, 57.1
opt-out agreements, 57.7
police, 57.3
railway workers, 57.36
records, 57.8
Regulations
coverage, 57.3
definitions, 57.4
introduction, 57.2
relevant agreement, 57.4
relevant workers, 57.3
rest breaks
generally, 57.17
monotonous work, 57.18

Working time – *contd*
rest periods
daily, 57.15
introduction, 57.14
weekly, 57.16
road transport workers, 57.34–57.35
seafarers, 57.31–57.32
transport workers, 57.34–57.35
unfair dismissal, and
generally, 57.24
introduction, 54.3
unmeasured working time, 57.28
victimisation, 57.23
weekly rest periods, 57.16
workforce agreement, 57.4
young persons, 57.3
Working under direction of third party
health and safety, and, 27.10
'Workless days'
guarantee payments, and, 34.24
Workplace nurseries
tax-free benefits, and, 46.23
Workplace standards
health and safety, and, 28.29
Work-related training
tax-free benefits, and, 46.23
Work-related upper limb disorders
health and safety, and, 28.31
Works councils
confidential information, 18.26
employment protection, 18.27
establishment, 18.25
European law, and, 25.12
implementation, 18.21
introduction, 18.4
number of employees, 18.22
requests, 18.23
special negotiating body, 18.24
time off work, and, 49.16
unfair dismissal, and, 54.3
Written particulars of contract
alternatives to inclusion, 8.6
changes, 8.7
directors, and, 9.6
European law, and, 25.7
excepted employees, 8.8
introduction, 8.4
remedies for failure to provide, 8.9
requirements, 8.5
Written statements of reasons
dismissal, and,
generally, 48.14

Index

Written statements of reasons – *contd*
  dismissal, and – *contd*
    remedy for failure to give, 48.15
  part time workers, and, 32.17
Wrongful dismissal
  acceptance of employer's breach, 58.7
  anticipatory breaches of contract, 58.22
  apprentices, and, 58.44
  cessation of existence of employer, 58.8
  change of employer's identity, 58.8
  choice of court, 58.38
  claims procedure
    choice of court, 58.38
    compromise of claims, 58.42
    hearings on liability and quantum, 58.41
    interim payments, 58.41
    limitation periods, 58.40
    payments into court, 58.41
    relationship with tribunal proceedings, 58.39
    summary judgment, 58.41
  compromise of claims, 58.42
  constructive dismissal, 58.6
  contrast with other modes of termination, 58.4
  Crown servants, and, 58.43
  damages
    accelerated receipt, 58.31
    accommodation, 58.28
    assessment approach, 58.25
    bonuses, 58.28
    cars, 58.28
    collateral benefits, 58.30
    commission, 58.28
    distress, 58.29
    holidays, 58.28
    insurance cover, 58.28
    intangible loss, 58.29
    interest, 58.31
    'liquidated damages' clauses, 58.26
    mitigation, 58.30
    pensions, 58.28
    rights in period of notice, 58.27
    salary, 58.28
    share options, 58.28
    taxation, 58.32
    unfair dismissal compensation, and, 58.33
    valuation of benefits, 58.28

Wrongful dismissal – *contd*
  defences
    exclusion clauses, 58.37
    illegality, 58.35
    invalidity of contract, 58.36
  'dismissal'
    acceptance of employer's breach, 58.7
    cessation of existence of employer, 58.8
    change of employer's identity, 58.8
    constructive dismissal, 58.6
    contrast with other modes of termination, 58.4
    dismissal with notice, 58.5
    dismissal without notice, 58.11–58.17
    insolvency of employer, 58.9
    introduction, 58.3
    removal of director from board, 58.10
  dismissal in breach of other requirements, 58.19
  dismissal in breach of procedures, 58.18
  dismissal with notice, 58.5
  dismissal without notice
    directors' notice periods, 58.14
    express notice periods, 58.11
    fixed term contracts, 58.12
    implied notice periods, 58.15
    justification, 58.17
    rolling contracts, 58.13
    statutory minimum notice, 58.16
  effect on other obligations, 58.34
  garden leave, 58.21
  hearings on liability and quantum, 58.41
  injunctions, 58.23
  insolvency of employer, 58.9
  interim payments, 58.41
  introduction, 58.1–58.2
  limitation periods, 58.40
  pay in lieu of notice, 58.21
  payments into court, 58.41
  reason for dismissal, and, 58.20
  remedies
    claims in debt, 58.24
    damages, 58.25–58.33
    injunctions, 58.23
  removal of director from board, 58.10

Wrongful dismissal – *contd*
  summary dismissal
    directors' notice periods, 58.14
    express notice periods, 58.11
    fixed term contracts, 58.12
    implied notice periods, 58.15
    justification, 58.17
    rolling contracts, 58.13
    statutory minimum notice, 58.16
  summary judgment, 58.41
  waiver of notice, 58.21

Y
Young persons, employment of
  breaks, 4.6
  contracts of employment, 4.10
  definitions, 4.1

Young persons, employment of – *contd*
  health and safety
    breaks, 4.6
    introduction, 4.5
    night work, 4.6
    rest periods, 4.6
  local authority powers, 4.3
  night work, 4.6
  rest periods, 4.6
  restrictions
    generally, 4.2
    local authority powers, 4.3
    other provisions, 4.4
  time off for study or training
    introduction, 4.7
    remedy for refusal, 4.8
    right not to suffer detriment, 4.9
  working time, and, 57.3